THE VOLUME LIBRARY

A Modern, Authoritative Reference for Home and School Use

Clear and Complete • Colorfully Illustrated • Totally Indexed
Special Atlas Section

THE SOUTHWESTERN COMPANY

Nashville, Tennessee

THE VOLUME LIBRARY

Copyright 1990 by The Southwestern Company.

Copyright under the Universal Copyright Convention, the International Copyright Union; Pan-American Conventions of Montevideo, Mexico, Rio de Janeiro, Buenos Aires, and Havana

The Volume Library copyright 1989, 1988, 1987, 1986, 1985, 1984, 1983, 1982, 1980, 1979, 1978, 1977, 1976, 1975, 1973, 1972, by The Southwestern Company. Cowles Volume Library copyright 1969, 1968, by Cowles Book Company, Inc. Cowles Comprehensive Encyclopedia—The Volume Library copyright 1967, 1966, 1965, 1964, 1963, by Cowles Education Corporation. The Volume Library copyright 1962, 1961, 1960, 1959, 1958, 1957, 1956, 1955, 1954, 1953, 1952, 1951, 1950, 1949, 1948, 1947, 1946, 1945, 1944, 1943, 1942, 1941, 1940, 1939, 1938, 1937, 1936, 1935, 1934, 1933, 1932, 1931, 1930, 1929, 1928, 1927, 1926, 1925, 1924, 1923, 1922, 1921, 1920, 1919, 1918, 1917, by Educators Association, Inc.

ISBN 0-87197-208-5

THE VOLUME LIBRARY

PREFACE

What is the Volume Library?

The Volume Library is a respected home reference book that has been published for more than 70 years, bringing knowledge and information to generations of readers. Its 2.5 million words and countless illustrations provide clear introductions to all major fields of study and bring together in two convenient volumes important and hard-to-find information.

The Volume Library, which is revised and updated annually, was designed for interested, well-informed people—students and adults who need an authoritative reference book for their home bookshelves, and parents who want to keep abreast of the subjects their children are studying in school.

Its uses can be summarized in four categories:

• *Learning.* In contrast with many other reference works, *The Volume Library* offers detailed and clear instruction in such practical skills as mathematics and writing. Readers can learn new skills or brush up on old ones without searching out many separate volumes.

• *Reference.* Thousands of important names, dates, places, and events are easily available; they can be looked up quickly and conveniently.

• *Research.* Students, business people, and others who are preparing reports on special subjects will find useful information in clear, understandable form.

• *Browsing.* Many successful people report that their first source of information as young readers was an interesting reference work to pore over while gathering miscellaneous information simply for enjoyment. *The Volume Library* offers introductions to many fields of interest and can often lead even a reluctant learner to further reading in more specialized books, magazines, and other materials.

How is The Volume Library organized?

Each of the 26 subject volumes is complete in itself. The volumes are arranged alphabetically, beginning with ANIMALS and ending with UNITED STATES AND CANADA. In addition, there are a full-color ATLAS of the world and a thorough INDEX, which provides detailed guidance for the use of *The Volume Library.*

Many of the volumes are related. Covering the broad areas of history and geography, for example, are five large volumes, each treating a major region of the world. Six other volumes cover the major subdivisions of science. In a similar way, social studies are considered under such broad volume headings as CHILD AND FAMILY and GOVERNMENT AND LAW. Several volumes outline such important practical fields as business, economics, and technology. Three volumes cover arts and letters, providing histories of painting, sculpture, music, dance, and literature. Finally, two important volumes provide detailed material on practical learning skills. The MATHEMATICS volume gives clear instruction from elementary arithmetic through to geometry and calculus. The LANGUAGE volume considers the skills of speaking, reading, and especially writing. It includes full sections on spelling, grammar, and research for school reports.

The following table shows the relationships of all the volumes and may be helpful for the reader who wants to know where to look first.

How to use The Volume Library

In most encyclopedias, information is broken into small entries and then arranged alphabetically. By contrast, in *The Volume Library* all information on a large topic is found in one place and is described in a way that makes comprehensive sense. This means that a reader with an interest in mathematics, for example, can find a connected account of arithmetic within a few pages; he will not have to look up separate entries on *addition, fractions, measurement,* and so on.

In some cases, of course, a reader will be looking for information that is separated. For example, a reader who has an interest in France will find a long entry on the country in the EUROPE volume, but he will also find an account of French art in the ART volume, of French literature under LITERATURE, of prominent Frenchmen under PEOPLE, and so on. He will even find a brief review of the French language in the LANGUAGE volume. Such a reader will find great usefulness in the INDEX at the back of the book. It is a valuable guide to any researcher seeking to understand the connections and relationships between the many aspects of knowledge in many fields of interest.

Only you, the reader, can decide which of the many attractive features of *The Volume Library* makes it most useful for your purposes. Whether you use it for learning skills, for looking up facts, for research, or for browsing, you will find it a convenient and endlessly fascinating source of knowledge.

TABLE OF CONTENTS

EDITORIAL STAFF
THE HUDSON GROUP, INC., PLEASANTVILLE, N.Y.

Editor in chief: GORTON CARRUTH
Sponsoring editor: EUGENE EHRLICH
Managing editor: HAYDEN CARRUTH
Art and production: PAM FORDE GRAPHICS
Copy editing and indexing: FELICE LEVY and CYNTHIA CRIPPEN/AEIOU, INC.

Contributors

ACOCELLA, NICHOLAS
M.A. Political writer and columnist.
GOVERNMENT AND LAW.

ADAMS, JANET
Ph.D. Candidate. Instructor, Rhode Island School of Design.
ART.

BAHLMAN, DUDLEY W. R.
Ph.D. Professor of History, and Dean of the Faculty,
Williams College.
EUROPE.

BAINER, ROY
M.S. Dean of Engineering, University of California at Davis.
FOOD AND AGRICULTURE.

BAKER, LAURENCE H.
Ph.D. Director, Computing Department, Pioneer Hi-Bred
Corn Company.
FOOD AND AGRICULTURE.

BARTELMEZ, ERMINNIE H.
Ph.D. Professor of German, Case Western Reserve
University.
LANGUAGE.

BARTH, FRANCES F.
Freelance medical writer.
HEALTH AND LIFE SCIENCES.

BARZANTI, SERGIO
Ph.D. Associate Professor of Social Sciences, Fairleigh
Dickinson University.
EUROPE; MIDDLE EAST AND AFRICA.

BAYES, MARJORIE
Ph.D. Clinical psychologist.
CHILD AND FAMILY.

BERLAND, LAURA
B.A. Writer and legal aide.
GOVERNMENT AND LAW.

BERRY, E. WILLARD
Ph.D. Late Professor of Geology, Duke University.
EARTH SCIENCES.

BIRMINGHAM, LLOYD
Freelance educational illustrator.
CHEMISTRY AND PHYSICS; INVENTION AND TECHNOLOGY.

BOARDMAN, FON W.
A.B. Former Vice President and Marketing Director of
Oxford University Press, N.Y.; author of books for
young people; freelance writer.
FOOD AND AGRICULTURE; PEOPLE; UNITED STATES AND CANADA.

BOCIAN, PHYLLIS R.
B.A. Freelance editor.
CHILD AND FAMILY; LANGUAGE.

BROWN, LEON CARL
Ph.D. Associate Professor of Oriental Studies,
Princeton University.
MIDDLE EAST AND AFRICA.

BUNCH, BRYAN H.
B.A. Writer, textbook consultant; former Editor in Chief,
American Book Company.
ANIMALS; ASTRONOMY AND SPACE; INVENTION AND
TECHNOLOGY; MATHEMATICS; PLANTS; RELIGION;
SOCIAL SCIENCES.

BUSHNELL, DAVID
Ph.D. Associate Professor of History, University of Florida.
SOUTH AND CENTRAL AMERICA.

BUTTFIELD, HELEN
A.M. Nature writer and photographer.
PLANTS.

BYAM, GUY R.
M.A. Vice President and Director of Personnel,
Bankers Trust Company.
BUSINESS AND FINANCE.

BYERLY, THEODORE C.
Ph.D. Administrator, Cooperative State Research Service,
United States Department of Agriculture.
FOOD AND AGRICULTURE.

BYRNES, ROBERT F.
Ph.D. Distinguished Professor of History,
Indiana University.
EUROPE.

CAREY, GEORGE W.
Ed.D. Associate Professor of Geography, Teachers College,
Columbia University.
SOUTH AND CENTRAL AMERICA.

CARTER, CHARLES H.
Ph.D. Professor of History, Tulane University.
EUROPE.

COHEN, MARSHALL H.
M.A. Economist, U.S. Department of Agriculture.
FOOD AND AGRICULTURE.

COHN-HAFT, LOUIS
Ph.D. Professor of History, Smith College.
EUROPE.

DALRYMPLE, DANA G.
Ph.D. Economist, International Agricultural
Development Service, U.S. Department of Agriculture.
FOOD AND AGRICULTURE.

DAVIS, FRANCIS K., JR.
Ph.D. Head, Physics Department, Drexel Institute of
Technology.
EARTH SCIENCES.

DELURY, GEORGE
M.A. Political science editor.
GOVERNMENT AND LAW.

DETWILER, SAMUEL B., JR.
M.A. Assistant to the Deputy Administrator for Nutrition,
Consumer, and Industrial Use Research, Agricultural
Research Service, U.S. Department of Agriculture.
FOOD AND AGRICULTURE.

DICKINSON, RICHARD
M.A. Lecturer and writer on fine arts.
ART.
DIPPEL, JOHN
Ph.D. Freelance writer.
LANGUAGE.
DIRKS, J. EDWARD
Ph.D. Professor of Christian Methods, Yale University
Divinity School; Founder and Editor, *Christian Science
Quarterly*.
RELIGION AND PHILOSOPHY.
DITTRICK, DIANE K.
M.A. Author and freelance writer on science subjects.
HEALTH AND LIFE SCIENCES.
DOWLING, KENNETH W.
Ph.D. Science Supervisor, State of Wisconsin.
INVENTION AND TECHNOLOGY.
DRAPER, EVERETT T.
M.A. Adjunct Lecturer, LaGuardia Community College,
City University of New York.
MATHEMATICS.
DUNBAR, ROBERT G.
Ph.D. Professor of History, Montana State University.
FOOD AND AGRICULTURE.
DUPREE, LOUIS
Ph.D. Research Associate in Anthropology,
American Museum of Natural History.
ASIA AND AUSTRALASIA.
EHRLICH, HENRY
B.A. Communications specialist, Assistant Vice
President, Citibank.
LANGUAGE.
EMBREE, AINSLIE T.
Ph.D. Associate Professor of History, Columbia University.
ASIA AND AUSTRALASIA.
EMILIANI, CESARE
Ph.D. Professor, Institute of Marine Sciences,
University of Miami (Florida).
EARTH SCIENCES.
ENNIS, THOMAS E.
Ph.D. Late Professor of Far Eastern History,
West Virginia University.
ASIA AND AUSTRALASIA.
EPPERT, RAY R.
D.Sc., LL.D. Chairman and Chief Executive Officer,
Burroughs Corporation.
BUSINESS AND FINANCE.
FABRICANT, MONA
Ed.D. City University of New York.
MATHEMATICS.
FAJARDO, FERNANDO U.
B.S. Chemist, freelance writer.
CHEMISTRY AND PHYSICS.

FELDMAN, ROBERT J.
Freelance writer.
SOUTH AND CENTRAL AMERICA.
FINAN, JOHN J.
Ph.D. Professor of Latin American Studies, School of
International Service, The American University.
SOUTH AND CENTRAL AMERICA.
FISCHMAN, JEROME
Ph.D. Associate Professor of History, Adelphi University.
SOUTH AND CENTRAL AMERICA.
FOREMAN W. L.
Director of Public Relations, National Cotton Council of
America.
FOOD AND AGRICULTURE.
FRANKLIN, PAULA
B.A. Writer and editor of school and college texts.
SOCIAL SCIENCES.
FUSSELL, G. E.
Formerly in the British Ministry of Agriculture.
FOOD AND AGRICULTURE.
GILBERT, SARA
Freelance writer.
ASIA AND AUSTRALASIA; MIDDLE EAST AND AFRICA.
GOLUB, MARCIA H.
B.A. Freelance writer and editor.
LANGUAGE; LITERATURE; RELIGION AND PHILOSOPHY.
GRAHAM, GORDON F.
B.A. Secretary, National Association of Wool Manufacturers.
FOOD AND AGRICULTURE.
GRIFFIN, CHARLES C.
Ph.D. Professor of History Emeritus, Vassar College.
SOUTH AND CENTRAL AMERICA.
HAMBURG, MORRIS
Ph.D. Professor of Statistics and Operations Research,
University of Pennsylvania.
BUSINESS AND FINANCE.
HARRINGTON, JOHN P.
Ph.D. Writer and editor of reference works.
UNITED STATES AND CANADA.
HEIMSATH, CHARLES H.
Ph.D. Professor of South Asian Studies, The School of
International Service, The American University.
ASIA AND AUSTRALASIA.
HELLEMANS, ALEXANDER
B.A. Freelance science writer.
ASTRONOMY AND SPACE, CHEMISTRY AND PHYSICS.
HERDER, RONALD
M.A. Adjunct Professor of Music, Manhattanville College.
PERFORMING ARTS.
HERON, S. DUNCAN, JR.
Ph.D. Associate Professor of Geology and Department
Chairman, Duke University; Editor in Chief,
Southeastern Geology.
EARTH SCIENCES.

HESS, CARL W.
Ph.D. Chief, Poultry Research Branch, U.S. Department
of Agriculture.
FOOD AND AGRICULTURE.
HESTER, ALBERT S.
B.S. Market Research Analyst, American Cyanamid
Company.
FOOD AND AGRICULTURE.
HOOLIHAN, CHRISTOPHER T.
M.A. Former Professor of French and Latin,
St. Meinrad College.
LANGUAGE.
HYNEK, J. ALLEN
Ph.D. Professor of Astronomy and Department Chairman,
Northwestern University; Director, Dearborn Observatory
and Lindheimer Astronomical Research Center.
ASTRONOMY AND SPACE.
INABA, M. G.
Ph.D. Chairman, Department of Geography,
Hofstra University.
ASIA AND AUSTRALASIA.
ISSAWI, CHARLES
M.A. Ragnar Nurkse Professor of Economics,
Columbia University.
MIDDLE EAST AND AFRICA.
JANOWSKY, OSCAR I.
Ph.D. Professor Emeritus of History, City University of
New York; Visiting Professor of History,
Brandeis University.
MIDDLE EAST AND AFRICA.
KAHKONEN, SHARON
M.S. Freelance science writer.
INVENTION AND TECHNOLOGY.
KAREL, MARCUS
Ph.D. Associate Professor of Food Engineering,
Massachusetts Institute of Technology.
FOOD AND AGRICULTURE.
KISH, GEORGE
Ph.D. Professor of Geography, University of Michigan.
EUROPE.
KLINE, HIBBERD V. B., JR.
Ph.D. Professor and Chairman, Department of
Geography, University of Pittsburgh.
MIDDLE EAST AND AFRICA.
KOCZY, FRIEDRICH F.
Ph.D. Late Professor and Chairman, Physical Science
Division, Institute of Marine Science, University of Miami.
EARTH SCIENCES.
KOMINUS, NICHOLAS
B.S. Director of Information, United States Cane Sugar
Refiners' Association.
FOOD AND AGRICULTURE.

KREN, GEORGE M.
Ph.D. Associate Professor of History,
Kansas State University.
EUROPE.
LAGUARDIA, ROBERT.
Freelance writer.
LITERATURE.
LEITH, JAMES A.
Ph.D. Associate Professor of French History,
Queen's University, Ontario.
EUROPE.
LEVY, STEPHEN H.
Ph.D. Assistant Professor, Computer and Information
Systems, Pace University.
RELIGION AND PHILOSOPHY.
LEY, WILLY
L.H.D. Late Professor, Long Island University.
ASTRONOMY AND SPACE.
LICHTENSTADTER, ILSE
Ph.D., D.Phil.Oxon. Lecturer on Arabic, Center for
Middle Eastern Studies, Harvard University.
ASIA AND AUSTRALASIA.
LINDROTH, DAVID
M.F.A. Cartographer and graphic designer.
ASIA AND AUSTRALASIA.
LINDSAY, MICHAEL
M.A. Professor of Far Eastern Studies, American University.
ASIA AND AUSTRALASIA.
LISS, HOWARD.
Freelance writer.
SPORTS AND RECREATION.
LOEWER, H. PETER
B.F.A. Author and illustrator.
ART; CHEMISTRY AND PHYSICS; CHILD AND FAMILY; FOOD AND
AGRICULTURE; GOVERNMENT AND LAW; HEALTH AND LIFE
SCIENCES; LANGUAGE; MATHEMATICS; PERFORMING ARTS;
SOCIAL SCIENCES; SPORTS.
LORIMER, DONALD
B.A. Freelance writer.
ART; CHILD AND FAMILY.
LORIMER, LAWRENCE T.
M.A. Author, editorial consultant.
ART; CHILD AND FAMILY; LANGUAGE; LITERATURE.
MACKAY-SMITH, ALEXANDER
L.L.B. Editor, *The Chronicle of the Horse*.
FOOD AND AGRICULTURE.
MARR, ANNE W.
M.A. Teacher of mathematics and computer science;
freelance writer.
INVENTION AND TECHNOLOGY.
McCARTHY, E. JEROME
Ph.D. Professor of Marketing, Michigan State
University.
BUSINESS AND FINANCE.

McGREGOR, SAMUEL E.
M.S. Chief, Apiculture Research Branch, Entomology Research Division, U.S. Department of Agriculture.
FOOD AND AGRICULTURE.

McHUGH, JANET
B.A. Writer and editor of school and college texts.
UNITED STATES AND CANADA.

MELAMID, ALEXANDER
Ph.D. Professor of Economics, New York University.
MIDDLE EAST AND AFRICA.

MERRILL, DAVID G.
M.A. Freelance writer.
ASIA AND AUSTRALASIA; EUROPE; MIDDLE EAST AND AFRICA; SOUTH AND CENTRAL AMERICA.

MILLER, PAUL W.
M.B.A. Management Consultant. Department of Management, Western Illinois University.
BUSINESS AND ECONOMICS.

MILNE, LORUS J.
Ph.D. Professor of Zoology, University of New Hampshire.
ANIMALS; PLANTS.

MILNE, MARGERY
Ph.D. Lecturer in Nature Recreation and Zoology, University of New Hampshire.
ANIMALS; PLANTS.

MITCHELL, JOHN W.
Ph.D., D.Sc. Leader, Plant Hormone and Regulator, Pioneering Laboratory, U.S. Department of Agriculture, Crops Research Division.
FOOD AND AGRICULTURE.

MURRY, PAUL B.
Freelance writer.
FOOD AND AGRICULTURE.

MYERS, SARAH K.
Ph.D. Geographer and freelance writer.
INVENTION AND TECHNOLOGY.

NOWELL, CHARLES E.
Ph.D. Professor of History, University of Illinois.
EUROPE.

O'BRIEN, ROBERT
B.A., author.
PERFORMING ARTS.

OLIVER, JOHN E.
M.A. Instructor of Geography, Columbia University.
MIDDLE EAST AND AFRICA.

PAVELIS, GEORGE A.
Ph.D. Chief, Water Resources Branch, Natural Resource Economics Division, U.S. Department of Agriculture.
FOOD AND AGRICULTURE.

PLUMMER, SAMUEL C.
B.A., M.B.A. Freelance writer and editor.
PERFORMING ARTS; SOCIAL SCIENCES.

RANDALL, BERNICE
M.A. Author and editor of educational materials in Spanish and English.
LANGUAGE.

RASMUSSEN, WAYNE D.
Ph.D. Chief, Agriculture History Branch, U.S. Department of Agriculture.
FOOD AND AGRICULTURE.

REILLY, E. M.
Ph.D. Curator Emeritus, Zoology, New York State Museum. Author and freelance writer.
HEALTH AND LIFE SCIENCES.

ROGERS, CHARLES E.
Ph.D. Former Information Officer, U.S. Department of Agriculture.
FOOD AND AGRICULTURE.

ROTBERG, ROBERT I.
D.Phil. Associate Professor of History and Political Science, Massachusetts Institute of Technology.
MIDDLE EAST AND AFRICA.

ROWNEY, DON KARL
Ph.D. Associate Professor of History, Bowling Green State University.
EUROPE.

SACERDOTE, MARC
M.A. Teacher of film animation; freelance writer.
INVENTION AND TECHNOLOGY.

SACKS, RICHARD
Ph.D. Assistant Professor of English and Comparative Literature, Columbia University.
LANGUAGE.

SCOTT, FRANKLIN D.
Ph.D. Professor of History, Northwestern University.
EUROPE.

SCOTT, FREDERICK
M.S. Chemical engineer; Consulting Editor, International Scientific Communications, Inc.
INVENTION AND TECHNOLOGY.

SHANER, DORIS D.
B.A. Vice President, Shaner-Grandelis Associates.
EARTH SCIENCES.

SHERIDAN, BARBARA
B.Sc. Mathematics and physical sciences writer.
MATHEMATICS.

SMITH, DAVID A.
Ph.D. Associate Professor of Geography, State University of New York at Buffalo.
ASIA AND AUSTRALASIA.

STUART, NEIL W.
Ph.D. Research Plant Physiologist, U.S. Department of Agriculture.
FOOD AND AGRICULTURE.

TARAPOR, MAHRUKH.
Freelance writer.
ART.

TESAR, JENNY
M.A. Freelance science and medical writer.
COMPUTERS.

THOMPSON, JOHN M.
Ph.D. Professor of History, Indiana University.
EUROPE.

VAN RIPER, JOSEPH E.
Ph.D. Professor and Chairman, Department of Geography,
State University of New York at Binghamton.
EARTH SCIENCES.

VARCHAVER, MARY
B.A. Freelance writer.
PEOPLE.

WAGNER, HARRY L.
B.A. Freelance education writer.
LANGUAGE.

WAHBA, ISAAC J.
Ph.D. Senior Research Chemist, General Mills, Inc.
FOOD AND AGRICULTURE.

WEARNE, ROBERT A.
M.S. Horticulturist, Extension Service, U.S. Department
of Agriculture.
FOOD AND AGRICULTURE.

WEBB, KEMPTON E.
Ph.D. Associate Professor of Geography, and Associate
Director of Latin American Studies, Columbia University.
SOUTH AND CENTRAL AMERICA.

WEISSMAN, GARY A.
Freelance writer.
MIDDLE EAST AND AFRICA.

WHEELER, DONALD H.
Ph.D. Principal Scientist, General Mills Central
Research Laboratories.
FOOD AND AGRICULTURE.

WHITE, DONALD A.
Ph.D. Associate Professor of History, Temple University.
EUROPE.

WHITE, ROBERT M.
Ph.D. Chief, U.S. Weather Bureau; Chief, Meteorological
Development Laboratory; Research Associate,
Massachusetts Institute of Technology.
EARTH SCIENCES.

WILLIAMS, L. PEARCE
Ph.D. John Stambaugh Professor of History and
Chairman, Department of History, Cornell University.
EUROPE.

YARRIS, LYNN
M.A. Science Writer for Lawrence Berkeley Laboratory.
INVENTION AND TECHNOLOGY.

ZOBLER, LEONARD
Ph.D. Professor and Chairman, Department of Geology
and Geography, Barnard College, Columbia University.
EARTH SCIENCES.

ZOLBERG, VERA L.
B.A. Assistant Professor of Sociology and Anthropology,
St. Xavier College.
MIDDLE EAST AND AFRICA.

Animal Life 3
Animal Behavior 13
Animals Glossary 17
For Further Reference 66

APPEARANCE OF ANIMAL LIFE ON EARTH (from earliest known fossils)
(in ''days'' relative to one year)

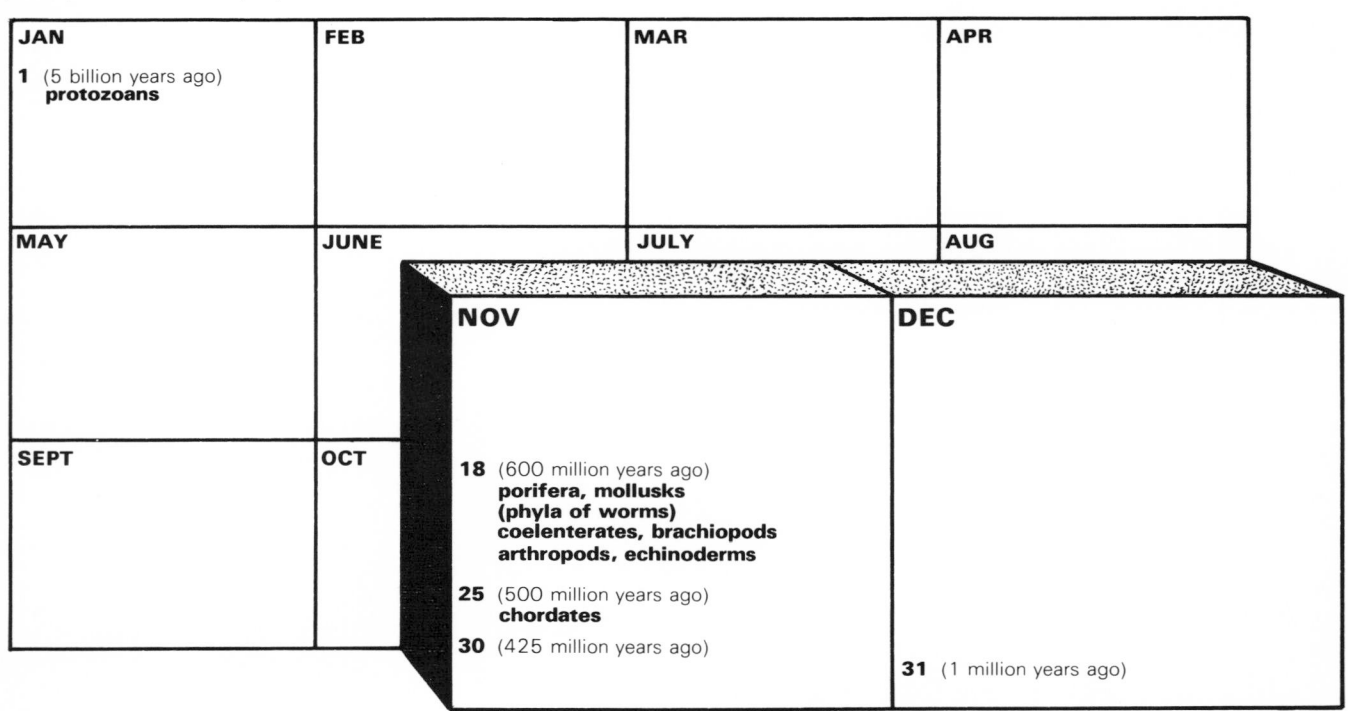

JAN	FEB	MAR	APR
1 (5 billion years ago) **protozoans**			
MAY	JUNE	JULY	AUG
SEPT	OCT	**NOV** **18** (600 million years ago) **porifera, mollusks** **(phyla of worms)** **coelenterates, brachiopods** **arthropods, echinoderms** **25** (500 million years ago) **chordates** **30** (425 million years ago)	**DEC** **31** (1 million years ago)

Animals

ANIMAL LIFE

The branch of science that deals with animals is called Zoology. Although it deals with the structures and functions of animals, perhaps its best-known aspect is the orderly classification of animal life, from the simplest to the most complex.

Although it is easy to see that a bear is an animal and that a pine tree is a plant, some of the smaller animals and plants are not obviously members of their respective kingdoms. Most animals can be distinguished by movement; yet there are microscopic water plants that swim as freely as animals do.

All animals large enough to be seen with the naked eye obtain energy by eating plants or other animals. Surprisingly, a few microscopic animals are like green plants in that through the process of photosynthesis they can capture energy from sunlight and can use simple chemical compounds dissolved in water as food.

Thus, it is obvious that methods must be found to distinguish animals from plants and to separate one kind of animal from another. One way to do this is an analysis of food habits. Another way is by studying habitat, or where an animal lives. The most important factors, however, are structure and function—how an animal moves, digests its food, breathes, and reproduces.

FOOD HABITS. The food habits of an animal will give information concerning its structure and function, some of the animals related to it, and a general idea of the environment in which it lives. Sometimes a broad category of food habits will cover a wide variety of creatures.

Herbivores. Any animal that eats only vegetable matter is a *herbivore,* or plant-eater. Herbivores eat grasses, leaves, twigs, succulent plants, and other types of vegetation. The classification encompasses such different creatures as caterpillars and cows.

Carnivores. Animals that eat the flesh of other animals are called *carnivores,* or meat-eaters. Animals as different as lions and ladybird beetles are in this category. When a cat pounces on a mouse, kills it, and eats it, the cat becomes a predatory carnivore, or *predator.*

Animals such as the vulture and hyena are also carnivores, although they usually prefer to feed on dead animals; this makes them *scavengers.* Domestic animals also become scavengers at times, such as when they rummage through refuse.

Omnivores. The most familiar *omnivores,* creatures that eat both animal and vegetable matter, are man himself and the domestic pig. There are, however, less familiar omnivores that are far more numerous.

The *aquatic omnivores* subsist on food so small that they must strain it from the water. Clams and oysters do so by producing a current within the shell, filtering out the food, and expelling the water. Worms that burrow in the ocean floor build U-shaped tubes, then wiggle in order to draw water in at one end; after they have strained the food from the water, they force the water from the other end of the tube.

Even the giant whales, which may be as long as 110 feet, filter their food. They swim, mouth opened, until small crustaceans, plankton, and other types of food are caught between thin plates known as whalebone that hang down in the mouth cavity. Then they close their mouths and swallow the contents.

Symbionts. Animals that form a beneficial partnership with animals of some other kind or a similar partnership with a living plant are *symbionts.* If both partners in a symbiotic arrangement benefit equally, the relationship is *mutualistic.* If one benefits without harming the other, it is a *commensal* relationship; if one gains at the expense of the other, it is *parasitic.*

Many termites illustrate mutualism. They chew and swallow wood but cannot digest the wood fibers until they are predigested by minute animals that inhabit the termites' digestive tract. These minute animals could not obtain wood fibers without the termites; the termites could not utilize wood fibers if the minute animals did not first digest them.

The shark sucker, also called pilot fish or remora, has a commensal relation with sharks. It attaches itself to the shark by means of a suction disk and is carried from place to place to share the shark's food. The shark sucker detaches itself while the shark is feeding, eats, and reattaches itself, to be carried elsewhere. Occasionally a shark sucker will be found attached to a sea turtle or a small boat.

Most parasites are harmless unless they have become numerous. One chicken louse will cause a bird mild discomfort; hundreds will cause a bird to scratch itself constantly, weaken, and grow ill. Such parasites as lice, fleas, ticks, and mosquitoes are called *ectoparasites.*

There are also *endoparasites,* which are internal parasites. They include tapeworms, which inhabit the digestive tract; flukes, which inhabit the lungs; and malaria parasites, which attack the red cells in the blood.

Certain minute insects parasitize plants by producing chemicals that irritate the plants into forming unnatural swellings on the leaf or stem, producing deformed terminal buds. These *galls* provide a place for the insects to live while they suck sap from the plant. Each type has a distinctive shape and inner structure.

HABITAT. The oceans are the home of the greatest variety of animals. Near the sea's surface, sunlight penetrates and enables the small, drifting plants called *phytoplankton* to carry on photosynthesis. Swimming weakly through the phytoplankton and feeding on them are *zooplankton.* Larger animals, called *nekton,* swim strongly and feed on the smaller forms of life. The largest of the nekton are the whales, which may migrate from the Arctic to the Antarctic and back again in a period of a single year.

Deep-sea Dwellers. Many inhabitants of the dark ocean depths are scavengers, dependent on material that sinks from the surface; a few are predators. Even in the muddy ooze that covers the sea floor at the greatest depths, there are animals utilizing the organic materials in the ooze. Many of them eat the bacteria that decompose material that sinks from the surface. Some animals at the deepest levels produce their own light; its function is not certain.

Coastal Dwellers. Much animal life is found near the shores, where the seaweeds are larger and more plentiful because the water is rich in minerals washed from the land. Wave action incorporates air bubbles in the water, thus providing more oxygen for the animal life.

The main danger to coastal dwellers is that of being thrown ashore by the waves. Some, like the sea urchins and sea stars, attach themselves to rocks by means of suction disks. Others burrow, or they live only in areas protected from wave action.

Marsh Dwellers. Animals that live in salt marshes and river estuaries must be able to tolerate great fluctuations of the water's salt content—from very low after a heavy rain to very high after a long drought. This is also true of the plants and animals on which they feed.

Freshwater Dwellers. Fresh water, whether flowing or still, supports fewer forms of life than salt water because it contains fewer dissolved minerals. It is often muddy, however, from undissolved particles. These reduce the amount of light penetrating the water and thus reduce the amount of plant food available to animals.

Fresh waters change level rapidly during floods and droughts, thereby altering the habitat of many creatures. They also freeze over in the winter, thereby greatly reducing the available oxygen and forcing some creatures, such as frogs and turtles, to hibernate.

Land Dwellers. There are many types of habitats to be found on the land, and various types of animals live in each. In the soil there are, among others, earthworms, moles, and many insects. Such animals as bears and deer choose forests or their edges.

The "edge" may grade off into willow or alder swamp, or into grassy field or pasture. In either case, there will be plants for herbivores, small herbivores for medium-sized carnivores, and large herbivores, such as deer, for large carnivores, for example, pumas.

Open plains, covered chiefly by grasses, have inhabitants like antelope, prairie dogs, rabbits, prairie chickens, and vast numbers of grasshoppers and ants. Wolves, coyotes, badgers, and snakes formerly were the main carnivores, but the spread of civilization has greatly reduced their numbers. Summer droughts have also served to curb predators, as well as to keep the herbivores from overgrazing the range.

Water is so scarce in deserts that few animals live there; those that do are generally small and have bodies specially adapted to their habitat. Only a few insects can live on ice or in hot springs. Maggots of one or two kinds of flies have been found at the bottoms of shallow petroleum pools in oil fields, feeding on insects that happen to fall in.

Caves also have special animals that exist as external parasites on bats or eat the mold that grows on the bat droppings. Some of these animals prey on other cave creatures.

STRUCTURE AND FUNCTION. Any animal that is to continue to exist must at some time in its life perform the activities common to all animals: movement; food handling, that is, digestion, absorption, and excretion; respiration; coordination, both chemical and nervous; and reproduction, followed by the growth to maturity of new individuals able to carry on the same activities as the parents.

Structure. *Unicellular* (single-celled) marine animals are believed to have been the first form of life. Today there are about 30,000 species of animals that carry on all of their life processes within the one cell.

Most modern animals are *multicellular* (composed of many cells). Among these, the sponges are unique in that any cell can take over the function of any other cell. A sponge may evolve into a different kind of sponge, but it can never become any other kind of organism.

Function. All multicellular animals except sponges have their cells arranged in layers called *tissues;* each tissue is composed of cells with a definite structure and function. In the higher animals, the tissues are connected in *organ systems.*

A man is composed of organ systems, such as the digestive system; this system in turn is composed of such organs as the esophagus, stomach, intestines, and colon. The stomach is composed of a lining layer, muscle layers, and a covering layer; each tissue layer is composed of a definite type of cell. All multicellular animals have the same general types of tissues.

Contractile tissue, composed of tissues that shorten and lengthen, does the work of the body. This type of tissue forms either muscles moving the body or continuous sleeves around cavities, such as the digestive organs or the blood vessels.

Connective and *supporting tissue* is composed of cells that produce nonliving secretions between themselves. The tissue may be a solid mass in cartilage or bone; or tough strands in tendons, which connect bones; or it may be in ligaments, which connect muscle and bone. Connective tissues form the walls of capsules that hold the lubricant in each joint, as well as fine fibers resembling cobwebs that hold organs in place.

Epithelial tissue is composed of thin tilelike, cuboidal, or close-packed columnar cells that are on the surface of the body or are the lining layer of body cavities, ducts, and tubes. Epithelial cells produce such important nonliving substances as shells, hair, antlers, feathers, milk, sweat, and digestive juices. Some epithelial cells have microscopic extensions called *cilia,* which pulsate and propel fluids over the tissues.

Circulating tissue, or *blood,* is a fluid made of blood cells suspended in plasma. It is circulated by the pulsation of the heart muscles and of the blood vessel walls; it may also move incidentally when the body moves.

Endocrine tissue consists of cells that secrete hormones into the blood, to be carried throughout the body in order to coordinate its activities. The pituitary and thyroid glands are endocrine glands, or glands of internal secretion. *Exocrine* glands, or glands of external secretion, such as sweat glands, are epithelial tissue.

Conducting tissue is characteristic of the nervous system. Its individual cells, known as *neurons,* conduct impulses of electrochemical charge and help to coordinate the body by linking *receptors,* such as the light-sensitive cells of the eye, to *effectors,* the muscle cells or glands that respond. Large units of conducting tissue are *ganglia,* which are clusters of neurons, and such centers as the brain and spinal cord, from which many neurons extend in bundles known as *nerves.*

Reproductive tissue consists of egg cells produced in the female's *ovaries* and sperm cells produced in the male's *testes.* An egg is normally fertilized only by union with a sperm cell, becoming a new individual.

CLASSIFICATION

Animals are identified and grouped into a scheme of classes on the basis of their physical structure and the development of the body parts.

BINOMIAL NOMENCLATURE. The system of naming animals by specifying two names was developed in 1758 by Karl von Linné, a Swedish physician and naturalist. He is better known by his Latin signature, Carolus Linnaeus.

Under von Linné's system, a *species* is a group of creatures that can interbreed with complete fertility; several species may be included in a *genus* if they are very similar in structure, but crosses between two species either result in no offspring or in offspring with incomplete fertility. A familiar example is the mule, which is comparatively sterile. It is produced by a mating between a horse *(Equus caballus)* and a donkey *(Equus asinus).*

Von Linné also saw the need for levels of classification between the animal kingdom and the binomial nomenclature of the individual creature. He therefore set within the animal kingdom, in descending order, the *phylum,* the *class,* the *order,* and the *family,* which is composed of the *genus* and the *species.*

For example, the full classification of man is: phylum *Chordata* (vertebrates and near kin), class *Mammalia* (mammals), order *Primates* (mammals with nails and opposable thumbs or big toes or both), family *Hominidae* (man and manlike primates), genus *Homo,* species *sapiens.*

In some cases, additional levels of classification are added to show differences that are considered important. These include *subphyla,* each with one or more classes; *subclasses,* each with one or more orders; *suborders,* each with one or more families; and *subfamilies.*

TRINOMIAL CLASSIFICATION. Geographical divisions of a species are *subspecies,* also called *races.* The distinction among the members of a species is made by using *trinomial nomenclature.* Thus, for example, the white-footed mouse of Vermont is *Peromyscus maniculatus gracilis;* the white-footed mouse found in Canada north of Lake Superior is *Peromyscus maniculatus maniculatus,* the "typical" or "standard" member of the species. These and all other races of the species will interbreed freely if brought together.

EVOLUTION. The idea of evolution received little attention for more than a century after von Linné established the binomial classification. In 1859 Charles Darwin's *On the Origin of Species by Means of Natural Selection* gave evidence and explanation of change in body form over time.

Darwin pointed out that all animals reproduce faster than is necessary merely to maintain a stable population. Competition develops for food and habitat, and the weaker members of the species, unable to compete effectively, are likely to die before being able to reproduce. Only the fittest survive, and they pass on to their offspring any inheritable advantages.

Gradually a species adapts, splits into races, or dies out. Many extinct species, known only through their fossil records, have been classified through their similarities to living animals. All the animals of today are descended from those of the past and are ancestors of all future animals.

PHYLA

Of the more than one million species that have been named, all but 2 percent are classified in 14 phyla. Small additional phyla have been established for the remaining 2 percent, most of them inconspicuous deep-sea dwellers or parasites.

PHYLUM PROTOZOA. There are about 30,000 species of unicellular "first animals," most of them too small to be seen with the naked eye. They are commonly called *protozoans*.

Class Mastigophora. Because they propel themselves through the water by means of one or more whiplike projections from the body, these "whip-carriers" are called *flagellates*. Some, such as *Euglena*, have a single extension, or *flagellum*. Others have two or as many as ten.

Euglena is a large genus, including many species that contain chlorophyll and carry on photosynthesis. Some of these are so numerous in still water that after a period of heat and drought, the water appears bright green. Many colorless flagellates feed on bacteria. Still others are symbionts of termites, living in their digestive tracts and predigesting the wood fibers the insect swallows.

African sleeping sickness is caused by a parasitic flagellate, *Trypanosoma gambiense*, which is transmitted to man through the bite of the tsetse fly. Ordinarily the parasite lives in various wild animals, which seem to be unaffected.

Class Sarcodina. The most famous sarcodinians are the *amoebas*, the *radiolarians*, and the *foraminiferans*. All move about by extending lobes or networks of protoplasm, called *pseudopodia*, or false feet. Amoebas are extraordinary in that they have no definite shape; they flow into one pseudopodium after another as they travel in fresh water or in the digestive tract of an animal.

Radiolarians and foraminiferans, which live on bacteria and microscopic green plants, produce minute skeletons or chambered shells of either silica or lime, from the surface waters of the oceans. When these sarcodinians die, their skeletons sink to the bottom and build up great thicknesses of ooze. Radiolarian ooze becomes an inert powder suitable for making filters and bonding material in dynamite. Foraminiferous ooze gradually becomes a type of limestone.

Class Sporozoa. All sporozoans are parasites of multicellular animals and absorb their food in dissolved form directly from the *host*, the animal to which they attach themselves. They have no means of moving by themselves but must be transferred from one host to another by the activities of *carriers*, such as mosquitoes.

Perhaps the best-known sporozoan is *Plasmodium falciparum*, the cause of the most dangerous type of malaria in man. It penetrates the red blood cells, reproduces, and causes the cells to break open, releasing more parasites to attack other red cells. Plasmodia are spread by mosquitoes of the genus *Anopheles*, which feed on blood. If an *Anopheles* consumes infected blood, the parasites undergo changes and then migrate to its salivary glands. If the mosquito bites a healthy person, the plasmodia, which go with the saliva into the victim's blood stream, start a new infection.

Class Ciliata. Ciliates are named for the many hairlike *cilia* that project from their microscopic bodies, beating in rhythmic waves and driving the cell through the water. The animals are unique in possessing two different kinds of cell nuclei—*macronuclei* and *micronuclei*.

Ciliates live in water and feed on bacteria and small protozoans. Among the best-known are the slipper-shaped *Paramecium*, the bell-shaped *Vorticella*, and the trumpet-shaped *Stentor*. In a strong light, all of these *animalcules* are large enough to be seen without a microscope.

PHYLUM PORIFERA. Phylum *Porifera* contains some 4,500 species of colonial animals that remain attached to the bottom of the sea or to other solid objects, while cells, known as *flagellated collar cells*, draw water and minute particles of food through small holes that lead to a central chamber or system of chambers. After the collar cells have caught the food particles, the water is released through one or more large openings.

Most of these animalcules, commonly known as *sponges*, are marine; a few live in fresh water.

Class Calcarea. *Calcarea* are marine sponges whose cells secrete needle-shaped or branching *spicules* of lime. The spicules usually project from the surface of the colony and mesh, giving it structural support; however, they are regarded as an internal skeleton. Common genera of this class include *Grantia* and *Leucosolenia*, some of whose species grow to an inch in length.

Class Hyalospongiae. *Hyalospongiae* are deep-sea sponges, often of great beauty, that produce a skeleton of silica. *Euplectella* is the Venus' flower basket sponge.

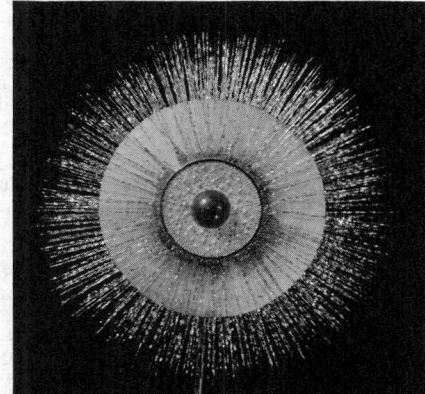

THE RADIOLARIA has an inner skeleton of silica that houses the spherical nucleus.

Class Demospongiae. *Demospongiae,* the commonest sponges, either lack a skeleton or have one composed of a plastic-like secretion called *spongin*. Most of them live in relatively shallow seas, but one family lives in fresh water. The old-fashioned bath sponge is *Spongia*.

The freshwater sponges belong to the genus *Spongilla*; they are usually bright green or golden-green because they have microscopic plants as mutualistic symbionts.

PHYLUM COELENTERATA. The phylum *Coelenterata* is composed of some 9,600 species of aquatic animals, most of them marine, that have a saclike digestive cavity with a mouth opening at one end. The bodies of the coelenterates are radially or biradially symmetrical, with a ring of tentacles surrounding the mouth. On the tentacles, and often elsewhere, there are unique cells with which smaller animals are stung and paralyzed before they are thrust into the digestive cavity of the coelenterate.

Class Hydrozoa. Hydrozoans are characterized by their method of reproduction. Usually a *polyp* (hydroid) stage reproduces by asexual budding and releases free-swimming *medusae* (jellyfishes), which reproduce sexually; the embryos resulting from this mating settle to the bottom, become attached as polyps, and repeat the cycle.

Colonial hydroids include *Obelia* and *Plumularia*, also known as sea firs, and *Millipora*, or stinging coral. Freshwater hydras have no medusa stage, and some of the larger marine hydrozoan medusae have no known hydroid stage. Freshwater medusae are usually *Craspedacusta*.

Hydrozoans also include such free-floating colonies as the Portuguese man-of-war (*Physalia*), the by-the-wind sailor (*Velella*), and the porpita (*Porpita*).

Class Scyphozoa. Scyphozoans, the larger marine medusae, have armlike tentacles extending from the four corners of the pendant, tubular mouth. *Aurelia*, the moon jelly, is commonly found near shore; it is usually about eight inches in diameter. *Cyanea*, a giant medusa of the open ocean, may be seven feet across.

Class Anthozoa. All anthozoans, which are marine, lack a medusa stage; many are colonial. The most familiar are the sea anemones, the true corals, the sea fans, and the sea whips. They differ from other coelenterates in that they have additional cells in the usually noncellular *mesoglea*, or jelly, that separates the outer epithelium (epidermis) and the inner epithelium (gastrodermis). This additional cellular material makes the anthozoans' bodies firmer than those of other coelenterates.

The reef-forming corals obtain lime from seawater through their symbiotic relationship with microscopic green plants. Since reef-making corals depend on green plants, they occur only where sunlight penetrates warm seas.

PHYLUM CTENOPHORA. About 80 species of free-swimming marine animals with transparent, biradially symmetrical bodies make up the phylum *Ctenophora.* Comb jellies, as they are also known, swim by rhythmically beating eight lengthwise rows of paddle-like comb plates.

Ctenophores feed on small planktonic animals that they usually capture by means of tentacles studded with adhesive cells. Many, such as *Mnemiopsis,* are thimble-shaped and glow in the dark when disturbed. *Cestus,* known as Venus' girdle, is ribbon-shaped and can be three feet long and two inches wide.

PHYLUM PLATYHELMINTHES. *Platyhelminthes* phylum is composed of 15,000 species of flat-bodied animals known as flatworms, which are bilaterally symmetrical and have well-organized muscle bands and muscle sheets. Flatworms also have a distinct nervous system consisting of at least one anterior ring of nerve fibers and lengthwise nerve cords.

Class Turbellaria. Turbellarians are free-living flatworms that glide on a ciliated lower epidermis or swim by bodily undulations. Most of these scavengers have a straight, Y-shaped, or multibranched blind digestive cavity. Although they are chiefly marine, turbellarians are also found in fresh water and in very moist soil. Freshwater turbellarians are known as *planarians.*

Class Trematoda. Trematodes are cilialess, parasitic flatworms that have one or more circular suckers with which to attach themselves to a host animal. The blind digestive tract is Y-shaped; the mouth, anterior.

The trematodes include flukes, such as the destructive liver fluke (*Fasciola*) found in sheep; intestinal and pulmonary parasites; and the dangerous African blood fluke *Schistosoma.* Some of the flukes, including *Schistosoma,* undergo a series of complex bodily changes that requires a sequence of hosts, one of which is usually a freshwater snail.

Class Cestoda. Cestodes, also known as *tapeworms,* are parasitic flatworms without digestive systems. They attach themselves to the intestine or body cavity of a vertebrate and absorb food directly.

Most tapeworms consist of an anterior individual (*scolex*) with suckers and hooks, and a series of posterior individuals. The latter are produced asexually by the anterior individual but can develop sex organs and produce fertilized eggs and embryos before breaking away from the oldest part of the chain and emerging from the host's body with the wastes.

Taenia solium, the tapeworm that attacks man when he eats improperly cooked, infected pork, can reach a length of 25 feet.

PHYLUM NEMATODA. The phylum *Nematoda* consists of about 10,500 species of cylindrical, unsegmented animals called roundworms with a straight digestive tube from anterior mouth to posterior anus. Between the outer body wall, which has only lengthwise muscles, and the digestive tract is a bloodlike fluid that churns back and forth as the animal moves.

Some of these roundworms are free-living in moist soil and other aquatic situations, including hot springs and glaciers. However, parasitic nematodes are the best known. *Necator* and *An-*

cylostoma are hookworms that attack man; *Enterobius* is the pinworm; *Trichinella* is a dangerous parasite acquired by eating infected improperly cooked pork. *Filaria* causes elephantiasis.

PHYLUM ROTIFERA. Some 1,500 species of unsegmented aquatic animals, none over 1/16 inch long, compose the phylum *Rotifera.* The head region has a mouth with a muscular grinding mill nearby; two whorls of cilia move food particles toward the mouth and aid in swimming. Posterior to the anus, the wheel animalcule usually has a two-toed foot with cement glands that temporarily anchor the rotifer to a solid object.

Most rotifers are free-living freshwater dwellers. Although they are multicellular, rotifers are approximately the same size as the larger protozoans.

PHYLUM MOLLUSCA. There are about 100,000 living and 40,000 extinct species in the phylum *Mollusca.* All mollusks have a soft muscular, usually unsegmented body with a dorsal mantle that generally secretes a limy shell. Usually the anterior head has a unique rasping instrument, called the *radula,* inside the mouth.

Class Amphineura. The class *Amphineura* consists of the *chitons,* all of which are marine. Most have a dorsal shell consisting of eight transverse overlapping plates. In dangerous situations, chitons curl up to protect the muscular ventral foot, exposing only the hard shell. The class name refers to the two pairs of ventral nerve cords that extend lengthwise from a nerve ring around the chiton's mouth.

Class Scaphopoda. Belonging mainly to the genus *Dentalium* and known as tooth shells, scaphopods are marine mollusks that have a slender, slightly tapered, tubular shell open at both ends. They use their muscular foot, somewhat resembling a horse's foot, to dig themselves into the ocean floor, leaving only the smaller opening of the shell exposed. Through this opening they draw in and expel water and minute particles of food.

Indians on the western coast of North America once used tooth shells as money; natives of New Guinea often wear them as ornaments in pierced ears, noses, and lips.

Class Gastropoda. Some two-thirds of the known species of mollusks are gastropods, known as snails if they have coiled shells, or slugs if they lack shells. All of them creep or cling on a flat, bilaterally symmetrical ventral foot; above the foot is a spiral body covered by the mantle.

Most gastropods are marine herbivores; but some, such as the whelk *Busycon* and the oyster drill *Urosalpinx,* are carnivorous predators.

Physa is a freshwater snail; *Helix pomatea* is the edible garden snail that has been cultivated in Europe for centuries.

Class Pelecypoda. Pelecypods are the *bivalves,* which have two-part limy shells hinged and controlled by muscles between them. These aquatic mollusks are chiefly marine; they are unique in that they lack a head region and a radula. The best-known genera include the scallop *Pecten;* the mussel

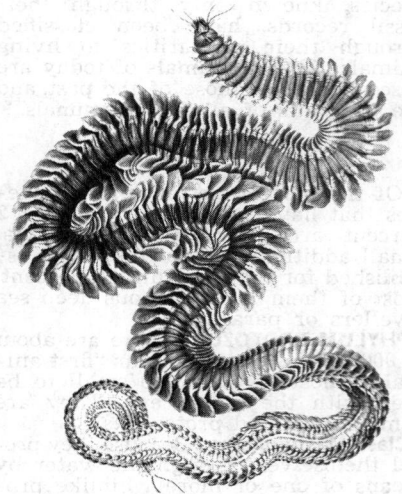

CLAM WORM, *Nereis virens,* shows an evolutionary link between mollusks and annelids.

Mytilus; the oyster *Ostraea;* the freshwater clam *Unio;* and *Tridacna,* the huge bear's-paw clam of the South Pacific reefs.

Class Cephalopoda. Cephalopods are marine mollusks that are "head-footed" in the sense that from eight or ten to as many as ninety tentacles extend from the part of the foot that contains the mouth; the rest of the animal is almost hidden by a high, conical mantle. Among fossil cephalopods a chambered shell was common; today, however, only the pearly *Nautilus* of the East Indies produces such a shell, in whose outermost chamber it lives.

Other living cephalopods have a greatly reduced shell, such as the "cuttlebone" of the cuttlefish *Sepia,* or none at all, as in the eight-tentacled *Octopus.* Most modern cephalopods have a pair of very large, camera-style eyes, which are much like those of vertebrates, and a highly developed brain.

All cephalopods are predators, most of them grasping their victims with suction disks on the tentacles, then rasping out flesh with the radula. Others are equipped with a special pair of concealed horny jaws, like the beak of a parrot, used for biting their prey.

Class Monoplacophora. Monoplacophorans, discovered alive for the first time in 1957, differ from all other mollusks in that they show signs of segmentation. A low, conical, one-piece shell characterizes and names this class, and is attached to the animal by from eight to twelve pairs of muscles. The sides of the flat foot bear a corresponding number of paired gills and excretory organs; the latter resemble those of the segmented worms.

Living species of Monoplacophorans are members of the genus *Neopilina.* Regarded as "living fossils" because they show an evolutionary link between mollusks and annelids, they are found in the deep waters of the eastern Pacific. Fossils of this class have been found in stratified rocks of the early Paleozoic Era, covering a period from the Ordovician Age to the Devonian Age.

PHYLUM ANNELIDA. Some 7,000 species of cylindrical or flattened segmented worms are included in the phylum *Annelida*. The body cavity of annelids is transversely divided into definite segments, each of which usually contains a portion of the straight digestive tract that extends from anterior mouth to posterior anus.

The body cavity also contains a ganglion of the ventral nerve cord; branches of the closed blood-vessel system; a pair of excretory organs, called *nephridia;* and a set of bristles used in locomotion.

Class Polychaeta. Most members of the class *Polychaeta* are marine worms with a distinct head and a fleshy paddle on each side of most body segments. The paddles are supported and moved by the body bristles embedded in them, and both paddles and bristles are controlled by muscles within the body wall.

Many of these annelids, such as the clam worm *Nereis,* are free-swimming predators and scavengers. Others build U-shaped burrows in the bottom mud and use their paddles to create a current that brings a constant supply of food and oxygen through the burrow. Polychaetes include the lugworm *Arenicola* and the parchment worm *Chaetopterus.*

Class Oligochaeta. The best-known oligochaetes are the terrestrial earthworms, which burrow and scavenge in the soil for decaying plant material. Earthworms have no distinct head and no lateral paddles; they creep or cling by means of bristles that can be extended from each body segment.

The body usually has a swelling, the *clitellum,* about one-third of the way along the body from the head. The clitellum provides a sheathlike case for the eggs.

The most common earthworms are *Lumbricus, Allolobophora,* and *Eisenia,* which can be distinguished by the location of the paired pores that connect to the sex organs, Other smaller oligochaetes live in fresh water, where they burrow into bottom sediments.

Class Hirudinea. The class *Hirudinea* is made up of predatory bloodsuckers whose bodies are composed of exactly 34 segments that are concealed among transverse wrinkles. All these annelids have a large posterior sucker; many also have an anterior one surrounding the mouth, which has three horny jaws to capture prey or to cut through the skin of a victim in order to reach the blood vessels.

Most leeches live in fresh water, but a few are marine; there is also one that lives in the rainy Malayan jungles. The medicinal leech, *Hirudo medicinalis,* has long been used in the bloodletting thought to be a remedy for many diseases in various parts of the world.

PHYLUM ONYCHOPHORA. The onychophores are the "velvet worms" or "walking worms" of humid climates, chiefly the tropics. Their cylindrical bodies, which may be as much as eight inches long, have from 15 to 43 pairs of soft legs, each ending in two claws. The anterior head region is indistinct and bears a pair of simple eyes, a pair of short, flexible tentacles, and a pair of blunt *papillae* through which large salivary glands open near the mouth.

Distinct impressions of onychophorans have been found among the oldest fossils, and those species alive today are referred to as "living fossils" because they show features of both arthropods and annelids.

Like other arthropods, they have the periodically shed exoskeleton of chitin; the reduced body cavity, which is mainly replaced by large *sinuses,* or cavities, through which blood flows in an open circulatory system; the system of fine *tubules* through which air reaches inner organs; and claw-tipped legs.

Like annelids, they have paired excretory organs (nephridia) and simple eyes; they also lack a distinct head (or head plus thorax). The best-known of the Onychophores belong to the genus *Peripatus.*

PHYLUM ARTHROPODA. There are more than 770,000 species of arthropods, of which almost 700,000 are insects. Typically, each arthropod has a segmented body enclosed by an external skeleton containing the polysaccharide *chitin;* this *exoskeleton* is shed periodically. Many of the body segments have a pair of jointed appendages, from which the phylum takes its name.

Almost 80 percent of the known animals are included in this phylum, which includes marine, freshwater, and terrestrial creatures of many types: free-living, *sessile* (attached by the base), commensal, and parasitic.

Class Trilobita. Extinct marine arthropods, of which over 2,000 species are known from Paleozoic times, compose the class *Trilobita.* Each had a flattened, elliptical body marked by lengthwise furrows that separated a central lobe and two lateral lobes (the three lobes gave the class its name).

Transversely, the body was divided into a head with a pair of joined antennae, four pairs of jointed *maxillae* (mouth parts), and a pair of compound eyes; a thorax of 2 to 29 segments, each with a pair of jointed appendages used in swimming and creeping; and an abdomen made up of several segments fused into one plate.

All trilobites, the longest of which were 26 inches long, seem to have been scavengers. Their numbers decreased when fishes with jaws, their natural enemies, proliferated.

Class Crustacea. Although generally marine, crustaceans can also be found in fresh water and on land. A few are parasites that attach themselves to fishes. All crustaceans have a head region with two pairs of *antennae,* a pair of *mandibles* (jaws), and at least two other pairs of maxillae. Both the thorax and the abdomen may have paired appendages for swimming and walking.

Familiar genera of these creatures include *Artemia,* the brine shrimp of alkaline lakes; *Balanus,* the acorn barnacle of seacoasts; *Lepas,* the goose barnacle; *Oniscus* and *Porcellio,* terrestrial pillbugs; *Homarus* the Atlantic lobster; and *Callinectes,* the blue crab.

Class Diplopoda. The diplopods are the *millipedes,* or "thousand-legged worms." Each has a pair of antennae, a pair of jaws, and a pair of maxillae on the head; four segments and three pairs of legs on the thorax; and from nine to more than a hundred segments on the trunk. Each of these segments is really two that have been fused in the course of evolution; thus, as the class name indicates, each segment has two pairs of legs.

Most diplopods are harmless terrestrial scavengers that inhabit moist places.

Class Chilopoda. Terrestrial predators commonly known as *centipedes,* chilopods have flattened bodies and only one pair of legs per segment—there may be from 15 to 181 pairs of legs. The head has a pair of jointed antennae; a pair of jaws; and two pairs of maxillae, the second pair partially joined to form a lower lip that gives the class its name.

The first pair of legs are hooklike and have poison glands that open at the sharp tip of each; these poisonous hooks inflict painful or dangerous wounds.

Class Insecta. Almost 700,000 species of insects, the only flying animals without backbones, are known today; and more are discovered every year. Insects are primarily terrestrial arthropods whose bodies are distinctly divided into head, thorax, and abdomen.

The head has a pair of jointed antennae, a pair of mandibles, a pair of jointed maxillae, and a *labium* (lower lip) that evolved from another pair of maxillae; the maxillae may be modified for chewing, sucking, or lapping. Typically, each of the three thorax segments has a pair of legs, in adult insects the second and third segments may also have a pair of wings apiece.

Insects may be classified by structure and by development. Structurally, the details of the maxillae and the wings are considered. The ancient insects are wingless, and change little in body form from hatching to maturity.

The most advanced of modern insects undergo indirect metamorphosis, a spectacular transformation from a specialized *larva* that spends most of its time eating and growing, to a quiet, non-feeding *pupa* that encases the larva, to an adult that reproduces. The wings develop internally during the pupal stage.

Less advanced modern insects experience direct metamorphosis, an incomplete transformation that lacks a pupal stage; the animal progresses from immature stage to mature stage. The wings of these insects develop as pads on the back.

Of the 16 orders described here, the first two are ancient, the next nine have direct metamorphosis with no pupal stage, and the last five have a pupal stage and indirect metamorphosis.

Order *Collembola* is made up of the *springtails,* minute insects that are rarely more than ⅛ inch long and have chewing mandibles. They leap by flipping a special ventral springing organ on the fourth abdominal

THE MONARCH BUTTERFLY is one of roughly 122,000 species of *Lepidoptera*. The butterfly shown is just emerging from its chrysalis.

segment from under a hook on the third segment. The order includes some 2,000 species that live on land, in soil, and over water.

Order *Thysanura* is composed of about 700 species of *bristletails*, including the silverfish *Lepisma*. They grow to 1¼ inches long, and their bodies are covered with overlapping scales. Thysanurans have chewing mandibles and long, threadlike antennae. There is also a pair of antenna-like structures on the posterior end, and the last body segment of thysanurans may extend as a third antenna-like "tail."

Order *Dermaptera* includes the *earwigs,* which may grow to two inches in length and have chewing mandibles and, at the end of the abdomen, a pair of strong forceps. Some are wingless; others have a short pair of leathery wings that, when the animal is at rest, cover a large pair of membranous, semicircular hind wings. Dermapterans include about 1,100 species, some of them harmful to crops.

Order *Orthoptera* includes some 23,000 species of insects, including cockroaches, stick insects, short-horned grasshoppers (locusts), long-horned grasshoppers (including katydids), and crickets. Some of these insects reach a length of 12 inches.

Most of them have as adults a pair of narrow forewings that cover the hind wings when the animal is at rest. The hind wings are folded fanwise. Certain species cause considerable damage to crops.

Order *Isoptera* is made up of the social insects called *termites* or "white ants." All of the some 1,800 species of this class have chewing mandibles and may reach a length of two inches. Only adult sexual individuals have wings, of which there are two narrow membranous pairs. The wings lie flat on the back when the termite is at rest and are detached after the nuptial flight. The thorax and abdomen are joined broadly; there is no "waist" like that of a true ant.

Termites that eat wood depend upon intestinal flagellates to predigest the fibers. Some tropical termites cultivate fungus plants on chewed vegetation, then eat the fungi.

Order *Odonata* contains about 6,000 species of damselflies and dragonflies, which in their immature stages are freshwater predators. Members of the order have chewing mandibles and may reach a length of six inches, with a wingspread up to one foot—fossil dragonflies had wingspreads of as much as 28 inches. Adults have two pairs of membranous wings crisscrossed with many veins; a head with huge compound eyes; and a long, slender abdomen.

Order *Ephemeroptera* consists of the mayflies, of which there are approximately 1,500 species. They have chewing mandibles in the immature aquatic stages, but these become only vestigial at maturity. Mayflies reach a length of as much as two inches but may look longer because the abdominal tip has two or three filamentous "tails."

Mayflies are unique in that they develop wings and emerge from the water before becoming adult; they must shed their skins once more —even over the wings. The wings consist of a large forepair and a small hind pair, both pairs membranous and crisscrossed with veins. Mayflies rarely survive more than a day as an adult, but may require a year or more to reach this stage of development.

Order *Mallophaga* is composed of the biting lice, which grow to ¼ inch long and have chewing mandibles. Their bodies are flat and wingless, and they have either no eyes or small eyes. There are about 2,700 species of biting lice, all of them external parasites on birds and mammals. The genus *Menopon* includes the hen lice.

Order *Anoplura* includes some 200 species of sucking lice, whose flat, wingless bodies may be up to ¼ inch long. These lice have sucking mouthparts and small eyes—or no eyes. *Pediculus capitis* is the head louse, or "cootie," which transmits typhus fever and other diseases; *Haematopinus suis* is the hog louse.

Order *Heteroptera* is the order of the true bugs, which may grow to a length of four inches and have piercing, sucking mouthparts that arise far forward on the head. Some heteropterans are wingless as adults; those

with wings have a forepair that is thick and horny at the base but membranous at the tips, where they overlap when held flat and slightly crossed at rest. The hind wings are membranous and fold slightly below the forewings.

Among the order's approximately 45,000 species are such water striders as *Gerris,* the stinkbugs *Pentatoma,* the milkweed bug *Lygaeus,* and wingless bedbug *Cimex.*

Order *Homoptera* contains the cicadas and their kin, about 25,000 species in all. These insects, many of them injurious to plants, grow to five inches long and have piercing, sucking mouthparts that rise far back on the head. Winged adults have forewings larger than the hind wings; both sets are membranous and at rest are held in tent fashion over the back. Some of the better-known homopterans are the cicadas, aphids (plant lice), scale insects, leafhoppers, and spittle bugs.

Order *Lepidoptera* consists of the moths and butterflies, insects that may have a length of four inches and a wingspread of almost one foot. A caterpillar usually has biting mandibles, three pairs of thoracic legs, up to four pairs of soft abdominal prolegs, and labral openings of silk glands, used in spinning the cocoon. Adults have maxillae joined to form a coiled sucking tube, or *proboscis.* They also usually have two pairs of broad, membranous wings covered by overlapping scales.

There are roughly 122,000 species of lepidopterans, including many that, as caterpillars, eat man's crops or possessions.

Order *Diptera* is composed of the two-winged, or "true," flies. These insects may attain a length of two inches and have a wingspread of three inches. The larval stages are usually legless maggots, some of which have chewing mouthparts. The adults have piercing and sucking, or lapping, mouthparts and one pair of membranous wings; the hind wings are represented by a pair of short, knobbed balancers.

Some of the roughly 90,000 species in the order are the mosquitoes *Anopheles, Aedes,* and *Culex;* the

FULLY EMERGED from its pupa case, the butterfly is in the final stage of its metamorphosis from egg to larva and finally to butterfly.

black flies *Simulium;* the beneficial tachinid flies that parasitize caterpillars; the fruit fly *Drosophila;* the housefly *Musca domestica;* and the wingless sheep tick or sheep ked *Melophagus.*

Order *Coleoptera* is made up of the beetles and weevils, which have biting mandibles in both larval and adult stages and may grow to six inches in length. The larvae are usually wormlike creatures with well-developed legs. Adults have a pair of thick, veinless forewings that, at rest, meet along the midline above the membranous hind wings, whose tips are folded when the wings are not in use.

Coleopterans are the largest order of insects, containing some 260,000 species. Many, such as the ladybug beetle *Coccinella*, are beneficial to man; others, such as the boll weevil *Anthonomus grandis*, are destructive.

Order *Siphonaptera* includes the fleas, which in the adult stage are external parasites on birds and mammals. The minute, legless larvae are scavengers with biting mandibles. The adults, about ¼ inch long, have laterally compressed, wingless bodies; their mouthparts are adapted for piercing and sucking.

Of the approximtely 300 species, two of the best known are *Pulex irritans*, which attack rats and humans, and *Xenopsylla cheopis*, the Indian rat flea, which transmits bubonic plague.

Order *Hymenoptera* takes in the ants, bees, wasps, and their kin, some 103,000 species. Some hymenopterans grow to three inches in length and may have a five-inch wingspread. Their larvae may be either legless maggots or caterpillar-like creatures; the latter are distinguished from caterpillars of the order Lepidoptera by having more than four pairs of fleshy prolegs. Some larvae are parasitic, usually attaching themselves to other insects, or living inside them.

Adults usually are solitary, but some species build colonies and organize societies that show distinct castes. Those adults that can fly have membranous forewings longer than the hind wings; the latter are hooked together in flight. The female's ovipositor is commonly modified as a saw, drill, or stinger.

Among the better-known species of the order are sawflies, with herbivorous, caterpillar-like larvae; beneficial *ichneumon* flies and *chalcids*, which parasitize harmful insects; gall wasps, ants, such as *Formica;* wasps, such as *Vespa* and *Polistes;* bees, such as the bumblebee *Bombus* and domesticated honeybee *Apis mellifera.*

Class Merostomata. Only four "living fossil" species of horseshoe crabs remain of the ancient "divided mouth" class, Merostomata. All of them dwell in shallow, offshore seas, where they scavenge on seaweeds, sea worms, and young mollusks.

Merostomates are armored creatures with an unsegmented *cephalothorax* joined broadly to an abdomen that ends in a bayonet-like tail spine; they lack antennae and true jaws. Food is chewed between the spiny bases of the four pairs of walking legs that flank the elongated mouth slit. Also near the mouth are two pairs of appendages, the usually pincer-like *chelicerae* and the *pedipalpi.*

Perhaps the best-known species is *Limulus*, of the American eastern coast, which comes to shore each spring to lay its eggs in beaches from Maine to Yucatan.

During the Paleozoic Era, the merostomates included sea scorpions, up to six feet long, whose clearly segmented, flexible, tapering abdomens suggest that they may have been the ancestors of land scorpions. Horseshoe crabs, by contrast, have an abdomen fused into a single unit; however, like the sea scorpions, they have a ventral series of five or six pairs of plates that are used in swimming and as protection for the gills.

Class Arachnida. The class *Arachnida* includes some 30,000 species of spiders and their kin. All species have a cephalothorax and an abdomen, a pair of chelicerae, a pair of pedipalpi, and four pairs of legs, but lacks antennae, jaws, and paired appendages on the abdomen.

The class arachnida includes the scorpion *Scorpio*, the house spider *Theridion*, the orb-web spider *Argiope*, the harvestman *Phalangium*, the tick *Dermacentor*, and the spider mite *Tetranychus*. Scorpions, spiders, and many of the mites are predators; ticks and the rest of the mites are external parasites of animals or plants and may transmit diseases from infected hosts to healthy ones.

PHYLUM BRACHIOPODA. Brachiopods, known as lamp shells because of a resemblance between one type of shell and ancient oil lamps, are marine bivalves that secrete the dorsal half and the ventral half of the shell from the mantle. There are 260 living species and over 5,000 fossil species.

Most adult brachiopods remain permanently attached to their surroundings by means of a short posterior stalk that emerges through an opening in the ventral valve of the shell, near the hinge. The unsegmented body has two *lophophores*, spiral or V-shaped arms, from which the phylum takes its name; the lophophores bear ciliated tentacles that create currents to bring oxygen and microscopic food particles into the shell.

One class of brachiopods has a largely chitinous shell and no hinge teeth; these animals include *Lingula* and *Crania*, genera with the longest fossil histories in the animal kingdom. A second class has a limy shell and teeth that keep the halves of the shell in alignment. These include *Terebratulina* and *Rafinesquina.*

PHYLUM ECHINODERMATA. There are roughly 5,700 species of echinoderms (or "spiny skins"), which begin life as bilaterally symmetrical embryos, then take on a false radial symmetry, and still later may become conspicuously biradial or even bisymmetrical; the symmetry usually has five parts.

If the creature has a skeleton, it is internal, composed of limy spicules or plates. Part of the large body cavity is separated to form a unique water-vascular system with special tube-like feet used in feeding and locomotion.

Echinoderms include the sea lilies and feather stars (class *Crinoidea);* sea cucumbers (class *Holothuroidea);* sea urchins, heart urchins, and sand dollars (class *Echinoidea);* sea stars, or starfishes (class *Asteroidea);* and serpent stars, or brittle stars (class *Ophiuroidea).*

PHYLUM CHAETOGNATHA. Roughly 50 species of arrow worms, all of them very slender, cylindrical, and unsegmented, compose the phylum *Chaetognatha*.

The lateral cranial lobes of these three-inch marine predators have chitinous bristles with which prey is captured and pushed into the mouth (hence the phylum name of "bristle jaws"). The digestive tract is straight, and the anus is just anterior to the tail. A pair of lateral fins, supported by fine chitinous rods, give the creature better stability and allow it to dart after minute crustaceans.

The arrow worms' remarkable transparency often causes them to be overlooked. They are plentiful, however, and provide an important source of food for whalebone whales.

PHYLUM CHORDATA. Chordates, of which there are some 45,000 species, are distinguished from all other animals by the development of a flexible supporting rod, called the *notochord*. This lies immediately below the hollow dorsal nerve cord and gives the phylum its name.

At some stage in development, gill slits connect the pharyngeal area to the outside of the body. Usually the body is bilaterally symmetrical and has a complete digestive tract, a closed circulatory system, and a tail posterior to the anus. Four subphyla are recognized.

Subphylum *Tunicata* is composed of about 1,600 marine species that have a notochord and a nerve cord only during the larval stage; the adult is a degenerate form surrounded by a secreted tunic, usually of cellulose.

The most familiar members of this subphylum are the sea squirts (class *Ascidiacea*). They are small and tadpole-shaped as larvae. The adult is permanently attached to the sea floor, where it draws in water, filters out microscopic food and absorbs oxygen, and expels the water.

Subphylum *Cephalochordata* includes about thirty marine species that retain the notochord and the nerve cord; both extend the full length of the body. Cephalochordates are the lancelets, or *amphioxi*, of the class *Leptocardii* and mainly of the genus *Brachiostoma*. They are slender, pointed at each end, and laterally compressed; they swim freely or make shallow burrows in the sandy sea floor near shore.

Subphylum *Agnatha* originally contained the earliest vertebrates, which are known through the fossilized covering of armor-like, bony scales over the head and much of the body; these members of the class *Ostracodermi* apparently were freshwater bottom dwellers during Ordovician, Silurian, and Devonian times.

Class Cyclostomata. Modern agnathans have a cartilaginous troughlike skull and a series of cartilaginous bars protecting the nerve cord. These smooth-skinned, cylindrical, unarmored creatures have horny teeth in their cup-shaped mouths, but no paired fins. They propel themselves by sinuous swimming movements of the whole body.

The hagfishes or slime eels, such as *Myxine,* are direct-developing marine scavengers that eat dead and dying fishes; the lampreys, such as *Petromyzon,* spend at least their larval stage in fresh water and then may move out to sea, where they attack living fishes. *Petromyzon marinus* spread through the Great Lakes in recent years and almost destroyed commercial fishing.

Subphylum *Gnathostomata* consists of chordates with an upper and lower jaw and blocks of cartilage or bone that serve as *vertebrae* and largely or completely replace the notochord in stiffening and supporting the body.

Usually these creatures have paired appendages—a pectoral pair of fins, legs, wings, or arms, and a pelvic pair of fins or legs. If the appendages are fins, the chordate is a fish; if they are limbs, it is a *tetrapod*. Six of the seven classes in the subphylum are represented by living species, the familiar vertebrates.

Class Placodermi. Placoderms (skin of plates) are extinct, jawed fishes that usually had an armor of bony plates or bony scales and two or more pairs of fins. These ancient fish are known from both freshwater and marine fossils of Upper Silurian to Devonian times; the best-known are *Dinichthys* and *Acanthodes*.

Class Chondrichthyes. About 275 living species, all primarily marine, compose this class of cartilaginous fishes that includes the sharks, skates, rays, and chimeras. All of them have cartilaginous rather than bony skeletons (hence the class name); in some, the cartilage is calcified. The scales are minute and usually have an enamel covering over a dentine base, similar to that of teeth.

Class Osteichthyes. A skeleton at least partly of true bone rather than of cartilage characterizes the approximately 25,000 marine or freshwater bony fishes in this class. Their bony scales either fit together in a diamond pattern or overlap like shingles.

Included in the class are the sturgeon *Acipenser,* whose eggs are caviar; the herring *Clupea;* the eel *Anguilla;* the sea horse *Hippocampus;* the cod *Gadus;* the freshwater perch *Perca;* the lungfish *Protopterus;* and the coelacanth *Latimeria,* sole known survivor of the lobe-fin fishes that are close to the ancestral line from which the tetrapods sprang.

Class Amphibia. Most of the nearly 2,000 species of amphibians transform from a gill-breathing immature stage (such as a tadpole) in fresh water to a lung-breathing, terrestrial adult stage. Most adults have forelegs and hind legs, the latter linked by way of a pelvic girdle to a specialized sacral vertebra. Unlike fishes, which have a two-chambered heart, adult amphibians have a three-chambered heart.

Common genera include the mud puppy *Necturus*, the salamander *Ambystoma*, the frog *Rana*, and the toad *Bufo*.

Class Reptilia. Some 5,000 living species of tetrapod chordates that have a dry skin, usually covered with overlapping scales, belong to the class *Reptilia* (creepers). Their skeletons are completely bony, and the pelvic girdle, if present, is linked to two sacral vertebrae.

These turtles, snakes, lizards, and crocodilians all obliterate the gill slits while developing within the egg; at no stage do they possess gills. Special membranes extend from the embryo to the eggshell and enable the embryo to breathe while surrounded by a watery egg "white" provided by the mother. Presumably the dinosaurs and all other extinct reptiles, including some that flew, were similar in general structure and development to modern reptiles.

Class Aves. More than 8,600 living species of birds are known, all of them warm-blooded and covered with feathers. They have a four-chambered heart and a system of blood vessels that carries all blood from the heart to the lungs for aeration before pumping it through the body again.

Other characteristics of birds are a mouth with a specialized beak; one pair of wings; and one pair of legs, which are linked to several vertebrae by way of a light but strong pelvic girdle. All birds lay eggs. Most can fly, but some—such as the ostrich *Struthio,* the kiwi *Apteryx,* and the penguin *Spheniscus*—are flightless and apparently had completely flightless ancestors.

Some well-known genera of class *Aves* are the domestic duck *Anas,* the fowl *Gallus,* the pigeon *Columba,* the crow *Corvus,* and the sparrow *Passer.*

Class Mammalia. There are more than 4,500 species of living mammals, all of them warm-blooded and at least partly covered with hair. The four-chambered heart pumps the blood through the lungs before it is circulated through the body. The pelvic girdle is fused to five vertebrae. Mothers secrete milk from special *mammary glands,* from which the newborn young gain nourishment. Twelve of the eighteen orders are of special interest.

Order *Monotremata* is composed of the egg-laying mammals. Some five genera belong to this order, all being found in Tasmania, New Guinea, and Australia; they include the duckbill or platypus *Ornithorhynchus* and the spiny anteater *Tachyglossus.* Only the young have teeth; adults have a horny beak. The large, yolky eggs are unique among mammals, as is the practice of incubating them.

The order is named to draw attention to the single body opening (cloaca) that serves the digestive, urinary, and reproductive tracts.

Order *Marsupialia* is made up of the pouched mammals, of which all but the American opossums inhabit Australasia. Unlike class Monotremata, the adult marsupials have teeth. The females have a pouch on the undersurface of the abdomen; the extremely immature newborn young creep in, attach themselves to a nipple, and remain attached until fully formed.

In all other orders of mammals (except Monotremata), the young are linked to the mother by a special membrane *(placenta)* formed by the embryo and used to transfer food and oxygen from the mother to the embryo, and wastes, including carbon dioxide, from the embryo to the mother. Such mammals are placental mammals.

Order *Insectivora* contains the insect-eating moles and shrews and their kin. These small mammals have pointed snouts and sharp teeth that are less specialized than those of other orders. The upper jaw has six to eight incisors, one pair of canine teeth, and three to four pairs of grinding teeth (molars and premolars); the lower jaw has no canines and often has fewer incisors.

Widely known genera are the mole *Talpa*, the shrews *Sorex* and *Blarina*, and the European hedgehog *Erinaceus*.

Order *Chiroptera* is composed of the bats, the only mammals that are capable of flapping flight. They fly by using their modified forelimbs, whose second to fifth toes are greatly elongated and support a thin, leathery membrane that extends to the hind legs, and usually to the short tail as well. The upper jaw often has one pair of incisors; the lower jaw, three.

Order *Primates* includes the monkeys and apes and their kin. Usually there are fewer incisors on both upper and lower jaws. Nails, rather than claws, are found on at least some fingers and toes. Characteristically, either the thumbs or great toes—or both—are opposable, and the shoulder girdle is linked to the breastbone by a collarbone on each side.

Modern man, *Homo sapiens*, and species of fossil man belong to this order, along with the chimpanzee *Pan*, the gorilla *Gorilla*, the orangutan *Pongo*, the rhesus monkey *Macacus*, the capuchin monkey *Cebus*, and the lemur *Lemur*.

Order *Edentata* includes the anteaters, sloths, and armadillos, about 30 different kinds of which live in tropical and warm-temperate America. The name means "without teeth," but actually only the anteaters are toothless. No kind has incisor or canine teeth, and there is no enamel on the premolar and molar teeth with which sloths and armadillos chew their plant food.

Order *Pholidota* consists of seven different kinds of pangolins, or scaly anteaters, of tropical Africa and Southeast Asia. These mammals are also toothless. They capture insects, particularly ants and termites, with a long, slender, sticky tongue and swallow the prey whole.

Order *Lagomorpha* includes rabbits and their kin. These animals may be distinguished by their teeth: two pairs of incisors in the upper jaw, one pair behind the other; one pair of incisors in the lower jaw; no canine teeth. The lower jaw can move from side to side but not from front to back; the jaws are not opposable. The tail is short. Some common genera are the pika or coney *Ochotona*, the hare *Lepus*, and the cottontail rabbit *Sylvilagus*.

Order *Rodentia* is made up of gnawing mammals that have only two incisors in the upper jaw and two in the lower; they have no canine teeth. Rodents have opposable jaws, and their lower jaws move forward and backward as well as from side to side.

Common rodents include the squirrel *Sciurus*, the marmot *Marmota*, the rat *Rattus*, the mouse *Mus*, the beaver *Castor*, the porcupines *Hystrix* and *Erethizon*, and the South American capybara *Hydrochaerus* (the largest rodent, which grows to four feet in length).

Order *Carnivora* comprises land mammals with well-developed canine teeth used in tearing the flesh of their animal food. They have six small incisors above and below. Included in the order are the dog, wolf, and coyote *Canis*, the bear *Ursus*, the cat *Felis*, and weasel *Mustela*.

Order *Pinnipedia* consists of swimming mammals similar in many ways to carnivores, such as the seal *Phoca*, walrus *Odobenus*, and sea lion *Zalophus*.

Order *Tubulidentata* contains only the aardvark *Orycteropus* of Africa south of the Sahara. It resembles a large-size pig with teeth of a strange, tabular form found only in the sides of the mouth.

Order *Proboscidea* is now represented by only one type of animal, the elephant. These massive, thick-skinned mammals have a nose and upper lip that extend into a trunk tipped with nostrils.

The two upper incisors are elongated as tusks, and only one or two molars at a time are on each side of the upper and lower jaws; there are no canines or premolars. The teeth are large and have many folded rows of enamel.

An elastic pad behind the toes bears the animal's weight; the toes have nail-like hoofs on three to five digits, depending on the species.

Order *Artiodactyla* contains the even-toed hoofed mammals. These animals have two or four toes; on each toe is a horny hoof that reaches the ground. *Sus*, the boar or pig, and *Hippopotamus* have four toes on each foot. They also have a simple stomach.

Other artiodactyls have two toes on each foot and a four-part stomach; they chew regurgitated food in the form of a cud. Included in this second group are the camel, the caribou, the deer, the cow, the giraffe, the antelope , the sheep, the goat, and the musk ox.

Order *Hyracoidea* contains nine kinds of African and Near Eastern animals known as conies, dassies, or hyraxes, whose toes bear flattened nails resembling hoofs—four on the front feet and three on the rear. The

BIRTH OF AN OSTRICH. The egg, which is the largest laid by any living bird, is deposited in the sand and incubated by the heat of the sun. The ostrich, a flightless bird, lives in many parts of Africa.

EARL THEISEN

soles of the feet have special suction cups that help the animals climb on rocks and trees.

Order *Sirenia* is composed of four kinds of sea cows, large animals of the seacoasts that are said to have confused homesick sailors into believing in mermaids.

Order *Perissodactyla* is composed of the odd-toed hoofed animals. They bear their weight on either the middle toe or the three middle toes; there is a hoof on each functional toe. There are no canine teeth, but there are incisors and molars in both jaws. The stomach is simple, so no cud is formed. The best-known genera include the horse and zebra *Equus*, the tapir *Tapirus*, and the rhinoceros *Rhinoceros*.

Order *Cetacea* contains the whales and their kin. Toothed whales, such as the sperm whale *Physeter*, the killer whale *Orcinus*, and the dolphin *Delphinus*, have identical enamel-less teeth and are carnivorous, preying on fishes, squids, and other marine animals.

Toothless (whalebone) whales, such as the great blue whale *Balaenoptera* (which, at 110 feet and 150 tons, is the largest animal of all time) and the right whale *Balaena*, strain food from the sea between parallel fringed plates of whalebone that hang from the inside of the upper jaw.

Both types of whale have a body highly adapted for swimming and diving: the forelimbs are reduced to flippers, the hind limbs have disappeared (although a pelvic girdle remains), and the tail is flattened into a pair of transverse fleshy flukes.

ZOOLOGY IN PERSPECTIVE

The scientific study of animals, with information carefully arranged, began with the works (336–323 BC) of Aristotle—the "Father of Zoology"—a Greek physician and naturalist who studied under Plato and served as tutor to the prince who later became Alexander the Great. Through his works, Aristotle showed himself eager for knowledge for its own sake and ready to relate his knowledge of nonhuman creatures to man.

For some 1,800 years after Aristotle, few people realized that some ideas and information in his works were incomplete and erroneous, and that new discoveries could be important. Among the first to correct Aristotle's mistakes was Andreas Vesalius (1514–1564), a Belgian physician, whose illustrated work on human anatomy appeared in 1543 and earned him the reputation of the "Father of Modern Anatomy." A Swiss contemporary of Vesalius, the naturalist Konrad von Gesner (1516–1565), compiled information on the known kinds of animals in a five-volume encyclopedia he published between 1551 and 1587.

In the 1600s, 1700s, and 1800s, discoveries came so quickly that it was hard for zoologists to fit them all together, and some facts remained unappreciated for many years. Even details visible through the microscope did not lead to immediate understanding.

Milestones in this period included William Harvey's (1578–1657) proof that the human heart circulates blood (1628), Robert Hooke's (1635–1703) discovery and naming of cells in cork (1665), Jean Baptiste de Lamarck's (1744–1829) conclusion that living things are evolving (1801—his theory that evolution came about through use and disuse was disproved), and Mattias Schleiden (1804–1881) and Theodor Schwann's (1810–1882) theory that all living things are either cells or composed of cells. Many zoologists after 1760 were content to improve upon the classification system established by Karl von Linné (1758).

EVOLUTION. Just as Schleiden and Schwann's cell theory provided a unifying concept among living things, so the theory of evolution provided an explanation for Sir Richard Owen's (1804–1892) principles of homology and analogy, set forth in 1843. Overwhelming evidence that evolution had occurred and a theory of its method through natural selection was provided in 1859 when Charles Darwin (1809–1882) published his book *On the Origin of Species*.

Darwin's lack of information on genetics forced him to assume that the visible variations he saw in each species followed an inheritable pattern. This first book and his later works stimulated zoologists all over the world to fresh research, which uncovered a wealth of new evidence supporting the theory of organic evolution.

The first experimental work to support Darwin's work came during his lifetime, in the statistical studies of inheritance in garden peas by the Austrian monk Gregor Mendel (1822–1884). This work, published in 1865, was not "discovered" until 1900, when three different research scientists brought it to the world's attention. In the meantime, W. Kuhne had discovered the nature of enzyme action (1878), W. Flemming had gained a consecutive understanding of the events in the cell division (1882), E. Van Beneden had discovered *meiosis* (1887), and Henry F. Osborne (1857–1935) had recognized the evolutionary principle of adaptive radiation.

MOLECULAR STUDIES. Many recent discoveries and theories have drawn attention to chemical similarities among animals, among plants, and between plants and animals. They have focused attention at the molecular level, leading to a greater appreciation of the steps in organic evolution—particularly those that occurred before the animals that have left fossils.

In 1916, Thomas H. Morgan (1866–1945) presented his theory of the gene; in 1953, the nature of the genetic code, in terms of the molecular structure of the DNA in the chromosomes, was visualized from the work of M. H. F. Wilkins, F. H. C. Crick, and J. D. Watson; today the fine details of the code are being worked out.

In 1929, K. Lohmann discovered ATP, the carrier of energy in living systems; in 1937, Sir Hans Krebs accounted for the citric acid cycle in the mitochondria of each cell as it carries on respiration, using oxygen and producing ATP.

Wendell Stanley (1904–1971) discovered in 1935 that a virus can be purified until it becomes a nonliving crystal without losing its ability to cause a disease; this reopened the question of the line between the living and the nonliving and led to new considerations of the origin of life and the chemical evolution that preceded the appearance of recognizable plants and animals. In 1953, in Harold Urey's laboratory, Stanley L. Miller demonstrated that organic compounds can form spontaneously under conditions very similar to those that geologists envision for the Earth during the Archeozoic Era.

NEW PERSPECTIVES. With all of this information, the zoologist is able to interpret the range of animal life, both extinct and living, in a new way. He sees the first long period after life began as one during which chemical systems evolved. To survive, each system had to meet the fundamental requirements for life: the ability to absorb from its environment the chemical substances and energy it needed and the ability to reproduce. The zoologist assumes that an almost infinite number of combinations was tried and that each successful one progressed by adding slight variations that improved its chances of survival.

Until a modern form of photosynthesis released quantities of oxygen into the atmosphere, it is believed that there was no basis for *aerobic respiration* on Earth. It is possible that some ancestors of protozoans lived without oxygen, and the same may be true of unicellular ancestors of other phyla.

Predatory animals could not have existed until oxygen was present, for only aerobic respiration allows rapid expenditure of energy for more than a few seconds. Multicellular parasites can thrive without oxygen, but only so long as they have larger, multicellular hosts that carry on aerobic respiration.

Since the Cambrian Age, which began some 550 million years ago, when animals reached a size and firmness of body that made fossils possible, essentially all the phyla—and many of the classes—are represented. Each ancestral line is of about the same length, but some animals have changed more in structure than others. To a great extent, the ones that have changed most have spread from the sea to fresh water and onto the land, into deserts, hot springs, and petroleum pools; today, the seas hold most of the animals that have changed least.

Although all animals have become more specialized in structure and function, some have become too specialized to survive a change in environment. An example is the dinosaurs, which became extinct with the advent of the Ice Age. Thus, the phyla of modern animals are regarded as alternative ways of living, all equally successful in their respective environments and all incorporating general features of life that evolved before the Cambrian Age.

—*Lorus J. Milne and Margery Milne*

ANIMAL BEHAVIOR

People speak of animal behavior, but not usually of plant behavior. This is because the word *behavior,* as applied to animals, refers to the movements of animals — what people can observe animals doing. While some plants, such as the mimosa or Venus flytrap, can move a little, and a few animals, such as oysters or sponges, do not seem to move very much, the most noticeable difference between plants and animals is movement, and movement is behavior.

This noticeable behavior in animals is a direct result of the basic difference between plants and animals. Plants, in general, obtain their energy from sunlight and nonliving sources. (Again, the Venus flytrap is one of the exceptions, as it obtains part of its energy from eating insects.) Animals, on the other hand, obtain their energy from living sources — plants, other animals, or remains of plants or animals. A plant can stay in one spot for all of its life. If the spot is reasonably sunny and if rain washes the right chemicals to it, a plant can survive with limited and slow movements or none at all. To obtain the energy animals need, however, most animals must move through their environment, searching out that energy. Animals such as oysters, which do not move much, live in an environment that moves through them. Oysters force water through their bodies, carrying food with it.

Not all animal behavior consists of moving through the environment, however. Because animals can move, they can develop behaviors other than the simple search for food. For example, because they are moving through the environment, animals of one sex must seek out animals of the other sex to mate. Complex mating behaviors are one result. Also, if all the animals of one type were to move to the same place, they would soon run out of the food source at that place. Therefore, animals have developed behaviors designed specifically to keep members of the same species apart. However, since some animals eat other animals as energy sources, the animals that are the victims may have developed behaviors that keep them together, for better protection from their predators; or the victims may have developed other means of avoiding predators. In turn, the predators have developed behaviors that help them overcome the defenses of their prey.

Understanding Animal Behavior

In addition to movement, animals have had to develop senses to locate their food. We human beings are animals, and we commonly recognize the five human senses as sight, hearing, taste, smell, and touch (although there are also some other human senses, such as the sense of knowing where the parts of your body are in space). Most animals have developed similar senses, but they are not necessarily the same. As a result, the behavior an animal exhibits may be caused by some feature in its environment of which humans are unaware. It is not always easy to understand why an animal behaves as it does. For example, some animals are color blind, so they see the world very differently from human beings that are not color blind. To a dog, the environment is all shades of gray.

When you observe that bees get their energy from nectar in flowers, and that most flowers are brightly colored, it is easy to assume that bees' behavior is governed by the fact that they are *not* color blind. Careful tests, however, show that bees do not see the same colors that human beings do. Bees can see ultraviolet light, which is invisible to human beings, but they cannot see pure red, which is a very bright color for humans. (In fact, we see red and yellow better than we see other colors.) If flowers were pure red, they would be black to bees. A poppy that we see as pure red, however, also reflects ultraviolet light that the bee can see and we cannot.

Since bees (and some other insects) can see ultraviolet light, it is natural to ask if some animals can see infrared light. So far as is known, no animals can see infrared light with their eyes. Some snakes, however, including rattlesnakes, have pits below their eyes that can detect infrared radiation. This enables them to "see" and attack prey in the dark, just as modern soldiers use infrared-detecting devices to see in the dark.

Just as some animals can see light that human senses cannot perceive, other animals can hear sounds that we cannot hear. For example, bats have very poor eyesight, yet they fly in total darkness and even catch small insects in the air in the darkness. They are able to behave this way because they have the ability to make and hear sounds that are higher in pitch than humans can detect. They use the echoes of their high-pitched squeaks for navigation just as the echoes from radio waves are used in radar.

Other animals can smell odors that

THOUGH NEARLY BLIND, *a bat navigates safely through the air by means of its "radar."*

humans cannot. The color-blind dog, whose visual world is all shades of gray, lives in a world of smells that we can only imagine.

Just as some human beings are color blind, and others are not, some human beings cannot taste some substances that others taste. This kind of difference in taste surely extends to the animal kingdom. For example, the caterpillar of the monarch butterfly eats nothing but milkweed. The juice of the milkweed is very bitter and poisonous to most other animals, yet it must taste good to a monarch caterpillar. One result of the caterpillar's milkweed diet is that the monarch is bitter and poisonous itself, even after it has turned into a butterfly. So one consequence of the feeding behavior of the monarch is protection from predators.

Other animals have senses that are not just different in degree from ours; they are different in kind. Fish, for example, have a sense organ on the sides of their bodies called the *lateral line*. Lateral lines can detect small changes in the pressure of water, but scientists are not sure what fish use these organs for. Some fish also have sense organs that detect electric currents. These fish include those, such as electric eels, that can also produce large amounts of electricity; but other fish, which cannot produce much electricity, also have organs to detect it. Perhaps such fish use their ability to detect electricity to avoid fish that produce it, for the fish that produce strong electric currents use these currents to stun their prey. On the other hand, it appears that some fish use the weak electric currents as a means of finding their own prey in the dark.

Other senses that have been found in animals include the ability to sense magnetic fields and to tell polarized from unpolarized light. The ability to detect the magnetic field of Earth may be used by some birds to navigate in their great migrations. The ability to tell polarized from unpolarized light is used by bees to find their way back to their hives on cloudy days.

Not only do we not know exactly how animals perceive the world, but also we do not know what internal reactions animals are having to what they perceive. Animals cannot tell us directly why they behave as they do. It is, then, unsafe to assume that an animal that behaves the way a human does is doing so for the same reasons.

For example, if a goose's egg rolls out of the nest, the goose stretches its neck out and rolls the egg back in with its bill. This appears to be parental concern, but experiments show that the egg-rolling behavior is a chain of movements stimulated by seeing the egg outside the nest. In fact, if the egg is removed after the chain has begun, the goose continues the movements until the chain is complete.

Purposes of Behavior

Although there are many barriers to understanding animal behavior, scientists from many nations have made considerable progress in recent years. In particular, a group of scientists known as *ethologists* have specialized in this work. These include Konrad Z. Lorenz from Austria, Karl von Frisch, who is also from Austria, and Niko Tinbergen from the Netherlands, who does most of his research in England.

These ethologists found that the behavior of animals is extremely varied. The "problems" of finding food, avoiding predators, and reproducing seem to have as many "solutions" as there are species. What follows is just a sampling of how different species have "solved" these problems.

Food. Everyone has observed a robin or other bird pecking at the lawn or a squirrel hiding nuts in the ground. These are relatively simple behaviors that locate, capture, or store food. Many animals have developed more complex behaviors for these purposes. As might be expected, the most complex behaviors tend to be those of animals that eat other animals.

Among the insects, for example, there is the ant lion. This creature digs a pit and buries itself at the bottom. It is waiting for ants to fall into the pit where they can be eaten. Some wasps, on the other hand, actively seek their prey, limiting themselves to just a few species of prey. Some ants keep herds of aphids in shelters that the ants make. As the aphids feed on plants, the ants stay with them and consume sweet juices that the aphids give off. While one generally thinks of predators killing their prey, insects such as female mosquitoes of some species attack large mammals and feed from their blood. (The males of these species feed on plant juices.) Lice are parasites; they live on the animals from which they feed. Even in this one animal group, then, there are many different behaviors for obtaining food.

Often the nature of the food sought determines the behavior. Most members of the cat family eat fairly small animals. They hunt alone. Lions, on the other hand, eat animals that are bigger than they are. Female lions work together in cooperative groups to kill their prey. The males join in the eating, but not the killing. Thus, in the case of the cat family, the difference in prey size determines whether the species will tend to be solitary or to live in small groups.

Stabilization. The first task for a moving animal is to orient itself to its

environment. A bird would not fly very far upside down, so it must develop a behavior that will cause it to fly rightside up.

Fish have the same problem of keeping upright in water. Most fish have small internal pads covered with sensitive hairs on which a small object rests. If the fish leans very far from the upright position, the object moves. This movement produces a sensation in the fish that causes it to right itself.

Sometimes an animal will use more than one sense to orient itself. Fish that swim near the surface of clear water may also use the direction that light comes from to keep upright.

Not only must the external environment be kept stable by behavior, but also the internal environment of an animal must be stabilized. Reptiles, for example, do not have the kind of internal devices that birds and mammals have for keeping blood at the right temperature. Lizards often solve this problem by moving from sun to shade to sun with just the right frequency to stabilize their blood temperature.

Protection. Many animals have developed behaviors that help them avoid becoming prey. These range from the obvious strategy of hiding in holes, as many small mammals do, to unexpected strategies. The opossum "plays 'possum"; that is, it pretends to be dead if it is frightened. Another strategy, widely practiced, is the release of unpleasant chemicals. This protective behavior occurs in ants, bugs, and skunks, among others.

One of the most common protective behaviors is camouflage. A caterpillar may match exactly the color of the leaves on which it feeds. In fact, in some species, the caterpillar will match the topside of the leaf. If placed on the underside of a leaf, which is a slightly different shade of green, the caterpillar will move quickly to the top. One of the champions of camouflage is the chameleon, which changes colors to match its environment. Less well known for changing colors are the cichlid fish, which can change not only their colors but even their patterns of color.

The true champions of camouflage, however, are insects. There is a tropical katydid whose wings look exactly like a leaf; a walking stick, an insect that looks like a twig; and a twig caterpillar, whose behavior consists largely of remaining motionless. In fact, if a twig caterpillar is dislodged from the branch of its tree, it continues to remain motionless on the ground. Therefore, it continues to look like an inedible twig instead of like an edible caterpillar.

Some insects even disguise themselves as other insects. This practice is called mimicry. The robber fly, which has no sting, mimics the bee, which

PROTECTIVE BEHAVIOR *in the opossum and in the Kallima butterfly (far left). The opossum "plays dead" when threatened; the butterfly in resting position mimics a leaf.*

protects itself with a poisonous sting. A toad that knows about bees (from having been stung) avoids not only bees, but also robber flies. On the other hand, a toad that knows only about robber flies is happy to eat as many as it can.

As noted earlier, the monarch butterfly is protected because of its bad taste, acquired from milkweed. Like many poisonous or bad-tasting animals, the monarch is brightly colored. Another butterfly, which does not taste bad, mimics the bright orange-and-black pattern of the monarch. The viceroy butterfly looks and behaves enough like a monarch to escape predation by birds that have had the unpleasant experience of eating a monarch butterfly.

Reproduction. Many specialized behaviors are connected with mating. For animals whose behaviors spread them over a wide area, there is a need for behavioral methods to bring the males and females together when they are ready to mate. One method that has been studied since the 18th century is the one used by many species of moth.

When a female moth is ready to mate, male moths from miles around fly unerringly to where the female is. Careful experiments have shown that this behavior in male moths is caused by an odor produced by the female. Extremely tiny amounts of her chemical in the air are perceived by the male moth. The odor causes him to fly toward its source, the female.

Raising young. While for many animals mating behavior is over when eggs are laid or young are born, for others there are complex behaviors involved in feeding and caring for the young. Birds and many fish build nests in which the eggs are laid. If the young are helpless, as baby gulls are, the parents must bring food to the young. They must also protect their young from predators. One unusual behavior for protecting the young is

found in certain cichlid fish. When danger threatens, the young swim into the mouth of their parent. The young are released unharmed when the danger has passed.

Dispersal. If all of one kind of animal stayed in the same place or moved together, they would soon exhaust the food supply. Also, the species would not have the diversity it needs if the young interbred for several generations. Special behaviors prevent these possibilities. In baboons, young males are regularly expelled from troops when they are no longer dependent on their mothers. They live on their own until they are old enough to win acceptance in another troop or to start a troop of their own.

Separation of species. Other special behaviors ensure that two members of related species do not breed with each other or do not compete for exactly the same source of food. For example, related species of insect-eating birds may be separated because one always feeds on the ground, another catches insects in the air, and a third eats insects it finds on the trunks of trees. Two closely related species of moth, which can breed with each other in a laboratory, do not do so in nature. In nature they emerge from their cocoons at different times of the year. In fact, the two species of moth never meet each other except in the laboratory.

Reduction of conflict. Other behaviors protect the members of one species from each other. Female spiders have a tendency to treat male spiders as food. In some species, the male spider has developed a behavior to prevent this. When the male spider wants to mate, he kills an insect and brings the remains to the female. The female eats the dead insect instead of the male spider.

Among mammals and birds, special postures are used to indicate that an

animal does not want to fight. When a male bison turns its head to one side, he is accepting dominance by another male bison. In that case, conflict is avoided. A dog wanting to avoid conflict lowers the front part of his body and points his nose in the air, exposing his throat. In species whose members fight with one another, most fights end when one member uses such a signal. As a result, animals seldom kill members of their own species.

Complex Behavior

In developing behaviors for various purposes, many animals use complex behavior patterns. These patterns, which are repeated in different ways throughout the animal kingdom, often combine several purposes. Some complex behaviors are so ingrained in animals that the behavior seems to become the purpose.

Communication. How animals communicate with each other and the extent of their abilities in communication has always been of interest. Wrapped up in these issues is the question of how much an animal really understands. When you call your dog's name and he comes to you, you are communicating with your dog. But does the dog know that the sound you make is his name?

The most sophisticated system of animal communication known (outside of the human system), is the dance of the honeybee. When a honeybee finds a food source, it returns to the hive to perform a complex dance that tells 1) that it has found food, 2) the direction of the food, and 3) the distance to the food. The dancing bee uses a figure 8 to show that food has been found. It uses a straight run to show the direction of the food; the length of the straight run indicates how far away the food is. Bees in the hive that see the dance leave the hive within minutes and fly directly to where the food source is located.

In other animals, communication rarely carries as much specific information as the honeybee's dance. Animals may use either one or both of two types of communication: the discrete signal or the graduated signal. A discrete signal is one with a specific meaning. For example, the vervet, an African monkey, makes one alarm cry for snakes or other ground-based danger and a different alarm cry for threatening birds of prey. These are discrete signals. If a troop of vervets hears the alarm for snakes, they look to see where the snake is, since it can be avoided if its location is known. When they hear the alarm for birds of prey, they scatter into hiding in the forest.

Graduated signals are more common than discrete signals. For example, squirrels signal hostility by waving their tails. The faster the waving, the more hostile the squirrel is.

While human beings communicate largely with sounds and body positions or movement, many animals use chemicals for communication. The odor that attracts males given off by the female moth is a form of communication. Ants use chemicals as graduated signals to indicate such things as amount of alarm, or the amount of food they have located. Many mammals use chemicals to indicate the limits of a region they feel in possession of — their territory.

Territory.

From the time of Aristotle, at least, it has been recognized that some animals defend a particular territory from other members of the same species. In recent years, the behavior called *territoriality* has been closely studied in many different animals.

Territoriality usually involves some combination of the following features: 1) the behavior tends to involve males more than females; 2) there is a specific location that is defended; 3) the defender of the territory usually succeeds in its defense; 4) special and often dramatic behaviors are developed for territory defense; and 5) neither the defender nor the attacker is injured during the process. In many cases, particularly among birds and fish, all five of these characteristics are present.

Frequently, the songs of male songbirds are intended to warn other males not to invade the territory of the singer. The same song has the additional function of welcoming female songbirds of the same species into the territory. Many species are territorial only during the mating season.

There are many different functions for territorial behavior, but one of the most common is the spreading of the species out over its range. When all the territories are occupied, the species has a kind of built-in population control.

Social space.

Some animals, such as leopards, travel alone except when involved in mating and raising young. Others, such as American bison, travel in great herds. Yet, even in herds, a minimum space between animals is usually kept. This space is different for different species of animal. (Among human beings, social scientists have also discovered that the socially acceptable minimum distance varies from culture to culture.) For example, it has been shown that swallows do not like to roost less than 15 centimeters apart, while flamingos prefer to keep 60 centimeters apart. If such birds are kept closer artificially,

they will move apart as soon as the restraint is lifted.

When the socially accepted minimum distance is small, animals may live together in organized societies. Depending on the species of animal and the size of the society, these groups may be called bands, troops, herds, or swarms. Since members of such societies interact with each other on a more or less continuous basis, they develop behaviors to control these interactions. One particular behavior that is quite common is the dominance hierarchy.

Dominance.

Dominance is sometimes known as the pecking order, since the hierarchy in domestic chickens is formed by pecking. A more dominant chicken is permitted to peck a less dominant one. Every chicken can peck the bottom chicken on the ladder.

Other dominance relationships are not necessarily so linear. For example, among the spider monkeys of South America, males tend to be dominant over females and adults over juveniles, but changes among the relationships occur frequently. The pecking order for chickens, however, once established, tends to remain stable. In general, the dominant animals have better access to both food and to choice of partners in mating.

Migration.

Whether found in fish, such as eels and salmon, or in birds, such as geese and swallows, the mysteries of animal migration have proved to be an excellent way to understand how animals perceive the world. Eels take two years to get from their birthplace in the middle of the Atlantic Ocean to their freshwater adult homes in Europe and North America. They use the tides as one means of guidance. Salmon, which return to the small stream of their birth, hundreds of miles inland, rely on smell. When the river branches, the salmon smell that the water in the correct branch comes from the stream of their youth, something that they may not have smelled for as many as five years.

The mechanisms that migrating birds use to find their way can be studied conveniently with homing pigeons. Pigeons use at least three different ways to find directions: 1) the position of the sun; 2) Earth's magnetic field; and 3) some mysterious method that no one, as yet, understands. This third method can be inferred from experiments in which pigeons cannot see the sun, have magnets attached to their bodies, and yet still find their way.

Innate or Learned?

A major question about animal behavior concerns whether animals are born knowing how to behave or whether

A CHIMPANZEE *uses a "tool" on an anthill. Its behavior is probably learned.*

their behaviors are learned. In some species, particularly insect species, experiments show that most behavior is innate; animals are born knowing how to walk or even how to perform complex acts such as spinning a particular kind of spider web. For birds and mammals, however, the situation is usually more complex.

For example, young geese believe that the first thing they see moving as they emerge from the egg is their mother. In normal circumstances, this innate tendency makes it appear that the gosling recognizes its mother. But the experience of researchers such as Konrad Lorenz suggests a different explanation. If the young goose sees Lorenz first, it believes that he is its mother, and acts accordingly. (This behavior is called *imprinting.*)

Similarly, all chaffinchs in nature sing the same song. But if a chaffinch is raised in the laboratory without hearing its parents sing, it does not learn the song. Its innate behavior is to sing, but it needs a model to learn how to do it.

Some animals use tools. When wasps use a small pebble to pound their nest entrances shut, the behavior is almost certainly innate. When sea otters use rocks to open mussels (while floating on their backs in the sea), the mechanism for the behavior may be innate, but the behavior itself is probably learned. And when chimpanzees use sticks as levers to pry open boxes, the behavior is generally learned from older chimpanzees. Thus there is wide variation in the mix of innate and learned behavior. For human beings, it is probable that only the simplest reflexes, such as blinking when a moving object approaches the eye, are innate. The complexity of human culture is certainly learned.

AARDVARK, an insect-eating mammal of Africa south of the Sahara and the Sudan. The aardvark (Dutch for earth pig) is about 5 feet long, including the tail. It uses its strong claws to burrow into the ground and to tear down the nests of termites (white ants). It licks up the termites with its long, sticky tongue. Although often called ant boar or earth pig, its small eyes and long snout are its only piglike features. Order Tubulidentata, specifically *Orycteropus afer.*

ABALONE, a sea snail of rocky coasts, which produces a low oval shell as much as 12 inches across. Abalones eat seaweeds, foraging for them while clinging to rocks by means of a large flat muscular foot. Only the edges of the foot project beyond the shell, which shows a slight spiral and usually a series of breathing holes near one side.

When disturbed, an abalone holds on like a suction cup, by contracting a strong muscle from the center of its foot to the center of its shell. This muscle has a high commercial value because of its delicate flavor. For their flesh and for the shells, which are lined attractively with mother-of-pearl, they are harvested in large numbers. Order Prosobranchiata, various species of genus *Haliotis.*

ADDER. See *Viper.*

AGOUTI, any of about 24 different rabbit-sized mammals native to the West Indies, South and Central America, and southern Mexico, For the most part, agoutis live on the ground eating roots, fruits, and foliage. They do not climb or dig to any great depth. When at rest or eating, they commonly sit on their haunches and hold food between their paws. They are considered good to eat and are sometimes domesticated. Agoutis can damage crops by eating the plant roots. Order Rodentia, member of genus *Dasyprocta.*

ALBATROSS, any of 13 different kinds of giant petrel-like sea birds. The extended wingspread may measure up to 12 feet, and the weight may exceed 20 pounds, making it the largest of all pelagic birds. Its plumage is white with black bands on the wings and back.

It has a strong, hard, long bill of a pale-yellow color with its nostrils near the tip; the flesh-colored feet are short and webbed, and the wings are long, narrow, and strong. Many species are frequently encountered in the South Pacific. Others have great nesting grounds on Laysan, an islet in the Hawaiian Islands Bird Reservation. Still another kind of albatross is seen in immense flocks about Bering Strait, in early summer, attracted by vast schools of migrating fish. Order Procellariiformes, the tube-nosed birds; members of genus *Diomedea.*

ALEWIFE, or sawbelly, a valuable herringlike fish as much as 15 inches long, with sharp projecting scales along its undersurface. Alewives are common near land along the western side of the North Atlantic Ocean from the Gulf of St. Lawrence to the Gulf of Mexico. Some are landlocked in the Great Lakes and the lakes in New York State.

In spring, alewives from the ocean enter coastal shallows and streams in large numbers to spawn. The young, hatched from the eggs, remain in fresh water until they are about 4 inches long (usually by autumn), at which time they go downstream to the sea and mature there. Order Isospondyli, specifically *Pomolobus pseudoharengus.*

ALLIGATOR. See *Crocodile.*

ALPACA, the domesticated South American camel, which stands about 2 feet high at the shoulder, native to the higher portions of the Andes.

The Peruvians keep vast flocks of alpacas and esteem the silky luster and fineness of their wool. Order Artiodactyla, specifically *Lama huanaco.*

AMOEBA, any of several different microscopic one-celled animals, or protozoans, which move by flowing slowly. An amoeba has no head end, covering, or skeleton. Freshwater amoebas (chiefly of genus *Amoeba,* from a Greek word meaning change) flow around and digest smaller animals and plants. A few kinds of parasitic amoebas, such as the dysentery amoeba (*Entamoeba histolytica*) of man, found in contaminated water, reach the intestine and cause severe inflammation. Class Sarcodina, order Amoebida.

ANACONDA. See *Boa.*

ANCHOVY, a bony fish about 4 inches long, belonging to the herring family. It abounds in the Mediterranean, particularly along the coasts of Italy, Greece, Spain, and France. It is bluish brown on the back and silvery white on the belly. Order Isospondyli, specifically *Engraulis encrasicholus.*

ANGELFISH, any of several different kinds of tropical bony fishes in which the body is so narrow and high that they can hide easily behind a plant stem. Their dorsal and anal fins are usually elongated, giving the body the appearance of having a long wing above and below. Marine angelfishes as much as 2 feet long are conspicuous in the shallow waters of coral reefs, where they display their bright colors

CRANDON PARK ZOOLOGICAL GARDEN
YOUNG AARDVARK

and gay stripes when not busy reaching with their small mouths among the crevices for food.

The freshwater angelfish (*Pterophyllum scalare*) has long been a favorite for tropical aquariums, but it is active mostly at night, very nervous by day, and fights with others of its own kind; it is a native of the Amazon River. Order Acanthopteri; various genera in family Cichlidae.

ANT, a social insect of the order Hymenoptera, family Formicidae, found in most temperate and tropical regions. Small and powerful, these insects have long been noted for their remarkable activities and interesting habits. Theirs is a well-defined community consisting of males, breeding females (much larger than the males), and sterile females called neuters, workers, or nurses.

The workers are wingless, and the males and breeding females acquire wings only for the nuptial flight, after which the males and females divest themselves of their wings and either return to established nests or found new colonies. The workers perform all the labor of the anthill, the community abode; they excavate the galleries, procure food, and feed the larvae or young ants, which have no organs of locomotion.

Some ants live on animal food, picking clean the skeletons of dead animals. Others live on saccharine matter, being very fond of the sweet substance called *honeydew,* which exudes from the bodies of aphids, or plant lice. These the ants keep in their nests or tend on the plants where the aphids feed; sometimes they even superintend their breeding. By stroking the aphids with their antennae, they cause them to emit the sweet fluid. Other insects are found living with ants in different types of association.

In temperate climates most of the male and female ants survive until cold weather. The next brood of ants appears in the spring from eggs laid the preceding summer. In colder climates the workers pass the winter in a state of torpor and require no food. They need food only during the season of activity, when they have a vast number of young to feed. Some species have stings as weapons, others have only their powerful mandibles or an acrid and pungent fluid (formic acid) that they emit.

ANTEATER, any of three different tropical mammals related to armadillos and sloths, which capture insects as food by means of their long, slender, sticky tongues, extensible over a considerable distance. All three have powerful front legs with strong hooked claws, which they use in climbing and in ripping apart the nests of termites and ants. They walk on the sides of their feet, with the claws incurved. Anteaters live in South and Central America.

The great anteater (*Myrmecophaga tridactyla*), which lives in humid forests from northern Argentina to southern British Honduras, weighs up to 50 pounds and is almost 7 feet long, counting the long bushy tail. The collared anteater (*Tamandua tetradactyla*) and the silky 2-toed anteater (*Cyclops didactylus*) are smaller, with short hair, and a long naked tail which is used like a fifth hand in climbing; both are found mostly in trees, from southern Mexico to Brazil and Bolivia, and become most active at night. Order Edentata.

ANTELOPE, any of more than 100 kinds of graceful, plant-eating, cud-chewing mammals, which resemble deer but have permanent hollow horns instead of solid antlers that are shed annually. Africa south of the great deserts is the home of most antelopes—the various gazelles, gnus, hartebeests, and the springbok (*Antidorcas euchore*) and two kinds of elands (species of *Taurotragus*). Europe and Asia have two species: the chamois (*Rupicapra rupicapra*), which inhabits the Alps; and the saiga (*Saiga tartarica*) in the Soviet Union.

Antelopes have a timid and restless disposition and are among the swiftest runners in the animal kingdom. Most are gregarious, associating in herds. Order Artiodactyla, family Bovidae.

ANT LION, or doodle bug, any of several dozen kinds of larval insects with soft, egg-shaped bodies and large flat heads, equipped with sickle-shaped projecting jaws. An ant lion digs a funnel-shaped pit in the driest and finest sand it can find, using its big head to toss out the sand. When the pit is about an inch deep, with smoothly sloping sides, the ant lion buries itself at the bottom, projecting only its jaws. If an ant or other luckless insect stumbles into the pit, it skids down the sides into the jaws of the ant lion.

Generally the ant lion reacts to the sandslide produced by the skidding insect, confusing its victim by tossing still more sand. A full-grown ant lion pupates in the sand, and transforms to a flying insect resembling a dragonfly. Order Neuroptera; various members of genus *Myrmeleon*.

APE, the most highly developed wild members of the mammalian order Primates. All inhabit the Old World. They include baboons, mandrills, macaques, orangutans, chimpanzees, and gorillas. The nostrils of an ape are separated by a narrow septum; both fore- and hind-feet have opposing thumbs; the callosities on the rump are generally naked; some species have cheek pouches.

APHIDS, or plant lice, any of several hundred different kinds of small, soft-bodied insects with slender, sucking mouthparts. They are found all over the world, sucking the juices from the buds, leaves, flowers, young stems, or tender roots of plants. Growing rapidly, they attain adulthood by direct development and generally reproduce by parthenogenesis (virgin birth).

In the late summer, aphids develop wings and fly feebly to new locations. Toward winter, males are produced. Mated females lay eggs that can survive cold weather, whereas all young and adults die when frozen.

Generally an aphid reaches into the veins or conducting tubes where the plant is transporting sugary solutions and other organic substances. Excess water and sugar are excreted by the aphid in droplets, known as *honeydew*.

To get honeydew to eat, some ants carefully carry the aphids to suitable locations on plants, as though these "ants' cows" were domestic animals. Aphids that ants place in underground chambers on the roots of crop plants often cause serious loss to farmers, without being seen. Order Homoptera; various genera in family Aphididae.

ARMADILLO, any of about 20 different kinds of burrowing mammals encased by an armor of bony material divided into small, separate bands. The bands are connected by a membrane, except on the forehead, shoulders, and haunches, rendering the armor flexible and enabling the animal to roll itself into an armored ball.

Armadillos live mostly in Central and South America. They burrow in the earth, where they lie in the daytime, seldom going out except at night. They subsist chiefly on fruits and roots, sometimes on insects and flesh. They are inoffensive and can be eaten.

The largest (*Priodontes giganteus* of eastern South America) is 3 feet in length, with an 18-inch tail; the smallest (*Chlamyphorus truncatus* of Argentinean deserts) is 6 inches long with a 1-inch tail. The nine-banded armadillo (*Dasypus novemcinctus*), more than 2 feet long with a 12-inch tail, has spread recently through Mexico into Oklahoma and Florida. Order Edentata; various species in 9 genera.

ASS, either of two horselike mammals with conspicuous ears, an erect mane, a dark stripe along the back, and hair covering the hind legs where a horse has bare, horny areas. The African wild ass, or donkey or burro (*Equus asinus*), is native to Ethiopia, Somaliland, and adjacent areas of East Africa. It is easily domesticated.

The Asian wild ass (*E. hemionus*), which once ranged over the deserts and high plains from Asia Minor to Central Mongolia, has small differences in color and markings that can be used to distinguish the Syrian wild ass (Syrian deserts) from the onager (Iran to Turkestan), the Indian wild ass (western India and Baluchistan), the kiang (Tibet), and the kulan (Central Mongolia). Of these, the Syrian wild ass is almost extinct.

The long-legged and slender-headed tarpan, from which the domestic horse (*E. caballus*) was derived, is extinct. A related animal with shorter legs and thick head is the Mongolian wild horse (*E. przewalskii*).

Of the zebras, or striped horselike mammals, the one with the least markings is already extinct. It was the quagga (*E. quagga*) of southern Africa. Surviving zebras include the mountain zebra (*E. zebra*) of South Africa and Angola; Burchell's zebra (*E. burchelli*), which is common from the Transvaal to Uganda; and Grévy's zebra (*E. grevyi*) of Somaliland, northern Kenya, and parts of Ethiopia. Order Perissodactyla; family Equidae.

AUK, any of more than 20 different kinds of heavy-bodied sea birds of the Northern Hemisphere. They fly and swim many miles out to sea, feeding mainly on fishes, squids, crustaceans, and sea worms. Auks are most numerous in Atlantic waters from Newfoundland to Iceland and south to Scotland, and in the Pacific from northern California to Bering Strait and southeast along the Soviet coast. They come to land only in times of bad weather and during the breeding season.

The great auk (*Plautus impennis*) is now extinct; the last survivors were killed about 1845. It stood about 3 feet tall. The great auk could not fly, but used its wings to guide its underwater swimming. Like all auks, it propelled itself by paddling with its webbed feet.

Among the smaller auks still alive, the razor-billed auk (*Alca torda*) stands about 16 inches tall. Various auklets (genus *Aethia*) are barely 6 inches high. Other auks, all of which belong to family Alcidae, include the guillemots and the puffins. Order Charadriiformes.

AVOCET, any of 4 different kinds of long-legged shore birds, about 18 inches in length with a peculiar up-curved beak. The avocet of Eurasia and Africa is black and white; the two avocets of North America and Australia have a tan head and neck; the fourth species lives around salt lakes in the Andes of Chile and Bolivia. All of these birds wade sedately, swinging their slender beaks from side to side in shallow water to capture aquatic insects and small mollusks. Order Charadriiformes; species of genus *Recurvirostra*.

BABOON, any of eight different kinds of powerful apes distinguished by having an elongated, abrupt, doglike muzzle, fairly long tail, and naked pads on the buttocks. All but one kind—the most famous—are restricted to Africa. The exception, whose range extends from northeastern Africa to Arabia, is the Arabian baboon (*Comopithecus hamadryas*), which was sacred to the ancient Egyptians, who depicted it on their monuments, and mummified and entombed it. Old males have a heavy mane around the neck and shoulders.

More widespread in Africa are the Chacma, or pigtailed baboon, (*Chaeropithecus ursinus*) of eastern and southern areas; the yellow baboon (*C. cynocephalus*) of central and southern parts of the continent; the western baboon (*C. papio*) of central and western Africa; and the Doguera baboon (*C. doguera*) of Kenya and Ethiopia. West African forest areas are the preferred territories for the bearded mandrill (*Mandrillus sphinx*) and drill (*M. leucophaeus*), which have particularly colorful skin on the face and buttocks. Ethiopian mountains have the distinctive Gelada baboons (*Theropithecus gelada*), whose nostrils open on the sides of the nose.

All of these animals run and sit on the ground. They rarely climb trees or stand upright. They travel by day in troops of 25 to 300 individuals of all ages hunting for edible roots, fruits, eggs, reptiles, and insects. Sometimes they attack sheep or vege-

U.S. DEPARTMENT OF THE INTERIOR
BEARS

table crops, despite the efforts of herders and farmers. If pursued, they defend themselves, often by throwing stones and dirt. Order Primates, family Cercopithecidae, which includes also the monkeys of the Old World.

BADGER, any of 9 different short-legged mammals, related to weasels and skunks, which dig for their food with large forepaws armed with strong claws. The American badger (*Taxidea taxus*), found in dry open country from southwestern Canada to central Mexico, is somewhat smaller than the Eurasian badger (*Meles meles*) of wooded country from Scandinavia to southern China, which attains a weight of as much as 40 pounds and a length up to 3 feet.

The hog badger (*Arctonyx collaris*) of China, India, and Malaya, is equally large but more slender and has a long naked snout. Three kinds of ferret badgers (genus *Melogale*) and two of stink badgers (genera *Mydaus* and *Suillotaxus*) are found in the East Indies and adjacent parts of Southeast Asia. A honey badger, or ratel (*Mellivora capensis*), ranges over most of Africa and in Asia from Arabia to Turkestan and India.

Badgers feed on roots, fruits, insects, frogs, and ground squirrels. Most species have anal glands that secrete a malodorous fluid. Order Carnivora, family Mustelidae.

BARNACLE, any of about 800 different kinds of marine crustaceans that spend most of their lives permanently attached to rocks, submerged timbers, steel pilings, and ship bottoms. Their eggs hatch as free-swimming larvae, which feed, grow, and change their form. Soon each attaches itself to a firm support and begins to produce its limy shell of overlapping plates.

Shells of acorn barnacles (chiefly of the genus *Balanus*) are fixed directly to the support. Those of goose barnacles (genus *Lepas*) enclose the major parts of the body, which is held away from the support on a flexible, rubbery stalk.

Barnacles of all kinds cease feeding when exposed to air or when the water around them is muddy. In clear water, even during the crash of a wave, they extend from a gap in the shell several feathery extensions from their feet. In a combing motion, the barnacle captures minute sea animals as food and sweeps them into its shell, where it can get them into its mouth. Ships' hulls and wharf pilings often must be treated to prevent growth of barnacles on them. Order Cirripedia.

BASS, edible, perchlike bony fishes found throughout the world, most of them valued as food. Sports fishermen prize the American striped bass (*Roccus saxatilis*), which is native to the entire Atlantic coast from Florida north, and has been introduced successfully from California to Washington; it often reaches a weight of 60 to 70 pounds.

Almost as prominent among game fishes of freshwater are the small-mouthed and the large-mouthed black bass (species of *Micropterus*), which attain record weights of from 12 to 22½ pounds. The small-mouthed bass is sturdily built and dark in color; it frequents rivers and clear, cold water, and it is more active than the much heavier large-mouthed bass, which prefers quiet water and attains its greatest weight in semitropical regions. Order Percomorphi, the sea basses in family Serranidae, the freshwater basses in family Centrarchidae.

BAT, any of about 770 different kinds of mammals capable of flapping flight through use of wings formed from a thin webbing of skin stretched between the body and the elongated toes of the forelegs. Almost all land areas of the world, including remote islands, have their native bats or are visited by bats on migration. Most of these animals live in the tropical and subtropical regions, but a few kinds travel in season as far from the Equator as Scotland and Alaska.

Most bats are covered with short fur, have a pair of mammary glands in the chest region, and show their most distinctive features in the head—small eyes, small and numerous teeth, large ears, and nostrils often equipped with sensory lobes of peculiar shapes. Bats find their way about at night and in the dark places they choose for sleeping during the day by listening to the echoes of their own ultrasonic chirping. They can avoid obstacles as small as a stretched wire 1/16th of an inch in diameter, and pass through narrow openings without touching by the most dexterous use of their wings.

The majority of bats use the same type of echolocation to find flying insects and capture these as food. Tropical bats include a large number of kinds that seek out flowers that offer nectar at night, and unwittingly attend to pollination; others locate ripe fruits and crush them to get the juices. The largest of all bats is an Australian fruit-eating bat (the flying "fox" or kalong, *Pteropus giganteus*) weighing nearly 2 pounds and with a wing span of about 5 feet; it does much mischief in orchards.

Far more feared are the small vampire bats (*Desmodus* species) of tropical America, which use their razor-sharp front teeth to cut through the skin of sleeping people and large animals, add a saliva that prevents clotting of the blood, and lap up the blood as food. Still other bats in tropical America fly back and forth over the surface of quiet water, finding fishes of small size within reach of their long-clawed hind legs; these fish-eating bats (*Noctilio* species) either eat the fish in flight, or carry it home to the roost cave.

In caverns where many kinds of bats take shelter, each species clusters by itself, every bat suspended upside

down. In cold regions, the bats either spend the winter hibernating where the temperature will always be above the freezing point, or they migrate toward the equator, where they can still be active and find food. All bats can bite in self-defense, and may be carriers of rabies. Order Chiroptera.

BEAR, any of 9 different mammals with large heads, large heavy bodies, short strong legs, and short tails. All except one (the polar bear, *Thalarctos maritimus*) live in temperate or tropical regions and tend to be active at night, sleeping by day.

All except one (the spectacled bear, *Tremarctos ornatus*, of northern South America) are animals of the Northern Hemisphere. The giants are the Alaskan brown bear (*Ursus arctos*) of the mainland and adjacent islands, which grows to almost 8 feet long with a weight of over 1,700 pounds, and the slightly smaller grizzly bear (*U. horribilis*) of the Rocky Mountains. Formerly, grizzlies ranged over much of western North America.

The Kodiak bear (*U. middendorffi*) is a brown bear larger than the grizzly, found only on Kodiak Island, Alaska. American black bears (*Euarctos americanus*), which may be chocolate-brown, cinnamon-brown, blue-black, or even white, live in the forests all over North America except where they have been eliminated.

Asia has a black bear (*Selenarctos thibetanus*) in forests of the Himalayas, China, Japan, and Formosa; usually it has a white, crescent-shaped mark on the chest. The sloth bear (*Melursus ursinus*) lives in forests of Ceylon and of India as far as the foothills of the Himalayas, whereas the Malayan sun bear (*Helarctos malayanus*) is found in wooded areas of Southeast Asia from Burma to Indonesia.

All of these animals feed on fruits, roots, insects, and whatever small mammals they can catch. Grizzlies and the giant Alaskan brown bear are experts at flipping salmon out of streams during the annual spawning run. Polar bears eat seaweeds and carrion when other food is scarce; they swim readily, often from one ice floe to another in pursuit of seals. Unlike the other bears of the far northern regions they do not hibernate.

Hibernation, for a bear, consists of lying quietly, sleeping but capable of instantly being aroused, in a den of some kind during the winter months. The one or two young are ordinarily born at the end of this period of inactivity. Order Carnivora, family Ursidae.

BEAVER, either of two different gnawing mammals of the North Temperate Zone, with a broad flat naked tail and webbed hind feet. The European beaver (*Castor fiber*) and the American one (*C. canadensis*) are closely similar; both now occupy a small fraction of their previously wide range. In escaping from the attention of people who want to kill beavers for their fur, these animals have become nocturnal.

The European species makes its home inconspicuously in burrows along the banks of rivers, whereas the American beaver continues to construct a lodge of sticks and mud in the pond behind a special dam of the same construction. Beavers dive into the water for safety, propelling themselves with the hind feet while using the tail as a rudder, front paws folded against the chest.

Their food is exclusively vegetable matter, particularly the young twigs and thin bark of trees such as aspen and willow. A supply of this food is ordinarily collected during late summer and pushed into the muddy bottom of the beaver pond, where the beavers can go for it under the ice during the coldest weather. Order Rodentia, family Castoridae.

BEDBUG, a flat-bodied wingless insect that hides in cracks and bedding until night and then crawls out to suck human blood. Its saliva is poisonous to some people, its odor objectionable to almost everyone. It can live without a meal for as much as a year.

Related insects attack bats, swallows, and poultry, emerging from crevices in roosting sites to feed in darkness on their victim's blood. Order Heteroptera, specifically *Cimex lectularius.*

BEE, any of several thousand different wasplike insects with 4 membranous wings, the second pair much smaller than the first pair. The bee differs from the wasp in having a hairy body and mouthparts specialized for sucking as well as biting. Bees of many kinds inhabit virtually all land areas.

The bees eat and store honey made from the nectar of flowers and a material called "bee bread" made from pollen. On these nourishing materials the female bees feed the maggotlike larvae that hatch from their eggs.

Full-grown larvae transform to a pupa stage, during which their bodies are converted into the structure of the adult insect. While visiting flowers to gather nectar and pollen, bees unwittingly attend to pollination—usually cross-pollination—and hence are responsible for the efficient production of seeds and many kinds of fruits.

Bees differ greatly in their nesting habits. A majority of these insects make solitary nests, and are comparatively inconspicuous. Carpenter bees (of genus *Xylocopa*), which are as big as bumblebees, cut tunnels in timber, stock them with food and an egg in each of many chambers, and close up the opening afterwards. Leaf-cutter bees (of genus *Megachile)* snip out almost circular pieces of leaves and petals, particularly of roses, with which they line the burrows and construct the partitions separating one egg and its food store from the next.

Mason bees (such as the metallic green, bluish or purplish insects of genus *Osmia*) construct earthen cells under stones, in small holes in decaying wood, in deserted snail shells, and elsewhere. The cuckoo bees (species of *Nomada*) lack a means to collect pollen, and place their eggs in the nests of other kinds of bees. Social nesting is characteristic of bumblebees (of the genus *Bombus)* and honeybees (genus *Apis*). The bumblebees include about 50 different kinds in the North Temperate Zone and the Arctic, where they are the only bees present; they are rare in the Tropics.

Usually a bumblebee is about 1 inch long, heavier and larger than a honeybee, and covered with golden and black hair. Females build small separate cells on the ground, each one called a honeypot. Generally a few dozen bumblebees nest close together, building 200 to 300 honeypots.

Like most female bees, the female bumblebee has an effective sting. She can use it repeatedly until her supply of venom is temporarily exhausted, whereas a worker honeybee can sting only once because the act of stinging tears the stinger out of the honeybee's body. Bumblebees differ also from the honeybee in that the females of one colony never try to destroy one another; they do not swarm, and are regarded as showing only a simple social habit.

Few bees show so complex a social organization as the domesticated honeybee *(A. mellifera).* The most distinctive feature of this bee is its habit of continuing to store honey and bee bread not only for the breeding season but also to sustain the hive during the winter.

During the greater part of the year, the population of a honeybee hive is composed exclusively of two sorts of individuals—the mother, or queen bee, and the workers, or neuter bees, which are sterile females. The males, or drones, generally appear in May and are all dead by the end of July. The queen lives for several years, the workers only 1 to 2 months in seasons of activity, and the drones 1 to 2 months.

The queen has a longer body and shorter wings than the workers. She can use her sting repeatedly without rupturing herself, and normally will use it within minutes after escaping from her pupal cell. She will explore the hive thoroughly and sting to death all other queens present, even those that have not yet emerged as adults.

The old queen, with a large number of worker bees, has already left in a swarm, to find a new place for a colony. The young queen soon goes out on her nuptial flight, pursued by dozens of drones. Within 2 days, she is back in the hive, prepared to lay eggs at the rate of about 200 a day for the rest of her life. She lays each egg in a separate cell in the brood region of the hive, a short distance away from cells in which honey or bee bread is stored.

Development and hatching of the eggs, growth of the larva, pupation and transformation into an adult ready to emerge take an average of 24 days for the unfertilized eggs that mature into drones, 21 days for the fertilized eggs that mature into sterile workers on a low-protein diet, and 15½ days for the fertilized eggs that mature into new queens on a high-protein diet.

The life of a worker follows a regular schedule, with tasks changing to match development of various glands in her body. She produces saliva as a varnish for the cells in which the queen will lay eggs. She visits the honey stores and cells with bee bread to get food she can regurgitate for the larvae of different ages. The wax glands below her abdomen begin to secrete, and she takes wax scales in her jaws to work them into a material with which she builds new cells in the comb. Eventually, she

crawls to the doorway of the hive and uses her wings there to create a current of air to ventilate the hive.

After a few days of this chore and of guarding the doorway from intruders, such as spiders or bees from other hives (which have the wrong "hive odor"), she becomes a field bee. Until their wings wear out, field bees daily gather nectar, pollen, resinous materials for sealing cracks in the hive, and water in hot weather when the inside temperature must be lowered by evaporation. A single hive may contain 60,000 workers at one time.

Only the workers possess special features on each of their 3 pairs of legs, which make these efficient tools in collecting and transporting pollen. The hind pair of legs—longer than the others—have on the outer surface a triangular depression (the palette) surrounded by stiff hairs; this forms a "pollen basket," into which the insect presses pollen combed from the surface of the body. The first segment of the feet on these legs is larger than the others, and bears on its inner surface a large number of short stiff bristles, forming a "pollen brush." The front pair of legs have notches through which the feelers are drawn carefully to clean them of pollen grains; an "eye brush" is on each front foot. Most of these and other special features are used by the bee while hovering in flight.

Worker honeybees appear to change their behavior according to the amount of a "queen substance" produced by their queen, and the amount of food stored in the hive. They communicate with one another in the darkness of the hive by special dances and sounds that tell other workers the direction and approximate distance to food they have found, as well as some measure of its abundance.

Order Hymenoptera, suborder Apoidea, and more than a dozen families.

BEETLE, any of more than 300,000 different kinds of insects in which the first pair of wings are hard, tough, and capable of meeting along the midline over the back to protect the membranous second pair of wings, which are used for flying. Beetles outnumber in variety all other insects, and are found on every continent, from forest to desert and fresh water.

Each beetle has a pair of strong jaws. Its eggs hatch to active larvae, which feed on living and dead parts of plants or on the remains of dead animals. Some bore in wood or live in tunnels eaten from the inner bark of trees. Upon reaching full size, a beetle larva pupates and transforms to the adult insect. Order Coleoptera.

BIGHORN, or mountain sheep, a wild sheep of the western mountain ranges of North America from New Mexico and California northward to British Columbia. It stands about 3 feet high at the shoulder; its horns are curved and spiraled back and outward, often to a full circle, and may measure from 32 to 40 inches in length. Its color varies from white to buffy brown to black with a large whitish rump patch. Order Artiodactyla, specifically *Ovis canadensis.*

BIRD OF PARADISE, any of 43 different kinds of perching birds related to crows, in which the adult male develops extraordinary feathers on the tail, wings, back, or head, used in courtship display. Females and young birds are inconspicuous and plain. Birds of paradise inhabit the remote forests of New Guinea and neighboring islands, and northeastern Australia. Field research has not yet provided full information on these magnificent birds. Order Passeriformes, family Paradisaeidae.

BISON, either of 2 kinds of large, cud-chewing mammals, remarkable for the great hump or projection over the fore shoulders, at which point the adult male is almost 6 feet high, and for the long shaggy rust-colored hair over the head, neck, and forepart of the body. In summer, from the shoulders backward, the surface is covered with very short, fine hair, soft and smooth as velvet. The tail is short and tufted at the end.

One, called the wisent (*Bison bonasus*), was once widespread in forested parts of Europe but survives now only in captivity. The other, the American bison (*B. bison*), was formerly numerous on the western plains of North America but is now present only in a few herds protected by law. The American bison is often incorrectly called a buffalo. Bison breed readily with domestic cattle, and their issue are fertile among themselves. Order Artiodactyla, family Bovidae.

BLACKBIRD, any of several American perching birds, related to orioles and meadowlarks. The red-winged blackbirds (*Agelaius phoeniceus*), which nest in marshes, often congregate in great flocks; the genus name *Agelaius* means gregarious. The related grackles are often called blackbirds. The unrelated European blackbird and the New Zealand blackbird are both songbirds of the thrush family. Order Passeriformes, family Icteridae.

BLACK DUCK, a common water bird of eastern North America, and a favorite with hunters. It is about 2 feet long and has dark-brown plumage with an iridescent bluish patch on the wings, and bright orange feet. It breeds from the Middle Atlantic States north to Labrador. The black duck and the closely related mallard are the two most abundant species of U.S. ducks. The nest of the black duck is a large structure made of weeds and grass; the 6 to 12 eggs are a pale greenish color. Order Anseriformes, family Anatidae, specifically *Anas rubripes*.

BLACK WIDOW, or hourglass spider, a small black spider with a black globular abdomen; a scarlet mark the shape of an hourglass on the abdomen's underside; and slender legs, the first and last pairs longer than the second and third. It is found in damp places from New England to Patagonia, more commonly in eastern North America and the far west.

The ¼-inch male is too small to be venomous, but the ½-inch female can puncture human skin where it is thin and soft, and inject a dangerous poison. She does so chiefly while guarding her 3 or 4 cocoons, each containing about 300 eggs, hung in a loose web in dark places such as cellars and outhouses. No deaths have been reported from such a bite in a healthy adult person. Related spiders with a similarly dangerous venom are found in Australia and New Zealand. Order Araneae, family Theridiidae, specifically *Latrodectes mactans*.

BLUEBIRD, any of 3 small perching birds of North America, with a soft twittering call and with blue feathers on much of the body. The eastern bluebird (*Sialia sialis*) was formerly much more common and was widely regarded as the harbinger of spring. Its breast and throat are earthy red, the rest of the body a solid blue. The western bluebird (*S. mexicana*) is similar except that the back is rusty red. The mountain bluebird (*S. currucoides*) is found from Mexico to Canada in high country; the male is azure blue, and the female is dull brownish with a blue rump, tail, and wings.

Bluebirds catch insects on the wing, but generally descend to the ground to eat them. They also eat fruits in season. Order Passeriformes, family Turdidae.

BLUEFISH, a mackerel-like marine fish, steely blue in color and beautifully shaped for speed and strength. It is widely distributed and abundant along the eastern coast of the United States.

Some individuals up to 20 pounds have been taken, but the average weight is from 3 to 8 pounds, and the length 20 to 30 inches. In addition to its food value, the fish is notable for the tremendous schools in which it congregates and for its feeding capacity. Young bluefish, called snappers, weigh about half a pound. Order Acanthopteri, family Pomatomidae, specifically *Pomatoma saltatrix*.

BLUE JAY. See *Jay.*

BOA, any of several dozen different nonvenomous snakes that resemble pythons in the way they capture and kill their prey, and in the possession of two functional lungs, not just the right lung as in snakes of other families. Unlike pythons, which lay eggs and are found only in the Old World, boas bear active young and most kinds inhabit the tropics of America.

In most boas and all pythons, a remnant of a hip girdle is attached to the backbone; in the male, further evidence of vestigial hind legs can be seen in a pair of protruding claws, one on each side of the vent. Like pythons, the boas lie in wait for prey, trying to capture mammals and birds far larger in diameter than the snake's head. Holding firmly with its mouth, the snake throws two or three coils of its body tightly around the victim and tightens still more every time the animal exhales. Prevented from breathing, the victim suffocates.

The snake swallows its prey whole, then seeks out some secluded spot in which to rest for a week or more while digesting its huge meal. Snakes with this habit are called constrictors. One referred to often as "the boa constrictor" is common from coastal Mexico to northern Argentina; it rarely exceeds 10 feet in length, but bears the name *Constrictor constrictor*.

The giant among boas is the anaconda (*Eunectes murinus*) of northern South America, which is reported to attain a length of 29 feet. It waits to prey along riverbanks, catching mammals and birds as they come to drink.

Beyond the New World, boas are represented in North Africa, Madagascar, the Mascarene Islands of the Indian Ocean, New Guinea, and some islands of the South Pacific. Order Squamata, suborder Serpentes, family Boidae.

BOBOLINK, an American perching bird of southern Canada and the northern United States, except the west coast. It is related closely to the oriole, the blackbird, and meadowlark, and is known also as reedbird or ricebird in the southern states, through which it migrates to and from its winter home in central and southern South America.

The male bobolink is almost 7½ inches long. In spring and summer he is black and white on top and solid black underneath. By mid-summer, when bobolinks start south, and through the fall and winter, his plumage becomes buffy olive streaked with black, and the underparts olive or yellowish. Throughout the year the smaller female resembles the male in autumn plumage.

Order Passeriformes, family Icteridae, specifically *Dolichonyx oryzivorus*.

BOBWHITE, a quail native to the United States and Canada, named for its clear, loud two-part whistle. Both Rhode Island and Oklahoma have chosen the bobwhite as state bird. It has a conspicuous white patch on the throat and a pale mark from the beak over the eye and down the neck. At maturity the bird may be 11 inches long, including the short tail, and weigh 9 ounces.

Bobwhites benefit man by eating insects in summer and weed seeds in winter. They seldom fly far, but may

AMERICAN BISON

22   **Boll Weevil**

ANIMALS

attain more than 50 miles per hour. Order Galliformes, family Perdicidae, specifically *Colinus virginianus*.

BOLL WEEVIL. See *Weevil*.

BONY PIKE. See *Gar*.

BOTFLY, a parasitic fly often mistaken for a honeybee buzzing about the head and front legs of horses, mules, or donkeys. The female botfly keeps the tip of her long pointed abdomen curled under her until she alights, usually on a leg, and begins attaching her yellowish eggs to hairs of a horse. The horse gets the eggs into its mouth when it licks the hairs; the eggs hatch quickly, releasing legless maggots called bots. These find their way to the horse's stomach and attach themselves to the lining.

For about 8 to 10 months of the year the bots absorb what they need of the horse's food, grow to maturity, and pass through the digestive tract. From the manure they enter the ground, where they pupate and transform into adult flies. Related flies attack deer, moose, rabbits, squirrels, and other mammals. Order Diptera, family Gastrophilidae, specifically *Gastrophilus intestinalis*.

BRISTLETAIL, any of several similar wingless insects in which the head bears two long, slender feelers and three similar appendages extend from the opposite end of the body; these are the "bristles" for which the animals are named. Best known are the cosmopolitan silverfish, or fishmoth, (*Lepisma saccharina*) and the European firebrat (*Thermobia domestica*), which inhabit human homes.

Like the firebrat, the silverfish uses its biting mouthparts in scavenging for food. Not content with crumbs, it dines on the glue that holds books together, or the sizing on coated paper, or the starch in clothes—often eating holes in garments and causing extensive damage. Lacking any transformation in body form as they mature, the bristletails are regarded as among the most primitive of insects. Order Thysanura.

BROWN THRASHER, a handsome songbird slightly larger than a robin and with a longer tail, a dark cinnamon-colored back, and rows of brown spots on its gray breast. Native to North America east of the Rockies, it hunts for insects, spiders, and worms among the fallen leaves below shrubs and woodland trees. Related to the mockingbird and catbird, the brown thrasher often sings loudly, mimicking other birds, usually repeating each phrase twice in quick succession.

For the winter, the brown thrasher migrates to the southeastern United States and eastern Mexico. Order Passeriformes, family Mimidae, specifically *Toxostoma rufum*.

BUFFALO, wild cattle of marshy places in the Old World tropics and subtropics. They are about 5 feet high at the shoulder. Some have been domesticated and used as beasts of burden.

The Indian or water buffalo (*Bos bubalus*) has been domesticated throughout Asia. The Cape or Kafir buffalo (*B. caffer*) of southern Africa is a larger, more powerful animal with a deserved reputation for being dangerous because it will charge and attempt to kill anyone who wounds it or threatens its young. The name buffalo was transferred by the early explorers to the bison of North America, a very different kind of animal. Order Artiodactyla, family Bovidae.

BUFFLEHEAD, or butterball, one of the diving ducks of North America, seen on lakes, rivers, and ocean bays, where it flies into and out of the water, pursuing fish and aquatic insects. In flight it displays conspicuous white patches on each wing. On the water, the dark back is often invisible and the body appears all white. The male's head is blackish green except for a large white area on the top. The female has a small slanting white patch on each cheek.

Buffleheads nest to the west and north of Hudson Bay, but spend the winter in most of the United States and Mexico. During migration, when they are hunted, each bird weighs 1 pound or less. Order Anseriformes, family Anatidae, specifically *Glaucionetta albeola*.

BULLHEAD. See *Catfish*.

BUNTING, any of several sparrow-sized birds with plump bodies and conical beaks. Europe has about a dozen different members of the genus *Embiriza*, including the corn bunting, the reed bunting, and the yellowhammer. In Eurasia and North America, the name "bunting" is used also for the snow bunting (*Plectrophenax nivalis*), which is the whitest of small land birds.

North America has 3 kinds of native buntings (*Passerina*), all spending the winter in Mexico but flying to separate nesting areas each spring. The indigo bunting (*P. cyanea*) goes to the central and eastern United States and Canada, where the males are the only all-blue birds; the mate is brown, faintly streaked below. The lazuli bunting (*P. amoena*) stays west of the Great Plains; the male is sky blue above and on his throat, but has a chestnut breast band and white wingbars; his mate is brown, sparrowlike. The painted bunting (*P. ciris*) nests in the Gulf States and as far north as Missouri; the male is red, purple, and green, his mate all green. Order Passeriformes, family Fringillidae.

BURRO. See *Ass*.

BUSHMASTER. See *Pit Viper*.

BUTTERFLY, any of a large group of scaly-winged insects with knobbed or hook-tipped feelers (antennae). They are closely related to moths, and develop in comparable stages: from an egg, to a plant-eating caterpillar, to a pupa, and to an adult with 2 pairs of wings and sucking mouthparts. The most conspicuous and useful of the mouthparts is a tube, which is coiled up like a watchspring when not in use.

Butterflies are active by day, and rest usually with the wings folded together vertically over the back, whereas moths are usually active at night, and rest with the wings more horizontal and to the rear. Most butterflies lay a single egg or a few in a place, and leave them unprotected. The caterpillars that hatch out are usually hairless, and pupate exposed, with no cocoon.

Of the 11 families of butterflies, 2 are composed of large insects found in the American Tropics: the brilliant iridescent blue *Morpho* butterflies (family Morphoidae), which conceal their display color when they close their wings; and the owl butterflies (*Caligo*, family Brassolidae), which have enormous eyespot markings on the underside of the rear wings, conspicuous when the insect is at rest.

Much more cosmopolitan are the skippers (most in family Hesperiidae), which are unique in having hooked, rather than knobbed, feelers, and of pupating in a cocoon; the swallowtails and their relatives (family Papilionidae), which include the giant birdwing butterflies of the Far East (*Troides*) and the familiar swallowtails (*Papilio*); the sulphurs, oranges, and whites (family Pieridae), including the cabbage butterfly (*Pieris rapae*); the blues, coppers, and hairstreaks (family Lycaenidae); the metalmarks (family Riodinidae); the huge family of brush-footed butterflies (Nymphalidae), such as the painted lady or thistle butterfly (*Vanessa cardui*), whose front legs, hairy and brushlike, are useless as legs; the wood-nymphs and satyrs (family Satyridae); the milkweed butterflies (family Danaidae), such as the migratory monarch (*Danaus plexippus*) of the Americas; and the heliconiids (family Heliconiidae), such as the zebra butterfly (*Heliconius charithonius*) of Florida, most of which are found in tropical America. Order Lepidoptera, suborder Rhopalocera.

BUZZARD. See *Vulture*.

BY–THE–WIND SAILOR, a colonial marine coelenterate, resembling an oblong floating jellyfish but related to the Portuguese man-of-war. Native to warm waters of the Atlantic and Pacific oceans, by-the-wind sailors are often carried north and south to temperate latitudes and cast ashore, where they die. Unlike the Portuguese man-of-war, by-the-wind sailors are harmless to people.

Each colony is supported by a thin purple float containing gas chambers and bearing a low upright sail diagonally across the top. From below a healthy colony, a central tube hangs down, ending in a mouth. Around the rim of the float, small individuals of the colony bear many tentacles with which they capture food. This consists of miniature crustaceans and other small marine animals that drift in surface waters. The food is passed to the mouth, where it enters the diges-

UNITED NATIONS

CAMEL

tive cavity. Additional individuals below the float attend to reproduction. Class Hydrozoa, order Siphonophora, specifically *Velella mutica*.

CADDIS FLY, any mothlike adult insect with 4 hairy wings and soft nonfunctional mouthparts. Caddis flies are found in great numbers near lakes and streams because their caterpillar-like larval stages, called caddisworms, are all aquatic. Caddisworms usually are less than 1 inch long, are important food for fish, and are used as bait by anglers. The worms build cylindrical, portable cases of mineral or plant material or spin nets in swift waters to catch food particles carried by the current. Order Trichoptera.

CAMEL, a large cud-chewing mammal of North Africa and the Near East. There are two kinds — the Asiatic camel (*Camelus bactrianus*), which is about 9 feet tall and has two humps; and the African camel, or dromedary (*C. dromedarius*), which has only one hump. Camels can go for a long time without water but will lose weight and strength. When they are well fed, the hump is erect and plump, but when the camel is inadequately fed, the hump shrinks and falls over.

Fossil camels have been found in North America. The alpaca and llama of South America are closely related to the camels of the Old World. Order Artiodactyla, family Camelidae.

CANARY, a small songbird related to the sparrow, native to the Canary, Azores, and Madeira islands but domesticated in many countries for 300 years. Their acceptance of life in a cage and their sweet and powerful song have made canaries popular as household pets. The best singers, notably those raised in the Harz Mountains, bring high prices. Cage birds are usually yellow (canary color is a brilliant reddish yellow, named from the bird), but wild birds are a dull green with brown streaks. Order Passeriformes, family Fringillidae, specifically *Serinus canarius*.

CANKERWORM, either of 2 kinds of North American moth caterpillars that attack shade trees, orchard trees, and other woody plants. Both are described as measuring worms or inchworms because they move along by holding to the support alternately with the legs at the forward and the rear end of the body. When full grown, they let themselves down to

the ground on long fine strands of silk, and burrow 1 to 4 inches into the earth before transforming into the adult stage—the moth.

Male moths have a wingspan of 1 to 1½ inches; the females are practically wingless, and merely crawl out of the ground, up a stem or tree trunk, and wait for a male to find them. Adults of the fall cankerworm (*Alsophila pometaria*) emerge in October or on warm days through the winter to as late as April. Adults of the spring cankerworm (*Palaeacrita vernata*) may appear as early as February or as late as May. The eggs of both species, laid in masses containing as many as 400, hatch about the time the leaves appear. Order Lepidoptera.

CANVASBACK. See *Duck.*

CARDINAL, or redbird, one of the most beautiful of American songbirds, the adult male being brilliant red, like a cardinal's hat, with a sharp crest of vermilion. The female and young are yellowish brown with some red, and with the same crest and heavy, red beak, which is black around the base. Its beautiful whistling song has given it the name, Virginia nightingale. The cardinal nests in bushes and thickets and constructs its nest of bark and twigs. Its food is almost equally divided among weed seeds, fruits, and insects. Order Passeriformes, family Fringillidae, specifically *Richmondena cardinalis*.

CARIBOU. See *Deer*

CARP, a coarse bony fish of the minnow family. Carp are native to freshwaters in Europe and Asia, where they are raised in ponds as a source of protein for human use. In American streams and lakes, to which the carp was introduced many years ago, it causes serious damage by muddying the water, uprooting vegetation, and devouring the young of native fishes.

Usually a carp is brown in color, darker along the back. Close to its mouth are 4 soft projections, called barbels, which help the carp find vegetable food in muddy water. It also eats snails, worms, insects, and eggs and young of other fishes.

The carp attains maturity when about 12 inches long, and the female lays as many as 2 million eggs during the late spring. In ponds fertilized with farm manure, carp sometimes grow to 40 inches long and a weight of 60 pounds. Order Eventognathi, family Cyprinidae, specifically *Cyprinus carpio*.

CAT, any of several different mammals with retractile claws, teeth specially adapted for cutting, and vertically elongated pupils of the eyes. The name is used particularly for members of the genus *Felis*, which includes the domestic cat, the jaguar, leopard, lion, ocelot, and puma, and the genus *Lynx*, which includes the Canada lynx and the bobcat. Order Carnivora, family Felidae.

Domestic Cat. The common cat (*Felis domestica*) is probably a native of Egypt. Domesticated there, it was an object of worship and was frequently

mummified. It was not known to the ancient Greeks and Romans who used domesticated martens to destroy rats and mice.

Domestic cats are fastidious animals, constantly washing their fur and paws. Different breeds vary widely in color, markings, size, shape, and length of tail. Notable are the tailless Japanese and Manx cats (coming from the Crimea as well as from the Isle of Man), the Angora or Persian cats with long silky fur, and the Siamese variety, a semialbino with blue eyes, a long pointed head, slender legs, and a long thin tail. The nose, ears, paws, and tail are darker than the body. The ancestor of the domestic cat was probably marked with black bars on a ground of tawny and white, these colors rendering it inconspicuous among the grasses and shrubbery where it ranged.

Wildcat. The name wildcat is applied in America to almost any cat (other than the domestic house cat). The lynx and puma are most commonly called wildcats. The true wildcat (*Felis catus*), however, is found only in Northern Europe and Asia. It is a striped animal, similar to other members of the cat family.

In the New World, the ocelot (*Felis pardalis*) is native to tropical America and has a limited range in the southern United States. Large specimens are about 3 feet long, excluding the 1-foot tail. The color is generally tawny-gray, barred or spotted with brown or black, with chin and underparts almost white. The ocelot preys mostly on birds in the deep forests. Individuals have been partly domesticated and trained for hunting, like the Asian cheetah.

The puma (*Felis concolor*), a little larger than the ocelot, is also native to America. It has a 2-foot tail. Slender, with long legs and small head, the puma is a fairly uniform tawny brown. This is the species referred to as mountain lion in the western United States, where it is notorious as a predator of young cattle and sheep. Elsewhere it is known as panther, painter, catamount, or cougar but the correct name is puma.

Leopard. The leopard (*Felis pardus*) is native to both Africa and Asia. The body of this fierce and rapacious animal is about 4 feet long. It is a superlative leaper, can swim and climb trees. The larger leopards are often called panthers, as are the American puma and jaguar. The leopard differs from the jaguar in having small spots thickly set; the jaguar's are large and open, making a beautiful pattern of dark rosettes on a tan or brown skin.

Jaguar. The jaguar (*Felis onca*), somewhat larger than the leopard, is one of the most formidable beasts of prey found on the American continent. It is typically South American but is found as far north as Texas. The banks of rivers are its favorite haunts, where it preys on such animals as the tapir and water hog or capybara. It kills by leaping on its victim's back, then twisting the neck with its heavy powerful paws until it breaks.

A noisy, heavy animal, it roams abroad at night, especially before the

---

approach of bad weather. It is an expert climber and swimmer and sometimes catches fish for food.

Lion. The lion (*Felis leo*) is the most majestic member of the cat family. It is nearly a uniform tawny or yellowish, paler on the underparts; but the immature lions show stripes like a tiger's and some spots like a leopard's. The male usually has a great shaggy flowing mane and a long tufted tail. The whole frame is extremely muscular, and the foreparts, in particular, are remarkably powerful. The heavy shoulders, large head, bright eye, and copious mane give the animal a noble appearance that has led to its being called the king of beasts.

A lion of the largest size is not so big as a tiger. It measures about 8 feet from the nose to the tail, and the tail measures about 4 feet more. The lioness is smaller, has no mane, and is of a lighter color on the underparts.

The strength of the lion is such that it can carry off a heifer as a cat carries a rat. It is chiefly an inhabitant of Africa, although it is also found in Asia, particularly in the Gir Peninsula forests of India. It was anciently much more common in Asia and was found in some parts of Europe (Macedonia and Thrace), according to Herodotus and other authors. The lion is an inhabitant of open plains in which the shelter of occasional bushes and thickets may be found. It hunts mostly at night and has a terrifying roar. It is easily tamed if it is taken young and abundantly supplied with food.

Tiger. The tiger (*Felis tigris*) is the largest and most dangerous of the cats, slightly exceeding the lion in size but far surpassing it in destructiveness. An Asian animal, the tiger reaches its highest development both in size and color on the hot plains of India. The full-grown male Indian tiger measures from 9 to 12 feet, and the tigress from 8 to 10 feet, from the nose to the tip of the tail, which has no tuft. The ground color is rufous or tawny yellow, white on the ventral surface, with vertical black stripes or elongated ovals and brindlings.

Although possessed of immense strength and ferocity, the tiger rarely attacks armed men, unless it is provoked, but often carries off women and children. When it is pressed by hunger or enfeebled by age and incapable of dealing with larger prey like buffalo, the tiger prowls around villages and, if it learns what easy prey humans are, it often becomes a habitual man-eater. Two varieties are the Bengal, or southern, type with short hair, and a northern variety, ranging as far north as Siberia, which has longer, softer hair. See also *Lynx*.

CATBIRD, a well-known American songbird, about 9 inches long, dark slate gray in color except for a rusty red area under the tail. During the summer it is found throughout the Middle Atlantic and New England States. During the winter it inhabits the extreme south of the United States, and is found also in Mexico and Central America. Order Passeri-

formes, family Mimidae, specifically *Dumetella carolinensis*.

CATERPILLAR, the wormlike immature stage in the development of a moth or butterfly. The name is said to be from the Latin *cata pilosa* (hairy cat), referring to the many caterpillars that are covered with hair. Most butterfly caterpillars are hairless.

Usually the head of the caterpillar, with its biting jaws, is followed by a portion of the trunk with 3 pairs of jointed legs. More posteriorly, the cylindrical body is generally supported on 6 pairs of stumpy, soft prolegs with many minute hooks; the last pair of prolegs are at the hind end of the caterpillar.

Some kinds of caterpillars do great damage to crops and other vegetation. An exception is the silkworm, which feeds on mulberry and grows to 1 inch long; it is economically valuable because commercial silk can be unwound from the cocoon it spins before pupating. Order Lepidoptera.

CATFISH, any of about 2,000 kinds of scaleless bony fishes with large, toothless mouths. Usually two or more long, soft, slender projections, called barbels, arise from the underjaw or from both jaws near the mouth. They help the catfish find food in muddy water.

Some kinds of catfishes have bony, platelike armor; other kinds are soft skinned. Generally the dorsal and pectoral fins have a stiff strong spine at the leading edge, which can serve as a dangerous weapon for self-defense. A species of catfish native to the Nile River and tropical Africa is capable of discharging an electric shock reaching 100 volts.

Most catfishes can live out of water for a few hours. Their flesh, which may be dark in color, is highly regarded in many parts of the world for human food. A common kind, attaining 20 inches long in American waters, is called the bullhead or horned pout (*Ameiurus nebulosus*), of order Ostariophysi, family Ameiuridae.

CATTLE, any of several kinds of large cud-chewing mammals useful to mankind as a source of power, meat, milk, hides, and horns. In India and other southern Asian countries, the zebu (*Bos indicus*) is used much as domestic cattle are in Europe or the United States. Zebus are humped animals with a great tolerance for hot weather. For meat, milk, and hides, they are less desirable than European and North African cattle (*B. taurus*), which have been bred into many particularly valuable lines of inheritance.

European cattle are especially productive of high-quality milk, and form the basis of the dairy industry. Among the dairy cattle, the Holstein breed (black and white) is perhaps the most important. Holstein cattle are great milk producers, but the percentage of its butter fat is somewhat less than in milk from other cattle. This variety originated in Holland, but has been imported to a considerable extent to the United States and

now forms an important part of the milk industry.

Jersey cattle yield milk rich in butter fat. This breed originated in the Isle of Jersey, off the coast of France. Guernsey cattle are reddish, with white markings. They also originated on one of the Channel Islands. Their milk is probably the richest in fat, but the quantity is not so great as in other breeds.

Of the beef cattle, the English Shorthorns are a very sturdy breed. These vary from red to almost pure white. Shorthorns orginated in England, but later were introduced into North America, South America, and to Australia. Another valuable beef animal is the Hereford. This has a red body and white head. Herefords are not so widely distributed as Shorthorns.

Sometimes male cattle are castrated to render them more amenable for draft or agricultural work. These are called oxen. When this is done to improve the quality of the beef for eating, the cattle are known as steers. Order Artiodactyla, family Bovidae, genus *Bos*.

CAVY. See *Guinea Pig*.

CAYMAN. See *Crocodile*.

CENTIPEDE, literally "hundred legged," any of about 2,000 different kinds of segmented terrestrial arthropod animals with biting jaws, one pair of feelers (antennae) on the head, and one pair of walking legs on each of 14 to 180 segments of the body. Centipedes are found on all continents and most major islands. North American kinds are mostly small and inconspicuous, living under stones or in and under decaying logs. In the tropics they often attain great size, some growing to 10 inches in length.

Most centipedes have the first pair of legs modified into poison claws. With them they can inject venom, which kills their prey. It causes considerable pain but rarely death to a person. Centipedes can run forward or backward with almost equal ease. Several orders of class Chilopoda.

CHAMELEON, any of about 80 different Old World lizards with independently roving eyes, a long tongue that can be shot out to capture insect prey, grasping feet, and a curled, prehensile tail. Half of the species are confined to the island of Madagascar, the rest living in Africa south of the Sahara, except one (*Chameleo chamaeleon*) found from Spain across North Africa to Asia Minor.

Chameleon is a Greek word meaning lion-on-the-ground, that is, a low or dwarf lion. These animals are famous for changing their color either in accordance with the environment or when disturbed. The change is due to the presence of clear or pigment-bearing contractile cells placed at various depths in the skin, their contractions and dilations being under the influence of the nervous system.

Chameleons can fast for weeks. When disturbed they inflate themselves with air. These habits gave rise to the fable that they live on air. In general they are slow-moving and completely harmless.

Unrelated lizards show less spectacular but still surprising changes of color, and the name chameleon has been applied also to them, especially the American chameleon (*Anolis carolinensis*) of the iguana family in the southeastern states. Order Squamata, suborder Sauria, family Chamaeleonidae.

CHAMOIS, a goatlike cud-chewing mammal closely allied to antelopes, native to high, inaccessible mountains in Europe and western Asia. A chamois stands 25 to 30 inches high at the shoulders, and wears horns 6 or 7 inches long, which are round, almost smooth, perpendicular and straight until near the tip, where they suddenly terminate in a hook directed backward and downward.

The hair is brown in winter, fawn in summer, and grayish in spring. The head is pale yellow, and a black band from the nose to the ears surrounds the eyes. The tail is black.

Its agility, the nature of its haunts, and its powers of smell render the pursuit of the chamois an exceedingly difficult and hazardous occupation. It can jump 20 feet and is proverbially sure-footed. A very soft yellow leather for linings and cleaning cloths is made from chamois skin and from inferior and less expensive hides. Order Artiodactyla, family Bovidae, specifically *Rupicapra rupicapra.*

CHEETAH, or hunting leopard, a large catlike mammal with nonretractable claws, and circular pupils in the eyes. It is native to the high plains and savannas of Africa and Iran. Longer legged than true cats, cheetahs race after antelopes and other prey; the world's fastest runners, they often attain a speed of 60 miles an hour.

Generally, however, a cheetah watches a herd of antelopes for an hour or more to select the weakest member as prey. During this time, the cheetah remains almost invisible because its sand-colored short fur and pattern of small black spots let it blend with its surroundings.

Unlike other cats, a cheetah cannot retract its claws. It growls, snarls, spits, mews, and makes a birdlike chirp, but can neither roar like a lion nor purr like a house cat. In Africa, cheetahs are often kept as pets. Order Carnivora, family Felidae, specifically *Acinonyx jubatus.*

CHICKADEE, any of several small plump active songbirds named from the sound of its cheerful call, *chick-a-dee-dee.* The common black-capped chickadee (*Parus atricapillus*) of Canada and the northern United States occurs also in Europe and Britain, where it is called the willow tit. Like the closely related titmice (singular, titmouse), chickadees eat many kinds of small insects, which make up about two-thirds of their diet, and various wild fruits. When offered suet, peanut butter, or sunflower seeds at a window feeder, chickadees become very tame.

All chickadees nest in small holes, such as in a decayed tree or branch, and lay 5 to 8 eggs finely spotted with reddish brown. Order Passeriformes, family Paridae, members of genus *Parus.*

CHICKEN. See *Fowl.*

CHIMNEY SWIFT, a fast-flying North American bird related to hummingbirds. It spends most of its life in the air and is often mistaken for a swallow. Its slender, cigar-shaped body is supported by narrow curved wings that seem very far forward because the beak is so short. The mouth is wide, and the bird uses it to catch insects and to drink while flying.

Originally, chimney swifts roosted for the night and built their nests in hollow trees and caves. With the arrival of Europeans in Canada and the United States, they changed to using chimneys and wells that are open.

The nests are of twigs, collected on the wing, held in place by a gluelike saliva. The birds cling with sharp claws, propping themselves up with their short stiff tail feathers. At the approach of cold weather, they migrate to a remote area of Peru.

Order Micropodiformes, family Micropodidae, specifically *Chaetura pelagica.*

CHIMPANZEE, a great ape with large conspicuous ears and short forearms, native to west and central Africa. A full-grown chimpanzee is almost 5 feet tall and weighs up to 150 pounds. It is not so large or powerful as a gorilla. The chimpanzee walks erect better than most apes, but not so well as the gorilla; when walking on all fours the feet are flat, whereas the fingers touch the ground with the knuckles.

The chimpanzee is more a tree-dweller than the gorilla. It feeds on fruits, often robs the gardens of the natives, and constructs a sort of nest among the branches of the trees. Order Primates, family Pongidae, specifically *Pan troglodytes.*

CHINCH BUG, a sucking insect less than ¼ inch long, with a black or dark gray body and white wings, if mature. Chinch bugs suck so much juice from corn and grain crop roots that they annually destroy thousands of dollars worth of crops. The adults seek protection near the roots and spend the winter under the soil. They emerge in the spring and lay eggs, which hatch in about 2 weeks.

When the young hatch, they start to feed at once. In about 3 months the adult stage is reached, and the insects lay eggs for a second brood. The young are yellow at first, then red, and later black. They are killed by heavy rains but survive from one year to the next in dry places. Order Heteroptera, family Lygaeidae, specifically *Blissus leucopterus.*

CHINCHILLA, a small South American rodent, strongly resembling a ground squirrel. The chinchillas inhabit the Andes of Chile and Bolivia, where they live gregariously in deep burrows, feeding on roots. They are more than 10 inches long and are highly prized and hunted for their lustrous gray pelts, which can be made into costly garments. An attempt has been made to domesticate them on fur farms in the United States. Order Rodentia, family Chinchillidae, specifically *Chinchilla laniger.*

CHIPMUNK, any of about 18 different kinds of small ground squirrels marked above with 5 lengthwise black or dark brown stripes separated by 4 paler stripes. One (*Tamias striatus*) inhabits most of the eastern United States and southeastern Canada. Another, the Siberian chipmunk (*Eutamias sibiricus*), is familiar from northern Japan westward through the northern Soviet Union.

The 16 others of this genus are denizens of forests and brushlands in western North America. Each chipmunk generally lives in a burrow, which it enlarges at intervals to make storage rooms for nuts, acorns, and seeds of many kinds. Four to 6 young are born in the burrow in early spring. Order Rodentia, family Sciuridae.

CICADA, any of about 1,500 different kinds of sucking insects with a short, heavy body and, when adult, 2 pairs of strong wings, the first pair much larger than the second. At rest, the wings are held tentlike over the body. Every continent and most large islands have cicadas; about 75 kinds are found in the United States, and 1 in Britain.

The call is among the most characteristic sounds of hot summer days in temperate zones, and a daily feature of the tropics. These loud sounds are produced by male cicadas, by means of a special pair of drumlike organs with resonators about midway back in the body. Females are attracted to the source of the sound and, after mating, lay eggs in slits cut into the bark of twigs on trees by means of a sawlike organ below the tip of the abdomen.

When the young cicadas hatch, they drop to the ground and spend the next 3 to 17 years (depending on the species) feeding on the sap from underground roots of trees and shrubs. Eventually the fully grown young

AMERICAN MUSEUM OF NATURAL HISTORY
CHIMPANZEE

cicadas climb to the soil surface, walk up a tree trunk or other support, and shed their skins to emerge as winged adults. Order Homoptera, family Cicadidae.

CIVET CAT, any of about 21 different kinds of weasel-like mammals related to mongooses, with a slender body and long tail, and a head suggesting that of a cat, with short rounded ears and sharp muzzle. The various kinds are widespread in the Old World, but one (the African civet, *Civettictis civetta*) from Africa south of the Sudan and the great deserts is best known for the musky substance it secretes in a sac near the anus. This substance, called civet, is used in making perfumes. Probably the civet cat uses the substance for marking out its territorial boundaries. The animal feeds on reptiles, small mammals, birds' eggs, and large insects. Order Carnivora, family Viverridae, several different genera.

CLAM, any of about 11,000 different kinds of bivalve mollusks, known in British countries simply as bivalves. Mostly they live on sandy or muddy bottoms, in both salt and fresh water, all over the world. They create a current of water containing oxygen and microscopic food particles, which enters the gaping shell at one opening, is used for respiration and feeding, and then passes out carrying wastes through a second opening.

In the United States, an important industry has grown up around freshwater clams (species of genera *Lampsilis*, *Margaritana*, and *Unio*), from whose hard shells are manufactured such articles as buttons and knife handles.

Many marine clams are of considerable economic importance, chiefly for food. Along the U.S. Atlantic coast, a favorite is the Venus clam (or little neck, or quahog, *Mercenaria mercenaria*), which is rounded and thick shelled, a source of wampum, which formerly was used as money among Indians; another is the soft-shelled or sand clam (*Mya arenaria*), oval in shape, about 2½ inches long, with shells that are almost paper thin. The soft-shell has been introduced on the Pacific coast, and now rivals in popularity the native Pismo clam (*Tivela stultorum*).

Other clams include the giant bear's-paw clam (*Tridacna*) of coral reefs in the South Pacific, which is the largest shelled mollusk; and the edible cockle (*Cardium*) of British and European shore waters, which provides food for man and bait for fish; a cockle can jump several inches by using its long powerful foot. Class Pelecypoda, various orders.

COBRA, any of several different venomous snakes of the Old World, with fixed fangs at the front of the mouth and a more or less distensible neck region. Best known is the Oriental common cobra (*Naja naja*), which ranges throughout Africa and tropical Asia; it can spread its "hood" in the neck region more widely than any other cobra. It has been used extensively by snake charmers during the day largely because at that time it strikes (if at all) with its mouth shut, and hence does not bite.

The king cobra (*Naja ophiophagus hannah*), native to Asia from India to the Philippines, attains a length of 12 feet and often stands its ground when disturbed; it eats other snakes as well as lizards, small mammals, and birds. South Africa has spitting cobras (of genus *Hemachatus*), which can discharge their venom with astonishing accuracy to a distance of 6 to 10 feet, apparently aiming for the eyes of prey or of people, and causing temporary blindness.

The asp of Egypt is a small deadly cobra (*Naje haje*), whose likeness is found on the headdresses of ancient Egyptian royalty. Order Squamata, suborder Sauria, family Elapidae.

COCKATOO. See *Parrot.*

COCKLE. See *Clam.*

COCKROACH, any of a large number of different flat-bodied insects with long threadlike feelers (antennae), biting jaws, long spiny legs used in running rapidly, and usually a pair of short, sensitive projections from near the hind end of the body. Winged adults have two pairs of thin membranous wings, held flat over the back at rest.

Primarily tropical insects, they occur also in temperate woodlands. A few have adopted a life in human dwellings, stores, and factories where they can find food of many kinds. They require moderate or high humidity and are rare in very dry situations. Household pests include the 1-inch European cockroach (*Blatella germanica*), the 2-inch Oriental cockroach (*Blatta orientalis*), and the 3-inch American cockroach (*Periplaneta americana*). Order Orthoptera, family Blattidae.

COD, a marine bony fish with a projecting lower jaw, a barbel on the chin, a ductless air bladder, and soft-rayed fins. Formerly abundant in cold waters near shore on both sides of the North Atlantic Ocean, cod are still found in great numbers off the coast of Newfoundland.

The back of the cod is olive-green with darker spots, and the belly is white. At 4 years of age, the fish is about 2 feet long; at 5 years, it begins to mate and reproduce, a female laying as many as 9 million eggs.

The average length of cod caught for commerce is about 3 feet. Until about 1950, large quantities of oil were extracted from cod livers for medical use, because of the rich supply there of vitamins A and D. Now artificial vitamins can be made more cheaply and reliably.

Closely related to the cod (*Gadus callarias*) is the whiting (*G. merlangus*), a silvery fish with a black mark on the base of its pectoral fin but with no barbel on the chin. It is harvested from Norway to the Mediterranean and in Atlantic waters from Maine to Florida. Also lacking the barbel is the North Atlantic pollack (*G. pollachius*), which is greenish and has a jutting lower jaw. The coalfish (*G. virens*) is blackish and has a bar-

COYOTE

bel but otherwise resembles the pollack.

A freshwater member of the cod family is the burbot (*Lota lota*), a slender fish of cold deep water found in the Great Lakes in North America, in Europe from the Arctic to mountain lakes in Italy, and in the far north of Asia. Order Anacanthini, family Gadidae.

CONCH, any of the large marine snails with heavy shells, which are powerful predators, seizing and eating the flesh of smaller snails, oysters and other bivalves, and sea urchins. Among the largest are the king conch (*Strombus gigas*) and the queen conch or cameo shell (*Cassis cameo*) of the Gulf of Mexico and warm waters of the Atlantic and Caribbean. A five-pound animal of this kind may have a shell 12 inches long.

The shells of the queen conch are shipped to Europe, particularly Italy, as the material from which cameo jewelry is carved. The trumpet shell (*Charonia tritonis*) is similar but more slender, with a higher spire and a long taper at the opposite end; it is sometimes made into a trumpet or shown as the musical instrument of the Greek sea demigods called Tritons. Class Gastropoda, order Prosobranchiata.

CONDOR. See *Vulture.*

CONE SHELL, any of a large number of different sea snails with smoothly conical chinalike shells. The spire of the shell is a short cone, and the opening is narrow. Cone shells live as vigorous predators in coastal waters of the tropics and the temperate zones, and are particularly numerous among the coral reefs of the South Pacific.

One of the most valued shells in the world is that of the fabulous glory-of-the-sea cone (*Conus gloria maris*) of the South Pacific, which combines beauty with extreme rarity. A collector of living cones must handle a snail with great care because it can jump part way out of its shell and drive into a person's hand a venomous organ, which normally is used to subdue fishes and other prey. A cone is very alert, watching with two eyes on long stalks for prey to come within reach. Order Prosobranchiata, family Conidae, various species of genus *Conus*.

CONY (known also as coney, cunny, and cunney), an ancient European name for a rabbit, a rabbitlike animal, or rabbit fur. The European rabbit *(Oryctolagus cuniculus)* has a diminutive, Latinized form of the word as its species name. The "coney" of the Bible (Leviticus 11:5) was probably the rabbit-sized hyrax or dassie *(Heterohyrax syriacus)* of Asia Minor and Africa, which is a hoofed animal of the order Hyracoidea, although it does not chew a cud and does not have a cloven hoof.

The rock cony or pika of northern Asia and the western mountains in North America *(Ochotona* species), which has no visible tail, and ears about as wide as they are high, is a member of the same order (Lagomorpha) as rabbits, but does not hop. The word is also used by fishermen for the burbot *(Lota* species), a codlike fish, and for a reef fish, the red hind *(Petrometopon cruentatus)* of the West Indies.

COOT, any of 10 different plump, short-tailed wading birds about 1½ feet long, whose individual toes have webbing on each side instead of between adjacent toes. Seven of the species are South American. Of the remaining 3, one breeds in southern Europe and winters in Africa south of the great deserts, another nests across Eurasia from Japan to the British Isles, and the third is found from southern Canada to northern South America.

All are expert swimmers and divers, inhabiting ponds and open water in marshes and swamps where they can find vegetable food. They pile up masses of vegetation in the water as the base for a nest. Coots are poor food, unsuspicious, and easily shot. This has led to the expressions "silly coot" or "queer as a coot" applied to persons who appear simple. Order Gruiformes, family Rallidae, members of genus *Fulica*.

COPPERHEAD. See *Pit Viper*.

COQUINA, or pompano shell, or butterfly shell, or variable wedge shell, a small marine bivalve 1 inch or less in length, living in sandy beaches from North Carolina to Florida and Texas. Rays of color mark the shell, diverging from the hinge region, often crossed by eccentric bands of the same or a different hue, in pink, yellow, green, blue, or lavender.

People collect them wholesale by scooping up the sand just below the edge of the tide, and passing it through a sieve. The coquinas are then cooked in their shells to make coquina soup. Other persons gather particularly colorful shells in pairs for use in jewelry. Order Teleodesmacea, family Donacidae, specifically *Donax variabilis*.

CORAL, any of a large number of lime-secreting, colonial marine coelenterates, or the limy external skeleton they secrete. Coral animals are mostly tropical. When the animals die, their skeletons remain so abundant and massive as to build up into the form of coral reefs and islands. The precious coral of the Mediterranean and of Japan is very solid and takes a high polish. Class Anthozoa.

CORMORANT, or shag, any of about 30 different large water birds which resemble geese when flying and loons while swimming. They are found all over the world, seldom out of sight of land, chiefly along coasts, inland lakes, and rivers. They dive and swim underwater in pursuit of fish, or to escape. Most kinds nest on cliffs and offshore islands in great colonies.

Most famous are the guanay birds (the white-breasted Peruvian cormorant, *Phalacrocorax bougainvillei)* off the Pacific coast of South America, whose nest areas provide guano as agricultural fertilizer. In China and Japan, trained cormorants are used for fishing, a brass ring being placed around their necks to prevent them from swallowing the fish.

Closely related are the 4 different kinds of snakebirds *(Anhinga* species) in which the beak is straight and sharp, not hooked at the tip. They are the original spear fishermen, impaling the fish or frog they catch on the closed beak, then tossing the victim into the air and catching it in the opened mouth. Both snakebirds and cormorants lack the usual water-proofing on their feathers, and must hold out their wings to dry after emerging from water. Order Pelecaniformes, families Phalacrocoracidae and Anhingidae.

CORNBORER, or corn-ear worm, the caterpillar of a moth native to Europe and now an introduced pest in America. It eats into the corn and makes it unsalable. Fermentation of the cornstalks in silos kills the overwintering insect; otherwise it lives through the winter in the plant, and emerges to reproduce the following summer. Order Lepidoptera, family Pyralidae, specifically *Pyrausta nubilalis*.

COTTONMOUTH. See *Pit Viper*.

COUGAR. See *Cat*.

COW. See *Cattle*.

COWBIRD, any of about 6 different kinds of dark-colored birds of medium size, which associate commonly with buffalo and cattle, eating insects disturbed by the grazing mammals. Most cowbirds lay their eggs in the nests of other birds (more than 90 species) and leave them there to be hatched and raised by the foster parents. Order Passeriformes, family Icteridae, chiefly members of genera *Molothrus* and *Tangavius*.

COWRIE, any of a large number of different sea snails with an egg-shaped shell, whose narrow aperture extends almost the full length. Through this opening, the animal puts out its foot and two short feelers, and two extensive folds of its soft mantle then expand, completely covering the shell.

Most cowries are tropical, living in shallow water. Each kind has a distinctive color pattern on its glossy shell, hence a collection of different cowries is particularly attractive. One of the smaller kinds in the South Pacific *(Cypraea moneta)* has been used for centuries as a kind of money by the inhabitants. Order Pectinibranchia, family Cypraeidae, members of genus *Cypraea*.

COYOTE, a medium-sized wolflike mammal of the western plains in North America. It eats chiefly rabbits, ground squirrels, and other small mammals, but occasionally attacks domestic sheep, particularly when lambs are being born or are very young and helpless. Order Carnivora, family Canidae, specifically *Canis latrans*.

CRAB, any of several hundred different crustaceans that spend their larval stages in the sea and then transform to possess 5 pairs of legs and a small abdomen folded under the anterior part of the body (the cephalothorax). The vast majority are marine, but a few come out on land after transforming and, as land crabs, return to the water only in breeding season to lay their eggs in the sea.

The edible blue crab *(Callinectes sapidus)* of the Atlantic coast of America south of Cape Cod is often kept captive until it sheds its hard outer covering, molting to grow larger. It is then a "soft-shell crab" for a few hours, and much easier to open for the table.

A similar crab of the Pacific coast is *Cancer magister,* with rounded sides to the cephalothorax instead of extended sharp spines there. Among land crabs, those with a huge pincer on one side in the male sex are called fiddlers *(Uca* species); at low tide they emerge from their burrows in the beach and search for small particles of food, often in armies of several thousand 1-inch individuals.

Hermit crabs differ in having a soft abdomen, which they conceal in the empty shell of a snail, carrying this shelter around with them wherever they go. A giant hermit crab *(Birgus latro)* of tropical islands in the South Pacific grows larger than any snail shell it can find; thereupon its abdomen becomes hardened, and the crab begins climbing coconut trees to feed on the fruit. Some of these coconut crabs weigh 20 pounds. Order Decapoda, several families and many different genera. See also *Horseshoe Crab*.

CRANE, any of 14 different long-legged birds that fly with the neck extended, not curved over the back in an *S* as among herons, and that stand on 3 toes on each foot because the fourth toe is raised well above the ground; herons have all 4 toes at the same level. The windpipe (trachea) of a crane is extensively convoluted, giving the voice resonance and letting the birds' calls be heard for great distances.

DEER

Cranes are native to all continents and major islands except South America, Malaya, New Zealand, and the Pacific Islands. They frequent large plains and marshes, where they can find insects, frogs, worms, mollusks, reptiles, fishes, and even small mammals. Cranes everywhere are becoming scarce. Those of North America are the rare whooping crane (*Grus americana*) of Great Slave Lake region, which winters in Texas, and the sandhill crane (*G. canadensis*) of northwestern and southeastern prairie country.

The European crane (*G. grus*) breeds in northern Europe and Siberia, but migrates south in winter, far into Africa. Order Gruiformes, family Gruidae.

CRAYFISH, or crawfish, a freshwater crustacean related to and resembling the North Atlantic lobster, but smaller (3 to 6 inches in length) and with claws proportionately smaller. The second syllable of the name was not originally fish, as the word is derived from French écrevisse and is like our word crevice—possibly from the burrows it digs. Originally applied to only one kind in Europe (*Astacus fluviatilis*), the name now refers to all fresh-water relatives in America.

Crayfishes in the southern United States are considered a table delicacy. Their extensive burrowing causes considerable damage to levees and dams. Blind crayfishes are found in the river of Mammoth Cave, in Kentucky. Order Decapoda, family Astacidae.

CRICKET, any of more than 900 different insects related to grasshoppers, with long threadlike feelers (antennae) and cylindrical bodies; those adults that have wings hold the fore pair flat over the back, with the sides turned down sharply. Females with long ovipositors seem to have thick needles projecting from the rear of their bodies; the ovipositors are never bladelike, as in the longhorned grasshoppers.

Only adult males produce the familiar chirping sounds, by rubbing together the bases of their forewings. Crickets are found all over the world, generally hiding during the day but emerging at night to feed on decaying plant material. The American black cricket (*Gryllus assimilis*) occasionally enters houses in cold weather. The European kind (*G. domesticus*) is the "cricket-on-the-hearth," which prefers living indoors on crumbs, and hiding in little chinks in the masonry of fireplaces.

Tree crickets (*Oecanthus* species) are slender, pale green, and stand on bushes while trilling continuously. Mole crickets (species of genus *Gryllotalpa*) have the front legs adapted for burrowing in soft soil. Cave crickets, known also as camel crickets because of their humped backs, are wingless members of a different family (Tettigoniidae), and remain permanently wingless; often they are found under bark or in cellars. Order Orthoptera, family Gryllidae.

CROCODILE, any of about 13 different formidable lizardlike reptiles whose long jaws gape widely and display strong teeth in bony sockets. They include the largest of living reptiles, and are found in tropical and subtropical shore waters and rivers in both hemispheres. They prepare nests of sticks and mud on shore, and guard their eggs until the young hatch.

Little crocodiles feed on insects and other small animals, but gradually change, as they grow, to larger food, often gorging on carcasses in a state of putrefaction.

Often a crocodile floats just below the surface, with only its prominent eyes and nostrils protruding into air. The nostrils at the end of the snout can be closed to keep out water.

The long compressed tail forms a strong swimming organ. The legs are short, with 5 toes on the front pair and 4 on the hind, which are somewhat webbed. The skin is armored with square bony plates.

Best known is the Nile crocodile (*Crocodilus niloticus*), which was worshiped and embalmed by the ancient Egyptians. Today it has been exterminated from the Nile except in the Sudan and Uganda, but it is present in other rivers, such as the Congo and the Zambezi, and in Madagascar. The longest measured specimen was 16 feet; presumably it was old. The salt-water crocodile (*C. porosus*) of Indian, Malayan, East Indian, and north Australian coasts, is more dangerous and generally larger, the biggest known being 20 feet long. It swims from island to island, and often becomes a man-eater. Like other adult crocodiles, it seizes large prey in shallow water and then rolls over and over to subdue it, often drowning it in the process.

The American crocodile (*C. acutus*) of southern Florida, the West Indies, and northern South America often enters salt water. It and the long-snouted Orinoco crocodile (*C. intermedius*) have been measured at 23 feet long, which is the maximum that can be regarded as authentic for any of these animals.

The closest relatives of crocodiles (family Crocodilidae) are the alligators and caymans (family Alligatoridae) and gavials (family Gavialidae), all of which have cavities or pits in the upper jaw into which the long canine teeth of the lower jaw fit. Alligators and caymans have broadly rounded snouts, whereas the snout of a crocodile is pointed, and that of a gavial is very long, narrow, and ends in a soft tip that can be expanded at will. Alligators have a relatively soft skin, easily distinguished by touch from the skin of caymans, which have hard bony plates below the surface.

Of the two kinds of alligators, the larger is the now scarce American species (*Alligator mississippiensis*), which has been nearly exterminated for its hides, and a Chinese representative (*A. sinensis*). Of the 5 kinds of caymans, all inhabit swamps of northern South America and Central America. The sole species of gavial (*Gavialis gangeticus*) is a fish-eater of Indian rivers. Order Crocodilia.

CROW, any of about 10 different large perching birds about 20 inches long, with mostly black feathers and beaks. They are distributed throughout the world. The common North American crow (*Corvus brachyrhynchos*) is remarkable for its gregarious and predatory habits, as well as for its intelligence and cunning.

Crows pair in March; the old repair their nests, the young frame new ones; but they are such thieves that while the one is fetching materials the other must keep watch to prevent the rising fabric from being plundered by crow neighbors. As soon as the nest is finished and five bluish-green eggs with dark blotches are laid, the male starts to provide for his mate; he continues this during the period of incubation.

Crows frequent the same rookeries for years, but allow no intruders into their community. They feed chiefly on worms and the larvae of insects, consequently during outbreaks of insects the crows are beneficial; but they also eat grain and seeds and are thus injurious to the farmer. Chiefly because they destroy beneficial wild birds and their eggs, crows are often regarded as enemies of mankind.

The raven (*Corvus corax*) is the largest of perching birds and the most widespread of crows in the Northern Hemisphere. Because they destroy so many different crops, they have been driven out of the whole of the United States except the western region.

The fish crow (*C. ossifragus*) frequents the Atlantic and Gulf coasts of the United States. The carrion crow (*C. corone*) and the hooded crow (*C. cornix*) are closely related European birds. Most gregarious are the somewhat smaller rooks (*C. frugilegus*), which lose most of the feathers on the face as they mature. Well-populated nest sites in Britain and northern Europe have been used continuously for centuries. Order Passeriformes, family Corvidae, members of genus *Corvus*.

CUCKOO, any of about 200 different kinds of slender-bodied, long-tailed birds with downcurved beaks and pointed wings. They are widely distributed on land, and are of diverse habits. Literary references are generally to the common Eurasian and African cuckoo (*Cuculus canorus*) which has the familiar call of a striking cuckoo-clock. Like many other cuckoos, it is a parasite, laying its eggs in the nests of other birds.

Among the 40 kinds of cuckoos in the New World, the most familiar are the black-billed (*Coccyzygus erythrophthalmus*) and yellow-billed (*C. americanus*) cuckoos, which are shy, inconspicuous, about 1 foot long, and grayish-brown above, white below. They build their own nests, look after their own young, and make guttural, unmusical calls that have earned them the name of "rain crows," because some farmers claim that the sound generally precedes a rain. The cuckoos of both the Old and the New World are regarded as helpful to farmers, because they consume large numbers of caterpillars and other crop-damaging insects.

Ten of the 13 different ground cuckoos are American birds, the others living in Malaya and nearby Southeast Asia. One is the roadrunner bird, or chaparral cock (*Geococcyx californianus*), of the southwestern deserts in the United States and Mexico, where it runs about in search of lizards and snakes to eat.

Also related are the most sociable of the cuckoos, the three different coal-black anis (*Crotophaga* species) of the American Tropics, which make communal nests. Even immature anis appear to help in incubation and feeding of nestlings. Order Cuculiformes, family Cuculidae.

CUTTLEFISH, a squidlike cephalopod mollusk with 10 arms around the mouth and an enclosed, limy shell called a cuttlebone. Cuttlefishes are abundant in the Indian Ocean, and common in the Mediterranean Sea. They prey on fishes and grow to a length of 18 inches. Many persons in southern Europe eat cooked cuttlefish or use pieces for fish bait. When disturbed, a cuttlefish can discharge a black ink from an inkbag, clouding the water around its body. The pigment sepia originally was obtained from this source. Order Dibranchia, specifically *Sepia officinalis*.

DADDY LONGLEGS. See *Harvestman*.

DAMSELFLY, any of a large number of extremely slender adult insects with four slender membranous wings, ordinarily folded together at rest above the long abdomen, while the insect clings to some support, such as a plant stem. Damselflies are found near freshwater on most continents and large islands. Their flight is weak, yet rapid enough to capture some other small insects, such as plant lice and midges.

Damselflies lay their eggs under the surface film of ponds and streams. When full grown, each immature damselfly (called a naiad) creeps up a stem or a rock out of the water and then transforms into the adult. Order Odonata, suborder Zygoptera, several families and genera.

DEER, any of more than 50 different kinds of long-legged, cud-chewing mammals with long necks, small heads carried high, large ears, and large prominent eyes. Usually the male produces solid, branching antlers that fall off annually and are replaced.

Deer are native to the Northern Hemisphere and as far south in South America as Uruguay, in Africa to the great deserts, and in Asia to the East Indies. They have been introduced in New Guinea, Australia, New Zealand, Hawaii, and reintroduced into the British Isles, where they had been exterminated.

Largest of existing deer is the American moose (*Alces americanus*), which is very similar to the smaller European animal (*Alces alces*) called an elk. Both have broad blades with tines as antlers, and inhabit spruce bogs.

The large wapiti or American elk (*Cervus canadensis*) and the smaller European red deer (*C. elaphus*) are similar animals with heavy antlers and many upturned tines on mature bulls. Eastern North America is the home of the white-tailed or Virginia deer (*Odocoileus virginianus*), which has as western counterparts the large-eared mule deer (*O. hemionus*) in the Rocky Mountain states, and the blacktail (*O. columbianus*) near the Pacific coast.

The Old World has small roe deer (*Capreolus capreolus*), which can bark like dogs, and fallow deer (*Dama dama*), which retain their juvenile pattern of pale spots for life. The only deer in which both sexes wear antlers are the reindeer (*Rangifer tarandus*) of the Eurasian Arctic, where it is domesticated and herded by nomads, and the caribou (*R. caribou*) of the Far North in Canada and Alaska, which form herds that wander continually. Order Artiodactyla, family Cervidae.

DINGO. See *Dog*.

DOBSONFLY, a North American insect, of which the larval stage is an aquatic predator known as a hellgrammite. The eggs are laid at the edge of a stream or river, which the larvae enter as soon as they hatch. They need 3 years to attain full size, at which time the mature larvae creep out of the water and pupate among fallen leaves or in the upper levels of the soil, there transforming into the winged adult.

The dobsonfly's wings are gray, with many veins, and spread to as much as 6 inches, making this the largest member of the order Neuroptera in the United States and Canada. The male has enormously extended jaws, held crossed in front of the head. The female has much smaller and more powerful jaws, similar to those of the larva.

Fishermen collect hellgrammites as a favorite bait for trout and other fishes of running water. Order Neuroptera, family Corydalidae, specifically *Corydalis cornuta*.

DOG, any of about 12 different kinds of wolflike mammals popularly regarded as distinct from wolves, jackals, and foxes. The domesticated dog (*Canis familiaris*) is presumed to have been derived from tamed wolves, and now is remarkable for the almost infinite variety in size, shape, color, and hair.

A domestic dog will live on cooked vegetables, but prefers meat. To drink, it laps with its tongue. It never perspires, but loses heat through its moist nose and by panting with its dripping tongue hanging from the mouth. The female (bitch) goes with young 63 days, and usually has 6 to 8 puppies in a litter. Blind at birth, they do not acquire sight until the tenth day. A dog is full grown at the end of its second year, is old at 15, and seldom lives beyond 20 years.

The main types of domestic dogs are: Eskimo, sheep dogs, greyhounds, mastiffs, terriers, hounds, spaniels, and poodles. In Australia, the dingo (*C. dingo*), which has yellowish brown fur, is semiwild. It was probably introduced in prehistoric times by the aboriginal people. Asia has a single kind of raccoon dog (*Nyctereutes procyonoides*), which is valued for its meat and fur but has become rare in Japan and adjacent parts of the mainland, and a red dog (or Indian dhole, *Cuon alpinus*) which associates into hunting packs in Java, Sumatra, Malaya, India, and parts of east Asia far into Siberia. Similar habits are shown by the small African hunting dogs (*Lycaon pictus*), which hunt game animals systematically over most of the continent south of the great deserts.

South America has bush dogs (*Speothos venaticus*) on the savanna areas of Paraguay northward to the Guianas and Panama, and small-eared dogs (*Atelocynus microtis*) in tropical forest areas of the Amazon basin, but both are short-legged, nocturnal, secretive animals about which little is known. Order Carnivora, family Canidae.

DOGFISH, any of several different small sharks that swim in schools along seacoasts, often destroying fish that have been caught in nets and tearing the nets as well. Dogfish rarely grow longer than 5 feet, or heavier than 30 pounds. They seldom attack bathers along beaches. But the spiny dogfish (*Squalus acanthias*) of North Atlantic coasts often severely wounds fishermen who are freeing dogfishes from tangled nets.

This dogfish has a strong sharp spine with a venom gland at the leading edge of each of its two dorsal fins, and while struggling to escape, may drive these spines into a human limb. Order Selachii, several families.

DOLPHIN, any of about 41 different kinds of small sea mammals with pointed noses, many teeth, streamlined bodies, flippers as forelimbs, a distinct fleshy dorsal fin, and transverse tail fin, or flukes, whose total length does not exceed 13 feet. They are found in all oceans.

Frequently dolphins accompany ships, displaying by leaping singly or in groups, coming out of the water in a graceful arc and plunging in again with scarcely a splash. Sometimes they ride the bow wave of a ship for hours at a time. Best known is the bottle-nosed dolphin (*Tursiops truncatus*) of the eastern coast of North America, which feeds on a variety of fishes and squids.

Formerly caught commercially as a source of fine oil for clocks and chronometers, they are now being studied in detail to discover how they navigate, echolocate food and obstacles underwater, and communicate with one another. Order Cetacea, family Delphinidae.

DONKEY. See *Ass.*

DOVE. See *Pigeon.*

DRAGONFLY, any of nearly 4,000 different strong-flying predacious insects with biting mouthparts, prominent compound eyes, four similar membranous wings with many crossveins, and a slender abdomen. They are found near freshwater all over the world. They lay their eggs in water where the young hatch and live as predators. The fully grown young crawl up the stem of an aquatic plant and transform into the adult dragonfly.

The adults destroy mosquitoes and other small insects. Some of the larger kinds are reputed able to fly at a speed of about 60 miles an hour. Popularly called "devil's darning needles" and thought to be dangerous, they are in fact harmless. Order Odonata, suborder Anisoptera.

DROMEDARY. See *Camel.*

DUCK, any of about 115 kinds of web-footed, swimming birds related to geese and swans, but of smaller size and with necks shorter than the body. Most gooselike are the whistling or tree ducks, of Central America and the Southern Hemisphere, of which one from Mexico and Brazil called the Muscovy duck (*Cairina moschata*) has been domesticated as the largest of barnyard ducks.

Some of the shelducks, native to the Old World, are large enough to be called geese; they include the Egyptian goose (*Alopochen aegyptica*) of the Nile valley and Africa south of the great deserts. Most familiar are the smaller ducks of rivers and ponds, which tip their bodies tail up to reach food on the bottom; they include the mallard duck (*Anas platyrhynchus*) of northern North America and Eurasia, from which the all-white Peking duck (*A. platyrhynchus*) became a favorite domestic breed. The tipping or dipping ducks are often called "true ducks," or freshwater ducks; they include also black ducks, pintails, shovelers, widgeons, and various kinds of teal.

The larger bay ducks, which include the canvasback and scaup ducks, dive for their food. The perching ducks. such as the handsome wood duck of North America and the decorative mandarin duck of Japan and eastern Asia, generally nest in a hollow tree or on a horizontal limb high above the water. The eider ducks nest in communities along arctic and sub-arctic rocky coasts, covering their eggs and young in the nest with a heavy layer of down feathers that have been pulled from the mother's winter coat.

The sea ducks, which include the mergansers, scoters, and goldeneyes, are fish eaters whose meat is generally considered inedible. Now extinct, the Labrador duck was formerly abundant along shores of the North Atlantic Ocean.

Most ducks and geese are expert fliers and highly migratory. But the stiff-tailed ducks, such as the ruddy duck (*Oxyura jamaicensis*), tend to be labored in flight, to be residents, and nonmigratory. Yet they swim and dive superbly and perform distinctive courtship displays with the tail stiffly upright, moving the head quickly up and down. Order Anseriformes, family Anatidae.

DUCKBILL, or platypus ("broad foot"), an Australian web-footed mammal whose toothless jaws have the form of a beak, like that of a duck. This animal lives in streams, feeding on worms and insects from the mud at the bottom. At maturity, a duckbill is about 1 foot long. The male has a horny spur on each heel, connected to a poison gland. The female lays eggs with a soft shell in a burrow dug from a stream bank, and takes the young that hatch out into a pouch. She has no nipples on her mammary glands, but the young lap the milk as it oozes out onto her fur. Order Monotremata, specifically *Ornithorhynchus anatinus.*

EAGLE, any of 27 different large birds of prey with broad rounded wings, feathers over most of the head and face, and well down on the feet almost to where the strong toes spread apart. Eagles fly and used to nest in most parts of the continents.

Largest and most widespread is the golden eagle (*Aquila chrysaetus*) of the Northern Hemisphere, which soars high above mountainous terrain, watching with sharp eyes for rabbits, marmots, woodchucks, ground squirrels, and other prey upon which to dive and snatch aloft. The spread of its wings is nearly 10 feet, although the length of the bird from beak to tail tip is only 33 inches. The eagle was the symbol of power of the Roman Empire, and it was trained like a falcon by Jirghiz Tatars to hunt antelope.

The emblem of the United States, the bald eagle (*Haliaeetus leucocephalus*, the "white head"), is actually a sea eagle, close relatives of which live in Africa, in Madagascar, in Malaya and the East Indies, the South Pacific islands, and in the northern regions from Siberia to Iceland and on to Greenland. Tropical jungles have their eagles in the powerful crested birds known as the harpy eagle (*Harpia harpyja*), which hunts for sloths and large parrots in southern Mexico, Central America, and south to the Argentine, and the monkey-eating eagle (*Pithecophagus jefferyi*) of the Philippines.

The harrier eagles, which specialize in catching reptiles, are native to Eurasia, Africa, and Madagascar; they include the splendid, short-tailed bateleur eagle (*Terathopius ecaudatus*) of African highlands. Almost all of these birds are in need of protection to keep them from becoming extinct. Order Falconiformes, family Accipitridae.

EARTHWORM, any burrowing segmented worm that swallows soil and digests out the organic matter before discharging the inert mineral particles as castings. These worms are found in practically all land areas of the world, with the exception of Madagascar and Antarctica.

Earthworms lack eyes and appendages, but are sensitive over their entire body surface and hold to the substratum by means of bristles under muscular control. They work through and loosen the soil, aiding the agriculturalist. In winter they burrow beneath the frost line.

Because they are used as bait by fishermen, earthworms are sometimes called angleworms. The common earthworms (usually *Allobophora foetida* or *Lumbricus terrestris*) are 3 to 5 inches long; in some tropical countries giant earthworms are 5 or more feet long. Class Oligochaeta, order Megadrili, family Lumbricidae.

EARWIG, any of about 1,100 different kinds of insects with biting mouthparts, a slender and somewhat flattened body, and a prominent pair of pincers at the posterior end. They live in temperate and tropical areas, subsisting chiefly on plant material, for which they scavenge at night. By day, earwigs hide among fallen leaves, under boards, in beach drift, or even in clothing that can provide shade. They use their pincers in self-defense, and to help adult earwigs in folding their transparent hind wings to fit under the opaque and horny forewings.

The European earwig (*Forficula auricularia*) has become established along both coasts of North America and in other parts of the world, where it often feeds on fruits, flowers, and garden plants. Females of the European and some other earwigs commonly guard their eggs and newly hatched young, which are called nymphs. Order Dermaptera.

EEL, any of about 350 different kinds of slender, bony fishes of snakelike form, the best known of which mature in brackish estuaries or fresh water but reproduce in the depths of the sea. The common eel of the North Atlantic coasts (*Anguilla anguilla*) is a valuable food fish 2 to 5 feet long. For breeding and egg laying they migrate from Europe and America to deep water near the Bahama Islands, where the spawning takes place.

The infant is a ¼-inch-long, ribbon-like creature so unlike the adult that it was long considered a different fish. When they are large enough, the young eels swim up and westward until they are carried along in the Gulf Stream. Young American eels leave to enter rivers along the coast. European eels remain longer in the Gulf Stream, until they can easily reach Europe's river mouths. Six to 12 years later these eels are mature, and return to the spawning place and apparently die there.

Eels usually have minute scales, but the conger eel (*Conger conger*), a larger, strictly salt-water fish, is quite scaleless; it sometimes grows 8 feet long. Lampreys are sometimes called lamprey eels. Order Apodes, several families, especially Anguillidae.

EGRET. See *Heron.*

EIDER, any of 4 different kinds of large sea ducks, strikingly marked in the male with black and white. They are found in northernmost Europe, Asia, and America, going south beyond the limits of sea ice only in winter. Most species live wholly in the water and go to land only for breeding.

The female lines her nest with her own soft, downy breast feathers. In Iceland and many other arctic areas, people gather these feathers as soon as the nest is deserted, and use them to line pillows and quilts. Order Anseriformes, family Anatidae.

ELEPHANT, either of two gigantic land mammals in which the nose is greatly elongated to form a cylindrical prehensile trunk with the nostrils at the tip. Once widespread, the Asiatic (Indian) elephant (*Elephas indicus*) is now confined to forested regions of tropical India, Burma, the Malay Peninsula, and adjoining islands; and the African elephant (*Loxodonta africanus*) to Africa south of the Sahara.

The Indian elephant has a concave forehead and small ears; the African elephant has a convex forehead and large ears and is chiefly hunted for its ivory. A pygmy race of elephants (4 or 5 feet high, half the size of the regular African elephant) is found in the Congo.

In both species the two upper incisors or front teeth are often enormously developed, constituting long tusks. The lower incisors are lacking, and there are no other teeth in the jaws except the molars, or grinders, of which two are usually in use at one time on each side of each jaw. The molars are very large and expose a number of transverse plates or enamel united by dentine. As each molar is worn out, another succeeds it. The feet have five toes, but these are barely indicated externally; the animal walks on the soles of its feet, each cushioned by a thick pad of skin.

Elephants are vegetable feeders, living almost entirely on the foliage of shrubs and trees, which they strip off by means of the prehensile trunk. As the tusks prevent the animal from drinking in the ordinary way, the water is sucked up by the trunk, which is then inserted in the mouth, where the contents are emptied.

Many species of extinct elephants are known, the most familiar of which are the mammoth and the mastodons. The mammoth (*Elephas primigenius*) formerly ranged over much of North America, Europe, and Siberia. In Siberia whole carcasses have been found preserved in the ice. Unlike the elephants of today, the mammoth was covered by long, thick hair. Its tusks reached a length of 15 feet, some weighing 250 pounds. The young of the Indian elephants have a hairy

covering that sometimes lasts for several years—a vestigial remain of their remote ancestors which lived in colder climates.

The mastodons (*Mammut* species) at one time spread into South America. Some mastodons had a small pair of tusks on the lower jaw in addition to the large pair on the upper jaw. Order Proboscidea.

ELK. See *Deer.*

EMU, a flightless Australian running bird, similar in habits and appearance to the ostrich and second only to the ostrich in size, sometimes standing 7 feet high. The emu grazes in small groups on the level plains, relying upon keen vision and long legs to escape from danger. Order Casuariiformes, family Dromiceidae, specifically *Dromiceius novae-hollandiae*.

ERMINE. See *Weasel.*

FALCON, any of 58 different birds of prey with long-pointed wings, bare shanks and feet, loose-looking feathers on the thighs and, usually, a notch in the cutting edge of the upper beak. They are found on all major continents and large islands except New Zealand.

Largest of falcons is the powerful gyrfalcon (*Falco rusticolus*) of arctic tundras in both hemispheres; smallest is the Philippine falconet (*Microhierax erythrogonys*), which resembles a swallow. Most famous, and perhaps the most skilful flier, is the peregrine falcon (*F. peregrinus*), known in America as a duck hawk; the male is called a tercel. These falcons are the favorites of falconers, men who catch and train the birds to pursue and capture wild game. Order Falconiformes, family Falconidae.

FER–DE–LANCE. See *Pit Viper.*

FINCH, any of several hundred small seed-eating perching birds with heavy beaks, related closely to sparrows. Those of family Fringillidae are of New World origin and include the cardinal of the United States, Darwin's finches of the Galápagos Islands, and the Saffron finch of the West Indies and South America. Those of family Ploceidae come from the Old World, and include the bullfinch, goldfinch, house finch, and weaver finch.

The sexes may or may not be differently colored. Finches are to be found in all types of places, but especially in forests and open meadows. Seeds, insects, and fruits form the greater part of their food. Order Passeriformes.

FIREFLY, a nocturnal beetle with light-producing organs on the lower side of the abdomen used to bring potential mates together. The light is described as "cold" bioluminescence, since it includes little energy in the form of heat. It is caused by the oxidation of a secretion called *luciferin.* The larvae are luminous and called *glowworms.* In some species the eggs are luminous. Order Coleoptera, family Lampyridae.

FISHER. See *Marten.*

FLAMINGO, any of 4 different kinds of wading birds with longer legs and necks than any others. Their beaks have an angular downward turn, adapted to their use in filtering minute particles of food from shallow saline or alkaline water in which the birds stand.

Most widely distributed is the greater flamingo (*Phoenicopterus ruber*) of southernmost Florida, the Bahamas, Yucatan, northern South America, and the Galápagos Islands, and locally in Eurasia and Africa; those of tropical America have the brightest pink color. The Andean and James' flamingos inhabit alkaline marshes at high altitudes in South America. The lesser flamingo is found only in Africa south of the great deserts.

Flamingos nest in colonies of 4,000 to 5,000, on small isolated islands. They build volcano-shaped mud nests about 1-foot high, patting them into shape with feet and beak. One or 2 eggs are laid in the crater. For a time the young birds wear grayish white down and have difficulty standing up. Order Ciconiiformes, family Phoenicopteridae.

FLATFISH, any of a large number of bony fishes that swim or lie on the bottom with one side of the body regularly downward. During their development from symmetrical hatchlings, these fishes grow distorted. Both eyes come to be situated on the upper side of the head.

Flatfishes are found to moderate depths in all oceans, and ascend estuaries into almost freshwater. The one side that becomes the "belly" of the flatfish is usually white; the other side ("the back") often possesses remarkable powers of changing color and pattern. The fish matches the color of its surroundings so well that it is overlooked by small fishes of other kinds that it eats.

Largest of the flatfishes are the halibuts, the name meaning holy fish; they commonly weigh 50 to 120 pounds, and sometimes up to 720 pounds; much of this is white flesh of excellent flavor. Flounders are smaller and possess teeth in their twisted mouths; soles are still smaller and generally lack teeth. Order Heterosomata.

FLEA, a wingless jumping insect with a body strongly flattened from side to side, and mouthparts fitted for piercing flesh and sucking blood. Fleas are found all over the terrestrial world, as external parasites on particular kinds of warm-blooded animals. They lay eggs on the host or in its vicinity. Larval fleas hatch out, and scavenge for food, often in the bedding or nests of the host, or among organic matter in cracks. After transforming during a pupal stage, the adult flea emerges.

The human flea (*Pulex irritans*) is about $\frac{1}{10}$-inch long. Fleas of cats and dogs (*Ctenocephalus* species) sometimes bite people when very hungry.

In the West Indies and other tropical areas, a small flea called the chigoe (*Tunga penetrans*) burrows into human skin, freeing her eggs and breathing through a small hole reaching the body surface. Order Siphonaptera.

FLOUNDER. See *Flatfish*.

FLUKE, any of about 5,800 different kinds of parasitic flatworms that are found all over the world and that cling to their host animals by means of two or more suckers. About 700 different kinds have a simple life history, attacking only a single host animal. They usually attach themselves externally to the skin or the gills of fishes. But some flukes have become adapted to living in the mouth, the nasal cavities, or the urinary bladder of amphibians and aquatic reptiles, such as turtles.

More than 5,000 different kinds of flukes have complex life histories, involving two or more hosts. Generally they live in the intestine of a vertebrate animal or in organs, such as the liver, that are connected to it.

The Chinese liver fluke (*Opisthorchis sinensis*), which reaches a size of ¾-inch in the bile passages of the human liver, lays eggs that reach the outside world in the feces. If an egg gets into freshwater and is eaten by an aquatic snail of the correct kind, the egg hatches into a parasite of a slightly different form, which goes through several larval stages. In the last larval stage it escapes from the snail and swims actively in the water, ready to penetrate the body of a fish in which it can go dormant.

Man becomes infected with the parasite by eating the dormant stage of the fluke in the flesh of fish that has been inadequately cooked. In many tropical countries a more serious parasitic fluke enters the human skin and reaches maturity in the blood vessels of the intestine. It is known as a blood fluke (*Schistosoma* species). Various orders of class Trematoda.

FLY, any of about 85,000 different kinds of insects in which the adult has 1 pair of membranous wings and 1 pair of knobbed balancers (halteres). Flies live on all land areas of the world. Most lay eggs that hatch into active maggots, which grow until they can pupate to transform to adult flies. Some, such as the flesh flies (species of *Sarcophaga*), whose maggots feed on carrion, and the biting tsetse flies (species of *Glossina*) of Africa, deposit active larvae that have hatched inside the body of the mother.

The larvae of mosquitoes, called wrigglers, are active aquatic insects, feeding on microscopic animals and plants. The floating pupae, called bullheads, can swim when disturbed.

Fly maggots of many kinds serve importantly as decomposers of dead plants and animals. Those of the tachina flies (members of family Tachinidae) are internal parasites of caterpillars, and help control infestations upon crop plants. The house fly (*Musca domestica*) and others that eat and drink food used by humans can transmit diseases; they can pick up infections because they seek out manure and other wastes as the places in which their maggots can find food for growth. Order Diptera.

FLYCATCHER, any of a large number of small to medium-sized perching birds with weak feet, which dart from perches on tree branches to capture insects on the wing. Flycatchers of the New World include 365 different kinds from northern Canada to Patagonia, including the eastern kingbird (*Tyrannus tyrannus*) of eastern and central North America, the tail-wagging phoebe (*Sayornis phoebe*) of the eastern United States and Canada, the spectacular scissor-tailed flycatcher (*Muscivora forficata*) of south central United States, the brilliant red vermilion flycatcher (*Pyrocephalus rubinus*) of Mexico, Central America, and the southwestern United States, and the great kiskadee (*Pitangus sulphuratus*), which calls out its name from southern Texas to Brazil.

Flycatchers of the Old World include 378 different kinds, chiefly tree-dwellers, of Africa, Europe, Southeast Asia, and Australia, among them the 5 friendly gray birds with a reddish breast that Australians call robins (*Petroica* species). Order Passeriformes, families Tyrannidae (New World) and Muscicapidae.

FLYING FISH, any of many specially adapted bony fishes that can glide for considerable distances in air, either with the aid of enlarged pectoral fins (the "two-winged flying fishes") or with both pectoral and pelvic fins expanded (the "four-winged flying fishes"). All have the lower lobe of the tail fin enlarged as a sculling organ.

Flying fishes probably take to the air to escape from larger sea animals that are pursuing them in the water. Order Synentognathi, family Exocoetidae.

FLYING LEMUR, or colugo, either of 2 kinds of gliding mammals about 15 inches long with a 9- or 10-inch tail with a gliding membrane linking the neck to the tips of fingers, toes, and tail. They live in the forests of Malaya and the East Indies, where they climb slowly but skilfully head up, or cling suspended by their front claws.

They feed on seeds, fruit, buds, flowers, and leaves. Although quite helpless on the ground, they are active in the trees, leaping from branch to branch with remarkable agility, and gliding as much as 450 feet for each 40-foot loss in altitude. Order Dermoptera, family Cynocephalidae, specifically *Cynocephalus volans* in the Philippines and *C. variegatus* in Southeast Asia and the East Indies.

FOWL, a term originally referring to any bird, but now generally restricted to members of the Order Galliformes, which includes the domestic fowl (rooster and hen), the peafowl (peacock and peahen), the pheasant, turkey, partridge, grouse, quail, and the moundbuilder of Australia. Most of these are rather heavy in the body, with short wings and an ability to fly short distances only. Generally they run on the ground, using their strong feet to scratch for food. Most nest on the ground, laying numerous eggs, which the hen bird incubates alone.

Wildfowl, however, are now regarded as ducks, geese, and swans, all members of the Order Anseriformes. Waterfowl include pelicans and all other swimming birds, but not the herons and other wading birds.

FOX, any of about 15 different kinds of small to medium-sized doglike mammals with a sharp muzzle, long bushy tail, and a "foxy" odor arising from special glands near the base of the tail. They inhabit most of Africa, Eurasia, and the Americas. The pupil of a fox's eye is generally elliptical in strong light; ears are usually triangular and pointed.

The red fox (*Vulpes fulva*) inhabits most parts of Europe and America and extends also into northern Asia. Its senses are extremely acute, and it has learned to use them to avoid man. It usually remains concealed in a burrow during the day and ventures abroad chiefly at night in search of food.

It is one of the principal predators on voles and mice, but eats also insects, eggs, fruit, grass, and whatever small birds and mammals are easy to catch.

The arctic, or white, fox (*Alopex lagopus*) is remarkable for changing its color with the season, being brown or bluish in summer and white in winter. The soles of its feet are hairy. The gray fox (*Urocyon cinereoargenteus*) is common from southern Canada to northern South America, and often climbs trees when pursued, or to rest inconspicuously. The furs of all foxes are valuable, especially the silver foxes and blue mutant strains of arctic foxes now raised for the market on fox farms. Order Carnivora, family Canidae.

FRIGATE BIRD, or man-of-war bird, any of 5 different tropical, web-footed birds with a long hooked beak, very long wings that are bent at an angle while soaring or flying, and a deeply forked tail. The magnificent frigate bird (*Fregata magnificens*) ranges from the Bahamas and Baja California to Brazil and Ecuador; the male is solid black, except for the brilliant red chest pouch that he inflates at mating season; the female has a white neck and throat.

The great frigate (*F. minor*), also measuring 40 inches from beak tip to tail tip, and whose wingspan is about 7 feet, patrols coasts of the western South Atlantic, the central and western Pacific, and the Indian Ocean.

Smallest is the 32-inch-long lesser frigate bird (*F. ariel*) of the South Pacific, Australian shorelines, Madagascar, and the coast of Brazil. These birds are all expert fliers, but can scarcely walk or swim. They pick food from the ocean surface, or snatch unguarded chicks from the nests of other sea birds, or like pirates attack any gull, booby, or cormorant that has caught a fish, forcing it to give up its prey. Order Pelecaniformes, family Fregatidae.

FROG, the common name for adult tailless amphibians that have smooth skin and webbed hind feet. Frogs inhabit moist places, near freshwater, all over the world. Females lay their eggs in long strings in the water. From these, fishlike larvae called tadpoles or polliwogs hatch out, each with a broad, swimming tail and gills on the sides of its head.

Tadpoles feed upon small aquatic plants that they scrape from sticks and stone with their horny jaws. As they increase in size, the legs grow out and the tail is absorbed. The anterior pair of legs forms first but remains concealed beneath the skin until the hind pair is well developed and conspicuous. With the growth of legs and the loss of tail, the gills disappear and the lungs come into use; nevertheless most species always remain in close proximity to water throughout life.

Adults live on animal food such as insects, mollusks, and small fishes. Some do not hesitate to eat members of their own species. Frogs are useful to man in keeping down certain species of insects. They are caught for the flesh in their hind legs, which is white meat of mild flavor.

The largest North American frog is the bullfrog (*Rana catesbiana*), 5 to 8 inches long, found almost everywhere east of the Rocky Mountains. The pickerel frog (*R. palustris*) is brown with green spots, and the leopard frog (*R. pipiens*) is brilliantly marked with black spots outlined in white on its bright-green skin. Order Salientia, family Ranidae.

FRUIT FLY, any of nearly 1,000 different kinds of 2-winged insects less than ¼-inch long, commonly found around bananas and other fruits in which its maggots can develop, feeding on yeasts in the fermenting juice. The Mediterranean fruit fly (*Ceratitis capitata* of family Trypetidae) is a destructive pest, especially on citrus fruits. Much that we know today about heredity has been learned from a study of fruit flies of the genus *Drosophila* (literally "honey-lovers"), of family Drosophilidae. Order Diptera.

GALLINULE, a marsh bird closely related to the coots and rails, with a plump body, suggesting that of a domestic fowl. Gallinules are found in many parts of the world, usually close to freshwater, in which they often swim about. Except on migration, they seldom fly far. They nest on platforms built of vegetation in the middle of marshes.

The common, or Florida, gallinule (*Gallinula chloropus*) of eastern North America and Central America is native also to Europe and Britain, where it is called a moorhen. The larger, purple gallinule (*Porphyrula martinica*) is a more conspicuous bird, with a purple breast and a blue shield on the forehead contrasting with a bright red, yellow-tipped beak, and with lemon-yellow legs.

Gallinules live along the Atlantic and Gulf coasts and in Central and northern South America. Similar, but flightless, birds in New Zealand are the pukeko (*Porphyrio melanotus*) of marsh edges and the rare takahe (*Notornis mantelli*) of valley tussock land, which until recently was believed to be extinct. Order Gruiformes, family Rallidae.

GAR (from an Anglo-Saxon word meaning pike or spear), any of about 8 different kinds of armored fishes with cylindrical bodies and needle-sharp teeth. They inhabit rivers and lakes of North America east of the Rockies and southward to the Isthmus of Panama.

Their covering is of rhomboidal scales, each with an enamel surface so hard that a fish spear will scarcely penetrate. The common gar, or bony pike (*Lepisosteus osseus*), sometimes attains a length of 5 feet and is easily distinguished by the long beaklike extension of the mouth region. The alligator gar of the lower Mississippi and of Mexico (*L. spatula*) is larger than the common gar, occasionally reaching 12 feet in length and a weight of 350 pounds. Order Ginglimodi, family Lepisosteidae.

GAZELLE, any of about 12 different exceedingly slender and long-legged antelopes, renowned for their long necks and graceful movements. They inhabit Africa, Asia Minor, and as far east as northern India and Mongolia. They include the dibatag or Clark's gazelle (*Ammodorcas clarkei*) of Somaliland, the gerenuk or Waller's gazelle (*Litocranius walleri*) of East Africa, the springbok (*Antidorcas marsupialis*) of South Africa and Angola, the Mongolian gazelles (species of *Procapra*), and various gazelles (genus *Gazella*) in which lyre-shaped horns develop in both sexes.

The common gazelle (*G. dorcas*), 3 to 4 feet tall, is fawn or dun colored on the back; a brown or black line separates this coloration from the white hair on the belly. The horns, stronger in the male than in the female, were used for lyre frames in early days.

The gazelle inhabits the large plains and the Saharan region of northern Africa, as well as Arabia and Syria, and lives in herds. Order Artiodactyla, family Bovidae.

GECKO, any of about 300 kinds of slender lizards with special suction discs on their toes, permitting them to creep on smooth vertical surfaces or even ceilings in pursuit of insects as food. Geckos sometimes bask in the sun, watching for danger through slit pupils suggesting those of a cat. Like cats, they prefer to hunt in twilight and darkness, capturing their food by sudden extension of a long, sticky tongue with an extended tip. Often geckos produce loud calls, which may sound like geck'-oh or like the chirp of an insect.

The banded gecko (*Coleonyx variegatus*) of the North American southwest, from Texas to California, is pale brownish gray, banded or speckled with dark reddish brown, and attains a length of 4 inches. Like all geckos it is harmless, despite superstitions to the contrary. Order Squamata, suborder Sauria, family Gekkonidae.

GIBBON, any of about 7 kinds of tailless anthropoid apes with extremely long arms and legs, enabling them to exceed all other mammals in the agility with which they swing through the tree tops from branch to branch. They

SATOUR

GNU

are native to southeastern Asia and the East Indies.

Rarely more than 3 feet high when standing erect, a gibbon usually balances itself by stretching its arms overhead. Let hang for a moment, the hands almost touch the ground. Gibbons have buttock pads and long canine teeth. They eat mostly fruit, leaves, buds, and whatever birds, eggs, and insects they can catch. By day they are active, but by night gibbons sleep upright in little groups, leaning on one another, and some crouch in big trees. Order Primates, family Pongidae.

GILA MONSTER. See *Lizard.*

GIRAFFE, the tallest mammal, a solid-horned cud-chewer with extraordinarily long neck and long legs. It inhabits African highlands, where it browses on the sides and tops of thorny trees. Formerly it was called the camelopard, because the neck was thought to resemble that of a camel, and the pattern of the skin the spots of a leopard. Actually it is related both to the antelopes, which have hollow horns, and the deer, which have solid antlers. In the giraffe the antlers are never shed, but continue to grow slowly under the hairy skin atop the head.

The giraffe uses its unusually long cylindrical tongue for stripping off the leaves from the trees on which it feeds. When the giraffe drinks it must spread its front legs wide apart to get its mouth to the water. Order Artiodactyla, family Giraffidae.

GNU, or wildebeest, e i t h e r of 2 kinds of hollow-horned, cud-chewing African antelopes with a conspicuous beard, mane, tuft of hairs between the forelegs, and tuft of long hairs at the tip of the tail. Commonest and widespread on the African savannas is the brindled gnu or blue wildebeest (*Connochaetes taurinus*) which often forms mixed herds with zebras, each benefiting from the association. The white-tailed gnu (*C. gnou*), which has been exterminated except in South Africa, is about the size of a horse and has structural features suggesting a bison and a deer.

In both male and female the horns taper to points, curving forward from the skull and turning up at the ends. Order Artiodactyla, family Bovidae.

GOAT, any of 5 different hairy cud-chewing mammals, similar to sheep but differing in that the forehead is convex, rather than concave; in the possession of a beard and scent glands on the body of the male; and in the absence of scent glands on the feet of both sexes.

Goats inhabit Eurasia from Spain to Siberia, south to the Sudan, Ethiopia, and the Arabian peninsula. Mostly they are found in wild mountainous countries where they scramble among the high rocks. The domestic goat (*Capra hircus hircus*) may have been derived in ancient times from the bezoar goat (*C. hircus aegagrus*) of Asia Minor. It has been bred into many distinctive lines, such as the Angora, whose hair is woven into the fabric called mohair, and the Kashmir goat, whose hair becomes fine cashmere for India shawls.

The flesh, especially that of the kid or young goat, is used as food, despite its rather poor quality. The milk is very rich and nutritious, and, because it is free from tuberculosis germs, it is often fed to tubercular and other patients. Many cheeses are made from goats' milk. Some goats yield about 2 quarts. The skin is dressed as leather for many uses, particularly for gloves and other fine kinds of shoes. The horns, which are worn by both sexes, are used to make knife handles, and the fat to make candles.

The Rocky Mountain goat (*Oreamnos americanus*) is really a closer relative to the European chamois, intermediate between the antelope and the goat. It is about as big as an ordinary sheep, and it looks like a sheep of the Merino breed with long straight hair and spiky horns. Order Artiodactyla, family Bovidae.

GOLDENEYE, or whistler, a diving duck that nests in tree holes in the northern United States, Canada, Scandinavia, and northern areas of Europe and Asia. When feeding, it frequents lakes, broad rivers, and bays of the ocean, in which it can dive for crustaceans, plants, and aquatic insects. In flight, its wings make a characteristic high-pitched whistling sound.

Goldeneyes are dark colored toward the tip, with white patches above and below toward the body. In both sexes the body itself is white below and dark above. The male has a black head with a white spot between eye and beak, and a white neck. His mate has a brown head and a gray neck with a white collar. In the common goldeneye (*Bucephala clangula*), the white patches on the head of the male and the beak in both sexes are smaller than in Barrow's goldeneye (*B. islandica*), which nests farther north and at higher altitudes in North America, and only in Iceland in the Old World. Order Anseriformes, family Anatidae.

GOLDFINCH, a small songbird with a short, strong beak suited to opening seeds, and a quick, undulating flight. The American goldfinch (*Spinus tristis*) is common over most of settled Canada and all except the southernmost states of the Union in summer; it ranges down into eastern Mexico for the winter.

In summer the male goldfinch is often called a "wild canary," because he is then brilliant golden yellow with a black forehead, a black forked tail, and black wings marked with a white bar. His coloration in autumn and winter more closely resembles that of his mate and young goldfinches, which are brownish olive-yellow, darker above, with black tail and black wings similarly marked.

The European goldfinch (*Carduelis carduelis*), introduced into America in 1852 on Long Island, New York, is even more brightly colored, and equally in both sexes. Its face is brilliant red, snow-white at the sides; the crown of the head is jet-black, as are the nape of the neck, most of the forked tail, and the wings except for a broad band of bright yellow and white spots along the trailing edge. The body is brown except on the rump and belly, which are white. The call of the European goldfinch is usually a canarylike twitter.

In Europe and Asia, goldfinches are permanent residents of gardens, orchards, and cultivated land. They are rare or absent in Iceland, northernmost Scotland, and similar latitudes across the great continent of Eurasia. Order Passeriformes, family Fringillidae.

GOOSE, any of about 14 different kinds of web-footed birds related to swans, which are bigger and have longer necks, and to ducks, which are smaller and have shorter necks in proportion to the body. With the exception of the Australian magpie goose (*Anseranas semipalmata*), which is black and white, they are birds of the Northern Hemisphere. The legs of a goose are farther forward than a duck's, and thus better adapted for walking.

Geese spend much of their time on land, feeding on grass and other herbage, berries, seeds, and various kinds of vegetable food. Although large and bulky, they have great powers of flight. They strike with their wings in fighting; at the bend of the wings there is a hard callous knob or tubercle, which in some species becomes a spur.

Gray geese of 5 kinds include the domestic goose (*Anser domesticus*), which probably originated from the European graylag goose (*A. anser*), which is almost 3 feet long from the tip of the bill to the extremity of the short tail; the wingspread is about 5 feet. The weight of the largest bird is about 10 pounds. The other gray geese are the lesser white-fronted goose, the bean goose and the swan goose of Eurasia and the greater white-fronted of the North American arctic.

Three white geese are the snow goose (*Anser caerulescens*) of northern Asia and the American arctic, the blue goose of Baffin Land, and Ross' goose which comes from the Arctic Circle to winter in California.

The black geese include the Canada goose (*Branta canadensis*) and the smaller brant of North America, the barnacle goose of far northern Europe, the bar-headed goose of the Himalayas, and the rare nene of Hawaii.

Geese are kept for their eggs, for their flesh (a favorite Christmas dish), and for their feathers that are used for pillows and beds. Quill pens were made from goose feathers. Order Anseriformes, family Anatidae.

GOPHER, any of 21 different kinds of squirrel-like burrowing rodents of the open plains in the Northern Hemisphere. The name is from the French *gaufre* (honeycomb), alluding to the burrow.

Gophers search by day for seeds, nuts, roots, soft stems and leaves, insects, bird eggs, and whatever mice and birds they can catch. Near cultivated fields, they may raid by night, making themselves troublesome pests in some localities. They carry home dry foods to storage chambers, but also become very fat by midsummer and often go early into winter dormancy. Order Rodentia, family Sciuridae, species of genus *Citellus*.

GORILLA, the largest of the manlike apes, which may reach a height of 5½ feet and a weight of 400 pounds. Gorillas live in the bamboo forests of tropical West Africa. Their arms in relation to the body are shorter than those of any other ape. Gorillas are very strong, but they usually retreat before man. When grown to more than 100 pounds, they rarely climb. Usually they make beds of leaves and boughs.

Little was known of them until 1859 when Paul Du Chaillu, a French-American explorer, brought skins and skeletons to Europe. He brought back to the United States the first gorillas ever seen there. Order Primates, family Pongidae, specifically *Gorilla gorilla*.

GRACKLE, either of 2 large blackbirds, about 14 to 17 inches long, including the long tail, found in Canada and the United States east of the Rocky Mountains. The bronzed grackle (*Quiscalus quiscula*), sometimes called crow blackbird, nests as far north as Great Slave Lake and Newfoundland, and winters in the southeastern United States. The boat-tailed grackle (*Cassidix mexicanus*), which is slightly larger (up to 16 inches long), is a bird of Atlantic coastal states and Mexico. Order Passeriformes, family Icteridae.

ROTHSTEIN/LOOK

GORILLA

INSECTS AND ARACHNIDS

TARANTULA

WOLF SPIDER

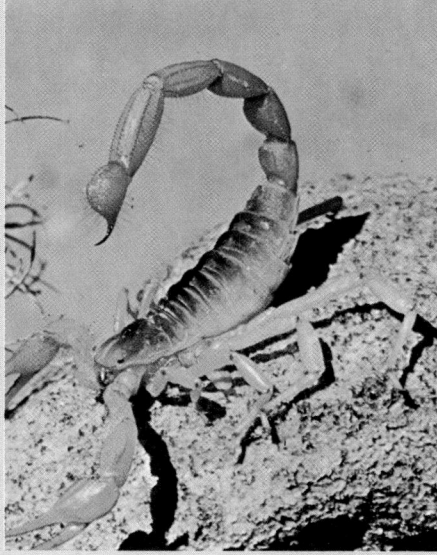

SCORPION

HORNED BEETLE

RED-BANDED LEAFHOPPER

PRAYING MANTIS

BEE AT FLOWER

GRASSHOPPER ON THISTLE

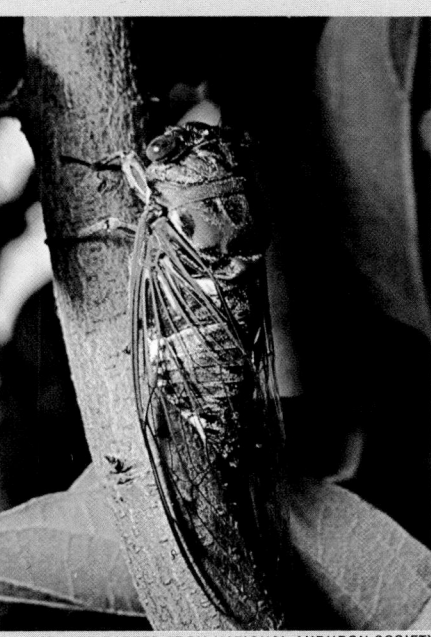

CICADA

OCEAN LIFE

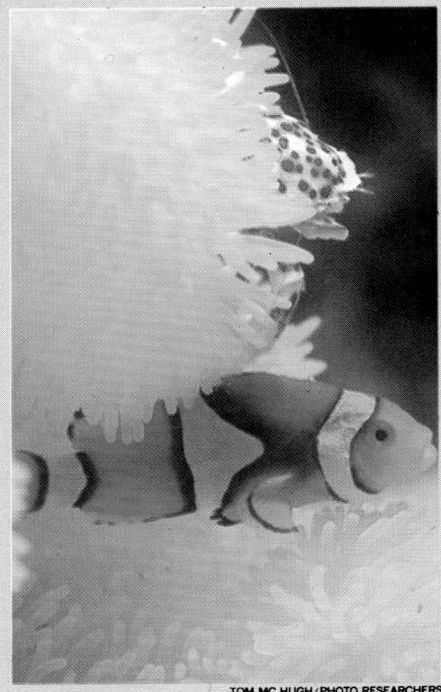

ARTHUR AMBLER/PHOTO RESEARCHERS
PURPLE STURGEON

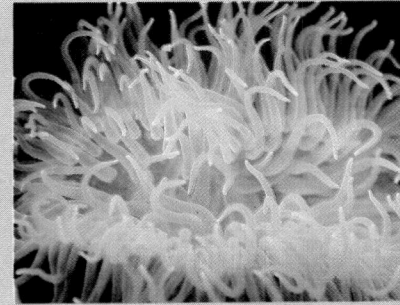

TOM MC HUGH/PHOTO RESEARCHERS
FLUORESCENT ANEMONE

TOM MC HUGH/PHOTO RESEARCHERS
CLOWNFISH, CRAB, ANEMONE

PETER DAVID/PHOTO RESEARCHERS
ABRALIA

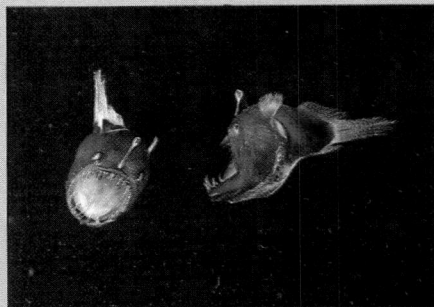

PETER DAVID/PHOTO RESEARCHERS
ANGLER FISH

SOAMES SUMMERHAYS/PHOTO RESEARCHERS
RED CORAL FISH

RUSS KINNE/PHOTO RESEARCHERS

DOLPHINS

TOM MC HUGH/PHOTO RESEARCHERS

BELUGA WHALE

TOM MC HUGH/PHOTO RESEARCHERS

REEF SHARKS

FRESHWATER SPECIES

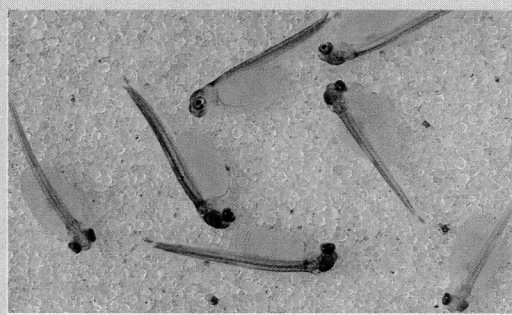

W. TREAT DAVIDSON/PHOTO RESEARCHERS

BROOK TROUT EGGS

TOM MC HUGH/PHOTO RESEARCHERS

GOLDEN TROUT

PREHISTORIC ANIMALS

FIN-BACKED EDAPHOSAURUS, a giant, plant-eating reptile, roamed through forests of exotic plants more than 300 million years ago.

TRIO OF ORNITHOMIMUSES, *left*, called "ostrich dinosaurs," around a drying water hole as the rain forests give way to desert lands.

GIANT PTERANODONS, *right*, flying lizards with leathery 25-foot wings and three-foot beaks, lived over 150 million years ago.

REPTILES AND AMPHIBIANS

CORAL SNAKE

BRAZILIAN HORNED TOAD

LAND IGUANA

GILA MONSTER

MUSSERANA

RATTLESNAKE

TEJU LIZARD

MAMMALS

BIGHORN MOUNTAIN SHEEP

GIRAFFES

RACCOON

ANTEATER

RINGTAIL CAT

MUSTACHED TAMARING

JAGUAR

RHINOCEROSES

KOALA

BEARS

BIRDS

YOUNG TOUCANS

FRIGATE BIRDS

SANGUE-DE-BOIS

JANDAIA

B. A. LEERBERGER, JR.

PENGUINS

RED-FOOTED BOOBY CHICK

HARPY EAGLE

GREBE, any of 18 different kinds of diving water birds, each of whose toes has horny flaps at the sides, like individual webbing, used particularly in swimming underwater. Grebes are found on all continents as inhabitants of slow streams and ponds. When disturbed, grebes usually dive below the surface where they swim long distances. They are good flyers, however, but have some difficulty in leaving the surface of the water because of their small-sized wings.

They feed mainly on small fish, frogs, crustaceans, and insects. They build nests near or on the water and the matted plant material sometimes actually floats. Grebes carry their young pick-a-back, sometimes even diving to escape with the young birds still hanging on. Order Podicipediformes, family Podicepedidae.

GROSBEAK, any of several songbirds with a conical, heavy beak well adapted to opening thick-shelled seeds. They are distinctly larger than sparrows, and frequent trees and brush, seldom coming to the ground. They are birds of the Northern Hemisphere. Generally the two sexes are unlike in coloration; the males are much more brilliantly marked. Many individuals associate together in winter, often showing little fear of man.

Among the grosbeaks of North America are the cardinal (*Richmondena cardinalis*), which has a crest; the rose-breasted grosbeak (*Pheucticus ludovicianus*); the black-headed grosbeak (*P. melanocephalus*); the blue grosbeak (*Guiraca caerulea*); the evening grosbeak (*Hesperiphona vespertina*); and the pine grosbeak (*Pinicola enucleator*), which is found also in coniferous forests of northern Europe, where a much smaller bird (*Carpodacus erythrinus*) is called the scarlet grosbeak, although it is a close relative of the American purple finch (*C. purpureus*). Order Passeriformes, family Fringillidae.

GROUSE, any of 18 different kinds of fowl-like birds with thick soft feathers, usually brown and reddish in inconspicuous patterns. Grouse are widely distributed in the Northern Hemisphere. Their short wings beat very rapidly in flight with a whirring sound, giving them great speed and agility over distances up to a few hundred yards. In general grouse prefer the deep woods and spend most of their lives on the ground where they find seeds, fruits, buds, and insects.

The ruffed grouse (*Bonasa umbellatus*), sometimes called partridge in the northern states, is regarded as the finest of all upland game birds over its whole area of distribution, coast to coast in Canada, and southward to Georgia and northern California.

During the mating season, the male ruffed grouse drums with his wings at some open spot on or near the ground, the sound sometimes carrying more than a mile, and serving as a call to the female or as a challenge to combat for other males.

Spruce grouse (*Canachites canadensis*) occupy much the same area in coniferous woods rather than in cutover forests. Most beautiful is the black grouse (*Lyrurus tetrix*) of forests in northern Eurasia, and largest among grouse the capercaillie (*Tetrao urogallus*) of Scandinavia, which is almost as large as a turkey. The heath hen (*Tympanuchus gallo*), which became extinct on the American mainland about 1835 and on Martha's Vineyard Island in 1932, was an eastern race of the prairie chicken (same name) which is growing scarce over its range from the Canadian prairies to the Appalachians and Arkansas. Order Galliformes, family Tetraonidae.

GUINEA FOWL, any of 7 different kinds of short-tailed, pheasantlike birds that run, rather than fly. They are native to Africa and Madagascar. Because of their tasty meat they are now widely domesticated even though they are almost too noisy to be raised on a small farm. They are mainly vegetarian, digging and scratching for seeds and roots. The common domestic guinea fowl (*Numida meleagris*) prefers grassy areas in which to hunt for seeds, fruits, slugs, and insects, but it needs trees in which to roost at night. In Africa, flocks sometimes number 2,000. Order Galliformes, family Numididae.

GUINEA PIG, or cavy, any of about 20 different kinds of stout-bodied, tailless, vegetarian rodents about 10 inches long. They are native to brushlands in mountainous South America, where one kind (*Cavia cobaya*) was domesticated in pre-Columbian times by the Incas as a convenient source of meat. In the wild, this guinea pig produces small litters, but in captivity it is extremely prolific: it begins to breed when 10 months old, and produces several families in a year, each family consisting of about 8 young. The popular name is inappropriate; the animal is not a pig and it does not come from Guinea. Order Rodentia, family Caviidae.

GULL, any of 43 different kinds of web-footed, scavenging birds, larger than terns, with a hooked tip on the upper beak and the habit of directing the beak forward, not down, while in flight. Gulls are common along seacoasts and large bodies of inland water, and on garbage dumps all over the world. They are usually white below with the upper parts varying from a light gray to black.

They can run and walk readily and often help in controlling plagues of grasshoppers and crickets. The Pacific gull (*Larus pacificus*) patrols the shores of Australia and the Great Barrier Reef for young turtles as they hatch and scamper over the beach toward the water. The herring gull (*L. argentatus*) and others of North and Central America drop mussels and sea urchins on rocks, paved areas, and parked cars to break open the shells and get at the meat inside. Order Charadriiformes, family Laridae.

GUPPY, or mosquito fish, a small top minnow from freshwaters of northern South America and the islands of the West Indies. It is named for Robert J. L. Guppy, who in 1866 discovered fishes of this kind in Trinidad.

At 1 inch in length the male guppy attains full size, and develops a long anal fin that shows his sex. The female grows twice as large, with an anal fin of normal size. During courtship, the male uses his special fin to transfer sperm cells to the female. Fertilization is internal, and the embryos develop into active little fish before emerging from their mother. From a single mating, a female guppy may produce 200 young in a month, and 200 more each month thereafter for about 8 months.

Because young fish can take care of themselves if the parents do not eat them, and reach maturity quickly, guppies have become popular as the "million fish" for tropical aquariums in the home. Supposedly a pregnant female guppy could give rise to 1 million descendants in a year or less, if the offspring were supplied with enough food and space that includes vegetation wherein the young can hide from older fish.

The common name mosquito fish refers to the readiness of the guppies to eat small aquatic insects. In captivity they may be supplied with water fleas (*Daphnia*) or young brine shrimp raised for the purpose. Order Cyprinodontes, family Poeciliidae, specifically *Gambusia affinis*.

HADDOCK, a marine bony fish resembling a cod in having the dorsal fin divided into 3 parts and the anal fin into 2, but with only a white line along the side instead of a pattern of markings. Haddocks are common in cold waters of the North Atlantic, where they eat virtually anything edible, especially mollusks. Haddock is one of the most important of the food fishes, and exceeds all other fishes in tonnage caught and sold annually. It is often smoked for sale as "finnan haddie." Order Anacanthinae, family Gadidae, specifically *Melanogrammus aeglefinus*.

HAKE, any of several different marine food fishes differing from cod in details of the skull bones and ribs; the dorsal fin consists of a long forward part and a shorter rear part (not three parts, as in the cod), and the lower jaw bears no projections (barbels) with which to detect smaller fishes and other animals as prey upon the sea bottom.

Despite this lack, hake, which are widely distributed, catch fishes, crustaceans, and squids in large numbers. Apparently they do so with little exertion, for their flesh remains soft. Like the cod, hakes have soft fins and an air bladder with no connection to the outside world.

The European hake (*Merluccius merluccius*) inhabits deep water in the Mediterranean Sea and along Atlantic coasts from Norway to northwestern Africa; it attains a weight of 20 pounds, and is fished for silver at depths as great as 2,400 feet. The silver hake (*M. bilinearis*) along the Atlantic coast of North America and the Pacific hake (*M. productus*) are of smaller size. The South African hake, or stockfish (*M. capensis*), grows to as much as 4 feet in length, and is caught at depths to 1,800 feet by trawling, as the most valuable single commercial fish of that region. Order Anacanthini, family Merluccidae.

HAMSTER, any of several different kinds of small burrowing rodents from Mediterranean countries and Asia. The common, or black-bellied, hamster (*Cricetus cricetus*) is a short-tailed species, which makes extensive burrows in which to spend the day and the winter. A hamster may store as much as 200 pounds of grass seeds, dry small fruits, and even potatoes in its burrow. In summer these animals eat large numbers of insects as well as frogs, worms, and other smaller animals.

In some areas of Europe and Asia Minor, hamsters are trapped for their furry skins, which are usually light brown above, marked with white on the sides, and black below. During recent years, large numbers of common hamsters have been raised in captivity on a diet of dog biscuits, corn, and lettuce. They make interesting pets, and have become a valuable experimental animal for medical science. Order Rodentia, family Cricetidae.

HARE, any of about 30 different kinds of short-tailed, long-eared, jumping mammals with a short palate and the habit of bearing young that are fully haired, open-eyed, and ready to run with the mother. Native to North America and Eurasia as far south as Malaya, they have now been introduced into South America, Australia, New Zealand, islands off the northwest coast of Africa, and the northeastern United States.

The popular names hare and rabbit are often incorrectly used interchangeably. For example "jack rabbits" and "snowshoe rabbits" are not rabbits, but hares, whereas the "Belgian hare" is a rabbit.

Most kinds of hares live in open grassy country, but the varying hare (*Lepus americanus*) inhabits evergreen forests, where its fur is white in winter and dark brown in summer; its large feet make huge prints in the snow, hence the name "snowshoe rabbit" for this animal. The arctic hare (*L. arcticus*) is not found south of Hudson Bay. The black-tailed jack rabbit (*L. californicus*) occupies the U.S. southwest and Mexico.

All of these animals supply important food for the larger predators, and might contribute important meat and fur for mankind if raised in captivity, as is the European hare (*L. europaeus*) in many parts of Europe, to keep the animals free of disease. In the wild, they carry tularemia, a severe bacterial disease to which people who handle infected hares are susceptible. Order Lagomorpha, family Leporidae.

HARVESTMAN, or daddy longlegs, a spiderlike land animal with extremely slender long legs and a small, compact, often hard body bearing a pair of eyes on an elevated turret on its back.

Harvestmen are abundant in field and forest in all parts of the world from May to October. Eggs are laid in the fall and hatch the following spring. A few species sleep through the winter, but the majority of the adults die each fall after the breeding season. Their food consists mainly of small insects and other minute animals. They are harmless, but may produce an unpleasant odor when molested. Order Phalangida of class Arachnida.

HAWK, any of about 80 different medium-sized birds of prey, larger than falcons, smaller than eagles, kites, and vultures. Hawks are found in all parts of the world except New Zealand and Oceania. They are almost wholly carnivorous and rarely take food that has not recently been killed. The plumage is usually brown or white, although gray is not uncommon. The nests are built in trees and on rocky cliffs; occasional ground nests are found.

The principal kinds are the sharpwinged members of genus *Accipiter,* and the broad-winged hawks of genus *Buteo.* The sharp-shinned hawk (*A. velox*) is small, measuring only 11 to 13 inches in length, grayish on the back with bars of brown, whitish underneath, and with yellow legs and feet. Cooper's hawk (*A. cooperi*) is similar in plumage to the sharp-shinned, but larger.

The goshawk, originally goose-hawk (*A. gentilis*), is circumpolar and a great favorite with falconers for hunting marsh birds and rabbits. The marsh hawk (*Circus hudsonius*), one of the harriers, is a highly beneficial and almost cosmopolitan bird which kills such pests as rats, mice, and grasshoppers; it rarely feeds on birds.

The broad-winged hawks prefer reptiles, amphibians, and small mammals no larger than a rabbit; they include the red-shouldered hawk (*Buteo lineatus*) of eastern North America, which winters in southern Florida and Cuba, and the birds called buzzards (*Buteo buteo* and *B. lagopus*) in Europe. Order Falconiformes, family Accipitridae.

HEATH HEN. See *Grouse.*

HEDGEHOG, any of about 12 different small mammals bearing barbless spines among the fur on the back and sides, and able to roll up into a ball surrounded by spines when disturbed. They are Eurasian and African animals, which feed on animal matter, live or dead, although they willingly eat bread and milk or other food put out for cats and dogs.

Hedgehogs measure from 10 to 12 inches in length; the legs are short; the snout is long; and the spines are usually about 1 inch long. They are nocturnal in habits; during the day they hide in logs and stumps. In winter hedgehogs hibernate in protected places. Their flesh is sometimes eaten in Europe. There are no true hedgehogs native to the western hemisphere: the North American porcupine (*Erethizon*) is sometimes erroneously called a hedgehog. Order Insectivora, family Erinaceidae, particularly the Eurasian *Erinaceus europaeus.*

ROTHSTEIN/LOOK

HIPPOPOTAMUS

HERON, any of the long-legged wading birds that have straight or slightly downcurved beaks, toothlike points on the side of the claw on each middle toe, and carry the head and neck in an S curve, particularly during flight. They are widespread, and commonly seen standing on one leg in shallow water, although they fly when disturbed.

Herons are generally subdivided into the bitterns (12 kinds), the tiger herons (6 kinds), the night herons (9 kinds), the day herons (35 kinds), and the agami heron of central and northern South America. Egrets are day herons with snowy plumes, the aigrettes of the milliner. The snowy, the white, and the reddish egrets live in the southern United States.

There are 2 American blue herons —the great blue (*Ardea herodias*), sometimes called blue crane, about 50 inches high, with a black crest; and the little blue heron (*Hydranassa caerulea*), only about 24 inches high. The European heron (*A. cinerea*) is so swift and strong that it was the favorite prey of trained falcons. Herons nest in high trees, in structures built of grass and twigs, sometimes in communities called heronries. The bitterns live in marshy places and the British species are becoming rare as marshy grounds are reclaimed.

The Old World bittern (*Botaurus stellaris*) is about 30 inches in length and about 44 inches in wingspread. Its usual color is a dull yellowish brown, with spots and bars of black or dark brown. It has long, loose breast feathers, a short tail, and a bill about 4 inches long. It is remarkable for its booming or bellowing cry, from which come the provincial names, miredrum, butterbump, and stakedriver. The eggs are 4 or 5 in number.

The North American bittern (*Botaurus lentiginosus*) resembles the common European bittern, and is 26 inches long. The little bittern (*Ixobrychus minutus*) of Eurasia to New Zealand and South Africa is not more than 15 inches in length. Order Ciconiiformes, family Ardeidae.

HERRING, any of about 175 different kinds of small, soft-finned, bony fishes with deciduous scales and a knifelike ridge along the undersurface of the compressed body. Some live in the freshwaters of Africa and the Amazon basin, but most are marine and commonly come to river mouths at spawning time.

These fishes occur in large schools; they swim through the sea with open mouths, scooping up the minute life for food. Immense numbers are caught. The young herring, also taken in quantity, are preserved as American sardines. Order Isospondyli, family Clupeidae.

HIPPOPOTAMUS (Greek for river horse), either of 2 kinds of large mammals with a broad snout, large mouth, bulky body, and short stout legs ending in 4 toes. The large hippopotamus (*Hippopotamus amphibius*) is a river dweller of many parts of Africa, whereas the pygmy hippo (*Choeropsis liberiensis*) lives only in swamp forests of West Africa.

The large hippo adult weighs about 4 tons, the pygmy about 550 pounds. Both feed on shrubs, grasses, and other vegetation, and spend most of each day almost submerged in a favorite water hole. The stomach is 3-parted, but the animal does not chew a cud. Order Artiodactyla, family Hippopotamidae.

HOG. See *Swine*.

HONEYBEE. See *Bee*.

HOOKWORM, any of several different small parasitic intestinal roundworms, which have special attachment spines around the mouth. They attain maturity while firmly anchored in the wall of the human small intestine where they often cause severe bleeding, with consequent anemia and weakness. Their eggs pass out with undigested wastes, and hatch if exposed to air on the soil.

The active larvae can bore through bare human skin, particularly along the sides of the foot, between the toes, and around the ankles, thus reaching the bloodstream. The blood carries them to the lungs where they bore through into the air cavities, opening an avenue for infection by tuberculosis bacteria and other diseases. The larval hookworms ride the mucous film up to the throat, are swallowed, and thus reach the intestine.

Millions of persons are infected by hookworms, primarily in warm countries where sanitary conditions are poor and bare feet are usual. Order Rhabditida, particularly genera *Ancylostoma duodenale* and *Necator americanus*.

HORNET, any of a number of wasplike insects about 1 inch long with conspicuous white or yellow markings on a brown or gray body. The name hornet is loosely applied to a number of stinging wasps, but referred originally to the European brown kind (*Vespa crabro*), which is justly noted for the virulence of the sting and the irritability of the female insects so equipped.

The widely distributed European hornet, now introduced accidentally near New York City, builds com-

munal nests in hollow trees, constructing the nest itself of wood fibers chewed to form a gray papery material.

The large gray hornet (*V. maculata*) found in eastern North America builds a similar "carton" nest, but suspends it from the limbs of trees. Inside the nest are cells like those of a honeycomb. The smaller yellow jackets (*V. communis* and *V. diabolica*) usually nest underground.

Hornets eat sweets of all kinds and steal honey from bees; they also feed on other insects. Order Hymenoptera, family Vespidae.

HORSE, either of 2 kinds of large herbivorous mammals that stand or run on a horny hoof capping the single elongated toe on each foot. Compared with the related asses and zebras, horses have small ears; they grow long hairs from the outer half of the tail, not at all from the end of the tail in a tuft as in these related animals.

Living horses are native to Africa north of the great deserts, and to central and eastern Asia. The only wild horses today are Mongolian, named *Equus przewalskii* after their discoverer the Russian explorer Nikolai Przhewalski; they are short-legged, thick-headed, stocky horses with an erect mane. The domesticated horse (*E. caballus*) is longer legged, more slender in the head, and graceful in body and legs. It probably is the descendant of an extinct horse of the same scientific name, the tarpan, which was an important source of food for mankind in prehistoric times.

Like other domestic animals, the horse has been bred into many special breeds, such as the Arabians for riding, the percherons for draft use, thoroughbreds for racing, and ponies for work in mine passageways. Order Perissodactyla, family Equidae.

HORSESHOE CRAB, or king crab, any of 4 different marine arthropod animals, in which the heavily armored body as seen from above shows conspicuous subdivisions into a front division that is the shape of a horse's hoof and as much as 22 inches wide, a rear division that is roughly triangular, and a terminal long tapering tail spine.

The front division of the body bears a large compound eye on each side, and 2 small simple eyes near the midline far forward. Below this portion of the body are 4 pairs of walking legs, arising from the sides of the mouth, and 2 pairs of special appendages used for tasting and handling food, anterior to the mouth.

The rear division of the body bears below it a series of hinged plates to which the leaflike gills are attached. Waving these hinged plates and beating with its legs, a horseshoe crab swims upside down. After swimming, it often sinks to the bottom back downward and must turn over to walk along in search of worms and other soft food. It uses its tail spine to turn itself over onto its feet. Order Xiphosura of class Merostomata, family Limulidae.

One kind of horseshoe crab (*Limulus polyphemus*) lives along Atlantic and Gulf coasts of North America. The other 3 are found along coasts of Southeast Asia and the East Indies. These animals are not true crabs, but distant kin of scorpions and spiders (Class Arachnida); all of their nearest relatives, the sea scorpions, have been extinct for more than 200 million years.

HOUSE SPIDER, a small dust-colored spider not over ¼ inch long with slender legs 3 times the length of the body and several dark chevron markings on both the upper and lower surfaces of the egg-shaped abdomen. House spiders seldom live outdoors, having adopted human dwellings. They spin loose silken webs that catch small insects as well as dust; the spider flings strands of silk at its prey, using a special comb on its last pair of legs to handle the silk. Order Araneae, family Theridiidae, mostly *Theridion tepidariorum*.

HUMMINGBIRD, any of 319 different kinds of small day-active birds, with long slender bills and very small feet, which hover while sipping nectar from flowers and produce a humming sound by rapidly vibrating their wings. They are natives to the New World from southern Alaska and northern Nova Scotia to Tierra del Fuego. They are represented by the largest variety in tropical South America.

About 18 species are found in the United States, many of them only on the borders of the country. Only one species, the ruby-throated *Archilochus colubris*, is found east of the Mississippi River. It is 3¼ inches long and beautifully colored. Their beaks are long and curved allowing the birds to reach into deep-throated flowers, many of which they pollinate. Order Apodiformes, family Trochilidae.

HYDRA, any of several freshwater coelenterate polyps with a cylindrical, contractile body some ¾ inch long and about the diameter of the lead in an automatic pencil. It is ordinarily attached at one end to underwater vegetation; from the free end, which bears the mouth, 8 or more long threadlike tentacles extend into the water like fishing lines waiting for minute animals. Each tentacle is studded with microscopic nettling cells, which discharge when suitable prey touches them. Some of these cells inject a poison that quiets the prey, such as a water flea (*Daphnia*), while lassolike extensions of other cells hold on to the victim.

Slowly the hydra pushes the prey animal into its mouth, which opens into a sac-shaped digestive cavity. After all digestible materials have been absorbed, indigestible remains are ejected through the mouth in a spitting movement.

Well-fed hydras may develop from the side of the body new small individuals called buds, or produce sex cells in simple sex organs. Fertilized eggs grow to become swimming embryos, which eventually attach themselves somewhere and transform into the polyp form of the adult hydra.

The name hydra refers to a monster in Greek mythology, which grew new heads when old heads were cut off. The name was given to these polyps because of their powers of regeneration when mutilated. Class Hydrozoa, order Hydroidea, species of *Hydra* and other genera.

HYENA, any of 3 kinds of doglike mammals with disproportionately large head and forequarters but weak hindquarters. They inhabit the semiarid portions of Africa and Asia, the spotted or laughing hyena (*Crocuta crocuta*) being widespread in Africa south of the great deserts, the brown hyena (*Hyaena brunnea*) in southern Africa, and the striped hyena (*H. hyaena*) from Asia Minor to West Pakistan.

The hyena is covered with coarse, bristly hair, short over most of the body, but forming a mane along the ridge of the neck. The hind legs are shorter than the forelegs, giving the body a slope from the withers to the haunches. The hyena is somewhat larger than a shepherd dog. The cheek muscles are greatly developed, and the large grinding teeth have great conical crowns that enable them to smash the thighbones of animals as large as the horse.

All hyenas are nocturnal in their habits. They are useful scavengers. Order Carnivora, family Hyaenidae.

IBIS, any of 23 different kinds of medium-sized, long-legged wading birds, which have no feathers on the face. Some lack feathers on the entire head and neck. Ibises are found in all warm and temperate regions except Oceania.

The sacred ibis (*Threskiornis aethiopica*) of Africa and Madagascar was worshiped in ancient Egypt; many legendary powers were ascribed to it. Today the bird has been virtually exterminated north of the great African deserts, although it is still common to the south. Far more widely distributed is the glossy ibis (*Plegadis falcinellus*) of southern Eurasia, Africa, Madagascar, Australia, the West Indies, and southern Florida.

The white ibis (*Eudocimus albus*), whose face and long down-curved beak and legs are reddish orange, is over 2 feet long with pure white plumage and a few black wing feathers. It nests generally by the thousands in immense rookeries in Florida, the West Indies, central and northern South America.

The scarlet ibis (*E. rubes*) of South and Central America has bright scarlet wings tipped with black. The American bird called a wood ibis is actually a kind of stork. Order Ciconiiformes, family Threskiornithidae—literally birds of worship, referring to the sacred ibis.

IGUANA, any of a number of tropical herbivorous lizards with a laterally compressed body and tail, and a number of soft spines that extend from the head to the tip of the tail, giving a crested appearance.

Iguanas are native to tropical America, including islands of the West Indies. A Galápagos iguana (*Amblyrhynchus cristatus*) lives on the lava rocks along the seashore and is partly aquatic, feeding on seaweeds, and growing to be 4 feet long. Even larger is the common green tree iguana (*Iguana iguana*) of Central and South America, which is sometimes 6 feet long.

Iguanas resemble more the legendary Chinese dragons than real animals. Their flesh has a delicate flavor, and their eggs, almost all yolk, are eaten in Latin America. Order Squamata, suborder Sauria, family Iguanidae.

JACKAL. See *Dog.*

JAY, any of about 50 different kinds of perching birds, smaller and more brightly colored than the closely related crows and magpies. They are found throughout the temperate and tropical zones, except in New Zealand and some oceanic islands. The common blue jay (*Cyanocitta cristata*) of eastern and central North America has beautiful bright-blue plumage, a conspicuous crest on its head, and a very harsh cry.

The Canada jay (*Perisoreus canadensis*) has sooty plumage, a black cap, white forehead, throat, and collar, but no crest. It is an accomplished thief, frequenting hunters' and prospectors' camps; it is called moose bird and whisky jack. Steller's jay (*Cyanocitta stelleri*) of America west of the Rockies is dark blue and black, with a crest, and inhabits coniferous forests. If they have a chance, nearly all jays will eat nestlings of smaller birds and their eggs. Otherwise they live on a wide variety of food, preponderantly of vegetable origin. Order Passeriformes, family Corvidae.

JELLYFISH. See *Medusa.*

JUNCO, any of several different sparrow-sized birds, characteristically slate-gray above, white below, and with white along each side of the tail. The feathers show no streaks or spots, but in some species provide red or pink color to the sides and some areas of the back. All are North American. Most widespread is the slate-colored junco (*Junco hyemalis*), which has a pink beak; it nests in Canada and the northern United States and winters throughout the United States and northern Mexico.

The western yellow-pine forests of the American Southwest are the sole home for the white-winged junco (*J. aikeni*), which has 2 white wing bars. Dry mountain forests and adjacent plains of the southwestern United States and northwestern Mexico have a gray-headed junco (*J. caniceps*), which has a gray head and a red-brown back. More widespread along the provinces and states of the Pacific slope and over the Rocky Mountain area into northern Mexico is the Oregon, or pink-sided, junco (*J. oreganus*).

All juncoes are often called "snowbirds," because they hop around on the winter snow while searching for dry seeds. During the summer they

AUSTRALIAN NEWS AND INFORMATION BUREAU
KANGAROO

eat large numbers of insects and feed their young exclusively on insects until the young birds leave the nest. Order Passeriformes, family Fringillidae.

JUNE BUG, or May Beetle, any of several kinds of flying adult beetles, which often fly to lights in late spring. Some are scarabs, such as *Phyllophaga* and *Cotinus;* others are stag beetles (*Pseudolucanus*). These types emerge from the ground where their larvae, called white grubs, pass a year or more feeding upon roots of grasses, vines, and trees. The adults, usually about an inch long, often chew vegetation; they are, however, most noticed when they fly through open windows and tumble to the floor. Order Coleoptera, chiefly families Scarabaeidae and Lucanidae.

KANGAROO, any of about 52 different kinds of mammals with a particularly strong, long tail serving as a third leg or as a prop while seated, with large, strong hind legs and small forelegs, and with a small head bearing a deerlike snout and large ears. Kangaroos and tree kangaroos, rat-kangaroos, wallabies, and wallaroos are found in Australia, Tasmania, New Guinea, and some adjacent islands. Females carry their young in a pouch (marsupium).

The largest kangaroo is the great gray (*Macropus giganteus*), which may stand 8 feet tall and weigh 150 pounds. Formerly plentiful over Australian plains, it is being eliminated to make space for cattle. While grazing, kangaroos walk on all fours. When alarmed or in a hurry, they leap along on their hind legs, 10 to 15 feet at a hop, the body being carried in a nearly horizontal position, and the tail extended to balance it. The forepaws are chiefly used for handling, and with these the females lift their young and place them in the pouch. The kangaroo skin is very soft and pliable and is used in making shoes and gloves. Order Marsupialia, family Macropodidae.

KATYDID, the popular American name for several different, large long-horned grasshoppers, which are active and make distinctive calls at night. In many parts of the country their loud, persistent "katy-did" notes are the most familiar sounds of a summer evening, being audible for ¼ mile or more on quiet nights. The sound is produced by the male rubbing the base of one forewing against the other. The katydids resemble common field grasshoppers in structure but are larger—almost 3 inches long—with bright-green bodies. Order Orthoptera, family Tettigoniidae.

KINGBIRD, any of several tyrant fly-catcher birds of North America, about 9 inches long. The common eastern kingbird (*Tyrannus tyrannus*) is crested, dark gray with white underparts, and has a white band across the end of its black tail. It is famous for fighting off any attacker at its nest, and in chasing crows from the vicinity.

Yellow underparts are distinctive of the western or Arkansas kingbird (*T. verticalas*) and of Cassin's kingbird (*T. vociferans*) of the American southwest. Kingbirds are commonly seen on bare limbs of trees from which they dart to catch flying insects. The call note is rather harsh and shrill. Order Passeriformes, family Tyrannidae.

KINGFISHER, any of 84 different kinds of stout carnivorous birds with long strong beaks, large heads, short necks, short tails, and short legs on which the front toes are joined for more than half their length. Kingfishers are found all over the world, except in the Arctic and on some oceanic islands. Europe has only one kind, the Eurasian kingfisher (*Alcedo atthis*) of northern Africa, and from Portugal eastward to the Solomon Islands. Only the belted kingfisher (*Megaceryle alcyon*), a crested blue and white bird, lives in America north of Mexico.

Kingfishers eat mainly small fish, which they get by diving. Sometimes they also eat insects. Their nests are usually built in tree trunks or in the banks of streams.

The laughing jackass, or kookaburra (*Dacelo gigas*), of eastern and southern Australia is a kingfisher as large as a crow, feeding chiefly on reptiles and insects and seldom going near water. The popular name comes from the bird's loud braying cry, which is like a noisy laugh. Order Coraciiformes, family Alcedinidae.

KINGLET, a very small plump bird of the forest, with a brilliant streak of feathers on its crown when mature. In the golden-crowned kinglet (*Regulus satrapa*) of North America and the goldcrest (*R. regulus*) of Britain and Europe the crest is bright orange-yellow bordered with black. In the ruby-crowned kinglet (*R. calendula*) of North America and the firecrest (*R. ignicapillus*) it is red.

All kinglets build nests in cone-bearing trees other than pine, suspending the nest below a branch or twig. In summer, these birds flit quickly through the dark evergreen forests, hunting for insects for themselves and their young. In winter, kinglets are more often seen on bare trees and evergreens around suburban homes. Order Passeriformes, family Sylvidae.

KINKAJOU, a tropical American mammal with a rounded head, short face, sharp claws, and a strong, prehensile tail. It lives in trees, hunts by night, eats insects, eggs, and honey, and is sometimes called a honey bear. A kinkajou is about as big as a house cat; it has soft wooly fur and is easily tamed. Order Carnivora, family Procyonidae, specifically *Potos flavus*.

KITE, any of about 25 different kinds of long-winged birds of prey with weak feet, which restricts their diet to small prey and carrion. All are strong fliers, graceful in the air.

Largest of the four kinds in the United States is the swallow-tailed kite (*Elanoides forficatus*), about 25 inches long, which spends most of its life on the wing, often in flocks of 20 or so. It hovers before pouncing on snakes, lizards, frogs, and other small reptiles, as well as grasshoppers, caterpillars, and grubs.

The other American kites, which differ in plumage but are similar in form and habits, are the white-tailed kite (*Elanus leucurus*), the Mississippi kite (*Ictinia mississippiensis*), and the Everglade kite (*Rostrhamus sociabilis*), which is dwindling toward extinction—perhaps because it feeds almost exclusively on one kind of snail. Order Falconiformes, family Accipitridae.

KITTIWAKE, a middle-sized gull of the open sea, which nests in colonies on steep rocky cliffs of Britain, Scandinavia, Iceland, and arctic Canada as far south as Gaspé peninsula of Quebec. Adults are distinctive because each wingtip appears to have been dipped in black ink, and the feet are black, not brown as in the immature bird.

Kittiwakes are rare inland, but common far out at sea, where they frequent the northern fishing areas. Often they pick food from the waves without stopping. At times they swim on the surface or dive deeply, apparently swimming underwater in pursuit of fishes. Order Charadriiformes, family Laridae, specifically *Rissa tridactyla*.

KIWI, any of 3 different plump-bodied flightless birds with virtually no wings and with a long slender beak at the tip of which the nostrils open. All kiwis are New Zealand birds, about the size of a domestic hen. They use the beak to reach into soft forest soil for earthworms and insects, locating them by scent. The wing stubs end in a claw; the feathers are hairy. The legs are strong, and used both for running and defense.

The female lays 2 eggs, each weighing about a third as much as she does after her laying is completed; her eggs are larger relative to her body than those of any other bird. Order Apterygiformes, family Apterygidae, species of genus *Apteryx* ("wingless").

KOALA, an Australian mammal as much as 33½ inches long, 33 pounds in weight, with a large head, big rounded hairy ears, a black bare nose, strong legs with opposable claw-bearing toes, and a vestigial tail. Native only to eucalpytus forests in eastern Australia, it feeds on about 12 different kinds of these trees, eating foliage, buds, and flowers. It clings tightly, using remarkable hands with thumb and forefinger both opposable to the other three fingers.

The young koala is carried in the mother's pouch for about 6 months and then on her back until it is a year old. Both appeal to people as living toylike "teddy bears." Order Marsupialia, family Phalangeridae, specifically *Phascolarctos cinereus* ("the ash-gray pouched bear").

KUDU, either of 2 African antelopes, second in size only to the eland. They frequent forests, where they browse on shrubbery. Unlike most other antelopes, they are heavy and rather ungainly.

The greater kudu (*Tragelaphus strepsiceros*, meaning twisted horn) inhabits southern Africa from Angola to Ethiopia, and stands almost 5 feet at the shoulder, 8 feet long not counting the long tufted tail; the male has massive horns up to more than 4 feet long, spirally twisted and beautifully curved. Both sexes are grayish brown with a white stripe down the middle of the back and numerous vertical white stripes on the sides.

The lesser kudu (*Strepsiceros imberbis*) of Somalia and East Africa is about 3½ feet tall at the shoulder, and its horns grow to more than 2 feet long. Order Artiodactyla, family Bovidae.

LAC BUG. See *Scale Insect*.

LACEWING, or goldeneye, or green fly, any adult insect that develops from an aphis lion. Lacewings are worldwide on land areas. Their 4 broad wings are pale green, with many cross veins, held at rest like a tent over the body; when spread, their span is about 1 inch. The head bears two large, bulging, golden-colored compound eyes and a pair of long threadlike antennae (feelers), as well as a pair of strong small jaws with which the insect attacks and devours aphids (plant lice).

Female lacewings lay their white eggs singly atop ½-inch slender stalks, seemingly to prevent the first larva that emerges from eating all unhatched eggs. The larva, called an aphis lion, devours large numbers of aphids. It attains full size in about 2 weeks, and spins a cocoon in which to transform to the winged adult lacewing. Often winter is spent in the cocoon. Because aphids cause so much damage to plant crops, lacewings are regarded as extremely beneficial insects. Order Neuroptera, families Chrysopidae and Hemerobiidae, members of *Chrysopa* (literally "golden eye").

LADYBEETLE, or ladybird beetle, or ladybug, a small hemispherical beetle, often orange or red with black spots, and ½ inch or less in diameter. It is a harmless beetle found in temperate and tropical climates. Lady beetles lay eggs on plants. The larvae that hatch out are usually black with a flattened pear-shaped body, the head with biting jaws, and six legs at or near the larger end.

In the Middle Ages, when it was seen that these insects and their larvae destroyed aphids (plant lice) and scale insects, they were dedicated to the Virgin and became "Beetles of Our Lady," hence ladybeetles. Most ladybeetles benefit agriculture, although a few kinds, such as the Mexican bean beetle (*Epilachua varivestis*) eat plants.

An Australian ladybeetle (*Vedalia cardinalis*) was introduced in California to control the cottony cushion scale, a mealy bug (also from Australia), which threatened the orange orchards. The countless descendants from 500 ladybeetles checked the pest in a few years. Order Coleoptera, family Coccinellidae.

LAMPREY, a cylindrical, jawless fish with a circular sucking mouth and no paired fins. Most lampreys live in the sea but ascend freshwater streams to lay eggs. They make nests by moving rocks on the pebbly bottom. The young hatch as small slender larvae, called *ammocoetes*. For 3 or 4 years, each larva burrows shallowly in mud or sand, drawing in water for respiration and filtering out microscopic particles of food. When ready to transform to the adult shape of body, it migrates to salt water to finish growing. Finally it returns to a stream to mate and die.

At maturity, a sea lamprey (*Petromyzon marinus*) is nearly 3 feet long. It uses the horny teeth in its mouth and suction to fasten itself as an external parasite on larger fishes, on whose blood and flesh it feeds. It has a single nostril and seven gill openings on the side of the neck.

Allied to the lampreys are the scavenging hagfishes or slime eels (genus *Myxine*), which sometimes burrow into the body of a dead or dying fish and eat it from the inside. Hagfishes, although uncommon along the Atlantic coast of North America, are abundant in European and Californian waters. Order Hyperoartia of class Cyclostomata.

LANCELET, or amphioxus, any of about 30 kinds of slender marine animals 2 to 3 inches long, about the shape of a willow leaf, sharp, pointed, and thin like a lance at both ends. Lancelets live near shore along temperate coasts all over the world, usually burrowing shallowly in sandy bottom materials during the day and emerging to swim about rapidly at night. The sexes are separate, but fertilization occurs in the open sea. Fertilized eggs develop into free-swimming larvae, which are distributed widely by water currents before they settle to the bottom and transform slightly to adult form.

At one end of the adult body is a narrow oval mouth opening into an extensive throat region (pharynx), which has multiple slits through which sea water passes. These slits allow the lancelet to filter from the water microscopic particles of food, and to absorb oxygen and get rid of carbon dioxide. The food, caught in sticky mucus, proceeds onward through a straight intestine.

Lancelets in some features resemble vertebrate animals in their embryonic development. They have a hollow dorsal nerve cord, a lengthwise supporting rod called a notochord, slits in the side walls of the pharynx that resemble gill slits in fishes, a closed circulatory system with arteries, capillaries, and veins, and a body cavity lined by a thin layer of cells called a peritoneum. But there are no indications of head or brain, nor of the blocks of cartilage or bone that form the internal skeleton of a vertebrate animal. Presumably lancelets represent an ancestral form of chordate animal, relatively unchanged for the last 600 million years or more. Subphylum Cephalochordata of phylum Chordata.

LARK, any of about 75 different kinds of songbirds the size of a large sparrow, noted for the song flights of the males. Most larks are African, but the group is represented in Eurasia, Australia, and North America.

The skylark of temperate Eurasia and North Africa (*Alauda arvensis*) begins its song early in the spring and continues to sing the whole summer. It is quietly colored in brown, buff, and creamy white, and in many countries is prized as food. The horned lark (*Eremophila alpestris*) of the same areas and the New World as far south as Colombia, has a black collar, yellowish throat, black tail, and black head "horns."

Meadowlarks of North America are about the size of a robin, with a black V on the yellow breast. They thrive, as the Old World larks do, on developed farmland and are highly regarded as destroyers of insect pests. The western meadowlark (*Sturnella neglecta*) is slightly smaller than the eastern (*S. magna*), and its whistled call is lower in pitch and less shrill. Meadowlarks are, however, totally different from true larks; they are related to blackbirds in family Icteridae, whereas the true larks comprise family Alaudidae, both families of order Passeriformes.

LAUGHING JACKASS. See *Kingfisher*.

LEAFHOPPER, any of more than 2,000 kinds of small insects resembling miniature cicadas, with a short head (often pointed) and compact body, and the 4 wings held tentlike lengthwise above them at rest.

They are found in all terrestrial parts of the world. With sucking mouthparts, they get nourishing juices from leaves, young stems, flower buds, and soft fruits, often doing much damage by introducing the agents of disease.

The largest leafhopper is less than an inch long when mature, and most do not exceed ¼ inch in length. The eggs hatch into small wingless insects of the same body form and similar habits. Development is direct, with no pupal stage.

In some species, such as the rose leafhopper (*Empoa rosea*), two generations attain maturity in vast numbers each year, the first generation attacking one kind of plant (in this case almost any type of rose) and the second generation a quite different plant (in this case apples). Adults of the second generation generally fly back to plants suitable as food for members of the first generation, there to lay eggs that will survive the winter. Order Homoptera, family Cicadellidae.

LEECH, a flattened segmented worm with a sucker surrounding the mouth at the front end, where the animal has 3 knifelike jaws, and usually a second sucker at the hind end. Leeches mostly inhabit freshwater shallows, where they catch small crustaceans and snails, and have a chance to attach themselves to fish, turtles, or a mammal that is drinking or wading. With their jaws, leeches can cut through the skin and reach blood, making a quick meal of it before dropping off.

Half a century ago freshwater leeches (*Hirudo medicinalis*) 2 or 3 inches long were used extensively by physicians to relieve certain diseases by bloodletting, but since it was found that the human system is weakened by bloodletting, the use of leeches has diminished.

A few kinds of leeches live in the ocean, attacking fishes and turtles. In wet forests of Southeast Asia, one kind of leech waits for victims along game trails on land. Several orders of class Hirudinea, phylum Annelida.

LEMMING, any of about 12 kinds of small, short-eared, short-tailed rodents found in tundras, coniferous forests, and mossy bogs of northern Eurasia and North America. The lemming (*Lemmus lemmus*) of Scandinavia and northwestern Russia, about 5 inches long with a heavy, rounded body, short legs, and a large head, is famous for its periodic migrations suddenly every 8 to 10 years. At these times, huge numbers of lemmings travel downhill from overpopulated and food-scarce high country. If their migratory urge persists, they do not stop even when they reach the ocean but plunge in and drown.

Normally lemmings eat reindeer moss (a lichen) and other plants, and serve as the principal food of predatory animals in the Far North. Order Rodentia, family Cricetidae.

LEMUR, any of about 16 kinds of long-tailed monkeylike mammals, from 5 to 17 inches long not including the tail. They are native to Madagascar and the Comoro Islands. Most are arboreal, associating in troops of up to 20 individuals. Their very large eyes, staring appearance, and nocturnal habits earn them their name—*lemures* is Latin for ghosts. Lemurs eat fruit and insects. Lemurlike but unrelated animals (order Demoptera) that glide from tree to tree are known as flying lemurs. Order Primates, family Lemuridae.

LEOPARD. See *Cat*.

LIMPET, any of a large number of marine gastropod mollusks having a low, conical shell widely open below, where the body of the animal expands into a large flat foot with which it clings by suction to solid supports. They are common along rocky shores between high-tide mark and a few feet below low tide. Those most abundant in this location around Britain and Europe belong to genus *Patella*, named for a fancied resemblance to the bone in the tendon of the human knee; the most familiar limpets along American shores belong to genus *Acmaea*. Keyhole limpets, which have a hole at the tip of the shell and use it for discharge of water from which they have taken their oxygen, often belong to genus *Fissurella*.

All limpets browse on the film of minute seaweeds that grow on rocks along coasts, and resist both the pounding of waves and the combination of dry air and sun when exposed by the tide. They arch the central portion of the soft muscular foot to create a vacuum like that in a suction cup; they can be dislodged easily by pressing a thin knife blade between the rock and the foot, thus releasing the vacuum. Large numbers of limpets are collected along British and European coasts for use as food and fish bait. Order Aspidobranchia.

LING, or lingcod, a large marine bony fish resembling the closely related cod in having short soft projections (barbels) from the lower jaw, used to detect small fishes, crustaceans, worms, and other food on the sea bottom. Ling are caught in the North Atlantic Ocean off the coasts of Europe and Greenland. Like a hake, a ling has a dorsal fin divided into a small forward part and a much more extensive hind part, whereas a cod has a three-part dorsal fin.

Ling is a term derived from a Middle English word, meaning long, and refers to the proportions of the body. In some parts of the world remote from Europe, the same name is given to quite different fishes in which the body appears longer in proportion to height than is customary among familiar fishes. Order Anacanthini, family Gadidae, specifically *Molva molva*.

LION. See *Cat*.

LIZARD, any of about 3,140 different kinds of scale-covered reptiles in which the 2 sides of the lower jaw are joined together, not merely linked by a flexible ligament as among snakes. Usually the eyelids are movable and an external opening of the ear can be found; most commonly a lizard has 4 legs with distinct toes, but a few are legless and often mistaken for snakes.

Lizards live in temperate and tropical countries all over the world. Largest are the monitor lizards of Africa and tropical Asia to Australia; one, the Komodo dragon (*Varanus komodoensis*) discovered in 1912 on the small Komodo Island in the East Indies, grows to a length of 9½ feet and is a formidable predator. Only the 2 kinds of beaded lizards in deserts of southwestern North America are venomous: the Gila monster (*Heloderma suspectum*) of Arizona and Mexico, and the Mexican beaded lizard (*H. horridum*) have a poisonous saliva that seeps into wounds made when the animal bites.

The tree iguanas (*Iguana iguana* and near relatives) of tropical America eat foliage high among the tall trees of the rain forest. Most other lizards are insectivorous or eat small invertebrate animals. This is the habit of the nocturnal geckos, the horned lizards (or horned "toads"), the fence lizards, the chameleons, and most of the legless lizards known as "worm" lizards or as "glass snakes" from their habit of breaking off the tip of the tail into separate twitching fragments when handled. Order Squamata, suborder Sauria (or Lacertilia).

LLAMA, a deer-sized, cud-chewing mammal of the Andes of South America. Although lacking a hump, it is related most closely to camels and, like them, has been domesticated as a beast of burden, capable of carrying 200 pounds for 17 miles in a day over mountain trails.

When annoyed, a llama spits and bites. From its long hairy coat, fine cloth can be made. The Andean Indians depend greatly on the llama for milk and meat. Order Artiodactyla, family Camelidae, specifically *Lama peruana*.

LOBSTER, a large marine "long-tailed" crustacean whose strong abdominal muscles are sought for food. At the front of the head are two pairs of sensitive feelers (antennae) and a pair of eyes on the end of short stalks.

The North Atlantic lobster (*Homarus americanus*) along coasts of both the Old and New World is distinguished by the exaggerated size of the front pair of legs, each ending in pincers, and one being larger than the other. Lobsters scavenge for decaying fish, and may be caught in large traps called *lobster pots,* made of lath and baited with decaying fish.

The number of lobsters taken is enormous, but overfishing has so greatly reduced their numbers that laws have been enacted almost everywhere to protect them. The annual catch on the New England coast is estimated at about 30,000,000 pounds, the weight of an average lobster being between 2 and 3 pounds.

The spiny, or rock, lobster, or sea crayfish (*Palinurus*), has no pincers on its 5 pairs of legs, but defends itself with antennae that are particularly thick and strong. They generally project from the rock crevices where the animal takes shelter. In the Mediterranean is found *P. vulgaris*, the langouste of French menus; similar animals are caught in the West Indies, southern Florida, Bermuda and the Bahama Islands, and along the coast of South Africa. Order Decapoda.

LOCUST, a loosely used word applied to (1) short-horned grasshoppers, (2) cicadas, and (3) several kinds of trees with edible seeds, belonging to the pea family. No one is sure which of these is referred to in the Bible as a food approved for Israelites (Leviticus 11:22) and as the food eaten with wild honey by John the Baptist (Matthew 3:4; Mark 1:6). Those that came in swarms and ate the crops were certainly the migratory grasshoppers (*Schistocerca peregrina*) of North Africa and Asia Minor.

LLAMA

A similar habit is shown by the smaller short-horned grasshoppers (*Melanoplus spretus*) of prairies near the Rocky Mountains in North America. Order Orthoptera, families Locustidae and Acrididae.

LOON, or diver, any of 4 large, handsome, fish-eating water birds whose legs are enclosed within the body all the way to the ankle joint. They normally come ashore only to nest, for their long, heavy body and short neck, as well as the position of the legs, make them clumsy and awkward on land. They cannot take flight from land at all, and even from the water they must run along the surface, frantically flapping their short wings.

Loons frequent coastal salt water and inland lakes, particularly far north in the Northern Hemisphere. They are rather solitary birds, and their favorite haunts are mostly in wild places unfrequented by man.

Most widespread is the red-throated loon (*Gavia stellata*) which nests around small arctic pools and winters as far south as Formosa and California around the Pacific, and the Gulf of Mexico and Mediterranean Sea around the Atlantic Ocean. The arctic loon (*G. artica*) and the yellow-billed loon (*G. adamsi*) are circumpolar but rarely come near human communities even in winter. The common loon (*G. immer*) of northern North America, Greenland, and Iceland is best known for its eerie calls, sometimes likened to the laughter of the insane. Order Gaviiformes, family Gaviidae.

LOUSE, any of a large number of wingless parasitic animals that cling to the body of a host animal or plant and feed from the surface. The blood-sucking lice that attack man and other mammals are classified in the insect order Anoplura. They include the worldwide head louse (*Pediculus humanus*), or cootie, which has often been the principal carrier of typhus fever, trench fever, and relapsing fever; and the hog louse (*Haematopinus suis*), which infests uncared-for domestic pigs, and occasionally spreads to people who walk among the pigs, causing intense itching but no harm.

The biting lice that feed on the feathers of birds are insects of the order Mallophaga; they include the common chicken louse (*Menopon gallinae*). So numerous do the chicken lice often become that the tickling by their feet on a fowl so distracts the bird from eating, sleeping, and social activities that its health declines. The whale lice that crawl over the surface of whales, feeding on the skin, are crustaceans of order Amphipoda.

These diverse parasites show remarkable adaptations in their legs, which help them hold to hairs or among feathers. Most lice are highly specialized to feed on one or a few closely related kinds of animals; they soon die if they cannot find the correct host.

Plant lice, or aphids, are insects that feed by placing their beaks into leaves and stems and sucking the juices; they are members of the family Aphididae in order Homoptera.

LOVEBIRD, any of several kinds of small plump parrots (*Agapornis*) of Africa and Madagascar, so named because they apparently choose a mate for life at a very early age and thereafter stay close together in pairs, giving frequent evidence of affection for one another.

In their native countries, lovebirds fly in large flocks, and generally nest close together. Like other members of the parrot family, they feed principally upon seeds and soft fruits, and produce a great deal of noise by their frequent chirps and calls and by the whir of their short wings as they fly from one branch to the next.

Each kind of lovebird has its distinctive color pattern, which usually is almost identical in the two sexes, and its own method for making a nest from plant fibers collected or cut with the beak in the forest.

The name lovebird is sometimes applied also to the Australian budgerigar (*Melopsittacus undulatus*) and to various South American parakeets (*Psittacula* species), all of which are attractive as cage birds. Order Psittaciformes, family Psittacidae.

LUNGFISH, any of about 5 different kinds of bony fishes in which the nostrils connect with the mouth cavity, instead of ending as blind pits, and the long slender body contains one or two lunglike air sacs opening into the throat region. They are river fishes of Australia, South America, and Central Africa, living where the water dries up for part of the year. When the dry period comes, the fish burrows into the damp earth and breathes by means of its air sacs. When water again appears in the river, the fish leaves the burrow, and the gills function as they do in other fish.

Only the Australian lungfish, called the barramunda (*Neoceratodus forsteri*), has leaflike fins; the South American one (*Lepidosiren*) and the African kinds (*Protopterus*) possess only filamentous paired fins. Order Dipnoi, families Ceratodontidae and Lepidosirenidae.

LYNX, any of 4 different kinds of shortbodied, strong-legged, short-tailed, catlike mammals with conspicuous tufts of fur on the ears. Formerly these powerful predators ranged more widely in Europe and North America, and in Africa and Southern Asia. The European lynx (*Lynx lynx*) and the North American lynx, or catamount (*L. canadensis*), are forest animals, which attain a length of 3 feet and weigh as much as 40 pounds. The northern variety, larger and darker in color than its southern relative, is trapped in large numbers for its fur.

The bobcat, or bay lynx (*L. rufus*), which is pale brown with black streaks and spots, differs from other lynxes in having a slightly longer tail (6 inches, instead of 4) with a black mark only above at the tip; it occurs in southern Canada, northern Mexico, and most of the United States. The caracal lynx (*L. caracal*) of Africa and southern Asia prefers hilly country and scrub-covered plains. All lynxes are efficient killers of rodents, but sometimes attack poultry and livestock. Order Carnivora, family Felidae.

LYREBIRD, either of 2 different shy, solitary songbirds about the size of a domestic hen. The mature male possesses a spectacular array of showy tail-covert feathers as much as 25 inches long; in a courtship display, he turns them forward over his back and head in the shape of a graceful lyre. The female has a long straight tail and no special covert feathers.

Lyrebirds are forest dwellers in eastern Australia, the superb lyrebird (*Menura novae-hollandiae*) occurring farther south than the Albert's lyrebird (*M. alberti*). They live on the ground, scratching among the leaf litter for insects, centipedes, snails, and other small animals as food. Lyrebirds whistle sweetly, and mimic expertly the calls of many other birds. Order Passeriformes, family Menuridae.

MACKEREL, any of about 10 different tunalike marine bony fishes with smoothly contoured bodies, widely forked tails efficiently linked to the last part of the backbone, and a series of dorsal and ventral finlets just in front of the tail. They are found in all oceans, from cold to tropical; many migrate along routes well known to fishermen.

Most important economically is the North Atlantic mackerel (*Scomber scombrus*), weighing up to 4 pounds, which is caught on hooks and with seine nets. A mackerel fleet from Gloucester, Mass., follows these fish yearly from Chesapeake Bay in April to the St. Lawrence River, which they reach in May. Among Spanish mackerels (species of *Scomberomorus*) in the North Atlantic, the largest is the king mackerel, or kingfish (*S. cavalla*), which grows to 100 pounds and a length of more than 5 feet. Frigate mackerels, such as the common *Auxis thazard* found in tropical seas around the world, are less valuable because their meat is dark. Order Acanthopteri, family Scombridae.

MAGPIE, or pie, any of a number of medium- to large-sized birds with predominantly black-and-white plumage in a bold design, and long oval tails. The name is given to birds of this appearance on all continents, following an old English tradition. There the black-billed magpie, or pie (*Pica pica*), of Eurasia and western North America long ago became a favorite cage bird, enjoyed because of its crafty behavior and its ability to imitate words; they were called Margaret or Mag (just as a parrot is Polly), hence magpie.

Wild magpies take a wide variety of food, animal and vegetable, often robbing other birds' nests of eggs and young. The Old World has also redbilled blue magpies, Ceylon blue magpies, and in Australia black-and-white magpies that are actually crow shrikes (*Gymnorhina* species). Western North America has a yellow-billed magpie (*P. nuttalli*), chiefly in the central valleys of California. Order Passeriformes, chiefly family Corvidae.

MALLARD, a large handsome dabbling duck with a glossy green head (purplish in some lights), a broad yellowish-green beak, a white ring around the neck, a brown back, and a whitish tail; the underparts are mottled gray, and the feet an orange red. Mallards are among the commonest ducks of the Northern Hemisphere, often flocking with black ducks in North America.

Mallards feed on plant rootlets, mussels, snails, small fish, frogs, fruits, and grain and other seeds. They nest inconspicuously in marshland near water, laying 6 to 12 olive-colored eggs. Domesticated mallard ducks have given rise to a number of hardy and prolific breeds for the barnyard. Order Anseriformes, family Anatidae, specifically *Anas platyrhynchos* (meaning broad-beaked duck).

MAMMOTH. See *Elephant.*

MANATEE. See *Sea Cow.*

MANDRILL. See *Baboon.*

MAN–OF–WAR. See *Portuguese man-of-war.*

MANTA. See *Ray.*

MARLIN, any of about 5 different kinds of spearfishes, in which the head is prolonged into a slender, sharp beak with a fancied resemblance to a marlinspike—a pointed metal tool used to splice rope. They are giant fishes of temperate and tropical seas, the largest being the black marlin (*Istiompax marlina*) of the Indo-Pacific, which grows to as much as 14½ feet long and 1,560 pounds. The striped marlin (*Makaira mitsukuri*) of the Pacific and blue marlin (*M. ampla*) of both the Pacific and Atlantic are slightly smaller. Order Percomorphi, family Istiophoridae.

MARMOSET, any of about 33 different kinds of small, monkeylike mammals in which the great toe is opposable and bears a flat nail, but the thumb is not opposable and, like the other fingers and toes, bears a sickle-shaped claw. They live in the forests of tropical South America and Panama, where they climb and leap jerkily from branch to branch in small groups, hunting for insects, spiders, and fruits. They have long, silky fur, elongated hind legs but short arms, and generally tufts of hair on their ears.

The one most often kept as a pet, called the common marmoset (*Callithrix jacchus*), has gray fur and produces a variety of birdlike chirps. Order Primates, family Callithricidae.

MARMOT, or woodchuck, or groundhog, any of about 16 different kinds of large burrowing rodents with pointed heads, small ears, short legs, and a tail about one third as long as the rest of the body. They inhabit cooler parts of the Northern Hemisphere, at lower elevations in the north and higher in the south.

When numerous in any area, woodchucks are the bane of the farmer. They devour many garden crops and are very fond of alfalfa and red clover. The burrow is deep and has several compartments in which the woodchuck hibernates from September to March. February 2, Candlemas, is known as Ground-hog Day or Woodchuck Day from the popular belief that then the animal comes out of his burrow and if he sees his shadow runs back again—cold weather will continue. Order Rodentia, family Sciuridae, species of genus *Marmota*.

MARTEN, any of 8 different kinds of tree-climbing, weasel-like mammals with a long bushy tail. In the New World they are denizens of coniferous and mixed forests; in the Old World they are found from the northern limits of forests to the Mediterranean and Malaya and the East Indies. Martens eat mice and squirrels, which they pursue relentlessly, and carrion, insects, and fruit. They have been trapped extensively for their fine fur.

In the New World, the larger of two kinds is the fisher, or pekan (*Martes pennanti*), sometimes 3 feet in length; the smaller is the pine marten (*M. americana*). Old World martens are often called sables, although one (*M. zibellina*), resembling the pine marten, is the only true sable; it is found chiefly in Siberia and Kamchatka where it is hunted for its fur, the darker shades being the most desired. Order Carnivora, family Mustelidae.

MASTODON. See *Elephant*.

MAY BEETLE. See *June Bug*.

MAYFLY, or shadfly, any of about 1,500 different kinds of adult flying insects with 2 or 3 long filamentous "tails" from the tip of the abdomen, and ordinarily 2 pairs of membranous wings, the front pair much larger than the rear pair. Mayflies are found near freshwater on all continents and major islands. As adults, very few have functional mouthparts or live beyond a few days, during which time they fly about, find mates, and deposit eggs.

The immature mayflies that hatch out are naiads or, incorrectly, nymphs. They have biting mouthparts, but feed principally on minute plant matter adhering to underwater vegetation or to rocks, or buried in the bottom sediments among which they burrow.

After a period of growth that lasts from 1 to 5 years according to the species, the naiad comes to the surface of the water and molts, freeing into air a flying individual that still is not mature. No other kind of insect includes in its development this winged stage, called a subimago, which has wings but must molt again. Mayfly subimagoes and adults are consumed in great numbers by bats, swallows, and other insect-eating birds; the naiads form an important food for fish. Order Ephemeroptera.

MEDUSA, or jellyfish, any of several hundred different kinds of solitary, free-swimming coelenterates, whose soft body has a jellylike consistency and the shape of a bell with a pendant tube where the tongue of the bell would be. These animals are widespread in the oceans; a few live in freshwater.

The mouth, at the end of the pendant tube, leads into a digestive cavity which branches out toward the edges of the domed body. Around the rim of the bell are pendant tentacles, studded with nettling organs used to subdue or kill small animals as prey. These writhing tentacles led to the use of the name medusa, from the mythical Greek gorgon whose hair consisted of writhing snakes.

The venom of some medusae can cause severe irritation to human skin. Medusae produce eggs that hatch into minute swimming larvae. The larvae settle to the bottom and there transform into colonial polyps (in class Hydrozoa) or special reproductive individuals (in class Scyphozoa) from which new medusae arise by asexual budding. After becoming free, they transform into little medusae, and swim away by expelling water from under the bell through muscular contractions.

MENHADEN, a large marine fish with a large head and special strainers on the gills used to filter from sea water the minute plankton animals and plants that form its diet. Menhaden live in coastal waters of the Atlantic Ocean from Nova Scotia to Brazil.

Mature fish, which average about 12 inches in length, are generally caught in the fall of the year while they are migrating to spawning grounds that remain unidentified. Their eggs float up to the surface and are carried along by oceanic currents, as are also the young fish when they hatch out.

Adult menhaden form large schools and are easily caught, but they are little used for human food because the flesh is very oily. The oil and eggs are often made into poultry food; the flesh from which the oil has been extracted is used for fertilizer. Order Isospondyli, family Clupeidae, specifically *Brevoortia tyrannus*.

MERGANSER, any of several fish-eating ducks with a slender beak that is hooked at the tip, and saw-toothed along the sides. They are waterfowl of the Northern Hemisphere, along coasts and in freshwaters. The bird (*Mergus merganser*), known as the American merganser in the New World and as the goosander in the Old World, is slightly larger than a mallard duck, and has a conspicuously red bill and feet; unlike other mergansers, it lacks a crest; it prefers freshwater lakes, reservoirs, and large rivers, and builds its nest in proximity to water, usually in a hollow tree or a hole in the bank, chiefly in Canada and northern Eurasia to beyond the tree-growth limit.

The red-breasted merganser (*M. serrator*) is smaller, with a rakish crest, and red or pink low on the neck; it generally remains close to the ocean, nesting among grass or trees near water in Canada, Alaska, Eurasia, Iceland, and Ireland. A hooded merganser (*Lophodytes cucullatus*) in many of the same regions lives more often along slow streams, and nests in wooded areas, generally in a hollow tree or stump; its diet includes fish, but also frogs, tadpoles, crayfish, insects, and vegetable matter. Order Anseriformes, family Anatidae, subfamily Merginae.

MIDGE, in general any small, 2-winged fly of feeble flight. More specifically, a member of the family Chironomidae, especially those of *Chironomus*, which resemble mosquitoes but do not bite. Midges often form immense swarms over shrubs or over water, within which the individual flying insects seek out mates; the combined humming of their wings can sometimes be heard for a considerable distance.

Generally midges lay their eggs in large masses at the edge of the water, into which the cylindrical larvae go. Some of these larvae are bright red with hemoglobin, and are known as "bloodworms."

Most midge larvae are scavengers; some live so often where there is an almost complete lack of dissolved oxygen that they are indicators of organic pollution. After 1 or 2 years of growth as larvae, these insects transform into a pupal stage that floats near the water surface until the adult insect is ready to emerge, using the floating pupal case as a raft while escaping into air.

Midge larvae are an important food for many kinds of fish, and the adults provide nourishment to bats, swallows, and other insect-eating birds. Order Diptera.

MINNOW, a popular name for small fishes that swim in schools, are easily netted, and serve as live bait for fishing. Scientists reserve the word minnow for about 1,200 different kinds of fishes from 1½ to 10 inches long, found in all watery habitats in the temperate and tropical regions except South America, Madagascar, and Australia.

Minnows lack teeth in the jaws, but have teeth in the throat; they have soft rays in their fins, and lack an adipose fin (between the dorsal fin and the tail fin on the back). Among the more familiar minnows are the silvery-scaled shiners (genus *Notropis*), and the goldfish (*Carassius auratus*) and carp (*Cyprinus carpio*) of Eurasia. Order Ostariophysi, family Cyprinidae.

MITE, or spider mite, any minute globular arthropod with 3 or 4 pairs of legs and an apparently unsegmented body. They are found all over the world as predators on microscopic animals in the soil or on the surface of plants, or as parasites on or in many kinds of animals and plants. Like the larger and closely related ticks, mites hatch from eggs as active creatures with 3 pairs of legs; at the first molt they gain another pair; the 4 pairs of legs are characteristically present for the rest of their lives.

In the itch mite (Sarcoptes scabiei) and similar species, the first two pairs of legs on the female are adapted into the form of suckers with which she pulls herself into a hair follicle on a person or other mammal. Protected within the skin, she extends her mouthparts to draw blood as food. In this position she can be reached for mating by male mites, which creep over the skin surface, and can extrude oval eggs, which she forces into furrows cut into the skin.

The skin develops an intense itching, and often scales off in large areas, partly from being scratched. The condition is commonly called sarcoptic mange or scab disease. It can be transferred easily to other individuals by contact or by infected cloth, since the mites themselves are less than 1/50 inch long and easily overlooked. Order Acarina of class Arachnida.

MOCCASIN. See Pit Viper.

MOCKINGBIRD, an inconspicuous ash-gray songbird slightly larger than a catbird, showing white on its wings when it flies. It is native to the southern United States, where it rivals the Eurasian nightingale in the variety of its song both day and night. It mimics other birds with special skill, but has a song of its own as well, full and varied. Order Passeriformes, family Mimidae, specifically Mimus polyglottos.

MOLE, any of about 40 different kinds of burrowing mammals with a pointed nose, small eyes, many tiny teeth, powerful forelegs, a cylindrical body, and usually a short tail or none. About half of them are golden moles (family Chrysochloridae) of Africa, with a metallic luster to their fine fur; they burrow by pushing their noses into the soil. The remaining moles (family Talpidae) live in Eurasia and North America, and dig with their front feet; they are grayish black.

For all moles, earthworms and insects provide the main diet. Moles build amazing subterranean fortresses or nests, consisting of an intricate system of chambers connected by tunnels at varying depths.

Largest of moles is the Eurasian desman (Desmana moschata), as much as 8½ inches long with a tail of equal length; except for the long flexible nose, it might be mistaken for a muskrat. The common Eurasian mole (Talpa europaea) is less than 6 inches long, as is the American star-nosed mole (Condylura cristata), which burrows in damp or muddy soil. The eastern mole of North America (Scalopus aquaticas) has partly webbed feet, but seldom swims. Order Insectivora.

MONGOOSE, any of about 30 different kinds of weasel-like mammals with pointed muzzles, mostly about the size of a house cat. They are persistent predators of the Old World, roaming alone or in small groups by day or night.

The Indian mongoose (Herpestes griseus), a 15- to 18-inch animal with a furry tail of almost equal length, has thick reddish-gray fur, and special agility used in killing poisonous snakes such as cobras. It was introduced as a rat- and snake-killer into Jamaica, Hawaii, and many other islands. In those places, it turned its attention to reptiles that were easier to catch and to native birds, often endangering the survival of rare kinds. In 1902 a law was enacted to forbid the bringing of a live mongoose into the United States.

The ichneumon (H. ichneumon) is a mongoose of North Africa and Asia Minor, that was kept like a house cat in ancient Egypt because of its efficiency in devouring rats, mice, crocodile eggs, and other pests. Order Carnivora, family Viverridae.

MONKEY, any of a large number of small tropical mammals with long tails, having opposable thumbs and great toes, and nails instead of claws. Most New World monkeys can support themselves by their tails; they have widely separated nostrils that open sidewise. Old World monkeys do not have prehensile tails; their nostrils open forward and downward, as in man.

Most monkeys anywhere choose fruits and soft greenery for their diet; however, they also eat insects, young birds, and eggs whenever they can. Order Primates, superfamilies Cercopithecidae in Africa and Asia, and Cebidae in America.

MOOSE. See Deer.

MOSQUITO, any of about 1,500 different kinds of delicate flies with long, slender sucking mouthparts. They are found in most parts of the world, feeding on sap from plants and blood from vertebrate animals.

Only the females "bite" animals. Usually they lay their eggs on the surface of water or in it, where larvae called wrigglers hatch out. These are unusual among fly larvae, in that they have eyes, well-developed biting mouthparts, and the ability to swim by wriggling until they can suspend themselves from the water's surface film while inhaling a fresh supply of air. With their mouthparts, mosquito wrigglers collect small particles of food from the water.

When fully grown, the wrigglers transform into pupae called bullheads, which are buoyant and float at the surface with breathing tubes reaching the air. If disturbed, a bullhead swims downward, but soon rises again. Inside the bullhead skin, the insect continues its transformation (metamorphosis) until it can break through into air as an adult mosquito, winged and ready to fly.

Males live on plant juices. Females of some species seek blood meals only and cause irritation and transmit disease. As a lubricant, anesthetic, and anticoagulant, a small amount of saliva is pumped into the wound made with the mosquito's mouthparts. The saliva contains proteins that later cause itching and often induce local swelling of the skin. Often the saliva contains live parasitic agents, such as the protozoan of malaria, the bacteria of myxomatosis (a disease fatal to European rabbits), the virus of yellow fever, and the filaria worm causing elephantiasis. Each of these diseases is carried only by a particular kind of mosquito; eradication of the disease can be achieved by elimination of the carrier mosquitoes, or by preventing the mosquitoes from becoming infected by "biting" people with the disease. Order Diptera, family Culicidae.

MOTH, any adult insect with 2 pairs of wings covered with overlapping scales and during flight linked together (as those of butterflies are not) by a special bristle or group of bristles on the leading edge of the hind wing. Moths are found on all habitable land areas of the world. They are usually recognized by having threadlike or feathery feelers (antennae), not knobbed or hooked ones as among butterflies; in folding their wings horizontally over the back at rest, not vertically as do butterflies; and in being active by night, rather than by day.

Like butterflies, however, moths lay eggs that hatch into caterpillars, most of which feed on foliage and other parts of plants. A large number of moths are regarded as major pests because of the damage their caterpillars do. After the caterpillar pupates, however, it no longer eats. Usually moth pupae lie in cocoons spun by the full-grown caterpillar. The moth that emerges from the pupa generally uses its long tongue to sip nectar from flowers that are open at night, and thus pollinates many of these plants, ensuring that seeds will form. Order Lepidoptera, suborder Heterocera.

MOUSE, the popular name for any small rodent. Mice are native to all continents except Australia and Antarctica, and of many islands, but not New Zealand. The house mouse (Mus musculus) of Eurasia has adopted man and gone with his belongings everywhere; in captivity the albino genetic strain has proved valuable in medical research. In Britain, most of Europe and parts of Asia, the wild harvest mouse (Micromys minutus) lives among tall undergrowth, while the various wood or field mice (species of Apodemus) frequent grasslands and open woods.

In North America the deer or white-footed mice (Peromyscus species) with very large eyes, occupy the woodland areas, while the short-tailed, short-nosed meadow mice or voles (species of Microtus) live in pasturelands and grain fields. Order Rodentia, family Muridae.

MULE, a hybrid bred from the horse and the ass, differing in size, strength, and beauty, according to the predominance of its parental species. Hybrids from a male ass and a mare are far superior to those from a she-ass and a horse, which are sometimes called hinnies to distinguish them from the other mules.

MULES

In mountainous countries mules are highly serviceable, for no beast of burden is more sure-footed or more capable of enduring fatigue. In beauty of form they fall short of the horse, and usually cannot reproduce. The mule has a large, clumsy head, long erect ears, a short mane, and a thin tail. Order Perissodactyla, family Equidae.

MULLET, the popular name given to several types of fishes that are unrelated. In Britain, fishmongers distinguish between gray mullets of family Mugilidae, and red mullets of family Mullidae. In the western United States, plain mullets are actually suckers, of family Catostomidae.

Gray mullets are bottom feeders, living close to shore along seacoasts or in brackish estuaries. Most of them are small, weighing 3 pounds or less, with small mouths and a special muscular gizzardlike stomach used in grinding up the vegetable matter they swallow. The striped mullet (*Mugil cephalus*) reaches a weight of 15 pounds and length of 3 feet, growing faster than other mullets and supporting commercial fisheries at many places around the world — chiefly where the water is warm.

Red mullets are generally called goatfish because they have two tactile projections (barbels) under the chin. The common red mullet (*Mullus barbatus*) of the Mediterranean and Atlantic coasts northward was once a great favorite among Romans, who kept them in salt ponds and trained them to respond to the sound of a bell or a voice at feeding time. Orders: Percomorphi (Mullidae) and Mugiloidae (Mugilidae).

MUSK OX, a hairy arctic cud-chewing mammal about the size of a small ox but with shorter legs, a shaggy brown coat of long hair hanging almost to the ground, and thick hollow horns that curve and taper down and forward below the eyes. Its range in glacial times was over the whole of Europe and in the United States as far south as Kentucky; now it is confined to the arctic regions of Greenland and North Amer-ica, where the steadily decreasing herds are hunted by Eskimos.

The animal is named for its musky odor, which—apparently not emitted by scent glands—is noticeable at a considerable distance from a herd and also in the flesh, which the Eskimo eats. The musk ox has gregarious habits, runs in herds of 30 to 40, and feeds on grass, shoots, moss, and lichens. Order Artiodactyla, family Bovidae, specifically *Ovibos moschatus*.

MUSKRAT, or musquash, a medium-sized rodent with a small round head, close-set ears, short neck, and bulky body covered with soft dense fur, brown on the back and gray below; the feet are partially webbed, the tail bare, round, and tapering. A marsh animal of North America, the muskrat has been introduced in Europe with mixed results. The fur, called Hudson seal, is useful. But the animal digs holes in dikes and shows a liking for vegetable gardens near water.

Normally muskrats eat aquatic roots, fish, worms, mollusks, vegetables, insects, and fruits. They are especially fond of apples and mussels, often traveling a considerable distance to procure them. Mostly nocturnal in habits, muskrats are not often seen, but their abundance is proved by the millions that are annually trapped for their skins. They do not seem to be on the decrease despite constant persecution by man and natural enemies.

The muskrat's home is built near water, usually burrowed into the bank of a stream with the entrance under the surface of the water. Order Rodentia, family Cricetidae, specifically *Ondatra zibethica*.

MUSSEL, a name loosely applied to members of 2 unlike types of bivalved mollusks. Marine mussels attach themselves to solid objects or to one another by means of strong threads of secretion. Often they form a wave-resistant "scalp" over sandbars and other soft bottom sediments, preventing erosion by storms.

In Europe the edible mussel (*Mytilus edulis*) is harvested from natural mussel beds, and also cultivated by driving leafless trees into the sea bottom to give mussels a place to cling.

Freshwater mussels, of which nearly 1,000 kinds are known, are widely distributed. Some are abundant in tributaries of the Mississippi River, attaining a length of 8 inches. They are used less for their meat and as a source of occasional pearls than as shells from which pearl buttons can be cut; shell waste is ground up to make lime fertilizer. Order Filobranchia, family Mytilidae, and order Eulamellibranchia, family Unionidae.

NAUTILUS, any of several shell-bearing cephalopod mollusks, distantly related to the octopus and squids. They live in the warm waters of the Indian and Pacific oceans close to the Equator, propelling themselves by squirting out sea water through a special nozzle. A nautilus has 4 gills instead of the 2 on all other cephalopods, and a large number of tentacles for capturing food. Unlike the tentacles or arms of an octopus or a squid, however, those of a nautilus lack suction cups which would give it a stronger grip.

The shell of a nautilus is a flat spiral, divided at intervals by curved partitions into a number of chambers. The animal lives in the outermost and largest chamber, but maintains control of the mixture of sea water and gas in the smaller chambers, using the mixture as a flotation device with which to rise or sink through the tropical sea in search of food.

The eyes of a nautilus lack a lens, and resemble a pinhole camera. Unlike most other cephalopod mollusks, the animal lacks an ink sac, and consequently cannot cloud the water about it while escaping from a predatory fish. About 300 different fossil species of nautilus are known, but only 4 remain alive today. Order Tetrabranchiata, genus *Nautilus*.

NEWT, or eft, any of several small aquatic, tailed amphibians or salamanders, with narrow compressed tails. The giant newt (*Triturus torosus*) of humid western parts of North America grows to be 6 inches long; it has red or orange underparts. The red eft (*T. viridescens*) is brick-colored with red and black spots. It is found in ponds and damp woodlands of eastern North America. A crested newt (*T. cristatus*) and a spotted one (*T. vulgaris*) are common in similar sites in Britain and Europe. Eft and newt are the same word; "an eft" was misdivided to "a neft" and rewritten "a newt." Order Caudata.

NIGHTHAWK, or bullbat, a medium-sized bird of the United States and Canada, allied to the whippoorwill and the nightjars. It has a short beak, an enormous mouth with which it catches flying insects while on the wing, pointed wings with a white spot near the tip, and a forked tail. The feet are so small and weak that the bird seldom walks. Instead it flutters to a stop on the ground, a rooftop, or the tip of a fencepost, or a horizontal branch of a tree. On a branch it turns parallel, and appears to be only a swelling of the wood, its mottled brown feathers matching bark of many kinds of trees.

Nighthawks build no nest; they lay their 2 eggs in some open area where they can see any animal or person approaching. On dull days, in twilight and at night, nighthawks fly erratically in search of food, often beating their wings 3 times in quick succession and uttering a harsh *peenk*. At intervals, a bird closes its wings for a sudden dive, then, with a loud *zing-g-g*, spreads them again to check its descent. For the winter, nighthawks migrate to South America, some of them as far as Argentina. Order Caprimulgiformes, family Caprimulgidae, specifically *Chordeiles minor*.

NIGHTINGALE, either of 2 different small, inconspicuous brown thrushes of Europe, whose sweet melodious song from dense cover is enjoyed by night and by day. The nightingale (*Luscinia megarhyncha*) that visits Britain in summer is widespread in Europe south of Scandinavia. The thrush nightingale (*L. luscinia*), which has a few streaks on its underparts, visits eastern Denmark and southern Sweden in summer, but it is an eastern European and western Asian bird. The song resembles that of the American hermit thrush, which is a distantly related bird.

Nightingales build a nest of dry leaves, lined with grass, fine roots, and hair, and lay 4 or 5 eggs of olive-brown color. Order Passeriformes, family Turdidae.

NIGHTJAR, any of several kinds of Eurasian birds related to the whippoorwill of America, with short beaks, enormous mouths, and long wings. The nightjar is active only at night, feeding in flight, eating large moths and smaller insects, which are caught in the widely open mouth as though the bird were trawling through the sky. By day the nightjars crouch motionless on the ground or on a tree branch, their mottled brown feathers camouflaging them well.

They build no nest, laying their eggs on the bare ground. The name refers to the loud jarring night song that rises and falls continuously for as much as 5 minutes at a time. Order Caprimulgiformes, family Caprimulgidae, members of genus *Caprimulgus*.

NUTHATCH, any of several small perching birds with strong beaks like those of woodpeckers, and large powerful feet, used in climbing down and up the bark of trees while searching for hidden insects to eat. Nuthatches do not use their short stubby tail as a prop the way a woodpecker does. They live principally in the coniferous forests of Eurasia (as far south as Malaya) and North America.

Nuthatches get their name from the habit of pecking at nuts that are wedged in the bark, probably to reach insects inside the nut. They do eat some fruits and many seeds, especially in winter, and will often visit a feeding shelf to get sunflower seeds.

Nuthatches nest in holes such as the abandoned cavities cut by woodpeckers, sometimes making their own holes by excavating the rotting wood in a dead tree. The female, whose size and coloration are closely similar to those of the male, attends to most or all of the incubation of the eggs; both sexes, however, bring insects as food for the nestlings.

Often the owner of the nest can be guessed before the bird is seen, because nuthatches commonly smear resin from coniferous trees or mud around the 1-inch opening to their nest. Order Passeriformes, family Sittidae, members of genus *Sitta*.

NUTRIA, or coypu, a South American rodent resembling a large rat, with a body weighing as much as 20 pounds; it is about 22 inches long and bears a 14-inch tail covered by scales and short hairs. The fur is long, grayish or brownish when seen at a distance, but thick because of a dense yellowish underfur visible when the outer guard hairs are parted. The large incisor teeth are bright orange-yellow. Only the hind feet are webbed. With them a nutria swims well. These animals dig burrows in the banks of rivers and marshes, and emerge principally at night to feed on many kinds of vegetation. Order Rodentia, family Myacastoridae, specifically *Myacastor coypus*.

OCELOT. See *Cat*.

OCTOPUS, or devilfish, any of a number of soft-bodied, shell-less marine cephalopod mollusks with 8 sucker-studded arms. These animals are found along most of the world's seacoasts, where they catch crabs and other animals as food. The common octopus (*Octopus vulgaris*) of the Mediterranean Sea, which is caught for food, often grows arms that can stretch 8 feet tip to tip. One (*O. apollyon*), found along the Pacific coast of North America from northern California to Alaska, is almost twice as large. Small ones are surprisingly abundant in tide pool and reef crannies in the tropics.

When it senses danger, the octopus squirts a dark inklike substance from a sac. It seems to have a high-domed head, although this actually is its body—above the head. The mouth is below, where the arms come together; in it is a pair of horny jaws and also a rasping organ (*radula*) with which an octopus can make a hole right through a heavy conch shell to reach the meat inside. Order Dibranchia, family Octopodidae.

OKAPI, a large cud-chewing mammal standing 4 feet high at the withers, with head and ears like those of a giraffe but a much shorter neck. It is found only in humid forests of Africa's Congo River basin. Its body is a curious mixture of deep red and black; the legs are cream-colored below and striped black and white where they join the body.

Sir Harry Johnston discovered the okapi in 1900. Order Artiodactyla, family Giraffidae, specifically *Okapia johnstoni*.

ONAGER. See *Ass*.

OPOSSUM, or possum, any of about 101 different kinds of short-legged, long-tailed marsupial mammals, most of which have a clawless, opposable big toe and a prehensile tail. All but one of the New World representatives live in the Tropics or in temperate South America; the exception is the Virginia opossum (*Didelphis marsupialis*), which is about the size of a housecat, occurring now from Florida north to eastern Canada and west to the Missouri River. When disturbed, it "plays possum," going into a sort of trance and giving no sport to animals that want live prey.

Possum is the official spelling for the Old World representatives, all members of family Phalangeridae, inhabiting Australia and New Guinea. The brush-tailed possum (*Trichosurus vulpecula*), which occurs in all humid forests of Australia, was introduced into New Zealand in 1900 as a fur bearer; too late was it recognized as a serious defoliater of native New Zealand trees.

All except 7 of the New World opossums belong to family Didelphidae. The 7 are small "rat" opossums from western South America, which have claws on their big toes and cannot grasp objects with their feet or their very long tails; they are grouped in family Caenolestidae. In these 7, as in some representatives among opossums and possums, a distinct pouch (marsupium) is lacking; the young must cling to the underside of the mother between two lengthwise folds of skin. Order Marsupialia.

ORANGUTAN, the Malay name (meaning man-of-the-woods) for a large manlike ape with dark brown skin and scanty reddish-brown hair. It is found in lowland swamps and forests of Borneo and Sumatra, where it grows to a height of slightly more than 4 feet. The arms of one big male, 4 feet 2 inches tall, spread 7 feet 9 inches; and when he stood erect, his hands nearly touched the ground. Such an orangutan weighs 250 to 300 pounds.

Orangutans live almost entirely in trees. They eat fruits, flowers, buds, and insects, and build for each night a new nest of leaves and boughs. The animal never jumps, but progresses through the forest by swinging itself from limb to limb. Order Primates, family Pongidae, specifically *Pongo pygmaeus*.

ORIOLE, any of about 65 different kinds of starling-sized birds that frequent tree tops, build saucer-shaped or sac-like nests suspended from high branches, and are brightly colored, with yellow or orange generally conspicuous on the plumage. Oriole is a variant spelling of aureole, from the Latin *aureus* for golden. In Europe, Asia, and parts of Africa, more than 30 kinds of such birds are found, all members of the Old World family Oriolidae. Only the golden oriole (*Oriolus oriolus*), which winters in Africa, is common in Europe and comes as far as Britain. Australia has 2 members of this family, called figeaters (*Sphecotheres* species).

Curiously, unrelated birds in the New World show similar body form, coloring, and nesting habits. They are the 30 kinds of American orioles, including the Baltimore oriole (*Icterus galbula*), the male of which is bright orange with a black head and throat; this bird nests over much of the eastern United States and Canada, and winters in southern Mexico and Central America. However, American orioles are related closely to the blackbirds, grackles, and cowbirds, in family Icteridae. Order Passeriformes.

OSPREY, or fish hawk, a large hawk with a wingspread of as much as 72 inches, which eats fish exclusively, catching them by a spectacular plunge into the water and then grasping the prey in its strong feet. Ospreys were at one time numerous about large rivers and lakes and along coasts of North America, Central America, parts of South America (Peru, Chili, Paraguay), Asia, Australia, Europe, and Greenland. Now their numbers are reduced; and the bird is disappearing or has disappeared from many of these regions.

Ospreys generally return year after year to nest at the same site, adding sticks to a bulky mass built atop a dead tree, a utility pole, or even on the ground. Both parents defend the nest and tend the 2 to 4 eggs, the young that hatch out blind and helpless, and the young birds that grow rapidly on fishes brought to them all day long.

The female osprey is larger than her mate, weighing between 4 and 5 pounds; a male bird rarely is heavier than 3 pounds 3 ounces. In flight, both appear to hold their wings in a bent position. Often an osprey with a fish in its grasp is robbed of its prey by an eagle that attacks it in mid-air. Order Falconiformes, family Pandionidae, specifically *Pandion haliaëtus*.

OSTRICH, the largest of living birds, males growing 8 feet tall and reaching 250 pounds in weight. They graze on grasses and other low plants on African savannas south of the great deserts.

Ostriches are flightless because of their great size, but not wingless although their wing muscles are small and weak. Feathers from wings and tail formerly were used for decorating hats, but today the chief uses for ostrich plumes are in feather dusters and feather boas for stage costumes. To supply these, and ostrich meat and ostrich eggs, ostrich farms have been developed in South America, South Africa, and California.

A hen ostrich lays 10 to 12 eggs on the sand. Two or 3 hens of a single male may lay eggs in the same nest. The male stands guard over them by day, shielding them from the sun or warming them with his body, depending on the temperature. At night the females take turns incubating the eggs. Each egg has about the volume of 24 eggs of domestic fowl. Order Struthioniformes, family Struthionidae, specifically *Struthio camelus*.

OTTER, any of about 17 different kinds of short-legged, heavy-bodied, swimming mammals with durable, valuable fur. Most are river otters (species of *Lutra*), playful animals that live on fish in the Americas, much of Africa and Eurasia, including East Indian islands. They slide down mud banks and snow banks, headfirst into streams. One kind is the rare sea otter (*Enhydra lutris*) of kelp beds along North Pacific coasts from California to Alaska and Kamchatka, where it feeds on sea urchins, sea snails, and mussels. The mother sea otter plays with her pups for hours and sometimes is seen asleep on a tangle of seaweed in the water, lying on her back with the little otter in her front paws. Order Carnivora, family Mustelidae.

OWL, any of about 123 different kinds of predatory birds with extremely large heads; huge eyes directed forward; short, stout beaks hooked at the tip; and very large ear openings. Owls have feathered legs and 4 toes, the outer one capable of being directed backward to make a clutching fist. Their plumage is remarkably soft, and the feathers of the face form disks around the eyes.

Owls are found over the whole globe. Species vary in size from 5 inches to 2 feet in length. They feed on small mammals, birds, fishes, and insects, swallowing the prey whole. Afterward they disgorge the hair, bones, feathers, and scales in the form of pellets. They nest on the ground, among rocks, in hollow trees and in buildings; some resort to the old nests of other birds. They lay from 2 to 5 roundish, white eggs.

Several species have feathered tufts of either side of the top of the head and are called horned owls or cat-owls — notably the eagle owl (*Bubo bubo*) of Europe and Asia and the North American great horned owl (*B. virginianus*), both about 25 inches long. The snow owl or snowy owl (*Nyctea scandiaca*), despite its scientific name meaning nocturnal, hunts in the long daylight of the Arctic in both hemispheres; it occasionally winters in northern United States; it has no horns and is almost snow-white.

One of the smallest owls is the 5½-inch elf owl (*Micropallas whitneyi*) of the American Southwest and Mexico, which often nests in abandoned

OWL

woodpecker holes in large saguaro cactuses. The burrowing owl (*Speotyto cunicularia*) of the American plains lives in the deserted holes of prairie dogs and viscachas. It is 9 or 10 inches long, and its legs are longer and barer than those of other owls. Order Strigiformes, family Strigidae.

OX. See *Cattle*.

OYSTER, any of a number of different marine bivalved mollusks that, at an early age, cease swimming and attach themselves by the left shell valve to the ocean bottom or a mangrove root or a wharf piling. Oysters live near shore along most coasts. Most valuable as a source of luxury food is the Atlantic-coast oyster (*Ostraea virginica*) of the United States from Cape Cod to the Gulf of Mexico. Formerly it extended to the coast of Maine, and even now there are scattered beds in the Gulf of St. Lawrence.

The European oyster (*O. edulis*) is smaller than the American and has a coppery taste. Both sexes are united in the same individual, whereas in the American species the sexes are separate.

In tropical waters, divers seek pearl oysters, *Avicula* and *Pinctada*, which are especially abundant around Cey-

lon, and *Margaritophora* near Bermuda. These oysters habitually secrete mother-of-pearl, which is the ordinary lining material for their shells, around sand grains, small worms, or other foreign particles that get between the body and shell. Layer after layer is added until a hard lump is formed; if it is spherical or of some interesting shape and suitably lustrous, the lump is a precious pearl. Order Prionodesmacea, family Ostreidae.

PANTHER. See *Cat*.

PARROT, any of about 315 different kinds of brightly colored birds in which both upper and lower beak are hinged movably to the skull, and the foot grasps strongly with 2 toes forward and 2 in back. Parrots live in all countries and major islands in the Tropics and also in some adjacent temperate lands.

In the southeastern United States there formerly lived a Carolina paroquet (*Conuropsis carolinensis*), but it was exterminated before 1910; tropical American parrots include 25 kinds of large macaws (species of *Ara*) with long slender tails, and another 25 of green parrots with short tails (species of *Amazona*), as well as numerous conures, parakeets, and parrotlets.

Africa is the home of the gray parrot (*Psittacus erithaceus*) with a red tail, which is particularly desirable as a cage bird because it excels in imitating human speech; other African relatives are the small colorful lovebirds (*Agapornis* species) of many kinds. Australia and New Guinea have numerous kinds of cockatoos, lorikeets, and the popular budgerigars (*Melopsittacus undulatus*) that now rival canaries as house pets.

New Zealand parrots include three plump kinds that are almost as big as a chicken: the flightless owl parrot, or kakapo (*Strigops habroptilus*), a rare ground bird of forest glades; the equally rare kaka (*Nestor meridionalis*), which feeds on fruit, nectar, and insects; and the mountain kea (*N. notabilis*), which now stays near camps and sheep-butchering stations, feeding on scraps and waste fat from sheep carcasses. No other parrot seems to have changed thus far from a diet of seeds and fruits in the treetops. Order Psittaciformes, family Psittacidae.

PARTRIDGE, any of several fowl-like birds with short beak, short legs, and short tail, and which produce a loud whirring sound when frightened into flying away.

Originally the word partridge referred to particular birds of Eurasia and Africa, specifically the Hungarian, or European, gray partridge (*Perdix perdix*), and the red-legged, or Chukar, partridge (*Alectoris rufa*) of Europe, Corsica, and the Canary Islands; both have been introduced widely into North America, New Zealand, and elsewhere as upland game birds that offer good targets and good eating.

In North America, the word partridge is often applied to quail in the southern states, and to the ruffed grouse farther north. Order Galliformes, family Phasianidae.

PEAFOWL, any of 3 different large pheasantlike birds with a slightly curved beak, a small distinctive crest on the head, short wings, long stout legs and, in the male, a magnificent set of long gold and green tail coverts that the peacock during courtship raises vertically like a semicircular screen extending from the ground on one side to the ground on the other.

The domesticated peafowl (*Pavo cristatus*) is native to India and Ceylon; both peacock and peahen have a blue neck and crest feathers with the little vanes only at the tips; the tail-covert feathers of the male are elaborately patterned with large eyespots, which show even when the plumes are lowered to make a "train" behind the bird. White peafowl, with no markings, are not uncommon in domestic flocks.

A Javanese peafowl (*P. muticus*) with a green neck and crest feathers with vanes the whole length lives in humid forests of Java and adjacent Southeast Asia. A Congolese peafowl (*Afropavo congensis*) is a glossy black bird with a patch of white in its crown. Order Galliformes, family Phasianidae.

PECCARY, either of 2 different kinds of New World wild pigs, whose tusks point downward instead of outward or upward, whose 2-chambered stomach shows special complexity, and whose long slim legs are peculiar in that the hind feet have only 3 toes, instead of the usual 4 among pigs.

Native to the New World, peccaries are forest animals, usually seen in bands containing both sexes and all ages. The larger white-lipped peccary (*Tayassu pecari*), which associates in groups of 50 to 100 or more, may if threatened, counterattack, slashing effectively with its sharp tusk.

Peccaries live from Paraguay to southern Mexico. The collared peccary (*T. tajacu*), found from Arizona and Texas to Patagonia, travels in bands of 5 to 15, often roaming desert regions as well as tropical forests.

Members of both species use their snouts to dig for vegetable food, grubs, snakes, and other small animals; sometimes they raid cultivated fields and inflict damage. Generally the presence of peccaries in an area is indicated by the strong-smelling substance their musk glands secrete whenever they are excited. Order Artiodactyla, family Tayassuidae.

PELICAN, any of 6 different kinds of fish-eating, swimming birds with a large pouch of skin between the halves of the lower jaw.

In the New World, the brown pelican (*Pelecanus occidentalis*) ranges along coasts from the southern United States to Venezuela and Chile; the white pelican (*P. erythrorhynchus*) is an inland bird, nesting from British Columbia to Ontario, and migrating to Mexico and the Gulf States in winter. Old World pelicans are largely white and venture far inland in Africa, southern Europe, southern Asia, to southeastern Australia.

All pelicans can hover, fold their wings, and plunge into water after fish. Sometimes they fish in groups.

They scoop the fish into the pouch and swallow it while flying again or after returning to the shore. Order Pelecaniformes, family Pelecanidae.

PENGUIN, any of 15 different short-tailed swimming birds of the Southern Hemisphere, in which the strong wings lack flight feathers and are stiff, moving only at the shoulder as paddles for underwater propulsion or as weapons in self-defense. Except for the Galápagos penguin (*Spheniscus mendiculus*), which lives on the Equator surrounded by icy water, they are birds of the Antarctic and the southernmost coasts of Africa, Australia, New Zealand, South America, and remote islands.

Tallest is the emperor penguin (*Aptenoides forsteri*), 4 feet high, which lays its eggs and raises its chicks on Antarctica during the winter night there. The only other penguins on Antarctica are the Adélies (*Pygoscelis adeliae*), 30 inches tall. Of medium size and with a call like a donkey's bray is the jackass penguin (*Spheniscus demersus*) of South America and South Africa. The smallest is the fairy penguin (*Eudyptula minor*) of Australia and New Zealand, 16 inches tall.

Newly hatched penguins are covered with down, but the grown birds have stiff scalelike feathers. Their food consists chiefly of fish and squids. Order Sphenisciformes, family Spheniscidae.

PERCH, either of 2 small, edible, freshwater fishes in which the pelvic fins are far forward, close to the pectoral fins, the dorsal fin has its spiny and its soft portions separated from one another, and there are 3 anal spines instead of 2, as in sunfishes.

The European perch (*Perca fluviatilis*), found through most of Europe to Siberia and in brackish waters of the Black Sea, sometimes grows to weigh 6 pounds. The yellow perch (*P. flavescens*) of North America lived only east of the Rocky Mountains until it was introduced elsewhere; a 15-inch fish weighing 2 pounds is a large one. Its orange-yellow sides have 6 to 8 dark vertical stripes, and its pelvic fins are reddish. Order Percomorphi, family Percidae.

PERIWINKLE, or winkle, any of several different kinds of small snails of the seacoast, with a compact top-shaped shell and a horny plate on the side of its foot with which to block the shell opening after the animal has withdrawn inside. Originally native to European coasts, periwinkles have now been introduced widely around the world. Periwinkles feed almost exclusively on small seaweeds, and their meat is delicately flavored.

Unlike many snails, a periwinkle has its foot divided into a right side and a left, and creeps by swinging alternately from side to side with a peculiar rolling gait. To reach its food, a periwinkle extends its tonguelike rasping organ (radula), which sometimes is twice as long as the 1-inch foot of the animal. Order Aspidobranchia, family Littorinidae, members of genus *Littorina*.

PETREL, any of 26 different kinds of small, web-footed sea birds, which have their nostrils opening at the end of a tubelike part of the upper beak. Four are plump-bodied diving petrels (family Pelecanoididae), resembling auks, flying with rapidly whirring wings, which they use also in swimming underwater in pursuit of fish. The others are slender-bodied storm petrels (family Hydrobatidae), which flutter over the sea surface but seldom alight, while feeding on squid, floating mollusks, surface shrimp and other crustaceans, or the galley scraps from passing ships.

Petrels are found far out at sea on all oceans, except at nesting time, when they return to offshore islands or the slopes of coastal mountains, generally coming in at dusk or after dark to burrows 2 to 3 feet deep or crannies under loose rocks. Leach's petrel (*Oceanodroma leucorhoa*) of the North Atlantic and North Pacific has a forked tail, the storm petrel (*Hydrobates pelagicus*) of European coasts, a rounded or square tail; both have become well known from their habit of following ships day after day, and are called Mother Carey's chickens—from the Latin *mater cara*, the divine virgin, referring to the Virgin Mary who is guardian of all seafarers. Petrel is believed to be a diminutive of St. Peter, alluding to the apparent ability of petrels to walk on water.

The name petrel is often given also to a shearwater, the giant fulmar or giant petrel (*Macronectes giganteus*) of southern oceans, a bird 3 feet long with an 8-foot wingspan. No true petrel is longer than 10 inches; they are the smallest of all pelagic birds. Order Procellariiformes.

PEWEE, or wood pewee, a small inconspicuous woodland flycatcher whose olive-gray body blends with the shadows while it perches on a branch, awaiting a flying insect. The pewee flits out quickly, catches the insect, and returns to the same or another branch, often calling *pee'-a-wee'* or *pee'-wee* in a plaintive way.

The bird has a forked tail, 2 pale wing bars, and often raises the feathers on its head to form a low crest. It builds its nest on an outstretched branch of a deciduous tree, constructing it of rootlets and other plant fibers, frequently covering it with lichens as though for camouflage.

For the winter, pewees migrate to northwestern South America, where they mingle with closely related birds from western North America. The western wood pewee (*C. sordidulus*), which inhabits more open woodlands and calls *dear* or *dear-me*, often sings at night. Order Passeriformes, family Tyrannidae, specifically *Contopus virens*.

PHALAROPE, any of 3 different shore birds of the Arctic, resembling large sandpipers, in which the female is larger than the male, with a wingspread from 14 to 16 inches, and does the courting; she is more brightly colored but often leaves the building of the nest and incubation of the eggs she lays in it to her mate. All nest in the Arctic, their small pear-shaped eggs hatching in about two weeks, and the young birds hiding themselves among grasses near the simple nest.

The northern phalarope (*Lobipes lobatus*), known as the red-necked phalarope in Britain and Europe, flutters over salt water, using its long beak to catch minute crustaceans and other small plankton animals as food. The red phalarope (*Phalaropus fulicarius*), called the gray phalarope in the Old World, swims more frequently in freshwater and performs characteristic spinning movements that appear to disturb insects, snails, and other prey into moving and being seen.

The Wilson's phalarope (*Steganopus tricolor*) of Arctic America nests farther south, to California and Indiana, feeding itself and young on terrestrial insects, crustaceans, spiders, and snails found near the marshlands where it nests. As soon as their young are ready to fly, all phalaropes migrate far south to cold waters off the coasts of South Africa and South America, particularly where ocean currents from the Antarctic enrich the surface waters and support large numbers of plankton, crustaceans, and small fishes. Order Charadriiformes, family Phalaropodidae.

PHEASANT, any of about 50 different kinds of large, long-tailed, grouselike birds. They are native to central and southern Asia and the East Indies, but many of them have been introduced elsewhere. The ringneck, or English or Mongolian pheasant (*Phasianus colchicus*) probably reached Britain during Roman times; it is a well-known and popular game bird. The argus pheasant (*Argusianus argus*) of Southeast Asia is almost as big as a peacock. Female pheasants are dull and plain compared to the males. In some parts of the United States, the name pheasant is used loosely for grouse and quail. Order Galliformes, family Phasianidae.

PHOEBE, a medium-sized flycatcher, is olive-gray in color, slightly paler below; continually wagging its tail up and down, it frequently calls its name *phee'-be* or (more insistently) *phee'-beee'*. Like other flycatchers it perches on bare branches where it can see flying insects coming, and dart out to catch them. It builds its nest under a cover, such as alongside an overhanging bank above a stream or under a bridge or porch roof.

In winter it migrates to Florida, the Gulf States, and Mexico. It was a nestful of young phoebes that John James Audubon marked along a stream in Pennsylvania, using loose bracelets of silver wire, in the first experimental study to determine whether birds return after a winter's absence to the region where they were hatched. Of 5 phoebes marked in this way, 3 returned the following spring to nest along the same stream. Order Passeriformes, family Tyrannidae, specifically *Sayornis phoebe*.

PICKEREL. See *Pike*.

PIG. See *Swine*.

PIGEON, any of almost 300 different kinds of small-headed, stout-bodied birds with short, rounded beaks topped by a fleshy part (the cere) through which the nostrils open. They are represented on every continent and most islands. Generally the term pigeon refers to birds with square or rounded tails, and the term dove to more slender-bodied related birds with pointed tails.

Domesticated and city pigeons are derived from the common rock pigeon (*Columba livia*), about 13 inches long, native to southern Eurasia and north Africa. Careful breeding has produced from this bird distinctive strains excelling in racing speed, homing ability, aerial acrobatics, showy feathers, and quick production of meat for people who enjoy eating young birds (squabs) that have just reached full growth.

The extinct passenger pigeon (*Ectopistes migratorius*) that vanished in the wild about 1899 had occupied vast oak and beech forests in central and eastern North America. Colonists destroyed their habitat, and also netted, shot, and trapped the birds for shipment to market until there were no more.

The giants are the 3 kinds of crowned pigeons in New Guinea, as much as 33 inches long. They have a crest of lacy feathers, and 16 instead of the usual 12 tail feathers. Nearby Australia has big, metallic-colored pigeons called bronzewings (the common one is *Phaps chalcoptera*), which eat so many seeds from a poisonous plant that their bones and internal organs are deadly to predatory animals, although their flesh is unharmed and edible. Order Columbiformes, family Columbidae.

PIKE, any of about 8 different kinds of predatory fishes of northern freshwaters, with a long pointed head, large mouth with formidable teeth, no spines in any of the fins, the dorsal fin far back—behind the pelvic fins and above the anal fin—and with a body slender and spear-shaped, as the name pike suggests.

Most widespread is the northern pike (*Esox lucius*) of Eurasia and the northern United States and Canada, a fish that has been recorded as attaining 54 inches in length and a weight of 46 pounds. It is exceeded in both ways by the muskellunge (*E. masquinongy*) of the upper Great Lakes and adjacent waters, which may grow to 102 pounds.

Smaller relatives of these large fish are called pickerels ("little pikes"), and differ in details of the scale pattern on the head and body, as well as in distribution and habits. Aside from the northern pike, the only member of this group in Eurasia is the black-spotted pike (*E. reicherti*) of Siberia. Order Haplomi, family Esocidae.

The fish called a walleyed pike (*Stizostedion vitreum*), found in eastern North America, and the pikeperch (*Lucioperca lucioperca*), found in Eurasia, are members of the perch family.

PIGEON

PINTAIL, a dabbling duck of freshwaters, in which the male has 2 long middle tail feathers 5 to 9 inches long stretching out behind his 28-inch body. Pintails breed in northern Eurasia, Canada, and the northwestern United States, migrating southward and to the Pacific coast in winter.

The male has a reddish-brown head, gray back, and white throat and underparts. The female is smaller and is streaked with brown. They nest on the ground, concealed in bunches of grass or weeds, usually near water. Seven to 10 greenish eggs are laid in March or April. Order Anseriformes, family Anatidae, specifically *Anas acuta*.

PIRANHA, any of several South American freshwater fishes 7 to 24 inches long, with elliptical bodies, strong lower jaw, and many razor-sharp teeth. Four kinds of piranha are greatly feared in their native rivers and lakes, because they attack in large numbers any person or mammal that enters the same water—particularly if it falls in and splashes about.

Most widely distributed is the 4-inch *Serrasalmus nattereri* of the Brazilian river systems, particularly the Amazon, whose normal diet consists of other fishes. This piranha might be mistaken for a small sunfish until it darts at a victim and uses its incredibly strong jaws and sharp teeth to cut out pieces of flesh and bone. Fishermen seek piranhas, an excellent food, but use strong wire leaders on fishing lines to prevent the piranha from cutting itself loose and swimming away with the baited hook. Order Ostariophysi, family Characidae, species of *Serrasalmus*.

PIT-VIPER, any of several poisonous snakes, which possess between nostril and eye a distinctive pit that is sensitive to radiant heat. They live in eastern Asia and the New World. Using its paired pits, the snake even in complete darkness, can find animals as prey because these are warmer than their surroundings—as a sleeping bird or a mammal would be, or cooler—as a frog would be because of evaporation from its wet skin. The pit-viper strikes its prey with two erectile fangs in its upper jaw, within which venom canals are connected to large glands that secrete the poison.

Most feared of these snakes is the bushmaster *(Lachesis muta)* of northern South America, Panama, and parts of Costa Rica, which lies in wait for small mammals along their trails through forest and scrubland where its mottled brown color makes it almost invisible. No less deadly is the smaller fer-de-lance *(Bothrops atrox)* which sometimes attains a length of 8 feet and frequents coconut plantations from southern Mexico to southern Peru, through all of northern South America. Like most pit vipers, but unlike the bushmaster which lays eggs, the fer-de-lance mother brings forth active young, as many as 71 at a birth, each with its sensory pits and venom apparatus fully developed.

Far less dangerous are the copperhead *(Ancistrodon contortrix)* of forest regions in eastern North America, the cottonmouth moccasin *(A. piscivorus)* of swamplands in the southern United States, and related members of the same genus in Mexico and the Old World from the southern edge of the Russian steppes to Ceylon, Malaya, and Japan.

Rattlesnakes *(Crotalus* and *Sistrurus)*, which are exclusively North American, represent a more venomous group of pit vipers. In these snakes, only part of each old skin is shed at molting time, and the remainder contributes to the accumulated loose sections of the "rattle" at the end of the tail. Because the terminal "button" and additional parts of the rattle commonly break away and the snake may shed its skin more than once a year, it is impossible to learn the age of a rattlesnake by counting the pieces in its rattle.

The amount of venom that a rattlesnake can inject, and hence the danger offered by the snake, is roughly proportionate to the length of the animal. This varies from one species to another, the giant being the eastern diamondback rattlesnake *(C. adamanteus)*, one of which was found to be 98 inches long. Next in size, so far as known, are the western diamondback (84 inches), the western Mexican rattlesnake (80 inches), and the South American rattlesnake (78 inches).

The famous timber rattlesnake *(C. horridus)*, which was the first kind encountered by the English colonists, sometimes reached a length of 75 inches. It is still found in many parts of the area from northern New England to northern Florida, west to eastern Texas and north to Wisconsin. From this territory westward to the Pacific coast and northward into Canada, the prairie rattler *(C. viridis)* is found. Sometimes it grows to a length of 60 inches. Order Squamata, suborder Serpentes, family Crotalidae.

PLATYPUS. See *Duckbill.*

PLOVER, any of 38 different kinds of shore birds with legs of moderate length and beaks no longer than the head, slightly enlarged toward the tip. They are found almost all over the world, nesting on open beaches and fields, where their spotted eggs blend inconspicuously and are easily overlooked. In England and on the Continent plovers' eggs are a great delicacy.

As a group, plovers are noted for covering enormous distances on their migratory flights. The golden plover *(Pluvius dominica)*, about 11 inches long, a beautiful but fast-diminishing species, breeds on the Arctic coasts but winters in southeastern Brazil and Argentina; its annual southern flight takes it many hundreds of miles out to sea, although it takes an overland route flying north.

One of the most familiar plovers is the killdeer of North America *(Charadrius vociferus)*, so called because the Latin word *vociferus* (loud) describes its noisy, reiterated cry. Killdeers, often found in the uplands many miles from water, are recognizable by their brown back, tail and wings. They are 10 inches long, brownish above and with 2 black bands on the white breast and 2 on the head.

The pale-backed, 7-inch piping plover *(C. meloda)* is nearly always found on the beach where it is often difficult to distinguish from the sand whose color it matches; it has a plaintive, melodious whistle, as indicated by its name. Order Charadriiformes, family Charadriidae.

POLECAT, any of several weasel-like predatory mammals in which the anal musk glands are well developed, producing a fetid secretion when the animal is threatened. Native to northern Africa and Eurasia, they have contributed one member that can be domesticated—the ferret, which is usually an albino and is valuable in driving rabbits from burrows or in destroying rats.

The wild form of the ferret is the most widespread polecat *(Mustela putorius)*; it grows to 20 inches long with a 7-inch tail, is dark brown to black in color with a yellow patch on each side of the head between ear and eye. Its pelt is sold in the fur trade as "fitch." A marbled polecat *(Vormela peregusna)* lives in steppes of southeastern Europe and across to Mongolia, differing markedly from other polecats in its mottled dark and pale coloration. Order Carnivora, family Mustelidae.

POLLACK. See *Cod.*

PORCUPINE, any of about 43 different kinds of rodents in which the back, and often the head and tail as well, bear large hollow barbed quills that pull out easily from among the shorter fur. In the Old World, 20 kinds in family Hystricidae live mostly on the ground, eating carrion and plant materials, in Africa, southern Europe to southern China, Indonesia, and the Philippines. In the New World, 23 kinds in family Erethizontidae are more tree-dwellers, as vegetarians, ranging from coast to coast and from the Arctic to southern South America.

When disturbed, a porcupine tries to hide its unprotected and sensitive nose, while presenting its quills by raising them at right angles from the body. The North American porcupine

AMERICAN MUSEUM OF NATURAL HISTORY
PORCUPINE

(Erethizon dorsatum) may back up, swatting vigorously with its quill-studded tail. Porcupines in Central and South America have prehensile tails that help them hold on while eating leaves high in the trees. The porcupines of Europe and Africa are as much as 32 inches long, weigh as much as 56 pounds, and have some quills 12 inches long. At birth, the quills are soft, but they harden in a few hours. Order Rodentia.

PORPOISE (from old French for hogfish), any of about 7 different kinds of small-toothed whales less than 6 feet long, with a blunt nose. Almost all of the world's coasts, estuaries, and harbors are visited by these animals as they hunt for unarmed fishes of modest size, squid, and crustaceans; sometimes they are seen following schools of fish, singly or in pairs or in groups of nearly 100. Unlike dolphins, they rarely follow ships.

Formerly they were caught in Europe for meat and an oil useful for lubrication and for burning. Porpoise fisheries still operate along the coasts of some Oriental countries. Order Cetacea, family Delphinidae, chiefly genus *Phocaena.*

PORTUGUESE MAN-OF-WAR, a dangerous colony of marine coelenterate animals, 1 member of which at a time grows to become a pinkish blue, gas-filled balloon as much as 8 inches long and 5 high. The float provides buoyant support for the colony; floating high in the sea surface, it catches the wind and hence pulls the colony along. Below it dozens of other members of the colony extend slender contractile tentacles, deep blue in color and as much as 60 feet long.

The tentacles hang down like fishing lines, waiting for fishes and other edible animals to bump into them. Special nettling cells on the tentacles can inject poison into a victim, stunning or killing it, while other cells cling to the prey and the whole tentacle (or group of tentacles) shortens to haul up the victim right under the float. There other individuals with soft flexible mouths begin digesting the prey. The digested food is then shared throughout the colony. In season, special reproductive individuals are formed, providing eggs and sperms for sexual multiplication.

The Portuguese man-of-war is common in tropical American waters, and is often carried northward by the Gulf Stream, to be blown ashore. Even dead colonies on the beach can sting painfully if their tentacles are touched, and live ones in water can sting a human swimmer worse than a nestful of wasps. Order Siphonophora, family Physalidae, specifically *Physalia pelagica*.

PRAIRIE CHICKEN. See *Grouse*.

PRAIRIE DOG, any of 5 different kinds of short-tailed, short-legged burrowing squirrel-like mammals. They live sociably in prairie-dog "towns" where bison used to roam, on the plains east of the Rocky Mountains, from the Canadian prairie provinces to northern Mexico. Like their relatives, the marmots, prairie dogs have well-developed claws on all the toes of the forefeet and shallow cheek pouches. They feed on herbs and grasses but store little.

The best-known species is the plains prairie dog (*Cynomys ludovicianus*), about 1 foot long with a 4-inch tail, reddish-brown above, variegated with gray. The name refers to their alarm cry, which suggests the barking of a small dog. Order Rodentia, family Sciuridae, all members of genus *Cynomys*.

PRAYING MANTIS, any of about 1,500 kinds of predatory insects with special grasping forelegs, thought to be the only insect with a neck so flexible it can turn its head and look backward. For hours a praying mantis may remain motionless or may sway slightly on the 4 long slender legs that support it, waiting for some other insect to come within snatching distance. Victims are held firmly by the forelegs, which are folded once again in a prayerful attitude, while the head is moved and the jaws are brought into play.

A female mantis may even eat her mate and incorporate his nourishment into the mass of eggs she will lay. As many as 1,000 eggs go into each mass, which is affixed to a plant stem or other support and coated with a brown froth that hardens as it dries. In the spring, miniature praying mantises emerge and are distributed by the wind. Those that survive will grow slowly, molt by molt, until they acquire wings and become mature—usually by autumn.

The largest mantises in the United States are the kind introduced from China (*Paratenodera sinensis*), of which females may be nearly 6 inches long. The introduced European mantis (*Mantis religiosa*) is rarely more than 2 inches long. There is only 1 mantis (*Stagmomantis carolina*) native to the United States. Order Orthoptera, family Mantidae.

PRONGHORN, a handsome antelope-like mammal, which differs from all true antelopes in possessing on the head of both sexes an unusual kind of armament—a pair of horns with a bony core, covered by a horny sheath that is shed each year. This is the swiftest mammal of the New World, able to run at least 65 miles per hour and to "cruise along" at 48 mph, often traveling 20 miles a day in its native western North America.

A full grown male (buck) pronghorn weighs about 125 pounds and stands 3 feet high at the shoulder. A female (doe) may reach 90 pounds. Both are marked alike, the back, 3 collars, and a streak down to each leg being reddish brown, the hind-quarters shining white, and the rest of the animal sand-colored.

Pronghorns feed on a wide variety of vegetation in open country, in herds and as individuals at short distances from one another. When alarmed they flash their white rumps in many directions, alerting all pronghorns in sight. Order Artiodactyla, family Antilocapridae, specifically *Antilocapra americana*.

PTARMIGAN, any of 4 different kinds of grouselike birds with feathers all the way down the legs and out on the toes. They live in the Arctic and on high mountains, nesting in thickets on the ground, eating buds, insects, berries, and roots.

Ptarmigans, with one exception, are reddish-brown in the summer, but turn snow-white in winter—a remarkable example of protective coloration. The exception is called the red grouse (*Lagopus scoticus*), and is found now only in Ireland and England. Britain has also the rock ptarmigan (*L. mutus*) and the willow ptarmigan (*L. lagopus*), both of which are circumpolar. A distinctive white-tailed ptarmigan (*L. leucurus*) living above the snowline in Alaska and the Rocky Mountains retains the white color of its tail in summer. Order Galliformes, family Tetraonidae.

PUFFIN, or sea parrot, any of 3 kinds of sea birds with heavy bodies, short tails, short-pointed wings, short necks, and enormous triangular beaks marked with red, yellow, and blue. At the end of the breeding season, the bright covering of the beak is shed, and a new one grown, bearing an extra ridge and colored stripe by which the age of a puffin can be estimated. A puffin feeds mostly on fish, crustaceans, and small mollusks.

Nesting in colonies on offshore islands along northern coasts, these birds produce a single large egg, then tend the single young in a hole in the ground or a natural crevice among boulders. The young bird becomes enormously fat, heavier than the parents, and is then deserted. It completes its development, taking on adult form, finds its way to the coast, and dives into the sea to get its food.

The Atlantic puffin (*Fratercula arctica*) is abundant in Iceland and breeds in smaller numbers as far south as Maine and Britain. Pacific puffins of the Far North include the horned puffin (*F. corniculata*) which has a small, fleshy appendage like a horn on its upper eyelid, and the tufted puffin (*Lunda cirrhata*), named for the yellow plume of feathers extending backward like a great eyebrow on each side of the head. Order Charadriiformes, family Alcidae.

PUMA. See *Cat*.

QUAIL, any of about 40 different kinds of small, grouselike birds with short beaks, wings, and tails, but strong legs and plump bodies. The 33 in the New World are nonmigratory, lack spurs, and have a notch in the cutting edge of the upper bill. They include the 4 different bobwhite quails (*Colinus* species) that live in fields and woodland edges from Canada to South America, whistling loudly the 2-note call for which they are named; and the valley quail (*Lophortyx californicus*) of the American Southwest and Mexico, in which the male has a fancy little recurved plume over his forehead.

The 7 kinds of quails in the Old World are migratory, lack the notch in the beak, and mostly have spurs. One is the European quail (*Coturnix coturnix*), which ranges widely over Eurasia and Africa. Three others have spread from Southeast Asia all the way to Australia and New Zealand: the Australian brown quail (*Synoicus ypsilophorus*), the Chinese painted quail (*Excalfactoria chinensis*) no bigger than a sparrow, and the stubble quail (*Coturnix novae-zealandiae*) which vanished in New Zealand in 1870. Order Galliformes, family Phasianidae.

QUETZAL. See *Trogon*.

RABBIT, any of about 18 different kinds of long-eared, long-legged, short-tailed mammals similar to hares but differing in being born naked, blind, and helpless in a nest prepared by the mother. They are generally smaller than the hares and live only on grasses or other herbaceous matter.

In the New World they are represented by 13 kinds of cottontails, marsh rabbits, and tropical forest rabbits (all in genus *Sylvilagus*) from southern Canada to Argentina and by the volcano rabbit (*Romerolagus diazi*) of highland Mexico, which trots rather than hops.

In the Old World, the most widespread kind of rabbit is the European rabbit (*Oryctolagus cuniculus*), which makes extensive burrows in the wild, and is raised for food, fur, experimental medicine, and for esthetic purposes; the "Belgian hare" is one true-breeding strain.

Additional kinds of rabbits are found locally in the Ryukyu Islands near Japan, in the foothills of the Himalayas, in forests of Sumatra, and in African equatorial forests. Order Lagomorpha, family Leporidae.

RACCOON, or coon, any of several different kinds of doglike forest mammals with a black masklike mark across the eyes, fore paws that are almost as flexible and versatile as a monkey's, hind feet that make footprints like a child's, and a well-furred tail marked with 5 to 10 black rings.

Raccoons are forest dwellers from southern Canada to northern South America. They climb and swim well, and prefer food found close to water, in which they habitually manipulate it, perhaps to free it of grit. From this comes the name of the most widespread species, *Procyon lotor*—the

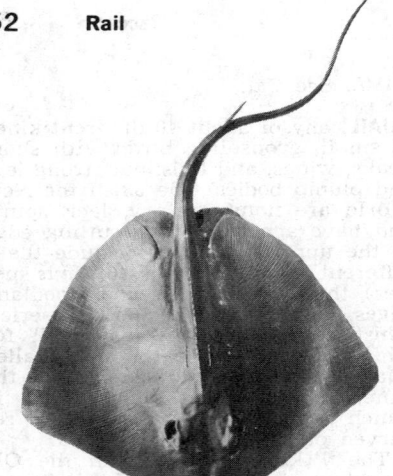

AMERICAN MUSEUM OF NATURAL HISTORY
STING RAY

washer. During the day the raccoon curls up in a tree to sleep. Order Carnivora, family Procyonidae, all members of genus *Procyon*.

RAIL, any of about 100 different kinds of running, swimming, and wading birds of marshes and tussock land, distinguished from the closely related coots and gallinules by the narrowness of their bodies, which helps when they run through thick marsh vegetation. They are "thin as rails."

Rails are found throughout the world except in polar regions. Living almost exclusively in marshlands, they are shy and use their wings only as a last resort, when they fly feebly for a short distance, immediately settling back into the swamp grass from which they were flushed.

Long-billed rails include the largest kind, the king rail (*Rallus elegans*) of the eastern United States. It grows to about 19 inches long, is dusky brown in color, and similar to the 11-inch Virginia rail (*R. virginianus*). Short-billed rails, called crakes in Europe, include the common American sora rail (*Porzana carolina*), 9 inches long, brown above and gray below. Rails are largely nocturnal in habits, and so elusive by day that gunners generally try to approach them silently by boat. Order Gruiformes, family Rallidae.

RAT, a vague term applied to almost any medium-sized rodent with a pointed nose, unspecialized legs, and long, usually naked tail. New World rats include rice rats, water rats, climbing rats, vesper rats, Andean rats, web-footed rats, cotton rats, pack rats, wood rats, fish-eating rats, mole rats, maned rats, and sand rats, all in family Cricetidae. Old World rats include climbing rats, spiny rats, tree rats, thick-tailed rats, shaggy-haired rats, bush rats, swamp rats, soft-furred rats, water rats, pouched rats, prehensile-tailed rats, cloud rats with bushy tails, shrewlike rats, and the two most destructive rats—the Norway rat (*Rattus norvegicus*) and the black rat (*Rattus rattus*).

The Norway rat probably is native to Japan and eastern Asia, and reached Europe about 1730 and America by 1775, to both by ship. The black rat

comes from Asia Minor, and came to Europe with the returning Crusaders. It is a better climber than the Norway rat, and lives better under tropical conditions. Both kinds harbor and carry bubonic plague, typhus fever, trichinosis, rabies, tularemia, and other diseases deadly to man. The laboratory white rat is a domesticated variety of the black rat. Order Rodentia, family Muridae.

RAVEN. See *Crow*.

RAY, any of about 340 different kinds of cartilaginous marine fishes in which the body is flattened or extended to the sides, the pectoral fins greatly enlarged, the gill slits on the lower surface, the pelvic fins small, and the tail often long and whiplike.

Rays are most abundant and varied in the Tropics, but are found also along cold coasts and in the great abysses. The giant manta rays, or devilfishes, measure as much as 22 feet from side to side, and probably weigh more than 3,500 pounds; they cruise slowly near the surface, using a special pair of feeding fins to drive small crustaceans and other food toward the cavernous scooplike mouth.

Sawfishes have the head prolonged into a flat "saw," studded on each side with sharp teeth; they use this strange tool to dislodge edible animals from sandy bottoms, and to slash sideways through schools of fishes, maiming and impaling many victims, which they can then eat at a leisurely pace. Rays of 2 different families have venom spines on their tails, and are called stingrays. Perhaps 25 different kinds of rays can discharge jolts of electricity in self-defense or to stun prey; they are called torpedoes or electric rays. Most rays, however, are relatively harmless, feeding on mollusks, crustaceans and small fishes they catch along the sea bottom and crush with teeth that have flat surfaces fitting together like tiles in a mosaic.

All rays swim with special grace, undulating their large pectoral fins (which form the edges of the body) as though they were the wings of a bird in leisurely flight. In Europe, some of the smaller and flattest rays, called skates, are sought as food. Order Batoidea, several different families.

REDSTART, any of several small, active dark-colored birds in the Northern Hemisphere. Redstarts in Eurasia are members of the thrush family (Turdidae), related closely to the nightingale; they continually flicker their rust-colored tails and display a rusty rump patch; they are classified in genus *Phoenicurus*.

Colonists to America, who were used to seeing Eurasian redstarts transferred the name to American birds of similar size, color, and behavior, without realizing that those of the New World were essentially different, being wood warblers of family Compsothlypidae. The common American male redstart (*Setophaga ruticilla*) is mostly black, with bright orange areas on wings and tail, and a white belly; the female is olive-brown where the male is black, and yellow where he is orange.

Members of both sexes continually droop their wings and display their colorful tail feathers while they hunt among the foliage for small insects. In the Southwest, a painted redstart (*S. picta*) is found in high mountains; it is black with white patches on the wings and tail, and a bright red patch on the breast. Order Passeriformes.

REINDEER. See *Deer*.

RHINOCEROS (from Greek words meaning nose horn), any of four kinds of massive, thick-skinned, 3-toed, hoofed mammals. Equatorial and South Africa have the largest two kinds, both with 2 nose horns: the square-lipped or white rhino (*Ceratotherium simus*), which is slate-gray and a grazer, and the slightly darker black rhino (*Diceros bicornis*)—both names mean two-horned—with a more pointed, prehensile lip, used in browsing. Next to the elephants, these are the largest land animals.

The Asian rhinos are smaller: the one-horned Indian rhino (*Rhinoceros unicornis*), often seen in zoos, comes from marshes of Southeast Asia and Java, and is threatened with extinction; the two-horned Asiatic rhino (*Didermocerus sumatrensis*), which is the smallest, is rare now in Southeast Asia, Sumatra, and Borneo, where it inhabits dense forests near streams. Order Perissodactyla, family Rhinocerotidae.

ROBIN, any of several different kinds of plump-bodied birds that are dark on the back, red or orange on the chest, and seen commonly near homes. The European bird (*Erithacus rubecula*), for which all the others were named, is about 5½ inches long; it is distinguished from the native redstart mostly by appearing neckless and having dark brown instead of chestnut-colored feathers in the tail. The British introduced "their" robin in Africa, India, Australia, and North America; it became naturalized in all except North America.

The New World robin (*Turdus migratorius*) is a bigger bird, 10 inches long, gray on the back, reddish on the breast, with the outer corners of the tail white; it nests throughout Alaska, Canada, the continental United States, Mexico, and the West Indies, migrating south well into the continent for the winter, except in regions along the coasts.

The European and American robins are both members of the thrush family (Turdidae). The Pekin robin (*Leiothrix lutea*), 6 inches long, in southern China and the Himalayan foothills, and five Australian robins (of genus *Petroica*) are unrelated babblers (Timaliidae) and flycatchers (Muscicapidae), respectively. Order Passeriformes.

SABLE. See *Marten*.

SALAMANDER, any of about 240 different kinds of Eurasian and North American amphibians with a distinct head, a trunk, and permanent tail, usually with clawless-toed limbs of about equal size. The young have gills and resemble the adults, having teeth in both jaws. From the characteristically moist cool skin has come the superstition that a salamander can live in fire, and the use of the name "salamander furnaces" for heating buildings during construction.

The common European spotted salamander *(Salamandra maculosa)* is 6 to 8 inches long, black with yellow or orange patches, sluggish, very shy, and perfectly harmless. The olm *(Proteus anguinus)* of caves in southeastern Europe is pink, unpigmented, and blind, its eyes covered by skin. The related mud puppy, or water dog *(Necturus maculosus)*, of eastern North America grows to 17 inches long in rivers, but never loses its gills, although at maturity it develops lungs.

North America also has many kinds of lungless salamanders, mostly under 6 inches long, that respire through their moist skins after they lose their larval gills. The axolotl *(Ambystoma mexicanum)* of Mexican lakes and marshes is sought as food, and interests scientists because in places where water is permanent it becomes sexually mature and reproduces while still a larva in body form—8 to 10 inches long, with gills on each side of the neck region. Given hormone treatment, it transforms and develops adult body pattern and other features not normally acquired.

The giants among salamanders are the Japanese *Cryptobranchus maximus*, sometimes over 5 feet long, and the related hellbender *(C. alleganiensis)*, about 18 inches long, which is found in streams of the Ohio Valley. Order Caudata.

SALMON, any of a number of different kinds of edible carnivorous fishes with a small soft adipose fin between the dorsal fin and the tail, directly above the anal fin, with pink or red flesh, and with a habit of migrating at spawning time. They are native to the Northern Hemisphere, particularly along seacoasts and in landlocked lakes that once were connected to the oceans by rivers up and down which the salmon could swim.

Atlantic salmon (species of genus *Salmo)* are large trout, which make seasonal spawning runs into rivers of eastern North America and western Europe, returning to the sea afterward. Pacific salmon (6 species of genus *Oncorhynchus)* enter rivers on the west coast of North America and the east coast of Asia, and die there after mating and laying eggs. All of these salmon commonly attain a length of 3 to 4 feet, and a weight of about 30 pounds; record individuals weigh 100 pounds or more. The king, or chinook, salmon *(O. tschawytscha)* has been successfully introduced into New Zealand, where it has set up a new migration pattern.

Only the landlocked salmon feed in freshwater. The others enter rivers full fed and in fine condition, but fast while they swim and leap past rapids and small waterfalls to reach the headwaters where they lay their large eggs.

The hatchling salmon, known as parr, feed in freshwater for various lengths of time from 1 to 7 years,

depending upon the species and the latitude. They descend to the ocean, losing their crossbands and becoming silvery as they go, and are known as grilse when the change is completed; they are almost indistinguishable, except for size, from full-grown salmon.

The remainder of their feeding is done in the ocean, over a period of 6 to sometimes more than 7 years, and while traveling 1,000 to 2,500 miles away from the coast. Eventually, many of them find their way back to the same tributaries of the identical streams in which they spent their immature lives. Order Isospondyli, family Salmonidae.

SAND DOLLAR. See *Sea Urchin.*

SANDERLING, a small, active, 3-toed sandpiper, seen virtually wherever in the world waves break against sandy shores. Feeding in small flocks on mollusks, worms, crustaceans, and insects, it follows each receding wave onto the wet sand, probing for food until the last moment before being overwhelmed by the next wave.

A conspicuous white stripe shows on the wing when the bird flies, helping give it a common name of *whitey.* The sanderling lays its eggs in a slight hollow, lined with grass or leaves, on the upper beach. Usually there are 4 eggs, which hatch to downy chicks that hide among the nearby grasses. Order Charadriiformes, family Scolopacidae, specifically *Crocethia alba.*

SANDPIPER, any of 23 different kinds of small wading birds in which the slender, straight, or slightly downcurved beak is as long or longer than the head; all except the sanderling have 4 toes on each foot. Almost all breed in the Northern Hemisphere, mostly in the arctic and subarctic barren grounds. They seldom are found far from water, even on their long migrations, which take them to the limit of land in the Southern Hemisphere.

Largest is the 10-inch knot *(Calidris canutus),* sometimes called the robin sandpiper because its breast is red in spring and summer; it nests in the arctic and antarctic barrens, visiting western Europe and the North American Atlantic and Gulf coasts on migration.

Smallest is the least sandpiper, or stint *(Erolia minutilla),* a 6-inch bird seen frequently on marshes and along the open beach; it nests from Newfoundland to Alaska, and winters in the southernmost United States, Mexico, Central and northern South America.

The best-known in America is the spotted sandpiper *(Actitis macularia),* a 7-inch bird that teeters its tail up and down, bobbing its head at the same time. The Eurasian common sandpiper *(A. hypoleucos)* has the same habit. Order Charadriiformes, family Scolopacidae.

SAPSUCKER. See *Woodpecker.*

SARDINE. See *Herring.*

SAWFISH. See *Ray.*

SAWFLY, any adult insect with 4 membranous wings, the fore pair larger than the hind pair, and biting mouthparts, differing from the ant, bee, and wasp in that its abdomen is broad where it joins the thorax portion of the body, never constricted to a narrow waist. Female sawflies possess a sawlike egg-laying organ, with which they produce narrow slits in plant stems that hold the eggs securely.

From the eggs, larvae resembling caterpillars emerge. They are leafeaters, and usually can be distinguished by having soft paired appendages (prolegs) on almost every body segment, not just 4 pairs in the middle region of the abdomen and a pair at the rear, as in a caterpillar. Commonly the full-grown larva of a sawfly creeps down into the soil to pupate, and emerges for a relatively brief period of adult life. Order Hymenoptera, family Tenthredinidae.

SCALE INSECT, any of a large number of soft-bodied sucking insects that secrete over themselves a hard protective scale or a series of fluffy projections that fend off ants and hungry birds. Found on all continents and most islands, scale insects attach themsleves to plant stems while sucking the juices. For most of the year they produce young by the process of parthenogenesis, one female often giving birth to thousands of offspring during one summer season. Generally the young remain for a while close to the mother, benefiting from her shelter; then they go off on their own to grow quickly.

The pernicious San José scale insect *(Aspidiotus perniciosus),* which attacks citrus and shade trees, is individually only about 1/16-inch long; it produces infestations so dense that the bark of the tree appears covered with dark-gray scurfy patches of overlapping sucking insects. The cottony scale of maple, Virginia creeper, and other plants *(Pulvinaria innumerabilis)* places its eggs in a mass of cottony secretion.

The cochineal insect *(Coccus cacti)* of tropical America sucks the juice from stems of prickly pear cactus, and was the source of a famous red dye called cochineal, now replaced by synthetic colors from coal tar. The lac insect *(Tachardia lacca)* of Asia secretes a substance from which shellac and also several dyes can be prepared.

In the Near East, the manna scale insect *(Gossyparius manifera)* on tamarisk trees produces an edible secretion, which is said to have been the food called manna, used by the Israelites as described in Exodus 16. Order Homoptera, many genera of family Coccidae.

SCALLOP, any of more than 100 different kinds of marine bivalved mollusks, in which the shell valves are shallowly saucer-shaped, almost circular, and serve in swimming to expel jets of water from the ends of the hinge at the back. Scallops live along most of the world's seacoasts, below low-tide mark and to depths of about 100 feet.

Around the edge of a scallop's shell, minute eyes look out, attached to the edge of the soft mantle. Generally the shell has ridges radiating from hinge to edge, which is wavy in the pattern said to be scalloped, from the name of the mollusk. Scallops are caught with nets and dredges, chiefly during July and August, after their spawning is completed. The edible part is the strong muscle that pulls the two valves together. Order Filobranchia, family Pectinidae.

SCAUP, either of 2 very similar ducks of northern latitudes in America and Eurasia, feeding and swimming along seacoasts except when nesting in the far north.

The distinctive markings of the male scaup include a pale blue beak, dark head, neck, and tail, and pale gray back and wings. The female is brown where the male is black, and has a white face. The greater scaup *(Aythya marila)* is 19 inches long, the lesser scaup *(A. affinis)* 17 inches, with a more angular head and less white on the wing.

Scaups fly swiftly and erratically in large flocks; they are often seen sitting on the water in so-called *rafts* that number several thousand; many are shot each year by hunters. Order Anseriformes, family Anatidae.

SCORPION, any of a large number of terrestrial arthropod animals walking on 4 pairs of legs, with a pair of pincers on the most anterior appendages, and with a slender elongated jointed portion of the flexible abdomen ending in a venomous stinger.

They live in tropical and warm lands, on all continents, preying upon insects and spiders, holding them in their pincers and often stinging a struggling captive to subdue it before bringing it to the mouth. Like spiders, scorpions lack both jaws and feelers (antennae). They crush their animal prey, squeezing out drops of liquid they can take in through the small, sucking mouth.

After an elaborate courtship and mating ceremony, female scorpions give birth to as many as 60 young of identical appearance, and carry them about on their backs for a week or so until the growing youngsters become independent. Scorpions are active chiefly at night, and often hide by day in shoes and clothing. Particularly in the tropics, where scorpions are often large and venomous, it is wise to shake out every garment before putting it on. Order Scorpionida of class Arachnida, family Scorpionidae.

SEA ANEMONE, any of about 1,000 flowerlike, marine, coelenterate animals found attached to piles and floating timber. Sea anemones usually do not have a free-swimming jellyfish stage. From their attached positions they extend arms or tentacles in all directions to find food, which consists of microscopic organisms. When a sea anemone is irritated, it contracts violently, expelling water from its central digestive cavity. Several orders in subclass Zoantharia of class Anthozoa.

SEA COW, any of 4 different massive aquatic mammals with a rounded head, small mouth, short neck, paddlelike forelimbs, no hind limbs, and a tail that is horizontally flattened. They are found in tropical waters along coasts, estuaries, and marsh-bordered rivers on both sides of the Atlantic and Indian oceans, from the Red Sea to the Philippines and the northwest coast of Australia.

The Indian Ocean representative is the dugong *(Dugong dugon)*, which usually feed in groups of 2 or more, eating marine plants in shallow waters; they grow to 9 feet in length and a weight of nearly 400 pounds.

The Atlantic Ocean sea cows, called manatees, include one *(Trichechus manatus)*, which inhabits the coast from Florida and the West Indies to northern South America; another *(T. inunguis)* in the Amazon and Orinoco River drainage areas of South America; and one *(T. senegalensis)* in West Africa. Manatees have a rounded tail, rather than a notched one, and feed mostly at night.

Sea cows are hunted in many areas for their tasty flesh and for a clear oil that does not turn rancid. Order Sirenia, families Dugongidae and Trichechidae.

SEA CUCUMBER, or bêche-de-mer, or trepang, any of about 500 different kinds of sausage-shaped, soft-bodied echinoderms that maintain their shape through hydraulic pressure of liquid in their voluminous body cavities. They are exclusively marine and occur in all oceans, but most commonly in the tropics. Their only skeletal support consists of tiny limy plates in the outer part of the body wall.

Many sea cucumbers are regarded as food; others are used as the source of a fish poison with which to force edible fishes in tide pools to come out of hiding, anesthetized and helpless. Many orders of class Holothurioidea.

SEA FAN, a colonial coelenterate animal of shallow warm seas, attached to a rock or some dead coral or other solid support, and growing upward in the form of a branching tree with all the branches in one plane. In the large sea fans *(Gorgonia)* of semitropical waters, the branches grow together to form a lacy network, upon the surface of which the individual polyps live. Each is a tiny, soft-bodied sac with a microscopic mouth at the center of a ring of tentacles.

Nettling cells on the tentacles help the sea fan catch and subdue equally small swimming animals in the nearby water, and to pull each victim into the mouth for digestion inside the body. Each polyp contributes toward the growth of the tough, hornlike protein which forms the core of the fan, and toward secreting the surface coating of limy spicules, which may be pastel yellow, lavender, pink, or purple.

In season, sea fans produce reproductive cells and liberate free-swimming larvae that eventually settle to the bottom where they may begin new colonies. Each colony grows toward whatever currents come regularly in the water, letting the polyps on both sides of the fan benefit equally from food in the passing water. Order Gorgonacea of class Anthozoa.

SEA HORSE, any of about 50 kinds of small, marine, bony fishes with a head strongly resembling that of a horse or the knight chessman. The mouth is round, at the end of a tubular snout, and used for sucking in minute animals and plants for food. The whole body is covered with bony plates. Generally a sea horse swims in an almost vertical position. It prefers quiet brackish waters and coils its long, prehensile tail around seaweeds and sea grasses to keep from being swept away by the currents.

The female sea horse lays her eggs in a pouch on the belly of the male, where they develop to the hatching stage, at which time he expels them. The common sea horse of the east coast of North America *(Hippocampus hudsonius)* is about 5 inches long; the Pacific coast sea horse *(H. kuda)* grows almost twice as large. Order Solenichthyes, family Syngnathidae.

SEAL, any of 18 different kinds of fin-footed marine mammals with only a wrinkle to show where the ear opens, with a tail of moderate length that is inconspicuous between hind legs so specialized for sculling through water that they cannot be folded forward, but merely drag when the animal hauls out on land. The harbor seal *(Phoca vitulina)*, found along Pacific and Atlantic coasts of the Northern Hemisphere, sometimes follows shad and other fishes far into rivers. Leopard seals *(Hydrurga leptonyx)*, which grow to 11½ feet long, prey on penguins and other birds. Order Pinnipedia, family Phocidae.

SEA LILY, any of about 630 different kinds of marine echinoderms in which the body is cup shaped, protected by limy plates that fit together closely just under the skin, and bearing 5 arms that divide close to the base into 2 equal feathery extensions. Almost all sea lilies live at great depths in temperate and tropical oceans, but those of polar seas live in shallower water.

All of the deep-water sea lilies seem permanently attached by long cylindrical armored stalks with rootlike clasping parts that can hold to firm objects on the sea bottom. Some shallow-water sea lilies, called feather stars, live in the Tropics on coral reefs, where they soon free themselves from their short stalks and move about from time to time; some can even swim feebly. Fossil sea lilies of the Paleozoic era are found in great numbers. Several orders of class Crinoidea.

SEA LION, any of about 12 different kinds of fin-footed marine mammals with a small protruding ear, a short tail, and hind legs sufficiently flexible to be folded forward and used for awkward walking or running on land. They live along coastlines of western North America and South America, Australia, New Zealand, some oceanic islands, and southern Africa.

ANIMALS

The trained "seals" of circuses and vaudeville shows are California sea lions (*Zalophus californianus*), which are found also along the shores of the Galápagos Islands and Japan. Related are the fur seals (*Callorhinus ursinus*) of the Aleutian Islands and Alaska, of which about 90,000 of an estimated 2 million are harvested annually for their fur; and the Antarctic fur seals (6 species of genus *Arctocephalus*), of which about 30,000 are taken each year. Order Pinnipedia, family Otariidae.

SEA SQUIRT. See *Tunicate*.

SEA STAR, or starfish, any of about 2,000 different kinds of marine echinoderms in which the body is star-shaped, 5-angled, and generally extended into from 5 to 50 flexible arms below which are grooves containing tubefeet used for locomotion and for holding to the substratum. Sea stars are found in all oceans, and some kinds tolerate being exposed to air a few hours while the tide is out. Most are predatory, feeding on mollusks and sand dollars. Many orders of class Asteroidea.

SEA URCHIN, any of about 860 different kinds of marine echinoderms in which the body is made firm by interlocking limy plates just beneath the skin, and protection is given by movable spines operated by muscles and located on ball-and-socket joints on the limy plates. These animals are found in all oceans, at many depths, but rarely where they are exposed by the receding tide.

A sea urchin holds on and moves about by means of a large number of fine flexible tube feet. Its mouth, on the surface next to the substratum, has 5 hard, sharp limy jaws with which it can bite out pieces of seaweed to swallow. Most sea urchins are circular, and their shells show impressive detail in a radially symmetrical pattern. Some urchins, mostly burrowing kinds, are heart shaped. Others, known as sand dollars, are very flat-bodied and live in the surface ooze over sand bars below low-tide level. Many orders of class Echinoidea.

SECRETARY BIRD, a long-legged, fast-running hawk about 4 feet high, with a crested head that gives the bird its popular name—as if it were a secretary with several pencils stuck in her hair. It is common in Africa south of the great deserts, and protected because of its fearless attacks on snakes, even large and poisonous varieties, which it kills with its talons and wings. It is sometimes domesticated as a snake-killer. Order Falconiformes, family Sagittariidae, specifically *Sagittarius serpentarius*.

SHAD, any of several edible, herring-like fishes about 2 feet long, which in spring seek out freshwater shallows to mate and lay their eggs. Many, such as the American shad (*Alosa sapidissima*) of the Atlantic coast, return to the sea, where they feed on plankton. Others, such as the Ohio shad (*A. ohiensis*), are restricted to river life.

Although the meat is full of small bones, shad are caught in large numbers for table use. Their eggs (roe) are also a delicacy. Order Isispondyli, family Clupeidae.

Related gizzard shad (6 kinds in genus *Dorosoma*, family Dorosomidae) live in salt water and freshwaters as forage fish. Their name refers to the specially modified muscular stomach with which they grind up their food.

SHARK, any of more than 250 different kinds of cartilaginous fishes with a torpedo-shaped body, a wide mouth underneath the head, separate gill slits on the sides, and a two-lobed tail of which the upper lobe is much the longer. They are found in all seas, and occasionally ascend rivers into freshwater, as in Lake Nicaragua.

The giants among sharks are the whale shark (*Rhincodon typus*), sometimes 45 feet long, and the giant basking shark (*Cetorhinus maximus*), which is nearly as big; both eat only tiny sea animals. The slender blue shark (*Prionarce glauca*), 12½ feet long, and the great white shark (*Carcharodon carcharias*, named from Greek words meaning sharp tooth because its teeth are shaped like arrow-head flints), up to 36½ feet long, are fast-swimming predators of open oceans, and the most famous of the man-eaters. They can swallow a 100-pound sea lion, a 50-pound seal, or a Newfoundland dog at a single gulp.

Almost as dangerous to skin divers and men overboard (or in flimsy life rafts) are the tropical Atlantic, 18-foot, mackerel shark, or porbeagle (*Lamna ditropis*), which is sharp-snouted, and the hammerhead shark (species of genus *Sphyrna*), whose head is extended on both sides like the top of a T, with the eyes at the extreme corners. Many tales of man-eating sharks are exaggerated and overdrawn.

Small sharks include some called dogfishes, which destroy fish caught in fishnets; spiny dogfishes, with a spine in front of each of the 2 dorsal fins, include many species of the genus *Squalus*. Smooth dogfishes lack these spines, and may be species of genus *Mustelis*. Both are caught for sale in Europe and the Orient, often as "grayfish" with edible flesh. Order Selachii, many families.

SHEEP, any of 9 different kinds of hollow-horned, cud-chewing mammals with narrow noses and pointed ears, distinguished from goats by the lack of a scent gland at the base of the tail. They are native to northern mountains of Eurasia and North America, and to Sardinia and Corsica, North Africa and the Sudan across to the north bend of the Niger River. The largest are the African aoudads, or Barbary sheep (*Ammotragus lervia*), which have a mane of long hairs on the throat, chest, and upper parts of the forelegs.

Slightly smaller are the Rocky Mountain sheep, or bighorns (*Ovis canadensis*) and Dall sheep (*O. dalli*) of western North America, and the argali, or Marco Polo sheep (*O. ammon*), of the central U.S.S.R. to Nepal and western China. The massive horns

MONTANA HIGHWAY COMMISSION
SHEEP

on the males reach impressive size, and are used in ceremonial butting activity at mating season. The mouflon (*O. musimon*) of Mediterranean islands has been introduced widely.

The original of the domestic sheep (*O. aries*) is no longer known in the world. It probably originated in Asia, and has been bred into many distinctive races. The Shropshire is a popular breed in the Middle States and is a good mutton sheep. The most important wool sheep is the Merino breed, Spanish in origin but found today largely in America and Australia, where its fine wool is a product of great importance.

In addition to their furnishing of wool and meat products, sheep are of considerable importance to farming because of the manure that they produce. Order Artiodactyla, family Bovidae.

SHINER. See *Minnow*.

SHIPWORM, any of several highly specialized marine bivalve mollusks that settle on wood soaked with seawater and spend most of their lives burrowing into this material. They are found in most parts of the world, doing great damage to wooden ships and pilings by weakening their structure.

The shipworm, also called teredo, uses its small valves as boring tools, while its elongated siphon (part of the mantle) extends to the surface of the wood to get seawater containing microscopic food and oxygen, and to discharge wastes, carbon dioxide, and reproductive cells. A thin limy tube is secreted around the wormlike siphon. Order Eulamellibranchia, family Teredinidae, chiefly members of genus *Teredo*.

SHREW, any of more than 200 different kinds of small, short-legged mouselike mammals with long-pointed noses and many small teeth; only the upper middle incisors are enlarged, and they are not fitted for gnawing. Shrews are found in most land areas, but not on arctic islands, the West Indies, Australia, Tasmania, New Zealand, or South Pacific islands. They include the smallest known mammal, the dwarf shrew (*Suncus etruscus*) of Mediterranean coastal countries, 1½ to 2 inches long with a 1-inch tail, weighing about 1/15 ounce.

Except in breeding season, shrews are solitary, voracious predators, spacing out their meals on insects, snails, and worms with seeds and other plant materials. The commonest shrew in the United States and Canada is the short-tailed *Blarina brevicauda*, which might be mistaken for a mole except for its delicate legs and feet. Order Insectivora, family Soricidae.

SHRIKE, or butcherbird, any of 73 different kinds of small to medium-sized birds with large heads, stout beaks hooked and notched at the tip, strong legs, short rounded wings, and, usually, long tails. They are found in both hemispheres, with 39 bush shrikes and 9 helmet shrikes in Africa.

Only 2 of the other shrikes live in America; one (the loggerhead shrike, *Lanius ludovicianus*) migrating from southern Canada to Mexico and central America, the other (the northern shrike, *L. excubitor*) ranging farther north and also across Eurasia. Like many shrikes, they are gray above, white below, black and white on wings and tail, and have a mask mark across the eyes.

Shrikes have the peculiar habit of impaling insects, frogs, and small birds on thorns or barbed wire fences, perhaps because the shrike's feet are not strong enough to hold its prey while its powerful bill tears the food apart. Order Passeriformes, family Laniidae.

SHRIMP, or prawn, any of a number of different aquatic crustaceans, 6 inches or less in length, with laterally compressed bodies or abdomens. Most shrimps are marine, and some 1½ to 3 inches long are caught in enormous numbers for human food. Those from the Gulf of Mexico (especially *Penaeus setifer*) are a delicate gray-green color spotted with brown; when cooked they turn pink and white. Order Decapoda.

The name shrimp is given to unrelated crustaceans: brine shrimps (*Artemia salina*) of salt lakes and fairy shrimps (*Eubranchipus vernalis*) of freshwater ponds in early spring belong to order Anostraca; freshwater shrimps, or scuds (species of *Gammarus*), live in shallows of streams and ponds, and belong to order Amphipoda; opossum shrimps, most of which are marine (species of *Mysis*), belong to order Mysidacea.

SILKWORM, any of a number of different moth caterpillars that spin a viscous secretion from their salivary glands into a single, continuous, fine silk strand with which to construct the egg-shaped cocoon that is to protect them during their pupal transformation.

Only one, the oriental silkworm (*Bombyx mori* of family Bombycidae), has achieved commercial importance. It supports an industry where cheap labor is available to keep captive caterpillars fed with fresh mulberry leaves, and to unravel and wind up the silk strands from the finished cocoons.

The caterpillar itself is yellowish gray, about 3 inches long when fully grown, with a hornlike projection on the last segment of the body. After the cocoon is complete and has hardened, it is plunged into hot water to kill the enclosed pupa and to free the silk fibers. As reeled, the raw silk fiber may be bright orange, tan, or almost white. Order Lepidoptera.

SILVERFISH. See *Bristletail*.

SKATE. See *Ray*.

SKIMMER, any of 3 coastal birds in which the lower bill is longer than the upper and used in a peculiar method of fishing. The black skimmer (*Rhynchops nigra*), which ranges along the Atlantic coast of North America from Long Island southward, and down both sides of Central and South America, is the largest. Its wingspan may be as great as 50 inches, and the lower jaw of its red beak 4½ inches long and the upper jaw 3 inches long.

The African skimmer, found along the coasts and larger rivers of Africa, has a bright yellow beak. The Indian skimmer, with a bill black at the base and yellow at the tip, patrols the rivers of India and Southeast Asia.

All skimmers cruise low over the water by steady beating of their long-pointed wings, while they lower the underbill into the water. If the tip of the bill encounters an obstacle, such as a fish or a crustacean at the surface, the bird quickly bends its head and closes its mouth, picking up the trophy as food. Skimmers feed mostly in the early evening and before dawn, when the water is calm and prey tend to come to the surface.

By day, skimmers roost in flocks on open beaches, and withstand the intense light by closing to a narrow slit their unusual pupils, which suggest those of a cat. Their nests are mere unlined depressions in a sandflat or beach near the water, with 4 eggs blotched with brown. The young birds have both bills equal until almost full grown. Order Charadriiformes, family Rhynchopidae.

SKUNK, any of 10 different kinds of short-legged, bushy-tailed mammals marked strikingly in black and white, and armed with a special gland under the tail, secreting an ill-smelling fluid that can be squirted to 10 to 15 feet with fair accuracy.

Skunks live only in the Americas, where they seek under logs and stones for insects, and catch mice and frogs; occasionally skunks attack birds, including poultry. Hog-nosed skunks (6 species of *Conepatus*) are the only ones in South America; their range extends to the southern United States. Spotted skunks (*Spilogale* species) are found from British Columbia to Central America, and striped skunks (*Mephitis* species) from eastern Canada to Central America. Order Carnivora, family Mustelidae.

SLIPPER SHELL, or boat shell, or quarterdeck, any of several kinds of marine snails that increase the surface area for attaching themselves to their oval shells by producing one half a horizontal shelflike platform.

Boat shells feed on minute animals and plants that become stuck in a film of mucus over the gills on each side of the foot. At intervals of about 4 minutes, the snail twists its head to right or left and sucks up the loaded mucus into its mouth. It swallows small particles at once but stores larger ones in a pouch for a later meal. The snail can feed on these at low tide when it must clamp its shell down tightly and hold on.

Often slipper shells are found holding on to horseshoe crabs or larger snails, or even to other slipper shells in a cluster of several dozen, all rolling together on the sea bottom. Female boat shells produce about 50 membranous egg cases, each containing about 250 eggs, and stand guard over these until the young hatch out. The young swim freely for about 2 weeks, then settle on some firm surface where they can become more or less permanently attached. Order Prosobranchiata, family Crepidulidae, species of genus *Crepidula*.

SLOTH (meaning slowness, laziness), any of 7 different kinds of tropical mammals with round heads, ears that are barely visible, eyes directed forward, and all feet with long, curved strong claws from toes not exceeding 3 in number, bound together for most of their length. Sloths live only in the Americas.

Sloths hang by their claws below horizontal branches, progressing slowly while feeding upon the leaves. The young, only 1 at a birth, holds tight to the mother's back and is almost hidden by her long hair.

There are 2 genera: *Bradypus* (which means slow foot), having 3 claws on the front feet; and *Choloepus* (lame foot), having 2 claws on the front feet. On the ground, sloths are practically helpless. They are usually 1½ to 2 feet long. Order Edentata, family Bradypodidae.

SLUG, any snail-like mollusk that is unprotected by a limy shell. Some of the land slugs that are classified in Order Pulmonata because they breathe air through a lunglike organ, have concealed a small shell that they secreted at a very early age and then outgrew. These slugs glide about on a large flat foot, chiefly at night or during rains when they are in less danger of desiccation. If attacked, they eject a thick slime that discourages birds and insects from coming closer.

Eating vegetable matter, both living and decaying, some land slugs (such as *Limax maximus* of the Olympic National Park forest in Washington state) grow to a length of 8 inches.

Sea slugs lack a shell altogether, and are classified in Order Opisthobranchiata. They also lack gills and breathe by means of highly decorative plumes upon the back. Sea slugs commonly creep over corals, sea fans, and other coelenterates, browsing on the polyps; they also crawl among seaweeds, eating the moss animals (bryozoans). One kind (*Glaucus eucharis*) has a deep blue color, and creeps along the underside of the surface film on the warm water of tropical oceans, capturing minute crustaceans and other animals as food.

SMELT, any of 13 different kinds of slender, bony, salmon-shaped fishes, with a small soft adipose fin in front of the tail, directly above the large anal fin. Smelt are fish of the Northern Hemisphere, especially Pacific Ocean coasts.

Tons of Sacramento smelt (*Spirinchus thaleichthys*) are caught annually in San Francisco Bay and the mouth of the Columbia River. The small surf smelt (*Hypomesus pretiosus*), which lives mostly close to shore, is a favorite bait for both surf fishermen and commercial operators.

The 1-foot Atlantic smelt (*Osmerus mordax*) of the American east coast was introduced into the Great Lakes in 1912 and is thriving in fresh water. The Atlantic smelt, or sparling, of Europe (*O. eperlanus*) is a valuable fish of northern waters, reaching a length of 8 inches. Order Isospondyli, family Osmeridae.

SNIPE, any of 25 different kinds of small- to medium-sized shore birds with short legs, and long beaks used for probing for small edible animals in muddy shores. They nest in arctic muskegs and freshwater marshes of all continents except Australia.

The circumpolar common snipe (*Capella gallinago*) nests over the northern United States, most of Canada, and much of northern Eurasia, but winters in the Americas from the middle United States to southern Brazil, and in the Southern Hemisphere of the Old World. The Japanese snipe (*Gallinago hardwicki*), which nests only on the northern islands of Japan, winters in New Zealand and eastern Australia, where it is called the Australian snipe. Order Charadriiformes, family Scolopacidae.

SOLE. See *Flatfish*.

SOWBUG, or slater, any of a large number of terrestrial crustaceans with a jointed oval body. On all continents, they scavenge in damp places, under fallen logs, stones, and the bark on rotting trees, eating principally decaying vegetation.

Some sowbugs, such as members of the common genus *Armadillidium*, are able to curl up into a ball when disturbed. In this position, their delicate legs and the vestigial gills with which they breathe in air are well protected by the hard armor of the body's upper surface. These particular sowbugs are often called "pill bugs."

Other kinds are unable to curl so tightly. Sometimes one that does not curl is seen to be a female carrying a batch of eggs with her, in a brood sac formed by flat projections from her legs. The young that hatch out are of the same body form as the parents. Order Isopoda.

SPARROW, or bunting, any of about 265 different kinds of 4½- to 8-inch perching birds, usually of a dark brown inconspicuous color and with a beak smaller than that of a finch. Found all over the world but most commonly in the American tropics, they generally frequent grasslands or open woodlands, hunting for seeds and insects on or near the ground. They nest on the ground or in low bushes. The snow bunting (*Plectrophenax nivalis*) and several kinds of longspurs (species of *Calcarius*) are circumpolar, nesting southward in mountain regions.

Temperate North America has about 50 different kinds of native sparrows, of which the largest is the fox sparrow (*Passerella iliaca*), 7 inches long, with a streaked breast and a reddish brown tail; it nests across Canada and in the western United States, wintering in the southern states. Its pleasant song is heard only in spring and fall, while the bird is migrating. The song sparrow (*Melospiza melodia*) is more widespread and sings much of the year; its white underparts have brown markings that fuse in the center of the breast to form a large blotch.

The white-throated sparrow (*Zenotrichia albicollis*), which nests in Canada and New England and winters in the southern United States, has a particularly sweet, clear whistle. The chipping sparrow (*Spizella passerina*), 5 inches long with a rusty stripe on the top of the head, nests near houses.

None of these native sparrows damages crops or drives away other birds as does the house sparrow (*Passer domesticus*), which was introduced into the United States in 1850, supposedly to eat insect pests. House sparrows spread to all parts of the continent, and became pests themselves. In their native northern Eurasia, they appear helpful to farmers, devouring insects and weed seeds.

Eurasia and Africa have 30 different kinds of very similar birds, which are called buntings (*Emberiza* species), and the most common sparrow of all—the chaffinch (*Fringilla coelebs*). All are primarily seedeaters, although the name seedeater is ordinarily reserved for about 30 kinds of birds in tropical America (species of *Sporophila*). Order Passeriformes, family Fringillidae.

SPRINGTAIL. any of a large number of widely distributed minute, wingless insects in which the hind-most abdominal segments (the "tail") are held in a curled position, turned forward under the more anterior abdominal segments. There the tip of the tail is held by a sort of catch, under voluntary muscular control. When alarmed, a springtail tenses its abdomen as though to straighten it out, then slips the catch. The tail strikes the surface, land or water, on which the springtail is standing, with enough force to toss the insect itself high in the air. It falls somewhere else and may be able to scurry away before being discovered.

Often large numbers of springtails scavenge for microscopic particles of food along the edge of a stream, on the water surface, giving the combined appearances of a gray-blue line ¼ inch or more in width. At the slightest disturbance, all of these insects toss themselves into the air, and the line vanishes as though by magic. Order Collembola.

SQUETEAGUE, or sea trout, or weakfish, any of several different kinds of marine bony fishes related to the croakers, with a triangular front dorsal fin and long rear dorsal fin. Squeteagues travel in schools along both the Atlantic and Pacific coasts of North America, attracting both commercial fishermen and sportsmen. The name weakfish refers to the ease with which the jaws can be torn from the head with a fisherman's hook while the fish is fighting for its life.

The Atlantic kinds attain lengths to 32 inches and weights to 17½ pounds. The closely related California sea bass (*Cynoscion nobilis*) is larger; largest is the totuava (*C. macdonaldi*) of the Gulf of California, which grows to 225 pounds. Order Percomorphi, family Sciaenidae, members of genus *Cynoscion*.

SQUID, any of about 300 different kinds of free-swimming, predatory, marine, cephalopod mollusks with 10 long arms projecting from the head end of the barrel- or cigar-shaped body. Squids are common in all oceans from the surface down to the greatest depths. They have 2 well-developed eyes, quite similar in form to those of vertebrate animals.

When disturbed, a squid gives off an inky substance that provides an underwater smokescreen and apparently dulls the sense of smell for fishes that are pursuing the squid. Squid themselves eat smaller fishes, young fishes, and crustaceans of many kinds; in turn, squid are eaten in large numbers by large fishes, seals, and toothed whales. Most squids are less than 2 feet long, but a giant squid (*Architeuthis harveyi*) of the North Atlantic attains a length of 52 feet, including both body and arms. Order Dibranchia.

SQUIRREL, any of about 280 different kinds of active rodents, mostly with bushy tails and tree-dwelling habits. They are found in most land areas except southern South America, Madagascar, Australia and New Zealand, and major deserts. Many are ground

SQUIRREL

squirrels with less conspicuous tails, living underground except while hunting for food. All except the flying squirrels, which do not fly but glide by means of a parachute of skin extending between the legs of each side, are active during the day and sleep at night.

Squirrels eat seeds and fruits, as well as some insects and snails, and occasionally birds' eggs. When numerous and hungry, they may attack corn and other crop plants. In the United States and Canada, red squirrels (2 species of *Tamiasciurus*) are common in evergreen coniferous forests, whereas the gray (*Sciurus carolinensis*) and fox (*S. niger*) squirrels live among hardwoods. Gray squirrels are larger and drive away red squirrels when the two meet.

The fur of a number of larger kinds of squirrels is valuable, and their meat is delicious. In both North America and Eurasia, ground squirrels (*Citellus* species) are plains animals, whereas chipmunks (*Tamias* in eastern North America and *Eutamias* in the West as well as in Asia) inhabit brush land and growing forests. Order Rodentia, family Sciuridae.

STARFISH. See *Sea Star.*

STARLING, any of about 106 different kinds of Old World perching birds with short tails, strong beaks and legs, and stout bodies. Most of them walk, instead of hopping. Starlings are chiefly African and Oriental birds of open country, but one of the Eurasian kinds is known as the common starling (*Sturnus vulgaris*). A vigorous, 8½-inch bird with a yellow beak, black iridescent feathers, and pointed wings, it provides important control over insect pests in its native regions.

Introduced into New York around 1890, it has spread over almost the entire United States and become a major menace, descending in enormous flocks to eat cereal crops, cultivated fruits, and berries. It competes for food and nesting places with many native birds, nearly all of which are more beneficial to man than the introduced starling. In many cities, the clamor of roosting starlings and the filth from their droppings have led to campaigns to destroy these birds, never with any success. Order Passeriformes, family Sturnidae.

STICK INSECT, any of a large number of biting insects with a long slim cylindrical body, long feelers (antennae), long slender legs, and wings (if any) similar to those of grasshoppers. Most stick insects, and all of the large ones—some to a length of 10 inches—live in the Tropics.

Stick insects move very slowly, eating green leaves on shrubs and trees, and remain motionless or slightly swaying if alarmed. In this way they resemble dead sticks or twigs and are overlooked by animals that eat insects. In the middle and northern United States and southern Canada, a completely wingless stick insect (*Diapheromera femorata*) is fairly common, and grows to a length of 4 to 5 inches, larger in the female. Order Orthoptera, family Phasmidae.

STICKLEBACK, any of several small fishes of the Northern Hemisphere. The 3-spine stickleback (*Gasterosteus aculeatus*), which has 2 or 3 sharp stiff spines on its back in front of its dorsal fin, occurs in both freshwater and salt water in North America and Eurasia. The brook stickleback (*Eucalia inconstans*), which rarely exceeds 2½ inches in length, has 4 to 6 spines and is restricted to fresh waters in the northernmost United States and southern Canada, coast to coast.

In breeding season, the male stickleback builds an elaborate globular nest with a front and back door. He courts a female and induces her to lay her eggs in his nest. After fertilizing the eggs, he stands guard over them and aerates them by fanning water through them with his fins. After the eggs hatch, he tries to keep the young fish together near the nest but they soon wander off. Despite their spines, many sticklebacks are eaten by birds. Order Thoracostei, family Gasterosteidae.

STILT, either of 2 shorebirds, related to avocets, with long, slender, straight beaks and very long legs. Only flamingos have legs longer in proportion to the body. In temperate and tropical regions all over the world, the black-necked, or pied stilt (*Himantopus mexicanus*) wades with a peculiar gait, as though skating on the water. Its back is black, its belly white, and its legs blood red.

The banded stilt (*Cladorhynchus leucocephalus*) of Australia and Tasmania stands slightly taller, and is white except for a brown band across the wing; its belly is light brown, and its legs red. Stilts swim if necessary and are strong fliers. All of them migrate to the Tropics for the winter. Order Charadriiformes, family Recurvirostridae.

STOAT. See *Weasel.*

STONE FLY, any insect (more than 200 kinds in North America) with biting mouthparts, 2 pairs of similar wings held flat over the back at rest, 2 "tails" (cerci) at the end of the abdomen, and aquatic young. The adults mate soon after emerging from the water, and live only a few days. Females deposit masses of eggs in the water of streams and rivers, where they hatch into immature stone flies, called naiads or nymphs.

The naiads are carnivorous, preying upon smaller water animals found while prowling along the bottom. Each naiad has strong jaws, strong legs, visible gills in pads just behind the base of the legs, and two tails. It may need 1 to 3 years to reach full size. Both naiads and adults are favorite food of trout and other fishes. Order Plecoptera.

STORK, any of 17 different kinds of large heronlike birds with comparatively short toes, which are partially webbed, and no voice. They communicate by gestures and by clapping the beak together. Storks live in most temperate and tropical countries, but not in northern North America, New Zealand, and islands of the South Pacific. They inhabit the vicinity of marshes and rivers, where they find food consisting of frogs, lizards, fishes, and even young birds.

The white stork (*Ciconia alba*) is migratory, arriving at nesting areas from the Mediterranean to Scandinavia, departing for the winter to warm areas of Africa all the way to the Cape of Good Hope. The black stork (*C. nigra*) is a swamp bird of Europe and Asia. The adjutant birds, or marabou, storks (*Leptoptilus* species) of tropical Africa and Asia, 60 inches tall, feed on carrion and snakes and are protected as useful scavengers by Indian law.

The wood stork, often misnamed an ibis (*Mycteria americana*), of the Gulf coast of the United States and as far south as Argentina, sometimes migrates after the breeding season to both California and Canada. It is one of the most striking of the group; it stands 4 feet high, is white with black tail and wing-tips, and has long, bluish legs and a long probing bill; the head and neck of the adult are entirely bare. Order Ciconiiformes, family Ciconiidae.

STURGEON, any of 21 different kinds of large fishes whose elongated body is clad in 5 rows of platelike scales, each with a raised ridge down the center; the upper half of the tail is longer than the lower, and the snout bears 4 barbels, somewhat resembling whiskers, beside the small sucking mouth. Sturgeons are native to the Northern Hemisphere, some in the ocean but entering fresh water to spawn, others in lakes and streams for their entire lives.

The American lake sturgeon (*Acipenser fulvescens*), once plentiful in the Great Lakes, reaches a weight of 200 pounds; it has blotched, reddish sides. The common sturgeon (*A. sturio*), a marine fish found on both sides of the North Atlantic Ocean, grows to 10 feet long and a weight of 500 pounds. The largest in North America is the white sturgeon (*A. transmontanus*) of freshwaters along the Pacific coast, weighing as much as 1,800 pounds. In Eurasia, the giant is the famous beluga (*Huso huso*) of the Caspian Sea, Black Sea, and Volga River, where it is believed to attain an age of 200 years; the record for size is 28 feet long and 2,860 pounds.

All sturgeons are sluggish fish, resting on the bottom, and sucking in vegetable matter plus any animals in it from the debris around marshes and near shore. Smoked sturgeon meat is widely appreciated as a delicacy. The eggs, preserved with salt, form caviar; the best quality comes from a small Russian sturgeon, the sterlat (*A. ruthenus*), usually 2 to 3 feet long. Air bladders from sturgeons were formerly sold as transparent plastic, called isinglas. Order Chondrostei, family Acipenseridae.

SUCKER, any of about 100 different kinds of minnowlike freshwater bony fishes in which the thick-lipped mouth is set low in the head and is toothless.

The fish was named from its habit of sucking mud and organic matter from the bottom. Most are North American fishes. The commonest, the white sucker (*Catostomus commersonnii*), is 28 inches long, with soft, bony, edible flesh. Order Eventognathi, family Catostomidae.

SUNFISH, any of more than 25 different kinds of small- to medium-sized freshwater fishes and 3 of enormous oceanic fishes, which have compressed bodies that appear oval or almost circular from the side. Freshwater sunfishes are all native to North America, although they have been introduced into Europe and elsewhere to delight fishermen. They differ from perches in having the spiny and soft-rayed portions of the dorsal fin continuous or separated by no more than a narrow notch, never as entirely separate fins.

Some sunfishes, such as the pumpkinseed (*Lepomis gibbosus*) which is common in ponds and streams from Maine to Florida and the Mississippi valley, have an earlike lobe from the rear edge of the gill cover, blood red in the pumpkinseed and bright blue in some other species.

Largest is the largemouth bass (*Micropterus salmoides*), recorded at 22½ pounds and 32½ inches in length, which eats smaller sunfishes, including the bluegill (*L. macrochirus*). In the southeastern United States, two kinds of sunfishes called crappies (species of *Pomoxis*) are favorites with fishermen. All freshwater sunfishes are edible, and belong to family Centrarchidae of order Acanthopteri.

Ocean sunfishes include one (*Mola mola*) as much as 11 feet long, weighing a ton; as a young fish, it swims in the normal vertical position, but as it ages it lazily cruises with one side up, swallowing medusae and other slow animals of the sea surface. Order Plectognathi, family Molidae.

SWALLOW, any of 79 different kinds of small, slender, long-winged birds with 12 tail feathers and short, broad beaks that open widely, surrounded by stiff facial bristles. Swallows are almost cosmopolitan over land, being absent chiefly from polar regions, oceanic islands, and New Zealand. All are noted for their graceful flight, and for their regular migrations in great flocks. They feed almost exclusively on insects, which they catch on the wing.

The name swallow is often mistakenly applied to the swifts, which have 10 tail feathers and no facial bristles. The American barn swallow (*Hirundo rustica*), 7½ inches long and with a deeply forked "swallow tail," is known in Britain as "the swallow" and elsewhere in Europe as "the chimney swallow"; it builds a nest of mud and grass atop the rafters of barns.

The cliff swallow (*Petrochelidon pyrrhonota*), 6 inches long, of America from Canada to central Mexico, constructs bottle-shaped nests of mud under eaves or cliffs; those nesting at the San Juan Capistrano Mission in California have earned a reputation for returning, generally on the same date each spring. Largest of the swallows in America is the sociable purple martin (*Progne subis*), 8 inches long, which alternately soars and flies rapidly. Order Passeriformes, family Hirundinidae.

SWALLOWTAIL, any of a number of large butterflies found all over the world, in which the hind wings are abruptly extended into a "tail" as much as ½ inch long. The eggs of swallowtails are laid on plants, where they hatch into caterpillars that eat the leaves.

Generally, swallowtail caterpillars are able to repel birds by suddenly extending from the head region a pair of long soft tentacles that release a disagreeable odor and probably a bad taste. When full grown, each caterpillar spins both a button of silk in which to anchor its posterior end and an open loop of silk to give extra support to the body after it transforms into a chrysalis (pupa). Within its loop, the chrysalis remains head up, leaning back like a professional window washer into his safety belt.

Among the best-known swallowtail butterflies of America, where it is widespread except along the West Coast, is the tiger swallowtail, or lilac butterfly (*Papilio glaucus*), which has a wingspan of about 5 inches, and a caterpillar that feeds on foliage of ash, birch, cherry, and poplar; it spends the winter in the chrysalis stage, and emerges in late spring, seemingly just in time to visit lilac flowers for nectar. Order Lepidoptera, family Papilionidae.

SWAN, any of 7 different large, long-necked water birds, with webbed feet and a beak about as long as the head. All but 2 swans are white birds of the Northern Hemisphere. The black swan (*Cygnus atratus*) of Australia has a little white on the wings; the black-necked swan (*C. melanocoryphus*) of South America is white except for the black neck.

European swans include the Polish swan (*C. olor*) of Eurasia which is the domesticated species, the whooping swan (*C. cygnus*) and the smaller Bewick's swan (*C. bewicki*), both of which nest in the Arctic. The domesticated swan is often called the mute swan, although it does make several different calls. In the United States there are 2 wild species: the whistling swan (*C. columbianus*) of arctic barrens, which winters southward along the Atlantic coast and the trumpeter (*C. buccinator*) of Montana

SWAN

and Wyoming, which does not migrate. Trumpeter swans were on the verge of extinction when they were made a protected species, and in their sanctuary their number has begun to increase.

The legend that the swan sings before it dies—a farewell song—is not true. Formerly swans were bred for the table but they are now raised solely as ornamental birds for lakes and pools. Order Anseriformes, family Anatidae.

SWIFT, any of 67 different kinds of small, fast-flying, insect-eating birds in which the tail contains only 10, not 12, feathers, and the short beak and wide mouth have no fringe of bristles such as distinguish the swallows. Swifts are primarily tropical and subtropical birds. Even the American chimney swift (*Chaetura pelagica*) journeys to Colombia, South America, for each winter.

Swifts are usually seen in groups. Nests are placed in inaccessible places, such as the sides of rocks, chimneys, and caves and are fastened in place by the birds' saliva. The edible birds' nests of Asia, especially China, are built by small swifts, particularly *Collocalia inexpectata*; and these nests are almost entirely composed of a salivary secretion. Order Apodiformes, family Apodidae.

SWINE, any of about 9 different medium-sized, thick-skinned mammals with barrel-shaped bodies, short necks, long heads ending in a flat snout, and a 2-chambered stomach. They are native to Eurasia, Africa, and Madagascar. The Eurasian wild hog (*Sus scrofa*) was hunted for centuries for sport and meat, and to prevent it from destroying crops; later it was domesticated, and true-breeding strains were selected for smallness of tusks, large production of meat, and other qualities.

In the wild form, the young are marked with brown stripes that remain for several months after birth. The African wart hog (*Phacochoerus aethiopicus*) received its name from the large facial growths that resemble warts. In this species there is a growth of long hair down the middle of the back, and the tusks are well developed in both jaws. Order Artiodactyla, family Suidae.

SWORDFISH, a very large bony fish in which the head is prolonged into a sharp, straight projection one-third as long as the body. These fishes are widely distributed in open waters of both the Atlantic and the Pacific oceans. The body itself is cylindrical in form, tapering toward the strongly notched tail. There are no scales, the sides being naked and grayish in color. This fish has no teeth and no ventral fins, and the dorsal fin is very long, often projecting above the surface of the water when the fish is sunning itself. The maximum weight of specimens is about 800 pounds, but the average is about half that size.

The beak of the swordfish can be a dangerous weapon and there are instances on record of its having been thrust through the planking of ships, so crippling them that they were forced to turn home for repairs. In feeding, the swordfish, capable of great speed, swims in among a school of fishes, lashing out from side to side with its beak, crippling or killing its food. Order Percomorphi, family Xiphiidae, specifically *Xiphias gladius*.

SWORDTAIL, a handsome freshwater fish with an extraordinary extension (the "tail") shaped like a sword, from the lower portion of the normal tail on the male fish; females are swordless. These fishes live in rivers along the Atlantic slope of southern Mexico and Guatemala. The body is shining olive-brown above, shading to blue or green on the sides, marked lengthwise and often vertically with red brown.

As a popular aquarium fish, a male swordtail will mate with 4 to 6 females, who produce living young in 6 to 8 weeks. The parents are likely to eat their own young if the 100 to 200 little fishes cannot find hiding places among tangled vegetation in the aquarium. Female swordtails are generally larger than males, and may attain a length of 4 inches. Order Cyprinodontes, family Poeciliidae, specifically *Xiphophorus helleri*.

TANAGER, any of about 200 different kinds of small- to medium-sized perching birds with a slightly downcurved conical beak that is notched in the cutting edges just before the slightly hooked tip. All live in tropical and subtropical America, except 4 that have become migratory and have spread as far north as Canada.

The best-known tanager is the handsome scarlet tanager (*Piranga olivacea*), 7 inches long, which nests from the Atlantic coast to Manitoba and Oklahoma, migrating for the winter to western South America. The male in summer is flaming red with jet-black wings and tail, but in fall and winter changes the red to olive-green shading to yellow underneath; the female resembles the winter male except that she is brownish gray where he is black.

The summer tanager (*P. rubra*), which migrates from the southern United States to Cuba, Mexico, and Central America for the winter, is slightly larger; the male is a uniform, dull red, and the female is yellowish green above, dull yellow below. In the western tanager (*P. ludoviciana*), which prefers open woodlands from the Rocky Mountains to the Pacific coast, the male is variegated yellow, black, and red; the female is undistinguished except that she has 2 yellow wing bars which are lacking in other similar birds.

The hepatic tanager (*P. flava*) nests as far north as Arizona and New Mexico, south to Guatemala. Many of the tropical tanagers belong to the genera *Tanagra* and *Tangara*, names derived from the language of the Tupi Indians of the Amazon basin. Order Passeriformes, family Thraupidae.

TAPEWORM, any of a large number of parasitic flatworms living in the digestive tract of vertebrate animals, each worm consisting of a single anchoring individual (the scolex), which holds to the wall of the intestine by means of hooks or suckers or both, and an indefinite number of flat individuals that appear to be mere segments of the tapeworm, called proglottids.. The scolex individual absorbs food from the intestinal contents, and reproduces asexually, forming one proglottid after another from the free end by the process of budding.

The proglottids remain connected to one another and to the scolex for a long while, and give the appearance of a continuous ribbon, constricted at intervals where one proglottid joins the next younger or next older one. The proglottids also absorb food and grow, becoming sexually mature and mating within the intestine. Eventually each proglottid is old and full of fertilized eggs that have already developed through many embryonic stages. The old proglottid breaks free and is carried out with the feces.

The embryos hatch into larvae which can wait a few days or weeks to be swallowed by a host of another kind, such as a cow or a fish. In this secondary host, the larvae move to the muscles and become dormant. If the beef or fish flesh is eaten uncooked, the dormant larvae of the tapeworm become active and soon attach themselves to the lining of the digestive tract in the meat-eating animal (the primary host), growing there into the scolex stage that can produce a whole tapeworm. Nine different orders in class Cestoda.

TAPIR, any of 4 different large tropical mammals somewhat resembling donkeys with close-clipped fur, short tails, and a long flexible nose bearing the nostrils at the tip. The Brazilian tapir (*Tapirus terrestris*) inhabits water edges in rain forests from northern South America to Paraguay. The mountain tapir (*T. roulini*) travels in its search for vegetable food even higher than the limit of forest in the Andes. Baird's tapir (*T. bairdi*) is found northward from Ecuador through Central America into southeastern Mexico.

Largest of all is the Malayan tapir (*T. indicus*), 6 to 8 feet long, which, unlike the dull reddish or brownish black animals of the New World, is white on the back and sides. All young tapirs are striped and spotted with yellow and white. Tapirs have 3 toes reaching the ground on both the fore and hind feet. Order Perissodactyla, family Tapiridae.

TARANTULA, originally the name given to a moderately poisonous wolf spider (*Lycosa tarentula*) of Taranto in southern Italy, with a striped tan and brown body about 1 inch long and legs spreading about 2½ inches. In North America, tarantula became the name for large and relatively harmless hairy spiders (*Avicularia* and *Eurypelma* species particularly), which arrived in shipments of tropical fruit. Order Araneae.

TARPON, either of 2 different kinds of marine bony fishes with a large bony plate under the head between the two sides of the lower jaw, and a long filamentous extension from the last ray of the dorsal fin. The smaller Pacific tarpon (*Megalops cyprinoides*), which ranges from Guam to the east coast of Africa, rarely exceeds 40 inches in length.

The Atlantic tarpon (*M. atlanticus*), which is caught from Cape Cod in summer to Brazil, grows as much as 8 feet long and to 240 pounds or more. The large overlapping silver scales of such a fish are more than 3 inches across.

No fish fights harder for its freedom than a hooked tarpon; it often makes explosive leaps as much as 8 feet out of the water, 15 to 20 times in succession before becoming exhausted. At each leap, its greenish blue upper back and shining silver sides gleam in the light. Order Isospondyli, family Elopidae.

TEAL, any of about 15 different kinds of small diving ducks with particularly rapid flight. They are found in the Americas, Eurasia, Africa, Australia, New Zealand, Hawaii, and other oceanic islands. One of the world's vanishing birds is the little teal of Laysan Island (*Anas laysanensis*), which nests nowhere else. The common teal in Eurasia (*A. crecca*), 14 inches long, is Europe's smallest duck; it visits North American coasts regularly. The Hottentot teal (*A. punctata*) of Ethiopia is Africa's smallest duck.

North American teals come in several sizes: the 14-inch green-winged teal (*A. carolinensis*), which has a chestnut-brown head, nests across Canada and in the northwestern United States; the 15-inch blue-winged teal (*A. discors*), which has chalky blue patches on the wings, nests over most of Canada and the United States; and the 16-inch cinnamon teal (*A. cyanoptera*), with a cinnamon-colored head and body, nests in the western provinces of Canada and states southward into Mexico. Order Anseriformes, family Anatidae.

TENT CATERPILLAR, the destructive larval stage of a North American moth (*Malacosoma americana*) found commonly east of the Rocky Mountains. Tent caterpillars hatch in early spring from thick, crusty masses of about 200 eggs which surround the twigs of trees, particularly apple and cherry. At once the caterpillars set about spinning an unsightly protective tent of silk, into which they retire by day. At night, when birds are less active, the caterpillars walk out of their tent and feed on the foliage, often stripping a tree in a few days.

When fully grown, a tent caterpillar is about 2 inches long, with a continuous white stripe down its black back, and with blue and white spots on each side. After about 6 weeks of feeding, the larvae spin cocoons, often on the bark of the same tree, and pupate. In about 3 weeks the moths emerge, each rather heavy bodied, with a wingspread of 1¼ inches in the male to 2 inches in the female.

A related moth and caterpillar (*M. disstria*) which is widespread in forested areas of Canada, the United States, and Mexico, is often called a "forest tent caterpillar" moth, although its caterpillars produce silken carpets only—never a voluminous tent in which to hide. Order Lepidoptera, family Lasiocampidae.

TERMITE, or white ant, any of about 1,800 different kinds of insects with biting mouthparts, the thorax of the soft body broadly joined to the abdomen, and 2 pairs of similar, narrow membranous wings carried flat over the back and detached after the nuptial flight. Termites are mostly tropical, social insects, living in social communities with an elaborate system of castes and functional varieties.

Immature individuals of both sexes assist in the work of the colony, gathering and sharing food. The queen lays millions of eggs, sometimes 4,000 in a day. Many termites eat wood, which they digest with the help of single-celled protozoans in their intestines. Their damage to wooden buildings, books, and other human possessions causes enormous losses in tropical countries and, until extermination methods were improved recently, in many temperate regions of the United States.

In Africa and Australia, certain termites build huge nests, or termitaries, 20 to 40 feet high, piled up a grain of earth at a time. The earth is cemented by saliva. Order Isoptera.

TERN, or sea swallow, any of 39 different kinds of slender, gull-like seabirds 8 to 23 inches long, with slender pointed beaks, webbed, weak feet, and a pattern of feather coloration that is usually gray above and white below, with black markings on the head; some kinds are pure white.

Although all terns are migratory, the circumpolar Arctic tern (*Sterna paradisaea*), which is grayish white with a red beak and red legs, is probably the champion migrant. Most of the Arctic terns breed in the Arctic in summer, and winter in the Antarctic, 11,000 miles away. They travel more than 25,000 miles a year; many cross the Atlantic Ocean in their migration. Order Charadriiformes, family Laridae.

TERRAPIN. See *Tortoise.*

THRUSH, any of 306 different kinds of medium-sized perching birds, 8 to 12 inches long, many of them renowned for their melodious song. They are native to all temperate and tropical lands except New Zealand and some oceanic islands. Thrushes include the nightingale (*Luscinia megarhynchos*) of Europe and southwestern Asia, the song thrush (*Turdus ericetorum*) of Eurasia, the familiar and widespread North American robin (*T. migratorius*), and the smaller, more slender wood thrush (*Hylocichla mustelina*) of the eastern United States, and the widely distributed hermit thrush (*H. guttata*).

Opinion is divided as to whether the nightingale, the hermit thrush, or the shama thrush (*Kittacincla macrura*) of India has the sweetest song. All are birds of the underbrush, eating insects and fruits, and raising young whose breast feathers are spotted. Order Passeriformes, family Turdidae.

TICK, any of about 2,000 different kinds of external parasitic arthropods larger than mites, which attach themselves to vertebrate animals and suck the blood, often becoming greatly engorged before voluntarily dropping off. They are found all over the world. Immature mites have 3 pairs of legs, but add a fourth pair at the molt that brings them to mature form. Several different diseases, such as tularemia in rabbits and Texas fever in cattle, are transmitted from infected animals to uninfected ones by ticks. Order Acarina of class Arachnida.

The name tick is used also for several degenerate kinds of insects that are external parasites, such as the sheep tick (*Melophagus ovinus*) of Order Diptera, family Hippoboscidae.

TITMOUSE, any of about 65 different kinds of small, active songbirds similar to chickadees. Most are Eurasian, but several live in Africa and in America south to Guatemala. In Britain and Europe they are called tits. All are extremely energetic and trusting, as they hunt for insects in bark crevices and on foliage; they also eat some small fruits and seeds. The tufted titmouse (*Parus bicolor*) of the southeastern United States, which has a crest and is about 6 inches long, often visits feeding shelves around homes for suet, peanut butter, and sunflower seeds. Order Passeriformes, family Paridae.

TOAD, any of several hundred different kinds of amphibians that, like frogs, develop from aquatic tadpoles, have a protusible tongue fitted for catching insects, and large hind legs fitted for leaping. Toads differ from frogs in having a rough skin, more suited for life on land far from water. Toads are common in most parts of the world except the Australasian region, living even in some deserts. Many kinds have glands in the skin that secrete an acrid or poisonous fluid, which protects them from attack. They cannot cause warts. Several orders in subclass Salientia.

AMERICAN MUSEUM OF NATURAL HISTORY
TURTLE

TOOTH SHELL, or tusk shell, any of about 200 kinds of marine mollusks that produce a slightly curved and gradually tapered conical shell open at both ends. The common tooth shell (*Dentalium entale*) found on both sides of the Atlantic Ocean below low tide in sandy bottoms attains a length of about 2 inches.

The precious tooth shell (*D. pretiosum*) of the Pacific coast of North America served until recently as a form of money and status symbol among west coast Indians; the abundant 1-inch shells had little value, but a 2-inch specimen had the buying power of a shilling, and a 3-inch shell could be owned only by a major chief, who generally wore it around his neck on a loop of woven plant fiber. In New Guinea, mountain people still use large tooth shells for personal adornment, pushed through holes made in lower lip, nose, and ear lobes.

A living tooth shell keeps the small end of its shell above the sediments of the bottom, to breathe water in and out through the hole at the end; it has no gills. The body is extended from the lower, larger opening of the shell to extend the foot—shaped like a horse's hoof—and a number of threadlike tentacles. The tentacles push among the sand particles, find and capture small bits of organic matter as food, and bring it back to the mouth. Class Scaphopoda, family Dentalidae.

TORTOISE, or turtle, any of about 265 different kinds of broad-bodied, slow-moving reptiles with horny jaws instead of teeth, and usually with some vertebrae and ribs fused to a shell-like armor consisting of an upper, convex carapace and a lower, flat plastron, which are joined at the sides. The shell protects the head, legs, and tail when these are retracted into special cavities.

Tortoises are found worldwide, except for western South America and New Zealand. Some are marine, coming ashore only to lay their eggs; others live in arid lands and deserts; most live near freshwater or frequent moist forests. Most tortoises eat both plant and animal food, including small dead animals.

Among the largest are the giant tortoises of the Galápagos Islands and islands in the Indian Ocean, where individuals attain a length of 4 feet and a weight of 400 pounds. Notable among the sea turtles are the green (*Chelonia midas*) of tropical Atlantic and Gulf of Mexico coasts, the loggerhead (*Caretta caretta*) of the Atlantic, and the hawksbill (*Eretmochelys imbricata*) of all tropic seas, which provides the best quality of horny plates from the shell, known commercially as "tortoise shell." All of these large sea turtles are sought for meat, and their eggs are collected for people to eat.

In the southeastern United States, the diamondback terrapin (*Malaclemys centrata*) was formerly raised in pens as one of the most expensive luxury foods; this turtle of muddy marshes, both brackish and salt, grows to 5½ inches long in about 9 years, then more slowly; for a while, a 7-inch terrapin brought $7 on the market, with an extra dollar for each ½ inch additional length.

Painted turtles (*Chrysemys marginata* and related species), 5 to 6 inches long, are common in freshwater ponds of eastern North America; the box turtle (*Terrapene carolina*), on the other hand, frequents open woodlands in the same area. This turtle can draw its body completely within its shell and close the ends by raising hinged portions of the plastron. Order Testudinata.

TOUCAN, any of 37 different kinds of tropical, fruit-eating birds with a beak nearly as long as the body, not including the tail. They are birds of forests and clearings from southern Mexico to Paraguay. Although the beak is strong, it is lightweight and does not make the bird awkward. Toucans use their beaks to pick fruit and in elaborate courtship displays. They fly with beak ahead, almost like woodpeckers—flapping vigorously 8 to 10 times, then gliding with wings stiffly spread. They nest in holes in trees.

The toco (*Ramphastos toco*) of the Guianas and Brazil is 25 inches long, of which 8 inches is beak and 8 inches is tail; its black plumage is set off by a white throat, red under the tail, and an orange-red, black-tipped beak. Many smaller toucans are called araçaris (species of *Pteroglossus*), and live in large flocks. In the Andes they are found to 10,000 feet elevation. Order Piciformes, family Ramphastidae.

TRAP-DOOR SPIDER, any of a number of black or brown spiders with long stout legs, on which the third pair bear a claw used in digging. They live in the western and southern United States and Latin America, and on other continents.

Most are 1 inch or more in length, and dig vertical burrows 6 inches or more deep, topped with neatly fitted trapdoors made of mud and silk. Below the doors, the spiders rest, ready to jump out and seize passing insects, then drag them back into the burrow and close the door again. New Zealand trapdoor spiders make similar lairs in the thick bark of trees. Order Araneae, family Ctenizidae, many different genera.

TROGON, any of 34 different kinds of brightly colored tropical birds with long tails or tail-covert feathers. The New World has 20 kinds from the southwestern United States to northern Argentina. Africa has 3 kinds south of the great deserts. Asia has the others, chiefly in Malaya and the islands of Sumatra, Java, and the Philippines.

The most famous trogon is the quetzal (*Pharomachrus moccino*), the national symbol of Guatemala and the name used for their coin. It is now almost extinct there. In former times the native chiefs used the long, green tail-covert feathers of the male for decorations. The bird was worshiped by the Aztecs and Mayas in the cult of Quetzalcoatl, the mythical king, part bird and serpent (coatl).

The female trogon is brownish except for green back and wings and red under the tail; the male is brilliant green on head, chest, and wings, blue on the back, and scarlet underneath. Order Trogoniformes, family Trogonidae.

TROUT, a common name for several bony fishes closely related to salmon, with soft, rayed fins and a small soft adipose fin without rays on the back behind the large dorsal fin. They have very small scales. All are excellent eating and are regarded as game fish.

The North American brook trout (*Salvelinus fontinalis*) thrives in the coldest and clearest streams, laying its eggs in December or January. Other species in North America are the lake trout (*Cristivomer namaycush*) and the salmon trout (species of *Salmo*) in the East, and the rainbow and Dolly Varden trout in the West. Sea trout is a general term for any salt-water trout that enter freshwater only to spawn.

All species belong to the Northern Hemisphere, but they have been introduced into Australia and New Zealand. Order Isospondyli, family Salmonidae.

TUBE-NOSED BIRD, any of the large or medium-sized sea birds in which the beak provides a tubular extension for the nostrils, making these breathing holes open separately almost at the tip of the beak or open together as a single hole above the tip of the beak. They include the albatrosses, shearwaters (or mutton birds), the storm petrels, and the diving petrels. All of these birds remain at sea, feeding on fishes and squids from the surface water, except during the breeding season. Order Procellariiformes.

TUNA, any of about 10 large marine bony fish, resembling the smaller but closely related mackerels in having a streamlined body that narrows to a slender stalk just before the large tail, which is almost T-shaped. Tunas are found in all oceans, and are hunted by both sportsmen and commercial fishermen; tuna flesh is valuable food.

Largest of tunas is the great bluefin (*Thunnus thynnus*), which reaches a length of 14 feet and weight of 1,800 pounds, following a migration pattern from the Tropics to far northern waters off Norway. The albacore (*T. alalunga*), which has particularly long pectoral fins, is a favorite because its meat is white.

Yellowfin tunas (*T. albacares*) of the Indian and Pacific oceans grow as much as 60 pounds in a year; those at 90-pound size are sought for canning. They feed in great schools and are netted or caught with a short line on heavy poles. Of recent years this fish has become recognized by sportsmen for its strength and fighting ability, and specimens weighing around 800 pounds have been landed by rod and reel. One of the favorite grounds for tuna fishing is off Nova Scotia. Order Acanthopteri, family Scombridae.

TUNICATE, or sea squirt, any of about 1300 kinds of soft-bodied marine animals that attach themselves to solid objects in sea water and secrete a stiffening tunic of cellulose within the skin. They are found along most seacoasts in water to 200 feet deep. Most of the space in the body of a tunicate is occupied by an enormous throat region (pharynx) of the digestive tract. Water entering the mouth passes out through a large number of pores in the pharyngeal walls, while oxygen is exchanged for carbon dioxide and particles of food are captured in a film of mucus. The loaded mucus goes on to the intestine. If a tunicate is disturbed, it contracts suddenly, expelling water from its mouth in a forceful jet, hence the name sea squirt.

In season, tunicates develop reproductive organs and release into the sea small larvae that resemble tadpoles. Each has a pharynx with gill openings, a hollow dorsal nerve cord, and a supporting rod called a notochord in the propulsive tail.

These features indicate that tunicates are degenerate members of the same phylum to which the vertebrate animals belong. Degeneration occurs when the larva settles to the bottom, attaches itself permanently, and absorbs its tail, its notochord, its propulsive muscles, and transforms into the form of the adult. Order Ascidiacea of the chordate subphylum Urochorda.

TURKEY, either of 2 different large pheasantlike birds with naked heads. They are native to woodlands in America from Canada to Central America, where they search along the ground for food by day and roost each night in trees.

The common turkey (*Meleagris gallopavo*), a 48-inch bird of southeastern United States and Mexico, was domesticated in Mexico at least 500 years before Columbus discovered America. Spanish conquistadores introduced them into Europe, and colonists brought them to New England. The tame birds differ somewhat in appearance from the birds in a wild state. In Yucatan, British Honduras, and Guatemala, the ocellated turkey (*Agriocharis ocellata*) still runs wild; it is a 36-inch bird, which lacks the beardlike chest tuft of feathers characteristic of the male common turkey. Order Galliformes, family Meleagrididae.

TURTLE. See *Tortoise*.

VAMPIRE, any of several different kinds of blood-sucking bats in which the incisor and canine teeth are shearlike, specialized for cutting through the skin of warm-blooded animals. Vampire bats alight gently on sleeping mammals such as horses, cattle, and even man, or creep along to a vantage point from which they can use their teeth to get blood flowing. They then lap the fresh blood with the tongue.

The teeth are so sharp that often considerable blood is lost and the bat has departed before the victim becomes aware that anything has happened. Order Chiroptera, family Desmodontidae.

VIPER, any of a large number of poisonous, stout-bodied Old World snakes in which the venom is discharged through 2 erectile fangs at the front of the upper jaw. They are widespread in Eurasia and Africa, and differ from the pit vipers of America in lacking the heat-sensitive pits between eye and nostril.

The adder, or common viper (*Vipera berus*), widely distributed in Eurasia, is the only British venomous snake. Its bite rarely proves fatal. It attains a length of 25½ inches, is brown with a black zigzag line down the back, feeds chiefly upon mice and, like most vipers, is viviparous (bears young alive —not from eggs).

The puff adders (*Bitis arietans*) of Africa south of the great deserts lie in wait for rat-sized rodents, which they strike with incredible speed and then slowly pursue for the few seconds needed until the victim dies. Largest is the Gaboon viper (*B. gabunica*), nearly 6 feet long and 6 inches in diameter. It rarely bites people, even in self-defense. Order Squamata, suborder Serpentes, family Viperidae.

VOLE, or meadow mouse, a small, short-tailed rodent (*Microtus pennsylvanicus*) of orchards and pasturelands in North America. The head and body are chestnut-brown above, gray beneath, marked with black above and cinnamon color below. A vole eats approximately its own weight daily of many kinds of plants, and cuts down a great deal that it does not eat.

Since a female vole begins producing young when only a month old, and may bear 13 litters of 4 to 8 young within a year, the population can increase spectacularly if not controlled by foxes, hawks, and other predators. Voles are the basic food for most of these flesh-eaters. Order Rodentia, family Cricetidae.

VULTURE, any of 6 different carnivorous, scavenging birds of the New World, and of 4 in the Old, all capable of soaring for hours with no apparent motion of their wings. With incredibly keen eyesight, they watch from high up for carcasses of dead animals or mammals that are dying or badly injured. Circling down, they alight near the carcass, then, using their strong hooked beaks, tear it into strips small enough to swallow.

Largest is the Andean condor (*Vultur gryphus*), 52 inches long with a wingspan of 10 to 12 feet and a weight of 20 to 25 pounds; it is one of the world's largest flying birds, and is becoming increasingly rare although it nests and perches from 10,000 to 15,000 feet above sea level on inaccessible cliffs. Under stress of hunger, it descends to the plains in search of sick and dead domestic animals, and is shot by ranchers.

A somewhat similar bird, the California condor (*Gymnogyps californianus*), is threatened with extinction in its last retreat—some relatively inaccessible mountain regions of California.

In the Old World, the only vulture of comparable size is the bearded vulture, or lammergeier (*Gypaetus barbatus*), named for a tuft of bristly feathers on its chin, which has the reputation of stealing lambs over the mountains from the Pyrenees and North Africa to eastern India. However, its feet are too weak to hold a struggling animal and it ordinarily waits until other scavengers have cleaned a carcass before descending to get the bones; it can crush these or drop them on crags and pick up the pieces to get at the marrow inside.

The griffin vulture (*Gyps fulvus*), a 41-inch bird with a ruff of white feathers into which it can withdraw its bare head and neck, watches over the same area surveyed by the lammergeier for animals to die; flocks of griffin vultures stand near the burning ghats in India, waiting to feast on the remains of human corpses that are thrown into the sacred Ganges. The smaller, white, Egyptian vulture (*Nephron percnopterus*), sometimes called pharaoh's chicken, ranges all over countries bordering the Mediterranean, often staying close to villages to eat whatever meat scraps it can find.

In the New World, the turkey vulture, or turkey buzzard (*Cathartes aura*), is the common scavenger from southern Canada to Tierra del Fuego. It gets its name from the reddish color of the naked head and upper neck; its body plumage and wings are drab gray-brown, but its wingspan of 6 feet lets it soar gracefully all day. Its services as a scavenger have earned it rigorous legal protection.

The black vulture, or black buzzard, or carrion crow, or urubu (*Coragyps atratus*), is a heavier bird of smaller size, residing in the southern United States and southward to Argentina. From southern Mexico southward it competes to some exent with the king vulture (*Sarcorhamphus papa*), a 32-inch bird whose naked head and neck bear many bright colors—white, yellow, red, and black— in a pattern made more startling by the bird's white eye.

New World vultures all belong to family Cathartidae, distinguished by longitudinal instead of round nostrils, lack of a voice, beaks so weak they cannot tear flesh until it rots, slightly webbed toes, and the hind toe somewhat elevated. Old World vultures belong to family Vulturidae. All vultures are classified in order Falconiformes.

WALLABY, any of about 35 different kinds of small- and medium-sized grazing and browsing marsupial mammals similar to but smaller than kangaroos. They inhabit Australia, New Guinea, and adjacent islands, often taking refuge among boulders. Often they emerge to sunbathe, but they feed mostly at night. The many genera are classified in order Marsupialia, family Macropodidae.

WALRUS, an arctic marine mammal (*Odobenus rosmarus*), closely related to seals and sea lions, distinguished by its bristly whiskers and enormous, down-turned tusks, or canine teeth, projecting from the upper jaw. Those of the male are larger and longer and sometimes reach a length of 16 inches beyond the sockets. The generic name means tooth walking, for it was once supposed that the walrus used its tusks to help drag its heavy body along land and ice. Actually, the tusks are used by the walrus to free mollusks from the sea bottom when feeding. The female walrus has smaller tusks.

Walruses have a heavy body, deepest at the shoulders, and limbs that are adapted for swimming. They reach a length of 12 feet or more, and a weight of 2,200 pounds. They are hunted for their hides, their tusks, and their blubber that produces 25 to 30 gallons of oil from each walrus. Order Pinnipedia, family Odobenidae.

WARBLER, any of 300 different kinds of small birds, mostly dull colored, in the Old World, all members of family Sylviidae, and nearly 120 of small, mostly bright-colored birds in the New World, all members of family Parulidae. To prevent confusion, the New World warblers are now referred to often as wood warblers. The name warbler is deceptive, in that very few of them are singers of any ability. In spite of this, the warblers are among the most charming and useful citizens of our wildlife. Their insect- and larvae-destroying activities are worth millions of dollars yearly.

Widespread in Eurasia are the grasshopper warbler (*Locustella naevia*), whose song is more distinctive than its plumage; the reed warbler (*Acrocephalus scirpaceus*) of reed beds and waterside shrubbery; the sedge warbler (*A. schoenobaenus*) of similar habitats; the blackcap (*Sylvia atricapilla*) of woodlands; the garden warbler (*S. borin*) of bramble patches; the whitethroat (*S. communis*) of more open country; and the chiffchaff (*Phylloscopus collybita*) of evergreen woodlands.

Familiar warblers in North America include the black-and-white warbler (*Mniotilta varia*) that creeps around tree trunks searching for insect food in crevices; the yellow warbler or yellowbird (*Dendroica petechia*), yellowish green above and bright yellow beneath; the myrtle warbler (*D. coronata*), slate gray, with conspicuous yellow patches at the base of the tail, the crown, and on either side of the breast; the redstart (*Setophaga ruticilla*), with brilliant red wing and tail marks contrasting with its jet-black plumage; and the yellowthroat (*Geothlypis trichas*), olive above and bright yellow below, with a black mask over its face. Order Passeriformes.

VULTURE

WASP, a member of any of several families of insects that, as adults, have biting mouthparts, 2 pairs of membranous wings of which the fore pair is much the larger, a narrow waist between thorax and abdomen, and in females and sterile workers, a well-developed stinger and poison gland at the hind end of the body.

Wasps differ from bees in having slenderer bodies and no pollen-gathering specialized apparatus on the hind legs. Some are solitary; others form colonies in which the individuals work together for the common good. Solitary wasps include the digger wasps (family Bembecidae), which excavate holes in the soil or in wood and there store insects that they have paralyzed with their stinger, as food for the maggotlike young that will hatch from their eggs.

The thread-waisted wasps (family Sphecidae) include mud daubers (genus *Sceliphron*), which collect spiders to fill the cells of nests built by sticking mud to beams in barns or similar places. The social wasps, chiefly members of family Vespidae, are commonly called simply wasps, or hornets.

Some wasps make a nest in the earth; others make paper nests from bits of decaying wood that they chew into a real paper pulp. In the colonies the male wasps die when winter approaches; but the females live to start a new colony in the spring. Order Hymenoptera.

WATER BOATMAN, any of a large number of aquatic insects (*Corixa*), ¾ inch long or less, that swim actively in fresh and stagnant water, propelling themselves with oarlike hind legs. They are found all over the world. The front legs are adapted for scraping microscopic algae from leaves, stones, and other firm surfaces. Females lay top-shaped yellow eggs on submerged objects. The immature water boatmen that emerge have the same blunt, boat-shaped body as the adults, but gain wings only at the final molt when they are mature.

Water boatmen often fly to lights, as well as to colonize new bodies of freshwater, including bird baths and public fountains. The adults are eaten by many kinds of birds, and the aquatic individuals by fishes and water birds. Order Heteroptera, family Corixidae.

WATER FLEA, a small crustacean of fresh and brackish water, not more than ⅛ inch long, which appears to dance as it swims by lashing its 2 feathery antennae. Most water fleas belong to genus *Daphnia*. They are found all over the world.

The sides of the flattened body of the water flea are extended ventrally to provide protection for the gills and for clusters of developing eggs. For favorable parts of the year, sexual reproduction is unnecessary; females reproduce by parthenogenesis, freeing a new brood of minute young with the same body form every 7 to 11 days.

Males develop toward the end of the summer or when a pond becomes too stagnant; the fertilized eggs have a heavy shell and can survive desiccation or frost. In this dormant condition, water fleas pass periods of drought, of winter, and get carried from one pond to another in mud on the feet of wading birds. Water fleas are raised in enormous numbers by fanciers of tropical fish, as a suitable food to add to aquariums. Subclass Branchiopoda, order Cladocera.

WATER STRIDER, or pond skater, any of a large number of insects with a compact, canoe-shaped body that support themselves on 4 long outstretched slender legs atop the surface film over ponds and streams. They are found in the Americas, Eurasia, and Africa, but not in Australasia or most oceanic islands.

Waxy hairs of microscopic size prevent the water from wetting the feet of a water strider. The insect holds its body well above the surface film as it sculls along with its middle pair of legs, riding its slight weight on the long hind legs and short front legs, which are held close together below the head.

Water striders are scavengers, investigating as possible food all objects of modest size that float up to the water film from below or that float in it after falling from above. In winter and during rain storms, most striders crawl out on the shore and hide under leaves. One that cannot often do so is the sea-going water strider (*Halobates*) that is common among the mangroves on quiet tropical lagoons, but ventures also far out at sea. It is believed to lay its eggs on the floating feathers dropped by sea birds. No one knows how it survives during storms. Order Heteroptera, family Gerridae.

WATER THRUSH, either of 2 short-tailed wood warblers (*Seiurus*), closely related to the ovenbird, which seem nervous as they teeter while walking along the edges of streams and rivers in North America and northern South America.

The northern water thrush (*S. noveboracensis*) is slightly smaller than the Louisiana water thrush (*S. motacilla*), and differs in that it has a yellowish line above the eye rather than a white one, and dark streaks on the greenish yellow breast instead of none. The northern water thrush prefers northern bogs and swamps or near quiet water as a nesting site; the Louisiana water thrush prefers flowing streams and rivers.

Both birds eat insects and crustaceans picked up along the edge of the water but, unlike the water ouzel, they do not venture into the water itself. Order Passeriformes, family Parulidae.

WAXWING, any of 3 different kinds of sleek, crested, fruit-eating, tree-dwelling birds 6 to 8 inches long, which have a yellow band across the end of the tail and red tips to the secondary flight feathers that show when their wings are folded at rest. The largest is the Bohemian waxwing (*Bombycilla garrulus*), found from northern Eurasia into the western United States.

The cedar waxwing (*B. cedrorum*) nests from coast to coast in Canada and the northern United States, flying south into Central America and the West Indies for the winter. A Japanese waxwing (*B. japonica*) has red-tipped wing feathers, but not the small pellets of waxy bright-red material found in the New World birds. Order Passeriformes, family Bombycillidae.

WEASEL, or stoat, any of 10 different kinds of short-legged predatory mammals so slender that they can follow a mouse to the end of its burrow or pass through a knothole into a chicken coop. They are found in North Africa, Eurasia, and America as far south as the rim of the Amazon basin. The longtailed weasel (*Mustela frenata*) of southernmost Canada southward into South America has brown feet even in winter when, in northern latitudes, its coat becomes completely white except for the feet and the black tip of the tail.

The ermine (*M. erminea*) of the northern United States, Canada, and northern Eurasia similarly has a black tip to its tail, turns white elsewhere in winter, and brown on the back in summer. Its pelt has been sought for centuries to line the robes of royalty and magistrates and, more recently, to make expensive fur coats for wealthy people.

Closely related are the two semi-aquatic minks, the European (*M. lutreola*) being found from Scandinavia into Siberia, and the American (*M. vison*) over all of North America except the southwestern states and Mexico. Unlike other weasels, minks have some webbing between their toes and a white patch on the chin; otherwise they are dark brown or black. Young minks are sometimes kept as pets and used like ferrets for hunting. Order Carnivora, family Mustelidae.

WEEVIL, or snout beetle, any of a large number of beetles, in which the forward part of the head is prolonged into the form of a snout, with the jaws at the tip. They are found all over the world, often as pests causing extensive damage to fruits and grains. With its jaws, a weevil cuts a cylindrical hole the length of its snout into fruits of many kinds, both to obtain food and to prepare a deep pit in which it can have some protection for the eggs it lays there. Order Coleoptera, family Curculionidae.

WHALE, any of about 34 different kinds of large marine mammals in which the forelimbs have the form of flippers, the hind limbs are completely concealed within the body or absent, and the tail is expanded widthways into flukes used in sculling along. Only the little white whale (*Delphinapterus leucas*) of shallow waters and large rivers in the Arctic, and the narwhal (*Monodon monoceros*)—named for the single long spirally-twisted tusk that grows straight forward from the male's head—of Arctic seas are less than 15 feet long; these two mature at 11 to 12 feet in length, and are placed in the same family (Monodontidae).

Twenty other kinds of whales have teeth of some kind, and are referred to as "toothed whales." They include the gregarious pilot whales, or blackfish (species of *Globicephala*), which are harvested off Newfoundland for oil and for meat to feed foxes on fur farms; and the dreaded killer whale, or orca *(Orcinus orca)*, of all seas but especially the Arctic and Antarctic, which attack in packs, often tearing even the biggest whales to pieces; these are members of family Delphinidae. Beaked whales of 14 different kinds (family Ziphiidae) and of all oceans are less famous than one of the 2 kinds of sperm whales—the cachalot *(Physeter catodon)* made familiar by Melville's *Moby Dick*; it attains a length of 60 feet, a weight of 50 tons, provides the teeth carved by sailors and called "scrimshaw," and is placed in family Physeteridae.

The whalebone, or baleen whales, which have row upon row of fringed horny plates ("whalebone") hanging from the roof of the enormous mouth, include the gray whales of the North Pacific *(Eschrichtius glaucus)*, many of which migrate within sight of the California coast to calving and breeding areas along the coasts of Baja California and mainland Mexico; and 5 different "right" whales (family Balaenidae) represented in all oceans, so named because they floated and could be flensed by old-time whalers, whereas "wrong" whales—the 6 kinds in family Balaenopteridae—sank when harpooned. The latter include the largest of whales: the blue or sulphur-bottom *(Sibbaldus musculus)*, to 100 feet long and 100 tons—the largest mammal that ever lived; 4 kinds of finback whales (members of genus *Balaenoptera)*; and the humpback whale *(Megaptera novaeangliae)* that often swims near coasts and inlets on its migration between tropical and polar seas north and south. Whalebone whales use their strange plates to strain from the water the 1- to 2-inch crustaceans and the squids and fishes that form their food. The blubber of whales, which underlies the smooth shining skin, is rich in oil and serves both to insulate the body from losing heat too rapidly in icy water and to buoy up the whale, saving it from expending extra effort to stay near the water's surface.

All whales dive, holding their breath for many minutes. The champion diver is the sperm whale, which dives to such great depths that it sometimes is caught and drowned by becoming entangled with transoceanic telephone cables. To these depths the sperm whale plunges in pursuit of the giant squid that form its favorite food. Undigestible beaks from these squids may irritate the lining of the whale's digestive tract until it forms a cheesy material called ambergris, which is much sought as a fixative for perfumes. Order Cetacea.

WHIPPOORWILL, an American bird *(Caprimulgus vociferus)* related to the nighthawk and the European nightjar, or goatsucker, named for its loud cry that sounds like "whip poor Will" with the last syllable heavily accented. The bird is not often seen, even where it is abundant, as in damp woods of the eastern United States. It usually rests on the ground during the day and searches for insects at early nightfall.

It is about 10 inches long and of plain colors, being grayish, much variegated with black and buff. Its bill is very broad, its mouth large (hence the genus name meaning cave mouth) and provided with a tuft of long bristles. It builds no nest but deposits its eggs on leaves or in a slight depression in the ground. Order Caprimulgiformes, family Caprimulgidae.

WHITEFISH, any of several freshwater fishes *(Coregonus)* of cool clear lakes and deep rivers in the Northern Hemisphere, distantly related to shad and herring. Whitefishes have few or no teeth, possess a pair of flaps between the nostrils, and are characteristically meaty and clad in silvery scales. They feed principally on insects and bottom animals, but come to shallow water to lay their eggs on rocks. These eggs are often gathered for sale as edible fish roe. The Great Lakes whitefish *(C. clupeiformis)* was formerly an important commercial species, attaining a length of 24 inches and a weight to 23 pounds. Invasion of the lakes by sea lampreys has ruined the fishery. Order Isospondyli, family Coregonidae.

WHITING. See *Cod.*

WIDGEON. See *Duck.*

WILDEBEEST. See *Gnu.*

WOLF, either of 2 different kinds of doglike, flesh-eating mammals, 42 to 54 inches long, with a tail 12 to 22 inches in length that is held high when the animal runs. Formerly, wolves were widespread in Eurasia and in North America from the Arctic to south of Mexico. Now the small, tawny red wolf *(Canis niger)* is restricted to a few areas of Oklahoma and Texas. The formerly widely distributed timber wolf, or gray wolf *(C. lupus)*, has been restricted to parts of the United States and eastern Canada. In the northernmost parts of its range, it remains white most or all of the year. Farther south it is usually gray, sprinkled with black.

A wolf differs from other members of the genus *Canis* in its larger size, longer legs, narrower but deeper and heavier body, and wider nose pad. Wolves can be crossed successfully with some breeds of domestic dogs, especially Eskimo sled dogs. Probably the preference for sled dogs that are part wolf has continued for thousands of years, keeping the fertility high despite the fact that the domestic dog has a separate, Asian origin. Order Carnivora, family Canidae.

WOLVERINE, or glutton, a heavy-bodied weasel-like mammal with a squarish head, short legs, and bushy tail, and very dark brown except for a pale stripe along each side and across the back at the base of the tail. It inhabits the northern coniferous forest

AMERICAN MUSEUM OF NATURAL HISTORY
WOLF

near the arctic tundra of Eurasia and North America. Usually solitary, it lives in dens or burrows, emerging when hungry to seek carrion or to feed on live animals, birds' eggs and nestlings in spring, and fruits in autumn. It is notorious for its skill in robbing traps of the meat used to bait them, without getting caught despite the most ingenious devices set for that purpose.

On a full-grown wolverine, nearly 3 feet long, the fur is coarse. Yet, better than any other fur, it repels condensation of moisture in freezing weather and, for that reason, is in large demand to trim parkas and reduce the formation of frost from moisture in the breath. Order Carnivora, family Mustelidae, specifically *Gulo gulo.*

WOMBAT, either of 2 different kinds of bearlike marsupial mammals, 2 to 3 feet long, with small eyes, short legs, and chisel-like incisor teeth that continue growing like those of rodents. Wombats live in Australia and Tasmania, hiding in burrows by day and feeding on grasses and roots in the forest by night. Both the coarse-haired wombat *(Phascolomis ursinus)* and the soft-furred wombat *(Lasiorhinus latifrons)* compete with livestock, and are in danger of being exterminated by stock raisers. Order Marsupialia, family Phascolomidae.

WOODCHUCK. See *Marmot.*

WOODCOCK, either of 2 different kinds of heavy-bodied birds with extraordinary adaptations to concealment on the ground against a pattern of fallen leaves, making a strange whirring courtship flight in twilight, and probing in the soft soil of swamps for earthworms. The Eurasian woodcock *(Scolopax rusticola)*, 14 inches long, migrates from temperate regions southward for the winter. The American woodcock *(Philohela minor)*, an 11-inch bird known also as the timberdoodle, nests in eastern Canada and the United States, and winters in the southeastern States.

Both kinds arrive in their nesting territories in early spring, and prepare a place for their eggs on the ground close to an alder swamp, into which they lead the young as soon as these hatch out. All during the mating and nesting season, the male woodcock performs at twilight his rapid, whizzing flights, rising high into the air and descending again close to his mate. She seems so confident that her soft mottled brown feathers match her background that she will not move if approached on the nest, until actually touched.

A woodcock's beak is well adapted to probing for and catching worms and insects deep down in the soft soil of the swamp. At all times when the beak is down, the bird can see in all directions because its large eyes are positioned unusually high on its head. The flesh of woodcock is delicious, and the birds are challenging targets, for they ascend almost vertically when flushed from the thick cover of vegetation, and fly off at high speed, dodging branches in a zigzag flight path. Many gunners swear a woodcock can fly sideways. Order Charadriiformes, family Scolopacidae.

WOODPECKER, any of 210 different kinds of birds with strong, straight, pointed beaks, long extensile tongues having barbs at the tip, short legs with 2 long toes forward, 2 backward and sharp curved toenails, and tailfeathers that are stiff, strong, and pointed at the tip. Woodpeckers live on all major land areas where there are trees, except Madagascar, Australia, and the oceanic islands. They fly strongly, undulating by beating their wings 4 or 5 times in quick succession to gain altitude, then closing the wings and curving downward like a projectile until the next series of wingbeats.

Most woodpeckers perch on tree trunks and branches, clinging to the bark while propping themselves with their special tail feathers. They hammer with the beak to expose insects, then spear each on the barbed tongue. Flickers, which often stand on the ground to pick up ants, and sapsuckers, which drill for sap and also eat nuts and fruits, match their food supply by migrating regularly. Other woodpeckers rarely fly far or on a schedule corresponding to the seasons. All except the South African ground woodpecker (*Geocolaptes olivaceus*) use the beak to make nest cavities in large trees.

The largest woodpeckers, which feed on carpenter ants in large, dead standing trees, are in danger of extinction because suitable forests are getting fewer: the imperial woodpecker (*Campephilus imperialis*), a 22-inch bird with a crest in Mexico; the ivory-billed (*C. principalis*), which once made the chips fly in the southeastern United States and Cuba; and the magellanic woodpecker (*C. magellanicus*) of southern South America. The sparrow-sized woodpeckers, such as the downy (*Dendrocopos pubescens*) of North America and the lesser spotted woodpecker (*D. minor*) of Europe are much more widespread and common.

The yellow-bellied sapsucker (*Sphyrapicus varius*), an 8½-inch bird of temperate North America, and

the 6 kinds of flickers (genus *Colaptes*) of America from Alaska to southern Chile are seen as transients in many regions between their nesting and wintering grounds. Two North American woodpeckers show peculiar habits, the red-headed (*Melanerpes erythrocephalus*) often pursuing insects on the wing in the manner of a flycatcher, and the California woodpecker (*Balanosphyra formicivora*) often embedding acorns in telephone poles. Order Piciformes, family Picidae.

WREN, any of 59 different kinds of small brownish birds with slender, slightly downcurved, pointed beaks, short, rounded wings, and comparatively large strong legs and feet. They fly fast, straight, and with a buzzing sound, and stand characteristically with tail upright. All but one are birds of the New World. The one (*Troglodytes troglodytes*), called the winter wren in America, is found in Eurasia from Iceland to Siberia, south to northern India and northwest Africa. The house wren (*T. aedon*), a 4½- to 5½-inch bird that nests readily in bird houses close to people, is distributed all the way from southern Canada to Tierra del Fuego.

The song of the wren is very melodious but exasperatingly repetitious and amazingly loud for so small a bird. The male is a good protector for nesting territory and young, often attacking birds much larger than itself, such as a bluebird or a swallow. Most wrens live on or near the ground, feeding on insects and worms that they find in the dense underbrush. Order Passeriformes, family Troglodytidae.

YAK, or grunting ox, a long-haired, heavy-bodied, cud-chewing mammal (*Bos grunniens*) native to the high regions of Tibet. A full-grown male may be 6 feet high at the shoulder and weigh nearly a ton, with widespreading horns. Wild yaks are blackish brown with a pale mark over the eye that gives them a sleepy appearance. Domesticated yaks are more varied in color, and serve docilely as beasts of burden; they are also a source of meat and milk. Yak hair is woven into fabrics and rope, and the tails are used for fly swatters. Order Artiodactyla, family Bovidae.

YELLOWLEGS, either of 2 American shorebirds with long, yellow legs. They are seen most often on migration or near the water of coastal marshes during the winter, for their breeding territory extends in a narrow band from Alaska across the southern end of Hudson Bay to southern Labrador and Newfoundland.

The greater yellowlegs (*Totanus melanoleucus*) winter along both oceanic coasts of the United States around the Gulf of Mexico and well down into the West Indies and Latin America. The lesser yellowlegs (*T. flavipes*), which have a straight rather than an upturned beak and are 11, not 15 inches long as are the greater yellowlegs, spend the cold months around the Gulf coast and in the West Indies southward to Patagonia. In

flight, these birds extend beak and long neck forward, and their legs stretch out behind. They wade about, capturing mollusks, aquatic insects, crustaceans, and some small fishes among water plants near shore. Order Charadriiformes, family Scolopacidae.

YELLOWTHROAT, an active olive-brown wood warbler with a yellow throat and a buff-colored breast, of which the male has a distinctive black mask on the face; both sexes differ from similar birds in having a whitish belly. Yellowthroats live in North America, frequenting the edges of swamps, marshes, and streams. They build a large cup-shaped nest of grasses and leaves, usually under a bush in a marsh.

The northern yellowthroat (*Geothlypis trichas*), formerly called the Maryland yellowthroat, has a loud song, *witchity-witchity-witch*, heard over most of the United States and Canada; it winters in the Gulf States, California, Latin America, and the West Indies. A Mexican bird that does not migrate, the Rio Grande yellowthroat (*Chamaethlypis poliocephala*) is larger and vireolike; the black mask of the male is so small that it does not reach beyond the eye. Order Passeriformes, family Parulidae.

ZEBRA. See *Ass.*

—Lorus J. Milne, Margery Milne

For Further Reference

Allen, Glover M. *Birds and Their Attributes.* Peter Smith, 1962.

Bellairs, Angus d'A. *Reptiles* (2nd Ed.). Hillary House, 1968.

Buchsbaum, Ralph M., and Lorus J. Milne. *The Lower Animals: Living Invertebrates of the World.* Doubleday, 1960.

Burton, Maurice. *University Dictionary of Mammals of the World.* Crowell, 1968.

Cochran, Doris M. *Living Amphibians of the World.* Doubleday, 1961.

Herald, Earl S. *Living Fishes of the World.* Doubleday, 1961.

Kevles, Bettyann. *The Females of the Species: Sex and Survival in the Animal Kingdom.* Harvard University Press, 1986.

Mitchell, Larry. *Zoology.* Benjamin-Cummings, 1988.

Nowak, Ronald M., and John L. Paradiso. *Walker's Mammals of the World* (4th Ed.). Johns Hopkins University Press, 1983.

Palmer, Ephraim Laurence. *Fieldbook of Natural History.* McGraw-Hill, 1949.

Rothschild, Nathaniel Meyer. *Classification of Living Animals.* Wiley, 1961.

Schmidt, Karl P., and Robert F. Inger. *Living Reptiles of the World.* Doubleday, 1957.

Sussman, Maurice. *Growth and Development* (2nd Ed.). Prentice-Hall, 1964.

FRICK COLLECTION

TIME-LINE OF WESTERN ART

Period	Year	Painting	Sculpture	Architecture
MIDDLE AGES	1100			St. Sernin Church (1100) Chartres Cathedral (1150)
	1200			Ste. Chapelle (1250)
RENAISSANCE	1300	*Lamentation,* Giotto (1300)		
	1400	*February,* Limbourgs (1400) *Holy Trinity,* Masaccio (1425) *Arnolfini Wedding,* van Eyck (1434)	*David,* Donatello (1432)	Pazzi Chapel, Brunelleschi (1440) Palazzo Rucellai, Alberti (1457)
	1500	*Birth of Venus,* Botticelli (1490) Leonardo da Vinci (c 1505) Raphael (c 1505) Michelangelo (c 1510) *Madonna,* Parmigianino (1535) *Hunters,* Breughel (1560)	*David,* Michelangelo (1504) Fontainebleau (1540)	
BAROQUE	1600	*Daughters of Leucippus,* Rubens (1617) *Las Meninas,* Velasquez (1656) *Burial,* Poussin (1660) Rembrandt self-portraits (c 1660's)	*David,* Bernini (1640)	
ROCOCO AND NEOCLASSIC	1700	*Voyage to Cythera,* Watteau (1717) *Back From Market,* Boucher (1760's) *Lion & Horse,* Stubbs (1700) Gainsborough portraits (1770's)		Vierzehnheiligen Church (c 1745) Petit Trianon (c 1755) Monticello, Jefferson (1769)
ROMANTIC	1800	*Don Manuel Osorio,* Goya (c 1780) *Death of Marat,* David (1795) *Raft of Medusa,* Géricault (1818) *Woman & Parrot,* Manet (1866) Cezanne landscapes (1880's)	*The Dance,* Carpeaux (1860's) *Walking Man,* Rodin (1890's)	Crystal Palace (1850)
MODERN	1900	*Demoiselles D'Avignon,* Picasso (1907) *Red Studio,* Matisse (1911) Mondrian (1920's) *Harlequin's Carnival,* Miró (1930's) *Autumn Rhythm,* Pollock (1945)	*Bird in Space,* Brancusi (1918)	Fallingwater, F. Lloyd Wright (1920's) Seagram Bldg., Mies van der Rohe (1955) Notre Dame du Haut, Le Corbusier (1955)
	2000	*Protractor Variation V,* Stella (1960's)	*Cubi XVIII,* Smith (1964)	

YOUNG WOMAN WITH A WATER JUG, JOHANNES VERMEER (1632-75): THE METROPOLITAN MUSEUM OF ART, GIFT OF HENRY G. MARQUAND, 1889

VOLUME **2**
Art

METROPOLITAN MUSEUM OF ART
BEQUEST OF MRS. H.O. HAVEMEYER, 1929

METROPOLITAN MUSEUM OF ART
THE CLOISTERS COLLECTION, PURCHASE, 1925

FRENCH GOVERNMENT TOURIST OFFICE

NATURHISTORISCHES MUSEUM, WIEN

MUSEUM OF FINE ARTS, BOSTON
GIFT OF HORACE L. MAYER

The origins of art are cloaked in mystery and magic. About 20,000 years ago, in the period called the Old Stone Age, people painted images of wild animals on the walls of the caves in which they lived. Man had not yet learned how to plant crops or raise livestock, and had to depend on hunting for food. Armed with only crude wooden and stone weapons, men spent their days stalking ferocious wooly bisons, mammoths, and wild cattle. Their success was essential: if they failed in the hunt, they would starve.

Gradually, cavemen progressed from crude scratchings in stone to huge and spectacular color paintings, some of which are over 18 feet long. By outlining the figures with the end of a charred stick and shading them with natural colors from the earth (reds, yellows, and browns), cavemen produced some of the most powerful works of art in all of man's history.

Many of the paintings are located so far away from the mouths of the caves that they can only be reached by crawling great distances through dark, winding tunnels. In fact, many have only recently—and accidentally—been discovered. The paintings of Lascaux in France, for example, were found in 1940 by a group of boys searching for their lost dog. The pet

had fallen through a hole in the ground into the cave.

Since these paintings were too inaccessible to be mere decoration, we believe they formed part of a hunting ritual. There is evidence that cavemen actually hurled spears at these paintings. Primitive man probably believed that by conquering the painted image, he somehow gained control over the animal itself. At the same time, perhaps the caveman conquered his own fear of the beast.

Once the image was "killed," it had no more value. An animal could not be killed twice, and neither could a painted image. So each time the cavemen set out on a hunt, they had to repeat the whole process. This explains the more than 500 different animals painted on the cave walls at Lascaux.

In addition to their "killing" power, these paintings also may have had "creating" power. Europe's climate was growing warmer and the great animal herds were migrating north. Cavemen may have painted animals with the hope of increasing their dwindling supply.

At any rate, it took a great deal of talent to paint such lifelike pictures, and there may have been certain people who specialized in creating these vivid images. These artists may have

worked their magic in the caves while others did the actual hunting.

Cavemen were also concerned with reproducing. Since life was short and uncertain, and success in the hunt depended on numbers, men and women knew the importance of having children. They made small stone fertility figures to help assure the propagation and birth of healthy offspring. The most famous of these magical charms is the Venus of Willendorf. She is four and a half inches long and can be held easily in the palm of one's hand. Her big hips, heavy breasts, and protruding belly make her appear pregnant. She is only one of about 60 similar figures that have been discovered by archaeologists. No two of these statuettes are exactly the same, but they all emphasize female sexuality. They represent the Great Mother who was entrusted with giving birth to the next generation.

About 8000 B.C. the Old Stone Age was ended by a slowly developing revolution. In the past, men had to hunt and gather food wherever they could find it. But gradually they learned to control their environment. They grew crops and raised cattle. And with their food supply assured, they settled in small communities, and so began the long history of civilization.

WESTERN ART

Western art is the name we give to the long, continuous tradition that began with ancient civilizations around the Mediterranean Sea. In the 5000 years since the birth of civilization in Egypt and Sumeria, many nations and peoples have produced works of art that still influence our ideas today.

The spirit of innovation passed from the Egyptians and Sumerians to the ancient Greeks and later to the powerful Romans. From them, the disciplines of painting, sculpture, and architecture passed to the new countries of Europe and eventually to the New World as well. At every step, new tribes and peoples made their own contribution. The art of the West is wonderfully various, yet at the same time it is the product of a single long and distinguished tradition.

Ancient Art

Egypt

"Egypt is the gift of the Nile." That is how Herodotus, the ancient Greek historian, described the land of the pharaohs. The Nile is the longest river in the world, and it was Egypt's major means of transportation and communication. More important, it left rich deposits of alluvial soil along its banks each spring, giving the Egyptians fertile land to plant.

Egypt, protected from her enemies by thousands of miles of desert, developed in secure isolation. There was a sense of permanence and order in this land of blazing sun, and this sense is clearly reflected in the art of the ancient Egyptians.

The history of the Egyptian nation begins about 5000 years ago when King Menes (also called Narmer) began the first of Egypt's 31 dynasties (ruling families). He did this by uniting its many small kingdoms under his own powerful rule. This important event is recorded on his palette, a ceremonial plate used for mixing eye makeup (the Egyptians painted their eyes to protect them from the glare of the sun).

The back of the palette (shown here) represents the victorious king wearing the tall crown of Upper Egypt. He prepares to kill his fallen enemy, while two other captives sprawl at his feet. To the right of the king, a hawk (who represents the god Horus) perches on a clump of papyrus (symbolizing Lower Egypt), and holds an enemy's head by a rope. This pictogram is another symbol of Menes's conquest over Lower Egypt. At the top of the palette, the king's name is written in hieroglyphics between two images of Hathor, the cow goddess.

On the opposite side of the palette,

the situation is reversed and Menes, now wearing the crown of Lower Egypt, conquers the Upper Kingdom. The Narmer palette thus symbolizes the union of the country, and from this time forward, all pharaohs wore double crowns and called themselves "kings of Upper and Lower Egypt."

CULVER PICTURES

THE PALETTE OF NARMER, *Egypt, created c 3000 B.C., portrays the ancient king about to kill an enemy. Showing human faces in profile is characteristic of early Egyptian art.*

The palette is important both as a historical document and as a work of art. It set a standard for all future paintings and relief sculptures of important Egyptian people. The king's eye and shoulders are seen from the front, but his head, waist, and legs are

viewed from the side. The artist adopted this formula so that he could show the most important parts of the body as he *knew* them to be, not just as he *saw* them in a fleeting glance. As a result, the figure has a peculiar, but permanent, look about him.

This concern with permanence can be traced to the Egyptians' view of eternal life. They believed that when a person died, his soul would continue to live as long as his body was preserved. This explains why the Egyptians made mummies. Life in the next world was to be a happier existence. To insure this, the Egyptians filled their tombs with all manner of goods including furniture, clothing, games, and even food. They also painted the tomb walls with beautiful and realistic pictures of the dead person's land, family, and slaves so that his spirit would never be in want. Of course, the most lavishly appointed tombs were those of the pharaohs, or kings.

The Egyptians believed that their pharaoh was a god. They also believed that everything, from the rising of the sun to the flooding of the Nile, depended on divine favor, so they took great measures to assure that the pharaoh's spirit would be content.

The Egyptians poured their nation's wealth into the construction of tombs for their kings. These great royal tombs went through a long period of evolution. They probably began as great mounds of earth and gradually grew into the standard form of *mastaba* (the Arabic word for "bench"). A *mastaba* is a rectangular flat-topped monument with sloping sides and a deep shaft leading to the subterranean burial chamber.

The next step was a giant one, and it came circa 2750 B.C. when King Zoser planned his eternal dwelling at Saqqara. King Zoser's resting place was built by Imhotep, the first known architect in history. By stacking six mastabas on top of one another, with the largest on the bottom and the smallest at the top, Imhotep created a "stepped pyramid": a staircase to heaven 195 feet high.

Amazing as this was, the pyramid was still only one part of the most imposing architectural complex the world had ever seen. Imhotep surrounded the pyramid with duplicates of the temples, chambers, and courtyards that King Zoser had used in his lifetime, but now their purpose was purely magical. Most of the buildings were stone dummies and were completely filled with earth and debris. The huge wall that encloses the complex, for example, has 14 massive gates, but only one of them is real. The others serve the spirit by magic.

In this brilliant architectural complex, Imhotep created the first monumental stone buildings in the world. The durability of stone was ideally suited to the eternal preservation of Zoser's body, and it became the standard building material for all future tombs. Stone was never used for houses of the living. At Saqqara, Imhotep united the past, the present, and the future for all eternity. His accomplishment was considered so great that the Egyptians came to consider him as a god.

Roughly a century after Saqqara, geometric purity was achieved during the Fourth Dynasty by smoothing out the sides of a stepped pyramid. The result was the Great Pyramid of Cheops, the first and largest of the three pyramids of Giza near present-day Cairo. Unlike Zoser, who built his stepped tomb in the center of his magical palace, Cheops set great gateways and temples in front of the pyramid where he was to purify his soul before its journey to the next world.

The sheer size and perfection of the pyramid give us some idea of the incomparable Egyptian genius for design and engineering. More than 2,300,000 limestone blocks were cut from nearby quarries, floated across the Nile at high tide, and then dragged by slaves to the building site. Most of the stones weigh about two and a half tons, but there are some that reach the staggering weight of almost 50 tons!

Because the wheel had not yet been invented, huge gangs of laborers were forced to drag these heavy stones up temporary ramps and to lay them one on top of the other, course by course. When all the blocks were in place, the entire pyramid was faced with gleaming white limestone, so finely finished that one can barely detect the joints between the stones.

After many long years of work by untold thousands of slaves, the pyramid was completed. It was a man-made mountain measuring 755 feet on a side, and so perfectly oriented that each of its corners was exactly aligned with one of the four cardinal points (north, south, east, and west). The towering mass of the pyramid, so simple and so pure, soared almost 500 feet into the sky and totally dominated the surrounding desert. It was a symbol to all the world of the ultimate power of the pharaoh who lay buried in the center of the gigantic tomb.

Cheops's building activities were continued and even surpassed by his successor Chephren, who built the second pyramid at Giza. Chephren also created the famous 240-foot-long sphinx. This monumental stone figure, with the body of a lion and the head of a king (probably Chephren himself), was carved from a rocky bluff near the tomb. But what is the significance of this great monster? The answer is probably to be found in an ancient Egyptian myth that tells of a ferocious lion who guarded the gates of the underworld. Chephren adopted the body of the king of beasts in order to keep an eternal guard at his own tomb.

Despite all of their precautions, the Egyptians were not always successful in protecting the pharaoh's body, and in many cases the pyramids were broken into almost immediately after they were sealed. This, of course, destroyed the entire purpose of the pyramids. Their massive size was supposed to protect the pharaoh's body. In practice, they told thieves exactly where the royal treasures were buried. By the end of the Fourth Dynasty, fewer pyramids were being built, and these were generally smaller and much less conspicuous than those at Giza.

PYRAMIDS: top, *the plan for Zoser's pyramid with its surrounding temples and courtyards, c 2750 B.C. Below, a 19th-century view of the Sphinx and the great pyramids at Giza, c 2615–2500 B.C. The men on the foot of the Sphinx give an idea of its enormous size. The largest of the pyramids covers an area equal to 19 football fields and is nearly fifty stories high.*

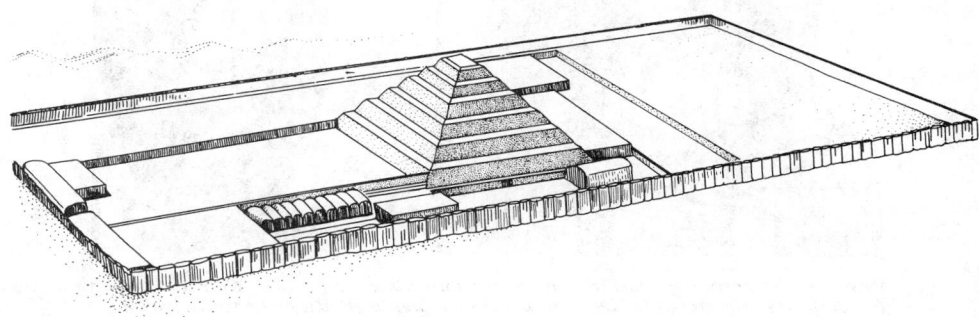

DON LORIMER

PHARAOHS: *portrait statues of Mycerinus and his wife (c 2575 B.C.) and of Amenhotep (c 1350 B.C.). Mycerinus is idealized, but Amenhotep is shown as he really looked.*

The third and last of the pyramids at Giza was built by Mycerinus, who is seen here with his wife Kha-merer-nebty. The king and queen take a step forward, but they are held captive in the stone block from which they were carved. Stone even fills in the spaces that we might normally expect to be open (like those between the pharaoh's arm and body). This "extra" stone strengthened the statue and protected it against breakage. Today we can appreciate how effective this measure was because the statue is still intact after more than 4000 years.

The stiff and immobile formality of the king and queen expresses the Egyptian ideal of royal majesty. All imperfections like scars or wrinkles have been eliminated in order to portray the couple as perfect. This was only appropriate for an Egyptian pharaoh, who was a god and was thus perfect by definition.

About 2300 B.C. the pharaohs lost their claim to absolute authority. Many powerful officials fought for control of the government and Egypt was plunged into a dark age. During these dark years the Hyksos, an Asiatic people, attacked and subdued the country. They introduced horses, chariots, and new weapons.

In about 1570 B.C. the Egyptians cast out the invaders and ushered in the New Kingdom, characterized by great geographic expansion for Egypt and unparalleled brilliance in the arts. At first, painting, sculpture, and architecture in the New Kingdom generally adhered to the rigid standards set up some 2000 years earlier.

Then, circa 1370 B.C., Amenhotep IV became pharaoh. In an absolutely revolutionary gesture, he forbade worship of the hundreds of Egyptian gods except for one. This was Aten, the sun god. The pharaoh closed all of the old temples and built an entirely new city (near the present Tel el-Amarna) for the exclusive worship of the sun god.

One of the effects of this religious revolution was a new interest in life in this world. And there was a consequent change in art. We can see this immediately when we compare the portrait of Amenhotep with the earlier one of Mycerinus and his queen. Previously, the pharaoh was seen as a divine king, with a strong and perfect body. But Amenhotep was depicted as he really looked: strangely shaped, with full hips, flabby belly, and a dreamy expression on his egg-shaped face. He was an impersonal and ideal king no longer. The flail and scepter,

symbols of royalty, were now possessed by a man with imperfections. The pharaoh was portrayed with real emotions and his own individual personality. Realism had taken the place of idealism.

After the death of Amenhotep, this naturalistic phase in Egyptian art gradually came to a close, and artists returned to the traditional styles of stiff and monumental depiction.

After 1100 B.C., the kingdom fell into decline, and Egypt became a group of competing states. For the next 2000 years, the country was often controlled by foreign powers. It was conquered in its turn by the Assyrians, the Persians, the armies of Alexander the Great, and the Romans. After the fall of Rome, Egypt became a part of the Byzantine Empire. Finally, in 642 A.D., it fell to the Arabs and gradually became a part of the Islamic world.

Few of the conquerors of Egypt were left untouched by its heritage of art. In all the centuries of foreign domination, the beauty of Egypt's art was prized throughout the Western world, and its ideals influenced the art of many other nations.

The Middle East

Even as the civilization of Egypt grew and prospered, another center of civilization was developing some 500 miles to the north and east. It was the first of a succession of Middle Eastern civilizations that would deeply influence the future of art.

Mesopotamia. Where was the birthplace of civilization? Egypt is one possible place, but an equally strong case can be made for Mesopotamia, the plain between the Tigris and Euphrates rivers in present-day Iraq. Both of these early civilizations relied on agriculture made possible by fertile river valleys. By 3000 B.C., both had produced wealthy and highly sophisticated cultures. But this is where the similarities end.

Egypt was well protected by its desert boundaries, but Mesopotamia had no natural defenses. Its luxuriant plain was open to attack from all sides. Over the centuries, one nomadic tribe after another swept down on Mesopotamia and conquered it. The history of the region is a seemingly endless story of upheavals, invasions, and wars.

The "Mesopotamians" were not a distinct people. They were a mix of conquering and conquered tribes who settled in this rich land. The earliest of these tribes was the Sumerians. The Sumerians settled in the northern part of Mesopotamia before 3000 B.C.

They were a fascinating and inquisitive race: they invented the potter's wheel and one of the earliest forms of

A SUMERIAN STELA, *an illustrated legal document with cuneiform writing.*

writing known to man. This is cuneiform, a language written by making small wedge-shaped marks on a soft clay tablet. Clay, in fact, was the only material available to the Sumerians in any quantity. Unlike Egypt, Mesopotamia had no stone or timber, so its inhabitants had to build their homes and temples with sun-dried mud bricks.

Great temple complexes that were dominated by ziggurats, enormous brick "stairways to heaven," were most characteristic of Sumerian architecture. Rising several stories, and reached by steep flights of steps, these gigantic manmade mountains were crowned by religious shrines. They were the Mesopotamian counterpart of the Egyptian pyramids. But the only remains of these once glorious structures are crumbling piles of earth. Unfortunately, mud bricks are far less durable than stone.

If we are lacking in Sumerian architectural remains, we are not lacking in their precious musical instruments, finely crafted goldwork, and small statuettes of gods and worshippers. The Sumerians were a deeply religious people, and the success of their civilization required them to spend great amounts of time praying to their gods. But they were also businessmen whose schedules would not permit their constant attendance at temple. The solution to this rather sticky problem was "worship by proxy." That is, the Sumerians deposited small statues in the temples to substitute for the absent person. The effect was the same as if the businessman were there himself. These little figures were often inscribed with short prayers, and they communicated with the gods through their enormous staring eyes.

By about 2360 B.C., the Sumerians had united with the Akkadians to establish an illustrious and powerful empire. But within a few hundred years, it was destroyed by the Amorite Semites who, in turn, were overcome by new waves of invaders. After centuries of turmoil, the great city of Babylon came into being. It introduced a magnificence previously unknown to Mesopotamia. Babylon was founded by Hammurabi, author of the world's first written code of laws, circa 1780 B.C. Civilized, powerful, and spectacular, Babylon became the cultural center of Mesopotamia.

Within a few short centuries, however, this brilliant civilization was devastated by the ruthless Hittites. Subsequent invasions brought the ferocious Kassites and later, the most terrifying of all, the dreaded Assyrians. The warlike Assyrians also built enormous fortresses in order to consolidate their widespread conquests. Strangely, the Assyrians produced some very great artists who brought the art of carving in low relief to unprecedented heights.

The favorite themes of the Assyrians were military campaigns and animal hunts, which show noble beasts collapsing under Assyrian attack. Exquisitely carved wild horses attempt escape and caged lions are mercilessly slaughtered. The Assyrians delighted in showing pain, and they used their unparalleled skills of observation to portray agonized animals, bleeding and weak, their energies exhausted from the chase. Assyrian art was cruel, but it was more realistic and more vividly rendered than any other in the ancient world; it introduced emotion into art.

This is seen most compellingly in the sculptural relief on this page. The *Dying Lioness,* pierced by arrows and bleeding heavily, attempts to stand. But her back legs are paralyzed and they drag heavily behind her. Powerful forepaws bulge with exertion. She lets out a final roar; in a moment she will die.

After roughly three centuries of unthinkable atrocities, the Assyrians were defeated in the sixth century B.C. by the combined forces of their abused subjects and neighbors. Babylon rose again, more fabulous than ever. Under the rule of King Nebuchadnezzar, the city enjoyed great prosperity as an international trade center, and it became the greatest metropolis of the East. The king created the famous Hanging Gardens of Babylon, one of the Seven Wonders of the World. This spectacular structure was built of mud bricks, and like all Mesopotamian architecture, almost nothing of it remains.

One of the very few extant structures is the Ishtar Gate, the major entrance to Babylon. It, too, was made of mud bricks, but it was protected by a covering of brightly colored glazed bricks, boldly ornamented with lions, bulls, and dragons.

In the sixth century B.C., the Persians became the dominant Eastern power, and essentially ended the complicated, but brilliant, history of ancient Mesopotamia.

The Persians had been a seminomadic tribe with no great interest in art. But when their leader was proclaimed the new "king of Babylon" he sought an art worthy of the distinction. Gradually, an authentic imperial art evolved, combining Mesopotamian traditions, the native Persian love of ornament, and inspiration from Greek artists. The effects of this marriage can be best appreciated at Persepolis, the site of the most ambitious Persian palace.

The palace is an enormous structure, more than a quarter-mile long and nearly 1000 feet wide. It is approached by a broad staircase, the walls of which are carved with an endless procession of figures paying tribute to the king. Inside, the palace's

DYING LIONESS, *an Assyrian relief sculpture, c 650 B.C., shows the wounded animal with both realism and a sense of admiration.*

gold and silver ceilings rest on gigantic animal figures that are carved atop lofty columns.

Persian power and wealth were world renowned. In less than 50 years, the Persians were transformed from a nomadic tribe into the most powerful people on Earth. In 525 B.C. they conquered Egypt; they might have taken possession of Europe as well had it not been for the heroic resistance of the Greeks. The Persians were finally humbled in the fourth century B.C. by Alexander the Great.

The Minoans. According to a Greek myth, the island of Crete was once ruled by a powerful king named Minos. (It is from him that the Minoans take their name.) The king's wife had given birth to a Minotaur, a terrible monster that was half man and half bull. The king was so embarrassed that he imprisoned the beast in a large maze, or labyrinth. Every seven years, the minotaur required the sacrifice of 14 young men and women. Finally, according to the myth, the Greek hero Theseus killed the Minotaur and ended his tyranny over the island.

This was virtually all that the later Greeks knew about the Minoans. Until about 80 years ago, there was not much that could be added to this. Then, in one of the most spectacular discoveries ever made, the British archaeologist Sir Arthur Evans uncovered the vast Minoan labyrinth!

It did not contain a Minotaur, but it did contain a wealth of information about this ancient culture. As the excavation proceeded, it became clear that the legendary maze was, in fact, the sprawling palace of King Minos in the capital city of Knossos. The palace

covered over four acres and included a marketplace and even a town, all arranged in a helter-skelter pattern. It's no wonder that the Greeks called it a labyrinth.

The palace was unfortified. It seems that the Minoans, unlike almost every other ancient peoples, were not warriors. Instead, they were sailors and merchants. They lived prosperous and happy lives, and enjoyed singing, dancing, and games. Their standard of living far surpassed that of any contemporary civilization. The palace had flush toilets, running water, and a sophisticated system of ventilation. It was decorated with colorful paintings which, in their gaily flowing lines, expressed the Minoan joy of life. These paintings are strikingly different from those of the brooding Egyptians who painted the walls of tombs for the sake of the dead.

The so-called *Toreador Fresco* on this page gives some idea of the Minoans' life-loving attitude. Surrounded by a highly decorative border, two girls stand behind and before a charging bull as a boy somersaults over its back. This dangerous display was part of a religious ceremony (perhaps related to the Minotaur). But rather than stressing the hazards involved, the artist has concentrated on the playful and ornamental vitality of the scene. The same feeling characterizes virtually all Minoan art, including its beautiful pottery.

By about 2000 B.C., the Minoan civilization was already highly sophisticated. In the following centuries, it suffered several serious earthquakes, but the people were resilient and the Minoans continued to thrive—that is, until circa 1400 B.C., when the Minoans mysteriously disappeared.

The Mycenaeans. Minoan traders often traveled to the shores of mainland Greece. Their art and civilization influenced its inhabitants, the people we call the Mycenaeans.

The Greek mainland did not have rich deposits of gold, yet the Mycenaeans amassed such vast treasures of this precious metal that 700 years later, the Greek poet Homer would describe it as "Mycenae, rich in gold." But where did the gold come from? All indications point to Egypt. It seems that the Mycenaeans were good fighters and had been paid in gold to fight as mercenaries for Egyptian warlords. The Mycenaeans' fame as warriors was later celebrated by Homer in his great epics, the *Iliad* and the *Odyssey*.

Much of our knowledge about the Mycenaeans comes from their tombs, which were filled with sumptuous treasures. These included beautiful gold cups imported from Crete, daggers inlaid with gold and silver, and death masks attached to the heads of mummified princes. These masks of finely beaten gold are powerful portrait studies of the deceased. The Mycenaeans' elaborate concern for their dead suggests that they were strongly influenced by the Egyptians.

Unlike Minoan sovereigns who lived in free-flowing unprotected palaces, Mycenaean kings lived in massive fortresses. In fact, one Mycenaean city was known as "Tiryns of the Great Walls," and was revered by the ancients as the birthplace of the legendary hero of strength, Hercules. These walls, built with huge boulders, were often 20 feet thick! This caused later Greeks to assume that they were built by the Cyclops, a mythical race of one-eyed giants.

When one approaches Mycenae, the

MINOAN AND MYCENAEAN: *the* Toreador Fresco (left) *was painted by the Minoans c 1500 B.C., but was only rediscovered in the present century. The* Lion Gate (right) *was the entrance to the Mycenaean capital in Greece, c 1300 B.C.*

capital of the Mycenaean world, he is confronted by the monumental Lion Gate. Colossal stones, some weighing as much as 18 tons, were used to construct this grand entrance. On top of the doorway is a triangular panel sculpted with mighty lions on either side of a column. This is the first example of large stone sculpture in Greek art.

Guardian lions were a common feature in both Egyptian and Mesopotamian sculpture, but combining these lions with massive defensive walls probably finds its origins with the Hittites, one of the ferocious tribes that invaded Mesopotamia. In the hands of the Mycenaeans, this motif becomes a coat of arms appropriate to conquering soldiers. It shows an alliance of the great: the kings of beasts protecting the kings of men.

Passing through the Lion Gate, a visitor would follow a path to the king's palace, or megaron. This great rectangular hall was the basic form from which the Greek temple evolved.

Mycenaean civilization flourished until the twelfth century B.C., when, during the Dorian invasion, barbarian tribes swept across Europe. Even the invincible Mycenaeans crumbled under the force of this onslaught.

The Dorian invasion signaled the end of Mycenaean power and introduced the Dark Age of Greece. People fled frantically from the invaders: some sailed to Asia Minor, others escaped to the Greek mountains, while still others simply met their deaths. Civilization all but came to an end. No buildings were constructed, almost no painting or sculpture was produced, and even the art of writing was lost. But in these bleak centuries, some important developments were taking place behind the scenes.

The Greeks

From the twelfth to the eighth century B.C., the inhabitants of present-day Greece settled into small communities for their common protection. Gradually, these scattered settlements developed into city-states. Each city-state was a separate entity, with its own government, its own code of laws, and its own distinct personality. There was no great king to unite them, so throughout their long history the city-states intermittently fought each other on the most bitter terms. But they had formed a sense of national identity based on a common language and some common values. In 776 B.C., these Greek-speaking city-states held their first Olympic games. From then on, all wars and rivalries were suspended temporarily every four years so they could once again compete in the sacred games.

Greece is a rugged country with mountains that touch the sky and ra-

vines that seem to plunge to the center of the earth. It is of little surprise, then, that the earliest Greeks worshipped these natural wonders. But during the Dark Age a very important change took place: the gods were given human forms and personalities. In fact, they were frequently only distinguishable from humans by their immortality.

GREEK VASE, *c 750 B.C., is decorated with a stylized funeral scene shown in detail below.*

METROPOLITAN MUSEUM OF ART, ROGERS FUND

In the past, man had lived in a world dominated by wild beasts. He fought them, ate them, was fearful of them, and worshipped them. But in Greece, man was elevated above the entire animal kingdom because of his intelligence. This recognition of man's innate worth changed the course of history, and laid the foundations for democracy, philosophy, poetry, medicine, and law, not to mention a totally humanistic style of art.

Man the rational being became the primary focus of Greek art. The Hellenes (as the Greeks called themselves) attempted to create the perfect mind and body, and thus paved the way for the concept of beauty held by the Western world. We still hold these same values, 2500 years later.

The creation of an ideal human form did not take place overnight. It evolved slowly over the course of centuries. We might expect to trace this development in painting styles, but unfortunately almost all Greek paintings have been lost to time. Instead, we must look to pottery.

The Greeks used clay vessels for many different purposes. Some were used to carry water, others contained oil, and still others were used to store wine, honey, or grain. Each of these vases had its own name and characteristic shape. For example, the vase on this page is called a "krater." It was designed with a large opening at the top to facilitate the blending of wine and water (the Greeks never drank their wine undiluted).

This krater is one of the earliest Greek vases to come down to us. Al-

most the entire surface is covered with geometric ornament, horse-drawn chariots, and people with triangular torsos. It shows an ancient funeral, with the deceased person lying on a bed, surrounded by mourners who tear at their hair in despair. At this early date, the artist is still treating human form as an element of geometric decoration, but more important is the fact that he is attempting to show human emotion. From the beginning, Greek artists were interested in the way man feels.

In the following centuries vase paintings were constantly refined, and more and more attention was paid to the realistic portrayal of people. Ultimately, convincing scenes of men and gods constituted the entire decorative scheme, and abstract ornamentation was used only sparingly for borders. By the fifth century B.C., painted Greek ceramics had reached their peak of popularity and were collected throughout the ancient world.

Architecture. Like vase painting, Greek architecture went through an evolutionary process that began in the Dark Age. Once the gods were given human form, they had to be sheltered in human houses. But the homes of ordinary mortals were entirely too humble. So the Greeks looked to their ancient ancestors, the Mycenaeans, and took the form of the king's megaron from them. It was a very simple structure with upright tree trunks topped by horizontal beams. This is a basic post and lintel

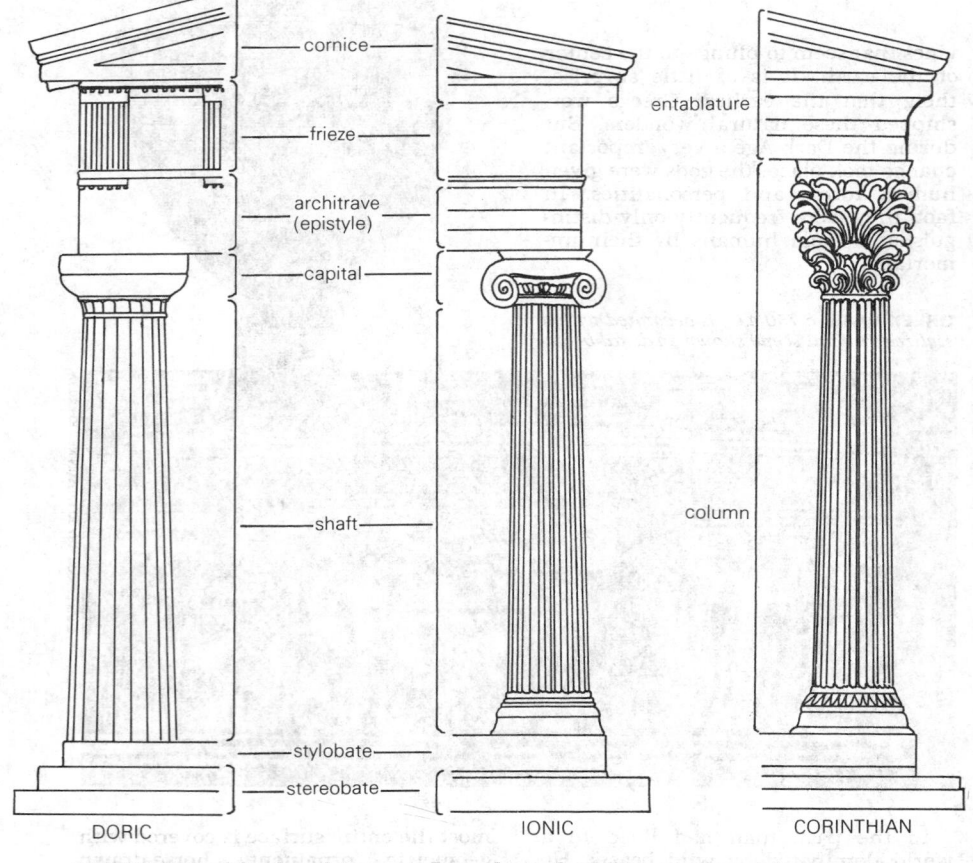

cornice
frieze
architrave (epistyle)
capital
shaft
stylobate
stereobate

entablature

column

DORIC   IONIC   CORINTHIAN

THE ORDERS of Greek architecture—Doric, Ionic, Corinthian—governed the proportions and decoration of columns as well as the design of whole structures.

system of construction. It was the standard for future Greek architecture.

The crudeness of early Greek temples was gradually refined. Under Egyptian influence, stone was substituted for wood, and an elaborate system of proportions was established. The Greeks believed that "all things were in the measure of man." This applied to their gods, paintings, sculpture, and also to their architecture.

Man's body is proportional. That is, the size of his arms, legs, head, etc., are all related so that none is too big or too small. The Greeks planned their temples in much the same way, with every part related to all the others, and all parts related to man. For example, the base of a column is equivalent to man's foot, the column itself is equal to his body, and the uppermost portion relates to his head. These relationships gave Greek buildings life and the hope of perfection. The concept of proportion was as important to the Greeks as "eternity" was to the Egyptians.

Greek temples are based on the Doric, Ionic, and Corinthian orders. The very fact that they are called "orders" tells us that they are sets of rules that control the entire arrangement or order of a temple.

Each order has its own characteristics, which determine not only the size and shape of the columns and capitals (the uppermost portions of the pillars), but also the spacing of the columns, and even the type of ornaments applied to the building. The orders are based on complex systems of geometrical proportion, but they also have human correspondences. For example, the Doric order, which is austere and generally undecorated, was considered to be the masculine warrior. The delicate Ionic, with its gently spiraling capital, was the matron, and the slender and ornate Corinthian was the young maiden.

The Greeks used the orders to regulate and give life to their temples. They were considered so important that Greek architects rarely deviated from them. Indeed, the orders still continue to exert their influence after 2500 years. Even the most casual glance will find their influence on our government buildings, banks, courthouses, and churches.

The most brilliant use of the orders is seen in the Parthenon, an enormous temple built in the fifth century B.C., the Golden Age of Greece. In plan and construction, it is as perfect a building as is humanly possible to create. It stands on the acropolis ("high city") above modern Athens.

The original Parthenon was destroyed by the Persians in 480 B.C., but it was rebuilt by the Greek tyrant Pericles upon their defeat. No expense was spared. Built entirely of pure white marble, the temple cost more than 18 tons of gold. But it is not just the materials or cost that make the Parthenon so famous.

The architects, Ictinus and Callicrates, created a building where all elements are in perfect harmony. They did this by using curved lines. Had they used straight lines, the temple, high on the hill, would appear distorted when approached from below. So they "adjusted" every part. For instance, the columns slant back even though they look straight, and the roof and floor are not really level, but actually convex. There are dozens of similar adjustments in the Parthenon, all of which give it the appearance of perfect equilibrium. The architects created the near-perfect humanistic building by combining the best materials, the most careful planning, and the sacred orders with a profound understanding of the way man sees.

THE PARTHENON, the most brilliant surviving example of Greek architecture, was completed in 433 B.C. It is shown here in a photograph from the early 1900's. The floor plan, showing columns and interior walls, is at left.

Sculpture. The humanistic qualities of Greek art are most clearly seen in sculpture. As early as the seventh century B.C., Greek artists, under the influence of Egypt, were producing large standing statues of people, one of their favorites being the kouros, a standing male youth. These figures were not quite gods, but neither were they mere men. They were heroes, semidivine figures who, like the gods, possessed perfect bodies.

The kouros on this page is from an early stage of Greek sculpture. Like Egyptian sculpted figures, this figure has broad shoulders, a pinched waist, an extended left foot, and a general anatomical rigidity. Instead of gently modeling the youth's muscles, the sculptor has outlined them with stiff, almost geometric boundaries. This is particularly visible in the way the stomach and kneecaps are treated. The position of the arms, held close to the body, adds to the figure's stiffness. But if this kouros shares strong similarities with earlier sculpture, it also looks forward to a totally new style.

One of the most obvious differences is the figure's nakedness (Egyptian statues were always clothed). Even at this early stage, Greek sculptors were interested in the beauty of the human form. But even more important is the fact that all the "extra" stone has been cut away from the figure, leaving it to stand free. Unlike Egyptian statues, it has no reinforcing stone slab behind it, and no stone fill between the arms and body and between the legs. This archaic kouros has taken a giant step toward "modern" free-standing forms of sculpture.

We can follow the growth of this humanizing tendency in the early classical image of the *Charioteer*. Originally, the *Charioteer* was part of a group statue with horses and a chariot. The statue was probably made to celebrate a victorious horse race. Admittedly, there is still a certain stiffness here, and the lower part of the athlete's skirt looks almost like a Greek column. But in every other respect, the figure has come to life. His arm reaches out to hold the reins of the now-missing chariot while his curly hair falls delicately to the sides of his face. His dark eyes are made of glass paste, and they warm his serious expression. Even the top part of his dress suggests a certain natural movement. His shoulders are slightly tilted and the drapery falls into soft folds. Natural textures of hair, skin, and cloth are realistically distinguished.

By the middle of the fifth century B.C., Greek sculpture had reached its Golden Age. The ever-threatening Persian troops were finally defeated, and Athens started to rebuild her temples on the acropolis. It was an era of wealth and optimism, a period when democracy flourished and art matured. By now sculptors had solved their early problems of naturalistic depiction. In place of former stiffness, muscular bodies gracefully bend. Sculptures are noble and quiet. A period of classical calm has set in.

The statue of Doryphorus by Polyclitos exemplifies this peak in Greek sculpture. Because Doryphorus rests his weight on only one leg, his hips and shoulders tilt slightly and a long fluid S-shaped curve runs from his head down to his extended toes. He is a great athlete, perfectly formed and impressively powerful. There is no awkwardness or clumsiness here, just grace and beauty. Doryphorus was considered so perfect by the ancients that they established him as their standard of harmony and proportion.

The classical period of Greek art was short-lived. Old city-state rivalries between Athens and Sparta erupted into the devastating Peloponnesian War. By its end circa 400 B.C., Athens was

GREEK SCULPTURE: *from the early kouros (c 600 B.C.) to the charioteer (474 B.C.) to the great Doryphorus by Polyclitos (c 440), the Greeks moved from stylized figures toward lifelike perfection, mastering the human form.*

CULVER PICTURES

CULVER PICTURES

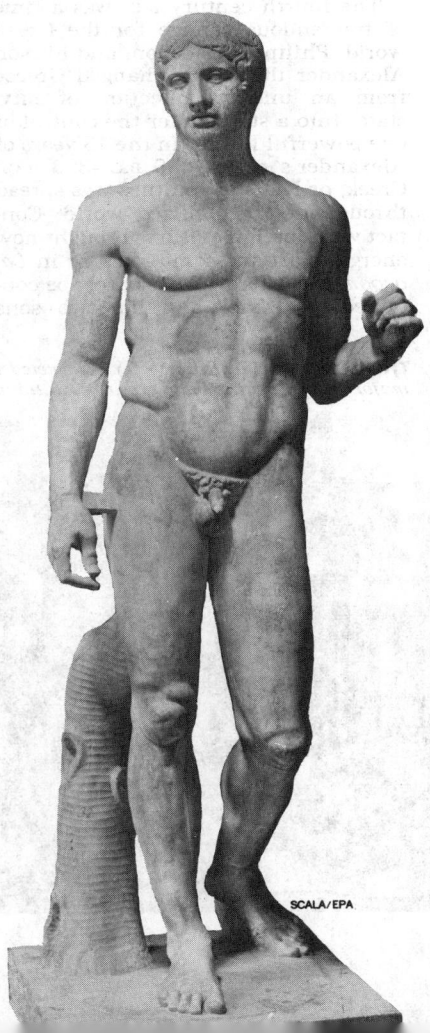

SCALA/EPA

LAOCOÖN, *made in Greece after 100 B.C., shows the Hellenic talent for dramatic sculpture.*

exhausted, the prosperity of Greece was on the decline, and art took a turn toward self-conscious grace and delicacy. The most famous sculptor of this time was Praxiteles, who created works of unparalleled charm and intimacy. But there were other artists of the fourth century B.C. who worked in a very different manner: they stressed explosive action and excitement.

The fourth century B.C. was a time of tremendous change for the Greek world. Philip of Macedon, and his son Alexander the Great, changed Greece from an uneasy collection of city-states into a state under the control of one powerful leader. In the 13 years of Alexander's reign (336 B.C.–323 B.C.) Greek, or Hellenic, culture was spread throughout the civilized world. Contact with foreign cultures brought new energy to art and sometimes, as in *Laocoön,* this energy could barely be contained. A father and his two sons

writhe in pain as they are attacked by serpents. They can barely maintain their balance in their desperate attempts to free themselves.

The sculptor's skill is extraordinary here, but he uses it emotionally to produce a work of violent contrasts and extravagant gestures. Unlike earlier Greek sculpture, where faces were idealized and expressionless, those of Laocoön and his sons are distorted by anguish and fright. Every part of the sculpture is electrified, even the clumps of hair that stand on end. Gone is the classical calm, gone is the ideal of man's control over nature. The height of Greek art and culture had passed. New forces were at work, and the world turned its eyes to Rome.

The Romans

Both Greece and Rome had their starts at roughly the same time. But Greek culture peaked with a brilliant climax in the fifth century B.C., while Rome was still a slowly developing hill town. In the following centuries, however, Roman military power grew and Rome began a systematic conquest of its neighbors. By the first century B.C., Rome was the leader of the world.

Early Roman life was dominated by the powerful Etruscans, who were fearsome warriors and inspired engineers. They were also gifted teachers who found receptive students in the Romans. In 509 B.C., the Romans defeated the Etruscans, using Etruscan weapons and military tactics.

One military victory followed another, until in 30 B.C. Rome became the unchallenged power of the entire Hellenistic world. The Greeks were totally subjected to Roman rule, but their culture exerted such a pervasive influence on Rome that one might well ask "who conquered whom?"

Architecture. The extent of Greek influence can be measured in the crowning glory of Roman architecture: the Pantheon in Rome. At first glance, the Pantheon looks exactly like a Greek temple, with eight huge columns crowned by a triangular pediment. But a closer look reveals that behind this classical facade are a large square block and an enormous domed cylinder. In typical fashion, the Romans took what they liked from Greek art and adapted it to their own needs. Greek and non-Greek forms are married here to produce something totally Roman and totally new: a vast interior space.

Previously, architects were only concerned with the exteriors of their buildings. Even the great temples of Greece were used like expensive stage sets. They were to be appreciated from the outside only. The interior was reserved for the gods. Today we are so accustomed to usable interiors that it is often difficult for us to imagine a time when this was not the case. With the development of interior space, the Romans turned architectural interest inside out, thus revolutionizing the course of building. Hereafter, architects would lavish considerable attention on how their buildings "worked."

When one passes through the great "Greek" porch of the Pantheon, one enters a different, totally unexpected world. The interior is a vast enclosed space, 140 feet high and just as wide. The ceiling is formed by a gigantic dome made from more than 5000 tons of poured concrete, pierced in the center by an oculus (round window), which is the only source of illumination. The entire composition is based on a complex relationship of circles and squares masterfully integrated through color and design.

The oldest roofed building in the world, the Pantheon is an eloquent expression of Roman culture: it reflects

THE PANTHEON *at Rome* (left), *completed in 125 A.D., resembles a Greek temple from the outside. But its vast interior space* (right) *was both a major feat of engineering and a revolutionary step in architecture.*

the passion for organization, the in-comparable engineering and architectural genius, and the authoritarian pretensions of the empire. Technically, the Pantheon was dedicated to all the gods, with its concrete dome as the dome of heaven. But it also symbolized expansive imperial extension.

Unlike the Egyptians and Greeks, who almost exclusively used stone in a post and lintel construction system, the Romans developed arches and vaults. Lacking natural stone, the Romans used brick and concrete. These materials were cheap and readily accessible, and the arches allowed great distances to be spanned safely. These were critical concerns for an empire that had to service the needs of millions of people. Roads, bridges, and sewers had to be built, and an elaborate system of aqueducts was built to insure sufficient water supplies.

Whereas Greece had lavished its architectural attentions almost solely on temples, and Egypt on tombs, the Romans used their new construction methods to erect a great variety of buildings. The empire is filled with palaces, apartment buildings, warehouses, and courts of law, not to mention great entertainment centers like the public baths and theaters. One of the most famous of these is the Colosseum, where architecture and engineering combine to create a vast structure with a seating capacity of more than 50,000. The walls of the Colosseum are composed of an endless series of brick and concrete arches, faced with a veneer of stone. In this instance, the structure has been exposed, but in many others, such as the Pantheon, thin layers of stone were used to hide the arched honeycomb wall structures.

The Romans were a practical, military people. They united a diversified world through systematic conquest, and through the imposition of a unified body of laws and culture. They were less concerned with Greek theoretical ideals than with day-to-day functionalism. This is apparent not only in their usable architecture, but in their sculpture as well.

Sculpture. The portrait of a Roman admirably demonstrates Roman practicality. Unlike idealized Egyptian or Greek sculpture, which erased all traces of age and imperfection, early Roman portraits depended on exacting realism for their impact. The sculptor here includes every wrinkle and every sagging muscle in his aged sitter's face. No attempt has been made to improve him. It is a portrait of a specific hard-working man, austere and iron-willed.

The realism of early Roman portraiture is related to religious practices. When the leader of a Roman family died, a wax mask was made of his face. It was carried in the funeral pro-

ROMAN SCULPTURE: *the portrait of a Roman* (above) *c 80 B.C., shows the Roman love of realism. The Emperor Augustus, c 20 B.C., shows the continuing appeal of idealized forms.*

cession and then stored in a domestic shrine for ancestor worship. A full collection of these images formed the ancient Roman's family tree. Gradually, stone portraits were substituted for the more perishable wax masks.

Even while the Romans created works of such compelling realism, they were still intrigued by idealized Greek sculpture. Their houses and public buildings were flooded with Greek imports or with Roman copies of them. (In fact, it is frequently only through Roman copies that we know of lost Greek originals.)

Rome had long felt culturally inferior to the brilliant Greek civilization. This explains why it borrowed Hellenic forms so extensively. Throughout the second century B.C., the Roman love of Greek things blossomed, reaching its peak during the next hundred years or so, particularly under Augustus, the first Roman emperor. We can see the results in *Augustus of Prima Porta,* in which Augustus is portrayed as a barefoot Greek god.

Egyptian and Mesopotamian ideas of divine kingship had reached Rome by the first century B.C. It was easy, especially in the distant parts of the empire, to conceive of the great ruler, surrounded by glory, as a divine or superhuman being. As a result, emperors were worshipped as gods in their own lifetimes. Augustus, for example, claimed descent from Venus. Reference is made to this by the small cupid (Venus's child) next to his right leg.

Augustus's semidivine nature is further suggested by his idealized form. His heroic pose is a direct imitation of the famous Greek Doryphorus, and his face, while clearly a portrait, is beautified and ageless. It is a far cry from

the ruthless realism of earlier Roman images.

Augustus of Prima Porta set the standard for the representation of the ideal Roman emperor. He is a god, a hero, and a great warrior whose military victories are recorded on his armor. These qualities, together with Augustus's confident and authoritative pose, made this statue an important piece of political propaganda.

If Greek influence can be found in Roman architecture and sculpture, then we might also expect to find it in painting. We should not be surprised to learn that the Romans copied Greek subjects and techniques, and perhaps even used Greek pattern books as their guides.

Painting. The most popular method of painting in early Rome was fresco, in which the artist applied watercolors to walls covered with wet plaster. A large number of frescoes have survived in the buried cities of Pompeii and Herculaneum.

When Mt. Vesuvius erupted in 79 A.D., these two cities were buried under volcanic ash. Silently they lay below the surface of the earth for more than 1700 years before they were uncovered. Then, within the course of a

SCALA/EPA

PEACHES AND GLASS JAR, *a Roman still life buried for 1800 years by a volcano.*

few short years, the secrets of Roman life were revealed. We discovered Roman forms of work, play, and worship, as well as how Romans dressed and what they ate. But perhaps most significant was the new insight provided into the Roman house. Undisturbed for hundreds of years, these homes still had their walls covered with brilliantly painted frescoes.

These paintings covered a wide variety of subjects. There were mythological and religious scenes, convincing architectural compositions, and delightfully naturalistic landscapes with trees, flowers, and fluttering birds. There were also vivid still-life compositions where everyday objects were isolated for their decorative effects.

One example of a Roman still life is the *Peaches and Glass Jar* fresco from Herculaneum. Unlike Egyptian tomb paintings that show flat, almost abstract objects stacked on top of each other, Roman frescoes are illusionistic. That is, the painter used perspective, light, and shade to make the objects appear three-dimensional. Using delicate greens and warm browns, the artist captured the natural beauty of fresh fruit. By the careful handling of shadows and highlights, he was able to represent a transparent glass jar partially filled with water. The painting is a casual record of the contents of a Roman cupboard, but its mastery of shape, modeling, and light marks the highest point of Roman representational skills.

Throughout the second century, the Romans continued to make advances in the arts, and the boundaries of the empire stretched farther across the globe. But even at its height of power, the great Roman state was already showing signs of strain. The empire had grown fabulously and could no longer be governed effectively. Thousands of troops were needed to guard its far-flung borders, now under constant attack by northern barbarians. The cost of maintaining such a large army brought about currency devaluation and rampant inflation.

To make matters worse, there were constant civil wars. At one point, there were 18 different claimants to the imperial throne! In such turmoil, the Romans could have little faith in a "divine and unerring" emperor.

The situation was further compounded by the incredible growth of Christianity. The new religion promised hope and salvation when the empire could only offer suffering. It told of truth and justice, and a merciful and loving God. It offered life instead of death. The resultant response to Christianity was overwhelming, culminating in mass conversions.

The existence of a new religion usually posed no particular problem for the empire. There had always been dozens of different cults peacefully coexisting. Christianity, however, was the only one to offer a direct threat to the government, not only by its sheer numbers but by its denial of the emperor's divinity. The government was undermined by this religion's insistence on exclusive devotion to the one true God. Despite its ruthless persecution by the Romans, Christianity continued to thrive. Ultimately, it succeeded the crumbling empire as the guardian of civilization.

The Early Christians

After a war-torn century, the fragmented Roman Empire was reunited by Constantine in 312 A.D. This emperor made two decisions that changed the course of world history. In 313 he made Christianity the official religion of the Roman state, and in 330 he moved the capital of the empire from Rome to Constantinople (present-day Istanbul, Turkey).

Christians at Rome. During the periods of persecution before 313, Christians did not, and could not, have public buildings for worship. Their art was hidden, and was designed only for other Christians. Yet it showed a remarkable resemblance to other Roman art. Christians and pagans differed in their beliefs, but in other ways they were much the same. They spoke the same language, performed the same jobs, and lived next door to one another. Christians, like pagans, were Roman. The result of this common tradition can be seen in Early Christian art.

A Christian painter or sculptor naturally drew on the artistic conventions with which he had grown up. Inevitably, these were pagan. So the artists simply "Christianized" their themes while maintaining many of their older motifs. Thus, the sun-god Apollo was transformed into Christ, the light of the world. The grapes and vines of

Bacchus, the pagan god of wine, were baptized for Christian use and made to represent the connectedness of the Christian community.

Notable examples of Christian transformations can be found in the catacombs. These caverns under the streets of Rome were primarily used as Christian cemeteries, but they also served as hiding places during periods of persecution. Their walls were carved out to receive the bodies of the faithful, many of whom had been martyred. It has been estimated that the catacombs of Rome alone accommodated more than 4 million dead.

Frequently, small chambers were included in the catacombs for use in the celebration of Christian rites. These were decorated with religious paintings. The Early Christian artist had a difficult task because he had to represent invisible things. He solved this problem by using symbols to portray intangibles like hope, faith, and the goodness of God. His paintings became a kind of coded message, representing the most profound beliefs of the Christian faith.

In comparison with Roman frescoes, Early Christian painting is perhaps a poor affair. Its figures are frequently flat and poorly drawn, and they seem stiff and lifeless. But the Early Christian artist was not concerned with things of this world. Here the simple and clear expression of Christian belief is more important than the Roman ideal of realism. The Early Christian artist wanted to depict the permanence of life in the next world, and the triumph of the soul over the body. These same nonnaturalistic qualities can be found in all facets of Early Christian art, including mosaics, manuscript illumination, and sculpture.

Byzantine art. When Constantine moved the capital of the Roman Empire to Constantinople, Christian art was injected with a new burst of energy. Influences from the East now entered the Christian repertoire and gave rise to a new sumptuousness. Unhappily, most of the works from the early years of Christian Constantinople have perished, and we have to look to the sixth century, under the reign of Justinian, to gain some idea of its splendor. The new style came to be known as Byzantine, after Byzantium, the ancient name of Constantinople.

By far, the most important enterprise was the construction of Hagia Sophia, the Church of Divine Wisdom. Constantine had built the first church by this name, but it was destroyed by fire. It was replaced by Justinian in the sixth century by the biggest and most structurally complex building in the world. Nonetheless, it was built in the span of only five years. The still extant church covers an area larger than three football fields and it could easily accommodate a 15-story skyscraper under its lofty dome. But it was not size alone that distinguished Hagia Sophia.

Early Christian churches in the West (that is, Rome) were based on Roman assembly halls, or basilicas. (Architects consciously avoided modeling them on the Roman temples dedicated to pagan gods.) These were low, horizontal buildings with open timber roofs that had plain brick exteriors, but they had beautifully decorated interiors. This was an architectural reflection of the inner worth of man (that is, his soul) and the lesser importance of his body.

When the imperial court moved to Constantinople, the Eastern tradition of domical buildings fused with the Western form of these elongated basilicas, thus creating the domed basilica of Hagia Sophia. By a series of daring engineering feats, the architects Anthemius of Tralles and Ictinus of Miletus managed to flood the church with light. The effect was so dazzling that people in the sixth century described the dome as being suspended from heaven by a golden chain.

The question of how to decorate the new churches posed a serious problem because large sculpture was now all but taboo: the statues in a Christian church could too easily be confused with pagan idols by the newly converted communicants. A similar, but more slowly developing, controversy was to surround painting, although it really became manifest only during the great iconoclastic battle of the eighth century. The West favored images as "books for the illiterate," while the East forbade their use as graven images. So great was the dispute that a schism developed between the two parts of the empire—a break that has never been totally repaired.

In the sixth century, however, the controversy had not yet fully developed and fabulous mosaic programs illuminated Byzantine church interiors. Tiny glass or stone cubes, set at angles in plaster-coated walls, picked up the reflections of light and bathed the churches in a heavenly glow.

Some of the finest mosaics of this period are found in Ravenna, Italy, which had been used at times by later emperors as the seat of the empire. The mosaic program at the church of San Vitale is a beautiful example. The small segment seen here portrays the emperor Justinian and his court. There is no question that a very skilled artist executed this panel; it was, after all, an imperial commission of the greatest significance. Yet we see none of the Greek mastery of human form; nor is the Roman concern with realism apparent. Instead, we find figures with wide-staring eyes whose stiffness and rigidity remind us of Egyptian art. In contrast to that ancient style, however, these figures are hidden by flat, but sumptuously patterned robes. There is

CULVER PICTURES

HAGIA SOPHIA, *built 532–37 A.D. at Constantinople (now Istanbul, Turkey) by the Emperor Justinian, was for centuries the largest and most elaborate temple in the world.*

no sense of bodily weight here, and the figures seem to float above the ground on their pointed toes.

All movement is denied in favor of total clarity. All incidentals are omitted in favor of the clear expression of a solemn message: Justinian in dead center is the only figure to wear a halo. He is a Christ symbol surrounded by twelve soldiers and clerics (counterparts to the twelve apostles).

This mosaic panel has a companion piece that shows the empress Theodora with her ladies in waiting. Her dress embroidered with an image of the Three Magi, Theodora is cast in the role of the Blessed Mother. Both Justinian's and Theodora's panels are located in the choir of San Vitale, in the most sacred part of the church. The message is clear: the emperor and empress symbolize Christ and his mother; they are the vicars of God on Earth. Art has fused in the double service of the church and state, blending political and spiritual authority.

THE EMPEROR JUSTINIAN, *builder of Hagia Sophia, appears as a saint in a mosaic at the church of San Vitale in Ravenna, Italy, c 540 A.D.*

SCALA/EPA

The Middle Ages

While Byzantine art flourished in the East, the Western empire collapsed under successive barbarian invasions. Vandals, Goths, and Huns, as well as Saxons, Danes, and Vikings, swarmed down from the east and the north, destroying Roman law and order, and thereby initiating the so-called Dark Ages.

For centuries this unflattering term was used to describe the period from about 500 A.D. through 900 A.D. (although sometimes it was used to describe a full 1000 years from 400 to 1400). This period was thought to be a bleak time, a void between the brilliant cultural achievements of the Roman Empire and the revival of learning and art in Europe. Most often, the period from about 900 to 1300 is called the Middle Ages, or the medieval period, the time that separates modern Europeans from the barbarian tribes from which they originated.

More recently, we have come to understand that the Dark Ages seem dark partly because of our own ignorance. The barbarian tribes were illiterate, but they were hardly lacking in skill or creative power. We have also come to see that there is no clear division between the "Dark" and "Middle" ages. For convenience, we will consider the period from about 400 to 1300 the Middle Ages.

Early Medieval Art

Because the early invaders of Europe were wandering peoples, their art concentrated on small, easily portable objects such as weapons, harnesses, belt buckles and jewelry. Skilled metalworkers ornamented these pieces with complicated patterns of interwoven lines and twisted animal bodies. One of their favorite techniques was cloisonné, in which strips of gold were soldered to a metal background. The spaces in between the upraised strips were filled with precious gems or enamel to produce highly colored and densely ornamented abstract designs.

Another early medieval style is called interlace. It may have come from Asia, or it may have arisen naturally from barbarian experience with woven leather thongs. Whatever its source, interlace resembles the animal style of ancient Mesopotamia and the art of the nomads of central Asia during the Early Christian era. Interlace was used to produce highly charged decorative pieces, such as snarling animal heads covered with vigorous patterns of interwoven lines. The ultimate significance of these fierce beasts leaves us puzzled; but there is some

suggestion that they were used to frighten demons away. Thus, art was once again employed in the service of magic, just as it had been by hungry cavemen and Egyptians seeking eternal life.

The interlaced animal style was put to new use in Ireland. As early as the sixth century, Christian monks had settled this land and established monasteries throughout the British Isles. These became vibrant centers of learning. When the rest of Europe was rav-

aged by wandering tribes, these monasteries were left as the sole guardians of civilization. Ireland escaped attack because of its isolation from the continent.

Under the combined influence of Saxon England and Celtic Ireland, barbarian interlace was Christianized for the decoration of Bibles and church manuscripts. The *Lindisfarne Gospel* is one of the most sumptuous of these early books.

The page shown here fully illus-

THE LINDISFARNE GOSPEL is decorated with elaborate abstract patterns, revealing the artistic talent of the "uncivilized" Celts and Saxons, c 700.

BRITISH LIBRARY

trates the pulsating new use of interlace. Dense coils in red, blue, green,
and gold are compressed within a rigid
geometric frame, and are overlaid by
the symbol of the cross. These formal
borders contrast markedly with the
throbbing lacelike maze and emphasize its rhythmic motion. Fantastic
beasts curl back on themselves and devour neighboring serpents, changing
size and color like elastic chameleons.
The intricacy of the pattern almost defies us to follow a line from beginning
to end as it tirelessly threads its way
through the woven net. But complexity is not confusion. The patterns are
strictly controlled by symmetry, each
part corresponding to the others, and
all combining to form a harmonious
balance of line, shape, and color.

This intricate style was also used to
portray men in other contemporary
manuscripts. The results were curiously knotted bodies, stiff and abstract, with all sense of human form
hidden under a riot of interwoven ribbons. The barbarian craftsman, so
accustomed to nonrepresentational
jewelry designs, had little practice in
the depiction of people. His life and
art were in every way different from
Roman order and realism.

Carolingian Art

The Dark Ages seemed to come to an
end on Christmas Day, 800 A.D., when
Pope Leo III placed a crown on the
head of Charlemagne (Charles the
Great) and proclaimed him emperor of
the Holy Roman Empire. Charlemagne
had been King of the Franks since 768,
and had created the empire through
war and diplomacy. It united modern
France, Germany, the Netherlands,
much of central Europe, and parts of
Spain and Italy. Under a dual allegiance to the secular power of the emperor and the spiritual leadership of
the Pope, it revived and Christianized
the concept of the Roman Empire. The
empire survived, at least in name, for
just over 1000 years. During much of
that time it was "neither holy, nor Roman, nor an empire," and it soon became just one of many competing
European powers. But during the life
of Charlemagne, it brought a great
change to Europe.

Charlemagne was a lover of learning, and during his reign he tried to
revive the splendors of ancient Rome.
His biographer said that he transformed a dark and barbarous kingdom
into one radiant with the blaze of
knowledge. Charlemagne saw himself
as the successor to the ancient Caesars
and he invited all the best minds and
finest artists to join his court in the
German city of Aachen (near the modern border between West Germany,
Belgium, and the Netherlands).

Charlemagne himself could not
write, but he could speak Latin and

CULVER PICTURES

understand Greek, and he enjoyed
learned discussions with the scholars
he summoned to court. He instituted
great monastic schools and encouraged the production of church manuscripts and books of psalms, all
beautifully illustrated. Some of these
were painted in realistic classical style
while others showed the vibrant influence of Irish ornament. To protect
these expensive parchment books,
craftsmen created sumptuous gold and
ivory covers, frequently adorning
them with precious gems.

Of all his projects, the emperor was
perhaps most interested in correcting
the text of the Bible. For centuries it
had been copied by ignorant scribes
whose mistakes had corrupted the
original text. The project was directed
by the brilliant monk from England,
Alcuin of York. Alcuin reformed the
shape of the letters of the alphabet,
and the results of his work can be seen
on this page. Our own clear and readable script is a direct descendant of his
improvements.

In architecture as in sculpture,
Charlemagne looked to the imperial
past. He wanted to combine the solidity and monumentality of ancient Roman buildings with the splendor of
Byzantium. The masterpiece of the period is his palace chapel, Aix-la-Chapelle. Its debt to the Byzantine style of
Ravenna is unmistakable. Charlemagne imported iron railings and marble from Ravenna, and he borrowed
the plan of its church of San Vitale.
The end result, however, could never
be confused with its Byzantine model.

Densely forested Germany had always built with timber; therefore,
Charlemagne's craftsmen were not totally prepared to construct a great
stone building. This is clearly seen in
Aix-la-Chapelle, where the fine spatial
qualities of Eastern architecture were
lost to a heavy-handed manipulation
of stone. Gone are the delicacy and in-

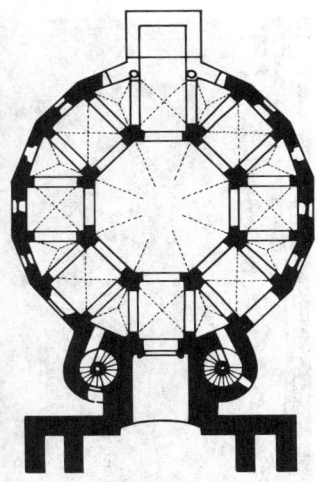

AIX-LA-CHAPELLE, *the palace
chapel of Charlemagne, was built
in 810 near the modern city of
Aachen, Germany.*

tricacy of fluid interiors, omitted are
the walls of glittering mosaics. The entire composition has been simplified
and restated in stiff geometric terms.
But if the sophistication of Byzantine
architecture was absent, Charlemagne's chapel was still a dignified
monument. It established a strong tradition of stone construction in northern Europe that was carried on for a
thousand years.

Ottonian Art

When Charlemagne died in 814, his
dream of a unified imperial culture
died with him. His successors divided
the kingdom among themselves only
to have it crumble under the invasions
of the Vikings, Magyars, and Saracens.
Once again Europe was plunged into a
dark age, perhaps more so than ever
before. A glimmer of light came only
in the tenth century, with the emergence of the kings of Saxony, the most
extraordinary of whom was Otto I
(ruled 936–973).

Determined to restore imperial traditions, Otto began a new Golden Age.
Great stone churches were built on
Early Christian and Carolingian models, and illuminated manuscripts were
painted with new confidence and expressive power.

Shortly before the year 1000, Bishop
Bernward, a distinguished patron of
the arts, supported the building of a
church at Hildesheim in northern Germany. In 1001 he went to Rome and
gained firsthand knowledge both of
classical and Christian antiquities. He
may well have seen and studied the
great doors of the Pantheon and of the
church of Santa Sabina. Upon his return to Germany, he commissioned
two bronze doors for his church.

Each of these 15-foot doors was cast
in a single plate, the first of their kind

THE EXPULSION OF ADAM AND EVE, *cast in bronze for the church doors of St. Michael's, Hildesheim, Germany, c 1000, tells the biblical story with great emotional force.*

since ancient Rome. Fearing confusion with pagan idols, Christian sculpture had previously been restricted to small works in metal or ivory. The bold monumentality of the bishop's doors broke with this tradition and looked forward to a time when large-scale sculpture would be reintroduced.

The bronze panel on this page is one of 16 Biblical scenes included on the doors. Having eaten of the forbidden fruit, Adam and Eve are reproached by the angry Lord. With the force of his entire body, God jabs His accusing finger at Adam, who, crouching and hiding his nakedness, points to Eve. She in turn passes the blame to the lowly serpent that snarls back at her as it cowers under the fateful tree. The drama of guilt and the origin of evil is staged theatrically against a blank ground. Gestures are exaggerated, giving the scene an air of intense pantomime. The aim of the artist was to depict the episode as clearly and as forcefully as possible. Nothing is included to distract the viewer. So strong is the emotional impact that one tends to overlook the fact that the figures are crudely ill-proportioned. The sculptor was more concerned with the portrayal of faith and divine justice than he was with convincing likenesses. In this, the medieval artist was distinct from most who had gone before. The Egyptians had portrayed things as they *knew* them to be, the Greeks as they *wished* them, and the Romans as they *saw* them. The medieval artist, on the contrary, depicted things as he *felt* them.

By about 1050, the rule of the Holy Roman Emperor had been limited to Germany alone. No monarch could claim universal control of the rapidly changing continent. Cities were growing, commerce was booming, and a new merchant class had arisen. Lands beyond the German borders were therefore governed by feudal lords who could deal with local requirements more effectively. It was a time when Europe as we know it began to take shape.

Romanesque Art

Feudalism was a set of complex relationships among the lord, his vassals, and peasants. In its simplest form, the lord offered protection and land in return for loyalty and agricultural and military service. Each of the many feudal kingdoms had its own problems and interests, and, as a result, each developed independently. The only true unifying force was the church. Feudal lords pledged allegiance to the church hierarchy (the bishops and the pope), and a vast international network of monasteries further unified the various regions and kingdoms. These religious communities were centers of agriculture, industry, and learning. In fact, they offered virtually the only means of receiving an education.

Cluny. The grandest of all monasteries was the Benedictine Abbey of Cluny, from which important church reforms were initiated in the 900's. Its magnificence was such that a twelfth-century chronicler described it as "shining on earth like a second sun." Founded in the sixth century, the Benedictine Order prospered and reached its peak around 1157, when it could count over 1200 houses from Scotland in the north and Portugal in the south to Jerusalem in the east.

Cluny's tremendous growth was directly related to the medieval preoccupation—even obsession—with eternal salvation. Crusades and pilgrimages were seen as the most effective means of insuring it. People traveled hundreds and sometimes thousands of difficult miles to visit the most sacred shrines in Christendom. With this they satisfied their desire for personal sacrifice. They believed they would be absolved of their sins as a result.

Pilgrimage churches. The most popular pilgrimage centers were Christ's tomb in Jerusalem, that of St. Peter in Rome, and Santiago da Compostela (the church of St. James the Apostle), located in the westernmost part of Spain (called "Finistera" or land's end).

Four major overland routes to Santiago da Compostela sprawled across France, merging near the Spanish border. These roads were dotted with scores of lesser churches, each possessing its own venerable relics. Roughly every 20 miles (the length of an average day's journey), there was a hospice or priory that offered food, lodging,

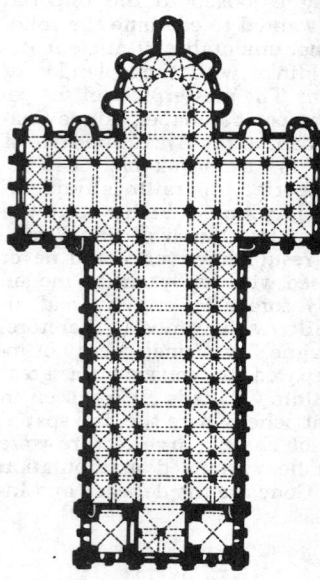

ST. SERNIN, *a pilgrimage church at Toulouse, France, c 1100, is built in the shape of a cross.*

and medical and spiritual attention to the weary pilgrim. In a sense, these way stations were the medieval Howard Johnsons along the highway.

The religious structures that developed along these routes are appropriately called "pilgrimage churches." Despite local differences in building materials, towers, and ultimate size, they share a remarkable uniformity. Their design was a calculated response to the need to accomodate large numbers of pilgrims. Their crisp logic is apparent in the plan of St. Sernin, which, like all pilgrimage churches, is characterized by extreme regularity.

The basic shape is a bold cross with a long nave (central vessel) intersected by transepts or arms. The round head or apse is the most sacred part of the church. For symbolic reasons, it almost always faces east (Christ was born in the East, the sun rises in the East, and Christ is the light of the world). Attached to the apse and the eastern sides of the transepts are a series of small chapels that hold additional relics, the central or axial one being elongated to emphasize its greater importance. The whole is surrounded by side aisles (distinguished by dotted x's on the plan) through which pilgrims could walk without disturbing the services being held at the high altar in the apse.

The logic of the plan is carried even further in the modular use of square bays. Every portion of the church is based on a square of set size. For example, each side aisle (there are two on either side of the nave) is made up of square bays or units. One nave bay equals two of these squares, and four of them would make up the crossing (the place where the arms of the cross intersect). The result is that the entire church is interrelated. Not only did this lead to harmony and balance in design, but it offered a very practical method of construction at a time when there were no standardized yardsticks.

The length of a foot might be twelve inches in Paris, but only ten inches in another part of France. We can well imagine what disastrous consequences this could have for architecture! If, for instance, two different masons were told to build a wall 30 feet long, one would be 360 inches while the other was only 300 inches. By using a modular bay system, the medieval master mason (architect) avoided the whole problem. After determining the size of his square, he could simply tell each of two masons to build a wall ten modules long. Working from the same basic square, the two masons would produce the exact same wall. This practical means of modular construction was to have a long and rich history. In fact, we still use a similar method in erecting modern skyscrapers with prefabricated materials cut to standard or modular lengths.

Two major problems confronted church architects in the eleventh cen-

tury: how to fireproof structures whose open timber roofs were often set aflame by candles, and how to give them a dignity suitable to a house of God. Both solutions were found in the rediscovery of stone vaulting, the secrets of which had been lost during the Dark Ages. Lofty barrel vaults were now built above tremendously thick walls. The sheer weight of these supports insured vault stability, but it reduced the size of windows, making the churches very dark. The answer to the lighting problem was only found later in technological developments accompanying the Gothic style.

The interior of a pilgrimage church is as regular as its plan, with vertical bays marching down the length of the building in orderly fashion. The result is so compelling and so unified that it clearly distinguishes the type from earlier, more helter-skelter structures. St. Sernin and other pilgrimage churches of the eleventh century are worthy successors of Roman architecture. For this reason, this massive style is called Romanesque.

Sculpture. The development of architecture went hand in hand with the revival of sculpture. It was only natural to want to beautify the new churches. On the one hand there were movable objects and church furniture; on the other there were large-scale stone sculptures. The purpose of these pieces, however, was not merely ornamental. In each case, decoration had the specific function of expressing Christian beliefs. It was used as a teaching tool by the church. Bronze baptismal fonts, for example, showed scenes of Christ's baptism; gold and ivory book covers depicted the authors of the four Gospels or Christ en-

throned. But it was with architectural sculpture that the Romanesque had its greatest development.

Initially, architectural scupture was confined to column capitals. Among their leaves were carved monsters, demons, and other fantastic creatures. The profound and unquestioning faith of medieval men led them to believe in the existence of such unlikely beasts and to fear them as agents of the devil. Biblical scenes were carved on other capitals to remind worshippers of miracles and other hopeful events in Christian history.

By the late eleventh century, architectural sculpture was concentrating on church portals, particularly on the tympanum (the semicircular panel above the door). No one who entered could miss the dramatic religious scenes carved above his head.

Of all themes, the Last Judgment was the most popular. Its visionary qualities gave full license to the fertile imaginations of Romanesque sculptors, as can be seen in the church of Autun. Surrounded by an almond-shaped mandorla (body halo), a flat and elongated Christ presides over the awesome process. In the lintel below, terror-stricken souls answer the summons of trumpet-blowing angels and rise from their graves to hear their final judgment. On Christ's right, calm angels lead the saved to Heaven, but on his left, hideous demons tilt the fateful scales of the damned. Insect-like devils force weeping souls into the mouth of Hell, while one unhappy figure is actually plucked from Earth by giant hands. The sculptor's skillful organization and balance of forms increase the impact of this frightful scene. Autun's tympanum was created and signed by Giselbertus, one of the earliest known medieval sculptors.

THE LAST JUDGMENT *was created by the sculptor Giselbertus, c1130, over the doors of the cathedral at Autun, France. The creation is dominated by the stylized Christ at center.*

GIRAUDON

Gothic Art

The decoration of church tympanums and capitals is only one example of the growing integration of medieval architecture and sculpture. This was to reach its greatest height in the Gothic cathedrals of the twelfth and thirteenth centuries.

These were times of great change for the Middle Ages. Pilgrimages and crusades had introduced new ideas into the West and fostered the growth of a large merchant class. Interest in education became more pronounced, universities were established, and cities (as opposed to monasteries) became the focus of medieval life. Amid this bustling activity Gothic cathedrals emerged.

Compared with Romanesque architecture, the Gothic style differs in almost every respect. Where Romanesque churches force us to our knees by their tremendous weight, Gothic buildings encourage our spirits to soar upward by their light and airy frameworks.

The Gothic style was the result both of technical developments and of a new religious and artistic vision. They first came together in Abbot Suger's Parisian church of Saint Denis (1144), and thereafter quickly spread throughout France, into England, Germany, Spain, and even reluctant Italy.

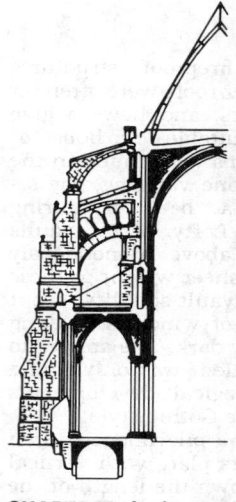

CHARTRES, *built c1150, used the flying buttress* (left) *to eliminate heavy wall supports and allow great windows, giving its interior a new kind of light and grace.*

Chartres.

One of the purest early Gothic buildings in France is the Cathedral of Notre Dame at Chartres. It has an enormous vertical interior, planned from the inside out. Its walls have been reduced to thin curtains pierced by tall arcades and frighteningly large windows.

Unlike Romanesque churches, Gothic cathedrals are characterized by their pointed arches. These can be seen at Chartres in the ground floor, second-story arcade, high (clerestory) windows, and even in the vaults. Pointed arches are more versatile than round arches because their height can be adjusted and they can span variable distances. (The principle is somewhat similar to opening a pair of scissors and extending its blades to any desirable distance.) Round arches, on the other hand, are inflexible: they are always half as high as they are wide. If, for example, an architect tried to vault a rectangular bay with round arches, the differing length and width of the bay would result in arches of conflicting heights. However, by using pointed arches and the "scissors principle," the architect would be able to bring all arches up to the same level and vault the nave uniformly.

Chartres' vaults tower 118 feet above the ground, pressing down and out with incredible force. But the cathedral's walls are little more than stone lattices opened by vast window

expanses. How could they possibly withstand such fabulous lateral pressure? The answer lies in flying buttresses, huge piers surmounted by arches that brace the wall from the outside and channel the vault thrusts safely to the ground. Gothic interiors were thus transformed into glorious "religious greenhouses," ablaze with the mysterious colored glow of huge stained glass windows.

Ste. Chapelle.

This achievement is seen most dramatically in Ste. Chapelle, the small two-story chapel that St. Louis built to house Christ's Crown of Thorns. The supporting structure has been reduced to 14 extremely slender piers between vast windows, measuring roughly 49 feet by 15 feet each.

These glazed panels (which were then the largest ever produced) form a veritable illustrated Bible with thou-

STE. CHAPELLE *in Paris, c 1250, shows the inspired combination of graceful Gothic architecture and the perfection of stained glass for the giant windows.*

sands of figures in 1134 different scenes from the Old and New Testaments. The jewel-like interior sparkles as the sun radiates through its multicolored stained glass.

So completely were the weight-bearing walls of Ste. Chapelle's dissolved that the architect took an unusual precaution: he stretched two iron link chains around the church, binding it against the collapse of its walls.

Gothic ideals of light and linearity were totally realized in Ste. Chapelle. Later 13th century architects strove for similar achievements, extending the skeletal principle to its very limits in their quest for skyscraping buildings. Boldly they challenged the force of gravity with vaults of ever-increasing height: 80 feet at Laon, 118 feet at Chartres, 123 feet at Reims, and 144 feet at Amiens. In 1272 they delivered the terrifying final statement of Gothic height in the awesome 156-foot vaults of Beauvais. Twelve years later, the vaults collapsed.

The disaster of Beauvais was the end of Gothic development. New churches tended to be fewer and more modestly sized. The Gothic building boom came to an end.

Sculpture. The beauty of Gothic architecture depends on the harmonious balance of parts. This includes sculpture, for in the twelfth and 13th centuries it was not applied to a wall, it was integrally related to the surrounding masonry.

As in Romanesque churches, sculpture was still concentrated around the portals. But now the field was extended to include complex iconographic programs that stretched over much of the exterior of the cathedral. Chartres, for example, has over 2000 carved figures distributed among its major entrances in the west and its transept portals in the south and north.

Initially, sculpture had been subservient to its bold architectural setting. Elongated early Gothic figures, like the jamb statues around Chartres's western doors, were shaped by the tall colonettes to which they were attached. The figures are stiff and cylindrical. At first glance, they may even seem to belong more to the building than to sculpture proper. But even while these Old Testament kings and queens are encased in their architectural strait jackets, they have a life of their own. Unlike Romanesque sculpture, which was cut back into the wall, these early Gothic figures stand out in front of it. They are treated three-dimensionally, with a spatial depth new to medieval sculpture. Draperies are still handled as inscribed lines, but now they have a direct correspondence to the bodies underneath. For example, the folds fall from waists and shoulders. This, too, is a development over the purely linear patterns of earlier medieval art.

PAULA GERSON/EPA

Perhaps most significant, however, is the incipient naturalism of the faces at Chartres. The abstract features of Romanesque masks have been softened by a faint human quality.

This naturalistic tendency is fully matured in the jamb statues of Reims, created 75 years later. These statues reveal the astonishing influence of classical sculpture. Inspired by antiquity, the artist replaced the rigid verticality of columnar figures with convincing life-sized statues. He used the heavy folds of realistic drapery to reveal the bodies underneath. The figures turn easily toward one another, freed almost entirely from architectural restraints. Now, after hundreds of years, people were once again thought worthy of critical artistic attention. In *The Visitation,* shown here, the two women are clearly distinguished by their ages and personalities. Mary is the youthful virgin, the ideal of feminine beauty. Pregnant with Christ, she is visited by her aged and careworn cousin, Elizabeth, soon to be the mother of John the Baptist.

Nature had been reinstated in Christian art. In the following centuries, portraits of recognizable individuals would emerge. Sculpture would break its last ties with architecture to become fully freestanding for the first time since the Roman Empire.

GOTHIC SCULPTURE: *early figures on the exterior of the Chartres cathedral (1150) are stiff and stylized compared with those on the cathedral at Reims (c 1230), which show two scenes from the life of Mary, the annunciation by the angel, at left, and her visit with Elizabeth.*

LAUROS-GIRAUDON

The Renaissance

Late Gothic naturalism began a process that, in the following centuries, was to culminate in a new kind of art. While artists in Northern Europe redirected their talents to stained glass windows (almost the only broad surfaces left in the Gothic cathedral), important changes were taking place in Italy.

As heirs to the Roman Empire and Early Christian basilicas, the states of the Italian peninsula were less devoted to the Gothic cathedral, and so had not turned their attention to stained glass. The naturalism of late Gothic times was a great influence, but it showed itself in a lively tradition of mosaic and fresco wall decoration inherited from the Byzantine culture to the east. In the 1200's, a new wave of Eastern influence washed over Italy, merging with late Gothic naturalism. This marriage of East and West set off the first artistic revolution of the new era. We have come to know this revolution as the Renaissance.

The Early Years

The leader of the revolution was a painter named Giotto.

Giotto. Shortly after 1305 Giotto began work on the small Arena Chapel in Padua. Several years later, its walls were covered with frescoes depicting the life of Christ. The *Lamentation* on this page is part of Giotto's work.

The actual dimensions of the painted figures are little more than half life size, yet they seem monumental. Giotto used large and simple forms to give his boulderlike humans a tremendous sense of weight. Like the creator of Bishop Bernward's bronze doors, Giotto avoided distracting incidentals; he focuses all attention on the tragedy of Christ's death. But unlike the Ottonian craftsman who confined his sticklike figures to an airless foreground, Giotto orchestrated his scene like a virtuoso stage director. He cast his characters so that they actually *occupy* space. Two seated figures dominate the foreground. Behind them Mary embraces her dead son. Behind Mary and her son cluster grieving mourners. A background of rocky hills and expansive sky acts as a great theater curtain and limits spatial depth to the middle- and foreground. For the first time since antiquity, the two-dimensional painted surface was treated like an open window through which we can look at the world. Instead of flat patterns on a flat plane, we are encouraged to see the drama as it might actually occur in space. And what drama it is!

When Giotto planned the frescoes, he considered some fundamental questions about man. How does he move? How does he relate to other people? How would he react to the death of his Savior? With these and similar questions, Giotto breathed a new naturalism into painting and created what are perhaps the first "modern" works of art.

Giotto made his native city of Florence a center of artistic activity. But the city of Siena made important contributions too. Its favorite son, Duccio, introduced a new refinement and elegance into painting, while his compatriot, Simone Martini, developed linear expression. Also from Siena were the Lorenzetti Brothers, who brought spatial illusion to a level previously thought to be impossible.

The international style. For the better part of the 1300's, the papacy was divided. One line of popes lived at Avignon in southern France. At Avignon Italian and French styles of art met and blended, creating the so-called International Style. This type of painting concentrated on the glamour of courtly life, with its use of brightly colored costumes and richly decorated surfaces to convey the splendors of chivalry.

One of its finest productions was the *Très Riches Heures* of the Duke of Berry, a sumptuous prayer book illustrated by the Limbourg Brothers with the labors of the twelve months. Some of these miniatures depicted the genteel life of the aristocracy, while others were dedicated to the less fortunate lot of the peasants.

EARLY RENAISSANCE: *the* Lamentation *by Giotto, c 1305, and the* February *scene by the Limbourg Brothers, c 1415, show two important Renaissance characteristics: a new interest in drama and a new interest in portraying everyday happenings.*

Calendar paintings had been popular throughout the Middle Ages, but the Limbourgs used their incomparable powers of observation to produce paintings of startling reality. In fact, they studied nature so closely that they even painted shadows. This had not been done since antiquity. Their naturalistic view of the world is apparent in their *February* scene.

The top of the page (not shown here) holds the astrological chart of the month and its zodiac signs (Aquarius and Pisces). In the center is the chariot of the sun making its rounds. Below, a delightful winter scene presents one of Europe's earliest snowscapes. Its freezing temperatures are warmed by a wealth of narrative detail. Inside a small house (one wall of which has been omitted for our convenience) chilled peasants cluster around a fire. Their companion in the barnyard breathes on her frostbitten hands while sheep huddle in the fold and hungry birds scratch for food. Beyond the wicker fence a man chops trees for firewood as another drives a mule to the distant town.

The scene seems to provide an almost encyclopedic record of winter: snowy fields, leafless trees, smoke spiraling from the chimney, and even the steam of human breath lingering in crisp February air. With their calendar paintings the Limbourgs made a brilliant advance toward the artistic conquest of atmosphere. From now on artists would abandon the medieval practice of copying pattern books; they would study nature firsthand.

By extending traditional subject matter to include everyday events, the Limbourgs also broke philosophically with medieval paintings. Instead of telling sacred stories, they were concentrating on the realistic depiction of ordinary events. The very fact that paintings of this genre were included in a prayer book signals a new time. During the next century, religious and secular themes would blend inseparably. The Middle Ages had ended and the Renaissance had begun.

The new spirit. By 1400, the Renaissance was fully launched in Italy and Southern France. It was a complex phenomenon, and it affected virtually every aspect of human activity. The ineffective feudal system of the Middle Ages gave way to the modern state and to a cash economy. It was an age of discovery. During the new century, navigators would greatly expand the concept of Earth's size and complexity. For the first time since the pre-Christian era, science was uncovering new secrets. Copernicus advanced his revolutionary theory that Earth revolved around the sun. Advances in optics led to new explorations of the stars through the telescope. It was a time of almost limitless possibility, encouraged by technological advances in navigation, transportation, metallurgy and warfare. But even more important, the Renaissance was a time of profound change in human attitudes.

Medieval man was in search of supernatural truths. He lived a fretful life constantly threatened by the Devil and plagued by worldly temptations. In the 1200's, however, St. Francis preached the goodness of God and the beauty of His earthly creations. Such teachings invited man to enjoy life in this world. It was not a rejection of Christian devotion, but a reinterpretation of it. Relieved from guilt and freed from church domination, Renaissance man began to think for himself. He looked to antiquity as the model of a more human existence. And he came to see the arts and literature as celebrations of man's intellect, achievement, and physical beauty.

In one way the Renaissance was an attempt to revive the classical age in all its glory. But in another way, the men of the Renaissance sought to produce a new and original classical age. Men sought not just a restoration of old ways, but a rebirth—a renaissance. It was during the 1400's that the preceding centuries come to be called the Middle Ages.

The School of Florence

The spirit of the new classical age was nowhere more intense than in Florence, the illustrious home of Giotto. In the late 1200's this city had begun an enormous Gothic cathedral that was to have a great dome over its 140-foot crossing. But for a century it had remained incomplete because no one knew how to build a dome of such fabulous proportions.

Brunelleschi. Then Brunelleschi appeared on the scene. This genius was originally a goldsmith. He turned to architecture after losing a design competition in 1401 for the doors of the cathedral's baptistry. Shortly afterward, he visited Rome and was awestruck by the beauty and power of ancient ruins. He studied them closely and made hundreds of accurately measured drawings. The result of Brunelleschi's Roman visit was a new understanding of ancient architecture. When he returned to Florence, he began plans for the cathedral's dome. Within 20 years, the immense project was complete. Brunelleschi had transformed a white elephant into Florence's most celebrated landmark.

The cathedral's dome is known throughout the world as a brilliant example of Brunelleschi's engineering

THE PAZZI CHAPEL *of Brunelleschi, c 1440, reflects a break with earlier church design.*

abilities. His powers as an architect are best seen in the chapel he built for the Pazzi family. Its small size and relatively simple structure freed Brunelleschi from complex building problems and allowed him to concentrate on the design.

His break with the Gothic is now complete. A simple stone box has replaced the soaring verticals and huge windows of the Gothic church. Great round arches, medallions, and stone pilasters (thin flat columns attached to the wall) show classical influence, but these elements are used in a new way to achieve a grace and lightness foreign to antiquity. Brunelleschi carefully broke the cool white walls into precisely defined segments, and then crowned the central space with a dome. He was the first great Renaissance architect, favoring crisp geometric clarity over Gothic complexity, and transforming the heavy classical style.

Brunelleschi's interest in geometry also led him to a momentous discovery: perspective, a system of mathematical laws that determine the diminishing size of objects as they recede farther back into space. This discovery radically altered the entire future of painting.

Masaccio. The discovery of perspective was quickly appreciated by Masaccio, the second (and the youngest) of the three great geniuses of the Early Renaissance. Masaccio grew up in the International Style. But rather than conform to its sumptuously detailed surfaces and brightly colored costumes, Masaccio brought about a revolution. He died prematurely, but in the six short years of his working life, Masaccio contributed more to art than most painters do in 40.

His last painting was the *Holy Trinity* in the church of Santa Maria Novella. By using perspective, Masaccio made the flat wall appear as if it opened into a square chapel of the kind that Brunelleschi might have built. He placed the viewpoint at the level of the viewer's eye as he stands before the fresco (about five feet from the floor) so that the viewer looks up and into the great coffered vault. The illusion is so convincing that modern scholars have been able to calculate the dimensions of the room as if it actually existed. When the painting was unveiled, it created a tremendous stir in Florence. Nothing like it had ever been created before, not even by the ancients.

The Florentines must have also been surprised by the massive figures that inhabit the chapel. Masaccio's people are not the graceful and elegant forms of the still popular International Style; they have a solidity and weight that recall the monumental work of Giotto. Masaccio uses light and shadow to model his figures, especially Christ's powerful body. Each of the figures seems to be a three-dimensional statue that could actually be touched; this adds to the illusion of

spatial depth. The whole composition is based on a human pyramid, with God the Father at the top and the kneeling patrons at the bottom. All is quiet and solemn; Mary makes the only movement as she stares at the viewer and points to her crucified son.

Masaccio's *Holy Trinity* was a total statement of Early Renaissance ideals. It used perspective, light, and shadow, and a great architectural framework to portray essential Christian beliefs with a new and compelling realism.

When Masaccio died, he left no students behind. His older contemporaries developed painting in slightly different directions. Uccello and Piero della Francesca were intrigued with perspective and used it as an end in itself, creating works of austere geometric clarity. Fra Angelico, however, remained conservative. He stayed closer to the International Style and produced religious paintings of unparalleled charm and decorative effect.

Another important painter was Fra Filippo Lippi. Like Fra Angelico, he was a Dominican monk, but he shared none of Fra Angelico's piety. He was quite unsuited to religious life and was constantly in trouble, for everything from forgery to the abduction of

an attractive nun (who later bore him a son). Despite his troubled life, Fra Filippo Lippi was still able to make major contributions to painting. He combined a heightened color sense with a brilliant use of line in his intensely sensuous religious paintings. Other artists, like Domenico Veneziano and Andrea Castagno, further explored the wonders of color, light, and sculptural modeling.

Donatello. The 1400's were a period of experiment in all the arts. In sculpture, the greatest personality was Donatello, who, with Brunelleschi and Masaccio, completes the Early Renaissance trio of outstanding geniuses. As a youth, Donatello was apprenticed to a stonecutter. By the age of 20 he was revered as the finest sculptor in Florence and one of the best in all of Italy. What gave Donatello this distinction? The answer is found in the authority, flexibility, and profound understanding of human nature that characterize his work.

Most sculptors of the time specialized in particular types of commissions. Some concentrated on portraits, others on relief panels, and still others on large free-standing statues. Donatello did them all. He worked in bronze, marble, and wood in both large and small scale, and he was equally at ease portraying the real, the ideal, and the spiritual. He carved moving Biblical scenes, innocent children, austere soldiers, saints, sinners, and despots. Never before had the variety of human experience been so fully treated by a single artist.

A solitary example will illustrate Donatello's brilliance. In the early 1430's he visited Rome and fell under the spell of antique sculpture. When he returned to Florence, he created the bronze statue *David* for the powerful Medici family. The sinuous David differed markedly from Donatello's earlier, more powerful work. It shows the influence of Hellenistic sculptors like Praxiteles (whom Donatello could have known through Roman copies). With this one work the classical ideal was reborn. It was the first time that this Biblical hero had been portrayed nude. Even more important, it was the first free-standing nude since antiquity. For a thousand years nakedness had been considered indecent. Only rarely was it permitted, and even then it was only as a necessary illustration to a Biblical or moral theme, as in the story of Adam and Eve. Donatello revolted, and thus began the impassioned Renaissance quest for physical beauty.

Holding a sword in his right hand and a stone in his left, David pokes at Goliath's severed head with his foot. His graceful adolescent body rests in a classical contrapposto stance that recalls the calm of Greek gods and athletes. But Donatello has replaced classical calm with a penetrating psy-

NEW REALISM *was brought to painting by Masaccio's use of perspective in the* Holy Trinity *(1425) and to sculpture by Donatello's natural yet beautiful* David *(1432).*

chological drama. The brim of David's hat shadows his moody face as he casts his eyes downward. In the moments after victory he has realized his strength, ability, and personal beauty. It is a moment of self-awareness after a millenium of sleep.

The last phase of Donatello's career saw a turning away from the beautiful to intentional distortion. In statues like his *Mary Magdalene* the sculptor extended his psychological repertoire to include the corrupting effects of sin and the power of spiritual remorse.

The length and brilliance of Donatello's career deserve the limelight, but other sculptors were also hard at work. One of the most notable was Ghiberti (whose victory in the baptistry door competition led to Brunelleschi's abandonment of sculpture for architecture). His personal grace and gift for spatial illusion made Ghiberti's studio the major training ground for the next generation of sculptors, the most outstanding of whom was Verrocchio. Other contemporaries of Donatello, including Nanni di Banco and Luca della Robbia, developed the expressive power of sculpture via their studies of antique drapery. By the late 1400's, the quest for sculptural truth had so evolved that Pollaiuolo was supplementing the authority of antiquity with his own studies of human anatomy. He even dissected corpses to gain a better understanding of bone and musculature.

Alberti.
The scientific interests of Pollaiuolo were typical of Renaissance art. Everywhere men were trying to develop valid theories on which to base their actions. Piero della Francesca's treatise on the theory of perspective was an early effort at such theory-making. With the invention of the printing press, Renaissance theory spread throughout all Italy and gradually through all of Europe through books and pamphlets.

By far the most influential spirit was Leon Battista Alberti, who wrote three treatises, *"On Painting," "On the Statue,"* and *"The Ten Books of Architecture."* As no man before him, Alberti codified Renaissance thought and established the theoretical basis of beauty. He defined it as "the harmony and concord of parts, achieved in such a manner that nothing could be added, taken away, or altered." Alberti was the first person to seriously study the first century architectural treatise of Vitruvius, and he used it to develop his ideal system of proportions. For Alberti, contact with antiquity was not just a mental exercise. It was a way of life. We can see its results in the palace that he designed for the powerful merchant family Rucellai.

As far as the Italians knew, there were no antique houses extant. Even if there had been, their value would have been minimal as a model. Times

THE PALAZZO RUCELLAI *in Florence (1457) shows Alberti's use of classic decoration: arches and pilasters inscribed on a flat wall.*

had changed, and Renaissance homes had to accommodate modern needs. Alberti solved the problem with a compromise: he built a traditional three-story house with windows, doors, and overhanging cornice, and then he decorated it with the classical elements that Brunelleschi had reintroduced. Alberti chose the Colosseum as his model. He copied its blend of arches and vertical pilasters. But the Colosseum's numerous openings were inappropriate for a private house, so Alberti simply indicated them by inscribed lines without changing the structure of his building. In fact, the facade is just a flat wall on top of which a linear net of classical details has been overlaid. In the Palazzo Rucellai, Alberti adapted antiquity to

modern needs. It was a theme to which he dedicated his entire career, reviving Roman barrel vaults, triumphal arches, and especially the orders as living parts of the new architectural vocabulary.

Alberti was a stellar intellect, but his situation was not unlike that of most artists of the later 1400's. They were confronted with the problems of how to infuse the new art with ancient spirit, how to make the teachings of antiquity their own, and in short, how to bring about a Renaissance of the classical past. Their interest led them to study classical philosophy, literature, and poetry. They were convinced of the ancients' superior wisdom, and they scoured their texts for profound universal truths.

Botticelli.
The most fertile center of humanistic thought was the circle of Lorenzo de Medici, the great Florentine prince, poet, and patron of the arts. He surrounded himself with the most enlightened scholars and artists of the day, including Sandro Botticelli. Of all the painters of the age, it was he who most effectively sought to reconcile pagan and Christian philosophies. In 1480 he painted the famous *Birth of Venus.*

Born of the sea, the goddess of love is driven to shore upon a cockle shell. She is propelled by embracing wind gods who fly behind her in a perfumed shower of roses. On land, a nymph extends a floral robe to the naked Venus. The painting has been variously interpreted. Some see it as an allegory for the birth of beauty, while others feel it represents the innocence of the human soul about to be draped in the robe of reason.

Such allegories were common in Renaissance thought. Botticelli, however, used them in a way that rejected

THE BIRTH OF VENUS *by Botticelli, c 1490, introduces a classical subject to painting.*

the illusionistic breakthroughs of his predecessors. Instead of painting a convincing expanse of sea, he provided a flat plane with little V-shapes for waves. The heavy figures of Giotto and Masaccio were abandoned by him for weightless beings who delicately float on their toes. Strength and emotion are sacrificed to linear patterns of fluttering hair and draperies, radiating shell segments, and isolating contours. Venus is like a cut-out doll pasted on top of the painting. Even attempts at perfect human proportion have given way to graceful exaggeration. But if Venus's long neck, sloping shoulders, and drooping left arm are unnatural, they emphasize the ethereal refinement of the beautiful naked goddess (the first nude Venus since antiquity). Unlike earlier Renaissance artists who strove to portray the natural world, Botticelli's mystical approach was based on the humanistic belief that man could reach God by the contemplation of beauty.

Such ideas were denounced by the fanatical monk Savonarola, who railed against the pagan attitudes of the Medici court. His puritanical attacks dampened humanistic fires and deprived Florence of its cultural leadership. Already the focus was shifting.

In Umbria, Signorelli was following up the work of Pollaiuolo and Verrocchio with violent paintings of muscular bodies; and his compatriot Perugino was laying the essential groundwork for High Renaissance spatial compositions. In Northern Italy, the literary and archaeological artist Mantagne exploited perspective in overwhelmingly realistic paintings. His influence would be felt in the later Venetian school. It crossed the Alps where it was enthusiastically received by Albrecht Dürer, the father of the Northern Renaissance.

The High Renaissance

The true successor to Florentine preeminence was Rome. The papacy was on the rise once again, and the promise of papal patronage attracted Italy's greatest talents. Architects, painters, and sculptors flocked to the Vatican to glorify the church and to satisfy the increasingly sumptuous tastes of the popes. Thus began the High Renaissance, the most illustrious period of Italian creative genius.

The new era was ushered in by men of such extraordinary genius that nothing seemed impossible. Their broad intellectual and creative horizons elevated them from lowly craftsmen to respected celebrities, reversing traditional patron-artist relationships in the process. In the past, the artist was flattered by a commission from a

MONA LISA, *c 1503, by Leonardo da Vinci, is perhaps the most famous portrait in the world.*

great prince. But now *he* bestowed the honor by agreeing to do such work. His new status gave respectability to the artistic profession and secured its place among the "fine" arts.

Leonardo. The prophet of the new age was Leonardo da Vinci, a man of such intellect that we can scarcely comprehend the breadth of his achievements. His voluminous notebooks show that he was interested in everything: the effects of atmosphere, the growth of babies in the womb, the nature of sound, and the motion of waves and currents. His insatiable curiosity led him to explore botany, zoology, anatomy, geology, hydraulics, psychology, physiology, and optics. He also studied the flight of birds and designed a flying machine. Moreover, Leonardo was a skilled military engineer, stage designer, architect, musician, and poet. He was the universal man.

The aim of Leonardo's unbounded pursuits was the discovery of nature's eternal laws. When he was confronted by a problem, he never turned to the ancients, but used his own mind and eyes to come up with a solution. All of his scientific experiments were conducted as a means of gaining more information about the visible world. To Leonardo, man's eyes were the "windows of his soul." It was only through them that he could find truth.

The significance of Leonardo's vision is apparent in his paintings. His *Last Supper* goes far beyond the mere recounting of a Biblical story. It combines perfect harmony, balance, and spatial illusion with a profound knowledge of human nature. It is a

model of psychological drama revealed by artistic genius.

Leonardo's celebrity soared to an even greater height with his *Mona Lisa,* the most famous portrait in the world. Seated quietly, she stares at the viewer with a smile that has both captivated and confused her admirers for nearly 500 years. Her mysterious expression, sometimes seeming happy, other times sad or even jeering, is the result of *sfumato.* Leonardo invented this technique of blurred contours to obscure the transition from one plane to another. Unlike his exacting psychological studies in the *Last Supper,* he intentionally disguises Mona Lisa's true character in fuzzy shadow. The absence of precise boundaries makes her face seem to merge with the hazy landscape behind. How different she is from the cold linear figures of Botticelli.

Leonardo's superb handling of light and shade gave *Mona Lisa* the warm fleshiness of a living person. She is at once eternal and immobile, yet fleeting. Leonardo himself must have been enchanted with this dreamlike painting because he could never part with it. He carried it with him to France and kept it in his possession until his death in 1519.

Bramante. While Leonardo was in Milan he met Donato Bramante, the greatest architect of the generation. Like Brunelleschi and Alberti, Bramante was dedicated to the revival of antiquity. But he was no slavish imitator. He distilled the essence of classical architecture (symmetry, clarity, geometry, proportion, and the orders) and used it to develop the centralized church plan. Its significance can hardly be overstated. A circle is appropriate to the eternal God because it has no beginning or end. As pure geometry, it was sanctioned in antiquity as the ideal symbol of perfection, beauty, and truth. Leonardo had made sketches of centralized churches; his influence is undoubtedly at work in the *Tempietto,* or little temple, by Bramante.

Bramante erected this small shrine on the site where St. Peter was believed to have been crucified. Its parts are so finely proportioned and so perfectly integrated that it stands in its courtyard like an inspired piece of monumental sculpture. Its austere Doric colonnade (appropriate to the masculine St. Peter) contrasts with the balustrade above, while its walls and niches play off each other with great three-dimensional complexity. The contrasting rhythms of solid and void, large and small, and projection and recession are orchestrated with such skill that the *Tempietto* can be likened to a beautiful symphony in stone.

It is little wonder that the creator of this architectural gem was selected by the pope to design the new church of

St. Peter. The church was destined to become the most important undertaking of the 16th century, employing the greatest talents in Italy. Bramante began the process with a centralized plan, but he died before his plans were carried out. He was succeeded by a host of architects (including Raphael and Michelangelo), only some of whom recognized the importance of his scheme. Ultimately, Bramante's centralized plan was rejected as too pagan and the more traditional form of an elongated basilica was adopted.

Raphael. If Bramante achieved ideal architectural form in the High Renaissance, then it was Raphael who attained it in painting. As a child he was apprenticed to Perugino, but he quickly surpassed his master, transforming his rigid spatial compositions into works of effortless grace. Raphael's genius was already far advanced at age 21 when he painted *The Marriage of the Virgin.*

In general format, the painting owes a great deal to Perugino. But Raphael softened his master's formality, creating the delicacy and grace of a visual ballet. Sweetly the Virgin extends her hand to receive a wedding ring from St. Peter. There is no excitement, just the flow of true classical calm. The quiet is not even disturbed by the rejected suitor who breaks his rod over his knee. On the contrary, his delicate balance only adds to this scene of ideal harmony. Raphael's figures epitomize High Renaissance goals of human conduct in a logically ordered world.

The theme is continued in the piazza and dominating temple (which recalls Bramante's centralized architecture). Space curves around its circular walls and penetrates its central door to an infinite vista behind. The whole composition transcends worldly limitations. So effective is its poise, so uncluttered its space, that it exists in the spiritual realm of supernatural ideals.

The effortless grace of Raphael's paintings makes it easy for us to forget that they were the result of countless hours of unrelenting work. He learned from everyone, but adapted borrowed ideas to his own style, which stressed simplicity, dignity, and charm.

In his short life, Raphael painted some of the world's most sensitive Madonnas. He also created frescoes of such power that they are without equal in the history of art. The finest of these are in the Vatican and were executed for Pope Julius II. *School of Athens* is a complete artistic and spiritual statement of the High Renaissance. Unified by a complex iconography, it shows a meeting of the greatest ancient philosophers and scientists. It is an eloquent celebration of classical and Renaissance ideals, the ultimate union between pagan and Christian thought.

Michelangelo. Raphael's grace, Leonardo's science, and Bramante's geometric perfection were offset by the brooding figure of Michelangelo Buonarroti. He was a wily recluse, intolerant, jealous, and short-tempered. But he had a deep understanding of man, and his explosive genius claimed for man an almost Godlike strength.

The extent of Michelangelo's skill was so great that he refused to be restricted by laws. Indeed, he even abandoned mathematical rules for perfect proportion. As far as he was concerned, beauty was in the "idea," and it was the task of the sculptor to release such slumbering concepts from their stone prisons. Removing excess stone freed the image locked inside.

Michelangelo's extraordinary talents were early recognized by Lorenzo de Medici, whose famous court introduced the youth to the most elevated humanist scholars and artists. However, Medici power collapsed in 1494 and Michelangelo fled to Bologna, and then to Rome, where he created the *Pietà.* It was his earliest masterpiece. Never before had cold white marble been transformed into such a warm and poignant vision. The Virgin Mother, beautiful and ageless, extends her left hand as she contemplates her dead son. Only the crumpled drapery across her breast reflects her grief. The wrinkled cloth simultaneously acts as a foil to the smooth refinement of Christ's body. His anatomical accuracy is the result of Michelangelo's dissection of human corpses. The crucified body shows no sign of pain. In fact, Christ's wounds are barely visible, and his dreamy face bespeaks the achievement of final peace.

When the sculpture was first exhibited in St. Peter's, no one in the awestricken crowd could believe that it was created by the 23-year-old Michelangelo. When they left, he stole back into the church and proudly carved his name on the strap across Mary's bosom. It is the only genuine signature on any of Michelangelo's sculptures.

After a six-year absence Michelangelo returned to Florence, where he tackled the "Giant," an enormous marble block that no one else had been able to carve. Out of this impossible challenge emerged the statue of *David,* the vibrant and battle-prepared youth who became the city's symbol. A quick look at *David* deceives us. We get an initial impression of relaxation. He is the Biblical hero standing at ease, slingshot over his shoulder. But closer study reveals pulsating muscles and bulging veins that suggest tremendous pent-up energy.

IDEAL AND NATURAL *blend in these High Renaissance masterpieces: Raphael's* The Marriage of the Virgin *and Michelangelo's* David, *both completed c 1504.*

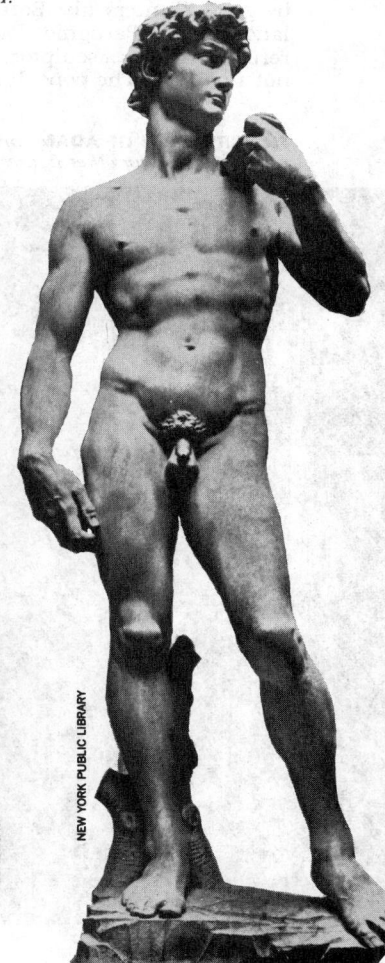

ALINARI/EPA

NEW YORK PUBLIC LIBRARY

With the tension of a spring about to uncoil, *David* acutely watches his approaching enemy. His penetrating stare and flaring nostrils give him a ferociousness that the Italians call *terribilita*. How different he is from Donatello's sweet young *David*. Michelangelo's statue is more closely related to those of Greek athletes like *Doryphorus*. Both celebrate the heroic physique, but next to the explosive *David*, the classical work seems feeble. This quality of pent-up passion characterized Michelangelo's life and work. It separated him totally from Raphael and other artists who were dedicated to the portrayal of calm and ideal beauty.

Michelangelo was next summoned to Rome to work on the colossal tomb of Julius II. But after six months the pope lost interest in the scheme, partly because of his construction of St. Peter's. Frustrated and sorely disappointed, Michelangelo returned to Florence. He was persuaded to come back to Rome only by the most skillful diplomacy. (The Florentines were actually afraid that the pope would blame them for harboring the artist and therefore encouraged his return.) When he finally submitted, an unhappy commission awaited. The pope wanted Michelangelo to paint the ceiling of the Sistine Chapel. The walls of the chapel already had been decorated by great painters like Botticelli, Ghirlandaio and Perugino. Michelangelo refused. He was a sculptor, he insisted, not a painter. The pope finally had his

way, and Michelangelo began work, still hoping he would soon be allowed to resume his work on the tomb.

Julius II envisioned paintings of the twelve apostles. But again, Michelangelo refused. In the end, the pope let him paint what he wanted, although Michelangelo must have had a theological advisor to guide him through complex Biblical iconography. After arranging for a crew of assistants, the artist locked himself in the chapel and allowed no one else to enter.

The ceiling was huge, covering 5800 square feet (the equivalent of a canvas 100 feet long and 58 feet—nearly six stories—high). During the next four years, this lonely genius painted the ceiling single-handedly, lying on his back 70 feet above the ground, a candle balanced on his head.

In 1512 the doors were opened to an astonished world. Over 300 figures in every imaginable posture dramatically stretch across the vault in a narration of man's creation, fall, and redemption. The achievement was nothing less than superhuman!

Seated in massive thrones on either side of the ceiling are the Old Testament prophets and sibyls who predicted the coming of the Messiah. Between them are triangular scenes of Christ's ancestors. In the center of the ceiling large and small panels alternate as the story of Genesis unfolds. Hosts of lesser figures appear: tiny putti (cherubs), standing sculptural figures, and muscular youths seated at the corners of the central scenes of the

Creation. There is no decoration other than the human body in encyclopedic postures. The human form is the source of expressive power and the beautiful creation of God, but it is also the prison of souls yearning to be free.

One of the most famous scenes from the Sistine ceiling is the *Creation of Adam*. Beautiful and potentially strong, the first man is still one with the unformed earth. He limply extends his hand to receive the vibrant spark of life from God the Father, who approaches in a billowing robe amid an angelic escort. All attention is focused on the outstretched fingers of the two heroic figures. The Creation of Adam had been painted many times before, but never with such a profound understanding.

Upon the completion of the Sistine ceiling, Michelangelo eagerly resumed work on Julius's tomb, only to be interrupted once again. The remaining 50 years of his long life were filled with the most important painting, sculpture, and architectural commissions of the century, including the construction of St. Peter's. By the time Michelangelo died at age 89, he had become the prototype of artistic genius: the supreme intellect who transcended law and tradition, the paramount talent who invested man with grand dignity. This artist was known by his contemporaries as the "divine" Michelangelo.

Mannerism

The extraordinary achievements of Leonardo, Raphael, and Michelangelo tend to obscure the accomplishments of other 16th century artists; for example, the lustrous color schemes of Andrea del Sarto and the unsurpassed sensuality of Correggio's religious and mythological scenes. But change was in the air.

By about 1520 High Renaissance art had reached its peak. All problems of space, color, composition, and human form seemed to have been solved. The towering geniuses of the era had succeeded in reviving antiquity and, indeed, they were confident that they had even surpassed it.

This presented the new generation of artists with an irksome question. If all artistic problems had already been solved, what was left for them to do? They decided to improve on the High Renaissance, especially the work of Michelangelo, which had taught them the benefits of artistic freedom. They rejected nature as their model and chose instead the art of their forebears. They hoped to recreate this art in a new and interesting manner. If the High Renaissance had achieved calm, harmony, balance, and naturalism, the new "Mannerists" sought restless discord, instability, and bizarre fantasy.

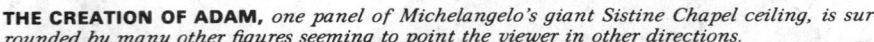

THE CREATION OF ADAM, *one panel of Michelangelo's giant Sistine Chapel ceiling, is surrounded by many other figures seeming to point the viewer in other directions.*
EPA

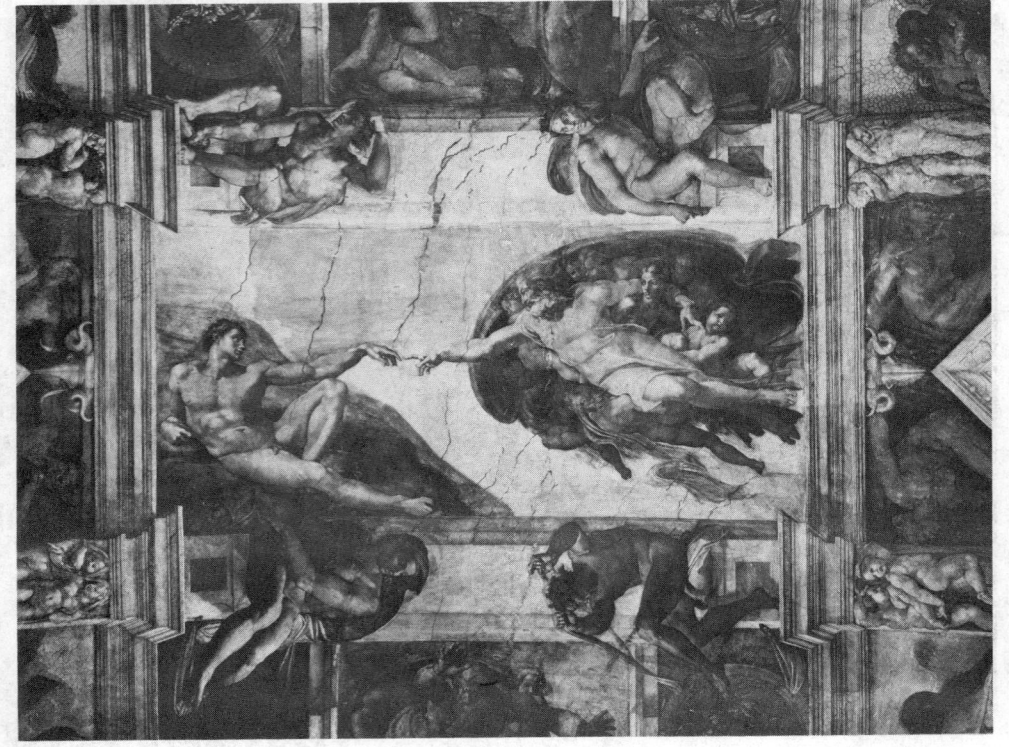

MADONNA WITH THE LONG NECK by *Parmigianino (1535) uses crowding and lack of visual balance for dramatic effect.*

Clarity and simplicity were replaced by ambiguous complexity, and paintings assumed the form of deliberately intricate puzzles. With a bold disregard of artistic conventions, the Mannerists concentrated on artificiality, distortion, and exaggeration. Pontormo, Bronzino, and Il Rosso Fiorentino ("the red head") produced strange works with clashing colors, nervous movement, and enamel-skinned people in disturbing spatial vacuums. Many of the same qualities are apparent in Parmigianino's *Madonna with the Long Neck.*

Seated with the ungainly Christ sprawled on her lap, the Madonna has been unnaturally elongated. To emphasize her elegance, Parmigianino gave the giantess a tiny oval head atop a swanlike neck, and delicate fingers that stretch like pulled taffy. She is worlds apart from Raphael's graceful Madonnas. To the Virgin's right a cluster of angels is compacted into an uncomfortably small space, only to be cut off abruptly by the picture frame. Unlike Renaissance paintings, where figures are evenly distributed across the surface, Parmigianino's paintings intentionally contrast the two sides of his work. Our eyes pass without transition from the congested foreground to the deep background, where a haggard prophet reads an outstretched scroll. An ominous colonnade that supports nothing adds a surreal note to the painting.

The artificial and extreme sophistication of Italian Mannerism spread to France when Il Rosso, Primaticcio, and Cellini were invited to Fontainebleau by King Francis I. With them came the full repertoire of Mannerist ornament. Cellini, sculptor and gold-smith, became a court favorite with his exquisite works in precious metals. The other two artists redecorated the interior of the king's chateau. The supreme example of their achievement is the bedchamber of the duchess of Etampes, where paintings of Alexander the Great are framed by slender female stuccoes. The origin of such human supports can be traced to antiquity, but in the hands of the Mannerists classical purity was replaced by a complicated network of garlands, cherubs, grotesques, and interlocking strapwork.

As work continued at Fontainebleau, more artists were enlisted from Italy and France. So powerful was Mannerist impact that it spread beyond the royal court. Its influence is best seen in the turbulent work of Jean de Boulogne, the French sculptor who traveled to Italy to receive further training. He Italianized his name to Giovanni de Bologna and settled down in Florence to become one of the most important sculptors of the latter 1500's.

As the Mannerist vogue spread, eventually influencing even architecture, it reached the highest peak of sophistication. Architects like Zuccari exploited its caprice with windows that look like human faces. Giulio Romano, on the other hand, worked in a more traditional idiom. His brand of Mannerism consisted of classical elements used in a most nonclassical manner to produce great architectural parodies of ancient and High Renaissance styles. His most famous work is the Palazzo del Te in Mantua, where deliberate irregularities violate the fundamental principles of humanistic architecture. A similar passion for distortion was indulged by Ammanati in the courtyard of the Pitti Palace in Florence.

The School of Venice

Throughout the 1400's, the powerful republic of Venice remained somewhat aloof from the other Italian states. It was distinguished as a separate country, culturally as well as politically, and one of its distinctions was its continued contact with the Byzantine Empire to the east.

The appeal of the great movements in art and architecture finally made their impact after 1530, and the result was a brilliant new flowering of Renaissance thought and sensibility.

Palladio. Classical architecture was introduced to Venice in the 1530's by Jacopo Samsovino. Within two decades, the new style had been perfected by Andrea de Pietro, known as Palladio (after Pallas Athena, the ancient goddess of wisdom). In Palladio, northern Italy could claim the world's greatest architectural classicist.

Palladio began as a stonemason and sculptor, but at age 30 he turned to architecture. During several trips to Rome he digested the lessons of antiquity and the theoretical writings of Vitruvius and Alberti. In 1570 he published the *Quattro Libri (The Four Books on Architecture),* a treatise whose significance can hardly be overstated. It was eagerly seized upon by architects throughout Europe, and it later formed the basis of a classical revival in England and North America during the 1700's. Few persons in all history have had such wide ranging effects as Palladio.

Palladio is best known for his villas and churches, most of which center around his hometown of Vicenza. The most famous is the Villa Capra, known by its nickname, Villa Rotunda.

In adapting antique forms to modern residences, Palladio erroneously assumed that ancient houses were fronted by great temple porticoes, and so he incorporated one on each face of the Villa Rotunda. He used the Roman Pantheon as a model for both the porticoes and the central dome.

Centuries later, the elegance of Palladio's "classical" design, and its practical advantages (protection from the sun and ventilation), appealed to plantation owners in the southern United States. Thus Palladian designs became popular for the great plantations.

ELABORATE DECORATION of a bed-chamber at *Fontainebleau, c 1540, reflects Mannerist tastes.*

The austerity of Palladio's rational architecture is considerably relieved by the soft northern light of Venice. His church of San Giorgio Maggiore, for instance, might appear rigid and formal somewhere else. But here, against the brilliant blue sky, and lit by the flickering play of reflections from the water, it seems relaxed and "at home."

Painting. Palladio's interest in light was typical of Venetian artists. In fact, the Venetian school of painting was dedicated to understanding and using light and color. A distinctly Venetian style emerged with Giovanni Bellini, whose long career spanned the three generations from International Style through to the High Renaissance. He is most famous for his paintings of Madonnas, which seem to radiate with supernatural light.

To Bellini and his followers light and color were not merely something *added* to a drawn image; they were the major ingredients of painting. By contrast, the earlier Florentines and the High Renaissance masters were more concerned with draftsmanship and with depicting space, especially through perspective.

Bellini's interest in color was extended even further by his student Giorgione. Although only five paintings can be absolutely attributed to Giorgione, he ranks among the great painters of the Renaissance. His idyllic scenes of tranquil love were bathed in mysterious soft shadows.

Titian. The advances made by Bellini and Giorgione peaked in the art of Titian, the supreme colorist. A brilliant draftsman, he challenged Michelangelo as the most popular Renaissance artist.

Titian was of the first painter to totally free his brush stroke from the literal description of tactile surfaces. He was not concerned with making an exact replica of how things look. He was more interested in capturing the subjects' energy and emotion as they were transformed by light. To achieve this effect, Titian used oil paints on rough-textured canvas (in place of earlier wooden panels). He began by painting the entire surface red. On top of this warm ground he added brilliantly colored figures. (A contemporary of Titian described his painted highlights as "drops of blood.") Next the painter applied layers of glaze—30 or even 40 of them—to unify his composition and to modulate the jarring effects of his exuberant colors.

The results of this technique are apparent in the *Rape of Europa,* which Titian painted in his old age. The *Rape* shows a final stage in Titian's ever-loosening use of the brush stroke. The mythological scene depicts the god Zeus (in the guise of a white bull)

RAPE OF EUROPA, *c 1560, illustrates Titian's use of new effects of light and color and a new sensuousness in portraying mythological stories.*

abducting the lovely maiden Europa. Surging forward, her red mantle waves dramatically against the sky as her friends cry out from the distant shore. Two flying cherubs and one astride a fish emphasize the compelling diagonal thrust of the painting. Titian's loosely applied paint melts the background into an indistinct multicolored haze.

During the course of his six-decade career, Titian dominated Venetian art with his portraits and his mythological and religious paintings. His achievements served as both a source and a foil to his competitors. The impetuous Tintoretto, for example, tried to emulate his color but opposed his slow and careful method of working. He was impatient with the many months that Titian lavished on his works. Tintoretto tried to combine the best of Titian with the power of Michelangelo.

The other great Venetian painter was Veronese, creator of enormous canvases that often used grand architectural settings from antiquity. Veronese's intoxicating colors and extreme illusionism bring Venetian Renaissance painting to a close. His works look forward to the theatrical productions of the upcoming Baroque period.

The Northern Renaissance

In Italy the period from 1300 to 1600 was zealously dedicated to the revival of antiquity. Ever since Giotto, architects, painters, and sculptors had worked to reinstate classical ideals. By about 1520 total victory was theirs. In just over 200 years Italian artists had established the rules for a scientific approach to the representation of nature. Treatises on science and art abounded, and theoretical standards of perfection were thoroughly explored. Unleashed from church domination and encouraged by classical philosophy, Renaissance man came into direct contact with his physical world. He became an achiever and an independent thinker. He established the basis of modern individualism.

A simultaneous revolution was taking place north of the Alps, but its character was quite different. Whereas Italy was filled with ancient ruins, ready inspiration for the modern imitators, the north had no such ties to antiquity. Consequently, this area (consisting of modern France, Belgium, Luxembourg, most of Holland, and part of Germany) remained under Gothic influence well into the 1400's.

This is most readily apparent in Northern architecture, where the pointed Gothic look became even more elaborate. It culminated in the flamboyant style of fantastic ornament and effusive overlays.

Painting. Northern painting had a parallel development. In Italy the International Style was quickly dispelled by the new classicism. In the North, by contrast, it became a rich point of departure for several generations of painters. The movement was led by the Master of Flamalle (most probably Robert Campin). Working in the tradition of the Limbourg Brothers, Campin and his followers maintained a style of two-dimensional decoration. But they addressed a more bourgeoise audience. Northern wealth was now in the hands of successful merchants and bankers, so art had a more popular appeal. Instead of preparing illuminated manuscripts for wealthy patrons, the Northern artist came to produce large painted panels to be set above church altars. There they appealed to a broad public, rich and poor, educated and simple.

This more democratic approach also changed the artists' subject matter. In place of splendid court scenes, early Northern painters depicted middle-class domestic interiors, complete with an encyclopedic record of everything inside. This could be a serious problem for the painter of religious scenes. How could he portray supernatural events in an everyday setting? His solution was "disguised symbolism," in which almost every detail, regardless of how casual or insignificant, was imbued with a symbolic message. For example, Campin's *Merode Altarpiece* depicts the Annunciation.

An angel appears in a common Flemish home to announce to Mary her selection as the mother of Christ. Virtually all the ordinary domestic accessories are analogies for some aspect of this sacred event. Particular flowers in the painting refer to Mary's humility, chastity, and love, while a water basin denotes her purity. Towels, candles, books and other objects all play similar symbolic roles.

With his humanization of divine events, the Northern painter deprived the holy characters of their supernatural distance from man. The characters appear just like ordinary people; even their halos have been omitted. By showing an extraordinary event in an ordinary environment, the artist could indulge his delight in tiny details. The Northern painter was totally committed to the accurate *appearance* of objects (in this he opposed his Italian counterparts who used perspective, mathematics, and proportion to discover the structure behind appearances). Thus the bases of the two artistic revolutions were different. In Italy, it was centered around the revival of antiquity. In the North, it concentrated on the discovery of man in his visible world.

Jan van Eyck.

The conquest of appearances was achieved by Jan and Hubert van Eyck. Their greatest combined effort was the *Ghent Altarpiece,* composed of 20 separate panels hinged together to form an enormous double-register altarpiece. It was signed by both artists and dated 1432. It is not clear what each brother contributed, but there is no doubt about the consummate skill of Jan van Eyck. So exacting was his microscopic record of the world, that even a contemporary Italian humanist called him the "prince of painters in our age." He is universally acknowledged as one of the greatest painters of all time.

Jan's acclaim stems from the almost photographic quality of his paintings, a revolutionary effect achieved through his invention of oil paints. Before the modern age, artists had to mix their own colors. They used stone to grind solid pigments into a fine powder and then they added a binding agent. Egg was the most popular. Its only drawback was that it dried quickly and so limited the artist's flexibility. Jan van Eyck substituted oil for egg. This allowed him to work much more slowly and to add many details with razor sharp accuracy.

Northern artists applied thin layers of transparent glaze on top of their pictures. This solution of oil and turpentine was mixed with color to unify the painting with a resonant glow. (We have already seen the effect of glazes on the works of Titian.) These enamel-hard layers made it seem as if one were looking at the painted image through tinted panes of glass. The effect it produced was revolutionary. Glazes tend to capture light, and thus Northern paintings seem to be lit from within. Their sparkling highlights, transparent shadows, intense tonalities, and minute accuracy distinguish them from contemporary Italian work. Executed in tempera, Southern paintings appear heavy and opaque.

Jan van Eyck used his new invention to catalog reality with scrupulous honesty. His achievements are apparent in the *Arnolfini Wedding*. It shows the Italian silk merchant Giovanni Arnolfini holding his young wife's hand. He takes the vows of matrimony and raises his right hand in an oath of fidelity. The quiet ceremony takes place in his Netherlands-like bedchamber. (It was common for Italian merchants to keep a business residence in the Northern centers of international banking and trade.)

At first glance it may seem a little strange for a wedding to take place outside a church. After all, marriage is a sacrament. But if Jan has omitted conspicuous religious imagery, he has charged every household item with a symbolism that participates in the sanctity of the occasion. The dog in the foreground represents fidelity (the original meaning of Fido). The nearby shoes identify the area as sacred. Fruit near the window symbolizes fertility, as does the small sculpted figure on the bedpost. It is St. Margaret, patron of childbirth.The small whisk brush on the back wall denotes domestic care, and the single candle burning in the chandelier (shining in broad daylight) signifies the all-seeing eye of God. Thus, while Jan has not included images of saints or angels, the spiritual exists in his symbols.

Another curious aspect of the *Arnolfini* portrait is the seeming privacy of the ceremony. Who and where are the witnesses? They are Jan van Eyck and his assistant! They are reflected in the mirror on the back wall and verified by the florid script above: "Johannes de Eyck fuit hic. 1434" (Jan van Eyck was here. 1434). The artist presented an exact depiction of what he saw; thus, the painting assumes the role of a visual marriage certificate, signed, dated, and witnessed.

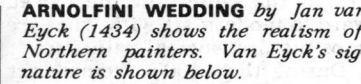

ARNOLFINI WEDDING *by Jan van Eyck (1434) shows the realism of Northern painters. Van Eyck's signature is shown below.*

NATIONAL GALLERY

Jan's techniques were irreproachable. Indeed, they were so perfect that very few painters attempted to improve on—or even imitate—his style. Instead, they sought new approaches to replace his exhaustive symbolic details. They aspired to human drama, action and a relief from overbearing disguised symbolism. The great leader of this expressive movement was Rogier van der Weyden, whose large emotional paintings became even more monumental through his contact with Italy.

After van der Weyden's death in 1464, the leadership of the Northern school of painting fell to the introspective Hugo van der Goes. His paintings, sometimes melancholy and other times passionate, infused Flemish art with an unprecedented internal drama. His greatest work, the *Portinari Altarpiece,* was installed in a Florentine church. It created a great stir among Southern artists who were mesmerized by its tremendous realism. Van der Goes' contemporary, Hans Memlinc, was also held in high regard, but his genial nature led this follower of Rogier van der Weyden to concentrate on pretty religious paintings.

The 1400's came to a disruptive close with the fantastic work of Hieronymus Bosch, one of the most intriguing and puzzling artists the world has known. Are his strange dreamlike paintings, filled with frightening beasts, hideous hybrids, and erotic plant forms, stern moral "lessons"? Or are they merely the pornographic creations of a perverse mind? Might they be the satirical work of a brazen heretic? Bosch's images are so complex that modern scholars still cannot answer these questions.

Bosch's grim view of life led him back to the old pagan animal style. Yet, at the same time, he looked forward to modern art with what are perhaps the first surreal paintings.

During the 1400's Flemish art had great impact in Germany. Scores of minor masters responded to the achievements of van Eyck, van der Weyden, and their followers. But the number of truly great talents was limited. Among the distinguished roster must be included Stephan Lochner and his charming religious paintings, Conrad Witz and his realistic landscapes, and Michael Pacher and his monumental compositions emphasizing perspective. The latter was the first to establish important contacts with Italy, and thus prepare the way for what would be a veritable flood of Southern influence in the 1500's.

Graphic arts. While national isolation was beginning to dissolve, a monumental event took place in Germany: the invention of the printing press by Gutenberg. Because it permitted the inexpensive publication of books, it provided the perfect avenue for the diffusion of foreign ideas, binding the various European countries ever more closely together.

The printing press also encouraged significant changes in the graphic arts. Previously, pictures were reproduced by means of woodblocks. Designs were first drawn of the face of a block; then the background was carved away. The lines left projecting were inked and pressed onto paper. The process could be repeated as many times as desired. The technique was simple enough and Northern artists developed its expressive potential. But by 1450, even the most refined woodblocks could not accommodate the new interests in microscopic detail. Consequently, they were replaced by engravings.

The engraving process was the opposite of the woodblock process. It called for the artist to trace lines on a copper plate with a special tool called a *burin.* When the design was completely drawn, the whole plate was covered with ink. The next step was to wipe the untooled areas clean, leaving ink only in the deep linear impressions made by the burin. From this point on, it was merely a process of pressing the plate against a sheet of paper.

It took great skill to handle a burin. Lines had to be of uniform depth and thickness, and mistakes were almost impossible to correct. But in the hands of skilled craftsmen, engravings provided much more subtlety and much finer detail than even the most developed woodcut. The greatest 15th century engraver was Martin Schongauer, whose mastery of the burin let him distinguish a tremendous variety of tones and textures, ranging from furry monsters and scaly beasts to wispy feathers, human hair, and coarse crumpled cloth. Moreover, his expressive and spatial powers gave him the title "the Rogier van der Weyden of engraving."

Italian influence. As notable as Schongauer's advances may have been, they hardly prepared one for the revolutionary achievements of the early 1500's. After years of only minor contact with Italy, Northern artists were seized by a sudden awareness of developments beyond the Alps. They were overcome by a desire to assimilate the Italian style as thoroughly and as quickly as possible. Many went to Italy to experience the Italian Renaissance at first hand. Scores of others learned of its wonders through engravings like those of Marcantonio Raimondi, who graphically reproduced Raphael's works. The ensuing creative explosion brought the Northern Renaissance to a peak. It developed simultaneously with the Italian High Renaissance, and it ended about 1530, ten years after the decline in Italy. The greatest Northern talents were contemporaries of Bramante, Raphael, Michelangelo, Giorgione, and Titian.

Outstanding among German artists was Matthias Grünewald. He painted scenes of horrifying intensity, such as the flesh-torn Christ in the *Isenheim Altarpiece.* However, his talent lies less in his ability to portray repulsive carnage than in his ability to transform events to the level of high human drama. Grünewald's contemporary, Albrecht Altdorfer, chose a totally different vehicle for his powerful expression. He concentrated on sweeping, passionate landscapes. A third German, Lucas Cranach, developed in yet another direction. He imitated Italian sensuality, but totally rejected its classical trappings. He remained steadfast in his provincial, oddly proportioned figures, oblivious to the scientific laws of Italian art.

Dürer. Of all German personalities, there is none who could compare with Albrecht Dürer, the "da Vinci of the North" (unlike Leonardo, Dürer devoted his research almost exclusively to artistic problems). Dürer was the first Northerner to travel to Italy for the sole purpose of studying art (1495), the first Northerner to establish an international reputation, and the first to fully comprehend the aims of the Italian Renaissance. He dedicated his life to their diffusion in the North.

Dürer wrote treatises on such diverse topics as military engineering, perspective, and proportion. He was also a great painter. But it is through the graphic arts that Dürer revealed his genius. His woodcuts and engravings are unsurpassed in their beauty and excellence.

A suggestion of his extraordinary talents is provided by his engraving *Adam and Eve,* the final result of a series of preparatory drawings in which

ADAM AND EVE *by Dürer (1504) puts classic figures in a Northern European setting.*

HUNTERS IN THE SNOW *by Pieter Breughel (1560) is a vast panorama of winter activities in Breughel's Netherlands. The painting reasserts the importance of the everyday life of simple people as a subject for art.*

Dürer experimented with ideal proportions. Both figures are based on classical models, although Eve retains the ungainliness of an overly fleshy German matron. Adam and Eve are still somewhat awkward foreigners in the North, Southern nudes shivering in the cold Northern forest that outlines them so dramatically. Nevertheless, they represent the first serious attempt to transplant Italian ideals beyond the Alps.

If the religious theme seems merely an excuse to show heroic nudes, it is balanced by Dürer's intellectual brand of symbolism, in which he emphasizes the conflicts of original sin. The branch that Adam holds signifies the tree of life, but the fig tree around which the serpent coils represents damnation. The elk symbolizes greed, the ox gluttony and sloth, the cat pride, and the rabbit lechery. On another level, these animals are an analogy for the diseases that man inherited as a result of Adam's and Eve's sin. In short, the engraving is a sophisticated combination of Northern and Southern, spiritual and secular motifs.

Dürer spent most of his life struggling to reconcile the Italian ideal of simple classical forms with the Northern penchant for exacting detail. The result Dürer sought was almost effortlessly achieved by Hans Holbein, whose compellingly realistic portraits assumed the monumentality of the Italian High Renaissance.

Around 1530 the tide of the Northern Renaissance was abruptly stemmed. Constant wars had drained the economy and the crisis of the Protestant revolt had challenged the very existence of art. The only area in which art developed unhampered was the Protestant Netherlands.

Breughel.
Jan Gossaert, Joachim Patinir, and hosts of other minor artists came to light, but it was Pieter Breughel who led the way. Like many of his contemporaries, Breughel traveled to Italy, where he spent almost two years exploring the Mediterranean countryside. But unlike his contemporaries, he was little affected by Italy's mania for antiques. In fact, the only specific reference to his trip is the occasional appearance of a bit of Southern landscape in otherwise Northern settings. Breughel avoided the classical nude. Instead, he assimilated a sense of monumental Italian harmony into his purely Netherlands-like subject matter. He is best known for his sprawling landscapes, which might be called genre pieces.

Hunters in the Snow is one of his most popular works. In the grand tradition of the *Très Riches Heures of the Duke of Berry,* Breughel painted the labors of the twelve months (only five of which are still extant). This winter scene (January or February) shows weary hunters trudging through the snow as they return home with their dogs. To their left, women tend an outdoor fire; beyond them stretches a vast Alpine landscape enlivened by skaters and a lonely flying crow.

Breughel captured the chill of winter air with a palette of gray-greens. His simple portrayal of peasants bound to the will of nature is no more than an objective record. The peasants are as much a part of the landscape as the barren trees or snow-covered fields. With his detached observation, Breughel was able to depict the awesome power of nature. Universal peace is disturbed only slightly by the muffled crunch of snow beneath the hunters' feet. Never again did the Netherlands produce a painter so totally in communion with nature. Never again was the peasants' simple humanity portrayed with such profound dignity.

The Baroque Era

The 16th century was a period of artistic genius, but it was also a time of contradiction and conflict, an epoch of tremendous upheaval in virtually every sphere of human activity. The church itself was convulsed by internal abuses. The papal throne was held by a succession of despotic and unscrupulous men, including Leo X, who squandered church funds on lavish pageants and gambling. Surrounded by Renaissance splendor, and battling for secular power, the popes were as much the successors of the Roman Caesars as they were the vicars of Christ.

The relaxation of moral and religious standards provoked a reaction in Northern Europe. Martin Luther, then Zwingli and John Calvin, protested the abuses of Rome and called for reforms. The great movement that these three began is called the Protestant Reformation. It resulted in a great schism in the Western church. From this time on the one Catholic (universal) Church became the Roman Catholic Church, to distinguish it from the Lutheran, Reformed, Calvinist, and other churches of the Reformers.

The Roman church responded to this movement with its own Counter Reformation. Under the pontificates of Pius IV, Sixtus V, and their successors, Christian zeal was rekindled. New religious orders were established, and there was a determined effort to directly involve the individual in the dynamism of religious experience.

The early Protestants, whose faith spread rapidly through the Northern half of the European Continent, were suspicious of the arts. In fact, some reformers made it a point to destroy statues, stained glass, and other religious works of art. The Counter Reformation saw the arts as an important part of its plan, however. So for much of the next century, the great work in the visual arts was in the Catholic South. Only gradually did art reassert itself under the Protestants.

The period, however, was more than just a time of religious turmoil. Royal families in France, Spain, and the North were well on their way to establishing absolute power. At the same time, the early Renaissance view that man was at the center of creation was being undermined by the very scientific research the reawakening had encouraged. Copernicus, Galileo, Kepler, and Newton demonstrated that man was a tiny creature on a small planet, in a corner of the universe. Exploration of the Americas, Africa, and Asia, further undermined men's sense of certainty and security.

Amid such religious, social, political, and scientific turmoil, it is no wonder that the character of art changed profoundly. The style that developed is known as Baroque. The origin of the name is not clear, but it may derive from the Portugese *barocco* meaning "irregular" or "rough." It was first used unflatteringly by critics in the 1800's who condemned the style as debased classicism. Their attacks against its over-ornamented theatricality have since been moderated, and we now use Baroque to simply designate the period from 1600 to 1750.

Architecture

The seeds of Baroque theatricality first appeared on Giacomo della Porta's facade for the church of Il Gesu in Rome. As the home of the Jesuits, it exerted considerable influence, and in succeeding centuries the facade was copied around the world. But it was at Saint Peter's, the greatest project of the 16th and 17th centuries, that a truly Baroque character matured.

Pope Paul V directed Carlo Maderna to extend Bramante's and Michelangelo's centralized plan by adding three bays to the nave. (The centralized format was now considered entirely too pagan for the seat of the Catholic Church.) Maderna was also commissioned to complete the facade, but his plans were never thoroughly executed. His work, as it stands today, is somewhat less than satisfactory. The front of the church is uncomfortably squat. It is too long, and its entrance is woefully understated. Worse yet, its horizontal sprawl tends to dwarf Michelangelo's magnificent dome.

THE PIAZZA AND COLONNADE OF ST. PETER'S *in Rome, designed by Gianlorenzo Bernini in the 1650's, set the great church in a heroic surrounding, directing all attention toward the church itself and toward the great dome designed earlier by Michelangelo.*

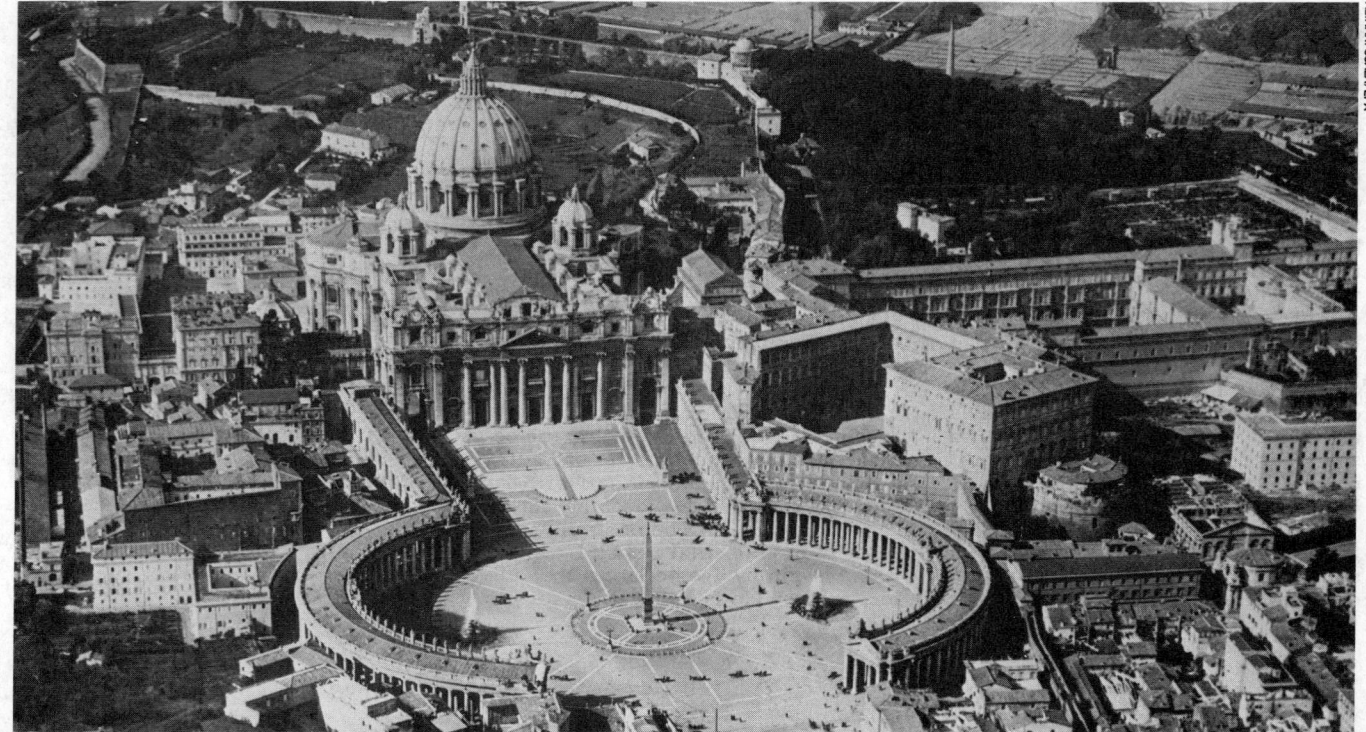

Giotto di Bondone (1266-1337), St. Francis Breaks With His Father, Upper Church of San Francesco, Assisi, Italy

Botticelli, Sandro (1444-1510), Primavera (detail), Uffizi Gallery, Florence

Brueghel, Pieter (1525/1530-1569), The Beggars, the Louvre, Paris

Velásquez, Diego (1599-1660), Juan, a servant, Earl of Radnor's Collection, Salisbury, England

Rembrandt van Rijn (1606-1669), Self-Portrait, Wallraf-Richartz Museum, Cologne, Germany

Degas, Edgar (1834-1917), The Tub, The Hill-Stead Museum, Farmington, Conn.

Gauguin, Paul (1843-1890), Maternity, A Private American Collection.

Toulouse-Lautrec, Henri (1864-1901), G. Celeyran,
Cousin, Musee Toulouse-Lautrec, Albi, France

Van Gogh, Vincent (1853-1890), Self-Portrait, Musee du Jeu de Paume, Louvre, Paris

·**Klee, Paul** (1879-1940), Fish Magic, Arensburg Collection, Philadelphia Museum of Art

Modigliani, Amedeo (1884-1920), Jeanne Hebuterne, Collection of Mr. and Mrs. Sidney F. Brody, Beverly Hills, California

Rouault, Georges (1871-1958), The Holy Face, Gallery Umeda, Osaka, Japan

Picasso, Pablo (1881-1973), Portrait of Madame Z, Home of the Artist

Bernini. These unpleasant effects were alleviated by Gianlorenzo Bernini, who built the piazza (courtyard) in front of St. Peter's. The undisputed genius of the Baroque age, he was an inspired sculptor, architect, dramatist, painter, and composer. Bernini combined his many skills at the Vatican, where he created the glorious *Throne of St. Peter* and carved much of the statuary for the interior of the church. He also constructed the dramatic exterior colonnade, which reaches out like gigantic arms, embracing the entire Christian world. The colonnade transformed St. Peter's from an isolated block into one vibrantly integrated with the surrounding neighborhood. More important, Bernini's great arms (each composed of four rows of colossal Doric columns) make the facade seem taller. He accomplished this by pinching in the colonnades' straight flanks so that they mask the ends of the facade. With the terminal bays thus hidden, the facade seems more lofty and elegant as one approaches it through the sweeping piazza.

Bernini's solution was based on dramatic spatial manipulation. He used classical columns in a most theatrical way, producing a swirling tension and compelling illusion, the very hallmarks of the Baroque style. He brought these qualities to absolute refinement in his *Scala Regia* (stairway leading to the papal apartments) and in his church of Sant' Andrea in Rome.

The same spatial elements were exaggerated by Francesco Borromini, Bernini's rival and the most daring architect of the 17th century. In his little church of San Carlo alle Quattro Fontane, Borromini twisted and turned his facade as if it were rubber. Its walls project and recede like rising ocean swells, dramatically confronting the unsuspecting viewer. He replaced Renaissance static balance with pulsating energy, and Renaissance logic with unbridled emotion. Similar sensations (though considerably modified) were sought by contemporary Baroque architects like Guarino Guarini and Carlo Rainaldi.

Bernini epitomized the goals of contemporary sculptors. His *St. Theresa in Ecstacy* is the most sensuous and sublime statue ever created for the church. Wafted off her feet on a bed of clouds amid golden rays of sun, Theresa swoons as an angel thrusts an arrow of divine love into her bosom. The intimate scene is so constructed that painting, sculpture, and even the surrounding architecture command the viewer's full participation. Like most 17th century religious sculpture, it exists in the realm of mystical theater.

Bernini's artistic genius was already apparent in his marble *David,* which he carved at age 25. A supreme example of Baroque drama, it emphasized the essential break with Renaissance ideals. Unlike Donatello's sweet ado-

BERNINI'S DAVID *is in motion, contrasting with earlier Davids by Donatello and Michelangelo.*

lescent *David* or Michelangelo's brooding giant, Bernini's explosive figure springs into action. Balancing on his toes, David lunges back to hurl his stone at Goliath. His entire body strains with the thrust of physical exertion. So determined is the youth that he even bites his lip. This level of psychological tension had never been achieved before, not even in passionate Hellenistic works like Laocöon. Whereas Renaissance sculpture reveled in eternal stasis, Bernini's *David* is caught in split-second action. In another second the slingshot will be released; moments later, David will stand to watch his opponent fall. The viewer is thus irresistibly involved in completing the heroic sequence. With torpedolike force, *David* dominates his surrounding space, defying the containment of a stone block. Calm perfection, the classical ideal, has been abandoned for the fiery passion of the Counter Reformation.

Painting

A different situation is apparent in Baroque painting. Tired of Mannerist extremes, 17th-century painters returned to nature and classical ideals. They reacted against pictorial distortion and turned to Michelangelo, Raphael, Titian, and to a lesser extent Correggio, for their essential artistic truth. Interestingly, their quest only emphasized the gap that separated

them from Renaissance models, for Baroque painters were equally committed to visual truth—even when it conflicted with standards of ideal beauty. Moreover, the Counter Reformation encouraged the expression of impassioned Christianity and demanded viewer involvement.

These multiple influences gave rise to as many painting styles, all of them heroic and all of them Baroque. The Carracci Brothers, for example, combined Raphael's grace, Michelangelo's drama, and Titian's color in their animated mythological paintings in the Farnese Palace. Instead of exaggerating or distorting their High Renaissance models, the brothers tried to recapture some of their simplicity and grandeur. Guido Reni had similar aims, although he concentrated more heavily on Raphael's fluid grace in paintings on ceilings where figures seem to dance across the clouds.

Strides toward the depiction of unlimited space gained tremendous momentum with Guercino, Pietro da Cortona, and especially Andrea dal Pozzo. In the latter's *Allegory of the Missionary Work of the Jesuits,* painted on the vaults above San Ignazio in Rome, exuberant figures thrust into the heavens with such force that they appear to surge beyond the limits of the roof. With sweeping action they thunder into the clouds, theatrically denying the distinction between real and painted space.

Baroque painters took High Renaissance models and gave them a kind of frenzied life. Heroic ease became Herculean effort, sweet love restless passion. The power of painted movement overcame human reason and established itself as the ultimate goal of art. The viewer is drawn irresistibly into a sense of violent, but often sensuous movement.

Caravaggio. Baroque painters believed that the Renaissance and the ancient masters had captured the essence of art. It merely remained for them to reinterpret and electrify it. This applied to all Italian painters except one: Michelangelo de Merisi, called Caravaggio, who openly denounced High Renaissance achievements. He was a rebel, an antisocial rowdy who had to flee Rome to escape charges of murder. Caravaggio spent his tragic career among the lower elements of Rome. He knew the ugly, the seamy, the dark side of human experience. And he drew on it to explore uncharted territories in art. It is not surprising to learn that he was feared and hated by more than one of his contemporaries.

After an early period of mythological and genre painting, Caravaggio turned almost exclusively to religious works. His *Calling of St. Matthew* provides a compelling example of his unconventional style. The subject matter

SPACE AND ACTION, *major Baroque concerns, are studied in* Las Meninas *by Velasquez (1656)* and Rape of the Daughters of Leucippus *by Rubens (1617).*

had been represented countless times before, but never with such profound psychological impact. The scene is a dingy Roman tavern. Seated among common people and young dandies, the bearded Matthew points to himself in disbelief. Why would he be chosen as an apostle? Christ's outstretched hand is a direct descendant of Michelangelo's figure of God in the Creation of Adam from the Sistine ceiling.

Caravaggio explored the power of coarse men in an unrefined environment. He abandoned decorum for cold truth. Consequently, he was charged with irreverence and disrespect. His paintings were regularly refused by the clergy who commissioned them. Still, Caravaggio refused to yield in his portrayal of grim reality. Within ten years of his death, Caravaggio's soul-searching paintings had become the major source of inspiration for Baroque painters in Italy, Spain, France, and the Netherlands. Chief among these were Velasquez, Rubens, and Rembrandt van Rijn.

During the late 1500's and early 1600's, Spain devoted herself to Counter Reformation in the form of the Inquisition, a determined effort to stamp out heresy by punishing (and often killing) the heretics. Isolated and even mysterious by nature, Spanish artists translated Italian Mannerism into a fiery brand of mysticism that agreed with the aims of the Iberian church. El Greco's flickering paintings, ablaze with Byzantine color, were the greatest expression of such religious ecstacy. But by the 17th century, Mannerist distortion was abandoned for the new Baroque style.

Caravaggio's imitators, the *Tenebrisi* (the shadowy ones) carried his influence across the Pyrenees where painters like Zurbaran and Diego de Ribera enthusiastically adopted his technique of contrasting intense light and shadow. They used it to paint gruesome religious paintings wherein Christian devotion soared to unprecedented peaks.

Velasquez. The greatest painter of the day responded to Caravaggio in a totally different way. Instead of exploiting darks and lights in sacred dramas, Diego Rodriguez de Silva y Velasquez applied them to his own brand of portraiture.

In 1623 Velasquez was appointed court painter to King Philip IV, and for the next 37 years he was devoted to painting portraits of the royal family. In this time before photography, portraits provided the most important record of the royal family. Moreover, they were used to help arrange marriages and thus came to affect international relations. Needless to say, royal portraits were supposed to be flattering. But for Velasquez this was no small task. With few exceptions, Philip's family was not blessed with an attractive appearance. The situation was only compounded by the stiff and awkward costumes they wore at court. Velasquez rose to the challenge, transforming mere painted likenesses into penetrating character studies. He was one of the most gifted portraitists the world has ever known.

In two lengthy trips to Rome, Velasquez studied Italian achievements. He

held no esteem for Raphael, little for the Renaissance as a whole, and perhaps even less for his Baroque contemporaries. He seems to have been influenced only by Titian's brush stroke and Caravaggio's liberating realism. But Velasquez never surrendered his Spanish individuality.

His acclaimed masterpiece is *Las Meninas* (the ladies in waiting). It is an enormous painting, the largest Velasquez ever produced. The painter represents himself inside his studio working on a large canvas (perhaps *Las Meninas* itself). To his left is the Infanta Margarita, whose kneeling maid offers a glass of water. Another maid stands between the royal child and her favorite dwarfs. Velasquez shared none of the court's perverse delight in these "human toys" and painted the dwarfs with dignity and compassion. Two more servants stand in middle ground, while a court official pauses in the door to observe the activities. To his left is a mirror that reflects the king and queen. Indeed, it might also reflect our own images because the royal couple views the scene from our own position outside the room. Brush and palette in hand, the painter stares at them (and us).

Las Meninas is one of the most complex illusionistic paintings ever created. By distributing his figures within and beyond the artist's studio, Velasquez establishes different layers of space and reality. He does this with such finesse that the studied group portrait appears to be no more than an informal gathering. The whole is transformed by diffuse shadows that dissolve distinct edges and by orchestrated highlights that dance from satin dresses to the reflected mirror image. Unlike van Eyck, who painted every tiny detail with exacting precision, Velasquez used quick brush strokes to suggest different textures. He used splashes of light, color, and shadow to create the illusion of form.

Quite aside from being a brilliant exploration of optical mysteries, *Las Meninas* is a testament to the artist's new professional status. Velasquez sought recognition as a noble in the illustrious Order of Santiago. At first, he was denied entry because painting was considered manual labor and below the dignity of nobility. But two years before he died, Velasquez's dream came true, and at the hand of King Philip he was inducted into the prestigious society. This honor is recorded by the red cross on the painter's doublet, which, according to tradition, was painted by the king himself. At last the respectability of the artistic profession had been realized.

Rubens. Velasquez's patronage by the Spanish court was typical of the 1600's. It was an age when royal monarchs glorified their reigns with sumptuous palaces and magnificent works of art. Foremost in royal esteem was Peter Paul Rubens, whose bouyant energy, brilliant color sense, and vibrant love of life made him the perfect instrument of royal pomp and ceremony.

Like Velasquez, Rubens studied in Italy. But unlike his Spanish friend, he fully adopted Italian art as the basis of his personal style. He studied antiquity, the Renaissance, and the works of his Baroque colleagues, drawing on Michelangelo's explosive power, Titian's color, Carracci's classicism, and Caravaggio's drama. He combined these influences with his native Flemish dedication to appearances. So successful was his synthesis that Rubens established a virtual monopoly over Baroque royal painting. Commissions flooded in from all over Europe.

In many cases Rubens only prepared quick color sketches for his students, who actually executed the paintings in his bustling studio. The master supervised their work and periodically stepped in to correct certain flaws or to provide glowing finishing touches.

Some idea of Rubens' universal appeal can be gained from his *Rape of the Daughters of Leucippus,* which recounts the abduction of two female mortals by the gods Castor and Pollux. Amid rearing horses and fluttering drapery the divine sons of Jupiter satisfy their love. The theme recalls Titian's *Rape of Europa,* as do the overly fleshy maidens. But Titian's work seems subdued in comparison with this dynamic sensuality. Rubens' work is violent. It is not the violence of struggle that activates the painting, for the gods hardly strain, and the maidens do not really resist. Instead, it is the motion of voluptuous passion rendered in sensuous tones of pearly flesh and glittering satins. Rising from a low horizon the interwoven figures sweep upward to a thundering climax. The splashing sea of female flesh reveals Rubens' primary interest: the human body in all of its healthy exuberance. More than any other painter, Rubens summed up the radiant pleasures of love.

The Baroque art scene in Flanders was totally dominated by Rubens. The only other major painter was Anthony van Dyck, who concentrated on refined aristocratic portraits. But in neighboring Holland the situation was completely different. Constrained by sober Protestant reforms, Dutch painters shrank from any form of religious art. Nor was there a strong monarch interested in glorifying his court. When painters were thus deprived of their primary stimuli, they turned to the open market. They relied on the new class of merchants who wanted paintings as symbols of their wealth.

With the new market came a change in attitude and subject matter. There were no paintings of sacred visions or royal portraits, no saints in ecstacy or rapturous nudes. Instead there were small studies of everyday life. Over 40 "little masters" supplied the demand of the middle classes with landscapes, shipping scenes, views of domestic interiors, and great numbers of still lifes. Jacob van Ruisdael, Pieter de Hooch, and Jan Steen are among the most famous of these painters, but many others produced works of extremely high quality. In a class by themselves are Frans Hals' engaging portraits and the studied interiors of Vermeer, which imbued Dutch life with an eternally quiet dignity.

Rembrandt. The supreme talent, however, was Rembrandt van Rijn. Rembrandt's early life was a wonderful success story. His arresting powers of observation, his mysterious sense of light, and his incomparable graphic skills flooded him with more commissions than he could possibly hope to execute. But by the time he was 50, Rembrandt's luck had soured. He fell into disastrous financial difficulties and the two women he loved most had died. He abandoned his earlier robust style, in which he combined the influence of Rubens and Caravaggio. He withdrew to quiet visions bathed in silent light. He turned increasingly to contemplative religious scenes and sympathetic studies of human affliction. The same spirituality is apparent in the series of self-portraits that Rembrandt executed in the last decade of his life.

One of the most moving appears on this page. In form it derives from Raphael's portrait of *Baldassare Castiglione,* but how different this is from its aristocratic beauty. Old, tired, and plagued by bankruptcy, the artist peers into the depths of his own character. The paint of his careworn face was laid on thickly with a knife, its rough texture adding to the sense of wrinkled old age. Rembrandt used light to reveal his innermost concerns, allowing it to merge with the gloomy ground behind. There are no stiff outlines, just patches of light and shadow. With profound understanding, Rembrandt completes the Renaissance conquest of illumination. It was begun by Masaccio, developed in Leonardo's *sfumato,* and dramatized by Caravaggio. To Rembrandt light was the painter's most important tool.

In the second half of the 1600's, Rembrandt's Holland and Velasquez's Spain fell to the power of France. Under the absolute monarchy of Louis XIV, the Sun King, France replaced Rome as the artistic center of the world. It established itself as the leader in the visual arts, a position unchallenged for nearly 300 years.

Italian influences were initially strong. Bernini was invited to France and carved a swirling marble portrait of the Sun King. He also submitted a design for the royal Louvre palace. But Italian exuberance found no home in the elegant and refined French court. Bernini was dismissed and under Louis and his chief minister, Colbert, French art was systematically organized for the aggrandizement of the king. The palace at Versailles was the crowning triumph of his absolute kingship. Never before or since has the impact of one man had such a pervasive influence over every aspect of human life.

There were, of course, outside influences, but in each case they were translated into something categorically French. For example, Dutch interpretations of Caravaggio filtered into the art of Georges de la Tour. But

LATE SELF-PORTRAIT *by Rembrandt (1669) contrasts with the earlier portrait in color plate.*

NATIONAL GALLERY

he simplified and abstracted them to a point of classical symmetry. So too with Louis LeNain's paintings of French peasants. But it was Nicolas Poussin who really established the classical character of French Baroque painting.

Poussin. Interestingly, Poussin spent most of his life in Rome. He had little patience with court intrigues and preferred to accept private commissions from sophisticated Frenchmen. He entertained no interest in the Renaissance (except for Raphael, whom he admired), and none at all in Italian Baroque. Instead, he skipped back to antiquity directly. His *Burial of Phocian* shows the results of Poussin's classical nostalgia. After reading the ancient writings of Plutarch, Poussin illustrated the story of Phocian, an Athenian hero who was unjustly executed by his countrymen. Denied burial in his mother country, the outcast was carried past its boundaries to a site of eternal isolation. Poussin chose to represent this painful tale objectively with the distance of classical logic. The lone corpse and its bearers do not evoke poignant response from the viewer; they are almost incidental to the rolling landscape dotted with classical buildings stretching back in time

and place. Unlike his contemporaries, Poussin had no interest in merely recreating nature; he harbored no desire to update antiquity. He tried instead to reverse the process, and attempted to bring the 17th century back to ancient Rome.

He longed for the time when men painted only the most elevated themes. Battles, heroic actions, and religious scenes provided the stage for his classically balanced works. Poussin's style totally opposed Caravaggio's vulgar, or Rubens' vibrating, works. He strove not for emotional, but intellectual response. Accordingly, Poussin distilled his painting technique to a formula for classical calm. He omitted all distracting incidentals and concentrated on the almost mathematical balance of his composition. Even color was reduced to a position of secondary importance.

Poussin's concerns with austere regularity so strongly opposed the mainstream of 17th-century art that it may seem illogical to classify him as a Baroque artist. But his classicism provided a true view of France under Louis XIV. He was not so much deflating Baroque energies, as redirecting their expression and purpose.

Now all things centered on the Sun King. Pulsating shapes and restless colors were harnessed for his supreme

glory. Jarring contrasts were replaced by Louis' passion for rigid symmetry. Louis used art as an international expression of his absolute power over France, a good deal of Europe, and even nature itself. Through the brilliant work of Louis Le Notre, the gardens at Versailles were made to obey the will of the king. To his great delight, natural irregularities were "corrected." Trees, bushes, lawns, and flowers were transformed into green geometry.

The binding regulations of French Baroque art were loosened in Louis' old age. By the time he died in 1715, the pendulum had swung and France joyously embraced the playful Rococo style.

But if French classicism was fated to die with Louis, it would thrive on British shores. Under the influence of Sir Christopher Wren and John Vanbrugh, classical logic replaced the last vestiges of the Middle Ages. Wren's St. Paul's Cathedral in London combined Italian Renaissance and French Baroque classicism into something thoroughly English. Still somewhat concerned with nonclassical spatial problems, St. Paul's nevertheless anchored English interest in the past. The splendor of antiquity would be the absolute preoccupation of the following century. —*Janet Adams*

BURIAL OF PHOCIAN by *Poussin (1660) brings a new kind of balance and repose to Baroque art, reflecting the stately court of King Louis XIV of France in its attempt to bring back the calm of classical art.*

GIRAUDON

Rococo and Neoclassic Art

The prevailing style of the early 1700's is called Rococo. The word derives from the French *rocaille,* or pebble, referring to the decoration of grottoes that were encrusted with pebbles and shells. Some of the most fanciful decoration in Italy had been done in the late Renaissance in the artificial grottoes of such palaces as the Pitti in Florence. It is this unrestrained decoration that is the essence of the Rococo style. The Rococo is a development of the earlier Baroque style in France, and the two share the same exuberance and energy, in contrast to the weight and stability of classic art.

Painting and Decoration

In France, the Rococo remained an interior style. It was developed and used extensively in the great *hotels,* or private houses, of the French aristocracy; these houses were built in Paris in the first part of the century. When Louis XIV died in 1715, the nobles who had been constrained to live at the court were free to build houses in Paris. These houses, or *hotels,* are found today in the section of Paris called the Marais. The exteriors of the houses are often of simple, even sober, design. The plots of land available at the time were both irregular and limited in size.

The interiors of the *hotels,* however, were lavishly decorated, reflecting the gaiety of a new age. The Regency in France (the early years of Louis XV when France was ruled by his regent) repudiated the austerity and formality of Louis XIV, both in manners and in artistic taste. Louis XV lived until 1774, and in France the Rococo style is called Louis XV.

Paris was a major center of intellectual and artistic life of Europe in the 1700's. Much of its activity centered on the salons of the great *hotels.* The Rococo style was carried out in the furniture, in the woodwork and plastering, in the ornaments, and in the painting and sculpture.

One of the most beautiful of these Rococo rooms is the Salon de la Princesse in the Hotel de Soubise. It was decorated by Germain Boffrand between 1737 and 1740. The overwhelming impression is of lightness and movement. The cornices of the room have disappeared, lost amid the gilded woodwork, mirrors, and painting. The entire room seems to rise to the richness of the ceiling, and the whole is unified by a repetition of forms—foliage, tendrils, scrolls, and

shells—that are found in the furniture as well. This decorative, flowing style is very feminine, perhaps because the salons of Paris, as well as many of the courts of Europe, were dominated by women. Maria Theresa ruled in Austria; Elizabeth and then Catherine were the first empresses of Russia; and Madame de Pompadour, Louis XV's mistress, was a major power in France. The development of taste for the Rococo, however, has as much to do with the place women had begun to assume in the 1600's when, long before the death of Louis XIV, they began to pursue their own interests.

The French school. Painting in France in the early 1700's is dominated by Jean Watteau (1684–1721). Watteau's student Boucher, and his successor Fragonard, carried on the Rococo tradition in painting until the French Revolution in 1789.

Watteau helped invent the Rococo style, but his paintings tower above it. He died at the age of 37, yet painted some of the most beautiful and mysterious canvases ever to be produced in France. *The Voyage to Cythera,* completed in 1717, won his admission to the French Academy, but the academy had to create a new category for it. From then on, such paintings were called *fetes galantes,* which means courtly or romantic entertainments.

This spirit characterizes most thoroughly French Rococo painting; as a literary form, it had flourished in the

preceding century. In *The Voyage to Cythera,* eight couples form a cortege across the canvas. They are departing from the island of Cythera, which was holy to Venus. A statue of the goddess of love is seen on the right, adorned with garlands. The painting seems an anthology of the rite of love. Its mood is of lingering tenderness, clearly evoked by the woman at the center of the picture who is looking back over her shoulder. The couples are variations on a single theme, expressing the most graceful attitudes of love. Their movement away from the statue of Venus describes a long horizontal, gently curving line that is continued by the boat and the cupids. The whole seems to lead to an apotheosis in the figures of the cupids in the sky. This sensuous line illustrates the essential Rococo sense of movement. The setting is the most ideal of landscapes, luminescent, ephemeral, and vast. Nature is at its most benign and seems to shelter the shrine and the last couple, who have not yet gotten up.

Watteau's particular poetic powers would not be equaled again in his century. He was unique in being willing to confront delicate feelings of sadness and uncertainty, and his pictures suggest deep, but undefinable, emotion. His other well known works—a portrait called *L'Indifferent* and a portrait of the clown Gilles—also reflect this emotional depth.

Watteau's successors, François Boucher and Jean Honoré Fragonard, perpetuate the painter's genre, the *fetes*

THE VOYAGE TO CYTHERA *by Jean Watteau shows the new warmth and emotion Rococo painters introduced into their "entertainments."*

GIRAUDON

ROCOCO AND REALISM: The Swing *by Jean Honoré Fragonard* (left) *continues the gentility of the Rococo; at the same time, Jean Baptiste Chardin introduced a new realism to painting, choosing an everyday event in* Back from the Market *(right).*

galantes, but it becomes a kind of Rococo decoration, and Watteau's psychological questioning is lost. Boucher (1703–1770) was commissioned as a young man to engrave Watteau's paintings. He helped transform Watteau's style into the full-blown Rococo. Boucher was the favorite painter of Madame de Pompadour, and later the "first painter of the king." Consequently, his influence was enormous.

Boucher's royal style can be seen in his portrait of Madame de Pompadour. The king's favorite is seen as both languorous and dignified. Her surroundings are of soft luxury and exquisite, refined taste.

More important, Boucher perpetuated the *fetes galantes,* developing the convention of amorous idylls in a protective, rich natural world. A typical painting is the *Shepherd Piping to a Shepherdess.* It is one of Watteau's couples caught in a graceful and ideal moment of love in a setting that mirrors in its flowers and luxuriant growth the love of the human couple.

Boucher's figures, however, have little to do with Watteau. They have rather the fleshy opulence of Rubens. This is even more evident in the *Cupid a Captive* (1754). Nudes of distinct, Rubenesque proportions intertwine with the natural elements to create an atmosphere of sensuality from which any hint of human care is banished. The title of one of his allegorical

pictures, *The Triumph of Venus,* indicates Boucher's philosophy: the goddess of love commands and dominates the natural world. To later viewers, this idealized state has little to do with real life.

Fragonard (1732–1806) was Boucher's pupil, and like his teacher, he was patronized by the French court. He was the last and most appreciated painter of the Rococo style in France, but his prosperity vanished with the style. After the French Revolution, the Rococo was identified with the overthrown monarchy. Fragonard died a poor man in Naples, forgotten in his native country.

The great exuberance of the Rococo style survives in Fragonard's paintings, however. They are, if possible, more sensual than Boucher's. Fragonard was a great colorist, and owes more to Rubens even then Boucher. In the *Bathers* (1765), the viewer is transported into a world that is constructed of round, sensual, human forms, foliage, and water. But Fragonard has dispensed with even a semblance of a rational, natural ordering of his elements. The foliage, the water, and the women's bodies interweave in a vision of ecstatic and unrestrained joy of the flesh. At the center of the picture is a piece of brilliant pink drapery that seems to be a kind of flag that floats like the clouds and echoes the shapes of the sheltering foliage. The play of

the brilliant pink and the bright greens against the blues of the sky is intense. The enthusiasm of the bathers creates an atmosphere of excitement that is an aesthetic counterpart of pornography.

Fragonard's painting is always unashamedly sensual. In another of his well known paintings, *The Swing* (1766), the erotic element is the crux of the picture. The scene is no longer of bathing nymphs, but of a woman whose position in a swing is an unexpected, or perhaps planned, good fortune for her lover hidden in the foliage beneath her. There is an element of humor since the young woman is pushed in her swing by an elderly bishop who cannot see the young man. The woman's dress is the same brilliant floating drapery that one sees in the *Bathers.* Orange-pink, it stands out against the dark but brilliant greens of the background. The picture is an intense dramatization of woman as an object of desire. She floats in her swing as a vision that is both idealized and humorously honest.

Realism. The style of Boucher and Fragonard was not the only possibility for painters in 18th-century France. In at least one case, great painting had nothing to do with the Rococo. Jean Baptiste Siméon Chardin (1699–1779) produced paintings of the solid bourgeoisie: interior scenes with women and children, even servants, portraying the intimacy of family life. His subject matter recalls the earlier Dutch painters such as Vermeer. The rapid, curving line of Fragonard and Boucher is absent in Chardin. He composes his pictures around large geometrical shapes, and there are many rectangles and circles in his pictures. The flat surface of the canvas, the picture plane, is divided by these shapes into distinct areas that give the illusion of stability—the moral and artistic value that the pictures extol. Chardin bathes his subjects in a gentle light that further emphasizes the calm of the pictures and makes them objects suitable for contemplation.

The picture reproduced here, *Back from the Market,* shows a servant still holding what she has brought from her shopping. She seems uncertain what to do next, and Chardin has arrested our attention on a moment without drama or grandeur. In a picture only 18 by 14 inches, Chardin renders the solidity of the walls and furniture, a fully developed space, a particular atmosphere, and the woman's passing mood. Chardin's art seems to reflect one aspect of the Enlightenment in its particularly reasonable and sane search for truth and value. It is noteworthy that Chardin was most admired by Diderot, a great figure of the Age of Enlightenment.

Much less subtle than Chardin and much more patently moralistic is Jean Baptiste Greuze (1725–1805). He is best known for his scenes of moral rearmament, as in *The Return of the Prodigal Son.* Greuze does not hesitate to improve on the Christian parable—his prodigal son returns to his father's deathbed. The dramatic grief of the painting seems melodramatic and overdone. Another typical painting by Greuze is *The Village Bride,* which is a scene from the life of the lower classes. Again the sentiment of the painting is without subtlety. Greuze's paintings of this kind are perhaps most interesting as documents of a France that both exalted the common people and condemned the frivolous immorality of the upper classes. These are the views that triumph in the French Revolution.

Italy. Outside of France the greatest Rococo painter was Giovanni Battista Tiepolo (1696–1770). He was a Venetian but he worked mostly in Austria, Germany, and Spain. Unlike French Rococo pictures, the paintings of Tiepolo are enormous; often he painted frescoes as part of architectural schemes for churches and villas. His style was well adapted to its architectural function, and perhaps no one has ever painted such airy and limitless skies. They seemed to open the ceilings of the buildings themselves.

His painting is distinguished by his economical and sure draftsmanship. Tiepolo needed only minimal line and shadow to create illusions of great space animated by moving figures and brilliant light.

Two other Italians of the 18th century were also adept at capturing great spaces. They were Antonio Canaletto (1697–1768) and Francesco Guardi (1712–1793). Like Tiepolo, they were Venetians, but they continued to paint easel pictures. Their main subject was their native city, of which their paintings make up an illustrated history. The festivals, lively citizens, canals, and splendid squares of Venice were recorded by both painters with care and feeling.

England. English painting of 18th century is dominated by the portraits of English lords and ladies, as its architecture is dominated by their great houses. The first major painter of the century, William Hogarth (1697–1764), is, however, best known for his dramatic, satirical paintings. In intent, these paintings are as apt to moralize as those of Greuze, with the fundamental difference that Hogarth's are immensely humorous and entertaining. They read like scenes from novels. Engravings were made from the paintings and widely sold, the most famous series being the *Rake's Progress* (1735). The individual scenes are characterized by great detail and incident and reveal a fully developed story that the viewer can spend much time in deciphering. A typical scene is *The Orgy,* where overindulgence in wine and pleasure cost the rake his purse, which one of his lady friends deftly steals.

MRS. ELLIOT, *one of Gainsborough's great portraits of English ladies.*

METROPOLITAN MUSEUM OF ART/ BEQUEST OF WILLIAM K. VANDERBILT, 1920

As are many of Hogarth's heroes, the rake is from the English upper classes. Hogarth's eloquence in exposing the weaknesses of the upper classes is overshadowed, however, by the accomplishments of other English painters in showing their strengths. Never before or since has painting so effectively and so extensively created an image of a class. The immensely rich upper classes could afford to commission the painters' work, of course, but the quality of the resulting work is a tribute to the artists' talents.

Before the 1700's, the English had imported painters from Europe. Holbein and Van Dyck, for example, made famous portraits of English kings. But the great portraitists of the 1700's were native-born.

Sir Joshua Reynolds (1723–1792) was the more conservative of two great painters, and served as president of the Royal Academy. His theory of art was deliberately classical, and he ennobled his portraits with classical motives. Thomas Gainsborough (1727–1788) began his career as a landscape painter. In one of his early pictures, the double portrait of Robert Andrews and his wife, the figures are placed in a broad expanse of English countryside that is painted with great skill and love.

Gainsborough, however, became the most sought after of portrait painters, and in the portrait of Mrs. Elliot reproduced here, it is easy to see what attracted his clients. It is hard to imagine a portrait of more elegance. At the time the portrait was made, Mrs. Elliot was the mistress of a great English lord who payed for the painting. Like most of the portraits of the time, it is life size and was meant to adorn the hall of a very large house as a guarantee of the elegance of its owners. Gainsborough gave himself wholeheartedly to the depiction of this elegance. Mrs. Elliot's tall and graceful figure is emphasized by the column behind her, and one sees the painter's delight in the shimmering splendor of her clothes and shoes. In contrast to the light concentrated in her figure and hair, all tones of silver, gray, and gold, is the dark landscape that forms the left of the picture. Mrs. Elliot seems to come in from that landscape, and her presence is a kind of rich, brilliant light that dominates both the architecture and the natural world.

Gainsborough's subjects are not always rendered with icy brilliance. In his portrait of Mrs. Richard Sheridan he treats his subject differently. Mrs. Sheridan is placed in a luxuriant and soft natural setting, and her hair, dress, and sash are of the same hues as the landscape. The woman's mood seems also a reflection of the landscape, almost melancholy. Gainsborough at his best seems to anticipate English Romantic poetry. He was also brilliant in revealing great psychological insight in purely visual terms.

LION ATTACKING A HORSE *by George Stubbs illustrates the menace that artists of the 1700's began to see in the world of nature.*

New directions. Gainsborough reached the highest technical level of any English painter, but his subject matter remained conservative. At the same time in England, one of the earliest manifestations of the new Romantic feeling appeared. One of the great themes of Romantic painting and literature would be the violence and passion of nature, and one of the ways of portraying that violence would be through the depiction of animals. George Stubbs (1724–1806) was a portrait painter who often painted racehorses. In 1770 he painted a picture that prefigured the new Romanticism. His *Lion Attacking a Horse* was the result of his having seen a horse killed by a lion in North Africa. His painting is much more than a recording of the event; it is its recreation in terms that allow the expression of the greatest emotion and psychological violence.

Earlier painters of the 1700's portrayed nature as a haven for man. In Stubbs's picture, nature is a threat. The lion, the rocks, the clouds, and even the trees are dark manifestations of forces that destroy, lit peculiarly red by a storm. The horse, in its movement and in the violent contrast of its whiteness, is not so much a victim as an opposing, and also potentially frightening, force. Its mane is fire, and its teeth and head are the focus of the violence of the picture. The indulgence of this kind of violent feeling is one of the distinguishing features of Romanticism.

The painting has the same force as the poetry of William Blake (1757–1827), another Englishman of the

same period whose work was also part of the early development of Romanticism. Blake's lines recall Stubbs in their concentration of an image, in their reliance on strong contrasts of dark and light, and in their awe of violence:

> Tyger! tyger! burning bright
> In the forests of the night,
> What immortal hand or eye
> Dare frame thy fearful symmetry?

Blake was also an artist of some accomplishment. His drawings are outside the technical mainstream of art and were meant to illustrate his poems in a way reminiscent of medieval illuminations. Yet Blake and his friend Henry Fuseli (1741–1825) were proponents of the cult of the imagination that deeply influenced the Romantics in their desire to explore the world of feeling.

At the end of the 1700's, human emotion was seeking a direct outlet in art. Strangely, it was in France, where the old style had been most securely rooted, that the new art broke forth with the most violence.

Architecture

The architecture of the 1700's in Europe saw the growth of a new classicism. The baroque style ended with a great flourish of Rococo in southern Germany and Austria in the early part of the century. But in England and France, a very pure classic style developed that quickly overcame rival styles.

Rococo. The Rococo style in France remained always decorative and was seen particularly in the interiors of the *hotels* of Paris. In southern Germany and Austria, however, the Rococo was used for a great number of churches and palaces that are Rococo in architecture as well as decoration. The Rococo architectural style owed much to earlier Italian styles, in particular the work of Francesco Borromini and Giovanni Guarini. The classic clarity of function and space is abandoned, and the decoration of the German and Austrian churches of this period is the most exuberant development of the Rococo line.

Fine examples of the style are found all over Germany and Austria, and one of the very best is the Vierzehnheiligen (Fourteen Saints) Pilgrimage Church by Balthasar Neumann (1687–1753). The surface of the facade of the church undulates and its corners are rounded, recalling the work of Borromini. The interior of the church is perhaps the highest point ever reached by the Rococo style. The altar is placed in the center of the church, allowing the various spaces to intersect; the decoration almost completely avoids horizontal and straight lines. The effect is one of continuous flow and movement with an opulence and lightness rarely achieved in architecture. The colors of the decoration are white, gold, pale yellow, coral, blue, and pink, with the whole bathed in light. The painted ceiling completes the effect, as the upper reaches seem lost in the clouds.

Neoclassicism. In the rest of Europe the 1700's brought a style of architecture that is the antithesis of the Baroque and Rococo. Versailles, built in the second part of the 1600's, was a monument of French classicism, and the taste that determined its construction never waned in France. If anything, this taste become purified of any extraneous elements.

The architecture of Jacques Ange Gabriel (1698–1782) is a simplified, more rudimentary version of the classicism of the preceding century. Gabriel built the École Militaire and the Hotel Crillon in Paris and the Petit Trianon at Versailles, which is illustrated here. The small palace, built in the park, shows the values of weight and solidity and the clear organization of elements that are the basis of any classic art. One also sees the paring down of ornamentation, compared even with the main palace at Versailles. The Petit Trianon was built only a few years after the Vierzehnheiligen Church, and the contrast illustrates the wide variations in taste during this period.

Another of the great neoclassic monuments of Paris is the Pantheon by Jacques Germain Soufflot (1713–1780). The Pantheon is a huge cross-

MARBURG/ART REFERENCE BUREAU

UNIVERSITY OF VIRGINIA LIBRARY

shaped church on the Mont Saint Ge-
nevieve surmounted by a dome that
overlooks Paris. Scholarly arcaeology
grew up in the 1700's, bringing a renewed interest in the buildings of
Greece and Rome. The immense por-
tico of the Pantheon is modeled on
that of a Roman temple. The dome,
however, is modeled on St Paul's in
London, and its proportions are those
of Baroque Italy. Despite these varied
elements, the effect is a classic sense
of order and simplicity.

Town planning was one of the most
noteworthy feats of French neoclassicism. In Nancy, the capital of the
province of Lorraine, the center of the
town was rebuilt along a new north-
south street, with a series of beautiful
squares and a palace, all in proportion
to one another and unified by classical
details. In Russia, too, the sense of order of classicism prevailed, and St. Petersburg (now Leningrad) became an
ordered classical city.

England had had a great classic architect in the person of Inigo Jones in
the 1600's, but the first great monument of 1700's England is Blenheim
Place by Sir John Vanbrugh (1664–
1726). Blenheim is a mixture of Baroque and classical styles on a mammoth scale. Many of the other great
country houses show a search for a
new, but not necessarily classical,
style. Strawberry Hill, built by Horace
Walpole, is in eclectic Gothic style, following a fashion of imitating Gothic
ruins. In urban planning, the classic
triumph on a grand scale in the architecture of John Wood and his son, who
rebuilt the city of Bath, designing
squares, streets, and crescents in vast
classical orders.

America makes its first contribution
to art history in architecture. Particularly in Virginia, the classically based
Georgian style predominated. Thomas
Jefferson's designs for Monticello
(1769) and later for the University of
Virginia modified the plain and very
clear style that had already developed
along Palladian lines in large houses
such as Carter's Grove.

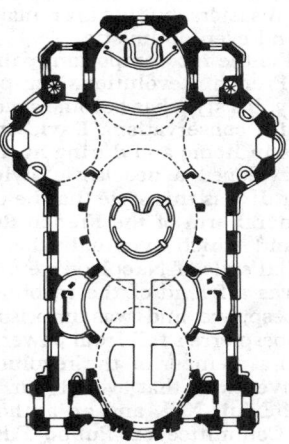 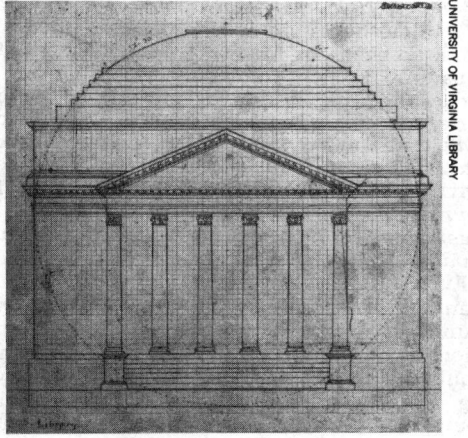

ROCOCO AND NEOCLASSIC: *the differences between the two competing styles are most clearly seen in architecture, where the irregular and ornate Vierzehnheiligen Church* (above and left) *contrasts sharply with the Petit Trianon in France* (below) *and Thomas Jefferson's carefully proportioned plans for the library at the University of Virginia* (right).

CULVER PICTURES

Sculpture

The 18th century was not a great age
for sculpture. There were few commissions for monumental works, and the
Baroque style of the preceding century
was transformed into the much less serious Rococo. Rococo sculpture is
small, intended to be viewed inside
and close at hand. It is not without
quality, but it does not rival the earlier
schools. An excellent example of its
charm is the *Satyr and Bacchante* of
Clodion (c 1775). The statue is in terra
cotta, and the movement and complicated relations of the figures are faithful to Baroque ideals despite the
smaller scale.

Romantic Art

It is common among historians to think of the 18th century as ending in 1789 with the French Revolution. This date is fitting in the history of art as well; soon after the revolution, France became the center of the artistic world. Paris in the 1700's was an intellectual center, but not necessarily the city where the most important artistic creation took place. Beginning after the revolution and well into the 1900's, Paris was unquestionably the most important center in the world for painting and sculpture. With few exceptions, the history of art became the history of French art. In many ways a movement as vigorous as the Italian Renaissance took place in France in the 125 years after the revolution, and that movement led to our modern conception of art.

GOYA AND DAVID: *The two great painters of the late 1700's produced the portrait of Don Manuel Osorio* (Goya) *and* The Death of Marat (David).

Painting

Goya. The greatest painter to bridge the 18th and 19th centuries, however, is not French but Spanish. Francisco Goya (1746–1828) is an isolated figure, generally considered outside the various schools of painting. He acknowledged his indebtedness to Velasquez and Rembrandt, but his painting is unlike anyone else's, and younger artists did not follow his lead. He arrived in Madrid in 1766, when Tiepolo was working there, and Goya's early painting has something of the lightness of the Rococo.

As his career developed, however, his style became increasingly his own. He was the court painter to Charles IV of Spain. He did many fine portraits, one of which is that of the king's entire family, painted in 1800. The picture recalls Velasquez's *Las Meninas* because Goya places himself in the picture in the act of painting. Indeed, the most fitting comparison for Goya is with Velasquez. The two handled paint and the use of highlights in similar fashion. There are also certain similarities of attitude in the two pictures cited. Goya's picture is famous, however, for the completely unflattering manner in which the members of the royal family are portrayed. Splendidly dressed, the adult members are at best plain and their attitudes undistinguished. The children are treated from a more hopeful point of view, and the young prince in the center of the picture has some of the mixture of fear and pride that one sees in the portrait of Don Manuel Osorio reproduced here.

Goya's themes become increasingly morbid and fantastic as he grows older. In response to the invasion of Spain by Napoleon, Goya used his painting to recall political events, as in the famous war picture *The Third of May, 1808,* a violent and emotion-filled depiction of the execution of the citizens of Madrid by a firing squad of French soldiers. Goya depicted the same kind of atrocities in a series of etchings called *Horrors of War,* and another series called *Disasters.* At the end of his life, he painted horrible fantasies, such as *Saturn Devouring His Children;* one of his etchings is called *The Dream of Reason Produces Nightmares.*

Even in his early portrait of Don Manuel Osorio, one can see Goya's profound sensitivity to the human situation and the fragility of feeling that would result in a morbid and consuming preoccupation with evil. The young child, like the prince in the portrait of the family of Charles IV, is both intently aware of the world around him and ready, it seems, to withdraw from it. He is an easy prey, like the magpie on its string. The picture has a symbolic function; the caged birds are traditional symbols of innocence, yet the child and the birds are surrounded by shadow. In the child's gaze and in his surroundings there is a brooding presence of something that is neither childlike nor beautiful. The picture seems to anticipate the disasters that Goya (and the child) would see in his own life.

David. Goya's contemporary in France was Jacques Louis David (1748–1825), who also painted political pictures. David, too, was an official painter of a government, but his masters were republican revolutionaries rather than royalty. David saw his share of disasters, but his art remained public and even optimistic.

David is the most important painter of the French Revolution, yet paradoxically, his style has become synonymous with conservatism. David spent six years in Rome and during his time there developed a neoclassic style of painting. It was this style that he used as the moral arm of the French Revolution and which eventually became the official style of Napoleon's empire. David was a friend of the revolutionary Robespierre and was imprisoned after Robespierre's fall from power. He was also a member of the revolutionary convention that voted for the death of Louis XVI, and an authority on the Committee on Public Education, which was in charge of the art of the new republic.

In *The Death of Marat* David's style and message are clear. One sees first the absolute clarity of form: the perfectly modeled torso and drapery, which have the precision of sculpture, and the clear description of shallow illuminated space. But the picture is more than an exercise in form; it is a dramatic and impressive vehicle for a message. David's picture pays homage to the revolutionary hero and martyr Marat, who had been assassinated in his bath by the young Charlotte Corday, who was opposed to his politics. David's portrayal of the dead hero (who was his friend) is clearly a political message, stark and simple as his signing of the picture, "To Marat."

Marat's fate is illuminated in this picture as if a spotlight were brought to bear upon it. David saw his painting as a clear means of communication derived from the mastery of form. His style is a return to the classical rules of Poussin, but he puts his art to the service of his political convictions. His classicism becomes a means of teaching and communication, even propaganda, in the real world of historical events.

Ingres.

David's classicism was the official style of the French Academy until late in the 1800's. It was propagated most effectively by his greatest pupil, Jean Auguste Dominique Ingres (1780–1867), who himself became head of the academy. Ingres's actual study with David was not a success, and in his early years he was considered a rebel and his style a deformation of classic art. With time, however, it was seen that he, more than anyone else, was faithful to David's principles. Chief among those principles was the preeminent importance of drawing in painting.

Classic art—architecture, painting, and sculpture—relies on the clear rendering of form, mass, and weight. In painting, the only way to convey these values is through drawing. Ingres as a draftsman was second to none, and whereas the actual forms he chose to paint differed considerably from those of David, he relied on the same careful modeling and the emphasis on contour that characterized David's style. Drawing is taught by academic discipline. Ingres more than any painter in the 1800's was the master of that discipline. Yet the classicism of Ingres was very different from that of David. Ingres used his mastery of technical means not to convey a message, but to create art that is an end in itself. Besides his portraits and a number of mythological paintings, Ingres is known for his pictures of the "odalisques," or Turkish harem slaves. These pictures are unique in the history of art for their splendor and precision. Human shapes, jewels, cloth—all contribute to give the completely convincing illusion of reality. It is a reality that has little to do with the day to day. In this sense Ingres is closer to Boucher and Fragonard than to David.

In his portrait of Joseph Antoine Moltedo, the great gifts of Ingres are visible despite a seemingly necessary contradiction. The subject of the portrait is in no way handsome, and Ingres renders the man's plainness with scrupulous and masterful drawing. The man's clothes, of a rich brown velvet and the whitest linen, are painted with the same care. In contrast to the man's person are objects of great, almost miraculous, beauty. The setting against which the man is painted, a distant cityscape of Rome, is of the same intense beauty. This portrait

documents Ingres's particular genius: the mastery of perfect illusion. Ingres used this mastery to record the intense visual beauty he saw and obviously enjoyed, creating one of the most refined styles that ever existed in painting.

The early 1800's are commonly referred to as the Romantic era, and critics traditionally spoke of neoclassicism and Romanticism as opposites. In a sense, however, the neoclassicism of Ingres is but one school of Romanticism. His painting of the odalisques, his love of the opulent, and his treatment of landscape, are all manifestations of the Romantic view of the world. The Romanticism of David and Ingres seems calm and reasonable, but it shares with the more turbulent Romanticism a desire to make visible a world that is exotic and far beyond the banality of ordinary existence.

One of the painters whose work helps shape what is commonly called Romantic painting is another of David's pupils, Baron Antoine Jean Gros (1771–1835). His best known painting, *The Pest House at Jaffa,* shows Napoleon visiting his plague-stricken troops. The painting pays homage to the emperor and, like some of David's works, carries a political message. The picture is also an attempt to describe the harrowing experience of the pest house. It is filled with dying and agonizing nudes in an exotic setting of Moorish arches, dramatic light, and a battle-ridden city. Emotionally, the picture's intention is similar to that of Stubbs's *Lion Attacking a Horse.* This emotional violence will characterize much of the work of the later thoroughly Romantic painters Géricault and Delacroix.

Géricault.

Jean Louis Géricault (1791–1824) is the prototypical Romantic artist. He died at the age of 33 as the result of a riding accident, and horses were one of the obsessive subjects of his paintings. At 21 he had painted the *Mounted Officer of the Imperial Guard* which is a glorification of the violence of war and horses. Superhuman power concentrated in a human figure is portrayed in the movement of the horse and the rider; the rider seems to reach for a new definition of human aspiration. Géricault successfully combines a classic mastery of form and an intensely dramatic sense of color and light. The mounted officer and his rearing, turning horse are silhouetted against a fiery battlefield, and the reds of the fire in the background are reflected in the jacket, sash, and plumes of the mounted officer.

The mounted officer was painted in 1812. By 1818, when Géricault created his masterpiece, *The Raft of the Medusa,* his assumptions about life seem to have changed. The mounted officer showed power within human reach. The raft and the survivors of the sunken ship *Medusa* are a depiction of human catastrophe, where man is helpless in a natural world that can engulf him. In the exaggerated and turbulent movement of the picture, one sees the same great technical skill that characterized the earlier painting, but the sense of color has changed. *The Raft of the Medusa* is a very dark picture, and the brilliantly lit nudes of the foreground, which recall Gros's figures in the pest house, play against the darkness of the sea, which is all the more somber and frightening because

THE RAFT OF THE MEDUSA *by Géricault shows the intense sense of visual drama shared by the early Romantic painters.*

ALINARI/EPA

of the dramatically lit sky. The picture is enormous, 23 feet 6 inches by 16 feet 1 inch, almost exactly the same size as Gros's monumental picture of the pest house. Romantic painting used size as well as form and subject to create a world of violent emotion.

After *The Raft of the Medusa,* Géricault studied the heads of the victims of the guillotine and painted many portraits of madmen, seeking to understand something beyond ordinary human reason (as did Goya in the same years). Romanticism in its violent manifestations eventually led to the birth of an important new discipline, the study of human psychology. Both Géricault and Goya recognized that the human mind is a place of violence.

Delacroix. Géricault's successor in the Romantic tradition was Eugene Delacroix (1798–1863). Delacroix inherited his subjects and his outlook from Géricault. The career of the younger painter was a continuation of Géricault's concern with the possibilities of portraying violence and drama. Delacroix's *Massacre at Chios* first won him notoriety. Depicting the disaster and violence of a real event, the massacre of Greeks by Turks on the island of Chios, it expressed the deep sympathies of the Romantics for the Greeks in their war for independence.

Delacroix is especially remembered as the proponent of a new kind of painting that saw as its prime concern the development of color. His technique is profoundly different from that of Géricault and Ingres, who was his artistic enemy for a quarter century. Géricault and Ingres were master draftsmen, but for Delacroix drawing was not as important as color. He composed his pictures with color, and his later career was a long experimentation with the possibilities of color and its application. He never gave up his preferred Romantic subjects of violence, combat, and animals, but these subjects were painted with an increasing scientific interest in the way color functions. Delacroix kept a journal of his observations that is considered to be the most important artistic research in the art of color painting up to his time. Delacroix was immensely admired by the younger painters, who would become known as Impressionists, and by the young Van Gogh, because of his concentration on the problems of color.

Painting in England. While the French were creating their heroic and violent versions of Romantic painting, another school of painting was developing in England; it was to have a profound effect on later painting. Joseph Turner (1775–1851) sought in many ways the same effects as French Romantic painting, but his pictures never portrayed the same intense human and animal violence. Rather, he made use of color and the grandiosity of nature to produce exalted and fantastic pictures that present a kind of expressive and emotional landscape painting. Like Delacroix, he experimented with color, but it is atmospheric, light-filled color that interests him, and his pictures lose almost all relation to reality, becoming exercises in color harmonics.

The painting of Turner's contemporary John Constable (1776–1837) was also of landscapes, but of landscapes as faithful as possible to reality. He painted recognizable views of the English countryside in great calm panoramas. Emotionally, his pictures are the opposite of those of the younger Delacroix, although an exposition of Constable's paintings in Paris in 1824 influenced both Delacroix and later French Romantics.

Constable did many oil sketches of the sites he painted, and these sketches were done out of doors. His painting is a study of nature, particularly as it undergoes the changes of weather and light. As his career progressed, he placed increasing confidence in the sketches; his finished pictures, even if painted indoors, preserve the quality of outdoor impressions. Painting directly from nature with scientific scrutiny was Constable's great contribution, along with his great poetic gifts.

Courbet. Gustave Courbet (1819–1877) began a movement that is also characterized by a faithful rendering of reality. But his concern was more with the subjects of painting than with the style. His style incorporated deliberate carelessness and simplicity of surface to achieve dramatic effects of light and shade, using a palette knife as well as a brush in applying paint. His approach appealed to the later Impressionists, but his freedom in choosing his subjects was a major inspiration for younger painters. His picture *The Stone Breakers* caused a scandal when it was first shown in 1854 because the subject was considered not "artistic," even dangerously subversive.

Manet. Painters before the time of Impressionism had been interested in the technical and stylistic problems of painting. But painters of the late 1800's changed the rules. The illusion a painter created of some real object or view had always been an important part of judging a painting. Edouard Manet (1832–1883) was perhaps the first to free painting from complete devotion to representing objective reality. This break invigorated the world of painting in Paris with an energy of creation that has rarely been equaled in the history of art. Many young painters of great talent, dedication,

THE WOMAN WITH A PARROT *by Manet pointed to new developments in art.*

and intelligence made the second half of the 1800's and the early years of the 1900's a period that for painting may equal the Renaissance in Italy or 17th-century Dutch painting.

The major subjects of Manet and the later Impressionists were the unadorned scenes of the life they found around them. Manet's first great painting, *Le Déjeuner sur l'Herbe* (Luncheon on the Grass) exploited the new freedom to paint the subject of his choice, no matter its seeming inappropriateness. Two ordinarily dressed men sit on the grass in the company of a nude woman. The picture caused a scandal. Manet's style only heightened the shock. The light is so brilliant as to minimize any modeling of the figures. They seem at the same time to be as flat as the canvas itself and to have exaggerated depth.

This is also true of the painting *Woman with a Parrot* (1866). The woman is brilliantly lit; her dressing gown reads illusionistically against the dark background, yet any particular part of it examined separately is an abstract—simply paint on canvas. Manet is less concerned with creating an illusion of a three-dimensional object than with the visual beauty of his paint, its color, the shapes it creates, and finally the brilliant light it seems to suggest. *Woman with a Parrot* is far from an abstract picture. The picture works in two ways: as a brilliantly illuminated picture of a beautifully dressed woman and as a study of the application of paint to a surface. The lemon at the bottom of the picture gives the illusion of a lemon, but also draws attention to the paint itself and to the inherent beauty of the painted surface. Other earlier painters had done similar things, particularly Velasquez, whom Manet admired. But

Manet carries this double approach further than earlier artists. He is not considered an Impressionist, but in his treatment of objects like the lemon and the woman's sleeves, his breaking down of an object into highlights and patches of pure color approaches the Impressionistic style.

Degas. Manet's friend and contemporary, Edgar Degas (1834–1917), was also only on the edge of the Impressionist movement. His artistic concerns were quite different from those of the Impressionists, yet he also contributed to the movement.

Degas was in many ways the most conservative of his contemporaries, and in his work the values of the classic tradition remain intact. He was a student of Ingres and he never ceased to admire the older man's teachings. Degas was the greatest draftsman of his age. His pictures are remarkable because they preserve classical ideas of space and figure, yet experiment at the same time with flat, two-dimensional composition.

In the painting *The Tub*, reproduced in the color plates, one sees the value of form and Degas' skillful manipulation of three-dimensional volumes within an illusion of space. At the same time, one sees a desire for abstraction and two-dimensional design in the way the surface of the picture divides easily into flat areas of color.

Degas, for all his insistence on drawing, was also an important colorist. His painting, like that of Monet and Cézanne, is responsible for the development of a new kind of space that is dependent on color. The blues of *The Tub* create an illusion of great space that is independent of the laws of perspective, having more to do with the fullness and density of color. Gauguin, Matisse, and later painters exploited this particular quality of uniform color surfaces.

The Impressionists. The Impressionist movement was the work of Manet's and Degas' slightly younger contemporaries, Monet, Pissarro, Renoir, and Sisley. The movement was the culmination of many ideas and practices begun by other individual artists. The Impressionists made these ideas and practices into a major school in painting. Courbet's realism and its dedication to the real, observable world; Constable's studies of sky, atmosphere, light, and landscape; and Delacroix's studies of color all came to fruition in the Impressionists' work. Their ideas were also influenced by scientific thought. A French chemist, Eugène Chevreul, had published *The Principles of Harmony and Contrast of Colors, and Their Application to the Arts* in 1839. Many of the laws discovered by Chevreul helped form the

CÉZANNE *painted a series of views of the Gulf of Marseilles from Estaque, studying the relationship between form and color in landscape.*

methods of Impressionism. Light was seen in its component hues; shadows were painted with their aureoles of complementary colors; contrast or fusing were used to evoke particular optical impressions. These optical effects were achieved with unmixed pigments painted on a white ground with visible brush strokes. The hope was to recreate the effects of light and its instantaneous changes.

Claude Monet (1840–1926) went the furthest with Impressionism. *Morning on the Seine Near Giverny* is a late painting, at a time when his particular form of Impressionism had advanced well beyond naturalistic landscape painting. But even during this period Monet was pursuing the natural phenomena of light and color. He arose before dawn to station himself in his boat in different parts of his water garden at Giverny or along the Seine, choosing carefully his viewpoint and recording the light at different moments. He painted many series employing these techniques: of snow and breaking ice in winter, of London in the fog, of the facade of Rouen cathedral, of rows of poplar trees, of haystacks. His painting gradually evolved to the state where color and its dynamics were the determining agents of the form of his pictures, yet they maintain a delicate equilibrium between observation of the real world and the purely aesthetic need of two-dimensional composition. The atmospheric space of these pictures was new in painting, and Monet's last works were enormous pictures of water and water lilies, where any constraint of composition or form had disappeared in favor of an overall color space.

Cézanne. Paul Cézanne (1839–1906) was less successful as an Impressionist, but his use of the Impressionists' methods contributed to a new synthesis of color and structure that is one of the highest points ever reached in painting. Cézanne is as great a colorist as Monet; at the same time, his pictures are the most highly and deliberately structured of all the work of the Impressionists. Cézanne developed a style of painting in which neither form nor color was sacrificed, and in which each intensified the other. Traditional three-dimensional form was relatively unimportant to the Impressionists—even two-dimensional design was absent in Monet's last pictures. But Cézanne wanted not only strong two-dimensional composition but also the classical solidity of three-dimensional form. Like Monet and the other Impressionists, Cézanne studied nature and painted series of views, such as the one shown from L'Estaque. His landscape paintings, like his still lifes, present an intense experience both of form and of light and color.

Cézanne's pictures suggest the depth and solidity of the world through a clear division between the planes and surfaces that compose it. Through his use of color, which is the most vibrant of 19th-century painting, he transforms the solidity into the movement and brilliance of light. These apparently conflicting approaches create an intense optical tension between the reading of a flat surface design and the experience of depth. This tension was taken up and developed further by the later school called cubism.

Gauguin and Van Gogh.

Manet, Degas, and the Impressionists were all working toward realism and away from it at the same time. Yet the Impressionists were still concerned with the depiction of visual reality. Two of the painters who followed were more concerned with another kind of reality. Like Blake or Géricault, they sought a deeper psychological level of meaning. Paul Gauguin and Vincent Van Gogh used the Impressionist techniques to explore more than visual perception. They made their own inner needs and desires the subject of their paintings and left the objective world behind.

Paul Gauguin (1848–1903) lived as a child in Peru. Later he was a sailor and traveled again to South America. He was also a stockbroker, who at the age of 35 devoted himself full-time to painting for the first time. He exhibited with the Impressionists and learned from Pissarro and Degas. His *Vision After the Sermon* (1888) is a depiction of Jacob wrestling with the angel as imagined by the peasant women whose backs and headdresses form the front of the picture. The emotion of the picture is heightened by the colors, which are completely freed from any necessity to be true to life. The angel is a kind of refutation of realism (Courbet had said that he could not paint an angel because he had never seen one).

He eventually abandoned France for the South Seas island of Tahiti. The emotional or spiritual values that Gauguin sought are expressed in the figures of the exotic island women. They are a far cry from the "scientific" observation of the Impressionists. The large decorative shapes and lines of the pictures and the opaque and flat, yet hot, colors show a complete repudiation of the naturalistic goals of Impressionism. Gauguin's work returns painting to the world of human expression.

Vincent Van Gogh (1853–1890), like Gauguin, painted to express his own experience. He came to France from Holland in 1886 and learned to adapt Impressionist techniques to his own purposes. The prominent use of his brush, often in small separate strokes, is his most significant technical trait. Though he was a friend of Gauguin's, both his style and his experience of reality were quite different. Van Gogh was hospitalized for mental illness, and he eventually committed suicide. In his paintings of the most unassuming objects, there is an eerie kind of intensity that one sees in his self-portraits (see color plates). The intensity is conveyed by the brushwork and the creation of an intense atmosphere of color and pattern. His intensity served strictly human goals, and is a projection of his interior, turbulent world. His last painting is a picture of the field where he killed himself, a vision of yellow wheat and vivid dark blue sky. The field and the sky are empty except for the small black wings of several crows.

Seurat.

Gauguin and Van Gogh are commonly called Post-Impressionists, as is another slightly younger painter, Georges Seurat (1859–1891). After the 1880's, even the painters most closely associated with Impressionism, including Monet, Renoir, and Pissarro, changed their styles in some way to seek new goals. But the techniques and works of Seurat are the most conspicuous.

Like Cézanne, Seurat wanted to create an art that was solid and durable. Of all the painters of his age, he worked in the most carefully controlled fashion, trying to make a science of his technique for the analysis of form in terms of color. He worked for as long as a year on a single picture, and there are 34 known oil studies for his largest picture, *Sunday Afternoon on the Island of La Grande Jatte.*

Early in his career he learned to compose a whole picture from the smallest of brush strokes. Later he used dots of pure color. He was seeking to create volumes and space like those of Renaissance pictures while remaining faithful to Impressionists' understanding of light and color. But his technique, sometimes called *pointillism,* had side effects. The immobility of the figures and the patterns of *La Grande Jatte* and its almost bizarre color make the painting an emotional experience more akin to a Gauguin or a Van Gogh painting than to those of the early Impressionists. The life in *La Grande Jatte* seems arrested, as if all motion and emotion were ordered stopped by the painter's will. The figures are both volume and silhouette. The painting itself reads both as a three-dimensional composition and as a flat, designed surface. This ambiguity makes it both arresting and mysterious.

Henri de Toulouse-Lautrec (1864–1901) also painted to express his emotions. He was an aristocrat and a dwarf, and he chose to live in and paint the world of Parisian nightlife. He exaggerated Degas' flat-colored planes and Manet's silhouetted figures to depict a world of extravagantly illuminated cafe and theater interiors. His color and his bold composition are instruments of strong yet tightly controlled emotion.

The 19th century in France began with the Romantic depiction of violence and grand public emotion, passed through the serene adoration of nature and light in Impressionism, and ended with the more subjective violence of the Post-Impressionists. This new subjectivity and search for a new meaning in art continued into the 20th century.

SEURAT *painted this large canvas,* Sunday Afternoon on the Island of La Grand Jatte, *using only tiny dots of color (see close-up). The technique came to be called pointillism.*

Architecture

The neoclassic style that had developed in Europe in the 1700's continued well into 1800's. Both Europe and America saw some of their finest public buildings built in the Greek and Roman orders. The Gothic revival style that grew alongside neoclassicism was an acceptable alternative for public and private buildings by the early 1800's. When Benjamin Latrobe (1764–1820) submitted plans for the Catholic Cathedral in Baltimore he offered designs in both a neoclassic and a Gothic style. The neoclassic plan was accepted and America owes one of its most beautiful interior spaces to Latrobe's plan. Latrobe had emigrated from England, but the cathedral in Baltimore owes something to the Pantheon in Paris, and in its proportions to the original Pantheon in Rome.

Jefferson's plan for the University of Virginia complex, which was executed by Latrobe, derived again from the Roman Pantheon. The Capitol of the United States in Washington is also a neoclassic building of impressive scale; it was designed by William Thornton at the end of the 1700's.

The flourishing of the neoclassic style in these still young American cities is an indication of its strength. In Europe, such buildings were built on a grand scale. Parts of Paris were rebuilt in the classical orders with monumental buildings dominating the vistas for which the city is famous. The Arc de Triomphe is a major monument of neoclassic Paris. Parts of London, too, were rebuilt in the neoclassic style by the architect John Nash (1752–1835).

The British Museum, which was finished in 1847 by Sir Robert Smirke, was the culmination of the neoclassic style. Its Ionic colonnade makes one of the largest expanses of classical architecture in the world. In Berlin the architect Karl Friedrich Shinkel built the Altes Museum between 1824 and 1828 on the same principle of an enormous Ionic colonnade. Even in small cities, such as Edinburgh, extensive classical facades changed the look of the city. Each city, and each architect, created different and sometimes eccentric versions of the style, but the architecture of Greece and Rome never failed as a source of inspiration.

By the time of the construction of the Paris Opera in 1861, the style was no longer truly neoclassical, but eclectic. Jean Louis Charles Garnier's architecture is a mixture of classical, Baroque, and Renaissance styles, combined to suggest great opulence. This old and overelaborated form is in stark contrast to the Impressionism that was sweeping the world of painting at the same time, illustrating the great gulf between official taste (the Paris Opera) and that of the avant-garde (the Impressionist painting).

THE CRYSTAL PALACE *in London made use of new construction techniques that permitted the lavish use of glass.*

In England, the greatest public building of the early 1800's is also eclectic in style, but it leans toward the Gothic. The old house of Parliament had burned in 1834. The architect of the new Parliament building, Sir Charles Barry, was famous for his neoclassic architecture, and it is to his assistant Augustus W. Pugin that the Gothic overlay of the building is due.

The form of the building—the clear and careful delineation of the elements and its symmetry—owes much to the classic despite its Gothic ornamentation. The building reflects the prosperity of the most powerful country in the world.

Parallel to the grand public architecture, there developed a much more simple and functional architecture, one that relied on a new building material—iron. Libraries, railroad stations, and commercial buildings were built using cast iron (later steel) frames. This engineering revolution made possible a whole new architecture. The strong but light metal frame allowed the extensive use of glass. And the standardization of structural elements made it possible to build large buildings far more quickly and cheaply. In London, the exposition building called the Crystal Palace was built in 1850 almost completely out of iron and glass in only six months. In Paris, in 1889, the Galerie des Machines and the Eiffel Tower showed the possibilities of a metal superstructure using a whole new concept of style. These innovative ideas and methods would culminate in a completely new aesthetic for public buildings in the 1900's.

Sculpture

Early 1800's sculpture was dominated by neoclassicism and its most successful proponent, Antonio Canova (1757–1822). Canova repeated and sometimes reworked the forms and attitudes of Roman sculpture, but he was capable of a refined sensuality that resembled that of Ingres.

Much more dynamic sculpture was done in France by François Rude (1784–1855), who is responsible for the gigantic figures on the Arc de Triomphe. The group, *La Marseillaise,* is approximately 42 feet by 26 feet; it shows a group of warriors being led to the defense of France by a winged figure, the goddess of liberty.

The work of Antoine Louis Barye (1795–1875) shows another Romantic preoccupation, that with animals. His *Jaguar Devouring a Hare* has the same ferocity as Stubbs's lion and horse or one of Delacroix's similar subjects.

The taste of mid-century France that produced the Paris Opera found a sculptor of exuberant vitality in Jean Baptiste Carpeaux (1827–1875). His group, *The Dance,* which was designed for the facade of the Paris Opera, is a monumental version of the taste of 100 years earlier, resembling the Rococo sculpture of Clodion. The forms, however, are more attenuated and less controlled by classic norms than Clodion's. Carpeaux's figures suggest exploding energy unrestrained by classic norms of balance and stability.

Rodin. The great sculptor of the 19th century was Auguste Rodin

ROMANTIC SCULPTURE: The Dance *by Carpeaux (left)* shows the continuing influence of Baroque and Romantic models in sculpture. Rodin's Walking Man *(right)* looks forward to the figurative sculpture of the 20th century.

(1840–1917). He worked briefly with Barye, and like the older sculptor, he preferred working in bronze. Rodin's use of the malleability of his wax and clay models also shows Barye's influence. Both men's bronzes show the same broken and irregular surfaces that come from the modeling of the soft materials of the casts.

Rodin said, however, that the great influence on his art was Michelangelo. He admired the unfinished and fragmentary state of Michelangelo's marble groups—an aspect not admired by earlier artists. Rodin used this admiration to justify his own work, which

shows a tension between realism and abstract form that recalls the Impressionist painters. Rodin felt less obliged than earlier sculptors to create a facsimile of reality. He studied the reality of form and movement, as one can see in the *Walking Man*. But he used his observations to focus on the abstract problems of sculptural expression. *Walking Man* is more a study of movement and weight than it is the sculptural portrayal of a man.

At the same time, Rodin desired his work to equal the great sculptured figures of the past. He worked for many years on figures for the monumental

Gates of Hell, which he never finished. *The Kiss* was to form one of the groups that made up the gates, and it is the clearest, most unpretentious, and most effective sculptural depiction of human love from the 1800's. Others of his sculptural groups were in a much more tragic vein, and the dominating figure of the *Gates of Hell* was to be *The Thinker.* The man, lost in brooding and merciless thought, may be the last direct expression of human emotion on the scale of Michelangelo. Like Michelangelo's sculpture, *The Thinker* makes of the human situation a philosophical and even tragic question.

Modern Art

Painting

To the end of the 1800's painting remained representational, despite tendencies of major painters toward more abstract or nonrepresentational painting. Between 1901 and 1906 there were several large exhibitions in Paris of the works of Gauguin, Van Gogh, and Cézanne, the three painters who

would most strongly influence the painting of the new century.

One sees in the late work of Cézanne in particular a concern with form and color for their own sake, even though he still refers directly to the real, perceived world. It was the nonconcrete, nonrepresentational aspects of his painting that impressed younger artists, however, and helped set the direction in which painting would move.

Modern art is a movement toward nonrepresentational and abstract values; painters after 1900 divorced themselves from ties to the real world in favor of creating their own space, forms, and experience. In a sense, artists have always done this. Greek sculpture portrayed ideal rather than real human form. Renaissance paintings idealized space, exaggerating perspective in the interests of illusion.

The liberties 20th-century painters took with the appearance of their subjects were only more extreme than those of earlier times. They left the idea of representation behind and sought to create visual art from the abstract elements of form, color, and design.

Matisse.

The first great liberation for 20th-century painting was in the area of color, and its liberator was Henri Matisse (1869–1954). Matisse had been trained as an academic painter, but he entered the history of art with a group of painters whose exhibition in Paris in 1905 so shocked the public and the critics that they were given the name "Fauves," or wild beasts. What caused the scandal was the paintings' extreme simplicity of form and extreme brilliance of color. Impressionist painting had made freer use of color and had maintained both harmony and subtlety. Gauguin, Van Gogh, and Lautrec had been the first to use much brighter greens, reds, and oranges. For the Fauve painters, violent use of color became the meaning of the picture itself.

Matisse's *The Red Studio* is from 1911, after the Fauve group had disbanded and individual painters were seeking their individual styles. Matisse remained faithful to the original stance of the Fauves, however. The color of *The Red Studio,* although more sober than that of some of Matisse's earlier paintings, is obviously the most expressive element of the picture. The larger part of the surface of the canvas is painted a rich brick red. Only very minimal drawing indicates the perspective of the room, yet it seems spacious partly because of the density of the color. The colors in the pictures on the walls are predominantly other reds and pinks, and the bits of blue in the pictures and the green of the plant on the table in the foreground heighten the intensity of the overall color red.

Two years earlier, Matisse had titled another painting *The Red Room (Harmony in Red).* Harmony of color was the basis of Matisse's painting. Color was both a means of expressing feeling and the basis of his pictures' design. He learned his use of color from Cézanne and Van Gogh, but he preferred a flatness and uniformity of hue untouched by Van Gogh's brushwork or Cézanne's description of planes. Matisse's color appeared in large calm segments, often animated, as in *The Red Studio,* by smaller bits of complementary colors. After the early Fauvist years, his use of color was never frenetic or disturbing, even when he depicted great movement, as in the large paintings of his dance series.

Matisse's drawing always remained minimal, but effective. He was able to indicate the human form in motion with the most economical lines. At the

THE RED STUDIO *by Henri Matisse makes color the dominant element of expression, while draftsmanship is simplified and de-emphasized.*

end of his long life, when he was no longer able to paint, he cut and pasted bits of colored paper to form pictures that were the most advanced of his time. Matisse more than anyone else of his era combined the classical values of painting with consistent innovation in the expressive uses of color.

Georges Rouault (1871–1958) was another painter of the original Fauve group, and he used his color and his training as a worker in stained glass to produce emotional, often religious, painting. It is a descendant of Van Gogh's early work in its portrayal of human pathos.

German expressionism.

Rouault's sensibility is entirely different from Matisse's, but it found reflection in a school of painting that developed after the Fauve period in Dresden and Munich and that is called German expressionism. Emil Nolde (1867–1956), Max Beckmann (1884–1950), Ernst Ludwig Kirchner (1880–1938), and many other German and Eastern European painters were liberated from more traditional painting by the Fauves' use of color and preference for rapid, "crude" brushwork. German painting more than any other was the inheritor of Van Gogh's subjective approach. The painters working in Germany just before 1914 made Germany's one great contribution to the history of painting. German expressionism is intensely social art and it is filled with psychological and philosophical or religious meaning. Its techniques were developed from the abstract French tradition, but it was

committed in a new way to the painful psychological realities of existence. In a sense, it is a generalization and broadening of Van Gogh's subjective psychological style.

It was from the German expressionist movement that the first completely nonrepresentational painting emerged. Wassily Kandinsky (1866–1944) came to Munich from his native Russia in 1896. He brought with him the clear desire to create a new kind of painting without subject matter. He had seen one of Monet's haystack paintings in Moscow, and the painting, which to him seemed to have no subject, was a revelation of his own desires. At first his painting was mostly of landscapes in Fauve colors applied in a strong and distinct fashion, a kind of modeling of the picture surface. By 1909, his painting called *Mountain* retained only the bare suggestion of a hill-like shape. By 1912, Kandinsky was painting pictures that he called "improvisations" or "compositions" and to which he gave numbers rather than titles. He sought to let his work emerge from his unconscious mind without conscious creation.

There is no recognizable subject in Kandinsky's later painting, only a maze of lines, planes, and bright colors. Yet they still read as a kind of landscape. In a sense, they are the depiction of the fantastic landscape of Kandinsky's imagination, where color and line replace the visible objects of nature. The pictures exist primarily as color, but Kandinsky also sought a sense of movement and incident. In contrast, Matisse's world is calm and ordered.

Cubism. In France in the years immediately following the Fauve exhibition another kind of painting developed that pointed in a second important direction. Pablo Picasso was born in 1881 and settled permanently in Paris in 1904. Between 1907 and 1914 he and George Braque (1882–1963) developed the style that was called cubism. At times they worked together so closely that it is difficult to tell the pictures of one from those of the other. Cubism grows out of Cézanne's interest in the picture surfaces. Picasso was deeply impressed by the retrospective show of Cézanne's paintings in 1907, the year after Cézanne's death. The beginning of cubism can be seen in Picasso's *Les Demoiselles d'Avignon* of 1907. Cézanne had talked of treating nature in terms of geometrical shapes—the cylinder, sphere, and cone. Now in the paintings of Picasso and Braque the critics could see only geometrical shapes and so they called the paintings "cubist." The crux of cubism, however, is not its geometrical shapes but the tension between the illusion of depth and the actual flatness of the canvas. That tension had already existed in major paintings of the late 1800's, but the cubists developed it as an independent value. They adopted Cézanne's methods to fracture the flat space of their pictures.

Les Demoiselles d'Avignon, along with its violence of feeling (Avignon was the red-light district of Barcelona), is equally violent in fracturing space and volume. The women's bodies are broken sharply into planes and contours that have no relation to reality yet that indicate volume and space. The space itself remains extremely shallow, the energy of the picture seemingly concentrated on the flat surface. Certain parts of the picture, such as the masklike faces of the women on the right, are drawn. Other planes are shaded to suggest depth, but the illusion is always denied.

This crowding of the picture surface with contradictory readings of depth and flatness are the basis of cubism. From its beginning through its later development in the works of Picasso, Braque, Leger, and Duchamp, the movement was a formal study of picture space, of the function of planes, and of two-dimensional depictions of volume. In a sense, it was a return to classical concerns about form, line, and contour. The influence of the cubists was immense, and its marks can be seen in the later works of Matisse, Kandinsky, and the German expressionists. As late as the 1940's and '50's, American abstract expressionism was using the same shallow, almost two-dimensional space.

The great disadvantage of cubism was its lack of interest in color. In *Les Demoiselles d'Avignon* the colors are earthen brown and shades of blue. In cubism's most intense phase, almost all color was banished. Later, color was used again, but it always remained of secondary importance. For years, painting seemed polarized between the apostles of form (the cubists) and the apostles of color (Matisse and his followers), the very division that Cézanne had worked so hard to deny.

Mondrian. Cubism always referred, at least indirectly, to the perceptible world, and even Kandinsky's compositions and improvisations retain the feeling of landscapes. Piet Mondrian (1872–1944) believed that cubism had not gone far enough toward formalism. After an initial cubist period, he created pictures that used a simple geometry to produce complete abstraction.

Mondrian, a Dutchman, was influenced by Van Gogh and later by cubism. During World War I, he meditated on the theory and meaning of painting. The paintings that developed from this meditation were constructed from rectangles and squares on an asymmetrical gridlike structure. Mondrian's use of color was similarly austere and restricted to the primary colors, which, painted in uniform flat surfaces, filled some of the rectangular spaces. His colors read on the same plane with the white surfaces and the black bands of the grid, causing his paintings to seem flat, solid, and infinite. Mondrian was seeking what he called "true reality," and his paintings are a contemplation of that reality. They are, in a sense, a philosophical quest, a variation of the spirit that animated Van Gogh, Gauguin, and Seurat.

Mondrian's was one of many attempts to make of painting a means of exploring realities that were not immediately perceptible in ordinary experience. Out of Italy had come futurism and its belief in movement as the universal principle. From Russia came suprematism, which, like Mondrian, saw painting as a means of perceiving a reality beyond natural forms. From Zurich came Dadaism, with its contempt for society and conventional art. Dadaism was one of the symptoms of deep disillusionment caused by the horrors of World War I. In revolt against established values, Dadaism created nonart, works that were a denial of art. The movement, contradictory as it was, helped liberate artists from old assumptions and encouraged them to explore new directions. This new freedom resulted in still another school, called surrealism.

Surrealism. The French poet André Breton wrote the manifesto of surrealism. The movement owed much to the thought of Sigmund Freud, the

LES DEMOISELLES D'AVIGNON, *an early painting of Picasso, is a step toward cubism, rendering the women as geometrical shapes.*

COLLECTION, THE MUSEUM OF MODERN ART, NEW YORK/LILLI P. BLISS BEQUEST

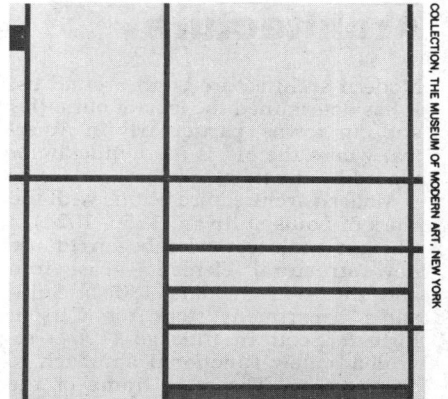

ABSTRACTION AND SURREALISM: *Mondrian achieved complete abstraction in* White, Black and Red, *calling attention to the design above all.* The Harlequin's Carnival (right) *by Miró is amusing yet ominous, a dreamlike composition whose style is called surreal.*

psychologist who first studied man's subconscious thoughts and desires. Surrealism sought to discover the inner truths of the subconscious and to promote the communion of man and the natural world. The poets of surrealism practiced automatic writing, and the painters tried to give form to the images of their subconscious minds.

Joan Miró (born 1893) was a leading surrealist painter, creating a unique personal world in his pictures. Other surrealist painters, including Dali and Max Ernst, used the means of traditional realist painting to describe personal dream images and fantasies. Miró's world was inhabited by flat floating creatures in a timeless undetermined space. In *The Harlequin's Carnival,* a room is filled in all dimensions by creatures that seem to be both animals and toys. There is a certain gaiety in Miró's paintings, and as in much surrealist art, the meanings and superstitions of the artist's childhood find life in his work. Another painter associated with surrealism, the Swiss-German Paul Klee (1879–1940), painted and drew small pictures in delicate and diverse styles, all of which depict a rich life of fantasy.

Surrealist painting was anticipated by the work of Henri Rousseau (1844–1910), a man who had no training as a painter but who created exotic and mysterious landscapes inhabited by magical figures who seemed to proclaim a new age of innocence or a return to the Garden of Eden. Less optimistic but equally mysterious were the cityscapes of the Greek-Italian Giorgio de Chirico (born 1888), who had been one of the first artists to devote his painting to the depiction of a world of his own making. His scenes of empty streets and squares of an imagined classical city seem full of prophecy and esoteric meaning. De Chirico and Rousseau have in common with the surrealists who followed

them the belief that truth must proceed from the depth of a man's interior world.

Surrealism was the last major artistic movement in Europe. In the late 1930's, World War II began, and when it was over, the center of the art world had shifted. Young American artists had made New York City the center of a new movement in painting, and for the first time in history American painting became the most advanced in the world.

Abstract expressionism.

The first important painting in postwar America is called abstract expressionism, although individual artists differed considerably in style and approach. Many of them were influenced in their formative years by Arshile Gorky and Hans Hofmann. Gorky (1904–1948) developed a style that was related to Miró's and that showed

the influence of Kandinsky and the cubists. Hofmann (1880–1966) was a great colorist, but his painting also remained within the cubist style.

Jackson Pollock (1912–1956), the most innovative of the abstract expressionists, is best known for what is called action painting. The term describes Pollock's method, which was to pour, throw, and splatter paint onto a canvas tacked to the floor. The result, as one can see in *Autumn Rhythm,* is not completely left to chance. The line Pollock created is no longer a drawn line; it is closer to a kind of figuration without any notion of plane or volume. The entire surface of the picture is animated by a dense, yet airy, chaos of line and color through which one can see into a kind of infinite space. Pollock's painting is the first that can be called post-cubist, since it is the first to go beyond the cubist dilemma of flatness versus depth. One sees also in Pollock's painting new possibilities

AUTUMN RHYTHM *by Jackson Pollock, a giant painting more than 17 feet wide, is a masterpiece of abstract expressionism, which flourished in New York in the 1940's and '50's.*

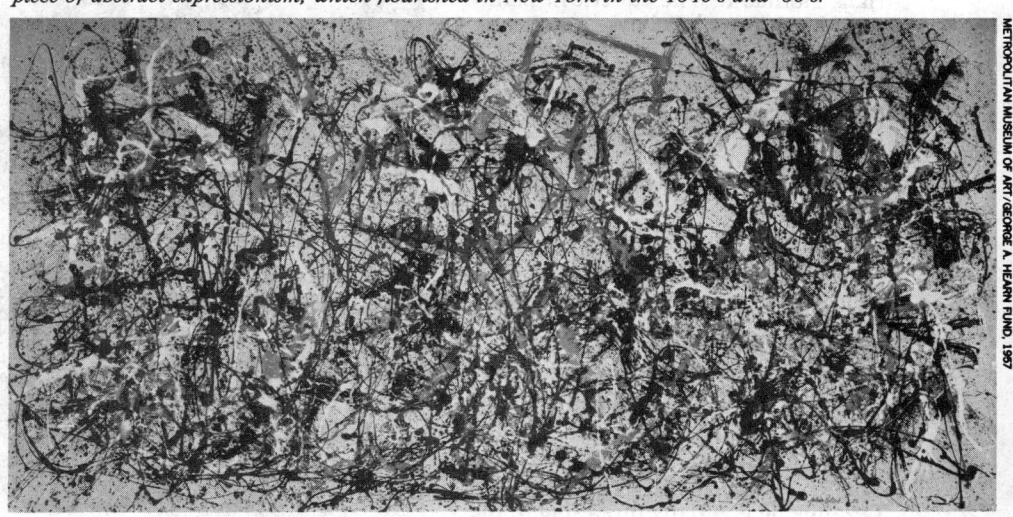

LEO CASTELLI GALLERY

PROTRACTOR VARIATION V *by Frank Stella combines geometric structure and brilliant color to produce a kind of flat sculpture.*

Architecture

Modern architecture is all around us. It has determined the look of our cities and our towns, particularly in America, where the old is more quickly replaced by the new.

Modern architecture begins with the work of Louis Sullivan (1856–1924), a Chicago architect who began to use new structural elements—cast iron and steel—in the late 1800's. Sullivan's department store for Carson, Pirie & Scott in Chicago (1904) revealed a new functional approach to architecture. The steel frame of the building became a part of the design itself, and Sullivan came to be recognized as the father of the modern skyscraper.

At the turn of the century, there was a flourish of style called Art Nouveau. It emphasized surface decoration that was composed of curved lines in long continuous patterns and that had no precise historical model. The new methods of construction with iron and glass aided its development, making possible the curvilinear facades still visible in Brussels and Paris. Some of the best examples on a small scale were the metro (subway) stations in Paris. On a larger scale, Victor Horta (1861–1947) constructed the Maison du Peuple in Brussels. The facade is one long assymetrical curve of steel and glass. A similar concern with curves and organic forms characterized the work of the most individual of 20th-century architects, Antonio Gaudi (1852–1926). He worked primarily in Barcelona, Spain and designed both an Art Nouveau version of

for color. His dribbled lines and splotches, though always of relatively sober hues, present color in a new, different way. Pollock used raw canvas, housepaint, and metallic paints that saturated the canvas and stained it. The paint becomes a kind of dye, and the viewer sees the paint as part of the canvas rather than on top of it. Pollock did not exploit his innovation, but the generation that followed made of it a new kind of painting, which, like Matisse's, had color as its prime value.

Part of the importance of American painting after World War II was its concentration on the problems that had been developed in painting in the previous hundred years in France. American painting is the continuation of a tradition that began with Delacroix and Manet. Pollock fits squarely in that tradition. The composition of his drip technique pictures, where he refuses to favor any part of the surface of the picture or to design the surface, is related in intent to Manet's enormous late pictures of water lilies.

Impressionism was a great liberating movement for color, taken up by Matisse, and brought to America by Hans Hofmann. The American painters who followed Pollock are characterized by their attempts to make pictures that develop the fullest possibilities of color. Morris Louis (1912–1962) was one of the first painters to realize the possibilities of Pollock's stained canvases, and Louis made entire pictures of veils and stripes of pure color stained into unprimed canvas. The optical effect of these pictures had never been seen before; the color is intense and luminescent, a pure experience free of any reference to the world as it is observed. Louis was followed by other painters, notably Kenneth Noland (born 1924) and Jules Olitski (born 1922), both of whom continued this intense color painting.

Frank Stella (born 1936) also shares Louis's concern with color, but like Cézanne he is equally interested in the

structure of his picture. Stella's first pictures denied color in favor of form. In his concern for form he changed the traditional rectangular shape of the canvas, using its shape to reflect the internal structure of the picture. In the picture reproduced here, *Protractor Variation V,* color emerges as one of Stella's concerns, but it is painted in a strict geometry that recalls Mondrian. Like Mondrian's, Stella's painting is a kind of two-dimensional sculpture, and like Cézanne's it is an attempt to endow color with structural strength and to make of it a kind of form. The great virtue of American painting has been its attempt to expand the traditional values of painting; its greatest achievement has been in the intelligence and the brilliance of its use of color.

FALLING WATER *in Pennsylvania is a famous example of Frank Lloyd Wright's pioneering style in the design of homes.*

FAYETTE COUNTY DEVELOPMENT COUNCIL

a Gothic cathedral and apartment buildings of undulating facades and stonework that simulated natural forms. Art Nouveau was short-lived, however, and its influence superficial. It quickly was supplanted by an international style of architecture from which the curve is absent.

Frank Lloyd Wright.

An American and a pupil of Sullivan, Frank Lloyd Wright (1869–1959) was an important influence in 20th-century architecture. Wright's buildings are characterized by a concentration on clean, sharply accented lines and interior spaces that flow into one another. He often stripped architecture of all unnecessary surface detail, and made the blocks of the structure itself the elements of design. In domestic architecture, he sought to integrate a building and its site. One fine example is seen in the Kaufman House, which is called "Falling-water." The house is built out over a waterfall, and the broad, horizontal planes of the decks and roofs make the building a kind of suspended sculpture in a natural setting of trees and water. It is noteworthy that in Wright's last building, the Guggenheim Museum in New York, he placed amid the city's exclusively right-angled buildings a series of bulbous curves, as if trying to relieve the standardized shapes of contemporary architecture.

The international style.

It is, however, the strictly rectilinear, hard-edged elements and the functionalism of Wright's style that were continued in Europe. The look of his buildings coincided exactly with the taste that is seen in Mondrian's painting and the design work of the school that grew up around it. In Germany the desire for pure forms is seen best in the work of Walter Gropius (1883–1969), who founded and designed the Bauhaus, a school of design in the town of Desau. Gropius's designs for the school itself, the most advanced of their time, established the principles of Sullivan and Wright—that a building's form should follow its function and that the structure itself should show through its style. The materials used were glass, steel, and concrete. The major facade of the studio building formed a kind of cage of glass that extended out from the steel supports and allowed a maximum of natural illumination for studios within. The clarity, precision, and symmetry of the Bauhaus and its regular volumes make it a triumph for classical principles, even in a modern style.

With the advent of Nazism in Germany, Gropius came to America as head of the Harvard Architecture School. At the same time, Miës van der Rohe (1886–1969) who was Gropius's associate at the Bauhaus, also came to America. He was responsible for applying Bauhaus principles to the American skyscraper, which he had always admired. The Seagram's Building in New York City, completed in 1956, is the realization of a plan he had made 30 years previously. This elegant skyscraper is faithful in every detail to the concept of pure form and line of the Bauhaus style. The building's facade is made of bronze and glass, and it is raised on piers in an open space. It has had countless imitators, and is perhaps a symbol of modern American technology and commercial wealth.

In Europe, two other architects were working on equally impressive and different buildings. Le Corbusier (1887–1965) designed the Church of Notre Dame du Haut at Ronchamp in France between 1950 and 1955. The great curves, the lack of right angles and symmetry, and the closed surfaces of the walls are the opposite of Bauhaus art and the purist international style that Le Corbusier had earlier helped to develop. Notre Dame du Haut reflects a desire for something more than the rectilinear.

In Italy, another kind of architecture was developed by Pier Luigi Nervi (born 1891), who as an engineer used the strength of prestressed concrete to create the great dome of the Palazzetto dello Sport in Rome. His style had developed in the 1930's when he designed similar buildings for use as hangars and stadiums. In America Eero Saarinen (1910–1961) used similar forms and the same precast concrete in the TWA terminal at New York's Kennedy airport.

The achievements of modern architecture in scale and technology are almost wondrous, and modern cities look from a distance like fabulous dreams of the imagination. However, the actual pleasure that architecture can give is often lacking, since the delights of decoration and intimacy have largely disappeared from modern construction. Architecture manifests the impersonality that is one of the byproducts of the technological society.

EZRA STOLLER © ESTO

MODERN DIRECTIONS: *The Seagram's Building in New York, designed by Miës van der Rohe, demonstrates the cool, simple lines of the international style. The Church of Notre Dame du Haut in France, designed by Le Corbusier, is a reaction using irregular lines.*

EPA

Sculpture

Twentieth-century sculpture follows the same course as painting—toward abstraction and purity of nonrepresentational form. The development in sculpture was rapid and took place largely in the lifetime of the great Rumanian sculptor Constantin Brancusi (1876–1957). Brancusi worked in Paris most of his life. His early work owes something to Rodin, but Brancusi quickly developed his own ideas of a sculpture that would be nonrepresentational. Brancusi created and reworked a limited number of sculptures, such as the head of Mademoiselle Pogany, which in the succeeding versions became more and more simplified. By the time of *Bird in Space* (1919), Brancusi had left any detail of representation behind in favor of a sculpted shape that was an image of flight. In the idea of sculpting movement *Bird in Space* follows Rodin's line of thinking in his *Walking Man*. Rodin's sculpture, though representational, was a step toward Brancusi's abstract rendering of flight, from which any representation of the bird had disappeared.

Most of Brancusi's sculptures were fairly small, and only in the works called *Endless Columns* did he approach the monumentality that had always been one of the aspects of major sculpture. The cubist sculpture of Picasso and Jacques Lipchitz, and almost all European sculpture before World War II, remained on a small scale. Even the futurist sculptor Umberto Boccioni (1882–1916) worked in a scale that was less than life-size.

Larger sculpture was made by Henry Moore (born 1898) of groups of human forms that were meant to be seen out of doors. Moore's sculpture also moved toward a more abstract rendering of the body but remained always representational.

Abstract sculpture on a monumental scale was the achievement of the American sculptor David Smith, who just before his death in 1965 initiated his Cubi series of blocks of polished stainless steel. Perhaps of all the geometric art of the 20th century, his is the most successful. Because of the beauty of their light-reflecting surfaces, Smith's Cubis are visually almost sensual. They are close to an experience of painting in three dimensions, just as Stella's painting was a kind of sculpture in two dimensions. The addition of color to sculpture, begun by Picasso early in his career, added a new dimension to a traditionally monochromatic medium.

Modern sculpture, in the diversity of its styles and forms—from attenuated, eroded figures by Giacometti to minimal constructions by Richard Serra—brought new life to a medium that had lacked serious development impersonality that is one of the by-products of the technological society.

MODERN SCULPTURE *approaches pure abstraction in Brancusi's* Bird in Space *and David Smith's* Cubi XVIII; *they were created nearly 50 years apart, in 1918 and 1964 respectively.*

New Directions

Even as American abstract expressionism gained international recognition in the 1950's, younger American artists went further. They questioned the conventional distinction between art and everyday life, seeking to bring art into the world of everyday experience.

One of the results of the new questioning came to be known as pop art. Robert Rauschenberg began to use everyday objects as part of his paintings. Jasper Johns shocked the art world with his straightforward painting of an American flag that filled his canvas. Was it a flag or a picture of a flag? Was it an everyday object or an art object? Johns seemed to be saying that the answer made no difference.

Pop art flourished for a dozen years, and succeeded in raising questions about art among artists and art viewers. Claes Oldenburg made giant "soft" sculptures of everyday objects. *Hamburger with Pickle* measured nearly eight feet across and was made of stuffed canvas painted in realistic colors. Andy Warhol painted a lovingly exact copy of a well known commercial soup can. George Segal peopled whole rooms with life-size plaster people doing everyday things. Roy Lichtenstein made enlarged, vividly colored frames from comic books. Many artists of the pop era sought to create new environments for audiences to experience. Some went even further and scheduled "happenings." In one famous happening, the Swiss artist Jean Tinguely gathered a group of viewers to watch one of his objects destroy itself. On schedule, it blew up, leaving only a powder mark on the floor of the museum to commemorate the event.

Many came to see art as a process rather than a product. Some who considered themselves artists wrote long plans for the construction of their work, complete with diagrams, and considered the documents themselves the product of their work. Others carried out their grand plans, sometimes modifying the very landscape to do so. Robert Smithson (1938–1973) built a long spiral-shaped jetty out into the Great Salt Lake in Utah. It has often been photographed and has a pleasing shape from the air. But what Smithson was really pointing to was the experience of walking out along the jetty, with the viewer perceiving the steady turning of the mountainous horizon as he circles inward toward the center of the spiral.

How recent art movements will affect the future is difficult to predict. Every generation uses art for its own purposes and needs. The only certainty is that art will continue—as an expression of the artist's being, a reflection of an audience's desires, or as pure and uncomplicated decoration.

—*Richard Dickinson*

American Art

Until the 1940's the work of most American artists was outside the mainstream of European art. A few American painters in the 1700's and 1800's left their homeland and established important reputations in England or France; but by leaving, they gave up the American experience.

In colonial times, an American artist was likely never to have seen the classic paintings and sculptures of Europe, and the social climate was indifferent or even hostile to the visual arts. As an anonymous writer in Boston wrote, "The Plowman that raiseth Grain is more serviceable to Mankind, than the Painter who draws only to please the eye."

The art that existed in the early years of white settlement was of two kinds. The first was portraiture designed to keep alive the memory of a great or wealthy person. The second was folk art practiced by a wide variety of craftsmen who made items such as weathervanes, furniture, quilting, and other useful items. A handful of untrained folk painters were also at work, producing flat two-dimensional portraits, often of women or children. These paintings are often called "primitives." Folk art underwent a great renaissance in the 1800's, and it survives even to the present day.

The federal period.
The first American to gain wide recognition at home was John Singleton Copley (1738–1815). He was a painter of great technical gifts, yet he followed the prevailing aesthetic of New England portraiture—that a good likeness was the first measure of a portraitist. In 1774, on the eve of the American Revolution, Copley visited Europe. When war broke out, he decided to stay, settling in England.

In London, Copley met two other American expatriates, Benjamin West (1738–1820), and Gilbert Stuart (1755–1828). West pursued his career in England. Stuart returned home and established a studio in New York City. One of his early New York portraits of Mrs. Richard Yates is shown here. It demonstrates the realistic, yet formal quality of Stuart's best work. He became most famous, however, for his portraits of the Founding Fathers. He painted the most famous likenesses of George Washington.

Discovering the landscape.
During the years of national expansion, in the early 1800's, Americans began to appreciate the artistic possibilities of the landscape all around them. In 1825, a painter named

NATIONAL GALLERY OF ART

MRS. RICHARD YATES, *a portrait by colonial portraitist Gilbert Stuart.*

Thomas Cole (1801–1848) first displayed his large romantic paintings of the Hudson River valley, less than 100 miles from New York City. Later, he traveled through New England, making drawings and oil sketches that he would finish in his studio. Cole succeeded in capturing the hazy light and the sense of timelessness that hangs over a great river. Soon there was an enthusiastic band of other painters working along the Hudson; they came to be known as the Hudson River School.

The rugged terrain and inspiring vistas of America appealed to the romantic taste of viewers both in America and Europe. Albert Bierstadt (1830–1902) traveled extensively through the western United States af-

ter mid-century, gathering material for canvases that would dwarf those of the Hudson River painters even as the Rocky Mountains dwarfed the Catskills. Another American, Frederick Church (1826–1900), went even further afield, seeking out the wilderness of South America, Labrador, Europe, and the Middle East.

Realism.
Contemporary with Bierstadt and Church, other painters sought to portray everyday life with a new kind of realism. Among the leading painters of this group were William Sidney Mount (1807–1868) and George Bingham (1811–1879). Bingham's works depicting life along the great rivers of the Midwest became especially popular through reproductions and imitations. Even as they were working, an older artist, George Catlin (1796–1872), was pursuing a similar style, portraying the American West, especially the Indians, whose way of life was rapidly disappearing.

The power of realism was most thoroughly realized, however, by two great American painters of the last half of the 1800's. Winslow Homer (1836–1910) was essentially a solitary man, and as he grew older, he became deeply fascinated with the sea and with men who relied on it for their livings. One of his late and most pessimistic paintings is *The Gulf Stream*. Homer leaves little hope for the black sailor here. The mast of his little boat has broken, the rudder is gone; a waterspout can be seen in the distance, and closer at hand, sharks circle the boat. In this battle of man against the elements, the man seems sure to lose.

THE GULF STREAM, *by Winslow Homer, shows the American devotion to realism, yet also suggests a symbolic interpretation.*

METROPOLITAN MUSEUM OF ART/WOLFE FUND, 1906

Homer's contemporary, Thomas Eakins (1844–1916), was a less isolated man. His paintings often featured his family and friends. He was an insatiable student; in his eagerness to master the human anatomy, he studied at a medical school in Philadelphia. His most famous painting, *The Gross Clinic,* vividly portrays a surgical operation in progress. Eakins sought to display the painting at the Centennial Exposition in 1876, but its subject matter shocked the judges and they refused it.

Many other approaches to art were developing in the same period. Albert Pinkham Ryder (1847–1917) rejected the realism of both Homer and Eakins for a deeply individual style that anticipated later expressionistic painting. George Harnett and others developed a style of almost photographic exactness, concentrating on still-life subjects. In the far West, Frederic Remington (1861–1909), preserved the images of Indians and cowboys of the vast plains in paintings that were both realistic and filled with action.

The major contrast to the works of Homer and Eakins, however, was to be found in the art of three American expatriates in Europe. The first of these was James McNeill Whistler (1834–1903). His famous painting of his mother, called *Arrangement in Gray and Black No. 1,* reveals his intense concern with design—a concern that sometimes overcame his interest in the subjects of his portraits.

John Singer Sargent (1856–1925) was born in Italy of American parents. Although he lived in Paris most of his life, he became increasingly involved with American artists. He is most famous for his elegant portraits, many of which are engaging both as character studies and as studies in composition and color.

The third expatriate master was Mary Cassatt (1845–1926). She began to exhibit with the French Impressionists in the 1870's and became closely associated with them. Among her special interests were portraits of mothers with children.

The Ashcan School.
Up to the 1890's, the subjects of most American paintings were either genteel (influential people, "noble" landscapes) or exotic (Indians, fur traders, cowboys). A group of younger painters from Philadelphia in the 1890's was determined to break into new subject areas. They wanted to show life as it was really lived in the city as well as in the countryside and wilderness.

Led by Robert Henri, whose book *The Art Spirit* came to serve as a kind of manifesto, this group, which called itself "The Eight," extended the subject matter of painting to the lives of the middle and lower classes. The painters came to be known as "The

SECOND STORY SUNLIGHT *by Edward Hopper portrays a warmly American scene, yet suggests a sense of isolation.*

Ashcan School." The individual artists had quite different styles and interests, but they did share a new openness to extending the subject matter of art and an antipathy to the "art for art's sake" approach championed by Whistler.

The Armory Show.
Members of The Eight were eager to gain a broader audience for their work. They finally arranged to sponsor a large art show in New York City and to bring over a wide representation of modern European art, including works of Gauguin, Van Gogh, Cézanne, Matisse, Picasso, and others. The Armory Show marked the beginning of modern art in America. Critics were shocked at the abstract art from Europe, but young artists were deeply influenced. Ironically, The Eight, the sponsors of the event, were largely ignored.

America against modernism.
From 1913 on, American artists were increasingly forced to choose between abstraction and the older home-grown realism. Regional painters of the 1920's and '30's adopted a modified kind of realism, using some new techniques but holding to American values. Thomas Hart Benton, John Stewart Curry, and Grant Wood were among the more successful.

Edward Hopper (1882–1967) was a loner who took something from each school. He began by painting seascapes and landscapes in the old tradition, yet his interest in composition and especially in showing light made his work both less engaged and more formal. He

produced haunting city scenes and seemed to revel in clearly American settings. His *Second Story Sunlight* demonstrates his deep interest in light and shade but also illustrates the separation and loneliness of his people. The scene is beautiful and yet somehow bleak—both characteristics that appear again and again in Hopper's work.

During the Great Depression of the 1930's, artists came to use their canvases as a medium for social comment and criticism. The most significant event of the decade was the establishment of the Works Progress Administration (WPA), which gave government-supported employment to visual artists, musicians, and writers. In its years of operation (1935–1943), the WPA employed more than 3500 artists; among them were Jackson Pollock, Willem de Kooning, and others whose works would make New York the art center of the world by 1950. By giving artists the chance to paint fulltime, the WPA allowed them to develop their skills and to form a sense of professionalism they had never felt before.

While Pollock and the abstract expressionists gained a secure place in the modernist tradition, the older American tradition of realism stubbornly survived. The paintings of Georgia O'Keeffe (herself trained in the international school) and the work of such painters as Andrew Wyeth attracted wide attention and admiration. The battle between abstraction and realism never really ended, and new skirmishes may arise in the future.

—*Lawrence Lorimer, Donald Lorimer*

EASTERN ART

Although the impulse to create may have sprung from the same roots in the East and the West, the development of art took very different paths over the centuries. Only in recent times have Western students taken a deep interest in the artistic traditions of Asia. They have discovered Asian arts to be profoundly impressive, while difficult to fully understand.

Just as a Chinese observer would have to understand much about Christianity to fully appreciate the art of medieval Europe, so a Western observer must come to Eastern art with some knowledge of and sympathy for the religious and cultural past of Asia. The effort to cross cultural barriers serves as a reminder that artistic expression is closely tied to cultural values and aspirations.

The following pages offer a brief summary of artistic development in the three great centers of Asian civilization: the Indian subcontinent, China, and Japan. The arts of other Asian countries were deeply influenced by the arts of India and China.

The art of Islam has been included here even though it is not confined to Asia. Rising from the peoples of North Africa and the Arabian Peninsula, it was influenced by many older traditions as Islam itself spread. Yet it developed its own traditions, separate from those of Europe and of Asia.

India

The art of India is primarily religious. Its temples are among the world's most impressive sacred monuments in stone. Its sculpture depicts a vast array of gods and goddesses, many of which decorate the temple walls; many others are ritually worshiped in shrines and monasteries. Its paintings illustrate the mystical and mythical texts that, through the centuries, have colored the Indian imagination. Despite its religious inspiration, however, Indian art is vigorous, exuberant, and often ravishingly sensual.

The beginnings of Indian civilization reach back to the highly developed, urban Indus Valley culture that flourished in northwest India between about 3000 and 1500 B.C. The earliest known examples of Indian sculpture date from this period. Around 1500 B.C., however, the native inhabitants of the Indus Valley (Dravidians) were forced by Aryan invaders to move southward. The Aryans brought with them new forms of ritual worship, concepts of caste, and a priestly class. They also adopted elements of Dravidian worship, and from these foundations, the religious system known as Hinduism later evolved.

Buddhism. Almost no artifacts exist from the period of the Aryan invasion to the rise of Buddhist monuments after 400 B.C. Buddhism was a powerful force in India from the 300's B.C. until about 900 A.D., when it largely disappeared from India. But its impact on all the arts of Asia was and continues to be enormous. After its decline in India, it survived in many different forms throughout the rest of the Asian continent.

Buddhism was the teaching of Gautama Siddhartha, a prince, probably from Nepal, who lived between 563 and 483 B.C. According to legend, the prince as a young man was so moved by the miseries of the human condition that he renounced his worldly life and possessions to become a simple monk. He meditated under the Bodhi Tree for 49 days, until he received understanding and became the Buddha, "he who is enlightened." The historic

A BODHISATTVA *from Gandhara (c 100 A.D.) shows a blend of Indian and Greco-Roman styles.*

sermon of the Buddha in the Deer Park of Benares (now Varanasi in north central India) formulated an eightfold path of conduct as a means of release from the agonizing cycle of birth and rebirth *(samsara)*. The path led to the attainment of nirvana, the extinction of all worldly desires.

The earliest Buddhist art in India dates from the Maurya period (322–185 B.C.), particularly from the reign of the Emperor Asoka, a devout Buddhist who dedicated his rule to the propagation of the Buddhist law. The characteristic monument of Buddhist art is the *stupa,* a large, solid, hemispherical relic mound that was built over the ashes of the Buddha, and later over the ashes of his disciples as well. The *stupa* was meant to be circumambulated, or walked around. The railings that enclosed the sacred area were elaborately decorated with narrative stories of previous lives of the Buddha *(Jatakas).*

During the dynasty of the Kushans (50–320 A.D.), Buddhist iconography was codified and the story of the Buddha's life and the miracles he performed were repeated in countless numbers of reliefs decorating vast numbers of *stupas* and monasteries in the ancient province of Gandhara, in northwestern India. Here, in the wake of the invasions of Alexander the Great around 330 B.C., there flourished a hybrid art that combined Greek (and later, Roman) and oriental elements. Greco-Roman styles brought by craftsmen from the West mingled with traditional Indian subjects. Many of the images of the Buddha and other deities recall the classic Apollo or a toga-draped citizen of Rome. The standing Bodhisattva image is an early example of this mixed style. A Bodhisattva is a compassionate, semidivine being who chooses not to enter nirvana in order to assist the faithful on Earth in finding salvation. As befits his fortunate station in life, he is always shown in elaborate dress and heavily jeweled. The emphasis on the volume and folds of the Bodhisattva's garment, his hair arrangement, and the necklace with animal head finials are typical of Hellenistic and Roman sculpture. At the same time, much of the symbolism is purely Indian. Note especially the pedestal where devotees worship the pillar of Buddhist law, rather than the Buddha figure itself.

But the principal image of Buddhist art is, of course, the Buddha himself. Anthropomorphic representations of the Buddha appeared in the early centuries of the Christian era, and can probably be linked to the rise of new Buddhist sects that emphasized *bhakti,* or devotion; these sects required the Buddha's representation in more accessible human form. The creation of the Buddha image occurred in two roughly parallel lines of development: one in Gandhara, where an Apollo type evolved; and the other in the southern Kushan capital of Mathura, near Delhi, where a more native style of Indian sculpture flourished.

The Mathura workshops produced some of ancient India's finest sculpture in the characteristic red sandstone of the region. This area was less susceptible to foreign influences than the outlying provinces of Gandhara, and its style derived from earlier, purely Indian traditions. The fertility goddesses *(yakshi)* were a popular subject for the decoration of railings and pillars in early Buddhist art. These images were a survival of the mother-goddess cult of pre-Aryan India, and in their robust and self-assured female form, with its suggestion of sensuous repose, we have the flowing grace and plastic ease characteristic of the native tradition of Indian sculpture. In contrast to the naturalism of Gandharan Buddha images, the Mathura Buddha and Bodhisattva types display idealized abstract proportions combined with deep spiritual qualities.

During the reign of the imperial Guptas (325–647 A.D.), a classic Buddha image was developed, an image of idealized perfection in proportion and form. Combining and harmonizing the styles of Gandhara and Mathura, Gupta sculptors developed an image that suggested both spiritual power and physical sensuousness; that image became the classic Buddha figure of southern Asia, exported throughout Southeast Asia and Indonesia.

The Gupta Buddha type was produced at Sarnath, the site of the Buddha's first sermon. As shown here, the Buddha is always represented as a transcendental being. Marks of his divine status are usually the elongated earlobes; the *urna* between the eyebrows, like a "third eye," to suggest wisdom; and the *ushnisha* crowning the head, to symbolize his high degree of spiritual enlightenment. He is clad in a monastic robe devoid of any ornament to represent his renunciation of all earthly wealth and desires, and his right hand is raised in *abhaya mudra,* a formal gesture denoting reassurance and protection; the lowered left hand, in *varada mudra,* confers blessings and favors.

In the Sarnath images, the heavy folds of Gandharan drapery are dispensed with and a youthful human frame seems to shine with a soft smoothness and an almost transparent luminosity of texture. The lotus-shaped eyes and the full compassionate lips recall the distinctly Indian ideal of the Mathura Buddhas.

The Gupta period was India's golden age, and its achievements in art, literature, and learning became a touchstone for the artists and literati of succeeding generations. The famous Buddhist frescoes in the cave temples of Ajanta perhaps best exemplify the luxurious, artistocratic brilliance of Gupta court and secular life. The first images of Shiva and Vishnu, the great gods of Hinduism, also date from this period.

Medieval India. Despite the brilliance of Buddhist art during this period, Buddhism began to decline after 700, and it eventually disappeared from India. Only in the northeast provinces of Bihar and Bengal did a hybrid form of Buddhism—mixed with many Hindu practices—survive. This form, with its worship of the Tantra (Manual of Ritual), magical formulas, and mystic diagrams, was transmitted to Nepal and Tibet, Southeast Asia, and eventually to China and Japan.

Hinduism, revived and reformed, became—and remained—the domi-

NINE CENTURIES OF ART: *The* yakshi (left) *was made in the second century* A.D. *at Mathura. The classic Buddha* (center) *is a product of the Gupta dynasty (325-647) at Sarnath. The Kandariya Mahaveda temple* (right c 1000) *illustrates the resurgence of Hindu religious art.*

WILLIAM ROCKHILL NELSON GALLERY OF ART/ ATKINS MUSEUM OF FINE ARTS

ASIA SOCIETY; MR. & MRS. JOHN D. ROCKEFELLER 3RD COLLECTION

GEORGE HOLTON/PHOTO RESEARCHERS

nant way of life and worship in India. Even during its highest period of ascendancy, Buddhism had never completely eliminated popular Hindu beliefs. It was the ability of Hinduism to absorb diverse approaches and philosophies that accounted for its resurgence and triumph.

The so-called medieval period in India dates roughly from 600 to 1200. As was the case in medieval Europe, the period was characterized by tremendous architectural activity. The collapse of Gupta power resulted in the emergence of many regional semi-feudal political dynasties, and a correspondingly varied number of art styles.

The Hindu temple, as it evolved during this period, was considered to be a replica of the cosmic world mountain, a microcosm of the universe. Its great soaring spires were decorated with a profuse array of all the divine, demonic, and mortal beings who were supposed to inhabit the universe. Gods, goddesses, musicians, dancers, ascetics, nymphs, animals, fabulous creatures, and plants were all part of the richly adorned temple walls.

The Kandariya Mahadeva temple at Khajuraho is one of the most famous of all Hindu temples. It was built some time between 950 and 1050, and the effect of its height—more than 116 feet—is greatly increased by its deep platform base and by the vertical lines of the recreations of the tower upon itself. A path of circumambulation is included in the whole mass of the structure. The intent was to lead the devotee through a celebration of life in all its abundant forms, to the innermost sanctum, the *garbhagrha,* where he worships his god alone. This symbolic union with the divine was expressed on the outside walls by the *mithuna* motif of eternally embracing figures representing earthly and divine love. At its best, medieval sculpture represented a natural and lively style, recalling the early Mathura emphasis on vigorous, fleshy forms. But by the beginning of the 1200's, over-refinement and a more rigid, angular style became increasingly evident; it marked the beginning of the long, slow decline of the medieval tradition.

In south India, at centers like Tanjore and Trichinopoly, the powerful Chola dynasty (850–1150) embarked on an impressive program of architectural activity; it became the creator of a new classic style. The Cholas were exceptional bronze casters. Their bronzes were not intended for decoration; they were cult images to be placed in the innermost recesses of shrines as aids for contemplation of the divine form. These images, like the earlier Buddha figures and images of all Indian gods, were composed according to certain fixed proportions that were prescribed in numerous texts *(sastras)* compiled for the technical guidance of sculptors and painters.

SHIVA, *a major Hindu god shown as Lord of the Dance, from the Chola period (c 1000).*

The Hindu pantheon is bewildering in its diversity, but it is given structure by an underlying faith in one divine being whose energy is manifested in varied forms—contemplative *(sattvic),* active *(ragasic),* and fearsome and destructive *(tamasic).* The basic Hindu trinity comprises Brahma, the Creator; Vishnu, the Preserver; and Shiva, the Destroyer.

Of these three, Vishnu and Shiva are by far the most important. Vishnu is a solar deity and is intimately associated with kingship. Shiva's most famous representation is perhaps as Nataraja, Lord of the Dance. This is one of the great creations of Indian art, perfected by the Chola masters. Shiva reveals his divinity in dance; he is Creator, Preserver, and Destroyer at once, in perpetual motion and eternal stasis.

His upper right hand holds the drum, symbolizing sound, one of the five elements that announce creation. The corresponding left hand carries the flame, symbol of the created world. The other right hand is raised in the gesture granting freedom from fear,

while the other left arm stretches across his body and points to the raised left foot, a symbol of release. The right foot holds firmly beneath it a dwarflike figure, the demon of ignorance. A flaming arch rises out of the lotus-based pedestal that supports the god, and from his high crown a fanlike arrangement of hair and leaves emerges and flows outward toward the nearly circular arch. The head, slightly tilted back, maintains an aloof serenity within the total rhythm of the dance.

The modern era. Many local schools of Indian miniature painting flourished in north India between the 16th and 19th centuries, growing out of the earlier illustrated manuscript tradition of western India. The great patrons of Indian painting were the local Rajput rulers who dominated most of northwestern India and the hill states in the western Himalayas. Rajput themes were largely drawn from the mythology of the Hindu epics.

The Mughals (1526–1857) were the Muslim conquerors of India, and during the reigns of the three great Mughals, Akbar, Jahangir, and Shah Jahan, between 1556 and 1658, Persian and Hindu artists worked together to create new styles in painting, architecture, and the decorative arts. In painting, they introduced realistic portraiture. Their achievements in architecture are crowned by the most sublime of all funerary monuments, the Taj Mahal, and decorate much of the present-day city of Delhi. The Mughal interlude was brilliant, but even at the peak of their power, the Mughals never ruled a unified India. The Rajput chieftains of the north and local Hindu rajahs in the south waged intermittent war against the Muslim invaders, so that native Hindu cultural and artistic traditions, though in decline, were never completely obliterated. India remains Hindu to this day. Predominantly Islamic Pakistan and Bangladesh are independent countries.

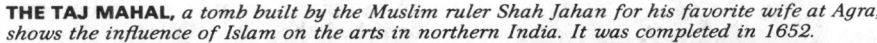

THE TAJ MAHAL, *a tomb built by the Muslim ruler Shah Jahan for his favorite wife at Agra, shows the influence of Islam on the arts in northern India. It was completed in 1652.*

UNITED NATIONS

China

The origins of Chinese culture reach back more than 4000 years. Large numbers of ceramic burial jars, apparently produced between 2500 and 1700 B.C., have been unearthed in Kansu Province in western China; they are the earliest records we possess of Chinese civilization. These painted jars were made without the aid of a potter's wheel, and their refined forms and fluid calligraphic patterns in red, white, and black suggest the interests that were to shape much of the course of later Chinese art.

Early dynasties. In the course of the second millennium B.C., at roughly the same time as the Aryan invasion of India, the Shang dynasty (1523–1027 B.C.) emerged; it is the first recorded dynasty of China. Elaborate underground burial chambers excavated in the Shang capital of Anyang in northern Honan contained large quantities of bronze, jade, and other sacrificial objects.

Ancestor worship has always been of great importance in Chinese life, as elaborate Chinese burial practices and tomb artifacts attest. Ancestors had special powers to mediate between this world and the world beyond.

Most of the archaic Chinese bronzes, like the one shown here, were buried in the tombs of an obviously wealthy ruling elite. The ritual bronze vessels of the Shang, and of the succeeding Chou dynasty (1027–256 B.C.), served both religious and social functions. They were used to pour libations, to store food in sacrifice to an ancestor, and as gifts.

By about the tenth century A.D., vessels were classified according to their form and use into about 17 basic types, of which this Shang *Hu* is one.

SHANG VASE (*before 1000 B.C.*) *was buried in the tomb of a prominent person.*

WILLIAM ROCKHILL NELSON GALLERY OF ART/ATKINS MUSEUM OF FINE ARTS

The *Hu* is decorated with a favorite Shang motif, a mythical monster mask, the *t'ao-t'ieh,* whose distorted features and large protruding eyes were perhaps meant to ward off evil. Its precise iconographic significance is not known. Other animal images, such as the water buffalo and ram appearing in high relief on the handles and neck of this vessel, and the winged and beaked striding dragon along its base, probably enhanced its magical properties.

In the late Chou period, sweeping curvilinear designs began to appear, and patterned motifs, often set in flat ribbon bands, decorated the surfaces not only of sacred vessels, but also of items of everyday use such as mirrors, chariot fittings, and belt hooks. Long inscriptions honoring the patrons who had commissioned the objects were frequently included. Eventually, vessels approximating the ancient ritual shapes were absorbed into the traditional ceremonial ritual of Confucian temples and ancestral shrines. Under the Sung and other later dynasties, they were copied in jade, porcelain, and marble and served a wholly decorative function.

The late Chou (771–256 B.C.) period was also the great age of Chinese philosophy. Under Taoist influence, it developed the ideals for a harmonious world order. Tao means "way"; it signifies the invisible law that governs all of creation. The great ethical teacher and reformer in ancient China was Confucius (K'ung Fu-tse, 551–479 B.C.), who stressed such ethical values as moderation, piety, and familial respect. His teachings reinforced the ancient belief in ancestor worship, which, in the succeeding Han period (206 B.C.–220 A.D.), raised tomb art to new heights.

During the long period of Han rule, both Confucian ancestor worship and Taoist myths found expression in art. All the stone sculpture that survives from this period belongs to funerary monuments. The tombs of high-ranking dignitaries were guarded by large lions, rams, and other beasts, and bold and animated scenic compositions embellished the tomb walls. All the implements that the dead person had used in this life and might have need of in the next accompanied him into the tomb.

Buddhism. It was also under the Hans that Indian missionaries first brought Buddhism to China, but it was not until the fourth century, during the rule of the Six Dynasties (220–589), that the Buddhist faith became the official state religion.

In the centuries following the death of the Buddha in India in the fifth century B.C., two major schools of Buddhist doctrine emerged. The more orthodox of these was the Hinayana tradition, which spread to the coun-

tries of Southeast Asia. The other tradition, Mahayana, spread from India and Nepal, through central Asia, to Korea, China, and Japan. Central to Mahayana philosophy is the ideal of the compassionate *bodhisattva* ("enlightened being"), who, with a number of other legendary Buddhas and lesser deities, assists both monks and laymen in the search for eternal truth.

The earliest Buddhist monastic centers sprang up in China during the Wei dynasty (386–554). They centered around cave temples, of which the most famous are the Yun-kang caves in Shansi; the Lung-men caves in Honan; and the caves of the Thousand Buddhas at Tunhuang in the far interior of northwest China, just inside the Great Wall. Votive stelae and wall paintings found in these caves show that the Buddhas were modeled on Gandharan images. These images probably traveled to China with missionary monks and traders in the form of small portable icons in gilt bronze.

In the course of the Sui dynasty (581–618), Buddha images from

KUAN-YIN, *a bodhisattva made during the classic T'ang dynasty (618–906 A.D.)*

CLEVELAND MUSEUM OF ART/PURCHASE, LEONARD C. HANNA, JR. BEQUEST

Gupta India seem to have inspired a movement away from the austerely draped Wei Buddhas to more sinuous and fleshy forms. This new interest in exploring and revealing body contours culminated in the work of the great T'ang sculptors (618–906), who, like the master craftsmen of Gupta India, endowed their creations with both spiritual grace and human warmth. In this beautiful image of the bodhisattva Kuan-Yin, a deity of mercy and compassion, we see the characteristic Chinese taste for linear and conventionalized form.

In the vital and cultured urbanity of the classic T'ang period, all the arts and sciences flourished in China. The T'ang capital, Ch'ang-an, was a large cosmopolitan city that attracted large communities of Jews, Muslims, and Christians, as well as traders and merchants from the Near East, the Caucasus, and central Asia. Large workshops existed for the manufacture of tomb figurines whose subjects reflected the diversity and vigor of the times. Musicians, merchants, dancers, implements, animals, and mythical creatures were produced in marble, jade, lacquer, and clay painted in the typical T'ang yellow, green, and white glazes.

Painting. The vibrant expansiveness of the T'ang spirit gave way in the 900's to the more conservative and isolationist Sung dynasty (960–1279), which revived much of the old Confucian ethic. The introspective mood of the new age found its richest expression in painting.

Painting was always an important art form in China, but unfortunately little has survived from the early periods. Although painters drew their subjects from a rich variety of themes and traditions, it was in landscape painting that the Chinese particularly excelled. This genre provided the painter with a special insight into the *tao,* the unity of all things. The Chinese word for landscape painting is "mountain-water picture," and the basic motif is comprised of soaring vertical mountain peaks (yang, the male principle) and water (yin, the female principle), running down to the fertile earth. Within this lofty scale, human figures and dwelling places are of no more importance than trees and rocks.

In the *Buddhist Temple Amid Clearing Mountain Peaks,* among the most famous of all landscape paintings, the eye is first drawn to the foreground detail of trees, rocks, a bridge, water, and a monastic complex. Then the viewer's eye is slowly guided upward by the pinnacled top of the temple itself. Behind loom massive mountain heights that dominate and dwarf the entire composition yet seem to recede into the infinite distance.

Chinese paintings were typically done on scrolls, which were treasured objects to be studied and contemplated at leisure. Scrolls in the vertical format were intended for hanging on walls, while horizontal scrolls, which varied in length from two or three to as much as 40 feet, were meant to be slowly unrolled, starting at the right and moving gradually to the painting's conclusion at the left.

Not surprisingly, the arts of calligraphy ("beautiful writing") and ink painting are closely related in China, for they both demand the same decisive strokes and sensitivity to nuances of line. Conventions existed for rendering trees, figures, and mountain formations, and these conventions formed part of the basic training of any artist. Under the Mongol rule of the Yuan dynasty (1280–1368), a new type of painting, known as the *wen jen,* or literati, style combined the arts of painting, poetry, and calligraphy. This continued to be popular well into the 18th and 19th centuries.

Ceramics. Native rule was restored by the Ming emperors (1368–1644), who initiated a new interest in China's past, and especially in the achievements of the old T'ang dynasty. The capital was moved to Peking, and artisan workshops were actively patronized by the imperial court. The decorative arts flourished. New techniques, such as cloisonné, were developed, and pottery and porcelain were produced in unprecedented quantities. The latter are so important in the history of ceramics that even today we continue to refer to fine dishes as "china."

In the early period, celadons (ceramic wares with gray-green or blue-green glazes) and monochromes predominated. But by the early 1400's, porcelain, a much harder and more refined ware, had become the most favored type of ceramic in China. Particularly prized were blue-and-white wares decorated with underglaze designs painted in cobalt blue, such as the large spherical flask shown here. A powerful, three-clawed dragon strides across a delicate floral background in a composition that is an extraordinary combination of calligraphic brushwork, virile line, and brilliant color. Such masterpieces, as well as vast quantities of commercial ware, were made at Ching-te Chen, the center of porcelain manufacture from the 1300's on. As early as the 1400's, blue-and-white porcelains had a wide market as far afield as Europe, where the art of making porcelain was not mastered for another 300 years.

The Manchu conquerors who succeeded the Ming dynasty tried to continue the high traditions they inherited in painting, ceramics, and other decorative arts. The Ch'ing dynasty (1644–1912) brings us well into the modern period. Under the Ch'ings, old designs were revived and the imperial factories produced porcelains of superb quality and exceptional brilliance. Another ancient Chinese art, jade carving, was also revived. Perhaps it was in the demands of this exacting art that the characteristics of the Ch'ing style—impersonality, technical virtuosity, and delight in the ornate — found their most perfect expression.

SUNG PAINTING *(960-1279):* Buddhist Temple Amid Clearing Mountain Peaks.

PORCELAIN VASE *(c 1400) shows exquisite design sense in blue and white.*

Japan

As in China, Japan's prehistoric age is known to us through rich finds of ceramics. The greater part of this age is called the Jomon period (4500–200 B.C.), and derives its name from the twisted-cord type of relief decoration of its pottery. The Jomon people had migrated to the island chain from Siberia.

The next migration of peoples, the Yayoi culture (200 B.C.–250 A.D.), came to Japan from the south. The use of the potter's wheel was known to these peoples, as was the art of bronze and iron casting, most notably seen in the large ceremonial bells they designed called *dotaku.*

From the Kofun, or Tumulus, period (250–552), mound tombs survive. These tombs were surrounded by simple clay figures of humans or animals known as *haniwa.* The *haniwa* were placed in the soil around the tombs, perhaps as a means of preventing erosion. Objects found in the tombs included, among other items, three that were to assume a special importance in Japanese culture. These were the mirror; a special type of curved jewel called *magatama;* and the sword. All three later became sacred symbols of imperial authority. Many of the tombs of this period are associated with historical emperors who were considered the direct descendants of the sun goddess Amaterasu. This belief was reinforced by the native Shinto (meaning the way or teaching of the gods) religion. Combining animistic beliefs in the beneficent spirits of nature with ancestor worship, the Shinto reverence for the pure and simple beauty of nature has survived through the centuries alongside Buddhism. It permeates Japanese culture even today.

Buddhism. The official date of the introduction of Buddhism into Japan is traditionally given as 552 A.D., when the ruler of the Korean kingdom of Paekche sent a bronze image of the Buddha and scriptures to the Japanese court. Adoption of the new religion encouraged official missions to China, especially during the long and splendid rule of the T'ang dynasty, which was established in 618. This exposure to China at the full height of her creative power was the backdrop against which early Buddhist art in Japan developed.

The popular divinities of China's Mahayana Buddhism were enthusiastically adopted by the Japanese, as were the artistic styles and conventions of the T'angs. The Japanese dependence on mainland traditions can be seen in the famous bronze Shaka Triad (that is, Shakyamuni, the historical Buddha), one of the treasures of early Japanese art, in the Horyu-ji monastery at Nara.

The Nara period (645–794) was an age of vast temple and monastery building, modeled after Ch'ang-an, the T'ang capital of China. This ambitious building program culminated in the magnificent temple of Todai-ji, where a colossal bronze image of Vairocana, the supreme Buddha of the universe, 53 feet high, was housed in a massive wooden temple 284 feet long, 166 feet wide, and 152 feet high. Innumerable icons, paintings, precious ritual objects, and votive gifts, all executed in the classic T'ang style, are still preserved in Nara today.

From the Mahayana ideals that shaped the early history of Buddhism and Buddhist art in Japan, there emerged three major strands of doctrine to dominate Japanese religious life in subsequent centuries.

The first, esoteric Buddhism, emphasized that Buddhahood could be attained in this world by penetrating the mysteries of body, speech, and mind through incantations, spells, and magic symbols. The esoteric pantheon is vast, and its most characteristic visual representation is the *mandala,* an abstract and geometric diagram of the universe that shows the relationships between the various heavens and their countless deities. Esotericism introduced to Japan many terrifying deities who subdued the physical obstacles to enlightenment.

Pure Land Buddhism came to Japan from China in the twelfth century, offering a single salvationist faith based on worship of the Amida Buddha—the Buddha of the Western Paradise. Pure Land mandalas evoked the paradise dwellings of Amida by showing well known shrines and landscapes. Paintings began to take on a more narrative character in an effort to provide pictorial aids in the instruction by monks of the common people. As new temples

THE AMIDA BUDDHA (*after 1000 A.D.) is shown in deep, peaceful meditation.*

WILLIAM ROCKHILL NELSON GALLERY OF ART/ATKINS MUSEUM OF FINE ARTS

sprang up, the demand for sculptures to furnish them rapidly increased, and the assembled woodblock (*yosegi*) system of manufacture was devised and perfected by the twelfth century.

The Amida Buddha shown here is an example of this technique; it has a hollow interior. The image is over nine feet high. It is calmly and impassively seated in the cross-legged position, with its hands in the *mudra* position, denoting profound meditation. The rows of small shell-like curls that form the Buddha's *ushnisha* (one of his transcendental properties) recall the Buddha images of Gupta India, while the formal folds of the robe clearly have a Chinese prototype.

It was during the long Heian period (794–1185) that both esoteric and Pure Land Buddhism dominated Japanese culture. At the capital of Heian-kyo, modern Kyoto, the powerful Fujiwara family ruled as state ministers, controlling the emperor and court politics for more than 250 years.

Heian court painters developed a specifically Japanese mode of painting and calligraphy known as *Yamato-e,* literally, "Japanese pictures." This style of painting on horizontal scrolls often had subject matter drawn from Japanese literary narrative.

In the succeeding Kamakura period (1185–1392), Japanese society took on a clearly feudal, hierarchical structure, based on the personal loyalty of vassal to master. The Kamakura *shogun* or guardians of the throne and nation dominated this hierarchy. Sculpture in the Kamakura period is distinguished by a sturdy naturalism, in contrast to the ideal beauty of the Nara period. Large portrait statues in the round emphasize true-to-life physical features, their heroic proportions reflecting the martial spirit of the Kamakura warriors.

The art form known as *e-makimono* or "painted scrolls" was one of the great achievements of this period. These are long hand scrolls, Chinese in origin, on which the Japanese painted genre subjects in continuous narrative, often ingeniously shifting perspective, tempo, and mood to suit the action of the story. Unlike the Chinese, who mainly used their scrolls for landscapes, the Japanese revealed a flair for the dramatic.

During the subsequent Muromachi (1392–1568) and Momoyama (1568–1614) periods, new warrior classes arose, creating a military rather than a feudal society. The arts came under the influence of yet another Buddhist doctrinal tradition called Zen. Zen insisted on personal self-discipline and introspection as aids to meditation, ideas that appealed to the newly emerging military clans and that found rapid acceptance.

Ink painting was favored by the Zen artists because it enabled them to illustrate in brush and ink the moment of spontaneous creativity in which

LANDSCAPE *was a particular interest of the Japanese.* The River Bridge at Uji *(c 1500) is 11 feet long. The* Poem Scroll with Bamboo, *below, completed 100 years later, combines pictorial and calligraphic elements.*

spiritual enlightenment may also be achieved. This accounts for the explosive, highly dramatic flavor of many Zen paintings.

By the time Kano Masanobu founded his school in the late 15th century, the tradition had become wholly secular and decorative. The Kano were commissioned to carry out large-scale decorations of rooms in new palaces and monasteries. The pair of sixfold screens, each more than five and a half feet high and eleven feet across, entitled *The River Bridge at Uji,* is an example of such decorations. The designs are bold and sweeping, against a gleaming gold ground, and the result is one of grand but unruffled magnificence.

The modern era. The Edo period (1615–1868), which ushered Japan into the modern age, takes its name from the remote village of Edo, modern Tokyo, to which the militant Tokugawa shoguns moved their capital at the start of their long rule. A rising merchant and middle class became the real wielder of power and arbiter of taste. Edo became a city where fortunes could be quickly made and spent, and the decorative arts—textiles, lacquer ware, ceramics—of this period are famous for their brilliance of design and perfection of technique.

A distinctive style of decorative painting called *Rimpa,* a term applied to a school of painters and calligraphers, originated in the early Edo period. Its founders were the painter Sotatsu, active from about 1596 to 1623, and the distinguished calligrapher Honami Koetsu. The vigorous and sensitive *Poem Scroll with Bamboo* is a superb example of the collaborative work of these two masters. This long hand scroll is one of the rare examples of Rimpa work on silk rather than on paper. The calligraphy, at once dynamic and delicate, recalls the elegant scripts of the Heian scrolls, and appears interspersed in a carefully balanced composition of bamboo stalks and leaves. Energetic line and unerringly effective spacing are the essence of Sotatsu's style, which here boldly projects the bamboo stalks beyond the borders of the silk.

At first glance, the popular art known as *Ukiyo-e,* "paintings of the Floating World," appears to express a completely different aspect of the Japanese temperament, one that we have encountered with neither the Kano nor the Rimpa traditions. But the origins of this style, which drew its subject matter from the bravura and colorful vitality of the theatrical life of Edo, reach as far back as the lively genre scenes of the early Kamakura scrolls. Courtesans and actors were the main theme; they were depicted with humor, irony, outrageous flattery, and even undertones of sadness. This mirror of their own world had a natural

appeal for the prosperous middle classes. As the market for these paintings expanded, a cheap method of reproduction by means of mass-produced polychrome woodblock prints was developed. It was through this peculiar art form of the color print that the world of Japanese art was first opened to the West in the late 1800's.

TWO ACTORS *in the Ukiyo-e style is a caricature of the two stage heroes.*

Islam

In the history of religions, Islam is relatively young. It was a monotheistic faith, founded by the Prophet Muhammad, who was born in Mecca about 570, and upon whose death in 632 an immense empire began to grow with extraordinary speed. The Arab tribesmen who were the followers of Muhammad embarked on extensive conquests, overcoming Palestine and Syria in 636, and North Africa and Persia a few years later. Eventually, the empire was to include virtually all the territory between Spain and Morocco in the west and India and Samarkand in the east. These lands were otherwise dissimilar in origin, ethnic character, and artistic tradition.

Islamic art is too vast and varied a subject to be easily condensed. Its origins lie in the Near East, roughly in the area of the Nile, Tigris, and Euphrates rivers. The influences it absorbed were thus Sumerian, Assyrian, Babylonian, and Hellenistic, to say nothing of the Christian arts of the East—Greek, Coptic, and Syrian. From this center, as the empire spread, Muslim art extended toward Iran and central Asia in one direction, and toward the Maghreb and Spain in the other.

Unifying these extremely diverse components and traditions, however, was the revealed message of the Koran, the book of God, dictated in its entirety by Muhammad. The Koran and the other sacred text, the Hadith (the "sayings" of the Prophet), formed the basis of the holy law that regulated all aspects, social and spiritual, of the life of every Muslim. The Koran was written in the Arabic script that may be considered the most typical and

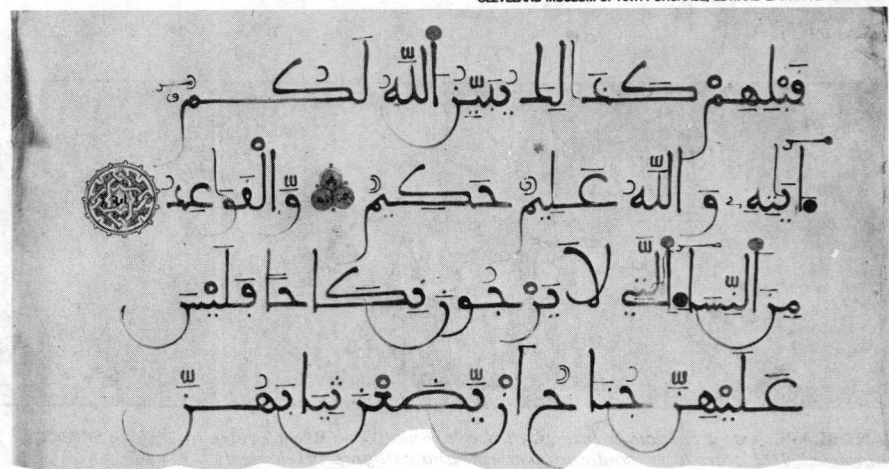

CALLIGRAPHY, often the text of the sacred Koran, is a characteristic Muslim art form, showing a deft sense of line and form. See also the Taj Mahal, page 127.

widespread art form in Islam. As the conveyor of the divine message, it is invested with a nobility and an excellence that surpasses every other art. Written from right to left, along a horizontal line, the script consists of 28 letters, punctuated by diacritical marks and vowel accents. The art of Islamic calligraphy had an almost endless range of possibilities. It inevitably merged with new decorative schemes, such as floral motifs and scrolls. The exquisite *maghribi* style seen here evolved in North Africa, parts of Spain, and Islamic Africa. Gradually, calligraphic designs covered the surfaces of monuments, textiles, ceramics, paintings, and jewels, thus transferring to the objects they decorated some of the sanctity of the script itself.

In the early centuries of Islam, human forms were excluded from manuscript illuminations, wall decorations, murals, and mosaics. But the strong pictorial traditions of Hellenistic, Byzantine, and Sasanian art eventually asserted themselves, so that later Islamic art was characterized by skillful depictions of human and animal figures in a dense landscape of vegetal, geometric, or epigraphic patterns. Many Persian, Turkish, and Indian (Mughal) carpets, for example, reflect this technique.

No mention of Islamic art is complete without a reference to its architectural achievements. The Muslim place of worship is the mosque, derived from the Arabic *masjid*, "a place where one prostrates oneself [before God]." Here again, the early Muslims borrowed elements from cultures they had conquered—Christian churches, Roman basilicas, Hellenistic columns—fusing them ultimately into uniquely successful and wholly Islamic creations. The great flowering of mosque architecture between 1500 and 1700 in Ottoman Turkey, Safavid Iran, and Mughal India, was the result of a long process of experimentation with existing forms. —*Marukh Tarapor*

For Further Reference

General

Arnheim, Rudolf. *Art and Visual Perception*. University of California Press, 1974.

Gardner, Helen. *Art Through the Ages* (6th Ed.). Harcourt, Brace, and Jovanovich, 1975.

Gealt, Adelheid M. *Looking at Art*. Bowker, 1983.

Gombrich, Ernst H. *Art and Illusion*. Pantheon Books, 1972.

Hauser, Arnold. *A Social History of Art*. 2 volumes. Alfred A. Knopf, 1957.

Janson, H.W. *History of Art: A Survey of Major Visual Arts from the Dawn of Civilization to the Present Day* (3rd Ed.). Harry N. Abrams, 1986.

Masters, Janet F., and Joyce M. Smith. *Art History: A Study Guide*. Prentice-Hall, 1987.

Read, Herbert E. *Art and Society*. Pantheon Books, 1950.

Ancient and Eastern Art

Boardman, John. *Greek Art*. Oxford University Press, 1973.

Frankfort, Henri. *The Art and Architecture of the Ancient Orient*. Harcourt, Brace, and Jovanovich, 1970.

Munsterberg, Hugo. *The Arts of Japan: An Illustrated History*. Charles E. Tuttle, 1978.

Powell, Thomas G.E. *Prehistoric Art*. Oxford University Press, 1966.

Rowland, Benjamin. *The Art and Architecture of India*. Penguin Books, 1981.

Wheeler, Robert E.M. *Roman Art and Architecture*. Oxford University Press, 1964.

Western Art

Barr, Alfred H., Jr., editor. *Cubism and Abstract Art*. Museum of Modern Art —New York Graphic Society, 1974.

Berenson, Bernard. *Italian Painters of the Renaissance*. Cornell University Press, 1980.

Focillon, Henry. *The Art of the West in the Middle Ages*. Cornell University Press, 1980.

Geldzahler, Henry. *American Painting in the 20th Century*. Metropolitan Museum of Art, 1965.

Grodecki, Louis. *Gothic Architecture*. Rizzoli International, 1985.

Hamilton, George H. *19th and 20th Century Art*. Harry N. Abrams, 1970.

Levey, Michael. *High Renaissance*. Penguin Books, 1978.

Pool, Phoebe. *Impressionism*. Thames Hudson, 1985.

Read, Herbert E. *A Concise History of Modern Painting*. Oxford University Press, 1974.

White, John. *Art and Architecture in Italy Twelve Fifty–Fourteen Hundred*. Penguin Books, 1988.

Zarnecki, George. *Art of the Medieval World*. Harry N. Abrams, 1976.

VOLUME **3**

Asia and Australasia

ASIA

H. ARMSTRONG ROBERTS

Introduction 135
Countries 140
Dependencies 201
Cities 203
Glossary 207
For Further Reference 214

For national flags see VOLUME 12: GOVERNMENT AND LAW.

DAVID LINDROTH

SOVIET UNION

Amu Darya R.

Ulan Bator ⊛
MONGOLIA

Kurile Islands

Aleutian Islands

Beijing ⊛ | NORTH KOREA
Pyongyang
Sea of Japan

JAPAN

NORTH PACIFIC OCEAN

Kabul ⊛
AFGHAN-ISTAN
Islamabad ⊛
PAKISTAN

Indus R.

CHINA

Huang He

Seoul
SOUTH KOREA ⊛
Shanghai

Tokyo ⊛

New Delhi
NEPAL ⊛ BHUTAN
Ganges R.
Brahmaputra R.
Yangtze R.

East China Sea

Tropic of Cancer

Dacca ⊛
INDIA
Bombay

BANGLA-DESH
BURMA
LAOS ⊛

Taipei ⊛
TAIWAN

International Dateline

Hanoi ⊛
Hong Kong

Mariana Islands

MARSHALL ISLANDS

Arabian Sea

Rangoon
THAI-LAND ⊛
Vientianne
CAMBODIA
VIETNAM

PHILIPPINES
Manila

Philippine Sea

Bay of Bengal
Bangkok ⊛
Andaman Islands
Phnom Penh

South China Sea

Caroline Islands
PALAU

FEDERATED STATES OF MICRONESIA

Nicobar Islands
MALDIVES
Colombo ⊛ SRI LANKA
BRUNEI
MALAYSIA
Kuala Lumpur ⊛ SINGAPORE

Equator

Celebes

Equator

NAURU

KIRIBATI

Sumatra

Borneo

INDONESIA

PAPUA NEW GUINEA

SOLOMON ISLANDS

TUVALU

WESTERN SAMOA

INDIAN OCEAN

Jakarta
Java

Timor

Port Moresby

VANUATU

FIJI

TONGA

Timor Sea
Darwin

Coral Sea

NEW CALEDONIA

Tropic of Capricorn

AUSTRALIA

Brisbane

SOUTH PACIFIC OCEAN

Perth

Sydney ⊛
Melbourne
Canberra ⊛

NEW ZEALAND ⊛
Wellington

Tasmania

Tasman Sea

PAGODA IN KAOSHIUNG, TAIWAN: STEVE VIDLER/LEO DE WYS INC.

134

Asia and Australasia

Asia has been traditionally defined as being those lands bounded on the west by Europe, including that part of the Soviet Union east of the Ural Mountains and the Middle East from Saudi Arabia north to Turkey.

However, in political, historical, and cultural terms, the Soviet Union is usually considered part of Europe. For this reason, *The Volume Library* contains information on the Soviet Union in the EUROPE volume. Similarly, the countries of western Asia have come to be discussed as a separate region. Therefore the countries from Iran west to the Mediterranean Sea are discussed in the volume entitled MIDDLE EAST AND AFRICA. The discussion of Asia in this volume covers the area south of the Soviet Union and east of Iran to the Pacific and Indian oceans.

This volume also discusses that part of the world known as Australasia, which includes the continent of Australia and the islands of the Pacific, sometimes called Oceania.

Asia and Australasia are by far the most populous regions of the world. Their population in 1989 was estimated to be 2,899,280,000, or about 55 percent of the world's total population living on only 22 percent of the world's land area. The land ranges from tropical island paradises to fro-

zen mountainous wastelands to lush rain forests. This large population and the geographical variety of the region have promoted the development of many different cultures.

The land. Asia is generally divided into several subregions, which tend to be unified not only geographically but also climatically and culturally. These subregions are South Asia, which includes Pakistan, India, Bangladesh, Bhutan, and Nepal; Southeast Asia, which includes the Indochinese peninsula, Indonesia, and the Philippines; East Asia, which includes the eastern third of China, Korea, and Japan; and Central Asia, which includes the western two-thirds of China, Mongolia, and Afghanistan.

The Pacific islands are generally divided into three groups. Melanesia is the group of islands just to the north and east of Australia, from New Guinea southeast to Fiji. The group of islands north of the equator and east of the Philippines is called Micronesia. Polynesia includes those islands to the east of a line drawn between Hawaii and New Zealand. Australia, a continent in its own right, is usually considered separately from the Pacific islands.

Asia is dominated by a large mountain mass at its center. The Himalayas form the southern edge of this mass, running 1500 miles along the northern edge of India, from the Indus River in the northwest to the Brahmaputra River in the southeast. The range contains the highest mountains in the world, including the 29,028-foot Mt. Everest, the highest mountain in the world. The Himalayas are a formidable barrier between northern and southern Asia.

North of the Himalayas is the huge Tibetan Plateau. This region of about 471,000 square miles has an average elevation of about 16,000 feet. Its northern edge is formed by the Kunlun Mountains, which join the Karakorum Mountains in the west, and by the Hindu Kush in eastern Afghanistan.

From the Hindu Kush a series of mountain ranges, including the Tien Shan and the Altai, extend from the northern borders of China and Mongolia. Between these mountains and the Kunlun Mountains lie the Gobi and Taklamakan deserts and the Mongolian plains.

In Southeast Asia mountain ranges spread like fingers southward from the eastern end of the Tibetan Plateau. Of these, the Annam Cordillera in Vietnam and Laos, the Tanen Taungghi in

Burma and Thailand, and the Arakan Yoma in Burma are most important.

Rivers. Asia's river valleys have been extremely important to its development. Population tends to be concentrated along the fertile valleys and deltas of the many rivers that rise in the central mountain core.

The Indus and the Brahmaputra rivers, two of the most important of South Asia, rise very near each other on the southern edge of the Tibetan Plateau, then run in opposite directions. The Indus flows first northwest around the northern end of the Himalayas, then south to the Arabian Sea. The Brahmaputra flows to the eastern end of the Himalayas and then south to the Bay of Bengal. Another important South Asian river, the Ganges, rises in the Himalayas in northern India and flows southeast to the Bay of Bengal.

The principal rivers of Southeast Asia are the Irrawaddy and the Salween of Burma; the Chao Phraya of Thailand; the Red in northern Vietnam; and the Mekong. The Mekong rises in eastern Tibet and flows southward 2600 miles through China and into Laos, where it forms much of the Lao border with Thailand. It then flows across Cambodia and into southern Vietnam, where it forms a large, fertile delta.

In China the principal rivers are the Huang He and the Chang (Yangtze), both of which also rise in Tibet and flow into the Yellow and East China seas, respectively.

The islands. The islands of Asia and the Pacific are generally of three types: mountainous, volcanic, and coral. Most of the islands of Southeast and East Asia are mountainous or volcanic or a combination of the two. They are arranged in several arcs that are associated with mainland ranges.

The arc formed by the Andaman and Nicobar islands, Sumatra, Java, and the Lesser Sunda Islands is a continuation of the Arakan Yoma range in Burma; it is volcanically active. Borneo is an extension of the Malay peninsula. All of these islands are located on an extension of the Asian continent called the Sunda Shelf. The Philippines, Sulawesi, and the Moluccas are essentially the tops of mountains situated on the edge of the shelf. The arc of the Japanese islands follows the juncture of several mainland and oceanic ridges.

Most of the Pacific islands are either volcanic, formed by the top of a volcanic peak thrust above the sea, or coral, built up by colonies of coral on a low-lying volcanic base. Sometimes an atoll is formed when the volcanic center of an island collapses into the sea, leaving a ring of small coral islands.

Climate. Asia's weather is dominated by the climatic pattern known as monsoon. The monsoon is typified by strong seasonal winds.

During the winter, high-pressure areas over Siberia create a flow of dry arctic winds toward the lower pressure areas over the oceans. In the summer, the opposite occurs. Low-pressure areas form in the interior, and high-pressure, moistureladen air flows toward them from the oceans.

This weather pattern, however, is greatly affected by the huge mountain barriers in the center of the continent. The Himalayas block much of the flow of the monsoon, moderating their effect on the lands beyond. In the winter southern Asia, from Pakistan to southeastern China, is protected from the Siberian cold. However, in areas that are not protected, such as northern and central China, Korea, or Mongolia, winters are quite bitter.

In the summer the monsoon winds bring a great deal of rain and hot weather to most of southern and eastern Asia. The bulk of the mountains, however, prevents this moist warm air from reaching the Tibetan Plateau or the rest of the interior of the continent.

Those parts of the continent that are within the equatorial belt, including the islands of the Pacific, experience a much more regular climate. Temperatures in southern Sri Lanka and much of Indonesia vary little from one season to another.

People. Asia's cultural and ethnic variety is the result of centuries of migration and invasion.

Asia's population is a mixture of three primary racial types: caucasoid, negroid, and mongoloid. Peoples of caucasoid descent are found primarily in Afghanistan, Pakistan, and northern India. The people of Central, East, and Southeast Asia are principally mongoloid. The negroid influence appears in the southern reaches of the continent, such as in southern India, the Malay peninsula, Indonesia, and across the islands of Melanesia. After many thousands of years of population migration, however, these racial divisions are no longer distinct.

Certain migratory patterns are known because they have continued into recent times. For example, in India the population tended to migrate from the northwest toward the south and east. Southeast Asia was repeatedly invaded by various southern Chinese tribes. The Philippine islands were settled in waves from Indonesia and the Malay peninsula. From Central Asia the Mongols pushed westward as far as Europe, south into Afghanistan and India, and east into China.

Asia's large number of ethnic groups vary widely in size and cultural development. For instance, the Han Chinese are numerous and enjoy a rich and complex civilization, whereas peoples like the hill tribes of Southeast Asia, or similar groups from the interior of Borneo or New Guinea, live in an isolated and primitive fashion.

ASIAN LANGUAGES *can be grouped into several major families, spoken for the most part in distinct portions of the continent.*

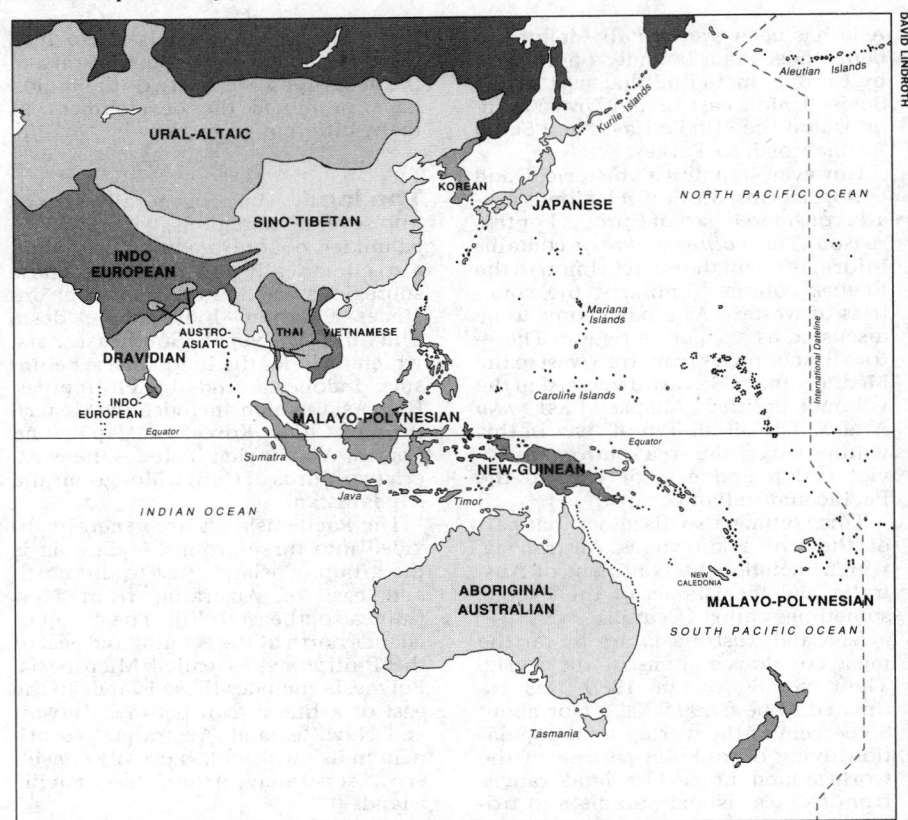

Language. There are many hundreds of languages spoken in Asia. Most are related, although sometimes distantly, to other languages in the region.

One of the largest language groups is the Indo-European. This includes many of the languages spoken in South Asia, including Pashto, Hindi, and Bengali. In southern India, Dravidian is a group of languages that seems to be unrelated to languages anywhere else.

Central Asia is dominated by languages of the Ural-Altaic family, which includes Mongol and Manchu. Chinese is part of the Sino-Tibetan group of languages, which also includes Tibetan, Burman, and Thai languages. The Austro-Asiatic family includes Cambodian and the languages of the Nicobar islands. Vietnamese, Korean, and Japanese do not appear to be related to any other languages.

The languages of most of the islands of Southeast Asia and the Pacific and the Malay peninsula belong to the Malayo-Polynesian group of languages. Malay, Bahasa Indonesia, Tagalog, Samoan, and Hawaiian are among these languages.

The many languages of New Guinea do not appear to be related to any other group of languages. This is also true of the aboriginal languages of Australia.

Religion. Most of the great organized religions are represented in Asia. The religion with the most followers is Hinduism, which is practiced primarily in India and Nepal but also in Burma and in enclaves such as Fiji, where sizable numbers of Indians have settled.

Buddhism, though it has fewer followers, is more widespread. It is practiced over almost all the continent, although it is most heavily concentrated in Tibet, Mongolia, and Southeast Asia.

The third most widespread organized religion in Asia is Islam. It is the primary religion of Afghanistan, Pakistan, Bangladesh, Malaysia, and Indonesia. There are also significant communities of Muslims in western China and in the Philippines. Other influential religions include Confucianism and Taoism in China and Shinto in Japan.

Christianity is predominant in Australia, New Zealand, and on many of the Pacific islands. Throughout the rest of Asia, small communities of Christians survive where the religion had been fostered by colonial rulers.

Population distribution. Asia's average population density is about 250 people per square mile. However, its population is not evenly spread out over its total surface. Because the terrain and climate of much of Asia is so harsh, the majority of the population live in a relatively small portion of the continent. Population is heavily concentrated in the fertile areas of the major river valleys and deltas, such as the Brahmaputra in Bangladesh and the Huang He in China.

Economy. In economic development, as in many other things, Asia is a continent of contrasts. Countries that are desperately poor exist side by side with countries that are wealthy. Australia, Japan, South Korea, and Singapore, among others, have developed economies with relatively high per capita incomes. Countries like Bangladesh, Burma, Laos, Vietnam, and Nepal, however, have undeveloped economies and low per capita incomes.

During colonial times, the Asian economies were geared primarily toward producing raw materials for the industries in the colonizing country. Today, despite efforts by governments to promote the domestic processing of locally produced raw materials, a large part of Asian exports still are processed in Europe, North America, and Japan.

Agriculture. Asia's economy is dominated overwhelmingly by agriculture. More than 60 percent of the population is involved in farming. Most of the farming is done on small individual holdings. In some parts of Asia, large plantations that grow a single crop, such as tea, bananas, or rubber, are common. In China and Vietnam, a large part of the farming is communal.

Farming methods remain, for the most part, very crude, with little or no mechanization or application of modern farming techniques. This contributes to low total crop production, to poverty, and to hunger in many Asian countries. One factor that has helped to increase production has been the so-called Green Revolution. This refers to the introduction, beginning in the 1970's, of new strains of rice, wheat, and other grains that produce much higher yields. Partly because of this development, some countries, like India, which have long suffered shortfalls in their domestic production, are now producing surpluses.

Rice is a staple throughout much of Asia and as a consequence is also the principal crop. It is one of the main items of trade between Asian countries; those nations with crop surpluses sell to those that do not produce enough to satisfy domestic demand.

Other important crops include wheat, produced principally in China and India, barley, corn, millet, and sorghum. Important export crops include tea, rubber, cotton, jute (a fiber from which burlap is made), and sugar cane. Copra, the dried meat of the coconut, is an extremely important export for many Pacific island nations.

Natural resources. The continents of Asia and Australia are richly endowed with natural resources.

Forests provide a valuable export product for a number of countries, particularly in South and Southeast Asia. However, overcutting of forests is leading to serious problems for the region. The denuding of the mountain slopes in Nepal has been partially blamed for the periodic flooding that occurs in

FLOODING IN BANGLADESH *is blamed by some on ecological damage upriver.*

Bangladesh. Ecologists are becoming increasingly concerned with the destruction of the rain forests in Southeast Asia, particularly in Indonesia, because of their important role in the cleansing of the air.

Fish are a very important resource in many parts of Asia and Australasia. In the Pacific, fishing is not only important to the diets of the islanders but also an important source of foreign exchange. The island nations earn not only from the export of fish they have caught themselves, but also from the sale to foreign fishermen of rights to fish within their territorial waters.

Asia is also rich in mineral and fossil fuel resources. China and Indonesia both produce large quantities of oil and natural gas, and other countries, such as India and Thailand, are just beginning to exploit their oil reserves.

Asia contains major reserves of almost all the minerals required by the industrial world; their exploitation is important to the Asian economy. However, exploitation is limited primarily because of the minerals' inaccessibility. Papua New Guinea is believed to hold large reserves of important minerals, but the harshness of the island's terrain makes mining very difficult.

Manufacturing. Asian industry has been handicapped by its colonial past and by its relatively late start in industrialization. The colonial powers primarily were interested in importing from Asia the raw materials necessary to their own industries. There was little incentive during colonial rule to introduce manufacturing to the colonies. By the time most Asian countries achieved independence, they were far behind the Western countries both technologically and educationally.

Not surprisingly, Asian industry is chiefly concerned with the processing of its raw materials and agricultural products. For example, fish and fruit are canned and cotton and jute are woven into textiles.

Not all Asian countries are industrially deficient. Japan was never a colony of a European power, but itself held colonies. Today it has the third largest economy in the world, after the United States and the Soviet Union. Other Asian countries are also having considerable success in industrializing and competing in the world marketplace. Australia, New Zealand, Taiwan, Singapore, and South Korea all have economies that are considerably stronger than those in the rest of Asia.

The most successful economies in Asia are those, like Japan's, that produce manufactured goods for export. Due in part to their much lower labor costs, these Asian nations are able to price their products very competitively in world markets. Products such as automobiles, textiles, and electronics are all competitively produced in Asia.

History. Many civilizations and cultures have flourished in Asia in different places at different times. Human fossils, dating from 1 million to 300 thousand years ago, have been found, indicating that man inhabited Asia long before the civilizations with which historians are familiar.

Two areas, especially, are believed to have fostered early civilizations. These are the Indus River valley in modern Pakistan and the Huang He (Yellow River) in northern China. Comparatively advanced and urban civilizations existed in the upper Indus River valley by at least 2000 B.C. and in the Huang He by 1500 B.C., during the Shang dynasty.

China. China expanded greatly during the Chou dynasty (about 1027–256 B.C.), and Chinese influence spread through eastern Asia by the third century A.D. Territories as far north as Korea and as far south as Annam (Vietnam) came under Chinese rule.

The Chinese inventions of writing, printing, paper, and gunpowder were spread throughout eastern Asia, including Mongolia, Tibet, and the kingdoms of the southeast. Equally important was the social and political model the Chinese extended of a settled agricultural society dominated by the mediating influence of Confucianism. This religion taught the value of ethical conduct, exemplified by a virtuous ruler, a father figure to whom the people paid reverence.

Japan received the influence of Chinese culture through its contacts with Korea. By the seventh century A.D., the Japanese had imitated the Chinese political system based on bureaucratic administration. Nevertheless, Japan remained at the mercy of the warring factions of its great landed nobility.

India. The early civilization in the Indus valley was overrun by invaders from central Asia, called Aryans, before the twelfth century B.C. The synthesis of Aryan culture with the earlier culture led to Hinduism.

Hindu civilization remained for the most part a loose confederation of many different kingdoms. The lack of a centralized political development in India meant that cultural unification was largely in the hands of the high priests of the Hindu religion. A great cultural tradition soon developed around this powerful religion.

After the fifth century B.C., Hindu priestly power was challenged by a closely related religion called Buddhism. Buddhism never overpowered Hinduism, and indeed largely died out in India, but it became very influential as it spread throughout Asia.

While Hinduism was fostering a strict caste system in India that led to some social and political stability, and while Confucianism was having a similar effect in eastern Asia, lawless bands of barbarians from the hill regions of central Asia were stirring.

The Turks, Mongols, and Huns spread fear into the civilized regions of Asia, and in the third century B.C. the Chinese constructed the Great Wall to form a barrier against invasion from the barbarians. Nevertheless, Mongol invaders conquered and ruled China in the 13th and 14th centuries A.D. India, protected from central Asia by the nearly impenetrable barrier of the Himalayas, was more accessible from the west. Muslim Moguls invaded India and ruled there from the 16th to 18th centuries.

Southeast Asia. This region is sometimes called Indochina, and the name reflects its position as the meeting place of Chinese and Indian culture. Indian influence predominated in most of Southeast Asia, however. The spread of Chinese culture was restricted primarily to Vietnam. In the 12th and 13th centuries, ships from Islamic northwestern India began to visit the Malay peninsula and Indonesia. Conversion of the inhabitants of those areas to Islam followed.

In 1275 Marco Polo, a Venetian trader and adventurer, traveled to the magnificent Chinese empire ruled by the Mongols under Kublai Khan. Polo's tales of Asian wealth and splendor spread throughout Europe, but it was not until the 16th century that a substantial European presence was felt in the Orient. In 1498 the Portuguese explorer Vasco da Gama rounded Africa to reach India, thereby opening a new route for European exploration and commerce. In the following centuries a fierce commercial rivalry developed in Asia among the European powers—the Dutch, English, Spanish, Portuguese, and French. Trading companies fanned out across all areas of Asia. By 1788 even Australia, hitherto isolated from European civilization, as had been most of Australasia, was being settled by the British.

The British took control of India from the Mogul empire, and most of

BY 1900 *most of Asia and Australasia was dominated by European powers. Although most of Asia now is independent, the influence of former colonial powers is still evident.*

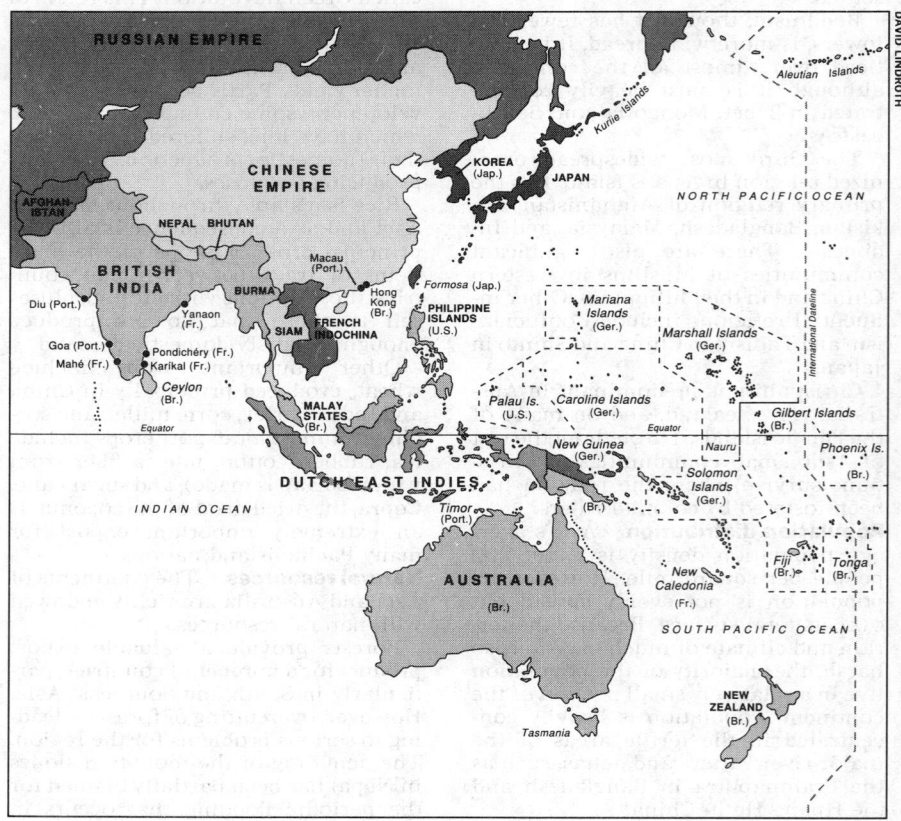

South Asia, including Pakistan, and much of East Asia, including Burma and Malaysia, were soon dominated. In the 19th century the French carved a colonial empire out of Laos, Cambodia, and Vietnam, and the Dutch took control of Indonesia. Most of the Pacific islands were claimed by one European power or another.

Japan, which had developed its own distinctive culture as early as the ninth century A.D., fought off Portuguese attempts to Christianize the empire in the 16th and 17th centuries. Thereafter, Japan embarked on a course of isolation to protect itself from European imperialism. China had been traditionally hostile to foreign influence, but by the mid-19th century, both China and Japan were forced to open their ports to eager merchants from the West.

Japan modernized rapidly and, having adopted the Western concepts of political and economic nationalism, built up a formidable military machine and embarked on its own policy of imperialism. Japan defeated China in 1894 and Russia in 1905, in the process beginning its own colonial empire by taking control of Manchuria, Korea, and Taiwan.

Japan invaded China in 1937, several years before entering World War II on the side of Germany and its ally Italy. At the height of its strength, Japan held a large part of Asia, including much of China, Southeast Asia, Indonesia, and the Philippines. Japan was defeated in large part by American forces during World War II. However, the war was a bitter one, and much of Asia and the islands of Australasia emerged battered and exhausted.

The first stirrings of Asian nationalism had appeared by the end of the 19th century. The nationalist Indian National Congress had been formed in 1885; the Philippine revolt against its Spanish colonizers had begun in 1896. By the end of World War II, the movement for national self-determination was widespread.

World War II left the European powers financially and militarily drained, and without the power to restore their control over their former colonies. As a result, many colonies became independent shortly after the war, although not always without a struggle. In Indonesia and Indochina, the Dutch and French, respectively, gave up their colonies only after local insurgencies made it impossible for them to stay.

After World War II the United States was the preeminent power in Asia. Because the former colonial powers were unable to resume their prewar positions, the United States began to assume some of their responsibilities.

In the decades following World War II, Asia became a battleground in a struggle between communist and non-communist forces. A terrible civil war raged in China before the Communist forces defeated the Nationalist forces

THE BALLOT BOX *is becoming an increasingly common sight in Asia.*

in 1949. Wars between Communists and anti-Communists in Korea in the early 1950's and in Vietnam in the 1960's prompted the Western nations, led by the United States, to support one side while the Communist governments of China and the Soviet Union supported the other. The Vietnam War spread into Laos and Cambodia and caused a great deal of destruction. Most of Southeast Asia was left in poverty and ruin following about 30 years of continual warfare. A number of other countries, the Philippines and Malaysia among them, faced problems caused by internal Communist insurgencies.

The postwar years in Asia were marked not only by wars of ideology and independence, but also by violence caused by religious and ethnic hatred. Civil war in Pakistan in the 1970's led to the creation of the separate Muslim state of Bangladesh. India has vacillated between authoritarian and democratic governments in its attempt to achieve Western-style industrial-economic success and at the same time

manage the tensions caused by its unstable mix of religions. In Indonesia and Malaysia, animosity toward the minority Chinese populations has several times erupted into violence.

Asia today. The 1970's and 1980's have seen a number of encouraging changes in Asia, both economic and political.

Led by the example of Japan and the other successful export economies, governments are abandoning some of the disastrous economic policies of their post-independence years. Even the two principal Communist countries, China and Vietnam, have shown signs of encouraging private enterprise to spur their economies.

Politically, there are also encouraging signs that the countries of Asia are instituting elements of democracy into their systems of government. This trend was exemplified by the Philippine overthrow of the Marcos dictatorship in 1986, and also by the reinstitution of democratic processes in South Korea soon after.

However, despite the gains of the past decades, the countries of Asia and Australasia still have many problems to deal with. Even with the economic gains that the regions have made, existence is still precarious for the vast majority of the people.

The huge numbers of people, and the rapid rate at which the population is growing, necessitate that the economies of Asia and Australasia perform exceptionally well just to stay abreast of the growth.

Natural disasters still have a huge effect on the fragile economies. Each flood or cyclone that strikes impoverished Bangladesh drives its people into an indebtedness from which they may never recover. Drought in China can still mean famine for many.

The developing nations of Asia face a great challenge in their drive to become economically and politically secure. They must struggle to be competitive in a world overwhelmingly dominated by Western ideas of politics and culture, and yet still maintain their own ancient cultural values and heritage.

NOTE ON THE COUNTRY LISTINGS

Most of the information included in the following section is self-explanatory; however, some of the recurring statistical information requires a word of explanation about its importance.

Population growth rate. This is the annual rate of natural increase in population when both births and deaths are taken into account. This is a crucial figure for many developing countries. A high growth rate can offset even spectacular economic growth because of the number of additional people to feed and jobs to find.

Literacy. The literacy rate, that is, the percentage of people who can read out of the total population, gives an important indication of the level of education in a country.

Life expectancy. This figure represents the average number of years a person born in the indicated year can expect to live. Life expectancy figures are a good indication of the quality of health care in a country.

Per capita GNP. This is the gross national product divided by the total population; it provides an indication of the standard of living in each country.

Exports/imports. Trade figures give an indication of the vitality of a country's economy and show in particular if a country exports enough goods to pay for the goods it imports.

COUNTRIES OF ASIA AND AUSTRALASIA

Afghanistan

The land. Afghanistan is a high country, with an average elevation of about 6000 feet above sea level. A great central mountain core dominates the landscape. In the east, the Hindu Kush ranges rise to more than 20,000 feet. The Koh-i-Baba and Paropamisus ranges, with elevations of 10,000 to 15,000 feet, fan out toward the west.

Near the western border the land drops to Seistan, a barren plateau at an elevation of 1500 feet. East of Seistan are two deserts, the Dasht-i-Margo and the Registan.

Four large rivers flow from the central mountains through the country's major inhabited regions. The Amu Darya (Oxus) drains the hilly northeast and forms part of the border with the Soviet Union. The Hari Rud flows west from the Paropamisus. The richest regions are the valleys of the Helmand and its tributaries, in the southwest, and the valley of the Kabul, which flows east to the Indus.

Afghanistan's climate is characterized by extremes. In the lower regions average temperatures range from over 115°F in summer to −10°F in winter. Mountain temperatures may vary by as much as 50°F in one day, although south of the mountains temperatures are more moderate. Winds are high throughout the country. Average precipitation ranges from 2 inches a year in the west to 12 inches in the east.

The people. Afghanistan's central position in Asia has given it a varied population. Over half the people are Pukhtun (also called Pashtun or Pathan), a tribal group related to the Persians and Indians. Their language is Pushtu. Other major groups are the Hazara, who speak a mixed Persian-Turkish dialect, the Turkic-speaking Uzbek and Turkoman, and the Tajik, whose language is Dari, a dialect of Persian.

Most Afghans live in rural villages. The urban population is about 15 percent of the total population. The major cities are Kabul in the east, Herat in the west, and Kandahar in the south.

Some 3 million Afghans have taken refuge in Pakistan since the Soviet invasion in 1979.

Economy. Afghanistan's economy is based on farming and herding, although no more than 25 percent of the land can be cultivated and only about 12 percent is farmed. Mineral resources include coal, oil, gas, iron, salt, copper, gold, and lapis lazuli.

Karakul sheep are Afghanistan's most valuable agricultural commodity, providing meat, milk, and fat for domestic consumption and skins for export. Goats, cattle, horses, donkeys, and camels also are raised. The leading crops are wheat, corn, barley and other grains, cotton, sugar beets, and a great variety of fruits and vegetables.

Leather processing, textile weaving, and flour milling are the only well established manufacturing industries.

Projects have been initiated to develop coal and hydroelectric resources; to expand transportation and communications facilities; and to improve education and health services.

Following the 1978 Communist coup and the 1979 Soviet invasion of Afghanistan, Western financial aid virtually dried up. The Soviet Union and the Comecon countries became the primary providers of technical and financial assistance.

Due principally to sales of natural gas, Afghanistan maintains a favorable balance of trade. Gas accounts for about 35 percent of total exports. Other exports include fruits and nuts, carpets, karakul skins, and cotton. Imports include food, petroleum products, and manufactured items.

Principal trading partners are the Soviet Union and other members of Comecon, the United Kingdom, West Germany, the United States, and The Netherlands.

Government. The head of state is the president of the 65-member Revolutionary Council. The council chooses a seven-member Presidium, and its chairman is the head of government.

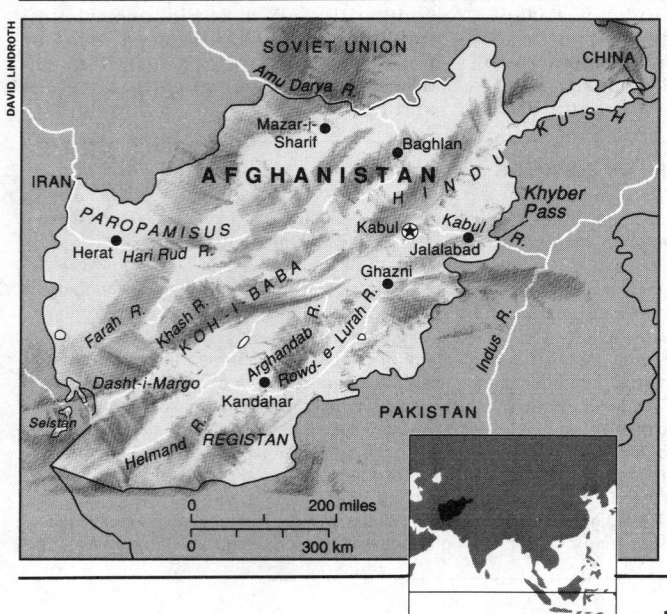

DAVID LINDROTH

Afghanistan

Official name: *Democratic Republic of Afghanistan*
Area: *249,999 sq. mi., 647,497 sq. km.*
Type of government: *People's republic*
Head of state: *President of Revolutionary Council, Haji Mohammad Tsamkani*
Head of government: *Chairman of Council of Ministers, Soltan Ali Keshtmand*
Population: *14,825,000 (1989 est.)*
Population growth rate: *2.3%*
Capital and largest city: *Kabul (Pop., 1987 est., 1,400,000)*
Languages: *Dari, Pushtu*
Religions: *Sunni Muslim 80%, Shi'ah Muslim 20%*
Ethnic groups: *Pathan 50%, Tajik 25%, Uzbek 9%, Hazara 9%*
Literacy: *10%*
Life expectancy: *42 years (1987)*
Currency: *Afghani*
Per capita GNP: *$220 (1986)*
Exports: *$565 million (1986)*
Imports: *$848 million (1986)*

The government is dominated by the People's Democratic Party of Afghanistan (PDPA); its general secretary holds primary power in the country. The PDPA is governed by a 36-member Central Committee and a nine-member Politburo.

History. Afghanistan lies at the crossroads of ancient Asian migration routes, and its early history is a story of invasions and conquests. The country has been inhabited since prehistory, but the first known settlers were Aryans, who passed through Afghanistan on their way to India in about 1500 B.C.

By the 500's B.C., Aryana, as the area was then called, was part of the Persian Empire. In 328 B.C. it was conquered by the Greek armies of Alexander the Great. After Alexander's death, it was divided between the Seleucid Empire of Persia and Bactria, a kingdom in the north. In the 100's B.C. these kingdoms fell before invasions from the north by nomadic tribes from central Asia.

Islam. At the end of the 600's and in the early 700's Arab armies invaded the country and converted the people to Islam. During the next several centuries many small kingdoms arose in Afghanistan, most of them ruled by Muslims. These kingdoms were dominated in the 900's by Turkic tribes, who made Afghanistan a center of culture and learning.

In the 1200's the Turkic kingdoms were destroyed by the Mongol armies of Genghis Khan. The Turkic-Mongol conqueror Tamerlane (Timur) made Afghanistan part of his empire in the 1300's. Two hundred years later Tamerlane's descendant Babur founded the vast Indian Mughal (Mogul) empire.

The Mughals lost most of Afghanistan to the Safavid rulers of Persia in the 1600's. But in the early 1700's Afghanistan asserted its independence and drove the Persians out. In 1747 the Afghan tribes jointly chose Ahmad Shah Durrani, of the Sadozay section of the Abdali tribe, as ruler of the united country. Many tribes were dissatisfied, however, and in the early 1800's rebellions toppled the dynasty.

Foreign interference. Several civil wars were fought for control of the throne, leaving the country vulnerable to foreign invasion. By the 1800's control of Afghanistan, long sought by Persia, had also become a goal of Russia and of Great Britain, whose Indian territory bordered Afghanistan. By 1839 Dost Muhammad, a Barakzay tribal leader strongly opposed to foreign control, held the throne. To protect its position in India and the Near East, Britain sought to place a more friendly ruler in power. This led to an Anglo-Afghan war between 1839 and 1842.

The British captured Dost Muhammad, but they could not put down a rebellion in the country and withdrew. For the next 36 years, Afghanistan's history was marked by civil war, Russian advances, Persian invasions, and,

in 1878, by renewed war with Britain. In 1879, having won the war, Britain in effect made Afghanistan a buffer state between British and Russian imperialist ambitions.

In 1880 a new emir, Abd-ar-Rahman, came to the throne and cooperated with the British whenever it benefited Afghanistan. During his reign rebellious tribesmen were pacified and the boundries were set between Afghanistan, Russia, and British India.

Afghanistan remained neutral during World War I, but anti-British sentiment spread, a spirit of nationalism developed, and in 1919 nationalists led a war against Britain. Neither side was able to win the war, but the British allowed the country to conduct its own foreign affairs. Afghanistan's right to domestic self-rule had already been promised in an Anglo-Russian agreement in 1907.

Modernization. After the war a new king, Amanullah, began to modernize the country. His reforms proved extreme, costly, and unpopular, and in 1929 he was deposed during a widespread tribal rebellion. Mohammed Nadir, a Pashtun leader, defeated rival contenders for power. Afghanistan was neutral during World War II.

Under Nadir Shah and his son, Mohammed Zahir Shah, Afghanistan was modernized very gradually. Many democratic forms and processes were introduced, the economy was developed, and the traditional society began to change as Western ideas were adopted.

In 1964 the Afghans received a written constitution that provided for many democratic reforms. However, the constitution was abolished when Zahir Shah was overthrown in 1973 by a group of army officers.

In 1978 another military coup brought the Communist People's Democratic Party of Afghanistan (PDPA) to power. The new government's unpopular policies led to widespread civil unrest. In September of 1979 President Noor Mohammad Taraki was killed during a bloody coup led by Hafizullah Amin, his prime minister. The Soviet Union, claiming to be bound by a 1978 Treaty of Friendship to protect the Taraki government, invaded the country in December.

Amid strong international protest, the Soviets deposed Amin and installed a new government. The new government, headed until 1986 by Babrak Karmal, and then by Najibullah, was highly unpopular. A strong guerrilla movement, supplied by Western and Middle Eastern countries, forced the Soviets to maintain a heavy military presence in Afghanistan.

The Soviet military presence in Afghanistan grew increasingly costly to the Soviet economy and in terms of casualties. In 1988 an accord was worked out between Afghanistan, Pakistan, the Soviet Union, and the United States. It established a time table for Soviet withdrawal.

Australia

The land. The Commonwealth of Australia is composed of six states and two mainland territories. The states are New South Wales, Queensland, South Australia, Tasmania, Victoria, and Western Australia. The two internal territories are the Northern Territory and the Australian Capital Territory.

Australia's external territories and colonies are mostly former British colonies. They include Christmas Island and the Cocos (Keeling) Islands, both once incorporated in the British colony of Singapore; Norfolk Island, an old British penal colony that was inhabited in 1856 by descendants of the mutineers of the HMS *Bounty;* Heard and McDonald islands, Ashmore and Cartier islands, Coral Sea Island Territory, and the Australian Antarctic Territory.

Australia contains some of the oldest and most stable portions of Earth's surface. It may once have formed part of an ancient continent known as Gondwanaland, consisting of Africa, parts of the Indian subcontinent, and Brazil, as well as Australia.

Regions. Australia has three main land regions—the Western Plateau, the Central Lowlands, and the Eastern Highlands. The Western Plateau occupies approximately the western half of the continent. It has an average elevation of about 1200 feet above sea level. It is flat for the most part, but there are some isolated mountain ranges, such as the Macdonnell Range and the Musgrave Range in the eastern part of the plateau, which rise to almost 5000 feet above sea level, and the Hamersley Range in the northwest. The central portion of the plateau is mostly desert.

The Central Lowlands, lying east of the Western Plateau, has an average elevation of about 500 feet, although Lake Eyre, in the southern part of the region, lies about 40 feet below sea level. Marine sediments, laid down about 50 million years ago, cover much of the region.

Sedimentary rocks in the northern part of the Central Lowlands form the Great Artesian Basin, an important source of underground water in an area that receives very little rain. The Murray-Darling-Murrumbidgee Basin, Australia's most extensive river system, occupies the southeastern portion of the lowlands.

The Eastern Highlands, sometimes known as the Great Dividing Range, is a collection of many mountain ranges and plateaus that run parallel to Australia's east coast. Among the ranges are the Australian Alps, Hunter Mountains, Blue Mountains, Liverpool Range, and Darling Downs. Mount Kosciusko, which rises more than 7300 feet in the Australian Alps, is Australia's highest peak.

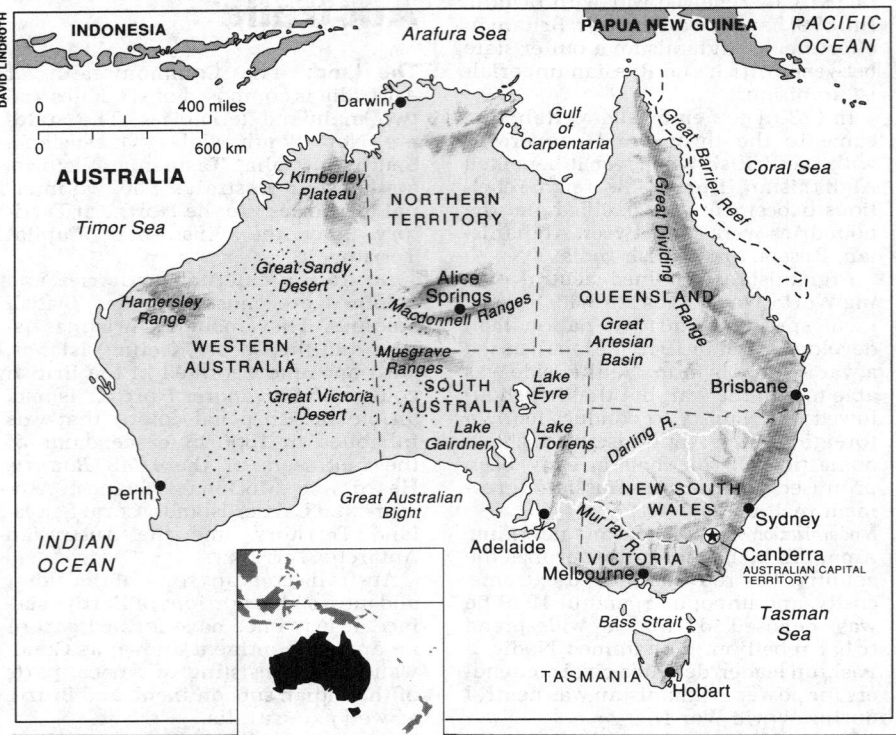

DAVID LINDROTH

Australia

Official name: *Commonwealth of Australia*
Area: *2,967,894 sq. mi., 7,686,845 sq. km.*
Type of government: *Parliamentary democracy*
Head of state: *Queen Elizabeth II*
Head of government: *Prime minister, Bob Hawke*
Population: *16,452,000 (1989 est.)*
Population growth rate: *0.8%*
Capital: *Canberra (Pop., 1986 est., 265,000)*
Largest city: *Sydney (Pop., 1986 est., 3,400,000)*
Languages: *English (official), aboriginal*
Religions: *Anglican 26%, Roman Catholic 26%*
Ethnic groups: *European 95%, Asian 4%, aboriginal 1%*
Literacy: *98%*
Life expectancy: *76 years (1987)*
Currency: *Australian dollar*
Per capita GNP: *$11,910 (1986)*
Exports: *$22.6 billion (1986)*
Imports: *$26.1 billion (1986)*

The island of Tasmania, about 130 miles from the Australian mainland, contains an extension of the Eastern Highlands. The highlands on Tasmania form a central plateau containing many natural lakes.

The Great Barrier Reef, a collection of islands, cays, and reefs, stretches for some 1250 miles along the northern half of the east coast. Some parts of the reef are formed from the same rocks as the adjacent mainland; others are made up of the skeletons of millions of tiny coral polyps that have solidified into reefs and islands.

Climate. Australia's winter season extends from June to August, and summer from December to February. Winters are mild almost everywhere; summers are warm to hot.

The interior parts of the Central Lowlands and Western Plateau are extremely arid, and Lake Eyre is usually completely dry. The northern coastal region receives heavy seasonal rainfall. Australia's southwestern corner receives winter rain. The only area to receive year-round rain is the southeastern corner. Rainfall over most of the interior averages less than 10 inches a year, creating constant concern over drought.

Plant life. Because of Australia's dryness, forests are found only in the southwest and along the eastern and northern coasts. Almost half the continent is covered with semidesert scrub or sand dunes. Another large portion has mixed grass and tree cover.

Australia's dryness, coupled with the continent's long isolation from the rest of the world, have led to the development of many unique species of plants and animals. Typically Australian are the eucalyptus and acacia types of plants, which together account for more than a thousand different species. These plants form the dominant nongrass vegetation.

Animal life. The continent is famous for its distinctive animal life, especially the platypus, kangaroo, wallaby, and koala. Rabbits, although not native to Australia, are so numerous that they have been labeled pests.

The kookaburra, emu, Australian lyrebird, and black swan are among the more famous of some 650 species of birds found in Australia.

The people. When the first European settlers arrived in Australia in the late 1700's, they found an estimated 300,000 aborigines living there. The aborigines are related to small groups of people living in other areas of southern Asia. Many of the aborigines died as a result of diseases introduced by the Europeans. Today there are about 150,000 aborigines living in Australia, mostly in the north, west, and central parts of the country.

About 95 percent of the Australian population is of British origin. After World War II Australia sought to double its immigration rate. Immigration restrictions were eased and over 2.5 million people came to Australia between 1947 and 1975, causing the native-born population composition to drop from 90 to 80 percent. The overall population increase between 1970 and 1976 was 1.5 percent.

The population of Australia is unevenly distributed. Eighty-five percent of the population lives in urban areas that are, for the most part, on or near the coast. The extremely arid interior of the continent has almost no permanent population.

Sydney, the capital of New South Wales, is the largest of Australia's cities and an important economic center. Melbourne, the capital and largest city of Victoria, is also a major economic center. Canberra, the national capital, is located in the Australian Capital Territory.

Economy. The Australian economy traditionally has been heavily dependent on agriculture and on the processing of raw materials. In recent decades, however, there has been a shift toward the manufacturing and service industries. Together they represent about 93 percent of employment.

Agriculture. Even though agriculture now employs only about 6 percent of the Australian population, and produces only about 5 percent of the nation's gross domestic product (GDP), it still accounts for about 40 percent of export earnings. The primary agricultural products are wheat and other grains, meat, wool, fruits and vegetables, and wine.

Farming is located mostly in the south, east, and southwestern parts of the country, while ranching is found throughout most of the central lowlands, across the north, and in the far west.

Mining. Australia is the largest exporter of coal in the world; it contains

AUSTRALIA *is one of the most heavily urbanized countries in the world, with a great majority of its people living in a few large cities. The interior of the country, or "outback," is very lightly populated.*

one-quarter of the world's proven reserves of bauxite (the primary source of aluminum). Also extracted are iron, nickel, lead, tin, and uranium. Petroleum production now supplies about 80 percent of domestic oil needs.

Manufacturing. About 20 percent of Australia's workforce is employed in manufacturing. Major industrial products include transport equipment and other machinery, food products, textiles, processed metals, and petrochemicals.

Trade. Australia's biggest trading partner is, by far, Japan, followed by the United States and Great Britain. Principal exports include coal, wheat, wool, iron ore, and beef. Imports include industrial equipment, consumer goods, and transport equipment.

Government. Australia's federal system of government is patterned on the governments of Great Britain and the United States. The nominal head of state is the British monarch, who is represented by a governor-general. Actual executive power is wielded by a cabinet, formed from the party with the majority in the House of Representatives, and headed by a prime minister responsible to Parliament.

Parliament has two houses—the 76-member Senate, with members elected to six-year terms, and the 148-member House of Representatives, popularly elected to three-year terms.

Each of Australia's six states has its own parliament and premier to deal with local matters. The organization of the state parliaments varies from state to state. The Northern Territory is self-governing, and the Australian Capital Territory is administered by the federal government.

Australia is a member of the Commonwealth of Nations, and close ties are maintained with Britain and other Commonwealth countries. Australia is also a member of the Colombo Plan in Asia and the Organization for Economic Cooperation and Development (OECD); it plays an active role in the United Nations.

History. The original settlers of Australia, the aborigines, arrived on the continent about 12,000 years ago from Southeast Asia. These people lived at an extremely primitive level, with very little in the way of material culture, but with a highly developed ability to survive in a hostile natural environment.

In the 1600's Portuguese, Spanish, and Dutch navigators explored the southern hemisphere. In 1606 a Spanish commander, Luis Vaez de Torres, sailed through the strait that now bears his name, off the northeastern tip of the mainland. In the same year Willem Jansz explored the region around the Gulf of Carpentaria.

Abel Tasman discovered the island of Tasmania in 1642. In 1770 Captain

James Cook made extensive explorations of the continent's east coast, and later claimed it for England.

Settlement. Britain made the first settlement in Australia in 1788, when Arthur Phillip led 1030 people (including 726 convicts) to Port Jackson, which eventually became the great city of Sydney. Britain established a second colony in 1803–1804 in Tasmania.

The early history of the settlements was dominated by the convict system, and by the struggle of the free settlers to establish their rights as Englishmen. The colony's first economic objective was agricultural self-sufficiency, and when a convict's time expired, he was encouraged to set up a small farm.

By 1796 Merino sheep had been introduced into the colony; wool soon became an extremely important industry. The dynamic wool industry spread rapidly after the 1820's and provided an export commodity that has since been basic to the Australian economy.

Because sheep ranching requires broad fields and a small workforce, each colony tended to develop a single urban center, usually near a port. In 1829 settlers founded Perth, in Western Australia; in 1835, Melbourne, in the Port Phillip district of what was then New South Wales; and in 1836, Adelaide, in South Australia. Except for Western Australia, these new colonies were for free men only.

The early 1800's were also marked by the further efforts of former convicts to establish their civil rights and of the colonies to achieve self-government. Many Australians and Englishmen strongly attacked the convict system on the grounds that it morally damaged Australian society, had ceased to be a punishment for English criminals, did not rehabilitate prisoners, and unfairly competed with free labor. Britain ceased sending convicts to New South Wales in 1840, to Tasmania in 1853, and to Western Australia in 1868.

Self-rule. Progress toward self-rule developed as the number of free colonists grew. In 1850 the British Parliament passed the Australian Colonies Government Act, which allowed the Australian colonies to organize legislatures. The act also formed the Port Phillip district of New South Wales into the separate colony of Victoria, and provided for the separation of Queensland from New South Wales in 1859. Western Australia waited until 1890 for responsible government, however.

In 1851 gold was discovered in eastern Australia, and the ensuing gold rush brought a rapid rise in the population, from some 400,000 in 1850 to 1,146,000 in 1860.

Also in the 1890's, in the midst of a worldwide financial depression, a serious shipping, shearing, and mining strike erupted in Australia. The effects of the strike were intensified by a severe drought, which reduced the numbers of sheep and cattle. At that time trade unions grew in importance, and the first politically oriented labor parties emerged.

Commonwealth. In 1897–1898, a convention met to draft a federal constitution. In 1900 Britain accepted a federal framework for Australia, and the Commonwealth of Australia came into being on January 1, 1901.

A significant development between 1901 and the outbreak of World War I was the impact of the Labour Party, organized in 1891. Trade unions saw the need for political support for social welfare legislation, but the Labour Party, representing the unions, entered federal politics reluctantly. It felt the best prospects for success lay in influencing the state governments.

In 1902 the Labour Party allied itself with Alfred Deakin, who became prime minister. Labour supported a white Australia position: they wanted to keep out Orientals, whom they feared as cheap labor.

At the outbreak of World War I, Australia was weak in manufacturing. After foodstuffs and raw materials, its major export for war was manpower. Of a total population of about 4 million people, Australia mobilized some 400,000 men and sent 332,000 volunteers overseas.

In 1915 William Morris Hughes, leader of the Labour Party, became prime minister. Hughes advocated conscription for overseas service, but a popular referendum twice defeated his attempts. A rift developed within the party following the defeats. Hughes broke from the Labour Party and organized a National War Government. His followers formed the Nationalist Party in opposition to the Labour Party.

Interwar era. After the war, the Commonwealth came under the rule of a coalition of the Nationalists and a new group, the Country Party. The Country Party was formed in 1918 by farmers who felt that rural areas were not adequately represented.

With war production over, the government emphasized land industries, but the markets failed. There was a postwar recession, exports declined, and tremendous imports left companies without means to finance purchases. The rural industries, except for wool, had to be supported by high, government-fixed domestic prices.

The worldwide Depression of the 1930's hit Australia hard because of the sharp drop in prices for its exports. Former Nationalist and Labour Party members formed the United Australia Party to meet the results of the Depression with sound finance.

World War II. At the onset of war in Europe in 1939, Australian troops were sent to fight Axis forces in the Middle East. However, following the Japanese attack on Pearl Harbor, Hawaii, in 1941, and then the fall of Singapore and the bombing of Darwin in 1942, troops were recalled from the Middle East to defend home territory. As military reverses forced Great Britain to reduce its role in the defense of Australia, the Australian government fostered closer ties with the United States. Australian forces were involved in the Battle of the Coral Sea and in land battles in New Guinea and Borneo.

After 1945. The war had provided a big boon to industrialization, helping to lift Australia out of the Depression of the 1930's. In 1941 Australia had elected a Labour government, and it enacted a series of important social welfare programs. It also introduced a program of aid to immigrants, prompting a huge influx from Europe.

In 1949 a coalition of the Liberal and Country parties, led by Robert Menzies, defeated the Labour Party in a national election. Menzies emphasized free enterprise and opposition to communism. One consequence of the election of Menzies was the further strengthening of ties with the United States. Australia joined with New Zealand and the United States to form the ANZUS defensive alliance, and sent troops to fight alongside United Nations forces in Korea and United States forces in Vietnam.

During the four decades following the end of World War II, Australia has experienced rapid economic expansion. The discovery of important deposits of metals, coal, and petroleum boosted manufacturing growth and introduced a period of prosperity.

The Liberal-Country coalition remained in power under five successive prime ministers. In 1972, however, the Labour Party attained the majority in the House of Representatives but failed in the Senate. Prime Minister Gough Whitlam's attempts to pass legislation were often balked by the Senate. In 1975 the Senate refused to approve the budget, hoping to force an election. When Whitlam refused to call one, the governor-general, in an unprecedented move, dismissed him, and called for new elections.

The Liberal Party, led by Malcolm Fraser, won the subsequent election. The economic situation in the late 1970's and early 1980's was marked by high unemployment and inflation, low export prices, and ineffective management by Fraser.

In 1983 elections the Liberals were turned out of office by the Labour Party, led by Robert Hawke. Hawke proved skillful at building a consensus between business and labor. His government focused on reducing government expenditures and increasing exports. In 1987, for the first time, Labour won three successive elections.

An important recent trend in Australia has been the growing realization of the importance of Asia to Australia's future. As a result, Australia has become increasingly active in regional trade and political affairs.

Bangladesh

The land. The land is dominated by the Ganges, Brahmaputra, and Meghna river deltas. The rivers branch into many small tributaries that weave throughout the land. They flood frequently, leaving rich deposits of soil, but also causing great loss of life and damage to land and property.

Land elevations in northwest Bangladesh seldom exceed 300 feet above sea level. Eastern Bangladesh is dominated by the Chittagong Hill tracts, which rise sharply as high as 3000 feet.

Bangladesh has a monsoon climate, with mild winters and hot summers. It is one of the rainiest areas in the world, with annual rainfall ranging from 50 to 200 inches.

The people. The population currently increases nearly 3 percent a year, and the country's density of 1969 people per square mile is one of the highest in the world. Ninety-one percent of this population is rural. Most of the people are Indo-Aryan Bengalis. There are also many Biharis, who migrated from India after 1947, and native tribal peoples living in the hill areas. Seventy percent of the labor force is engaged in agriculture, mostly on a subsistence level.

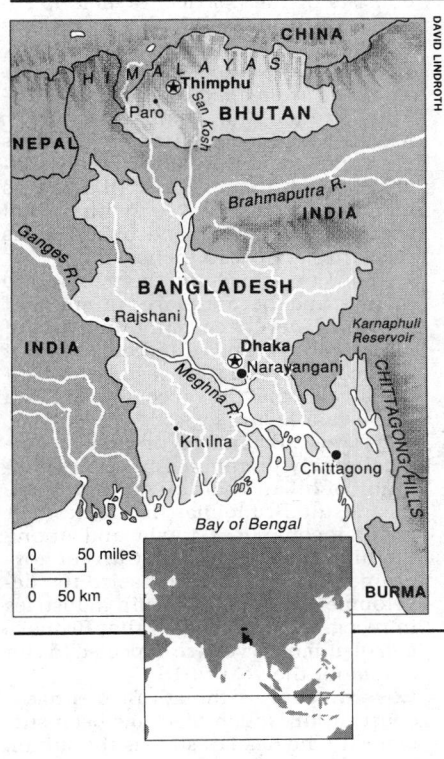

DAVID LINDROTH

Bangladesh

Official name: *People's Republic of Bangladesh*
Area: *55,598 sq. mi., 143,999 sq. km.*
Type of government: *Parliamentary democracy*
Head of state: *President, Hussain Mohammad Ershad*
Head of government: *Prime minister, Mizanur Rahman Chowdhury*
Population: *112,855,000 (1989 est.)*
Population growth rate: *2.7%*
Capital and largest city: *Dhaka (Pop., 1986 est., 3,500,000)*
Languages: *Bangla (official), English*
Religions: *Muslim 83%, Hindu 16%*
Ethnic group: *Bengali*
Literacy: *29%*
Life expectancy: *51 years (1987)*
Currency: *Taka*
Per capita GNP: *$160 (1986)*
Exports: *$820 million (1986)*
Imports: *$2.3 billion (1986)*

Bhutan

Official name: *Kingdom of Bhutan*
Area: *18,000 sq. mi., 46,620 sq. km.*
Type of government: *Monarchy*
Head of state: *King, Jigme Singhe Wangchuk*
Population: *1,534,000 (1989 est.)*
Population growth rate: *2.0%*
Capital and largest city: *Thimphu (Pop., 1986 est., 15,000)*
Languages: *Dzongkha (official), Sharchop*
Religions: *Mahayana Buddhist 75%, Hindu 25%*
Ethnic groups: *Bhotia 60%, Nepalese 25%*
Literacy: *12%*
Life expectancy: *48 years (1987)*
Currency: *Ngultrum*
Per capita GNP: *$160 (1986)*
Exports: *22.2 million (1985–1986)*
Imports: *$72.6 million (1985–1986)*

Dhaka, the capital, is also the largest city in Bangladesh. Chittagong, in the east, is the country's largest port.

Economy. Bangladesh is an extremely poor country with an unskilled labor force. Most of the population is engaged in traditional subsistence farming. The most important crops are rice, jute, tea, and sugar.

Manufacturing contributes only about 8 percent of the gross domestic product. The manufacture of products from raw jute, such as burlap sacks and carpet backing, is important. Increasingly important is textile manufacture, both for domestic consumption and for export.

Bangladesh imports far more than it exports; the difference is made up primarily from the aid it receives from other countries. Primary exports are jute and jute products, textiles, frozen fish, leather, and tea. Imports include industrial goods, food, petroleum, and consumer goods.

Government. The head of government in Bangladesh is a president popularly elected every five years. Legislative power rests with a popularly elected parliament of 320 members. The president chooses a cabinet from among the members of the parliament.

History. The history of Bangladesh is closely tied to that of the rest of the Indian subcontinent. Though there were periods of independence for Bengal (the region of which Bangladesh is a part), its history is largely one of invasion and domination by outside powers.

In 1193 the first of several invasions that eventually converted much of the region to Islam occurred. In 1576 Bengal was conquered by the Mughal Empire, which was centered in Delhi, India.

In 1514 the Portuguese built several trading posts in Bengal, but they were driven out in 1632. They were followed by Dutch, French, and British traders. By the end of the 19th century, the British had pushed the other European powers out of the area.

Bangladesh was administered as part of British India until 1947, when the region was partitioned into separate Hindu and Muslim nations and India and Pakistan were created. Pakistan consisted of present Pakistan plus the eastern portion of Bengal, which was known as East Pakistan.

From the beginning there were tensions between the eastern and western halves of the country. East Pakistan felt neglected by the West Pakistan-dominated government.

In December, 1970, the Awami League (a Bengali nationalist party), led by the enormously popular Sheik Mujibur Rahman, won a majority of the seats (167 of 313) in the Pakistan National Assembly. This unexpectedly large showing in the first national elections held in Pakistan since independence emphasized the fissure between the Bengali-speaking people of East Pakistan and their rulers in Islamabad.

On March 1, 1971, Pakistan's President Ayub Khan announced that the convening of the National Assembly would be postponed. Leaders of the Awami League claimed they were being cheated of the fruits of the election. Widespread rioting in the Bengali province ensued, and strikes crippled many cities, including the key port of Chittagong.

On March 25, President Ayub Khan ordered the Pakistan national army into the Bengali province to crush dissent. Sheik Mujibur Rahman, who had in a radio broadcast declared the independence of Bangladesh, was arrested. The death toll of this phase of the civil war was estimated by some observers to be in the hundreds of thousands. In addition, several million Bengalis fled to neighboring India, which thereafter gave extensive aid to Bangladesh. In December, 1971, India entered the war on the side of Bangladesh, and the Pakistani forces were quickly defeated.

Bangladesh was proclaimed an independent state with Sheik Mujibur Rahman as its prime minister.

Incensed by economic chaos and governmental corruption, a military group seized power on August 15, 1975. Mujibur Rahman and his family were killed. Parliamentary government was reinstated by the constitution of 1977 and in 1979 Ziaur Rahman was elected to the presidency.

Rahman was killed during an attempted coup in 1981. A second coup in 1982 succeeded in installing a military government, led by Hussain Mohammad Ershad. In the following years, martial law was lifted slowly and democratic processes restored gradually. Ershad was elected president in 1986 in an election that was boycotted by the opposition parties.

Bhutan

The land. Bhutan is no more than 190 miles long and 90 miles wide, but it has three distinct geographical zones. Within 20 miles of its northern border is a wild and snowy region, where peaks of the eastern Himalayas tower to almost 25,000 feet. A central zone, about 40 miles wide, ranges in elevation from 3500 feet to 10,000 feet; it is forested with evergreens. The southern region, which grades into the valley of the Brahmaputra River, is low and mostly covered with dense semitropical forest.

Several rivers flow south through Bhutan. The most important are the Amo Chu, the Sankosh, and the Dangme Chu.

Bhutan's climate varies with elevation. In the north, where alpine tundra conditions prevail, the cold is extreme, and glaciers fill the higher valleys. The central zone is temperate, and rainfall averages 40 to 60 inches a year. The southern region has a semitropical climate—heat and humidity are extreme, and up to 300 inches of rain may fall in a year.

The people. Bhutan's population is concentrated in the river valleys of the temperate central region. About two-thirds of the people are Bhotia, a Tibetan-speaking group. A Nepali minority makes up about one-quarter of the population.

Economy. Agriculture is the basis of Bhutan's economy, employing 90 percent of the population. Bhutan's forests are valuable. Deposits of dolomite, coal, gypsum, limestone, and other minerals have been unexploited.

Farms are concentrated in the rich river valleys, and although small, they produce a surplus of food. The major crops are rice, wheat, corn, barley, and millet. Fruits and vegetables are also raised. Yaks, goats, and cattle are herded.

Bhutan is one of the least developed countries in the world. Manufacturing accounts for only 1.5 percent of employment. Products include weaving, woodwork, cement, textiles, and plywood. There is some hydroelectric production and more is planned for the future. Tourism is a big contributor to the economy.

India is Bhutan's largest trading partner and donor of aid, accounting for 90 percent of Bhutan's exports. Exports include cement, fruit, cardamon, timber, and handicrafts. Imports include food, textiles, and machinery.

Government. Bhutan is a monarchy ruled by a hereditary king. The king is advised by a Council of Ministers and a Royal Advisory Council.

Legislative functions are handled by the National Assembly. The assembly has 151 members, of which 101 are popularly elected; the remainder are monastic representatives, or appointed by the king.

History. Little is known of Bhutan's early history. In the 1500's Tibetans conquered the Mongol tribes that inhabited the land and placed it under the spiritual authority of the Dalai Lama of Tibet. In the 1700's China conquered Tibet and assumed control over Bhutan jointly with the Dalai Lama, but the country actually was governed by local tribal chieftains.

In 1774, after several raids by Bhutanese hill tribesmen on British India, the English East India Company forced Bhutan to grant it trading privileges through the important Himalayan passes that Bhutan controlled. But the raids continued, and in 1865 British troops subdued the hill tribesmen and annexed Bhutan's eastern region.

In 1885, after years of feuding among tribal chieftains, one leader, Ugyen Wangchuk, gained dominance over all the tribes. He cooperated with the British and by 1907 established himself as the maharaja of Bhutan. During the early 1900's China tried unsuccessfully to reassert control over the country, but in 1910 an Anglo-Bhutanese treaty recognized Bhutan's sovereignty. Its foreign affairs were to be managed by Britain, which also agreed to pay compensation for the territory annexed in 1865. Bhutan remained largely isolated from the rest of the world for half a century. In 1949 India agreed to assume Britain's responsibilities in Bhutan.

The Chinese Communist conquest of Tibet in 1950 greatly increased Bhutan's strategic importance to China and India. Bhutan in recent years has begun to assert its independence a bit more strongly. It joined the United Nations in 1971, and in 1985 was a founding member of the South Asian Association for Regional Cooperation. In 1984 Bhutan opened talks with China in order to define their border.

Brunei

The land and people. Brunei is split into two separate sections by an offshoot of the Malaysian state of Sarawak. The western and larger section consists of the districts of Belait, Tutong, and Brunei and Muara. In the east is the district of Temburong.

Much of the land is rugged and hilly. The land is drained by the Belait, Tutong, Brunei, and Temburong rivers. Much of the land in these river valleys is swampy, and little of Brunei is suitable for cultivation. Rainfall averages about 150 inches per year, with coastal areas receiving less, and inland areas receiving up to 200 inches.

About two-thirds of the people are Malays, and there is a large minority of Chinese. There are small minorities of native peoples and of Indians. Most of the people live in the coastal areas, especially around the oil centers of Seria and Kuala Belait.

Economy. Brunei's economy is overwhelmingly dominated by the exploitation of oil and natural gas resources. As a result, Brunei has the highest per capita income in east Asia, and among the highest in the world. Current government objectives emphasize the development of nonpetroleum industries in recognition of the fact that Brunei's petroleum reserves are expected to run out about the year 2015.

Government. Although Brunei has a constitution, much of it has been suspended. The head of state is the sultan, and he holds complete authority over the country. He is assisted by a Council of Ministers.

History. Very little is known of the early history of Brunei. There were early contacts with both China and India, and through the latter Brunei's rulers were converted to Islam. By the beginning of the 16th century, the Brunei sultanate controlled all of the island of Borneo as well as a part of what is now the Philippines.

In 1600 the Portuguese established a trading post at Bandar Seri Begawan,

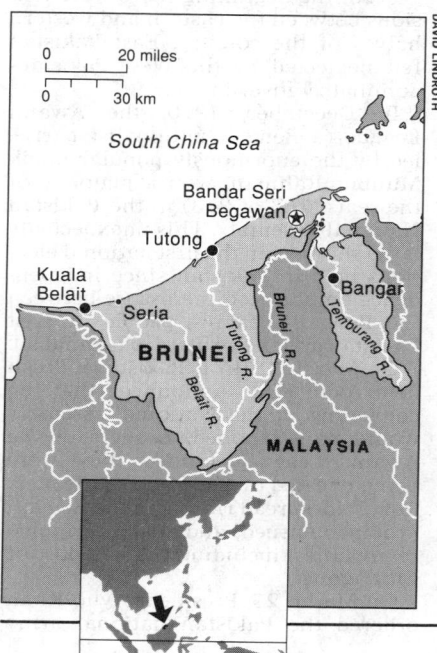

Brunei

Official name: *Brunei Darussalam*
Area: *2235 sq. mi., 5789 sq. km.*
Type of government: *Sultanate*
Head of state: *Sultan and Yang Dipertuan, Sir Muda Hassanal Bolkiah Mu'izzaddin Waddaulah*
Population: *268,000 (1989 est.)*
Population growth rate: *2.3%*
Capital and largest city: *Bandar Seri Begawan (Pop., 1985 est., 119,000)*
Languages: *Malay (official), English, Chinese*
Religion: *Muslim*
Ethnic groups: *Malay 65%, Chinese 20%*
Literacy: *95%*
Life expectancy: *71 years (1987)*
Currency: *Brunei dollar*
Per capita GNP: *$15,400 (1986)*
Exports: *$2.2 billion (1986)*
Imports: *$625 million (1986)*

and over the next two centuries the city became a center of European trade for the area.

During the 18th and 19th centuries, Brunei lost more and more territory to European traders and adventurers. Finally, in 1888, the sultan appealed for aid to the British, who responded by making Brunei a protectorate.

The discovery of oil in 1929 increased the importance of Brunei. In 1959 a new constitution was promulgated; it returned full executive power to the sultan. In 1963 the sultan declined an invitation to join the new Malaysian federation.

In 1979 Brunei and Great Britain signed an agreement granting Brunei total independence. On January 1, 1984, that agreement went into effect.

Burma

The land. Burma is a diamond-shaped country with a long, narrow extension stretching southward into the Malay peninsula. The Tenasserim coast, in the south, and the Arakan coast, to the north, are rocky and steep. The central coast is shallow and filled with sandbars. Many small islands dot the long coastline.

Along the coast the densely forested Arakan mountain range rises more than 10,000 feet and extends into a region of hills in the country's northwest corner. Central Burma is a low basin through which flows the Chindwin and Irrawaddy rivers and, east of a low range of hills, the Sittang River. In the east is the hilly Shan Plateau, about 3000 feet in elevation, threaded by the Salween River and its tributaries.

The Irrawaddy River dominates Burma's terrain. It rises in the far north and flows southward for approximately 1400 miles before entering the Gulf of Martaban at the head of the Andaman Sea. It is navigable for about 875 miles inland, and it leaves a deposit of rich soil in its valley and delta. The delta is 150 miles wide and extends about 180 miles inland from the sea.

Burma has a tropical climate. Average winter temperatures range from 70°F along the coast, where humidity is very high, to 60°F in the interior. Summer temperatures rise above 100°F. In southwestern and northeastern Burma, monsoons are common and rainfall is generally heavy—about 80 inches a year in the northeast and up to 200 inches in the southwest. Tropical forests cover these wet regions. Central Burma is a treeless, grassy plain that receives only about 25 inches of rainfall a year.

The people. The people of Burma are divided into a number of traditional tribal and language groups. The dominant people are the Burmans, who speak Burmese, a Sino-Tibetan language, and use an alphabet similar to

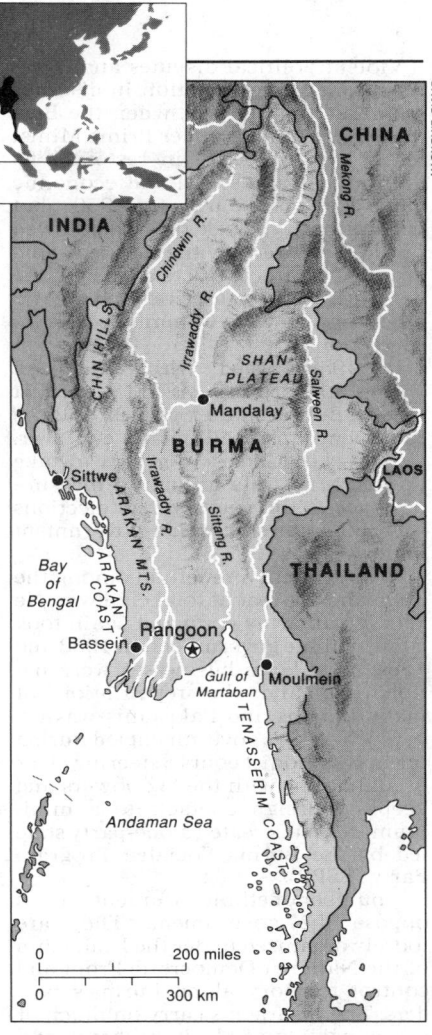

Burma

Official name: *Socialist Republic of the Union of Burma*
Area: *261,217 sq. mi., 676,552 sq. km.*
Type of government: *Socialist Republic*
Head of state: *U Saw Maung*
Population: *40,452,000 (1989 est.)*
Population growth rate: *2.1%*
Capital and largest city: *Rangoon (Pop., 1987 est., 2,600,000)*
Language: *Burmese*
Religions: *Buddhist 85%, Muslim and others 15%*
Ethnic groups: *Burman 68%, Shan 9%, Karen 7%*
Literacy: *66%*
Life expectancy: *53 years (1987)*
Currency: *Kyat*
Per capita GNP: *$200 (1986)*
Exports: *$407 million (1987)*
Imports: *$627 million (1987)*

that of Sanskrit. The larger minority groups are the Chin, Shan, and Kachin peoples of the hill regions, and the Karen of lower Burma.

Buddhism is the major religion of Burma, although there is also an active Muslim minority.

Population is densest in the river valleys. Seventy-five percent of the population is rural. Rangoon is the largest city in Burma. Other important cities include Mandalay, Pegu, Bassein, and Moulmein.

Economy. Burma is a country with rich natural resources. Over half of the country is forested, and there are valuable stands of teak and ironwood. Burma's mineral riches include petroleum, lignite, lead, tin, tungsten, copper, iron, nickel, zinc, silver, gold, jade, amber, and rubies. All are mined to some extent but none has been fully exploited.

Burma's most valuable resource is its soil, which is extremely fertile in the river valleys. Agriculture employs about 70 percent of the population. The chief crop is rice, which is grown on approximately two-thirds of the cultivated land, mostly in the rich, moist delta region. Peanuts, sugar, sesame, cotton, and tobacco are also raised. Fishing is important along the coast.

Most of Burma's few industries are concerned with the processing of agricultural goods or the extraction of such natural resources as timber and oil. Light industry has increased recently, but Burma's economic planning is geared mainly toward the increased exploitation of agriculture and petroleum. Industry has been heavily nationalized since the early 1960's.

Burma's exports consist mainly of rice, teak, and ores and metals. Most of these exports go to Indonesia, Singapore, Sri Lanka, and Japan. Burma's imports consist mainly of finished goods and machinery. One-third of these imports come from Japan, while China, the United States, and Great Britain also contribute significantly. A large black market provides goods that are unavailable in official markets.

Government. Burma is a one-party socialist state. A 489-member People's Assembly is elected to a four-year term. The assembly elects the members of the chief policy-making body, the Council of State, as well as the Council of Ministers, which is responsible for the administration of the government. The head of state is the chairman of the Council of State, and the head of government is the head of the Council of Ministers.

History. The easy migration and invasion routes along the Sittang and Irrawaddy river valleys have helped make Burma's history turbulent. The earliest known settlers were the Pyu, probably a Tibetan people, who had moved into the region by the late 600's. In the late 700's a more powerful people, the Mon, settled in the delta region of lower Burma; in the 800's they conquered the Pyu.

The Burmans. The Burman people immigrated from northeastern Tibet during the 900's. They came in such large numbers that they were able to occupy all of central and southern Burma and parts of Thailand, and they soon dominated the entire region. At first the Burmans were divided into many small clans, but in the mid-1000's one clan chieftain, Anawrahta, united all the Burmans.

The Burmans conquered the Mon and adopted much of their culture, which focused on warfare and religion. The king was deified, and many great temples were built in their fortresslike capital, Pagan, in central Burma.

In 1287 Pagan fell to the Mongols, and the empire collapsed. The Mongols took over central Burma, the Mon reestablished their southern kingdom, and a newly powerful people, the Shan, established a group of states in the northeastern hills. The Shan led the Burmans in resistance to the Mongols and drove the Mongols out of the region in the early 1300's.

In the 1750's a powerful Burman dynasty arose under Alaungpaya, who reunited the Shan, Burman, and Mon kingdoms and conquered portions of India and Thailand. The destruction wrought by centuries of violence, and the stagnation created by an archaic system of government, weakened the country, and it was unable to meet a strong challenge from British merchant interests.

British rule. Between 1824 and 1826 the British drove the Burmese out of northeastern India and occupied the Arakan and Tenasserim coasts. The Burmese refused to grant trading privileges to the British, and by 1886 the British had conquered all Burma and made it a part of British India.

Burma's economy and government were modernized under British rule. Burma became the world's leading exporter of teakwood, and the Irrawaddy delta became one of the world's leading producers of rice. Missionaries, especially from the United States, began working in Burma's upland areas, and many of the hill peoples were converted to Christianity and brought into contact with the modern world.

Many Burmese resented the British and the Indians, who had come to play a prominent role in economic affairs. After World War I a wave of nationalism led to strikes, riots, and, in 1931, to a brief but large-scale rebellion. The British introduced democratic forms of government in the 1920's and 1930's, and in 1937 granted a constitution separating Burma from India and permitting some self-government.

By the beginning of World War II, Burma had a prosperous economy and a fairly stable political system, but Japanese occupation in 1942 and British reconquest in 1944 caused great economic destruction.

Independence. After the war a group of nationalists who had organized an anti-Japanese army and a political network during the occupation led a drive for independence. As the Anti-Fascist Peoples Freedom League (AFPFL) they emerged as the dominant political party after the British granted Burma its independence in 1948.

Violent political disputes and tribal rebellions kept the nation in disorder from 1948 until 1952, when the Burmese government, under Prime Minister U Nu, succeeded in restoring its authority. Some social and economic gains were made during the 1950's, but corruption and lack of skills slowed progress. Moreover, the national government was too weak to cope with the demands of the minorities for greater autonomy or with Communist-led insurrections.

In 1958, faced with dissension within the ruling AFPFL, conflict among Burma's other parties, and the imminence of rebellion and civil war, U Nu asked General Ne Win to take power. Army rule brought a measure of peace to the country, and elections in 1960 restored civilian government under U Nu.

In 1962, with a rebellion among the Shan and a threat of total civil war, Ne Win led an army coup and again took control of the government. In 1963 and 1964 most large businesses were nationalized and the repatriation of many Indians and Pakistanis was ordered. Ne Win's government led Burma on an isolationist course, steering clear of affiliations with the big powers and keeping foreign contacts to a minimum. Ne Win created a one-party state led by the Burma Socialist Program Party (BSPP).

A number of ethnic insurgent groups oppose the government. They are loosely organized under the leadership of the National Democratic Front and control territory along Burma's borders. The insurgents carry on much of the smuggling of black market goods, and are also greatly responsible for the drug production in the area known as the Golden Triangle, the region where the Thai, Lao, and Burmese borders meet.

In 1988 Ne Win resigned from leadership of the BSPP, citing a need for economic and political change. However, a hardline conservative, Saw Maung, assumed control of the country, taking the leadership of the BSPP and the presidency for himself.

Cambodia

The land. Cambodia occupies the mountain-rimmed basin of the lower Mekong River. At the center of the basin, only a few feet above sea level, is Tonle Sap, a lake that serves as an overflow basin for the floods of the Mekong. It has an area of about 1000 square miles and a depth of 5 feet during the dry season, but it increases to four times that area and ten times that depth during the rainy season.

Cambodia's highest point, in the Cardamom Mountains along the southwest border of the basin, is only slightly under 6000 feet. Separated from the Cardamoms by a narrow lowland corridor in the northwest are the Dangrek Mountains, which rim the basin on the north. East of the basin, the Moi plateau rises to between 1500 and 4000 feet.

Cambodia has a tropical climate, with rainy summers and dry winters. Year-round temperatures range from 70°F to 100°F, and the humidity is high. An average of 60 inches of rain a year falls in the basin, and the mountains receive about 80 inches a year.

The people. Cambodia's population is quite homogeneous. Most of the people are Khmers, or native Cambodians. They are Theravada Buddhists and speak Khmer, or Cambodian. There are minorities of Vietnamese, Chinese, and Chams, and some small tribal groups in the hills.

Cambodia (Kampuchea)

Official name: *People's Republic of Kampuchea*

Area: *69,898 sq. mi., 181,035 sq. km.*

Type of government: *Communist*

Head of state: *President of the Council of State, Heng Samrin*

Head of government: *Prime minister, Hun Sen*

Population: *6,838,000 (1989 est.)*

Population growth rate: *2.3%*

Capital and largest city: *Phnom Penh (Pop., 1985 est., 650,000)*

Languages: *Khmer, French*

Religion: *Theravada Buddhism 95%*

Ethnic groups: *Khmer 90%, Chinese 5%*

Literacy: *48%*

Life expectancy: *47 years (1987)*

Currency: *Riel*

Per capita GNP: *$159 (1975)*

Exports: *$3.2 million (1985)*

Imports: *$27.6 million (1985)*

Population is concentrated along the Mekong River and around the shores of Tonle Sap.

Economy. The Cambodian economy has been in a shambles since the beginning of civil war in the early 1970's. Until then, Cambodia had a self-sufficient economy, producing enough rice and other agricultural products to be a net exporter of food.

Agriculture is still the backbone of the economy though at much reduced levels. The principal products are rice, rubber, cotton, tobacco, pepper, beans, and kapok. The Tonle Sap and the Gulf of Thailand yield large catches of fish.

Cambodia's principal natural resource is its rich soil, but valuable hardwood forests, high-grade iron ore deposits, and phosphate deposits are also important.

Even before the onset of war, Cambodia had little industry, though a beginning was being made. Tobacco, rubber, lumber, textile, and food processing plants were being built. Since 1975 some of the plants that were destroyed have been rebuilt.

Foreign trade has remained at a very low level. Cambodia's main exports are rubber, rice, timber, pepper, and semiprecious stones. Imports include food, medicine, machinery, and military equipment. Most trade is with Vietnam and the Comecon countries.

Government. Cambodia has two governments. One, the People's Republic of Kampuchea, is in actual control of the country, but it is recognized by few international organizations. It consists of a seven-member Council of State, a 16-member Council of Ministers, and a 117-member National Assembly. The head of state is the president of the Council of State.

The other government, Democratic Kampuchea, is a government in exile; it is recognized by and is a member of the United Nations. Democratic Kampuchea supports a guerrilla movement that has had little success.

History. Cambodia's history extends back at least as far as the 100's A.D., when the Kingdom of Funan, in southern Cambodia, was established. It gained power over territory in present-day Thailand, Malaya, Vietnam, and Laos. During the 500's, the kingdom of the Chenla, to the north, overthrew the Funan Empire.

By about 800, the Khmers, inhabitants of southern Cambodia who may have been descended from Indians, united with the Cham, an Indonesian people of the northern Malay peninsula. They conquered the Chenla and established an empire centered at Angkor, on the plain northeast of Tonle Sap. Their culture was predominantly Indian and their religion similar to Hinduism.

For the next 400 years Khmer god-kings ruled an empire that included large areas of Southeast Asia. Their rice-growing civilization was quite advanced, and evidence remains of great temples, roads, irrigation projects, and public buildings at Angkor, including the magnificent Temple of Angkor Wat. Khmer power declined during the 1300's. In 1431 the Siamese conquered Angkor, and the Khmer kings retreated to the region near Phnom Penh.

During succeeding decades, the Khmers fought several disastrous wars with their former subjects, the Cham, the Thais, and the Vietnamese, and lost much of their territory. By the mid-1800's, when French colonists began to settle in Indochina, Cambodia was a minor state plagued by dynastic disputes and in danger of being divided between the Siamese and the Vietnamese.

French control. In 1863 France made Cambodia a protectorate. Except for preventing its partition, the French generally ignored Cambodia. They fostered little social or economic change and allowed the Cambodian monarchy to continue to function. During the 1930's Cambodian nationalism began to grow, and it turned into anti-French feeling during World War II, when Vichy France allowed Japan to use bases in Cambodia and permitted Thailand to occupy some Cambodian territory.

In 1945 Japan briefly took direct control of the Cambodian government, but King Norodom Sihanouk proclaimed his country's independence. In 1953 the French, having allowed Cambodia complete internal self-government after the war, turned control of the military over to the Cambodians. In 1954 Vietnamese Communist forces invaded Cambodia, joining anti-French guerrillas who had been active there since 1945. A Geneva conference held late in the year ended the fighting, and the troops were withdrawn.

Independence. In 1955 King Sihanouk abdicated in favor of his father and assumed the title of prince. He consolidated the nation's political strength and founded a political party, the People's Socialist Community. In 1960, when Sihanouk's father died, the prince was elected chief of state. He was chosen to lead a council to act as regent for his mother.

The country concentrated on social and economic development and remained at peace despite violent conflicts raging in neighboring Southeast Asian nations. In the early 1960's, however, when the Vietnam War intensified, Cambodia feared for its safety and sought international guarantees of its neutrality.

Although Cambodia did not become directly involved in the Vietnam War, for five years it was ravaged by a civil war between government forces, backed by the United States and South Vietnam, and the United National Cambodian Front, supported by North Vietnam and China.

In 1975 Sihanouk, who had been ousted by General Lon Nol in 1970, came out of exile in Beijing to lead the Khmer Rouge in a Communist invasion of Phnom Penh, which fell to him on April 17.

But he soon lost power to Pol Pot, the prime minister of the new government, who directed mass evacuations of cities and towns as the nation's population was set to work in the fields and clearing forests. An extraordinary policy of isolation tried to hide from the world the facts of forced labor, mass executions, and the near total destruction of culture, education, and civilization that ensued.

The Vietnam-backed Kampuchean National United Front for National

TENS OF THOUSANDS OF REFUGEES *have fled the turmoil in Cambodia since 1975. Many live in neighboring Thailand in camps run by one of the antigovernment factions.*

CHAUVEL/SYGMA

Salvation drove Pol Pot into exile when it captured Phnom Penh on January 7, 1978. A new government headed by Heng Samrin was formed; it maintained its power with the assistance of Vietnamese troops.

A government in exile, led by Sihanouk, Khieu Samphan, and Son Sann, the leaders of the three largest guerrilla movements, supports a guerrilla army in Cambodia.

In 1988 peace talks were held between the Cambodian government and the rebel coalition. The Vietnamese, as well as members of the Association of South East Asian Nations, also participated, but the talks ended without any real progress being made.

China

Republic of China
See Taiwan

People's Republic of China

The land. China is an immense country, and only the Soviet Union and Canada are larger in area. Mainland China's length from east to west is approximately the same as that of the United States, and its range from north to south is equivalent to that from Puerto Rico to Labrador.

The huge area of mainland China is divided into 21 provinces, five autonomous regions, and two municipalities —Beijing, the capital, and Shanghai. The autonomous regions are more than administrative units. Each of the five—Guangxi-Zhuang, Tibet, Xinjiang-Uygur, Ningxia-Hui, and Inner Mongolia—contains a majority of non-Chinese people, and each has a history and culture different from China's.

Regions. Geographically, it is conventional to divide China into five regions—China Proper, Manchuria, Tibet, Xinjiang, and Mongolia. China Proper, the region south of the Great Wall and east of Tibet, occupies a third of the land. It is the geographical and historical core of the country, containing the bulk of the population and the roots of Chinese civilization in the Huang He (Yellow River) valley.

The other four regions comprise what is often called Outer China. Manchuria, northeast of China Proper, is more sparsely populated and contains rich mineral deposits. Tibet, in the southwest, lies high in the Himalayas and has a very small population. Xinjiang, in the northwest, is arid and inhabited mainly by Uygur peoples. The Mongolian region, Inner Mongolia, north of China Proper, is arid and peopled primarily by Mongols.

China's provinces serve as administrative subdivisions; some provinces include parts of two major regions. The provinces and the regions also have distinctive cultures with recognizable dialects, if not individual languages, and customs, social patterns, and traditions that exist independently within the larger framework of Chinese culture.

Highlands dominate China's terrain. High mountains thrusting eastward from the southwest include the Himalayas and their foothills.

These mountain systems and the high, barren plateau of Tibet in their center form the world's most formidable land barrier, separating the Hindu civilization of South Asia from the Chinese civilization of East Asia. The eastern edge of these mountains also contains the sources of China's two great rivers, the Yangtze and the Huang He.

Between this mountainous mass and a northern spur, the towering Tien Shan in Xinjiang, is the Taklimakan desert. Along the northern rim of China are the Ordos desert and the eastern fringe of the Gobi desert, bound on the east by the Greater Khingan range, which marks the western edge of Manchuria.

China Proper and Manchuria are crisscrossed by less formidable highlands that follow two major sets of intersecting structural areas, one trending northeast to southwest and the other intersecting it east to west.

The northeast-southwest axis is marked in the east by the Fujian Massif, the Shandong and Liaodong peninsulas, and the Manchurian highlands bordering Korea in the northeast. The central portion of this axis is formed by the Greater Khingan range in Manchuria and the Wutai and Luliang ranges in Shanxi province farther south.

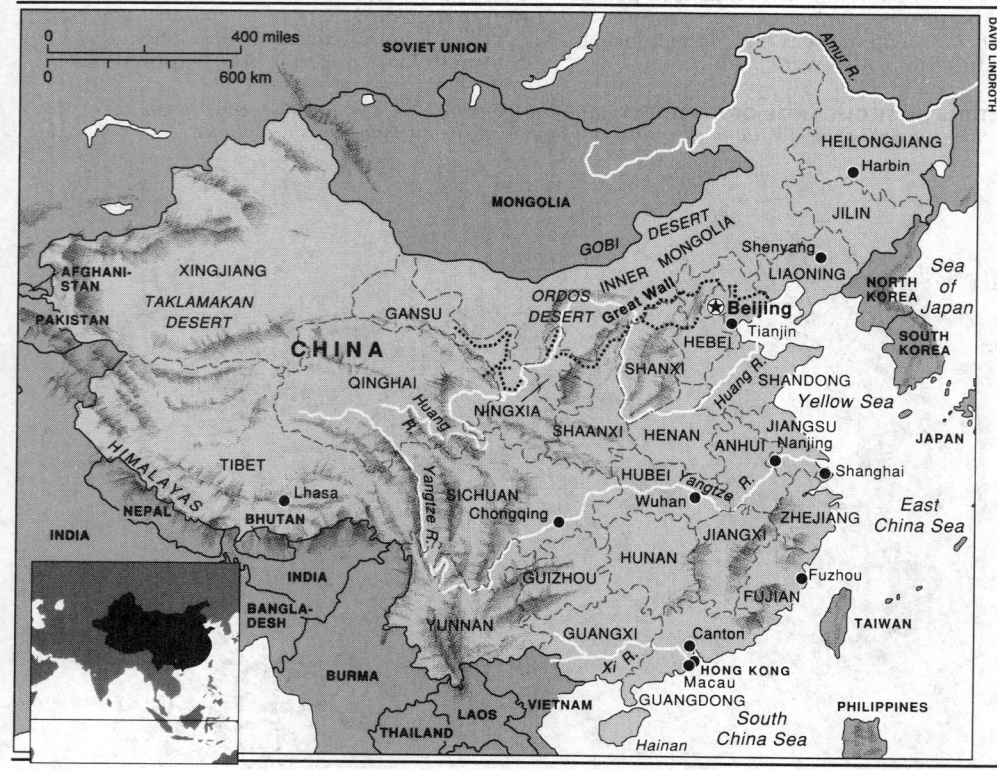

DAVID LINDROTH

China

Official name: *People's Republic of China*
Area: *3,705,390 sq. mi., 9,596,960 sq. km.*
Type of government: *People's republic*
Head of state: *President, Li Xiannian*
Head of government: *Premier of the State Council, Li Peng*
Population: *1,101,742,000 (1989 est.)*
Population growth rate: *1.3%*
Capital: *Beijing (Peking) (Pop., 1986 est., 4,860,000)*
Largest city: *Shanghai (Pop., 1986 est., 6,980,000)*
Languages: *Mandarin (official), Shanghai, Canton, dialects*
Religions: *Buddhist, Muslim, Lamaist, Christian*
Ethnic group: *Han Chinese 94%*
Literacy: *70%*
Life expectancy: *68 years (1987)*
Currency: *Yuan*
Per capita GNP: *$280*
Exports: *$31.1 billion (1986)*
Imports: *$43.2 billion (1986)*

This line is a major physical and cultural division of eastern Asia. To the west of it elevations are from 3000 to 6000 feet higher than to its east. The west is arid, the east is humid; the western economy is based on pastoral activities, the eastern on sedentary agriculture.

The series of east-west trending chains is represented at the far north by the Lesser Khingan mountains, at the southern edge of Mongolia by the Yin Shan, and in the far south by the Nan Ling mountains, a series of hills and low mountains between the Yangtze and the Xi rivers. By far the most important mountains of the east-west axis are those of the Qin Ling, which bisect China Proper.

The Qin Ling has a physical and cultural significance similar to that of the north-south Khingan divide. South China, below these mountains, is generally warm and humid, whereas north China tends to be cold and dry.

China's few major lowlands and plateaus lie in China Proper and Manchuria, among the intersecting lines of highlands. In the northeast the Manchurian Plain's grasslands contain some of China's most fertile soils.

The flat and fertile North China Plain is essentially a giant compound delta of the Huang He, the Huai, and the Yangtze rivers. The 100,000-square-mile Yangtze Basin is rich with alluvial soils. The mountain-ringed Sichuan basin on the upper Yangtze River includes about 75,000 square miles of rolling terrain.

The most important region in south China, the Canton lowlands, the compound delta of the Xi, Bei, and Zhu (Pearl) rivers, is a key agricultural, industrial, and commercial center.

Rivers. Almost all of China's rivers, which are concentrated in the eastern portion of the country, flow east or south toward the sea. The most important in the south is the Xi, formed by streams flowing from the eastern Tibetan foothills.

The Yangtze rises in the eastern Tibetan Plateau and twists some 3200 miles through south-central China, passing through deeply etched gorges in Sichuan and emptying into the East China Sea at Shanghai.

The Huang He rises near the Yangtze and flows north along a winding course, making a great bend northward around the Ordos desert and on eastward between Shanxi and Henan provinces. It empties into the Bo Hai gulf, an inlet of the Yellow Sea.

Both the Huang He and the Yangtze are subject to frequent and vicious floods and sudden changes of course, but both supply the water and the soil to raise food for the huge concentration of people in their valleys.

Climate. China's climate is determined by the winter and summer monsoons. Cold dry air from Siberia moves across China in the winter, and hot moist winds from the Pacific flow inland during the summer, bringing the heavy rains.

Most of China lies in the temperate zone, but climate varies extensively from region to region. North China and Manchuria have long, severe winters. Rainfall is under 20 inches a year, and the growing season is less than 200 days. But farther south, the growing season lengthens, ultimately permitting year-round agriculture in the southernmost parts of China. Precipitation also increases greatly, averaging 40 to 80 inches annually.

The people. China contains approximately one-quarter of the world's people. About 90 percent of the people live in the eastern third of China. The overall population density of China is about 293 people per square mile, but this figure can vary greatly, from near zero in portions of the west, to over 2000 people per square mile along the coast. About 20 percent of the population live in urban areas.

Although many ethnic groups make up China's population, more than 90 percent of the people are of the Han group, the people commonly considered "Chinese." The Han have great cultural unity and share the same written language, but they speak many regional dialects of Chinese. The Beijing dialect, or Mandarin, is the national language; it is taught in the schools throughout China. The Chinese language is written in ideographs, or "characters," that carry the same meaning no matter how one pronounces the word or phrase they represent.

About 6 percent of China's people are non-Han Chinese. They belong to more than 50 ethnic groups that live in the areas surrounding China Proper. The Zhuang, a Thai-speaking people in southeastern China, are the largest minority. The Yi, also in the south, are another large group. Along the western and northwestern frontiers Tibetans, Uygurs, and Mongols are in the majority, and the Manchu people are in the northeast.

The Chinese religious tradition is an amalgam of primitive animistic beliefs linked to the agricultural nature of Chinese society and to the literate religious traditions of Confucianism, Taoism, and Buddhism. Confucianism provides the philosophic, moral, and ethical underpinnings of Chinese society and culture; however, aspects of Confucianism have religious overtones for the average Chinese.

Economy. China traditionally has been an agricultural land, and this remains true today, despite considerable industrialization since the advent of the Communist regime in 1949.

Until 1979 the government maintained strict control over the economy. Agriculture was collectivized and industrial output centrally planned. Following the death of Mao in 1976, the new leadership followed a more pragmatic approach to the economy, allowing more individual initiative. A long-range 20-year plan provides for a 10-year period of transition to a less centralized economy, and calls for, among other things, the development of light industry, tourism, agriculture, energy, and a rising standard of living.

Natural resources. Exploration and development of China's mineral resources was not undertaken on a large scale until the 1950's and 1960's.

CHINA IS STILL A DEVELOPING NATION. *Despite the recent advances in industrialization in many parts of China, much of the country is still relatively undeveloped and rural, and and much of the labor is still done manually.*

China has large reserves of coal, enough to last some 400 years at present usage rates. Oil is found in Manchuria, Xinjiang, and in the central Yangtze basin, as well as along the continental shelf. In 1986 China produced 911 million barrels of oil, making it the sixth largest producer of oil in the world.

Agriculture. Poor climate, rough terrain, and inadequate soil or water prohibit farming in a large part of China. With an estimated 270 million acres, or about 11 percent of China's total area, under cultivation, there is still less than half an acre of farmland per person.

Starting in 1979, some of the farms that were collectivized in the 1950's were returned to family control under the new program of economic liberalization. Households contracted with the government to produce a certain amount of a crop. Anything above that amount could be sold either to the government at a higher price or on the open market.

Agricultural production rose an average of 7.9 percent per year from 1979 to 1983, in contrast to a rise of about only 3 percent per year from the 1950's through most of the 1970's. Though much of the credit for this rise must be given to the new economic reforms, and to new pricing policies, some credit must go to earlier state investment in pesticides, fertilizer, farm equipment, and large-scale works such as irrigation projects.

China's chief crops are wheat, raised chiefly in north China and Manchuria, and rice, grown mainly in the Yangtze basin and south China. Other important crops include barley, millet, kaoliang, soybeans, cotton, tobacco, and tea. There is little livestock raising, but there is some fishing off the coasts and in the rivers.

Industry. In 1984 the government brought about sweeping changes in the industrial sector. A move was made away from centralized control of all manufacturing toward more control by local management. The government will continue, as it has in the past, to provide policy and long-range planning for some products. For many other products, however, it appears that the government intends to let the marketplace regulate production.

Trade. Foreign trade historically played a small role in the Chinese economy. Because of a desire for self-sufficiency and a shortage of export commodities, until the 1980's the Chinese adopted a conservative policy toward foreign trade, using it primarily to obtain technology.

Recently, however, trade restrictions with the West have loosened considerably. Special economic areas have been set up in which foreign investment is encouraged.

Principal exports include petroleum, light industrial goods, chemicals, and agricultural goods. Imports include grain, consumer goods, textiles, and advanced technology. Ninety percent of China's trade is with noncommunist countries, principally Hong Kong, Japan, and the United States.

Government. The government established by Communist China in 1949 and embodied in a constitution in 1954 is a people's republic, which is democratic in form but dominated by the Communist Party.

Supreme legislative and executive power is vested nominally in an elected National People's Congress. The congress chooses a standing committee to act for it between sessions. The congress also elects a state council, led by a prime minister, to administer the government, and a chairman of the government, who acts as head of state.

The actual seat of power is the Chinese Communist Party's Political Bureau, or Politburo, of the party's Central Committee. It determines national policy, and its chairman is usually the key figure in the government. Only party-supported candidates are elected to public office, although party membership is not required for election. Most important government posts are held by party leaders.

History. China has a long continuous history. The remains of prehistoric "Peking man," found in north China, date back as far as 1 million years. The valley of the Yellow River on the North China Plain was the site of one of the earliest human societies, which developed its own, unique culture.

First dynasties. Heroic legends tell of a Hsia dynasty founded by an emperor Yü in 2205 B.C. There is no concrete evidence of its existence, however, and the first documented Chinese dynasty is the Shang, or Yin. Exact dates of ancient Chinese events are often disputed, but the Shang dynasty was founded in 1766 or 1523 B.C. on the North China Plain.

The Chou. During the Chou dynasty (about 1027–256 B.C.) a loose confederation of feudal states was organized. Wealth was based on land ownership and the economy was based on agriculture. Warrior nobles formed the upper class, and village peasant society was communal.

Agricultural and military technology improved, canals were built, a monetary economy developed, population grew, contact was made with western Asian countries, and trade prospered. Art, music, and literature all flourished, but the Chou is known primarily for its philosophers.

Three of the most important philosophers who founded schools of thought between 600 and 300 B.C. were Lao Tzu, Confucius, and Hsüntzu. Lao Tzu, who was probably several writers, taught that there is a natural order to the universe, of which man is a part. Confucius and his student and interpreter Mencius laid the foundation for much of China's subsequent social order, moral code, and political development.

CHINESE DYNASTIES

Hsia (Xia)	c 22nd–16th centuries B.C.
Shang (Yin)	c 16th century–c 1027 B.C.
Chou (Zhou)	c 1027–256 B.C.
Ch'in (Qin)	221–206 B.C.
Han	206 B.C.–220 A.D.
Three Kingdoms	220–265
Tsin (Chin)	265–420
Sui	581–618
T'ang	618–907
Five Dynasties and Ten Kingdoms	907–960
Sung	960–1279
Yüan	1271–1368
Ming	1368–1644
Ch'ing (Manchu)	1644–1912

Confucius taught that a perfect moral order can be realized if one follows certain norms of social behavior (li) set forth by ancient sages. His idea of a well ordered, well educated, and mutually cooperative society stood as the Chinese ideal for many centuries. Hsüntzu laid the basis for the "legalist" school of thought, which provided the philosophical foundation for an authoritarian state led by an absolute ruler and ordered by strict laws.

The legalist doctrine found followers when the Ch'in conquered the Chou and established leadership over the Chou subject states. This semibarbarous, authoritarian state (221–206 B.C.), following its unification of the formerly warring states, contributed to agricultural prosperity through the construction of an elaborate irrigation system. Its strong central government permitted the growth of social stability and military strength. The Ch'in dynasty, which gave China its name, extended Chinese rule south to modern Canton and west across the Plateau of Yunnan, founding the first Chinese empire. The Ch'in ruler soon after began construction of the Great Wall to keep out invaders from the north, the only exposed frontier. Political chaos followed his death (210 B.C.). The eventual succession of Liu Pang marked the beginning of the long-lasting native Han dynasty (206 B.C.–220 A.D.).

The Han. The Han emperors built an empire that became one of the world's greatest states. Political order was maintained by the concession of local rule to outlying regions of the empire. Foreign invasions were thwarted, and during the expansionist reign (141–87 B.C.) of Wu Ti, the empire absorbed most of the territory that is now part of modern China.

Under the later Han emperors, who introduced state control over parts of the economy, China grew prosperous.

Public works as well as cultural and educational achievements marked the period.

The dynasty was interrupted (9–23 A.D.) by the revolutionary rule of Wang Mang. Concerned about social and economic inequality, he championed land reform and the nationalization of the great landed estates.

The Han dynasty was restored, but tensions between the ruling class and the peasants increased. Peasant rebellions and fighting between rival lords were frequent in the 100's A.D. Professional armies moved into local areas to keep the peace and soon came under the control of the local lords.

Three leaders of these armies grew to such power that they divided the empire into three semi-independent kingdoms—the Wei, the Wu, and the Shu Han. Imperial power disintegrated, and the last Han emperor died in 220.

The six dynasties. For the next 370 years China was merely a collection of petty states, most of them at war with one another, and none able to dominate the others. The period was known as the era of the "six dynasties," as six houses in succession managed to gain the throne, but none actually ruled China.

In the 300's and 400's nomads conquered China's northern frontier region, although the natural mountain and desert barriers prevented them from penetrating farther. Many northern Chinese migrated southward, and during the 300's and 400's they spread their culture into Southeast Asia.

While military invasion from the north disrupted China, the spread of Buddhism, the Indian religion, altered China's traditional social base. Confucianism had fallen from favor because of the failure of the Han dynasty, which had been built on it. Taoism also grew in strength and soon rivaled Confucianism in importance.

During the brief Sui dynasty (581–618) the central government was restored to its former power, the Great Wall was rebuilt, the economy was revitalized, and the northern territories were reconquered. In trying to expand Chinese territory the Sui met disastrous defeats at the hands of the Koguryo people of Korea in the north and Turkic tribes in the west. Following these defeats, a rebellion toppled the Sui.

A brief period of turmoil followed the end of the Sui. Li Yüan, a Sui bureaucrat of Chinese and "barbarian" descent, with the support of Turkic tribes from central Asia, became emperor of China in 618, founding the T'ang dynasty (618–907).

The T'ang. The 300-year T'ang era was one of China's most brilliant. In the 600's T'ang rulers consolidated their control of the government and made China's borders secure against further invasion by forming an alliance with the powerful, warlike Uygurs. T'ang government was efficient, economical, and more just to all classes.

ARTS LIKE SCULPTURE *were highly advanced during the T'ang dynasty.*

Agriculture and trade prospered. Chinese thinkers assimilated Buddhism, Taoism, and Confucianism and developed a unified philosophical base for society. Under the T'ang, poetry, painting, sculpture, scholarship, and science flourished and attracted artists and scholars from other lands.

T'ang peace and prosperity were interrupted in the mid-700's by a revolt led by An Lu-shan, a "barbarian" who had the command of some Chinese armies. The uprising resulted in a bloody civil war. Thus weakened, the empire was left open to attack by its neighbors, and the late 700's were marked by invasions by such peoples as the Uygurs and Tibetans.

The Sung. The Sung dynasty (960–1279), which finally won the competition for power in 960, led China into the modern age. Sung leaders reformed the military and reorganized the government by creating a large, well salaried, honest, and efficient civil service. They won the support of the masses by reducing taxes, abolishing the traditional forced labor, providing loans to farmers, and initiating public works projects.

The arts and sciences continued to advance, spurred by the widespread use of printing. The Sung empire was not a strong military state, however. By 1234 the north had fallen before the Mongols, who had begun in the 1100's to conquer an empire that eventually included all of Asia north of India.

The Yüan. In 1260 Kublai, a leader of the Mongols, was elected khan, ruler of the Mongol empire. Eleven years later he proclaimed the Yüan dynasty (1271–1368) in northern China. By 1279 the dynasty controlled the entire country, and China became a subdivision of the Mongol empire. One European adventurer, Marco Polo of Venice, visited Kublai Khan's court, and his reports excited European interest in the unknown empire.

Despite rule by non-Chinese, central China retained its traditional culture and social organization and remained remarkably unified. In the 1300's Chinese antagonism to foreigners sparked rebellions against the Mongols. These

THE GREAT WALL *was constructed in the third century* B.C. *as a protection against invaders. It runs for about 1500 miles across northern China, and averages about 25 feet in height.*

THE AVENUE OF ANIMALS, *statues of, among mythical beasts, lions, camels, elephants, and horses, is part of the Sacred Way, which leads to the tombs where the Ming emperors are buried.*

rebellions, and rivalries among the Mongols themselves, led to the disintegration of the Yüan dynasty in the mid-1300's.

The Chinese leaders of the rebellion against the Mongols competed among themselves for the throne. Chu Yüan-chang, a Buddhist from northwestern China, emerged dominant and in 1368 established himself as the first emperor of the Ming dynasty (1368–1644).

The Ming. By 1382 Ming rulers had driven the Mongols out of China Proper, and by the 1400's they had regained control of all but the western third and the northern fringe of present-day China. In 1421 Yung-lo moved the capital from Nanking, where it had been since the founding of the dynasty, to Beijing, where a walled "forbidden city" became the center of imperial rule.

The Ming emperors proclaimed China supreme in all the world, and indeed China wielded great power throughout Asia. From its Asian neighbors China demanded tribute, emphasizing its preeminence; in return it offered financial aid and military protection. Ming expansion of foreign contacts improved Chinese prosperity and influenced the country's cultural growth. For the first time, large numbers of Christian missionaries and Western merchants visited China.

Largely due to paralyzing internal corruption, diverse opposition to the dynasty surfaced in the early 17th century. In the 1630's a bandit, Li Tzu-ch'eng, gained control of northern China, and his rebellion soon spread. He gained the support of many groups in society, won control of most of China, and soon conquered Beijing.

By the 1640's the Manchus, a non-Chinese people who lived in the region northeast of China Proper, had begun to penetrate China. They joined the government troops in defeating the rebels and then used their position of power to establish the Ch'ing dynasty (1644–1912).

The Ch'ing. Much of the early Ch'ing period was spent in putting down resistance by supporters of the Ming regime and in subduing the non-Chinese neighbors of China Proper and annexing their territory.

By about 1800 the Ch'ing had expanded to the boundaries of present-day China and beyond, to Taiwan in the east, across Mongolia and coastal Siberia in the north, and to Tibet in the west.

The Manchus did not attempt to replace Chinese customs; rather, they continued the political and economic policies of their Ming predecessors, maintaining strict state control over all areas of Chinese life. Chinese culture and scholarship continued to flourish in the traditional pattern through the 1700's.

At the same time, the Western world was beginning to take an active interest in the Far East. European states were beginning to establish trading colonies in the nations near China.

The Portuguese in the 1500's were the first to trade with China; they were followed by the Dutch and the British. The English East India Company established a trading station at Canton in the late 1600's and throughout the 1700's carried on a brisk trade in tea through Canton.

As Western influence began to challenge traditional concepts of Chinese society, Chinese leadership entered a decline. The Ch'ing rulers became mired in fruitless military activity, and their court became riddled with corruption. Prosperity began to wane as the population level began to soar and the traditional economy could not support it.

Western impact. Ch'ing policy confined foreign trade to the one port of Canton, in the south. There foreign traders were only allowed contacts with a licensed monopoly group of Chinese merchants. The British, dissatisfied with the trading conditions, tried to establish diplomatic relations in the 1790's. But the imperial authorities insisted that any country wishing to establish relations with China must accept the status of a tributary state.

By the end of the 1700's, foreign traders found a large Chinese demand for opium and local officials ready to cooperate in smuggling it into China. Efforts to suppress the trade by an able imperial official led to the Opium War in 1839. The British, with complete naval superiority and small parties of Indian troops under British officers, defeated the Chinese armies.

Under the Treaty of Nanking (1842), ending the war, China ceded Hong Kong to Britain and opened five more ports to foreign trade. Later treaties established extraterritoriality (putting foreigners under the jurisdiction of their own consuls, not Chinese laws), the most-favored-nation principle (a concession to one foreign power shared by all), tariff restrictions, and the right of missionaries to work in China.

The result was a system that survived until the 1940's, under which foreigners in China had a privileged position largely exempt from Chinese control. The treaty ports under foreign jurisdiction became the main commercial and industrial centers, and the customs service, from which developed the post office, came under foreign control.

The Manchu regime was further weakened in the mid-1800's by the Taiping rebellion (1850–1864). Led by a religious mystic with the aid of a military officer, a large force of rebels marched toward Beijing conquering the territory along their route.

The Taiping leaders overran large parts of central China and set up a totalitarian state with a distorted Christianity as a religion. The Taiping and later rebellions in northern and western China were suppressed only when local officials raised new armies that remained loyal to their organizers rather than to the central government.

The able officials who rose in this period of crisis realized that China must modernize to survive, but they had to contend with very strong conservatism. After 1860, moreover, the court was dominated by the empress dowager, skilled at intrigue but an extreme conservative and ignorant of the outside world. Thus, attempts at modernization were slow and halfhearted, and often ended when sponsoring officials moved to other positions.

Treaty system. Problems raised by the presence of foreigners worsened. Canton, where most of the Westerners were concentrated, was especially rebellious because of its resentment of the British conquest in the Opium War. Friction between the Cantonese and the foreigners grew so intense that in 1857 and 1858 French and British troops, using the need to protect their interests as an excuse, seized and occupied the city.

In settlement of this conflict, the treaties of Tientsin opened more ports to foreigners, legalized the importation of opium, permitted the establishment of European diplomatic missions at Beijing, allowed missionaries and traders to enter the interior of the country, and exacted further indemnities from the Chinese.

The Ch'ing rulers, giving the matter second thought, refused to admit foreign ambassadors to Beijing. In reprisal, British and French armies stormed Beijing in 1860 and burned the summer palace.

Having thus proved the weakness of the imperial government, the British and French saw an advantage in maintaining a weak dynasty that they could control, and they assisted the Ch'ing rulers in putting down the bloody rebellions throughout the country. The Ch'ing remained on the throne, but they and China were dependent on the Westerners who flooded the once isolated empire after 1860.

The imperial government still made no major attempts to reform its administration or modernize its economy and society, and China continued to be humiliated as it became weaker and more and more subservient to the foreign powers.

Renewed conflict. In 1874 the Ch'ing proved unable to prevent Japan from invading Taiwan. They avoided losing the island only through Western diplomatic maneuvers. In the 1880's France occupied Indochina, part of the traditional Chinese tribute system. In 1887 Portugal was granted Macao, a port near Hong Kong.

Relations with Japan, which had made a rapid transition from its traditional ways to the technological and political sophistication of the 1800's, grew tense. Korea, long a tributary of China, slipped into Japanese control in the 1860's and 1870's, when China did not protest Japan's recognition of Korea as an independent state.

In 1885 both China and Japan agreed to withdraw their troops from Korea, but continuing intrigue and growing Korean nationalism led in 1894 to war between Korea and China and to a Sino-Japanese war.

By early 1895 Japanese forces had all but destroyed China's army and navy. China was forced to recognize Korean independence, cede Taiwan, the Liaotung peninsula, and the Pescadores to Japan, pay a huge indemnity, and open more ports to foreigners.

Reform efforts. In 1894 Dr. Sun Yat-sen (Sun Wen) organized one of the earliest secret revolutionary societies whose goal was the overthrow of the Ch'ing. Students organized "study societies" to develop theories of reform. Philosophers reinterpreted Confucianism to permit modernization and reform within Chinese traditional ideology.

A new style Chinese army was organized under Yuan Shih-k'ai with German instructors, and an officers' training school was established. Its cadets later rose to dominant positions. Chiang Kai-shek went to this school and then to an officers' training course in Japan.

In 1898 the emperor started a program of drastic reforms guided by advisers who were Confucian scholars but who realized the need to modernize. The conservatives rallied around the empress dowager who, with the support of Yuan Shih-k'ai, imprisoned the emperor and reversed the reforms.

The reactionaries who came to power with the defeat of China's attempts at domestic reforms hoped to restore China to its position of isolation. Thus, in 1899, when Italy sought concession of a port, the demand was rejected violently. An antiforeign militia, called the "Righteous and Harmonious Fists," or "Boxers," was organized in eastern China.

The Boxer Rebellion. The Boxer Rebellion in 1900 was the last major uprising against foreign intervention in China. The Boxers, assisted by some imperial army units, besieged the foreign diplomatic quarter in Beijing. The empress dowager declared war on all the major foreign powers, although local officials in south and central China promptly negotiated neutrality for the areas they controlled. An international expedition captured Beijing and the powers imposed further restrictions on Chinese sovereignty.

Republican revolution. By that time a new opposition was developing under leaders educated outside the traditional system. Sun Yat-sen (1865–1925) became the leader of a revolutionary republican movement, winning support from Chinese students in Japan, overseas Chinese communities, and secret societies. He also had some powerful Japanese supporters.

After several unsuccessful attempts, the revolution succeeded in 1911. The Manchu court called on Yuan Shih-k'ai to suppress the uprising. After winning some battles, he then negotiated to join the revolution if he were first made president of the republic. As president, he made himself independent of the parliament in which Sun Yat-sen's Kuomintang Party had a majority, defeated a Kuomintang uprising against him, and finally tried to make himself emperor.

In place of the constitution, which was to have been ratified by the parliament, Yuan ruled under a "constitutional compact," which he announced in 1914 and which gave him a ten-year term as president.

The establishment of the republic did not lessen the financial and political power wielded by foreign nations, however, and Chinese political instability left China even more unprepared to cope with foreign interference. When World War I broke out in 1914, China became the diplomatic and occasionally the military battleground for Russia, Japan, and Germany.

Nor was the war the only source of violence in China. A successful rebellion broke out in 1915 in Yunnan, led by Yuan's opponents in response to his assumption of the title of emperor.

Yuan's death in 1916 left all real power in the hands of local military commanders, and a period of continual civil wars began. The warlords gave first priority to their own power, but otherwise differed greatly.

With China itself divided, the end of World War I also found Manchuria in the hands of Japan and Mongolia under Russian domination. The Versailles Treaty, which ended the war, allowed Japan to retain Shantung, and China refused to sign the document.

At the Washington Conference in 1922, the Allied powers agreed to reconsider their demands for extraterritorial rights, to respect China's territorial integrity, and to assist China in the formation of a stable government. A Sino-Japanese treaty was arranged by which Japan was to withdraw from Shantung.

This official end to foreign intervention came too late, however. No one government led China, and in 1920 the country was plunged into open civil war among the warlords.

Kuomintang. By 1920 the old Confucian order was discredited and parliamentary democracy had failed. The Western democracies seemed to have betrayed their principles by helping Yuan Shih-k'ai to destroy the parliament and by backing Japanese claims on China after World War I. In this situation, Chinese intellectuals were attracted by what the Soviet Union claimed to offer. The Chinese Communist Party was founded in 1921 but, until 1924, it had only a few hundred members.

Also in 1924 a Kuomintang congress met to plan the party's future. It accepted Communists as members and employed Soviet advisers to train members in military and political tactics. Sun Yat-sen died in 1925, and leadership of the Kuomintang passed to Chiang Kai-shek.

With Soviet aid, Chiang suppressed the warlords and gained control of northern China. Soon, however, a split opened between the conservative Nationalists, led by Chiang, and the radicals and Communists. The radicals and Communists established a government at Wuhan, and the Nationalists set up a government at Nanking.

After a brief reconciliation, the two factions split widely apart. In 1927 Mao Tse-tung, a Communist Party leader, organized a peasant uprising in Hunan Province. When the uprising was suppressed, the Communists retreated into the interior and organized an anti-Kuomintang revolutionary army. In June, 1928, Chiang and a purged Kuomintang captured Beijing and proclaimed a single government for the whole of China with its capital at Nanking.

Between 1928 and 1937 the new Kuomintang National government made real though uneven progress in national reconstruction. It had full control only in the lower Yangtze valley. Elsewhere local warlords remained powerful and often challenged the central government. The Japanese seized Manchuria in 1931, fought at Shanghai in 1932, and tried to extend their influence in north China. The national government gave a high priority to modernizing its army with the help of German advisers, but tried to postpone a showdown with Japan until it had some chance of fighting successfully. This gave the appearance of an appeasement policy, which became increasingly unpopular. In civil affairs, there was great improvement in administration and a well managed currency reform. There were fairly successful experiments in rural reconstruction in some local areas, but several innovative laws were not effectively enforced.

When, in 1936, it became apparent that Japan was preparing for total war with China, Chiang was kidnapped by Nationalists who attempted to force him to postpone internal struggles to meet the threat posed by Japan. After his release, Chiang concluded a truce with the Communists, and the Nationalists and Communists formed a united front against Japan.

War with Japan. In 1937 Japan opened a major offensive against China. Japanese troops met surprisingly strong resistance from Communist and Nationalist forces, but by 1939 they had conquered and occupied the eastern third of China, the country's heartland. From this large mainland base, Japan entered World War II.

During the war, the British, Soviet, and U.S. governments aided the Chinese by sending supplies through western China. In 1943 Britain and the United States abrogated all treaties giving them special rights in China and promised President Chiang that they would force Japanese restitution of Chinese territories after the war.

Although the Chinese Communists did not change their theoretical beliefs, their practical policies from 1937 to 1946 were reformist. They initiated sweeping agricultural reforms and effectively reorganized local government and the system of taxation in the areas they held.

The National government, on the other hand, failed to use the surge of patriotic enthusiasm in the early war years to put through the essential reforms that could have increased its efficiency and enabled it to compete with the Communists for popular support. Failure to reform the tax system led to accelerating inflation, with all its demoralizing effects. Late in the war, Soviet troops occupied Manchuria and stripped the industrially developed area of its machinery.

When the war ended in 1945, civil war again broke out between the Nationalists and the Communists. A U.S. mission, led by General George C. Marshall, tried without success to mediate the conflict.

Renewed struggle. At the outset, the National government had a larger and much better equipped army than the Communists, and was backed by a larger population and greater resources. It threw away these advantages by inept strategy, poor army leadership, and bad civil administration. The leaders reacted to increasing

difficulties by a growing reluctance to face unpleasant realities. American advisers could never induce them to admit that drastic reforms in both military and civilian affairs were essential for their survival.

The Communists won most of the battles and in 1949 captured the Nationalists' restored capital, Nanking, and proclaimed the People's Republic of China from Beijing. Chiang Kai-shek and his government fled to the island of Taiwan, where they established themselves at Taipei.

Communist regime. The outbreak of the Korean War (1950–1953) aided the Communist government. It rallied popular support against the United States and United Nations forces and gained prestige by successfully repelling an invasion across the Yalu River and pushing back U.S.-UN forces led by General Douglas MacArthur.

By 1952 the Communist Party had consolidated its control of the mainland, and in 1953 it announced the first five-year economic plan to industrialize China. However, plans for enacting the program were not drawn up until 1955. With aid from the Soviet Union, Communist China's strong central government and well disciplined party, backed by a strong army, made great strides in repairing the damage done by years of warfare. The Communist government collectivized agriculture and worked for the rapid industrialization of China.

In 1956 the government called for a "Great Leap Forward," which aimed at replacing family and village life with communal life, and which hoped to have each citizen participate in all phases of the economic development program.

But the first plan and the subordination of agriculture to industrial growth proved to be disastrous mistakes. Combined with floods and poor initial organization, they caused a great decline in crop production. Moreover, industrialization did not proceed at the pace the Communist planners had hoped, and it was not until the early 1960's that China's economy seemed based on a firm foundation.

In foreign affairs Communist China concentrated on extending its influence throughout eastern and Southeast Asia. Communist Chinese troops had aided North Korean forces in the Korean War and supported Communist guerrilla bands in Laos, Vietnam, Cambodia, and elsewhere. Also, despite its own need for food and funds, the Communist government sent financial and technical aid to other nations.

China's progress was interrupted in the mid-1960's by events stemming from an ideological conflict that had been growing between the Soviet Union and China since the mid-1950's. The dispute became an open break in the early 1960's.

The Chinese government declared itself ideologically purer than the Soviet

JAPAN MAINTAINED *strong military pressure on China in the early 1930's, even before the Sino-Japanese War began in 1937.*

THE BETTMANN ARCHIVE

CHINESE INDUSTRY RELIES *heavily on collectivized production, like this concrete fabrication commune* (left). *Deng Xiaoping* (above, with Mao Zedong) *tried to reduce China's dependence on state-organized production in order to stimulate economic productivity and growth.*

Union, which it claimed had compromised communism with Western ideas. China felt that the Soviets' withdrawal from Cuba during the Cuban missile crisis in 1962 was just one example of the U.S.S.R.'s soft-line approach to the noncommunist nations.

Chairman Mao carried his ideological campaign further in 1966 by proclaiming a "proletarian cultural revolution" to purge China of "revisionist," or regressive, tendencies. He charged that China's party apparatus had become a privileged ruling group "taking the capitalist road," and organized the Red Guards from university and middle-school students to attack the party apparatus.

Schools were closed, agricultural and industrial production interrupted, and the government's administrative machinery disrupted. Nonetheless, China successfully continued its research and development programs in atomic weapons, and exploded its first thermonuclear device in 1964.

Beginning in the early 1970's, Mao began to lead China out of the cultural revolution. His death in 1976 led to a struggle for power between the radicals and moderates in government. The radicals, led by Mao's widow and three others, made a bid for power that failed. Labeled the "Gang of Four," they were arrested and denounced.

In July, 1977, they were expelled from the Communist Party while Deng Xiaoping, an able administrator who himself had been purged, was restored to the Politburo.

The new party leadership pursued a more pragmatic approach to the country's problems. The economy was liberalized over a number of years, making it more responsive to the laws of supply and demand. Some of the reforms instituted included providing long-term leases on individual farms and more realistic prices for products, and reducing the level of state ownership of industry.

The reforms were not without opponents. However, during the 1980's, the reformers consolidated their hold on power. In 1987 a number of old-line Maoists were forced to resign from the Politburo. Deng Xiaoping gradually turned over leadership to his protégé, Zhao Ziyang. In late 1987 Deng became the first top Chinese Communist leader to retire voluntarily. Zhao Ziyang succeeded him as general secretary of the Communist Party. Li Peng became acting prime minister, and was confirmed to that post in April, 1988.

In 1979 the United States and China began diplomatic relations. China has also worked to establish better relations with its Asian neighbors, including South Korea and Japan. In 1984 an agreement was reached with Great Britain providing for the return of Hong Kong to China in 1997.

A LEADER INSTRUCTS HER CLASS IN TAI CHI, *an ancient Chinese system of movements used as an exercise, in a park in Shanghai.*

Fiji

The land and people. Fiji, or the Fiji Islands, consists of two large islands, Viti Levu and Vanua Levu, many islets, and numerous atolls. The islands are coral-rimmed and consist primarily of densely forested volcanic mountains deeply etched by rapidly flowing rivers. The climate is tropical, with high year-round temperature and humidity.

Nearly three-quarters of the people live on Viti Levu. The population is divided between Fijians, a Melanesian people, and people of Indian origin. There are also small groups of Europeans and Chinese. English is the official language.

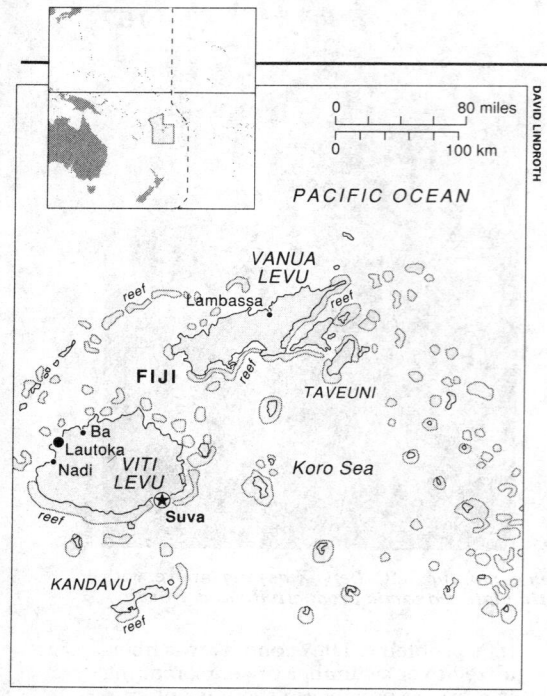

Fiji

Official name: *Fiji*
Area: *7095 sq. mi., 18,376 sq. km.*
Type of government: *Republic*
Head of state: *President,
  Penaia Kanatabatu*
Head of government: *Prime minister,
  Kamisese Mara*
Population: *757,000 (1989 est.)*
Population growth rate: *2.4%*
Capital and largest city: *Suva
  (on Viti Levu)
  (Pop., 1986 est., 64,000)*
Languages: *English (official),
  Fijian, Hindustani*
Religions: *Christian 49%, Hindu 40%,
  Muslim 8%*
Ethnic groups: *Indian 50%,
  Fijian 45%*
Literacy: *80%*
Life expectancy: *67 years (1987)*
Currency: *Fijian dollar*
Per capita GNP: *$1810 (1986)*
Exports: *$246 million (1986)*
Imports: *$368 million (1986)*

In 1987, following an election that appeared to increase the influence of the Indian majority, a coup removed the government. The leader of the coup, Sitivena Rabuka, a Melanesian army officer, promised a new constitution that would guarantee Melanesian control of the government and make Fiji a Christian nation.

India

The land. India, approximately one-third the size of the United States, stretches about 2000 miles from north to south. The country has three major land regions: the Himalayas and associated mountain ranges in the north, the Indus-Ganges-Brahmaputra plain in north-central India, and the Deccan Plateau in the south.

Land regions. The Himalayas extend from east to west for 1500 miles, interrupted by the Indus and Brahmaputra rivers. The mountains range from 150 to 200 miles in width, from north to south.

The vast Indus-Ganges-Brahmaputra plain, which lies between the Himalayas and the Deccan Plateau, is formed by the Indus, the Ganges, and the Brahmaputra rivers and their many tributaries, stretching from the western border with Pakistan across northern India to Bangladesh.

The Deccan Plateau, which forms the triangle-shaped peninsular portion of the Indian subcontinent, is bounded by the Vindhya and Satpura mountains in the north. Running southwest to northeast for about 800 miles, they rise from 1500 to over 4000 feet. Unlike the great plains, where the rivers are fed by mountain snows and flow all year, the rivers of the plateaus flow seasonally and depend on the monsoon rains. Since less rain falls in the Deccan Plateau, it is much more arid and supports a less dense population.

The plateau is bounded along the Arabian Sea coast by the Western Ghats and along the Bay of Bengal by the Eastern Ghats. Near the southern tip of the peninsula, the Western Ghats have peaks of over 8000 feet. The Eastern Ghats have an average height of 1500 to 2000 feet.

The northern edge of the plateau is drained by a series of rivers flowing northward to the Gangetic plain. The Narbada and Tapti rivers in the northwestern portion of the plateau drain westward into the Gulf of Cambay. The major rivers of the plateau rise on the eastern flanks of the Western Ghats, flow eastward across the plateau, and drain into the Bay of Bengal. The largest of these rivers are the Godavari, Krishna, and Cauvery.

Climate. The Himalayas shield the Indian subcontinent from the main body of the Eurasian land mass. As a result, the climate of the subcontinent is unique. In winter, high pressure sys-

Economy. The islands have good forest resources, some gold and copper deposits, and rich farmland in river deltas. Agriculture is the mainstay of the economy, with fruits, sugar cane, coconuts, cacao, and rice the chief commercial crops.

Timber milling, gold mining, and the processing of sugar and copra are the chief industries. There is some boat building and repair. Tourism is an important source of income.

Agricultural products are the main exports, and manufactured goods, fuels, and equipment are imported. Great Britain, Australia, and Japan are the islands' major trading partners.

Government. Until 1987, when a coup toppled the government, Fiji was a parliamentary democracy whose head of state was the British monarch. Fiji is being ruled by decree while a new constitution is drafted.

History. Little is known of the islands before they were visited in the 1600's by the Dutch. They were virtually ignored by Europeans until the 1700's, when traders came in search of sandalwood, coconut products, and other exotic goods. The traders were followed by Christian missionaries.

Tribal warfare raged on the islands in the mid-1800's, and in 1874 the tribal chiefs ceded power to Great Britain. Plantations were established in the late 1800's, and Indian laborers were imported to work them. The islands' economy prospered on farming and forestry. The Indians soon grew to be a majority of the population, and disputes between the Indians and Melanesians continued into the mid-1900's. In 1966 a constitution came into effect that divided representation between the Indians and Melanesians in an effort to settle the ethnic conflict.

THE INTERIOR OF FIJI'S ISLANDS, *somewhat protected by the mountains from the tropical rains, are good for agriculture. They produce, among other crops, sugar cane.*

tems in the Punjab region of central Pakistan and northwestern India produce winds that move down the Gangetic plain into the Bay of Bengal. Winters are generally dry in most of the subcontinent.

During March, April, and May, there is little air movement and the subcontinent begins to heat up, creating low pressure conditions in the north. By the end of May or the beginning of June, the summer monsoons arrive, bringing rain into the Ganges valley.

Rainfall varies considerably. On the Ganges-Brahmaputra delta, in the Khasi and Chittagong hills, Assam, the southern zone of the Himalayas, and along the Malabar coast, the total rainfall may exceed 80 inches a year. In the northeastern portions of the Deccan, along the southeast coast, and in parts of the Western Ghats and the Punjab, the total ranges from 40 to 80 inches. In Kathiawar and the western half of the Deccan, the annual rainfall is 20 to 40 inches.

In the southern half of the country, temperatures are tropical and vary little from month to month. In northern India, however, the annual range is considerable. In January the average temperature in the north may be 30°F lower than in the south.

The people. There have been movements of peoples into India since prehistoric times. The result is a wide variety of physical types. Major ethnic groupings, however, are much less important in tracing cultural and historical developments than those based on language and religion.

The majority of Indians belong to either Indo-Aryan or Dravidian language groups. In northern India, the Indo-Aryan groups are prevalent, while in the south Dravidian languages are most common. Tribal people who live in the Himalaya regions speak a number of languages.

Fourteen major languages are spoken in India, and these are broken up into hundreds of local dialects. Hindi is the official national language, although English is still widely used in government and is the common means of communication among educated Indians.

The vast majority of Indians are Hindus, but India has one of the world's largest Muslim communities. In addition, there are minorities of Christians, Sikhs, Buddhists, and Jains.

India is second only to China in population, and there is great geographic variation in its distribution. Most Indians live in the Gangetic lowlands and the coastal areas. There, rural population densities approach 2000 persons per square mile in the more crowded districts. Overall, India's population density is 644 persons per square mile.

The most recent census showed an increase in population of nearly 25 percent during the decade since the previous census, and in recent years there has been a striking decline in the death rate. This is generally attributed to better sanitation and health care, the control of epidemics, increased food production, and general economic improvement. This rapid population growth places a heavy burden on the nation's economy. The government has embarked on a family planning program in an attempt to sharply reduce the rate of population increase.

About 25 percent of India's population live in urban areas. India's most populous cities are Calcutta, Bombay, Delhi, and Madras.

Economy. India has great economic problems. There is not enough cultivated land or industry to support the country's population, and unemployment and underemployment are high.

Natural resources. India has most of the mineral resources required for industrial expansion. It has one of the largest high-grade iron ore reserves in the world, as well as large deposits of coal. Other important deposits include bauxite, chromite, lead, manganese, and tin.

Agriculture. India traditionally has had great difficulty feeding its population. Since independence, however, agricultural production has averaged a growth rate of about 3 percent per year. A yearly rise in production of at least 2 percent is necessary to keep pace with the population increase.

A large majority of India's people, about 68 percent, are employed in agriculture, though agriculture accounts for only 38 percent of India's gross domestic product. It is estimated that roughly 50 percent of India's total area is cultivated.

Despite the gains in agricultural production, there are still great numbers of subsistence farmers. The average size of a farm is 6.5 acres; at least 34 percent of rural households possess less than half an acre.

One of the chief hazards to Indian agricultural development is lack of water. Much of the Indian government's effort to improve agriculture has been invested in increasing irriga-

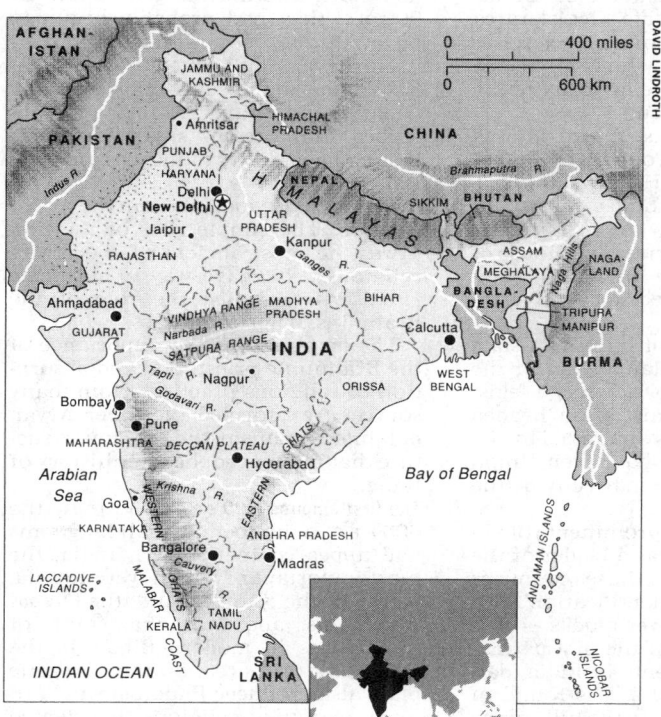

India

Official name: *Republic of India*
Area: *1,269,339 sq. mi., 3,287,588 sq. km.*
Type of government: *Federal republic*
Head of state: *President, Ramaswamy Venkataraman*
Head of government: *Prime minister, Rajiv Gandhi*
Population: *833,422,000 (1989 est.)*
Population growth rate: *2.1%*
Capital: *New Delhi (Pop., 1981, 272,000)*
Largest city: *Delhi (Pop., 1986 est., 5,700,000)*
Languages: *16 official, including Hindi and English*
Religions: *Hindu 83%, Muslim 11%, Christian 3%, Sikh, Jain, Buddhist, Parsi*
Ethnic groups: *Indo-Aryan 72%, Dravidian 25%*
Literacy: *40%*
Life expectancy: *56 years (1987)*
Currency: *Rupee*
Per capita GNP: *$270 (1986)*
Exports: *$11.7 billion (1987)*
Imports: *$17.1 billion (1987)*

INDIA IS A NATION OF CONTRASTS. *Impressive new technology, such as that involved in running a power station, exists side by side with older industries, like clothing manufacture.*

tion. India is surpassed only by China in the acreage under irrigation.

Increased use of chemical fertilizers and the sowing of high-yield and drought-resistant strains of grain also have contributed greatly to the rise in production. Principal crops include rice, wheat, coffee, sugar cane, cotton, jute, and tea.

India has one of the largest cattle herds in the world, and though religious beliefs forbid their slaughter for meat, better management of dairy farming has resulted in India becoming self-sufficient in dairy products.

Industry. Industrial production contributes about one-fifth of the domestic product. The government is seeking ways to increase the role of manufacturing in the economy.

Manufacturing in India can be divided into two groups. The first group consists of handicraft industries organized on a household or guild basis. These industries are small, producing light consumer goods such as cotton cloth, jewelry, sugar, and soap. The second group is made up of modern factory industries that manufacture cotton and silk textiles, mill iron and steel, produce chemicals and pharmaceuticals, and refine part of the domestic production of crude oil.

An increase in electric power generating facilities has been a major target of the various five-year plans. By 1985 there was a capacity of about 40 million kilowatts. The sources for this energy are hydroelectric, thermal, and, to a limited extent, nuclear.

Trade. India generally has suffered an unfavorable trade balance, importing more than it exports. Since independence India has moved away from a dependence on traditional exports such as tea and textiles, although they still constitute a large part of its exports, and toward the export of manu-

factured goods. India's exports include crude oil, engineering goods, precious stones, and handicrafts.

In the past, India has been a large importer of food, but as it has achieved self-sufficiency in food production, these imports have declined. India's principal imports are petroleum, machinery, fertilizers, and steel.

India's trade is carried on chiefly with the United States, Japan, the Soviet Union, and Great Britain.

Government. India is a democratic republic and has a parliamentary system of government. The head of state is the president, who is elected to a five-year term by the members of the national and the state legislatures. Effective executive power is exercised by a prime minister, who is almost always the leader of the majority political party in parliament.

Parliament consists of two houses, the *Rajya Sabha* (Council of States) and the *Lok Sabha* (House of the People). The Council of States consists of up to 250 members, who are indirectly elected to six-year terms. The House of the People may have up to 544 members, most of them elected by universal suffrage.

The organization of India's 24 state governments is similar to that of the federal government. Each has a legislature and an administration headed by a governor, who is appointed by the president. India also has seven Union Territories, governed indirectly by the president.

India has played a prominent role in international affairs as a leader of the nonaligned nations—those countries that seek to avoid identification with the world's great power blocks.

History. Evidence of the first permanent village settlements in India, dating from about 3000 B.C., is found in what is now Pakistan, in the hilly areas

of southern Baluchistan. Some time after the appearance of these settlements, a great urban civilization developed in the Indus Valley, which lasted from about 2500 to 1500 B.C. It is probable that this civilization was related to the great river valley civilization of Sumer that had already appeared in Mesopotamia, but there is little evidence of direct borrowing.

Between 2000 and 1500 B.C., Aryans, or Indo-Europeans, spread from their homeland (probably western Russia) to Europe, Mesopotamia, and India. The Aryans gradually advanced from northwestern India through the Punjab, down into the Gangetic plain. By 900 B.C. they had probably begun to penetrate the Deccan Plateau.

The Aryans subjugated the native inhabitants, and by the 600's B.C., the tribal communities were being absorbed into various small kingdoms that had hereditary monarchs and capital cities.

Changes also took place in the Aryan religion. The simple rites of the *Rig-Veda,* the most ancient of the Aryan religious texts, gave way to elaborate rituals that exalted the role of the Brahmins, or priestly class.

The emphasis on the importance of the Brahminic priesthood and absorption of religious practices from many sources transformed the older Aryan cult into Hinduism, the religious structure that influenced the later history of India.

The first empires (600 B.C.–300 A.D.). By the 600's B.C., a number of small kingdoms had appeared in northern India, the most important of which were Kosala, between the Ganges and the Nepal mountains, and Magadha, south of the Ganges in modern Bihar. In the 500's B.C. this area of the Gangetic plain also produced Buddhism and Jainism, two great religions that denied the authority of the old Vedic scriptures and the supremacy of the Brahminic priesthood.

By the beginning of the 300's B.C., Magadha, ruled by the Nandas, had become the dominant power in the Gangetic plain. In about 322 B.C. the Nanda dynasty was overthrown by Chandragupta Maurya, who embarked on a policy of conquest that brought under his control most of northern India, including part of modern Afghanistan, and much of southern India.

The Mauryan Empire was ruled from the splendid capital of Pataliputra (modern Patna). Asoka (about 273–232 B.C.), Chandragupta's grandson, turned his back on territorial expansion and sought to make Buddhist ethics the guiding force for a kingdom of righteousness.

On rock walls and pillars all over the kingdom, he had engraved the principles of conduct that his people were to follow. In these edicts he emphasized honesty, obedience to parents and teachers, religious toleration, and service to others. The beginning of the Buddhist shrines that were to provide many of the great masterpieces of Indian art date from Asoka's reign, when Buddhism became the religion of kings and merchants and made important contributions to philosophy.

The Mauryan Empire disintegrated soon after Asoka's death, when foreign invaders entered from the northwest. The invaders included the people known as Sakas, or Scythians, and the Kushan, a Central Asian people who were the most influential. They established a strong kingdom in northern India in the first century A.D. that lasted for nearly 200 years. Their greatest king, Kanishka (about 78–110 A.D.), supported Buddhism, and during his reign missionaries carried Buddhism to central Asia. From there it was eventually transmitted to China and other parts of East Asia.

In most of southern India Mauryan control had probably never been very strong, and in the extreme south three kingdoms—the Chola, the Pandya, and the Chera—had existed independently during Asoka's reign. These three kingdoms, with periods of decay and obscurity, continued to exist up to the 1100's A.D. Following the disintegration of the Mauryan Empire, the history of southern Indian tended to be quite separate from that of the north. From the first century B.C. to about 200 A.D., most of the Deccan was controlled by the Satavahanas, who ruled from Andhra Pradesh.

Guptas and Rajputs (300–1200 A.D.). After the downfall of the Kushan, no empire developed in northern India until the 300's, when the Guptas, a family from the Magadha region (modern Bihar), built up a powerful new kingdom. Under Samudragupta (about 330–375 A.D.) and his son Chandragupta II (about 375–413 A.D.), the dynasty's power spread all over northern India.

AKBAR THE GREAT *was one of the earliest Indian rulers to deal with European traders.*

The principal cities of the empire were Pataliputra and Ujjain.

The Gupta period was an age of great activity in literature, the fine arts, religion, science, and philosophy. Its intellectual and artistic accomplishments reflected a prosperity and state of material well-being perhaps never again matched in India's history. During this golden age, Buddhism and Jainism remained important, but Hinduism, which had developed its characteristic social laws and devotional rituals, had become dominant.

A central Asian people, the Huns, invaded northern India in the 400's, and although their empire was short-lived, it destroyed the power of the Guptas.

Attempts were made in the following century, notably by Harsha (606–647), to recreate a single political authority in northern India, but none of these efforts was particularly successful. By the 800's northern India was split up into many kingdoms ruled by Rajputs, members of the Hindu warrior class.

Developments in southern India. During the period of Gupta and Rajput ascendancy in northern India, southern India was controlled by various regional kingdoms. The Chalukyas, who ruled from Badami in the western Deccan, were dominant from about 600 to 750 A.D. Their major enemies were the Pallavas, whose capital was Kanchipuram. The Pallavas ruled from the 300's until the end of the 700's, when they were overthrown by the Chola kings of Tanjore.

The Cholas maintained control of all the territory south of the Tungabhadra River from about 850 to 1200, when they were usurped by the revived power of the Pandyas at Madura.

The southern kingdoms were the centers of cultural and religious movements. Most of the rulers were great

builders, and they adorned their kingdoms with magnificent temples and palaces. The Pallavas were responsible for the series of rock-carved temples at Mamallapuram and the great temple complex at Kanchipuram. The Cholas built numerous temples, the most famous of which is at Tanjore, and decorated them with stone and bronze sculpture.

Muslim dominance (1200–1700). The first impact of Islam on India came in 712, when Arab control was established over Sind, in the lower Indus River valley. The Rajput kings of northern India prevented the Arabs' further expansion.

A dynasty of Afghan Turks from Ghor overcame the Rajputs in 1192 at Taraori. They established a sultanate at Delhi and from there gradually extended their control over all northern India. Under Ala-ad-din Khalji (1296–1316), the Turks conquered southern India. This new empire, the greatest in India since that of the Mauryas, fell apart after Ala-ad-din's death.

Weakened by Tamerlane's raids from central Asia in the late 1300's, the Delhi sultanate lost all but parts of the Punjab and the Gangetic plain by 1500. But permanent changes had been effected in the pattern of Indian civilization by the 300 years of Muslim occupation. A large Muslim minority had been created, and Islamic ideas and values had begun to influence Indian life. Orthodox Hinduism remained the most popular religion, however.

A new group of invaders entered India in 1526, led by Babur, a Mongol chieftain who had founded a kingdom at Kabul. He defeated the Delhi sultan at Panipat in 1526 and made himself master of the Gangetic plain up to Patna. He was succeeded by his son Humayun, who was driven out of India in 1540. Humayun was succeeded by his son Akbar (ruled 1556–1605), the founder of the Mughal Empire. Akbar pursued an aggressive policy of expansion that brought all of northern India under his control.

Akbar's reign is one of the most vital in Indian history, for he initiated policies that had a lasting influence. At the very beginning of the conquests, the Muslims had been faced with the problem of the proper treatment of the Hindus. Akbar enunciated a policy of universal toleration, the most obvious sign of which was the abolition of the *jizya,* the discriminatory tax. Akbar also instituted far-reaching administrative reforms, including the expansion of the revenue system, careful surveys of all cultivated land, and reforms of the taxation system.

Akbar's successors continued his policy of consolidation and expansion up to the middle of the 17th century. The Taj Mahal and the Pearl Mosque at Agra were built at this time.

Aurangzeb (1658–1707) reversed the religious policy initiated by Akbar.

As a devout Muslim, he looked with disfavor on the growing power and prosperity of the Hindus, and as a statesman he probably questioned the possibility of holding the empire together without the loyalty of a Muslim ruling class. The discriminatory taxes were reimposed on the Hindus, the building of new temples was forbidden, and an attempt was made to replace Hindu government officials with Muslims.

Aurangzeb also embarked on a policy of territorial expansion and acquisition that brought all of India, except the extreme southern tip, under Mughal control.

Aurangzeb's vast empire began to crumble within a generation of his death. Rebellions broke out everywhere in the Mughal Empire, and a series of weak successors to the throne were unable to control the administration effectively. In 1739 northern India was invaded by Nadir Shah of Persia. By 1750 the empire was reduced to the territory around Delhi.

Western dominance and unification. The Marathas were the most important of the regional powers that emerged from the wreckage of the Mughal Empire. By 1760 they controlled all of central India and much of the south. Their expansion was checked in 1761 with their defeat at Panipat by a combined Mughal and Afghan army, and further halted in the 1780's by the rising power of the English East India Company.

The English had been in India since 1600 as traders, but the company became important as a political power only after the decline of Mughal power. In 1757 it interfered in a succession dispute over the throne of Bengal, and by 1765 it was in effective control of Bengal's resources, which it used to pay for the cost of expansion. By 1820 it was the paramount power in India, and soon all of India was brought under its control.

In 1857 the Great Mutiny, also called the Sepoy Mutiny, in northern India was instigated by the company's Indian soldiers, but it was abetted by other groups in the population that had special grievances against the new power.

The rebellion was crushed, and the East India Company lost its power to rule. A new administration was created, directly responsible to the British Crown. It directly ruled Bengal, Bombay, Madras, the Punjab, and the United Provinces (modern Uttar Pradesh). Indirect control was exercised over the remaining two-fifths of the territory through about 600 Indian princes. Although these rulers had internal autonomy, they had no control over their relations with other states.

The political unity achieved in the 1800's was made possible by a number of factors. The development of modern communications and transportation brought all India under the immediate control of the central government through telegraphs, railways, and steamships.

An efficient civil service was also created for the first time. A uniform legal system introduced Western ideas and methods of jurisprudence. Finally, English was the language used not only in administration but also in higher education. Colleges and universities gave Indians a common means of communication as well as a common knowledge of Western thought.

The rise of nationalism. The emergence of a nationalist movement in the late 1800's was the direct result of political unification. Educated Indians became aware simultaneously of the Western tradition of political freedom, the dependent state of their own country, and the glory of their past history. The nationalist movement had its formal beginnings in 1885 with the founding of the Indian National Congress by Allan Octavian Hume and a small group of Indian intellectuals.

The nationalist movement, with its demands for responsible government and a larger degree of independence, was complicated by Hindu-Muslim relations. Muslim leaders argued that responsible government based on direct popular representation would mean that Muslims, who constituted 25 percent of the population, would be a permanent minority ruled by Hindus. This led to the founding in 1906 of the Muslim League.

The British responded to the demands of the nationalists in 1909 through the Morley-Minto Reforms. They allowed the direct election of a number of Indians to provincial legislatures, and gave the Muslims separate electorates to ensure their adequate representation. The Indian National Congress denounced this as an attempt by the British to continue their hold over India by turning one religion against another.

The next response to nationalist demands came in 1919, when a new constitution, called the Montagu-Chelmsford Reforms, increased the power of the elected representatives in the provinces and widened the franchise. Indian political leaders were disappointed with the constitution, for they felt the British had, through the control of finance, kept all the important sources of power in their own hands.

The Indian National Congress, under the leadership of Mohandas K. (Mahatma) Gandhi, passed a resolution in 1920 condemning the new system of government, it began a campaign of nonviolent noncooperation. This became the characteristic method of the congress in its struggle against the British from that time on. Gandhi's great achievement was to make the demand for independence a mass movement through the use of terminology and symbols drawn from traditional Indian religion and culture rather than from Western political thought. His chief lieutenant was Jawaharlal Nehru, who appealed to the intellectuals of India as well as to the country's masses.

Gandhi's success tended to alienate the Muslims, who increasingly argued that when freedom came, provision should be made for the Muslims to control their own destinies. Muhammad Ali Jinnah emerged as the leader of the Muslims.

The Government of India Act of 1935 was another unsuccessful attempt to give the Indians a sense of responsibility in government. When World War II broke out in 1939, the congress leaders resigned their government posts to protest their country's involvement in the war.

In 1945 a new Labour government in Britain entered into negotiations with the leaders of the congress and the Muslim League. Jinnah insisted that Nehru's demands for British withdrawal and the election of a constituent assembly to decide the future of the country would leave the Muslims without any protection against the Hindu majority. Following outbreaks of Hindu-Muslim violence in 1947, the congress consented to the creation of a separate Muslim state.

Independence. On August 15, 1947, British rule ended in India. A Muslim state, Pakistan, was formed from territories in the west and east, with Jinnah as governor-general and Liaqat Ali Khan as prime minister. The remainder of British India became the Dominion of India, which inherited British India's organization and international obligations and rights. Nehru became prime minister and Lord Mountbatten governor-general.

With partition, violence flared along the border, particularly between West Pakistan and the Indian part of Punjab, as Hindus fled to India and Muslims to Pakistan. The two governments finally succeeded in stopping these bloody riots, but as the bitterness lingered. Gandhi was assassinated (January 30, 1948) by a Hindu extremist. Nehru then became leader of the new India.

The memory of violence on both sides, and dislike by most Indians of the fact of partition, have strained relations between the two countries. Other issues include the use of the Indus River for irrigation, payment of compensation for property left behind by refugees, and disputes over Kashmir.

On January 26, 1950, India adopted a new constitution, by which it became a sovereign republic but remained a member of the Commonwealth of Nations. In 1952 and in elections in 1957 and 1962, the Indian National Congress won a majority of seats in the national legislature. Jawaharlal Nehru, as head of the Congress Party, remained prime minister until his death in 1964.

Contemporary India. Since independence, one of India's major foreign policy concerns has been its relationship with

RELIGIOUS VIOLENCE, *such as that which has recently occurred between Hindus and Sikhs, has long been a problem in India. India's revered early leaders, Jawaharlal Nehru and Mahatma Gandhi, were unable to prevent the tension that caused the partition of India into separate Muslim and Hindu states in 1947.*

Pakistan. Relations between the two were never good but they worsened during 1962, when Pakistan agreed to negotiate a treaty with China to define a part of the frontier west of the Karakorum Pass held by Pakistan but claimed by India.

A new quarrel broke out in April, 1965, over the boundaries between the two in the Rann of Kutch, a desolate territory on the western coast. Fighting broke out, but a truce was arranged in June, 1965. Two months later fighting again erupted between the two nations, this time along the border between Indian- and Pakistani-controlled parts of Kashmir.

In 1971 the civil war between East and West Pakistan, in which India supported the rebellious East (Bangladesh), resulted in some 10 million refugees crossing into India.

Indira Gandhi, the daughter of Nehru and an important figure in the Congress Party, became prime minister in 1966. She won a landslide victory in 1971, even though Gandhi had dissolved the lower house of Parliament the year before.

In 1975 political unrest led Gandhi to suspend civil liberties and arrest hundreds of political opponents. She also imposed "emergency rule" and postponed scheduled national elections. She initiated an unpopular program of forced sterilization and population control. When elections were finally held in 1977, she was defeated in her bid for reelection.

Morarji Desai and then Charan Singh served as prime ministers before January, 1980, when Indira Gandhi led her Congress Party to a stunning upset. Gandhi was reinstated as prime minister amid hopes that she could curb inflation and restore order to the increasingly fragmented Indian society.

The 1980's brought an upsurge in religious violence. In 1984 militant Sikhs, agitating for more political autonomy for the Punjab, were ejected from the Golden Temple by the Indian army. It is estimated that about a thousand people died during the two-day battle.

In October of 1984 Indira Gandhi was assassinated by two Sikh members of her bodyguard. Her death touched off a period of violence by Hindus against Sikhs. In December another terrible tragedy struck India. A leak of highly toxic gas at a Union Carbide pesticide plant in Bhopal caused the deaths of more than 2000 people; hundreds of thousands more were injured.

Indira Gandhi's son Rajiv was chosen by the Congress Party to succeed her as prime minister. Despite high expectations when he took office, Gandhi has proved unable to live up to his promises to clamp down on governmental corruption and on religious violence between Sikhs and Hindus.

In 1987 Gandhi helped to negotiate a cease-fire between the government of Sri Lanka and the Tamil rebels. He sent Indian troops to Sri Lanka to help enforce the peace.

Indonesia

The land. Indonesia consists of over 13,500 islands and stretches some 3000 miles from east to west and some 1500 miles from north to south across the equator. The islands are divided into three main groups—the Greater Sundas in the west; the Lesser Sundas in the south; and the Moluccas in the east.

The Greater Sundas include Indonesia's largest and most important islands—Java, Sumatra, Borneo, and Sulawesi (Celebes). The western part of New Guinea, West Irian, is also part of Indonesia.

A typical Indonesian island consists of a core of high mountains and hills ringed by coastal plains. The islands are divided into three geologic regions. The largest islands, in the northwestern portion of the archipelago, are outcroppings of the Sunda Shelf, a submerged extension of the continent of Asia. The southeastern islands are part of the Sahul Shelf, the continental shelf of Australia and New Guinea.

Between these two stable geologic regions lies a third region still in formation. It is marked by a semicircular band of some 300 volcanoes, of which 60 are considered active.

Indonesia has an equatorial climate moderated by the influence of the sea. Temperatures are high, but not excessively so, and stable throughout the year, usually ranging between 75°F and 90°F. Rainfall is generally heavy, between 40 and 100 inches a year.

The people. Indonesia is ranked fifth among the nations in population. Almost two-thirds of the people live on Java, which accounts for only one-tenth of the country's area. Population is extremely dense near Djakarta, the capital.

The two next largest Indonesian cities are also on Java—Surabaja, the leading port, and Bandung, a cultural and educational center. Parts of Sumatra and Bali are also heavily populated, but elsewhere population is sparse.

Most Indonesians are Malays, but the population is divided into many ethnic and cultural groups. It is estimated that there are over 250 languages spoken in Indonesia. At independence, Bahasa Indonesia was chosen as a national language to be used in government and taught in the schools. The language is based on a form of Malay widely used in trade. Approximately 90 percent of Indonesians are Muslims; most of the rest are Hindus, Christians, and Buddhists. There are Chinese and Arab minorities.

Eighty-two percent of the Indonesian population live in rural areas and 74 percent of the labor force is employed in agriculture.

Economy. Indonesia has made important progress since the dark years of the 1950's and 1960's, when political instability and mismanagement left the economy a shambles.

The largest reserves of petroleum in the Far East are in Sumatra, Borneo, Java, and Ceram. In 1986 Indonesia produced nearly 445 million barrels of oil and accounted for about 2 percent of the world's oil production. Indonesia's economy is dependent on oil, which accounts for almost 70 percent of export earnings and about 55 percent of government revenue.

Indonesia is also a leading world producer of tin, mining 22,000 metric tons in 1985.

There is also bauxite on Bintan, sulfur and manganese on Java, nickel on Sulawesi, and abundant iron ore and low-grade coal in Sumatra, Java, and Borneo. In addition to their rich resources, the islands are covered by valuable forests, which provide teak, sandalwood, bamboo, resins, and oils.

Most of Indonesia's resources are undeveloped, however, and agriculture is the mainstay of the economy, providing about 25 percent of gross domestic product (GDP). The equatorial climate permits year-round farming. Agricultural products raised primarily for export include cinchona (source of quinine), rubber, coffee, tea, copra, palm oil, sisal, tobacco, sugar, cocoa, indigo, and pepper and other spices. The basic food crops include rice, corn, sweet potatoes, peanuts, soybeans, bananas, manioc, and vegetables.

Manufacturing industries make up only about 13 percent of GDP. The government has encouraged the development of industries based on the exploitation of Indonesia's own natural resources. A recent ban on the export of logs has encouraged the processed lumber industry and helped make Indonesia the leading exporter of plywood. Indonesia is also the world's largest producer of liquefied natural gas. Other manufactures include textiles, motorcycles, petro-chemicals, and paper.

Indonesia's imports include machinery, transport equipment, and textiles. Its largest trading partners are Japan, the United States, and Singapore.

Government. Executive power is held by a president who is both chief of state and head of government. The president is elected every five years by a People's Consultative Assembly, which meets only once and sets state policy. Legislative authority rests with the 460-member House of People's Representatives.

Although Indonesia is nominally a democracy, the army has held considerable influence since independence. This influence is felt not only in the government, where members of the military hold a number of important posts, but also in important national industries, where army personnel often hold top positions. This situation is formalized in the philosophy of "two functions," which holds that the armed forces have a social role as well as a military one.

History. Indonesia has been inhabited since prehistoric times, and remains of one of the earliest humans have been found on Java. By the 100's B.C., Malay people had developed on the islands of the archipelago simple societies based on fishing, agriculture, and seafaring. In the 100's A.D., Indian peoples began to come to the islands, first as traders and then as settlers.

Early kingdoms. By the 500's and 600's many small Indian-Malayan Buddhist and Hindu kingdoms had been established on the islands, and a variety of cultures and societies developed. These societies built up a vigorous trade with nearby island and mainland states, and with India and China.

The first of these kingdoms to achieve significance beyond its own island territory was Srivijaya, on Suma-tra. It developed a high Buddhist culture and an advanced civilization, and by the 800's it controlled an empire that included part of the Malay peninsula as well as most of the Indonesian islands.

In the 1100's internal conflicts and threats of attack from the mainland weakened Srivijayan control over the islands, and a new kingdom centered at Majapahit, on Java, gained power. After leading a defense of the islands against an attack by the Mongols in the late 1200's, the Javanese kingdom became the dominant influence in the archipelago.

In the 1300's and 1400's Muslim Arabs began to settle in Indonesia, and by the late 1400's Islamic influence had weakened the older Hindu and Buddhist kingdoms. By the early 1500's there was no single powerful state governing Indonesia. In the 1400's and 1500's European traders began visiting the islands, attracted by the fame of the spices, woods, and other goods of the "East Indies" and the "Spice Islands," as Indonesia was called.

European control. The Portuguese were the first Europeans to establish trading posts in the islands. By the mid-1500's they held military control over most of the islands, and they attempted to convert the islanders to Christianity. Islam spread rapidly through the islands as one weapon against the European invaders.

Portugal held a virtual monopoly of the islands' trade by 1580, when Spain acquired the Portuguese crown. Spain's European rivals, especially England and The Netherlands, redoubled their efforts to break the monopoly after 1580. The Dutch, with the assistance of Muslim islanders, gained a foothold on the islands.

In 1602 the Dutch formed the Dutch East India Company. During the 1600's

DAVID LINDROTH

Indonesia

Official name: *Republic of Indonesia*
Area: *782,659 sq. mi.,*
  2,027,087 sq. km.
Type of government: *Republic*
Head of state: *President, Suharto*
Population: *187,651,000 (1989 est.)*
Population growth rate: *2.0%*
Capital and largest city: *Jakarta*
  (Pop., 1980, 6,503,449)
Languages: *Bahasa Indonesian*
  (official), Javanese
Religions: *Muslim 90%, Christian 5%*
Ethnic groups: *Javanese 45%,*
  Sundanese 14%, Madurese 7%
Literacy: *67%*
Life expectancy: *58 years (1987)*
Currency: *Rupiah*
Per capita GNP: *$330 (1987)*
Exports: *$15 billion (1987)*
Imports: *$11.1 billion (1987)*

THE PROMOTION OF HIGH-TECHNOLOGY INDUSTRY, *like the manufacture of aircraft, receives increasing attention from the Indonesian government.*

the company drove out the Portuguese and other European traders and subdued the islanders. The Dutch trading center of Batavia (modern Jakarta), on western Java, grew into a prosperous center for the rich trade of the islands. The Dutch were joined in the 1700's by Chinese immigrants, whose plantations first developed the islands' agricultural potential and who began investing in the colony's business.

Dutch rule. In 1798 The Netherlands took direct control of the colony from the East India Company. The company's government had grown corrupt and inefficient, and The Netherlands needed the islands as a naval base during the Napoleonic wars. Moreover, the colony had proved even richer than expected. In the early 1800's the French and the British briefly occupied The Netherlands East Indies, but the Dutch resumed control in 1816.

During the 1800's the Dutch reaped great riches from the colony through a system of state-regulated, privately owned plantations. The Europeans' concentration on producing export crops to the exclusion of subsistence crops led to frequent famines and to the misuse and depletion of the islands' resources.

Although the Dutch encouraged and educated some islanders and did not prohibit them from owning their own businesses or farms, the majority of Indonesians were illiterate, poor, and powerless. And although colonial regulations protected native workers from mistreatment, most of them were severely exploited.

In the early 1900's Indonesian nationalist movements grew out of the resentment of colonial inequities. Led by Dutch-educated Indonesian intellectuals, the movements grew rapidly. In 1916 these groups succeeded in obtaining from the Dutch a *Volksraad,* or people's council, in which Indonesians could participate. The council had little authority, however, and did not satisfy the nationalists.

As the nationalists grew stronger and more active in the 1920's and 1930's, they met with repression. Their leaders were jailed and the colony's limited social welfare and educational programs were curtailed.

In 1942, during World War II, Japanese forces invaded Indonesia. They quickly crushed the Dutch defenses and occupied the islands. The Japanese encouraged Indonesian nationalism by allowing the Indonesians to participate in the occupation government. One government leader, Sukarno, founded the National Indonesian Party, one of the country's major nationalist organizations.

Indonesian leaders who opposed the Japanese established a government-in-exile in Australia. There they outlined a plan for a gradual postwar separation of Indonesia from control of The Netherlands.

In 1945, three days after the Japanese surrender, Sukarno and Muhammad Hatta, another nationalist leader, proclaimed the independence of the Republic of Indonesia.

Independence. Several years of political conflict and warfare followed, with Sukarno's government fighting not only the Dutch, who attempted to reestablish their control, but more conservative nationalist groups as well. In 1949 The Netherlands yielded sovereignty over the islands.

An independent federal union was established, loosely united with The Netherlands. However, dissatisfaction with this organization led in 1950 to the abolition of the federal state and the creation of the centralized Republic of Indonesia, which included all the islands.

The new country was faced from the start with the problem of unifying a large number of islands with a variety of cultures and no tradition of unity. It tried to solve this problem with a strong central government. Between 1950 and 1955, Sukarno, the nation's first president, held great power, appointing all local officials and all members of parliament.

The country held its first elections in 1955 for both a parliament and a constituent assembly, which was to draft a permanent constitution. Of Indonesia's 29 political parties, the Communists emerged from the elections as one of the four strongest, along with two Muslim parties and Sukarno's Nationalist Party.

The army objected to the influence of the Communists in the government, and in 1958 army officers on Sumatra rebelled, sparking an uprising that spread to Sulawesi and many smaller islands. The rebellions were not quelled until 1961.

Between 1957 and 1959 Dutch property was seized, Dutch businesses harassed, and all Dutch citizens were ordered out of Indonesia. The resulting economic crisis compounded the problems created by the rebellion and left the government very weak. Moreover, the constituent assembly was unable to agree on plans for a new constitution. In 1959 it was dissolved and a government reorganization was begun.

By 1960 the country was under a system that Sukarno called "Guided Democracy"—with an executive so powerful that popular participation was effectively stifled—but dissension among the islanders did not end. Conflicts with the Dutch also continued, with Indonesia demanding sovereignty over The Netherlands' New Guinea colony, called West Irian by the Indonesians. In 1963 The Netherlands agreed to surrender the territory.

Contemporary Indonesia. In 1963 a new, more violent dispute erupted when the Sukarno government moved to block the establishment of the nearby Federation of Malaysia, formed by the union of four former British colonial areas—Malaya, Singapore, Sarawak, and Sabah (North Borneo).

A "Crush Malaysia" campaign soon became the prime concern of the Indonesian government. Border fighting was frequent, and in 1965 Indonesia announced its withdrawal from the United Nations after Malaysia was admitted to membership.

Hostility to Malaysia was one aspect of Sukarno's general opposition to all European involvement in Southeast Asia. In 1965 Indonesia nationalized all foreign-owned businesses in the country, and although it officially remained neutral in foreign affairs, the government strengthened its ties with Communist China as its opposition to Western nations stiffened.

Indonesia's pro-Beijing Communist Party grew in power, and in October, 1965, attempted to seize the government. The coup attempt was crushed by the army, and it is estimated that more than 100,000 Indonesian Communists were killed in the aftermath. Many thousands of Indonesia's Chinese residents were murdered or driven from their homes. Some of Sukarno's top aides were convicted of complicity in the Communist plot.

The army officially took control of the government in 1966 and Lieutenant General Suharto became prime minister. Sukarno retained the post of president until March, 1967, when the Peoples' Consultative Assembly dismissed him and appointed Suharto acting president. Elections in 1968, 1973, 1978, 1983, and 1988 have kept Suharto in office.

Japan

Official name: *Japan*
Area: *143,750 sq. mi., 372,312 sq. km.*
Type of government: *Parliamentary democracy*
Head of state: *Emperor, Hirohito*
Head of government: *Prime minister, Noboru Takeshita*
Population: *123,197,000 (1989 est.)*
Population growth rate: *.5%*
Capital and largest city: *Tokyo (Pop., 1986, 8,200,000)*
Language: *Japanese*
Religions: *Shinto, Buddhist*
Ethnic group: *Japanese*
Literacy: *100%*
Life expectancy: *78 years (1987)*
Currency: *Yen*
Per capita income: *$21,820 (1986)*
Exports: *$210 billion (1986)*
Imports: *$127.5 billion (1986)*

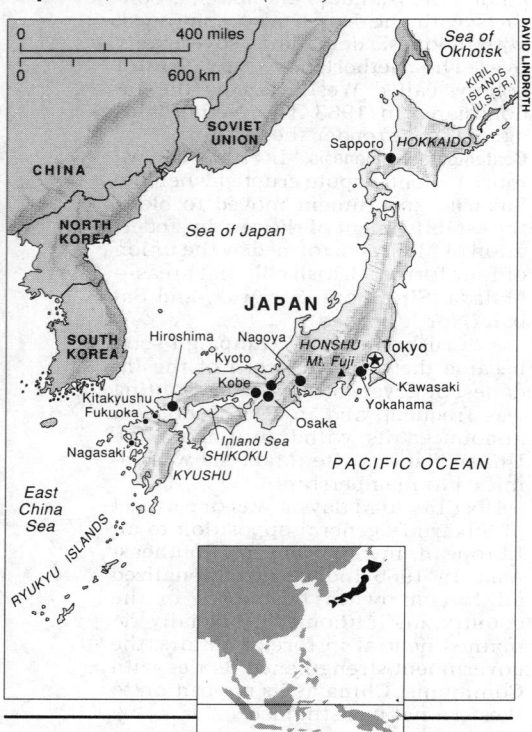

Suharto's military government has concentrated on rebuilding the economy, ravaged by years of violence and political upheavals. Although oil income since the 1960's strengthened the economy, there was an uneven distribution of this new wealth, accompanied by charges of unfair economic advantages to Chinese and Japanese minorities. Student riots erupted over the issue in 1974, and even though they were readily put down, the government pursued a course of reform.

Suharto also sought closer ties with noncommunist nations. Japanese and U.S. financial aid and investments were significant outcomes of this policy.

Indonesia also has taken a more active role in regional affairs. In 1966 friendly relations were reestablished with Malaysia. In 1988, as a member of the Association of South East Asian Nations, Indonesia was host to talks between the various warring factions in Cambodia. Indonesia broke relations with China in 1967, and remains strongly anticommunist.

In 1976 Indonesia annexed the former Portuguese colony of East Timor during a civil war on the island. Thousands of civilians were reported killed during the takeover.

Japan

The land. The Japanese archipelago consists of over 3000 islands and extends 2000 miles from northeast to southwest. But 98 percent of the area lies within the four major islands of Honshu (87,300 square miles); Hokkaido (30,300 square miles); Kyushu (16,200 square miles); and Shikoku (7200 square miles).

Most of the country is mountainous, with only about 15 percent of the land sufficiently level for cultivation. The country's limited plains areas are concentrated on Honshu. Japanese civilization, not surprisingly, has developed primarily in the limited space occupied by four major plains, those around Tokyo, Nagoya, Kyoto-Osaka, and Kitakyushu. Roughly half of the nation's population lives in these areas.

Many of the mountains are folded ranges upthrust from the Pacific floor. Japan is crossed by seven principal volcanic chains containing 192 major volcanoes, 58 of which are active. An average of four seismic shocks a day are recorded. Volcanic masses produce the highest peaks in the country. Mount Fuji, a dormant volcano on Honshu, has an elevation of 12,389 feet.

Japan's rivers are short and swift with greatly varying water levels. The Inland Sea serves Japan as a major waterway. It is about 250 miles long and is connected with the Pacific Ocean and with the Korea Strait.

The coastline of the Sea of Japan has few indentations and consequently has

few good harbors. The southern coast of Honshu contains Japan's most important harbors and ports, such as Tokyo, Yokohama, Nagoya, Osaka, and Kobe.

Climate. Japan's climate, subtropical in the south and cooler in the north, is generally mild and pleasant. The average mean January temperature is 45°F in southern Kyushu and 14°F in Hokkaido. August is usually the hottest month of the year, with a mean of 81°F in the south and 69°F in the north.

Western Hokkaido, eastern Honshu, and the Inland Sea region receive 40 to 60 inches of rain a year. In central Honshu and along the Sea of Japan 100 to 120 inches of rain is not uncommon. In most parts of the country maximum rains occur in the early summer.

The people. The Japanese are a Mongoloid people with a mixture of Malay and Caucasoid stocks. The only important minority group consists of about 600,000 Koreans. There are small groups of Chinese and Europeans, and remnants of the aboriginal people, the Ainu.

The indigenous religion of Japan is Shinto, which emphasizes ritual cleanliness and the living, moving spirit of nature. The second important religion is Buddhism, which came to Japan in the sixth century from China.

Education is very important to the Japanese. The level of literacy is one of the highest in the world. The school dropout rate is very low, and nearly one-third of all high school graduates attend college.

The Japanese inhabit one of the world's most heavily populated lands, with a density of about 850 people per square mile. Moreover, because the nation is so mountainous, more than 4000 persons live in each arable square mile. In 1980 Japan had eleven cities of more than 1 million inhabitants, the largest being Tokyo, Yokohama (2.9 million), Osaka (2.6), Nagoya (2.1), Sapporo (1.5), Kyoto (1.4), and Kobe (1.4).

Economy. Japan's economic performance since World War II has been phenomenal. Despite a poverty of natural resources, Japan has become a leading nation in the world economy. The country's economy expanded at an annual rate of about 11 percent from 1947 to 1952, slowed during the 1950's, and then grew by 10 percent a year during the 1960's. Growth was slower during the 1970's owing to soaring oil prices, but it still remained stronger than in other major nations. By 1980 the gross national product (GNP) had passed the trillion-dollar mark, the third highest in the world, and average family income approximated that of the United States. In the 1980's the GNP was growing at about 4 percent, keeping it one of the highest in the world.

Natural resources. Japan has a large variety of mineral resources, but the deposits are small and inadequate for

Japan's advanced level of industrial development. Coal is the main mineral resource, but most of it is of low grade. Most basic industrial materials must be imported.

Materials in which domestic production is sufficient are lead, zinc, arsenic, bismuth, pyrite, sulfur, limestone, gypsum, barite, silica, and dolomite. Vanadium, chromium, molybdenum, tungsten, titanium, tin, manganese, mercury, antimony, and iron ore also are produced, but large imports still are required to meet the economy's needs.

Japan's mountainous terrain and abundant rainfall help make the country the fourth largest producer of hydroelectricity in the world.

Agriculture. Agriculture's position in Japan's economy has declined since World War II, even though production has increased. Agriculture contributed 21 percent to the gross domestic product in 1953, but less than 5 percent at the beginning of the 1980's. At the same time, Japanese farmers, despite a decrease in their actual numbers, are increasingly affluent; their income increased fivefold in the 20 years from 1955 to 1975.

The average Japanese farm of about $2\frac{1}{2}$ acres is intensively cultivated. Such techniques as fertilizer use, irrigation, multiple cropping, and terracing place Japan's crop yields per acre among the highest in the world.

About half the cultivated land is used for the production of paddy rice, the staple of the Japanese diet. Barley, wheat, potatoes, pulses, vegetables, and fruits also are grown.

Fishing. Fish ranks second to rice in the Japanese diet and is the principal source of protein. Japanese coastal waters contain a great variety of fish.

The sardine catch leads in both volume and value, although herring and mackerel are important in northern waters. In addition to coastal fishing, Japan has a large fleet that goes to distant fishing grounds in the north and south Pacific.

Forestry. About two-thirds of Japan is covered by productive forests, which are the source of building materials, fuel, paper, and other articles. Oak, laurel, and bamboo grow in southern Japan. A mixed forest, including maple, ash, birch, cypress, and pine, is found in central Japan. Conifers such as spruce, fir, and hemlock grow in mountain areas in northern Japan. However, domestic production of timber provides only about 40 percent of Japan's needs.

Industry. Despite its limited resources, Japan is an industrial giant, having invested heavily over the last three decades in the construction of both light and heavy industrial plants.

A telling index of the magnitude of Japan's industrial success is a list of areas in which the country is a world leader: rayon and acetate fabrics, plastics, aluminum, synthetic rubber, resins, raw silk, crude steel, cotton fabrics, watches, cameras and lenses, pianos, calculators, television and radio sets, wood pulp, motorcycles, ships, automobiles, and chemicals.

Textile production has experienced a transition in recent years, as synthetic fabrics have challenged Japan's silk and cotton industries. As a consequence, Japan's synthetic fiber production increased nearly twentyfold from the war era to the late 1970's, enabling Japan to continue as the world's second leading producer of fabrics.

A major growth industry has been the manufacture of transportation vehicles. Since the war, Japan's motorcycle industry has become dominant in the world market; its shipbuilders have produced more tonnage than all other nations combined, despite recent cutbacks owed to European pressures; and in 1980 Japan passed the United States as the largest automobile producer in the world.

Another important postwar development has been Japan's rise as a producer of electronic equipment, such as television sets, videocassette recorders, and computers. Japan ranks with the United States as a leader in the futuristic "smart machine" industry that has grown from the electronics-computer revolution.

Trade. Deficient both in arable land and natural resources, Japan is heavily dependent on foreign trade. Raw materials, foodstuffs, and fuel are Japan's principal imports, especially cereals, sugar, raw cotton and wool, iron ore, bauxite, copper ore, coking coal, crude rubber, and crude petroleum. Almost all of Japan's exports are manufactured goods. Markets for these goods are found in Canada and Australia, but mostly in the United States, where Japan has concentrated its foreign investments in recent years.

Government. Japan is a constitutional monarchy with a parliamentary system of government. The emperor is the symbol of the state, and executive power is wielded by a prime minister and cabinet responsible to the legislature, the Diet. The prime minister, chosen by the Diet from among its members, appoints the cabinet ministers, at least half of whom must be members of the Diet.

The Diet is composed of the House of Representatives, whose 512 members are elected to four-year terms, and the House of Councillors, with 252 members elected to six-year terms. One hundred of the councillors are elected by the nation at large, and the other 152 councillors are elected from local constituencies.

JAPAN HAS ADOPTED MANY WESTERN CUSTOMS, *particularly those that are American. The Japanese are as passionate about baseball as most Americans and Western dress has become the norm for most working men and women.*

History. Although the first inhabitants of Japan were ancestors of the modern Ainu, a Caucasoid people, archaeological evidence indicates that most of the early Japanese were Mongoloid invaders from Korea, who first appeared in Japan in the early centuries A.D. They brought with them a bronze and iron civilization and founded the Japanese state.

Early Japan was ruled by numerous clans, one of which, the Yamato, gained supremacy by the 300's or 400's. From the Yamato descended the Japanese royal family, although Japanese tradition maintained that the Sun Goddess of the Yamato chiefs was the progenitor of the imperial family.

An emigration of Chinese artisans and scholars in the first century A.D. introduced Japan to the advanced civilization of China. The introduction (mid-sixth century) of Buddhism particularly revolutionized Japanese arts and architecture.

Between 607 and the mid-800's, a series of Japanese missions went to the Chinese court. The missions included officials, scholars, artists, and Buddhist monks. They remained in China for periods of study and many became influential on their return to Japan.

A complex centralized administration in the Chinese manner was established and Chinese-style cities were built. Nara was built as the capital in 710. It was replaced by Kyoto in 794. Less successfully imitated by the Japanese were China's provincial administration and land distribution systems, which were strongly opposed by the clans.

Such cultural borrowings as Buddhism and Buddhist art were the most enduring. Attempts to adapt the Chinese writing system to the Japanese language were largely unsuccessful and made writing unnecessarily difficult. After 200 years of imitation, a native Japanese culture began to emerge, and in 838 the last Japanese embassy was sent to China.

A brilliant Japanese court life developed, which came to be dominated by the Fujiwara family. The Fujiwara gained control over the imperial family through intermarriage, and from about 850 on its head acted either as regent or as civil dictator.

While the Fujiwara dominated the court in the 900's and 1000's, real power came to reside in the provincial knights and their families. Of all these families, the Minamoto emerged as the most powerful in 1185. Its chief, Yoritomo, settled in Kamakura and gave himself the title of shogun, or generalissimo.

Kamakura era. By appointing its men as estate managers throughout the country, the Kamakura group was able to control both peasants and court nobles, whose incomes came from the Kamakura-managed estates. The Kamakura group became the only real central government in Japan.

Upon Yoritomo's death, the Hojo family assumed power, ruling through a puppet shogun from the Fujiwara family and then from the royal family.

By the late 1200's the Kamakura system had begun to disintegrate, although Kamakura soldiers were able to repel Mongol invasions ordered by Kublai Khan in 1274 and 1281. The strain of warding off Mongol invasion attempts had weakened the Kamakura shogunate, and in 1331 a retired emperor, Daigo II, led a revolt against the Kamakura. The result was a bitter struggle. In 1338 Ashikaga Takauji had himself proclaimed shogun; his successors ended the conflict in 1392. The Ashikaga shoguns never acquired the same degree of authority as the Kamakura shoguns, but they preserved a measure of stability until 1467. During this period of political collapse, commerce and manufacturing prospered and trade with China expanded.

Political reunification came in the late 1500's when Oda Nobunaga, a feudal lord, seized Kyoto in 1568 and became ruler of central Japan. His successor, Hideyoshi, assumed power in 1582 and reunited the entire country. He attempted an invasion of Korea in 1592, but was repulsed by Chinese forces. Hideyoshi was succeeded in 1598 by Tokugawa Ieyasu, who took the title of shogun in 1603.

Tokugawa era. Tokugawa and his successors created a political system that remained unchanged for 250 years. The price of stability and peace, however, was an oppressive and reactionary government. Social stability was achieved by the creation of a strict class system. Foreign relations and Western influence, especially Christianity, had flourished in the late 16th century. Both now became the targets of bitter reactionary politics. The Spanish and Portuguese were expelled,

and in 1638 the Japanese were forbidden to go abroad. In the same year, the thriving Christian community was liquidated by fierce oppression and persecution.

By the 18th century a wealthy merchant class, merged through intermarriage with the warriors, began to undermine the austere Confucianism encouraged by the Tokugawa shoguns. There was also a revival of interest in the West.

Commodore Matthew Perry conveyed (1853 to 1854) strong American insistence on establishing trade; this underscored demands to end Japan's isolation. In 1858 a full commercial treaty with the United States was signed, and similar agreements with European countries followed. Foreign businesses were set up in Yokohama, which soon became a major world port.

Meiji restoration. The Tokugawa regime lost national confidence by negotiating a treaty with a foreign power, and in 1867 the new shogun voluntarily surrendered control of the country to the emperor, a return to royal rule called the Meiji restoration.

The new Meiji government quickly set Japan on a course that would bring two generations of breathtaking transformation. Leaders went abroad to study Western institutions and invited Western advisers to Japan. From what they learned, the Japanese created new structures suited to Japan's goal of modernization. Compulsory education, a standard land tax, universal military conscription, and a constitution that made Japan a constitutional monarchy in 1889 were among the acquisitions.

The costs of modernization were borne mostly by the peasants, who paid new land taxes instead of feudal dues. Foreign investment, with its risk of for-

JAPAN RETAINS ITS TRADITIONS, *like this Shinto wedding ceremony, despite the country's affinity for modernization.*

KALVAR/MAGNUM PHOTOS

eign control, was limited, and new industries developed by the government were sold cheaply to private Japanese firms. With a strong army and navy, and a large industrial complex, Japan was ready to test itself as a world military power.

Expansionism. A quarrel with China over Korea provoked the Sino-Japanese War of 1894–1895, which was easily won by Japan. Clashes of interest with Russia over Korea and Manchuria led to the Russo-Japanese War of 1904–1905, a war won by the Japanese after a series of stunning victories on land and on sea. Korea was annexed in 1910. Japan now had the opportunity to become the leader of a modernizing pan-Asian movement, but the movement was neglected in favor of attempts to secure dominance in Asia by military force.

In 1914 Japan, as Britain's ally, declared war on Germany in World War I. Seeking to take advantage of the situation, Japan attempted to dominate China. These plans were upset largely through diplomacy initiated by the United States. Thereafter, extreme nationalism flourished in Japan. Japan's "divine mission" to rule Asia and, ultimately, the world, was preached. Meanwhile, the world economic crisis of the 1930's increased support for nationalist extremism.

To maintain its economy and large population, Japan was desperately in need of foreign markets where it could obtain supplies and sell its exports. With the Depression, Japan became subject to the will of other nations' tariff policies.

By the 1930's many Japanese, especially the militarists, were eager to engage in a policy of colonial expansion to obtain sources of raw materials and markets. Although the emperor and many leading statesmen disliked the

PEACE PARK in Hiroshima commemorates the dropping of the first atomic bomb.

army extremists, they were unwilling to produce a public scandal by acting decisively against them. This culminated in the invasion of Manchuria in 1931. Full-scale war with China started in 1937.

World War II. Meanwhile, in 1936, Japan had signed with Germany the Anti-Comintern Pact. Finally, in 1940, the Rome-Berlin-Tokyo Axis was established. To break the economic blockade set up by the Western nations, especially the United States, in protest against Japanese aggression, Japan attacked Pearl Harbor on December 7, 1941, without warning.

After many important initial Japanese successes, the United States and its allies counterattacked. By 1943 Japan was in retreat. Yet Japan did not surrender until August 14, 1945, after the United States dropped the world's first atomic bombs on the Japanese cities of Hiroshima and Nagasaki.

Japan was occupied by U.S. forces under the command of General Douglas MacArthur, and attempts at a thorough democratization of the country were started. Emperor Hirohito disclaimed his divinity, and in 1946 a new constitution gave power to a parliament chosen by universal suffrage, with the emperor as a constitutional monarch. The constitution also included effective civil liberties clauses. Reforms to strengthen labor unions, break up business cartels, and end the rural landlord system also supported democracy.

Contemporary Japan. Economic recovery was slow after the destruction wrought by the war, but the rapidly changing international situation provoked sharp modifications in U.S. policy in regard to Japan. Since Japan regained its independence (September 8, 1951), Japan and the United States have maintained exceptionally close ties. A mutual security treaty (also September 8, 1951) promised American protection of Japan in return for the right to maintain U.S. bases there. Though trade competition has created strains, basic cooperation has never diminished. A symbol of this close relationship was America's return to Japan in 1972 of the Ryukyu Islands won in World War II.

The Korean War, from 1950 to 1953, sparked a startling increase in Japan's industrial output. This growth has been somewhat slowed since 1970 because of inflation caused largely by high oil prices.

One key to Japan's postwar adjustment has been a stable government dominated by the conservative Liberal Democratic Party, which has held the office of prime minister, and has won almost every election since its formation in 1955. Under prime ministers like Yoshida Shigeru (1946–1947, 1948–1954) and Sato Eisaku (1964–1972), the party has given Japan both political stability and a highly business-oriented climate.

The party suffered reverses in the 1970's because of corruption scandals that beset Prime Minister Tanaka Kakuei and several years of economic slowdown; but it still retained power, and by the end of the decade had won back its strong majorities.

In 1982 Yasuhiro Nakasone became prime minister. During his terms in office he worked to improve Japan's status as a world power, responding to the perception that Japan was not accepting fully its responsibilities as a world economic leader. Under his administration, Japan increased development aid to Southeast Asia and the

VENDING MACHINES are one expression of the Japanese love of gadgetry. Almost anything can be bought from them, including jewelry and clothing.

Pacific basin and improved ties with neighbors such as China and the Philippines. Japan has also increased its share of the costs of maintaining a U.S. military presence, a move that sparked some controversy, as Japan is forbidden by its constitution to maintain any but a purely defensive force.

Japan has come under fire from many of its trading partners, particularly the United States, for what is seen as unfair trading practices, including tariffs and quotas that restrict imports.

Kampuchea

See Cambodia

Kiribati

The land and people. Kiribati is scattered across more than 2 million square miles of the west central Pacific. It consists of four groups of atolls, including the 16 Gilbert Islands, eight Phoenix Islands, eight Line Islands (one group of five and another group of three), and Banaba, or Ocean Island.

All of the islands are low-lying coral atolls, except Banaba, which is of volcanic origin with a rugged, mountainous terrain. The islands' climate is hot and humid, with rainfall ranging from 40 to 120 inches annually.

Most of the people of Kiribati are Micronesian, but there is also a small minority of Polynesians. Over 90 percent of the population live on the Gilbert Islands, and about one-third on the single island of Tarawa. The Phoenix Islands are not permanently inhabited.

Economy. Banaba once had rich phosphate deposits, the mining of which was the economic mainstay of the islands until deposits were depleted in 1980. Since then Kiribati has been faced with the challenge of developing

a diversified economy. Coconuts are grown, and copra is the main export. Kiribati also exports fish and fish products and receives income from the sale of the right to fish in its waters.

Government. The head of both state and government is the president. The legislature of the republic is a unicameral House of Assembly. It has 35 elected members.

History. The first Europeans to sight the islands may have been Spanish sailors in the 1500's, but most were discovered in the late 1700's and early 1800's by British seamen.

Great Britain proclaimed the Gilbert and Ellice islands a protectorate in 1888, and added Ocean Island in 1900. At the request of the inhabitants, it annexed the islands as a colony in 1916. The other islands were added to the colony between 1916 and 1938. British settlers established copra plantations, and the British government has used the islands as cable stations, ports, and radar stations.

The Gilbert Islands were the scene of heavy fighting in World War II. After the war, efforts were made to expand the economy of the islands, to extend self-government, and to relieve population pressure on the crowded islands.

In 1975 the Ellice Islands severed ties with the territory and became a separate territory under the name Tuvalu, which is now independent.

Kiribati became an independent republic on July 12, 1979. Banaba has actively sought separation since the inception of the new republic.

Korea

North Korea

The land. North Korea is mostly mountainous. The northern end of the Taebaek mountains, which extend

down the Korean peninsula, and the Hamgyong mountains, which run southwest to northeast, dominate the country. Lowlands occupy the western part of the country, along the Yellow Sea.

North Korea's most important rivers are the Yalu and the Tumen, which form most of the border with China, and the Taedong, which flows through the capital city of Pyongyang.

The climate in North Korea is dominated by a long cold winter and a short summer, although along the western coast temperatures tend to be more moderate.

The people. North Korea's population is both ethnically and linguistically homogeneous. Nearly all the population are believed to be Korean, although there may be a small minority of Chinese.

The population of North Korea is unevenly distributed, with a much higher density along the west coast than in the interior or the east coast. Pyongyang is by far the largest city. Other important cities include Hamhung (480,000), Chongjin (300,000), Sinuiju (300,000), and Wonsan (275,000).

Although the constitution permits North Koreans to practice religion, in reality the government actively discourages any religious participation.

Economy. The North Korean economy is patterned on the Soviet model. Industrial capacity is mostly owned by the state, and agriculture has been collectivized.

North Korea is rich in natural resources. Mineral resources include coal, manganese, iron ore, uranium, and zinc. Because of the many swift streams and rivers, hydroelectric potential is high.

Heavy industry is well developed in North Korea. Significant manufactures include products such as steel, cement, and fertilizer. The severe climate

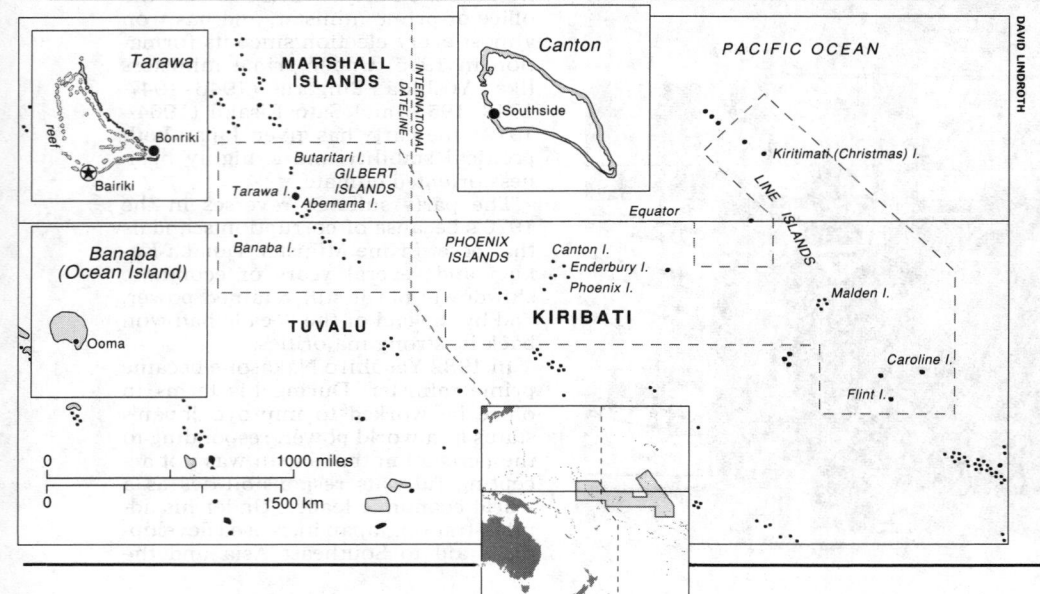

Kiribati

Official name: *Republic of Kiribati*
Area: *278 sq. mi., 720 sq. km.*
Type of government: *Democracy*
Head of state: *President, Ieremia Tabai*
Population: *69,000 (1989 est.)*
Population growth rate: *2.0%*
Capital: *Baikiri (Pop., 1988 est., 1800)*
Languages: *I-Kiribati, English (both official)*
Religions: *Roman Catholic 50%, Protestant 44%*
Ethnic groups: *Micronesian, Polynesian*
Literacy: *20%*
Life expectancy: *54 years (1987)*
Currency: *Australian dollar*
Per capita GNP: *$417 (1984)*
Exports: *$1.4 million (1986)*
Imports: *$11.7 million (1986)*

DAVID LINDROTH

Korea (North)

Official name: *Democratic People's Republic of Korea*
Area: *46,768 sq. mi., 121,129 sq. km.*
Type of government: *Communist*
Head of state: *President, Kim Il Sung*
Head of government: *Prime minister, Kang Song San*
Population: *22,521,000 (1989 est.)*
Population growth rate: *2.5%*
Capital and largest city: *Pyongyang (Pop., 1986 est., 2,000,000)*
Language: *Korean*
Religions: *Officially atheist, Buddhist*
Ethnic group: *Korean*
Literacy: *99%*
Life expectancy: *69 years (1987)*
Currency: *Won*
Per capita GNP: *$910 (1986)*
Exports: *$1.7 billion (1986)*
Imports: *$2 billion (1986)*

Korea (South)

Official name: *Republic of Korea*
Area: *38,031 sq. mi., 98,500 sq. km.*
Type of government: *Democratic republic*
Head of state: *President, Chun Doo Hwan*
Head of government: *Prime minister, Lee Han Key*
Population: *43,347,000 (1989 est.)*
Population growth rate: *1.4%*
Capital and largest city: *Seoul (Pop., 1986 est., 9,581,000)*
Language: *Korean*
Religions: *Buddhist 37%, Protestant 26%, Roman Catholic 5%*
Ethnic group: *Korean*
Literacy: *90%*
Life expectancy: *69 years (1987)*
Currency: *Won*
Per capita GNP: *$2800 (1987)*
Exports: *$46.9 billion (1987)*
Imports: *$40.5 billion (1987)*

found in most of North Korea means that the growing season is quite short. However, investments in fertilizers and mechanization have recently made the country self-sufficient in food.

Most of North Korea's trade is with other socialist countries. Principal exports include machinery, steel, metal ores, textiles, and chemicals. Imports include petroleum, food, rubber, and machinery.

Government. North Korea is nominally ruled by a Supreme People's Assembly that elects a Central Committee to act for it between its short sessions. In actuality the Communist Party dominates political life. Its central political committee determines national policy and its chairman is the key figure in government.

History. *Note: For Korean history prior to the end of the Korean War, see article on South Korea.*

Postwar. Following World War II, a government based on the Soviet pattern was established in North Korea. It was dominated by a newly formed Communist Party, and was greatly influenced by China's new Communist government. Kim Il Sung became its leader. Following the Korean War, Kim established a degree of independence from both China and the Soviet Union. He has carried a "cult of personality" to extreme lengths in one of the most tightly regimented and closed Communist societies.

No peace treaty was ever signed between North and South Korea following the Korean War. Reunification remains one of Kim's central goals, and North Korea has pursued that goal using both diplomacy and violence.

Talks between the two Koreas on normalizing relations have been held periodically, however little progress

has been made. Recently, talks were held to work out participation by North Korea in the 1988 Summer Olympic Games held in Seoul, but no agreement was reached.

North Korea has periodically used violence to try to destabilize the South Korean government. Among its acts of aggression have been attempts in 1968 and 1974 to assassinate South Korean president Park; the 1968 seizure of the U.S.S. *Pueblo* in international waters; and a 1983 bombing of South Korean officials in Rangoon, Burma.

South Korea

The land. The eastern part of South Korea is dominated by the Taebaek mountains, and the center of the country by an offshoot called the Sobaek range, which runs from northeast to southwest. The most fertile areas of the country are the lowlands along the west coast between the mountains and the Yellow Sea. The Han, the Kum, and the Naktong are South Korea's most important rivers. The south and west coasts are dotted by numerous small islands. The larger island of Cheju is located about 50 miles off the south coast.

The climate is generally temperate. Summers are hot and humid, and winters are cold and dry. Yearly rainfall averages about 60 inches along the west coast, falling mostly during the summer months.

The people. South Korea has a very ethnically homogeneous population. There is, apart from Koreans, only a small minority of Chinese origin. Most South Koreans are either Confucian or Buddhist, but there are also many Christians. Ch'ondogyo, a mixture of

Confucian, Taoist, and Buddhist teachings, also has numerous adherents.

South Korea is quite densely populated, with 1121 people per square mile. In 1988 about 65 percent of the population lived in urban areas. Seoul is by far the largest city, but other important cities include the ports of Inchon and Pusan and the interior cities of Taegu and Kwangju.

The economy. South Korea is one of the so-called "little dragons" of Asia. Driven by high levels of exports, the country achieved an astonishing growth rate of about 10 percent per year during the 1960's and 1970's.

The division of the Korean peninsula in 1945 left the South Korean economy in terrible shape. The south had little in the way of natural resources and most of the industrial development to that time had taken place in the north.

Light industry has grown rapidly in South Korea since the 1950's. Textiles, clothing, paper, and electronic equipment are produced. Heavy industry also has increased, including such products as steel, motor vehicles, chemicals, and ships.

Agriculture's importance to the South Korean economy has declined as the importance of industry has increased. Today agriculture and industry each employ about one-quarter of the population. Principal agricultural products include rice, barley, potatoes, and fruits and vegetables. Forestry is important, but many forests have been depleted.

Major exports include transport equipment, textiles, electrical products, and steel. Imports include oil, food, machinery, and raw materials. Japan and the United States are by far South Korea's largest trading partners.

Government. Following revision of the constitution in 1987, South Korea has as head of state a president popularly elected every four years. Legislative power rests with the National Assembly, which has 276 members elected to four-year terms.

History. Korea was settled more than 3000 years ago, probably by peoples from Manchuria or northern China. They lived by hunting, fishing, and herding, and over many centuries developed a culture unique to the peninsula. The first known state of any significance was the kingdom of Choson, which was founded in the 190's B.C. By 108 B.C. Han Chinese had conquered Choson and established Chinese colonies in Korea, one of which, Lolang, survived until the 300's A.D.

Agriculture and iron smelting appeared in southeastern Korea by the first century A.D., but the area was not politically unified until the 300's, when three native Korean kingdoms had developed—Koguryo in the north, Paekche in the southwest, and Silla in the southeast.

Silla grew in power under the strong leadership of a political and military elite, and in the 600's, with aid from China, it conquered Paekche and Koguryo. Silla ruled a unified peninsula for almost 250 years, a period considered the golden age of Buddhism. The government was efficiently run, society was well organized and peaceful, trade prospered, the arts flourished, and Buddhist culture and learning took firm root. By the 800's, however, Silla began to collapse.

In the period of confusion that followed, some powerful merchant communities developed trade relations with China and Japan.

By the 900's, rebel leaders had revived the Koguryo state, conquered the rest of Korea, and in 918 founded the Koryo dynasty. The Koryo restored order by establishing a centralized, bureaucratic government. The new government did nothing to remedy the inequitable division of land and power that had split Korean society, however.

By the mid-1000's the court was dominated by a succession of powerful families, and by the mid-1100's the whole system was in a state of collapse as a result of factional fights and revolts. By 1258 Korea had fallen to the Mongols and the Koryo kings became Mongol vassals.

Korea suffered greatly under the Mongols, but by the late 1300's it was independent again, under the Yi.

The era of the Yi dynasty is considered the golden age of Confucianism in Korea. Confucian emphasis on learning produced an elite of scholars and was responsible in the 1400's for the development of an alphabet, called *hangul,* for the Korean language. Confucian ethics served to widen the divisions within the traditional social and economic order, and factionalism severely weakened the country.

In the late 1500's Korea was devastated by Japanese invasions. An inva-

sion in 1592 led to the Japanese conquest of most of Korea, but China came to the aid of its vassal state and the Japanese were driven out. A second invasion in 1597 led to further destruction, and Korea never fully recovered. In the 1620's and 1630's, it was overrun by Manchu armies and became totally dependent on China for support and protection.

New influences. The destruction of the old social and economic orders, and the weakening of traditional values, left Korea open to new influences. Christian missionaries began to visit the country in the 1600's, and by 1800 they had won many converts and had introduced Western learning and ideals into the peninsula.

Also by the 1800's, a new middle class of craftsmen and merchants had replaced the old feudal landlords as the dominant and most prosperous group in society. Trade with Japan thrived, and the appearance of trading ships from Western nations in the 1800's promised even greater prosperity.

The Korean government tried unsuccessfully to maintain traditional society by repressing Western learning and banning foreign trade. Moreover, by the mid-1800's China had lost much of its power and was unable to serve as Korea's protector or as its agent in foreign affairs.

Foreign rivalries. Japan and China vied for political, commercial, and diplomatic control of Korea. To back its position, China invited the United States, Britain, Germany, Italy, France, and Russia to enter into trade and diplomatic relations with Korea, and in the 1800's Korea became a diplomatic battleground for the world's great powers. The government was sharply divided into rival factions and became extremely unstable.

An antiforeign and nationalistic religious uprising in 1894 opened the door

for Japanese troops to move into Korea to protect Japanese interests. This precipitated the Sino-Japanese War that ended in 1895 in victory for Japan, forcing China to relinquish all claims to Korea.

Russia, with interests and influence in Korea second only to those of China, challenged Japanese dominance over Korean affairs. Russo-Japanese rivalry led to war between the two in 1904. The treaty ending the war in 1905 recognized Japan's dominant position in Korea, and in 1910 Japan annexed Korea, making it a colony.

Japanese rule. Korea was ruled despotically, and Japan was concerned only with economic exploitation of the land and the people. The Japanese developed the country's industries and resources by using forced labor, gave the best land and jobs to Japanese, and tried to impose Japanese culture on the people of Korea.

Japan's rule was bitterly resented, and an independence movement soon developed. Although it was able to do little against the Japanese, its leaders aligned themselves during World War II with the Allies, who were fighting Japan—China, Britain, the United States, and, at war's end, the Soviet Union.

Divided land. In 1945 Soviet and U.S. troops liberated the peninsula from the Japanese. To facilitate acceptance of the Japanese surrender and to prepare the country for independence, the two agreed to divide their authority in Korea at the 38th parallel. U.S. and Soviet representatives could not agree on the formation of a provisional government for a reunited country, or on the withdrawal of their troops. In the south, a constituent assembly was elected and a constitution adopted. Syngman Rhee, a leader of the independence movement, was elected to the presidency.

SOUTH KOREA, FOLLOWING IN JAPAN'S FOOTSTEPS, *has begun to make a name for itself as a producer of inexpensive and reliable products, like motor vehicles.*

In 1949 Soviet and U.S. forces withdrew and the 38th parallel became the boundary between rival Korean states. The division of the country added to the difficulties it faced in recovering from years of war and colonial rule, and Korea became a focus of the worldwide confrontation between the United States and the Soviet Union.

In June, 1950, the North Koreans tried to unify Korea by conquering the South, and they certainly would have succeeded but for United Nations-sponsored U.S. intervention. General Douglas MacArthur came near to unifying Korea by conquering North Korea, but he was driven back by Chinese intervention. A truce negotiation in 1953 left the frontier between the two Koreas not far from the prewar one.

In the postwar years President Syngman Rhee became increasingly dictatorial. He was overthrown in 1960 in a revolt started by student demonstrators. An ineffective civilian government that was overthrown by the army in 1961 ensued.

The government became dominated by General Park Chung Hee. Although he allowed the restoration of some democratic systems, the power of the presidency, which Park assumed, was strengthened, and little dissent was permitted. Park was elected to the presidency five times before he was assassinated in 1979. During Park's tenure great emphasis was placed on the reform and modernization of the South Korean economy. As a result, South Korea has one the strongest economies in Asia.

In 1980 the army, led by Chun Doo Hwan, again imposed martial law, sometimes brutally. The reaction by the military to a protest in Kwangju left 170 people dead and put a stain on the government that it has not yet overcome. Martial law ended in 1981, and South Korea returned to a strong indirectly elected presidential system of government, with broad powers to limit dissent.

In 1983 South Korea was rocked by two tragedies. In September the Soviet Union shot down a Korean passenger plane, killing 269 people. In October a bomb blast in Burma killed 17 South Korean officials, including four cabinet ministers and two principal advisers to Chun.

Popular antigovernment demonstrations in 1987 forced Chun's resignation. His successor, Roh Tae Woo, supported a referendum on a new constitution that provided for direct election of the president. The constitution was approved.

In the presidential election that followed, however, the opposition candidates were disorganized and disunited, and Roh won the election. In the year following the election South Korea focused on organizing the 1988 Summer Olympics, which were held in Seoul.

Laos

The land. Laos is a long, narrow country, broader in the north, with a southern panhandle that narrows at one point to little more than 50 miles in width. In the northern region sandstone and limestone plateaus are deeply etched by the Mekong River and its tributaries. The long, almost impassable range of mountains called the Annam Cordillera forms nearly the entire eastern border of Laos. The western border is formed primarily by the Mekong River; its fertile valley supports most of the population.

Laos has a tropical climate, with high humidity and temperatures averaging between 80°F and 90°F.

The people. Laos is an ethnically diverse country. The Lao and the Tai are related to the Thai people of Thailand, and they speak related languages. The Meo and Man in northern Laos are related to peoples in southern China. The Kha are most closely related to the Mon-Khmer peoples of Cambodia. Buddhism is the principal organized religion in Laos, but animist beliefs and practices are widespread.

Laos is sparsely populated and 85 percent of the population live in rural areas. There is no large metropolis. Vientiane, the administrative capital, is the largest city. Luang Prabang, the royal capital, ranks second, with a much smaller population.

Economy. Laos is a poor country with an undeveloped economy and an unskilled, largely illiterate labor force. It is thought to have deposits of iron ore, manganese, gold, coal, and copper, but these have not been explored. Tin, gypsum, salt, and limestone are mined in small amounts.

Almost all of the country is forested with potentially valuable timber, and the soil is very rich, especially in the valleys of the Mekong River and its tributaries.

Subsistence agriculture dominates the economy. The major crop is rice, but yields are very low. Vegetables, spices, and some fruits, including bananas, mangoes, and pineapples, are grown throughout the country. Cotton is widely raised, and there is some commercial tobacco farming around Vientiane.

Many upland tribes still follow the "slash and burn" form of farming. These farmers clear the forest by cutting down the smaller trees and burning the refuse. In the fields thus cleared, they plant a variety of crops for a few seasons and then abandon the field to the forest to start over again at another clearing. When all the land within a certain radius of the village has been exploited, the people migrate to a new area.

Foreign trade is of little importance in the economy, and the balance of trade is very poor. The main exports are hydroelectric power, tin, coffee, soybeans, leather, and forest products such as wood, cardamom, benzoin, and lac. Petroleum, machinery, manufactured goods, and foodstuffs are principal imports.

Government. Laos is a republic with a president as titular head of state. The basic power rests with the prime minister, who is also the secretary-general of the Lao People's Democratic Party (the only political party).

History. The aboriginal Kha people of Laos were joined in the mid-1200's A.D. by the Lao, one tribe of the Thai people who fled the Mongol invasion of south-central China and settled the

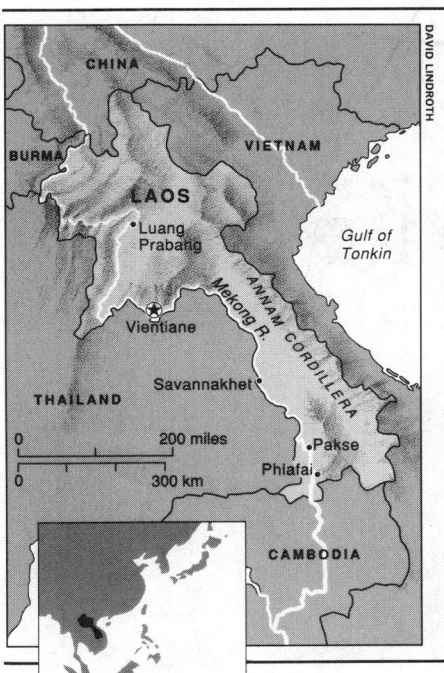

Laos

Official name: *Lao People's Democratic Republic*
Area: *91,430 sq. mi., 236,803 sq. km.*
Type of government: *Communist*
Head of state: *President, Phoumi Vongvichit*
Head of government: *Prime minister, Kaysone Phomvihan*
Population: *3,936,000 (1989 est.)*
Population growth rate: *2.3%*
Capital and largest city: *Vientiane (Pop., 1987 est., 300,000)*
Languages: *Lao (official), French*
Religions: *Buddhism 58%, indigenous 34%*
Ethnic groups: *Lao 48%, Mon-Khmer 25%, Thai 14%, Sino-Tibetan 13%*
Literacy: *41%*
Life expectancy: *48 years (1987)*
Currency: *Kip*
Per capita GNP: *$180 (1986)*
Exports: *$58.5 million (1986)*
Imports: *$205 million (1986)*

northern edge of the Indochinese peninsula. They established many small kingdoms that were in almost constant competition for control of the entire region.

Lan Xang. In the mid-1300's, Fa-Ngum, ruler of a kingdom centered in Muang Swa, on the upper Mekong River, conquered most of the kingdoms of Laos and northern Siam (Thailand) and united them in the empire of Lan Xang, the "Land of a Million Elephants." The culture and religion of India, transmitted through tribes south of Laos, heavily influenced Lao culture. Fa-Ngum adopted Buddhism and made his capital a center of Buddhist culture.

His son, Sam Sene T'ai, consolidated the kingdom and established an efficient administration. By the late 1300's Lan Xang was a powerful, peaceful kingdom that had grown prosperous as a producer of forest products and as a center of trade in Southeast Asia.

During the 1500's attacks by powerful neighbors of Laos—Annam to its east, and Siam (present Thailand) and Burma to its west—weakened Lan Xang and lowered its prestige. During this period the Lao capital was moved south, to Vientiane, and Muang Swa was made a temple city and renamed Luang Prabang.

Civil strife. In the late 1500's Laos was torn by violent dynastic struggles that left it poverty-stricken and defenseless against tribal rebellions and attacks by its neighbors. By the early 1700's, this civil strife had split Laos into three rival states, one ruled from Luang Prabang, one from Vientiane, and the third from Champassak in southern Laos.

No state could regain the former power, prosperity, and prestige that the unified kingdom had enjoyed, and each sought the aid of Siam, Annam, and Burma in conquering the others. As a result, Laos continued to be torn by conflict throughout the 1700's. By the early 1800's Siam had conquered the kingdoms and had annexed Laos.

During the 1800's European explorers, traders, and missionaries began to visit Laos. Although Laos itself, with few riches and no access to the sea, held little attraction for the Europeans, competition was keen among the European states for control of all the territory in Southeast Asia.

French control. By the late 1800's only Siam, which included Laos, separated British Burma from French Cambodia. The British wanted Siam to remain independent, and the French wanted to gain control of Siam. In 1893, in an effort to hold off French conquest, Siam ceded to France all its territory east of the Mekong, which included most of Laos. In 1904 most of the remainder of present-day Laos became French.

The French imposed peace on the warlike Lao tribes and kingdoms, and they allowed Lao leaders to participate in the government. They modernized the government, abolished slavery, and brought education and medical care to the Lao. The French also attempted to develop the country's natural resources and improve its economy, but the world economic Depression of the 1930's hindered any real economic progress.

Japan occupied all of Indochina during World War II, and during the Japanese occupation Lao nationalism began to grow. A "Free Laos" government was organized and it took over when the Japanese withdrew. After the war, the French made an unsuccessful attempt to reestablish their control. In 1947 the Lao adopted a constitution establishing a monarchy and a parliament. In 1949 Laos became an independent state within the French Union.

Opposition to the French was quite violent elsewhere in Indochina. In Vietnam open war, supported by Communist forces, was raging against the French, and in 1953 the Communist-dominated Vietminh forces of Vietnam invaded Laos. In 1954 the French gave up the struggle in Vietnam.

Independence. A peace conference held at Geneva later in 1954 officially ended the war and recognized Laos as a sovereign state.

Political and economic chaos reigned in Laos after 1954, as the governments that came to power were too unstable to deal with the many factions within Laos or to repair the social and economic damage of years of warfare. In addition, Communists from Vietnam organized a rebel army, the Lao People's Liberation Army, originally called the Pathet Lao.

Numerous conflicts between the Pathet Lao and neutralist royal forces resulted in almost constant civil war after 1960. The situation was aggravated by the war in neighboring Vietnam, as the Vietminh established invasion bases in Laos.

The United States and South Vietnam frequently bombed Vietminh bases in Laos before the Vietnam War ended in 1973. At that time a coalition Communist-Royalist government was formed in Laos. In August, 1975, the Vietminh-backed Pathet Lao took control of Laos. The king was forced to abdicate and a Communist government, strongly influenced by Vietnam, was instituted.

Laos continues to be closely tied to Vietnam and the Soviet Union, although in the mid-1980's there were signs that an effort was being made to improve relations with Thailand, China, and the United States.

Malaysia

The land. Malaysia includes West Malaysia (the former British colony of Malaya) on the southern end of the Malay peninsula, and East Malaysia, consisting of the states of Sarawak (on northwest Borneo) and Sabah (north Borneo).

West Malaysia consists of a narrow central core of low, jungle-covered mountains rising up from swampy mineral-rich coastal plains. East Malaysia has a mountainous interior and a narrow border of swampy coastal plains. Small islands lie off the

FISHING THE MEKONG RIVER *provides much food in Laos. For this reason, many Laotians live along the river's banks.*

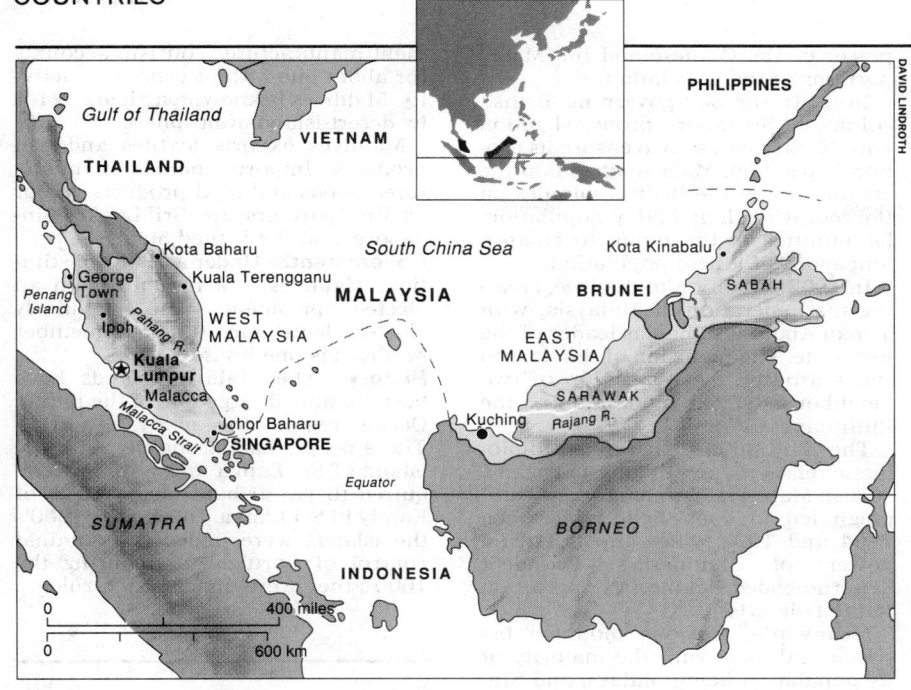

DAVID LINDROTH

Malaysia

Official name: *Malaysia*
Area: *128,400 sq. mi., 332,556 sq. km.*
Type of government: *Constitutional monarchy*
Head of state: *Yang di-Pertuan Agong Mahmood Iskandar*
Head of government: *Prime minister, Mahathir Mohamad*
Population: *16,727,000 (1989 est.)*
Population growth rate: *2.1%*
Capital and largest city:
Kuala Lumpur
(Pop., 1986 est., 977,100)
Languages: *Malay, Chinese dialects, English, Tamil*
Religions: *Muslim, Hindu, Buddhist*
Ethnic groups: *Malay 59%, Chinese 32%, Indian 9%*
Literacy: *75%*
Life expectancy: *67 years (1987)*
Currency: *Ringgit*
Per capita GNP: *$1850 (1986)*
Exports: *$13.9 billion (1986)*
Imports: *$10.8 billion (1986)*

coasts of both West and East Malaysia. Of the many rivers that thread Malaysia, the most important are the Pahang, in West Malaysia, and the Rajang, in East Malaysia.

The Malaysian climate is equatorial. The year-round temperature averages 80°F, and an annual average of 100 inches of rain falls on the country as a whole.

The people. The Malaysian population is quite varied. Just under half of the people are Muslim Malays who speak Malay. Slightly more than one-third are Chinese. The Chinese are primarily urban; the Malays are predominantly rural. Indians and Pakistanis make up about 10 percent of the population; the remainder consists of a variety of native islanders, mostly in East Malaysia.

Population is concentrated in the coastal regions. It is densest in the western half of West Malaysia, where the country's largest cities are located —Kuala Lumpur, the Federation's capital, Ipoh (300,000), and George Town (250,000), a port city on Penang Island in the Malacca Strait.

Malaysia's population has urbanized considerably since World War II. Today, 35 percent of the population live in urban areas, with many people living in urban centers that exist as planned agricultural settlements.

Economy. Malaysia has a prosperous and growing economy, largely because of its wealth of natural resources, especially rubber and tin. Malaysia is the world's leading producer of natural rubber, with an output of over 1.5 million metric tons in 1984. Most of the rubber comes from West Malaysia.

Malaysia's abundance of high-grade tin ore, concentrated on the west coast of the Malay peninsula, has made it the world's largest producer of tin, mining 41,000 metric tons in 1984. Forests cover more than 75 percent of Malaysian territory and are one of the most valuable resources, supplying timber, palm oil, hemp, and coconut products. Bauxite, iron ore, and petroleum also are found in Malaysia.

Rubber processing and tin smelting are the country's major industries. In an effort to lessen its economic dependence on two commodities—rubber and tin—that fluctuate sharply in value, the government in the mid-1960's encouraged the development of diversified manufacturing industries.

Very little of Malaysia's cultivable land is devoted to subsistence crops. Rice paddies, concentrated in the coastal lowlands, account for most of the farmland, and the country's farmers raise less than half of the rice they need. Fish, the other staple of the Malaysian diet, are abundant off the coasts.

Malaysia has a favorable balance of trade, with West Malaysia making a much larger contribution to the country's trade than East Malaysia. Important exports include petroleum and natural gas, electric and electronic equipment, rubber, and tin. Imports include transport equipment, machinery, and food products. Malaysia's major trading partners are Japan, Singapore, and the United States.

Government. Malaysia is a constitutional monarchy. The paramount ruler, or king, is elected to a five-year term by the nine hereditary rulers of the states of West Malaysia from among themselves. He serves as chief of state and as Muslim religious leader. Actual executive power is wielded by the prime minister and cabinet, who are responsible to a parliament.

The 68-member Senate, the upper house of parliament, is partly elected by the state legislatures and partly appointed by the king. The more powerful 154-member House of Representatives is popularly elected. Parliament shares legislative power with the state legislatures.

History. The territory of present-day Malaysia was inhabited in ancient times by Malay peoples who lived in many small coastal kingdoms and whose economies were based on fishing, farming, and trading. From the 800's to the 1200's they were controlled by the far more powerful Sumatran Buddhist Srivijayan empire, and in the 1300's by the Javanese Hindu kingdom of Majapahit.

In about 1400 a Malay ruler founded the state of Malacca, on the western coast of the peninsula. Its capital, the port city of Malacca, soon became the most important trading center in Southeast Asia. During the 1400's Arab traders and missionaries converted the ruler and the people of Malacca to Islam. The state became a center for the spread of Islam throughout the area.

Malacca's port interested European nations that were establishing colonies in southern Asia in the late 1400's. In 1511 Malacca fell to the Portuguese, but in 1641 the Portuguese were ousted by the Dutch. The Europeans did not develop the territory or attempt to bring all of Malaya under their authority. Malacca gradually declined in importance except as a stopping-off point on the sea route between Asia and Europe.

British role. In 1795 Britain took Malacca from the Dutch. In 1826 it was consolidated with the British settlements at Penang, at the northern end of the Strait of Malacca, and with Singapore, at the southern end of the peninsula, to form the Colony of the Straits Settlements.

In the mid-1800's an English adventurer, James Brooke, gained control of Sarawak in northwest Borneo. In 1881 a British chartered company took over what is now Sabah in north Borneo. Thus an arc of British influence developed across the northern edge of the island world at the same time that Dutch influence was slowly growing in what is now Indonesia. The Dutch and the British formally apportioned sovereignty over the area by treaties in 1824 and 1891.

After the opening of the Suez Canal in 1869, Southeast Asian trade became more profitable and important, and competition increased among European states for territory in the region. Also in the late 1800's, the wealth of Malaya's tin mines was realized, and the tin industry grew prosperous and attracted the interest of the British.

By 1914 Britain had concluded treaties making protectorates of the sultanates on the Malay peninsula. Once the British presence guaranteed their security, Chinese miners came in large numbers to Malaya. These workers formed the nucleus of the state's large Chinese minority.

Malaya soon was the world's leading producer and exporter of tin. In the early 1900's the British also developed rubber plantations on the peninsula. The rubber industry was manned largely by Indian labor, and the Malay states soon ranked as the world's leading producers of rubber.

By the 1920's, with a well-ordered government under British administration and a prosperous economy run by Chinese and Indian labor, Malaya was economically, politically, and socially unique in Southeast Asia. The great alien immigration that had left the native Malays and their sultans a bare majority in their own land inhibited the development of any nationalist movements.

Malayan nationalism grew during World War II, when the country was occupied by Japanese forces. Under Japanese direction, the Malayans were largely self-governing, and a desire for full independence followed liberation from the Japanese.

In 1948, after two years of an unsatisfactory trial union, the protected Malay states were united to form the Federation of Malaya. In June, 1948, guerrilla fighting broke out, instigated by Chinese Communists with the support of part of the Malayan Chinese population. Rivalries and conflicts between the Chinese and the Malays within Malaya helped to keep the war going. With the aid of British troops, the federation government gradually defeated the guerrillas.

Independence. In 1957 Malaya became fully independent under a constitution that attempted to balance carefully the power of the Chinese and the Malay portions of the population.

In 1961 the self-governing British colony of Singapore proposed union with Malaya as a step to ensure its economic position. Malaya agreed on the condition that the British colonies on Borneo, with their Malay population, be admitted to the union to balance Singapore's Chinese population.

In 1963 the union took place, creating the Federation of Malaysia, with Tunku Abdul Rahman as leader of the new state. The inclusion of the Borneo states aroused the opposition of two neighboring states, Indonesia and the Philippines.

The Philippines suspended diplomatic relations, and Indonesia began a "Crush Malaysia" campaign. The campaign led to open fighting between 1964 and 1966, when the fall from power of Indonesia's President Sukarno ended Indonesia's opposition to the federation.

Meanwhile, tensions mounted between Malaysia, with the majority of its population being Malays, and Singapore, ruled by its Chinese majority. In 1965 Singapore seceded.

Perhaps Malaysia's most persistent problem since independence has been the uneasy relationship among its three main ethnic groups. In 1969 riots broke out against Chinese Malaysians because of their disproportionate control of wealth. As a result, the constitution was suspended until 1971, and legislation was passed that assured ethnic Malays preferential treatment in education and employment. In the 1980's the government has used the security laws enacted at that time to restrict political opposition.

Maldives

The land and people. The country is formed of some 2000 islands in the Indian Ocean grouped into twelve atolls, or island groups. Most of the islands are small and low-lying, and only about 220 are inhabited.

The Maldivians are an amalgam of people from Sri Lanka, India, Southeast Asia, the Middle East, and Africa. They speak a language similar to Elu, or old Sinhalese, the language of ancient Sri Lanka. Almost all the people are Muslim. Population is densest near the center of the island group, on Male Atoll, which is the site of the capital and largest city, Male.

The overall population density on the crowded islands is 1753 people per square mile, although most islands have fewer than 1000 inhabitants.

Economy. The Maldives, for such a tiny country, has a relatively diverse economy. Fishing is one of the most important industries, employing about 45 percent of the population and supporting a canning and drying industry. The country also supports some garment manufacture. Tourism accounts for about one-fifth of economic activity. Maldives is known particularly for its desert-island atmosphere.

Maldives exports textiles and fish products. Imports include manufactured goods and food products. Major trading partners are Sri Lanka, Singapore, and the United States.

Government. Under a 1968 constitution, Maldives is a republic with an elected president. The popularly elected legislature, the 48-member Majlis, has one house.

History. The Maldive islands have been inhabited by people of the Indian Ocean region for many centuries. These people had strong ties with the island of Sri Lanka and were long required to pay tribute to the kings of Kandy in Sri Lanka. During the 1500's the islands were under the nominal control of Portugal, and during the 1600's they were under Dutch rule.

Maldives

Official name: *Republic of Maldives*
Area: *115 sq. mi., 298 sq. km.*
Type of government: *Democratic republic*
Head of state: *President, Maumoon Abdul Gayoom*
Population: *211,000 (1989 est.)*
Population growth rate: *3.7%*
Capital and largest city: *Malé (Pop., 1985 est., 46,000)*
Languages: *Dhivehi, English*
Religion: *Sunni Islam*
Ethnic groups: *Indian, Sinhalese*
Literacy: *82%*
Life expectancy: *59 years (1987)*
Currency: *Rufiyaa*
Per capita GNP: *$310 (1986)*
Exports: *$22.5 million (1986)*
Imports: *$52 million (1986)*

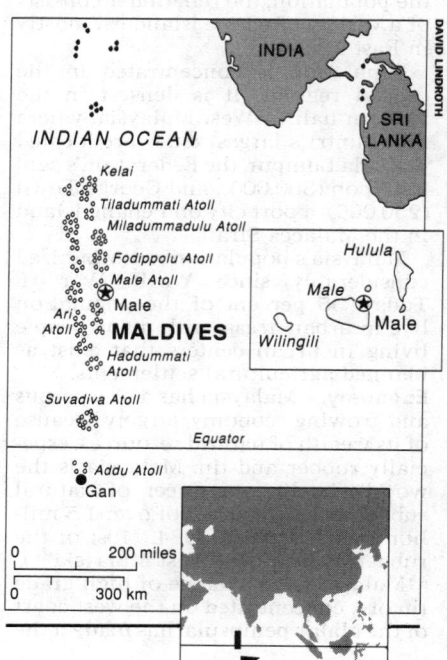

Great Britain made Sri Lanka a crown colony in 1789 and assumed indirect authority over the Maldive islands. In 1887 the islands became a British protectorate. During World War II, Britain built an important air base on Gan Island, in the southern Addu Atoll.

The 1950's were years of great unrest for the islands. In 1953 the national assembly abolished the sultanate and proclaimed a republic, but in 1954 an insurrection resulted in the restoration of the sultanate. British attempts to reactivate its air base on Gan led to clashes between those opposing and those favoring the British presence on the islands. Moreover, the government was unable to deal with the islands' severe food shortage.

Discontent in 1958 led to an insurrection in Suvadiva, south of Male. A rebel leader declared Suvadiva a republic and requested aid from Britain. Britain granted the aid, arousing strong anti-British feeling in Male. In 1959 the Suvadiva rebellion ended and the British were allowed to reopen their air base.

During the early 1960's the Maldivian government and Great Britain negotiated the islands' future, and in 1965 a treaty between Great Britain and the Maldive islands granted full sovereignty to the country. Britain was allowed to retain control of the Gan Island base, although they abandoned it in 1976, and agreed to provide aid to the new nation. In a referendum held in 1968, the Maldive islands voted to become a republic. Ibrahim Nasir, the former prime minister, became the Maldives' first president.

Maumoon Abdul Gayoom was elected to the republic's highest office in November, 1978. In 1980, a coup using mercenaries was attempted and the subsequent investigation implicated former president Nasir.

MAJURO ATOLL is the capital of the Marshall Islands and its largest population center. The islands are very flat, low-lying, and rarely more than about 400 yards wide.

The Marshall Islands

The land and people. The Marshall Islands are a group of 34 islands in the Pacific Ocean east of the Philippines. The islands consist of two roughly parallel chains of coral atolls: the Ratak chain, with 16 atolls, and the Ralik chain, with 18 atolls. The most populous atolls are Kwajalein and Majuro.

The population is Micronesian. Most of the population is Christian, principally Roman Catholic.

Economy. The majority of the Marshall islanders are subsistence farmers and fishermen. The principal crops are coconut, taro, yams, breadfruit, and vegetables. Most of the small amount of industry is involved in processing the coconut and fish harvests.

Fish products, copra, and coconut oil are the principal exports. Imports include food, machinery, and textiles. Rent for the U.S. missile tracking base on Kwajalein Atoll and aid from the United States are important contributions to the economy.

Government. The head of state is the president, who is elected by the 33-member legislative Nitijela from among its members. The members of the Nitijela are elected to four-year terms. A 12-member Council of Iroij (traditional chiefs) advises the president and cabinet.

History. The Marshall Islands were probably originally settled from islands to the west and south. They were first sighted by Europeans in the 16th century, when the Spanish explored the region. However, little value was placed on the islands, and no formal claim by a European power was established until 1886, when Spain and Britain recognized German control over the islands.

At the beginning of World War I, Japan took control of the Marshalls from Germany, and in 1920 obtained a League of Nations mandate to administer the islands. The Marshall Islands, in particular Kwajalein Atoll, saw heavy fighting during World War II.

After the war, the islands were administered by the United States under a United Nations mandate as part of the Trust Territory of the Pacific. From

Marshall Islands

Official name: *Republic of the Marshall Islands*
Area: *70 sq. mi., 181.3 sq. km.*
Type of government: *Democracy*
Head of state: *President, Amata Kabua*
Population: *38,000 (1989 est.)*
Population growth rate: *3.4%*
Capital: *Majuro (Pop., 1985 est., 14,000)*
Languages: *English, Marshallese (official)*
Religion: *Protestant*
Ethnic group: *Micronesian*
Literacy: *90%*
Life expectancy: *66 years (1980)*
Currency: *U.S. dollar*
Per capita GDP: *$1000 (1981)*
Exports: *$2.5 million (1985)*
Imports: *$29.2 million (1985)*

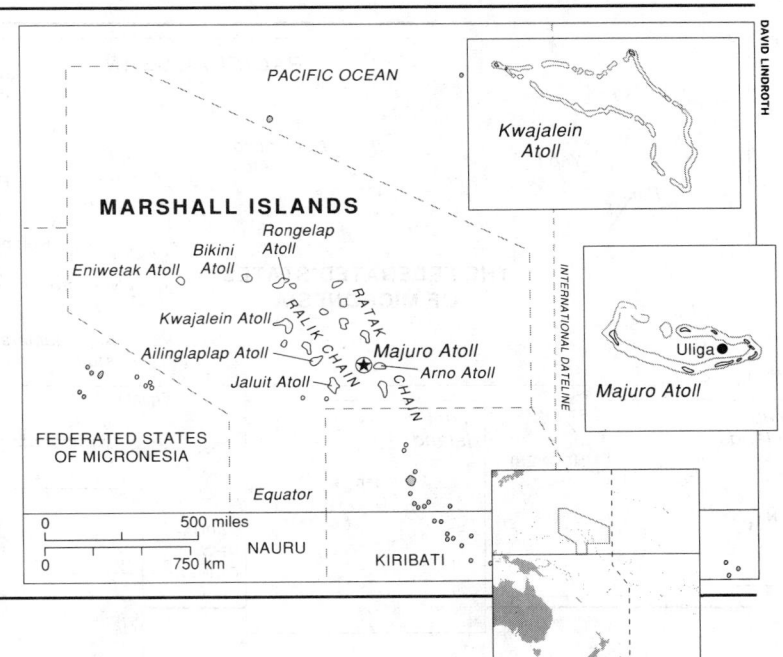

1946 to 1958 the United States used the Bikini and Enewetak atolls as testing sites for nuclear weapons.

After a failed attempt to unite all of the Trust Territory into one independent nation, the Marshall Islands became the Republic of the Marshall Islands in 1979. The islands became a sovereign nation in 1986 when a Compact of Free Association took effect. The compact leaves defense and foreign policy matters in the control of the United States.

The Federated States of Micronesia

The land and people.   The Federated States of Micronesia comprises 607 islands spread across the southern Pacific Ocean. Consisting of most of the Caroline Island chain, the Federated States is about 2000 miles across, from Yap Island in the west to Kosrae Island in the east.

The islands are of coral and volcanic origin. The island groups of Yap and Truk, and the islands Kosrae and Ponape, are the most densely settled parts of the nation. The Yap group has four large, hilly islands and seven smaller islands. The Truk island group consists of eleven islands encircled by a coral reef.

Most of the population of the Federated States is Micronesian. However, the islands are culturally and linguistically diverse. There are eight major indigenous languages spoken in the Federated States, although English is the official language.

Economy.   A large part of the population of the Federated States is employed in subsistence agriculture. The principal crops include coconuts, cassava, yams, and fruits. Fishing is also extremely important to the economy.

The small amount of industry in the Federated States is concentrated in the processing of coconuts and fish. The principal export is copra, though some vegetables and fruit also are exported. Imports include food and manufactured products. The Federated States relies heavily on aid from the United States.

Government.   The head of state is the president, who is elected by the 14-member congress from its members.

The Federated States of Micronesia achieved independence in 1986 with the ratification of the Compact of Free Association. This compact leaves defense and foreign policy matters in control of the United States.

History.   The Carolines were probably first settled from the Philippines, Indonesia, and the Solomon Islands.

The first European visitors to the islands were the Spanish in the 16th century; they established a colony in 1668. In 1899 Germany bought the Carolines from Spain and held them until World War I. Japan received a League of Nations mandate over the islands in 1920.

During World War II the islands saw heavy fighting between U.S. and Japanese forces. In 1947 the United Nations joined the Caroline, Northern Mariana, and Marshall islands as the Trust Territory of the Pacific Islands, under U.S. administration.

An attempt to create a constitution to unite the trust territory pointed up regional differences and led to its division into four separate political entities. The districts of Yap, Truk, Ponape, and Kosrae ratified a constitution creating the Federated States of Micronesia in 1979. The Federated States became sovereign in 1986 when the Compact of Free Association with the United States became effective.

Mongolia

The land.   Much of Mongolia occupies the grassy, rolling Mongolian Plain, which ranges in elevation from 3000 to 6000 feet. Mountains in the north and west rise to between 5000 and 11,000 feet. Along the southwestern border, the Altai range towers over 12,000 feet. In the south and southeast, the Mongolian Plain becomes the barren desert of the Gobi Depression, which extends into Inner Mongolia.

All of Mongolia's principal rivers flow northward, toward the Soviet Union. They include the Selenge and the Orkhon, which empty into Lake Baykal, and the Kerulen, an important tributary of the Amur River.

Mongolia's climate is generally dry and is characterized by long, cold winters and short, cool summers. Precipitation increases from south to north, ranging from less than 5 inches to 15 inches a year.

The people.   The population is almost entirely Mongol, divided into a number of groups, of which the Khalkha is by far the largest. There are minorities of other Mongols, and some Russians and Chinese. Lamaist Buddhism is the dominant religion, but its practice has been restricted since the 1930's.

Over half the population is rural, and some is seminomadic. Population is concentrated in the northern half of the country. About 25 percent of the people live in Ulan Bator, the capital, in east central Mongolia.

The population density is an extremely sparse three persons per square mile.

Economy.   Livestock herding, the Mongol's traditional way of life, remains the mainstay of the country's economy. The country's huge herds of sheep, goats, cattle, horses, and camels provide most necessities, including

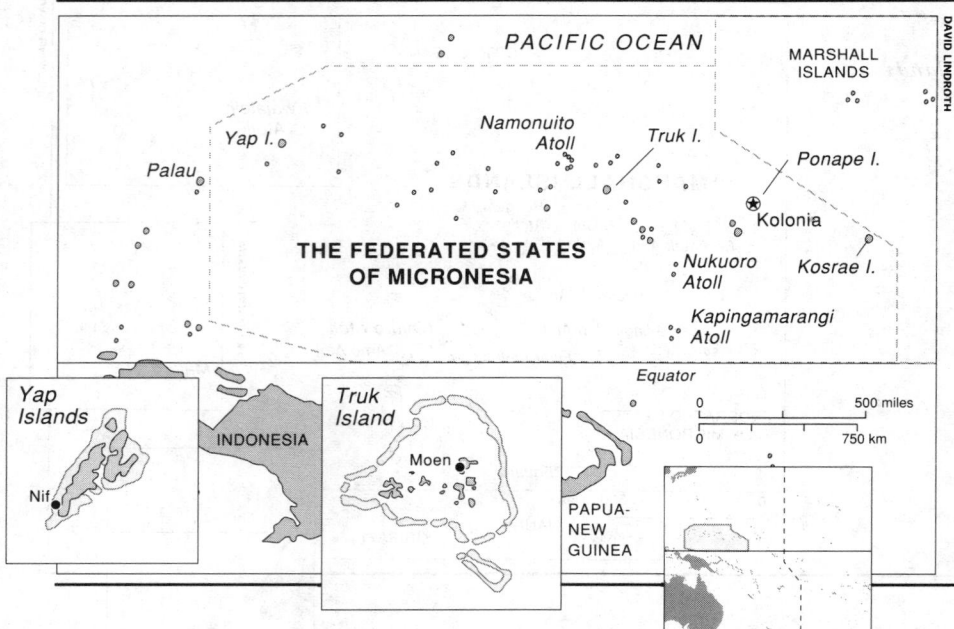

DAVID LINDROTH

PACIFIC OCEAN

MARSHALL ISLANDS

Palau

Yap I.

Namonuito Atoll

Truk I.

Ponape I.

Kolonia

THE FEDERATED STATES OF MICRONESIA

Nukuoro Atoll

Kosrae I.

Kapingamarangi Atoll

Equator

0   500 miles

0   750 km

Yap Islands

Nif

INDONESIA

Truk Island

Moen

PAPUA-NEW GUINEA

Federated States of Micronesia

Official name: *Federated States of Micronesia*
Area: *271 sq. mi., 702 sq. km.*
Type of government: *Democracy*
Head of state: *President, John R. Haglelgam*
Population: *91,000 (1989)*
Population growth rate: *2%*
Capital: *Kolonia*
Languages: *English, local languages*
Religions: *Roman Catholic, Protestant*
Ethnic groups: *Micronesian, Polynesian*
Literacy: *Not available*
Life expectancy: *61 years (1987)*
Currency: *U.S. dollar*
Per capita GNP: *$1300 (1983)*
Exports: *$1.6 million (1983)*
Imports: *$48.9 million (1983)*

MANY MONGOLIANS STILL LIVE *as nomadic herdsmen, much as their ancestors did when their greatest leader, Genghis Khan* (left), *led them to conquer a large part of Asia.*

food, clothing, shelter, and transport, as well as goods for export. The main crops are grain, potatoes, and some vegetables. Agriculture is collectivized on the Soviet model.

Mongolia's resources include coal, copper, gold, iron, molybdenum, and petroleum. The country's considerable hydroelectric capacity is being developed. Industrialization has been recent and relatively rapid. Manufactures include building materials, textiles, and processed foodstuffs.

Mongolia exports farm and animal products and some metal ores. Consumer goods, raw materials, and machinery are imported. Mongolian trade is primarily with communist countries, especially with the Soviet Union. Mongolia receives large amounts of aid from the Soviet Union.

Government. Although Mongolia is constitutionally a republic in which supreme power is vested in a popularly elected assembly, the Khural, political power actually rests with the country's Communist Party, officially called the Mongolian People's Revolutionary Party.

The party proposes all candidates for the Khural, and its political bureau, or politburo, sets national policy. The party's first secretary is the key figure in the government. The chief of the presidium, a council elected by the Khural to govern between its short sessions, serves as the head of state.

History. The early Mongols were divided into many rival nomadic tribes. They lived by herding and raiding neighboring tribes and states. By the beginning of the 1200's, the Mongols held the territory all around the Gobi.

Expansion. The first leader to unite the Mongol tribes was Genghis Khan, the "very mighty king," in 1203. He led the Mongols in the conquest of northern China, eastern Russia, and the Islamic lands of the Near East.

After Genghis Khan's death in 1227, his son, Ogotai, led the Mongols across Hungary and Poland and as far west as Vienna. Ogotai's death in 1241 forced the Mongols to retreat to elect a new khan. Kublai Khan, their choice, conquered all of China and Korea and controlled much of Southeast Asia.

The Mongols proved less skillful at governing than at conquering, however, and in eastern Europe and the Middle East effective Mongol rule ended as soon as the Mongol armies were withdrawn. In China, where the Mongols had established the Yüan dynasty, government corruption eroded Mongol authority and scattered revolts broke out in the Chinese provinces.

Decline. After Kublai Khan's death in 1294, the empire was divided, with the east Asian portion coming under the Mongol-Chinese Chin dynasty. In the late 1300's, under Tamerlane, a second Mongol empire briefly ruled western Asia. But Mongol power and influence had declined greatly, and the Mongols gradually were pushed back to the Mongolian Plain.

In the 1500's Lamaist Buddhism spread to Mongolia and became a powerful force. Buddhist monasteries came to hold much of the land, and a large proportion of the male population became monks.

In the 1600's Inner Mongolia came under the control of the Manchus, who conquered China in 1644 and established the Ch'ing dynasty. Despite Mongol resistance, the Manchus had conquered almost all of Outer Mongolia by the 1680's, and Mongolia became a province of China. In the early 1700's, Russia began to exert a strong influence on northwestern Mongolia.

Apart from its contacts with China and Russia, during the 1700's and 1800's Mongolia remained isolated from the outside world. Mongolians came to resent their Chinese adminis-

trators, who governed the region as though it were a colony, and Chinese settlers, who appropriated grazing land for farm use.

Mongolia

Official name: *Mongolian People's Republic*
Area: *604,100 sq. mi., 1,564,619 sq. km.*
Type of government: *Communist*
Head of state: *Chairman of the Presidium of the Khural, Jambyn Batmönh*
Head of government: *Prime minister, Dumaagiyn Sodnom*
Population: *2,125,000 (1989 est.)*
Population growth rate: *2.8%*
Capital and largest city: *Ulan Bator (Pop., 1987, 515,129)*
Languages: *Khalkha Mongolian 90%, Kazakh*
Religion: *Tibetan Buddhist*
Ethnic group: *Mongolian*
Literacy: *80%*
Life expectancy: *64 years (1987)*
Currency: *Tugrik*
Per capita GNP: *$940 (1978)*
Exports: *$520 million (1984)*
Imports: *$750 million (1984)*

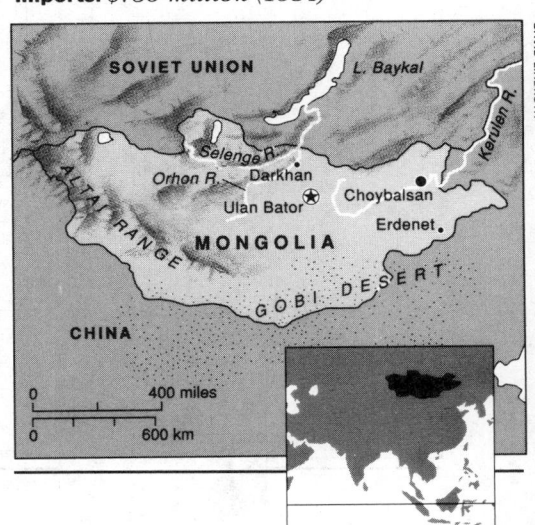

Autonomy. Manchu power had declined by the early 1900's, and Japan and Russia agreed to share influence in Mongolia, with Japan controlling eastern Inner Mongolia and Russia dominating Outer Mongolia. In 1911 a revolution in China overthrew the Manchu dynasty, and the people of Outer Mongolia, with Russian support, toppled the Chinese provincial government and proclaimed the autonomy of Outer Mongolia. The Mongolians chose a lama, the *hutukhtu,* or "living Buddha," as nominal ruler.

The country was far from independent, however. China did not recognize Mongolia's autonomy, and it remained under the protection of Russia. In 1919, during the upheaval accompanying the fall of the monarchy in Russia, China resumed rule over Mongolia. By 1921 Soviet troops had occupied Outer Mongolia, however, and in 1924, when the reigning hutukhtu died, Mongolia was renamed the Mongolian People's Republic.

People's republic. During the 1920's and 1930's, the government promoted radical and rapid economic and social change. The economic power of the Chinese in Mongolia was destroyed, and the power of the Buddhist lamas was crushed. All opposition to government programs was suppressed.

Inner Mongolia had remained a Chinese province, and in the 1930's it was occupied by Japanese forces. Japanese occupation posed a threat to the Mongolian People's Republic, and in 1939 Soviet and Mongol troops drove the Japanese from the border area.

The Mongolian People's Republic participated briefly in World War II. In 1945, as part of the war settlement, the people of Outer Mongolia confirmed in a referendum their desire to be independent of China; in 1946 China, under Chiang Kai-shek, recognized Outer Mongolia's independence. In 1950, after a Communist government had been established in China, the Chinese Communists and the Soviets agreed to guarantee the independence of the Mongolian People's Republic.

In the late 1950's Mongolia began to expand its diplomatic and commercial contacts with the West, and in 1961 Mongolia became a member of the United Nations. In the early 1960's, when a split developed between Communist China and the Soviet Union, Mongolia sided with the Soviets. In 1966 Mongolia and the Soviet Union reaffirmed their close relations in elaborate ceremonies accompanying the signing of a 20-year treaty of friendship, protection, and aid. This pact was expanded further by an agreement signed in 1976. Thousands of Soviet troops are currently reported to be based in Mongolia.

Nauru

The land and people. Nauru is ringed by coral reefs. The island consists of a narrow coastal plain encircling an upland region, most of which is occupied by phosphate-bearing rock. The climate is hot and humid throughout the year.

Native Nauruans are a mixture of Micronesian and Polynesian stock. Most are Christian. Chinese and other foreign workers and European administrators and managers make up about half the population.

Economy. The island's economy is almost totally dependent on phosphate mining, although coconuts and other fruits and a few vegetables are raised on the coastal plain. The production of phosphates is Nauru's chief industry, and the island is one of the world's leading producers of phosphate rock, exporting about 2 million metric tons a year. The Nauruans took control of the phosphate industry from the British Phosphate Corporation in 1970. The Nauruan people now enjoy one of the world's highest standards of living.

Phosphates are the only exports, and food, machinery, and consumer goods are imported. Most trade is with Australia, New Zealand, Japan, and Britain. Efforts are currently under way to diversify the economy in preparation for the predicted depletion of the phosphate deposits in the 1990's.

Government. Nauru's government is headed by a president, who is chosen by a popularly elected legislature from among its members. The legislature's 18 members are elected to three-year terms.

History. Nauru was discovered in 1798 by a British explorer, but for over a century it remained a beachcombers' refuge and a minor source of copra. In 1888 possession passed to Germany.

In 1900 Nauru was found to be rich in phosphate rock, the basis of a fertilizer then coming into extensive use in Australia and New Zealand. By agreement with the Germans, phosphate mining was undertaken by an Australian-based British company.

After World War I, in 1919, Nauru was made a League of Nations mandate entrusted to Great Britain, but Australia administered economic and political affairs. Phosphate production was shared by Australia, New Zealand, and Great Britain. Occupied by the Japanese in World War II, the island was reoccupied in 1945 by Australian troops.

Following the war, it became a UN trust territory under joint Australian, British, and New Zealand authority, with Australia administering the island. In 1964, as exhaustion of the phosphate rock was foreseen, Australian and Nauruan officials discussed relocating the islanders, but the Nauruans wished to remain on Nauru.

In 1966 the UN General Assembly recommended that the trustee nations make the island habitable again when the phosphate is depleted by replacing all soil that had been removed with the rock. The UN also recommended independence for Nauru, and the island became an independent nation on January 31, 1968.

Much of the 1980's was marked by instability in Nauru as no party was able to gain a clear majority in parliament until 1987.

Nepal

The land. Nepal can be divided into three distinct geographical regions, each extending east to west. The Great Himalayas dominate the northern region, an area of spectacular alpine scenery with many of the world's tallest mountains. There are eight peaks with elevations of over 26,000 feet, and Mt.

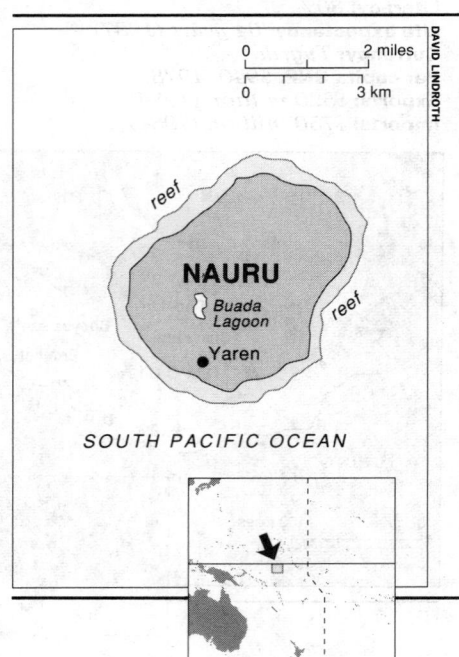

0   2 miles

0   3 km

DAVID LINDROTH

reef

NAURU

Buada Lagoon

reef

Yaren

SOUTH PACIFIC OCEAN

Nauru

Official name: *Republic of Nauru*
Area: *8 sq. mi., 21 sq. km.*
Type of government: *Democratic republic*
Head of state: *President, Hammer DeRoburt*
Population: *9000 (1989 est.)*
Population growth rate: *1.7%*
Languages: *Nauruan (official), English*
Religions: *Protestant 58%, Roman Catholic 24%*
Ethnic groups: *Nauruan 58%, other Pacific islanders 26%, Chinese 8%, European 8%*
Literacy: *99%*
Life expectancy: *67 years (1987)*
Currency: *Australian dollar*
Per capita GNP: *$20,000 (1985)*
Exports: *$93 million (1984)*
Imports: *$73 million (1984)*

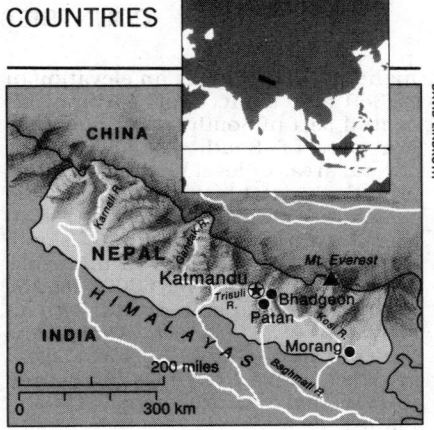

Nepal

Official name: *Kingdom of Nepal*
Area: *54,359 sq. mi., 140,790 sq. km.*
Type of government: *Monarchy*
Head of state: *King,*
  Birendra Bir Bikram Shah Dev
Head of government: *Prime minister,*
  Marich Man Singh Shrestha
Population: *18,700,000 (1989 est.)*
Population growth rate: *2.4%*
Capital and largest city: *Kathmandu*
  (Pop., 1986 est., 422,000)
Language: *Nepali*
Religions: *Hindu 90%, Buddhist 7%*
Ethnic groups: *Indo-Caucasian,*
  Tibeto-Mongoloid
Literacy: *29%*
Life expectancy: *49 years (1987)*
Currency: *Rupee*
Per capita GNP: *$160 (1986)*
Exports: *$130 million (1987)*
Imports: *$365 million (1987)*

Everest, on the Nepal-Tibet border, with an elevation of 29,028 feet, is the tallest mountain in the world. The lower portions of this region are forested. The climate is very cold and rather dry.

The second region, in central Nepal, is also mountainous. Elevations range from 4500 in the valley bottoms to 10,000 feet. Most of the lower slopes and valleys are cultivated.

The most important part of the central region is the Katmandu Valley, the heart of the country. Only 18 by 15 miles in area and surrounded by high mountains, it contains Nepal's main towns—Katmandu, the capital, Patan, and Bhadgeon. The valley is well watered, receiving about 58 inches of precipitation annually, and has a moderate climate.

The third region, called the terai, is a narrow belt 10 to 20 miles wide next to the Indian border. Most of the terai is heavily wooded. Its climate is hot and humid, with rainfall averaging 60 inches a year. Winters can be quite pleasant, however.

Many rivers flow from the Himalayas through Nepal, including the Kosi, the Trisuli, the Baghmati, the Gandak, and the Karnali.

The people. Nepal's population is concentrated in the central region, especially the Katmandu Valley, and in the southern region, the terai. The north is sparsely populated.

The Nepalese are descendants of Mongols and peoples of northern India. They are traditionally divided along tribal lines, with the Gurkha the dominant group. The minority Newar and Sherpa peoples are Mongol-Tibetan. The Nepalese speak Nepali and a variety of hill dialects. Nepal is officially a Hindu country, although there is a Buddhist minority. Ninety-three percent of the population is rural and 93 percent of the labor force works in agriculture.

Economy. The Nepalese economy is based on agriculture, but the country is rich in natural resources. Nepal's mineral resources include copper, iron, sulfur, coal, hematite, and bauxite, but they remain virtually untapped because of Nepal's isolation and lack of transportation facilities.

Because of its many rapid rivers, Nepal has a large hydroelectric potential. A number of joint Indian-Nepali hydroelectric projects have been undertaken.

The country's best farmland is in the south, where farmers grow rice, jute, mustard, tobacco, wheat, linseed, and some sugar cane. The south produces a surplus of cereal grains. There are also many acres of valuable forest. The majority of farmers in the central region eke out a subsistence living by intensively cultivating small, terraced plots of irrigated land.

Herding is the main activity of the Sherpa in the north, who graze sheep, goats, and yaks on the Himalayan slopes. Wheat and barley are grown in the valley bottoms of the north.

An important source of income and foreign exchange traditionally has been the service of Gurkha soldiers in the British and Indian armies. Nepal relies on financial and technical assistance from the United States, China, and the Soviet Union.

Nepal's international trade is limited. The main exports are rice, jute, wool, timber, linseed, and hides. Textiles, fuels, medicines, footwear, and industrial raw materials are imported. Most trade is with India, although Japan has figured increasingly as a trading partner.

Government. Nepal is a constitutional monarchy, with the king as chief executive and head of state. The king appoints a council to advise him and chooses a council of ministers from among the members of the Panchayat, the legislative assembly. Most members of the 140-member Panchayat are popularly elected to five-year terms and some are appointed by the king.

History. The earliest inhabitants of the Katmandu Valley were the Newars, who lived under a tribal form of government and developed a religion and customs representing a blend of Buddhism and Hinduism. In the first centuries A.D., the valley came under the rule of Indian kings, who consolidated Indian influence in Nepal in the form of the Hindu religion and culture and monarchical government.

When the last of the dynasty of Indian kings, the Malla, began to weaken in the 1400's, the country returned to tribal government. In the 1500's a western principality, Gurkha, gained strength under the Shah dynasty, whose most famous ruler, Prithvi

THE HIMALAYAS *dominate the landscape of Nepal. The mountains cover most of the country and make travel within the country difficult.*

Narayan, conquered the Katmandu Valley in 1769 and created the modern Nepalese state.

Expansionism. Combining military ambition with an unusual talent for administration, Prithvi Narayan extended his rule eastward to Darjeeling, now in India, and his descendants expanded Nepalese hegemony to the east as far as Kashmir and to the south into present-day India.

Two Nepalese invasions of Tibet, in 1788 and 1791, brought retaliation from China, which had gained suzerainty over Tibet. Nepal was forced to withdraw from Tibet and to pay tribute to China. The payments ceased in 1908.

Nepalese expansionism soon turned southward and confronted the British, who were extending their control of India northward in the Ganges valley. The Nepalese refused to negotiate with the British and permitted frequent raids into the Indian plains.

The British were able to subdue the Nepalese marauders and reach a settlement with Nepal in 1816, in the Treaty of Sagauli. The treaty established Nepal's boundary with India and gave Britain a deciding influence in Nepalese foreign relations. Gurkha soldiers began to be used by British armies.

Rana rule. Struggles for power in the early 1800's weakened Nepal and in 1846 resulted in the establishment of rule by the prime ministers, the Ranas. Rana rule, supported by the army and the British in India, was marked by conspiracies and assassinations within the extended Rana family and the isolation of Nepal from modernizing influences.

In the 1900's in India, Nepalese intellectuals laid the groundwork for a movement supported by the titular ruler, King Tribhuvana, to unseat the Ranas and institute a program of reform and advancement. After India achieved independence in 1950, the Nepalese National Congress, modeled on the Indian Congress Party, led a reform drive that was backed by the new government in India.

The Ranas responded with legislative concessions in 1950, but revolts broke out and with Indian encouragement King Tribhuvana was able to end Rana power in 1951. The political and administrative turmoil accompanying the downfall of the Ranas lasted for eight years, while the country was held together by the newly found power of the king. Tribhuvana died in 1955 and was succeeded by his son, Mahendra.

Contemporary Nepal. With Chinese power increasing in Tibet, threatening the security of both Nepal and India, King Mahendra, in 1959, promulgated a new constitution, giving himself supreme executive powers but also providing for a legislature.

In 1960 King Mahendra reinstated direct royal rule, but it included a new delegation of authority to village councils. The king's provisions for what he

called "democracy from below" led to a resurgence of popular support for the monarch.

The king attracted a progressive body of supporters in the government with a program directed toward modernization of the still largely traditional society and economy. In 1963 the caste system and childhood marriages were abolished.

Although Nepal has traditionally been closely allied with India, it canceled an arms agreement with India in 1969, charging that nation with harboring Nepalese political fugitives. Meanwhile relations have improved considerably with China. Recently, China financed a major highway project connecting Tibet with Katmandu. Nepal also has become more closely linked, by highways and airline service, with India and Pakistan.

King Mahendra died in 1972 and was succeeded by his son, Birendra Bir Bikram Shah Dev, who put down serious student riots in 1974 and 1979.

In 1980 a revision of the constitution made provision for direct popular election of representatives to the national legislature.

New Zealand

The land.   New Zealand is made up of two main islands, North Island and South Island, and several smaller islands, including Stewart Island and the Chatham Islands.

New Zealand is a relatively mountainous country. The southern Alps extend along the length of South Island, and there are 28 peaks with elevations over 10,000 feet above sea level. The

highest peak, reaching an elevation of 12,349 feet, is Mt. Cook, in the west-central part of South Island. The eastern part of South Island contains several areas of level land at fairly low elevations, notably the Canterbury and Southland plains. Cook Strait separates North Island from South Island.

North Island has four volcanic peaks with elevations of over 6000 feet, the highest of which is Ruapehu, with an elevation of 9175 feet. Among the larger lowland regions of North Island are the Waikato-Thames Plain and the Manawatu-Horowhenua Coastal Plain.

There are many rivers on the islands, including the Waikato, Wanganui, and Rangitaiki on North Island, and the Waitaki, Oreti, and Clutha on South Island.

Climate. New Zealand has a damp, mild climate, which is strongly influenced by the small size of the islands in relation to the vastness of the surrounding ocean. The waters surrounding the country tend to moderate its temperatures, so that the winters are relatively mild and the summers comparatively cool.

Only a small area of South Island receives less than 20 inches of rain a year, whereas many parts of both North and South islands receive over 50 inches of rain a year. The greatest rainfall occurs in the western part of South Island, where some areas receive over 200 inches a year.

Dependencies. New Zealand is responsible for several former British colonies. Tokelau has been one of New Zealand's overseas territories since 1949. Ross Dependency in Antarctica attained the same status in 1923. New Zealand is responsible for the external

New Zealand

Official name: *New Zealand*
Area: *103,736 sq. mi., 268,676 sq. km.*
Type of government: *Parliamentary democracy*
Head of state: *Queen Elizabeth II*
Head of government: *Prime minister, David Lange*
Population: *3,373,000 (1989 est.)*
Population growth rate: *0.8%*
Capital: *Wellington (Pop., 1986, 325,697)*
Largest city: *Auckland (Pop., 1986, 882,754)*
Languages: *English, Maori*
Religions: *Anglican 29%, Presbyterian 18%, Roman Catholic 15%*
Ethnic groups: *European 87%, Maori 9%*
Literacy: *99%*
Life expectancy: *75 years (1987)*
Currency: *Dollar*
Per capita GNP: *$7110 (1986)*
Exports: *$5.88 billion (1987)*
Imports: *$6.1 billion (1987)*

COUNTRIES

affairs and defense of its two self-governing territories, the Cook Islands, self-governing since 1965, and Niue Island, self-governing since 1974 (see page 201).

The people. About 85 percent of New Zealanders are of British descent. A small percentage of New Zealanders are descended from other European settlers. The Maori, a people of Polynesian stock, migrated to New Zealand from the Pacific islands beginning in the 900's. Maoris now make up about 9 percent of the population.

About three-quarters of the people live on North Island. Eighty-four percent of New Zealanders are urban dwellers, and two cities, Auckland and Wellington, along with their suburbs, account for over one-third of the population.

Economy. New Zealand is primarily an agricultural country. At one time all of North Island and most of South Island were forested. In the 1800's European settlers cleared large areas to establish farms, and today only about 20 percent of New Zealand is forested.

Agriculture. The country's mild climate and its grasslands provide excellent conditions for pastoral industries, and agriculture employs about 10 percent of the population. Sheep are raised in most parts of the country, and New Zealand is one of the world's largest exporters of wool. Dairying is also an important agricultural industry in New Zealand. Most of the dairying is confined to North Island. The principal products are butter and cheese.

On South Island, wheat, oats, barley, and turnips are grown. Fruits and vegetables are grown mainly on North Island and on the northern tip of South Island.

Mining and manufacturing. New Zealand is not an important mining country, but enough coal is mined to meet local needs in most years and some gold is produced. Because of a lack of major mineral resources and a limited home market, New Zealand did not develop a great number of manufacturing industries in the past. Today, however, in an attempt to diversify its economy, New Zealand is building up the manufacturing sector. Increased steel and aluminum manufacturing has been particularly significant. Most manufacturing is still concerned with the processing of dairy products, the canning and freezing of vegetables, and leather and wool preparation.

Industrialization has called for increased energy sources. The Maui offshore gas field was discovered in 1969, and recently an oil refinery was built in the country. Hydroelectric power provides almost 80 percent of the country's electricity needs.

Auckland is the principal manufacturing center, with woodworking, textile, brewing, and light engineering plants. Both Auckland and Christchurch have automobile assembly plants that use some components of New Zealand manufacture.

Trade. New Zealand's trade structure has changed drastically since the 1950's. Great Britain, which for many years accounted for approximately 60 percent of New Zealand's exports and imports, is now involved in less than 20 percent. On the other hand, trade with the United States and Australia has increased greatly, and trade with

Japan has gone from practically zero to about 15 percent of the country's total.

There has also been a change in the products exported, with agricultural products dropping from 95 to 60 percent of the total and manufactured goods, including unwrought aluminum, rising to approximately 40 percent. The major exports, however, are still meat, dairy products, and wool. Principal imports are fuels, chemicals, food, machinery, and other manufactured goods.

Government. New Zealand has a parliamentary system of government. The head of state is the British monarch, who is represented in New Zealand by a governor-general. Actual executive power is vested in a prime minister and a cabinet responsible to the legislature. Legislative power is held by a 92-member House of Representatives. House members are popularly elected to three-year terms.

History. The Maori migrated to New Zealand between the 900's and 1300's. In 1642 the Dutch navigator Abel Tasman sighted the islands of New Zealand, but they were not visited by Europeans again until 1769, when Captain James Cook accurately charted the coasts.

Only after European settlement in Australia in the late 1700's and early 1800's did Europeans develop an interest in New Zealand. From the 1790's to the 1840's, Europeans exploited New Zealand's timber, seals, whales, and flax and established a port of call at the Bay of Islands, on North Island.

Missionaries worked among the Maoris while Britain sought to maintain order on the islands and stimulate trade without assuming governmental responsibility. Perhaps 2000 Europeans then lived in New Zealand.

British rule. In 1840 settlement began in earnest. In that year the British signed the Treaty of Waitangi with the Maoris. By this treaty Britain extended its sovereignty over New Zealand and promised protection of Maori land rights and equality in a biracial society. In 1841 New Zealand became a crown colony.

In quick succession, settlements were made at Wellington and Auckland, and at Nelson, Dunedin, and Christchurch on South Island. The British settlers intended to develop an economy based on crop production, but sheep grazing and wool production proved more feasible and profitable. In 1852 Britain granted a constitution providing for a loose federation of six provinces, and in 1856 a parliamentary system of government was permanently established.

Federal government. Gold was discovered in the 1860's on South Island, and gold rushes brought men and capital. In that same decade North Island was preoccupied with wars between Maori tribes and settlers over land. The Maoris were defeated in 1872; after that

WELLINGTON, *the capital of New Zealand, nestled between the Tararua Mountains and Cook Strait, is a major metropolitan center and port.*

UPI/BETTMANN NEWSPHOTOS

184
COUNTRIES

many Maoris refused to cooperate with the government.

The Maori population declined from about 100,000 in 1840 to 40,000 at the end of the 1800's. After that, however, under educated Maori leadership, the Maoris developed into an influential minority, and today they number over 290,000.

New Zealand stagnated in the 1880's and people left the island. Technological changes solved New Zealand's problems, however, as the introduction of refrigerated shipping made possible the export of meat and dairy products to Britain. This development diversified pastoral exports and triggered a rapid growth of dairying on North Island.

In 1891 the Liberal Party, supported by small farmers and city workers, came to power. Prime Minister Richard Seddon launched a program of social and economic experimentation. The government introduced land reforms, compulsory labor arbitration, and social services. Trade unions grew in importance. Reforms, along with technological changes and improved export prices, provided a system that benefited the common man, farmers in particular. In 1907 Great Britain granted New Zealand dominion status. **Dominion.** Between 1912 and 1935 a more conservative government, supported mainly by North Island farmers, remained in office almost continuously.

New Zealand gained new importance within the British empire as a supplier of dairy products, meat, and wool to Great Britain. New Zealand soldiers campaigned with British

forces against the Central Powers in World War I.

Politically important in the years from 1916 to 1935 was the rise of the Labor Party, supported by a growing industrial working class. In 1935 Labor came to office and held power continuously for 14 years.

The world economic depression of the 1930's hit New Zealand hard. The Labor government arranged guaranteed prices for farmers, and took control of exports and imports, foreign exchange, and banking. It emphasized the redistribution of income, elaborated a social security system, and promoted factory industries to balance the economy. In effect, the government sought to socialize national income rather than the means of production. **Contemporary New Zealand.** In 1939 New Zealand entered World War II, collaborating with the United States in the Pacific and with Great Britain in Europe. After the war, cooperation with the United States continued, especially in the area of defense.

The two major political parties, Labor and National, have been working to advance social welfare policies. When Labor was in power from 1935 to 1949, it carried through a broad program of social and economic legislation, including a comprehensive Social Security Act. During the period from 1949 to 1957, when the National Party held the government, it moved cautiously in discarding economic controls set up by Labor. Since then, both parties, Labor (1957–1960, 1972–1975, 1984–) and National (1960–1972, 1975–1984) have been careful in removing economic controls.

The main problems facing New Zealand today are its loss of a protected market for its agricultural products, caused by Britain's entry into the European Economic Community in 1973, and the worldwide problems of inflation and petroleum supplies.

In elections in 1984 the Labor Party ousted the more conservative National Party from the majority in parliament. It won an unprecedented second term in 1987. During its first term, Labor was successful in privatizing several industries that had been government run, such as the electrical distribution system. It was also able to substantially deregulate many areas of the economy.

In 1986 the government began a new policy of refusing to allow visits by United States nuclear warships to New Zealand ports, thereby breaching the ANZUS defense alliance.

Pakistan

The land. Pakistan can be divided into five separate geographic regions. Baluchistan, in the southwest, is an arid region of mountains and valleys. The Makran Coast forms a narrow corridor connecting the Indus valley with Iran. The Northwest Frontier is a mountain and hill region whose many mountain passes, including the Khyber Pass, historically have been the gateways to the Indian subcontinent. Punjab, in the upper Indus valley, is the traditional economic, political, and cultural heart of Pakistan, a land rich in wheat and with a growing industrial capacity. Sind, a desert region, occupies the lower Indus valley.

The people. The people of Pakistan are a mixture of many groups. Two-thirds of the population is Punjabi; the rest is mostly Sindhi, Pushtun, Urdu, or Baluchi. Urdu is the national language, but English is widely used.

Over 95 percent of the people are Muslims, but there are significant Christian and Hindu minorities.

Aggressive government educational policies in recent years have raised Pakistan's literacy rate significantly, but it is still quite low.

Pakistan's natural population increase is high. Three-quarters of the population is rural. Only three cities have populations over 1 million: the major port of Karachi (7 million), the industrial city of Lahore (3.5 million), and Faisalabad (2 million).

Economy. Over half the labor force is employed in agriculture. Pakistan has an extensive system of irrigation. The principal crops include wheat, cotton, rice, corn, and sugar cane.

At Pakistan's partition from India in 1947, the country had almost no industrial base, but after substantial investment, industry accounts for about 13 percent of employment. Manufactures include textiles, carpets, steel, fertilizer, cement, and petroleum products.

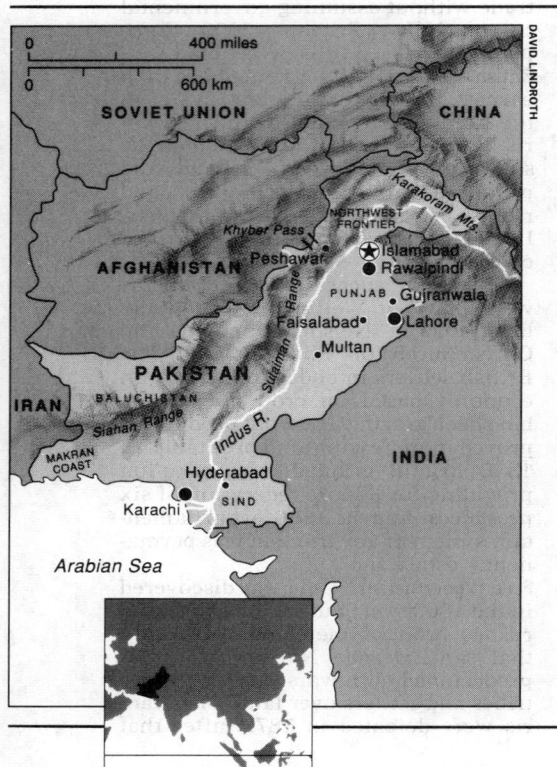

DAVID LINDROTH

Pakistan

Official name: *Islamic Republic of Pakistan*
Area: *310,403 sq. mi., 803,943 sq. km.*
Type of government: *Parliamentary democracy*
Head of state: *President, Ghulam Ishaq Khan*
Head of government: *Prime minister, Benazir Bhutto*
Population: *110,407,000 (1989 est.)*
Population growth rate: *2.9%*
Capital: *Islamabad (Pop., 1986 est., 400,000)*
Largest city: *Karachi (Pop., 1986 est., 7,000,000)*
Languages: *Urdu (official), English, Punjabi*
Religion: *Muslim 97%*
Ethnic groups: *Punjabi 66%, Sindhi 13%, Pushtun 9%, Urdu 8%*
Literacy: *26%*
Life expectancy: *54 years (1987)*
Currency: *Rupee*
Per capita GNP: *$330 (1987)*
Exports: *$3.7 billion (1987)*
Imports: *$5.4 billion (1987)*

Pakistan's largest export is cotton, both raw and processed. Also exported are rice, leather, and fish products. Imports include machinery, fuels, and consumer goods. An important contribution to the economy is made by Pakistanis working abroad, especially in the Middle East, who send a portion of their wages home to their families. Japan, the United States, and Saudi Arabia are principal trade partners.

Government. Following a 1977 military coup, democratic processes were only gradually restored. A constitutional amendment in 1986 bound Pakistan to observe Islamic law.

According to the constitution, the president is head of state and is elected by an electoral college. The head of government is the prime minister, who is chosen by the president and confirmed by the popularly elected National Assembly. The National Assembly consists of 217 members elected to five-year terms. The upper legislative house is the 84-member Senate, indirectly elected by provincial and tribal leaders for a term of six years.

History. Pakistan's existence as a separate Muslim state is rooted in the early history of northern India. Islam began to influence northern India in the early 600's, when Muslim sailors from Arabia visited the coast of Sind, at the mouth of the Indus. Muslim conquerors ruled Sind from the 600's and spread Islam there.

In the 1000's Muslims from Afghanistan began extending their rule over territory in northwest India. Until the 1800's Afghans, Turks, Arabs, and finally the Mughals (or Moguls) ruled all or part of northern India, establishing many small kingdoms and princely states that at times were unified into empires. In addition to their religion, the Muslims brought Persian and Arabic art, literature, learning, and customs to produce a way of life different from that of Hindu India to the south.

Britain began extending its influence over India in the 1700's. By the early 1900's the British controlled most of the Muslim territories, and by the mid-1800's, with the addition of Punjab and Sind, the British were in firm command of all of India.

In the late 1800's, when Indian leaders began to demand a stronger voice in their country's government, Muslims made up about one-quarter of India's population. The Indian National Congress, formed in 1885 to work for self-government, spoke for all India and included prominent Muslims. Its composition, however, was predominantly Hindu.

Muslim autonomy. The positive movement toward autonomy for Indian Muslims began soon after the Indian nationalist movement was organized, and in part as a result of its organization. Sir Sayyid Ahmad Khan and other Muslim leaders argued that there was a distinct Muslim nation in India that should not be submerged in the Hindu

ISLAM *has a strong influence on the culture, laws, and government of Pakistan.*

VIKANDER/WEST LIGHT

majority. This, they contended, would happen if the British left the country and a fully representative government was introduced.

While urging Muslims to improve their relatively backward condition through education and commerce, Sir Sayyid recommended that they not participate in the activities of the Indian National Congress.

Muslim League. In 1906 Muslims founded the All India Muslim League to press for protection and advantages for Muslims. Although its overall goal, self-government for India, was the same as that of the National Congress, the two organizations could not agree on a plan for dividing power and protecting Muslim interests.

Violence between Hindus and Muslims in the 1920's and 1930's, as well as continued sponsorship of a Hindu revival, widened the split within the nationalist movement. The final blow to unity came in 1937, when the Indian National Congress gained control of most provincial legislatures popularly elected on a broadened franchise. The Muslim League believed that the policies of these Congress majorities discriminated against Muslims.

It was after 1937 that Muhammad Ali Jinnah, a former Indian National Congress leader and advocate of Hindu-Muslim unity, began a drive for the creation of a separate Muslim state. By 1940, under Jinnah's leadership, the Muslim League resolved that a Muslim state should be created when India gained independence.

In 1946 negotiations took place for a transfer of power to Indians, but the Congress and the League could not agree on terms for establishing an interim government, or for drafting a constitution for the new state. The British had strongly supported a unified India, but they had also sponsored separate religious electorates and had encouraged Muslim ambitions.

Partition. In 1947, when the Hindu-Muslim stalemate could not be broken,

Britain acquiesced to Muslim demands for a separate state. It was to consist of all contiguous areas with Muslim majorities in British India. Bengal in the east and the Punjab in the west were divided and the princely states adjacent to Pakistan were given the choice of joining one of the new states. This resulted in the creation of a country with two nonadjoining sections.

On August 15, 1947, Pakistan became an independent nation within the British Commonwealth. Muhammad Ali Jinnah became Pakistan's first governor-general.

Partition created serious problems for both India and Pakistan. Communal rioting, especially in the Punjab, killed thousands. The economies of the two countries were disrupted by large migrations of Muslims to Pakistan and Hindus to India.

The cultural difference between the eastern and western parts of the new state also caused much antagonism and sharpened struggles for political power. In addition, Pakistani political leadership faltered after the death in 1948 of Jinnah and the assassination in 1951 of Liaqat Ali Khan, Pakistan's first prime minister. Delays in formulating a constitution extended the period of governmental instability.

The republic. A republican constitution was adopted in 1956. But years of political turmoil had weakened the economy, and the decentralized federal system established by the constitution could do little to solve the country's economic problems.

Relations with India, bitter after decades of religious conflict, grew especially hostile in the mid-1950's over the issue of Kashmir. India gained control of the bulk of Kashmir, but the region had a Muslim majority, and Pakistan argued that Kashmir should be made part of the Muslim state. This dispute worsened Pakistan's internal political and economic situation.

In 1958 a group of military leaders under General Muhammad Ayub Khan took over the government. The new government took firm control of economic activity and initiated modernization programs that improved the economy.

In 1962 a new constitution was adopted; martial law was gradually lifted and civil rights restored. In 1965 President Ayub Khan won reelection by a large majority. The country's economy continued to improve in the mid-1960's under government development programs using aid from abroad. In 1965 the dispute over Kashmir again broke into open warfare.

Violent protests erupted in East Pakistan in 1969 as its population demanded political autonomy. Ayub Khan was forced to resign and martial law was declared under General Yahya Khan. In December, 1971, East Pakistan ended the civil war that had broken out in March by declaring itself the independent state of Bangladesh. Yahya

Khan resigned and Zulfikar Ali Bhutto, leader of the Peoples' Party, became Pakistan's first civilian president.

Bhutto sought to reestablish peaceful relations with India, which had aided East Pakistan during the war. He initiated land reforms and government control of industry. In 1973 he permitted the formation of a parliamentary form of government.

Bhutto was deposed during a military coup in 1977 and was executed in 1979. The new president, Muhammad Zia ul-Haq, announced the end of elections and sessions of parliament and instituted absolute military rule. Martial law was lifted in 1985 and democratic processes were revived.

Zia was killed in 1988 in an airplane explosion along with the U.S. ambassador. The subsequent parliamentary elections were regarded as a test of the return to democracy. Benazir Bhutto, daughter of former president Zulfikar Ali Bhutto, won a decisive victory to become prime minister.

Papua New Guinea

Official name: *Independent State of Papua New Guinea*
Area: *178,259 sq. mi., 461,691 sq. km.*
Type of government: *Parliamentary democracy*
Head of state: *Queen Elizabeth II*
Head of government: *Prime minister, Paias Wingti*
Population: *3,736,000 (1989 est.)*
Population growth rate: *2.4%*
Capital and largest city: *Port Moresby (Pop., 1987 est., 132,000)*
Languages: *Melanesian Pidgin, English, Motu*
Religions: *Protestant 63%, Roman Catholic 31%*
Ethnic groups: *Melanesian, Australian, Chinese*
Literacy: *32%*
Life expectancy: *54 years (1987)*
Currency: *Kina*
Per capita GNP: *$690 (1986)*
Exports: *$1.03 billion (1986)*
Imports: *978 million (1986)*

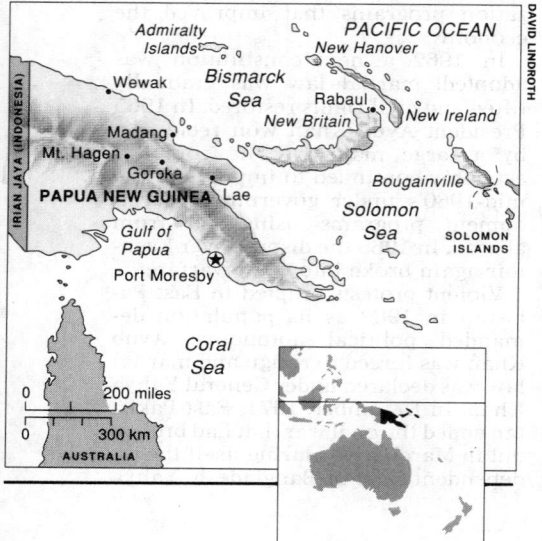

Papua New Guinea

The land and people. The country of Papua New Guinea consists of the eastern half of the South Pacific island of New Guinea, the islands of the former territory of New Guinea, and several other island groups east of New Guinea, including the islands New Britain, New Ireland, and Bougainville. The interior and eastern tip of Papua proper are extremely mountainous, but there are lowlands in the north, south, and west. There are many rivers. The outlying islands are mountainous, and coral reefs ring Papua and most of the islands.

Indigenous Melanesian peoples form the bulk of the population. There are also Europeans, Asians, and many extremely isolated tribal groups of the western hill regions. There are several hundred languages spoken in Papua New Guinea. Two languages, Hiri Motu and a form of pidgin English, are widely spoken. Standard English is the official language.

Economy. The economy is based on agriculture. Coconuts, cacao, coffee, and rubber are the chief commercial crops. There is also commercial forestry and fishing. Most industry is involved in the processing of the country's agricultural products, but light manufacturing is developing. Papua New Guinea has some important mineral deposits, including copper and gold, which, because of their inaccessibility, are only beginning to be exploited.

Government. Papua New Guinea is a member of the British Commonwealth, and the British monarch is head of state. Executive power is held by the prime minister, who is the leader of the majority party in the 109-member parliament.

History. Human remains found in New Guinea date back at least 10,000 years. New Guinea and the adjacent islands were inhabited by Melanesian peoples when they were first visited by the Spanish and Dutch in the 1600's. No European settlement was made until 1828, when the Dutch occupied the western half of New Guinea. In 1883, after a German company had begun trading in eastern New Guinea, Australia occupied Papua without British approval. In 1884 Britain made southeastern New Guinea a protectorate as British New Guinea. Australia was given full sovereignty over the area in 1905.

New Guinea was occupied by Japanese forces in the 1940's, during World War II, and the area was the site of bitter fighting. After the war, economic development projects were begun. Forestry and fishing were developed and new industries were started. Popular participation in government also increased. The country became self-governing in 1973 and achieved full independence in 1975.

Bougainville, rich in copper deposits, tried to secede several times in the mid-1970's, but its attempts were crushed. Indonesian border conflicts with West Irian flared in 1978. In 1979 a state of emergency was declared in the wake of severe labor strikes and tribal warfare.

Philippines

The land. There are more than 7000 islands within the Philippine archipelago, but the eleven largest islands account for 94 percent of the country's total land area. The largest islands are Luzon (40,420 square miles) and Mindanao (36,537 square miles). Each of the remaining islands is less than 6000 square miles in area.

Most of the islands are hilly or mountainous, with only limited areas of level land. In the northern half of Luzon, the principal island, there are several mountain ranges running from north to south. The Sierra Madre range runs parallel to the northeastern coast, and the Central Cordillera forms the spine of the island. Between the two ranges is the Cagayan Plain, one of the two sizable lowlands on Luzon.

The temperature is warm year-round. Average monthly temperatures at sea level range from 76°F to 84°F. Although it is cooler at higher altitudes, temperatures below 60°F rarely occur. Typhoons strike the Philippines every year. Most of the Philippines receive at least 60 inches of rain a year, some up to 125 inches.

The people. Most people in the Philippines are of Malay stock, but there are also people of Chinese, American, and Spanish origin. The population is unevenly distributed. Luzon, Cebu, Negros, Bohul, Leyte, and Panay are the most heavily populated islands. The largest city is Manila, on Luzon.

Most Filipinos are Christian, but there are also minorities of Muslims in northern Luzon and western Mindanao. Many local languages are spoken in the Philippines. Pilipino, the official language, is derived from Tagalog, the language spoken around Manila. English is also widely spoken.

Economy. The economy of the Philippines is based on agriculture, and about 50 percent of the labor force is dependent on agriculture for its livelihood. About one-third of the land is arable, and about three-quarters of that is devoted to domestic food crops.

While rice and fish are the two mainstays of the Filipino diet, the islands do not catch enough fish for their own population's demands. Self-sufficiency in rice production was only recently attained. Rice occupies almost one-half of the cropped land. Corn and coconuts are also important crops. Other crops of some significance include root crops, fruits, nuts, sugar cane, abaca, tobacco, ramie, kapok, and rubber.

The number of persons engaged in fishing is second only to the number in agriculture. Fishing is becoming an increasingly important industry.

Forests cover about 50 percent of the country and are among the most important resources of the Philippines.

The Philippines has considerable mineral wealth, and is a leading producer of copper and gold. Also extracted are nickel, zinc, cobalt, coal, and silver.

Before independence in 1946, industry was confined largely to processing

Philippines

Official name: *Republic of the Philippines*
Area: *116,000 sq. mi., 300,440 sq. km.*
Type of government: *Republic*
Head of state: *President, Corazon Aquino*
Population: *64,907,000 (1989 est.)*
Population growth rate: *2.8%*
Capital and largest city: *Manila (Pop., 1980, 1,630,485)*
Languages: *Pilipino, English*
Religions: *Roman Catholic 83%, Protestant 9%, Muslim 5%*
Ethnic groups: *Malay 95%, Chinese 2%*
Literacy: *88%*
Life expectancy: *65 years (1987)*
Currency: *Peso*
Per capita GNP: *$570 (1986)*
Exports: *$5.2 billion (1987)*
Imports: *$6.2 billion (1987)*

agricultural products. Since independence, the government has promoted industrialization, and by 1986 manufactured goods contributed nearly one-quarter of the gross national product. A number of consumer goods industries have been established or expanded, and some heavy industry has been established. In the 1980's an emphasis was placed on developing export-producing industries.

The main imports are machinery, chemicals, food, iron and steel products, and petroleum. The major exports are electronic goods, clothing, coconut oil, copper, gold, and bananas. Most trade is conducted with the United States and Japan. The Philippines receives economic aid from the United States.

Government. Under the new 1987 constitution, the head of state is the president, who is popularly elected to a six-year term. Legislative authority, as in the United States, rests with a 24-member Senate and a 250-member House of Representatives.

History. The earliest arrivals to the Philippine archipelago are thought to have been a dark-skinned people who migrated across land bridges from Southeast Asia 20,000 to 30,000 years ago. The next migrants to arrive on the islands were Malay peoples from the Indonesian islands.

The Philippine islands were known to traders from China and Southeast

Asia at least as early as the 14th century. During this period, Arab traders introduced Islam to the islands.

Ferdinand Magellan visited the Philippines in 1521 and claimed the islands for Spain. In 1571 Miguel López de Legazpe, a Spanish soldier, established the first Spanish settlement in the islands and extended Spanish control over Cebu, Leyte, Mindanao, Panay, and central Luzon. In 1571 he took possession of Manila and made it the capital of the territory.

Long before the Spanish conquest, the Philippines traded with China. Later, Spanish galleons brought silver to Manila from the port of Acapulco in Mexico to trade with the Chinese for luxury goods, and Manila became an important trading center.

Under Spanish rule, Christianity and Western legal concepts and customs were introduced into the Philippines, and a centralized government was established. In the 1800's resentment against Spanish rule grew, and by the end of the 1800's the Filipinos had staged a number of revolts.

In 1896 José Rizal, a leading Filipino patriot, was executed for his part in uprisings that broke out in that year. His death spurred the revolutionary movement. Spain promised to grant Filipino representation in Madrid and to permit wider autonomy for the islands, but it failed to keep these promises, and the Filipinos, led by General

CATHOLICISM, *brought to the Philippines by the Spanish in the 16th century, took strong hold; it is practiced by more than 80 percent of the population.*

VIDLER/LEO DE WYS

DAVID LINDROTH

Francisco Makabulas, renewed the struggle against Spanish rule.

U.S. rule. In April, 1898, the United States declared war on Spain, after the U.S. battleship *Maine* was destroyed in Havana harbor, in Cuba, which was also under Spanish rule. By that time the Filipinos were battling hard against the Spanish in the Philippines. In August, 1898, U.S. forces occupied Manila. In the Treaty of Paris, signed on December 10, 1898, Spain ceded the Philippines to the United States for $20 million.

In 1899 a war of insurrection against the United States was led by Emilio Aguinaldo, head of the anti-Spanish rebellion of 1896. In 1901 Aguinaldo was captured and the uprising was ended.

Between the summer of 1900 and the summer of 1901 the islands were administered by a military governor while the Taft Commission, established by President William McKinley and headed by William Howard Taft, drew up plans for a civil government. The commission plan provided for a legislature to be made up of an appointed upper house and an elected assembly. In 1907 the first elections were held for the assembly.

In 1934 President Franklin D. Roosevelt signed the Tydings-McDuffie Act, stipulating that independence was to be granted the Philippines in 1946. Under the terms of the act, the Philippines, in 1935, became a self-governing commonwealth headed by an elected president. Manuel Quezon was chosen the first president.

On December 7, 1941, Japanese forces struck the islands, and on January 2, 1942, Manila was occupied by the Japanese. Valiant defensive battles were fought on Bataan peninsula and Corregidor, an island in Manila Bay, but the Philippines were forced to surrender in May, 1942.

Japan established a puppet government in the Philippines in which many Filipinos served. Quezon established a government-in-exile in Washington, D.C., and Americans and Filipinos organized a large-scale guerrilla movement to fight the Japanese in the Philippines.

Early in the war the peasant farmers struck back by creating an army, the Hukbalahap, commonly called Huk, led by Luis Taruc. The Huks rallied the rural population and killed some 25,000 Japanese and their Filipino supporters.

On October 20, 1944, U.S. troops, supported by Filipino guerrillas, landed on the island of Leyte, and on February 23, 1945, after a fierce three-week battle, the Allied forces captured Manila.

Independence. On July 4, 1946, the Philippine Islands became independent. The new government faced the problems of rebuilding the country's economy; of dealing with the rebellion of the Huk, which had become a Communist-dominated group; and of handling the unpopular abuse by American businesses of what was called "parity," or equal rights with their Filipino counterparts.

Under the leadership of President Ramón Magsaysay, who was elected in 1953, the Huk rebellion was suppressed by a newly strengthened army, which also acted to control political corruption and abuse. Magsaysay was killed in a plane crash in 1957. His successors were beset by economic problems aggravated by sharp population increases, stress over the Americans' privileged position in the nation, and renewed political corruption.

Ferdinand Marcos became president in 1965. Problems continued and were heightened by the nation's military involvement with the United States during the Vietnam War. In the face of rising criticism and terrorism, Marcos declared martial law in 1972.

The assassination, in 1983, of Benigno S. Aquino, an opposition leader, provoked a national crisis. Allegations that the Marcos government was involved in the assassination caused widespread rioting.

In 1986, within weeks after Marcos declared himself the winner in presidential elections widely believed to be fraudulent, popular demonstrations and defection of military units forced him into exile. The opposition candidate, Corazon Aquino, Benigno Aquino's widow, became president.

Samoa

See Western Samoa

Singapore

The land. The nation of Singapore consists of the large island of Singapore and some 55 low-lying islets within 10 miles of its eastern and southern shores. On Singapore Island, a coastal plain surrounds a central plateau that has a peak of 581 feet. Once swampland and jungle, most of the island has been cleared for farming and building. The island is about 26 miles long and 14 miles wide.

Singapore's climate is hot and humid. The average year-round temperature is about 81°F, and an average of 96 inches of rain falls each year.

The people. Singapore is very densely populated, with over 11,789 persons per square mile. An extremely high rate of population growth was slowed down by a determined government program of birth control. Approximately two-thirds of the people live in the capital and largest city, Singapore, on the southern coast of Singapore Island.

About three-quarters of Singapore's people are of Chinese descent. Malays and Indonesians make up some 14 per-

Singapore

Official name: *Republic of Singapore*
Area: *239 sq. mi., 619 sq. km.*
Type of government: *Parliamentary democracy*
Head of state: *President, Wee Kim Wee*
Head of government: *Prime minister, Lee Kuan Yew*
Population: *2,674,000 (1989 est.)*
Population growth rate: *1.1%*
Capital: *Singapore City*
Languages: *English, Mandarin Chinese, Malay, Tamil*
Religions: *Buddhist, Taoist, Muslim, Hindu*
Ethnic groups: *Chinese 77%, Malay 15%, Indian 6%*
Literacy: *85%*
Life expectancy: *73 years (1987)*
Currency: *Dollar*
Per capita GNP: *$7410 (1986)*
Exports: *$22.5 billion (1986)*
Imports: *$25.5 billion (1986)*

cent. About 8 percent are of Indian and Pakistani origins, and there are small groups of Europeans and people of mixed ethnic backgrounds.

Malay is the national language, and Malay, Mandarin, Chinese, English, and Tamil, an Indian language, are official languages. Many of the dominant Chinese adhere to Confucianism, Taoism, and Buddhism. Most of the Malays and Pakistanis are Muslim, the Indians are largely Hindu and Sikh, and there are many Christians.

Economy. Singapore is one of Asia's "little dragons," so called because of the strength of its economy in relation to the size of the country. Singapore's prosperity is based on its location on important sea routes between the Indian Ocean, the South China Sea, and the Pacific and on its large, industrious population. Singapore is the commercial and financial center of Southeast Asia, and a large share of the region's trade passes through its port, the second largest in the world. This economic activity has given Singapore the third highest per capita income in Asia.

Singapore's industry traditionally has been based on processing Southeast Asia's natural products, such as tin, rubber, spices, copra, coffee, and timber. Attempts have been made to develop heavy industry to broaden Singapore's economic base. As a result industries like petroleum refining and shipbuilding have become important. A more recent trend has been a move toward producing high value-added goods for export, such as consumer electronics.

Trade. Commerce, especially transshipment trade, remains a major factor in Singapore's economy, however. The country processes Asian goods for export and distributes imports to Asian market centers.

A large part of the value of Singapore's trade is for transshipped goods. Electronics, machinery, petroleum products, and rubber are principal exports. Imports include crude oil, foodstuffs, machinery, and many types of manufactured goods. The United States, Japan, and Malaysia are primary trading partners.

Government. Singapore is a republic with a parliamentary system of government. The head of state is the president, who is chosen by a popularly elected legislature, the parliament. Executive powers are exercised by a cabinet, headed by a prime minister, responsible to the parliament. The parliament has one house with 79 members elected under a system of compulsory universal suffrage. The People's Action Party is the only political party with power.

History. Singapore had become an important commercial center by the 1100's A.D. In 1377 Singapore city was destroyed by Java, and it lost its trading importance. In 1819 Sir Thomas Stamford Raffles, a British East India Company agent, established a trading post on the island. Commerce flourished, and in 1824 the British purchased Singapore.

British rule. In 1826 Britain established the "Straits Settlements," combining Singapore with two former rival trading centers, Malacca and Penang. In 1867, as their prosperity and importance increased, the settlements were raised to the status of British crown colony.

The opening of the Suez Canal in 1869 and the development of steamships increased Europe's trade with the Far East and further bolstered Singapore's prosperity. In the late 1800's profitable tin smelting and rubber processing were added to the island's trading activities.

In the 1920's the British established a major naval base at Singapore, and in the 1930's an air base. In 1942, during World War II, Japan captured Singapore and occupied it until the British recaptured it in 1945. In 1946 Singapore was separated from Penang and Malacca and made a separate crown colony.

In the 1950's Singapore moved toward self-government, and in 1959 it was granted full internal autonomy. The major political force in the country became the largely Chinese People's Action Party.

Independence. In 1963 Singapore joined the new nation of Malaysia, formed of Malaya, Sabah (North Borneo), and Sarawak. Singapore's dominant economic position and its Chinese majority led to friction between it and Malaysia's federal government. As a result, in 1965 Singapore reluctantly withdrew from the federation and became a sovereign state.

Lee Kuan Yew, who had been prime minister before federation, remained so afterward. Although regarded as greatly responsible for Singapore's remarkable economic growth in the 1960's and 1970's, Lee has been criticized in the 1980's for his increasingly dictatorial rule.

The nation pursues close economic and political relations with Malaysia and its other Asian neighbors, while attempting to maintain nonalignment with the world's major powers.

Solomon Islands

The land and people. The Solomon Islands consists of about a dozen large islands and many small islets. The islands are of two types, mountainous and volcanic, and low-lying coral atolls. The climate is warm and rainfall is heavy.

Melanesian, Polynesian, and Micronesian people make up the bulk of the population, and there is a small group of Europeans. English is the official language, but pidgin English is more widely spoken.

Economy. The islands' forests are a rich source of valuable hardwoods, and there are deposits of gold and other minerals that are only partially exploited. Most people live by subsistence farming and fishing. Coconuts and cocoa are the chief commercial crops.

Coconut products, fish, cocoa, and timber are the chief exports, and manufactured goods, fuels, and food are imported. Japan and Australia are the principal trade partners.

Government. The Solomon Islands is a member of the British Commonwealth, and the British monarch is its head of state. The head of government is the prime minister, who is elected by a 38-member parliament.

History. Little is known of the islands before they were visited by the Spanish in 1567. They were soon lost to Europeans again, and were rediscovered by the French only in 1792. The islands served Europeans as a source of copra and cheap labor. In the 1880's and 1890's Great Britain assumed control of the islands and established a protectorate. British authorities took steps to halt "blackbirding," the forcible recruiting of island labor. At the same time, British settlers established plantations, Christian missions, and trading posts.

THE BUSY PORT OF SINGAPORE *handles a major portion of the trade of Southeast Asia. It contributes to the city's role as commercial center for the region.*

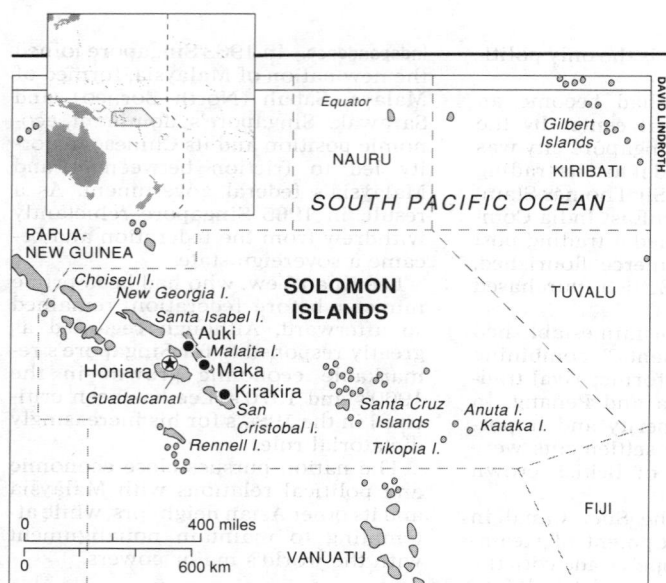

Solomon Islands

Official name: *Solomon Islands*
Area: *11,500 sq. mi., 29,785 sq. km.*
Type of government: *Parliamentary democracy*
Head of state: *Queen Elizabeth II*
Head of government: *Prime minister, Ezekiel Alebua*
Population: *324,000 (1989 est.)*
Population growth rate: *3.6%*
Capital and largest city: *Honiara (Pop., 1987 est., 26,000)*
Languages: *English (official), Pidgin*
Religions: *Protestant 76%, Roman Catholic 19%*
Ethnic groups: *Melanesian 93%, Polynesian 4%*
Literacy: *13%*
Life expectancy: *68 years (1987)*
Currency: *Dollar*
Per capita GNP: *$530 (1986)*
Exports: *$65 million (1986)*
Imports: *$59 million (1986)*

The islands, especially Guadalcanal in the southwest, were the scene of fierce fighting between Japanese and Allied troops in World War II. In the decades after the war, Great Britain concentrated on raising the islanders' standard of living and expanding the local economy by developing natural resources.

From the end of the war, the Solomon Islanders began to press for self-government. After a short period of representative councils, the islands received a constitution in 1974 and became an independent member of the Commonwealth on July 7, 1978.

Sri Lanka

The land. Sri Lanka's coastline is low and sandy except for the area around the Jaffna Peninsula, in the north, and at Trincomalee, in the east. Both have excellent natural harbors. In the interior of southern Sri Lanka, mountainous highlands rise from the coastal plain to a peak of over 8000 feet. The north is largely a flat plain with an elevation only slightly above sea level.

Sri Lanka has a tropical climate, with average year-round temperatures ranging between 80°F and 100°F. It is cooler in the mountains. Humidity is high throughout the country, but especially in the southwest, where as much as 200 inches of rain a year may fall. About 50 inches fall yearly on the rest of the country.

The people. More than two-thirds of the people of Sri Lanka are Sinhalese, and speak Sinhala, an Indic language. Most are Buddhist. Almost one-quarter of the people are Tamils, a people of southern Indian origin who speak Tamil, a Dravidian language. Most Tamils are Hindus. The Tamils are divided between Sri Lanka Tamils, those who have been Sri Lankan for many

generations, and Indian Tamils, the descendants of Indian laborers brought to the island in the 1800's.

Smaller minorities include Muslim Arabs, Burghers—descendants of Dutch colonists—Eurasians, Muslim Malays, and Veddas, descendants of the island's first settlers. Relations among the various groups have not always been good, and there have been bitter conflicts between the Sinhalese and the Tamils.

The population is concentrated in the southwestern corner of the island and in places along the coasts. It grew at a rapid rate of about $2\frac{1}{2}$ percent a year between 1963 and 1971. Since then, however, a national birth-control program has helped to reduce the annual increase. The most populous cities are the capital, Colombo; Dehi-

wela-Mt. Lavinia (173,000); Jaffna (151,000); Kandy (122,000); and Galle (100,000).

Economy. Sri Lanka's economy is based almost completely on agriculture, which employs 45 percent of the labor force. The soil is Sri Lanka's most important natural resource. The leading crops of tea, rubber, coconuts, and spices are grown on large plantations. Tea is grown in the highlands, rubber in the wet lowlands, and coconuts in drier coastal regions. Small farms produce ample supplies of rice and vegetables. Fish are abundant off the coasts.

Sri Lanka's few industries are mainly concerned with processing tea, rubber, and coconuts. There are also factories producing textiles, cement, soap, and other consumer items.

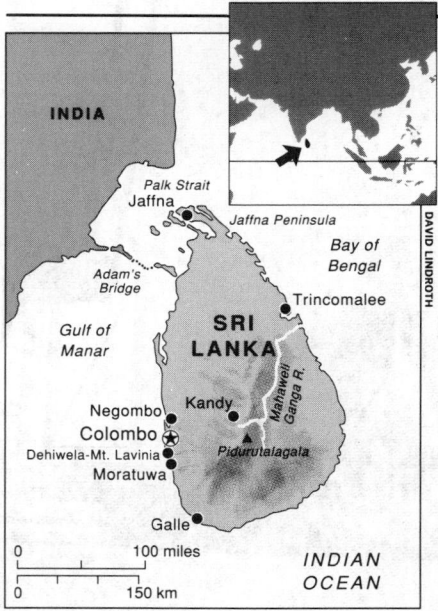

Sri Lanka

Official name: *Democratic Socialist Republic of Sri Lanka*
Area: *25,332 sq. mi., 65,610 sq. km.*
Type of government: *Republic*
Head of state: *President, Ranasinghe Premadasa*
Population: *16,870,000 (1989 est.)*
Population growth rate: *1.7%*
Capital and largest city: *Colombo (Pop., 1987 est., 700,000)*
Languages: *Sinhala (official), Tamil, English*
Religions: *Buddhist 69%, Hindu 15%, Christian 7%, Muslim 7%*
Ethnic groups: *Sinhalese 74%, Tamil 18%, Moor 7%*
Literacy: *87%*
Life expectancy: *70 years (1987)*
Currency: *Rupee*
Per capita GNP: *$400 (1986)*
Exports: *$1.2 billion (1986)*
Imports: *$1.95 billion (1986)*

Sri Lanka relies heavily on foreign trade for many commodities. Tea, textiles and garments, rubber, and coconut products account for most of the exports, which are shipped mainly to the United States, Egypt, and West Germany. The major imports, including foodstuffs, petroleum products, textiles, fertilizers, and machinery, come mainly from Saudi Arabia, Japan, and the United States.

Government. In 1978 Sri Lanka received a new constitution that provided for a strong popularly elected president as head of state. The president appoints the prime minister and cabinet and can dismiss them.

Legislative power is held by a unicameral parliament with 196 members. The president also has the power to dismiss the parliament.

History. Sri Lanka's first known inhabitants were a primitive people, the Veddas. In the 500's B.C., they were conquered by the Sinhalese, an Aryan people from northern India. The Sinhalese established a kingdom in the north central portion of the island, and constructed irrigation works to enable them to grow rice in the dry region. By the 200's B.C. Sinhalese civilization was quite advanced, and its culture, centered on Buddhism, had produced many magnificent temples, especially in the capital at Anduradhapura.

The kingdom was subjected to repeated attacks and invasions by people from southern India, and it was conquered in the 900's A.D. by the Chola empire. The Chola were driven out in the 1000's, but some Chola cultural influences remained. During the 1000's Arab traders began to stop at Sri Lanka, and some settled on the island.

Between the 1200's and the 1400's the island was attacked repeatedly by Malay and Chinese adventurers, as well as by Indians. In the 1300's the Hindu Tamil people of southern India invaded Sri Lanka and settled in the northern part of the island, forcing the Sinhalese to the south.

European influence. In the 1500's Portuguese traders arrived in Sri Lanka, drawn by the high quality of the cinnamon that the islanders grew. They soon destroyed the Tamil kingdom and established control over the coastal regions. The Sinhalese retreated to the highland interior, around Kandy. In 1638 traders of the Dutch East India Company arrived.

By 1658, aided by the king of Kandy, the Dutch had driven out the Portuguese and had taken over the spice trade. The Dutch exerted little control over the island's government. During the 1600's and 1700's the Sinhalese kingdom of Kandy underwent a cultural revival and grew in power, controlling some smaller islands in the Indian Ocean.

In 1796 the British replaced the Dutch in the coastal areas, and in 1802 made the island the crown colony of Ceylon. By 1815, with the aid of some of the Kandyans, the British took control of the entire island, including Kandy. The British expanded the area of cultivated land, planted tea and rubber, and improved irrigation facilities in the drier north. They established schools and introduced Western forms of government.

In 1931 Ceylon was granted limited self-government. Parliamentary elections were held in 1947, and on February 4, 1948, Ceylon was granted sovereignty as an independent member of the Commonwealth of Nations.

Independence. Independent Ceylon concentrated on developing its economy and improving the lot of its people through social welfare programs. From the mid-1950's to the mid-1960's, Ceylonese politics was dominated by the socialist Sri Lanka Freedom Party (SLFP). S.W.R.D. Bandaranaike, leader of the SLFP, was prime minister from 1956 until his assassination in 1959. His widow became prime minister in 1960 and the country followed strongly socialist policies, with many businesses being nationalized. The government's methods were unpopular, and it fell in 1964.

Under the more moderate United National Party (UNP), elected in 1965, the socialist program continued, but encouragement was given to private business in an effort to speed economic growth. The UNP government concentrated on uniting the many factions of Ceylon's society.

Mrs. Bandaranaike was elected prime minister again in 1970. She severely suppressed left-wing rioters who wanted more rapid socialization and an end to the nation's economic problems.

In 1972 a new constitution was adopted; it declared Ceylon to be the Republic of Sri Lanka, and ended the role of the British queen as monarch. Sri Lanka remained, however, a member of the Commonwealth.

Another new constitution in 1978 provided for a presidential government after the UNP had ousted Mrs. Bandaranaike in the election of 1977. Junius Jayewardene, leader of the UNP, then became president.

The Sri Lankan government has had little success in coming to terms with a violent separatist movement among the minority Tamils. In 1987 the government signed an agreement with India, which was representing the

THE RECLINING BUDDHA STATUE *is typical of principally Buddhist Sri Lanka. Tea is an important plantation crop on the island, with harvesting done by hand.*

HOLBROOKE/MONKMEYER

H. ARMSTRONG ROBERTS

Tamil population, that provided increased autonomy for the Tamil-dominated provinces in the north and east. Indian peacekeeping forces moved into the disputed areas, but they quickly became embroiled in battles with Tamil guerrillas opposed to the plan.

Taiwan

The land. The island of Taiwan is mountainous. Its major range, the Chungyang, runs from north to south in the eastern third of the island. It contains many peaks over 10,000 feet high, and its highest peak, Yü Shan, is more than 13,000 feet high. To the east, across a narrow rift valley, a coastal range rises to a maximum of 7000 feet and then drops sharply into the sea. Many rivers flow east and west from the Chungyang range.

Taiwan

Official name: *Republic of China*
Area: *12,456 sq. mi., 32,261 sq. km.*
Type of government: *One-party democracy*
Head of state: *President, Lee Teng-hui*
Head of government: *Prime minister, Yu Kuo-hua*
Population: *20,233,000 (1989 est.)*
Population growth rate: *1.2%*
Capital and largest city: *Taipei (Pop., 1987 est., 2,500,000)*
Language: *Mandarin Chinese (official)*
Religions: *Buddhist, Confucian, Taoist*
Ethnic group: *Han Chinese 98%*
Literacy: *90%*
Life expectancy: *73 years (1987)*
Currency: *Dollar*
Per capita GNP: *3640 (1986)*
Exports: *$39.8 billion (1986)*
Imports: *$24.2 billion (1986)*

To the west of the mountains the land slopes to a fertile coastal plain that is the heartland of the island. It is only some 25 miles at its widest, but its width is being extended by continuous sedimentation along the shallow west coast. The west coast contains the island's best harbors.

Taiwan's climate is semitropical. Annual precipitation varies from 50 inches in the mountains to 200 inches on the coasts. During winter, from October to April, north to northeast winds bring much rain to the northern areas. In summer, the winds are chiefly from the south and southwest, and it is during this period that most of the south receives its maximum rain. From May to November, the island may be struck by typhoons.

Temperatures in the lowlands rarely drop below 60°F. The higher elevations are colder, and the higher peaks have prolonged snow cover.

The people. Taiwan was settled by Chinese from Fukien and Kwantung provinces during the period from the 1600's to the 1900's. There was a large influx of people from all parts of the mainland in the late 1940's and early 1950's. There are also small numbers of aborigines who are considered to have come from Polynesian stock. Mandarin Chinese is the official language of Taiwan; however, many native Taiwanese speak the Amoy dialect of Chinese.

Taiwan is densely populated, with over 1422 people per square mile in 1988. Sixty-seven percent of the population is urban. The most populous cities are the capital, Taipei; Kaohsiung (1.6 million); Taichung (700,000); and Tainan (650,000).

Economy. Taiwan has one of the world's fastest growing economies, and the second highest per capita income in East Asia, after Japan.

The island's natural resources are limited to coal, natural gas, hydroelectric power, and its main resources, fertile land and abundant water.

Agriculture continues to play an important role in the economy. As only one-quarter of the island's land can be cultivated, farming is intensive and two or three crops a year are raised on the same land. Rice is the major crop, and the staple of the diet. Sugar cane, raised primarily for export, is second in importance. Sweet potatoes, soybeans, tea, peanuts, and fruits are also significant items.

Taiwan's real economic success, however, has come from light manufacturing geared to the export market. Heavy industry has also been successful, including steel, shipbuilding, and oil refining.

Taiwan relies heavily on its export market for the strength of its economy. Exports include electronic equipment, plastics, footwear, toys, textiles, and other consumer goods. Imports are largely raw materials and capital goods to support industry and food. Its major trading partners are the United States, Japan, and Hong Kong.

Government. The Republic of China (also called Nationalist China) is the continuation of the nationalist government that fled mainland China under Chiang Kai-shek in 1949. It claims to be the legitimate government of all China, but its authority is confined to Taiwan. The People's Republic of China insists that Taiwan is an integral part of Chinese territory. Taiwan has a republican form of government. The island has two elected legislatures—one theoretically for all China, and one provincial assembly for Taiwan.

The executive branch of government is quite strong. It consists of a president and vice president elected by the National Assembly, and a premier, or

TAIWAN'S FERTILE LAND *is intensively farmed, and a favorable climate permits several harvests per year.*

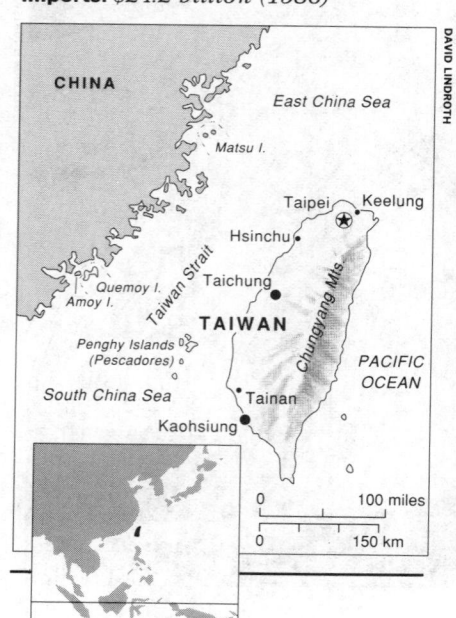

prime minister, appointed by the president and responsible to the assembly.

The National Assembly is responsible for electing the president and amending the constitution. Primary legislative responsibility rests with the legislative Yuan. Both bodies are dominated by Nationalist Chinese leaders. In recent years many changes have been made to permit greater Taiwanese representation.

The Kuomintang, or Nationalist Party, is the island's dominant political organization.

History. Most of Taiwan's history prior to 1949 is coincidental with China's, now known as the People's Republic of China.

In 1624 the island of Taiwan, inhabited by aborigines and a small number of Chinese, was seized by the Dutch. In 1661 a Ming dynasty loyalist, Cheng Cheng-kung (Koxinga), drove out the Dutch and made Taiwan a base from which he hoped to reconquer the mainland from the Manchus, but Manchu armies regained control in 1683.

In 1896, following the first Sino-Japanese war, Taiwan was ceded to Japan. For a half-century, until the end of World War II, Japan invested heavily in the Taiwanese economy, preparing the island for its later, great economic success.

In 1945, when the Nationalists took over the government of Taiwan, they were faced immediately with difficulties in governing the island. Descendants of the mainland Chinese who had settled Taiwan in the 1600's regarded themselves as native Taiwanese, different from the mainland people. Some had hoped for complete independence for Taiwan after the Japanese withdrew.

The sufferings of the Taiwanese under outside rule, their unmet demands for independence, and the ineptitude and harshness of the Nationalist government after 1945, combined to create severe friction between the Taiwanese and the mainlanders. The situation worsened, and in 1947 the Taiwanese rebelled. The revolt was crushed ruthlessly.

When the Nationalists lost to Communist forces on the mainland in 1949, they moved their government, their army, and some 3 million of their citizens to Taiwan. There, President Chiang Kai-shek proclaimed a government of all China and declared his intention to return to the mainland.

In 1950 Communist China declared Taiwan to be a part of its territory and announced its intention to reclaim it. The U.S. Navy protected the island and prevented any contemplated mainland invasion attempt.

Taiwan's history in the 1950's and 1960's was shaped by the claim of both Chinas to be the sole representative of the Chinese people. Because of the rivalry, low-level military activities continued between the two Chinas in the 1950's and 1960's, flaring up into sev-

THE BETTMANN ARCHIVE

CHIANG KAI-SHEK *led China's Nationalist government to exile in Taiwan.*

eral crises—the battle for the tiny offshore islands of Quemoy and Matsu in the late 1950's, and the large-scale buildup of Communist and Nationalist troops on facing coasts in the early 1960's.

The division radically affected the nation's foreign affairs as well. Taiwan committed itself to maintaining its position in the noncommunist world as the sole legal government of China, and it refused to deal officially with any nation that recognized Communist China.

The United States not only protected the island with U.S. naval forces, but gave the Nationalists their main diplomatic support, trained the Nationalist army, and provided the aid that made possible Taiwan's economic growth.

The Kuomintang claim to all China affected Taiwan's domestic politics in other ways. Full-scale national elections were postponed until the return to the mainland, and the republic's affairs remained in the hands of the National Assembly, which elects the president. Twice it amended the consti-

TAIPEI, *the capital of Taiwan, has much thriving commerce and industry.*

H. ARMSTRONG ROBERTS

tution to permit President Chiang Kai-shek to be reelected.

In the early 1960's the Kuomintang moved to strengthen its control over Taiwan's politics in response to a widening of opposition activities. In 1966 the National Assembly greatly increased the powers of the presidency, at the same time promising that elections would be held for the assembly on Taiwan.

In 1971 Taiwan lost its seat in the United Nations to the People's Republic of China. In 1979 the United States recognized the People's Republic as China's legal government. In 1980 it failed to renew the mutual security and defense pact it had signed in 1954 with Taiwan, but it continues to maintain a "privileged relations" status.

President Chiang, the center of the Nationalist movement for over 50 years, died on April 5, 1975. His son, Chiang Ching-kuo, the premier, was named chairman of the Central Committee of the Kuomintang Party. In 1978 he was elected president.

In 1987 Chiang Ching-kuo lifted martial law, beginning the slow process of turning Taiwan into a true democracy. Chiang died in 1988 and was succeeded by Lee Teng-hui, the first native Taiwanese president. Lee continued the process of reform, thus increasing the representation of native Taiwanese in the government and relaxing controls on contact with the mainland government.

Thailand

The land. Thailand has several distinct land regions. The north-south trending Bilauktaung mountain range follows the border with Burma. It extends southward across the Kra Isthmus into peninsular Thailand, which forms the backbone of the great Malay peninsula.

In northwestern Thailand, a mountainous upland area, with an elevation of 600 to 3000 feet above sea level, lies between the Salween and the Mekong river basins. It contains the major tributaries of the Chao Phraya, the principal river system of the country.

The basin of the Chao Phraya, which contains the fertile Bangkok Plain, is the core region of Thailand. The basin has an inverted U-shaped outline, with the Dawna and the Bilauktaung mountain ranges on the west, the uplands of the hilly Shan Plateau on the north, and the Phetchabun Mountains on the east.

The Phetchabun Mountains form the western margin of the Khorat Plateau, a rolling basin with elevations generally below 700 feet. Rising in the Khorat Plateau is the Mun River, the chief Thai tributary of the Mekong River. The Dang Raek scarp establishes the southern boundary of the Khorat Plateau; between this scarp and

Thailand

Official name: *Kingdom of Thailand*
Area: *198,772 sq. mi., 514,819 sq. km.*
Type of government: *Constitutional monarchy*
Head of state: *King, Bhumibol Adulyadej*
Head of government: *Prime Minister, Chatichai Choonhavan*
Population: *55,524,000 (1989 est.)*
Population growth rate: *1.8%*
Capital and largest city: *Bangkok (Pop., 1987 est., 7,000,000)*
Language: *Thai*
Religions: *Buddhist 95%, Muslim 4%*
Ethnic groups: *Thai 75%, Chinese 14%*
Literacy: *84%*
Life expectancy: *64 years (1987)*
Currency: *Baht*
Per capita GNP: *$810 (1986)*
Exports: *$8.8 billion (1986)*
Imports: *$9.2 billion (1986)*

the Cardamom Mountains on the Gulf of Thailand coast, a narrow lowland connects the Tonle Sap basin of Kampuchea with the delta of the Chao Phraya.

Climate. Thailand lies within the monsoon area of Southeast Asia, but due to the rain shadow effect of the surrounding mountains, annual precipitation is limited in the lowlands. Temperatures are generally quite high.

The people. Almost all of Thailand's people are Thai, related to the people of Laos and eastern Burma. They speak Thai, and most are Buddhists. The largest minority group is Chinese.

Compared with most Southeast Asian countries, Thailand, with a population density of about 276 people per square mile, is rather thinly settled.

Population is concentrated in the river valleys, especially that of the Chao Phraya. Bangkok (Krung Thep), the capital and by far largest city, is located near the mouth of the Chao Phraya.

Economy. Thailand is a relatively prosperous country. Agriculture is the basis of economic life, but industry based largely on the exploitation of Thailand's rich natural resources has increased in recent years.

Forestry, mining, and related operations are the country's leading nonagricultural activities. Thailand is the world's second greatest producer of tin, although mining as a whole employs only 1 percent of the total labor force. In the early 1970's, a substantial amount of petroleum and gas was discovered in the Gulf of Thailand; the production from these fields is helping to reduce Thailand's dependency on imported oil.

One of Thailand's most valuable resources is timber. About one-quarter of the country is covered by forests. Tropical evergreen rain forests in the mountains contain a great variety of hardwoods, and dense monsoon forests contain teak, of which Thailand is one of the world's leading producers. However, overexploitation is leading to rapid depletion of the forests. There is an abundance of fish in the waters off Thailand's long coast and in its many rivers.

Agriculture. Thailand has rich soil and agriculture employs about 60 percent of the labor force. Although farming methods tend to be rather primitive, so much land is under cultivation, about 44 percent of the total area, that Thailand is a large net exporter of food and agricultural products.

Most Thai farms are small and individually owned, except for the rich Bangkok region estates, which use tenant farmers to cultivate rice. Rice is by far the largest crop.

Other agricultural activities include rubber production, both on large estates and on small holdings. Some short-staple cotton is produced on the peninsula in the northern sections of the central plain. Other crops include tobacco, sugar cane, corn, fruits, cassava, peanuts, soybeans, coconuts, sesame, castor beans, silk, and peppers.

Manufacturing is becoming an increasingly important part of the Thai economy. Although most industry is involved in the processing of Thailand's natural resources and agricultural products, the government is actively promoting export industries like electronics assembly and textile manufacture, and its heavy industries like cement production and natural gas liquefaction.

Trade. Thailand's international trade depends primarily on the country's

farms, forests, and mines. Rice, rubber, tapioca, electronics, and textiles are major exports. Fuels and manufactured goods are the major imports. Japan, the United States, and the European Economic Community are Thailand's major trading partners.

Government. Thailand is a constitutional monarchy with the king as head of state. The king appoints a prime minister to head the government. Legislative power rests with a bicameral National Assembly, consisting of a 347-member House of Representatives and a 260-member Senate. The House is popularly elected; the Senate is appointed by the king on the recommendation of the prime minister.

History. The Thai have a long history. People speaking closely related dialects of the Thai language have been living throughout the hilly region of southern China and northern Southeast Asia since nearly the beginning of recorded history. Modern Thailand has its origins in a state created by small warring bands of Thai-speaking people who moved down into the lowlands of the Chao Phraya valley in the 1200's A.D.

In the late 1200's, under their first important kingdom, Sukhothai, the Thai conquered most of the area of present-day Thailand from Mon and Khmer peoples. They adopted the Theravada Buddhism of their Mon subjects and the political system of the Khmer rulers whom they displaced.

Between the 1300's and the 1700's, the Thai ruled from a capital located at Ayutthaya, about 75 miles north of modern Bangkok. The Thai state, like others in Southeast Asia at that time, had no real boundaries. The king ruled his palace-city and its surrounding area directly.

The king exercised some control over most of the Chao Phraya plain through semiautonomous noble-officials. At times Thai kings were strong enough to exact tribute from more distant vassals in Malaya, Cambodia, Laos, and northern Thailand. Wars were common and generally were fought to enforce claims to tribute or to capture new subjects rather than to acquire territory.

Chakri dynasty. In the 1500's the Burmese overran the kingdom and sacked Ayutthaya. The Thai recovered, only to suffer another crushing defeat by Burma in 1767. A powerful Thai revival led to the founding of a strong, new dynasty, the Chakri, in 1782. The Chakri kings established their capital at the port city of Bangkok, and it was from there that Thailand—called Siam by Westerners—faced European imperialism in the 1800's.

The Chakri kings, unlike their Burmese, Vietnamese, and Chinese counterparts, were actively interested in commerce and aware of what was happening in the world outside. In 1855 King Mongkut willingly signed a treaty with the British opening Siam to inter-

THOMPSON/TAURUS PHOTOS

THAILAND, *one of the few Asian countries not colonized by a European power, has a long cultural history that is relatively intact today.*

national trade; he took the first step to modernize the monarchy.

Mongkut's first son, Chulalongkorn, ruled from 1868 to 1910. He carefully steered the country toward modernization while avoiding the dangers presented by European imperialists and Siamese reactionaries.

Slowly but steadily Chulalongkorn abolished slavery, replaced traditional forced labor with monetary taxes, drawn in part from rapidly rising exports of rice and teak, and reorganized the administration with the help of European advisers. He was obliged to yield control of large vassal areas to the British and French, but at the same time he greatly extended the area effectively ruled by Bangkok.

During Chulalongkorn's reign, old Siam was transformed into a recognizably modern nation-state. It was the only country in Southeast Asia not to fall under colonial rule, thanks in part to its position as a buffer state between the British colonial territory in Burma and India and the French colonies in Indochina. The name Thailand was adopted in 1939.

In the early 1900's Siam's prosperity grew as demands for its rubber, tin, and timber increased. The country's progressive social, economic, and educational policies enabled all classes of Thais to share in its prosperity.

Constitutional monarchy. Chulalongkorn's successors were less able men, and the changes he inaugurated created a new class of Western-educated administrators and army officers who were in-

creasingly restive under the rule of absolute monarchy. In 1932 a small group of civilians and officers seized power in a swift and bloodless coup.

The Chakris were reduced to the status of constitutional monarchs. The king's willingness to give up absolute rule contributed to the stability of the constitutional system despite frequent changes of administration.

In a continuation of Chulalongkorn's "survival diplomacy," the Thais joined Japan as a passive ally during World War II to avoid invasion and occupation. When Japan's defeat became inevitable, Thailand quietly let it be known that it supported the Allies. After 1945 Thailand was actively pro-Western, and in 1954 was a founding member of the Southeast Asia Treaty Organization (SEATO), although, following its well-established neutralist tradition, it also attempted to maintain informal, friendly contacts with Communist China.

Modern Thailand. King Bhumibol Adulyadej ascended the throne following the death of his older brother in 1946. In the decades after the war Thailand concentrated on industrializing and modernizing its economy and on protecting itself from the military conflicts that still raged in Southeast Asia.

Internal conflicts and persistent Communist guerrilla activities have resulted in several military coups. While these takeovers often resulted in the suspension of constitutional and civil rights, they did not weaken Thailand's political stability. Although the

governments were autocratic, they were not oppressive.

A bloody military takeover in 1976 was followed by another in 1977. A democratic constitution was provided in 1978, and in February, 1980, the prime minister resigned in the face of rising oil prices, inflation, and unemployment; he was succeeded by Prem Tinsulanonda who remained in office until 1988. There has been guerrilla activity in several areas, and border clashes with Laos and Cambodia.

Thailand is host to several hundred thousand refugees from Cambodia, Vietnam, and Laos. Most of these live in camps near the Cambodian border.

Tonga

The land. The Tonga, or Friendly, Islands include about 170 small islands that form three major groups—Tongatapu, the largest, in the south; Ha'apai; and Vava'u, in the north. Some of the Tonga Islands are volcanic in origin and have a mountainous, rugged terrain. Others are coral formations and are flat and low. Coral reefs ring most of the islands of the group. The climate is mild throughout the year and rainfall is moderate.

The people. Tongans, a Polynesian people, make up a large majority of the population. There are small groups of Europeans and other islanders. Tongan, a Polynesian language, and English are spoken. Most of the people are Protestant.

Economy. The Tongan economy is based on agriculture. Coconuts, bananas, vanilla beans, and pineapples are the main commercial crops, and taros, yams, fruits, and corn are grown for local consumption. Pigs and cattle are raised, and there is some fishing.

With no mineral resources other than a small quantity of building stone, and no important fuel resources, the islands' only industry is copra production. Tonga exports copra, vanilla beans, and fruit and imports foodstuffs, fuels, and machinery. Australia, New Zealand, and Japan are Tonga's principal trading partners.

Government. Tonga is a constitutional monarchy with a hereditary king who appoints the prime minister. The legislative assembly consists of nine nobles who are elected by their peers, nine popularly elected people's representatives, and the ten members of the cabinet.

History. Tongan history extends back to the 900's or earlier, when the first Tongan ruling dynasty is considered to have been founded. Europeans reached the islands in the 1600's, and in the late 1700's European ships began to visit Tonga. In the 1820's European Christian missionaries arrived on the islands, and by the mid-1800's most of the islanders had been converted to Christianity.

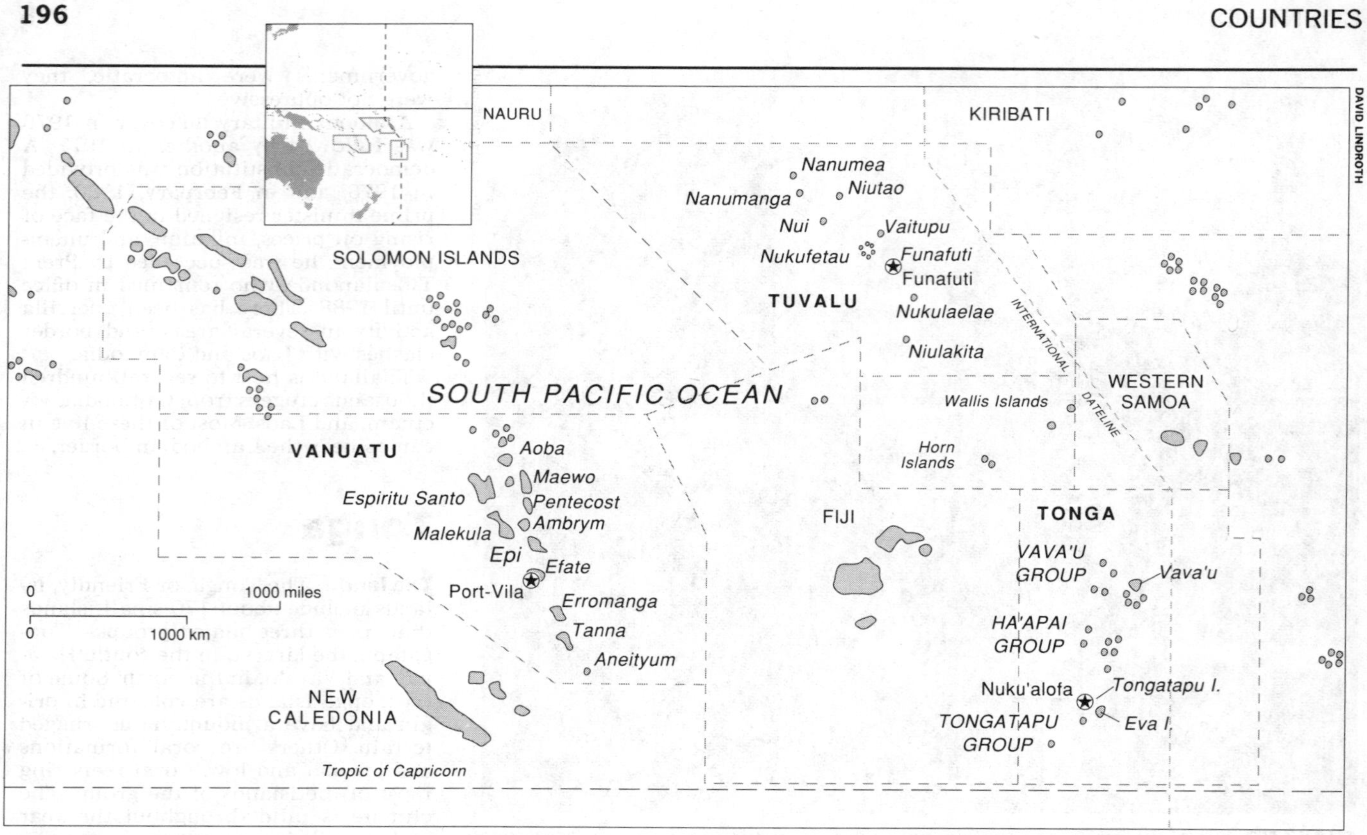

Map showing the South Pacific Ocean region, including Solomon Islands, Nauru, Kiribati, Tuvalu (Nanumea, Niutao, Nanumanga, Nui, Vaitupu, Nukufetau, Funafuti, Nukulaelae, Niulakita), Western Samoa, Wallis Islands, Horn Islands, Vanuatu (Aoba, Maewo, Espiritu Santo, Pentecost, Ambrym, Malekula, Epi, Efate, Port-Vila, Erromanga, Tanna, Aneityum), Fiji, Tonga (Vava'u Group, Vava'u, Ha'apai Group, Nuku'alofa, Tongatapu I., Tongatapu Group, Eva I.), New Caledonia, and the International Dateline.

Tonga

Official name: *Kingdom of Tonga*
Area: *385 sq. mi., 997 sq. km.*
Type of government: *Constitutional monarchy*
Head of state: *King, Taufa'ahau Tupou IV*
Head of government: *Prime minister, Fatafehi Tu'pelehake*
Population: *100,000 (1989 est.)*
Population growth rate: *2.3%*
Capital and largest city: *Nuku'alofa (Pop., 1984 est., 27,800)*
Languages: *Tongan (official), English*
Religions: *Protestant, Roman Catholic, Mormon*
Ethnic groups: *Tongan 98%*
Literacy: *93%*
Life expectancy: *71 years (1987)*
Currency: *Dollar*
Per capita GNP: *$580 (1986)*
Exports: *$5 million (1985)*
Imports: *$41 million (1985)*

Tuvalu

Official name: *Tuvalu*
Area: *10 sq. mi., 26 sq. km.*
Type of government: *Parliamentary democracy*
Head of state: *Queen Elizabeth II*
Head of government: *Prime minister, Tomasi Puapua*
Population: *9000 (1989 est.)*
Population growth rate: *1.7%*
Capital and largest city: *Funafuti (Pop., 1985 est., 2800)*
Languages: *Tuvaluan, English*
Religion: *Protestant*
Ethnic group: *Polynesian*
Literacy: *50%*
Life expectancy: *61 years (1987)*
Currency: *Australian dollar*
Per capita GNP: *$450 (1984)*
Exports: *$1 million*
Imports: *$2.8 million*

Vanuatu

Official name: *Republic of Vanuatu*
Area: *5700 sq. mi., 14,763 sq. km.*
Type of government: *Republic*
Head of state: *President, Ali George Sokomanu*
Head of government: *Prime minister, Walter Lini*
Population: *160,000 (1989 est.)*
Population growth rate: *3.3%*
Capital and largest city: *Port Vila (Pop., 1986 est., 20,000)*
Languages: *Bislama, English, French (all official)*
Religions: *Protestant 54%, Roman Catholic 16%, animist 15%*
Ethnic group: *Melanesian*
Literacy: *15%*
Life expectancy: *68 years (1987)*
Currency: *Vatu*
Per capita GNP: *$350 (1981)*
Exports: *$14.3 million (1986)*
Imports: *$58 million (1986)*

THE KINGDOM OF TONGA *has long had close ties with Great Britain.*

The islands were most recently united into a single kingdom in 1845, when Taufa'ahau Tupou, the king of Ha'apai, won the thrones of Vava'u and Tongatapu as well. The king granted a democratic constitution in 1875. In 1900 Tonga and Great Britain signed a treaty and the islands became a British protectorate, retaining their autonomy while leaving defense and foreign affairs to Britain.

Tongan troops participated in World War II alongside Allied forces in the Solomon Islands, and Allied bases were established in Tonga.

Under a new treaty ratified in 1959, Tonga received greater local autonomy, and in 1965 Britain further relaxed its authority over Tonga. The islands became fully independent in 1970.

Tuvalu

The land and people. Tuvalu (formerly the Ellice Islands) is a group of nine coral atolls in the west central Pacific, just south of the Gilbert Islands. The islands are generally low, with some rising to 90 feet, and have a hot and humid climate. The people are Polynesian; their language is called Tuvaluan.

Economy. There are many pandanus groves and coconut groves on the islands. The natives engage in fishing, farming, and the production of copra, which is the chief export. The economy also relies on income from the sale of postage stamps and on remittances from overseas workers. A trust fund has been set up by Australia, New Zealand, and Great Britain to provide income for the future.

Government. Tuvalu is a member of the Commonwealth, and its head of state is the British monarch. The 12-member parliament elects a prime minister.

History. The islands were discovered in 1764 by Captain John Byron, grandfather of Lord Byron. They were made a British protectorate in 1892 and were included in the colony of Gilbert and Ellice Islands, which was created in 1916. In a referendum held on the islands in 1974, a large majority of the islanders voted to separate from the Gilbert and Ellice territory. This separation took place in October of 1975; at that time the name of Ellice Islands was changed to Tuvalu. Independence was obtained on October 1, 1978.

Tuvalu receives extensive British economic aid, but it remains basically dependent on its single cash crop, copra. Many of its citizens seek employment overseas in the phosphate industry in the Republic of Kiribati.

Vanuatu

The land. Vanuatu consists of about 80 islands. The islands are of volcanic origin and have rugged, mountainous interiors rimmed by low coastal plains. The climate is hot and humid throughout the year.

The people. Most of the islanders are Melanesian, and there are people of British and French origin. Vanuatu is 18 percent urban with a density of only 27 people per square mile. It is a primitive and technologically backward nation with a low literacy rate. Most of the labor force consists of peasant farmers.

Economy. The economy is agricultural, with coconut and cocoa the chief commercial crops. Yams, bananas, breadfruit, and manioc are grown for local consumption. Large herds of cattle are raised, and there is considerable fishing. Industry is limited to the processing of farm products, hides, and fish. The country exports copra, beef, fish, and cocoa. Imports include manufactured goods, food, and fuel. Principal trading partners include Australia and the Netherlands.

Government. The republic has a unicameral legislature, the Representa- tive Assembly. It has 46 elected members. The head of state is the president, who is indirectly elected to a five-year term. The assembly elects a prime minister from among its own members.

History. Vanuatu has been occupied for many centuries by Melanesians. European planters and traders began visiting the islands after their discovery in 1606 by the Spanish.

By the mid-1800's, British and French settlers outnumbered other Europeans, and in 1887 the two nations formed a commission to protect their mutual interests. In 1906 joint control of the islands was established. In the mid-1900's, projects were undertaken to modernize and expand the islands' economy and to improve the health and welfare of the islanders.

The constitution, which was granted in 1979, provided for pre-independence elections. A fear of the nationalization of the plantations and the possibility of creating a tax-free haven led to a controversy over the desirability of independence.

Separatist movements on both Espiritu Santo and Tanna led to violence after elections that favored the pro-nationalist party. In May, 1980, Jimmy Stevens led a revolt on Espiritu Santo, which attempted to declare independence as Vemarana.

Anglo-French forces crushed the revolt, and the nationhood of a united Vanuatu was preserved. Papua New Guinea forces have been stationed in the country since its independence, to maintain peace and control separatist violence.

In 1987 the Western powers were alarmed when the Vanuatu government signed a one-year agreement with the Soviet Union allowing Soviet fishing boats to operate in Vanuatu's territorial waters.

Vietnam

The land. Vietnam is a narrow S-shaped strip of territory that consists of two large river deltas—the Red and Mekong—and a connecting mountain range—the Annam Cordillera.

Lying entirely within the tropics, all the lowlands of Vietnam have warm, moist, frost-free weather. The total amount of rainfall and the maximum period of rainfall depend upon exposure to the northeast and southwest monsoons. The average range of temperatures is from 60° to 90°F.

From mid-September to March, the northeast monsoons bring cool weather to the Red River delta area, rain to the entire east coast, and sunny skies to the Mekong delta. From June to September, the southwest monsoons bring high humidity and rain to all of Vietnam. From July to November, the country is subjected to irregular and sometimes damaging typhoons.

The core of northern Vietnam is the Red River delta, in the eastern part. It is the compound delta of the Red, the Black, and other lesser rivers, most of which originate in adjacent China and Laos. Mountains and highlands dominate the landscape throughout the entire western and northern parts of the region.

Vietnam

Official name: *Socialist Republic of Vietnam*
Area: *127,300 sq. mi., 329,580 sq. km.*
Type of government: *Communist*
Head of state: *President, Vo Chi Cong*
Head of government: *Prime minister, Pham Hung*
Population: *66,821,000 (1989 est.)*
Population growth rate: *2.6%*
Capital: *Hanoi (Pop., 1985 est., 1,750,000)*
Largest city: *Ho Chi Minh City (Pop., 1985 est., 3,500,000)*
Languages: *Vietnamese (official), French, Chinese*
Religions: *Buddhist, Hoa Hao, Cao Dai, Roman Catholic*
Ethnic groups: *Vietnamese 84%, Chinese 2%*
Literacy: *78%*
Life expectancy: *63 years (1987)*
Currency: *Dong*
Per capita income: *$200 (1986)*
Exports: *$785 million (1986)*
Imports: *$1.6 billion (1986)*

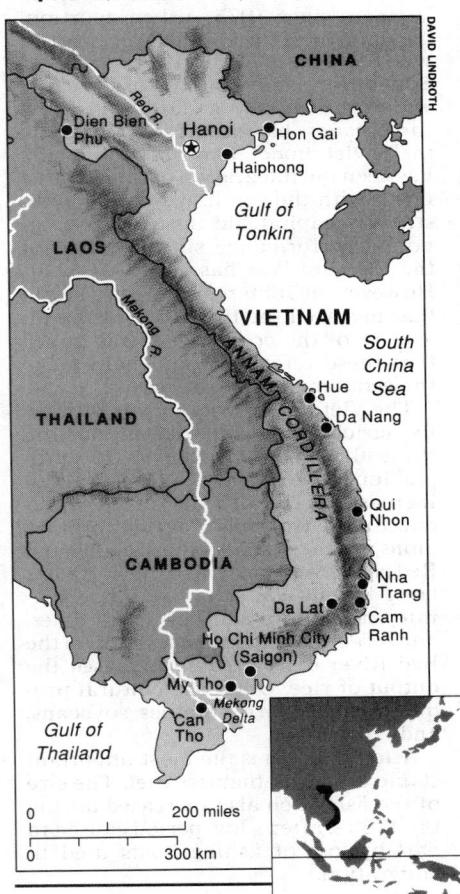

South of the 17th parallel, the Annam Cordillera and its foothills form a central massif. It occupies some two-thirds of the southern area and leaves room for only a few small, enclosed coastal plains. The south's only major lowland lies in the swampy delta of the Mekong River at the southern tip of the country.

The people. Almost all of the people are Vietnamese, descended from Mongol and Indonesian peoples.

The largest minority group is the Chinese, most of whom live in Hanoi, Haiphong, and Ho Chi Minh City.

The second largest minority consists of Montagnards, the aboriginal people of the country, who are of Malay-Indonesian or Mon stock, and who lead seminomadic lives in the mountains.

The third largest group is the Khmers, who are concentrated mostly along the Cambodian border. There are also minorities of Cham (remnants of a 16th-century kingdom), Indian, and Malay peoples, and in the mountainous areas of the north and northwest are members of the Muong, Tai, Meo, and a number of smaller tribes.

In the northern section of the country, the population is concentrated in the Red River delta. In the southern section, the most densely settled area is in the Mekong delta region, especially around Ho Chi Minh City. The overall population density for Vietnam in 1988 was 512 persons per square mile.

Large numbers of people have fled Vietnam since 1975. A disproportionate number of these are ethnic Chinese who have claimed discrimination.

Economy. The economy of Vietnam, which has been in a state of disarray for decades, has been reorganized on the Soviet model. Part of the difficulty has been the integration of the socialist north with the south, which had been strongly capitalistic until 1975. Economic performance since the end of the Vietnam War has been very poor. However, in 1986 reforms were begun that loosened the tight controls on all aspects of the economy. It was hoped that these reforms would help make the economy more productive.

The Vietnamese economy is primarily agricultural, with rice production the leading activity. After very low production in the 1970's, the 1980's saw an increase in the amount of rice produced. The two major agricultural regions are the deltas of the Mekong and Red rivers. Agriculture in the north has been largely collectivized. An elaborate irrigation system of dams, dikes, and reservoirs put into operation in the Red River delta greatly increased the output of rice. Other agricultural products include corn, potatoes, soybeans, and coffee.

After rice, fish is the most important staple of the Vietnamese diet. The size of the fish catch also increased during the 1980's, after a low period caused in part by loss of fishing boats used in emigration.

Manufacturing is plagued by equipment failure and unreliable sources of raw materials. Important industries include food processing, textiles, cement, fertilizers, and chemicals.

Most of Vietnam's trade is with the Soviet Union, but a small amount of trade takes place with Hong Kong and Japan. Principal exports include raw materials, agricultural products, handicrafts, and seafood. Imports include petroleum, transportation equipment, chemicals, and fertilizers. The Soviet Union contributes a huge amount of aid to Vietnam.

Government. Vietnam's government is democratic in form, but it is basically controlled by the Communist Party. The constitution vests supreme governmental authority in the popularly elected National Assembly, which chooses a standing committee to act for it between its short sessions and elects a president as head of state. The president appoints the prime minister and other cabinet members.

The Communist Party, however, nominates all candidates for the National Assembly, and government leaders are usually top officers of the party. The politburo of the party's central committee determines national policy.

History. Vietnam has been inhabited for many centuries, but little is known of its early history. It is thought to have been settled by people from elsewhere in Indochina and from neighboring islands, and by people moving southward from China.

By about 500 B.C. a kingdom had been established by these Viet peoples, as they called themselves. It extended from present-day northern Vietnam across the modern southern Chinese province of Kwangtung. In the 200's B.C. the Viet began to feel the cultural influence of China, and their kingdom was conquered by generals of the disintegrating Ch'in dynasty of China.

Chinese rule. The Ch'in ruled until 111 B.C., when armies of the Han dynasty, the successor to the Ch'in, conquered Vietnam and annexed it to China. It remained Chinese for about 1000 years. The Vietnamese managed to retain their own culture despite the influences of Chinese economics, religion, and language.

The T'ang dynasty came to power in China in 618 and asserted strict authority over the "pacified South," or An-Nam, as Vietnam came to be called.

Independence. In 907 the T'ang dynasty collapsed, and the Vietnamese successfully rebelled. In 939 a rebel leader, Ngo Quyen, founded a Vietnamese dynasty that by 940 had regained control of all the territory from the 17th parallel to the southern Chinese province of Yünnan. China never recognized Annam's independence, and the country remained under nominal Chinese control.

The first strong dynasty was the Li (1009–1225), which launched a successful drive to regain territory from the Chams of Champa. In 1471, after the Chams had been severely weakened by civil war, the Vietnamese were able to conquer the entire Champa kingdom and extend their Annamese empire across Cochin China, in the south, and into present-day Cambodia. Annam had become a great power in Southeast Asia, but its era of unity, power, prestige, and peace, was short.

Dissension. The 1500's were years of political upheaval. In 1620 civil war erupted between two powerful families—the Trinh in the north, or Tonkin, and the Nguyen in the south, or Annam. Each supported and controlled rival dynasties.

While the Vietnamese were fighting each other during the 1700's, Europeans began establishing colonies in Southeast Asia. Missionaries, explorers, and merchants arrived in Vietnam from Great Britain, France, the Netherlands, Portugal, and Spain. Despite their internal warfare, the Vietnamese successfully prevented any of the foreigners from establishing colonies. But Roman Catholic missionaries, most of whom were French, were successful in converting and influencing many people.

Unification. One of the missionaries, Pigneau de Behaine, had become a close adviser of Nguyen Anh, the emperor of Annam. Through him, in 1787, the emperor first requested French aid in conquering all of Vietnam. French volunteer sailors and soldiers helped reorganize and train the Annamese army. They helped Nguyen Anh put down a rebellion in Annam and then assisted him in a successful attack upon Tonkin.

By 1802 the Annamese had conquered all of Tonkin, and in 1802 Nguyen Anh proclaimed himself Emperor Gia-Long of all Vietnam, which included much of present-day Cambodia as well. Gia-Long restored peace to his newly unified country. He practiced toleration of all religions and permitted friendly Westerners to live in the country. His death in 1820, however, brought to the throne Minh-Mang, who was anti-Western and anti-Christian.

France tried to open Vietnam to trade by offering to negotiate commercial and diplomatic treaties with Minh-Mang. He rejected all offers and in 1826 broke off formal relations with France. In the 1830's he ordered the persecution of Christians.

Minh-Mang's successor, Thieu-Tri, practiced even harsher persecution of the missionaries and merchants, most of whom were French. It worsened under Thieu-Tri's successor, Tu-Duc, and when, in 1857, a Spanish bishop was executed, France joined Spain in attacking Vietnam.

French conquest. France's emperor, Napoleon III, seized the opportunity to increase French influence in the area. Following the occupation in 1859 of Saigon and French military success in

1861 in Cochin China, Tu-Duc ceded control of the southern region to France in 1862.

Tu-Duc obtained Chinese protection for his remaining kingdom (Annam and Tonkin) in the 1870's, but the French still captured Tonkin. In 1884 the Treaty of Hue placed all of Vietnam under French protection.

China protested but was not prepared to fight. France established its control over the region and in 1887 united Cambodia, Cochin China, Annam, and Tonkin into the colony of French Indochina.

Rebellions were frequent. In the 1920's France granted the Vietnamese a partially elected council to advise the colonial government. Vietnamese representation was not effective, however, and in 1930–1931 more violent rebellions occurred. They were put down harshly. Opposition to French rule grew and Vietnamese nationalist groups were organized.

World War II. In 1940, after the outbreak of World War II, Japan invaded and occupied Vietnam, and took control of the colony from the Vichy French regime. The Japanese permitted Vietnamese leaders to participate more fully in the government than the French had, and although the Japanese exploited the country economically, they gave the people greater freedom.

During the war, the Communist Viet Minh, led by Ho Chi Minh, became the first anti-Japanese guerrilla force in Vietnam. In March, 1945, near the end of the war, Japan declared Vietnam independent.

In August, 1945, Ho's forces seized Hanoi and demanded the abdication of the emperor, Bao Dai. In September Ho proclaimed the independence of the Democratic Republic of Vietnam. A

HO CHI MINH *fought to oust the French and Japanese and to unify Vietnam.*

struggle for power followed among the Viet Minh, the non-Communist Vietnamese, and the French forces.

Division. In December, 1946, full-scale war broke out between French soldiers and Viet Minh forces. The people tended to support the Viet Minh. Communist countries aided the rebels, especially after 1949, when a Communist regime came to power in China.

Finally, in 1954, at the Battle of Dien Bien Phu, the French suffered a shattering defeat and decided to withdraw. The 1954 Geneva Conference, which arranged for a cease-fire, provisionally divided Vietnam into northern and southern sectors at the 17th parallel. The unification of Vietnam was to be achieved by general elections to be held in July, 1956, in both sectors under international supervision. In the north, the Democratic Republic of Vietnam was led by its president, Ho Chi Minh, and was dominated by the Communist Party.

In the south, Ngo Dinh Diem, a Roman Catholic who was prime minister under Emperor Bao Dai, took over the government when Bao Dai left the country in 1954. As the result of a referendum held in 1955, a republic was established in South Vietnam, with Diem as president. Diem refused to participate in the elections mandated by the Geneva Conference.

Diem's government proved unable to solve South Vietnam's problems. Political power was concentrated in Diem's family, and his brother, Ngo Dinh Nhu, organized a secret police force to enforce Diem's policies. Hostility toward the increasingly repressive regime aided the organization of Communist-supported rebels, the Vietcong, who opened guerrilla activity in the late 1950's.

Vietnam War. The United States committed itself to supporting the Diem regime and sent military and political advisers to train the South Vietnamese army and to assist the government. Little headway was made against either the insurgents or the country's pressing social and economic problems, due in part to widespread corruption in the government.

Resentment against the government increased, especially among Buddhist leaders, who believed the government discriminated against Buddhists. Antigovernment riots, led by the Buddhists, broke out in Saigon and Hue. In November, 1963, a military group seized power and killed Diem.

The war intensified as the United States expanded its role from training and advising to actual combat in the early 1960's. Also assisting the South Vietnamese army were Australian, Filipino, Korean, New Zealand, and Thai forces. Air raids began carrying the war to the north in 1965. U.S. troop strength reached its peak in April of 1969.

In January of 1973, in Paris, an agreement was signed providing for a cease-fire in place and calling for a political settlement of the conflict. The United States began withdrawing its last remaining troops, but hostilities continued between North and South Vietnam. In early 1975 the North Vietnamese opened a successful offensive, which brought about the complete defeat of the South Vietnamese forces. In June, a Provisional Revolutionary Government established an administration in Saigon.

Steps were undertaken to transform the society along the lines of the North. Vietnam was officially reunified in 1976.

Vietnam joined the United Nations without incident in 1977, and in 1978 joined the Soviet trading bloc, known as Comecon.

Vietnamese forces invaded Cambodia in 1977, and heavy fighting lasted for two years. China, already disturbed by Vietnam's domestic discrimination against Chinese residents,

VIETNAMESE FISHERMEN *not only make an important contribution to their country's economy, but also supply a means of transport for refugees leaving the country.*

cut financial aid to the new Communist government and invaded some of the country's northern provinces on February 17, 1979. Relations with China remained tense through the mid-1980's.

Vietnam continued to maintain a large force in Cambodia to support that nation's government against guerrilla forces trying to overthrow it. Vietnam's presence in Cambodia was a great drain on the Vietnamese economy; it also proved an obstacle to achieving better international relations. In 1988 Vietnam participated in a round of talks sponsored by the Association of South East Asian Nations in an unsuccessful search for a solution to the conflict in Cambodia.

Western Samoa

The land. Western Samoa is made up of two large islands, Savai'i (660 square miles) and Upolu (430 square miles), and several small islands, including Manono and Apolima. The islands are volcanic in origin and are almost entirely surrounded by coral reefs. Mountains form the core of the two major islands, reaching an elevation of 3608 feet in Upolu and 6094 feet in Savai'i.

Western Samoa has a tropical climate. Temperatures average about 80°F, and yearly rainfall is 112 inches.
The people. Most of the people of Western Samoa are of Polynesian stock, and most are Christian. About 70 percent of the people live in Upolu, and about 28 percent live on Savai'i. Apia, on Upolu, is the commercial center of the islands and the only city of any size.

THE ROYAL TOMBS *illustrate the long cultural history of the Samoan islands.*

Most Samoans live in traditional extended family communities in small coastal villages.
Economy. The economy of Western Samoa is based on agriculture. Sixty-seven percent of the labor force are agricultural workers. Most of these people are engaged in crude subsistence farming. The basic food crops are taro, yams, breadfruit, and papaya. Fish are also important in the diet of the people, and poultry and pigs are raised. Cocoa, coconuts, and bananas are grown for export. The islands have few mineral resources, and there is little industry apart from some processing of agricultural products.

The major imports are food, fuel, textiles, and machinery. The major exports are bananas, coconut oil, timber, cocoa, and copra. Most trade is with New Zealand and Australia.
Government. The constitution of Western Samoa provides for a head of state, known as *O le Ao o le Malo.* The present head of state rules for life but future heads of state will be elected by the legislature to a five-year term. Ex-

ecutive power is exercised by a cabinet headed by a prime minister responsible to the legislature.

Legislative powers are held by the Legislative Assembly. In the assembly, 45 members are elected by the chiefs of clans, and two members are popularly elected to a three-year term. New Zealand represents Western Samoa in foreign affairs.
History. Archaeological evidence suggests that the Samoan islands were first settled before 1000 B.C., perhaps from islands farther south. It is believed that much of the eastern part of Polynesia may have been settled from Samoa.

The first European to visit Samoa was a Dutch explorer, Jacob Roggeveen, in 1722. The islands were later visited by other explorers, but European penetration did not begin until 1830, initiated by British missionaries. British, U.S., and German traders came to the islands in the following years.
Foreign interests. The British were interested in the islands as a place for missionary work, trade, and the development of plantations. U.S. interest centered on trade and control of the exceptional harbor at Pago Pago, in present-day American Samoa. The Germans came first to trade and then developed the largest plantation interests on the islands. New Zealand also held an interest in the islands.

The last three decades of the 1800's saw periodic clashes arising from efforts of the three great powers to settle the Samoan question. Much of the time they assumed that Samoa would be independent, but with one of the powers exercising a dominant political influence in the islands. The United States, firmly in control of Pago Pago, was most consistently concerned with Samoan independence. Germany and Great Britain favored an agreement to leave a single power in control.

By an international agreement in 1900, the islands were divided. Germany gained control of present-day Western Samoa, and granted Great Britain territories elsewhere in the Pacific. The United States annexed eastern Samoa. From 1900 to World War I, Western Samoa was a German colony.

New Zealanders occupied the islands of Western Samoa early in the war, and in 1920 began to administer them as a League of Nations mandate. In 1946 Western Samoa became a United Nations trust territory under New Zealand's administration, and in 1959 it became self-governing.
Independence. In 1961 a plebiscite was held under UN supervision, and the people voted overwhelmingly for independence. On January 1, 1962, Western Samoa became the first independent Polynesian state of modern times. Close ties were maintained with New Zealand, which continues to provide economic aid and educational assistance.

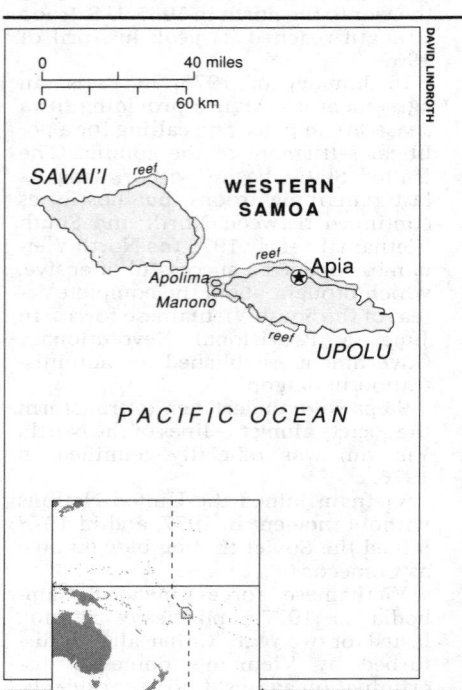

Western Samoa

Official name: *Independent State of Western Samoa*
Area: *1133 sq. mi., 2933 sq. km.*
Type of government: *Constitutional monarchy*
Head of state: *King, Malictoa Tanumafili II*
Head of government: *Prime minister, Vaai Kolone*
Population: *182,000 (1989 est.)*
Population growth rate: *2.7%*
Capital and largest city: *Apia (Pop., 1987 est., 37,000)*
Languages: *Samoan, Polynesian, English*
Religions: *Protestant 70%, Roman Catholic 20%*
Ethnic groups: *Polynesian 88%, Euronesian 10%*
Literacy: *99%*
Life expectancy: *65 years (1987)*
Currency: *Tala*
Per capita GNP: *$680 (1986)*
Exports: *$10.5 million (1986)*
Imports: *$43 million (1986)*

DEPENDENCIES IN ASIA AND AUSTRALASIA

Australian Dependencies

Australian Antarctic Territory (2,472,000 square miles), in Antarctica, is uninhabited except for scientific research stations.

Christmas Island (52 square miles), with 2000 people (1986), is 230 miles south of Java, in the Indian Ocean. Phosphate extraction, the economic mainstay, is expected to end in the 1990's, when the deposits will be exhausted.

The Cocos (Keeling) Islands (5.4 square miles) have 616 people (1986). Located in the Indian Ocean, 1700 miles northwest of Australia, they consist of two atolls with 27 small islands. Home, with three-quarters of the population, is the main island. West Island, at about 6 miles from end to end, is the largest. The Cocos were purchased by Australia in 1978.

The Coral Sea Islands Territory (8.5 square miles) is virtually uninhabited. Located east of Queensland, Australia, it is administered from Norfolk.

The Heard and McDonald Islands (113 square miles) are uninhabited islands in the Indian Ocean 2575 miles southwest of Australia.

Norfolk Island (13.5 square miles), with 1977 people (1986), is located in the South Pacific, 900 miles northeast of Australia. It is inhabited largely by descendants of the *Bounty* mutineers, who went there in 1856. It received limited domestic rule in 1979. The islanders live mainly from tourism and the sale of postage stamps.

Chilean Dependencies

Easter Island (63 square miles) has 1867 people (1982). It is in the Pacific Ocean, 2300 miles west of Chile. Sheep grazing is its economic mainstay.

Sala y Gomez Island (.05 square mile) is an uninhabited island in the Pacific Ocean, 250 miles east of Easter Island.

French Departments and Territories

Clipperton Island (2 square miles), formerly part of French Polynesia, was separated from it in 1979. Located 700 miles southwest of Mexico in the East Pacific, it is uninhabited.

French Polynesia (1359 square miles) has a population of 166,753 (1983). It includes about 130 islands in the South Pacific. Its most important member is Tahiti, one of the Society Islands group, which includes the Windward and Leeward island groups. Tahiti was discovered by Captain James Cook in 1769. It is a beautiful island with a large tourist industry. Over half the population of French Polynesia lives on Tahiti. Also part of French Polynesia are the Tuamotu Archipelago, the Marquesas Islands, and the Austral or Tubuai Islands. Nuclear testing on the islands has instigated an international dispute since it began in 1966. The capital is Papeete on Tahiti.

EASTER ISLAND *is home to large statues, called moais, whose origins are unknown.*

LARRAIN/MAGNUM

The French Southern and Antarctic Lands (169,805 square miles) include Adelie Land on Antarctica and four island groups in the Indian Ocean, south of Australia: Kerguélen and Crozet archipelagos, each discovered in 1772, and Saint-Paul and Amsterdam islands. All the islands are mostly uninhabited. Adelie Land, discovered in 1840, has several research stations.

New Caledonia (7172 square miles) has a population of 145,368 (1983). It is a group of islands in the western Pacific Ocean, 110 miles east of Australia. New Caledonia is the largest of the islands, which include the Isle of Pines, the Loyalty Islands, the Huon Islands, and the Chesterfield Islands. Discovered in 1774, New Caledonia was a French convict station from 1871 to 1896. It is the world's third largest producer of nickel. Its capital is Noumea.

Réunion (969 square miles) is the only French Department in this area of the world, while New Caledonia, the Wallis and Futuna Islands, French Polynesia, and French Southern and Antarctic Lands are French Territories. Réunion has a population of 515,798 (1982). It is a volcanic island in the Indian Ocean, 420 miles east of Madagascar. It has been a French possession since 1653. Its capital is St. Denis.

The Wallis and Futuna Islands (106 square miles) have a population of 11,943 (1982). Located in the southwest Pacific between Fiji and Samoa, the islands were dependencies but elected in 1961 to become a French overseas territory. The capital is Mata-Utu.

New Zealand Dependencies

The Cook Islands (93 square miles) have a population of 17,754 (1981). They are in the South Pacific, 2000 miles northeast of New Zealand. They include the Northern Group, with seven atolls, and the Southern Group, with eight atolls. They accepted domestic self-government in 1965.

Niue (100 square miles), with a population of 2442 (1987), is in the South

Pacific, 400 miles west of the Cook Islands. It was given internal self-rule in 1974.

Ross Dependency (160,000 square miles) in Antarctica was established in 1923. It is uninhabited but has several research stations. The principal station, Scott Base, is manned year-round.

The Tokelau Islands (4 square miles) have a population of 1690 (1986). They are in the South Pacific, 300 miles north of Samoa. They include the atolls of Atafu, Nukunonu, and Fakaofo. The population is principally Polynesian and has close ties to Western Samoa.

Norwegian Dependencies

Peter I Island (69 square miles) is an uninhabited Antarctic island south of the South Shetland Islands. The island was first explored by a Norwegian expedition in 1929, and was made a dependency in 1933.

Queen Maud Land is an uninhabited region of Antarctica that had been visited only by Norwegian explorers before it was claimed by Norway in 1939.

Portuguese Dependency

Macao (6 square miles) is an enclave on the south China coast, 40 miles west of Hong Kong. It includes a province and two small islands and has 261,680 people (1981). Broad autonomy was granted it in 1976. Macao is a thriving urban commercial center. Its free gold trade, tourism, and fishing are other major sources of income. Macao will pass into control of the People's Republic of China in 1999.

United Kingdom Dependencies

The British Indian Ocean Territory (23 square miles), formed in 1965, has 2000 people (1977) and includes the five atolls of the Chagos Archipelago, of which Diego Garcia is the most important member. The other atolls are Peros Banhos, Salomon, Eagle, and Egmont. The territory is 1180 miles northeast of Mauritius. Major U.S. air and naval bases are stationed on Diego Garcia.

Hong Kong (413 square miles) has 5,431,200 people (1986). A Crown Colony at the mouth of the Canton River in southern China, it is 90 miles south of Canton. The British annexed it in 1841, then added the islands of the New Territories and leased it from China in 1898 for 99 years. Hong Kong receives a heavy flow of Chinese refugees and is a commercially thriving colony. Shipping, banking, textile and electronics industries, and tourism do very well. The colony is 80 percent urban. Hong Kong has become one of the most important trading centers of Southeast Asia. Victoria is its capital. In 1984 Great Britain and the People's Republic of China signed an agreement by which Hong Kong will pass into control of the People's Republic in July, 1997, as a Special Administrative Region. Under the agreement, China agreed to permit Hong Kong's social and economic system to remain unchanged for another 50 years.

The Pitcairn Islands (17 square miles), located in the South Pacific Ocean about midway between Peru and New Zealand, includes Pitcairn Island and the uninhabited Henderson, Ducie, and Oeno islands. Pitcairn Island has a population of 57 (1986), most of whom are descendants of the *Bounty* mutineers. The only community is Adamstown.

United States Dependencies

American Samoa (76 square miles), 1600 miles northeast of New Zealand, in the Pacific, has 39,254 people (1988). It includes six small islands of the Samoan group, plus Swains Island. It has been American since 1899, except for Swains, which was added in 1925. The territory's constitution, ratified in 1966, provides for a bicameral legislature and a popularly elected governor. The capital is Fagotogo on the Island of Tutuila.

Guam (212 square miles), the largest and southernmost of the Mariana Islands, has a dense population of 130,266 (1988). Located in the western Pacific, it is about 1500 miles south of Japan. First colonized by the Spanish in the 17th century, it is now a manufacturing and oil-refining center. U.S. military bases are on the island, which is also a popular resort. In 1979 its U.S. citizens voted down a proposed constitution that would give the island more self-government but would deprive the citizens of U.S. citizenship rights. Agana is the capital.

Howland, Baker, and Jarvis Islands (2.7 square miles) are uninhabited South Pacific islands, 1500 to 2000 miles south and southwest of Hawaii.

Johnston Atoll (91 square miles), with a population of 1000 (1987), is located in the Pacific, 715 miles southwest of Hawaii. American-controlled since 1858, it is now administered by the U.S. Air Force. It has been used for nuclear tests.

Kingman Reef (.4 square mile) is an uninhabited American dependency (since 1922) in the Pacific, 35 miles northwest of Palmyra Island. It became a U.S. naval station in 1934.

The Midway Islands (1.9 square miles), with a population of 1500 (1987), are in the Northern Pacific, 1200 miles northwest of Hawaii. They include an atoll plus the two islets called Sand and Eastern. Controlled by the U.S. Navy since 1903, Midway was the scene of several famous World War II air and sea battles.

Commonwealth of the Northern Mariana Islands (184 square miles) approved commonwealth status in 1975 and a new constitution went into effect in 1986. The islands were formerly part of the Trust Territory of the Pacific Islands. The 16 islands are located north of Guam, and there are 20,591 people (1988). The chief island and governmental center is Saipan.

Republic of Palau (192 square miles) is located about 530 miles southeast of the Philippines. Palau is the last state remaining in the UN-mandated Trust Territory of the Pacific Islands, which was established after World War II and included some 2100 islands in the area commonly known as Micronesia. Palau includes 26 islands and several hundred islets; it has a population of 14,106 (1988). Its capital is Koror, on the island of Babelthaup. Palau signed a Compact of Free Association with the United States in 1986, but its implementation was delayed because of a constitutional provision establishing Palau as a nuclear-free zone. The United States maintained that this provision conflicted with U.S. defense authority under the compact.

Palmyra Island (4 square miles), an atoll with over 50 islets, is in the Pacific, 1000 miles southwest of Hawaii. It is privately owned and uninhabited, but is administered by the Department of Interior. It became American in 1898 along with Hawaii, from which it was separated in 1959, when Hawaii gained statehood.

Trust Territory of the Pacific Islands. See Republic of Palau.

Wake Island (2.5 square miles), an unincorporated territory administered by the U.S. Air Force, is an atoll of three small islands located 2300 miles west of Honolulu, Hawaii. It has a population of 302 (1988).

For more information on the U.S. Pacific territories see the UNITED STATES AND CANADA volume.

CITIES OF ASIA AND AUSTRALASIA

Agra, in northern India, on the Yamuna River in Uttar Pradesh State. One of the oldest cities in India, Agra is famous as the site of the Taj Mahal, the Red Fort, and other historic monuments. It is an important agricultural center and is well known for metal inlay work. Pop., 770,000.

Allahabad, in Uttar Pradesh State in northern India, at the confluence of the Ganges and Yamuna rivers. The city is a shipping and trade center for local agricultural produce, especially sugar cane and cotton. Allahabad is also a holy city for Hindus. It was built in 1583 by the Mughal emperor Akbar the Great on the site of ancient Prayag and has many historic monuments. Pop., 642,000.

Amritsar, in northeastern India, the capital of Amritsar District in Punjab State. The city is an important commercial and manufacturing center, especially for textiles and chemicals. Amritsar is the site of the Golden Temple, the major shrine of the Sikh religion. Pop., urban area, 589,000.

Apia, the capital, largest city, and chief port of Western Samoa, on the north coast of the island of Upolu. Chief exports are copra, bananas, and cocoa. Pop., 37,000.

Auckland, the chief port of New Zealand, located on North Island between the harbors of Waitemata and Manukau. Auckland is New Zealand's largest industrial center. It is the site of the University of Auckland and the Auckland War Memorial Museum, noted for its Maori collection. Pop., 882,754.

Bandung, the capital of West Java Province, Indonesia, located on Java, about 75 miles (120 km.) southeast of Jakarta. The city is an important resort because of its cool climate. It is the site of many medical and educational institutions, including the Pasteur Institute and a nuclear research center. Nearby Malabar radio station is one of the most powerful in the world. Pop., 1,462,637.

Bangkok, the largest city and capital of Thailand, located on the Chao Phraya River about 20 miles (32 km.) inland from its mouth on the Gulf of Siam. The city is Thailand's industrial center and major port and handles most of the country's foreign trade. It is an important rail center and has one of the most modern airports in Southeast Asia. Pop., 7,000,000.

Bassein, a port of Burma, on the Bassein River, which flows from the Irrawaddy River to the Bay of Bengal. It lies in a rice-growing region, and rice is its chief export. Pop., 144,092.

Beijing, or Peking, the capital of China, situated in northeastern China at the northern end of the Grand Canal. The city is an air and rail center, with links throughout China and connections with the Soviet Union and Korea. Its major industries produce steel, transportation equipment, agricultural machinery, and textiles. Beijing, the political, financial, cultural, and educational center of the country, is an ancient walled city that comprises the Inner City in the north, the Outer City in the south, and recently annexed suburban areas. Pop., 9,470,000.

Bombay, the capital of Maharashtra State, located on the west coast of India. The city is a major commercial, financial, and industrial center. As a port, Bombay ranks second only to Calcutta. Bombay has many educational institutions, including the University of Bombay. Pop., 8,227,000.

Brisbane, the capital and principal port of Queensland, Australia, on the Brisbane River, 14 miles (23 km.) from Moreton Bay. Brisbane is a commercial and manufacturing center and is the seat of the University of Queensland. Pop., 1,171,300.

Calcutta, the largest city in India, about 80 miles (130 km.) north of the Bay of Bengal. It is the capital of West Bengal State. Calcutta is one of the world's busiest ports. Pop., 9,166,000.

Canberra, the capital of Australia, in the Australian Capital Territory, in the southeastern corner of New South Wales. A model city, Canberra was founded in 1913 and became the seat of government in 1927. The Australian National University is located there. Pop., 265,000.

Canton. See Guangzhou.

Chengdu, in south-central China, on the Min River, a branch of the Yangtze, about 170 miles (275 km.) northwest of Chongqing. It is the capital of Sichuan Province and one of China's oldest cit-

A TYPICAL STREET SCENE *in Bombay, India, presents a striking contrast between rich and poor, and between West and East.*

ies. Chengdu is an important agricultural and commercial center and a river port. It is also a major industrial center. Pop., 2,580,000.

Chittagong, in southeastern Bangladesh. It is a district capital and the most important port of Bangladesh. Pop., 1,391,877.

Chongqing, in southeastern Szechwan Province, southern China, at the junction of the Yangtze and Chia-ling rivers. The city is the major river port and industrial center of southwest China. It was the capital of China from 1937 to 1945. Pop., 2,780,000.

Colombo, the capital, largest city, and chief port of Sri Lanka. It is located on the island's southwestern coast. Colombo exports most of Sri Lanka's tea, coconut products, cotton, and rubber. It is the site of several Buddhist and Hindu temples and of Colombo University. Pop., 700,000.

Da Nang, a seaport in east-central Vietnam. It has an excellent harbor and is Vietnam's fourth-largest city. Pop., 492,194.

Delhi, or Old Delhi, a city in north-central India close to New Delhi, the capital, in the union territory of Delhi. It has served as the capital city of various conquerors and is an important rail and trade center. It is famous for its handicrafts in metals and ivory. Pop., 5,700,000.

Dhaka, or Dacca, the capital of Bangladesh, between the Meghna and Ganges rivers. The city is a trade and processing center and is noted for the production of gold and silver jewelry, textiles, tea, paper, carved shells, and jute. It is the seat of the University of Dacca. Pop., 3,500,000.

Djakarta. See Jakarta.

Fushun, in northeastern China, 30 miles (48 km.) east of Shenyang, in Liaoning Province. The city has one of the largest coal strip mines in the world and is connected by rail with Shenyang and Luta. It processes oil shale deposits, and its manufactures include aluminum, machinery, automobiles, chemicals, and synthetic fibers. Pop., 1,240,000.

Fuzhou, a seaport on the southeast coast of China, at the northern end of the Formosa Strait. It is the capital of Fujian Province and has many beautiful temples, pagodas, and monasteries. It is the seat of several institutions of higher learning. Pop., 1,190,000.

Guangzhou, formerly Canton, in southern China, on the Pearl River, about 80 miles (130 km.) from the South China Sea. It is the capital of Kwantung Province. A major river

HONG KONG'S *Nathan Road, on the Kowloon peninsula, is an indication of the mixed Chinese and British heritage of the Crown Colony.*

port, it manufactures chemicals, paper, textiles, cement, and machinery. Pop., 3,290,000.

Hanoi, the capital of Vietnam, situated on the Red River delta. The city is an important commercial and industrial center. Pop., 1,750,000.

Hiroshima, a Japanese seaport, the capital of Hiroshima Prefecture, lying on the Inland Sea. The city is an important industrial, commercial, and cultural center for the surrounding area. Its manufactures include textiles, machinery, tools, and canned goods. Hiroshima was the target of a U.S. atom bomb attack at the end of World War II. The city, which was almost completely destroyed by the bomb, has been rebuilt. Pop., 1,044,000.

Ho Chi Minh City, formerly Saigon (the capital of South Vietnam from 1954 to 1976), near the southeastern coast of Vietnam. It is a commercial and transportation center, and with its suburb, Cholon, is a major port and industrial complex. Pop., 3,500,000.

Hong Kong, officially Victoria, a seaport and capital of Hong Kong Colony. The city overlooks one of the world's finest natural harbors and is the commercial and banking center of the colony, which has become a thriving industrial region. Pop., 1,026,870.

Hue, a port city in central Vietnam. The city was once the capital of the Vietnamese empire in Indochina, and of the French colonial state of Annam. It was a major battleground of the Vietnam War. Pop., 199,900.

Hyderabad, a major city of south-central India, the capital of Andhra Pradesh State, situated on the Musi River.

The city is noted for the production of pottery, paper, textiles, and rugs. Pop., 2,528,000.

Islamabad, the capital of Pakistan, just northeast of Rawalpindi in northern Pakistan. The city has light manufacturing industries. Pop., 400,000.

Jakarta, or Djakarta, seaport and capital of Indonesia, on the northwest coast of Java. It is the largest city of Indonesia. Pop., 6,503,449.

Kabul, the capital of Afghanistan, situated on the Kabul River about 50 miles (80 km.) from the Pakistani border and the Khyber Pass. The city is a commercial center and the seat of Kabul University and other educational institutions. Pop., 1,400,000.

Kamakura, a Japanese resort and historic city, on Honshu Island. It was the capital of Japan from the late 1100's to the early 1300's. Kamakura is known for its large statue of Buddha. Pop., 165,520.

Kandahar, the capital of Kandahar Province in southeastern Afghanistan. The city is a trading center and is noted for the production of silk and felt. Pop., 178,409.

Kandy, the capital of Sri Lanka's Central Province. The capital of the former kingdom of Kandy, the city contains many temples, mosques, palaces, and crypts. Pop., 97,872.

Kaohsiung, a seaport on the southwest coast of Taiwan, its chief port and a major industrial and manufacturing center. Pop., 1,028,334.

Karachi, the largest city and most important port of Pakistan, situated on the Arabian Sea near the delta of the Indus River. The city has excellent air, rail, and shipping facilities. Its industries produce textiles, chemicals, transportation equipment, steel, and ships. Pop., 7,000,000.

Kathmandu, the capital and commercial center of Nepal. The city is a marketing center for rice, fruit, vegetables, and livestock raised in the area. Kathmandu has some small industries. Pop., 422,000.

Khulna, in southwestern Bangladesh, near the Ganges delta, a river port that exports timber and forest products from the surrounding forested area. It processes agricultural products, especially jute and rice. Pop., 646,359.

Kobe, a seaport on western Honshu, Japan, on Osaka Bay. The city is a shipping, railway, and industrial center. It is also a cultural center with many colleges, shrines, and temples. Pop., 1,411,000.

Kuala Lumpur, the capital of Malaysia, situated on the western part of the Malay peninsula, about 200 miles (320 km.) northwest of Singapore. It is a transportation center with industries based on rubber and tin production. Pop., 977,100.

Kyoto, the former capital of Japan, situated on west-central Honshu Island. Kyoto is a cultural and artistic center known for its handicraft industries. There are many temples and shrines in the city, and parts of the old imperial palace are preserved. Pop., 1,479,000.

Lahore, capital of Punjab Province in east-central Pakistan, located on the Ravi River. The second largest city in Pakistan, Lahore is an important railroad junction and industrial center. Lahore has many cultural institutions and is the site of the University of the Punjab. Pop., 2,922,000.

Lanzhou, capital of Gansu Province in northwestern China, located on the Hwang He, near the Great Wall. An important rail and industrial center, the city produces machinery, refined petroleum, plutonium, textiles, plastics, and chemicals. Pop., 1,500,000.

Lhasa, capital of Tibet Autonomous Region, southwestern China, on a tributary of the Brahmaputra River. It was long known as the Forbidden City because of the hostility to foreigners of its many lamas, who have now been suppressed and dispersed by the Chinese. It is the site of magnificent palaces of the former Dalai Lama and impressive temples and monasteries. Pop., 310,000.

Lüda, an urban complex in northeastern China, at the tip of the Liaotung Peninsula. It consists of the seaports of Lüshun (formerly Port Arthur) and Dalian. It is a leading Pacific port and an industrial, commercial, and naval center. Its manufactures include machinery, electrical and mining equipment, ships, and machine tools. Grapes, winter wheat, and cotton are grown within its municipal boundaries. Pop., 4,000,000.

Madras, a port on the southeastern coast of India with a wholly artificial harbor. Madras is the capital of Tamil Nadu State and one of India's largest cities. It is a transportation and commercial center. Pop., 4,277,000.

Makasar. See Ujung Pandang.

Mandalay, on the left bank of the Irrawaddy River in central Burma, about 350 miles (565 km.) north of Rangoon. Mandalay is an important religious and cultural center. The leading industry is silk weaving. Pop., 532,985.

Manila, the largest city, chief port, and capital of the Philippines. It lies on Luzon Island on Manila Bay. The city is a transportation, manufacturing, cultural, and educational center. Its products include chemicals, coconut oil, textiles, tobacco, drugs, paints, and rope. Pop., 1,630,485.

Melbourne, the capital, largest city, and chief port of Victoria State, Australia, located at the mouth of the Yarra River on Port Phillip Bay, in southeastern Australia. The city is an important railroad terminus and one of Australia's leading commercial centers. Manufactures include electrical goods, motor vehicles, textiles, and processed foods. Pop., 2,942,000.

Nagasaki, a seaport on the west coast of Kyushu Island, Japan. Opened to foreign trade in 1568, it has had the longest contact with the Western world of any Japanese city. A large steel rolling mill and nearby coal fields have made it an important shipbuilding and industrial center. The inner city was destroyed on August 9, 1945, by the second U.S. atomic bomb used in warfare. Pop., 449,000.

Nagoya, a city of Japan, located on the south coast of Honshu Island at the head of Ise Bay. A major port and industrial and rail center, the city produces pottery and porcelain, textiles, machine tools, automobiles, and chemicals. Pop., 2,116,000.

Nagpur, a city in Maharashtra State, India, 420 miles (675 km.) northeast of Bombay. An important rail center, the city also has many cotton and woolen mills and an important weaving industry. Pop., 1,298,000.

Nanjing, formerly Nanking, the capital of Jiangsu Province, China. It is on the Yangtze River, which seagoing vessels can navigate to the city. Rail lines connect it to Beijing and Shanghai. Traditional industries include the manufacture of silk and cotton cloth and a durable cotton fabric called nankeen. Iron, oil, and food-processing plants also have been established. Manufactures include textiles, machinery, chemicals, trucks, and electronic equipment.

An important cultural and educational center, Nanjing is the site of scientific research institutes and several institutions of higher learning, including Nanjing University. It was the capital of Nationalist China from 1928 to 1937 and again from 1946 to 1949. Pop., 2,250,000.

Nara, a Japanese city within 50 miles (80 km.) of Kyoto and Osaka. It was the first capital of Japan, from 710 to 784. Nara is the site of a national museum. Pop., 328,000.

New Delhi, the capital of India, situated in the north-central part of the country on the west bank of the Yamuna River. New Delhi lies south of Delhi. It is a transportation and trade center with some light industries, textile mills, and printing plants. New Delhi was constructed as an administrative center. The seat of government was transferred from Calcutta to Delhi in 1912 and to New Delhi in 1931. Pop., 272,000.

Osaka, a Japanese port, situated on the southwestern coast of Honshu Island. Osaka is one of the most important industrial and commercial centers of Japan. Its industries produce a wide variety of goods, including cotton textiles, automobiles, steel, and chemicals. Pop., 2,636,000.

Palembang, a river port of Indonesia, situated in southeastern Sumatra on the Musi River. It is the most important trade center and the largest city of Sumatra. Palembang, which has important oil refineries, exports oil and petroleum products, rubber, coffee, spices, and coal. Pop., 787,187.

Patna, a city on the Ganges River in northeastern India, the capital of Bihar State. It is a transportation and trade center that produces grains, oilseeds, and sugar cane. The city is considered sacred by the Sikhs and is the seat of two universities. Pop., 916,000.

Peking. See Beijing.

Peshawar, in Pakistan, strategically situated near the Khyber Pass. The city serves as a gateway to Afghanistan and central Asia. Peshawar, a road and rail junction, is the trade center for a region that produces grain, oilseed, cotton, and sugar cane. Pop., 555,000.

Phnom Penh, the capital and commercial center of Cambodia, situated at the junction of the Tonle Sap and Mekong rivers. Phnom Penh is a rail center and a river port. Pop., 650,000.

Port Moresby, the capital of Papua New Guinea, in the South Pacific Ocean. Port Moresby lies on the southern coast, on the Gulf of Papua. It is a commercial center that exports copper, rubber, and wood products. Pop., 132,000.

Pune, or Poona, a city in west-central India, about 80 miles (130 km.) southeast of Bombay. Pune is a transportation and commercial center and has a number of military facilities. Its manufactures include machinery, textiles, chemicals, munitions, and paper. Pune is a major cultural and educational center. Pop., 1,685,000.

Pusan, a seaport in southeastern South Korea, about 200 miles (320 km.) southeast of Seoul on the Korea Strait. Pusan is a major commercial and industrial center. It has several colleges and the National Museum and Art Gallery. Pop., 3,516,768.

Pyongyang, the capital of North Korea, situated on the Taedong River in the western part of the country. The city is a center of heavy industry and manufactures steel, rubber, cement, and chemicals. Pop., 2,000,000.

Rangoon, the capital of Burma, on the Rangoon River, 21 miles (34 km.) from the Gulf of Martaban. It is Burma's largest city and chief port. The city is the seat of the University of Rangoon. The skyline is dominated by the 368-foot Shwe Dagon Pagoda, which is covered with gold leaf. Pop., 2,600,000.

Saigon. See Ho Chi Minh City.

Seoul, the capital of South Korea, situated near the Han River in the northwestern corner of the country. The cultural and economic center of South Korea, it is the site of several colleges. It is connected by a railway with its port, Inchon. Pop., 9,581,000.

Shanghai, a port city on the eastern coast of China, near the mouth of the Yangtze River. It is the largest city in China and is a major industrial and commercial center. It is an important cultural and educational center with many universities and scientific institutes. It also has several museums and theaters. Pop., 6,980,000.

Shenyang, formerly Mukden, in northeastern China, on the Hun River. It is the capital of Liaoning Province and a major industrial city. It is also an educational and cultural center with historic buildings and monuments. Pop., 4,200,000.

Singapore, a seaport and capital of Singapore, on Singapore Island off the

southern tip of the Malay peninsula. It is a major commercial and industrial center. Pop., 2,413,945.

Surabaya, a seaport on the northeast coast of the Indonesian island of Java. It exports rubber, oil, sugar, spices, tobacco, and other local goods, and has shipyards, oil refineries, textile mills, rubber processing plants, and chemical factories. Pop., 2,027,913.

Suva, the capital of Fiji, situated on the southeastern coast of Viti Levu Island. It is a port of call on international shipping routes, and it processes and exports fruits, sugar, coconuts, cacao, and timber. Pop., 64,000.

Suzhou, a port city in eastern China, on the Grand Canal in Jiangsu Province. Silk and cotton textiles are its chief manufactures, along with handcrafted items. Famous for its natural beauty and its many canals, it is called the Venice of China. Pop., 1,300,000.

Sydney, the capital of New South Wales, on the southeastern coast of Australia. It is the country's largest city and chief industrial and commercial center. It has a deep natural harbor and an excellent port. Sydney is the site of several colleges and of the national art and history museums. Pop., 3,400,000.

Taipei, the capital of Taiwan, situated at the northern end of the island. The city is the commercial and industrial center of Taiwan, with good transportation facilities. Taipei is the seat of National Taiwan University. Pop., 2,500,000.

Taiyuan, a city of east-central China situated on the Fen River, about 265 miles (425 km.) southwest of Beijing. Taiyuan is an industrial and rail center, lying near important iron and coal fields. Its industries produce iron and steel, agricultural equipment, and chemicals. The city also has machine shops, textile mills, and oil refineries. Pop., 2,725,000.

Tianjin, a port of northeastern China, situated at the junction of the Pie River and the Grand Canal, about 80 miles (130 km.) southeast of Beijing. Tianjin is a commercial and industrial center that handles much of the import-export trade of the surrounding region. It is also the seat of several institutions of higher education. Pop., 5,380,000.

Tokyo, the capital of Japan and one of the largest cities in the world, situated on Honshu Island in Tokyo Bay. The city is the administrative, economic, and industrial center of Japan. Tokyo is served by an excellent port, many railroads, an international airport, an extensive highway system, and a rapid transit system. It is also Japan's cultural, educational, and religious center. It is the seat of Tokyo University and

has many museums, theaters, and religious shrines. Pop., 8,200,000.

Ujung Pandang, a port in Southeast Asia, on the island of Celebes, or Sulawesi, in Indonesia. It is one of Indonesia's largest cities. Exports include coffee, copra, rice, and spices. Pop., 709,038.

Ulan Bator, capital of the Mongolian People's Republic, located on the Tuula River. It is connected by a branch of the Trans-Siberian railroad and by air with the Soviet Union and China. Pop., 515,129.

Varanasi, formerly Benares, in north-central India, on the Ganges River in Uttar Pradesh State. One of India's oldest cities, it is the holiest city of the Hindus, who visit it as pilgrims to bathe in the sacred waters of the Ganges. The city is also sacred to Jains, Sikhs, and Buddhists. A cultural center, the city is the seat of Benares Hindu University and Benares Sanskrit University. Pop., 794,000.

Vientiane, the administrative capital of Laos, on the Mekong River near the border with Thailand. The city is a commercial center, dealing in textiles and wood products. Pop., 300,000.

Wellington, the capital of New Zealand. It is located at the southwestern tip of North Island, overlooking Cook Strait. Wellington has a large harbor and is the financial, commercial, and transportation center of New Zealand. Pop., 325,697.

Wuhan, in east-central China, at the confluence of the Han and Yangtze rivers. It was formed by the merger of three cities, Hankow, Hanyang, and Wuchang, and is the capital of Hubei Province. Wuhan is central China's industrial, administrative, and transportation center. Pop., 3,400,000.

Yogyakarta, in southern Java, Indonesia, at the foot of volcanic Mt. Merapi, 175 miles (280 km.) southwest of Surabaya. The city is the cultural center of Java and is noted for its drama and dance festivals, the Islamic University of Indonesia, and its colleges. The Buddhist temple, Borobudur, and the palace of the sultans attract many tourists. Pop., 398,727.

Yokohama, a seaport in southeastern Honshu, Japan, in Tokyo Bay. The city is part of the urban-industrial complex around Tokyo and is the seat of four universities. It also has many churches, temples, shrines, gardens, and parks. Pop., 2,993,000.

Zhengzhou (Chengchow), the capital of Henan Province in east-central China, an important railroad junction and the center for a large textile industry. Pop., 1,590,000.

GLOSSARY OF ASIA AND AUSTRALASIA

Amur, a river of northeastern Asia marking part of the boundary between China and the Soviet Union. The Amur flows eastward and then turns northeastward for about 1780 miles (2866 km.) before emptying into the Tatar Strait.

Annam Cordillera, a mountain range of Southeast Asia. It extends northwest to southeast along the central portion of the border between Laos and Vietnam. The peaks are between 5000 and 9000 feet high.

Ashikaga dynasty, the reigning Japanese dynasty from 1336 to 1568. The name is derived from the city of Ashikaga, located north of Tokyo, which was the ancestral home of the Ashikaga shoguns, or military rulers.

Asian Development Bank, a development bank funded by member states. The bank lends money to member Asian countries and private businesses to fund projects that aid the development of those countries. The bank has 32 members including the United States, Canada, and European nations.

Association of Southeast Asian Nations (ASEAN), an organization formed in 1967 that seeks to promote the stability, cultural development, and economic progress of the Southeast Asian region. Its members are Brunei, Indonesia, Malaysia, the Philippines, Singapore, and Thailand.

Ava, the capital of Burma and the name given to Burmese rulers from 1364 to 1555. Ava was located on the Irrawaddy River, about six miles south of Mandalay. The Ava rulers had cultural and military relations with rulers as far away as China and Ceylon.

Bandung Conference, also known as the Asian-African Conference, a meeting of delegates from 29 nations of Asia and Africa held in April, 1955, at Bandung, Indonesia.

The conference was an attempt by African and Asian states to increase their influence in international affairs by acting together on issues of mutual concern. They agreed on closer economic and cultural cooperation and endorsed the principles of self-determination and human rights as expressed in the UN Charter. The conference condemned colonialism, and several of the Asian leaders condemned communism as well.

No machinery was set up to implement the proposals of the conference, and the states remained divided in their attitudes toward both communism and cooperation with the West. The conference did, however, draw attention to Asian and African nations, their problems, and their potential strength as a nonaligned unit in world politics.

Borneo, an island lying between the South China Sea on the north and the west, the Java Sea on the south, and the Makasar Strait, Celebes Sea, and Sulu Sea on the east. The island, about 290,000 square miles (751,000 sq. km.) in area, is the third largest in the world. Indonesia, Malaysia, and Brunei share the island. The Indonesian part is called Kalimantan.

A SAMURAI *followed the code of conduct and honor called bushido.*

METROPOLITAN MUSEUM OF ART/FLETCHER FUND

Brahmaputra, a river on the Indian subcontinent that rises in the Kailas Mountains of southwestern Tibet and flows for 1800 miles (2900 km.) before merging with the Ganges in Bangladesh to flow into the Bay of Bengal. As the Tsangpo, it flows eastward through Tibet for about 700 miles (1130 km.) before turning sharply southward into the Assam Valley and then into Bangladesh, where it is called the Jamuna. Its southern course is navigable for 800 miles (1288 km.), and it waters a vast valley.

Bushido, the unwritten feudal code of conduct for the Japanese samurai, or warrior class. The code, the "way of the warrior," developed during the Kamakura period (1185–1333) and was based on Zen Buddhist and Confucian tradition. It emphasized courage, physical and mental toughness, loyalty, and filial piety. With the abolition of the feudal system in the early 1870's, the code became a general ethical standard for all Japanese.

Caste, from the Portuguese word *casta,* "breed" or "race," the system of hereditary social units in Indian Hindu society. There are four major caste divisions—Brahmans, priests and scholars; Kshatriyas, warriors and administrators; Vaisyas, shepherds, merchants, and artisans; and Sudras, laborers and servants. The four main castes are divided into numerous subcastes. Outside the caste system are the untouchables, or outcasts. They occupy the lowest social, economic, and religious position in traditional Hindu society. The importance in India of the caste system has diminished. Since the 1930's, largely as a result of the work of Mohandas K. Gandhi, the government of India has taken steps to place the untouchables on an equal footing with the rest of Hindu society.

Champa, an ancient Southeast Asian kingdom that existed in the coastal region of present-day central Vietnam from the 100's to the 1700's. It was founded by the Chams, a people related to the Indonesians who had been strongly influenced by Indian culture. Descendants of the Chams are still to be found in modern Kampuchea and Vietnam.

Chao Phraya, the principal river of Thailand, formed from the Ping,

MOUNT EVEREST, *the highest mountain in the world, is located in the Himalayas, a mountain range that dominates the center of the Asian continent. The Ganges River, which rises in the Himalayas, is sacred to Hindus, who bathe in its water to purify themselves.*

Wang, Yom, and Nan tributaries, which rise in the northern mountains and then merge at Nakhon Sawan. The river's total length is about 225 miles (362 km.) from the mountains to its mouth on the Gulf of Thailand.

Ch'ondogyo, a Korean religious sect founded in the 1860's, known first as Tonghak (Eastern learning). Ch'ondogyo, which means "society of the heavenly way," incorporated many concepts of other religions and philosophical systems, including those of Buddhism, neo-Confucianism, Taoism, and Roman Catholicism. The founder of the Tonghak movement, a scholar named Ch'oe Che-u, was executed in 1864 on charges of heresy, but the movement grew after his death. Most of its followers were oppressed peasants.

Ch'ondogyo was a traditionalist and antiforeign movement that developed in opposition to Roman Catholic Christianity, known in Korea as Sohak (Western learning). The hostility between the followers of Tonghak and the followers of Sohak became the basis for a major uprising in 1894, the Tonghak Rebellion, which was crushed only after Chinese and Japanese troops intervened on opposing sides. The immediate consequence of this intervention was the struggle between China and Japan for control of Korea in the Sino-Japanese War of 1894–1895. This war led to Japanese domination of Korea after 1896. Despite continued persecution under the Japanese until 1945, Ch'ondogyo survived, and in 1979 there were 1,100,000 members.

Colombo Plan, a plan for cooperative efforts to raise standards of living and strengthen the economies of the devel-

oping nations of South and Southeast Asia. It was published on November 28, 1950, by a committee of Commonwealth ministers; it came into effect on July 1, 1951. It has several times been extended. The member nations assist each other on a bilateral basis. The aid includes technical assitance, loans, equipment, educational programs, and food supplies.

In 1981 the members were Afghanistan, Australia, Bangladesh, Bhutan, Burma, Cambodia, Canada, Fiji, India, Indonesia, Iran, Japan, Laos, Malaysia, Maldives, Nepal, New Zealand, Pakistan, Papua New Guinea, the Philippines, Singapore, South Korea, Sri Lanka, Thailand, the United Kingdom, and the United States.

Comprador, a term applied to Chinese men who served as intermediaries between the Chinese and foreign firms trading with China after Chinese ports were opened to foreign trade in the 1840's and 1850's. The compradors were commissioned and paid salaries by the foreign firms. They hired a Chinese staff that included money experts, servants, translators and interpreters, watchmen, and laborers. Because of their knowledge of the Chinese language, as well as Chinese law and business customs, the compradors virtually controlled the trade in China of the firms that they represented. Some compradors eventually established their own trading firms.

Coromandel Coast, the southeastern coast of India extending from the eastern end of Palk Strait, separating India and Sri Lanka, north of the mouth of the Krishna River. Madras lies at about the center of the coast, which lacks the good natural harbors so vital to commerce.

Daimyo, Japanese feudal chiefs, or territorial lords. The origins of the daimyo can be traced to the local lords of the 1000's, who can properly be called daimyo after the 1500's. The daimyo became especially prominent during the later portion of the Ashikaga period (1336–1568) and the early part of the Tokugawa period (1603–1867).

After 1600 most of Japan was divided into feudal domains, called *han,* of which the daimyo were rulers. Although the daimyo were allowed virtual autonomy within their own realms, the central Tokugawa government developed an intricate system of controls to prevent the daimyo from becoming a military threat to their central authority.

In 1871 an imperial decree abolished feudal domains and marked the end of the daimyo as feudal lords. The daimyo were given governmental pensions and were classified as nobles. In 1876 they were given lump-sum payments in the form of government bonds. Many became members of Japan's growing commercial class.

Everest, a mountain in the Himalayas, between Nepal and Tibet. It is the highest mountain in the world, rising to 29,028 feet (8848 m).

Examination system, a system of nationwide examinations by which Chinese men became eligible for appointment to the Chinese civil service and thus members of the ruling group in traditional Chinese society.

By about 100 A.D., China had developed a civil-service system based on merit. Under the Sung dynasty (960–1279), the examination system became the most important means of recruiting civil servants, and during the Ming dynasty (1368–1644) methods were developed to ensure complete impartiality in the grading and selection process. The system remained virtually unchanged until the 1900's.

The examinations were held every three years. They were given at three successive levels—the local, or prefectural, level; the capital; and the royal palace. About 10 percent of the candidates passed at each stage. After passing the last stage, candidates were eligible for official positions.

Although the examinations were theoretically open to all, success depended on years of study and, often, tutoring by scholars. This effectively limited candidates to the sons of well-to-do families. Sometimes extended families or clans sponsored bright students in their preparation for the examinations.

One of the weaknesses of the system was the heavy emphasis given to the Four Books, considered the most important works of Confucianism, and the Five Classics, five ancient works on songs, documents, prophecy, historical annals, and rituals. Literary style was very important and little attention was given to practical affairs.

Between 1901 and 1906 the examination system was gradually abolished and a modern school system instituted in which Western subjects were taught.

Ganges, a river of South Asia that rises in the Himalayas and flows south and east for about 1500 miles (2496 km.) through northern India and Bangladesh to the Bay of Bengal. It is heavily used for transportation and provides power for industries and water for irrigation. The Gangetic Plain is formed by the river in northern India. The Ganges is a sacred river for Hindus.

The major southern tributaries of the Ganges are the Son and the Jamna. Major northern tributaries are the Kosi, the Gogra, and the Gandak. As it flows through Bangladesh, the Ganges is joined by the Brahmaputra River about 100 miles (160 km.) from its mouth to form the Padma and the world's largest delta.

Genro, a group of elder statesmen who helped govern Japan in the early Meiji period. From about 1890 to about 1910, the Genro, composed of a core numbering about ten men, were the ultimate source of executive authority in Japan.

Ghaznavids, an Islamic dynasty that arose in Ghazni, Afghanistan, in the late 900's. It ruled northeastern Iran, Afghanistan, and northern India.

In 977 the Turkish slave commander Sebuktigin became governor of eastern Afghanistan. He established a tradition of raiding the plains of India, but remained a subject of the Samanid empire. Sebuktigin's son Mahmud (998–1030) became fully independent and greatly enlarged Ghaznavid territory.

AUSTRALIA'S GREAT BARRIER REEF, *the longest coral reef in the world, creates a shallow lagoon between itself and the mainland.*

He raided deep into India, moving down the Ganges River to sack the cities of Mathura and Kanauj, and into the Kathiawar (Saurashtra) Peninsula. Mahmud set the northern frontier at the Amu Darya and annexed an area southeast of the Aral Sea. In 1029 he seized Hamadan, in western Iran.

Under Mahmud's son the western portion of the empire fell to the Seljuk Turks. By 1059 the Ghaznavids held only eastern Afghanistan and northwestern India. Attempts to reassert Ghaznavid influence led to the sack of Ghazni by Ghurids, a dynasty based in central Afghanistan, or Ghur. In 1151 a Ghurid, Ala ad Din Husayn, destroyed the city. The Ghurids extinguished the Ghaznavid line in 1186.

Gobi, a desert region in northern China and southeastern Mongolia. Asia's largest desert, the Gobi covers about 500,000 square miles (1,295,000 sq. km.).

Great Barrier Reef, a coral reef that extends 1250 miles (2000 km.) off the coast of northeastern Australia and southeastern New Guinea at the edge of the continental shelf. It protects the coastline and forms a channel that contains many small coral islets.

Great Dividing Range, a series of mountain ranges bordering the eastern coast of Australia. The mountains are generally below 5000 feet (1525 m) but Mt. Kosciusko, in the south, rises 7316 feet (2230 m).

Hainan, a large Chinese island, about 13,200 square miles (34,190 sq. km.) in area, lying about 15 miles (24 km.) south of the mainland. The island is mountainous, thickly forested, and rich in minerals.

Hari Rud, a river that rises in the mountains of central Afghanistan and flows for about 700 miles (1130 km.), ending in the Kara Kum desert. The Hari Rud flows west through the Herat Valley and then north along the Iranian border into the Soviet Union.

Himalayas, a mountain system in southeastern Asia containing the world's highest peaks. The range extends for about 1600 miles (2575 km.) from Kashmir in the west to Assam in the east. It forms an arc separating the subcontinent of India from the rest of Asia.

The system may be divided into three sections—the Greater Himalayas in the north, with an average elevation of about 20,000 feet; the Lesser Himalayas in the center, averaging about 11,000 feet; and the Outer Himalayas in the south, with average elevations of about 3500 feet. The Greater Himalayas contain Mt. Everest.

The Himalayas are primarily responsible for the extreme dryness of western China, because they block the wet monsoon winds before they can reach the interior. By contrast, the southern slopes of the mountains receive a considerable amount of rain and snowfall.

The Himalayas hold the sources of several of Asia's important rivers, including the Ganges, the Brahmaputra, and the Indus.

Hindu Kush, a mountain range in northeastern Afghanistan that extends for about 600 miles (965 km.) along the border with Pakistan as far as Kashmir. The mountains form a barrier between the Soviet Union and Afghanistan, Pakistan, and India. The highest peak is Tirich Mir, 26,000 feet (7700 m) above sea level. The Hindu

Kush is a watershed between the Amu and Indus river systems.

Hong, or Cohong, a small group of Chinese business firms licensed to carry on trade with the West. This merchant guild enjoyed a monopoly of Chinese trade with Western nations. The Hong monopoly came to be located in Canton in the 1700's, and the Hong merchants were involved in worldwide trade, much of it with the English East India Company. By the 1830's the Canton system had become antiquated, and the Treaty of Nanking, which ended the Opium War (1839–1842) between Britain and China, abolished the Hong monopoly at Canton.

Huang He, or Yellow River, the second longest river of China. The Huang He rises in the Kunlun Mountains of northwestern China and flows in a generally easterly direction for 2900 miles (4670 km.), emptying into the Gulf of Chihli. Its tributaries include the Fen, Huai, and Wei rivers. The river has been the cause of numerous floods.

Hwarang, bands of warriors prominent during the 600's in the state of Silla in southeastern Korea. The hwarang groups were led by young members of the nobility, who emphasized moral and military training. The hwarang were the core of Silla's armies and produced future national leaders. By the 700's, however, their military prowess had degenerated.

Indochina, a general name for the peninsula of Southeast Asia occupied by Vietnam, Laos, Cambodia, Thailand, Burma, and the mainland portion of Malaysia. French Indochina was a French colony that included present-day Cambodia, Laos, and Vietnam.

Indus, one of the major rivers of South Asia. Rising on the northern slopes of the Kailas range of southwestern Tibet, it flows northwest into Kashmir, then southwest through central Pakistan to the Arabian Sea—a total of more than 1800 miles (2900 km.). Its major tributaries include the Chenab, the Sutlej, the Jhelum, and the Ravi.

Irrawaddy, a major river of Burma that rises in the north and flows for more than 1300 miles (2090 km.) to empty into the Gulf of Martaban of the Bay of Bengal near Rangoon. The delta of the Irrawaddy is about 150 miles (240 km.) long. The river's chief tributaries are the Nmai and the Chindwin.

Jajmani system, an Indian practice by which the land-holding families of a village give a portion of the annual crop to the artisans and laborers in payment for their services during the year. This barter system has increasingly come to be replaced by cash transactions, weakening traditional rural economic and social patterns.

Katipunan, a secret society founded in 1892 in the Philippines by Andres Bonifacio with the aim of winning independence from Spain for the Philippines. When the Spanish authorities discovered the organization and tried to capture its leaders in August, 1896, a nationwide rebellion erupted.

While trying to suppress the revolt, the Spanish authorities accused the Filipino patriot and writer José Rizal of sedition. His execution in December, 1896, spurred the revolt, which came to be led by Emilio Aguinaldo. Aguinaldo held out until December, 1897, when a truce was signed.

Khyber Pass, a pass in a range of the Hindu Kush on the border between Afghanistan and Pakistan, about 33 miles (53 km.) long and between 50 and 600 feet (15 and 183 m) wide. The pass has had continuing strategic and historical importance since the fifth century B.C.

Konbaung dynasty, the last Burmese dynasty, ruling from 1752 to 1885. The dynasty was founded by a north Burmese leader who took the name Alaungpaya (1752–1760), meaning "embryo Buddha." His conquests formed the basis for the modern Burmese state.

By the mid-1700's the Toungoo dynasty (1486–1752), whose court was at Ava in central Burma, had fallen into decline. The Toungoo had been defeated by the Mon, whose power was centered in the south, at Pegu, the Manipuri of the northwest, and the Shan of the northeast.

Between 1752 and 1757 Alaungpaya succeeded in reuniting Burma. In 1753 he cleared the capital city, Ava, of its Mon conquerors, and built a new capital at Shwebo. In 1757 he took Pegu, which completed his conquest of the

THE KHYBER PASS *highway is the main route between Afghanistan and Pakistan.*

Mon. In 1760 he invaded Siam (Thailand), but was wounded and returned to Burma, where he died.

Alaungpaya's successors, Hsinbyushin (1763–1776), Bodawpaya (1781–1819), and Bagyidaw (1819–1837), continued his policy of conquest. By 1824 the Burmese advance threatened the interests of the British East India Company in India. In 1824 the British declared war on Burma, initiating the first Burmese war (1824–1825). The Burmese were defeated, and by the Treaty of Yandabu of 1826 Britain annexed Assam, Arakan, Manipur, and the Tenasserim coast. In a second Burmese war (1852–1853) the British annexed Pegu, and with the third Burmese war (1885–1886), the Konbaung dynasty came to an end. In 1885 the British took Mandalay, then the Burmese capital. On January 1, 1886, Burma was officially annexed by Great Britain.

Korean War, an undeclared war, officially termed a "conflict" by the U.S. government, fought from 1950 to 1953 by South Korea and various members of the United Nations, primarily the United States, against North Korea and Chinese Communist troops aided by the Soviet Union.

Korea, which was part of the Japanese empire from 1910 to 1945, was partitioned at the end of World War II. Under the terms of the 1945 Yalta agreement between the United States and the Soviet Union, Korea was divided at the 38th parallel. Soviet forces occupied the northern part of the country, and United States forces occupied the south.

In 1948 a Communist regime was established in North Korea, the Democratic People's Republic of Korea, with Kim Il Sung as prime minister. In South Korea, elections held in 1948 resulted in the establishment of the Republic of Korea, with Syngman Rhee as president. In June, 1950, a year after U.S. occupation forces had been withdrawn from South Korea, North Korean troops invaded the south.

The United States was the first to aid South Korea, but it quickly received support from the United Nations. The UN Security Council was able to pass a measure authorizing a police action in Korea partly because the Soviet delegation had boycotted the meeting and was unable to veto the resolution.

At the beginning of the war the South Korean and UN forces were driven southward, almost off the peninsula. In September, 1950, an amphibious landing by U.S. troops at Inchon forced the North Koreans into retreat. During the next 70 days North Korean forces were pushed back almost to the Yalu River, which forms the Chinese-Korean boundary.

In November, 1950, a well equipped Chinese Communist army of 200,000 crossed the Yalu to counterattack. They drove the UN divisions steadily back, and by January, 1951, Communist forces were 70 miles below the 38th parallel. The UN troops then began another offensive, which carried them across the 38th parallel on March 31.

On July 10, 1951, the first of many negotiating sessions began at Kaesong. The fighting continued, however. An armistice was finally signed at Panmunjom in 1953. Korea remained divided, with roughly the same boundary between north and south as that observed before the conflict. An international inspection team was established to maintain the armistice.

Krakatoa, or Krakatau, a volcanic island between Sumatra and Java whose eruption in 1883 was the most violent ever recorded. The sound of the explosion was heard as far away as Japan and Turkey. Nearly five cubic miles (21 cu. km.) of fragmented material was ejected into the atmosphere by a series of explosions.

Malabar Coast, India's southwestern coast, lying between the Western Ghats and the Arabian Sea.

Malay Archipelago, the world's largest island group extending east from the Malay peninsula between the Pacific and Indian oceans. It includes the islands of the Philippines and Indonesia, and, sometimes, New Guinea.

Malay peninsula, a projection of mainland Southeast Asia between the Andaman Sea, on the west, and the Gulf of Thailand, which is an arm of the South China Sea, on the east. It is occupied by Burma, Thailand, and Malaysia.

Manchuria, a northeastern region of China, consisting today of the provinces of Jilin, Liaoning, and Heilongjiang. Rich in natural resources, it was coveted by both Russia and Japan. Japan seized it in 1931 and created the puppet state called Manchukuo.

Mandarins, the name given to Chinese officials by Westerners before the Chinese revolution of 1911. After passing a rigorous series of examinations, the mandarins were made responsible for all aspects of government.

The mandarins were prevented from accumulating power by not being allowed to serve in their native provinces, by serving only three years in any one area, and by being subject to review by a board of censors, which investigated the administration of provincial governments.

Mandate of heaven, a theory used in China to justify a ruler's power. The term was first used in ancient China by the Chou at the time of their conquest of the Shang in 1122 B.C. or 1027 B.C. The Chou justified their conquest by claiming that they had received the mandate of heaven to rule. Those who

A MANDARIN, *the traditional Chinese official appointed by examination, in 1889.*

rose in rebellion against a dynasty often claimed that the ruler had lost the mandate.

Mataram, a kingdom in central Java that rose to power in the 1600's, after the fall of the Majapahit kingdom.

The Mataram kingdom was threatened by the Dutch, who had established trading posts in Indonesia. When the Matarami leader, Sunan Agung, sought to expand his influence into northwestern Java, he met resistance from the Dutch and was eventually defeated.

In 1646 the Dutch signed a trade treaty with Agung's successor, Amangkurat I. Dutch relations with Mataram remained more or less stable until 1674, when a rebellion broke out threatening Amangkurat's reign. In this first Javanese war of succession, Amangkurat was forced to flee his capital and seek Dutch protection.

The Mataram kingdom was further weakened in the 1700's by two more wars: the second Javanese war of succession (1719–1723) and the third Javanese war of succession (1749–1757). The third war eventually turned into a rebellion against Dutch control and resulted in the partition of Mataram in 1755.

May Fourth Movement, an intellectual movement in China that was at its height from about 1917 to the early 1920's. During this period Chinese intellectuals were attracted by Western ideas; they were critical of traditional Chinese values that were based on Confucian teachings.

An important attack on the Confucian tradition was a demand by Chinese intellectuals that the traditional Chinese literary language be abandoned. Written Chinese was very different from spoken Chinese, and Chinese intellectuals considered it inadequate for scientific studies, for

popular education, and for a literature expressing new ideas. A new written language based on the spoken language was created, and, soon after, textbooks in the new writing began to be used in primary schools.

The May Fourth Movement takes its name from the May fourth incident of 1919, in which university students and professors in Peking demonstrated in protest against the refusal of the Paris Peace Conference to return Shantung to China. Shantung had been seized by the Japanese during World War I.

Mekong, a major river of southeastern Asia, rising in the Tangkula Mountains in eastern Tibet. It follows a twisting, generally southeasterly course for 2600 miles (4185 km.) before emptying into the South China Sea through a wide delta at the southern tip of Indochina in Vietnam.

The Mekong's major tributaries include the Mun, the Hou, the Khong, the Srepok, and the Chinit.

The river marks parts of the Burma-China, Burma-Laos, and Thailand-Laos borders. It is navigable to north-central Laos and has a fertile valley and delta.

Metsuke, a Japanese word for censors or spies. The metsuke were employed by the Tokugawa shogunate (1603–1868) to keep a check on the affairs of each *han,* or feudal territorial unit.

Murray, Australia's principal river rising near Mt. Kosciusko in southeastern Australia and flowing westward for 1609 miles (2590 km.) to Encounter Bay, off the Indian Ocean on the south Australian coast. With its tributary, the Darling River, it forms a watercourse 2310 miles (3719 km.) long.

Nerchinsk, Treaty of, signed in 1689, the first treaty between China and Russia and the first Chinese treaty with a European power. It settled conflicts over possession of the Amur River region and was the basis for Chinese-Russian relations until the mid-1800's.

New democracy, a political phrase originated by the Chinese Communist leader Mao Zedong in a 1940 essay entitled "On the New Democracy." The document announced that the goal of the new democracy was the creation of a "democratic" state ruled by several revolutionary classes under the control of the working class, or proletariat.

In 1941 Mao announced that a "new democratic" government should be composed of all parties in addition to representatives from nonpartisan groups. In 1945 a Chinese Communist party conference again advocated coalition government. In 1949 Mao stated that the new government should be a "democratic coalition" under Communist leadership and should also be a dictatorship directed against the "enemies of the people." The people were categorized into four classes—proletariat, peasantry, petty bourgeoisie, and national bourgeoisie.

New Guinea, the world's second largest island, lying in the southwest Pacific Ocean, north of Australia. The island, with an area of 320,000 square miles (829,000 sq. km.), has a mountainous interior and swampy coastlands. New Guinea has extensive mangrove and sandalwood forests and contains deposits of gold, oil, cobalt, and nickel. New Guinea is shared by West Irian, a province of Indonesia, and Papua New Guinea.

Open-door policy, a policy of allowing equal commercial opportunity to all nations in a particular foreign region. The policy, which came to refer particularly to China in the late 1800's and early 1900's, was designed to counter the development of spheres of influence, in which one country has exclusive trading privileges in a specific area.

The term "open door" was first used by U.S. Secretary of State John Hay in 1899. Hay joined with Britain in opposing plans by France, Germany, and Russia to establish areas of exclusive interest in China. Hay won partial agreement for an open-door policy from the powers.

In 1900 the Boxer Rebellion broke out in China, and the possibility arose that China would be partitioned among the powers. Again the United States proposed an open-door policy to the other major powers, and once again it met with limited success.

The Washington Conference of 1921 had as one of its aims the formal recognition of the open-door policy in China. Among the conference participants who agreed to the plan was Japan. The open-door policy remained more or less in effect until 1931, when Japan invaded China and took the rich northeastern region of Manchuria.

Opium War, a conflict between China and Great Britain from 1839 to 1842. Britain, wanting to force China to open up to more trade, used the pretext of a Chinese ban on the import of opium and the destruction of a British supply of the drug. Britain won the war easily. By the Treaty of Nanking, China was forced to give the British important trade concessions and cede them the island of Hong Kong, as well as pay a large indemnity.

Pamir, a mountain range in the southern Soviet Union in central Asia, lying along the borders of Pakistan, Kashmir, and China, north of the Hindu Kush and Karakorum ranges. Peaks in the Pamirs rise to almost 25,000 feet (7620 m) above sea level.

Panchayat, a village tribunal in India. In the period from about 800 to 1200, each caste had a separate panchayat, which exercised authority over it. The panchayat probably derived from the *panchakula,* a committee that collected revenues and judged disputes in a village.

In modern India, the panchayat is an organ of local government in about half of the country's villages. Its members are elected, and its duties are both administrative and judicial.

Plassey, Battle of, a battle fought June 22, 1757, between a small British force and the army of Suraja Dowla (Sirajah-daulah), Muslim ruler of Bengal, which resulted in the reduction of French influence in India and the beginning of the British Indian empire.

The battle took place shortly after the outbreak of the Seven Years' War (1756–1763) between Britain and France. When the war began, Robert Clive of the British East India Company decided to oust the French from their trading stations in Bengal. The French, however, were protected by Suraja Dowla, who expelled the British from Calcutta.

After capturing the city, he ordered 146 Englishmen locked up in a small windowless room (later known as the Black Hole of Calcutta) for one night, during which most of them died of suffocation.

Soon thereafter Clive's small force defeated Suraja Dowla at Plassey, about 80 miles north of Calcutta. Clive put a puppet ruler on the Bengal throne, and the English rapidly established complete control of the Bengal region.

Rites controversy, a dispute between Jesuit missionaries and other Roman Catholic religious orders in China during the 1600's and 1700's. It concerned the compatibility of traditional Chinese rites with Christianity.

The Jesuit missionaries believed that Confucianism and Christianity were compatible. They considered Confucian practices as civil rites and therefore not in conflict with Christianity. To members of other orders, this duality seemed heretical.

The controversy continued from 1640 to 1742, when a papal bull was issued forbidding Roman Catholic missionaries to allow the practice of Chinese rites. The bull caused increased persecution of missionaries and a decline of Christianity in China.

Ronin, Japanese aristocratic warriors who owed their allegiance to no particular lord. Many participated in the political upheavals that shook Japan in the 1800's. The ronin joined in terrorist attacks against Westerners in Japan and were instrumental in bringing about the imperial restoration of 1868.

Salween, a major Asian river that rises in the Tangkula Mountains of Tibet. It flows east and south for about 1500 miles (2400 km.) through China and Burma into the Gulf of Martaban, an arm of the Andaman Sea.

Samil Movement, a peaceful national demonstration held throughout Korea on March 1, 1919. It is sometimes called the March First Movement. Korean patriots, whose country had been annexed by Japan in 1910, announced Korean independence in a proclamation read in every town. The demonstrators were harshly suppressed, however, and the movement failed.

San-Min Chu-I, or Three Principles of the People, a political statement written by Sun Yat-sen in the early 1900's to guide a republican revolution in China. The three principles were nationalism, democracy, and socialism.

Sun's "nationalism" was anti-Manchu and anti-imperialist. Sun's "de-

THE OPIUM WAR (1841), fought to keep the trade open, led to foreign domination of China.

CULVER PICTURES

mocracy" involved a constitution with five powers—executive, legislative, judicial, examination, and censorial. Sun's "socialism" meant merely the application of a single tax to put a limit on the accumulation of capital. The three principles became part of Kuomintang ideology.

Satsuma Rebellion, an uprising in Japan in 1877 in the former province of Satsuma. The rebellion was led by conservative samurai (aristocratic warriors) who opposed the movement of Japan's new government, established by the Meiji Restoration, toward a constitutional monarchy.

The samurai, having been stripped of many of their traditional privileges and sources of income, attacked an army installation at Kagoshima. Government forces rushed to the area. Heavy fighting ensued, and the samurai were eventually defeated.

The Satsuma Rebellion, which was the last armed insurrection against the Meiji regime, marked the end of the feudal powers and prerogatives of the samurai.

Shogun, a short form for *Seii-tai-shogun,* Japanese for "barbarian-quelling generalissimo," a title first given to outstanding generals in Japan in the 700's. By the 1100's a feudal system had developed in Japan and a hereditary clique headed by a warrior, Yoritomo, came to govern much of the country. Although the official seat of government was the court at Kyoto, Yoritomo's private government was more powerful. The title of shogun came to apply to all the hereditary military dictators who were to rule Japan for the next 600 years. The shoguns' administrations were known as shogunates.

South Asian Association for Regional Cooperation (SAARC), a regional organization that attempts to promote economic cooperation among member nations. In 1988 its members were Bangladesh, Bhutan, India, Maldives, Nepal, Pakistan, and Sri Lanka.

South Pacific Form, an informal regional organization of independent and self-governing states. Representatives of the member governments meet to discuss issues of importance to the South Pacific region. In 1988 the members were Australia, the Cook Islands, Fiji, Kiribati, the Marshall Islands, the Federated States of Micronesia, Nauru, New Zealand, Niue, Papua New Guinea, the Solomon Islands, Tonga, Tuvalu, Vanuatu, and Western Samoa.

Tasmania, an island 150 miles (240 km.) off the southeastern coast of Australia, lying between the Indian Ocean and the Tasman Sea. About 180 miles by 190 miles (290 by 306 km.), Tasmania is geologically a continuation of the Australian continent. A high cen-

tral plateau is surrounded by forested mountains in the west and agricultural lands in the north and southeast.

Tibet, a plateau region in southwestern China of about 471,700 square miles (1,221,700 sq. km.), bordered on the south by the Himalayas and on the north by the Kunlun Mountains. Both the terrain and climate of Tibet are quite harsh, and it supports only a small population (1,970,000 in 1985). Tibet maintained its independence for much of its history; however, China several times tried to gain dominance over the area, with mixed success. The most recent invasion came in 1950, when the new Chinese Communist regime annexed Tibet. Tibet has not submitted easily to Chinese rule, and there have been several uprisings, notably in 1959 and 1987.

Turtle ships, ironclad naval vessels used by the Korean admiral Yi Sun Sin to fight the Japanese, who had invaded Korea in 1592. Yi's "turtle ships" defeated the Japanese navy and the Japanese were forced to withdraw. Some consider the turtle ships the world's first armored warships.

Vietnam War, a guerrilla war dating from the collapse of the French colonial empire in Southeast Asia in 1945, following World War II. Initially a nationalist struggle, the conflict grew and eventually involved both Asian and non-Asian nations.

The war in Vietnam began in 1945 as a struggle between Vietnamese nationalists seeking independence and French colonial forces attempting to reestablish French rule after the defeat of Japan, which had invaded and occupied the area during World War II. The Viet Minh, as the Vietnamese forces were known, were led by Ho Chi Minh, a long-time Communist.

A crucial battle in the French struggle to retain control of Vietnam was fought in 1954 at Dien Bien Phu. The Viet Minh won a decisive victory and the French agreed to withdraw.

An international conference was held in Geneva, Switzerland, in 1954. The terms of the Geneva agreement provided for the division of Vietnam at the 17th parallel. The north became a Communist-controlled republic led by Ho Chi Minh, and the south became a monarchy with a weak emperor, Bao Dai, and a strong prime minister, Ngo Dinh Diem. In 1955 a republic with a powerful president was established in the south. Diem served as the first president and won U.S. support.

Almost immediately after the partition of Vietnam, South Vietnam began to be infiltrated by guerrilla forces, known as the Vietcong, from the north.

The Diem government was unable to cope with domestic problems or conduct a successful campaign against the insurgents. Resentment against the Diem regime culminated in a bloody coup in November, 1963. Diem was killed and the government was seized by a military junta.

A change in the nature of the war came in 1965, when U.S. air attacks on North Vietnam were begun and U.S. combat troop strength in South Vietnam was sharply increased.

Late in January, 1968, the Vietcong launched the Tet offensive, a major attack that caused heavy loss of life and equipment in the south and weakened morale.

World pressure for settlement of the conflict brought a meeting of both sides in Paris in May, 1968, but the fighting continued until January 23, 1973, when a peace settlement was finally announced. In early 1975 North Vietnamese and Vietcong forces launched a new offensive and the South Vietnamese military effort col-

THE WAR IN VIETNAM *caused a terrible destruction from which it will take the country long to recover.*

lapsed. On April 29 U.S. President Gerald Ford ordered the complete evacuation of all remaining U.S. personnel. On April 30 the South Vietnamese president surrendered unconditionally to the Vietcong.

Warlords, Chinese military leaders who controlled many large areas of China and competed with one another for increased power and territory. The period 1916 to 1928 is often called the warlord era in modern Chinese history. Warlords remained in control of some areas of China until the advent of the Communist regime in 1949.

Yalu, a river that rises in northeastern Korea and forms part of the North Korea-China border. It flows for 500 miles (800 km.), emptying into Korea Bay.

Yangban, a Korean term meaning "two groups" and referring specifically to the civil and military branches of the bureaucracy. The term generally designates the whole landowning official class, however. During the Yi dynasty (1392–1910), important official posts were held exclusively by the landowning class, or *yangban.* Although Korea, like China, used an examination system to recruit competent men for government service, the examinations were usually open only to members of yangban families. After Korea became a Japanese protectorate in 1905, the Japanese abolished the yangban's status.

Yangtze, one of the principal rivers of China and of the world. It rises in the Kunlun Mountains and follows a twisting course for 3434 miles (5530 km.)

before it empties into the East China Sea. The portion east of its rugged gorges—about one-sixth of its length —is navigable by ocean vessels.

Zamindar, a Hindu landholder in northern India. During the period of Muslim rule of Hindu northern India, from the late 1100's to the 1700's, the zamindars formed a group roughly equivalent to territorial chiefs. The Muslim rulers feared the power of the zamindars, but generally let them serve as administrators.

During the period of British rule in India, from the late 1700's to 1947, the zamindars, with their extensive administrative experience, served as intermediaries between the peasants and the British authorities. Among their duties were the assessment and collection of taxes.

For Further Reference

General

Area Handbook Series. *Afghanistan, A Country Study; Burma, A Country Study;* etc. Government Printing Office.

Bingham, W., H. Conroy and F. Ickle. *A History of Asia* (2nd Ed.). 2 volumes. Allyn and Bacon, 1974.

Darling, Frank C. *The Westernization of Asia: A Comparative Political Analysis.* Schenkman, 1980.

Dudley, Guilford A. *A History of Eastern Civilizations.* John Wiley & Sons, 1973.

Pieries, Ralph. *Social Development and Planning in Asia.* South Asia Books, 1976.

Scalapino, Robert A. *Asia and the Road Ahead: Issues for the Major Powers.* University of California Press, 1975.

Stroup, Herbert Hewit. *Four Religions of Asia.* Harper & Row, 1968.

Australasia

Alkire, William H. *An Introduction to the Peoples and Cultures of Micronesia* (2nd Ed.). Cummings Publishing, 1979.

Cameron, Ian. *Lost Paradise: The Exploration of the Pacific.* Salem House, 1987.

Clark, C.M.H. *A Short History of Australia* (3rd Ed.). New American Library, 1987.

Gordon, Bernard K. and Kenneth J. Rothwell, editors. *The New Political Economy of the Pacific.* Ballinger Publications, 1975.

Jeans, D.N. *Australia: A Geography.* St. Martin's Press, 1983.

Kolde, Endel. *The Pacific Quest: The Concept & Scope of an Oceanic Community.* Lexington Books, 1976.

Mamak, A. and Ali, editors. *Race, Class & Rebellion in the South Pacific.* Allen Unwin, 1979.

Sahlins, Marshall David. *Islands of History.* University of Chicago Press, 1985.

Terrill, Ross. *The Australians.* Simon & Schuster, 1987.

East Asia

Barnett, A. Doak. *Communist China: The Early Years, 1949–1955.* Frederick A. Praeger, 1964.

Carter, Alden R. *Modern China.* Franklin Watts, 1986.

Coye, Molly J. and Jon Livingston, editors. *China, Yesterday and Today* (3rd Ed.). Bantam Books, 1984.

Fitzgerald, C. P. *China, A Short Cultural History.* Westview, 1985.

Forbis, William H. *Japan Today.* Harper & Row, 1975.

Hinton, Harold C. *Three and a Half Powers: The New Balance in Asia.* Indiana University Press, 1975.

Hulbert, Homer B. *History of Korea* (Revised Ed.). 2 volumes. Hillary House, 1962.

Li, Dun J., translator. *The Civilization of China.* Charles Scribner's Sons, 1975.

Reischauer, Edwin O. *The Japanese Today: Change and Continuity.* Belknap, 1988.

Reischauer, Edwin O. and John K. Fairbank. *A History of East Asian Civilization.* 2 volumes. Houghton Mifflin, 1962, 1965.

Rupen, Robert A. *The Mongolian People's Republic.* Stanford University Press, 1966.

Schwartz, Benjamin. *Chinese Communism and the Rise of Mao.* Harper Torchbooks, 1967.

Topping, Seymour. *Journey Between Two Chinas.* Harper & Row, 1977.

Webb, Herschel F. *Introduction to Japan* (2nd Ed.). Columbia University Press, 1957.

Wright, Mary C., editor. *China in Revolution: The First Phase, 1900–1913.* Yale University Press, 1968.

South and Southeast Asia

Beckett, I.F.W. *Southeast Asia from 1945.* Franklin Watts, 1987.

Brown, William Norman. *The United States and India, Pakistan, Bangladesh.* Harvard University Press, 1972.

Hall, D. G. *A History of South-East Asia.* (4th Ed.). St. Martin's Press, 1981.

Isenberg, Irwin, editor. *The Nations of the Indian Subcontinent.* H. W. Wilson Co., 1974.

Lengyel, Emil. *Pakistan and Bangladesh.* Watts, 1975.

Lye, Keith. *Asia and Australasia.* Gloucester Press, 1987.

Meyer, Milton W. *South Asia: A Short History of the Subcontinent* (2nd Ed.). Littlefield, 1976.

Naipaul, Vidiadhar Surajprasad. *India: A Wounded Civilization.* Alfred A. Knopf, 1977.

Sihanouk, Norodom. *War and Hope: The Case of Cambodia.* Pantheon Books, 1980.

Thapar, Romila. *A History of India. Volume 1.* Penguin Books, 1965.

Uppal, Jogindar S. *Economic Development in South Asia.* St. Martin's Press, 1977.

Veit, Lawrence A. *India's Second Revolution: The Dimensions of Development.* McGraw-Hill, 1976.

Williams, Lea E. *Southeast Asia: A History.* Oxford University Press, 1976.

Ziring, Lawrence, editor. *The Subcontinent in World Politics: India, Its Neighbors, and the Great Powers* (2nd Ed.). Frederick A. Praeger, 1982.

Astronomy and Space

THE BETTMANN ARCHIVE

FACTS ABOUT THE SOLAR SYSTEM

	DISTANCE FROM SUN	LENGTH OF YEAR	DIAMETER (MILES)	LENGTH OF DAY	MASS RELATIVE TO EARTH	SURFACE TEMP.	WEIGHT OF 150 LBS.	NUMBER OF MOONS	ATMOSPHERE
Mercury	36,000,000	87.96 days	3030	58.65 Earth days	0.054	660 F	55 lbs.	0	helium, hydrogen
Venus	67,270,000	224.70 days	7517	243 Earth days	0.815	800 F	130 lbs.	0	carbon dioxide, nitrogen
Earth	93,000,000	365.25 days	7921	23 hrs., 56 min.	1.0	60 F	150 lbs.	1	nitrogen, oxygen, water
Mars	141,710,000	687 days	4215	24 hrs., 37 min.	0.108	−67 F	55 lbs.	2	carbon dioxide, nitrogen
Jupiter	483,880,000	11.86 years	88,803	9 hrs., 50 min.	317.8	−240 F	380 lbs.	16	hydrogen, helium
Saturn	887,140,000	29.45 years	74,520	10 hrs., 14 min.	95.2	−290 F	160 lbs.	21+	hydrogen, helium
Uranus	1,783,980,000	84.01 days	32,168	10 hrs., 49 min.	14.5	−360 F	155 lbs.	15	hydrogen, helium, methane
Neptune	2,795,460,000	164.79 years	30,739	15 hrs., 48 min.	17.2	−380 F	210 lbs.	2	hydrogen, helium, methane
Pluto	3,675,270,000	248.4 years	2,173	6.39 Earth days	0.18	about −460 F	unknown	1	methane
Sun	—	—	860,000	25 Earth days	333	10,000 F	4200 lbs.	—	hydrogen, helium

HALLEY'S COMET: DENNIS DI CICCO/PETER ARNOLD, INC.

Astronomy and Space

HALE OBSERVATORIES

PHOTO RESEARCHERS

PHOTO RESEARCHERS

MOUNT WILSON AND PALOMAR OBSERVATORIES

RAPHO/PHOTO RESEARCHERS

Astronomy occupies a singular position among the sciences in that its benefits to society are not directly apparent. Physics and chemistry benefit the development of technology, and biology often results in enormous assistance for medical and agricultural research. In this sense, astronomy is an exception: astronomical knowledge has no direct impact on our life. Astronomy does not aid technology or further defense. Most assuredly, it does not help increase people's standards of living.

Notwithstanding this absence of direct applications, universities and governments expend large sums on giant optical and radio telescopes, and on special astronomical spacecraft. Astronomers and astrophysicists devote entire careers to further the understanding of phenomena observed directly or indirectly in the sky.

This leads inevitably to the fact that astronomy plays an important role in society, comparable to that of literature, scholarship, or music. Research in astronomy is fueled by the desire to understand the world we live in, to satisfy our never-ending thirst for knowledge.

Throughout history, astronomy has played an important role in the advancement of the science of physics.

Isaac Newton discovered his laws of gravity by trying to understand the force that held the planets in their orbits around the sun. Albert Einstein's theory of relativity has been verified through astronomical observation. It is probable that high-energy physicists at work now will learn much about the universe from high-energy processes observed in the sky.

Astronomy divides into a number of disciplines. *Classical astronomy* refers to the description of the celestial sphere and the location of stars using celestial coordinates. It also deals with the motions of the moon, sun, and planets and their satellites, as well as celestial objects such as comets.

Classical astronomy from the start has had important practical applications. Celestial observations were used to keep time and construct calendars. Knowledge of the exact positions of stars has served as the basis of navigation.

Newton's discovery of the laws of gravitation enabled scientists to make precise calculations of the trajectories of celestial bodies in space; this field became known as *celestial mechanics*. Today the knowledge of celestial mechanics is of great importance for the computation of the trajectories of spacecraft.

With the introduction of the spectroscope in the 19th century, astronomers began to investigate the chemical makeup of the sun, stars, planets, and nebulas. Such investigation, called *astrophysics,* today comprises the study of stellar interiors, the evolution of stars, and the processes that govern energy production in stars and extragalactic systems. The field also covers the study of the nature of such objects as black holes, supernovas, pulsars, and quasars.

New observational techniques have revolutionized astronomy since World War II. Radio telescopes and observations in infrared light and x-rays have greatly extended the observable universe. These new observational techniques have given rise to entirely new fields: radio astronomy, ultraviolet and infrared astronomy, and x-ray astronomy.

Cosmology is the study of the structure and evolution of the universe as a whole. Modern scientists base their conception of the universe on two important discoveries: the recession of galaxies, discovered by Edwin Hubble in the 1920's, and the presence of cosmic background radiation, which tends to confirm the theory that the universe began with a huge explosion, the big bang.

FOUNDATIONS OF ASTRONOMY

Astronomy is an observational rather than an experimental science. Astronomers can only observe phenomena; they cannot perform experiments, as physicists and chemists can do. However, astronomers today do not feel limited because they are peeking directly into the greatest laboratory of all: the universe. With present-day observational techniques, astronomers

THE TELESCOPE *has been the single most important instrument for helping us understand the universe.*

are witnessing processes that cannot possibly be created in a laboratory on Earth. For example, black holes and neutron stars are states of matter that no one can experiment with on Earth. Because of this, the exchange of information between physics and astrophysics has increased in recent years. In fact, many physicists become astrophysicists during their careers.

History of Astronomy

Astronomy: The Oldest Science

To the ancients the stars appeared as points of light attached to a large sphere that rotated slowly around Earth. Very early in history, probably 5000 years ago, ancient peoples noticed that not all the stars appeared to be fixed to this sphere. Instead, a small number of them moved on more erratic paths and seemed to wander through the sky. These stars became known as wandering stars or planets. The term "planet" is derived from the Greek verb *planan,* to lead astray or to wander. The other stars became known as fixed stars; they are still called that today to distinguish them from planets.

The Babylonians, in the reign of King Hammurabi, about 1800 B.C., prepared the first known star catalogs and records of planetary motion. They used a number system with 60 as the base. About 450 B.C., they began using these sexagesimal numbers for indicating the position of stars on the celestial sphere. Today we still are using this number system to divide a degree into 60 minutes of arc and a minute into 60 seconds of arc.

The Egyptians were less interested in recording stellar and planetary positions. Astronomical observations, especially of the stars that rose or set with the sun, served mainly for timekeeping.

The Chinese very early introduced accurate recordkeeping of astronomical events. Like the Babylonians and the Egyptians, the Chinese grouped

patterns of stars in constellations. Many Chinese records have been helpful to present-day astronomers. For example, the Chinese recorded in 240 B.C. the appearance of what later became known as Halley's comet. This information became useful for calculating the degree of perturbation of the comet's orbit. The Chinese also reported several novas and the supernova of 1054, the remnant of which in recent times has been identified with a pulsar in the Crab nebula.

The zodiac. The ancients noticed that the sun also seemed to wander against the background of fixed stars. During the day, stars are not visible, but just before and after sunset they become noticeable. The ancients perceived that the sun again occupied a

THE ZODIAC *is the area in the sky through which the sun appears to travel. It is divided into twelve sections, each containing a constellation.*

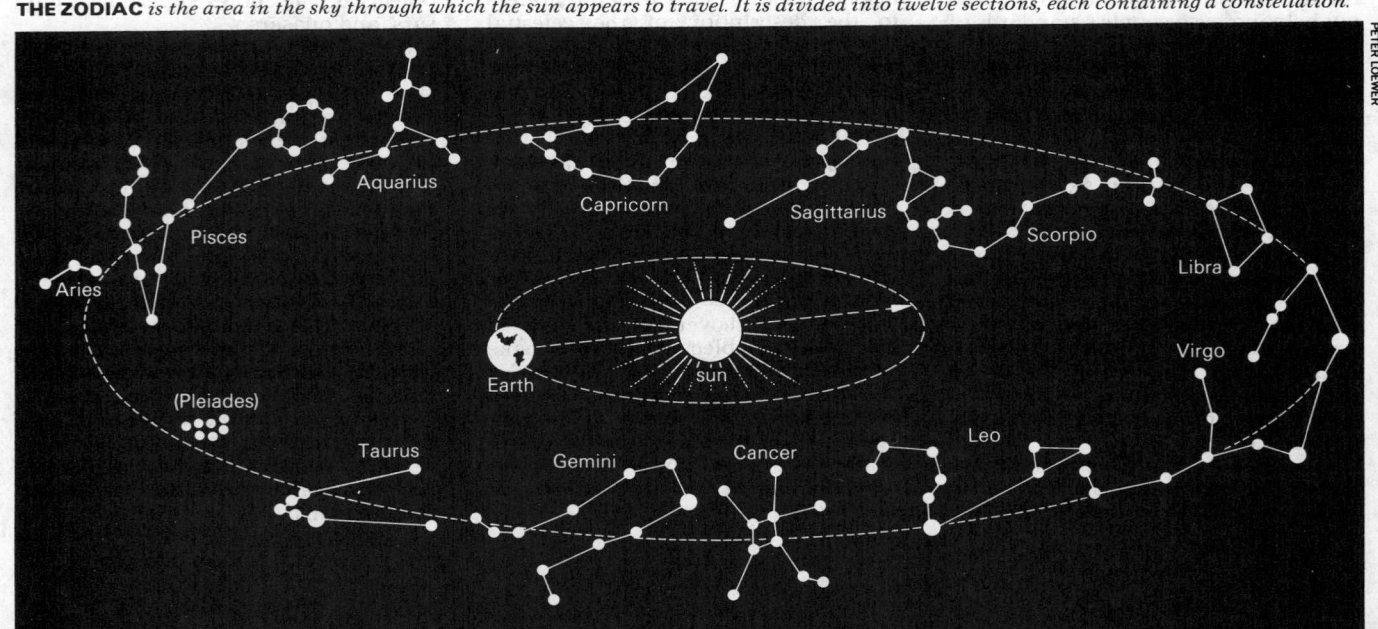

position in the same constellation after approximately 365 days and thus traveled a full circle in that time. The path the sun describes on the celestial sphere (the *ecliptic*) passes through twelve constellations. Early astronomers and astrologers, especially the Assyrians, attached special importance to these constellations, which they named after mythical people and animals. The band across the sky that contains these constellations is called the zodiac, literally, circle of animals.

Archeoastronomy. Several ancient populations have left traces of their concern with astronomy. In some Egyptian temples, such as the great temple of Amen-Ra at Karnak, corridors and doorways are aligned with the direction of the setting of the sun on the longest day of the year, the summer solstice. Only during that day, predicted by the priests, would sunlight flash throughout the temple.

More positively related to astronomy are the large numbers of remnants of rings of stones found in many parts of the British Isles. Best known is the site at Stonehenge in southern England. At the monument at Stonehenge, massive stones are placed in concentric circles. The stones are aligned with the rising and setting position of the sun at the summer and winter solstices (the longest and shortest days of the year, respectively). Certain stones on the site are aligned with the two farthest points on the horizon, at which the moon can be seen rising or setting.

Calendars. Early man used the daily motion of the sun and stars across the sky, as well as the monthly cycle of the phases of the moon, to keep time. Scientists have found bones in Zaire, approximately 25,000 years old, that carry marks believed to be recordings of months and lunar phases. Early in prehistory, man noticed the relationship between the path of the sun through the sky and the regularly recurring seasons.

When man began cultivating land for food, about 12,000 years ago, keeping track of time became a necessity. Planting and harvesting had to be done at the right time of year. In the Nile valley in Egypt, accurate timekeeping was critical for predicting the annual flooding of the Nile valley and delta region, for this was the area that supplied most of the food for Egyptians. Early calendars were based on the motion of the sun through the zodiac or on the phases of the moon.

Solar calendars. The Egyptians used a calendar of 365 days and determined the time of year by observing the positions of stars at the spot where the sun would rise. The Egyptian calendar, however, had a problem: after four years it would be one day out of step with the seasonal variation of the sun's

path because the sun actually returns to its starting position every $365\frac{1}{4}$ days.

Lunar calendars. The Babylonians based their calendar on the phases of the moon. The length of the month was defined as the period from one new moon to the next. The Babylonians divided the year into twelve lunar months. Like the Egyptians, they soon noticed that their calendar was not in tune with the seasons (a solar year equals twelve lunar months plus eleven days), so in sporadic years they inserted an extra month. The Babylonians were accurate in administering their calendar, with the result that today we can trace historical events from 636 B.C. to 45 A.D. with an uncertainty of one day at most.

Astrology. Administration of the Babylonian calendar was in the hands of the priests, who made the astronomical observations and announced changes in seasonal occurrences of flooding. Babylonians also believed that the positions of the moon and the planets could influence human and political destiny. Thus, astrology, as still practiced today, has its roots in early Mesopotamian astronomy.

Early Concepts of the Universe

The structure of the universe usually is described by a cosmological model, a mathematical or physical description. The early cosmological models were static, holding that the universe does not change with time. They generally placed Earth at the center of the universe. Because of new insights gained during the 17th century, the idea of an unchanging universe was replaced by a belief that the universe had undergone some form of development.

Today, the most widely accepted cosmological model is that of the *big bang*. According to this model, the universe started from a *primeval atom;* that is, the concentration of all the mass of the universe in a single point that exploded. Most scientists now believe that the entire universe is the result of that explosion, and that the fragments are still flying in all directions.

Egyptian and Babylonian cosmologies.
Concepts of the universe in the great civilizations of about 1000 B.C. were straightforward: Earth is flat and is covered by a large dome carrying the stars. The Babylonians believed that Earth floats on an ocean. The Egyptians and Chinese believed Earth to be square.

Greek cosmologies.
Science, as we know it now, was born in ancient Greece. Before the Greeks, natural

phenomena were explained in legends and stories. For example, the Egyptians believed that each star is inhabited by a god who travels with the star in a boat over the celestial rivers. The Greek natural philosopher Thales of Miletus (624–546 B.C.) is considered to have been the first to apply rational methods instead of myths to the explanation of natural phenomena. He held that Earth is a flat disk floating on a vast ocean. Thales thus believed in the necessity of some support for Earth, an idea that was abandoned by Parmenides of Elea (c 540–470 B.C.), who believed Earth to be spherical and talked about "up" and "down" relative to Earth's center.

Pythagoras of Samos also viewed Earth as spherical. During an eclipse of the moon, he observed the round form of Earth's shadow on the surface of the moon. He also noticed that at sea the masts of a ship become visible before the hull. This supported his idea that Earth is spherical.

Aristotle, who became one of the most influential Greek scholars, taught that Earth is the center of the universe. His influence was so great that the idea of an Earth-centered, or *geocentric,* universe went practically unchallenged for the next 2000 years.

Aristarchus of Samos, however, challenged Aristotle and suggested about 280 B.C. that Earth and other planets move around the sun, and that the sun occupies the center of the universe; such a universe is termed *heliocentric.* In his book *On the Sizes and Distances of the Sun and Moon,* Aristarchus maintained that the moon shines because it reflects the light of the sun and that the sun is much larger than the moon and 18 to 20 times farther away. These ideas of Aristarchus were not widely accepted because he could not supply proof that Earth is moving.

The Ptolemaic system. Most of our knowledge of Greek astronomy is provided by *Megale Syntaxis tes Astronomias,* a book written by Ptolemy (127–180 A.D.), the last great astronomer of the Alexandrian school in Egypt. Arab scholars translated this book during the ninth century; it is now known by its Arabic title, *Almagest.* The book contained a catalog of stars compiled by Hipparchus in 130 B.C. Most important, it contained the description of the Ptolemaic system, a synthesis of Ptolemy's own ideas and the ideas of other Greek scholars, including Aristotle, Pythagoras, Apollonius of Perga, and Hipparchus, all of whom believed in a finite, geocentric model of the universe.

According to the Ptolemaic system, Earth is at the center of the universe, while the sun and moon move around Earth on perfect circles at a constant rate. It was obvious to Ptolemy that the planets could not move on perfectly circular orbits at a constant rate because of their irregular and sometimes retrograde motion (they appear to move backward at times) through the sky. Ptolemy solved the problem by placing each planet on a small circular orbit, called an *epicycle.* The planet rotates on the epicycle around a point called the *deferent,* which in turn rotates around Earth in a circular orbit. The combined motions of the planet on the epicycle and the rotation of the entire epicycle around Earth was held to explain the irregular motion of the planets.

Ptolemy rejected the idea of Earth rotating around the sun, as was proposed by Aristarchus. Like some Greek scholars before him, Ptolemy argued that if Earth orbited around the sun, in one year the fixed stars would exhibit a small yearly shift, called *parallax.* To understand this, imagine that you are on a merry-go-round. While you are going around, look at the buildings around you and forget for a while that you also are moving. The buildings will appear to move to the right and then to the left for every turn of the merry-go-round. Ptolemy could not observe the stellar parallax and therefore believed that Earth had to be in a fixed position. However, Ptolemy had underestimated the distance to the stars. They are so distant and the effect is so small that astronomers could not discover stellar parallaxes until 1838, when the German astronomer Friedrich Wilhelm Bessel (1784–1846) discovered the parallax of 61 Cygni, a double star.

Ptolemy also rejected the idea that Earth would rotate around its axis. He argued that all clouds would then appear to move in one direction, opposite to the rotation of Earth. Ptolemy's book remained the standard text for astronomy throughout the Middle Ages. The Arabs revived astronomy by studying the ancients and repeating their observations. Al Ma'mun (786–833) founded the first astronomical observatory, in Baghdad. The Toledan tables, compiled by al-Zarkali (c 1029–1087,

also known as Arzachel), became the basis of the Alphonsine tables that were published in Spain by order of Alfonso El Sabio (Alfonso X of Castile–Leon, 1252–1284). This compilation of planetary and stellar positions was to remain in use for three centuries.

Astronomy and the Scientific Revolution

The influence of Aristotle on scientific thinking throughout the Middle Ages was so great that most scholars contented themselves with teaching his theories and elaborating on them without attempting much innovation. Most of the teaching was in the hands of the church, and religious thinkers believed that Aristotle's ideas were in accordance with the Holy Scriptures. Around 1507, Nicolaus Copernicus (1473–1543), himself a church official, became convinced that Ptolemy's system was wrong. He proposed the idea that Earth, instead of being the fixed center of the universe, is a planet circling the sun. Copernicus completed his famous book *De Revolutionibus Orbium Coelestium* (Concerning the Revolutions of the Celestial Orb) c 1533, but he postponed publication of it until shortly before his death, since he feared being accused of heresy.

Similar to Ptolemy's system, Copernicus's system uses perfect circles and deferents to describe the motions of the planets, with the difference that Earth revolves around the sun. Copernicus explained that the discrepancies between his model and actual observations were caused by observational errors; he tried to account for the errors by adding circles.

A great advance in observational astronomy came from the experimental skills of Tycho Brahe (1546–1601), a Dane who was supported through most of his active career by Denmark's King Frederick II. Brahe not only developed instruments of novel design that greatly increased observational accuracy, he also introduced sound observational procedures. The improved determinations of stellar and planetary positions served as ideal material for Johannes Kepler (1571–1630), a young German whom Brahe appointed as his assistant not long before Brahe's death.

Kepler used Brahe's splendid data to devise a heliocentric system that would agree with the observations. His outstanding finding was that the true shape of the orbit of a planet around the sun is not a circle, but an ellipse with the sun at one of the foci of the ellipse, not at its center. (Ironically, Arzachel, about 1080, had suggested ellipses rather than circles for planetary orbits, but no one listened.)

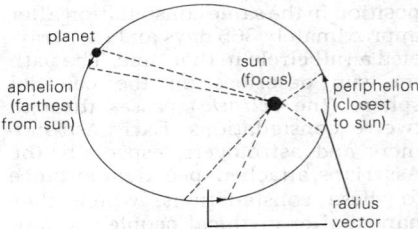

A RADIUS VECTOR *sweeps the same total area in the same time, no matter what its length.*

Kepler's laws. Kepler's first law states that the orbit of every planet is an ellipse with the sun at one focus. In his second law, Kepler stated that the *radius vector,* an imaginary line joining the sun to a planet, sweeps over equal areas in equal times. In 1609, in his book *Astronomia Nova,* Kepler applied these two laws to the planet Mars.

In 1619 Kepler published his third law, which states that the square of the time any planet takes to complete its orbit is proportional to the cube of its distance from the sun. When a planet is closer to the sun, it moves faster; when it is farther from the sun, it moves slower. With these three laws, a planet's path and orbital velocity can be determined.

Galileo's discoveries. A contemporary of Kepler was Galileo Galilei (1564–1642), an Italian physicist and astronomer. In 1609, while Galileo was staying in Venice, he heard about a system of lenses, invented in Holland, that magnify distant objects. Galileo set about assembling his own instrument. When Galileo directed his telescope to the night sky, he made more discoveries than had been made by all the astronomers who had lived before him. In a few months he discovered the craters on the moon, the moons of Jupiter, and the phases of Venus.

Newton. If Kepler showed *how* the planets move, it was Isaac Newton (1642–1727) who showed *why* they move in elliptical orbits. Before he was 24, Newton had deduced from Kepler's laws that the force keeping a planet in its orbit must be inversely proportional to the square of the distance between the planet and the center about which it revolves. Newton did little with his result until 1684, when the physicist Edmund Halley (1656–1742) urged him to write out his mathematical demonstration that a body moving under a force inversely proportional to the square of the distance moves on an elliptical path. The resulting manuscript, *Philosophiae Naturalis Principia Mathematica* (the *Principia*), published in 1687, sets forth the physical principles for the motion of bodies under the influence of gravitational forces.

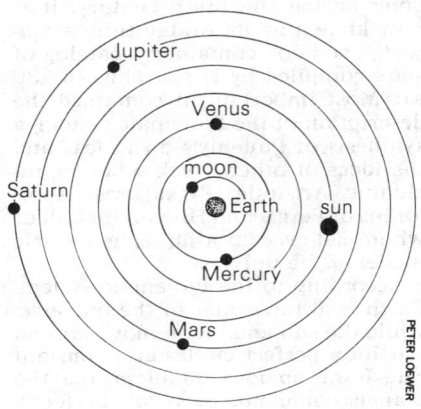

ACCORDING TO PTOLEMY, *the sun and other planets revolved around Earth.*

Jupiter
Venus
moon
Saturn
Earth
sun
Mercury
Mars

PETER LOEWER

FINDING YOUR WAY IN THE STARS

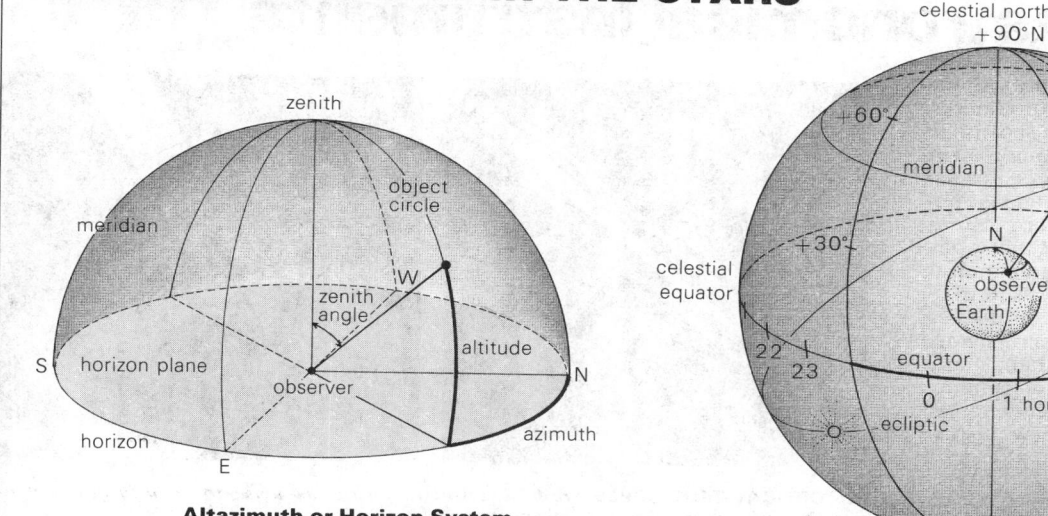

Altazimuth or Horizon System

Equatorial System

In order to communicate with each other, astronomers need a system of coordinates to pinpoint celestial objects in the sky. It is convenient to assume that all the celestial objects are placed on a sphere surrounding Earth. The point just above us is called the *zenith*.

Distances on this sphere, such as the distance between two stars, are expressed in angles. These *angular distances* are not to be confused with real distances between celestial objects. Two stars that appear close on the celestial sphere can actually be very far apart. We can measure the angular distance between two stars by pointing a stick toward each one and measuring the angle between the two sticks. We express angular distances in arc degrees, minutes, and seconds. A full great circle on the celestial sphere comprises 360 arc degrees. (A great circle is a circle whose center coincides with the center of the sphere.) One arc degree is subdivided in 60 arc minutes, and one arc minute is divided in 60 arc seconds.

Celestial coordinates. The position of a star on the celestial sphere is expressed in *celestial coordinates*. The simplest coordinate system is called the *altazimuth*, or *horizon* system. The observer projects the visible horizon onto the celestial sphere to form a great circle, called the *astronomical horizon*. Starting from the zenith one can draw an arc, called a *vertical circle*, so that it intersects the astronomical horizon. The height of the star in degrees on the vertical circle above the astronomical horizon is called the *altitude* or *elevation* of the star. The altitude of the zenith is precisely 90 degrees. The angle along the astronomical horizon from the direction of the North Pole to the vertical circle of the star is called the *azimuth* of the star. The azimuth is counted turning from east to south to west. For example, the azimuth of a star exactly in the east is 90 degrees, and that of a star exactly in the west is 270 degrees.

The altitude and the azimuth together determine the position of the star on the celestial sphere. The altazimuth system has, however, two disadvantages: first, the position of the star depends on the location of the observer on Earth; second, as Earth rotates, the coordinates of the star change continuously with time.

Equatorial coordinates. Astronomers prefer to use equatorial coordinates, a system that is independent of the rotation of Earth and of the location of the observer on Earth. Consider a celestial sphere that rotates around Earth and on which the stars occupy fixed positions. (Of course, the sun, moon, and planets move on this sphere, just as they do through the sky.) The celestial sphere is assumed to rotate around the same axis as Earth's axis. The *celestial poles* are the points around which the celestial sphere seems to rotate. The *celestial equator* is the projection of Earth's equator on the celestial sphere. The *ecliptic* is the apparent path of the sun around the celestial sphere. The ecliptic intersects the celestial equator in two points, called *equinoxes*. On the first day of spring, March 20 or 21, the sun crosses the celestial equator at the *vernal equinox*; the sun crosses the celestial equator at a point called the *autumnal equinox* on September 22 or 23, the first day of autumn.

Starting from the celestial pole, one can draw a great circle, called an *hour circle*, so that it intersects the celestial equator. The *declination* of a star is its angular distance north or south of the celestial equator, measured along the hour circle passing through the star.

The angular distance between the hour line of a star and the vernal equinox is called the *right ascension* of the star. The right ascension is measured, turning west-south, in hours, minutes, and seconds rather than arc degrees. The choice of time units is easily understandable if one remembers that it takes a star 24 hours to describe a full circle in the sky.

Constellations. Since ancient times, astronomers have used constellations to indicate groups of stars on the celestial sphere. Ptolemy listed 48 constellations, 21 in the northern hemisphere, 12 in the zodiac, and 15 in the southern hemisphere. Several new constellations, especially in the southern hemisphere, were added by Tycho Brahe, the German lawyer Johann Bayer (1572–1625), Augustine Royer, the German astronomer Johann Hevelius (1611–1687), and the French astronomer Nicolas Louis de Lacaille (1713–1762). Today, 88 constellations are recog-

nized internationally. They not only indicate the visible stars forming the constellations but also define areas of the sky with internationally agreed on boundaries.

Astronomers generally use the Latin names of constellations. Although a large number of bright stars have proper names, many of them Arabic in origin, astronomers indicate stars by the letters of the Greek alphabet, followed by the Latin genitive (possessive) form of the name of the constellation to which the star belongs. This method was introduced by Johann Bayer, the publisher of *Uranometria*, a star atlas. The brightest star is designated with an {α}, the second brightest star with a {β}, and so on. For example, the brightest star in the Great Dog (Canis Major), Sirius, is {α} Canis Majoris. The second brightest star in Orion, Rigel, is called {β} Orionis.

As there are more stars in a constellation than Greek letters, fainter stars are indicated by a number in a catalog compiled by John Flamsteed (1646–1720), the astronomer royal of England. Variable stars often are indicated by one or two capital letters between R and Z; for example RR Lyrae.

A CONSTELLATION *can change shape as its stars move in different directions.*

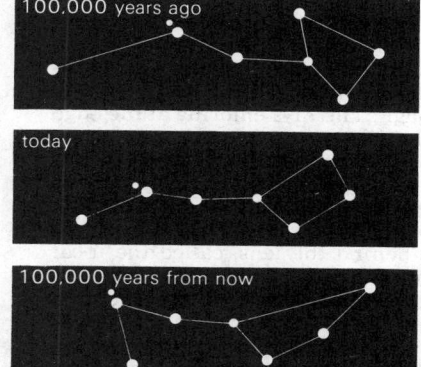

100,000 years ago

today

100,000 years from now

PETER LOEWER

Astronomical Instruments

Astronomers performed observations until the 17th century with the eye alone. They determined the positions of celestial objects using angle-measuring instruments, such as quadrants or sextants. Tycho Brahe, the last observational astronomer before the era of the telescope, attained an accuracy of one arc minute with his great mural quadrant. Brahe's observations were so accurate that Kepler could deduce from them his famous laws of planetary orbits. Perhaps more than in any other science, advances in astronomy have been the direct consequence of the introduction of one new instrument: the telescope.

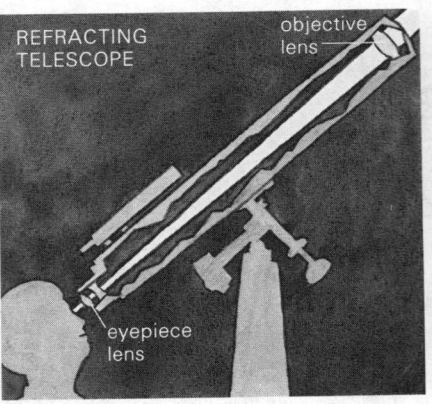 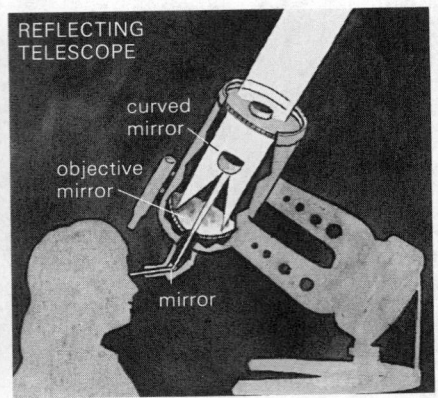

ALL OPTICAL TELESCOPES *are either* refracting, *which use lenses to magnify an object, or* reflecting, *which use mirrors to magnify.*

Telescopes

When Galileo directed his telescope toward the Milky Way, he saw that it consisted of numerous stars. He also noticed that he could see many more stars than with the naked eye. With this he had discovered the most important aspect of the telescope to astronomy, its great light-gathering power. Because the objective lens is much larger than the pupil of an eye, it can capture much more light from the star in its focus than the eye on the retina.

The second important aspect of the telescope is its magnifying power. But the magnifying power is useful only for the observation of extended objects. In 1610 Galileo already had noted that when he pointed his telescope at the fixed stars themselves, they remained pointlike objects. The stars are so distant that even in the largest telescopes, they remain pointlike, although images have been obtained of very large and close stars using a technique called *speckle interferometry* (see page 224).

Refracting telescopes. The telescopes built by Galileo were refracting telescopes, consisting of a tube and two lenses: a large objective lens and an eyepiece. The objective is a convex lens. When light from a star reaches the lens, it bends slightly toward the optical axis as it passes through. The rays entering at the edge of the lens are refracted at a larger angle than those closer to the center of the lens. The curvature of the lens is designed so that all the light passing through the lens is bent toward a single spot behind the lens, called the focal point or focus. The distance between the objective lens and the focus is called the focal length. An observer sees the image formed by the objective in the focal plane with the eyepiece, which works like a magnifying glass.

The objective lens in early telescopes was a single lens. Since glass bends light of different colors differently, the objective lens will focus red light, for example, at a different point from blue light. This effect, called *chromatic aberration,* degrades the quality of images that can be obtained with a single-lens objective. Isaac Newton, while experimenting with the refraction of light in prisms, discovered this effect. Believing that chromatic aberration was unavoidable in refracting telescopes, Newton in 1668 designed a reflecting telescope. Instead of a glass lens, a concave mirror gathers the incoming light and focuses it at the focal plane. Because a mirror reflects light of any color in exactly in the same way, reflecting telescopes are free of chromatic aberration.

In 1729 the inventor Chester More Hall (1703–1771) discovered that by combining two lenses of different types of glass, it is possible to construct an objective lens for a refracting telescope in which chromatic aberration is largely eliminated. Such lenses are called *achromatic.*

Because large lenses were easier to produce than large mirrors, most of the telescopes used throughout the 18th and 19th centuries were refractors. The world's largest refractor was completed in 1897 at Yerkes Observatory in southern Wisconsin. The telescope, still in use, has an objective lens of 102 centimeters (40 inches) in diameter.

The construction of lenses larger than one meter (three feet) in diameter becomes impracticable because the required thickness of glass results in too much light absorption and the large lenses distort under their own weight. It is easier now to construct large telescope mirrors. Since the end of the 19th century, most large telescopes are reflectors.

Reflecting telescopes. The reflecting telescope was invented independently by the mathematician James Gregory (1638–1675) in Scotland in 1663 and the physician N. Cassegrain (fl. 17th century) in France in 1672. In a reflecting telescope, the light from a celestial body passes down a tube to the surface of a mirror mounted at the bottom of the tube. The surface of the mirror is ground to a precisely convex shape, which reflects the light back up the tube toward the prime focus, where all the light passes through a single point.

Because the focus is directly in the path of the incoming light, the image at the focus usually cannot be observed directly. The light is reflected by a secondary mirror inside the tube to bring the focus to a convenient location.

Newton used a flat secondary mirror to reflect the light to one side of the tube. In a Newtonian reflector, the eyepiece is mounted on the telescope tube at a right angle to the incoming light from a star. Cassegrain used a convex secondary mirror to reflect the light back through a circular opening in the center of the primary mirror; thus, the eyepiece was placed behind the mirror.

In very large reflecting telescopes, such as the Hale telescope at Mount Palomar Observatory, the eyepiece or a photographic plate can be placed in a cage with room for the observer at the prime focus inside the tube itself. Though the observer's cage blocks off a small amount of the incoming light, this does not interfere with the quality of the telescope.

Multiple-mirror designs. The primary mirrors of telescopes can be made much larger than objective lenses; however, problems arise in building telescopes with mirrors larger than six meters (19.5 feet) in diameter. The mirrors become deformed by their own weight.

FOUNDATIONS OF ASTRONOMY

One solution to this problem is to combine a number of smaller mirrors in one telescope. For example, the multiple-mirror telescope built in 1979 on Mount Hopkins, near Tucson, Arizona, consists of six 1.8-meter (72-inch) mirrors that are kept in alignment by a laser beam; the mirrors work as one. Together they have the same light-gathering capacity as a 4.5-meter (177-inch) mirror.

Angular resolution.
The diameter of the objective lens or of the primary mirror is called the *aperture* of the telescope. A large aperture increases the light-gathering power of the telescope. Very faint stars and nebulas invisible with small telescopes become visible with telescopes of large apertures.

Another important specification of a telescope is the degree of sharpness with which it can render images. The sharpness of an image can be expressed as the resolving power, or *angular resolution,* of the telescope. Angular resolution is defined as the angle between two points that still can be seen as distinct. The smaller this angle, the sharper the image.

The human eye has an angular resolution of one arc minute, meaning that with the unaided eye, humans can tell apart two stars that are separated by one arc minute. Tycho Brahe's measurements of planetary positions were that accurate.

The Hale telescope, which has an aperture of 500 centimeters (about 16.5 feet), in theory has an angular resolution of 0.02 arc second. In principle, it should be possible to resolve directly the images of a few very large stars, such as Betelgeuze (Alpha Orionis), which has an angular diameter that varies between 0.034 and 0.047 arc seconds. But turbulence in the atmosphere limits the angular resolution to about one arc second. The Hale telescope illustrates the limit in performance that can be attained with an Earth-based telescope.

Atmospheric turbulence causes the twinkling of stars. In contrast to stars, planets do not twinkle. Because of their great distance from Earth, stars are pointlike, so their images are affected by small turbulent elements that are only a few inches across. This causes their images not only to move quickly in all directions, but also to change rapidly in size.

Telescopes in space.
Earth's atmosphere spoils the quality of the images of celestial objects. It also absorbs or blocks large parts of the radiation that reaches Earth, especially infrared and ultraviolet light. For this reason, astronomers have placed telescopes for observation in the infrared or ultraviolet spectrum in orbits around Earth.

The largest telescope to be placed in orbit during the late 1980's is expected to be the space telescope, also called the Hubble telescope, scheduled to be launched by NASA aboard the space shuttle. Although the aperture of the Hubble telescope is less than half that of the Hale telescope—2.4 meters (94 inches)—it will enable astronomers to take full advantage of its angular resolution of 0.05 arc seconds, resulting in pictures approximately 20 times sharper than those obtainable with the Hale telescope.

Magnifying power.
The magnifying power of a telescope depends on its focal length. When a telescope is pointed at an object with a visible angular diameter, such as the moon or a nebula, the size of the image at the focus depends on the distance from the lens or mirror to the focus. If the focal length of a telescope is 3 meters (10 feet), the image of the moon at the focal plane will be about 2.5 centimeters (1 inch) across, but it would be 25 centimeters (10 inches) across if the focal length were 30 meters (100 feet). Therefore, telescopes used for observing or photographing the surface features of the sun, moon, and planets are always long-focal-length instruments.

Telescope mounts.
Two types of telescope mountings exist: altazimuth and equatorial. In an *altazimuth* mount, the telescope is free to move up and down or horizontally on two axes. One is perpendicular and the other is parallel to Earth's surface.

THE HALE TELESCOPE (below) *is one of the most powerful telescopes on Earth. However, turbulence in the atmosphere limits the resolution the telescope can achieve. The Hubble telescope* (above) *should solve this problem when it is placed in orbit above Earth.*

The tracking of celestial objects requires the simultaneous control of two drive motors, now simplified by the use of computers.

In an *equatorial* mount, the telescope is free to move about the polar axis, an axis parallel to the axis of Earth's rotation. When observing a specific star, the telescope is first set to its *declination,* a position corresponding to the star's distance above or below the plane of Earth's equator. Once the telescope is pointed at the star under investigation, it can track the star by slowly rotating about the polar axis, compensating for the rotation of Earth.

Solar telescopes.

For observation of the sun, astronomers use special telescopes with long focal lengths. Because of their lengths, these telescopes remain fixed in a vertical or inclined position while the image of the sun is projected on the telescope's objective by a *coelostat.* A coelostat consists of a mobile and a fixed mirror; the mobile mirror is clockwork-driven and follows the sun throughout the day.

Photographic processes and special detectors.

The photographic plate was introduced quite early as an astronomical tool. The image recorded on a photographic emulsion represents all the light accumulated over any length of time, often several hours, provided that the telescope accurately tracks a star throughout the exposure. The intensity of the image on the photographic emulsion builds up as long as it is exposed to light, making the faintest objects in the sky visible. Thus, stars and galaxies can be recorded that could never otherwise be observed visually.

Electronic images.

Even more sensitive than photographic emulsion are the recently introduced charge-coupled devices (CCDs) and charge-intensified devices (CIDs). These devices are light-sensitive silicon chips.

CCDs detect up to 70 percent of the photons falling on them, while photographic emulsions have an efficiency of only 1 percent. Besides a higher sensitivity, these devices are capable of dealing with much bigger differences in light intensities. The lowest and highest intensities that can be recorded can differ by a factor of 10,000. This means that these devices can record, for example, simultaneously faint parts of a nebula as well as parts that are 10,000 times more luminous. For photographic film, this factor is limited to 100.

Images obtained from CCDs and CIDs can be studied and manipulated using a computer with image-processing capabilities. Because the cathode-ray tubes used in the visual display units of computers also are limited in showing relative light intensities,

 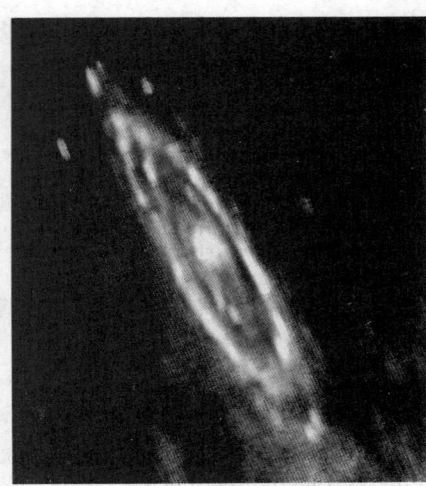

THESE IMAGES OF THE ANDROMEDA GALAXY *were made in the visible* (left) *and the infrared* (right) *spectra, providing different kinds of data.*

image-processing techniques are valuable in enabling astronomers to display just the intensity ranges they desire.

Photometry.

Accurate measurement of the brightness, or magnitude, of stars is of prime importance to astronomers. A characteristic of photographic emulsion is that it renders a star (which in reality is pointlike) as a small disk because of the diffusion of light within the light-sensitive layer. The size of the disk depends directly on the star's brightness. An astronomer can measure the brightnesses of stars by comparing the sizes of their images on a photographic plate with those of the images of certain reference stars whose brightnesses have been determined accurately.

A more precise method of measuring the brightnesses of stars is achieved by photoelectric photometers placed at the focus of the telescope.

Speckle interferometry.

Even the closest stars have apparent diameters that fall within the limits of angular resolution caused by turbulence in the atmosphere. However, this turbulence does not seem to affect images obtained during short exposure times, approximately $\frac{1}{100}$ second. By electronically recording thousands of images and combining them with a computer (speckle interferometry), astronomers have created speckle photographs of a few large nearby stars.

Spectroscopy

The most important source of information about a star is its light spectrum. Isaac Newton was the first to study the spectrum of the light of the sun. He directed a beam of sunlight from a small hole made in window shutters through a glass prism, producing a rainbow spectrum: a band of colors ranging from the red to the blue. Newton then theorized that white light is a mixture of all the colors of the rainbow. In 1802 English chemist and physicist William Wollaston (1766–1828), using a prism that received sunlight through a narrow slit, discovered the dark lines in its spectrum. He believed these lines to be the boundaries between the colors of the spectrum.

In 1814 the German optician Joseph Fraunhofer (1787–1826), analyzing sunlight with a similar setup, observed a large number of dark lines. In 1859 the German physicist Gustav Kirchhoff (1824–1887) noticed that he could observe these dark lines when white light was passed through a gas. He also noticed that when a gas was heated so that it glowed, it would emit a spectrum of narrow bright lines seen against a dark background. But Kirchhoff found that gases under high pressures, liquids, and solids emit a continuous spectrum when brought to high temperatures; that is, a spectrum containing the colors of the rainbow without any dark or bright lines. Low-pressure gases that are heated or through which an electric current is passed in the form of an arc or spark emit a spectrum of bright lines against a dark background. These bright lines are called *emission lines.* When white light (light of all wavelengths) is passed through a relatively cool gas, only dark lines appear in the spectrum. These dark lines are called *absorption lines.* The gas absorbs the light selectively at certain wavelengths; the obtained spectrum is called an absorption spectrum. (For more information on emission and absorption lines, see CHEMISTRY AND PHYSICS volume, page 466.)

Kirchhoff established that these *Fraunhofer lines* were the fingerprints of elements present in the gas under observation. Each element produces a number of absorption or emission lines at certain wavelengths specific to it. By studying the absorption lines in the solar spectrum, Kirchhoff and the German chemist Robert Wilhelm Bunsen (1811–1899) were able to identify a number of elements in the solar atmosphere. Kirchhoff completed the first map of the solar spectrum in 1862.

Spectra. The spectrum of a celestial body provides us with information on chemical composition and many other properties of celestial bodies, such as the presence of magnetic fields, temperature, and velocity in relation to Earth. Thus, the spectroscope became the most important instrument of the optical astronomer. But not only do optical spectra form invaluable sources of information, so also do spectra in electromagnetic radiation of other wavelengths, such as ultraviolet, infrared, and radio waves.

The Doppler effect. Just as the pitch of a sound source changes when the source (for example, a train or airplane) moves toward or away from a listener, so does the wavelength of light waves change when a light source moves toward or away from a viewer at high velocity (see CHEMISTRY AND PHYSICS volume, page 449). When the light source is moving away, its light becomes shifted to longer wavelengths; that is, the red end of the spectrum (red shift). Light of sources moving toward us are shifted toward the blue end of the spectrum.

Astronomers can detect these small shifts in the spectra of celestial bodies by comparing the spectra with spectra photographed on the same film.

The determination of red shifts in the spectra of galaxies has played a key role in establishing that the universe is expanding. Doppler shifts also are used for measuring local velocities on celestial objects, such as the velocities of moving gas masses on the sun.

Zeeman effect. The Dutch physicist Pieter Zeeman (1865–1943) discovered in 1897 that the spectral lines of a gas placed in a magnetic field are split. In 1908 the American astronomer George Ellery Hale (1868–1938) discovered split Fraunhofer lines in the spectra of sunspots, proving that sunspots are magnetic phenomena.

Electromagnetic Spectrum

Light is an electromagnetic wave, as are radio waves, infrared radiation, ultraviolet radiation, x-rays, and gamma rays. These forms of radiation differ from each other only in their wavelengths, which can be several miles for radio waves to 10^{-11} centimeters (cm) for gamma rays. Under the rubric *electromagnetic spectrum* we place the entire range of electromagnetic radiation between those two extremes. For more information on the electromagnetic spectrum, see CHEMISTRY AND PHYSICS, pages 459–460.

Absorption by the atmosphere. Although a good deal of infrared and ultraviolet light from the sun reaches Earth, most of it is absorbed by Earth's atmosphere. The atmosphere is transparent only to visible light and to some of the infrared radiation and most radio waves. Ozone and other components of the atmosphere absorb ultraviolet radiation and x-rays almost completely, while water vapor and oxygen absorb large parts of infrared radiation and radio waves at wavelengths shorter than 1 millimeter.

The regions in the spectrum where the atmosphere is transparent are called *windows.* The radio window is largest. Radiation with wavelengths between 2 centimeters and 30 meters passes almost unhindered. Radio waves with wavelengths between 30 and 100 meters are partially reflected by the ionosphere, while waves above 100 meters are reflected completely.

Radio astronomy. Galileo's telescope revolutionized astronomy. Another breakthrough in astronomy was brought about by the introduction of

sensitive radio technology. The two major discoveries in radio astronomy —the discovery in 1931 that the Milky Way transmits radio waves and, in 1965, of the existence of cosmic background radiation—were the result of attempts by engineers and physicists at Bell Laboratories to pinpoint the sources of interference that disturb radio communications.

Between 1928 and 1930, the radio engineer Karl Jansky (1905–1949) was assigned by Bell Laboratories to track down the source of radio static that interfered with shortwave communications. By using a rotatable directional antenna, he found that the static came from one area in the sky, the center of the Milky Way galaxy.

From World War II, radio astronomy developed rapidly, taking advantage of the newly developed radar technology. (The first radio telescopes were the famous Wurzburg antennae, high-precision radar antennae developed by the Germans during the war.) A typical modern radio telescope consists of a huge metal paraboloid-shaped dish that functions like a mirror and an antenna placed in the focus of the dish. Because radio telescopes gather electromagnetic radiation of much longer wavelengths than light, the requirements for the exact shape of the dish are much less demanding than for the mirrors of an optical telescope. Therefore, the diameter of a radio telescope with a mobile dish can be quite large, as much as 100 meters (300 feet). The largest single-dish radio telescope is at Arecibo, Puerto Rico. It consists of a fixed metal mesh reflector, 304.8 meters (1000 feet) in diameter, suspended horizontally in a circular valley. The receiving antenna is suspended in its focus by a system of cables.

Radio interferometers. Since the angular resolution of a telescope is directly proportional to the wavelength

---

RED SHIFT

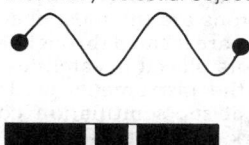

stationary celestial objects

normal spectograph

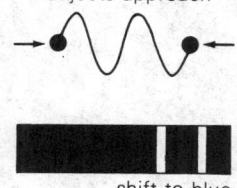

objects approach

shift to blue

objects part

shift to red

PETER LOEWER

A spectrograph provides information about the composition of celestial bodies by producing lines that mark the frequencies corresponding to particular elements found in the body being observed. Astronomers compare the pattern of these lines with reference patterns produced in a lab to determine the composition of the body.

If a celestial body is not moving toward or away from Earth, its spectral lines will match up closely to those produced artificially. If it is, however, the movement can cause a shift in the lines because of the Doppler effect. If the body is moving toward the observer, the light waves become compressed, changing their frequency

and shifting the object's light and the pattern of its spectral lines toward the blue end of the light spectrum. If the body is moving away from the observer on Earth, the light waves become elongated, shifting the spectral lines toward the red end of the spectrum.

it gathers, the angular resolution of a single radio telescope is much inferior to that of an optical telescope, ten arc seconds at best as compared with one arc second for the best optical telescopes. But the angular resolution of a telescope is inversely proportional to its aperture; that is, the diameter of the primary mirror or dish. Therefore, the larger the aperture of a radio telescope, the better the angular resolution. Radio astronomers have employed a simple trick to increase synthetically the aperture of a radio telescope. Two identical radio telescopes, both pointing exactly in the same direction but 1000 meters (3000 feet) apart, will together have the same angular resolution as a giant radio telescope with a dish 1000 meters in diameter.

A setup of two or more radio telescopes operating in tandem is called a radio interferometer. The distance between the two farthest telescopes is the *baseline.* The baseline corresponds, in matters of angular resolution, to the aperture of the radio telescope.

The largest and most sensitive radio telescope in the world is the Very Large Array telescope on the Plains of San Augustin in New Mexico, operated by the National Radio Astronomy Observatory. It consists of 27 movable antennae, each 26 meters (85 feet) in diameter, placed in a Y-shaped pattern.

The baseline (distance between the two farthest dish antennae) of the Very Large Array is nearly 30 kilometers (18.6 miles). The angular resolution of this system is 0.2 arc seconds, better than the resolution achieved with any optical telescope.

Even greater resolution can be achieved by combining existing radio telescopes at different places in the world. This technique is known as *very long baseline interferometry.* An international setup with telescopes in North America, Europe, and the Soviet Union achieved an angular resolution of 0.001 arc second.

By scanning an object, radio astronomers can construct an electronic image similar to the ones obtained by charge-coupled devices (CCDs) in optical telescopes. These images can be processed electronically, for example, by using colors to represent differing intensities.

Telescopes in space.
Astronomers have tried to counteract the effects of the atmosphere on observations by moving their instruments as high as possible into the atmosphere. The first observations in the space age were made shortly after World War II with instruments placed in V-2 rockets recovered from Germany.

THE IRAS, or Infrared Astronomy Satellite, scans space for sources that emit infrared rays.

During subsequent years astronomers have also made observations from manned space stations, such as Skylab, and have launched a number of satellites dedicated to astronomical observations.

Infrared astronomy. The transition between radio waves and infrared astronomy is not well defined. For example, observations at 0.5 millimeter wavelength can be made with radio telescopes or with special infrared detectors placed in the focus of optical telescopes.

The atmosphere does not absorb all the infrared radiation, and some observations in the window of 1 to 20 microns (10.000–200.000 Å) are possible from dry observatories at high altitudes. Since much of our galaxy is obscured by enormous interstellar dust clouds, one great advantage of infrared radiation is that it passes easily through these dust clouds, making visible large parts of the galaxy.

X-ray astronomy. In recent years, several of the important discoveries in astronomy, such as possible *black holes,* have been made with x-rays. The atmosphere entirely absorbs x-rays (rays with wavelengths between 0.1 and 100 Å); thus, all observations have been made with instruments aboard rockets and satellites.

Several dedicated x-ray satellites have been launched during the past years. The first one, *Uhuru* (the Swahili word for freedom), was launched in 1970. It discovered 339 new x-ray sources in the sky. The Einstein Observatory (HEAO-2), launched in November, 1978, was equipped with an x-ray telescope with angular resolution of two arc seconds.

Gamma-ray astronomy. Gamma-ray photons are the most energetic of all. They are located through the use of detectors placed in satellites that resemble the instruments used by particle physicists: scintillation counters and spark chambers. The first gamma-ray pulses from space were detected by a series of Vela satellites. These satellites were designed to monitor nuclear explosions on Earth (a nuclear explosion produces a strong burst of gamma rays). By using triangulation methods (simultaneous detection by at least three satellites), the extraterrestrial origin of the pulses could be established. Several astronomical spacecraft, such as the Einstein Observatory and the Pioneer–Venus Orbiter, have been equipped with gamma-ray detectors.

DANNER/PHOTO RESEARCHERS

THE VERY LARGE ARRAY of radio telescopes in Socorro, New Mexico, comprises 27 dish antennae mounted on railroad tracks.

EXPLORATION OF THE UNIVERSE

The study of astronomy and astrophysics can be divided into a number of topics. *Planetary astronomy* deals with the observation and study of the planets. It also includes the study of satellites of planets and other objects in the solar system. The sun and the stars are the subjects of *stellar astronomy. Galactic astronomy* is the study of all objects in the galaxy, including stellar clusters and galactic nebulas. *Extragalactic astronomy* is the youngest branch of astronomy. It was born when powerful telescopes became available during the 1920's and astronomers dis-

DUST ORBITING THE SUN *scatters its rays to produce the zodiacal light.*

covered that the universe not only consisted of the Milky Way galaxy but of millions of other galaxies as well.

Radio telescopes became important tools for extragalactic astronomers. Quasars, which are the most distant objects from Earth known in the universe, were discovered with these instruments. Extragalactic astronomy is closely related to *cosmology,* the study of the creation and evolution of the universe. By observing distant galaxies and quasars, astronomers have increased their understanding of the overall structure of the universe.

The Planets

The sun, moon, and planets are our closest neighbors. Their exploration began with the invention of the telescope early in the 17th century. Knowledge of the planetary system increased steadily with the perfection of telescopes, but it made an enormous leap forward when astronomers sent space probes into the solar system to investigate the moon and the planets from close by.

Discovery of New Planets

When in 1609 Galileo directed his telescope at the planets, only Mercury, Venus, Mars, Jupiter, and Saturn were known. No one suspected that there might be more planets until the English astronomer William Herschel (1738–1822) discovered Uranus during one of his systematic surveys of the sky. On March 19, 1781, he observed an object in the constellation Gemini that did not have the appearance of a star. At first he believed it to be a comet because when he observed the object four days later, it had moved against the background of stars. However, a study of its orbit showed it to be almost circular instead of elongated. The object thus had to be a planet.

Before Herschel's discovery, the planet had been recorded as a star 20 times by a number of observers, including the English astronomers John

Flamsteed (1646–1720) in 1690 and James Bradley (1692–1762) in 1753. With these observations astronomers could map the orbit of Uranus. By 1820 the observed position of Uranus differed markedly from the calculated orbit. Even precise determinations of its position after 1781 could not remedy the discrepancy between observed and calculated positions. In 1845 astronomers John Adams (1819–1892) in England and Urbain Joseph Le Verrier (1811–1877) in France independently calculated that the anomalies in the orbit of Uranus could be explained by the gravitational force exerted on it by a planet having an orbit beyond its own. J.G. Galle (1812–1910), the head of the Berlin Observatory, discovered Neptune in 1846 after receiving a letter from Le Verrier indicating the planet's position.

The perturbations of Neptune largely explained the irregularities of the orbit of Uranus, but not completely. Astronomers started looking for another, still unknown planet that might provide the explanation. American astronomer Percival Lowell (1855–1916), who had carried out the calculations predicting the existence of a so-called planet X, began searching for the planet at the observatory he had founded in 1894 in Flagstaff, Arizona. Clyde Tombaugh, an assistant, found Pluto on March 13, 1930. He used a *blink comparator* or *blink microscope,* an optical device that enables one to see two photographs in quick, alternating succession. By comparing

two photographs of the same part of the sky taken on different nights, Tombaugh could spot objects that move against the fixed background of stars: they appear to jump back and forth.

Pluto takes 248.5 years to revolve once around the sun. Only a small part of its orbit has been tracked in the last 60 years. Again, Pluto's orbit deviates from the predicted one, so it is possible that its path is perturbed by a tenth planet.

GALILEO *made important contributions to our knowledge of the solar system.*

Planetary Orbits

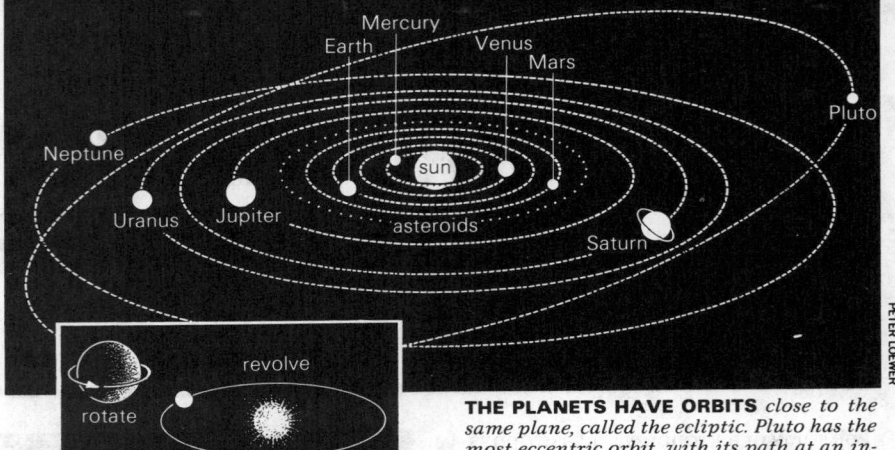

Besides the sun and the planets, several other types of celestial bodies make up the solar system: satellites of planets, asteroids, comets, meteoroids, and interplanetary dust. All the planets move in almost circular elliptical orbits around the sun. Seen from the "north side" of the solar system (that is, from the direction to which the North Pole of Earth points), the planets revolve counterclockwise. They all move approximately in the same plane of orbit as Earth. Because of this, when seen from Earth, all the planets occupy positions near the ecliptic.

The planets rotate on their own axes counterclockwise, or in a *prograde* direction, except for Venus and Uranus, whose rotations are defined as *retrograde.*

Astronomers use *astronomical units* to indicate distances in the solar system. One astronomical unit (A.U.) is defined as the average distance between Earth and the sun. The internationally accepted value of 1 A.U. is 149,790,000 kilometers (92,870,000 miles).

Titius-Bode law. In 1766 the German astronomer Johann Daniel Titius (1729–1796) discovered a simple mathematical relationship between the distances between the sun and the planets. The relationship later was published by the German astronomer Elert Bode (1747–1828); hence, it is sometimes referred to as the Bode law or the Titius-Bode law. It states, to a series of fours, add the number three to the second four; six to the third; twelve to the fourth; and so on, doubling the number each time. By dividing each of the sums by ten, the result is a series of numbers corresponding approximately to the distance between each planet (except Neptune and Pluto) and the sun in astronomical units.

No theoretical basis has ever been found for this law. Unlike other relationships, it does not follow from either the law of gravitation or the laws of motion. In addition, it cannot be applied strictly, since Neptune's orbit clearly does not follow the law.

In 1781, when Uranus was discovered in an orbit predicted by Bode's law, a search was begun for a missing planet at 2.8 A.U., between the orbits of Mars and Jupiter. Astronomers discovered hundreds of tiny planets, or asteroids, orbiting in the region, possibly remnants of one or more larger bodies.

Origin of the solar system.

The study of the origin of the solar system often is termed *cosmogony* (in contrast with *cosmology,* which refers to the study of the origin and evolution of the universe in its entirety). Several different types of theories to explain the origin of the solar system have been proposed:

1. *Catastrophe theories,* which involve catastrophic events such as a close encounter between the sun and a passing star or the explosion of a nearby supernova.

2. *Capture theories,* which state that the sun captured the planets or planetary matter in its gravitational field.

3. *Evolutionary theories,* which propose that the whole solar system has evolved from a slowly condensing nebula.

The first two types of theories have been largely rejected because they are too improbable or because they can explain only part of the known properties of the solar system.

A theory of the origin and evolution of the solar system has to satisfy two requirements. First, the theory must explain the dynamic (motion of the

THE PLANETS HAVE ORBITS *close to the same plane, called the ecliptic. Pluto has the most eccentric orbit, with its path at an inclination of about 17° to the ecliptic.*

planets and sun), physical, and chemical properties of the solar system. Second, it has to explain the mechanisms for formation of planets from a contracting nebula.

There are nine important properties that the theory has to account for:

1. All planets orbit around the sun in almost circular orbits and in planes very close to the plane of the ecliptic (the plane that contains Earth's orbit).

2. The axis of the sun's rotation is approximately perpendicular to the plane of the ecliptic.

3. The planets all revolve around the sun in the same direction, which is also the direction of the sun's rotation.

4. The sun possesses more than 99 percent of the mass of the total system.

5. The planets possess the preponderant angular momentum of the system. (The sun rotates slowly in relation to the revolution and rotation of the planets.)

6. The majority of the planets rotate in a prograde direction around their axes.

7. Almost all the satellites of planets revolve around their primaries in the same direction as the primaries rotate around their axes.

8. A host of smaller objects, such as comets and meteoroids, often of low density, with orbits that are elongated, exist. The inclination of the orbits to the plane of the ecliptic varies widely.

9. The chemical composition of planets close to the sun (terrestrial planets) is different from those that are distant from the sun (Jovian planets).

These major properties of the solar system must be explained in a way consistent with the estimated age of the solar system (4.6 billion years).

Past theories. One of the earliest theories, the *nebular hypothesis,* proposed by the German philosopher Immanuel Kant (1724–1804) and French mathematician Pierre Simon Laplace (1749–1827), stated that the sun condensed from a primordial gas cloud. As it shrank, it spun faster and faster, throwing off rings of material from its equatorial regions. These rings were thought to have condensed into the planets. This theory is untenable for two reasons. First, the rings would disperse rather than condense; second, the sun would still be spinning rapidly.

RELATIVE SIZES OF THE PLANETS (diameter in miles)

Mercury (3030)
Venus (7517)
Earth (7921)
Mars (4215)
asteroid belt
sun
Jupiter (88,803)
Saturn (74,520)
Uranus (32,168)
Neptune (30,739)
Pluto (2173)

The English theoretical physicist James H. Jeans (1877–1946) supported a catastrophe theory in 1917. He proposed that the sun once had a close encounter with another star, causing huge tidal effects on its surface, pulling long filaments of material from it that later condensed to form the planets. The major objection to this theory is that such a close encounter would be an extremely rare event since the stars are so far from each other. Astronomers have estimated that no more than ten such encounters have occurred throughout the entire lifetime of the galaxy (15 to 18 billion years). This theory also is unable to account for the large angular momentum of the planets.

Present theories. Most current explanations of the origins of the solar system are evolutionary theories that revert to the original nebular hypothesis, but with several important differences. These models all postulate a large nebula, or cloud, containing much more material than now constitutes the solar system. Such parameters as initial mass, temperature, and composition of the nebula may differ, so astronomers feed into a computer different values of these parameters to test the various models.

The slowly rotating cloud contracts because of the mutual attraction between the particles making up the cloud. This process is termed *gravitational collapse* and is believed generally to be the initial stage of star formation. Because it preserves its angular momentum, the rotation speeds up. (The phenomenon is similar to that of a figure skater spinning faster and faster as he brings his arms and legs closer to the axis of rotation.) The rotation causes the cloud to flatten. Because gas heats up when it is compressed, the center region of the nebula, where the gravitational collapse is the strongest, begins heating up and forming the sun. Because of the increase in temperature, however, the contraction of the sun stops and it remains surrounded by a less dense cloud. The material in this cloud begins to condense, forming small solid aggregations circling the sun.

It is in this stage that the separation may have occurred to cause the difference in chemical composition between the terrestrial and the Jovian planets. Materials that are solid at high temperatures, such as iron, nickel, and magnesium silicate, condense in the hotter areas of the cloud, close to the sun. The volatile compounds, such as hydrogen and helium, condense at greater distances from the sun, forming the matter of the Jovian planets.

The small solid aggregates begin to form larger ones under the influence of gravitation and collisions. These are the *protoplanets*. Volatile materials, such as hydrogen and helium, are driven off by the hot sun from terrestrial planets, while Jovian planets keep

MODERN THEORY *proposes that a cloud of matter condensed to form the sun and planets.*

accreting these compounds, thus increasing their mass and size.

None of the evolutionary models offers a satisfactory explanation of why the sun has retained so small an angular momentum. A possible solution was given by the English astrophysicist Fred Hoyle, who assumed that a large proportion of the initial cloud was ionized, forming a plasma. It is known that magnetic field lines become "frozen" in a plasma, so it was postulated that the rotation of the sun became coupled by its magnetic field to the surrounding cloud, speeding up the nebula's rotation and slowing down the sun's rotation.

A discovery in favor of the nebular hypothesis of planet formation is that of the *disk star,* a star surrounded by a disklike structure with a diameter 20 times that of the star. Astronomers at the Steward Observatory of the University of Arizona made the discovery in 1977.

Terrestrial Planets

Because of certain similarities in their physical characteristics, the planets are divided into *terrestrial planets* and *Jovian planets.* The terrestrial planets, Mercury, Venus, Earth, and Mars, are rocky in nature, relatively small, and have high densities. Only Venus has a dense atmosphere. The Jovian planets, Jupiter, Saturn, Uranus, Neptune, and Pluto are, with the exception of Pluto, quite large, with dense atmospheres and low densities.

Mercury. Mercury is the planet closest to the sun. It has almost no atmosphere; its surface temperature is 440K (332°F). The planet orbits around the sun with a period of 88 terrestrial days. By bouncing radar signals on its surface, astronomers have measured a rotational period of 59 terrestrial days.

Because the rotational period is two-thirds that of the orbital period, the apparent rotation of the planet, as seen from the sun, is much slower. A day on Mercury lasts 176 terrestrial days.

The planet was explored in March, 1974, by the *Mariner 10* probe, which performed three flybys and returned images of its surface to Earth. Except for many elongated ridges, Mercury's surface features resemble the craters, basins, and plains found on the moon. The *Mariner* probe also discovered that Mercury has an extremely tenuous atmosphere and a weak magnetic field, although stronger than the magnetic fields of Venus and Mars. This field hints of the existence of a large molten iron core.

Venus. Venus, whose diameter is 12,104 kilometers (7516 miles), is about 644 kilometers (400 miles) smaller in diameter than Earth and nearly as massive and dense. Like Earth, Venus has an atmosphere; its cloud cover has long been known.

The planet revolves around the sun in 224.7 terrestrial days. Its rotation is very slow—243 days—and retrograde. The Venusian day is equal to 118 terrestrial days.

Exploration. Venus is the closest planet to Earth and the brightest object in the sky. For this reason, Earth and Venus often were considered to be sister planets. Spacecraft exploration has changed this view. Early in the space programs of the Soviet Union and the United States, Venus probes were launched. The probes either flew by Venus or landed on its surface. The

THIS IMAGE OF MERCURY *is a composite of a series of photographs.*

Mariner 10 probe flew by Venus in 1973. A small radiometer aboard measured the surface temperature at more than 400°C (750°F).

Beginning on February 12, 1969, the Soviet Union launched a series of Venera probes that landed on the planet's surface. The first probes of the series were not designed to withstand high external pressures and were crushed by the planet's atmosphere before they could send pictures. *Venera 7* measured a pressure of 90 atmospheres (1 atmosphere equals the pressure on Earth's surface) and functioned for 20 minutes before being destroyed by heat. *Venera 8* operated for 40 minutes, and *Venera 9* returned the first pictures of the surface of Venus on October 22, 1975. *Venera 10* landed three days later and returned pictures from an area 2000 kilometers (1242 miles) from the landing site of *Venera 9*. The images showed a landscape resembling that of Mars: rocks and pebbles and traces of erosion.

The Venusian atmosphere consists almost entirely (97 percent) of carbon dioxide (CO_2), some nitrogen and water, and minute amounts of hydrogen chloride (HC1) and hydrogen fluoride (HF). The atmosphere absorbs a large fraction of the infrared radiation from the planet's surface, causing the heating of the atmosphere, known as the greenhouse effect.

The cloud cover is at an altitude of 50 kilometers (31 miles) and consists of droplets of sulfuric acid. The upper clouds move at very high speeds, 350 kilometers (224 miles) per hour, and circle the planet in four days.

On December 4, 1978, NASA launched the *Pioneer Venus* into an orbit around the planet. *Pioneer Venus* studied the atmosphere and ionosphere of the planet and mapped its surface with a radar altimeter. It was placed in such an orbit that it mapped 93 percent of the surface of Venus in the 243 days it took to complete the

THE SWIRLING CLOUDS of *Venus are seen here in an image taken from Mariner 10.*

scan. The planet was shown to be very flat compared with Earth. About 60 percent of the surface has variations of less than half a mile in height, and nearly 80 percent has variations of less than a mile. There is a large mountain, named Maxwell, that is 11 kilometers (7 miles) high, and two highland regions, named Ishtar and Aphrodite.

In 1982 the Soviet Union landed two probes on Venus. *Venera 13* and *Venera 14* sent back to Earth the most sophisticated and detailed analyses of the surface of Venus to date. The probes also sent back the first color photographs of Venus. Analyses of the soil of Venus showed that its chemical composition is similar to that of volcanic rock on Earth.

Earth. Earth is by far the most interesting celestial body of the solar system. Its geology, biosphere, and other features, including its position in the universe, are discussed elsewhere (see volume 9, EARTH SCIENCE).

The moon. Except for Earth, the moon is the most extensively explored object in the solar system. Twelve American astronauts have landed on the moon, performing experiments and returning a total of 382 kilograms (842 pounds) of rock. Three Soviet Luna spacecraft have brought back 310 grams (11 ounces) of soil.

The moon's orbital period is 28 days. It also rotates around its axis once every 28 days, so one side of the moon is always turned toward Earth.

The side facing Earth consists of two-thirds light colored, highly cratered highlands and one-third dark, fairly smooth, less cratered plains. The plains are sometimes called *maria* because of their resemblance to seas,

TAKEN FROM APOLLO 8, *this photograph shows the moon's cratered surface.*

especially as seen through early telescopes. The far side of the moon consists almost entirely of highlands. The plains were formed by the flooding with lava of lunar basins (depressions). The size of the craters in some cases reaches 1000 kilometers (620 miles) in diameter. The craters are thought to have been formed by the bombardment of the moon by meteorites.

Lunar exploration. During the 1960's the Soviet Union started exploration of the moon's surface with its Luna series of spacecraft. Lunas 4 through 8 attempted lunar landings. *Luna 9,* on February 3, 1966, made the first intact landing on the moon. A panoramic view from its television cameras was relayed to Earth before its batteries ran down. Lunas 10 to 14 were orbiters that measured the lunar magnetic field, radiation from the moon, cosmic ray background, and meteoritic impacts. *Luna 13* also relayed a succession of television pictures.

In July, 1969, while the *Apollo 11* astronauts were on the moon, the Soviet Union put *Luna 15* into lunar orbit to initiate a third, even larger series of Luna spacecraft. In September, 1970, *Luna 16* soft-landed a 4100-pound spacecraft on the moon. Besides carrying a variety of scientific instruments, this craft drilled a 30.48-centimeter (1-foot) core sample of the moon, packaged the 101 grams (3.5 ounces) of material in a sealed container, and launched it back to Soviet territory.

Luna 17 was essentially like *Luna 16,* except that instead of the drilling arm and ascent stage, it carried *Lunokhod 1,* a roving vehicle. The vehicle was directed and operated via radio from a base on Earth. This device, which operated for almost a year, not only revealed lunar features but also took pictures of star fields, measured solar-flare protons, and analyzed the lunar soil for chemical constituents with an x-ray spectrometer.

The United States lunar program started with the eight Pioneer spacecraft launched before 1960, but only one Pioneer was successful in flying past the moon and measuring particles and fields near that body. Nine Rangers were launched in the early 1960's to transmit close-up black and white pictures of the moon before crashing on it; three succeeded. Surveyor spacecraft were designed to soft-land on the moon, relay color photographs, test the soil, and perform chemical analyses of the soil. Five of the seven Surveyors launched in the last half of the 1960's were successful. In 1966–1967, five Lunar Orbiters, all successful, mapped almost all of the lunar surface with detailed photographs from low orbit. Data from the Surveyors and Orbiters helped select landing sites for the teams of Apollo astronauts that landed on the moon. (For information on the Apollo missions, see pages 256–257).

From samples, scientists have determined that the moon's surface contains only igneous rock and no sedimentary rock, indicating that at one time the moon's surface was completely molten and that no seas filled with water ever existed on the moon.

Scientists have found that the moon's gravity is not constant over its surface. Especially in large circular plains, there are *mascons*, concentrations of higher than normal density causing local increases of gravity.

Very little geological activity, such as erosion or eruption, takes place in the lunar crust. Seismographs placed on the moon's surface by the Apollo crews registered "moonquakes" of one or two points on the Richter scale. From the travel times of seismic vibrations, scientists have been able to calculate that the crust is approximately 60 kilometers (37 miles) thick. Underneath the crust is a solid mantle about 1000 kilometers (621 miles) thick. The central core is probably molten: in 1972 seismographs registered only pressure waves from a meteor impact at the opposite side of the moon (transverse waves do not pass through liquid).

Origin of the moon. Radiocarbon dating of soil samples indicates that the moon was created about 4.6 billion years ago, but there is no certainty as to how or where the moon was formed. Many scientists lean to the view that the moon was formed at the same time as Earth and the other planets from one large cloud of dust and gas. A recent proposal, however, suggests that a large planetary body collided with Earth, ejecting material that soon formed the moon.

Mars. With about half the diameter (6788 kilometers or 4218 miles) and a tenth the mass of Earth, Mars has a very thin, transparent atmosphere. Its surface is directly observable. Mars has two small satellites, Phobos, about ten miles in diameter, and Deimos, about six.

Exploration. Space probes have demonstrated that Mars's atmosphere consists mainly of carbon dioxide, with nitrogen making up 2 percent and argon about 1.5 percent. Minute quantities of oxygen and water vapor also are present. The atmospheric pressure is 0.006 times the pressure of Earth's atmosphere.

Magnetometers aboard *Mariner 4,* the first spacecraft to reach Mars, launched on November 28, 1964, and aboard Soviet spacecraft of the Mars series, have measured a very weak magnetic field that may be induced by the solar wind. The absence of a magnetic field supports the theory that Mars lacks a metallic core, even though its density approximates that of Earth.

In 1969 *Mariner 6,* and in 1971–1972 *Mariner 9,* returned large numbers of images of the Martian surface. Mars exhibits at least three distinct types of surface features. It has a cratered terrain that resembles the surface of the moon and that appears to be very old. It has a chaotic terrain that seems more recent, has no craters, but includes a jumble of short ridges and depressions. And it has a third terrain that seems featureless, lacking craters, ridges, or valleys.

Over half of the Martian surface is desertlike, and vast planet-wide dust storms occur. These storms have probably been responsible for the development of the featureless type of terrain. Several very large volcanoes, which may have been active in the early history of Mars, have dark, lavalike floors. The largest volcano, Olympus Mons, is more than 580 kilometers (360 miles) across and is 24.2 kilometers (15 miles) high. It has a caldera 80.5 kilometers (50 miles) across. The planet's crust supports these large volcanoes without any deformation, suggesting to scientists that in certain areas the crust must be from 50 to 200 kilometers (30–125 miles) thicker than Earth's.

Search for life. In 1877 the Italian astronomer Giovanni Schiaparelli (1835

–1910) caused a sensation when he announced his discovery of a network of canals on Mars. Thus was born the theory of Martian inhabitants, the builders of the canals. No canals have been revealed by photographs taken by space probes, but several large canyons are present, suggesting that water, long since escaped from the planet, once flowed on the surface. The polar caps, which show seasonal activity by growing and receding, are composed almost completely of frozen carbon dioxide. The daily variation of surface temperature is about 140°C (284°F). The maximum temperature at the equator is about 17°C (63°F) at noon; it drops to about −118°C (−180°F) at night.

Scientists for a long time have suspected that some form of life may exist on Mars. Experiments aboard two spacecraft, *Viking 1* and *Viking 2,* launched in 1975, showed no trace of life on the Martian surface. Each of the two Viking spacecraft combined a 2356 kilograms (5190-pound) orbiter with a 1180 kilograms (2600-pound) lander. Both made safe landings on Mars in July and August of 1976, after a 10-month, 800-million kilometer (496 million miles) journey. The orbiters photographed the surface and relayed data and commands between the landers and Earth. The landers reported the weather, analyzed the air and soil, photographed the terrain, and performed biological experiments in a search for life.

A seismograph aboard the *Viking 2* lander—the seismograph of *Viking 1* had failed—detected quakes with an intensity of three on the Richter scale. Because at least two seismic detectors are required to investigate the internal structure of the crust, not much can yet be said about the thickness of the crust.

IMAGES OF MARS *show the planet's surface* (below) *and its polar ice cap.*

Scientists estimate it to be approximately half that of Earth's.

The *Viking 2* lander operated for four years before ceasing to provide data in 1979. The *Viking 1* lander is programmed to operate through 1990.

Viking's main purpose now is to provide a long-term data base on Martian weather patterns. Weather appears to be less variable than on Earth. Indeed, the wind patterns, pressure, and temperature vary extremely regularly throughout the day. An important discovery was the seasonal variation in atmospheric pressure of 30 percent—a very large amount—probably caused by the condensation of large amounts of carbon dioxide at the poles.

Viking also continues to send back an occasional photograph of the surface of Mars in the immediate vicinity of the lander, so that scientists can see what changes, if any, occur over the years.

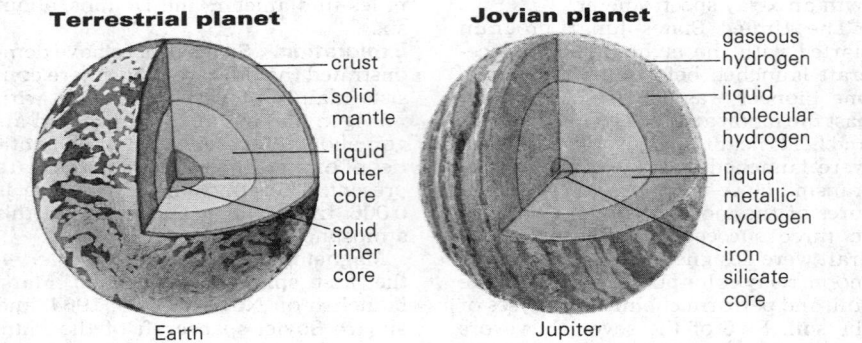

The rocky nature of Earth and the low density of Jupiter mark them as representative of terrestrial and Jovian planets respectively.

Jovian Planets

The Jovian planets are quite different from the terrestrial planets. All, except Pluto, have a composition very similar to that of the sun, consisting mainly of hydrogen.

Jupiter. Jupiter is a giant planet, larger and heavier than all the other planets combined. With a diameter of 142,800 kilometers (88,679 miles)—about eleven times larger than Earth's—its volume is more than 1000 times that of Earth and its mass 318 times that of Earth. Its density is very close to that of the sun. Its strong surface gravity enables it to hold an atmosphere many hundreds of miles deep. Jupiter's rotation period is 10 hours; it takes the planet 11.9 years to complete one revolution around the sun.

Visible on Jupiter's surface are multicolored bands of clouds and numerous red and brown spots. The most conspicuous mark, the Great Red Spot, is 25,000 kilometers (15,500 miles) long. It is oval shaped and is easily observable from Earth with even a small telescope.

Exploration with spacecraft. Data from flybys by *Pioneer 10* and *Pioneer 11* in 1973 and 1974, and from *Voyager 1* and *Voyager 2,* which flew by in 1979, have provided detailed information about Jupiter and its moons. Pictures show that the multicolored bands of clouds are continuously interacting, sometimes transferring material, sometimes simply disintegrating. The pictures also show that the clouds contain centers of great turbulence moving at nearly 320 kilometers (200 miles) per hour.

The Great Red Spot appears in high-resolution pictures to be a giant, long-lasting storm. The gas masses in the cloud make a full rotation every twelve days, rotating even faster closer to the center. Several smaller red spots have been photographed by the Pioneer and Voyager spacecraft, showing astronomers that the Great Red Spot is not a unique phenomenon.

Atmosphere. The atmosphere of the planet Jupiter is composed of 82 percent hydrogen, 17 percent helium, and 1 percent other substances. Much of the hydrogen is locked up in ammonia, water, and ammonium hydrosulfide molecules. Other compounds found in Jupiter's atmosphere are methane, ethane, acetylene, phosphine, hydrogen cyanide, carbon monoxide, and germane (GeH_4). The temperature at the cloud tops is 125K ($-235°F$).

Unlike Earth's weather, Jovian weather is internally driven; twice as much heat is radiated from the planet than is received from the sun. The heat source is the remaining heat from the gravitational contraction that occurred when the planet was formed.

Internal structure. Astronomers consider Jupiter to be a failed star: nuclear fusion would have started in its core if the planet had been ten times more massive. The planet has no solid surface, but a gradual transition from gas (atmosphere) to the liquid, molecular hydrogen surface.

When subjected to very high pressure, liquid hydrogen becomes metallic; that is, the electrons can move freely from one hydrogen atom to another. Therefore, at a depth of about 25 percent of Jupiter's radius, there is an abrupt transition from the molecular liquid to the metallic liquid. Jupiter has the strongest magnetic field of all planets, 20,000 times stronger than that of Earth. Astronomers believe it is generated by electric currents in this zone. Just as Earth's magnetic field traps charged particles (in Van Allen's belts), so does Jupiter's. Jupiter's radiation belts are 10,000 times stronger than Earth's; they pose a serious threat to visiting spacecraft. The magnetosphere extends outward up to 100 Jupiter radii.

Moons. Jupiter has 16 known moons. The largest four, Io, Europa, Ganymede, and Callisto, have been photographed by the Pioneer and Voyager probes. Io has an unscarred surface, but at least seven large active volcanoes whose plumes have been photographed by the Voyager probes. Europa also has no craters, but its surface is crosshatched by long, narrow fractures extending for hundreds of miles. Ganymede is dotted with very large, ancient ringed craters. Callisto

THE GREAT RED SPOT *of Jupiter and two of Jupiter's moons, Io,* left, *and Europa,* right, *were photographed by the space probe* Voyager 1 *in 1979.*

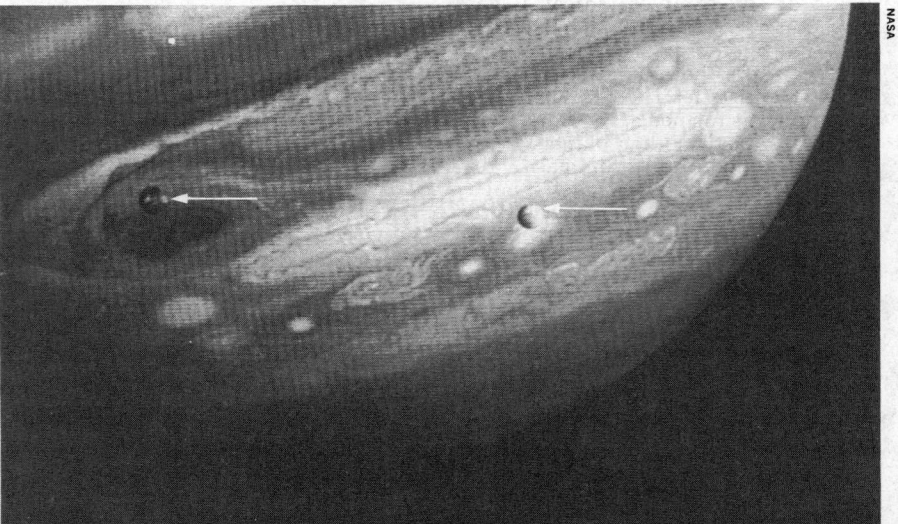

displays ten times as many craters as Ganymede.

Voyager 1 discovered Jupiter's ring system, which extends from 122,000 kilometers (75,800 miles) to 129,000 kilometers (80,150 miles) from the planet's center.

Saturn.

Saturn is second only to Jupiter in size, mass, and speed of rotation. Its diameter is 120,000 kilometers (74,520 miles), and its mass is 95 times that of Earth. The mean distance from the sun is 1507 million kilometers (936.4 million miles), and its rotational period is 10 hours, 39.4 minutes. It orbits the sun in 29.5 years.

Except for Pluto, Saturn is the least dense of all planets. Many features of Saturn's atmosphere and inner structure are similar to those of Jupiter.

Saturn's ring system.

By far Saturn's most outstanding feature is its ring system. Galileo observed it in July, 1610, but the resolving power of his telescope was insufficient to enable him to identify the system as rings. The Dutch astronomer Christiaan Huygens (1629–1695), using a much better telescope, identified the ring system.

Even when observed with a small telescope, Saturn's ring system appears to consist of several concentric rings. Giovanni Cassini (1625–1712) discovered a wide gap, called Cassini's division, separating two bright rings, A and B, of which B is the brighter. The fainter C ring, also called Crepe ring, is inside the B ring. The rings are believed to consist of small particles of water and ammonia ice.

Exploration with spacecraft.

Much has been learned about Saturn from space probes. *Pioneer 11* reached Saturn in September, 1979, and approached the planet as close as 20,880 kilometers (12,974 miles). *Voyager 1* reached the planet in November, 1980, and *Voyager 2* in August, 1981. *Voyager 1* passed close by Titan, Saturn's largest satellite. *Voyager 2* was programmed to continue its voyage to Uranus and Neptune.

The pictures of Saturn's ring system taken by these spacecraft count among the most spectacular ever obtained in astronomy. The A, B, and C rings proved to consist of thousands of smaller rings, called ringlets, resembling the grooves on a phonograph record. The F ring, never observed from Earth before, became visible in the photographs. The Cassini division proved not to be empty but to contain a number of rings, of which some are eccentric. In the B ring, a number of spokes—radial darker zones—become visible and persist for hours. Their nature is not yet understood, but they may consist of small particles lifted from the plane of the ring by electrostatic or magnetic forces. *Voyager 2* performed measurements that showed that the ring system is very thin, at most 150 meters (490 feet) thick.

SATURN'S RINGS

Distance from center of Saturn to inner edge of ring.

NAME	DISTANCE (MILES)
D	42,000
C	45,500
B	57,300
Cassini division	73,000
A	75,200
Encke division	83,000
F	87,400
G	106,000
E	130,000

Moons of Saturn.

With the discovery of new satellites by spacecraft, the total known moons of Saturn grew to over 20. The largest one, Titan, was discovered by Huygens in 1655. Voyager photographs of Titan show that it is covered by a thick orange atmosphere mainly containing nitrogen. The atmospheric pressure is 1.6 times that of Earth. Mimas, Enceladis, Tethys, Dione, and Rhea are much smaller than Titan and consist mainly of water ice. All their surfaces show cratering. An interesting discovery was the existence of shepherding satellites. The orbits of moons S 13 and S 14, two such shepherding satellites, are on each side of the F ring. Their gravity sweeps back into the ring any stray particles.

Uranus.

With a magnitude of 5.5, Uranus is barely visible to the naked eye and so remained unidentified as a planet until the 18th century.

Uranus is half the size of Saturn, with a diameter of 52,000 kilometers (32,292 miles). The mean distance from the sun is 2900 million kilometers (1801 million miles). Uranus orbits the sun in 84 years and rotates around its axis in 16.3 hours. Like Venus, the planet rotates in a retro-

THIS PHOTOGRAPH *was overexposed in order to capture an image of the five satellites of Uranus.*

grade direction, but its axis is tilted over 98° to its orbital plane. Consequently, unlike the other planets, Uranus does not know day and night. Its northern and southern halves are pointed toward the sun alternately every 42 years. Uranus has been found to have five to nine rings that are similar to Saturn's rings.

Voyager 2 visited the planet in December, 1985. Pictures taken by the probe show that Uranus is covered by a thick atmosphere that is colored greenish blue by trace amounts of methane. The atmosphere contains 75 percent hydrogen and about 25 percent helium. The planet's surface may be covered with water 8000 kilometers (5000 miles) deep. The central part of the planet may consist of a rocky core the size of Earth. *Voyager 2* discovered ten smaller moons, making 15 the total of known moons. Two are shepherding satellites to one of Uranus's rings.

The five largest moons are Ariel, Miranda, Oberon, Titania, and Umbriel. They consist of about 60 percent water ice and 40 percent rock. Pictures of Miranda revealed structures never seen on other celestial bodies in the solar system. Rectangular and circular features cover large parts of its surface, hinting that Miranda never completed the process in which heavier elements sank to form the core and lighter elements formed the crust. *Voyager 2* also photographed the ring system and discovered two more rings.

Neptune.

Neptune is far from Earth. With a magnitude of eight, Neptune is invisible to the naked eye, but can be observed through binoculars. The average distance from the sun is 4500 million kilometers (2795 million miles). The planet completes an orbit around the sun in 165 years. Neptune rotates around its own axis with a period of 18 hours, 12 minutes. Until the flyby by *Voyager 2,* data about the planet's composition will remain tentative, but it is thought to be similar to Uranus in structure, temperature, and atmosphere. With a temperature of

55K (−361°F), methane and ammonia would be frozen solids.

Neptune has two satellites. Triton describes a retrograde orbit while Nereid has an extremely elliptical orbit.

Pluto.

Pluto is the most remote and smallest of the known planets. At present it is inside Neptune's orbit. (The orbits of the two planets intersect.) The planet's average distance from the sun is 5900 million kilometers (3660 million miles). It takes Pluto almost 248 years to circle the sun.

In 1978 a moon was discovered orbiting Pluto at a distance of about 19,300 kilometers (12,000 miles). The period of revolution of this moon, called Charon, is the same as the period of rotation of Pluto. The plane of Charon's orbit was parallel to our line of sight from 1983 to 1987. Thus, Charon and Pluto occult each other periodically. From these occultations astronomers have determined that Pluto is 2420 kilometers (1500 miles) in diameter and Charon 1180 kilometers (730 miles).

The Minor Members

Besides the large planets, a host of smaller bodies circle the sun. The largest among them are the asteroids, also called planetoids—literally, small planets—followed in size by the comets. The smallest bodies are the meteoroids. The number of meteoroids is very large, and many of them fall on Earth.

Asteroids.

Asteroids are considered small, solid bodies found mainly between the orbits of Mars and Jupiter. The largest known asteroid, Ceres, has a diameter of 1003 kilometers (623 miles). The smallest one known is Hathor, with a diameter of 500 meters (1525 feet). These asteroids are thought to be remnants of a large body or bodies that disintegrated. They also are thought to be the most likely source of meteorites. Orbits of more than 2000 asteroids have been computed; their total number probably exceeds 40,000.

In 1977 the American astronomer Charles Kowal discovered an asteroid that, unlike common asteroids, orbits the sun on a very eccentric path between the orbits of Saturn and Uranus. The asteroid is about 650 kilometers (404 miles) in diameter and has been named Chiron.

Comets.

The most spectacular phenomena in the night sky are comets. In antiquity, comets were viewed as harbingers of changes in royal succession or leadership. For example, the

THE COMET KOHOUTEK *was visible from Earth during 1973 and 1974. As a comet passes close to the sun, the solar wind exerts pressure so that the comet's tail always points away from the sun.*

birth of Alexander the Great in 356 B.C. and that of Mithradates VI, king of Pontus, in 132 B.C. occurred during the appearance of comets. The death of Charlemagne in 814 was announced by a comet, and Halley's comet appeared in 1066, when William the Conqueror invaded England. The association of comets with disaster was made in the late Middle Ages and early Renaissance.

Nature of comets. For a long time comets were believed to be phenomena occurring close to Earth's surface. The German astronomer and mathematician Petrus Apianus (1501?–1552) showed that the tail of a comet is always directed in a path away from the sun. Tycho Brahe showed that the comet of 1577 had to be farther away than the moon because it had no measurable parallax. These two findings contradicted Aristotle's universally accepted theory that comets are atmospheric and sublunar phenomena.

Edmund Halley developed a method for calculating cometary orbits. He proved that the comet of 1682 was the same one observed in 1531 by Apianus and in 1607 by Kepler. Halley predicted that the same comet would return again in 1758. Later calculations by the French mathematician Alexis Claude Clairaut (1713–1765), in which

he accounted for the perturbations on the comet's orbit by Jupiter and Saturn, predicted the return of the comet in 1759. The calculations proved to be precise within one month. When the comet, now named after Halley, showed up in 1759, the last remaining doubts—especially in France—of the validity of Newton's theory of gravitation were lifted.

Halley's comet made a spectacular return in 1910, when it could be observed by astronomers for more than 20 months. During its latest return, in 1986, the comet was observed from five spacecraft: the Soviet *Vega 1* and *2*, which after visits to Venus were redirected to the comet; the European Space Agency's *Giotto;* and Japan's *Suisei* and *Sakigake.*

Structure of comets. Comets consist of a nucleus, coma, tail, and halo. The American astronomer Fred Whipple introduced the term dirty snowball to describe the constitution of the nucleus. The matter emanating from the nuclei of several comets, especially Halley's comet in 1986, has been analyzed spectroscopically. The nucleus appears to contain water ice, carbon dioxide, formaldehyde, carbon monoxide, and nitrogen.

At great distances from the sun, comets do not have a tail and appear as fuzzy spots in telescopes. As a comet approaches the sun, matter from the nucleus becomes heated and dissociates, forming the luminous and extensive tail. The tail shines partly by directly reflected sunlight and partly by reradiated sunlight absorbed by gases in the comet's atmosphere.

Light also exerts pressure, much too slight to affect more substantial celestial bodies, but strong enough to affect the microscopic particles that make up a comet's tail. This, plus the additional driving force provided by the solar wind, explains why comets' tails generally point away from the sun.

With each new approach to the sun, some of the comet's material is driven away from its nucleus and left strewn along the comet's orbital path. Because of this, after many return trips, any comet that orbits close to the sun will eventually waste away entirely. When Earth crosses a comet's orbit, even though the comet may have passed many years before, the bits of cometary material left behind collide with Earth's atmosphere and cause a meteor shower.

Planets can disturb the paths of comets with very large orbits and make an elliptical orbit hyperbolic. When this happens, the comet leaves the solar system, presumably forever.

Investigation with space probes. The first space probe ever to visit a comet was the *International Cometary Explorer* (ICE). It passed near Comet Giacobini-Zinner on September 11, 1985, approaching it at a distance of 7800 kilometers (4850 miles). The probe flew through the comet's tail and found that the tail contains ionized water vapor.

On March 14, 1986, the *Giotto* flew by Halley's comet at a distance of 605 kilometers (376 miles). It returned photographs of the nucleus; however, the spacecraft was hit by a large particle and started gyrating. The closest picture, taken from 1703 kilometers (1058 miles) from the nucleus, showed that the nucleus has the shape of an avocado pear, 16 kilometers (9.5 miles) long and 8 kilometers (5 miles) across at its widest. The surface of the nucleus was found to be extremely dark, suggesting that it is covered by a layer of dust. It reflects only a small percentage of the sunlight. From the observations, astronomers have determined that the nucleus continually loses mass—about 6 tons per second. At this rate the comet would have lost 300 million tons since 1910, corresponding to a surface layer of 1.4 meters (4.5 feet) if matter were to leave the nucleus evenly.

THE ARIZONA METEOR CRATER *is believed to be the result of the impact of a small asteroid with Earth's surface. The crater is about three-quarters of a mile in diameter.*

Meteors. A meteoric particle traveling in space is known as a *meteoroid*. The same particle, after it enters Earth's atmosphere and is made luminous by friction with the upper air, is called a *meteor*. Meteors are visible as falling stars; they usually burn up before reaching Earth. Any part of a meteor that reaches Earth's surface is known as a *meteorite*.

Many meteors are cometary debris and do not reach Earth's surface. The large meteors that do hit Earth have a different origin. They are really tiny asteroids composed largely of iron and nickel or stone. They are capable of withstanding the enormous heat of entry into Earth's atmosphere.

The great pit in Arizona known as the Arizona Meteor Crater is the result of a prehistoric collision of Earth and a small asteroid.

ANNUAL METEOR SHOWERS

NAME	DATES
Quadrantid	Jan. 1–6
Lyrid	Apr. 19–24
Alpha Scorpiid	Apr. 28–May 12
Eta Aquarid	May 2–7
Delta Aquarid	July 15–Aug. 15
Perseid	July 27–Aug. 17
Orionid	Oct. 12–16
Taurid	Oct. 26–Nov. 25
Leonid	Nov. 15–19
Geminid	Dec. 7–15

The Sun and Stars

The Sun: A Typical Star

The sun, our own star, is a glowing sphere of gas about 1,392,000 kilometers (864,000 miles) in diameter with a mass of 332,000 Earths. It is an average, or typical, star for it is about halfway between the faintest and the brightest and the smallest and the largest of known stars. The sun was formed about five billion years ago.

The sun rotates very slowly about its axis. In 1863 the English amateur astronomer Richard Carrington (1826–1875), by carefully observing sunspots over a period of ten years, concluded that the sun does not rotate as a solid body. Its period of rotation varies with latitude, a phenomenon known as *differential rotation*. At the solar equator, the rotation period is 24.8 days and at 40 degrees latitude it is 26.7 days.

Structure of the sun. The visible layer of the sun, or solar atmosphere, is called the photosphere. The chromosphere, which is the thin outer layer of the sun, and the solar corona are visible only during an eclipse or with a special instrument, called a coronagraph.

The photosphere. The photosphere is a layer of gas about 500 kilometers (310 miles) thick. It has a temperature at the outer edge of 4300K (7280°F); the temperature at its inner boundary is 6600K (11,420°F). Most of the light we receive from the sun, which is generated in the photosphere, has the same energy spectrum as that of a black body at a temperature of 5900K (10,160°F) (see page 252).

Solar light consists of a continuous rainbow spectrum, discovered by Isaac Newton in 1666. The dark lines in this spectrum were first observed by Wollaston and Fraunhofer at the beginning of the 19th century. Kirchhoff started the systematic study of these lines in order to identify the elements present in the solar atmosphere. Hydrogen, with 71 percent of the total, is the most abundant, followed by helium with 27 percent. Sixty-six other elements and a number of their ions (atoms that have lost one or more electrons) have been identified and make up the remaining 2 percent of the sun's atmosphere.

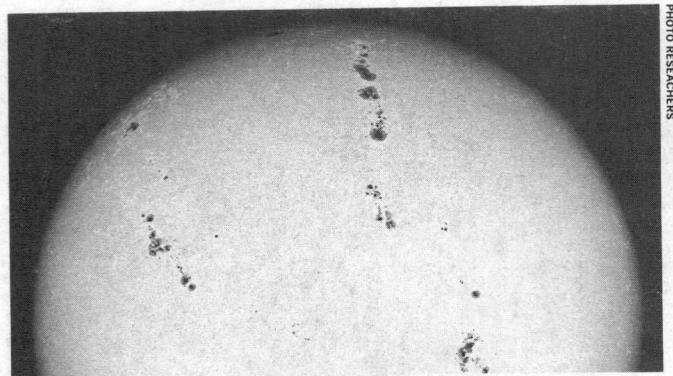

MOUNT WILSON AND PALOMAR OBSERVATORIES/
PHOTO RESEARCHERS

SUNSPOTS *appear dark against the brilliance of the surface of the sun because they are areas of lower temperature.*

NASA

THE SUN'S CORONA *can only be photographed during a total eclipse or with a special instrument called a coronagraph, which blocks out the bright disk of the photosphere.*

NASA/TAURUS PHOTOS

A PROMINENCE *is a huge eruption of gaseous hydrogen or helium. This photo was taken during an eclipse in 1919.*

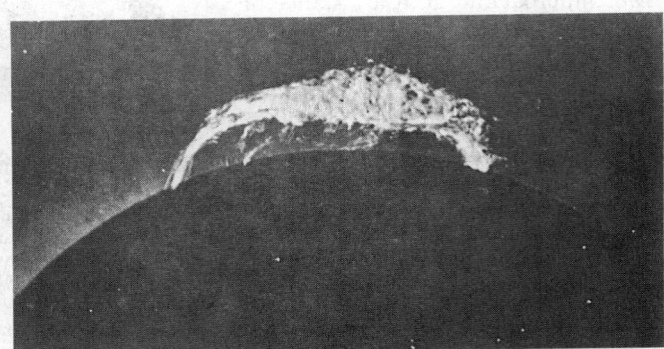

PHOTO RESEARCHERS

SOLAR FLARES, *shown here in a spectroheliogram, can cause disruptions in Earth's magnetic fields.*

Granulation. Photographs of the brilliant surface of the disk taken with a telescope under good atmospheric conditions show that the surface of the sun looks granular. This phenomenon, called *granulation,* is caused by the convection of hot matter just under the visible layer. As in boiling water, hot gas elements rise to the surface while cooled elements sink. The difference in temperature between the cool and hot elements is not large, but it is enough to cause a difference in brilliance that is easily observed from Earth.

The chromosphere. The chromosphere is the layer above the photosphere. Because it is much less luminous than the photosphere, it is visible only during an eclipse, when it is seen as a reddish glow around the sun. The chromosphere extends from the photosphere to an altitude of several thousand kilometers. It consists of numerous gas jets, called *spicules.* They are typically 1000 kilometers (620 miles) across and rise up to heights of 10,000 kilometers (6200 miles). The gas masses rise upward with velocities of about 25 kilometers (15 miles) per second; each mass has an average lifetime of about 15 minutes. Going toward the outer edge of the chromosphere, the temperature of the gas rises from about 4500K (7640°F) to 400,000K (720,000°F). The increase in temperature is caused by the increasing speed of the particles that are flowing away from the sun.

The corona. The corona is a very thin envelope of gas surrounding the sun and extending far from the sun, a distance as great as several solar radii.

Because the corona gives off a million times less light than the photosphere, it can be observed with the naked eye only during an eclipse or with a coronagraph, a special instrument invented by the French astronomer Bernard Lyot (1897–1953).

The temperature in the corona is believed to reach 2,000,000K (3,600,000°F). The corona, however, radiates very little heat. The high temperature is only a measure of the high average speed of the individual particles. Because of the high temperature, the corona is a strong emitter of x-rays.

Solar wind. A constant stream of particles, known as the solar wind, mainly electrons and protons, flows from the sun into interplanetary space. The particles originate in the solar corona. There, because of the high temperature, individual particles have enough energy to escape into space. The corona is replenished continuously by the gases escaping through the spicules in the chromosphere.

Material weighing approximately 100 billion tons escapes from the sun every day. Although this figure seems enormous, it would take at least 55 trillion years for the sun to evaporate completely. The solar wind particles reach Earth with a speed of 600 kilometers (375 miles) per second. Because the solar wind carries a magnetic field with it, it strongly influences the magnetosphere of Earth and other planets.

Sunspots. The most conspicuous markings on the sun are sunspots. Even without a telescope, sunspots can sometimes be observed at sunset.

Sunspots appear as dark regions on the photosphere that start out as tiny specks and grow, sometimes to diameters of 50,000 kilometers (31,000 miles). Their lifetime is usually a few weeks to a few months, after which they gradually disappear. They occur in pairs, groups, or strings and appear to move slowly across the sun because of the sun's rotation. A typical sunspot consists of a central dark region called the *umbra* surrounded by a brighter region called the *penumbra.* The temperature in a spot is approximately 4500K (7640°F), or 2000K (3600°F) cooler than the surrounding photosphere. In contrast to the surrounding hotter photosphere, the spot appears dark.

The German pharmacist and amateur astronomer Heinrich Schwabe (1789–1875) began observing the sun regularly in 1826. He discovered that the number of sunspots varied from a minimum of almost no spots to a maximum of over 200 in a cycle lasting an average of eleven years. The German astronomer Friedrich Wilhelm Gustav Spörer (1822–1895) discovered in 1861 that the latitude at which the sunspots appear also depends on the progress of the cycle. After a sunspot minimum, the first spots appear at latitudes between 30° and 45° on both sides of the equator. As the cycle progresses toward a maximum, the zone with spots appears to move toward the equator, reaching it when the number is again at a minimum.

George Ellery Hale discovered that the spectral lines in the light coming from sunspots show *Zeeman splitting,* which indicates the presence of strong magnetic fields. The strong magnetic field present in a sunspot may explain why the spot is cooler than its surroundings: the field may impede convection in the layer below the spot.

Solar activity.

The number of sunspots is an indicator of solar activity. Several other phenomena occur as well when the sun is active. Some regions of the sun, especially those near sunspots, become hotter and brighter. Those areas are called *plages.* Plages are often the precursors of *prominences,* large tongues of gas that seem to project from the surface of the sun.

The most spectacular events on the sun are solar flares, sudden short-lived outbreaks releasing large amounts of energy, sometimes equivalent to the explosion of ten billion one-megaton hydrogen bombs. Flares transmit a large amount of ultraviolet light, x-rays, radio waves, and streams of charged particles. Flares often have strongly noticeable effects on Earth: the radiated x-rays and ultraviolet rays cause disturbances in the ionosphere that result in auroras, disruptions of short-wave radio communications, and voltage surges in long-distance electrical transmission lines; cause magnetic storms; and can pose radiation hazards to astronauts and passengers aboard planes flying at very high altitudes.

The energy source in the sun.

Although a number of theories had been advanced, the nature of the sun's energy source remained a mystery until the development of nuclear physics in the years before World War II. The American physicist Hans Bethe worked out the theory that nuclear fusion reactions furnish the enormous amounts of energy liberated by the sun and the stars.

In such a process, four hydrogen atoms combine into one helium atom and release energy. This reaction can occur only under conditions of extremely high temperature, when the particles have high kinetic energy, and extremely high pressure, when the particles have a reasonable chance of colliding (see CHEMISTRY AND PHYSICS, page 470).

The fusion of hydrogen into helium in the sun occurs in a relatively small central region with a radius 20 percent of that of the sun. The released energy is transported by radiation through the sun toward the outer layers. The photons leaving the sun's core, however, are absorbed, reemitted, and scattered in the sun's interior on their path to the outer layers. It takes a million years for the photons to reach the outer layers of the sun. In the region closer to the sun's surface, the energy is transported by convection.

Solar neutrinos.

The nuclear reactions in the core of the sun produce neutrinos as well as photons. Neutrinos have a unique property: because they have no mass or electric charge, they pass almost unhindered through matter. In contrast to the photons produced in the sun's core, which take a million years to reach the photosphere, neutrinos pass through the sun instantly.

Since neutrinos hardly interact with matter, they are difficult to detect. One way of detecting neutrinos is to enable them to interact with chlorine-37 atoms, thus producing a radioactive argon atom that can be detected. Such a neutrino detector has been placed 1600 meters (5250 feet) below the surface of Earth at the Homestead Mine, in Lead, South Dakota. The detector is placed deep underground to shield it from cosmic radiation. It is a huge tank containing 380,000 liters (100,000 gallons) of tetrachloroethylene.

One of every 10^{21} neutrinos entering the tank reacts with a chlorine atom, forming a radioactive argon atom. It was predicted that, on average, three radioactive argon atoms would be produced each week, but on average only one argon atom a week has been detected. Astronomers have not yet explained the discrepancy between predictions and experimental findings.

Stars

Like the sun, stars are huge spherical masses of gas that began radiating energy because of nuclear reactions occurring deep within their interiors. Stars do, however, differ greatly in size, luminosity, temperature, and composition, and the nuclear reactions in their cores also can be different. When the hydrogen in the core is depleted, stars can begin to convert helium into carbon and carbon into heavier elements.

Stars begin their lives through the gravitational contraction of clouds of gas and dust. The collapsing mass heats up because the pressure increases. (This is exactly the same process that heats up the air in a bicycle pump when it is being used.) After a while the mass of gas becomes spherical and glows red: a *protostar* is formed. As the gravitational contraction continues, the confined temperature and pressure at the center of the gaseous mass initiates the nuclear reactions that supply the energy of a fully formed star.

Star formation is an ongoing process in areas of the galaxy rich in dust and gas, such as the Orion nebula. The heated dust clouds radiate strongly in infrared light. Several areas of active star formation have been photographed by means of the *IRAS* satellite.

Stellar distances.

Because stars are so far away, it is impractical to use kilometers, miles, or even astronomical units to express their distances. One of the units used is the *light-year.* One light-year is equal to the distance light travels in one year: 94607×10^9 kilometers, or 5878×10^9 miles. The closest star to the sun, Proxima Centauri, is about 4.5 light-years away, corresponding to 284,750 A.U. The most distant stars in our galaxy are more than 50,000 light-years away.

It is interesting to note that when we look across huge distances, expressed in thousands of light-years, we also look back in time thousands of years. For example, quasars are at distances of billions of light-years, so when we examine them, we are observing phenomena that occurred not long after the big bang.

Measurement of distances.

The basic way of measuring the distance to a star is by the *trigonometric parallax method.* As Earth moves around the sun, a star relatively nearby will appear to shift its position in the sky relative to more distant stars. By measur-

A CONSTELLATION *can comprise stars that are a great distance apart, even though they may appear to lie relatively close together.*

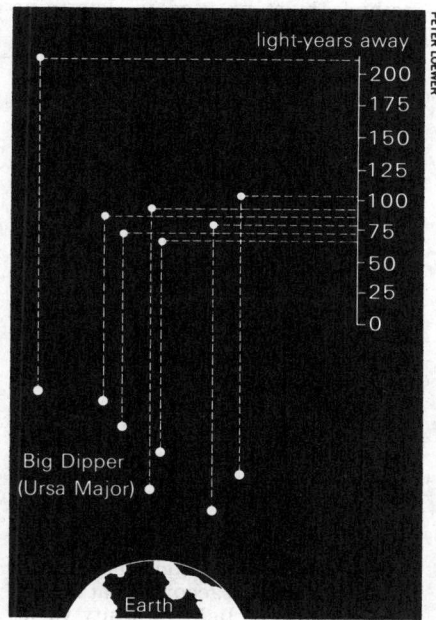

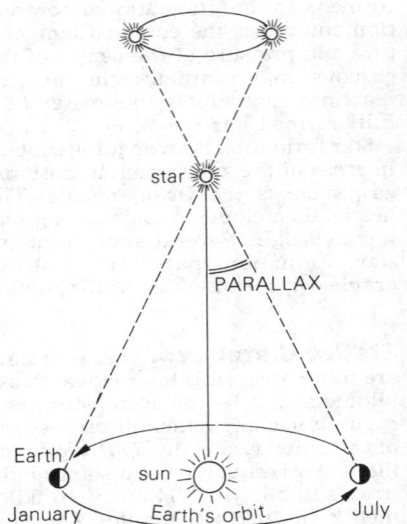

PETER LOEWER

MOUNT WILSON AND PALOMAR OBSERVATORIES

PARALLAX SHIFT *is caused by Earth's revolution around the sun.*

THE STAR CLUSTER PLEIADES, *also called the Seven Sisters, is in the constellation Taurus. Some of its stars have magnitudes between three and four.*

ing these minute angular shifts, the distance of the star can be determined trigonometrically. Half the total apparent shift of the star with respect to the background is called the star's *trigonometric parallax*. It follows that the parallax of a star is the angle formed at the star by the triangle formed between the star and each end of the radius of Earth's orbit.

By definition, a parallax of one second of arc corresponds to a distance of one *parsec* (*par*allax of one *sec*ond). The distance of a star in parsecs is thus 1/parallax. One parsec is equal to 3.26 light-years. For example, the parallax of the star 61 Cygni is 0.35 seconds of arc. Its distance is then 1/0.35 = 2.85 parsecs, or 9.3 light-years.

The trigonometric shifts of distant stars are virtually negligible, so other methods must be used to determine their distances. One method is based on the fact that the intensity of light varies inversely as the square of the distance. In other words, when we look at two stars of the same intrinsic, actual brightness, but one of them is twice as far away as the other, the more distant star will appear four times fainter than the closer one. The intensity of certain absorption lines in stellar spectra depends strongly on the intrinsic brightness of the star. In many cases it is possible to derive the intrinsic brightness of a star from its spectrum; its distance can then be derived simply by noting how bright or faint it appears. Distances so determined are called *spectroscopic parallaxes*.

Stellar magnitudes. A star's brightness as it appears to us is measured by its *apparent magnitude*. The scale of stellar magnitudes is logarithmic and takes into account that the visual sensation of light intensity varies

logarithmically; that is, the difference of light intensity between the brightest stars and the faintest stars seems to the human eye not to be very great, even though we receive from the brightest stars about 100 times more light than from the faintest stars.

Hipparchus categorized stars in six classes of brightness, the brightest having a magnitude of one and the faintest a magnitude of six. Astronomers have preserved this definition of the magnitude scale; about the middle of the 19th century they agreed to a scale in which the difference of five magnitudes corresponds exactly to a ratio of 100 in brightness. If five steps correspond to a ratio of 100, one step corresponds to the fifth root of 100, which is 2.5. Each step in the magnitude scale corresponds to a factor of 2.5 in brightness.

Although this method of indicating the brightness of stars seems cumbersome, astronomers have maintained this system because the response of photographic emulsion is also a logarithmic function of light intensity.

Astronomers have extended the magnitude scale to include objects brighter than the brightest stars: the planets, the sun, and the moon. For this the scale has been extended to negative numbers: the sun has a magnitude of −26.7; the moon −12.6; and Venus at its maximum brightness a magnitude of −4. When photometry became more accurate, it was found that two stars also have negative magnitudes: the magnitude of Sirius is −1.4, and of Betelgeuse −0.7.

With good binoculars we can see stars with magnitudes of 9. The photographic limit of the Hale telescope is 24.

Using photoelectric detectors and exposure times of 2000 seconds, the space telescope should reach stars of magnitude 27. Although the telescope

has a smaller aperture than the Hale telescope, the stellar image is concentrated in a smaller area of the detector because of the absence of atmospheric turbulence, thus increasing the number of photons reaching a unit area of the detector.

The truly bright, giant stars can be seen at enormous distances, while the fainter ones must be relatively close to be seen at all. The stars we see when we glance up at the night sky are predominantly intrinsically bright, faraway stars—beacons far out in space. For every star we can see with the naked eye, there are 100 or more closer to us that we cannot see, even at moderate distances, because they are intrinsically faint.

Absolute magnitude. Because the apparent magnitude depends both on the intrinsic brightness and the distance of the star from Earth, astronomers have introduced the concept of *absolute magnitude:* the magnitude a star would have if it were at a distance of 10 parsecs.

Luminosity and temperature.

The luminosity of a star depends directly on its size (surface area) and on how brightly each unit of area shines (i.e., luminosity = surface area × luminosity per unit area). A big star can appear bright even though it is relatively faint per unit area. A small, intensely brilliant star will appear as bright as an enormous but faint star.

The total luminosity of a star, therefore, reveals nothing of the star's size unless we also know the star's surface brightness. To find this, the star's temperature must be known.

Colors of stars. Most observers have noticed that stars do not appear to have the same colors, some appearing reddish while others appear bluish.

STELLAR CLASSIFICATION

Spectral Classes

TYPE	TEMPERATURE RANGE (KELVIN)	COLOR
O	100,000–30,000	blue-white
B	25,000–12,000	blue-white
A	11,000– 8,000	white
F	7,800– 6,200	creamy
G	6,000– 4,600	yellow
K	4,900– 3,350	orange
M	3,400– 2,600	red

Luminosity Classes

Ia	bright supergiant
Iab	less bright supergiant
Ib	supergiant
II	bright giant
III	giant
IV	subgiant
V	main sequence
VI	subdwarf
VII	white dwarf

The color of a star is a fairly good indicator of its temperature. The hotter the temperature, the bluer the color. We can compare this to a piece of metal that is heated: at first, it glows a dull red; then, as its temperature rises, it becomes brighter. It also becomes, in turn, orange and bright yellow. If the metal does not melt and vaporize, it will become green and then blue. Stars, of course, are completely vaporized, but they still conform with the laws of radiation. An orange-yellow star such as Arcturus has a temperature of about 4100K (6900°F); our yellow sun has a temperature of about 5800K (9900°F). The bluish star Rigel has a surface temperature of some 12,000°C (21,600°F).

Stellar spectra. Like the sun, stars are surrounded by a gaseous atmosphere consisting mainly of hydrogen, a lesser amount of helium, and a small amount of other elements. Absorption in this layer produces the Fraunhofer lines that are superimposed on the continuous spectrum of the star (see also page 235). The spectra of hotter stars contain a smaller number of Fraunhofer lines than the spectra of cooler stars.

Stellar classification. In 1890 the American astronomer Edward C. Pickering (1846–1919) introduced the so-called Harvard classification of stars. Stars were arranged in classes named A, B, C, D, and so on. This classification system underwent several modifications, causing certain assigned letters to become superfluous or misplaced. The standard spectral classes used today are, more or less in order of decreasing temperature, O, B, A, F, G, K, M, R, N, S. American astronomer Henry Norris Russell (1877–1957) provided a useful mnemonic: Oh Be A Fine Girl Kiss Me Right Now, Smack. In use, each major spectral class is subdivided into ten decimal parts. The spectral class of the sun is G2.

The Hertzsprung-Russell diagram.
At the beginning of the 20th century, the Danish astronomer Ejnar Hertzsprung (1873–1967) and, independently, Henry Russell, wondered whether there might be a relationship between the color and the absolute magnitude of a star. Hertzsprung had already noticed in 1905 that the hotter blue stars had much larger absolute magnitudes than the cooler red stars.

In 1911 Hertzsprung published a graph of the relationship between the color and luminosity of a number of stars in the Pleiades and Hyades. In 1913 Russell published a similar graph. Instead of using the color of stars, Russell used the spectral class of stars. The latter type of graph is called the *Hertzsprung-Russell diagram*. This graph showed that the great majority of stars fall on the *main sequence,* a nearly straight line running from highly luminous, hot, bluish stars down to faint, relatively cool, reddish stars. A given temperature and size go together. Thus, along the main sequence, any stars having the same temperature will also be of the same magnitude.

Mass-luminosity relation. From the study of binaries we know that the more massive stars are also the brighter stars. Measurements of a small number of stars have shown that the luminosity L is proportional to the third power of the mass of a star; this relationship is called the *mass-luminosity relation.* It implies that for the stars in the main sequence, the bright stars are much more massive than the faint stars.

The Hertzsprung-Russell (H-R) diagram is one of the most important graphs of astrophysics. From the spectrum of a main sequence star, one can derive directly its absolute magnitude, termed spectroscopic absolute magnitude. Together with the star's apparent magnitude, it can be used to calculate the star's distance.

Not long after the introduction of

HERTZSPRUNG-RUSSELL DIAGRAM

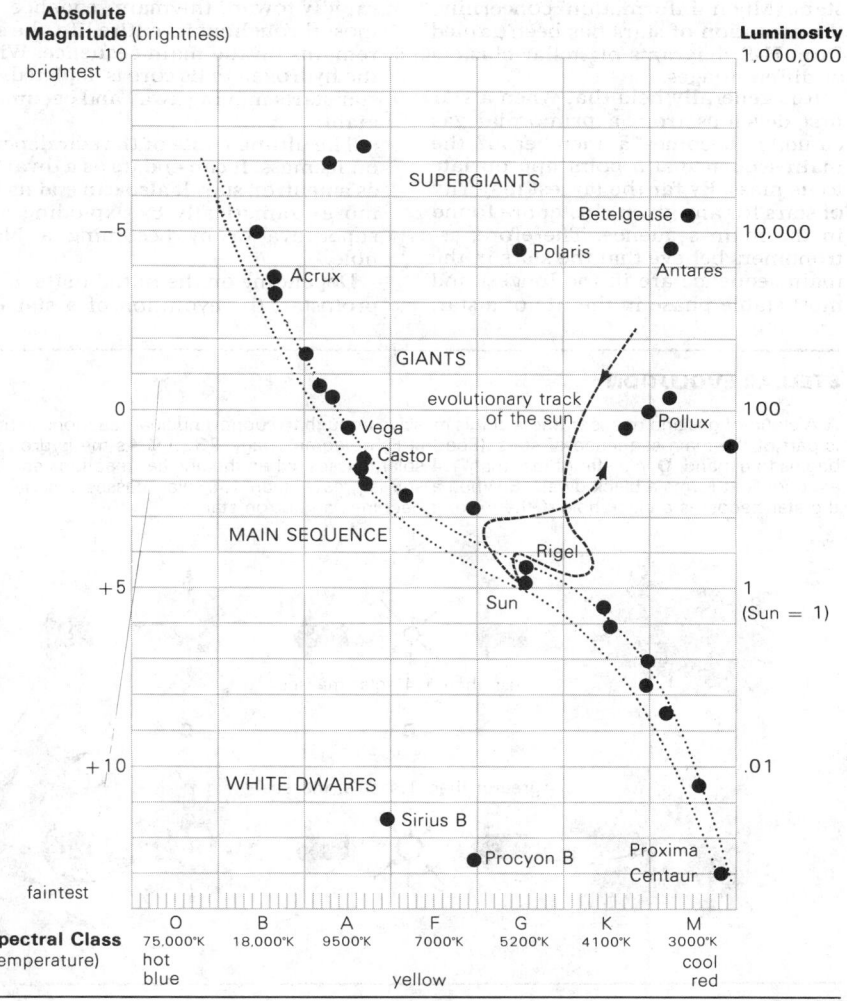

PETER LOEWER

their diagram, Hertzsprung and Russell discovered there were exceptions to the rule that each spectral type corresponds to only one absolute magnitude. For example, the stars Alpha Aurigae and Alpha Centauri are both G-type stars, but they differ strongly in absolute magnitude, 0.3 and 4.4, respectively. Alpha Centauri has an absolute magnitude close to that of the sun and is thus in the main sequence, while Alpha Aurigae is much more luminous.

Since the surface temperature has to be approximately the same, the much higher luminosity can only be explained by assuming that the star is much larger. Hertzsprung introduced the term *giant* for these large stars. The stars that lie above the main sequence in the H-R diagram include the red and yellow giants and the very large supergiants. Similarly, there are groups of stars that are much fainter than their counterparts in the main sequence. These stars are much smaller and are called *white dwarfs.*

Stellar evolution.
The H-R diagram is useful not only for drawing conclusions about the size, temperature, composition, and evolution of stars. Much information concerning the evolution of stars has been gained from H-R diagrams of stellar clusters of different ages.

It is generally held that when a star first develops from a primordial gas cloud, it becomes a member of the main sequence at a point appropriate to its mass. By far the largest majority of stars for any given cluster are found in the main sequence. Therefore, astronomers believe that the stars in the main sequence are in the longest and most stable phase in the life of a star.

When the hydrogen supply becomes depleted, the star's surface temperature drops and the star expands greatly in size and becomes more luminous. Astronomers assume that all the members of a stellar cluster were formed at approximately the same time.

The H-R diagram of an old cluster, such as Messier 3, shows that only the lower half of the main sequence is densely populated with stars. The stars in the upper half of the main sequence appear to have migrated to the right of the main sequence. They are cooling but retain their luminosity. In other words, they are evolving to become giants. The older the cluster, the lower in the main sequence is the turning point toward the giant phase.

These examples confirm the theory that more massive stars evolve faster than their less massive counterparts. This can be understood if one considers that the temperature in the cores of more massive stars becomes higher because of greater compression; consequently, the nuclear reactions proceed much faster.

The plot of the successive positions of an evolving star in the H-R diagram is called an *evolutionary track.* The protostar starts somewhere on the right of the main sequence and evolves rapidly toward the main sequence. Almost throughout its entire life, the star remains on the main sequence. When the hydrogen in its core is depleted, the star starts moving away and becomes a giant.

The ultimate fate of the star depends on its mass. It can end up as a dwarf or as a neutron star. It also can end its life more dramatically by exploding as a supernova or by becoming a black hole.

Depending on the initial mass of the protostar, the evolution of a star can

take different courses. Protostars of less than 0.1 solar mass never become stars. The temperature in the core does not reach the required temperature and pressure for nuclear reactions. These objects quickly fade away as faint red dwarfs and become invisible. Many consider Jupiter to be such a failed star.

Protostars between 0.1 and 1.4 solar mass contract slowly until the core reaches a temperature of about 10,000,000K and the nuclear reactions begin. In stars of lower mass, the proton-proton cycle is the most important mechanism for conversion of hydrogen into helium. In hotter stars the carbon cycle is the more important reaction mechanism. When the hydrogen in the core is depleted, the star leaves the main sequence and begins to convert helium into carbon. The volume of the star increases enormously while the surface temperature decreases, but because of the increased volume the star becomes much more luminous. The giant phase is relatively short. It has been calculated that for the sun, it will last only 100 million years. Even in the giant phase, the temperature in the core is not high enough for nuclear reactions beyond the formation of carbon and oxygen. When the nuclear fuel becomes exhausted, the star begins to contract.

With no thermonuclear reactions to stave it off, gravitation wins the battle. The core of the star goes on contracting until a white dwarf is formed.

Final stages of a star.
White dwarfs were first discovered as the fainter companions in double star systems. The bright star Sirius, also known as the Dog Star, has a companion, called the Pup, with a mass similar

STELLAR EVOLUTION

A A cloud of gas and dust contracts. If it is massive enough to support nuclear reactions, it becomes a star. **B** The star through most of its existence is part of the main sequence of stars. (See the H-R diagram, page 239.) **C** As the hydrogen that fuels the nuclear reaction is depleted, the star begins to expand. **D** In a star of less than 1.4 solar masses, when the nuclear reactions end, the star again contracts, forming a white dwarf. Then, as it cools, it forms a black dwarf. **E** When a star is greater than 1.4 solar masses, a supernova occurs. If the remaining core is massive enough, the star becomes a black hole. Otherwise, it becomes a neutron star.

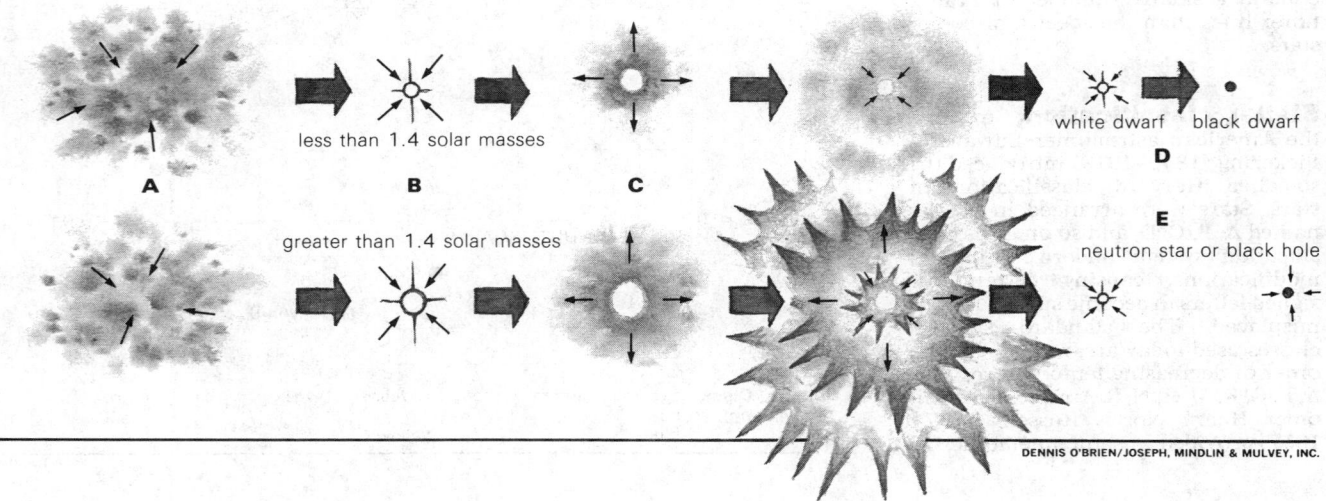

less than 1.4 solar masses

A   B   C

white dwarf   black dwarf

D

greater than 1.4 solar masses

E

neutron star or black hole

DENNIS O'BRIEN/JOSEPH, MINDLIN & MULVEY, INC.

to that of the sun but with a size smaller than that of Neptune. The density of the star must be very high; in fact, the Pup is so dense that a cubic inch of it would weigh ten tons on Earth.

In 1930 the astrophysicist Subrahmanyan Chandrasekhar showed that a white dwarf could be formed only if the mass left over when the nuclear reactions ended was less than 1.4 times the mass of the sun. Below that mass, the star would be held up by electron pressure. The movement of electrons is restricted by the Pauli exclusion principle, which states that only two electrons with the same energy but different spin can occupy a given energy level. In a white dwarf, the compression of matter is so high that all of the allowed energy levels are fully occupied with electrons and there is no room for further compression. Electrons in that condition are said to be *degenerate*.

According to estimates, 99.9 percent of all stars end their careers as white dwarfs. The white dwarfs continue to radiate energy and cool down slowly. They become fainter and fainter and become black dwarfs, huge chunks of crystalline and extremely dense matter unobservable from Earth.

Supernovas. The 1.4 solar-mass limit is called the Chandrasekhar limit. But what happens to the 0.1 percent of stars that have masses exceeding that limit? Because of their greater mass, they spend less time as main sequence stars. In the giant phase the core temperature becomes much higher. When the hydrogen becomes depleted, the star begins converting helium into carbon and oxygen; carbon into neon; even oxygen into silicon; and finally silicon into nickel, cobalt, and iron. The fusion reactions stop with iron because the fusion of iron into heavier elements would consume energy instead of producing it.

The nuclear reactions can proceed simultaneously in different layers of the star. Conversion of the heavier elements requires more pressure and higher temperatures and takes place in deeper layers of the star.

As soon as the nuclear reactions stop, the core collapses catastrophically in a fraction of a second. Gravity crushes it together into a small sphere about 16 kilometers (10 miles) across. The pressure is so enormous that the electrons are forced to combine with protons to form neutrons. Neutrons can be more compressed than electrons, but neutron pressure eventually builds up to the point at which it can resist further gravitational collapse. The result is that the core is transformed into a *neutron star* or, if the remaining core exceeds about two solar masses, it is transformed into a black hole. Matter in a neutron star is said to be *neutron degenerate*.

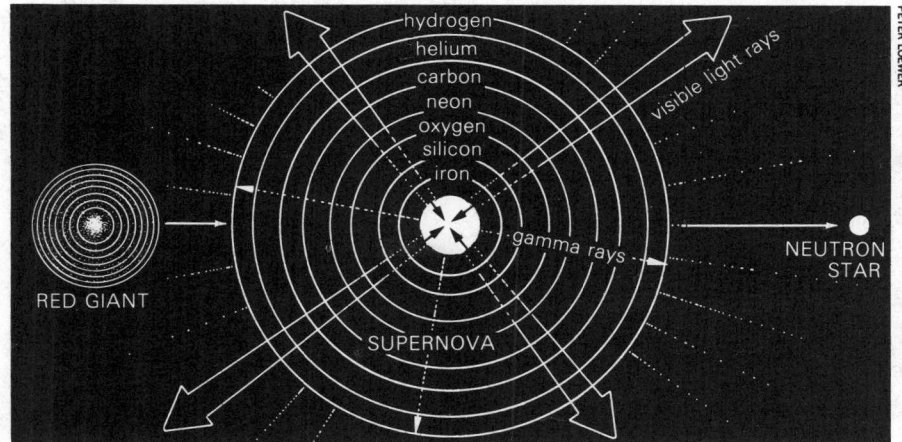

A STAR IN THE GIANT PHASE *has an onionlike structure, with different elements formed at different pressures and temperatures. When a star becomes a supernova, the outer layers are blown off, leaving the core.*

During the resulting collapse of the core, the outer layers of the star are blown off by a shock wave traveling from the core outward. Some astronomers believe that this phenomenon is the result of an enormous flux of neutrinos coming from the collapsing core and dispersing the outer layers of the star into space.

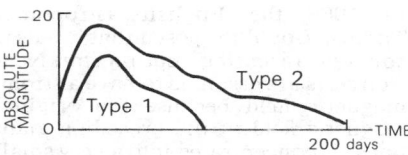

A TYPE I SUPERNOVA *is brighter and visible longer than a type II.*

Supernovas are of two types. The most luminous ones, type I, can reach a brightness as much as ten million times that of the sun. During the explosion, a relatively small amount of mass is ejected into space. Type II supernovas are less bright, up to only one million times the brightness of the sun, but they are characterized by a much larger proportion of stellar mass that is blown into space. It is believed that type II supernovas are explosions of much more massive stars than those of the first type. It is also believed that the remaining core collapses into a black hole.

Supernovas are extremely rare. Astronomers estimate that they occur in our galaxy, on average, every 30 to 100 years. Most of them are not seen because they probably remain hidden from us by galactic clouds. The last supernova in our galaxy was recorded in October, 1604, and was described by Kepler in his book *De stella nova*. The Chinese recorded a supernova that appeared in Taurus in the year 1054; that one was visible in daylight for a time. It now can be seen as the well-known Crab nebula.

In recent times supernovas have been observed only in other galaxies; they can outshine the entire galaxy.

SUPERNOVA 1987A

 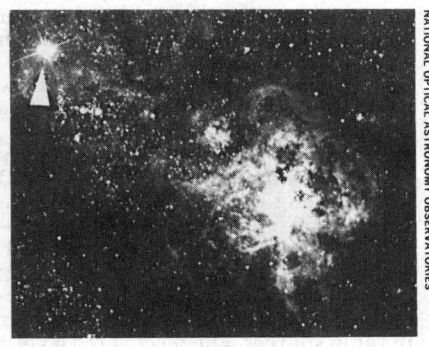

In recent times supernovas have been observed only in other galaxies; they can outshine the entire galaxy. The only supernova visible to the unaided eye since 1604 appeared on February 24, 1987. The explosion of this star, having a mass 30 times that of the sun, occurred in our closest neighboring galaxy, the Large Magellanic Cloud, at a distance of 160,000 light-years. The supernova explosion also was detected by teams of particle physicists operating neutrino detectors, confirming the theory that a supernova produces a large number of neutrinos.

Astronomers believe supernovas are the source of the heavier atoms found in stars like the sun and that constitute Earth, planets, and even living matter. During the explosion, atoms are accelerated to such energies that they are able to combine to form the heavier elements.

The heavy elements created in supernovas are blown into space and become incorporated in new generations of stars. The sun is believed to be a second- or third-generation star. All the heavier elements present in the solar system, and thus also in living matter, are believed to have been formed during supernova explosions long before the birth of the sun.

Novas.

Novas are also explosions of stars, but they are less violent. A nova can brighten up to nine magnitudes in a few days and can reach luminosities of 100,000 suns. Forty novas occur in a given year in our galaxy. They have been observed only in double-star systems and may be caused by matter flowing from one component onto another. The component receiving the matter heats up because of the additional gravitational contraction. Suddenly, new nuclear reactions begin in the star's core and cause the explosion.

Neutron stars.

Neutron stars are believed to have even more dense structures than white dwarfs. Matter is crushed to such a degree that the electron pressure is not sufficient to withstand the pressure. Electrons begin combining with protons to form neutrons. Matter in that form consists, then, of neutrons packed side by side. Its density, comparable to that of the nucleus of an atom, is incredibly high, 10^{15} times the density of ordinary matter. There are 20 times more neutrons than protons in a neutron star. The star can be viewed as a huge atomic nucleus containing a very large number of nucleons. One spoonful (1 cm³) of matter of a neutron star on Earth would weigh about 200 million tons. The neutrons form a rigid crystalline structure, making the star behave like a solid sphere.

Pulsars.

The concept of neutron stars remained a matter of conjecture until 1967, when radio astronomers at Cambridge University discovered a peculiar new object in the sky. The English astronomer Jocelyn Bell was analyzing data obtained by a special radio telescope designed to measure variations in radio sources. She discovered a very regular series of short radio pulses that were emitted every 1.33730115 seconds, with an accuracy resembling that of an atomic clock.

It was clear only very small objects could produce pulses at such a high frequency. The obvious candidates were neutron stars, because they were

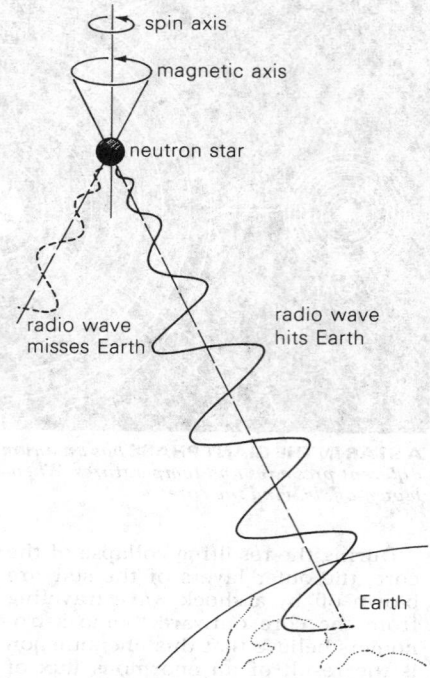

A PULSAR *emits a stream of radio waves from its magnetic poles.*

spin axis
magnetic axis
neutron star
radio wave misses Earth
radio wave hits Earth
Earth

PETER LOEWER

assumed to be only a few miles across. In 1968 the English astronomer Thomas Gould proposed that a pulsar could be a rotating neutron star. Neutron stars are assumed to have a strong magnetic field because the original magnetic field of the preceding giant phase is concentrated into a very small space. Perhaps currents of neutrons and protons inside the star contribute to the magnetic field. Because the rotation impulse also is preserved, the slow rotation of the preceding giant star is transformed into the fast spinning of the neutron star. If the magnetic poles are not aligned with the rotation axis, the magnetic field lines will sweep through space surrounding the neutron star, accelerating electrons that emit radio and light waves. The result, a beam of radiation rapidly rotating with the neutron star, causes a flash when the beam points in our direction, like the flashes observed from the warning lights of a police car.

In 1968 a pulsar was discovered in the middle of the Crab nebula. The remnant of the supernova observed in the year 1054, it transmits radio pulses with a period of 30 milliseconds. Until 1982 it was the fastest spinning pulsar known. In 1969 this pulsar was identified in optical light by observing it through a rotating shutter tuned to the period of the pulsar. Since then, the optical pulses also have been recorded with charge-coupled devices.

The rotation period of most pulsars ranges between 100 milliseconds and 4 seconds. The fastest pulsar known has a period of 1.5 milliseconds. It is named 1937+214 and was discovered in 1982 in the constellation Vulpecula. In all known pulsars, the pulsation period increases by a very small amount. The rotation period typically will dou-

ble in a million years. This slowing down of pulsars is attributed to the conversion of rotational energy into electromagnetic radiation.

Today, computers are used to help in the search for new pulsars. Signals captured by radio telescopes scanning the Milky Way are recorded on magnetic tape. Computers analyze these data in the search for faint periodic signals. This method of computer search is especially useful for pulsars with periods of about one millisecond.

Black holes.

Just as there is a limit to the mass of a dwarf star consisting of electron-degenerate matter, there is an upper mass limit to the existence of a neutron star. Called the Landau-Oppenheimer-Volkoff limit, this limit is estimated to be about three solar masses. Above that value, the stellar core of neutron-degenerate matter cannot support itself and begins collapsing even further into a state of matter called a black hole.

The existence of black holes was first predicted in 1798 by the French mathematician Pierre Simon Laplace (1749–1827). He argued that if a body becomes massive enough, the gravity on its surface will be so great that not even light will be able to escape it.

Laplace's description of a black hole was not entirely accurate, since he could not take into account the curvature of the space-time continuum caused by large masses. The theory of general relativity describes gravity as the degree of curvature of space-time (see MATHEMATICS volume, page 1480). A more exact mathematical description of black holes was developed shortly after publication of Einstein's work on gravity.

The German astronomer Karl Schwarzschild (1873–1916) did the major work on the subject shortly before his death. His most surprising conclusion was that the region around the central mass from which no information could escape beyond that mass to a distance that has come to be known as the *Schwarzschild radius*. The radius depends on the amount of mass that has collapsed. For example, if Earth were to collapse into a point, its Schwarzschild radius would be about 10 centimeters (4 inches). If a star ten times as massive as the sun were to collapse, its Schwarzschild radius would be about 29 kilometers (18 miles). The surface of the sphere, 18 miles in radius, is called the *event horizon*. At the center of the event horizon is the region into which the mass has collapsed. The curvature of space-time there becomes infinitely great and forms a space-time *singularity*. Once anything comes inside the event horizon, it can never escape and no information about it can reach the outside world.

There are two x-ray sources that may be black holes. The most promising candidate, discovered by the *Uhuru* satellite, is called Cygnus X-1. The Vela satellites have also discovered gamma rays coming from this object. It is at a distance of 6000 light-years from Earth and consists of a blue supergiant star of about 30 solar masses around which rotates a highly condensed object of about 14 solar masses.

Cygnus X-1 emits x-rays quite irregularly, but a periodic variation of 5.6 days is noticeable. It is believed that the x-rays are produced by matter flowing from the supergiant to the black hole. The matter spirals in a disklike region around the black hole before being swallowed by it. As the matter swirls toward the black hole, it becomes more and more concentrated and heated, and it begins emitting x-rays.

Double stars.

Optical pairs are stars that seem to be near each other in the sky, but actually are light-years apart. Star pairs that show evidence of orbital motion are known as *visual doubles* or *visual binaries*. Approximately 50 percent of all stars belong to double or multiple star systems.

In 1802 William Herschel, after years of careful determination of star positions, was the first to describe this type of binary. About the time Herschel made the first observations of visual double stars, astronomer J. Goodricke (1764–1786) made observations of the periodic variations in the luminosity of Algol (Beta Persei). He noticed in 1782 that the luminosity of this star reached a sharp minimum every 70 hours. Goodricke explained these variations by assuming that Algol is a double star viewed along the orbital plane and that one of the components periodically eclipses the other and shuts off some of its light. Such double systems are called *eclipsing binaries*.

The existence of close binaries is also revealed by the spectrograph. When, in its motion, a component approaches Earth, its spectral lines are shifted by the Doppler effect toward the blue end of the spectrum and reduced in wavelength. Half a cycle later, when this component recedes from Earth, the lines shift toward the red and the wavelengths increase. This Doppler shift can easily be measured. It has led to the discovery of many *spectroscopic binaries*.

IN A BINARY SYSTEM, *one star will sometimes spill matter through the Lagrange point to the other star.*

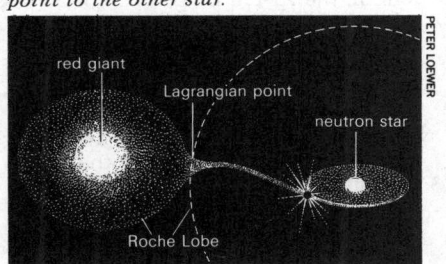

red giant

Lagrangian point

neutron star

Roche Lobe

PETER LOEWER

Evolution of binaries.

Because in many cases the masses and sizes of the components of binaries can be determined, they are interesting objects for the study of stellar evolution. In most binaries the masses of the components are different and are considered to be in different evolutionary stages. For example, W Ursae Majoris consists of two giants, while Algol contains a giant and a main sequence star. In both systems the components are close to each other. In W Ursae Majoris the components, in fact, are so close that they touch. Such systems are called *contact binaries.*

A more detailed study of Algol during the 1960's revealed an interesting contradiction between theory and observation. That contradiction was known as the Algol paradox. The mass of the main sequence star is 3.7 times that of the sun, while the mass of its giant companion is only 0.8 solar masses. Astronomers assume that the components of binaries form at the same time and that the binaries start their evolution together. Thus, the more massive component should evolve faster and should now be in the giant stage. However, the less massive star reached the giant stage first.

A solution to this paradox was suggested by the German astronomers R. Kippenhahn and A. Weigert in 1966. Both stars begin to evolve normally on the main sequence. The more massive star converts helium to hydrogen faster and develops into a giant first. It begins increasing its volume considerably until its outer surface so closely approaches the other star that it comes into its gravitational field.

Now let us examine the Earth-moon system. Imagine a line joining the center of Earth with the center of the moon. At a certain point between Earth and the moon, called the Lagrange point, the gravity of Earth and the moon cancel out. If from this point we move a small distance toward the moon, we will become attracted by the moon and will fall onto it.

All the points in space around a celestial object where gravity has a certain given value are called *equipotential surfaces*. The equipotential surfaces close to the surface of Earth are almost spherical. The equipotential surfaces passing through the Lagrange point are called *Roche surfaces* or *Roche lobes*. There are two Roche lobes, one around each component of a double system, such as Earth and the moon or a double star. In a close binary, a star becoming a giant will swell until it completely fills its Roche lobe. If the interior of the star keeps expanding, the actual star will not increase in size; it will begin spilling matter on its companion through the Lagrange point.

IDENTIFYING CELESTIAL OBJECTS

Since celestial objects are classified by size and brightness, astronomers have used these characteristics and the locations of celestial objects for devising systems for naming and identifying them.

Various catalogs have been in use for some time to aid astronomers in identifying stars and nebulas. These catalogs also help to establish whether celestial bodies have already been identified and named.

General location and brightness are both considered in naming stars. Letters of the Greek alphabet are used in devising names for the brighter stars. Under this system, the Greek letter *alpha* is used for the brightest star in a constellation as seen by the astronomer. The Greek letter *beta* is used for the next brightest, and so on. The name of a star also identifies the constellation in which it appears. Thus, the star called *alpha* Crucis is the brightest star in the constellation Crux (the Cross), and *beta* Orionis is the second brightest star in the constellation Orion.

Variable stars are given names in the Roman alphabet; thus R Andromedae identifies a star in the constellation Andromeda.

Catalogs of stars, besides giving the names of stars, also supply their positions (by coordinates on the celestial sphere), brightnesses, motions, parallaxes, spectral types, and velocities, as well as other stellar properties.

Several catalogs are in use for identifying nebulas, galaxies, and star clusters. Most widely used are the catalogs devised by Charles Messier and Johan Dreyer. The Messier catalog, first compiled in the late 18th century, now has 109 entries. It identifies the brightest nebulas, galaxies, and clusters visible from France, Messier's native land. Dreyer's catalog, first compiled in the late 19th century, and now known as the *New General Catalogue* (augmented by two supplements), has almost 13,000 listings.

The various catalogs have their own identification numbers for nebulas, galaxies, and star clusters. Astronomers use these numbers to refer to the celestial bodies. In Messier's catalog, for example, the Crab Nebula is known as M 1. In the *New General Catalogue*, the Crab is NGC 1952.

Other catalogs are also in use. The Cederblad identifies diffuse nebulas; the Minkowski identifies new planetaries; and the Palomar charts show many faint extended nebulas. Amateurs are helped particularly by consulting the Skalnate-Pleso charts.

Galaxies

The Milky Way

It was Galileo who discovered that the Milky Way, viewed through the telescope, consists of a great number of stars. Astronomers gradually were forced to give up the idea that stars are placed on a spherical shell, as was still believed by Copernicus and Kepler. The mathematician Thomas Wright (1711–1785) proposed in 1750 that the solar system belongs either to a thin spherical layer of stars or to a ring of stars evolving around a heavier body. The German philosopher Immanuel Kant (1724–1804), taking up this idea, said in his 1755 book *General Natural History and Theory of the Heavens* that our solar system belongs to a flat, rotating system and that it is only one of the many other "island universes" that exist.

William Herschel was the first astronomer to try to divine the shape of the Milky Way galaxy from systematic observations. He assumed that the number of stars in any direction would be proportional to the extent of the galaxy in that direction. He constructed a map of the Milky Way by plotting points at distances proportional to the number of stars in that direction, thus outlining the boundaries of the Milky Way galaxy.

In 1918 the American astronomer Harlow Shapley (1885–1972) discovered that, contrary to what had been assumed, the sun is not at the center of our galaxy. Astronomers already had observed a large number of globular clusters—large, spherical associations of between ten thousand and one million stars that are found in all directions, not only in the plane of the galaxy. Assuming that these globular clusters are evenly distributed around the center of the galaxy and that the center of the system of clusters would coincide with the center of the galaxy, Shapley found that the clusters are arranged in a spherical system with the center of the galaxy at a distance of about 30,000 light-years in the direction of Sagittarius.

In 1927 the Swedish astronomer Bertil Lindblad (1895–1965) and the Dutch astronomer Jan Hendrik Oort deduced the rotation of the galaxy by observing the distribution of the radial velocities of the stars relative to the sun. Along one axis the stars move away from the sun, while in the direction perpendicular to that axis they move toward the sun. This motion can be explained by the *differential rotation* within the galaxy: the stars closest to the galactic center rotate fastest, while the stars far away rotate very slowly.

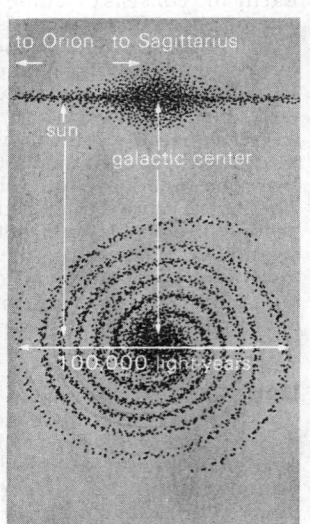

THE MILKY WAY GALAXY *is believed to be a spiral galaxy. Seen edge on, the galaxy would appear rather flat with a bulge at the center.*

The galaxy rotates very slowly. The sun travels around the galactic center at a speed of 250 kilometers (155 miles) per second and completes one revolution in 210 million years. In the sun's lifetime of 4.5 billion years, it has revolved 20 times around the galactic center.

Structure of the galaxy. During the 1920's it became clear that our galaxy was one among many, and that its structure should be similar to the many spiral galaxies that had already been observed. Astronomers, assuming that our galaxy looked especially like the Andromeda nebula, began looking for ways to observe the spiral structure of our galaxy. Our star, the sun, is located far from the galactic center, near one of the spiral arms. Consequently, if we look outward, we see relatively few stars, along with many open spaces through which we can peer toward the realm of the myriad other galaxies. If, however, we look along the plane of the galaxy, our view of the universe outside our own galaxy is completely blocked by the concentration of stars, cosmic dust, and gases that lie largely in the plane of our galaxy. This obstruction is so great that before light from stars within the central regions of the galaxy reaches us, it is absorbed and scattered by the intervening material.

Certain types of stars are clearly visible in the spiral arms of the Andromeda nebula: the very bright and hot O- and B-type stars. Because these stars are massive, they have relatively short lifetimes. Therefore, they should be young stars, formed recently from

dust and gas in the spiral arms of the galaxy. Astronomers surmise that such stars should be visible in our galaxy over great distances, and that they could serve to delineate the spiral arms. By plotting the directions and distances of O-type and B-type stars within our galaxy, astronomers have been able to map three distinct parts of spiral arms in the neighborhood of the sun.

21-cm radiation. Astronomers can penetrate farther into the galaxy with radio waves because these waves can penetrate clouded and obscured regions far better than light waves. One particular frequency received from the galaxy is the 21-cm line that radiates from neutral atomic hydrogen. Atomic hydrogen consists of a proton around which one electron circles. Radio waves are produced by changes in the spin of this electron. The spin of the electron can occupy only two positions: aligned with the spin of the proton, or opposite to this spin. When the electron flips from one state to the other, it emits or absorbs a quantum of relatively low energy. Because the two energy levels associated with the two spins are very close together, the result is radiation of relatively long wavelength, the 21-cm line.

Because neutral hydrogen is concentrated mainly in the spiral arms, radio astronomers have been able to map the structure of the galaxy by monitoring the 21-cm radiation in the galactic plane. Some of the galactic arms are moving toward us while others are moving away. We observe the 21-cm line slightly shifted toward shorter or toward longer wavelengths because of the Doppler effect.

THE MILKY WAY, *of which a portion is shown here, is a spiral galaxy. It consists of billions of stars, one of which, appearing toward the outer rim of the galaxy, is our sun.*

From optical and radio observations made of our galaxy, and from comparisons with observations made of other galaxies, such as Andromeda, astronomers have been able to construct a precise image. The galaxy is a huge disk about 100,000 light-years in diameter. The five or six spiral arms emerge from a central bulge. This is a flattened spheroid about 6000 light-years in diameter and 3000 light-years thick. It surrounds the *galactic nucleus* and has a diameter of about 20 light-years. The entire galaxy is surrounded by the *galactic halo,* a spherical region with a diameter comparable to that of the galaxy. The halo contains very thin gas, mainly hydrogen, and globular clusters. The globular clusters are distributed quite evenly throughout the galaxy and the galactic halo.

Galactic corona. The existence of the galactic corona, a giant but tenuous cloud of gas surrounding the galaxy and its halo, has recently been established. The corona around our galaxy is believed to extend outward a distance of about 300,000 light-years. Its existence was predicted from the gravitational effects it exerts on stars within the galaxy. Some of the stars at the visible edge of the Milky Way move faster than inner stars, and high-velocity stars that seem to have escape velocity do not leave the galaxy. Although the gas in the galactic corona is very thin, the corona contains an enormous amount of mass because of its size. Some scientists have estimated it at more than one trillion solar masses. Astronomers suspect that the extra mass from the corona probably explains why galaxies influence each other gravitationally.

The galactic nucleus. The galactic nucleus is in the direction of Sagittarius, hidden from Earth behind dense clouds of gas and dust.

Radio telescope observations made at a high angular resolution by intercontinental baseline interferometry reveal a very small region, the size of Jupiter's orbit around the sun, as a strong radio source. The same area also radiates strongly in infrared light. Taking all the radiation together, the nucleus emits as much radiation as would be emitted by no less than 100 million suns.

The nature of the energy source in the galactic center is still a mystery. The nucleus may be a massive black hole, perhaps formed by the sudden merging of millions of stars, or it may be a region of annihilation of matter and antimatter. Annihilation reactions produce gamma rays. This radiation coming from the nucleus has been detected by gamma ray telescopes aboard satellites.

Stellar populations. The spiral arms of galaxies are regions of active star formation. The newly formed stars and those formed within the last several billion years are known as *Population I* stars. Older stars, whose histories go back to the early stages of the galaxy, are called *Population II* stars. Population II stars are found chiefly between the spiral arms, outside of the galactic plane, in globular clusters, and in the galactic nucleus.

Because of their greater age, Population II stars differ somewhat in chemical composition from Population I stars. The latter have on average a concentration of metals 100 times greater than their forerunners. The metals and heavy elements were formed in the first-generation stars, blown into galactic space by supernova explosions, and then recycled by Population I stars.

Stellar clusters. There are many subsystems of stars within our galaxy, notably the *open clusters* and *globular clusters.*

Open clusters. Open clusters, such as the Pleiades and the Hyades in Taurus, contain Population I stars. Often they can be observed easily with binoculars or small telescopes. They consist of several hundred stars, apparently formed from one large gas cloud in the recent astronomical past. Clusters gradually lose stars because some of the stars are accelerated by the gravitational pull of stars passing nearby. Stars that escape become *field stars,* found throughout the disk of the galaxy. Astronomers believe that many, if not all, stars are born in clusters.

Globular clusters. Globular clusters are spherical collections of very densely packed Population II stars. Each cluster contains thousands to millions of stars. Their sizes range from 20 to about 100 light-years across. Several hundred globular clusters close to and in our galaxy are known. Globular clusters do not follow the general flattening of the galaxy; they are found evenly distributed in the spherical halo. Some globular clusters, quite distant from the galaxy, are termed intergalactic tramps. Globular clusters, like open clusters, lose stars continually, which may account for the presence of stars in the galactic halo.

A GLOBULAR CLUSTER *is a closely packed grouping of stars.*

THE GREAT ORION NEBULA *is an example of an emission nebula. A nearby star ionizes the nebula so that it emits light.*

NASA

tons reach each square meter (9 square feet) of Earth's atmosphere each second. The abundance distribution, that is, the relative amount of the elements, is similar to the abundance distribution of the sun and the solar system, with the exception of the elements lithium, beryllium, and boron. These elements have much higher abundance distributions.

THE TEN MOST COMMON ELEMENTS IN THE UNIVERSE
(atoms per million atoms)

Hydrogen	927,000
Helium	72,000
Oxygen	500
Neon	200
Nitrogen	153
Carbon	81
Silicon	23
Magnesium	21
Iron	14
Sulfur	9

Interstellar matter. About 10 percent of the mass of our galaxy consists of gas and dust. Much of the dust absorbs light, thus obscuring large parts of our galaxy from the view of optical astronomers.

The absorption and scattering of starlight by dust is called *extinction.* The extinction is not the same in all directions, but on the average it makes a star at a distance of 1000 parsecs appear one magnitude fainter.

Galactic nebulas. Some interstellar clouds are visible either because they reflect starlight or because they absorb ultraviolet light and reemit visible light. An example of the first type of cloud, a *reflection nebula,* is the nebula surrounding the Pleiades. The stars light up the gases in a way similar to that of automobile headlights illuminating dense fog.

The second type of cloud is called an *emission nebula.* An example is the Great Orion Nebula (M42). This nebula is located close to the tip of Orion's sword and can be seen easily even with binoculars or a small telescope. Emission nebulas are irradiated by very hot stars that are located nearby, usually O-type and B-type. These nebulas emit light by a process called *fluorescence.*

Their spectra mainly contain emission lines of hydrogen.

The composition of interstellar matter is about two-thirds hydrogen, one-third helium, and about 2 percent heavier elements. Few of these elements have aggregated into dust particles. It is estimated that the dust particles are about 100 meters (300 feet) apart, but there are enough of them in a line of sight to cause substantial extinction. An important recent discovery is that a large number of more complex, and even organic, molecules exist in interstellar space. More than 40 such molecules have been discovered, including those of carbon monoxide, water, ammonia, hydrogen cyanide, ethanol, hydrogen sulfide, and formaldehyde.

Cosmic radiation. The largest part, about 89 percent, of cosmic rays consists of hydrogen nuclei (protons); about 9 percent is helium nuclei (alpha particles); and 1 percent is electrons. Another 1 percent consists of atomic nuclei of heavier elements, mainly those that have atomic numbers of less than 26 (iron), but some heavier elements also are found. About 1000 pro-

Cosmic ray particles, which come toward Earth from all directions, possess *relativistic* velocities; that is, velocities close to that of light. Some of the particles possess enormous energy, much higher than the the energy imparted to particles by the largest particle accelerators on Earth.

The most energetic particles possess the energy required to lift 2.5 kilograms (5.5 pounds) of weight to a height of 1 meter (3.28 feet). As soon as the cosmic ray particles enter Earth's atmosphere, they fragment because of collisions with atoms and molecules. On Earth's surface, we can detect these fragments, termed *secondary particles* or *secondary radiation.* The stream of particles before interaction with Earth's atmosphere is called *primary cosmic radiation.*

Origin of cosmic rays. Because magnetic fields in space deflect cosmic ray particles, they reach Earth from all directions. Therefore, it is not possible at present to pinpoint the source of most of this radiation.

A small fraction of cosmic radiation is produced through great eruptions on the sun. Supernovas and pulsars are considered by astronomers as other possible sources of cosmic radiation. In addition, the center of the galaxy may be a source of cosmic rays.

Extragalactic Systems

For a long time, astronomers believed that everything observable in the sky is located within the Milky Way. The limits of the Milky Way were viewed as the limits of the universe. Only recently did astronomers realize that our galaxy is one of many star systems visible in telescopes as faint nebulas or patchy objects. Only during the 1920's did it become possible to prove that these objects are far away, outside the Milky Way.

With the discovery that we can observe celestial objects that are outside our galaxy, a new field in astronomy has opened up, *extragalactic astronomy.* Astronomers now can observe some systems that are believed to be

THIS SPIRAL GALAXY, *similar to the Milky Way, is located in Ursa Major.*

more than ten billion light-years away. This means that light coming from these systems has taken ten billion years—almost the entire lifetime of the universe—to reach us. Thus, we can see systems the way they looked shortly after the birth of the universe.

Island universes.

The nebula known as Andromeda, visible to the unaided eye as an elliptical patch in the constellation Andromeda, was recorded by the Persian astronomer Al-Sûfi in the tenth century; it was noted next in 1612 by Simon Marius (1570–1624). During the 18th and 19th centuries, with the improvement of telescopes, a large number of patchy objects became visible. The French astronomer Charles Messier (1730–1817) published in 1781 a list of 103 nebulas, mainly to help comet hunters distinguish comets from nebulas. This catalog contained several kinds of objects: star clusters, planetary nebulas, and 35 objects now known to be extragalactic systems.

The catalog is still used for indicating these nebulous objects. For example, the Andromeda nebula, which was listed as the 31st object in Messier's catalog, is still called Messier 31, or more simply, M 31. William Herschel in 1786 compiled a catalog of 1000 nebulas, to which were added 1000 more nebulas in 1789 and 500 more in 1802.

His son, who was the astronomer John Herschel (1792–1871), published in 1864 his *General Catalogue of Nebulae,* which listed 5079 celestial objects from both the northern and southern hemispheres.

With the general introduction of wide-aperture reflectors and long-exposure photography in observational astronomy, the structure of a large number of Messier's and Herschel's nebulas became visible. Many were recognized as large associations of stars, but the nature of many of the fuzzy objects remained a mystery.

Galactic or extragalactic? Like most stars, these fuzzy objects were too far away to measure their distance by methods used to find distances to nearer stars. Many astronomers suspected that these systems might be much farther away than the stars in our galaxy.

The beginning of the solution to this problem came as an unexpected result of the work of American astronomer Henrietta Leavitt (1868–1921) on Cepheid variables in 1912. Cepheids are pulsating stars whose period of luminosity is related to their absolute magnitude. From observing these stars in the Large and Small Magellanic Clouds, she discovered their period-luminosity relation. Using statistical methods, Shapley determined the absolute magnitudes of Cepheid variables and, with this information, calculated the distance of the Magellanic Clouds. He found that they are 70,000 parsecs away, a distance corresponding to about twice the diameter of our own galaxy, making the clouds close neighbors.

The problem of the distance of the spiral nebulas remained unsolved until 1923, when the American astronomer Edwin Powell Hubble (1889–1953) discovered Cepheid variables in the great nebula in Andromeda and other nebulas. From the apparent magnitudes of these variables, Hubble was able to show that the Andromeda nebula and a number of other nebulas are well outside our galaxy. They are island universes, like our own galaxy.

This discovery also eliminated the confusion in terminology that existed.

Until their true nature was discovered, island universes were called nebulas because of their fuzzy appearance. Now we know that the nebulas are large star systems, like the Milky Way. Today they are also called galaxies.

Three galaxies are visible to the unaided eye, the Andromeda galaxy in the northern hemisphere and the Large and Small Magellanic Clouds in the southern hemisphere. Because the light-gathering power of our eyes is so weak, only the central bulge of the Andromeda galaxy can be seen as a faint elliptical patch, although the whole galaxy extends over an area of 1.25° by 4°, about 20 times the apparent area of the moon. With binoculars with a wide aperture, we can see a larger number of galaxies.

Because of its proximity, (2 million light-years) the Andromeda galaxy is one of the best studied galaxies. Like the Milky Way, its spiral arms are rich in dust and gas and contain young, Population I stars. Observed at radio frequencies in the 21-cm line, the neutral hydrogen gas in the arms becomes visible, while the central bulge remains dark. The rotation speed of the galaxy can be derived from the Doppler shifts in the 21-cm line. The galaxy rotates around its nucleus with a period of about 200 million years. The Andromeda galaxy is 1.5 times the size of our own galaxy and is believed to contain 100 billion stars.

Classification of galaxies.

The number of galaxies in the universe is estimated to be about ten billion. Approximately 100 million are within range of the 5-meter (16.4 feet) Hale telescope.

There is a wide variety of sizes and shapes of galaxies. The smallest ones, called *dwarf galaxies,* are 2000 parsecs in diameter and have a mass ten million times that of the sun. The largest galaxies, the *giant ellipticals,* are 100,000 parsecs in diameter and have a mass 1000 billion times that of the sun. About 17 percent of galaxies that astronomers can observe through a telescope have a structure with spiral arms comparable to that of our own galaxy or to that of the Andromeda galaxy. However, among the 1000 brightest galaxies, almost 70 percent have a spiral structure. Eighty percent of all galaxies are elliptical, with no spiral arms and little or no visible structure. A small percentage of galaxies have irregular shapes; among them are the Large and Small Magellanic Clouds. One group of galaxies has a barred structure, consisting of a central bar from whose ends emerge two spiral arms.

Edwin Hubble in 1925 introduced a classification system for galaxies based on their forms and structure. *Elliptical galaxies* are designated with the letter E followed by an index suggesting the ellipticity of the galaxy. E0 is used for spherical galaxies and E7 for very

TYPES OF GALAXIES

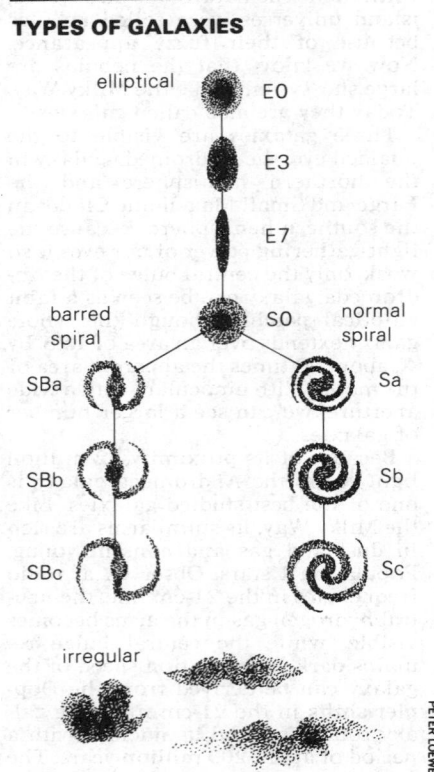

GALAXIES ARE CLASSIFIED *according to their shape.*

elongated ellipses. *Spiral galaxies* are denoted by S, and barred spirals by SB. Both are subdivided as a, b, and c types. The a types have large and very bright nuclei or central bars; the b types have a less pronounced nucleus; the c types have most of their light coming from the spiral arms. S0-type galaxies are an intermediate form between elliptical and spiral galaxies. They have a bright nucleus surrounded by an elliptical zone with little evidence of spiral arms. Spiral galaxies range in size from 50,000 to 200,000 light-years.

In contrast with elliptical galaxies, spiral galaxies and irregular galaxies contain large amounts of interstellar gas and dust and large numbers of newly formed stars. Spiral galaxies emit strongly in the 21-cm line, indicating a large presence of atomic hydrogen. Elliptical galaxies are almost invisible at the 21-cm frequency. It is believed that supernovas, which occur much more frequently in elliptical galaxies, keep these galaxies clean of interstellar gas and dust and thus prevent the formation of new stars.

Distribution of galaxies.
The galaxies are not evenly distributed throughout the universe but occur in *clusters,* forming sheets and filaments of galaxies around large areas that are almost devoid of galaxies. Our galaxy has several neighbors, of which the Small and Large Magellanic Clouds

are the closest. These galaxies are members of the so-called *Local Group,* which also includes the Andromeda galaxy and at least 25 smaller galaxies located in a sphere of three million light-years. These galaxies are so close that they interact gravitationally. For example, the plane of the Andromeda galaxy is somewhat warped by the presence of two satellite galaxies and, under mutual gravitational attraction, it approaches our galaxy with a speed of 500 kilometers (310 miles) per second.

Over 2000 clusters of galaxies are known, and it is believed that billions exist. Most of the clusters contain at least 50 members. *Regular clusters* are more or less spherical, with a higher concentration of galaxies toward the center. They contain mainly E (elliptical) and S0 (between elliptical and spiral) galaxies and have a total mass about 10,000 times the mass of our galaxy.

The Hercules cluster, in the Hercules constellation, is an example of an *irregular cluster.* Such clusters are less symmetrical than regular clusters and contain fewer galaxies. They usually contain about 100 times the mass of our galaxy. Irregular clusters with a small number of galaxies generally contain spiral galaxies. Those with a large number of galaxies generally contain elliptical galaxies.

The Local Group, the Virgo Cluster, and the Coma Cluster are relatively close and form a *supercluster.* About 50 superclusters, which are clusters of clusters, have been identified in the universe.

Distances of galaxies.
Cepheid variables, visible only in galaxies closer than ten million light-years, play a role in proving the extragalactic nature of spiral galaxies. By contrast, the very bright O- and B-type stars, which in our galaxy delineate the spiral arms, are clearly visible in other galaxies at distances up to 75 million light-years. These stars have approximately the same absolute magnitude; thus, by measuring their apparent magnitude, astronomers are able to estimate the distances of the galaxies that contain them.

For distances beyond 75 million light-years, supernovas can be used to estimate distances. Supernovas are so bright that they can be observed in galaxies at enormous distances. Supernovas occur sporadically, so they are not suitable for systematic determinations of distance in the universe. It is reasonable to assume that in clusters the brightest or largest galaxies are comparable in brightness or size. The distance of these clusters can be estimated by comparing the brightest or largest galaxies with those in clusters whose distance has been determined by other means.

Hubble's law.
The spectra of the light from distant galaxies contain the same absorption lines as do the sun and stars.

The American astronomer Vesto Melvin Slipher (1876–1939) was hired in 1914 by Percival Lowell to study the spectra of the spiral nebula in order to find out whether nebulas rotate. If they

THE MILKY WAY *galaxy and other nearby galaxies form a cluster of galaxies called the Local Group.*

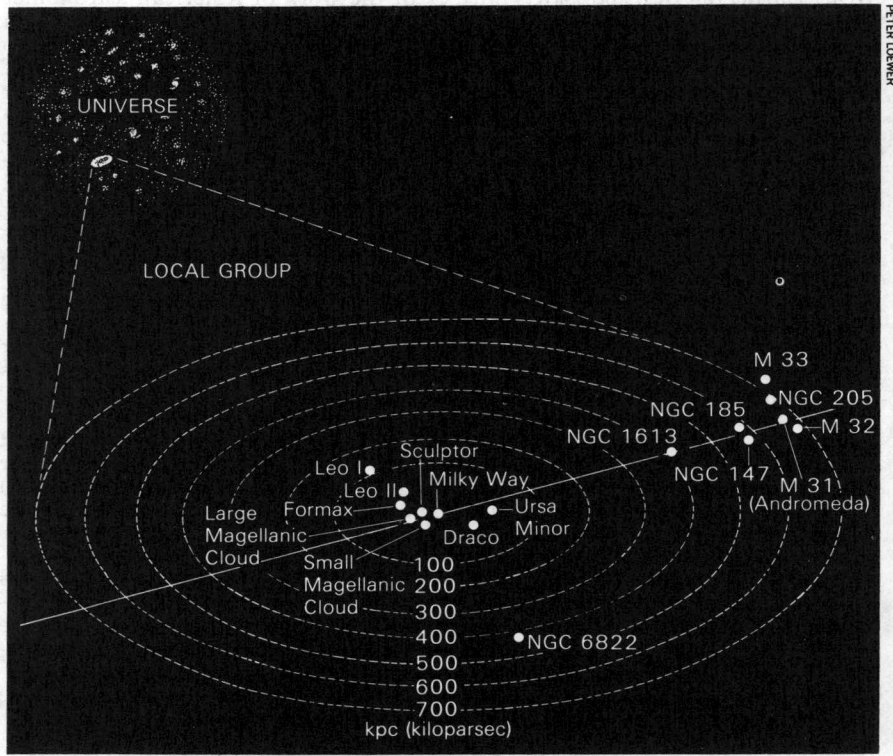

do, it was argued, the absorption lines in the spectra from one side of the galaxy would be shifted toward the red; those coming from the other side of the galaxy would be shifted toward the blue. Slipher noted that the absorption lines were shifted to the red in almost every galaxy. He also found that this red shift was generally larger in the fainter galaxies.

If one assumes that the red shift is caused by the Doppler effect, it appears that the fainter galaxies—the farthest ones—move away from us at higher speeds than the brighter, or closer, ones.

Hubble started his systematic study of galaxies during the early 1920's and established the extragalactic nature of galaxies in 1923. As early as 1919, having studied 86 novas and 40 Cepheid variables, Hubble established from their apparent magnitudes the distance of about two dozen galaxies. When Hubble compared his results with the red shifts measured by Slipher, he reached a surprising conclusion. The recession velocity of galaxies is directly proportional to their distance. In other words, the farther away a galaxy is from Earth, the faster it moves away from Earth.

The relationship between the recession velocity V and the distance D of a galaxy is given by Hubble's law:

$$V = H \times D$$

H is a constant called Hubble's constant. This constant indicates the increase in velocity with distance. Hubble initially found that the velocity of galaxies increases by 15 kilometers (9.3 miles) per second for each million light-years that they are farther away from us.

Hubble's discovery led to a new method for measuring the distance of galaxies. Most important, it revolutionized the understanding of the structure of the universe. The fact that galaxies appear to move away from us in all directions became the basis of the theory of the expanding universe and the big bang.

Active galaxies.
A number of galaxies are said to be *active* because they are very powerful transmitters of radiation in certain ranges of the electromagnetic spectrum.

Seyfert galaxies.
A group constituting 1 percent of spiral galaxies is called the *Seyfert galaxies,* after the American astronomer Carl Seyfert, who first identified them in 1943. Seyfert galaxies have bright, very compact nuclei that exhibit violent activity. In contrast with the spectra of the nuclei of normal spiral galaxies, which contain only absorption lines, the spectra of the nuclei of Seyfert galaxies contain broad emission lines, indicating the presence of hot gas. The nuclei are powerful infrared transmitters and have been identified as x-ray sources.

The x-ray emission of some sources

CENTAURUS A *is one of the strongest radio galaxies known.*

shows a variability in output of less than ten minutes. Variations over such short times are possible only if a source is less than ten light-minutes across. Yet, the total output can be ten times larger than that of our own galaxy. Astrophysicists have not yet been able to explain the production of so much energy in so small a space, but the possibility of an enormous black hole accreting matter has not been ruled out.

Radio galaxies.
During the early years of radio astronomy, shortly after the World War II, astronomers discovered a number of strong radio sources in the sky. One of these sources is in the constellation of Cygnus; it is called Cygnus A. It was discovered in 1946 by James Stanley Hey with radar equipment. In 1951 the German astronomer Walter Baade (1893–1959) identified this source with the 5-meter (16.4 feet) Hale telescope as a galaxy at a distance of 700 million light-years.

Centaurus A, a galaxy in the southern sky, is only 16 million light-years away. It occupies an area in the sky several times that of the moon and can easily be observed with binoculars. Observed at radio frequencies, the radiation comes from two huge lobes stretching over 9 degrees in the sky, about 20 times the width of the moon. The lobes stretch out over 2.5 million light-years, making Centaurus A one of the largest radio galaxies known. The energy production at radio wavelengths is about 1000 times that of our own galaxy.

The nucleus of Centaurus A is hidden by a dark lane of dust that seems to cut the galaxy in two halves. Observed at infrared wavelengths, the nucleus appears to be a compact area with a high stellar density.

Cygnus A and Centaurus A are examples of *extended* radio sources. Radio sources with angular diameters of less than one second of arc and diameters of less than ten parsecs are termed *compact* sources.

Quasars.
During the 1960's, astronomers studied a number of radio sources with very small angular diameters that did not match any galaxies

THE 3C 273 QUASAR *appears in this x-ray image as a very high-energy object.*

that could be seen. Because the angular resolution of radio telescopes was limited, it was difficult to pinpoint their exact locations. In 1962 one of these radio sources, called 3C 273 (Number 273 in the *Third Cambridge Catalogue of Radio Sources*), became occulted by the moon. Cyril Hazard, an astronomer at the Parkes Radio Observatory in Australia, determined its position accurately. The occultation also showed that the object has two components with a separation of 20 arc seconds.

With this information, the astronomer Maarten Schmidt, in 1962 at Mount Palomar Observatory, identified on photographic plates taken with the Hale telescope a radio source with a starlike object of magnitude 12.8 with a jetlike appendage. This object had an absorption spectrum that was shifted toward the red by a very large amount. If the red shift were caused by the Doppler effect, 3C 273 would have a speed 0.146 times the speed of light. Another starlike object, 3C 48, had an even larger red shift; thus, it would be moving away from us at 0.303 times the speed of light.

Astronomers estimated that if these speeds correspond to that of the expansion of the universe, quasar 3C 273 is at least 1.6 billion light-years from Earth, and 3C 48 more than three billion light-years away. Today it is believed that each one is probably twice that far away. Yet 3C 273 can be seen through a fairly ordinary 10-centimeter (4-inch) telescope. This means that 3C 273 must be five trillion times as luminous as the sun.

The red shift controversy.
The red shift of an extragalactic object is termed cosmological when it is caused by the velocity of the object resulting from its participation in the expansion of the universe. The quasar with the largest red shift is an object called PKS 3000-330. The lines in its spectrum are shifted toward longer wavelengths by a factor of 3.78. If this red shift is cosmological, this quasar would move at a fantastic speed, equal to 0.91 times that of light. According to Hubble's law, this object would be over twelve billion light-years away.

From the amount of radiation received, astrophysicists can calculate the total energy output of quasars. If we assume that quasars have cosmological red shifts, then the amount of energy produced by them is enormous. Several quasars radiate more energy than 2000 ordinary galaxies.

In some quasars the radiation has varied strongly in a period of one week or one month. Intensity variations of such short durations are possible only if the region emitting the radiation is small. If a quasar shows variability over one week, the size of the quasar cannot be larger than one light-week. Astrophysicists thus far have no satisfactory theory for explaining such energy production.

Because of these problems, some astronomers have raised doubts that the red shifts of quasars are caused by the Doppler effect. If quasars were closer, then their energy could be explained more easily. However, one would also have to explain the large red shifts by some other mechanism than the Doppler effect.

The American astronomer Halton C. Arp identified a number of quasars that seem to be physically linked to other quasars or to galaxies, but have fundamentally different red shifts than their companions have. Arp believes that these systems prove that quasars do not follow the general expansion of the universe, but may be closer by, although they are flying away from us at very high velocities.

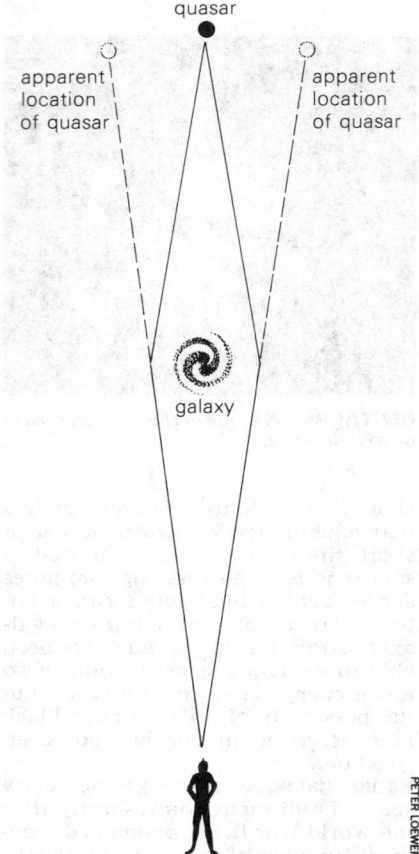

A GALAXY'S GRAVITATION *can act as a lens, bending light and causing a distorted image.*

Gravitational lenses. In 1979 a phenomenon was discovered that may contribute to settling the issue of how far away quasars actually are. Astronomers found a pair of identical quasars separated by only six arc-seconds with similar spectra, red shift, and color. It seemed improbable that two quasars with identical red shifts and spectra could be found so close together as to be hard to separate even with the best telescopes under the best conditions.

The explanation is that the double quasar is really just one quasar, with the gravity of an intervening galaxy bending the light as a lens does, so that astrophysicists see two images of the same quasar. If a gravitational lens is to produce two images, it should be approximately halfway between Earth and the quasar. Absorption lines stemming from the intervening galaxy have been observed in the spectra of the two components. These absorption lines have a lower red shift than those of the quasar, showing that the galaxy is closer than the quasar.

The nature of quasars. At present, no universally accepted theory explains quasars. Many astrophysicists believe that quasars are early stages in the evolution of galaxies. Most astronomers believe that an enormous black hole may be the energy source. But no theory exists that would give a detailed description of the processes resulting in the enormous amounts of energy produced by quasars.

Cosmology

Cosmology, as a branch of astronomy, is the scientific study of the general structure, origin, and evolution of the universe. It differs from cosmology as a branch of philosophy or metaphysics in that it concerns itself only with the categories proper to physics; that is, space and time, matter, radiation, energy, and their interactions.

By the end of the 19th century, the concept of the universe was as follows: The universe contains stars and nebulas that are vast distances apart. There is a large concentration of these stars in an area known as the Milky Way. There are also stars scattered throughout space, and their number is infinite. The universe is thought always to have looked as it looks now, and will remain the same indefinitely.

Olber's paradox. Yet there was an observational fact that made these ideas about the universe untenable. Let us assume, as astronomers did in the past, that the number of stars is infinite. If so, when we look at the sky in any direction, we will see a star, and the sky will radiate with a brightness comparable to that of the solar disk, because every space will be filled with the disk of a star. Obviously, this is not the case.

At first there seem to be two possible explanations for this paradox. Either the number of stars is finite, and where the sky is black we peek into empty space, or the universe has existed for a finite time, and only the light of stars that has traveled for less than the age of the universe reaches us. The presently accepted solution, formulated by the American astronomer Edward Robert Harrison in 1964, is somewhat different: "Light travels at finite speed, and when looking out in space we also look back in time. . . . The look-back time is much greater than the luminous lifetime of stars."

Modern theories. At the end of the 19th century, two scientists, Carl Gottfried Neumann ((1832–1925) and Hugo von Seelinger (1849–1924), tried to apply Newton's laws of gravitation to the entire universe. Their calculations showed that all the moving particles of matter in the universe would either keep moving apart from each other indefinitely or would slow down and begin falling toward each other under the influence of mutual gravitational attraction.

At that time a description of the universe as an entity undergoing large-scale changes seemed philosophically unacceptable. In order to create a model of a static universe, Neumann and Seelinger introduced a universal repulsion force that would increase with the distance between particles and keep the universe from collapsing.

Modern cosmology. In 1915 Einstein published his new theory of general relativity, in which time is stated to be the fourth dimension. He described gravitation as the curvature of this four-dimensional space. In 1917 Einstein applied his theory of general relativity to the entire universe. Again he found no static solution. The universe he described would either collapse or expand forever. At that time, it was not known that the universe is expanding, and Einstein, who believed that the universe is static, tried to solve the problem by introducing a cosmological constant; that is, a force acting over long distances that would prevent the universe from collapsing.

The Russian mathematician Aleksandr Friedmann (1888–1925) developed another model of the universe by applying Einstein's theory of general relativity. He found that the universe had expanded from a state in which all matter was originally concentrated in a small space.

Friedmann's cosmological model predicted that the universe can be either open, flat, or closed. In an open universe, the gravitational attraction between fragments that are flying in all directions is too small to slow them down, and the expansion of the universe will be expected to go on forever. If, however, the mass of the universe or, better, the average density, is high enough, then the gravitational forces between fragments will be great enough to slow the expansion down. This is the explanation known as the closed universe theory. In the closed universe, fragments will eventually begin falling together toward other fragments. The entire universe will collapse gravitationally, constituting a big bang in reverse: the big crunch. The average density below which the universe is open is called the *critical density*. The critical density is about 10^{-29} gram/cm^3, which corresponds to a few hydrogen atoms per cubic meter. If the density of the universe is above that value, the universe becomes closed. A universe in which the average density equals the critical density is called a *flat universe*. A flat universe will expand forever, but at a lower rate than expected in an open universe.

Astrophysicists have not yet been able to determine whether the universe is closed, open, or flat. It is certain that gravitational forces slow down the expansion of the universe. This slowing down is expressed by cosmologists in terms of a *deceleration parameter*.

The geometry of the universe.
Cosmologists over many years have tried several approaches to determine whether the universe is closed, open, or flat. One of the methods employed consists of determining how much expansion is slowing down by trying to quantify the deceleration parameter. In another method, cosmologists have tried to evaluate the density of the universe by counting the galaxies in certain areas and multiplying those numbers by the average mass per galaxy. Most of the resulting calculations yield the strong inference that the visible mass of the universe repre-

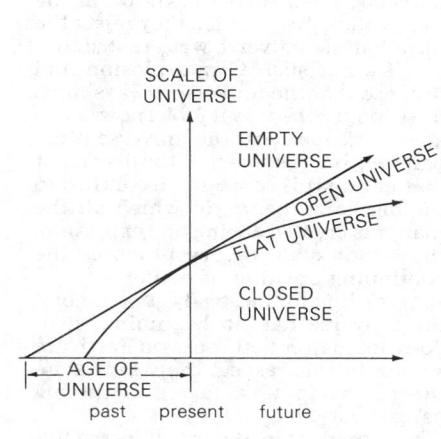

OPEN OR CLOSED?

To illustrate the evolution of the universe, cosmologists construct a graph whose axes are time and the size of the universe. On the graph are plotted two lines. The upper line is the dividing line between the possibility of a completely empty universe and one in which some matter exists. The lower line represents the *critical density* below which the universe is considered closed. In a closed universe, the *average density* of matter is high enough to produce sufficient gravity so that the universe will eventually collapse in on itself.

Between the two lines the universe is considered open: the average density of matter in such a universe would not produce enough gravity to reverse the expansion of the universe. A universe in which the critical density equals the average density is called a flat universe; the line for such a universe is the same as that for the lower line.

sents only about 10 percent of the critical mass (the total mass of the universe at critical density).

The hidden mass. Recent estimates based on motions of galaxies in clusters indicate that the average density is close to the critical density; thus, many astronomers believe that the universe is flat. The 90 percent of the mass that remains invisible is referred to as the hidden mass or missing mass. Some astrophysicists have suggested that the hidden mass may consist of very faint, small dwarf stars, or cool objects the size of Jupiter. Black holes, when they do not interact with surrounding matter, are perfectly invisible. This could also account for the hidden mass.

The big bang. In 1927 the Belgian priest Georges Lemaître (1894–1966) published a paper in which he linked the observation of the red shift in distant nebulas by astronomers to a model of the universe based on relativity. Lemaître proposed that the universe began with the explosion of a primeval atom. This explosion subsequently became known as the big bang. The primeval atom would be a single mass from which all the mass now present in the universe would have been formed.

In 1929 came Hubble's publication of his research on the velocity-distance relationship of galaxies, with observational evidence that the universe is expanding. By 1936, based on the red shift, Hubble had enough data to give a numerical value to the distance of galaxies. Some problems with the big bang theory remained, however. According to the value calculated for Hubble's constant in 1936, the big bang

took place 1.8 billion years ago. This, then, could be taken as the age of the universe: if it is known how fast the galaxies are flying apart (Hubble's constant), then it can be determined when the expansion began. But geologists have established that the oldest rocks on Earth are at least 3 billion years old. Clearly Earth could not be older than the universe. If, then, the geologists were correct, something was wrong.

The age of the universe. Walter Baade, who had discovered that there are two stellar populations, found that the short-period variables used by Hubble and Milton La Salle Humason (1891–1972) to determine the distance from Earth to Andromeda and other galaxies are Population I stars rather than Population II stars. Therefore they are twice as far away as first believed. This implies that they are also twice as luminous as originally assumed. Consequently, all distance determinations based on the short-period variables were wrong by a factor of two, and the galaxies in which they were observed are also twice as far away.

Because the galaxies are much farther away than previously thought, they must have taken much longer to get where they are. Thus, the universe is much older than 1.8 billion years. Current estimates by scientists of the age of the universe fall between 10 and 20 billion years. Harvey Butcher, an astronomy professor at the University of Groningen, the Netherlands, analyzed light from the sun and from 20 other stars and concluded, in July, 1987, that the universe is 11 to 12 billion years old.

Steady state cosmology.

In 1948 the British astronomers Fred Hoyle, Thomas Gold, and Hermann Bondi advanced another model of the universe. Their theory is known as the steady state theory. In it, they reject the idea that the universe was created by a single event, such as an explosion, and propose that the universe always must have looked the way it looks now. They accept the idea that the universe is expanding, but assume that the density of matter remains constant. In contrast to the big bang theory, in which all the matter is created during one explosion, the steady state theory proposes the continuing creation of matter.

According to the steady state theory, the universe has no beginning, so it does not matter that rocks on Earth are so old. In this respect the steady state theory has an advantage over the big bang theory.

The steady state theory offers the following explanation of the expansion of the universe. As the galaxies moved farther and farther apart, over millions or billions of years, new galaxies formed from the hydrogen that was continuously being created. Not much hydrogen was required, perhaps one atom formed per cubic mile per century. With enough empty space and enough time, there would be enough hydrogen available to form many galaxies. If, then, the steady state theory is true, on average the galaxies in the universe would always be the same distance from each other, even though always flying apart. In the big bang theory, the distances between the galaxies would become greater and greater over time. However, the amount of time for these differences to show up is so great that it is difficult to tell which theory is right.

Cosmic background radiation.

Until 1965 the only existing proof for the big bang theory was the red shift in the spectra of distant galaxies and quasars. However, the red shift of quasars was so great that some astrophysicists of that era believed it was caused by some other, still unknown mechanism.

In 1948 the Russian-American physicist George Gamov (1904–1968) stated that the universe as a whole should be emitting radio waves that are the remnants of the big bang. If the universe had started with a big bang, it should have cooled down, just as an expanding gas does, to a temperature of about 5K (−450.7°F). Gamov believed that this radiation would not be perceived with a radio telescope because it would be extremely weak.

About 1965 two physicists from Bell Telephone, Arno H. Penzias and Robert W. Wilson, were experimenting with a horn antenna installed in Holmdel, New Jersey, not far from where Jansky made his first observations of radio waves coming from space. The antenna had been used for communications with Telstar satellites, and was readied for use as a radio telescope. Using a very sensitive receiver to test the sensitivity of the antenna, the researchers picked up a hiss at a wavelength of 7.35 centimeters with an intensity that seemed independent of the orientation of the antenna. Penzias and Wilson first assumed that the radiation was produced by the antenna itself. The antenna had been a roosting place for pigeons, so it was possible that pigeon droppings were the source of the radio signal. (Any matter at a temperature above absolute zero emits radiation, known as black body radiation.) After thorough cleaning of the antenna, the signal was still present and the two researchers concluded that the radiation came from the universe. The most puzzling fact was that this radiation appeared to be isotropic—coming from every direction in the universe with the same intensity.

The physicists Robert H. Dicke and James E. Peebles, both unaware of Gamov's 1948 statement, identified this radiation with the equivalent of the radiation of a black body at a temperature of 3K (−454°F).

Black body radiation.

Any object at a temperature above absolute zero radiates electromagnetic waves. Very hot bodies mainly produce radiation of relatively short wavelengths. Cooler objects emit radiation of longer wavelengths. The entire universe can be viewed as a gas that has expanded and therefore cooled down to a temperature of 3K (−454°F).

In reality, the cosmic background radiation received on Earth comes from matter that is much hotter, but that is moving away from Earth at high velocity because of the expansion of the universe. Because of the Doppler shift, this radiation is strongly shifted toward longer wavelengths and thus appears to be coming from matter at 3K.

The cosmic background radiation is very weak. If we were to place an ice-cream cone in front of Penzias and Wilson's horn antenna, we would pick up a microwave signal about 22 milion times stronger than the cosmic background radiation.

Several astronomers have measured the intensity of the background radiation at different frequencies; its intensity fits closely with that of a black body at a temperature of 3K.

Astronomers consider cosmic background radiation the strongest evidence for the occurrence of the big bang about 15 billion years ago.

In 1969 and 1971 astronomers discovered that cosmic background radiation is not entirely isotropic. In one direction the radiation seems to come from matter that is slightly hotter. More precise measurements made high in the atmosphere aboard a U-2 airplane in 1976 confirmed the earlier measurements. Radiation coming from the direction of the constellation Leo is less Doppler shifted toward longer wavelengths. From the difference in red shift, astronomers could calculate that the solar system, and probably the entire galaxy, is moving in the direction of Leo with a velocity of about 600 kilometers per second.

The inflationary universe.

Three observational facts, the red shift of distant galaxies and quasars, cosmic background radiation, and the abundance of helium, are viewed by cosmologists as confirmation of the big bang. Most of the helium present in the universe would have been formed by fusion during the first minutes following the big bang. For this reason, scientists believe that the present abundance of helium provides confirmation of this theory.

Certain properties of the universe have been highly perplexing to cosmologists, however. One of them is the large-scale homogeneity of the universe, which is best demonstrated by the apparent homogeneity of the measured background radiation. Except for a small difference that is caused by the Doppler effect, resulting from the motion of our own galaxy, the background radiation is highly isotropic. The intensity of the radiation coming from different parts in the sky is the same to about one part in 10,000. Homogeneity in a system is usually considered to be the consequence of the exchange of matter or energy. (This can be understood readily by observing how water of different temperatures poured into a bucket will soon reach a uniform temperature because the cooler and hotter masses readily mix with each other.) However, this exchange of energy cannot have taken place everywhere in the universe. Certain parts of the universe are so far from other parts that light has not had sufficient time to travel from one part to the others.

The noted American physicist Alan H. Guth has proposed a model for the first moments following the big bang that would explain the large-scale uniformity of the universe. Before the universe reached the age of 10^{-35} seconds, according to Guth's model, it is suggested that there occurred an enormously rapid expansion, or inflation. During the sudden expansion, according to the model, any irregularities that would have prevented the universe from becoming uniform were smoothed out.

The inflationary theory also predicts that the universe is flat. The curvature of space can be compared to the curvature of the surface of a balloon. When a balloon suddenly inflates to a very large size, its surface becomes flatter, almost indistinguishable from a plane surface. Cosmologists believe that the sudden inflation of the universe right after the big bang caused space to become rigorously flat.

THE SEARCH FOR EXTRATERRESTRIAL INTELLIGENCE

Although astronomers have tried to find the artifacts of intelligent beings on other planets (for example, the elusive canals on Mars), an active search for extraterrestrial beings became possible only with the advent of radio astronomy. Because the operation of radio telescopes is expensive and each instrument is continually in demand for astronomical programs, it is mandatory that the search for extraterrestrial intelligence be based on scientific reasoning.

Scientists agree today that life in the universe will only be found in surroundings similar to our own. It would begin on a planet that circles a star very similar to the sun. A hotter star would radiate too much deadly ultraviolet radiation. A cooler star would not radiate enough energy, and processes basic to life, such as photosynthesis, would not occur. The planet would rotate fast enough so that its temperature would not vary too much between day and night. The planet would have to be at the right distance from the star so that the temperature would not deviate too much from the 10° to 38°C (50° to 100°F) range, the optimal temperature range for the occurrence of complex chemical reactions. Molecules that make up living organisms, such as proteins, react very slowly at low temperatures and disintegrate at high temperatures.

We know that a large number of stars similar to our sun exist in our galaxy. As a matter of fact, the sun belongs to the most common group of stars in our galaxy. These are the main sequence stars. Astronomers believe that many stars have planets circling them, although such stars with planets have not yet been observed directly. Some stars appear to wiggle as they travel, indicating that both the star and an invisible companion are rotating around a common center of mass. Even if the stars having planets that satisfy the conditions for life comprise an extremely small fraction of the total number of stars in the Milky Way (200 billion), their number could still be substantial. Of course, not all these planets will have civilizations that will reveal themselves by the transmission of radio waves. Some might not be advanced enough (as we were not 100 years ago), and others might be so advanced that they consider us too primitive and not worth contacting.

In 1961 Frank Drake devised a formula that expresses the chance of existence of an extraterrestrial civilization:

$$N = R \cdot f_g\, f_p\, n f_l\, f_i\, f_c\, L$$

in which R is the average rate of star formation, f_g is the fraction of stars that could support life, f_p is the fraction of stars that have planets that could be inhabitable, n is the number of such planets per solar system, f_l is the fraction of suitable planets on which life has developed, f_i is the fraction of these planets on which life has taken intelligent forms, f_c is the fraction of these intelligent civilizations that have reached the stage in which they are able to communicate, and L is the duration of that stage. Some of the factors in Drake's formula, such as R and f_g, can be estimated fairly well, while some of the others are open to conjecture. It is, therefore, not surprising that astronomers have come up with results for N ranging between 1 (Earth is the only planet with intelligent life) and 100,000,000.

Since 1960 radio astronomers have pointed their radio telescopes at targets on the celestial sphere in the hope of detecting

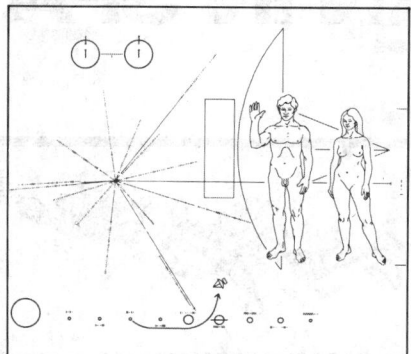

PIONEER 10 *carried this drawing, a message to alien life.*

signals produced by intelligent beings. These signals would be expected to differ from the radio waves transmitted naturally by celestial objects. Natural signals look much like the noise and static that interfere with radio reception. The signals astronomers are looking for would be characterized by certain regular patterns, such as coded transmissions or transmissions similar to the radar signals produced on Earth. (Some radars on Earth are powerful enough to be received by a civilization many light-years away.) In 1967 the English astronomer Jocelyn Bell discovered such signals—very precisely timed pulses. This discovery was kept secret for a few months, until it became clear that the pulses were transmitted by a new type of celestial object, the very fast spinning pulsars.

For their search programs, radio astronomers have selected one portion of the radio spectrum, radio waves with wavelengths between 18 and 21 cm. That portion is relatively free of radio noise from natural cosmic sources. A more important reason is that the hydroxyl radical (—OH), as found in water, emits radio waves with 18 cm-wavelengths, and neutral hydrogen emits 21-cm waves. These two wavelengths are used extensively in radio astronomy because they indicate the presence of hydrogen and water. Therefore, it is considered likely that extraterrestrial civilizations would also be scanning or transmitting in these frequencies.

Drake directed the first large SETI (search for *extraterrestrial intelligence*) project, called Ozma, in 1960. With the 305-meter (1000-foot) reflector at Arecibo, Puerto Rico, project members tried to detect 21-cm radio signals from two nearby stars, Epsilon Eridiani and Tau Ceti. Since then, more than a dozen such search programs have been undertaken. The most advanced instruments for this research consist of special receivers that scan the heavens automatically at a very large number of frequencies. Researchers at the University of California use a system that listens simultaneously to 65,536 channels. Computers search the signals from these channels for certain regularities, polarization, or pulses. NASA is planning a system that will automatically analyze eight million channels. It is expected to be in operation by the end of this decade.

Astronomers so far have gathered more than 120,000 hours of observations, but no signal has been received that can clearly be identified as originating from an advanced civilization. The absence of such signals is one of the arguments used by a group of scientists who believe that this search is a waste of money.

THE RADIO TELESCOPE AT ARECIBO, *Puerto Rico, has been used to listen for extraterrestrial radio signals.*

MAN IN SPACE

The idea of space travel appeared early in literature. Bishop Francis Godwin (1562–1633) wrote *The Man in the Moone,* published in 1638, in which huge birds carry the hero to the moon. Cyrano de Bergerac de Savinien (1619–1655) described the use of rocket propulsion in *Voyage to the Moon* (1656). In the late 19th century, Jules Verne (1828–1905), in *From the Earth to the Moon* (1865), employed a huge cannon to fire a manned projectile fitted with rockets to steer it. By the turn of the

MAN HAS LONG DREAMED *of leaving the ground, as did the mythical Daedalus.*

century, H. G. Wells's (1866–1946) romantic novel, *The First Men in the Moon* (1901), presaged countless tales to come based on interplanetary travel.

The first steps in space were short flights in the upper atmosphere and orbits around Earth. Then followed the longer journeys in space, and finally man landed on the moon. The space shuttle has increased man's mobility in space, and will probably enable the building of permanently manned space stations during the 1990's. This, in turn, will open the way to manned exploration of the planets during the first decades of the 21st century.

Rockets

The first mention of rockets appears in ancient Chinese writings. The Chinese used rockets in warfare and in fireworks as early as 1232. The key to rocket operation was gunpowder, a mixture of nitrate salt, probably saltpeter, which served as an oxidizing agent, along with a combustible. Arabs, Greeks, Italians, and Germans later developed mixtures of sulfur, charcoal, saltpeter, petroleum, and turpentine for rockets used in warfare.

Modern rocket technology.

The Russian physicist Konstantin Tsiolkovsky (1857–1935) was the first to investigate seriously the use of rockets for space travel. Tsiolkovsky published in 1903 an extensive work, *Exploration of Planetary Space by Means of Reaction-Powered Equipment.* In this book Tsiolkovsky introduced the word *sputnik,* literally co-traveler, for an artificial satellite.

The American physicist Robert H. Goddard (1882–1945) during his student years devoted time to rocket experiments and detailed calculations. Years of experimenting with various explosive charges as propellants led to the publication, in 1919, of Goddard's revolutionary treatise, *A Method of Reaching Extreme Altitudes.* During his career he obtained over 200 patents that embraced liquid-propellant-fed combustion chambers, thrust modulation, and staged-rocket vehicles. He ran rocket tests in a vacuum and proved that thrust and propulsion could take place in an airless environment. From 1920 on, Goddard worked at developing liquid-propellant engines. At Worcester, Massachusetts, in 1926, he first launched a rocket with such an engine. The propellants were liquid oxygen and gasoline.

The German physicist Hermann Oberth in 1923 published *The Rocket into Interplanetary Space.* This work contained many important concepts, including the advantages of staged rockets, self-cooled rocket thrust chambers, improved thrust outside Earth's atmosphere (citing Goddard's experiment as proof), the theory of gas flow through nozzles, and the selection of hydrogen and oxygen as a preferred propellant for high performance. In 1927 the *Verein für Raumschiffahrt* (Society for Space Travel), under the presidency of Oberth, began rocket experiments with liquid oxygen and gasoline. Werner von Braun (1912–1977) joined the society in 1929. Army influence infiltrated the society in 1932, resulting in the development of the world's first large rocket missile, the V-2. It first flew in 1942. By the end of World War II, more than 3000 had been produced. This 12,925-kilogram (28,500-pound) vehicle, 14 meters (46 feet) long and 1.7 meters (65 inches) in diameter, took off with 25,400 kilograms (56,000 pounds) of thrust and carried a 998-kilogram (2200-pound) warhead. It traveled 290 kilometers (180 miles) in just five minutes. The V-2 was to become the first tool for research beyond the atmosphere in the United States, the Soviet Union, France, and the United Kingdom.

After the collapse of Germany in 1945, Russian forces acquired considerable equipment, as well as complete and partially assembled V-2s. A number of German technicians earlier had gone to the Soviet Union to further the development of rockets, initiated at the Gas Dynamics Laboratory in Leningrad during the 1930's. By the end of the war, the Russians had developed long-range rockets on their own.

ROBERT H. GODDARD, *shown here* (second from left) *with one of his later rockets, was one of the most important pioneers in the field of rocket design.*

A boost to progress in U.S. rocketry was the postwar defection of key German scientists, engineers, and technicians. Components of about 100 V-2s were brought to the United States and assembled and launched at White Sands Proving Ground, New Mexico, between 1946 and 1952. Photographs taken from these V-2s gave U.S. scientists a glimpse of Earth from 97 kilometers (60 miles) up and, with the addition of a second stage, from 402 kilometers (250 miles) up. At this time, small animals were also carried aloft.

Postwar developments. After the war, both the United States and the Soviet Union instituted programs to develop long-range guided missiles. Both developed a series of missiles, first intermediate-range with typical ranges of 2400 kilometers (1500 miles); then some intercontinental missiles with ranges over 10,000 kilometers (6000 miles).

By 1960 both nations were well under way with programs of space exploration. Hundreds of satellites, space probes, and manned spacecraft were to be launched in the next decades.

Principles of rocket propulsion.
Airplanes are not usable in space because the presence of air is necessary to create the forces on the wings that keep an airplane aloft and to supply the oxygen needed by its engine. The ability of a rocket to provide adequate thrust even when air is absent makes it a suitable propulsion system for space flight.

Rocket engines. In its simplest form a rocket engine consists of a combustion chamber and a nozzle. The fuel and the oxidizer are pumped into the combustion chamber and burned. The hot, high-pressure gas produced by this combustion escapes through the nozzle at high velocity and forms the jet that provides thrust.

Newton's third law describes how a rocket engine produces thrust. This law states that for every action there is an equal and opposite reaction. This law can be visualized easily. Imagine that you are throwing a bowling ball while wearing roller skates. When you throw the ball (action), a force will cause you to roll back in the opposite direction (reaction). This law also works for liquids, as with the recoil of a garden hose to its jet of water. That it works for gases is seen in the flight of an inflated toy balloon when its stem is released.

The reaction force, or thrust, produced by a rocket engine depends on the amount of gas ejected through the nozzle and the velocity of the gas particles. The conventional measure by which propellants are rated is *specific impulse.* It is defined as pounds of thrust produced per pound of propellant burned per second.

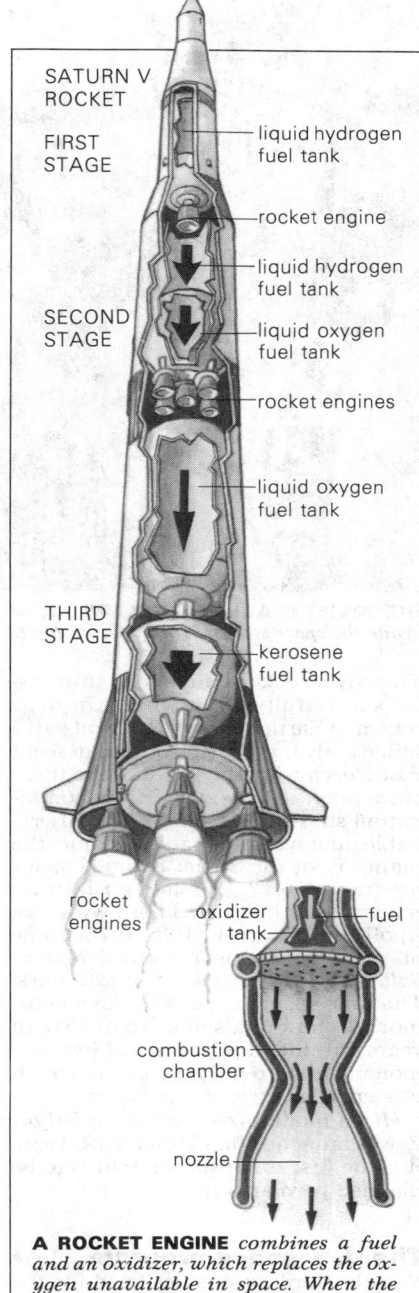

A ROCKET ENGINE *combines a fuel and an oxidizer, which replaces the oxygen unavailable in space. When the two are ignited, the resulting hot gases leave the combustion chamber at high speed, providing thrust.*

Rocket fuels. Selection of a propellant for a specific application depends on several factors such as flight performance, storability, reliability, safety, servicing requirements, and cost.

Solid propellants. Largely because they are simple and ready to go, solid rockets are useful for the propulsion of military missiles and as booster rockets. The two reusable booster rockets of the space shuttle are solid-fuel rockets. One kind of propellant is called a *double-base propellant,* because it is mainly a mixture of nitrocellulose and nitroglycerine with small amounts of plasticizer and other additives. The oxygen for the reaction is contained in

the molecular structure of the main ingredients.

A *composite propellant* consists of two main ingredients, a fuel and an oxidizer. The oxidizers are either chlorates or nitrates of sodium, potassium, or ammonium. The fuels are usually such hydrocarbon materials as asphalts, plastics, or synthetic rubbers that bond the propellant into solid form.

Liquid propellants. The liquid-propellant rockets may use a *monopropellant,* like hydrazine or hydrogen peroxide, which decomposes when a suitable catalytic agent is present to produce high-temperature gas. Such systems are useful for the control of motions of a spacecraft, but their performance is not adequate for use as primary propulsion.

A *bipropellant* system provides the highest propulsion performance. Commonly used oxidizers are liquid oxygen and nitrogen tetroxide. The fuels include kerosene and ethyl alcohol. The most efficient fuel is liquid hydrogen, which powers the engines of the space shuttle.

Nuclear propulsion. Much higher performance, with a specific impulse of 750 pounds of thrust per pound of propellant per second, about twice as good as with chemicals, has been demonstrated with a test-stand version of a U.S. nuclear rocket. In this test a nuclear reactor was fueled by graphite-moderated, uranium-heated hydrogen gas, which expanded to produce a high specific impulse. Nuclear rockets are not feasible for launching spacecraft from Earth because they would require shielding and be too bulky. They can be used for powering spacecraft already in orbit around Earth.

Electric propulsion. Electric propulsion, like nuclear propulsion, is still in an experimental stage. A still higher specific impulse than with nuclear propulsion can be obtained by electric rockets. In one design, an electric arc heats hydrogen or another gas to very high temperatures to obtain high exhaust-jet velocities.

The ion engine is a very effective form of electric thruster. An easily ionized propellant, such as mercury or cesium, is ionized and then accelerated by an electrostatic field. The ions leave the thruster with a specific impulse up to 20 times that of a chemical rocket.

Thrusts are small, and electric power requirements are large, but the high efficiency of propellant utilization makes the ion device attractive either for keeping satellite stations and attitude control or for long, deep-space missions.

Principles of space flight.
Newton suggested that if a projectile were shot fast enough from a mountain in a trajectory parallel with the surface of Earth, it would assume a circular orbit. The velocity required to

put a space vehicle in orbit around Earth close to its surface is 27,360 kilometers (17,000 miles) per hour. At that velocity, the centrifugal force is balanced by gravity. Satellites placed in higher orbits have lower velocities because gravitational attraction diminishes with altitude. The moon orbits Earth with a velocity of 3681 kilometers (2287 miles) per hour.

The velocity required to leave Earth or another celestial body is called the *escape velocity*. Escape velocity is determined by the kinetic energy required to overcome the gravitational field. Escape velocity for Earth is 11.2 kilometers (36,700 feet) per second. Escape velocity of the moon is much less because of the moon's lesser mass.

Manned Spaceflight

The first manned flight took place on April 12, 1961, when Major Yuri A. Gagarin (1934–1968) went into orbit aboard the Soviet *Vostok 1* spacecraft. Gagarin circled Earth once; his total flight time was 1 hour, 48 minutes. On May 5, 1961, the United States sent up its first astronaut, Alan B. Shepard, Jr. In a Mercury capsule, boosted by a Redstone rocket, Shepard made a 15-minute flight to an altitude of 188 kilometers (117 miles). The first American orbital flight was the three circuits made by John H. Glenn, Jr., in *Mercury-Atlas 6* on February 20, 1962.

The Soviet space program.

The first series of manned spaceflights, the Vostok program, consisted of six flights between 1961 and 1963, including the first manned flight, the first mission of more than 24 hours in space *(Vostok 2)*, and the first spacecraft piloted by a woman, Valentina V. Tereshkova *(Vostok 6)*. The Vostok, like all the other manned U.S.S.R. spacecraft, landed on Earth by parachute, although the cosmonauts were ejected at a low altitude and parachuted to Earth separately.

The second generation of Soviet manned spacecraft, the Voskhod, was the first capable of carrying more than one person. The spacecraft was designed to stay in space for up to two weeks, and an airlock system permitted the cosmonauts to leave the craft for space walks.

The Soyuz spacecraft became the third-generation manned space vehicle. Soyuz was a three-module spacecraft, more than 10.4 meters (34 feet) long; it weighed 5900 kilograms (13,000 pounds).

From 1971, Soyuz craft had the opportunity to dock with a space station, Salyut. The 19.8-meter (65-foot) space station had several compartments, including an airlock transfer tunnel.

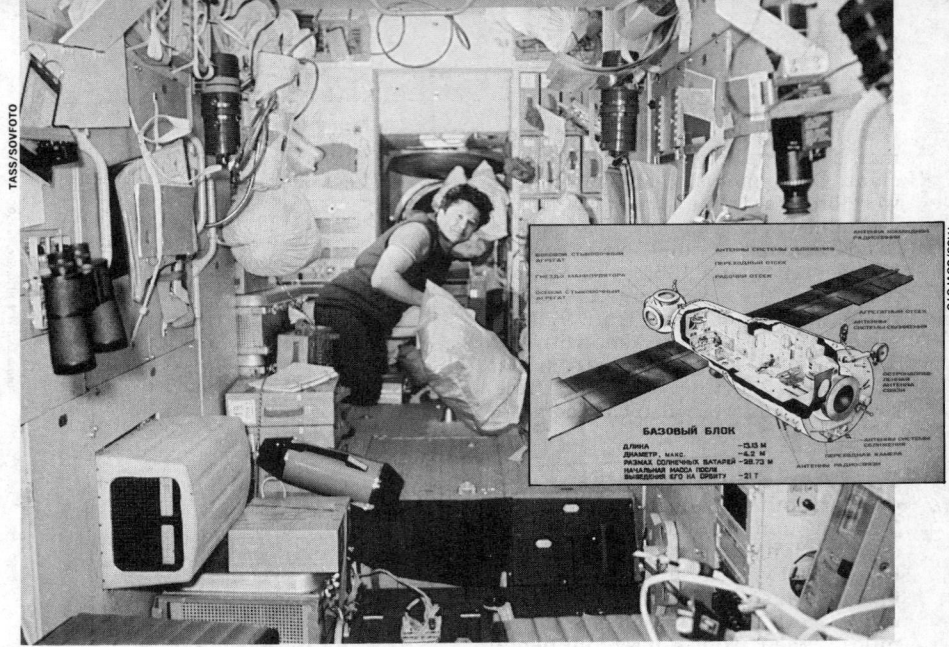

THE SOVIET SPACE STATION *MIR* is to be permanently manned. Pictured is a cosmonaut inside the space station. Inset is a schematic for Mir.

Tragedy struck the first crew to transfer successfully to *Salyut 1.* On their return to Earth in *Soyuz 2,* a vent valve failed and air escaped from the descent module, causing the death of the three cosmonauts. The Soyuz-Salyut combination subsequently proved highly reliable and versatile and became the mainstay of the Soviet manned space program. *Soyuz 19* made an historic rendezvous and docking with an Apollo spacecraft in July, 1975. Some of the cosmonauts remained aboard *Salyut 7* for periods up to 237 days. The time spent in space by Soviet cosmonauts now totals more than 25 man years. In June, 1985, a crew of two cosmonauts repaired the *Salyut 7,* which was crippled by a power failure.

Mir, a modernized version of *Salyut 7,* was launched on February 19, 1986. It is the first space station that is to be manned permanently.

The U. S. space program.

Like Vostok, Mercury was designed for the initial steps of manned spaceflight. Compared with today's spacecraft, the Mercury was tiny and was therefore called a capsule. It was bell-shaped, 2.9 meters (9 feet, 7 inches) long, and 2 meters (6 feet, 7 inches) wide at its widest point. It weighed approximately 1360 kilograms (3000 pounds) and landed on water. There were six flights between 1961 and 1963, four of them orbital.

The second generation of manned spacecraft, Gemini, was designed for two-man crews. The spacecraft consisted of two parts, a reentry module housing the crew and an adapter section containing fuel and equipment. Like Mercury, the Gemini spacecraft landed on water. NASA launched the first Gemini on March 23, 1965, and the program continued through ten manned flights. The last was launched

November 11, 1966. The program included a number of highlights: the first orbital maneuvering by a manned spacecraft *(Gemini 3);* the first flight by an American crew of two, and the first American space walk *(Gemini 4);* a flight of exceptionally long duration for that time, $330\frac{1}{2}$ hours *(Gemini 7);* the first rendezvous between two spacecraft *(Gemini 6* and 7*);* and the first docking in space *(Gemini 8,* with an unmanned capsule).

The Apollo program. Spurred by a long series of Russian firsts and by an eager industry, President John F. Kennedy, on NASA's word that it could fly men to the moon, said, on May 25, 1961, "... that this nation should commit itself to achieving the goal, before this decade is out, of landing a man on the moon and returning him safely to Earth."

Kennedy's speech initiated one of the most ambitious enterprises in the history of science and technology: the development of the Apollo program. The project culminated in several landings on the moon, beginning in 1969 and lasting until 1972—a feat that probably will not be repeated until the last years of the 20th century.

The Apollo had three modules: the command module, the reentry capsule that also served as crew quarters and command post; the lunar module, in which two of the astronauts descended to the lunar surface; and the service module, a jettisonable segment that contained much of the fuel, the expendables, and other equipment. Fully assembled, Apollo was 18.3 meters (60 feet) long and weighed about 45.4 tons (100,000 pounds). Weights varied from mission to mission. A main propulsion engine, located in the service module and producing 9300 kilograms (20,500 pounds) of thrust, together with 16 small thrusters mounted around the cylindrical wall of the spacecraft, gave

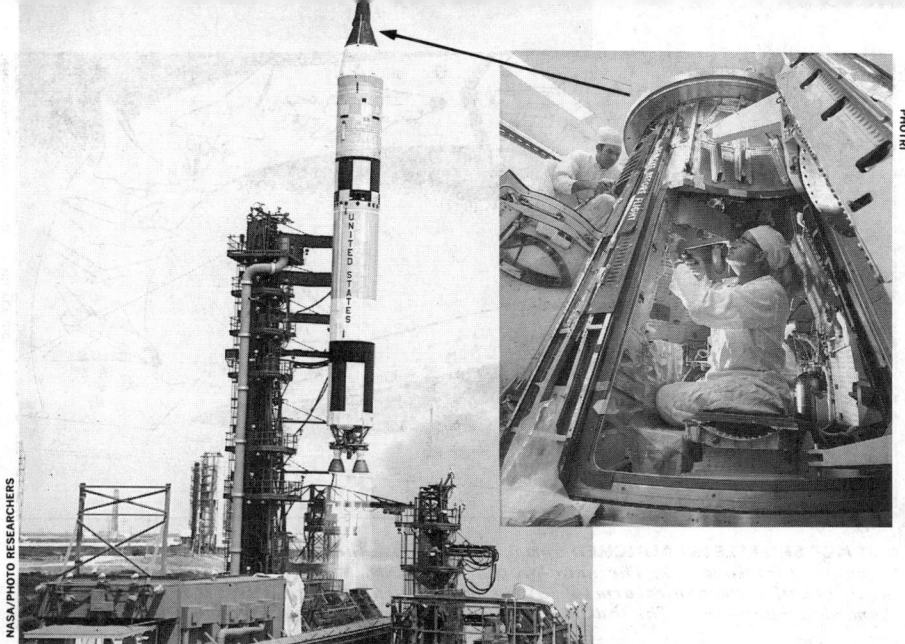

THE GEMINI *rocket was an important precursor of the Apollo program. The flight capsule held two astronauts.*

Apollo extraordinary maneuverability.

On January 27, 1967, a tragic fire during a ground test of an Apollo command module killed three astronauts and delayed the program. By December, 1968, a lunar orbital flight was tried, and on Christmas Eve, an Apollo crew read the first ten verses of Genesis to the world from a lunar orbit. The first manned lunar landing came on July 20, 1969, when *Apollo 11* astronauts Neil A. Armstrong and Edwin E. Aldrin, Jr., set foot on the moon. Michael Collins waited for them in orbit.

Armstrong and Aldrin performed a solar wind experiment; set up a seismometer to measure vibrations of the moon's surface; assembled a reflector to bounce back laser beams sent from Earth, thus enabling scientists to measure the distance between moon and Earth to within inches; and collected 22 kilograms (48 pounds) of surface material from the Sea of Tranquility, where they had landed.

On November 19, 1969, the *Apollo 12* lunar module landed on the moon. On one of their two trips outside the lunar module, the astronauts walked to the lunar probe, *Surveyor 3,* which had landed on the moon in April of 1967. Some parts of *Surveyor 3* were brought back to Earth so the effects of the moon's environment on them could be studied. The astronauts also performed several experiments. After they had boarded the command module for their return trip to Earth, the lunar module was crashed into the moon's surface so that the vibrations it created could be studied.

Apollo 13 was launched on April 11, 1970, nine months after *Apollo 11,* but the mission had to be aborted because of a leak in an oxygen tank when the craft was 330,000 kilometers (205,000 miles) from Earth. By employing the engines of the lunar module, the team of astronauts was able to make a safe return to Earth. The remaining four Apollo missions were of increasing duration and complexity. In the last missions, an electric car greatly increased the productivity of the scientific exploration by roving several miles on the moon's surface with the astronauts and their gear.

Experiments were left operative on the moon and in orbit around it. *Apollo 15* visited Hadley Rille, up north, at the foot of the Apennine Mountains. *Apollo 16* visited other terrain, at Descartes, south of the *Apollo 11* site. *Apollo 17,* which landed at Taurus-Littrow, north of *Apollo 11,* completed the program.

Skylab. The follow-up to Apollo was Skylab, a program that used modified Apollo hardware to create a prototype manned space station. The large, unmanned orbital laboratory, 6.7 meters (22 feet) in diameter, more than 30.5 meters (100 feet) long, and weighing 85 tons, was put in a 435-kilometer- (270-mile-) high orbit by a Saturn V rocket on May 14, 1973. The laboratory consisted of a 12.2-meter- (40-foot-) long workshop and living area, an instrument unit, an airlock module and docking port, and a solar observatory. Three crews visited the orbital laboratory for stays of 28, 59, and 84 days. Skylab yielded much data about the sun, cosmos, and Earth, and about living and working conditions in space.

Spacelab. Spacelab is a laboratory designed to be carried in space in the cargo bay of the space shuttle. It was developed and built by the European Space Agency (ESA) and consists of a pressurized cabin 7 meters (23 feet) long. The flights were joint enterprises of NASA and ESA. The first mission, aboard the shuttle *Columbia,* flew on November 28, 1983. The crew had six members, two of whom were scientists assigned to perform experiments in the space laboratory. Their work included astronomical observations, solar physics and atmospheric studies, biological experiments, and experiments with the mixing of metals and growth of crystals in the absence of gravitational forces.

Spacelab flew for the second time aboard the *Challenger* shuttle from April 29 to May 6, 1985. On October 30, 1985, Spacelab started its third mission —a joint operation of NASA and Germany—again aboard *Challenger.* Several other Spacelab missions were planned for the second half of the 1980's, but they were delayed indefinitely by the *Challenger* disaster in January of 1986.

THE LANDINGS ON THE MOON *during the Apollo program are often considered the crowning achievement of the U.S. space program.*

Space shuttle.

The most versatile spacecraft designed by NASA is the space shuttle, a vehicle that can take off from the surface of Earth, execute its mission in an orbit around Earth, reenter the atmosphere, and glide, supported by its wings, back to Earth. The main reason for development of the space shuttle was the high cost of launching satellites and spacecraft with conventional rockets that are not reusable.

A new design.

The official name for the space shuttle is Space Transportation System (STS). The STS consists of an orbiter, an aircraftlike spacecraft that returns to Earth; two reusable solid-fuel rocket boosters; and an external tank containing the ascent propellant, liquid hydrogen and oxygen, for the main engines of the orbiter.

The orbiter is comparable in size and weight to a DC-9 aircraft. It is 37.2 meters (122 feet) long with a 23.8-meter (78-foot) wingspan. It can carry as much as 29,500 kilograms (65,000 pounds) in its 18.3-meter by 4.5-meter (60-foot by 15-foot) cargo bay. Its crew compartment is fitted out for seven people, usually three astronauts and one to four scientists, also called payload, or mission, specialists.

Three main propulsion engines in the aft of the orbiter are used from launch until orbit. At sea level, the thrust of each engine is 170,000 kilograms (375,000 pounds). On takeoff, the main liquid-fueled engines are assisted by two solid-fuel rocket boosters that supply a thrust of 1,202,000 kilograms (2,650,000 pounds) each for two minutes. The spent boosters parachute into the ocean for recovery, refurbishing, and reuse. The external fuel tank for the liquid-fuel engines, which holds 526,000 liters (139,000 gallons) of liquid oxygen and 1,400,000 liters (370,000 gallons) of liquid hydrogen, is the only part that is not reusable. It is discarded when empty and burns up when entering the atmosphere.

A SPACE SHUTTLE IS LAUNCHED *upright (1). After use, the solid-fuel boosters separate from the shuttle for recovery (2). The liquid-propellant tank is jettisoned (3). The shuttle can deploy satellites with a mechanical arm (4). (5) The shuttle turns so its rockets face forward and fires them, slowing the ship. The shuttle then flips over again so it can glide to Earth (6).*

The orbiter itself is protected from burning when it enters the atmosphere at a speed of 22,500 kilometers (14,000 miles) per hour by a shield consisting of more than 30,000 glazed silica tiles that cover the entire fuselage and wings. After reentry into the atmosphere, the orbiter becomes an 80-ton glider. While it can be maneuvered, it is no longer powered. It lands like a conventional airplane.

Missions.

Many scientific experiments and observations have been performed during shuttle missions. STS crews have also placed satellites in orbit and retrieved satellites for repair. Several secret military missions commissioned by the Department of Defense also have been flown. Crew members of the second flight of *Atlantis,* in October, 1985, experimented with the assembly in space of large aluminum structures, similar to those that will be used in future manned space stations.

The *Challenger* disaster.

The worst accident in the history of manned spaceflight occurred on January 28, 1986. The shuttle *Challenger,* with a seven-member crew on board, exploded 73 seconds after takeoff from the Kennedy Space Center at Cape Canaveral, Florida. The crew, consisting of mission commander Francis R. Scobee; pilot Michael J. Smith; mission specialists Ronald E. McNair, Ellison S. Onizuka, and Judith A. Resnick; payload specialist Gregory B. Jarvis; and teacher-observer Christa McAuliffe, perished.

Study of photographs that were taken during liftoff revealed that the seal between segments of the solid state boosters leaked. A flame escaped, burned through the outer skin of the external fuel tank, and ignited the liquid oxygen and hydrogen.

Subsequently, all shuttle flights were halted, pending the correction of the design of the solid booster.

A LARGE PART OF A SPACE SHUTTLE'S *length is taken up by its 60-foot payload bay. The payload bay can either carry satellites to be placed in orbit or a special module containing Spacelab, a laboratory where astronauts can perform experiments. Near the nose of the ship is the cockpit from which the shuttle is controlled, and on the lower level are the crew quarters.*

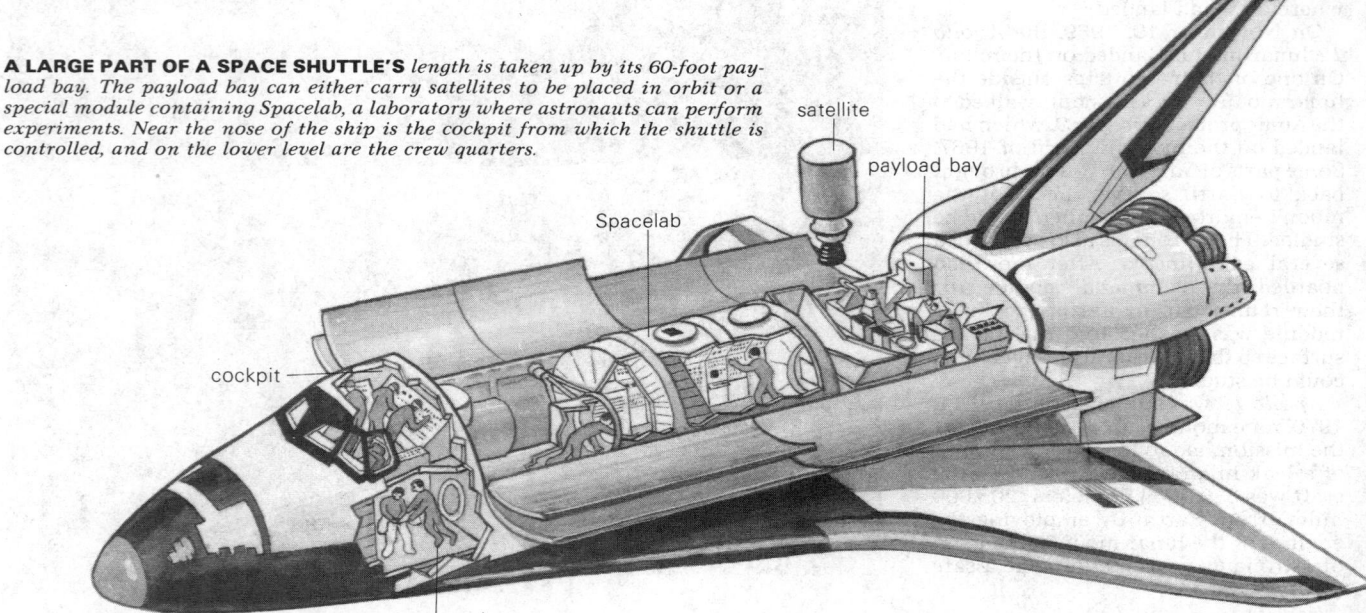

satellite

payload bay

Spacelab

cockpit

crew quarters

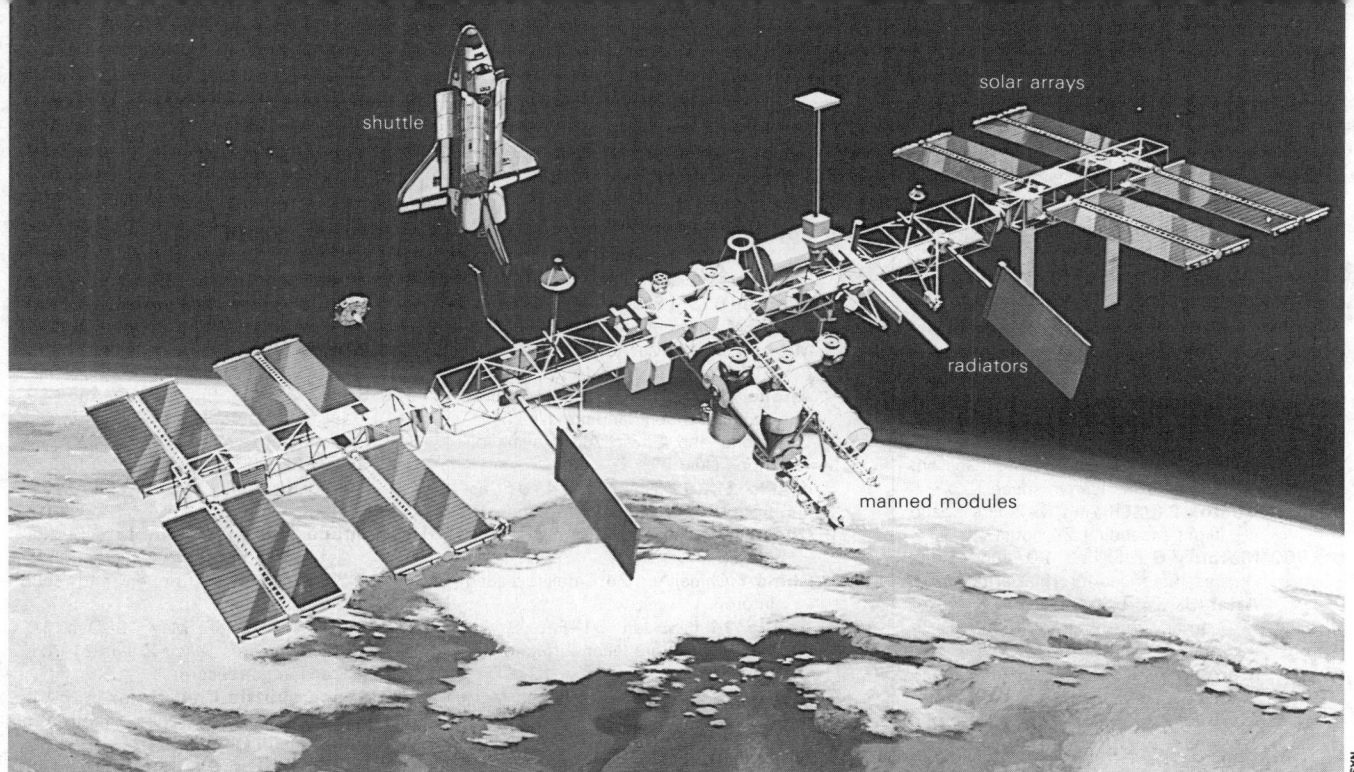

THE SPACE STATION *will carry a permanent crew of six astronauts when it is built, probably in the mid 1990's. Power for the station will be supplied by huge solar panels, and people and supplies will be delivered by space shuttle.*

Space station. The space shuttle also plays a key role in NASA's plans for a permanently manned space station, to be assembled in an orbit around Earth in the 1990's. NASA's plans include a so-called power tower, a 400-meter- (1200-foot-) long structure to which are attached solar panels, modules with living quarters and laboratories, instruments, and antennae. All the components will be transported into orbit by space shuttles. Shuttles also will dock with the living quarters for crew changes. Several plans are now under study for supplying modules to be based on the design of Spacelab.

—*Alexander Hellemans*

SPACE PROGRAMS OF OTHER NATIONS

The world no longer has to depend for space exploration and research exclusively on the capabilities of the United States and the Soviet Union. As a result of vigorous and well-funded scientific and technological research and development programs, the European Space Agency, the Chinese Ministry of Astronautics, and the Japanese Space Development Agency now provide space facilities and capabilities.

European missions.   The European Space Agency (ESA), strongly committed to research, consists of a group of 13 nations. Despite problems with the Ariane rocket, the ESA had dramatic success with its Giotto probe to Halley's comet in March of 1986. Its planned missions for the next two decades are to be made as a result of the Ulysses and Soho projects. The Ulysses spacecraft, with a launch scheduled for 1990, will see parts of the sun that are now unknown, including the uncharted polar regions. The Soho spacecraft will study the sun's surface and make measurements of the temperature of its corona.

Chinese missions.   China's space efforts have concentrated as far as is known to the rest of the world on development of the Long March booster rocket. China is believed to have three launching sites, the third completed in 1987. China is also developing a manned space program in cooperative efforts with other nations. It is planned that Chinese astronauts will fly as crew members aboard the U.S. space shuttle in the 1990's. China hopes, however, that its own astronauts will pilot a Chinese spacecraft by the year 2000. Plans also call for China to launch a polar-orbit weather observation vehicle in 1988 or soon thereafter.

Japanese missions.   Japan's National Space Development Agency is responsible for the growth of Japan's space technology. Evidence of progress came in 1986, when two Japanese craft flew close by Halley's comet and transmitted technical data to help in analyzing the comet's cloud and tail. The launch in 1987 of the Marine Observation Satellite (MOS-1), known as "Peach," was another significant achievement of Japan's space program. It was the first Japanese satellite to circle Earth over the poles.

Japan plans to develop a three-stage booster rocket, with first launch set for the early 1990's. The vehicle will be used as a low-orbit spacecraft for collecting scientific data and for missions to Venus and other distant bodies in our solar system. It will be developed by the Japanese Institute of Space and Astronautical Sciences, which has launched about one scientific satellite annually for more than a decade.

HIGHLIGHTS OF SPACE EXPLORATION

1957 **Sputnik 1** (USSR) Oct. 4. First man-made satellite.

Sputnik 2 (USSR) Nov. 3. Carries dog in Earth orbit.

1958 **Explorer 1** (US) Jan. 31. Discovers Van Allen radiation belt.

1961 **Vostok 1** (USSR) Apr. 12. Yuri Gagarin first to orbit Earth.

Mercury 3 (US) May 5. Alan Shepard first American in space.

Mercury 4 (US) July 21. Virgil Grissom second American in space.

Vostok 2 (USSR) Aug. 6–7. First space flight exceeding 24 hours.

1962 **Mercury 6** (US) Feb. 20. John Glenn first American to orbit Earth.

Ariel (UK and US) Apr. 26. U.S. rocket carries British satellite into Earth orbit.

Mercury 7 (US) May 24. Scott Carpenter second American to orbit Earth.

Mariner 2 (US) Aug. 27. Space probe within 22,000 miles of Venus (Dec. 14).

Mercury 8 (US) Oct. 3. Walter Schirra orbits Earth six times.

1963 **Mercury 9** (US) May 15–16. Gordon Cooper exceeds 24 hours in space.

Vostok 6 (USSR) June 16–19. Valentina Tereshkova becomes first woman in space.

1964 **Ranger 7** (US) July 28. Photographs moon.

Voskhod 1 (USSR) Oct. 12–13. Three-man crew in orbit.

Mariner 4 (US) Nov. 28. Photographs Mars from 6000 miles (July 14).

1965 **Voskhod 2** (USSR) Mar. 18. First space walk.

Gemini 3 (US) Mar. 23. Manned spacecraft alters orbital path.

Gemini 4 (US) June 3–7. Edward White in space walk.

Gemini 5 (US) Aug. 21–29. Endurance record for manned spacecraft.

A-1 Diamant (France) Nov. 26. First French satellite in orbit.

Gemini 7 (US) Dec. 4–18. James Lovell and Frank Borman remove spacesuits in orbit.

1966 **Gemini 9** (US) June 3–6. Eugene Cernan successfully performs 2-hour, 9-minute space walk.

Gemini 10 (US) July 18–21. Docks with Agena target vehicle.

Gemini 11 (US) Sept. 12–15. First landing directed solely by on-board computer.

1967 **Apollo 1** (US) Jan. 27. Launch pad fire kills Virgil Grissom, Edward White, and Roger Chafee.

Surveyor 3 (US) Apr. 17. Lands on moon to test soil samples.

Soyuz 1 (USSR) Apr. 23. Crashes after reentering Earth's atmosphere; kills cosmonaut.

Mariner 5 (US) June 14. Passes within 2500 miles of Venus (Oct. 19).

1968 **Apollo 8** (US) Dec. 21–27. First manned flight to orbit moon.

1969 **Soyuz 5** (USSR) Jan. 15–18. Crew members transfer to *Soyuz 4* after space docking.

Mariner 6 (US) Feb. 25. Passes within 2000 miles of Mars (July 31).

Mariner 7 (US) Mar. 27. Passes within 2000 miles of Mars (Aug. 5).

Apollo 11 (US) July 16–24. First manned moon landing; Neil Armstrong and Edwin Aldrin walk on moon (July 21).

Apollo 12 (US) Nov. 14–24. U.S. astronauts' second moon landing.

1970 **Ohsumi** (Japan) Feb. 11. Satellite is placed in orbit.

China 1 (China) Apr. 24. Satellite placed in orbit.

1971 **Apollo 14** (US) Jan. 31–Feb. 9. Astronauts explore lunar surface for 9 hours.

Mariner 9 (US) May 30. Orbits Mars (Nov. 13).

Soyuz 11 (USSR) June 6–30. Docks with *Salyut* space station; two orbit Earth together for 23 days; crew dies in reentry.

Apollo 15 (US) July 26–Aug. 7. First use of lunar roving vehicle.

1972 **Pioneer 10** (US) Mar. 3. Passes Jupiter; becomes first manmade object to leave solar system (June 13).

Apollo 17 (US) Dec. 7–19. Makes record 75-hour lunar stay.

1973 **Skylab** (US) May 14. First U.S. space station.

Skylab 2 (US) May 25–June 22. First crew on U.S. space station.

Skylab 3 (US) July 28–Sept. 25. Second crew aboard space station.

Mariner 10 (US) Nov. 3. Reaches Mercury (Mar. 29, 1974).

Skylab 4 (US) Nov. 11–Feb. 8, 1974. Crew aboard space station for 84 days.

1975 **Apollo 18** (US) July 14–25; **Soyuz 19** (USSR) July 15–21. After docking, U.S. and Soviet crews cooperate in experiments.

1977 **Voyager 1** (US) Sept. 5. Passes Jupiter (Mar. 5, 1979), Saturn (Nov. 13, 1980).

Voyager 2 (US) Sept. 20. Passes Jupiter (July 9, 1979), Saturn (Aug. 26, 1981), Uranus (Jan. 8. 1986).

Soyuz 26 (USSR) Dec. 10–Mar. 16, 1978. Crew boards *Salyut 6* space station; sets 96-day endurance record.

1978 **Pioneer Venus 1** (US) May 20. Enters orbit of Venus (Dec. 4).

Soyuz 29 (USSR) June 15–Nov. 2. Crew boards *Salyut 6;* sets 139-day endurance record.

Pioneer Venus 2 (US) Aug. 8. Reaches Venus (Dec. 9).

1979 **Soyuz 32** (USSR) Feb. 25–Aug. 19. Crew boards *Salyut 6;* sets 175-day endurance record.

1980 **Soyuz 35** (USSR) Apr. 9–Oct. 11. Crew boards *Salyut 6;* sets 185-day endurance record.

1981 **Space shuttle Columbia** (US) Apr. 12–14. Reusable spacecraft flies; crew: Robert Crippen and John Young.

1982 **Soyuz T-5** (USSR) May 13–Dec. 10. Crew boards *Salyut 7;* sets 211-day endurance record.

1983 **Space shuttle Challenger** (US) Apr. 4–9. Second space shuttle on maiden flight.

Space shuttle Challenger (US) June 18–24. Sally Ride first U.S. woman in space.

Space shuttle Challenger (US) Aug. 30–Sept. 5. Guion Bluford first black person in space.

1984 **Space shuttle Challenger** (US) Feb. 3–11. Bruce McCandless and Robert Steward first to fly free of spacecraft.

Soyuz T-10 (USSR) Feb. 8–Oct. 17. Crew boards *Salyut 7;* sets 237-day endurance record.

Ariane 3 (European Space Agency) Aug. 4. Launch vehicle developed by French deploys two satellites.

Space shuttle Discovery (US) Aug. 30–Sept. 5. Third space shuttle launched.

1985 **Giotto** (European Space Agency) July 2. Passes within 335 miles of Halley's comet nucleus (Mar. 14, 1986).

Space shuttle Atlantis (US) Oct. 4–7. Fourth space shuttle launched.

1986 **Space shuttle Challenger** (US) Jan. 28. Explodes shortly after launch, killing entire crew: Francis Scobee, Michael Smith, Judith Resnick, Ronald McNair, Ellison Onizuka, Gregory Jarvis, and Christa McAuliffe.

1987 **Mir** (USSR) Feb. 6–Dec. 29. Yuri Romanenko sets 326-day endurance record.

VOYAGER 2

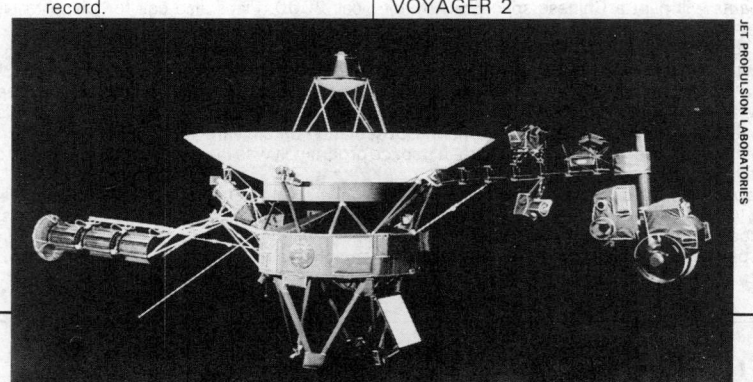

GLOSSARY OF ASTRONOMY

Aberration. The apparent change in the position of a celestial body resulting from the finite velocity of light and the orbital motion of Earth.

Albedo. The fraction of light reflected by the surface of a celestial body that is not self-luminous, such as a planet. The albedo depends on the atmosphere and the constitution of the surface of the body.

Altitude. Of a celestial body as seen from Earth, the angular distance from the horizon to that body measured along the vertical circle passing through the celestial body.

Angular distance. As seen from Earth, the angle subtended between two celestial bodies on the celestial sphere.

Angular resolution. A measure of the sharpness of an image obtained by a telescope. It is expressed as the angle, as seen from Earth, between two points on the celestial sphere that can be seen as distinct.

Aperture. The diameter of the objective lens or of the primary mirror of a telescope. The larger the aperture, the better its light-gathering power and angular resolution.

Aphelion. The point in the orbit of a planet, or any member of the solar system, such as a comet, that is farthest from the sun. Compare *Perihelion.*

Apogee. The point in the orbit of the moon or artificial satellite that is farthest from Earth. Compare *Perigee.*

Astronomical unit (A.U.). The mean distance from Earth to the sun. It is the unit of measurement for distances within the solar system and equals 149,780,000 kilometers (92,887,000 miles).

Big bang. The initial explosion of a very high concentration of matter and energy that is thought to have given rise to the formation of the universe.

Black-body radiation. The radiation given off by a black body. A black body is a perfect radiator in that it reradiates all the radiation incident upon it, and its temperature can be derived from the color of the emitted light.

CONJUNCTION *of the moon, Venus (at bottom), and Jupiter occurs every ten years.*

Black hole. The concentration of matter in so small a space that the gravity on its surface is so great that light cannot escape from it.

Celestial equator. The circle formed by the intersection of the plane that passes through Earth's equator with the celestial sphere.

Celestial sphere. The concept of an imaginary sphere of indeterminate radius that rotates around Earth and on whose surface all celestial bodies seem to be fixed.

Cepheid variable. A star that regularly increases and decreases in brightness over a short period. Because the absolute magnitudes of Cepheids are related to their periods, they are used for computing the distances of galaxies from Earth.

Chromatic aberration. A defect in lenses caused by the differences in refraction of light of different colors.

Chromosphere. On the sun, a layer above the photosphere visible as a reddish glow during an eclipse.

Circumpolar star. A star that always remains above the horizon. The angle between the star and the celestial pole must be less, or equal to, the latitude of the observation point.

Cluster. An association of stars. *Globular clusters* are spherical associations of stars found in galaxies that contain up to several hundred thousand stars. Large associations of galaxies are also called clusters.

Color index. A number that indicates the color of a star. It is equal to the difference between the magnitudes of a star measured in blue light and in yellow light.

Coma. Pertaining to a comet, the cloud of gas and dust surrounding the cometary nucleus.

Conjunction. One of two planetary configurations. The *superior conjunction* is the one in which the sun is between Earth and the planet. The *inferior conjunction* occurs when the planet is between Earth and the sun.

Constellation. A group of stars that seem to form the outline of a figure. The stars appear to be close to each other, but in reality they may be very far apart.

Cosmic background radiation. Microwave radiation coming from all directions in the universe. It is believed to be a remnant of the big bang.

Cosmic radiation. A vast stream of atomic nuclei and electrons moving at very high speeds that reach Earth from all directions.

Cosmogony. Study of the origin of astronomical systems, specifically the origin of the solar system. The term is sometimes used to mean cosmology.

Cosmology. Study of the general structure, origin, and development of the universe.

Doppler effect. The change in wavelength of sound or light produced by a moving object. When an object moves toward an observer, the wavelength decreases. When the object moves away from the observer, the wavelength increases (or shifts toward the red).

Dwarf. A very small and faint star, considered to be the final stage in development of stars of little mass.

Eclipse. The obscuring of light from one celestial body by another. In a *solar eclipse,* the moon moves between the sun and Earth so as to obscure the sun as seen from Earth. In a *lunar eclipse,* Earth moves between the sun and the moon so that the moon is in Earth's shadow.

Ecliptic. The apparent path of the sun around the celestial sphere.

Ephemeris. A published table of the daily positions of the sun, moon, planets, artificial satellites, and selected stars. It also provides other data necessary for astronomical and navigational observations.

Equinox. A point of intersection of the celestial equator with the ecliptic. There are two equinoxes. The sun crosses the celestial equator at a point called the *vernal equinox,* or *first point of Aries,* on March 20 or 21, the first day of spring. The sun also crosses the celestial equator at a point called the *autumnal equinox* on September 22 or 23, the first day of autumn.

Escape velocity. Velocity required for a spacecraft to overcome the gravity of Earth or other body in the solar system.

Event horizon. The boundary of the region around a black hole from which no light or matter can escape.

Extinction. The scattering and absorption of starlight by interstellar dust.

Field stars. Stars in our galaxy that are found outside stellar clusters.

Flare. A sudden and brief outburst on the surface of the sun that releases a large amount of energy.

Focus. In an elliptical orbit of a body revolving around a primary, one of the two points that the primary can occupy. In a telescope, the point at which the light rays converge after being refracted by the objective lens or reflected from a mirror.

Fraunhofer lines (absorption lines). Dark lines in the spectrum of the sun or a star caused by selective absorption of light in its atmosphere.

Free fall. Any condition in which the force of gravity is not opposed by another force. In space, free fall occurs when the propulsion system of a space vehicle is turned off.

Galactic halo. The spherical region that surrounds the galaxy and contains gas and globular clusters.

Gegenschein. Sometimes called *counterglow,* a faint illumination of the sky seen at night in the ecliptic opposite to the position of the sun. It is produced by the scattering of sunlight by dust particles in space, and is related to the zodiacal light.

Giant star. A star of very large size and great luminosity. It is a stage in the development of a star after it leaves the main sequence.

Gravitational collapse. The collapse of matter into a very small region because of the mutual attraction of mass particles. The end result of gravitational collapse is believed to be a black hole.

Gravitational lens. An effect produced when a galaxy, because of its gravitation, bends light rays coming from systems that are in the same direction as, but more distant from, Earth than the galaxy.

Great circle. The circle on a sphere whose center coincides with the center of the sphere.

Hertzsprung-Russell diagram. Graph of the relationship that can be found between the color and the luminosity of any group of stars.

Interferometer. A telescope in which light from a celestial object is gathered by two mirrors separated by a known distance. Light reflected from the two mirrors produces an interference pattern that enables determination of stellar diameters. A *radio interferometer* is a combination of two or more dish antennas.

Jovian planets. The planets with orbits beyond that of Mars: Jupiter, Saturn, Uranus, Neptune, and Pluto.

Lagrange point. The point between two celestial bodies at which the gravitational pulls of the two bodies on a third body cancel each other out.

Libration. The oscillation in the motion of a celestial body traveling about another body. The term is most commonly applied to the oscillations of the moon around its axis of rotation, as seen from Earth. Because of the moon's libration, more than half its surface is visible from Earth.

Light-year. A unit of measure of stellar distances. One light-year is equal to the distance light travels in one year: 9.46 trillion kilometers, or 5.9 trillion miles, or 63,290 astronomical units.

Longitude. On Earth, the angle measured at the center of Earth between the points at which the meridian through Greenwich, England, and the meridian through any other place on Earth cross the equator.

Magnitude. The brightness of a star or other celestial object. *Apparent magnitude* is the brightness of a star as it appears to an observer on Earth. *Absolute magnitude* is the apparent magnitude that a star would have if it were observed from a distance of 10 parsecs.

Mean sun. For convenience in measuring time, a fictitious sun that is considered to move around the celestial equator at a uniform rate.

Meridian. The great circle on the celestial sphere that passes through the zenith and both the north and south poles. On Earth it is the great circle that passes through the north and south poles and any given point.

Meteor. A celestial body observed as a streak of light in the night sky as the body burns up because of frictional heating by Earth's atmosphere.

THIS METEORITE, *which was found in Antarctica, is believed by many to be of Martian origin.*

Meteorite. The portion of a meteoroid that survives as it passes through Earth's atmosphere.

Meteoroid. Any mass of rock in the solar system. When a meteoroid enters Earth's atmosphere, it can be observed as a meteor.

Nebula. Any luminous patch seen among the stars. More specifically, a cloud of dust or gas that can be seen because of the emission of absorbed light or the reflection of light.

Neutron star. A star composed solely of neutrons packed very closely together. Pulsars are neutron stars.

Nova. A star that flares from obscurity to great brilliance and then sinks back to obscurity. See also *Supernova*.

Nutation. A small periodic movement of Earth's axis that causes the celestial pole to trace a wavy path as it moves among the stars.

Objective lens. The lens mounted at the front end of a telescope. It gathers light from a celestial object and focuses it on a photographic plate or in front of the eyepiece.

Occultation. The hiding of one celestial body by another. Eclipses of a star or planet by the moon are occultations.

Orbit. The path, usually an ellipse, that is traveled by a celestial body as it moves about another under the influence of the gravitational attraction of a second body.

Parallax. The apparent change of position of a celestial body against the celestial sphere when viewed from two different points in Earth's orbit.

Parsec. A unit of measure of stellar distance. A star having a parallax of one arc second is at a distance of one parsec. One parsec equals 206,265 astronomical units, or 3.26 light-years.

Perigee. The point in the orbit of the moon, or of any artificial satellite, that is closest to Earth. Compare *Apogee*.

Perihelion. The point in the orbit of a planet or of any other member of the solar system that is closest to the sun. Compare *Aphelion*.

Perturbation. Disturbance in the orbit of a celestial body caused by the gravitational force of another body. Perturbations in orbit of Uranus led to discovery of Neptune and Pluto.

Phase. The apparent change in the illumination of the moon or inferior planet over a month that is caused by the changes in the relative positions of the sun and moon, or planet, as seen from Earth.

Photosphere. The layer on the sun that gives off light, also called *solar atmosphere*. Compare *Chromosphere*.

Planetary nebula. A nebula that resembles a planet. It is formed by ejection of the outer layer of a star.

Plasma. A gas that is almost completely ionized, that is, one or more electrons are split off each atom. Most of the matter in the universe, such as that inside stars, is plasma.

Pole. One of the ends of the axis of rotation of a sphere. Earth's axis passes through Earth's surface at the north and south poles and touches the celestial sphere at the north and south celestial poles.

Primary. The larger object around which a smaller object revolves. In a binary star, the primary is the more massive component.

Primeval atom. In the big bang theory, the original concentration of mass and energy from which the universe is thought to have been created.

Prograde. Counterclockwise, when viewed from north of the ecliptic, rotation of a celestial body around its axis.

Prominence. Large tongues of incandescent gas that project from the solar surface during solar activity.

Quasar (quasi-stellar radio source). An extragalactic system with the appearance of a star but exhibiting a large red shift. Quasars are believed to be at very great distances and to emit very large amounts of radiation.

Radiation belt. A zone around Earth or a planet containing high-speed charged particles. The radiation belts around Earth are called *Van Allen belts*.

Radiation pressure. A force exerted by electromagnetic radiation. Radiation pressure is one of the two forces that direct a cometary tail away from the sun. The other force is caused by interaction with the solar wind.

Red shift. Shift of spectral lines in the visible spectrum toward longer wavelengths, caused by Doppler effect.

Retrograde motion. The apparent motion of a planet from west to east among the stars, caused by a combination of its true motion with the motion of Earth. Retrograde rotation is rotation around its axis of a celestial object in the clockwise direction as viewed from north of the ecliptic.

Revolution. The orbital motion of a planet or satellite about its primary.

Roche's limit. The closest point to which a satellite can approach its primary without being pulled apart by the tidal effects of the gravitational field of the primary.

Rotation. The turning of a celestial body about its axis.

Schwarzschild radius. The radius of a hypothetical sphere at which a contracting mass becomes a black hole.

Scintillation. The irregular variation in the brightness of a star caused by variations in the density of different layers of Earth's atmosphere.

Shooting star. See *Meteor*.

Singularity. A region in space at which some physical quantity reaches an extreme value. For example, a black hole is a singularity because its gravitational field reaches an infinite value.

Solar activity. The occurrence of prominences and eruptions on the sun.

RADIATION BELTS *around Earth consist of charged particles trapped in Earth's magnetic field. The magnetic field is distorted by pressure from solar winds.*

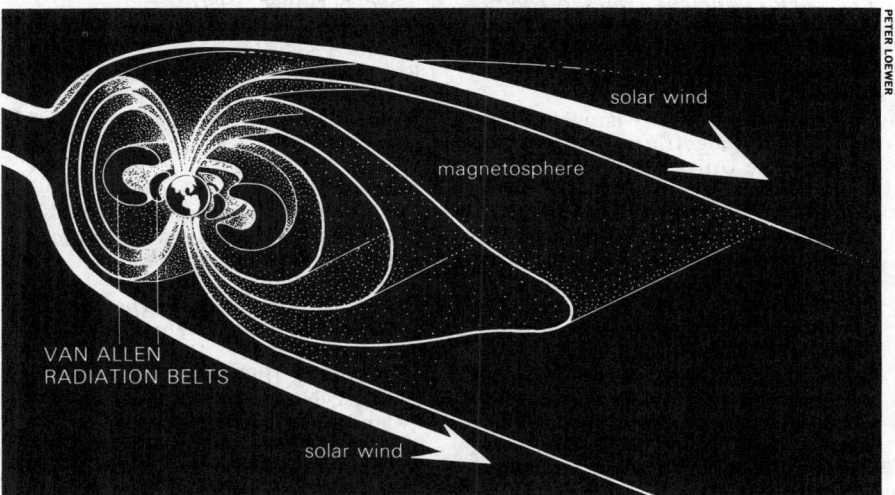

solar wind

magnetosphere

VAN ALLEN
RADIATION BELTS

solar wind

PETER LOEWER

The sun is said to be active when these phenomena occur frequently.

Solar wind. A stream of charged particles caused by the expanding corona of the sun.

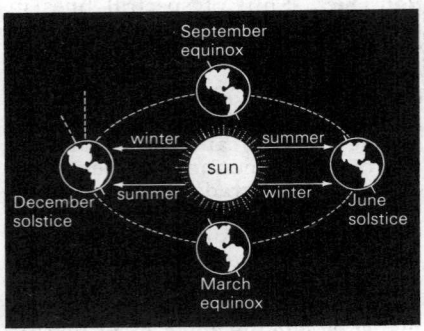

Solstices. The two points on the ecliptic at which the sun is at its maximum distance from the celestial equator. These two points correspond to the longest and shortest days of the year.

Steady-state theory. A cosmological theory that contends that the universe has always existed the way it does today, and that matter is continuously created to account for the expansion of the universe.

Supercluster. A cluster of clusters of galaxies.

Supernova. An exceptionally bright nova. It is considered to be the explosion of a star during the final stage of its development.

Terminator. The line separating the illuminated and dark parts of the moon or a planet.

Terrestrial planets. The planets with orbits within the orbit of Jupiter: Mercury, Venus, Earth, and Mars.

Trajectory. The path a rocket or spacecraft takes, especially the path after the propulsion engine has been stopped and the spacecraft is in free fall.

Transit. The apparent passage of a celestial body across a meridian. It is also the passage of a celestial body across any other body as seen from Earth.

Van Allen belt. See *Radiation belt.*

Zenith. A point on the celestial sphere directly above the observer on Earth and directly opposite the nadir, the point below the observer.

Zodiac. A band on the celestial sphere extending about 9 degrees on either side of the ecliptic that contains the orbits of the sun, moon, and all the planets except Pluto. It also contains the twelve constellations that gave their names to the signs of the zodiac.

Zodiacal light. A cone-shaped bright region in the night sky seen in the west shortly after sunset during spring or in the east shortly before sunrise during autumn. The zodiacal light is caused by reflection or scattering of sunlight by interplanetary dust.

For Further Reference

History

Aschbrook, Joseph. *The Astronomical Scrapbook: Skywatchers, Pioneers, and Seekers in Astronomy.* Sky Publishing, 1984.

Dreyer J.L.E. *A History of Astronomy from Thales to Kepler.* Dover Publications, 1953.

Herrmann, Dieter B. *The History of Astronomy from Herschel to Hertzsprung.* Cambridge University Press, 1984.

Moore, Patrick. *Explorers of Space: The Story of the People Who Chartered the Heavens and the Discoveries They Made.* W.H. Smith, 1986.

Tauber, Gerald E. *Man and the Cosmos: Evolving Concepts of the Universe from Ancient Times to Today's Space Probes.* Greenwich House, 1982.

General

Audouze, Jean and Guy Israel, editors. *The Cambridge Atlas of Astronomy.* Cambridge University Press, 1985.

Dixon, Robert J. *Dynamic Astronomy* (4th Ed.). Prentice-Hall, 1984.

Friedlander, Michael W. *Astronomy: From Stonehenge to Quasars.* Prentice-Hall, 1985.

Harwit, Martin. *Cosmic Discovery: The Search, Scope and Heritage of Astronomy.* Basic Books, 1981.

Moore, Patrick. *The Guinness Book of Astronomy: Facts and Feats* (2nd Ed.). Guinness Superlatives, 1983.

Rogers, Eric M. *Astronomy for the Inquiring Mind.* Princeton University Press, 1982.

Solar System

Briggs, Geoffrey and Frederic Taylor. *The Cambridge Photographic Atlas of the Planets.* Cambridge University Press, 1982.

Giovanelli, Ronald. *Secrets of the Sun.* Cambridge University Press, 1984.

Ritchie, D. *Comets: Swords of Heaven.* New American Library, 1985.

Smoluchowski, Roman. *The Solar System.* W.H. Freeman, 1984.

Star Guides

Burnham, R. *Burnham's Celestial Handbook.* 3 volumes. Dover, 1978.

Holt, Terry. *The Universe Next Door: A Complete Guide to Exploring the Skies and Understanding What You See.* Scribner, 1985.

Mayer, B. *Starwatch.* G.P. Putnam's Sons, 1984.

Ridpath, Ian. *Universe Guide to Stars and Planets.* Universe, 1985.

Ronan, Colin. *The Skywatcher's Handbook.* Crown, 1985.

Astrophysics

Field, George B. and Eric J. Chaisson. *The Invisible Universe: Probing the Frontiers of Astrophysics.* Birkhäuser Boston, 1985.

Gribbin, John. *Spacewarps: A Book About Black Holes, White Holes, Quasars, and Our Violent Universe.* Delacorte, 1983.

Henbest, Nigel. *The New Astronomy.* Cambridge University Press, 1983.

Tucker, Wallace and Giacconi Ricardo. *The X-Ray Universe.* Harvard University Press, 1985.

Stars and Stellar Evolution

Clark, David H. *Superstars: Celestial Explosions Shape the Destiny of the Universe.* McGraw-Hill, 1983.

Cohen, Martin. *In Darkness Born: The Story of Star Formation.* Cambridge University Press, 1986.

Greenstein, George. *Of Pulsars, Black Holes and the Fate of Stars.* Freundlich Books, 1983.

Extragalactic Astronomy

Hodge, P. *The Universe of Galaxies.* W.H. Freeman, 1984.

Kaufmann, W. *Galaxies and Quasars.* W.H. Freeman, 1979.

Cosmology

Ferris, Timothy. *The Red Limit.* William Morrow, 1983.

Harrison, Edward R. *Masks of the Universe.* Macmillan, 1985.

Trefil, James S. *Space, Time. Infinity: The Smithsonian View of the Universe.* Pantheon Books, 1985.

Weinberg, Steven. *The First Three Minutes.* Basic Books, 1977.

Space Research

Horowitz, Norman H. *To Utopia and Back: The Search for Life in the Solar System.* W.H. Freeman, 1986.

Lewis, Richard. *The Voyages of Columbia: The First True Spaceship.* Columbia University Press, 1984.

Shapland, David and Michael Rycroft. *Spacelab: Science in Earth Orbit.* Cambridge University Press, 1984.

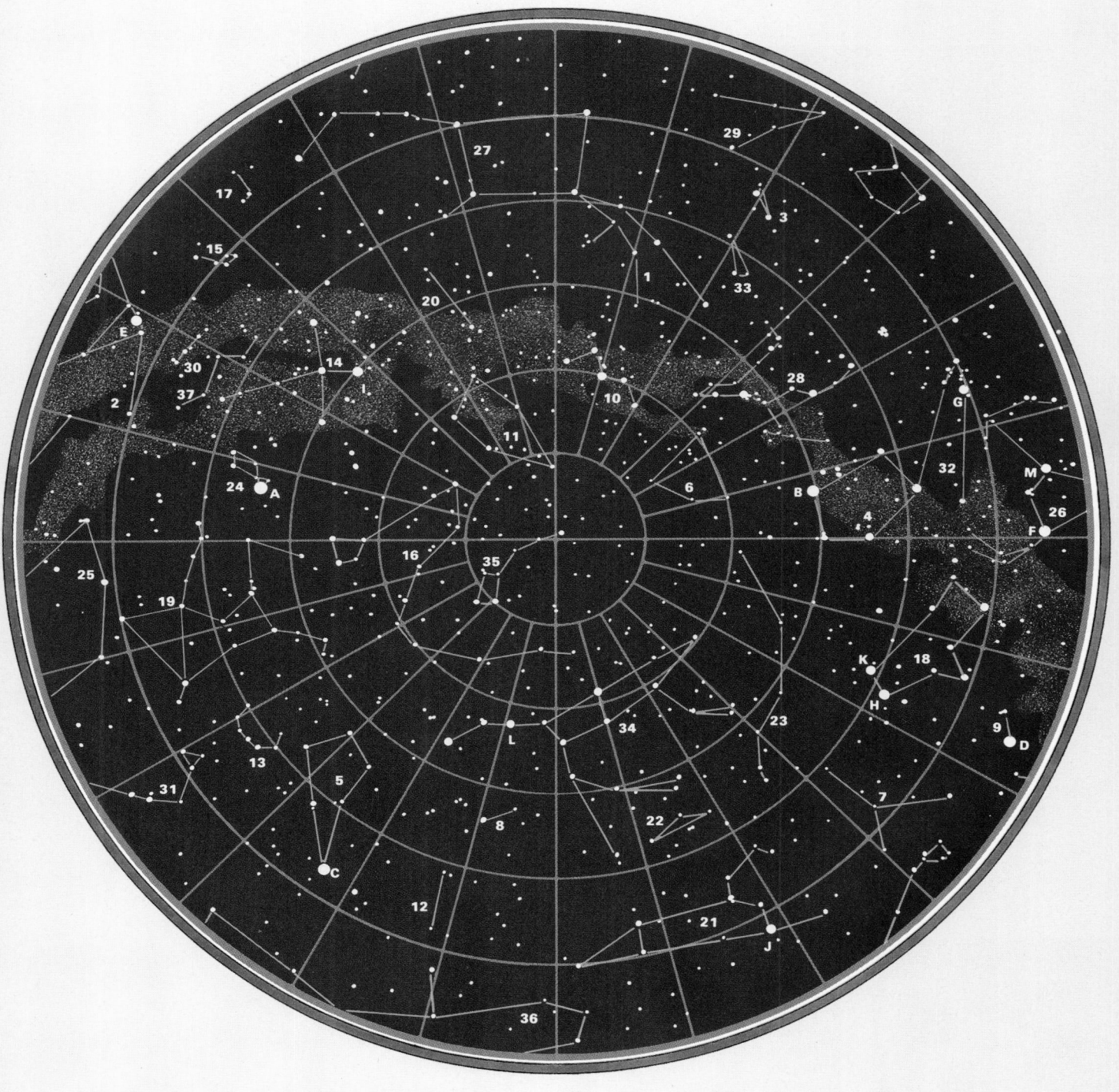

THE NORTHERN HEMISPHERE

The Constellations

LATIN NAME	ENGLISH NAME
1. Andromeda	The Chained Lady
2. Aquila	The Eagle
3. Aries*	The Ram
4. Auriga	The Charioteer
5. Boötes	The Herdsman
6. Camelopardalis	The Giraffe
7. Cancer*	The Crab
8. Canes Venatici	The Hunting Dogs
9. Canis Minor	The Lesser Dog
10. Cassiopeia	The Lady in the Chair
11. Cephus	Cassiopeia's Consort
12. Coma Berenices	Bernice's Hair
13. Corona Borealis	The Northern Cross

LATIN NAME	ENGLISH NAME
14. Cygnus	The Swan
15. Delphinus	The Dolphin
16. Draco	The Dragon
17. Equuleus	The Lesser Horse
18. Gemini*	The Twins
19. Hercules	Hercules
20. Lacerta	The Lizard
21. Leo*	The Lion
22. Leo Minor	The Lesser Lion
23. Lynx	The Lynx
24. Lyra	The Lyre
25. Ophiuchus	The Serpent Holder
26. Orion	The Hunter

LATIN NAME	ENGLISH NAME
27. Pegasus	The Winged Horse
28. Perseus	Persons
29. Pisces*	The Fishes
30. Sagitta	The Arrow
31. Serpens	The Serpent
32. Taurus*	The Bull
33. Triangulum	The Triangle
34. Ursa Major	The Great Bear (The Big Dipper)
35. Ursa Minor	The Little Bear (The Little Dipper)
36. Virgo*	The Virgin
37. Vulpecula	The Fox

*Located in the Zodiac.

Brightest stars

A. Vega
B. Capella
C. Arcturus
D. Procyon
E. Altair
F. Betelgeuse
G. Aldebaran
H. Pollux
I. Deneb
J. Regulus
K. Castor
L. Alioth
M. Bellatrix

THE LUNAR MODULE (*left*) rests on the moon's surface after landing with the Apollo 12 crew. Working near the LM (*above left*), the crew begins setting up scientific equipment. The nation's first manned lunar landing mission was Apollo 11, shown on the take-off (*above right*) of the Apollo/Saturn V space vehicle. The earth (*right*) was photographed by the ATS-III scientific satellite. Portions of North and South America, Africa, Europe, and the Greenland ice cap can be seen.

MOON ROCK SAMPLE from the Apollo 12 mission (*above*) weighs 133.9 grams and is a fine-grained igneous rock with needles of feldspar up to 3 mm long. The Apollo 12 crew sets up experiments (*above right*) on the moon near the Sea of Storms. The picture of the full moon (*below*) was taken by the Apollo 11 crew on their way back to Earth. They were about 10,000 nautical miles away from the moon when the picture was taken. Astronaut David Scott salutes the U.S. flag (*below right*) on the Apollo 15 mission. Hadley Delta Mountain, in the background, is about 5 kilometers away.

A MANNED ORBITAL SPACE STATION designated Skylab *(above)* was occupied by three different crews in 1973-74. The Skylab program carried out scientific experiments leading to the development and construction of permanent space stations. During the landing of Apollo 15, the command and service modules *(below)* passed over the lunar surface, as seen from the Apollo 15 lunar module. The lunar Rover *(right)* sits on the moon's surface during the Apollo 15 mission. Astronaut Irwin is just behind the Rover, and Hadley Delta Mountain is in the background.

PHOTOGRAPHS COURTESY OF NASA

JPL

NASA

SATURN WITH ITS FAMOUS RINGS. In 1980–1981 the Voyager space probes flew close to Saturn, taking photographs such as this. Instead of the expected clearly defined bands, the rings turned out to be exceedingly complex structures.

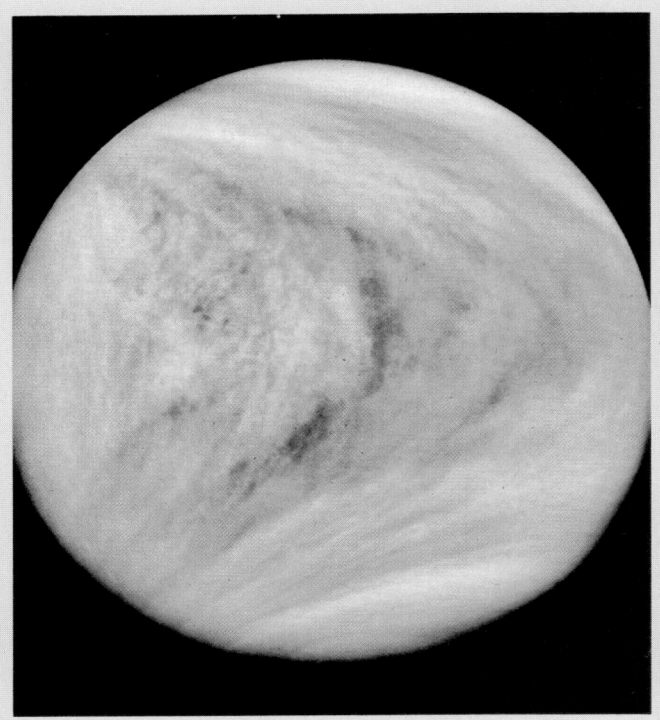

PHOTOGRAPHY REVEALS THE PLANETS. The full disk of Venus is seen *(upper left)* shrouded by its opaque cloud cover brightly illuminated by the midday sun. The colored clouds that surround the Great Red Spot of Jupiter *(lower left)* apparently swirl around it at various altitudes. This view *(lower right)* of the Great Red Spot also shows the part of Jupiter that extends from its equator to its southern latitudes. A computer-enhanced Martian sunset *(upper right)* was taken by Viking 1 just after the sun had dipped below the horizon. The inset shows the rocky soil of Mars, taken by Viking 2 on the Utopian Plain.

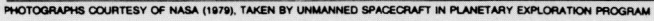

ASTRONOMY IS MAKING RAPID PROGRESS. This computer-enhanced image of Halley's Comet *(top)* was created from a photograph taken December 9, 1985. The comet was 67.6 million miles from Earth; its tail exceeded 3 million miles in length. Io, a moon of Jupiter *(top left)*, has circular features that may be meteorite impact craters or internal in origin, especially because it has a number of active volcanoes, one of which *(lower right)* is erupting on the horizon of this color representation. The photograph of Europa *(lower left)*, the brightest of the Galilean moons of Jupiter, shows the long, narrow fractures extending for hundreds of miles that are typical of its surface.

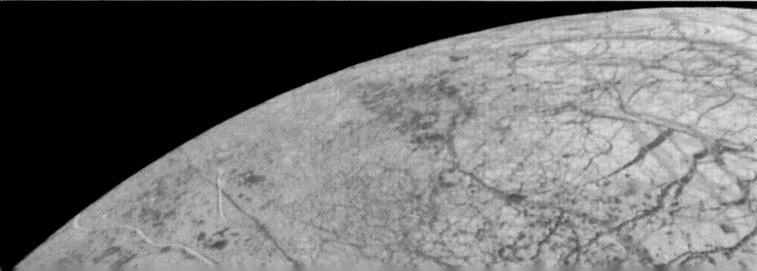

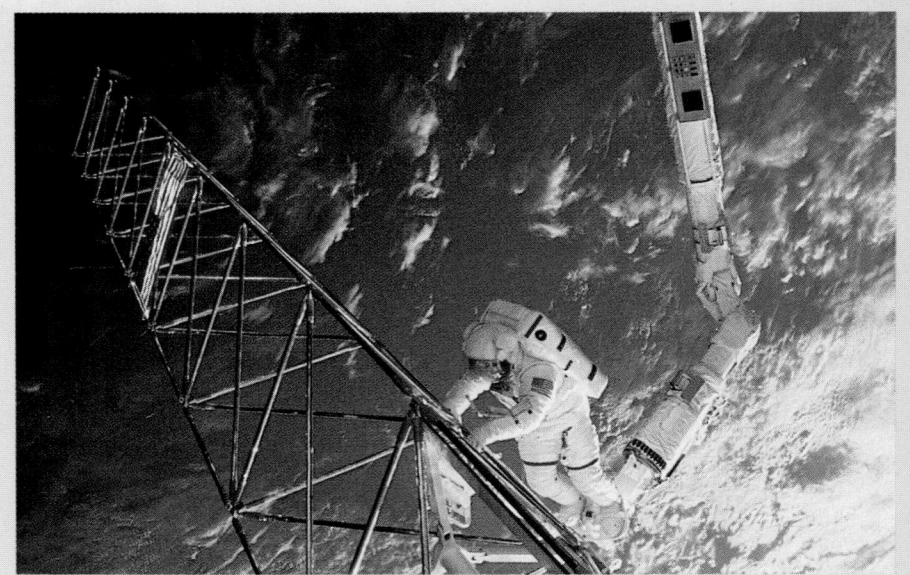

NASA (The National Aeronautics and Space Administration) conducts an ambitious program in the weightlessness of space, carried out by Shuttle crews. They launch space satellites *(top left)*, conduct experiments *(lower left)*, and test techniques for building structures above Earth *(upper right)*. NASA's newest orbiter is *Atlantis (lower right)*, launched first on October 3, 1985.

PHOTOGRAPHS COURTESY OF NASA

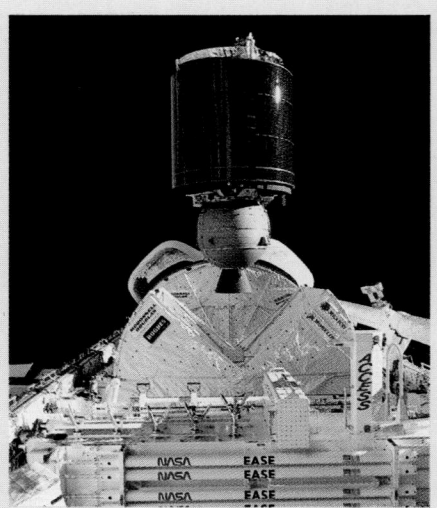

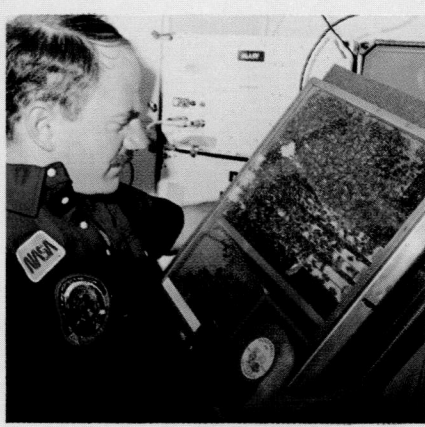

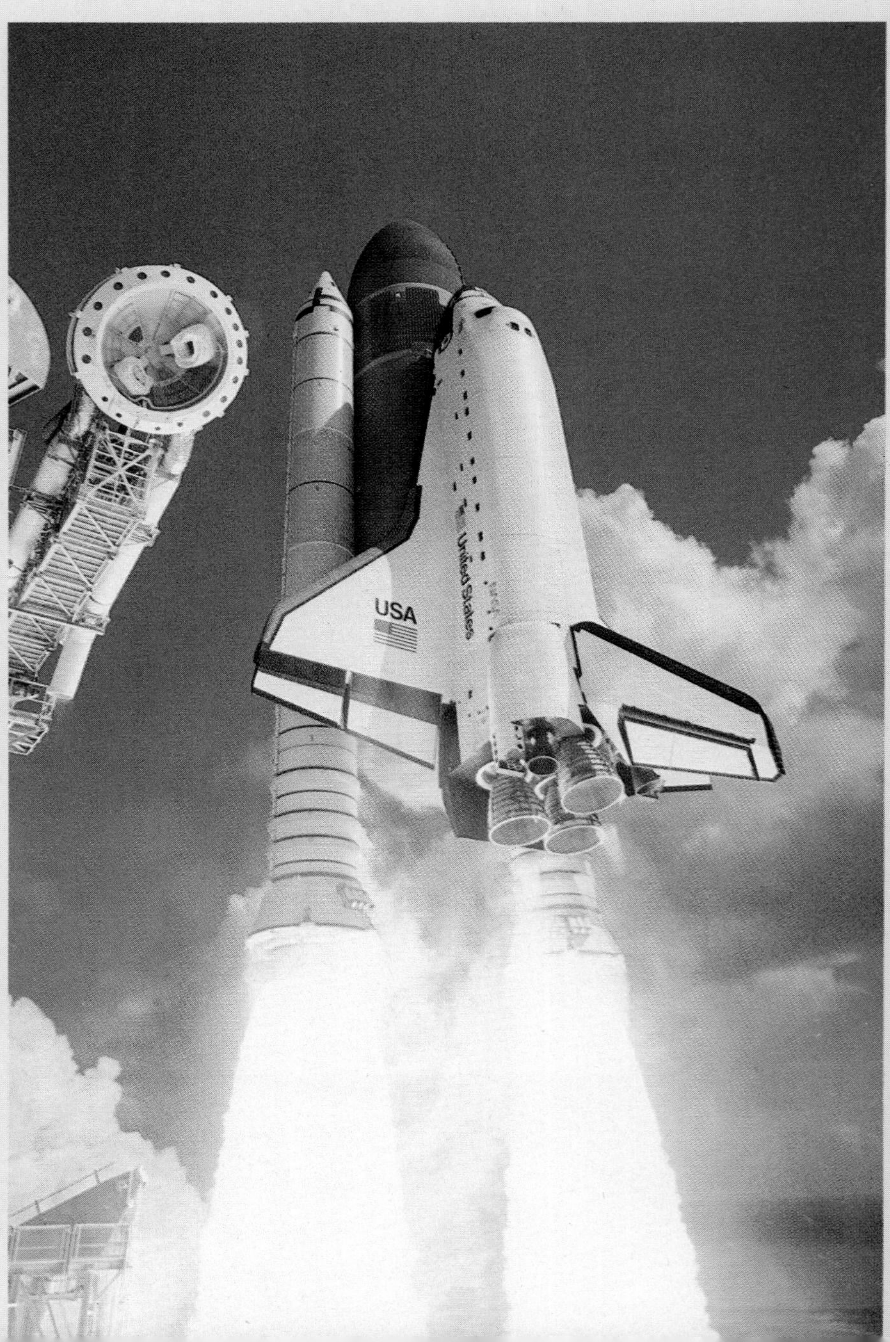

Business and Economics

ERIC KROLL/TAURUS PHOTOS

LARGEST U.S. BUSINESSES		SALES
1.	General Motors	$102,813,700,000
2.	Exxon	69,888,000,000
3.	Ford Motor	62,715,800,000
4.	International Business Machines	51,250,000,000
5.	Mobil	44,866,000,000
6.	General Electric	35,211,000,000
7.	American Telephone & Telegraph	34,087,000,000
8.	Texaco	31,613,000,000
9.	E. I du Pont de Nemours	27,148,000,000
10.	Chevron	24,351,000,000
11.	Chrysler	22,513,500,000
12.	Philip Morris	20,681,000,000
13.	Amoco	18,281,000,000
14.	RJR Nabisco	16,998,000,000
15.	Shell Oil	16,833,000,000
16.	Boeing	16,341,000,000
17.	United Technologies	15,669,157,000
18.	Procter & Gamble	15,439,000,000
19.	Occidental Petroleum	15,344,100,000
20.	Atlantic Richfield	14,585,802,000
21.	Tenneco	14,558,000,000
22.	USX	14,000,000,000
23.	McDonnell Douglass	12,660,600,000
24.	Rockwell International	12,295,700,000
25.	Allied-Signal	11,794,000,000

Source: The Fortune 500 © 1987 Time Inc. All rights reserved.

LARGEST COMPANIES OUTSIDE THE UNITED STATES			SALES
1.	Royal Dutch/Shell Group	Netherlands/Britain	$64,843,217,000
2.	British Petroleum	Britain	39,855,564,000
3.	IRI	Italy	31,561,709,000
4.	Toyota Motor	Japan	31,553,827,000
5.	Daimler-Benz	West Germany	30,168,550,000
6.	Matsushita Electric Industrial	Japan	26,459,539,000
7.	Unilever	Netherlands/Britain	25,141,672,000
8.	Volkswagen	West Germany	24,317,154,000
9.	Hitachi	Japan	22,668,085,000
10.	ENI	Italy	22,549,921,000
11.	Philips' Gloeilampenfabrieken	Netherlands	22,471,263,000
12.	Nestlé	Switzerland	21,153,285,000
13.	Siemens	West Germany	20,307,037,000
14.	Nissan Motor	Japan	20,141,237,000
15.	Fiat	Italy	19,669,581,000
16.	Bayer	West Germany	18,768,914,000
17.	BASF	West Germany	18,640,985,000
18.	Renault	France	17,661,021,000
19.	Hoechst	West Germany	17,509,344,000
20.	Elf Aquitaine	France	17,287,058,000
21.	Samsung	South Korea	16,522,664,000
22.	Mitsubishi Heavy Industries	Japan	15,932,973,000
23.	Peugeot	France	15,152,869,000
24.	Toshiba	Japan	15,036,390,000
25.	Imperial Chemical Industries	Britain	14,867,911,000

Source: The International 500 © 1987 Time Inc. All rights reserved.

Business and Economics

Business has been a dominant force in the development of American society, helping the country achieve an enviable position in the family of nations. Businesses provide goods, services, and jobs, but they also establish the standard of living of the members of society and influence human values and beliefs. The factors that combined to enable the United States to develop into a prominent industrialized nation evolved from European economic philosophies. Over the years, the American influence has added to these principles, resulting in a unique society in which business plays a major role.

According to the traditional view, businesses had no responsibility to society or its individual members. Business managers concentrated on increasing efficiency and productivity in order to maximize profits. Resources were exploited, and there was little thought given to conservation. There was an equal lack of concern for the environment, and employees were viewed as just another resource to be used in the most productive manner possible.

This philosophy was consistent with the attitudes of previous times. Following the Industrial Revolution, in the late 1800's and early 1900's, businesses flourished as they produced the vast quantities of goods and services society wanted. Most people showed little concern about how such productivity was to be accomplished.

As time went by and businesses grew, they also grew in power. In many cases this power was abused, and the cost of unrestrained production became high. Working conditions in factories became unhealthy and dangerous. Working days of 16 hours were common. Children were a source of cheap labor. Eventually, the public demanded that businesses be restrained in their activities.

Concern about business abuses increased rapidly early in the 20th century. By the 1930's, the United States had passed from the profit maximization phase of business to the trusteeship management phase. According to the trusteeship theory, businesses were seen as having a greater responsibility than merely to return maximum profits to shareholders. Companies began to recognize their responsibility to employees and customers, and to the communities in which the companies did business.

The Great Depression ushered in an era of change regarding the way in which employers treated employees. During the 1930's, several federal laws were passed protecting workers. The Wagner Act of 1935 gave employees the right to unionize and bargain collectively with employers. The Social Security Act of the same year provided for retirement pensions and disability benefits. The Wage and Hour Law of 1938 set minimum wages for workers employed in interstate commerce and established maximum hours that employees could be made to work.

The Equal Pay Act of 1963 required that employers pay all employees equally who perform jobs requiring substantially the same abilities or skills. The objective was to ensure that women and others would receive equal pay for essentially equal work. The Civil Rights Act of 1964 prohibited discrimination against employees on the basis of race, religion, color, creed, sex, national origin, age, or disability. Employers must hire, promote, and terminate on a nondiscriminatory basis. They are often required to seek employees among groups that have been subjected to discrimination.

Despite the strides that have been made to ensure equal employment opportunities, inequities still exist. While business has done much to improve the economic life of the nation, challenges still face us, and much work remains to be done.

ECONOMIC DEVELOPMENT

MERCANTILIST *policy favored establishment of a balance of trade favorable to a mother country at the expense of a colony.*

Mercantilism

By the 15th century, mercantilism was the prevailing economic policy of most European nations. Under mercantilism, nations strove to increase their wealth, primarily by establishing a favorable balance of trade to ensure that more wealth flowed in than flowed out. Nations that were able to realize a favorable balance of trade could accumulate gold and silver, the primary measure of wealth at the time.

Businesses were strictly controlled under this policy, producing the goods that each government wanted and exporting only those goods approved for export. It was generally illegal to export gold, silver, and other precious metals. Imports were also controlled, usually through high tariffs, to protect domestic industries.

Aggressive exploration and colonization were integral parts of mercantilism. Colonies were needed to provide the mother country with resources and raw materials. Colonies also provided a market for surplus goods, being required to buy what the mother country needed to sell at prices dictated by the mother country. American colonies, for example, provided England with tobacco and cotton and were forced to buy English tea and sugar. To preserve the captive market, colonies were often forbidden from trading with other nations.

Although mercantilism survived well into the 18th century, it was not without its opponents. In the same year as the American colonies' independence from Great Britain, Adam Smith (1723–1790), a British economist, advocated an economic system far different from that of mercantilism. Smith felt that a highly directed economy, with most of the profit accruing to national treasuries, provided little incentive for individual businessmen. He advocated a free economy in which businesses would be allowed to produce at will and to sell goods wherever they could realize the best price. Smith further emphasized the importance of private ownership of capital to enable individuals to exert greater control over their business destinies.

Smith's doctrine of free trade held that businessmen acting in their own best interests and constrained only by competitive forces would, in the long run, benefit society more than the highly controlled businesses under mercantilism. Smith's laissez faire philosophy eventually became the cornerstone of U.S. economic policy after the Revolutionary War.

Colonization of the New World.

The religious motivation for colonization of the New World is well documented. Equally important, however, were economic reasons. The colonization policy that developed under mercantilism helped lead to the settling of America. The early settlements of Jamestown, Plymouth, and Massachusetts Bay were financed by independent investors seeking profit.

Although mercantilism provided the early basis for American business, it became one of the main factors leading to England's loss of colonies.

England's relationship with the colonies became severely strained following the French and Indian War (1754–1763) as England tightened commercial restrictions affecting American business. Although there was considerable commercial regulation prior to the French and Indian War, restrictions were not vigorously enforced and were commonly ignored by the colonists. Smuggling of molasses to support American rum production in violation of the Molasses Act of 1733, for example, was common, and little was done by the British to stop this practice.

The attitude of the English government changed significantly following the war. The war had been costly and the expense of administering the newly acquired territory was significant. By the mid-1760's, the British national debt was about 140 million pounds. The English felt that the war had benefited the colonists more than the taxpayers at home, who had financed it. As a result, the English turned to the colonies as a source of tax revenues to offset these expenses through the Sugar Act (1764), the Stamp Act (1765), and the Townshend Revenue Act (1767).

American independence. English mercantilistic policies and oppressive taxation finally resulted in the American Revolution. At the time of the war, most Englishmen did not consider the colonies particularly important. England was experiencing trouble elsewhere and did not commit a significant amount of resources to fighting the Americans.

Significant factors in American development were the vast amount of arable land and the existence of extensive natural resources, particularly iron ore and timber. Fertile farmland had made the new nation agriculturally independent even before the Revolutionary War, freeing labor for other uses, such as factory work during the 1800's.

In addition, many immigrants to the New World brought skills and capital with them. Many were merchants with business and entrepreneurial skills. In the South, an extensive slavery system provided a large work force, numbering over 500,000 by the outbreak of the Revolutionary War.

The new economy. When the framers of the new government met to write the Constitution, a favorable business climate was a primary concern. Although few men of the time had heard of Adam Smith, the new republic embraced many of the free enterprise principles. Article Five of the Bill of Rights, for example, guarantees the right of private ownership of property. This right was later strengthened by the addition of the 14th Amendment, which guarantees that no person may be deprived of property without due process of law.

The Constitution united the colonies into a single economic entity, thus eliminating the trade tariffs that had existed between colonies before the revolution.

The Industrial Revolution

The Industrial Revolution did not make its way to the United States until about 1790, but when it did arrive, it ushered in an era of increased productivity and economic growth.

The textile industry. One of the first technological advances in the United States was the development of the machinery necessary to run a textile mill. Samuel Slater (1768–1835) came to the United States from England. There, he had worked in a textile mill where a mechanized spinning machine, as well as other mechanized equipment, had been invented by one of the owners, Richard Arkwright. Slater helped build a mill in Pawtucket, Rhode Island, using Arkwright's designs. The mill, fully mechanized by 1793, was the first true factory in the United States. It helped the textile industry play a major role in the industrialization of the United States.

Eli Whitney (1765–1825) invented the cotton gin, enabling the cotton industry to expand to national prominence. In 1798 Whitney made an even greater contribution. To fulfill a government order for 10,000 muskets, he broke down the production process into specialized tasks and divided those tasks among his workers, who performed a single task repeatedly. He then designed the equipment to produce all parts of a musket in such a way that individual parts would be identical and interchangeable. The specialization of labor and interchangeability of parts laid the groundwork for the factory system that was to develop over the next century.

Steam power. Since early industrial America relied on waterpower, all factories had to be located close to rivers. Introduction of steam engines enabled factories to be built anywhere, so factories could be built closer to available labor, raw materials, and markets.

Transportation and communication. Steam power also made a national transportation system possible. Earlier, because goods were shipped by water or transported overland by wagons, the movement of goods to areas far from rivers was difficult and extremely slow. Railroads, however, could be built to go virtually anywhere. By the 1830's, railroads linked together major business centers of the eastern seaboard. In 1869 the Union Pacific Railroad and the Southern Pacific Railroad met in Utah, linking the East and West coasts. This achievement enabled goods to be shipped across country in a week. Thus, it opened new markets to manufacturers and made raw materials more accessible. For example, consumers in San Francisco had access to goods produced in New England. The U.S. economy, which had previously been regional in nature, was in the process of being integrated.

Invention of the telegraph also assisted economic growth by making information regarding markets more available to producers, who could then take advantage of those markets through improved transportation facilities.

The American Civil War further fueled the fire of industrial development. The necessity of producing a large amount of war goods in a relatively short period of time required technological advancements in production processes. Factories became more productive and efficient to meet the needs of the war. After the Civil War, these factories and their technology were applied to the production of peacetime goods.

Responsible in no small part for the phenomenal growth in industrialization and economic output during the 19th and early 20th centuries was a relatively small group of bold, sometimes ruthless, entrepreneurs referred to as robber barons. Nevertheless, they helped establish an industrial system that served as the foundation for future prosperity.

The rise of corporations. Although the corporate form of business was known in colonial times, it was not common. Most corporations were educational or religious organizations or groups responsible for the operations of public facilities such as toll bridges and canals. Many of the large firms in the 1800's were partnerships, but as the 19th century came to a close, corporations came into prominence. Advocates of the partnership form felt that executives would be more firmly attached to a company as partners rather than as corporate officers. As long as profits provided sufficient funds for business expansion, the partnership form worked well. By the late 1800's, many firms found that profits alone were not sufficient to finance expansion. The corporate form of business provided greater access to capital markets than did partnerships.

By the 1890's, large manufacturing businesses, such as Procter & Gamble, P. Lorillard, and Westinghouse Electric, had adopted the corporate form. By the beginning of the 20th century, corporations dominated major industries such as manufacturing, mining, transportation, and utilities.

Monopolies and trusts. As a result of the technological advances of the 19th century, abundant resources, a favorable political climate, and entrepreneurial skills, virtual monopolies existed in the major industries by the end of the century. Monopoly conditions also existed in industries that were not dominated by a single company, often through the use of business pools. A *business pool* was an agreement among companies in an industry that limited competition among them. Marketing areas were divided into territories, each assigned to a specific company that sold its product free of competition from other producers. Pools were common during the 1880's and 1890's in steel, explosives, meat products, tobacco products, and other industries.

Eventually, many pools evolved into *business trusts,* the arrangements whereby the stockholders of compet-

THE PRODUCTION LINE, *a development introduced in 1798 by Eli Whitney, revolutionized the mass production of manufactured goods.*

ing companies turned over their shares to a group of trustees who controlled the companies in such a manner as to eliminate competition among the formerly independent firms. By the late 1800's, trusts existed in the sugar, whiskey, cottonseed oil, lead, and salt industries. Trusts were declared illegal in many states and were replaced by holding companies, which still exist today in many industries.

Industrial expansion of the 19th century was not without its costs. The labor force paid the highest price. At the time when John D. Rockefeller was becoming a billionaire, working conditions in the factories were poor and wages were low. Children worked 70 hours a week in the coal mines for $2 a day. Between 1865 and 1900 the disparity between the rich and the poor grew. By 1900 10 percent of the population owned 90 percent of the wealth.

These deplorable labor conditions contributed to the considerable economic growth of the time. Low wages enabled incredible capital formation to take place; without this, the expansion of the 19th century would not have been possible. Instead of using profits to increase wages and improve working conditions, companies were able to use these funds for business expansion.

By 1900, however, as monopolies continued to grow, so did public and government concern. In 1890 Congress passed the Sherman Antitrust Act. Under this act, contracts, conspiracies, and combinations in restraint of trade were prohibited, as were monopolies and attempts to monopolize. Although it was years before monopolies were effectively controlled, passage of the Sherman Act marked the beginning of greater involvement by government in the affairs of business.

Technology continued to advance during the 20th century, with bold entrepreneurs again playing a major role. The most important entrepreneur of this period was Henry Ford. In 1913 he introduced a production breakthrough in the manufacture of automobiles that changed the nature of American manufacturing. His assembly line increased worker productivity and made mass production possible.

The rise of consumer credit.

The 1920's saw a boom in consumer purchases as wages grew and consumer credit became important for the first time. Prior to 1913, banks had generally lent money only to businesses in need of capital. There were few installment sales and even mortgages were rare.

In the late 1800's and early 1900's, there was a significant increase in the supply of money. This was primarily the result of vast gold discoveries in the West. (The United States adopted the gold standard in 1900, and more gold essentially meant more money.) From 1890 to 1914, the supply of gold in the United States virtually tripled. The resulting rapid increase in the supply of money drove interest rates down and made loans more widely available to the public.

Decline of the tycoons.

The period between 1900 and 1929 was a period during which ownership of the giant companies became diffused. Ownership passed from the hands of a few men into the hands of thousands of corporate shareholders and their professional managers. Productivity and business expansion continued during this period, but the structure of American industry had changed forever.

The Great Depression

Although there were recessions and depressions in the first 150 years of the United States, the Great Depression of the 1930's represented a true economic collapse. One reason for the collapse was a rapid expansion in installment buying. In response, businesses overproduced consumer goods and investment declined.

Stock market crash.

In 1929 there was a great deal of speculative investment, and many companies were not financially sound. The stringent listing requirements that the major stock exchanges have today did not exist then, and speculation drove up the prices of many stocks far beyond their actual value. Much of this buying was done on margin: the buyer needed to pay only a small portion of the actual purchase price and, in effect, borrowed the rest. When the prices of some overpriced stocks began to fall, many investors could not come up with the funds needed to cover their investments. They were forced to sell stock to satisfy margin requirements. The increased selling led to further price declines, which continued until prices on the exchanges hit bottom.

Bank failures.

Even more significant than the stock market crash were the bank failures. During October of 1930, March of 1931, and the last quarter of 1932, banks failed because of panic on the part of depositors. Since banks did not keep 100 percent of deposits on hand, they soon ran out of money and closed. Millions of people lost their life savings. The economic collapse of 1929 and 1930 ushered in a depression that was to last until World War II.

The New Deal.

When President Roosevelt took office in 1933, unemployment had reached 25 percent, production of goods and services had declined by half, and corporate profits were a third of earlier levels. Roosevelt's New Deal policies for economic recovery targeted banking reform and unemployment. The New Deal worked to a degree, but by 1939, 9 million American workers, 20 percent of the work force, were still unemployed.

Increased government involvement.

Until 1930 businesses were primarily responsible for the production of goods and services and government played a minor role. The Depression convinced many that, contrary to the economic philosophies of Adam Smith, an economy will not automatically adjust in the long run to

WORLD WAR II, *because of the demand for war materiel such as tanks, provided a boost to the U.S. economy that helped lift it out of the Depression.*

meet the best interests of society. Many felt that a strong central government was essential to direct the economy through active monetary and fiscal policy. The result was an increase in government involvement in business operations that has continued to this day.

Economic Recovery

When World War II began, factories converted to the production of war goods, and people went back to work. Production of consumer goods was curtailed so the industrial might of the United States could be directed toward providing war goods. Not being able to afford consumer goods was no longer a problem: such goods simply were not available. Shoes, gasoline, and even meat were in short supply and had to be rationed.

Following World War II, there were fears that a depression would return, but demand increased for consumer goods virtually unavailable during the war, and consumers had savings to support their purchases. Industry quickly turned to the task of satisfying the demand.

The postwar years were years of rapid technological advancement. One of the major advancements was the development of the computer, which came into widespread business and scientific use during the 1950's. There were also technological advancements and modernizations in such important industries as plastics, electronics, and aeronautics.

In the postwar years, thanks to favorable legislation and the growing power of labor unions, workers realized increased wages and benefits.

The very nature of the economy was also changing. An increasing number of workers were involved in service industries rather than manufacturing. One factor leading to this increase in service occupations was advanced technology. As industry became more capital intensive, using machines more and people less, there was a greater demand for technicians to service this modern equipment.

The increasing standard of living of the American people also stimulated service-oriented industries. Many Americans had disposable income, and they spent a portion of that income on entertainment, travel, and other leisure-time activities. Americans were also living longer. As the average age of American citizens increased, so did their need for services in the health care industry. By 1960 more than half of all American workers were involved in supplying services.

The Modern Era

During the 1960's, the economy generally prospered, but Americans were introduced to a new problem, inflation. The 1960's also saw growing public concern over the environment, conservation of resources, and individual rights. Again the federal government assumed an active role in addressing problems in these areas. Among other significant measures, Congress passed the Clean Air Act in 1963 and the Water Quality Act in 1965, and established the Environmental Protection Agency in 1970 to preserve and improve the environment. A number of measures were undertaken to encourage industry to conserve scarce resources, such as requiring timber producers to replace the trees they harvested. The Equal Pay Act of 1963, the

THE OIL CRISIS *in 1973 provided a great shock in the U.S. economy.*

Civil Rights Act of 1964, and the Age Discrimination in Employment Act of 1967 were passed to ensure equal employment opportunity.

The post-World War II boom ended in the 1970's. One reason for the boom had been the availability of cheap resources. But resources, particularly petroleum, became scarcer and more expensive. The oil crisis of the mid-1970's, during which the Organization of Petroleum Exporting Countries (OPEC) dramatically increased the price of crude oil, further aggravated inflation, which exceeded 10 percent. By the 1970's, the purchasing power of the dollar was half what it was in 1940.

The rate of inflation was generally considered acceptable if it was accompanied by increases in economic output. But in the 1970's, economic output could no longer keep pace with inflation. There were also marked changes in the nature of the work force in the 1970's. Its size increased dramatically, largely because of the increased number of women in the work force. Although business activity was still increasing, business expansion was insufficient to absorb additional workers. The result was high unemployment. This unemployment coupled with inflation, known as *stagflation,* was a problem into the 1980's.

By the 1980's, the nature of business had changed. Many companies had become multinational to take advantage of foreign markets and cheap resources, especially labor. There was also a wave of corporate mergers that created diversified companies involved in many, often unrelated, industries. Improved technology continued to be a major trend and American businesses became still more involved in service industries. The eventual outcome of these changes is yet to be seen.

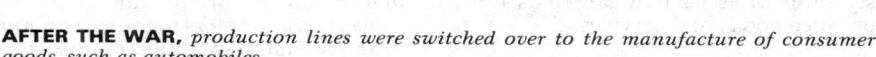

AFTER THE WAR, *production lines were switched over to the manufacture of consumer goods, such as automobiles.*

ECONOMICS

Decisions of the government as well as private enterprise are often made in response to economic problems or conditions. To understand such decisions and their impact, it is necessary to have an understanding of the economic factors that underlie them.

On a personal level, an understanding of economics may help us select savings and investment plans that will safely provide income in our later

![The New York Times front page]

STOCKS PLUNGE 508 POINTS, A DROP OF 22.6%; 604 MILLION VOLUME NEARLY DOUBLES RECORD

Does 1987 Equal 1929?

THE STOCK MARKET *can both reflect and affect the health of the economy.*

years, or choose an occupation that will continue to be in demand during periods of unemployment.

Businessmen rely on an understanding of our economy in making decisions about new products, business expansion or contraction, and personnel policies. Their analyses of the impact of economic factors enable them to keep their businesses headed in the direction of maximum profitability.

The Study of Economics

What Is Economics?

Economics is the study of the process by which scarce resources are allocated and organized to maximize the satisfaction of human wants and needs. Although the resources of nearly any society are limited, human wants and needs are basically unlimited. The problem, then, is to employ available resources in such a manner as to maximize the satisfaction of society as a whole.

Factors of production. In an economic sense, there are several types of resources that may be utilized in satisfying these needs. Economists group these resources into four categories known as factors of production. It is the bringing together of these factors of production that results in economic productivity.

Land. The first of these factors of production is *land,* which includes raw materials, such as minerals, soil, and water.

Labor. The second factor of production, *labor,* is the effort provided by the people of a society. The effectiveness and efficiency of labor in the production process are functions of two variables, the amount of labor and the quality of that labor. The first variable, the amount of labor, tends to have a greater impact on effectiveness (the ability to produce goods and services) than on efficiency (the production of goods and services with a minimal waste of resources). In other words,

adding labor to a production process normally will increase the amount of output, but it will not necessarily increase efficiency. The second variable, the quality of the workers involved, affects both effectiveness and efficiency. A highly skilled labor force makes for greater productivity and less waste than a labor force that is less skilled.

Capital. The third factor of production is *capital.* Most people think of capital as money. To an economist, capital refers to the instruments, tools, machines, factories, and other assets used in the production process. When economists speak of capital formation, therefore, they are referring to the assembling of assets that can be used to produce goods and services.

CAPITAL *can be a truck or factory building as well as money.*

Capital also includes processed raw materials, that is, raw materials to which some amount of labor has already been applied. Steel, for example, is an element of capital, while iron ore, from which steel is produced, is a natural resource. Note that it is the function of an item, rather than its form, that distinguishes capital goods from consumer goods. A car used to satisfy personal needs is considered a consumer good. If the same car is part of a fleet used by a corporate sales staff, for example, it is considered a capital good, since its function is to produce sales for the company.

Entrepreneurship. The fourth and final factor of production is *entrepreneurship.* It refers to the ownership initiative and assumption of risk that bring the other factors of production together. An entrepreneur is one who initiates a business, assumes the risk of a failure, and receives the rewards of a success.

Entrepreneurs are generally motivated, in part at least, by the possibility of making a profit. If an entrepreneur produces goods or services that consumers want, and does so in an effective and efficient manner, the profit will reflect the value that his or her effort has added to the products made and sold.

Economic Analysis

Economic analysis is divided into two broad disciplines, macroeconomics and microeconomics.

272

Macroeconomics.

Economic theory and analysis applied to an entire economy is called macroeconomics. Major concerns of macroanalysis are the total level of employment rather than employment in specific industries or companies, the level of national income as opposed to the distribution of that income, national productivity as opposed to productivity within various industries, and the general level of prices rather than the prices of specific commodities.

In recent years, as international trade has increased, macroeconomic analysis has become more complex. For example, the impact of foreign imports and international financing has made it difficult to study any single nation's economy independently of foreign considerations. The expansion of macroeconomic analysis to include global factors is sometimes referred to as *international economics* or *global economics.*

Policy economics refers to government regulation and activities designed to influence various areas of an economy. Consideration of a tax cut to stimulate a sluggish economy, for example, falls in the area of policy economics. It involves not only analysis of economic activity but value judgments about that activity.

Microeconomics.

Microeconomics is concerned with analysis as it applies to economic subunits, such as

MACROECONOMISTS *study the whole of an economy while microeconomists study one particular unit of the economy, for instance the food industry.*

individual industries and companies, workers, and consumers. It studies how resources are allocated among various industries and companies rather than what is the total amount of resources available. It deals with the distribution of products and income rather than with aggregate productivity and total national income. In microeconomics it is the relative prices of individual goods that are considered rather than the general price level of the economy.

As practiced by business managers in the operation of their companies, microeconomics is often referred to as *managerial economics.* Managerial economics is concerned with such factors as the level of output that maximizes profit, efficiency in production,

the optimal number of workers, and the establishment of appropriate selling prices for products.

Although separate disciplines, macroeconomics and microeconomics are highly related. For example, although inflation is a macroeconomic concern, it has a significant impact on the operations of individual businesses.

At the same time, individual businesses have a great impact on the overall economy. If companies foresee a strong economy and high consumer demand, they may increase levels of production and thus affect total national productivity and income. In fact, macroeconomics is sometimes viewed as the aggregate of all microeconomic activity.

Economic Objectives

A basic function of government is to promote the general welfare of the people. Since economic factors significantly affect the quality of life of the members of any society, most governments promote economic growth, full employment, and price stability.

Economic Growth

Depending on the nature of an economy and the degree of its development, economic growth is important for various reasons. In underdeveloped nations, it is often necessary for the economy to become more productive in order to provide people with the basic requirements of life, such as food, clothing, and shelter. For these nations, economic growth is not only the key to a higher standard of living, it may be the key to survival for a significant portion of the population. For nations sufficiently advanced to provide the basic necessities, growth still serves valuable functions, the most no-

table of which is an improved standard of living.

Not everyone, however, considers economic growth desirable. Critics point out that proliferation of goods and ser-

vices does not guarantee a higher quality of life, and material growth may lead to degradation of the environment and to factory systems that provide workers with little job satisfaction.

THE GROWTH RATE *is measured as percent change in the gross national product, adjusted for inflation.*

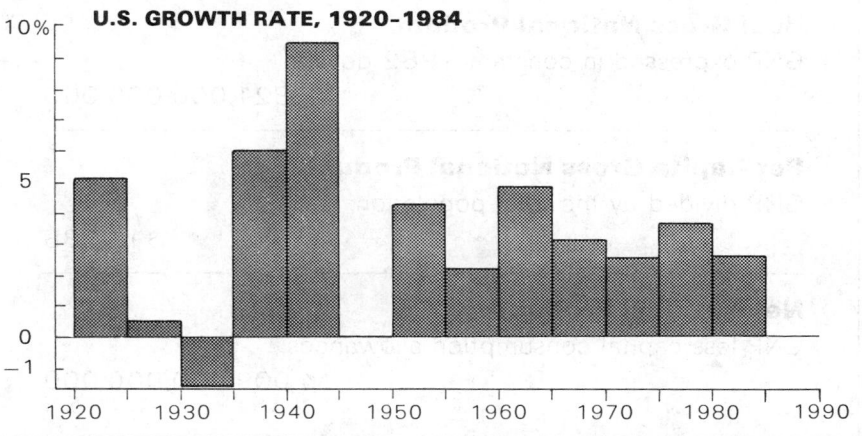

U.S. GROWTH RATE, 1920-1984

PETER LOEWER

Gross national product. The most common measure of economic productivity is the *gross national product* (GNP). GNP is the total value of all goods and services produced in final form during a specified period of time, usually one year. GNP is, however, not the only measure that economists use for analyzing and estimating economic productivity.

Real GNP. On the surface, it would seem that an increasing GNP indicates growth. It is not that simple, however, since GNP is determined using the market price of goods and services; thus, inflation may cause a GNP to increase simply because the price of goods is increasing, not because more is being produced. This problem can be corrected by statistically adjusting GNP for changes in overall price levels. Unadjusted GNP is referred to as *nominal GNP* or *money GNP,* while adjusted GNP is referred to as *real GNP.* Real GNP measures economic output in terms of the dollars of a base year, typically 1982, which serves as a standard of comparison.

Per capita GNP. To provide a better measure of the standard of living in a society, GNP is often stated as *per capita GNP,* which is calculated by dividing GNP by the total population. This provides a measure of output per person and eliminates the effect that an increasing or decreasing population may have on GNP.

Net national product. Although GNP provides an acceptable measure of economic productivity, it still leaves something to be desired as a measurement of growth. Some of the goods produced by an economy are used to replace other goods. Industrial equipment, for example, wears out and must be replaced. These replacement goods are counted in the GNP but they do not represent true growth. To allow for this, another measure of economic productivity is used, *net national product* (NNP). NNP is calculated by subtracting from GNP the value of goods that are produced to replace other goods (called *capital consumption allowances*). The result is closer to a measure of true growth rather than productivity.

Productivity and efficiency.

The key to economic growth is productivity, the ability of businesses to produce goods and services that satisfy needs. As the resources available to increase productivity become scarcer, it becomes more important to increase efficiency, that is, to eliminate waste in production processes. Without this efficiency, economic growth cannot be sustained.

Recessions and depressions. *Recessions* and *depressions* are almost always tied to decreased productivity. This was never more apparent than during the Great Depression. Economic productivity was high in 1929, but by 1933 the production of goods and services had declined by 31 percent. Business investment had also dropped, to almost zero, and the value of shares on stock markets dropped to one-sixth of their 1929 value. Unemployment went from 3 percent to an almost incredible 25 percent.

Foreign competition. The ability of an economy to produce goods and services in an efficient manner is highly related to international competitiveness. In recent years the level of international trade has greatly increased as U.S. companies have sought markets, sources of raw materials, and cheap labor overseas. The result has been an increase in the importance of the economic characteristics of foreign nations.

Furthermore, U. S. companies have increasingly had to compete at home and abroad with foreign companies whose costs of production, particularly labor, have been substantially below those of U.S. firms. At home, some advocate protective tariffs and trade restrictions to protect U.S. industries and jobs from foreign competition. Others feel that the most effective way to meet this competition is for the private sector in the United States to become more efficient. Increased efficiency, resulting in greater productivity, would enable retention of the high wage rates prevalent in the United States.

Full Employment

Creating the opportunity to make full use of people's abilities is a major objective of most economic systems, regardless of their forms. The goal of full employment, however, is not achieved easily or without cost.

There have been periods of mass unemployment in the United States that have threatened the viability of the economy as well as the quality of life of the American people. Unemployment during the Great Depression of the 1930's, for example, was so severe that it brought poverty to millions of people, not only in the United States but throughout the world. The recession of the 1970's, although not as severe as the Great Depression, added 2.5 million Americans to the poverty rolls.

Costs of unemployment. Unemployment exacts a heavy toll. During the 1930's there was widespread hunger, illness, and even premature death. There also is evidence that high levels of unemployment are accompanied by anxiety, emotional difficulties, and higher crime rates. When an economy does not create jobs for all those who want to work, a valuable resource is wasted. The goods that could have been produced by the unemployed are lost to society forever. In 1975, for example, the unemployment rate in the United States was 8.5 percent. It has been estimated that this resulted in a $115-billion loss in real GNP (1972 dollars).

Causes of unemployment. When a nation enters a period of high unemployment, the reasons are not always apparent. Many claim that in re-

U.S. NATIONAL PRODUCT (1987)

Gross National Product (GNP)
total value of all goods and services:
$4,488,500,000,000

Real Gross National Product
GNP expressed in constant 1982 dollars:
$3,821,000,000,000

Per Capita Gross National Product
GNP divided by the total population:
$18,388

Net National Product
GNP less capital consumption allowances:
$4,009,400,000,000

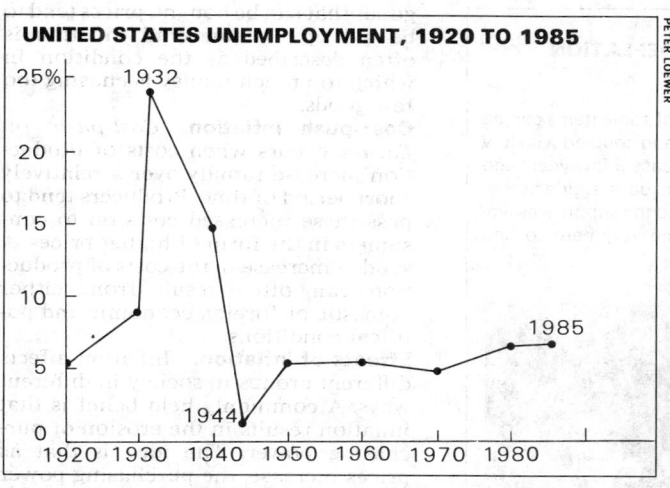

UNITED STATES UNEMPLOYMENT, 1920 TO 1985

PETER LOEWER

TRESS/PHOTO RESEARCHERS

UNEMPLOYMENT *can have many different causes, from the mechanization of certain kinds of jobs to the collapse of an industry. In the history of the United States, the highest rate of unemployment came in 1932, during the Great Depression, and the lowest rate in 1944, during World War II.*

cent years competition from foreign producers has been one of the major causes of unemployment in the United States. Another possible explanation is the changing nature of the U.S. work force. In 1960 women constituted approximately 32 percent of the U.S. civilian work force. By 1985 this percentage had increased to 44.

Technology also has been blamed for unemployment. The argument is that automation and computerization have reduced the need for human labor. The opposite viewpoint asserts that technology creates more jobs than it eliminates. The problem is that the jobs created are usually different in nature from those eliminated. People who have lost their jobs as a result of the introduction of new technology are usually not qualified to perform the newly created jobs.

Government intervention.
Although the unemployment problem has not recently been as severe as it was during the Great Depression, unemployment continues to be a major governmental concern. In 1946 Congress passed The Employment Act; it states that "maximum employment, production, and purchasing power" are important objectives of government policy. In 1978 the Full Employment and Balanced Growth Bill, called the Humphrey-Hawkins Bill, officially established 4 percent as the nation's target maximum unemployment rate.

Frictional unemployment.
One of the problems in attaining full employment is the definition of employment. It is unrealistic to strive for 100 percent employment because a certain amount of unemployment is unavoidable. There will, for example, always be a number of people who are temporarily between jobs because they are changing occupations, moving to a

new locality, or working for a firm that is going out of business. To a great degree, this type of *frictional unemployment* is unavoidable.

Structural unemployment.
As long as technology advances and the nature of jobs changes, a certain number of people will be displaced because their skills are no longer needed. This is referred to by economists as *structural unemployment.*

Acceptable unemployment.
An appropriate societal objective, then, is to achieve a level of employment that takes these unavoidable circumstances into consideration. At various times certain target levels of employment have been established as objectives of the government. The relatively low unemployment rates of the 1940's and 1950's led President John F. Kennedy to establish 4 percent as a national goal. This was the first time that the federal government had formally quantified unemployment goals. The Humphrey-Hawkins Bill made the 4 percent goal the law of the land.

Price Stability

In general, the market price of goods and services determines how those goods will be distributed among the members of society. Those who can afford to pay the market price of goods are those who will end up with them. The market price of goods and services is also the major mechanism by which income is distributed. Those who own the most valuable goods and services, including personal labor, will receive the greatest income. Since market prices affect both the allocation of goods and services and the distribution of income, the level of prices has wide-

spread impact. Because rapidly increasing or decreasing prices tend to be accompanied by other economic problems, such as recession or depression, price stability is a major objective of economic regulation.

The consumer price index.
The degree to which prices increase or decrease over time can be measured in a number of ways. One of the most common methods used in the United States is the *consumer price index* (CPI). The CPI compares current price levels with those of a given base year, commonly 1967.

PETER LOEWER

THE CONSUMER PRICE INDEX AND THE PURCHASING POWER OF THE DOLLAR

The consumer price index is a measure of inflation. As the index rises, reflecting a rise in prices, the amount that each dollar will buy decreases. That is, its purchasing power decreases.

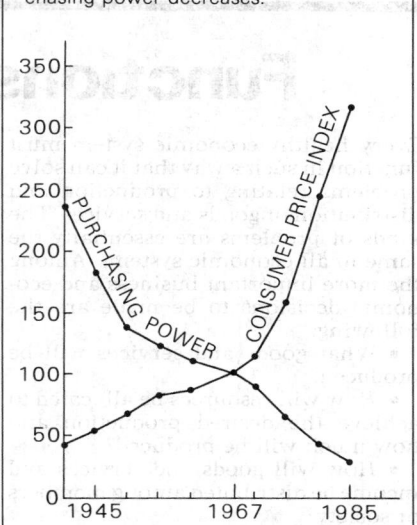

The CPI is compiled by the Bureau of Labor Statistics (BLS), a division of the U.S. Department of Labor, which computes the CPI from a sampling of products called a *market basket* of goods. The current prices of the goods in the market basket are compared with the prices of the same items in the base year, and the relationship is expressed as a percentage of that base year. A current CPI of 150, for example, means that the current level of prices is 150 percent of the level of 1967, if that is the base year in use.

Although a useful statistic, the CPI has certain shortcomings. Not all consumers purchase goods in the proportion represented by the market basket. Individual consumers, therefore, may experience inflation rates above or below those indicated by the CPI.

Deflation.
Deflation, a condition of generally declining prices, tends to result in hardship for sellers of commodities, such as farm products, since the prices of farm and other commodities tend to fall before other prices. Debtors also are likely to suffer during deflationary periods, because they must repay their loans in more valuable money.

Inflation.
Inflation, a condition of generally increasing prices, has been the predominant trend in the United States since 1940. Inflation takes more than one form.

Demand-pull inflation. One major problem associated with the control of inflation is that rising prices may result from various causes. Inflation resulting from increased consumer demand is called *demand-pull inflation.* It occurs when disposable income or the supply of money grows significantly faster than the supply of goods available to the consumer. Since there is more money available than

INFLATION AND DEFLATION

Inflation of the price of some items can be due to very high demand coupled with low supply. This was the case a few years ago when Cabbage Patch dolls suddenly became very popular and the supply was limited; the dolls became very hard to find and their price rose.

BARBARA ALPER

Conversely, when the supply of a commodity is high but demand for it is low, its price tends to deflate. In 1980 the price for a bushel of corn was $3.11, but due to oversupply and lack of demand, the price fell to $1.45 a bushel in 1986.

1980: $3.11   1986: $1.45

MARILYN BASS

goods that can be bought, prices tend to be bid up. Demand-pull inflation is often described as the condition in which too much money is chasing too few goods.

Cost-push inflation. *Cost-push inflation* occurs when costs of production increase rapidly over a relatively short period of time. Producers tend to pass these increased costs on to consumers in the form of higher prices. A sudden increase in the costs of production can often result from either domestic or foreign economic and political conditions.

Effects of inflation. Inflation affects different groups in society in different ways. A commonly held belief is that inflation results in the erosion of purchasing power. The idea is that as prices increase, the purchasing power of the dollar declines, so it takes more money to buy the same products. In actuality, this effect is only partially true. Those on fixed incomes, for example, feel the squeeze because their incomes do not keep pace with rising prices. The work force in the aggregate, however, usually does not experience a loss in purchasing power as a result of inflation, since for the past 40 years, increases in general wage levels have outpaced inflation.

Creditors and debtors are two groups that are affected differently by inflation. Periods of high inflation usually benefit debtors more than creditors, since debtors are repaying their debts in cheaper dollars. Conversely, creditors tend to lose, since they are the ones who are likely to be receiving the cheaper dollars.

Those with savings accounts and other savings instruments that pay relatively low rates of interest may also lose during an inflationary period. When savers are receiving a return below the rate of inflation, as time goes by, their investments or deposits become progressively less valuable in terms of purchasing power.

Functions of an Economic System

Every healthy economic system must function in such a way that it can solve problems relating to production and distribution of goods and services. The kinds of problems are essentially the same in all economic systems. Among the more important business and economic decisions to be made are the following:

• What goods and services will be produced?

• How will resources be allocated to achieve the desired production and how much will be produced?

• How will goods and services and income be distributed among members of society?

What Will Be Produced?

One of the functions of an economic system is to allocate available resources to the various production possibilities. In a free enterprise system, such as that operating in the United States, the determination of what to produce begins in the marketplace. Individual consumers interact in the marketplace to decide what will be produced. They do so through a kind of voting process in which the dollars they spend on products act as votes.

How Will Resources Be Allocated?

Resources are allocated to those who will pay the most for them. Those who are willing to pay the most are those who can derive the greatest value from them. If the market is efficient, producers of products in high demand can realize the greatest prices from the sale of those products; therefore, they are able to pay the suppliers of resources more than other producers. It follows

LLOYD BIRMINGHAM

DEMAND BY CONSUMERS *for a particular item requires a retailer to order more of the item and the manufacturer to produce more of it.*

that in this way, resources end up in the hands of those who can generate the most consumer satisfaction from their use.

Reallocation. When consumer demand changes, the process works to reallocate resources away from industries experiencing declining demand into industries experiencing increasing demand. As consumers spend more on some products and less on others, producers of goods in high demand are willing to spend more to procure the necessary resources to meet the increased demand.

Labor. Although shifting physical resources, such as raw materials, from one industry to another may be relatively simple, shifting labor poses a more difficult problem. Theoretically, growth industries would be willing to pay more for labor than nongrowth industries, and workers would shift to the growth industries to take advantage of the higher wages.

If the skills required in growth industries are the same as those required in nongrowth industries, the problem of shifting jobs may be minimal. When the skills required are markedly different, reallocation of labor becomes more difficult.

How Much Will Be Produced?

The appropriate quantities of each commodity to be produced are determined hand in hand with the determination of what to produce. Again, consumers cast their votes for appropriate quantities with their purchasing dollars. When demand exceeds supply, industries react to provide greater quantities to meet the demand.

In addition to an increase in production by firms already in an industry, other companies will be enticed to

enter the industry in order to take advantage of the high profits that typically accompany the production of goods that are in high demand.

The opposite effect takes place in industries in which supply is in excess of demand. If businesses see their inventories swelling as a result of too little demand, they are likely to reduce production in order to liquidate inventories. Some businesses will leave the industry as prices and profits drop. Eventually, supply will be reduced to a level that is more in line with demand.

How Will Goods and Services Be Distributed?

In addition to providing a mechanism whereby resources are allocated and levels of production are established, economic systems must also decide who will receive the fruit of the production process. As already noted, in a free enterprise economy operating without interference, it is the price of the item that primarily determines who will obtain it. Those who want the goods and have sufficient money to buy them will be the ones who obtain them.

Distribution of goods through the market-price mechanism, however, is not free of problems. For one thing, the question of need is not considered. Some people may have a great need for certain products but lack the money needed to acquire them. All members of a society, for example, must have food, clothing, and shelter. Without some intrusion on the free enterprise system, some people would go without the needed goods and services. An economic system should be efficient, but most people believe it should also be humane. Allotting goods and services to those who cannot afford them is the function of the social systems, such as Social Security and unemployment compensation, that have been implemented in the United States.

How Will Income Be Distributed?

The distribution of income in an economy is the other side of the resource allocation and goods distribution process. For every dollar spent, a dollar of income is received. Income accrues to the holders of resources and products when they are sold. Those who have the greatest number of resources to sell or the most valuable products will receive most of the income.

In a perfectly efficient economy, the seller of resources will receive an amount exactly equal to the value that those resources add to the product being produced. For example, consider the production of an automobile. If the automobile is worth $75 more after the battery is installed, the seller of the battery would receive exactly $75 for the battery. The automobile manufacturer would be unwilling to pay more since, in effect, the manufacturer would be losing money on the transaction.

Automobile manufacturers also receive income for the value they add to their products. A pile of automobile components, tires, a battery, a steering wheel, etc., can be considered to be worth less than a finished automobile. The services provided by the manufacturers in the assembly of the individual parts into functioning automobiles have value, just as the individual components do. The difference between the total value of the individual components and the value of a finished car is the value added by the manufacturer.

Labor. In the context of income distribution, labor is also a resource. Workers, again in a perfectly efficient market, would receive a wage exactly equal to the value that their labor adds to the value of the product produced. If

THE LABOR *that goes into manufacturing a product adds value to it.*

HAYMAN/PHOTO RESEARCHERS

a worker's labor could add more to the value of another product, the worker could earn more by changing jobs: the new employer would be willing to pay more for the worker's labor.

Workers, however, seldom have perfect knowledge as to where their labor would be worth the most. Additionally, some types of labor, such as management, are difficult to quantify. Although the effort of a manager certainly adds value to the production process, exactly how much it adds is generally impossible to determine. In such instances, subjective judgments become part of the economic process. Nevertheless, it can still be said in a general sense that workers receive a wage that employers believe equals their contribution to the production process.

Evolution of Economic Theory

Although a distinctive U.S. economy has evolved over the years, much of its philosophical basis came from foreign economists, many of whom were British. The influences of Adam Smith, David Ricardo, and John Maynard Keynes are evident today, as are the theories of American economists, such as John Kenneth Galbraith and Milton Friedman.

Adam Smith

Adam Smith (1723–1790) was born in Kirkcaldy, Scotland, at a time when *mercantilism,* a system that would be attacked by Smith in his writings, was still the prevailing economic policy of the nations of Western Europe. Although the Industrial Revolution was still 50 years away, Great Britain was emerging as the leading trade and manufacturing nation of Europe.

In 1759 Adam Smith published his first book, *Moral Sentiments,* in which he introduced his principles of human nature. This was a psychological investigation of human behavior that served as the basis of his later, more famous work, *An Inquiry into the Nature and Causes of the Wealth of Nations.* In *Moral Sentiments,* Smith advanced the theory that men acting in their own self-interest are often led unknowingly by an "invisible hand" to "advance the interest of society." He would later apply that theory to economic behavior in *Wealth of Nations.*

Despite his considerable reputation, Smith desired to provide a more complete work on economics and politics. For the next twelve years, he worked on *An Inquiry into the Nature and Causes of the Wealth of Nations,* which was published in 1776. Although *Wealth of Nations* was basically a description of the forces that direct an economy, Smith's rejection of mercantilism in favor of *laissez-faire* policies provided the basis for the model of classical capitalism. It earned Smith the title of the father of modern economics.

Self-regulating economy.
Smith believed that the free market and an individual desire for profit

> *. . . men acting in their own self-interest are often led unknowingly by an "invisible hand" to "advance the interest of society."*
>
> ADAM SMITH

ECONOMIC THEORIES *seek to explain and predict the fluctuations of interest rates, unemployment levels, inflation, and other important economic factors.*

would direct the flow of scarce resources in a more efficient and effective manner than a government could. Unburdened by government interference, the "invisible hand" of the economy would allocate the factors of production in such a way as to maximize the greatest good for all. Self-interest, restrained by competition, would result in full employment, price stability, and economic growth.

Interest rates. Two keys to Smith's self-regulating economic model were fluctuating interest rates and wage-price flexibility. Classical economists believe that interest rates determine the level of savings and investment. Depository institutions will lower interest rates to make borrowing more attractive to businesses. If businesses borrow, the level of investment—the purchase of machinery, equipment, and other productive assets—will increase.

If, on the other hand, the level of savings is less than businesses want to borrow, interest rates will increase, since the demand for funds is greater than the supply. These higher rates will discourage some potential borrowers, and investment will decline to a level commensurate with savings. Equilibrium will ultimately be reached when the interest rate is such that the level of savings equals the level of investment.

Wage-price flexibility. The second major key to the classical self-regulating model is flexible wages and prices. When an economy is operating at full employment, total income is sufficiently high to enable people to purchase the goods and services provided by businesses. If demand declines, producers are forced to lower prices to liquidate growing inventories. Because of the lower prices, businesses will have to decrease wages or lay off workers to remain profitable.

As unemployment increases, competition for jobs increases. Some workers will be willing to work for less rather than not work at all, and businesses will be able to hire additional workers at the lower wage. As more and more workers are hired at the lower wage, wages in general will fall. Ultimately, all workers will return to work. Since there is no longer a pool of inexpensive labor to draw on, wages will gradually increase to a point at which all who are willing to work at the prevailing wage rate are employed. The higher wages mean that greater consumer demand can be supported. Once again the economy will reach a point where all production can be bought and all workers are employed. In this manner, the market will react automatically to cure the unemployment.

If, instead of a decrease in demand, there is an increase in demand, prices will increase, but so will wages because businesses can afford to pay more and there is no available pool of labor to draw from. As wages increase, the supply of labor will increase. Adam Smith believed this would occur because higher wages would result in a higher standard of living, which would in turn decrease infant mortality. The end result is an expansion of the economy, more production, and higher wages.

Influence on other economists.

Smith's work had considerable influence. Jean Baptiste Say (1767–1832) built on Smith's basic concept that a market economy is self-regulating in developing his theory that "supply creates its own demand." This principle, known as "Say's law," holds that production always results in income to owners of resources. Workers receive income. Sellers of raw materials and equipment are paid for their contribution to the production process. Owners receive income that they spend on other products. Thus, an increase in production in one industry will increase the demand for the products of that industry as well as other industries because of the additional income it generates. Say believed that the total income received by the resource owners as a result of increased production would always be sufficient to pay for the additional output. Say's law became one of the basic tenets of supply-side economic policy (see The Role of Government section, page 287).

Alfred Marshall.

Alfred Marshall (1842–1924) based his pricing theory on the free market concepts developed by Smith. Marshall believed that of the two major determinants of market price, demand and supply, demand is more significant in the short run and supply is more significant in the long run. In the short run, Marshall contended, demand can change quickly but supply is relatively fixed. New factories cannot be built overnight, nor can more productive equipment be developed at once. In the long run, however, supply can be adjusted in response to demand.

Karl Marx

Even the philosophy of Karl Marx (1818–1883) had elements in common with that of Smith. Smith felt that the self-interest motivation of individuals shaped the nature of social institutions and the way in which society was organized. In the preface to *A Contribution to the Critique of Political Economy,* Marx wrote: "The mode of production in material life determines the general character of the social, political, and spiritual processes of life." The two differed widely, however, in what they felt the ultimate result of such a process would be. Smith saw the process acting in the best interests of society. Marx, by contrast, believed that wealth would accrue to the owners of the factors of production, and that the workers would be increasingly exploited. The resulting class struggle would inevitably result in revolution and the downfall of capitalism.

RICARDO *believed that all goods have a natural price, and that the flow of gold into a country is related to the level of profit of businesses.*

David Ricardo

During the time of Adam Smith, production was the major concern, since productivity was low. By the time of David Ricardo (1772–1823), the Industrial Revolution had arrived and productivity had increased markedly. Although Ricardo adopted many of Smith's principles, he concentrated on the distribution of goods and wealth within the economy of a society rather than on productivity.

Ricardo's interest in economics began in 1799, when he read Adam Smith's *Wealth of Nations.* For the next ten years he studied economics, adopting many of Adam Smith's principles and developing many of his own.

Prices. According to Ricardo, commodities derive their value from two factors: scarcity and the amount of labor required for their production. Since most commodities can be produced in quantity, Ricardo believed scarcity applies only in nonreproducible items such as paintings or rare books. For most commodities, therefore, labor time is the major factor that determines the value, or *natural price.* Ricardo's *labor theory of value,* as this concept is called, ignores the impact of technology. If two companies, for example, produce the same product but one uses more machinery and less labor than the other, the product produced by the non-labor-intensive firm would be less valuable because of the smaller amount of labor time involved in its production.

Ricardo believed that the market price of goods would differ from the natural price only in the short run, and as the result of temporary fluctuations in supply and demand. The self-regulating nature of the economy would always be pushing market prices toward natural prices.

Wages. According to Ricardo, labor is bought and sold like any other commodity. As such, the short-run market price of labor is determined by the demand and supply of labor, but in the long run, the natural price of labor prevails.

Ricardo believed that the natural wage level is that which is sufficient to enable workers to acquire the bare necessities of life. If wages rise above the subsistence level, the size of the work force will grow because of the lower mortality rates associated with a higher standard of living. The increased supply of labor will drive wages back down to or below their natural level.

If wages fall below the subsistence level, the work force is reduced owing to higher mortality rates. As the pool of available labor shrinks, wages will increase. Like Malthus (discussed below), Ricardo felt that the tendency is for workers eventually to receive subsistence wages, a concept known as the *iron law of wages.*

Profits. There is, according to Ricardo, an inverse relationship between wages and profits. If wages increase, profits must fall. Higher wages cannot be passed along in the form of higher prices because of the impact of foreign trade. If prices did increase, the supply of money in the economy would have to increase to support the higher prices. Since the gold standard was in effect during Ricardo's time, the supply of money could only be increased by increasing the supply of gold. With domestic prices increasing, however, the purchase of foreign goods would increase. To satisfy the balance of payments, gold would flow out of the country, thus reducing the supply of gold rather than increasing it. The higher prices required to maintain profitability, therefore, could not be maintained. Employers would have no choice but to bear the burden of higher wages themselves, thus reducing their profits.

A decline in wages, on the other hand, would result in an increase in profits. Prices would not fall, again because of the impact of foreign exchange. Falling prices would attract foreign buyers, resulting in gold flowing into the country to pay for those purchases. Under the gold standard, an increase in gold means an increase in the supply of money, which stimulates demand and drives prices back up.

Ricardo also felt that profits in various industries equalize over time. If one industry is more profitable than another, capital will move into the more profitable industry, thus increasing the supply of goods in that industry and driving prices and profits down.

John Maynard Keynes

Through the first quarter of the 20th century, the classical theories of Adam Smith, Jean Baptiste Say, and David Ricardo provided the framework for capitalism. Then came the Great Depression. According to the classical perspective, occasional imbalances and fluctuations in economic activity were to be expected. The market mechanism would correct such imbalances, if not immediately, then certainly in the long run.

As the years wore on and the Great Depression lasted from 1930 until 1941, the United States, as well the rest of the world, remained mired in a severe depression. Many began to wonder how long it would take to correct the imbalances, that is, how long the long run would be. It was beginning to appear that John Maynard Keynes (1883–1946) was right when he said: "In the long run we're all dead."

In 1935, against the background of pervasive depression, John Maynard Keynes published his famous book, *The General Theory of Employment, Interest, and Money.* He cast doubt on the viability of the classical capitalist model and provided a new conception of the workings of a mature capitalist economy. Keynes's view of the relationship between the various economic elements—national income, employment, savings, and investment—differed significantly from that of classical economists.

Interest rates. Keynes challenged the classical view that interest rates determine the level of savings and investment in society, proposing that interest rates do not significantly affect the level of either. Personal savings represent the bulk of savings, and individuals save for a variety of reasons, many of them completely unrelated to interest rates. They save to accumulate funds for a special purchase, for retirement, to provide for emergencies, or simply out of habit. Is it reasonable to assume that individuals will withdraw their savings from savings accounts, or cash in their certificates of deposit and spend the proceeds if interest rates

KEYNES *argued savings and investment are unrelated to interest rates.*

decline? Do low interest rates make people suddenly unconcerned about the proverbial rainy day or a comfortable retirement? The Keynesian answer to these questions is a resounding negative.

At most, Keynesians believe, savers will alter their savings vehicle; that is, they may switch from one form of savings to another in response to changing interest rates, but the total amount of savings will remain relatively unaffected. The real determining factor in the level of savings, asserted Keynes, is the level of national income. People have a tendency to save, and to consume, a relatively stable and predictable proportion of any additional money they may acquire, whether through tax cuts, increased income, or other means.

Keynes also believed that interest rates do not regulate investment more effectively than they regulate savings. Businesses borrow, Keynes believed, because they think they can make a profit from the borrowed funds. Even if interest rates are as low as 5 percent, businesses will not borrow if they feel they can make only 4 percent from the borrowed funds. On the other hand, businesses will borrow even at high rates if they feel they can realize a return that is greater than the interest they have to pay. It is not the interest rates themselves that regulate investment, Keynesians insist, but the expectations of businesses regarding returns on investment compared with interest rates.

Wages and prices. Another major classical precept challenged by Keynesian economic philosophy is the assertion that wages and prices adjust in response to market conditions. For example, because of the high unem-

ployment rate associated with a recession, downward pressure is exerted on wages. In the classical model, as wages adjust downward, employment increases. During expansionary periods, when labor is in great demand, wage rates increase. In the classical model, prices also fluctuate to correct imbalances in supply and demand.

Keynesians argue that these reactions to price levels simply do not occur. Wages do not readily decline for a number of reasons, including union collective bargaining contracts, minimum wage laws, and the general reluctance of workers to accept pay reductions. Neither do prices respond to economic imbalances in the manner the classicists propose. Many prices are established by contract, while others are influenced by government regulation or the general reluctance of businesses to cut prices.

Keynesians assert that the key elements of the self-regulating market mechanism, interest rates and wage-price flexibility, are ineffective. For Keynes, the Great Depression was proof that an economy could come to an equilibrium without achieving full employment.

Income and employment. Keynes believed that national income and employment are highly correlated. He demonstrated that income is a function of personal consumption, business investment, and government spending. Since personal consumption is relatively stable, in Keynes's opinion, and government spending is controllable, the level of business investment is left as the most volatile of the three determinants of national income. Therefore, the government must intervene, primarily through fiscal policy, to make up for insufficient investment by businesses. Deficit spending is far preferable to allowing an economy to languish in a recession while waiting for the "invisible hand" to correct deficiencies. When private sector investment is high, on the other hand, the government should cut back spending.

Keynes argued that fiscal policy, particularly government spending, is the key to offsetting fluctuating business investment. His insistence that the government has a legitimate role in a nation's economy earned him the title of father of the mixed economy, an economic system in which business and government combine to achieve economic goals.

Critique of Keynesian economics. Critics argue that Keynes failed to recognize that spending and consumption patterns change over time, particularly in response to growing levels of income. They further argue that his model is oriented to the short run and virtually ignores the question of economic growth.

THE WPA, *the Works Progress Administration, was an important agent of fiscal policy during the New Deal. It provided jobs, which created a demand for construction material, giving a boost to the economy.*

While the administrations from Kennedy through Carter all embraced the Keynesian approach, the Reagan administration favored a more classical approach dominated by supply-side and monetarist principles. Even President Reagan, however, did not completely disdain Keynesian techniques (see The Role of Government section, page 287).

Thomas Malthus

Unlike Adam Smith, who was a predecessor of Malthus, and unlike Keynes, who came later, British clergyman and economist Thomas Malthus (1766–1835) is best remembered for an economic theory that is basically unrelated to savings, investment, and interest rates. In 1798 he published *An Essay on the Principles of Population,* in which he asserted that the ultimate lot of mankind depends on the relationship between two factors—population and resources.

Population and resources.
Malthus contended that population tends to expand geometrically, for example, 2, 4, 8, 16, 32, while the resources of the world are limited and productivity from those resources grows arithmetically: 1, 2, 3, 4, 5. People have children and populations grow, Malthus contended, for reasons unrelated to economics. As populations grow, more food is needed to feed the growing numbers. While new land can be cleared to increase the food supply, at some point in time there will be no land left to clear. Productivity increases can then be achieved only by means of more advanced and productive agricultural technology.

Law of diminishing returns. The problem, according to Malthus, is that once all arable land has been cultivated, each subsequent application of technology yields an increase in production that is less than the preceding increase. For example, if an improved fertilizer is developed, the resulting increase in agricultural output will be less than that realized from the introduction of previous fertilizers. Eventually, maximum productivity is reached and no further increases are possible. This so-called law of diminishing returns cannot be denied, Malthus claimed, for if productivity could be increased without limit, the entire food requirements of the world, as the old adage puts it, could be grown in a flowerpot.

Malthusian trap. According to Malthus, as world population grows faster than the means of supporting it, the world's standard of living can be expected to decline as the food supplies of the world are divided into increasingly smaller shares. Eventually, the food supply would be insufficient to support the world's population. As a result, many people would starve, and malnutrition and squalid living conditions would cause disease and death. World population would eventually be reduced to a level that can be sustained.

If the reduction in population results in a standard of living for the survivors that is above the subsistence level, human reproduction would again drive the population above a level that can be maintained, and the cycle would begin again. According to Malthus, populations will always increase if there are sufficient resources to sustain additional members, even at a subsistence level.

The ultimate fate of mankind, therefore, is to live in abject poverty, ravaged by disease and starvation. Malthus did concede that people could exercise some control over this eventuality by voluntarily limiting family size or by marrying at an older age. Eventually, however, the ultimate fate of economic stagnation at the subsistence level could not be avoided. Reduction of the human standard of living to the subsistence level as a result of geometric population growth and arithmetic resource growth is referred to as the *Malthusian trap.* This scenario contributed in no small part to the fact that economics is often referred to as the *dismal science.*

Critique of Malthusian philosophy.
The prophecies of Thomas Malthus have thus far failed to materialize, at least on a global scale. Undeniably, population growth is a severe problem in many of the underdeveloped nations of the world, and Malthusian predictions of famine, disease, and starvation have come true in some of these areas.

In other areas of the world, however, the world envisioned by Smith or Keynes is much more a reality than that foreseen by Malthus. Population has not increased geometrically. In fact, many nations of the world have experienced moderate population growth over the past decade. Productivity has continued to increase, and the nearly two centuries since Malthus's time have witnessed capital formation and increases in standards of living that would undoubtedly astound the great pessimist.

In defense of Malthus, however, it should be noted that his predictions were made about a world that no longer exists. The settling of the United States, Canada, and Australia added significantly to the world's available agricultural land. The total amount of available resources is significantly more than seemed available in 1798. Neither could Malthus have foreseen the advances in technology and agricultural processes that have increased productive capacity so significantly.

Could it be that Malthus will ultimately be proved correct? Just as Malthus could not have foreseen the circumstances that apparently prevented his prophecies from coming true, we cannot foresee with certainty the events of the next two hundred years.

Milton Friedman and Monetarism

In contrast to the Keynesian view of the economy, the monetarist model, developed by the American Milton Friedman while at the University of Chicago, holds that monetary policy, not fiscal policy, is the most effective manner of guiding an economy toward its goals, since only monetary policy can affect GNP.

Equation of exchange.
At the heart of monetarist theory is the *equation of exchange,* which holds that the level of national income is equal to the supply of money multiplied by the velocity of money. (The velocity of money refers to the number of times that a given dollar is spent during a particular time period.) In other words, total income depends not only on how much money there is in circulation, but on how often it is spent. The monetarists also hold that the velocity of money is relatively stable. Therefore, the supply of money is the only variable remaining that can be manipulated to affect national income.

Changes in the supply of money can only be achieved through actions of the Federal Reserve Board. Fiscal policy, according to monetarists, is ineffective. Consider, for example, deficit spending by the government that is designed to increase capital formation and productivity. Monetarists argue that borrowing by the government to finance a deficit will crowd out private investment to the same extent. Instead of placing their savings in banks and other savings institutions or buying corporate stocks and bonds, people will buy government bonds and other federal debt instruments.

Supply of money.
Monetarists contend further that changes in the supply of money affect spending directly, not just indirectly as a result of changes in interest rates. Monetarists believe that individuals have a tendency to keep a fixed proportion of their income in the form of cash or other liquid financial assets. If the money supply is increased, therefore, most of the extra money infused into the economy will be spent. According to monetarists, as one might expect, reduced supply of money will result in decreased spending.

In order to maintain a growing economy, monetarists advocate automatic and continuing increase in the supply of money, not just when deemed necessary by the Federal Reserve. Monetarists reason that Federal Reserve actions are often ill-timed, based on outdated information, or put into effect too late. This is why they advocate expansion of the money supply regardless of the state of the economy at any time. In the long run, according to monetarists, an ever expanding money supply will provide for economic growth in a steady fashion rather than in the erratic fashion historically experienced.

Critique of monetarism.
Critics of monetarism argue that there is little evidence to support the position that changes in the money supply will always affect spending. Businesses, for example, often operate within negotiated credit lines with their banks. Changes in the money supply have no effect on these contractually established rights to borrow. Tight money may drive interest rates up, but it has little effect on access to credit.

These critics also deny monetarist claims regarding the money supply's relationship to investment. They point to the Great Depression, when efforts on the part of the Federal Reserve failed to encourage business investment. If businesses have machines standing idle, it seems ridiculous to presume that they would borrow money to buy additional equipment even if additional funds were available. Although critics of monetarism generally agree that steady economic growth is desirable, they doubt that a continually increasing money supply will achieve steady growth. The demand for money, they contend, is not steady but erratic.

Critics also point out that the Federal Reserve has no control over the ability of large banks to make Eurodollar deposits. These are U.S. dollars on deposit in banks outside the United States and available to American businesses. Since Eurodollar balances are greater than the entire supply of M1 (see page

MONETARISTS *believe a steadily increasing money supply is the best way to maintain a stable, healthy economy.*

LAFFONT/SYGMA

287), there is a significant supply of available money outside the control of the Federal Reserve. At any rate, although controversial, monetarism is not without support as the dispute between the relative merits of monetary and fiscal policies continues.

John Kenneth Galbraith

In every area of human endeavor there are mavericks who advance their beliefs in the face of traditional thought. John Kenneth Galbraith admirably and willingly fulfills this role in the field of economics.

Economic power.
Galbraith began in the mainstream of economic thought, but his first book, *American Capitalism,* published in 1952, signaled his departure from his contemporaries. In this book Galbraith chastised his contemporaries for what he believed to be their overemphasis on the supply-demand relationship as a primary factor in the workings of an economic system.

Galbraith believes that other economists have overlooked the influence of economic power, particularly that held by big businesses, and have, in general, ignored the real workings of the economy. He believes that the traditional view of the importance of the three pillars of a free economy—consumer sovereignty, the free-market mechanism, and profit-maximization incentive—is more a part of an economics dream world than the true basis of a capitalist economy. There is no true consumer sovereignty, Galbraith argues. *Producer sovereignty* is closer to reality. Rather than responding to consumer demands, businesses produce products and then convince consumers to buy them, principally through the use of advertising. Do consumers, for example, really dictate clothing fashions to which manufacturers respond? Not in Galbraith's world. The clothing industry changes fashions in order to encourage consumers to continually replace serviceable clothing. It is the power of the industry that dictates demand, not the power of the consumer.

The technostructure.
Galbraith believes that the real directors of a market economy are the major power groups: big labor, big government, and, most significantly, big business. In his book *The Affluent Society* (1958) Galbraith maintains that rather than being controlled by the market, big business replaces the free market to a great extent. The major power groups actually plan the movement of the economy. This societal planning system is run by the managers, accountants, lawyers, and even economists of

GALBRAITH *believes that businesses manipulate demand, creating fads, like the hula hoop, and fashions, like the miniskirt, to sell more products.*

the world. These so-called technocrats, collectively called the *technostructure* by Galbraith, manipulate the economy, especially in the area of consumer demand. Galbraith further asserts that, since these corporate giants could use their profits to finance their own activities and investments, they are largely immune to the workings of the capital market, such as the impact of fluctuating interest rates.

It is also big business that decides which goods will be produced. Because of the power of the large corporations, the goods produced by these corporations will overpower smaller companies and their products, regardless of the relative value to society of the goods involved. The goods produced will typically be for personal consumption rather than public goods, such as highways or educational systems. Proliferation of goods, says Galbraith, will be "on behalf of more beer but not of more schools."

Business managers. In addition to denying the existence of effective con-

sumer sovereignty, Galbraith denies that the profit motive controls business activities. He argues that the shareholders of the major corporations are far removed from the day-to-day operations of the businesses. Companies are actually run by managers, and their goals are far different from those of the shareholders. Managers are guided by their own self-interest, not the profit motive, Galbraith maintains. More often than not, the interests of the professional manager are better served by corporate growth than by profit maximization. As long as the managers produce a satisfactory return for the stockholders, they can ensure their continuing place in the technostructure and pursue their own interests.

Monopolies. Galbraith also believes that traditional economists have misunderstood the nature and impact of monopolies. The traditionalists view monopolies as an inferior method of business operation from the standpoint of society. Without competitive pressures, the traditional theory goes,

monopolies restrict output to maintain higher prices than would prevail under pure competition; in addition, they are inefficient in their use of resources. Galbraith points out that it is the corporate giants that seem to be most efficient. Rather than underproducing, they produce goods in great excess which they then convince consumers to buy through advertising.

Galbraith's solution. J. K. Galbraith's solution to the economic and social problems that exist does not comprise a unified, comprehensive theory, and he has been criticized on that ground. Galbraith does offer some suggestions. He believes that a permanent system of wage and price controls is needed. He also contends that increased government spending for social projects is necessary, since such items are not sufficiently provided for in an economy geared to producing goods for consumption. He has expressed great concern for the degradation of the environment, another area in which he feels government intervention is required.

Critique of Galbraith. One of the most prominent of Galbraith's critics has been Robert Solow of the Massachusetts Institute of Technology. In regard to Galbraith's claim that advertising robs consumers of their sovereignty, for example, Solow speculates about what would happen if rental car agencies cut their advertising in half and deodorant manufacturers did not. Solow doubts that consumers would buy deodorant rather than rent cars. He argues that advertising by one company simply cancels out the advertising of competitors.

Solow also doubts that the profit motive plays the small role in business that Galbraith contends. Solow suggests that if managers do not seek to maximize profits, they may find themselves replaced by other managers.

Types of Economic Systems

Nearly all countries differ significantly in the manner in which they strive to achieve economic objectives. The basic differences lie in the areas of ownership of property and allocation of resources and production.

Capitalism

The economic system in operation in the United States is known as *capitalism*. Capitalism relies on the interplay of buyers and sellers in a relatively free

marketplace for the basic determinations relating to price, levels of production, and income distribution. Other terms used to refer to capitalism reflect some of the basic characteristics of capitalism. *Free enterprise*, for example, reflects the discretion allowed the participants in the economic system to decide what to buy, what to produce, how much to produce, and how much to charge for that production. *Private enterprise* suggests that capitalism relies on private ownership of property rather than on central or communal ownership. *Laissez-faire*, which means

let people do as they please, implies a minimal role for government to play in the economy.

Classical capitalism. The basics of what is now called *classical capitalism* come from the theories of Adam Smith. In *The Wealth of Nations*, Smith advocates an economic system in which the market answers basic economic questions and the government plays virtually no role. Smith believed that businessmen motivated by self-interest and contrained only by

CAPITALISM

Like all economic systems, capitalism has strengths and weaknesses. It encourages individuals to take a chance on making a success of their own businesses. A capitalist economic system is especially good at supplying the products that consumers want by keeping store shelves full of the merchandise consumers buy, and at providing a great deal of choice among different brands of the same product. On the negative side of capitalism, producers sometimes misjudge what consumers want and spend enormous amounts developing a product, like Ford Motor Company's Edsel, that consumers will not buy. The most serious failing of capitalism, however, is that unassisted it can be cruel to the poorest members of society.

```
  + profit
  - loss
  + profit
  - loss
  + profit
  ─────────────
  = The Bottom Line
```

competitive forces would, in the long run, provide for the needs of society better than a more directed economy. Private ownership of property, in Smith's view, is the basis on which such an economic system is built (see Evolution of Economic Theory section, page 278, for further details on Smith's philosophy).

Although no economic system in the world complies exactly with classical capitalism as envisioned by Adam Smith, its basic premises have greatly influenced economic theory and practice in the United States. The government of the United States plays a greater role than Smith advocated, but the American system is still considered capitalistic because of the far greater role played by the marketplace than by the government.

Capitalism in practice.

Part of the divergence between classical capitalism and capitalism in practice can be attributed to the changes that have taken place since the time of Adam Smith, principally changes that have occurred since the Industrial Revolution. Businesses are larger and more powerful than in Smith's time. Labor unions have also grown and have become a powerful force in the economy. As a result, the concepts of classical capitalism, from time to time, have been challenged by more contemporary economists, such as John Maynard Keynes (see Evolution of Ec-

onomic Theory section, page 278).

Nevertheless, there are some basic characteristics still considered intrinsic to capitalist economies.

Private property. In true capitalistic economies, ownership of the factors of production as well as personal property rests largely with individuals. The ownership and exchange of this property are unique characteristics of capitalism. It is the freedom to exchange goods in the marketplace that enables the market mechanism to work.

Capital formation. Private ownership of property is also a key factor in capital formation. Companies owned by private citizens bring together the land, labor, and entrepreneurial skills that produce the goods and services needed by society. These companies decide the best way to combine the factors of production to make goods and provide services that will satisfy consumers and return a profit to the owners of the companies.

Self-interest motivation. The catalyst in the capital formation process that unites the factors of production is the self-interest of those who combine resources. Businessmen and women combine resources in a manner that they anticipate will result in the greatest possible profit.

Self-interest is not confined to business enterprises. Workers are also continually trying to improve their situations. They strive for higher wages, better fringe benefits, job satisfaction, and security.

As businesses and workers pursue their individual economic interests, both groups benefit from what they receive from the other. Workers tend to be employed in the area in which they will be most valuable and contribute most to the production process. Proper use of labor leads to production efficiencies that increase profits and lower prices for consumers.

Consumers also are involved in the pursuit of self-interest. They attempt to spend their dollars in such a manner as to maximize satisfaction, that is, get the best deal possible. This forces businesses to compete for consumer patronage by providing goods and services that consumers want at a price and quality superior to that of other producers.

Consumer sovereignty. It is consumers, through their purchases, who direct the allocation of resources and, therefore, determine what will be produced. Although consumers can be influenced, for example, by advertising, no one can direct consumers to spend their money in a certain manner. Sellers must satisfy the wishes of consumers in order to realize a profit.

Competition. Competition is generally defined as the efforts of two or more companies striving for the patronage of the same customers. In order to remain profitable, businesses must continually strive to increase or maintain their shares of the market. They are motivated to do so by the desire to make a profit. In most cases, the greater the sales, the better the chance for a large profit. Competition, then, tends to make those firms the most profitable that do best in producing what consumers want.

Competition benefits the public in a number of ways. First, it ensures that the goods and services the public wants will be produced. Secondly, competition usually results in lower prices and better service as companies strive to make their products more appealing than those of their competitors. Thirdly, competition leads to efficient use of resources. Usually, the company that offers a product at the lowest price can do so, at least in part, because its production costs are lower than those of competing firms. Reducing waste in production means that more products can be produced from the same amount of resources, thus increasing the productivity of a society and hence its standard of living. Finally, competition may force businesses to increase the quality of their products as they strive to gain increased market shares.

Limited government intervention. Although there is no economy in the world in which the government plays no role, some economies are more directed than others. In the United States, the role of the government is secondary to that of the free market. Most decisions relating to production and pricing are left to business, with the government intervening only in areas in which the free enterprise system does not act in the best interests of society as a whole. For example, the United States has implemented various social welfare programs to ensure that the poor or unemployed realize a subsistence standard of living. The degree to which the government should intrude on the free enterprise mechanism is a source of constant debate in capitalistic economies.

Critique of capitalism. Even though most economists would agree that ideal, or classical, capitalism is impossible to achieve, the degree to which reality matches theory is a continuing subject of debate. Some economists believe that the theoretical framework of capitalism closely parallels the actual workings of the market mechanism. These economists advocate the least possible governmental interference with a system that they feel will work well if left to operate free of government constraints. These economists generally advocate governmental participation only in those areas in which the private sector is unable to effectively or efficiently provide necessary services, such as national defense, education, or expensive public projects such as highway systems.

At the other extreme are those economists who believe that capitalism, as it is theorized, bears little relation to reality and that there are forces and conditions that the market mechanism cannot mediate. The result, assert such economists, is a system that does not automatically maximize consumer satisfaction or allocate resources in the most efficient manner.

With respect to the profit motive, critics point out that major U.S. corporations are owned by stockholders who take little part in the management of the company. In such companies the daily decisions and the operational directives emanate from a group of professional managers who can perhaps best fulfill their own personal goals by striving for corporate growth rather than profitability because growth, more consistently than profits, leads to increased salaries and promotion.

Some economists argue that producer sovereignty, rather than consumer sovereignty, is what actually exists in the United States, as well as other capitalistic nations, because of the influence of advertising on consumer choice.

The concept of competition assumes that there are so many sellers in the marketplace that none can exert a significant influence over price levels, and each must continually strive to improve product quality. Critics argue that this picture of capitalism is observably false. Many major American industries, such as the automotive and steel industries, are dominated by a few large producers. Under such conditions, fierce competition resulting in higher quality, better service, and lower prices does not occur often. The competition that does exist is more likely to be in the marketing arena than in the research laboratory. Product changes often are simply cosmetic in nature and are intended to influence consumer preferences.

The truth regarding the nature of capitalism probably lies somewhere between the two extremes. There is little doubt that classical capitalism as envisioned by Adam Smith does not exist, nor could it. On the other hand, to deny that profits, consumer sovereignty, and competition play a role in the capitalistic economy is equally absurd.

Socialism

The modern socialist perspective arose primarily from the harmful effects of the Industrial Revolution, a period of technological advancement that increased the productive capacity of many nations. Although the Industrial Revolution ultimately aided in raising the general standard of living in most nations, it was not without severe social impact. Working conditions in early factories, to say the least, were unpleasant; working hours were long, and the use of child labor was extensive. Workers' wages were low, since most of the wealth accrued to the owners of capital. The sudden growth in the size of cities brought health problems and crowded slums.

Criticisms of capitalism. Private ownership, according to socialists, rather than improving the overall standard of living, concentrates the wealth of a nation in the hands of the resource owners. The rich get richer, and the poor get poorer. This concentration of wealth further results in a concentration of power, which, in turn, perpetuates and aggravates an already inequitable system. Further, it is argued, the concept of private ownership places property rights ahead of human rights.

Socialists deny that the profit motive results in the most satisfactory combination of production and resource allocation. Rather, they argue, it results in the production of goods and services that the rich want rather than goods that the poor need. This waste of scarce resources further widens the gap between the rich and the poor. Pursuit of the profit motive, according to socialists, eventually leads to imperialism because capitalistic nations ultimately have to look abroad for sources of raw materials.

Competition is viewed by socialists as counterproductive, because duplication of effort in the form of many companies producing the same product is wasteful. It also results in the imprudent use of natural resources as companies endeavor to realize profits. Resources are wasted on such things as advertising, which adds nothing to the value of a product but increases the price, or on excessive production of unneeded consumer goods.

Characteristics of socialism. The basic precepts of socialism revolve around curing the alleged ills of capitalism. Since private ownership of property is the major culprit, the logical solution is to eliminate massive concentrations of privately held property. In socialist economies, the government owns or controls a large portion of the capital of the economy.

Labor. Although physical resources can be placed under government control fairly easily, labor resources present a more difficult problem for socialist economies since a worker's labor cannot be separated from the worker.

Production. The determination of which basic goods and services will be produced and in what quantities is normally accomplished through government planning agencies. Although socialism does not advocate that government own or control all factors of production, government can and should, according to the socialist perspective, allocate them according to the priorities established by central planning agencies. Luxury goods are often assigned low priorities, resulting in few resources being allocated to their production. Production is sometimes further controlled through the establishment of targets and quotas.

SOCIALISM

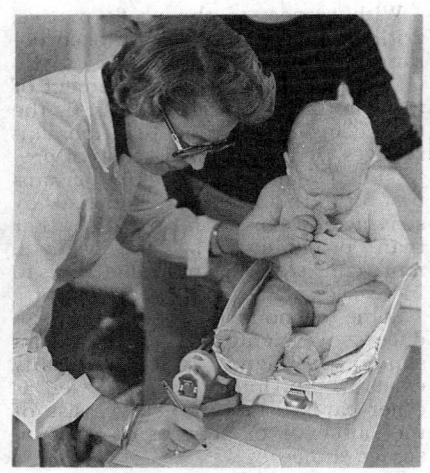

Socialism has problems that are almost the direct opposite of those of capitalism. One of the best features of a socialist economy is that it tends to minimize the extremes of poverty found in capitalist societies. Health care, among other services, is usually provided free of charge to all citizens. Most socialist societies, however, have experienced difficulty in matching product supply to consumer demand, often leaving shelves empty of essential items.

Prices. The market price mechanism is similarly restricted. Although it may be allowed to function for some products, the government is likely to control prices to reflect the priorities set by the central planning agencies. These price controls, along with wage controls, also serve to distribute the economy's production among its citizenry. Price subsidies may also be employed to stimulate consumption of certain goods.

Foreign trade. Under socialism, international trade tends to be more restricted than in capitalistic nations. The intent is to protect native businesses and ensure the continued employment of the nation's citizens.

Advocates of the socialist system claim that socialism can eliminate income inequalities, overproduction, and waste better than capitalism can. They further claim that elimination of private ownership and major concentrations of capital, and thus elimination of the power that results from that ownership, ultimately results in an economic egalitarianism impossible to attain under capitalism.

Critique of socialism.
Opponents of socialism argue that the typical socialist system provides poor incentives for improved performance. The profit motive, intrinsic to capitalism, points the members of society in the direction of greater rewards. Socialism, on the other hand, rewards the productive and nonproductive members of society alike. The more productive members of society subsidize the efforts of the less productive members.

Central planning. Opponents of socialism also see a major problem in the central planning advocated by socialists. They contend that the free market mechanism more accurately and more quickly anticipates the will of the public. Consumers receive the goods they want rather than the goods that a governing body decides should be made available.

Efficiency. Opponents of socialism contend that the waste associated with duplication of effort in a capitalistic economy is more than offset by the efficiency and improved products that result from a truly competitive environment.

Costs of advertising are also justified, since advertising results in greater demand. This enables companies to take advantage of economies of scale. Such economies can be passed along to the consumer in the form of lower prices. They also contend that advertising fulfills a valuable informational function, alerting people to the availability of goods and services that can make their lives more comfortable and satisfying.

Socialism in practice.
The socialist nations of the world differ markedly in the degree to which the socialistic doctrine is practiced. Some nations, such as Sweden, Denmark, and Great Britain, are politically democratic, but finance most public welfare programs, such as medical care, from tax dollars.

Communism

The distinction between communism and socialism is more political than economic. Although the philosophies of both socialism and communism advocate the abolition of capitalism, socialism advocates an orderly transition from capitalism to socialism as members of capitalistic societies realize the superiority of the socialist system. Communists, on the other hand, advocate the abolition of capitalism through revolution, which they feel is inevitable in all capitalist nations. Communists believe that with the capitalist class eliminated, class antagonism would cease, and society could turn its efforts to economic productivity. People would contribute to the economy according to their ability and receive the fruits of the economic system according to their need. The ultimate result would be abundant production capable of providing for the needs of all the members of society.

Mixed Economies

No contemporary economy is purely capitalistic or purely socialistic. The economies of the world are a continuum between the two theoretical extremes. Although the United States and the Soviet Union occupy positions close to each end of the spectrum, neither is a pure form.

Although the Soviet Union is predominantly socialistic, private enterprise does exist in a limited way. In the United States, on the other hand, most of the output of the economy originates in business rather than in government. Most resources are privately owned, and capital formation is primarily an activity of the private business sector.

Nevertheless, government in the United States, as well as in other capitalistic economies, contributes significantly to the output of the economy, primarily in the area of services. At the federal level, providing for national defense typically represents a major portion of federal expenditures. The United States Postal Service provides a service that would be difficult to accomplish by the private sector. At the state and local levels, fire and police protection as well as education normally fall within the responsibility of the government. The public and private sectors contribute to an economy in varying proportions. For this reason, all contemporary economies are, to some degree, mixed.

Some economists assert that the economies of the world have been evolving toward each other for many years. The United States economy, for example, was much closer to pure capitalism prior to the New Deal program of President Franklin D. Roosevelt. Since that time, many social welfare programs have been implemented. The Soviet Union, at the other extreme, has experienced a type of consumer revolution wherein Soviet citizens are demanding more consumer goods.

The Role of Government

Action taken by the U.S. government to manipulate the economy can be divided into two categories—monetary policy and fiscal policy.

Monetary Policy

Monetary policy refers to actions taken by the Federal Reserve System to control the supply of money. Expansion and contraction of the money supply are designed to control business cycles, maintain price stability, and contribute to full employment (see Central Banking, pages 301–303, for further discussion of the Federal Reserve System).

When an economy is experiencing a recession, an increase in the supply of money can stimulate consumer demand. Stimulation, in turn, may result in increased productivity and employment as producers endeavor to meet the higher level of demand. As more people go to work, they spend more money, and the cycle continues. Also, as more people are put to work, tax revenues increase and welfare payments decrease, thus reducing the amount of money the government needs to borrow in order to operate. When the Federal Reserve System increases the supply of money, however, inflation may result unless the supply of goods expands quickly enough to meet increased consumer demand.

Decreasing the supply of money, on the other hand, can be an effective method of combatting inflation. With less money available in the economy to purchase goods and services, demand declines, bringing it in line with supply. As producers experience declining, or at least stabilizing, sales, they are less inclined to raise prices.

Unfortunately, efforts to reduce inflation may result in higher unemployment. Businesses, experiencing a decreased demand for their products, may cut back production. Typically, as businesses lay off unnecessary workers, one of the first results of reduced output is unemployment.

Reserve requirement. Three techniques are used by the Federal Reserve System to control the supply of money. One technique is to change the reserve requirement, which is the percentage of funds deposited with a bank that it must keep on hand in its vault or on deposit with the Federal Reserve Bank to meet transactional demands. For example, if a bank has $100 million in deposits and the reserve requirement is 20 percent, the bank has to keep $20 million on hand or on deposit with the Federal Reserve. The remaining $80 million may be lent by the bank. If the Federal Reserve decides to reduce the supply of money, it can increase the reserve requirement. If the reserve requirement is increased to 30 percent, for example, the hypothetical bank would have to keep an additional $10 million on hand in its vault or on deposit with the Federal Reserve to bring its total reserves up to $30 million, leaving it with only $70 million in loanable funds. The result is a $10 million decrease in the supply of money.

Decreasing the reserve requirement has the opposite effect. A reduction from 20 to 10 percent, for example, would reduce the level of required reserves from $20 million to $10 million. The hypothetical bank now would have $10 million more on deposit than is required. This is referred to as *excess reserves* and may be lent by the bank. The result is an increase in the amount of loanable funds from $80 million to $90 million.

Manipulation of the reserve requirement has the most dramatic effect on the supply of money of any method available to the Federal Reserve, since it affects all commercial banks. The Federal Reserve will normally use this mechanism only when the supply of money is seriously insufficient or excessive.

Discount rate. A second method is available to the Federal Reserve to control the supply of money, that of manipulation of the discount rate. The *discount rate* is the interest rate paid by commercial banks when they borrow money from Federal Reserve banks. Commercial banks may receive such loans when they are short on their required reserves. By raising or lowering the discount rate, the Federal Reserve can make it either more attractive or less attractive to borrow funds.

Unlike manipulation of the reserve requirement, changing the discount rate tends to be a relatively weak mechanism, since it only affects banks that wish to borrow from the Federal Reserve. Also, commercial banks may borrow only to cover small reserve deficiencies. Even in the aggregate, therefore, borrowing for such purposes is small.

Open-market operations. The third, and most frequently used, method of controlling the money supply is open-market operations. *Open-market operations* are the buying and selling of government securities by Federal Reserve banks. If the Federal Reserve, for example, feels that the money supply should be expanded to combat an economic slump or recession, it will buy government bonds in the bond market. The key to the system is that the Federal Reserve will pay the bond dealers with checks drawn on the Federal Reserve Bank. These checks are not drawn on an account in any commercial bank. When the checks are deposited by the bond dealers in their accounts at commercial banks, the process of increasing the supply of money begins.

As the checks clear the banking system, the Federal Reserve Bank credits the reserves of the commercial bank in which the checks were deposited. This creates excess reserves for the bank, since these checks are not drawn on any commercial bank and there is no offsetting reduction in reserves at another bank. The result is that the bond dealer's bank has gained reserves that it may lend out or invest, but no other bank has lost reserves. Thus, the supply of money has been increased.

MEASUREMENT OF MONEY SUPPLY

There are several measures of the money supply of the United States. The most common measurement used by economists is called M1. It includes the most liquid forms of money. The following are the components of the various measurements of the money supply:

M1:
1. Currency and coin held by the public.
2. Travelers' checks.
3. Total checking account balances.
4. Balances of NOW and super-NOW accounts.
5. Balances in Automatic Transfer Service (ATS) accounts.
6. Credit union share draft balances.

M2:
1. M1 plus:
2. Small savings and time deposits (less than $100,000).
3. Overnight repurchase agreements (RPs) at commercial banks.
4. Specified Eurodollar deposits.
5. Money market mutual fund shares held by individuals and small businesses.

M3:
1. M2 plus:
2. Large time deposits (over $100,000).
3. Repurchase agreements at commercial banks and savings and loans institutions with maturities in excess of one day.
4. Institutional and corporate money market mutual fund shares.

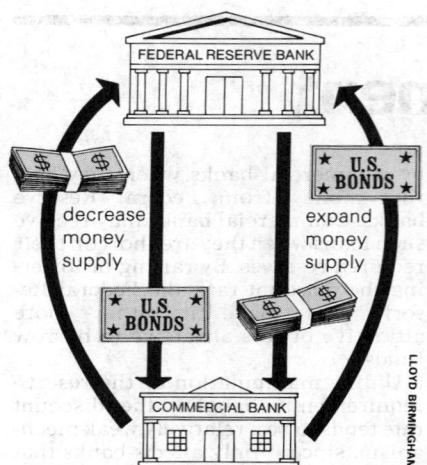

THE FEDERAL RESERVE *can increase or decrease the money supply through buying or selling of bonds.*

If the Federal Reserve believes that the supply of money is too great and needs to be contracted, it buys bonds and the process works in reverse. The Federal Reserve can use open-market operations to make much finer adjustments in the money supply than can be achieved by changes in the reserve requirement, which tend to have widespread effects.

Investment impact.
Increasing or decreasing the supply of money affects prevailing interest rates and, as a consequence, the level of business investment in new or expanded production facilities and capital goods, such as machinery and other equipment. Interest rates can be thought of as the price paid for the use of money. The price of money is determined in the same way as the price of any other commodity—by supply and demand.

If the supply of money is contracted, through any of the three methods available to the Federal Reserve, funds for loans are decreased, causing interest rates to rise. Companies faced with higher financing costs may postpone or abandon new investment projects. As interest rates increase, more and more investments fall into the marginal or unprofitable category. Restraining the supply of money is often referred to as a *tight money policy;* the technique generally is used to combat inflation. The danger is that with reduced investment, productivity and the level of employment may suffer.

Expansion of the supply of money has the opposite effect on both interest rates and investment. The increased supply of money relative to demand lowers the price of money as banks seek to lend out their excess reserves.

Consumer purchases.
Interest rates affect consumer purchases just as they do business investment. The impact is generally most noticeable in the purchase of homes and durable goods, because these items are relatively high in price and often are purchased with borrowed funds. High interest rates will discourage many consumers from such purchases, and low interest rates will stimulate sales.

A change in consumer interest rates can have a significant impact on an economy. High interest rates, for example, generally result in a reduction in the number of mortgages for new housing starts. This reduction affects many areas of the U.S. economy, notably the construction and building materials industries.

Effectiveness of monetary policy.
Many economists believe that monetary policy is far more effective in controlling inflation than in controlling unemployment or reversing recessionary trends. Contracting the supply of money can be particularly effective in reducing demand-pull inflation, which often accompanies rapid economic expansion. The cause of this type of inflation is too much buying power compared with the amount of goods and services available to satisfy demand.

Monetary policy is less effective in stimulating sluggish business activity. If the money supply is increased to stimulate business investment, there is no guarantee that businesses will take advantage of the available funds and attractive interest rates. If businesses remain pessimistic about the state of the economy, they may be unwilling to increase their investment in plants and equipment despite the efforts of the Federal Reserve. Also, during recessions, many businesses have unused capacity. It is unlikely that they will increase their level of capital investment until current capacity is fully used.

Some economists believe that of the three spending groups in our economy —consumers, businesses, and government—only business spending is significantly impacted by a tight money policy. Government spending is normally unaffected by interest rates, and consumer spending, except for real estate expenditures, is more a function of income than of interest rates. Some economists even argue that high interest rates have little effect on business borrowing and investment. If a firm desires to expand, it may pass the costs of financing on to customers. Other companies may have large cash reserves that can be used for investment. Interest rates have virtually no effect on investments financed from these funds.

Critics also argue that monetary policy is ineffective against cost-push inflation, which is the type of inflation caused by rapidly rising costs of production; it is often accompanied by more and more unemployment. A tight money supply has the effect of using up cash reserves held by businesses as they strain to meet increased costs. With less money in circulation, dwindling reserves, and higher costs, investment is discouraged, and firms may lay off workers to reduce operating costs. The result may be that the economy is pushed into a recession characterized both by high inflation and high unemployment. Some economists, for example, blame the Federal Reserve's tight

---

INDEX OF LEADING ECONOMIC INDICATORS

The Bureau of Economic Analysis (BEA) of the Commerce Department computes and publishes 300 economic indicators on a monthly basis. Sixty-five of these indicators are *leading indicators,* measurements of certain economic activities that tend to change direction prior to general economic changes. In addition to these individual indicators, the BEA also computes a composite index, which is made up of twelve leading indicators:

1. **Average work week,** in hours, of nonsupervisory workers in manufacturing industries.
2. **Average weekly claims** for state unemployment insurance.
3. **Inflation-adjusted new orders** for consumer goods and materials (1982 dollars).
4. **Vendor performance,** that is, the percentage of companies receiving slower deliveries from suppliers.
5. **Index of net business formation,** that is, the number of new businesses that are incorporated.
6. **Inflation-adjusted contracts** and orders for plants and equipment (1982 dollars).
7. **Number of new building permits** issued for private housing.
8. **Inflation-adjusted change in inventories,** including inventories on hand and on order (1982 dollars).
9. **Change in index of prices** of 28 sensitive materials.
10. **Index of 500 common stock prices** (Standard & Poor's Corporation).
11. **Money supply**—M2 adjusted for inflation (1982 dollars).
12. **Change in business and consumer borrowing** (installment credit, business loans, real estate loans, etc.).

Movements of the index of leading economic indicators are used to predict general movements of the economy. For example, a downturn in the index indicates that a recession may be coming. Conversely, an increase in the index during a recession may indicate that a recovery is coming. The Department of Commerce generally regards two consecutive months of decline or increase as significant.

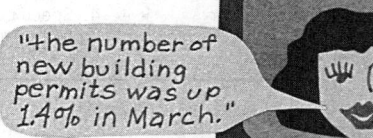

"the number of new building permits was up 1.4% in March."

money policy for the recession and high unemployment of the early 1980's.

There are other arguments against the effectiveness of monetary policy. Critics point out that the Eurodollar market (U.S. dollars on deposit in foreign banks) is a vast source of money beyond the control of the Federal Reserve. During a tight-money period, banks may draw on this source of funds, thus defeating the Federal Reserve's policy.

Even if monetary policy works in the way it is intended, many feel that there is a considerable lag between the time a tight- or easy-money policy is adopted and the time it takes effect. During this time lag, matters may get worse so that the effect of the policy is not sufficient by the time it affects the economy. Conversely, if the economy improves, the impact may turn out to be too dramatic.

Although not all economists and policymakers agree as to the effectiveness of monetary policy, many believe that it is a powerful tool. They believe it is particularly powerful in expansionary times, and far more flexible than fiscal policy (see below) because the Board of Governors, which is the directing authority of the Federal Reserve System, can normally react to economic trends quicker than the legislature.

Fiscal Policy

The alternative to monetary policy in the regulation of the economy is fiscal policy. *Fiscal policy* involves using taxation, government spending, or a combination of the two to achieve economic objectives.

Taxation. Taxation, to some degree, is an automatic economic stabilizer. This is particularly true of progressive taxes, those that increase percentagewise as the base amount increases. One of these progressive taxes is the federal income tax. Larger incomes result in larger tax revenues not only in amount but in the percentage of income taken in taxes. As income increases, the proportion of that income that is paid in taxes increases. Rapid economic growth, therefore, is automatically dampened somewhat by taxation, since disposable income increases less rapidly than gross income.

In recessionary times, when unemployment is high or workers accept wage concessions, tax revenues decrease proportionately. Percentagewise, disposable income does not decline as rapidly as total income, thus reducing recessionary effects.

Active tax policies. If income taxes are increased, purchasing power diminishes. This is because a greater portion of earnings is siphoned off for

$1.02	Gasoline
.17	State and federal excise tax
.07 1/10	Sales tax
$1.26 1/10	Total

AN EXCISE TAX *is a tax levied on a commodity, for example, petroleum products.*

taxes. Tax increases, then, can be used to combat inflation, particularly demand-pull inflation, which results from excess purchasing power.

Tax decreases, on the other hand, can be used to stimulate a sluggish economy. The increased disposable income that results from decreased taxes can have the effect of higher levels of demand; the higher demand may stimulate businesses to increase production and hire additional workers. Decreased taxes may also increase savings and, therefore, the level of business investment (see Reaganomics heading, page 291).

Since there are many types of taxes in our economy, tax policies may be applied selectively. During inflationary times, excise taxes, which are taxes imposed on commodities, may be raised on a great number of goods or on only those experiencing the greatest demand-supply disparity.

Effect of tax policies. Taxation does not affect everyone equally. Taxes that

affect higher income groups have a minimal effect on consumer spending, since wealthier people tend to meet new tax obligations by reducing savings rather than reducing consumption. Under such conditions, an increase in taxes to control inflation is of minimal effectiveness in curbing demand; it could, in fact, have an adverse impact on business investment by reducing the amount of funds available for loans. Reduced investment in an inflationary economy aggravates the problem, because fewer goods are produced to meet demand.

Investment can be stimulated by reducing corporate tax rates to give businesses additional funds for capital expansion. There is, of course, no guarantee that businesses will use the funds for this purpose, but at least some of the enterprises receiving such funds are likely to do so.

Government spending. Government spending is the other arm of fiscal policy. During a recession, a government may increase spending in an effort to increase total consumption, to which businesses may respond by increasing production and hiring more workers. An increase in total demand, however, can only be accomplished if the changes in government spending result in a budget deficit. An increase in government spending that is offset by an increase in taxes will reallocate national income but have little effect on the total amount of income. Taxpayers end up with a decrease in disposable income, but government suppliers realize an increase in income.

TYPES OF TAXES

Governments levy taxes for three reasons: to finance the operations of the government, to control various elements of the economy, and to regulate trade.

Capital gains tax. A tax on profit realized from the sale of capital assets, such as machinery and equipment, stocks and bonds, and real estate. The tax is imposed on the difference between the sale price and the cost of the asset.

Consumption tax. A tax imposed on consumer goods, such as a retail sales tax or excise tax. Import duties are considered consumption taxes as well, since the amount of such taxes is included in the sale price of the good.

Direct tax. A tax that cannot be passed along to subsequent purchasers of the item taxed, for instance, a property tax.

Estate tax. A tax levied on the total value of a decedent's estate. It differs from an inheritance tax in that it is imposed on the estate prior to distribution, while an inheritance tax is imposed on the individual shares of the beneficiaries.

Excise tax. A tax imposed on the sale of a specific commodity.

Flat-rate income tax. An income tax that taxes all levels of income at the same rate.

Flexible tariff. A tax on goods produced abroad that can be raised or lowered without the consent of Congress. The President has the authority to institute flexible tariffs without congressional approval. The basic purpose of a flexible tariff is to protect domestic industry.

Import duty. A tax on imported goods.

Income tax. A tax levied on the incomes of individuals and corporations, the major purpose of which is to generate revenue for the government.

Indirect tax. A tax that can be shifted to subsequent purchasers of the item taxed, such as sales tax, excise tax, and import duty.

Inheritance tax. A tax levied on a beneficiary's share of an estate.

Payroll tax. A tax imposed on employers and based on the total amount of wages and salaries paid by that employer. The U.S. Social Security tax is a payroll tax.

Progressive tax. A tax, such as income tax, that taxes higher incomes at higher rates.

Property tax. A tax on real estate, including land, improvements, and buildings.

Sales tax. A flat-rate tax imposed on the selling price of an item.

Tariff. A tax on imported or exported goods. Export tariffs are rare, since the usual purpose of a tariff is to protect domestic producers by raising the price of imported goods.

Effectiveness of fiscal policy.

Fiscal policy alone is generally a somewhat clumsy mechanism for achieving economic goals. Part of the problem is that governmental policy reflects efforts to achieve social as well as economic goals. Federal budget and taxation policies not only must address economic issues, but defense requirements, foreign aid, and social welfare objectives as well as a myriad of demands of interest groups. Government spending and taxation programs reflect a compromise of these various demands.

Since budget approval and tax reform often are debated for a long time before they are implemented, the economic situation may change before the full effect of governmental action is realized. The result often is too little too late, or too much too late.

Although tailoring federal budgets with an eye toward countering unfavorable business cycles has been a popular administrative policy since World War II, predicting the course of business activity is not easy. Predicting the best course of action for the future presents an enormous challenge.

State and local fiscal policies may aggravate the problem. To counteract declining tax revenues encountered during recessionary times, local gov-

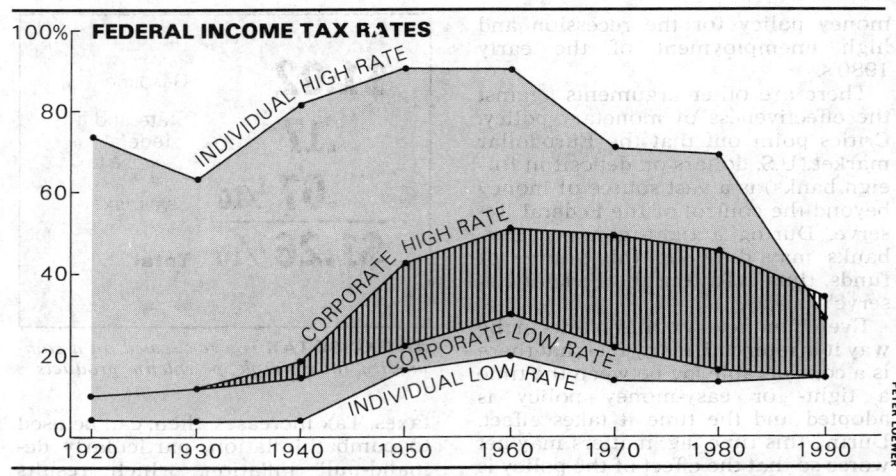

FEDERAL INCOME TAX RATES

INDIVIDUAL HIGH RATE

CORPORATE HIGH RATE

CORPORATE LOW RATE

INDIVIDUAL LOW RATE

PETER LOEWER

CORPORATE TAX RATES *have historically shown less of a difference between the highest tax bracket and the lowest than have individual tax rates.*

ernments tend to cut back on expenditures and/or increase taxes. During boom periods, these local governments are likely to increase spending, since there are more funds available. Such actions tend to aggravate recessionary or inflationary trends rather than alleviate them.

Demand-Side vs. Supply-Side Economics

Whether the government uses monetary or fiscal policy to manipulate the economy often depends on whether the approach is based on demand-side economics or on supply-side economics. The basic difference between these two philosophies is that demand-side economics relies on the manipulation of total demand to guide the economy toward desirable objectives. By contrast, the supply-side approach attempts to stimulate business productivity. During inflationary times, for example, a demand-side approach would involve restricting the money supply to curtail demand. This would alleviate the traditional cause of inflation, too many dollars chasing too few goods. If, on the other hand, an economy is mired in a recession, the money supply would be increased, thus stimulating demand. Businesses would respond by increasing production. This increased production would lead to more jobs and alleviate unemployment, which usually accompanies recessions.

Using a supply-side approach to counter inflation might involve decreasing corporate taxes in the hope that companies would use the additional funds for capital investment and increased output. Such an increase in production would bring supply more in line with demand and thus alleviate the upward pressure on prices.

Stagflation.

Until the 1970's it was commonly thought that inflation and unemployment could be played off against one another. If inflation was the big problem, a tight money policy could be used to reduce inflation at the cost of somewhat higher unemployment rates. Much of the economic history of the United States reflects swings from unemployment to inflation as each problem was addressed at the expense of the other. During the 1970's, however, this inverse relationship changed considerably. Inflation was increasing and the unemployment problem was getting worse at the same time. This new situation, referred to as *stagflation,* did not seem to respond to demand-side techniques. It was time to try something new; that something was a supply-side approach to economic policy.

Demand-side economic policies became ineffective during the 1970's because the nature of the U.S. economy was changing. Although many factors

SCARCITY *of a product, often because of high demand, can lead to high prices.*

$125 each

$50 each

LLOYD BIRMINGHAM

IMPACT OF TAX REFORM

The ultimate impact of the Tax Reform Act of 1986 is uncertain at this time. Some economists feel there will be little if any impact, at least in the aggregate. Consumption patterns may change, but overall consumption and aggregate production will remain relatively unaffected.

Others feel the impact could be considerable. Since the 1986 tax law will result in an estimated $120 billion in tax savings over the next five years, they argue that this will result in greater consumption. Ultimately, this could lead to increased productivity as businesses increase output to satisfy increased demand.

The lower tax rates could also lead to an increase in savings, since most individuals will have more disposable income. Since many economists feel that the level of business investment in an economy is closely linked to the level of savings, increased capital formation could result. Increased capital formation usually leads to higher levels of production.

Other economists feel that savings may actually decrease. Lower tax rates mean that consumers can keep a greater portion of interest income. Reduced savings would therefore be required to provide the same amount of after-tax return. A pension plan, for example, would require lower contributions to return the same income at retirement. If this happens, the level of aggregate investment could decline with the level of savings.

The effect of tax reform on interest rates is equally open to debate. If the level of savings declines and/or businesses increase their investment in capital goods, interest rates could increase as the demand for money exceeds the supply. On the other hand, if savings increase, interest rates could decline as a result of excess loanable funds.

could be cited, a major one was the rapidly expanding size of the work force during this period. Over 2 million new workers joined the work force each year, most of them relatively unskilled. The inability of the economy to absorb these additional workers resulted in increased unemployment. The money supply was expanded in the hope that the resulting increase in demand would stimulate business to expand production and hire more workers, but increased energy costs and the unskilled nature of new workers made capital formation very expensive. The total effect was a situation that a demand-side approach could not handle.

Reaganomics. Supply-siders believed that the expanded money supply of the 1970's contributed to the inflationary problems of the time. The answer, supply-siders contended, was not in demand management but in the stimulation of productivity. This approach is based, at least in part, on Say's law, which asserts that supply creates its own demand. If productivity can be increased, Say's law contends, employment will also increase. This results in more disposable income, some of which will be spent on goods and services. This additional spending stimulates productivity, and the cycle continues until full employment is reached.

The supply-side approach to economic policy also holds that the best way to increase productivity is to transfer resources from the public to the private sector. In this way, the market mechanism can act to achieve price stability and full employment. When President Reagan took office in 1980, supply-side economics, dubbed *Reaganomics,* became the prevailing economic policy.

National Debt

As long as governments are able to levy sufficient taxes to meet expenditures, they can maintain a balanced budget and avoid a national debt. This is not always possible, however, because tax revenues as well as expenditures are not perfectly predictable. Unexpected unemployment can result in lower tax revenues and increased transfer payments. (Transfer payments are payments made by the government for which no goods or services are received in return, such as Social Security payments, farm subsidies, and unemployment compensation.) This imbalance between money coming in and money going out, called a *budget deficit,* can be corrected only by borrowing.

Reasons for borrowing. Governments borrow for reasons other than to correct imbalances between income and outflow. Large public works projects, such as interstate highways or mass transit systems, produce benefits for society over many years. If the government were to wait until it had sufficient funds to finance such projects, society would meanwhile be deprived of the benefits. Emergencies and unexpected events also force governments to borrow. A war, for example, is a costly endeavor that must be financed immediately. Governments also use deficit spending, spending in excess of revenues, to stimulate a sluggish economy (see Fiscal Policy in The Role of Government section, page 289).

The total of all outstanding financial obligations of the federal government is called the *gross federal debt* or *gross national debt.* The *net federal debt* includes only that debt held by individuals and organizations outside the government. It does not include obligations of one government agency held by another. Since payments between government agencies have little effect on the economy, the net national debt is the more relevant and reliable measure of indebtedness.

Impact of national debt. Common beliefs regarding a large national debt are that it decreases the wealth of a nation, adversely impacts the standard of living, and places a large financial burden on future generations. The actual effect depends on many factors, including who owns the debt and the size of the debt compared with the gross national product. If most of the U.S. national debt is held by U.S. citizens or domestic organizations, it has little effect on the wealth of the nation. When this is true, interest on the debt and principal repayment remain, for the most part, within the United States.

Redistribution of wealth. Since individuals in the United States do not hold bonds and other government debt instruments in the same proportion as they pay taxes, the debt has the effect of redistributing wealth. The interest that the government pays to those who hold government bonds and other government debt instruments comes from tax revenues. Therefore, if taxpayers do not own any government securities, through taxation, part of their income is transferred to those who do own such securities. Although this affects

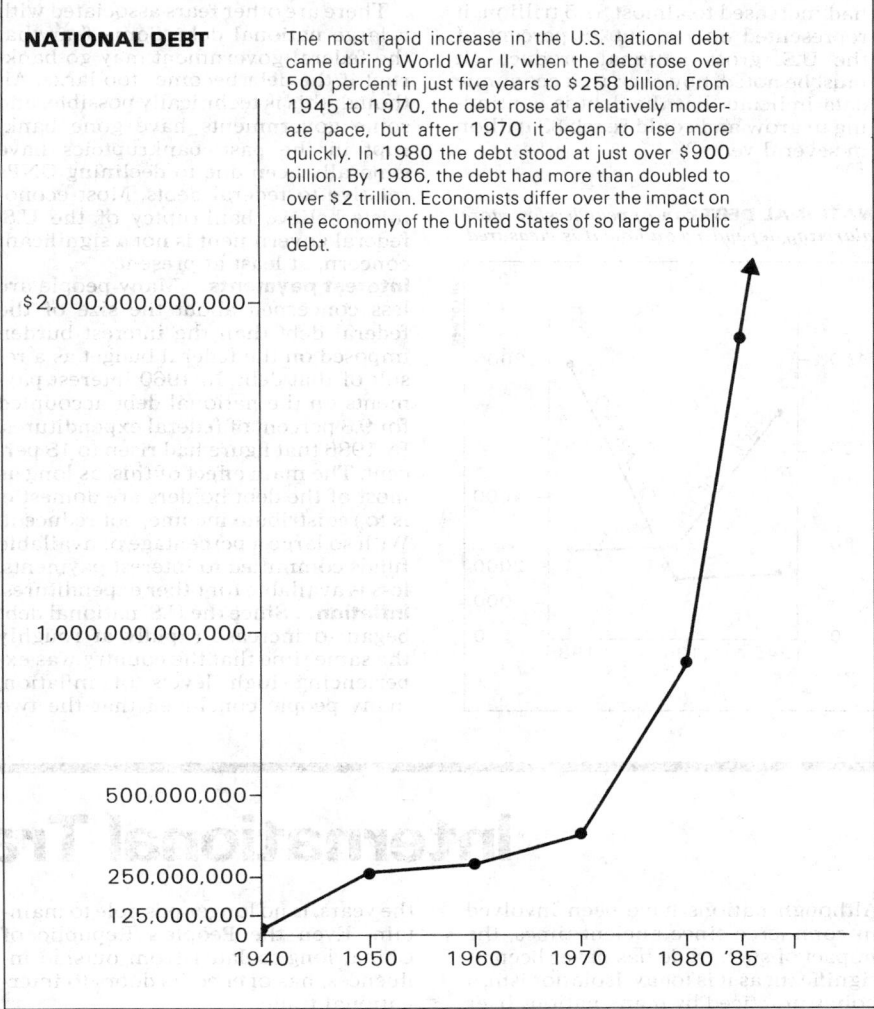

NATIONAL DEBT

The most rapid increase in the U.S. national debt came during World War II, when the debt rose over 500 percent in just five years to $258 billion. From 1945 to 1970, the debt rose at a relatively moderate pace, but after 1970 it began to rise more quickly. In 1980 the debt stood at just over $900 billion. By 1986, the debt had more than doubled to over $2 trillion. Economists differ over the impact on the economy of the United States of so large a public debt.

$2,000,000,000,000 —

1,000,000,000,000 —

500,000,000 —

250,000,000 —

125,000,000 —
0

1940   1950   1960   1970   1980 '85

the relative wealth of some people, it has no effect on the total wealth of the nation.

Although most of the U.S. federal debt is currently held domestically, the percentage held by foreigners has increased since 1970. If this trend continues, it could become a cause for alarm as interest payments on foreign-held U.S. debt leave the country.

Debt and the GNP. The impact of any debt, public or private, must be considered relative to income. An individual who earns $100,000 a year usually can afford a higher level of debt than someone who earns $25,000 a year. Similarly, a nation with a high gross national product can sustain a higher level of debt than a nation with a low GNP.

Although budget deficits increased from 1955 to 1980, they increased at a slower rate than did the gross national product. Since 1980, however, the national debt has been increasing at a faster rate than the GNP. Despite this, the federal debt as a percentage of gross national product is still fairly moderate. In 1945, after World War II, for example, the net federal debt was $252.5 billion, 119 percent of the GNP. By 1985, although the net national debt had increased to almost $1.5 trillion, it represented only about 38 percent of the U.S. gross national product. (It must be noted, however, that economic data indicate that the debt is continuing to grow and could reach $3 trillion in several years.)

NATIONAL DEBT *can appear less or more alarming depending on how it is measured.*

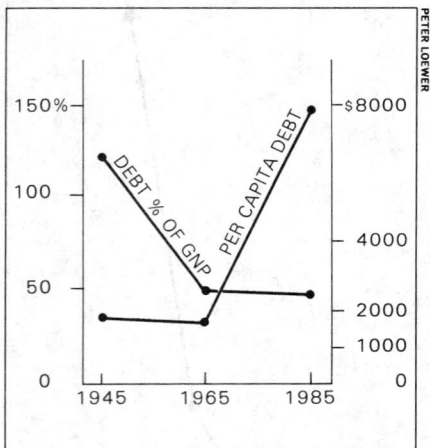

U.S. GOVERNMENT EXPENDITURES

National defense, income security (which includes Social Security payments, unemployment insurance payments, and retirement benefits), and interest on debt account for about 74 percent of the federal budget. Since 1980 net interest has risen about 6 percent, national defense has risen about 4 percent, and income security expenditures have dropped about 3 percent.

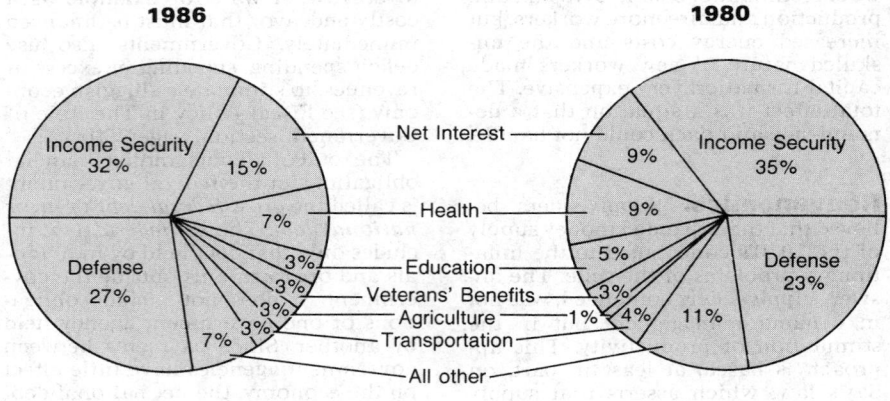

PETER LOEWER

There are other fears associated with a large national debt. Some fear that the federal government may go bankrupt if the debt becomes too large. Although this is technically possible, and some governments have gone bankrupt in the past, bankruptcies have generally been due to declining GNPs relative to federal debts. Most economists believe bankruptcy of the U.S. federal government is not a significant concern, at least at present.

Interest payments. Many people are less concerned about the size of the federal debt than the interest burden imposed on the federal budget as a result of that debt. In 1960 interest payments on the national debt accounted for 9.3 percent of federal expenditures. By 1986 that figure had risen to 15 percent. The main effect of this, as long as most of the debt holders are domestic, is to redistribute income, not reduce it. With so large a percentage of available funds committed to interest payments, less is available for other expenditures.

Inflation. Since the U.S. national debt began to increase rapidly at roughly the same time that the country was experiencing high levels of inflation, many people concluded that the two were related. A large national debt may or may not be inflationary. If, for example, the government sought to pay off its debt by printing and circulating a large amount of additional money, the increased demand created by this sudden influx of currency would almost certainly be inflationary.

A large government deficit when businesses are operating at full capacity might also result in inflation if insufficient investment funds were available, or interest rates were too high to enable capital formation. Lack of investment, which impedes increased productivity, coupled with increased demand resulting from deficit spending, might result in inflation.

Balanced budget. Although a large federal debt is of concern to many, few would suggest that the federal budget should always be balanced. The need to stimulate a sluggish economy, fund a needed public works project, or finance a war may be more important than a balanced budget. The size and rate of growth of a deficit, however, are a major political as well as economic issue.

International Trade

Although nations have been involved in commerce since ancient times, the impact of such trade has never been as significant as it is today. Isolationism, a policy practiced by many nations over the years, is no longer possible to maintain. Even the People's Republic of China, long isolated from outside influences, has opened its doors to international trade.

Specialization. A main factor contributing to increased trade over the decades is the specialization that exists at all levels of human endeavor. Prehistoric people were fairly self-sufficient. They hunted or gathered their own food, found or built their own shelter, and provided for their own defense. Modern people, by contrast, are specialists. They provide only a small fraction of their own individual needs, and much of what they do provide is in component form, needing other components to be of benefit. Since modern people specialize, they must trade with other specialists to acquire what they need.

Nations also specialize. No nation on Earth produces all the different types of products its people need or desire. Trade between nations enables nations to obtain products they do not produce.

Comparative advantage.

Even nations capable of producing certain goods often import them. This occurs when nations are more efficient in the production of certain goods and services than others and trade some of them for goods that they are relatively less efficient in producing. This is referred to as *comparative advantage*. The petroleum situation in the United States is a good example. Although there are sources of fossil fuel in the United States that could be exploited, oil from the Middle East has typically been less expensive than petroleum from domestic sources.

International trade based on comparative advantage not only enables nations to obtain goods they do not produce, it enables them to increase the overall satisfaction of society. Consider what would happen if the United States could not export any of the wheat it produced. The price of a bushel of wheat would drop to virtually nothing. Similarly, if Germany could not export any cameras, the price of cameras in Germany would decline considerably. Since Germany does not produce an abundance of wheat, wheat has a high value in Germany. Cameras, likewise, have a high value in the United States. Trade between the two nations enables each to obtain items they value in exchange for goods of less domestic value. The satisfaction and standard of living of the citizens of both nations have thus been increased. Furthermore, the wheat that has not been traded is worth more domestically, since there is not as much of it.

Balance of Trade

The relationship between a nation's imports and exports is called its *balance of trade*. If the total value of a nation's imports exceeds the total value of its exports, an unfavorable balance of trade *(trade deficit)* exists. Such a situation is considered unfavorable, since it results in money flowing out of the country. The opposite situation, total value of exports exceeding

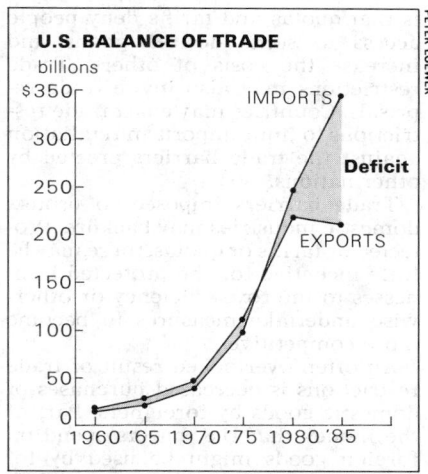

U.S. BALANCE OF TRADE

U.S. EXPORTS declined by 3 percent from 1980 to 1985, while imports climbed by 41 percent.

imports, results in a favorable balance of trade *(trade surplus)*. That is, more money is spent by foreigners in the purchase of U.S. goods than is being spent on foreign goods by people in the United States.

Impact of foreign trade.

A nation's balance of trade has a significant impact on the economies of other nations. If one country has a trade surplus, one or more other nations must be experiencing a trade deficit. It is, of course, impossible for all nations to operate in such a manner as to avoid deficits and still maintain a relatively free international market. Only through the strictest control of the international marketplace could such a balance be achieved, and virtually no one would support such stringent control. In reality, deficits and surpluses do exist, some of significant magnitude. In 1987, for example, the United States trade deficit exceeded $160 billion.

Large deficits or surpluses can pose serious problems. Nations with large deficits may experience unemployment problems, since most of the goods and services have been produced by foreign rather than domestic workers. Nations with large surpluses may experience inflationary pressures as demand for their goods increases.

Exchange rates. One of the most significant impacts of a trade imbalance is its effect on the foreign exchange rates of various national currencies. Since goods imported from other nations must be paid for in the currency of the exporting nation, a large demand for that nation's goods also means a large demand for its currency. This may drive the price of that currency up on the foreign exchange market. This is the situation in which Japan found itself in the mid-1980's. The high level of Japanese exports, coupled with the large U.S. deficit, resulted in a strong yen. This meant that the yen would buy more dollars on the foreign exchange market or, conversely, the dollar would buy fewer yen. The weak dollar, as compared with the yen, meant that Japanese imports became more expensive for Americans.

Changes in import quotas or tariffs can also affect the demand for goods produced in foreign nations. If quotas are relaxed, more goods are made available. More people may become aware of the availability of such goods with a resultant increase in demand. Reduction of tariffs makes the imported goods less expensive, which tends to stimulate demand much as any other price decrease would. A technological breakthrough that enables goods to be produced less expensively also tends to stimulate demand. Rapid income growth in a particular nation may increase overall purchases by the people of that country.

The currency of nations with large trade deficits often becomes weak as the demand for that nation's currency

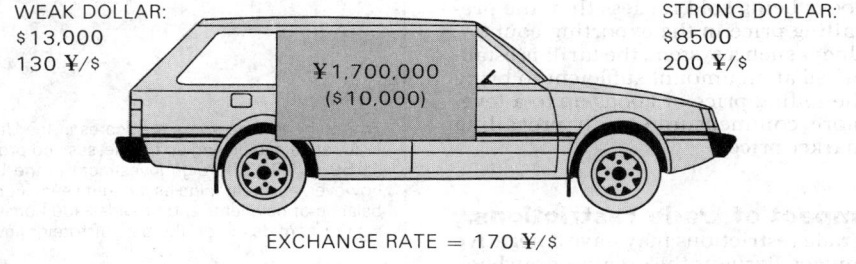

EFFECT OF EXCHANGE RATES ON IMPORTED GOODS

Exchange rates can greatly affect the competitiveness of countries' products in foreign markets. For instance, at an exchange rate of ¥170 (170 yen) to $1, an automobile that costs ¥1,700,000 to produce in Japan would cost about $10,000 in the United States. With an exchange rate of ¥200 to $1, the same automobile would be more competitively priced at $8500. At an exchange rate of ¥130 to $1, the same car would be much more expensive, about $13,000.

WEAK DOLLAR:
$13,000
130 ¥/$

STRONG DOLLAR:
$8500
200 ¥/$

¥1,700,000
($10,000)

EXCHANGE RATE = 170 ¥/$

decreases. This was the situation of the United States during the mid-1980's. Some U.S. economists hoped that since the dollar was weak, the purchase of imported goods would decline. It was also hoped that purchases of U.S. goods by foreigners would increase as they became less expensive in the currencies of other nations. If both of these events occurred, the balance of trade would become more favorable. Experience has shown, however, that although a weak currency may reduce a trade deficit somewhat, it does not provide the entire solution.

Trade Restrictions

Although the buyers of goods and services could maximize the purchasing power of their money if the international trade market was free of restrictions, virtually every country in the world, to some degree, imposes trade restrictions on imported goods. Such restrictive actions may be undertaken to preserve a favorable balance of trade or correct a trade deficit. They also may be used to protect domestic jobs or shelter infant industries until they can become competitive. Often, trade restrictions are imposed in response to pressure from special interest groups. Trade restrictions may be imposed during recessionary times to stimulate domestic productivity.

Quotas. Two major methods are used to restrict the flow of imports, *import quotas* and *tariffs*. Quotas establish upper limits on the amount of goods that may be imported. While some quotas are mandatory, others are voluntary. During the 1980's the United States negotiated an agreement with Japan whereby Japan agreed to voluntarily restrict the number of automobiles exported to the United States.

Tariffs. Protective tariffs do not restrict the amount of goods imported, but impose a tax on them when they are imported. Tariffs essentially amount to a sales tax on imported goods.

Some countries have *antidumping laws* that may be invoked against goods being sold for less than the prevailing price in the exporting country. Under such a system, the tariff is established at an amount sufficient to bring the selling price of goods up to a level more commensurate with prevailing market prices.

Impact of trade restrictions. Trade restrictions may have a negative impact. Perhaps the greatest drawback

is that quotas and tariffs deny people access to some desired goods and increase the costs of others. Trade restrictions may also invite trade reprisals. Countries may enact trade restrictions to limit imports in retaliation against the trade barriers erected by other nations.

Trade barriers imposed to protect domestic industries may backfire. Protected by tariffs or quotas, there may be little incentive for the protected businesses to improve efficiency or otherwise undertake measures to become more competitive.

An often overlooked result of trade restrictions is decreased purchases of domestic goods by foreigners. Part of the money that U.S. buyers spend on foreign goods might be used by foreigners to purchase U.S. exports. This would have the effect of creating employment and stimulating U.S. industry. If foreign producers sell less on American markets, income available to purchase U.S. goods may also decline. If this occurs, the objective of the quota or tariff is defeated.

If a country decides to erect trade barriers, tariffs may be preferable to quotas. Both actions raise prices but, under a quota, it is the seller of the product who receives the benefits of the higher price. Tariffs, on the other hand, result in income to the government. Rather than solving problems, restrictive tariffs and quotas often shift the economic and competitive burdens of the depressed areas of an economy to the exporting industries and to the consumer.

Balance of Payments

A nation's balance of trade is only part of the international economic picture. The balance of trade refers to merchandise trade, which accounts for only part of the money transferred between nations. In addition to purchases of goods, money flows into and out of

a nation as the result of gifts, foreign aid, and foreign investment. This affects the foreign exchange rate just as purchases of goods and services do. The relationship between the total amount of money flowing into and out of a nation, its *balance of payments*, represents a more comprehensive picture of a nation's international economic and monetary position.

Foreign investment. The most significant flow of funds that occurs between nations, in addition to that resulting from purchases of goods, is due to foreign investment. Large multinational corporations, such as General Motors and Exxon Corporation, have large investments in foreign countries. Although this may also seem to result in an unfavorable balance of payments, since U.S. firms are investing in foreign land and equipment and hiring foreign workers, the long-run impact of foreign investment may have exactly the opposite effect. Since the stockholders of these companies are predominantly U.S. citizens, the profits made in these foreign countries flow back to the United States.

Americans also buy stocks and bonds issued by foreign companies. The dividends and interest paid on these investments represent another source of money flow into the United States. In 1982, U.S. investors realized income from these foreign investments of $28.7 billion, an amount nearly sufficient to offset the merchandise trade deficit. Since 1982, the trade deficit has increased much more than income from foreign investments.

Foreign investors also invest funds in the United States. The degree to which foreign funds are invested in U.S. companies depends on a number of factors. If interest rates in the United States are high compared with interest rates in other countries, foreign investors will tend to invest in U.S. firms or in U.S. government securities in order to take advantage of the higher rates of return. This has a favorable impact on the balance of payments and increases the demand for U.S. currency.

FOREIGN INVESTMENT

JAPANESE BUY MANHATTAN

From time to time, there are scares in the United States that foreigners are investing too heavily in America and buying up businesses and property that ought to remain in American hands. From 1980 to 1985, foreign investment in the United States more than doubled. This trend is not, however, as threatening as it might seem. Foreign money flowing into the United States helps the balance of payments and provides additional capital for economic expansion. Additionally, it is a sign of confidence on the part of foreign investors in the health of the U.S. economy.

FINANCE

T BILLS Blue Chips MONEY MARKET munis CDs

EACH FINANCIAL INSTRUMENT *has a particular use for which it is especially suited.*

For an individual company, financial planning encompasses those activities designed to manage the firm's cash flow and ensure that sufficient funds are available to meet its objectives. A company must estimate future financial requirements, not only for its day-to-day activities, but for major capital expenditures, and so it must initiate programs that will provide the necessary funds when needed.

For the economy as a whole, governmental financial planning must meet a number of objectives. First, it must develop sufficient revenue for the government to operate and to provide such services as education and national defense. Governments must establish stable monetary and banking systems that can facilitate the free flow of goods and services. During the late 1970's and 1980's, moreover, as budget and foreign trade deficits increased, governments became increasingly involved in managing the federal budget and correcting trade imbalances.

Money

Historical Development

Before the invention of money, trade and commerce were accomplished through the barter system, the trading of one type of goods for another. Three major problems are associated with the barter system. First, trade can occur only if each of the trading parties has something the other wants. Second, the purchase and sale transactions cannot be separated, but must be simultaneous. The sale or purchase of goods cannot be deferred. The third major problem relates to perishable goods. If the owner of perishable goods cannot trade those goods immediately, they soon lose their value.

Mediums of Exchange

Something that would be considered valuable at any time was needed to solve these problems; that is, a universal medium of exchange or a commodity that would make it possible to express the value of all other items.

Over the centuries many items have served as mediums of exchange. The American Indians used beads made from shells, called wampum. Early colonists of North America at one time used tobacco. Cigarettes and liquor were used in Germany immediately after World War II because of the extremely low value of the official currency. Fur pelts, whale teeth, grain, salt, and livestock are but a few of the other commodities that, at one time or other, have been used as mediums of exchange.

Metals eventually became the prevailing medium of exchange because of their intrinsic and relatively stable value. When a purchase was made, an appropriate amount of metal, determined by weight, was shaved off an ingot as payment. It was from this use of metal as a medium of exchange that coins evolved.

Coins. The earliest recorded use of coins was in the seventh century B.C. in the Greek state of Lydia. These coins were made from a metal called *electrum,* a combination of silver and gold. The use of coins facilitated transactions since payment could be made by counting rather than by weighing.

Although trade was facilitated by the use of coins, so was fraud. Individuals could shave small bits of precious metal from the edges of coins and pass these debased coins for full value. As a result, the coins became lighter and lighter. As the coins became worth less

MONEY has taken many different forms, from shells to tobacco to gold coins.

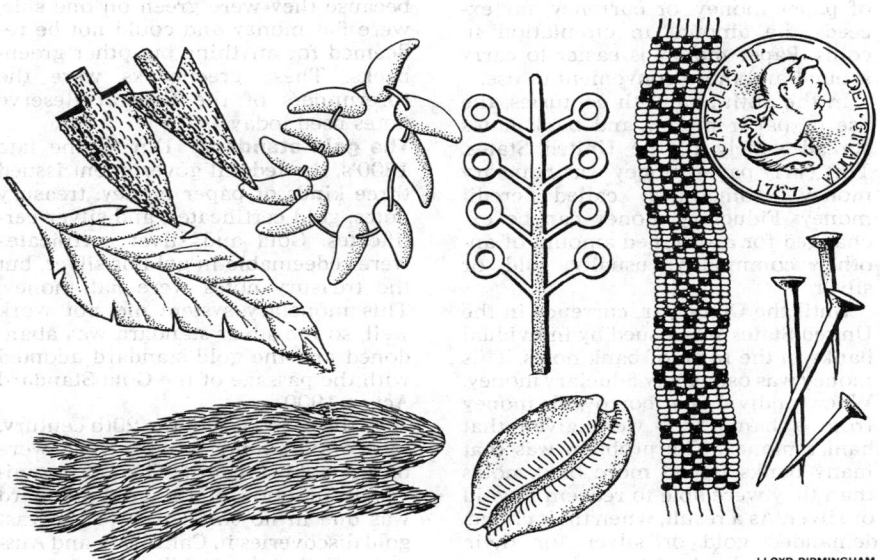

LLOYD BIRMINGHAM

and less, the ultimate effect on the economy was inflation. Eventually small grooves were cut into the edges of coins to combat fraud. This milling made it possible to tell whether a coin had been debased.

When settlers came to America, they brought their money with them, mostly in the form of silver and gold coins from their native countries. One common coin in use at the time was the Spanish piece of eight. One piece of eight was worth eight smaller coins, called bits. To this day some people still refer to a quarter as two bits. The first coins actually made in America were issued in 1652 in Massachusetts Colony.

In 1792 Congress established the United States Mint, which made coins in gold, silver, and copper. Among these coins were copper cents and half cents, silver dimes and half dimes, quarters, half dollars, and dollars. Gold coins included the quarter eagle (two and one-half dollars), half-eagle (five dollars), and eagle (ten dollars). Other early coins made by the U.S. Mint included two-cent, three-cent, and twenty-cent coins. In 1866 the nickel was introduced to replace the half dime.

Early coins were commodity money; that is, they contained metal worth the face value of the coin. A silver dollar, for example, contained a dollar's worth of silver. Thus, coins were intrinsically worth their stated value. Today's coins, however, are fiat money, which does not contain its face value in metal. Thus, a dime does not contain ten cents worth of silver but it will still buy ten cents worth of goods, since people are willing to accept it in payment for that amount of goods. It is the willingness of people to accept fiat money that makes it valuable.

Paper money. The amount of money in circulation today in the form of paper money, or currency, far exceeds the amount in circulation in coins. Paper money is easier to carry around and more convenient to use.

In the 18th and 19th centuries, the use of paper money and bank notes spread widely in the United States. This early paper money was fiduciary money, sometimes called credit money. Fiduciary money can be exchanged for a specified amount of another commodity, usually gold or silver.

Until the Civil War, currency in the United States was issued by individual banks in the form of bank notes. This money was ostensibly fiduciary money. When individuals borrowed money from a bank, they were given that bank's money. The problem was that many banks issued more bank notes than they were able to redeem in gold or silver. As a result, when their clients demanded gold or silver for their notes, many banks failed.

GOLD RESERVES AT FORT KNOX, *Kentucky, backed the dollar when the United States was on the gold standard.*

During the U.S. Civil War, the federal government issued money to finance the war. These bills, called greenbacks because they were green on one side, were fiat money and could not be redeemed for anything but other greenbacks. These greenbacks were the forerunners of the Federal Reserve notes used today.

The gold standard. During the late 1800's, the federal government issued three kinds of paper money: treasury notes, gold certificates, and silver certificates. Gold and silver certificates were redeemable in gold or silver, but the treasury notes were fiat money. This monetary system did not work well, so the silver standard was abandoned and the gold standard adopted with the passage of the Gold Standard Act in 1900.

By the early part of the 20th century, most of the countries of the world were on the gold standard. The nearly universal adoption of the gold standard was due in no small part to the vast gold discoveries in California and Australia during the 1800's.

Under the international gold standard, shipments of gold were made between nations to balance trade deficits. If, for example, the United States imported more goods from Great Britain than Great Britain did from the United States, gold would be shipped from the United States to Great Britain to make up the difference. World War I and the Great Depression eventually brought an end to the international gold standard. Since free trade ceased between the warring nations, shipments of gold could not be made to compensate for trade imbalances. This, in effect, amounted to a suspension of the gold standard.

Following the war, the world attempted to return to the gold standard. Britain was the first major power to do so, readopting it in 1925. By 1929 most Western nations had followed suit. The development of central banking systems in many nations, however, impeded the flow of gold from country to country. The U.S. Federal Reserve System, like other central banking systems, manipulated the supply of money; this prevented the adjustment mechanism of international gold flow from working as it had prior to World War I.

During the Great Depression, countries found it necessary to exert greater control over their economies; being tied to an international gold standard impeded that effort. Great Britain abandoned the gold standard in 1931, and the United States followed suit in 1933.

Dollar standard. From the end of World War II until 1971, the world operated under a dollar standard. In international trade, goods were often bought and sold in U.S. dollars rather than in the currencies of the trading nations.

Characteristics of Money

Whatever is used for money, whether it be shells, cattle, or Federal Reserve notes, it must have certain characteristics for it to serve its purpose.

Negotiability. Money must be readily accepted. Gold and silver certificates were readily accepted because they could be redeemed in gold and silver, which was valued by virtually everyone. Federal Reserve notes, while not redeemable, still act effectively as money because people know they can pass them on to others in payment for goods and services.

Scarcity. Money must also be relatively scarce. This ensures that the supply will not change radically in a short period of time. A sudden increase could result in a dramatic reduction in the value of the currency, while a decrease could impede economic growth. Such a situation caused the downfall of the use of tobacco as money in colonial America. When crops were good, the money supply increased dramatically, thus reducing the value of tobacco. When the harvest was poor, the value of tobacco increased significantly.

Other characteristics.
Money must also be easily recognized. It must wear well so that the supply is not automatically reduced through use. It must be readily divisible into smaller units, and small enough to carry around, a problem with the use of cattle or other livestock as money.

Functions of money.
The most obvious function of money is to serve as a medium of exchange. People must be willing to accept it in payment for goods and services.

Money must also serve as a measure of value; this allows the values of different items to be compared. A $50 item is more valuable than a $10 item, regardless of the nature of the two items.

The third function of money is to act as a store of value. Money enables people to sell an item today and use the proceeds at a future date, with full confidence that the money will keep its value.

Foreign Exchange Rates

When people or businesses buy goods from producers in a foreign country, it becomes necessary to obtain that country's currency to pay for the goods. This creates demand for the currencies of foreign nations. The more goods that are imported from a nation, the greater the demand for that nation's currency.

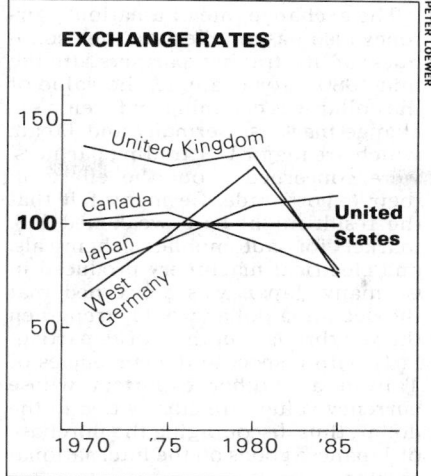

EXCHANGE RATES

THE EXCHANGE RATE *of a currency tends to reflect its level of demand.*

Floating exchange rates.
Just as increased demand for goods tends to result in an increase in the market price of those goods, an increase in the demand for a particular currency tends to increase the price of that currency as measured by the currencies of other nations. It is this supply/demand relationship between currencies that esta-

blishes the various international exchange rates.

The foreign exchange rate refers to the number of units of one currency that it takes to buy one unit of another currency. Assume, for example, that the price of the yen in U.S. dollars is $0.005. This means that one dollar will buy 200 yen, and five dollars will buy 1000 yen. If U.S. goods are in high demand, the resulting high demand for the dollar creates a strong dollar and makes it more valuable compared with other currencies. A currency that is declining in value compared with other currencies is referred to as weak. For example, a weak dollar might make the price of a yen $0.007. This means that one dollar will buy only 142 yen.

Strong dollar.
Strong currency is not always good, and weak currency is not always bad. A strong dollar is generally a positive situation for those buying foreign goods. Since the dollar is more valuable compared with foreign currencies, the dollar will buy more. Importers of goods as well as people on vacation abroad will be able to buy more goods for the same amount of money than if the dollar were weak. A strong dollar is also advantageous to those investing abroad. Foreign securities become less expensive in terms of U.S. dollars, and companies can buy

IN GERMANY, FOLLOWING WORLD WAR I, *currency was so nearly worthless that it made more sense to burn it than to use it to buy firewood.*

MONEY FUNCTIONS *as a measure of value in an exchange of goods.*

resources or build plants abroad for less money.

For exporters, however, a strong dollar may not be beneficial. Foreigners buying U.S. goods have to pay more, in terms of native currency, than they would if the dollar were weak. This results in a higher price for U.S. goods abroad. Those U.S. companies that rely heavily on foreign markets tend to suffer competitively when the dollar is strong. A strong dollar also acts as a disincentive to foreign investment in the United States, again because the cost would be greater in terms of the foreign investor's currency.

Weak dollar. A weak dollar can contribute to inflation as foreign demand for U.S. goods increases. Interest rates may also increase, since inflation is typically accompanied by high interest rates. A weak dollar may also have positive effects. Increased foreign purchases of U.S. goods, for example, can lower trade deficits.

The exchange rate of a nation's currency also has an effect on the economies of its trading partners. In the mid-1980's, for example, the value of the dollar was declining on foreign exchange markets. Germany and Japan, which are major U.S. trading partners, were concerned about the effect on their export trade. Germany felt that the result might be a weakened U.S. market for automobiles, chemicals, and electrical machinery produced in Germany. Japan was concerned that the declining dollar would strengthen the yen throughout the world, particularly with respect to the currencies of Taiwan and other exporters whose currency values are closely tied to the dollar, thus discouraging the purchase of Japanese goods on the international market.

Managed exchange rates. Although foreign exchange rates are de-

cided in a basically free market, nations can exert some influence on the value of their currencies. They may, for example, buy foreign currencies if they desire to devalue their own currency. The increased demand for the foreign currencies drives up the price of those currencies compared with the currency used to purchase them.

Some nations, particularly developing nations, have chosen to peg the exchange value of their currencies to a major foreign currency or to a basket of currencies. This is done to stabilize the international exchange rate of such currencies, since the currencies of developing nations tend to experience severe fluctuations in value on foreign exchange markets. The exchange values of currencies pegged in such a manner still float, but do so in response to fluctuation in the foreign exchange value of the currency or currencies to which they are pegged.

Banking

The Development of Banking

Banking, in its many and various forms, has existed since ancient times, although not much is known about banks prior to the 13th century. Early banks were heavily involved in facilitating foreign trade, and a major part of their business was to supply foreign coin and bullion for international trade. Without a ready means of payment for goods and services, international trade would have been extremely difficult and cumbersome.

The merchant banks of medieval times were located along trade routes; they provided payment for the goods that were traded along those routes. Since they existed all along trade routes, the banks could provide payment without actually shipping bullion from one place to another. This was the earliest use of *bills of exchange*. Through these bills of exchange, bankers would pay money to a merchant at one place at the direction of another merchant at a separate location. Banks made a profit as a result of the different exchange rates of the different currencies.

By the 17th century, English bankers had begun to accept deposits, as did the money scriveners, who were actually notaries, and the goldsmiths, who kept money and valuables for their customers. As the depository function grew, these early institutions found that the deposits tended to create a fund of idle cash. Withdrawals from some ac-

counts were generally offset by deposits in others, resulting in little change in total balances. New accounts usually increased the total amount of idle funds, which was lent to borrowers at an interest rate that was designed to provide a profit for the depository institutions.

Creation of the Bank of England in 1694 solidified the English banking system, and banks began to replace scriveners and goldsmiths as depository institutions. They held money and valuables for safekeeping, accepted deposits of funds for transfer to others, and created current accounts through extending and collecting loans. For centuries these were the principal functions of banks all over the world.

At about the same time, banks began allowing their depositors to transfer funds in their accounts to the accounts of others. This was the beginning of the checking system. These banks also allowed their customers to borrow by check. This occurred as depositors would draw checks in excess of their balances. The banks would honor the overdrawn checks and charge interest on the amount of the overdraft. These early checks, unlike modern checks, were actually claims against the bank itself. The bank, in turn, held an equivalent claim against the depositor.

In addition to the checks drawn by merchants, banks also created claims against themselves by issuing bank notes. Bank notes are promissory notes payable to the bearer and acceptable as money. The first such notes were issued by the Bank of Stockholm in 1661.

Banking Systems

As time passed, the banking systems of the world evolved somewhat differently. Although most systems serve basically the same functions, they differ in the manner in which they are organized. Banking in the United States, for example, unlike banking in other countries, is regulated both at the state and federal levels. As a result, the U.S. banking system has evolved more slowly than in other countries.

Banking in the United States.
The first bank in the United States, the Bank of North America, was chartered by the Continental Congress in 1781. Prior to this time, banking had been fairly informal, with individuals, merchants, and colonial governments all involved in making loans. By 1790, the Bank of New York and the Bank of Massachusetts began operations under state charters. Other state banks soon followed.

In 1791 Congress chartered the first Bank of the United States. It was chartered to operate for 20 years and had the power to issue its own bank notes. It was a large bank by the standards of the time and competed with state banks in the issuance of currency and the making of loans. It was also the forerunner of the central banking system, since it acted as fiscal agent for the federal government. By the time its charter had expired, a number of state banks had been established. These state banks, not relishing competition from the Bank of the United States, put pressure on Congress not to renew its charter. As a result, the charter expired, and the first Bank of the United States passed out of existence.

In the absence of the Bank of the United States, state banks grew rapidly in number, from 88 in 1811 to 246 by 1816. These state banks also issued their own notes, but they often overissued and did not have sufficient gold or silver with which to back their notes, many of which became worthless. As a result, Congress granted a charter for the second Bank of the United States in 1816. The second Bank of the United States eventually prospered, but it too passed out of existence when its charter expired in 1836 and President Andrew Jackson vetoed a bill to recharter it.

Growth of banking. One of the major forces that contributed to the growth of the U.S. banking system was the westward movement during the 1800's. As the population grew in the West, it required extended banking services. In addition to serving the banking needs of individuals, banks were needed to supply the capital requirements associated with western expansion. Since communications facilities were inefficient, large numbers of banks sprang up to meet local needs.

The turmoil of the mid-1800's caused considerable change in the banking system. The Civil War required financing and a more stable

BANKS PROVIDE MANY SERVICES, *including checking accounts, consumer loans, and the rental of safety deposit boxes, in which valuable objects and important papers can be stored.*

banking environment. In 1864 Congress passed the National Banking Act, which provided for a system of national banks to be chartered by the federal government. This act also established a standard currency system and stabilized the banking system by limiting the amount of notes that national banks could issue, requiring them to redeem notes of any national bank at full value and to maintain sufficient reserves to meet their depositors' demands.

The system of national banks grew rapidly because of the more stable environment it provided and, by 1866, 1600 of the 2000 banks in existence were national banks. They accounted for 75 percent of all bank deposits. The growth in the banking industry continued into the 20th century. By 1899 there were 13,000 banks in existence and by 1913 there were 27,000. Most of the new banks in the early part of the 20th century were state banks—national banks tended to grow in size more than in number.

Federal Reserve System. The early stability provided by the national banking system did not persist, and severe financial panics occurred in 1893 and 1907. In an effort to stabilize the system, Congress passed the Federal Reserve Act in 1913, creating the Fed-

eral Reserve System to act as the central banking authority. The act called for the creation of twelve regional Federal Reserve banks and required all nationally chartered banks to become members of the Federal Reserve System. State banks could also become members by meeting Federal Reserve requirements (see Central Banking section, page 301).

FDIC. The panic of the 1930's caused many bank failures. As a result, the Federal Deposit Insurance Corporation (FDIC) was established in 1933 to provide depositors with more security and shore up confidence in the banking system. The FDIC, like the Federal Savings and Loan Insurance Corporation (FSLIC), established in 1934 for deposits in savings and loan associations, insures deposits up to $100,000 per account.

Canadian banking. The oldest commercial bank in Canada is the Bank of Montreal, established in 1817 and chartered in 1822. Until 1867, Canadian banks were chartered by the provincial governments. Since 1867, banking activities have been chartered and regulated by the Canadian federal government.

The 14 years between 1867 and 1881 saw expansion of commercial banks. In that period, the number of chartered banks increased from 28 to 48. The period that followed was one of amalgamation, and by 1931 the number of chartered banks had dwindled to ten. But branch banking had developed by that time, and the total number of branch banks exceeded 3000 by 1931. These early commercial banks not only conducted standard banking activities but also issued notes that constituted the chief currency of Canada until the Bank of Canada, in 1934, was granted the exclusive right to issue notes.

In contrast with the banking system of the United States, the Canadian banking system still relies heavily on branch banking. Although there are only a few chartered banks in Canada, there are over 7000 branches. As a result of this extensive branch banking system, Canada has a much more national credit market than is the case in the United States. Money deposited in a local bank in the United States, for example, is generally available for loans to local or regional enterprises only. A deposit in a Canadian branch bank, on the other hand, becomes part of a pool of funds that can be drawn upon by borrowers in any part of the country in which that bank has a branch. In the United States, it is common for one regional bank to have an excess of loanable funds while another has a shortage. Under an extensive branch banking system, this imbalance is less likely to develop.

Commercial banks are licensed under, and are subject to, the provi-

THE CANADIAN BANKING SYSTEM *has relied historically on a relatively few large national banks with many local branch banks.*

Commercial Banking

In modern industrialized countries, commercial banking generally entails the handling of money and money equivalents, such as checks and bills of exchange. Commercial banks realize profits by accepting deposits and lending money at an interest rate higher than that which they pay depositors. Additional profit is earned by charging for other services, such as the rental of safe deposit boxes. Banks are different from other types of businesses in that the bulk of funds used for activities is not supplied by stockholders but by depositors.

The amount of money a commercial bank has available for loans is directly proportional to the amount of deposits. Although the level of deposits may vary somewhat as depositors add to and withdraw from accounts, total deposit fluctuations usually are minor.

Reserves. Banks may not lend out their total deposits, but must keep a percentage of deposited funds available to meet day-to-day transactional demands. These funds are referred to as *reserves*. The amount of reserves kept on hand depends on the judgment of the bank and the requirements of the central bank. In the United States, the Board of Governors of the Federal Reserve System sets the reserve requirement (see Federal Reserve System heading, page 302).

Virtually no bank could meet the demands of its depositors if all of them decided to withdraw their money at the same time. Confidence on the part of the depositors keeps this from happening, since depositors generally feel their money is secure when deposited in a bank.

If a bank does experience an extraordinary demand for funds, there are several ways for the bank to meet its obligations. It may call in its outstanding loans or sell some of the negotiable

sions of the Bank Act, originally enacted in 1871 but revised many times since. The operations of all commercial banks in Canada are subject to review by the inspector general of banks, a federal official.

The Bank of Canada. The Bank of Canada, the central bank, was established in 1934. It began operations on March 11, 1935, and was nationalized in 1938. According to the preamble to the Bank of Canada Act, the function of the central bank is "to regulate credit and currency in the best interests of the economic life of the nation, to control and protect the external value of the national monetary unit and to mitigate by its influence fluctuations in the general level of production, trade, prices, and employment, so far as may be possible within the scope of monetary action, and generally to promote the economic and financial welfare of the Dominion."

Consistent with this general function, the Bank of Canada serves as fiscal agent for the Canadian and the provincial governments. It has the exclusive right to issue currency, as has been stated previously.

The central bank also affects monetary policy in much the same way as the Federal Reserve System does in the United States. First, the Bank of Canada sets the bank rate, which is the interest rate charged on loans made to chartered banks. The Bank of Canada may also make loans to the federal government and the provincial governments. The central bank holds the required reserves deposited by the chartered banks. It also regulates the supply of money through open-market

operations, and the buying and selling of government securities. The Bank of Canada also manages the gold and foreign exchange reserves of Canada.

A paramount objective of Canadian monetary policy has been economic growth and a stable Canadian dollar. To meet this objective, the Bank of Canada has relied extensively on achieving desired growth rates in the supply of money. Although fairly successful in this endeavor in the late 1970's, this approach to economic stabilization encountered problems in the early 1980's, primarily as a result of federal budget deficits, high unemployment rates, persistent inflation, and an adverse balance of trade. Canada has learned, as has the United States, that monetary policy alone is seldom sufficient to achieve national economic objectives.

HOW A BANK MAKES A PROFIT

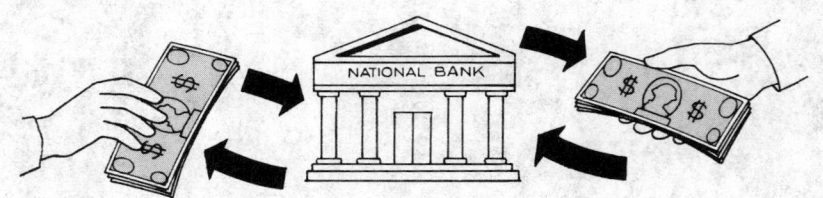

The bank pays 5 percent on money deposited.

The bank makes 3 percent profit.

The bank charges 8 percent on money it lends.

securities it typically holds. It may also borrow from the central bank to meet short-term requirements, using its outstanding loans as collateral.

To avoid having to employ any of these techniques, banks try not only to maintain sufficient cash reserves, but to balance their investment portfolios in such a manner as to always have sufficient maturing investments to meet withdrawal demands.

Interest rates.

In the United States, interest rates charged by banks are largely a function of the supply of and demand for loanable funds. If demand is high and the amount of funds low, interest rates will be high. Supply in excess of demand usually results in low interest rates.

Since the 1930's, the relatively free market mechanism with respect to loan rates has been significantly affected by government expenditures based on borrowing. Large-scale borrowing by the government affects private sector interest rates in a manner similar to that of Federal Reserve activities.

Chartering.

In the United States, banks can be chartered by either the federal government or the state governments. Although the operations of state and national banks are generally the same, there are some differences. All federally chartered banks and state banks that are members of the Federal Reserve System, for example, must be members of the FDIC. Banks chartered by states may become members of the Federal Reserve System if they meet certain financial standards.

NONBANK FINANCIAL INSTITUTIONS

Trust company. An organization that holds title to property for the benefit of another. The trustee's responsibilities include estate planning and careful investment of trust funds.

Credit union. A not-for-profit cooperative financial institution, usually organized by employees of an organization. Deposits are obtained through sale of shares to members. All earnings of a credit union go to its membership as dividends. The National Credit Union Administration monitors federally chartered credit unions.

Finance companies. Organizations that lend money to individuals and businesses. Their financing comes from banks and other financial institutions, rather than from deposits. A personal finance company makes small short-term loans to consumers.

Other financial institutions.

In addition to commercial banks, other financial institutions have a significant effect on the financial activities of the United States. Savings and loan associations, for example, engage in many of the same types of activities performed by commercial banks. Savings and loans, however, have typically channeled a greater portion of their loanable funds into mortgages and real estate loans. Since passage of the Deregulation and Monetary Control Act of 1986, differences between commercial banks and savings and loan associations have been diminishing.

Other financial institutions, such as trust companies, insurance companies, credit unions, and finance companies, are sometimes referred to as *near banks,* since they serve basically as financial intermediaries and do not create loanable funds.

Central Banking

Capitalistic nations sometimes experience significant fluctuations in economic activity, particularly in output, employment, and prices. Since such problems often are exacerbated by the ability of commercial banks to create money through their lending operations, most capitalistic nations have established a central banking system to monitor and exert control over money supply fluctuations resulting from commercial bank operations and other economic factors. The concept of central banking was first employed in England during the 19th century; it soon spread throughout Europe and, more recently, spread to the United States.

Banking activities.

Yet another major function of a central banking system is to provide a stable banking structure. Among other services, central banking authorities may provide advice and counsel to commercial banks.

In some countries, particularly developing nations, the central banking authority intervenes to establish banks where they are needed.

Control of commercial banking. Central banks also exert a degree of control and regulation on commercial

---

FEDERAL DEPOSIT INSURANCE CORPORATION

Prior to 1933 bank failures were not uncommon. Over 8000 banks failed between 1929 and 1933 alone. The major reason for bank failures is a run, which occurs when depositors fear that the bank does not have enough money to pay them and they rush to withdraw their deposits. Since no bank has enough cash on hand to meet the claims of all of its depositors at the same time, the bank soon is out of cash and is forced to close.

To restore public confidence in banks during the Great Depression, Congress passed the Banking Act of 1933, which established the Federal Deposit Insurance Corporation (FDIC). The FDIC insures deposits up to $100,000 per account in commercial and other qualifying banks entitled to coverage under the Federal Reserve Act and Federal Deposit Insurance Act.

FEDERAL DEPOSIT INSURANCE CORP.

Each depositor insured to $100,000

FDIC

FEDERAL DEPOSIT INSURANCE CORPORATION

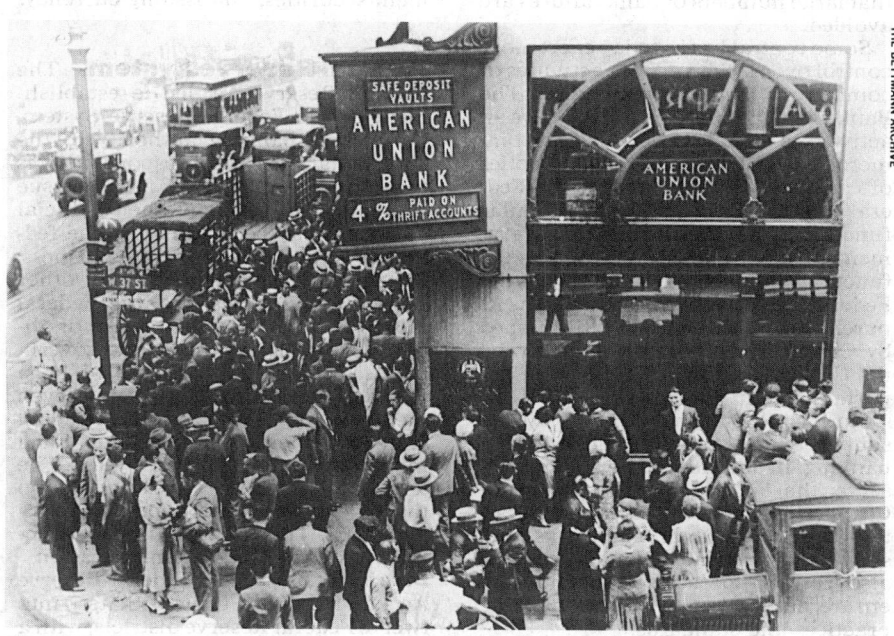

THE BETTMANN ARCHIVE

FEDERAL RESERVE SYSTEM

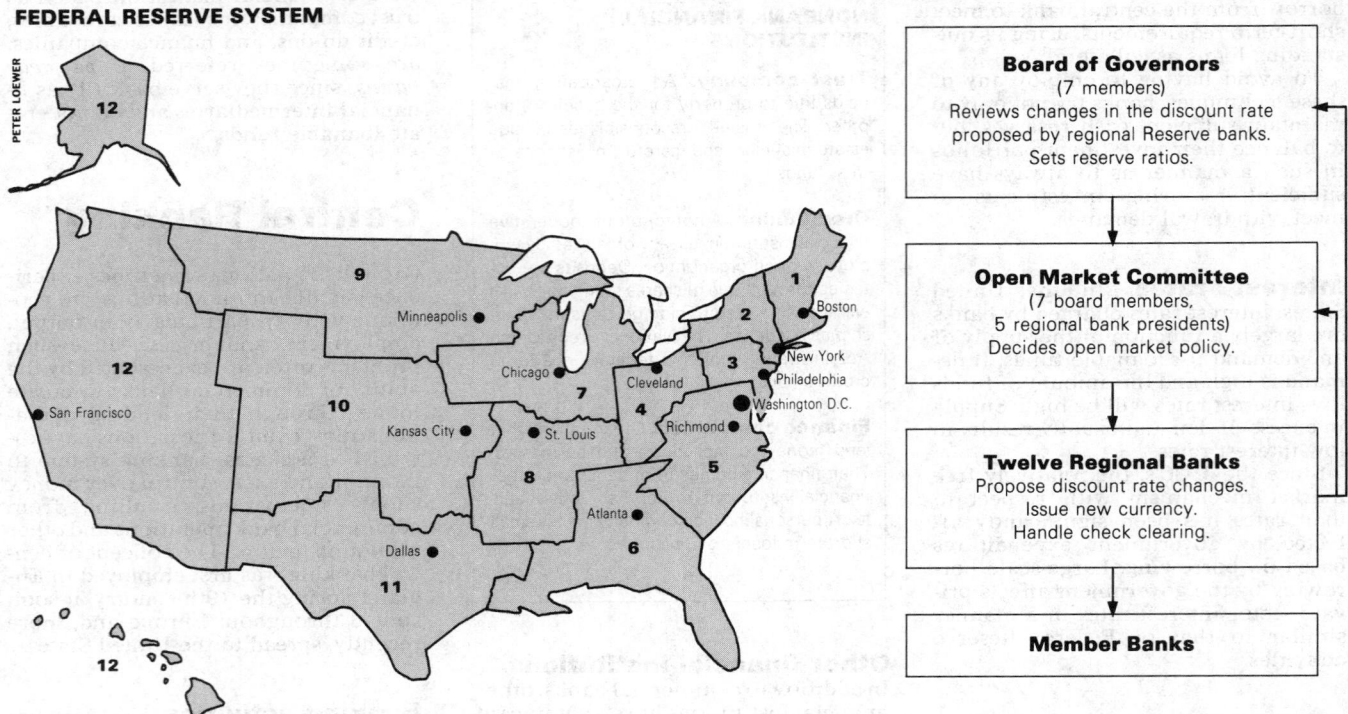

PETER LOEWER

banks. As is the case in the United States and Canada, they may set legal reserve requirements with which commercial banks must comply.

In the United States, the Federal Reserve examines the financial records of commercial banks to ensure viable operations. The central banks of developing countries often establish agencies to maintain close supervision over banking activities. The objective of such activities is to ensure that bank procedures are financially sound and that large numbers of bank failures are avoided.

Some central banks today exert more control over the day-to-day activities of commercial banks than do others. The Bank of England, for example, plays an active role in making certain that commercial banks have sufficient supplies of cash. In the United States, the Federal Reserve System serves a similar function by buying and selling government securities. The Bank of Canada functions in much the same way as the Federal Reserve System through its purchase and sale of securities issued by Canada, the United Kingdom, and the United States. Thus, it plays an important role in commerce.

No business in the United States is subject to greater regulation than is banking. In addition to the Federal Reserve, the Federal Deposit Insurance Corporation and the Comptroller of the Currency (for national banks) and state bank examiners (for state banks) also conduct periodic inspections to ensure observance of proper banking practices and standards.

Even banks that employ sound fiscal practices and keep adequate reserves on hand occasionally will experience shortfalls as a result of unexpected withdrawals. Central banks protect such banks from runs and failure by acting as lender of last resort, lending funds to commercial banks to help meet temporary shortages.

Central banks generally act also as banks for the national government, holding its accounts, acting as intermediaries for distribution of government securities, and issuing currency.

Federal Reserve System. The Federal Reserve Act led to establishment of the Federal Reserve System, the central banking authority of the United States. Its basic responsibility is to regulate the supply of money, issue currency, and perform other financial duties as may be required by the federal government and private business.
Board of Governors. Unlike other central banking systems, the Federal Reserve System is not owned or directly controlled by the federal government. Its activities are guided by a Board of Governors, comprising seven members appointed by the President and confirmed by the Senate. Each member serves a term of 14 years. The terms of the members are staggered so that a new governor is appointed every two years. This is to minimize the influence of any single administration.
District banks. The Federal Reserve Act divides the United States into twelve Federal Reserve districts, with a

Federal Reserve bank located in each district. Most districts also have one or more branch banks. The individual Federal Reserve banks are owned by the commercial banks in each district that are members of the Federal Reserve System. This ownership is significantly different from ownership by private corporations. The commercial banks have no control over the operations of the Federal Reserve banks, although they receive small dividends from the profits of the Federal Reserve banks. Since Federal Reserve banks were not established as profit-making institutions, funds remaining after dividend payments and operating expenses are turned over to the United States Treasury.

Each Federal Reserve bank has a nine-member board of directors responsible for the operations of the bank. Six of these directors are chosen by the member commercial banks of the district, and the other three are selected by the Board of Governors. To help ensure that the board acts in the public interest, only three of the nine board members may be bankers. The operations of the Federal Reserve banks at all times must be consistent with the policies established by the Board of Governors.
Federal Open Market Committee (FOMC). The buying and selling of government securities is a primary function of the Federal Reserve System as regulator of the supply of money. The body responsible for conducting these open-market operations is the Federal Open Market Committee

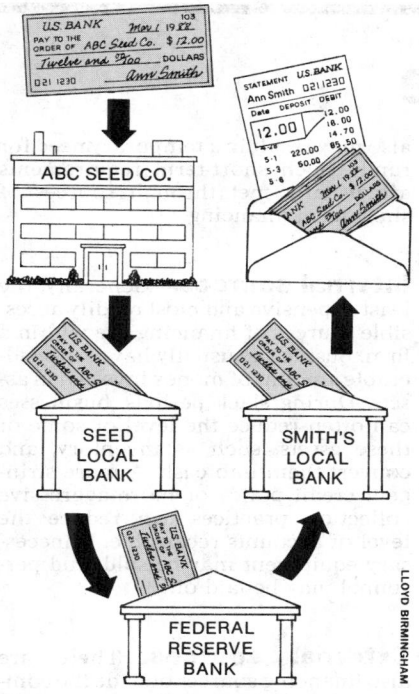

THE FEDERAL RESERVE *acts as a clearinghouse for checks, moving them between member banks.*

(FOMC), the most important subgroup within the Federal Reserve System. It has twelve members, seven of whom are the members of the Board of Governors. The other five positions include the president of the Federal Reserve Bank of New York, who is a permanent member, and four positions that rotate among the presidents of the other Federal Reserve banks. The Federal Open Market Committee has complete control over the implementation of monetary policy with respect to the timing and amount of purchases and sales of government securities. The Federal Reserve Bank of New York acts as the agent for open-market operations.

Federal Advisory Council. Another subgroup of the Federal Reserve is the Federal Advisory Council, which provides liaison between commercial bankers and the Board of Governors. It meets in Washington at least four times a year and serves in an advisory capacity. Its membership is made up of commercial bankers selected by the Federal Reserve banks.

Banking functions. The Federal Reserve System provides a number of banking services for the federal government and for the banking community. It establishes the *discount rate,* which is the interest rate at which member banks may borrow from Federal Reserve banks. It also sets the reserve requirement with which all depository institutions must comply, including institutions that are not members of the Federal Reserve System. To comply with these reserve requirements, member banks maintain

reserve accounts with the Federal Reserve banks.

One of the most important functions served by the Federal Reserve is to assist in check-clearing operations. When checks are written on accounts in one bank and deposited in another, there must be some process by which the checks find their way back to the bank of origin so that the appropriate customer account can be adjusted. Many large cities have clearinghouses, which sort out the checks and route them to the appropriate banks. Out-of-town checks present a more difficult problem. It would be impractical for each bank to send collected checks to each originating bank. Therefore, these checks are turned over to the Federal Reserve bank located in the district. That bank adjusts member bank reserve accounts to reflect the transactions and forwards the checks to the appropriate banks.

Because neither the federal government nor the U.S. Treasury has a bank of its own, the Federal Reserve System acts as the federal government's fiscal agent. In this capacity, the Federal Reserve maintains all the federal government's financial accounts. Tax receipts and other collections are handled by the Federal Reserve, as are federal payments, such as Social Security and federal employee payroll checks.

International Banking

As international trade has increased, the need for an international banking system has increased. Currencies of every nation must be made available to purchase goods that are produced in other countries. There must be an easy method of transferring payments between traders of different countries. In addition, companies often require loans to engage in international commerce.

Commercial banks. The most important segment of the international financial community is the worldwide network of commercial banks. Many large U.S. banks, such as the Bank of America, Citibank of New York, and the First National Bank of Chicago, have substantial foreign operations. These commercial banks, through branches and correspondent relationships, facilitate international trade in a number of ways. They hold funds for international traders, investors, and other banks that may be drawn upon for the purchase of goods produced abroad. A British firm involved in importing goods from the United States, for example, may have balances in U.S. banks from which it draws to pay for goods it purchases in the United States.

Commercial banks also lend funds to finance the purchase of goods or to invest. Since 1950, this function has become increasingly important as U.S. banks have lent large sums of money to foreign interests, often to finance the purchase of U.S. products. In the 1980's, however, the amount of outstanding foreign debt became a source of concern for many banks in the United States and around the world.

Many developing nations continue to incur more debt than their economies seem able to support. If foreign nations do default on a large portion of this debt, there could be severe economic repercussions. The banks involved would suffer a loss in earnings as they write off the unrepaid debt. Thus, fewer funds would be available for loans. This condition would drive interest rates up and discourage business investment.

Other organizations. In addition to the network of commercial banks, several national and international organizations have been established to facilitate international financial activities. Among the more important of these organizations are the Export-Import Bank, which helps finance foreign trade, and the International Monetary Fund, which makes loans to trading nations and countries experiencing balance-of-trade problems (for more information on these international organizations, see the International Trade section, page 292).

MOST LARGE AMERICAN BANKS *maintain branches in foreign cities.*

Business Finance

The general purpose of business financial activities is to make certain that a business has sufficient funds to meet day-to-day operating expenses and to fund major capital expenditures, for example, in expansion. The financial planning process is the procedure by which a company's financial resources and requirements are identified and strategies are developed for obtaining needed funds. Although companies differ in the way they perform this procedure, there are several steps that generally are taken in financial planning.

The first step is to determine the financial needs of the firm for the period under consideration, often called the planning period or planning horizon. These needs are frequently divided into long-range and short-range requirements, since they are often financed through different mechanisms. The company may decide, for example, that it will need to expand its production facility in five years. This would be considered a long-range requirement. Having sufficient cash to pay salaries, on the other hand, is an example of a short-range requirement.

For most companies, the primary source of funds is through the sale of the company's product. The company may also hold marketable securities or other investments from which it derives income. The company must estimate the amount of money that it will be taking in during the period that is being planned.

Once the requirements and sources of funds have been determined, the two can be compared. This tells the firm when income will be sufficient to meet requirements and when it will not. It also reveals the amount of additional funds that will be needed at various times. It is important that money is available when needed but, if borrowing is involved, it is also important not to secure funds before they are required: interest payments on money not put to use are an unnecessary expense.

After financing has been arranged, a system for recording relevant financial and accounting data must be established. Such a system is not only a legal requirement; it assists the firm in future financial planning.

The final step involves the implementation of a control system. Feedback on operations is necessary to determine whether activities are going as planned. If unexpected financial shortages should occur, the financial manager may react to this situation by securing additional financing. Similarly, if financing requirements are less than anticipated, the financial manager may cancel financing plans or arrange for the short-term investment of cash surpluses.

Short-Term Financing

Most companies experience fluctuations in revenue during the year. Their products may be seasonal, such as swimwear or ski equipment, or they may depend on other businesses that experience fluctuating sales, such as auto tire producers who depend on the production of new cars for much of their business.

Since expenses do not always vary directly with income, most firms find it necessary to obtain extra funds to finance their operations during slack periods. If such financing is accomplished through debt, these loans can be repaid when business picks up. Emergencies and unexpected events also may result in a temporary need for funds. Such short-term requirements are usually met through sources of short-term financing.

Internal sources. Generally, the least expensive and most readily accessible sources of financing are within a firm. Businesses usually have a considerable amount of money invested in assets. During slack periods, businesses can often reduce the level of some of these assets, such as inventory, and convert them into cash. A more stringent credit policy or more aggressive collection practices can reduce the level of accounts receivable. Unnecessary equipment may be sold, and personnel may be laid off.

External sources. There are also financing sources outside the company. One such source is trade, or mercantile, credit. Businesses generally buy inventory or raw materials on credit rather than for cash, and most suppliers invoice purchases once a month. Such bills normally must be paid within a specified period of time, typically one month. By taking advantage of such credit terms, companies can retain the use of their funds longer before paying for purchases.

Commercial loans. Loans from commercial banks are another external source of short-term financing. Next to trade credit, bank loans, either in the form of direct loans or lines of credit, are the most important external source of short-term business financing. A *line of credit* is a borrowing limit set by the bank. Banks offering a line of credit to a business usually require that the company maintain an account with the bank and guarantee a minimum balance. The borrower can borrow any amount up to the credit limit. This is a popular form of financing, since it can be arranged in advance, thus eliminating the need for costly emergency financing.

Commercial loans may be either secured or unsecured. A *secured loan* is one that is supported by specific assets of the company, called collateral. It gives the lender the right to take ownership of the collateral in the event that the borrower defaults on the loan. Common types of collateral for such loans are machinery, inventory, and accounts receivable.

An *unsecured loan* is backed by the general good credit of the borrower rather than a specific item of collateral. Unsecured loans, which are generally made in smaller amounts than secured loans, are normally available only to businesses with very good

---

A FINANCIAL PLAN FOR MAJOR PURCHASE

Object: Purchase of new equipment costing $1,000,000.

Money needed		Money source	
NOW		NOW	
Down payment of	$550,000	Loan (to be paid back over 10 years)	$550,000
LATER		LATER	
Due in 1 year	$150,000	From sales in year 1	$150,000
Due in 2 years	$150,000	From sales in year 2	$150,000
Due in 3 years	$150,000	From sales in year 3	$150,000
TOTAL NEEDED	$1,000,000	TOTAL SUPPLIED	$1,000,000

The company expects annual sales plus the increased profit from the use of the new equipment to cover the annual payments for the equipment as well as repayment of the initial loan plus interest.

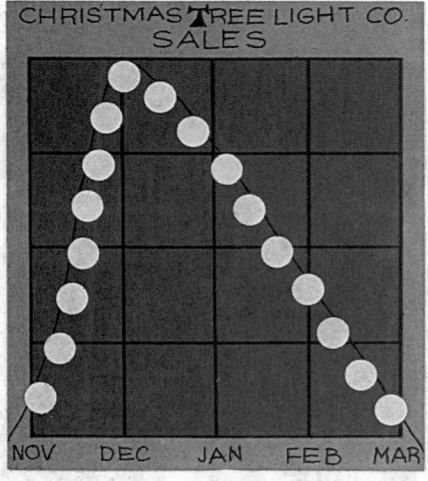

SHORT-TERM FINANCING *is intended for meeting immediate needs, such as cash flow problems resulting from slow sales. Long-term financing is intended for use in major projects, such as the building of a new factory.*

credit ratings or to those with which the bank has had previous satisfactory relations.

Factoring. Instead of using accounts receivable as collateral for a loan, a business may decide to sell its accounts receivable. This is called *factoring.* The factor, the business to which the receivables are sold, pays the company in cash for the accounts receivable. The amount paid is less than the face value of the receivables, usually between 50 and 80 percent of face value. Payments made on the accounts receivable go directly to the factor. The difference between the face value of the accounts receivable and the amount paid by the factor represents an allowance for profit and uncollectable accounts.

Commercial paper. A method of financing available only to the most creditworthy of firms is commercial paper. *Commercial paper* is unsecured promissory notes normally ranging in face value from $25,000 to $1 million; they generally mature within 270 days of issuance. An issuer usually must have a line of credit with a bank sufficient to redeem the notes in the event that the issuing company does not have sufficient funds at maturity of the notes.

Since commercial paper can be used only by the most financially secure firms, it represents a very low-risk investment for those who buy the commercial paper. Therefore, the interest rates are normally lower than those for bank financing. Buyers of commercial paper normally are those looking for a temporary and safe place to invest excess cash.

Long-Term Financing

If a company needs funds for a major project, such as the building of a new plant or the acquisition of a subsidiary, long-term financing is required. Long-term financing refers to funds that will be paid back over periods longer than a year or, as is the case with common stock, not paid back at all.

Internal sources. Among general sources of long-term financing, the major internal source is the retained earnings of the firm. Such funds represent profits that have been put back into the company rather than paid to the owners. By reducing or eliminating the distribution of profit to owners, firms can increase their retained earnings and, therefore, their working capital. If the firm is a corporation, this entails reducing or eliminating common stock dividends, something that companies often are reluctant to do. Such a move may erode investor confidence in the company and result in a decrease in the market price of the company's stock. It also may make future financing difficult or expensive to obtain.

External sources. The other two sources of long-term financing, both external, are debt financing and equity financing. *Debt financing,* as the name implies, involves borrowing. *Equity financing* entails the sale of stock to raise needed funds.

Debt financing. Bank loans constitute one of the major sources of longterm debt financing, just as they do for short-term financing. A common debt instrument is a mortgage loan, which involves the pledge of a fixed asset, such as land or equipment, to guarantee the loan.

Another common corporate form of long-term debt financing is issuance of corporate bonds. A bond is basically a long-term IOU, with maturities ranging from 5 to 40 years, whereby the issuer agrees to pay the holder a specified annual interest rate based on the face value of the bond rather than on the market value, which fluctuates. A $1000, 8 percent bond, for example, would return $80 a year to the bond-

holder regardless of the market value of the bond at any moment in time. The issuer also has the legal obligation to pay the face value of the bond at maturity. Many bond issues reserve to the issuing company the right of redemption; this means that the company may buy the bond back from the holder prior to maturity under specified conditions. Through the issuance of bonds, corporations can raise larger sums of money than would generally be made available through various lending institutions.

Two common types of bonds are mortgage bonds and debenture bonds. *Mortgage bonds* are bonds that, like mortgage loans, have a specified asset as collateral. *Debenture bonds,* on the other hand, are unsecured and backed only by the creditworthiness of the issuing company.

Equity financing. The most significant form of business financing is the capital committed to the firm by its owners. In corporations, ownership is acknowledged by shares of stock (see Capital Markets section, below).

There are two types of stock that a corporation may issue, common stock and preferred stock. *Common stock* represents the basic capitalization of the firm. Common stockholders have certain rights, including the right to attend stockholder meetings, vote on issues brought before the stockholders at those meetings, and elect the members of the board of directors. Common stockholders also have the right to inspect the financial records of the company, since they are the owners, and to share in the profits of the company in proportion to the number of shares held. Common stockholders are not guaranteed a dividend but have the right to receive a dividend should one be declared.

Preferred stock, as the name implies, entitles holders to special treatment. Unlike common stock, preferred stock has a stipulated dividend. There is no guarantee that the dividend will be paid, but if dividends are paid at all, preferred stockholders are entitled to the full amount of their stated dividend before any dividend may be paid to common stockholders. If the firm does not pay the stated dividend, the dividend typically accumulates and remains a liability of the firm until such time as it is paid. Preferred stockholders also have preferential rights to the assets of the company if the company is dissolved.

Although preferred stockholders have special privileges, they typically have fewer rights than common stockholders. Preferred stockholders, for example, have no voting rights at stockholder meetings and cannot participate in the election of the board of directors. The fixed annual return that is due to preferred stockholders puts them in a position similar to that of bondholders. The major difference is that preferred stockholders are not

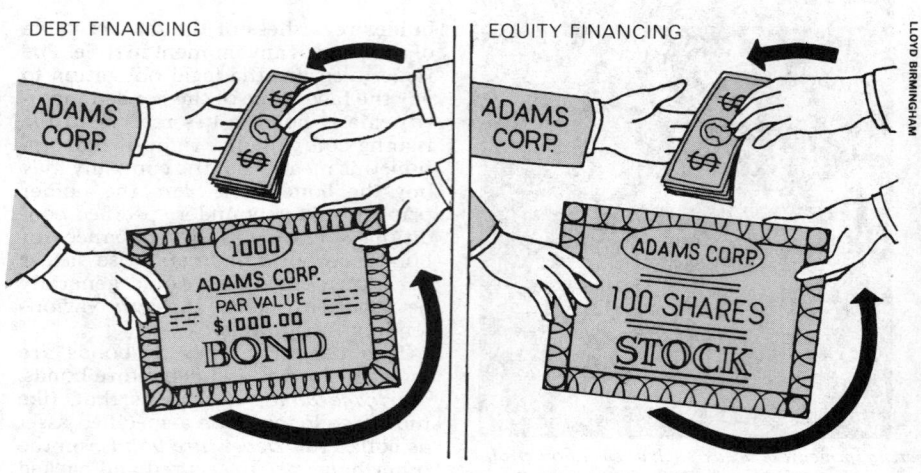

DEBT FINANCING

EQUITY FINANCING

ADAMS CORP.

1000
ADAMS CORP.
PAR VALUE
$1000.00
BOND

ADAMS CORP.
100 SHARES
STOCK

LLOYD BIRMINGHAM

IN DEBT FINANCING, *money received from sale of bonds must be repaid. In equity financing, sale of stock means partial loss of ownership.*

GRANT/PHOTO RESEARCHERS

AS OWNERS, *stockholders can have a say in the way a company is run.*

guaranteed an annual return on their investment.

Debt vs. equity financing. There are advantages and disadvantages to both debt and equity financing. One advantage of debt financing is that debtholders are creditors of the company rather than owners. As such, they have no say in the management of the company. A firm incurring debt normally retains full managerial control, although banks in some cases may place restrictions on operations as a condition of indebtedness.

A second advantage of debt financing is that the cost of debt service, the interest on the debt, is tax deductible. Dividends paid to stockholders must be paid with after-tax dollars. Another advantage of debt financing is leverage. *Leverage* occurs when borrowed funds are used for a purpose that yields a return that is greater than the cost of the debt. If a company can put borrowed funds to use in such a manner that it will return more than the interest charges, the firm is experiencing leverage. (See Mergers heading in Business section, page 312, for discussion of leveraged buyouts; that is, the use of leverage in corporate acquisitions.)

There also are disadvantages to debt financing. One is that the debt must eventually be repaid, while capital raised through the issuance of stock need never be repaid. A second disadvantage is that the interest payments on debt represent a fixed and inescapable expense. In the event of default, the bondholders may claim the collateral behind the debt. Common stock dividends, on the other hand, may be reduced or even eliminated if insufficient funds are available.

Equity financing, nevertheless, has certain advantages over debt financing. As has been said, the investment of the stockholders need never be repaid. Furthermore, payment of dividends is left to the discretion of the firm and does not represent a legal obligation. Issuing stock rather than incurring

debt also makes the firm appear more financially sound.

There also are disadvantages associated with equity financing. Since common stockholders are essentially the owners of the company and have the right to vote at stockholders' meetings, management activities are ultimately subject to the wishes of the stockholders. The management of a company, for example, may be convinced that profits should be reinvested to promote growth. Stockholders, however, may be much more interested in dividends.

Long-term debt and stock, taken together, are referred to as a firm's *capitalization structure,* the means by which the firm acquires its permanent financing. Selecting the appropriate capitalization mix, that is, the combination of debt and equity, is extremely important, since it may affect the price of the firm's stock and its creditworthiness as well as its long-term viability.

Capital Markets

The markets in which corporate securities (stocks and bonds) are sold are known as *primary markets* and *secondary markets*.

Primary markets. When a company wishes to raise money by selling stocks or bonds, it generally does not try to sell the securities directly to the public. It relies instead on an intermediary, called an *investment banker* or *underwriter,* who buys the securities from the issuing corporation and resells them in smaller lots to other investment bankers or individual investors through securities exchanges. If the dollar amount of the stock or bond issue is particularly large, several underwriters may join together to buy the securities. Under-

writers make a profit by selling securities for more than they paid for them.

Secondary markets. Once any securities have been sold to an underwriter, the issuing company is no longer involved, except when redeeming bonds at maturity or when redeeming preferred stock. Subsequent sales are made between individual buyers and sellers.

To fulfill the need to bring buyers and sellers of securities together, securities exchanges have developed. A securities exchange is an auction in which, through brokers, buyers and sellers negotiate the selling prices of stocks and bonds. Despite the formal and computerized nature of modern exchanges, the hectic activity of the auction house remains a distinctive characteristic of securities exchanges.

The New York Stock Exchange (NYSE). The largest securities exchange in the United States is the New York Stock Exchange, established in 1792 by a group of merchants who met daily to buy and sell securities. Initially, they met beneath a buttonwood tree on Wall Street, but eventually the New York Stock Exchange moved into a building at the corner of Wall and Broad streets. The New York Stock Exchange handles over 2000 securities of more than 1500 corporations. In order to be listed on the Big Board, companies must meet stringent requirements, the strictest of any U.S. exchange. Highly speculative securities or the securities of financially unsound companies cannot be listed on the NYSE, and only listed securities may be traded on the exchange.

Only members of the New York Stock Exchange may trade on the exchange, and membership is limited to 1366 members. To become a member of the NYSE, one must buy a seat, as a membership is called, from a member who wants to sell (see box on page 307).

THE NEW YORK STOCK EXCHANGE— WHO ARE THE PLAYERS?

When the bell rings at 9:30 A.M., Eastern time, trading begins on the floor of the New York Stock Exchange, the largest securities market in the United States. Many of the brokers have already been there for more than an hour, getting a feel for the market and preparing for the activities of the day.

There are four types of members: specialists and three kinds of floor brokers—commission brokers, independent floor brokers, or registered competitive market makers.

Specialists. *Specialists,* who are either officers or partners of member firms, act as catalysts in the trading process. Each of the more than 300 specialists is assigned one or more stocks, depending on the size of the company or companies whose stock the specialist handles. Each specialist works at one of the trading posts located on the floor of the exchange, the only place on the floor where a particular stock may be bought or sold. The tall posts that once marked the specialists' positions on the floor have been replaced with electronic equipment that has greatly improved the speed with which customer orders are processed. Television screens above the specialists' positions now provide financial data.

Specialists receive no commission for their service. They make a profit by trading on their own portfolios. They may not, however, buy or sell stocks for their own accounts until all orders from the floor brokers have been satisfied.

In addition to facilitating the trade of stocks assigned to them, specialists provide another valuable service for the securities market. It is their responsibility to maintain a degree of stability in the price of the stocks they sell by buying or selling against the trend when trading becomes unbalanced. For example, if many more shares of a stock are offered for sale than investors want to buy, the price of that stock might be driven down sharply. Under such circumstances, the specialist who handles that stock must buy shares to bring the trading more closely in balance. If more people want to buy than sell, the specialist is required to sell shares to balance the market.

Commission brokers. The largest group of floor brokers is made up of *commission brokers,* who buy and sell stocks on behalf of their clients. Assume, for example, that Mrs. Smith wants to buy 100 shares of XYZ Company at a certain price. She contacts her local stockbroker, who relays Mrs. Smith's order to the brokerage firm's commission broker on the floor of the exchange. The commission broker then takes Mrs. Smith's order to the post at which XYZ Company is traded and gets a quote of the current market price from the specialist. If another floor broker has left an order with the specialist to sell 100 shares of XYZ at the price specified by Mrs. Smith, the commission broker may buy the shares through the specialist. The commission broker may also buy directly from another floor broker who has come to the trading post to sell 100 shares of XYZ.

Computerized trading. In addition to the face-to-face interaction between floor brokers and specialists, many transactions are executed electronically through the NYSE's SuperDot system. This system enables orders to be routed automatically from the broker to the trading post where the computerized system matches sell orders with buy orders and executes the transaction without the personal intervention of the commission broker. For example, if Mrs. Smith's order to buy 100 shares of XYZ was a *market order,* an order to buy at the current market price, the commission broker would probably not be personally involved. Computers would match the buy order with an order to sell at the market, and the transaction would be electronically executed.

Independent floor brokers. *Independent floor brokers* are entrepreneurs who execute orders for the companies that are their clients. If a company does not have its own floor broker, for example, it may engage an independent floor broker to execute orders on its behalf.

Registered competitive market makers. *Registered competitive market makers* are securities dealers who buy and sell for their own accounts. They make no purchases or sales for customers.

The members of the exchange, their support staff, and the approximately 700 NYSE employees bring the total number on the floor during business hours to about 2700, all crammed into 30,000 square feet of floor space.

The exchange has many rules regarding behavior on the floor. Running is prohibited, squirt guns are outlawed, sneakers may not be worn, and food and drink are not allowed.

By the time the buzzer rings at 4:00 p.m., when trading stops, the floor of the exchange indicates that there is no rule against littering. Before computerization reduced the need for brokers to carry around great numbers of notes, it was not unusual for janitors to remove three tons of debris after a vigorous trading day.

STOCK PRICES *are quoted on an electronic board* (above). *Brokers use hand signals* (below left) *to communicate transactions that they then record* (below right).

Stock information. Here is how *The Wall Street Journal* lists the daily information about the New York Stock Exchange. Most daily newspapers provide stock tables in the same format.

1. The highest and lowest prices paid for the stock over the previous year.
2. Abbreviated name of the company.
3. Amount of last quarterly dividend; "pf" means preferred stock; no indication means common stock.
4. Yield, or the percentage of the stock price returned in its annual dividend.
5. Price-earnings ratio, the ratio between the stock's current value and the company's most recent report of earnings per share.
6. Shares traded in 100's.
7. The day's high price.
8. The day's low price.
9. The day's final price.
10. Change over the previous day; no indication means zero change.

1		2	3	4	5	6	7	8	9	10
$61\frac{1}{2}$	$26\frac{5}{8}$	GnInst	.50	1.0	15	4179	53	$50\frac{1}{2}$	$52\frac{1}{4}$	$+2\frac{1}{4}$
$54\frac{3}{4}$	33	GnMills	1.84	4.0	10	799	$46\frac{3}{8}$	$45\frac{5}{8}$	$45\frac{7}{8}$	$-\frac{1}{4}$
$65\frac{1}{2}$	34	GMot	2.40e	3.9	21	7362	$62\frac{1}{2}$	$61\frac{1}{8}$	$61\frac{3}{4}$	$+1\frac{5}{8}$
$49\frac{3}{4}$	37	GMot	pf5	11.	...	6	$47\frac{1}{2}$	47	47	$-\frac{1}{4}$
$32\frac{7}{8}$	$8\frac{3}{4}$	GNC	.16	.6	27	62	28	$26\frac{7}{8}$	$27\frac{1}{4}$	$-\frac{1}{8}$
$8\frac{1}{8}$	$4\frac{1}{2}$	GPU		...	15	816	8	$7\frac{3}{4}$	$7\frac{7}{8}$	$+\frac{1}{8}$
$65\frac{1}{2}$	$33\frac{7}{8}$	GenRe	s1.08	1.9	13	554	$57\frac{1}{4}$	$56\frac{5}{8}$	57	....
$4\frac{7}{8}$	$2\frac{3}{8}$	GnRefr		...	...	55	$4\frac{3}{8}$	$4\frac{1}{4}$	$4\frac{3}{8}$	$+\frac{1}{8}$
47	28	GnSignl	1.68	3.7	11	247	$46\frac{3}{8}$	46	46	$-\frac{1}{4}$
$11\frac{5}{8}$	8	GTFI	pf1.25	11.	...	z100	11	11	11	....
12	$8\frac{3}{4}$	GTFI	pf1.30	11.	...	z10	$11\frac{1}{2}$	$11\frac{1}{2}$	$11\frac{1}{2}$	$+\frac{3}{4}$
70	53	GTFI	pf8.16	12.	...	z200	70	70	70	$+2\frac{1}{8}$

STOCK INDEXES

A stock index is a composite of the prices of a selected group of stocks. It reflects the general movement of the stock market during a day, week, month, year, or any period of time. The most commonly used indexes are the Dow-Jones Industrial Average, the Dow-Jones Transportation Average, the Dow-Jones Utility Average, and the Dow-Jones Composite Average.

Dow-Jones.   The Dow-Jones Industrial Average is computed from the prices of 30 well-established industrial stock issues, stocks that are in the *blue chip* category and have a stable record of performance. The composition of the 30 firms changes from time to time, as does the composition of the stocks used to compute the other indexes.

The Dow-Jones Transportation Average is computed from the prices of 20 transportation stocks; the Utility Average from the prices of 15 utility stocks; and the Composite Average from the 65 stocks used to calculate the other three indexes.

These averages have been used for many years, the Industrial Average dating back to 1896, when it included twelve stocks. The Transportation Index, also dating back to 1896, was a railroad average until 1970, when it was expanded to include the stocks of other transportation firms. The Utility Average was first used in 1929, and the Composite Average was first computed in 1933.

Standard and Poor's.   Another commonly used stock index is the Standard and Poor's 500 Composite Index. More broadly based than the Dow-Jones averages, it is computed from the prices of 500 stocks: 400 industrial stocks, 20 transportation stocks, 40 utilities, and 40 financial stocks. Generally, the Standard and Poor's Composite Index and the Dow-Jones Composite Average move in the same direction.

Stock indexes are used not only as measures of overall stock market performance but as predictors of business activity. They experience ups and downs that generally precede similar swings in business activity.

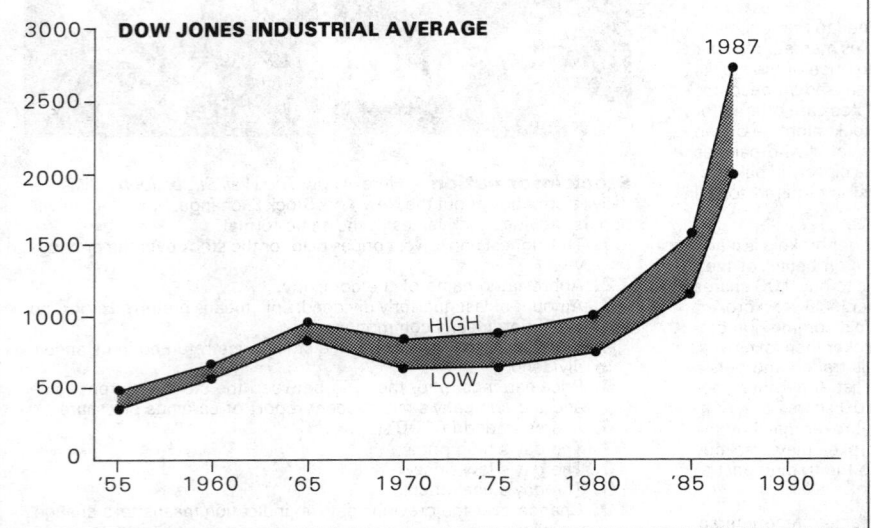

DOW JONES INDUSTRIAL AVERAGE

American Stock Exchange (AMEX).
The American Stock Exchange, also located in New York City, is not as large as the New York Stock Exchange. It handles the securities of about 600 companies that are not listed on the New York Stock Exchange. Although the listing requirements are not as stringent as those for the NYSE, the AMEX does carry the securities of many reputable firms.

Regional exchanges.   In addition to the New York Stock Exchange and the American Stock Exchange, there are seven regional exchanges. These include the Mid-West Stock Exchange in Chicago; the Pacific Coast Stock Exchange, with operations in San Francisco and Los Angeles; the Boston; Cincinatti; Intermountain, located in Salt Lake City; Philadelphia; and Spokane exchanges. These regional exchanges normally trade the securities of small, sometimes local companies.

Over-the-counter market (OTC).
The OTC market is somewhat unusual in that, unlike the exchanges, it does not have a physical location. Instead, a computerized communications system developed by the National Association of Securities Dealers links together 3700 dealers across the United States. There are no listing requirements in the OTC market. The stocks traded are normally those of small and medium-sized firms, many of which do not meet the requirements of the NYSE or AMEX. The OTC market has grown considerably over the years; more than 4000 stocks of over 3600 companies now are traded on the OTC market.

Regulation of securities exchanges.
Securities exchanges are regulated by state and federal statutes and regulatory agencies. The primary federal regulatory agency is the Securities and Exchange Commission (SEC). Any company desiring to sell its securities to the general public must first file a registration statement with the SEC; the statement contains information regarding the issuing company, its management, and operations. It must include a description of the securities the firm would like to sell as well as copies of the firm's financial statements.

Securities described in registration statements are called *registered securities*. Registration does not constitute an endorsement by the SEC or a guarantee that the securities will return a profit to investors. The SEC does not even guarantee that the information contained in the registration statement is true. The primary purpose is to provide the public with information upon which to make investment decisions. If the registration statement is found to be false, the person or persons responsible may be subject to fine or imprisonment or both. Numerous federal statutes regulate the securities industry. The Securities Act of 1933 provides for the filing of registration statements with the SEC, outlines conditions under which securities are exempt from the requirement, and contains antifraud provisions that apply to unregistered securities as well as to registered securities.

The Securities Exchange Act of 1934 gives the SEC sweeping regulatory powers with respect to the operation of securities exchanges. Under this act, securities exchanges are required to register with the SEC, which has the power to oversee the self-regulatory practices of national exchanges and regulate the activities of securities dealers and brokers.

The Investment Company Act of 1940 requires investment companies to register with the SEC and gives the commission the power to regulate management fees, composition of boards of directors, and capital structure of such firms.

The Investment Advisors Act of 1940 requires that all dealers or other persons engaged in the business of giving advice with respect to securities transactions register with the SEC.

State regulation.   State governments also regulate the purchase and sale of financial securities. Most states have enacted *blue sky laws,* which are designed to protect potential investors against fraud and unscrupulous securities dealers.

Foreign stock exchanges.   In
addition to the stock exchanges in the United States, there are many large and important secondary markets in other countries. In Canada, there are five major exchanges: the Alberta Stock Exchange, the Montreal Stock Exchange, the Toronto Stock Exchange, the Vancouver Stock Exchange, and the Winnipeg Stock Exchange.

There are also major exchanges in Tokyo, London, Frankfort, Sydney, Paris, Zurich, Hong Kong, Milan, Amsterdam, and Singapore.

BUSINESS

The term *business* refers to the totality of activities of profit-seeking organizations involved in the development, production, and distribution of goods and services. Some businesses provide tangible goods, such as automobiles or clothing, while others provide services, such as hotel rooms or insurance policy coverage.

Although the desire for profit is the main objective of business enterprises, a number of other objectives are also important, for example, growth. Growth makes some businesses more profitable because overhead costs can be spread over more units of production. Growth is also viewed as a sign of success. Entrepreneurs see their businesses grow and feel a strong sense of satisfaction.

STRATFORD/PHOTO RESEARCHERS

KROLL/TAURUS PHOTOS

THESE TWO BUSINESSES *are different, but their owners have many of the same objectives.*

Forms of Business Organization

The three major forms of business organization are sole proprietorships, partnerships, and corporations. Each type of business has distinctive characteristics and advantages and disadvantages compared with the others.

Sole Proprietorships

The simplest form of business organization is the sole proprietorship, a business owned and operated by one person. It is the most common form of business, accounting for about three-fourths of all the businesses in the United States. Since sole proprietorships are usually small, they account for only about 10 percent of all business revenues and only about 5 percent of all business profits.

Advantages. The sole proprietorship is the easiest type of business to initiate. One reason is that there is no legal distinction between a sole proprietorship and the sole proprietor. There is relatively little red tape involved in the initiation of a sole proprietorship, as there is with other forms, such as the corporation. Anyone

may initiate a sole proprietorship. The cost involved is usually low compared with the cost of initiating other types of businesses.

A sole proprietorship may be dissolved as easily as it was formed, primarily because there are no obligations to stockholders. The owner simply satisfies all outstanding debts and discontinues the business.

The sole proprietor may run a business without having to answer to higher management, a board of directors, or stockholders. The owner, therefore, can respond to changing business conditions more quickly than can partnerships or corporations. In addition, all the profits from the business go to the sole owner, not to a partner or to stockholders.

Disadvantages. There are some disadvantages associated with a sole proprietorship. One of the most significant is the unlimited liability of the owner. Just as a sole proprietor is entitled to all of the profits, the proprietor is also personally responsible for all of the debts of the business.

Since a sole proprietorship is usually small, arranging for financing may be a problem. A sole proprietorship is typically financed by the savings and borrowing power of the proprietor.

Debts often must be secured by the personal assets of the owner, such as the owner's home or personal investments. The creditworthiness of the business is thus restrained by the creditworthiness of the owner. Therefore, the availability of credit is not as great as with a corporation, or with a partnership.

Once the business starts up, financing requirements are usually met primarily from profits. There may not be an abundance of funds available for business expansion, modernization of equipment, or other needs associated with an ongoing business.

A sole proprietorship normally does not have available an abundance of specialized management expertise. Its small size and limited resources result in the owner making most of the management decisions. Since few entrepreneurs are experts in all areas of management, the result may be less than effective management of some aspects of the business.

Partnerships

A partnership is a business owned by two or more persons. It has some of the characteristics of a sole proprietorship, including the fact that it is legally indistinguishable from its owners.

Partnership agreement. The rights and responsibilities of the partners are generally specified in a *partnership agreement.* Such an agreement may be either oral or written, but it is sound business practice for it to be in writing and signed by all of the partners. Written partnership agreements are referred to as *articles of partnership* and typically include the following: names of the partners and amount of money or other property that each has invested; procedures for distributing profits and covering losses; duties of each partner; procedures for dissolving the partnership; and the circumstances under which new partners may be admitted.

Types of partnerships. There are two types of partners, general partners and limited partners. A *general partner* is one who is actively involved in the management of the business and receives a share of the profits. A general partner is personally responsible for the debts of the business.

A *limited partner* is one whose liability is limited to the amount the partner has invested. A limited partner does not take the active management role that the general partner does. The limited partner is more of an investor than an entrepreneur, that is, someone who initiates and assumes the risk of running a business.

The limited partnership arrangement is one method of attracting capital to a small business. An individual who fears the high risk associated with being a general partner may be willing to invest when liability is limited.

A partnership in which all partners are general partners is referred to as a *general partnership,* whereas a partnership consisting of both general and limited partners is referred to as a *limited partnership.* Even in a limited partnership, at least one of the partners must be a general partner.

Advantages. A partnership has many of the same advantages as a sole proprietorship—ease of formation, management flexibility, and profit incentive for the owners. It has the added advantage of being able to attract more capital than a sole proprietorship because the fact of having more than one owner generally increases the creditworthiness of the business. Additionally, the ability to admit limited partners makes possible additional capital contributions from the new partners.

Disadvantages. Like a sole proprietorship, a partnership has a limited life. Its existence is even more precarious than that of the sole proprietorship. If any one of the general partners should die or withdraw from the business, the partnership is considered to be legally terminated. If the remaining partners desire to carry on the business, it must be reorganized as a new business.

Joint ventures. A special type of partnership that became increasingly popular during the 1980's is the *joint venture,* in which two or more companies combine to accomplish a common objective. The companies nevertheless retain their own independence and, if the project is established as one of limited life, will sever their relationship after its completion.

Corporations

The largest and most powerful companies in the world are *corporations.* They account for over 80 percent of all business income in the United States, although they represent only about 15 percent of the total number of known businesses.

Legal entity. A corporation is significantly different from either a sole proprietorship or a partnership. One of the major differences is that a corporation is a legal entity separate from the owners, who are called *stockholders* or *shareholders.* Chief Justice Marshall described a corporation as "an artificial being, invisible, intangible, and existing only in contemplation of the law."

As a legal entity, a corporation has many of the same rights and responsibilities as a person. Corporations pay taxes, borrow money, sue, hire people, fire people, and sell goods and services.

Although a corporation is only an "artificial" person, the distinction between a corporation and a person has diminished over the years. In the late 1970's, Ford Motor Company became the first corporation to be criminally charged and tried. It was charged with, but found not guilty of, reckless homicide as a result of the deaths of three girls who died when the gas tank of a Ford Pinto exploded.

Advantages. The corporate form of business has several advantages over other forms. One of the most significant advantages is that the liability of the stockholders is limited to the amount of their investment. If a corporation goes bankrupt, the stockholders lose their investment but cannot be held liable for the debts of the company beyond that amount. (There are some exceptions to the limited liability protection. Investors may be held liable, for example, for Social Security taxes withheld from employees' wages yet not paid to the government.)

A corporation generally has far greater ability to raise capital than either a sole proprietorship or a partnership: it can sell stock and issue bonds to the general public. Another advantage of a corporation is that it is able to hire managers with specialized expertise because it is generally larger and has greater financial resources than a partnership or a proprietorship. Unlike a partnership or a proprietorship, when a stockholder dies or sells stock, the corporation continues to exist.

Disadvantages. The corporate form is not without drawbacks. One of the most significant is what is known as *double taxation.* When a partnership or a proprietorship makes a profit, that profit is taxed as part of the owners' personal income. Since a corporation is a legal entity, its profits are taxed just as the incomes of other legal persons are. When the corporation pays out a portion of its profit to the stockholders in the form of dividends, the dividends are also taxable as personal income of the recipients. Thus, the same dollars are taxed as income twice, once as corporate profit and once as personal income.

PARTNERSHIPS are called general *when all partners are actively involved in the business, and* limited *when one or more partners are not.*

GENERAL PARTNER

LIMITED PARTNER

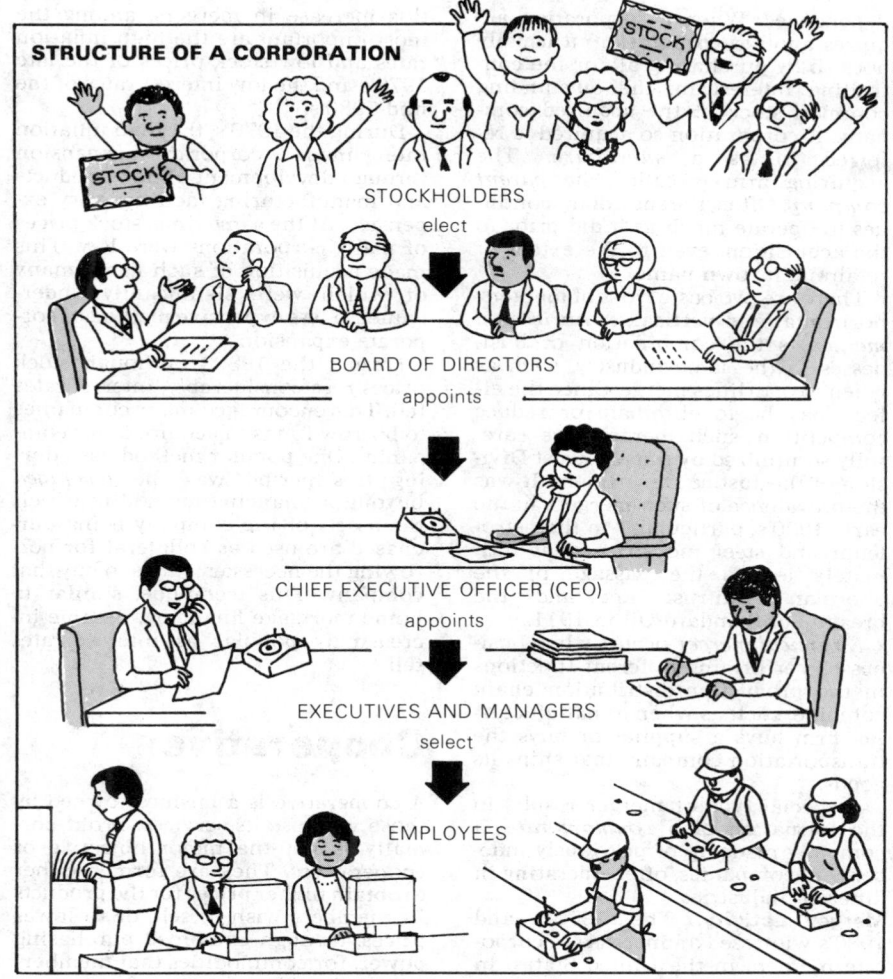

STRUCTURE OF A CORPORATION

STOCKHOLDERS

elect

BOARD OF DIRECTORS

appoints

CHIEF EXECUTIVE OFFICER (CEO)

appoints

EXECUTIVES AND MANAGERS

select

EMPLOYEES

A special type of corporation, called a *subchapter S corporation,* avoids the disadvantage of double taxation. The profits of such a corporation are not taxed at the corporate level but flow straight to the individual stockholders; they are taxed as personal income only. Not all corporations qualify for the subchapter S classification because there are a number of restrictions. Subchapter S corporations, for example, may have no more than a total of 25 stockholders.

A corporation is also much more difficult to initiate or terminate than a proprietorship or a partnership. There are significantly more legal requirements, such as the obtaining of a corporate charter from the state. Because of its size, a corporation is also subject to considerably more regulation and government scrutiny than are partnerships and proprietorships. The operations of a corporation are restricted not only by the government, but by its own charter. A corporate charter, which is the company's legal authorization to conduct business as a corporation, limits the power of the corporation and restricts its activities to those generally described in the charter. If a corporation wishes to alter any aspect of its charter, it must obtain stockholder approval. Thus, a corporation may have less flexibility than a sole proprietorship or a partnership.

Because the owners of a corporation are generally not the managers, much of the incentive that drives a sole proprietor may be missing from the management of a corporation.

Structure of a corporation.
The owners of a corporation become owners by purchasing shares of ownership in the company. They generally receive a document called a *stock certificate,* which indicates the type of stock and number of shares owned (see Capital Markets section, page 306).

Board of directors. The stockholders elect the board of directors, the chief governing body of the corporation. The board of directors' role is to represent the stockholders' interests. In fact, the stockholders may hold board members personally liable if they fail to execute their responsibilities properly. The board of directors appoints the corporate officers, who conduct the day-to-day activities of the company.

A board of directors often includes both inside and outside directors. An *inside director* is one who works for the firm, usually as a senior officer, and

serves on the board. An *outside director* is one who is not employed or otherwise associated with the company except in the capacity of board member. The responsibilities of the board of directors typically include defining corporate goals and objectives; evaluating corporate officers; formulating corporate policies; and deciding on major corporate strategies, compensation for top managers, and stock dividends and stock splits.

Corporate officers. The officers of the corporation manage the day-to-day operations of the company in accordance with the policies established by the board. They are also responsible for staffing the organization and supervising its employees.

Types of corporations.
The distinctions made between types of corporations are generally based on ownership.

Private corporations. *Private corporations,* also referred to as privately held corporations, are corporations whose stock is owned by members of the public. Private corporations can be further divided into *open corporations* and *closed corporations.* The stock of an open corporation is generally widely dispersed and available to anyone who wishes to buy it. The stock of such companies is usually traded on one of the securities exchanges or over the counter.

The stock of a closed corporation, on the other hand, is generally not available to the public. The stock of such companies is usually held by a small group of stockholders, sometimes family members or the employees of the firm, and not traded on any securities exchange. A *closely held corporation* is similar to a closed corporation in that its stock is generally not widely dispersed. The stock of such companies may, however, be available to the general public on a limited basis.

MANY COMPANIES *are privately held, unlike most well-known companies.*

Public corporations. Unlike private corporations, a *public corporation,* such as the Tennessee Valley Authority, is owned by the federal, state, or local government. It is not organized for the purpose of making a profit, but for the benefit of the public.

Quasi-public corporations are corporations whose ownership is divided between the government and private citizens. Such corporations typically provide a needed public service, but they may be exposed to a great degree of risk, as with railroad corporations.

Nonprofit corporations. *Nonprofit corporations,* which include many hospitals and state universities, are incorporated to acquire the limited liability of the corporate form, but they are not operated for the purpose of returning a profit to the owners.

Mergers. As has been said, one objective of most corporations is growth, which is desirable for many reasons. If a business is capital intensive, greater size means greater economies of scale: large overhead expenses may be spread over more units of production, thus lowering the unit costs. This serves to make the firm more competitive and adds to profits as well. Firms also grow to reduce the risk associated with business cycles. By expanding into many industries, a corporation becomes less prone to the cycles existing in any one industry. It is believed unlikely that a highly diversified firm will experience business downturns in all areas of operations simultaneously.

One way to accomplish growth is through a *merger;* this occurs when one company acquires another with the acquiring company retaining its independence. When a corporation acquires another corporation, it usually does so by purchasing all, or the controlling interest in, the outstanding common stock of the acquired company. A corporation so acquired is referred to as a *subsidiary.* The acquiring firm is called the *parent company.* Often, the subsidiary continues to operate much as it did prior to the acquisition, even to the extent of retaining its own name.

There are two basic types of mergers, horizontal and vertical. A *horizontal merger* is the combination of businesses in the same industry, such as when two airlines merge. Since the effect may be to eliminate or reduce competition, such mergers are carefully scrutinized by the Antitrust Division of the Justice Department. It was the prevalence of such mergers in the early 1900's, particularly in the petroleum and steel industries, that ultimately led to the passage of the Sherman Antitrust Act and the breakup of Standard Oil in 1911.

A *vertical merger* occurs when businesses performing different functions in the production/distribution chain combine, such as when a manufacturing firm buys a supplier or buys the transportation company that ships its goods.

A special type of merger results in the formation of a *conglomerate,* a company made up of previously independent companies, often operating in different industries.

Merger activity. The 1970's and 1980's witnessed an increase in corporate mergers in the United States. In 1981, for example, there were about one-third more mergers than in 1980. Although many reasons are cited for this increase in mergers, among the most important are the high inflation rates and low stock prices of the late 1970's and the low interest rates of the mid-1980's.

During the 1970's, the high inflation rate made corporate expansion through development of new products and manufacturing facilities very expensive. At the same time, stock prices of many corporations were low. This made acquisition of such firms, many of which were significantly undervalued, a less expensive method of corporate expansion.

During the 1980's, although stock prices rose considerably, interest rates fell. This encouraged many companies to borrow funds to acquire other companies. One popular method used during this period was the *leveraged* buyout, a financing method in which the assets of the company being purchased are used as collateral for borrowing the necessary funds to buy that company. This technique, similar to home mortgage financing, became increasingly popular as interest rates fell.

Cooperatives

A cooperative is a business owned by those who use its services. Profit normally is not the major objective of cooperatives. They are formed either to obtain higher prices for the products its members wish to sell, or to lower prices, through combined purchasing power, for commodities that members wish to buy. The earnings of a cooperative are distributed to the members in proportion to the shares they own.

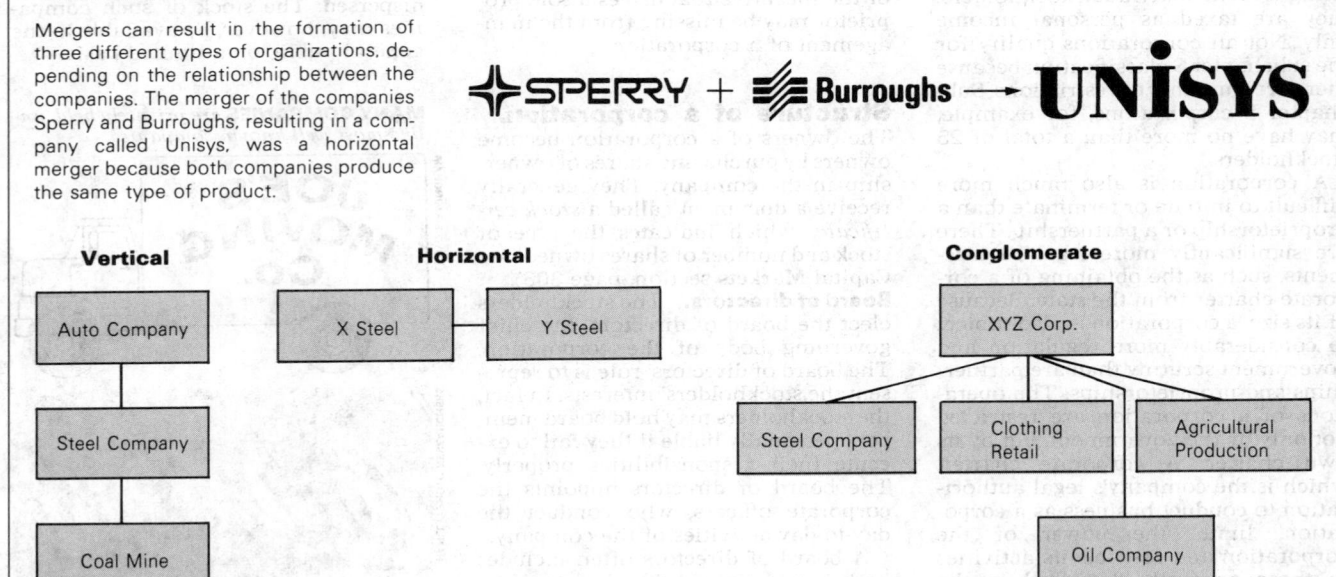

TYPES OF MERGERS

Mergers can result in the formation of three different types of organizations, depending on the relationship between the companies. The merger of the companies Sperry and Burroughs, resulting in a company called Unisys, was a horizontal merger because both companies produce the same type of product.

Since cooperatives are regulated by state statutes, their forms vary from state to state.

Cooperatives first appeared in the agricultural industry, but they have since expanded into other areas, such as utilities and credit unions. Some cooperatives incorporate to take advantage of corporate tax laws. A major advantage of the cooperative form of business organization is that a cooperative may deduct from taxable income the dividends paid to shareholders. Even unincorporated cooperatives tend to be managed much like corporations, since shareholders seldom participate actively in management.

Franchising

A franchise is an arrangement in which a parent company, called a *franchiser,* grants permission to a private person, called a *franchisee,* to market a product or service of the franchiser, using the name and goodwill of the franchiser. The franchisee may also receive marketing and management assistance, as well as other operational assistance, from the franchiser.

In exchange, the franchisee agrees to abide by the rules set forth by the franchiser. The franchiser may require that the franchisee use a standardized building reflecting the name of the parent company, buy stipulated supplies from the franchiser, market only the goods of the franchiser, and return a specified percentage of the franchisee's earnings to the franchiser. The franchisee usually must pay an initial franchising fee.

Although franchises exist in many types of businesses, they are particularly common in the hotel/motel and food service industries. Best Western, Ramada Inns, and Holiday Inns are all franchise operations, as are McDonald's Corporation, Pizza Hut, and Ponderosa Steaks.

Franchises are unlike chain-store operations in that the franchisee is le-

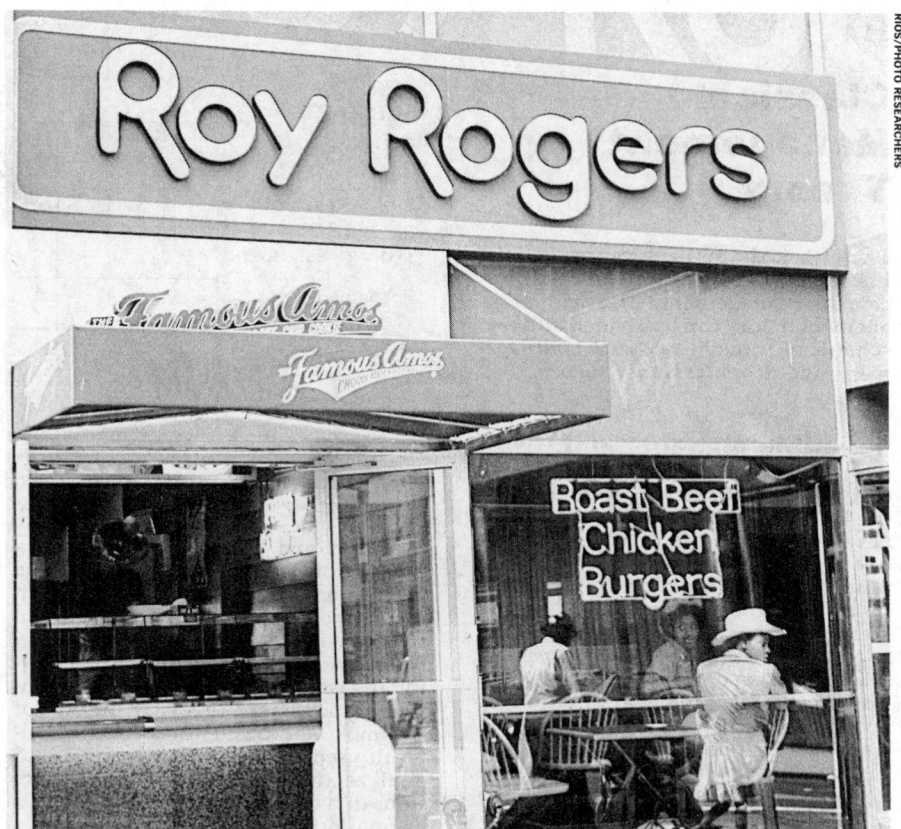

A FRANCHISE *can be like a Roy Rogers restaurant, in which many functions are regulated by the franchiser, or like Famous Amos cookies, in which the franchiser may only distribute the cookies.*

gally considered an independent business person. Although often strictly controlled by the franchise agreement, the franchisee is nonetheless an entrepreneur who pays taxes and assumes the liability associated with operating as an independent business person.

Franchises have been successful for a number of reasons. One advantage of franchises is that they combine many of the benefits of a large corporation with the benefits of local ownership. Since the franchiser is usually a large corporation, the franchisee often benefits from the purchasing power of the franchiser. The local business also benefits from national advertising that

it would not be able to afford on its own.

Local ownership provides management that is knowledgeable about the marketing area. There is also a high degree of motivation, since local managers run their own businesses. A franchise is also a business that a local entrepreneur can enter with a minimum of capital and still have an instant market, since people are already familiar with the product or service that is offered. This results in a much higher success rate, since one of the major problems associated with a new business is establishing a customer base.

Management

Management, the process of organizing resources and directing people in such a manner as to achieve the objectives of a company, generally reflects the needs and demands of society as well as those of business. During the period following the Industrial Revolution, for example, the demand for goods and services increased at an unparalleled rate. As a result, those managers were most successful who could combine large amounts of raw materials, labor, and capital in such a

manner as to meet this demand. There was little concern at the time for the rights of the individual worker; society as a whole was more concerned with production. Thus, the stern taskmasters who could cajole, coerce, or otherwise motivate their subordinates to higher and higher levels of productivity were highly rewarded in salaries, shares of ownership, housing, expense allowances, and other perquisites.

In contrast, in the last two decades, society has made it clear that produc-

tion of abundant goods and services is not the only responsibility of the business community. Businesses also have the responsibility not to discriminate when hiring or promoting employees, not to pollute, and to create a working environment in which employees can realize their potential and be satisfied in their work. This change in the perception of the purpose of business has brought about changes in the functions of those who run businesses, the managers.

Classical Management Theory

The classical approach represents the first formal attempt to study the process of management. Classical management theory can be divided into two schools of thought, *scientific management* and *organizational theory.*

Scientific management. Even though there are many examples of early use of management techniques in the United States, the most significant developments in the theory and practice of management came after the Industrial Revolution. For the first time in history, the technology existed to couple large amounts of labor with capital to form a new *factory system.*

This new type of business organization allowed greater proliferation of goods and services, but such advances were not without problems. Coordinating the efforts of large groups of people and doing so in such a manner as to realize the greatest degree of efficiency became crucial. Thus, many of the early management theorists and practitioners concentrated on productivity and efficiency.

Frederick Taylor. One management pioneer was American engineer and management consultant Frederick Taylor (1856–1915), who used time studies in an attempt to determine the "one best way of performing a task." Working primarily in the U.S. steel industry, Taylor was able to break down many work tasks into the their essential components and develop the quickest way to perform them. This method of increasing productivity became known as the *scientific approach to management.* To encourage employees to meet work standards, Taylor also developed incentive wage plans designed to reward those employees who were most productive.

Henry Gantt. Henry Gantt (1861–1919) and Frank Gilbreth (1868–1924), American engineers, and Lillian Gilbreth (1878–1972), an American psychologist, also made contributions to the scientific school of management during the latter part of the 19th century and the beginning of the 20th century. Gantt, who once worked with Taylor, developed bonus systems for production employees and added a new dimension to incentive programs by suggesting that foremen should receive bonuses if their employees surpassed production standards.

Gantt also made significant contributions in the area of production scheduling with the *Gantt chart,* still used today. A Gantt chart is a visual technique for planning work flow. Time is depicted along the horizontal axis of

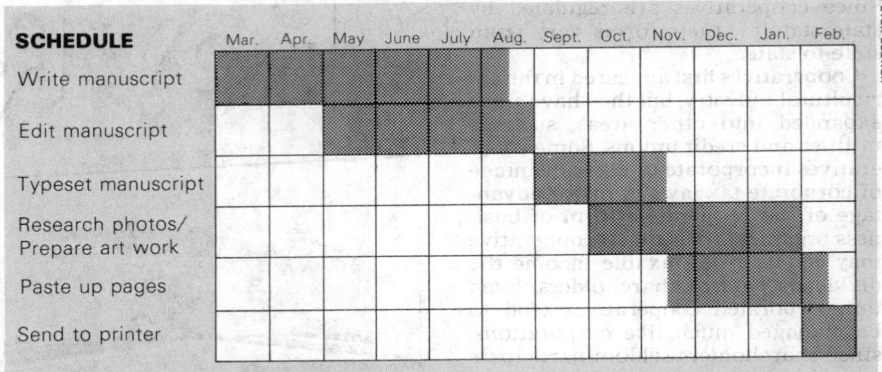

SCHEDULE	Mar.	Apr.	May	June	July	Aug.	Sept.	Oct.	Nov.	Dec.	Jan.	Feb.
Write manuscript	■	■	■	■	■	■						
Edit manuscript		■	■	■	■							
Typeset manuscript						■	■	■		■		
Research photos/ Prepare art work								■	■	■	■	
Paste up pages										■	■	
Send to printer												■

A GANTT CHART *is used as a way to visualize the work flow over the life of a project in order to promote more accurate scheduling.*

the chart and the different steps in a production process are shown on the vertical axis. The chart is used to plan when and how long the indicated activities will run.

Frank and Lillian Gilbreth. Like Taylor and Gantt, the Gilbreths were scientific management theorists. In one of his most famous efforts, Frank Gilbreth used motion picture cameras to analyze and eliminate the wasted motions of a bricklayer. This resulted in a dramatic increase in productivity and a decrease in the fatiguing nature of the job.

Critique of scientific management. Although the school of scientific management made significant contributions to management theory, it left many problems unresolved. Its failures were due partly to its limited scope, concentrating primarily on individual workers' tasks and shop productivity, and partly to the selective adoption by management practitioners of the concepts of Taylor et al. Taylor, for example, not only worked to increase productivity, but espoused the need for a *mental revolution* in business and management. He believed that management and labor should cooperate to increase productivity rather than fight over the profits made. In this way, Taylor believed, profits would increase and the two groups would no longer have to compete for them because there would be enough for everyone.

A significant oversight in the scientific methodology, or at least in the way it was applied, was the presumption that workers are totally rational in that they will respond to demands for higher productivity only in return for higher wages. This assumption proved to be an oversimplification of worker motivation. Even though wages may increase, workers may still go on strike over working conditions and move from job to job for reasons unrelated to wage rates.

Organizational theory. *Organizational theory,* which grew substantially from the efforts of Henry Fayol

(1841–1925), a French mining engineer, adopted a wider perspective than scientific management. Fayol investigated management functions and activities that could be applied universally. His concern was more with the complexity of large organizations than with specific problems, such as productivity. His presumption was that productivity will follow if management tasks are performed correctly.

Fayol, unlike many others of the period, believed management to be a skill, and therefore able to be learned. He was the first to suggest that management be taught as a formal discipline in schools. Fayol was responsible for the development of the now famous *five functions of management.* He asserted that all management activity falls into one of five categories. *Planning,* the first of the five functions, involves developing courses of action that will enable the company to reach

FAYOL'S 14 PRINCIPLES OF MANAGEMENT

FAYOL BELIEVED *that it is important for a manager to promote team spirit among his employees.*

its objectives. *Organizing* refers to obtaining the necessary physical and human resources and combining them in such a manner as to carry out the plans the company has developed. *Commanding* involves motivating employees and guiding their efforts toward accomplishment of the individual tasks necessary to achieve the company's objectives. *Coordinating* is making sure that the activities of the company are working together to accomplish desired goals. *Controlling*, the final function of management, entails monitoring the activities of the company to make sure that plans are being followed and objectives are being accomplished.

Human Relations Movement

Although the theorists of the classical school did not completely ignore the needs of the worker, their emphasis was primarily on productivity and efficiency. Indeed, Robert Owen (1771–1858), a classical theorist who saw workers as *vital machines,* stressed the prime importance of the manager's role as a reformer and strove for improved working conditions and for a generally more humanitarian approach to management.

Mary Parker Follet. The first half of the 20th century witnessed the emergence of other theorists. Mary Parker Follet (1868–1933), a British management theorist, believed that

Taylor was right when he claimed that management and labor share a common purpose. But she also believed that the artificial distinction set up between labor and management, that is, the order-givers versus order-takers, is detrimental to this partnership. She believed that management and labor should work together as a single unit and that authority should be given to those with the greatest expertise. Henry Ford expressed this same philosophy when he said: "The question of 'Who ought to be the boss?' is like asking 'Who ought to be the tenor in the quartet?' Obviously, the one who can sing tenor."

Chester Barnard. Chester Barnard (1886–1961), who based his management theories on psychology and sociology, used his approach to management as he rose to become president of New Jersey Bell in 1927. He claimed that formal organizations are formed because people cannot accomplish many of their goals individually. Therefore, a successful organization, according to Barnard, balances the needs of the organization and the needs of the individual.

Barnard was one of the first to recognize the existence of the *informal organization structure* in business. He noted that cliques and unofficial hierarchies form in business organizations that can significantly affect the efforts of managers. If the leaders of these cliques are highly motivated, their followers are likely to be equally motivated. If, on the other hand, these leaders are not committed to the objectives of the company, the efforts of

managers to motivate their subordinates will likely be less successful.

Elton Mayo. Elton Mayo (1880–1949), an American researcher in the area of industrial development, and his experiments at the Hawthorne Western Electric plant near Chicago from 1924 until 1933, provided further insights into worker motivation. Initially concerned with productivity, Mayo's experiments involved varying the amount of light in work areas to determine what effect increased illumination would have on productivity. As expected, when the level of illumination was increased, worker productivity increased. Paradoxically, however, when the level of lighting was decreased, productivity still increased. Mayo conducted further experiments using other variables thought to be related to worker productivity and found similar results. Ultimately he concluded that it was not the manipulation of working conditions that brought about changes in worker performance at the Hawthorne plant, but the fact that the workers were given special attention. The attention itself was the motivating factor: workers interpreted it as concern on the part of management for their welfare. The researchers concluded that employees will work harder if they believe that management cares about them. This important discovery became known as the *Hawthorne effect.* It became an important principle of what is known as the human relations school of management philosophy.

Management Style

Many management theorists of the mid-1900's concentrated their study on the activities of managers, attempting to isolate the attitudinal and behavioral factors that affect employee performance positively.

Douglas McGregor. American management theorist Douglas McGregor (1906–1964) believed that managers hold certain opinions about the character of their employees, and that these opinions are reflected in their management styles. In his Theory X/Theory Y analysis of managerial behavior, McGregor asserted that some managers (Theory X managers) believe that employees are basically lazy and disdain the idea of work. Other managers (Theory Y managers) believe employees think work is natural and desirable, are self-motivating, and readily accept responsibility. According to McGregor, Theory X managers are likely to be highly directive, even coercive in their relations with their subordinates. Theory Y managers, on

1. **Division of labor.** Workers are more efficient when they specialize, as on an assembly line.
2. **Authority.** It is the function of managers to get things done. They do so by giving orders to subordinates. Although all managers have formal authority, authority granted by the company, to be effective, managers must also develop personal authority, such as that resulting from technical expertise.
3. **Discipline.** For an organization to accomplish its objectives, its members must observe the rules and regulations of the organization. According to Fayol, discipline will result only from good leadership, one of the major elements of which is rewarding superior performance and penalizing those who do not adhere to the policies of the organization.
4. **Unity of command.** Each employee must report to and receive orders from one and only one superior. Fayol believed that an employee who is responsible to more than one manager will experience conflicts and confusion.
5. **Unity of direction.** Those operations within an organization that have the same objective must be guided by one plan under the supervision of one manager.
6. **Subordination of individual interest to the common good.** The interests of the organization as a whole should have priority over the interests of individual employees.
7. **Remuneration.** Compensation plans should be fair to both employees and employer.
8. **Centralization.** Managers should retain the final responsibility for making decisions, but they must also give subordinates enough authority to perform their jobs.
9. **Hierarchy.** There must be a line of authority in an organization that ranks individuals in the organizational structure from the lowest to the highest positions.
10. **Order.** People and physical resources must be in the right place at the right time if the objectives of the organization are to be met. It is particularly important that employees perform the jobs for which they are most suited.
11. **Equity.** Managers should treat employees fairly.
12. **Stability of staff.** High employee turnover adversely affects the efficiency and effectiveness of the organization.
13. **Initiative.** Employees should be given sufficient autonomy to develop and implement thier own plans.
14. **Esprit de corps.** Organizational unity will result if a feeling of team spirit is developed.

the other hand, are more likely to allow their subordinates freedom in the performance of their jobs. McGregor further asserted that, in most cases, the Theory X manager will be more effective than the Theory X manager.

McGregor's approach to management and the motivation of employees opened up a new perspective in the evolution of management thought. McGregor, through his Theory X and Theory Y analysis, sought to explain what managers actually do, explaining management behavior in terms of the managers' beliefs about their employees. Thus, the topic of *management style* entered the forum of management theory.

Henry Mintzberg. Canadian researcher Henry Mintzberg, who has concentrated much of his study on top level management, has made some interesting observations on the actual nature of management. Mintzberg notes, for instance, that the manager is less the systematic planner than classical management theorists would lead us to believe. Today's managers work at a breakneck pace and are most involved in short, action-oriented activities. Managers seem to jump from project to project in an almost random fashion. In general, Mintzberg suggests that a manager's work is significantly more fragmented than the organized

coordinated efforts described by classical theorists.

Mintzberg has provided some interesting and often controversial comments on management behavior. Mintzberg suggests, for example, that the nature of a particular manager's style may depend on which side of the brain is more developed. Sometimes called the *hemispheric theory of management,* it has its roots in the specialized nature of the various areas of the brain. The logical functions occur in the left side of the brain and the relational functions occur on the right. In other words, most planning takes place on the left side of the brain, and most action is initiated by the right side. The most effective manager, naturally, is the one who can integrate effectively the functions of the two sides of the brain.

Contemporary Management

To be sure, many of the concepts of classical management theory and the human relations school have their adherents in business enterprise. What is also clear is that prevailing concepts regarding the nature of managerial work, or opinions regarding methodologies that best accomplish the

management function, are ever-changing. Not only do opinions change, the business environment is constantly changing. These changes necessitate the continual reevaluation of the role of management.

Employee involvement. Perhaps the greatest movement in the past two decades has been toward a more people-centered approach to management. The efforts of Peter Drucker, American management consultant and author, and others have led to the development of such programs as *MBO (management by objectives).* Although the precise forms of these programs vary from organization to organization, they are generally designed to get employees more involved in the decision-making process of the company and engender greater job satisfaction and productivity.

The MBO process begins with a commitment on the part of top management to involve employees in the decision-making and objective-setting process. Under most systems, supervisors and subordinates jointly set performance goals for the subordinates. Since employees have a voice in determining their own performance standards, they tend to be more committed to them than if they were dictated by management. After the performance goals are established, supervisors meet with subordinates regularly to review performance compared with the established standards.

THE QUALITY CIRCLE, *where owners and managers meet to discuss problems, is typical of the Japanese management style.*

WHEELER/BLACK STAR

Japanese management. Many feel that the impressive productivity achieved by Japanese companies in the 1980's was a result of their unique management style. As a result, *Japanese-style management* has received considerable attention from management researchers, one of the most prominent of whom is William Ouchi, author of *Theory Z: How American Business Can Meet the Japanese Challenge* (1981). Studies such as this have revealed that typical Japanese managers differ significantly from their American counterparts. Whereas American managers have traditionally been decision-makers, Japanese managers encourage the *bottom-up process* of problem-solving, in which problems are solved by those closest to the problem rather than by those in the management ranks.

Visibility. Japanese managers tend to be highly visible to their employees and work alongside them. Many American managers maintain offices in work areas separate from their subordinates. One observer noted that when looking at a Japanese business department, it is impossible to identify the boss since all work together in the same area.

Consensus decision-making. Japanese management style emphasizes *con-*

sensus decision-making, in which managers and subordinates jointly solve problems and develop policy. American managers have traditionally tended to be much more competitive and individualistic.

Theory Z. Since many Japanese companies have achieved very impressive productivity and efficiency, the application of Japanese principles to U.S. businesses operations, referred to as *Theory Z,* has received considerable attention. The Japanese style of management, however, has not been wholeheartedly accepted by all American theorists and practitioners. Many point out that the considerable cultural differences between the United States and Japan may make adoption of the Japanese style by American managers difficult.

On the other hand, Peter Drucker points out that many aspects of the so-called Japanese style are American in origin; that the idea of *participative management* (getting the employee involved in the decision-making process) was originated by American managers and theorists long before it was practiced in Japan. The difference, according to Drucker, is that the Japanese implemented participative management techniques much more widely than did American managers.

U.S. management today.

Many of America's most successful managers bear little resemblance to the stereotypical hard-nosed, "I'll make the decisions around here" type. Many are involving their employees in the decision-making process to a significant degree.

Entrepreneurial spirit. More and more managers are trying to instill in their employees an entrepreneurial spirit, showing employees how to take charge of certain operations of the company and, in effect, run those operations as if they were their own businesses. These managers hope that such an approach will lead not only to pride of accomplishment, but to greater creativity and innovation.

Corporate culture. What has sometimes been called a caring climate is another characteristic of many successful companies as managers begin to realize that the corporate culture can have as great an impact on employee satisfaction and productivity as the individual actions of managers.

Management visibility. Increasing management visibility is another trend that has surfaced in recent years. The traditional manager, particularly the high-echelon manager in a large corporation, was often aloof. Today more and more managers are realizing the benefits of getting out among their employees and interacting more with the public. Such visibility is thought to have a humanizing effect on the corporate culture as employees and consumers alike begin to view the chief

LEE IACOCCA, *the chairman of the Chrysler Corporation, is for many people the embodiment of the action-oriented, successful manager.*

executive officer or chairman of the board of a major corporation as a real person rather than some vague entity responsible for many of their woes.

Successful managers. Despite the significant number of management theories that have been developed over the years, no one has ever been able to come up with a list of qualities, policies, or practices that will always work better than another list of such items. As a matter of fact, with the possible exception of the general statement that the effective manager gets the job done, there may not be even one characteristic that all good managers have in common. It is possible, however, to analyze what many effective managers do and what characteristics seem to be exhibited by many successful organizations.

Hard work. Effective managers seem to work extremely hard. Today's top-notch managers eat, sleep, and drink their jobs. They put in long hours, evaluate mountains of information, talk to great numbers of people, and move quickly from one item of concern to another.

Commitment. Successful managers have a strong belief in what they are doing and in their ability to do it. Once committed to a task, the effective managers of today do not waiver in their resolve to get the job done.

Action-oriented. Thomas Peters, co-author of *In Search of Excellence: Lessons from America's Best Run Companies,* points to three major factors that separate the good manager from the also-ran. One such factor is a *bias for action,* the ability to move quickly and, even more important, the ability to be innovative and creative.

Consumer-oriented. Peters also observes that well-run companies are in tune with consumer desires and respond to those desires. This principle of management seems obvious, but Peters points out that the Japanese have done a far better job of giving the consumer what he or she wants than have American firms.

Productivity through people. The third factor observed by Peters is the ability to achieve productivity through people. This may be the most complex managerial skill of all. It includes such elements as treating employees with dignity, stimulating creativity, and instilling the spirit of entrepreneurship.

Recognition. Use of recognition and reward ranks high on the list of effective management techniques. Financial rewards are important, but companies have found that other rewards can also be extremely effective. Whether it is through the Golden Circle of IBM (those marketing people who have exceeded their sales goals) or North American Tool and Die's Superperson Ceremony, effective managers recognize the efforts of those employees who contribute to the success of the firm.

Corporate climate. The corporate climate in many respects may be viewed as management in the aggregate. Many managers find that when they embody the ideals of the company, and become a living representative of what the firm is trying to accomplish, employees respond. Peters points out that truly effective organizations have leading executives who exemplify the values of the organization. They have the ability to transmit to others the essential values of their company.

Employee creativity. Effective managers continually strive to stimulate creativity among employees. Most realize that people are the most important resource that a firm possesses, and that the degree to which this resource is effectively and efficiently used will be reflected in the company's success. Some companies go to elaborate lengths to stimulate creativity. At 3M, for example, employees are unofficially encouraged to take time and money from approved projects to use on unapproved projects. Although the techniques for encouraging creativity vary considerably, the objective is a common one, to get the most out of all the human resources available.

Marketing and Advertising

Marketing refers to all activities involved in the movement of goods and services from producer to consumer. The process begins with determining the needs and desires of the customer. Following this initial step, a firm must develop products to satisfy those needs and wants. It must make certain that the desired goods are available, know when and where customers want them, and inform potential customers of their availability. Marketing also includes financing activities that facilitate the exchange of goods and services.

Advertising is one of the most important elements of marketing. It includes all forms of nonpersonal communication. Its purpose is to promote a product or service or otherwise influence public opinion.

Marketing

Marketing is sometimes viewed as the creation of utility, referring to the ability to satisfy consumer desires. From the marketing perspective, four kinds of utility must be provided by a successful marketing system: form utility, place utility, time utility, and ownership utility.

Form utility. *Form utility* refers to the production of goods that consumers want. This includes consideration of product quality, aesthetic appeal, functional characteristics (what the product will do), and support services, such as repair facilities.

Since the creation of form utility begins with determining what products or services people want, market research is a key element. Firms use a variety of techniques to determine consumer desires, including surveys, consumer panels, and test marketing.

Place utility. *Place utility* refers to the distribution of goods. It is important to produce commodities that consumers want, but it is also equally important to make those products conveniently available. Physical distribution is the key element in creating place utility. Firms must develop effective transportation and storage facilities and have an efficient network of wholesalers, retailers, or other middlemen to effect the transfer of goods to customers.

Time utility. *Time utility* refers to placing goods on the market when customers want to buy them. Attempting to sell snowmobiles in July is a difficult marketing situation.

Warehousing is an important element in the creation of time utility, just as it is in the creation of place utility. Firms involved in the production of seasonal goods usually try to produce year round and store goods during periods of low demand so that the goods will be available during periods of high demand.

Ownership utility. *Ownership utility* involves facilitating the transfer of ownership from seller to buyers. Advertising, personal selling, and other promotional activities inform potential buyers of the availability of goods.

The marketing concept. In the relatively prosperous times preceding the Great Depression, American businesses generally followed the *production concept.* The idea was that virtually any useful product could be sold provided that the price was reasonable. The emphasis was more on production and efficiency than on marketing. Businesses tended to produce products that fit well with their production processes and then rely on their sales departments to sell whatever the company decided to make.

Rise of the consumer market. The Great Depression marked the beginning of the end of the production concept. No longer could firms sell their products relatively easily. Consumer spending decreased dramatically, competition for the remaining consumer dollars increased, and many firms went out of business.

Following World War II, the great race for the consumer dollar began. The American economy had excess capacity, developed during the war for the production of war goods, which then turned to the production of peacetime commodities.

As excess capacity geared up to produce peacetime goods, and as American citizens returned to a normal life, businesses were forced to compete for the consumer dollar. The businesses that were most successful were the ones that adopted the *marketing concept* of business operations. According to this concept, it is the consumer, not the production process, that is at the forefront of product development and distribution.

Competitive advantage. According to the marketing concept, each company seeks a *competitive edge*—something it can do or a service it can provide better than its competitors—a niche in the market that it can defend (see Target Marketing section, page 319). To accomplish this, the firm must constantly be on the alert for changes in the needs and desires of the consuming public. The history of the American economy since World War II is replete with companies that felt so secure in their operations that they ignored clues that consumer desires were changing. For example, the American automobile industry in the 1970's largely ignored clues that the American public was becoming attracted to smaller, more efficient cars and continued to produce large automobiles primarily.

Marketing research. When the marketing concept replaced the production concept, it became essential to determine the needs and desires of the consumer. To accomplish this, a new area of marketing emerged. *Market research* involves the collection and analysis of data relating to consumers and their buying behavior. It attempts, among other things, to determine trends in sales and sales potential for specific products; to identify those customers who are the most likely purchasers of the firm's products; and to identify those factors that motivate consumers to buy certain goods and services.

Market research also assists in determining how and where a product is purchased, thus enabling a firm to develop the appropriate channels of product distribution.

Market research often interests a firm in taking a broader perspective of its business. Motion picture theaters, for example, may see that they are in the entertainment business rather than just the movie business. As such, they are in competition with amusement parks, nightclubs, and television as much as with other theaters.

Demographics. One of the most important determinations to be made in market research is who buys the company's product, that is, who may benefit from its purchase and why. Researchers have found that consumer demographics play a significant role in this process. *Demographics* refers to

SLOGANS are one method used in marketing to gain a marketing niche.

"fewer calories"

"Just Like Mom's"

"60,000 mile warranty"

"100% PURE"

AGE AND CONSUMER SPENDING
Book vs. total entertainment expenditures

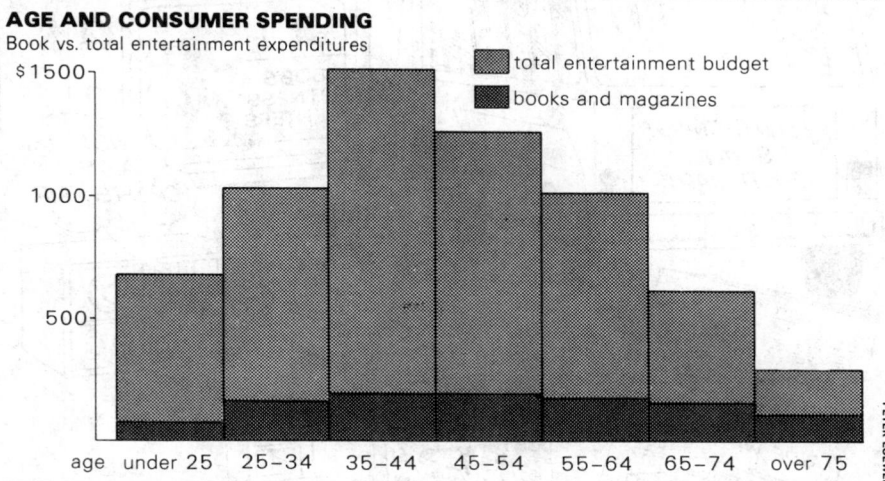

AGE *is considered to be an important factor in the purchase of many products and is therefore studied.*

characteristics of populations, such as geographic distribution, age, family structure, and income.

The geographic distribution of the population, particularly those members of the population who are potential buyers of the company's product, is important for a number of reasons. Even when a firm has a viable product, it is necessary to market the product where the consumers are. Knowing the geographic distribution of potential customers is also important because residents of different regions often have different tastes and preferences.

Another important influence on the nature of consumer purchases is the age of consumers. Between 1966 and 1987, the average age of the population increased from 21 to 32, a trend that is expected to continue. Different age groups have different consumption patterns. A population typified by a relatively young average age tends to buy toys, baby food, and other child-oriented products. Teenagers are significant consumers of clothing, sports equipment, and stereo equipment. Adults purchase homes, major appliances, and automobiles. Older adults, in addition to spending more on medical care, also account for a significant proportion of travel expenditures and luxury purchases.

The changing nature of the American family is another factor that is of considerable importance in marketing. For example, people are marrying at a later age than in the past. This could have a negative impact on such items as life insurance, typically first purchased when people marry, but a positive impact on the sale of such things as sporting equipment and entertainment systems, which are purchased more by single individuals than by married couples.

Perhaps the most obvious factor that affects consumer spending is the amount of disposable income in the hands of potential buyers. As income

increases, as it generally has in the United States since 1940, expenditure patterns as well as expenditures themselves change. With more income, the purchase of nonessentials and more expensive goods tends to increase.

Companies have become aware that psychological factors also play a part in consumer spending. The desire to keep up with the Joneses, for example, or drive a prestigious car, can influence spending. Companies often market to psychological rather than rational desires. A homeowner buys insurance for the security of his family, a young professional may buy a sports car because of the image it reflects, and a traveler may fly first class because of the impression it creates. An old adage in marketing asserts that successful companies "sell the sizzle, not the steak."

Target Marketing

Successful firms realize that they cannot be all things to all people. No company has yet developed a product of completely universal appeal. Therefore, companies direct their product development and marketing activities toward a portion of the market in which they believe they will be the most successful. This subgroup within society is called a target market.

A *target market* may be defined by income, educational level, sex, age, family status, recreational pursuits, or any other factor that influences buying behavior.

A company arrives at potential target markets through a process known as *market segmentation*. This process entails dividing the total market into several groups, each of which has unique characteristics. The company then selects the market segment or segments that it believes will contain the most probable purchasers of its product.

Promotion. Once a company has selected a market and developed a product that it believes will appeal to that market, it must make the members of that market aware of the product's existence and convince them to buy it. This is the role of *promotion.* There are three major methods of promoting a product: personal selling, advertising, and sales promotion.

Personal selling. *Personal selling* involves one-on-one contact between the company's marketing representative and the potential customer. It is the oldest form of product promotion and has the greatest flexibility, because the salesperson can adapt his or her message immediately to fit the customer.

Personal selling techniques vary with the type of product. Those involved in retail selling primarily help customers make their selections and take orders. They generally do nothing to solicit customers as do other types of salespersons.

Business selling, selling to businesses rather than consumers, by contrast, generally involves the solicitation of new customers as well as service to those customers who already buy from the company.

Advertising. *Advertising,* the dissemination of information through various types of media, such as newspapers, radio, television, direct mail, signs, and billboards, is the most common type of product promotion (see Advertising section, page 320).

Sales promotion. *Sales promotion* includes a variety of mechanisms, such as advertising specialties (rulers, pens, etc., with the name of the company on them), coupons, and sales contests. One of the most important categories of sales promotion techniques is point-of-purchase displays, which include window displays, merchandise racks, store displays, and in-store signs.

The use of advertising specialties has increased significantly in recent years. Traditionally, such items were small and inexpensive, such as calendars or pens; their major purpose was to keep the name of the company in front of the customer. Today, however, a wide variety of advertising specialties are available, including beach towels, coolers, glasses, T-shirts, hats, jackets, and even shower curtains. One of the unique aspects of such advertising specialties is that people often pay for the privilege of promoting a company's product, such as when they buy a hat or a T-shirt with a company's name on it.

Types of goods. The type of goods that a company sells affects the choice of marketing strategy. Goods can be classified as either durable or nondurable.

Durable goods. Durable goods, such as cars, television sets, refrigerators, stereos, and other major appliances last a fairly long time and are generally more expensive than nondurable goods. Although extensively advertised, they may also require intensive personal selling. Customers generally have questions that must be answered before they decide to buy. Consumers usually give more thought to, and require more information related to, the purchase of an automobile than the purchase of a shirt.

Nondurable goods. Most nondurable goods, such as food and clothing, are normally consumed quickly and have a relatively low cost. Customers usually do not spend as much time in the consideration of such purchases as they do for durable goods. Advertising is generally more important than personal selling.

Industrial goods. Goods can also be classified as industrial goods or consumer goods. *Industrial goods* are those purchased by companies for business use, such as typewriters or copying machines. The sale of industrial goods relies more heavily on personal selling than on advertising.

Consumer goods. *Consumer goods* are purchased for personal, family, or household use. There are three basic types of consumer goods—convenience goods, shopping goods, and specialty goods, each of which has unique characteristics that may dictate the appropriate marketing strategy.

Convenience goods are purchased without a great deal of advance thought. Newspapers, candy bars, and dishwashing soap are convenience goods for most consumers. Ease of purchase is of primary importance. Therefore, mass marketing through many retail outlets is usually the best way to sell such products.

Shopping goods, such as clothing and major appliances, are goods that are purchased less frequently than convenience goods. The customer spends more time in shopping and comparing the relative advantages of different brands. Shopping goods are more expensive than convenience goods and usually require more personal selling than convenience goods.

Specialty goods are relatively expensive items that the customer buys only after much investigation and comparison. Convenience is relatively unimportant. Consumers looking for a new car are willing to travel out of their way to get the best deal or the exact features they want.

Advertising

The most pervasive form of product promotion is advertising. *Advertising* is any form of nonpersonal communication designed to sell a product or service or otherwise influence public opinion. Its purpose is to disseminate information to a large group of people, generally through the use of such mass media as television, radio, magazines, and newspapers.

AN ADVERTISER *will choose various media, such as newspapers, magazines, and television, to reach specific types of consumers.*

Advertising media. Every year billions of dollars are spent on advertising. These advertising dollars are allocated among the various methods of dissemination, called *advertising media:* handbills, direct mail, outdoor signs, and even the sides of buses and taxis as well as mass media.

Print media. In terms of total expenditures, newspapers are the most common advertising medium in the United States. Newspapers provide local, yet fairly broad, coverage at reasonable rates. Although some newspapers have national coverage, most are regional. As such, they have the advantage of being able to carry a message tailored to a particular geographic area. Newspapers are particularly useful to small businesses, which may not be able to afford the higher expense of television.

Next to newspapers, magazines are the most important print medium for advertising. Although there are a number of general interest magazines, the most important magazines, from an advertising standpoint, are those that are directed to special markets. Such magazines enable advertisers to direct their advertising to those most likely to benefit from their product. A producer of hunting equipment might choose to advertise in *Field and Stream* to pinpoint the readers most likely to buy hunting equipment.

Professional journals also represent an important advertising medium. There are journals addressed to physicians, attorneys, architects, and other occupational groups who may depend on these publications to keep abreast of new developments in their respective professions.

One of the fastest growing print media is *direct mail*, which includes catalogs, fliers, pamphlets, and other advertising pieces mailed directly to consumers' homes or places of business. The major advantage of direct mail is that markets can be targeted even more specifically than would be possible through magazines, because mailing lists have been developed that provide the names of potential customers with similar characteristics or buying patterns.

Outdoor advertising includes advertising that is located at a fixed location; exposure is basically random. Signs and billboards are the most significant forms of outdoor advertising. Since outdoor advertising relies on random exposure, it is most often employed as a supplement for other advertising techniques.

Broadcast media. In addition to print media, advertisers make significant use of broadcast media, which include radio and television. The fastest growing as well as the newest of the broadcast media is television. Its major advantage over other types of media is that it can reach millions of people at one time. It is this broad market penetration that makes television appealing. Advertisers not only achieve national exposure, they can target specific geographic markets through local programming. Thus, television can assist both the local and the national advertiser.

The major use of television advertising is in the promotion of consumer products. Traditionally, industrial products have been advertised less often on television because they are usually too technical and difficult to explain in the limited time available during a television commercial. In recent years, however, some companies in the industrial market have turned to television advertising. The computer industry, for example, has made extensive use of television in selling information processing systems. Manufacturers of office equipment, such as copying machines, have also used television to promote products.

The other major broadcast media, radio, is not as expensive and does not normally cover as large a marketing area as television. Radio is a significant advertising media, however, and does offer some advantages over television advertising in addition to its lower cost. One advantage is that radio stations can target markets better than television stations. Rock stations, for example, usually have an audience with different characteristics than do classical music stations.

Radio has the further advantage of reaching people at times when no other media is appropriate, such as when driving, at work, or during picnics and other outdoor activities.

Product advertising.
The two major types of advertising are product advertising and institutional advertising. *Product advertising,* by far the more common of the two, is designed to sell a specific product or product line by delineating the characteristics, quality, and capabilities of the product.
Product life cycles.
Many factors are considered when developing advertising for a product. One of the most significant is the stage of the product's life cycle. Products generally progress through four stages—introduction, growth, maturity, and decline. During the introduction stage, advertising is generally informational in nature. Since consumers are unaware of the product or its capabilities, advertisers must acquaint potential customers

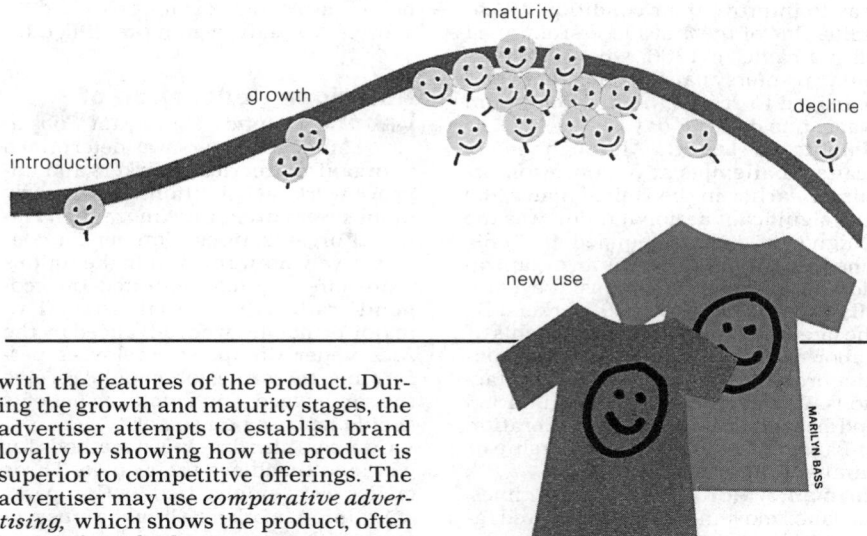

LIFE CYCLE OF A PRODUCT'S SALES

introduction · growth · maturity · decline · new use

MARILYN BASS

MOST PRODUCTS *tend to follow a cycle of increasing then decreasing sales. One way to regain profitability is to find a new use for the old product.*

with the features of the product. During the growth and maturity stages, the advertiser attempts to establish brand loyalty by showing how the product is superior to competitive offerings. The advertiser may use *comparative advertising,* which shows the product, often in side-by-side demonstrations, as superior to specific competitors. (The law requires that such claims be verifiable and documented.)

During the later stages of the product's life cycle, the advertiser may use *reminder advertising* in an attempt to rejuvenate or sustain demand. Such advertising often points out that, although the product has been around for a while, it is still superior to other products on the market.

Another technique used during this stage is to develop new uses for old products or aim new advertising at different market segments. During the mid-1980's, for example, coffee, traditionally seen as a product for older age groups, experienced declining demand. In an effort to stimulate sales, the coffee industry aimed a considerable amount of advertising at the young adult market segment.

Institutional advertising.
Institutional advertising, in contrast to product advertising, is designed to promote a company rather than a product by fostering goodwill or a positive image. Insurance companies sometimes inform people of ways to save on insurance premiums and utility companies publish brochures on how to save energy. Advertisers hope that the favorable impression created by institutional advertising will lead to more sales because people tend to patronize companies they trust.

Labor-Management Relations

Although the objectives of managers and employees generally differ, they must find a way to work together. The relationship between labor and management in the United States has often been adversarial, yet both have cooperated to support the highly productive U.S. economy.

Historical Evolution

The improved technology of the Industrial Revolution, along with division of labor, made manufacturing more efficient and resulted in the development of the factory system. As a result, workers became specialists. Work was divided into small tasks, each of which was performed repeatedly by a worker. Rather than making an entire shoe, as a cobbler would, one worker in a shoe factory would cut the uppers, another would attach the heel, etc.

Specialization of labor, although it increased efficiency, made workers dependent on the factories in which they worked. If there was no factory work, employees lost their jobs and were not trained to move into other kinds of jobs.
Worker exploitation.
Dependence of workers on the factory owner gave employers considerable power over their workers, who were in a poor bargaining position and had little control over the work place. As a result, working conditions were often poor, the length of the workday was long, and safety programs were virtually nonexistent. By 1900, the average work week was about 60 hours. In some industries, such as steel production, it was even longer—twelve hours a day, seven days a week. Child labor was extensively used, as were women, since employers could usually pay them less. Children often earned as little as a dollar a week for twelve- to fourteen-hour days. There was little or no job security. Workers who became sick or were injured on the job were fired and replaced. There were no pensions or workers' compensation programs.

Early organization.

Most workers eventually learned that the only way to improve their condition was to unite. One of the first successful united efforts came in 1786, when Philadelphia printers banded together and managed to secure the first minimum wage, one dollar a day.

Knights of Labor.

Although many scattered attempts at organization occurred earlier in the United States, the first significant national union was the Knights of Labor, founded in 1869. The Knights of Labor was an organization of several craft unions; it eventually grew to over 700,000 workers. By the late 1880's, however, the Knights of Labor became fragmented, and conflict broke out among the various factions. One faction split away in 1886 and became the American Federation of Labor (AFL) under the leadership of Samuel Gompers (1850–1924).

Haymarket riot.

During these times, the labor movement was not viewed favorably by a majority of the population. Unions were generally viewed as socialistic, often violent, organizations. This image became solidified by incidents such as the famous Haymarket riot in Chicago. On May 4, 1886, a riot broke out as police attempted to break up a union rally. A bomb was thrown, and eleven people, including seven police officers, were killed. Eight participants in the rally were arrested, charged, and found guilty of being accessories to the crime. One of the eight received a fifteen-year prison sentence and the other seven were sentenced to death. Of the seven sentenced to death, four were hanged, one committed suicide, and two had death sentences commuted to life in prison. Public outrage made the attempts of unions to secure better working conditions and a shorter workday even more difficult.

American Federation of Labor.

Despite significant obstacles, Samuel Gompers was determined to organize American workers and improve working conditions. While early unions were often little more than fraternal organizations, Gompers, a conservative who wanted to make unions more effective, concentrated on economic rather than social issues. Two major principles were advanced by the AFL under Gompers: employees performing the same job should receive the same wage, and employee benefits should be based on seniority.

Gompers also developed methods for workers to achieve their goals. Three tactics were emphasized by Gompers:

1. Union workers should refuse to work with nonunion workers.

2. Collective bargaining and strikes should be used to achieve improved working conditions and better pay.

3. Union members, as well as the union itself, should support political candidates with platforms favorable to unions.

Gompers' bread-and-butter unionism, concentrating on economic issues such as wages, hours, and working conditions, kept the union movement growing into the 20th century. From 1900 to 1920, the union movement flourished and achieved important gains. Union-backed Presidential candidate Woodrow Wilson was elected in 1912, creating a favorable political environment for unions. In 1913 the Labor Department was created. In 1914 the Clayton Act was passed; it exempted unions from prosecution under the Sherman Antitrust Act. By 1920, three out of every four workers who belonged to a union belonged to the AFL.

Depression era.

The Great Depression significantly hampered union activities. With over one-fourth of the labor force unemployed, unions could hardly press for higher wages and better working conditions.

Further hampering the growth of unions during this period was the lack of growth in the number of skilled factory workers. As factory operations became mechanized, more and more unskilled workers, such as machine operators, were employed instead of skilled craftsmen. Since the AFL was essentially an organization of craft unions, the vast numbers of unskilled workers in the United States were not members of the AFL.

Some of the unions within the AFL sought to solve slackening growth rates by organizing workers in major American industries, such as the automotive and steel industries. Organization was on the basis of industry rather than craft; skilled as well as unskilled workers were accepted as members. In 1935 the industrial unions split from the AFL and formed the Congress of Industrial Organizations (CIO) under John L. Lewis (1880–1969). Since the CIO accepted unskilled as well as skilled workers, it soon approached the AFL in size.

The modern era.

In 1933, 2.5 million American workers belonged to labor unions. In the 20 years that followed, thanks to favorable legislation and increased demand for workers during the years of World War II, union membership grew to over 14 million. During this time the AFL and the CIO competed for membership. In 1955 the conflict ended as the AFL and the CIO merged under George Meany (1894–1980) to form the AFL-CIO.

White-collar workers.

Even though early unions sought to organize basically blue-collar workers, they have since sought out other groups as the pool of unorganized blue-collar workers has shrunk. In the 1960's, government employees began to organize. Certain groups of white-collar workers, such as teachers, have also formed unions. The two largest teachers' unions, the National Education Association (NEA) and the American Federation of Teachers have a combined membership of over 2 million members. (Technically, the NEA is a teachers' association, but it is also considered a union since it often acts as a collective bargaining agent and organizes strikes and pickets.) By the mid-

WIDESPREAD MISTREATMENT *of workers in many industries, for example in the garment industry, contributed to the rise of unions.*

THE BETTMANN ARCHIVE

1980's, over 35 percent of all union members were white-collar workers.

Declining membership. The late 1970's were troubled years for organized labor as double-digit unemployment made it more difficult for unions to demand increased benefits. Many workers were laid off and others had to give up benefits to preserve their jobs. Despite continued efforts to organize professional and white-collar workers, union membership continued to decline into the 1980's. By 1985, total union membership in the United States had dipped below 17 million.

Union Organization

There are four levels of union organization common in the United States: local unions, regional organizations, national or international unions, and federations.

Local unions. At the worker level are the local unions, which represent workers in a given geographic area. It is these local unions to which workers actually belong. The officers of local unions, as well as representatives to regional and national conventions, are elected by the members of the locals. At the regional level, most unions have state or district offices that coordinate the activities of local unions.

National unions. National unions are made up of all the local unions of a given craft or industry. It is the national unions that give local unions their charter to operate. In return, local unions must operate in accordance with the national union's constitution and bylaws. In large national industries, such as automotive or steel, it is often the national union that negotiates major issues with employers. Some unions, such as the United Auto Workers, have locals in Canada as well as the United States, making them international unions.

Federations. The highest level of union organization is the federation, the most significant of which in the United States is the AFL-CIO. The AFL-CIO is not itself a union, but an organization of unions. Federations mediate disputes between individual unions and provide a united labor front. They also perform a political function by trying to get candidates elected to state and federal governments who are sympathetic to labor, and by lobbying or otherwise pressuring for favorable legislation. Representatives of the AFL-CIO may also advise Congress or the President on labor affairs.

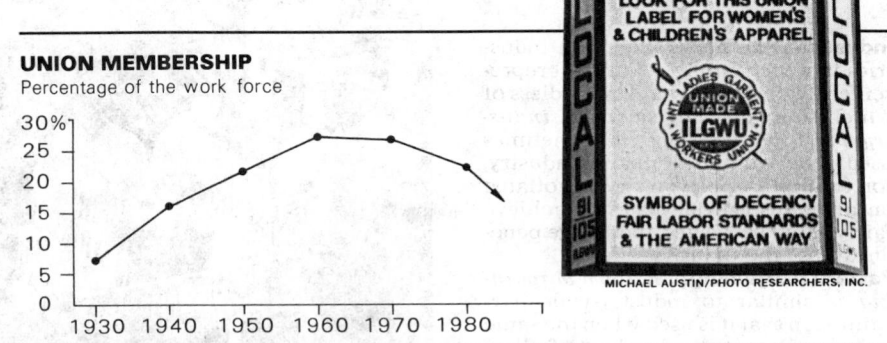

UNION MEMBERSHIP
Percentage of the work force

UNION MEMBERSHIP, *after rising steadily from the 1930's through the 1960's, began to level off and then decline in the 1970's and 1980's.*

Canadian federations. In Canada, the major national federations are the Canadian Labor Congress (CLC) and the Canadian Federation of Labor (CFL). The CLC is the Canadian counterpart of the AFL-CIO. The CFL, which split from the CLC in 1982, is a federation of building trade unions.

Union certification. The means by which employees are represented by a union are specified by law. The first step is the contacting of employees by union organizers, or vice versa. The union attempts to get employees to sign a union recognition card. If 30 percent of the employees sign such a card, the company may decide to recognize the union voluntarily, or an election is held to determine whether the union will become the official bargaining agent for the employees.

Union elections, which are conducted by secret ballot, are supervised by the National Labor Relations Board. If a majority of the employees eligible to vote are in favor of union representation, the union becomes the official bargaining agent for the employees. Once the union is officially elected by the employees, the union is certified by the National Labor Relations Board. The company then has no choice but to bargain with the union rather than with the employees individually.

Collective Bargaining

Contract negotiations between the union and the company are referred to as *collective bargaining.* In this process, the emphasis is generally on such issues as wages, working conditions, grievance procedures, and fringe benefits. The law requires that both sides bargain in good faith and make every effort to reach an acceptable agreement, which will be embodied in a formal contract signed by union and company representatives.

Once a tentative agreement has been reached between union representatives and company management, the contract must be presented to the union membership for ratification. If the workers vote in favor of the contract, it becomes legally binding on both parties to live up to the agreement for its duration, usually from one to three years. When the contract is about to expire, the process starts over again. Each party is required by the Taft-Hartley Act to notify the other party prior to the expiration of the contract of any changes in the current contract that it anticipates requesting.

Resolving disputes. If negotiations between union and management are not progressing toward a satisfactory settlement, the parties may decide to use mediation or arbitration to settle unresolved issues.

Mediation. *Mediation* involves the use of a disinterested third party to offer assistance and suggestions. The mediator or panel of mediators reviews the unresolved issues and proposes possible solutions. Mediators do not have the power to settle disputes. Their role is to make recommendations. Either or both of the parties may decline to accept the suggestions or compromise solutions offered by the mediator.

Arbitration. Like mediation, *arbitration* entails using a disinterested third party, called an arbitrator, to listen to evidence presented by both labor and management. The arbitrator then makes a decision. Arbitration differs from mediation in that the decision of the arbitrator is binding.

Types of collective bargaining. Most collective bargaining agreements are arrived at through negotiations between a single employer and a bargaining representative of the employees of a single facility. Other agreements, however, are negotiated between the employer and a representative of all the employees in all of its plants. If several unions represent the employees of a particular company, *coalition bargaining* may be used. This entails having all the unions bargain as if they were a single unit with the employer.

Industry-wide bargaining. In industries in which employees are all represented by the same union, regardless of which company they work for, *industry-wide bargaining* is sometimes used. The women's apparel industry, for example, has typically negotiated on an industry-wide basis to achieve fairly standard wages and fringe benefits across the industry.

Pattern bargaining. *Pattern bargaining* is similar to industry-wide bargaining in that it is used when the same union represents the workers of all of the companies in a particular industry. In pattern bargaining, the union negotiates an agreement with a target company and then requires that the other companies in the same industry accept the same contract, although those other firms are under no legal obligation to do so. If no agreement can be reached, a strike is called against the target company.

Collective bargaining agreement.
Contracts between employers and employees generally cover a wide variety of items, including wages, seniority, working conditions, hours, personnel policies, and grievance procedures.

Cost-of-living clause. During the inflationary period of the 1970's, a popular part of many collective bargaining agreements was a *cost-of-living adjustment* (COLA) clause. Such a clause calls for automatic wage increases when the cost of living increases significantly prior to expiration of the contract.

Job security. During the recession of the early 1980's, high levels of unemployment made job security a bigger issue than income in collective bargaining agreements. Unions pressed for job security guarantees. Management, on the other hand, was concerned with survival and pressed for union concessions, claiming that without such concessions their companies could not compete, particularly against foreign producers, and that many jobs would be lost. As a result, management often pressed for and received union concessions, sometimes called *givebacks.* Unions would agree to give up benefits and even accept lower wages to preserve jobs. Most collective bargaining agreements that included givebacks also included provisions that stipulated the conditions under which benefits would be reinstated.

Grievance resolution. Despite the comprehensive nature of employment contracts—some can be over 200 pages—there is always the possibility that a dispute will arise during the term of the contract. To handle these disputes, most collective bargaining agreements include a *grievance procedure,* a specified process by which complaints and disputes are aired and reconciled.

A STRIKE *has traditionally been the most powerful means of persuasion available to a union during bargaining with an employer.*

Union Tactics

The vast majority, about 98 percent, of all labor-management negotiations result in a ratified contract without work stoppages. When a satisfactory agreement is not reached, however, both labor and management have tactics available to them to pressure the other side into a settlement.

Strikes. The most dramatic union tactic is the strike. A strike deprives the employer of the services of its employees and draws public attention to the issues. In most cases, neither side wants or benefits from a strike. The company loses a significant amount of productivity, possibly even market share, and the loyalty of its customers. Profits generally suffer dramatically.

A prolonged strike usually results in considerable hardship for the striking employees as well. Although most large unions provide strike benefits, payments made to striking employees during a strike, they are far less than the wages of the employees and are limited in duration.

Because of the adverse effect on both the employer and the employees, a strike is usually implemented only as a last resort.

Picketing. Picketing is a way of informing the public that a dispute is in progress. Picketing attempts to discourage people from crossing the picket line for the purpose of working for, or conducting business with, the company with which the employees are in dispute. Picket lines may be employed independently or in conjunction with a strike. Normally, the most effective aspect of picketing is that members of other unions refuse to cross the lines.

Boycotts. The third major tactic used by union members is the *boycott.* A boycott involves the refusal of workers to use or buy the products of the company with which the employees are in dispute. There are primary boycotts and secondary boycotts. When employing a primary boycott, striking workers try to persuade union members and others not to buy the products of that company.

A secondary boycott is aimed at firms other than the one with which the workers have a grievance. In the late 1960's, the United Farm Workers went on strike against California grape growers. In an effort to put pressure on the growers, the union asked airlines and restaurants not to purchase grapes from them. The union also threatened to boycott businesses that did buy these products. Cesar Chavez, head of the United Farm Workers Organizing Committee, made a national appeal asking individuals not to purchase grapes grown by California growers who did not use union workers. This was one of the most widespread secondary boycotts in American history. The Taft-Hartley Act and the Landrum Griffin Act prohibit most types of secondary boycotts. The secondary boycott of the United Farm Workers was legal, however, since farm workers are excluded from secondary boycott prohibitions.

THE NFL *used strikebreakers to put pressure on striking players in 1987.*

Management Tactics

Management also has weapons that it may use in the event of a labor dispute. The four major techniques available to management are lockouts, strikebreaking, court injunctions, and combined efforts through employer associations.

Lockouts. A *lockout* is management's counterpart to a strike. It occurs when the employer closes the business and refuses to allow the employees to work. Lockouts are rare and are generally used only when a strike has already closed the plant.

Strikebreakers. Employers may try to replace striking union workers with nonunion personnel. Sometimes management personnel will be used in production jobs until the dispute is solved. On other occasions, the company may hire new workers to replace striking workers. These nonunion employees are called *strikebreakers* or *scabs.* The use of strikebreakers is designed to put pressure on striking employees by making them believe that they will lose their jobs if they do not return to work.

Injunctions. In some instances employers may be able to secure a court order, called an *injunction,* forcing employees to cease certain activities. Excessive picketing or the use of pickets to intimidate those who attempt to cross picket lines are activities that may lead to court injunctions, as are activities that may result in damage to the property of the employer. The court may order that the number of pickets on a picket line be limited to a specific number at any one time.

Employers' associations. On occasion, a number of companies may form an employers' association to bargain with a union on an industry-wide basis. Using a single representative in this way increases the power of the employers. The result is often an industry-wide negotiation with one agent bargaining for all of the employees and one agent negotiating for all of the employers.

Other tactics. There are other tactics that management may use. During a strike or other labor dispute, the company may *outsource,* or contract work, to other companies that was performed by its own employees prior to the strike. Companies may also transfer work from one of its plants to another or even declare bankruptcy to end a union contract.

Employers may even take their case to the public through advertising. When airline pilots went on strike in the early 1980's, some of the airlines published the salaries of their pilots in newspapers. The objective was to show the public how much the pilots were making, which in most cases was far more than the average American worker. In this way, the airlines hoped that the public would support their stand not to increase salaries.

The Regulatory Environment

One hundred years ago government regulation of American business was minimal. Giant corporations, at least by the standards of the time, evolved and prospered in the laissez-faire environment. Monopolies and near-monopolies existed in many industries, such as railroading and oil. Abuses during these early years gave rise to pressures for regulation of these industrial giants. Creation of the Interstate Commerce Commission (ICC) in 1888 was the first major step in the evolution of the contemporary business regulatory environment. Although its powers have been greatly expanded over the years, the Interstate Commerce Commission was originally designed to correct abuses in the railroad industry.

Today there are thousands of regulations and hundreds of laws and precedent-setting court cases that regulate the activities of businesses. The most important areas of regulation include competition, employee relations, consumer protection, and environmental protection.

Regulation of Competition

One of the first major concerns of the federal government was protection of the competitive environment. Following creation of the Interstate Commerce Commission, Congress enacted its first major piece of antitrust legislation, the Sherman Antitrust Act of 1890. The Sherman Act is a broad statute prohibiting contracts and conspiracies in restraint of trade and banning monopolies and efforts to monopolize industries.

Clayton Antitrust Act. Following the Sherman Act, and more specific in nature, was the Clayton Act of 1914, which prohibits specific actions when the effects of the actions are to restrain trade. The prohibitions of the Clayton Act include:

1. *Tying contracts.* A tying contract requires the seller of a product to carry other products of the manufacturer whether or not the seller wants to carry those products. The danger of a tying contract is that it may limit the seller from buying from competitors, thus reducing the level of competition.

2. *Interlocking directorates.* When one or more members of the board of directors of a company also serves on the board of a competing firm, the danger of collusion or other competition-restricting activities may exist.

3. *Acquiring stock in competing firms.* If one company acquires a sufficient portion of the ownership of a competing firm, it may be able to guide the operations of that firm toward noncompetitive ends.

Celler-Kefauver Antimerger Act.

The Celler-Kefauver Antimerger Act of 1950 expanded the prohibitions of the Clayton Act to include the purchase of major assets that would tend to decrease competition, such as the purchase of a production facility of a competing company.

A.T.&T. TO SPLIT UP, TRANSFORMING INDUSTRY

THE COURT-ORDERED BREAKUP *of American Telephone & Telegraph into several independent companies was one of the largest antitrust actions ever taken.*

Robinson-Patman Act. The Robinson-Patman Act of 1936 prohibits price discrimination on the part of wholesalers and manufacturers, except on specific legally allowed bases. Price differentials are allowed, for example, if there is a difference in the quality or grade of products sold to different purchasers.

Federal Trade Commission Act.

The Federal Trade Commission Act of 1914 created the Federal Trade Commission (FTC), charging it with the responsibility of enforcing the various federal statutes and regulations relating to business operations. Its powers are broad, and it generally may investigate any "unfair methods of competition in commerce." The original purpose of the Federal Trade Commission was to protect competing businesses from each other. Today, the scope of the FTC includes consumer protection as well as the protection of competitors (see Consumer Protection section, page 327).

Employee Relations

The passage of the Sherman Antitrust Act in 1890 left the status of labor regulation in doubt. According to the Sherman Act, combinations and conspiracies in restraint of trade were illegal. Whether or not this prohibition applied to labor was unclear.

In 1908 the Supreme Court, in the case of *Loewe* v. *Lawler,* commonly referred to as the *Danbury Hatters case,* ruled that the activities of labor unions are subject to the prohibitions of the Sherman Act. In 1921, the case of *Duplex Printing Press Co.* v. *Deering,* also decided by the Supreme Court, confirmed the High Court's stance that labor unions are subject to antitrust legislation. The reasoning was that since a strike could impede the flow of goods, restraint of trade could result from labor activities. Thus, in the early 1900's, unprotected by legislation, unions were subject to injunctions if they attempted to strike.

Norris-LaGuardia Act. As the use of injunctions increased during the early part of the 20th century, the call for reform became more intense. The result was the passage in 1932 of the Norris-LaGuardia Act, which significantly restricted the use of injunctions in labor disputes. Norris-LaGuardia also prohibited *yellow-dog contracts,* agreements under which an employee, as a condition of employment, agrees not to join a union.

Wagner Act. Even though the Norris-LaGuardia Act restricted the activities of employers, it did little to establish affirmative rights for employees. To affirmatively establish and clarify the rights of employees, Congress passed the National Labor Relations Act of 1935, commonly called the Wagner Act.

Essentially, the Wagner Act states that employees have the right to unionize and bargain collectively. Congress empowered the National Labor Relations Board to rule on alleged unfair labor practices under the Wagner Act.

Taft-Hartley Act. In the ensuing years, under the protection of the Wagner Act, unions increased in power. A decade after the passage of the Wagner Act, there was concern that unions had become too powerful. To curb potential union abuses, in 1947 Congress passed the Labor-Management Relations Act, commonly called the Taft-Hartley Act. The Taft-Hartley Act amended the Wagner Act by adding certain provisions. Primary among those provisions were ones limiting the use of strikes.

The Taft-Hartley Act affirmed the legally binding nature of an employment contract. If either party does not live up to its contractual obligations, the aggrieved party can sue.

The Taft-Hartley Act defines six unfair labor practices applicable to union activities:

1. A union cannot interfere with the right of employers to choose employees' supervisors.

2. A union cannot seek to have an employee fired, except in the event of nonpayment of union dues and fees.

3. A union cannot fail to collectively bargain in good faith with employers.

4. A union cannot set high initiation fees for the purpose of discriminating against certain potential members.

5. Featherbedding cannot be used to force employers to pay for services that have not in fact been rendered.

6. Secondary boycotts, refusing on an organized basis to deal with an organization other than the one with which the union has a dispute, cannot be employed.

Right to work. One provision of the Taft-Hartley Act that caused organized labor considerable concern was the prohibition against *closed shops,* businesses in which union membership is a precondition of employment. The Taft-Hartley Act made such arrangements illegal. The *union shop,* a work place where an employee need not be a union member before being employed but must become one after being hired, is not prohibited, but Taft-Hartley gives individual states the right to ban them. State laws that ban closed shops are called *right-to-work laws;* they currently exist in 21 states.

Fair Labor Standards Act.

The Fair Labor Standards Act of 1938, commonly called the Wage and Hour Act, establishes the standard work week at 40 hours for employees of firms involved in interstate commerce. Hourly workers who work more than 40 hours in any given week are entitled to time and a half pay for the overtime hours. It further prohibits the use of children under the age of 14.

Equal Pay Act. In the United States, the decade of the 1960's witnessed mounting concern for civil rights. Between 1963 and 1973, Congress enacted several important pieces of legislation relating to fair employment and discrimination. The first was

THE MINIMUM WAGE *has been raised periodically to reflect increases in the cost of living.*

MINIMUM WAGE IN U.S.

Year	Rate per hour
1938	$ .25
1950	.75
1956	1.00
1961	1.15
1963	1.25
1967	1.40
1968	1.60
1974	2.00
1975	2.10
1976	2.30
1978	2.65
1979	2.90
1980	3.10
1981	3.35

the Equal Pay Act of 1963, which requires that pay rates be the same for both sexes. A woman, for example, must be paid the same wage as a man working for the same company if they perform equal work, defined by the act as "jobs the performance of which requires equal skill, effort, and responsibility, and which are performed under similar working conditions." Equal work does not, under the Equal Pay Act, mean identical work.

It is important to note that the Equal Pay Act does not require equal pay for jobs of equal value. This concept, called *comparable worth,* became an issue 20 years later.

One of the shortcomings of the Equal Pay Act is that it only requires that women who hold the same job as a man be paid the same wage, or vice versa. It does not legislate against discrimination that prevents women from acquiring such jobs in the first place.

Civil Rights Act.
In 1964 Congress passed the Civil Rights Act. Title VII of that statute deals with business practices that tend to discriminate against individuals because of personal characteristics. The act provides that:

1. It is unlawful for employers to fail or refuse to hire or to discharge any individual, or otherwise to discriminate against any individual with respect to his or her compensation, terms, condition, or privileges of employment because of the individual's race, color, religion, sex, or national origin.

2. It is unlawful for an employer to limit, segregate, or classify his or her employees or applicants for employment in any way that would deprive or tend to deprive any individual of employment opportunities or otherwise adversely affect status as an employee on the basis of that employee's race, color, religion, sex, or national origin.

Pregnancy Discrimination Act.
A question left unresolved by the Civil Rights Act was whether pregnant women were protected from differential treatment. Many argued that since pregnancy related only to women, such a classification was indeed in violation of the Civil Rights Act. The Supreme Court, however, in the case of *General Electric Co.* v. *Gilbert,* held in 1976 that a company disability plan that excluded pregnant employees from benefits does not violate the provisions of Title VII of the Civil Rights Act.

The resulting furor caused Congress to pass the Pregnancy Discrimination Act of 1978, which amended Title VII to include pregnancy and childbirth. As a result, employers' disability plans cannot exclude benefits for disabilities related to pregnancy and childbirth.

Age Discrimination in Employment Act.
Another area left unregulated by the Civil Rights Act was discrimination on the basis of age. In 1967 Congress passed the Age Discrimination in Employment Act, which expands the provisions of Title VII of the Civil Rights Act to include discrimination on the basis of age. Originally, the act protected only those workers between the ages of 40 and 65. The upper age limit was subsequently raised to 70 and eliminated altogether in 1986. The Age Discrimination in Employment Act protects only people over 40. It provides no protection for younger workers, so companies are free to establish minimum ages for certain jobs.

Reverse discrimination.
An issue that developed in the 1970's and 1980's was that of *reverse discrimination.* What happens, for example, if a company, in its efforts to make sure that women are given equal opportunity, discriminates against men? The issue of reverse discrimination reached the Supreme Court in 1979. The United Steelworkers of America and Kaiser Aluminum had developed and implemented an affirmative action program that reserved for blacks one-half of the positions in a training program. As a result, some blacks were accepted into the program over whites with more seniority. The practice was challenged and in *United Steelworkers of America* v. *Weber,* the Supreme Court ruled that the plan was legal and fulfilled one of the Civil Rights Act's main objectives, the elimination of a traditional form of employee discrimination, race. Although most reverse discrimination suits have not been successful, the courts and the legislature

THE CIVIL RIGHTS ACT *helped open many professions to women.*

KROLL/TAURUS PHOTOS

have yet to develop a definitive policy on how far businesses may and are expected to go in ensuring the rights of minority groups.

OSHA.
The Occupational Safety and Health Act was passed in 1970 to ensure safe and healthy working conditions in American businesses. The Occupational Health and Safety Administration (OSHA) was established by the act to enforce its provisions. OSHA has the authority to conduct periodic inspections to ensure that safety standards are being observed. OSHA is empowered to issue citations for non-compliance and may impose fines.

Consumer Protection

Historically, the concept of *caveat emptor,* let the buyer beware, was the basic principle governing relationships between buyers and sellers. It was up to buyers to look out for their own well-being.

The rationale for consumer protection under the law is based on the precept that accurate information is a requirement if the free-market mechanism is to benefit society. False and misleading product claims rob consumers of such information.

Modern consumer protection statutes relate to four major areas of consumer affairs:

1. unfair and deceptive retail trade practices,
2. sales to consumers of goods, services, and property,
3. consumer credit, and
4. consumer safety.

Federal Trade Commission.
The primary federal regulatory agency involved in the investigation of unfair or deceptive trade practices is the Federal Trade Commission (FTC). Specific powers granted the FTC include the power to issue injunctions, cease and desist orders, for the following ends:

1. Prohibiting a firm from continuing to engage in certain activities considered unfair or deceptive by the FTC, such as false or misleading advertising.
2. Requiring that a firm perform some specific act, such as rewording certain commercials or airing corrective advertising.
3. Requiring that a firm provide proof of advertising claims.
4. Requiring that a firm make certain trademarks available on a royalty basis to anyone desiring to use them.
5. Requiring that a firm rescind a particular contract, such as one entered into as a result of unsubstantiated product claims.
6. Ordering refunds or awarding compensatory damages.

THE FTC: AFFIRMATIVE DISCLOSURE

In 1976 the Federal Trade Commission took action against the National Commission on Egg Nutrition (NCEN). NCEN, through its advertising, had attempted to combat information alleging that the cholesterol in eggs can contribute to the likelihood of heart disease and other circulatory diseases. The NCEN launched an advertising campaign asserting that "there is no scientific evidence that eating eggs increases the risk of heart and [circulatory] disease. . . ."

The FTC ruled that the advertising campaign was deceptive and ordered affirmative disclosure. Specifically, the FTC required that in future ads, the NCEN include a statement to the effect that many medical authorities believe that ingesting cholesterol can increase the likelihood of heart and circulatory disease. It also required that future ads refrain from making disparaging comments regarding the scientific evidence linking cholesterol with such disease.

Deceptive advertising.

In recent years, advertising practices have come under particular scrutiny by the FTC. In the broadest sense, the FTC prohibits deceptive advertising. What constitutes a deceptive advertisement, however, has been open to debate. The test generally used by the FTC is whether the advertisement may have the effect of deceiving the reasonable consumer. This does not mean all consumers or even necessarily the average consumer. It also does not mean that the ad need be false. (A half-truth or partial truth that tends to mislead is considered deceptive.)

In a policy statement issued by the FTC in 1983, the commission solidified its stance on deceptive advertising. This policy statement reaffirmed earlier rulings by the FTC that establishing actual deception or intent to deceive is not a requirement for declaring an ad deceptive. The requirement is that there be a "tendency" to deceive. This means that even an ad that is basically truthful can sometimes be considered deceptive.

Affirmative disclosure.
FTC may use three specific remedies with respect to advertising practices. One such remedy is the power to order affirmative disclosure. *Affirmative disclosure* requires that an offender include certain information in his or her advertisements.

Corrective advertising.
Yet another remedy available in the event of deceptive advertising is corrective advertising. *Corrective advertising* is an even more powerful remedy than affirmative disclosure, because it requires that an advertiser reveal in future ads that prior claims were not true or were not substantiated.

Multiple product orders.
Multiple product orders represent yet another remedy available to the FTC. *Multiple product orders* require advertisers to modify advertising related not only to the product in question, but to all products sold by the company.

Consumer purchases.
Another major area of legislative and judicial involvement in consumer protection relates to purchases of goods, services, and property. With respect to such purchases, warranties play a major role.

There are two types of warranties relative to sale of goods contracts. *Express warranties* arise out of specific statements, written or oral, made by the seller or manufacturer, while *implied warranties* are created by law.

Express warranties.
Any statement made by a seller regarding the characteristics, quality, or capabilities of a product constitutes an express warranty. If the product fails to live up to the express warranty, a breach of warranty exists and consumer remedies are available.

Implied warranties.
An implied warranty differs from an express warranty in that it arises out of law rather than from any specific statements made by the seller. One such warranty is the *warranty of title:* a seller of goods guarantees that the goods are free of liens and that the seller has the legal right to convey ownership.

Another implied warranty is the *warranty of merchantability*, which guarantees that the goods sold are fit for the purpose that such goods normally serve. The warranty of merchantability applies to used as well as new goods, but the degree of protection is less than would be the case with new goods. The age, price, and condition of the used goods are all factors in determining the degree of merchantability that is warranted. The implied warranty of merchantability applies to merchant sellers only.

The implied *warranty of fitness* for a particular purpose applies to all sellers, merchant and nonmerchant. This warranty, however, applies only if the seller is aware of the use to which the buyer intends to put the product and the buyer relies on the advice and knowledge of the seller to provide an appropriate product.

Warranty disclaimers.
Sellers may exclude or limit certain warranties provided that the language of the contract is clear and explicit in its exclusions or limitations. Although the exact wording of disclaimers may vary, a typical disclaimer may read, "The warranties herein are expressly in lieu of any other express or implied warranty, including any implied warranty of merchantability or fitness."

Consumer credit.
A consumer credit transaction is one in which the credit obtained is for the purpose of acquiring consumer goods, services, or property. In 1968, Congress passed the Federal Consumer Credit Protection Act. This statute set the stage for considerable consumer legislation in the 1970's.

There are five major areas of legislation related to consumer credit: (1) access to credit, (2) disclosure of credit information, (3) regulation of the terms of the credit contract, (4) reporting of consumer credit information, and (5) creditor remedies.

MAGNUSON-MOSS WARRANTY ACT

The major federal statute dealing with warranties is the Magnuson-Moss Warranty Act. Passed by Congress in 1974, the statute requires that sellers provide buyers with adequate warranty information. Enforced by the Federal Trade Commission, the act provides that:

1. Written warranties must be worded clearly.

2. Written warranties must be identified as either "full" or "limited." To be considered a full warranty, it must state that: (a) the warrantor will fix, without charge, the defective product; (b) the warrantor will replace the product or provide a refund if the original product cannot be repaired; (c) consequential damages (such as food spoilage resulting from the malfunctioning of a freezer) are not excluded or limited unless such exclusion or limitation is conspicuously indicated on the face of the warranty; (d) no implied warranty is excluded or limited in its duration. A limited warranty is one that does not comply with all of the above conditions.

3. Implied warranties cannot be disclaimed by written warranties. Such implied warranties, however, may be limited in their duration if there is a written statement to that effect.

The Magnuson Act applies only to the sale of consumer goods accompanied by a written warranty. Contracts for sale of industrial or commercial products are not covered.

UNIFORM COMMERCIAL CODE

The Uniform Commercial Code is perhaps the most important set of laws governing relations between merchants, and between merchants and consumers, in the United States. The code is a body of laws and legal principles drawn up in 1952 in order to standardize the law of commercial transactions. The code replaced several acts that covered some of the same subjects. Among them were the Uniform Negotiable Instruments Act, the Uniform Sales Act, and the Uniform Stock Transfer Act. The Uniform Commercial Code has been ratified by every state except Louisiana.

The code is divided into several parts, each dealing with a different area of commercial law. The section on sales discusses such matters as sales contracts, warranties, terms of delivery, auctions, and breach of contract. Sections concerning commercial paper and banking deal with checks, drafts, and other negotiable instruments; letters of credit; and bank deposits and collections. The code also contains sections concerning sales of items in bulk; documents of title, such as warehouse receipts and bills of lading; investment securities; and personal property security.

Access to credit. The Equal Credit Opportunity Act of 1974 prohibits lenders from discriminating against potential borrowers on the basis of sex, marital status, race, color, religion, national origin, or age. Creditors are required to act on credit applications within 30 days of receipt and give consumers who are denied credit detailed reasons for the denial.

Disclosure of credit terms. The Truth in Lending Act (Title I of the Federal Consumer Credit Protection Act) provides that the consumer must be provided with specified information prior to formalizing a credit arrangement. Required disclosures under the Truth in Lending Act include the following: interest and finance rates must be stated on an annual percentage rate (APR) basis; consumers applying for open-ended credit accounts (revolving charge accounts) must be told how the finance charges are computed; consumers entering into closed-end credit arrangements (a credit arrangement, such as an installment purchase, where only one purchase is included in the contract) must be told the cash price of the item, the total amount subject to finance charges, the number, amount, and due dates of the payments, the applicable delinquency charges, and the collateral securing the loan.

Billing errors. The Fair Credit Billing Act of 1974 provides a specified procedure that a consumer may follow in the event that any billing errors have been committed relative to the credit contract.

The creditor is required to respond to complaints filed by consumers; until the creditor does so, he or she may not take action to collect amounts in dispute. The creditor is also barred from restricting the consumer's use of a revolving charge account or reporting the account as delinquent until the dispute is resolved.

Fair credit reporting. Before a business grants credit to a consumer, the business generally conducts a credit check on the applicant. This credit check includes obtaining information about the applicant from credit bureaus that collect such information for the express purpose of supplying it to potential creditors.

To ensure that such information is collected and disseminated appropriately, Congress passed the Fair Credit Reporting Act in 1970. Under this statute, credit information agencies are required to correct all erroneous information and eliminate outdated information from a consumer's credit record. Upon request, all consumers have the right to know the contents of their credit file, the sources of information contained therein, and the names of those to whom the information has been disseminated. If the consumer feels that any of the information is incorrect, the agency must conduct an investigation to ascertain the truth. If the agency is unable to resolve the dispute, it may leave the disputed information in the consumer's file, but the consumer has the right to have his own statement included in the file.

Creditor rights. By statute and regulation, creditors have remedies available to them in the event that a credit agreement has been breached. Subject to limits established by law, the creditor has the right to exact penalties for late payments. In the event of default, the creditor has the right to declare the entire balance remaining due.

If there is a cosigner to a credit agreement, the creditor has the right to collect the amount outstanding from that cosigner in the event of default by the debtor. If the debt is secured by specific collateral, the creditor may claim that collateral and sell it to satisfy the remainder of the obligation.

The right of the creditor to collect amounts due is not without constraints. The Fair Debt Collection Practices Act of 1978 was passed in order to prevent abuses in collection practices. Under this act, creditors are forbidden from harassing a debtor in an attempt to collect overdue amounts. If the debtor is represented by a lawyer, the creditor must deal with that attorney and is forbidden from contacting the debtor directly.

Consumer safety. In the contemporary marketplace, consumers have the right to expect that they will not suffer injury because of negligently manufactured products.

Tort law. Much of this right to safety rests in tort law. A tort is a willful or negligent act that results in harm to another. Persons who assault others can be held liable under tort law for the damage that they cause. The concept of tort law has been extended through statute and court cases to the area of product liability.

Many states have extended the concept of tort law to include situations in which harm is sustained even if negligence on the part of the manufacturer is not established. Under this principle, the aggrieved party must establish that the product was defective; that the product defect was the cause of some injury or damage; and that the product defect made the product unreasonably dangerous.

Pure Food and Drug Act. In addition to the protection of tort law, many statutes have been passed to protect consumers from dangerous or potentially harmful products. As early as 1906, the Pure Food and Drug Act prohibited adulteration of food and drug products. In 1938 this statute was expanded through passage of the Food, Drug, and Cosmetic Act. It prohibited false and misleading labels and established quality standards for food and cosmetic products. The Kefauver-Harris drug amendments passed in 1962 further expanded the Pure Food and Drug Act.

Fair Packaging and Labeling Act. In 1966 Congress passed the Fair Packaging and Labeling Act, requiring that manufacturers provide certain information on product labels. According to its provisions, manufacturers must identify the product, provide the name and address of the manufacturer, and provide other information relating to the quality of the product.

RALPH NADER *has been influential in promoting consumer rights legislation.*

UPI/BETTMANN NEWSPHOTOS

Consumer Product Safety Act. One of the most significant statutes passed in the interest of consumer safety in recent years is the Consumer Product Safety Act of 1972. Enforced by the Consumer Product Safety Commission, the express purposes of this statute include:

1. Protection of consumers from risk of injury associated with the use of consumer goods.

2. Assistance in evaluating the relative safety of various product offerings.

3. Development of safety standards for consumer products.

4. Promotion of investigation into the causes and prevention of injury, illness, and death caused by consumer products.

The Consumer Product Safety Commission, created by the act to enforce its provisions, has the power to ban or order the recall of products that it considers hazardous. It may also order the manufacturers of the products to issue a public notice of the hazard and to notify all known purchasers.

Environmental Protection

In the early years of the development of the United States, resources seemed unlimited. Since additional resources could always be procured by moving west or tapping vast reserves, conservation was not viewed as important. An equal lack of concern existed with regard to the environment. Since the United States was primarily an agrarian society with a modest population, pollution was minimal and the manufacturing activity that did exist posed little threat to the ecological balance.

As the United States became more industrialized, however, the impact of industrial pursuits became more severe. It was not until the 1960's, however, that it became apparent that unrestrained industrial activity was harming the quality of the environment. Some of the damage, it was felt, was irreversible. Social pressure mounted to bring a halt to potentially harmful business activities.

Clean Air Act.
Although the first piece of federal environmental legislation was the Refuse Act of 1899, which prohibited the dumping of waste into navigable waters without a permit, the Clean Air Act of 1963, the first modern statute, ushered in the era of environmental concern. Although the Clean Air Act dealt only with air pollution, it was later expanded to include solid waste pollution, toxic substances, nuclear energy, and water pollution.

National Environmental Policy Act.
In 1969 Congress passed the National Environmental Policy Act, which committed the government to enhancing and maintaining the environment. The act states it is the responsibility of the government to use all practical means to:

1. Fulfill the responsibility of each generation as trustee of the environment for generations to come.

2. Provide a safe, healthy, productive, and aesthetic environment for all Americans.

3. Use the resources of the environment in the best possible way without health or safety risk and without degrading the quality of the environment.

4. Preserve the cultural, historic, and natural elements prevalent in the environment.

5. Achieve a balance between the use of resources and a high standard of living.

6. Enhance the quality of renewable resources and use recycling of resources to the greatest extent possible.

Perhaps the most significant aspect of the act was that it established the Environmental Protection Agency (EPA) to formulate and enforce regulations to meet its objectives.

Comprehensive Environmental Response, Compensation, and Liability Act.
In 1980 Congress passed the Comprehensive Environmental Response, Compensation, and Liability Act (CERCL) to regulate hazardous waste sites, a problem of paramount importance in the 1980's. CERCL requires that hazardous waste sites in the United States be inspected to ensure that they present no risk to health. The act further established a hazardous waste fund to be used to eliminate or curtail the expansion of existing sites.

Environmental Protection Agency.
The primary federal regulatory agency for protecting and enhancing the environment is the Environmental Protection Agency (EPA). Since its creation in 1970, the EPA has been involved in establishing emissions standards for automobiles, factories, and other sources of pollution that result from the activities of an industrialized economy. The specific activities of the EPA include:

1. Directing and regulating the use of pesticides (it may also order the removal of hazardous pesticides from the market).

2. Establishing noise level standards for vehicles, commercial equipment, and appliances.

3. Determining which chemicals present an "unreasonable risk of injury to health or the environment" and prohibiting or controlling their manufacture, distribution, and disposal.

4. Regulating the disposal of toxic and nontoxic waste.

5. Enforcing provisions of the 1970 Clean Air Act related to automobile emissions standards, and granting extensions to compliance deadlines if the technology is not available to meet requirements of the act and if auto manufacturers are making good-faith efforts to meet such standards.

6. Establishing air quality standards for stationary sources, such as factories, and regulating emissions from such sources.

THE PROTECTION OF THE ENVIRONMENT *from hazardous wastes has become an increasingly important part of governmental regulation of business.*

NATION/SYGMA

7. Setting guidelines and ensuring compliance with water pollution regulations, including thermal pollution from nuclear reactors.

8. Setting standards for an acceptable overall level of radiation in the environment.

9. Establishing standards and guidelines for disposal of radioactive waste.

Deregulation

During the late 1970's and early 1980's, pressure mounted to decrease the amount of government regulation to which businesses were subject. Those who favored deregulation argued that large-scale government intervention in the private sector often makes it difficult for businesses to accomplish their primary function, the production and distribution of goods and services. They further argued that compliance with regulatory constraints can be excessively costly, makes businesses unable to meet foreign competition, and ultimately costs jobs. In short, it was said, the government had gone too far in interfering with the free market system.

One of the major campaign positions of the Republican Party in 1980 and 1984 was a promise to reduce the size of government and its role in business regulation. The move toward deregulation actually started before then, with moves toward deregulation of the financial and transportation industries in 1978.

Airline Deregulation Act.
The Airline Deregulation Act of 1978 was one of the first significant statutes aimed at reducing government intervention in a major industry. It gave individual carriers greater control over the rates they charge, the services they offer, and the routes they maintain.

Financial institutions.
In 1979 the federal government began the process of removing interest rate ceilings on deposits in financial institutions. The objective was to make savings and loan associations, as well as other financial institutions, more competitive with banks. Deregulation was almost complete by 1986 and has resulted in a more competitive financial industry.

Staggers Rail Act.
The Staggers Rail Act of 1980 gave railroads more control over their rates and allowed them to discontinue unprofitable routes and to sign long-term contracts with customers. Similar relaxation of controls has been applied to the trucking industry.

Not everyone considers deregulation to be beneficial. Some fear, for example, that deregulation of the airline industry will actually make it less competitive as many small airlines are forced out of business. Some also fear that decreased regulation and the resultant fierce competition may result in unsafe flying conditions if airlines skimp on necessary maintenance in order to reduce operating costs.

Small Business

Small businesses play a vital role in maintaining the competitive nature of the U.S. economy. Small businesses constitute over 97 percent of all nonfarm businesses in the United States. Over 80 percent of all firms in the United States have annual sales of $100,000 or less. They employ nearly one-half of nonfarm employees and create more new jobs annually than do large businesses. According to the Small Business Administration, small businesses are also more likely to hire women, part-timers, and older or younger workers.

The Small Business Act of 1953 defines a small business as one that is independently owned and operated and not dominant in its field of operation.

The Committee for Economic Development defines small business as one that is characterized by at least two of the following:

1. Independently managed, with the managers often owning the firm.

2. Ownership resting with one or a few individuals.

3. Primarily local operations.

4. Representing only a small proportion of the entire industry.

Types of Small Businesses

Although small businesses exist in virtually every sector of the economy, as one might anticipate, they are most prevalent in service industries and retailing.

Service businesses.
Over 60 percent of all workers employed in the United States work in service businesses, large and small. It is estimated that this figure will increase to 86 percent by the year 2000. Although some suppliers of services are large national or international organizations, such as insurance companies and some banks, most businesses supplying services are small. Television and radio stations, barber and beauty shops, repair shops, restaurants, collection agencies, accounting firms, moving and storage companies, real estate companies, theaters, and rental companies are all typically small service businesses.

Retailing.
Although large national retailers, such as discount and department stores, are more significant in terms of sales than smaller retail firms, small firms far outnumber large national chains. Clothing, jewelry, drugs, and thousands of other products are marketed primarily through small businesses.

WHAT IS A SMALL BUSINESS

A common definition of a small business is one that is owned and operated by an entrepreneur. The Small Business Administration, however, is more precise in its definition, making distinctions between types of businesses in deciding which businesses are large and which are small. For instance, a wholesaling business can be considered small with annual sales up to $22 million, while a retailing business is considered small up to $7.5 million in annual sales. Manufacturing businesses are measured by the number of people they employ and can be considered small with up to 1500 employees.

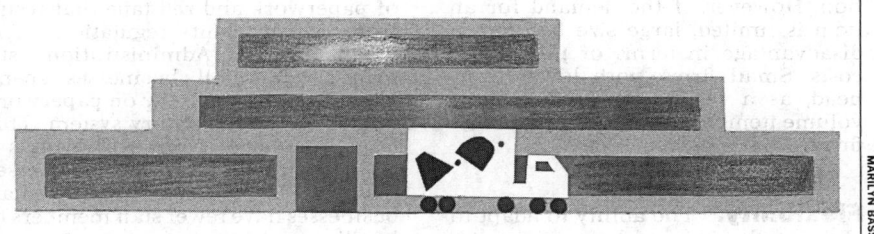

MARILYN BASS

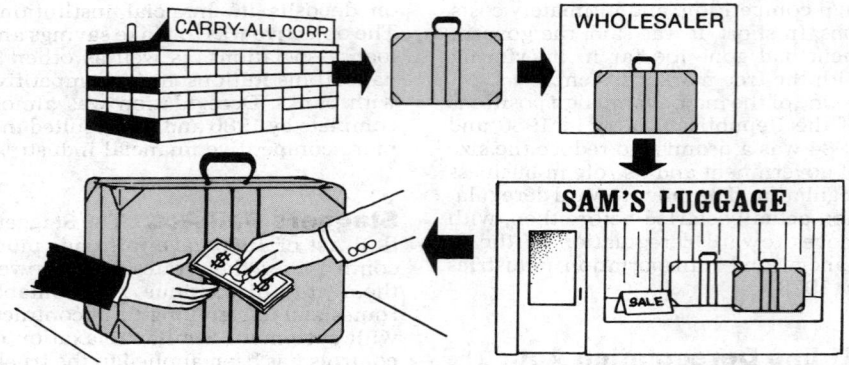

WHOLESALERS *act as middlemen between the producer of an item and the retailer, often distributing the products of several producers.*

Wholesaling. Wholesalers may buy finished goods from manufacturers and sell them to retailers or to other businesses, which resell them to consumers. Wholesalers are important in both the consumer and industrial markets. Such consumer products as hardware, drugs, clothing, automotive parts, and food products are typically distributed by wholesalers.

Construction. Builders of homes and other structures are important to overall business activity. They are so significant that the level of construction activity is often used by the government as a key economic indicator. Most construction companies are small, concentrating their activities in a small geographic area.

Manufacturing. Because of the capital required and the relatively high operating costs of heavy manufacturing, most manufacturing companies in key industries, such as automotive and steel, are large businesses. Small firms often exist, however, as suppliers for the larger firms or in the production of custom-made or low demand products.

Advantages of Small Businesses

Small businesses have an important role in the American economy because of their special advantages over large firms and the benefits they provide society. It is hard to imagine life without barber shops, the corner gas station, or the local machine shop.

Innovation. Small firms are often leaders in developing new or innovative technology. Since large firms usually rely on economies of scale to earn a profit, they often prefer to produce their current product lines rather than spend additional sums in the development of new and improved products.

IBM, for example, although now the leader in the production of data processing equipment in the United States, was not responsible for the development of the electronic computer. A small company, Univac Corporation, developed the first commercial electronic computer and ushered in the computer age. At the time, IBM had a considerable investment in the punch-card equipment business. Since it controlled 97 percent of this industry, IBM had little incentive to develop revolutionary products, especially products that would replace its major business.

Because small businesses are unencumbered by the large bureaucracy that often accompanies large business operations, they have the flexibility necessary to adopt new and creative ways of doing things.

Employee development. Since small businesses generally do not have the high degree of job specialization typical of large companies, their employees usually have the opportunity to learn a wide variety of skills and become involved in the overall operations of the company. As a result, they may find their jobs more satisfying than similar jobs in large companies. Workers who are trained in many areas tend to become effective managers: they have a good understanding of the overall operations of the business and how the pieces fit together.

Costs of production. One of the reasons why large companies become large is to take advantage of economies of scale, that is, spread overhead costs over large numbers of units of production. However, if the demand for an item is limited, large size becomes a disadvantage in terms of production costs. Small firms, with lower overhead, as a result can produce low-volume items at lower costs than large firms.

Flexibility. The ability to adapt to changing business and economic con-

ditions often means the difference between business success and failure. Large corporations, because of their size and bureaucratic structure, are often unable to react quickly to changing conditions. The small business owner, on the other hand, can generally react quickly, because a small business does not have a large and complicated organizational structure.

Disadvantages of Small Businesses

Most of the approximately 250,000 new businesses formed every year do not survive. Thirty percent fail within the first year of operation. One-half do not survive past the second year. Eventually, about two-thirds will either close their doors voluntarily or be forced into bankruptcy. The vast majority of business failures are small businesses. According to the Small Business Administration, the typical failing business has fewer than 20 employees and outstanding debt between $25,000 and $100,000.

Management limitations. A significant factor in the failure of many small businesses is lack of expert management. Many entrepreneurs start their own businesses because they have grown tired of their jobs or are unemployed. They often have little training or experience in running a business. Although they may be technically knowledgeable about the product they produce, they may have had no experience in finance, personnel, management, or marketing.

Research indicates that those entrepreneurs with management experience have more than twice the chance of success of entrepreneurs who lack such experience.

Lack of financing. The most common cause of small business failure is lack of adequate financing. Many small businesses start with too little capital and are unable to make it through rough times without experiencing a shortage of funds.

Government regulation. One of the most common complaints of small business managers is the amount of paperwork and red tape that result from government regulation. The Small Business Administration estimates that small businesses spend about $13 billion a year on paperwork related to the regulatory system. This large amount of paperwork causes a greater burden for small businesses than for large firms because small businesses have fewer staff members to handle regulatory requirements.

LENNON/PHOTO RESEARCHERS

BUSINESSES CAN FAIL *for reasons as varied as poor location, bad inventory control, or an attempt by the owner to draw from the business more income than it can support.*

Reasons For Failure

Lack of experience. Although most first-time entrepreneurs have experience in the type of business they are initiating, they may not have experience in running that type of business. Managing a business is quite different from working for one.

As a business grows, problems surface. Developing an organization to handle increasing sales is an experience that few first-time entrepreneurs have. Hiring additional employees, developing an effective management structure, managing cash flow and working capital, and controlling larger inventories are problems associated with growth. Many businesses that survive for years may eventually fail because they cannot manage growth.

Insufficient capital. When a new business is launched, many expenses accrue before the business ever serves its first customer. Even if the entrepreneur has calculated these expenses and has enough money to meet them, there are still two pitfalls to contend with.

First, expenses are invariably higher than anticipated, and there are expenses that the entrepreneur failed to consider. No one can think of everything. Some experts recommend that when budgeting start-up expenses, businesspeople should arbitrarily add 25 or even 50 percent to allow for unanticipated expenses.

The second major pitfall associated with financing is that start-up costs are not the only expenses that must be met. Most business are not immediately profitable, and some take years to become financially viable. During this period, operating expenses must be met, at least in part, by funds provided from sources other than sales revenue.

Wrong location. In order to minimize start-up costs, an entrepreneur may choose a business location because it has an attractive purchase price or low rent. In some cases, the location of the business may not be important, but if the business is a retail store or other business that relies on easy accessibility, the proper location may mean the difference between success and failure.

Successful entrepreneurs suggest that the future be considered in the selection of a location. Although a business generally is small when it is initiated, many businesses grow. Expanding a facility is often less expensive than moving to a larger one. Entrepreneurs should ask themselves such questions as: Is there sufficient room for building an addition to the building? If my business grows, will there be sufficient parking for my employees and customers?

Inventory management. Since small businesses generally have little excess cash, tying too much of it up in inventory can be disastrous. On the other hand, not having goods available when customers want them is equally undesirable. The key to inventory management is simple—keep enough inventory on hand to meet demand, but no more. In practice, determining proper inventory levels is difficult. It is an important factor, however, because a small business cannot afford to have funds tied up unnecessarily.

Another major mistake regarding inventory management, in addition to buying too much or too little, is buying improperly. Carrying a large stock of fast-moving goods is usually necessary. Inventory levels of slow moving goods, however, should not be as large. Complicating the problem is the fact that customer tastes change, sometimes abruptly. Obsolete inventory items are worth very little and can quickly erase the profit of a small business, which may be only 2 or 3 percent of sales in any case.

Excess capital assets. When a business buys a piece of equipment, it loses its market value quickly. This means that the business is essentially stuck with it. Since limited funds are almost always a problem, it is important to make large expenditures wisely. Consider small manufacturers whose businesses are growing. To meet the demands of their customers, the manufacturers may buy automated and expensive equipment. They are relying on continued sales growth to justify the purchase of the equipment. If sales decline, however, they may no longer need the equipment but still have to make the payments on the loans they have obtained to buy it.

From time to time, all businesses must buy new equipment or replace obsolete machinery with more efficient models. The key is to make such investments only when they are necessary and will pay benefits. Small business owners must be particularly careful when purchasing equipment that does not add directly to productivity or profits. Sophisticated computer equipment and word processing systems can be helpful in running a business, but they can also represent an unnecessary expense and should not be purchased unless they will add to the profitability of the company.

Poor credit policies. The ideal situation, from a cash flow perspective, is for a small business to sell only on a cash basis. To remain competitive, however, many feel compelled to grant credit. Although a common business practice, the extension of credit can be costly, since uncollectable accounts can quickly eat up the modest profits of a small business.

Excess withdrawals. A natural temptation to a business owner is to live like a proprietor. A small business, however, often cannot support a large salary for an owner or owners who would like to have a boat and a cottage on the lake. The prudent move is to put as much profit back into a business as possible, particularly during the early years. As the business grows, it will be better able to provide the level of salary the owner wants.

Overstaffing. For many small businesses, employee wages represent the highest cost of business operations. In many cases, one unnecessary employee is enough to erase the total annual profits of the company. An employee who is paid $20,000 a year must contribute more than that to the total revenue of the firm.

Tips for Success

Plan ahead. Small businesses cannot afford surprises. Planning is necessary for effective development of marketing strategies, production scheduling, purchasing, and the hiring of personnel. One of the most important planning areas is finance. Expenses, as well as anticipated revenues, must be budgeted. In this way, businesses can plan for loans if, for example, the businesses experience seasonal fluctuations. A financial plan also gives the businesses a control mechanism, allowing variances from the budget to be corrected before they get out of hand.

Find a niche. Small businesses do not have the resources to be all things to all people. Because businesses are eager to please customers and increase sales, a small business might try to do too much. The owner of a restaurant located near a college campus, for example, may have difficulty appealing

---

THE SMALL BUSINESS ADMINISTRATION

The primary federal agency involved in assisting small business enterprises is the Small Business Administration (SBA). Founded in 1953, the SBA provides financial assistance, assistance in procuring government contracts, and consulting and training services.

Financial assistance: Two types of loan programs are administered by the Small Business Administration. Some loans are made directly by the SBA to small businesses; others are made by private lenders but guaranteed up to 90 percent by the SBA.
 The SBA also makes loans to handicapped people and other specifically designated groups, such as minorities and business people who have suffered losses resulting from natural disasters or civil disorders.

Help in obtaining government contracts: By law, small businesses are entitled to a share of all government contracts. Although the SBA does not guarantee success in obtaining such contracts, it does provide guidance on how to go about applying for and bidding on them.

Training and consulting: The SBA publishes hundreds of publications containing advice for the small business manager. The SBA has also established a number of management consulting programs, such as the Service Corps of Retired Executives and the Active Corps of Executives. These groups have volunteers who provide management consulting services to small businesses.

---

to both college students and families because of the different tastes of the two groups.

Get help. The owner of a small business must often be sales manager, personnel director, and production manager. There are areas of the business, however, that cannot be managed by one person. Since the financial aspect of a small business is crucial, small businesses should obtain the services of a professional accountant who can advise not only on matters related to the overall financial health of the business, but on expansion programs or the undertaking of other projects.

Small businesses should also seek the assistance of an attorney to make certain that contracts are executed legally and that zoning laws, licensing requirements, and other aspects of the business meet legal requirements.
 Since a small business usually needs financial assistance from time to time, a reliable banker is also a must.

Stay lean. Because of their limited resources, small businesses must be as streamlined as possible. Unnecessary personnel, large offices, and nonessential equipment represent drains on the moderate profitability realized by most small businesses.

International Business

THE UNITED STATES *is both the largest importer and the largest exporter in the world and has trading ties with almost every country.*

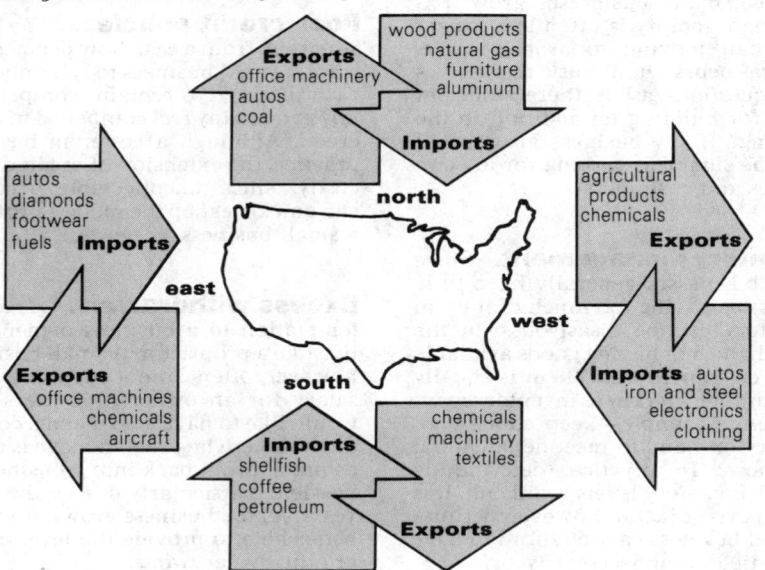

As a country develops, it usually becomes specialized in the goods it produces. This specialization has two major effects. First, the country becomes efficient in the production of those goods and develops a *comparative advantage;* it can produce and sell those goods at a lower cost than other countries. The second major effect of specialization is *surplus production.* Since the country becomes efficient in the production of certain goods and allocates resources to their production, it creates a surplus of goods that cannot be consumed by its own people.

Just as a country produces more of some types of goods than it needs, it produces less of other types of goods. The logical solution is for countries of the world to trade goods they have in abundance for goods they need. This is the basic reason for international trade.

Comparative advantage leading to surplus production may result from a number of causes. Australia, for example, because of its climate and other factors, is ideal for raising sheep. As a result, Australia is one of the world's leading exporters of wool. Saudi Arabia, Iraq, and other Middle Eastern countries have a comparative advantage in petroleum because of their vast oil reserves. Canada is a leading exporter of wheat because of its favorable climate and rich soil, and Argentina produces an abundance of beef because of its vast amount of open grazing land. Switzerland, although it does not possess abundant resources, does have many highly skilled craftsmen. As a result, Switzerland's comparative advantage lies in the production of high-value crafted items. Each of these countries uses its comparative advantage in the production of goods to trade for commodities it does not produce in abundance.

U.S. International Trade

Despite the fact that the United States is a highly productive economy, it is not self-sufficient and is highly involved in international trade. The United States is the world's leading importer of goods as well as the world's leading exporter. Although the U.S. trades with many nations throughout the world, Canada is the leading trading partner of the United States.

In recent years, the U.S. advantage in the production of manufactured goods has diminished. Plants and equipment in some industries, such as steel, have become outdated and inefficient. Labor costs have increased, as has government regulation. The result has been a growing ability on the part of other nations to compete with U.S. businesses. The U.S. balance of trade has reflected this trend, since the U.S. now imports far more than it exports.

In the early 1980's the demand for foreign goods grew significantly as a result of the strong dollar, which bought more goods on foreign markets than foreign currencies did on U.S. markets. In addition, increased dependence on foreign petroleum increased, and petroleum became the leading U.S. import.

Despite growing competition from foreign countries on the world market, U.S. companies are more involved in foreign trade than ever before. Over 25,000 U.S. firms are involved in international commerce in some form. One reason is that many firms now operate foreign subsidiaries to produce goods to be sold overseas as well as in the United States. In this manner, companies can take advantage of less expensive sources of labor and have easier access to foreign markets. Such foreign investment also benefits the host nation, since it brings needed technology, capital, and employment into the country, often a developing nation whose

economy is in need of such economic assistance. In 1970 U.S. investment in foreign nations totaled approximately $75.5 billion. By 1987 this total had increased to $308.8 billion.

Even firms that do not build production facilities in foreign nations often find that overseas markets are very profitable, particularly in industries in which the United States still holds an advantage. There is significant demand for U.S. agricultural products, aircraft, machinery, and computer equipment.

Trade Restrictions

Most countries strive for a favorable balance of trade, that is, a situation in which a nation's exports exceed its imports. This is considered favorable because under such conditions more money is coming into the country than is leaving it. It also results in greater employment, as the net monetary inflow stimulates domestic productivity. It has been estimated that each billion dollars in U.S. exports creates 40,000 jobs in the United States.

It is impossible for every nation to achieve a favorable balance of trade. If a nation's balance of trade becomes highly unfavorable and threatens to harm its economy, the nation may attempt to impede the flow of foreign imports. The two major techniques that have been used to reduce the flow of imports are protective tariffs and import quotas.

Tariffs. A *protective tariff* is a tax on imported goods. Such tariffs have the effect of increasing the price of imported goods, as importers pass the cost of the tariff along to customers, and of making domestically produced goods more competitive.

Quotas. An *import quota* is a limit on the amount of goods of a certain type that may be imported into a country. The objective of import quotas is basically the same as that of tariffs—to

TARIFFS *may have the effect of making cheaper imported goods more expensive than domestically produced goods.*

protect domestic producers or restore a favorable balance of trade. The United States imposes import quotas on many goods, including sugar, apparel, steel, machine tools, dairy products, automobiles, and over 100 categories of textiles.

Orderly market agreements. Some quotas result from negotiations between the United States and foreign governments. Such was the case in the 1980's, when President Reagan induced Japan to limit the number of automobiles it exports to the United States. Such agreements are called orderly market agreements.

Tariff wars. Countries must be careful about imposing tariffs and quotas; they may invite retaliation in the form of tariffs and quotas by other nations. The possibility of a tariff war is something that all countries try to avoid. Although all-out tariff wars are rare, tariff retaliation occurs with some frequency. In 1986, for example, the United States imposed a 35 percent tariff on imported Canadian cedar shingles and shakes. In retaliation, Canada imposed import tariffs on U.S. computer parts.

Dumping. One practice that most nations discourage is dumping. *Dumping* occurs when goods are sold abroad at a price less than the same goods bring in the producing nation or at a price significantly below the market price for such goods in the country to which they are exported. Countries may dump goods for a number of reasons. One is to gain a competitive foothold in the country to which the goods are exported. Companies may also dump products on a foreign market to dispose of excess production. Or they may dump products that are considered to be obsolete in their economy but still of value in less industrially advanced nations.

GATT. Despite the fact that at least some foreign trade restrictions exist in virtually all trading nations, efforts have increased to reduce trade barriers and make foreign trade more free and therefore more equitable.

A major step in this direction was the adoption in 1947 of the General Agreement on Tariffs and Trade (GATT). Since then the members of the GATT accord have engaged in many rounds of trade negotiations in an effort to reduce tariffs and eliminate other trade restrictions. The so-called Tokyo round of negotiations, conducted from 1975 to 1979, were particularly effective, and tariffs were reduced by nearly one-third on about 6000 products. By 1987, 94 countries had become members of the GATT accord, including the United States, Canada, and Japan and most of western Europe.

Foreign trade zones. A technique used to reduce the impact of tariffs and stimulate foreign trade is the establishment of foreign trade zones (FTZ), also referred to as customs-free zones, free ports, export processing zones, and free trade zones. An FTZ is an area in a nation that is considered to be part of a foreign country for trade purposes. Goods can be imported into foreign trade zones tariff free and reshipped to other countries. They may be processed within the FTZ and shipped abroad or to other parts of the country in which the FTZ is located, where import duties are then applied. For example, if a manufacturer builds a factory in a U.S. foreign trade zone, it may import raw materials and components duty-free as long as the materials are used within the FTZ. If the finished product is then shipped to a foreign country, U.S. tariffs are avoided altogether. If the product is sold in the United States, the tariff is levied when the product leaves the FTZ.

Although there are foreign trade zones located inland, many are located near ports of entry, such as Newark and Houston, to take advantage of shipping facilities. Additionally, companies may have their production facilities licensed as subzones, as U.S. automakers and other manufacturers have done.

The major advantage of an FTZ is that it provides jobs for American workers, jobs that would otherwise be performed by foreign workers. It also attracts business that U.S. companies would not otherwise be able to attract because of tariffs. Although the first foreign trade zone in the United States was established in 1934, the concept has seen significant growth only since the late 1970's. In 1980 there were about 50 FTZs compared with over 130 in 1987. The number of subzones increased from ten to over a hundred during the same period.

FACTORIES *are sometimes made foreign trade zones to promote exports.*

Trade Facilitating Organizations

Over the years many organizations have been established to stimulate foreign trade or assist companies in international operations.

The Export-Import Bank. The Export-Import Bank (EXIMBANK) of the United States was established in 1934 by the federal government to help facilitate foreign trade, particularly by financing export activities. Financed by the federal government, the bank lends money to foreign borrowers who wish to buy U.S. products, particularly capital goods. It also extends credit to U.S. exporters to facilitate distribution of goods to foreign countries. The Export-Import Bank also guarantees commercial loans that are made to U.S. exporters.

International Monetary Fund (IMF). The IMF was established in 1945 to promote international monetary cooperation and foreign exchange stability. It has developed into an important element of the international banking system. As of 1986, membership in the IMF totaled 151 nations, including virtually all those heavily involved in international trade. Exceptions are Switzerland, which cooperates with the activities of the IMF, the Soviet Union, and some countries of Eastern Europe.

Each member nation contributes a share to the IMF according to an assigned quota based on a number of factors, including the size of the nation's economy and the degree of its involvement in international trade. The pool of funds created by these contributions is used to facilitate international trade, support the creditworthiness of member nations, and provide currency liquidity.

The IMF, with headquarters in Washington, D.C., is directed by a board of governors that includes representatives from every member nation, 22 executive directors, and a managing director.

Sale of foreign currencies. If a member nation wishes to buy goods from another country, the IMF will sell that nation the foreign currency it requires in exchange for that nation's currency. This sale is actually a loan, because the nation that buys the foreign currency must repurchase its own currency at a date negotiated with the IMF. In this way, a perpetual pool of currencies is maintained.

Drawings. The IMF also assists nations that are experiencing temporary balance-of-payments difficulties resulting from export price declines by lending those nations funds to compensate for declining export revenues.

If, for example, the price of coffee declines significantly on the international market, resulting in a severe decline in export income for Brazil, Brazil may borrow from the IMF to offset the deficit. In the mid-1980's, several Latin American nations borrowed heavily from the IMF. One of the heaviest borrowers was Mexico, which sought to offset declining revenues from oil exports.

The amount that a country may borrow, called *drawings,* is based on the amount of its subscription and must be repaid within the time negotiated with the IMF, generally no longer than five years. Loans made by the IMF are normally contingent on the borrowing nation's compliance with certain IMF requirements, the object of which is to promote fiscal stability in the debtor nation. For example, loan agreements executed with Mexico in the 1980's required that Mexico take steps to reduce its rate of inflation, which had reached an annual rate of 85 percent.

In the mid-1980's, the IMF became concerned over the inability of some debtor nations to repay their debts. Peru alone owed over $600 million, of which $134 million was in arrears. By the end of 1986, five member nations were so far in arrears on their debt repayments that they were declared ineligible for additional loans. Many feared that the IMF would collapse. Additional contributions by member nations, however, and a more conservative loan policy on the part of the IMF combined to forestall financial collapse. Repayment of loans in 1986 also provided the IMF with additional funds. In the first five months of 1986 alone, the IMF collected $774.7 million more from debt repayment than it loaned out.

The Foreign Credit Insurance Association. (FCIA). The FCIA was established in 1961 as an agent of the Export-Import Bank. It works with the EXIMBANK in order to provide insurance coverage for exporters to cover such risks as foreign creditor default and expropriation.

World Bank. An agency of the United Nations, the World Bank was established along with the IMF by the Bretton Woods Agreement in 1944; it began operations in 1946. It is financed by the contributions of member nations, the interest it earns on loans, and funds borrowed through the sale of its bonds. It makes loans to member nations for public works projects, such as roads, power facilities, and transportation systems, and for projects related to economic development, such as agricultural and industrial projects. Since its basic function is to stimulate economic development, most loans are made to developing nations.

GLOSSARY OF BUSINESS AND ECONOMICS

Properties, net	**1,852.3**	1,007.1
Cost in excess of net assets acquired	**962.6**	
Investments at equity	**539.5**	49.1
Other assets	**838.8**	136.3
Total	**$9,408.8**	$4,556.4
Liabilities and stockholders' equity		
Current liabilities		
Notes payable	**$ 155.9**	$ 157.2
Current maturities of long-term debt	**373.5**	14.0
Accounts payable	**1,098.3**	511.7
Other accrued liabilities	**1,326.3**	447.6

A BALANCE SHEET *totals up a company's assets and liabilities, comparing the current year's figures with the previous year's figures.*

Ad valorem tax. A tax, such as a sales or real estate tax, based on the value of an item.

Affirmative action program. A program established by a business or other institution or government agency to increase the number of women, minorities, or any other underrepresented categories of workers.

Annualized interest rate. Interest expressed as an annual rate. Credit card interest of $1\frac{1}{2}$ percent per month, for example, is 18 percent on an annualized basis.

Appreciation. An increase in the value of an asset.

Arbitrage. The simultaneous purchase and sale of securities, currency, commodities, or other items in two different markets. The objective is to make a profit by taking advantage of temporary price imbalances between the two markets. The activities of arbitrageurs may bring such markets back into balance.

Arbitration. The use of a disinterested third party, called an arbitrator, to settle disputes between two parties.

Asset. Any item of value owned by an individual, business, or other organization. An asset may be a physical object, such as land or equipment, or a right, such as a patent or copyright.

Balance of payments. The difference between the total payments made by a nation to all foreign creditors and payment receipts from all foreign debtors for a specified period of time. The major category of transaction resulting in international payments is the purchase and sale of goods and services. However, such payments also result from investment transactions, shipping, and insurance underwriting. If a nation's receipts exceed its payments a *balance of payments surplus* exists. Payments in excess of receipts, on the other hand, create a *balance of payments deficit.*

Balance of trade. The difference between a nation's total imports and total exports of goods for a specified period of time. A *favorable balance of trade* exists when the exports exceed the imports. An *unfavorable balance of trade* exists when total imports exceed total exports.

Balance sheet. An accounting statement that depicts the status of a company at a specific moment in time. It shows the firm's assets and its liabilities as well as the net worth of the firm. See also *Income statement.*

Bankruptcy. A legal condition of insolvency. Bankruptcy may apply to individuals or businesses. Once declared bankrupt, the debtor is discharged from all debts except those specified by law as still binding. Bankruptcy may be either *voluntary,* initiated by the debtor, or *involuntary,* initiated by the debtor's creditors.

BANKRUPTCY: CHAPTER 11

One of the most common forms of bankruptcy today is referred to as "Chapter 11" because it is covered by the eleventh chapter of the Bankruptcy Reform Act of 1978. Chapter 11 describes the situation of an individual, partnership, or corporation that has been declared bankrupt but still continues to control its business under the supervision of the court. Generally, the debtor is in charge of reorganization, but creditors and other parties have a voice. The stress in Chapter 11 is on reorganization rather than on the distribution of assets to creditors. Chapter 11 provides an opportunity for a business to borrow additional money to stave off its creditors and regroup its finances.

Chapter 11 is often appropriate when businesses are having temporary difficulties because of economic conditions.

Bear market. A condition of a market, such as a stock market or foreign exchange market, in which prices are generally falling. One who believes that prices on a securities exchange will fall is referred to as a bear. Such an individual will normally be selling securities rather than buying. Contrast with *Bull market.*

Behavioral economics. Economic analysis that concentrates on the attitudes, motives, tastes, and preferences of people that widely influence economic factors.

Block trading. Buying or selling of corporate stock in amounts of 10,000 shares or more.

Blue chip. Something of high value or quality. Thus, a *blue chip stock* is the stock of a company with a reputation for profitability and a history of consistent dividend payments.

Board of directors. The chief governing body of a corporation, comprising members who are elected by stockholders. The board of directors generally is concerned with planning and developing general corporate policy. Duties of the board of directors usually include the selection of top officers, the determination of the amount of dividends to be paid, the establishment of executive compensation plans, and the planning and conducting of stockholders' meetings. The board of directors may include *inside directors,* individuals who also function as managers of the business, and *outside directors,* individuals who have no connection with the company except in their capacity as members of the board of directors.

TYPES OF BONDS AVAILABLE TO INVESTORS

Several types of bonds are traded.

U.S. Treasury bonds are considered free of risk because of the country's economic power and taxing capacity. While the interest of these bonds are subject to federal income taxes, it may not be taxed on the state and local levels.

Municipal bonds are bonds of both state and local agencies. There is a big tax advantage for buyers of municipal bonds because the interest paid is exempt from federal income taxes and usually from state and local taxation as well.

Corporate bonds are issued by corporations that pay interest and repay principal. Holders of corporate bonds are generally entitled to receive payment before stockholders are paid dividends.

Convertible bonds are issued by many corporations. They are exchangeable for common stock at a stipulated rate of exchange and within a specified period of time.

Debenture bonds are a type of corporate bond, but they are not backed up by collateral of any kind. Instead, they are backed by the "full faith and credit" of their issuer. Thus, they represent a promise to pay depending on the future prospects of the issuing corporation.

A New York City municipal bond

MURRAY GREENBERG/MONKMEYER PRESS PHOTO SERVICE

Bond. An interest-bearing debt instrument by which the issuer, a government or corporation, promises to pay the owner of the bond a specified sum of money on a specified future date. The issuer also promises to pay interest periodically. See also *Debenture.*

Book value. The value of a corporation as calculated by subtracting total liabilities from total assets. Also, the value of an asset as carried on the financial records of a company, computed by subtracting total accumulated depreciation from the initial purchase price of the asset.

Bottom line. In accounting, the last line of the income statement, the net income of the company.

Brand loyalty. The degree to which purchasers prefer a specific brand of merchandise. The strongest degree of brand loyalty is *brand insistence:* the consumer not only prefers a particular brand, he or she will accept no other.

Brand name. The name associated with a product or line of products that identifies that product as being produced by a specific company. A brand name is often distinguished from a trade name in that a brand name refers to a product and a trade name refers to a company.

Breakeven point. That level of sales and expenses at which the revenue earned by a company exactly equals its costs, resulting neither in a profit nor a loss.

Bull market. A condition of generally rising prices on an exchange, such as a stock market or foreign exchange market. One who believes that prices on a stock exchange will rise is referred to as a *bull.* Such an individual usually is buying securities rather than selling them. Contrast with *Bear market.*

Business. An organization whose major purpose is to return a profit to the owners by producing and/or selling desired goods and services to its customers.

Business barometer. An index or other measure of activity, such as the producer price index or the number of new housing starts, that is used to evaluate some aspect of national business activity or the general health of the nation's business sector.

Buyer's market. A market in which supply significantly exceeds demand. When such a situation exists, sellers may cut prices or offer attractive financing in order to reduce inventories. Contrast with *Seller's market.*

Call. An option to buy a specified amount of corporate stock at a set price within a specific period of time.

Call loan, callable loan. A loan payable on demand of the lender.

Capital. The money and other property owned by a company used in the operation of its business. Also, the *net worth* of a company, that is, the sum of the various capital stock accounts, surpluses, and undivided profits. In accounting, the excess of assets over liabilities.

Capital asset. See *Fixed asset.*

Capital expenditure. Money spent for a fixed asset, such as a piece of equipment. Also referred to as a *capital investment.*

Capital formation. The addition to the total amount of capital during a specified period less reductions to capital stock resulting from depreciation, destruction, or other causes. The term is used with reference to individual companies or to nations as a whole.

Capital gain, capital loss. The difference between the amount paid for a security and the amount realized on the sale of that security. If investors sell a security for more than they paid for it, they have realized a capital gain. If they sell the security for less than they paid for it, they have suffered a capital loss.

Capital goods. Machinery, buildings, equipment, and rolling stock used in the production of other goods.

Capital market. A financial market offering long-term investment funds. Common stock and corporate bonds are instruments of the capital market.

Cartel. A combination of individual businesses acting together to create a monopolistic business environment. See also *Monopoly.*

Cash flow. In general, the movement of cash in and out of a business. If more cash is coming into a business than is going out of it, a positive cash flow exists. If more cash is flowing out of the business than is coming into it, a negative cash flow exists.

Caveat emptor. Latin for "Let the buyer beware."

Caveat venditor. Latin for "Let the seller beware."

Certificate of deposit. A document representing a sum of money on deposit in a commercial bank for a specified period of time and earning a specified interest rate.

Cheap money. Condition in a financial market characterized by low interest rates and wide credit availability.

Collective bargaining. Negotiation between the management of a company and representatives of its employees in order to arrive at a mutually agreeable employment contract.

Commercial paper. Short-term, unsecured promissory notes issued by corporations with high credit ratings.

Commodity. A tangible good available for sale.

Commodity exchange. An organized group of traders who specialize in the sale of commodities contracts. Most transactions involve the sale of futures rather than spot transactions. Markets exist for many commodities, including such food items as wheat and soybeans and such precious metals as gold and silver.

A certificate for five shares of common stock

Common stock. Evidence of ownership in a corporation. Common stockholders have unlimited interest in the earnings and the assets of the corporation. They also have the right to attend stockholders' meetings, vote on issues, and participate in the election of the board of directors.

Comparable worth. The theory that an employee should be paid as much as anyone else for performing work that is comparable even if the job itself is different.

Competition. The classic model of *pure competition* describes a system in which buyers meet sellers in an unrestricted and perfectly efficient marketplace, a marketplace typified by several characteristics, including perfect market information and ease of reallocation of resources from one use to another.

Complementary goods. Any products related to the extent that demand for both tends to move in the same direction. For example, if the sale of

COMPETITION *for customers among retailers helps reduce prices.*

cameras increases, the sale of photographic film usually increases as well.

Concentration ratio. The percentage of the total sales in a given industry accounted for by its major firms.

Conglomerate. A corporation made up of previously independent companies. Conglomerates are highly diversified, often producing a wide variety of unrelated products.

Consumer finance company. A financial institution specializing in loans to private citizens. Interest rates are generally higher than those of commercial banks and savings and loan associations.

Consumer price index. A statistical measure that indicates changes in the prices of goods and services as compared with prices of a base year. The measure includes the cost of such items as food, housing, and automobiles. Sometimes referred to as the *cost-of-living index.*

Consumption tax. A tax levied on purchased consumer goods. Two of the most common consumption taxes are import duties and sales taxes.

Convertible debenture. A corporate bond that may be exchanged, according to stipulated conditions, for a specified number of shares of other securities of the same company within a specified period of time.

Corporate merger. The process by which two or more independent corporations join to form a single corporation, generally through the acquisition of all, or the controlling interest, of one firm by another. See also *Leveraged buyout.*

Corporation. A form of business organization in which the liability of the owners is limited to the amount of their investment. Corporations may be either public or private. A *private corporation* is operated for the purpose of generating earnings for the stockholders. A *public corporation* is one established and owned by a government for the benefit of the public.

Cost of living adjustment. A provision in a labor contract specifying that employees will automatically receive a wage increase as a specified index increases. The consumer price index is often used as the measure to which wage increases are tied.

Cost-push inflation. A general increase in prices resulting from rising business operating costs (labor, raw materials, interest rates). Inflation results as the increased costs are passed on to consumers in the form of higher prices. See also *Demand-pull inflation; Inflation.*

Craft union. A labor union whose membership is limited to those who practice a specific trade.

Debenture, debenture bond. In general, a *debenture* is a debt instrument that is not secured by a specific item of collateral. A *debenture bond* is a bond issued by a corporation that is secured by the general credit of the corporation but is not backed by specific collateral.

Debt capital. Borrowed funds used to finance the operations of a company, as contrasted with *equity capital,* which refers to funds obtained through the sale of stock.

Defensive stock. Common stock whose price does not vary as much as that of other stocks. As the general price level of stocks on stock exchanges move up and down, the prices of defensive stocks exhibit less volatility.

Deficit. A situation in which liabilities exceed assets; also, expenditures that exceed budget allocations. *Deficit spending,* a term generally applied to governments, refers to spending in excess of revenues.

Deflation. A general decline in the level of prices; the opposite of inflation. Deflation is usually accompanied by recession or depression and high levels of unemployment. The last deflationary period in the United States occurred during the Great Depression. See also *Inflation; Stagflation.*

Demand deposit. A bank deposit that may be withdrawn on demand by the depositor without advance notice.

Demand-pull inflation. Inflation resulting from demand for goods and services that is in excess of supply. See also *Cost-push inflation; Inflation.*

Demand-side economics. Economic theory holding that the best way to influence critical elements of an economy is through manipulation of consumer spending. For example, if an economy is experiencing inflation, the demand-side economic cure might involve decreasing government spending or increasing taxes to decrease the spending power of the economy and so bring demand in line with supply.

Demographics. The study of the characteristics of populations, such as geographic distribution, family size, age distribution, and income. Such information is useful both in economics and in marketing.

Depreciation. The portion of value of a fixed asset, such as machinery and equipment, that is used up during a designated period of time. Depreciation may be viewed also as the decrease in the productive value of an asset.

Depression. A period of decreased business activity characterized by decreasing prices, high unemployment, and a low level of business investment. The deepest depressions in the United States occurred from 1873 to 1879 and 1929 to 1933. See also *Recession*.

Deregulation. The reduction or elimination of governmental constraints or regulations governing the operations of businesses. Generally, the objective of deregulation is to stimulate aggressive competition among businesses in an industry in order to achieve the benefit of lower prices or improved services for consumers.

Devaluation. A reduction in the foreign exchange value of a nation's currency. For example, if the U.S. dollar is devaluated, it will buy fewer units of foreign currency.

Discretionary income. The portion of an individual's disposable personal income remaining after taxes and expenses for necessities have been deducted. It represents the money people can spend on nonessential items.

Disposable personal income. Personal income less taxes and other payments to the government.

Diversification. In finance, spreading investments over a number of types of investments to reduce risk. In business operations, expanding into more than one area of business. The major objective of business diversification is to reduce risk.

Divestiture. The selling of a portion of a business or the splitting of a company into two or more new companies,

DIVESTITURE is being used in a campaign against South Africa.

UPI/BETTMANN NEWSPHOTOS

such as occurs when a division of a corporation becomes an independent company.

Dividend. A distribution of a portion of the profits of a corporation to its stockholders.

Double taxation. Any situation in which the same dollars are taxed twice as a result of two different taxes. One of the most common examples of double taxation is the taxing of corporate profits. They are taxed when the firm earns them and they are taxed again as personal income when distributed to stockholders in the form of dividends. Double taxation may also occur as the result of taxes imposed by two levels of government.

Dow-Jones averages. Barometers of price trends among major classes of businesses listed on the New York Stock Exchange.

Dumping. The selling of a product in a foreign country at a lower price than the price that prevails in the exporting country in order to gain a competitive advantage or to dispose of excess production.

Durable good. A consumer or industrial good with a relatively long anticipated life, usually three years or longer.

Earnings per share. The net income of a company divided by the total number of shares of common stock issued and outstanding. Earnings per share should not be confused with dividends. Companies may earn more or less than they pay out in dividends.

Econometrics. A branch of economics that uses mathematical models and statistical techniques as a means of analyzing the relationship between economic variables.

Economic indicator. A measurement or statistic that evaluates or predicts economic conditions.

Economies of scale. Production efficiencies and per-unit cost reductions realized as a result of mass production.

Effective interest rate. The actual interest rate paid on an installment loan as opposed to the stated, or nominal, interest rate. The effective rate on installment loans is higher than the nominal rate because the principal is paid back during the life of the loan.

Elastic demand. Demand for a product or service that tends to respond significantly to price changes. If the price increases, the demand drops off sharply. A decrease in price, on the other hand, generally results in a significant increase in demand. See also *Inelastic demand*.

Entrepreneur. A person who initiates, owns, and manages a business and assumes its risks.

Equity. The amount by which a firm's assets exceeds its liabilities. Also, the degree of ownership in property or in a company as contrasted with the claims of creditors. For example, if a person's home is valued at $100,000 and has an existing mortgage in the amount of $30,000, the amount of equity would be $70,000.

Equity capital. The total investment in a business by its owners. Equity capital in corporations is acquired through the sale of stock.

Escalator clause. A provision in a contract that calls for an adjustment in the amount of a payment in the event of changing circumstances, usually changes in prices.

Eurodollars. Dollar deposits in banks or bank branches outside the United States. A Eurodollar deposit is created when dollars deposited in a U.S. bank are transferred to a foreign bank or a foreign branch of a U.S. bank.

Excise tax. A tax imposed on an item of merchandise. Excise taxes differ

BUSINESS CYCLES are shown here as a series of peaks and troughs. This graph does not indicate the magnitude of the swing, only its duration.

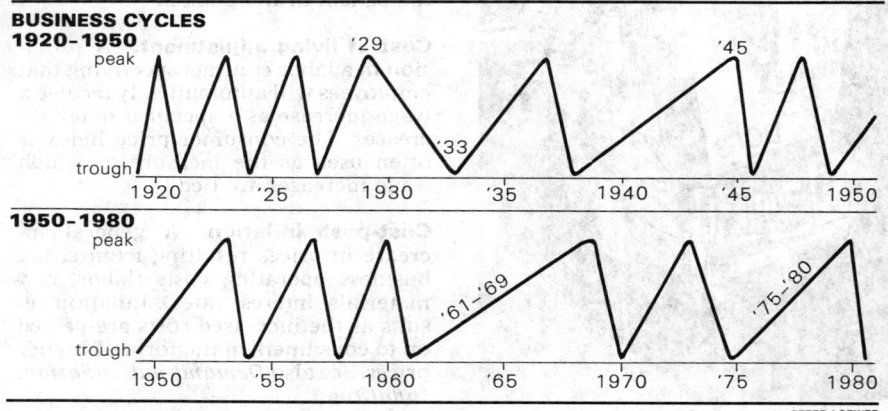

PETER LOEWER

from sales taxes in that they are imposed only on selected items. They are usually levied at the manufacturing level and then passed on to customers as part of the selling price. See also *Sales tax.*

Factoring. The selling of accounts receivable to another party who assumes responsibility for collection and assumes the risk of uncollectability.

Factor of production. An element that contributes to the production of goods or services. There are considered to be four factors of production that lead to productivity—land, labor, capital, and entrepreneurship.

Featherbedding. Employing people for a task beyond the number that is necessary. A work rule requiring two operators for each piece of equipment, although only one operator is necessary, is an example of featherbedding.

Financial intermediary. Any financial institution that receives funds from one source and lends them to another party. In the broadest interpretation of the term, financial intermediaries include commercial banks, savings and loan associations, mutual savings banks, insurance companies, finance companies, and trust companies. In a narrower sense, financial intermediaries often exclude commercial banks.

Financial statement. Any one of a number of documents depicting the financial condition of an individual, business, or other organization. Two of the most common financial statements are the profit and loss statement and the balance sheet.

Fiscal policy. Taxation and spending activities undertaken by a government to manipulate or control aspects of an economy.

Fixed asset. An asset that is permanent or of long life. Land, buildings, and equipment are considered fixed assets. For accounting purposes, a fixed asset is generally any asset with an expected life in excess of one year.

Fixed cost. Cost incurred by a business that does not fluctuate with the level of production or sales. Such costs generally include insurance, administrative salaries, and property taxes. Synonymous with overhead. Contrast with *Variable cost.*

Float. The amount of money in transit, usually in the form of checks, from payers to payees. For example, if a purchaser of raw materials sends a check for payment to a supplier, the amount is deducted from the payer's balance, but is not received immediately by the payee or added to his or her cash balance. During this period of time, the money is considered to be float.

Foreign exchange rate. The value, or price, of one nation's currency in terms of the currency of another nation. This exchange rate is established by the demand, supply, and stability of the currency of the respective nations.

Frictional unemployment. The unemployment of workers who are between jobs. Frictional unemployment results from two causes. One is the voluntary changing of jobs by workers. The other is a change in the nature of business operations that results in some jobs disappearing and new ones appearing. See also *Unemployment.*

Fringe benefit. Nonwage compensation received in addition to regular pay. Common fringe benefits include paid vacations, pension plans, company-paid hospitalization, and profit-sharing plans.

Full employment. A situation in which all persons who are willing and able to work are employed. See also *Unemployment.*

Futures market. A market in which contracts for the sale of commodities or foreign exchange are for future, rather than immediate, delivery. Many who buy futures contracts never intend to take delivery. They buy such contracts as an investment and hope to resell them prior to the delivery date.

Gantt chart. A chart used in production planning or scheduling in which time is depicted on the horizontal axis and the various activities involved in the production process are depicted on the vertical axis.

Gresham's law. The concept that if an economy has two kinds of money in circulation, even though both kinds may possess the same exchange value, the public will tend to hoard one kind to a greater extent than the other. The result of hoarding the good money is that it will be driven out of circulation, leaving the so-called bad money as the remaining primary medium of exchange.

Gross national product (GNP). The total dollar value of all goods and services produced in a country in final form during a specified period of time, usually one year.

Gross private domestic investment. The total of all expenditures for income-producing assets, such as buildings, machinery, equipment, vehicles, and inventories, as well as all new private housing and construction by individuals and private businesses.

Group banking. An arrangement in which the operations of two or more independent banks are brought under control of a holding company. The holding company may be a bank or a business organized solely to control other banks.

Hidden tax. A tax paid by consumers without their knowledge. Excise taxes and import duties, for example, are reflected in the selling price of a commodity, but the consumer is normally unaware of the amount of the tax or even of its existence. See also *Excise tax.*

Holding company. A company that owns controlling stock in one or more other firms. A holding company owns stock in other companies in order to control the operations of those other companies. The stock is not held as an investment.

Housing start. The beginning of new construction of a residential unit. The structure is usually considered started when the foundation is dug. The number of housing starts is an indicator of economic activity.

Imputed income. The measure of goods or services received that need not be paid for. Imputed income is included in the computation of the gross national product.

Income statement. A financial statement that summarizes the operations of a business or other organization for a given period of time. It shows revenue generated, expenses incurred in generation of revenue, and profit realized during the period. See also *Balance sheet.*

Indirect costs. Costs of conducting business, such as maintenance, taxes, insurance, and wages of supervisors, that cannot be associated with the production of a product. Generally synonymous with overhead.

Industrial revenue bond. A bond issued by a local government to finance construction of a production facility that is then leased to private industry. The revenue from the leasing of the facility is used to pay the interest and principal of the bond.

Industry. A group of businesses that produce the same or similar products.

Inelastic demand. Demand for a product that does not respond significantly to price changes. See also *Elastic demand.*

Inflation. A general upward movement in the level of prices in an economy. Economists generally consider that inflation exists when prices are increasing on average more than 3.5 percent per year for a sustained period of time.

Inflationary gap. The value of unsatisfied demand for goods and services; demand that cannot be fulfilled at the full-employment level of production of an economy.

Infrastructure. All communication, transportation, and power facilities as well as other public services, and the skills, education, and attitudes of the people that serve as the foundation of a nation's economic activities.

Installment credit. Credit that entails the gradual repayment of principal and interest through periodic payments. Installment credit is most often used in the purchase of relatively expensive consumer goods, such as automobiles or major appliances.

Interest. The cost of credit, usually expressed as a percentage of the loan or credit line.

Investment banking. The process of marketing newly issued corporate securities. An investment bank will buy large blocks of stock from the issuing company and resell the stock in smaller amounts to many individual investors.

Joint venture. The combined effort of two or more individuals or companies in the execution of a business activity. A joint venture differs from a partnership in that the firms that participate in a joint venture retain their separate identities.

Labor force. Defined by the U.S. Bureau of Census as all persons 16 years of age or older who are willing and able to work and are either employed or seeking employment.

Labor mobility. The ease with which workers can change jobs or professions within the work force.

Laissez-faire. The theory of governmental economic and business policy asserting that government should intrude to the least extent possible in the affairs of the private sector.

Law of diminishing returns. The theory that at a certain level of production, the use of additional amounts of capital, land, and labor will not increase productivity as much as was the case with the addition of previous units of these elements.

Law of supply and demand. The economic theory that the price level of goods will rise as demand rises and fall as demand falls.

Leverage. The use of debt to increase profits or earnings per share. When a business can increase profits or earnings per share by more than the cost of the debt, leverage is being used. A company that borrows funds at 10 percent, for example, and earns 12 percent from the use of those funds is realizing the benefits of leverage.

Leveraged buyout. The purchase of a company by another with borrowed funds, for which the assets of the acquired company serve as collateral.

Limit order. An order placed by an investor with a broker for the purchase or sale of a specified amount of stock at a stipulated price.

Liquid assets. Assets readily convertible into cash, such as marketable securities.

Liquidity. The ease with which an asset can be converted into cash. Some assets, such as marketable securities, are considered highly liquid, since they can readily be sold. Other assets, such as inventory, can be converted less easily and are therefore not as liquid.

Listed security. A stock or bond that has been registered and is traded on an organized securities exchange, such as the New York Stock Exchange or the American Stock Exchange.

Lockout. The refusal of an employer to allow employees to report to work.

Loss leader. An item sold by a retail store at a low price, perhaps below cost, in order to increase store traffic. The retailer's hope is that some customers who come to the store to purchase the loss leader will also purchase other goods.

Manchester school. A classic economic theory emphasizing the benefits of free trade and laissez-faire government policies.

Margin. In banking, the difference between the market value of collateral pledged to secure a loan and the face value of the loan itself. Within limita-

tions established by the Federal Reserve Board, each bank sets its own margin. In stock dealings, buying on margin refers to the purchase of stocks or bonds without tendering the entire amount due at the time of the purchase. In essence, the purchaser is borrowing money from the brokerage firm.

Marginal cost. The cost associated with an increase in production. For example, if a firm can produce 100 units of a product at a total cost of $10,000 and 101 units at a total cost of $10,090, the marginal cost of the one additional unit is $90.

Marginal revenue. The additional revenue realized as a result of an increase in sales.

Marginal-revenue product. The additional income that results from increased production as a result of the employment of one additional unit of a resource, given that the level of other resources remains the same.

Marketing mix. The combination and coordination of the elements of a marketing plan toward the end of maximizing the marketing effort at the least cost.

Market segmentation. The process of dividing a total market into subdivisions, the members of each having certain common characteristics that are different from the characteristics of other market segments. Such a procedure enables marketers to select that group or groups of individuals for whom their product is thought to have the greatest appeal.

Market share. The percentage of total industry sales, either in dollars or units, accounted for by one producer.

A LOW PRICE ON GOLD *is being used by this merchant as a loss leader to draw customers into the store.*

TYPES OF MORTGAGES

Fixed rate. These mortgages have monthly payments and an interest rate that remains the same for the life of the loan.

Flexible rate. Also called *adjustable* and *variable* rate, these mortgages have an interest rate that can change to reflect changes in market conditions.

Balloon. These are generally short-term mortgages with relatively small monthly payments and a very large final payment. Often the monthly payments are repayments of interest only; the principal is repaid in the last payment.

Graduated payment. These mortgages start out with relatively smaller monthly payments that grow gradually until they reach a level where they remain for the rest of the life of the mortgage.

Assumable. This is a mortgage that can be transferred to a subsequent buyer of the property.

Seller-financed. This mortgage is arranged privately and is financed by the seller. Such a mortgage can be advantageous for someone who is having a hard time selling a property and is willing to offer a below-market interest rate, or for someone who wants to defer income for tax purposes.

Markup. The difference between the cost of a good and the resale price.

Maturity. The date on which a loan or bond becomes due and payable.

Mediation. In labor relations, the use of a disinterested third party to assist management and labor in reaching a collective bargaining agreement. A mediator has no power to impose action on the parties involved and acts only to provide suggestions and keep the two parties actively negotiating.

Mercantilism. An economic philosophy with the objective of increasing the wealth of a nation by exporting goods in exchange for gold.

Monetary policy. Actions taken by a central bank, like the Federal Reserve, to influence the supply of money or the cost of credit in a nation's economy.

Money. Anything that serves as a medium of exchange, a measure of value, and a store of value.

Money market. The network of financial institutions that executes transactions for purchase and sale of short-term credit instruments, such as commercial paper, short-term promissory notes, bankers' acceptances, and Treasury bills.

Money supply. The amount of money in circulation in an economy. In the narrowest sense, the money supply consists of the total of all currency and demand deposits.

Money wages. The amount of money received by workers in exchange for labor services. See also *Real wages*.

Monopoly. A business that is the only seller of a good or service.

Mortgage. The transfer of ownership of property without the transfer of possession. A mortgage is executed in conjunction with a loan, the repayment of which cancels the mortgage. A mortgage represents a lien on the financed property.

Most favored nation clause. A provision in a commercial treaty that guarantees all signing nations the most favorable tariff rates from the other signatories.

Multinational company. A company that has investments abroad or that markets its products abroad.

Multiplier effect. The effect of increased government spending or decreased taxes on the total amount of spending in an economy. The money is spent over and over again in the economy. Thus, the effect is multiplied.

Municipal bond. A bond issued by a state or local government, usually to finance public projects, such as the building of a bridge or low-income housing. One of the advantages of municipal bonds is that interest earned on such bonds is not generally taxable.

Mutual savings bank. A bank operated for the benefit of its depositors.

Although the depositors have no say in the operations of the bank, they receive a proportionate share of the earnings.

National bank. A bank chartered by the federal government.

National income. The total compensation received by the sellers of factors of production as a result of the production of goods and services. It consists of wages, interest, rent, business profits, and the net income of those who are self-employed.

Nationalization. The act of a government taking over ownership of a business or industry previously owned by private individuals.

National wealth. The total value of all assets, excluding military assets, of a nation.

Net national product. Total value of goods and services produced in final form in an economy during a specified period of time, generally one year, less the amount of capital expended in the production process during that same period of time.

Net worth. The amount by which assets exceed liabilities for a business or for an individual. The net worth of a business represents the equity of the owners.

Odd lot. A number of shares of stock that is less than the standard trading unit. On the New York Stock Exchange, the standard trading unit is 100 shares. Any number of shares less than 100 is considered an odd lot.

Oligopoly. The control of a market by few suppliers. See also *Monopoly*.

Open-market operations. The buying and selling of government securities in the bond market by the Federal Reserve System for the purpose of expanding or contracting the supply of money. Buying securities has the effect of expanding the money supply. Selling securities has the effect of contracting the money supply.

Overhead. See *Fixed cost.*

Par value. The value printed on the face of stock and bond certificates. The par value does not necessarily reflect the market value of any security.

Personal income. Defined by the U.S. Department of Commerce as the total income received by people, including transfer payments from businesses and the government.

Planned economy. An economy in which economic decisions regarding resource allocation, investment, and distribution of goods and services are made by a central planning agency.

Plant. In accounting, a financial classification of fixed assets, including factories, warehouses, and all other buildings.

Portfolio. The mix of security holdings of an individual, company, or other organization.

Preemptive right. The right of common stockholders to retain their proportionate share of ownership if the corporation issues additional stock. A preemptive right gives the current stockholders the right to purchase additional shares in proportion to their current proportion of ownership before the shares are made available to the general public.

Price earnings ratio. The ratio of the current market price of a share of stock to its annual earnings.

Price-support program. A governmental program designed to maintain market prices above what would normally prevail if the market were left free to determine the market price.

Prime interest rate. The interest rate charged by commercial banks for short-term financing extended to their best and most creditworthy institutional borrowers.

Producer price index. A measure of the change in prices charged by producers of approximately 3000 commodities, including cotton, oil, apparel, and machinery.

Progressive tax. A tax that takes a higher percentage of higher tax bases than of lower ones. The United States federal income tax is progressive, since those in higher tax brackets pay a higher percentage of their incomes in taxes than do those in lower income tax brackets. See also *Regressive tax.*

Promissory note. A written promise to pay a stated amount on or before a specified date or on demand.

Proportional tax. A tax with a constant rate regardless of the size of the base. Property taxes are proportional, since the tax rate is the same regardless of the assessed value of the property.

Protectionism. Activities by a government to restrict imports and thus shelter domestic businesses and industries. The primary protectionist techniques are import quotas and tariffs.

Proxy. An individual who is authorized by the owner of voting corporate stock to vote in his or her place at a stockholders' meeting. A proxy is also the authorization itself.

Proxy fight. The efforts of competing factions to acquire sufficient proxies to influence votes at a corporation stockholders' meeting. The ultimate purpose of a proxy fight is to obtain voting control of the board of directors.

Public sector. The portion of an economy represented by federal, state, and local governments.

Pump priming. Spending by the government in order to stimulate private sector activity.

Quality circle. A work group, normally consisting of between eight and ten employees and supervisors, working in a common area, who meet regularly to discuss quality problems encountered on the job.

Real wages, real income. Earnings expressed in terms of purchasing power rather than nominal value. Real wages are computed by adjusting money wages by an inflation indicator, such as the consumer price index.

REAL WAGES VS. MONEY WAGES

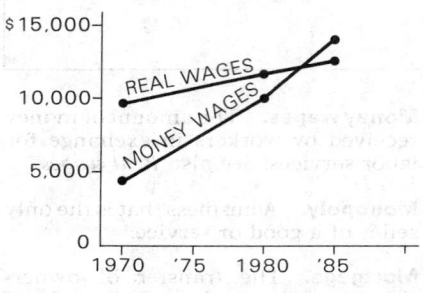

PETER LOEWER

Recession. A period of general decline in business activity. A recession is usually typified by little capital investment and high unemployment. The difference between a recession and a depression is basically one of degree.

Regressive tax. A tax whose rate decreases as the tax base increases. Sales taxes and property taxes are sometimes considered regressive because they tend to take a larger percentage of the incomes of low-wage earners than of high-wage earners.

Repurchase agreement. A short-term loan, usually made by a bank to a securities dealer, in which the lender buys securities and agrees to sell them back at the same price within a specified period of time.

Research and development. Design and development of new or improved products and procedures by businesses, governments, and other organizations.

Restraint of trade. Any activity that tends to reduce the amount of competition in an industry. Collusion and mergers may cause restraint of trade.

Return on equity. The net income of a business for a given financial period divided by the average total owner's equity for that same period.

Return on investment. The amount of money earned as a percentage of the amount invested, usually expressed as an annual return.

Revenue bond. A bond issued by a municipality that is secured and liquidated by the project it finances.

Revenue sharing. The policy of distributing a portion of federal tax revenues to individual states and to municipalities according to a formula.

Risk management. A broad function of management concerned with reducing the potential loss a company may incur as a result of unpredictable or varying circumstances. Probably the most common risk management technique is obtaining insurance, by which a company transfers the risk of loss to an insurance company.

Sales tax. A flat-rate tax based on the selling price of an item, normally levied at the time of purchase.

Seasonal unemployment. The unemployment resulting from seasonal conditions, such as weather, rather than business or economic downturns.

Secondary boycott. Union attempts to discourage outside parties from buying products of the company with which the union has a dispute.

Seller's market. A market characterized by demand that is in excess of supply. Such a situation is generally favorable to sellers, since it usually means that they can raise their prices and still sell all of their output. Contrast with *Buyer's market.*

Services. Intangible items sold in the marketplace, such as transportation, communications, and education.

Short sale. A contract to sell stocks, bonds, commodities, or foreign exchange that the seller does not yet own. Sellers will *sell short* in the hope that the price of the item will decline prior to the stipulated delivery date. They can then buy the commodity to cover the short sale and thus make a profit from the difference between the purchase price and the sale price.

Spending unit. A group of people living together who make major purchases as a group rather than as individuals. Families consisting of spouses and children under the age of 18 are always considered a spending unit. Other individuals who may live with the family are considered part of the spending unit if they do not earn more than a specified amount per week. An individual living alone is also considered a spending unit.

Stagflation. Inflation coupled with economic stagnation. Stagflation is generally accompanied by an increasing money supply and spiraling wages, which cause excess aggregate demand. This type of economic situation is difficult to combat because inflation and high levels of unemployment exist simultaneously.

Stock. Ownership interest in a corporation, evidenced by shares held. *Common* stock represents a right to earnings and assets of the corporation that is subordinate to the rights of creditors and *preferred* stockholders. Common stockholders generally have voting rights at stockholders' meetings. Preferred stock represents a claim on earnings and assets that is superior to that of common stockholders but subordinate to creditor claims. Unlike common stock, preferred stock has a specified dividend rate. Preferred stockholders generally may not vote at stockholders' meetings.

Structural unemployment. Unemployment resulting from changes in the nature of jobs or in the demand for goods and services.

Subsidiary. A business that is controlled by another company through the ownership of its shares of stock. The subsidiary remains a separate company.

Subsidy. A payment made for which no goods or services are received in exchange. The objective of a subsidy is to make a particular good or service available at a price that consumers can afford to pay, or to support inordinately low prices.

THE U.S. GOVERNMENT SUBSIDIZES *certain farm products, including dairy products, in order to maintain a particular price.*

Supply-side economics. A theory intended to fight inflation and stimulate economic growth that holds that the most effective mechanism is the stimulation of production through tax cuts and other incentives, such as depletion allowances and accelerated depreciation plans.

Target market. A segment of a market toward which a marketer directs advertising, promotional, and other marketing activities.

Tariff. A tax levied on imported goods. There are generally two types of tariffs, revenue tariffs and protective tariffs. A *revenue tariff* is designed to provide income to the government. A *protective tariff* is designed to protect domestic producers by making imported goods more expensive than otherwise is the case.

Tax avoidance. Reducing tax liability by taking advantage of legal methods of arranging assets and evaluating income. Unlike tax evasion, tax avoidance is not illegal.

Tender offer. The offer of an outsider to purchase a certain amount of a company's outstanding shares of stock. This is usually done to obtain control of the company. Also, an offer made by a corporation to buy back shares of its own stock or other outstanding securities, such as bonds and debentures.

Theory X. A theory of human behavior holding that most people are lazy, dislike work, and will avoid it whenever possible. This theory also holds that most people must be directed, coerced, or even threatened to get them to exert adequate effort toward the accomplishment of corporate goals. See also *Theory Y; Theory Z.*

Theory Y. A theory of human behavior that asserts that most people accept work as natural, are self-directed when allowed to be, and seek out responsibility. This theory further holds that individuals will commit to the goals of the organization to the extent that rewards accompany accomplishment. See also *Theory X; Theory Z.*

Theory Z. A management style that emphasizes many of the features of Japanese business management. It has such characteristics as long-term employment, frequent performance review, formal planning, use of management by objectives, and decision making that involves all members of the organization. See also *Theory X; Theory Y.*

Thrift institution. A savings institution whose major objective is to accumulate the savings of individuals and lend those funds to borrowers.

Tied loan. A loan made to a foreign nation with the stipulation that the money be spent in the lending country.

Time deposit. A deposit in a bank that requires prior notice before its withdrawal.

Trade barrier. Any impediment to the free exchange of goods between nations. The primary barriers to trade are foreign exchange agreements, trade quotas, and tariffs.

Trademark. A symbol that identifies a business or a product.

Trade name. See *Brand name.*

Transfer payment. A government expenditure for which no goods or services are received in exchange. Major transfer payments made by the U.S. government include Social Security payments, welfare, and unemployment compensation.

Treasury bill. The shortest-term security issued by the federal government. Treasury bills are sold to the public at auction and mature in either 91 or 182 days. Treasury bills, because of their short maturity and the good credit of the federal government, are among the most secure investments available.

Treasury bond. A U.S. government long-term security having a maturity of more than five years.

Treasury note. A U.S. government long-term security having a maturity of from one to five years.

Unemployment. In the United States, all persons 16 years of age or older who are not working but are looking for jobs are considered unemployed. Unemployment statistics also include those who have been temporarily laid off and are waiting to be recalled, those who are not working but will be reporting to new jobs within 30 days, and those who are not working and are not seeking employment because they are sick or because they believe that no jobs are available for them in their line of work.

Variable cost. A cost that fluctuates with the level of some business activity, generally production or sales. The costs of raw materials and sales com-

missions are examples of variable costs.

Venture capital. The portion of the total capitalization of a company that is not secured by a lien or mortgage. Also funds available as the result of the sale of new stock and reinvested earnings of a company. Synonymous with risk capital.

Warrant. A document that gives the holder the right to buy specified securi-

ties at a stipulated price within a given period of time.

Yellow-dog contract. An agreement between an employer and a prospective employee under which the employee agrees not to join a union.

Yield. The profit earned from an investment. Also the percentage rate of return on an investment in securities or property.

—Paul W. Miller

For Further Reference

General

Buckley, William F., Jr. *Overdrive.* Doubleday, 1983.

Deal, Terrence E. and Allan A. Kennedy. *Corporate Cultures.* Addison-Wesley, 1982.

Holbrook, Stewart H. *The Age of the Moguls.* Harmony Books, 1985.

Mayo, Elton. *The Human Problems of an Industrial Civilization.* Macmillan, 1933.

Nader, Ralph and Mark Green. *Corporate Power in America.* Grossman Publications, 1973.

Naisbitt, John. *Megatrends.* Warner Books, 1984.

Peters, Thomas J. and Robert H. Waterman, Jr. *In Search of Excellence: Lessons from America's Best-run Companies.* Harper & Row, 1982.

Sloan, Alfred P., Jr. *My Years with General Motors.* Doubleday, 1964.

Tarrant, John P. *Drucker: The Man Who Invented Corporate America.* Warner Books, 1976.

Business Operations

Ball, Donald A. and Wendell H. McCulloch, Jr. *International Business: Introduction and Essentials* (2nd Ed.). Business Publications, 1985.

Gibson, James L., John M. Ivancevich, and James H. Donnelly, Jr. *Organizations: Behavior, Structure, Processes.* Business Publications, 1982.

Miner, John R. *Theories of Organizational Structure and Process.* Dryden, 1982.

Mintzberg, Henry. The Structure of Organizations. Prentice-Hall, 1979.

Robock, Stefan H. and Kenneth Simmonds. *International Business and Multinational Enterprises* (3rd Ed.). Irwin, 1983.

Van Voorhis, Kenneth R. *Entrepreneurship and Small Business Management.* Allyn & Bacon, 1980.

Management

Barnard, Chester I. *The Functions of the Executive.* Harvard University Press, 1938.

Chandler, A. D. *The Visible Hand: The Managerial Revolution in American Business.* Harvard University Press, 1977.

Drucker, Peter F. *The Effective Executive.* Harper & Row, 1967.

Drucker, Peter F. *Management: Tasks, Responsibilities, Practices.* Harper & Row, 1974.

Drucker, Peter F. *Managing in Turbulent Times.* Harper & Row, 1980.

Fayol, Henri. *General and Industrial Management.* Sir Isaac Pitman & Sons, Ltd., 1949.

Fiedler, Fred and Martin Chemers. *Leadership and Effective Management.* Scott, Foresman and Company, 1974.

Grove, Andrew S. *High Output Management.* Random House, 1983.

Herzberg, Frederick, Bernard Mausner, and Barbara Snyderman. *The Motivation to Work* (2nd Ed.). Wiley, 1959.

Kotter, John. *The General Managers.* The Free Press, 1982.

McGregor, Douglas. *The Human Side of Enterprise.* McGraw-Hill, 1960.

Mintzberg, Henry. *The Nature of Managerial Work.* Harper & Row, 1973.

Ouchi, William. *Theory Z: How American Business Can Meet the Japanese Challenge.* Addison-Wesley, 1981.

Quinn, James Brian. *Strategies for Change.* Richard D. Irwin, 1980.

Sayles, Leonard R. *Managerial Behavior.* McGraw-Hill, 1964.

Steiner, George A., John B. Miner, and Edmund R. Gray. *Management Strategy and Policy* (2nd Ed.). Macmillan, 1982.

Banking and Finance

Hutchinson, Harry D. *Money, Banking and the U.S. Economy* (4th Ed.). Prentice-Hall, 1980.

Keown, Arthur J., David F. Scott, Jr., John D. Martin, and J. William Petty. *Basic Financial Management* (3rd Ed.). Prentice-Hall, 1985.

Welshans, Merle and Ronald Melicher. *Finance, an Introduction to Financial Markets and Institutions.* South-Western Publishing, 1980.

Marketing and Advertising

Horton, Raymond L. *Buyer Behavior: A Decision-making Approach.* Charles E. Merrill, 1984.

Kotler, Philip. *Principles of Marketing* (3rd Ed.). Prentice-Hall, 1986.

Packard, Vance. *The Hidden Persuaders.* Pocket Books, 1980.

Pope, Daniel. *The Making of Modern Advertising.* Basic Books, 1983.

Weilbacher, William M. *Advertising.* Macmillan, 1984.

Economics

Browne, M. Neil. *Modern Economics: Principles, Goals, and Trade-offs.* Prentice-Hall, 1987.

Brue, Stanley L. and Donald R. Wentworth. *Economic Scenes: Theory in Today's World* (3rd Ed.). Prentice-Hall, 1984.

Galbraith, John Kenneth. *The New Industrial State* (3rd Ed.). Houghton Mifflin, 1979.

Heilbroner, Robert L. and James K. Galbraith. *The Economic Problem* (8th Ed.). Prentice-Hall, 1987.

Heilbroner, Robert L. *The Worldly Philosophers.* Simon & Schuster, 1980.

Leftwich, Richard H. and David E. R. Gay. *A Basic Framework for Economics.* Business Publications, 1987.

Peterson, Wallace C. *Income, Employment, and Economic Growth.* W. W. Norton & Co., 1978.

Samuelson, Paul A. *Economics* (10th Ed.). McGraw-Hill, 1976.

Simon, Julian L. *The Economics of Population Growth.* Princeton University Press, 1977.

Smith, Adam. *Wealth of Nations.* Modern Library, 1937.

Business and Society

Ackerman, Robert W. *Managing Corporate Responsibility.* Harvard University Press, 1975.

Diebold, John. *The Role of Business in Society.* Anacom, 1982.

Smith, Len Young, Richard A. Mann, and Barry S. Roberts. *Business Law and the Regulation of Business* (2nd Ed.). West Publishing, 1987.

Steiner, George A. and John F. Steiner. *Business, Government, and Society.* Random House, 1980.

Weidenbaum, Murray. *Business, Government, and the Public* (2nd Ed.). Prentice-Hall, 1981.

VOLUME **6**

Computers

THE SCIENCE MUSEUM, LONDON

TODAY'S COMPUTERS

The computers available today are versatile tools that can perform a broad range of tasks accurately and quickly. They have four basic parts, each devoted to one of the four steps of the computing process: input, processing, output, and storage. These computers are inventions of the 20th century, but their history goes back hundreds of years and includes such precursors as Charles Babbage's Difference Engine (*above*), conceived in the 1820's to handle one type of calculation.

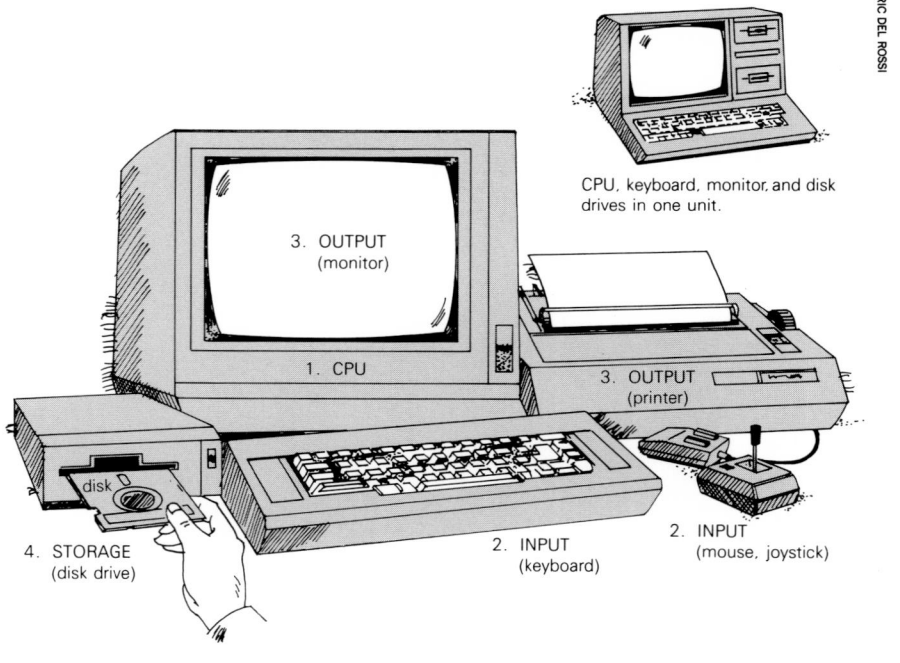

RIC DEL ROSSI

CPU, keyboard, monitor, and disk drives in one unit.

3. OUTPUT (monitor)

1. CPU

3. OUTPUT (printer)

4. STORAGE (disk drive)

disk

2. INPUT (keyboard)

2. INPUT (mouse, joystick)

Computers

PIERRE VAUTHEY/SYGMA

Hello, new, user... What, is, your, name?

THE PHOTO WORKS/PHOTO RESEARCHERS

AP/WIDE WORLD PHOTOS

MICHAL HERON/WOODFIN CAMP

TANNENBAUM/SYGMA

The computer has revolutionized our lives. When a telephone call is made, a computer helps place the call. When an airplane soars into the sky, a computer helps the pilot fly the plane. When a school gives standardized tests, a computer scores them. When a patient has an electrocardiogram, a computer reads the printout.

Computers are being used for complex tasks that would take humans a lifetime to complete, even tasks that would otherwise be impossible.

What is a computer? It is nothing more than a tool, though a more versatile tool than any other ever created. It can teach, play games, do paperwork, give a view of the interior of a living brain, and provide access to information stored far away. It does these things at lightning fast speeds, and does them accurately.

Computers remember and instantly recall enormous amounts of information. They work hour after hour without making a mistake.

This volume is designed to familiarize readers with computers and how they are being used. It provides the basic information needed to be truly "computer literate"—that is, to understand how computers work and to feel comfortable about using them. There are four main sections:

How computers work. Most modern computers are digital computers. Whether large or small, they operate on the same general principles. The first section covers all the basic concepts of computer science, describing the computer process and the major functions of the various components of a computer system. Readers then are introduced to the major aspects of programming, which consists of writing the algorithms, developing the flowcharts, selecting the computer-appropriate languages, and using commands to write an actual program. Finally, the section describes the major types of computers and provides information on how to choose among the variety of hardware and software available on the market.

The evolution of computers. Several thousand years ago, people invented the abacus, a device consisting of beads on a string that could be used for simple arithmetic computations. Today, descendants of this crude device are guiding ships, running factories, and talking to people over telephones. And this is merely a sampling of the things they do. This section traces the development of counting devices—from abacuses to

supercomputers—and shows how the pace of technological improvements has quickened since the development of microelectronics.

Applications software. Almost every occupation is affected by just five types of computer applications: word processing, database management, electronic spreadsheets, graphics, and communications. These types of programs, or software, have a major impact not only on businesses but also on consumers, students, volunteer organizations, and other groups. This section discusses in detail the capabilities of these applications programs and explains how each can be used to perform a variety of tasks.

Computers in society. Computerization has affected health, communications, employment opportunities, manufacturing processes, indeed, every aspect of life. This section describes how computer technology has permeated all aspects of society, from homes to schools, hospitals, factories, and farms. Computers have enriched lives but, as the section points out, they have also created legal, social, and ethical problems.

HOW COMPUTERS WORK

A computer once was defined as a device that helped one to compute—that is, add, subtract, multiply, divide, and perform other types of mathematical calculations employing these four types of computation. Today, computers can perform a much broader range of tasks and can better be described as electronic machines that store, manipulate, and analyze information.

A computer cannot function without a set of instructions. The instructions are called programs, or software.

There are numerous kinds of programs, each providing the computer with instructions for different tasks—for example, chess programs provide instructions on how to play chess; spreadsheet programs, on how to set up financial spreadsheets and do requested calculations with figures entered into the spreadsheets; graphics programs, on how to create animated full-color drawings.

The computer itself is a piece of hardware, as is any equipment connected to the computer, such as a printer, joystick, or monitor. Any hardware connected to the computer is called a peripheral. Taken together, the computer and its peripherals constitute a computer system.

Most modern computers are digital devices, meaning they translate all data into discrete numbers. This volume focuses primarily on digital computers, though the second kind of computer, the analog computer, is described later in this section.

The Computing Process

The computing process involves four steps, each handled by different parts of the computer system:
- *Input.* Entering a program and data into the computer. A keyboard is the most popular input device.
- *Processing.* Executing the steps of the program. This is done by the computer's central processing unit.
- *Output.* Getting the results of the computer's operations to the user. The two most common ways of getting output into readable form are by displaying it on the screen of a monitor or by printing it on paper via a printer.
- *Storage.* Saving programs and data until they are needed for processing. This is done internally, in the computer's memory, or externally, on disks or tapes.

Binary Code

A computer can handle all sorts of input, can follow many different instructions, and can create output consisting of printed words, pictures, and even musical sounds. But within the computer itself, all the data exist in the form of electric signals.

A computer comprises thousands of electrical circuits. Within each circuit, there are two possibilities: an electric current is either flowing or not flowing. When electricity flows, the circuit is on; when no electricity flows, the circuit is off. These two states can be represented by the digits 0, for off; and 1, for on. Modern digital computers

use the binary number system, which consists of only two digits—0 and 1—for all calculations and processing. (For an explanation of the binary system, see MATHEMATICS volume, Glossary). The two digits are called bits, from *b*inary dig*its*.

ASCII code.
Computers store and process characteristics (letters, numbers, and symbols such as %, $, and +) as code numbers. Most computers use a standard code, called the American Standard Code for Information Interchange, or ASCII (pronounced ass-key), which assigns a number between 32 and 127 to standard symbols, digits

0 through 9, and upper- and lower-case letters. Codes 128 to 255 are used by many computer systems for graphics and other special characters. ASCII numbers 0 through 31 do not print but are used as control codes for peripherals; for example, code 13 controls the carriage return, moving the print head of the printer or the cursor of the display screen to the left margin.

In today's computers, an ASCII character is represented by an eight-bit number, these eight bits equal one byte—the basic unit of information storage in a computer. For example, the ASCII code for the letter A is 65, or the byte 01000001. When a person types the letter A on the computer keyboard, a program within the computer translates it into 01000001. If

"21 ORANGES"

is typed, the computer translates it to

```
00110010
00110001
00100000
01001111
01010010
01000001
01001110
01000111
01000101
01010011
```

Note that digits and the space, like letters, are treated as ASCII characters.

The process sounds complicated and time-consuming, but it really is very fast; in a millionth of a second, a computer can switch thousands of bits on and off.

BINARY EQUIVALENTS OF ASCII CODES

	ASCII CODE	BINARY NUMBER		ASCII CODE	BINARY NUMBER
A	65	01000001	N	78	01001110
B	66	01000010	O	79	01001111
C	67	01000011	P	80	01010000
D	68	01000100	Q	81	01010001
E	69	01000101	R	82	01010010
F	70	01000110	S	83	01010011
G	71	01000111	T	84	01010100
H	72	01001000	U	85	01010101
I	73	01001001	V	86	01010110
J	74	01001010	W	87	01010111
K	75	01001011	X	88	01011000
L	76	01001100	Y	89	01011001
M	77	01001101	Z	90	01011010

Chips and Buses

A computer circuit consists of transistors and other devices that act as on-off switches to control the flow of electricity. The circuit is printed on a small wafer called a chip. Thousands of circuits can be manufactured on a single chip less than 1 inch square. Circuit parts may be only 3 microns wide, 3 millionths of an inch (a human hair is about 100 microns thick). Because the circuits are connected, or integrated with one another, they are called integrated circuits, or ICs.

Integrated circuits. An IC is made of a semiconductor, a material that transmits electricity better than a resistor or an insulator but not as well as a true metal conductor. Silicon is the material most commonly used to make chips. The ability of a semiconductor to conduct electricity can be changed by temperature variation or by adding impurities.

The chip is embedded in a package made of epoxy and metal and connected to a series of pins embedded in the side of the package to make it easier to connect the package electrically with other components. The package is then attached to a circuit board together with other IC packages.

There are hundreds of kinds of chips. Some are designed to store data, others to turn parallel streams of data into serial streams. Some do arithmetic, turn written words into spoken words, and so on. Even within each category, there are different designs.

The more components there are on a chip, the faster a computer can operate. One of the most powerful chips currently available is the Intel i486, which has 1.2 million transistors on a square of silicon the size of a baby's fingernail. This chip can execute up to 20 million operations a second.

Making a chip. First, an engineer designs a chip to perform the desired function. Increasingly, powerful computer programs, known as silicon compilers and logic synthesizers, are used to draw and test chips. The programs automatically handle much of the detail, such as where to place the transistors and how to best connect them for maximum efficiency and speed.

The finished design is transmitted to a semiconductor factory, where a mask outlining the circuitry is made. This mask is similar to a stencil or a photographic negative. The circuitry is etched onto very pure silicon. Through a series of chemical steps, tiny amounts of certain impurities are added to the silicon, creating regions that conduct electricity under some conditions but impede its flow under others.

Because the circuits are so tiny and so close together, malfunctions may be a serious problem. To reduce the reject rate and the possibility of later malfunctions, many chips are designed with redundant circuits. Then, if one part of the chip is faulty, the extra circuits can perform the same function.

Circuit boards. Chips for a unit of the computer, such as memory or the CPU (central processing unit), are attached to a printed circuit board, a thin plastic board that varies in size from a few square inches to several square feet. Metallic tracks printed on both surfaces of the board conduct signals from one part of the board to another. Mounted on the board are a number of discrete components plus sockets designed to receive the chips. All the wires that leave or enter the board are drawn to an edge of the board, which fits into a receptacle connecting it with other components of the computer.

Connecting components. Electrical conductors connect the components of a computer and computer system, enabling them to communicate with one another. There are two basic types: unidirectional, which can carry signals in one direction only; and bidirectional, which can carry signals in either direction.

Conductors linking components within the computer are called buses (short for "omnibus," meaning for every device). Three basic types of buses constitute a system bus:

An address bus enables the CPU to address any memory location or I/O (input/output) port.

A data bus carries information between the CPU and memory, between the CPU and an I/O port, or between memory and an I/O port.

A control bus conveys signals between chips. These include clock signals, which control the timing of system operations; initiating signals, which activate units, prepare them to send or receive data, and determine the direction in which the data lines are to operate; and interrupt signals, which coordinate input and processing activities.

A CHIP, *shown magnified 56 times, contains thousands of circuits. It is embedded in an epoxy-metal package, mounted on a circuit board.*

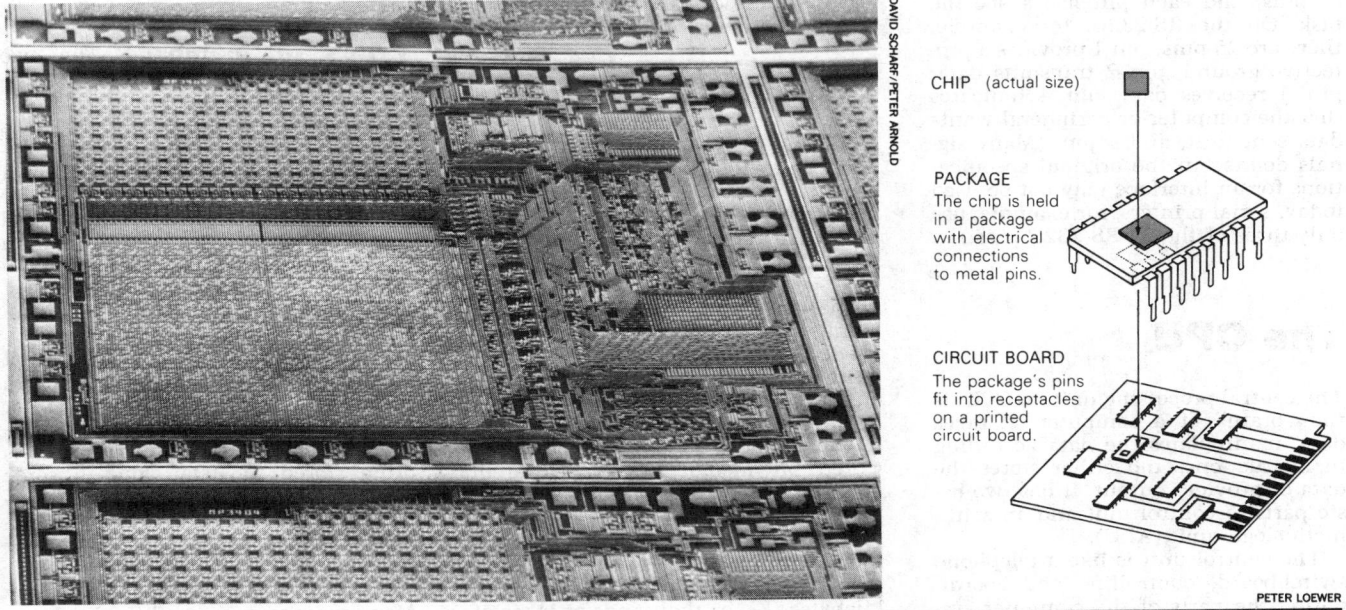

DAVID SCHARF/PETER ARNOLD

CHIP (actual size)

PACKAGE
The chip is held in a package with electrical connections to metal pins.

CIRCUIT BOARD
The package's pins fit into receptacles on a printed circuit board.

PETER LOEWER

An interface connects a peripheral to a computer. Interfaces are of two types: parallel and serial. Within a computer, information travels in parallel; that is, the eight bits that form a byte travel in a parallel stream on eight paths. If the peripheral has a parallel interface, the parallel arrangement is not altered; the interface transfers each character to the peripheral as a complete unit, with each bit traveling along its own path, in parallel with the other seven.

In a serial interface, the eight-bit-wide stream is funneled into a one-bit-wide stream, with the eight bits in a precise order. The bits are sent to the peripheral in series, that is, one at a time. The peripheral must collect all eight bits before it can process them, then collect the next eight bits for the next character, and so on. This happens very quickly, but not nearly as quickly as data transmission in a parallel interface.

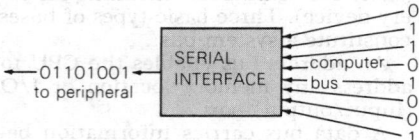

To use a peripheral with a computer, the two devices must be compatible, that is, capable of being interfaced with one another. Several standard interfaces are available, and any device made to a particular interface standard should be compatible with any other made to the same standard. A common parallel interface is the Centronics, which is widely used for connecting printers. The standard serial interface on microcomputers is RS-232C (Recommended Standard 232 Version C).

The interface connector has a series of pins, and each pin has a specific task. On the RS-232C, for example, there are 25 pins: pin 1 provides a protective ground, pin 2 transmits data, pin 3 receives data, pin 4 indicates that the computer or peripheral wants data sent to it, and so on. (Many signals defined in the original specifications for an interface may not be used today; serial printers, for example, use only three of the 25 RS-232C pins.)

The CPU

The central processing unit, or CPU, is the "brain" of a computer. It takes data, manipulates the data according to instructions, and either stores the data or provides output. It has two basic parts: a control unit and an arithmetic/logic unit (ALU).

The control unit is like a telephone switchboard, controlling and coordinating the parts of the computer system as directed by instructions in the program that is being run. It sends binary data to the arithmetic/logic unit, to memory, or out of the computer.

The ALU changes binary data according to the program instructions. It carries out arithmetic operations: addition, subtraction, multiplication, and division; and logical operations, such as determining the truth or falsity of sentences using *and, or,* and *not*; and it makes comparisons, such as determining whether one number is equal to, greater than, or less than another, or whether two alphabetic characters are the same.

Microprocessors. In microcomputers, the entire CPU is placed on a single chip, called a microprocessor. Most microcomputers now on the market have either a 16-bit or a 32-bit microprocessor, which means that the CPU can handle either 16 or 32 bits of data at a time. The more bits a CPU can manage simultaneously, the faster it can access memory and execute instructions. Intel's 16-bit 8086 microprocessor can find a word buried anywhere within a 29-volume encyclopedia in about 5 minutes. The 32-bit 80386 processor can find the same information in 7 seconds.

Memory

Memory enables a computer to store program instructions, data awaiting processing, and intermediate results of mathematical and logical operations it has performed. Without memory the CPU would be virtually helpless. Information would have to be fed in manually every time the computer needed it, and the user would have to write down intermediate results of calculations, then key them in when the computer was ready for them.

Today, most computer memory is stored on memory chips. Different chips are designed for storing different types of data.

The size of a computer memory is indicated in bytes. The memory of microcomputers is generally stated in kilobytes (K), or thousands of bytes of data. One kilobyte equals 1024 bytes, which is rounded off to 1000 bytes. Thus, a machine with 64K of memory can store approximately 64,000 bytes of data. Larger computers can store millions or even billions of bytes. One megabyte (MB) equals 1 million bytes. One gigabyte (GB) equals 1 billion bytes.

The limits on the memory of a computer are inherent in its CPU. Ordinarily, an 8-bit computer can handle a maximum of 64K. This does not, however, mean that the computer will actually have that capacity. For example, an 8-bit computer may have only 48K of usable memory; the other 16K will be needed by the machine to operate itself. Even with 48K of usable memory, it would not be possible to run a 48K program, for some memory is needed for the movement of data. (Otherwise, program execution could not occur and a situation analogous to traffic gridlock at a city street intersection would result.) The memory requirements printed on the packaging of commercial software take into consideration these factors; if a package indicates that the program requires 64K of memory, it will run on a 64K machine.

Types of memory. The two most common types of internal memory are RAM and ROM.

RAM, or Random Access Memory, is temporary memory; when the computer is turned off or when there is a power failure, any data in RAM are lost, scrambled into random 1's and 0's. RAM is used to store information entered from a disk, a keyboard, or any other input device.

ROM, or Read Only Memory, is manufactured with data permanently written in each memory location. It cannot be changed, users cannot store data in it, and it will not be erased by either turning off the computer or power failure. The computer operating system is often stored in ROM, and in some computers ROM contains an interpreter for a computer language, enabling users to write programs in the language.

PROM, or Programmable Read Only Memory, is a memory chip closely re-

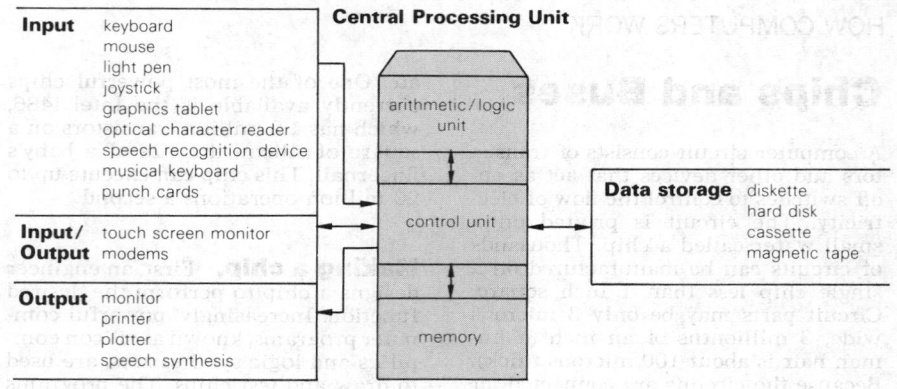

THE CPU *controls movement of information between parts of the computer.*

lated to ROM that can be programmed by the user. Once programmed, however, it cannot be altered, for programming involves applying voltage and burning out fusible metal links at specific locations on the chip. PROMs are used by people who wish to program their own read-only devices to hold specialized programs. PROMs are available in various sizes and tend to have extremely fast memory-access times.

EPROM, Erasable Programmable Read Only Memory, combines the benefits of user-programmable read only memories with the ability to correct mistakes. The fusible links consist of a conductive crystalline substance; exposing the chip to high-intensity ultraviolet light causes the substance to flow and bridge previously created gaps, thereby erasing the program and allowing the user to reprogram the chip. An EPROM may be reprogrammed several hundred times.

Memory addresses.   To enable the CPU to find specific data in memory quickly, every byte is stored in a

INFORMATION STORED *at memory addresses can be thought of as letters in numbered mailboxes.*

coded memory location. These locations are given addresses—that is, they are numbered, in binary code, from zero upward, much as houses on a street are numbered to ease identification of a specific dwelling. Addresses are generally assigned in ascending numeric order, as data are entered into memory.

A 64K computer actually contains 65,535 addressable memory locations. It uses a 16-digit binary number to address each memory location.

Bubble memory.   Another approach to data storage is bubble mem-

ory. Chips, usually made of garnet, are coated on both sides with a thin magnetic film that can be magnetized to form negatively charged regions (bubbles) in positively charged strata. The presence of a bubble—which has a width of only one one-millionth of an inch—represents a binary 1, while the absence of a bubble is a binary 0. Electrical charges are used to control the generation, storage, detection, and movement of the bubbles.

The biggest drawback of bubble memory is that data are only accessible serially, which results in significantly slower access times than with the comparable RAM.

A major advantage of bubble memory is that it is nonvolatile; that is, because of the presence of a permanent magnetic field, bubble memory retains data even when power is not supplied. Bubble memory chips are rugged and dependable, and consume very little power. One use of bubble memory is storage of recorded telephone messages. Another use is made in some portable computers. But the slow access speeds and high cost of the chips have limited wider use.

Input Devices

Input devices are used to enter data into computer memory or to give instructions to the computer to enable it to do a specific job. In order for an input device to function, the computer must have instructions on how the device is to be used. In the case of a keyboard, such instructions are usually built into the computer operating system. Other input devices generally can be used only with software that contains the necessary instructions. Most business and educational software is written with keyboard control in mind, whereas most game software is written to be used with a joystick.

Keyboard.   A computer keyboard resembles a typewriter keyboard but also has special function keys unique to computing. The central part of a computer keyboard has the same QWERTY layout of keys that is found on a typewriter. (The name is based on the order of letters on the upper left-hand corner of the keyboard.) The arrangement and functions of the special keys vary from one computer model to another.

When a key is pressed, a coded electrical impulse is sent from the keyboard to the operating system, which translates it into machine code. This code is stored in RAM until it is needed by the CPU, and is sent to the monitor to be displayed.

A key may be labeled with as many

as four symbols. Which symbol is produced depends on whether the key is pressed by itself or in conjunction with another key. For example, if a user presses only the "A" key, lowercase "a" is produced. If "A" is pressed while the shift key is depressed, capital "A" is produced. If "A" is pressed while the control key or another function key is depressed, still other symbols may be produced or a specific action may occur. In some word-processing programs, for example, pressing "A" while the control key is depressed will cause the cursor to move to another location in the text.

Mouse.   A mouse is a palm-sized device that, like the directional keys on a keyboard, controls the position of the cursor on the display screen. Moving the mouse on a flat surface, such as a desk top, moves the cursor a proportionate distance. The user moves the mouse until the cursor is on the desired item, such as an option on a menu, then pushes a button on the top of the mouse to select that item.

"Pointing" with a mouse cannot replace the keyboard for data entry, but many people consider it a superior tool for manipulating data already in the computer, since it is generally faster to

A TYPICAL COMPUTER KEYBOARD *has standard typewriter keys; function keys that give programming commands; and a numeric keypad similar to a calculator keyboard.*

FUNCTION KEYS   TYPEWRITER KEYBOARD   NUMERIC KEYPAD

BAR CODES

A bar code consists of a series of parallel lines of various widths and spacing that can be read by a specialized type of OCR called a bar code reader.

The best-known application of bar codes is on items sold in supermarkets. In the United States, the code used for this purpose is the Universal Product Code, or UPC. It decodes into two five-digit numbers, each of which is printed in text below the code. The one on the left identifies the manufacturer; the one on the right is the product number. Separating the numbers are two thin punctuation lines. The outermost thin lines indicate to the bar code reader the outer limits of the bar code. The 0 at the left of the code, and the thick line and thin line in from the right, indicate that the item is a grocery product.

A scanner at the checkout counter reads the code and matches it against codes in a computer to determine the price of the item, which is then printed on the tape that is given to the purchaser. The information read by the scanner can also be used to update inventory records and to provide sales statistics.

DAVID R. FRAZIER/PHOTO RESEARCHERS

use and easier to master than a keyboard. Numerous software packages permit a mouse to be used to complement the computer keyboard. For example, a word-processing program may permit use of the mouse to perform editing functions. Some graphics software uses a mouse to choose shapes from a menu, place them at any location on the screen, move them around, change their size or color, and so on.

Joystick. A joystick consists of a base on which is mounted a plastic or metal rod that can be moved in a circle. The joystick contains two potentiometers, instruments that measure voltage in steps between 0 and, typically, 255. One reads for the x direction, the other for the y direction. When the joystick is pushed, the x and y values of its position will be transferred as data to the computer and acted upon. The joystick also has one or more fire buttons, usually simple switches that input information in a yes-no mode.

Joysticks do not afford the precise positioning obtainable with a mouse, but they do move the cursor around the screen much more easily than can be done with cursor-control keys. Joysticks are used primarily for playing games.

Similar to the joystick is the paddle, which works in one direction only, and the trackball, which has a rolling ball that can be moved with greater precision than a joystick.

Light pen. A light pen enables the user to input data or commands by pointing at the display screen. The pen, which is about the size of a bulky ballpoint, contains a phototransistor that sends the computer a signal indicating the x,y value of the pen location

on the screen. Instructions in the program tell the computer what the user wishes to do when the pen is at that position. For example, the screen may display a menu with six choices labeled A through F. The position of each of the six letters is part of the program instructions. If the user touches one of the letters, the computer will act on the input; if any other part of the screen is touched, the computer will not respond.

Light pens vary considerably in precision and response time. Some can indicate their exact location on the screen; others indicate only an approximate location. The speed with which the pen responds is measured in nanoseconds. Precision-grade pens respond within 300 to 500 nanoseconds, while less expensive pens may take 700 nanoseconds or more.

Graphics tablets. A graphics tablet or pad has a flat surface on which the user can draw. What is drawn is entered into memory and appears on the display screen. Depending on the model, the user draws with a special stylus, an ordinary pen, or even a finger.

Different tablets offer different features, depending not only on the physical hardware but also on the accompanying software. Some have a grid on the surface, which makes it easier to draw parallel lines and objects with precise dimensions. Some are shaped like the display screen, making it easier for the user to size drawn objects. Many offer a variety of colors, textures, and magnification options. A mirroring option gives users the ability to create mirror images of a drawn object.

Some tablets are designed for home and school markets. More sophisticated models are intended for professional applications.

Scanners. A scanner is a device that converts words, numbers, pictures, and other images into digital form. Once the information is in the computer, it can be viewed on screen, printed onto paper, sent to another computer, or stored.

One type of scanner is the optical character reader (OCR). It reads and converts printed text into ASCII code that can be read by the computer. A typical system has a rotating drum that moves paper past an optical scanner that can distinguish between white and black patterns of reflected light. The light patterns are converted into electrical impulses, which are analyzed and matched to a character pattern in the reader circuits. The character is then sent to the computer for whatever further processing is needed.

Some OCRs can recognize printed handwriting, but script, or cursive handwriting, is beyond the capabilities of current technology.

OCRs are used in publishing, law, and other businesses. They also are used by schools and educational testing organizations to grade standardized tests; students make marks in specific areas of a score sheet and the marks are read by an OCR.

Page recognition systems can read multiple columns of text and distinguish among text, drawings, and photos. These systems make it easy and comparatively inexpensive to convert into computer data anything from job resumes to illustrated magazine articles or books.

Image scanners copy photographs, charts, signatures, fingerprints, and all other kinds of pictures originating on paper. They also can convert CAT scans and pictures from still and video cameras.

A scanner breaks up an image into dot patterns, much as photographs are broken up for magazine reproduction. The greater the number of dots per inch (DPI), the higher the quality of the stored image and any subsequent printed image. Six hundred and 800 DPI black-and-white scanners have been introduced; among color scanners, 300 DPI is the standard.

Unlike an OCR, a scanner does not convert into ASCII; it lets the computer do any needed processing. Also, images require much more storage than OCR data: a color photograph may need 18 to 24MB, and even a black-and-white image can use 3 to 6MB.

Magnetic ink character reader (MICR).

This resembles an OCR system but uses a magnetic reading head instead of optical components. Characters are printed on documents in a black ink that contains finely ground magnetic material. As a character passes under the reading head, it induces an electrical current that is proportional to its magnetic ink content.

MICR technology is widely used in the banking industry. Account numbers are printed on checks in MICR characters, and the face amount is encoded on the check after the check is deposited. The document is then fed into an MICR that reads the data into the computer for processing.

Speech recognition devices.

Devices that can recognize words spoken by humans have limited capabilities at the present time, but great potential. Current speaker-independent systems can recognize short commands given in a very limited vocabulary that has been programmed into the system. For example, a system used to sort baggage at airline terminals can understand the codes for cities used as flight destinations—for example, JFK for John F. Kennedy Airport in New York City—and respond by moving the baggage along the proper pathway.

Other devices are speaker-dependent: they can be taught to recognize the voice of a specific individual. First, the person records key words; as the words are spoken the device converts them into digital signals, which then are converted to binary numbers and stored. Later, when the device hears the person speak one of these words, it matches the word with the appropriate code and converts it into instructions. The process uses up a great amount of memory. For example, it takes about 8000 bytes to store the spoken word "republican," as compared with 10 bytes for the typed word. Also, the system may not recognize the person's voice if the voice changes, as happens when someone has a cold.

Researchers hoping to achieve unrestricted speech recognition face several challenges:

A. Ordinary speech is continuous; that is, there are no obvious breaks between words. The computer must have some way of determining where one word ends and the next begins.

B. Different speakers pronounce the same words in different ways; that is, regional and national speech patterns differ.

C. Many words sound alike but have different meanings. Among these are words that derive their meanings entirely from the context of the sentences in which they are spoken.

D. A language contains hundreds of thousands of words, and there is great variation in the words people use and the structure of their sentences.

E. A normal environment is usually filled with sound. The device must be able to isolate the human voice from background sound.

F. To be useful, the system must be able to analyze speech in something approaching real time—that is, almost instantly.

Musical keyboards.

Electronic keyboards that can be interfaced with a computer may mimic a dozen or more instruments, ranging from piano organ to trumpet and bagpipe. Systems vary in the features provided. Some enable users to record different instruments on separate tracks and then combine tracks. For example, a musician might record the melody line using a flute sound, play it back and, while doing so, add harmony in a violin voice, then repeat the process and add a bass line in a piano voice.

Although designed to mimic pianos and other instruments, there are interesting differences between the real instruments and the electronic device. For example, a computer can hold a chord indefinitely.

Punch cards.

Before disks and tapes, punch cards were the primary method of communicating with a computer. Today they have been replaced by other devices. Still, an understanding of how punch cards work is helpful in gaining an understanding of modern computers.

The standard punch card has 80 vertical columns with twelve punching positions in each column. The positions can be assigned to record almost any kind of data; the data are entered by punching holes in the appropriate positions. Data punching is accomplished on a keypunch, a machine much like a typewriter; as characteristics are typed, the configuration of punches is made.

Punch cards are fed into a card-reading machine, which converts the data into electrical signals that are sent to the computer. In one system, the presense or absence of holes is determined by metallic brushes that can complete an electric circuit through a hole but not through an unpunched position. In another system, a light shines through holes and activates photoelectric cells.

Output Devices

Output devices handle information that comes out of the computer. Like input devices, they are activated by instructions within the program or instructions provided by the user.

Monitors.

Monitors have screens for displaying information in the computer memory. Monitors are much like television sets and, in fact, some personal computers are designed to use television sets instead of monitors.

The dominant display technology is the cathode ray tube (CRT), in which a narrow beam of electrons generated by

an electron gun in the base of the tube is directed at a display screen that is coated with a phosphorescent chemical. Wherever electrons hit the chemical, a small dot of light appears.

One of the most important features of a monitor is the resolution, or quality, of the image on the screen. The higher the resolution, the sharper the picture. The screen is made up of a series of tiny units called pixels (PICture ELements). A pixel can be lit (turned on) or not lit (off). Resolution is expressed by the number of pixels the monitor can display; the greater the number, the higher the resolution.

DISPLAY SCREENS *are divided into tiny dots called pixels. The greater the number of pixels per unit of area, the more detailed a drawing or other image can be.*

An ordinary television set has a resolution of 256 pixels horizontally by 192 pixels vertically, yielding a total of 49,152 pixels. In comparison, many monitors have 1000 by 800, for a total of 800,000 pixels. Monitors with ultrahigh resolution—1600 pixels per horizontal line—display a near-photographic quality image.

(Television sets must limit their bandwidth, or the amount of space available to carry the signal, to prevent interference between adjacent channels. The narrower bandwidth affects text as well as graphics displays. Generally, television sets display 40-column text, whereas monitors display 80-column lines.)

Monitors are either monochromatic (black and white, black and green, or black and amber) or full color. The important features to look for are resolution, picture brightness (which determines how much detail can be seen), and scan rate (which sharpens pictures and reduces eyestrain).

Touch-sensitive screens. These are screens that enable users to perform tasks by touching pictures or other images on the screen. The touch creates a signal that can be read electronically. For example, to change the color of a wedge in a pie chart, a user would point to the wedge and then to a box containing the desired color.

At present, touch screens have limited applications. Reaching out to touch the screen temporarily obscures at least part of the screen. It can dirty the screen and, if frequent touching is needed, a person's arm can tire.

Liquid crystal displays (LCDs). Liquid crystals are substances with unstable molecular arrangements. When a slight electric current is applied to a crystal, the crystal molecules rearrange themselves in such a way that the normally opaque crystal becomes transparent to light. A liquid crystal display (LCD) consists of a layer of liquid crystal sandwiched between two layers of glass. Each segment of the display has a pair of electrodes that can activate the molecules in that seg-

ment, resulting in various light patterns on the display.

The first LCDs, developed in the mid-1970's, were small, with approximately 20 pixels per square centimeter, and used primarily for watch and calculator displays. Today's large-area LCD displays, displaying the same number of lines as a traditional CRT monitor, have resolutions approaching those of CRTs. Because of their light weight, they have found broad use in laptop computers.

Printers. A printer is a device used to make a printed copy of information in the computer. It is much like a typewriter but without a keyboard. It receives electronic signals from the computer via the connecting cable, specifying which characters to print, when to advance the paper, where text should end on a page, and so on.

There are several types of printers, each with its own advantages in terms of speed, print quality, noise level, graphics capabilities, and so on. Printers can be divided into two main groups: impact printers (daisy wheel, dot matrix), in which the print head physically strikes the paper through an inked ribbon; and nonimpact printers (laser, thermal, ink jet), which form characters without contact between the print mechanism and the paper. Nonimpact printers are significantly quieter than impact printers and, because they have fewer moving parts, are less susceptible to breakdown. However, they cannot make carbon copies and most require special papers, which cost more, are harder to write on, and subject to fading.

Daisy wheel printers. These printers use a rotating plastic or metal print wheel that resembles a daisy, with a character at the end of each "petal." The wheel is removable, enabling a person to change typefaces easily.

Daisy wheel printers produce high-quality documents that resemble those produced by electric typewriters. They

are relatively slow, however, typically printing at 15 to 40 characters per second (15 to 40 cps).

Dot matrix printers. These printers create characters by making tiny dots close together in a grid or matrix, much in the way that characters are formed on a CRT screen. The closer together the dots, the better the quality of the printed characters. The best quality dot matrix printers use 24-pin print heads, while most of the rest use 9 pins. Some dot matrix printers can make multiple passes over each line of text for higher print quality but this process reduces the speed of the printer.

Dot matrix printers are fast, printing between 80 and 200 cps. They are compact and relatively inexpensive.

Laser printers. Laser printers direct a highly focused beam of light at photographic film or paper, burning the characters onto the paper. They are very quiet and capable of producing high-quality documents at speeds approaching 500 cps. Some models come equipped with a page description language, which is helpful in designing brochures, documents, and newsletters. Although laser printers are significantly more expensive than impact printers, prices are declining.

Thermal printers. One type of thermal printer forms characters by burning dots onto special heat-sensitive paper. Another type uses a technique called thermal transfer, in which the printhead electrodes heat a film ribbon and "melt" ink onto ordinary paper. The print quality is generally inferior to that of other printers.

Ink jet printers. In an ink jet printer, the printhead sprays tiny ink particles onto the paper to form the characters. The text may be slightly fuzzy, because the printer cannot precisely control the trajectory of the ink drops. But ink jet printers are fast (up to 150 cps), quiet, and capable of producing high-quality color graphics.

Color ink-jet printers can mix colors on paper, thereby providing a wide range of hues and intensities. One high-priced model generates 125

INPUT DEVICES *such as light pens* (left) *and touch-sensitive screens* (right) *are highly interactive devices that enable computer users to give instructions by touching the screen.*

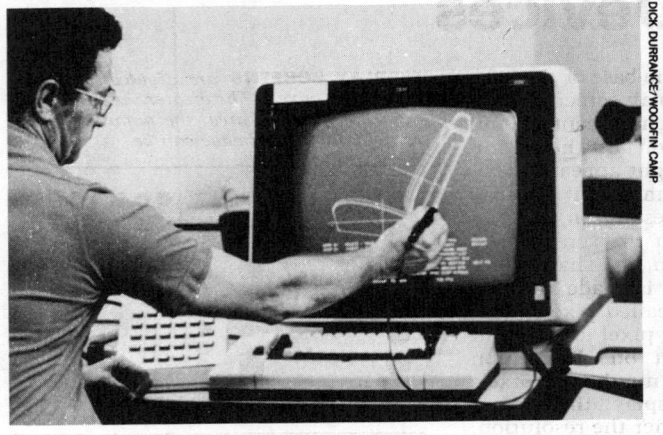
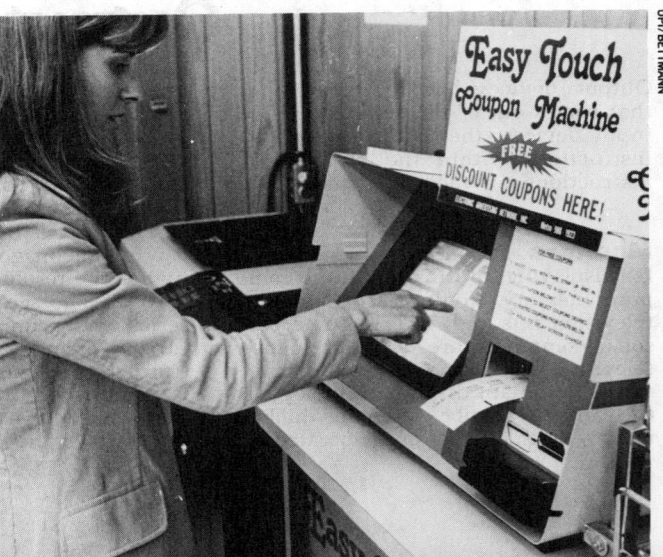

shades, produces images with resolutions up to 1200 by 1024 dots in 90 seconds, and prints every page at the same speed, regardless of the mix of text and graphics. Another model uses three inks to print up to seven colors, uses halftone patterns for color shading, and prints at the rate of 20 cps.

PRINTER FEATURES

Even basically similar printers can vary widely in the features they offer. People interested in buying a printer should consider which of the following features are best suited to their needs.

Speed. Printers vary greatly in the number of characters they print per second. Some operate at speeds of less than 20 cps, others at speeds approaching 500 cps. (At 40 cps, a printer will print a double-spaced page of text in approximately 1 minute.)

Print quality. The sharpness of printed characters or how they actually look on the paper determines print quality. "Letter-quality" printing resembles that produced by an electric typewriter and is considered desirable for business letters and other important documents.

CHARACTERS *produced by a daisy wheel letter quality printer* (left) *are cleaner than those produced by a dot matrix printer* (right). *Dot matrix printers generally are more versatile and faster.*

```
Letter quality printers
characters required for
Though still expensive,
of the dot-matrix units.
such as underlining, emb
of type, subscripts₂ and

These printers provide a
print wheels or elements
characters needed for sc
work or foreign language
And many printers will e
basic graphics such as l
```

LETTER QUALITY (A)

```
Dot-matrix printers
very quick, and inex
But in gaining spe
Letters are formed f
The dots can be used
style can be changed
get really fancy us
gothic type might be

In any case, dot-mat
for low cost.  And
where the dots can b
```

(A) DOT MATRIX

Proportional spacing. In printers that offer this feature, wide characters such as "w" and "m" take up more space than narrow ones such as "i" and "l". This makes documents look more professional.

Print pitch. The width of the characters determine print pitch. The higher the pitch (measured in characters per inch, or cpi), the more compressed the characters. Pitch affects the number of characters that can fit across a sheet of paper. Many printers can print at a variety of pitches.

Character sets. In addition to the usual characters, some printers offer a variety of special characters and may enable users to program their own special characters and symbols.

Graphics. Printers that can produce graphics vary in dot resolution. Some can also produce color graphics.

Paper feed. Paper is fed into a printer by one of two methods: friction feed or tractor feed. The friction method is best used for feeding in one sheet of typewriter paper at a time, as would be desirable for printing letters and other short documents. Tractor feed uses sprockets to feed in continuous-form paper with holes punched along the sides. Tractor units may feed paper in one or both directions; the latter type is preferable for printing graphics, superscripts, and subscripts. Many printers offer both friction feed and tractor feed.

Carriage width. An 8-inch carriage is adequate for letters and most other documents. A wide carriage is useful for spreadsheets and financial reports.

Buffer. An area for storing excess data in electronic form until the printer is ready to print the data. A page of single-spaced text requires about 3K of memory, but a page of high-resolution graphics may use a megabyte. Many printers have a small buffer, typically 4K. New laser printers can be equipped with 1MB or more.

Cost. Printer prices vary widely. Speed, type quality, and availability of special features are generally proportional to the cost of the machine. (Cost comparisons should also include the price of ribbons, specially coated paper, and so on.)

Electronic typewriters. Some electronic typewriters can be connected to a computer and used as a printer, thereby serving a dual purpose. They either have a built-in RS-232 interface or require additional circuitry before being connected to the computer. Most print using a daisy wheel, but some models use a form of thermal-transfer printing. Quality and speed are comparable to that of daisy wheel printers.

Plotters. These devices are designed to draw lines on paper. Unlike printers, they can draw continuous lines. A plotter can also print alphanumeric characters, but this is a slow process since the machine must draw each letter or number.

A plotter has one or more pens. Some models use a range of pens of different colors. Signals from the computer raise or lower the pens over the paper.

Plotters are used in many applications that require printed graphics, including charts, maps, and engineering drawings.

Modems. A modem (*MO*dulator/*DEM*odulator) is an input/output device used to send and receive information over telephone lines. It changes (modulates) the digital signals generated by a computer into analog signals that can travel over telephone lines; when these signals reach another computer, the demodulator part of the modem converts the signals back into digital form.

Modems that fit inside the computer are called internal, or board, modems. External modems that plug directly into telephone line are called direct-connect modems. Other external modems, called acoustic couplers, have a pair of rubber cups into which the handset of a telephone fits. The cup for the mouthpiece contains a speaker to generate audible tones, and the cup for the earpiece has a microphone to receive tones.

MODEMS *enable computer users to send and receive information via telephone.*

The speed at which a modem sends and receives data is measured in units called baud. One baud equals approximately one bit per second (bps). Currently, 300-, 1200-, and 2400-baud models are the most commonly used modems, though companies that make extensive use of electronic data transmission are switching to 9600-baud modems. Because of data compression techniques, some types of 9600-baud modems can actually send up to 19,200 bits per second.

A modem that operates at 300 baud sends about 30 characters per second—a rate slow enough to enable a person to read the material as it moves across the display screen. A person cannot read data moving at 1200 baud but this speed and higher speeds are useful for sending long files or programs.

The advantages are obvious: a 10,000-word document takes less than a minute to send at 9600 baud, about 3 minutes to send at 2400 baud, 6 minutes at 1200 baud, and almost 25 minutes at 300 baud.

Transmitting and receiving modems must operate at the same speed; a 1200-baud modem must go down to 300 baud to communicate with a 300-baud modem (most higher speed modems contain electronic circuitry for lower speeds as well as for their highest speed.)

Speech synthesis. All devices that enable a computer to speak in a natural language produce speech in one of two ways. One type of synthesizer contains a built-in list of words.

Users can instruct the computer to produce individual words or to string together a number of words to form a sentence. Though speech quality is comparatively high, each word must be "taught" to the synthesizer and stored separately in memory. The second type of synthesizer generates words by stringing together individual speech sounds, called phonemes or allophones, which are part of memory. The user types in words, and the synthesizer responds by combining the appropriate sounds to produce spoken words.

A major use of computer-produced speech has been in readers for the visually handicapped. Computer games and educational programs for young children also incorporate speech-synthesis chips.

Storage Devices
Disk Storage

Since a computer may not hold all the data that must be stored and accessed, auxiliary, or secondary, storage is an extremely important part of a computer system. Such storage enables a user to save information held in RAM before the computer is turned off. There are two major aspects to auxiliary storage: the type of media on which data are stored and the manner in which the data are accessed.

At present, magnetic tapes and magnetic disks are the primary storage materials. These components are made of plastic coated with ferrous oxide or other compounds that are easily magnetized. Data are stored in the form of magnetic pulses, which the computer can translate into binary 0's and 1's. Up to 10,000 of these bits can be stored on 1 inch of disk or tape. The direction, or polarity, of each magnetic field determines whether the bit of data is interpreted as a 0 or a 1.

To create and read magnetic fields on tape or disk, a device with a read/write head is used. For both types of media, reading is nondestructive; that is, the data can be read repeatedly. However, writing onto tape or disk is destructive, erasing data previously present on that part of the medium.

The primary difference between tapes and disks is the manner in which data are accessed. Tape is a sequential medium; data are stored—and must be read—one record after another. Accessing a file at the end of a tape can take several minutes. On disks, data are stored in concentric rings in such a way that the data can be accessed directly and at random, making access very rapid. Primarily because of the far greater access speeds, disks have largely superseded tapes, although tapes are still in general use.

The two types of disks, floppy and hard, work in a similar fashion. Information is written in circular tracks arranged like the rings of a tree. The number of tracks per inch along the radius is called the track density of the drive. Increases in track density have been the major source of increased storage capacity on disks; densities of up to 1000 tracks per inch are now possible.

Each track is divided into sectors, a sector being the smallest amount of data that can be transferred in response to a read or write command. All tracks can hold the same amount of information, even though the inner tracks have a considerably smaller circumference than the outer tracks.

Before it can be used, a disk must be formatted. This involves defining tracks and sectors on the disk, and is done by the operating system. Once the disk has been formatted, it can be recorded on over and over again; reformatting is necessary only if the disk is to be used with another operating system, or if it develops an error.

Floppy disks. The standard storage device in small computer systems is the floppy disk, sometimes called a diskette but most commonly referred to as a disk. It is a flexible, flat platter

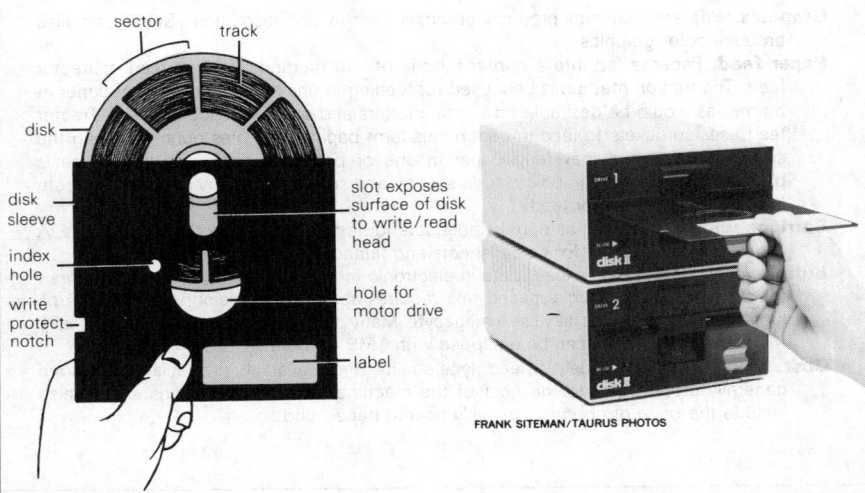

FLOPPY DISKS

Floppy disks are enclosed in protective vinyl jackets, with an access window through which the drive head creates and reads files.

sector

track

disk

disk sleeve

index hole

write protect notch

slot exposes surface of disk to write/read head

hole for motor drive

label

PETER LOEWER

FRANK SITEMAN/TAURUS PHOTOS

permanently enclosed in a protective jacket to prevent fingerprints, dust, or other contaminants from damaging the disk surface. The most common floppy disks are 5.25-inch and 3.5-inch. Current versions of the 5.25-inch disk can store up to 1.2MB (1.2 million characters). For 3.5-inch disks, 720K and 1.44MB are standard. The former is the equivalent of 520 double-spaced typewritten pages of text.

To read or write to the disk, it is inserted into a disk drive through a door in the front of the case. Closing the drive door pushes the disk over a spindle. The disk rotates within its jacket; a slot in the jacket enables the drive read/write head to move from track to track across the disk to perform the desired task.

Floppy disks are inexpensive, so users may easily make back-up copies of information. However, the disks are easily damaged if they are subjected to careless handling.

Hard disks.

A hard disk is a stiff, round aluminum platter, usually hermetically sealed in the disk drive. Hard disks capable of storing up to 40MB of data are now standard; advanced systems have a capacity of 760MB. Data are accessed extremely quickly from a hard disk, and the need to repeatedly swap floppy disks is eliminated. Hard disks are also more reliable than floppy disks, and more expensive.

Hard disks are rotated in a disk drive at a constant high speed. Depending on the system, the drive contains one or more disks, all stacked on a common spindle. The disks may be single- or double-sided; there is a read/write head for each side and these move together, accessing a stack, or cylinder, of tracks simultaneously.

Data usually are stored in terms of cylinders. When a particular track on one disk side, or surface, is filled, the next track to be filled is the same track on the next disk surface; for example, after track five on surface one is filled, track five on surface two is filled, then track five on surface three, and so on until the entire cylinder has been filled. The access arms then move to the next cylinder. This avoids the necessity of moving the entire set of access arms from one cylinder to the next each time a track is filled.

Today, most hard disks are based on the Winchester systems developed by IBM in the early 1970's. These systems got their name from the first one, which had the same model number—3030—as the Winchester rifle. The disks and read/write heads are in a sealed unit to prevent contamination from airborne particles. Until recently, the disks were permanently built into the drives, but now removable cartridges containing the disks and in some cases the read/write heads are available, making it possible to expand storage by buying more cartridges.

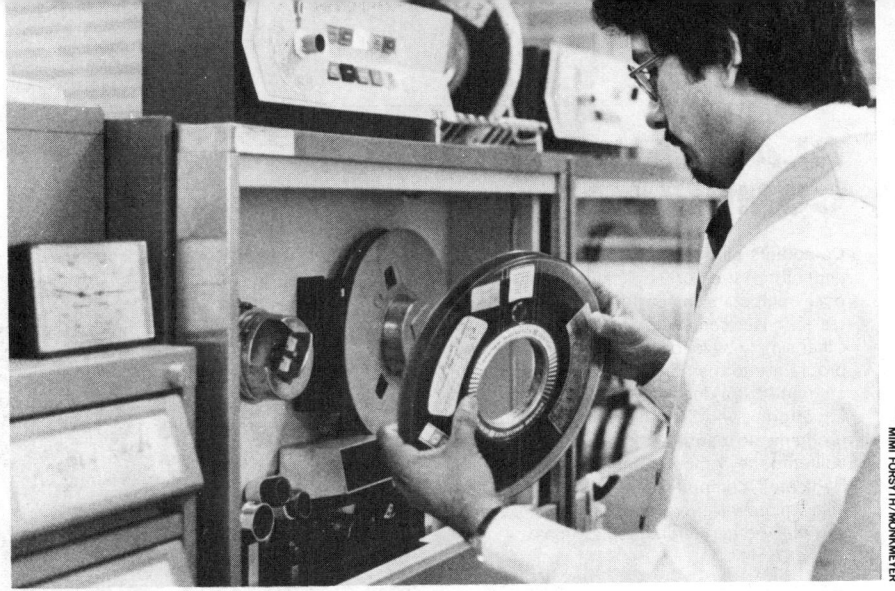

MAGNETIC TAPE *similar to that used for recording music can be used to store computer data. However, the suitability of tape for many chores is limited by its sequential nature.*

Tape Storage

Magnetic tape used to record computer data is similar to that used to record music. Once the most common storage medium, tape has largely been superseded by disk storage.

The amount of data a tape can hold depends on the recording density, or closeness, of the vertical rows of bits along the length of the tape. Common densities are 800 bytes per inch (bpi); 1600 bpi; and 6250 bpi. A typical 2400-foot reel of tape can store 150 million characters (150MB).

Tape drive units.

Reels of tape used on mainframe computers and minicomputers generally hold 2400 feet of 1/2-inch tape, but minireels holding about 600 feet are common.

Cartridges.

Cartridges look like eight-track audio tape cartridges. They are used to store commercially produced programs. The programs are stored in ROMs and cannot be erased without physically destroying the chips in the cartridge. The primary advantages of cartridges are convenience and speed. As soon as the cartridge is inserted into the computer, the program loads and is ready to use. Cartridges are used primarily for games and for educational programs designed for children.

Optical Storage

Instead of magnetic media, it is possible to use a laser beam to store and retrieve data. A laser encodes binary data as a pattern of pits on a disk. Another laser reads that pattern, translating it back into the binary 0s and 1s understood by a computer.

The newest storage technology, optical disk technology, is comparatively expensive, but it allows the storage of enormous amounts of data in very little space.

Magneto-optical drives.

In a magneto-optical system, data are stored on a cartridge the size of a 5.25-inch floppy disk. The cartridge can hold up to 1GB. As with floppies and hard disks, a user can repeatedly store, alter, and erase files.

WORM (write once, read many).

This system allows a user to store data once, but not erase or change it. A 12-inch WORM can store 1GB per side; it is two-sided. A 5.25 WORM stores 300MB per side. WORM is being used to archive large databases in legal and medical organizations.

CD-ROM (compact disk-read only memory).

The same compact disks used in the music industry can be used to store words, graphics, and other computer data. A disk 4.72 inches in diameter can store almost 600MB of data on one side (no data are etched on the reverse side). The data on a CD-ROM are placed there by the manufacturer and are permanent.

CD-ROM is being used to store financial data, encyclopedias, and other large databases. Much of the medium's growth during the 1990's, however, is expected to be in multimedia uses such as interactive video. Interactive video combines full-motion video, 3-D graphics, audio, and text on a single CD-ROM disk. For example, one prototype program lets a user "walk" through an ancient Mayan site. Realistic background sounds are heard, and the user can retrace steps, enjoy panoramic views of the area, or switch to text about the Mayans.

CLASSIFYING COMPUTERS

Computers can be classified according to architecture, size, or application. General-purpose computers can perform a great variety of tasks; a user can switch from one task to another simply by loading a different application program into memory. In contrast, dedicated computers are designed for special purposes, to perform a very limited set of operations. The programs to carry out these operations are built into the computer and cannot be altered. Dedicated computers are found in automobiles, microwave ovens, navigational systems, and many other helpful applications.

DEDICATED COMPUTERS *are designed to perform specific functions. The computer in this car contains travel maps that can be called up by the driver.*

Analog computers. An analog computer is designed to measure something that changes continuously and smoothly, such as voltage or temperature. Data are coded according to voltage rather than by the presence or absence of a current and are represented as a continuous quantity. The drawback is the lack of precision. A good comparison is an old-fashioned watch with hands that move smoothly around the face, mimicking the smooth passage of time. It is easy to determine when an hour has passed, but not as easy to know when half a second has passed.

Analog computers generally are dedicated devices. They are most commonly used in working engineering problems.

Digital computers. A digital computer processes discrete numbers. A digital signal is noncontinuous (discrete) but specific—either a 0 or a 1. This is identical to what happens in digital watches, which divide time into tiny bits, making it easy to measure seconds, microseconds, and even nanoseconds.

Divisions among digital computers have been blurred by technological developments, but four broad categories are still generally recognized.

Microcomputers. A microcomputer has a microprocessor as its CPU and it is designed to serve a single user. However, like other computers, microcomputers can be connected in a network with other microcomputers. This enables communication and the sharing of data among many computer users.

Microcomputers are the most common computers; they are widely used in all types of businesses as well as in homes and schools. They range in size from desktop models to models as small as a credit card. There also are broad ranges of internal memory, speed, and cost. One microcomputer used in many homes and schools has 256K of memory and costs about $1000. At the other end of the scale is a work station that has 32MB of memory and costs $50,000 or more.

Work stations are fast, powerful microcomputers originally meant to handle engineering and scientific tasks; however, newer models are showing up in other work environments—just as more traditional desktop microcomputers are becoming powerful enough to handle engineering and scientific jobs.

Many work stations are based on a relatively new and simpler chip design called RISC (reduced instruction set computing). This design eliminates instructions that are rarely used, putting them in software if needed. This enables RISC computers to execute instructions much more rapidly than traditional computers. Already, RISC computers can outdistance the processing speed of the fastest mainframe computers, and at a lower cost.

Minicomputers. A minicomputer is larger, more powerful, and more expensive than most microcomputers. It is designed to be used by more than one person at a time. For example, the cash registers in a grocery store can be connected via a network to a minicomputer, which has a large enough memory to store data on sales of the thousands of different products sold by the store.

Mainframe computers. These are large, powerful computers that may fill an entire room, with a CPU as large as a refrigerator. They are designed to be used by many people simultaneously. Because of their cost, which may be several million dollars, mainframe computers have been used primarily by government agencies, scientific organizations, and businesses that require massive record and data storage facilities. For example, mainframes play a central role in airline reservation systems. The ability to network computers, coupled with the dramatic increase in microprocessor speed, is causing many organizations to move away from mainframes. Instead, they are using microcomputers linked together by a network.

Supercomputers. The fastest digital computers in existence are called supercomputers. In many ways, they are the harbingers of the future: supercomputers of 25 years ago were less powerful than the microcomputers of today; the supercomputers of today will probably be considered dinosaurs 25 years from now.

Most supercomputers, as well as other computers, are vector machines: they operate serially, reading sequential bytes with a single processor, and perform most efficiently when handling repetitive calculations. Today scientists are developing parallel supercomputers, which operate on the principle that two processors are better than one, four better than two, 1000 or more better yet. Parallel computers divide a problem into parts, assigning portions to multiple processors operating simultaneously; each processor calculates subtotals and returns them to a central processor for combining. Such a system is much more flexible than the vector system. The major problem to be solved is keeping synchronization among the processors.

Supercomputer speed is measured in gigaflops, or billions of floating point operations per second. Speeds of 10 gigaflops are now possible, and researchers developing parallel machines predict that speeds measured in teraflops, or trillions of operations per second, will be attained in the mid-1990's.

Supercomputers are 40,000 to 50,000 times faster than a typical microcomputer. Their great speed makes it possible to solve problems that would take years on conventional mainframes. Supercomputers are being used to design bridges, airplanes, and nuclear power plants; to do basic research in science and engineering; to conduct weapons research and code cracking; to forecast weather and assist in petroleum exploration; and to create complex graphics and special effects for motion pictures.

Software Concepts

How—and what—a person communicates with a computer is determined by the software, or programs, used. Every program must be written in a language understood by the computer or written in a language that can be translated into one understood by the computer. This is not dissimilar to what takes place in conversations between two people: you either speak in a language the other person understands or you use an interpreter to translate what you are saying.

Computer Languages

There are three types of computer languages: machine, assembly, and high-level. Machine language is sometimes referred to as object code; assembly and high-level languages, as source code.

Languages vary greatly in complexity but have two important features in common: every language has a very limited vocabulary and a simple, but very strict, syntax.

Machine languages.
The only language a CPU can understand is machine language, which consists solely of binary 0's and 1's. An instruction telling the computer to add 5 plus 2 would look like this:

```
11001110
00000101
11001110
00000010
```

Additional instructions would be needed to have the computer display the sum. Many hundreds of numbers would be needed for the computer to print "The sum of 5 plus 2 is 7."

Programming in machine language has one advantage: the program can run at blinding speed. But such programming is tedious and subject to error; a single misplaced numeral will prevent the entire program from working properly. Also, it is almost impossible for a person to read and comprehend a program written in machine language.

Early computers were programmed entirely in machine language. Then, in 1951, the first translator was developed, allowing the creation of languages that are easier to use.

Assembly language.
Assembly language is similar to machine language, obeying exactly the same rules as machine language but using sym-

bols instead of binary code to describe the instruction. For example:

ADC means "add with carry"
CLC means "clear carry"
LDA means "load accumulator"
STA means "store accumulator"

To have the computer add 5 plus 2, these instructions might be given:

```
CLC
LDA #5
ADC #2
```

The actual instructions vary somewhat from one microprocessor to another, which is one disadvantage of assembly language. For example, the instruction for adding two numbers is ADD on the 8088 microprocessor and ADC on the 6502. Programming in assembly language takes much longer than programming in a higher level language. But it enables the programmer to create programs that use much less memory and that run much faster than equivalent programs written in other languages.

High-level languages.
High-level languages use letters, words, and numbers that are easily understood by people. To have the computer add 5 plus 2 using the BASIC language, a person would type this instruction:

```
PRINT 5+2
```

This simple statement causes the computer not only to add the numbers but to print the result on the screen.

More than 150 high-level languages now exist, each suitable for different applications. Some are general-purpose languages, intended for a variety of applications. Others are designed for specific uses, such as COBOL for data processing, and FORTRAN for mathematical and engineering applications. Even within the language there are variations, or dialects. For example, CBASIC is a structured version of BASIC that runs on the CP/M operating system; MBASIC is a version that lacks the structure of CBASIC but is easier for novices to learn.

Another difference among languages is their degree of structure. Some are very structured, which means that programs must be logically organized and strictly follow established rules in order to run. In PASCAL, for example, each program must begin with the word PROGRAM followed by the program's name. Next must come the word VAR followed by a list of variables used throughout the program. Then must come the word BEGIN, and so on. Other languages, such as BASIC, give programmers much more leeway. Generally, struc-

tured programs are easier to design, read, and debug than relatively unstructured programs.

Some languages are easier than others to learn to use, in part because they are interactive; in such languages it is easy to switch back and forth between writing and testing a program. An interactive language will immediately report any error that it detects, so that programmers can correct errors while the purpose of the program line is still clear in their minds. Noninteractive programs will indicate errors only after the entire program has been typed in. BASIC is a very interactive language; COBOL is not.

A COMPARISON OF LANGUAGES

Each of these programs instructs the computer to print this message on the monitor.

```
I CAN COUNT!
0
1
2
3
4
5
6
7
8
9
10
I AM VERY SMART!
```

BASIC	10 PRINT "I CAN COUNT!" 20 FOR A=0 to 10 30 PRINT A 40 NEXT A 50 PRINT "I AM VERY SMART!"

PASCAL	PROGRAM 1COUNT:
	VARA: INTEGER
	BEGIN
	  WRITELN ('I CAN COUNT!');
	  FORA:=0 TO 10 DO
	  WRITELN (A);
	  WRITELN ('I AM VERY SMART!');
	END.

FORTH	:ICOUNT "I CAN COUNT!" CR 10 0 DO A1 + .CR LOOP "I AM VERY SMART!" CR;

COBOL	PROCEDURE DIVISION.
	MAIN ROUTING.
	  DISPLAY "I CAN COUNT!".
	  PERFORM PRINT-OUT-A
	  VARYING A FROM 0 BY 1
	  UNTIL A>10.
	  DISPLAY "I AM VERY SMART".
	  STOP-RUN.
	PRINT-OUT-A.
	  DISPLAY A.

POPULAR HIGH-LEVEL LANGUAGES

ADA. Named in honor of Lady Augusta Ada Lovelace (1815-1852), ''the first programmer.'' Developed for the U.S. Department of Defense for use in control systems such as aircraft navigation systems. It is a very efficient language; programs written in ADA can be run at very fast speeds.

APL (A Programming Language). Developed by Kenneth Iverson at IBM in the early 1960's, APL uses a special character set and functions that require a knowledge of mathematics. It is particularly suitable for mathematical applications and is widely used on large computer systems.

BASIC (Beginner All-purpose Symbolic Instruction Code). An easy-to-use general-purpose language that relies on such familiar English words as *print, let, read,* and *return.* BASIC is an interactive language that is one of the most popular for use in personal computers.

C. A general-purpose language invented by Dennis Ritchie at Bell Laboratories in 1972 for use on the UNIX operating system. C is structured and not interactive. It is well suited for systems software and widely used for everything from software for 16-bit computers to sophisticated graphics seen in films such as *Star Trek II.* C facilitates the transfer of programs between computers with different microprocessors without sacrificing the use of specific features of a given machine.

COBOL (Common Business-Oriented Language). Developed in 1959-1960 by a committee with representatives from the U.S. Department of Defense and major computer corporations specifically for use by businesses. COBOL is procedure-oriented, self-documenting, and not interactive. It is well suited for large-scale data manipulation, and the most popular business language.

FORTH. Developed in the 1960's by Charles Moore at the National Radio Astronomy Laboratory in New Mexico. FORTH is general purpose, interactive, unstructured, and difficult to read and write. It is widely used in industry to enable computers to run other machines, and is the standard control language for many astronomical observatories.

FORTRAN (FORmula TRANslator). The first high-level language, developed in the 1950's by John Rackus and others at IBM for writing programs to solve problems that can be stated in terms of arithmetic procedures. Statements are expressed in algebraic form and symbolic language. FORTRAN is not interactive and is popular for scientific and mathematical computations.

LISP (LISt Processing). Created in 1959 by John McCarthy and others at MIT. LISP can manipulate symbols as well as numbers, including non-numerical data that change considerably in length and structure during the course of program execution. Both the programs and the data they manipulate are expressed as lists. LISP is a large, difficult to learn language. It is widely used in artificial intelligence research because of its ability to represent such data as sentences, formulas, logic theorems, and game positions.

LOGO. Developed in the late 1960's by Seymour Papert and others at MIT. The basic feature of LOGO is the turtle, a small movable triangle that appears on the screen and enables users to draw and experiment with geometric angles. The language is especially popular for introducing young children to mathematical and programming concepts.

PASCAL. Named for the 17th-century French mathematician Blaise Pascal and developed by Niklaus Wirth of the Federal Institute of Technology at Zurich, Switzerland, in 1973. PASCAL is a highly structured language that requires programs to conform to a rigorous format. Programs are easy to read and change. PASCAL is not interactive and is widely used in high-school, college, and university computer science programs.

PL/1 (Programming Language One). A combined algebraic and business language developed by IBM in the mid-1960's as a middle position between FORTRAN and COBOL. PL/1 is a large, complex language; finding and correcting errors is fairly difficult.

Types of Software

There are three types of software: operating systems, translation programs, and application programs.

Operating systems.
An operating system (OS) comprises the programs that enable a computer to manage all of its internal housekeeping tasks. An OS interacts with memory, controls input and output functions, controls peripherals, and communicates with the computer user. All parts of the computer system—hardware and software—must

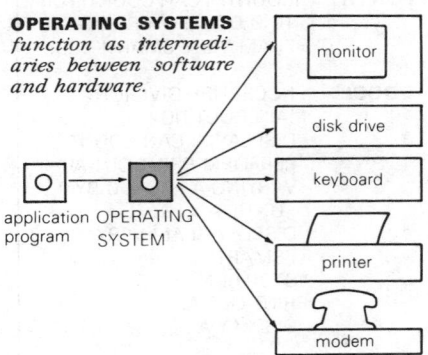

OPERATING SYSTEMS *function as intermediaries between software and hardware.*

application program → OPERATING SYSTEM → monitor / disk drive / keyboard / printer / modem

be compatible with the OS. Thus, all programs are written to interact with a specific OS, and all machines that use it should appear identical to the programs. For example, a person with a Compaq computer with a hard disk and a daisy wheel printer can send data via telephone lines to a person with an IBM PC, a floppy disk drive, and a dot matrix printer. The common operating system of the two computers masks their differences, so applications programs perceive the different computers as identical.

If a computer system uses a disk drive, the OS coordinates the transfer of information to and from the disk. It may also include programs, called utilities, which rename files, copy files from one disk to another, indicate the amount of available disk space, and report on the size of the files on a disk.

Usually, the OS is built into the computer. Some computers contain more than one OS, enabling them to run a wide variety of software. In other cases, add-on operating systems are available on disks, to load into the computer memory.

Operating systems can be either specific—designed to work with one particular machine or group of machines—or generic. A generic operating system is one designed to function on a variety of models. Microcomputer operating systems currently in widespread use include the following:

CP/M (originally, Control Print/Monitor, now Control Program for Microcomputers), written by Gary Kildall at Digital Research in the mid-1970's, was the first widely used generic system; it is supported by a large library of software. CP/M was designed for 8-bit computers, but more recent versions work with 16-bit machines.

MS-DOS (MicroSoft Disk Operating Systems, called PC-DOS by IBM), is

DEFINITION OF "FILE"

A file is a collection of information stored on a disk. It can range in length from a few characters to a complex program to text consisting of millions of words. Each file is given a short name, the format of which varies from one OS to another but which typically consists of a group of letters followed by a period and an extension. For example: LOUIS.TEXT might be the name given to a file consisting of a letter to someone named LOUIS; IRS.DATA might be a file consisting of income tax data. A list of all the files on a disk is called the directory.

easier to use by novices than CP/M; it is designed for 16-bit computers.

UNIX, developed by Bell Laboratories in the early 1970's, can be used on everything from microcomputers to supercomputers. Written in C, UNIX contains hundreds of utility programs for file manipulation and makes programming comparatively easy.

Translation programs.

To do programming in a language other than machine language, a translator is needed to convert the so-called human language into one the computer can understand. There are several types of translator programs.

An assembler translates assembly-language programs into binary code.

A compiler translates a high-level language into binary code or assembly language; if assembly language is produced, then an assembler is needed for final translation into machine language. Compilers translate and store (usually on tape or disk) all program statements at once; execution occurs only after the entire program has been translated. Since the program is stored in machine language, the compiler does not have to be used again. COBOL and FORTRAN are examples of compiler-oriented languages. Programming procedures in these languages may be comparatively complex, but the final programs run very quickly.

An interpreter is another type of program that translates a high-level language into machine language. Unlike compilers, interpreters translate statements one at a time and execute one statement before reading the next. Every time the program or part of the program is executed, it must be reinterpreted; thus, in a loop that repeats five times, each statement in the loop is translated five times. This allows a programmer to start running a program immediately and to change it immediately if there is an error. But programs translated by an interpreter may run as much as 20 times slower than compiled programs. Most languages that come with interpreters, such as BASIC, also have compilers.

This enables programmers to use the interpreter for program development, then compile the finished program to create fast, compact machine code.

Applications programs.

The programs that are loaded into the computer by a user and that consist of a set of instructions to perform a particular job or application are called applications programs. Tens of thousands of such programs are available, with new releases almost daily. They fall into such categories as education, word processing, data management, home productivity, and entertainment. Later sections of this volume are devoted to applications programs and how they are used.

An application program is written to work with a specific operating system and to run on a specific model or brand of computer. Because of incompatibilities among operating systems and computers, most application programs are sold in different versions for different computer models.

Programming

At one time, the only way to get software was to write it oneself. Today, computer users can depend on commercial software to perform myriad tasks without their ever needing to know how to program. Yet programming continues to be a useful skill. Knowing how to program enables people to get computers to perform specialized functions for which little if any commercial software exists, such as solving esoteric engineering problems. Programming encourages clear, precise, logical thinking, hence its popularity among educators. Programming also is enjoyable, enabling people to be creative in much the same way that gardening, woodworking, and other hobbies are rewarding.

Flowcharts

To write a program, a person must first have a step-by-step plan that details how to go about solving a problem. Such a plan is called an algorithm. After the algorithm is written, its steps can be translated into a programming language to create a program that will enable a computer to solve a problem. Essential features of any algorithm are a clearly defined goal; proper organization of a series of precise, unambiguous steps that lead toward that goal; explicitly defined data in each step; and the absence of extraneous information or superfluous instructions.

Most problems can be solved in more than one way. Which algorithm is chosen depends at least in part on the amount of usable memory and other hardware limitations.

Programmers frequently create flowcharts to reflect the logic or the steps in an algorithm. A flowchart is a map-like drawing consisting of a series of symbols, each representing a logical step in the program. To facilitate the exchange of information, standard flowchart symbols have been adopted by the American National Standards Institute and the International Organization for Standardization. The four most common symbols are:

— terminal symbol; indicates where the program begins and ends

— process symbol; indicates any type of calculation or processing of data

— decision symbol; indicates that a decision is made or a test performed

— input/output symbol; indicates any type of input or output

Flowcharts are drawn so that they can be read from top to bottom and from left to right. Although the flow sometimes goes in a reverse direction, flow lines should never cross one another. Arrows are used to indicate the paths followed by the program.

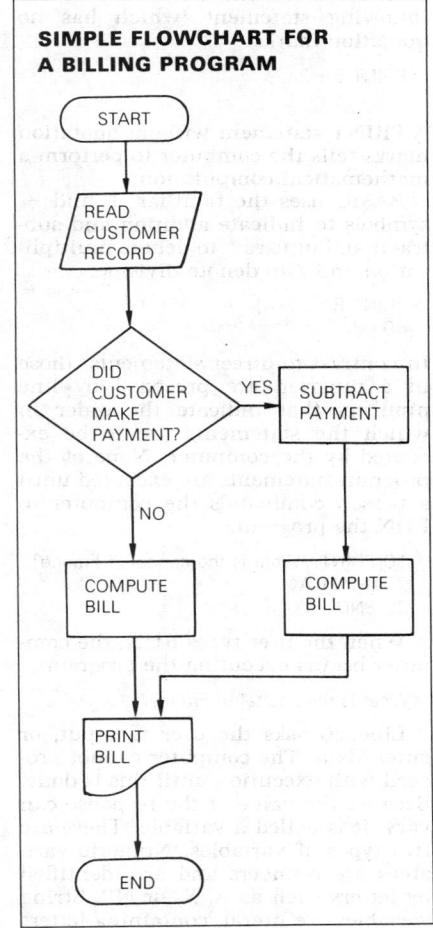

SIMPLE FLOWCHART FOR A BILLING PROGRAM

BASIC Programming

Because BASIC is comparatively easy to learn and use, it is one of the most popular programming languages. This section introduces a number of BASIC statements and shows how to use them to build a simple program. (Note: Because each brand of personal computer understands a slightly different dialect of BASIC, the program may not run on a particular computer without modifications.)

The simplest way to communicate with a computer is through the use of direct statements:

```
PRINT "I am a computer."
```

As a person types this statement on the keyboard, it appears on the display screen. When the person presses the RETURN key, the computer immediately acts on the command:

```
PRINT "I am a computer."
I am a computer.
```

The computer prints whatever is between the two quotation marks. Here is another example:

```
PRINT "5+2"
5+2
```

Contrast this with the results of the following statement, which has no quotation marks:

```
PRINT 5+2
7
```

A PRINT statement without quotation marks tells the computer to perform a mathematical computation.

BASIC uses the familiar + and − symbols to indicate addition and subtraction, but uses * to denote multiplication and / to denote division.

```
PRINT 8*(20/4)
40
```

In contrast to direct statements, those in a program are preceded by line numbers that indicate the order in which the statements are to be executed by the computer. None of the program statements are executed until a person commands the computer to RUN the program.

```
10 PRINT "What is the capital of France?"
20 INPUT A$
30 END
```

When the user types RUN, the computer begins executing the program:

```
What is the capital of France?
```

Line 20 asks the user to input, or enter, data. The computer cannot proceed with execution until this is done. Because the value of the response can vary, it is called a variable. There are two types of variables. Numeric variables are numbers and are identified by letters such as A, X, or NP. String variables are literal, containing letters or words, and are identified by a letter followed by a dollar sign.

```
What is the capital of France?
Washington
```

The problem with the program is obvious: the computer accepts any answer typed by the user. This can be corrected by using IF . . . THEN statements, telling the computer that IF a certain condition is met, THEN it should carry out the rest of the statement. Four types of conditions are possible with numeric variables: = means equal, < means less than, > means greater than, and < > means not equal to. With string variables, two conditions are possible: = and < >.

```
10 PRINT "What is the capital of France?"
20 INPUT A$
30 IF A$="Paris" THEN PRINT "Correct!"
40 IF A$< >"Paris" THEN PRINT "Wrong"
50 END
```

If the user inputs Paris, the condition in line 30 is met and the computer prints Correct! If the user inputs anything other than Paris the condition in line 30 is not met; the computer cannot execute the rest of the line and it proceeds to line 40.

The program can be made more complex by adding GOTO statements that tell the computer to proceed to a specific line in the program.

```
10 PRINT "What is the capital of France?"
20 INPUT A$
30 IF A$="Paris" THEN GOTO 100
40 PRINT "Wrong. Please try again."
50 GOTO 10
100 PRINT "Correct!"
110 PRINT "What is the capital of Japan?"
120 INPUT B$
130 IF B$="Tokyo" THEN GOTO 200
140 PRINT "Wrong. Please try again."
150 GOTO 110
200 PRINT "Correct!"
210 END
```

If the user answers the first question correctly, the program skips from line 30 to line 100. If the user's answer is incorrect, the program cannot execute line 30 and proceeds to line 40. At line 50 it goes back to line 10 and prints the question again. It will continue to do this until the user enters the correct answer. To limit the number of times this part of the program is repeated, a loop using LET statements can be incorporated into the program.

```
5 LET A=0
35 LET A=A+1
40 IF A<4 THEN PRINT "Wrong. Please try again."
50 IF A<4 THEN GOTO 10
60 PRINT "Wrong. Paris is the capital of France."
70 GOTO 110
```

Replacing line 40 in the program with these six lines limits the user to three chances to answer the question. The LET statement in line 5 assigns the value 0 to the variable A. This value is increased by 1 every time the program reaches line 35. As long as that value remains less than four, the computer will execute lines 40 and 50. But on the fourth try, it will jump to line 60.

The program could incorporate this loop after every question, and could be expanded to ask users for the capitals of dozens of countries, but it would be a very long and very inefficient program. Instead, capitals and countries can be assigned to variables through the combined use of READ and DATA statements. Here is a simple program using a READ-DATA loop:

```
10 READ X$
20 IF X$="X" THEN GOTO 50
30 PRINT "One of my favorite foods is "X$"."
40 GOTO 10
50 END
100 DATA pizza, ice cream,
110 DATA yogurt, apple pie, X
```

When this program is run, the computer reads the first value in the DATA statements and assigns the value to X. It executes the statement in line 30, then returns to line 10 and reads the *next* value in the DATA statements. It continues to do this until X$ equals X.

```
One of my favorite foods is pizza.
One of my favorite foods is ice cream.
One of my favorite foods is yogurt.
One of my favorite foods is apple pie.
```

The DATA statements can be placed anywhere in the program; the computer will automatically go to them after reading the READ statement.

The READ statement can instruct the computer to read more than one piece of DATA at a time. READ X,Y tells it to read two numerical values and store the first in X and the second in Y. This concept can be used to rewrite the capitals quiz:

```
10 READ X$, Y$
20 IF X$="STOP" THEN GOTO 300
30 LET A=0
40 PRINT "Name the capital of "X$"."
50 INPUT A$
60 IF A$=Y$ THEN GOTO 200
70 LET A=A+1
80 IF A<4 PRINT "Wrong. Try again."
90 IF A<4 GOTO 40
100 PRINT "Wrong." "Y$ is the capital of "X$"."
110 GOTO 10
200 PRINT "Correct!"
210 GOTO 10
300 PRINT "This is the end of the quiz. Thanks for playing!"
310 END
1000 DATA France, Paris, Japan, Tokyo, England, London, Egypt, Cairo
1010 DATA Canada, Ottawa, Norway, Oslo, Peru, Lima, STOP, STOP
```

A person reading a listing of a program will be helped if the program contains remarks, or REM statements.

These clarify the purpose of the program or sections of the program. The sample program might include these REM statements:

```
2 REM Capitals Quiz
5 REM X$=country, Y$=capital
25 REM A=counter
```

BASIC includes other statements, but the ones introduced here provide the rudiments for creating a wide variety of original programs.

Bugs and debugging.

A mechanical flaw in a computer system or an error in a computer program is called a bug. (The term originated in 1947, when mathematician Grace Hopper, working for the U.S. Navy, tried to determine why one of the Navy's computers had stopped. She discovered a moth crushed to death in one of the machine relays; removing the moth cleared up the problem. Hopper taped the moth into her log and next to it wrote, "First actual case of bug being found.")

There are various types of software bugs. Syntax errors occur when a person gives the computer an instruction it cannot understand. Typing a word that has no meaning in the language is a syntax error. So is a misspelling, such as typing PRIMT instead of PRINT; a punctuation error; sometimes even incorrect spacing between words. Often, the computer will detect such an error and print an error message for the programmer:

```
10 PRINT "What is your name?"
20 INPET A$
SYNTAX ERROR
```

Such an error can be corrected simply by retyping the incorrect line:

A BASIC VOCABULARY

BASIC commands tell the computer to do something with a program

RUN	execute the program
LIST	print all program lines in ascending numerical order
NEW	delete the program in memory
SAVE	save the program currently in memory
LOAD	load a file from disk
EDIT	make changes to a section of the program
RENUM	renumber program lines

BASIC statements make up a program

PRINT	outputs answers and messages
INPUT	prepares the computer to receive data from the program user
LET	names a variable and tells the computer to find or compute the value of whatever is to the right of the equal sign and assign that value to the variable
IF . . .	THEN indicates that if a certain condition is met, the computer should execute whatever is specified by the THEN part of the statement
GOTO	tells the computer to go to a specific line in the program
GOSUB . . .	RETURN tells the computer to go to a subroutine, execute it, and then return to the next line in the main part of the program
FOR . . .	NEXT limits the number of times a part of the program is repeated
READ	tells the computer to find the DATA list and read one or more data items into memory so the computer can use it (them)
DATA	identifies a list of data
REM	a remark; documentation; does not affect the program logic or operation but explains what the program or a section of the program does
CLS	clears the screen
END	tells the computer to stop executing the program

```
10 PRINT "What is your name?"
20 INPET A$
SYNTAX ERROR
20 INPUT A$
LIST
10 PRINT "What is your name?"
20 INPUT A$
```

When the program is run or compiled, the computer may pick up other errors, such as a GOTO statement that directs the computer to a nonexistent line. The computer will not detect logic errors or errors in data. For example, if the capitals quiz listed Washington as the capital of France, the computer would not know that this is incorrect.

Special debugging programs that can be used to find and correct bugs are useful programming tools. A debugger allows a person to set stopping places, or breakpoints, in a program; type out a record of program variables, called a trace; and in other ways ease program debugging.

Selecting Hardware and Software

Buying a computer is much like buying an automobile or an audio system: the right buying decision depends on a number of factors. The following steps are advisable when considering purchase of a computer.

1. Identify the primary uses to which the system will be put. These should determine the kind of system needed, even though it may be used for additional activities. The most suitable system for a small accounting business may not be the best system for a graphics artist or for an elementary school or for a family with two college-bound teenagers.

2. Identify the software that best meets your needs. If, for example, word processing will be a primary use,

determine which features you *must* have and which would be totally superfluous.

3. Determine which computer systems can run that software. The best computer in the world is worthless if it cannot run the required software.

LEARN *what software is available for a computer system before making a purchase.*

Define the specific hardware features needed: which peripherals (and, therefore, interfaces), which operating system, how much memory. Remember, all parts of the system must be compatible, and always keep in mind the primary uses of the system. A business that plans to use the computer for business correspondence will want a letter-quality printer; a student using a computer for school may choose a faster and less expensive dot-matrix printer.

4. Try to determine future computing needs. A hard disk drive or 512K of RAM may not be needed at present, but if it is probable that such features will be needed in a year or two, it may be wise to purchase them with the initial system.

If a system is expandable, it is more likely to meet future as well as present needs. Expandability refers to the ability to add new features, such as increased memory, a hard disk drive, or networking capabilities. Many manufacturers build expandability features into their computers, allowing upgrading with only minor modifications or additions to the hardware. For example, some 8-bit machines provide the option of installing an additional 16-bit CPU so that the system can function at both levels. The cost of upgrading a system that offers built-in expandability features is significantly less than the cost of replacing the system with a newer model.

The newest technology may not always be the best choice; when new technology is introduced, older models often drop sharply in price, yet they may more than meet one's needs.

5. Gather information. Prepare a list of currently available hardware and software that meet your needs. Try to find out whether suitable products are scheduled to be marketed soon.

6. Set a price target for the entire hardware system and for specific software packages. If applicable, include furniture, training costs, and installation charges.

7. Try before you buy. Whenever possible, ask for a thorough, hands-on demonstration. Reputable retailers will allow customers to test hardware, and will usually have demonstration programs of costlier software packages. Do not rush this process; operations that seem easy to experienced computer users may seem complicated to neophytes, who need to spend more time familiarizing themselves with basic procedures. If possible, have a specific task for the computer to do. If one's primary use for the computer will be word processing, it is useful to bring some words to process; if spreadsheeting, some figures to project.

Pay particular attention to those features that will be used most: the feel of the keyboard and the ease of reading text on the monitor if the system will be used primarily for typing; the

READ *the fine print before deciding which computer best meets your needs.*

screen resolution and color quality if it will be used primarily for graphics. Also, check the documentation to make certain that is easy to understand and complete.

8. Read the terms of the warranties and guarantees that come with the product. If a disk develops a flaw, can it be returned for a free or low-cost replacement? Is a backup copy of a program provided?

9. Determine the maintenance that is to be done by the user. Owners usually are responsible for such preventive maintenance chores as removing dust from the keyboard and screen, changing ribbon cartridges and type elements in the printer, and cleaning the disk drive heads. But most repairs and adjustments have to be done by computer technicians.

If repairs are needed, where will they be done? Some dealers perform on-site service, others use regional service centers. Computers purchased from mail-order firms may have to be shipped thousands of miles, perhaps even abroad, for repairs. Find out whether the dealer will lend you a computer free or at reasonable cost while repairs are being made.

Service contracts, either from the dealer or the manufacturer, are generally available and sold on a yearly basis. These vary in price, depending on which equipment is covered; for example, the contract may specify service for the computer but not for the printer, especially if the latter is of a different manufacture than the rest of the system.

10. Find out what kind of support can be expected from manufacturers and dealers. Are they available to answer questions and assist with troubleshooting? Do they maintain toll-free or other special telephone lines to increase accessibility?

Documentation. Users of any product, whether a simple word game, a complex graphics program, or a piece of hardware, should become familiar with the documentation, or printed instructions, that come with the product. The documentation explains the capabilities and intricacies of a system and makes it possible for users to take advantage of all of the capabilities of the system.

Good documentation is easy to read, well organized, and accurate. It explains the purpose of the product and describes its features. Instructions for set-up and basic housekeeping procedures (such as backing up a disk) are described step by step. There are explanations and practice drills to familiarize users with the product. Lengthy documentation, which accompanies most hardware and large software packages, includes a table of contents, an index, and perhaps a glossary for easy reference. Thus, documentation is invaluable for the user.

Sources of Information

Many information sources exist.

Magazines and books. Contain much information about computing in general and about specific hardware and software products. Many publications provide evaluations of products and tips on how to best use them.

Retailers. Good salespeople are able to answer questions clearly and are willing to spend time familiarizing customers with products sold. Most salespeople tend to know more about one aspect of computer use than another; find a business expert if you are planning to buy a business system, a games expert if you want the most challenging adventures. Some stores offer training programs and other educational support. (Note: retailers are generally more willing to offer help to people to whom they have sold equipment than to people who have bought their equipment elsewhere.)

Computer shows. Provide an opportunity to see a wide variety of hardware and software all at once. Some are geared to the needs of average consumers, others toward business people, and some toward specific audiences, such as physicians or publishers. Local dealers generally have information on consumer shows; professional organizations and magazines can provide information on shows relevant to specific interests.

Users. People who have had experience using a particular system or software product are valuable sources for discovering whether a product does what it says it can do, if it holds up under heavy use, and so on.

Computer clubs (users groups). Clubs offer a mixture of information, support, and camaraderie. Members range from prospective buyers and beginners to computer enthusiasts (hackers) and professionals. Meetings generally include product demonstrations and topic discussions of general interest to the membership. Some clubs are special-interest groups, designed for people who use a specific computer or work in a particular profession. Others are broader, often with subgroups that focus on specific interests, such as programming, business uses, or CP/M systems. Many clubs have their own newsletters and libraries of public-domain software that members may borrow or copy. Information on local clubs can usually be obtained from computer stores. Electronic bulletin boards and manufacturers may also be helpful.

Schools and camps. Offer computer-related courses ranging from general overviews to how to program a specific computer in a specific language. Computer camps, primarily for children, offer computer instruction together with more traditional camp activities.

THE DEVELOPMENT OF COMPUTERS

Though computers are inventions of the 20th century, their history actually began many centuries before, when people first developed methods of counting. As societies formed and became progressively more complex, the need for rapid counting grew, and people invented machines to help them. Gradually, over hundreds of years, these counting machines became ever more sophisticated, but the objective of the inventors was always the same: to develop machines that perform calculations quickly, precisely, and accurately.

No one person can be credited with the invention of the computer. Many people contributed to the development of today's machines, and many more are working to create even more powerful and more useful computers. Computers are still evolving, and just as black-and-white television helped pave the way to color television, so are today's computers building a path toward the more advanced computers of tomorrow.

JOHN ISAAC/UN PHOTO 152,802

FROM ABACUS TO COMPUTER: *In a computer center in China, both the oldest and the newest counting tools are used to process census data.*

Early Counting Devices

At first, people may have used their fingers and toes to count. They could have made marks in the sand to indicate how many people lived in their community. Knots tied in a length of some sort of string may have served to record the number of sheep in a herd. Stones in a pile could have kept track of the number of days until the next new moon. Later, as trade between advanced societies grew, merchants began scratching records of transactions on clay tablets.

The oldest known counting tool is the abacus. It consists of beads strung on parallel wires or wooden rods in a rectangular frame. Each bead is a "counter" and represents a value of one, ten, or some multiple of ten; the beads's value depends on its position on its rod. By moving the beads back and forth, one can use the abacus to add, subtract, multiply, and divide.

The abacus is between 2000 and 5000 years old. Its place of origin is unknown, though various forms of the device were used in ancient China, Egypt, and Greece. Today, the abacus

is still widely used in some parts of the world. In China, for example, it is common to see children heading for school with their abacuses tied to their wrists.

One major advantage of the abacus is that it can be used with any counting system. It became a popular tool throughout Europe, which used the Roman number system (a system without a symbol for zero) until about 800 A.D., when invading Moors introduced the Hindu-Arabic zero to nine number system. The switch to this system occurred slowly; it was not until the 16th century that the Hindu-Arabic system was in common use throughout Europe.

In the early 1600's, John Napier, a Scottish mathematician, devised a way to multiply and divide numbers by adding or subtracting their "secret corresponding numbers," his name for logarithms. This system was useful for mathematicians, as well as astronomers, navigators, and surveyors.

In 1621, an English mathematician, William Oughtred, developed the slide

rule, a device that made it easy to use logarithms. The slide rule was in wide use until the 1970's, when it was made obsolete by the introduction of electronic calculators and computers.

Napier also developed a calculating device that sped the multiplication of large numbers. The device consisted of a set of rods on which numbers were engraved in certain positions. By turning the rods to the appropriate combination of numbers, the answer to a multiplication problem was easily found. Because the rods were made of ivory, people called the device Napier's bones (see page 1486).

Mechanical Calculators

The first mechanical calculating device was built in 1623 by Wilhelm Schickard, a German professor greatly interested in science and mathematics. This was just at the time when the

368

Thirty Years' War was spreading havoc and disease across much of Europe. Schickard died during the war, and details of his calculating clock lay buried until 1935, when a researcher discovered references to it among letters written by Schickard to the astronomer Johannes Kepler. Thus, the device had no influence on the development of calculating devices.

The Pascaline. The world has generally credited 19-year-old French mathematician Blaise Pascal with invention of the first mechanical calculator. In 1642, to help his father, tax commissioner for Upper Normandy, calculate taxes, Pascal invented a machine that came to be called the Pascaline. Depending on the model, the Pascaline had from five to eight interlocking gears, each with ten notches, numbered zero through nine. Above the gears was a row of small windows.

A user dialed in the numbers to be added, and the sum appeared in the windows. The Pascaline could easily add numbers and could handle subtraction, though less efficiently; the gears turned in one direction only, so subtraction was performed by a method that is called the nines complement, which transforms subtraction into addition.

The Stepped Reckoner. A more sophisticated, gear-driven calculator was invented in the early 1670's by Gottfried Wilhelm von Leibniz, the German mathematician, scientist, and philosopher. His machine, the Stepped Reckoner, used eight cylindrical gears, all connected to a central shaft. Each cylinder had nine rows of teeth. The first row, containing one tooth, was one-tenth the length of the cylinder. The second row had two teeth and was two-tenths the length of the cylinder. And so on up to the ninth row, which had nine teeth and was nine-tenths the length of the cylinder. Using a combination of dials and metal pegs, a person was able to add, subtract, multiply, divide, and find square roots. However, the Stepped Reckoner could not carry or borrow numbers automatically, and the inability to machine precisely made parts—a problem that plagued many early inventors—meant that the Stepped Reckoner did not always give correct answers. Most of the calculating machines developed during the next 150 years were inspired by the Stepped Reckoner.

Leibniz made two other important contributions to computing: he introduced the concept of breaking a mathematical problem down into a series of small steps, each easier and faster to compute than the problem in its entirety; and he was among the first Europeans to study the binary system and its potential applications.

THE SCIENCE MUSEUM, LONDON

THE ANALYTICAL ENGINE, a steam-powered, gear-driven machine designed by Charles Babbage, was never completed, but many of its features are used in modern computers.

The Analytical Engine. One of the most creative thinkers of the 19th century was the English mathematician Charles Babbage, who developed the concepts that underlie today's computers. He is often considered the father of computers.

Irritated by the inaccuracies in mathematical tables and by the time that had to be spent finding and correcting them, Babbage conceived of a steam-driven calculating machine and set to work designing what he called a Difference Engine. He built a model of the engine and in 1823 received a grant from the British government to construct it.

The Difference Engine was designed to calculate to the twentieth place and print out answers on paper. Its dimensions were approximately 10 feet high by 10 feet long by 5 feet deep. Its weight was about 2 tons. Obtaining parts with the required precision was difficult and expensive. Progress was discouragingly slow, and in 1833 the British government stopped funding the project. Perhaps Babbage still could have completed his Difference Engine, but his interests had moved on to a radically new kind of machine.

The Difference Engine was designed to handle a specific type of calculation. But Babbage had conceived of a machine, which he called the Analytical Engine, that could perform any computation. This machine would be programmable; that is, it could be given instructions on the kind of calculations desired. It had the same basic parts found in a modern computer: an input device, calculating unit, control unit, memory, and printer to produce the output.

The instructions would be coded and punched onto cards. Babbage borrowed the idea of punch cards from Joseph-Marie Jacquard, a French silk weaver who in 1801 had devised a way to use patterns of holes punched into cards to control the operation of weaving looms. Different patterns of holes on a card produced different woven designs.

For the next 40 years, until his death in 1871, Babbage worked on his Analytical Engine—at great personal expense, since the British government had no interest in funding the project. Only parts of the Analytical Engine were ever built; the machine was too advanced for the engineering techniques of its time.

One of Babbage's strongest supporters was Lady Augusta Ada Lovelace, a mathematician and the daughter of the English poet Lord Byron. She persuaded Babbage to use the binary system instead of the decimal system and suggested ways to program the machine so that it could repeat the same set of instructions and carry out instructions as long as certain conditions existed.

Though Babbage never completed the machine, a machine inspired by his Difference Engine was built during his lifetime by two Swedes, Pehr George Scheutz and his son, Edvard. Though of simpler design than Babbage's proposed machine, it was able to process large numbers faster and more accurately than any previous machine—or any human being. In 1855, the Scheutz's Tabulating Machine was awarded a gold medal at the Great Exhibition in Paris—history's first computer prize.

Hollerith's Tabulating Machine.

During the latter part of the 19th century, the United States began to equal and then surpass the European nations both industrially and technologically. Like the countries of Europe, the United States faced a growing need for faster calculating devices. The 1880 census of America's 50 million people took eight years to tabulate. Unless something were done, it was estimated that the 1890 census would not be completed until after the 1900 census began.

A young engineer named Herman Hollerith designed an electromechanical machine that could count and sort punch cards. Called the Tabulating Machine, it was the first such device to use electricity and the first to use punch cards for calculations. A card was prepared for each person counted in the census. Punching out holes in specific locations on the card indicated such information as the person's age, marital status, income, and occupation. For example, a hole in one location indicated that the person was a farmer; in another location, a hole would indicate that the person was a banker.

The card was then fed into a press on the tabulating machine. The upper surface of the press (the part that touched the upper side of the punch card) was covered with small pins. On the lower surface were small depressions, each one corresponding to a pin on the upper surface. When the card was put into the press, pins would pass through all its holes and touch the underlying depressions. Each such contact completed an electrical circuit which, in turn, caused one of the tabulator counters to advance by a count of one. Say, for example, that occupational information was being tabulated. A card fed into the press has no hole for "banker," so no electrical circuit can be completed at that point. But there is a hole for "farmer," so contact is made, and the counter for farmer moves ahead by one.

The Census Bureau tested Hollerith's machine against two other systems, both of which involved counting cards by hands. The machine was eight to ten times faster, so the Census Bureau used them in the 1890 census. It took six weeks to determine the nation's population: 62,622,250. Over the following years, a mass of other 1890 census data was tabulated.

Many nations soon ordered Hollerith's machine to tabulate census returns, and large companies began using it for accounting and inventory. In 1896, Hollerith founded the Tabulating Machine Company. In 1911, the company merged with several other small firms to form the Computing-Tabulating-Recording Company (CTR), which in 1924 became International Business Machines Corporation—known today as IBM.

The Rise of Computers

In the 1930's, the first computers in the modern sense of the word were built in the United States. They were huge electromechanical devices, much larger than any of the calculating machines built theretofore. One was an analog computer, the other a digital computer.

Differential analyzer.

An analog device had been built by the British scientist Lord Kelvin in 1873. It was a special-purpose machine, used to predict the rise and fall of tides and to draw a chart representing this information. Kelvin realized, however, that such a "differential analyzer" could be built to solve any type of problem involving differential equations, and he described this concept in a paper published in 1876. Because the technology of that time was still limited, Kelvin never attempted to build a machine of this type.

The first differential analyzer, or large-scale analog computer, was built in 1930 by Vannevar Bush, at the Massachusetts Institute of Technology (MIT). It had six computing elements, called Thomson integrators, and six electric motors, plus a system of shafts that relayed the calculations to an output unit.

The capabilities of the computer were impressive. A later model was able to handle problems with as many as 18 variables. Though useful for certain specific jobs, analog devices proved not to be the wave of the future, because they lacked the versatility and the accuracy of digital computers.

The Mark I.

In 1937, Harvard mathematician Howard Aiken began work on the first digital computer. The machine was completed in 1943 with the help of students and IBM engineers. Called the Automatic Sequence-Controlled Calculator, or Mark I, it stood more than 50 feet long and 8 feet high. It had some 750,000 parts, including almost 500 miles of wire. To perform the computing, Aiken used approximately 3300 electromechanical switches instead of vacuum tubes. He realized that vacuum tubes would have speeded up operations, but they were less reliable than the switches and created a great deal of heat, which would have necessitated a cooling system, making Mark I even bigger.

Instructions were coded on punched paper tape. When operators wanted to give the computer new instructions, they removed the tape and inserted a new one that contained the desired program.

Mark I could add, subtract, multiply, divide, and create mathematical tables. It could perform about three additions per second. It was first used by the U.S. military during World War II, for computing ballistic data. For example, firing tables made by Mark I could be used to determine where to aim a gun so that the shell would reach its target. Taken into consideration were such factors as distance, air density and temperature, and shell construction.

THE MARK I *was driven by a long metal shaft powered by an electric motor. It sounded "like a roomful of ladies knitting," remarked one scientist.*

First-Generation Computers

While Aiken and his associates were completing Mark I, other computers were incorporating concepts that would make the Mark-type computers obsolete. Instead of relays, these computers used only electronic circuits, thereby providing much greater operating speeds.

Since the 1940's, there have been four main stages, or generations, in the evolution of computers, distinguished by the type of electronic circuitry used and the resulting advances in speed, memory capacity, and size reduction.

First-generation computers had circuits containing vacuum tubes. Invented by Lee De Forest in 1906, vacuum tubes can amplify electronic signals and can be used as switches. Since they can switch an electronic signal on and off in much the same way that a light bulb is turned on and off, it is possible to use vacuum tubes for binary operations—an on signal representing 1 and an off signal representing 0.

In the late 1930's and early 1940's, several researchers were working toward development of electronic computers. In England, Alan Turing headed a team that designed Colossus, a machine used to decipher German messages during World War II. In Germany, Konrad Zuse built a programmable computer that used the binary system for calculations. And in the United States, John Atanasoff, a theoretical physicist at Iowa State University, built a prototype of a digital computer he envisioned. The machine worked well and was able to add and subtract the binary equivalents of decimal numbers having up to eight places. Together with Clifford Berry, Atanasoff then proceeded to build the full-sized computer, which was completed in 1942. It incorporated some of the basic concepts that would eventually be found in all modern computers. It was relatively slow, however, and it could not he programmed. But Atanasoff's work greatly influenced the efforts of the men who invented ENIAC, the computer that demonstrated to the world the potential of these machines.

ENIAC. The *E*lectronic *N*umerical *I*ntegrator *a*nd *C*alculator (ENIAC) was built at the University of Pennsylvania under the direction of John Mauchly and J. Presper Eckert. Begun in 1943, ENIAC was funded by the U.S. Army, which planned to use it to develop firing tables. But the computer was not completed until 1946, after World War II had ended and, with it, the urgency for improved firing tables. Instead, ENIAC was used to design the hydrogen bomb.

ENIAC was gigantic: 80 feet long, 8 feet high, and some 30 tons in weight. It contained approximately 18,000 vacuum tubes, 70,000 resistors, and 500,000 hand-soldered connections. It was programmed by setting 6000 switches and plugging wires into three walls of plugboards similar to those used in telephone switchboards. Changing a program could take several days, since the operator had to reset the switches and replug the wires.

ENIAC could perform 5000 additions or 300 multiplications a second. By contrast with Mark I, which took 15 to 30 minutes to compute a ballistic trajectory, ENIAC needed only 20 seconds to do the job.

Stored programs. By 1944, Mauchly and Eckert were designing another computer: the *E*lectronic *Di*screte *V*ariable *C*omputer, (EDVAC). It would be a stored-program computer; that is, operating instructions would be in its internal memory rather than read into the machine from punch cards or perforated paper tape.

Mathematician John von Neumann, a professor at the Institute for Advanced Study in Princeton and a consultant on EDVAC, made major contributions toward the development of the stored-program concept. In 1945 he wrote a report describing the design of the machine—the first paper describing the design of a general-pur-

ENIAC programmers had to feed in operating instructions by setting thousands of switches and plugging numerous wires into huge plugboards, a process that could take several days. In today's computers, operating instructions are stored internally, on a tiny memory chip.

UNIVERSITY OF PENNSYLVANIA

pose digital electronic computer. Because of this paper, many people mistakenly credited von Neumann with inventing the concept of stored programs, but Babbage, Zuse, and others, including of course Mauchly and Eckert, also were involved in the development of stored programs.

The first stored program was run in 1948, on the Manchester Mark I, a computer built in Manchester, England, under the direction of mathematician Max Newman. The program, a search for the factors of a number, was stored as charge spots on cathode ray tubes (CRTs). Electron guns in the bases of a tube shot beams of charged electrons at the face of the tube, thereby storing bits in the form of charge spots. The Manchester Mark I had six CRT memory tubes, each capable of storing 1K to 2K of information.

EDVAC, completed in 1952, stored programs in mercury delay lines. A delay line consisted of quartz crystals mounted at opposite ends of a tube filled with mercury. When one crystal was activated with electric pulses representing the binary digits to be stored, it created ultrasonic signals that moved through the tube and struck the second crystal, causing it to oscillate and regenerate the original electric pulses—rather in the way that a canyon holds an echo. In this manner, a continuous stream of digits could be stored indefinitely. The system was slower and costlier than CRTs, but more reliable and capable of holding more information.

UNIVAC. In 1951 Mauchly and Eckert completed the *UNIV*ersal *A*uto-matic *C*omputer (UNIVAC), the first computer designed for commercial purposes. The first model was delivered to the Census Bureau, which used it for tabulating the 1950 census. Over the following years, businesses bought 46 UNIVACs.

UNIVAC had a memory of 1.5K and was the first computer to use magnetic tape for input. It could process up to ten tapes simultaneously, each storing more than 1 million characters. As they had done with ENIAC, Mauchly and Eckert made UNIVAC a decimal machine, which required many more vacuum tubes (over 5000) and much more space than a comparable binary computer. The processor was approximately 15 feet long, 7.5 feed wide, and 9 feet tall, and weighed about 5 tons. Connected to the processor were a printer, magnetic tape drive, tape copier, and other equipment.

Other developments. In 1951, Grace Murray Hopper, a mathematician working on the UNIVAC project, devised the first compiler, an internal program that converts, or compiles, a programmer's instructions into machine language. It could understand ordinary words and could perform certain operations automatically, such as those involving floating-point numbers (fractions multiplied by a power), thus eliminating the need for writing lengthy subroutines detailing how to perform such operations.

In the early 1950's, MIT engineer Jay W. Forrester developed magnetic core memory, a new form of internal memory, composed of tiny doughnut-shaped ferrite cores strung on a grid of wires. Each core had its own coordinates and could be magnetized in one direction for "on" and in the other direction for "off." The system was much faster and required far less maintenance than earlier systems. The first full-scale computer to use core memory was MIT's Whirlwind, originally built with a CRT memory. The switch doubled Whirlwind's operating speed, quadrupled the input data rate, and greatly reduced maintenance time and costs.

IBM introduced its first computer—the IBM 701—in 1953. It was a binary computer with a CRT memory of 2K. The first commercial computer to use magnetic-core memory was the business-oriented IBM 705, which appeared in 1955. That year also saw the introduction of the IBM 704, a scientific computer and the first machine that could automatically perform certain operations. No longer, for instance, did a programmer have to spend time writing a floating-point subroutine for every calculation. (This computer gave birth to the first formal computer users' group, SHARE, which met to exchange homemade software for the 704.)

In 1957, the first high-level language appeared: FORTRAN, a scientific and engineering language developed by a team of IBM programmers headed by John Backus. FORTRAN allowed people to write programs in mathematical terms rather than in machine language, making programming easier and significantly reducing programming errors. Other high-level languages soon followed, including ALGOL (1958) and COBOL (1960).

COMPUTER GENERATIONS

	First	Second	Third	Fourth
DATES	1946–1959	1958–1964	1964–1971	1971–present
CIRCUITRY	vacuum tubes	transistors	integrated circuits	large-scale integration
CIRCUITS PER CU FT	1000	100,000	10 million	trillions
SPEED (INSTRUCTIONS PER SECOND)	up to 10,000	up to 1 million	up to 10 million	up to 10 billion
MEMORY	up to 8K	up to 64K	up to 4MB	up to 32MB
EXTERNAL STORAGE	punch cards	magnetic tape	disks	mass storage disks

Second-Generation Computers

The second generation began about 1958, when transistors replaced vacuum tubes. Invented in 1947 at Bell Telephone Laboratories by a team headed by physicist William Shockley, the transistor could do everything the vacuum tube could, but it was 1/200th the size, used much less energy, generated less heat, and was much faster and more reliable (see INDUSTRY AND TECHNOLOGY volume, Machines and Processes section). As a result, second-generation computers were ten times faster and had more memory capacity than first-generation computers.

The first completely transistorized computers were IBM's 7090 and 7070, introduced in 1958. The use of transistors led to much lower costs. In 1958, it is estimated that there were approximately 2550 computer systems in the United States; by 1964, as a result of transistorization, the number had jumped to 18,200.

Magnetic-tape storage became common during this period, largely replacing punch cards for input and output. Disk file storage was introduced in 1962 with the IBM 1440 series. In 1963 Digital Equipment Corporation introduced the first successful minicomputer, the PDP-8. About the size of a refrigerator, it used transistors and core memories, and contained 4K of memory.

This period also saw the development of time-sharing and on-line systems, which also helped broaden the market for computers. In 1961, the National Institutes of Health Clinic Center in Bethesda, Maryland, initiated the first computerized patient-monitoring system. In 1962, American Airlines launched SABRE, the first computerized airline reservation system. In 1963, General Motors Research Labs produced the first computer-designed auto part: the

TODAY'S COMPUTERS *range from small battery-powered portables, such as the one being used by biologists in an African wildlife park* (left), *to supercomputers capable of tackling immensely complex tasks* (right).

trunk lid for 1965 Cadillacs. In 1964, Sara Lee, a producer of frozen pastries, opened the first fully automated factory in Deerfield, Illinois.

The first general-purpose language, BASIC, invented at Dartmouth College by John Kemeny and Thomas Kurtz, was demonstrated in 1964. Also in 1964, IBM introduced System/360, the first family of compatible computers. Initially, it included six processors and 40 different input/output and auxiliary storage devices. Designed for both business and scientific use, it was a tremendous success and made many then-existing computers obsolete. The logic circuits of the first System/360 computers were printed in small ceramic blocks—a compromise between transistors, which were on their way out, and integrated circuits, which were coming onto the market.

Third-Generation Computers

In third-generation computers, integrated circuits (ICs) replaced transistors. The first IC was created in 1958 by Jack Kilby, an engineer with Texas Instruments. Kilby connected the circuit components with tiny wires, a process that had to be done by hand under a microscope. The following year, Robert Noyce and Jean Hoerni, physicists at Fairchild Semiconductor, developed an IC in which photoengraving was used to connect the circuit components.

ICs are smaller, faster, more powerful, and more reliable than transistors. Furthermore, a single IC can do the

work of thousands of transistors. The first ICs were very expensive and were used primarily in space and military equipment. Commercial computers with ICs began appearing in the mid-1960's; the first models using only ICs were introduced in 1968: Control Data's CDC 7600 and NCR's Century Series. In the early 1970's, IBM replaced its System/360 with the System/370, based entirely on ICs.

ICs also replaced magnetic-core memories, particularly after 1968, when 1K RAM chips were introduced. ICs not only led to a substantial decrease in the price of storage but also increased access speed. Access to data stored in core memories was measured in microseconds (millionths of a second), whereas access to data stored in ICs is measured in nanoseconds (billionths of a second).

Fourth-Generation Computers

In the late 1960's, scientists discovered that more than one circuit could be put on a single chip, thereby giving birth to large-scale integrated circuits (LSIs), the basis of fourth-generation computers. In 1969, Marcian E. Hoff, an engineer at Intel, put all the logic circuitry of a calculator CPU on a single chip less than 1/6-inch long and 1/8-inch wide. This first microprocessor, named the Intel 4004, paved the way for most of the major developments of the 1970's and 1980's.

Technical advances also led to a major change in data processing. Prior to the 1970's, data were generally pro-

cessed in a group, or batch. For example, all the sales orders for a day would be collected, taken to the organization's data processing department, and fed into the computer in a batch. Updating of individual records could not be done quickly and the process was often costly. Now, because of improved software, time-sharing systems, and direct-access storage devices, it was possible for a person using a terminal at a remote site to enter orders or other data individually, as they developed. Transactions did not have to be sequenced, they were easier to correct or update, and users had faster access to data.

Personal computers. Microprocessors make it possible to build computers small enough to sit on a desk or to carry around. The first such computer on the market was the Altair, introduced in 1975 and developed by Edward Roberts and his associates at MITS (Micro Instrumentation and Telemetry Systems), a small electronics firm in New Mexico. Available in kit form, the Altair had 256 bytes (1/4K) of memory and was an instant success, astonishing everyone and providing impetus to others investigating the economic potential of small computers. What happened from that point on is business history. Two years later, Apple introduced the Apple II, Radio Shack the TRS-80 Model I, and Commodore the PET. In 1981, Commodore introduced the VIC-20, which was the first microcomputer to sell more than 1 million units, and Osborne Computer introduced the 24-pound Osborne 1, which was the first portable microcomputer.

During the 1970's, software became

as important a part of the computer industry as hardware. In 1975, Harvard student William Gates and his associate Paul Allen adapted BASIC for the Altair. They went on to market their version of the language and develop other software. In 1979 Personal Software began selling *VisiCalc*, developed by Harvard Business School student Daniel Bricklin with Robert Frankston at MIT. This spreadsheet program is largely credited with ending people's perceptions of microcomputers as hobby and toy machines.

By 1990 personal computers had become an essential part of every type of business. An increasing need to move information easily from one computer to another fueled a rapid growth in networks that connect anywhere from two to hundreds of computers. The networks offer power previously available only on minicomputers and mainframes. Network software even allows communication among computers with different operating systems.

COMPARISON OF ENIAC COMPUTER (1940s) WITH MACINTOSH COMPUTER (1980s)

	ENIAC	Macintosh SE
CIRCUITRY	18,000 vacuum tubes	32-bit microprocessor
SIZE	80' long × 8' high	10.9″ × 9.6″ × 13.6″
WEIGHT	60,000 lbs	21 lbs.
PROGRAMMING	set thousands of switches + cables	type in program
INTERNAL MEMORY	100 bytes (.1K)	256K ROM, 2MB RAM
INPUT	punch cards	81-key keyboard, mouse, disk, modem
OUTPUT	punch cards	monitor, printer, disk, modem
STORAGE	none	disks (800K per disk)
SOUND	none	4-channel sound/music
GRAPHICS	none	512×342 pixel graphics resolution

The Future

Enormous advances are anticipated in computer speed, reliability, and ease of programming, coupled with dramatic decreases in cost and size. Ultra-large-scale integrated (ULSI) chips holding millions of circuits will become common, making small desk-top computers as powerful as today's supercomputers.

Dedicated computers the size of credit cards may herald the cashless society. People will use their card for all purchases and other financial transactions, with credits and debits instantly appearing on the person's bank account balance, even if the account is miles away. Cards will carry appropriate identification so that they will be useless if lost or stolen.

Sophisticated computer-communication links will permit personal telephone numbers and miniature wireless devices that people could wear, like pins or buttons. These would enable people to telephone and be telephoned wherever they may be.

Supercomputers. In the future, supercomputers will have much larger memories, faster speeds, and more performance per watt of power used. They will enable researchers to design, rather than discover, new materials that meet specific needs of the marketplace. Simulations will approach reality, even in situations involving thousands of constantly changing variables, such as studies of atmospheric pollution or the life cycle of a thunderstorm. When providing statistical estimates, these supercomputers will also be able to indicate the reliability of the estimates.

Such applications will be possible in part because of a change in computer architecture—that is, in the internal structure and organization of the machines. Serial processing, the design used for almost all computers to date, involves doing one thing at a time; a single processor reads and processes all information bit by bit. Many of tomorrow's supercomputers will have parallel architecture, with two or more processors operating simultaneously, either on different problems or different portions of the same problem. Several dozen extremely promising computer research projects that are now under way envision large-scale parallel processing involving thousands of processors, reducing processing on a given project from a month to perhaps a day.

Molecular computers. Each circuit on a silicon chip consists of thousands of molecules. How much smaller a circuit would be if it consisted of a single molecule! Researchers are studying the possibility of using protein molecules such as the compounds porphyrin and bacteriorhodopsin as the building blocks (biochips) of molecular computers. Such molecules could be created by genetically engineered bacteria or other organisms. Computers with capabilities surpassing those of today's supercomputers would be microscopic in size. One potential application for molecular computers would be to restore sight to blind people; the computer could process data from a miniature camera and directly stimulate the visual cortex of the brain.

Artificial Intelligence

Some of the most significant advances are expected to be in the area of artificial intelligence, or AI, the branch of computer science devoted to programming computers to perform tasks considered to require human intelligence. AI had its beginnings in the early 1950's, after Alan Turing published a paper entitled "Computing Machinery and Intelligence," in which he raised the question, Can machines think? Some important advances in AI occurred during the 1950's and 1960's, including the development by John McCarthy of Stanford of LISP (*LISt Processing*), the language most commonly used in AI programming because it can manipulate other types of symbols as well as numbers. The first expert systems appeared in 1973, and by 1980 applications companies were being formed. In 1981, Japan announced an ambitious project to develop fifth-generation computers—computers that will be able to learn, make inferences and decisions, converse with humans, and recognize objects and pictures. The computers will handle all symbols other than numbers and carry out many tasks at once.

AI techniques. Simulating how people do things and mimicking human reasoning are complex goals posing many challenges. The attainment of these goals will require new techniques, superfast processors, huge amounts of memory, and specialized languages. Ultimately, however, AI will make computers easier to use and extend their applicability.

Many computers will be goal-directed: told *what* to do rather than *how* to do it. For example, a goal-directed robot, with the ability to correct anything that goes wrong along the way, could be placed in an unknown environment, such as a distant planet; it would be able to see its environment, build its own model of the world, and function appropriately. Robots, tanks, and automobiles with sensors and AI processors would be able to operate without human help, recognizing obstacles and maneuvering to avoid them. (Automobiles, freed from human fallibility, could safely travel at speeds four or five times the current limitations.)

One AI technique is pattern matching. When today's computers execute programs, they look for similarities between strings of characters and stop short whenever they come to a spelling error in the instructions. In the future, computers will not be stopped by small errors. They will compare a given pattern with patterns in their memory, and match it with the one that is most similar ("North Dakata" with "North Dakota," for example).

Another AI technique is hierarchically structured tree searches, dubbed tree pruning. In a chess-playing program, for example, rather than have the computer search through every possible move, the program decides which moves can be ignored and which are promising and to be explored. Rules of thumb are incorporated in the program to help narrow and guide the search.

Sensory systems.

AI projects concerned with sight and speech involve not only creating physical representations of what is seen or heard but also involve interpreting and using the data. Mobile robots are being developed that integrate perception and distance; AI techniques are used to interpret the sensor input and coordinate robot response. The Terregator, an autonomous vehicle developed at Carnegie-Mellon University, uses the technologies of sonar rings and stereo vision to find the edges of a road. If the edges are curved, the vehicle figures out the change mathematically and adjusts its course to follow the road.

Another current vision system enables robots to inspect crackers and reject those that are burned. A camera focuses on the crackers; the image is digitized as a series of light, shaded, and dark dots to which numbers are assigned. Lightly shaded areas have a high numerical value, and dark areas have a low number. If the cracker has a high percentage of dark areas, the robot recognizes the lower numbers and rejects the cracker.

Natural language programs enable computers to communicate in English or other natural, that is, human, languages. Ideally, people will be able to enter requests using whatever words and phraseology they desire, either aural or written, and the computer will understand the requests and respond accordingly.

It is considerably easier to develop computers that can talk than it is to produce ones that can understand human speech. The tremendous variations in people's pronunciation, inflection, sentence structure, and speed of talking, together with semantic ambiguities, make the development of

powerful speech recognition devices a long-term endeavor. Today's most advanced systems can distinguish a vocabulary of 20,000 words when they are separated by pauses.

Expert systems.

Expert, or knowledge-engineering, systems are designed to simulate the judgment of experts in a given field of knowledge. Such a system has a knowledge base and a set of rules for using that knowledge. The system draws conclusions and gives advice based on the stored knowledge and new information provided by the user. It can explain how it reached its conclusions and why other possible conclusions were rejected. Limitations include the system's narrow knowledge base and an inability to check whether its conclusions are reasonable.

Expert systems are developed by transferring knowledge and decision-making rules (usually in an IF . . . THEN format) from human experts to machines. This results in a program that can be copied and used by an unlimited number of people, many of whom might not have access to the human experts. Expert systems are being used successfully in a variety of fields in which knowledge can be classified into neat factual categories.

PROSPECTOR, based on the accumulated knowledge of nine geologists, contains a huge data base of geological information and a series of rules about how to locate the presence of minerals from observations made in the field. When given information on the types of rocks and configurations found in a region under study, PROSPECTOR indicates the types of ore deposits that might be present and asks a series of increasingly narrow questions about the region. With this system, geologists were able to locate a $100 million deposit of molybdenum ore under Mount Tolman, Washington—a deposit they were convinced existed but had been unable to find despite digging dozens of mines and drilling hundreds of test borings over a period of 60 years.

ACE (Automatic Cable Expertise) locates faults in telephone cables, and recommends and monitors repairs and maintenance. It can do a job in an hour that would take a team of technicians a week to complete.

CADUCEUS, an internal-medicine diagnostic system, contains information on 500 diseases, 350 disease manifestations, and 100,000 symptomatic associations, and can be extended by users to include other diseases and symptoms. A doctor using CADUCEUS is asked for specific information about the patient's medical history, disease symptoms, test results, and so on. Like a highly skilled physician, CADUCEUS uses the information to discard some diagnostic possibilities and explore others.

THE TERREGATOR is an autonomous vehicle that uses vision and sonar guidance systems to enable it to follow a path. It is shown here navigating through a mine tunnel.

THE ROBOTICS INSTITUTE, CARNEGIE MELLON UNIVERSITY

APPLICATIONS SOFTWARE

Programs designed to perform a specific task are called applications software. The most widely used types enable word processing, data base management, electronic spreadsheets, graphics, and communications. In each category, many commercial packages are available, most of which are general-purpose programs, usable by many people in a wide variety of situations. A general-purpose word-processing program, for example, can be used by students to write reports, by business people to write letters, and by authors to write books. People who have very specific needs may create their own applications programs or purchase programs that have been designed for those needs. Mathematicians and engineers, for instance, may choose a scientific word processor that offers an assortment of Greek, mathematical, and chemical characters, making it possible to write equations.

Some people need several different applications programs that can interface with one another—for example, a program that makes graphs, incorporated into a report written with a word-processing program. Software that combines several applications is called integrated software. The user can move back and forth among the applications. Software systems called operating environments enable users to assemble individual programs and make them operate as though they were part of an integrated package.

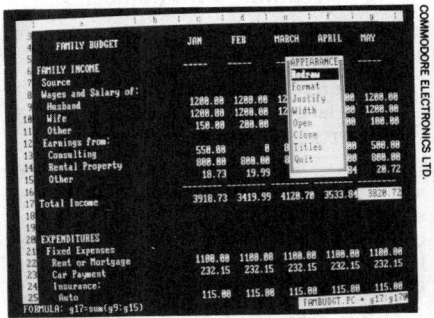 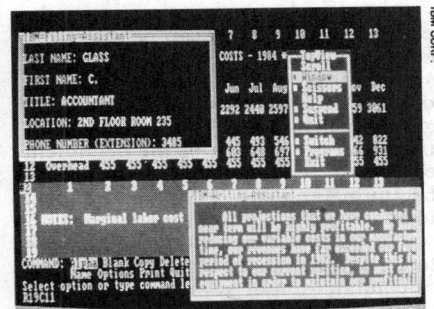

WINDOWING *enables information to be obtained from other files* (right), *or program instructions to be displayed* (left), *without interrupting work in progress.*

Integrated programs use a windowing system, which splits up the display screen into two or more areas or boxes, called windows. The windows enable a user to call up and display information from different programs or different parts of the same program at the same time. If desired, the user can move data from one window to another. While preparing a report with a word-processing program, for example, a user can display a spreadsheet in a second window and a graphing program in a third. Figures from the spreadsheet can be moved to the graphing program to create a graph of the data, which can then be incorporated into the written report. Some windowing systems overlap windows on the screen, partially, though temporarily, obscuring other windows.

Other systems use a technique called tiling, in which the size of a window is limited by the total number of windows on the screen at one time. Each time another window is opened, the existing windows shrink in size, thus displaying less of the contents of that program.

Windowing has also led to the development of so-called accessory programs, which perform such tasks as notetaking, calculating, dialing a phone, and checking or updating an appointments calendar. These programs "hide" in the computer memory until needed. With one keystroke a user can open a window and switch the computer from its main chore to an accessory chore; another keystroke sends the computer back to where it was.

Word Processing

The most widely used application is word processing—the composing and editing of text, and then the saving or printing of it on paper. The process has several advantages over writing by hand or with a typewriter. Making changes and corrections is easy and quick; revisions can be made in seconds, without having to rewrite or retype an entire document. A document can be formatted in different ways and printed again without retyping.

A general-purpose computer can be used for word processing by loading word-processing software into its memory. Word processing can also be done at a terminal connected to a mainframe containing the appropriate

software. Word processors themselves are dedicated computers designed specifically for this application. They perform faster and more efficiently than a general-purpose computer, can usually be expanded into a network, and may also serve as electronic mail terminals. They cannot be used, however, for any functions other than those that are permanent parts of the system.

Creating a document. Any piece of text created with a word-processing program is referred to as a document, whether it is a letter, poem, or report. It must be given a file name, or short title, for use by the computer

in identifying it and retrieving it at any time. There generally are rules for file names—no blank spaces or question marks, a limited number of characters, and so on.

As the user types, the words enter into RAM and appear on the screen. The cursor on the screen indicates where the next character typed will appear. When the cursor reaches the end of a line, it moves to the beginning of the next line. If it is within a word, that word also moves to the next line. This is called word wrap:

As a person types on a computer key■

As a person types on a computer keyb■

Word wrap speeds typing, since carriage returns are not required at the end of each line. The user presses the RETURN or ENTER key only when a new paragraph is desired.

Typically, a screen displays 24 lines of text at a time. When the screen is full, the top line scrolls up and off the screen, so that the new material being typed will be visible at the bottom of the screen. Pressing specified keys enables the user to scroll back and forth through the text.

Once text has been entered into the computer memory, it can be revised or edited. With only two or three keystrokes, text can be changed, added, or deleted. Most word-processing programs permit blocks of text to be moved to other parts of the document or copied. This requires marking the beginning and end of the block of text to be moved or copied, moving the cursor to the position where the block is to go, and then pressing a specified key or combination of keys.

Deleted text is usually kept in a temporary memory, called a buffer, and can be retrieved if users change their minds. However, material is stored in the buffer only until something else is deleted; the new material then replaces the old material, and the original text in the buffer is permanently erased from the computer memory.

Another standard feature is "search and replace," which enables users to locate words or short phrases each time they occur in the text. When users give the search command and type the word or phrase to be located, the program searches through the document; each time it finds the group of characters that matches the request, it stops and highlights them. Suppose, for example, a user discovers that "ROM" has been written rather than the intended "RAM". The computer is told to look for ROM. It hunts for this sequence of letters in the text and marks it each time it occurs. Users then decide whether to change the word or leave it as it is. To prevent the computer from also marking words that begin with these letters, such as "romance," a space must be typed before and after the word.

If a user wants every instance of a word or phrase replaced with the same new word or phrase, the replace, or global change, function can be used. The computer is told what to search for and given the replace command. A prompt asks what word or phrase is to be used as a replacement. The program then searches for the request and replaces every occurrence of it.

Formatting a document. A document can be saved to disk or printed on paper. The latter requires that the text be formatted—that is, the computer must be told how the printed document should look. This is done by typing formatting commands.

Here are examples from one program:

.m:1	tells the computer to single space the text
.l:56	tells the computer to print 56 lines on a page
.h. . .	Page $ $ $. . . tells the computer to print a header in the center of each sheet consisting of the word "Page" followed by a number, with pages numbered consecutively beginning with number 1.

Most programs permit the user to justify the printed text:

This paragraph is unjustified. It has a straight left margin but the right margin varies from one line to the next.

This paragraph is justified, with straight left and right margins. The computer adjusts the spacing between words so that all the lines are of the same length. This may look more attractive than unjustified text but may be considered more difficult to read.

Other commands may indicate that certain words should be underlined or printed in **boldface** type; where margins should be set; and what line height (number of lines per inch) is desired. Such commands appear on the screen but are not printed out. Some word-processing programs have on-screen formatting, showing the results of formatting decisions on the screen so that users can see how the printed document will appear. Other programs have off-screen formatting: they store the formatting commands in memory but do not show the results of formatting decisions until the document is printed.

A merge feature enables users to combine information from two or more files into one printed document.

This makes it possible to create standardized paragraphs and to move them into various documents. So-called personalized letters, for example, take names and addresses from one file, the body of the letter from another.

Accessory Programs

A spelling checker finds misspelled words in a document by checking each word in the document against a list of words, called a dictionary, in the program. Any word that does not agree with the dictionary is displayed, preferably in context. The user decides whether to change the word or, if it is spelled correctly, to add it to the spelling checker's dictionary. Most dictionaries contain between 20,000 and 100,000 words; the larger the dictionary, the more effective the program. Because a spelling checker only matches combinations of letters, it cannot determine whether words are being used correctly. It makes no distinction, for example, between *too* and *to* or *their* and *there*. Nor will it flag the three errors in "Sum boys walked passed the candy stare."

An electronic thesaurus, like its printed counterpart, lists synonyms. When a user marks a word in the text, the thesaurus displays synonyms for the word in a window on the screen. If the user chooses a new word, it automatically replaces the old word in the document, retaining the same capitalization and punctuation and making the necessary adjustments in line spacing.

A SPELLING CHECKER *compares each word in a document with words on its dictionary list. If a word is not found, the program flags the word and asks the user how to proceed.*

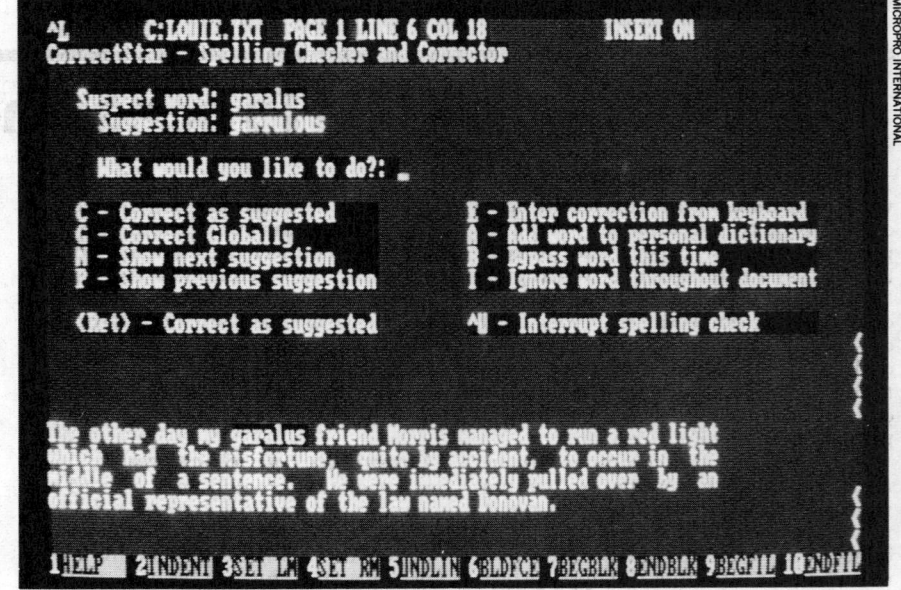

Punctuation and style programs make certain that sentences begin with capital letters, have balanced quotation marks and parentheses, and end with proper punctuation. They may also point out the use of sexist terms, redundancies, and clichés. And they may mark exceptionally long sentences or indicate whether a particular word, in the opinion of the programmer, has been used too frequently.

Indexing programs assist in creating indexes for long documents. Words can be chosen automatically by a program: the program scans the document and displays all commonly used words and phrases that might be candidates for indexing. The user indicates which of these words should appear in the index, and the program automatically compiles an alphabetized listing. Alternatively, the user can tell the program which words and phrases to look for and index.

Data Base Management Systems

A data base is a collection of data having a certain logical organization. File cabinets, dictionaries, telephone directories, cookbooks, thesauruses, and encyclopedias are familiar noncomputerized examples.

Today, many data bases, including the examples just cited, are being computerized. A set of computer programs that enables a user to manipulate the information in the data base and to extract data from it for report preparation or for analysis is called a data base management system (DBMS).

Computerized data bases assist users in doing much more than merely locating information. A user can instruct the computer to search through a file and locate all records that meet certain criteria, such as the records of all employees in a company who have been employed there for more than 25 years, all receivables over 30 days, all checks written to a given firm, all patients over the age of 65, or all people who live in a certain state or zip code area. The user can instruct the computer to print mailing labels from a prospective client file, address purchase orders from a vendor file, or prepare due notices from an accounts receivable file.

The most significant advantages that computerized data bases offer over traditional filing systems are quicker, easier access to information; economy of space; and improved ease of maintaining records. With traditional filing systems, the larger the file, the greater the time needed to locate information—and the greater the possibility of misfiled or misplaced information. A DBMS enables records to grow without sacrificing efficiency in finding information. Data are compactly stored on small disks instead of in rows of file cabinets. Records can be added, changed, or deleted quickly and without retyping or messy erasure, making it easy to keep the data base current and ready for use.

Setting up a computerized data base may be time-consuming, particularly if large quantities of information must be transferred from printed files to computer files. But once the system is established, a great deal of time will be saved in the long run. Perhaps the major disadvantage of computerized data bases is the need to sacrifice a certain amount of flexibility and freedom in recordkeeping. All the records in a data base must be standardized, containing exactly the same types of information in exactly the same format.

Organizing a Data Base

Information in a DBMS must follow a logical, consistent structure that the computer understands. The structure has three basic building blocks:

1. a *field,* an item of information— for example, a person's name
2. a *record,* a collection of related fields—for example, a person's name, address, and telephone number
3. a *file* (or data base), a group of records—for example, an address book

The first step in using a DBMS is to develop a format—that is, a form for the information. All records in a file must have the exact same set of fields; categories of information included in one record must also be included in every other record. Here is a sample

COMPUTERIZED CARD CATALOGS *are replacing library drawers filled with 3-by-5 cards.*

format for a computer store's customer data base:

CUSTOMER NAME:
ADDRESS:
CITY:
STATE: ZIP:
TELEPHONE:
COMPUTER BRAND:
COMPUTER MODEL:
PRINTER:
MODEM:
PRIMARY USE:

This sample format contains eleven fields. The total number of fields allowed in a format depends on the DBMS. In some systems, adding fields at a later time requires the user to reenter all the data from the original format.

After designing the form and defining the data fields, that is, indicating the labels and number of spaces needed to accommodate the information to be entered in the data base, the user enters the data. To enter data into the system, the user calls the format to the screen, moves the cursor to the first field, and types in the requested data. The procedure continues until the fields in the record are complete:

CUSTOMER NAME: Leslie Jamison
ADDRESS: 14 Chestnut Avenue
CITY: Barnum Square
STATE: CT   ZIP: 06806
TELEPHONE: 203-212-8773
COMPUTER BRAND: Apple
COMPUTER MODEL: IIc
PRINTER: Epson FX80
MODEM: none
PRIMARY USE: education

Within a field, information must always be entered the same way. A telephone number, for example, might always be entered in this way: area code, a hyphen, three numbers, a hyphen, then four more numbers. The user may not write one telephone number following this format, then another using parentheses for the area code. Furthermore, some programs limit the length of each field, allowing, say, two characters for state abbreviations and five for postal codes.

Most systems use fixed-format screens for the entry of information, allowing users to fill in blanks. Most also allow various validity checks on the information typed in, thereby

AN INVENTORY DATA BASE

A data base is an extremely efficient and convenient way to keep product records. A bookstore, for instance, might have a data base with records in this format:

TITLE:
AUTHOR:
PUBLISHER:·
COST:
PRICE:
QTY IN STOCK:

Here is a partial listing of the database:

Kidnapped	Stevenson	Bantam	.68	1.50	5
King Lear	Shakespeare	Penguin	1.62	3.75	8
Leaves of Grass	Whitman	Bantam	1.47	2.95	1
Leaves of Grass	Whitman	Doubleday	8.30	17.95	4
Lincoln	Tice	Rutgers	18.25	37.95	2

This data base enables store employees to determine instantly which books are available and which are out of stock. It indicates which works by a particular author are carried, their retail price, and so on. The data base helps the store maintain inventory at the desired level, as well as answer customer inquiries about particular books.

catching potential errors before they become part of the data base. Typing an alphabetic character in a numerical field is one example of an error; typing a zip code that is too long is another.

After all the records have been entered, data can be retrieved, sorted, or searched. If, for instance, customer records indicate date of first order, the user might sort customers chronologically. If the program permits a search for more than one item at a time, the user might request new customers in 1986 from the state of Idaho.

Both complete and partial matches can be made. If the manager of the computer store in the above example asks for a listing of customers with Epson FX80 printers, the record shown will come up. It will also come up if the manager asks for a listing of customers with Epson printers; since this is a partial match, customers with other Epson models will also come up.

DBMS Features

DBM systems vary considerably in the types of information they will accept, the formats they will allow, and the amount of information they can accommodate. If a system cannot sort by telephone numbers, or if it only accepts three-line addresses, this may be a serious flaw for a potential user.

One measure of capacity is the maximum number of records allowed per file; some systems permit as few as 5000 records, others more than 10 million. Another measure of capacity is the number of fields a record can contain; systems range from less than 20 to more than 250 fields per record.

Another important factor is speed, of which there are two key measures: retrieval time and processing time. Retrieval time is the amount of time needed by a system to find and display

or print out a requested item. Processing time is how long it takes for a program to complete a task, such as sorting a file in a specified sequence.

Many data base managers have a calculations feature that enables users to compute totals, and averages, and make other basic calculations. Such systems can compute sales commissions, total dollar value of all receivables over 60 days, total sales for a quarter, and so on.

Another useful feature is report production, which enables a user to extract information from the data base, organize it in a useful, attractive format, and then print it out.

Advanced DBM systems enable multirecord access, so users may alter several or all records in the data base in a single step. For example, with a single instruction, the list price of every product in an inventory file can be increased by 5 percent. Another advanced feature is the ability to simultaneously access records in several different files. For example, by searching the new order file and the customer file at the same time, a user can retrieve data needed to create an invoice. The product number and quantity would be taken from the new order file, the customer's shipping address and customary terms of sale from the customer file. A multilevel security feature makes it possible to restrict access to certain information in a data base, and determine who is authorized to alter information and who may erase it.

Some systems allow information from the data base to be incorporated into work from another type of application program. For example, information from a data base might be entered into a worksheet being created with an electronic spreadsheet. Finally, some packages store files in such a way that the files can be transmitted over telephone lines to another computer.

Electronic Spreadsheets

An electronic spreadsheet combines the functions of a paper spreadsheet, pencil, eraser, and calculator. Like a paper spreadsheet, it consists of a display area and a work area with rows and columns. Unlike a paper spreadsheet, formulas can be built into an electronic spreadsheet, enabling the computer to perform calculations on numeric data. Changes in any data are quickly made, and the user does not have to erase or change other data affected by the changes.

Spreadsheets are widely used in budgeting, accounting, forecasting, and other financial tasks. They can also be used, for example, by coaches

to calculate team statistics, teachers to figure grade averages, borrowers to determine interest charges at various percentages, families to compute taxes, and joggers to keep track of calories burned.

Using an Electronic Spreadsheet

Like a paper spreadsheet, the electronic version consists of a matrix of rows, columns, and cells. Columns run

vertically and are generally labeled with letters; rows run horizontally and are generally labeled with numbers. The intersection of a column and a row is called a cell; its location is defined by its coordinates (for example, A2 or M27). A cell may contain a number, a label, or a formula that defines the value of that cell. Here is a typical example:

	A	B	C	D	E
1					
2		12.00	14.00	8.50	34.50
3					
4					
5					

In this example, the user has defined cell E2 as B2+C2+D2. If the value in cell B2 is changed from 12.00 to 10.00, the program instantly recalculates the value of cell E2 and changes the display to 32.50. This spreadsheet can be made more realistic by adding labels and information:

	A	B	C	D	E
1		JAN	FEB	MAR	1st Q
2	Paper	12.00	14.00	8.50	34.50
3	Postage	42.00	32.45	56.60	
4					
5	Totals	54.00	46.45	65.10	34.50

Cell B5 contains the formula B2+B3+B4, permitting addition of another expense category in row 4. Cells C5, D5 and E5 contain similar formulas. At present, cell E3 contains nothing; here is what happens as soon as the formula B3+C3+D3 is entered into cell E3:

	A	B	C	D	E
1		JAN	FEB	MAR	1st Q
2	Paper	12.00	14.00	8.50	34.50
3	Postage	42.00	32.45	56.60	131.05
4					
5	Totals	54.00	46.45	65.10	165.55

Both cells E3 and E5 are affected by the addition of the formula to cell E3. Every spreadsheet has its own combination of financial, scientific, and mathematical functions. Here are some typical formulas from a general-purpose program:

SUM(B2 . . . B18)	the sum of the values of cells B2 through B18
MAX(B2 . . . B18)	the largest number from the values in cells B2 through B18
MIN(B2 . . . B18)	the smallest number from the values in cells B2 through B18
B2*B7	multiply the value of B2 by the value of B7
AVE(B2 . . . B18)	the average of the values in B2 through B18

A program may provide for thousands of cells, with a grid so large that only part of the spreadsheet can be viewed at one time. In such a case, any cell can be brought to the screen by specifying its coordinates, or the user can scroll vertically and horizontally until the desired area of the spreadsheet is visible.

Both letters and numbers can be entered into a cell, and any information already in a cell can be altered or deleted. There usually is a limit to the number of characters a cell can contain. Programs also offer flexibility in formatting column widths, displaying decimals, and using commas and dollar signs.

Some programs can sort spreadsheet data by numerical or alphabetic values, which is particularly useful for analyzing large amounts of data and for producing reports. Some programs permit users to link or combine several worksheets, some come with templates (prefabricated standard worksheet formats), and some have a graphics option that enables users to produce bar charts directly from the data. Also helpful are logic functions, which allow users to say IF a certain thing has happened THEN do such and such (for example, IF a check has cleared THEN do not include it in the outstanding balance).

Forecasting

Because spreadsheets are often used to predict outcomes—that is, to answer "what if" questions—they are widely

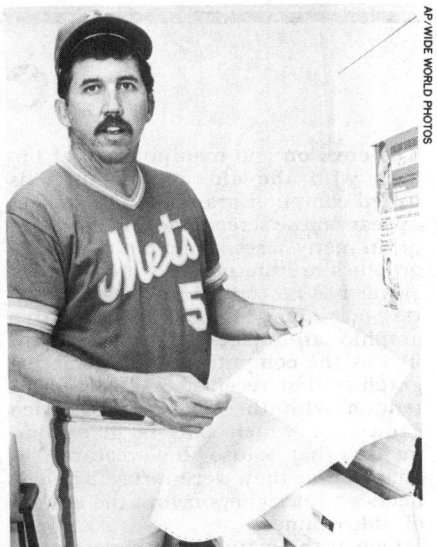

COMPUTERS *are used successfully for many tasks. Davey Johnson, New York Mets manager, keeps player statistics in a computer.*

used by financial planners. Consider a spreadsheet that contains a company's sales figures and trends; production, administrative, and advertising costs; and so on, with formulas relating them. Varying any one parameter—say, the cost of a raw material—causes the program to recalculate all the other relevant figures, instantly showing the effect the change will have on unit costs, profits, and even taxes.

The goal of forecasting is to enable people to see the ramifications of a change they are thinking of making, a change already made, or no change at all. Forecasting calls attention to a wide range of future possibilities and forces people to look at details and dynamics that might otherwise be overlooked. It stimulates discussion and helps people weigh the risks of a course of action before committing to it.

SPREADSHEET PROGRAMS *automatically recalculate all relevant figures when a user changes data on the spreadsheet. In this example, a change in the Marina sales figure for October caused the program to instantly recalculate the Marina's total sales, monthly total, and grand total.*

```
          1         2         3          4          5
     Sales analysis by month for selected outlets
1
2
3               Marina    Downtown   The Plaza      Total
4
5  January      1,000.00  4,214.00   2,100.00     7,314.00
6  February     1,250.00  4,645.00   1,534.00     7,429.00
7  March        1,100.00  4,123.00   2,134.00     7,357.00
8  April        1,463.00  3,078.00   3,245.00     7,786.00
9  May          1,634.00  2,345.00   4,234.00     8,213.00
10 June         2,134.00  2,034.00   4,768.00     8,936.00
11 July         3,645.00  2,345.00   6,034.00    12,024.00
12 August       4,234.00  2,890.00   5,123.00    12,247.00
13 September     3,215.00  3,245.00   4,235.00    10,695.00
14 October      2,042.00  4,218.00   3,985.00    10,245.00
15 November     1,789.00  5,200.00   3,324.00    10,313.00
16 December     1,903.00  4,890.00   2,984.00     9,777.00
17
18 TOTAL:      25,409.00 43,227.00  43,700.00   112,336.00

Command list 5: Auto-Recalc  Beep  Confidence  Display  Execute  F-Calculator
                Macro  Parameters  Remember  Send  User-Menu
Worksheet: sales    Location: r14c2               FN:0    Font: Standard
AUTO-RECALC - specifies the method to be used in formula recalculation
```

```
          1         2         3          4          5
     Sales analysis by month for selected outlets
1
2
3               Marina    Downtown   The Plaza      Total
4
5  January      1,000.00  4,214.00   2,100.00     7,314.00
6  February     1,250.00  4,645.00   1,534.00     7,429.00
7  March        1,100.00  4,123.00   2,134.00     7,357.00
8  April        1,463.00  3,078.00   3,245.00     7,786.00
9  May          1,634.00  2,345.00   4,234.00     8,213.00
10 June         2,134.00  2,034.00   4,768.00     8,936.00
11 July         3,645.00  2,345.00   6,034.00    12,024.00
12 August       4,234.00  2,890.00   5,123.00    12,247.00
13 September     3,215.00  3,245.00   4,235.00    10,695.00
14 October      2,500.00  4,218.00   3,985.00    10,703.00
15 November     1,789.00  5,200.00   3,324.00    10,313.00
16 December     1,903.00  4,890.00   2,984.00     9,777.00
17
18 TOTAL:      25,867.00 43,227.00  43,700.00   112,794.00

Command list 5: Auto-Recalc  Beep  Confidence  Display  Execute  F-Calculator
                Macro  Parameters  Remember  Send  User-Menu
Worksheet: sales    Location: r14c2               FN:0    Font: Standard
AUTO-RECALC - specifies the method to be used in formula recalculation
```

Computer Graphics

The creation and manipulation of images with the aid of computers is called computer graphics. The images appear on the screen and can be stored or, in many cases, printed out. Passive graphics are those over which the observer has no control (for example, title or menu screens). Interactive graphics are images that can be modified by the computer user. Interactive graphics first received widespread attention with the invention of video games, in which players give commands that cause the pictures to change, but they were in use by engineers and designers before the advent of video games.

One of the main advantages of computer-generated art is the ability to instantly alter, or redraw, an image. A child can draw a house on the screen, paint it red, then with a keystroke or two change its color to green. More sophisticated programs enable an architect to draw a house, then see the effects of increasing the width of the kitchen by 2 feet. The new data are entered into the system, and the architect watches as the computer redraws the house and recalculates such data as total area, lumber and other material requirements, and cost.

How Computers Create Graphics

A computer screen may be thought of as a giant sheet of graph paper. It is composed of thousands of tiny squares or dots, called pixels, which are arranged in rows and columns. Each pixel can be individually addressed by its coordinates and designated to be a specific shade or color.

The greater the number of pixels a computer can generate, the finer the detail, or resolution, of the image. Depending on the model, personal computers generally divide a display screen into anywhere from 128,000 to 800,000 pixels. Supercomputers used to create graphics for motion pictures create pictures with millions of pixels.

The higher the resolution, the greater the amount of memory needed to store an image, and the greater the amount of time needed by the computer to create that image. A 500 x 500 pixel image may take half an hour to create: a 3000 x 3000 pixel picture may take as long as 18 hours—and, of course, much more memory is required to store all the information needed to display so many pixels.

Two methods are used to display images on a screen: raster graphics and vector graphics. Raster graphics is the more widely used method, and is the one used in commercial television sets. The screen is divided into a number of horizontal lines. Thirty times a second, the electron beam inside the cathode ray tube (CRT) scans across the lines, starting at the top and going to the bottom before moving to the top again. Each time the CRT scans, signals from the computer dictate the color and intensity of the beam at each point, or pixel, on each line, thereby creating an overall image.

In vector graphics systems, the electron beam does not move in a pixel-by-pixel, line-by-line pattern. Instead, it moves like a pencil over paper to draw images in the form of angled lines, or vectors. Since the vector system plots by angled lines, it is very difficult to create shading and other subtleties of detail.

Character graphics. Most personal computers enable users to create graphics by means of a standard set of characters incorporated in the machine ROM. The set generally contains 256 characters, of which about 100 are in the form of letters, numbers, punctuation marks, and essential symbols such as % and $. The remaining characters vary, depending on the manufacturer, but usually include such symbols as a solid square and various thicknesses of line that can be used as building blocks for borders and other designs. Since each of these graphics characters takes up the same amount of space as an alphanumeric character, finely detailed pictures are not possible. Thus, pictures created with graphics characters tend to have a boxy, or stepped appearance with boundaries between adjacent characters clearly visible.

Graphics Software

For a computer to draw a line, it must be given the coordinates of the pixels at the beginning and end of the line. For example, to draw a square, the computer must be given the coordinates of the four corners of the square. More complex drawings require more complex instructions. To simplify the process, various types of graphics software have been developed. There is software for programmers who wish to put professional-quality graphics into their own programming efforts, software for people who wish to create art on their home computers, and software for engineers and other professionals who design anything from bridges to running shoes.

Graphics software generally falls into three categories: drawing programs, graph programs, and computer-aided design (CAD) programs.

Drawing programs. Drawing programs make it possible to use the computer screen as a drawing board.

PALETTES *along the edge of the computer screen—accessible via a mouse—enable users of this paint program to choose from a variety of tools, line widths, and patterns.*

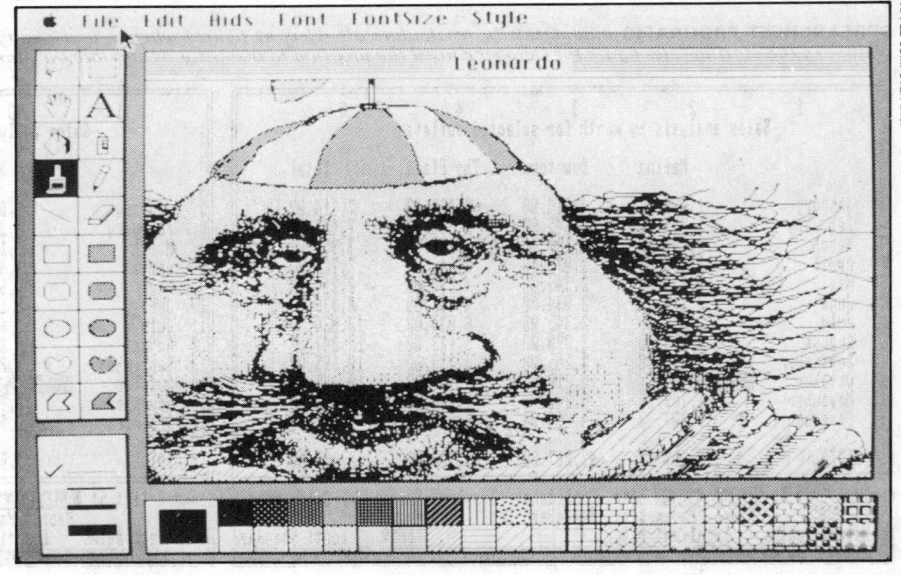

CAD PROGRAMS *are used to design, test, and analyze a broad range of facilities. Here, engineers study plans for a chemical plant.*

RICHARD WOOD/TAURUS PHOTOS

With a light pen, mouse, or other device, the user chooses from a menu that offers such options as:

DRAW	draw freehand
LINE	draw a line between two specified points
FILL	fill an area with color
MAGNIFY	enlarge a section of the picture (program replots section with maximum resolution rather than magnifying the pixels)
MIRROR	create a mirror image of an object
SCALE	enlarge or reduce the size of an image
ERASE	erase part of a drawing
CLEAR	erase the entire drawing

A storage submenu offers the possibility to print, save, or load a picture. A picture submenu has a dictionary of shapes that can be added to a drawing. A paint submenu enables the user to choose among various colors, textures, and paint brush shapes.

Graph programs.

Graph programs generally begin with a menu asking the user to indicate what is to be done: create a new graph, edit an existing graph, print a graph, and so on. To create a graph, the user enters the format, heads, and data that will appear on the graph. The screen may look like this:

U.S. ENERGY CONSUMPTION

Source	Percent of Total
1. Coal	23
2. Natural gas	21
3. Nuclear	8
4. Oil	43
5. Other	5

Next, the user indicates the type of graph desired: circle, bar, or line. (Depending on the program and the type of data to be graphed, other options may also exist, such as stacked bars and scatter graphs.) The computer then creates the graph. Most graph programs make it possible to change the graph form without reentering the data.

Graph programs frequently are integrated with or compatible with electronic spreadsheets. Composing graphs on the computer as opposed to drawing them by hand offers speed, consistency in quality, and low cost.

GRAPH PROGRAMS *make it possible to present information in eye-catching ways.*

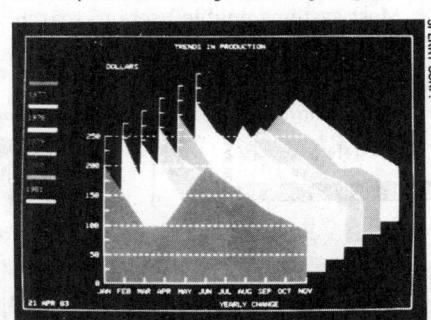

SPERRY CORP.

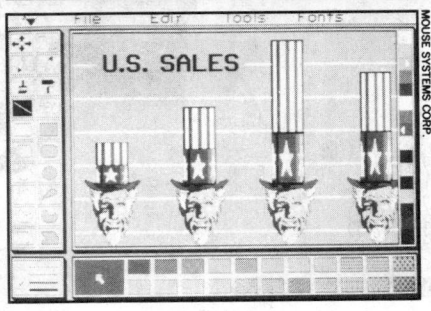

MOUSE SYSTEMS CORP.

Computer-aided design (CAD).

CAD programs are much more powerful and versatile than drawing and graph programs. A CAD system not only creates and stores an image, it can save and use related information, such as the size of an object, the formulas used to create the object, the raw materials and parts needed to build the object, the cost of such materials, and so on.

Combining CAD software with other applications software expands the capabilities. For instance, systems used by architectural engineers and construction firms can track inventories and reorder materials as needed. Aeronautical and automotive engineers can test their designs to identify areas of high stress, heat, and other conditions.

Some CAD systems are generic, while others are tailored to meet the needs of specific users. One microcomputer product, for example, is designed for use mainly in architectural engineering and facilities planning. At the other end of the scale is a supercomputer dedicated to producing special effects and extraordinarily realistic imagery for motion pictures and television programs.

Engineers use CAD systems to draw electronic circuits; fashion designers, to create next year's clothes; biologists, to produce pictures of viruses; and art historians, to restore priceless masterpieces.

Computer-aided design frequently is integrated with computer-aided manufacturing (CAM) to form a CAD/CAM system that can be used for everything from product conceptualization to fabrication to inventory control. Such systems have become essential tools of the automotive industry and many others.

Communications

Telecommunications, or the transmission of information between computers over telephone lines, enables users to access extensive reference libraries, participate in group conferences, play games with another user thousands of miles away, read stock-exchange tickers, send mail, buy toys, and carry out other activities quickly, conveniently, and often at a significant savings in cost.

To go on-line—that is, use a computer to communicate with another computer via telephone—a user needs a modem. This equipment translates computer signals into information that can be handled by the telephone system. The user also needs communications software. Program features that may be useful include automated dialing, auto-answering, data capture (saving on disk or in RAM the information received from another computer), printing out of data as it comes in from another computer, and text file transmission (the ability to send data previously typed).

Information Utilities

An information utility is an organization that offers, usually for a fee, both information and services. Information is available on an almost endless list of subjects from various sources: up-to-the-minute news from wire services; prices on the major stock exchanges, updated throughout the day; weather reports; movie reviews; and standard reference material from encyclopedias. Services include at-home banking, game playing, electronic mail, and the ability to write and run programs on mainframe computers.

Electronic utilities provide almost instantaneous access to information. The information is constantly updated and always there. (In a conventional library, the reference book desired may have been borrowed by another person.) Obtaining information is convenient—a person need not travel to it or use it only during certain hours; most services operate almost around the clock.

In addition to broad, consumer-oriented utilities, there are services that offer access to in-depth information. These are aimed primarily at professional researchers. For instance, one utility is designed mainly for lawyers who need to research court decisions; another enables health care professionals to check drug interactions; still another contains tens of thousands of abstracts of papers dealing with the sources, control, and prevention of air pollution.

Upon joining a utility, a user receives a password that is requested each time the service is used. Most of the organizations charge start-up fees plus monthly fees that are based on the amount of time actually spent on-line. Rates may vary depending on the feature accessed and the time of day the utility is accessed.

Services operate on a menu system. The main menu lists the main services available; submenus help zero in on the user's interests and needs. Alternatively, a user can use a specified command to go directly to a particular option.

Most systems enable users to search for a key word or words, and to connect these words with AND, OR, or NOT. For example, a person searching a listing of news items for articles on the relationship between smoking and cancer might request articles on "smoking AND cancer." The system would then list all articles containing both key words. Requesting "smoking OR cancer" would provide all articles related to either smoking or cancer (including, say, one on asbestos-induced cancer). Requesting "smoking NOT cancer" would provide all articles on smoking except those dealing with the relationship between smoking and cancer.

Transaction-based services.

Electronic shopping enables users to purchase items from the comfort and convenience of home or office. Because the services generally do not have high overhead, many offer products at prices significantly lower than those found in retail stores and even in mail-order catalogs. A potential customer would indicate the type of item being considered for purchase—for example, a television set. The service prints a series of questions on the user's screen, such as whether a color or black-and-white set is desired, the size of screen desired, price, and so on. The service then lists all the options available that meet those requirements. If a user orders an item, payment is made via credit card number.

On-line supermarkets, already operational in several areas in the United States, enable shoppers to send orders via modem to a central computer that processes the orders. The purchased items are then delivered C.O.D.

Travel services give consumers ac-

TELECOMMUNICATIONS *enable people to send and receive information electronically. Stock prices and sports scores are among the types of data available to information utility subscribers. This information can be displayed on the computer screen, saved on disk, or printed.*

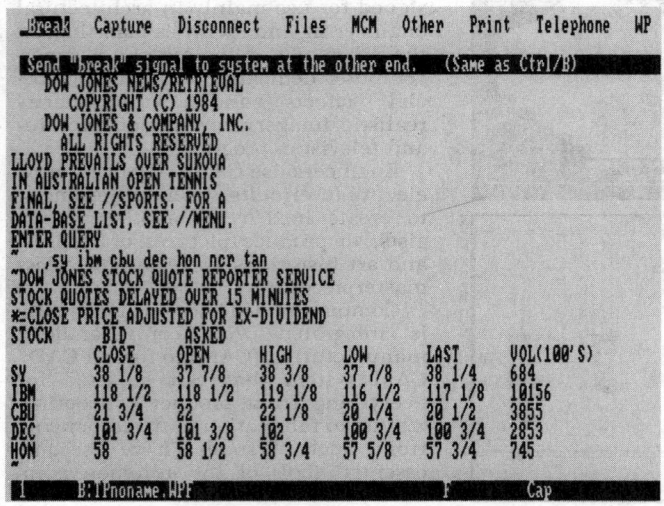

cess to much of the same information that is available to travel agencies, including hotel room, car rental, and plane seat availability and cost. A traveler can make reservations and receive confirmations on-line, then pay with a credit card.

Electronic Mail

Messages sent from one person to another through computerized channels are called electronic mail. A person can send a message to anyone else who uses the system. The message is placed in the recipient's mailbox, a storage area in the system's computer, where it remains until a user signs onto the system. It is also possible to send the same message to several people by instructing the system to forward copies to a designated list. A recipient can reply to a message, forward it to someone else, delete it, or save it for future reference.

If messages are waiting in someone's mailbox, most systems will so inform the person when he or she signs on. Some systems will also inform the sender when a recipient has read the message.

Electronic mail is much faster and more efficient than writing letters and posting them in traditional mailboxes. Often, the only real cost is telephone time. In addition, electronic mail provides both sender and recipient with a record of the communication on disk or as a printout. (If the mailboxes are part of an information utility or bulletin board system, access time fees may also be incurred.)

For letters addressed to people who do not have computers or compatible communications software, or who do not regularly check their electronic mailboxes, a combined electronic and conventional system may be used. Such a system converts the electronic message to a printed form before delivery via mail or courier.

Computer Conferences

A computer conference links people on-line; it is a meeting place within a computer system rather than in a single geographic location. Thus, instead of traveling to a particular place to hold a meeting, participants enter their reports, ideas, comments, and suggestions into a central computer. These can be called up, read, and commented on at the convenience of the participants. Since everything is stored in the computer, it is always possible to go back to exactly what was reported earlier in the conference. If necessary, final decisions can be made and confirmed by voice telephone.

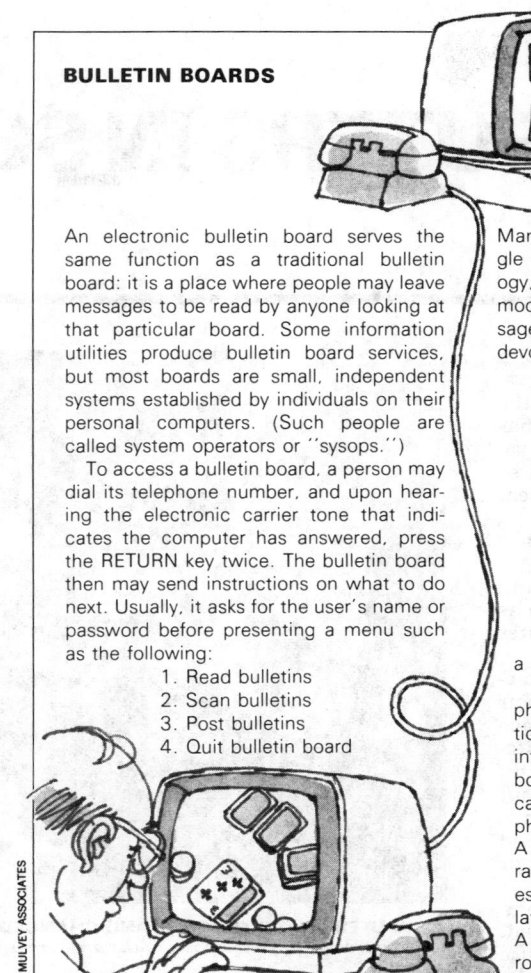

BULLETIN BOARDS

An electronic bulletin board serves the same function as a traditional bulletin board: it is a place where people may leave messages to be read by anyone looking at that particular board. Some information utilities produce bulletin board services, but most boards are small, independent systems established by individuals on their personal computers. (Such people are called system operators or "sysops.")

To access a bulletin board, a person may dial its telephone number, and upon hearing the electronic carrier tone that indicates the computer has answered, press the RETURN key twice. The bulletin board then may send instructions on what to do next. Usually, it asks for the user's name or password before presenting a menu such as the following:

1. Read bulletins
2. Scan bulletins
3. Post bulletins
4. Quit bulletin board

BILL COLRUS/MULVEY ASSOCIATES

Many bulletin boards are devoted to a single subject, such as photography, genealogy, health, or a particular computer model or application. Here are two messages posted on an urban bulletin board devoted to restaurants:

Barker's on Newton Ave. has a superb Italian buffet on Fridays from 6 to 10, for $10.95 per person. If you plan to get there after 7, be sure to make reservations.

I'm new in town . . . and addicted to ice cream. Where can I find really good chocolate ice cream for takeout?

Anyone wishing to respond can post a message on the bulletin board.

Most bulletin boards list the telephone numbers of other boards. National boards are generally part of an information utility. Local bulletin boards, often focusing on local issues, can be accessed for the cost of a telephone call and are usually free to users. A high-school bulletin board in Colorado has been used to display student essays and post news about school-related issues before the state legislature. A board in Los Angeles specializes in role-playing games. A board in Washington, DC, reports on developments in the fabric and carpet industries.

Computer conferences avoid many of the problems associated with traditional meetings: conflicting schedules that make it difficult to bring all conferees together, cost and time involved in traveling, and limited interaction, since only one person speaks at a time.

Institutions can use computer conferencing to plan meetings, hold meetings, conduct surveys, share information, present educational seminars, link geographically dispersed employees who have common problems, and so on.

Local Area Networks

A local area network, or LAN, is used to connect all the computers in an organization, whether in a single building or, less commonly, dispersed over a wide area. An LAN enables all of an organization's computers—from mainframes to microcomputers—to interact and share files, applications, and equipment. LANs improve inter-office communications and may substantially reduce computer expenses, since workers may share peripherals, such as high-speed printers and hard disk drives.

The computers and other devices in an LAN are linked by cables. Special adaptors serve as interfaces to the cables, and special software is needed, including both an operating system and utility programs to handle such chores as auditing the use of the LAN.

The network operating system runs the network and controls how each piece of hardware communicates on the network. The operating system can be resident in every computer in the network, or it can reside in a single computer, which then becomes the "server" for all of the applications installed on the network. Data move through a network at very high speeds, from 256K to over 100MB per second.

LANs vary in the way components are electrically connected, the maximum number of computers allowed, the ease of expansion, and the design of the network software. In the future, most networks are expected to conform to international standards.

COMPUTERS IN SOCIETY

In the 1950's, it took several days for a person to make a confirmed reservation for a plane trip. Since then, the number of flights and passengers has increased tremendously, but reservation systems now are computerized so it takes only seconds to reserve a seat on a plane.

Until recently, updating road maps was a laborious process. Redrawing a map to add new street names and highway route numbers could take as long as two weeks. Now, a computer can complete the task in minutes.

For most people, the most spectacular use of computers has been their role in the space program. A space mission requires so many computations of such things as flight path, thrust, and engine firings that without computers humans would not have been able to walk on the moon or send craft to explore the surface of Mars or the rings of Saturn.

The growth in the number of computer systems has been phenomenal. In 1955, the computer systems in use in the United States totaled 244. By 1980, this number had increased to over 600,000. By 1985 it had surpassed 30 million. Microcomputers, which did not exist until the mid-

PAUL CONKLIN/MONKMEYER

COMPUTERS HAVE TOUCHED AND CHANGED *people in all areas of life, from education to law enforcement, from sports to the arts, from firefighting to manufacturing.*

1970's, are more powerful and efficient than the computers of the 1950's and account for 75 percent of all computers in use. Computers have filtered into so many different aspects of our lives that almost all human activities are being changed to some extent by these machines.

How People Use Computers

Computers are considered essential for the smooth functioning of a complex society. They enable people to handle and make sense of large amounts of information. They help extend the frontiers of knowledge by making it possible to study phenomena far more complex than those that could previously be considered. They keep people abreast of important advances in their field. They make it possible to produce goods and provide services efficiently and economically.

Versatility is perhaps the greatest asset of computers. They can process large volumes of data rapidly and accurately, perform in seconds calculations that would take humans years to complete, analyze and correct problems in automated systems, communicate with humans and with other computers, and do myriad other tasks.

Computers are used to make motion

pictures and television programs, specify dance movements, compose music, and inventory a museum's holdings. Artisans use computers to analyze and copy weaves of antique fabrics, calculate the chemical properties of ceramic glazes, and create three-dimensional pictures of woodworking projects. Astronomers use computer systems to determine the orbits of newly discovered comets and to simulate the evolution of stars. Professional sports teams use computers to analyze opponents' games and to devise their own strategies.

Most computers and software are mass produced. Some computer applications, however, require tailor-made products. The U.S. Air Force, for example, requires that many of its computers be made resistant to radiation and wide temperature fluctuations, making them suitable for use under

extreme combat conditions. Computers designed for manufacturing environments also must withstand temperature extremes, as well as vibration, voltage transients, and dust.

Business and Industry

Computers teamed with software such as word-processing programs, electronic spreadsheets, and data base management systems have changed the way most businesses operate. Organizations use computers in a wide variety of applications: planning, decision-making, accounting, inventory management, sales forecasting, product design, project management, employee training, and so on.

In such systems, communication is primarily between human and computer, with the human usually determining the pace of operations. By contrast, there are real-time systems that monitor control processes, such as electric power distribution, elevator operation, and aircraft flight. These systems communicate primarily with the physical world, rather than with humans, and the pace of operations is determined by events in the world they monitor. For example, such a system can be used to control a process in a petroleum refinery. Information on temperature, pressure, and other conditions are sent to the computer; if changes are needed, the computer instantaneously issues appropriate commands. Input and output devices may be part of the system, enabling human operators to reprogram the system or to monitor what is happening.

Banking.

The trend toward a so-called cashless society is being fueled by the increasing use of electronic funds transfer systems (EFTS), which instantly transfer funds between financial institutions and between these institutions and their customers. Automatic teller machines (ATMs) enable customers to make deposits and withdrawals 24 hours a day, seven days a week, by inserting a plastic card into a machine and punching in a personal identification number. Many ATMs are hooked into large networks and can access a variety of banks. ATMs handle more than 375 billion transactions a month. Similar, but less widespread, are point-of-sale systems, in which the cost of a purchase is instantly transferred from a customer's account to a merchant's account.

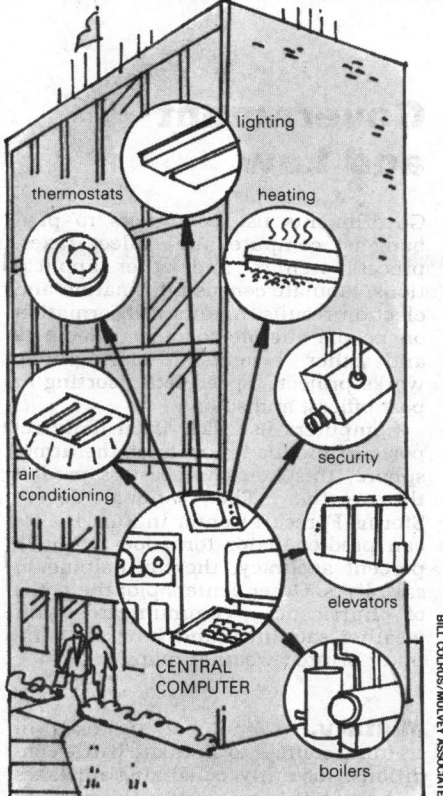

"SMART" OFFICE BUILDINGS *use computers to control and monitor a wide range of systems.*

BILL COLRUS/MULVEY ASSOCIATES

The traditional credit card that employs magnetic strip technology may soon be replaced by a so-called smart card with an embedded microprocessor that can handle all types of financial transactions. Such a card will contain a digitized picture of the card user's signature (and perhaps of the user), credit information, and a record of transactions that will be updated with each purchase.

Manufacturing.

Robotics, computer-aided design, vision systems, and other specialties are causing a radical restructuring of many industries, improving efficiency, safety, quality control, and other aspects of the production process.

Industrial robots can be programmed to perform a variety of repetitive tasks, including spot welding, spray painting, die casting, machine loading and unloading, and fabric cutting. Some have been designed to do dirty and dangerous work, such as nuclear power plant maintenance and repair, surveillance, and space and deep-sea exploration. As the capabilities of robots increase, their applications are expected to increase.

CAD systems are used to design robots, factories, and products of all kinds, including hair dryers and fire hydrants. They also are used to produce orthopedic shoes and other customized products. One firm uses computer-produced cross-sectional images of a cancer patient's diseased bone as the basis for the design of an artificial bone. A computer then directs a machine that cuts an artificial bone in titanium alloy. Because the entire process takes only a fraction of the time needed by noncomputerized procedures, some cancer patients have been spared amputations.

Vision systems are used to spot flaws in materials and to align product parts prior to assembly by robots.

Transportation.

Computers are used to design safer roads, simulate the aerodynamic behavior of planes and cars, coordinate traffic signals, schedule maintenance, help pilots fly safely, and monitor air and rail traffic.

MODERN RAPID TRANSIT SYSTEMS *use computers to monitor traffic, make routing decisions, schedule maintenance actions, and handle ticketing for passengers rapidly and efficiently.*

ROGERS/MONKMEYER

Airline reservation systems enable clerks throughout an airline's service area to communicate with a central computer; within seconds, a clerk can obtain information on seat availability on a specific flight, then sell a seat to a passenger and key into the computer the passenger's name, address, telephone number, method of payment, and so on. The computer immediately updates seat availability for that flight, enabling assignment of seats right up to the time of departure.

A computer that controls the mix of air and gasoline entering the engine is commonplace on many automobiles. Also available are computerized display maps on dashboard screens, antiskid braking, and traction control. Under development are systems that continuously monitor the safe distance to a vehicle ahead and, if needed, decelerate or even brake a car.

Agriculture.
Farmers use software for farm accounting, livestock records, and crop planting and fertilizing schedules. Electronic feed systems monitor how much food animals eat and alert the farmer if a particular animal is off its feed, a sign of possible illness. Other systems, used to monitor milk production and temperature, help spot mastitis infections and tell farmers when cows are in estrus.

A program that simulates soybean growth under a variety of conditions can predict the final yield, helping farmers obtain optimal crop yields without sacrificing long-term soil fertility or resorting to excessive amounts of fertilizer. A computerized irrigation system automatically delivers just enough water to plants, and can also apply herbicides, fertilizers, and mulch.

Government and Law

Governments use computers to plan budgets, compute and collect taxes, process welfare and other applications, tabulate census information and election results, maintain information on people eligible for Social Security and other benefits, design public works projects, speed letter sorting at post offices, and so on.

Computers use data from daily reports to produce models of the atmosphere; this helps forecasters predict the weather. The National Severe Storms Forecast Center in Kansas City can predict major tornadoes with 88 percent accuracy, thereby helping to save lives. Other centers plot the paths of hurricanes, communicate with weather satellites, and generate computer-printed weather maps.

Military.
Computers are used in training courses to simulate battle conditions, instantly penalizing mistakes and enabling military personnel to analyze the performance of soldiers and equipment. Electronic instruments enable computers to track the location and movement of tanks, armored personnel carriers, and other vehicles. The use of computer-directed harmless, low-power laser beams, instead of live ammunition, makes it possible to score the firing of a wide range of weapons.

Computer systems provide air and sea surveillance, weapons control (for example, controlling the flight of a rocket), and data communications. Computer simulation of explosive devices, sensor systems, and other equip-

ment enables the military to test designs before building equipment.

Law enforcement.
Computers are used to keep detailed information about crimes and known criminals. In seconds, law enforcement officers can learn whether a suspect is dangerous, a car or other property stolen, or a child reported missing. Computers are also used to map and analyze trends in the incidence of crimes.

A fingerprint identification system recognizes and matches the small identifying characteristics that make each person's fingerprints unique. It quickly and accurately can search tens of millions of prints, and can even read smudged or partial prints that may be found at the scene of a crime, highlighting areas of prints difficult to read. The system, instituted in San Francisco in 1984, has already enabled police officers to solve crimes in which a fingerprint is the only clue.

Health and Medicine

Medical practitioners use computers to meet needs in three broad areas: administration, patient management, and test evaluation.

Administrative purposes include recordkeeping, billing, accounting, and patient scheduling.

Patient management includes prescription writing and monitoring, behavior modification techniques (to control smoking or overeating, for example), and monitoring the critically ill. On-line medical data bases provide health-care professionals with up-to-date information on diseases and their treatment. One data base matches donors with patients needing organ transplants. Another provides information on about 100 types of cancer, including prognosis, survival rates, stages the cancer may enter, how fast the cancer moves, and treatment options. Recently introduced are cards similar in size and appearance to credit cards that can store up to 800 pages of medical history, x-rays, and electrocardiograms. The cards can be read and written on with a computer designed to accept them.

Physicians use computers to analyze laboratory samples, electrocardiograms, and pulmonary function tests. Some diagnostic techniques enable examination of the inside of a human body without surgery. Computer assisted tomography (CAT) scanners use computers and x-rays to produce three-dimensional images of the body. The nuclear magnetic resonance (NMR) scanner is a computerized tool that uses radio waves and powerful magnetic fields to measure the distribution and chemical bonds of hydrogen nu-

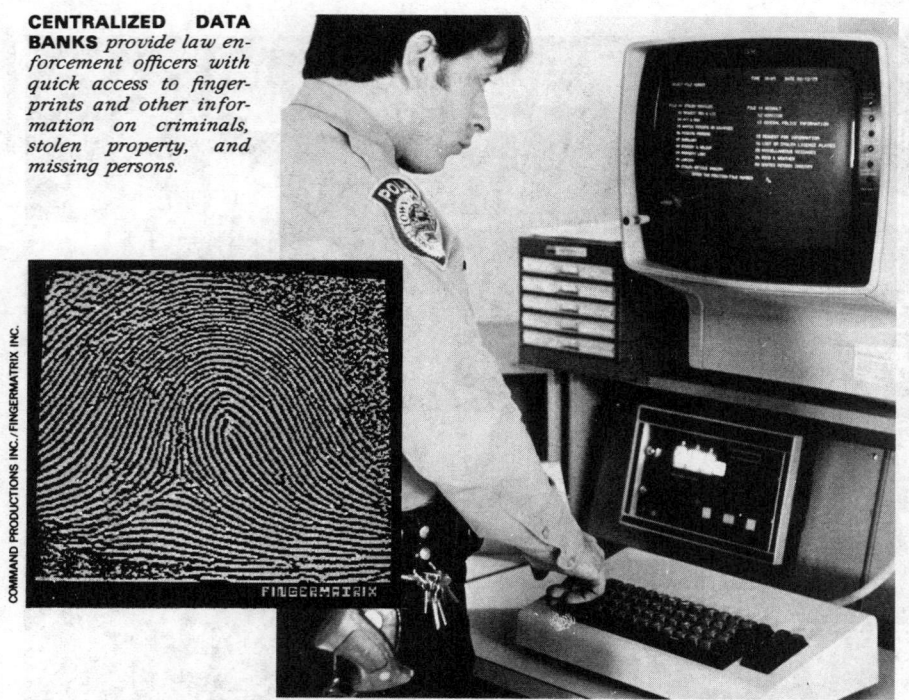

CENTRALIZED DATA BANKS *provide law enforcement officers with quick access to fingerprints and other information on criminals, stolen property, and missing persons.*

COMMAND PRODUCTIONS INC./FINGERMATRIX INC.

SYBIL SHACKMAN/MONKMEYER

FINGERMATRIX

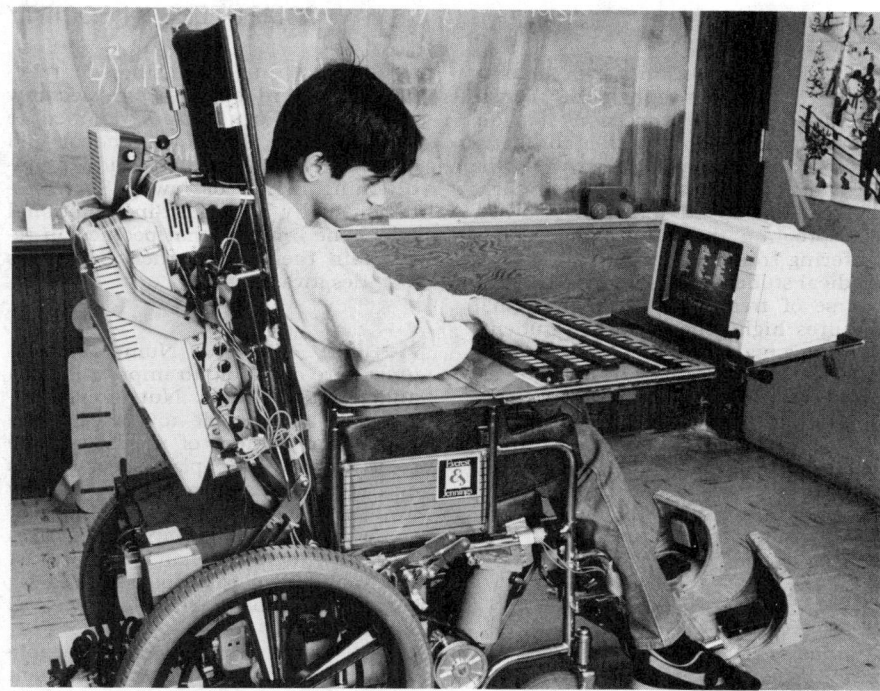

CUSTOMIZED KEYBOARDS *and other specialized equipment enable handicapped people to use computers, and computerized wheelchairs provide increased mobility.*

clei and then translate those measurements into three-dimensional images of body tissue.

Computers and the handicapped.

Computer technology is enabling many severely handicapped people to circumvent their disabilities. Speech recognition systems enable paralyzed people to ask a computer to lower the heat, dial a telephone number, or display headline stories from a news service. Wheelchairs that respond to voice direction give quadriplegics greater mobility. A machine that almost instantly turns printed text into Braille broadens the range of reading materials available to the blind. Computer-controlled eyeglasses help the deaf read lips.

Various switches can be connected to computer hardware to enable disabled people to use a computer system. A "sip and puff" switch, for example, makes it possible to operate a computer by inhaling or exhaling. Inhaling sipping causes the computer to do one thing, perhaps scan a menu; exhaling puffing activates another function, perhaps indicating a choice on the menu. Another type of switch lets people input instructions by making clicking sounds with their tongues. There also are switches that react to the wrinkling of the brow and to back and forth head movements and feet movements.

In the past, the limbs of paralyzed individuals often atrophied from lack of exercise. Today, computer stimulation can be used to build up muscles and bones. Electrodes may be connected to paralyzed legs, for example, and the computer told which muscles

are to be exercised, how much weight is to be lifted, and how far and how fast the legs should move. The computer controls leg movement, providing exactly the right amount of stimulation to make the muscles move through the indicated range. It also keeps track of heart rate and muscle fatigue.

Numerous educational programs are available to help people who are learning disabled or mentally handicapped. Specially designed systems enable teachers and parents with no programming experience to create picture recognition exercises, spelling tests, and other teaching activities tailored to the needs and abilities of a particular handicapped student.

Education

Among many preschoolers, students, adults—in schools, homes, and industry—computers are playing an increasingly important educational role. Computers are helping people learn everything from how to read and write to how to conduct an interview or read a blueprint. Students routinely use computers to write reports, take tests and receive grades, publish school newspapers, and keep track of athletic statistics.

An increasing number of educational institutions are offering electronic courses in which instructors and students may never meet: they communicate solely via modem. In some on-line learning systems, students study from textbooks and other printed materials, then take tests via computer. In other systems, students

receive lectures on disks or directly from the teacher over telephone lines. When they complete a lesson, they may send it to the teacher's electronic mailbox, to be read, corrected, and returned to the students' electronic mailboxes.

Educators are also using computers to handle administrative chores, including scheduling, maintaining attendance records, scoring tests, and calculating grades. Data banks on colleges and scholarships are used by guidance counselors. Computerized card catalogs and on-line data bases in libraries speed access to information.

Computer-assisted instruction.

The use of computers to help people learn, practice, and improve skills is frequently referred to as computer-assisted instruction, or CAI. A substantial body of research indicates that CAI improves students' retention of information and reduces the amount of time needed to master a subject.

CAI permits students to work at their own pace rather than at the pace of quicker or slower students in a class. Computers have infinite patience: they will repeat instructions or information over and over again if necessary, without yawning or showing signs of impatience. The system is interactive, requiring the student to react and participate in a dialogue with the computer. It provides constant, immediate feedback to the student. It encourages experimentation, removing the fear of being reprimanded for mistakes. Finally, the student is in control and has the computer's undivided attention.

Incorporating computer-based materials in a classroom can significantly

MANY SCHOOLS *teach computer literacy— how computers work and how they can be used.*

alter the way learning takes place, freeing teachers to provide individual and small-group instruction in ways never before possible.

The primary concern raised by the presence of computers in schools has been that of accessibility. Funding disparities among school districts mean that some students may have little opportunity to use computers, thus failing to benefit from the technical revolution.

There are three main types of educational programs: tutorials, drill and practice, and simulations.

Tutorials. A tutorial is designed to teach facts, skills, or concepts through step-by-step interactive instruction. It takes a student through such subjects as algebra, punctuation, human anatomy, and musical notation. Information is presented in small units, each followed by questions that test the student's comprehension. If a student answers correctly, new information is introduced. If incorrect answers are given, the program reviews the material, perhaps presenting it in a different way.

Many programs contain branching, which makes it possible to meet individual needs. In such programs students who do substandard work can be given expanded explanations and extra review questions, while students who give evidence of understanding the subject being taught can be provided with more advanced problems.

Drill and practice. Drill-and-practice programs are designed to review material already learned and to reinforce skills. Many of these programs are given the appearance of games. There are, for example, programs that help people learn to type, providing the repetitive practice needed to become a proficient typist. As a student types a sequence of letters or words, the computer immediately indicates errors, helping to prevent incorrect habits from becoming ingrained. In addition, the computer monitors (in thousandths of a second) and records the time needed by the student to respond to each key. The resulting data are used to customize later drills so that practice time is directed to those letters and key combinations that are found to be most difficult for a particular individual.

Most drill-and-practice programs have several levels of difficulty; when users master one level they can move on to a more challenging one. Some programs are self-paced, and others involve a time factor. In almost every case, however, students receive instant feedback indicating that their answers are correct or incorrect.

Simulations. A simulation program engages students in a real situation in order to teach or reinforce facts and concepts. Such a program might require a student to operate a nuclear power plant or to navigate a ship through narrow straits. Users must make decisions within a complex scenario while observing the consequences of the decisions made. Simulations make it possible for learners to experience events that would be too time-consuming, costly, complex, or dangerous to experience in real life.

A program that simulates patients suffering from lung disorders requires medical students to determine the best course of treatment. A program that requires high school biology students to bring a malaria epidemic under control teaches facts about mosquitoes, pesticides, and treatment of disease plus important ecological concepts. A program that simulates a political campaign requires students to develop campaign strategies and decide how to allocate campaign funds.

Home

Computers in the home are used for many of the same activities as computers in other environments. People use them for educational purposes, to access information services, order merchandise, write letters, prepare budgets, analyze investments, organize records, and so on.

Home banking services enable people to link home computers to a bank's central computer to check account balances, transfer funds between accounts, examine monthly statements, and pay bills. If bills are of the recurring type, such as mortgage payments, payments can be made automatically month after month. Some banks offer additional services, such as electronic mail and access to financial data bases.

Computerized thermostats can be programmed for different temperature settings—one temperature at night, another in the morning, still another while people are away from home during the day, thus increasing energy efficiency. More complex are security systems that can be programmed to turn heat up and down, indoor and outdoor lights on and off, and air conditioning higher or lower. Such systems usually have built-in or optional telephone links, so that people can reprogram them even when thousands of miles away.

Healthy living. Numerous programs are available to improve health and physical fitness. Nutritional programs enable people to compute the nutritional content of meals, analyze foods and recipes, plan special diets and menus, and determine activity levels for weight gain or loss. Many of these programs have large data bases of foods—including name brands, fast foods, and even baby foods—enabling users to monitor nutritional as well as caloric intake.

Biofeedback programs enable people to monitor and change levels of tension and relaxation as a means of reducing stress. One such system has sensors that perceive galvanic skin response (GSR), or changes in electrical characteristics of the skin. With the appropriate software in the computer, users place their fingers on the sensors, and a GSR reading is displayed on the screen. Exercises teach users self-control. As the exercises are performed, users receive instant visual feedback signaling the degree of success of their efforts to learn to relax. This system also has several games; the calmer the player remains while playing a game, the better the score. Each game can be played on several levels of difficulty, thereby challenging a user's ability to relax even while under pressure.

Self-hypnosis and subliminal reprogramming software is available, de-

COMPUTERS IN THE HOME *are used to count calories, plan nourishing meals, regulate appliances, keep financial records, compute taxes, and design exercise programs.*

TONY KORODY/SYGMA

signed to modify behavior and habits. One program constantly flashes messages at a high speed on the screen while the user performs other computer tasks. The messages appear too briefly for the person to be conscious of them, but persist long enough to be perceived at a subconscious level. The user chooses the positive messages desired and the frequency with which they are to appear. For example, a user might enter messages such as "I can stop smoking!" or "I can lose weight!"

Physical fitness software is designed to help users monitor and carry out personalized exercise regimens. Aerobic exercise programs may teach routines and track factors such as time elapsed, beginning and end pulse rate, and calories burned. Running programs may help a person set goals; suggest training schedules; record times, distances, and calories consumed; and graph progress over a period of time.

First aid and safety programs, often written in accordance with standard Red Cross guidelines, present step-by-step instructions on how to recognize, prevent, or treat medical problems. These programs cover everything from routine problems such as falls, cuts, and burns to life-threatening emergencies, such as coronary attacks and epileptic seizures.

Recreational software.

The major types of recreational, or game, software are arcade, adventure, simulation, and traditional. Hybrids, however, are also common, melding aspects of two or more of the above. A strategy game based on the 1941 German invasion of the Soviet Union has simulation and artificial intelligence routines. Another depicts the classic struggle between good and evil, combining the strategy of a board game with the action of an arcade-style game.

Arcade games were initially the dominant games, and they played an influential role in early computer sales to the home market. Most of these

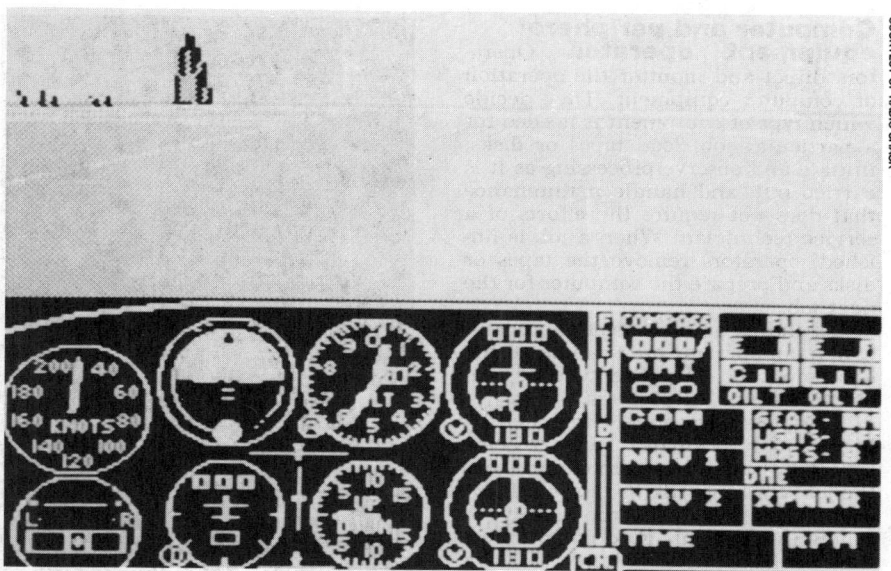

RECREATION SOFTWARE *is not limited to arcade-type games. Programs like this one, which simulates operation of an airplane from the cockpit, can be educational as well as fun.*

games stress hand-eye coordination and have several levels of speed and complexity, to adjust to the increasing skill of the player. Most have exceptionally fine graphics plus music.

Adventure games are games of strategy, with emphasis on character and plot. They match the wits and imagination of a player with those of the game creators. The player must analyze a situation, understand or discover the rules that govern the environment, and develop a strategy to achieve a goal. Adventure games may be extremely intricate, requiring days, weeks, or months of play.

Simulations recreate real-life situations: baseball games, geopolitics in the nuclear age, space travel, real estate speculation, investment in the stock market, and so on. One of these adventure games simulates airplane flight, including takeoffs and landings. Players must monitor an array of gauges on the instrument panel and take into consideration such factors as

the weather, cloud cover, and wind velocity.

Traditional games include games such as chess and poker, trivia and word games. The quality of the game may well depend on the amount of memory it requires. Chess programs for home computers cannot compete at the level of Deep Thought, a chess program developed at Carnegie-Mellon University. Deep Thought can examine 720,000 possible arrays of chess pieces on a board each second. It plays at the grandmaster level and has beaten some of the world's best human chess players.

In addition to their entertainment value, most games have some learning value, if only because they require players to solve problems. Many games help develop logical thinking and other important intellectual skills. For instance, adventure games demand inductive reasoning, formulation of hypotheses, and other thinking skills like the ones required in everyday life.

Computers and Careers

Almost all workers will come in contact with computers at one time or another during the course of their careers. But in addition to the use of computers in traditional jobs, there are computer-related careers that did not even exist a few years ago. These careers are found not only in the computer industry itself, but in government, banking, manufacturing, publishing—in fact, in every sector of the economy.

The demand for computer workers

will continue to grow. Salaries are comparatively high, advancement can be rapid, and there is great potential for job involvement and satisfaction. Computer occupations are excellent choices for people with logical minds.

Here are brief descriptions of the work and educational requirements for some of the major occupations available in the computer field. Within each job category, there are various positions, from entry-level to managerial.

Data entry operator. Data entry clerks and operators are responsible for entering data into files that will be processed by a computer. They may enter data directly on magnetic media via a keyboard or use OCR (optical character reader) devices. They may work with mainframe computers, minicomputers, or microcomputers.

Usually, a high-school diploma and good typing skills are required for an entry-level position, but the ability to work carefully is also essential.

Computer and peripheral equipment operator.

Operators direct and monitor the operation of computer equipment. They decide which type of equipment is needed for a particular job, load tapes or disks, initiate and observe processing as it is carried out, and handle maintenance that does not require the efforts of a service technician. When a job is finished, operators remove the tapes or disks and prepare the computer for the next job.

Depending on the size of the organization, an operator may handle all the equipment or only one type of machine, such as the printers.

Entry-level personnel are generally high-school graduates, who receive several weeks of classroom and on-the-job training. Skills essential for advancement include the ability to follow instructions, good communications skills, and the ability to solve problems as they arise.

Computer technician.

Technicians install, maintain, and repair equipment. They must be familiar with basic mechanics, basic electronics, and common tools and test equipment. Many are employed by manufacturers and thus are required to be familiar with the models produced by their employers. They must also keep up to date on equipment changes. Entry-level positions generally require at least one or two years of technical training in electronics.

Telecommunication technicians monitor and maintain the hardware in a communications network. They need a strong background in electronics plus special training in communications networks. They complete vocational electronics programs and acquire additional skills through on-the-job training and special classes.

Programmer.

Programmers write the software that instructs a computer on how to accomplish desired tasks. They also test and debug programs. Some programmers work individually, handling the development of entire programs, but programmers more commonly are members of programming teams, in which each member works on particular segments or aspects of a program.

Applications programmers prepare applications software; scientific programmers work on scientific and engineering problems; and systems programmers develop operating systems software, write programs that can be used to detect hardware problems, and develop and improve programming languages. An area that is expected to grow significantly in the next decade is robotics programming, which gives robots the capabilities needed for performing specific types of work.

TEST MANAGERS *examine new computer boards to make certain they meet quality standards.*

In the past, some programmers had formal training, while others learned programming as a hobby. Today, employers are selective, often requiring a college degree in computer sciences plus special training in a particular field, such as business applications or graphics. Programmers must continue their technical training throughout their careers, to keep informed about changes in equipment, programming languages, and systems and programming concepts.

Systems analyst.

Systems analysts respond to the needs of an organization by developing plans for meeting those needs by computer. They study how tasks are currently being handled, consider alternative means of performing the tasks, and review equipment available to aid the process. For instance, they may analyze a firm's manual payroll operation, then develop a plan for a computerized system that will perform all the same tasks—plus additional tasks such as computing taxes, insurance premiums, and retirement benefits.

Sometimes, analysts develop proposals for expanding computerized systems that already exist. Once management approves a proposal, the analysts supervise its development, help install it, and monitor its operation to make certain it does all that it should.

Many systems analysts begin their careers as programmers. Others begin as trainees, working under the direction of an experienced systems analyst. Most employers require analysts to have a college degree in computer science, mathematics, or data processing. Additional training in a special field, such as banking or hospital administration, may also be required, depending on the nature of the organization's work. All systems analysts continue their technical training throughout their careers to keep abreast of new developments.

Other occupations.

Other occupational categories that deal directly with computers include *computer scientists*, who study the theoretical aspects of computers, such as programming theory and artificial intelligence; and *computer engineers*, who design and help develop computer equipment.

Data base managers build and maintain data base management systems. They devise ways to make sure that information can be accessed easily by those who need it, and to prevent unauthorized personnel from retrieving confidential data.

Large data processing departments generally include *librarians*. Their function is to maintain, and distribute tapes, disks, and other records in the department. Librarians must be able to locate any record in the library rapidly, check it out, inspect it for damage on its return, and store it where it can be retrieved easily when needed again.

Technical writers interpret information and put it in a form that can be understood by people with either technical or nontechnical backgrounds. Some prepare documentation that explains how to assemble a machine or set up a hardware system. Others write documentation that describes a software program: what it does, how it works, and how it is used. The writers may also develop promotional materials and news announcements.

Computer security specialists have the job of protecting computer systems against improper use. Their goal is to deny unauthorized access to computer centers, communications lines, data bases, and so on. They design, implement, and supervise control systems that protect against fraud, theft, sabotage, natural disasters, and other types of vulnerability.

Computer training specialists help identify and meet an organization's training needs, ranging from orientation for new employees to technical courses for experienced personnel. They may teach courses themselves, hire instructors, or make arrangements for employees to take college courses or other outside courses.

Marketing and sales personnel who have selling talents plus an understanding of and familiarity with computer technology are employed by manufacturers of hardware and software, distributors, and a great number of retail operations.

Computer Ethics

Like any other new development, computers can be misused, leading to legal, ethical, and social problems that society must address. Of particular concern are issues of privacy, crime, and unemployment, all of which have existed for centuries, but which seem to have been magnified by the development of computers.

Privacy

A basic tenet of a democratic society is that individuals have rights of privacy regarding their personal beliefs and activities. Among these is the right to control the circulation of information about oneself, deciding when, how, and to what extent such information may be communicated to others. Computerized data systems may have endangered such rights, for they make it easier to collect, store, retrieve, and disseminate personal information. This trend may accelerate as a result of the growing use of computers by all types of government and private agencies. The development of networks, on-line systems, electronic mail, and electronic funds transfer systems also makes it easier to gain unauthorized access to records.

It is often difficult, if not impossible, for people to discover what information has been collected about them, how accurate it is, and who has access to it. For example, in the United States, some motor vehicle licensing agencies have sold the names and addresses of licensed drivers to business organizations that solicit customers.

Computer Crime

The most lucrative form of computer crime is embezzlement. Manipulation of computerized financial accounts for personal gain has led to million-dollar losses for government agencies, banks, insurance companies, and others. Other problems include unauthorized retrieval, reproduction and use of data, and damage to or alteration of records. For example, there have been incidents of alteration of student grades and tampering with election results.

Sabotage is another concern, particularly for defense, police, banking, and medical systems. Water, fire, induced magnetic fields, and chemicals can destroy millions of dollars worth of hardware and software in minutes.

Piracy. Unauthorized copying of software, called piracy, is a major problem plaguing the computer industry. It costs software publishers billions of dollars in lost sales each year. The problem is particularly acute with business software.

There are several types of pirates. Some make extra backup copies for their personal use. Some make illegal copies for others. Some organizations buy one set of software, then make a dozen copies on their various machines. "Professionals" exist, whose business it is to copy software they have acquired and sell it to others, illegally, for profit.

Software is protected by the U.S. copyright law, which allows program duplication only for personal backup purposes. Many software publishers protect their programs to fight piracy. The most common protection methods involve encryption—using code words and programs to scramble a program, making it difficult to copy.

Viruses. Computer viruses are bits of computer code designed to reproduce, much like their biological counterparts. Some are innocuous. Many, however, are designed to destroy or scramble data and programs or damage monitors and disk drives.

A virus originates with a programmer who writes the code. This code is attached surreptitiously to existing software, such as a utility or word-processing program. The program is

THE PERVASIVENESS *of computers raises questions of privacy and security.*

SOLOMON/MONKMEYER

disseminated, perhaps via a network or an electronic bulletin board. Once in a new host, the virus reproduces. Then, at a preset time, it activates itself and works its mischief.

Security measures. Keeping a computer system secure against unauthorized access becomes increasingly difficult as the number of remotely located terminals increases. Large networks accessible by telephone by the public are particularly vulnerable. Intruders may be able to obtain information they are not entitled to have or damage information in the system.

Many abuses can be prevented by making it difficult for unauthorized personnel to gain access to a system. Organizations can establish rules specifying who has the right to use a system and to what extent. Under such rules, users must identify themselves by a name or number that is kept secret. Users may also be required to give a password before gaining access to the system; this password is changed frequently.

Physical security measures can be undertaken to protect rooms and buildings where sensitive computer data are housed. Telecommunication lines can be equipped with electronic scramblers. Programmed time locks can be placed on accounts and files. Data and programs can be fragmented so that they cannot be accessed through a single account. Antiviral programs can detect or "vaccinate" against computer virus infections.

Employment

Computers and automation enable advanced nations to remain competitive in world markets, but often at the cost of displacing human workers. Demand for machine operators, laborers, lower and middle managers, and clerical personnel is expected to fall over the coming years. Even agricultural workers can by affected by automation and their livelihoods threatened.

To date, however, most information indicates that people who lose their jobs because of computers usually find other jobs within a short period of time. Also, the number of jobs that has been eliminated by computers has been offset by the number of new jobs created in computer-related fields. The jobs created by expanding computer usage, however, generally require education and skills beyond the capabilities of many displaced workers. Thus, there will continue to be a need for job counseling and retraining programs.

GLOSSARY OF COMPUTER TERMS

Access code. A password that permits access to a computer file.

Address. A specific location in the computer's memory, identified by a number. Also, the location of a cell on an electronic spreadsheet.

AI. *See* Artifical intelligence.

Algorithm. A set of instructions for solving a problem. The steps of the algorithm can be translated into programming language to create a program that enables a computer to solve the problem.

Alphanumeric. Consisting of letters and numbers and often punctuation marks and other symbols.

American Standard Code for Information Interchange (ASCII). A standard computer code representing letters, numbers, punctuation, and other symbols; used to convert alphanumeric characters into binary numbers, and vice versa.

Analog computer. A computer that handles data coming from sensing devices that measure quantities that change continuously.

Applications software. Computer programs that enable a computer to perform tasks, such as word processing, accounting, graphics, training, or chess playing.

Arithmetic/logic unit (ALU). The part of the central processing unit that combines and compares numbers.

Artificial intelligence. The branch of computer science devoted to designing computers so that they have attributes associated with intelligence. Also describes the ability of computers to reason and "think."

ASCII. *See* American Standard Code for Information Interchange.

Assembler. A computer program that translates programs written in assembly language into binary code.

Assembly language. A low-level computer language that is similar to machine language but that is written in symbolic form rather than zeroes and ones.

Backup. The practice of copying computer data to protect against loss. Also the name given to such duplicate disks or files.

Bar code. A set of printed parallel lines of varied width and spacing that can be read by a computer. A common application is the coding of price and inventory information for merchandise sold in supermarkets.

Batch processing. A method of processing data in which the computer performs the same computation or computations on a number of similar records at one time.

Baud. A unit of measurement used to indicate the speed of data transmission. Baud is usually figured in bits per second.

Binary number system. The base-two number system used by computers. It has only two digits, 0 and 1.

Bit, binary digit. Either 0 or 1, the two digits in the binary system. A bit is the smallest unit of data recognized by a computer.

Boot. To turn on the power in a computer system and bring in the operating system so that the computer is available to the user. Derived from the expression "he lifted himself up by his bootstraps."

Bubble memory. A storage method that uses areas of negative charges—bubbles—in positive strata to represent binary 0 and 1.

Buffer. A temporary storage area for data located between two areas, such as between the computer memory and the printer.

Bug. An error in a computer or computer program. Getting rid of an error is called debugging.

Bus. Conductors that connect the parts of a computer so that data flow between them. A unidirectional bus can carry signals in one direction only; a bidirectional bus, in either direction.

Byte. A group of adjacent binary digits processed as a unit; usually equals eight bits, the number required to encode one symbol.

CAD. *See* the entry for Computer-assisted design.

CAI. *See* the entry for Computer-assisted instruction.

CAM. *See* the entry for Computer-assisted manufacture.

Cartridge. A device used to store a recorded program. To run a program, the cartridge is inserted into a special slot in the computer.

CASE. *See* Computer-aided software engineering.

CAT. *See* Computer-assisted tomography.

Cathode ray tube (CRT). A video display unit used in television sets and computer monitors; an output device used to display information.

CD-ROM (compact disk-read only memory). A compact disk used as a storage device for computer data. A CD-ROM player reads the data and sends it to the computer.

Central processing unit (CPU). The part of the computer that interprets and carries out instructions. It consists of an arithmetic/logic unit and a control unit.

Character. A letter of the alphabet, number, or other symbol.

Chip. A tiny wafer of semiconductor material on whose surface is etched electronic circuitry. In a computer, chips with different functions are wired together.

Clone. A computer that is compatible with another computer, usually an IBM computer. It can run the same software used by the IBM computer.

Code. Type of programmed instructions: source code is in the language in which the program is written; object code is in machine language.

Command. An instruction given to a computer.

Communications software. The programs that enable a computer, modem, and telephone to work together to send or transmit data.

Compatibility. The capability of a computer system to accept and process data prepared by another system without modification. Also, the capability of a software program or hardware component to be used by a computer system.

Compiler. A program that translates a high-level programming language into binary code, an assembly language, or an intermediate language, which is sometimes called pseudocode.

Computer-aided software engineering (CASE). The use of computer software to help in the design and development of new computer programs.

Computer-assisted design (CAD). The use of computer programs to create designs, especially engineering designs.

Computer-assisted instruction (CAI). The use of computer programs in training and education; also educational software, including tutorials, drill-and-practice, simulations, and other programs.

Computer - assisted manufacture (CAM). The use of computer programs to direct factory machines.

Computer-assisted tomography (CAT). The use of computer programs to make a special type of medical x-ray photograph.

Computer graphics. Graphs, charts, drawings, and other pictorial displays generated by a computer.

Computer language. A defined set of characters and words and the rules for their use in writing programs. Examples include BASIC and COBOL.

Computer piracy. The unauthorized copying of software.

Computer system. The computer and its attached peripherals, such as printer, disk drive, and monitor.

Copy-protection codes. Instructions added to programs that prevent or make it difficult to copy the programs; done to limit computer piracy. Adding such codes is also called encryption.

CPU. *See* Central processing unit.

CRT. *See* Cathode ray tube.

Cursor. A spot of light on the display screen that indicates where the next entry will appear.

Data. Information. A general term for information consisting of characters, numbers, and symbols that can be processed by a computer.

Data bank. *See* Information utility.

Data base. An organized collection of information, especially one stored in a computer and made accessible electronically.

Data base management system. Software that enables a computer to create a data base and then to organize, store, and retrieve the data therein.

Data processing. Operations carried out on data, such as entering, storing, retrieving, and manipulating.

Desktop publishing. The use of personal computers in conjunction with laser printers to produce typeset-style text and graphics.

Digital computer. A computer that operates with numbers expressed directly as digits.

Disk. General name given to a flat, round storage device. *See also* CD-ROM; Floppy disk; Hard disk.

Disk drive. A device that holds and rotates a disk at high speed. The drive contains a read/write head that can read data from the disk and write data onto the disk in the form of magnetized patterns.

Display. A monitor screen or the image produced on it.

Documentation. The written instructions that explain how to use computer hardware or software.

DOS (disk operating system). A program needed to use disks. It manages space on a disk, formats data for storage and retrieval, and tells the computer how to interact with the disk drive.

Electronic Funds Transfer. A method of receiving and paying for goods and services by which funds are transferred electronically from one account to another.

Electronic mail. The transmission of messages and other information from one computer to another, usually via telephone lines.

Emulator. A device that translates programs written for a computer so that they will run on a computer of another type.

EPROM (erasable, programmable read only memory). A type of ROM that can be altered by using specially designed equipment.

Expansion slot. A place inside a computer to receive a board with additional memory or other capability.

Expert system. A program or group of programs designed to simulate the judgment of experts in a specific field. It comprises a knowledge base and rules for using the knowledge.

Feedback. In interactive programs, the computer's response to an input.

Floating point operation. A mathematical operation involving fractions multiplied by a power; a convenient way to express very small and very large numbers. A measure of computer speed is the number of floating point operations flops performed per second.

Floppy disk. A flexible magnetic disk used to store information.

Flowchart. A drawing showing the logical sequence of a solution or operation. Several types of symbols are used in designing a flowchart, including ovals, rectangles, and diamonds.

Forecasting. Making financial predictions based on "what-if" questions. A popular application of electronic spreadsheets.

COMPUTER-ASSISTED MANUFACTURE, *such as the use of robots to weld automobile chassis, improves output while reducing costs, thereby improving plant productivity.*

TOM McHUGH/PHOTO RESEARCHERS

Formatting. Preparing a blank disk to receive and store information; also called initializing. In word processing, the laying out of the appearance of a printed document to be produced.

Function key. Any key on a computer keyboard that has been or can be designated to perform a specific task. For example, *reset, return,* and *locate* keys.

Giga-(G). One billion. Computer memory can be measured in gigabytes (GB), or billions of bytes of data.

Graphics tablet. An electronic drawing board connected to a computer. Whatever is drawn on the tablet is entered into computer memory and appears on the display screen.

Hard copy. Text or graphics printed by the computer on paper. Also called "printout."

Hard disk. A rigid magnetic disk in a sealed housing; used for storing information. A hard disk can store many times the data that a floppy disk can.

Hardware. The physical components of a computer system, such as circuit chips, disk drives, monitor, and keyboard.

High-level language. A programming language that uses instructions and expressions similar to human language to direct the computer. Examples include BASIC, COBOL, LOGO, and PASCAL.

Icon. A pictorial image on a computer menu indicating a computer function, such as a drawer to indicate storage and retrieval, or scissors to indicate file editing.

Information utility. An organization that offers, usually for a fee, access to computerized data bases, bulletin boards, and other services. Some utilities are referred to as data banks or information retrieval services.

SAMPLE ICONS

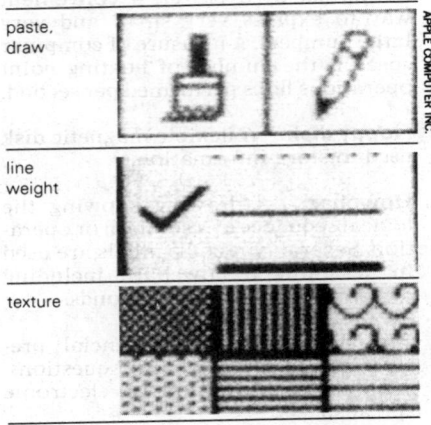

Input. Information to be transferred from an external source, such as a disk, modem, or keyboard, into the internal memory of a computer. Also, instructions given to a computer to enable it to perform a useful function.

Integrated circuit (IC). A microscopic electronic circuit etched on a chip.

Integrated software. Two or more programs packaged together that have a common set of commands and that can share data. For example, an integrated package may contain word-processing, spreadsheet, and data-base programs.

Interactive. Enabling two-way communication between the computer and user. Also, in programming, enabling a user to switch back and forth easily between writing and testing a program.

Interface. The circuitry between the computer and an I/O device. Enables the computer to communicate with a peripheral, such as a monitor, printer, or storage device.

I/O (input/output). The process of transferring data into or out of the central processing unit.

Joystick. An input device resembling an airplane joystick that enables a user to move words, numbers, or graphics from one point to another on the computer display screen.

K. *See* Kilo-.

Keyboard. A device used to input characters into the computer. It resembles a typewriter keyboard but also has certain special function keys unique to computing.

Kilo-. Thousand. Computer memory can be measured in kilobytes (K or Kb), or thousands of bytes of data.

LAN. *See* Local area network.

Laptop. A small, portable computer. It is battery powered and has a full typewriter-style keyboard and a built-in display screen.

LCD. *See* Liquid crystal display.

Light pen. A penlike device with a light-sensitive detector at its tip; when pointed at the monitor screen, it enables the user to select, input, or delete data.

Liquid crystal display (LCD). A screen consisting of a layer of liquid crystals encased in glass. Used as an output device for some computers, especially portables.

Load. To transfer a program and its data from a storage device to RAM.

Local area network (LAN). A system for connecting computers within a limited area, such as a building, to permit communication among the computers.

Machine language. Language that is understood by the internal circuitry of a computer. Consists of sequences of numbers. The lowest level in the hierarchy of computer languages.

Mainframe. A large, powerful type of computer capable of processing large amounts of data very rapidly.

Mega-. Million. Computer memory can be measured in megabytes (Mb), or millions of bytes of data. Computer speed can be expressed in megaflops, or millions of floating point operations per second.

Memory. The part of a central processing unit used to hold a program that is being executed and the data upon which the program works. The most common types of computer memory are RAM and ROM. Storage media, such as disks, provide off-line memory.

Menu. A list of functions or commands offered by a program. These are displayed on the monitor, and the user indicates the option desired. A program with such a feature is often called menu-driven.

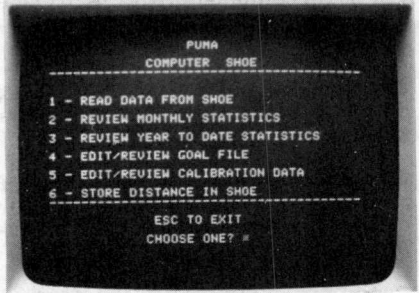

SAMPLE MENU

Microcomputer. A small computer that uses a microprocessor for its central processing unit. Also called a personal computer, home computer, or desk-top computer.

Microprocessor. A chip that contains all the electronic circuitry of a computer central processing unit.

Minicomputer. A medium-sized computer, smaller and less powerful than a mainframe but larger and more powerful than a microcomputer.

Modem (*mo*dulator *dem*odulator). A device that enables computers to communicate with one another via telephone. It converts digital signals into acoustic signals and vice versa.

Monitor. A unit with a screen used for displaying information produced by the computer.

MOUSE

Mouse. An input device that is moved around the desk top to control the position of the cursor on the display screen. It is used to select data and commands.

Nano-. A prefix denoting billionth. Computer speed can be measured in nanoseconds, or billionths of a second.

Natural language. Human language, such as standard English. One goal of artificial intelligence research is to develop computers that can communicate in natural language.

Network. A group of computers linked together.

Numeric keypad. A group of number keys on some computer keyboards, arranged like the keys on a calculator. In addition to enabling the user to input numerals, the keys may perform other functions.

OCR. *See* Optical character reader.

On-line. Connected to a working computer. Usually refers to the connection of a personal computer to a mainframe, via modem and telephone.

Operating system. A complex program that controls the operation of a computer system, for example, controlling signals to the monitor or disk drive. It acts as an intermediary between hardware and software, loading and supervising all other programs.

Optical character reader (OCR). A device that reads letters, numbers, and other symbols and converts them to electronic signals that can be recorded on magnetic disk or tape and processed by a computer. A bar code reader is one type of OCR.

Output. Information processed by a computer and sent to a peripheral, such as a monitor, disk drive, or printer.

Parallel processing. A type of computer architecture, found in some supercomputers, that enables the computer to do multiple tasks simultaneously. The central processing unit comprises two or more microprocessors linked together, with each capable of working on separate problems or separate portions of the same problem at the same time.

Peripheral. Any hardware that is attached to the computer; for example, a printer, modem, disk drive, light pen, or monitor.

Personal computer (PC). *See* Microcomputer.

Pico-. Trillionth. Computer speed can be measured in picoseconds, or trillionths of a second.

Pixel (*picture element*). The tiny dots of light on a display screen. The greater the number of pixels per square inch, the higher the resolution of an image.

Plotter. An output device that uses one or more moving pens to produce inked drawings, graphs, or text on paper.

Port. A connection point on a computer that allows I/O devices to be connected to the microprocessor. A port is either serial or parallel.

Printed circuit board. A board on which is printed interconnecting circuitry and which has holes for chips and other components that are soldered to the board.

PRINTED CIRCUIT BOARD

Printer. An output device used to make a hard (paper) copy of information in the computer.

Printout. *See* Hard copy.

Program. A set of instructions for the computer. *See also* Software.

Programming. Writing instructions, or programs, for a computer.

QWERTY. The name given to the standard layout of keys on a typewriter or computer keyboard. The name is based on the order of letters on the upper left-hand portion of the keyboard.

Random access memory (RAM). The area of computer memory in which users can store information. Temporary storage; information in RAM is lost when the computer is turned off.

Read. To copy information from a storage device, such as a disk, to the computer memory.

Read only memory (ROM). Permanent memory built into a computer. It can be read but not altered.

Resolution. The quality of the image on the display screen. The higher the resolution, the sharper the picture. Resolution is expressed by number of pixels per square inch.

RISC (reduced instruction set computing). A chip design that eliminates instructions that are rarely used, putting them in software. The result is greater speed at lower cost.

Save. Store information from RAM in a disk or tape so that it can be used again at another time.

Scroll. Move information horizontally or vertically on the screen.

Semiconductor. A material, such as silicon, that transmits electricity better than a resistor or an insulator but not as well as a true conductor. The ability of a semiconductor to conduct electricity can be changed by temperature variation or by adding impurities. Used to make memory chips, microprocessors, and various other integrated circuits.

Serial processing. The most common type of computer architecture, in which a single processor performs all tasks sequentially.

Simulation. A computer program that imitates a real event. For example, a program that simulates the operation of an airplane or a power plant.

Soft copy. Nonpermanent output, such as text and graphics that appear on a display screen.

Software. Computer programs. The instructions that tell a computer what to do. There are two main types: systems and applications. Systems software, also called operating systems, gives the computer general instructions on how to operate. Applications software tells the computer how to perform a specific task, such as writing a document or playing a game.

Speech recognition. The ability of a computer to understand spoken words.

Speech synthesis. The artificial production of speech.

Spelling checker. A program that checks the words in a file against a stored dictionary, questioning or correcting words not in the dictionary. Usually part of a word-processing package.

Spreadsheet. A program used primarily for accounting and other financial functions.

Telecommunications. The transmission of data from one computer to another via telephone lines and other communications links.

Terminal. An input/output device connected to a computer. Sometimes refers to the screen on which computer data are displayed. A "dumb terminal" can accept data and transmit to a computer but has no processing capabilities. A "smart terminal" can edit, store data, and so on.

Transistor. A semiconductor device that can amplify or switch a flow of electrons.

User friendly. In computer jargon, a computer or an item of software that is easy to use.

User groups. Clubs of computer owners, usually organized around one particular type of computer or software. Club meetings are often good sources of information and help. Some user groups maintain libraries of software that members may copy, and use.

Utilities. Programs that are part of the operating system and are used to perform special tasks, such as formatting a disk.

Videotex. An interactive system that provides information, buying, and other services to users via a television set and a terminal.

Virus. A computer program or part of a program which is designed to reproduce itself, much like a biological virus, and spread from one program or computer to another. The person who creates the virus may design it to destroy data and programs or damage computer equipment.

Window. An area on the display screen used to show data from another program or from other parts of the same program. Some programs enable simultaneous use of multiple windows, each showing different information.

Word processing. A program used for writing that enables a user to compose and edit text on the screen, then save it or print it on paper.

—Jenny Tesar

For Further Reference

General

Consumer Guide Computer Buying Guide. Publications International, 1989.

Dewdney, A.K. The Armchair Universe. W.H. Freeman & Co., 1988.

Freedman, Alan. The Computer Glossary (4th Ed.). American Management Association, 1989.

Gebhart-Seele, Peter A. Computer and the Child: A Montessori Approach. Computer Science, 1986.

Gilmore, Charles M. Beginner's Guide to Microprocessors. Tab Books, 1984.

Gookin, Dan. How to Understand and Buy Computers (2nd Ed.). Computer Publishing Enterprises, 1988.

Graham, Ian and Helen Varley. The Home Computer Handbook. Simon & Schuster, 1984.

Rosch, Winn L. The Winn Rosch Hardware Bible. Simon & Schuster, 1989.

Turkle, Sherry. The Second Self: Computers and the Human Spirit. Simon & Schuster, 1984.

Weintraub, Joseph. Exploring Careers in the Computer Field (Rev. Ed.). Rosen Publishing Group, 1988.

Computer Languages

Helms, Harry L. Computer Language Reference Guide. Howard W. Sams, 1984.

Taylor, Charles F. The Master Handbook of High-Level Microcomputer Languages. Tab Books, 1984.

Wyatt, Allen L. Using Assembly Language. Que, 1987.

Programming

Crawford, Chris. The Art of Computer Game Design: Reflections of a Master Game Designer. Osborne/McGraw-Hill, 1984.

Curnow, Ray and Susan Curran. Games, Graphics & Sound. Simon & Schuster, 1984.

Downing, Douglas. Computer Programming in BASIC The Easy Way (2nd Ed.). Barron's Educational Series, 1989.

Fisher, Alan S. CASE: Using Software Development Tools. John Wiley & Sons, 1988.

Hartnell, Tim. Creating Adventure Games on Your Computer. Ballantine Books, 1984.

Kochan, Stephen G. Programming in C (Rev. Ed.). Hayden Books, 1988.

Lammers, Susan. Programmers at Work. Microsoft Press, 1986.

Lampton, Christopher. COBOL for Beginners. Franklin Watts, 1984.

Roberts, Ralph. Computer Viruses. Compute! Books, 1988.

History

Aspray, William, Jr., editor. Computing Before Computers. Iowa State University Press, 1989.

Augarten, Stan. Bit by Bit: An Illustrated History of Computers. Ticknor & Fields, 1984.

Freiberger, Paul and Michael Swaine. Fire in the Valley. Osborne/McGraw-Hill, 1984.

Ritchie, David. The Computer Pioneers: The Making of a Modern Computer. Simon & Schuster, 1986.

Slater, Robert. Portraits in Silicon. MIT Press, 1987.

Artificial Intelligence

Berry, Adrian. The Super-Intelligent Machine: An Electronic Odyssey. Salem House, 1985.

Frenzel, Louis E., Jr. Crash Course in Artificial Intelligence and Expert Systems. Howard W. Sams, 1987.

Harmon, Paul and David King. Expert Systems. John Wiley & Sons. 1985.

Hsu, Jeffrey and Joseph Kusnan. The Fifth Generation: The Future of Computer Technology. Windcrest Books, 1989.

Hyde, Margaret O. Computers That Think? Enslow Publishers. 1986.

Johnson, George. Machinery of the Mind: Inside the New Science of Artificial Intelligence. Microsoft Press, 1986.

Waldrop, M. Mitchell. Man-Made Minds: The Promise of Artificial Intelligence. Walker, 1987.

Applications

Brand, Stewart. Whole Earth Software Catalog. Doubleday, 1984.

Fox, David and Mitchell Waite. Computer Animation Primer. McGraw-Hill, 1984.

Glassner, Andrew S. Computer Graphics User Guide. Howard W. Sams, 1984.

Goldmann, Nahum. Online Research and Retrieval with Microcomputers. Tab Books, 1985.

Holtz, Herman. How to Make Money with Your Micro (Rev. Ed.). John Wiley & Sons, 1989

Hsu, Jeffrey. Guide to Commercial Telecommunications Services. Prentice-Hall, 1989.

Noble, David F. and Virginia Noble. Improve Your Writing with Word Processing. Que, 1984.

Parker, Roger C. Looking Good in Print: A Guide to Basic Design for Desktop Publishing. Ventana, 1988.

Prueitt, Melvin L. Art and the Computer. McGraw-Hill, 1984.

Sanders, D. Computer Concepts and Applications. McGraw-Hill, 1987.

VOLUME 7

Chemistry and Physics

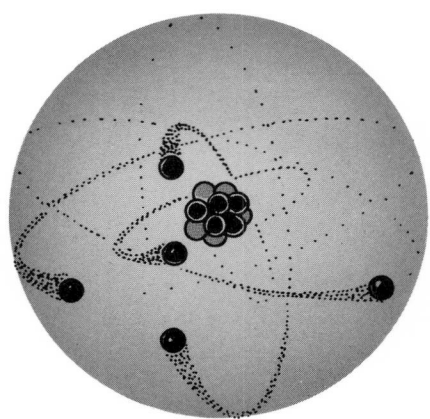

MAJOR BRANCHES OF CHEMISTRY AND PHYSICS

Chemistry

PHYSICAL	INORGANIC	ORGANIC	SILICONE
theory and principles	noncarbon hydrogen compounds	carbon hydrogen compounds	silicone hydrogen compounds
• periodic law	• mineral acids, bases, and salts	• alkanes	• silicon raw materials
• structure	• gases	• alkenes	• silanes
• thermo-dynamics	• liquids	• alkynes	• halosilanes
• oxidation/reduction	• solids	• carbo-hydrates	• silanols
• kinetics	• electro-chemistry	• aromatics	
• reactions		• proteins	
• phases of matter		• enzymes	
• measurements		• polymers	
		• alkaloids	

MAJOR APPLICATIONS

• testing and analysis	• metals	• fuels	• sizing agents
• heating	• ceramics	• sugars	• surfactants
• cooling	• refractories	• wines	• elastomers
• separation	• glasses	• spirits	• lubricants
• crystallization	• cements	• medicines	• oils
• evaporation	• plasters	• pesticides	• molding compounds
• liquification	• concrete	• coolants	• sealants
• catalysis	• reactive gases	• dyes	• water repellents
• nucleonics	• noble gases	• monomers	• computer chips
• colloids	• dry cells	• plastics	
• solutions	• batteries	• soaps	
	• fuel cells	• paints	
	• fertilizers	• rubbers	
		• adhesives	
		• biochemicals	

Physics

MECHANICS	PROPERTIES OF MATTER	THERMO-DYNAMICS	SOUND	ELECTRICITY/MAGNETISM	LIGHT	NUCLEAR PHYSICS
kinematics	solids	temperature	waves	static electricity	wave theory	atomic nucleus
statics	• crystal structure	• measurement	resonance	• Coulomb's law		accelerators
dynamics			Doppler effect	• conductors and insulators	geometrical optics	
• time	liquids	heat	ultrasonics		• mirrors	elementary particles
• measurements	• surface tension	• heat capacity		electric currents	• lenses	• fundamental forces
• velocity	• viscosity	• heat conduction			physical optics	• Grand Unification theories
• acceleration		• convection		magnetism	• interference	
• force	gases	• radiation		• magnetic fields	• diffraction	
• gravitation	• kinetic theory of gases			• electromagnetic induction	• polarization	
		thermodynamics				
		• conservation of energy			atomic spectra	
		• cryogenics				

MAJOR APPLICATIONS

• machines	• materials science	• power generation	• room acoustics	• electrical engineering	• optical instruments	• nuclear power
• structural engineering	• solid state devices	• engines	• electro-acoustics	• electric power	• illumination	• radiation therapy
• calculation of orbits	• hydraulic devices	• heating	• ultrasonics	• semiconductors	• lasers	• beam weapons
	• pneumatic devices	• cooling	• ultrasonic imaging	• electronics	• holography	

Chemistry and Physics

RUSSELL A. THOMPSON/TAURUS PHOTOS

RICHARD MEGNA/FUNDAMENTAL PHOTOGRAPHS

Looking back to the earliest days of science, we can only marvel at the insights achieved. Before the birth of Christ, Greek philosophers formulated the brilliant concept of elements and compounds. Aristotle defined a simple body as "one into which other bodies can be decomposed," adding that a simple body "itself is not capable of being divided." Aristotle's definition is not far from the modern definition of an element. In the eras following Greek antiquity, people occupied themselves with magic, occultism, and alchemy. They searched for a process to transmute base elements into gold, a potion to enable them to live forever; and a way to create valuable gems.

By the 17th century, however, chemists were directing their research toward the behavior of gases; this led to an understanding of the relationship between pressure and volume. Scientists thus were able to explain the phenomenon of combustion, though they were misled at times by false notions about the nature of matter. Nevertheless, the identification of elements began to move ahead, and the groundwork was laid for modern chemistry.

What was true of ancient chemistry also held true for ancient physics. Early philosophers formulated concepts to explain various phenomena, for example, the solar system. They also made important early forays into mathematics, so important in physics, and into numbering systems. Moving closer to modern times, Sir Isaac Newton gave the world the renowned three laws of motion and the concept of gravity, so necessary for the explanation of celestial motion and the behavior of falling bodies. And it was Newton who devised a form of calculus, essential for modern mathematics.

As recently as 100 years ago, scientists had not identified many of the elements that now appear in the Periodic Table of Elements. Laboratory instruments were crude. Atomic structure and the interaction of atoms were not understood. Space travel was the realm of the dreamer and the writer of fiction. And the synthesis of molecular structures was far off.

Chemists of the recent past were extremely limited in the laboratory work they could undertake, but today's researchers can call on a wide variety of advanced equipment. For example, they can create precisely controlled vacuums; establish conditions of extreme cold with cryogenic equipment; and employ precise measuring instruments, thanks to the development of electronics.

A century ago, physics was also in a relatively primitive state. Scientists could only guess at the nature and behavior of structures too small to be visible to the naked eye. There was little opportunity for researchers to verify their assumptions and inferences. Today physicists have the electron microscope, the cyclotron, and powerful computers to assist in their work. In addition, developments in mathematics have moved physicists closer to a full understanding of matter and energy.

Despite a lack of adequate instrumentation, 19th-century scientists believed they had explained the mysteries of matter and its behavior. They were confident that only a few details remained to be explained. Although their optimism was mistaken, physics was poised for a breakthrough.

Much is known today about the fundamental characteristics of matter and energy, but all the mysteries have not been solved. There is still much to be learned. Each day brings scientists closer to full understanding of the nature of the universe, thanks in part to the expansion of their activities into space, but in the truest sense resulting from the unquenchable curiosity and persistence exhibited by the men and women of science.

CHEMISTRY

Chemistry exists everywhere. All animals breathe in oxygen (O_2) from the air and almost immediately exhale carbon dioxide (CO_2). Plants, in turn, absorb carbon dioxide and by the action of sunlight and photosynthesis release oxygen. This quick and efficient reaction is called *chemical change*. A pot of liquid water is heated to 100° C and turns into gaseous steam, but still remains water. It cools, condensing back to a liquid; but as the temperature keeps dropping, it turns into solid ice or frozen water. This process, by which a material undergoes different changes in phase (gas to liquid to solid and vice versa) without losing its identity, is known as *physical change*. The science of chemistry is concerned with chemical and physical changes. After briefly describing the branches and history of chemistry, this section will present a synopsis of what causes these changes, why they occur, and how they are used to man's benefit.

Branches of chemistry.

Physics, chemistry, and mathematics form the core of science. In the last

BILL COLRUS/MULVEY ASSOCIATES

CHEMICAL CHANGES *occur when carbon dioxide and oxygen recycle.*

hundred years, each has divided into specialized disciplines that will, no doubt, again branch off. Currently, chemistry is divided into the following six branches.

• *Physical chemistry* applies the principles of Newtonian and atomic physics to chemical and physical changes.

• *Analytical chemistry* develops techniques and equipment to monitor reactions and to identify the nature and composition of materials.

• *Nuclear chemistry* is concerned with the study and use of radioactive and subatomic reactions. Most of nuclear chemistry deals with atomic physics rather than conventional chemistry. (See page 467.)

• *Inorganic chemistry* is dedicated to the chemical and physical changes of all solids, liquids, and gases that are not the hydrogen compounds of carbon and silicon.

• *Organic chemistry* is concerned with the hydrogen compounds of carbon and their derivatives. This includes biochemistry (the chemistry of life), the synthesis of carbon-based fuels, (oils and gasoline), organic solvents (alcohols, ethers, aldehydes, ketones, and esters), drugs (antibiotics, pain-killers, and hormones), and plastics (polyethylene, polystyrene, epoxies, and many more).

• *Silicone chemistry* is concerned with the hydrogen and carbon compounds of silicon that are used to make adhesion promoters (sizing agents), surfactants, lubricants, elastomers, rubbers, paints, and sealants that are highly resistant to heat and to weathering.

History

Alchemy

If the universe lacked energy it would be "dead." All energy is convertible to the equivalent of heat, that is, the change in temperature produced by fire. All matter that is not at 0° K (Kelvin) or absolute zero ($-273°$ C) is at some level of heat. Chemical and physical changes are totally dependent on available heat. Although man discovered fire at least 1.4 million years ago, he had no understanding of why it occurred. But man was clever enough to know how to start fire, save it, and use it as a heating medium.

It was not until 10,000 years ago that the primitive rudiments of chemistry began to be developed in Asia and the Middle East. By mixing and pouring different combinations of materials, and then applying heat, man was able to create reproducible chemical and physical changes. However, these

ALCHEMISTS *mixed materials at random, without knowing why changes occurred.*

CULVER PICTURES

required a multitude of hit-and-miss experiments. For instance, the extraction of iron from its ore, the selective blending of sand with fluxes to make glass, the selection of clays, fluxes, metal oxides, and water to produce ceramics, and the processing of lime mortars and cements, not only required careful preparation (segregation and weighing) but also temperatures in excess of 1000° C. Additionally, our ancestors developed techniques to refine gold, silver, mercury, copper, zinc, and tin. They learned to ferment beers and wines, and by distilling the latter, to get alcohol. Astonishingly, ancient man had no thermometers or pyrometers.

The Romans referred to this craft as "alchimia," meaning "to pour together." Alchemists, the practitioners of this craft, were like excellent chefs. They could "cook and bake," but they did not understand the nature of matter or the chemical changes that occurred. Even if they had accepted the concept of Democritus (Greek, c 460–c 370 B.C.) that matter is made up of indivisible particles called atoms, modern advances in physics and chemistry would not have been made in ancient times. The geniuses that transformed craft into science were yet to be born. The methods of objective inquiry and of systematic analysis did not exist. So alchemists continued to extend their craft by trying to convert metals into gold and wines into restorers of youth.

It was not until the 16th century A.D. that old "truths" were contradicted. Earth was not flat nor the center of the universe. Beginning with such men as Galileo Galilei (Italian, 1564–1642) and Sir Isaac Newton (British, 1642–1727), brillant and inquisitive men transformed the world of science. It was from their technique of inquiry that the scientific method of analysis was developed. This method required rigorous experimentation based on a stated principle that led to the establishment of other principles that could be corroborated by independent scientists.

Modern Chemistry

The rise of modern chemistry began in the 17th century. Hundreds of physicists and chemists (as they began to be known) contributed to the foundation of this science. Only a few of them will be discussed in this section. The chronological order of their contributions, rather than their births, will be highlighted, since many of these scientists happened to be born within the same generation.

Robert Boyle (British, 1629–1691) reintroduced the concept of the atom. He is best known for Boyle's law, which states that the volume of a gas varies inversely upon the application of pressure at a constant temperature, or

$$P(final) \times V(final) =$$
$$P(initial) \times V(initial)$$

where P and V stand for pressure and volume.

Joseph Black (British, 1728–1799) discovered that the temperature of melting ice remains constant at 0° C while it first absorbs a fixed amount of heat, the heat of fusion. After this absorption, the ice becomes liquid. He similarly described the "heat of vaporization" as the fixed amount of heat absorbed by liquid water at its boiling point prior to its transformation into gaseous steam. These absorption values were found to be reversible—steam gives up the same amount of heat of vaporization before it is cooled into a liquid. The latter also yields the same quantity of heat of fusion at its freezing point before converting into ice. Black's work led others to measure the thermal properties of materials and the physical changes associated with them.

Henry Cavendish (British, 1731–1810), without realizing it, discovered hydrogen gas in 1781. He ignited the unknown gas (which he called inflammable air) released by sulfuric acid (H_2SO_4) when it was acted upon by iron filings. The ignition caused the hydrogen to react with the oxygen in the air and, thereby, produce water. His subsequent experiments with oxygen in 1785 suggested that the atmosphere contains 78 percent nitrogen and roughly 20 percent oxygen, with the balance unidentified. This result was considered doubtful. More than 100 years later, Cavendish's experiments were repeated. The questionable portion was identified as consisting of trace amounts of the noble, rare, or inert gases (helium, neon, xenon, argon, and krypton).

Karl Wilhelm Scheele (Swedish, 1742–1786) and **Joseph Priestley** (British, 1733–1804) independently discovered oxygen, which they identified as a gas that burns better than air, by heating mercuric oxide (HgO). Priestley made his discovery in 1774; Scheele published his findings in 1777. Cavendish, Scheele, and Priestley were searching for phlogiston, a nonexistent material that was thought to be responsible for combustion.

Antoine Lavoisier (French, 1743–1794) correctly identified Cavendish's gas as hydrogen and Priestley's as oxygen. In 1775, he showed that one-fifth of the volume of air is "lost" when mercury (Hg) is heated in the atmosphere. He then demonstrated that upon reheating the burned mercury (Hg0), a gas equal to the volume originally lost is recovered. Finally, Lavoisier showed that the ignition of oxygen not only caused combustion but also supported life upon inhalation. He thus not only disproved the phlogiston theory, but on learning of Cavendish's work on inflammable gas (1781), he proved that the combustion of oxygen and hydrogen results in the creation of water.

Alessandro Volta (Italian, 1745–1827) discovered how to make electricity from a chemical reaction. The principles of the wet- and dry-cell battery are based on his work.

Jacques Charles (French, 1746–1823) is best remembered for Charles's law: at constant pressure, the volume of a given weight of a gas varies directly with absolute temperature—

$$V(Initial) \times T(Final) =$$
$$V(Final) \times T(Initial).$$

ANTOINE LAVOISIER *pioneered many of the basic analytical methods used in chemistry to explain and predict changes in reactions between materials.*

Joseph Gay-Lussac (French, 1778–1850) observed that a gas initially at 0° C contracts by 1/273rd of its original volume for each degree it is cooled. This suggested that at −273° C, the gas would have no volume or that it would have reached an absolute zero point because no more volume exists for further cooling. This theory became the basis for the Kelvin or absolute temperature scale, that is, 0° K = −273° C. He is also known for Gay-Lussac's gas law, which asserts that at a constant volume, the pressure exerted by a given weight of gas varies directly with absolute temperature:

$$P(Initial) \times T(Final) = P(Final) \times T(Initial).$$

John Dalton (British, 1776–1844) introduced an atomic theory and the atomic scale, which describes the known elements as having different relative weights that produce new compounds when the atoms of one element react with those of another. Dalton showed that the elements always react with each other in fixed proportions. For example, one part by weight of hydrogen reacts with eight parts by weight of oxygen to yield nine parts by weight of water.

Jons Berzelius (Swedish, 1779–1848) established shorthand notations (subscripts and coefficients) and symbols to describe chemical reactions. He introduced the concept of electrically charged atoms, called ions, and coined the word "catalyst" to describe a substance that speeds up or slows down a reaction without itself being altered.

YEAR OF INTRODUCTION

PRODUCT OR PROCESS	YEAR
Celsius thermometer	1735
Portland cement	1824
Carbon electrodes	1850
Safety matches	1856
Aluminum	1886
Acetylene chemistry	1890
Coal tar chemistry	1895
Synthetic dyes	1900
Phenolic plastics	1900
Amines/amides	1920
Polyvinyl chloride	1936
Polystyrene	1938
Oxygen furnace	1938
Antibiotics	1940
Polyethylene	1942
Glass fibered plastics	1942
Silicones	1943
Petrochemicals	1948
Polypropylene	1959
Polycarbonate	1964
Microchips	1965
Optical fibers	1972
Nuclear Magnetic Resonance	1980
Making of anticancer cells	1985

Humphry Davy (British, 1778–1829) held that electrolysis (a battery or generator charging two electrodes in a salt solution of water) is the best way to reduce compounds to their respective elements. He discovered several elements and also disproved Lavoisier's notion that oxygen is the universal constituent of mineral or inorganic acids. (Hydrogen is actually that universal constituent.)

Amedeo Avogadro (Italian, 1776–1856) accurately hypothesized that equal volumes of different gases, while not weighing the same, contain the same number of particles, which can be either uncombined atoms or two of the same atoms combined as molecules (like H_2 or O_2).

Stanislao Cannizzaro (Italian, 1826–1910) showed the validity of Avogadro's argument, and in 1858, the relative atomic weight of oxygen was arbitrarily designated as 16.0000; all other atomic weights were calculated relative to it. (See page 406 for an explanation of relative weights.) On this basis, the correct reaction for making water is

$$2H_2 + O_2 \rightarrow 2H_2O,$$

and not

$$H + O \rightarrow OH,$$

as Dalton had insisted. Dalton believed that the relative atomic weight of oxygen was 8. His conclusion that one part by weight of hydrogen combines with eight parts by weight of oxygen to give nine parts by weight of water is correct, but reactive gases like hydrogen and oxygen exist in pairs (as diatomic molecules). Dalton would have been right if the equation had been

$$\tfrac{1}{2}H_2 + \tfrac{1}{4}O_2 \rightarrow \tfrac{1}{2}H_2O.$$

In 1909, **Robert Andrews Millikan** (American, 1868–1953) corroborated Avogadro's hypothesis by showing that 22.4 liters of any gas at 0° C contains 6.024×10^{23} molecules. This is known as Avogadro's number.

Michael Faraday (British, 1791–1867) discovered the law for electrolysis. It states that in an aqueous electrolytic solution, the application of 96,500 ampere-seconds of electricity to two electrodes will cause the reduction of one element in the solution at the cathode; the corresponding oxidation occurs at the anode. If the element has a valence of one, then 96,500 ampere-seconds separates the exact relative atomic weight of the element. If the element has a valence in excess of one, then the amount deposited or liberated is equal to its atomic weight divided by its known valence (valence means reacting capacity). This is called its equivalent weight. (See page 406.)

Friedrich Wöhler (German, 1800–1882) made urea (an extract of living tissue) from an inorganic substance, ammonium cyanate. His synthesis accelerated the development of organic chemistry.

Friedrich Kekule (German, 1829–1896) correctly identified the ring structure for benzene and also introduced the concept of tetravalent carbon atoms joined to each other. (See page 421 for an explanation.) His work was pivotal in the later corroboration of the structure of molecules in organic chemistry.

Emil Fischer (German, 1852–1919) received the Nobel Prize for Chemistry in 1902 for his work on sugars, proteins, depsides, and purine compounds. His contributions helped to lay the foundation for biochemistry.

Henry Le Châtelier (French, 1850–1936) is famous for his work on reactions involving equilibrium. Le Châtelier's principle states that if the conditions of a system initially at equilibrium are changed, then the equilibrium will shift in a direction that tends to restore the original conditions. This principle is vital in the design and operation of industrial chemical plants.

Lothar Meyer (German, 1830–1895) and **Dmitri Mendeleev** (Russian, 1834–1907) independently discovered the basis for the Periodic Table of the Elements. The short or consolidated form is shown on page 405. In 1871, Mendeleev arranged the known elements in relation to their then-accepted atomic weights, combining powers (valences) and properties. His correlations not only revealed correctable errors, but also predictions about the existence of other unknown elements. The discovery of the electron and the proton by **J. J. Thomson** (British, 1856–1940), of the noble gases by **William Ramsay** (British, 1852–1916), and of x-rays by **Wilhelm Roentgen** (German, 1845–1923) culminated in the work of **Henry G. J. Moseley** (British, 1887–1915) in 1913 that proved the validity of Mendeleev's interpretations of his proposed Periodic Table. Moseley diffracted x-rays from a large series of elements, showing that the number of electrons they contained corresponded to their sequential positions in the Periodic Table. Subsequent work in the 20th century by **Niels Bohr** (Danish, 1885–1962), **Werner Heisenberg** (German, 1901–1976), **Erwin Schrödinger** (Austrian, 1887–1961), **Max Planck** (German, 1858–1947), **Paul Dirac** (British, 1902–1984), **Wolfgang Pauli** (Austrian, 1900–1958), **Albert Einstein** (American, 1879-1955), and **James Chadwick** (British, 1891–1974) literally divided the atom into its component parts. The most significant impact of this scientific milestone may be the further deciphering of the genetic chemistry of living matter in the 21st century to help cure diseases and prolong life. The discovery of DNA (deoxyribonucleic acid) in 1953 by **James Watson** (American, 1928–) and **Francis Crick** (British, 1916–) is the cornerstone for this pursuit.

Physical Chemistry

Physical chemistry uses the principles of physics to explain how the atoms of different elements are structured, and how they interact with each other or themselves to create chemical or physical changes. For example, anthracite coal, consisting mostly of the element carbon, produces heat and light when ignited in air. But what is the makeup of carbon and of the oxygen in air that causes this to happen on the atomic level? What is the quantity of heat that is given off? Suppose the burning takes place in a closed container. Why does pressure form against the sides of the container? The dynamics of motion and the impact between the interaction of particles are involved in each of these instances.

Physical chemistry also forms the foundation for the design and construction of chemical factories and for the equipment to test and monitor chemical and physical changes.

Today, each branch of chemistry depends on physical chemistry. In this segment, chemical nomenclature will be explained. A description of how atoms are structured and of the way they interact to create new products will follow.

Notation

Nomenclature. Understanding chemical nomenclature requires learning the names and corresponding symbols of the elements as found in the Periodic Table on page 404 or in the detailed chart at the end of this section. The elements are further identified as to type (metal, nonmetal, or gas) and their major uses described. The names of many elements have Latin roots; for example, ferrum means iron and has the symbol Fe; aurum means gold and has the symbol Au. By universal accord (the International Union of Pure and Applied Chemistry), the symbol for any element can have no more than two characters. (Note: those elements starting with atomic number 104 now have three characters in some tables.) The name and symbol for each element stand for the atoms of one kind that make up that particular element.

Compounds. In all, seven major classes of compounds exist. They are known as oxides, acids, bases, salts, silicates, organics, and silicones. The latter two are discussed on pages 419–424. A compound is created when the atoms of two or more elements join together to form a completely new

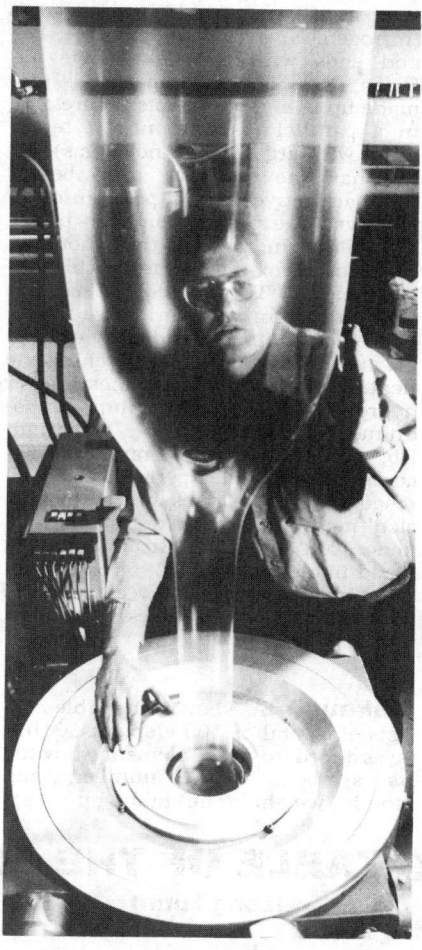

POLYETHYLENE *is produced under strictly controlled manufacturing conditions to achieve high quality.*

material. For example, water is formed when atoms of oxygen, an element, react, or are joined together, with atoms of hydrogen, another element. This new union of atoms is also called a *molecule*. The molecules of the metal oxides are generally easy to name. For instance, the oxides of calcium, magnesium, and aluminum are respectively known as calcium oxide, magnesium oxide, and aluminum oxide.

In naming some metals, however, the word stem is changed to indicate their oxidation state. Two forms of iron oxide exist. The first is ferr*ous* oxide (one atom of iron, Fe, joined to one atom of oxygen, O, as FeO); the second is ferr*ic* oxide (two atoms of iron, Fe, combined with three atoms of oxygen, O, as Fe_2O_3). In general, the oxide of a metal is designated by first naming the metal and then using the word "oxide." The ending "ous" means "less or

lower" while "ic" means "greater or higher." Iron, Fe, in ferrous oxide has a valence or oxidation state of +2, while in ferric oxide, it has a valence or oxidation state of +3. (See pages 406 and 410 for an explanation of valences and oxidation.) An in-depth study of chemistry enables one to recognize when each stem should be used. The nonmetal oxides follow the same pattern. The name of the nonmetal comes first, followed by a Latin numerical prefix and the ending oxide. Some examples are carbon *mon*oxide (chemically designated as CO), carbon *di*oxide (CO_2), and sulfur *di*oxide (SO_2). Many exceptions exist. Water is not called *di*hydrogen oxide (H_2O), and H_2O_2 is known as hydrogen *per*oxide.

The bases are the easiest to name because they always end with the word "hydroxide" preceded by the name of a metal. Some common ones are sodium hydroxide (NaOH), calcium hydroxide ($Ca(OH)_2$), and potassium hydroxide (KOH). In contrast, the mineral acids consist of hydrogen atoms combined with a nonmetal oxide or a nonmetal. Hydrosulfuric acid (H_2S), hydriodic acid (HI), and hydrochloric acid (HCl) are examples of hydrogen atoms combined with nonmetals. Sulfuric acid (H_2SO_4), nitric acid (HNO_3), and sulfurous acid (H_2SO_3) represent hydrogen atoms combined with nonmetal oxides. It is best to memorize their names.

Salts are the reaction products of a base and an acid. For example, mixing sodium hydroxide (a base) with hydrochloric acid in the correct proportions yields sodium chloride, table salt, plus water. Salts contain the metal portion of the base joined to the nonmetal radical or ion of the acid. Sodium sulfate (Na_2SO_4), sodium sulfite (Na_2SO_3), potassium chloride (KCl), calcium sulfate ($CaSO_4$), and magnesium chloride (MgCl) are salts. SO_4^{-2}, Cl^{-1}, NO_3^{-1}, SO_3^{-2}, and S^{-2} are known as ions or charged radicals. Notice that the endings, "ate," "ite," and "ide," when preceded by a metal's name, indicate a salt, while "ic," and "ous" preceded by hydrogen indicate an acid.

The silicates are fused oxides of silicon with other metal oxides that are usually combined with water. There is no pattern to their naming. Consequently, we shall only identify the molecule for white clay, which is

$$Al_2O_3 \cdot 2SiO_2 \cdot 2H_2O,$$

or hydrated aluminum silcate, also known as kaolin clay. (Notice that two molecules of water—$2H_2O$—are joined or combined with the oxides of aluminum and of silicon. The word "hydrated" means containing water.)

The Periodic Table

The Periodic Table is a matrix of the first 89 elements found in nature and of the 19 other elements thus far synthesized by man. Element 108 has yet to be made. The table is like the map to a city. Each element resides in a "house" or box, as determined by its atomic number and its relationship to other elements. It is this ordered relationship that allows scientists to understand how elements react with each other and to probe further into the nature of the universe.

Two formats of the table are the short form, found on page 405 and the long form, shown below. Although many versions exist and future revisions will occur, the sequence of atomic numbers and relationship of the elements remain constant.

Organization. The Periodic Table is a catalog of how the elements are related to each other in nature. The horizontal rows from left to right are called periods; the vertical columns are known as groups. Of the latter, group 18 (group 0 in other tables) is the pivotal one because it indicates the end of a period. This allows the elements to be arranged in a pattern prescribed by nature, not man. For example, the first period consists of gaseous hydrogen and immediately ends with helium, a noble gas, which is the first element in group 18. Note that all the elements in group 18 are noble gases. The second period, consisting of eight elements, starts with a highly reactive metal (lithium, Li), progresses through two other metals (beryllium, Be; boron, B), passes to a nonmetal (carbon, C), proceeds to three gases (nitrogen, N; oxygen, O; fluorine, F;), and ends with the next noble gas (neon, Ne). The third period is also made up of eight elements progressing in a parallel fashion until it terminates with argon, Ar (a noble gas). After that, the sequence again begins with an active metal, potassium, K. However, the progression then passes through 14 metals and three nonmetals before reaching the next noble gas, Kr. The subsequent periods again all begin with an active metal, while continuing to add heavier metals and nonmetals before reaching the next noble gas. The active metals after hydrogen in group 1 (lithium, Li; sodium, Na; potassium, K; rubidium, Rb; cesium, Cs; and francium, Fr) commence all other periods. The corresponding noble gases terminate a period (neon, Ne; argon, Ar; krypton, Kr; xenon, Xe; and radon, Rn). The metals listed under groups 3, 4, 5, 6, 7, 8, 9, 10, 11, and 12 are less reactive than their metallic countertypes in groups 1 and 2.

Makeup. As shown, the table consists of a total of 109 elements. A box is assigned to each element showing its symbol, atomic number, and atomic weight. The table on pages 425–433 additionally lists the valences, name, discoverer, and year of discovery of each element. Only two elements exist as liquids at room temperature. These are mercury and bromine. The rest are solids or gases.

All the elements listed are in a neutral state. They have a zero electrical charge. The valences found in the table on pages 425–433 represent electrical charges that a given element can assume. A "+1" is a positive charge of one; a "+ or −4" is either a positive or negative charge of 4, and a "−1" is a negative charge of one. Positive and negative charges attract each other. On contact, they "stick." The oppositely charged atoms of the elements do the same, as a result, they produce a union of their atoms, a molecule. In a real sense, they give birth to a form of matter (the molecule) that did not exist prior to their chemical reaction. A charged atom is called an ion. Na^{+1} and O^{-2} are respectively the ions of sodium and oxygen.

The table can also be considered as a matrix consisting of hydrogen, the electropositive metals, nonmetals (metalloids), electronegative reactive gases, and noble gases. The most versatile elements are the nonmetals, chief of which are carbon, C; silicon, Si; phosphorus, P; sulfur, S; and nitrogen, N. They can become either electronegative or electropositive. Also note that the noble gases are always neutral, that each element in group 1 has a positive valence of +1, and that the elements in group 17 have a negative valence of "−1."

PERIODIC TABLE OF THE ELEMENTS
(Long Form)

GROUP ↓

Note: Atomic masses shown here are the 1983 IUPAC values (maximum of six significant figures).
* Symbols based on IUPAC systematic names.

Key: atomic number — chemical symbol — atomic weight or mass

	1 alkali metals	2 alkaline earth metals	3	4	5	6	7	8	9	10	11	12	13	14	15	16	17	18 inert gases
PERIOD 1	1 H 1.0079																	2 He 4.00260
PERIOD 2	3 Li 6.941	4 Be 9.01218											5 B 10.81	6 C 12.011	7 N 14.0067	8 O 15.9994	9 F 18.9984	10 Ne 20.179
PERIOD 3	11 Na 22.9898	12 Mg 24.305				transition metals							13 Al 26.9815	14 Si 28.0855	15 P 30.9738	16 S 32.06	17 Cl 35.453	18 Ar 39.948
PERIOD 4	19 K 39.0983	20 Ca 40.08	21 Sc 44.9559	22 Ti 47.88	23 V 50.9415	24 Cr 51.996	25 Mn 54.9380	26 Fe 55.847	27 Co 58.9332	28 Ni 58.69	29 Cu 63.546	30 Zn 65.39	31 Ga 69.72	32 Ge 72.59	33 As 74.9216	34 Se 78.96	35 Br 79.904	36 Kr 83.80
PERIOD 5	37 Rb 85.4678	38 Sr 87.62	39 Y 88.9059	40 Zr 91.224	41 Nb 92.9064	42 Mo 95.94	43 Tc (98)	44 Ru 101.07	45 Rh 102.906	46 Pd 106.42	47 Ag 107.868	48 Cd 112.41	49 In 114.82	50 Sn 118.71	51 Sb 121.75	52 Te 127.60	53 I 126.905	54 Xe 131.29
PERIOD 6	55 Cs 132.905	56 Ba 137.33	57 La ★ 138.906	72 Hf 178.49	73 Ta 180.948	74 W 183.85	75 Re 186.207	76 Os 190.2	77 Ir 192.22	78 Pt 195.08	79 Au 196.967	80 Hg 200.59	81 Tl 204.383	82 Pb 207.2	83 Bi 208.980	84 Po (209)	85 At (210)	86 Rn (222)
PERIOD 7	87 Fr (223)	88 Ra 226.025	89 AC ▲ 227.028	104 Unq* (261)	105 Unp* (262)	106 Unh* (263)	107 Uns* (262)	108	109									

other metals

★ Lanthanide series	58 Ce 140.12	59 Pr 140.908	60 Nd 144.24	61 Pm (145)	62 Sm 150.36	63 Eu 151.96	64 Gd 157.25	65 Tb 158.925	66 Dy 162.50	67 Ho 164.930	68 Er 167.26	69 Tm 168.934	70 Yb 173.04	71 Lu 174.967
▲ Actinide series	90 Th 232.038	91 Pa 231.036	92 U 238.029	93 Np 237.048	94 Pu (244)	95 Am (243)	96 Cm (247)	97 Bk (247)	98 Cf (251)	99 Es (252)	100 Fm (257)	101 Md (258)	102 No (259)	103 Lr (260)

PERIODIC TABLE OF THE ELEMENTS
(Short Form)

Legend:
AN — atomic number
Element
Symbol AW — atomic weight
Valences
Discoverer
Year
a, b, = subgroups

PERIOD → / GROUP

	0	1	2	3	4	5	6	7	8	8	8
SHORT SHORT PERIOD 1–2		1 Hydrogen, H 1, ±1, Cavendish 1766									
FIRST SHORT PERIOD 3–10	2 Helium, He 4, 0, Ramsay 1895	3 Lithium, Li 7, 1, Arfvedson 1817	4 Beryllium, Be 9, 3, Vauquelin 1797	5 Boron, B 11, 3, Davy 1808	6 Carbon, C 12, ±4, (Antiquity)	7 Nitrogen, N 14, −3,+5, Rutherford 1772	8 Oxygen, O 16, −2, Scheele 1774	9 Fluorine, F 19, −1, Moissan 1886			
SECOND SHORT PERIOD 11–18	10 Neon, Ne 20, 0, Ramsay 1898	11 Sodium, Na 23, 1, Davy 1807	12 Magnesium, Mg 24, 2, Davy 1808	13 Aluminum, Al 27, 3, Oersted 1825	14 Silicon, Si 28, ±4, Berzelius 1823	15 Phosphorus, P 31, −3,+5, Brand 1669	16 Sulfur, S 32, −2,+6, (Antiquity)	17 Chlorine, Cl 35, −1,5,7, Scheele 1774			
FIRST LONG PERIOD 19–36	18 Argon, A 40, 0, Ramsay 1894	19 Potassium, K 39, 1, Davy 1807 [a]	20 Calcium, Ca 40, 2, Davy 1808 [a]	21 Scandium, Sc 45, 3, Nilson 1879 [b,a]	22 Titanium, Ti 48, 2,3,4, Gregor 1791 [b,a]	23 Vanadium, V 51, 2,3,4,5, Sefstrom 1830 [b,a]	24 Chromium, Cr 52, 2,3,6, Vauquelin 1797 [b,a]	25 Manganese, Mn 55, 2,3,4,6, Gahn 1774 [b]	26 Iron, Fe 56, 2,3, (Antiquity)	27 Cobalt, Co 59, 2,3, Brandt 1735	28 Nickel, Ni 59, 2,3, Cronstedt 1751
(subgroup b)		29 Copper, Cu 64, 1,2, (Antiquity) [b]	30 Zinc, Zn 65, 2, (Antiquity) [b,a]	31 Gallium, Ga 70, 2,3, Boisbaudran 1875 [b,a]	32 Germanium, Ge 73, 2,4, Winkler 1886 [b,a]	33 Arsenic, As 75, 3,5, Schroder 1649 [b,a]	34 Selenium, Se 79, 2,4,6, Berzelius 1817 [b,a]	35 Bromine, Br 80, −1,5, Balard 1826 [b]			
SECOND LONG PERIOD 37–54	36 Krypton, Kr 84, 0, Ramsay 1898	37 Rubidium, Rb 85, 1,3,5, Bunsen 1860 [a]	38 Strontium, Sr 88, 2, Crawford 1790 [a]	39 Yttrium, Y 89, 3, Gaddlin 1794 [b,a]	40 Zirconium, Zr 91, 4, Klaproth 1789 [b,a]	41 Niobium, Nb 93, 1,2,4,5, Hatchett 1801 [b,a]	42 Molybdenum, Mo 96, 3,4,5,6, Scheele 1778 [b,a]	43 Technetium, Tc 99, 6,7, Perrier 1937 [b,a]	44 Ruthenium, Ru 101, 3,4,6,7, Klaus 1844	45 Rhodium, Rh 103, 2,3,4, Wollaston 1844	46 Palladium, Pd 106, 2,4,6, Wollaston 1803
(subgroup b)		47 Silver, Ag 108, 1, (Antiquity) [b]	48 Cadmium, Cd 112, 2, Stromeyer 1817 [b,a]	49 Indium, In 115, 1,3, Richter 1863 [b,a]	50 Tin, Sn 119, 2,4, (Antiquity) [b,a]	51 Antimony, Sb 122, 3,5, Valentine [b,a]	52 Tellurium, Te 128, 2,4,6, Reichenstein 1782 [b,a]	53 Iodine, I 127, −1,3,5,7, Courtois 1811 [b]			
THIRD LONG PERIOD 55–86	54 Xenon, Xe 131, 0, Ramsay 1898	55 Cesium, Cs 133, 1, Bunsen 1860 [a]	56 Barium, Ba 137, 2, Davy 1808 [a]	57–71 Lanthanide Series (■ Below) [a,b]	72 Hafnium, Hf 178, 4, Coster 1922 [b,a]	73 Tantalum, Ta 181, 2,4,5, Ekeberg 1802 [b,a]	74 Tungsten, W 184, 2,4,5,6, De Elhumars 1783 [b,a]	75 Rhenium, Re 186, −1,4,6,7, Noddack 1925 [b,a]	76 Osmium, Os 190, 2,3,4,6, Tennant 1804	77 Iridium, Ir 192, 3,4, Tennant 1804	78 Platinum, Pt 195, 2,4, Scaliger 1557
(subgroup b)		79 Gold, Au 197, 1,3, (Antiquity) [b]	80 Mercury, Hg 201, 1,2, (Antiquity) [b,a]	81 Thallium, Tl 204, 1,3, Crookes 1861 [b,a]	82 Lead, Pb 207, 2,4, (Antiquity) [b,a]	83 Bismuth, Bi 209, 3,5, Valentine 1450 [b,a]	84 Polonium, Po 209, 2,4, Curies 1898 [b,a]	85 Astatine, At 210, −1,3,5,7, Segre 1940 [b]			
FOURTH LONG PERIOD 87–	86 Radon, Rn 222, 0,2,4, Dorn 1900	87 Francium, Fr 223, 1, Perey 1939	88 Radium, Ra 226, 2, Curies 1898	89–103 Actinides (▲ Below)	104 Transactinides (● Below)						

■ LANTHANIDE SERIES FROM GROUP 3 / RARE EARTHS 57–71

57 Lanthanum La 139, 3, Mosander 1839	58 Cerium Ce 140, 3,4,6, Berzelius 1803	59 Praseodymium Pr 141, 3,4, Welsbach 1885	60 Neodymium Nd 144, 3,4, Welsbach 1885	61 Promethium Pm 145, 3, Marinsky 1947	62 Samarium Sm 150, 2,3, Boisbaudran 1879	63 Europium Eu 152, 2,3, Demarcay 1896	64 Gadolinium Gd 157, 3, Marignac 1886
65 Terbium Tb 159, 3, Mosander 1843	66 Dysprosium Dy 167, 3, Boisbaudran 1886	67 Holmium Ho 165, 3, Cleve 1879	68 Erbium Er 167, 3, Mosander 1843	69 Thulium Tm 169, 3, Cleve 1879	70 Ytterbium Yb 173, 3, Marignac 1878	71 Lutetium Lu 175, 3, Welsbach 1907	

▲ ACTINIDE SERIES FROM GROUP 3 89–103

89 Actinium Ac 227, 3, Debierne 1899	90 Thorium Th 232, 4, Berzelius 1828	91 Protactinium Pa 231, 5, Hahn 1917	92 Uranium U 238, 2,3,4,5, Klaproth 1789	93 Neptunium Np 237, 3,4,5,6, McMillan 1940	94 Plutonium Pu 244, 3,4,5,6, Seaborg 1940	95 Americium Am 243, 3,4,5,6, Seaborg 1944	96 Curium Cm 247, 3, Seaborg 1944
97 Berkelium Bk 247, 3,4, Seaborg 1949	98 Californium Cf 251, 3, Seaborg 1950	99 Einsteinium Es 254, 3, Seaborg 1952	100 Fermium Fm 257, 3, Thompson 1953	101 Mendelevium Md 256, 3, Thompson 1955	102 Nobelium No 264, 3, Ghiorso 1958	103 Lawrencium Lr 260, 3, Ghiorso 1961	

● TRANS-ACTINIDES FROM GROUP 4 104–

104 Unq * Ghiorso 1969	105 Unp * Ghiorso 1970	106 Unh *	107 Uns *	108 (Can Be Made)	109 *

* Unstable

Atomic structure.

The word "valence" is derived from the Latin word *valentia,* which means power. In chemistry, valence refers to an atom's ability or power to combine or react with another atom. Consequently, the structure of an atom determines its power or valence, which is electrical in nature. Scientists have taken atoms apart and determined the differences in electrical makeup and valences that exist between the atoms of different elements.

The atom of any element has three dimensions and occupies space. Our bodies are made up of molecules that are in turn made up by the arrangement of different atoms. We occupy space, so our atoms must also. An atom has a superstructure consisting of a heavy central core that is surrounded by negatively charged particles known as electrons. In contrast, two massive particles reside in the core. One is called a neutron, which is electrically neutral. The other is called a proton; it has a positive charge that is equal in value to the negative charge of an electron.

By indirect but accurate measurements, scientists have found a proton weighs 1.68567×10^{-24} gram, .00000000000000000000168567 gram. In contrast, an electron is 1/1836th as heavy as one proton. Because these numbers are exceedingly cumbersome, they can be converted into smaller atomic mass units (AMUs). One AMU equals 1.6735×10^{-24} gram. On this basis, a proton weighs 1.007276 AMUs; a neutron is generally heavier at 1.008665 AMUs, and an electron weighs 0.0005486 AMU. While helpful, AMUs are also impractical to use.

The charge on an electron has been measured as -1.6021×10^{-19} coulombs. A proton has the same charge, but positive $(+1.6021 \times 10^{-19})$. A neutron is "neutral" (the reason for its name).

Measurements of the diameter of the nucleus are uncertain. At best, the nucleus of an atom is 1/100,000th of the atom's diameter. The nucleus is very dense because it holds most of the atom's mass. In contrast, the electrons occupy most of the space taken up by an atom as they orbit the core in imaginary spherical paths or zones. These paths are designated as major shells; they, in turn, are divided into subshells. It is as if each atom consisted of spherical territories that are constantly traversed by electrons assigned to those spaces.

Electrons are under constant strain because they are simultaneously being attracted by their protons in the nucleus and being repelled by each other. As a result, they are spinning on their own axes while orbiting the nucleus at varying distances from it. This causes the electrons to display magnetic and wavelike properties. No two elements have the same number of electrons or protons. This serves to account for the differences in properties and reactivities between any given elements.

Atomic weights.

Early in the 19th century, some chemists believed that the correct chemical formula for water was HO, because when one part by weight of H (hydrogen) was reacted with eight parts by weight of O (oxygen), nine parts by weight of water resulted. Subsequently, it was shown that reactive gases like hydrogen and oxygen exist in pairs (H_2 and O_2) and not as single atoms. It was also proved that two volumes of hydrogen react exactly with one volume of oxygen to create two volumes of water vapor. The equation was changed to:

$$2H_2 \quad + O_2 \rightarrow \quad 2H_2O$$
$$2 \text{ vols} \ + 1 \text{ vol} \quad = 2 \text{ vols}$$
$$4 \text{ parts} + 32 \text{ parts} = 36 \text{ parts}$$

Since one atom of oxygen equals $1/2$ (O_2), its correct weight must be 16 parts and not eight. Thousands of experiments proved this to be the case. In 1858, oxygen was assigned an atomic weight of 16, and the weight of all other elements was calculated relative to it. Keep in mind that combining weights (eight parts of oxygen react with one part of hydrogen, or 16 parts of oxygen react with two parts of hydrogen, etc.) do not directly reveal the makeup of atoms. Measures are relative and based on an agreed supportable standard.

For example, on an equal volume basis, oxygen was found to be 1.332 times heavier than carbon, which meant that the latter had a relative weight of 12.011. Because carbon is involved in more reactions than oxygen, chemists decided to use it as the relative weight standard instead of oxygen. They arbitrarily set the value of carbon at 12.000, which is 11.905 times heavier than hydrogen. This resulted in a relative weight value of 1.0079 for hydrogen (12/11.905) as compared with 1.008 when oxygen was employed as the standard. The relative weights of all the other elements were subsequently recalculated accordingly.

Isotopes.

An isotope is an atom of an element that is heavier or lighter than the normal distribution of atoms for a given element. For example, investigations showed that a small percentage of a given distribution of atoms of an element had variances in weight and stability. Some were lighter, others were heavier, because they had either more or fewer neutrons in their nuclei. This caused these atoms to display varying degrees of stability as they attempted to rearrange their structures to the more stable ones of atoms having an equal number of neutrons and protons.

Manmade elements tend to be very unstable; as a result, half of their mass decays in seconds. Some isotopes emit radiation, or half of their atoms decay over a given period of time (some in seconds, others in millions of years). Such a time frame is called the half life of an isotope. The atomic weights shown for the elements in the Periodic Table are an average, which is heavily influenced by the preponderance of stable atoms. All isotopes of a given element have the same number of protons and electrons. The number of neutrons in a stable atom is equal to the difference between its atomic weight and its atomic number.

How atoms react.

The atomic number of an element in the Periodic Table is equal to the number of electrons it contains, which is also equal to the number of protons it holds in its nucleus. The element is, therefore, neutral. For example, the elements in group 18 show the following atomic numbers: 2 for He; 10 for Ne; 18 for Ar; 36 for Kr; 54 for Xe; and 86 for Rn. These numbers represent the total number of electrons each of these noble gases holds around its nucleus. Each also contains an equal number of protons in its nucleus. Neon, Ne, has ten orbiting electrons but also has ten protons in its nucleus. The chart on page 407 shows the simple structures for the first three elements in the ta-

CARBON DATING

Carbon dating is a method of determining the age of prehistoric objects by measuring the amount of the radioisotope carbon-14 in them.

Carbon-14 enters tissue of living organism.

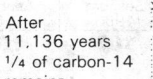

Intake of carbon-14 stops at death.

After 5,568 years only 1/2 of carbon-14 remains.

After 11,136 years 1/4 of carbon-14 remains.

THE STRUCTURE OF ATOMS

Atoms contain an equal number of protons (+) and electrons (−). Electrons circle the nucleus in orbits called shells.

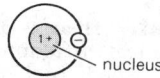

HYDROGEN
(H)
one proton

nucleus

HELIUM
(He)
two protons

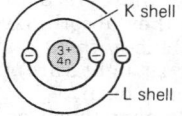

LITHIUM
(Li)
three protons

K shell

L shell

OXYGEN $1s^2 + 2s^2 + 2p^4$

shorthand
notation

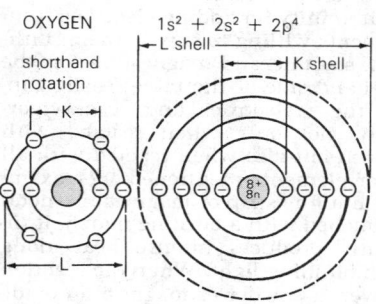

NEON

$1s^2 + 2s^2 + 2p^6$

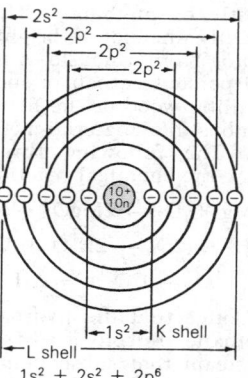

NOTE: Though represented here as circles, electron shells are actually spherical.

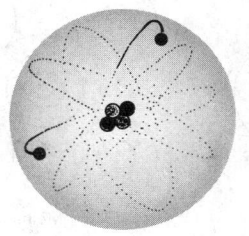

ble, hydrogen, helium, and lithium. The pictorial reveals that the nuclei of these atoms are surrounded by imaginary spherical shells containing orbital paths for the electrons. The first, or K, shell has but one orbital path, 1s. When it is filled with two electrons, as is the case with helium, it results in a stable electron configuration. The next imaginary spherical shell is L, which has four subshells designated as 2s plus *three* 2p's. When all the L subshells are filled, they contain a total of eight electrons. A stable configuration is again achieved. Neon has an atomic number of 10 and has its K shell filled with two electrons and its L shell with eight, which makes it extremely inert and stable.

The hydrogen atom has but one electron in its K shell, while lithium has two electrons in its K shell but only one in the 2s orbital of its L shell. What happens if lithium loses its solitary outer electron and hydrogen loses its electron? As the chart shows, on losing an electron, hydrogen becomes charged positively because its single proton is no longer neutralized. When lithium loses its outer electron in its L shell, it exposes a stable K shell just like the one in helium, except that it still has three protons and now only two electrons. It becomes a charged ion, Li^{+1}, having one positive charge. Its K shell cannot lose electrons; neither can helium's.

What happens if hydrogen gains an electron? Its K shell becomes filled, but now it has two electrons to one proton. The hydrogen atom turns into a negatively charged ion, H^{-1}. What would happen if a positively charged lithium ion (Li^{+1}) and a negatively charged hydrogen ion (H^{-1}) were to meet? Each would have the "power" to react one-to-one to neutralize its charges. The result is lithium hydride, LiH. Remember, however, that the preponderance of reactions involving hydrogen are with its positively charged ion, H^{+1} (also referred to as a proton because hydrogen has only one proton in its nucleus).

What are the configurations of some heavier elements? The illustrations at right show the electronic configurations for neon and oxygen found in the second period. A top view of the three-dimensional configuration is displayed. For simplicity, the shorthand notation (as shown for oxygen) may be used to consolidate the L shell electrons into one outer shell. Notice that the K shells of both atoms are filled with two electrons spinning in opposite directions around their axes (one spins clockwise; the other counterclockwise). The L shell occupies space around the K shell. The space within the L shell is further divided into four orbital paths or subshells, that is, 2s, 2p, 2p, and 2p. In the case of neon, each subshell is completely filled. Superscripts indicate the number of electrons in each subshell. Therefore,

neon's electronic structure is represented as

$$1s^2 + 2s^2 + 2p^6.$$

(This is a not a mathematical notation.) These "extra" subshells exist because only two electrons having opposite spins can exist in the same elliptical path. This is known as the Pauli exclusion principle.

If the L shell in an oxygen atom gains two electrons, its structure becomes like neon's. However, the oxygen atom is no longer neutral, for it now has a total of ten electrons (eight in its outer L shell and two in its K shell) and eight protons in its nucleus. Therefore, it becomes a charged oxygen atom represented as O^{-2}, or with an excess negative charge of −2. Where does oxygen get its excess electrons? From any other element, with the exception of the noble or inert gases, whose structure makes them unreactive. What happens if four atoms of hydrogen are each induced to give up one of their outer electrons (for a total of four electrons) to two oxygen atoms that they contact? Water is formed. A spark induces the reaction. The hydrogen atoms are oxidized. The two oxygen atoms gain or share the four electrons from the hydrogen atoms. The reaction is summarized in the following set of equations.

A. $2H_2 - 4e- \rightarrow 4H^{+1}$

B. $O_2 + 4e- \rightarrow 2O^{-2}$

Add A. and B. to get C.

C. $2H_2 + O_2 \rightarrow 2H_2O$

IONS

Ions are atoms that have become charged through the gain or loss of electrons.

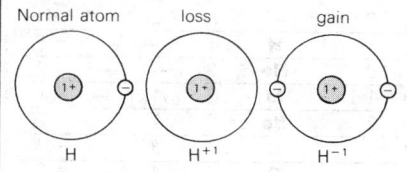

Normal atom   loss   gain

H H^{+1} H^{-1}

ISOTOPES

Isotopes are atoms with a smaller or larger number of neutrons than normal. Hydrogen has three isotopes.

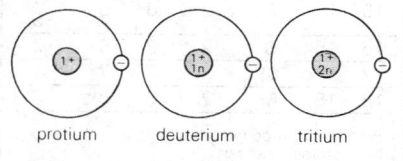

protium   deuterium   tritium

The examples suggest that only atoms having unfilled outer shells are capable of creating a reaction. In the process of the reaction, electrons may be gained or lost to imitate a stable configuration. As a result, the atoms involved become charged or ionized. It is the charged state of an ion that determines its valence or power to combine with other oppositely charged ions. In order to create a neutral molecule, the number of negative and positive charges must add up to zero, as shown in equations A. and B. on the previous page. The table below summarizes the electrons in the K, L, and some in the M, shells for the atoms of the first 18 elements in the Periodic Table. Note that this chart contains all of the reactive gases that exist as paired or diatomic molecules at 25° C. These gases are hydrogen (H_2), oxygen (O_2), fluorine (F_2), and chlorine (Cl_2). Nitrogen (N_2) becomes reactive at high temperatures.

How is the chart used? For example, fluorine is shown as having a negative valence of -1 because it can gain one electron to fill its outer L shell to the stable configuration of eight electrons. When it does so, it achieves a charged state and becomes a fluoride ion, F^{-1}. In contrast, sodium (Na) has a valence of $+1$ because it can lose an electron from its M shell so that it has a stable configuration of eight outer electrons in its L shell. This turns it into a positively charged ion, Na^{+1}. Each atom of fluorine can attract one electron from a sodium atom if they are in contact. Since fluorine gas exists as F_2, two atoms become ionized as $2F^{-1}$ while two atoms of sodium (a solid at 25°C)

become ionized to $2Na^{+1}$. They react to form sodium fluoride, NaF. The equation is properly shown and balanced as follows:

A. $2Na - 2e- \rightarrow 2Na^{+1}$

B. $F + 2e- \rightarrow 2F^{-1}$

C. $2Na + F \rightarrow 2NaF$

Carbon and silicon can each have a positive valence of $+4$ or a negative valence of -4. If they gain four electrons, they achieve a stable outer configuration of eight electrons, and both become negative ions, C^{-4} and Si^{-4}. But if they lose four electrons, they become positively charged ions, C^{+4} and Si^{+4}. Carbon achieves a stable configuration of two electrons in its exposed K shell, while silicon exposes the eight electrons in its L shell. Some of the major reactions of both elements are separately covered in the segments on ''Organic Chemistry'' on page 419 and ''Silicone Chemistry'' on page 424.

The potential valence numbers or charges of the elements in the long periods of the table are best accepted from published values. As elements get heavier, the number of their major shells and contained orbits increases. Seven major shells exist (K, L, M, N, O, P, and Q). The M shell has the following subshells; 1s, 2s, 2p, 3s, 3p, and 3d. The Q shell is made up of 18 subshells.

Covalency and ionization.

Once reacted, certain atoms can also share electrons, either among themselves or with other atoms to achieve the simulated stability of a filled K or L shell. After it is formed, the water molecule is predominantly covalently bonded. Many organic molecules, like methane (CH_4), are completely covalently bonded because they do not conduct electricity. The reactive gases exist as diatomic molecules, which are covalently bonded. However, the molecules of strong metal salts (like lithium chloride) conduct electricity because they retain an ionic character (like $Li^{+1} Cl^{-1}$). Such combinations are said to have an *ionic bond*. Although water is mostly covalently bonded, it is a weak conductor of electricity. This

indicates that its bonding is partially ionic. Many other inorganic and organic compounds exhibit this dual behavior.

Heat and Gases

Heat. Heat is the byproduct of a chemical reaction. The burning of coal, wood, fuel oil, and natural gas are examples of chemical reactions that produce heat. However, intense light and heat are also created by igniting an active metal such as magnesium in the presence of air. All of these ignitions have one thing in common: they are oxidized. This means that they absorb oxygen from the air, combine with it, and produce heat as well as light (fire). Oxidation causes them to burn.

Elements such as oxygen, fluorine, sulfur, and phosphorus (on the right-hand side of the Periodic Table) have a great affinity for adding electrons from elements willing to supply them. Lithium, sodium, and magnesium (on the left-hand side of the table) easily supply these electrons and react vigorously, not only when reacted with oxygen but also when reacted with all other elements mentioned. For example, if a fine strip of magnesium metal is touched with a burning match, it instantly produces intense heat along with blinding light. When the reaction is over, a powder of magnesium oxide (MgO) remains. On the other hand, after ignition, natural gas (consisting mostly of methane, CH_4) will burn steadily and not so brightly when escaping from a nozzle. Anthracite coal (80 percent carbon or more) requires kindling wood or the firing of a more combustible material before it flares up. The following three equations show the chemical reactions involved.

$2Mg + O_2 \rightarrow 2MgO - \Delta H$

$CH_4 + 2O_2 \rightarrow 2H_2O + CO_2 \uparrow - \Delta H$

$C + O_2 \rightarrow CO_2 \uparrow - \Delta H$

Notice that the hydrogen atoms of methane are converted into molecules of steam that subsequently may con-

ELECTRONS IN SHELLS K, L, AND M; FIRST 18 ELEMENTS

GP	AN	AS	K	L	M	V
1	1	**H**	1	—	—	±1
18	2	**He**	2	—	—	0
1	3	**Li**	2	1	—	+1
2	4	**Be**	2	2	—	+2
13	5	**B**	2	3	—	+3
14	6	**C**	2	4	—	±4
15	7	**N**	2	5	—	−3 +5
16	8	**O**	2	6	—	−2
17	9	**F**	2	7	—	−1
18	10	**Ne**	2	8	—	0
1	11	**Na**	2	8	1	+1
2	12	**Mg**	2	8	2	+2
13	13	**Al**	2	8	3	+3
14	14	**Si**	2	8	4	±4
15	15	**P**	2	8	5	−3 +5
16	16	**S**	2	8	6	−2
17	17	**Cl**	2	8	7	−1
18	18	**Ar**	2	8	8	0

GP = group in periodic table
AN = atomic number
AS = atomic symbol

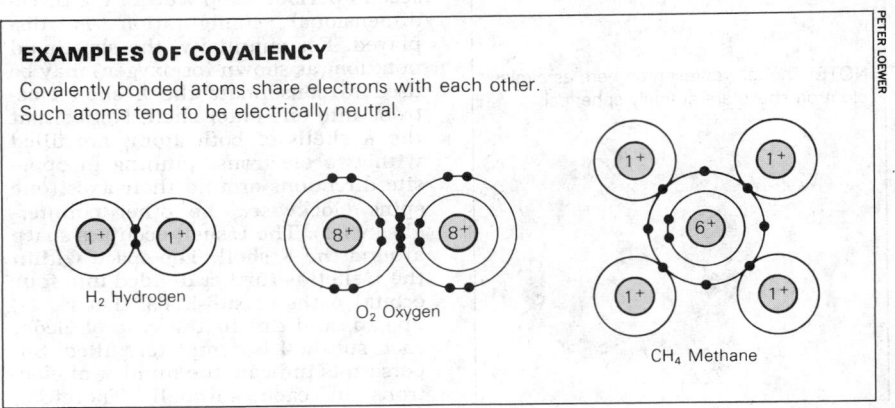

EXAMPLES OF COVALENCY

Covalently bonded atoms share electrons with each other. Such atoms tend to be electrically neutral.

H_2 Hydrogen

O_2 Oxygen

CH_4 Methane

PETER LOEWER

dense. The carbon dioxide (CO_2) escapes into the atmosphere as indicated by the upward arrows (↑). The evolution of heat in an equation is indicated by the symbol $-\Delta H$. Any reaction that produces heat is called exothermic, while one that absorbs heat from its surroundings is known as endothermic. In all three reactions, oxygen causes combustion along with the creation of light. The "burning" or reacting atoms of magnesium, carbon, and hydrogen combine with oxygen and are oxidized.

The heat of a reaction refers to the amount of heat liberated or absorbed during a chemical change. Most reactions produce only heat. The heat of combustion refers to reactions that yield both heat and fire (light). For example, the heat of combustion for burning 1 gram of carbon with 2.66 grams of oxygen is 7833 calories.

Scientists have measured the amount of heat necessary to raise the temperature of 1 gram of water by 1° C. This quantity of heat is called one *calorie;* it is also referred to as heat capacity or specific heat. The calorie is employed as a standard to measure the specific heats of materials. For instance, if two calories are required to raise the temperature of a gram of a given material by 1° C, then its specific heat is twice as great as that of water and is listed as 2 cals/g° C.

Specific heats are used in conjuction with heats of combustion to calculate the amount of fuel required to raise the temperature of a given quantity of matter. One hundred grams of water may be heated from 10° C to 90° C by burning 1.023 grams of carbon. The required heat is calculated as follows:

$$90° \text{ C} - 10° \text{ C}$$
$$\times 1 \text{ cal/g}° \text{ C}$$
$$\times 100 \text{ grams}$$
$$= 8000 \text{ needed calories.}$$

One gram of burning carbon supplies 7817 calories, therefore, 8000/7817 or 1.023 grams of carbon are necessary.

Physical changes.

A physical change occurs when an atom or a molecule is transformed to a different phase of matter, such as from frozen water (ice) to liquid, or liquid to gas (steam when water is involved), without a change in composition or in structural identity. No loss or gain of electrons occurs. The given particles of the same element remain the same during their physical transformation. The change can also be reversible, that is, from gas to liquid to solid. If the water molecule (H_2O) is involved, it remains as the same molecule regardless of how many transformations or physical changes it undergoes. The same applies to an atom of iron (Fe) or any other atom or molecule.

However, a material does undergo a change in its physical behavior. As-

sume that a cube of ice weighing 18 grams is at −10° C. What is the condition of the molecules that make up this piece of ice at this temperature? Not unlike other solids, the cube feels hard and has shape. If allowed to stand over a period of time, its surface dimensions would undergo some slight changes. If 18 calories of heat were added, the surface changes would accelerate as 0 ° C was reached. Then, surprisingly, the temperature would remain at 0° C until 1440 more calories were absorbed by the "sweating" ice. Eventually, it would completely lose its shape and become the familiar liquid we all recognize. The great amount of heat absorbed at 0° C (the melting point of ice) is called the heat of fusion. The temperature continues to rise quickly by 1° C for every 18 calories of heat consumed by the liquid. At 70° C, vapors more noticeably escape from the surface. Then, suddenly again, the temperature stops rising at 100° C until the water absorbs 9720 calories. Intense boiling occurs as the liquid turns into gas (steam), rising into the atmosphere, then condensing back to a liquid as it cools. The great quantity of heat consumed at 100° C is called the heat of vaporization.

No new molecules were formed; no chemical reactions occurred. It was the increased motion of the water molecules, and their huge absorption of calories at 0° C and 100° C that accelerated their motion as they passed from one phase of matter into another. On cooling, steam first gives up its heat of vaporization (540 cals/gram) before turning into a liquid. The liquid surrenders its heat of fusion (80 cals/gram) at 0° C before turning into ice. The molecules have dramatically slowed down. Yet, as long as molecules contain heat, they either exhibit motion or vibration. But not all molecules exhibit uniform movement. Those at the surface of ice or on a body of the liquid tend to pull away and evaporate. This is how clouds form and then condense into rain as atmospheric conditions change. These kinds of physical changes are common in varying degrees to all molecules and atoms.

Gases.

What do oxygen, hydrogen, nitrogen, and all other gases have in common? The answer is that the molecules of all gases are in constant motion and that an equal number of molecules of any gas occupy the same volume at standard temperature and pressure (STP); that is, at 0° C and at a pressure of one atmosphere or 760 torrs (1034 grams per square centimeter). At STP, 22.4 liters of oxygen weigh 32 grams, 22.4 liters of hydrogen weigh 2 grams, and 22.4 liters of nitrogen weigh 28 grams, or twice the known values of their atomic weights. In contrast, helium weighs 4 grams, neon 20 grams, and argon 40 grams, all of which are the exact atomic weights of these three noble gases. The explanation for this is that at STP, each 22.4 liters holds 6.024×10^{23} particles. In the case of hydrogen, oxygen, and nitrogen, two atoms of each are covalently bonded as a molecular particle. In contrast, because of their great stability and inertness, helium, neon, and argon exist as single atomic particles.

Another important feature that gases have in common is that their volume at 0° C contracts by 1/273rd of its original value for each degree Celsius that the temperature drops. This suggests that if the temperature were to drop to −273° C, a gas would have no volume. What this actually means is that no further heat exists below −273° C because the molecular motion of the gases no longer exists. Experiments have shown that this is actually the case.

The general relationship among the pressure, volume, mass, and temperature of a gas is expressed as

$$PV = nRT.$$

P is expressed in atmospheres of pressure (1 atm = 760 millimeters of mercury = 760 torrs; 1 torr = 1/760 mm); V is in liters; n = the mass of the gas in grams divided by its molecular weight in grams (n stands for moles); R is a constant having the value 0.08821 liters per degree Kelvin per mole; and T is in degrees Kelvin (degrees Celsius + 273 = degrees Kelvin). Other relationships are found on page 401 under "History."

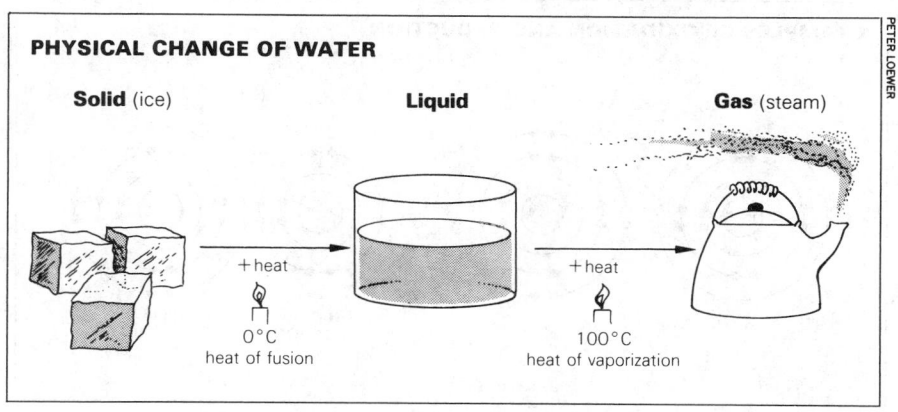

PHYSICAL CHANGE OF WATER

Solid (ice)   **Liquid**   **Gas** (steam)

+heat   0°C   heat of fusion

+heat   100°C   heat of vaporization

PETER LOEWER

Gases have many uses. For example, oxygen sustains life, causes combustion, and is needed to make metal oxides, sugars, oxygenated solvents, water, acids, bases, and a wide range of other organic and silicone compounds. Hydrogen is needed to make all organic and silicone compounds, ammonia, mineral acids, and water. Nitrogen forms an inert atmosphere at ordinary temperatures. It is also used to make ammonia, organic derivatives, and fertilizers. Fluorine is used to make refrigerants and fluoroplastics. With the exception of radioactive radon, the noble gases result in nonreactive environments. The atoms of neon can be electrically excited to produce "neon lights."

Oxidation and Reduction

Oxidation is defined as a loss of electrons by any atom to another in a chemical reaction. For example, in the course of reacting with chlorine, a sodium atom loses an electron and turns into a positively charged ion of sodium, expressed as Na^{+1}. Chemically, the neutral atom becomes an ion:

$$Na - e- \rightarrow Na^{+1},$$

where "e" stands for an electron.

Reduction is defined as a gain in electrons by an atom in a chemical reaction. In the above example, the chlorine atom pulls away and gains an electron from a sodium atom; it becomes a negatively charged ion, Cl^{-1}. Chemically this is shown as

$$Cl + e- \rightarrow Cl^{-1}.$$

By convention, chlorine is said to be reduced. The mechanism of the reaction is summarized below.

Oxidation: $2Na - 2e- \rightarrow 2Na^{+1}$
Reduction: $2Cl + 2e- \rightarrow 2Cl^{-1}$
Reaction: $2Na + Cl_2 \rightarrow 2NaCl$

The loss and gain of electrons by the atoms of elements are described on page 406. The valence number of an element identifies the possible charged state, $(+)$ or $(-)$, of its atoms either on losing or gaining electrons. Consequently, a knowledge of valence numbers helps the chemist to predict hypothetical reactions (chemical changes). The changes take place only by the sharing, gain, and loss of electrons.

The concept of oxidation and reduction that is stated above is broader and more correct than the traditional but narrow principle that an element becomes oxidized upon the addition of oxygen. All metals oxidize, although some oxidize more strongly than others (cesium reacts violently with oxygen; gold reacts very sluggishly with oxygen). The traditional principle also states that reduction occurs when a molecule loses its oxygen and some or all of its component atoms are returned or reduced to their original states. This is partially correct, for example, when mercuric oxide (HgO) is heated. Mercury is reduced to its original state as the metal mercury (Hg). However, oxygen is also liberated and returned to its original state as O_2. If the modern concept of oxidation and reduction is applied to this reaction, oxygen is actually oxidized because it loses electrons.

Oxidation: $2O^{-2} - 2e- \rightarrow O_2$
Reduction: $2Hg^{+2} + 2e- \rightarrow 2Hg$
Reaction: $2HgO \rightarrow O_2\uparrow + 2Hg$

Unlike mercury, some metals are very difficult to reduce. The active metals, like cesium and calcium, do not readily give up their oxygen. Others are easier to reduce. Silver and gold readily surrender their oxygen and take it back only slowly. Additionally, the traditional view could not account conveniently for reactions that did not involve oxygen. That is why the valence concept (the loss and gain of electrons by any atoms, instead of only the loss or gain of oxygen in a particular reaction) is considered more comprehensive.

Some rules. In judging whether an element has been oxidized or whether it has been reduced, the following assumptions must be made.

1. Any element that takes on oxygen is oxidized.
2. Any compound or molecule that loses oxygen is reduced (an element is separated from its combined oxygen in the compound).
3. Oxygen has a negative valence (excess electrons) charge represented as O^{-2}. Hydrogen has a positive valence (a free proton), shown as H^{+1}. However, if hydrogen is exclusively combined with a metal (for example, LiH or NaH), then it has a negative valence (an excess electron) charge of -1, displayed as H^{-1}.
4. Fluorine (F), chlorine (Cl), bromine (Br), and iodine (I) each has a negative valence of -1. (Exceptions exist for Cl, Br, and I.)
5. The noble gases (helium, neon, argon, krypton, xenon, and radon) are unreactive.
6. The reactive metals lithium (Li), sodium (Na), potassium (K), rubidium (Rb), cesium (Cs), and francium (Fr) each has a positive valence of $+1$.
7. Oxidation and reduction occur simultaneously as indicated in the above examples. The sum of all negative and positive charges must cancel out and be equal to zero.
8. The reactive gases (hydrogen, oxygen, nitrogen, fluorine, and chlorine) exist as diatomic molecules in their natural states (H_2, O_2, N_2, F_2, and Cl_2).
9. Elements in group 2 in the long form of the Periodic Table have a positive valence of $+2$. Aluminum (Al) and boron (B) each has a positive valence of $+3$.
10. Carbon and silicon may each have a valence state that is $+4$ or -4. Exceptions exist.

Consider the following example in calculating the correct molecular formula for calcium oxide (CaO). Ca is oxidized. The initial equation might be considered as $Ca + O_2$, because oxygen always exists as a diatomic molecule $\rightarrow CaO_2$. Does one atom of calcium combine with one molecule of oxygen to yield a molecule containing one atom of calcium joined to two atoms of oxygen? Check the Periodic Table. Ca is in the fourth period in group 2. It has a positive valence of $+2$, which means that an atom of calcium gives up two electrons. This is written as:

$$Ca - 2e- \rightarrow Ca^{+2}$$

But oxygen is assumed to have a negative valence of -2 per atom. Each atom accepts two electrons. However, a molecule of oxygen has two atoms of oxygen. Therefore:

$$O_2 + 4e- \rightarrow 2O^{-2}$$

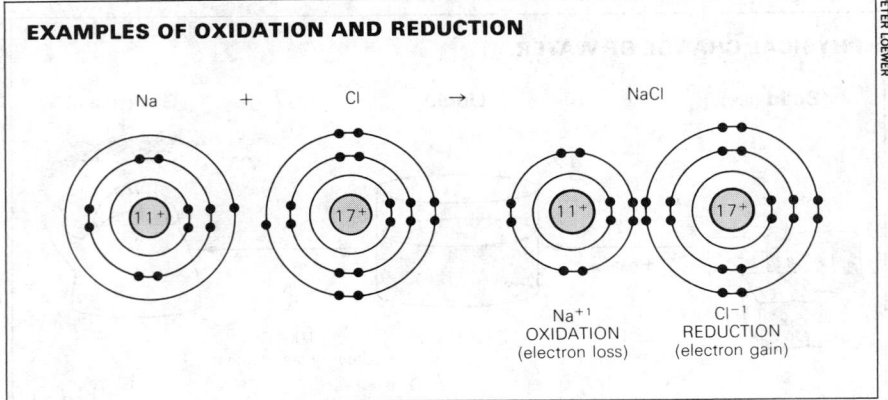

EXAMPLES OF OXIDATION AND REDUCTION

Na   +   Cl   →   NaCl

Na^{+1}
OXIDATION
(electron loss)

Cl^{-1}
REDUCTION
(electron gain)

PETER LOEWER

OXYGEN CORRODES *exposed metal. Electrochemistry is used to apply a protective coating to this car body.*

Combine the two ionic equations and examine them.

$$O_2 + 4e- \rightarrow 2O^{-2}$$
$$(2 \times (-2) = 4e-)$$

$$Ca - 2e- \rightarrow Ca^{+2}$$
$$(1 \times (+2) = 2e-)$$

The number of exchanged electrons between the two ionic equations does not add up to zero (they do not cancel out $4e- - 2e- = 2e-$). Another atom of calcium is needed.

Reduction:	$O_2 + 4e-$	$\rightarrow 2O^{-2}$
Oxidation:	$Ca - 2e-$	$\rightarrow Ca^{+2}$
Oxidation:	$Ca - 2e-$	$\rightarrow Ca^{+2}$
Reaction:	$2Ca + O_2$	$\rightarrow 2CaO$

Each atom of oxygen gains two electrons and is reduced while each atom of calcium loses two electrons and is oxidized. Four major reactions involving oxidation and reduction are further illustrated below.

Electrolytic. Aluminum metal is reduced from its oxide (Al_2O_3) when reacted with carbon. The latter is made into an electrode with one end of a high-power electrical line connected to it. The aluminum oxide is then dissolved in an electrolyte that conducts an electrical current. The electrolyte separates the carbon anode, or electrode, from its counterpart, the cathode. The other end of the high-power line is attached to the cathode. When a huge current is applied, a temperature of 1000° C develops between the electrodes because the electrolyte is a weak conductor of electricity. At that temperature, the carbon anode, which is positively charged, reacts with the oxygen combined with the aluminum. The latter is released as an ion, Al^{+3}, and is attracted to the other end of the electrical line, the cathode, which is negatively charged with the electrons lost by the carbon making up the anode. The aluminum ion (Al^{+3}) gains those electrons, is reduced to its original state, and is collected as molten aluminum. The reaction is summarized as follows:

$$2Al_2O_3 + 3C \rightarrow 4Al + 3CO_2$$

The carbon anode is oxidized and is progressively destroyed as it converts to gaseous carbon dioxide. A single atom of carbon loses four electrons as it is oxidized and combines with two atoms of oxygen, each of which already has a negative charge of -2.

Thermal. Iron ore in the form of ferric oxide (Fe_2O_3) is heated with carbon monoxide (CO) at 1500° C in a blast furnace to separate the iron from its combined oxygen.

$$Fe_2O_3 + 3CO \rightarrow 2Fe + 3CO_2 \uparrow$$

The iron is reduced from its oxide to Fe, and carbon monoxide is further oxidized to carbon dioxide, which escapes as a gas.

Low energy. At room temperature, iron is easily oxidized to ferric oxide or rust (it is the same ingredient as found in the ore).

$$4Fe + 3O_2 \rightarrow 2Fe_2O_3$$

The oxygen of the air is reduced while the iron that it is in contact with is oxidized.

Catalytic. A catalyst is an ingredient that may be used to speed up a reaction or, in some cases, slow it down. However, the catalyst itself does not become part of the reaction. It simply induces it. Enzymes, which are complex organic compounds, are valuable catalysts. Our bodies contain multiple varieties of enzymes to quickly, accurately, and painlessly convert the oxygen we inhale into the carbon dioxide we exhale. In a simpler fashion, the enzyme zymase converts sugar into an alcohol.

$C_6H_{12}O_6$ with zymase $\rightarrow$
$$2C_2H_5OH + 2CO_2 \uparrow$$

(C_2H_5OH is ethyl alcohol, while $C_6H_{12}O_6$ is the molecular formula for a sugar.)

In the above reaction, the sugar loses oxygen and is reduced to an alcohol, while part of the carbon that is contained in the sugar is oxidized to carbon dioxide.

Electrochemistry

Two major segments make up electrochemistry: the creation of electrical energy (voltage and current) as a result of a chemical reaction; and the application of electrical energy to create a chemical change. Flashlight and car batteries are examples of the first type of electrochemistry (creation of electrical energy); the plating of silver on iron is an example of the second (applying electrical energy). The processes of oxidation and reduction are involved in all of the reactions of electrochemistry.

Batteries. The principle of creating electricity from a chemical reaction is based on the ability of one metal to replace another from its oxides or its salts in a water solution. For example, zinc metal in the form of strips will replace copper from copper sulfate ($CuSO_2$); so will sodium, lithium, and any other metal more active than copper. The relative activity of some metals is found below in the chart of the electromotive series.

THE ELECTROMOTIVE SERIES

Elements are arranged in their capacity to reduce others from their salts.
Cesium (Cs) is the strongest reducer.

				EMF
Cs	$= Cs^+$	$+$	$e-$	$+3.02$
Li	$= Li^+$	$+$	$e-$	$+3.02$
K	$= K^+$	$+$	$e-$	$+2.92$
Ba	$= Ba^{++}$		$+2e-$	$+2.92$
Ca	$= Ca^{++}$		$+2e-$	$+2.87$
Na	$= Na^+$	$+$	$e-$	$+2.71$
Mg	$= Mg^{++}$		$+2e-$	$+2.34$
Al	$= Al^{+++}$		$+3e-$	$+1.70$
Zn	$= Zn^{++}$		$+2e-$	$+1.67$
Cr	$= Cr^{+++}$		$+3e-$	$+0.76$
Fe	$= Fe^{+++}$		$+3e-$	$+0.44$
Cd	$= Cd^{++}$		$+2e-$	$+0.40$
Co	$= Co^{++}$		$+2e-$	$+0.28$
Ni	$= Ni^{++}$		$+2e-$	$+0.25$
Sn	$= Sn^{++}$		$+2e-$	$+0.14$
Pb	$= Pb^{++}$		$+2e-$	$+0.13$
H₂	$= 2H^+$		$+2e-$	0.00
Cu	$= Cu^{++}$		$+2e-$	-0.34
Ag	$= Ag^+$	$+$	$e-$	-0.80
Hg	$= Hg^+$	$+$	$e-$	-0.85

A cell constructed from an electrode made of zinc metal, which is immersed in a solution of copper sulfate, and a second made from copper metal (Cu) provides a voltage of 1.1 volts when connected to a voltmeter. However, if zinc sulfate ($ZnSO_4$) is employed, no reaction occurs. In the first instance, zinc metal is oxidized,

$$Zn - 2e- \rightarrow Zn^{+2};$$

copper is removed from copper sulfate and reduced,

$$Cu^{+2} + 2e- \rightarrow Cu.$$

Similar experiments have shown the ability of other metals and nonmetals to become oxidized and to reduce other elements. This was firmly established in forming the electromotive series, a small segment of which is shown on page 411. The voltage values are relative to hydrogen set at zero. Any metal at the top of the list reduces any metal below it. The net voltage values for a reaction can be calculated as follows:

$$Zn - 2e = Zn^{+2} +0.76 \text{ volts}$$
$$\text{(oxidized)}$$
$$Cu^{+2} + 2e = Cu +0.34 \text{ volts}$$
$$\text{(reduced)}$$
$$Zn + Cu^{+2} =$$
$$Zn^{+2} + Cu +1.1 \text{ volts}$$

The chart shows the reaction for copper as

$$Cu = Cu^{++} + 2e- \quad -0.34 \text{ volt},$$

which indicates oxidation. Since copper is being reduced, the reaction as shown is reversed along with the voltage, which becomes +0.34 volt instead of −0.34 volt.

The differences in reactivities between metals and nonmetals are utilized to make batteries, which are either primary (nonrechargeable, for example, flashlight cells) or secondary (chargeable, for example, car batteries). All batteries have three major components: *electrodes* or poles that collect and pump electrons through an external circuit; *electrolytes* that conduct electrons through an internal circuit; and materials that supply *electrons*. The electrons are generated in an oxidation/reduction reaction such as the following in a standard flashlight battery.

When a flashlight or transistor radio is connected between the positive and negative terminals, the atoms of the outer zinc plate become ionized. They give up electrons that travel through the negative electrode, energize the flashlight or radio, pass on to the positive electrode, and become absorbed by manganese ions. The electrolyte completes the circuit; a permeable membrane between the electrolyte and the discharging zinc plate allows the passage of current, but prevents direct contact between the zinc plate and the electrolyte. This substantially increases the service life of the cell. The

PETER LOEWER

BATTERIES

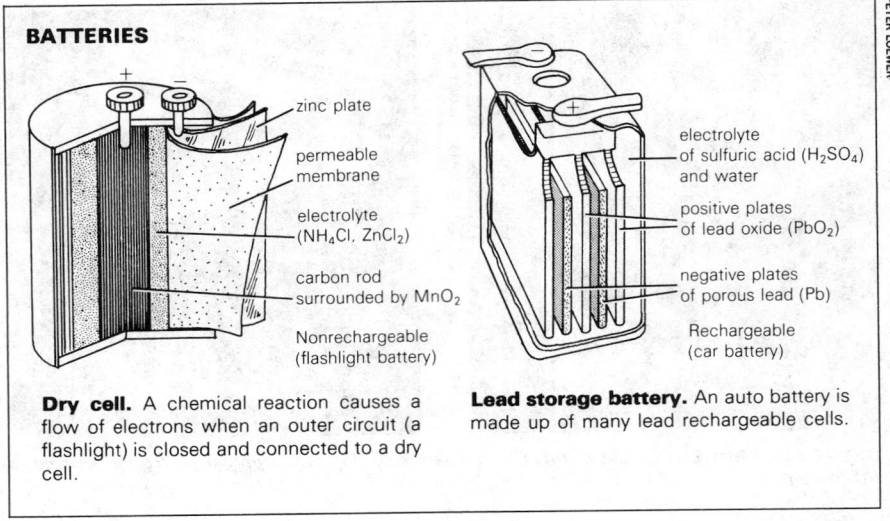

zinc plate

permeable membrane

electrolyte (NH_4Cl, $ZnCl_2$)

carbon rod surrounded by MnO_2

Nonrechargeable (flashlight battery)

Dry cell. A chemical reaction causes a flow of electrons when an outer circuit (a flashlight) is closed and connected to a dry cell.

electrolyte of sulfuric acid (H_2SO_4) and water

positive plates of lead oxide (PbO_2)

negative plates of porous lead (Pb)

Rechargeable (car battery)

Lead storage battery. An auto battery is made up of many lead rechargeable cells.

reaction that created the current is summarized as follows:

$$Zn + 2NH_4Cl + 2MnO_2 \rightleftarrows$$
$$Zn(NH_3)_2Cl + H_2O + Mn_2O_3$$

Oxidation: $\quad Zn - 2e- \rightarrow Zn^{+2}$
Reduction: $Mn^{+4} + 2e- \rightarrow Mn^{+2}$

The ammonium chloride is the electrolyte; it undergoes no oxidation or reduction but loses hydrogen that combines with the part of the oxygen lost by manganese dioxide to form water. This is called a dry cell. When the zinc is used up or insufficient MnO_2 exists, the cell is used up and cannot be recharged.

In contrast, a rechargeable car battery has an electrolyte that is a 38 percent mixture of sulfuric acid by weight in water. As the illustration below shows, the positive plate of a cell is lead dioxide (PbO_2), while the negative plate is "spongy" (porous) lead metal (Pb). The negative and positive terminals are connected to exterior devices that when "turned on" establish a circuit for the movement of electrons. This results in the flow of an electric current.

The reactions are as follows:

$$PbO_2 + H_2SO_4 \rightleftarrows$$
$$PbSO_4 + H_2O + 1/2)O_2$$

Reduction: $Pb^{+4} + 2e- \rightarrow Pb^{+2}$
$$Pb + H_2SO \rightleftarrows$$
$$PbSO_4 + H_2$$

Oxidation: $\quad Pb - 2e- \rightarrow Pb^{+2}$

The two reactions can be combined:

$$PbO_2 + Pb + 2H_2SO_4 \rightleftarrows$$
$$2PbSO_4 + 2H_2O$$

When all of the lead and lead dioxide have been reacted to lead sulfate, the cell ceases to yield an electric current. The battery is "dead." However, if an electric current is applied to its terminals from another battery or generator, the lead sulfate is reconverted back to lead, sulfuric acid, and lead dioxide. The battery is then recharged, or "alive." One cell in a car battery

provides 2 volts of electricity, while a flashlight dry cell provides 1.3 to 1.5 volts. Car batteries and dry cells supply only direct current. An automobile generator constantly keeps its battery recharged with direct current.

Electrolysis. In electrolysis, a direct current generator or battery is employed to separate a metal from its aqueous salt and to deposit it on an electrode (always the cathode or negative electrode). An inexpensive way of producing "silver" spoons is to stamp them out from iron and plate the latter with a thin coating of silver. In order to do this, an electrolytic cell is constructed as sketched on page 413.

The positive electrode or anode is made from silver; the aqueous salt is silver cyanide, which also acts as the electrolyte or current-conducting medium within the cell. The iron spoon becomes the cathode. A current of 1000 amps is applied for 96.5 seconds. The iron spoon becomes coated with 108 grams of silver, or exactly its gram atomic weight. For the next spoon, the current is reduced to 100 amps, but this time, it takes 965 seconds to plate 108 grams of silver. If copper were substituted for silver, a copper anode and copper sulfate (the new electrolyte) would replace the former anode and electrolyte. The iron spoons remain as the cathodes. A current of 1000 amps is reapplied for 96.5 seconds, and only 32 grams of copper are plated on the spoon, or one half the atomic weight (64) of copper. The current is reduced to 100 amps, and after 965 seconds, 32 grams of copper are again plated on the second spoon. Thus, 96,500 ampere-seconds (1000 amperes × 96.5 seconds or 100 amperes × 965 seconds) were required to plate one gram atomic weight (108 grams) of silver and one half of one gram atomic weight of copper ($\frac{1}{2}$ × 64). The chemical reactions are explained below.

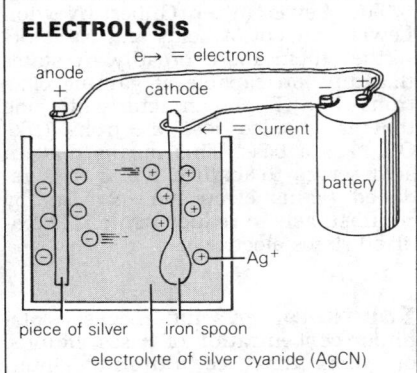

ELECTROLYSIS

anode +
cathode −
e→ = electrons
←I = current
battery
Ag⁺
piece of silver
iron spoon
electrolyte of silver cyanide (AgCN)

Electrolytic cell. A battery or direct current supplies electrons to an iron cathode that attracts and neutralizes silver ions (Ag⁺¹) that lose electrons at the cell's anode.

Oxidation: $Ag - 1e- \rightarrow Ag^{+1}$ (anode)

Electrolyte: $Ag^{+1} + CN^{-1} \leftrightarrows AgCN$

Reduction: $Ag^{+1} + 1e- \rightarrow Ag$ (plated iron spoon at cathode)

Oxidation: $Cu - 2e- \rightarrow Cu^{+2}$ (anode)

Electrolyte: $Cu^{+2} + (SO_4)^{-2} \rightleftarrows CuSO4$

Reduction: $Cu^{+2} + 2e- \rightarrow Cu$ (plated iron spoon at cathode)

The current supplies electrons to the cathode (the iron spoons), where the electrons are taken up by the silver

$$(Ag^{+1} + 1e- \rightarrow Ag)$$

and copper

$$(Cu^{+2} + 2e- \rightarrow Cu)$$

ions as they plate out as reduced metals on the spoons. Simultaneously, the silver and copper anodes become positively charged as the current strips away outer electrons

$(Ag - 1e- \rightarrow Ag^{+1}$ and
$Cu - \rightarrow Cu^{+2})$

from each metal and takes them away. This leaves the anodes positively charged. The metal ions then enter the electrolyte and await their turn to be reduced on the iron spoons. When both anodes are depleted, they are replaced to continue the plating reactions. The process of electrolysis is summarized in Faraday's law, which states that an electrolytic cell deposits or liberates 1 gram equivalent weight of a given metal or gas by applying 96,500 ampere-seconds or coulombs. *One gram equivalent weight is equal to the gram atomic weight of the metal or element involved divided by the number of electrons it loses or gains.* Therefore, 1 gram equivalent weight of copper in the above reaction is its atomic weight, expressed as 64 grams divided by the electrons it either gains or loses (in this case 2e's), which equals 32 grams. By the same reason-

ing, it may be stated that 1 gram equivalent weight of silver is equal to its gram atomic weight, 108 grams, because its electron gain or loss that is involved is only 1e.

One coulomb of current is equal to 1 ampere per second. The charge on one electron is equal to -1.6021×10^{-19} coulombs. One proton has a charge exactly equal in value, except that it is positive. However, 1 gram atomic weight of an element is made up of 6.024×10^{23} atoms. If each of these atoms exists as an ion (such as Ag^{+1}), then the total electrical charge of these charged atoms is equal to 6.024 $\times$ 10^{23} Ag+ ions multiplied by $+1.6021 \times 10^{-19}$ coulombs per ion, or 96,510 coulombs. This verifies Faraday's law. Consequently, one Faraday, or F, is equal to one mole of electrons (that is, 6.024×10^{23} charged atoms) or to 96,500 ampere-seconds (that is, 1F = 1e is also equivalent to 96,500 ampere-seconds). Therefore, in the ionic equation

$$Ag^{+1} + 1e- \rightarrow Ag,$$

the gram equivalent weight of silver is its atomic weight divided by 1e−. The equation also says 96,500 ampere-seconds will deposit 1 gram atom of silver or its atomic weight, 108 grams. However, the equation

$$Cu^{+2} + 2e- \rightarrow Cu$$

states that 2 × 96,500 ampere-seconds, or 193,000 ampere-seconds, will deliver 1 gram atom of copper, or 64 grams. Thus, 1 mole of electrons (1F) deposits only 32 grams of copper, which is then called the equivalent weight of copper. In other words, in electrolysis, it may be said that the equivalent weight of an element is its weight deposited for every 96,500 ampere-seconds used.

Important uses of electrolysis include the plating of automotive parts for corrosion protection and for decoration. Electrolysis is considered the most efficient method known for plating gold and silver on jewelry or on electronic components.

Acids, Solutions, and Colloids

Acids. A discussion of acids goes hand in hand with a discussion of bases and salts. The latter are found in ores and are a source for acids and bases. The distinguishing characteristics among these three classes of compounds are listed at right.

All acids contain ionizable hydrogen (hydrogen protons, H⁺¹) that dissociate in water. The concentration of the hydrogen ion determines the strength of an acid. The higher the ionization constant, Ka shown at top of next column, the stronger the acid.

Acid	Ka
Permanganic, $HMnO_4$	1.0×10^8
Sulfuric, H_2SO_4	1.0×10^3
Phosphoric, H_3PO_4	0.75×10^{-2}
Carbonic, H_2CO_3	0.45×10^{-6}
Boric, H_3BO_3	5.8×10^{-10}

Examples of strong bases include all the hydroxides of the alkali metals ("alkali" means basic) such as sodium hydroxide (NaOH), lithium hydroxide (LiOH), and potassium hydroxide (KOH). An ammonium hydroxide base (NH_4OH) is the only weak base that is considered. Salts are the reaction products between acids and bases, as the equations below indicate.

$$HNO_3 + NaOH \rightarrow NaNO_3 + H_2O$$
Nitric Sodium Sodium Water
acid hydroxide nitrate
salt

$$2HCl + Ca(OH)_2 \rightarrow CaCl_2 + 2H_2O$$
Hydro- Calcium Calcium Water
chloric hydroxide chloride
acid salt

Many metals replace hydrogen from an acid in an oxidation/reduction reaction

$$(2Fe + 3H_2SO_4 \rightarrow Fe_2(SO_4)_3 + 3H_2 \uparrow)$$

and, thereby, convert into a salt.

Acids and bases are used as intermediates to manufacture a variety of familiar products, as highlighted by the table below.

Acidity is related to the concentration of ionized and dissociated hydrogen protons (H⁺¹, a hydrogen ion without its lone electron in its K shell). Similarly, alkalinity also de-

DISTINGUISHING CHARACTERISTICS AMONG ACIDS, BASES, AND SALTS

	Acids	Bases	Salts
Bitter	No	Yes	No
Brackish	No	No	Yes
Soapy	No	Yes	No
Sour	Yes	No	No
Litmus Indicator	Red	Blue	None
Phase	Liquid	Liquid	Solid
Color	Clear	Clear	Many
Ionizable	Yes	Yes	Yes

SOME USES OF ACIDS AND BASES

Acids:

H_2SO_4 Sulfuric Acid	HNO_3 Nitric Acid	HCl Hydrochloric Acid
Explosives Dyestuffs Drugs Fertilizers Catalysts Gypsum	Plastics Dyes Fertilizers	Glues Gelatins Cleansers

Bases:

$Ca(OH)_2$ Calcium Hydroxide	NaOH Sodium Hydroxide	NH_4OH Ammonium Hydroxide
Cement Insecticides	Soaps Paper	Fertilizers

THE pH SCALE

The pH scale indicates the acidity of a solution. A solution with a pH value of 7 is neutral; less than 7 is an acid; more than 7 is a base.

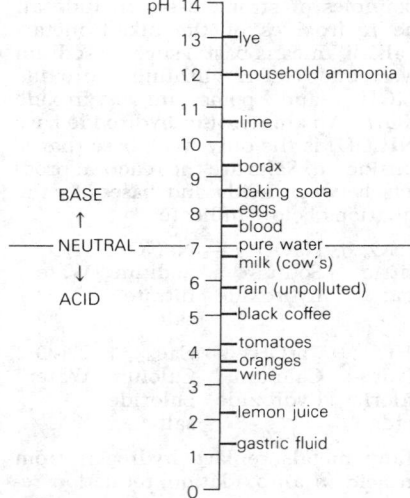

```
pH 14
   13 —— lye
   12 —— household ammonia
   11 —— lime
   10
    9 —— borax
            baking soda
BASE    8 —— eggs
  ↑         blood
— NEUTRAL — 7 —— pure water
  ↓         milk (cow's)
ACID    6 —— rain (unpolluted)
    5 —— black coffee
    4 —— tomatoes
            oranges
    3 —— wine
    2 —— lemon juice
    1 —— gastric fluid
    0
```

pends on the concentration of ionized and dissociated hydroxyl ions (OH^{-1}). The negative charge on the latter is due to the extra electron that the oxygen atom shares with a hydrogen atom. All bases (except ammonium hydroxide) and all strong acids are predominantly ionized and dissociated in water.

Dissociation means that their ions in water are very mobile. In the case of mineral acids, the proton (H^{+1}) is not tightly held by its nonmetal oxide ion or negatively charged radical (like the radical SO_4^{-2} in H_2SO_4 or Cl^{-1} in HCl). The same analogy applies to a base. The positive ions (that is, Na^{+1}, Ca^{+2}, Li^{+1}, NH_4^{+1}, etc.) are also loosely held by their negatively charged hydroxyls (OH^{-1}). These positive ions and their corresponding hydroxyl ions are in a state of equilibrium, as shown in the following ionic equations. For this reason, they are conductors of electricity and make desirable electrolytes.

$$2H^{+1} + SO_4^{-2} \rightleftarrows H_2SO_4$$
$$Na^{+1} + OH^{-1} \rightleftarrows NaOH$$

In contrast, weaker acids and ammonium hydroxide are poor conductors of electricity because the dissociation of their acid (H^{+1}) or basic (OH^{-1}) components is substantially less. The proton H^{+1} is tightly held, as is the hydroxyl OH^{-1} in ammonium hydroxide. Similarly, water is less than 2 percent ionized, as represented by the following singular equation:

$$H_3O^{+1} + OH^{-1} \leftrightarrows 2H_2O.$$

(The H_3O^{+1} ion is also referred to as a hydronium ion.)

The equilibrium between molecular water and its ions is more conveniently represented by

$$H_2O \rightleftarrows OH^{-1} + H^{+1},$$

in which complete reversibility is assumed. This indicates that the reactants are forming as rapidly as the product (H_2O in this case), so that the composition remains fixed at a specific temperature. Consequently, the ionization constant of water is calculated by the following expression.

$$\frac{[H^{+1}] \times [OH^{-1}]}{[H_2O]} = K$$

The mole coefficients in the above equation are each equal to one. Because, as stated previously, the ionization is very slight, the undissociated molecules of water are in great excess and constant. At 25°C, the ionization constant for water is 1×10^{-14}. If the concentration of H^{+1} and OH^{-1} are unknown but assumed to be equal, and that of H_2O is 1 mole per liter, then the acidity or alkalinity of water can be calculated by using the above expression. Let y = the proton and hydroxyl concentrations. Since they are equal, the net concentration of water will be 1 mole per liter − y, which can be disregarded because y is very small.

$$[y] \times [y] = 1 \times 10^{-14}$$

After taking the square root of the latter, y equals 1×10^{-7} moles per liter as the concentration of the proton and the hydroxyl respectively. This is the neutral point of water, at which it is neither acidic nor basic.

The acidity or alkalinity of a solution is more conveniently expressed by calculating the common logarithim of the reciprocal of the proton concentration (moles per liter). The calculated value may be specified as the pH of the solution.

If $(H^{+1}) = 10^{-7}$,
then $pH = \log 1/(H^{+1})$
           $= \log 1/(10^{-7})$
           $= \log 10$
           $= 7$.

Or, the pH of the solution = 7 (neutral): pH values of 1 to 7 indicate acidity (the lower the pH, the stronger the acid). Those values between 7 and 14 are basic; the higher the value the more alkaline the solution.

The ionization constants Ka of other weak acids are measured similarly. The proton and hydroxyl concentrations in a given solution are determined by first using an indicator to show the pH of the solution. If acidic, a solution of known alkaline concentration is prepared and injected drop by drop into the acid solution until it is neutralized. A potentiometer measures the change in conductivity and shows when the end point (neutralization) is reached. This technique is called titration. The calculation of pH values for a set of reactants is usually necessary because the small amounts of contained protons or hydroxyl ions can create large changes in the efficiency of a specific reaction.

The Lewis (after Gilbert Newton Lewis) concept of acids and bases describes them more broadly. It states that any ion capable of gaining electrons (like H^{+1}) is an acid, while one that is able to lose electrons (like OH^{-1}) is a base. This means that an acid serves to oxidize while it is reduced (gains electrons). A base, by contrast, acts to reduce while it is oxidized (loses electrons).

Solutions. A solution consists of a minor concentration of gases, liquids, or solids that are uniformly intermixed but not reacted with other gases, liquids, or solids that make up over 50 percent of a total mixture. Air is a homogeneous or uniform mixture of oxygen, nitrogen, and trace amounts of carbon dioxide plus noble gases. Since nitrogen makes up 78 percent of air, the other gases are dissolved in it. Nitrogen is called the solvent; the others (oxygen, carbon dioxide, and noble gases) are known as the solute. The ocean is also a uniform mixture, consisting predominantly of water (the solvent) and dissolved salts, such as sodium chloride, magnesium chloride, calcium carbonate, etc. (the solutes). An alloy of bronze may consist of 20 parts of tin dissolved in 80 parts of copper, which is the solvent. In its solid state, this mixture is known as an alloy. A gas like carbon dioxide can be dissolved in water to make "soda water." The gas is considered the solute.

The molecules of different compounds or the atoms of different elements are soluble to varying degrees because they have some similar structures or electrical properties. For example, the molecular structure of ethyl alcohol is

$$CH_3CH_2\text{—}OH,$$

that of glycol is

$$OH\text{—}CH_2CH_2\text{—}OH,$$

that of acetic acid is

$$CH_3COOH,$$

and that of sugar is

$$CH_2OHCHOHCHOHCHOHCHOHCHO.$$

These compare with water, H_2O, or

$$O\text{—}H\text{—}O.$$

Note that each of these molecules has oxygen and hydrogen groupings (OH^{-1}, called hydroxyls).

It is these common groupings (similar structures) that makes these molecules compatible with one another and capable of forming homogeneous solutions. For example, a cube of sugar is a solid at 25° C. When it is immersed in water, the molecules at the surface of the cube are disengaged by the molecules of water layer by layer until all the molecules of sugar occupy a large aqueous volume (the solvent). They are still in the solid state, but because they are so small, they go unseen. Table salt, NaCl, dissolves in water in similar fashion. (In this case, the salt is ionizable and the water is slightly ionic. Both have similar electrical properties.) If the water is evaporated, the salt remains behind as solid crystals. This method can be used to recover salt from sea water. Dissimilar molecules or atoms may only partially dissolve in a given solvent, or not at all. Oil forms a layered solution when mixed with water. The top layer floats on the heavier layer of water. Vegetable oil and fuel oils have molecules that are larger than the ones that are shown for sugar, but they contain few or no hydroxyl or oxygenated groups. When no compatibility exists, a uniform solution does not result.

A solution becomes saturated with a solute at the point when a portion of the solute begins to reappear, as if coming out of the solution. Chemists call this the saturation point, when an equal part of the solute leaves the solvent and an equal portion is dissolved. Additions made beyond this level result in excess undissolved solute. Supersaturation can be induced by heating the solutes and the solvent, and then charging in a greater amount of solute than used at the saturation point. On cooling, the solute stays in solution but in a precarious way. Jarring the solution or even introducing a fraction of solute will cause crystallization of the solute.

The concentration of a given solution is calculated at its saturation point and at a given temperature. It is expressed as grams of solute per 100 grams of solvent. For example at 0° C, 35.7 grams of table salt (NaCl) per 100 grams of water reach a saturation point; 39.8 grams of NaCl per 100 grams of H_2O saturate at 100° C. In contrast, at 20° C, 0.165 gram of $Ca(OH)_2$ per 100 grams of water reaches saturation, a very dilute solution. At 25° C, 200 grams of sugar per 100 grams of water achieves saturation, a very concentrated solution. Ethyl alcohol and water are infinitely soluble in each other; they have no saturation point.

Depending on the kind and concentration of a solute in a solvent, the resulting solution will have a different freezing and boiling point from that of the solvent. The addition of glycol to water raises its boiling point while it lowers its freezing point. This makes it an ideal antifreeze for autos during the winter. Increasing the amount of water dilutes the solution. The amount of glycol is unchanged, but the freeze point increases. The chemical concentration of a solution (made of solvent[s] plus solute[s]) may be determined in any of three ways, listed below:

Molar concentration = the weight of the solute divided by its molecular weight (moles) in 1 liter of solution.

Normal concentration = the equivalent weight of the solute contained in 1 liter of the solution.

Molal concentration = 1 mole of solute in 1000 grams of solvent.

For example, the molecular formula for sulfuric acid is H_2SO_4. Its molecular weight is the sum of the atomic weights in grams of the hydrogen, sulfur, and oxygen atoms that make up its molecule or 98 grams. The equivalent weight of an acid is its molecular weight divided by the total number of hydrogen atoms in its molecule. Therefore, the gram equivalent weight of H_2SO_4 is 98/2 = 49. A 1M (molar) solution contains 1 mole (98/98) of solute; a 1N (normal) solution contains 1 gram equivalent weight of H_2SO_4 or 49 grams, and a 1m (molal) solution has 1 mole (98/98) of the acid for every 1000 grams of solvent. Diluting a solution increases its volume and reduces its concentration. Chemical equations do not reveal the concentrations of the liquid or gaseous reacting solutes they contain. Thus, a chemist may have to first describe the equations of a given set of solutes, which at that point are not dissolved in any solvents. The chemist may then have to select compatible nonreactive solvents. Third, he or she must determine the concentrations of the solutions containing the amounts of solutes, as indicated by the equation, along with any desirable catalysts. The chemist must also consider the reaction conditions of time, temperature, needed mixing, and applied pressure or vacuum, so that neither the solutes nor the solvents are boiled off prematurely. Lastly, he or she must note whether the reaction releases or absorbs heat, and the extent of solubility of the resulting products in the unreactive solvents.

Colloids.

What is larger than a molecule but small enough to be "suspended" in a solvent? A particle having dimensions between 1 micron (u) and 1 millimicron (mu) (1u = 10^{-4} centimeters; 1mu = 10^{-7} centimeters). Such a particle cannot be seen with a microscope, but when carried in a solution, it will not diffuse through a membrane made from parchment paper. In contrast, salt molecules or sugar molecules will diffuse. A colloid may consist of grains of a solid, bubbles of a gas, or droplets of a liquid dispersed in three kinds of mediums.

Sols: Solid colloids in a liquid or a gas in a liquid.

Gels: Oblong shaped colloids forming a branched structure in a liquid.

Emulsions: Minute droplets of a liquid dispersed in a second liquid.

Colloids have a random motion (they zigzag) because of collisions with other molecules. They are stable while carrying the same electrical charge, which causes them to repel each other and literally disperse themselves in a solvent or gaseous medium. (This phenomenon is known as Brownian motion.) Colloids will provide a path for a sharp beam of light, but may otherwise reflect normal light as a color. (This is known as the Tyndall effect.) They are capable of adsorbing themselves on solid surfaces.

Solid colloids are prepared by very fine grinding or by controlled condensations, analagous to the way nature makes snow. A very small amount of an electrolyte or a surface wetting agent may be used to make colloids compatible with a specific solvent. For example, clay is a naturally occurring colloid. If water is treated with less than 1 percent of an electrolyte and

A LIGHT BEAM *passes freely through a solution but when penetrating a colloid the suspended particles scatter the light.*

FUNDAMENTAL PHOTOGRAPHS

clay is added in, the clay will disperse to a pourable fluid consistency, which can then be charged into plaster of Paris molds. The latter absorb the water but not the clay particles, which form into thin-walled clay parts. After removal from the molds, these parts are baked and fired into ceramic wares having thin walls.

Similarly, trace amounts of a surface active agent may be added to finely ground plastic powders, which then become compatible with water so that they can be transformed into paints or caulks. Because colloids carry an electrical charge, they may be sprayed onto an oppositely charged surface, where they become electrically bonded. The plate is then heated to smooth out the coating.

In a similar manner, colloidal particles being exhausted from industrial smokestacks can be conveyed between electrically charged plates to prevent the particles from entering the atmosphere. Solids, which would be impossible to react, could be ground to fine colloids, dispersed in solvent, and reacted.

Equations and Kinetics

THE CHEMICAL EQUATION

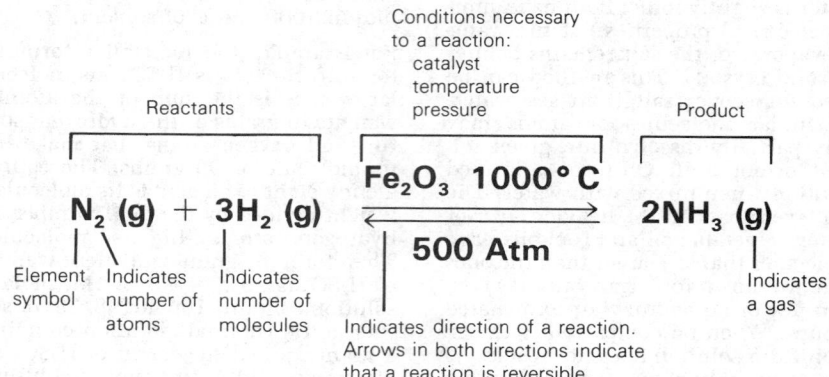

The coefficient values in an equation do not indicate amounts in any particular system of measure. The coefficients in an equation indicate a *proportion* of one reactant to another. For example, if the following values were assigned to the above equation, differing amounts of the same product would result.

1 molecule N_2 + 3 molecules $H_3 \rightleftharpoons$ 2 molecules NH_3

1 mole N_2 + 3 moles $H_2 \rightleftharpoons$ 2 moles NH_3

28 metric tons N_2 + 6 metric tons $H_3 \rightleftharpoons$ 34 metric tons NH_3

Equations. Chemical equations use symbols that allow the chemist to quickly identify the atoms of elements and the molecules of compounds that are reacted to create new ones. The symbols for the reactants are on the left side of the equation while those for the resulting products are on the right. An arrow from left to right indicates the direction of the reaction; that is, the combination of reactants yield the products on the right. A second arrow from right to left, below or above the first, states that the reaction is reversible. An arrow pointing to the top of the page and placed after a product identifies the product as a gas. An arrow pointing downward specifies that the product is an insoluble one (a precipitate), or the atom of a reduced element in solid form.

Coefficients placed in front of the reactants and products indicate the relative numbers of the elements or molecules participating in the reaction. Subscripts after an element or conjugate group like OH^{-1} in $Ca(OH)_2$ always specify a molecule. The symbol for each element in an equation represents its atomic weight as found in the Periodic Table. This weight may be expressed in any system of measure (grams or pounds).

The heat of reaction or of combustion that results from the reaction is shown on the right side and is indicated by a minus sign (meaning released) followed by the quantity of calories produced per mole or gram-

atom of a reactant. If heat is removed by the reaction, then the heat of absorption is also shown on the right side. A plus sign (meaning absorption) is placed before the amount of calories involved. It is important that all equations be balanced. The sum of all valences should equal zero. This is done by adjusting the coefficients of the atoms and the molecules involved. This requires a knowledge of some of the valence states of the atoms in the reaction so that the others can be calculated. The valence state of uncombined atoms or divalent gas molecules is always equal to zero.

Variable but important conditions, such as temperature, pressure, and catalyst, may be noted above or below the horizontal yield arrow. Likewise, the symbol (g) for a gas may be shown after a gas molecule, (l) after a liquid, and (s) after a solid. The equations do not assert the concentrations of liquids (that is, molar, normal, or molal); the partial pressures of reacting and resulting gases; or the ionization or equilibrium constants. They also do not assert that at standard temperature (0° C) and pressure (760 torrs or 1 atmosphere or 1034 grams/square centimeter), the molecular weight of a gas is contained in exactly 22.4 liters. Chemists are aware that reactions take place only between atoms and molecules and that these reactions can be represented by the correct relative values assigned to equations.

In describing the reaction, a chemist

might say that one molecule of nitrogen reacts with three molecules of hydrogen to produce two molecules of ammonia. (Volumes or moles could also have been chosen.) However, in industrial chemistry, the reaction is just as validly described by stating that 28 metric tons of nitrogen are reacted with 6 metric tons of hydrogen to make 34 metric tons of ammonia. In experimental chemistry, grams or liters will be selected as the units of measure. After whatever equivalent units are chosen, the heat of formation (kilocalories per mole of NH made) will be determined along with the yield or actual amount of ammonia that is recovered under the reaction and catalyst conditions used.

How is equation N_2 (g) + 3H_2 (g) $\rightleftharpoons$ 2NH_3 (g) balanced in the first place? Keep in mind that the total number of atoms on the left-hand side of an equation must equal the total number of atoms on the right. The sum of all valences must equal zero. If hydrogen is involved, assume that it has a valence state of +1 in its combined states. (However, if hydrogen is exclusively combined with a metal, it has a valence state of −1, as in lithium hydride [LiH] or sodium hydride [NaH].) If oxygen is involved, assume that it has a negative valence state of −2 in its combined states.

Note that an equation containing gases may use liters or volumes for the gases only. This is indicated for the above reaction to make ammonia.

HOW TO BALANCE AN EQUATION

1. Write down the unbalanced equation.

$N_2 + H_2 \rightleftarrows NH_3$
Unbalanced

2. Balance the partial equation involving only the hydrogen, oxygen, or atom whose valence combining state has been assumed.

Assume that each H has a positive valence, H^{+1}, but $3H^{+1}$ protons exist for each nitrogen (N) atom. Therefore, the latter should have three negative charges, N^{-3}. Now balance the hydrogens on the left with those on the right.

$[H_2]$ Unbal.	$\rightarrow$	$[3H^{+1} + 3e-]$
$3[H_2]$ Trial	$\rightarrow$	$2[3H^{+1} + 3e-]$
$3H_2$ Balanced	$\rightarrow$	$6H^+ + 6e-$

3. Assign the countervalence state that the other combined atom should have with H^{+1} or O^{-2}.

N in combined NH3 is assigned a valence state of -3 and represented as N^{-3}.

4. Balance the partial equation for the other combined atom.

$[N_2]$ Unbal.	$\rightarrow$	$[N^{-3} - 3e-]$
$[N_2]$ Trial	$\rightarrow$	$2[N^{-3} - 3e-]$
N_2 Balanced	$\rightarrow$	$2N^{-3} - 6e-$

5. Add up the positive and negative charges and see if they cancel each other out, as illustrated at the right.

Add up the partially balanced equations.

$$N_2 \rightarrow 2N^{-3} - 6e-$$
$$3H_2 \rightarrow 6H^{+1} + 6e-$$
$$N_2 + 3H_2 = 2N^{-3} + 6H^{+1}$$

The valences cancel out.
$$N_2 + 3H_2 \rightarrow 2NH_3$$
The total number of atoms on the left equals the total on the right. Nitrogen is reduced (gains electrons); hydrogen is oxidized (loses electrons to nitrogen).

Weight measures based on the molecular or atomic weight of the reactants or products must be used if they are in the solid or liquid state. However, an equation may contain all three forms of matter, as displayed below.

Zn	$+ H_2SO_4$	$\rightarrow ZnSO_4$	$+ H_2 \uparrow$
solid	liquid	solid	gas
g-atm	1 mole	1 mole	1 mole
65 gr.	98 gr.	161 gr.	22.4 liters at STP

Kinetics. The duration, speed, energy, and ultimate direction of a reaction describe its dynamics or kinetics. For example, a common adhesive found in hardware stores is a "5-minute epoxy" that becomes a solid warm mass in 5 minutes, or after equal amounts of the liquid epoxy resin and its liquid sulfide hardener have been well blended. Thereafter, regardless of how much heat is added to the solidified mass, it will not revert back to its liquid constituents. However, if the liquid epoxy and hardener are preheated, they will react in less than 5 minutes; if cooled, in more than 5 minutes. In all cases, the same amount of heat will be released by the reaction, which takes place in the forward direction, yielding in a solid.

Many reactions first take place in the forward direction. Unless reaction conditions are adjusted, the reactions then also begin in the opposite direction, until both reactions exist simultaneously and reach an equilibrium

point. Assume that at STP 67.2 liters of hydrogen and 22.4 liters of nitrogen are injected by a compressor into an insulated steel container, and that heat is applied to the container. The nitrogen and the hydrogen gases slowly begin to react with each other, releasing heat and forming ammonia. No heat is removed. This causes part of the ammonia to convert back to nitrogen and hydrogen until a point is reached when all three molecules are present and reacting to maintain a steady state that can be equated to an

TIME AND TEMPERATURE *are important factors in many chemical reactions, such as the mixing of an epoxy adhesive.*

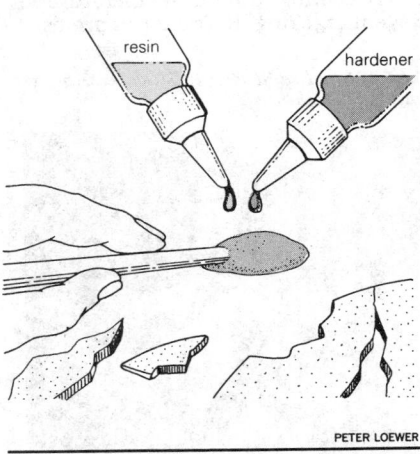

resin   hardener

PETER LOEWER

equilibrium constant. This is calculated as follows.

$$N_2 (g) + 3H_2 (g) \underset{S_2}{\overset{S_1}{\rightleftarrows}} 2NH_3 (g) -22000$$

1 mole	3 moles	2 moles	calories
22.4 L	67.2 L	44.8 L	released
.045 moles per L	.045 moles per L	.045 moles per L	

S_1 equals the rate with which 1 mole of N_2 reacts with 3 moles of H_2 to form 2 moles of NH_3. S_2 equals the rate at which 2 moles of NH_3 decompose to produce 3 moles of H_2 and 1 mole of N_2. S_1 and S_2 are dependent, respectively, on the concentrations (moles per liter) of N_2, H_2, and NH_3, and are proportional to the product of each raised to the power of the number of moles involved.

$$S_1 = K_1 \times [.045]^1 \times [.045]^3$$
$$S_2 = K_2 \times [.045]^2,$$

where K_1 and K_2 are rate constants that are dependent on temperature, pressure, and catalyst used. When equilibrium is achieved,

$$S_1 = S_2$$

or

$$K_1 \times 4 \times 10^{-6} = K_2 \times 2 \times 10^{-3}.$$
$$K_1/K_2 = 2 \times 10^{-3}/4 \times 10^{-6}$$
$$= 500$$
$$= K_c.$$

which is the concentration equilibrium constant.

To interpret the meaning of the K constant, it is better to express the kinetic equations as follows.

$$K_c = \frac{[NH_3]^2}{[N_2] \times [H_2]^3}$$

If the reacting system has reached equilibrium, adding in more nitrogen and hydrogen causes more ammonia to be made to maintain the equilibrium. Withdrawing ammonia and the heat of reaction increases the forward reaction to restore the constant K_c. Increasing the pressure will result in a greater proportion of ammonia because the forward reaction is accompanied by a reduction in volume (four volumes of reactants yield two volumes of NH_3). A catalyst will speed up the forward reaction to the equilibrium point, but will also speed up the reverse reaction when that point is reached.

In practice, the reaction is very sluggish at room temperature and 1 atmosphere. Very high temperatures (300 to 500° C) and pressures (500 to 1000 atm as suggested above) are needed. Additionally, a catalyst, Fe_2O_3, also has to be employed to economically speed up the reaction. Unfortunately, once the equilibrium point is reached, the reverse reaction is almost instantaneous. Ammonia and unreacted or formed nitrogen and hydrogen are quickly drawn off. The mixture is cooled; the ammonia condenses to a liquid; hydrogen and nitrogen remain as gases. They are drawn off and recycled back into the reacting chamber.

Engineering. Engineers apply the principles of physical chemistry to the design and operation of plants that are involved with producing chemical changes. Laboratory experiments are scaled up to produce tons of a given product, instead of grams. To accomplish this, a chemist or chemical engineer must understand the path of a reaction and how heavy-duty motors, compressors (to create high pressures), displacement pumps (to create vacuums), piping, reactors, and furnaces are put together to carry out a reaction. Usually, heat exchangers must be employed to remove heat; huge distillation columns to separate or purify gases; condensers and chillers to change gases into liquids; and crystallizers and centrifuges to purify and separate solids. Computerized sensing devices are used to monitor reactions as well as necessary and unwanted emissions. Spectrometers are used to quickly identify the formation of molecules. Other instruments examine the makeup of a product and its impurities. Pressurized and refrigerated bulk tanks may be employed to transport sensitive gases and liquids. Granular and powdered chemicals and plastics are packed in multiwalled sacks or are conveyed in bulk rail cars. Because of intense competition, all of these operations must be performed at the lowest possible cost and with highest achievable quality.

Inorganic Chemistry

Inorganic chemistry is devoted to the study of products not based on the hydrogen compounds of carbon (organic chemistry) and silicon (silicone chemistry). Such inorganic products include *gases* (oxygen, hydrogen, ammonia, carbon monoxide, etc.), *refractories* (silicon oxide, silicates, aluminates, etc.), *graphites* (carbon, diamonds, and metal carbides), *ceramics* (clays, fluxes, and metal oxides), *glasses* (silicas, borates, fluxes, and metal oxides), *cements* (concretes, mortars, and plasters), *acids* (nitric, sulfuric, phosphoric, etc.), *bases* (all metal hydroxides and ammonium hydroxide), *salts* (combinations of metals with nonmetal oxides or nonmetals), *fertilizers* (nitrates and phosphates), and *metals*. A few of these products will be described briefly.

Fuel sources. The reaction of carbon monoxide (CO) with three molecules of hydrogen ($3H_2$) at 250° C yields one molecule each of water and methane gas (CH_4), the major constituent of natural gas. A nickel catalyst is employed. Calcium carbonate ($CaCO_3$) is oxidized (burned with oxygen) to yield calcium oxide (CaO) and carbon dioxide (CO_2). One molecule of calcium oxide is then reacted with three molecules of carbon at 2000° C; it yields one molecule of carbon monoxide and one of calcium carbide (CaC_2). The latter is treated with water, and one molecule each of calcium hydroxide ($Ca(OH)_2$) and acetylene (C_2H_2) are produced. The latter can be further reacted to make benzene, plastics, organic compounds, and fuels. The carbon monoxide can be recycled to produce more methane.

The calcium hydroxide is hydrated lime that is added to concrete cement in order to harden it, or it is mixed with sand to make mortar cement for bonding bricks. Anthracite coal (containing over 80 percent carbon) or coke (containing over 90 percent carbon) may be used as sources of carbon.

This alternative method for making fuels is considered a standby for currently less expensive natural petroleum resources.

Clays, ceramics, and glass. Ceramics and refractories are made from clays, which are found as colloidal particles around bodies of water or in stationary deposits above or below ground level. Most clays are complex molecules of alumina (Al_2O_3), silica (SiO_2), and hydrated or bonded water that are chemically bonded in various proportions. For example, white kaolin clay is chemically represented as

$$Al_2O_3 \times 2SiO_2 \times 2H_2O.$$

Ceramics are made by mixing clays with fluxes (usually oxides of highly reactive metal oxides that control high temperature flow and that also bond the clays), silicas (flint or sand to control porosity and shrinkage), oxides of less reactive metals (to impart color), and water (to work and form the mixture at room temperature). The hard ceramic (used for tiles, pots, dinnerware, etc.) is then made by forming, drying, baking (to drive off all water), firing in an oven at temperatures that range from 800° to 1500° C, and then slowly cooling to room temperature to prevent cracking. Refractories are usually formed under pressure; less water and fluxes are used. "Fire clays" containing higher concentrations of alumina or silica are baked and then reacted at 1300° to 1500° C. Rocks and stones are natural ceramics and refractories.

In contrast, formulas for making glass products are rich in silica (SiO_2) or boric oxide (B_2O_3). They contain high concentrations (20 percent to 30 percent) of fluxes (like the oxides of sodium, potassium, lead, calcium, aluminum, magnesium and iron, which are used in combinations), but no water. The formulated mixture is directly heated to between 800° and 1300° C; withdrawn while hot, formed, and quickly frozen to an amorphous or random crystal structure that accounts for the transparency of glass.

Iron. Iron ore is a mixture of silica with fluxes plus ferric oxide (Fe_2O_3), which is first granulated, concentrated so that its ferric oxide content is over 60 percent, mixed with coke (almost pure carbon), and fed into a blast furnace along with limestone ($CaCO_3$) to lower the melting temperature of the prepared ore. The bottom of the furnace is at 1650° C. The fuel ratio is richer in coke than in oxygen from the air. The coke (carbon) first converts to carbon monoxide, which then removes the oxygen from iron oxide (Fe_2O_3) and turns to carbon dioxide (CO_2) while the iron (Fe) is liberated or reduced. The other ingredients of the ore form a glass known as a slag, which floats on the much heavier iron. The molten mixture is drawn off at the bottom of the furnace, where the slag is skimmed off while the iron is conveyed to billets or molds, where it is solidified. The reaction is summarized as follows.

$$Fe_2O_3 + 3CO \rightarrow 2Fe + 3CO_2 \uparrow$$

Carbon monoxide is oxidized to carbon dioxide while the iron oxide is reduced to iron.

GLASS, *fused sand rich in silica, can be reshaped when heated.*

KENNETH PARSONS/LEO DE WYS

Organic Chemistry

Of all the sciences that exist, none is more fascinating or more dynamic than organic chemistry. A countless number of carbon and hydrogen atoms are combined together with lesser amounts of oxygen, nitrogen, and trace metals to create programmable molecules. Some of these molecules, in turn, become living organisms that can feel, see, think, and duplicate themselves into variations of the same molecular species with uncanny accuracy and detail. The dynamics of organic chemistry has made all plant and animal life possible. All the coal and natural oil deposits on Earth are but the remains of ancient plant and animal life that underwent reactions. These deposits remain organic in structure and constitute an immense supply of raw materials for mankind.

Inasmuch as organic chemistry is so extensive, only an outline of its fundamentals can be presented in this segment. Organic chemistry is divided into two major categories: the aliphatics, or mostly linear molecules, and the aromatics, or benzene and its derivatives. Covalent bonding is the overriding structural feature of organic molecules. Over 1 million compounds already exist. For this reason, organic chemistry has a unique nomenclature that depends on knowing the molecular structure of organic molecules.

Structure. The Periodic Table on page 405 indicates that hydrogen has one electron. It can lose this electron or share it. In contrast, carbon has four electrons in its unfilled outer L shell. Like hydrogen, it can lose these electrons and achieve a more stable structure by exposing the two electrons in its K shell. Optionally, carbon can allow four electrons (supplied by four hydrogen atoms or other elements) to share orbiting positions in its L shell, so that eight electrons move through the space in its L shell as the latter interfaces with the outer shell of the other atoms around it. An outer shell has a stable configuration if it has two or eight electrons. In this process of sharing, or covalent bonding, neither carbon nor hydrogen becomes electrically charged. No electrons are gained or lost by either atom. The most fundamental organic molecule is a carbon atom sharing four hydrogen atoms. This molecule is called meth-*ane*. It is represented as CH_4. Each of the hydrogen atoms may be displaced by a member of the halogen family (chlorine, bromine, fluorine, or iodine), which would have an interfacing orbit with carbon.

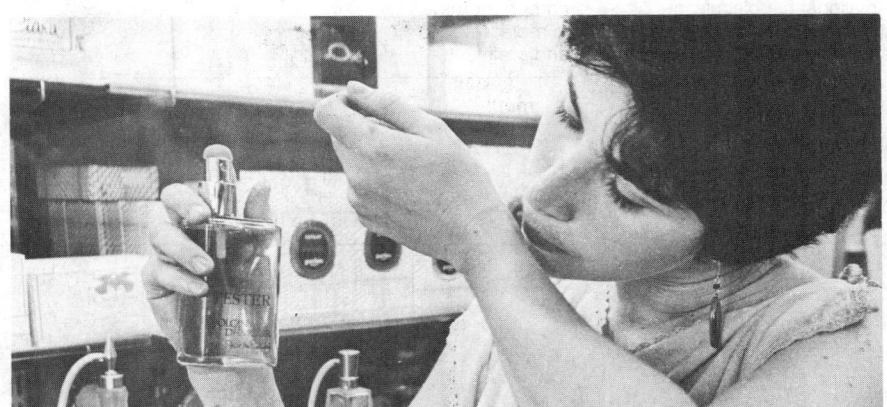

MANY ORGANIC CHEMICALS *are synthesized to create fragrances that are used in perfumes and cosmetics.*

In the laboratory, if one molecule of methane is reacted with one molecule of chlorine, they form chloromethane (CH_3Cl) and hydrochloric acid. A hydrogen atom is displaced by one atom of chlorine, as represented by the following equation:

$$CH_4 + Cl_2 \rightarrow HCl + CH_3Cl.$$

(If excess chlorine is used then more or all of the hydrogen atoms of the methane molecule may be replaced.) The reaction is carried out under sunlight. When two molecules of chloromethane are reacted with two atoms of sodium metal, they combine to form

$$eth\textit{ane} \ (CH_3CH_3),$$

$$[2Na + 2CH_3Cl \rightarrow 2NaCl + CH_3CH_3].$$

Ethane may be viewed as two methane molecules that have each lost one hydrogen atom. Chloroethane may be made in a similar fashion and then reacted with chloromethane and sodium metal to make

$$prop\textit{ane} \ (CH_3CH_2CH_3),$$

or three methane molecules joined together less the proper number of their displaced hydrogen atoms. Alternatively, two molecules of chloroethane may be reacted with two atoms of sodium metal to produce

$$but\textit{ane} \ (CH_3CH_2CH_2CH_3).$$

This laboratory preparation or synthesis (the Würtz reaction) indicates that a short linear molecule like ethane can become very long, or even branched, due to the possible displacement of one or more hydrogen atoms along the length of the chain. As the size and complexity of the molecules increase after butane, they exist as liquids at 25° C and turn into soft solids (fats) when 17 or more carbon atoms are joined together. A countless number of these compounds are extracted and refined from natural petroleum and coal deposits. Plant and animal life produce yet another array of complex linear and branched organic molecules by processes that are more sophisticated and exacting than the Würtz reaction. The pictorials below show that methane, like all molecules, occupies three-dimensional space. However, chemists prefer the structural or compositional formula representations.

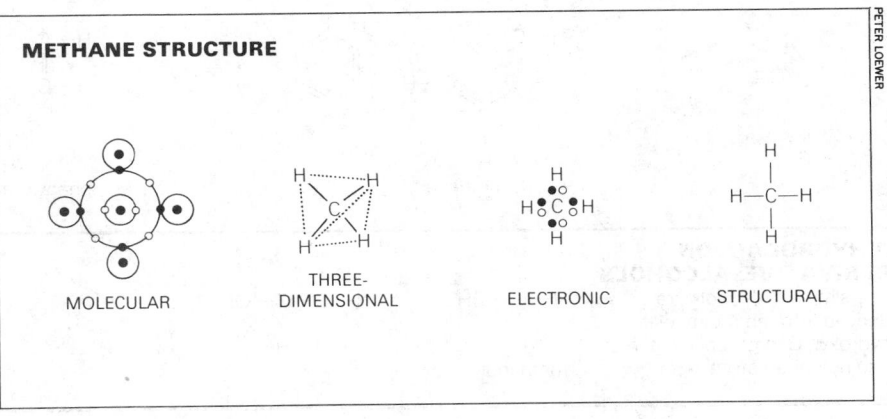

METHANE STRUCTURE

MOLECULAR   THREE-DIMENSIONAL   ELECTRONIC   STRUCTURAL

HYDROCARBONS

ALIPHATICS

An aliphatic molecule is one in which carbon atoms are linked in a chain.

Key: — single bond
$=$ double bond
$\equiv$ triple bond

Number of carbon atoms in molecule, and prefix	Alkanes (C_nH_{2n+2})	Alkenes (C_nH_{2n})	Alkynes (C_nH_{2n-2})
1 meth-	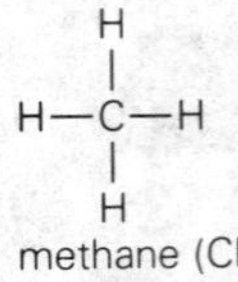 methane (CH_4)		
2 eth-	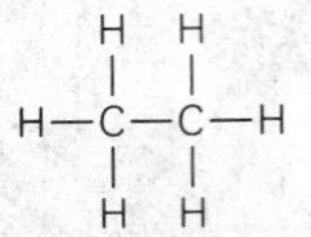 ethane (C_2H_6)	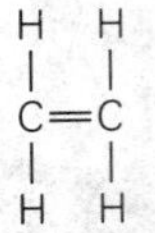 ethene (C_2H_4)	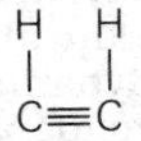 ethyne (C_2H_2)
3 prop-	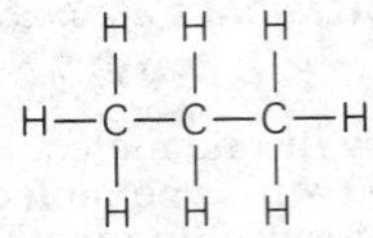 propane (C_3H_8)	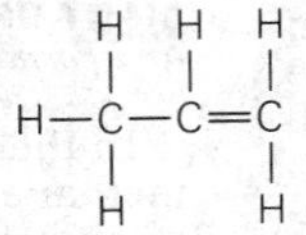 propene (C_3H_6)	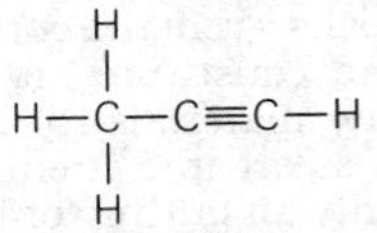 propyne (C_3H_4)
4 but-	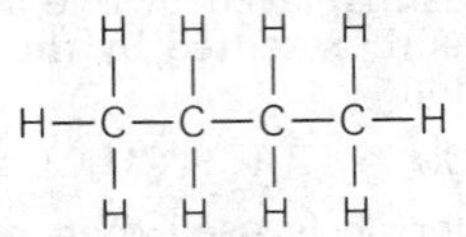 butane (C_4H_{10})	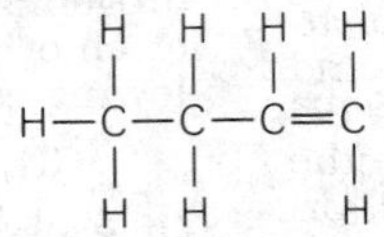 butene (C_4H_8)	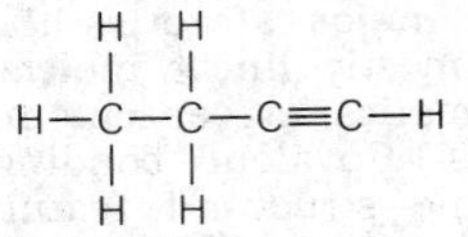 butyne (C_4H_6)

AROMATICS

structural representation

simplified representation

reactive positions
radical
ortho
meta
para

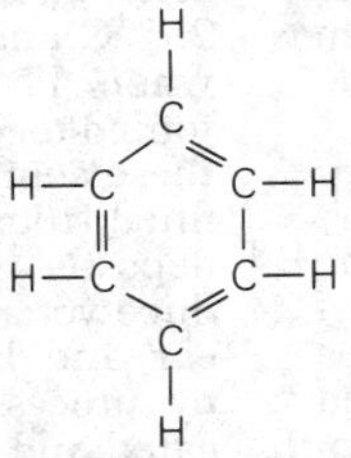

benzene (C_6H_6)

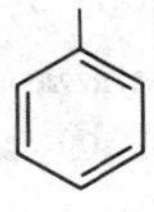

When a benzene molecule is joined to an alkane, both molecules lose one hydrogen atom.

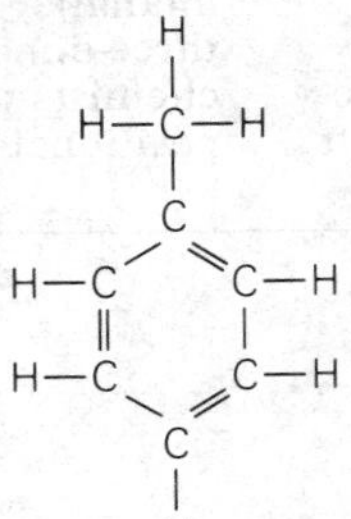

CH_3

phenylmethane

CH_2CH_3

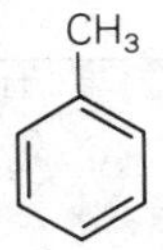

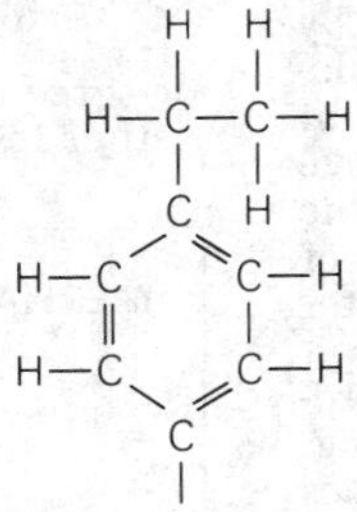

phenylethane

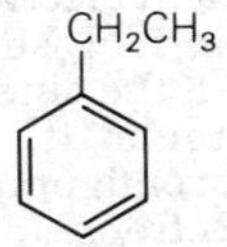

A HYDROCARBON DERIVATIVE: ALCOHOLS

The simplest alcohols are derived from an alkane with a hydroxyl (OH) group in place of one hydrogen atom.

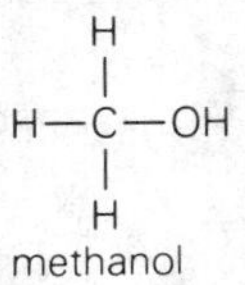

methanol

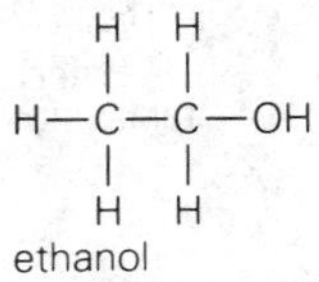

ethanol

Aliphatic names. This linear series consists of four major groups. The *alkanes,* or saturated hydrocarbons; the *alkenes* (also called olefins), or unsaturated double bond versions; the *alkynes,* or unsaturated triple bond types; and the *carbohydrates,* or alkanes, having a predominance of hydroxyl (OH^{-1}) groups along their chain length.

The saturated alk*anes* begin with

meth*ane,* (CH_4); proceed to
eth*ane* (C_2H_6);
prop*ane* ($CH_3CH_2CH_3$);
but*ane,* ($CH_3CH_2CH_2CH_3$), etc.

They have the general formula

$$C_nH_{2n+2},$$

as illustrated below.

C_5H_{12} pent*ane* C_8H_{18} oct*ane*
C_6H_{14} hex*ane* C_9H_{20} non*ane*
C_7H_{16} hept*ane* $C_{10}H_{22}$ dec*ane*

Beginning with butane, branched isomers (molecules having the same number of atoms but with different positions along a given chain) exist. The number of possible isomers increases geometrically as the number of carbon atoms becomes larger. Note the following simple examples.

$$CH_3$$
$$|$$
$$CH_3—CH—CH_3 \qquad \text{isobutane } C_4H_{10}$$

$$CH_3$$
$$|$$
$$CH_3—CH_2—CH—CH_3 \qquad \text{isopentane } C_5H_{12}$$

$$CH_3$$
$$|$$
$$CH_3—C—CH_3 \qquad \text{neopentane } C_5H_{12}$$
$$|$$
$$CH_3$$

The unsaturated alk*enes* begin with

eth*ene* (CH_2CH_2),

which is two hydrogen atoms short (one position in each of the L shells of each carbon atom is open for sharing); the next is

prop*ene* (CH_3CHCH_2),

followed by

but*ene* ($CH_3CH_2CHCH_2$),

etc. Starting with the latter, unsaturation may occur at both ends of the molecule or in between. The molecule is then referred to as a *diene,* as in

buta*diene* ($CH_2CHCHCH_2$).

Similar unsaturations can occur within the structures of isomers. The alkenes have C_nH_{2n} as a general formula (but not the dienes). The alk*ynes* have C_nH_{2n-2} as a general formula. The first alk*yne* is eth*yne,* or acetylene, $CHCH$, followed by prop*yne,* CH_3CCH, etc. Alkynes are not as prevalent as alkenes or alkanes because, with the exception of acetylene, they are difficult to make and limited in use.

Carbohydrates include sugars, starches, and celluloses. A representative structure is one for glucose, a sugar.

$$\begin{array}{ccccccc} H & H & H & H & H \\ | & | & | & | & | \\ CH_2—CH—CH—CH—CH—CH{=}O \\ | & | & | & | & | \\ OH & OH & OH & OH & OH \end{array}$$

A hydroxyl (OH^{-1}) on this chain may be positioned where a hydrogen atom is placed. It then becomes an optical isomer because it diffracts light at a different angle. In other words, a change in position in space of two different atoms or groups relative to the same carbon atom can alter the properties of the atom.

Aromatic names. The aromatic series is centered around the unsaturated ring structure of benzene, C_6H_6. Its easiest derivatives to name are the inorganic substitutions made on its three reactive positions, designated as ortho, meta, and para along the ring. Chloro benzene, bromo benzene, iodo benzene, nitro benzene, and benzene sulfonic acid are common designations. The benzene ring may also have alkane or alkene groups attached as side chains to its three reactive positions. The benzene molecule less one hydrogen atom may then be called by the term "phenyl," followed by the name of the attached alkyl group (an alkane less one hydrogen atom). For example, phenylmethane, $C_6H_5CH_3$, is a phenyl group joined to a methyl group. Phenylmethane is more popularly known as toluene.

IUPAC nomenclature. Since organic molecules can become quite complex, the International Union of Chemistry (IUC), now known as the International Union for Pure and Applied Chemistry (IUPAC), adopted the following system of nomenclature. First, an organic molecule is named as a derivative of the hydrocarbon corresponding to the longest continuous chain of carbon atoms in its formula. Then, the carbon atoms in the chain are counted, either from right to left or from left to right, to specify the position of a substituted group by the smallest possible figure. Additionally, the IUC adopted the conventions that C_nH_{2n+1} is any alkyl radical (that is, $CH_3—$, methyl, $C_2H_5—$, ethyl, etc.), and that the capital letter R may stand for either a substituted hydrogen or alkyl group so that a specific group is highlighted. For instance, an oxygen atom joining two of the same or alkyl groups is called an ether. This joining can be shown as

$$R—O—R$$

if the same alkyl groups are involved (for example, $CH_3CH_2—O—CH_2CH_3$, in this case, diethyl ether), or desig-

nated as $\qquad R_1—O—R_2$

if two different alkyl groups are meant to be involved. It is important to note that R without a subscript stands for any alkyl group that is the same. Subscripts indicate that the alkyl groups can be different. Many general equations can be written in this fashion.

Physical states. At and above 25° C, methane, ethane, propane, butane, ethene, propene, butene, and acetylene are gases. The next series containing carbon atoms in the range of 5 to 16 are liquids; those beyond become soft solids. Benzene is a liquid; the carbohydrates are solids.

Major uses. All organic molecules will burn and oxidize to carbon dioxide and water while giving up heat. Methane and propane are used as fuel gases. Gasoline is a blend of purified liquid fractions (predominantly consisting of shorter branched and unsaturated molecules), while fuel oil has longer and more linear molecules. After burning, the next prominent reaction is the cracking or splitting of heavy alkane and alkene fractions in unrefined oil, followed by reforming or rearrangement reactions to extract useful petroleum products and petrochemicals (alkanes, alkenes, and aromatics). The majority of our industrial chemicals and plastics are based on petrochemicals. The alkenes are the most reactive, followed by the alkynes, the aromatics, the carbohydrates, and the alkanes. All are susceptible to halogenation (chlorination, bromination, fluoridation, and iodonation) on exposure to sunlight. Chlorinated products are used as cleaning compounds or as intermediates to make other organic compounds. Fluoridated organic products are employed as refrigerants, propellants, and blowing agents in making foams.

INSECTICIDES *are often made from petrochemical hydrocarbons.*

STEVE RAYE/TAURUS PHOTOS

ETHANOL, *the alcohol found in wines and liquors, can also be used as a fuel supplement for gasoline.*

Major reactive groups.

Because the number of reactions is so extensive and complex, it is expedient to describe only the major reactive groups, as outlined below. In place of an R, substitute any alkyl group desired. If an extra carbon is attached to the R group, then convert it to the next alkyl group. Follow it with the name of the group shown.

Examples of reactions.

Simple addition reactions involve alkenes or alkynes; no byproducts are formed. For example, ethylene, $CH_2{=}CH_2$, plus hydrochloric acid, HCl, yields ethylchloride, CH_3CH_2Cl. Substitution reactions, like the halogenation of an alkane or benzene, result in a byproduct, a halogen acid. Oxidation predominantly involves the addition of oxygen along with the loss of hydrogen. Reduction occurs with the addition of hydrogen or the loss of oxygen. A halogenated alkane may be reacted or grafted to a benzene ring by using aluminum trichloride ($AlCl_3$) as a catalyst (that is,

$$ClCH_2CH_3 + C_6H_6 \text{ [AlCl}_3 \text{ cat]} \rightarrow C_6H_5{-}CH_2CH_3 + HCl).$$

This alkyl side chain may then be converted into many of the above reactive groups. The formation of some of these reactive groups is illustrated below using ethylene (CH_2CH_2) as a starting raw material. Catalysts are enclosed in square brackets.

Acytylene, propylene, butylene, alkylated benzene derivatives, etc., are reacted in a similar manner to give yet another assortment of alcohols, acids, aldehydes, etc. For instance, isopropyl alcohol, $CH_3CH{-}OH{-}CH_3$, is oxidized to yield a product known as acetone, $CH_3{-}CO{-}CH_3$. Commercially, ethyl alcohol is employed as a solvent, to make whiskeys, and as a gasoline additive. Ethylene glycol is usually blended with water for use as an automotive antifreeze.

Natural sugars are fermented to make wines that can then be distilled into ethyl alcohol. The latter can, in turn, be dehydrated back into ethylene. The aldehydes, ketones, and ethers are used mostly as paint solvents, while the acids and alcohols are reacted into esters, like ethyl acetate, that are also used as solvents. The amides, amines, and amino acids are widely employed as drug intermediates; they are also used for the production of plastics. Aminoacetic acid, NH_2CH_2COOH, is a fundamental unit of proteins, immensely long-chained molecules that are made by all living matter and essential to survival. Proteins are plastic in nature.

MAJOR REACTIVE GROUPS

REACTIVE GROUP	NAME OF GROUP
R—Cl	Rchloride
Cl—R—Cl	Rdichloride
$CH_2{=}CH_2$	Ethylene
CH≡CH	Acetylene
R—O—R	R Ether
R—ONa	Sodium Roxide
R—OH	R Alcohol
OH—R—OH	R Dialcohol
R—CH=O	R Aldehyde
R—C—R (with O double bond above C)	R Ketone
R—CN	R Cyanide
R—COOH	R Acid
R—C=O—O—C=O—R	R Anhydride
R—C=O—OR	R Acetate
HOOC—R—COOH	R Diacid
R—COONa	Sodium Rtate
R—COCl	Rnyl Chloride
R—CONH₂	R Amide
OH—R—CO—NH₂	R Amino Acid
R—NH	R Amine
NH₂—R—NH₂	R Diamine
R—NCO	R Isocyanate

EDDIE ADAMS/WOODFIN CAMP
DEAN/FREDERIC LEWIS

EXAMPLES OF ASSOCIATED REACTIONS

Ethylene is oxidized to ethyl alcohol.
$$CH_2{=}CH_2 \text{ [H}_2\text{SO}_4/\text{H}_2\text{O]} \rightarrow CH_3CH_2OH$$

Ethyl alcohol is oxidized to acetaldehyde.
$$CH_3CH_2OH \text{ [Cu]} \rightarrow CH_3CHO$$

Acetaldehyde is oxidized to acetic acid.
$$CH_3CHO + 1/2O_2 \rightarrow CH_3COOH$$

Acetic acid is reduced to acetyl chloride.
$$CH_3COOH \text{ [PCl}_3\text{]} \rightarrow CH_3COCl$$

Acetyl chloride is converted into acetamide by substitution.
$$CH_3COCl + NH_3 \rightarrow CH_3CONH_2 + HCl$$

Acetic acid is reacted with ethyl alcohol to make ethyl acetate by a condensation reaction (forms water).
$$CH_3COOH + CH_3CH_2OH \rightarrow CH_3C{=}O{-}OCH_2CH_3 + H_2O$$

Ethyl alcohol is condensed to diethyl ether.
$$CH_3CH_2OH \text{ [H}_2\text{SO}_4 \text{ @ } 130° \text{ C]} \rightarrow CH_3CH_2{-}O{-}CH_2CH_3 + H_2O$$

Ethyl alcohol is dehydrated back to ethylene.
$$CH_3CH_2OH \text{ [H}_2\text{SO}_4 \text{ @ } 190° \text{ C]} \rightarrow CH_2CH_2$$

Acetic acid is chlorinated and forms chloroacetic acid by substitution.
$$CH_3COOH + Cl \rightarrow ClCH_2COOH + HCl$$

Chloroacetic acid is ammoniated and yields aminoacetic acid by substitution.
$$ClCH_2COOH + NH_3 \rightarrow NH_2CH_2COOH + HCl$$

Acetic acid is ammoniated and yields methyl cyanide by substitution and condensation.
$$CH_3COOH + NH_3 \rightarrow CH_3CN + 2H_2O$$

Methyl cyanide is reduced by hydrogen addition to yield ethyl amine.
$$CH_3CN + 2H_2 \rightarrow CH_3CH_2NH_2.$$

Ethylene is oxided to ethylene oxide.
$$CH_2{=}CH_2 + 1/2O \rightarrow CH_2{-}O{-}CH_2.$$

Ethylene oxide is further oxidized in a water or a basic solution to ethylene glycol, a dialcohol.
$$CH_2{-}O{-}CH_2 \text{ [mild base]} \rightarrow OH{-}CH_2CH_2{-}OH$$

Ethylene oxide is oxidized to yield a diacid, oxalic acid.
$$OH{-}CH_2CH_2{-}OH + O_2 \rightarrow (COOH)_2 + 2H_2$$

Ethylene is oxychlorinated by addition to yield ethylene dichloride.
$$CH_2{=}CH_2 + 2HCl + 1/2O \rightarrow ClCH_2CH_2Cl + 2H_2O$$

Ethylene dichloride is ammoniated to yield ethylene diamine.
$$ClCH_2CH_2Cl + 2NH_3 \rightarrow NH_2CH_2CH_2NH_2 + 2HCl$$

Ethylene dichloride is subjected to high heat and converted into vinyl chloride. (The radical $CH_2{=}CH{-}$ is called vinyl.)
$$ClCH_2CH_2Cl \text{ [high heat]} \rightarrow ClCH{=}CH_2 + HCl$$

Ethylene is reacted with benzene to yield phenylethane or ethylbenzene.
$$CH_2{=}CH_2 + C_6H_6 \text{ [AlCl}_3\text{]} \rightarrow C_6H_5C_2H_5$$

Plastics.

Living tissue consists of a wide assortment of cells, vitamins, and enzymes (catalysts) that result in a colloidal gelatinous mass. Tissue also serves to nourish a host of amino acids that form long-chained helixially coiled molecules known as *polypeptides*, or living plastics. There are multiple varieties of polypeptides. Some make up hair, fingernails, and muscle fiber. In contrast, manmade plastics are far simpler, less elegant, and lifeless. A commercial plastic, like a polypeptide, is a very long molecule that is made up of repeating units. An example of a polypeptide is shown below.

$$-[RHS-C=O-NH-CHR-C=O-CHR-C=O-NH]_n-$$

The n stands for the number of molecular repeating units (shown inside the brakets). The n can range from one to over a million units.

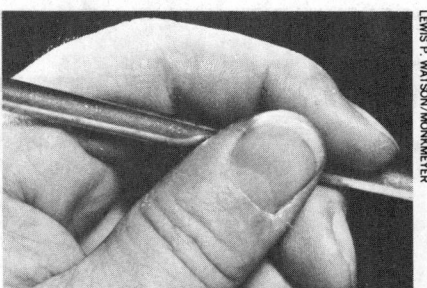

PLASTICS, *natural and man-made, surround us. A fingernail is a complex, replenishable polymer; plastic utensils are simple inert polymers.*

Thermoplastics.

As shown in the above example, it is important to realize that any plastic is produced from one kind of a repeating molecular unit that can react with itself or with a different molecular species. A single starting unit, like ethylene, is called a monomer. Many monomers that are reacted with themselves are referred to as polymers. Any molecule having a double bond can react with itself and form repeating units until the reaction is stopped. For example, an ethylene monomer lacks two hydrogen atoms. It has two reactive positions or bonds that it either shares with itself or with another monomer that is lacking two hydrogens:

$$(-CH_2CH_2- + -CH_2CH_2- \rightarrow -CH_2CH_2CH_2CH_2- \text{ or } nCH_2=CH_2 \rightarrow -[CH\ CH\ CH\ CH\ ]n-).$$

Special catalysts are used to conduct most polymerization reactions. Thermoplastics are generally flexible, but with the application of heat they will melt at their softening points into viscous liquids. They can be reformed into any desired shape by cooling. The chart below displays some of the most widely used thermoplastics.

Thermosetting plastics.

A plastic that is generally rigid but will not soften or reform on cooling is a thermosetting plastic. For the most part, thermosetting plastics are based on benzene (polyureas and melamines are notable exceptions). One part of a thermosetting reacting system consists of a liquid or solid *prepolymer* having two or more reactive positions. This prepolymer is then mixed with a hardener or catalyst, which reacts with the prepolymer to create repeating units or induces the prepolymer to react with itself. The structures of some reactive prepolymers appear at right.

Organic chemistry is older than mankind. Decomposed fossils (oil and coal) provide the world with a myriad of organic molecules that were once alive. Animals and plants produce molecules of the most advanced kind that genetically alter themselves, almost beyond credibility.

PLASTICS
Common thermoplastics

MONOMER	POLYMER	MAJOR USES
$n(CH_2=CH_2)$ ethylene	$-[CH_2CH_2CH_2CH_2]_n-$ polyethylene	packaging/ bottles
$n(CH_2=CHCl)$ vinyl chloride	$-[CH_2CHClCH_2CHCl]n-$ polyvinyl chloride	rigid water pipes
$n(CH=CH_2)$ | CH propylene	$-[CHCH_2CHCH_2CH]_n-$ | CH CH CH polypropylene	housewares
$n(CH_2=CHCH=CH_2)$ butadiene	$-[CH\ CH=CHCH\ ]_n-$ polybutadiene	rubber tires
$n(CH_2=C-CH_3)$ | C=O | O | CH_3 methyl methacrylate	$-[CH_2CCH_3CH_2CCH_3]_n-$ | | C=O C=O | | O O | | CH_3 CH_3 polymethyl methacrylate	plexiglass and paints
$n(C_6H_5CH=CH_2)$ styrene	$-[CHCH\ CHCH]_n-$ | | C_6H_5 C_6H_5 polystyrene	styrofoam and housewares

Common thermosetting plastics

REACTIVE PREPOLYMER	REACTS WITH	MAJOR USES
CH_3 | C_6H_3—NCO | NCO 2,4, tolylene diisocyante	The isocyante groups (NCO) react with organic acids and water.	flexible and rigid foams
CH_3 | $CH_2-O-C_6H_4CC_6H_4-O-CH_2$ | | HC CH_3 HC \\O \\O HC HC | | H H standard epoxy resin	An epoxy resin reacts with organic acids, alcohols, amines, and amides.	paints and adhesives
OH OH | | $OHCH_2-C_6H_3-CH_2-C_6H_3-CH_2OH$ phenolic resole resin	A phenolic resole resin reacts with inorganic acids, amides, and amines; it can also react with itself upon the application of heat.	laminating adhesives for plywood

Silicone Chemistry

Man developed silicone chemistry, for no natural organic derivatives of silicon exist. Silicon is in group 14 of the Periodic Table, just below carbon. Silicon is more than twice as heavy as carbon (atomic weight of 28 versus 12 for carbon), and has 14 electrons to carbon's 6. However, like carbon, silicon's outer shell can give up four electrons or accept four electrons in order to gain a stable configuration. This accounts for its valence states of +4 and −4. Also like carbon, it can share electrons in its outer shell to form covalent bonds. Unlike carbon, silicon is not found free in nature but as silicon dioxide, SiO_2 (sand, quartz, flint, as a component in clay, and in all rocks and stone minerals). In contrast, carbon dioxide (CO_2) is a gas. Pure silicon reacts vigorously with free and bound oxygen and is used as a deoxidizing agent to refine metals. It has a melting point of 1412° C and a boiling point of 3145° C. Carbon melts at 3700 +/− 100° C and boils at 4830° C. It is the most heat-resistant element known. Although both are nonmetals, silicon is more conductive and more of a "metalloid" at room temperature than carbon. Because it can share electrons, silicon may be joined to alkyl radicals, like CH_3— (methyl). The result is a family of plastics and molecules known as silicones.

Manufacture.
Crushed quartz (SiO_2) is mixed with charcoal in an electric furnace. The charge is placed between a negative graphite electrode and one positive graphite electrode. The application of 15,000 (average) kilowatt-hours of power per ton of silicon produced causes part of the carbon in the charcoal to combine with the oxygen contained in SiO_2 and to escape as carbon dioxide. Free silicon (98 percent pure) is made along with silicon carbide (SiC). The latter is used as a refractory material that is highly resistant to oxidation (recombining with oxygen). The impure silicon metalloid is then reacted under special conditions with methylchloride (a gas) to produce silicon tetrachloride ($SiCl_4$) or trichlorosilane ($SiCl_3H$). Both are gases. After further purification, either material is reacted with very pure hydrogen (H_2) at a temperature between 800° and 1200° C. Silicon metalloid then deposits on the walls of an extremely pure quartz container. The hydrogen reacts with the chlorine atoms attached to the silicon atom and is converted to gaseous hydrochloric acid. After careful removal, the metalloid is remelted and then "doped" with small amounts of elements having a valence of +3 (boron, alumi-

SILICONE *products are used in the manufacture of fiberglass boat hulls.*

num, indium, and gallium) and +5 (phosphorous, antimony, and arsenic). The elements having a valence of +3 are one electron short of completing the outer shell of silicon to a desired complement of eight shared electrons.

With respect to an electric current, a "hole" of a so called p-type positive junction develops. In contrast, the elements having a valence of +5 have one too many electrons when their outer shells become mutually joined with the outer shell of a silicon atom, and a negative or an n-type semiconductor is formed. After doping, the melt is carefully cooled to yield single crystals, which are then transformed into silicon wafers that are etched with electrical circuits. The positive and negative junctions of the crystals provide the circuit with the ability to use "coded" electrical currents that form fixed messages (ROM, read only memory) or variable ones (RAM, random-access memory) in a computer silicon chip.

Silicon can combine with four hydrogen atoms to form SiH_4 (sil*ane*) as compared with CH_4 (meth*ane*). However, unlike carbon, silicon is currently much more limited in the "infinite" number of compounds it can form. Longer chains than hexasilane (Si_6H_{14}) are not easily synthesized. However, the silanes, halosilanes, and most other silicone compounds are more reactive than their linear organic countertypes. As shown below, most industrial silicones use organic or carbon-based radicals as part of their molecular structure.

The materials for production of silicone compounds can include methylchloride (CH_3Cl) or chlorobenzene (C_6H_5Cl). Reaction conditions are maximized to yield dimethyldichlorosilane ($CH_3CH_3SiCl_2$) and diphenyldichlorosilane ($C_6H_5C_6H_5SiCl_2$), as noted below.

$$2CH_3Cl + Si \rightarrow (CH_3)_2Si(Cl)_2$$
A copper catalyst is used.

$$2C_6H_5Cl + Si \rightarrow (C_6H_5)_2Si(Cl)_2$$
A silver catalyst is used.

A Grignard reagent (RMgX; R is an al-

kyl radical, Mg is magnesium, and X is a halogen) may be reacted with a silicon halide, or the halide may be added to an alkene (like ethylene) to extend the chain length, as illustrated below.

$$(CH_3)_2SiCl_2 + CH_3MgCl \rightarrow$$
$$(CH_3)_3SiCl + MgCl_2$$
Tetrahydrofuran instead of ether is employed as a solvent for the reaction.

$$SiHCl_3 + H_2C{=}CH_2 \rightarrow CH_3CH_2SiCl_3$$
Trichlorosilane is reacted with ethylene to make ethyltrichlorosilane. A platinum catalyst is used.

These alkylchlorosilanes and many other variations like them are reacted with water (hydrolyzed) to convert them into silanols. These, in turn, are reacted into polymers or plastics for various applications. The following equations illustrate this.

$$(CH_3)_2Si(Cl) + 2H_2O \rightarrow$$
$$(CH_3)_2Si(OH)_2 + 2HCl$$

$$n[(CH_3)_2Si(OH)_2] \rightarrow$$
$$[(CH_3)_2SiO]_n + nH_2O$$
This is a self-polymerization reaction. Dimethylsilanediol, or $(CH_3)_2Si(OH)_2$, reacts with itself, and if n is 5 and the methyl radical (CH_3—) is R, the polymer is represented as

$$\begin{array}{ccccc} R & R & R & R & R \\ | & | & | & | & | \\ -O-Si-O-Si-O-Si-O-Si-O-Si- \\ | & | & | & | & | \\ R & R & R & R & R \end{array}$$

The value of n is controlled by using an "end stopper," such as a monosilanol (R_3SiOH) to terminate the reaction at the desired end point. A variety of polymers may be made by using phenyl (C_6H_5—) and other alkyl reactive groups, which are combined with additional hydroxyl groups.

Uses.
Low n values (under 4) are employed to make molecules that are water soluble on one end of their chain while oil soluble on the other. These kinds of products are used as surfactants in the manufacture of urethane foams. Specific reactive groups may be incorporated at the ends of each molecule so that they serve as sizing agents in the preparation of fiberglass composites to make insulation, boats, and cars. If the molecules are heavily alkylated (especially with CH_3— radicals), they become excellent water repellants and sealants. By using n values from 4 to 10, lubricants and oils are produced. Silicone oils exhibit stable changes in viscosity. For example, on cooling from 38° C to −37° C, the viscosity of hydrocarbon oils increases almost two-thousandfold, while that of silicone oils goes up only sevenfold.

TABLE OF ELEMENTS

At. wt., *atomic weight* (C = 12)
At. no., *atomic number*
Sp. gr., *specific gravity*
V. *valence*

M.P., *melting point °C.*
B.P., *boiling point °C.*
*All temperatures in the text
are in degrees Centigrade (°C.).*

C.S., *crystal structure*
C = *cubic, whether body- or face-centered unknown*
Cb = *cubic, body-centered*
Cf = *cubic, face-centered*
H = *hexagonal*
T = *tetragonal*

ELEMENT		OCCURRENCE, PREPARATION, DATE OF DISCOVERY, AND DISCOVERER	PROPERTIES	CHIEF COMPOUNDS AND USES
Actinium (Ac)	At. wt. 227 (?) At. no. 89 V. 3 Sp. gr. 10.1 M.P. 1,050° B.P. 3,200°	In uranium ores, resulting from radioactive decay of uranium. Bombardment of bismuth. 1899; Debierne.	Radioactive; half-life ranges from 20 years to 3.7 seconds. It is chemically quite similar to lanthanum.	Used in research.
Aluminum (Al)	At. wt. 26.9815 At. no. 13 V. 3 Sp. gr. 2.7 M.P. 660.2° B.P. 2,327° C.S. Cf	Cryolite, bauxite, impure emery, ruby, sapphire (Al_2O_3). Commercially, by electrolysis of Al_2O_3 from bauxite, dissolved in cryolite; water power usual source of electrical energy. 1825; Oersted.	Silver-white, ductile metal; malleable at 120°; tensile strength (wrought) 16 tons per square inch. Better conductor of electricity, weight for weight, than copper. Acted upon by dilute hydrochloric acid, slowly by sulfuric acid, but not by nitric acid or the acids in foods. Soluble in alkaline hydroxides.	Used for cooking utensils, boatbuilding, airplanes, small articles requiring lightness and strength, and electric leads. The powdered metal is used as a body for paint; its mixture with ferric oxide, called thermite, is used for producing very high temperatures (up to 2700°).
Americium (Am)	At. wt. 243.13 At. no. 95 V. 3, 4, 5, 6 Sp. gr. 13.67 M.P. 995°	Does not occur naturally. Bombardment of uranium-238 with very high energy electrons. 1944; Seaborg, James, Morgan, Ghiorso.	Radioactive, transuranium element. Alpha activity amounts to 70 billion alpha disintegratons per minute per milligram.	Its short half-life restricts use of this element to nuclear research.
Antimony (Sb)	At. wt. 121.75 At. no. 51 V. 3, 5 Sp. gr. 6.684 M.P. 630.5° B.P. 1,640° C.S. H	Free and as stibnite (Sb_2S_3). Roasting stibnite gives Sb_2O_4, which is then reduced by heating with carbon. 1450; Valentine.	White, brittle, crystalline metal. Its alloys expand on solidification, give very sharp castings for type. Does not tarnish, but may be burned in air; unites directly with the halogens.	Constituent of type metal, Britannia metal, Babbitt metal (used for bearings), and other alloys. Oxide (Sb_2O_3) is both basic and acidic. Trichloride, butter of antimony ($SbCl_3$), is easily hydrolyzed. Tartar emetic is used in medicine and dyeing.
Argon (Ar)	At. wt. 39.948 At. no. 18 V. 0 M.P. −189.2° B.P. −185.7°	Present in the air 0.94 per cent by volume. To isolate from air, carbon dioxide is removed by soda lime, water by phosphorus pentaoxide, oxygen by red-hot copper, nitrogen by magnesium and calcium; fractional distillation of residue yields argon. 1894; Rayleigh, Ramsay.	Monatomic gas, identified by its characteristic spectrum seen by examining light emitted when the gas is placed in a vacuum tube at low pressure and sparked. More soluble than nitrogen in water; 100 volumes of water dissolves 4 volumes of argon under ordinary conditions.	Forms no compounds, hence its name, argon, meaning 'inert.'
Arsenic (As)	At. wt. 74.9216 At. no. 33 V. 3, 5 Sp. gr. 5.7 M.P. 817° (under pressure) B.P. 613° (sublimes)	Free as arsenical pyrites (FeSAs), or pigment (As_2S_3), and realgar (As_2S_2). By heating arsenical pyrites to change as follows: (FeSAs → FeS + As). 1649; Schröder.	Steel-gray, dull metallic, crystalline element classed as a metalloid because it is between metals and nonmetals. Vapor density corresponds to As_4 at 644°, and to As_2 at 1700°. Burns in air and unites directly with the halogens, sulfur, and many metals.	Used for hardening lead shot. All compounds are poisonous. White arsenic (As_2O_3) is partly basic, forming a chloride, and partly acidic, forming arsenites. Scheele's green is a dangerous pigment used in wallpaper. Traces of arsenic may be detected by Marsh's test, in which intensely poisonous arsine (AsH_3) is formed.
Astatine (At)	At. wt. 210 (?) At. no. 85 V. 1, 3, 5, 7	Does not occur naturally. By bombardment of bismuth with a stream of alpha particles. 1940; Segré, Corson, MacKenzie.	Synthetic element similar to polonium. All the known isotopes are short-lived, the longest-lived isotope having a half-life of 8.3 hours.	Its limited stability restricts its use to nuclear research.
Barium (Ba)	At. wt. 137.34 At. no. 56 V. 2 Sp. gr. 3.5 M.P. 729° B.P. 1,637° C.S. Cb	As barite, or heavy spar, ($BaSO_4$) and witherite ($BaCO_3$). By electrolysis of the fused chloride ($BaCl_2$). 1808; Davy.	Silver-white, lustrous, malleable metal harder than lead. Like calcium, it reacts slowly with water to give barium hydroxide and hydrogen. The vapors of its compounds impart green color to the Bunsen flame.	Peroxide (BaO_2) is used in manufacture of oxygen and hydrogen peroxide; nitrate and chlorate in pyrotechnics to produce green fires; sulfate as the body for permanent white paint and for filling glazed paper. All its soluble compounds are poisonous.
Berkelium (Bk)	At. wt. 248 (?) At. no. 97 V. 3, 4 M.P. 1,278°	Does not occur naturally. By bombardment of americium-241 with alpha particles. 1949; Seaborg, Ghiorso, Thompson.	Radioactive, transuranium element. The longest-lived isotope has a half-life of several thousand years.	Expensive to make; restricted to radioactive research.
Beryllium (Be)	At. wt. 9.0122 At. no. 4 V. 2 Sp. gr. 1.8 M.P. 1,284° B.P. 2,970° C.S. H	In beryl [$Be_3Al_2(SiO_3)_6$]. By electrolysis of the fused double fluoride ($BeF_2 \cdot 2KF$). 1797; Vauquelin.	Hard, white metal that tarnishes when heated in air; soluble in dilute acids when powdered.	Hydroxide [$Be(OH)_2$] is feebly acidic as well as basic, thus resembling the hydroxide of zinc. Emerald is beryl colored green by chromium oxide. Used as nuclear reactor fuel-rod casing.
Bismuth (Bi)	At. wt. 208.980 At. no. 83 V. 3, 5 Sp. gr. 9.8 M.P. 271.3° B.P. −1,560° C.S. H	Free and as trioxide (Bi_2O_3) and trisulfide (Bi_2S_3). Ore is roasted, then heated with charcoal and metallic iron to remove traces of sulfur. 1450; Valentine.	Exceedingly brittle, crystalline, shiny metal, white with tinge of pink. Expands on solidification. Does not tarnish, and can be burned in air. Dissolves in oxygen acids. Most diamagnetic substance known.	Used for making fusible alloys such as Wood's metal (melting point 60.5°), used in plugs of fire sprinklers, boiler safety valves, and for taking casts. The oxynitrate is used in medicine and as a cosmetic.

(continued)

TABLE OF ELEMENTS *(continued)*

ELEMENT		OCCURRENCE, PREPARATION, DATE OF DISCOVERY, AND DISCOVERER	PROPERTIES	CHIEF COMPOUNDS AND USES
Boron (B)	At. wt. 10.811 At. no. 5 V. 3 Sp. gr. amorphous 2.4 crystalline 2.5 M.P. 2,300° B.P. 2,550°	Occurs as follows: boric acid (H_3BO_3), borax ($Na_2B_4O_7 \cdot 10H_2O$), and colemanite ($Ca_2B_6O_{11} \cdot 5H_2O$). Amorphous, by reducing B_2O_3 with magnesium; impure crystalline, by reducing B_2O_3 with excess aluminum. 1808; Gay-Lussac, Thénard, Davy.	Amorphous form is a greenish-black powder that burns in air at 700°, forming B_2O_3 and BN. Boron is oxidized by adding hot concentrated nitric acid or sulfuric acid to boric acid.	Compounds are analogous to those of silicon. Borax is used as a flux and, in solution, as a mild alkali because of its hydrolysis. Boric acid is used as a weak antiseptic and preservative.
Bromine (Br)	At. wt. 79.909 At. no. 35 V. −1, +5 Sp. gr. 3.12 M.P. −7.2° B.P. 58.78°	In sea water, as alkali bromide; in layers of salt deposits as sodium and magnesium bromide. By treatment of brine with sulfuric acid and manganese dioxide, or with chlorine. 1826; Balard.	Dark red liquid; smells like chlorine; vapor irritates eyes, throat, and nose. Dissolves in 30 parts of water (bromine water). Combines with most other elements, but less vigorously than chlorine.	Potassium bromide is used in pharmacy; silver bromide, in photography. Bromine is used in preparation of organic dyes and as a disinfectant and a bleach.
Cadmium (Cd)	At. wt. 112.40 At. no. 48 V. 2 Sp. gr. 8.6 M.P. 320.7° B.P. 765°	With zinc ores, as carbonate and sulfide. Comes over in first portions in distillation of impure zinc. 1817; Stromeyer.	Silver-white metal, more ductile and more malleable than zinc. Burns in air; is attacked by dilute acids.	All compounds are poisonous, little ionized. Sulfide is basis of cadmium yellow; iodide is used in pharmacy; metal as protective plating.
Calcium (Ca)	At. wt. 40.08 At. no. 20 V. 2 Sp. gr. 1.55 M.P. 850° B.P. 1,420° C.S. C	As carbonate (Iceland spar, calcite, aragonite, marble, chalk, limestone), sulfate, phosphate (apatite), fluoride (fluorspar), complex silicates (feldspars, pyroxines, amphiboles). By electrolysis of the fused chloride, or heating the iodide with sodium. 1808; Davy.	White crystalline metal, harder than lead. Can be cut, drawn, rolled, and turned. Reacts with water and burns in air at red heat, forming the oxide (CaO) and the nitride (Ca_3N_2). Unites with hydrogen to form CaH_2, whose reaction with water is source of hydrogen for balloons. Salts color test flame yellowish-red.	Oxide (quicklime) is used for mortar and to remove hair from hides. Hydroxide mixed with sand forms mortar; solution is limewater. Plaster of Paris is less hydrated sulfate; takes up water on setting to form gypsum. Phosphates are fertilizers.
Californium (Cf)	At. wt. 251 (?) At. no. 98 V. 3	Does not occur naturally. By bombardment of curium-242 with alpha particles. 1950; Seaborg, Thompson, Ghiorso, Street.	Radioactive; transuranium element.	Expensive to make; restricted to radioactive research.
Carbon (C)	At. wt. 12.01115 At. no. 6 V. 4, 6 Sp. gr. diamond 3.5 graphite 2.3 amorphous 1.9 M.P. not realized; volatilizes at 3652° B.P. 4,827°	Free as diamond and graphite; in combination with hydrogen as petroleum; with oxygen as carbon dioxide; with these and other elements as coal and in plant and animal tissues; as many carbonates. By dry distillation of wood or coal, yielding charcoal and coke, respectively. Known in antiquity.	Diamond is crystalline, and is the hardest of minerals; dark-colored bort used for cutting and grinding. Graphite has black metallic luster, is crystalline, and may be scratched by the fingernail. Charcoal is amorphous and can absorb gases and coloring matters. All three forms burn in oxygen to form carbon dioxide.	The carbon compounds form the substance of organic chemistry. Carbon dioxide results from burning coal, coke, wood, oil, or illuminating gases, from fermentation and decay (slow burning), and from exhalation. Carbon monoxide is a deadly gas. Graphite is a popular lubricant; diamond is a precious gem; coal, coke, and petroleum are fuels.
Cerium (Ce)	At. wt. 140.12 At. no. 58 V. 3, 4, 6 Sp. gr. 6.90 M.P. 804° B.P. 3,468° C.S. C	As silicate in cerite, along with neodymium, praseodymium, and lanthanum; also in monazite sand. By electrolysis of the fused chloride. 1803; Berzelius, Klaproth, Hisinger.	Rare earth metal with the color and luster of iron; like tin in hardness; very ductile and malleable. Burns in air more easily and more brightly than magnesium. Emits sparks when scratched with steel.	Welsbach incandescent gas mantles contain 1 per cent cerium dioxide (CeO_2). Alloys are used for gas and cigar lighters.
Cesium (Cs)	At. wt. 132.905 At. no. 55 V. 1 Sp. gr. 1.9 M.P. 28.5° B.P. 670° C.S. Cb	In certain micas, mineral waters, and the ashes of certain plants. By heating the hydroxide (CsOH) with magnesium or by electrolysis. 1860; Bunsen, Kirchhoff.	Silver-white metal resembling rubidium and potassium. The softest of all solid metals; one of the most active metals and the most electropositive. Reacts violently with water. Cesium gives two bright lines in the blue of the spectrum; its name comes from *caesius*, meaning 'sky-blue.'	Used in certain photoelectric cells; in vacuum tubes to eliminate traces of gases. One of its radioactive isotopes is used in medical radiation therapy.
Chlorine (Cl)	At. wt. 35.453 At. no. 17 V. −1, 5, 7 Sp. gr. (liquid) 1.5 M.P. −103° B.P. −34.6°	In sea water as chlorides of the alkalis and alkaline earths; in salt deposits as like compounds. By electrolysis of alkali chloride, fused or in solution; by the action of manganese dioxide (MnO_2) on hydrochloric acid (HCl). 1774; Scheele.	Greenish-yellow gas with characteristic odor. Acts violently on respiratory tract. Unites directly with all elements except oxygen, nitrogen, and the argon family. Displaces bromine and iodine from their compounds; substitutes for hydrogen in organic compounds.	Gas is used in extracting gold and in preparing bleaching and disinfecting agents. In presence of water it bleaches many coloring matters. Forms chlorides, such as NaCl, KCl, $CaCl_2$; hypochlorites, as solution of $Ca(OCl)_2$; chlorates, as $KClO_3$, used for matches and in pyrotechnics; and perchlorates, as $KClO_4$. Common table salt is NaCl.
Chromium (Cr)	At. wt. 51.996 At. no. 24 V. 2, 3, 6 Sp. gr. 7.2 M.P. 1,890° B.P. 2,480° C.S. Cb	As chromite [$Fe(CrO_2)_2$]. By reducing the oxide of chromic acetate (Cr_2O_3) with aluminum filings. 1797; Vauquelin.	Steel-gray, lustrous, brittle, very hard metal. At high temperatures it burns in air to form green Cr_2O_3. Attacked by dilute sulfuric acid or hydrochloric acid, but not by nitric acid.	Used in alloys of steel and nickel. Chrome green (Cr_2O_3) and chrome yellow ($PbCrO_4$) are pigments. Bichromates (such as $K_2Cr_2O_7$) are used in photo processes, tanning and dyeing, and as oxidizing agents, as in batteries. The metal, like nickel, is used as a protective and decorative plating.
Cobalt (Co)	At. wt. 58.9332 At. no. 27 V. 2, 3 Sp. gr. 8.71 M.P. 1,495° B.P. 2900° C.S. H (?)	As smaltite ($CoAs_2$) and cobaltite (CoAsS) found with iron and nickel. By igniting the oxide in hydrogen. 1735; Brandt.	White, malleable metal, less tenacious than iron. Turns pinkish on exposure to air. Less active chemically than iron.	Intensely blue silicates are used in coloring porcelain and constitute the pigment smalt. Used in commercial dyes; also used in medical radiation therapy.

ELEMENT		OCCURRENCE, PREPARATION, DATE OF DISCOVERY, AND DISCOVERER	PROPERTIES	CHIEF COMPOUNDS AND USES
Copper (Cu)	At. wt. 63.54 At. no. 29 V. 1, 2 Sp. gr. 8.93 M.P. 1,083° B.P. 2,336° C.S. Cf	Free as cuprite (Cu_2O), copper glance, chalcopyrite ($CuFeS_2$), and malachite [$Cu_2(OH)_2CO_3$]. After removal of iron and sulfur, the oxide is reduced by heating with carbon. It is refined electrolytically. Known in antiquity.	Red, lustrous, very ductile and malleable metal; high tensile strength (14 tons per square inch); second only to silver in electrical conductivity. In ordinary air it gradually becomes coated with basic carbonate. In absence of air, nitric acid alone among the dilute acids attacks it; in the presence of air, even acids in foodstuffs can dissolve it.	Used for coins, ornaments, electrical leads, electroplating, roofing, cooking vessels, and for making such alloys as brass, bell and gun metals, German silver, and the bronzes. The soluble compounds are poisonous and are used as agricultural germicides. Blue vitriol is $CuSO_4 \cdot 5H_2O$; the basic acetate is verdigris.
Curium (Cm)	At. wt. 247 (?) At. no. 96 V. 3 Sp. gr. 13.51	Does not occur naturally. By bombardment of plutonium-239 with alpha particles. 1944; Seaborg, James, Ghiorso, Morgan.	Radioactive, transuranium element. The longest-lived isotope has a half-life of a half-million years.	Expensive to make; restricted to nuclear and radioactive research.
Dysprosium (Dy)	At. wt. 162.50 At. no. 66 V. 3 Sp. gr. 8.56 M.P. 1,407° B.P. 2,564°	In monazite, in gadolinite, and in other rare minerals. By fractional crystallization of bromates. 1886; Boisbaudran.	Rare earth. The oxide, dysprosia (Dy_2O_3), is found with three other rare earths.	Salts are green or yellow and show characteristic absorption bands. They are the most magnetic of all salts.
Einsteinium (Es)	At. wt. 252 (?) At. no. 99 V. 3	Does not occur naturally. Prepared by intensive neutron irradiation of plutonium-239. 1952; Thompson, Harvey, Choppin, Seaborg, Ghiorso.	Radioactive, transuranium element. Half-life of longest-lived isotope is 280 days.	Expensive to make; limited to nuclear research.
Erbium (Er)	At. wt. 167.28 At. no. 68 V. 3 Sp. gr. 9.16 M.P. 1,497° B.P. 2,900°	In gadolinite and other rare minerals. 1843; Mosander.	Rare earth. The oxide erbia (Er_2O_3) is found with holmia, thulia, and dysprosia.	Salts are rose-colored and show characteristic absorption spectra.
Europium (Eu)	At. wt. 151.96 At. no. 63 V. 2, 3 Sp. gr. 5.24 M.P. 826° B.P. 1,439°	In monazite and other rare minerals. By electrolysis of the chloride. 1896; Demarçay.	Rare earth. This element so closely resembles samarium that the two elements are difficult to separate analytically.	Salts are pinkish and show a faint absorption spectrum. Sometimes used in control rods of nuclear reactors.
Fermium (Fm)	At. wt. 257 (?) At. no. 100 V. 3	Does not occur naturally. Prepared by intensive neutron irradiation of plutonium-239. 1953; Thompson, Harvey, Choppin, Seaborg, Ghiorso.	Radioactive, transuranium element.	Expensive to make; limited to nuclear research.
Fluorine (F)	At. wt. 18.9984 At. no. 9 V. 1 Sp. gr. (liquid) 1.1 at −187° M.P. −223° B.P. −188.14°	As cryolite (Na_3AlF_6), fluorspar (CaF_2), and very widely elsewhere in small quantities. By electrolysis of dry hydrogen fluoride at −23°. 1886; Moissan.	Pale yellowish-green gas that unites with every element except oxygen. Rapidly displaces oxygen from water, and displaces chlorine from hydrogen chloride.	Hydrogen fluoride is used for etching glass and in silicate analysis. Silver fluoride is soluble and calcium fluoride is insoluble, in contrast with the other halides of these metals.
Francium (Fr)	At. wt. 223 (?) At. no. 87 V. 1	Does not occur naturally. Disintegrates so rapidly that it is almost impossible to obtain in sufficient quantity to enable weighing. 1939; Perey.	Synthetic radioactive element; heaviest of the alkali metals.	Expensive to make; limited to radioactive and nuclear research.
Gadolinium (Gd)	At. wt. 157.25 At. no. 64 V. 3 Sp. gr. 7.94 M.P. 1,312° B.P. 2,800°	In gadolinite and samarskite. By electrolysis of the chloride. 1886; Marignac.	Rare earth. Closely resembles terbium in its compounds.	Salts are colorless and show absorption bands only in the ultraviolet.
Gallium (Ga)	At. wt. 69.72 At. no. 31 V. 2, 3 Sp. gr. 6.095 M.P. 30.150° B.P. 1,983°	In iron ores, zinc blende (ZnS), and bauxite (Al_2O_3). By electrolysis of an alkaline solution of its salts secured from zinc. 1875; Boisbaudran.	Bluish-white, tough metal that can be cut with a knife. Like aluminum, it is soluble in hydrochloric acid and caustic soda, but not in nitric acid.	Forms two chlorides, $GaCl_3$ and $GaCl_2$, that yield very characteristic spark spectra. Alloys with aluminum and cadmium are used for optical mirrors and cathodes.
Germanium (Ge)	At. wt. 72.59 At. no. 32 V. 2, 4 Sp. gr. 5.35 M.P. 947° B.P. 2,700°	In the rare mineral argyrodite. By the reduction of the dioxide (GeO_2) by the element carbon. 1886; Winkler.	Grayish-white, brittle, lustrous metal, insoluble in hydrochloric acid. Combines directly with the halogens.	Close relation of this element to carbon and silicon is shown in the compound germanium chloroform. Mendeleev described it before its discovery, calling it ekasilicon. The oxide is used to treat pernicious anemia.

(continued)

TABLE OF ELEMENTS *(continued)*

ELEMENT		OCCURRENCE, PREPARATION, DATE OF DISCOVERY, AND DISCOVERER	PROPERTIES	CHIEF COMPOUNDS AND USES
Gold (Au)	At. wt. 196.967 At. no. 79 V. 1, 3 Sp. gr. 19.4 M.P. 1,063° B.P. 2,600°	Chiefly free, but also a telluride; many specimens of iron pyrites are auriferous. From gold-bearing sands by washing away the lighter materials and dissolving the gold from the residue in mercury, which is subsequently separated from the gold by distillation. Known in antiquity.	Soft, bright-yellow metal, easily scratched by a knife; most ductile and malleable of the metals; excellent conductor of heat and electricity. Chemically, gold is rather inert and is not attacked by the oxygen of the air, by hydrogen sulfide, or by any single acid.	Pure gold is 24-carat gold. Jewelry is made in 18-, 14-, and 9-carat gold because alloying it with copper increases hardness and rigidity. Sodium chloraurate is used for toning in photography, and potassium auricyanide is used in electrogilding.
Hafnium (Hf)	At. wt. 178.49 At. no. 72 V. 4 Sp. gr. 13.3 M.P. 2,230° B.P. 3,200°	Associated with zirconium. By decomposing the tetraiodide. 1922; Coster, Hevesy.	Analogous to zirconium.	Similar to zirconium compounds, from which it is separated by fractional crystallization.
Helium (He)	At. wt. 4.0026 At. no. 2 V. 0 Sp. gr. (liquid) 0.15 M.P. −272.2° (at 26 atmospheres) B.P. −268.9°	In the air to the extent of 1 to 2 volumes per million; also occluded in certain minerals. First observed in sun's spectrum (1868; Lockyer, Jannsen). Neon and helium are boiled off crude argon, and the neon, when cooled, solidifies. 1895; Ramsay.	Lightest gas except hydrogen; transparent, odorless, and colorless.	Forms no compounds. Used for balloons; not flammable.
Holmium (Ho)	At. wt. 164.930 At. no. 67 V. 3 Sp. gr. 8.803 M.P. 1,461° B.P. 2,600°	Occurs with, and is separated from the erbium subgroup of the rare earths. Has never been isolated. 1879; Cleve.	Rare earth. Salts are orange-yellow and similar to those of dysprosium.	Used in glass to transmit radiant energy for wavelength-calibration instruments.
Hydrogen (H)	At. wt. 1.00797 At. no. 1 V. 1 Sp. gr. (liquid) 0.09 M.P. −259.1° B.P. −252.7°	In the air to the extent of 1 volume per 20,000 volumes of air; combined, in water (11.19 percent by weight), natural gas, petroleum, and animal and vegetable bodies. By treating zinc with hydrochloric or sulfuric acid; by electrolysis. 1766; Cavendish.	Lightest gas, transparent, odorless, and colorless. Soluble in water (2 volumes in 100 volumes of water under average conditions), in platinum, in palladium (502 volumes in 1 volume of palladium). Burns in air and in chlorine and unites with many other elements.	Its two oxides are water and hydrogen peroxide, the latter used in solution as a bleaching agent. Every acid contains hydrogen as an essential constituent. Its compounds with carbon and other elements number over 100,000.
Indium (In)	At. wt. 114.82 At. no. 49 V. 1, 3 Sp. gr. 7.3 M.P. 156° B.P. 2,000°	In zinc blende (ZnS) in small quantities. Electrolytically from solutions of its salts. 1863; Reich, Richter.	White, malleable metal, softer than lead; about as heavy as tin.	Compounds color the nonluminous gas flame blue and show a characteristic indigo blue line in the spectrum—hence its name. Sometimes used as a coating on bearings.
Iodine (I)	At. wt. 126.9044 At. no. 53 V. 1, 3, 5, 7 Sp. gr. 4.93 M.P. 113.7° B.P. 184.35°	In the ocean and certain seaweeds; always in the combined state. From iodides by displacement of their iodine by chlorine. 1811; Courtois.	Dark gray, brittle solid with a metallic luster. Vapor is violet, as are its solutions in chloroform and carbon bisulfide. Requires more than 5,000 parts of water for solution. Combines directly with many elements, but is much less active than chlorine or bromine.	Used in pharmacy as an antiseptic and in prescriptions for the treatment of goiter. Potassium iodide and iodoform likewise find application in medicine. The alkyl iodides are much used in synthetic organic chemistry.
Iridium (Ir)	At. wt. 192.2 At. no. 77 V. 3, 4 Sp. gr. 22.42 M.P. 2,454° B.P. 4,800° C.S. Cf	With platinum and osmium. Obtained from platinum ores by a complex series of operations. 1804; Tennant.	White metal, brittle when cold, very hard, and one of the densest substances known. Attacked by fused alkalis, but not by aqua regia.	Used for pointing gold pens. Its alloy with 9 parts of platinum is used for standard meter bars because of its unalterability. Used as a black color in china decorations.
Iron (Fe)	At. wt. 55.847 At. no. 26 V. 2, 3 Sp. gr. 7.86 pig 7.03−7.73 M.P. 1,535° wrought 1,600° steel 1,375° gray pig 1,275° white pig 1,075° B.P. 3,000° C.S. Cf, Cb	As magnetite (Fe_3O_4), hematite (Fe_2O_3), limonite ($2Fe_2O_3 \cdot 3H_2O$), siderite ($FeCO_3$), which are important ores; iron pyrites (FeS_2); in rocks as complex silicates; in plants and animals. Pig iron is prepared in blast furnace by reduction of the ore by means of carbon monoxide in presence of suitable flux. From pig iron, wrought iron is obtained by puddling, and steel by the Bessemer, or by open-hearth or other processes. Known in antiquity.	Malleable, ductile, magnetic metal, that is unchanged in dry air, but rusts in water and moist air. Easily attacked by dilute acids, but not by fused alkalis. Cast iron contains 2 to 5 per cent carbon and other impurities, and is hard and brittle. Wrought iron contains less than 0.2 per cent carbon and is softer and tougher, with tensile strength of 22 to 25 tons per square inch. Steel contains from 0.2 to 1.5 per cent carbon, and is permanently magnetic.	The metal is used as a structural material for rails, machinery, tools, etc. Jeweler's rouge and Venetian red consist of the oxide (Fe_2O_3). Rust is chiefly hydrated oxide. Hammer scale and lodestone have the composition Fe_3O_4. Ferric chloride ($FeCl_3$), ferrous iodide (FeI_2), and other iron compounds are used in medicine. Green vitriol ($FeSO_4 \cdot 7H_2O$) is used in making ink and in dyeing.
Krypton (Kr)	At. wt. 83.80 At. no. 36 V. 0, 2, 4 M.P. −156.6° B.P. −152.3°	In minute quantities in the air. From crude argon by fractional distillation. 1898; Ramsay, Travers.	Inert, colorless, and odorless gas resembling, but denser than, argon.	Once thought to be chemically inert; forms series of fluoride compounds, such as KrF_2 and KrF_4.
Lanthanum (La)	At. wt. 138.91 At. no. 57 V. 3 Sp. gr. 6.15	As lanthanite [$La_2(CO_3)_3 \cdot 8H_2O$]. By electrolysis of the fused chloride ($LaCl_3$). 1839; Mosander.	Rare earth; iron-gray metal; tarnishes in air to steel-blue; malleable and ductile. Attacked slowly even by cold water.	When heated in air, it forms a strongly basic oxide (La_2O_3) that is diamagnetic, and a nitride (LaN).

ELEMENT		OCCURRENCE, PREPARATION, DATE OF DISCOVERY, AND DISCOVERER	PROPERTIES	CHIEF COMPOUNDS AND USES
Lawrencium (Lr)	At. wt. 256 (?) At. no. 103 V. 3	Does not occur naturally. By bombardment of californium-252 with boron ions. 1961; Ghiorso, Sikkeland, Larsh, Latimer.	Radioactive, transuranium element.	Expensive to make; used in nuclear research.
Lead (Pb)	At. wt. 207.19 At. no. 82 V. 2, 4 Sp. gr. 11.34 M.P. 327.43° B.P. 1,515° C.S. Cf	End product of certain radioactive decompositions. As galena (PbS) and in silver ores. By calcination of partially roasted galena. Purification is effected by Parkes process. Known in antiquity.	Soft, gray metal; malleable and of low tensile strength, relatively impermeable to X rays and atomic radiation. In presence of air, water acts on lead to produce the hydroxide which, being slightly soluble, may cause lead poisoning. When heated in air, lead is oxidized to litharge and, under suitable conditions, to minium.	Used for water pipes, roofs and gutters, and storage batteries. For shot is alloyed with 0.4 per cent arsenic. Type metal contains 80 per cent lead. Babbitt metal, for bearings, contains over 70 per cent lead. Solder and pewter are alloys of lead and tin. The basic carbonate, white lead, is the basis of most oil paints.
Lithium (Li)	At. wt. 6.939 At. no. 3 V. 1 Sp. gr. 0.53 M.P. 179° B.P. 1,317° C.S. C	In amblygonite [$Li(AlF)PO_4$]. By electrolysis of the fused chloride (LiCl). 1817; Arfvedson.	Lightest metal; silver-white, softer than lead, tarnishes quickly in air, and easily reacts with water. When heated, it unites vigorously with nitrogen.	The carbonate (Li_2CO_3) is used in medicine as a solvent for uric acid, lithium urate being soluble. The salts give a carmine flame coloration.
Lutetium (Lu)	At. wt. 174.97 At. no. 71 V. 3 Sp. gr. 9.84 M.P. 1,652° B.P. 3,330°	In euxenite. By electrolysis of the chloride. 1907; Urbain, Welsbach.	Rare earth. Like ytterbium but has lower magnetic susceptibility.	Its compounds resemble those of ytterbium. It was once known as Casseopium.
Magnesium (Mg)	At. wt. 24.312 At. no. 12 V. 2 Sp. gr. 1.74 M.P. 651° B.P. 1,107° C.S. H	Occurs as magnesite ($MgCO_3$), dolomite ($MgCO_3 \cdot CaCO_3$), carnallite ($MgCl_2 \cdot KCl \cdot 6H_2O$), and in very many complex silicates. By electrolysis of dried, fused carnallite. 1808; Davy.	Silver-white, very lightweight metal, ductile when hot, and malleable. It tarnishes in air and reacts slowly with water, rapidly with steam. Burns in air to the oxide (MgO), emitting a very bright light. Unites directly with nitrogen.	Used as a reducing agent. Sulfate, known as Epsom salts, is used in medicine, as are the oxide (magnesia), the carbonates, and the citrate. The bright light emitted when the metal is burned in air is used in photography.
Manganese (Mn)	At. wt. 54.9380 At. no. 25 V. 2, 3, 4, 6, 7 Sp. gr. 7.2 M.P. 1,220° B.P. 2,152° C.S. CT	As pyrolusite (MnO_2), braunite (Mn_2O_3), hausmannite (Mn_3O_4), and manganese spar ($MnCO_3$). By heating Mn_3O_4 with aluminum filings. 1774; Gahn.	Steel-gray, hard, brittle metal with a pinkish tinge. Rusts in moist air and is attacked by dilute acids.	Ferromanganese and spiegeleisen are alloys with iron, used in making steel tougher. With copper it forms the tough, hard manganese bronzes, with tensile strength up to 30 tons per square inch.
Mendelevium (Md)	At. wt. 258 (?) At. no. 101 V. 3	Does not occur naturally. By bombardment of einsteinium-253 with alpha particles. 1955; Thompson, Harvey, Choppin, Ghiorso, Seaborg.	Radioactive, transuranium element.	Expensive to make; limited to nuclear and radioactive research.
Mercury (Hg)	At. wt. 200.59 At. no. 80 V. 1, 2 Sp. gr. 13.6 M.P. −38.87° B.P. 356.58° C.S. H	Free and as cinnabar (HgS). By roasting cinnabar: $HgS + O_2 \rightarrow Hg + SO_2$ Known in antiquity.	Silver-white, mobile liquid, 20 percent heavier than lead. Has vapor pressure of 0.0002 millimeter at 0°. Tarnishes slowly in air and is attacked only by nitric among the dilute acids. Vapor is monatomic.	Used in thermometers and barometers. Alloys, some of which are used in dentistry, are called amalgams. Calomel (HgCl) is administered internally in medicine; corrosive sublimate ($HgCl_2$) forms a solution with very powerful germicidal properties.
Molybdenum (Mo)	At. wt. 95.94 At. no. 42 V. 3, 4, 5, 6 Sp. gr. 10.2 M.P. 2,620° B.P. 4,507° C.S. Cb	As molybdenite (MoS_2) and wulfenite ($PbMoO_4$). By reducing the oxides with aluminum powder. 1778; Scheele.	White metal as malleable as iron; will not scratch glass. Insoluble in hydrochloric or dilute sulfuric acid.	Ferromolybdenum alloys are used in the manufacture of special steels.
Neodymium (Nd)	At. wt. 144.24 At. no. 60 V. 3, 4 Sp. gr. 6.9 M.P. 1,024° B.P. 3,027°	With cerium and lanthanum. By electrolysis of the fused chloride. 1885; Welsbach.	Rare earth; yellowish metal; tarnishes in air.	Salts are rose-violet; solutions show characteristic spectra.
Neon (Ne)	At. wt. 20.183 At. no. 10 V. 0 M.P. −248.67° B.P. −245.92°	Minute quantities in atmosphere. Neon and helium are boiled out of crude argon and the neon separated from helium by cooling with liquid hydrogen. 1898; Ramsay, Travers.	Colorless, odorless, transparent, monatomic, inert gas.	Forms no compounds; is recognized by its characteristic spectrum. Used in glow tubes for display signs.
Neptunium (Np)	At. wt. 237 At. no. 93 V. 3, 4, 5, 6 Sp. gr. 20.45 M.P. 640°	Does not occur naturally. By bombardment of uranium with neutrons. 1940; McMillan, Abelson.	Radioactive element. First transuranium element to be synthesized. Emits alpha particles. Half-life of longest-lived isotope is 2,200,000 years.	Oxide is dark brown; costly to make; limited to nuclear and radioactive research.

(continued)

TABLE OF ELEMENTS *(continued)*

ELEMENT		OCCURRENCE, PREPARATION, DATE OF DISCOVERY, AND DISCOVERER	PROPERTIES	CHIEF COMPOUNDS AND USES
Nickel (Ni)	At. wt. 58.71 At. no. 28 V. 2, 3 Sp. gr. 8.9 M.P. 1,455° B.P. 2,730° C.S. Cf	As nicollite (NiAs) and nickel glance (NiAsS). By igniting the oxalate in hydrogen. 1751; Cronstedt.	White, very hard, lustrous metal; malleable, ductile, and tenacious. Rusts slowly in air and is easily attacked only by nitric acid.	Metal furnishes protective coating when plated on iron. German silver is an alloy of nickel, copper, and zinc. Nickel chromium steel is used for armor. Manganin, containing nickel, copper, and manganese, is used for electrical resistors. It is a catalyst, especially in hydrogenation.
Niobium (Nb)	At. wt. 92.906 At. no. 41 V. 1, 2, 4, 5 Sp. gr. 8.57 M.P. 2,415° B.P. c. 3,300°	In the mineral columbite ($FeCb_2O_6$). By reduction of the dioxide (NbO_2) by paraffin. 1801; Hatchett.	Light gray, malleable, ductile metal, as hard as wrought iron; not affected by acids, even aqua regia. The hydride (NbH) burns in air.	Compounds occur with those of tantalum, which they closely resemble. It was originally called Columbium.
Nitrogen (N)	At. wt. 14.0067 At. no. 7 V. 3, 5 Sp. gr. (liquid) 0.808 M.P. −209.86° B.P. −195.8°	Free nitrogen forms about 79 percent of the air by volume. Also in Bengal saltpeter (KNO_3), Chile saltpeter ($NaNO_3$). By fractional distillation of liquid air. 1772; Rutherford.	Colorless, odorless, transparent gas, rather inactive chemically. At ordinary temperature and pressure, 100 volumes of water dissolve 1.5 volumes of nitrogen.	Nitrous oxide, or laughing gas, is used by dentists. Nitric acid has many applications in analytic and industrial chemistry. Ammonia is a very soluble gas. Many nitrogen compounds are used as fertilizers, explosives, dyes, and drugs.
Nobelium (No)	At. wt. 255 (?) At. no. 102 V. 2	Does not occur naturally. By bombardment of curium-246 with carbon-12 ions. 1958; Ghiorso, Sikkeland, Walton, Seaborg.	Radioactive, transuranium element.	Costly to make; limited to nuclear and radioactive research.
Osmium (Os)	At. wt. 190.2 At. no. 76 V. 2, 3, 4, 6, 8 Sp. gr. 22.48 M.P. 2,700° B.P. 530°	With platinum and iridium. By reducing the tetroxide (OsO_4). 1804; Tennant.	Gray metal, harder than glass; densest of the known elements.	Its alloy with iridium is used in tipping gold pens. Osmium tetroxide is used as a microscope stain for fat.
Oxygen (O)	At. wt. 15.9994 At. no. 8 V. 2 Sp. gr. (liquid) 1.13 M.P. −218.4° B.P. −183°	Free oxygen forms about 20 percent of air by volume. Water contains 88.88 percent oxygen. Rocks of earth's crust contain about 46 percent in combination, chiefly as silicates. In the laboratory, by heating potassium chlorate ($KClO_3$). Commercially, by fractional distillation of air. 1774; Priestley, Scheele.	Colorless, odorless, tasteless, transparent gas, slightly heavier than air. At ordinary temperature and pressure, 100 volumes of water dissolve 3 volumes of oxygen. Very active chemically, combining directly with all but a few elements to form oxides. Most substances burn more vigorously in oxygen than in air. Liquid oxygen is magnetic.	Gas is sold compressed in mild steel cylinders, and is used for the oxyhydrogen blowpipe, in medicine, and for chemical purposes. Necessary to support animal respiration and ordinary combustion. Enters as a constituent into all oxides, most salts, and many organic compounds. Liquid oxygen (LOX) is an important propellant for rockets.
Palladium (Pd)	At. wt. 106.4 At. no. 46 V. 2, 4, 6 Sp. gr. 11.97 M.P. 1,549° B.P. c. 2,200° C.S. Cf	With platinum and gold in nickel ores. By a complex series of processes from platinum ores. 1803; Wollaston.	Silvery, malleable, ductile metal, related to platinum, unlike which, however, it may be attacked by nitric acid. Under suitable conditions it can absorb over 900 volumes of hydrogen.	Since it does not tarnish, it is used for coating silver goods, and by dentists as a substitute for gold. Like platinum, it is used as a catalyst.
Phosphorus (P)	At. wt. 30.9738 At. no. 15 V. 3, 5 Sp. gr. white 1.82 red 2.2 M.P. (white) 44° B.P. (white) 280°	As phosphates, such as apatite [$Ca_5F(PO_4)_3$]; in bones, teeth, and brain; and in seeds of plants. By reduction of calcium phosphate by carbon with a suitable flux in an electric furnace. 1669; Brand.	Exists in two allotropic modifications: white phosphorus, which is waxy in consistency, soluble in carbon bisulfide, foul-smelling, and poisonous; and red phosphorus, which is a solid, insoluble in carbon bisulfide, odorless, and not poisonous. White phosphorus has a low ignition temperature.	Red phosphorus is used in the manufacture of matches, as is the compound P_4S_3. In the form of superphosphate of lime, phosphorus is an important artificial fertilizer. The chlorides PCl_5 and PCl_3 are much used in organic chemistry. Compounds are used in medicine. Phosphine, PH_3, is a poison gas.
Platinum (Pt)	At. wt. 195.09 At. no. 78 V. 2, 4 Sp. gr. 21.45 M.P. 1,773° B.P. 4,300° C.S. Cf	Free, alloyed with iridium and osmium, as nuggets in alluvial sands. Freed from the metals with which it is alloyed by a complex series of processes. 1557; Scaliger.	Silvery, tenacious, very heavy, ductile, malleable metal, unaltered in moist air and not attacked by any single common acid. Aqua regia, fused alkalis, alkali nitrates, and cyanides, however, do attack it. Platinum sponge and platinum black are finely divided forms.	Because of its resistance to acids, platinum is used for chemical vessels and electrodes. Since its coefficient of expansion is close to that of glass, platinum wires can be fused through glass without danger of breakage on cooling. The salts are used in photography. The metal is used in jewelry.
Plutonium (Pu)	At. wt. 239.05 At. no. 94 V. 3, 4, 5, 6 Sp. gr. 19.84 M.P. 640°	Present to a small extent in uranium ores. Produced in nuclear reactors starting with natural uranium. 1940; Seaborg, McMillan, Wahl, Kennedy.	Radioactive transuranium element. Emits alpha particles. Half-life of longest-lived isotope is 24,300 years.	Used as a pure nuclear fuel in reactors and weapons. It may be alloyed with carbon, iron, and aluminum, which are also used as nuclear fuels.
Polonium (Po)	At. wt. 210.05 At. no. 84 V. 2, 4 Sp. gr. 9.3 M.P. 254° B.P. 962°	With bismuth in uranium minerals. Metal has been isolated only in minute quantities because almost 13 tons of pitchblende ore yields only about one gram of the element. 1898; the Curies.	Radioactive element. Half-life is 138.7 days.	Compounds resemble those of tellurium.
Potassium (K)	At. wt. 39.102 At. no. 19 V. 1 Sp. gr. 0.86 M.P. 62.3° B.P. 760° C.S. Cb	As sylvite (KCl), carnallite ($KCl \cdot MgCl_2 \cdot 6H_2O$); in plant and animal ashes, and in many complex silicates. By reduction or electrolysis of fused potassium hydroxide (KOH). 1807; Davy.	Silver-white, lustrous, very lightweight metal, as soft as wax; tarnishes instantly in moist air. Chemically very active, decomposing in the cold and uniting violently with the halogens, sulfur, and oxygen.	Alloy (with sodium) is used in high-temperature thermometers. Bengal saltpeter is the nitrate and is used in pyrotechnics, for gunpowders, and as a preservative. Iodide, KI, is used in pharmacy. It is one of the three basic fertilizer elements, nitrogen and phosphorus being the others.

ELEMENT		OCCURRENCE, PREPARATION, DATE OF DISCOVERY, AND DISCOVERER	PROPERTIES	CHIEF COMPOUNDS AND USES
Praseodymium (Pr)	At. wt. 140.907 At. no. 59 V. 3, 4 Sp. gr. 6.78 M.P. 935° B.P. 3,127°	With cerium and lanthanum. By electrolysis of the fused chloride. 1885; Welsbach.	Rare earth; yellowish metal; remains untarnished in air.	Salts are leek-green, and their solutions have characteristic absorption spectra.
Promethium (Pm)	At. wt. 145 (?) At. no. 61 V. 3	Does not occur naturally. 1947; Marinsky, Glendenin, Coryell.	Rare earth metal, produced artificially. Recognized by its X-ray spectrum and optical absorption spectrum. Radioisotopes identified.	Compounds are similar to those of samarium and neodymium.
Protactinium (Pa)	At. wt. 231.10 At. no. 91 V. 5 Sp. gr. 15.37 M.P. 1,230° B.P. ?	In uranium ores. Metal has been isolated; about 70 milligrams may be secured from 1,000 kilograms of pitchblende. 1917; Hahn, Meitner, Soddy, Cranston.	Radioactive element, emitting alpha particles. Its half-life is 12,000 years.	Compounds resemble those of tantalum.
Radium (Ra)	At. wt. 226 At. no. 88 V. 2 Sp. gr. 5 (?) M.P. c. 960° B.P. 1,140°	In minute quantities in pitchblende and other uranium ores. Metal has been isolated; bromide is separated from the barium bromide prepared from pitchblende by fractional crystallization. 1898; the Curies, Bémont.	In all of its compounds, the metal has the power of emitting certain radiations. These can pass through materials that are opaque to light, render air a conductor, affect a photographic plate, and cause a zinc-sulfide screen to fluoresce visibly.	Rays from radium compounds (such as $RaBr_2$, $RaCl_2$, $RaCO_3$) during medical treatment act destructively on living tissues.
Radon (Rn)	At. wt. 222 At. no. 86 V. 0, 2, 4 Sp. gr. (liquid) 4.4 M.P. −71° B.P. −68°	Admixed with air. By passing air through solutions of radium salts. 1900; Dorn.	Inert gas of the helium family; radioactive, emitting alpha particles; half-life of longest-lived isotope is 3.83 days.	Forms fluoride salts. Used in treatment of cancer; enclosed in minute glass vessels the size of a small match head, it is inserted into the tumor.
Rhenium (Re)	At. wt. 186.2 At. no. 75 V. 1, 4, 6, 7 Sp. gr. 20.53 M.P. 3,167° B.P. c. 5,900°	In molybdenum and platinum ores. Hydrogen reduction of NH_4ReO_4. 1925; Noddack, Tacke, Berg.	Silver-white, hard metal, heavier than gold. Only tungsten is less fusible. Chemical properties are similar to those of manganese.	Used in electronics.
Rhodium (Rh)	At. wt. 102.905 At. no. 45 V. 2, 3, 4 Sp. gr. 12.4 M.P. 1,966° B.P. 2,500° C.S. Cf	In the ores of platinum. By a complex series of processes from platinum ores. 1803; Wollaston.	Silvery, malleable, ductile metal; does not tarnish in air; not attacked by aqua regia.	The red chloride ($RhCl_2$) is formed by the action of chlorine on the metal. Rhodium-platinum alloy is used for thermocouples to measure high temperatures.
Rubidium (Rb)	At. wt. 85.47 At. no. 37 V. 1, 3, 5 Sp. gr. 1.53 M.P. 38.5° B.P. 700° C.S. Cb	Found with cesium. Salts are associated with those of potassium. By heating the hydroxides with magnesium or by electrolysis of cyanides or hydroxides. 1860; Bunsen, Kirchhoff.	Silver-white metal resembling potassium; reacts vigorously with water.	Compounds show characteristic flame spectra with two red lines. Used in photocells and in pharmaceuticals.
Ruthenium (Ru)	At. wt. 101.07 At. no. 44 V. 3, 4, 6, 7, 8 Sp. gr. 12.3 M.P. 2,450° B.P. 4,150°	In the ores of platinum. By a complex series of processes from platinum ores. 1844; Klaus.	Hard, white, brittle metal, oxidized when heated in air. Scarcely attacked by aqua regia; very infusible. Chemical properties resemble those of osmium.	The following oxides are known: Ru_2O_3, RuO_2, RuO_4, as well as salts corresponding to RuO_3 and Ru_2O_7. Ruthenium red, an ammoniacal compound, dyes silk a beautiful yellow, but its high price limits its usefulness.
Samarium (Sm)	At. wt. 150.35 At. no. 62 V. 2, 3 Sp. gr. 7.536 M.P. 1,072° B.P. 1,900°	In monazite and samarskite. By electrolysis of the chloride. 1879; Boisbaudran.	Rare earth; whitish-gray metal; tarnishes in air.	Salts are topaz-yellow and are similar to those of lanthanum.
Scandium (Sc)	At. wt. 44.956 At. no. 21 V. 3 Sp. gr. 2.992 M.P. 1,539° B.P. 2,727°	In the minerals euxenite and gadolinite. Existence of this element was predicted by Mendeleev in 1869; he called it ekaboron. Leached from ores with sulfuric acid. 1879; Nilson.	Forms an oxide and a number of colorless salts.	An alloying element for nickel and nickel steels.

Selenium (Se)	At. wt. 78.96
	At. no. 34
	V. 2, 4, 6
	Sp. gr. amorphous 4.26
	    monoclinic 4.28
	    hexagonal 4.8
	M.P. amorphous 50°
	    monoclinic 170°
	    hexagonal 217°
	B.P. 684.9°
	C.S. THC
		Free in some specimens of sulfur and in combination with lead, iron, and other metals, as in pyrites.
		Amorphous, by reducing selenious acid (H_2SeO_3) with sulfur dioxide. With tellurium it is obtained from the anode slime occurring in copper refineries.
		1817; Berzelius.
			Three varieties are known: (1) red amorphous, soluble in carbon bisulfide from which it is deposited as (2) red translucent monoclinic crystals, soluble in carbon bisulfide; (3) blue-gray metallic selenium, insoluble in carbon bisulfide. This last form conducts electricity much better when exposed to light; conductivity increases with light intensity.	Selenium cells are used as indicators of intensity of illumination. The compounds strongly resemble those of sulfur. Hydrogen selenide is a foul-smelling, flammable gas. Selenic acid (H_2SeO_4) is a more powerful oxidizer than sulfuric acid and dissolves gold. The oxychloride is a valuable solvent for resins, fish oils, etc. Selenium is used in the manufacture of colorless and red-tinted glass, and in electronic rectifiers.

(continued)

TABLE OF ELEMENTS *(continued)*

ELEMENT		OCCURRENCE, PREPARATION, DATE OF DISCOVERY, AND DISCOVERER	PROPERTIES	CHIEF COMPOUNDS AND USES
Silicon (Si)	At. wt. 28.086 At. no. 14 V. 4 Sp. gr. amorphous 2.35 crystalline 2.4 M.P. 1,410° B.P. 2,355°	Silicon dioxide (SiO_2) occurs as flint, quartz, quartz sand, etc. Igneous rocks are composed largely of silicates, and silicon constitutes more than 27 percent of the earth's crust—more than any other element except oxygen. By reducing sand with coke in a furnace. 1823; Berzelius.	Amorphous silicon is a brown powder that burns when heated in air. Crystalline silicon forms black needles. It is less active than the amorphous variety and is attacked only slowly by a mixture of hydrofluoric acid and nitric acid. It unites with fluorine, however, at ordinary temperatures.	Silicon is used in steelmaking. Silicon steel is more magnetic than iron. Ornamental varieties of quartz find uses as gems, as do several natural silicates. Silicon carbide, or carborundum (SiC), is used as an abrasive. Sodium silicate solution is water glass, used to protect sandstone and to preserve eggs. Common glass is a mixture of sodium and calcium silicates.
Silver (Ag)	At. wt. 107.868 At. no. 47 V. 1 Sp. gr. 10.53 M.P. 960.8° B.P. 1,950° C.S. Cf	Native, as sulfide (AgS_2) often associated with galena; as chloride (AgCl). From lead alloys by the Pattinson process or the Parkes process; from the ores by the Mexican and other processes. Known in antiquity.	White, highly lustrous, tough, very ductile, malleable metal; best conductor of heat and electricity known. Liquid silver dissolves oxygen. It is unaffected by the oxygen of moist air; its tarnishing is caused by the action of hydrogen sulfide. It dissolves in dilute nitric acid and in hot concentrated sulfuric acid.	Used for tableware, ornaments, coins, etc. U.S. sterling silver contains 90 percent silver, 10 percent copper. Lunar caustic is silver nitrate. This salt and the halides of silver are used extensively in photography. For electroplating, a bath of potassium argenticyanide is used.
Sodium (Na)	At. wt. 22.9898 At. no. 11 V. 1 Sp. gr. 0.97 M.P. 97.5° B.P. 883° C.S. Cb	In the sea as chloride (NaCl); in salt deposits as chloride, borate, and nitrate; in many complex silicates in rocks. By electrolysis of fused sodium hydroxide (NaOH). 1807; Davy.	Silver-white metal, soft as wax. Immediately tarnishes at ordinary temperatures. Like potassium, it is very active, uniting directly with many other elements and vigorously reacting with cold water.	Used in manufacture of chemicals. Sodium chloride is a necessity of life for most animals, and is used in manufacture of hydrochloric acid, chlorine, and sodium compounds. Sodium carbonate and sodium hydroxide are used for cleaning and for manufacture of soap and chemicals. Sodium bicarbonate is baking soda. The sulfate is known as Glauber's salt; the thiosulfate, by photographers, as "hypo."
Strontium (Sr)	At. wt. 87.62 At. no. 38 V. 2 Sp. gr. 2.6 M.P. 774° B.P. 1,366° C.S. C	As strontianite ($SrCO_3$) and celestite ($SrSO_4$). By electrolysis of the chloride. 1790; Crawford.	White metal; harder than sodium, softer than calcium; tarnishes to a yellow tint. Like calcium, it is active enough to react vigorously with cold water.	The nitrate and chlorate are used in fireworks for red color. All volatile compounds color the Bunsen flame red.
Sulfur (S)	At. wt. 32.064 At. no. 16 V. 2, 3, 4, 6 Sp. gr. rhombic 2.07 monoclinic 1.96 M.P. rhombic 112.8° monoclinic 119° B.P. 444.6°	Native, in combination with most metals as sulfides, and with some metals as sulfates. By melting the free sulfur away from the rocky matrix (Frasch process), and subsequent purification by distillation. Known in antiquity.	Natural sulfur is rhombic in crystalline form, yellow, brittle, and of vitreous luster. It is a poor conductor of heat and electricity. This and the monoclinic variety are soluble in carbon bisulfide, while amorphous sulfur is not. When heated, sulfur unites directly with most other elements.	Used to prepare sulfur dioxide (SO_2), which is used in making sulfuric acid and sulfites and for bleaching; also for vulcanizing rubber and in manufacture of black gunpowder. Sulfuric acid (H_2SO_4) is to the chemical industry what iron is to engineering. Thiosulfuric acid and its salts are important in the processing of film.
Tantalum (Ta)	At. wt. 180.948 At. no. 73 V. 2, 4, 5 Sp. gr. 16.6 M.P. 2,996° B.P. 5,425°	In tantalite and many other rare minerals. By the action of sodium tantalofluoride (Na_2TaF_7). 1802; Ekeberg.	Hard, silver-white metal; ductile and malleable when hot; of very high tensile strength. The hot metal can absorb 740 volumes of hydrogen. Not attacked by aqua regia.	Used for filaments for electric lamps until tungsten replaced it; in surgical instruments and in rectifiers; and as a substitute for platinum.
Technetium (Tc)	At. wt. 97 (?) At. no. 43 V. 6, 7 Sp. gr. 11.50 M.P. 2,200° B.P. ?	Does not occur naturally. By bombardment of molybdenum with a stream of deuterons. 1937; Perrier, Segré.	The first artificially produced element. Resembles rhenium and manganese.	Used experimentally and for making technetium carbonyl $Tc_2(CO)_{10}$, which is stable, is soluble in organic compounds, and is reactive with halogens.
Tellurium (Te)	At. wt. 127.60 At. no. 52 V. 2, 4, 6 Sp. gr. rhombic 5.93 monoclinic 6.3 M.P. 449.5° B.P. 989.8°	Free and as tellurides. By reducing tellurous acid (H_2TeO_3) by means of sulfur dioxide. 1782; Müller von Reichenstein.	Crystalline variety is white, has metallic luster, and conducts heat and electricity. Precipitated variety is black and of lower density. Element is related to sulfur, but is more metallic.	Compounds find few applications; in coloring glass, gives silver a platinum finish. Telluric acid (H_6TeO_6) has basic as well as acidic characteristics, in keeping with the position of the element between the metals and nonmetals.
Terbium (Tb)	At. wt. 158.924 At. no. 65 V. 3 Sp. gr. 8.27 M.P. 1,356° B.P. 2,800°	In gadolinite, in samarskite, and in other rare minerals. By electrolysis of the chloride. 1843; Mosander.	Rare earth element. Closely resembles the element gadolinium.	Salts are almost colorless; oxide is almost black.
Thallium (Tl)	At. wt. 204.37 At. no. 81 V. 1, 3 Sp. gr. 11.86 M.P. 303.5° B.P. 1,457° C.S. T	In crookesite and in small quantities in many samples of iron pyrites. Precipitated by zinc from solution obtained by suitable treatment of flue dust from sulfuric acid works. 1861; Crookes.	Bluish-white, leadlike metal; rather soft and malleable, but of low tensile strength. Decomposes water rapidly at red heat and dissolves in dilute acids.	Forms two sets of salts, thallous and thallic. The salts, used in making optical glass, are poisonous. All the compounds show a characteristic green line in the spectrum.
Thorium (Th)	At. wt. 232.038 At. no. 90 V. 4 Sp. gr. 11.7 M.P. 1,845° B.P. 4,230° C.S. C	In monazite sand. By reducing potassium thorium chloride with sodium, or by electrolysis of fused potassium and sodium chlorides. 1828; Berzelius.	Metal has the color of nickel; can be burned in air. Hydrochloric acid attacks it slowly. Most isotopes are radioactive.	The nitrate $Th(NO_3)_4 \cdot 6H_2O$ is used in making Welsbach incandescent mantles, which consist of 99 percent thorium dioxide. Alloyed with magnesium for special purposes.

ELEMENT		OCCURRENCE, PREPARATION, DATE OF DISCOVERY, AND DISCOVERER	PROPERTIES	CHIEF COMPOUNDS AND USES
Thulium (Tm)	At. wt. 168.934 At. no. 69 V. 3 Sp. gr. 9.33 M.P. 1,545° B.P. 1,727°	In gadolinite and other yttrium minerals. 1879; Cleve.	Rare earth metal; has never been isolated.	Salts are a pale green that is destroyed very easily by minute quantities of erbium.
Tin (Sn)	At. wt. 118.69 At. no. 50 V. 2, 4 Sp. gr. 7.3 M.P. 231.89° B.P. 2,260° C.S. TC	As cassiterite (SnO_2). After roasting, the ore is reduced by heating with carbon. Known in antiquity.	Silver-white, rather soft, very malleable, ductile metal; practically unchanged in air. When heated, it may be burned in air. Dilute nitric acid is the only dilute acid that attacks it rapidly. When kept long at temperatures below 0°, ordinary tin changes to a brittle, gray, powdery form.	Much tin is used in coating iron as tinplate. A constituent of Britannia metal, pewter, solder, bronze, etc. Forms two sets of salts: stannous and stannic. Pink salt is used in dyeing. Mosaic gold is essentially stannic sulfide.
Titanium (Ti)	At. wt. 47.90 At. no. 22 V. 2, 3, 4 Sp. gr. 4.5 M.P. 1,675° B.P. 3,260° C.S. C	As rutile (TiO_2) and ilmenite ($FeTiO_3$). By reducing the chloride ($TiCl_4$) by means of sodium. 1791; Gregor.	Hard, brittle metal, resembling polished steel. May be forged at low red heat. Dissolves in dilute sulfuric acid and decomposes in steam at 800°. Unites easily with nitrogen.	Used in alloys, as a white pigment (paint and paper), and as a coloring for ceramics. Used as structural material in supersonic aircraft.
Tungsten (W)	At. wt. 183.85 At. no. 74 V. 2, 4, 5, 6 Sp. gr. 19.3 M.P. 3,410° B.P. 5,927° C.S. Cb	As wolframite ($FeWO_4$) and as scheelite ($CaWO_4$). By reducing tungstic acid (H_2WO_4) with carbon at high temperatures. 1783; the De Elhuyars.	Hard, brittle, gray metal, attacked by chlorine only at 250°, although it can be caused to burn in air. Slowly acted upon by dilute acids and even by water.	Used for filaments of incandescent electric lamps, giving an efficiency of 1.3 watts per candlepower. Tungsten steel has 5 percent tungsten. Sodium tungstates are used as mordants in dyeing processes. Was originally known as wolfram.
Uranium (U)	At. wt. 238.03 At. no. 92 V. 2, 3, 4, 5, 6 Sp. gr. 19.05 M.P. 1,132.3° B.P. 3,818°	As pitchblende, which contains U_3O_8. By reducing the oxides with aluminum. 1789; Klaproth.	White, lustrous metal; tarnishes in air and reacts slowly with cold water. Combines directly with many other elements.	All compounds are radioactive in proportion to their radium content. Glass to which uranium compounds have been added shows a greenish-yellow fluorescence. Used in nuclear weapons. Chief fuel for nuclear reactors.
Vanadium (V)	At. wt. 50.942 At. no. 23 V. 2, 3, 4, 5 Sp. gr. 5.96 M.P. 1,890° B.P. 3,000° C.S. Cb	In a few rather rare minerals. By reducing the dichloride (VCl_2) in hydrogen. 1830; Sefström.	Silver-white lustrous metal, harder than quartz. Does not tarnish or react with water at ordinary temperatures, but can be burned in oxygen.	Added to steel even in small quantities (0.2 per cent), it increases the tenacity and elastic limit without reducing ductility.
Xenon (Xe)	At. wt. 131.30 At. no. 54 V. 0, 2, 4 Sp. gr. (liquid) 3.52 M.P. −111.9° B.P. −107.1°	In minute quantities in the air, 1 volume in 170 million. By fractionation of liquid argon. 1898; Ramsay, Travers.	Transparent, colorless, odorless gas. Densest member of the noble gases.	Once thought to be chemically inert; forms fluorides (XeF_2, XeF_4, XeF_6), oxide (XeO_3), and hexafluoroplatinate (Xe_2PtF_6) compounds.
Ytterbium (Yb)	At. wt. 173.04 At. no. 70 V. 3 Sp. gr. 7.01 M.P. 824° B.P. 1,427°	In gadolinite, euxenite, and other rare minerals. By electrolysis of the chloride. 1878; Marignac.	Rare earth. Forms colorless salts.	Compounds exhibit a characteristic spark spectrum.
Yttrium (Y)	At. wt. 88.905 At. no. 39 V. 3 Sp. gr. 4.34 M.P. 1,495° B.P. 2,927°	In gadolinite, euxenite, and other rare minerals. By electrolysis of sodium yttrium chloride. 1794; Gadolin.	Gray, lustrous metal.	Chloride yields a characteristic, though complex spectrum.
Zinc (Zn)	At. wt. 65.37 At. no. 30 V. 2 Sp. gr. 7.14 M.P. 419.4° B.P. 907° C.S. H	As zinc blende (ZnS), calamine ($ZnCO_3$), zincite (ZnO), etc. After roasting, the ore is reduced by coal, the metal distilling off. Known in antiquity.	Bluish-white, lustrous, brittle metal; malleable and ductile at 120°; tarnishes in moist air. Reacts slowly with cold water, and rapidly when heated in steam. Dissolves in dilute acids and sodium hydroxide solution.	Used for roofs, gutters, galvanic batteries. Iron galvanized with zinc, preventing rust. Zinc alloyed with copper to make brass. In paint, zinc oxide is less toxic than lead oxide. Salts used in medicine, chloride and sulfate used in antiseptic solutions.
Zirconium (Zr)	At. wt. 91.22 At. no. 40 V. 4 Sp. gr. 6.4 M.P. 1,852° B.P. 3,578°	As zircon ($ZrSiO_4$). By reducing the oxide (ZrO_2) with carbon in an electric furnace. 1789; Klaproth.	Hard, gray metal remaining bright in air; oxidizes slowly at white heat. Dissolves in aqua regia and caustic potash solution.	Oxide is contained in some incandescent gas mantles; is used for furnace linings and as a cleansing agent in metallurgy. Increases tensile strength of armor plate. Carbide is an abrasive.

—Fernando U. Fajardo

PHYSICS

What is physics? Physics may be said to be the story of matter, radiation, and their interaction. Matter appears everywhere in various forms. It has such characteristic properties as mass, temperature, and hardness.

In a similar sense, radiation is omnipresent in the universe. We experience radiation in different forms, for example, as light or heat radiation. Radiation is not matter, although it has some of the properties of matter. Radiation can be described both as an electromagnetic wave and as a particle called the photon. Neither description alone is adequate. Niels Bohr was the first to point out that the descriptions are complementary: depending on certain conditions, radiation can behave as a wave or as a particle.

Scope of physics. Physics, once called natural philosophy, forms the underpinning of several other sciences. Astrophysics may be called the physics of the stars; geophysics, the physics of the earth. Chemistry may be considered a branch of atomic physics. The composition of substances and the transformations they undergo are determined by the properties of the atoms of the substances.

Engineering is now often called applied physics, since the demarcation between engineering and physics may be hard to distinguish. Engineering laboratories and courses in engineering now resemble those in physics, especially laboratories and courses that deal with the properties and structure of matter.

Divisions of physics.
The commonly recognized divisions of physics are mechanics, thermodynamics, electricity and magnetism, acoustics, optics, and a variety of topics often referred to as modern physics. The topics of modern physics include radioactivity and nuclear physics; atomic and molecular spectra; the quantum theory of matter and radiation; solid-state physics; relativity; high-energy physics, including the study of cosmic radiation; and the physics of fundamental particles.

The various categories are by no means separate and independent. Nature is not divided into nicely compartmentalized units, and it is our attempt to comprehend nature that leads to the division of physics into subjects based on types of phenomena.

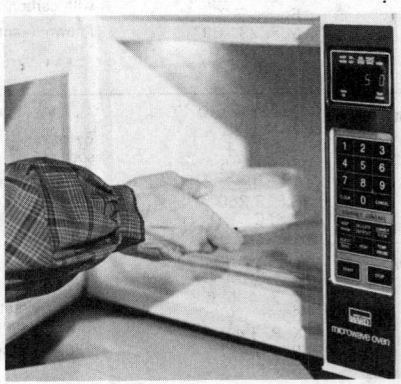

THE STUDY OF PHYSICS *has led to greater understanding of the physical world and the laws that govern it. It has enabled scientists to plot accurately the orbit of a space satellite and to develop many useful domestic devices, such as the microwave oven.*

Mechanics. Mechanics, the oldest of the subjects dealt with in a quantitative manner, has three branches. The first is kinematics, the geometry of motion without regard to forces or energy. Dynamics includes the forces acting and the energy involved when bodies are in motion. Statics deals with bodies in equilibrium. Mechanics is basic to much of engineering, certainly to structural engineering. Sir Isaac Newton developed mechanics to the stage where he was able to determine the velocity and energy needed to put a satellite into orbit.

Thermodynamics. Thermodynamics is the study of heat and of the behavior of matter with respect to thermal energy. The laws of thermodynamics include the conservation of energy and the decrease of available energy, the trend in nature that is termed increase of entropy.

Electricity and magnetism. Electricity and magnetism deal with the characteristics of electric charges, currents, electric fields, and magnetic fields. The practical application of this knowledge led to development of electric machinery and of electronics.

Optics. Physical optics deals with light as a form of electromagnetic radiation. Geometrical optics traces the paths of light rays through such devices as lenses and a variety of other optical instruments.

Acoustics. Acoustics deals with phenomena related to sound and might well have been called the study of elastic waves in solids, liquids, and gases.

Nuclear physics. Radioactivity was the first nuclear phenomenon studied by physicists, and this study established that not all atomic nuclei are stable. Atomic energy, which is more appropriately called nuclear energy, is the practical application of nuclear physics.

Quantum theory. The characteristic radiation, both visible and invisible, emitted by atoms and molecules under a variety of conditions is the major source of data on which are based our notions of atomic and molecular structure. The quantum theory of matter and radiation was initiated by Max Planck's hypothesis regarding the manner in which radiation is emitted from a solid. This was followed by the work of Niels Bohr, who recognized that the electrons in atoms occupy certain fixed energy levels, and that of Albert Einstein, who explained the photoelectric effect by proposing that light is made up of particlelike entities called photons.

Solid-state physics. Engineers and physicists have recently given much attention to the electrical and mechanical properties of solids. Although solids have always been a part of our environment, only recently has it been possible to relate the behavior and characteristics of solids to the properties of the atoms of which solids are composed.

Since 1900, physicists have been aware of a penetrating radiation coming to Earth from outer space. Although called radiation, the primary component that strikes the upper atmosphere is known now to be made up largely, if not completely, of atomic nuclei. Protons, the nuclei of hydrogen atoms, predominate and enter the upper atmosphere with extremely high energies. Their origin and the source of their energy are not known, but they are messengers that, with the radio signals detected by large radio telescopes, may yield new information about the stars and galaxies. The high energy of the primary components of cosmic rays has been approached but not equaled by the very large particle accelerators built in the United States, Western Europe, and the Soviet Union.

Role of physics. Before astronauts go into outer space, the energy required for launching, the direction of launching, and the direction of the final boost to the vehicle in which they ride must be determined precisely. Principles of physics are applied in providing the answers to these vital computations. Communication between the astronauts and their Earth-based controllers utilizes electronic apparatus and depends on an understanding of the behavior of electromagnetic radiation, which was developed in physics laboratories. It might be said that the ability to communicate instantly with all parts of the world is one result of the discoveries made by scientists.

Much of modern engineering is based on research performed in physics laboratories. For example, the x-ray machines, ultrasound imaging devices, radium, radioactive isotopes, computer assisted tomography (CAT scanners), proton-emission tomography (PET scanners) and electrocardiographs used in hospitals had their origins or were discovered in physics laboratories. Many of the conveniences in our homes—temperature controls, air conditioning, refrigerators, microwave ovens, and television sets—are byproducts of this same physical research.

The theory of relativity, with its requirement that mass and energy be equivalent, and the relation between them represented as $E = mc^2$, where E is energy, m represents mass, and c is the velocity of light, may be considered an achievement in physics that will characterize the present century. The theoretical work has been confirmed by experimentation achieving fission and fusion of atomic nuclei, in which a small amount of the mass of a nucleus changes to energy. The direct consequences of this research were the development of the nuclear bomb and design of fission reactors for electrical power stations.

Mechanics

Mechanics deals with force, motion, inertia, and energy. Of most interest are the laws governing the effect that a force—thought of as a push or a pull—will have on the form and motion of an object. Mowing a lawn, for example, requires a force to push the mower. A car engine exerts a pulling force to move its load. As was stated earlier, mechanics is divided into three areas. Statics is the area that deals with forces that are in equilibrium. Dynamics is the area that deals with the production and causes of motion. Kinematics is the area that treats motion without regard to the forces that produce it.

Measurement

For the expression of physical quantities, such as distance, mass, force, or time, scientists use an international system of units known under the French name of *Le Système International d'Unités* (SI), the International System of Units. It employs the metric system of measurement, first introduced in France in the 1790's and later in most other countries. The meter, the fundamental unit of length in the metric system, was then defined as one millionth of the distance between the north or south pole and the equator. More recently, the meter was defined as the length that is equal to 1,650,763.73 wavelengths of the orange-red radiation emitted by the krypton atom. In 1983, scientists redefined the meter with even greater precision as the length of the path traveled by light in vacuum during a time interval of 1/299,792,458 of a second.

Mass. The amount of matter of an object is called mass and is shown by its inertia, the measure of resistance to a change of motion. Our most common experience of the mass of an object is its weight, the force by which it is attracted to Earth. The fundamental unit of mass in the SI system is the kilogram (kg). Originally, the kilogram was defined as a mass equal to the mass of 1 liter of water at a temperature of 4° C. The kilogram is now defined as the mass of the International Prototype Kilogram, a platinum iridium cylinder preserved at the International Bureau of Weights and Measures at Sèvres, France.

Time. Time is universally measured in hours, minutes, and seconds. Scientists once relied on the rotation of Earth for the precise measurement of time: 24 hours was defined as the time interval between two passages of the same star through the cross hairs of a transit telescope. Because the rotation period of Earth is slightly irregular, however, a second, which is the fundamental SI unit of time, is now defined as the time it takes for the cesium atom to radiate 9,192,631,770 wavelengths of light at a specific wavelength.

Units expressed in meters, kilograms, and seconds are also called mks units. Since many scientists still use the centimeter, gram, and second for measurements, these units are called cgs units. In the United States, the foot, pound, and second, which are known as fps units, are still widely used, especially for mechanical engineering applications.

KEEPING TIME

Timekeeping once was based on the rotation of the Earth and observation of the passage of a star through the cross hairs of a transit telescope. After astronomers discovered that the rotation of the Earth is not constant, atomic clocks came into use as time standards. Atomic clocks like the one to the right are more accurate than other clocks because they use the natural vibrations of atoms rather than a pendulum or oscillating crystal as the timekeeping device. Most precise of all are the cesium beam clocks, with accuracy better than one part in 10^{13}. Coordinated Universal Time (UTC) is based on atomic clocks, but "leap seconds" are added periodically to keep UTC synchronized with rotation of the Earth.

U.S. NAVAL OBSERVATORY

Vectors

In mechanics, two systems of addition must be used. When adding two numbers that have identical units, an answer is easy. For example, 8 feet plus 2 feet equal 10 feet. But some answers also require a direction. If a direction is added, 8 feet north plus 2 feet east, the problem is no longer one of simple arithmetic.

A quantity specified by a number and its unit, 8 feet or 50 miles per hour, for example, is called a scalar quantity. A quantity that also specifies direction, for example, 8 feet north or 50 miles per hour east, is known as a vector quantity.

Examples of vector quantities are force and velocity. A force has a certain strength, represented by the length of the vector, and a direction. Velocity has a value, indicated by the length of the vector. It also has direction, the direction of motion, indicated by the direction of the vector.

Vector quantities and operations can be represented graphically. For example, an object initially at a point 0 may be moved 3 feet east and 4 feet north. The final position of the object is then distance B from the starting point 0, or it may be said to be displaced distance 0B. Displacement of the body is a vector quantity, the direction and distance from the origin.

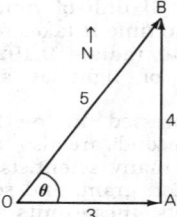

Equilibrium

Equilibrium is the state achieved when the resultant of all the forces acting upon a body is zero. When equilibrium is attained, there is no change in the motion of the body. The body may be at rest; it may be moving in a straight line at uniform speed; or it may be rotating about a fixed axis at a uniform rate.

Velocity and Acceleration

The discussion of equilibrium began with the supposition that the resultant, or summation, of the forces acting upon a body is zero. Equilibrium was defined as the state in which there was no change in the motion of a body. However, in mechanics one must also consider bodies upon which the resultant force is not zero, that is, upon which the forces do not result in a state of equilibrium. When the resultant force on a body is not zero, therefore, the motion of the body must change.

The motion of a body is described by its velocity. Velocity is the rate of change of position, or the rate of displacement. Velocity is usually expressed in meters or feet per second. Velocity is a vector quantity, so for complete specification, both its magnitude and its direction must be stated. Thus, when a body is not in equilibrium and its motion is changing, its velocity must also be changing. The rate of change of velocity is acceleration. Acceleration is usually expressed in meters or feet per second per second, or meters or feet per second squared.

When, for example, a car speeds up, it is accelerating; when it slows down, it is decelerating. Acceleration may be expressed algebraically as the final velocity, v_f, minus the original velocity, v_o, divided by the time interval, t, or

$$a = \frac{v_f - v_o}{t}.$$

Newton's laws of motion.

The relationship of force to motion was described in three laws formulated by Isaac Newton. These fundamental laws make possible the science of mechanics.

Newton's first law. Unless acted upon by an unbalanced force, a body at rest remains at rest, and a body in motion continues to move at constant speed along a straight line.

The first part of the law is simple enough to illustrate. Forces acting on a book that has been placed on a table cause it to remain at rest. Gravity pulls it down; the table pushes up. The

forces are in equilibrium, so the book remains stationary.

The second part of the law can be illustrated by the flight of a spacecraft in space. An initial force accelerates the spacecraft to a constant speed. Since there is no air in space, no opposing force is caused by friction. The spacecraft will follow a straight path at constant speed unless an external force acts upon it, for example, a gravitational field or an impulse created by a retro rocket.

Newton's second law. An unbalanced force acting on a body causes the body to accelerate in the direction of the force, and the acceleration is directly proportional to the unbalanced force and inversely proportional to the mass of the body.

Expressed algebraically, the law states that a varies as F/m, where a is the acceleration, F is the force, and m is the mass. This proportion may be expressed as

$$a = \frac{F}{m} \quad \text{or} \quad F = ma.$$

To illustrate the law, suppose two identical cars are driven along a road and that more force, in the form of push, is applied to the first car than to the second. This so-called push is really acceleration. Hence, the force acting on the car causes acceleration proportional to the unbalanced force in the direction of the force.

Now imagine that five passengers are added to one of two identical cars and that equal forces are applied to both vehicles. The car that has only a driver will have the greater acceleration. Generally, the greater the unbalanced force, and the less the mass, the greater the acceleration.

Newton's third law. For every action or force, there is an equal and opposite reaction or force.

Of all of Newton's laws, this is the easiest to understand. A book on a table presses down, the table pushes up. Action is the book pressing on the table; reaction is the table pushing against the book. Now consider a missile being launched. The rocket engines fire hot gases downward. This is the action. The reaction is the upward motion of the missile away from the accelerated gases.

Note that two bodies are involved in each case. Note also that action and

NEWTON'S LAWS ILLUSTRATED: *first law, the forces on the book are balanced; second law, the lighter car can accelerate faster; third law, reaction forces the missile upward.*

HALLEY'S COMET

Halley's Comet had been seen earlier, but Edmond Halley saw it in 1682 and suggested that the comet would return in 1758 or 1759. It arrived on schedule, reinforcing the validity of Newton's theory of gravitation.

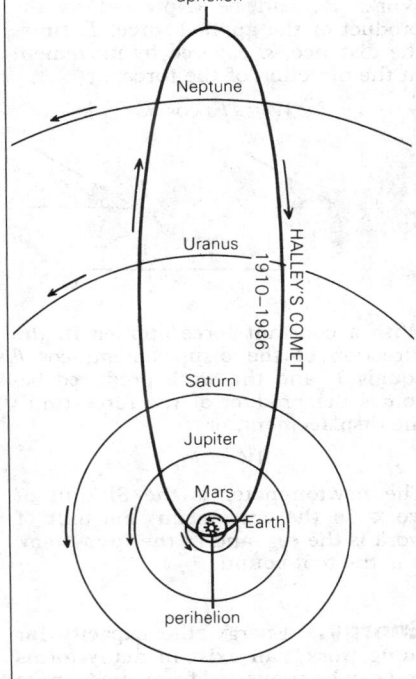

reaction, although equal and opposite, can never balance each other because, to balance each other, they must be exerted on the same body.

There are also forces at work on a body in circular or curvilinear motion. A body will move in a curve only when a lateral force is exerted upon it. The classic example is the stone whirled at the end of a string. The stone pulls outward on the string and, as the string becomes taut, it pulls inward on the stone. In the same way a spacecraft moves in an orbit around Earth because, as it is drawn inward by the pull of Earth's gravity, it maintains its position along a curved path due to its velocity.

Hence, the motion of a body traveling in a circular path with constant speed is of special interest. In such circular motion, the moving object is pulled toward the center of the circle by a force called centripetal force. Since, by the first law of motion, an object in motion tends to travel along a straight-line path, the inertia of the object opposes the inward pull. For many years it was thought that the opposition to centripetal force caused by the body's inertial tendency was actually a reaction force, called centrifugal force, as stated in the third law. However, to repeat, action-reaction pairs are never exerted upon the same body.

Force. Since the acceleration of a body is the result of a force acting on it, the acceleration is used to define the units of force. The SI unit of force is the newton: 1 newton is the force that gives a body of 1 kilogram an acceleration of 1 meter per second. The cgs unit of force is the dyne: 1 dyne gives a body of 1 gram an acceleration of 1 centimeter per second.

Gravitation

Each particle of matter attracts every other particle with a force, F, that is directly proportional to the product of their masses, m_1 and m_2, and inversely proportional to the square of the distance, r, between them:

$$F = G\,\frac{m_1\,m_2}{r^2}.$$

G is the gravitational constant, equal to 6.67×10^{-11} in SI units.

The most familiar example of universal gravitation is seen in the fall of an object when released. The amount of Earth's gravitation is different for different bodies, varying with their mass: this attraction is known as the weight of the body. Weight is proportional to mass; if the same force, gravitational attraction, produces the same acceleration on two bodies, the weights of the two bodies are equal. Since mass is the measure of quantity of matter, a quart of water, for example, must have twice the mass of a pint. By experiment, it can be shown that a quart of water weighs twice as much as a pint of water.

All bodies would fall with the same velocity if there were no air resistance. One can prove this by dropping a feather and a metal pellet in an evacuated glass vessel. Both objects reach the bottom at the same time.

The laws of falling bodies are based on the fact that their motion is uniformly accelerated, but in air the uniform acceleration does not continue indefinitely. If the body falls a sufficient distance, the gravitational force causing acceleration will be equaled by the increasing resistance of the air. At that point, acceleration ceases and

HENRY CAVENDISH, *using a sensitive torsion balance, found the gravitational constant by measuring the attraction between two equal small masses and two equal large masses.*

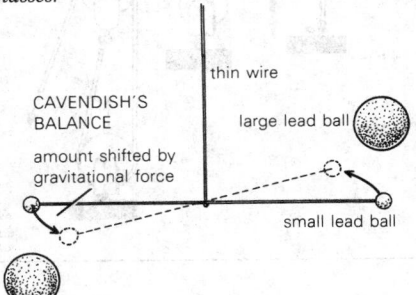

the body continues to fall at a uniform maximum velocity, called its terminal velocity.

A relationship exists between velocity, distance covered, acceleration, and time in uniformly accelerated motion. Based on the acceleration formula,

$$a = \frac{v_f - v_o}{t},$$

the formula for final velocity is

$$v_f = v_o + at.$$

The distance traveled by a body having constant acceleration is found by averaging its velocities during time interval t. Then distance traveled, s, may be found by the equations

$$s = v_{avg}t,$$
$$= \frac{v_o + v_f}{2}\,t.$$

Replacing v_f by $v_o + at$,

$$s = \frac{v_o + (v_o + at)}{2}\,t,$$
$$= v_o t + \tfrac{1}{2}at^2.$$

The third equation of uniformly accelerated motion is derived by eliminating time:

$$as = \left(\frac{v_f - v_o}{t}\right)\left(\frac{v_o + v_f}{2}\,t\right),$$
$$= \tfrac{1}{2}(v_f - v_o)(v_o + v_f),$$
$$v_f{}^2 = v_o{}^2 + 2as.$$

Substitution of gravitational acceleration, g, in these uniformly accelerated formulas yields

$$v_f = v_o + gt,$$
$$s = v_o t + \tfrac{1}{2}gt^2,$$
$$v_f{}^2 = v_o{}^2 + 2gs.$$

The only change is that acceleration due to gravity is substituted for acceleration. The value of g at the surface of Earth is 32.2 feet per second per second.

Friction

When two bodies in contact are in motion relative to one another, a force, called frictional force, opposes this motion; that is, the frictional force acts in a direction opposite to the direction of motion. There are several causes of friction. One is the roughness of the two surfaces in contact. No matter how smooth the surfaces may appear, when they are observed under magnification, irregularities can be seen. The irregularities tend to interlock and cause opposition to motion. A second cause of friction is found in the same atomic forces that hold molecules together in a solid. They also tend to hold the molecules of the two surfaces together. The magnitude of a frictional force depends on the materials in contact, the condition of the surfaces, and the forces that are pressing the surfaces together.

To illustrate frictional force, consider a box at rest on the ground. A rope is attached to the box and is pulled on with a 1-pound force. If the box does not move, the resultant force is zero, and the ground must be exerting a frictional force of 1 pound opposite to the force on the rope. If the pull is increased sufficiently, the box will eventually move, and at the moment it does move and continues to move at constant speed, friction has been overcome. Further increase in the pull will then cause acceleration of the box.

The coefficient of friction.

The accompanying figure shows a box being moved to the right at a constant velocity by a force, F. The box pushes against the ground with a force equal to its weight, W, and the ground pushes back with an equal force, called the normal, N. Since the box is moving at a constant velocity, the system must be in equilibrium, and frictional force f must therefore equal F.

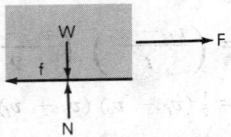

If a second box is placed on top of the first, in order to keep the system moving uniformly, the force to the right must be increased to a magnitude of F. The boxes are pressing against the ground with a force equal to their combined weights, W + W, and the

COEFFICIENTS OF FRICTION

MATERIALS	STATIC (NO RELATIVE MOVEMENT)	DYNAMIC (IN RELATIVE MOTION)
steel on steel	0.74	0.54
steel on lead	0.9	0.9
copper on steel	0.53	0.36
copper on glass	0.68	0.53
copper on cast iron	1.05	0.29
glass on glass	0.94	0.4
Teflon on Teflon	0.04	0.04
ski on snow at −10°C		0.2
ski on snow at 0°C		0.05

ground is pushing back with the equal force N. Since the system is still in equilibrium, the frictional force must have increased to f to remain equal to F. By experiment it has been shown that the frictional force increases in the same proportion as the normal force:

$$\frac{f'}{f} = \frac{N'}{N}$$

or

$$\frac{f}{N} = \frac{f'}{N'} = \text{constant}.$$

The constant, which is designated as μ, is called the coefficient of friction and has been determined for a large number of surface pairs. It can be used to determine the frictional forces in a system through the equation

$$f = \mu N.$$

Work

In physics, work is used to describe a situation in which an applied force produces movement in the direction in which the force is applied. A truck does not perform work in holding up a load of bricks, but it does perform work in moving the load up a hill. Work, W, can be expressed as the product of the applied force, F, times the distance, s, covered by movement in the direction of the force, or

$$W = Fs \cos \theta.$$

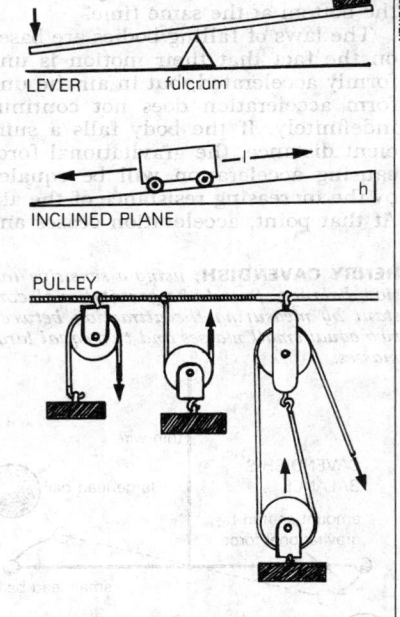

With a constant force applied in the direction of the displacement, cos θ equals 1, and the work produced becomes the product of the force times the displacement, or

$$W = Fs.$$

The newton-meter is the SI unit of work. In the cgs system, the unit of work is the erg, and in the fps system, it is the foot-pound.

Energy. Energy, the capacity for doing work, can exist in many forms and can be converted from one form to another. Potential energy is the energy a body has by virtue of its position. Kinetic energy is the energy a body has by virtue of its motion. Ignoring friction, the work done on a body equals the change in kinetic and potential energy. The energy change is expressed in the same units as work: newton-meters in the SI system, ergs in the cgs system, and foot-pounds in the fps system. It is converted or transformed by machines to a usable form. Although energy cannot be destroyed, it may be transformed into some usable form and dissipated. For example, electrical energy used to heat the coils in a toaster is irretrievably dissipated. Mechanical energy used to stop a moving car is converted into heat in the brakes and is dissipated. The energy used to operate any machine, therefore, can be said to follow a standard pattern: it is converted into a more usable or convenient form and finally dissipated as heat.

Potential energy. The energy a body possesses by virtue of its location was referred to earlier as potential energy. Water in a reservoir, or a weight lifted to an elevated position, has potential energy that can be converted by a machine into a more desirable or convenient form. Gravitational potential energy is the most common form of potential energy. Since Earth's gravity attracts every body, work is required to

MECHANICAL ADVANTAGE

Mechanical advantage is defined as the ratio of the force exerted by a machine to the force applied to the machine. With a lever, the mechanical advantage is the ratio between the lengths of the lever on either side of the fulcrum. For an inclined plane it is the ratio of l/h; only a small force is necessary to lift the car to a height of h. With gears, the mechanical advantage is determined by the proportion of teeth on each gear. With pulleys, the mechanical advantage is equal to the number of pulleys. In the arrangement shown here, a 100-lb. weight can be lifted with a force of 50 lbs., but the rope must be pulled twice the distance the weight moves.

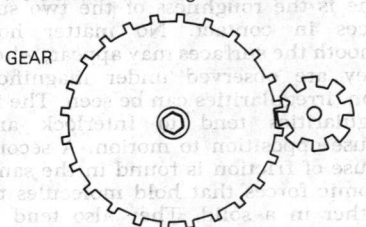

PETER LOEWER

elevate a body to a higher level. The work expended on the body (weight of the body times the elevation) represents energy that is stored and can be reconverted. This potential energy, P.E., is the product of the weight, W, and the height, h, to which the body was raised, and can be stated as

$$P.E. = Wh.$$

If W is given in newtons and h in meters, then the potential energy is expressed in newton-meters. The SI unit of work is the joule, and 1 joule is defined as 1 newton-meter. The unit of work in the cgs system is the erg, defined as 1 dyne-centimeter. When a mass is elevated, its potential energy is increased. When a mass is lowered, its potential energy is decreased. In either case, the potential energy is measured from an arbitrary zero point, such as sea level, a floor, or a table top. A stone on a table has no potential energy when the table top is selected as zero point. With the floor as zero point, the potential energy of the stone is equal to its weight times the height of the table. Potential energy can also be stored in a spring by stretching the spring. The energy can be released and put to work, for example, driving a spring-wound clock.

Kinetic energy. As has been said, the energy a body possesses due to its motion is called kinetic energy. A bullet in flight, a spinning flywheel, and a speeding automobile all possess kinetic energy. The amount of work a moving object can do while being brought to rest, or the work required to produce the velocity at which the body moves, is a measure of its kinetic energy, K.E.

A body at rest acted upon by an unbalanced force, F, through a distance, s, is accelerated, a, to a velocity, v. The work done to accelerate the body is equal to its kinetic energy, or

$$K.E. = Fs = mas.$$

From the earlier discussion of acceleration and velocity, it can be seen that the following substitutions can be made for a and s:

$$a = \frac{v_f - v_o}{t},$$

$$s = \frac{v_o + v_f}{2} t.$$

Thus,

$$K.E. = mas$$
$$= m \left(\frac{v_f - v_o}{t} \right) \left(\frac{v_o + v_f}{2} t \right).$$

Starting from rest, when v_o is zero,

$$K.E. = \frac{mv^2}{2}.$$

Accelerating or decelerating a body requires the application of a force that produces a change in the kinetic energy. The change in kinetic energy is

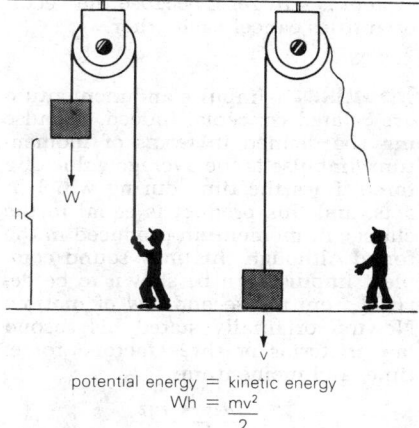

potential energy = kinetic energy
$$Wh = \frac{mv^2}{2}$$

THE POTENTIAL ENERGY *of the mass at rest becomes kinetic energy when the mass falls.*

equal to the total kinetic energy when the body is accelerated from rest or brought to a standstill.

To stop a moving object, its kinetic energy must be absorbed by work done in opposition to its motion. Since the kinetic energy of an object is proportional to the square of its velocity, doubling the speed increases the kinetic energy four times. Therefore, four times the amount of work is needed to bring the body to a stop. One consequence of this is that the braking distance of a car is not proportional to its speed but increases much faster. Assuming identical braking pressure, it takes much more than twice as long to stop a car traveling at 60 miles per hour than to stop a car at 30 miles per hour.

Power. Power is a measure of the amount of work that can be done per unit of time. By dividing the amount of work involved by the time required to complete the work, the average power can be determined. Both the work, W, and the time, t, must be measured in order to determine the average power, P.

$$P = \frac{W}{t} = \frac{Fs}{t}.$$

The SI unit for power is the watt, W, defined as the power of a system that produces 1 joule per second. A frequently used unit for power, especially for automobile engines, is the horsepower, a unit introduced by James Watt to relate the power of a steam engine to the rate of work of a horse. One horsepower equals 745.2 watts.

Torque

A body at rest or in uniform motion can be said to be in equilibrium. A body will remain in equilibrium as long as all forces acting on the body pass through a common point and the sum of their vectors is zero. When the forces do not pass through a common point, the rotation and the linear motion will be changed. Torque is the force that produces or tends to produce rotation.

When opposing but equal forces act on one point of a body, the resultant movement will be zero because the sum of the vector forces will be zero. If the same forces are applied to two different points of the body, the vector sum of the forces will again equal zero, but the body will rotate.

It must be noted that when the vector sum of the forces acting on a body is zero, the body will not move in a linear manner, but rotation is possible. Equilibrium is not assured, therefore, unless a second condition is satisfied. That condition requires that the sum of the torques generated by the applied forces also be zero.

The torque, L, about a selected axis is a product of the force, F, and the moment arm, s. (The moment arm is the perpendicular distance from a selected axis to the line of the applied force.) Then

$$L = Fs.$$

When combined into the single quantity torque, or moment of force, the magnitude of the force and the length of the moment arm are of equal importance. For a given moment arm, increasing the force increases the torque. For a given force, increasing the length of the moment arm increases the torque. Torque, a product of force, newtons, and measure of length, meters, is expressed in the SI system as $N \cdot m$, in the cgs system as dyne$\cdot$cm, and as pound-feet in the fps system.

Center of gravity. Center of gravity is the point at which the entire weight of a body may be considered to be concentrated. The sum of all torque produced by the weights of all parts of the body around a horizontal axis through the center of gravity must equal zero. The location of the center of gravity can be important for stability. For example, a car with a center of gravity close to the road will not tip over as easily as a vehicle with a center of gravity that is placed much higher, as in a double-decker bus.

THE TWO TUGBOATS *exert equal and opposing force (torque) on the ship, so it rotates.*

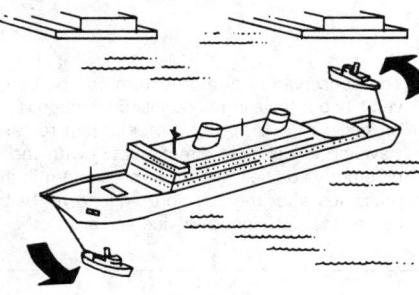

Momentum

During the study of basic mechanics, it must not be forgotten that the same laws apply to atomic particles that apply to larger objects. This is particularly true in the study of momentum, in which application of basic laws enabled scientists to predict the movement and properties of atomic particles years before their existence was verified.

The momentum, P, of a body is defined as the product of its mass, m, times its velocity, v, or

$$P = mv.$$

Momentum, a vector quantity, takes its direction from velocity. When two or more bodies are involved in a system, the momentum of each body must be added vectorially. If two balls of equal mass are rolled toward each other with equal velocity, the momentum of each is equal. Since the vectors are opposite in direction, the vector sum equals zero.

Conservation of momentum.

Newton's first law states that there is no change in the motion of a body unless an external force acts upon it. The mass of a body is constant; therefore, its momentum will remain constant unless an external force is applied. With this basic fact kept in mind, the behavior of everyday objects can be studied and analyzed. When a force is applied to a system of bodies, the momentum of the system is altered, but some other set of bodies will gain or lose momentum equal to the loss or gain produced in the first system. This conservation of momentum can be expressed simply as momentum lost equals momentum gained. If the balls discussed previously collide, they will rebound (if they are elastic). Since the law of conservation of momentum applies to the system, the velocity of the rebounding bodies will be equal to, but not necessarily the same as, the original speed. The total momentum of the system is still zero, because the vector quantities cancel each other.

Impulse. Impulse and momentum are related concepts. Indeed, impulse may be defined in terms of momentum. Impulse is the average value of a force times the time during which it acts, and this product is equal to the change in momentum produced in the force. Although this may sound complex, impulse can be shown to be derived from the second law of motion. Newton originally stated his second law in terms of three factors: force, time, and momentum:

$$F = \frac{mv - mv_o}{t},$$

where F is the force, m the mass, v the terminal velocity, v_o the starting velocity, mv and mv_o the terminal and initial momentums, respectively, and t the time. This equation can be changed to its more familiar form by factoring out mass:

$$F = \frac{m(v - v_o)}{t}$$

Since

$$\frac{v - v_o}{t} = a,$$

$$F = ma.$$

By multiplying the above equation by t, it becomes

$$Ft = mv - mv_o.$$

This is called the impulse equation. Ft is the impulse, and $mv - mv_o$ is the change in momentum.

As an illustration of impulse, consider a hammer of mass m accelerating at a rate a to a velocity v and striking a nail with a force F. This force, which lasts for a fraction of a second, drives the nail into the wood by impulse. The hammer has supplied an impulse equal to its loss of momentum. In the SI system, the unit of impulse is the newton-second. In the cgs system, the unit of impulse is the dynesecond, and in the fps system it is the pound-second.

Density

Liquids and solids share the property of density. A 1-inch block of lead is much heavier than a 1-inch block of wood. The difference reflects their different densities, ρ, or mass per unit volume:

$$\rho = \frac{m}{V}.$$

In the SI system, density is expressed as kilograms per cubic meter, kg/m^3. In the cgs system, density is expressed in grams per cubic centimeter, g/cm^3. The weight per unit volume is called the weight-density, D:

$$D = \frac{W}{V}.$$

Since

$$W = mg,$$

$$D = \frac{mg}{V}$$

$$= \rho g.$$

Density, ρ, is used when problems involving mass are being considered, while weight-density, D, is used when dealing with problems that involve taking into account the effects of force.

The ratio of the density of a substance to that of water at 4° C, which is 39.2° F, is called its specific gravity and is expressed as:

$$\text{specific gravity} = \frac{\rho}{\rho w},$$

where ρw is the density of water, and

$$\text{specific gravity} = \frac{D}{D_w},$$

where Dw is the weight-density of water. Specific gravity has no units because the densities of both substances have the same units. Since specific gravity is frequently tabulated, it is convenient to find densities of specific substances by the formula:

$$\rho = (\text{specific gravity}) (\rho w).$$

Pressure. A liquid confined in a container exerts a force on the walls and bottom of the container. With a still liquid, the force is normal or perpendicular to the surface. This perpendicular force, F, per unit area, A, is called pressure, P, and pressure is expressed as:

$$P = \frac{F}{A}.$$

Pressure, a scalar quantity, is exerted whenever force is applied over an area. Even people of very light weight can exert high pressure if they apply their weight over a small area, such as that of a shoe heel. The SI unit for pressure is newtons per square meter, N/m^2. The cgs unit is dynes per square centimeter, $dynes/cm^2$. Pounds per square inch is the most commonly used unit in the fps system.

MOMENTUM

The conservation of momentum can be demonstrated with pool balls. Two balls with equal velocity but traveling in opposite directions (1) have a total momentum of zero. After the head-on collision (2), the total momentum remains zero because the two pool balls will still be traveling in opposite directions (3) with the same speed. If the two pool balls initially have different velocities, the total momentum is then not zero. The total momentum will again be preserved after the collision. The slower ball will rebound with the speed the faster ball had before the collision, and vice versa. In other words, the balls exchange velocities.

SPECIFIC GRAVITY

One way of determining the specific gravity of a solid object is to compare the weight of an object in air with its weight in water. The following formula, where W is the weight of the object in air and W_1 is its weight in water, gives the specific gravity.

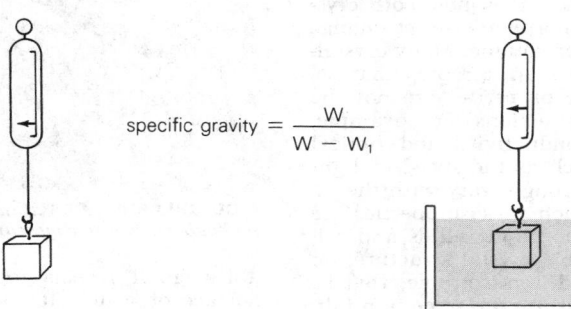

$$\text{specific gravity} = \frac{W}{W - W_1}$$

Specific gravity of some materials

SUBSTANCE		SPECIFIC GRAVITY g/cm³
SOLIDS	aluminum	2.70
	iron and steel	7.8
	copper	8.9
	gold	19.3
	concrete	2.3
	glass	2.6
	ice	0.917
LIQUIDS	water (4°C)	1.00
	blood, plasma	1.03
	mercury	13.6
	alcohol, ethyl	0.79
	gasoline	0.68
GASES	air	1.29×10^{-3}
	helium	0.179×10^{-3}
	water (steam) (100°C)	0.598×10^{-3}

Properties of Matter

Solids

A body is said to be a solid when it retains its shape and offers resistance to forces tending to deform it. A solid has perceptible strength and does not flow. A solid is characterized by its elastic properties.

Solids are commonly divided into two groups: those with a glassy, or amorphous, structure, such as glass or asphalt; and those with a crystalline structure, such as table salt or ice.

Crystal structure. The molecules in a crystalline solid are not arranged randomly. A geometrical spatial arrangement of molecules is found in all crystals, although different arrangements are found in different crystals. A three-dimensional pattern of some type, called unit cell, repeats itself regularly in all crystals.

Metals in the solid state are usually composed of a myriad of tiny crystals, more or less randomly oriented and interlocking with one another. It is possible to grow large single-metal crystals, each having dimensions of several centimeters. Such crystals have elastic properties differing markedly from the polycrystalline forms. For example, a single crystal of copper, 1 centimeter thick and several centimeters long, can be bent easily. In copper, the atoms in the crystal are arranged in one of the ways, face-centered cubic, that uniform spheres would be packed to occupy the smallest volume possible.

In common salt, sodium chloride, the atoms are not identical, as they are in copper. Sodium and chloride atoms are alternately placed in a cubic pattern, or lattice. The crystals may be very small or very large, but in every case the faces, or surfaces, of the crystals make definite angles with each other, which is 90° in the case of sodium chloride.

CRYSTALS

The shape of crystals reflects the arrangement of atoms in the crystal lattice.
1. Table salt has a cubic structure. Atoms in a unit all are placed at the corners of a cube.

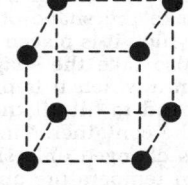

2. The atoms of calcite (calcium carbonate) are placed on the corners of a cube that has been stretched along a diagonal. The crystal is said to have a trigonal structure.

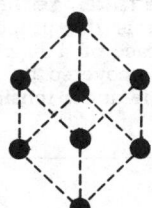

3. In quartz (silicon dioxide), the atoms are placed on hexagons. Such crystals have a hexagonal structure. The photo shows large quartz crystals that have been grown artificially. Crystals of such size occur rarely in nature.

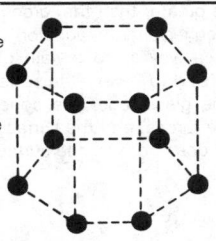
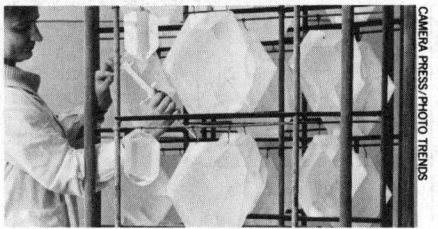

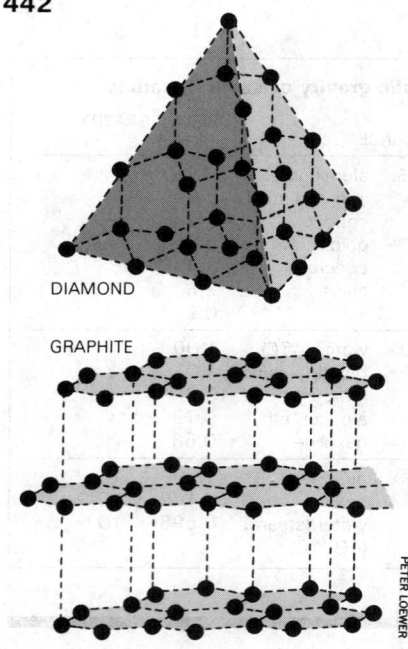

DIAMOND

GRAPHITE

PETER LOEWER

Two or more crystalline forms of a substance sometimes are found. For example, although both the diamond and graphite are pure carbon, they have different crystal forms. In the diamond, each carbon atom is surrounded by four other carbon atoms at the corners of a regular tetrahedron. In graphite, the carbon atoms lie in planes, or flat sheets, and each atom is attached to three others in this plane to form a series of flat hexagons. The flat sheets of atoms are relatively easy to separate or move over one another. As a result of their respective structures, graphite acts as a lubricant, while diamond is the hardest naturally occurring substance known.

Amorphous solids. Carbon is also found in the amorphous, noncrystalline, state as carbon black. Here, if crystals exist, they are microscopic, and the bulk substance does not behave as a crystal. In glassy substances, the atoms are not ordered. Numerous solids are not crystalline in structure.

Wood, for example, exhibits a spatial organization of its atoms, but is not crystalline in the sense that metals are.

Properties. All solids, both crystalline and amorphous, resist change of shape and of volume. Many crystalline solids are anisotropic; that is, many of their properties are not the same in all directions. For example, their heat conductivity and optical properties, such as the speed of light as it passes through, vary with the direction in which these properties are measured. Amorphous solids and solids with a cubic crystal structure, on the other hand, are isotropic; that is, their properties are the same in all directions. Crystalline solids melt at clearly defined temperatures. Glassy solids do not melt at defined temperatures, but instead gradually soften and become more fluid with increasing temperatures.

Liquids

A liquid generally is characterized as matter in which the molecules are free to move among themselves without being able to separate from one another, as molecules of a gas do. A liquid will take the shape of any container into which it is placed. Although a gas will also take the shape of any container into which it is placed, a gas will expand to fill all the available space in the container. The volume of a liquid is changed only slightly by variations in temperature and pressure. In addition, the atoms in a liquid are about as closely spaced as are those in a solid, but there is no long-range order, as in a crystal.

Surface tension. Surface tension is the property that causes the surface of a liquid to behave as if it were covered by a thin, elastic membrane under tension. This property en-

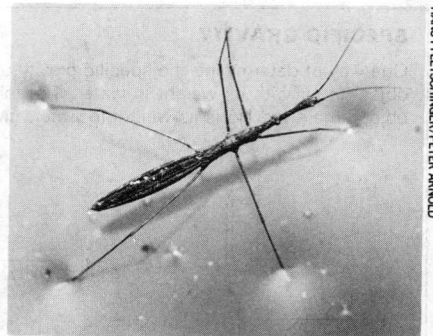

HANS PFLETSCHINGER/PETER ARNOLD

MOLECULAR FORCES *at the surface of water enable this water measurer to walk on it.*

ables small insects to walk on the surface of water. It results from the fact that the molecules in the surface layer of the liquid are attracted downward by the molecules within the liquid with a force greater than that exerted by the molecules in the atmosphere above. The surface of a liquid always tends to contract to the smallest possible area, so drops of liquid assume a shape as close to spherical as possible. The surface area thus becomes as small as possible for any given volume.

Viscosity. The measure of the resistance of a liquid to flow is called viscosity. Like surface tension, viscosity is caused by the attraction of forces between layers of molecules. The greater the attracting forces, the more difficult it is for one layer to flow over another, and therefore the greater the viscosity. The viscosity of a liquid usually decreases significantly with increasing temperatures.

Gases

A gas is a fluid that has neither independent shape nor volume. A gas will take the shape of, and expand to fill, any container in which it is placed. Gases are also characterized by their sensitivity to changes in temperature and pressure. The gas laws (page 401) describe the behavior of most gases on a macroscopic scale, that is, changes in volume, temperature, and internal energy.

Kinetic theory of gases. The macroscopic behavior of gases, as described by the gas laws, can be explained by the kinetic theory of gases. This theory is based on the assumption that a gas consists of a very large number of moving particles, or molecules. These particles are assumed to be very small and to occupy only a small volume of the total space that is occupied by the gas. The particles are also assumed to be in constant random motion and to behave as hard elastic

---

CAPILLARY ACTION

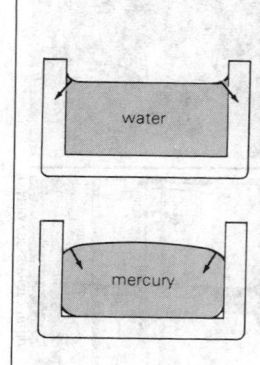

water

mercury

Capillary action is a phenomenon related to surface tension; it can be observed as the curvature of the surface of a liquid in a container or tube. For example, if water is contained in a glass tube, the attraction forces between the water molecules and the glass molecules (adhesion) will be greater than the forces between the water molecules themselves (cohesion). In addition, the surface of the water will bend in such a way as to remain perpendicular to the resultant force. Water is said to "wet" the surface of glass. If mercury is introduced in the glass tube, the cohesive forces will be greater than the adhesive forces, and the surface of mercury will be curved upward; mercury does not wet the surface of glass.

spheres. They collide with one another and with the walls of the container in which the gas is confined.

The idea that collisions of gas particles with the walls of a container could account for the pressure the gas exerts on the wall was first expressed by Daniel Bernoulli in 1738. During each collision of a particle with the wall, the particle transfers momentum to the wall, thus exerting a tiny force. Because the number of particles bouncing off the wall is very large, the effect is that of a continuous force on the wall. This force per unit surface is defined as the gas pressure. His theory also explains the fact that when the number of gas molecules is increased in a fixed volume, the pressure increases—more particles bounce off the walls per unit of time.

The kinetic gas theory also explains why gas pressure increases when a gas is enclosed in a fixed volume and its temperature is raised. The temperature of a gas is a measure of the average speed at which the gas molecules move about. When the temperature is

KINETIC GAS THEORY

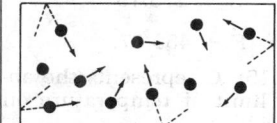

Low temperature.
Velocities of the molecules are low and transfer only a small amount of momentum to the sides of the box.

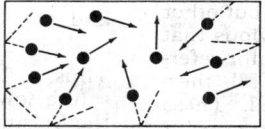

High temperature.
Velocities of the molecules are high and transfer more momentum to the sides of the box, resulting in higher pressure.

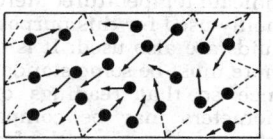

More molecules.
A larger number of molecules hit the sides, so more momentum is transferred, increasing pressure.

raised, the average speed of the particles increases, as does their energy. The particles strike the walls at a higher speed and thus exert a larger force on the wall.

The kinetic gas theory also accounts for the cooling of a gas that has been allowed to expand. For example, when a gas in a cylinder expands by pushing a piston, work is performed by the expanding gas. As a result, the kinetic energy of the gas molecules decreases, and the molecules slow down, resulting in a decrease in temperature. When a gas is compressed, the opposite happens. The molecules absorb the work delivered by the piston, thus increasing their kinetic energy and causing a rise in temperature. Anyone who uses a bicycle pump can observe the heating of the air in the pump when it is compressed.

Heat

Caloric Theory

For a long time, the manifestations of heat were attributed to an ethereal, invisible fluid called caloric. This fluid was believed to have the power of penetrating, expanding, solidifying, and dissolving various materials. It was also thought to have the power of converting the materials from solid to liquid or from liquid to vapor. The caloric theory pictured heat as a fluid able to flow into a body when the body was heated and out of a body when it was cooled.

Although the caloric theory was accepted by many scientists, certain observations could not be explained by the theory of an invisible, weightless, all-pervading fluid. For instance, the generation of heat by friction when two mechanical objects rubbed against one another was attributed to a loss of caloric: it was presumed to be ground or squeezed out of the objects. Many scientists of the late 18th century found this explanation inadequate.

In experiments conducted in a Bavarian arsenal, Benjamin Rumford demonstrated the inadequacy of this explanation and in so doing initiated the downfall of the caloric theory. Rumford had observed that when cannons were bored, a large temperature rise accompanied the boring. In his experiments, Rumford measured the heat generated by the boring process. He also attempted to measure the

weight of the caloric fluid picked up by the hot cannon. Finding none, he concluded that the heat was some form of atomic motion.

Rumford's experiments alone were not sufficient to disprove the caloric theory. Not until Joule was able to determine accurately the mechanical equivalent of heat was it recognized for what it is, energy in transit. Joule's experiments established beyond doubt that heat and work are different manifestations of energy.

Temperature

According to the kinetic theory of gases, the temperature of a gas is a measure of the random kinetic energy of molecules. If two bodies at different temperatures are brought together—a hot steel bar placed in a bowl of water is an example—the hotter body will begin to cool, and the cooler body will begin to warm. Soon both bodies will be at the same temperature. This temperature will lie between the temperatures both bodies had at the starting point. In this process, heat has been transferred from the hotter body to the cooler body. At the area of contact, the highly energetic molecules in the steel bar will transfer energy to the water molecules by colliding with them. Thus, in the contact area, the energy of the metal molecules decreases, and

at the same time the energy of the water molecules increases.

It is important to distinguish between heat and temperature. The heat content of a body is the total change of the kinetic energy of the molecules constituting that body. Temperature is the measure of the average kinetic energy per molecule.

For gases at low pressures, temperature is defined simply as being proportional to the square of the average molecular velocity. In high-pressure gases and in solids and liquids, the same general concept is accepted, although the reasoning is somewhat more complicated.

BROWNIAN MOVEMENT *describes the random path of a particle buffeted by collisions with surrounding molecules.*

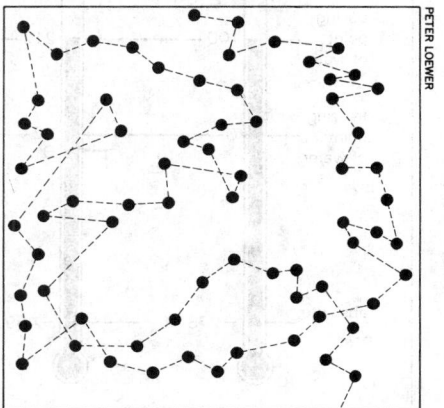

Thermometers.

Most thermometers use the expansion of a liquid to indicate temperature. Mercury is commonly used for this purpose, but other fluids are also used. It is obvious that there must be some standard for reference so that readings on all thermometers may be compared. These reference points are the freezing point of water, the boiling point of water at one atmosphere of pressure, and the boiling and freezing points of several other materials.

These reference states are assigned numbers in each temperature scale. The most familiar scales are the Celsius, C, and the Fahrenheit, F. Celsius is related to Fahrenheit thus:

$$9/5\ C + 32 = F.$$

The accompanying chart indicates the reference state temperatures. If the freezing point of water is chosen as 0° C, and the boiling point of water as 100° C, then each degree represents 1/100 of the scale between 0 and 100. Since the volume change for each degree of temperature change is not in fact constant over the entire scale, the actual distance between degree marks varies slightly on most liquid thermometers. To ensure that all thermometers give the same temperature readings when placed in the same environment, they are calibrated against a low-pressure gas thermometer. This type of thermometer is used because the volume change of the gas is very nearly the same for each degree change in temperature.

It was stated earlier that temperatures are indicative of molecular kinetic energy. As kinetic energy decreases, one might expect to find that at some lower limit of temperature, all motion of molecules or atoms would stop. This lower limit is referred to as absolute zero, and the scales that use this point as a basis are Kelvin scale, K, and the Rankine scale, R. These absolute temperature scales are related to the Celsius and to the Fahrenheit scales in this manner:

$$K = C + 273.15$$
and
$$R = F + 459.67.$$

Thus, −273.15° C represents the absolute lower limit of temperature on the Celsius scale.

Other measuring devices.

Numerous other techniques are used to measure temperature. A thermocouple is a circuit using two wires of different metals joined together. To measure temperature, two junctions are connected together. A voltage and current flow are generated in the circuit when one junction becomes hotter than the other. The voltage is indicative of the temperature difference that exists between the two junctions, and calibration charts are available for many common thermocouple circuits.

A resistance thermometer measures the change in electrical resistance as temperature changes, and calibration permits the resistance measurement to be converted to a temperature reading. This technique is useful in obtaining accurate measurements in laboratory conditions.

At very high temperatures, an optical pyrometer may be used for temperature measurement. This instrument uses as a basis for comparison the visible light emitted by a body at very high temperatures.

Units of Energy

The heat energy required to raise the temperature of 1 gram of water by 1 degree Centigrade is defined as one calorie of energy. If stated in terms of one pound of water and 1 degree Fahrenheit, then the unit is 1 British thermal unit, Btu. One Btu is the equivalent of 252 calories. Calories are used by most scientists and by the general public in countries employing the metric system. British thermal units are used by engineers in many English-speaking countries, including the United States.

Heat capacity.

We know that if we supply 1 calorie of heat to 1 gram of water, the temperature of the water will rise by 1 degree Centigrade. However, if we supply 1 calorie of heat to 1 gram of aluminum, the temperature of the aluminum will rise by 4.5 degrees. Thus, only 0.22 calorie is needed to raise the temperature of 1 gram of aluminum by 1 degree Centigrade, so it may be said that the heat capacity of aluminum is smaller than that of water.

The heat capacity of a substance is the change in energy needed for a 1-degree rise in temperature. Values of heat capacities are needed in order to determine how much heat transfer must occur to heat or cool a substance through a given temperature interval. Simply stated, the heat transfer requirement per unit of mass is the product of the heat capacity times the temperature change.

A calorie and a Btu were so defined that the heat capacity for water was approximately 1 in the units of calories/gram or Btu/lb. Heat capacities of other materials may be greatly different from that of water but are usually smaller. The term specific heat is the ratio of the heat capacity of a material to the heat capacity of water. Since heat capacity is near unity, 1, heat capacity and specific heat are often confused and used interchangeably. These terms are not synonymous, however, since specific heats have no units but are simply numbers.

One of the reasons why different materials have different values for specific heat is that heavier materials have fewer atoms per unit mass and consequently can store less of the energy transferred by heat.

Phase Changes

In most cases, materials expand when heated. For expansion to occur, the molecules constituting the material must move farther apart. In causing molecules to separate, work must be done against the forces with which they attract one another. If we stretch a spring too far, the spring may lose its ability to return to its original position. In fact, it may break. Similarly, if the molecules in other materials are moved far enough apart by heating, a point will be reached at which the influence of the attracting forces is almost completely overcome. The molecules would no longer be constrained.

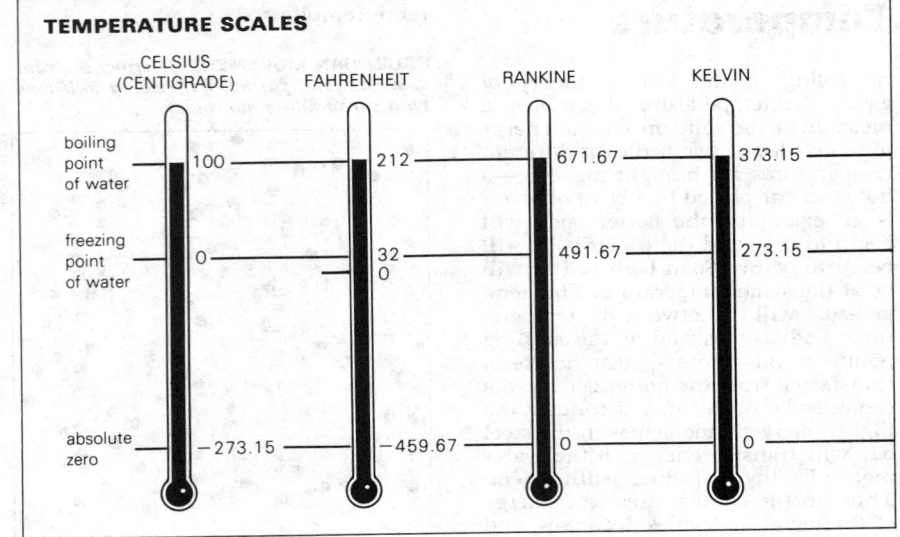

TEMPERATURE SCALES

	CELSIUS (CENTIGRADE)	FAHRENHEIT	RANKINE	KELVIN
boiling point of water	100	212	671.67	373.15
freezing point of water	0	32	491.67	273.15
absolute zero	−273.15	−459.67	0	0

In this condition, the molecules would be able to move about freely and completely fill the volume available. The random kinetic energies corresponding to the high temperatures in this condition are much greater than the potential energy of attraction between the molecules, and the material is a gas. Conversely, as a gas is cooled, the random kinetic energies of molecules decrease. Thus, when a gas is cooling, a point is reached at which the attracting forces predominate and the gas collapses. The molecules lose much of the potential energy of separation. When a substance changes from a gas to a liquid, the process is known as liquefaction.

In passing from a gas to a liquid, a substance loses energy. The energy changes accompanying the phase changes are known as latent heat effects and are quite large. For example, we know that the heat capacity of water is approximately 1 calorie/gram. The latent heat associated with the condensation of 1 gram of water is almost 1000 calories/gram. Clearly, a drastic change has occurred on the molecular level.

To extend this picture, if the liquid is further cooled, a temperature will be reached at which the attracting forces so dominate that another phase change occurs, solidification. Movement of molecules is now almost completely prevented, because the molecules have been locked in a semi-rigid structure. This change from liquid to solid is accompanied by another energy change, called the latent heat of fusion. Heats of fusion are usually much smaller than heats of vaporization. For instance, 133.5 calories of energy must be removed to freeze 1 gram of water.

To complete the picture, if the original pressure had been sufficiently low, the cooling process would have resulted in a phase change directly from gas to solid. The energy change associated with this process is termed the heat of sublimation, and the heat of sublimation is approximately equal to the sum of the heats of fusion and vaporization.

When certain liquids are cooled rapidly, there is no assignable freezing-point temperature. Instead, the ability of the liquid to flow freely decreases steadily until a glassy substance is obtained. This glassy state is characterized by the absence of a regular crystalline structure and by optical isotropy, transparency, when not in a state of strain. Over a period of time, especially under high temperature conditions, glasses may undergo crystallization. This state may be viewed as a condition lying between the liquid and solid states.

Vapor pressure of a liquid is the pressure at which a dynamic state of equilibrium is achieved, with continual interchange of molecules between the gaseous and the condensed phase.

The higher the temperature, the higher the average kinetic energy of the liquid molecules and, therefore, the greater the number of molecules that can break away from the strong attracting forces within the liquid. Vapor pressure increases with temperature, and vice versa, so by increasing the pressure above a liquid, one increases the temperature at which a liquid will boil.

Critical temperature. At what is called critical temperature, the kinetic energy of liquid molecules exceeds the attracting forces; no liquid phase can exist at critical temperature regardless of the pressure. At the critical point, the molecular energies of the liquid and gas are equal, and the latent heat effects are zero.

Phase diagrams. The phases of a compound may be represented in a pressure-temperature diagram, or phase diagram. A complete phase diagram contains three curves. The boiling point curve indicates how the boiling point depends on pressure. The solidification curve indicates how the melting point depends on pressure. A third curve indicates the temperature at which the gas and solid phases of a substance are in equilibrium. These three curves intersect at what is called the triple point. The triple point represents the temperature and pressure at which the solid, liquid, and gaseous phases can coexist in equilibrium (see diagram).

A PHASE DIAGRAM *indicates whether at a given temperature and pressure a substance, in this case water, is solid, liquid, or gaseous. At certain combinations of temperature and pressure, ice changes directly to steam without becoming a liquid first.*

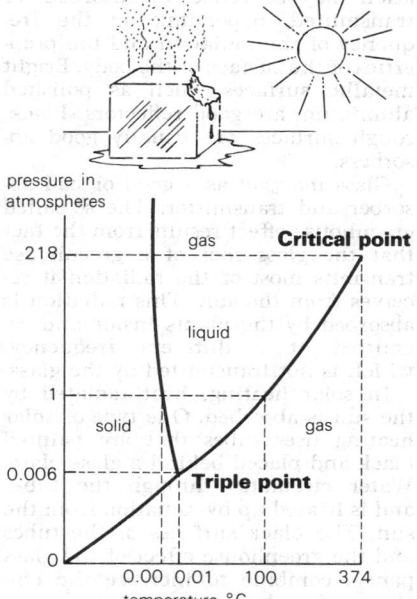

Heat Transfer Mechanisms

If one end of a copper bar is held in a gas flame, the temperature at the other end of the bar will quickly increase. Heat is transferred through the bar by conduction. In this process, heat is transferred mechanically from the hotter atoms to the cooler atoms by the transfer of vibrational energy. The strongly vibrating atoms shake the cooler atoms, which in turn begin to vibrate more strongly and thus become hotter.

If the copper bar is put into a bowl of water, the temperature of the water increases. The water molecules in contact with the copper bar heat up because of conduction. However, the water temperature increases almost equally fast in areas farther away from the copper bar than in regions close to it. The process responsible for this heat transport is convection. Since heated liquids expand, the liquid close to the hot copper bar becomes buoyant and rises. The space around the copper bar is replaced by cooler liquid, and the process is repeated. This explains the quick distribution of heat in the bowl of water.

Bodies that are not in contact with one another can also exchange heat. The heating of Earth by the sun is a dramatic example of this third mechanism of heat transfer, which is called radiation.

Conduction. The temperature of a solid is related to the amplitude of vibration of the molecules around some equilibrium position in the solid lattice. When two solid bodies of unequal temperatures are placed in contact, some of the excess vibrational energy of the surface molecules of the hotter body is communicated to the surface molecules of the colder body by collisions of the molecules at the point of contact. As a result of this exchange of energy, the surface molecules of the colder body acquire a higher average energy level—higher temperature—than the molecules in the underlying layers. Similarly, the surface molecules of the hotter body are now at a lower temperature than those in the underlying solid. This energy exchange process is repeated between the surface molecules and the molecules just below the surface in both solids, as well as between the original interacting surface molecules. This type of energy transfer is termed heat conduction, in which no gross movement of any part of the materials occurs.

Not all substances conduct heat equally well. If, instead of a copper bar, one end of a glass bar is held in a gas flame, it will take much longer for the other end of the bar to become hot.

THE THREE KINDS OF HEAT TRANSFER *are present in a pot of boiling water. Conduction transfers heat from the burner through the pot to the water; convection distributes the heat in the water; and radiation transfers heat from the pot to nearby objects. The solar collectors on this roof* (right) *capture the radiated heat of the sun.*

In general, solids that are poor conductors of electricity are also poor conductors of heat. Most metals conduct heat well. Insulators, such as glass, wood, or paper, are poor conductors of heat.

Thus, at identical temperatures, a piece of copper is much colder to the touch than wood. Since copper conducts heat much better than wood, the rate of heat loss from the hand is greater in the case of copper, and it will feel colder.

Handles of cooking pans are usually made of materials of low thermal conductivity, for example, wood. The pan bottoms, by contrast, are made of a metal with high thermal conductivity. Cold metal objects can actually freeze the moisture on a hand so rapidly that the hand will stick to them. Nonmetallic objects, which have low thermal conductivity, do not conduct body heat away at a sufficiently rapid rate to result in such freezing.

Conduction processes may occur in liquids and gases by an identical mechanism, but for these fluids, it is difficult to prevent motion of parts of the material.

Convection. The principal heat-transfer mechanism in fluids is convection. Because fluid molecules can move around quickly, temperature differences do not build up in fluids. Convection, for example, is the process that distributes warm air evenly in a heated room. Natural convection, which occurs in boiling water, depends only on the buoyant force of gravity to accomplish the mixing of the liquid. If a mechanical means is used to increase convection, for example, a pump or fan, the process is called forced convection. Forced convection is used in cooling car engines: a pump circulates water continuously along the cylinder walls to carry away excess heat. The cooling water, in turn, is cooled by a stream of air forced through the radiator by a fan.

Radiation. Radiation does not depend on molecules contacting molecules. Molecules, by their vibration, can emit electromagnetic waves. When these waves are absorbed by other materials, the energy transfer mechanism is termed radiation. In a vacuum, radiation is the most efficient means of heat transfer. All bodies with temperatures above absolute zero, $-273°$ C, radiate heat, but materials must be at a rather high temperature before much emission occurs. In fact, the intensity of the radiation, I, is proportional to the fourth power of the absolute temperature, or $I \alpha T^4$. In general, then, radiation is important only at very high temperatures, or where heat is transferred between surfaces that are separated by a vacuum.

Electric heaters transfer heat primarily by radiation from the glowing coils, although some natural convection occurs simultaneously. When heat radiation strikes a body, the radiation may be reflected, absorbed, or transmitted, depending on the frequency of the radiation and the properties of the surface of the body. Bright metallic surfaces, such as polished aluminum, are good reflectors. Black, rough surfaces are usually good absorbers.

Glass may act as a good or bad absorber and transmitter. The so-called greenhouse effect results from the fact that the glass roof of a greenhouse transmits most of the radiation it receives from the sun. This radiation is absorbed by the plants inside and re-emitted at a different frequency, which is not transmitted by the glass.

In solar heating, heat radiated by the sun is absorbed. One type of solar heating uses tubes that are painted black and placed behind a glass plate. Water circulates through the tubes and is heated up by radiation from the sun. The black surfaces of the tubes and the greenhouse effect of the glass panels combine to increase the efficiency of such systems.

Thermodynamics

All mechanical work performed by machines is obtained from the transformation of heat energy into mechanical energy. The steam engine and the internal combustion engine are examples of machines producing work from heat. Conversely, mechanical work can also be transformed into heat. One example of this process is the heating of car brakes caused by friction.

Joule, in a series of experiments (see accompanying diagram), measured the amount of heat generated by mechanical processes. He found that a fixed amount of mechanical work always produces a fixed amount of heat. This amount is called the mechanical equivalent of heat and equals 4.18 joules for the production of 1 calorie of heat.

JOULE'S APPARATUS *measures the amount of heat produced when the falling weights turn the paddles.*

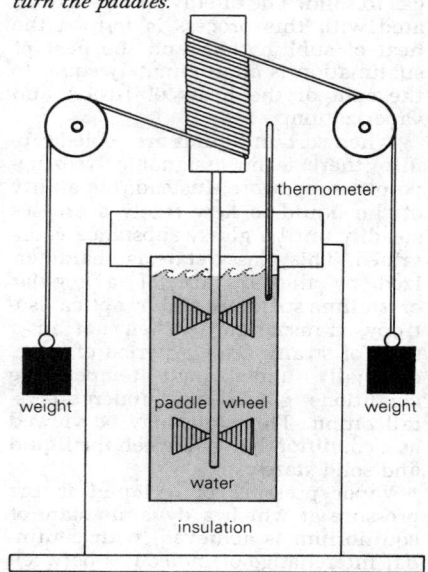

PETER LOEWER

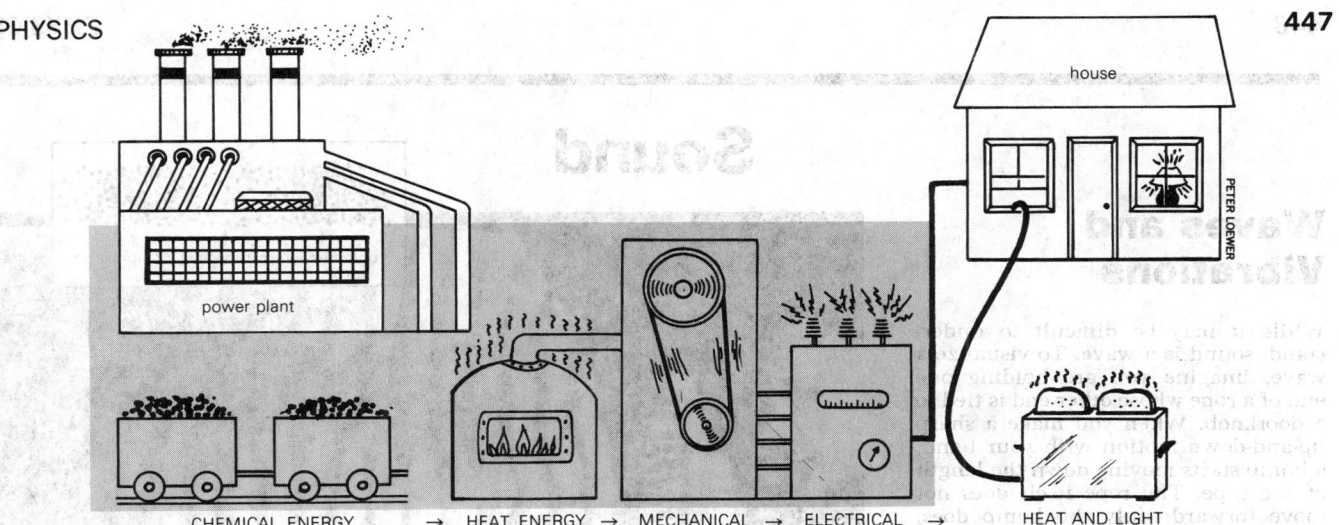

ELECTRIC POWER *reaching a home has had three transformations. Combustion of fuel produces chemical energy in the form of heat, transformed into mechanical energy by steam turbines, and transformed into electrical energy by electric generators.*

CHEMICAL ENERGY → HEAT ENERGY → MECHANICAL ENERGY → ELECTRICAL ENERGY → HEAT AND LIGHT

Conservation of energy.

When an object is lifted and then dropped, the potential energy it acquired through being lifted is changed into kinetic energy, and the sum of both forms of energy remains constant during the process. When the object falls to the floor, it stops moving, so its kinetic energy becomes zero. Because we assume that the potential energy is zero on the floor, the total energy of the body would seem to be zero. One of the most fundamental principles in physics, however, is that energy cannot be created from nothing, nor can it disappear. Energy can only be transformed from one form into another. Kinetic energy can be transformed into potential energy, and potential energy can be transformed into kinetic energy. Therefore, when the object hits the floor, its energy cannot disappear. The molecules in the object and in the floor begin vibrating faster, and the mechanical energy is transformed into heat energy.

In a closed system, mechanical energy can be transformed into heat, and the sum of both forms of energy remains constant.

The first law of thermodynamics:
The energy of a system can be changed by the transfer of heat.

In a closed system, heat can only flow from one part to another, but the total amount of energy will remain constant.

The second law of thermodynamics:
Heat flows spontaneously from a hot object to a cool object, but never from a cool object to a hot object.

This law is of fundamental importance for engines that transform heat into mechanical work. They can only produce work if heat can flow from a hot reservoir to a cool reservoir, or heat sink. An automobile engine is a good example. It can work only when heat resulting from combustion is allowed to flow to a heat sink, the radiator. Some of the heat from the radiator is used to warm the passenger compartment, but most of it is lost to the environment and cannot be converted to mechanical work. The second law of thermodynamics thus also implies that no machine can convert heat energy completely into mechanical energy, because part of the heat energy is always lost.

The third law of thermodynamics:
At absolute zero, the entropy of a system is zero.

Physicists define entropy as the amount of disorder in a system. Thus, entropy corresponds to the amount of random thermal motion of atoms or molecules in matter. As temperature is a measure for this random motion, one can understand that if we lower the temperature of a body, the random motion will slow down; to cease almost completely, absolute zero is approached. According to modern theory, even at absolute zero, a residual amount of random motion remains. This residual thermal motion corresponds to a state of minimal disorder, in other words, to a minimum of entropy, which may be set equal to zero.

THERMAL EFFICIENCIES

The thermal efficiency of an engine relates the amount of heat that is converted to work to the amount that is released as waste heat. When an engine is said to be 40 percent efficient, it means that 40 percent of the heat created by combustion, for instance, has been used, and 60 percent of the heat has been wasted.

steam turbine	40%
diesel engine	38%
gasoline engine	25%
steam locomotive	8–12%

Cryogenics

Cryogenics refers to various phenomena occurring at temperatures below about 150° K, some 125° C below the freezing point of water. At these temperatures, most substances are liquids or solids. The small number of materials that boil below 150° K at one atmosphere are often referred to as cryogenic fluids.

	NORMAL BOILING POINT (at 1 atmosphere)	
FLUID	(°F)	(°K)
Helium	−452.1	4.2
Hydrogen	−423.0	20.4
Nitrogen	−320.5	77.3
Oxygen	−297.3	90.1
Methane	−258.6	111.7

When the temperature decreases, molecular velocities decrease, and liquefaction and/or solidification occur. Several unusual changes in the thermodynamic and electrical properties of various materials also occur at these temperatures owing to the decrease in molecular motion. For example, the electrical resistance of some metals becomes zero below a certain temperature. This phenomenon is known as superconductivity. Practical application of cryogenics ranges from medicine to electronics to space research to transportation.

Superfluids. If liquid helium is cooled below 2.2° K, it becomes a superfluid, that is, its viscosity becomes negligible. Superfluid helium has some interesting properties: it can flow without resistance through microscopic holes, and if kept in an open container, it will escape from it by climbing up the sides and over the rim of the container. The motion of molecules of superfluid helium can be compared with the movement of electrons in a superconductor.

Sound

Waves and Vibrations

While it may be difficult to understand, sound is a wave. To visualize a wave, imagine you are holding one end of a rope whose other end is tied to a doorknob. When you make a sharp up-and-down motion with your hand, a bump starts moving down the length of the rope. The rope itself does not move forward; only the bump does. This is one of the important characteristics of waves. The medium through which the wave travels does not move forward or back. It swings up and down across the direction of wave motion. The wave in the rope demonstrates a one-dimensional wave; it moves on a plane.

When a pebble is dropped in the center of a pond, the waves move away from the point of impact in ever-widening circles. Sound, like the waves in the pond, is three-dimensional. The crests and troughs of sound are not bumps, but high-pressure areas—compressions—and low-pressure areas—rarefactions—of the compressible medium we know as air. Each compression forms the surface of an ever-growing sphere. Each following rarefaction is a slightly smaller sphere, just inside the pressure sphere, and is itself followed by another sphere of high pressure.

A sound wave moves forward even though the air compacts only a little. It then thins out a bit as the sound wave passes. The wave is started by the quick motion, a vibration, of an object. When a musician raps the head of a drum, it moves away from the stick, creating a partial vacuum in the layer of air touching the surface of the drum. The surrounding air rushes in to fill this vacuum, leaving a partial vacuum just above the drum head, and so on away from the surface. The drum head then returns from its depressed position and bounces to a level higher than normal. This compacts the air immediately above the drum, and the high-pressure area in this space also moves out into the air immediately behind the rarefaction. Thus, a wave is created by the back-and-forth motion of the drum head. A loudspeaker cone works in the same way. It is pulled sharply back and forth in a quick series of vibrations, oscillations, that move into the adjacent layers of air.

Sound waves move out on the surfaces of ever-growing spheres. Since the amount of energy carried by a single wave at the start remains with that wave throughout its existence, the

A SOUND WAVE, *illustrated in this photograph, consists of compressions and rarefactions of air molecules, which show here as an alternating pattern of light bands and dark bands.*

amount of compression and rarefaction decreases as the area of the sphere increases. In theory, the wave never disappears entirely. In actuality, the rubbing of air molecules against one another slowly absorbs all the initial energy and turns it into heat, so eventually the sound wave dissipates.

Dissipation of sound energy is more pronounced in enclosed areas. In an auditorium, the sound waves initiated on the stage strike the walls, ceiling, and floor. While some of the sound is reflected back into the room, causing reverberations, the rest is absorbed by curtains, rugs, and clothing.

Intensity and pitch. Sound has two important characteristics. The first is intensity, or loudness, which corresponds to the intensity of the pressure in the compression part of the wave and the reduction in pressure in the rarefaction. The greater the rise of

pressure and the thinner the rarefaction, the louder the sound will seem.

Intensity of a sound wave is defined as the power transported by the wave per square meter, and is expressed in watts per square meter, W/m^2. The human ear perceives sound intensities according to a logarithmic scale. For people to perceive that a sound is twice as loud as another requires a sound intensity ten times higher. To accommodate the subjective perception of sound intensity, a logarithmic scale representing intensity levels of sound has been introduced. The unit in this scale is the bel, named after Alexander Graham Bell. In practice, a unit ten times smaller is used, the decibel, or dB. A sound with an intensity of $0.468 \times 10^{-12} W/m^2$ is defined to have an intensity level of 0 dB. Ten dB corresponds to a sound intensity ten times as large; 20 dB, to a sound intensity 100 times as large; 30 dB, to a sound intensity 1000 times as large,

INTENSITY OF SOUND

SOUND	DECIBELS
threshold of hearing	0
whisper	10–20
very soft music	30
average home	40–50
automobile	40–50
conversation	60–70
heavy street traffic	70–80
loud music	90–100
threshold of pain	120
jet airplane engine	170

SPEED OF SOUND

MEDIUM	M/SEC
carbon dioxide	258
air	331
water	1440
seawater	1560
copper	3560
hardwood	4000
glass	4500
aluminum	5100
iron	5130
steel	5130

and so on. The faintest sound the ear can perceive is approximately 4 dB. We usually cannot bear to hear sounds louder than 120 dB.

The second characteristic of sound is pitch, which is the frequency of the waves. The more rapidly sound waves follow one another, the higher the pitch of the sound. A loudspeaker cone that moves back and forth very quickly produces a tone much higher in pitch than one that moves back and forth slowly.

Velocity. Regardless of the frequency of a wave, sound always travels through a given medium at the same speed. The speed depends on the stiffness, temperature, and density of the medium. Since air is a relatively soft material, at sea level at a temperature of 70° F, sound travels through air at the fairly slow speed of approximately 334 meters per second, or 1100 feet per second, or about 750 miles per hour. Water is stiffer and denser than air, so sound moves faster in the sea, 1464 meters, or 4800 feet, per second. Sound moves even faster in hard steel, over 4877 meters, or 16,000 feet per second, or more than 10,000 miles per hour.

Wavelength. Sound waves in air always travel at about 1100 feet per second, no matter how quickly a loudspeaker cone moves back and forth. Therefore, if a speaker completes one cycle in 1/30 of a second—forward in 1/60 of a second and back in 1/60 second—the wave that moves away from the speaker will have traveled about 11 meters, or 37 feet, by the time the cone is ready to start its second swing. The distance a wave travels during one cycle is called its wavelength.

Resonance

Resonance is the phenomenon by which sound waves are reinforced so that they are perceived as sounding louder. If the handle of a vibrating tuning fork touches a table, the sound emanating from the tuning fork becomes louder. The reason for this is that the tuning fork causes the table top to vibrate. Thus, the table top also produces sound waves of the same frequency as the sound waves coming from the tuning fork. This particular type of resonance is called sympathetic vibration.

Resonance can also be illustrated by holding one end of a long cardboard tube in a bowl of water. If a vibrating tuning fork is held near the open end of the tube, and the tube is moved slowly into the water, when the tube has reached the correct position, the sound will be amplified. For a certain length of the air column in the tube,

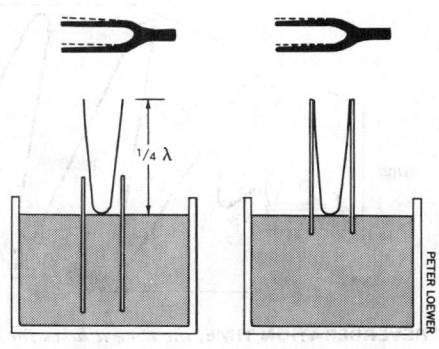

RESONANCE *will occur in a column of air when the length of the column equals a quarter of the wavelength produced by the tuning fork.*

that air column vibrates at the same frequency as the tuning fork (as shown in the diagram).

Doppler Effect

Consider an observer and a source of sound moving relative to one another. One or both may be moving, but they cannot be moving in the same direction at the same speed. The observed frequency or pitch of the sound waves differs from the emitted frequency or pitch. This is called the Doppler effect, after its discoverer, Christian Johann Doppler.

Consider sound waves coming from the horn of a car traveling at high speed on a highway and moving toward you. The pitch of the horn is raised when the car is moving in your direction. Each time a wave is emitted in the forward direction of the car, its maximum is closer to the maximum of the previously transmitted wave, because the car is moving in the same direction in which the waves are moving. The result is that the waves in the direction of movement of the car

are compressed. Their wavelength is shorter. Therefore, their pitch is higher. By the same reasoning, when the car moves past you, waves traveling in the direction opposite to the movement of the car are elongated, and the pitch drops.

The Doppler effect is used in a sonar device to help submarines detect the speed and direction of surface vessels and even of other submarines. It is also used in astronomy, where the change in the frequency of light waves is measured to determine the velocities of distant galaxies.

Electroacoustics

For hundreds of years, makers of musical instruments have been able to create instruments whose sole purpose has been the production of beautiful sounds. Yet their skill was and to a great extent is still largely the result of trial and error. The knowledge of how to shape the resonance chamber, select woods for construction, allow time for seasoning, and provide the thickness of varnish that will achieve the optimum sound quality reflects hundreds of years of experimentation.

Over the last hundred years, the study of sound has evolved into a science. Acoustic engineers know what sound is, how to detect it, and how to preserve it on records and tapes that can be played again and again. Microphones have been developed that work much as the ear does. A thin membrane in a microphone vibrates back and forth as the compressions and rarefactions impinge on it. The membrane may move a coil of wire in a magnetic field to create an electric voltage. Alternatively, it may move toward and away from a flat metal plate, changing the capacitance between the two and correspondingly affecting an electric circuit. Once the sound is transformed into an electrical

THE DOPPLER EFFECT, *the apparent change in pitch of a horn as the vehicle moves toward or away from the listener, is explained by the bunching and spreading of sound waves.*

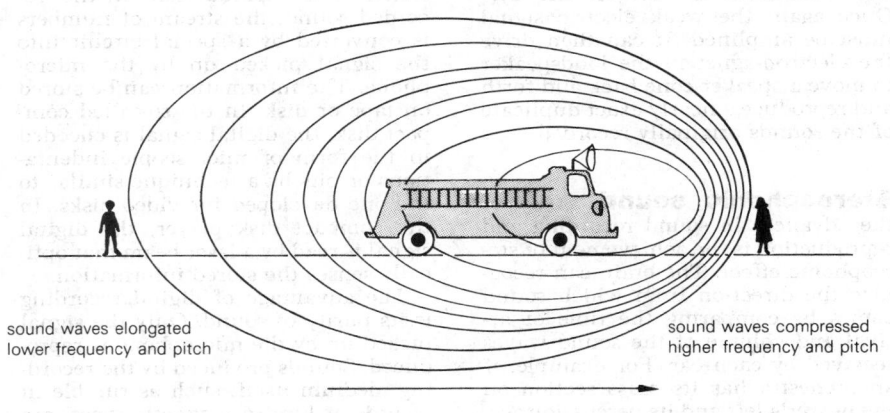

sound waves elongated
lower frequency and pitch

sound waves compressed
higher frequency and pitch

PETER LOEWER

signal, which oscillates in voltage as sound waves do in pressure, it can then be amplified. The voltage is increased while the relative strengths of loud and soft signals are maintained. Amplification is necessary because the electrical signal generated by the microphone is so weak that only sensitive electrical measuring instruments can detect any change at all.

Sound recording.

There are many ways to preserve the pattern of rising and falling voltage. For example, the signal can be made to move a pen back and forth over a moving strip of paper to create a jagged trace. The signal can also be used to swing a light beam back and forth across a moving photographic film, which is then developed to show the changing intensity and frequency by the sweep and density of lines. In addition, the signal can drive a stylus back and forth as a soft plastic disk turns under the point, leaving a wavy groove. The signal can power an electromagnet to create magnetized and reverse-magnetized areas on a strip of thin plastic tape coated with tiny iron oxide particles, or the voltage pattern can be stored as a series of digital numbers. All these methods are used in modern sound recordings. The photographic film method is used in motion pictures. The plastic disk is the master from which records are duplicated. The coated tape is used in tape recorders. Digital recordings are stored on compact disks.

Sound reproduction.

Sound is recreated by reversing the recording process. In a tape recorder, an electromagnet senses the changing magnetism of the coated tape passing across its face and reproduces the original electrical signal. A stylus rides in the groove of the record disk and moves back and forth. In this way, a tiny coil of wire placed in a magnetic field builds up a similarly varying voltage. A light beam directed at motion picture film dims and brightens a tube that functions like an electric eye. Once again the weak electric signal must be amplified. It can then drive the electromagnet in the loudspeaker to move a speaker cone back and forth and reproduce a nearly exact duplicate of the sounds originally recorded.

Stereophonic sound.

One of the advances in sound recording and reproduction is the achievement of stereophonic effect. The brain can recognize the direction from which sound comes by comparing the time of arrival and volume of the sound waves received by each ear. For example, if an orchestra has its brass section on the hearer's left and its percussion section on his right, the sound waves

from the trumpets will reach his left ear a fraction of a second before reaching the right ear. Those from the tympani will reach the right ear before the left. By interpreting the time of arrival and the intensity, or volume, of the sound reaching each ear, the brain can determine the locations of the musical instruments.

In stereophonic recording, two microphones are set a distance apart in front of the orchestra, one recording the sound waves emanating more strongly from the left side of the orchestra, and vice versa. The electrical signals produced by each of the microphones are recorded on a separate channel or track. When the sound is reproduced through two separated speakers, each channel is reproduced in only one speaker. Thus, the sounds recorded by the left-hand microphone are reproduced by the left-hand speaker, and those recorded by the right-hand microphone are reproduced by the right-hand speaker. In this way, the listener can sense the direction of the sound, experiencing a greater feeling of spaciousness and depth than possible with monaural reproduction.

Digital recording.

By electronically sampling the electric signal produced by a microphone thousands of times per second—typically between 44,000 and 55,000—one can create a stream of digital numbers that represent the amplitude fluctuations of the signal. For reproduction of the recorded sound, the stream of numbers is converted by a special circuit into the signal picked up by the microphone. The information can be stored on tape or disk. In the so-called compact disk, the digital signal is encoded in the form of microscopic indentations or pits by a technique similar to the one developed for video disks. In the compact disk player, the digital signal is read by a laser beam that optically senses the stored information.

The advantage of digital recording is its purity of sound. Only the signal picked up by the microphone is reproduced. Sounds produced by the recording medium itself, such as rumble in records or hiss in magnetic tapes, are absent.

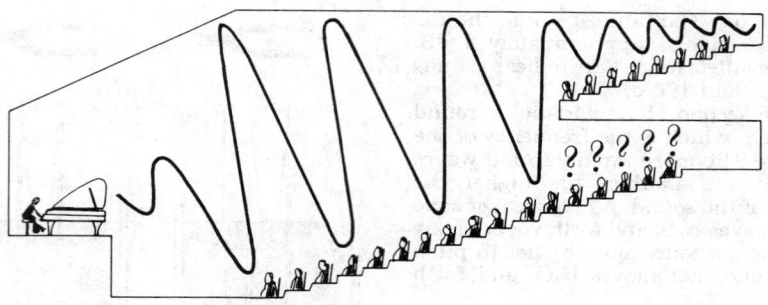

REVERBERATION TIME, *the time it takes for sound to die away, is important in the design of concert halls. Resonators are sometimes used to correct the sound.*

Room Acoustics

Sound engineers face enormously difficult problems in designing concert halls. In planning Philharmonic Hall at Lincoln Center for the Performing Arts in New York City, studies were made of all the world's great concert halls. The goal was to duplicate the best characteristics of each hall. The hall contemplated for Lincoln Center would distribute music equally to all parts of the auditorium. There would be no seats where the music would be inaudible or overly loud. Furthermore, there would be no preferential treatment of some instruments at the expense of others. The piccolos would be heard as well as the bass drums. In addition, the reverberation time, the time it takes for all echoes of a note to die out, would have to be close to the ideal of 1.7 to 2.0 seconds.

Not all of this was accomplished in the initial design, but subsequent modifications have brought the hall closer to the original goal.

Ultrasonics

Supersonic speeds are speeds greater than the speed of sound in air, above 700 miles (1100 km) per hour. Ultrasonic frequencies of sound waves are frequencies above the range of human hearing, that is, greater than 20,000 cycles per second, or 20 kHz (kilohertz). These high-frequency waves can be made with the equipment used to reproduce music in the home. For very-high-frequency waves, however, the area of the speaker face need not be as large, since a 1 MHz (megahertz) ultrasonic signal has a wavelength approximately the thickness of three pages of this book. Further, these very-high-frequency waves do not move from the sound producer in ever-widening spheres, but tend to remain in a narrow beam.

Certain crystalline materials, such as quartz and Rochelle salt, change shape when an electric voltage is applied across their opposite faces. This change in dimension is only a few thousandths of an inch, but that is all that is needed to start a sound wave in adjacent layers of air. These piezoelectric crystals are, therefore, used as sources of ultrasonic waves, or ultrasound.

When ultrasound moves through water, it creates billions of tiny bubbles when the rarefaction part of the sound wave tries to thin out a layer of water. Because the water cannot thin out in this fashion without losing its basic liquid character, it turns into a vapor. But the vapor bubble lasts only a fraction of a second before a pressure wave snaps the bubble with a bang. It is believed that local pressures in the range of hundreds of thousands of pounds per square inch are generated in these collapsing bubbles. Studies of cavitation, the creation and destruction of vapor bubbles, explain why high-speed ship propeller blades wear out faster than lower-speed propeller blades. With their extremely high local pressures, the collapsing bubbles quickly destroy the surfaces of the metal blades, much like striking the blades with a sharply pointed hammer. The destructiveness of ultrasound is not limited to marine propellers. Fish in the sea are killed in great numbers when their delicate nerve cells are exposed to high-frequency sound.

Ultrasonics has a number of important uses. These include removal of grease from tools and sterilization of surgical instruments. In medicine, ultrasound is used in obtaining images

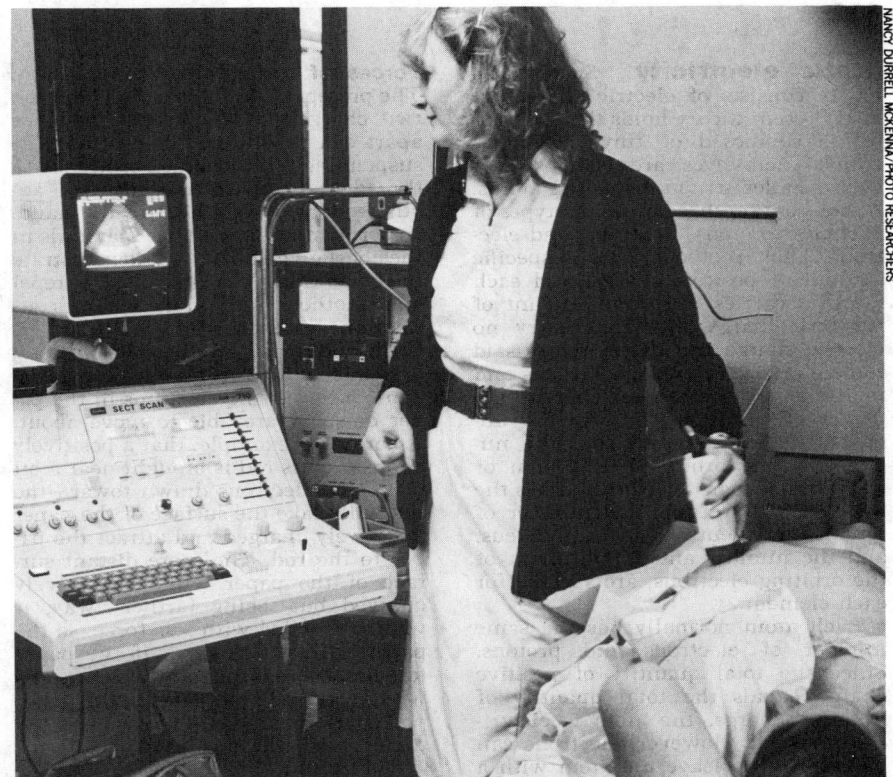

ULTRASONIC WAVES, *unlike x-rays, are not harmful, and their use in medicine is becoming common. Here, a fetus is examined using ultrasound.*

of bones and organs inside the human body. Transducers placed on the skin of the patient transmit ultrasonic waves. The reflected waves are picked

up by the transducer and fed into an oscilloscope, which reconstructs the image of the inner structures of the body.

Electricity and Magnetism

History. Electricity and magnetism are closely associated phenomena that play a vital part in nearly every aspect of modern life: at home, in transportation, in communications, and in industry. The impact on society of these phenomena has been far-reaching. Because their many applications have made them commonplace, it may be difficult to realize that electricity and magnetism have been harnessed for the benefit of mankind only within comparatively recent times. This is true despite the fact that three natural manifestations of electricity and magnetism are readily observable.

One of these manifestations is electrical attraction. Records indicate that as early as 600 B.C., it was known that a piece of amber, which was used for ornamental purposes and called electron, when rubbed with wool or fur could be made to attract small bits of straw. In 1600 William Gilbert discovered that many other substances could be made to exhibit the same effect. He called the effect "electric," from the word "electron."

Lightning, a second manifestation of electricity, has probably been observed since people first appeared on Earth. However, its electrical nature was not recognized until 1751, when Benjamin Franklin performed his kite experiment.

A third natural manifestation, involving magnetism, was known to early Greek philosophers. A lodestone was known to attract iron and, when suspended freely, to orient itself in a north-south direction. The magnetizing of a steel needle by a lodestone and use of the needle as a compass were recorded by the Chinese at the beginning of the 12th century.

The connection between electricity and magnetism was discovered by Hans Christian Oersted in 1819. Progress in the understanding of electric phenomena was made by Michael Faraday, who studied electrolysis in 1834 and became convinced that electricity consisted of "atoms of charge." James Clerk Maxwell studied the phenomena of electromagnetism in the 1860's and introduced the concept of the electro-

magnetic field. J. J. Thomson showed in 1897 that electrons are the carriers of electric charge. Robert Millikan, in his famous oil-drop experiment of 1912, measured the charge of the electron (see diagram).

THE ELECTRON'S CHARGE *was measured by injecting oil droplets between two charged plates. By adjusting the charge on the plates, the droplets were held suspended. The necessary charge was always a multiple of a basic charge, that of the electron.*

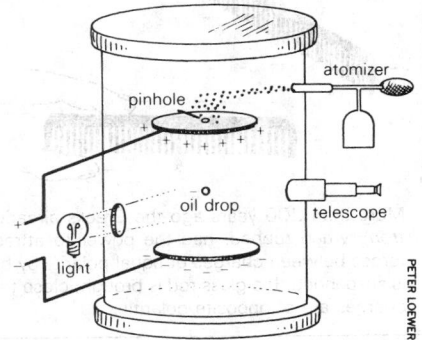

Static electricity.

Static electricity consists of electric charges at rest. Present theory holds that all matter is composed of tiny molecules, which themselves are composed of even smaller structures called atoms. Atoms contain three principal types of particles: protons, neutrons, and electrons. Each proton carries a specific amount of positive charge, and each electron carries the same amount of negative charge. Neutrons carry no electric charge and therefore are said to be electrically neutral. Protons and neutrons are located together at the center of the atom to form the nucleus; electrons move about the nucleus in tiny orbits. Each proton or neutron has more than 1800 times the mass of an electron. The number of protons and neutrons in the nucleus, and the number and arrangement of the orbiting electrons, are specific for each element.

Each atom normally has the same number of electrons and protons. Since the total quantity of positive charge equals the total quantity of negative charge, the atom is electrically neutral. However, electrons can be removed to leave the atom with a net positive charge, or they can be added to give a net negative charge.

The number of electrons in an atom can be altered by friction. Atoms have the ability to attract more electrons than the number normally moving about each nucleus. This attraction is of different strength for different materials. When two substances of different attracting power rub together, some of the electrons in one will leave their orbits and move to new orbits in the other. One substance will then have a net positive charge, and the other will have a net negative charge. Examples may be tabulated as follows:

RUBBED MATERIAL	CHARGE	RUBBING MATERIAL	CHARGE
Amber	−	Fur or wool	+
Rubber	−	Fur or wool	+
Glass	+	Silk	−

Forces of attraction and repulsion.

The presence of a force acting between two charged bodies a little distance apart can readily be demonstrated by suspending one charged body by a thread and approaching it with another charged body held in the hand. Experimentation with the materials in the chart given above will demonstrate the general law that like charges repel one another, and unlike charges attract one another.

An uncharged bit of paper or straw is attracted to the charged body because a few of the electrons in the paper or straw are able to move about. Assume, for example, that a positively charged glass rod is brought near a bit of paper. Electrons drawn toward the rod will make the surface of the paper negatively charged and attract the paper to the rod. The more distant surface of the paper will be positively charged but, being farther away, it will be repelled with less force, so the paper will be attracted. If the paper touches the rod, the movable electrons will go onto the rod, leaving the paper positively charged. The paper will then jump away.

Coulomb's law.

The French physicist Charles de Coulomb was the first to determine the forces between charged bodies. He found that the force between small charged spheres was inversely proportional to the square of the distance r between the two spheres and directly proportional to the product of the magnitudes q_1 and q_2 of the charges:

$$F = k \frac{q_1 q_2}{r^2}.$$

The constant k depends on the units used to express the force F and the charges. If two equal charges are separated by 1 cm and the repellent (or attracting) force between them is 1 dyne, the unit of force in the *cgs* system, then k equals 1, and each charge is said to have the value of 1 electro-static unit, abbreviated esu. The unit of charge in the SI system is the coulomb. One coulomb equals 3 billion electrostatic units.

Electric fields.

If we place an electron near an electric charge, the electron will experience a force, either toward the charge if the charge is positive, or away from the charge if the charge is negative. If an electron or an electric charge experiences a force, it is said to be placed in an electric field. Every electric charge has an electric field associated with it.

Conductors and insulators.

Rubbing a copper bar on wool or fur, will not give it an electric charge. The reason is that, unlike glass or amber, the electrons making up the electric charge of copper are free to move about in the material, and are able to flow away to earth through our hand and body. Amber and glass are thus said to be insulators, while copper and other metals are conductors of electricity. A stream of moving electric charges constitutes an electric current.

The electrons orbiting about atomic nuclei are not all unchangeably fixed in their orbits. In some materials, there are electrons that move readily from atom to atom. If such a material is placed in an electric field, the free electrons will begin moving rapidly, thus creating an electric current. Generally speaking, metals contain quantities of such free electrons and are said to be good conductors (see diagram). In most nonmetallic substances, all the electrons are tightly bound in their orbits and can move from atom to atom only with great difficulty. These substances are called nonconductors, or insulators. Metals differ in the ease with which electrons can move about and are said to differ in their electrical conductivity. The conductivities of several metals, relative to the conductivity of copper, are listed here.

STATIC ELECTRICITY

REPULSION

ATTRACTION

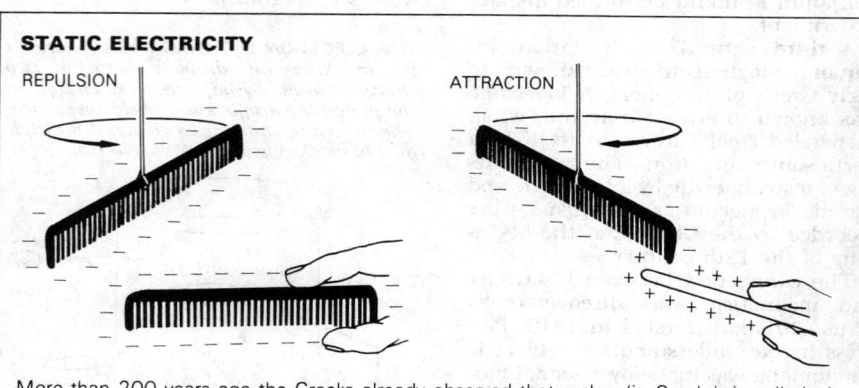

A CHARGED COMB *can attract electrically neutral pieces of paper.*

More than 200 years ago the Greeks already observed that amber (in Greek it is called *electron*), when rubbed, had the power to attract small objects. We can demonstrate repulsive forces between charges of equal polarity by bringing a charged rubber comb near a comb that is suspended. If a glass rod is brought close to the rubber comb, it will be attracted because the charges are of opposite polarities.

METAL	CONDUCTIVITY (percent)
Copper	100
Silver	105
Gold	71
Aluminum	61
Iron	18
Low-carbon steel	8–13
Some alloy steels	2

Of these metals, copper is the most widely used because it is relatively inexpensive and light in weight. High-power transmission lines frequently are constructed of stranded steel cable around which aluminum strands are spiraled. This combination provides high strength, light weight, and good conductivity at low total cost.

Resistivity, the converse, or reciprocal, of conductivity, often is used to describe the property of a material as a conductor. Good conductors have low resistivity. Good insulators have very high resistivity. For example, plate glass has approximately 10^{19} times, and porcelain approximately 10^{20} times, the resistivity of copper. It is this enormous difference in resistivity between good insulators and good conductors that makes possible efficient control and distribution of electricity.

Under certain conditions, a gas can become a conductor. A neon light is an example. Under the influence of an electric field, atoms of neon in the glass tube become positively charged ions and are drawn to the negatively charged conductor. At the same time, electrons that have left the neon atoms are drawn to the positive conductor (see diagram). A more spectacular example of an electric current through a gas, air, is a lightning flash.

NEON LIGHT

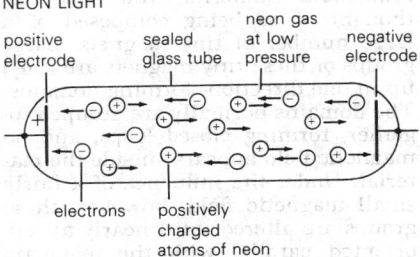

positive electrode | sealed glass tube | neon gas at low pressure | negative electrode

electrons | positively charged atoms of neon

Some liquids, principally water solutions of acids, bases, or salts, also are able to conduct electricity. A portion of the molecules of the solute (the acid, base, or salt) split, or dissociate, into two parts. One part has an excess of electrons, the other a deficiency, so that they are respectively negatively and positively charged. Under the influence of an electric field between two conductors in the solution, these charged particles move, constituting a current. The solution is called an electrolyte, and the conductors are electrodes. Pure water dissociates only to a slight extent and therefore is a poor electrolyte. (See Electrolysis, page 412.)

Direct and Alternating Current

The basic types of electric current are direct current and alternating current. Direct current is a stream of electrons past any one point in one direction. Alternating current alternates its direction, alternately flowing past a point in one direction and then in the opposite direction. The frequency of an alternating current is its number of cycles per second. A complete cycle is the interval during which a current starts from zero, pulses to a maximum in one direction, drops back to zero, pulses to a maximum in the opposite direction, and returns to zero once again. Batteries supply direct current. The current available in the home is alternating current, with a frequency of 60 cycles per second. Most electronic devices require direct current to operate, so television sets, stereo amplifiers, and personal computers contain special circuits that convert alternating current into direct current. The conversion of alternating current into direct current is called rectification, and the circuit for this process is called a rectifier.

Units of measure.
The unit of quantity of electricity is the coulomb. One coulomb is equivalent to the charge carried by 6.24×10^{18} electrons. Electricity flowing at the rate of 1 coulomb per second is a current of 1 ampere. Thus 1 ampere is equal to the passage through a given point of 6.24×10^{18} electrons per second.

The electric pressure, or electromotive force, e.m.f., which causes the flow of current, is measured in volts. The intensity of an electric field may be expressed as volts per centimeter or volts per inch.

The resistance of a conductor is measured in ohms. An e.m.f. of 1 volt applied to a resistance of 1 ohm will produce a current of 1 ampere. Ohm's law, named after its propounder, Georg Simon Ohm, states that current is proportional to the voltage applied and inversely proportional to the resistance. Ohm's law is stated in the form of an equation, $I = E/R$, where I is the current in amperes, E is the e.m.f. in volts, and R is the resistance in ohms. Conductance, the converse of resistance, is measured in mhos, which is ohms spelled backward.

Resistance and conductance refer to the properties of a material of a particular shape and size. The corresponding characteristics of the material itself, which do not depend on size or shape, are resistivity and conductivity. These are respectively the resistance and conductance of a cube of the material of unit size.

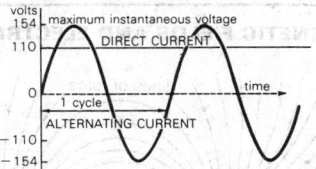

THE VOLTAGE *of direct current remains constant. In alternating current voltage changes polarity 60 times per second.*

The volt, ohm, ampere, and coulomb are named in honor of the following pioneers in the study of electricity and magnetism: Alessandro Volta; Georg Ohm; André Ampère; and Charles de Coulomb.

Production of electric current.
Aside from the transient discharges of static electricity, the first production of electric current was by chemical means. Chemical production of electric current is still important, as shown by the large number of battery-operated devices. The great bulk of electric power, however, is generated by electromagnetic induction in rotating machinery. Photoelectric cells are used to supply power in artificial satellites and certain small appliances, such as electronic calculators.

Chemical cells. When electrodes of two different materials, such as zinc and copper, are immersed in an electrolytic solution, one acquires a positive charge and the other a negative charge. If they are then connected externally by a wire, a current will flow through the wire. This arrangement constitutes a voltaic cell, which was discovered about 1800. Chemical action between the electrolyte and the electrodes causes atoms of one electrode to go into solution, each atom leaving behind one or more electrons. This leaves that electrode with a negative charge. The electrolyte takes electrons from the other electrode, thus giving that electrode a positive charge. The electrons flow through the external wire from the negative electrode to the positive electrode. Voltaic cells connected together form a battery. (See Electrochemistry, page 411.)

Magnetism

Magnets are generally defined as materials that attract iron. Permanent magnets always retain this capability, but an electromagnet requires an electric current to become magnetic. A magnet always has two poles. When the magnet is free to move, the poles orient themselves along the north-south direction. The pole that orients itself toward the north pole of Earth is called the north pole; the other pole is called the south pole. A magnet always retains its two poles. When we cut a magnet in two pieces, each piece will have a north pole and a south pole.

MAGNETIC FIELDS AND ELECTRIC CURRENT

THE MAGNETIC FIELD *around a magnet can be represented by lines of force joining the north and south poles. An electric current in a wire creates a magnetic field represented by lines of force in circles around the wire. The magnetic field created by a solenoid (a coil of wire) is identical to the magnetic field created by a bar magnet.*

Magnetic fields.

Attraction and repulsion between magnets follow a set of principles similar to those described previously for electrostatic forces. Consider the familiar magnetic compass, the needle of which orients itself in a north-south direction. For convenience, the end pointing north is marked N and the other end S. When another compass is brought near the first and is moved about it, the two needles deviate from their north-south direction and tend to point toward each other. The attracting and repelling forces reside in the ends of the needles, and ends that are marked alike repel one another. The ends of the needles, and of all magnets, are called poles. Just as like electric charges repel and unlike electric charges attract each other (see diagram), like poles repel one another, and unlike poles attract one another.

There is, however, an important difference between a magnetized bar and a charged body. The charged body may carry the same polarity of charge over its entire surface, whereas the magnetized bar always has two poles of unlike polarity and of equal strength. (The existence of a magnet with a single pole, however small, and termed monopole, has not been proved.)

The forces that act between magnets at a distance suggest that the magnets are surrounded by a magnetic field (see diagram). Like an electric field, a magnetic field is considered to consist of lines of force, a line of force being a line along which a magnet pole tends to move. The positive direction is that in which the N pole tends to move. Thus, a compass needle in a magnetic field will orient itself parallel with the lines of force, with the N pole pointing in the positive direction. There is an important difference, however, between the concepts of the magnetic field and the electric field. The electric lines of force do not terminate at the S pole but continue unbroken through the magnet to emerge at the N pole. Magnetic lines of force exist only as closed loops and never cross.

Force between current and fields.

In 1819 Hans Christian Oersted found that a compass needle was deflected when a conductor carrying current was held over it. Further experimentation demonstrated that there is a magnetic field about an electric current and that the lines of force form closed loops encircling the conductor in planes perpendicular to the conductor. The lines of force about two parallel wires carrying current produce a force between the two wires. They attract each other if the current flows in the same direction in both. They repel each other if the currents flow in opposite directions.

If a wire is bent into a closed loop and a current is passed through it, magnetic lines of force will form closed loops around the wire (see diagram). If a series of wire loops is joined to form a helix, or coil, lines of force will pass inside, parallel with the axis, and curving around outside to close upon themselves. Such a coil, which is called a solenoid, exhibits all of the characteristics found in a bar magnet.

When a bar of soft iron is put inside a solenoid and a current is then passed through the solenoid, the bar exhibits all the characteristics of a strong magnet. When the current is turned off, the magnetic properties of the bar disappear. This important device is called an electromagnet.

Discovery of the electromagnet and development of the chemical cell as a source of electricity opened the way for the invention of the telegraph by Samuel F.B. Morse in 1837. They were also essential for invention of the telephone by Alexander Graham Bell in 1875. Electromagnets are used in relays to open and close electric circuits, to operate valves, and to do a multitude of other mechanical tasks.

Ferromagnetism.

The magnetic characteristics exhibited when a core of soft iron is put into a solenoid are many times greater than those of a solenoid alone. The magnetic properties contributed by the iron are called ferromagnetism, and the iron is said to be ferromagnetic. Two other metals, nickel and cobalt, and a few nonferrous metal alloys, also are ferromagnetic, but to a lesser extent than iron. Some of the most widely used ferromagnetic materials are alloys of iron with nickel and cobalt.

The source of ferromagnetic properties lies in the electrons orbiting about the atomic nuclei of the material. The electrons spin about as they orbit, producing a magnetic field along their axis. In all materials other than ferromagnetic materials, the electrons in each atom are so oriented that practically no magnetic field is produced outside the atom. In ferromagnetic materials, however, there is a net imbalance in each atom so that the atom has a magnetic field about it. The ferromagnetic material, thus, can be thought of as being composed of a large number of tiny magnets. Large groups of these tiny magnets are lined up in one direction, forming domains. The domains normally are grouped together, forming closed loops, and no magnetic field appears outside the material. Under the influence of a fairly small magnetic field, however, these groups are altered until nearly all are oriented parallel with the magnetic field and add their own fields to it. The total field of all the tiny magnets in the material may be many thousand times greater than the field required to line them up. When the external field is removed, the tiny magnets revert approximately to their former orientations, producing no outside field.

In some ferromagnetic materials, the magnetic domains are reoriented with great difficulty, and a strong field is required to accomplish this. Moreover, when the field is removed, many of the domains do not revert to their initial orientations. The bar is said to be magnetized, and is called a permanent magnet. Early permanent magnets and compass needles were made of hardened carbon steel, but materi-

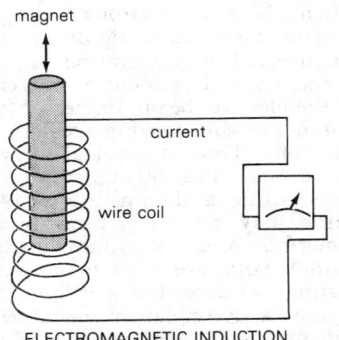
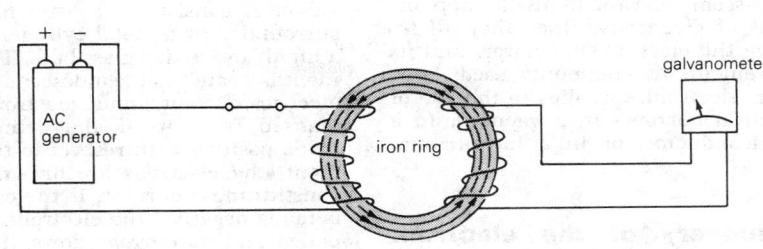

FARADAY DISCOVERED *that a varying magnetic field, such as one produced by a magnet moving inside a coil of wire, produces a current in the coil. The phenomenon is called magnetic induction. Faraday also discovered that if two coils are wound around an iron core, an alternating current applied to one coil will induce an alternating current in the other coil.*

PETER LOEWER

als have recently been developed offering vastly improved permanent magnet characteristics. These materials have made possible the development of many new instruments and devices. Permanent magnets, when properly prepared and treated, exhibit great stability of their magnetic fields and are used widely in instruments that measure electricity and in loudspeakers.

Electromagnetic induction.

In 1831, Michael Faraday discovered that when he plunged a magnet into a coil of wire, a current flowed while the magnet moved. The generation of current in a coil by a varying magnetic field is called magnetic induction. Electric generators make use of electromagnetic induction for the production of electricity. The current is created in coils mounted on an axis and moved through a magnetic field, thus generating electricity.

Conversely, when a coil of conducting wire is placed in a magnetic field and a current is applied to the coil, the coil will undergo a force (see diagram). Thus, in principle, the same device used for the generation of electricity from mechanical motion can also be used to produce mechanical motion from electricity. Electromotors are, therefore, very similar in construction to electric generators, and many designs may be used interchangeably.

The forces acting on a coil are also used to produce sound in a loudspeaker. A coil is attached to the diaphragm of the loudspeaker and placed inside the magnetic field of a strong permanent magnet. When the amplified sound signal flows through the coil, it will put the coil in motion and reproduce the sound waves that have been picked up by the microphone.

Transformers.

We know that an electric current passing through a wire coil wrapped around a bar of iron creates a magnetic field in the bar. If the current through the solenoid varies rapidly, the magnetic field in the bar will also vary. If another coil is wrapped around the iron bar, the varying magnetic field will create an electric current through this coil.

Generally, transformers have cores made of insulated iron sheets. This prevents the induction of electric currents in the core itself and thus limits the losses in the transformer. The coil to which current is applied is the primary coil; the coil in which the current is induced is the secondary coil.

Transformers work only with alternating currents, since the current in the secondary coil can only be created by a varying magnetic field. The voltage induced in the secondary coil is proportional to the number of turns in the coil. In a transformer in which the primary and secondary coils have the same number of turns, the voltage in the secondary coil is the same as that in the primary coil. Such transformers are used to separate electric appliances from house current.

Transformers are used mainly for changing the voltage of alternating current. For example, a transformer in which the primary coil has ten times as many turns as the secondary coil will transform 110 volts into 11 volts. Such a transformer is called a stepdown transformer. Many appliances are equipped with transformers that reduce high house voltage to a lower voltage suitable for operation of the appliances. Transformers in which the secondary coil has a much larger number of turns than the primary coil are called step-up transformers. Such transformers are used for the generation of high voltage. Large high-voltage transformers are used in long-distance transmission of electric power. Losses in transmission lines are proportional to the current passing through them. Since one can lower the current by increasing the voltage, transformers are used to increase the voltage generated by the generators to several hundred thousand volts.

Electric Circuits

Electric devices may be interconnected in a variety of ways with respect to the circuits the current follows. In a series circuit, the current flows in sequence through one device after another. There is only one path. One type of Christmas tree light string is an example. When one bulb burns out, the circuit is broken and all bulbs go out. In a parallel circuit, there are two or more paths. The current divides, and part flows simultaneously to each path. In another type of Christmas tree lights, the bulbs are connected in parallel. The full supply voltage is applied to each bulb, and the current through each bulb comes directly from the source and returns to it. Thus, when one bulb burns out, the other bulbs may not go out.

Many circuits used for street lights are in series, but most other circuits normally encountered are in parallel. House wiring consists of several parallel circuits. When an appliance is plugged into an outlet, it is put in parallel with other appliances.

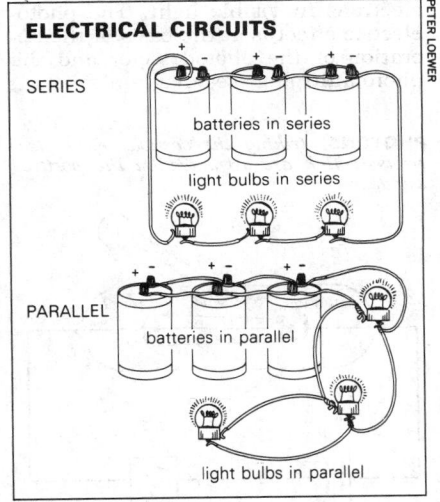

ELECTRICAL CIRCUITS

SERIES — batteries in series — light bulbs in series

PARALLEL — batteries in parallel — light bulbs in parallel

PETER LOEWER

Electronics

In a broad sense, the term electronics may seem relevant to all the applications of electricity, since they all involve the electron, its charge, and its movement. As commonly used, however, electronics applies to the use of electron currents in a vacuum, in a semiconductor, or in a low-pressure gas.

Discovery of the electron.

The discovery of the electron in 1897 by Joseph Thomson was a result of his study of the electric discharges in evacuated glass tubes. When the pressure is reduced in such a tube, the electric discharge first produces a blue glow. This changes to pink, and then dark areas appear as the pink discharge disappears. Finally, the glass itself glows with a faint greenish light. This light is caused by invisible rays coming from the cathode, the negatively charged electrode. The light rays first were called cathode rays.

Thomson showed that these rays were deflected both by magnetic and electrostatic fields. Because the rays were deflected toward positively charged plates, he concluded that they had to be negatively charged particles. These particles were given the name of electron, a term first used by the Irish physicist G.J. Stoney in 1881 to designate carriers of charge in electrolytic phenomena.

Electronic emission.

A very strong field is required to dislodge electrons from the atoms in the surface of a metal at room temperature. As the metal is heated, a temperature is reached at which electrons are emitted spontaneously. This is called thermionic emission.

Electrons also are emitted at room temperature when light falls upon a metal. This is called the photoelectric effect. Most metals exhibit this effect only under ultraviolet light, but such metals as rubidium and cesium emit electrons in visible light. The photoelectric effect is at the basis of the operation of the photodetector and the photomultiplier (see diagram).

PHOTONS *striking the cathode eject electrons, which are attracted by the positive anode.*

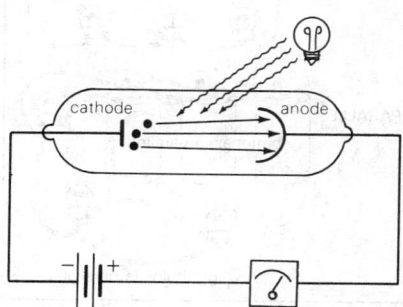

Electron tubes.

The first important, successful application of thermionic emission was developed by John Ambrose Fleming in his Fleming valve. It consists of a wire filament surrounded by a metal cylinder inside a highly evacuated glass bulb. The filament is heated to incandescence by an electric current, and electrons are emitted from it. If the cylinder is made positive with respect to the filament, the electrons are drawn to it, constituting a current. If the cylinder is made negative, the electrons are repelled and no current flows. The device that permits current to flow in only one direction is called a rectifier. It is also called a diode, because it has two electrodes.

An important invention was made by Lee De Forest in 1907, when he placed a wire grid between the filament and plate of a Fleming valve. He called the new tube an audion. Such a tube also is called a triode, indicating the use of three electrodes. A relatively small voltage applied to the grid has a strong controlling effect on the passage of electrons from the filament to the plate. The effect is much greater than when the voltage is applied directly to the plate. Through this effect, the triode functions as an amplifier, enabling very small amounts of power to control large amounts of power. Additional grids may be added, making a tetrode or pentode, to modify the characteristics of the tube.

Since the late 1950's, electron tubes have been gradually replaced by transistors in most electronic devices. Today, electron tubes are used in some specific cases, including the cathode-ray tubes in television sets and computer monitors.

X-rays.

X-ray machines are electronic devices. X-rays are produced when a beam of electrons impinges on a metal target in a highly evacuated chamber. The penetrating power of the x-rays is dependent on the energy of the electron beam, expressed as the number of volts used to accelerate the electrons. Thus, a surgical x-ray machine may use 50,000 to 100,000 volts, while a therapeutic x-ray machine may require several hundred thousand volts. Machines using 10 million volts are used to x-ray large castings for detection of internal flaws or cracks. Even larger machines, requiring hundreds of millions of volts, are used for scientific investigation and research.

Electron microscope.

The electron microscope is a device in which a beam of electrons is used to produce magnified images of objects that are many times smaller than those the best light-beam microscope can see. This has been useful, for example, in studying the structure of matter and the nature of viruses.

Illumination.

Several of the familiar types of electric lamps are electronic in nature. The neon lamp is a tube containing neon at low pressure through which an electric current passes. Mercury vapor lamps are widely used for highway lighting. Fluorescent lights are glass tubes filled with argon and mercury vapor at low pressure and coated on the inside surface with a phosphorescent material. An electric current in the gas produces ultraviolet light, which causes the phosphorescent material to glow brightly. Fluorescent lights produce several times more light for the same expenditure of power than do incandescent lights, which must dissipate relatively large amounts of heat.

THE NATURE OF THE INVISIBLE RAYS *produced during electric discharge in evacuated glass tubes eluded scientists until 1837, when Thomson proved they consisted of electrons.*

W.H. FREEMAN

Semiconductors

Classification. Solid substances are classified, on the basis of their electrical behavior, as conductors, insulators, superconductors, and semiconductors. Substances that offer little resistance to the flow of electrons are called conductors. Substances that offer a great deal of resistance to the flow of electrons are called insulators. Materials that offer more resistance to the flow of electrons than conductors, but offer less resistance than insulators, are called semiconductors. All metals show increasing resistance as temperature increases. In semiconductors and insulators, resistance decreases as temperature increases.

Semiconductor theory. In isolated atoms, electrons occupy stable orbits around the atomic nucleus. Each electron orbit corresponds to a fixed energy level of the electron. When individual atoms are assembled in a crystal lattice (see Solids, page 441), individual energy levels of the electrons merge into energy bands. Solids have several energy bands, which can be occupied by electrons. These energy bands are separated by gaps; electrons require extra energy to pass from one band to another.

The electrical properties of solids can be described by the mobility of electrons in these energy bands. In electrical conductors, the outermost energy band is called the conduction band. This band is not completely filled, and its electrons can move easily from atom to atom. These electrons, which are called free electrons, account for the current in a conductor.

The outermost energy level in an insulator is called the valence band. It is completely filled, and no electrons can move from atom to atom. Insulators can conduct electricity under certain extreme conditions. If, for example, electrons acquire enough energy by acceleration in a very strong electric field, they can reach an energy band placed higher, and conduction can occur. The gap between this higher energy band and the normally occupied valence band, called the forbidden gap, can only be bridged by highly energized electrons.

In certain elements, the forbidden gap is quite narrow, so electrons can easily acquire energies to bridge the gap, for example, by an increase of temperature in the solid. These elements, called semiconductors, conduct electricity more or less efficiently, but at low temperatures act as insulators. Their conductivity, contrary to that of conductors, increases with increasing temperature, because more electrons have enough energy to jump the forbidden gap. Germanium and silicon are examples of semiconductors.

Conductivity of a semiconductor can also be increased by adding minute amounts of different elements, called impurities, to the semiconductor material. Germanium has four electrons in its outermost shell and shares each one of them with the four neighboring germanium atoms in the crystal lattice, forming thus a completely filled valence bond. Arsenic atoms have five electrons in their outer shell. When arsenic atoms are introduced into the germanium crystal lattice, four of the arsenic electrons will be shared with the four neighboring germanium atoms. The fifth arsenic electron will not find a place and will forcibly occupy a place in the conduction band. These electrons flow through the material freely and can produce an electric current. Semiconductors of this type are called n-type semiconductors, the n indicating that the charge carriers are negative. The impurities are called electron donors.

Conduction in a semiconductor can also be enhanced by creating so-called missing electrons in the valence band. Boron atoms have three electrons in their outermost shell and thus can share only three electrons with the four surrounding germanium atoms. The missing electron is called a hole. Just as an electron can flow through a material, so can a hole (see diagram). A hole can be filled up by a neighboring electron, which in turn leaves a hole. This new hole can be filled up by an electron, and so on. When the semiconductor is subjected to an electric field, holes behave as positive charge carriers. Semiconductors containing holes are termed p-type semiconductors, with the p indicating that the charge carriers are positive. Impurities that produce holes are called electron acceptors.

MANY MICROCHIPS *are produced simultaneously on a semiconducting silicon wafer.*

Semiconductor devices.
Semiconductors had their first important application as rectifiers for low-frequency alternating currents.

About 1904, the rectifying properties of semiconductors were used to provide a detector of the high-frequency currents set up in circuits by radio waves. The crystal rectifier, a fine metal wire in contact with crystalline lead sulfide or silicon, was the best detector of radio waves in the early days of radio. Vacuum tubes replaced such devices, and during World War II metal point-contact silicon devices were used in radar.

P-N junctions. It is possible to produce both an n-type region and a p-type region in a single crystal of semiconductor material. Such a combination, called a p-n junction, is the basis for many semiconductor devices. In the n-region, donor impurity atoms give up electrons in greater numbers than acceptor atoms contribute positive holes. In the p-region, holes are in excess compared with electrons. Most of the electrons remain in the n-region, and most of the holes remain in the p-region. However, some electrons from the n-region diffuse into the p-region, leaving behind positive donor ions. Similarly, some holes from the p-region diffuse into the n-region, leaving negatively charged acceptor ions. Due to the impurity ions, an electric field is established at the junction, and this field inhibits additional electrons from diffusing out of the n-type material and additional holes from diffusing out of the p-type material.

When a battery is connected with its negative terminal on the n-type material and its positive terminal on the p-type material, electrons from the battery neutralize the positive ions on the n-side of the junction, and electrons enter the positive terminal of the battery from the p-region, thereby decreasing the negative charge on the p-side. As a result, the junction field is diminished and electrons can move from the n-type material through the junction to recombine with holes. The holes on the p-type side carry current from the positive battery terminal to

IN A P-N JUNCTION, *the zone without carriers (electrons and holes) is narrowed when the diode is forward biased, and widened when it is reverse biased.*

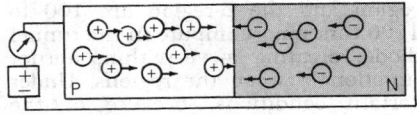

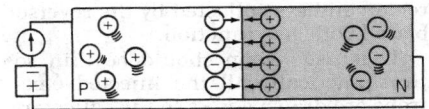

the junction. A p-n junction connected to a voltage source in this fashion is said to be forward biased, and the device can carry appreciable amounts of current.

If the p-n junction is reverse biased—negative voltage is applied to the p-side and positive voltage to the n-side—a field is present that causes the mobile holes and electrons to move away from the junction and one another toward the p-contact and n-contact respectively. Electrons are added to the p-region and removed from the n-region by the battery, leaving a wider region near the junction charged with immobile impurity ions but depleted of mobile charge carriers. The junction field is enhanced by reverse biasing, but because of the depletion of mobile charges, little current flows. The current that flows is attributable to thermal excitation of holes and electrons in the junction region. These carriers contribute a small but finite reverse current. A p-n junction passes electrical current when forward biased and opposes the flow when reverse biased.

A rectifier can be used to convert alternating current into direct current. Solid-state rectifiers have wide commercial applications as radar or microwave detectors, computer switching diodes, television and radio diodes, and power rectifiers for battery chargers and electronic power supplies. Although vacuum-tube rectifiers were widely used for 50 years, invention of the p-n junction rectifier and the vast needs of computer companies for reliable, small, efficient, and long-lived circuit elements have made semiconductor diodes predominant.

Transistors.
The most important development in the application of semiconductors came in 1948, when the germanium transistor was invented by William Shockley, John Bardeen, and Walter H. Brattain, at Bell Telephone Laboratories. The transistor is an electronic device that can be used to control or amplify electric current. The earliest type consisted of two metal-point contacts placed close together on the surface of a germanium crystal and a third soldered at its base. One of the point contacts is called the emitter; the other, the collector; the soldered contact, the base.

In 1949 Shockley outlined many of the theories that led to an understanding of semiconductors and subsequently, with his coworkers, developed the junction transistor. This device consists either of a thin section of p-type semiconductor between two parts of n-type semiconductor—known as an n-p-n junction transistor—or vice versa, the p-n-p junction transistor.

Modern electronic computers depend for their existence on transistors. Vacuum tubes are too unreliable, slow,

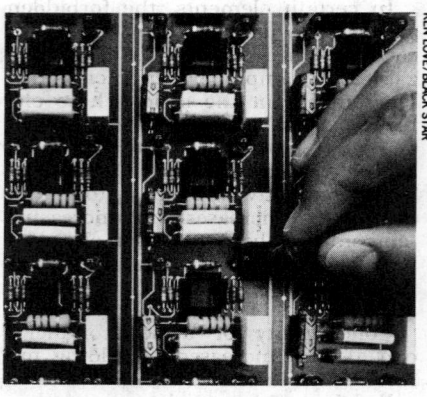

IN A TRANSISTOR, *the current from one n-region (emitter) to the other n-region (collector) can be controlled by applying a voltage to the p-region (base) between them.*

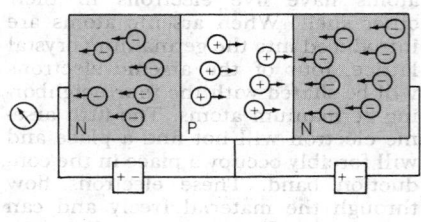

and bulky to be used in a large-scale computer. Radios, hearing aids, electronic systems, and space communications systems use transistors as active circuit elements because of the many advantages the transistor has over vacuum tubes.

Junction transistors. Silicon and germanium are the most important semiconductor materials for transistors. While both n-p-n and p-n-p transistors are used commercially, only the n-p-n will be discussed here. Two p-n junctions exist in an n-p-n transistor and share a common narrow p-region. Three contacts are made to the three regions: the emitter, base, and collector. The n-p junction between the emitter and the base contact is the emitter junction and it is forward biased. The junction between the collector and the base is the collector junction and it is reverse biased. Because the emitter junction is forward biased, electrons flow from the emitter contact through the n-region of the emitter to the emitter junction. There they are injected into the p-region. These injected electrons diffuse as minority carriers across the thin p-base region and are collected by the reverse biased collector junction.

The base region should be thin so that practically all the injected electrons are drawn across to the collector. They are swept into the collector by the large junction field of the reverse biased collector before they find their way to the base contact or recombine

with holes. The emitter current also includes holes injected from the base into the emitter region. By introducing impurities more heavily in the n-region of the base, the electron injection can be made to dominate as required for an efficient transistor. The fraction of the emitter current that crosses the collector junction is known as the alpha, α, of the transistor. For junction transistors α can reach 0.99.

When the emitter current is varied by a signal voltage introduced at the input terminals, there will be a corresponding variation of the collector current. Since the collector impedance, or resistance, is high compared with the impedance of the forward biased emitter, a large-load resistor can be used in the output to accomplish voltage amplification or power amplification. For example, if the impedances of the input and output circuits are 100 and 1,000,000 ohms respectively, there is a power gain and a voltage gain of about 10,000.

Field-effect transistors. In recent years, the field-effect transistor, FET, has come into use. In the FET a flow of current from a source to a drain is controlled by a transverse voltage impressed on a gate. The most common type of FET is the MOSFET, metal-oxide silicon. Its insulating layer of silicon oxide eliminates the need for physical isolation of the components. The MOSFET is favored for use in high-frequency applications and integrated circuits. Experimental versions of a more recent kind of FET, the Schottky variety, need no oxide gate-layer. They have produced oscillations in the microwave range.

Injection lasers. The injection laser was developed contemporaneously in 1962 by Marshall Nathan and coworkers at IBM and by Robert Hall and coworkers at General Electric. It consists of a p-n junction in a compound semiconductor, such as gallium arsenide, indium phosphide, or indium arsenide, that emits coherent light when sufficient electrons are injected into the p-region. The electrons recombine radiatively, that is, fill the holes, and emit light in the process. This device requires a specific geometrical configuration to permit electrical current to be converted directly into a highly directional and pure beam of light through laser action. Semiconductor lasers are used in optical communication systems.

Tunnel diodes. The tunnel diode was invented by Leo Esaki in 1957. A tunnel diode differs from an ordinary p-n junction diode in that both the n-region and the p-region are 100 to 1000 times more impure in the tunnel diode, creating a very thin, abrupt junction between the regions. Under certain conditions, because of the junction, electrons can go from the n-side directly to the p-side without having to climb over the junction barrier. This process is called tunneling. Because tunneling is inherently rapid, tunnel diodes are used in computer switching circuits, where high speed is essential.

Photocells. Semiconducting photocells are devices that conduct electricity better when exposed to light. There are three main types of semiconducting photocells. Photoconductive and photodiode photocells are used as light detectors, particularly infrared light. Photovoltaic photocells are used as power sources. An example of this type is the silicon solar cell, which has been used to power electronic circuits in satellites by direct conversion of solar energy into electrical energy.

Integrated circuits. The integrated circuit, also called a microchip, is a small chip of semiconductor on which are deployed microminiaturized diodes, transistors, resistors, capacitors, and the needed insulation and connections. Thousands to millions of elements can be created on a single chip.

HENRI BUREAU/SYGMA

THIS SOLAR PLANE *uses photocells to convert light into the electrical energy that turns the propeller.*

Superconductors

In 1911 the Dutch physicist Kamerling Onnes discovered that when mercury is cooled to 4.16° K, its electric resistance completely vanishes. Several other metals and alloys also lose their electrical resistance when cooled to close to absolute zero. This phenomenon is called superconductivity, and the temperature at which a metal becomes a superconductor is called its critical temperature. Not all metals become superconductors, some retaining their resistivity even when cooled to absolute zero.

Different superconductors have different critical temperatures. For certain metals, the critical temperature is very close to absolute zero. For lead, it is 7.22° K. An alloy of niobium and germanium has the highest known critical temperature: 23.2° K.

An explanation for the phenomenon of superconductivity was found in 1957, when the American physicists John Bardeen, Leon N. Cooper, and John Robert Schrieffer formulated their so-called BCS theory. According to this theory, coupled electron pairs appear in a metal when it is cooled below critical temperature. These electrons cannot give off energy through scattering, the usual mechanism responsible for resistivity in metals, so these coupled pairs can travel through the metal unhindered.

Several interesting applications of superconductivity exist. Large magnets in some particle accelerators use superconducting solenoids to create the magnetic field. Once the current flows, it continues to flow indefinitely, and no power, except for the power required for cooling the superconductor, is required to run the magnet. Superconducting electromotors and generators have long been operated experimentally, and studies are under way for the use of superconductors in long-distance transport of electricity.

Light

Light is the form of radiant energy that produces visual sense impressions by stimulating the retina of the eye. Ultraviolet and infrared light are physically the same as visible light, but cannot be seen by the human eye. Ultraviolet light is sometimes called black light, and infrared light is often called heat radiation, a misnomer.

Light is dualistic in nature, so its properties must be explained by two separate and distinct theories, wave theory and quantum theory.

Wave theory. The wave theory considers light as both electric and magnetic in character, and as transmitted through space as an electromagnetic transverse wave. This transverse wave motion may be compared to the motion of water molecules in a pond stirred by a stone thrown into it. Upon striking the water, the stone causes a series of ever-widening circles to ripple outward from the center of movement. Each circle consists of water molecules oscillating up and down, at right angles to the direction of wave movement. These waves form a series of crests and troughs. The distance between any two wave crests is the wavelength, and the frequency is the number of wavelengths passing a given point in a second. In a luminous body, such as an incandescent bulb, the light waves travel out spherically, in three dimensions, from the bulb. The water waves travel out in circles, in two dimensions, from the source of disturbance. However, an electromagnetic wave is transverse, like a water wave, and can be depicted as follows.

A represents the amplitude of the transverse wave, in the case of the electromagnetic wave, the maximum electric or magnetic intensity. The period, T, is the time it takes the wave to travel one wavelength, λ. Thus, λ equals velocity times time, or $\lambda = VT$. This can also be written $V = \lambda / T$. Since the frequency is equal to $1/T$, V can be equated to frequency times wavelength, or $f\lambda$.

TRANSVERSE WAVE

crest

amplitude

amplitude

trough

wavelength (λ)

ELECTROMAGNETIC SPECTRUM

The electromagnetic spectrum contains radio waves, microwaves, light, x-rays, and gamma rays. They are all the same type of radiation, differing only in wavelength.

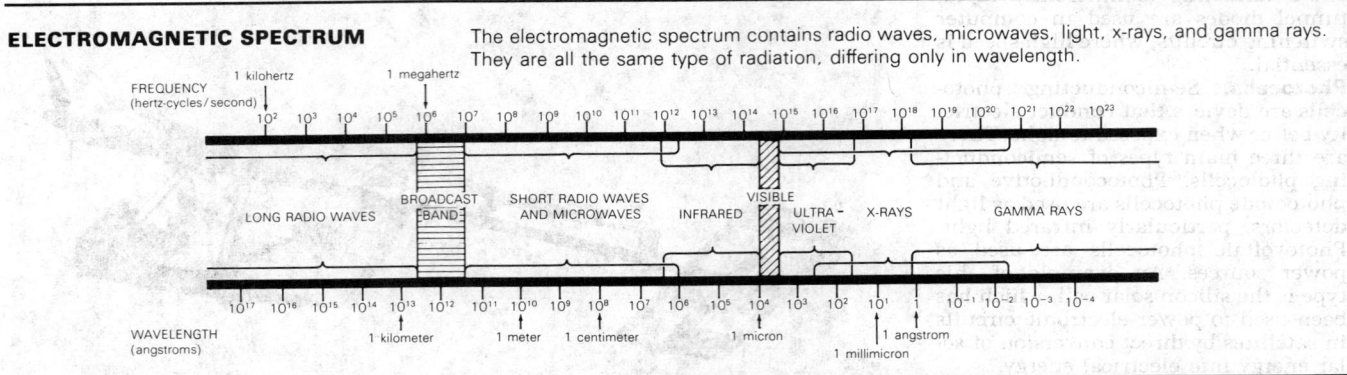

Electromagnetic waves are in the electromagnetic spectrum, which is divided into various regions. These regions, from long wavelengths to short, are radio waves, Hertzian waves or microwaves, infrared, visible light, ultraviolet rays, x-rays, and gamma rays. In the visible-light region, or visible spectrum, the waves are classified by the colors the human eye senses on receiving certain wavelengths. The wavelength is usually given in nanometers, abbreviated nm. One nm is equal to 10^{-7} (.0000001) centimeter. Wavelengths, especially in the visible region, are also denoted in angstrom units. One angstrom unit, or 1 Å, is equal to 10^{-8} centimeter, or 1 nm = 10 angstrom units. The visible region extends only from 760 nm (7600 Å), the red region, to 380 nm (3800 Å), the blue region. It is obvious, therefore, that the eye responds to a rather small portion of the overall spectrum.

Quantum theory. Quantum theory explains light effects left unexplained by electromagnetic theory. It regards electromagnetic energy as traveling in small packets. A single packet is called a quantum, or photon. The energy in a quantum is given by the expression $e = h\nu$, where e is the energy in the photon, h is a constant (called Planck's constant), and ν is the frequency. The existence of these discrete photons has been shown by the work of Niels Bohr, Albert Einstein, and Max Planck.

Velocity of light. Light travels at a velocity of approximately 299,793 km per second, or 186,283 miles per second, in a vacuum and at practically the same speed in the atmosphere. The velocity is lower in all other transparent media. In water, for example, it is approximately 225,500 km per second, or 140,000 miles per second. The distance light travels in one second is roughly equivalent to seven times around Earth at the equator. The American physicist Albert A. Michelson, using a mechanical device, made the first precise measurement of the speed of light.

Reflection and transmission.

Glass is said to transmit light almost perfectly. Only a small part of the transmitted light is absorbed. Other materials do not let light pass through them. They are said to either reflect the light or absorb it. Light is reflected when most of its energy is radiated back, as, for example, by a mirror. A sheet of black paper does not reflect light, but absorbs it. Carbon black absorbs almost all the wavelengths of light, so it appears to us as black.

Some materials only absorb a fraction of wavelengths and reflect light at other wavelengths. A surface will appear as red if it absorbs all wavelengths but red light. A white surface does not absorb light in any specific wavelength range, so it reflects all the wavelengths it receives. Transparent materials can also absorb selectively at certain wavelengths. For example, a filter that absorbs the wavelengths of light corresponding to green will appear red, since red light can pass without absorption.

MICHELSON *measured the velocity of light using a rotating mirror. At a certain rotational speed, light reflected to the plane mirror will be reflected back to the observer by another face of the mirror.*

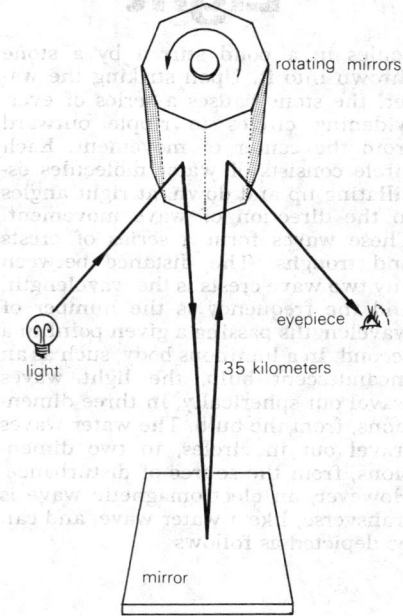

Geometrical Optics

Geometrical optics is concerned with the study of lightpaths through optical systems, more specifically the laws governing reflection and refraction. The basic assumption of geometric optics is that light travels in rectilinear paths.

The law of reflection states that when a ray of light is reflected from a surface, the incident ray, reflected ray, and normal all lie in the same plane. (The normal is a line drawn perpendicular to the surface at the point where the incident ray strikes the surface.) The law of reflection also states that the angle of incidence, which is the angle between the incident ray and the normal, is equal to the angle of reflection, which is the angle between the reflected ray and the normal.

When a ray of light from an object strikes a plane mirror, it does not change. It merely travels in a new direction. When looking at a plane mirror, therefore, the eye sees an image that is identical to the object and that appears to be at the same distance behind the mirror as the object is in front of the mirror. A line joining the object and the image would be perpendicular to the mirror. In addition, the image is said to be virtual. That is, the rays appear to be coming directly from the object, even though they are not.

Curved mirrors. A spherical mirror is the simplest curved mirror. Its reflecting surface is a section of a sphere. If the outer surface of the sphere segment is reflective, the mirror is convex. If the inner surface is reflective, the mirror is concave. Parallel rays reflected by a convex mirror diverge, that is, spread apart. Parallel rays reflected by a concave mirror converge, that is, come together. The point at which the rays converge is called the focus of the mirror. A spherical mirror focuses well only those rays that are close to the optical axis of the mirror. The optical axis is the line perpendicular to the surface of the mirror and passing through its center. Rays reflected at the mirror at

DISPERSION

white light → prism

wall
red
orange
yellow
green
blue
violet

A prism disperses white light into its component colors.

sunlight → red, orange, yellow, green, blue, violet

red, orange, yellow, green, blue, violet

If the sun shines during a rain, sunlight is refracted and reflected by the raindrops. Red light is reflected by drops higher in the sky, violet light by drops lower in the sky, and all the other colors by drops in between.

some distance from the optical axis meet at a point closer to the mirror. This phenomenon is called spherical aberration. A parabolic mirror will focus a beam of parallel rays perfectly at one point. Because of the absence of aberration, parabolic mirrors are used extensively in optical telescopes and in radio telescopes.

Refraction. When light passes into a denser medium from a less dense medium, its path is altered. This change in the direction of a light ray is called refraction. The velocity of light varies in different media, being greater in a less dense medium than in a denser medium. For example, the velocity of light is greater in air than in glass.

Every material that transmits light is said to have an index of refraction, which is defined as the velocity of

light in a vacuum divided by the velocity of light at the same wavelength in the material. The index of refraction, n, may be stated in the form of an equation:

$$n = \frac{\text{velocity of light in vacuum}}{\text{velocity of light in material}}$$

when the two velocities are for the same wavelength of light. The index of refraction depends, therefore, on the material and on the wavelength.

The law of refraction is in two parts. When a ray of light passes from a less dense medium into a more dense medium, the ray is bent toward the normal, that is, to the surface of the medium. Conversely, when the ray passes from a more dense medium into a less dense medium, it is bent away from the normal. Also, the incident ray, the normal, and the refracted ray all lie in the same plane. For any given wavelength, the index of refraction of

the first medium multiplied by the sine of the angle of incidence is equal to the index of refraction of the second medium multiplied by the sine of the angle of refraction. This is known as Snell's law.

Dispersion. Since the index of refraction of a medium is different for different wavelengths of light, the component wavelengths of white light are bent by varying amounts when the light passes through a prism. The light is then said to be dispersed. That is, it is separated into its component colors: red, orange, yellow, green, blue, indigo, and violet. Note that red light, which has the longest wavelength, bends the least when it is passing through a prism. Violet light, which has the shortest wavelength, bends the most when it is passing through a prism.

REFLECTION AND REFRACTION

Reflection

Light falling on a plane mirror is reflected so that the angle of incidence equals the angle of reflection.

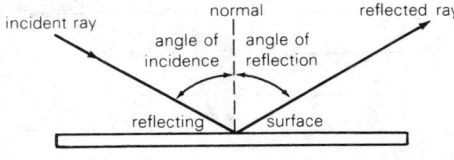

incident ray — normal — reflected ray
angle of incidence | angle of reflection
reflecting | surface

Refraction

The path of light rays passing from one medium, such as air, to another medium, such as water, changes direction.

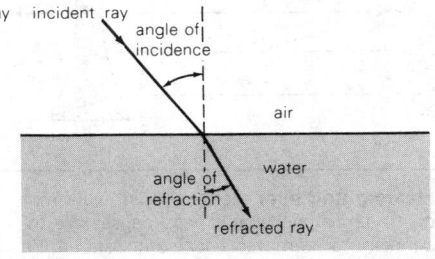

incident ray
angle of incidence
air
water
angle of refraction
refracted ray

MIRRORS   Plane

A beam of parallel rays remains parallel after reflection by a plane mirror.

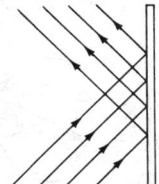

Concave

Parallel rays reflected by a concave mirror meet at a point called the focus.

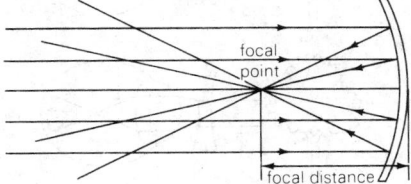

focal point

focal distance

Convex

In a convex mirror parallel rays diverge from a point behind the mirror.

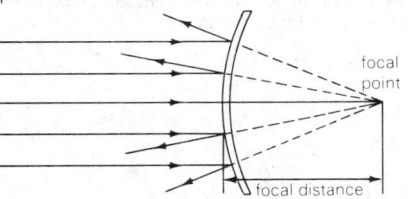

focal point

focal distance

Lenses. A lens is made of a material that transmits light. Its surfaces are shaped so that when light passes through the lens, the light will be refracted. Lenses, which are usually made to form images, are generally of two types: positive and negative. A positive lens is thicker in the middle than at the edges. A negative lens is thinner in the middle than at the edges.

Positive lenses and negative lenses are described by their optical axes, the positions of their focal points, and their lengths. This is true when a lens is considered to be thin, meaning that the thicknesses of the lens can be neglected in any computation involving the lens.

The optical axis is an imaginary line passing through the centers of the spherical lens surfaces. The focal point is the point through which will pass all incident rays parallel with the optical axis and entering the lens. The focal point for a positive lens is real: the rays actually pass through this point. For a negative lens, the focal point is imaginary. The light rays appear to be passing through this focal point but actually do not. The focal length is the distance of the focal point from a thin lens. The linear magnification of a lens is the image height divided by the object height.

It may be said that an image is real if it is on the side of the lens opposite to the object. That is, the image is real in the sense that if a screen is placed at the image distance, the image will be formed on the screen. In the case of a slide projector, for example, the slide is the object; the lens becomes the projection lens; and on the screen is produced a real image of whatever is on the slide. The real image produced by a single lens is inverted, that is, upside down and turned left for right, the right side of the object becoming, in effect, its left side in the image.

Virtual images only appear to be where they are seen. If a screen is placed at the point where the virtual image appears to be, no image is formed on the screen. However, to an eye looking through the lens, the image appears to be at that point.

With a positive lens, if the object is located between the first focus and the lens, the image is virtual, erect, and magnified. This is the principle of the simple magnifying glass. For an object located at a distance greater than twice the focal length of a positive lens, the image is real, inverted, and reduced. Magnified, inverted, real images will be produced by a positive lens when the object is at a distance from the lens greater than once, but less than twice, its focal length. At an object distance equal to twice the focal length of a positive lens, the image will be real, inverted, and the same size as the object.

Most lenses are made with spherical surfaces because such surfaces are the cheapest to produce. However, aspherical surfaces are available. Such surfaces are said to overcome certain image defects of spherical surfaces. These image defects include coma, spherical aberration, and distortion.

Coma and spherical aberration result from the fact that rays passing through the zones of the lens farther from the center are brought to a focus before the rays passing through the zones closer to the center are brought to a focus. In either case, no sharp image can be formed, and the image is always out of focus. Coma, a diffuse pear-shaped image, results when light rays originate from a point not on the axis of the lens. Spherical aberration occurs when the light rays originate from a point on the axis. In coma, light is spreading from a point source off the optical axis into a small, pear-shaped image because of the displaced, out-of-focus image rays from the outer zones of the lens.

Distortion, unlike coma and spherical aberration, does not refer to the inability of a lens to form a point image of a point source. Instead, distortion results from a variation of magnification with distance from the axis. In pincushion distortion, the magnification increases with increasing distance from the axis, and the outer parts of the object appear larger than they should. The result is, for example, that the sides of a square appear to be caving in toward the center. In barrel distortion, the magnification decreases with increasing distance from the axis, and the outer parts of the object appear smaller than they should. The result is, for example, that the sides of a square appear to bulge away from the center.

Aberrations generally are corrected in several ways: (a) careful selection of radii of curvature for lenses, (b) construction of lenses of parts that have different refractive indices, (c)

LENSES

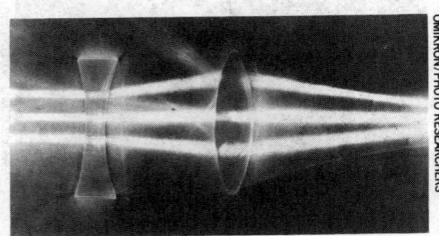

OMIKRON/PHOTO RESEARCHERS

Concave
NEGATIVE LENS

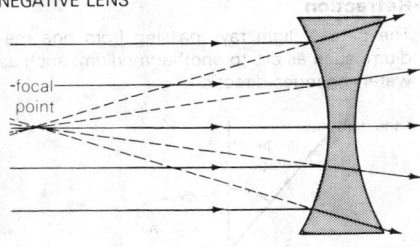

-focal point

Convex
POSITIVE LENS

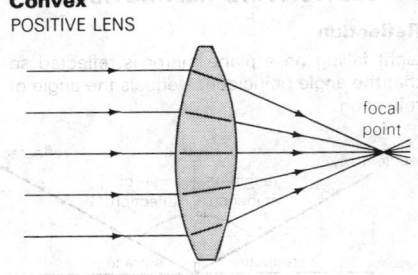

focal point

Normally the lens of the eye focuses an image on the retina. The lens adjusts itself to the distance of the object being viewed. When viewing a faraway object, the lens is nearly flat. To view a close object, the lens thickens. An eye that is nearsighted or farsighted is unable to focus an image properly on the retina. Corrective lenses, in the form of glasses or contact lenses, help focus the image.

Nearsighted eye: the focal point is in front of the retina. A negative lens causes the focal point to be moved back so it rests on the retina.

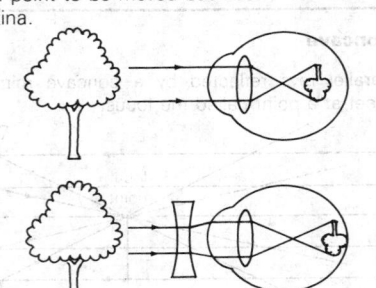

Farsighted eye: the focal point is behind the retina. A positive lens causes the focal point to be moved forward so it rests on the retina.

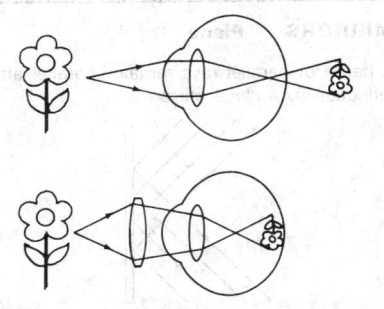

use of aspherical surfaces, and (d) control of the distances between lens elements. While it may be impossible to produce a perfect image, with careful lens design it is usually possible to obtain images within the limits desired.

While all the aberrations mentioned are monochromatic, occurring for any one wavelength or color, there is also a form of aberration that occurs only with light consisting of more than one wavelength. It is called chromatic aberration and is explained by the fact that the index of refraction of any substance varies with the wavelength of the light. When light of more than one wavelength passes through a lens, therefore, some wavelengths are bent more than others. The result is that each of the various colors, or wavelengths, has a different focal point. If a lens not corrected for chromatic aberration is used to form an image, the image will have a border of spectral colors. All single lenses, when used in light of more than one wavelength, exhibit chromatic aberration.

An achromatic lens is designed to correct chromatic aberration. Such a lens actually consists of two lenses, a convex lens of one type of glass and a concave lens of another type of glass. The chromatic aberration of one lens is neutralized by the other.

Prisms. Reflecting prisms find use in optical instruments for a number of reasons: (a) to displace a beam of light through a certain distance, (b) to deflect a beam of light through a known angle, (c) to rotate an image, or (d) to invert an image formed by a lens before the image enters another lens.

Prisms are often combined to make up a prism system. For example, two prisms may be combined so that the rays entering and exiting the system are parallel, although laterally displaced. The image formed by this system is inverted, so this system is commonly used in binoculars to reinvert the inverted image formed by the objective lens and eyepiece. This system also permits higher magnification without lengthening the binocular housing.

Physical Optics

Interference. When two or more light waves cross, they interact. This interaction is called interference. Consider two light waves of the same frequency (see diagram). If both waves are in phase, that is, if the troughs and crests occur at the same time, the amplitudes of the waves will add, the phenomenon being called constructive interference. If two waves of equal frequency and equal amplitude are out of phase, that is, if the trough of one wave matches the crest of the other

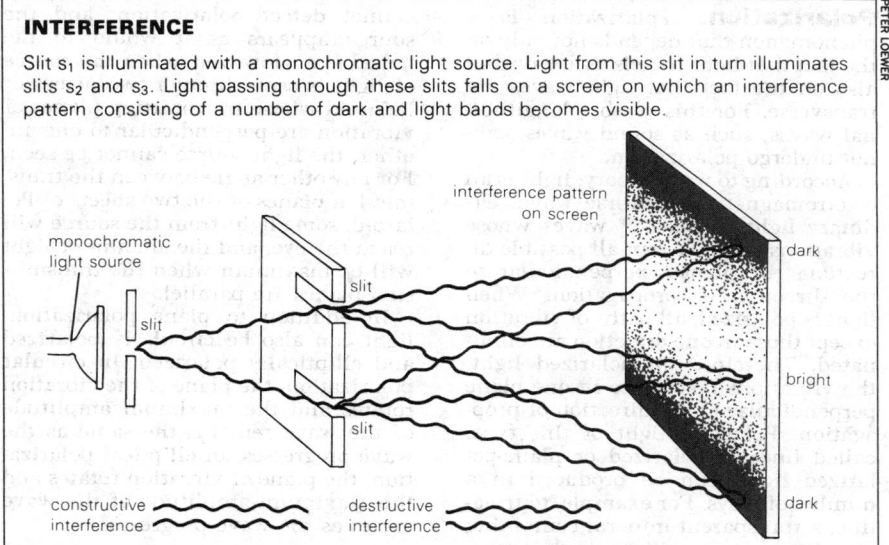

PETER LOWER

INTERFERENCE

Slit s_1 is illuminated with a monochromatic light source. Light from this slit in turn illuminates slits s_2 and s_3. Light passing through these slits falls on a screen on which an interference pattern consisting of a number of dark and light bands becomes visible.

monochromatic light source — slit — slit — slit — interference pattern on screen — dark — bright — dark

constructive interference — destructive interference

wave, the amplitudes will also add. However, the amplitude of a crest is considered positive, and the amplitude of a trough negative, so the amplitudes will cancel each other, and the resultant amplitude will be zero. This phenomenon is called destructive interference.

The colors observed when looking at a thin film of oil or a soap bubble are caused by interference effects at the surface of the medium. Since the light is reflected from the top and bottom surfaces of a film, interference takes place at the top surface and depends upon the wavelengths of the light, the index of refraction of the material, and the film thickness.

Diffraction. Consider light traveling in straight lines in a homogeneous material, one whose composition is identical throughout. One would expect that a beam of this light passing through a slit to a screen would form an illuminated image of the slit. If, however, the slit width is comparable to the wavelength of the light passing through the slit, a number of alternate light and dark areas will appear on the screen, similar to the light and dark areas produced by interference. What has happened is that the light has bent around the corners of the slit. This same diffraction effect takes place with sound waves. Sound will travel around obstacles, but since sound waves are longer than light waves, the effect is greater.

The diffraction pattern caused by a single slit can be explained. Light rays coming from the slit can be divided in two parts, rays coming from the upper part of the slit, and those coming from the lower part. Depending on the angle, the upper and lower parts of the rays interfere constructively or destructively, thus forming the light and dark bands.

To increase the number of slits through which the beam of light must pass, a diffraction grating may be produced by using a diamond point to cut very narrow parallel slits on a piece of glass. When a beam of parallel rays of white light strikes such a grating, the various wavelengths are spread out by the diffraction, and a spectrum is produced. This is similar to the color spectrum produced by a prism, except that in the case of diffraction the longest wavelength is bent most. In the case of prism refraction, red light is bent least.

Gratings can be produced with many thousands of lines per inch, and the surface that is cut does not have to be a transmitting surface. Lines can also be ruled on reflecting surfaces, which become known as reflection gratings, and the ruled surfaces can be either plane or concave. Many gratings of the latter type are used in spectrographic systems. A grating system has less light loss and greater dispersion than a prism, since the colors are spread out more.

INTERFERENCE FRINGES *are obtained by projecting the shadow of an object on a screen, using monochromatic light.*

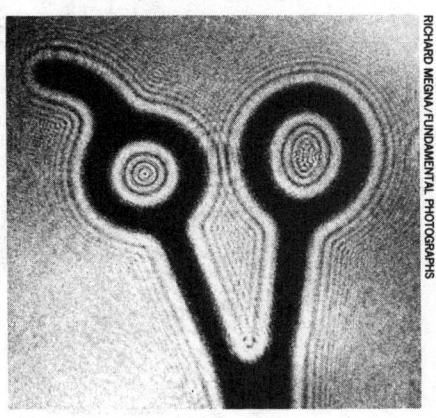

RICHARD MEGNA/FUNDAMENTAL PHOTOGRAPHS

Polarization.

Polarization is a phenomenon that depends not only on the fact that light travels as a wave but also on the fact that light waves are transverse. For this reason, longitudinal waves, such as sound waves, cannot undergo polarization.

According to wave theory, light is an electromagnetic transverse wave. Ordinary light consists of waves whose vibrations take place in all possible directions, or planes, perpendicular to the direction of propagation. When light is polarized, all paths of vibration except those in one direction are eliminated. Therefore, in polarized light, the vibrations take place in one plane perpendicular to the direction of propagation. Polarized light of this type, called linearly polarized or plane-polarized light, can be produced in a number of ways. For example, tourmaline, a transparent mineral containing aluminum, boron, silicon, and oxygen, transmits vibrations in only one plane. Polaroid, a manmade material developed in 1934 and consisting of transparent sheets resembling cellophane, possesses the same property. Materials such as these are called dichroic.

Other crystalline materials, such as calcite and quartz, split an ordinary light beam into two beams. These two beams are plane-polarized light beams, and the planes of polarization in the two beams are at right angles to one another. Such crystalline materials are called birefringent or, with the same meaning, double refracting.

Ordinary light can also be plane polarized by reflection. At a certain angle of incidence, vibrations in one plane predominate in the reflected beam. The angle of incidence at which this occurs depends on the index of refraction of the reflecting glass; the angle is called Brewster's angle. For ordinary glass, this angle is approximately 57 degrees. Since light reflected from a road surface on a sunny day is partly polarized, Polaroid eyeglasses will decrease the glare.

When a source of light is observed through a sheet of Polaroid, the eye cannot detect polarization, and the source appears as it would to the naked eye. However, when the source of light is seen through two pieces of Polaroid whose transmitting planes of vibration are perpendicular to one another, the light source cannot be seen. For any other angle between the transmission planes of the two sheets of Polaroid, some light from the source will reach the eye, and the amount of light will be maximum when the transmission planes are parallel.

In addition to plane polarization, light can also be circularly polarized and elliptically polarized. In circular polarization, the plane of the vibration rotates and the maximum amplitude of the wave remains the same as the wave progresses. In elliptical polarization, the plane of vibration rotates and the maximum amplitude of the wave varies as the wave progresses.

Units.

The definition of light is based on our visual awareness of radiation in a very narrow band of the electromagnetic spectrum, the visible region. The eye is not equally sensitive to all visual light waves, and variation in sensitivity to wavelengths may be graphed as a luminosity curve. The luminosity curve for the average eye shows how the eye responds to equal amounts of energy at the various wavelengths within the visible region. Since the eye is more sensitive to wavelengths in the yellow region, yellows appear brighter than reds and blues. The most sensitive wavelength is at 555 nanometers, and the curve is normalized by making the maximum ordinate at this point equal to one. Above and below, the maximum curve falls off sharply. It drops to practically zero at 400 and 700 nm, the limits of the visible region.

Units based on the visual interpretation of radiant energy are called photometric units or luminous units. Those based on the physical interpretation of radiation are called radiometric units. There would be no need for two sets of units if the eye responded equally to all the visible wavelengths. If this were the case, only the purely physical radiometric units would be needed.

The lumen is the unit of luminous flux or power. The watt is the unit of radiant flux. The two units are related by means of the luminosity curve. At 555 nm, 1 watt equals 685 lumens. At any other visible wavelength, 1 watt expressed in lumens will be less than 685 and will equal 685 times the luminosity curve ordinate at the particular wavelength.

The candle is the unit of luminous intensity. One candle equals 1 lumen per steradian. The steradian is the unit of solid angle, and the total number of steradians subtended at the center of a sphere is 4π. A point source of light having a uniform intensity of 1 candle in all directions, therefore, emits 4π lumens of luminous flux. This can be understood by thinking of the point source as being at the center of an imaginary sphere, and there are 4π steradians in the sphere. The analogous unit of radiant intensity is watt per steradian.

When light falls on a surface, the surface is illuminated. Illuminance, or illumination, is the unit of luminous flux per unit area. If the area is 1 square foot and the flux is 1 lumen, then there is 1 lumen per square foot, or one foot-candle. The analogous radiant term is irradiance, expressed in watts per square foot.

A source of light can be an extended source as well as a point source. For extended sources, the larger area of the source is thought of as being divided into smaller unit areas, each of them emitting light. The total luminous flux emitted per unit area is called the luminous emittance of the extended source, expressed as lumens per square foot, lumens per square meter, lumens per square centimeter, lumens per square inch, and so on. The corresponding radiant quantity is called radiant emittance, expressed as watts per square foot, watts per square meter, and so on.

POLARIZATION

A Polaroid sheet converts unpolarized light into polarized light. If a second Polaroid sheet is placed in the beam of polarized light and rotated so that its polarization plane becomes perpendicular to the polarization plane of the beam, no light will pass.

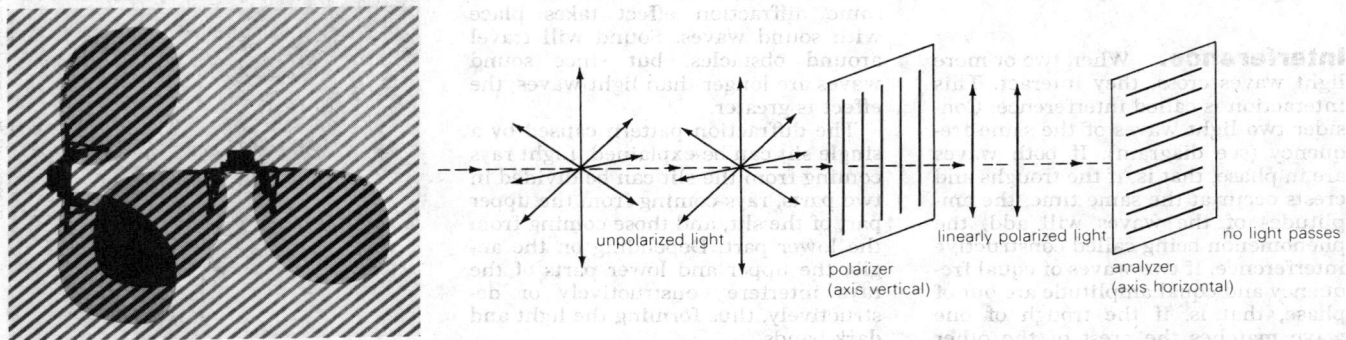

unpolarized light

polarizer
(axis vertical)

linearly polarized light

analyzer
(axis horizontal)

no light passes

PETER LOEWER

The last unit of significance correspondingly associated with an extended light source is brightness, or luminance. This is the luminous intensity per unit area of the source, expressed as candles per square foot, candles per square meter, and so on. Many surfaces appear equally bright no matter the direction from which they are viewed. Such surfaces obey Lambert's law and are called perfectly diffuse emitters. The sun is a good example, since the edge appears exactly as bright as the center. The analogous radiant quantity is radiance, or radiant intensity per unit area of an extended surface.

The inverse square law states that the illuminance on a surface varies inversely as the square of the distance from a point source. For example, if the illuminance on a surface is 1 lumen per square meter, when this surface is at a distance of 1 meter from a point source, the illuminance on the surface will be $\frac{1}{4}$ lumen per square meter when the object is placed at a distance of 2 meters from the same source. The inverse square law makes it possible to compare the intensities of two point sources of light, or if one intensity is known the other can be determined. In essence, the sources are so placed that the illuminance on the screen is the same from either source. By measuring the distance of the screen from the sources, the relative intensities, or the unknown intensity, can be calculated by employing instruments known as photometers.

Color.

The word *color* is commonly used in various ways. It may refer to the sensation received in the brain when the retina of the eye is stimulated by light of a particular wavelength. It may be used to describe a property of an object, for example, a red barn. Indeed, by definition, everything that is seen has a sensation of color associated with it. The only truly colorless things are those that are invisible, such as air.

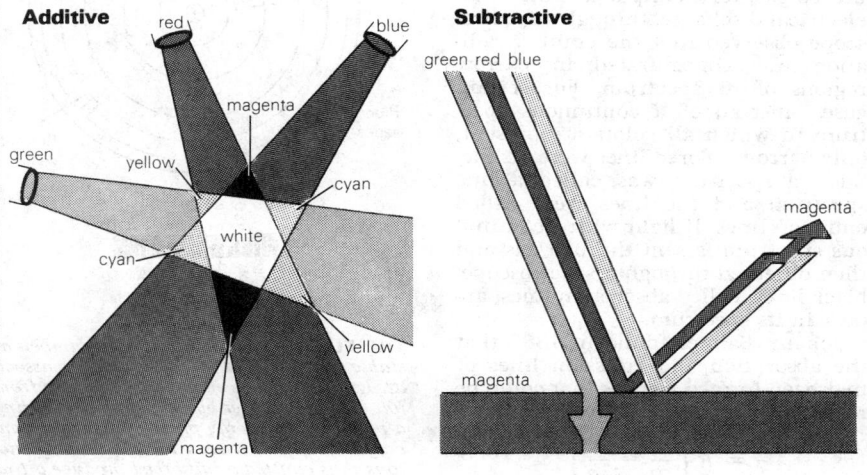

COLOR

Additive mixing can be demonstrated by mixing colored lights. The basic colors—red, green, and blue—combine to form white. Magenta, for example, is the result of mixing red and blue. Subtractive mixing occurs in pigment colors; for example, magenta is obtained by absorption of green.

Additive

Subtractive

PETER LOEWER

Additive process. In passing through a prism, sunlight is dispersed and broken down into its constituent colors: red, orange, yellow, green, blue, indigo, and violet. Sunlight, which is essentially white light, is therefore an additive color mixture of all the spectral colors. If all these spectral colors are added in the same amounts in which they are known to appear in the sunlight spectrum, white light will be produced.

When colors are projected on a screen simultaneously by two or more projectors, different colors are obtained in regions where the colored images overlap. Similarly, when a disk made up of different colored sectors is rotated rapidly in front of the eye, the eye sees a color different from that of any of the colored sectors. When half the disk is red and the other green, the disk appears yellow. If a third of the

disk is red, a third blue, and a third green, the disk appears to be grayish white.

A color other than a pure spectral color can be reproduced by adding three spectral colors together in the correct luminous amounts. All colors cannot be produced by an additive mixture of the same three spectral colors, but it is always possible to find three spectral colors that, when added together in the right amounts, will produce the color desired. Since the greatest number of color variations can be produced by additively mixing red, yellow, and blue, they are called the primary colors. In some cases, it is possible to produce white light by adding two colored lights instead of three. Such colors are called complementary colors. Purple and green, for example, are complementary.

Subtractive process. When white light is passed through an optical filter, the filter transmits a percentage of the incident light at each particular wavelength in the visible region. If the filter is yellow, it transmits a greater percentage of yellow light than light of other wavelengths. A blue filter transmits a larger percentage of light in the blue region, and so on. If the incident light is passed through a blue filter and yellow filter in combination, the light transmitted is of the wavelengths where the transmission curves of the two filters overlap. In the case of the blue and yellow filters, the greatest percentage of light transmitted is in the green region; thus, green light is observed through the two filters. Since each filter subtracts a certain amount of energy from the incident light, this method is called the subtractive method of color mixing.

LAW OF INVERSE SQUARES

The intensity of the illumination of a surface is inversely proportional to the square of the distance of the light source. In astronomy, this property is used to measure the distance of stars whose intrinsic luminosity is precisely known.

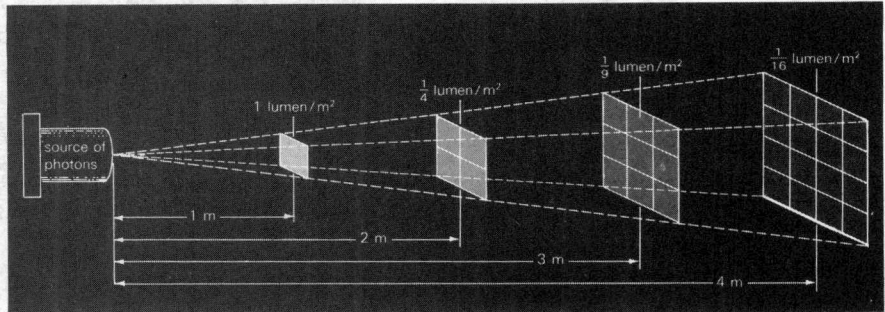

PETER LOEWER

Atomic Structure and Spectra

Spectra. During the 19th century, scientists observing the light of a heated gas, for example, a flame or an electrical discharge, through a spectroscope observed that the emitted radiation was concentrated in narrow regions of its spectrum. For certain gases, instead of a continuous spectrum in which all colors are present, only narrow colored lines were visible. Such a spectrum was called a line spectrum and the lines were called emission lines. If light with a continuous spectrum is sent through gas and then observed through a spectroscope, black lines, called absorption lines, appear in its spectrum.

Johann Balmer found in 1885 that the absorption and emission lines of hydrogen formed a series that could be represented by a simple formula:

$$\frac{1}{\lambda} = R\left(\frac{1}{2^2} - \frac{1}{n^2}\right),$$

in which λ is the wavelength, R the Rydberg constant, and n an integral number with value 3, 5, 7, etc.

In 1906 Ernest Rutherford postulated that the atom consists of a dense, positively charged nucleus surrounded by electrons moving in circular orbits, accelerated toward the nucleus by the coulomb force. According to classical electromagnetic theory, an accelerated charge emits radiation while losing energy. A consequence of Rutherford's model would be that the orbiting electrons would continuously radiate energy while slowing down to eventually fall into the nucleus. In 1915, Bohr proposed a model for the atom that circumvented this difficulty and also explained the occurrence of emission and absorption lines.

Atomic structure.
Bohr postulated that in an atom, the electrons can only occupy certain stable orbits. Each orbit corresponds to an energy

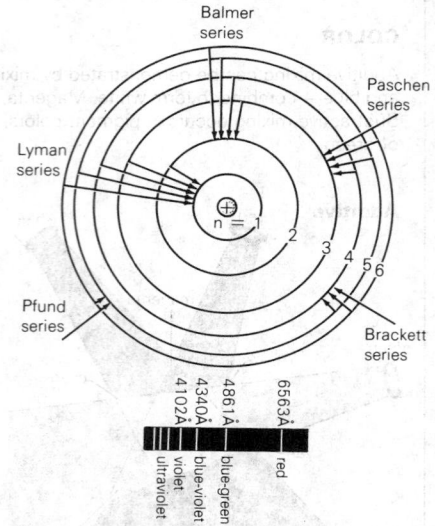

THE ELECTRON *can occupy a number of stable orbits around the nucleus, each associated with a certain energy. It can jump from one orbit to another by absorbing or emitting a photon with energy proportional to the energy difference between the two orbits. Photons thus emitted or absorbed produce a line spectrum.*

level of the atom. Electrons can jump from one orbit to another orbit either by absorbing or emitting energy in the form of a photon. The lowest energy level an electron can occupy is called the ground state. By absorbing photons the electron can jump to orbits with higher energy levels. These levels are called excited states of the atom. Above a certain level, the electron becomes separated from the atom, leaving the atom with a positive charge. Such an atom is called an ion. The energy of the emitted or absorbed photon, or the frequency of the associated wave, is proportional to the energy levels. If E_0 and E_1 are the lower and upper energy levels of the atom, the frequency of the emitted photon will be given by $(E_0 - E_1)/h$, where h is Planck's constant.

Each element has a characteristic line spectrum, so spectra are used to detect and identify chemical elements. For example, by studying the absorp-

tion lines present in sunlight, astronomers were able to determine the composition of the solar atmosphere.

Lasers and Masers

Lasers. A laser, *Light Amplification by Stimulated Emission of Radiation*, is an amplifier or generator of light. Light emitted by a laser is said to be coherent and monochromatic.

As has been said, a typical light source, for example, the glowing filament of a lamp, emits light in small wave packets in random directions and with no special phase relationships. That is, the light is not coherent. A consequence of this, for example, is that it is difficult to create interference phenomena, since light wave packets with random phase differences interfere with one another so that no clear-cut constructive or destructive interference is possible.

In coherent light, by contrast, all the wave packets are in phase. The amplitude of each wave packet goes through a crest and a trough at the same time. Laser light also has a high degree of monochromaticity. The wavelength of the radiated light lies in a very narrow frequency range. Because lasers produce coherent and monochromatic light, they are used in a large number of optical experiments and instruments, and in optical communication.

Stimulated emission. Atoms or molecules raised to a higher energy level, for example, by the absorption of a photon, usually fall down to a lower energy level spontaneously after a short time by emitting a photon. This process is called spontaneous emission. However, an atom or molecule raised to a higher energy level can also be induced to emit a photon when another photon with the same frequency interacts with the atom or molecule. This process is called stimu-

LASER TECHNOLOGY *is becoming increasingly important. It is being used in medicine for both surgical and diagnostic procedures (left). Lasers, like Nova (right) at the Lawrence Livermore National Laboratory, are also used in research. Nova, at more than 600 feet long, is the largest laser in the world.*

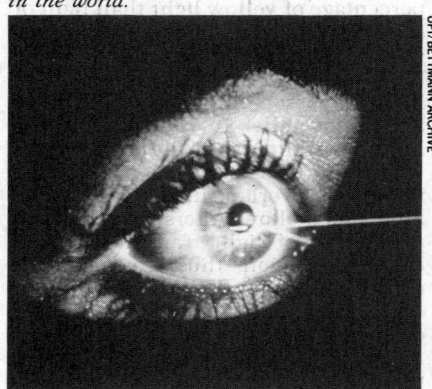

UPI/BETTMANN ARCHIVE

LAWRENCE LIVERMORE NATIONAL LABORATORY

lated emission. The emitted photon has exactly the same frequency, the same direction, and the same phase as the interacting photon. The creation of this extra photon underlies the amplifying principle of the laser.

Optical pumping. In a laser, a certain amount of matter, called lasing material, is used for light amplification. If the atoms are left undisturbed, most of them will be in the ground state. This means that the population of atoms in the ground state will be much larger than the population of atoms in an excited state. In order to obtain light amplification by stimulated emission, the population of excited atoms must be made larger than the population of atoms in the ground state. This condition is termed population inversion.

Several processes can create a population inversion. A common one is that of irradiating the lasing material (the gas, liquid, or solid) with a powerful light source at a frequency corresponding to the energy difference between the ground level and the excited level, also called laser level. In this process, called optical pumping, atoms are said to be pumped to a higher energy level by light. When a beam of light enters a chamber containing atoms in which population inversion is achieved, the photons interact with the excited atoms. These atoms, in turn, transmit photons of the same frequency and in the same direction as the incoming photons. Many of the newly created photons interact with other excited atoms, producing new photons in a manner resembling a chain reaction.

In most lasers, the chamber containing the lasing material is placed between two parallel mirrors, one of them semitransparent. The light beam bounces between the two mirrors several times and becomes amplified each time it travels through the lasing medium. The beam finally emerges from the laser through the semitransparent mirror.

A device that amplifies microwave radiation by stimulated emission is called maser, for *M*icrowave *A*mplification by *S*timulated *E*mission of *R*adiation. Masers are used as low-noise amplifiers for radio astronomy and in satellite communication.

Holography. An important application of lasers is in the creation of holograms. Holography is a special photographic recording technique for creation of three-dimensional pictures. In ordinary photography, light intensities are recorded on photographic film to reconstitute the original picture. Holograms, by contrast, are the result of recording the fringe patterns that are obtained by the interference of light produced by reflection of coherent light on an object with another beam of coherent light, which is called a reference beam.

In the most common holographic procedure, a laser beam is split into two beams by a half-silvered mirror (see figure). One beam illuminates the object, and the other beam is directed to the photographic plate. The photographic plate receives wave fronts from the reference beam and wave fronts reflected by the object. Both light waves produce an interference pattern on the photographic plate. That is, they produce dark and light fringes as a result of constructive and destructive interference.

When coherent light is shined through the photographic plate, a three-dimensional image, a hologram, of the photographed object becomes visible. The light and dark fringes on the photographic plate act as a diffraction grid and reconstitute the original wave fronts that reached the photographic plate. Viewing of the hologram in a beam of coherent light reveals that the same wave fronts are present as are present when the object itself is viewed.

Nuclear Physics

Characteristics of the Nucleus

An atom is about 10^{-8}, or .00000001 centimeter (cm) in diameter. You can understand how small an atom is when you realize that a drop of water contains 6 sextillion (6 followed by 21 zeros) atoms. The nucleus of the atom, which is composed of neutrons and protons—the nucleus of the commonest form of hydrogen consists only of a single proton—is much smaller. It is about 10^{-12} cm in diameter. Outside the nucleus, there are only electrons. The neutron and the proton have almost identical masses, 1.67×10^{-24} gram. This is approximately 1837 times the mass of an electron.

In the atom of the commonest form of hydrogen, therefore, which is composed of one electron and one proton, the mass of the nucleus is 1837 times greater than the mass of the region outside the nucleus. Since the region outside the nucleus is 100,000 times as large as the nucleus, it can be said that an atom typically is composed mostly of empty space, with only a very small region where all the mass is found. Although the neutron and proton have virtually the same mass, they differ in one important respect: the proton carries an electrical charge, and the neutron does not. The electron has an electrical charge of the same magnitude as that of the proton, but its charge is negative.

Nuclear structure. The nucleus of a hydrogen atom consists of one proton and therefore has a positive charge. The electron has a negative charge, so the net charge on the hydrogen atom is zero, because the positive charge is equal to but opposite the negative charge. The force holding the atom together, which binds the electron to the proton in some way, is the coulomb force, the attraction between positive and negative charges. The next smallest atom after hydrogen is that of helium, which has two protons and two neutrons in the nucleus. This results in a net positive charge of two units. In order for helium to be electrically neutral, therefore, two electrons must orbit the nucleus. Once again, the forces holding the electrons in the atom are the coulomb forces.

At this point, however, a question arises. Since there are two protons in the helium nucleus, with identical positive charges, why do they not repel one another and cause the nucleus to fly apart? What prevents this from occurring is the strong force, one of the fundamental forces in nature. (See page 472.)

Building elements. The building of the atoms of elements by adding protons and neutrons in the nucleus, and adding electrons outside the nucleus, continues in orderly fashion until uranium, the heaviest naturally occurring element, is reached. The uranium nucleus contains 92 protons and 146 neutrons. There actually are several different forms of uranium, called isotopes, which differ in the number of neutrons in the nucleus. It should be noted that isotopes are known for every element, even though some do not occur in nature but are created by man. Uranium electrons number 92, again preserving the zero net charge of the atom. Over a dozen elements have been created, with more than 92 protons in the nucleus, but they are relatively unstable and do not exist in nature. These elements are called transuranic elements, and two of the most familiar are plutonium and neptunium.

Scattering Experiments

Until this point, nothing has been said about how knowledge of the structure of the nucleus and the nucleons, the neutrons and protons, is obtained. The basic experiment of nuclear physics is the scattering experiment, pioneered by Rutherford. In scattering, neutrons, protons, electrons, gamma rays, and various other nuclear particles are accelerated to high energies and directed at a target consisting of atoms of a material to be studied. Scattering experiments offer the principal means by which physicists can comprehend the structure and interactions of matter on a subatomic scale. Detectors, or collectors, of various types are set up at positions around the target. This setup may be compared, in a simple way, to the game of pocket billiards. The cue ball serves as the projectile, one or more other balls as the target. The pockets are the collectors, and the pool cue is the accelerator.

Some features of scattering immediately emerge. As anyone familiar with pocket billiards knows, the effect of scattering several balls is different from that of scattering a single ball. It is also clear that scattering cubes instead of billiard balls would lead to a markedly different scattering pattern.

The scattering experiment in nuclear physics differs from billiards in that scientists do not know what the targets look like. They know what kind of accelerator they have. They know what the projectiles look like—the protons, neutrons, or other particles—since they come out at the end of the nuclear accelerator. They know what the collectors do because they are built for a specific performance. But, as has been said, they do not know what the target looks like. To see how they might deduce the appearance of the target, a simple case is shown in the accompanying illustration.

Thinking about a possible shape of the target leads to the following logical inferences. The dimensions of the target have to be about the distance from point A to E, because balls (1) and (4) passed straight through the target area without deflection. (This is an important concept in physics. The dimension d obtained is called the cross section of the target. Obviously, nuclear physics deals with three dimensions, so d, instead of being a length, is an area.) Ball (2) was deflected to the left, and ball (3) to the right. A possible way of accounting for the scattering of these balls might be a target shaped like the one shown. The scattered paths are indicated. Thus, by observing the scattered particles, the shape and dimensions of targets can be deduced, at least in principle.

Accelerators

One of the first accelerators used in a nuclear physics experiment was a naturally radioactive element that emitted alpha particles. An alpha particle consists of two protons and two neutrons bound together, and thus is a helium atom stripped of electrons. Rutherford used radium as his accelerator to bombard thin foils of materials. The results indicated that some of the alpha particles were scattered backward, although most went through relatively untouched. Backscattering could be explained only if the alpha particles were striking something with more mass than the alpha particles. It was in these experiments that the depiction of an atom as being composed of a small but massive nucleus surrounded by a relatively vacant space was first deduced and then confirmed by Rutherford.

Other types of accelerators include the Cockroft-Walton accelerator, invented by J. Douglas Cockroft and Ernest Walton in 1932; the Van de Graaff accelerator, proposed by Robert Jeminson Van de Graaff in 1931; the cyclotron, built by Ernest O. Lawrence in 1930; the synchrocyclotron; the synchrotron; the bevatron; the betatron; and the linear accelerator. In all these accelerators, the effect of electric and magnetic fields on charged particles is used to give the particles high velocities.

Cyclotrons. The effects of electric and magnetic fields can best be explained by considering the cyclotron, in which the effects of both types of fields are used to produce an energetic beam of particles. As shown in the accompanying diagram, charged particles (protons) are introduced at point A. B and C are magnets, called dees because they resemble the letter "d" in shape. An electrically charged particle is pushed on by the electric field, say, in the direction shown by the arrow. The particle then enters the magnetic field of C. While in the magnet, it is turned in a circular path, as shown, and finally is ready to emerge from the magnet. While the particle is completing the half circle, the voltage on the magnets is reversed. Once again the particle is accelerated, but now toward magnet B. Once the particle enters B, it again is turned in a circular path. Upon emerging from B, the particle finds that the direction of the electric field has again been reversed to cause acceleration toward C. This process continues until the particle emerges from the cyclotron.

One characteristic of the cyclotron is that the rate at which the voltage on the magnets has to be reversed is independent of the radius of the path of the accelerated particle or particles and of their velocity, provided that the mass of the accelerated particle remains the same. Relativity predicts that the mass of a particle will increase with its velocity, however, and this effect has been noted in the cyclotron. Such a change in mass means that the rate at which the electric accelerating potential is changed must change as the accelerated particle increases in velocity. An accelerator that does this is the synchrocyclotron, a device put into operation after World War II. Its operating principle and that of the cyclotron are basically the same. The electric field accelerates the particles, and the magnetic field steers them.

The basic operation of the synchrotron is also similar to the cyclotron and the synchrocyclotron. In the synchrotron, the particles travel in nearly circular orbits whose radii are kept constant by a changing magnetic field.

Other accelerators. A different type of accelerator is represented by the Van de Graaff, Cockroft-Walton, and linear accelerators. They do not

SCATTERING EXPERIMENTS *can help determine the size and shape of an unknown* (right). *Rutherford used the apparatus shown* (below left) *to determine the size of the nucleus of an atom. Rays of alpha particles were directed on a thin gold foil. The size of the nucleus could be found from the way the alpha particles were scattered.*

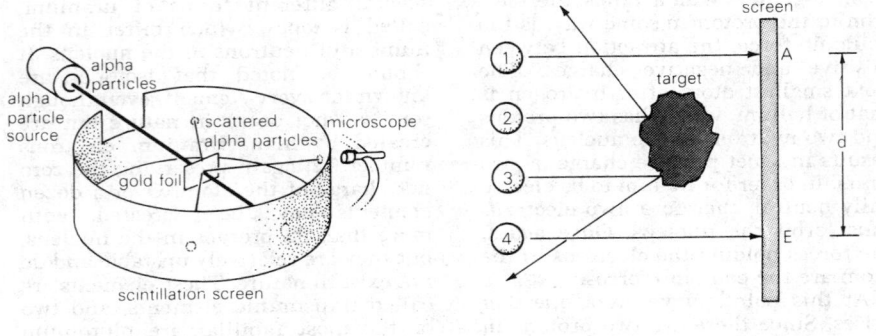

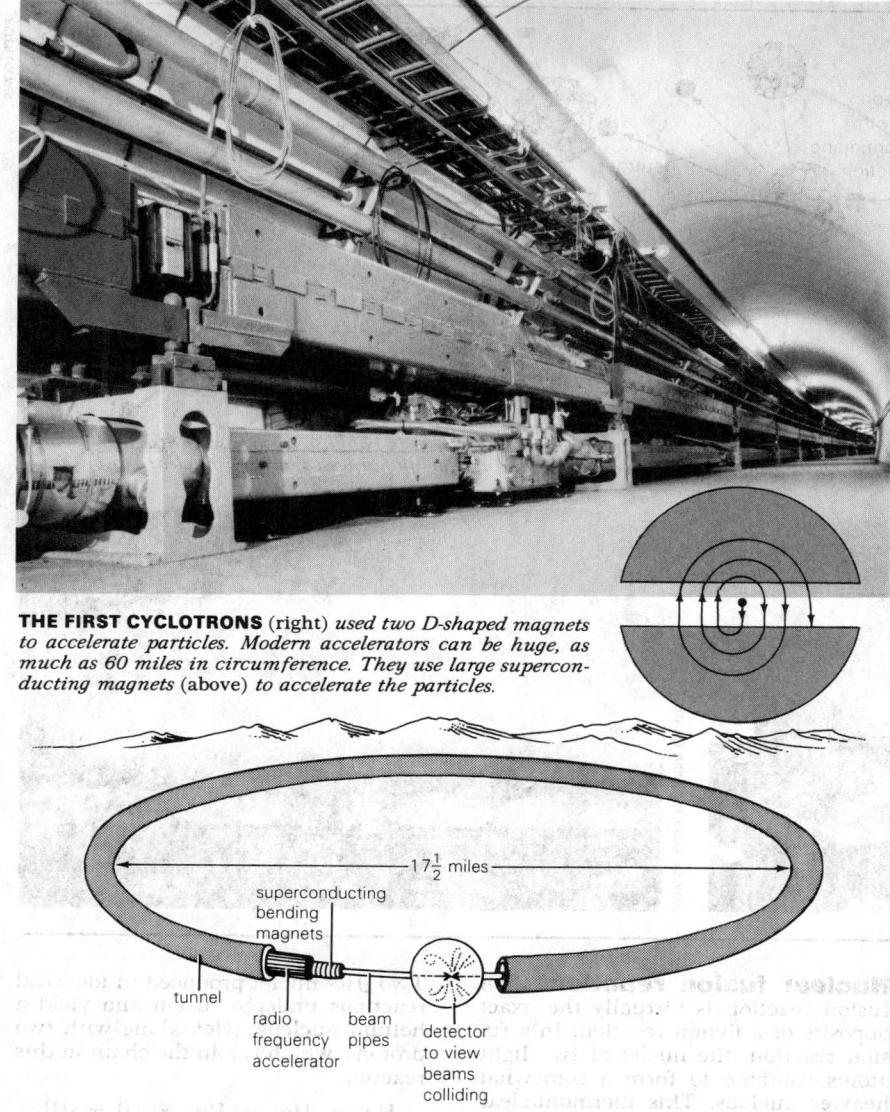

THE FIRST CYCLOTRONS (right) *used two D-shaped magnets to accelerate particles. Modern accelerators can be huge, as much as 60 miles in circumference. They use large superconducting magnets* (above) *to accelerate the particles.*

$17\frac{1}{2}$ miles

superconducting bending magnets

tunnel

radio frequency accelerator

beam pipes

detector to view beams colliding

PETER LOEWER

Scintillation counters make use of the fact that radiation produces flashes of light when it strikes certain crystals, such as those of sodium iodide. Electronic circuitry, in conjunction with photomultiplier tubes, is used to detect and count the flashes. These devices measure only the quantity of a certain type of event but do not give detailed information about the event. In some experiments in nuclear physics, this type of information proves extremely important, particularly where accurate measurement of large numbers of events is desired. This is true, for example, in observations made of the behavior and structure of the nucleus.

Cloud chamber. In research into the structure of the nucleus and the forces that hold it together, it is important to observe individual nuclear events. Detectors have been developed to do this. The first was the Wilson cloud chamber, designed by Charles Wilson in 1911. A gas-filled chamber containing supersaturated vapor is exposed to radiation. The incoming particles cause the excess moisture to precipitate along the trail of the particle, creating a visible trace. When the cloud chamber is used in conjunction with electric and magnetic fields and photographic films, the charge and momentum of the incident particles can be deduced. A difficulty with the cloud chamber is that relatively few events can be observed in a given time, since the chamber is sensitive only when the vapor is supersaturated. The process of supersaturation is a relatively long one, so the cloud chamber is unproductive during a good part of the time.

Bubble chamber. A device whose action is similar to that of the cloud chamber is the bubble chamber, designed in the 1950's. This chamber usually contains supersaturated liquid hydrogen, but other possibilities are liquid xenon and helium. The action of the incoming radiation causes a row of bubbles along the trail of the incoming particle, provided that the particle has an electrical charge. After supersaturation of the liquid is achieved, a light is flashed so that events of interest can be recorded on photographic film. The bubble chamber suffers from relative slowness and, since the picture does not necessarily coincide with a particular type of event, it is not very selective. Because the liquid hydrogen is dense compared with the gases used in the cloud chamber, many more events can be photographed in a given volume of liquid than can be observed in an equal volume of gas in the cloud chamber.

Furthermore, since the nucleus of hydrogen is a proton, scattering experiments are performed with the detector simultaneously. Much information concerning scattering of various primary beams off protons has been obtained in this way in recent years.

use magnetic fields to bend particles in a circular or almost circular path. Instead, the charged particles are accelerated in a straight line by the action of an electric field. In the case of the Van de Graaff and Crockroft-Walton accelerators, the electric field is static. In the linear accelerator, it travels. The 2-mile linear accelerator at Stanford University has produced energies of 20 billion electron volts.

Neutron production. After accelerated particles emerge from the accelerators, they are allowed to hit targets directly in order to study the targets themselves, or they are allowed to hit targets in order to produce beams of particles of other than the original type. For example, since neutrons have no charge, they cannot be accelerated or steered by electric and magnetic fields. Beams of neutrons must be produced by collisions of the primary beam with other targets.

Detectors. In the early days of nuclear physics, nuclear events were observed on photographic plates, just as radioactivity was discovered by Antoine Becquerel in 1895 through the darkening of photographic film—charged particles expose film in passing through it. The use of photographic plates and their descendants, nuclear track plates, continues to this day, yielding accurate and useful data. The methods are slow, however, and the plates require developing and processing, thus making data collection and processing more complex and more difficult.

Electronic techniques have also been used. The Geiger counter, invented by Hans Geiger, uses the effect of energetic radiation in making an enclosed gas electrically conductive in order to measure the nuclear processes. Details of the events are not visible in the Geiger and similar counters. Only the number of events taking place is known by the user.

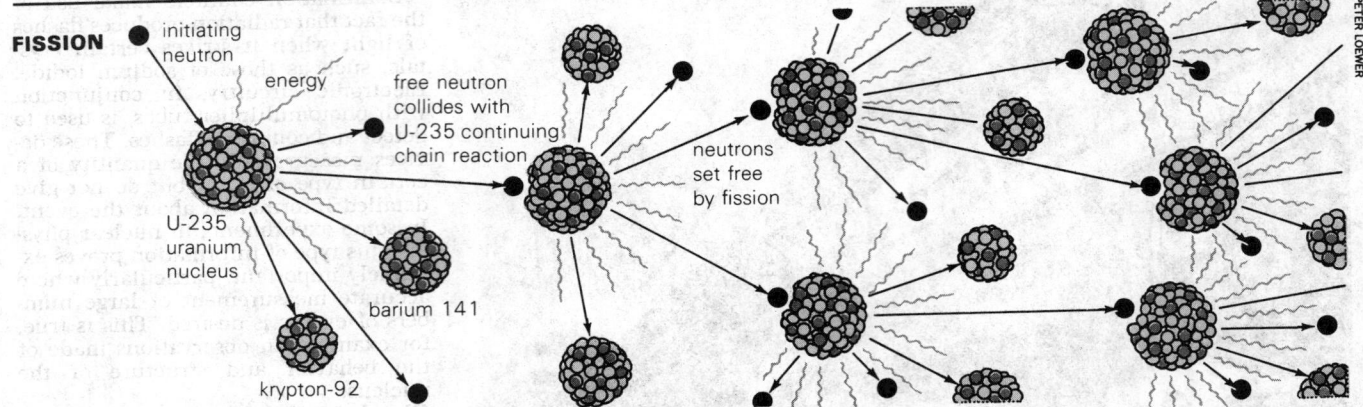

FISSION

initiating neutron

energy

free neutron collides with U-235 continuing chain reaction

neutrons set free by fission

U-235 uranium nucleus

barium 141

krypton-92

PETER LOEWER

A FISSION REACTION, *which requires splitting of a heavy atomic nucleus, can be made, under certain conditions, to sustain itself in a chain reaction involving a very large number of nuclei. The chain reaction can be controlled and its energy harnessed, as in a nuclear power plant, or it can be uncontrolled, as in an atomic bomb.*

TANNENBAUM/SYGMA

NATIONAL ARCHIVES/TAURUS PHOTOS

Nuclear fission reactions.

In nuclear fission reactions, the nucleus of a heavy isotope of an element ruptures into two segments of almost equal mass and releases large quantities of energy and of neutrons. The two segments into which the nucleus splits are the nuclei of other, lighter atoms. The rupture occurs when the nucleus absorbs a free neutron. The neutrons released during the fission process may, in turn, cause other atoms of the heavy isotopes to undergo fission in a chain reaction. When the chain reaction is not inhibited, an uncontrolled fission reaction takes place, releasing vast amounts of energy over a very short period. This is what happened in the atomic bombs exploded over Hiroshima and Nagasaki, Japan, in 1945.

When a chain reaction is inhibited, a controlled reaction takes place, and the same quantity of energy is liberated over a much longer period of time. This is what takes place in a nuclear reactor.

A typical fission reaction is the one undergone by uranium-235 to produce atoms of barium-141 and krypton-92, as shown in the following equation:

$$_{92}U^{235} + _{0}n^{1} \rightarrow$$
$$_{50}Ba^{141} + _{36}Kr^{92} + 3_{0}n^{1} + \text{energy}.$$

Nuclear fusion reactions.

A fusion reaction is virtually the exact opposite of a fission reaction. In a fusion reaction, the nuclei of two light atoms combine to form a somewhat heavier nucleus. This thermonuclear reaction results in the release of a tremendous amount of energy. It is believed by scientists that chains of uncontrolled nuclear fusion reactions produce the energy emitted by the sun and by other stars. The sun, for example, continuously radiates energy at the rate of 54 horsepower from each square inch of its surface. This energy is liberated when four hydrogen nuclei combine to form a helium nucleus. There is a consequent loss of mass, and this energy is then emitted. For the most part the energy is in the form of gamma rays that are rapidly transformed into heat.

Two series of fusion reactions are believed to be primarily responsible for energy generation in the sun, and the proton-proton chain is undoubtedly the most important source of energy production in hydrogen-rich stars, of which the sun is an example. The proton-proton chain follows this sequence:

$$_{1}H^{1} + _{1}H^{1} \rightarrow _{1}H^{2} + e^{+} + \text{energy}$$
$$_{1}H^{1} + _{1}H^{2} \rightarrow _{2}He^{3} + \text{energy}.$$

Two $_{2}He^{3}$ nuclei produced in identical reactions undergo fusion and yield a helium nucleus, $_{2}He^{4}$, along with two protons, which rejoin the chain in this reaction:

$$_{2}He^{3} + _{2}He^{3} \rightarrow _{2}He^{4} + _{1}H^{1} + _{1}H^{1}.$$

Or, in summary:

$$4(_{1}H^{1}) \rightarrow _{2}He^{4} + 2e^{+} + 26.740 \text{ Mev}.$$

The carbon-nitrogen chain follows this sequence:

$$_{6}C^{12} + _{1}H^{1} \rightarrow _{7}N^{13} + \text{energy}$$
$$_{7}N^{13} \rightarrow _{6}C^{13} + e^{+}$$
$$_{6}C^{13} + _{1}H^{1} \rightarrow _{7}N^{14} + \text{energy}$$
$$_{7}N^{14} + _{1}H^{1} \rightarrow _{8}O^{15} + \text{energy}$$
$$_{8}O^{15} \rightarrow _{7}N^{15} + e^{+}$$
$$_{7}N^{15} + _{1}H^{1} \rightarrow _{6}C^{12} + _{2}He^{4} + \text{energy}.$$

Thus, the chain is completed with the creation of both a helium nucleus and a new carbon nucleus that will serve as a catalyst for continuation of the cycle, or, in summary:

$$4(_{1}H^{1}) \rightarrow _{2}He^{4} + 2e^{+} + 26.740 \text{ Mev}.$$

Experiments are currently being conducted in an effort to produce a controlled fusion reaction. Such a reaction would become highly important as a commercial source of energy. Energy sufficient to meet the world's re-

FUSION

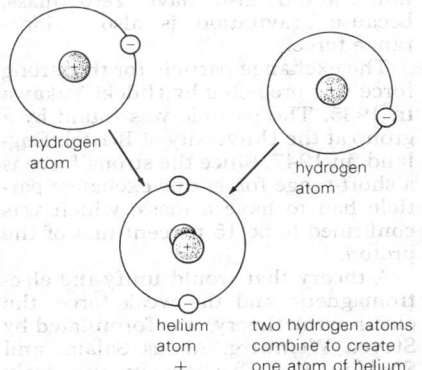

hydrogen atom

hydrogen atom

helium atom
+
energy

two hydrogen atoms combine to create one atom of helium, releasing energy

MIMI FORSYTH/MONKMEYER

A FUSION REACTION requires the joining of two light atomic nuclei to form one heavy nucleus, in the process releasing a great deal of energy. Fusion is the basic reaction producing the energy released by the sun. Scientists hope that research, such as that carried out at the Tokamak Fusion Test Reactor at Princeton University, will find a way to control a fusion reaction and use its energy. A fusion power plant would produce much less dangerous waste than does a fission plant.

DEPARTMENT OF ENERGY

DANGER
HIGH VOLTAGE
13,800 VOLTS

quirements for thousands of years would be readily available from the small amount of heavy hydrogen found in ordinary water. In addition, fusion reactions do not produce radioactive wastes that demand expensive treatment for safe storage and disposal by industry and government.

The major difficulty to be overcome in obtaining a controlled release of fusion energy is the extremely high temperature that must be maintained for long periods of time to sustain the reaction.

Elementary Particles

Until 1932, when the neutron was discovered, only the electron and the proton were known as the basic constituents of matter. In 1932, James Chadwick discovered the neutron, which was the missing link in explaining the stability of the atomic nucleus. Chadwick had previously observed that the electrons emitted in beta decay of radioactive nuclei did not have fixed values for their energy. The sum of the energy of the final particles— the proton and the electron—was less

than the energy of the neutron at the beginning of the reaction. To explain this difference, Wolfgang Pauli proposed the existence of another particle that would be emitted during the reaction. Pauli's hypothetical particle was called the neutrino, the little neutron. In 1933, Enrico Fermi formulated a theory in which a neutron during beta decay is transformed into an electron, a proton, and a neutrino. Since the neutrino barely interacts with matter, its existence was difficult to prove experimentally. In 1955, Clyde Cowan and Frederic Reines succeeded in showing the existence of neutrinos emitted by nuclear fission in a reactor.

Antiparticles. Paul Dirac, in the 1920's, suggested the existence of positive electrons, that is, particles with the mass of electrons, but with a positive charge. During 1932, the year of discovery of the neutron, Carl Anderson discovered Dirac's particles, called positrons, while studying cosmic rays in cloud chambers. Scientists subsequently discovered that all the other known particles have corresponding antiparticles. Antineutrinos are the antiparticles of neutrinos, and antiprotons are the antiparticles of protons. When a particle and its antiparticle

collide, they annihilate each other, that is, their masses are converted into energy.

New particles. With the advent of particle accelerators with higher energies, a large number of new elementary particles have been discovered.

Today, particles are divided into three groups: leptons, baryons, and mesons. Leptons are said to undergo weak interactions. Baryons and mesons, which together form the hadrons, undergo strong interactions. The most familiar baryons are the neutron and the proton. The pi-meson, a particle proposed by Hideki Yukawa to explain nuclear forces, is an example of a meson.

There are six different leptons: the electron, muon, tau-particle, and three varieties of neutrinos. Unlike hadrons, leptons are considered to be true elementary particles, in that they are not believed to be composed of smaller constituents.

Quarks. By the early 1960's so many hadrons had been discovered that it became clear they had to be composed of even smaller building blocks. In 1963, two physicists at the

California Institute of Technology, Murray Gell-Mann and George Zweig, proposed independently that all the hadrons would be made up of three even more fundamental particles. Gell-Mann named these particles quarks.

The most striking quality of quarks is their fractional charge: They have, respectively, $2/3$ $-1/3$, and $-1/3$ times the charge of the electron. Quarks combine in such a fashion as to form particles with a charge of 0, 1, or -1.

The three types of quarks were designated by u (up), d (down), and s (sharp). U, d, and s are known as flavors. Soon it became clear that antiquarks were required to explain the composition of hadrons. Baryons are now believed to consist of three quarks, and mesons to consist of a quark and an antiquark. To complete the scheme, colors were introduced in addition to flavors. Quarks may be red, green, or blue; their corresponding antiquarks are given complementary colors: cyan, magenta, and yellow. When quarks combine, the colors have to combine in such a way that white theoretically results. The proton is believed to consist of two u and one d quarks, with the condition that there is a quark of each color: red, green, and blue (their mixture results in white).

Fundamental forces. Four fundamental forces exist in nature. Gravitation is the force of attraction be-

tween masses. The electromagnetic force manifests itself as the attraction and repulsion forces between electric charges. The strong force holds the atomic nucleus together. The weak force is responsible for certain forms of radioactive decay. The gravitational and electromagnetic forces are long-range forces. Their magnitude decreases with the square of the distance, but they act, although weakly, over infinite distances. Strong and weak forces act only over very short distances, typically the distance between nucleons in nuclei. Over these short distances, however, the strong force is much stronger than gravitational or electromagnetic forces. The strong force is 1000 times stronger than the electromagnetic force, and 10^{38} times stronger than gravitation.

Grand unification theories. Several attempts have been made in recent years to explain the four fundamental forces by a single theory. Such theories are characterized as unification schemes, and a theory that would unify the strong, weak, and electromagnetic forces is called a grand unification theory, or GUT.

A basic concept in these theories is that forces between particles are mediated by exchange particles. The mass of these particles should be inversely proportional to the range of the force. Electromagnetic forces are transmitted by virtual photons, photons with a very short lifetime. Photons have no mass, which agrees with the

fact that the electromagnetic force has an infinite range. The exchange particle for gravity, the hypothetical graviton, would also have zero mass, because gravitation is also a long-range force.

The exchange particle for the strong force was predicted by Hideki Yukawa in 1935. The particle was found by a group at the University of Bristol, England, in 1947. Since the strong force is a short-range force, this exchange particle had to have a mass, which was confirmed to be 15 percent that of the proton.

A theory that would unify the electromagnetic and the weak force, the electroweak theory, was formulated by Steven Weinberg, Abdus Salam, and Sheldon Lee Glashow in the early 1970's. They predicted that three particles, the W^+, W^-, and the Z^0, would transmit the weak force in atomic nuclei. Since the weak force has a shorter range than the strong force, the masses of these particles had to be greater than the mass of the pi-meson, the Yukawa particle. They predicted that the two W particles would have a mass of 81 GeV, which is 80 times the mass of the proton, and that the mass of the Z particle would be 93.8 GeV. All three particles were discovered by Carlo Rubbia in 1983. The particles were formed in collisions of protons and antiprotons in the huge proton-antiproton collider at CERN, *Centre Européen de Recherche Nucléaire*, near Geneva, Switzerland.

—*Alexander Hellemans*

ATOMIC PARTICLES

ANTIPROTON-PROTON COLLISIONS *obtained at Fermilab's Tevatron in 1985 are recorded on a computer display. Antiprotons collided with protons at the point marked with an X. The tracks of the produced particles are detected by means of a three-dimensional detector and displayed in the rectangles above and below the collision point. The three-dimensional distribution is indicated by color coding on the screen.*

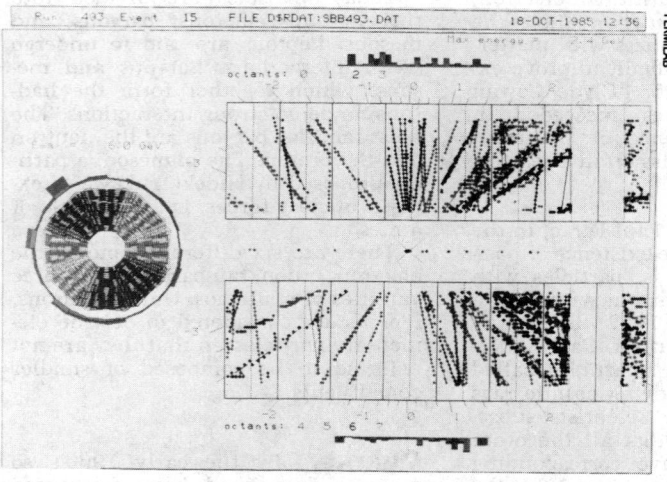

Some atomic particles				
NAME	SYMBOL	MASS (IN MEV)	CHARGE	AVERAGE LIFETIME (in seconds)
Photon	γ	0	0	Stable
LEPTONS				
Neutrino	ν	0*	0	Stable
Antineutrino	$\bar{\nu}$	0*	0	Stable
Neutrino (Muon type)	ν_μ	0*	0	Stable
Antineutrino (Muon type)	$\bar{\nu}_\mu$	0*	0	Stable
Electron	e^-	0.511	-1	Stable
Positron	e^+	0.511	$+1$	Stable
Muon	μ^-	105.7	-1	2.2×10^{-6}
Antimuon	μ^+	105.7	$+1$	2.2×10^{-6}
MESONS				
Positive Pi	π^0	139.6	$+1$	2.6×10^{-8}
Negative Pi	π^-	189.6	-1	2.6×10^{-8}
Neutral Pi	π^0	135	0	8×10^{-17}
Positive K	K^+	493.7	$+1$	1.2×10^{-8}
K-zero-short	K^0_S	497.7	0	9×10^{-11}
K-zero-long	K^0_L	497.7	0	5.2×10^{-8}
Negative K	K^-	493.7	-1	1.2×10^{-8}
BARYONS				
Proton	p	938.3	$+1$	Stable*
Antiproton	$\bar{p}$	938.3	-1	Stable*
Neutron	n	939.6	0	9.18×10^2
Antineutron	$\bar{n}$	939.6	0	9.18×10^2
Lambda Hyperon	Λ^0	115.6	0	3×10^{-10}
Lambda Antihyperon	$\bar{\Lambda}^0$	1115.6	0	3×10^{-10}

*Some theories challenge this.

GLOSSARY OF CHEMISTRY AND PHYSICS

Absorption. In physics, the taking up of energy from radiation by matter. Absorption occurs when an electron or atom is raised to a higher energy level by interaction with a photon. In acoustics, it is the decrease in energy of sound waves when reflected by certain substances, such as cloth.

Acid. Any soluble substance that dissociates in water and whose hydrogen ion (H^{+1}) concentration can be measured. A mineral acid is a compound containing hydrogen protons (H^+) joined either to a nonmetal (for example, HCl or H_2S) or to a nonmetal oxide (for example, H_2SO_4 or H_2CO_3). The positively and negatively charged ions of an acid conduct electricity when dissociated in water. The relative acidity of a substance is indicated by its pH value, which may range from 1 to 7, the neutral point. The lower the pH, the stronger the acid.

Adiabatic process. In thermodynamics, any change in a closed system in which no energy is transferred from or to the environment.

Alkali metals. Metals found in group one of the periodic table; metals in group two are alkaline earth metals. These metals are designated as alkali and alkaline because they form bases and dissociate in water into their respective positively charged metal and negatively charged hydroxide (OH^{-1}) ions, which are electrically conductive. A base has a pH value in the range of 7 to 14. The stronger the base, the higher its pH or hydroxyl concentration. Bases and mineral acids react to produce salts and water.

Alkane. In organic chemistry, any hydrogen compound of carbon having the general empirical formula C_nH_{2n+2}. Alkanes are aliphatic and have saturated bonds.

Alpha particle. The nucleus of a helium atom, consisting of two protons and two neutrons. Alpha particles are emitted by radioactive materials.

Anion. A negatively charged atom or molecule (radical) that collects at the anode (positive electrode) of an electrolytic cell and gives up its excess electrons to that anode. Positively charged atoms migrate to the cathode (negative electrode), where they ac-cept electrons and are designated as cations.

Antimatter. Matter whose atoms consist of antiparticles, that is, positrons, antiprotons, and antineutrons. Antimatter and ordinary matter annihilate upon collision to yield energy. Except for short-lived particles detected in cosmic radiation and during collisions of accelerated particles, antimatter is not found in the universe, although its existence is a possibility.

Antiparticle. Elementary particle corresponding to a normal particle but opposite to it in electric and magnetic properties. When brought together with its counterpart, the result is their mutual annihilation.

Atom. The smallest unit of matter having the characteristics of an an element, consisting of nucleus (containing neutrons as well as positively charged protons) and surrounded by revolving negatively charged electrons. Most of the mass of an atom is in its nucleus. The number of electrons (its atomic number) is equal to the number of protons it holds.

Avogadro's number. The cipher 6.024×10^{23}. Avogadro's law states that 22.4 liters of any gas at $0°$ C and 760 torr (standard temperature and pressure) contains 6.024×10^{23} particles existing either as atoms or as molecules whose weight in grams is equal respectively to the atomic or molecular weight of the gas in question.

Beta particle. An electron emitted during radioactive decay of such substances as thorium and uranium. Positive beta particles are positrons; they are emitted during the radioactive decay of certain elements.

Buffer. Any ingredient that suppresses a change in acidity (hydrogen ion, H^{+1} concentration) or alkalinity (hydroxyl, OH^{-1} concentration). For example, the pH of blood, about 7.4, changes slowly on the addition of an acid or a base. Serum proteins containing acidic and basic groups act as buffers because they react with the added acids and bases and tend to neutralize them.

Carbonyl radical. In organic chemistry, the molecular structure —C=O. Carbonyls differentiate the ketones and aldehydes from the other organic compounds.

Carboxyl radical. In organic chemistry, the molecular structure —COOH. The carboxyl radical differentiates all organic acids from other compounds.

Carnot cycle. The series of operations that is gone through by the Carnot engine, an ideal heat engine that operates at maximum efficiency. The four phases of the cycle are isothermal expansion, adiabatic expansion, isothermal compression, and adiabatic compression. Work is done only during the two expansion phases of the cycle; this accounts for the high efficiency of the engine.

Catalyst. Any substance that speeds up or slows down the reaction between atoms or molecules to produce new compounds. The catalyst remains unchanged at the end of the reaction.

Chemical change. The result of a reaction between two or more atoms or molecules to produce a new and different set of atoms or molecules.

Chemical equation. A balanced expression that uses the chemical symbols of the elements, coefficients, subscripts, and arrows to show a chemical change or reaction. The reactants are shown on the left-hand side of the equation; an arrow from left to right indicates that the reaction takes place in the forward direction to yield the products on the right-hand side of the equation. If the reaction is reversible, a second arrow, from right to left, indicates this.

Chemical formula. A formula that uses the chemical symbols of the elements, along with subscripts and brackets as needed, to show how atoms of the same kind or of different elements are combined as molecules (for example, O_2 is oxygen gas; $Ca(OH)_2$ is calcium hydroxide).

Colloid. Solid particles that have diameters in the range of 10 to 10,000 angstroms and that are suspended or dispersed in a gas, liquid, or solid. The particles repel each other because they have the same electrical charge and they do not affect the melting or boiling points of the medium.

Covalency. The sharing of the outermost electrons between two or more neighboring atoms of the same or different elements.

Diffraction. In optics, the deviation from a straight line of a beam of light when it passes along an object placed in its path. Diffraction is the phenomenon that causes perceptible fuzziness at the edge of a shadow and of interference patterns.

Diffusion. The scattering of light in all directions during transmission or reflection. During transmission, diffusion is caused by light waves striking minute particles. During reflection, diffusion is caused by irregularities in the reflecting surface.

Dipole. A pair of electric charges of opposite polarity a short distance apart.

Distillation. A separation process that occurs when the components of a liquid are separately converted to a vapor by the application of heat (a vacuum may be applied simultaneously to lower the boiling points of the components involved), drawn off, cooled or condensed, and collected.

Electric current. The flow of electric charge through a conductor. The current is measured in amperes; 1 ampere equals the flow of 1 coulomb (the unit of electric charge) per second.

Electrode. A terminal, pole, or conductor that conveys a flow of electrons through a solid, a molten solution, a gas, or a liquid. Electrodes are either negatively or positively charged. In an electrolysis cell, the negative electrode is called the cathode; the positive electrode is the anode. In a battery, the reverse holds true; the negative electrode is the anode and the positive electrode is the cathode.

Electrolysis. The application of a direct electric current through the positive electrode (anode), electrolytes, and negative electrode (cathode) of an electrolytic cell to produce a chemical reaction. The components of the electrolyte become ionized. Reduction takes place at the cathode, and oxidation takes place at the anode. Depending on selection, the electrodes may participate in the reaction.

Electrolyte. In electrolysis, any substance (usually an acid, base, soluble or molten salt) that dissociates into its respective cations (positive ions) and anions (negative ions) by the application of a direct electric current.

Electromagnetic spectrum. The entire range of wavelengths or frequencies according to which electromagnetic radiation is classified; the range is from about 10^{-14} meter (gamma rays) to about 10^7 meters (radio waves). The visible portion of the electromagnetic spectrum covers wavelengths from about 4×10^{-7} meter (violet light) to 7.5×10^{-7} meter (red light).

Electron. A subatomic particle with negative charge that commonly occupies the outer region of the atom. An electron has a mass 1/1800th that of a proton.

Electron volt (eV). A unit used to express the energy of elementary particles. One electron volt is defined as the kinetic energy acquired by an electron or proton when accelerated by an electromotive force of 1 volt.

Faraday. In electrolysis, a unit of charge that is equal to 1 mole of electrons (6.024×10^{23} charged atoms) or to 96,500 ampere-seconds. A Faraday liberates or deposits 1 gram-equivalent weight of a particular substance in the oxidation-reduction reaction involved.

Field. In physics, the area around a body in which another body undergoes an influence or force. A field can be represented by field lines. These lines indicate the direction of the force perceived by a body that is placed in the field.

Frequency. The number of times an event will take place in a given unit of time. Can be measured in cycles per second, revolutions per minute, pulses per second, and so on. In acoustics, the audiofrequency is any sound-wave frequency that can normally be heard; audiofrequencies range from 15 to 20,000 cycles per second. An infrasonic frequency is a frequency below the audiofrequency range; an ultrasonic frequency is a frequency above the audiofrequency range.

Gamma ray. Electromagnetic radiation of very short wavelength, typically 0.1 nanometer. Gamma rays penetrate matter easily and are emitted during radioactive decay.

Gram atom. A unit equal to the atomic weight of an element expressed in grams. One gram atom of oxygen is equal to 16 grams, which is its atomic weight in grams.

Gram mole. The molecular weight of a compound or molecule expressed in grams is equal to 1 gram mole. Water has a molecular weight of 18; 1 gram mole of water is equal to 18 grams.

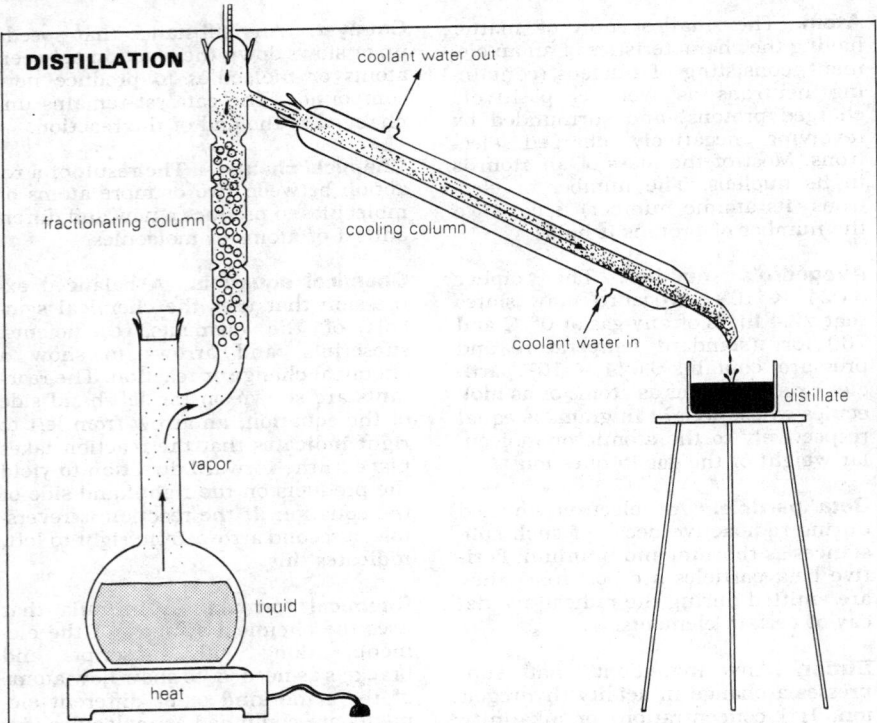

DISTILLATION

coolant water out

fractionating column

cooling column

coolant water in

vapor

distillate

liquid

heat

PETER LOEWER

Distillation is used to separate the components of a liquid. Each component has a different boiling point, so a component with a lower boiling point (A) will turn to vapor before a component with a higher boiling point (B). The vapor is cooled to return it to a liquid, called the distillate. When the process is complete, the remaining liquid has a higher percentage of component B, and the distillate has a higher percentage of component A. If the boiling points of the two components are close, many repetitions of this process might be required to achieve a pure or nearly pure result. A slightly more complicated apparatus involves the use of a device called a fractionating column. The variation in temperature over the length of this column causes the vapor to condense and be redistilled continuously. Use of such a column yields a much purer distillate.

HALF-LIVES OF SOME ISOTOPES

RADIOISOTOPE	HALF-LIFE
uranium 238	4.51×10^9 years
plutonium 239	24,000 years
carbon 14	5730 years
radium 226	1620 years
cobalt 60	5.3 years
iodine 131	8.07 days
potassium 42	12.4 hours
yttrium 88	2.0 hours
bismuth 212	60.5 minutes
silver 106	24.5 minutes
nitrogen 13	9.93 minutes
francium 229	27.5 seconds
lithium 8	.88 seconds

Half-life. A measure of radioactivity, different for each element or isotope, defined as the average time it takes for half the atoms of a sample to undergo radioactive decay. Half-lives vary from trillions of years to fractions of seconds. For example, the half-life of samarium 152 is 10^{12} years; that of polonium 212 is 3×10^{-7} seconds.

Harmonic. A frequency that is a multiple of another frequency to which it is related. A harmonic having a frequency four times that of the fundamental frequency, for example, is called the fourth harmonic. In acoustics, the harmonics of a sound that are heard simultaneously with the fundamental frequency are called overtones.

Heat. The energy that results from the vibrations, motions, reactions, and collisions of nuclear particles, atoms, and molecules.

Heat capacity. The amount of heat (calories) necessary to raise the temperature of 1 gram of a given substance by 1° C. The heat of fusion is the amount of heat needed to convert 1 gram of a solid into a liquid at its melting point. The heat of vaporization is the amount of heat required to convert 1 gram of a liquid into a vapor at its boiling point.

Heat of combustion. The amount of heat, along with light, that is released by a reaction. The reaction usually involves the ignition of oxygen with another substance at constant pressure and volume.

Heat of formation. The quantity of heat given off or absorbed when 1 mole of a compound is produced from its elements. Conversely, the heat of reaction is the quantity of heat liberated or absorbed during a chemical change.

Hydroxyl radical. In organic chemistry, the molecular structure —OH (also the charged hydroxide OH^{-1}).

Hydroxyl radicals distinguish phenols, alcohols, and sugars from other organic compounds.

Impedance. In electronics, the apparent resistance to the flow of an alternating current. Impedance can be equated with the resistance to the flow of direct current through a circuit.

Indicator. An indicator is any substance that changes color when affected by an acid or base. Litmus paper, the most common indicator, changes to red under acidic conditions and to blue under alkaline conditions.

Induction. The creation of an electromagnetic force (emf) in a conducting coil by a varying magnetic field. Electric generators produce electricity by induction. The emf created in a coil by its own varying magnetic field is termed inductance or self-induction. This emf is opposite to the emf applied to the coil, so it resists passage of an alternating current.

Ion. A charged particle that results when an atom or molecule gains or loses one or more electrons. A positive ion is an atom or molecule that has lost an electron; a negative ion is an atom or molecule that has gained an electron.

Isothermal process. Any change in matter that takes place at a constant temperature; thus, there is a resultant change in the pressure and/or volume of the substance.

Isotopes. Atoms of the same element with the same number of protons (and thus identical atomic numbers), but with different numbers of neutrons (and thus different mass numbers). Isotopes are chemically identical, but differ in nuclear properties. In nature, each element consists of a mixture of stable isotopes. Many isotopes can be created artificially. Unstable isotopes are used as radiation sources.

Kinetics. In chemistry, a term that refers to the direction and speed of a given reaction as it is influenced by the concentration of reactants and products formed along with the temperatures, pressures, and catalysts that are used.

Mach number. The ratio of the speed of a fluid to the speed of sound at that location. Generally used to designate the ratio of the speed of an aircraft in flight and the speed of sound at the altitude at which the aircraft is flying. Thus, an aircraft flying at Mach 2 would have a speed twice that of sound, or about 1400 miles per hour. If the Mach number is less than 1.0, the speed is called subsonic; if the Mach number is greater than 1.0, the speed is called supersonic.

Mass defect. The difference in mass before and after a nuclear reaction. In a fission reaction, the total mass of the formed nuclei is lower than the mass of the original nucleus. In a fusion reaction, the mass of the formed nucleus is less than the total mass of the nuclei forming it. This difference in mass is converted completely into energy according to Einstein's formula: $E = mc^2$, in which E is the energy, m the mass defect, and c the velocity of light.

Meson. Any of the subatomic particles belonging to the hadrons, and whose mass lies between that of the electron and that of the proton. Mesons have electrical charges of 0, +1, or −1, and are unstable. They are found in cosmic rays and are produced in nuclear reactors. The two most prominent species are called mu mesons and pi mesons.

Neutrino. An elementary particle without mass or electrical charge, but with spin. It always travels at the speed of light, hardly interacts with matter, and is considered to be formed in nuclear reactions.

Neutron. An electrically neutral particle, constituting with protons the nuclei of atoms. The mass of a neutron is equal to the mass of a proton.

Nuclear fission. A nuclear reaction in which the nucleus of an atom is split into two lighter nuclei. The total mass of the lighter nuclei is less than the mass of the original nucleus. This difference in mass, called mass defect, is converted entirely into energy. Nuclear fission is the power source in nuclear reactors.

THE CONCORDE, *a supersonic aircraft, can travel at speeds as high as Mach 2, or twice the speed of sound.*

Nuclear fusion. A nuclear reaction consisting of the combination of two light nuclei into one nucleus. The mass of the formed nucleus is less than the total mass of the nuclei before the reaction. This difference in mass, called mass defect, is converted entirely into energy. Nuclear fusion is the power source of the sun and of the hydrogen bomb.

Nucleon. Either of the two particles making up the atomic nucleus, that is, the neutron and the proton.

Optical pumping. The raising of atoms or molecules to a higher energy level by irradiation with light. Excited atoms or molecules are said to undergo a population inversion, that is, the population of excited atoms or molecules is higher than in the normal situation. Optically pumped matter is used in lasers to produce coherent radiation by stimulated emission.

Oscillator. Any physical system that produces oscillations. An example of a simple oscillator is the pendulum. In electronics, an oscillator is a device for producing an alternating current, such as radio waves.

Oxidizing agent. One that gains electrons in a chemical reaction and, therefore, undergoes reduction.

Oxygenation. The formation of an oxide through a chemical reaction. Carbon dioxide is formed when carbon is ignited with oxygen; it may also be made at high temperatures by burning it with iron oxide. The iron is liberated from its oxygen, which reacts with the free carbon and also yields carbon dioxide.

Periodic law. An assertion that all the elements are differentiated from each other by their atomic masses and the number of electrons and protons they contain in their atoms. Consequently, the elements can be arranged in predictable sequential periods that further reveal specific groups for elements that have similar chemical properties. The periodic table displays this periodic and group relationship among the elements.

Phase. Any of the states in which matter can exist: gaseous, liquid, or solid. In a wave motion, the phase is the portion of the cycle already completed by the oscillation. The phase is expressed as an angle representing the part of the 2 pi radians, or 360 degrees, that make up one complete cycle.

Photon. The smallest discrete unit (quantum) of electromagnetic radiation. The energy (E) of a photon is related to its wavelength v by the formula $E = hv$, in which h is Planck's constant.

Piezoelectricity. An electric current developed in some crystalline materials when they are subjected to a strain in an appropriate direction. This property is utilized commercially in ceramic phonograph cartridges.

Plasma. An ionized gas consisting of electrons, positive ions, and a variable amount of neutral particles. Gases heated to extremely high temperatures form plasmas. Plasmas can also be created by electrical discharges. Plasmas are widespread in the universe, especially in the interiors of the sun and stars, where fusion reactions occur. In experimental fusion reactors, plasmas are heated to temperatures high enough for spontaneous fusion reactions to occur.

Polymerization. A fundamental reaction that occurs in nature and is employed in organic chemistry, in which one molecule (called a monomer) can be made to react with different molecules (other monomers) to form repeating units (called polymers), which have properties different from those of the initial monomers. Plastics and proteins are two examples of materials made through polymerization.

Positron. An elementary particle with the same mass as the electron, but with a positive charge. The positron is the antiparticle of the electron.

Proton. An electrically charged particle that, with neutrons, is contained in the nuclei of atoms. The proton has a positive electrical charge equal in magnitude to that of the electron. Its mass is equal to that of the neutron and is about 1800 times as large as that of the electron.

Qualitative analysis. The division of analytical chemistry that uses techniques and equipment to identify the kinds of elements, radicals, and constituents of a given sample.

Quantitative analysis. The division of analytical chemistry that uses techniques and equipment to determine the precise quantities of elements, radicals, and constituents in a sample.

Quantum. The smallest unit of energy. Atoms can occupy only certain fixed energy levels. When an atom makes a transition from a higher energy level to a lower energy level, it emits a quantum whose energy is given by $E_2 - E_1 = hv$, in which E_2 and E_1 are the two energy levels of the atom, h is Planck's constant, and v is the frequency of the emitted radiation. Conversely, an atom can absorb a quantum by making a corresponding transition from a lower to a higher energy level.

Quark. The smallest building block of matter constituting the hadrons.

Reaction. The interaction of atoms and molecules, either with atoms and molecules of the same type or with other kinds of atoms and molecules, to form distinct and different kinds of products that have properties different from those of the original reactants.

Reducing agent. An atom that loses electrons to another atom or radical in a chemical reaction. As a result, the reducing agent is oxidized.

Reduction. The gain of electrons by an atom or ion in a reaction.

Refraction. The change in direction of a light ray as it passes between substances of different densities. Refraction results from the fact that the speed of light varies inversely with the density of the medium through which it is traveling.

Saturation point. When two or more soluble ingredients are mixed with each other, a homogeneous solution results. However, the point may be reached where an excess of one or more solutes causes slight crystallization or induces a small amount of one of the solutes to come out of solution. If at some point no further crystallization or separation takes place on standing, that point is designated the saturation point for a particular group of solutes at a given temperature and pressure.

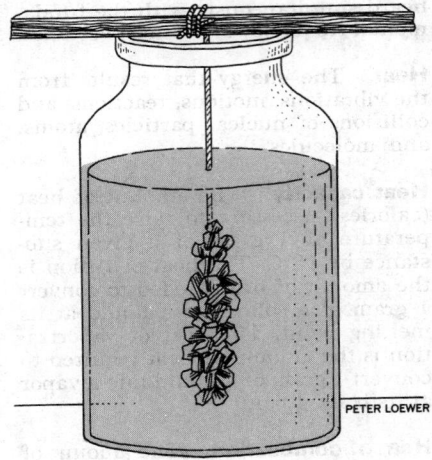

PETER LOEWER

CRYSTALLIZATION *can occur once the saturation point of a solution has been passed.*

Silane. A silicon hydride (having the general formula Si_nH_{2n+2}) that has no saturated or free bonds. In organic chemistry, silanes are analogous to alkanes. Depending on their chain length, silanes exist as gases or liquids at room temperature.

Silanol. Any hydroxyl (—OH) bearing silicon hydride. A silanol is analogous to an alcohol in organic chemistry. Silanols are largely used to make silicone polymers.

Solute. A soluble ingredient in a solid, liquid, or gas that is less than 50 percent of the total solution. The major component of the solution is the solvent, making up over 50 percent of the mixture by weight.

Surfactant. A substance that alters the surface tension of a liquid or solid in respect to another gas, solid, or liquid. Insoluble ingredients may become compatible with other solutes or solvents. In organic and in silicone chemistry, a molecule that has one part oil soluble, the other water soluble. Hence, an oil that may be incompatible with an alcohol may be made compatible by the action of the oil-soluble part of the surfactant. In turn, the water-soluble portion of the surfactant is compatible with the alcohol. The result is a uniform emulsion or latex.

Temperature. A relative measure of the heat energy contained in a given mass of matter as generated by the motion, vibration, interaction, and collision of its atoms or molecules. Because a hotter body loses heat to a colder one, mercury expands in a thermometer at a given rate. A colder body absorbs heat; the mercury in a thermometer loses heat to the colder body and, therefore, contracts. The temperature thus goes down.

Thermoplastics. These are plastic materials that soften at a particular range of temperatures, allowing them to be molded or formed into specific shapes. Careful cooling freezes the desired shape. Reheating to the softening point allows it to be reshaped.

Thermosetting plastics. The plastics that require heat or a chemical reaction to take a permanent shape in a particular mold. Unlike thermoplastics, once cooled, thermosetting plastics cannot be reshaped by the application of heat. Instead of softening, they will weaken, even disintegrate in some cases. In general, they are more diversified and can be exposed to higher service temperatures than thermoplastics.

Titration. A procedure that involves the determination of the unknown composition of a particular solution by adding known quantities of standardized solution until a specific reaction occurs, such as a change in color, conductivity, or precipitation.

Transuranium element. Any of the artificially produced elements, all having atomic numbers greater than 92, that of uranium. Transuranium elements with atomic numbers up to 108 have been obtained.

Uncertainty principle. A fundamental principle in physics first discovered by Werner Heisenberg in 1927. The principle states that because of the nature of matter, it is impossible to measure simultaneously the momentum and the position of a particle accurately.

Valence. The potential number of outer electrons that an atom of a given element can either gain or lose in reacting chemically with another atom. For example, hydrogen can either lose an outer electron and become electropositive (H^{+1}) or gain an electron and become electronegative (H^{-1}). Therefore, it has two possible valences, $+1$ and -1.

Velocity. The rate of displacement, or rate of change of position, per unit time. Velocity includes direction, but speed does not. Thus, an airplane that has a velocity of 600 miles per hour east will have a speed of 600 miles per hour. The distinction between velocity and speed is not always made, especially in nontechnical usage. For example, the velocity of light is generally given as 186,300 miles per second, but this is really its speed. Scientists are careful to make the distinction.

X-ray. X-ray is electromagnetic radiation with wavelengths ranging from 0.0001 nm to 100 nm. In the electromagnetic spectrum, x-rays occupy the region between gamma rays and ultraviolet rays.

RELATIVITY

Until the beginning of this century, scientists believed that Newton's laws of motion and of gravity offered a satisfactory basis for explaining the physical world. However, during the 1880's, physicists were faced with an enigma: Albert A. Michelson and Edward Williams Morley, in an attempt to measure the velocity of Earth relative to a hypothetical "ether," found that the measured velocity of the light coming from stars toward which Earth was moving was exactly the same as the velocity of light coming from stars from which Earth was moving away. In 1905, Albert Einstein published a theory based on the notion that it is impossible to determine the absolute motion of a moving object. Einstein's concern, however, was not the failure of Michelson and Morley to show the presence of an ether, but the validity of Maxwell's electromagnetic theory in systems that move at speeds close to the velocity of light. Einstein's theory is based on the following assumptions:

- Absolute speed cannot be measured; only speed relative to some other object can be measured.

- The measured value of the speed of light in a vacuum is always the same no matter how fast the observer or light source is moving.

- The maximum velocity possible in the universe is that of light.

From these assumptions Einstein could show that when the velocity of a body increases, its mass m increases according to the equation

$$m = \frac{m_0}{\sqrt{1 - \frac{v^2}{c^2}}}$$

in which m_0 is the mass of the object at zero velocity, v its velocity, and c the velocity of light. Also, its length changes: a body moving at high speed is shorter than a body at rest. However, these changes in mass and length will be perceived differently by observers moving at different speeds relative to each other; somebody traveling aboard a spaceship moving close to the velocity of light will not notice these changes. Time is also slowed down at high speed. A well known example of this time dilation effect is the twin paradox: One twin takes off in a spaceship and makes a trip through space at a speed close to the velocity of light; the other twin stays on Earth. When the first twin comes back from his trip, he will be younger than his brother who stayed behind.

One of the most important consequences of Einstein's theory is the equivalency of mass and energy, $E = mc^2$. This equation shows that whenever energy is created it is associated with a decrease in mass. In ordinary chemical reactions, the decrease in mass is not measurable, but in nuclear reactions a sizable fraction of the mass of atoms is converted into energy.

For Further Reference

General Chemistry

Asimov, Isaac. *Asimov's New Guide to Science*. Basic Books, 1984.

Boikess, Robert, and Edward Edelson. *Elements of Chemistry: General Organic and Biological*. Prentice-Hall, 1986.

Brown, Theodore L., and Eugene LeMay, Jr. *Chemistry: The Central Science* (3rd Ed.). Prentice-Hall, 1985.

Dean, John A., editor. *Lange's Handbook of Chemistry* (13th Ed.). McGraw-Hill, 1985.

Goldwhite, Harold, and John R. Spielman. *College Chemistry*. Harcourt Brace Jovanovich, 1984.

Grayson, Martha, editor. *Kirk-Othmer Concise Encyclopedia of Chemical Technology*. Wiley, 1985.

Hess, Fred. *Chemistry Made Simple*. Doubleday, 1984.

Maizell, Robert E. *How to Find Chemical Information: A Guide For Practicing Chemists, Teachers and Students* (2nd Ed.). Wiley, 1986.

Mascetta, Joseph A. *Chemistry the Easy Way*. Barron's, 1983.

Morgan, Alfred Powell. *First Chemistry for Boys and Girls*. Charles Scribner's Sons, 1977.

Nentwig, Joachim. *Chemistry Made Easy*. VCH Publishers, 1983.

Perlman, Philip. *Essentials of Modern Chemistry*. Barron's, 1979.

Richards, W. Graham. *The Problems of Chemistry*. Oxford, 1986.

Sax, N. Irving, and Richard J. Lewis, Sr., editors. *Hawley's Condensed Chemical Dictionary* (11th Ed.). Van Nostrand, 1987.

Schoenfeld, Robert. *The Chemists English* VCH Publishers, 1987.

Sherwood, Martin. *The New Chemistry*. Basic Books, 1974.

Sienko, M. J., and R. P. Plane. *Experimental Chemistry* (6th Ed.). McGraw-Hill, 1984.

Walmsley, Frank, and Kenneth Henold. *Chemical Principles, Properties, and Reactions*. Addison-Wesley, 1985.

Weast, Robert C., editor. *Handbook of Chemistry and Physics* (68th Ed.). CRC Press, 1987.

History

Asimov, Isaac. *A Short History of Chemistry*. Anchor Books, 1985.

Ihde, Aaron J. *The Development of Modern Chemistry*. Dover, 1983.

Physical Chemistry

Carpenter, Barry K. *Determination of Organic Reaction Mechanisms*. Wiley-Interscience, 1984.

Flurry, R. L., Jr. *Quantum Chemistry, An Introduction*. Prentice-Hall, 1983.

Gardiner, William C., editor. *Combustion Chemistry*. Springer-Verlag, 1984.

Hampel, Clifford A., and Gessner G. Hawley. *Glossary of Chemical Terms*. Van Nostrand Reinhold, 1982.

Jeans, James. *An Introduction to the Kinetic Theory of Gases*. Cambridge University Press, 1982.

Kuznetsov, V. I., editor. *Theory of Valence in Progress*. Mir (Moscow), 1980.

Laidler, Keith, and John H. Meiser. *Physical Chemistry*. Benjamin Cummings, 1982.

Levi, Primo. *The Periodic Table*. Schocken Books, 1984.

Linden, David, editor. *Handbook of Batteries and Fuel Cells*. McGraw-Hill, 1984.

Mantell, Charles L. *Batteries and Energy Systems*. McGraw-Hill, 1970.

Parker, Sybil, editor. *Dictionary of Chemical Terms* (2nd Ed.). McGraw-Hill, 1984.

Pauling, Linus. *The Chemical Bond*. Cornell University Press, 1967.

Petersen, Eugene E. *Chemical Reaction Analysis*. Prentice-Hall, 1965.

Spielberg, Nathan, and Byron D. Anderson. *Seven Ideas That Shook the Universe*. Wiley, 1987.

Inorganic Chemistry

Akhmetov, M., et al. *Problems and Laboratory Experiments in Inorganic Chemistry*. Mir (Moscow), 1982.

Cotton, Albert, and Geoffrey Wilkinson. *Basic Inorganic Chemistry*. Wiley, 1976.

Jolly, William L. *Modern Inorganic Chemistry*. McGraw-Hill, 1984.

Organic Chemistry

Knocke, W. Herman. *Essentials of Organic Chemistry*. Addison-Wesley, 1986.

Loudon, Marc G. *Organic Chemistry*. Addison-Wesley, 1984.

March, Jerry. *Advanced Organic Chemistry* (3rd Ed.). Wiley-Interscience, 1985.

Morrison, Robert T., and Robert N. Boyd. *Organic Chemistry* (4th Ed.). Allyn & Bacon, 1983.

Pine, Stanley H., and George S. Hammond. *Organic Chemistry* (5th Ed.). McGraw-Hill, 1987.

Traynham, James G. *Organic Nomenclature: A Programmed Introduction* (3rd Ed.). Prentice-Hall, 1985.

Silicone Chemistry

Rochow, Eugene G. *An Introduction to the Chemistry of the Silicones* (2nd Ed.). Wiley, 1951.

Runyon, W. R. *Silicon Semiconductor Technology*. McGraw-Hill, 1965.

Careers

Billmeyer, Fred W. *Chemical Engineering as a Profession*. Wiley-Interscience, 1975.

Taylor, L. *Chemistry Careers*. Franklin Watts, 1978.

General Physics

Asimov, Isaac. *The History of Physics*. Walker, 1984.

Asimov, Isaac. *Understanding Physics. Vol. 1: Motion, Sound and Heat*. New American Library, 1969.

Einstein, Albert. *Relativity: The Special and General Theory*. Crown, 1961.

Holton, Gerald. *Introduction to Concepts and Theories in Physical Science* (2nd Ed.). Princeton University Press, 1985.

Segre, Emilio. *From X-Rays to Quarks*. W. H. Freeman, 1980.

Mechanics

Gamov, George. *Gravity*. Doubleday/Anchor, 1962.

Machinnon, L. *Mechanics and Motion*. Oxford University Press, 1978.

Thermodynamics

Fenn, John B. *Engines, Energy, and Entropy: A Thermodynamics Primer*. W. H. Freeman, 1982.

Steffens, Henry John. *James Prescott Joule and the Concept of Energy*. Science History Publications, 1979.

Sussmann, M. V. *Elementary General Thermodynamics*. Addison-Wesley, 1972.

Sound

Pierce, John R. *The Science of Musical Sound*. W. H. Freeman, 1983.

White, Frederic A. *Our Acoustic Environment*. Wiley, 1975.

Electricity and Magnetism

Anderson, David L., editor. *The Discovery of the Electron*. Ayer, 1981.

Asimov, Isaac. *Understanding Physics. Vol. 2: Light, Magnetism and Electricity*. New American Library, 1969.

Gibson, W. M. *Basic Electricity* (2nd Ed.). Longman, 1976.

Optics

Van Heel, A. C. S., and C. H. F. Velzel. *What Is Light?* McGraw-Hill, 1968.

Particle Physics

Feinberg, Gerald. *What Is the World Made Of: The Achievements of Twentieth Century Physics*. Doubleday/Anchor, 1978.

Squires, Euan. *To Acknowledge the Wonder: The Story of Fundamental Physics*. Adam Hilger, 1985.

Trefil, James S. *From Atoms to Quarks: An Introduction to the Strange World of Particle Physics*. Charles Scribner's Sons, 1980.

Weinberg, Steven. *The Discovery of Subatomic Particles*. Scientific American Library, 1984.

Child and Family

S. ROTNER/ UNITED NATIONS

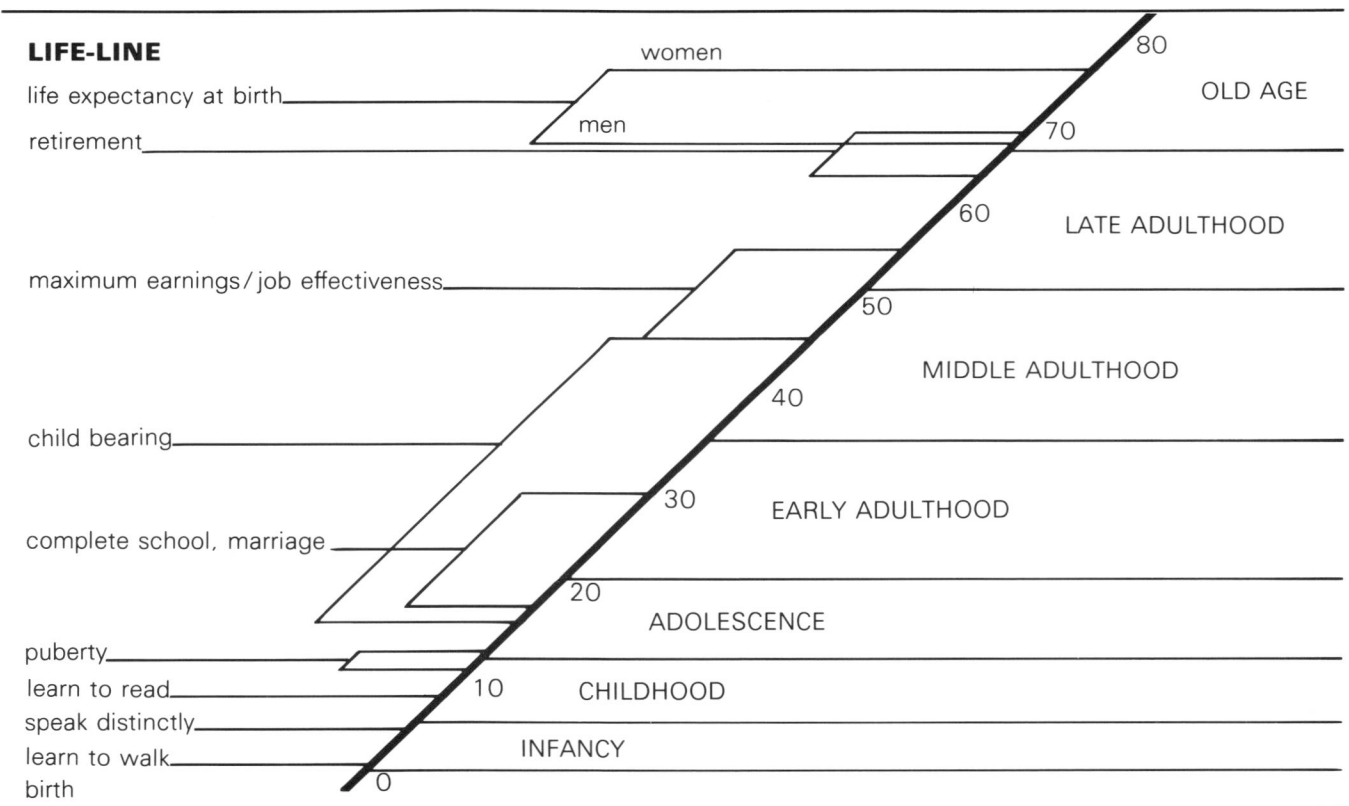

LIFE-LINE

life expectancy at birth _____ women

retirement _____ men

80

OLD AGE

70

60

LATE ADULTHOOD

maximum earnings/job effectiveness _____

50

MIDDLE ADULTHOOD

40

child bearing _____

30 EARLY ADULTHOOD

complete school, marriage _____

20

ADOLESCENCE

puberty _____

learn to read _____

10 CHILDHOOD

speak distinctly _____

INFANCY

learn to walk _____

birth

0

FATHER AND CHILD: S.J. KRASEMANN/PHOTO RESEARCHERS

Child and Family

WILL McINTYRE/PHOTO RESEARCHERS

BOB COMBS/PHOTO RESEARCHERS

IRENE BAYER/MONKMEYER

MIMI FORSYTH/MONKMEYER

Only one institution comes close to affecting every human being, and that institution is the family. Each of us has been influenced, for better or worse, by the quality and texture of our upbringing and by the care, example, and advice of our parents.

For those about to take on the responsibility of parenthood, the pervasive influence of the family is bound to be a sobering thought. Suddenly, a young man and woman are in a position to exercise the same deep influence on a small child that their own parents had on them. Can the new parents do better than their parents? Can more knowledge, careful study, or better surroundings make one generation more able than the one before? Perhaps, but in many respects, each generation learns child-raising all over again, making many of the same mistakes, and the same discoveries.

This volume is arranged to inform and assist those with an interest in family life, with special attention to parents. There are four main parts:

Child development. The first section begins with the birth of a child. It presents a wide range of information about the child's growth and development—physically, mentally, and emotionally. In addition, considerable attention is given to practical concerns, especially those of parents of the very young. The section follows the child's growth through adolescence to the edge of adulthood.

Adult development. Until recently, most people believed that development ended when a person achieved adulthood. Recent studies have shown, however, that adults also grow and change according to predictable patterns. A knowledge of these general patterns often helps to understand feelings or behavior that might otherwise seem frightening, strange, and unaccountable. The studies show, for example, that between major phases of life, most people go through a turbulent and often painful *transition* phase in which their lives to date are evaluated and their future may seem in doubt. Development seems to continue straight through adult life, perhaps even to the moment of death.

Marriage and family. Up to this point, the volume has been largely concerned with the growth of an individual. This section considers the growth of an intimate relationship between a man and a woman. It covers the time from early courtship through the child-rearing years to the quieter period after sons and daughters have left home.

The marriage relationship develops according to its own nature, depending in part on the changes that take place in the individuals. The development pattern does not restrict individual couples, but often it helps explain feelings that might otherwise be disturbing or unaccountable.

Individual and family problems. The final section considers the more common serious problems that confront individuals and families. Read by itself, this section may seem alarming. But the prevalence of such problems as alcoholism, drug abuse, and emotional illness make it seem important to include some discussion of them here so that readers may avoid these problems or be prepared if they encounter them.

Readers who seek further information on such social sciences as psychology and sociology should consult the volume on Social Sciences. Additional information on health and various diseases can be found in the volume on Health and Life Sciences.

CHILD DEVELOPMENT

Every parent, when faced with the incredibly complicated task of raising children, is bombarded with conflicting advice, all of it claiming to be critical for the child's future mental and physical health. It is no wonder that so many new parents feel overwhelmed by and ill-prepared for the task they have undertaken.

How do they know which expert is right? With such a variety of advice, which should they follow? The answer seems to be that there is no one right way to bring up a child. Different cultures and different eras have held widely varying views on child rearing; despite these differences, most children in all societies grow into healthy and functional adults.

Take, for example, the fashions in child rearing in the United States in the last two centuries. In the period between 1820 and 1860, parents were guided by moralistic, religious considerations, and no one doubted that to spare the rod was to spoil the child. Mothers were advised to breast feed (or hire a wet nurse), wean quickly (at about one year), and feed on demand. Children were dressed in many layers of warm clothing. Early toilet training

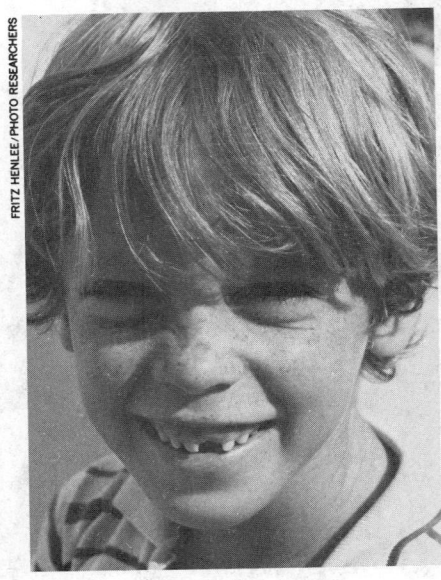

was seen as ideal, and enormous attention was given to the timing and frequency of bowel movements. Neatness and cleanliness were viewed as moral imperatives.

By the 1940's, mothers were advised to bottle feed infants, keep them on a rigid feeding schedule, and delay toilet training until the child was ready to cooperate. Today the emphasis is once again on breast feeding at the infant's demand and looser and lighter clothes are in vogue; the jury is still out on the best time for toilet training.

Some things, however, do not change. We know that parents transmit to their children the attitudes and skills necessary for success in their own society. We also know that such attitudes are delivered within the framework of a genetic timeclock; that is, we cannot teach a child something before he is developmentally prepared to learn it.

All infants in all cultures are born helpless and dependent on adults. Despite the influence of parents and society, there seems to be a genetic predisposition of babies in all cultures to achieve certain goals (for example, walking, talking, and toilet training) at roughly the same time. There are, of course, areas in which societal customs do have importance. These may be important for success within that society and are not universal.

Theories of Development

In the early part of the 1800's, child development became the subject of scientific study. Before that, religion and philosophy had been the two major influences on methods and styles of child rearing.

Philosophers. One school of thought, represented by the English philosopher John Locke, held that all knowledge is acquired from experience. The child was seen as a blank slate upon which all experiences could be written. If this were the case, then controlling the conditions under which the child was raised would lead to predictable results.

Such beliefs gave little weight to the child's inborn predisposition to become or do certain things. At the same time, they correctly recognized the role of cause and effect in the child's development.

MINIATURE ADULT: *in the 1880's children were dressed and treated as if they were small grownups.*

The German philosopher Immanuel Kant represented a school that believed that there are categories of thinking that do not come from experience. In this view, the infant is believed to have an inborn capacity to organize experience and information.

Observational method. Both philosophical schools came under scrutiny during the 1800's, when attempts were made to study the way in which children develop. Theorists focused attention on the child as a discrete entity rather than as a miniature adult. One impetus for this study was the theory of evolution as proposed by Charles Darwin. Psychologists became interested in the possible parallels between the development of children and that of animals. They compared stages of behavior and certain behaviors that encouraged survival.

Darwin's theory, with its focus on change, brought scientific study out of the laboratory and into the natural environment of its subjects. If animals could be studied by careful observation, it seemed logical that children could be studied in the same manner. Thus, the naturalistic—or observational—approach to studying children was developed.

 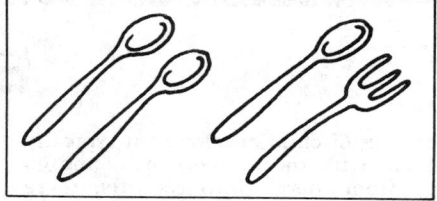

INTELLIGENCE TESTING *of young children tests their understanding of such concepts as "sameness"* (left) *and "difference"* (right).

Mental testing.

At approximately the same time there was an increasing interest in education in the Western world. The widening educational opportunities for greater numbers of children brought increased interest in the kind of education that would be appropriate for different children. The methods of selecting children for continued education had been haphazard and subjective. The desire to develop scientific criteria for evaluating students led to mental testing, a tradition that is still strong in educational circles today.

In France, Alfred Binet, a psychologist, was asked by officials of the Paris school system to devise a test that would screen out those unsuitable for further education. With Théodore Simon he developed a test that claimed to measure capacity to learn rather than present knowledge. This test, which was the first IQ (intelligence quotient) or mental-age test, was revolutionary in that it attempted to predict future performance.

In Germany Wilhelm Wundt was examining the senses as measures of intelligence. Although this method was highly controversial, it, too, had the aim of predicting behavior or development by establishing norms and measuring individual performance against them. This normative approach is one of the dominant themes of developmental psychology today. We use it even in informal assessment, as when we predict that an infant will learn to walk sometime around his first birthday.

Parents use normative standards when comparing a child with his brothers and sisters, or with the other children in the playground. The psychologist, however, uses it in a more rigid fashion, deriving statistical inferences about normal behavior, and at the same time allowing for individual variation. This last point is critical. No matter how carefully we compile data on normal development, there is *always* individual variation, and this must be allowed for within given limits. Not all babies walk at exactly a year, and the child who walks earlier as well as the child who walks later may both be considered normal.

Psychoanalytical theory.

At this point we must briefly consider the influence of psychoanalytical thought developed by Sigmund Freud.

The Freudian viewpoint, which was formulated in Austria during the late 19th and early 20th centuries, has provoked more passionate debate than any other theory of personality to date.

Freud believed that the human being is confronted by internal conflicts that must be resolved. These conflicts are between such primal forces as life and death, love and hate, and creativity and destructiveness. Freud related all development to the resolution (or lack of resolution) of such early internal conflicts.

What made Freudian theory so controversial was its insistence on the presence of such conflicts, including sexual ones, in childhood. Further, Freud saw the infant as a somewhat passive receiver of adult actions. Such a theory puts a tremendous burden on parents, who must judge their every action according to the emotional effect it might have on the growing child. Many parents who have some knowledge of Freudian theory have come to believe that the way to avoid future neuroses is to avoid imposing too many strictures on the child. From this concern comes the so-called permissive school of child rearing.

Interactive approach.

Perhaps the most useful method for parents to adopt is the interactive approach. In this theory, we see the infant as having some innate ability to organize experience. This ability, however, must be stimulated by experience. In this view, parents or caretakers play a vital role in the development of the child, for they provide the experiences that activate the child's physical, social, intellectual, and emotional development. Within this framework, one would also recognize the potential damage that might be caused by neglect.

In the end, a parent can never be guided completely by the experts. What is best for baby is probably what instinctively feels best and most suitable to the parents. When parents are comfortable, the infant will most likely respond to that comfort.

DOCTOR SPOCK

Originally published in 1946 as *The Common Sense Book of Baby and Child Care*, Dr. Benjamin Spock's baby book has sold 25 million copies, more than any book (except the Bible) in U.S. history.

In the 1940's, Spock advised parents to relax the tightly scheduled approach to childraising: his ideas seemed revolutionary at the time. He advocated considering each child as an individual whose needs are different from those of other children. His advice was important in the growth of a more relaxed—yet more child-centered—approach to children.

The fifth edition of *Baby and Child Care*, published in 1985, was revised to include topics such as single parenting. Spock himself had become a controversial figure for his activities opposing the war in Vietnam, but his book continued to be the most used manual for baby care. As its first title made clear, Dr. Spock was a firm believer in common sense, and millions of parents continued to rely on his calm, reasonable advice.

Expecting a Child

Studies of child development typically begin with the newborn baby and go on from there. Until recently, there was very little time or money devoted to the study of the fetus in the approximately 38 weeks from conception to birth. New technology—ranging from microsurgery in the uterus to ultrasound testing—has provided scientists and parents with a new awareness of the development of the fetus in the nine months before delivery.

Prenatal Development

Conception is the fertilization of an egg by a sperm. For the first two weeks of cell division following fertilization, there is little differentiation between the kinds of cells produced. After this remarkably short period, however, the embryo begins to develop clearly differentiated kinds of cells and primitive structures that will become the heart, veins, brain, kidney, liver, and digestive tract. Although the embryo is less than an inch long, it has begun to develop into a distinct human being.

During the rapid growth that follows, the embryo begins to take on the external configurations of a human baby, and by about 16 weeks it resembles a human baby of about six or seven inches in length. At about this time the fetus, as the embryo is now called, begins to move within the uterus, and such movement is perceptible to the mother.

Throughout the rest of the course of a pregnancy, the fetus grows both in size and complexity. Although the basic organic structure develops in the first few weeks, the internal organs now grow and prepare for the functions they will assume after birth. From the third month of pregnancy, the fetus exhibits primitive reflexes; by the end of the fifth month it can make grasping gestures, blink, suck, and swallow.

A fetus younger than about 24 weeks is generally not considered viable; that is, the fetus at that stage of development is unlikely to survive outside the uterus despite the most sophisticated medical care.

The question of when the fetus becomes a psychologically functional being has been hotly debated in recent years, but no definitive answers have been put forth. It is incontrovertible that biological life begins at the moment of conception, but the quality of that life is open to debate. Is the fragile, rapidly expanding cluster of cells a human being? Or is the fetus only hu-

REATHER/PHOTO RESEARCHERS

DO'S AND DON'TS OF PREGNANCY *change over the years. Today most doctors recommend continuing work and other normal activities up to the last few weeks. At the same time, concern for the effect of drugs, alcohol, tobacco, and other substances has greatly increased.*

FREDA LEINWAND/MONKMEYER

DURING PREGNANCY

Don't smoke. It's bad for you and bad for the baby. Ask your doctor for help in quitting.
Watch out for "junk food." Candy, soda, chips, and sweets have little that's good for you or the baby.
Don't drink alcohol. Even a drink a day might harm the baby. Get help from your doctor if you need it.
Don't take drugs or medication—not even aspirin—without asking your doctor.
Avoid caffeine. It's in coffee, tea, chocolate, and cola—and it might be bad for the baby.
Don't forget to tell every doctor or dentist who wants to x-ray you that you're pregnant. Then they can decide whether to go ahead.
Keep all your clinic or doctor's appointments. You need regular checkups.
Start eating right. Eat lots of fresh vegetables, fruits, and meat. Drink lots of milk, water, and juice.
Get plenty of rest.

man at such time as it begins to move in the mother's body? Or does the fetus become human when it has developed enough to survive outside of the uterus? Or is it only possible to talk about a human after the baby has been born?

Such questions are not merely theoretical, for they are at the heart of issues such as abortion, *in utero* surgery, genetic planning, amniocentesis, and the morality of using extraordinary life-saving measures.

Health of mother. What is less debatable is the influence of the fetal environment on the developing child. A mounting body of evidence exists to prove that the physical condition of the mother during pregnancy plays a critical role in the well-being of the baby.

We know that mothers who are malnourished are more likely to have babies who are smaller, more often malformed, and more vulnerable to disease than normal babies. In addi-

tion to these obvious disabilities, there is also evidence that children of malnourished mothers are more likely to develop learning disabilities. This is true even if a previously malnourished mother receives an adequate diet during pregnancy.

Other high risk factors in fetal development are excessive smoking or drinking, exposure to x-rays, narcotic addiction, and the use of many legal drugs. In fact, the safest course during the prenatal period is to avoid any drugs (even aspirin) unless specifically recommended by a physician for use during pregnancy.

The fetus can also be affected by many viral infections to the mother. This is especially true during the first twelve weeks of pregnancy, when the fetus is most at risk. Women who believe they may be pregnant should also avoid inoculations against viral diseases, such as rubella and measles, since the inoculations may be implicated in birth defects.

While we learn more and more about environmental factors that may affect the fetus, we know very little about how the mother's emotional state bears on the developing infant. There is some evidence, however, that severe anxiety, anger, or grief may be harmful.

Genetic factors.

We know that in the normal fetus each cell contains 23 pairs of chromosomes. One set of 23 comes from the father; the other set from the mother. These chromosomes contain the instructions that will determine the baby's genetic makeup. For example, chromosomes determine whether the fetus is male or female, the color of its eyes and hair, and a wide variety of other physical and emotional conditions.

Abnormalities in the chromosomes may result in any of a series of so-called genetic diseases. Best known among these are Down's syndrome (mongolism), cystic fibrosis, and muscular dystrophy. In the last decades, a test to determine whether an infant is afflicted by some of these illnesses has been developed. The test, known as amniocentesis, involves removing some of the fluid surrounding the fetus (amniotic fluid) from the mother, and then culturing the material in a laboratory. The test is generally used in mothers who are at high risk for Down's syndrome. If the test indicates that the baby will be afflicted, the mother may opt for a therapeutic abortion.

Despite all of these potential problems, the vast majority of infants are born healthy and able to cope with their new environment. On the whole, nature takes very good care of the unborn child. The best advice for the expectant mother is to avoid known or potential risks to the baby and to put herself in the care of a qualified physician early in her pregnancy.

Birth

In recent years, a great deal of attention has been given to birth. Perhaps the most important emphasis has been on making delivery as safe for both child and mother as possible. Another important concern has been the training of expectant mothers, to let them know what to expect during labor and to teach them to cooperate throughout the labor and birth process.

In the 1940's and '50's, most mothers were given a general anesthetic before the last stages of labor. They remembered nothing of the birth itself and awakened to their new baby. More recently, doctors have voiced several objections to the indiscriminate use of anesthetics. The most serious is the danger it poses for the baby. Any medication in the mother's bloodstream before birth soon passes into the baby's bloodstream as well. In some cases, the depressant effects of the anesthetic can cause a child to be born half unconscious and not able to breathe for itself. Heavy anesthesia also reduces the cooperation the mother can give in the birth process and may reduce the strength and effectiveness of the muscular contractions that push the baby out into the world.

In recent years, anesthesia has been used more sparingly (although it is still available and can be of great assistance in difficult cases). Many expectant mothers attend prenatal training classes in "natural childbirth." They learn how to cooperate during the birth process and are thoroughly advised on the stages of labor. Many women trained in this way are able to give birth with little or no medication. The experience of being awake and alert at the moment of birth more than makes up for the exertion and pain of the delivery itself.

Still another recent concern has been the effect of birth on the child. If (as we now suspect) the unborn infant is conscious and has feelings, birth must be the first great shock of life. The difficulty of passing through the birth canal leaves many babies bruised and exhausted. In addition, they are leaving a snug, thoroughly controlled environment for the uncertainties of the outside world. We can only speculate on what effect noises, bright lights, and cold air have on the newborn.

Some physicians have suggested that delivery might better be accomplished without the bright lights of the conventional delivery room. Other practitioners advocate delivery at home rather than in a hospital in cases where a normal delivery is expected. There are hazards to home deliveries—if a medical crisis develops, help is not close at hand. But it is true that a normal delivery can be accomplished at home if preparations have been made beforehand.

One ingredient of many natural childbirth programs has been the participation of the father. Rather than waiting nervously and helplessly in a hospital waiting room, he has been encouraged to learn about the process of childbirth and to be present at the delivery, both to help his wife and to share the excitement of the birth of their daughter or son.

Some doctors and hospitals are more sympathetic to natural childbirth than others. Parents who wish to use such methods should inquire well before the delivery date about training sessions and about hospital policies. They should also remain flexible; if there are complications during labor, natural childbirth may not be possible. The physician may prescribe anesthesia in such cases or may decide on delivery by Caesarean section. When complications arise, modern medical facilities and procedures are most welcome to protect the health of both child and mother. Parents should not feel they have failed in any way if such procedures are necessary.

The moment of birth seems one of great importance to expectant parents and is often the goal toward which they have aimed for weeks or months. Yet the moment of birth is much more a beginning than an ending, as all new parents soon discover.

NATURAL CHILDBIRTH *training often enlists the prospective father. Here, a woman does breathing exercises to prepare for childbirth with her husband's coaching.*

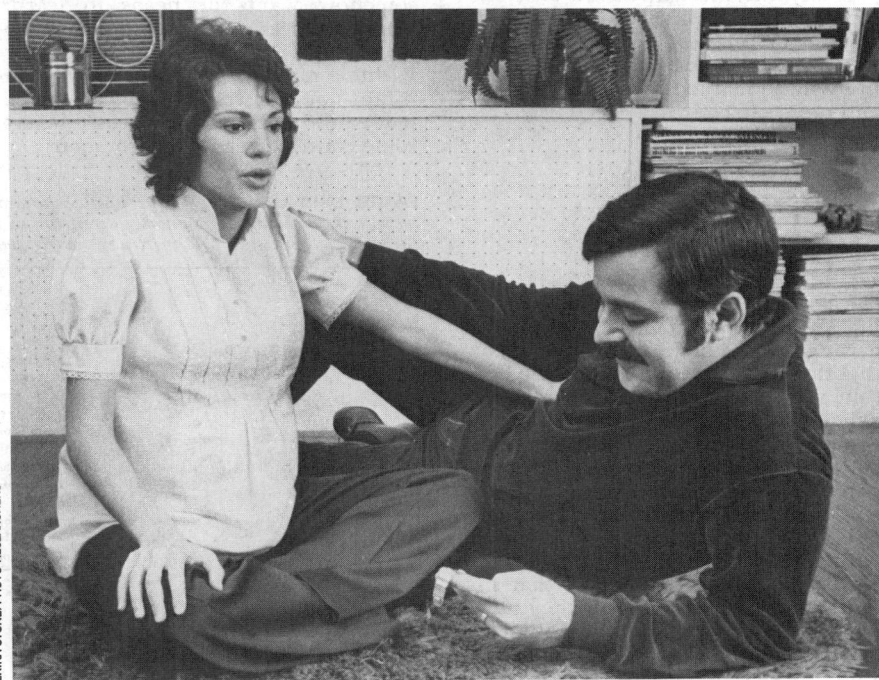

ERIKA STONE/PHOTO RESEARCHERS

The First Two Years

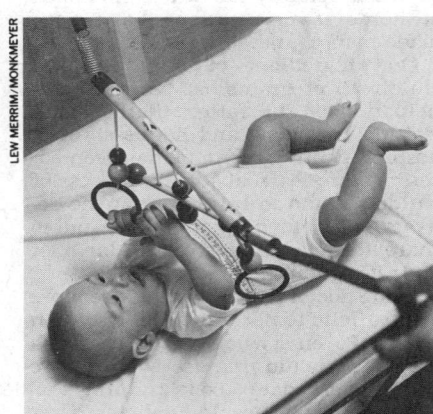

GRASPING *is one of the first tasks a baby masters.*

Anyone who says that infants are boring has not spent much time observing them. The popular idea that a newborn merely eats and sleeps ignores the complex and rapid development that is taking place.

The normal infant enters the world with its senses intact: it can see, hear, taste, feel, and smell. These senses are not fully developed, but they are present from the beginning. The baby also can move. Its bones, muscles, and nervous system are already formed and ready for use. Its task during the early weeks and months is to learn to coordinate its sensory and motor (movement) abilities, to learn to use the equipment it has effectively. This is probably the most awesome task one faces in life. Consider the tremendous amount of progress a child makes in its first year. No other period in all of life will be marked by such enormous and rapid changes.

Sensory Development

Not so long ago it was believed that the sensory development of the newborn was minimal. Today we know that the baby can see virtually the first time it opens its eyes, and there is evidence that it even has some depth perception. This means that a newborn baby can locate objects in space. Experiments have shown that infants will turn their heads and move their eyes in the direction of a loud sound within the first minutes after birth. Mothers have always known that infants respond to touch, but they have not always known that the baby can discriminate between bitter, sour, and sweet tastes. Babies will also turn

away from an unpleasant odor soon after birth.

These sensory mechanisms are the newborn baby's means of exploring the world. Different theorists have different explanations for how or why an infant responds to a stimulus.

In an experiment conducted by Robert Fantz, infants from the age of two months were shown pictures of a yellow disk, a white disk, a red disk, a bull's eye, a circle with newsprint, and a human face. The time the infants spent staring at each picture was carefully measured. It was soon determined that the babies responded most to a human face.

The babies fixed their gaze on the areas of highest black and white contrast. The youngest subjects concentrated on the hairline. Those several weeks older began to focus on the eyes. Other experiments showed that the infants were more interested in patterns than solid colors, and that they devoted more time to complex patterns than to simple ones.

Similarly, infants respond more to tones within the register of human speech. In fact, they are most responsive to high-pitched tones in the female speech register. The common gooing and babbling that adults use to "communicate" with a baby seem to correspond to the things the baby is really "interested in."

Some say the newborn responds to stimuli because it has been conditioned by the parents to do so. Others suggest the baby responds because it somehow wants or needs to learn. These theories are too complicated to debate here. Yet there is no doubt that within a matter of weeks or months an infant not only responds to the things it sees and hears but it learns to exert some control over its environment.

One fascinating question is how a baby chooses between the virtually overwhelming variety of stimuli the environment offers. If it responded equally and continuously to all stimuli, it would soon be overwhelmed. It appears that the infant becomes habituated to a given stimulus when it has been present for a long time; the child studies a new stimulus, responds to it, and then (if it continues) tunes it out. As soon as a change is made in the stimulus, even a minor one, the infant responds once again.

In one experiment, a group of infants was presented with a strong-smelling mixture of chemicals. At first they responded strongly to the smell. Gradually, however, they began to ignore the odor. Then the concentration of chemicals was reduced. Once again the infants responded to the odor. Apparently, this slight change (even in a negative direction) was enough to re-awaken their interest. Thus we can assume that infants are quite sensitive even to small changes in their environment. This sensitivity probably extends beyond the simple realm of sight, smell, and touch. Infants often seem able (perhaps through a combination of sensory clues) to sense the emotional climate around them. They may become fussy when mother is nervous or upset, for example. Parents are often not aware how sensitive a small baby can be.

Infants do not always wait for outside stimulus. Studies have shown that they actively seek experience. In one such study, two- and three-month-old infants were presented with a visual display that was controlled by a pacifier. By sucking at different rates the babies could control the focus of the picture. They soon learned to keep the pictures in focus.

FANTZ EXPERIMENT: *Robert Fantz showed discs like these to infants and recorded their responses, showing their greater attention to complex patterns, especially those that resembled faces. They focus on the hairline in early weeks; later they pick out the eyes.*

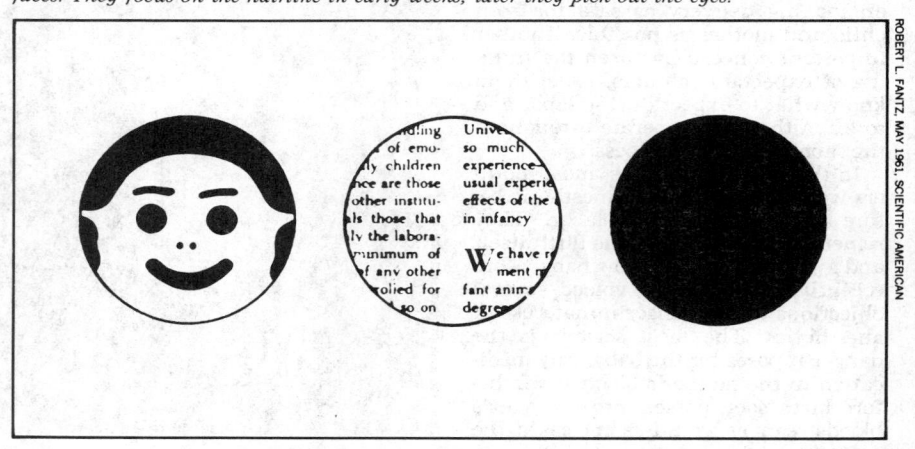

In another experiment, infants learned to turn on a motorized mobile by a specific sequence of arm and leg movements. When the correct sequence was changed, they soon learned the new sequence as well.

This is powerful evidence that babies are engaged in an active effort to make sense out of—and to exert control over—their environment. They seem to be self-motivated to solve problems and gain pleasure from a successful outcome.

Motor Development

It is hard to separate sensory development from motor development, since the two are closely connected. The baby relies on the senses for information. He then uses this information to help control his movements. For example, consider the infant grasping at an object. In order for him to reach for an object, he must first locate it in space, usually by seeing it. The first motor control needed is in the eyes: the muscles must be trained to focus on the object. Eventually the child begins to reach for the object with his hand, using a new set of muscles to touch or take hold of the object. This seemingly simple action is really an enormously complicated achievement, a coordination of sensing, elementary reasoning, and movement. Soon the child improves even on that skill, becoming able to anticipate where in space the object will be, and to reach for it in that location.

Blind babies do not develop reaching skills in the same manner as sighted infants. Not surprisingly, blind babies learn to reach and grasp objects later than their sighted counterparts, and they do so by relying on their other senses for information.

It may seem that a newborn's motor skills are totally undeveloped. But almost from birth, the baby is able to control its limbs and can move them in order to maintain balance. The infant is often able to place a finger or hand in the mouth in order to gratify the desire to suck, and is also able to imitate an adult's facial movements using eyelids, tongue, and mouth. Of course, these early efforts are not well coordinated, but within a matter of months the child integrates these movements and learns to turn over, to sit, to crawl, and to stand.

Infants follow a predictable sequence in the development of motor skills. The pattern is quite orderly, yet there is room for considerable individual difference. The developmental chart on this page shows the usual pattern and the ages at which an average infant first develops certain skills. It is important to note that every baby is different and that minor differences

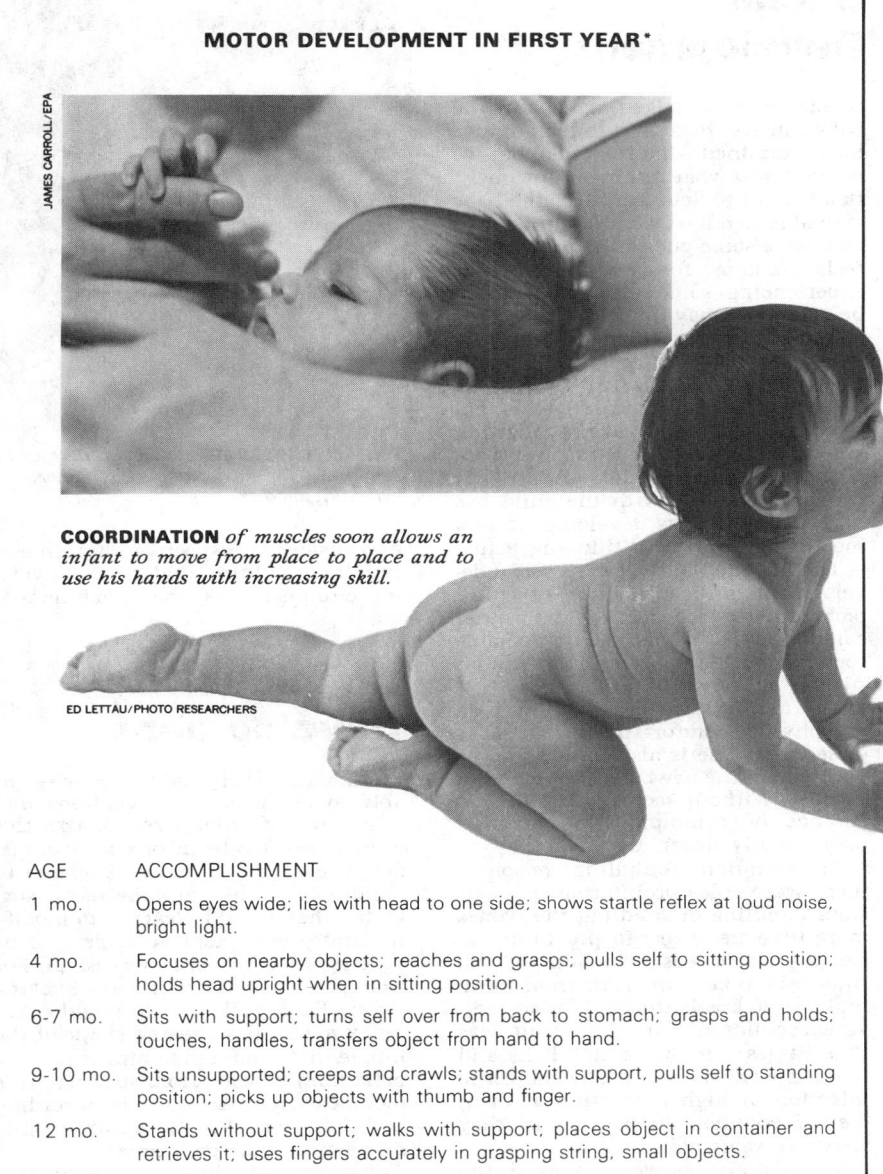

MOTOR DEVELOPMENT IN FIRST YEAR *

JAMES CARROLL/EPA

COORDINATION of muscles soon allows an infant to move from place to place and to use his hands with increasing skill.

ED LETTAU/PHOTO RESEARCHERS

AGE	ACCOMPLISHMENT
1 mo.	Opens eyes wide; lies with head to one side; shows startle reflex at loud noise, bright light.
4 mo.	Focuses on nearby objects; reaches and grasps; pulls self to sitting position; holds head upright when in sitting position.
6-7 mo.	Sits with support; turns self over from back to stomach; grasps and holds; touches, handles, transfers object from hand to hand.
9-10 mo.	Sits unsupported; creeps and crawls; stands with support, pulls self to standing position; picks up objects with thumb and finger.
12 mo.	Stands without support; walks with support; places object in container and retrieves it; uses fingers accurately in grasping string, small objects.

* Based on studies of Arnold Gesell, et al. A given child may learn somewhat earlier or later and in slightly different order.

both in sequence and in age are to be expected.

Among the landmark stages in an infant's motor development are the ability to roll from stomach to back, to sit unsupported, to crawl, to stand, and to walk. These developments usually occur within the first 15 months after birth. It is important to note that premature babies do not have a developmental age equal to their chronological age. For instance, when a child born two months premature is six months old, he will have a developmental age of about four months.

Many parents are so eager for their babies to learn to sit, stand, walk, and crawl, that they try to teach the baby these skills. There is perhaps no harm in being helpful, but these skills are largely unteachable. The infant needs

the opportunity to practice the skills, but given normal opportunities, the child will learn with no instruction.

In one study, researchers attempted to teach one identical twin to climb steps and gave no help to the other. Both twins were later allowed to play on the steps. Both twins achieved mastery over the steps at about the same time. The twin who had been "taught" seemed to have no advantage. The results would be different, of course, if the uninstructed twin were never allowed to explore the steps.

In practical terms, studies of this kind suggest that a parent should provide a child with opportunities to practice and perfect new skills, but need not feel responsible for teaching the skills to them. When the child is ready to walk, he will walk.

Social Development

So far, we have talked about how the baby can see, hear, and touch, and we have examined what it can do, but we do not know what it thinks. Obviously, this is hard to determine, for the baby is unable to tell us what he thinks. We can make some guesses about what he feels. We know, for example, that he is experiencing some discomfort when he cries. We may not know the cause of the discomfort—hunger, pain, exhaustion—but we recognize the distress signal. Similarly, sounds of cooing and gurgling indicate to us that the baby is content. Again, we may not know exactly why this is so, but we are receiving the message. This early "communication" with the child has to do both with its development as a social being and as a thinking being.

The first step in the baby's social development is the formation of an attachment to its mother (or other caretaker). How this occurs remains something of a mystery, but studies suggest its universal importance.

The mother provides not only food and physical comfort, but a basic sense of security. She is also the first being with whom the newborn baby communicates. Without security and the assurance of communication, a baby may literally sicken and die.

In Victorian foundling hospitals there were rules prohibiting the staff from handling or fondling the babies more than necessary in providing basic physical needs. The aim of the rules was to keep the staff from forming hard-to-break attachments to individual children. But the result was that babies who were not held and fondled seemed unnaturally subject to infection. A high proportion of them died of common diseases before they were two years old.

When the rules were changed, the mortality rate dropped sharply. Just how the physical handling of the infants increased their resistance to disease is not known. But the connection is clear.

In a more recent experiment, Harry Harlow demonstrated that infant monkeys could become attached to unresponsive terry cloth dummies which served as surrogate mothers by providing food. The monkeys seemed to thrive physically. But when they grew up they exhibited bizarre behavior and were not able to become normal monkey parents. This suggests that the responses of a mother to an infant are somehow of crucial importance to its emotional health and growth.

This attachment—the beginning of a child's social and cognitive life—involves both child and mother. Complex as it seems to researchers, it may be quite simple on an instinctive level. Neither baby nor mother "learns" to

ANIMAL EXPERIMENTS *suggest that an infant looks for food and softness even in a substitute mother.*

play his or her respective roles. In every human culture, under widely varying circumstances, the attachment is made.

Cognitive Development

From a very early age the baby seems able to organize its perceptions into some kind of order, even though this order may often be incorrect. Jean Piaget, one of the foremost students of children's thinking processes, suggested that a child "learns" to modify its strategies to achieve some goal by judging what action is successful. For example, every newborn has a sucking reflex. Each will have to modify that reflex to suit the size and shape of the nipple that is offered to him to provide maximum benefits from sucking. This modification of strategies is, according to Piaget, central to the child's gaining mastery over the environment.

Piaget based a great deal of his theory on the observation of his own children, and his detailed observations helped to explain what was seemingly mysterious behavior. Piaget noted that infants between four and eight months will not search for an item when it is removed from their view, even when they see where it is being hidden. At about eight months children begin to search for an item that is taken out of view. Piaget took this to mean that the younger child lacks the concept of object permanence. That is, the child does not understand that things continue to exist, even when out of sight. The older child has demonstrated a belief in the continued existence of the object, and will act on this belief by searching for that object. This is a major intellectual development, for one cannot make full sense out of the world until it is understood that objects have an existence of their own, independent of the observer.

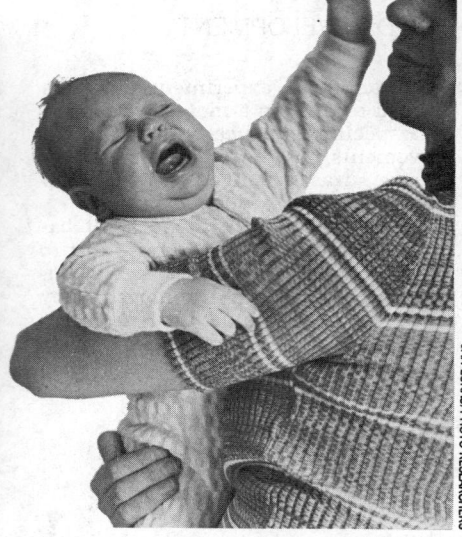

CRYING *is the baby's first means of communication, expressing pain, fear, or anger.*

Language. It is really impossible to talk about cognitive development without mentioning the beginnings of language. Language is a system of communication with rules shared by the participants. Language is both receptive and expressive—that is, it consists of both understanding what others say to us (receptive) and attempting to communicate with others (expressive). Language is, thus, more than just speech. It can be written or gestural. Sign language is not speech, but it is language. When speaking of language development, however, we often mean the development of communication through speech.

Although most children do not begin to speak during the first year of life, the roots of language go at least to early infancy, and some authorities believe that the structure of language is inborn. The ability to communicate starts with a baby's crying. This most primitive signal alerts the parent to the child's need. Researchers have discovered three distinct patterns of crying—rhythmic crying, angry crying, and painful crying. Each of these communicates a different need. By three months, normal babies are producing gurgles and coos, and by six months nonsense syllables and babbling. All babies in all societies appear able to make the sounds that are heard in all languages. By the time actual speech begins, however, a baby has confined himself more or less to the sounds of the language(s) spoken around him. Babbling often imitates the inflection and phrasing of the language the child hears.

The baby also learns to communicate by gesture. An outstretched hand generally means "give me" and repeated banging is a way of saying "pay attention to me." At about the age of one year, the first one-syllable words begin to appear. Most frequently—and this is true in a variety of languages—the earliest words are some variation on *ma* and *da*. It is not clear that the baby means to indicate his parents by these sounds. Possibly they are babble syllables to which adults attach the desired meaning. What is certain is that the baby eventually comes to understand that these sounds represent the parents. Thus begins spoken language.

By about 18 months, most children utter a number of single words. These words are called holophrases because linguists believe that they may indicate something more than the name of the object. For example, when a baby says the word cookie, the meaning may be "That is a cookie," or "Give me a cookie," or "Where is the cookie?" or "Is that a cookie?" Interpretation of the word is routinely made by the caretakers, who often try out different possibilities until hitting on the right explanation. Holophrases give way to two-word phrases around the second year, and at this point interpretation becomes somewhat easier. It must be pointed out here that language skills, like motor skills, are acquired at different rates by different children. Receptive language precedes speech, and many children with excellent receptive language are still delayed in speaking.

Practical Considerations

We have dealt with the physical and cognitive development of the child during the first two years, but we have not yet given much attention to the practical situations in which parents must deal with their baby's daily demands. It seems that there are four major areas of concern: food, sleep, socialization, and health and safety.

Feeding. As has been suggested earlier, styles of feeding vary from culture to culture and from generation to generation. One thing that does not change is the biological process that enables a mother to feed her baby. In virtually all cases, the mother who chooses to breast feed is able to keep her baby adequately nourished using the breast milk she produces.

Breast feeding. Breast feeding has certain advantages for both mother and child. Breast milk is believed to be the ideal nutritional food for the infant, and it carries with it the transfer of some natural immunities from the mother. Additionally, the act of nursing is believed to aid the mother's uterus in contracting back to its normal size. Finally, many professionals believe that nursing provides the best environment for the formation of an attachment between the mother and child, and is, in the bargain, an inexpensive and trouble-free method of providing the baby with optimum nutrition (no mixing, no sterilizing).

Clearly, however, not all mothers can—or choose to—breast feed. Working mothers, women on medication, and mothers of hospitalized babies cannot always be on hand to breast feed. Are they really harming their babies? While there are strong advocates for the superiority of breast feeding, the general opinion seems to be that properly prepared formulas provide an excellent substitute for breast milk. Moreover, the mother who holds and caresses her baby during a bottle feeding is likely to form an equally good attachment as the woman who breast feeds. There is no good evidence for the early psychoanalytic view that breast feeding is the *only* way to assure the baby's well-being. What now seems evident is that infants have a great deal of flexibility and can adapt to either style of feeding, as long as the mother is comfortable with it.

If you breast feed, it is important that you not feel pressured to succeed. Breast milk takes a few days to become plentiful. The baby rarely needs a supplementary feeding in the first few days of life. Remember that the baby is as inexperienced as you are. Not all babies feed voraciously at the start. Many need time to adjust to the complexities of fitting the nipple in the mouth, sucking vigorously, swallowing properly, and all the time continuing to breathe. These are complex tasks, and many an infant needs a patient mother while learning them. The first two or three days of life, during which the mother has little milk and the baby has little need of nourishment, are a good time to introduce the baby to the breast. It is almost as if nature has provided a practice period before the serious work begins. Once the baby is accustomed to the breast, the length of nursing time should be lengthened gradually.

Schedules. Determining a feeding schedule is a very individual matter, one which depends on both the temperament of the baby and the schedule of the mother. Some mothers prefer to let the baby nurse whenever it desires. Others find fewer but longer sessions desirable. This is a matter that should be discussed with a pediatrician, who can offer guidelines for the most effective nursing methods.

Whether to allow the baby to nurse from one breast or both at a given feeding is a matter of both preference and amount of milk. Some mothers find that the milk of one breast is sufficient for each feeding. If you choose this method, remember to alternate breasts at each feeding. If your baby appears to be hungry after emptying one breast, it is all right to offer the other breast. Again, one should alternate which breast is offered first.

If the baby cries after or between feedings, do not jump to the conclusion that it is hungry. Crying is not always a sign of hunger. Some babies are naturally fretful at certain times of day; others are irritable or colicky, and although continued feeding seems to pacify them for the moment, they will resume crying when feeding stops. This is a situation to discuss with your doctor.

The nursing mother can lead a normal life, but special attention should be paid to her diet. She should avoid hard-to-digest, "gassy" foods, for these seem to upset many babies. During nursing, the mother should avoid drugs and should consult with her doctor about nursing when drugs must be taken. Since the baby depletes the mother's calcium supply, it is especially important for the mother to eat foods—especially milk products—that are rich in calcium. Her diet should also include fresh fruits and vegetables, grain products, and high-protein foods such as meat, poultry, and eggs. The doctor may prescribe supplementary vitamins. Stringent dieting for weight loss while nursing should be avoided unless under the supervision of a doctor. Many mothers find the La Leche League a valuable source of advice on nursing.

Weaning. Weaning the baby from the breast should be done gradually. A baby is usually weaned from the breast to a cup, but there are times when a baby must be weaned from the breast to a bottle. This might occur if the mother develops a serious illness or must change her schedule and is no longer available for feedings. This is generally done by omitting one breast feeding per day and substituting a bottle at that time. After a few days, if the baby takes the bottle willingly, another breast feeding may be eliminated. Continue on this schedule until the baby is comfortable and the breast milk has diminished. If the mother is uncomfortable, she can express the milk manually or with a breast pump until the supply diminishes. Some babies balk when a bottle is first introduced. Do not be discouraged, however, for when the baby is hungry enough, he will accept the bottle.

Weaning a baby to a cup often takes place during the latter part of the first year. Once the baby sits in a high chair, a cup can be introduced. Use only a small amount of milk at a time, since young babies lack the coordination to swallow more than a tiny amount. Some babies seem to have little need for continued sucking, and are content to take nourishment from a cup. Others miss the gratification of sucking, and resist the cup. It is wise to take your cue from the baby. In some instances it may be better to defer weaning. In others, the substitution of a pacifier will give the baby additional sucking time, and milk can be offered from a cup.

Bottle feeding. If you choose to bottle feed your baby, you will find many kinds of formula available. Usually the baby is started on formula while in the hospital. If he is thriving on this formula, it is wise to continue with the same brand. Formula is available in powdered form, in concentrate, and in ready-to-feed disposable bottles. Although the disposable bottles are the most convenient, they are also the most expensive, and many mothers choose to use them only when away from home. If you are mixing formula, be sure to put it into sterile bottles and keep it refrigerated. Most pediatricians advise that the heat of an automatic dishwasher is equivalent to that of sterilizing, so bottles that go through a dishwasher need not be sterilized again. Disposable bottles can be kept at room temperature when unopened, but once the baby has nursed from a bottle, it should be refrigerated if it is going to be reused.

Giving the baby a bottle is not difficult. The bottle may be fed cold, at room temperature, or warmed, but it should be the same at each feeding. If you prefer to warm the bottle, test the milk on your wrist before offering it to the baby to be certain that the milk is not too hot. The baby should be held in the arms while being bottle fed, with the head slightly elevated. The bottle is held at an angle, so that the nipple remains full of milk and air is not swallowed. Propping the bottle in the crib is not a good idea, except in emergency situations. Part of the feeding situation is the interaction between the baby and the caretaker. Experiments have shown that touching is a crucial part of nurturing, and an ideal time to provide such tactile stimulation is during feeding. By the time the baby is about six months old, he may choose to hold his own bottle or be ready to use a cup. If this is the case, then holding is no longer a necessary part of the feeding experience.

Solid foods. The question of when to introduce solid foods into the baby's diet has no easy answer. Some pediatricians believe that a baby who is thriving on breast milk or formula needs no additional foods for the first year. According to this philosophy, children are less likely to develop allergic food reactions when foods are introduced in the second year. Other doctors are equally strong in the belief that solid foods can be introduced during the third or fourth month. They argue that babies seem to like such foods as cereals and mashed fruits, are able to digest them well, and are less resistant to new foods if offered a variety during the first few months. Babies who always seem hungry are particularly good candidates for early feeding. Cereals are usually offered first, and can be introduced between regular feedings. Fruits and strained meats are usually added after cereals. Eggs are a potential problem—many babies are allergic to them, so they should be introduced slowly and not offered every day.

By about one year all babies should be able to manage some solid foods.

EATING WITH A SPOON *requires complex hand-eye coordination.*

The infant should, by this time, be on a schedule of approximately three meals per day, and the diet should begin to resemble that of an adult. A baby's breakfast, lunch, and dinner should be nutritionally balanced, and composed of foods of different textures. The baby can chew some foods that are lumpy; it is important to get him used to them. For example potatoes, bread, and pieces of soft, cooked vegetables are fine. On the other hand, some foods can cause a baby to choke and should be avoided during the first two years. These include nuts of all kinds, small hard candies, and crisp raw vegetables like carrots. The use of vitamin supplements should be discussed with the baby's doctor. Some doctors feel that a balanced diet provides more than enough vitamins; others believe that a supplement cannot hurt.

Babies should not be offered foods with large amounts of sugar or salt, or such food additives as monosodium glutamate. Until recently, prepared baby foods had uncommonly high amounts of these items. Manufacturers have reduced the amount of flavor enhancers, but many mothers prefer (both for nutritional and economic reasons) to cook baby's meals themselves. Almost any food that is prepared for the rest of the family can be pureed with the help of a blender or food processor.

Sleeping. A baby's sleeping habits can be an even greater source of anxiety to a family than his eating habits. The mother who is awakened every two hours through the night is unlikely to find feeding times as intimate and enjoyable as the mother who has enjoyed a good night's sleep. A tired baby is a cranky baby; so, too, a tired mother is a cranky mother. Poor sleep habits can cause a downward spiral in the relationship between mother and child.

One of the things we ought to define here is sleep, for it is not quite as distinct from wakefulness as might be imagined. For all humans there are two kinds of sleep—active (or REM) sleep and quiet (or non-REM) sleep. REM is an acronym for the rapid eye movement that occurs during one stage of sleep. Newborn infants appear to be in a state of REM sleep almost half of their total sleep time; at the end of three months REM sleep is only one-third of total sleep time. Adults have even less REM sleep. Although the purpose of REM sleep is not clearly understood by researchers, one theory suggests that it offers a form of self-stimulation.

As there are different forms of sleep, so there are also different types of wakefulness. Often a baby is awake but quiet and inactive; parents may not even know that he is awake. During active wakefulness, the baby's noises are more likely to attract attention; and the baby seems to know from a very early age to cry if it requires attention. Because they are not always aware that babies can be awake but quiet, many parents have concluded that the baby sleeps a great deal more of the time than it actually does.

What are normal sleeping patterns for a baby? One study shows that newborns sleep an average of 16 hours 20 minutes per day during the first few weeks. By the 16th week, the time has decreased to 14 hours 50 minutes. The duration of sleeping episodes changes, too. Newborns tend to sleep for short periods and waken for short periods. As they get older, the periods of sleep increase in length, as do the periods of wakefulness. There are great variations in normal sleeping patterns, however. Some babies thrive on relatively little sleep, and others seem to need a great deal of sleep.

Most babies work themselves into a schedule that demands feedings at intervals from three to four hours. The rest of the time they either sleep or remain alert, but not in need of attention. The periods between feedings grow longer between the third and the sixth month, and by the seventh month many are ready to give up a nighttime feeding and sleep through the night. Babies who are reluctant to give up this feeding might be encouraged to do so by the addition of cereal to the evening meal. This usually gives the baby enough food to get through the night without hunger.

If the baby continues to cry during the night after the sixth month, it is a good assumption that hunger is not the cause. The baby may be uncomfortable, or he may just have gotten used to being held at four-hour intervals. Some authorities believe that an infant should never be left to "cry it out," while others fear that holding the baby will reinforce the desire to waken at night. Which course a parent chooses depends on philosophy as well as logistics. If your baby shares a room with two older siblings, or if your neighbors are banging on the walls for quiet, it is pretty difficult to let the baby cry it out. If, on the other hand, you are convinced that the baby is becoming more and more fixed in a bad pattern, perhaps it is worth a night or two of screams with the goal of eventual nighttime peace. Halfway measures might include rocking the baby in a cradle or carriage, as some infants are soothed by motion. This is not, however, always a practical solution. The baby may remain quiet as long as the motion continues, only to resume crying once it stops. Many parents have had the experience of a cranky baby falling asleep in the car, only to find that the shrieks begin with renewed vigor when the car stops for a light.

By about six months or so, the baby should be on a schedule in which his daytime sleep is consolidated into a morning nap and an afternoon nap. By about 12 to 18 months, these naps generally merge into one long afternoon nap. While one cannot influence how much sleep the baby needs, one can shape the timing of it. If you want your baby fed and in bed by 7:00 p.m., do not let him nap too late in the afternoon. If, on the other hand, you prefer to have the baby awake in the evening when the whole family is home, move his nap time to later in the day. Such moves have to be made gradually and consistently. Most babies do not take well to a schedule that changes daily.

Socialization. While we do not think much about an infant's social life, babies are intensely social creatures. As the period of wakefulness increases, babies begin to explore both the things and the people around

them. Both physical development and increasingly expressive language are part of the emerging social structure. Most significantly, these new-found abilities are used in play. Play is a form of activity that usually produces pleasure, is largely uncontrolled by others, and allows the child to express thoughts that cannot always be expressed in other situations. In addition, play is a form of preparation for adulthood. This becomes obvious when children use play to practice activities not yet integrated into the child's daily routine. More than one mother has reported watching a recalcitrant two-year-old toilet train his favorite teddy bear.

Obviously, there are many different kinds of play, and not all of them are well understood. In a child under the age of two, most play is exploratory. An infant's play may take the form of exploring his feet or fingers, or reaching for a mobile, or rubbing a favorite animal against his nose.

A child of about six months indulges in a more sophisticated form of play. This child not only explores, but seems to reinvent some of the laws of physics. Many observant parents will attest to their young Newton's discovery of gravity—everything and anything will be dropped repeatedly from high chair, crib, or playpen with great delight. The child cries until the objects are returned, then repeats the performance. The child is, in fact, learning that things fall when dropped. At the same time, there is also a social side to the game—it requires another person to retrieve the object.

Children under the age of two usually socialize more with adults than with other children. They do, how-

ever, like to see and be with other children. The play between very young children has been called parallel play, in that the children seem to enjoy playing side by side, but rarely interact in any meaningful fashion. Very young children will examine one another visually and make tentative efforts at touching, but that is usually the extent of their social behavior.

On the other hand, children under the age of two do a great deal of socializing with parents and older siblings. Babies react with smiles and coos when familiar adults approach them, and many appear to look forward to ritual games that are played—peek-a-boo, and the like. Babies also appear to socialize with adults through language. They will play with words or phrases in a sort of primitive joke form. Also, many babies will listen raptly to a story being recited or told, and it is not unusual for them to want to hear the same story repeatedly. Listening to familiar words, whether fully comprehended or not, is a form of social interaction for the baby.

Health and safety. All newborn babies are routinely visited by a pediatrician in the hospital shortly after they are born. The pediatrician will recommend a schedule of visits and of inoculations for the infant, and this should be closely followed. It is now possible to provide protection for a child against almost all of the childhood diseases of a generation ago. Unless a physician advises against it (for example, in the case of very premature or highly allergic infants), the schedule in the following box should be maintained.

There are also some basic precautions that should be taken in the

OTHER PEOPLE—*especially brothers and sisters—become more interesting as a child grows older. Relations between children are important to growth.*

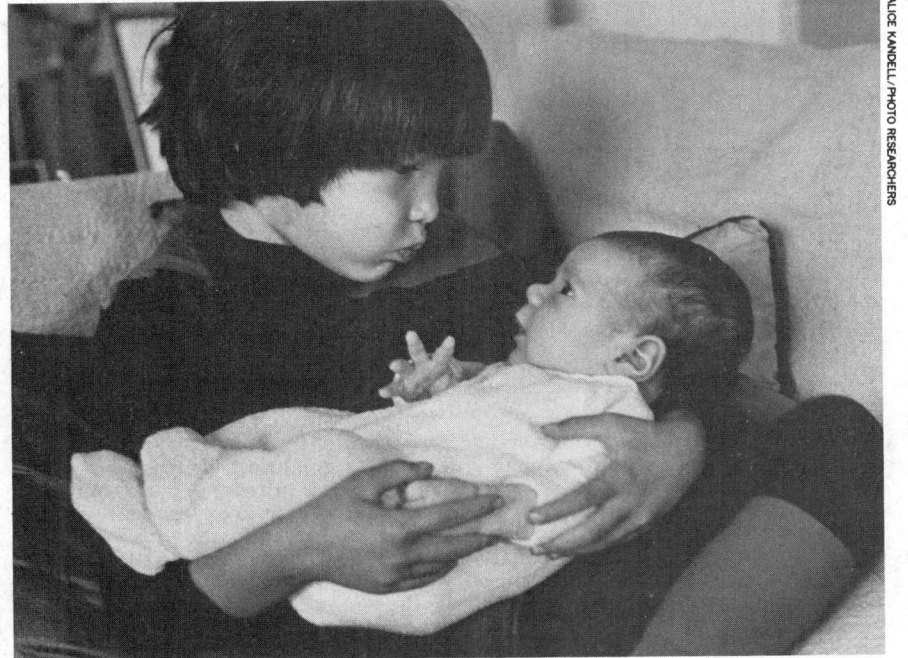

ALICE KANDELL/PHOTO RESEARCHERS

VACCINE SCHEDULE	
2 months	— DPT (diphtheria, pertussis, tetanus) shot
3 months	— oral polio
4 months	— DPT shot
5 months	— oral polio
6 months	— DPT
7 months	— oral polio
8-9 months	— tuberculin test blood test
15 months	— measles vaccine
18 months	— DPT booster polio booster
24 months	— mumps rubella (German measles) vaccine

Before entering school the child should receive an additional polio and DPT booster.

home. Although a newborn is unlikely to pose much of a safety hazard to himself, crawlers and toddlers can get themselves into very dangerous situations. The following rules should be observed:

- keep all medications in child-proof containers and out of the baby's reach
- remove all household cleansers and potentially toxic items from low cabinets; if this is impossible, install child-proof locks on such cabinets
- cover upper story windows (especially in apartment houses) with grates
- keep gates across open stairways
- cover electrical outlets or close them with plastic inserts
- keep matches out of the child's reach
- keep tools out of the child's reach

Remember that some young children are climbers, and merely putting an object on a shelf is not enough. Try to think of any potential for danger, and avoid it.

A final word on safety regards car trips with a child. Holding a baby on your lap is *extremely dangerous.* The safest place for a baby is in an approved car seat in the rear of the car.

SYBIL SHELTON/MONKMEYER

CURIOSITY CAN MEAN DANGER: *keep all medicines and dangerous substances, as well as objects small enough to swallow, secure from a toddler's reach.*

The seat should be properly installed and then secured with the auto's seat belt. A car bed is not an acceptable substitute. A child under six months should be kept in an infant seat. Once he is able to sit unsupported, a child safety seat may be used. No matter how uncomfortable a child may look, and no matter how much he protests, the car seat is the safest place.

The Preschool Child (Two to Five)

Children from the ages of two to five are especially endearing and especially exasperating. Their physical, social, and intellectual development is far enough advanced for them to participate in a variety of family experiences. At the same time, they remain maddeningly stubborn in their devotion to babyhood. It is as if the child were facing two ways at once—toward adulthood, and toward infancy.

Motor Skills

The two-year-old has mastered the basic motor skills: walking, running, climbing, and jumping. In the years between two and five he will refine these skills and become more adept at them. He will be able to combine such skills in order to ride a tricycle, hop, skip, and the like. By five, many children have enough motor coordination to swim, skate, or ride a bicycle. At the same time that the larger motor skills improve, the coordination between hand and eye movements becomes greater. This means that the child can learn to throw and catch, to bat a large ball, and do a multitude of tasks requiring visual judgment.

The smaller motor skills are also de-veloping during this period. The child learns how to control a pencil, to cut, and to do tasks that involve fine muscular control. In this instance, there appears to be a sex difference, for girls usually acquire small motor skills slightly earlier than boys.

The development of all motor skills continues throughout childhood, but in the preschool period we see an enormous amount of change.

Language

Volumes have been written about the development of language in the preschooler. The variety and complexity of expression is truly astounding. Language seems to almost explode from the toddler, with changes so rapid that even the most observant parent has trouble cataloging them. We left our two-year-old with two-word phrases; we return to find that only a few months later he is able to utter statements and ask questions in reasonably complete sentences. Grammar at this age is not well established, but the child does have a correct sense of word usage. Declarative sentences usually sound fine, but the structure of a question is often a statement with an in-flection on the end. The child may say, "The doll is broken?" rather than "Is the doll broken?"

The young toddler also lacks the proper strategy for making negatives, often just attaching no or not to a statement. Thus, "I no happy" for *I am not happy,* and "He not go" for *he is not going.* Despite the grammatical errors, the meaning is clear.

Around the age of three the child's sentences become longer and more complex. The grammar also becomes clearer, and the use of negatives and questions improves. A child of three and a half has a vocabulary of some 1000 words. Between four and five the child's language becomes much more complex in thought and construction, and the grammar becomes more and more correct. As children acquire larger vocabularies and more competence with grammar, they begin to tell stories and to delight in listening to stories. Children's expressive language is frequently imaginative and poetic, using a great deal of imagery.

As children become more competent they also begin to experiment with linguistic jokes and later with puns. Even a child of two or three will indulge in a joke by calling a well known item by the wrong name. The child who calls a cat a dog, will indicate that he is joking by the hilarity of his own reaction to this misstatement. As he gets older, the jokes become more sophisticated, and misnaming gives way to puns.

We have talked mainly about the development of the child's expressive language, but we have not yet talked about receptive language. How much does this creative linguist around us understand? We know, for instance, that he can follow simple directions. For example, "Go to your room" or "Bring mommy the book" seem clear enough to toddlers. But do they understand more abstract concepts? Do they know *more* and *less, bigger* and *smaller, near* and *far*? Experience with toddlers would say yes, they understand such things, but research has shown that abstract concepts are understood incompletely. A child might understand *more,* but not *less,* and he might not understand either consistently. It is not until around the age of five that abstract comprehension becomes well developed, and some children do not really understand such abstractions until six or seven.

Somewhere between the ages of two and five the child also learns to use language to classify. The two-year-old may call any four-legged animal a dog. By four or five he has learned to discriminate dogs as a class. Similarly, the two-year-old may make the classification too narrow, calling only the tree in his backyard "tree" and refusing that label for all other trees. The correct specific use of language is a reflection of the child's intellectual development during this period.

Parents cannot help but wonder whether they can teach their children to speak and to speak correctly. The question has never been satisfactorily answered, but we do have some clues. On the one hand the answer must be yes, for children who are not exposed to language do not learn to speak. What is more, the fact that the child of English-speaking parents learns to speak English and not Farsi is powerful evidence that we do, in fact, teach children to speak through imitation.

But this answer clearly cannot account for all language development. Children learn to create sentences they have never heard before. This means that while the child may learn words and their meaning through imitation of adults, they have the ability to take these words and combine them to form an infinite number of original sentences. Additionally, children seem to make the same kinds of grammatical errors as one another, despite not hearing them. This comes, in part, from overgeneralizing rules that they do understand. For instance, in English children make plurals by adding "s" to all words, including irregular nouns. In the same way, they make a past tense by adding "ed" to all verbs. Studies have shown that whether or not these errors are corrected, children learn the correct forms at about the same time. This, too, suggests influences other than imitation at work.

Finally, something might be said about the apparent inborn ability of young children to acquire language with ease. It has long been observed that small children learn languages more easily than adults, and children brought up in a bilingual atmosphere acquire competence in both languages at about the same time. They even appear to be able to distinguish between two languages by about the age of three. If one language is not heard or spoken around the child for any length of time, the child then appears to forget the language.

Cognitive Development

It is almost impossible to separate cognitive development from language, for it is through language that we are able to learn what and sometimes how the child thinks. On the other hand, we cannot rely totally on the child's language for this information. We must accept other evidence.

Piaget conducted many experiments to demonstrate the way in which the thinking of the preschooler differed from the thinking of the adult. In these studies Piaget attempted to show that the difference in thinking was not just a matter of degree, but of kind. In one famous experiment, he demonstrated that the thought of a young child is egocentric. This means not that the child is selfish, but that the child is unable to imagine the viewpoint of another. He demonstrated this by showing children a model of three mountains, some of which blocked the views of the others. Piaget then asked the children what the scene would look like from the other side. The children were unable to imagine that the view would differ from the one they saw.

Piaget also felt that preschoolers lack logic. Their reasoning was termed intuitive, since they make conclusions without correct reasoning. They lack the ability to draw a proper conclusion from the evidence. For example, a child is given a lump of clay. He is then told to roll the clay into a long snake. The child is then asked "Which is more, the lump or the snake? Invariably, the young child answers "the snake" for he is unable to draw the logical conclusion that it is the same piece of clay, no matter what the shape. The child is only able to concentrate on one dimension at a time, and so he uses the visual evidence of length without accounting for the difference in width.

In another experiment you might try with a preschool child, show the child two rows of beads, each with the same number of beads. In one row place the beads close together, in the other far apart. Ask which has more beads. The child who is still thinking in a nonlogical manner will conclude that the longer row has more beads.

OOOOO

O O O O O

Although the answers to these problems seem obvious to us, we should not disparage the ability of the child. The child is unable to look at two dimensions at one time, but he has acquired the skill of representational thought. This means that the child can not only imagine that an object exists when not in sight, but that the child can think about that item. This is a form of abstraction the infant lacks. Without it, the baby's thought is limited to those things in view.

PLAY AND LEARNING *are the same thing to young children. Playing with clay, for example, helps them grasp important physical ideas such as size and shape.*

Another characteristic of the thought of the preschooler is its lack of consistency. The child goes from one thing to another without any logical connection. As the child's thinking jumps from one thing to another, so does his interest. We recognize this when we say that the preschooler has a short attention span.

A final distinguishing characteristic of the preschooler's thought is his inability to make classifications correctly. As pointed out before, the tendency to overgeneralize a class (all four-legged animals are dogs) or to over-specify a class (only my brother is a brother) are seen in the preschooler. But even the child who correctly distinguishes dogs from horses has more to learn. Try this experiment. Show the child pictures of four horses and eight dogs. Ask which are dogs and which are horses. Are there more horses or dogs? So far the child has answered correctly. Then ask, "Are there more dogs or animals?" The child may say dogs. He understands the two sub-groups, dogs and horses, but he may not understand how these are related to the larger group, animals. An older child would not make this error.

In sum, the thinking of preschoolers is much more complex than that of an infant, but it differs from an adult's thinking in that it is neither systematic nor coordinated.

One final point is that thinking is connected to the culture in which a child grows up. There is evidence that children in nonliterate societies process information in a somewhat different way than those in Western societies. This suggests that some modes of thinking are more appropriate in one society than another. Cognitive development is approximately the same in all cultures, but there are many specific differences.

Social Development

Perhaps the largest element in the child's social development is play. Play is not, however, only an instrument of sociability. It is also an instrument of learning, for in play the child learns more and more to use objects abstractly. For example, in order for a two-year-old to play horsie, she may need some representation of a horse before her. Her four-year-old counterpart, though, can take a broom and use it to represent a horse.

Symbolic play is both a social and cognitive function. The child plays symbolically in order to fulfill wishes or to work out situations that are causing difficulty in the real world. In symbolic play, the child makes his own rules and is not dominated by other people or events.

SELFISHNESS AND SEPARATION FEARS *are two strong feelings children gradually learn to overcome as they develop socially and emotionally.*

Play also helps prepare the child for adult functions. Much play is modeled on the behavior of adults. We see this in the child who pretends to drive the car, to do the marketing, and to take care of the younger sibling. This type of play may be helpful in strengthening the child's sense of identity within the family or community. It also helps develop physical skills.

Play provides a release of energy; a strengthening of social bonds; a development of mastery; and, frequently, a source of pleasure for the child.

It is no coincidence that parents of three- and four-year-olds form play-groups or enroll their children in nursery school, for it is at about this age that the child begins to want the companionship of other children. Contact with other children is very important, for it is a means of practicing the social skills that the child will need in many future situations.

Observing a group of three-year-olds at play may prompt one to question the value of nursery school. The children tend to move rapidly from one activity to another, rarely completing what they have begun. In addition, there are many times when the children play side by side rather than with one another. Yet a closer look will reveal that children learn social behavior by watching others, and that they use social occasions to test out strategies for dealing with others. It is not by accident that children argue, fight, and occasionally bite one another. All of this is an effort to learn what actions are acceptable and what actions bring about the results the child wants.

Obedience is not automatic for a preschooler. The child is deeply torn between the desire to receive praise for doing the right thing and the desire for

gratification from doing what he wants. The child who grabs a toy from a playmate, all the while yelling "bad boy" knows that he is not going to get approval for his actions, but is unwilling or unable to control himself. At the same time, by voicing disapproval ("bad boy"), he is beginning to gain some control over the situation. With time and practice he will learn to share.

Separation from parents.
Along with play, nursery school offers the often unwelcome challenge of prolonged separation from parents and home environment. Separation anxiety is a much studied phenomenon that occurs in children who have developed an attachment to their mothers (or other caretakers). Such anxiety is exhibited by clinging to the adult, crying, and an unwillingness to be left with strangers. Separation anxiety is a normal and predictable stage, and one that is outgrown only slowly. In some senses it is a positive development, for it means that the child has formed a close and binding relationship with a significant adult. On the other hand, it is troublesome for the parent who wants or needs to leave the child in the care of others.

Different nursery schools have differing philosophies about how to treat separation. Some encourage parents to leave the child "cold turkey" on the theory that the child will never adjust until the parent leaves. Others prefer a gradual introduction of the child into the new situation. Often this is accomplished by having the parent accompany the child for the first week, and then slowly decreasing the amount of time spent with the child. Sometimes parents are asked to stay in a room ad-

SEX ROLES *are learned by example, but children can be helped to see that such roles are flexible and that they need not fear activities associated with the opposite sex.*

jacent to the classroom so that the child may be reassured that a familiar adult is nearby.

It is hard to say one method is better than another, for strong arguments can be offered for either side. Some find it cruel to leave a distressed child in an unfamiliar environment. Others believe that the gradual approach exacerbates the problem of separation, and makes the child feel that the parent is having difficulty separating. Probably there is no answer, but it is wise to ask about a school's policy before enrolling your child if you have a preference for one style or the other.

Children's social development is also influenced by gender and the place of the child in the family. The eldest (or only) child tends to have more social interaction with adults and less opportunity to model behavior on other children. This situation has both positive and negative effects. On the plus side, first (or only) children tend to be high achievers and to feel secure in their place in the family unit. On the other hand, they often have more difficulty separating from the parents and are less adept at dealing with other children.

Sex roles. Children's sex-role identification begins in childhood, although there is some debate as to how this is achieved. Clearly boys and girls are born with anatomical differences, but the child is unlikely to know much about this at first. It is not until the child is exposed to the anatomy of the opposite sex that there is a true awareness of the differences. Young children do, however, differentiate between boys and girls, usually on the basis of external clues—hair, clothing, style of dress, and even color of clothing.

How do children learn to identify with their same-sex parent? Freudian theorists suggest that the child's psychosexual development follows five clearly delineated stages (see box). Learning theorists disagree, claiming that the child learns by imitation, and that when he or she imitates the same-sex parent, society rewards the child with approval. Eventually the child makes an identification with the parent of the same sex and begins to model behavior on his or her role.

We might ask how children in single-parent families achieve gender identity. Learning theorists say that children need a model whose behavior they can imitate. Such a model might be a teacher, a camp counselor, a relative, clergyman, or family friend.

We have avoided the most problematic question of all: whether gender differentiation in childhood is responsible for sexist behavior in adulthood.

Some argue that children of both sexes should be offered identical opportunity and identical encouragement in the whole variety of human endeavors. This means that one should encourage boys to engage in what was once thought of as girls' play—caring for dolls, playing house, dressing up, and the like—and girls to engage in boys' play—playing with trucks, mechanics, pretending to be doctors and lawyers, etc. Indeed, our society's increasing acceptance of this view is even reflected in the curricula of our schools. No longer are girls required to take home economics while boys take shop. In many schools both sexes are required to try both types of courses. Moreover, it is now required that girls be given access to the same sports teams as boys.

Many thoughtful people are uneasy with this trend, and not completely without reason. Many parents protest that boys and girls are different, not only because they have been treated differently, but in some innate manner. Experiments have proved that men and women do employ different strategies in problem-solving. Male high school students consistently score better in math on college entrance examinations, while the females show greater strengths in verbal skills. But are these differences innate? Perhaps the differences merely reflect the emphasis and encouragement these students have received during their formative years.

Finally, one must ask whether nonsexist child rearing will produce adults with same-sex gender identification. More time and research will be necessary before we can even attempt to answer such questions.

Moral development. Another aspect of the child's socialization process is learning the difference between right and wrong. The preschooler is able to understand the difference between right and wrong in at least some

STAGES OF EARLY LIFE		
APPROX. AGES	PSYCHO- PHYSIOLOGICAL CONCERNS	MAJOR PSYCHOLOGICAL GOALS (ERIK ERIKSON)
0-1½	Mouth; senses of touch and sight	To develop a sense of *basic trust* instead of mistrust in parents, outside world.
1½-3	Excretory organs; large muscles	To develop a sense of *autonomy* or independence rather than a sense of shame or guilt.
3-6	Genital organs; locomotor skills (walking, running, jumping, etc.)	To develop a sense of *initiative* rather than guilt, finding constructive uses for aggressive impulses.
6-12	Latency: postpone interest in genitals, opposite sex	To develop a sense of *industry* rather than inferiority in the accomplishment of valued tasks at home and school.
12-18	Puberty and adolescence: renewed interest in physical gratification, opposite sex	To develop a sense of one's own sexual and psychological *identity* and resolve confusion of one's roles in life.

instances, and is also able to see a connection between his own behavior and the behavior of others. For instance, he knows that it is wrong to bite his sister. He may or may not be able to control his impulse to bite, but he is aware that biting people is forbidden and will bring a punishment. Similarly, he knows that sharing a toy with his sister will make her happy. Again, he may or may not act on this knowledge, but he is beginning to understand that his behavior affects the way others feel.

As in other areas of development, there are a variety of theories about how moral development occurs. Learning theorists claim that moral behavior is learned by imitation and is rewarded by adults. Freudians believe that moral behavior results from the resolution of an unconscious conflict between the impulse for immediate gratification of desires and the demands of reality. In this view, the id represents the instinctual aspect of personality, the ego represents the reality principle, and the superego, or conscience, develops as a sort of mediator between desire and reality.

The cognitive school has another explanation of moral development, which it sees as part of the child's general intellectual development. In this view, as the child's intellect develops, the understanding of moral behavior broadens, and eventually becomes internalized. When we say that moral behavior is internalized, we mean that the behavior is no longer done because of fear of punishment or in hopes of a reward. It is done because it is perceived as correct.

Can moral behavior be taught? No matter what theoretical school one follows, the fact remains that what is or is not considered moral is determined in general by the society and in particular by the family. The child is not born with the belief that it is wrong to bite his sister or to grab toys. Those beliefs are imposed upon him by the people around him. In fact, the child does not even have a sense that it is wrong to make another person sad. This, too, is taught. We must, therefore, conclude that however a sense of right and wrong develops, the definition of what is moral is learned. In this sense, adults do teach children how to behave. It must be emphasized, however, that a young child does not always or even usually have the self-control necessary to act on his knowledge of what is moral.

Practical Considerations

The practical problems of caring for preschoolers are often related to the stages of development.

Toilet training. All of what we know about how children develop may be of some help in practical application. We can see, for example, what a powerful influence Freudian theory has had on the way we toilet train and discipline children.

In the early part of the century, toilet training was considered one of the mother's most important tasks. The mother who could accomplish this task at the earliest possible time was greatly admired. Infants were held over potties from the earliest months, and lavish praise was accorded the child who managed to produce a bowel movement while in this position. As soon as the child could sit, he was placed on the potty for long periods and required to remain there until the job was accomplished.

When Freudian theory became generally known in the 1950's, there was an extreme reaction to the rigidity of early toilet training. Freud linked rigid toilet training to such later personality traits as stinginess, coldness, and compulsive behavior. In Freud's theory, the years from one to three were the years in which the child first had to accede to the demands of reality and to learn to delay gratification. If toilet training became a battle of wills between the powerful adult and the powerless child, the result would be a neurotic child.

Parents with some knowledge of Freudian theory reacted with horror at the thought of causing irreparable damage to their children. Many ignored that aspect of Freudian theory that claimed that a child who is overindulged is as likely to be neurotic as a child who is rigidly controlled. The pendulum swung to the opposite extreme, and parents were careful not to exert too much pressure on their children to use the toilet. The result was that many children remained untrained until the age of about three. This created practical problems—a child could not enter nursery school without being trained. Then the battle began in earnest, and many parents found themselves outwitted by a stubborn and resourceful preschooler.

What then, is a parent to do? Some clues should be taken from the child. As a first step, the parents should pay attention to when the child has his bowel movements. By the age of about one year, many children establish a regular schedule. Regular timing can be helpful, since it allows the parent to anticipate the movement.

Parents should also change the diaper as soon as it is wet or dirty. Children who are frequently changed are often uncomfortable being wet or dirty. These children become accustomed to being dry, and are often cooperative in their toilet training.

When the child has had a bowel movement or has urinated, comments should be made. A child cannot control his behavior until he is aware of it. By naming what the child has done (without any expression of approval or disapproval), parents are helping their child to make the connection between the end product and the behavior that produces it.

Most children, between the first and second year, begin to comment on their movements, usually after producing them. This is a cue that the child is aware of the behavior and is soon going to be ready to control it. Another cue is offered when a child wakes up from a nap with a dry diaper. This is a good time to begin to offer the potty to the child.

Parents often ask whether to use a potty seat or a seat attached to the toilet. This is a matter of individual preference, although it has been noted that many children are frightened of the toilet seat. The potty is closer to the ground, less wobbly, and does not require an adult's help in getting on and off. It is a little inconvenient for the parent, but probably worth it for the security it offers the child.

Once the child is introduced to the potty, he should be lavishly praised for producing either a bowel movement or for urinating. A toddler is both eager to assert his own identity and to please the adults around him. Do not turn toilet training into a battle of wills, for both child and parent will be the loser. Merely praise the child for successes and reserve comment on failures. *Do not expect instant success.* Even the child who wants to cooperate will have lapses.

Many parents have found that the promise of "big boy pants" is a reward the child will work toward. One chubby toddler who complained that his diapers were "too tight" was toilet trained virtually overnight when assured that underpants came in all sizes. Most children are proud of their success in toileting, and that alone is enough incentive to achieve. But when other issues intervene and the child's sense of controlling his own destiny is threatened, a battle ensues. Parents who have had the most success in toilet training are those who have taken the cues offered by the child, and who have made the child feel that the success belongs to the child himself.

It is worthwhile to note that bowel training usually precedes urine training, and that daytime success is often achieved before nighttime success. You can help your child to stay dry at night by not offering liquids just before bedtime. The child who goes to bed with a bottle is going to have a hard time staying dry during the night.

Child care. In earlier periods of American history, the issue of child care was not much considered. It was a general rule that the mother had responsibility for the care of the child. Even in affluent families where nurses

CHILD CARE *takes many forms: from hiring a private nanny* (top left) *to a nursery school with an emphasis on learning* (right) *to the regimented activities of a center in China* (below).

or nannies were employed, the mother was in charge both of hiring and supervising the child-care staff.

Things today are much more complicated. Many mothers are unable to assume the role of primary caretaker and other arrangements must be made. Arguments over who are the best caretakers and what are the best arrangements for the child have hardly proved conclusive. For every point of view, there is a study to support it. The fact that so many studies contradict one another goes unnoticed in the heat of battle. As in so many things, the decisions regarding child care are personal. Nobody seems to know what is best. Rather than offering opinions, we will try to discuss some of the options.

In the home. One obvious solution to the problem of child care is to hire a substitute mother-housekeeper. This solution supposes that the parents are financially able to pay for this kind of help. Assuming that they are able to pay, they must decide what kind of person is suitable for the job.

Many working mothers have found it extremely difficult to find competent, reliable child-care surrogates.

One of the problems is locating someone whose views about child rearing coincide with the parents' views. Unless the parents are willing to follow the philosophy of the person they hire, they must find someone willing to do things as the parents desire. Otherwise, the child is left with the confusion of two different standards for behavior.

Even when a good child-care worker is available, other problems arise. The preschooler is in need of playmates. If the family lives in an urban area, it may be possible for the babysitter to take the child to a park or playgroup within walking distance. If, however, the child lives in a suburban or rural area, finding playmates is much more difficult.

Babysitters. Some parents solve this problem by arranging for child care in the home of a babysitter. If the babysitter has children of her own, or if she cares for one or two other children, the companionship of peers is assured. On the other hand, the child may be less well cared for if there are too many children and too many distractions for the adult. In addition, many localities have strict laws governing the use of a private home for babysitting purposes.

Day care. An increasingly prevalent solution is the day-care center or all-day nursery. Day-care centers are usually licensed and must meet minimum standards of safety, sanitation, and supervision. The quality of day-care centers varies widely—with some providing only minimal custodial care and others providing superior programs. Clearly it is wise to observe a center for at least a day before deciding to enroll your child there.

In countries where two incomes per family are a necessity, both government and industry have taken an active role in providing quality day care. In the United States, the development of child care for working parents has been slow, and the number and quality of centers remains insufficient. Many parents find that better day-care centers have long waiting lists for admission. If you are contemplating enrolling your child in a center, application should be made as early as possible.

Nursery school. For the parents whose needs are less extensive, nursery school may provide a good alternative to child care in the home or day-care centers. Most nursery schools have classes for three- and four-year-olds, but some accept younger children. Some offer full-day programs, but many offer either morning or afternoon sessions. Nursery schools are often organized according to the philosophy of the founders. For example, Montessori schools stress the development of cognitive skills in a highly structured setting. Other schools offer development of the same skills through exploration and experimentation. Still others believe that socialization is the main goal of the preschool, and that the development of particular skills should be left for the regular school.

Parents with clear philosophies about preschool education have little difficulty in selecting a nursery school. For the majority of less certain parents, a visit to several schools provides the best means of assessment. Many schools will allow you to bring your child to visit, and this is a good idea, for you will be able to observe where your child seems most comfortable. Many parents assume that because the children are "just playing" no learning is going on. As we have seen, however, play is one of the most important ways in which a child learns. Preschoolers who spend their time with workbooks and ditto sheets may be missing the most valuable learning experiences of all.

Discipline. Discipline refers to the means by which we teach children self-control. It need not refer to punishment, although punishment is one means of maintaining discipline. In general, the young child is responsive to parental approval or disapproval as a means of maintaining discipline.

We have learned that the two-year-old understands the difference between right and wrong in terms of what the parents approve or disapprove of. Of course, the rules of approval change as the child gets older. For example, an infant is offered neither approval nor disapproval when he wets his diaper, so in his framework the behavior of wetting is not wrong. On the other hand, his five-year-old sister will meet with disapproval if she wets her pants.

The preschooler has not learned enough control to always behave in the approved manner. In addition, he may indulge in forbidden activity for other reasons. The two-year-old who bites his sister when she ignores him is aware that he will receive disapproval from his mother. He continues to bite because he is willing to risk that disapproval in order to gain the attention of his sister.

How do we discourage unacceptable behavior without damaging the child? In general, we do so by expressing disapproval. By so doing, we cause the child to accept responsibility for making us feel this way. The child feels less good about himself for that moment and, with repeated trials, realizes that the behavior should be altered.

There is, however, a danger. If we are constantly disapproving of a child, we diminish his self-esteem and cause him to be frightened of normal behavior. This can be a danger to normal emotional development. If, on the other hand, we ignore unacceptable behavior (or even reward it with amusement), the child never develops the controls necessary to function as a member of the community.

How much is too much? A child who never gets into trouble may be too frightened of disapproval to test the waters. This child is probably being disciplined too much. Similarly, the child who has constant temper tantrums is probably so frustrated by the extent of the discipline imposed upon him that he has lost all other means of expression. Most children have some tantrums; they often occur when the child is tired. But if a child is having several tantrums a day, discipline is probably too strict.

Punishment. What kinds of punishments are effective without being damaging? If disapproval is not enough, try confining a child to his room for a certain period of time, withholding a favorite privilege, or requiring the child to make amends for the damage done. An example of the latter would be to require the child who has dumped out all of her brother's toys to pick them up. Clearly, this kind of punishment depends on the age and abilities of the child, as well as the type of damage done.

Many parents wonder if a spanking would not be a better punishment for the child. Parents in favor of mild spanking say that it expresses disapproval and then ends the incident, allowing life to return to normal. Nearly all child-care authorities advise that spanking is not a good form of punishment. Many believe that it is too temporary to help the child develop a conscience. Others fear that spanking is a humiliating violation of the child's body or that spanking causes inappropriate sexual arousal. Nonetheless, surveys indicate that most parents spank a child sometimes, which leads one to the conclusion that parents are not convinced that spanking is harmful or ineffective.

There is no doubt in anyone's mind that excessive physical punishment is damaging to the child. Children who are beaten, burned, and otherwise mistreated develop severe emotional problems. Moreover, battered children are most likely to become abusive parents, perpetuating a chain of abuse and mistreatment for generations. Any adult who is unable to control impulses to physically abuse a child should seek immediate counseling. A family physician or community crisis center can help.

A NEW BABY in the house brings mixed feelings of love and jealousy.

Siblings. The way a preschooler feels toward brothers or sisters has a great deal to do with the birth order, but it is probably safe to say that no child views siblings without some degree of jealousy. The child who has older siblings is usually fairly secure with them, for he has never been without them. At the same time, he may be jealous both of the abilities they have and of the privileges they receive.

The arrival of a new baby is difficult for all children in the family, particularly the youngest. The new baby displaces the youngest, and this can be a cause of a great deal of jealousy. One strategy that seems to help somewhat is to stress to the preschooler that he is now old enough and able enough to be valued as a participating member of the family. Encourage his help whenever possible, both in tasks that relate to the baby and in regular household chores.

Never minimize the impact of a new baby. No matter how fair you try to be, the fact is that there is one more child—and a very dependent one at that—competing for the attention and love of the parents. While there may

CHILD ABUSE often leads to the death of a child, even when the parents protest that they "didn't mean to do it." Parents who injure their children should seek counseling.

Parents Beat Boy to Death for Lying

be enough love to share with all children, there is not always enough time. The toddler knows this and is understandably unhappy about his diminished share.

Do not expect the new baby to be loved and admired. An honest preschooler might admire the baby and then ask you to return it. Sometimes the jealousy is minimal while the new sibling is still an infant, but when the baby begins to crawl and elicit approval from the adults in the family, the trouble begins.

It is fine to encourage your preschooler to openly express his feelings toward the baby. You certainly can sympathize with his legitimate complaints, but when talk turns to physical abuse, it is the parents' obligation to intervene. Reasoning with a three-year-old who is poking her little brother with a stick is ridiculous. First remove the stick, then express disapproval and/or administer a punishment. Once the danger has been removed, the feelings that caused the incident can be discussed. Sometimes parents are so concerned with an older child's feelings that they jeopardize the younger child's well-being.

In families with more than one child, a certain amount of fighting and jealousy is inevitable. How much the parents intervene depends in part on the parents' tolerance for discord. Another guiding factor should be how able each member of the dispute is to fend for himself. In the beginning, most parents tend to take the part of the youngest child, feeling he is most likely to be victimized by the older ones. Eventually, however, the youngest learns to manipulate this situation in order to get the older child or children into trouble. At this point, the parents should examine each situation and decide each case on its merits. Gradually, they should learn to leave the children to work things out for themselves. This is particularly important when children have learned to use their disputes to demand the parents' attention.

An only child is in a different situation. People once assumed that only children were spoiled by their parents and socially handicapped by having no sisters or brothers. Today things do not seem so clear-cut. As in all situations, "onlies" have advantages and disadvantages. They get more adult attention, are spared endless petty battles with siblings, and often prove to be high achievers. On the other hand, they lack the companionship of siblings and are often exposed to more than their share of adult activities. Some complain that "only" is lonely.

Since the advantages and disadvantages of family size are about even in terms of the child's or children's development, the decision to have or not have more children should be based on other factors. Parents should not feel compelled to have a second child, for example, just to keep the first one company.

The Grade-School Child (Six to Twelve)

The years from six to twelve are the years in which school becomes a major occupation for the child, and learning becomes an activity largely directed by other people. Freud termed this period the latency period, suggesting that it was a period in which energies were directed away from emotional conflict and toward the acquisition of new skills and behaviors in other realms. Certainly, it is a period of intense activity in many spheres.

Intellectual Development

The school-age child in our culture is deeply involved in one activity that may have a major impact on the course of his adult existence—formal learning. While his emotional, social, and physical skills continue to be of great importance, his ability to learn and apply the lessons of school may be a major determinant of his future life.

The well known psychiatrist and theorist Erik Erikson has described the school years as a practice run for entrance into adult life. The child is offered the opportunity to master new tasks, and through this new mastery he begins to develop the competencies of an adult. The school-age child is, in a sense, an apprentice in life skills. If his apprenticeship is successful, he will emerge from it with a sense of identity and worth. If, on the other hand, he is unable to successfully ful-

ABSTRACT IDEAS *such as "number" become a major concern of elementary school children. Ability to use such ideas is an important skill in modern society.*

fill his own expectations, or the expectations of parents and teachers, he may emerge with a sense of inferiority and a diminished idea of his own worth.

The kind and amount of learning that goes on during these early and middle school years differ from what has gone before. The child is no longer engaged in a struggle to master the physical aspects of his world. Both gross and fine motor skills will improve during these years, but the major tasks (walking, running, jumping, and the like) have been mastered. Similarly, language is no longer a primary concern. Language continues to increase in scope and complexity, but the ability to communicate with others is now firmly established.

Learning is now dependent on organization and strategy. The school-age child is able to devise mental strategies for remembering things. These strategies increase with age, perhaps because of more exposure to problem-solving. The school-age child is also able to use mental imagery rather than physical objects to solve problems. A toddler might solve the problem of how to get a nursing bottle through the crib bars by experimentation, pushing the bottle into the bars until he hits the right way. A school-age child could solve that problem without a bottle and a crib being present. He would have enough information about those objects in his mind to solve the problem.

Piaget termed this kind of thinking mental imagery. By that he meant that the child could perform internal mental actions. Moreover, the school-age child could account for physical properties that remained the same and those that changed. He would know that two rows containing seven beads were equal in number, even though one row might be longer than the other. He would not be fooled into believing that a long piece of clay had greater quantity than the original ball of clay from which it was made.

The school-age child has another capacity that his younger siblings lack. He has formed a conceptual framework to account for time and space. He is able to understand the relationship of hours to days to weeks, etc.; and he knows that people and events exist outside of his view. He has clear notions of past and present, and can mentally imagine events taking place in other times and places.

A third area of expertise for the school-age child is the understanding of cause and effect. While his thinking is not yet abstract enough to deal with many variables, the child can understand that *a* causes *b*, and will always do so under identical circumstances. He is beginning to acquire a scientific framework of inquiry, and no longer believes that all events occur at random.

One of the strategies used by the school-age child is classifying. Classifying makes order out of the enormous amount of information that comes the child's way. The passion for classification is often exhibited in the collection and sorting of baseball cards, stamps, and dolls' clothes. The ability to classify and then to generate rules has enormous implications for success in school. The child who cannot do so will have great difficulty making sense out of numbers and letters. Both reading and mathematics depend on the ability to sort and classify.

GROUPING, ORDERING, ORGANIZING *are popular activities with 7–10 year-olds.*

As children learn to walk at different ages, so children learn to internalize abstractions at different ages. The child who cannot read in first grade may not be ready to read. If his scheme of organization is immature, he will be unable to sort out all those letters and form them into words. Sometimes, a child merely needs enough time and encouragement to blossom in school.

Learning disabilities. There are children who are termed learning disabled. Such a label implies that the child is unable to perform the tasks of the school years for reasons having nothing to do with intelligence. There may be many causes for such a disability. One child may lack the proper eye coordination to focus on the printed page and may perceive numbers and letters backward or in reverse order. Some experts believe that learning disabilities are caused by organic disabilities or by neurological problems that make the decoding of written material difficult or impossible.

A child with a learning disability has many obstacles to overcome. He may suffer a diminished self-image if he continually perceives himself as a failure in school. Many such children have been accused by parents or teachers of being lazy or stupid. It is crucial

that such a child receive a good educational evaluation from his school or from an outside agency. In many cases, early detection solves many of the learning problems and helps to avoid emotional problems. Nobody would think of disparaging a child who cannot tell red from green because he is color blind. Why, then, should the child who is unable to decode words suffer abuse?

There are many techniques for helping children with learning disabilities, and many learning disabled children become able and productive adults. If you are unable to get assistance from school personnel, ask your pediatrician for a referral.

Social Development

The school years are also a period of intense social development. Children are grouped in classes by age, and tend to form social relationships in groups rather than in pairs. Parents and teachers notice that children of six or seven begin to segregate themselves by sex. Relationships between boys and girls are often a source of amusement to the group and thus to be avoided. Boys and girls who have been the best of friends in nursery school will barely acknowledge one another in public by age seven. Their friendships might continue in the privacy of the home or neighborhood, but it is too risky to continue in school.

Cliques. Children at this age are eager to form groups. They belong to different groups at different times, and sometimes to several at the same time. An eight-year-old girl may play with others in her reading group during lunchtime, be part of the jump-rope group at recess, and associate with a group of budding gymnasts after school. Boys in the mid-school years often associate themselves with other boys who share nonacademic interests rather than those of like intellectual abilities.

Along with the constant shifting of

DYSLEXIA *often involves difficulty in telling direction. Here a dyslexic has written his numbers with every other line reversed in direction.*

THE ORTON SOCIETY

1 2 3 4 5 6 7 8 9 10 →

23 22 21 20 19 18 17 16 15 14 13 12 11 ←

24 25 26 27 28 29 30 31 32 33 →

FORMING FRIENDSHIPS *and becoming a member of a peer group can lead to negative (at left) or positive activities. The choice depends partly on a child's earlier experiences and self–confidence.*

groups, there is also a struggle for leadership. Both boys and girls tend to form cliques centered around an acknowledged leader. Changes in leadership or challenges to the current leadership are a source of conflict within the group. Parents and teachers frequently find it hard to keep up with the daily realignments of members. Yesterday's enemy is often today's friend.

Why is the formation of cliques so important at this age? For one thing, it occurs at a time when the child is further establishing his identity as a person who has an existence outside the family unit. He is spending more hours a day away from home and is eager to assert independence, but he is not confident of his ability to succeed independently. The clique offers a sort of substitute family—a group to which one can return for support and for confirmation of one's own behavior and attitudes.

By identifying himself as a member of a group, the child makes an implicit negative judgment about the members of another group. Sometimes this shows itself in territorial ways—this part of the playground is reserved for kickball players and others should keep away.

A child may experience a lot of conflict about the cliques. He may have friends in two different groups and find it impossible to belong to both. He may be unwilling to declare himself a part of one or the other, and yet feel forced to choose. Children may also wish that they were part of another group and find they lack the means of

admission. In some communities, informal cliques develop into more highly organized gangs or clubs.

School administrators spend a great deal of time trying to defuse the potential for conflict between groups. One reason for rearranging classes every year is to separate groups that have become too well established and powerful, and to allow new leaders to develop. When Tommy comes home distraught because he has been separated from his best friend, the perceptive parent might accept this as an opportunity for new friendships to develop. Tommy might also be reassured that if his friendship with Jimmy is solid, it will survive the classroom separation.

Moral development. Aside from the social skills in group relationships, other things are being learned. Perhaps one of the biggest areas of development is that of moral development. The emerging conscience that was so wobbly in the preschooler now has a chance to exert itself and be tested.

The school-age child no longer acts solely because of fear of punishment. Now there is a new factor directing his behavior—the approval or disapproval of peers—the kids his own age. The child knows that he is being judged by them and modifies his actions in accordance with their values. The problem is, of course, that the child is extremely vulnerable at this point and is not yet certain of his own values. If he becomes part of a group that values

vandalism or petty thievery, he may be tempted to suspend his own moral judgment in order to win the approval and acceptance of the group.

There have been many theoretical attempts to explain how the child develops a sense of moral behavior. Freud believed that a sense of morality developed through the resolution of conflict between the child and the same-sex parent. The child gradually forms an identification with that parent and takes the parent's values.

Learning theorists argue that ethical behavior is simply learned from others. Parents, teachers, and peers set standards of behavior and reward behavior that is "good." Good behavior is reinforced by praise; bad behavior is discouraged by disapproval or punishment. It depends on whose ethics and values are most reinforced. A child who places great value on the approval of peers might indulge in behavior that parents disapprove of in order to win the approval of friends. On the other hand, a child who is strongly influenced by parental approval might avoid associating with groups whose values displease his parents.

Another approach to moral development has been formulated by Lawrence Kohlberg. In his view, moral development occurs in stages that are roughly equivalent to the stages of cognitive development. In this view, all children follow the same pattern of development, although not all people reach the ultimate stage, in which moral actions are carried out because to do otherwise would violate one's own principles (see box on next page).

MORAL DEVELOPMENT

Recent studies have sought to understand how a child develops a sense of right and wrong. According to Lawrence Kohlberg, moral development occurs in much the same way as cognitive development. Kohlberg identifies three main stages:

1. *Preconventional.* One follows the rules of society to avoid a punishment or to earn a reward.
2. *Conventional.* One defines morality as the performance of good acts according to a set of principles (for example, the Golden Rule).
3. *Post-conventional.* One follows self-generated rules that are consistent with maintaining one's self-respect.

In judging what stage a person may be at, Kohlberg asks each one to consider dilemmas such as the following:

THE HEINZ DILEMMA

In Europe, a woman was near death from cancer. One drug might save her—a form of radium that a druggist in the same town had recently discovered. The druggist was charging $2000 for the substance, ten times what it cost him to prepare.

The sick woman's husband, Heinz, went to everyone he knew trying to borrow the money, but he could only get together about half of the cost. He told the druggist that his wife was dying and asked him to sell the radium for less or to let him pay for it later. The druggist refused both suggestions.

Heinz finally became desperate and broke into the druggist's store to steal the radium for his wife. Should the husband have done that? Why (or why not)?

Responses to the dilemma are evaluated not by the yes or no answer, but by the reasons a respondent gives for the choice.

Emotional Development

The emotional development of this period has not been as widely studied as that of early childhood or of adolescence. In fact, Freud's term *latency period* suggests that emotional development is somehow on hold while energy is diverted to intellectual tasks.

Parents of school-age children are likely to disagree. Emotional development may take second place, but the child is developing the traits that will be called personality. Emotional characteristics that were apparent in infancy and the preschool years are now being altered and modified to meet the demands of the child's social and intellectual environment. The style the child exhibits in dealing with peers, parents, and authority figures will be the models for the mature personality that will emerge in the next few years.

The child of eight or ten is working hard at the task of becoming an adult, but is not yet threatened by the reality of adulthood. He can ask for greater privileges and more responsibility and yet be sure that adults will not yet demand that he function as an adult in the world.

It is the ability to prepare for adult roles without the responsibility of assuming such roles that characterizes the early school years. The emotional conflicts that arise from both social and school situations, while terribly stressful when they occur, do not usually imply to the child that the rest of his life will be affected by the outcome. Perhaps it is this certainty that gives the child at least the appearance of emotional calm. Many parents see this period as the calm before the storm, for they know that puberty and adolescence bring with them emotional turbulence.

Practical Considerations

In dealing with school-age children, parents soon learn that their job becomes letting go—gradually giving up their emotional and practical control.

Granting Independence. This process began to some extent when the children were toddlers, but it accelerates quickly in the school years. Just how much independence to grant, and when, become major practical as well as emotional issues.

The extremes are easy to describe. Parents in one family may be overprotective. When other children are visiting friends and going to the store by themselves, the overprotective parents keep their children home or accompany them wherever they go. The children may react to such protection by beginning to doubt their own abilities and become timid about facing new situations. Others may become rebellious, provoking arguments by taking independent actions without asking permission.

Other parents may let go too soon. They may subject their children to situations they are too young to cope with. This may cause a child to feel abandoned—and he may either court dangerous situations to see how far his independence goes or withdraw, forcing his supposedly uncaring parents to protect him.

Just where the happy medium is depends on the child, on the parents, and on outside circumstances. Parents should recognize the double view a child has during the elementary school years. On one hand, he is away from home during the day, encountering new people and situations, and testing his independence. At the same time, he relies implicitly on his parents for guidance and for placing limits on his activities. He needs help in deciding from year to year how independent he can be and what social and emotional risks he can reasonably take. He listens carefully to his parents' reactions, judging how seriously they take a quarrel with a friend, a bad mark at school, a music recital, or a gymnastics meet.

Outside circumstances often determine what parents allow their children to do. A child in a small village may have more independence to come and go on his own than one in a busy city. Parents understandably feel a responsibility not to subject a child to serious safety risks. Yet the story of a young child's progress—first walk to school, first solitary trip to the store, first weekend away from home—is the

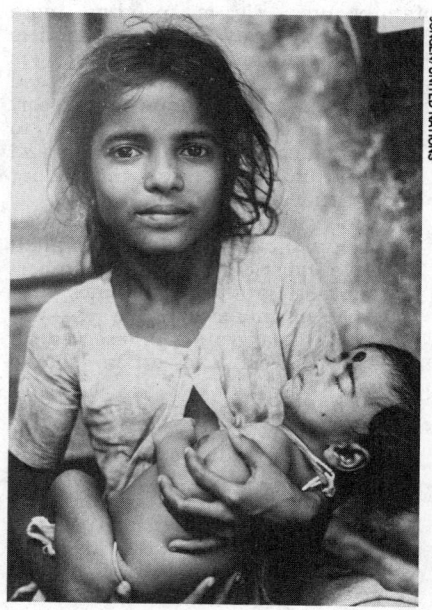

RESPONSIBILITY *comes early to many children. This East Indian girl has regular responsibilities caring for a younger child in the family. Learning to accept responsibility is important to growing up.*

JONGEN/UNITED NATIONS

story of one risk after another encountered successfully. In fact, children learn how to take chances (both in a good sense and a bad sense) from following their parents' leads.

Learning problems.
We spoke earlier about learning problems and failure at school. If a child begins failing in school, it is important for a parent to understand the source of the problem and to take steps to remedy it.

Since the adoption of Public Law 94–142 in 1975, parents have been guaranteed the right to testing and evaluation for children's special needs and suitable education in the least restrictive environment. Parents are also entitled by law to be provided with an individualized education plan for any child who has been evaluated as handicapped.

Parents of children who have more than transient school problems for either physical, emotional, or unknown reasons, should request a meeting with the school principal, psychologist, and special education teachers to devise the most appropriate educational plan for that child.

School phobia.
Another, and more subtle, form of school difficulty in these years is school phobia. This refers to the child who is tremendously afraid to go to school and devises any of a number of excuses to stay home. If a child has chronic headaches, stomach aches, or pains, of course, the first step is to consult a physician. But if no physical explanations are forthcoming, the child may have a school phobia.

Children with school phobia are neither lazy nor stupid. They avoid school because they are unable to solve a conflict about leaving home. In some cases, especially among young children who have not gone to preschools, the phobia is a case of delayed separation anxiety. Usually it will solve itself with time. Other phobias may be caused because something frightening has happened to the child at school (or on the way to and from). School authorities may be asked to help explain or solve such a problem. Still other cases occur because a child is fearful of what will happen at home while he is gone. A child whose mother is abused by his father may become phobic because he believes that he must stay home to protect his mother. Sometimes the assistance of a psychologist or psychiatrist may prove valuable. Your physician or school authorities can usually refer you to an appropriate counselor.

Bedwetting.
Another problem that becomes significant in the school years is bedwetting or enuresis. Children's lapses in the preschool years

GIFTED CHILDREN *often need special attention if they are to avoid becoming bored by the slower pace of others their age.*

tend to be dismissed, but the child who has reached school age without adequate urine (or, occasionally, bowel) control has a problem that requires professional help.

The first step is a complete physical examination. Your pediatrician can perform such an examination or refer you to a specialist in urinary disorders. In some cases, therapy with drugs is effective. In others, a program of behavior modification will prove valuable. Sometimes both techniques will be used in conjunction. Do not be discouraged. It often takes time and patience to break the cycle of wetting and soiling.

Hyperactivity.
Another disability is hyperactivity. This condition is characterized by an inability to sit still, an extremely short attention span, and generally disruptive behavior. The underlying mechanisms of hyperactivity are poorly understood. Some believe the condition reflects a neurological dysfunction; some that it is reflective of a biochemical imbalance; still others that it is a largely psychological phenomenon. Treatments include drug and diet therapy, neurophysiological training, behavior modification, and psychotherapy.

If you suspect that your child is hyperactive, you should discuss the matter with both your pediatrician and school authorities. Hyperactive children generally are recognized as such in the school setting, for they are unable to conform to the structure im-

posed by a classroom. Before undergoing any kind of therapy, the child should have a complete physical exam and an educational and psychological evaluation performed by professionals. The various treatments should be thoroughly evaluated before committing a child to a particular one.

The gifted child.
Children with extraordinary intellectual abilities often become bored with unchallenging classroom routines. They respond by showing little attention and becoming "turned off" to education. Unfortunately, the rights of gifted children are not clearly defined by law, and the amount of enrichment a child receives depends primarily on the school he or she attends.

It is even difficult to define a gifted child. Some school districts define gifted in terms of IQ scores. Others look for an outstanding talent in one specific area. Many others choose to simply ignore the problem. A parent who suspects his child is gifted and is not receiving adequate stimulation should first discuss the matter with school authorities and then request an educational evaluation. If the child meets any of the criteria for giftedness, and the school is unable or unwilling to provide assistance, outside sources of enrichment should be sought. Many universities offer programs for gifted school-age children. The education department of a nearby university may be able to suggest programs for gifted children.

Adolescence

Adolescence refers to the period that begins with puberty and ends with adulthood. In the United States puberty usually occurs sometime between the ages of ten and 14, with wide individual variation. Puberty is marked by the physical changes that accompany sexual maturity. In girls, puberty brings such changes as the development of breasts, the growth of pubic and underarm hair, and the onset of menstruation. In boys, there is growth of both facial and body hair, as well as the development of the sexual organs, which includes the ability to ejaculate.

Yet to define adolescence in purely physical terms is to miss the point, for the onset of puberty brings with it profound emotional, social, and even cognitive changes. For many, it is the most tumultuous and stormy part of life. Parents who say "Little children, little problems; big children, big problems," refer, no doubt, to the upheavals of adolescence.

When we speak of the developmental achievements of the adolescent, and his entry into the world of adulthood, this does not imply that development ends at the end of adolescence. Physical, intellectual, and emotional changes continue throughout life, and there is no one point at which we can stop and say, "Now I am a fully developed human being." Only the rapidity of the changes in adolescence make them dramatically different from those in the decades that follow.

Intellectual Development

The adolescent is, in many ways, continuing in the role that he began in school at the age of five or six, but a new dimension has entered into his thought processes. The adolescent has the ability to form a hypothesis and systematically examine whether or not it is correct. This kind of thinking involves the ability to try out many combinations and variables in a given situation to see which is correct. His understanding of cause and effect is more sophisticated, and he is equipping himself to participate fully in adult intellectual pursuits.

Another quality of adolescent thinking is reflectiveness. An adolescent can think about hypothetical situations, playing out various possibilities in his mind almost as if they were really happening. He may also become intensely (sometimes even morbidly) preoccupied with himself and his own thought processes.

Along with increased intellectual powers, the adolescent also has a longer attention span and a more finely developed sense of focus. He can use his intellectual abilities to concentrate on the problem at hand without being easily distracted by irrelevant material. At this stage, he is also beginning to use the resources around him to find what he wants to know. These abilities make it plausible for a 15-year-old to do a serious research paper. To ask a seven-year-old to do so would demand skills that he cannot yet possess.

Emotional Development

It is in the emotional and social arenas that the turmoil of adolescence is most apparent. We spoke earlier of the bodily changes that occur in the teen years. These profoundly affect the way the adolescent relates to his family, peers, and teachers.

The appearance of physical signs of maturity are received variously by different children. Some are overjoyed at the evidence that they are ready to enter the world of adults. Others are frightened at the inescapable signs that childhood is coming to an end. Most adolescents feel both emotions. Growing up is both exciting and threatening.

Similarly, parents react with mixed feelings to the evidence of their child's maturity. Some fear the end of their nurturing years and are upset by the imminence of sexual activity in their child. Others are thrilled by their child's passage through the straits that lead from childhood to adulthood. Like their children, most parents feel both excited and threatened by the onset of puberty.

More independence. For both parents and children the task at hand is the same—the completion of the separation that began in infancy. Now the task must be done with more finality. The child must learn to accept himself as a being separate from his parents, capable of functioning in the world as an adult. This is no small order, and although all of childhood prepares one for this task, the road is not an easy one.

The transition takes place in a series of advances and retreats. The child in the early teens makes small, tentative steps toward maturity and freedom, but usually runs back to the security of home. Over time, the steps forward become longer and more frequent; the retreats shorter and less intense. If all goes well, the adolescent manages to integrate the values and strengths of the parents, adapts to the demands of his own age group, and emerges at the end of adolescence as a capable and mature adult.

ROMANCE is an exciting—and somewhat frightening—experience for many adolescents; it is capable of bringing great happiness and sadness, sometimes in the same week.

PAUL CONKLIN/MONKMEYER

Family conflict.

The conflicting feelings of both the parents and the child in this period cause the innumerable conflicts that frequently characterize these years. Parents often feel they are in a "no-win" situation: if they allow the child too much freedom, they abdicate their responsibility. If they allow too little leeway, the child feels degraded and untrusted. Either situation can set the stage for rebellious behavior.

The child may also feel himself to be in a no-win situation. If he convinces his parents that he is trustworthy, he may feel overwhelmed by the freedom allowed. He may also feel that if his parents truly cared about him, they would not allow him to be in a position so fraught with danger. If, on the other hand, he does not seek the freedom to "try his wings" he feels doomed to a life of immaturity and dependency.

Nobody treads this road without some mishaps, but, in general, some kind of balance between dependence and independence seems safest. Parents should realize that age must bring increasing privileges to the child who has demonstrated the ability to handle freedom. Similarly, the child must accept that privileges must be earned through the demonstration of responsibility. If the balance can be struck, with a slow but constant increase in the child's handling of his own affairs, then the transition from childhood to adulthood should not be too painful.

That, of course, is the theory; in life, things rarely go so smoothly. Children and adults are often sidetracked by irrelevant issues. A minor argument over a largely unimportant matter can assume the proportions of a major battle. Soon the plan for a smooth transition is lost in the tangle of recriminations that ensue. Such battles are probably unavoidable, but if they become constant and disruptive, then an impartial counselor may be needed to provide the guidance necessary to defuse the issues.

What, in fact, are the major issues facing the adolescent and his family? Usually family disagreements focus on matters relating to academic performance, dating and sex, and the use of drugs and alcohol. Frequently, a combination of these issues is involved, and even in the most tranquil families some disputes arise.

School work.

In many families, the adolescent's academic performance is seen as the crucial link with future success. The child who does well in school will have many career options. According to this logic, the child who fails in high school has excluded himself from the benefits of higher education and the chance for a "good life."

From the adolescent's point of view, however, this may all seem irrelevant. First, he may still be unable to deal with the present, and is certainly not very concerned with the distant future. At a time when physical, social, and emotional turmoil is uppermost in his mind, academics may seem the last item on the agenda. What is more, if the adolescent is having a difficult time coping with separation and impending adulthood, he may unconsciously sabotage his academic future in order to delay taking the final step into adulthood.

Finally, many students reject the pressure to achieve in school as a means of asserting independence from their parents. By failing to achieve, they assert that the parents' values are not necessarily identical with their own, and that they have the right to make choices.

Dating and sex.

The adolescent, from the time of puberty, is capable of full participation in sexual activities. Yet he lives in a society that will not accept him as an adult for another five to ten years. This results in a conflict, for the adolescent is in some senses a child with the body of an adult. He lives in his parents' home, is financially dependent, is often emotionally dependent, and yet is physically a mature adult.

The parents are probably in as much conflict as the child. Having grown up in a world that demanded that sexual activity be postponed until marriage, they are now faced with an era of permissiveness that may conflict with their own religious and moral values. Parents are called upon both implicitly and explicitly to set values. For example, they may set curfews and limit dating to certain hours. They may demand that the young adolescent date only in groups, or they may ban dating entirely. No matter what explicit limits they set, however, they do not have complete control, for the young adult is generally able to circumvent rules, especially those seen as unjust.

The dilemma of the parents then increases. If they are too strict, they court defiance. If they are too lenient, they court disaster. And if they refuse to take a stand, they abdicate all responsibility for a youngster still in need of guidance. If the parents tell their daughter that they disapprove of premarital sex and therefore do not discuss the issue of contraception, they may be leaving her unprotected against pregnancy. If, on the other hand, they discuss birth control, they seem to offer implicit acceptance of premarital sex.

The child may be equally confused. Faced with conflicting physical and emotional demands, the adolescent is pushed into decisions he may not be ready to make. Peer pressure and rebellion are powerful forces, and both are partly responsible for the growing incidence of sexually active teenagers.

It seems clear that parents must offer their teenage children a clear explanation of their own moral and religious beliefs about sex and dating. They need also to set certain limits on the activities of their teenagers, if for no other reason than to express concern for the child's well-being. At the same time, the parent must realize that the child has, in fact, the ability to act according to his own wishes and desires. Moreover, the time is approaching when the child will be an adult who must negotiate the world of

CLAIMING INDEPENDENCE *from parents often means quarrels and anger on both sides. Teenagers may be most quarrelsome when they feel most reliant on their parents.*

ANN ZANE SHANKS/PHOTO RESEARCHERS

DRINKING, SMOKING, *and other forbidden activities appeal to teenagers. Such activities help them conform to the behavior of others their age and give the illusion of being adult. Learning to say no is an important test of a teenager's inner strength.*

sex and dating without any parental intervention. It is the parents' job, then, to offer guidelines and assistance where necessary, with the goal of having the adolescent develop his own rational and coherent set of moral standards.

Drugs and alcohol. Even more explosive than sex and dating is the issue of drug and alcohol abuse. Here, the parent fears not only for the child's emotional turmoil, but his very physical survival. In the years since most parents were, themselves, adolescents, the world has greatly changed, and drugs are almost universally available. No longer can one escape to a secluded town in the hopes of protecting one's children from the influence of drugs, both legal and illegal. How, then, can one protect them?

Again, the answer seems to lie in providing the adolescent with a value system strong and coherent enough to protect him from the twin temptations of peer pressure and rebellion.

Complicating the issue is the fact that so much of what has been written about drug and alcohol abuse is questionable. Adults who warn that experimentation with marijuana inevitably leads to heroin addiction are dismissed by adolescents as hysterical and illogical. Warnings about the illegality of drugs also meet with disbelief. The common response is that "everyone does it" and no one seems to have gone to jail for trying marijuana.

Parents who themselves use (or abuse) legally prescribed tranquilizers or amphetamines serve as very poor models for their teenage children. Similarly, those who drink excessively are likely to find an adolescent skeptical about their advice. Teenagers are sensitive to any suggestion of hypocrisy or double standards.

It is easier for a family with well regulated adult standards of drug and alcohol intake to impart their standards to their children. Furthermore, it is the adult's responsibility to point out that although the uses of alcohol and mind-altering drugs may be similar, the law does distinguish between them. At this time, alcohol is a legal substance, while mind-altering drugs sold without prescription are not.

In the end, there are no simple rules that guarantee that the adolescent will deal with the drug issue in a way that the parents find acceptable. Many, if not most, teenagers experiment with drugs at some point. While parents need not condone such experimentation, it is unwise to write off as a "junkie" the child who bows once or twice to peer pressure or pure curiosity. There are few adults who can honestly recall their own adolescence without remembering an intemperate experiment. It is wise to recall such instances when taking your teenagers' indiscretions to account.

Social Development

The social development of the adolescent reflects the desire for independence from the family and the need for acceptance into a group.

Teenage styles. While the teenager frequently asserts his independence by refusing to dress or style his hair in a manner that would suit the parents, he is, at the same time, conforming to a dress code that is rigidly prescribed by his peers. A classic example is the long-hair revolt of the 1960's. Many teenage boys took to wearing their hair in long and frequently unkempt styles. When their fathers began to adopt similar hair styles, however, the great hair revolt ended, for it no longer served to distinguish the adolescent from his father's generation.

CONFORMITY *among teenagers is often expressed in clothing as well as in gestures, pet phrases, and attitudes.*

Friendships.

Teenagers usually become attached to a particular group, but at the same time they begin to form intense friendships with one or two others. Such friendships may be with those of the same sex or the opposite sex. Frequently, such friendships include hours of discussion on the plight of adolescents—that is, the inability of their parents and teachers to understand them. Such discussions serve a valuable purpose, for they give the teenager a sense that his problems are less individual and more universal than he might have imagined. In a sense, peer relationships form a sort of loosely structured environment for group therapy.

Intimacy.

As teenagers pair off into intense one-to-one relationships, they are, in a sense, rehearsing the intimacy that marriage brings. The ability to form a close, personal relationship with another person is one that develops during the adolescent years. This close relationship usually takes place on several levels simultaneously. The relationship may be based on physical attraction, intellectual compatibility, and mutual social and emotional goals. A friendship that is based on only one of these factors, is usually short-lived under normal circumstances. Such limited relationships sometimes continue, however, if the parents disapprove of it, and continuing becomes a matter of principle for the teenager.

Parents often ignore the social, emotional, and intellectual bases of teenage pairs, and concentrate their attention on the physical or sexual side of the relationships. This is not a totally unreasonable concern, for adolescents, by definition, are in the throes of emerging sexuality, and sexual experimentation is surely a part of that experience. Parents are rightly concerned that the adolescent may not be emotionally ready to handle a sexual relationship. Many adolescents recognize this themselves, and voluntarily withdraw when a long-term physical relationship threatens. This may provide a temporary solution, but in the long-term, it is as unhealthy as that of the adolescent who responds to pressure by becoming promiscuous.

Professionals in adolescent psychology are often questioned as to the best approach for parents when their adolescent has formed an intense romantic attachment. No single answer serves in all cases, but in general professionals advise against extreme reactions. Forbidding the relationship may be no more effective than ignoring it—in either case the involvement becomes the adolescents' emancipation proclamation. A more successful approach seems to be the open and frank discussion of the situation, without value judgments. The adolescent may, in fact, be looking toward his parents

SELF-CONSCIOUSNESS *can make adolescents painfully awkward and shy, especially when they find themselves in situations that seem to call for mature social behavior.*

for support in extricating himself from a too intense situation.

In the last analysis, it is wise to remember that the adolescent is no longer the child he was. Parents can not impose change upon the teenager. They can help the young adult to modify his behavior, but the impetus must be his own. A teenager has both the physical and intellectual ability to guide his own life, and while his parents have the option of refusing to support that lifestyle, they no longer have absolute control over it.

Adolescence is the transition from childhood to adulthood, but it does not imply the end of development. The adolescent is groping toward a style of life that will serve him well in the adult world. The greatest gift parents can make to their child is that of support in helping him find an appropriate and comfortable style that will work for him. —*Phyllis Bocian*

ADOLESCENCE *is the period between becoming an adult physically and taking on adult responsibilities. The period of adolescence has grown increasingly longer in the 20th century, as shown here in the increasing gap between the age of puberty and the age of leaving school. In some cases, this in-between period can extend for 15 years or more.*

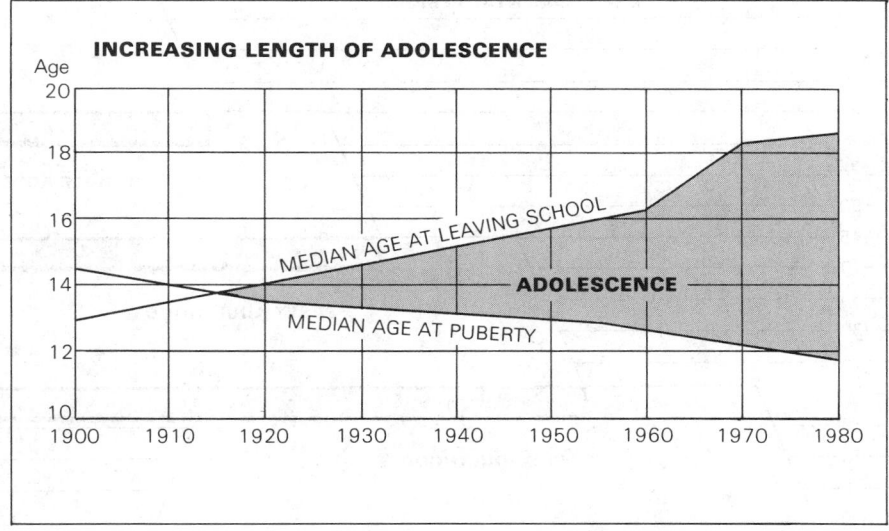

ADULT DEVELOPMENT

In the 1970's, a book called *Passages,* by Gail Sheehy, became a best seller. Its subject was adult development, and its popularity helped change people's thinking about adulthood. For decades the concept of development had been a great help in understanding childhood and adolescence. But the general feeling was that development ended with adolescence and that an adult was a *developed* person.

Passages helped popularize a new view of adulthood. This view suggests that human beings continue to develop and change in somewhat predictable ways throughout their lives. Until recently, most people had never thought of adulthood as a time of development. Things happened in the adult years, certainly, and we felt ourselves changing, but we did not think of this as a series of age-related changes, similar in nature to the changes that occur in childhood and adolescence. Perhaps because physical changes occur more slowly in adulthood, we believed that emotional changes were also slower and less significant after age 20 or so. However, researchers have recently discovered that there is a significant pattern of development all through the adult years. Not every individual changes in exactly the same ways or on the same schedule, but the study of adult development helps us understand our adult lives more completely. In many cases, we are relieved to see that our difficulties in adulthood are not peculiar to us but are normal—even predictable—problems faced by a majority of other adults.

Stages

We can consider the life cycle as a series of stages, or stable periods, with transition periods between them. Changes in behavior from one stage to the next occur in characteristic ways. Daniel J. Levinson and his colleagues at Yale University have studied men's lives, and are now studying women's lives, through an intensive interviewing and testing process. In their book, *The Seasons of a Man's Life,* these researchers present a broad theoretical framework for understanding development in the adult years.

First of all, they divide the life span into eras of about 20 years each. The *Preadult Era* lasts from birth to about age 20; the *Early Adult Era* covers the years from 20 to 40; the *Middle Adult Era* lasts from ages 40 to 60; and the *Late Adult Era* is age 60 and beyond. Levinson's research team concentrates on early and middle adulthood, and describes specific, shorter developmental phases within these eras.

What, then, is the sequence of these periods and the transitions between them? The following table presents a summary of these periods; we will investigate them more fully in this article.

Levinson believes that changes in adulthood can be understood as development of the *life structure.* The life structure is the underlying pattern or design of a person's life at any given time. The structure of a life includes a person's sense of self, relationships with other people, and connections with the world at large. It includes where one lives and works, and the relationships one builds with people, groups, organizations, places, objects (a piece of land, a painting), and all the things one chooses. The life structure remains stable for some years, then begins changing as a new era of life approaches. Stable periods are

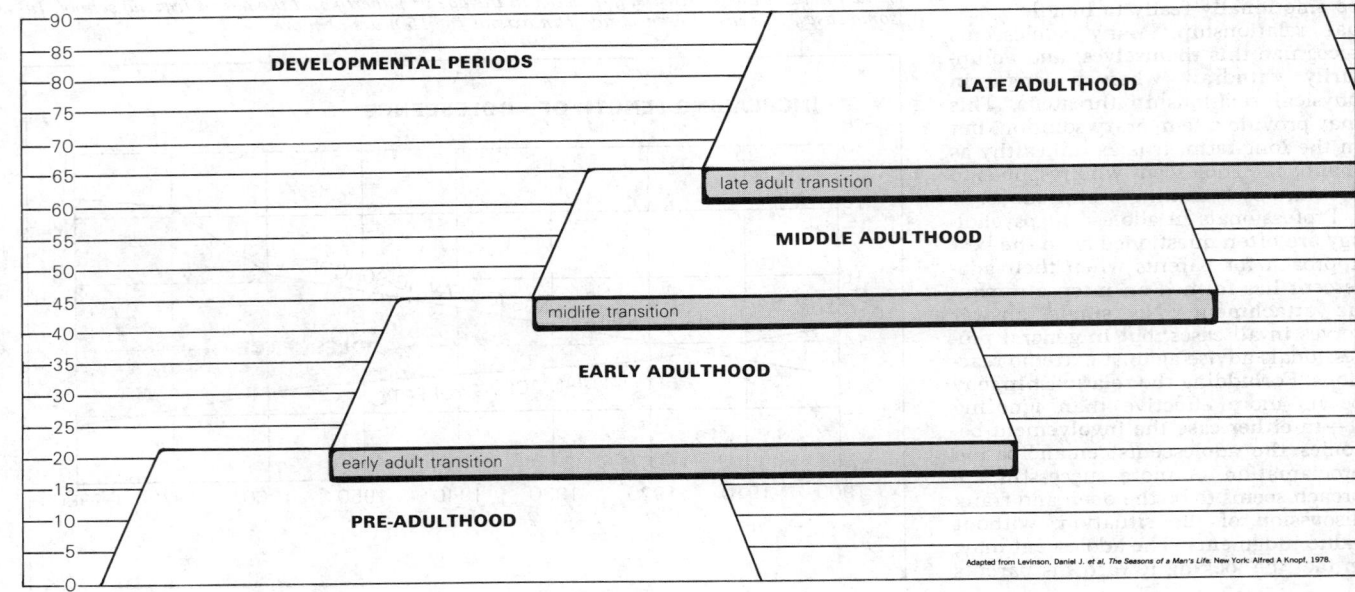

Adapted from Levinson, Daniel J. et al, The Seasons of a Man's Life. New York: Alfred A Knopf, 1978.

times of building a new structure and living within it, while transition periods are times of reassessing the structure and making the changes that may seem necessary.

Building a life structure involves making choices. You choose an occupation, a place of work, a place to live, a spouse, friends, and so on. During a stable period, the choices necessary for that period are made. Although there may be stresses and tension, the basic fabric of life is in place; commitments are made and carried out. A stable period usually lasts six or seven years, ten years at the most. A transition period usually lasts three or four years.

During a transition period, the previous life structure is ended and a new one is begun. At these times, we evaluate our lives and ask, "How am I doing? Am I doing what I want to do?

Do I need something I don't have? How can I get it?" We often decide to keep some elements of our former life structure and to give up or change others. We make new choices and reaffirm old ones. We place our bets and begin the next phase of our journey.

A transition time is difficult because it means judging oneself and exploring new possibilities. It can go relatively smoothly or it can be a time of crisis when a person feels hemmed in and the present seems intolerable but making changes seems impossible.

Why must a life structure be repeatedly modified over the years? There are two reasons. The first is that no one life structure can be built that allows total expression of our complex selves. Every life structure, no matter how thoughtfully created, is limited and must be modified to make room

for change and growth. The second reason is that we seem to have certain *developmental tasks* to accomplish at different times in our lives.

According to Robert J. Havighurst in his book *Developmental Tasks and Education,* a developmental task is one that is important to our future lives. "Successful achievement of [such a task] leads to [one's] happiness and to success with later tasks, while failure leads to unhappiness, disapproval by society, and difficulty with later tasks." Havighurst believes that these tasks are set for us by our biology (for example, having children must be accomplished during young adulthood) and by society, which "expects" us to play different roles at different ages. We will return to the particular tasks that Havighurst suggests for each era of adult life.

Early Adulthood

Early Adult Transition

The period of transition between preadulthood and adulthood is called the Early Adult Transition. It takes place between the ages of 17 and 22. These years are the bridge between adolescence and adulthood. The adolescent life structure is no longer appropriate. Now a person starts to form the first adult life structure and becomes a novice member of the adult world.

This is a time of dramatic change in a young person's life. Up to now, that person has been a student and has been taken care of by members of the older generation. While some independence is gained in adolescence, all of the early years have been a time of dependence on others. Now comes the task of leaving that kind of life behind. One is suddenly a fledgling adult, but still does not know how to be an adult.

The first major change is in relationships with parents. The young adult feels himself to be between families— too old to continue to live with parents, not quite ready or able to form a new family. He must separate from the family in which he grew up and form an identity separate from that family. Developing a new identity as an adult will allow him to move toward becoming fully responsible for his own life. Forming an identity means developing a view of one's strengths, accepting one's limitations, acknowledging one's needs and impulses, and living comfortably with one's body.

The ties with parents do not need to be severed, but they do need to be loos-

ened and changed. The young person needs freedom to take steps into the wider world, to explore possibilities, and to make independent choices.

When the relationship with parents has been changed, and the young person's independent identity formed, he can move toward increased self-sufficiency. The task of becoming an independent person is an important preparation for forming a new family. And so young adults begin to build their skills, to support themselves, and to give up their dependence on their parents.

Along with financial independence comes finding a new home base. College students may not be financially independent, but their new home base, the college, will be an important transitional home. They will be in charge of their own physical space for the first time. Many young adults choose to go to college far from home as a way of helping separate emotionally from their families.

During this transition period, the young person must make important and far-reaching choices—usually the choice of an occupation and sometimes the choice of a marital partner. The young adult can only get a limited amount of help with these choices, because the decisions depend on his understanding of his own most basic needs, interests, and talents.

The task of transforming interests into an occupation is not an easy one, and usually is not completed until one is past 30. Yet the basic choice must often be made early, especially when the occupation requires extensive training. Career choices made early in life often turn out to be a version of following in a parent's footsteps. For

example, a young man whose father had a civil service job and whose mother did mail-order work from home chose to work for the post office, a combination of both parents' work patterns.

Some young people choose occupations because their parents expect them either to follow a family pattern or to raise the family's social status. And some choose occupations because their parents oppose them. Others choose on the basis of earning power or current popularity. Ideally, in choosing a career, a person should assess his skills, talents, and aptitudes, learn about the advantages and disadvantages of possible choices, and finally choose one that will provide a high level of interest and satisfaction. Since very few people have sufficient experience to know such things before age 22, early occupational choices are often flawed and must be reexamined later in life.

Young women may make only tentative choices about their occupation, believing that the choice of a husband is more important to their future. This pattern is changing slowly, since society in the United States is coming to value women as independent adults.

The second major choice often made during this time is that of a lifetime partner. Young people have much yet to learn about intimacy with another person—not just sexual intimacy, but emotional intimacy, the everyday give and take of a close relationship with someone else beside parents, brothers, and sisters. The average age of a first marriage for women in the United States is 21; for men it is 23. According to the Population Reference Bureau in Washington,

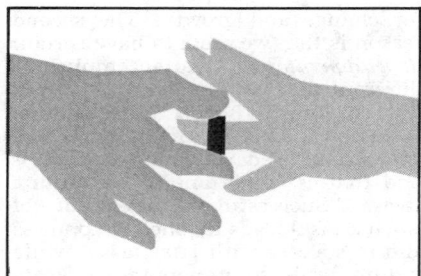

Median age at first marriage
is 21 for women and 23 for men.

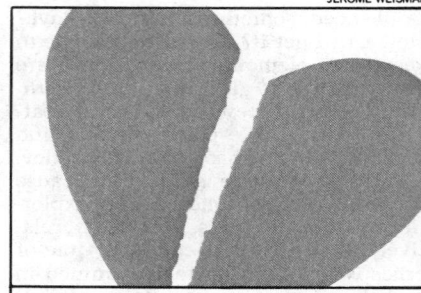

JEROME WEISMAN

Marriages between teenagers:
twice as likely to end in divorce
as later marriages.

D.C., 38 percent of women marry before they are 20. How do these young marriages fare? These women are twice as likely to divorce as are women who marry in their 20's. An early marriage may be an escape from one's family rather than a signal of real independence and choice.

Since 1970, more and more young people have been postponing marriage; women, especially, are choosing to marry later. Perhaps this is because of their understanding that there is much to learn about the process of intimacy before one can make a serious choice of a long-time partner.

Because these choices are so hard and of such major importance to the years that follow, some researchers think that young people should not be rushed into making them without sufficient preparation. Harvard psychologist Lawrence Kohlberg, for example, speaks of the importance of a "moratorium experience," a time during which the young adult can delay making major life decisions. This may be the time of the early college years, or it

may mean taking a year off to travel and to learn about the world.

However it is done, young people of this age have the developmental task of experimenting and exploring the world of adulthood. It is an exciting and stressful time; studies show that people of this age rate their life satisfaction as quite low, compared with older people's ratings. These young people have much to learn and are embarking on a journey filled with uncertainty. They will make a great many mistakes.

Entering the Adult World

The years between about 22 and 28 are a time to fashion the first adult life structure. While there is still time to continue exploring possibilities and to leave some options open, it is now also time to become more responsible for one's life. One must make at least ten-

tative commitments to occupation and to intimacy with another person.

Sometime in early adulthood, a person forms what Levinson calls the Dream—a sense of oneself as an adult, a vision of imagined possibility that generates excitement and energy. The Dream includes occupational ambitions, wishes for family or other close relationships, and other goals. The decade of the 20's is the time not only to form the Dream but to begin to live it out.

As a group, young adults are physically healthy, vigorous, and strong. Adolescence was a time of rapid physical change; now, for the first time, growth seems to cease. Physical energy and skills are at a peak. By the age of 25, a person has ended the adolescent growth time and entered the quiet plateau of young adulthood, the most stable time of life as far as physical functioning is concerned.

Young adults are more sexually active than any other age group. At the end of the teens and the beginning of the 20's, men feel strong sexual drives; it is the peak time for male sexuality. The peak of women's sexuality is said to be in the 30's. But some researchers believe that this is because it takes women some years of sexual activity to overcome their early training, which discourages them from exploring their sexual needs and interests. Women may need more time in adulthood to learn about and develop their own sexuality.

Psychoanalyst Erik Erikson describes the basic developmental task of young adulthood as acquiring a sense of intimacy with a loved person. A person emerging from adolescence with a firm sense of identity is ready to learn about intimacy. Since intimacy involves caring about someone else and

YOUNG ADULTHOOD *brings conflicting urges: one to pursue career goals energetically, the other to take some time out to explore or "find" oneself.*

sharing activities, thoughts, and feelings, one must have a strong sense of identity and worth before making a lasting commitment to a partnership. Intimacy involves significant sacrifices and compromises of one's own needs, and means the loss of some freedom. One must be able to recognize one's own and one's partner's imperfections and yet still desire a close human attachment.

Most people choose to marry before they are 30. However, statistics show that an increasing number of young adults are choosing to live alone, postponing the choice of a mate. A large number live with a partner of the other sex to whom they are not married. In 1977, for example, 2 million adults lived with a person of the other sex to whom they were not related.

Most young people believe they marry because they have met the "right" person. But studies show that the decision to marry is often influenced by family events. For example, people often decide to marry soon after the illness or death of a parent, after problems within the family, or after a loss of some kind. They may marry to avoid a deep sense of aloneness or to separate from the family and become independent.

The first years of marriage bring the highest sense of satisfaction *and* the highest rate of divorce. One of the peak times of divorce is in the early 20's. Many couples decide to have their first child, and thus they must also learn to become parents. Only recently removed from the shelter of their own parents' care, they may feel deeply inadequate as parents themselves or they may adopt their own parents' methods uncritically and find these methods do not work.

There are two parts to the task of parenting. The first has to do with the technical skills to be mastered if one is to care for an infant—diapering, bathing, nutrition, feeding, safety. The second is learning to interact with an infant on the social and emotional level—playing, talking, holding, giving warmth, support, and approval. Research psychiatrist Daniel Stern, in his book *The First Relationship,* emphasizes the importance of this task. New parents must learn how to do this from older people—usually from their own parents and family. Not much can be learned from courses or how-to books, Stern believes; one cannot really "teach" someone how to play with a baby. Young parents need on-the-job training and emotional support for the job of parenting, particularly during the difficult early months.

Women between the ages of 20 and 35 have fewer difficulties in pregnancy and labor than do either younger or older women. The reproductive system seems to function most efficiently during these years. The hormonal changes of pregnancy are the most extreme and sudden changes that ever occur in adulthood. During pregnancy, hormone levels may increase to several hundred times the level in nonpregnant women. Then, just before birth, the hormone levels drop quickly. These drastic changes are believed to be at least partly responsible for the common feelings of depression that come over a mother after her baby is born.

The issue for all adults, but particularly for young adult women, is how to divide their lives between marriage, children, and career. Women in their 20's have some hard choices. They may feel that they cannot do justice to a career and a family at the same time. It is during the 20's that women often alter their career plans to accommodate the needs of their husbands and their children.

This period, then, between 22 and 28, is a busy time, filled with new experiences, with learning about the world and one's place in it. Choices are made and carried out; the first adult life structure is built. A young adult learns about pleasures and responsibilities, costs and benefits, and the possibilities of adulthood. Havighurst summarizes the developmental tasks for the years from 20 to 40 as follows:

HAVIGHURST'S DEVELOPMENTAL TASKS FOR THE YEARS 20–40

1. choosing a mate
2. learning to live with that person
3. starting a family
4. rearing children
5. managing a household
6. choosing and entering an occupation
7. taking social responsibility
8. entering a social network of friends and colleagues

The decade of the 20's is a time of beginning the developmental work on all of these tasks.

CAREER OR FAMILY? *Young women usually go to work after their schooling, but many face the difficult choice of career or starting a family while in their early 20's. The conflict may persist through the child-bearing years.*

Age Thirty Transition

This transition time, the years between 28 and 32 or 33, is a link between two stable previous periods. It provides a chance to work on the flaws of the first adult life structure and to fix things that are not satisfying. It is a time to look at the structure built for the 20's and ask, "What have I done with my life so far? What do I want to change?"

The life structure of the 20's may have taken one of several forms. It may have been relatively stable and organized, but with important parts missing. Perhaps a major interest was left out. The structure may have included strong interest in more than one possible occupation, causing the person to work in several different directions at once, still not able to make up his mind. The structure may have been extremely unstable and incomplete, satisfying in its lack of responsibilities for a while, but now beginning to feel insecure. If a person does not have an occupation, a home, and a partner by age 30, he or she may begin to feel incomplete and rootless. The Age Thirty Transition is the time to do something about that, to make firm choices and commitments.

For many people, the 30th birthday is a shock. Time is passing. It is time to settle down to the serious business of achieving ambitions and goals. The few years around the age of 30 are a time for making adjustments in the framework of one's life, making major changes as they are needed. And, since major life changes are stressful, this can be a very tense time.

Settling Down

New choices are made and a new stable period begins, a period called Settling Down, which continues from about 33 to 40. This is the second adult life structure. A person invests time and energy in a few key choices, such as family, occupation, and perhaps a third area—a leisure-time activity, perhaps, or a political or religious cause. Seldom can a life structure support more than three major interest areas at any one time.

We have said that most physical functions change very little during the period of young adulthood, 20 to 40. Those changes that do take place are silent—that is, we do not notice that our bodies are changing very much. We may notice some lessening of energy between the 20's and the 30's; for example, we may no longer be interested in staying up all night just for fun. Beginning at about age 25, muscle strength begins to decrease. Beginning at about age 30, bones lose some

of their strength and density, becoming more brittle. Our joints are not as flexible as they once were. Vision and hearing are not as acute. The efficiency of our heart, lungs, and digestive system begins slowly to decrease after the 20's.

Mental abilities are beginning to change. Up to about age 30, people learn quickly, use information rapidly, and have a good memory for recent events. After 30, people do not score as well on tests that require speed and close concentration. These decreases are very small at first, but will continue slowly throughout life. To compensate for this decline in ability, there are increases in other abilities well into old age—vocabulary, fund of information, and wisdom and skill gained from experience.

Young adults are in an enviable position. They have passed through the childhood phase of many acute illnesses (colds, flu, childhood diseases) and have fewer of these than at any previous time in life. They are not yet old enough to be developing the chronic diseases of later life. According to the National Safety Council, the major cause of death for this age group is accidents—motor vehicle accidents, poisonings, drownings, shootings. Men more than women, and black men in particular, have the highest death rate from accidents and from violence, including homicide and suicide.

In their 30's, women who are childless feel the biological clock running down, and may have hard decisions to make—to interrupt their lives and have children now or to remain childless. A woman who has her first child when she is over 30 may have more difficulty than younger women because her body has lost some of its

elasticity and her pelvis is not as flexible for the passage of the baby through the birth canal. In addition, as a mother she may have less physical energy for caring for active youngsters, and she may be out of step with her friends, who may already have preteen or adolescent children. Yet there are advantages to having a first baby in the 30's. A woman is likely to have a stronger sense of her own identity after 30, in addition to greater financial security, and experience that will help her as a parent.

Parents in their 30's who have adolescent children face different stresses. Teenagers challenge the family in various ways and often put a strain on the marital relationship. These are years when all the skills of parenting are called into use.

At the beginning of the 30's, a person is still a junior member of society. As the decade progresses he is working toward becoming a senior member.

Harry L. Cross, 45, has been promoted to Vice President, Sales and Marketing, for the ZZZ Corporation. Mr. Cross began his career as a commission rep for the PLM Co., and moved to ZZZ three years later. With ZZZ he has served as assistant sales manager, director of international marketing, and director of national sales. James Norton, president of ZZZ, credits Cross with increasing ZZZ's share of the market in several product lines, and he anticipates further growth under his direction.

PROMOTION *to increasingly responsible positions may be a source of great satisfaction and great anxiety in middle age.*

TELEVISION *is a focus for family gatherings. At its best, it provides shared entertainment, but it may also provide an excuse for avoiding each other.*

This means developing competence in work and in family life and becoming more anchored in a community. People find that they have, and want, more responsibility. The demands are great; so are the rewards. If all goes well, it is a period with a sense of order, planning, pursuit of long-range goals. Important career decisions are made that may determine the course of occupational achievement for the rest of one's working life.

The 30's is a serious time of "making it." By the end of the decade, one wants to be senior, to speak more strongly with one's own voice, to have a greater measure of authority. Yet the experience is not all positive. Psychiatrist Roger Gould found that people in their 30's discovered life is more difficult and painful than it had appeared to them in their 20's. They lost the illusions that they could do anything or be anything and they began to realize vaguely that life would not last forever and that they themselves had important limitations.

Middle Adulthood

The Age Forty Transition

Forty seems like a milestone, the approximate midpoint of life. The Age Forty, or Midlife, Transition is a time when the life structure of early adulthood is evaluated. For most people, parts of the old life structure will not seem appropriate or satisfying for the future.

This transition is especially important because it is the link between the era of early adulthood and the era of middle adulthood. It is time for a review of all of early adulthood, sometimes with a sense of urgency, of time running out. The questions now, according to researcher Levinson, are "What have I done with my life? What do I really get from and give to my family, friends, work, community—and self? What is it I truly want for myself and others? What are my greatest talents and how am I using (or wasting) them? What are my central values and how are they reflected in my life? What have I done with my early Dream and what do I want to do with it now?"

Asking and answering those questions can be a great struggle.

One of the aspects of life that may trigger this far-reaching reappraisal is a sudden awareness of physical aging. You may feel stiff when you get out of bed in the morning. When you look in the mirror, you see a few wrinkles, gray hairs, a bald spot, a chin line that is not as firm as it once was. You find that your body is thickening. You feel less vigorous. You need reading glasses or bifocals in order to read small print. As psychoanalyst Elliott Jaques has said, "The individual has stopped growing up and has begun to grow old." In the cycle of generations, you have become next-to-the-old.

You may not have an illness, or feel particularly unhealthy, but physical functioning is gradually slowing down. You cannot move as quickly as you once could. Many of your body systems are less efficient. Hormonal output decreases. And your immune system, which fights off infections, is less effective.

AGING *happens to all, even the famous, as these two photographs of Frank Sinatra suggest, the first taken in the late 1930's, the second in the late 1970's.*

Why does all this happen? No one knows for sure. Some physical changes noticeable in the 40's seem to be universal, occurring in everyone. Other changes may be more closely linked to lifestyle, especially accumulated years of smoking, lack of exercise, overeating, overuse of alcohol, and tension.

With the experience of bodily decline and aging comes the sense of mortality. One must now come to terms with ambitions and goals. Will they ever be realized? Is it worth continuing to work toward them? Or should new dreams be built?

During the Age Forty Transition, one finds how much of life up to this point has been based on illusions—long-held assumptions about oneself and the world that are false. It is a time to recognize which of one's beliefs are false and to try to see more clearly, to be less childlike in one's view of the world. Recognizing one's illusions is painful, but it can often free one to strike out in new and more realistic directions.

At 40, we are also likely to reclaim and recognize parts of the self that have been neglected. Levinson and his colleagues found that development during the young adult period requires people to suppress certain aspects of the self in order to succeed in building a first adult life structure. There is not time or energy for everything at once. In the pursuit of some goals and ambitions, some personal needs and interests are put aside. A father with young children may not have time for the music he loves; a woman with heavy work responsibilities may have to forego activity in a political party or religious institution. But as a person enters the 40's, the wish to recover these lost interests becomes stronger.

Roger Gould points out that this period is often one of emotional instability and pain, resembling adolescence, the transition into early adulthood. There are important changes to be made; as Carl Jung said, "We cannot live the afternoon of life according to the program of life's morning."

"Wake up, Harold! It's 1971, and the children are grown and gone."

© 1971 *SATURDAY REVIEW*/HENRY MARTIN

Entering Middle Adulthood

Now, after a painful reassessment, we build a new life structure for middle age. Some of us try to pretend that there have been no changes, that we are as young and vigorous as ever. But both physical and psychological evidence is against us. Gradually we become aware of the distance between ourselves and young adults; we begin to feel closer to those who are old and who understand what life is like.

Havighurst lists the developmental tasks of middle adulthood as follows:

**HAVIGHURST'S
DEVELOPMENTAL TASKS
FOR MIDDLE ADULTHOOD**

1. assisting and allowing children to become adults
2. accepting and achieving a place in the community
3. maintaining a satisfactory work life
4. creating adult leisure activities
5. developing the relationship to one's spouse
6. accepting and adjusting to the physical changes of middle age
7. adjusting to aging parents

As one passes into the 40's, one becomes aware of how much has been gained in adulthood. Novelist T. H. White, in *The Once and Future King*, describes "the seventh sense—a thing called knowledge of the world, which people do not have until they are middle-aged. It is something which cannot be taught to younger people."

There are both gains and losses to be managed. On the side of losses come those physical changes noted in the section on the Age Forty Transition. All of us are concerned about these changes. In particular, all of us are concerned about our sexuality and our reproductive functions. These become a troubling issue during midlife.

For both men and women, there are decreases in sex hormones. These hormones are involved not only in reproduction and sexuality, but also in regulating many other bodily functions. We are more familiar with the changes that occur for women because there is a clear signal of hormone changes, the menopause. Usually occurring between the early 40's and the mid-50's, the menopause is the time during which menstruation and ovulation (the process of producing eggs in the ovaries) cease naturally. Menopause is a process that takes place over a period of from two to five years, signaling the end of the time in life during which a woman can bear children. Hormonal changes may play a part both in the physical discomfort and psychological distress some women feel.

Psychologist Bernice Neugarten studied women's feelings about menopause and found that most women were happy to have menstruation over. Some women feel that they are no longer sexually desirable because they can no longer bear children, but many have a stronger sex drive after menopause because they no longer fear an unwanted pregnancy.

The hormonal changes in men are gradual, without specific or dramatic signs. But male hormonal changes do have a negative effect on sexual performance. Men often feel depressed about these changes, and should be reminded that the skill and experience they have gained over the years of sexual activity make up for decreased physical ability.

Chronic diseases begin to appear in middle adulthood. Heart disease, lung disease, cancer now begin their attacks. Years of poor diet, drinking, smoking, and stress can bring on or worsen such diseases as hypertension, diabetes, and atherosclerosis. People who change their diets and their patterns of exercise to adapt to their changing physical status are likely to remain healthier.

Even under the best conditions of self-care, however, our chances of having a chronic disease increase after 45. Heart disease and cancer are the leading causes of death between 45 and 64. Their rates are sharply higher than in younger age groups. In general, men have a higher death rate from heart disease, while women have a higher death rate from cancer.

In their 40's, most people who have chosen to be parents are engaged in "launching" their children, helping them to leave the home and strike out on their own. It is a time of much coming and going. The almost-grown children are gone most of the time, but return occasionally; they come for holidays and at other times when they need a safe harbor. It is a period of "now I need you, now I don't."

It has long been thought that women suffer when their children leave home, that they are left with an "empty nest," and that they are likely to be depressed. This is true for some women, but many women feel a sense of relief and are delighted to help their children pack. (In fact, the child who does not leave home as expected can be a major problem.) Women feel that they can now turn their attention to their own needs. Most of the women studied felt a loss, but they rarely felt devastated. Men, on the other hand, may feel the loss more acutely, especially if they regret spending so little time with their children while they were growing up.

As the launching is accomplished and the children leave, the marital relationship may need revision. Some researchers have found that marital dissatisfaction reaches a peak just before the children leave, but this is followed for many couples by a sense of increased satisfaction when the last child is gone. Yet many others find this change so extreme that an entirely new marriage seems necessary for a new phase of life. The divorce rate reaches a high peak among couples in their 40's. Many people decide that the new relationship they want must be with a new partner, not realizing that a new relationship can be negotiated with the same partner. After 20 or 25 years of marriage, the relationship may still be reviewed and refocused.

RAY ELLIS/PHOTO RESEARCHERS

MID-ADULT LIFE *offers new and promising relationships such as those with one's young grandchildren.*

New attitudes and kinds of behavior may be needed. Whether the renegotiation takes place with the same partner or with a new one, it can be stormy and difficult.

When the children of a marriage, now young adults, begin to choose their partners, new people (in-laws) enter the lives of the parents and form important new relationships. As these new members of the family are added, emotional relationships become more complicated. When grandchildren are born, the person in middle adulthood takes on a whole new role, and now has to learn about how to be a grandparent. Part of the task of the 40's and 50's is to let go of the pleasures and satisfactions of parenting young people, to view one's children as being able to take care of themselves, and to build new affections, loyalties, and bonds with the new family members they bring in.

People in their 40's are caught in the middle; not only do they have to learn how to be good parents to adult offspring, but they also have to be good offspring to their own parents, who are now elderly and may be ill or dying. This is a difficult task at best, but the care of dying parents is worst when relationships have been troubled and old conflicts have never been resolved. For middle-aged people who have not resolved issues with their aging parents, who have not forgiven them or been forgiven by them for a lifetime of problems, the parents' illness and death brings an overriding sense of guilt.

Erik Erikson, author of *Identity and the Life Cycle,* believes that the major developmental task of middle adulthood is acquiring a sense of *generativity,* an interest in establishing and guiding the next generation. This may be accomplished through parenthood, by the care and guidance of young people other than one's own offspring, or

by creative and humanitarian accomplishments that affect the next generation. This task is often carried out through the organization in which one works. One becomes a mentor to younger colleagues.

A mentor is a person who is eight to 15 years older than the younger person he will guide, sponsor, and counsel, usually in career matters. Those who are in positions of authority are most appropriate to become mentors; a mentor generally has attained a senior position in the job world. Mentors are usually in their 40's and 50's. Junior adults, in their 20's and 30's, may have a mentor; senior adults must give up having a mentor and become mentors themselves. The role of wise, authoritative guide is a role of middle adulthood.

By middle adulthood, a worker has either made progress and is reaching career goals or has gotten stuck at a lower level, with a feeling that there is little chance of "making it" now. Sociologist Rosabeth Moss Kanter, in *Men and Women of the Corporation,* notes three ways a person can get stuck in an organization. First, a person may find that he or she has been following a career course that does not lead to higher positions. Second, a person may lose out in the competition. There are many competent people, but only a few top-level positions. Some qualified people will lose to others. Third, a person may have taken the wrong career path; his or her interests and abilities may not have been in the right direction, or training may not have been appropriate.

What happens to workers who get stuck in midlife? Some learn to be content with their place and their work; they may relax and enjoy their careers in a new way. Others feel sad and disappointed and may take out their unhappiness on coworkers or on their families. Still others launch themselves into new occupations, perhaps following a major interest that was put aside in early adulthood. Changing careers in middle age is far more common and possible today than it was decades ago.

Even those who are successful by their own standards and those of others may find that their occupational

victories are hollow, that the positions they worked so hard to attain are oppressive and dreary. They have to decide whether to stay with these choices, or to make others—either choosing a new career direction, or to expand some other interest that is not work-related.

It is during these middle years that many women renew their occupational interests, set aside during the years of parental responsibility. Studies show that women in their 40's and 50's feel less need to serve and please others and are freer to pursue their own needs and develop their abilities. Men at this age, on the other hand, become more aware of their own feelings and their connections with other people. This "crossing" of interests is a major cause of misunderstanding in midlife marriages.

Culmination of Middle Adulthood

The next transition stage, between 50 and 55, is called the Age Fifty Transition. This is often a smooth transition, used to make minor adjustments in life structure, but basically continuing on the same path. However, if major evaluation work was not done during the midlife transition, one may have to do it now. Therefore, if there is unfinished developmental work left over from earlier periods, this transition may be a time of stress and confusion.

The period between 55 and 60 is the final period of middle adulthood, the culmination of this 20-year era. It is similar to the Settling Down period of early adulthood, a time of stability and fulfillment.

Studies by Bernice Neugarten at the University of Chicago show that the 50's are a time of quiet thinking about life, a time of reorganizing how time is used, a period when people form new understandings of themselves, of time, and of death. Researcher George Vaillant at Harvard also finds that people report the 50's to be a quieter time than the 40's; they feel content, tranquil, with some mild regrets.

Changing careers in midlife is becoming increasingly common.

JEROME WEISMAN

The divorce rate reaches a peak among couples in their 40's.

Physically, the 50's are a time of slowly continuing decline of the functions first noticed in the 40's. After about 50, many men have problems with the prostate gland, located at the neck of the bladder. This gland stores the fluid that carries sperm. As a man grows older, the prostate often becomes enlarged; it may also become inflamed or infected. The result is painful, difficult, or frequent urination and difficulty with sexual intercourse. Cancer of the prostate is also one of the leading causes of cancer deaths in men.

For both men and women as they age, those who were sexually active when they were younger are likely to remain active in later life as well. Although men may be concerned with their diminishing sexual prowess, as measured by frequency, continued sexual activity is a major source of satisfaction well into old age.

Many couples find themselves increasingly satisfied with their marriage after launching their children. They find companionship and mutual caring; they have learned how to care for each other. Sexual intimacy, uninterrupted by children, is often more satisfying.

However, divorces after 30 or more years of marriage are becoming more common in the United States. Some of these marriages were created for and sustained by the task of parenting; when the years of active parenting are over, there is no glue to hold the relationship together and it cannot be renegotiated. When a divorce follows many years of marriage, the after-divorce period is especially painful. Children take sides and partners feel victimized. Long-term friendships are disrupted because friends of the couple either break off relationships with both parties or feel they have to choose

between the two. The fabric of the couple's lives seems to unravel, and they may doubt their ability to start over. Dating, after many years of marriage, may be particularly hard.

In career life, people in their 50's have reached maximum capacity and ability to handle complex issues. The knowledge and wisdom of middle age are highly valued, yet competition from younger colleagues may threaten the older worker. In George Vaillant's study, one man reported "I feel under attack by ambitious young people."

In general, people in their 50's report that this final period of middle adulthood is apt to be a period of calm and quiet satisfaction. They still have health and energy, although they may be feeling some elements of physical decline. Developmental tasks from the 40's continue to be important; for example, learning to be a grandparent may be an exciting new role.

Late Adulthood

As Carl Jung has observed, "Being old is highly unpopular." The transition to "being old," to late adulthood, takes place between 60 and 65, marking the end of middle age and creating the basis for the era of late adulthood. The task of this transition period is to come to terms with entering the final season of life.

This final broad period of life, age 65 and over, is called late adulthood. It has not yet been carefully studied in terms of stable and transition periods; we still have much to learn about development during these years.

Havighurst cites these developmental tasks for late life:

HAVIGHURST'S DEVELOPMENTAL TASKS FOR LATE LIFE

1. adjusting to decreasing physical strength and health
2. adjusting to retirement and reduced income
3. adjusting to death of a spouse
4. establishing an affiliation with one's age group; accepting one's age and status in society
5. meeting social and civic responsibilities; sharing wisdom, participating in public affairs
6. establishing satisfactory living arrangements

The physical aging process continues, with increased slowing down and loss of vigor, and decreased vision and hearing. Biological decline proceeds gradually and irregularly, with wide individual differences in timing and amount of change. Hair turns white or

gray and is thinner. Muscle tone is less firm. Tissues are less elastic and resilient. Skin wrinkles. Teeth are lost. Joints become stiff.

Sexual ability and interest can be retained, but hormonal secretions are less and older men experience some continuing decrease in sexual responsiveness and capacity for sexual performance. Both sexes experience a decline in intensity and duration of orgasm late in life. But more than physical limitations, the limitations of society often keep the elderly from enjoying all aspects of their sexuality. Society says in many ways that sex is only for the young. We joke about dir-

ty old men and women's loss of youthful attractiveness. We should not then be surprised that older people feel upset about their changing bodies and fear that they have lost their sexual ability and attractiveness.

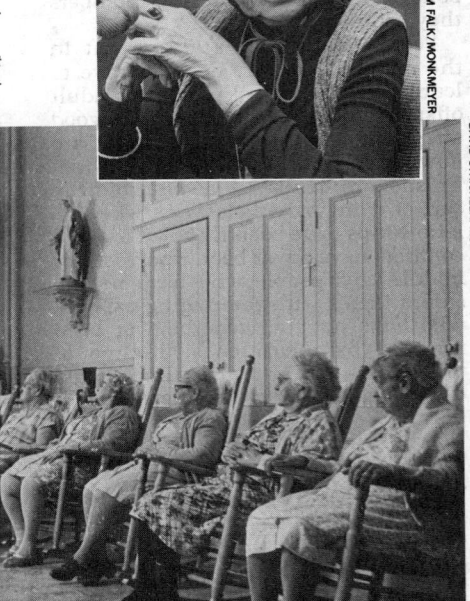

OLD AGE *brings infirmity to many, but many, like Maggie Kuhn* (inset) *remain active and useful for years past retirement.*

As we grow older, into the 70's and 80's, we must learn how to adjust to decreasing physical strength and health. We must learn how to manage what seem to be inevitable—ill health and physical decline. Elderly people have fewer acute illnesses, such as colds and flu, but when they do have these illnesses, they are sick for longer periods of time than are younger people. The body gradually loses some of its ability to heal itself, to return to normal after an illness or injury.

Chronic illness is a major problem for the elderly. According to the United States Public Health Service, the four major chronic illnesses of the elderly are heart disease, hypertension (high blood pressure), diabetes, and arthritis. Over half of all persons over 65 have some kind of heart problem, and half of the over-65 population suffer from some degree of arthritis. Some chronic illness can be kept under control with diet, exercise, and medication, but about 30 percent of elderly people report that they are limited in their daily activities as a result of chronic illness.

Aging brings with it a decrease in the general functioning of the heart and circulatory system. Veins and arteries lose their elasticity. Blood pressure goes up. Two conditions, arteriosclerosis (hardening of the blood vessel wall) and atherosclerosis (narrowing and closing of a blood vessel) interfere with the amount of blood that can reach the brain; as a result, mental ability may be impaired.

Scientists still do not agree that mental abilities decline naturally with age. It does seem that some mental processes slow down with age; for example, the speed with which a person can perform a mental task declines. This slowing down is particularly striking on complicated tasks that require decision-making. Short-term memory (memory for recent events) declines with age; long-term memory (for events in the past) shows no decline. Other kinds of skills, such as vocabulary and fund of knowledge, do not decline, and indeed may increase throughout life.

Older people must set priorities for their use of energy and recognize that there are new limitations that require adjustment. Some people deny that any changes are taking place and attempt to do all they did when they were younger. Unfortunately, many younger people admire this kind of unrealistic thinking because it makes their own aging seem less real. An older person must understand the realities of aging and tailor a new life structure to meet the new reality. Concretely, this may mean moving to a safer and more manageable home, changing household or job responsibilities, and hiring help for physical work.

Retirement from work can be both a gift and a burden. On the negative side, retirement removes a worker from a whole social and occupational network of other people, places, and happenings, a lively part of the world that may offer a great deal of stimulation and pleasure. Some older people, missing their work life, decide to embark on second careers as a way of fulfilling their need to feel productive and involved. Others involve themselves in volunteer work.

On the positive side, a retired person may find more time to spend on activities that take the place of work as a way of affirming identity and self-esteem. Many retirees enjoy their new life structure, and become full-time participants in leisure activities. One's financial situation, of course, determines what kinds of activities are possible. Some people look forward to this use of time with great pleasure, and enjoy these years fully. Others find that they cannot sustain an interest in recreation, but need other things to do.

Two kinds of retirement experiences seem most likely to lead to satisfaction. In the first, a person is finally able to satisfy some unmet need, to do something he or she wished to do but had never done—for example, a recreational activity or a second career. The second kind of experience occurs when a person concentrates on some service to others, on something larger than the self, something that will continue beyond one's own lifetime. This contribution to society may be large or small; the important thing is that it be a continuation of one's own connection with others.

Several studies, notably ones by psychologists Bernice Neugarten and David Guttman, show that older men and women show some personality changes. Older men become more interested in caring for and connecting with other people, while older women become more assertive. Men seek more closeness, women seek more independence. Older people who can allow the unsatisfied aspects of themselves to emerge and be satisfied have greater feelings of happiness and may live longer.

One of the stereotypes of people over 65 is that most of them live alone or in institutions. In fact, only four percent live in institutions at any one time, and 90 percent do not live alone. Twenty-five percent live with children and 80 percent live within one hour's travel from one of their children. Many older people strongly prefer to maintain their own households rather than live with their children. Increasingly often, several older people live together. Most older people and their children are in frequent contact, giving each other emotional support in a pattern that has been called "intimacy

LONELINESS *is a problem as friends die, but older people can and do make friends with members of the younger generation.*

UNITED NATIONS

LES MAHON/MONKMEYER

at a distance.'' Seventy percent of people over 65 have grandchildren, and 33 percent have great-grandchildren.

As the years pass, the older person loses more and more friends and associates to death. First, the last members of the preceding generation—parents, aunts, uncles—die. Then increasing numbers of contemporaries die. But the most stressful loss is the death of a husband or wife, the loss of intimacy and companionship of many years.

Older people do remarry and find new intimacy, but for many it is not easy. Older women in particular may have difficulty in finding potential spouses of their own age. Since men die at an earlier age than women on the average, there are many more older women than older men. In the United States, there are 80 men for every 100 women ages 55 to 64; 72 men per 100 women ages 65 to 74; and 63 men to 100 women after age 75. In addition, two-thirds of men over 65 are married, but only one-third of women over 65.

The developmental task designated by Erikson for older people, beginning in the 60's, is the establishment of a sense of integrity. Integrity here means the acceptance of one's own life as it has been lived; it includes giving up the wish that things might have been different, and accepting one's life as one's own responsibility.

People who accomplish this developmental task look back on their lives with understanding, with a sense of membership in a wider world, and a comradeship with other people. Without this sense of integrity, an older person looks back with feelings of despair and fears the end of life. The despair is for what might have been; and for the realization that there is now not enough time to try other ways of life that might have been more satisfying. Bitterness prevails.

One of the most important activities of old age is what Robert Butler, director of the National Institute of Aging, calls the life review. The life review is a process of recollection and reintegration of one's past life. The process begins when one realizes that life is almost over; it is a step in preparation for death and makes the acceptance of death easier. The review consists of a general survey of one's life, of remembered experiences, conflicts, feelings. It may proceed silently, or it may be discussed with others. It is partly conscious and partly unconscious, a lengthy process, taking place over a period of years. Memories, thoughts, dreams, nightmares—all have a place in the life review. Often there is a belated resolution of old conflicts, a mental reorganization of the past based on better understanding. The process stimulates feelings of regret, nostalgia, sadness, guilt, sometimes despair. It is most painful for those who find they have been, in Butler's words, ''thoughtless in their use of life.'' The

"Oh, it hasn't been all bad. There were parts of 1918, 1925, 1946, and 1947 that I liked."

© 1980 THE NEW YORKER/HENRY MARTIN

MARITAL STATUS AND LIVING ARRANGEMENTS OF PEOPLE OVER 65
(millions)

	TOTAL	MEN	WOMEN	MEN PER 100 WOMEN
All people over 65	23.1	9.5	13.6	70
Married, living with spouse	12.6	7.4	5.2	142
Not married (single, widowed, divorced)	10.5	2.1	8.4	25
Living alone	7.1	1.5	5.6	27

AMONG PEOPLE OVER 65, *there are four times as many unattached women (widowed, single, or divorced) as there are single men.*

end product of the life review, however, can be wisdom and serenity.

Younger people often do not help their elders with the review. Reminiscences of the elderly are often scorned by those who listen. Too often the preoccupation with memories of the past is regarded as a symptom of ''senility,'' and the process of life review does not meet with understanding and support.

In a study by Edwin S. Shneidman, most people reported that they preferred their death to be in old age, and that it be sudden, nonviolent, quiet, and dignified. Unfortunately, the reality is that most deaths are not sudden and are not likely to be dignified.

Death most often comes at the end of a chronic, debilitating illness. Such illnesses bring great stress to the dying person and to the family; toward the end it is not unusual for the patient and the family to wish for the death to come. In this situation, the whole family may close down communication,

refusing to talk to each other or to the dying person about the final developmental process, the process of dying. If people work at it, and are willing to tolerate the anxiety and emotional pain that have to be expressed, the dying person and the family can resolve leftover issues and say a loving goodby to each other before death.

Each of us hopes to arrive at our own time of dying with an appreciation of a life well-lived. The study of adult development seeks to understand the richness and complexity of human life and to introduce us to common patterns of life as well as to the uniqueness of each individual life. In this pattern of periods in the cycle of life, each period has its time and place, its structure to be created, its tasks to be done. Each period offers us growth, pain, satisfaction, and discovery. Our understanding of the pattern of our lives can enrich us.

—*Marjorie Bayes*

MARRIAGE AND FAMILY

Coming together for mutual comfort and for raising a family is universal among human beings. Although specific customs differ from culture to culture, in every society some form of marriage has been sanctioned and protected both by religious authorities and the state. Husband and wife acknowledge certain responsibilities to each other and to the family, and each receives both internal (emotional) and external (religious and legal) encouragement to carry out his or her individual responsibilities.

Anthropologists and sociologists have studied a wide variety of marriage customs and rituals in different cultures and ages. Even with a single society, there may be several models for marriage among people of different classes, or communities, and religious affiliations.

Observers believe that marriage in 20th-century America has been changing rather rapidly. Although being married once for life (monogamy) remains the accepted ideal, divorce has become so prevalent that some now describe the prevailing custom as serial monogamy—that is, having a succession of spouses, one at a time. The specific responsibilities of husband and wife in raising and supporting a family also show signs of change. Such changes can introduce new pressures and confusions to marriages, further complicating the already complex psychological relationships between men and women and between parents and children.

Earlier sections in this volume have outlined the developmental stages of childhood and adulthood. In a similar way, this section outlines the stages of marriage from the point of view of the partners. The emphasis is on the typical course of events rather than on the atypical. A later section, "Individual and Family Problems," considers some of the problems that may arise in a family.

Thinking About Marriage

Why do people marry? Although the reasons may seem obvious, many are in fact unconscious.

What is clear is that most people marry in order to meet some of their own needs. Some of these needs are emotional. It is important to feel that there is someone we can count on, someone who will have our interests at heart, who will love and cherish us and agree to be loved and cherished in return.

Other needs are physical. Young adults in particular are conscious of a need for physical lovemaking, both the act of sex itself and related kinds of close physical contact. Needs for physical closeness can be met outside marriage, but most men and women look for a permanent and stable relationship in which they can receive and give physical pleasure and comfort as well as emotional support.

Still other needs are material. In the traditional marriage, a man seeks a woman to help him set up and keep a house. A woman seeks a man who will be a provider and protector. These traditional roles are not as clearly defined today as in past generations, but it remains true that two people living together can help provide for each other's material needs, dividing the labor and making life easier. The need for mutual support is especially great when a couple has young children.

Marriage not only satisfies the needs of individuals, it also satisfies the

FALLING IN LOVE *is one part of preparing for marriage.*

needs of society. Society—through the laws of the state and through prevailing moral and religious codes—prefers marriage as the framework for lasting relationships between men and women and for raising children. Individuals see in marriage a fulfillment of the need to act in accordance with society's expectations.

Not all reasons for marriage are positive. Those who marry primarily because society expects it are overreacting to societal pressures. Teenagers sometimes marry to get away from unhappy homes, thinking more of what they are escaping than of what they are getting into. After an unhappy romance or a divorce, people sometimes marry to get back at the person who has rejected them. Still others may marry out of a deep fear of being alone.

If a person is contemplating marriage and realizes that most of his or her reasons are negative, it would be wise to reconsider. The problems of an individual are not often solved by getting married. In fact, in many cases, taking on the responsibilities of marriage can intensify them.

Choosing a Spouse

There is some truth in the notion of falling in love, and it can be an exciting experience. Some deep, almost unconscious, part of one person is drawn to another. Suddenly it may seem that anything is possible. People in love learn to take risks. Often their love teaches them about powers and attractions they scarcely knew they had.

Yet romantic love is not enough in itself to guarantee a happy marriage. Most teenagers learn that they can fall out of, as well as into, love. Romantic love may also include strong negative elements, notably the desire to dominate or possess the other person.

Because romantic love is so intense and emotional, it is often "blind," unwilling to recognize any negative aspects of the relationship. In many cultures, parents have made all the marriage arrangements for their sons and daughters. This would seem intolerable to most people today, but partners in such marriages seem to have had a fair chance for happiness. We do not necessarily choose better for ourselves than others might choose for us. But how are we to know what qualities a person should look for in choosing a marriage partner?

Compatibility. Perhaps the most important is compatibility. The word can mean many things. It suggests first that each partner is secure enough in his or her own identity to be able to recognize the identity of the other. Compatibility also means being able to give and to receive emotionally.

To many people, compatibility suggests that the partners should be of similar racial, religious, and social background. Studies have shown that there are many very happy mixed (racial, religious, and social) marriages. Yet partners of different backgrounds should realize that they begin with some handicaps and that their differences could one day lead to unhappiness. It is important, too, that partners agree at least on matters about which they feel strongly. For a deeply religious person to marry one who is an atheist could be disastrous.

Compatibility usually connotes some combination of similarities and differences. Those who seek a partner too like themselves risk eventual boredom; those who seek perfect opposites may come to find constant differences tiresome and irritating.

Stability. Another desirable quality in a prospective partner is stability. No one is a perfectly unshakable pillar of emotional strength; but those who fly into violent rages or who often are incapacitated by deep depressions are not likely to be cured by marriage.

Common views. In a sturdy partnership, the common views of the partners go beyond their love for each other. During courtship, there should be time for some serious explorations of each partner's values and aspirations. For example, the couple should be in general agreement on such questions as:

- How important is marriage compared to work, child-raising, possessions, religious or civic activities, hobbies?
- What should be expected from one's partner in pursuing a career or further study?
- How important is having children? How many? When?
- How important are money and possessions? How little could one be happy with?
- How important are other friendships and associations? Should a partner be willing to move away from family and friends? Is it right to take time away from a partner for a hobby or activity?

There are no "right" or "wrong" answers to such questions. But if prospective partners answer them very differently, chances are that their marriage will be troubled.

It is also important to remember that answers to such questions may change over time. Newlyweds may not expect to spend any spare time away from their partners; a year later, they may feel differently. A partner may want to have six children but have a change of mind after the arrival of the first. Even two partners in general agreement should remain flexible, allowing room for both their own answers and those of their partner to alter as conditions change.

Unconscious needs. It is often the "hidden" needs that people bring to their marriages that cause misunderstanding and disappointment. Problems are especially likely when unexpressed needs are unrealistic or contradictory.

For example, a woman may invite her husband to father her, then reject his fathering because it threatens her independence. By the same token, a man may feel a need for emotional support and comfort, yet not know how to express this need. Even though he never asks for support, he may be disappointed that his spouse does not provide it.

In the excitement of a whirlwind romance, such deep contradictory needs may pass unnoticed. When this happens, the needs appear early in marriage and must be dealt with then. A person contemplating marriage is wise to examine himself or herself carefully for signs of unrealistic or contradictory wishes. Those who see their own contradictions can tolerate contradictions in their partners.

People who have dated widely are likely to have a clearer and more real-

UNDERSTANDING ONE ANOTHER: *shared interests, such as a sport or activity* (left) *or discussion of campus events between classmates* (right), *help us understand the points of view and motivations of others.*

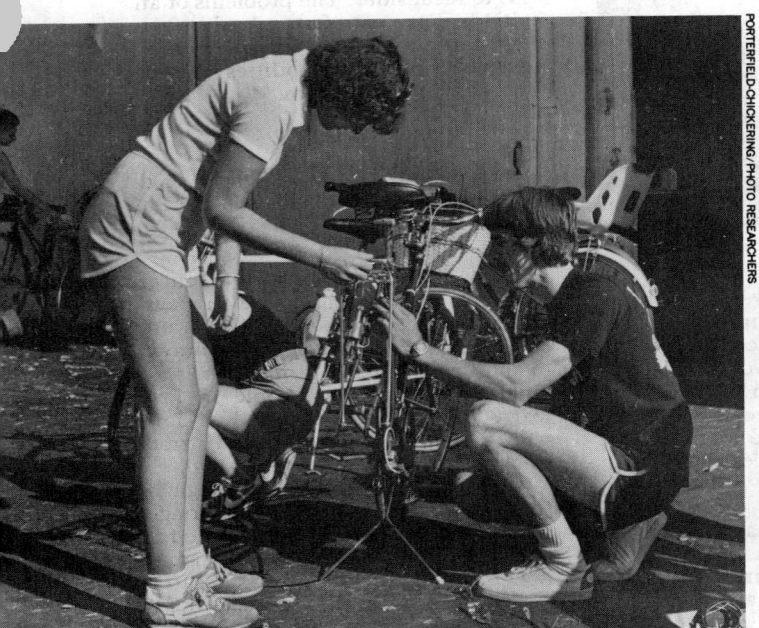

istic idea both of their own needs and of what they may reasonably expect from a partner. Those who marry with very little dating experience seem more likely to be disappointed in their spouse and in marriage.

Sense of humor.
A sense of humor can be the most important quality of all, for its basis is the ability to see oneself and others in perspective. If a couple cannot see the laughable side of love, perhaps the relationship is *too* serious. A sense of humor is a sign of emotional balance.

Religion and Society

Both religion and the state take marriage very seriously, their main concern being the maintenance of stable family life.

Prospective partners often are so involved with each other that they ignore the larger social significance of marriage. Only when they begin to prepare for the wedding do they realize its importance to society and to their parental families.

The view of marriage as a partnership designed to provide self-fulfillment for a man and a woman has developed only in the last hundred years. Before then, marriage was primarily a social arrangement for the proper and orderly raising of children and the passing of family values, religious and moral beliefs, and property from one generation to the next. Such considerations remain important.

Religious concerns.
Nearly all major religous groups stress the permanence of the marriage vow. In varying degrees, they frown upon divorce, instructing their members that the marriage relationship is intended to outlast other kinds of relationships. In the words of one traditional ceremony, the partners promise to remain faithful "for richer or for poorer, in sickness and in health, till death do us part." Some denominations do not allow remarriage for divorced persons.

Civic concerns.
In all modern societies, the state registers all marriages, recognizing them as civil agreements between the two parties. The state may also enforce certain terms of the marriage agreement, requiring a working spouse to support his or her family, for example.

The legal implications of marrying often do not occur to a couple until the marriage has reached a point of dissolution. Partners contemplating a divorce soon realize that the state also regulates all divorces by providing for child support and custody, dividing property, and the like.

What Kind of Relationship?

It seems likely that one major cause for separations and divorces is the failure of the partners to understand what each expects from marriage. Many couples contemplating marriage seem to assume that all good marriages are the same, thereby creating a perfect climate for later misunderstanding and bitterness. Three ideas or models of marriage illustrate the breadth of the choices to be made.

Traditional roles.
Until the last hundred years, people in Western societies largely agreed on the roles a man and woman were to play in marriage. In both a moral and legal sense, the man was the head of the household. The wife promised in her marriage vow to honor and obey him.

The man was expected to be the sole financial provider, and was often judged primarily on his success as a provider. The woman managed the house and cared for the children.

Although economic and social conditions have made it difficult for most couples to observe these traditional roles exactly, this model of marriage remains influential. It assumes a firm division of responsibility between men and women and often includes the suggestion that the man is the ultimate authority.

Equality.
In recent years, the emphasis has been more on the equality of men and women than on their different roles. Often both husband and wife are pursuing careers and thus share the role as provider. They may also share household tasks, including cooking, cleaning, child care, and domestic errands.

Some people see this model as an ideal. Others, who favor a more traditional separation of roles, share many responsibilities because of economic necessity.

MARRIAGE MODELS. *According to the traditional view of marriage, each partner specializes: the wife cares for the kitchen while the husband tends to other things* (left). *Many couples today share household tasks* (right), *income, and other responsibilities.*

Openness. The modern emphasis on women's equality has placed new demands on men and on women for openness and responsible freedom. Women must represent both themselves and their families in the outside world, working, engaging in their own leisure-time activities, and making their own social contacts. A woman's new attachments to career, hobbies, and people outside of the marriage require that she have a relationship that is more "open" than in the past, with room for both partners to make outside commitments. By the same token, the man often must accept new responsibilities within the "closed" system of the family, giving up some of his traditional freedom to come and go as he pleases.

Some couples have gone so far as to allow each other sexual activity outside the marriage. While this extreme is repugnant to most couples and seems practically difficult to maintain in any case, it does raise the serious question of exclusiveness.

A prospective couple should consider their views on all three of these models. No marriage is likely to be fully described by any of them, and it is likely that over the life of a marriage the balance between traditional and more modern roles will shift to meet changing conditions.

Forever, or for Now?

Surveys of newly married couples reveal that they married with the intention of achieving stability and permanence. A majority do not believe in divorce, and almost none expect to be divorced themselves. Yet statistics show that between one-third and one-half of marriages are likely to end in divorce.

This suggests that most prospective partners are not prepared for the many changes they are likely to experience both as individuals and as a couple. Their anticipation of forever living happily together mistakenly assumes that they will always be the same people, with the same needs and desires, as they were on their wedding day. To the contrary, both individuals (see "Adult Development" above) and married couples continue to develop and change through all of their lives.

This does not suggest that marriage should not be "forever"; it does suggest that those contemplating marriage should be more aware of the changes they are likely to experience in their lifetimes. If they understand some of these changes, their expectations of their partners, themselves, and of marriage itself will be more realistic, and they will be more likely to develop the flexibility and consideration that go a long way toward providing marital happiness.

The following sections discuss the major stages of courtship and marriage, from the first serious moment to old age.

Marriage and Family Development

Courtship and marriage may be thought of in four stages. The first stage begins at the point in a romantic relationship when the man and woman begin to consider each other as prospective marriage partners, and it ends with their final commitment to each other in marriage.

The second stage, early marriage, lasts from the wedding to the arrival of the first child, when the partners see themselves as a couple. The third stage consists of the years in which caring for and bringing up children is a major concern. During these years the couple becomes the nucleus of a family. The last stage begins as the children gain their independence and lasts into old age.

The length of these stages varies from marriage to marriage. In some cases, partners have been acquainted with each other for years before marrying, in other cases for only weeks. The early marriage period may last many years for one couple, only a few months for another. Similarly, the length of the family-raising stage depends on the number of children and the spread of their ages. (In a childless marriage, this stage does not exist.) Some couples may reach the last stage while still in their early 40's, while others will not see their youngest off until they are near retirement. Yet there remains a general pattern. It is this pattern—the particular pleasures, concerns, and problems of each stage—that we are concerned with here.

Getting Married

The decision to marry generally is made in three steps. The first is the serious decision of the partners to go out with each other exclusively—to "go steady."

Going steady is usually the time to explore the personality of a prospective partner without making any final commitment. Often a man or woman will go steady with several members of the opposite sex before seriously considering marriage. Such experiences are valuable because they permit comparing and contrasting several prospective partners.

A second stage begins when the couple begins to think seriously of marriage. They may first consider this question individually, silently measuring each other. Then they may discuss the possibility of marriage—often lightly at first—testing each other to see if their feelings are mutual. This is a new level of commitment, the time when observers say the relationship is "getting serious." Then the partners' explorations begin in earnest. Often it is a time of testing, with the couple quarreling, making up, then quarreling again. The two test each other's loyalty and their own abilities to trust the other and to disagree without feeling rejected.

The final premarital stage is the formal engagement, itself in three parts. The first part consists of the couple's making a deeper commitment. The

pair begins to say "When we get married," rather than "If we get married." The second part of the engagement is the public announcement. This tests the reactions of parents, family, and friends. Does "society" seem to approve? Or do people express doubts, directly or indirectly, about the match? The third and final part of the engagement period is the setting of the wedding date and the planning of the wedding. This period is often the first test of the couple's dealings with their own parental families and with their prospective in-laws.

Premarital sex. The whole period of dating, courtship, and engagement is often deeply complicated by the issue of sex. One ideal, still strong in many parts of society, is that sex is legitimate and fulfilling only within the bonds of marriage. Yet the same impulse that causes a couple to want to know each other emotionally also pushes them toward physical intimacy. More than 80 percent of married couples have had sexual intercourse prior to marriage.

How sex is treated by a given couple depends on how each individual has been brought up. If both have been taught to see sex as a symbol of ultimate commitment, premarital sex may cause intense guilt and shame. If both partners have had previous experience, it is less likely that engaging in sex will cause serious conflict.

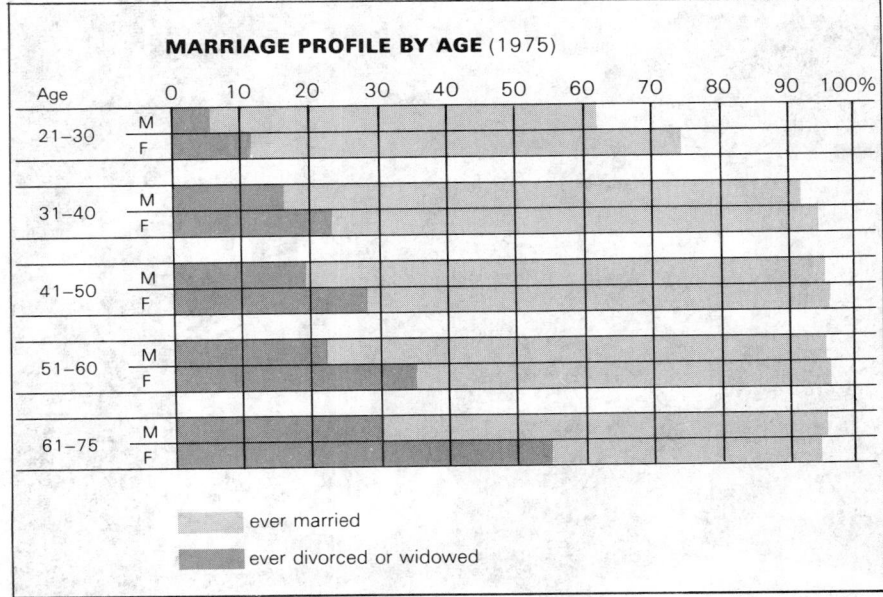

MARRIAGE PROFILE BY AGE (1975)

Age		0	10	20	30	40	50	60	70	80	90	100%
21–30	M											
	F											
31–40	M											
	F											
41–50	M											
	F											
51–60	M											
	F											
61–75	M											
	F											

ever married

ever divorced or widowed

MARRIAGE *is nearly universal: in 1975, 95 percent of men and women over 30 had been married at some time in their lives.*

The deepest problems arise between partners who have very different understandings of sex and its significance. In that case, the question of sex can be a constant irritation to both partners.

If sex were only a matter of physical desire, the problem would not be so severe. Because it is also related to a person's deepest emotional desires, it is often a topic difficult to deal with rationally. In addition, satisfying sexual relations must be learned, so that early sexual encounters are likely to be disappointing.

In some parts of society, cohabitation—living together prior to marriage—has become widespread. Defenders of this practice say that a couple may adjust to each other both emotionally and physically during this trial period and avoid an unhappy marriage if they find they cannot get along.

Premarital pregnancy. One of the frequent and difficult results of premarital sex is pregnancy. When the partners are engaged, the result of the pregnancy may be only to hurry the wedding. When pregnancy occurs before the couple is fully committed to each other, the results may be more serious.

Many pregnant young women are pressured to marry the father of the child to "give the child a name" and to avoid an illegitimate birth. Such marriages have poor prospects for success unless the couple had previously committed themselves to marriage. Prospects are especially unpromising if the partners are teenagers.

Many solutions have been suggested for this problem, but all have serious drawbacks. The first is to provide unmarried teenagers with birth control devices and information to prevent premarital pregnancy. Many people object that this implies that society approves of premarital sex. A second solution is to abort the pregnancy. Such abortions are now legal and have been advocated by social service professionals. But many others have strong objections to abortion, except in the most extreme circumstances. Still another solution is for the mother to give the baby up for adoption. This alternative is often difficult for the mother, who may want to keep the child after giving birth. Some unwed mothers keep the child and rely on their families to help care for it.

A woman who is unmarried and believes she is pregnant should seek advice from a family member, religious leader, or social service professional before deciding what to do. Marriage may at first seem the simplest choice, but it can make the problem more, rather than less, severe.

Breaking up. The drive toward marriage gains momentum as the couple passes from stage to stage. There comes a time when it seems easier to go ahead and get married than to decide not to. What should a person do, then, if he or she has second thoughts?

Some second thoughts during the months or weeks prior to marriage are natural. A man may feel his freedom slipping away and wonder if he is really willing to give it up. Many brides report that even on the day of the wedding, they have a strong impulse to run away.

On the other hand, there may be legitimate reasons to resist the rush to marriage even after the engagement. Some possible danger signs are:

- A steady increase in the frequency and seriousness of quarrels.
- An increasing feeling that one cannot say what he or she thinks.
- A growing feeling of boredom.
- An acute sense of embarrassment at how the partner acts or speaks.
- Serious concern about the partner's emotional stability.
- Increasing fear that the partner asks more than one is able to give, or more than he or she is willing to give in return.
- An increasing tendency to dwell on what changes one would like in a partner's behavior or attitudes.

When serious doubts arise, one possible course is to postpone the marriage. If the partners hope to maintain their relationship, they may want to seek counseling.

In some cases, however, it may be necessary to break off altogether. This is painful, but it is preferable to hoping that a marriage will improve a situation. Marriage rarely solves serious problems in a relationship or in an individual.

The wedding. The final premarital responsibility is to plan the wedding. Weddings can be expensive, time-consuming, and emotionally exhausting. Intense feelings both of joy and apprehension are experienced not only by the bride and groom, but also by their parents, for whom the wedding is an important milestone. Many couples, after exploring the economics and mechanics of weddings, feel a strong impulse to elope.

THE WEDDING, *whether informal or traditional, is a big day for the couple and their families.*

In most cases, elopements and private weddings cause more unhappiness than they prevent. The wedding is a chance both for the partners and for their families to celebrate the commitment of the couple to each other. Marriage customs, like birth and death customs, are durable and slow to change. Even when the bride and groom are too intent on each other to notice, the wedding is important to their family and friends.

Early Marriage

Never in their marriage will a couple be so intent on each other as they are late in their engagement and in the early days of marriage. By tradition, the marriage begins with a honeymoon, a time for the couple to be away from their everyday routines and free to concentrate on each other.

Intimacy. The main concern of the honeymoon period is the establishment of a bond of intimacy between husband and wife. Part of this bond is the physical act of love. Even if the couple has engaged in premarital sex, the honeymoon provides a chance to make love without fear of society's disapproval and often without the fear of unwanted pregnancy. Either a pregnancy is welcome, or the couple has settled on a means of birth control.

Although the physical part of the honeymoon is important, it is often overemphasized. Unless the couple has lived together prior to marriage, the honeymoon affords them the first chance to live in almost constant touch with each other. They not only sleep in the same bed but dress in the same room, use the same bathroom, eat every meal together. Sooner rather than later they learn that they will see each other in states of emotional as well as physical undress—in moods of irritation, anger, and sadness, as well as affection and love.

Romantic stories often portray the honeymoon as the culmination of the romance between newlyweds. It is more likely to be an intensive learning experience—not unpleasant, but filled with little surprises. The two best qualities newlyweds can bring to the first few weeks of marriage are flexibility and a sense of humor. Perhaps most important, they can remind themselves that the first few weeks are just that—the beginning of a long relationship.

Everyday life. Once the honeymoon is over, the couple settles into a routine. If all has gone well in previous months, this can be a happy period. Life becomes less intense, although there remains much to learn. At the same time, this may also be a

THE HONEYMOONERS, *a classic TV couple played by Jackie Gleason and Audrey Meadows, made comedy out of the stresses and strains of marital quarrels and misunderstandings.*

period of petty irritations. A husband may learn that his wife leaves wet nylons hanging all over the bathroom. A wife may learn that her husband has never in his life taken the garbage out. These small things—much smaller than the exalted concerns of courtship—often cause the first fight. How a couple fights and makes up may be one of the most important predictors of future happiness. Couples who can express their anger, tolerate the other partner's anger, and hold no grudges have the best prospects of success.

Gradually the couple sets patterns—agreeing on who brings in the money, who spends it, who cooks, who cleans, who decides what movie to go to, and so on. The pair are negotiating an unspoken contract that covers dozens of small, everyday concerns. Once the questions have been answered, both can relax, and the little jobs will be done out of habit. If the contract leaves one party unsatisfied, however, the little everyday matters can cause indefinite irritation. Even if the agreement is successful, it is important to remember that it is not graven in stone. Changing circumstances may require renegotiation later.

The spirit of these negotiations is another indication of the marriage's future. If both partners are genuinely considerate and yet able to stand up for their own interests, the outlook is good. If one partner is stubbornly selfish, or always gives in even to unreasonable demands, then some major readjustments may later be necessary.

Distance. Sometime in the first year, both partners begin rediscover-

ing parts of their own lives that they have ignored during their engagement and the early months of marriage. One partner may reestablish close ties with family or arrange to see old friends regularly. Another may throw himself into study or work in a way that has not been possible before.

Reestablishing earlier interests implies a certain moving away from one's spouse. Each partner may see certain aspects of life as belonging to the individual rather than to the partnership. The emphasis on the marriage itself may lessen, and marriage may become one of several relationships rather than the only one.

This new sense of distance is normal and healthy. Couples who accept each other's individuality adjust to it naturally and without losing their sense of intimate attachment. In some cases, however, one partner may be disappointed in the other's pulling away and may come to fear that he or she is being abandoned.

Competition. In cases of disagreement, partners may come to feel that they are competing to see who gets his way. When both partners want or need further education, for example, it may be impossible for both to study at the same time. Who goes first? Or one partner may have a good job when the other receives a promising offer in another city. Does the couple stay, move, or live apart during the week?

In such cases, one partner may have to sacrifice so that the other can advance. If all or most of the sacrifices fall to one partner, resentment builds up. Sometimes it may not be expressed openly, but it can poison a relationship all the same.

Some good-natured competition between husband and wife may be healthy and fun. The no-competition marriage, in which one partner is conceded everything, can become a trial for both partners. But if the competition becomes a fight in which neither partner is willing to compromise, the relationship will suffer.

Contradictory demands.
The understanding between the sexes has always been imperfect. Husbands and wives frequently say, "My wife/husband doesn't understand me." Often the speakers are confessing at the same time that they do not understand their partners.

A major reason for such misunderstanding is contradictory desires. A husband, for example, may want both to be acknowledged as head of the house and to be loved for his feelings of indecision and inadequacy. When his wife acknowledges his leadership, he seems oppressed and resentful of the responsibility. But when she tries to comfort him for his shortcomings, he gets angry and becomes head of the household again.

A wife may seek in a similar way to be both an independent career woman and a dependent, submissive wife. When her husband congratulates her on success at work, instead of being happy, she may feel guilty and wonder if he still loves her. But when her husband assumes that she is submissive, she may become resentful and act like the independent career woman again.

In this kind of situation, the partner loses no matter what he or she does. Such situations cannot always be avoided, but it is important for people to realize that everyone is sometimes irrational—even themselves—and that spouses are no exceptions.

Arguments.
During the early years of marriage, most couples settle on a style of arguing. In some marriages, quarrels are carried on for days without a word being spoken. Other couples argue verbally, either in long drawn-out discussions or in brief shouting matches.

Many marriage partners feel guilty when they are angry. People who are really in love do not quarrel, they believe, so their anger makes them doubt that they are still in love. Such people may refuse to recognize that they are angry, and they will try to avoid any argument.

No angry dispute is pleasant, but to deny anger and to bury it is destructive. In general, it is better to express anger quickly and to argue about an issue then and there. Marriage counselors report that people with the most serious marital problems are often those who have let anger and resentment build up for years.

People who are in love *do* argue. Disagreements are inevitable. But there is more than one way to argue. Surveys of married people show that what they most often admire in their spouse is consideration, a quality that is especially important in marital arguments. Disputes that lack this quality become vicious, and many things are said simply to injure the opponent. Marriage partners need to find ways to argue that are honest, even when honesty is painful, but not destructive.

Learning to argue constructively is a much greater achievement than avoiding argument. Couples who manage to avoid disputes in the early years of marriage often must deal with far more serious arguments later.

Planning for children.
The stage of early marriage lasts until the birth of the couple's first child. Until this century, children were conceived at the whim of nature, and many women went through ten or more pregnancies during their child-bearing years. Today, most married couples adopt some form of birth control. This enables them to plan for children, deciding not only how many children to have but also when they will be born.

Since having children is now a matter of choice, it becomes an important issue for young married couples. They may consider the career plans of both spouses, economic conditions, and their own sense of readiness when deciding to begin a family. There are arguments for having children early (when the wife is in her early or mid-20's) and counterarguments for having them later (in the wife's 30's). There is more physical risk, both to the child and the mother, in pregnancies of women under 18 and over 35.

The decision to have a child is much more than the decision to have a baby. The baby will grow to be a toddler, a schoolchild, a teenager, and finally an adult, a process requiring at least 18 years of care. Husband and wife become father and mother, and the child occupies a central position in the home. Having children can be a great and satisfying adventure, but it is also an immense responsibility.

Increasing numbers of married couples are deciding not to have children, a choice that is more often respected and admired now than in the past. Such childless marriages can allow both spouses to fulfill their own career ambitions and can be satisfying for both partners.

Having Children

When a woman becomes pregnant, she and her husband begin to prepare for a new era in their marriage. During the first period of excitement, attention is focused on the prospective mother's health. As the time for delivery comes closer, both parents begin to concentrate on the birth itself and on the equipment and knowledge required to care for the new baby.

With the birth of the child, the couple will have become a family, and the participants will need to fashion a new set of relationships and a new set of priorities.

Prospective fathers often participate in their wife's preparation for birth. They may help their wives learn exercises for natural childbirth and may be present at the delivery. Such fathers feel closer to the event than those who

LARGE HOUSEHOLDS, *those with 5 or more members, have become increasingly rare, reflecting fewer multigenerational households and fewer children per family.*

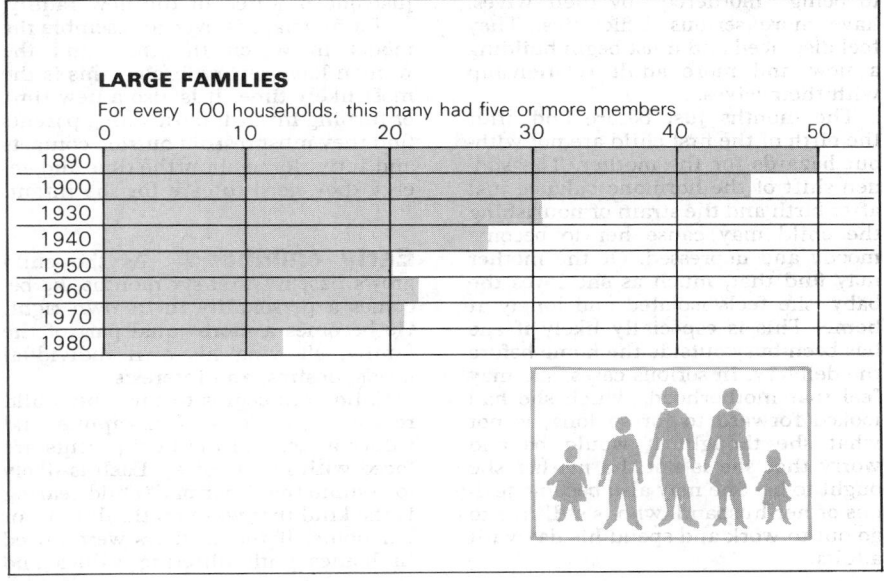

LARGE FAMILIES

For every 100 households, this many had five or more members

	0	10	20	30	40	50
1890						
1900						
1930						
1940						
1950						
1960						
1970						
1980						

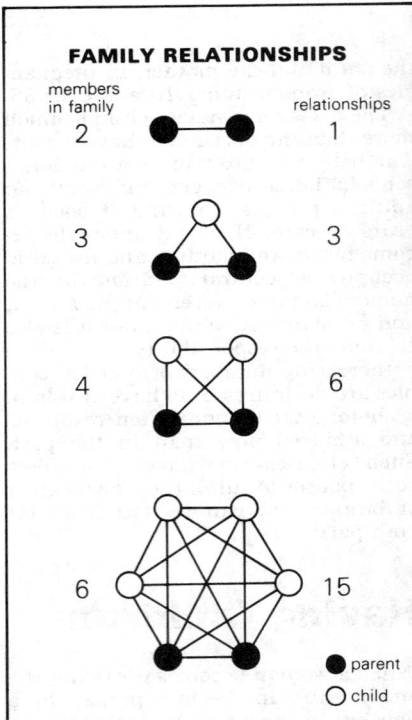

FAMILY RELATIONSHIPS

members
in family   relationships

2   1

3   3

4   6

6   15

● parent
○ child

SUZANNE SZASZ/ PHOTO RESEARCHERS

FAMILY SIZE *determines the number of relationships in a family. From one bond between a couple, the number rises rapidly—with four children, there are 15 separate one-to-one relationships, only 9 of which include either parent.*

pace nervously in a waiting room. But in an important sense, the father cannot participate fully. Biologically and emotionally, the mother does the work

Infancy.
The mothering instinct is strong. In the last months of pregnancy, the mother's attention focuses more and more on herself and her child. This concentration continues for some months after the child is born.

As reasonable and necessary as this may be, many husbands come to feel neglected during those months. Most manage to adjust to the situation, but a few, who may have been accustomed to being "mothered" by their wives, have more serious difficulties. They feel displaced and must begin building a new and more adult relationship with their wives.

The months just before and after the birth of the first child are not without hazards for the mother. The sudden shift of the hormone balance just after birth and the strain of nourishing the child may cause her to become moody and depressed. Or the mother may find that, much as she loves the baby, she feels isolated and lonely at home. This is especially likely if she has been busy outside the home before the delivery. In serious cases, she may feel that motherhood, which she had looked forward to for so long, is not what she thought it would be and worry that she is not the mother she ought to be. She may also become jealous of her husband, who is still free to go out to work and spend his day with adults.

Many mothers return to work within weeks or months of the birth. Some go out of choice, others from necessity. This keeps them from feeling the isolation of staying home, but they may feel guilty at leaving their child in the care of others.

For both husband and wife, the time of the child's infancy may seem both confining and exhausting. They are no longer free to stay up late or to sleep late. The household schedule is set by the child, who may require middle-of-the-night feedings or fuss and cry for long periods. The new parents are closer to each other in their mutual concern for the child, but also further away. Suddenly their relationship is just one of three in the new family.

If a marriage is ever to resemble the model in which the man and the woman have separate roles, this is the most likely time. It is also a new time of turning inward; most young parents find they must restrict outside contacts and activities to allow the time and energy they need to care for the infant.

Early childhood.
As the child grows past his first six months, he becomes a personality in its own right. He becomes a more equal part of the family, showing his own individual needs, desires, and interests.

Child care begins to turn into child rearing. Questions of discipline and values arise, and the new parents are faced with new choices. Each is likely to assume that "normal" child rearing is the kind that was practiced in his or her home. If the partners were raised in homes with differing values and

methods, they may find themselves disagreeing about how to deal with the child.

If both spouses grew up in fairly happy homes, they need only to compromise different values and styles. If either grew up in less than happy circumstances, things can be more complicated. A new mother who is unhappy with her own mother, for example, may go to great lengths to do things differently.

Much of what new parents have learned from their parents is quite unconscious, however. While they may work toward changing certain elements of their own upbringing, they will often surprise themselves by sounding like perfect echoes of their own parents. Attitudes toward child rearing are passed from generation to generation, and they change very slowly indeed.

More children.
The first child is usually treated cautiously. New parents worry about hazards to the firstborn and about their own methods. When a second or third child is born, the parents tend to be more relaxed.

The arrival of each new child greatly increases the emotional complexity of the household. One of the vexing problems of a growing family is equality. Not only are family members unequal in their ability to care for themselves, but they may also come to see themselves as unequal in the attention and affection they receive from their parents. Parents themselves find it difficult to love each child in exactly the same way, for each child is different. Often traditions grow up in a family as to who is most closely allied to whom. Some favoritism is hard to avoid, but too much can damage both children and parents. In basically happy families, both the reality and the inflated legends of favoritism fade over the years. In unhappy and disorganized families, however, such legends may carry down to still another generation.

Children grow up.

At birth, a child is helpless and dependent; but within the first year, the child begins to demand small tokens of independence. The demands continue in more and more areas of life until the child becomes an adult. The granting of independence gradually and lovingly is a principal task of parenthood.

Some parents, impatient with parenthood or unhappy for other reasons, ask their children to grow up to be independent too fast. Such children come to doubt that their parents really love them and feel threatened by the dangers of the outside world. Other parents cannot let go of their children, overprotecting them and encouraging them to remain dependent. These children often become rebellious, provoking quarrels and insisting on their independence in dangerous ways.

How does a parent know when and how much to let go? There is no simple answer, but making the right decisions seems to depend on the emotional health of the parents and often on the health of their relationship. If they have self-confidence and trust each other, they will probably have confidence and trust in their children. Often the general well-being of a child is a reflection of his parents' emotional well-being.

Adolescence.

When children reach sexual maturity, their parents also reach a new stage in married life. Despite the recommendations of many experts that families discuss sexual matters openly, the subject is still rarely mentioned in many households. But when the children reach the age of curiosity and eagerness to experiment, parents' attitudes toward and values about sex are tested anyway.

The questions revolve most often not around the physical aspect of sex but around the emotional. Adolescents want to know what sex "means," when and how it may be legitimately enjoyed, and why their parents often seem nervous and edgy about it. Parents may sometimes have to answer in words, but the deeper answers may come from their actions. Adolescents begin to wonder what kind of emotional relationship their parents have, and they begin to observe and draw conclusions.

A couple that is basically happy can withstand this questioning and scrutiny with only passing moments of embarrassment. In fact, their children's questions may prompt a re-evaluation of their own relationship. Perhaps the most helpful quality for dealing with adolescent questions and challenges is a sense of humor. Teenagers tend to have a melodramatic view of life, and a parent's ability to see the lighter side of a problem may be the best answer.

Adolescents challenge their parents in other ways. They have already gained considerable independence, and they are loudly demanding the rest of it—immediately. At the same time, they are not quite ready for it. Parents often notice that when they draw a line and say no, the teenager communicates a secret sense of relief even while appealing the decision.

Having nearly grown children gives a couple several reasons for concern. First, they begin to feel that they are being replaced in the world, realizing that they are neither as young nor as resilient as their sons and daughters. Second, they may be troubled by their teenagers' sense of rebellion—by assertions that the grown-up world is not as good or just as it might be.

Parents often fear that a child will seek to become their exact opposite. Yet at the same time, they may fear that a child will become too much like them, imitative in areas of life with which the parents are dissatisfied.

Finally, grown to be young men and women, children leave home. Parents often feel a mixture of sadness and satisfaction at the end of an era and anticipation for the new freedom they will have. Parenthood will not end, of course—parents usually follow their children throughout life with great concern and interest—but most of its responsibilities will end.

Children and continuity.

By the time their children have left home, many parents have the sense of having come full circle. They remember their own teenage and young adult years; now they are parents with their own adult children. This sense of repetition grows as life goes on. Husband and wife watch sons and daughters marry, establish homes, and give birth to another generation of children.

At the same time, the couple may be dealing with their own aged parents—without failing to note that old age brings physical infirmities and other problems. Looking at the aged on one hand and the young and soon-to-give-birth on the other may please or upset the middle-age couple. If they are content, they see themselves as the link between old and young. If they are unhappy, however, they may resent the dependency of their parents (and the reminder of approaching death that they represent) and feel envious of the young who are just starting out.

If middle age leads a couple to an acceptance of the cycle of life and of death, then the years ahead seem promising. But if middle age leads to regret of the past and fear of the future, the future may come to seem grim and discouraging.

After Children

By the time the last child has left home, the married couple has usually been married for between 20 and 40 years. If the children were born early in the parents' lives, the couple may have many active years ahead of them; if later, the couple may be near retirement. In any case, the marriage is entering still another phase.

The relationship between husband and wife has often settled into a routine. Just what the routine is and how satisfying it is depends on the individuals and on the quality of their lives together. There are probably more different types of marriages among couples in their 50's than among couples in their 20's, and the relationships tend to be more complex as well.

Mid-life adjustments.

Couples who have had a happy life together often look forward to the period after children as a time for renewing their acquaintance and concentrating on each other. The number of relationships in the household diminishes and life seems simpler. Two people who have come to see themselves first as father and mother are free once again to see themselves as husband and wife, to come and go as they please, and to give increased attention to their own needs and interests.

This stage is not without its confusions and chances for unhappiness, however. Beginning in his 40's, a man is likely to go through a period of re-evaluation and change. In many cases he has devoted much of his time and energy as a young man to achieving career goals, and any time he had left over went to necessary household or family activities. Now he may feel that during those years he did not have the time for an emotional life of his own. He may lose interest in his job or demote it to a less important place in his life. He may develop new hobbies or return to ones long neglected. Helping other people may come to seem more important. At the same time, he may be troubled that the world (including his own grown children) seems to be passing him by. He may be eager to make some kind of new start.

The woman whose children are leaving feels she must make up for lost time, too. She may have left a career to care for her children. Now that they are going or gone, she may feel a sense of urgency about getting back into the world of work. Many of her concerns point in a direction directly opposite

RETURNING TO SCHOOL *is increasingly common among women whose children are in school. Such classwork often helps women to reenter the job market.*

"completed" family, may resolve to try again, marrying a younger woman and fathering a second family. Or the wife, resentful of her dependence on her husband, may leave him to gain her independence before it is too late.

Other dissatisfied partners may not end their marriage but may settle for whatever practical advantages the relationship can bring. Burnt-out relationships between people who do not much like each other anymore may be characterized by rigid routine and silence or by constant quarreling. Such marriages are difficult for younger people to understand. But just as people in middle age develop a positive ability to accept a less-than-perfect relationship, they also may acquire the negative ability to settle for a bad relationship without letting go of their resentment and anger.

Physical changes. At the same time that the middle aged are working to understand and accept the past, they are beginning to accept the future. Part of the future is the gradual physical decline that comes with aging. Aches and pains increase, a chronic illness may take some of the pleasure from life, and the likelihood of major illness increases.

Many people are particularly troubled by the effect of aging on their sexual attractiveness and activity. At menopause, women sometimes feel that they have lost their attractiveness. Men may be troubled by a gradual loss of sexual ability. Yet among happy couples, sexual activity brings pleasure well into old age.

For many people, the aches and pains and restrictions are not intolerable in themselves, but they may be very difficult to accept emotionally.

from her husband's. Now she is interested in succeeding in a job or profession. She has less, rather than more, interest in helping others, having devoted many years to nurturing her family, and an interest in meeting her own needs.

This crossing of interests calls for some major adjustments between spouses. Unless both parties have a fair amount of self-confidence, each may be troubled or angered by the direction the spouse is taking. The man may feel that he is losing his wife to the outside world, and the woman may feel disappointed or resentful that her husband is softening. Both parties may be confused by the changes these developments suggest.

In reality, these changes are both natural and promising. Both partners can afford to give up the restrictions of their sex roles and become more human. They can acknowledge that a man may want to nurture and help others and that a woman may want to achieve in the outside world. When partners are willing to help each other in making these mid-life changes, they increase their chances for a contented marriage in the years to come.

On the less positive side, many couples in middle age are also wrestling with a sense of disillusionment. Looking back at their young selves, they are likely to conclude that married life— and life in general—has not been all they had expected. They may see some of their cherished dreams unfulfilled and realize that there is not time or energy left to correct everything.

A person may deal with his disillusionment by concluding that his early hopes and dreams were unrealistic (which they often were), or by understanding the circumstances that made their realization impossible. Most people gradually acquire a new sense of

acceptance in middle age. This consists partly of gratitude for the good things in their lives and partly of a wry (but not unhappy) sense of their own limitations and failures. Many marriages that have gone through stormy times settle down into relative peace and contentment in middle age, not because the partners have changed very much but because they have come to have different and more realistic expectations of each other.

For some, coming to terms with the past is more difficult. Realizing that past dreams have not come true, these people become bitter and cynical, seeking someone or something to blame. The husband, perhaps remorseful about spending too little time with his

COMMON ACTIVITIES *can be an important bond between partners at any stage of marriage, but are especially important in middle age and beyond.*

People are often frightened of growing old. Those who can accept aging are usually happier than those who fight it and deny it.

Old age.

As the partners approach their 60's, there are still other preparations to be made for aging. Plans for retirement must be made, a prospect that can be both welcome and frightening at the same time.

One of the major concerns may be money. Often a retired couple cannot afford to live in the style to which it has been accustomed. A move to a smaller house or apartment may make good sense both financially and physically, but this may make it difficult to entertain returning children and grandchildren, and make it seem that the couple is giving up part of its role in the family.

Giving up work can be the hardest part of all. Those who invest a great deal of themselves in a job find it difficult to find a replacement for the job in their lives. They may feel useless, unwanted, and discarded. Many retirees miss the day-to-day personal contacts on the job as well as the regular structure it provided.

This loss of outside contacts can put great strain on a marriage. Partners may find themselves seeing more of each other than ever before, and this may cause minor irritations to become serious arguments.

Some partners solve these problems with great ingenuity. They begin second careers or small businesses at home, take up demanding hobbies, or devote themselves to community service. The secret of being able to retire gracefully and happily may be the ability to plan for retirement before it arrives.

Dependence.

The retirement years are particularly difficult when one partner becomes ill or disabled and requires a great deal of care. Husbands are likely to age more quickly and die at younger ages than their wives. Often the aging man finds it difficult to entrust more and more responsibility to his wife. The man may have to give up driving at night, for example, because of poor eyesight, leave household maintenance to others, and so on.

In a marriage that has weathered other storms successfully, this situation will be difficult but not intolerable. In a less stable relationship, it can cause bitterness and unhappiness.

The problem of dependence often extends beyond the couple itself. As the partners age, they may reach a point where they are not able to provide and care for themselves, becoming increasingly dependent on grown children. This reverse dependence is often hard for both sides to accept, and it often revives conflicts that began when the children were growing up.

For the elderly couple, the challenge is to maintain a sense of emotional independence and yet learn to accept help cheerfully.

Death.

The final test in old age is preparing for death. Ironically, this preparation may be most difficult for the couple that has been happiest together. The death of one partner will mean a separation after decades together. Suddenly one must consider getting along without one's partner. The partners may feel a desire to separate themselves emotionally to prepare for the day when one of them will be left alone.

Looking back.

The whole progress of marriage, from courtship to old age and death, consists of two contrasting themes—dependence and independence. Learning to be gracefully dependent on and supportive of another is perhaps the first key to a happy marriage. At the same time, every person has the need to be independent, to be an individual in his or her own right. At its best, marriage can help its partners be both dependent and independent. The challenge of marriage, today as in the past, is to reach the balance that makes life richer and fuller for both partners.

The institution of marriage may change from era to era, and partners may look for different models and approaches, but the family—really the succession of families—continues as long as the human race survives. For the great majority of people, family is part of the human condition and the source both of their greatest satisfactions and of their greatest sufferings.

Other Family Groups

Up to this point, we have concentrated on the nuclear family—a married couple and their child or children. Yet there are many other groupings in which people live at some time in their lives. Some are made up of related people (elderly parent and grown child, for example). Others are made up of unrelated people; these are not technically families, because the attachment between the individuals is unofficial and informal. In many situations, however, such groups work much like a family, providing many advantages of a family—and some of the disadvantages as well.

Single-parent households.

This kind of family has become very common because of rising divorce rates. Commonly, the mother has custody of the children, although in an increasing number of cases, divorced parents may have joint custody. Single-parent families may also be created by the death of one spouse or by a long separation (as for military service or hospitalization).

Single-parent families encounter both practical and emotional problems. Often the parent must earn a living and maintain the household at the same time, leaving him or her little time and emotional energy to devote to the children. At the same time, the parent must take the part of both father and mother, complicating the situation further.

PARENTS WITHOUT PARTNERS *and similar groups provide support and assistance to single parents.*

When the single-parent family is a permanent arrangement, it may settle into an agreeable and happy routine. The relationship between parent and child is likely to be closer, and often a spirit of cooperation and comradeship prevails. Many single parents have found valuable support in Parents Without Partners and similar groups. Such organizations bring the single parents into contact with others who face similar challenges, and give them a chance to make new social contacts and reduce their sense of isolation.

Extended-family households.

In previous generations, households that housed three or more generations of the same family were common. Today, many people of all ages so value their independence that they consider such a multi-generational household undesirable. Only in times of serious need do such people agree to live with their extended families. An aging parent, perhaps widowed or ill and in need of care, may move in with his or her children. Less frequently, a married son or daughter with children may live with his or her parents.

The disadvantages of such arrangements are apparent. Often old family patterns reassert themselves, and parents and children adopt inappropriate roles. In families where independence has been prized, the need to depend on one's children or parents seems an admission of failure.

The advantages of the multi-generational household are less frequently mentioned. The generations can be helpful to each other in both practical and emotional ways. Psychologists believe, for example, that many children benefit from close relationships with their grandparents. The grandparents themselves may remain lively and happy longer when they live close to growing children and are able to contribute to their care.

Living at close quarters can also help parents and grown children understand and respect each other in new ways. When living together, the generations see each other as individuals rather than as symbols. While this may lead to disagreements and unhappiness, it may also lead to greater understanding.

The abandonment of the extended family household is a recent development. It may be that future generations will consider our emphasis on the separation of one generation from another to have been unwise.

Communal living.
Perhaps the most venerable form of living with unrelated individuals is the religious community. Monasteries and convents in the Middle Ages offered unmarried individuals security and companionship as well as the opportunity to accomplish worthwhile tasks. Such religious communities continue to exist, even though few are willing today to give up their individuality in the interests of such a group. The modern emphasis on sex also reduces the interest in such communities.

Military life offers a somewhat similar opportunity for communal living. For many, military service is a temporary style of life during young adulthood.

In the United States there have been other less conventional experiments in communal living. These range from religious and philosophical experimental communities in the 1800's to the hippie communes of the 1960's. Such communities require a strong common purpose or a talented and magnetic leader. They are usually unstable and disappear with the departure of the leader or the loss of the original sense of purpose.

Roommates.
One modern arrangement that resembles communal living is that of living with roommates. This is particularly common among young adults. Usually the roommates are of the same sex and have formed a rather simple relationship based on practical needs. In some circumstances, roommates may be of different sexes; sexual activity is usually not part of the agreement.

Cohabitation.
In some parts of society, a man and woman living together without benefit of marriage is a common practice. In certain cases the arrangement may be understood to be temporary, with neither partner making a lasting commitment. In other

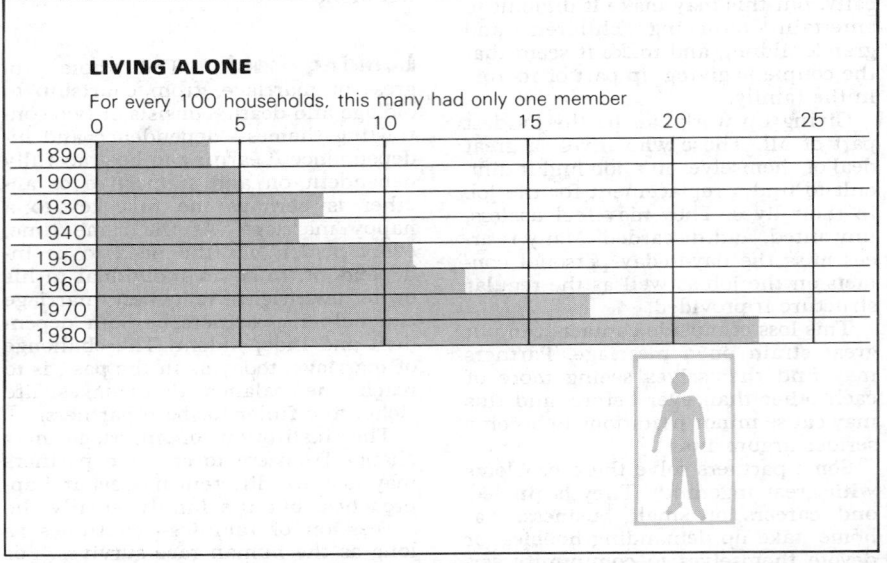

SINGLE-PERSON HOUSEHOLDS *in the United States have increased from 2.4 million in 1930 to 17.2 million in 1980.*

COMMUNAL LIVING *involves sacrifices of privacy and individuality in return for a sense of membership in the community.*

cases, cohabitation is considered to be a trial period before marriage. The couple may live together for months or years before agreeing to marry (or, if the arrangement proves unsatisfactory, agreeing to end the relationship).

Supporters of such arrangements claim that a trial period before a marriage can be helpful to both partners and that it will cause potentially unhappy partnerships to end prior to marriage. Others strongly oppose cohabitation, holding the traditional view that conjugal living is only sanctioned within marriage.

Whatever the ethical judgments on cohabitation, it can lead to difficult and painful misunderstandings. If one partner sees the living arrangement as a deep commitment and the other partner merely as a temporary expedient, the household may break up with hurt feelings and bitterness on both sides.

Same-sex partners.

Homosexuality, sexual and affectional preference for individuals of the same sex, has existed in all times and places. Even though many societies (including our own) have discouraged homosexual behavior, it continues to exist. Some men form deep emotional and sexual attachments to other men; some women form such attachments to other women.

There is no general agreement on what causes homosexuality. Evidence suggests that certain people may have a biological predisposition. Other evidence suggests that a homosexual orientation may be fostered by experiences in early childhood.

Whatever its cause and whatever one's views on the morality of homosexual behavior, there are many misconceptions about it. For example, a homosexual is no more likely to be a sex offender than a heterosexual. Homosexuals cannot usually be identified by their dress, their manner of speech, or their mannerisms. Homosexuals do not want to be members of the opposite sex; most would not change their sex if they could.

Many homosexuals form lasting relationships with a single partner, relationships that in many ways resemble marriage. Perhaps the most serious difficulty for most homosexuals is social disapproval. Where heterosexual marriage is an occasion for public announcement and celebration, even the most loving homosexual relationship may need to be hidden from public view. Members of many professions would risk their livelihoods if any but their closest friends knew of their lives as homosexuals.

The parents of a homosexual may have difficulty in understanding and dealing with their son's or daughter's preferences. Most authorities counsel families to seek a way to accept their child rather than deny or try to change

him. Efforts at redirecting the sexual orientation of homosexuals have generally met with little success. Most psychologists agree that homosexuality is not an emotional illness but a part of some people's makeup that is unlikely to change. In itself, homosexuality is no danger to others or to the homosexual himself, and many homosexuals lead lives as happy as those of their heterosexual counterparts.

Living alone.

Although the vast majority of people live with someone, whether in a family or in a less formal relationship, an increasing number live alone. Among them are those who are by themselves by necessity, through the death of a spouse or the breakup of a marriage, for example. For many, living alone will be only temporary, ending when the person finds a new relationship to substitute for the one that has been lost.

Many live alone by choice. The advantages of such independence are clear: privacy, space, and freedom. A single person is free to come and go as he chooses, to be eccentric, and to travel without encumbrance.

The disadvantages of living alone are also clear, however. Many who find themselves alone after a long marriage or other close relationship feel lost and isolated. They miss having someone with whom to talk and with whom they can share. Many find it difficult to cook only for themselves, and worry about who might come to their aid in a time of emergency.

Those who live alone for a long time often find themselves acquiring valuable resources: new interests, new activities (both solitary and social), and a new sense of independence.

Persons living alone may gradually acquire a large network of friends and acquaintances. They often compensate for their solitary living by leading active social lives. Their network may include others who live alone, and in times of illness or difficulty, single people often take care of each other.

Changing groups.

Conventional families tend to live in the same neighborhoods and to socialize with each other. It is not uncommon, for example, for a married couple to know only other married couples of the same age. By the same token, those who live alone or in less conventional groupings tend to live in the same neighborhoods and to socialize with each other.

Social commentators suggest that such segregation by family type is unfortunate. Most of us move at some time in our lives from the conventional family to a less conventional arrangement, as when moving away from home as a young adult or when divorce or death brings a marriage to an end. For those who do not know any people out of their immediate circle, making the adjustment can be difficult. The various kinds of formal and informal family groups have many things to teach each other that can only be learned by exposure to other groups.

LIVING ALONE *allows great independence, but it may also bring feelings of loneliness and isolation.*

INDIVIDUAL AND FAMILY CRISES

For many people, marriage and raising a family provide some of the happiest and most satisfying experiences of life. But when some member of the family is in trouble or when the family itself is falling apart, family life can be miserable indeed.

This section considers some of the problems that can provoke crises in family life. At first glance, many of the problems, such as alcoholism and mental illness, seem to be problems suffered by individuals. Yet as anyone knows who has lived in a household visited by such problems, the individual's trouble is difficult to contain. By the very nature of family life, the affliction of one of its members becomes the affliction of the whole family.

In many cases, a problem in the family may cause one of its members to develop an addiction or show signs of mental or physical illness. Deciding whether a parent's drinking caused the family to fall apart or whether the unhappiness in the family caused the parent to drink can be a difficult question. Perhaps the parent's drinking is *both* a cause and an effect of the family's problems. Individual and family troubles often reinforce each other.

The first section below considers the problems that appear to belong to an individual. The second section considers problems that grow out of a marriage or a family.

Individual Problems

Problems in which the individual may turn his unhappiness inward upon himself include alcoholism, drug addiction, mental or emotional illness, and psychosomatic illness. In other circumstances, the individual may turn his unhappiness on others in the family, often through physical violence. Finally, there are circumstances that may be beyond anyone's control that cause individuals and families to suffer. These include death, serious illness, loss of livelihood, and moving from one's home.

Alcoholism

Alcoholism is a form of drug addiction. From ancient times to the present day, alcohol, made from the fermenting of fruit juices or grains, has been the most common intoxicating drug. Chemically, it is a depressant of the central nervous system. It slows reflexes, deadens response to physical and emotional pain, and diminishes mental alertness. It also can produce a sense of euphoria and loosen inhibitions.

Like other drugs, alcohol has its uses. Taken in small doses, it relaxes the drinker and dilates blood vessels, aiding circulation. Before the introduction of modern anesthetics, alcohol was often used to deaden pain during surgery. In small amounts, it has few side effects and is not hazardous to the user (unless other drugs are used at the same time). In many parts of the world, large and small events are celebrated by the drinking of alcohol.

ALCOHOLISM, *traditionally an affliction of adult males, is increasing sharply among women and teenagers.*

Unfortunately, alcohol is subject to serious abuse. People who do not control their drinking cause thousands of auto accidents. Authorities estimate that more than half of all drivers involved in fatal accidents had been drinking. Alcohol is also associated with a high proportion of all family violence, robberies, assaults, and other crimes.

Some people abuse alcohol on occasion yet do not seem vulnerable to frequent and habitual use. Many others, however, become addicted to alcohol—that is, they become alcoholics.

Becoming an alcoholic is both a psychological and a physical process. Psychologically, as in many types of addiction, the alcoholic comes to see his drink as a sort of panacea. He uses it to banish his shyness, to ease loneliness or pain, to lighten his mood, and to make his troubles go away. Many alcoholics have trouble making or keeping emotional commitments to other people.

There are probably physical causes of alcoholism as well. Some people may have a biological predisposition to becoming addicted. There is evidence that for such people, even very moderate drinking causes changes in body chemistry that increase the body's need for more.

The line between the problem drinker—the occasional abuser of alcohol—and the alcoholic is vague. During the early phases of alcoholism, it may be impossible to tell the two apart.

Gradually, however, the difference becomes clear. The alcoholic slides into complete dependence on his bottle. The thought of the next drink rarely leaves his mind. He begins to drink early in the day. Hangovers become common and begin to interfere with his work and with his family relationships. He begins to black out from time to time, losing all memory of the period when he was drinking heavily. During this second stage of alcoholism, the drinker goes to great lengths to conceal his addiction.

The last stage of alcohol addiction is one of rapid physical and mental deterioration. The drinker becomes palsied; he may have terrifying hallucinations. The alcohol is doing permanent and irreversible damage to his liver, brain, and other organs. Often, the alcoholic will be malnourished, preferring drinking to eating.

One of the most painful consequences of alcoholism is the damage it does to the alcoholic's family. As the addiction progresses, the alcoholic becomes a different person. He may lie, steal, and hide behind other family members, using them to conceal his problem. He may be irritable or emotionally withdrawn. When angered, he may be violent.

The family reacts with confusion and guilt. If they admonish him and complain about his behavior, he gets angry and drinks. Yet if they leave him alone, he feels abandoned and still drinks. Soon the whole family may revolve around the alcoholic's addiction.

Alcoholism is no respecter of class. It appears in every level of society and among every age group. In recent years, the number of women and teenage alcoholics has risen rapidly. It is estimated that there are 12 million alcoholics in the United States, yet the number may be higher because so many drink only in secret.

No magic cure for alcoholism has been found. But in many cases, the disease may be arrested. Nearly all authorities agree that the first requirement is that the drinker abstain completely from further drinking. Ef-

> Give us
> serenity
>   to accept what
>   cannot be changed,
> courage
>   to change what
>   should be changed,
>   and
> wisdom
>   to distinguish
>   the one from
>   the other.

AA PRAYER *suggests that controlling alcoholism requires new personal resources.*

forts to cut down are nearly always doomed to failure.

Many major hospitals have detoxification centers where alcoholics may go to "dry out." This is a fairly brief (though painful) process of ridding the body of alcohol. But in most cases, this is only a first step. Without further treatment, there is a high likelihood that the drinker will return to his old habits. There are many residential treatment programs for alcoholics. Some use psychoanalytic techniques, seeking to identify the root cause of the drinker's addiction. Others use medication, both to treat the drinker's feelings of depression and to make his body antagonistic to alcohol.

The most prominent group in the treatment of alcoholism is Alcoholics Anonymous (AA), an organization composed of alcoholics who have stopped drinking. (AA members never say that they are "cured," only that their alcoholism has been arrested.) Chapters of AA in nearly every city and town have regular meetings where they offer group support to alcoholics trying to conquer their addiction. They encourage the drinker to accept help and to take responsibility for his own life rather than blame other people or circumstances.

AA has devoted increasing attention to helping the families of alcoholics. Chapters of Alanon (for families) and Alateen (for teenage children of alcoholics) exist in many areas.

Alcoholism is recognized today as a disease, not a character flaw. Seeing it as a disease is the first step toward dealing with it realistically. If the disease is recognized and treated in its early stages, the serious emotional and physical toll of the latter stages can often be avoided.

Even among families of arrested alcoholics, however, it is generally realized that the drinker may one day have a relapse and require further treatment. In this respect, alcoholism is best thought of as a chronic illness—one that can be controlled and managed, but never cured.

Drug Abuse

The most common of the illegal or so-called "street" drugs is marijuana, which is used in some circles much the way alcohol is used. It is smoked at parties or with friends on social occasions. Other street drugs are heroin (an opiate), cocaine, and psychedelics (such as LSD). Certain prescription drugs, such as barbiturates, amphetamines, and tranquilizers, are also subject to abuse and often are obtained illegally.

While most attention is directed at street drugs, a large part of the addiction problem is the result of the abuse of legally prescribed substances. Billions of doses of the major tranquilizers are made and legally sold each year.

Some drugs, such as heroin, are physically addicting. When an addict stops taking it, the withdrawal symptoms are extremely painful. Other substances are only psychologically addictive, but such addictions may be at least as difficult to break.

Many drugs cause serious medical problems in and of themselves. Users of amphetamines lose all appetite, do not sleep for long periods, and may go into a toxic psychosis, in which they believe they are being persecuted and have hallucinations. An overdose of many drugs can cause brain damage or death, especially if used in combination with alcohol.

ALCOHOL AND SEDATIVES *are a dangerous, even life-threatening, combination. Many celebrities have died from the accidental combination of alcohol and prescription sedatives.*

The greatest short-term danger in the abuse of most drugs is the risk of distorted perception, confused reasoning, and impaired judgment. In the long term, the problem is addiction. The stages of addiction to any strong mood-changing or perception-changing drug are similar to the stages of alcoholism listed above, as are the effects on the family. In the first stage, the drug is a panacea. In the second stage, it becomes the center of the addict's life, crowding out family, friends, work, and nearly all normal human pleasures. In the final stage, the addict has isolated himself and begins a process of psychological and physical deterioration.

There are many drug treatment centers in the United States run on a wide variety of principles. Alcoholics Anonymous now deals extensively with multiple addiction—to drugs and alcohol—which present serious medical and psychological complications. Physicians and local social service offices will provide referrals.

▶ Drug Abuse & Addiction-Information & Treatment

Cage Teen Center Incorporated
  4 Longvw Av Whi Plns - - - - - - - - - - - -946-4241
Cage Teen Center Incorporated
  4 Longvw Av Whi Plns - - - - - - - - - - - -946-5058
Cage. Teen Center Inc 5 New Whi Plns - - - 428-1600
Community Counseling Center
  234 Stanley Av Mamk - - - - - - - - - - - -698-7549
Daytop Village Inc 117 E 3 Mt Vern - - - - 664-4070
Hastings Drug Guidance Council
  545 Warbrtn Av Hstgs-On-Hdsn - - - - - - -478-2471
Hot Line Of Hastings
  545 Warbrtn Av Hstgs-On-Hdsn - - - - - - -478-1300
Hot Line Of New Castle
  270 Washngtn Av Plsntvl - - - - - - - - - - 238-8383
Human Connection Tri-Council Help Line
  74 Main Rd

FINDING HELP *for drug abuse: try the yellow pages of the phone book.*

Teenagers and drugs.
Teenagers and even grade-school children are likely to be exposed to drugs in many communities. This is often a major concern to parents. There are a few important points to remember:

- Experimentation with drugs, though dangerous, is not the same as addiction.
- Teenagers often base their attitudes toward drugs on their parents' behavior regarding drugs and alcohol; they are far more likely to follow what their parents practice than what they preach.
- Sudden changes in behavior—withdrawal from social activities and family concerns, loss of interest in friends and in school—may be signs of a drug problem. A doctor or other health professional should be consulted.
- If you suspect your child of using a specific drug, find out from an authoritative source what its long- and short-term dangers are; there are many inaccuracies and distortions both in anti-drug and pro-drug literature.

Severe Mental Illness

There are few things more difficult for most people to understand and deal with than mental illness. Until recently, it was believed that the mentally ill were possessed by devils. Today, we understand something about the causes of these illnesses, and drugs have been discovered that moderate some of their frightening symptoms. But serious mental disturbances are still not usually curable. They are painful not only for the sufferer, but for his family.

The two principal severe illnesses are schizophrenia and manic-depression. The schizophrenic loses the ability to perceive reality and to reason. At times, he may withdraw and show no emotional response to people or events. At other times, he may be wildly talkative and have serious delusions. Schizophrenics sometimes become so disorganized that they speak their own private language and act in wildly inappropriate ways.

The manic-depressive has greater control over his ability to perceive and reason but less over his moods. During the manic phase, he becomes wildly excited; his inner thoughts race faster than he can express them, and he may believe himself able to do extraordinary things. The manic phase soon gives way, however, to a period of shattering depression, in which the sufferer is guilt-ridden, fearful, and suicidal. Some manic depressives experience only the severe depressive phase.

In recent years, the principal treatment for the sufferers of these diseases has been drugs. These substances moderate the symptoms of the illness and often allow the sufferer to pursue normal activities. In some cases, electroshock therapy may also be helpful. Psychoanalytic treatment has not been successful in a majority of cases.

The progress of both diseases is unpredictable. Schizophrenia tends to appear first in the teenage years and to appear over and over again throughout the sufferer's life. In severe cases, the symptoms become gradually worse. In manic depression, the sufferer often seems to get better spontaneously and then to function normally for months or years. Severe episodes may recur, however.

The consequences of mental illness to the victim's family can be devastating. In cases where the person's behavior is erratic for extended periods, family members often organize their lives around the sufferer's behavior. The family may feel frustrated in not being able to communicate with the mentally ill individual and feel guilty because they resent having to live according to his dictates. They may also feel embarrassed by the sufferer's behavior in public. Many families need counseling to learn how to deal with the mentally ill member and to carry on their own lives at the same time.

Suicidal tendencies.
The person who threatens suicide may have a history of mental illness or of drug or alcohol addiction. In most cases, however, he is deeply depressed and sees suicide as the only way out of a crisis. He often does not understand that if he succeeds, he will not be around to enjoy his "solution."

Women attempt suicide three times more often than men, but the attempts are usually less serious. Of successful suicides, 70 percent are men and only 30 percent women. Nearly all potential suicides announce their intentions; family members or friends who receive such an announcement should make every effort to get help. Many cities have suicide or crisis hot lines, and the availability of a trained listener on the phone often helps a suicidal person through a crisis.

The family of a person who has attempted suicide is likely to have deeply contradictory feelings. On one hand, they will feel guilty that they could not prevent the act; on the other, they may be angry that the attempt was made at all, perhaps sensing that one of its motives may have

DRAWINGS *sometimes give clues to the type and severity of mental illness.*

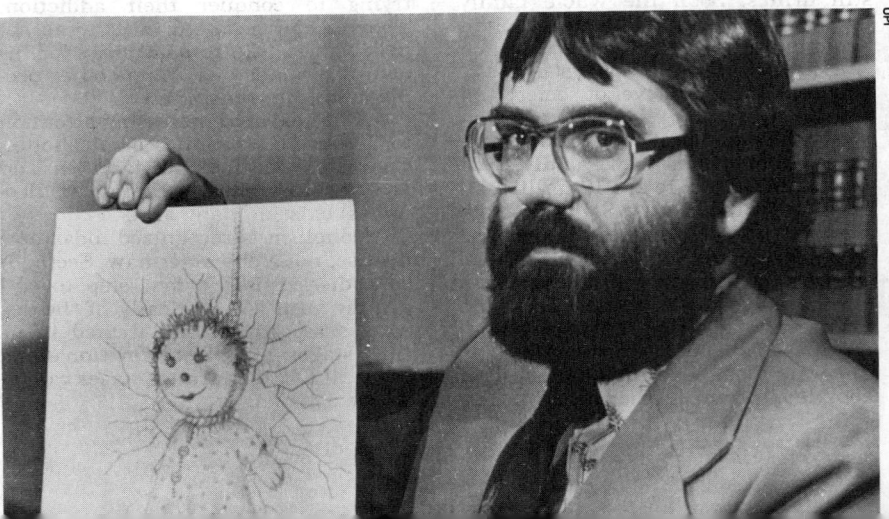

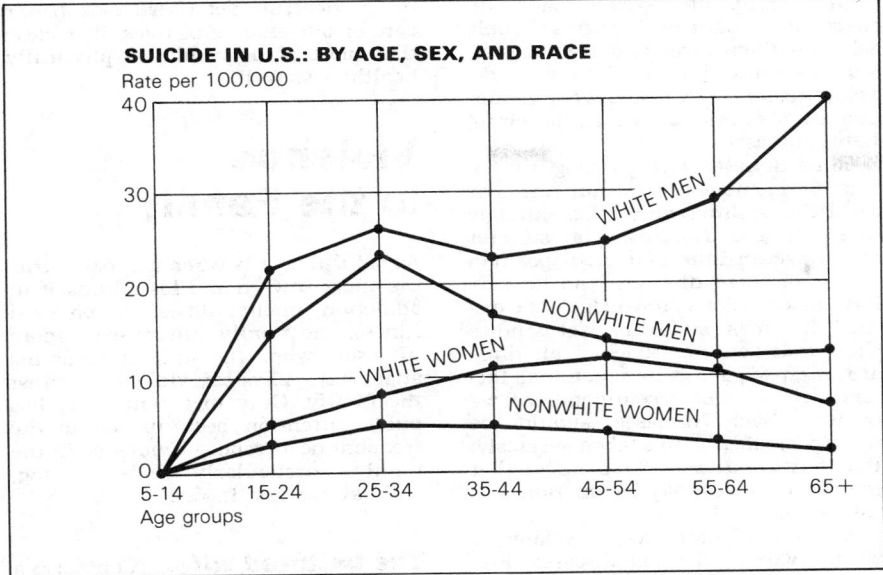

SUICIDE IN U.S.: BY AGE, SEX, AND RACE
Rate per 100,000

WHITE MEN

NONWHITE MEN

WHITE WOMEN

NONWHITE WOMEN

Age groups: 5-14, 15-24, 25-34, 35-44, 45-54, 55-64, 65+

THE SUICIDE RATE *is higher for men than for women and higher for whites than for non-whites. It is a serious problem among aging white men.*

been to punish them. Sometimes counseling both for the attempted suicide and for his family can help deal with these feelings.

Other Emotional Problems

Most families will not have to face the test of severe mental illness or suicide. But many of these families will be troubled by other, less severe emotional problems.

Depression. The most common problem is depression. The term has been used to describe conditions ranging from brief periods of vague unhappiness to severe and extended periods of deep hopelessness, often including thoughts of suicide. In its milder forms, depression has probably been experienced by more than half the adult population. It is particularly prevalent among women.

Depression can be disabling. The depressed person feels that life is not worth living, is unable to make any important decision or take any important action, and finds himself scarcely able to accomplish the minimum daily tasks. Although he feels exhausted, he sleeps poorly; he may either lose his appetite or eat compulsively; he may seek solace in alcohol (which often intensifies the depression) or addictive drugs.

Treatment with anti-depressant drugs can reduce the symptoms, and often this relief is enough to allow the depression to "cure" itself. In more severe cases, however, medication provides only temporary relief.

Many psychologists believe that most depression can be traced to feelings of anger or resentment—feelings that the depressed person has never felt free to express openly or even to acknowledge to himself. Such unrecognized anger is turned inward against the self. Periods of depression may become manageable or even disappear if the sufferer can recognize and come to terms with his anger.

Families of persons with serious depressions often feel angry themselves. They resent that one member has stopped functioning and seems to have dropped out emotionally. They may become depressed themselves or may strike out at the depressed person, seeking to raise a response. An important step toward relieving this grim, unhappy atmosphere may be for family members to work at expressing their feelings to each other—both the positive and the negative. In serious cases, the services of a psychologist or other counselor may be helpful.

The emotionally disturbed child.
A child who becomes a behavior problem in early childhood, has trouble concentrating and getting along with other children, or has trouble learning in school may have an emotional disturbance. He may cause considerable uproar and unhappiness at home. Parents are often baffled by his problem, yet they hesitate to seek help, feeling that this would be an admission of their failure as parents.

Some children may have a biological predisposition to behave in these disturbed patterns. They should be carefully examined for neurological problems. Educators have been particularly active in recent years in finding ways of identifying specific learning

and behavior problems and in developing effective ways to treat them.

In other cases, the child's disturbance may reflect some serious problem at home. Although the child probably does not understand the nature of such a problem—the emotional trouble of a parent or marital discord, for example—his behavior may be his way of coping with it. The parents may be unconsciously requiring contradictory things of a child, making it impossible for him to do the right thing or ever to be "good." They may be making a scapegoat of the child, finding it simpler to deal with "his" problem than to face their own.

Whatever the cause of the disturbance, the emotionally disturbed child can cause great unhappiness in the family. Both parents and other children may develop compensating troubles of their own to cope with the troubled child.

The parents of an emotionally disturbed child should seek a careful evaluation of the child's problems and should be prepared to participate in his treatment.

Compulsive behavior. There are many forms of compulsive behavior, and each has its own characteristics and consequences. Some, such as compulsive neatness, may be irritating to others but relatively harmless. Others may present a serious hazard either to the individual (as in overeating) or to the victim's family (as in compulsive gambling).

Such compulsions can distort the life of a family and cause serious strains to all its members. Although they are not as serious or as immediately threatening as severe mental illness, acute compulsions may require treatment. Many helping organizations, often patterning their work after Alcoholics Anonymous, have been established to help compulsive eaters, gamblers, etc.

Other compulsions may center around money or sex. Many families find themselves in serious financial trouble because they feel obliged to spend more than they earn, falling further and further into debt, even though their income seems adequate. At the other extreme, some people have a compulsion to save, finding the withholding of their money even from those closest to them a way of withholding affection or approval. Neither the spendthrift nor the miser is generally considered emotionally ill, but in extreme cases, serious emotional problems may be at the root of the person's behavior.

Similar extremes in sexual behavior may also be a sign of emotional trouble. There are both men and women who are promiscuous. They go from partner to partner, seeming to want to prove over and over again that they are desirable and wanted. Yet their promiscuity may also protect them from ever having to trust and make a commitment to another. At the other extreme, there are men and women who hold back on sexual activity because of deep anxiety or the fear of becoming vulnerable to another. As with the use of money, the use of sex is not in itself a sign of trouble, but extreme behavior may be a symptom or danger sign.

Psychosomatic illness.

A serious illness can cause dislocations in a family under any circumstances. But in some cases, the illness itself is a symptom of emotional trouble in the individual, the family, or both.

Psychosomatic illness is real and may even cripple or kill, but it is brought on in some measure by the sufferer's mental state.

The relationship between mind and body is a question that has been a major concern of philosophers for centuries and, more recently, of psychologists. The question has not yet been conclusively answered. We do know, however, that mental states have an important effect on the body.

One group of psychosomatic illnesses is brought on by stress. People who put themselves under great pressure to succeed or achieve may develop ulcers. They also have a greater chance of developing heart and circulatory diseases.

Other diseases with a strong psychosomatic element are certain forms of arthritis; asthma and other allergic diseases; and diabetes. The sufferer may have an inherited predisposition to one of these diseases, and he may have no conscious knowledge of "causing" his own suffering, yet studies show that acute episodes of all three are often triggered by emotional factors such as anger, resentment, or frustration. Such diseases should be treated medically and taken seriously. But it is important to remember that their root causes may be emotional as well as physical.

Emotional factors may be related to a wide variety of other diseases. Frequent illness can be a sign that there is some underlying emotional problem, yet the exact connection is difficult to identify. It would be useless in most cases to tell a seriously ill person that he would feel better if only he were

more cheerful. Yet if we took better care of our emotional lives, it is clear that most of us would be physically healthier as well.

Violence in the Family

As painful as it is when a person turns his anger inward and loses himself in addiction, mental illness, or physical illness, the family suffers even more intensely when the sufferer turns his anger into physical violence against the family. Only in recent years has public attention been turned to the frequent occurrence of violence in the family, particularly wife beating, child abuse, and incest.

The battered wife.

Conflict is a normal part of family life, and it is not uncommon for conflict to be expressed physically. Couples may stomp out of a room, slam a door, throw things, and even push and shove each other. But when physical violence becomes a regular part of the family's existence, something has gone seriously wrong.

There are occasional cases of wives beating their husbands, but violence in a marriage is most often committed by the man. His aggressive tendencies are usually more intense, and he is likely to be both bigger and stronger than his wife.

The wife batterer is generally a man with a low opinion of himself. Incidents of violence often occur when he has been drinking heavily. His anger may not be limited to his wife, but she is the most convenient and safest target. Others—even the police—hesitate to intervene, sensing that his anger may be turned on them. One policeman in five who is killed while on duty is slain while intervening in a family quarrel.

After the violent episode, the wife batterer may be filled with remorse and promise never to become abusive again; he rarely keeps his promises.

The wife batterer often considers his wife to be his property. If questioned about his behavior, he asserts that he "has the right" to abuse her. He is rarely willing to receive counseling, and his wife, out of her own fear or confusion, may support him.

Often the man's illness is shared by his wife. She may have strong practical reasons for fearing to leave her home. Her husband may have threatened to follow and even kill her if she leaves. She may also refuse to leave her children unprotected. Often she feels that in some way she deserves the punishment her husband gives her. In addition, she may refuse to acknowledge the danger she is in, hoping against hope that her husband will get better.

STRESS

Stress is defined as any change in life that causes the expenditure of emotional energy. Some people can tolerate more stress than others, but those who experience too much in a short time run a greater risk of major illness.

The following table compares the stress caused by various life changes. Research shows that a person who has experienced under 150 points of change in the past year is relatively safe. Those scoring between 150 and 300 points in the past year have a 50-50 chance of developing a serious illness in the coming year or two. Those scoring over 300 points have an almost 90 percent chance of serious illness.

LIFE EVENT	VALUE	LIFE EVENT	VALUE
1. Death of spouse	100	22. Change in responsibilities at work	29
2. Divorce	73	23. Son or daughter leaving home	29
3. Marital separation	65	24. Trouble with in-laws	29
4. Jail term	63	25. Outstanding personal achievement	28
5. Death of close family member	63	26. Wife begins or stops work	26
6. Personal injury, illness	53	27. Begin or end school	26
7. Marriage	50	28. Change in living conditions	25
8. Dismissed from job	47	29. Revision of personal habits	24
9. Marital reconciliation	45	30. Trouble with boss	23
10. Retirement	45	31. Change in work hours or conditions	20
11. Change in health of family member	44	32. Change of residence	20
12. Pregnancy	39	33. Change of schools	20
13. Sex difficulties	39	34. Change of recreation	19
14. Gain of new family member	39	35. Change of church activities	19
15. Business readjustment	39	36. Change of social activities	18
16. Change in financial state	38	37. Mortage or loan less than $10,000	17
17. Death of close friend	37	38. Change in sleeping habits	16
18. Change to different line of work	36	39. Change in number of family get-togethers	15
19. Change in number of arguments with spouse	35	40. Change in eating habits	15
20. Mortgage over $10,000	31	41. Vacation	13
21. Foreclosure of mortgage or loan	30	42. Christmas	12
		43. Minor violation of law	11

Reprinted with permission of Journal of Psychosomatic Research, Holmes, T. H., and Rahe, R. H., "The Social Readjustment Rating Scale," copyright 1967, Pergamon Press, Ltd.

Police and the courts have traditionally been reluctant to intervene in family violence. Even women who have sustained serious injuries have often been advised to return to their husbands. Today, however, there are support services for battered women in many parts of the country, offering both temporary shelter and legal and psychological assistance.

The effect of such family violence on children is incalculable. Children from violent homes are frequently seriously disturbed; they often develop learning disabilities and engage in disruptive behavior. In a large number of cases, the children grow up to perpetuate violence in their own homes.

Child abuse. Even more damaging is the phenomenon of child abuse. Many parents occasionally spank their children as a means of punishment, but for some, physical abuse of the child becomes an end in itself. Both husbands and wives can be involved.

Parents who batter their children do not have the patience or emotional energy to cope with their children's demands for attention and care. Such parents have a very low opinion of themselves and a low tolerance for stress. Injuring the child may be a means of proving their complete authority over at least one other creature in the world.

Outsiders who know of families who abuse and injure their children are often reluctant to intervene. This reluctance is shared by police and the courts, even when severe injury can be proved. When children are removed from homes where batterings occur, they are often returned there within months to receive further abuse. If they survive their childhoods, they are extremely likely to batter and abuse their own children.

Incest. A related problem is incest. Carried on most often between a father and daughter, it probably begins before the child is of school age. Although the child may profess no unhappiness about her relationship with her father, she has in reality no way to say no. On the father's part, it is an act of extreme emotional, as well as physical, violence against the child. Children who are the victims of incest often have serious emotional and sexual problems in later life.

In some cities, reported cases of incest are now referred to psychological counselors. There is some evidence that counseling can help end the perverse relationship and repair some of the damage it has caused.

Incest between a mother and her son is rarely reported. But some mothers do form deeply seductive emotional relationships with sons. These are likely to result in later emotional and sexual problems.

External Problems

The problems discussed so far develop in great part within the family. There are other circumstances, however, that seem to be imposed from the outside that can also cause great personal and family unhappiness.

Death. Everyone must at some time experience the death of a family member. An adult may be shaken by the death of a parent, even though the death might have been expected and prepared for. The death of a spouse, especially if premature and unexpected, can be a devastating blow and can cause serious problems for the couple's children. Perhaps hardest of all to deal with is the death of a child.

Death is difficult for most people to understand because they cannot quite believe in their own. Many people tend not to consider the subject at all until it is forced upon them. Recent studies suggest, however, that both people who know they are dying and their survivors must go through a process that will help them understand and accept dying. The five stages are:

- *Denial.* The victim and his family refuse to believe that death is on the way. They may claim there has been a mistake and go from doctor to doctor seeking encouragement.
- *Anger.* The dying person may strike out at those closest to him, who often respond in kind. In reality, they are angry at the inevitability of death itself. The family that cannot tolerate anger may isolate the dying person, making his situation even harder.
- *Bargaining.* The dying person may try to make a deal with God or with his doctors, promising to behave better or redress old grievances if he is granted the right to live a little longer.
- *Depression, grief, sorrow.* The dying person replays his life, feeling deep regret or sorrow over missed opportunities, over the loss of participation in the world that his death will bring, and over people and activities already lost to him. The family, although it may be going through a similar process, often tries to cheer the dying person up, unrealistically asking him not to accept his death.
- *Acceptance.* The last stage is not necessarily joyful, but it can be peaceful. The dying person begins to lose interest in the day-to-day activities of the world and to draw into himself emotionally. Families often misunderstand this stage, resenting the person's decreasing interest in life and in them. They may feel abandoned and think, "If only he would try harder, he might not have to die." For the dying person who has worked through these stages, however, dying may seem both natural and welcome.

The process of grieving and acceptance may go on for the survivors for some months after the death itself. Successfully completing the process can make life seem more precious and yet make dying seem less frightening and unnatural.

Catastrophic illness. Because of the high cost of medical care, any major illness may be catastrophic financially. The emotional costs are high as well.

During the acute stage of an illness, there is often a period of suspense while the family waits for some indication of the seriousness of the condition. Is the illness terminal? Will there be lasting disability? How long will the patient be in the hospital? How long will it be before he or she can return to normal activities?

During this period, adults prepare themselves emotionally for any eventuality. They may feel, however, that it is not fair to burden children with

---

THE HOSPICE

"The modern hospital is dedicated to saving lives; the dying are often an embarrassment to its staff. Heavily sedated, they are shunted off to one side. By contrast, the hospice—a name taken from the medieval way stations for travellers—sees death as a part of life and the dying as very special people who have something to teach the rest of us but who also need as much emotional and medical support as possible."

"A DEEPLY COMPASSIONATE BOOK A MOVING EXPERIENCE TO READ" —Anne Morrow Lindbergh

THE HOSPICE MOVEMENT A BETTER WAY OF CARING FOR THE DYING

Sandol Stoddard

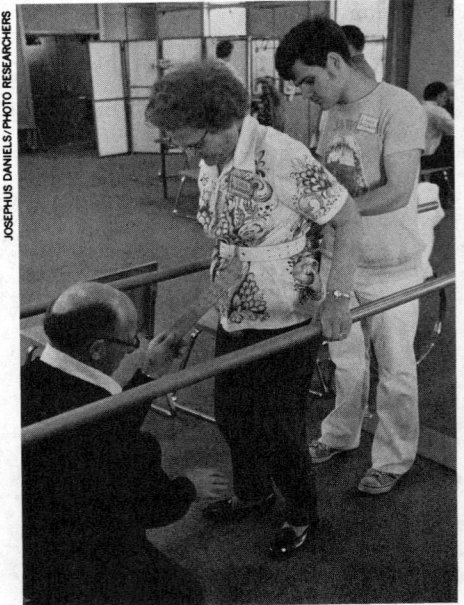

ILLNESS AND MOVING: *such major life changes cause stresses and strains in individual and family life. These changes often require learning new skills, seeking outside assistance, and going through a period of mourning for things left behind.*

the seriousness of the situation. This is often a mistake, since children need time to prepare as well. Otherwise they may be angry and feel betrayed if, for example, they are told that their grandmother is getting better, and she then dies.

Once the situation becomes clear, the family must make many practical arrangements, including plans that will allow frequent visits to the ill person and yet allow day-to-day life to go on. Then, when the patient improves, further plans will be required for home care during convalescence.

If the illness and convalescence last many weeks or months, the strain may begin to threaten healthy members of the family. Financial worries, additional household responsibilities, and the absence of a loved one can cause emotional problems for adults and children. Often, however, the family pulls together during the crisis, with the serious strain showing only after the ill person has recovered or died.

Chronic illness. Chronic conditions such as severe arthritis, multiple sclerosis, paralysis (from an accident, stroke, or other causes), and senility, present different problems. On one hand the family does not face the possibility of losing a member in the near future. On the other, there is usually little prospect of improvement, and the situation stretches into the indefinite future.

Many families have learned to deal with disabilities. Often they find a major difficulty to be the emotional state of the sufferer. He may have severe pain; he may become unreasonably demanding and dependent, expecting the household to revolve around his

condition; or he may be resentful and irritable.

The physical demands placed on other household members may be extreme as well and may cause the adult responsible for the sufferer's care to be exhausted and unhappy. If caring for the sufferer is more work than the household can manage, arrangements should be made for professional help either in the home or in a medical facility. Social service agencies can sometimes be helpful in solving practical problems and may also be able to offer suggestions aimed at reducing emotional tension.

Loss of livelihood. Another serious threat to both individual and family emotional health can be a loss of livelihood. The practical problems come to mind first—without its accustomed income, how will the family pay for housing, buy food, and meet its other obligations? If the period of unemployment is long, the emotional problems can also be severe.

Often the spouse who brings in most of the income gains a great sense of worth by successfully supporting his family. When he is laid off or can no longer work, he is likely to feel helpless and angry. Seeking other employment, particularly in jobs that seem below him, is an added strain. At the same time, the other spouse, on whom the burden of breadwinning has fallen, may respond with anger or deep disappointment at the turn of events. In extreme cases, the family may disintegrate under the strain.

In many cases, finding a new line of work can be difficult and threatening. Career counseling may help a displaced worker plan realistically for

finding satisfactory employment. In the meantime, the family should apply for unemployment or other government benefits to which they may be entitled.

Moving. Families move for many reasons. One spouse may be transferred from one company office to another, or the family may be seeking improved employment opportunities, a better climate, or increased distance from relatives.

Whatever the cause, moving can be a serious strain, both on individuals and on the family. This is especially true if the move takes a family far from its roots.

In the short term, a move often gives a family a sense of closeness. The members turn to each other for support in the new and unfamiliar environment. But this closeness soon evaporates under the strain of making a new start, especially in the demands of performing well at new jobs and at school, and of making new friends. Families who move primarily to leave old problems behind are often disappointed, discovering that they take their most serious problems with them. Usually the strain of the new environment slackens over a period of two or three years, and the new residence gradually becomes home.

If a family moves often, whether from desire or necessity, moving may cause permanent problems. Family members learn not to make close friends in a new community because breaking the ties will be too painful when the next move arrives. The resulting sense of rootlessness and isolation can be a serious strain and result in severe emotional problems.

FINDING HELP

Assistance for individuals and families in trouble is often available in the community. People seeking help should ask for referrals from a family physician, clergyman, or social service worker. The Yellow Pages of the phone book often list helping agencies under such headings as *Alcoholism, Drug Abuse, Marriage and Family Counseling, Social Service Organizations,* etc. The following list offers the names and addresses of national organizations that will send helpful information; in some cases, they may be able to refer inquirers to local programs.

CHILD-RELATED PROBLEMS
Child Abuse
CALM
P.O. Box 718
Santa Barbara, CA 93102

Parents Anonymous
22330 Hawthorne Blvd.
Torrance, CA 90505
Autism
National Society for Autistic Children
1234 Massachusetts Ave. N.W.
Washington, DC 20005
Mental Retardation
Association for Retarded Citizens
National Office
2501 Avenue J
Arlington, TX 76011
Learning Disabilities
Association for Children with
Learning Disabilities
4156 Library St.
Pittsburgh, PA 15234
Runaways
National Runaway Switchboard
Toll-free phone: 800-621-4000
Death of a Child
Compassionate Friends
National Headquarters
P.O. Box 1347
Oakbrook, IL 60521

FAMILY AND ADULT PROBLEMS
Counseling (*see also* Mental Health *below*)
American Association of Marriage and
Family Counselors
924 West 9th St.
Upland, CA 91786

Family Service Association of America
44 East 23rd St.
New York, NY 10010
Single-parent Families
Parents Without Partners, Inc.
7910 Woodmont Ave.
Washington, DC 20014
Family Planning
National Family Planning Council
5958 Whittier Blvd.
East Los Angeles, CA 90022
Unwed Mothers
National Conference of Catholic Charities
1307 Connecticut Ave. N.W., Suite 307
Washington, DC 20036
Aging
National Council on the Aging, Inc.
600 Maryland Ave. S.W.
West Wing 100
Washington, DC 20024

DEPENDENCY AND ADDICTION
Alcoholism
Alcoholics Anonymous
General Service Office
468 Park Ave. South
New York, NY 10016

Al-Anon and Alateen
(for families of alcoholics)
200 Park Ave. South, Rm. 1602
New York, NY 10003

The National Clearing House for
Alcohol Information
P.O. Box 2345
Rockville, MD 20855
Drug Abuse
Drug Abuse Council
Washington Area Council on Alcohol and
Drug Abuse, Inc.
1221 Massachusetts Ave. N.W., Suite A
Washington, DC 20005

Families Anonymous
P.O. Box 344
Torrance, CA 90501
Overweight
Overeaters Anonymous
World Service Office
2190 190th St.
Torrance, CA 90504

Tops Club, Inc.
P.O. Box 07489
Milwaukee, WI 53207
(over 1200 local chapters)
Gambling
Gamblers Anonymous
National Service Office
P.O. Box 17173
Los Angeles, CA 90017

MENTAL HEALTH (*see also* Family and Adult Problems *above*)
American Psychiatric Association
1700 18th St. N.W.
Washington, DC 20009

American Psychoanalytic Association
1 East 57th St.
New York, NY 10022

American Psychological Association
1200 17th St. N.W.
Washington, DC 20036

National Mental Health Association
1800 North Kent St.
Arlington, VA 22209

HANDICAPS
Physical Impairment
Institute for Rehabilitation Medicine
Publications Dept.
400 East 34th St.
New York, NY 10016

National Easter Seal Society for
Crippled Children and Adults
2023 West Ogden Ave.
Chicago, IL 60612
Hearing and Speech Impairment
Alexander Graham Bell Association
for the Deaf
3417 Volta Place N.W.
Washington, DC 20007

American Speech–Language–Hearing
Association
10801 Rockville Pike
Rockville, MD 20852
Sight Impairment
American Foundation for the Blind
15 West 16th St.
New York, NY 10011

MEDICAL PROBLEMS
Arthritis
Arthritis Foundation
3400 Peachtree Rd. N.E.
Atlanta, GA 30326
Asthma
National Foundation for Asthma
P.O. Box 50304
Tucson, AZ 85703
Cancer
American Cancer Society
777 Third Ave.
New York, NY 10022

Cancer Care, Inc.
(for care of patients with advanced cancer)
1 Park Ave.
New York, NY 10016

Candlelighters Foundation
(for parents of cancer victims)
2025 "I" St. N.W.
Washington, DC 20006
Diabetes
American Diabetes Association
2 Park Ave.
New York, NY 10016
Epilepsy
Epilepsy Foundation of America
4351 Garden City Dr., Suite 406
Landover, MD 20785
Multiple Sclerosis
National Multiple Sclerosis Society
205 East 42nd St.
New York, NY 10017
Muscular Dystrophy
Muscular Dystrophy Association
810 Seventh Avenue
New York, NY 10019
Parkinson's Disease
National Parkinsonism Foundation
1501 N.W. 9th Ave.
Miami, FL 33136

Marriage and Family Problems

The severe individual problems discussed above seem intimidating as a group, yet almost every family has faced one or another of them.

The same is true of the less specific but still painful problems that arise between married couples or within families and that lead at times to separation and divorce and the possible dissolution of the family itself.

Marital Problems

The earlier section on marriage mentioned many potential marital problems. Here we need only consider the most common issues, the means of finding help for difficulties, and the prospect of separation and divorce.

The issues. The most immediate cause of marital conflict is often the development of one of the individual problems discussed above (for example, alcoholism, depression, compulsive behavior). The misbehavior of a child may also be an immediate issue.

In addition, there may be other less specific causes. The couple may claim to be bored with each other or to have grown apart. Or they may complain that they fight all the time, seldom agreeing on anything.

Such conflicts tend to be emotional and subjective. It is difficult for any third party to judge who is responsible and even more difficult to see what can be done about the problems.

If the partners can discuss their disagreements with calm and reason, they may be able to understand each other better and to change their behavior. Often, however, the emotional level is too high for such discussion to be of much good. The partners may have to stay apart and cool off first.

This may give both a chance to consider deeper issues that may be troubling them. These issues constitute a second level on which marital conflict can be considered. They are the major themes about which discord often revolves.

The first of these is the issue of *blame vs. responsibility*. In a dispute, the instinct of most people is to determine who is to blame—to place the fault. In a marriage, the fault is usually placed squarely on the other party.

Most partners realize at least vaguely that they are most likely to find fault with their spouse when they themselves feel unhappy. Blaming can be a way of taking out one's own negative feelings on the nearest target. A man who is worried and upset about his job, for example, may come home and pick a fight with his wife, thereby placing some of the blame at her feet. A woman who is bored and unhappy at home may be unrealistically demanding on her husband in order to share her unhappiness with him.

In its extreme form, blame comes to explain not just one incident, but a whole year or a whole marriage. When one partner says, "I always knew you'd turn out to be no good," or "I always knew you'd leave me," he or she is using the partner to explain all past and present problems. This kind of blame can wound the partner who is being accused. More important, the accuser can avoid acknowledging his or her share of the responsibility.

Easy as it is to blame the other person, many persons will turn around unexpectedly and take all the responsibility on themselves, whether deserving it or not. Paradoxically, this may be as unhelpful as accepting none of the blame.

If a marriage runs into trouble on such issues, the partners are faced with learning how to share responsibility—not only for household chores but for the things that have gone wrong between them.

A second issue that often arises is *independence vs. dependence*. We all grow up with two strong but conflicting desires. One is to be independent—self-sufficient, self-determining, in control of our lives and surroundings. We fear being absorbed or taken over by another. On the other hand, we feel incomplete and in need of the affection, approval, and support of another person—we want to be somehow dependent.

It is important for couples to understand in what respects each partner is to be independent and dependent. If this understanding is not reached, there is likely to be conflict from the beginning. Later, changed circumstances may make the agreement seem out of date and in need of renegotiation. The discontent can be of four kinds:

- I feel trapped because I cannot pursue my own interests and ambitions (wants more independence).
- I feel trapped because my partner relies too much on me, wants too much from me (wants partner to be more independent).
- I feel abandoned because my partner does not care for me the way I would like (wants to be more dependent).
- I feel abandoned because my partner does not seem to need or rely on me anymore (wants partner to be more dependent).

People who want one or both of the first two conditions are struggling toward a new separateness—they want room within the marriage to be more themselves, and want their partner to behave accordingly. Those who feel one or both of the last two are seeking a new or more complete feeling of togetherness.

It is even possible to feel at once both trapped and abandoned—conflicting needs for independence and dependence can be felt at the same

ADVICE COLUMNS *like Ann Landers' show readers that their problems are not unique.*

dead marriage shoul

N: When a marriage has gone sour only thing that keeps you from filing rce is the promise, "Till death do us you split with a clear conscience? I able in this marriage for nd my mate feels the , but I am haunted by the would be a sin to break

ry Guilty in South Bend You already have been —the death of your love, our devotion, the joy of and the warm feelings want a lifetime partner- ning is dead it should be lieve God understands

ANN LANDERS

you will find between those covers is collection of columns. The subject mat organized skillfully in a way that makes ful and provocative reading.

It's the perfect gift for ar to 88. Buy a dozen while th sure to be a runaway best

Dear Ann: Tim and I married two years. We liv family dwelling with thre ples. At first, it was fun. We the same age, and postpone because we have good job save some money. We together almost every nigl like one happy family—un Now one couple gets every weekend. They hav

time. This is not rational, but it is human.

In a troubled marriage, it is often the case that one partner is growing and feels his or her needs changing, while the other partner clings desperately to the old agreement and the old way of looking at things. Sometimes such a conflict can be overcome with care and patience. In other cases it may lead to deeper unhappiness and to the end of the relationship.

The third theme that often runs through marital arguments is *selfishness vs. selflessness*. "All my husband ever thinks about is himself." "She's so busy with her activities that she never has any time for me." Such complaints are almost universal at one time or another.

The problem is that we have two different ideas of what selfishness is. On the one hand we see it as a sin and an obstacle to a satisfying relationship with another person. Yet in practice, we find it necessary to be selfish in many ways—to assert ourselves, to stand up for our rights, to be recognized as individuals.

In marriage, partners learn that if selfishness is knowing one's own mind and sticking up for oneself, it can be helpful to the partnership. Two individuals with a strong sense of themselves will have arguments, but they will also come to respect each other's individuality.

Selflessness, the opposite of selfishness, is sometimes seen as an ideal. If selflessness is being willing to compromise in the partner's favor and being considerate of him or her, then it too can be helpful in a marriage. On the other hand, if it means refusing to assert oneself, deferring always to the partner, it can be as damaging as self-ishness. A wife may always defer to her husband's wishes, for example, and yet never find any pleasure in what she has forced him to decide.

In fact, there may be no clear difference between the effects of extreme selfishness and selflessness. The partner who runs roughshod over others, always demanding that his needs be met first, is often a person who has painful doubts about who he is. Feeling inadequate, he makes selfish demands on others to prove that he is really someone. He has little time or energy to consider other people's needs because he is so busy trying to keep his own self together.

There is still another level on which marital conflicts can be considered, one still deeper. Psychoanalysts believe people are the result of experiences in early life, often those revolving around their parents. For example, a man who felt overprotected and smothered by his mother is likely eventually to feel smothered or trapped by his wife. A woman who never felt she could trust her father's love will likely have trouble trusting her husband's. In this way, certain kinds of problems are carried from generation to generation.

Getting at these deeper personal problems often requires the help of a trained psychologist or psychoanalyst, and working them out may take many months or even years.

Finding help. When things begin to go wrong in a marriage, the partners often refuse to acknowledge the fact for some months or years. They may be afraid to acknowledge the failure of the relationship or afraid to risk the stability that the partnership gives to their lives. In many cases, the problem may finally reveal itself in some severe and apparently unrelated problem such as alcoholism, depression, or psychosomatic illness. Often the treatment of that problem will bring the partners to realize and accept their marital problems.

However it occurs, acknowledging that the marriage is unhappy is the first step toward making changes—whether the changes lead ultimately toward improving the relationship or ending it.

Once they agree that they are unhappy, the partners may try on their own to patch things up, and if the problems between them are not too serious, they may succeed.

Often, however, the problems are so deep that self-help will not work—in fact, it may make things worse. This leads to a second step: an agreement by both partners to seek outside help. Then the question is where to look or whom to ask.

One of the most common courses is to seek out friends. Each partner may confide in a concerned friend or relative. The hardest part often is revealing the problem in the first place. Unhappy partners tend to assume that no one else has noticed their unhappiness and that friends will feel shock and disillusionment to learn that there is trouble, even though this is seldom the case.

Revealing unhappiness to a sympathetic listener often proves a great relief. It also forces the unhappy partner to think of the marital problem more objectively. Slights or injuries that seemed terrible and unforgivable begin to shrink when they are described to an outside party. A sense of perspective may be restored just in the telling.

EXPRESSING ANGER *is often a relief in a troubled family. Airing one's feelings with a counselor can help family members become more objective about their complaints.*

In addition, people who are chosen as confidants in such matters may have experience or understanding that can result in good advice.

Deeper problems may be beyond the help of friends, or may be of the sort that the partners are unwilling to discuss with any but a professional counselor or therapist.

Some couples turn to a religious leader for advice. Many clergymen have received training in marital counseling; some refer a couple to an appropriate counselor. Other couples ask their friends—particularly those who may themselves have had marital problems—for referrals to a marriage counselor or psychologist.

In general, it is wise to seek a counselor who can demonstrate some training in counseling. In many states, marriage counselors are licensed, and in some, clinical psychologists (those who do counseling) are licensed as well. Psychiatrists are medical doctors with advanced training in the diagnosis and treatment of mental and emotional disorders. Licensing and education do not necessarily guarantee that the counselor will be helpful, but they reduce the chances of unorthodox or dangerous treatment.

Counselors may use a wide variety of methods in dealing with an unhappy couple. Some concentrate on the outward behavior of the partners and try to correct it. Others may seek the root cause of the trouble by requiring lengthy individual counseling for one or both partners. Still others use a combination of approaches.

If the problem is clearly in a specific area, specialized therapy may be best. In recent years, for example, sex therapy clinics have been established in many parts of the country; they report a high rate of success in correcting some sexual problems.

It is often difficult to assess the effectiveness of the counseling. On one hand, couples should not expect overnight miracles. Improvement may require time and may, in fact, cause considerable pain and conflict in the short run. On the other hand, the unhappy couple should keep a sense of perspective. If they agree that a particular method or counselor is making no progress after a reasonable time, they should seek help elsewhere.

Separation and divorce.

There may come a time in an unhappy marriage when the partners agree that their relationship should end. This is almost always a painful realization, no matter how acrimonious and unhappy life together has become.

The first step usually is separation. One spouse moves from the family dwelling and takes up a separate residence. The couple will meet (usually represented by lawyers) to conclude a separation agreement. This agreed-upon separation is called *de facto*

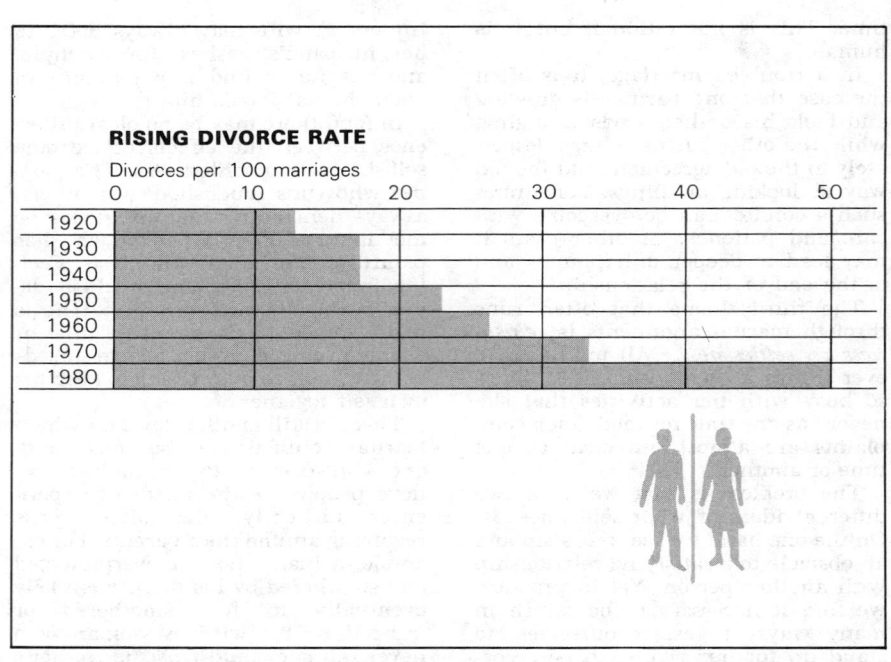

RISING DIVORCE RATE
Divorces per 100 marriages

	0	10	20	30	40	50
1920						
1930						
1940						
1950						
1960						
1970						
1980						

DIVORCES HAVE BECOME *increasingly common, rising from 171,000 during 1920 to 1.2 million during 1980, an increase of seven times.*

separation. If the couple cannot agree on the terms—the division of property, custody and support of children, for example—a judge may hear the arguments of both parties and render a judgment. This is called a *de jure* separation.

Any separation leaves the marriage technically in effect. Neither party is free to marry again. If the terms of the agreement or judgment are broken, either party may take the case to court. However, the separation may later become grounds for divorce in some states.

Ending a marriage is considerably more difficult than beginning one, in legal as well as emotional terms. Divorce laws differ greatly from state to state. Traditionally, the partner requesting the divorce was required to allege specific grounds—acts or failures to act on the part of the other partner that would justify dissolution of the marriage. In some states, until recent years, the only acceptable ground for divorce was adultery.

Gradually, states began to allow other grounds for divorce. The most common included abandonment (one partner leaving without the consent of the other and with intent not to return), cruelty (physical or mental), drug addiction, habitual intoxication, imprisonment, failure to provide support, legal insanity, and fraud (misrepresenting or concealing facts about prior marriages, children, serious illnesses, serious crimes, etc.). In applying for divorce on any of these grounds, it is the duty of the aggrieved party to prove his or her allegations. The other partner may seek to disprove them.

In recent years, however, more than half the states have added less specific and legalistic grounds for divorce. The grounds may be called incompatibility, irreconcilable differences, or irretrievable breakdown. Whatever the official name, neither partner must prove a case against the other so long as both agree to the divorce. Together, these nonlegalistic grounds are called no-fault laws.

In many states there is a waiting period between the application for a divorce decree and its final effect. Thus, partners cannot agree to be divorced one day and be free of the marriage the next. Some states also require efforts at reconciliation before a divorce decree will be granted.

The divorce decree resembles the separation agreement or judgment in that it makes provision for division of property, child custody, payment of child support and alimony, etc. The decree has the force of law, although its provisions are often hard to enforce. The laws governing division of property and other particulars vary considerably from state to state. Any person considering divorce should seek legal advice and assistance.

The emotional costs of separation and divorce are often greater than the financial or legal. Especially in cases where the couple has been married for many years, the adjustments that each will have to make are large. Very few couples get married expecting to be divorced, so when the day arrives, it usually seems a confession of failure. In addition, many former spouses do not realize how "married" they were until they resume life as single individuals. They may find dating and making new friends of the opposite sex especially difficult.

TELEVISION FAMILIES *like this one can give a false, idealized picture of family life—good for comedy, but not to be taken too seriously.*

Divorce also tends to break up friendships that a couple developed over many years. Old friends may feel awkward about inviting the divorced parties either separately or together and resolve the situation by not inviting them at all. Families of spouses may have a similar reaction.

Emotional difficulties may be compounded by practical ones. The separated or divorced partners may find it financially difficult to maintain two places of residence. Often there are deep resentments on both sides about the financial restrictions the divorce has placed on them. Lifestyles may have to change drastically.

Where young children are involved, the divorced parties may meet each other fairly regularly when exercising visitation privileges. They are often enjoined by the terms of the divorce decree not to seek to enlist the children against the other partner. The natural impulse to do just that can be very strong.

Still, in cases where life together has become intolerable for two people, all the prospective difficulties of divorce may be well worth the price. At best, divorce allows an individual to start fresh and make something better of the rest of his or her life. The important thing is that the partners come fully to terms with their failure in marriage. If they do, their future relationships and remarriage may be much happier. If they do not, they may find that they have carried their personal troubles with them rather than leaving them behind in the dissolution of their marriage.

Family Problems

Serious problems in families occur not only between spouses but also between parents and children. Although a child may not consciously seek to disrupt and trouble other family members, he may be extremely shrewd in the way he does so.

When trouble first arises, the question is often, "Whose fault is it?" Assigning responsibility for a problem to one family member can be convenient for other members, but it may often seriously misrepresent a situation.

One group of psychologists suggests that it is useful to consider the family unit rather than the individual. When a family is not working well, its members are unhappy. Placing the blame on one individual, whether a child or an adult, may make solution of the problem more, rather than less, difficult. Family therapy, in which all members of a family are seen either individually or together, has gained considerable support and may be more helpful in many cases than individual therapy.

Triangles. One important idea that is an outgrowth of family therapy will help explain its uses. When one family member is unhappy with another, he or she may express this unhappiness by forming a triangle. For example, a mother who feels insecure and unhappy with her husband may focus all her attention on one of her children. The father, feeling excluded

from this special relationship, may give the same child special attention and try to make his relationship with the child more important than his wife's. The child, sensing that his parents are competing for his affection, may take a hand himself. If he is unhappy with his mother, he knows he can anger her by seeming to favor his father.

The father might get back at his wife for being excluded by focusing his attention on a second child instead. In effect, this sets up a second triangle. The two children, resenting the special relationship the other has with one of the parents, may begin to compete—first for the mother's love and attention, then for the father's—setting up still another triangle. This set of interlocking and shifting triangular relationships demonstrates the complexity of family relations.

Triangles of this sort are formed in all families, and often they are very durable, lasting as long as the family is intact. Even reasonably happy adults carry the marks of their childhood triangles, and they often form similar patterns with their children.

In seriously troubled homes, these triangular relationships may take on unbearable intensity. If the pressure focuses on one individual, that person may break down in some way—by delinquent behavior in a teenager, for example, or serious emotional trouble in an adult. When triangles grow in atmospheres of distrust or competition, they become absolute—"you must either love him or me"—and this kind of impossible situation can do great damage, especially to a child.

Families and individual problems. The normal functioning of the family may be seriously disrupted by any of the individual problems listed above. It is the nature of family life that a crisis for one family member affects all members. Parents sometimes believe that when one of them faces a serious difficulty—illness, death of a parent, unemployment—or when the two of them have a troubled marriage, the children will not notice if they are not told. In fact, even children too young to understand the problem notice the changes in the family climate and may respond with anxiety or other symptoms. As children become old enough to understand, it becomes more and more important to tell them what is happening. Children find it far more troubling to know that something is wrong without being told what it is.

Dealing with chronic trouble in the family—alcoholism, illness—can be especially difficult. Yet parents are often surprised that children are more adaptable than adults. As long as there is an atmosphere of emotional support, children are far less concerned about physical inconvenience and about appearances than most adults.

Perhaps the most serious problem a family has in chronic situations is the feeling that nothing like this has ever happened to any other family. Mutual help groups such as Alanon (for the families of alcoholics) can quickly dispel this impression and can suggest that in some cases the most severe problems can be handled positively, even with humor.

Families and divorce. For a child, few events have as much significance as the divorce of his parents. There is no way in which pain and unhappiness can be avoided. Yet there is some evidence that children of divorced parents may be happier than children who have lived for years with two intensely unhappy parents. In many cases, separation and divorce may be preferable for the children— preferable to staying together "for the children's sake."

In the stages leading up to divorce, it is especially important to tell the children as much as they can reasonably understand about what the future holds. There should be no appealing to the child for support—choosing between the parents can be painful indeed—but the child should be assured that he is not responsible for the prob- lem between adults. Children who know something is wrong but not what is wrong often jump to the conclusion that the trouble is their fault.

The parent who has custody of the children must make plans for the children's practical and emotional care. If the parent is working full-time, this may mean babysitters or child care facilities. In the first months there may be a feeling of great closeness between the remaining parent and the children. But the children must be prepared gradually for their parent to strike out again into the world of adults. Children may resent their parents' dating and may be cool or even aggressively hostile. It is important for children to realize that adults, too, need friends of their own age.

The parent who leaves the home has different problems. He or she is likely to feel lonely and cut off from the children, who may seem more lovable at a distance than they ever seemed at close hand. Visits to children may be awkward and cool; the children may express their resentment toward the absent parent, and he or she may secretly agree with them.

Children learn more—or perhaps learn different things—about divorced parents. They are apt to see them in periods of loneliness and vulnerability; one day they may share in the ex- citement of a new friendship that will lead to a permanent relationship. The challenge for both parents is to forget the negative aspects of their divorce and make the most of the positive aspects. The divorce is most likely to cause serious trouble for the children when the parents themselves have not accepted the situation.

Parents Without Partners and similar groups are often as useful for children as they are for single parents. They give the children a chance to meet others who live in similar circumstances and to realize that they are not unique or even seriously handicapped.

The end of the story of a divorce (and the beginning of another story) is often the remarriage of the single parent. The months leading up to the new marriage may be hard. The children may resent the prospective stepparent and even try to dissuade their parent from marrying again. But if the new partnership is sound, both parent and children will adjust. The relationships in the new family may never approach those of the first family in intensity, yet everyone may look forward to the chance to recover many of the good things a family can offer while leaving some of the bad things behind.

—Lawrence Lorimer, Donald Lorimer

For Further Reference

Child Development

Ames, Louise. *Your Two-Year-Old* (1976); *Your Three-Year-Old* (1976); *Your Four-Year-Old* (1976); *Your Five-Year-Old* (1979); *Your Six-Year-Old* (1979). Delacorte Press.

Beaty, Janice J. *Observing Development of the Young Child.* Merrill, 1986.

Chess, Stella. *Know Your Child: An Authoritative Guide for Today's Parents.* Basic Books, 1987.

Elkind, David. *The Child and Society.* Oxford University Press, 1979.

Fraiberg, Selma H. *The Magic Years.* Charles Scribner's Sons, 1968.

Gesell, Arnold, et al. *Infant and Child in the Culture of Today* (2nd Ed.). Harper & Row, 1974.

Gesell, Arnold, et al. *The Child from Five to Ten* (Revised Ed.). Harper & Row, 1977.

Ginott, Haim G. *Between Parent and Child.* Macmillan, 1965.

Harris, Judith Rich. *The Child: Development from Birth through Adolescence* (2nd Ed.). Prentice-Hall, 1987.

Spock, Benjamin, and Michael Rothenberg. *Dr. Spock's Baby and Child Care* (Revised Ed.). E. P. Dutton, 1985.

White, Burton L. *The First Three Years of Life.* Prentice-Hall, 1975.

Adult Development

Ashley, Montagu. *Growing Young* (2nd Ed.). Bergin and Garvey, 1988.

Erikson, Erik H. *Identity and the Life Cycle.* W.W. Norton, 1959, 1980.

Geddes, Jim. *The Better Half of Life.* Broadman Press, 1987.

Gould, Roger. *Transformations.* Simon & Schuster, 1979.

Henig, Robin M. *How a Woman Ages.* Ballantine, 1985.

Levinson, Daniel J., et al. *The Seasons of a Man's Life.* Alfred A. Knopf, 1978.

Sheehy, Gail. *Passages: Predictable Crises of Adult Life.* E.P. Dutton, 1974.

Vaillant, George. *Adaptation to Life.* Little, Brown, 1977.

Marriage and Family

Bing, Elizabeth. *The Adventure of Birth.* Simon & Schuster, 1970.

Goldzband, Melvin G. *Quality Time: Easing the Children Through Divorce.* McGraw-Hill, 1985.

Gordon, Michael. *The American Family: Past, Present, and Future.* Random House, 1978.

Hunt, Bernice Kohn. *Marriage.* Holt, Rinehart & Winston, 1976.

Landis, Judson T., and Mary G. Landis. *Personal Adjustment, Marriage, and Family Living* (6th Ed.). Prentice-Hall, 1975.

Parker, Rolland S. *Living Single Successfully.* Franklin Watts, 1978.

Pietropinto, Anthony. *Husbands and Wives.* Times Books, 1979.

Problems

Gross, Ronald, et al., editors. *The New Old: Struggling for Decent Aging.* Anchor Books, 1978.

Gurman, Alan S., and David P. Kniskern. *Handbook of Family Therapy.* Brunner/Mazel, 1981.

Jaffe, Jerome, et al. *Addictions: Issues and Answers.* Harper & Row, 1980.

Kra, Siegfried J. *Aging Myths: Reversible Causes of Mind and Memory Loss.* McGraw-Hill, 1986.

Mann, Marty. *Marty Mann Answers Your Questions about Drinking and Alcoholism* (Revised Ed.). Holt, Rinehart & Winston, 1981.

Nathan, Peter E. *Psychopathology and Society.* McGraw-Hill, 1975.

Pincus, Lily. *Death and the Family.* Pantheon Books, 1974.

Scarf, Maggie. *Unfinished Business: Pressure Points in the Lives of Women.* Doubleday, 1980.

Silverstone, Barbara, and Helen Kandle Hyman. *You and Your Aging Parents.* Pantheon Books, 1976.

VOLUME **9**

Earth Sciences

BRUCE ROBERTS/PHOTO RESEARCHERS

GEOLOGICAL TIME

Era	Period	Epoch	Years ago	Years duration	Characteristics
Cenozoic	Quaternary	Recent	15 thousand		moderate climate; receding glaciers
		Pleistocene	1 million	1 million	warm and cold climates; glaciers
	Tertiary	Pliocene	10 million	9 million	cold; snow building up
		Miocene	25 million	15 million	temperate
		Oligocene	35 million	10 million	warm
		Eocene	55 million	20 million	very warm
		Paleocene	70 million	15 million	very warm
Mesozoic	Cretaceous		120 million	50 million	warm; swamps dry out; Rocky Mtns. rise up
	Jurassic		150 million	30 million	warm; lowlands and continental seas
	Triassic		180 million	30 million	warm, dry; extensive deserts
Paleozoic	Permian		240 million	60 million	variable climate; mountains rising
	Pennsylvanian (Late Carboniferous)		270 million	30 million	warm, humid climate; widespread swamps; coal age
	Mississippian (Early Carboniferous)		300 million	30 million	warm, humid; shallow inland seas; coal age begins
	Devonian		350 million	50 million	land rises; shallow seas and marshes and some arid areas
	Silurian		380 million	30 million	mild climate; inland seas
	Ordovician		440 million	60 million	mild; warm in Arctic; most of the land submerged
	Cambrian		500 million	60 million	mild; lowlands and inland seas
(Pre-Cambrian) Proterozoic			1.5 billion	1 billion	conditions uncertain; first glaciers; first life arises
(Pre-Cambrian) Archeozoic			3.5 billion	2 billion	conditions uncertain; probably no life

MT. ST. HELENS, WASHINGTON STATE, 1980: JAMES MASON/BLACK STAR

Earth Sciences

The earth sciences are *geology* and *physical geography*, studies of the lithosphere, or solid part of the earth; *oceanography*, a study of the oceans, which are included within the hydrosphere, or liquid part of the earth; and *meteorology*, a study of the atmosphere.

The earth sciences are grouped within the natural sciences, or sciences of natural phenomena; other natural sciences include zoology and botany. The earth sciences are largely concerned with inorganic substances, or nonliving matter.

Because the earth sciences are devoted to the study of natural objects, they are, almost by definition, interdisciplinary. The geologist, for example, uses chemistry to determine the composition of rocks and minerals, and biology to classify the fossils found in rocks.

GEOLOGY

Geology is divided into a number of somewhat separate branches of study. *Paleontology* is the study of ancient life—the evolution of animals and plants, their various adaptations and extinctions, and their environments. The need for metals and for fuels other than wood has led to *economic geology*, the study of commercially usable fuel and mineral deposits in the earth's crust. *Mineralogy* explains the origin of ores and minerals, the building blocks of rocks. The search for minerals and petroleum has led to *structural geology*, the study of rock structures and how they are formed. The study of rocks themselves is called *petrology*. The application of physical investigations to geology is known as *geophysics*.

The two general divisions of geology that include the branches mentioned above are physical geology and historical geology. *Physical geology* is the study of the earth as we see it around us; of the physical development of the face of the earth and its associated rocks. *Historical geology* is the study of the development of our planet and its life.

Physical Geology.—To understand the earth's surface we must know what it is made of, how it changes, and the processes that cause it to change. A number of processes can operate at the same time. Some operate quite abruptly with spectacular effect, but these are only occasional. Most act slowly but continuously, and have done so for billions of years.

■**WEATHERING.**—*Weathering* is one of the earth's slow and continuous processes. The crust of the earth is made up of many kinds of rock, each with a different chemical composition. The elements in rock may be attacked by elements in the atmosphere, with a resulting change in composition that may also alter the durability and size of the particles. On the other hand, physical forces may break up rocks, with little or no chemical change. The first process is called chemical weathering; the second, mechanical weathering.

In *chemical weathering*, or decomposition, certain minerals in rocks are affected by the carbon dioxide, oxygen, or water vapor in the atmosphere. For example, when feldspar —a silicate mineral common in granitic rocks—is attacked by carbon dioxide dissolved in water vapor, it changes to clay and soluble compounds. Oxygen and water vapor attack the iron in rocks, causing both a change in the size and composition of particles and a familiar rust-colored stain. Chemical weathering is more common in hot, humid climates than in cool, dry climates. In some places in the Arctic and Antarctic, unweathered rock is exposed at the surface; but toward the equator there is a thickness of overlying weathered rock. Weathering may extend several hundred feet below the surface in parts of the wet tropics.

Mechanical weathering, or disintegration, does not change the chemical composition of rocks or minerals, but breaks them into smaller particles. If water seeps into a crack in a rock, then freezes and expands, it may break the rock. This is especially common where freezing and thawing alternate rapidly. The roots of plants may push into cracks in a rock and grow, slowly forcing the sides of the cracks apart. Burrowing animals often expose rocks to the attack of mechanical weathering.

Where the earth's surface is relatively level, the layer of weathered rock gradually becomes thicker. The weathering processes become slower with depth, however, until they almost stop. If the surface is relatively vertical, the weathered fragments continually fall off and expose a fresh surface to the effects of weathering, the process continuing until the slope almost disappears. The weathered material and fragments usually accumulate at the bottom of the slope, forming *talus*, or *scree*.

■**EROSION.**—Weathering softens and loosens rocky material but does not move it. The process of wearing away and transporting weathered particles is called erosion. The agents of erosion are gravity, wind, water, and glacial ice.

Gravity erosion is called *mass wasting*. The most spectacular form of mass wasting is the *landslide*. Here thousands of cubic yards of rock, soil, trees, and other debris move downslope. Most landslides start on steep water-soaked slopes. Mass wasting also takes the form of the *mudflow*. The mudflow is usually a narrow tongue of mud that flows down a steep valley.

Wind erosion can occur only if the surface of the ground is composed of loose particles that are small enough to be moved. These conditions exist in deserts, along lake shores and seashores, and, less commonly, in fields where plant cover is scarce or absent. Fine dust blows entirely out of such areas, leaving only the heavier and coarser sand grains behind. The dust may accumulate elsewhere in a thick deposit called *loess*, which is usually very fertile. As it compacts, the loess develops a vertical, columnar structure, and water can pass downward through it easily. Therefore it does not erode readily, but tends to stand in high banks if cut into by a river or man-made excavation. Loess deposits, thought to have blown out of the Gobi Desert, are common in parts of China. In Europe there are deposits of loess that probably came partly from the Sahara Desert and partly from glacial debris deposited during the Ice Ages. Other loess deposits which are generally considered to be of Ice Age origin, occur in the upper Mississippi valley in the United States.

As desert sand is blown along the ground by the wind, the grains cut and shape the surfaces they move over. This action sometimes carves weird shapes in rocks by wearing away the soft material while leaving the harder rock standing out in relief. Where sand has been blown off the desert floor, there is *desert pavement*, usually covered with sand-blasted stones and bare rock. Elsewhere the sand accumulates in wind-deposited *dunes*, shaped much like snowdrifts. A dune is formed when the velocity of the wind is lessened by some obstacle, and the wind-borne sand is dropped. Oncoming sand is rolled up the windward side of the dune, and the grains drop down the lee side through the force of gravity. In general, the side toward the wind is less steep. Dunes are slowly moved before the wind; this movement often exposes objects previously buried. Where there is little shift in the wind's direction, the dunes tend to be *crescentic* as seen from above; but most dunes have an irregular outline.

STREAM EROSION. A stream with a steep gradient (left) has a high velocity and cuts downward to form a deep, V-shaped valley. A stream with a low gradient (center and right) has a low velocity and cuts sideways, forming a wide valley with a flat floor, or floodplain.

Stream erosion is among the most active agents in lowering the elevation of the land. Clear water is a poor cutting agent; but armed with fragments of weathered rock, it can cut even the solid rock of a stream bed. Very fine material, like mud, is carried in suspension; coarse material is pushed along the stream floor; and the intermediate sizes are rolled and bounced over the bottom. All of this material is the stream's *load.* Sediment in suspension may travel the river's entire course without being dropped; the largest fragments move only during floods, when the current is exceptionally strong.

A river valley is usually the product of the stream flowing through it. A narrow, V-shaped valley shows that the river has a steep *gradient,* or longitudinal slope. Such a river actively cuts downward as it flows and has waterfalls and many rapids. An example of a downward cutting river is the Colorado River in the Grand Canyon.

A river valley which is wide and flat is produced by a stream with a low gradient. Such a stream is close to its *base level,* the landward projection of the surface of the ocean or lake into which the river flows. The stream does not cut into its bed but into its valley walls. This may cause the river to *meander,* or wind back and forth, forming great meander loops. The river flows across a *floodplain* composed of sediment— sand, silt, and clay particles—deposited by the river in time of flood.

Natural *levees* may build up along the river channel where the initial decrease in velocity occurs when the river overflows its banks. Man may enlarge these levees in an effort to contain the river in its channel and prevent inundation of the floodplain.

The lower Mississippi River is an example of a stream with a broad, flat floodplain. Here one can see *oxbow lakes,* which are formed by parts of meander loops that are isolated when the river cuts across the neck of land at both ends of the curve.

The land surface drained by streams may not be stable, but move upward or downward. An upward moving land mass can cause a lateral cutting stream to cut downward and produce a narrow valley with steep walls. In such a case, great meander loops can be entrenched or cut down below the general level of the land. The incised meanders, or Goosenecks, of the San Juan River in southern Utah were once meanders on a broad, flat floodplain.

Where the land surface sinks downward, the river valley may be drowned by an apparent rise in sea level. Chesapeake Bay and its adjacent tributaries are part of such a drowned river system.

Groundwater.—Almost everywhere from a few feet to several thousand feet below the surface, water is present in the cracks and pore spaces of rocks and unconsolidated sediments. Called *groundwater,* it is the source of all well water. In some places the consumption of groundwater has been so great that the *water table,* or upper surface of the groundwater, has brought sea water into many wells. Inland, however, the salt water that is sometimes pumped from deep oil wells is usually water that was trapped at the time when the rocks were deposited in ancient seas.

Easily soluble rocks, such as limestone, are sometimes dissolved by circulating groundwater to form caves below the ground and *sinkholes,* or *swallow holes,* on the surface. In such areas, the drainage may be entirely underground, with no surface streams in evidence. The subterranean water may come to the surface elsewhere in large springs, like some of those in Florida. Where the rock is less soluble, instead of solution there may be commercial mineral deposits enriched by groundwater.

Oceans and Lakes.—On the shores of oceans, seas, and large lakes, waves constantly attack the land. When a wave recedes, it can cause a *rip tide,* or undertow. This continual bombardment by waves gradually erodes the shore. In areas where there are high tides, a wider vertical range of wave action is possible. Incoming waves sometimes force air into cracks in a rock and, in so doing, burst the rock apart. Waves may also carry rocks and pebbles that shatter the loose shoreline material and thereby cause erosion. The retreating waves then drag the finer debris into deep water and return the coarser material for another attack. This wave action gradually cuts back the shoreline, eventually forming a wavecut platform bordered on the land side by a cliff. The platform may become so wide that the waves hit the cliff only during storms. In general, this kind of erosion is more advanced along the coasts of oceans and seas than on lake shores.

Ocean currents can move sediments produced by wave erosion or deposited at the mouths of rivers. Material eroded from headlands can be deposited nearby, forming a *spit, bar,* or *hook* that extends from the headland. Such deposits are usually built and maintained by currents flowing parallel to the shore. As erosion progresses, the headlands are cut back, forming sea cliffs, and the shoreline becomes straighter.

Evidence of wave action is emphasized where the shoreline moves up or down in relation to the sea level. A shoreline that rises is called an *emergent shoreline,* and one that sinks is called a *submerged shoreline.* In some areas, there are features of both submerged and emergent coasts combined in a *compound shore development,* which may have both drowned valleys and long shore bars. The best harbors are usually found along submerged shorelines.

River water entering the sea is slowed down, and its sediment is deposited to form a large, low, flat, swampy area called a *delta.* A delta is roughly triangular, with the apex of the triangle pointing upstream, thereby splitting the river into a number of channels called *distributaries.* As the water slows down, the heaviest and coarsest sediment is dropped first; the finest, last. This forms a series of inclined layers of sediment, called *fore-set beds,* on the slope of the land margin. Beyond the fore-set beds are roughly horizontal layers of fine material called *bottom-set beds.* On top of the fore-set beds near the land margin are the finest sediments, the *top-set beds.* Deltas are fertile because of the constant addition of fresh soil.

Sea water contains many dissolved minerals. These include, in order of their abundance, sodium chloride, magnesium chloride, magnesium sulfate, calcium sulfate, potassium sulfate, and calcium carbonate. These soluble salts come from the chemical weathering of rocks on the land. They are carried by ground water to the rivers and then to the seas.

River water contains much more calcium in solution than sodium or chlorine. In the ocean, various organisms use calcium in the construction of external shells and internal skeletons. It is estimated that the calcium content of sea water would double in about 100,000 years if it was not precipitated in this way.

In contrast, the amount of sodium chloride, or salt, in sea water has increased through geologic time. Where the rate of evaporation is high, as in parts of the Indian Ocean, the salinity of sea water is higher than the average. Sodium chloride can be precipitated as the mineral halite when salinity exceeds the saturation point. This occurs in a restricted basin, such as a small lagoon or a large bay, where high-salinity sea water caused by evaporation cannot be exchanged for sea water of normal salinity.

Geologically speaking, lakes are temporary inland bodies of standing water. They may contain either fresh or salt water, depending on the presence or absence of outlets. A lake with no outlet eventually grows salty because the water that drains into it tends to evaporate, leaving behind an ever-growing concentration of dissolved minerals. Streams that empty into a lake bring sediment with them, and in the quiet water this sediment settles. This explains why water flowing out of a lake is usually clear. Lakes gradually fill with this sediment and turn first into swamps, then into level plains with streams wandering over them. Most lake deposits are thin-bedded clays and silts, which may contain remains of land-dwelling or fresh-water plants and animals. The world's coal deposits are the remains of lush vegetation that once grew in swamps that were cool enough so that the plant material did not rot, but was preserved in the form of carbon.

In the geologic past, large deposits of sodium chloride were precipitated in restricted basins. These salt deposits are mined in such states as Kansas, Louisiana, Michigan, New York, Ohio, and Texas, and in countries such as England, France, Germany, India, and China. The halite, or native salt, is ground to form rock salt and table salt. It is also used as a source of chlorine, sodium, and compounds of these elements.

Glaciation.—In Antarctica and Greenland, and on the upper slopes of high mountains elsewhere, there are *glaciers*—accumulations of snow and ice that move slowly over the ground. Some 10,000 to 20,000 years ago, during the Ice Age, the northern parts of North America, Europe, Asia, and much of southern South America were covered with ice just as Greenland and Antarctica are today. Such conditions result from a climate so cold that the winter's snows never melt entirely. The snow accumulates, and the lower layers gradually turn into ice under the increased weight.

Glaciers are generally divided into two types: *mountain,* or *alpine, glaciers* and *continental glaciers,* or *ice sheets.* Alpine glaciers have been compared to rivers of ice, but they are more like bulldozers that slowly plow down a valley, straightening it out and deepening it. When an alpine glacier eventually disappears, it leaves a U-shaped valley with steep sides and a *cirque,* or amphitheater-like depression, in the mountainside at its head; the cirque often contains a lake. Alpine glaciers produced the rugged landscapes of the Alps and Himalayas.

Continental glaciers, on the other hand, tend to smooth out the surface over which they move. At the margin of the ice, a continental glacier pushes up a mass of irregular, unsorted rock debris called an *end moraine.* On the side of the moraine away from the ice is a relatively level area, called an *outwash plain,* composed of fine material washed away from the end moraine by meltwater from the glacier. There are irregular *kettle holes* in both the end moraine and the outwash plain, caused by the melting of buried blocks of ice. Behind the end moraine is the *till plain,* or *ground moraine,* a wide, gently undulating area of unsorted debris called *till,* which was carried in and under the ice and was dropped when the glacier receded. Continental glaciers also form *eskers,* or winding ridges of sorted till, and *drumlins,* or long, narrow hills of unsorted till. When it melts back, the ice also deposits *erratics,* or single boulders composed of rock foreign to the area. There may be many lakes in end moraines, but few in ground moraines or outwash plains.

Rocks.—The crust of the earth is made up of three main kinds of rock: igneous, sedimentary, and metamorphic. *Igneous rock* has crystallized and hardened from a hot, liquid mass. *Sedimentary rock* is derived from fragmental material carried as sediment, or in solution by water. *Metamorphic rock* is formed by the alteration of other kinds of rock by pressure or heat. Igneous rock makes up the greatest volume of the crust, but is often hidden under layers of sedimentary or metamorphic rock. Compared with the bulk of the crust, the sedimentary rocks are relatively insignificant, but spread over a greater area. Metamorphic rocks are common in areas of mountain-building.

■**SEDIMENTARY ROCKS.**—There are three groupings of sedimentary rock, based on origin. Those that were carried in suspension are *clastic sediments;* those that were deposited from solutions are *chemical,* or *precipitated, sediments;* those that form such deposits as coal beds and coral reefs are *organic rocks*—that is, they are composed of the remains of either plant or animal organisms.

Clastic sedimentary rocks are classified largely according to the size of

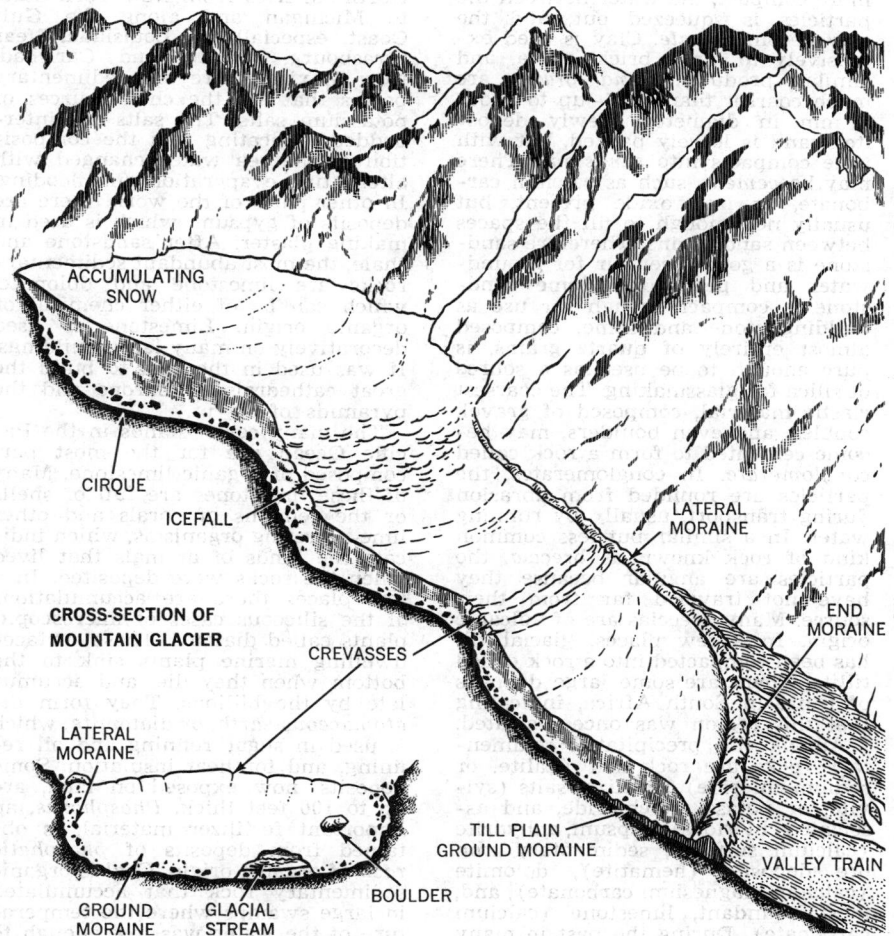

ACCUMULATING SNOW

CIRQUE

ICEFALL

LATERAL MORAINE

END MORAINE

CROSS-SECTION OF MOUNTAIN GLACIER

CREVASSES

LATERAL MORAINE

TILL PLAIN GROUND MORAINE

VALLEY TRAIN

GROUND MORAINE

GLACIAL STREAM

BOULDER

MOUNTAIN GLACIERS flow from high snowfields through mountain valleys, gouging boulders from mountain valleys and walls and changing the configuration of the terrain as they pass.

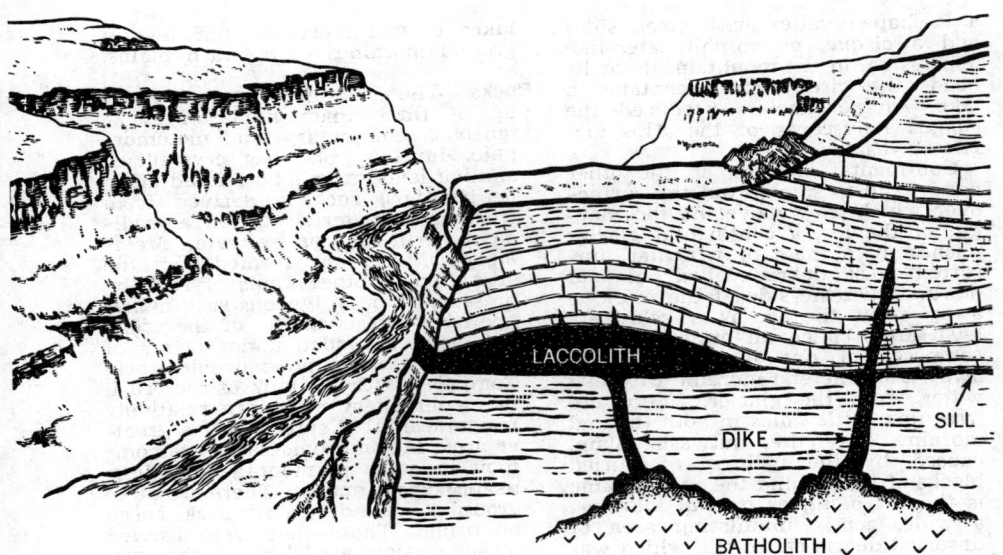

VOLCANIC INTRUSIONS such as the batholith extend deep beneath the earth's crust. From the igneous batholiths emerge lens-shaped laccoliths, vertical dikes, and horizontal sills.

the fragments of which they are composed. The finest sediments are deposited as *clay*—a soft, slippery, plastic, mudlike material that varies greatly in color. As clay becomes more compact, the water between the particles is squeezed out, and the clay becomes *shale*. Clay is used extensively to make brick, china, and similar products. *Sand grains* are much coarser than clay—up to about 2 mm in diameter. Newly deposited sand is loosely packed, but with time compacts into *sandstone*. There may be *cement*, such as calcium carbonate, or iron oxide present, but usually not enough to fill the spaces between sand grains. Therefore sandstone is a good reservoir for groundwater and petroleum. Some sandstone is compact enough for use as building stone and some, composed almost entirely of quartz grains, is pure enough to be used as a source of silica for glassmaking. The coarsest clastic material, composed of gravel, cobbles, and even boulders, may become cemented to form a rock called *conglomerate*. In conglomerates, the particles are rounded from abrasion during transport, usually by running water. In a similar but less common kind of rock known as *breccia*, the particles are angular because they have not traveled far from their source. Many breccias are of volcanic origin. In a few places, glacial till has been compacted into a rock called *tillite*. There are some large deposits of tillite in South Africa, indicating that this region was once glaciated.

Among the precipitated sedimentary rocks are rock salt (halite, or sodium chloride), fertilizer salts (sylvite, or potassium chloride, and associated chlorides), gypsum, anhydrite (calcium sulfate), sedimentary iron ore deposits (hematite), dolomite (calcium magnesium carbonate), and, most abundant, limestone (calcium carbonate). During the past in many parts of the world there have been times when great quantities of so-

dium chloride were precipitated as rock salt, or halite, in beds hundreds of feet thick. Halite, which has only to be crushed to be used as table salt, is mined in great quantities in North America from New York State to Michigan and along the Gulf Coast, especially in Louisiana. Near Strasbourg, France, and Carlsbad, New Mexico, there are sedimentary basins that are the chief sources of potassium salts. The salts are interbedded, indicating that the composition of the sea water changed with alternating evaporation and flooding. In other parts of the world there are deposits of gypsum, which is used in making plaster. After sandstone and shale, the most abundant sedimentary rocks are limestone and dolomite, which can be of either chemical or organic origin. Limestone is used decoratively on many large buildings. It was used in the past to build the great cathedrals of Europe and the pyramids of Egypt.

The many coral islands in the Pacific Ocean are for the most part composed of organic limestone. Many of these limestones are full of shells or the remains of corals and other lime-secreting organisms, which indicate the kinds of animals that lived when the rocks were deposited. In a few places there are accumulations of the siliceous cases of microscopic plants called diatoms. These surface-dwelling marine plants sink to the bottom when they die, and accumulate by the billions. They form *diatomaceous earth,* or *diatomite,* which is used in sugar refining and oil refining, and for heat insulation. Some deposits, now exposed on land, are up to 100 feet thick. *Phosphorus,* an important fertilizer material, is obtained from deposits of *phosphatic rock* of organic origin. *Coal* is organic sedimentary rock that accumulated in large swamps where the temperature of the water was low enough to keep the material from decaying completely. Coal seams range in

thickness from a fraction of an inch to over 400 feet. A few seams as thin as one foot have been mined, but those less than two feet thick are not usually worked by underground mining. If they are not too deep, however, they can be worked by *strip mining,* or surface mining. Other organic materials that originate in sedimentary rocks are *petroleum* and *natural gas* which, together with coal, are known as *fossil fuels*.

■**IGNEOUS ROCKS.**—By far the most abundant rocks are the igneous rocks that crystallized from hot liquids, such as *lava,* which flows from erupting volcanoes, cools, and hardens to form such rocks as *basalt* and *felsite*. Lava can be any color, and some types contain gas bubbles. The amount of bubbles in lava and its color and fluidity depend on its formation temperature and its composition. Lava that is viscous, dark, and full of large bubbles forms *scoria;* whereas lava that is light gray, relatively fluid, and full of small bubbles forms *pumice*. Scoria and pumice are types of volcanic glass that cooled so rapidly crystals could not form. Pumice is so lightweight that it will float on water. Volcanic glass that does not contain bubbles is called *obsidian*. Other volcanic rocks are crystalline, even though the crystals may be microscopic. These rocks are either *felsic* or *mafic,* depending on their composition. The felsic rocks are usually white to gray or pink; and the mafic ones are dark green to black. Felsic rocks are often called *felsites;* and the mafic rocks, *basalt*. Basalt is a fairly common rock, underlying such large areas as the Columbia Plateau in the northwestern United States and the Deccan Plateau in India. Basaltic rocks also underlie most ocean basins.

Underlying the lava flows and sediments on the continents are large quantities of igneous rock with easily visible crystals. If this coarse-grained rock is light-colored, like felsite, it is called *granite*. Granite is widely used as building stone and for curbstones and cobblestones. It is strong and durable. The corresponding mafic rock is *gabbro,* a coarse, black rock that differs little from basalt in composition. *Porphyry,* an igneous rock that contains relatively large crystals in a fine-grained matrix, may be either felsic or mafic.

Igneous rocks do not occur in beds like sedimentary rocks, since they are intruded, or injected, from below into preexisting rocks, or flow on the surface as lava. Tabular, relatively horizontal intrusions are called *sills*. Tabular intrusions that are more or less vertical are called *dikes*. Sills that have arched up the overlying rocks are known as *laccoliths*. The largest igneous intrusions are *batholiths,* which have no recognized floor and may have incorporated some of the overlying rock. These bodies underlie many mountain ranges.

■**METAMORPHIC ROCKS.**—Alteration, or *metamorphism,* is caused by heat or pressure. *Gneiss* is one of the most easily recognized metamorphic rocks. It can be altered granite, with the mineral grains so oriented that the rock is banded. *Slate,* or altered shale, is a fine-grained metamorphic rock that can be split into thin layers. This again is caused by orientation of the mineral grains. Slate is used for roofing and blackboards. *Schist* is similar to slate, but the mineral grains are larger and visible to the unaided eye. The grain shows foliation. Sandstone becomes *quartzite* when it is metamorphosed. The *carbonate rocks* are altered to *marble,* which may be fine-grained or coarse-grained. Very fine-grained marble is used in sculpture, and coarse-grained marble is often used as building stone. In marble, the original fragments have recrystallized, destroying any fossils. Partly recrystallized marble, which is sometimes used for interior decoration, usually contains some fossil remains.

At the boundary between many igneous intrusions and the surrounding rock there is a zone of contact metamorphism, where the surrounding rock has been baked or burned. There may also be a zone of chemical alteration caused by the movement of solutions from the igneous mass into the surrounding rock or by the dissolving of some of the preexisting rock by the molten intrusion. Valuable mineral deposits are formed in this manner.

Diastrophism.—The deformation of the earth's crust is called *diastrophism.* Beds of rock are sometimes bent, and rock materials sometimes abruptly change. These changes are caused by the *folding* or *faulting* (breaking) of the rocks in the crust by natural phenomena, such as internal pressure and strain. Uparched folds are called *anticlines,* downfolds are called *synclines,* and simple folds from one level to another are called *mono-clines.* When layers of rock are faulted, beds that were once continuous are offset laterally or vertically. Sometimes younger beds are found under older ones without evidence of overturning, indicating that the older deposits have been thrust over the younger ones. In all cases the opposite sides of the fault zone have been moved in different directions. More or less vertical faults often have displacements of up to a few thousand feet, whereas relatively horizontal faults may have displacements measured in miles. Where a fault intersects the surface there may be a definite *scarp,* but this, like all surface features, will eventually disappear through erosion. Some faults continue to be active, but a great many are stationary. Old fault zones may be filled with mineral veins of economic value because they often form channels for mineralizing solutions. The study of faults and folds is important because of the relation of geologic structures to the production of oil, gas, and various minerals. Other aspects of diastrophism are *volcanoes* and *earthquakes.*

■**VOLCANOES.**—Active volcanoes occur mainly in two belts. One follows the shores of the Pacific Ocean; the other extends around the earth from east to west, crossing the Pacific belt in Indonesia and Central America. However, traces of ancient volcanism can be found in many other parts of the world. Volcanoes are relatively quiet most of the time, but now and again they explode violently, ejecting thousands of tons of liquid rock and fragmental material, along with large quantities of water vapor and other gases. Many volcanoes form large, cone-shaped mountains, like Mt. Hood in Oregon. Some build cones of lava that have low, gently sloping sides, like volcanoes in the Hawaiian Islands. Others are combinations of lava and cinders and form steep cones, like Mt. Vesuvius in Italy. Some volcanic cones cave in or blow up to form *calderas,* like Crater Lake in Oregon. If a volcano becomes dormant, the cone starts to wear away, leaving a core standing alone or with dikes radiating from it. Ship Rock in New Mexico had such an origin. The estimate of active volcanoes in the world is 400 to 500.

■**EARTHQUAKES.**—*Earthquakes* are the result of a sudden release of strains in the earth's crust. If a strain is released slowly, there is little noticeable effect; but if the release is sudden, the rocks in the crust move against one another and set up vibrations. When these vibrations reach the surface, loose soil and surface objects are shaken, sometimes violently. The violent earthquake belts of the world are roughly the same as the volcanic belts, but no region is immune to earthquake shocks.

Conclusion.—The information quite literally dug out of the earth by geologists is used in many fields, from exploration for fuels and building materials to the location of power and water-storage dams. Even the disposal of atomic wastes involves geology, because it is essential that these wastes not leak through porous rocks or fault zones and cause harm to life. The earth's geological processes, such as erosion and diastrophism, are slow and continuous. Spectacular events, such as earthquakes and volcanic eruptions, are relatively infrequent, and they constitute only minor aspects of the continuing changes that affect the earth.

—E. Willard Berry;
S. Duncan Heron, Jr.

MINERALOGY

History.—Mineralogy, a branch of geology, is a systematic, integrated science intimately related to chemistry and physics. Historically, it is one of the oldest sciences practiced by man. Minerals were known to, and used by, early man throughout the Stone Age, the Bronze Age, and the Iron Age. As far back as 3400 B.C. the inhabitants of the valleys of the Tigris and Euphrates and surrounding areas were searching for, mining, and polishing many-colored gem stones. They were familiar with amethyst, carnelian, agate, beryl, turquoise, lapis lazuli, malachite, jasper, chalcedony, and garnet. In the societies of those days, gems were as much of a status symbol as they are today. They were of special importance to the Egyptians, who used them to adorn the bodies of their dead, which they considered sacred. These gem stones were also buried in ancestral tombs, to be taken along by the deceased and enjoyed in the afterlife. It was from such religious and social practices that mineralogy was born.

The first mineralogy textbook was the *Book of Stones,* written by Theophrastus (c. 372–c. 287 B.C.), a stu-

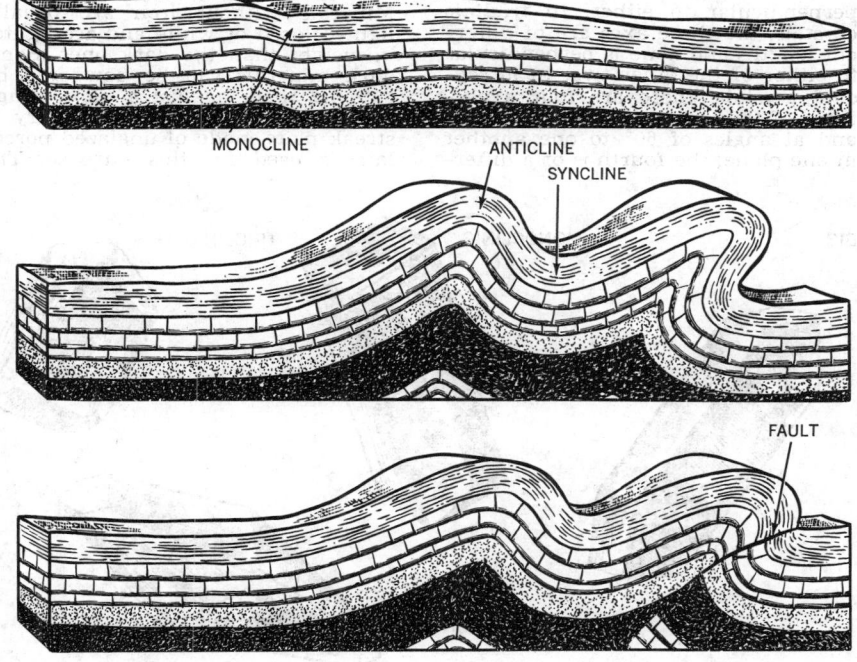

MONOCLINE ANTICLINE SYNCLINE FAULT

FOLDING AND FAULTING of the rocks in the earth's crust are part of the diastrophic process.

dent of Aristotle. In this book he classified 16 minerals under three groupings: metals, stones, and earths. Pliny the Elder (23–79) described minerals and mineral deposits in his books on natural history, and Georg Bauer (1494–1555), better known as Agricola, published an outstanding treatise on economic mineralogy over 400 years ago. Through the years, mineralogy has prospered, and its scope has enlarged to encompass many new areas.

Today mineralogy is divided into a number of branches, including chemical mineralogy, crystallography, descriptive mineralogy, determinative mineralogy, and physical mineralogy. The mineralogist employs geological methods to map rock formations, mineral deposits, and structures of the earth's crust. He collects mineral specimens, tests them by sight, touch, taste, and weight—and then examines them further in the laboratory, using the techniques of the chemist and the physicist.

Minerals.—A *mineral* is defined as a solid, homogeneous, natural substance with definite physical properties and a chemical composition that is fixed within narrow limits—its composition must be such that it can be expressed with a chemical formula.

In order to be classified as a mineral, a substance must be formed by inorganic processes. Thus coal, oil, amber, and pearls are not minerals, for they are produced from plant and animal substances. Also, materials such as the man-made sapphire are not minerals, even though they may be chemically, structurally, and physically identical with the natural substance.

Minerals are the building blocks of the earth's crust. Yet of all the known minerals, only about 50 are rock-making, and only about 20 of the 50 could be said to be essential constituents of rock.

Crystal Structure.—Minerals are crystalline; that is, their atoms or groups of atoms are arranged in a symmetrical, three-dimensional, geometric pattern called a *crystal lattice.*

When minerals are free and uncrowded, they develop as *crystals*—solid bodies having smooth plane surfaces, or *faces.* Crystals give minerals characteristic outward shapes that reflect the internal crystalline arrangement. The angle between corresponding faces of any given mineral is always the same, no matter what the size of the specimen or its origin. An important part of mineralogy consists of measuring these angles. This is done with an instrument called a *goniometer.*

All similar faces on a crystal constitute a *form.* The most common forms are cubes, prisms, and pyramids. Crystal faces on the minerals contained in rocks are seldom distinguishable because they are so closely packed.

■**CRYSTAL FORMS.**—The symmetry in the geometrical form of a crystal is due to regularities in the positions of the corresponding similar faces and edges. Because of this regularity, crystals have planes and axes of symmetry. A *plane of symmetry* divides the crystal into two similar halves, one the mirror image of the other. Crystal forms are divided into six systems: cubic, tetragonal, orthorhombic, monoclinic, triclinic, and hexagonal. The systems are identified by the relative lengths of the axes of symmetry and the angles that the axes make with one another. In *cubic* crystals, the axes are all of the same length and are perpendicular to one another. In *tetragonal* crystals, two axes are of the same length and different from the third; all three axes are perpendicular to one another. In *orthorhombic* crystals, the three axes are of different lengths and perpendicular to one another. In *monoclinic* crystals, the three axes are of different lengths; two of the axes are perpendicular to one another but the third is not perpendicular to either. In *triclinic* crystals, the three axes are of different lengths and none is perpendicular to either of the other two. In *hexagonal* crystals, there are four axes—three of them are of identical lengths and at angles of 60° to one another in one plane; the fourth is of a differ-

ent length and perpendicular to the plane of the other three. Often a seventh system, trigonal, is used. In *trigonal* crystals, the three axes are of equal lengths and the three angles are equal but are not 90°.

■**HABIT.**—The crystal form that a mineral characteristically takes in response to rate of growth, heat, and pressure is called its *habit.* In the case of a mineral made up of single and distinct crystals, its habit may be *acicular* (needlelike), *capillary* and *filiform* (hairlike and threadlike), or *bladed* (elongated and flattened).

If the mineral is made up of a group of distinct crystals, its habit may be *dendritic* (branchlike), *reticulated* (latticelike), *divergent* (or *radiated*), or *drusy* (covered with a layer of small crystals).

When a mineral is made up of parallel or radiating groups of single crystals, its habits may be *columnar, bladed, fibrous, stellated* (starlike), *globular, botryoidal* (grapelike), *reniform* (kidney-shaped), or *mammillary* (breastlike). A material consisting of scales could have a habit that is *foliated, micaceous* (capable of being split into very fine sheets), *tabular,* or *plumose* (featherlike). A mineral habit can also be *granular, stalactitic* (with pendant cylinders or cones), *oölitic* (like fish roe), or *pisolitic* (rounded and pea-sized).

Mineral Identification.—When the hand specimen of a mineral is examined, the first thing seen is its outward appearance. It can be granular, compact, or earthy. Other physical aids in identification are the color, luster, hardness, cleavage, tenacity, specific gravity, and magnetism.

■**COLOR.**—Among the rock-forming minerals, the color depends largely upon the presence of iron. Minerals that contain this element are dark: black, brown, deep red, rust, or green. Minerals without iron are usually light-colored or white and are lighter in weight than the dark ones. Some dark minerals can be powdered by rubbing them against a hard, rough surface. In the testing laboratory, a streak plate made of unglazed porcelain is used for this purpose. The

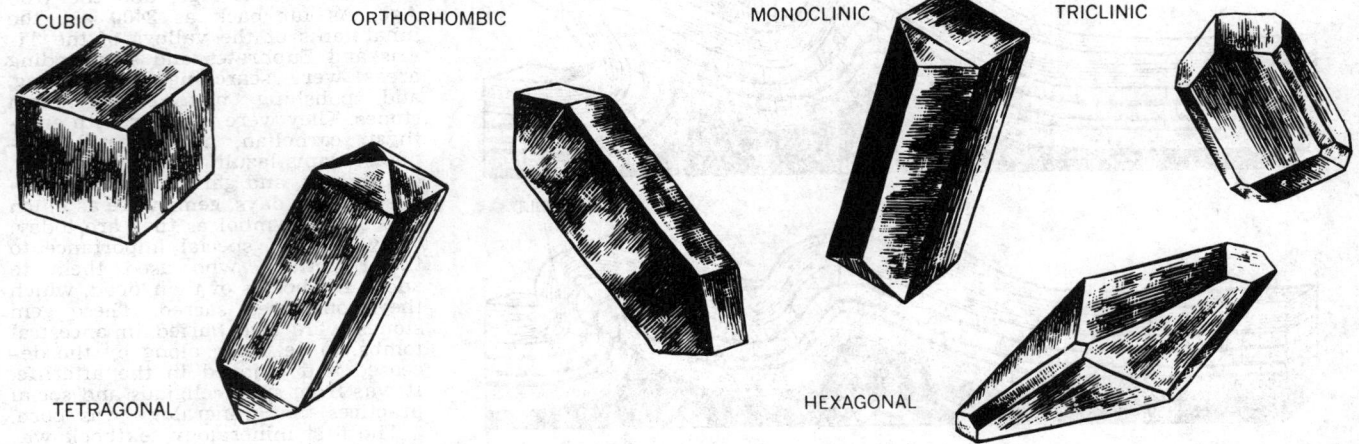

CUBIC ORTHORHOMBIC MONOCLINIC TRICLINIC TETRAGONAL HEXAGONAL

CRYSTAL SYSTEMS are characterized by their axial angles and ratios. Every crystalline substance can be classified according to structure.

color of the streak is, in most cases, characteristic of the mineral.

■LUSTER.—Luster is the quality and intensity of the light that a mineral reflects. Luster can be metallic (resembling iron or brass) or nonmetallic—pearly, greasy, silky, resinous, vitreous (glasslike), or adamantine (diamondlike). Some minerals will show a play of colors, or an iridescent effect.

■HARDNESS.—The hardness of a mineral is tested by attempting to scratch it with a series of minerals that have been chosen as a standard scale. This scale, called *Mohs' scale*, was proposed by the German mineralogist Friedrich Mohs in 1820. Mohs designated the softest known mineral, talc, as having a hardness of 1; and the hardest, diamond, 10. The ten minerals of the scale, arranged in order of increasing hardness (with their numerical designation on Mohs' scale in parentheses) are: talc (1), gypsum (2), calcite (3), fluorite (4), apatite (5), orthoclase (6), quartz (7), topaz (8), corundum (9), and diamond (10). Each of these minerals will be scratched only by minerals with a higher number on the scale and will scratch only those with a lower number; hence talc will be scratched by all (and will scratch none) and diamond will scratch all (and be scratched by none). Quick approximations of the hardness of minerals may be made by using handy substances to scratch them. These substances, with their numerical designation on the Mohs' scale, are: a fingernail (2½), a copper penny (3), the blade of a penknife or a piece of window glass (5½), and a steel file (6½).

■CLEAVAGE.—Many minerals have the tendency to split evenly or break in definite directions along the planes of weakness in their crystal lattice. This is called *cleavage*. The number and arrangement of cleavage planes provide a reliable clue to the identification of minerals. Mica, for instance, has only one direction of cleavage; orthoclase has two, at right angles; calcite has three, mutually oblique. Minerals that break irregularly are said to *fracture*. Fractures can be *conchoidal* (shell-like), as in glass; *hackly* (jagged-edged); *even*, if the break is smooth; *uneven*, if it is irregular; *fibrous* or *splintery*, if like wood; or *earthy*.

■TENACITY.—*Tenacity* is the resistance of a mineral to breaking, crushing, bending, or tearing. Some minerals are *sectile* (cutable), *malleable* (capable of being hammered into thin plates), *ductile* (can be drawn into wires), *flexible*, or *elastic*.

■SPECIFIC GRAVITY.—The *specific gravity* refers to a mineral's weight, expressed in a number that shows how many times heavier a given volume of that mineral is than an equal volume of water. The specific gravities of minerals range from 1.5 to 20.0, but most fall in the range between 2.0 and 4.0.

■MAGNETISM.—A few minerals, such as magnetite, an oxide of iron, will respond to an ordinary pocket magnet and can be identified by this property.

Common Rock-Forming Minerals.—A rock is an aggregate of minerals of different kinds in varying proportions. The following are some of the minerals more commonly found in rocks.

Quartz, whose chemical composition is silicon dioxide, is one of the most widely occurring minerals. It is the most common vein mineral, and makes up the largest part of most sands. Quartz is usually colorless or white; but it can be any color, depending upon its impurities. The colored varieties—amethyst, rose quartz, smoky quartz, citrine, chalcedony, and agate—are used in the manufacture of jewelry. Quartz is also used as an abrasive, in the manufacture of glass and porcelain, in paints, and in scouring soaps. As sand it is used in mortars and cements. Quartzite and sandstone—rocks made up largely of quartz—are used in the building trades.

Orthoclase feldspar, whose chemical composition is sodium-calcium-aluminum silicate, is usually found in various shades of gray, and sometimes white, although the latter is less common. It is a feldspar with a pearly to vitreous luster. Two distinctive subspecies are white *albite* and the dark *labradorite,* which often shows a play of colors when rotated in a good light. These subspecies occur in the same way as orthoclase.

Pyroxene is a silicate of calcium and magnesium, and also contains varying amounts of aluminum, iron, and sodium. It is the name of a group of minerals comprising many varieties that differ slightly in chemical composition. It is light green to dark green or black in color and commonly opaque. The most frequent member of this group is *augite,* which occurs in stubby, irregular crystals. It is a very abundant rockmaking mineral that occurs chiefly in dark-colored igneous rocks. It is rarely found in rocks that contain quartz.

Amphibole, like pyroxene the name of a group of slightly differing minerals, is a silicate of calcium and magnesium, with varying amounts of aluminum, iron, and sodium. It is similar to pyroxene in composition, but differs in that it also contains water of constitution. Amphibole has a brighter luster and longer crystals than pyroxene. This mineral is usually opaque. The most familiar member of this group is *hornblende,* which has a luster of silky to dull and a color of black, dark brown, or dark green. It is a common rock-forming mineral that occurs in both igneous and metamorphic rocks.

Mica consists of characteristically shiny, flexible, elastic flakes that are stronger than steel. *Muscovite* (white mica) is a complex silicate containing potassium and aluminum. It occurs in granite, together with quartz and feldspar. Muscovite is typical of mica *schists*—rocks that split in flakes and slabs parallel to the cleavage of mica. It is used in insulation materials and in the manufacture of electrical equipment. *Biotite* (black mica) is a complex silicate containing potassium, magnesium, iron, and aluminum. It is generally dark green, brown, or black. Thin sheets of biotite have a smoky color, which distinguishes it from muscovite. This common rock-making mineral is found in *gneisses*—laminated or foliated rocks—and schists.

Hematite is the most abundant ore of iron. Some specimens are metallic, others earthy and red. More than 90 per cent of iron in the United States comes from ores containing this mineral. Michigan, Wisconsin, and Minnesota are important hematite mining areas.

Limonite is the general name for all hydrous oxides of iron. It is an earthy material, reddish brown, yellow, or orange, that often forms crusts. Limonite, also a valuable source of iron, is formed by the oxidation and hydration of iron in previously existing minerals.

Pyrite, or iron sulfide, is also known as "fool's gold." It is metallic, brassy, and generally granular. It is the most common sulfide ore and an important vein mineral. Pyrite is often a carrier of gold or copper, thus becoming an ore for both of these metals. It is an important source of sulfur in the manufacture of sulfuric acid.

Chalcopyrite is a copper-iron sulfide. It is a golden yellow mineral, although it is generally seen tarnished to iridescent or bronze. It is the most important ore of copper, and is often an ore of gold or silver.

Sphalerite, the most important source of zinc, is a zinc sulfide. It is yellow-brown to dark brown, and has a resinous to submetallic luster. It is widely distributed, generally in veins or irregular bodies in limestone.

Galena, a lead sulfide, is the chief source of lead. Its color is lead-gray, and it has a bright metallic luster. Galena sometimes contains silver; therefore it is also an ore of this metal.

Cassiterite, a tin dioxide, is almost the sole source of tin. It usually occurs in pyramid crystals or rounded pebbles. It is brown to black, with a diamond to metallic luster. Cassiterite is mined on a commercial scale in Malaysia, Bolivia, Indonesia, the Congo republics, and Nigeria.

Bauxite, a mixture of hydrous aluminum oxides of indefinite composition, is the only commercial source of aluminum. Its color varies from white to gray, yellow, or red. Bauxite is translucent, with a dull to earthy luster. The chief deposits of bauxite in the United States are in Georgia, Alabama, Mississippi, and Arkansas. The principal world producers are Jamaica and Surinam.

Uraninite, or *pitchblende,* a uranium dioxide, is usually massive and grapelike in crystal structure. It is black, with a submetallic to pitchlike, dull luster. It is the most valuable source of uranium. The Congo republics and Canada are the most important producers.

Other important rock-forming minerals are *garnet* (a ferromagnesium silicate), used as a gem stone; *calcite* (a calcium carbonate), the chief constituent of marbles and limestones;

and *chlorite,* a complex hydrous magnesium-iron-aluminum silicate with micaceous cleavage. Chlorite is a common rock-forming mineral that gives a green color to many rocks. It is typical of schists and green roofing slates. *Serpentine,* a hydrous magnesium silicate, usually is the altered product of *olivine,* and is the chief constituent of the rock of the same name. *Gypsum,* a hydrous calcium sulfate, is used in the production of plaster of Paris. *Halite,* chemically sodium chloride, is common table salt and is used for seasoning food, as a preservative, and in the chemical industry. *Kaolinite,* chemically hydrous aluminum disilicate, is common clay. It occurs widely and is used in making pottery and brick.

—Doris D. Shaner

HISTORICAL GEOLOGY

Origin of the Earth.—Man's desire to explain the means by which the earth was formed extends to prehistoric times. From the early legends of mythology to the modern theories of cosmogony, numerous explanations of the earth's formation have been offered. Today almost all scientists agree on one point—that the earth and its sister planets are related in their origin. However, no theory yet presented has been generally accepted, for each has left many important questions unanswered.

■TWO-STAR HYPOTHESIS.—Probably the most popular theory prior to World War II was that proposed by the American geologist-astronomer team of Thomas Chrowder Chamberlin (1843–1928) and Forest Ray Moulton (1872–1952), called the *two-star,* or *collision, hypothesis.* Chamberlin and Moulton proposed that the planets were born when the sun and a larger star passed so closely that they almost collided. Great bolts of gaseous material were pulled from the sun by the larger star's gravitational attraction. This gaseous material assumed an elliptical orbit around the sun and then condensed to form the planets and their satellites.

■ONE-STAR HYPOTHESIS.—In recent years a number of new theories have been suggested. The general trend today is toward the acceptance of a modification of the oldest truly scientific hypothesis ever proposed, the *one-star,* or *nebular, hypothesis.* It was presented in 1755 by the German metaphysician Immanuel Kant (1724–1804), who based his theory on the work of Nikolaus Copernicus (1473–1543), Johannes Kepler (1571–1630), and Sir Isaac Newton (1642–1727). This theory was further refined some 40 years later by Pierre Simon de Laplace (1749–1827), a French mathematician and astronomer. The one-star hypothesis assumes that a hot gaseous *nebula,* or cloud, automatically developed into a solar system as it cooled, without interference by an outside star or other body. This theory was widely accepted during the nineteenth century, then fell into disfavor until it was reconsidered in recent years.

The one-star theory can be summed up in the following way: Eons ago a greatly diffused, spherical gas cloud, or nebula, existed, the radius of which was at least as great as the distance of Pluto, the outermost planet, from the sun today. The cloud rotated slowly, and as it cooled—and therefore contracted—its velocity increased in the same way that a dancer will whirl faster and faster as he draws his arms closer to the body. The gaseous mass developed a disk, or equatorial bulge, around it; indeed, the present appearance of the planet Saturn, with its equatorial rings, resembles this, although on an infinitely smaller scale. At critical points during its rotation, rings of fiery gas are assumed to have been thrown off from the whirling disk by centrifugal force. Each ring then broke up into fragments, which gathered into a sphere. In this way a planet, which began to revolve in the same orbit as the ring from which it had been formed, was produced. A comparable process accounts for the formation of satellites, such as the moon. The planet liquefied as it cooled, and with further cooling acquired a solid crust. The main body of the gas meanwhile condensed and became the sun.

In 1943 a German physicist, Carl von Weizacker, was able to answer the greatest objection to the Kant-Laplace one-star hypothesis. According to mathematical analysis, the forces operating to cause the dispersion of the gaseous nebula revolving around the sun should have been just as strong as those forces acting toward the nebula's formation into planets. Weizacker's addition to the one-star hypothesis was that the materials that went into the formation of a planet such as the earth would have constituted no more than 1 per cent of the entire revolving gaseous mass—which would have been composed mostly of hydrogen and helium. In this milieu, tiny particles of dense material, revolving with the greater part of the gaseous nebula, could have collided. The smaller particles would have been absorbed into the mass of the larger, resulting in the eventual depletion of the supply of particles and the formation of the giant aggregates we know as planets.

Age of the Earth.—Until recently most geologists, astronomers, and cosmogonists (specialists dealing with the origin of the universe), believed the earth to be about two billion years old. But new data seem to indicate that the earth and the solar system are at least four, and perhaps as much as five, billion years old.

■DATING METHODS.—One of the most valuable tools available to scientists today for dating the earth is *radioactive decay,* or *disintegration.* Certain radioactive elements, such as uranium, found in minerals and rocks are very unstable. Uranium breaks down into lead at a constant and measurable rate that apparently is unaffected by heat, pressure, or other conditions. If the amount of lead and the amount of uranium are known, the age of the rock can be determined. The ratio is 1/7,600,000,000. This means that the presence in a sample of one gram of lead to 76 grams of uranium indicates that the parent rock is 100 million years old. This method is good exclusively for igneous rocks, since uranium is not likely to be found in either metamorphic or sedimentary rock.

Scientists are experimenting with other ratios, too, such as the ratio between several different isotopes of lead (the isotopes of an element are distinguished by differences in their atomic weights). Scientists are also experimenting with the decay of potassium to argon, and of rubidium to strontium.

■GEOLOGIC PROCESSES.—The present is the key to the past—all changes in the earth's crust that occurred billions and billions of years ago are the result of the same physical laws that are in operation today. Thus, mountains have loomed, then have been leveled to nothing by erosion; and arid lands have been flooded by invading seas that later retreated, leaving behind traces of the marine life that inhabited them.

All of the methods of radioactive dating, however, have one disadvantage—they cannot be used to date "recent" events in geologic history; that is, events that occurred less than two million years ago. Only one technique, which uses the radioactive isotope carbon-14, has proved to be an accurate time gauge within this period. And even this technique, known as *radiocarbon dating,* has its limitations, for it can be used to date only organic material that is less than 40,000 years old. The principle of radiocarbon dating is as follows: When cosmic rays bombard nitrogen in the outer atmosphere, the nitrogen may be converted into carbon-14. This carbon-14 combines with oxygen to form a special carbon dioxide. The carbon dioxide circulates through the atmosphere, reaches the earth's surface, and is absorbed by living, or organic, matter. The distribution of this special carbon dioxide has been found to be constant throughout the world. Therefore, there is an identical—although very small—amount of carbon-14 in all living organisms. When death comes to an organism—whether it is an animal or a plant—it ceases to absorb carbon-14. Instead, the carbon-14 present in the organism begins to be converted back to nitrogen at a constant rate. Thus, the longer the organism has been dead, the smaller the amount of carbon-14 that will remain within it. By comparing the amount of carbon-14 present in a no-longer-living organism with the uniform amount of carbon-14 present in all living organisms, the amount of time that has elapsed since death can be calculated.

Geologic Time.—Geologic time is generally taken as the period extending from the end of the earth's formative period to the beginning of the historical period. Thus, geologic time did not begin when the earth was born, but much, much later. The hot gaseous jets thrown off by the sun had to cool into a liquid and then into a solid crust. There was upheaval beneath the earth's crust; the crust broke, and the fragments sank into the thick, molten rock underneath; then the crust solidified once more. Gradually, the earth cooled enough to allow the water vapor in the envelope of gas surrounding it to condense into rain, and the earth's surface was sufficiently cooled so that the rain could remain as water. It is with erosion that geologic processes, and consequently geologic time, started.

The geologic processes that have left their mark on the face of the earth during the period of geologic time fall into three categories: gradation, volcanism, and diastrophism. The process of *gradation* consists of *erosion,* which is the weathering (wearing away) of rocks and soil by the action of water, ice, and wind, and *deposition,* which is the building up of rock layers through the accumulation of sediments laid down by the action of water, ice, and wind; thus deposition is the converse of erosion. *Volcanism* includes all movements of molten rock, or *magma*—which is assumed to be the earth's inner core—and the formation of solid rock from the molten state, both within the solid crust and on the surface. *Diastrophism* is the process by which the earth's crust is deformed to produce continents, mountains, ocean basins, and plateaus; it therefore includes the processes of *epeirogenesis,* or continent building, and *orogenesis,* or mountain building.

■GEOLOGIC TIME DIVISIONS.—A logical way had to be found to divide the vast periods of geologic time. This was done by using the most obvious physical breaks in the biological record. Because the progress of life has been greatly affected by physical disruptions on the earth, a correspondence can be found between the radical changes that occurred on the earth and those that occurred in the development of plants and animals.

During periods of radical change or great diastrophism, tremendous upheavals of the earth's crust occurred, and the forces within the crust caused the rocks to fold like layers of soft modeling clay. The molten interior of the earth pushed into the overlying older rocks of the crust in the form of great *batholiths*—masses of intruded igneous rock—mountains were formed, and parts of the continents were lifted high above sea level. Then shorelines emerged, streams were rejuvenated, and a great amount of erosion took place.

This uplift of the continents caused a change in the climate, which became cold as the lands were removed from the tempering effects of the ocean. *Glaciation,* the formation of large bodies of ice over the land, occurred when the uplift was great enough; and life changed accordingly. Some of the forms of life adapted themselves to colder climates; some died out or migrated to warmer areas. The climate at times destroyed vegetation; and as a result, the animals feeding on it died out. Each new cycle—the uplift of the land, the retreating of the seas, the downwarp of the continents, and the encroaching seas—meant a new phase with new life.

The largest portions of geologic time are called *eras,* and are separated by periods of revolution. These revolutions were most likely worldwide in scope and profoundly affected plant and animal life. The rocks deposited during an era are called a *group.* Eras are divided into *periods,* which are separated by such minor diastrophism as folding, the advance or retreat of the sea, or simply a change in life. A *system* of rocks is deposited during one period. Periods are further subdivided into *epochs,* which are often separated by retreats of the sea on a local scale. A *series* of rocks is deposited during one epoch. Epochs are divided into *stages;* and the rocks deposited then constitute a *stage,* which can be broken down into *substages* and still further into *zones,* named according to the fossils they contain. Basic rock units are called *formations* and are made up of a single layer or several layers in which all sediments have been deposited continuously and under the same conditions.

■GEOLOGIC COLUMN AND TIME CHART.—The seas have flooded the land many times since the world began. This has occurred either because the sea level has risen generally or because the continent has warped downward. Consequently, the profile of the land and sea has been vastly different from age to age. All these movements of the continents and the seas have left their telltale marks in the rocks.

To trace the earth's history, records of local regions all over the world have to be painstakingly pieced together, like a jigsaw puzzle, in the proper chronological order. This way, geologists can construct a composite for the world—by superposing the major rock units from different parts of the world in the form of a *geologic column,* representing formations as they would appear in a well core, with the oldest bed at the bottom and the youngest layer on top. The counterpart of the geologic column is the *geologic time chart,* where major units of geologic time are arranged to correspond with the geologic column. Within this framework, geologists are reconstructing the history of the earth.

A complete record of all geologic time cannot be found in any single area. Because of the irregular warping of the earth's surface, the areas of deposition have shifted. However, deposition has always been going on in one place or another. Therefore, while no area contains a complete record, it is only necessary to discover and correlate enough of the scattered fragments to piece together a composite record of all geologic time. Geologists and allied scientists the world over have pooled their knowledge and skill in tagging and timing the earth's rocks. More than 500,000 feet of rock are classified.

Two laws of historic geology form the basis for the construction of the geologic column and time chart. These are the law of superposition and the law of faunal and floral (animal and plant life) succession.

The *law of superposition* assumes that layers of sediments are deposited one at a time, one on top of the other. Therefore, in any normal section—one that has not been deformed—the oldest bed is on the bottom and each bed in turn is younger than the one on which it rests.

The *law of faunal and floral succession* assumes that any grouping of remains of animal and plant life is a collection of organisms that existed together at one time and in one place. In addition, fossil floras and faunas succeed one another in a definite and determinable order.

Fossils.—Fossils are any recognizable organic structures or impressions of organisms preserved from prehistoric time. Referred to in former times as "devices of the Devil placed in rocks to delude men" and "relics of the accursed race that perished with the Flood," fossils were not universally recognized until 1800 A.D., as representatives of life in the geologic past. There were great controversies concerning fossils during the Dark Ages because men took their Scripture so literally. These men, who believed in a special creation, could not accept relics of a life older than 6,000 years. But there have been men through the ages who have recognized the significance of fossils. Herodotus, around 450 B.C., was one of the first to identify fossils. He found fossil seashells in Egypt and the Libyan desert during his African travels, and he came to the accurate conclusion that the Mediterranean Sea must have extended much farther to the south at some past time than in his day.

Fossils can be found in the state of original preservation, such as the woolly mammoth embalmed intact in the Arctic ice. They can also exist as molds, casts, and imprints, as well as footprints and trails. *Coprolites*—prehistoric excrement—are also considered a class of fossils. Although coal and petroleum are referred to as fossil fuels, they are not true fossils despite their age and organic beginnings because they have no recognizable structure. Remains of animals or plants recently dead are not considered fossils even though the species may be extinct because the word "fossil" necessarily implies antiquity. Fossils occur only when and where the environment was favorable for their existence and preservation, and two special conditions are of the utmost importance: the fossils must possess such internal or external hard parts as bones, teeth, scales, shells, or wood, which are left behind when the animal or plant decomposes; and the remains must be buried quickly to protect them against weathering, bacteria, and scavengers. Molds, casts, and imprints also must have quick burial if they are to be preserved. The sea bottom is by far the most important and favorable environment for the preservation of fossils because marine life is particularly prolific; and the shells are quickly, sometimes instantaneously, buried with mud and sand during storms. The beds of prehistoric lakes, bogs, the frozen tundra, asphalt or tar pits, volcanic ash, lava flows, and windblown sediment, such as loess,

CRYPTOZOIC — "Time Of Hidden Life"	PHANEROZOIC—						
PRE-CAMBRIAN	PALEOZOIC "Era Of Old Life"						
KEWEENAWAN, HURONIAN, TIMISKAMING & KEEWATIN	CAMBRIAN	ORDOVICIAN	SILURIAN	DEVONIAN	MISSISSIPPIAN	PENNSYLVANIAN "Age Of Cockroaches"	PERMIAN
?	100	70	15	43	40	45	40
4? BILLION	550	450	380	355	310	270	225

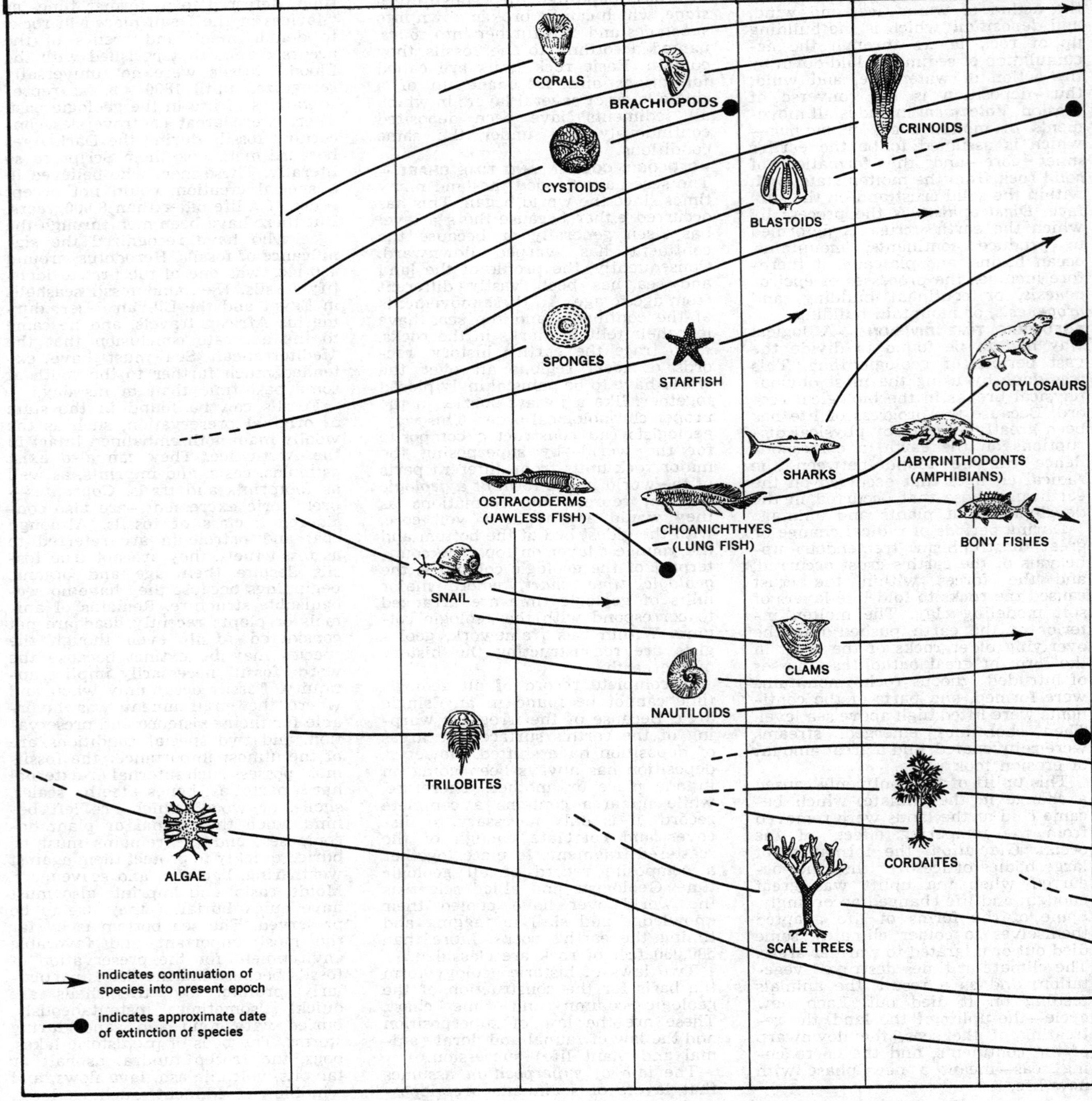

CORALS

BRACHIOPODS

CRINOIDS

CYSTOIDS

BLASTOIDS

SPONGES

STARFISH

COTYLOSAURS

SHARKS

LABYRINTHODONTS (AMPHIBIANS)

OSTRACODERMS (JAWLESS FISH)

CHOANICHTHYES (LUNG FISH)

BONY FISHES

SNAIL

CLAMS

NAUTILOIDS

TRILOBITES

CORDAITES

ALGAE

SCALE TREES

→ indicates continuation of species into present epoch

● indicates approximate date of extinction of species

										EON
"Time Of Visible Animal Life"										EON
MESOZOIC "Era Of Middle Life"			CENOZOIC "Era Of Recent Life"							ERA
TRIASSIC	JURASSIC	CRETACEOUS "Time Of Great Dying"	TERTIARY					QUATERNARY		PERIOD
			PALEOCENE	EOCENE	OLIGOCENE	MIOCENE "Golden Age Of Mammals"	PLIOCENE	PLEISTOCENE "The Ice Age"	RECENT	EPOCH
27	33	65	10	10	10	15	14	1	LATE ARCHEOLOGIC AND HISTORIC TIME	DURATION (Millions of Years)
185	158	125	60	50	40	30	15	1		BEGAN Millions of Years Ago

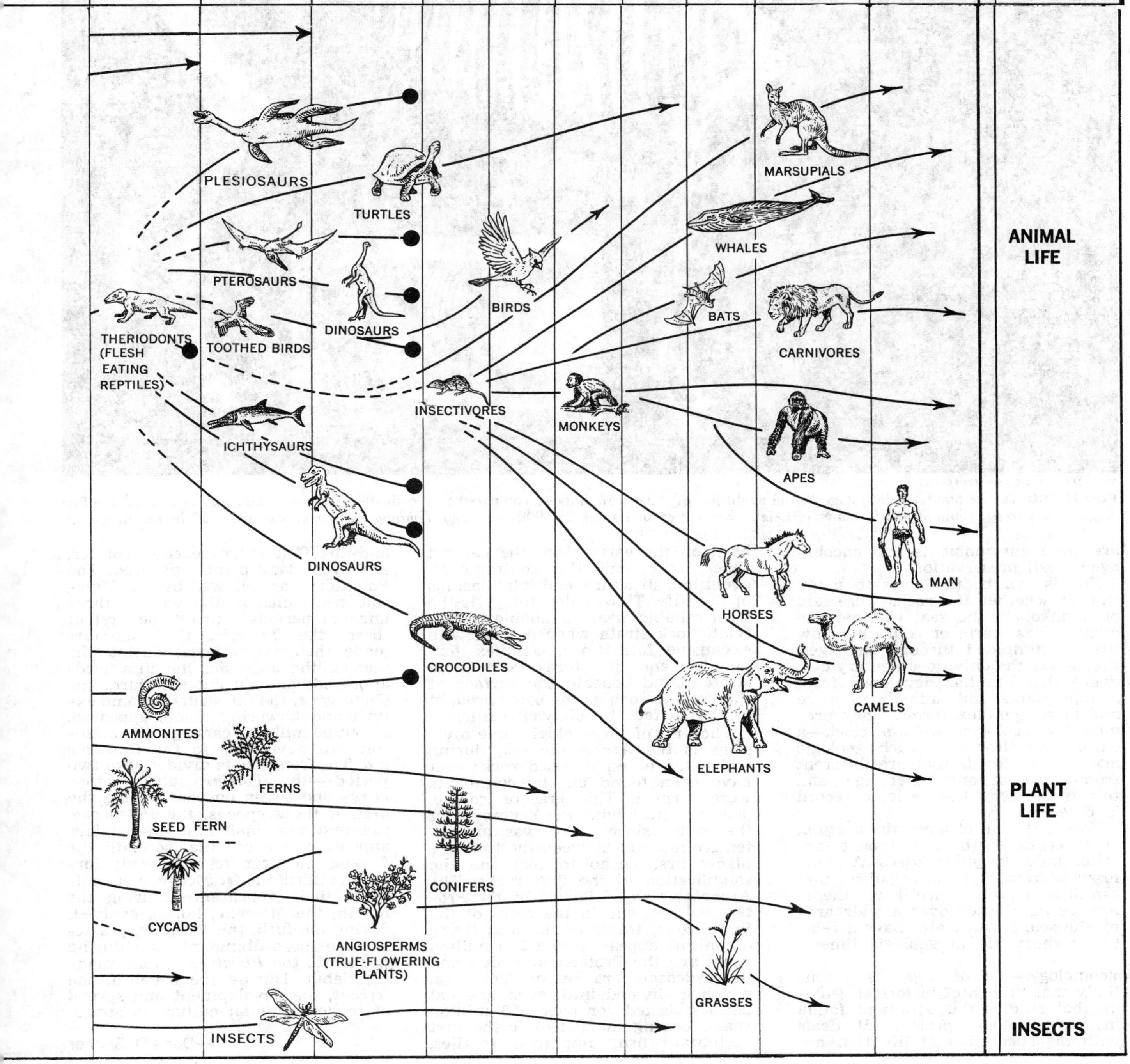

ANIMAL LIFE

PLESIOSAURS
TURTLES
PTEROSAURS
DINOSAURS
BIRDS
THERIODONTS (FLESH EATING REPTILES)
TOOTHED BIRDS
INSECTIVORES
MONKEYS
MARSUPIALS
WHALES
BATS
CARNIVORES
APES
ICHTHYSAURS
DINOSAURS
HORSES
MAN
CROCODILES
CAMELS
AMMONITES
ELEPHANTS
FERNS
SEED FERN
CONIFERS
PLANT LIFE
CYCADS
ANGIOSPERMS (TRUE-FLOWERING PLANTS)
GRASSES
INSECTS
INSECTS

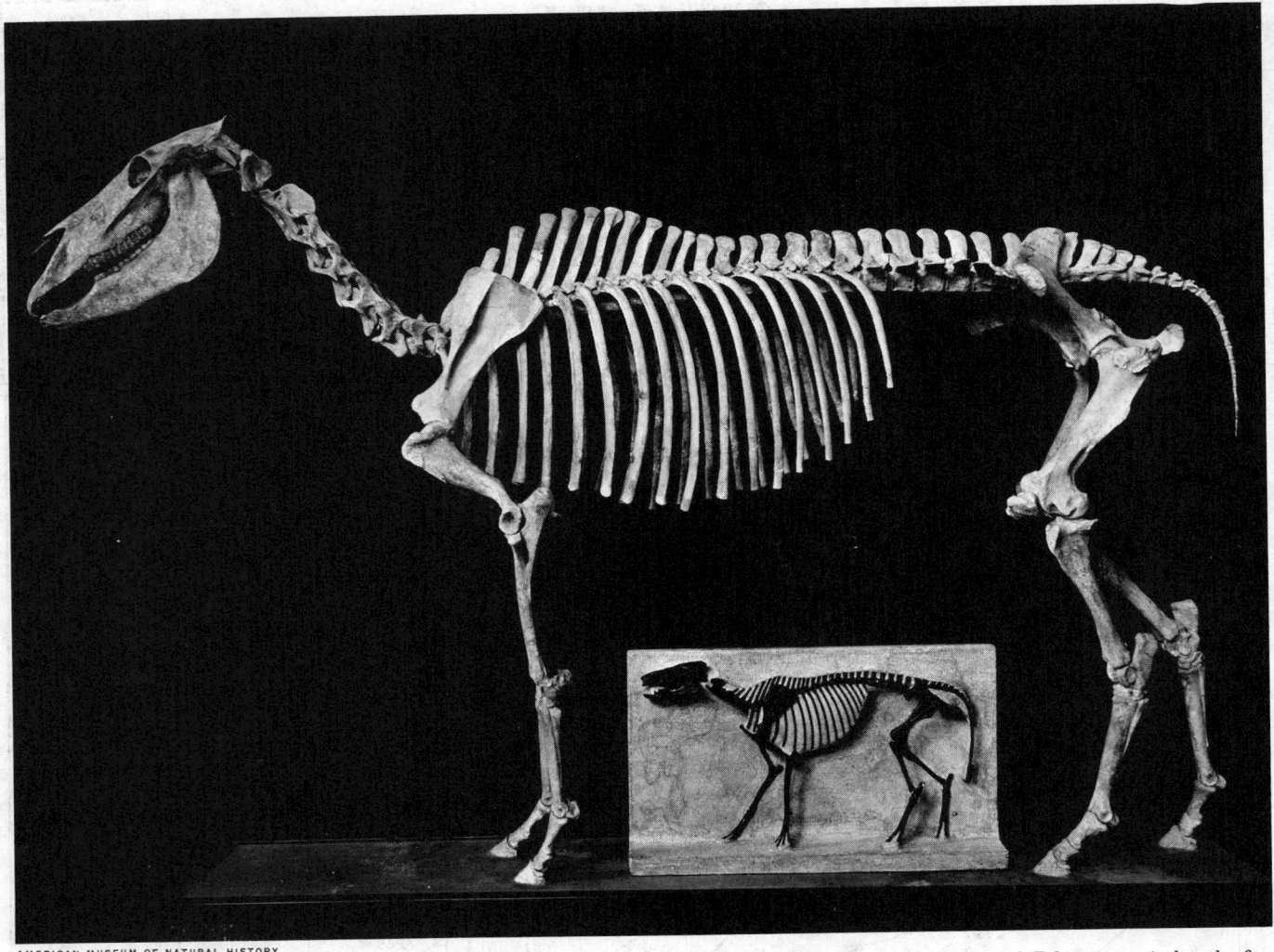

EQUUS SCOTTI, the one-toed, last stage in the evolution of American horses, compared to the smaller, four-toed *Eohippus venticolus,* the first stage. *Equus scotti,* about 3 feet 9 inches in height, became extinct some 250,000 years ago. *Eohippus venticolus* was about 12 inches in height.

are other environments that encouraged fossil preservation.

Fossils can be the clues to many things: whether the rocks were laid on land or in the sea; whether the climate was warm or cold; and how life has unfolded through the ages. Fossils are the only documentary evidence that life has developed from simple plants and animals to more and more complex forms. They provide the geologist with a clock—a chronology. Rocks of each geologic age contain fossils that are different from those of any other age, and this is the way the geologic record is dated.

Fossils typical of a certain *stratum,* or layer of earth or sediment, are called *index* or *guide fossils.* A guide fossil preferably is an organism that can float or swim, since it will therefore be distributed over a wide area by the sea. It must also have a relatively short life in geologic time.

Paleontology.—*Paleontology* is essentially that branch of historical geology that studies the flora and fauna in past geologic periods. It deals with the succession of life that has been on the earth since the earliest times, and with the environment, evolution, structure, and relationships of that life. Thus, paleontology is the most reliable means available to correlate rock strata when dealing with expansive formations, complex formations and structures, and those strata found beneath the surface of the ground, such as the cores brought to the surface by oil well drillers.

The first of the geologic time divisions is the *Archeozoic era,* during which the oldest exposed rocks that have been found on the continents were formed. This era, of course, does not start with the beginning of the earth, since there was an extensive interval between the time the planet first began to cool and the solidification of the first rocks. The Archeozoic was followed by the *Proterozoic era,* and in the rocks of the Proterozoic, traces of the first living organisms appear. About 550 million years ago the Proterozoic ended and the *Paleozoic era* began. This era, which is divided into seven unequal periods, lasted for over 350 million years. During the Paleozoic the first vertebrate fish, amphibia, reptiles, and the first spore-bearing, conifer, and cycad land plants appeared. The Paleozoic was followed by the *Mesozoic era,* which is divided into three unequal periods. During the first of these, the *Triassic,* the dinosaurs made their appearance; during the second, the *Jurassic,* the first birds appeared; and during the third, the *Cretaceous,* the dinosaurs became extinct and flowering plants appeared. About 60 million years ago, the Mesozoic era gave way to the *Cenozoic era.* The Cenozoic is divided into two periods—the *Tertiary* and *Quaternary*—and seven epochs. During the first of these epochs, the *Paleocene,* the first mammals, the marsupials, appeared; during the second, the *Eocene,* the primates appeared; during the third, the *Oligocene,* elephants made their appearance; during the fourth, the *Miocene,* horses evolved; during the fifth, the *Pliocene,* grasses became more abundant; and during the sixth, the *Pleistocene,* man made his debut. During the seventh, the *Recent,* the development and spread of modern human culture occurred.

—Doris D. Shaner

SCIENTIFIC OIL EXPLORATION in Saudi Arabia. A portable corer drills shallow holes in the desert floor and flushes rock fragments to the surface. Petroleum geologists study the rock fragments to learn whether, farther below, there is the type of strata that may contain oil.

ECONOMIC GEOLOGY

Scope.—The economic geologist is concerned with the mineral substances in the earth's crust that are necessary to man's survival and comfort. Only about 200 of the nearly 2,000 minerals that have been identified are of economic interest. The most

important of these in today's economy are the mineral or fossil fuels, such as petroleum and coal. (Technically, these fuels are neither true minerals, since their composition cannot be expressed by a chemical formula, nor fossils, since they have no identifiable structure.) Economic geology deals not only with ores and mineral deposits, but also with the rocks that contain them—how the rocks were formed,

their nature and structure, and the geological formations developed on them. An economic geologist uses all the principles and techniques of physical and historical geology.

Historical Development.—The early history of economic geology closely parallels that of mineralogy, since both sciences evolved from man's desire for ornamentation. One might say that economic geology, however, began when the first man used a rock to help him survive. The first known economic geologist was probably Haroeris—an Egyptian captain who led an expedition to the Sinai Peninsula around 2000 B.C. After prospecting for several months, Haroeris found and extracted large amounts of the semiprecious stone turquoise. The early Egyptians, the Greeks, and their various neighbors prized gems, gold, and silver highly for the ornamentation of their bodies, their homes, and their dead.

Mining as an industry began with the search for gems and decorative stones during the time when the Egyptian pharaohs were most powerful. Gems and ornaments were so much a part of religious belief in those days that they were considered a necessity of life. However, the gem minerals that were economically important at that time play only a minor role in our life today—they are our luxuries. At the conclusion of the Dark Ages, the chief mineral substances in use were iron, copper, lead, tin, gold, silver, mercury, precious stones, clay, and building stones—compared with more than 75 minerals traded internationally today. The chief minerals now are oil and gas, coal, iron ores, iron-alloy metals (chromium, manganese, molybdenum, nickel, tungsten, vanadium), nonferrous metals (copper, lead, zinc, tin, aluminum), the minor metals, metallurgical minerals, chemical minerals, ceramic materials, and abrasives. Gold is not considered as an industrial mineral because of its monetary value, but it plays an important part in affording means of purchasing needed mineral supplies.

Locating Minerals.—All the easy-to-find mineral deposits have already been exploited, and the search for new deposits has taken scientists to strange and hard-to-reach places, such as deep into the earth and far out over the oceans. One of the main jobs of the economic geologist is to use the principles of geology in searching for and helping to develop valuable mineral deposits. He also works with other scientists and technicians in finding new methods and developing new instruments that will aid in this search and lower production costs. In the future, such new techniques will help develop deposits that are considered too costly to exploit today.

The economic geologist has such powerful prospecting aids as the *seismograph,* a device for recording shock waves that travel through the earth, the airborne *magnetometer,* a device for measuring the strength and direction of magnetic forces, and the *gravity meter,* a device for detecting differences in gravitational attraction. He takes readings from these instruments, interprets them according to his knowledge of the geology of the area, and evaluates the results. From this information, he constructs a map of the geologic structures below the surface of the ground. Thus a geologist can select spots where economically exploitable mineral deposits are most likely to be found.

Mineral Products.— The principal mineral products in the United States, in order of value, are crude petroleum, natural gas, and coal—with petroleum contributing more than half of all the revenue received from the total mineral-fuel production. The U.S. produces annually more than 3 billion barrels of crude oil that is valued today at the wellhead at approximately $30 billion. About 6 million tons of anthracite (hard coal) are produced each year, with a value of $170 million, and 700 million tons of bituminous (soft coal), with a value of $14 billion. A ready yardstick to indicate the order of importance of mineral fuels in the American economy is the fact that three out of four geologists in the United States are petroleum geologists, employed by oil companies in the search for oil and natural gas. The greatest oil deposits are found in the Middle East, but significant new discoveries of deposits in North Africa in recent years indicate that this region, too, will continue to be a major source of production. Production from the North Sea and from Alaska will undoubtedly increase in the coming years.

Besides petroleum and coal, the nonmetallic minerals of economic value include cement materials, ceramic products, building stones, gems, and sulfur. The total value of these nonmetals (excluding fuels) is today over $10 billion in the U.S. The metallic minerals include the industrial and precious metals—gold, copper, lead, tin, zinc, titanium, uranium, and a host of others. Today in the U.S. these produce an annual revenue in excess of $5 billion.

■**PETROLEUM.**—Petroleum is a complex mixture of gaseous, liquid, and solid hydrocarbons (compounds containing hydrogen and carbon). The consensus among geologists is that petroleum originated from marine plant and animal life that died and fell to the bottom of the shallow prehistoric seas. Here it decomposed as the result of bacterial action, yielding carbon and hydrogen. The residue was buried by sediments and subjected to further chemical change. Finally, the weight of the sediments squeezed the oil and gas into porous rocks, from which they migrated to suitable reservoirs.

Four conditions are necessary for the formation of an oil deposit. First, a *source rock,* which contains the carbonaceous matter from which oil can be formed, must be present. The most common source rocks are marine bituminous shales. Next, there must be a *reservoir rock* in which the oil can collect. Sandstones are the most common reservoir rocks because they are porous and permeable —that is, they have connected pore spaces large enough to permit the oil to move through the rock. Limestones and dolomites are also important reservoir rocks. The third condition is a *structural* or *stratigraphic trap*—the rock strata must be arranged or deposited in such a way that there is a place where oil can collect in quantity. The simplest structure is an *anticline,* where the rock strata have been folded into the shape of an inverted soup bowl. This was the first type of trap recognized, but today more than a score of different traps are known. Finally, there must be an impervious layer called *cap rock*—generally shale or clay— that overlies the reservoir rock and seals in the oil.

■**COAL.**—Coal, another vitally important mineral fuel, is a compact mass of carbonized plant debris. It occurs in beds, which are usually sandwiched between layers of sandstone and shale. The great coal-making eras of geological history were the Mississippian and the Pennsylvanian periods, over 230 million years ago. During these periods, tropical climates and lush swamp vegetation encouraged great accumulations of vegetable matter, from which coal was later formed. Coal beds range in thickness from hardly more than a film to hundreds of feet. The grades of coal depend on the concentration of carbon, or how much of the volatile constituents of the carbonaceous mass have been driven off. The stages in coal formation are *peat, lignite* (brown coal), *bituminous* (soft coal), *anthracite* (hard coal), and under favorable conditions, *graphite.*

■**ORE DEPOSITS.**—Most ores (metal-bearing mineral deposits) are concentrations of metals brought about by igneous activity. *Magma,* the molten material underneath the surface of the earth from which the igneous rocks were formed, supplied the metals in the ore deposits. The metals were released from the magma at the time it solidified. Most deposits of metallic minerals are situated either in border zones of granite *batholiths* or *stocks,* or in the rocks immediately surrounding such intrusive masses.

However, other methods of concentration were also important. Iron ore deposits—iron is by far the most useful and abundant metal—were formed in more ways than deposits of any other metal. But the most important method was *sedimentation,* a process that has produced far larger accumulations of ore than any other process of concentration.

—Doris D. Shaner

For Further Reference

American Geological Institute. *Dictionary of Geological Terms.* Doubleday, 1960.

Calder, Nigel. *The Restless Earth: A Report on the New Geology.* Viking Press, 1972.

Dejong, Kees, and Robert Scholten, editors. *Gravity and Tectonics.* Wiley, 1973.

Foster, Robert. *General Geology* (4th Ed.). Merrill, 1983.

Longwell, Chester R., and Richard F. Flint. *Introduction to Physical Geology* (2nd Ed.). Wiley, 1962.

Rudman, Jack. *Geology.* National Learning, 1985.

Thompson, Henry Dewey. *Fundamentals of Earth Science* (2nd Ed.). Appleton-Century-Crofts, 1960.

As man reaches for the stars in his conquest of space, it is important that he understand his home planet, earth, in comparison with the other heavenly bodies. Unlike the stars, which are incandescent gaseous masses similar to our sun, the earth is a planet, a roughly spherical mass of material which describes a slightly flattened circle, or ellipse, around the sun along with eight other planets.

The word planet is derived from a Greek word meaning *wanderer*. The ancients recognized that a few stars in the heavens had paths across the sky that differed from the fixed circuits followed by nearly all of the other celestial bodies, including the sun. The planets seem to move across the background of stars because they are so much nearer and have paths comparable to that of the earth.

If the radius of the entire solar system, almost 3.7 billion miles, were reduced to one foot, the nearest of the millions of stars beyond the solar system that we have charted would be 7.6 miles away. If the sun were placed at the center of the same one-foot scale, the earth would have an orbit only ⅓ inch in radius, representing a mean distance of 92.9 million miles from the sun. Because the earth's orbit is an ellipse, it is about 3 million miles closer to the sun during January than in July.

EARTH

SIZE AND SHAPE. The earth is fifth in size among the nine planets, being larger than Mercury and Venus, the planets nearest the sun; Mars, between the earth and the sun; and Pluto, the planet farthest from the sun. The diameter of the earth is slightly greater at the equator (7,926.68 miles) than it is at the poles (7,899.99 miles), because of a slight flattening at the poles.

The earth is far smaller than the largest planet, Jupiter, which has a diameter over 10 times that of earth and a mass more than 300 times as great. The sun, however, is by far the largest body in our solar system, for more than 100 earths could be strung along its diameter.

The total weight of the earth has been calculated at about 6,000 million, million, million tons, with an average density approximately 5.5 times that of water. Because the average density of rocks at the surface is only about 2.7, it is obvious that the interior of the earth must contain extremely dense material.

The great accuracy of location required for intercontinental rocket flights has led to increased refinements in the determination of the shape of the earth. Precise measurements made with the use of satellite rockets have revealed that, in addition to being flattened at the poles, the earth bulges slightly a short distance north of the

TOTAL ECLIPSE, an awesome spectacle as the moon moves across the sun's face.

equator and is thus somewhat pear-shaped. Such distortions from a perfect spherical shape, are relatively small, however, and would be difficult to see were the earth to be viewed at about the same distance as we see the moon.

COMPOSITION. Although man has scarcely pricked the outermost skin of the earth, the deepest penetration being an oil well about five miles deep, he has a considerable amount of information concerning the interior of the earth through the careful study of earthquake shocks as revealed in seismograph records.

The earth's crust varies in thickness from more than 20 miles under the continents to as little as 3 miles under the oceans. Near high mountains, it is believed to be somewhat thicker, perhaps as much as 40 miles.

The crust consists of two layers: an outer, *sialic* (*si*lica and *al*uminum) or granitic, layer; and, below this, a *simatic* (*si*lica and *ma*gnesium) or basaltic layer. Under continents the sial and sima are each 10 to 15 miles thick; under the oceans the sial thins out, disappearing completely in areas under the Pacific.

The surface separating the earth's crust from the mantle is called the Mohorovičić discontinuity, after the Yugoslavian seismologist who discovered it. The mantle is a relatively solid region approximately 1,800 miles deep. It probably consists of ferromagnesian minerals or sima and may be glassy in its upper portion. Below the mantle is the core.

The core has two parts. An outer zone 1,300 miles thick is composed of iron and probably is in a plastic or liquid state. An inner core, with a radius of 800 miles, is probably composed of solid iron mixed with nickel and cobalt in the same proportions as in metallic meteorites.

EARTH-SUN RELATIONSHIPS. Considering the range of temperatures in the entire universe, from the absolute zero of outer space, −273°C or −459°F, to the tens of thousands of degrees within the hottest stars, it is amazing that the surface of the earth has an absolute range of only about 260°F, and there are broad areas on earth where the temperature rarely varies more than 20°.

The reason for this unique condition, as well as many other phenomena such as day and night and seasonal changes, lies in the positioning and motions of the earth with respect to the sun. Before discussing these relationships it would be well to know something of the sun itself.

SUN

The sun is a rather ordinary star among the countless millions that have been observed in space. By our standards it seems immense, but many stars are much larger and some are smaller. It is also somewhat average in its temperature. There seems to be a rough correlation between size and temperature, with the smallest stars tending to be the hottest and most dense.

We are most concerned with the role of the sun as a body radiating energy in every direction. This radiant energy moves outward through space in waves that have a wide range of frequency and length. One band of such waves stimulates our eye retinas in the form of visible light. But there are many that are both longer and shorter than the light we can see.

Also issuing from the sun are vast streams of electrons that at times produce wild bursts of static on radios and may even interfere with many surface communication systems. The brilliant displays of the *aurora polaris* (termed northern lights in the northern hemisphere) are caused by the ionization of upper air atoms by incoming streams of electrons.

The distance between the earth and the sun allows the earth to intercept just enough solar radiation for the development of life as we know it. The atmosphere screens out the dangerous short wave-length radiation. Once absorbed by molecules on the earth, radiant energy may be transformed into other types of energy.

Nearly all of the energy found in any form at the surface of the earth has been derived from solar radiation, including the chemical energy of coal and oil, the hydroelectric power generated along our streams, the power of draft animals, and the energy within our own bodies. Were it not for the sun, the earth would be a lifeless, rocky orb, without soil or water.

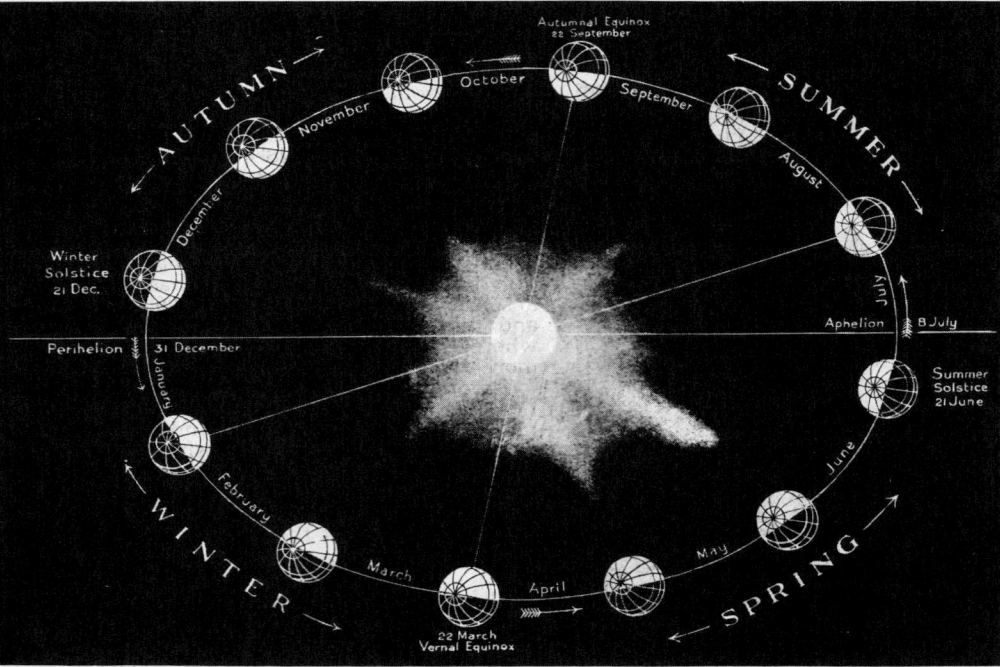

SEASONS SHIFT as the earth's position relative to the sun changes, as shown in this drawing.

While it is true that the entire earth receives slightly more energy from the sun in January than in July, the influence of global temperatures is slight and overshadowed by more important factors. Latitude determines the seasonal changes in temperature and variations in the length of day and night, which become greater with increasing latitude.

These changes and variations are caused by the combination of several factors: the rotation of the earth on its axis once every 24 hours, the tilting of the earth's axis 23½° from the perpendicular to the orbital plane, and the constancy of the axial tilt at all positions in the earth's orbit.

There is little seasonal temperature change at the equator because day and night are always of virtually equal length, and the sun at noon never varies more than 23½° from the vertical. At the poles, on the other hand, days and nights are approximately six months long, and the sun shifts from being 23½° above the horizon to 23½° below it during the course of the year.

TIME AND LOCATION

The rotation of the earth on its axis, and its revolution around the sun, also provides a basis for keeping track of time and for locating places on the earth's surface. Our year of 365¼ days represents an approximation of the time it takes for the earth to complete one revolution around the sun. The true solar year is 365 days, 6 hours, 9 minutes, and 9.54 seconds.

The Egyptians and Mayans both had surprisingly accurate calendar systems compensating for the odd period of revolution. Monthly divisions also have long been used in the attempt to fit the lunar orbital cycle into the solar year. The moon moves into the same relationship with the

earth and sun approximately every 29½ days. Thus, our 12 months represent divisions of the year that are close to the lunar cycle.

TIME ZONES. As the earth turns on its axis once every 24 hours, noon (when the sun is highest in the heavens) lies on the opposite side of the earth from midnight. The time of day, therefore, as measured by the position of the sun, changes continually as one passes around the earth in an easterly or westerly direction.

Appointments would be difficult to make and keep, except locally, were we to use solar time. For this reason, time zones approximately 15° of longitude in width have been arbitrarily determined.

Within each time zone the time remains constant. Adjacent time zones differ by one hour, since 15° represents 1/24 of the circumference of the earth. Because the earth rotates on its axis from west to east, the time zones are later to the east and earlier to the west of any given point. Eastern Standard Time, the time zone in the eastern United States, is one hour later than Central Standard Time, the next zone to the west.

INTERNATIONAL DATE LINE. Eventually, as one passes around the earth, a change in day must be made. This was first observed by the crew of the Portuguese navigator Ferdinand Magellan, who noted upon their return to Spain after traveling around the world from east to west that their ship's log had apparently lost a day. Had they sailed around the earth from west to east they would have gained a day. To correct this possible source of confusion, the international date line was established as the place where each calendar day begins.

The date line is located near the 180° meridian, one half of the world away from the Greenwich meridian,

and zigzags from north to south through the Pacific Ocean, avoiding island groups. When a traveler crosses the date line from east to west, he moves ahead one day to make up for the hours he has set his watch back while traveling west through the time zones. When crossing the line going east, the traveler drops one day.

LONGITUDE AND LATITUDE. By comparing local sun time with the sun time along the 0° meridian, the meridian passing through Greenwich, England, longitude may be determined. If the sun, for example, is one hour short of being at its highest point at the same time that solar time is noon at Greenwich, the local position is 15° west longitude. Keeping track of Greenwich time today is done either by radio signals or by accurate time pieces such as chronometers.

Latitude, the angular distance north and south of the equator, is calculated by comparing the elevation of the sun above the horizon with what it would be at the intersection of the equator and the same meridian during the same moment. At night selected stars can be used for similar calculations.

EARTH HISTORY

No one knows for certain exactly when or how the earth came into being. The age of rocks can be estimated by carefully measuring the quantities of certain substances known to result from the decomposition of such radioactive minerals as uranium, however. The oldest rocks dated so far are about 2.7 billion years old. Yet none of these were part of the original crust, for heat and pressure altered them in later eons of time.

The age of the earth is presently estimated to be about 4.5 billion years. This agrees closely with the age of some meteoric material as shown by their content decomposition products of radioactive minerals.

ORIGIN. Many theories for the origin of the earth and its planetary companions have been proposed, but few of them are sufficiently comprehensive to explain the many puzzling details of the solar system. One of the most widely accepted hypotheses involves the generation of giant tidal waves in the incandescent solar atmosphere by the gravitational attraction of a passing star.

A long filament of gas, tapering at both ends, was drawn out too far to be pulled back into the sun. Its oblique motion carried it some distance, but the greater mass of the sun prevented its total escape into space. A close analogy can be found in placing satellites in orbit around the earth.

Condensation of the gaseous material, and gravitational attraction exerted by the condensed material on smaller masses near its path, led to the gradual growth of the planets. The earth is still sweeping in some meteoric fragments, but it is likely that the present size of the earth was reached during the first billion years or so.

Gravitational compression of the earth material as it grew in total mass, and the accumulation of heat resulting from the decomposition of radioactive material, led to the development of a molten or liquid core. Convectional currents in this and in the semi-solid or plastic outer portion shifted some of the lightest constituents to the surface as a kind of scum to form the outer crust. Areas of the earth's surface exhibiting interior heat losses and gains seem to indicate that the convectional movement of heat and material still continues.

The atmospheric gases may have resulted from rock fusion and ejection from deep within the earth. Some gases may have been gained by gravitational capture in space.

LIFE. Water, oxygen, carbon dioxide, sunlight, and the first oceans occupying the major depressions in the earth's surface were the requirements for the beginning of life.

The actual beginning is hidden, but the remains of lime-secreting algae have been found in sediments that radioactive uranium dating shows to be about 2.6 billion years old.

It is believed that life first appeared in the seas, perhaps along some warm, sandy shore. There, water rich in mineral salts, air with its carbon dioxide and oxygen, sunlight, and the possible catalytic action of rare minerals in the adjacent sand grains combined in this natural laboratory to form the first protoplasm, cell structure, and the first blueprint for genetic reproduction.

EARTH PULSE. Earth history, or at least the history of the outer crust, is essentially a long succession of alternate periods of instability and rest. These cycles have sometimes been referred to as the "pulse" of the earth. During the periods of instability, the crust buckled and warped, especially along what became continental margins.

Mountains and plateaus were lifted high above sea level, and volcanic activity was widespread in the areas of crustal weakness and cracking. The seas were confined largely to the ocean basins, and climatic changes were drastic. Pronounced glaciation at times covered large portions of the continents.

Under the continually changing demands of, a dynamic environment, life forms changed rapidly. Some highly specialized forms were unable to adapt to the new conditions and died out completely.

These times of mountain-building, or orogeny, have been used as markers separating the divisions of geologic time. Major global orogenies separate the broad eras; the lesser ones, usually more local in occurrence, separate the periods and, within the periods, the epochs.

The intervening times of crustal stability were usually much longer than the orogenies. During these times erosion wore mountains down to plains, and deposition in other areas caused great troughs to subside under the weight of accumulated sediments. The seas frequently invaded the continental blocks along the coastal margins and through broad seaways into the interior plains.

Life forms spread over extensive areas of the earth and developed highly specialized characteristics in tune with the stable environments. Climates were much more uniform over the earth than they now are, and a distinct frozen polar region was rare.

GEOLOGIC TIME. The enormity of time measured on the geological time scale is difficult to comprehend. On such a scale mountains are but fleeting features on a continually changing stage. The Grand Canyon, awesome to behold as an example of the inexorable work of running water over vast periods of time, is a feature that has been developed only "yesterday" in the vastness of geological time, for it began to appear during the latter part of the Tertiary period, a mere 20 to 30 million years ago.

Using a base figure of 4.5 billion years for the age of the earth, and representing this as a quarter-mile race track, the length of time since glacial ice was rapidly receding from North America, about 10,000 years ago, would be equal to a distance on the track slightly less than the width of a dime standing on edge.

LITHOSPHERE

The solid outer crust of the earth has been altered many times since it was formed, and no remnant of the original unaltered crust has ever been found. Sometimes and in some places the crust was warped into huge folds or broad regional arches only to be worn down, or eroded, by running water, glacial ice, wind, or waves. At others, it was bent deep into the plastic sima, the dark, heavy sub-crustal material, under the weight of slow but continuous deposition, such as at the mouths of great rivers like the Mississippi or China's Hwang Ho, or Yellow River.

It is believed that such troughs or basins of deposition, subsiding for thousands of feet under the weight of erosional debris, at first push down on the underlying sima. After a certain critical point, the sima moves sideways toward the downward bulge, compressing its edges into great folds and slowly forcing up the entire basin.

This balancing process, termed isostatic compensation, has operated for billions of years to insure the continuation of the geologic processes of erosion, deposition, and crustal deformation, or tectonics. *Terra firma* (solid earth) is not an expression appropriate in the continuum of geological time.

Not all portions of the lithosphere are equally susceptible to tectonic forces. The most unstable portions have appeared to be the continental margins. Around the edge of the Pacific Ocean, for example, high mountains and ocean deeps are close together. The Pacific border is also the site of volcanic activity and earthquakes.

Some areas have been notably stable for long periods of time, however. Such areas are called shields because of their tendency to have broad, slightly convex surfaces somewhat similar to medieval European shields. The largest and most studied of these is

the Canadian Shield, a huge mass of granite and other sialic rocks that covers a large part of Canada, dipping into northern New York, Michigan, Wisconsin, and Minnesota. Much of Africa is an ancient shield block.

CONTINENTS AND OCEAN BASINS

Earth scientists have been intrigued for many years by the apparent "fit" between North and South America on one hand, and Eurasia and Africa on the other. An associated feature of this pattern is a submarine ridge that runs the length of the Atlantic Ocean from north to south, describing an elongated S, which corresponds to the Atlantic shoreline of these continents.

Furthermore, if the American and Eurasian-African blocks were placed together, there would be an astounding conjunction of rock structures, strata ages, glaciated areas, fossils, and alignment of magnetic mineral particles in rocks. This conjunction seems to fit from the northern tip of Norway to the southern tip of Africa.

Another "fit" is possible, with Australia and Antarctica tucked together in the space now occupied by the Indian Ocean.

CONTINENTAL DRIFT. Early in the 1900s, Alfred Wegener, a German geologist, proposed a theory of continental drift. He suggested that during the Mississippian and Pennsylvanian periods all the continents were joined. But a rent appeared, and during the early part of the Mesozoic era the continents slowly moved, or drifted, apart toward their present positions. This may have been caused by slow-moving convection currents in a dense, plastic zone below the earth's crust.

Many objections have been found to the details of the Wegener hypothesis, and until recently it was generally not accepted by geologists. During the past two decades, however, new techniques of geophysical investigation have turned up much additional evidence to support the theory of continental drift, although the time and causes of its occurence are still subject to considerable debate.

CHARACTERISTICS OF CONTINENTS. The continental blocks, with islands, make up less than 30 percent of the earth's surface. Except for the southern tip of South America, each block has an ocean at its antipodal position (opposite side of the earth). The continental blocks also tend to have a triangular shape, with a broad side to the north and tapering to the south. It may be noted on a world map how many peninsulas point southward and how few extend northward.

Generally, the edges of the continental blocks lie below sea level. With few exceptions, there is a pronounced shelf zone bordering the continents which averages some 30 miles in width, and slopes gradually to a depth of less than 600 feet before the start of the continental slope. The continental slope plunges steeply into the ocean basins.

Crossing the continental shelf and slope in many places are submarine canyons, which may be as much as 10 miles wide and more than 6,000 feet deep. Some of these canyons appear to be extensions of valleys on the land

PLATE TECTONICS

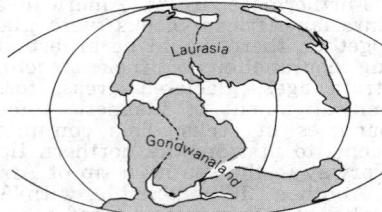

200 million years ago

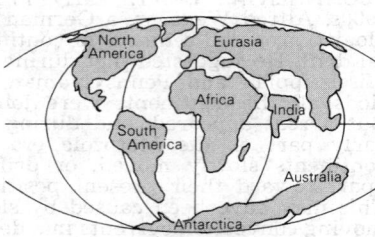

135 million years ago

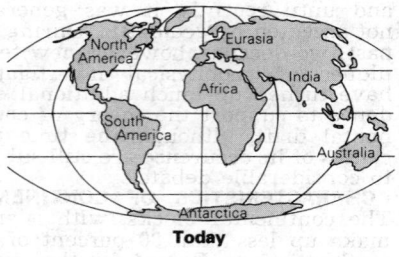

65 million years ago

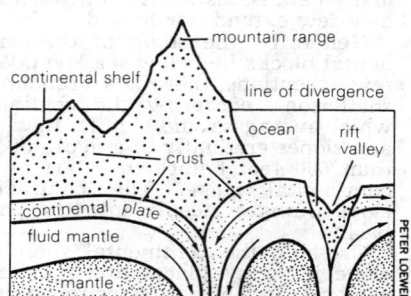

Today

Continental drift. Inspection of a map of the world reveals an apparent fit between the coastlines of Africa and South America. Fossil remains of the same animals have been found on both continents, and both share the same rock formations. Is this just coincidence?

Alfred Wegener, a German scientist, in 1912 proposed a theory of continental drift. According to Wegener, about 200 million years ago all the land on Earth was one large continent, which he called Pangaea. Approximately 180 million years ago, according to Wegener, Pangaea began to break apart to form three separate continents. The large block to the north (which later became Europe, Asia, North America, and Greenland) he called Laurasia. It broke away from the other two land masses, which together he called Gondwanaland.

The northern block of Gondwanaland was to become South America and Africa; the southern block would become Antarctica, Australia, and New Zealand. A small piece broke away between the northern and southern parts of Gondwanaland and began moving northward. According to Wegener's theory of continental drift, this became India.

The land masses continued to drift. About 65 million years ago, the continents began to look as they do today. South America and Africa had drifted apart, and soon North America and Greenland broke away from Laurasia. India was about to collide with Asia. The southern block of Gondwanaland would soon break apart into separate pieces, forming Antarctica, Australia, and New Zealand.

Although Wegener's theory of continental drift was not credited at first, it eventually came to be accepted in a modified form. Increasingly, geologists found geological, fossil, and magnetic evidence that the continents were no longer in the same relationship to each other as before. More recently, evidence has turned up to show that the continents themselves have been built in part from large islands that have drifted and stuck to the shorelines of the continents.

The moving crust. Today Earth's surface continues to be in motion. According to the *plate tectonics theory,* Earth's surface—or *crust*—is broken into pieces called plates. A crustal plate may carry only ocean floor, only continent, or some combination of both. Some plates are huge, such as the Pacific Plate, which carries most of the Pacific Ocean. Others are much smaller, like the Nazca Plate, which lies off the west coast of South America. These plates move around on a layer of molten rock beneath Earth's surface much as a boat floats on water.

Plates are involved in three different types of movement. On the floor of the Atlantic Ocean, the plates are moving apart in a process called *sea-floor spreading.* The amount of movement is about 2 inches a year, which means that the Atlantic is constantly growing wider, and Europe is moving farther away from the United States. As the plates move apart, molten rock wells up from beneath the surface to form new ocean floor.

Sea-floor spreading in the Atlantic occurs along a huge underwater mountain range called the *mid-ocean ridge.* Within the ridge is an opening called a *rift valley,* through which molten rock pours out. Rift valleys can be found in other parts of the world too. In East Africa a large rift valley has formed, perhaps indicating that the African continent is beginning to break apart. The Red Sea may have appeared as a result of separation of the Arabian Peninsula from Africa.

In some parts of the world, crustal plates are converging. Here crust is being destroyed, offsetting the new crust being formed in other regions, thus keeping the size of Earth's surface constant. When a plate carrying oceanic crust collides with a plate carrying continental crust, the sea floor sinks beneath the continent, forming a deep ocean trench. Such trenches are found along Japan and the Aleutian Islands. Volcanoes are common in these areas. For example, the volcanic Andes Mountains in South America and the deep trench in the nearby Pacific may have been produced when two plates converged.

Collision of plates carrying continental crust may also lead to the formation of huge mountain ranges. An example is the Himalayas, which were created when India collided with Asia millions of years ago.

When two plates carrying oceanic crust converge, one is forced beneath the other. This results in the formation of an ocean trench accompanied by undersea volcanic activity and earthquakes.

Instead of separating or coming together, two plates may simply move past each other. This type of movement is occurring along the San Andreas Fault in California.

14

and could have been formed during a glacial period when the sea level was lower than it is at present. There is also evidence that some of them could have been formed below the surface of the sea by turbidity currents or underwater avalanches.

VOLCANOES AND EARTHQUAKES

Volcanoes and earthquakes are associated with zones of crustal instability. Volcanoes occur where there has been a rupturing of the crust, permitting hot fluid rock, or magma, to rise along cracks or fissures. This magma originates within the crust itself.

It is not entirely understood why reservoirs of magma occur within the outer solid part of the earth, but suggested reasons include tensional stresses, which relieve the great rock pressures that normally keep the rock material solid despite temperatures of many thousands of degrees. There is also the possibility of the gradual accumulation of heat resulting from the breakdown of radioactive minerals.

VOLCANIC MATERIAL. The composition of volcanic material varies greatly, ranging from light-colored silicic lava that erupts explosively, contains large quantities of gases, has a relatively high temperature, is viscous or gluey, and piles up around the volcano, to the dark basic lava which erupts gently, has a low melting point, is relatively fluid, and may flow for miles.

The explosive volcanoes tend to build cone-shaped accumulations of ash and cinders, whereas the highly fluid and dark-colored lavas pour out onto the surface in broad sheets, forming immense dome-shaped masses such as the great volcanoes of Hawaii. During a volcano's eruptive period the composition of the lava may change and the volcano may produce both fragmental and fluid lavas during the same eruption.

EARTHQUAKES. The shock waves, or vibrations, produced by rock rupture are called earthquakes. When stresses accumulate over a long period, owing either to compression or tension, rocks eventually will break and slip along lines called faults. Certain fault lines may have active slippage along them for millions of years, and may produce cumulative displacements measuring miles in length and thousands of feet in height.

Most earthquakes take place well below the surface of the earth and their displacements may not be noticeable. Occasionally, however, a severe one near the surface produces sudden dislocations of roads, fences, or streams. Minor earthquakes also may result from severe volcanic eruptions or from the elastic rebound of the crust following the melting of huge continental ice sheets.

LANDFORMS

The physical features that make up the surface of the earth are the result of many different processes of change operating on a variety of materials for widely different periods of time. For these reasons no two hills or mountains look exactly alike, yet many of them have common proper-

ties by which they may be classified and understood.

Valleys, for example, may be produced by stream erosion, by the scouring action of a glacier, or by the solution of limestone by underground water. Each of these valley forms has distinctive characteristics whereby their origin can be deciphered. Furthermore, the pattern of stream valleys in a region of horizontal sedimentary rock layers will be different from the pattern in an area of metamorphic, or granite, rocks, or in Arctic climates the pattern will be different from that in the Sahara.

There is also a variation in the appearance of a stream from youth, when it has virtually no flood plain and the valley walls form a V in cross-valley profile; to maturity, when most of the falls and rapids have been eliminated and a flood plain begins to form; to old age, when valley-widening dominates downward cutting and oxbow lakes and natural levees are common.

Natural agents such as glaciers, waves, tectonic forces, weathering, and erosion produce specific types of landforms that can be recognized and classified.

The continental glacier that was retreating from North America 10,000 years ago left behind many characteristic landforms. Glacial deposition resulted in the hummocky belts of unsorted boulders and pulverized rock called moraines, the mounds of sand and gravel laid down by glacial meltwater called kames, the oval hills of unstratified clayey till called drumlins, and the low, winding ridges of sand and gravel that may extend for 100 miles or more in northern Canada and Scandinavia called eskers.

Glacial erosion also helped shape landforms such as the smooth, striated glacial pavements; the low, beveled rock mounds called roche moutonnées (sheep rocks), and the steep-walled basins called cirques formed by the headwall erosion of mountain glaciers.

Waves and currents in the sea produce their characteristic landforms such as notched sea cliffs; stacks, or rock columns left as erosional remnants; offshore bars or barrier beaches, such as the one on which Atlantic City, New Jersey is built; wave-filled terraces constructed off-shore by wave deposition; and spits and hooks, the sandy deposits extending out from the ends of coastal capes and promontories.

Tectonic forces produce anticlines, or upfolds; synclines, or downfolds; fault scarps, or cliffs resulting from slippage along earthquake faults; graben (from the German *Graben*, for ditch), or depressed crustal blocks bounded on at least two sides by faults. Volcanic activity may produce cinder cones, huge craters or calderas, sills or sheets of lava intruded horizontally between sedimentary rock strata, such as the New York Palisades, and dikes, lava intruded across and through rock strata.

Weathering and erosion in humid climates produce gently rolling plains or peneplains. In arid and semi-arid climates, plateaus with steep faces and pediments or slopes thinly veneered

with gravel are the common results. In the tropics isolated, steep-sided hills and mountains may rise abruptly from relatively flat landscapes. In desert areas temporary salt lakes, or playas, dunes, and broad, flat-topped hills, or mesas, are frequently encountered.

All these and many other landforms help to give variety to the surface of our planet, and to challenge scientists to interpret their various and changing shapes and compositions.

MINERAL DEPOSITS

Only a very small portion of the outer crust of the earth contains minerals that have an economic significance to man. In fact, of the thousands of individual minerals that man has found and identified, only a small number make up the bulk of the crust.

One single mineral, orthoclase, a pink or gray potassium aluminum silicate, is the primary mineral constituent of granite—the most abundant rock in the earth's crust. This one mineral probably constitutes one-fourth of the entire earth's crust. Although it has useful aluminum as one of its atomic elements, the aluminum is so tightly bound to its oxygen and silica companions that it is not commercially profitable to separate it.

Instead, nature performs this task by weathering and decomposing the shiny mineral into tiny clay particles. Under tropical or subtropical climatic conditions, most of the silica is leached out of the clay, producing an impure mixture of aluminum oxide and water known as bauxite, the principal ore of aluminum.

Most of the useful minerals are contained in relatively small exploitable deposits. As a general rule, the metallic minerals have more localized deposits than the non-metallic ones, and the richest metallic deposits are narrow veins of ore precipitated in rock fissures by thermal solutions.

In some localities valuable but lean materials have been concentrated into workable deposits. In one process of concentration the agents of erosion break down rocks, and as streams carry the sediment away, the heavier minerals fall to the floor of the stream channels. The placer deposits of gold, found in stream gravels, are an example of this.

Another process of concentration is secondary enrichment, in which new bodies of high-grade ore are derived from the oxidation of decomposed overlying masses of low-grade ore. Many copper and iron deposits are the result of this process.

Many valuable minerals are also scattered thinly in large rock masses, and as the small, localized deposits of high-grade ore are depleted, man has been forced to turn toward these massive deposits of low-grade ore. Some copper ores that are being worked economically today by mass-production techniques have such low-grade copper contents that they could scarcely be recognized as ore without careful quantitative analysis. For example, the average copper ore mined in the United States has a copper content of only about 0.9 percent. This is an indication of the world-wide scarcity of this metal.

Some minerals tend to be more concentrated in nature than others. Nickel, for example, is a fairly common mineral in the earth's crust, but it occurs in extremely small quantities and is mined in only a few widely scattered localities. Copper, on the other hand, is not so abundant, but it tends to be much more concentrated and is mined in many localities.

In general, the heavier metallic elements tend to be less abundant than such light metals as aluminum, sodium, or potassium. The heavier metallic elements, however, are likely to be more abundant in the sima rocks that have been brought to or near the surface by volcanic activity and are more easily separated from their compounds than the light metallic elements.

The mineral fuels—coal, petroleum, and natural gas—are almost always located in sedimentary strata. Coal represents ancient vegetation that accumulated under water in swamps and marshes and was later buried and compressed by sediments such as silt, clay, or sand. For this reason most coal occurs as broad sheets enclosed by sedimentary rocks.

Oil and gas are fluids and may flow from one place to another through permeable strata. They do not accumulate in commercial, exploitable quantities until they are trapped in some way, such as along the top of upfold or dome in rock strata which is overlain by shale or other impermeable rock.

SOILS

Solid rock forms the major portion of the earth's crust, but it is not in balance with environmental factors at the immediate surface. There nature tends to produce a balanced mixture of rock, air, water, and tiny life-forms which is called soil. Soil, therefore, is a natural substance that represents interaction among the four major global spheres—lithosphere, atmosphere, hydrosphere, and biosphere.

The properties of soils are exhibited not only at the surface but also for a variable distance below and are influenced by local variations in any of the environmental factors—climate, vegetation, bedrock, and relief of the land surface. Time is also a factor because the forces of erosion, weathering, and deposition are continually exposing new rock material or transferring fragmental rock debris to new locations.

Man himself has become an important agent in influencing the characteristics of soils in his search for food and fuel. So many factors influence soil characteristics that if one looks closely enough, soil differences may be seen every few feet.

SOIL CHARACTERISTICS. There are, however, broad features of soils that are similar over wide areas and that enable man to make, classify, and understand the development and best uses of soils.

In general, the youngest, or azonal, soils are composed of fragmental material that has recently been depos-

CANADIAN INFORMATION OFFICE
MINERAL DEPOSITS can be found by digging deep into the earth, as these uranium miners do.

ited. Their most distinctive properties are derived from the chemical composition of the included rock material. Intrazonal soils, somewhat older, have their principal properties largely determined by local conditions, such as wetness or limy parent material. The older, zonal, soils reflect the full effects of environmental factors and may be divided into major groups.

Tundra soil has a dark brown peaty surface over brownish-black soil, underlain by permafrost. Chernzem is a dark soil, high in organic matter, found in moderately humid regions under tall grasses. Desert soil is light-colored, porous, and low in organic matter. Podzol has a thick top layer of partially decayed organic material over a gray leached layer, underlain by a compact, dark reddish to yellowish brown layer. Podzols develop under forests or heaths in temperate to cold, humid climates.

Latosols are leached red and yellow soils which prevail in the tropics. Mildly acid solutions result from rainwater percolating through the soil, removing silica from the original rock particles and leaving behind concentrated iron and aluminum oxides common in crustal rocks, The reds and yellows are derived from iron oxides and are similar to the rust that forms on a piece of iron left outdoors.

In dry climates lime tends to accumulate in the subsoil, deposited by percolation from above or by capillary attraction from below. Evaporation releases this normally soluble and common substance and it accumulates much as the lime crust in a kitchen tea kettle. Poor drainage in dry areas often results in alkali or salty soils,

which are highly toxic to most plant growth.

Tropical soils are usually light-colored because bacteria destroy organic material. In temperate regions frost retards the development of bacteria so the soils generally contain more humus and are, therefore, dark.

ATMOSPHERE

The gaseous envelope that encloses the earth was little known until a few years ago when man decided to explore the rims of space. It is a highly complex part of the earth, and it is subject to continual change.

The atmosphere is many things. It is a huge heat-exchange mechanism, a filter for screening out dangerous short wave solar radiation, a means of transport for energy and water, a source of life-giving carbon dioxide for plants and oxygen for animals, an active agent in the breakdown of rocks and minerals, and a transportation medium for man himself.

The total thickness of the atmosphere is difficult to measure because the outer boundaries gradually blend into interplanetary space. We do know, however, that it extends at least 700 miles above the earth's surface.

At the earth's surface the average composition of the atmosphere by volume is about 75.5 percent nitrogen and 23 percent oxygen, plus small amounts of carbon dioxide, ozone, hydrogen, water vapor, dust, and gaseous impurities. There are also traces of several inert gases, such as krypton, neon, argon, xenon, and helium, which have no known function on the earth or in the behavior of the atmosphere.

VERTICAL DIVISIONS

Like the interior of the earth, the atmosphere is divided into layers.

TROPOSPHERE. The lowest layer, or troposphere, extends from the earth's surface to about 11 miles above the equator and to about 5 miles over the poles. The identifying characteristic of the troposphere is the decrease in temperature with altitude, or lapse rate, which averages about 3.3°F per 1,000 feet. Nearly all clouds and most of the mass of the atmosphere are contained in the troposphere.

A striking feature of the troposphere at increasing heights is the merger of the separate systems of the global wind pattern into one system of westerlies, although easterly winds persist to great heights in the low latitudes.

Tropopause. The upper boundary of the troposphere is called the tropopause. This boundary slopes downward near the poles and at times its surface is broken into step-like edges. There is a steep downward plunge of the tropopause in the midlatitudes which shifts between 25°F in winter and 40°F in summer.

Jet Streams. Near the slope is a narrow, westerly current of air called the jet stream. It averages 75 miles per hour (mph) in summer and 35 mph in winter, although it may reach speeds as high as 250 mph. Fluctuations in the speed of the jet stream appear to be related to the changes in solar energy accumulations on earth. The faster the jet stream flows, the more it kinks and loops. These irregular loops also seem to be linked to surface weather fronts.

There is some evidence for an easterly jet stream in equatorial regions. But it is not as strongly developed nor as regular in its occurrence.

STRATOSPHERE. The stratosphere, the layer above the troposphere, extends to approximately 50 miles above the earth. In the lower part of the stratosphere the temperature remains quite constant, near −67°F, as one ascends. Farther up the temperature tends to rise with increased altitude, and there is a tendency for the portion above the equator to have lower temperatures than portions over the poles.

It was believed for many years that the stratosphere was without much air movement because there is an unusually still zone in its lowest layer which is useful for high altitude flight. But rocket flights have revealed that this still zone is extremely narrow and that violent winds may be encountered above it.

Air flow patterns in the stratosphere seem to be almost the reverse of those in the troposphere. In the stratosphere easterly winds, complete with jets, prevail at middle and higher altitudes.

OZONOSPHERE. The ozonosphere is a zone lying between about 18 and 35 miles above the earth. It sometimes overlaps the stratosphere. The ozonosphere is characterized by an unusual concentration of ozone molecules, which are units of three ozygen atoms loosely linked together. Normally oxygen in gaseous form is in atomic pairs (O_2). Solar energy splits the ordinary double molecule into single atoms, which, in turn, combine with a double to form ozone.

Ozone has a strong affinity for absorbing ultraviolet radiation and re-radiating it at longer wave lengths. Thus the ozonosphere acts as an automatic filter for short wave-length radiation. The greater the radiation, the greater is the manufacture of ozone and the greater its absorption. When the radiation level drops, so does the ozone content.

IONOSPHERE. The ionosphere forms the outermost and by far the thickest of the atmospheric layers, with a lower limit of about 35 miles during the day and about 60 miles at night and extending to more than 300 miles above the earth's surface. The temperature ranges from −90°F at its lower limit to as much as 2000°F at its upper limit.

The primary identifying feature of the ionosphere is the presence of several distinct layers. In each of these layers a large part of the atomic particles are ionized, which means that they have extra electrons attached to them. There also appear to be bands of free electrons.

At the outer edges of the ionosphere there is a danger zone for man —the Van Allen radiation belt. This is a zone of high-energy electrons and protons of extreme intensity. It varies in its concentration and appears to be open above both poles. This doughnut-shaped zone, while not strictly a part of the atmosphere, presents a hazard to astronauts escaping the earth's gravitation.

GLOBAL THERMAL BALANCE

The earth not only receives radiant energy from the sun, but it also re-radiates this energy into outer space. There is a close balance between incoming and outgoing radiation.

Considering the many different alterations that incoming radiation may undergo in the atmosphere or at the surface, even being locked up in coal or oil deposits for hundreds of millions of years, the continued existence of this balance is a remarkable feature of the earth. Had this balance not existed, our planet would have become progressively either hotter or colder.

Even more striking is the fact that the ratio between input and output of energy varies greatly from place to place, not only at the earth's surface but above it. The equatorial regions at the surface, for example, receive considerably more radiation than they re-radiate, and the high latitudes release more than they receive from the sun. The reverse situation seems to be true within the upper stratosphere and ozonosphere.

At the surface, the boundary between surplus and deficient energy lies at about 40° north and south latitude, shifting somewhat with the seasons.

To maintain a total balance in the face of latitudinal imbalances, energy must flow from low latitudes to high latitudes at the surface and vice versa in the upper air. The transportation of this energy takes many forms. It may be transported by ocean currents in the form of heat.

The main carrier of energy, however, is the motion of air, which moves vertically in air currents and horizontally in winds. This may involve direct heat transfer or the flow of warm air toward the poles and cold air toward the equator. It may also utilize the transfer of kinetic energy, the energy of motion, for mild breezes wafting poleward can become concentrated into howling blizzards in polar areas and then lose some of this energy by friction.

EVAPORATION AND CONDENSATION. By far the most efficient and effective means of energy is the evaporation of water from the warm oceans of low latitudes, the transportation of this water vapor by winds or air currents, and its subsequent condensation into liquid water at higher latitudes. This mechanism of heat transfer is very important to the global heat balance.

To vaporize water requires a surprisingly great amount of energy. For example, it requires about 540 calories to change one gram of water into vapor form, or 540 times as much as is needed to raise the temperature of one gram of water one degree Centigrade. In other words, it takes over five times as much energy to change boiling water to water vapor without a temperature change than it does to raise the temperature of water from the freezing point to the boiling point.

Condensation of water in a thunderstorm releases fantastic quantities of energy. The rain that falls to a depth of one inch on one single acre, or a plot about 200 by 200 feet, releases energy during condensation equivalent to the heat energy contained in 15,000 tons of coal. This heat was taken on somewhere—perhaps over a warm tropical or subtropical body of water such as the Gulf of Mexico.

Rain, of course, does not fall only in middle and higher latitudes. In fact, the equatorial regions are among the rainiest places on earth. This is caused by the fact that in those regions the transportation of heat is vertical, and the columns of rising air necessary for rain clouds may tower to heights of 30,000 to 45,000 feet. This is far higher than in middle latitudes. Meteorologists refer to the regions of net outflow as heat sinks, and it is clear that although the frozen wastes of polar areas constitute major sinks at the surface, others occur in the upper air above the low latitudes.

GLOBAL WIND PATTERNS

Wind, the horizontal component of air motion, is caused by the equalization of horizontal differences in air pressure. Therefore, variations in air pressure and in time are of prime consideration in understanding the global wind system both at and above the surface of the earth.

The source areas for the major surface winds are huge cells of high pressure, into which air descends from near the top of the troposphere and from which air diverges at the surface in huge spirals. The air does not blow straight from the center of these pressure cells, or highs, but obliquely, because of the deflective effect of the earth's rotation. This gives a rotational movement to the entire cell that is clockwise in the northern hemisphere and counter-clockwise in the southern hemisphere.

HIGH PRESSURE CENTERS. The major high pressure centers are located in the subtropics with their centers roughly between 25° and 35° (the "horse latitudes"). They are permanent fixtures in the eastern third of the oceans, but tend to be located over the continental areas during the winter season.

The air flow along their equatorial sides is known as the trade winds (easterly winds); the flow along their poleward sides is known as the westerlies. Fluctuations in the number and shape of the subtropical highs determine the amount of wind that flows toward the equator on their eastern sides and poleward on their western sides.

There is a great interchange of air latitudinally when the cells are many and strong, as in the winter season, and little when the cells are few and elongated from east to west. The behavior of these subtropical highs is an important part of the heat exchange system of the earth.

Another high pressure source for surface air movement occurs during the winter over North America and Eurasia. The outward moving air there is extremely cold and shallow. It hugs the ground and moves into the westerly wind belt toward an area of lesser pressure. An analogy may be drawn with drops of water collecting under a dripping faucet and building up a mass that finally moves rapidly toward the drain.

FRONTS. The interaction between the cold air masses and the warm, often moist, westerly winds produce the storms and precipitation that release the energy that had been carried poleward. The fronts that appear on daily weather maps are the boundaries between air masses of different temperatures.

A cold front indicates that the strongest attacking air mass is the coldest of the two. A warm front occurs when warm air is attacking the weak side of a cold air mass. An occluded front is a situation in which one front overtakes another and destroys it, at least on the surface.

PRECIPITATION

Condensation and precipitation, or rain and snowfall, are important parts of the heat exchange system of the earth. The mechanics of precipitation are important in the understanding of this system for they greatly influence the distribution of precipitation over the world.

Condensation requires a tiny nucleus of some kind, such as a speck of dust, a tiny ice particle, or even a small bit of sea salt blown high into the air. It also requires cooling, because this decreases the capacity of air to hold moisture. If air is cooled enough, it may reach the dew point, which means that further cooling will cause the water molecules to pass from the vapor state to a liquid state,

WORLD CLIMATE REGIONS

Climatic Region	Characteristics	Location
Rainy Tropics	Enough rainfall for normal forest growth all year. Hot, little seasonal change in temperature.	5°S to 10°N, in places extending to 20-25° poleward on E. side of continents.
Wet and Dry Tropics (Monsoon Climates)	Pronounced seasonal variation in rainfall; dry season in low sun period (winter). Warm, little seasonal change in temperature.	Poleward of rainy tropics to about 15°.
Dry Climates (Arid and Semi-Arid)	Evaporation exceeds precipitation. Sharp daily changes in temp. Seasonal temp. changes increase with latitude.	15-30° on west side of continents, extending inland and poleward to 45-50°. Rare on E. side of continents.
Mediterranean Climates	Mild, rainy winters; arid summers.	West coast of continents to 50° and around Mediterranean Sea.
Humid Subtropical with Mild Winters	Rainfall throughout the year; hot summers, mild winters with occasional snow and frost.	E. third of continents between 25-40°.
Maritime West Coast Climates	Cool, drizzly summers; mild, rainy winters. Little sunshine. Thunderstorms rare.	West coasts of continents 40-65°.
Humid Continental with Hot Summers and Cold Winters	Rainfall throughout year; hot summers; cold, snowy winters.	N. Hemisphere only. N. Corn Belt and Lower Lake States in U.S.; NE China, Manchuria, and N. Japan.
Humid Continental with Cool Summers	Severe, snowy winters; cool, pleasant summers with some rainfall.	Northern U.S., southern Canada E. of 100° Long.; most of European Russia; Scandinavia E. of Atlantic coast; N. Manchuria.
Subarctic Climates	Long, very severe winters; short, cool summers.	A broad belt from N. Alaska to Labrador. N. Sweden and Finland east to most of Siberia.
Polar Climates	No frost-free season.	Antarctica; N. rim of N. Amer. and Central Eurasia. Extends south along E. coasts to 50°.

or condense. How much cooling is required depends on the amount of water in the air and its temperature.

Examples of condensation are seen on a glass of cold water in a warm room, on a bathroom mirror after a hot bath, and in the dew of early morning. Condensation in the free air by natural causes is represented by fog or clouds, the difference between the two being that fog occurs at ground level. The passage of warm air over a cloud surface may produce fog, and the rising of air, cooling as it rises, produces clouds.

In both of these examples little energy is involved because the amount of condensation is not great. The quantity of water in a fog blanket is not especially large because the droplets are so tiny.

A raindrop is quite another thing for it is usually a million times greater in total mass than the water vapor in fog or clouds. To obtain an increase in the rate of condensation in such a mass requires extremely rapid cooling by strong vertical air currents. The mechanism for such updrafts lies within the condensing water vapor. If very warm, moist air rises to the cloud level, the latent heat released will warm it, making it rise farther and faster to be further cooled, condensed, and so on in a chain reaction.

The air will continue to rise as long as condensing moisture maintains its temperature above that of the adjac-

ent air. This cumulative chain reaction produces the rapid growth of rain drops. In unusually high columns of rising air, the drops may grow into hailstones by a series of ascents and descents in turbulent air.

Snow does not require as much condensational lifting as rain, and only a few degrees of cooling may be needed to produce snow flakes directly from vapor. Because cold air cannot hold much moisture, winter snowfall does not involve as much heat transfer as summer rain. On the average, about 10 inches of snow is equivalent to one inch of rain.

Rain and snow, therefore, occur in those parts of the world where there is air containing water vapor and mechanisms for making saturated air rise to the condensation or cloud zone. Such places include the side of a mountain facing a strong prevailing wind, or the front between contrasting air masses where warm air rises, or is displaced upwards, by colder air, or by local updrafts caused by unequal surface heating, as over a hot city street or a plowed field.

Rain is rare where downward air currents prevail, as in the regions of the subtropical high pressure centers, or where the air is extremely cold, as in polar regions. Warm air that is being chilled from below is stable and resists upward movement, whereas cold air that is being warmed from below is unstable and is easily triggered into upward movement.

REGIONAL CLIMATE

Climate is the average condition of the weather at a particular place over a long period of time. The word climate is derived from the Greek *klima*, which means incline or slope. The ancient Greeks thought that climate depended almost entirely on latitude, believing that the earth sloped away from the sun north of the Mediterranean Sea and, therefore, that the climate became colder to the north.

Many kinds of classifications of climate have been used but most of them have been based on average conditions of temperature and precipitation near ground level. The following table shows the principal climates of the world, their major characteristics, and general location.

HYDROSPHERE

Water makes up about 70 percent of the earth's surface, and the water area is called the hydrosphere. This area includes the water and ice in the oceans, rivers, lakes, and marshlands; ground water; and the water vapor in the atmosphere. Water fills tiny openings in rocks and soils, making itself available to living organisms almost everywhere except in desert areas or in frozen polar wastes.

HYDROLOGIC CYCLE

In the section of the atmosphere, it was noted how important the alternate evaporation and condensation of water was to the regulation of global energy balance, like a thermostat. This same process is also part of the hydrologic cycle, which is our continental water supply and drainage system. In the hydrologic cycle, water begins as atmospheric water vapor, passes into liquid and solid form as precipitation, falls to the surface of the earth where evaporation and transpiration through plants return it to the atmosphere as water vapor. Of course, the details of this process are far more complicated.

There are many detours, wanderings, and shortcuts, but every gallon of water on the surface of the earth is involved in this eternal cycle. Because water is so essential to man and is becoming more so with every passing century, the behavior of this cycle is of great importance.

Just as energy from the sun accumulates and is stored in vast underground oil and coal deposits, so too are there traps to intercept a portion of the hydrologic cycle. The great ice sheets of Greenland and Antarctica, remnants of much greater ones that existed thousands of years ago, are trapped water.

If these ice masses were to be melted, the global sea level would rise by some 150 to 200 feet, which would completely submerge most of the great cities of the world. Water may also be trapped in sedimentary and igneous rocks, in soils, and in the bodies of living things everywhere.

GROUND WATER. The part of the hydrologic cycle contained below the surface of the earth is called ground water. As rain falls, much of it soaks into the soil, filling the openings in both soil and rock. In most places there is a point below which all openings are filled with water.

The top of this saturated zone is called the ground water table. Where the water table meets the surface of the earth there may be lakes, swamps, springs, and streams. The water table rises and falls with changes in the amount of precipitation and tends to follow the general slope of the land surface.

Ground water is an important source of water for human use mainly because it is somewhat more dependable, is colder during summer periods, is usually cleaner, and is less susceptible to pollution than surface water sources. Its main disadvantage is that mineral salts it contains may make the water too "hard" or too salty for use. The quantity of ground water is also more likely to be limited for massive municipal and industrial use than the flow of large surface streams or the supply from lakes and ponds.

THE OCEANS

Fully 96 percent of all the water on earth is contained within the oceans. Not only are the oceans far larger than the continents, but they are also much deeper than the continents are high. There is considerably less local irregularity on the floors of the oceans than on the continents, but the major features, such as canyons and mountains, are much more impressive.

Far from being a featureless plain, the ocean floors are dotted with towering isolated pinnacles, called seamounts, which rise 3,000 feet or more above the floor; elongated ridges miles high; and, in some places around the margins of the ocean basins, great chasms or ocean deeps, which may plunge 20,000 feet or more below the level of the ocean surface.

COMPOSITION. In sea water the proportions of the various contained soluble salts remains relatively constant, despite wide fluctuations in total salinity. Sodium chloride represents about 70 percent of the soluble salts in the ocean. It is noteworthy that the same proportion of elements, although much more diluted, appears in human tears and blood plasma as appears in sea water. The source of so much sodium in the seas is an unsolved riddle to ocean scientists because the average composition of the rocks in the lithosphere does not show sodium and chlorine to be such dominant ions.

The most important substances in sea water to organic development are the dissolved gases of oxygen and carbon dioxide, and certain potash, phosphate, and nitrogenous salts that form plant foods just as they do in soils. The content of dissolved gases decreases with an increase in temperature. Thus, the polar seas have more life-giving oxygen and carbon dioxide than tropical waters, and hence are more prolific of life, especially during the long summer days when sunlight is available for photosynthesis.

Nitrates are a major requirement for life in the seas. Especially fertile "pastures" are found where an upwelling brings toward the surface the nitrate-rich waters which originate from the decay of life on the ocean floor. Such areas are found off the west coast deserts of the continents and in polar waters.

CIRCULATION. The circulation of water in the sea is in a complex system of great circular currents, or gyres, similar to the great currents of air that surround the subtropical highs. The direction of movement of the ocean gyres also resembles that of atmospheric high pressure cells in that they move clockwise in the northern hemisphere and counter-clockwise in the southern hemisphere.

The centers of the gyres are especially barren waters, high in salt, low in contained gases, and a deep blue in color. They lack the greens which mark the presence of tiny organic particles that are a sign of fertile waters. The center of the North Atlantic gyre is called the Sargasso Sea. The masses of floating seaweed and flotsam that collect in the gyre led early mariners to fear this strange ocean region as the graveyard of lost ships.

Not all the waters of the gyre rotate with the same speed. The most rapid currents are found on the western sides of the gyres. The Gulf Stream which forms the western edge of the North Atlantic gyre, has a speed at times as much as 5 miles per hour and has been called an "ocean river."

Although most of the water in the gyres makes its way slowly around and around the great circuits, a portion of it is discharged toward the polar seas, sometimes as marginal tongues and drifts, sometimes as great eddies. As the Gulf Stream begins its eastern path away from the east coast of the United States, it forms great loops, or meanders, in rough proportion to its speed, much as a garden hose bends and twists when the water is turned on full force.

At times the loops may cut across themselves, the detached loops heading slowly into the bordering sea as giant eddies. In such ways warm surface water is injected into polar waters. Cold polar water drifting equatorward is forced against the eastern coasts of continents and deflected to form slow, coastal currents, such as the Labrador Current, which flows southward along the Labrador and Newfoundland coast, and the Falkland Current, which flows northward along the Argentine coast.

The cold water meets warm water moving poleward at about 40° and flows under the warm water, eventually being added to the great surface gyres as the cold water gradually becomes warmed in low latitudes. As in the atmosphere, there is a complex mechanism in the sea involving "wheels within wheels," which runs our global heat transfer system and which is needed to remove the surplus heat of low latitudes.

BIOSPHERE

The biosphere is the zone of living organisms at or near the earth's surface, including parts of the lithosphere, hydrosphere, and atmosphere.

Since the beginning of life billions of years ago, countless forms of living things have spread throughout the world. Perhaps the most wonderful thing about life is that it has adapted to almost every environment found on earth.

Simple algae (single-celled plants) thrive in the hot springs of Yellowstone Park. Lichens fasten themselves to bare rock surfaces, requiring no soil and extracting their nourishment from the atmosphere. Underwater flash cameras have revealed life forms living in the ocean deeps without sunlight and under enormous water pressures. The Arctic tundra, frozen and windswept in winter, has a rich flora and fauna that lies waiting for the short summer season when the darkness disappears.

In the atmosphere, tiny grass seeds and thousands of plant spores and pollen particles ride the air streams a mile above the earth to be deposited in regions far from their place of origin. A close microscopic examination of a typical cultivated soil would show it teeming with life, with individuals continually being born, feeding, reproducing, adjusting their forms and activities to their special environments, and finally dying and adding their remains to the organic debris on which others will feed.

Nature has a remarkable way of working toward environmental balances, and the surface of our planet is a varied mixture or fusion of the four great spheres—lithosphere, atmosphere, hydrosphere, and biosphere. All of them are subject to change, and every change produces sympathetic alterations in each of the others. Some changes are global in scale and require millions of years to evolve; some are minute, taking only minutes to occur and involving only the most miniature characteristics of the environment.

Balances are thus relative in time, but they are no less real. The trend toward balances is especially evident in the biosphere. Life forms are very sensitive to environmental change, tending to form complex assemblages or communities that are nicely adjusted to the soil, the climate, the water supply, sunlight, and to each other, whether plant or animal.

Man is a culmination of the biosphere in two ways. First, he is the first organism to comprehend the totality of the environment and his own place in nature; and second, he is the only living creature to be able to consciously alter the environment to suit his needs. He can, if he so desires, sleep in cool comfort in the tropics, grow fresh strawberries in frozen Antarctica, or turn desert sands into luxurious market gardens.

One of the most highly specialized living organisms ever to appear on earth, man has become an independent variable, modifying the face of the earth wherever his needs require. There is no such thing as a completely natural environment anymore, except perhaps in those rare parts of the earth that are not as yet worth man's efforts to change them, such as the ocean depths, and the frozen polar regions.

Yet, with all his power and knowledge, man has much to learn of the complexities of organic balances, and his battles with living competitors for food and feed never ends.

THE LIVING PYRAMIDS

The plant and animal kingdoms, whether on land or in the sea, both are numerically arranged in the form of a truncated pyramid, or a pyramid whose tip has been cut off. The base of the pyramid, usually comprising by far the greatest total mass, is formed by the micro-forms, the tiny dwellers in the soil or in the surface layers of the sea.

Tiny plants and animals live together and depend on each other for their life cycles. As the life forms become larger, they become less numerous, but are no less a part of the dependent mass. The pyramid has no tip, because the requirement of mobility to obtain food places an upper limit on the size of living things.

PLANT WORLD. And so, within the plant world, the pyramid begins with the simple, single-celled algae, members of which form the green scum on stagnant pools, or band together in the oceans to form huge masses of seaweed, such as kelp. Soils everywhere are rich in micro-plant life, including the moulds or fungi whose *mycelia*, or mass of slender white threads may be seen entangling the needle litter beneath many pine forests. Such plants do not require sunlight and extract their carbohydrates from dead organic material.

Above the ground are other plants that attain various sizes in the competition for sunlight, water, and mineral foods. Some develop special devices to make effective use of the dim light on a shaded forest floor. Others thrive only in open sunlight, but require little water and so can meet competition. Some are water lovers, thriving in saturated bogs or along the edges of ponds. Competition eventually produces a mixture of large plants, or dominants, and smaller ones in each local environment.

The size of the dominants varies in different parts of the world and is related largely to the amount of water taken in through roots and the volume of water going out by transpiration through leaf and stem surfaces. The rainy tropics have large trees as dominants because of a plentiful supply of water the year round combined with warm temperatures all year to insure high transpiration rates.

In the tundra of Arctic regions, on the other hand, the plant life is rich and varied, but the dominants are small because of both low intakes and low discharges. Birches and willows that would have been trees a few hundred miles to the south here are stunted shrubs, a foot or two high. There is no liquid water for intake during the frozen winters, and transpiration rates are low because of cool temperatures, even during the short growing season. Nitrate deficiencies also contribute to the stunted growth of arctic plants, since micro-life forms are the usual source of supply, and soils are acid and almost devoid of bacteria.

Some large portions of the continents have grasses and herbaceous (nonwoody) plants as dominants. Others have brush and scattered low trees—a woodland rather than a forest. Even the great deserts of the world are not without their flora and dominants, sparse though they may be.

The dominants are only at the tops of the pyramids. Living among them are the more numerous members of the assemblages, many of whom are too small to see or are hidden beneath the surface of the soil.

ANIMAL KINGDOM. The animal kingdom also has its pyramids which vary in constituent members with different environments. Some local pyramids are much larger than others and represent fertile regions, where conditions are favorable for life. Since most animal life feeds on plant life of one kind or another or on other animals, the animal pyramids closely parallel the plant pyramids on the land as well as in the sea.

Especially fertile regions, like the cold waters of polar seas, or the mid-latitude prairies (grass by virtue of fire and not climate), have supported massive communities of both plants and animals, especially before man inserted himself into the pyramid.

There are dominants and sub-dominants among the members of the animal communities as well as among the plant assemblages, and together they adjust themselves to each other in balanced relationships. Every plant and animal in an assemblage has its place and there are natural checks to their increase or decrease in numbers.

Man's experience in introducing new plants and animals into new environments without the customary checks and balances has forcibly illustrated this point. Some of his most serious ecological problems have been the result of such events, both intentional and accidental, as the introduction of the jackrabbit and prickly pear into Australia, the starling and Japanese beetle into the United States, and *lantana* (a flowering shrub) into the Pacific Islands.

MAN'S ROLE. The differences in plant and animal communities are somewhat like those of soils or climates. With close scrutiny, there are minute differences every few feet that can be noted, and these are changing rapidly as their micro-environments change. Then too, there are the great global plant formations—the tropical rain forest, the grasslands, the deciduous (leaf-shedding) forest, the coniferous (cone-bearing) forest, the tropical scrub woodland, the desert shrubs, and the tundra. Each has its own unique features, its own assemblage of animals, large and small. Man is the only organism that roams them all, selecting here, destroying there—an independent, conscious force that will continue to alter the entire surface and to insert himself into every areal balance, whether local, regional, or global in scale.

—Joseph E. Van Riper

OCEANOGRAPHY

Scope.—The ocean is the most striking physical feature of our planet, covering over two-thirds of the globe's surface. Without the waters of the seas, there could be no life. Since earliest time, man has used the ocean as a highway, as a great moat to protect him from enemies, as a source of food, and as a final resting place. Only recently, however, has man begun to delve deeply into the sea to learn its secrets.

Oceanography is an environmental science encompassing the study of all processes in the ocean and its boundaries. It includes the study of plant and animal life at all depths (*biological oceanography*, or *marine biology*); the study of the origin of the ocean, its structure, and the stratigraphy and composition of its bottom sediments (*geological oceanography*, or *marine geology*); the study of sea water and its composition (*chemical oceanography*); the study of currents, tides, waves, temperature, salinity, density, and the general circulation of the sea (*physical oceanography*); the study of the food, mineral, and energy sources of the sea and the uses of the ocean for recreation, navigation, communication, and war (*marine technology*).

The Oceans.—Billions of years ago the earth was a lifeless planet plummeting through the darkness of space. As the mass of gases and molten metals cooled, water was squeezed from its interior. The planet became a world unique, as far as we know, in the entire solar system; it had an ocean.

■**ORIGIN OF LIFE.**—For millions of years the sterile waves lapped against the cold, dead shores. Then, through a series of processes whose nature is still unknown, organic matter developed and became concentrated into a living cell capable of reproducing.

There is no way of knowing what this first life was like, or what the conditions were that produced it. Chances are that some of the earliest organisms were similar to the single-celled plants still found in the surface layers of the ocean. These contain chlorophyll, the substance that enables plants to utilize the energy of sunlight to produce organic material from water and carbon dioxide. Through this process, known as *photosynthesis*, the oxygen of the earth's atmosphere was created from the water in the ocean.

Over the countless generations, spanning millions of years, differences developed among the single-celled organisms. Some preyed on others, so organisms evolved different methods of finding food and of escaping from being eaten; in response to changing conditions they developed different tolerances and sensitivities to light and to chemical variations. Eventually, life in the sea made the jump from simple individual cells to complicated, highly specialized plants and animals. (For further information see *Origin of Life*, Volume 13, **Health and Life Sciences**.)

■**CURRENTS.**—Only recently has man

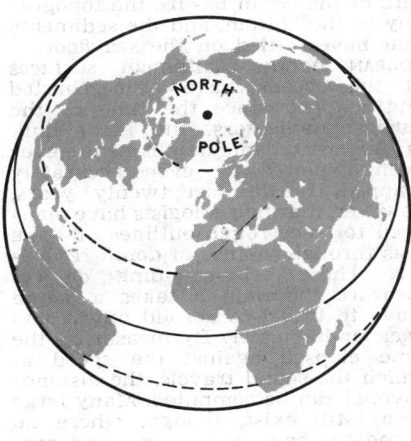

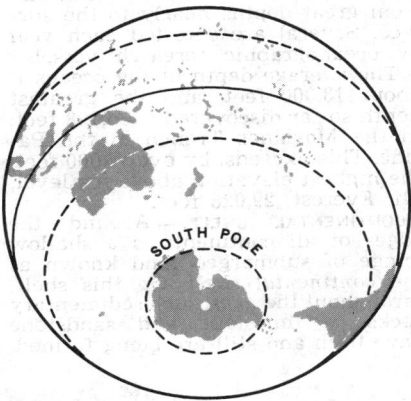

OCEANS, covering two-thirds of the earth, are our most striking physical feature.

known anything of the internal movements of the sea. The movement of water on the surface has been charted, but not the currents that flow beneath the surface. Now, however, through new techniques of measuring natural radioactivity, heat flow, and salt content, and by taking direct measurements of deep currents, a new picture of the ocean's circulation is being revealed.

Along with the horizontal currents in the ocean, there is a constant vertical motion. Practically nothing is known of this vertical movement, but it is vital to life in the sea, since it is the chief process by which the surface waters are constantly supplied with the nutrients required by the *phytoplankton*, the microscopic plants and animals without which no life could exist in the ocean.

Origin of Oceanography. — When man first ventured onto the sea to travel from one place to another, he began to navigate. He found that waves and currents would either help or hinder him in reaching his destination. He noticed that the tidal movements were greatest at certain times of the month, and he saw a correlation between the tidal movements and the moon phases. Going to the sea in search of food, he learned that certain

types of bottoms were apt to harbor certain kinds of fishes, mollusks, or crustaceans. As he became conscious of these things and began to search into their causes and relationships, he became, in essence if not in name, a student of oceanography.

The study of oceanography is as important today to navigation and shipping as it was to primitive sea-going man. Today oceanographic knowledge is vital not only to ships traveling on the surface of the sea, but also to craft that travel under the sea and in the air above. Information about currents, tides, and temperatures is necessary in both peacetime and wartime navigation and shipping, as are further studies of the strange behavior of sound and light under water. And today, more than ever before, knowledge of the ocean's circulation is of prime importance.

History of Oceanography.—Oceanography as a science began fairly recently. In 1750 the first scientific dredge was invented by Marsigli and Donati; a few years later, in 1769, Benjamin Franklin published the first chart of the Gulf Stream. During the following decade Captain James Cook, in his explorations of the Pacific, took a naturalist along to make observations and to record data. During Cook's second voyage, the first subsurface water temperatures were taken and were found to differ markedly from temperatures on the surface. On this voyage, too, some deep-water soundings were made, and a sample of blue mud was brought up from a depth of 683 fathoms.

■**DARWIN.**—It later became customary to take a trained naturalist on long survey or exploratory voyages. Charles Darwin's around-the-world voyage on the H.M.S. *Beagle* from 1831 to 1836 was one of the first purely scientific voyages. On this trip Darwin's two great theories were developed: the theory of natural selection and the less revolutionary but oceanographically more important theory of the origin of coral reefs.

■**MAURY.**—The first textbook on the subject of oceanography, entitled *The Physical Geography of the Sea*, appeared in 1855. The author, Matthew Fontaine Maury (1806–1873), was an American naval officer who was forced by an accident to retire from sea duty. He compiled and analyzed material from ships' logs; and the wind and current charts he drew from them soon became well-known throughout the world and greatly shortened sailing times between the continents. With the aid of a new sounding apparatus that employed a detachable weight, data were obtained from which Maury prepared the first bathymetric chart of the North Atlantic.

■**THOMPSON** — Until a century ago, most marine scientists believed the depths of the ocean to be utterly devoid of life. The absolute limit of life was thought to be about 300 fathoms. In 1860, however, the transatlantic cable, laid only two years before, was broken. Upon being brought up from a depth of 1,000 fathoms, it was found to be encrusted with living organisms, including a deep-sea coral. Subsequently Wyville Thompson made a series of deep hauls in North Atlantic waters—to a maximum depth of 2,435 fathoms— and in every case the dredge brought up living organisms.

The stage was now set for the first world-wide scientific investigation of the oceans. In 1872 Thompson's book, *The Depths of the Sea,* was published, and it stimulated the scientific world to renewed interest in the deep sea. In the same year the 2,000-ton British corvette H.M.S. *Challenger* embarked on a 70,000-mile voyage through the Atlantic, Pacific, and Indian oceans for the purpose of learning "everything about the sea." During the next three and a half years the *Challenger* scientists, under the direction of Wyville Thompson, and his assistant John Murray, collected animals at great depths, settling for all time the dispute over whether or not the depths are inhabited. Altogether they described a total of 4,417 new species of plants and animals. The *Challenger* expedition occupied 362 oceanographic stations and collected 77 water samples for total chemical analysis. Papers and reports of the voyage filled 50 volumes and required 20 years to complete. This mass of data, and the wide range of the samples collected, were vitally important to the development of modern oceanographic theory.

Geological Oceanography.—The marine geologist is interested in the structure of the ocean basins, the topography of the bottom, and the sediments that have settled on the sea floor.

■**OCEAN DEPTHS.**—Although surfaces of the oceans have been charted and mapped since the time of the earliest navigators, the great bulk of the vast oceanic depths have never been explored or even accurately mapped. In the last twenty years, however, marine geologists have managed to trace rough outlines of some seas through the use of *depth recorders.* These echo-sounding devices measure the time it takes a sound wave to travel to a solid object and back under water. By measuring the time elapsed against the speed at which the sound travels, the distance covered can be computed. Many large areas still exist, though, where no soundings have been made, and precipitous peaks still unknown may rise from great depths nearly to the surface. Several are detected each year by oceanographic research vessels.

The average depth of the oceans is about 13,000 feet, and the greatest depth so far discovered is 36,198 feet, in the Marianas Trench in the Pacific. This exceeds, by over 7,000 feet, the highest elevation above sea level, Mt. Everest, 29,028 feet.

■**CONTINENTAL SHELF.** — Around the edges of all continents is a shallow fringe of submerged land known as the *continental shelf.* On this shelf, throughout the ages, such sedimentary rocks as limestone and sandstone have been and still are being formed.

The continental shelf averages about 30 miles in width along most continents, although in some parts of Siberia it extends to 800 miles and along mountainous coasts it diminishes to almost nothing. The shelf is not a smooth, flat surface but is broken up into terraces, ridges, and hills.

Beyond the shelf, at a depth of about 600 feet, a more precipitous drop occurs. This is known as the *continental slope,* and it continues downward to the bottom of the sea— two or three miles, on the average. The deepest spots in the ocean, the ocean *trenches,* are found at the bottoms of the continental slopes.

The continental slopes are explained by the fact that the continental crust consists of rocks less dense than the oceanic crust. The continents can therefore be said to float, like ice floes, on the earth's mantle higher than the oceanic crust. Within the continental shelves and slopes are great canyons similar to deep river valleys, some as large as the Grand Canyon.

■**OCEAN FLOOR.**—The floor of the sea is quite different from the surface of the land. One reason is that the lack of erosion caused by wind, rain, and ice has preserved the submerged peaks, valleys, and canyons—just as the face of the moon has not been changed by weathering. However, there is also a tendency for sediment to very slowly drown these features on the sea floor.

■**SEAMOUNTS.**—All ocean basins have a mid-ocean rise and a range of moun-

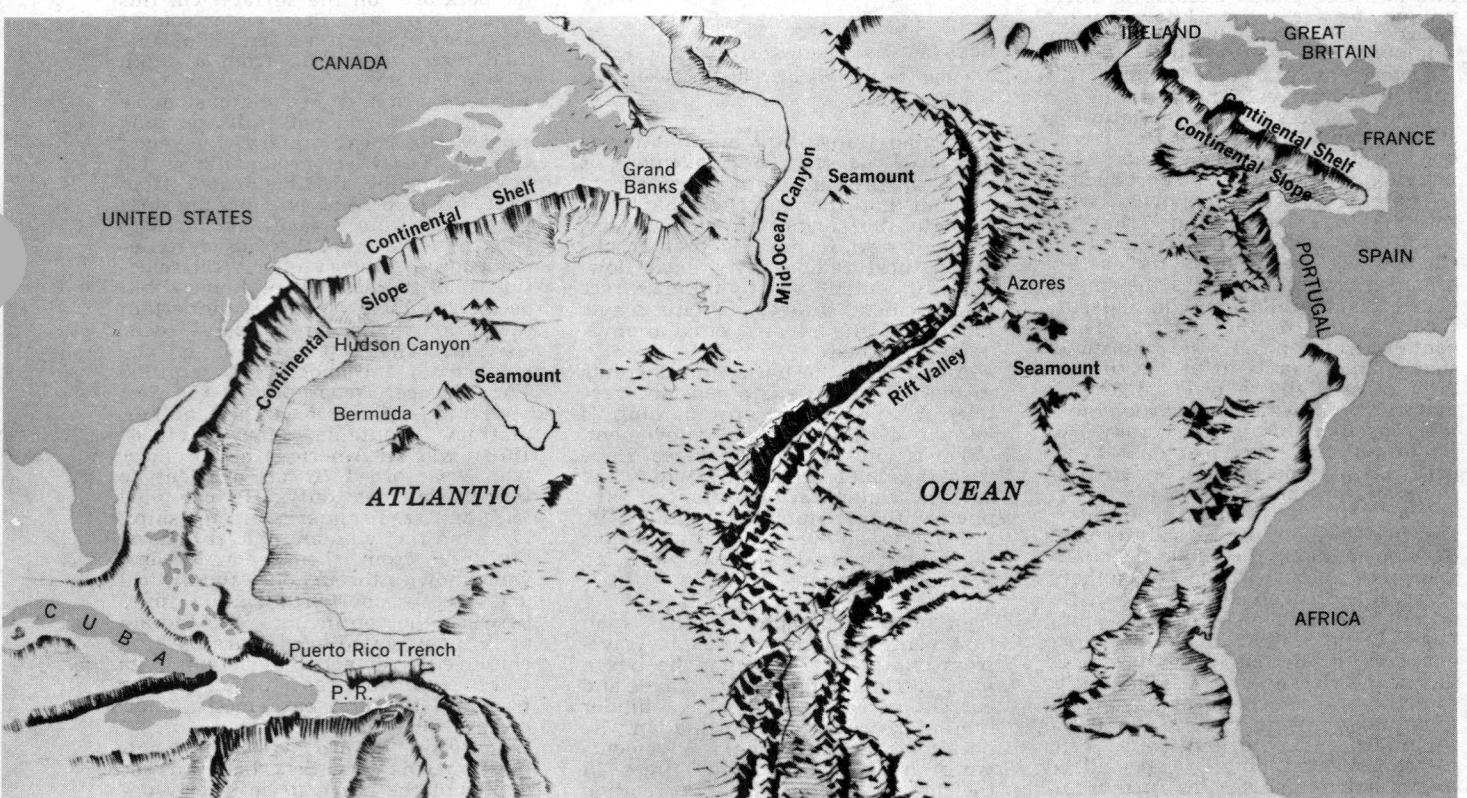

RELIEF OF THE OCEAN FLOOR. The floors of the oceans have their own valleys, mountains, and plains. Until recently, these regions could not be mapped. Today, scientists are discovering new regions at the ocean's bottom. Notice the 10,000-mile-long Mid-Atlantic Ridge.

tains down the middle. Thousands of volcanic peaks called *seamounts* dot the ocean floor. A comparative few of these peaks reach the surface to form islands, such as the Hawaiian chain in the Pacific or the Azores in the Atlantic. Many of the drowned peaks are the foundations of coral atolls, with the dead remains of reef-building corals and calcareous algae extending sometimes thousands of feet downward to the submerged peak. Since reef corals grow only in well-lighted waters (to a maximum depth of about 180 feet), a dead coral cap several thousand feet thick suggests that the atoll's base sank slowly over thousands or millions of years. This was first postulated by Charles Darwin and recently confirmed by deep drillings.

Many seamounts are flat on top, their peaks cut off at depths of 2,000 to 6,000 feet below the ocean's surface. These seamounts are called *guyots*. They were flattened by erosion at some period in the past when they were islands. Since the tops of these seamounts are found at various levels, it is unlikely that they were decapitated by a succession of great rises and falls of sea level. A more likely explanation is that they sank with the collapse of the earth's crust under their tremendous weight.

■SEDIMENT.—Much of the ocean floor is covered with a layer of sediment that has, in undisturbed regions, been accumulating for a hundred million years or more. This sediment contains a record of the earth's early history. Layers of volcanic ash are there, telling of great eruptions; ice-scarred stones from glaciers; and the remains of multitudinous planktonic plants and animals tell of climatic and evolutionary changes. Hollow tubes, or *corers*, are pushed into the sea floor to withdraw cross sections of the sedimentary carpet. An examination of the types of shells and other materials in these cores reveals the climatic variations of the past, and, by deduction, much information about the evolution of early life. Since some species of ancient marine life lived only in cold waters and others flourished in temperate or tropical waters, the sequence of fossils tells a great deal about sea temperatures and productivity millions of years ago.

Of primary importance in geological research on the composition of sediments is the determination of their specific origin. All sediments can be divided into three different groups according to their mode and place of origin. The first group is composed of material having its origin on land, such as soil, clay, and unweathered rock fragments. The second is made up of material formed in the ocean by inorganic precipitation. To this group belong some clays, manganese nodules, and other components of crystalline or gel consistency. The third group consists of organic material formed in the ocean, such as skeletons and other remains of animal and plant life. In addition to these sources, which account for most of the material, outer space contributes very tiny spherules of nickel-iron, remnants of meteorites.

By a careful study of the composition of the sediments, the relationship of the different components to one another, the shape of the particles, their chemical composition, grain size, and color, marine geologists are able to trace their origin and mode of transport before they were buried in the scientist's great treasure trove —the ocean floor.

There are several means by which sediments are transported to the ocean. The finest dust can be blown very long distances from the land (desert sand is found 2,000 miles from Africa in the Atlantic Ocean). Soil particles transported from North Africa across the Mediterranean may settle in rain on Germany, causing the landscape to be colored red. In many places on the ocean floor, the inorganic material consists nearly entirely of wind-transported matter.

The ocean currents also play a part. Their speed is much slower than the wind speed; on the other hand, the particles settle much more slowly in water than in air. Consequently, they may be carried across the ocean before they settle to the bottom. The greatest quantity of sediment, however, settles on the continetal shelf. There is evidence that on occasion large quantities of this unconsolidated material slide off the shelf and down the continental slope to the sea floor, spreading over large areas. Such large-scale movements, known as *turbidity currents*, may have played a part in forming the great canyons found on the continental slopes.

Chemical Oceanography.—The water that makes up the ocean probably had two sources. Some came as rain from the gases surrounding the earth; some from the earth's interior, forced from the rocks as they recrystallized to form the crust. Water is still being released from the interior of the earth through volcanic eruptions.

■SEA WATER.—Analyses of 77 water samples taken during the around-the-world cruise of H.M.S. *Challenger* established two vitally important properties of sea water: the *salinity*, or total content of salts, in sea water varies only slightly throughout the world; and, even where variations do exist, the relative quantity of the major dissolved salts remains constant. This property, known as the *constancy of relative proportions*, helps determine the salinity of water.

The major constituents of sea-water salts are sodium, chlorine, magnesium, sulfur, calcium, and potassium. In addition, sea water contains traces of all natural elements. Unlike the major constituents, these trace elements are found in widely differing proportions in different places and at different times. Studies of the concentrations of trace elements aid in understanding life processes in the ocean. Perhaps the appearance or

SEDIMENTS found on the ocean's floor are composed of many organic materials. When more than 30 per cent of a sediment consists of dead plant and animal life, it is called an *ooze*. Nearly half of the ocean floor is covered with Globigerina ooze.

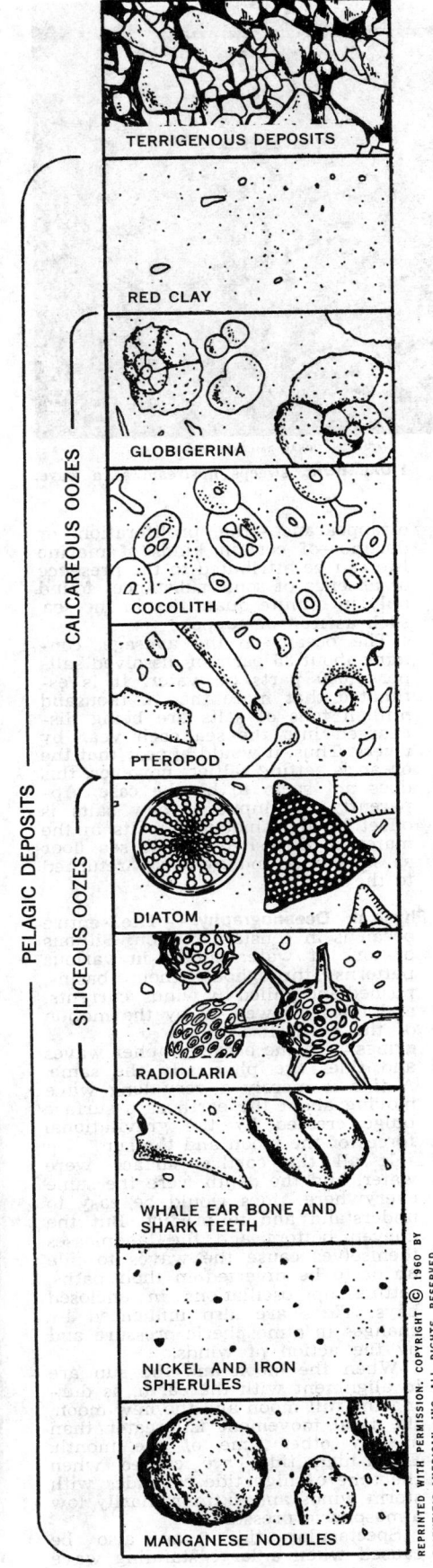

TERRIGENOUS DEPOSITS

RED CLAY

GLOBIGERINA

COCOLITH

PTEROPOD

CALCAREOUS OOZES

DIATOM

RADIOLARIA

SILICEOUS OOZES

PELAGIC DEPOSITS

WHALE EAR BONE AND SHARK TEETH

NICKEL AND IRON SPHERULES

MANGANESE NODULES

CANADIAN NATIONAL RAILWAYS
TIDAL BORE sweeps upstream as a wave.

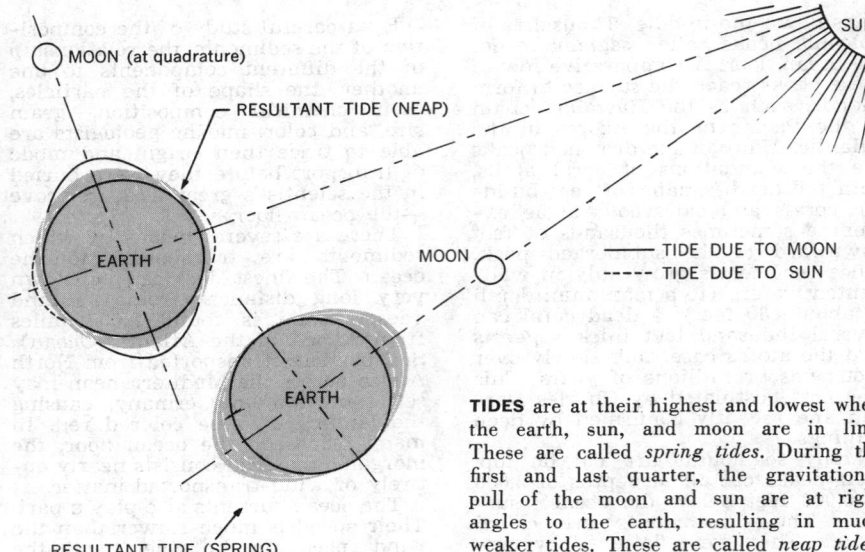

MOON (at quadrature)

RESULTANT TIDE (NEAP)

EARTH

EARTH

SUN

MOON

—— TIDE DUE TO MOON
---- TIDE DUE TO SUN

RESULTANT TIDE (SPRING)

TIDES are at their highest and lowest when the earth, sun, and moon are in line. These are called *spring tides*. During the first and last quarter, the gravitational pull of the moon and sun are at right angles to the earth, resulting in much weaker tides. These are called *neap tides*.

disappearance—the proliferation or decline—of certain kinds of marine life can be attributed to the presence or absence of some substances found only in minute quantities in the sea, such as iron or copper.

The ocean, on the average, contains about 35 parts of dissolved salts per 1,000 parts of water. It is estimated that more than a thousand million tons of salts are being discharged into the sea each year by rivers. Thus, it would appear that the ocean is getting saltier; however, this does not seem to be the case. Apparently the input of new salts is offset by the amount of salts in the materials deposited on the sea floor as sediments and by spray returned to the land.

Physical Oceanography. — The entire ocean is in constant motion. Billions of tons of water course in various patterns throughout their basins, pushed and pulled by winds, currents, and tides, as well as by the motion of the earth itself.

■**TIDES.**—To the oceanographer waves and tides are physically the same. A tide is merely a very long wave moving about the earth as a surface bulge created by the gravitational forces of the moon and the sun.

If all the earth's surface were water, and the depth were the same everywhere, tides would be easy to understand and to predict. But the uneven bottom and the landmasses themselves cause the waves to pile up or to be diverted in their paths, setting up oscillations in enclosed bays. Tides are also influenced by changes in atmospheric pressure and by the action of winds.

When the moon and the sun are in alignment with the earth, as during the full moon and the new moon, the tidal movement is greater than at any other time of the month. Extra-high tides are caused when the time of high tide coincides with storm winds and extraordinarily low atmospheric pressure.

Spectacular tides can also be caused when a large standing wave

arrives at the same time as a high tide. When the tide in some areas rises high enough to move against a river, it may sweep upstream as a thundering wave called a *tidal bore*. Tidal bores occur in certain rivers in Europe, North America, South America, and Asia. One of the highest tides is that which occurs in the Bay of Fundy in eastern Canada.

■**WAVES.**—There are two basic kinds of waves: standing waves and progressive waves. A *standing wave* moves back and forth in a confined space, its speed and size determined by the size and depth of the bay or estuary where it moves. A *progressive wave*, on the other hand, moves across an open area. In neither case do the particles of water themselves move very much. They may move in the arc of a pendulum, or they may travel in a circular motion, but they move very little horizontally.

This motion is the same in all waves, from the smallest ripple to the greatest ocean roller. The highest point in a wave is the *crest,* and the

lowest is the *trough;* the *height* is measured by the distance between these two points. The *length* is the distance from one crest to that of the following wave, while the *period* of a wave is the time it takes to pass a given point. In the open ocean, waves higher than 25 feet are rare, although waves of 60 and perhaps even 100 feet have been reported in the great unbroken expanses of the Pacific and Antarctic oceans.

The great waves commonly known as *tidal waves,* but more accurately called *tsunamis,* are of seismic, not tidal, origin. Caused by earthquakes on the sea floor or near shore on land, a tsunami wave is hardly noticeable at sea, but it may pile up to form tremendous crests on striking shore. Hawaii and Japan have suffered many devastating tsunamis. The speed of a tsunami wave is very great and is determined by the ocean depth.

Not all ocean waves are on the surface; the sea has internal waves as well. These waves develop on the interfaces between layers of dif-

EWING GALLOWAY
TSUNAMIS, or tidal waves, are caused by earthquakes. They are most common in the Pacific.

ferent density and are usually larger than surface waves, although they move more slowly. The existence of these waves has only recently been determined, largely because of their effect on submarines; and much more is still to be learned about their formation and movements.

■**CURRENTS.**—Surface currents of water are driven mainly by winds. Each hemisphere has three similar wind zones. Along the equator and extending north and south for some 30 degrees of latitude, the wind blows from the east. For the next 30 degrees, the wind is primarily from the west. Nearer the poles, the wind again comes from the east. The prevailing winds—equatorial easterlies and middle latitude westerlies—impart a clockwise circulation to the surface waters of the North Pacific and North Atlantic and counterclockwise circulation to those of the South Pacific and South Atlantic.

Where the wind blows steadily in the same direction the water mass, on the average, tends to move away at an angle 90 degrees to the right of the wind direction in the Northern Hemisphere and 90 degrees to the left in the Southern Hemisphere. The surface moves at 45 degrees. This angle of difference increases with depth. This effect, known as the *Ekman transport*, can produce upwellings when winds blow parallel to coastlines. As warm surface water is pushed away from a coast, colder water from underneath takes its place. The Ekman transport also creates *eddies*, or circular movements of water, such as the Sargasso Sea.

The direction of the ocean currents, as well as the great vertical movements in the sea, are also determined by the differences in the temperature of the water. All parts of the ocean are layered, with the warmer water at the surface. Deep water is always close to the freezing point, even at the equator. In tropical and temperate regions, the upper warmer layers tend to stay on top because they are less dense than the cold, deeper water. Near the poles, however, the surface layers are cooled by the frigid air, become heavy, and tend to sink underneath warmer layers. They then move in the direction of the equator.

Water flows toward areas of lower pressure. Cold water weighs more than warm water, and the higher the salinity, the greater the weight. A horizontal movement of water results as the water flows down a horizontal pressure gradient. As water flows from a high-pressure area to a low-pressure area, it follows a curved path. This curving path is caused by the rotation of the earth and is known as the *Coriolis force*. This phenomenon causes the paths of objects moving in the Northern Hemisphere to turn to the right, and those in the Southern Hemisphere to turn to the left.

Biological Oceanography.—It is almost certain that life began in the sea, for all animal phyla on earth have members living in the marine environment. Furthermore, the body

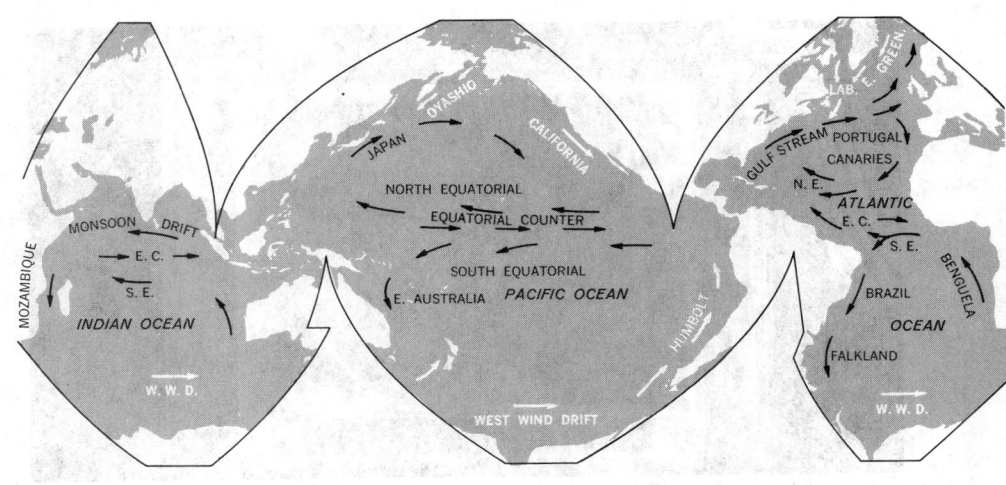

SURFACE CIRCULATION of the world's oceans is controlled mainly by winds. The flow is in a clockwise direction in the Northern Hemisphere and a counterclockwise direction in the Southern Hemisphere. The cooler surface currents are indicated with white arrows.

fluids of even the land animals are similar to the salty liquid known as sea water. Human blood, for example, is a saline solution that has many of the properties of sea water.

■**PLANKTON.**—All living organisms are either plants or animals. The tiny plants that drift free in the ocean are known as *phytoplankton*. "Phyto" means 'plants,' and "plankton" is from the Greek *planktos*, meaning 'wandering.' Since all plant life depends on sunlight, and sunlight penetrates only to about 600 feet, all chains of life in the sea are linked to the tiny organisms of the upper layers.

Plankton can be defined as those animals and plants that are carried by currents. Since they either drift without independent movement or swim weakly, they cannot move against the current.

The *diatoms* are among the most important forms of life in the sea. These single-celled plants are composed of two shells of silica that fit together like a box with a lid. Other forms of phytoplankton are the *dinoflagellates*, microscopic plants that swim about by beating appendages called flagella.

Mixed with the plants in the upper layers are the planktonic animals that are known collectively as *zooplankton*. Smallest and simplest of these are the *protozoa*, single-celled creatures of a wide diversity of form that feed on the single-celled plants and are themselves eaten by larger and more complex planktonic animals, such as copepods, jellyfish, crustaceans, mollusks, and the larval forms of fishes.

The surface waters of the colder seas hold prodigious quantities of plankton, which furnish food for the great schools of mackerel and herring, the sea birds, and even the herds of baleen whales that subsist on planktonic crustaceans known as krill. This abundance of plant and animal life is made possible by the mineral richness of the colder waters rising from deeper layers.

Although it is evident that cool waters provide more nutrient salts,

warmer seas show a much greater diversity of forms. While an area like the Grand Banks of Newfoundland might hold schools of millions of cod and haddock and support a great fishery, a coral atoll might hold thousands of species of marine animals but relatively few of any one species. The reason for this is that life cycles are speeded up in tropical waters; hence a greater number of genetic differences show up.

■**NEKTON.**—The term *nekton* covers the free-swimming creatures that are largely independent of tides, currents, and waves. This group includes most marine fishes, from the tiny sardines to the great whale sharks, which may exceed 50 feet in length. Also among nektonic creatures are the animals of the middle depths, those perpetually black regions thousands of feet down, inhabited by bizarre lantern fish and other grotesque creatures with luminous organs, cavernous mouths, and rapierlike teeth. Here there is no light, and no plants grow. All life must subsist on other living creatures or on the remains of dead animals and plants sifting down from the surface. Most creatures in the middle regions are small, but here are also found the giant squid and the massive sperm whale that pursues the squid in prodigious breath-holding dives of 2,000 feet or more.

■**BENTHOS.**—The *benthic* animals, the dwellers of the sea floor, are, in many cases, almost identical to bottom forms found in shallow water. There are brittle stars, sea cucumbers, sea spiders, crustaceans, flounderlike fishes, and others that would not look greatly out of place on any tidal flat. On the floor of the ocean, the pressure is thousands of pounds per square inch, but it is so evenly distributed throughout the bodies of these creatures that they feel no pressure at all. Except for certain animals with air spaces in their bodies (such as many fishes that have air bladders), the deep-water creatures can be raised from the greatest depths to the surface without injury due to changes in pressure.

GENERAL ELECTRIC RESEARCH LABORATORY

ARTIFICIAL GILL extracts air from the water but prevents the passage of the liquid.

■**TAXONOMY.**—Biological oceanography takes many forms. Most early students were primarily taxonomists who collected, pickled, classified, and described organisms. Many an outstanding authority on a certain group never saw a living member of that group. Now that the kinds of organisms found in the sea have become better known, biologists have begun to study these animals and plants as living organisms, not as museum specimens. Today studies are made in the undisturbed natural habitats of organisms, wherever possible.

Such environmental studies have been given great impetus by the development of undersea research vehicles and SCUBA (Self-Contained Underwater Breathing Apparatus). With SCUBA, almost any scientist can become a diver and observe marine life in its own habitat. Many shallow-water studies are made with no more than a diving mask, a snorkel, and a pair of flippers.

■**MARINE ECOLOGY.**—With this new ease of penetration into the sea—or at least into the upper sunlit layers—the scientific discipline known as *marine ecology* is coming into its own.

Ecology, or environmental biology, can be defined as a study of organisms in relation to their environment; it is also a study of the interrelationships of individuals and groups. There are many different approaches to ecology, of course. One biologist may be interested in the ecology of a particular taxonomic group—for example, fishes, crustaceans, worms—or even a single species of one of these. Others may be interested in pelagic, benthic, littoral, or coral reef ecology, and yet others in communities or populations. One kind of ecologist may be interested in *function,* the things that animals and plants do. The study of animal *behavior* is still in its infancy, especially as applied to marine animals, but several long-range projects are now under way.

Marine Technology.—Marine scientists and technicians are using the tools and techniques of the oceanographer to harvest many of the resources of the sea. Offshore drilling rigs in the Gulf of Mexico tap reservoirs of oil beneath the sea floor, while prospectors with aqualungs and dredges are bringing up diamonds from the continental shelf off Africa. The use of recorded mating sounds to attract food fishes to nets is under experiment by some fishing fleets. Another technological invention transferred from land is undersea television, which is in use as an important oceanographic research aid and also as a tool of the fishing and communications industries. Even the water of the sea and the invisible plankton that inhabit it are being put to man's service. Modern plants now extract magnesium from sea water, and new and cheaper methods are being developed for producing fresh water from the sea. Eventually we will find a way to utilize directly the vast supply of protein-rich plankton.

Researchers are working on ways to reduce the devastation of hurricanes and the perennial damage caused by beach erosion and by shipworms, barnacles, and other ocean pests. Investigators seek safe, clean methods for disposing of industrial, human, and atomic wastes, and for coping with increased oil pollution.

From a military standpoint, our greatest problem of national defense is an oceanographic one. More effective methods of communication under water must be found—from submarine to submarine and from submarine to surface craft and airplanes—and of detecting and destroying enemy submarines in time of war. Radar and radio cannot be used under water, so all detection and communications systems in the sea involve the use of sound.

The unknown regions and untapped resources of the sea present one of the greatest challenges to man's ingenuity and daring. As new methods of oceanic exploration are devised and craft descend for longer periods into the ocean depths, men will finally return to the seas from which they came, to explore, to work, and perhaps even to live in the last frontier regions of the earth.

—Friedrich Frans Koczy;
Cesare Emiliani

For Further Reference

Bascom, Willard. *Waves and Beaches.* Anchor Books, 1964.

Davis, Richard A., Jr. *Oceanography: An Introduction to the Marine Environment.* William C. Brown, 1987.

King, Cuchlaine Audrey Muriel. *Introduction to Oceanography.* McGraw-Hill, 1963.

Maury, Matthew Fontaine. *The Physical Geography of the Sea.* Harvard University Press, 1963.

Turekian, Karl K. *Oceans.* Prentice-Hall, 1968.

STANDARD OIL COMPANY, NEW JERSEY

WEALTH FROM THE SEA. The vast mineral reserves stored beneath the ocean's floor are only now being tapped. Here, an oil derrick is being set up in the Gulf of Mexico.

METEOROLOGY

Meteorology is the science of the atmosphere. The *meteorologist* deals with atmospheric processes. Although the meteorologist is often thought of as one who forecasts weather conditions, there is much more to meteorology than weather forecasting. Some meteorologists, for instance, are concerned only with the effects of the atmosphere on the flight of missiles and satellites. Some deal with atmospheric processes as they affect the health and behavior of plants, animals, and human beings. Other meteorologists work with weather conditions as they influence the operations of specific businesses and industries, and still others concern themselves entirely with seeking ways to modify and control the weather. These are only a few of the studies that make up the science of meteorology. In essence, the goal of the meteorologist is to be able to describe and predict the atmosphere's behavior. The first step is to learn everything possible about the properties of the air in which we live.

Historical Background.—The early attempts at weather forecasting related the condition of the surroundings, or the appearance of certain objects, to particular types of future weather. This type of weather prediction dates back to at least 700 B.C., when the Assyrians used the ring around the sun or moon as a sign of coming weather—a sign that is still used. The first book on meteorology was written by Aristotle in about 350 B.C., but no real progress was made in the development of meteorology as a science until the invention of the thermometer by Galileo Galilei in 1640 and of the barometer by Evangelista Torricelli in 1643. The use of these instruments led to recognition of the fact that high-pressure and low-pressure areas can be associated with certain types of weather. In 1743 Benjamin Franklin presented evidence that high-pressure and low-pressure systems move across the earth and carry the weather with them.

Composition of the Atmosphere.—We live at the bottom of a mixture of gases that envelops the earth. This mixture of gases is called *air. Pure, dry air* is made up of 78 per cent nitrogen, 21 per cent oxygen, less than 1 per cent argon, and very small amounts of carbon dioxide, hydrogen, neon, helium, krypton, and xenon. *Ordinary air* contains many other substances, the most important of which is water vapor. Depending upon prevailing conditions, the water vapor can be either liquid or solid, producing fog, clouds, rain, sleet, snow, or hail. Very small sea-salt and dust particles in the air provide nuclei around which rain drops form. Impurities in the air such as smoke and dust sometimes become great enough to cause the condition known as *smog.*

■**TROPOSPHERE.**—Although the atmosphere extends to great heights, most of it is contained in a six- to ten-

ATMOSPHERIC REGIONS

mile-high layer that is highest over the equator and lowest over the poles. Since almost all water vapor is distributed throughout this layer, most ordinary weather conditions occur within it. This region of the atmosphere is called the *troposphere.* The troposphere is characterized by a decrease in temperature with each increase in altitude—the greater the height, the lower the temperature. On the average the temperature in the troposphere drops slightly more than 1° F. with each 300-foot increase in elevation.

■**TROPOPAUSE AND STRATOSPHERE.**—The layer separating the troposphere and *stratosphere* is known as the *tropopause.* Within the stratosphere the atmosphere thins with each increase in altitude until, at a height of 60 miles, all but one-millionth of the atmosphere is below.

■**IONOSPHERE.**—The region above the stratosphere is called the *ionosphere* because it contains several layers of electrically charged particles known as *ions.* These particles reflect radio waves, thereby making world-wide radio communication possible. The colorful *aurora borealis,* or northern lights, produced by charged particles from the sun, also occurs in the ionosphere.

■**TEMPERATURE.**—The temperature of the atmosphere decreases through

the troposphere, becoming as low as −80° F. at the tropopause. It remains constant through the lower stratosphere until, at an elevation of from 12 to 15 miles, it begins to rise again. Above 30 miles the very thin air may become as warm as 70° F. This rise in temperature is due to absorption of ultraviolet rays from the sun by the *ozone,* a form of oxygen found in this region. Above this warm layer the temperature again decreases steadily until, at a height of 45 to 50 miles, it has fallen to as low as −90° F. There are indications that the temperature again begins to rise above the 50-mile level, but the atmosphere is so thin at this height that it is difficult to measure temperature in the usual manner.

Elements of Weather

■**ATMOSPHERIC PRESSURE.**—The expression "light as air" and the fact that air is invisible to the eye imply that, in a physical sense, there is nothing to the atmosphere. Air is quite heavy, especially near the surface of the earth. The weight of air over a unit area is called *air pressure.*

On the average the weight of the atmosphere over every square inch of the earth's surface at sea level is 14.7 pounds, or *one atmosphere.* Thus the total weight of air on a 100-foot square plot of ground is more than 10,000 tons. Buildings and other objects are not crushed by this weight because the same pressure inside them equalizes the outside pressure and makes the resultant force zero.

Air pressure is an important element of weather because, generally speaking, high pressure can be associated with fair weather and low pressure can be associated with clouds and precipitation. Pressure patterns and pressure changes are important, therefore, as indicators of future weather. In addition, it is the difference between pressure in one area and another that causes the air to move, thereby creating winds.

■**PRESSURE MEASUREMENT.**—An instrument used to measure air pressure is a *barometer.* The most direct method of measuring the pressure or weight per unit area of air is to balance it against the weight of some other substance. Mercury is usually used for this purpose because it is the heaviest of liquids.

A simple *mercury-in-glass barometer* consists of a glass tube about three feet long that is open at one end and closed at the other. The tube, filled with mercury, stands vertically in a dish of mercury, its open end submerged. Since the weight of the air pressing down on the surface of the mercury in the container will support a column of mercury of equal weight in the glass tube, air pressure is often spoken of in terms of the equivalent height of a mercury column. When barometric pressure is stated as 30.00 inches, it means simply that the weight per unit area of the air is equal to the weight per unit area of a column of mercury 30 inches high. This type of barometer is very accurate, but has numerous disadvantages. It is difficult to transport; the glass tube is easily broken; mercury can be harmful under certain circumstances and is subject to expansion and contraction with temperature variations.

The *aneroid barometer* is portable, liquidless, and automatically corrected for temperature contraction and expansion. Most aneroid barometers have a dial face with the descriptive words "stormy," "rain," "fair," and "dry" printed on it. Mechanically, it consists of a "dry" pressure-sensing element linked by a system of levers and gears to a pointer moving across the dial face.

The barometer is probably the most useful instrument in making a weather forecast, but should not itself be considered as a forecaster of weather. Although it frequently proves true that high pressure means "fair" weather and low pressure means "bad" weather, there are some exceptions. It is, therefore, important to realize that the function of the barometer is to read air pressure; the change in pressure is more important than the actual reading. A pressure change indicates that a change in the weather is imminent; the more rapid the change in pressure, the sooner the change in prevailing weather conditions will occur.

■**TEMPERATURE.**—The earth's atmosphere behaves much like a heat engine operating on energy supplied by the sun. *Temperature* is the measure of the intensity of heat energy supplied. Although as a concept temperature is technically more difficult to define than pressure, it is more easily understood because of the human body's temperature sense. The body can feel temperature differences (that some things are warmer than others), but it cannot ordinarily feel differences in atmospheric pres-

sure. The body sensations of hot and cold are very crude measurements, but accurate values of temperature can be established with instruments.

■**TEMPERATURE MEASUREMENT.** — Most objects change in size as the temperature changes, expanding as the temperature increases and contracting as the temperature decreases. This relationship is used to assign a definite numerical value to a temperature.

In 1724 Gabriel Daniel Fahrenheit, a German physicist, produced a *thermometer* similar to the instrument in use today, consisting of a thin glass tube with a bulb or "bulge" at one end. The bulb is filled with mercury; as the temperature rises, the mercury expands and is forced up into the tube. The level of the mercury in the tube, gauged on a calibrated scale, indicates the temperature—the higher the mercury rises in the tube, the higher the temperature.

Alcohol is frequently used in place of mercury because it has two advantages. Alcohol has a much lower freezing point and can therefore be used to measure air temperatures at which mercury would freeze; and it can be colored, making it readable.

There are many other types of thermometers used for special purposes. The *bimetallic thermometer* consists of two strips of different metals with different expansion characteristics—one expands more than the other as the temperature rises. When the two metals are fastened together, the resulting compound strip bends as the temperature changes because of the difference in rates of the metals' expansion. One end of the compound strip is fixed, and a pointer attached to the free end moves across a temperature scale as the strip changes shape. A pen is sometimes attached to the free end of the bimetal strip instead of a

pointer. The pen is positioned so that it touches a piece of graph paper wrapped around a slowly rotating cylinder. Such an instrument, called a *thermograph,* keeps a continuous record of temperature. Thermometers designed to read the highest and lowest temperatures over a given period of time are called *maximum thermometers* and *minimum thermometers,* respectively.

■**HUMIDITY.**—The amount of water in the air in vapor or gaseous form is referred to as *humidity.* Compared to the amount of oxygen and nitrogen in the atmosphere, the amount of water vapor is very small—usually only 1 to 2 per cent. The total volume of water vapor in the atmosphere, however, is substantial. The amount of water, for instance, carried in the atmosphere over the continent of North America is about six times the amount flowing in all the rivers on the continent.

Water vapor in the atmosphere sometimes condenses to form clouds, fog, or rain; sometimes it solidifies to form snow, sleet, or hail. Water vapor is, therefore, responsible for most of the conditions we commonly call "weather." Water vapor also affects the distribution of heat in the atmosphere by absorbing and reflecting solar radiation and by releasing heat during the process of condensation. The amount of water vapor in the air also governs, to a large extent, the degree of human comfort, especially in hot weather.

■**HUMIDITY MEASUREMENT.**—A *hygrometer* measures water vapor (humidity) in the atmosphere through the use of substances that vary in size with humidity. Hair, for instance, expands when the humidity increases and contracts when it decreases. Human hair is especially sensitive to such changes, and is used in an instrument called a *hair hygrometer.*

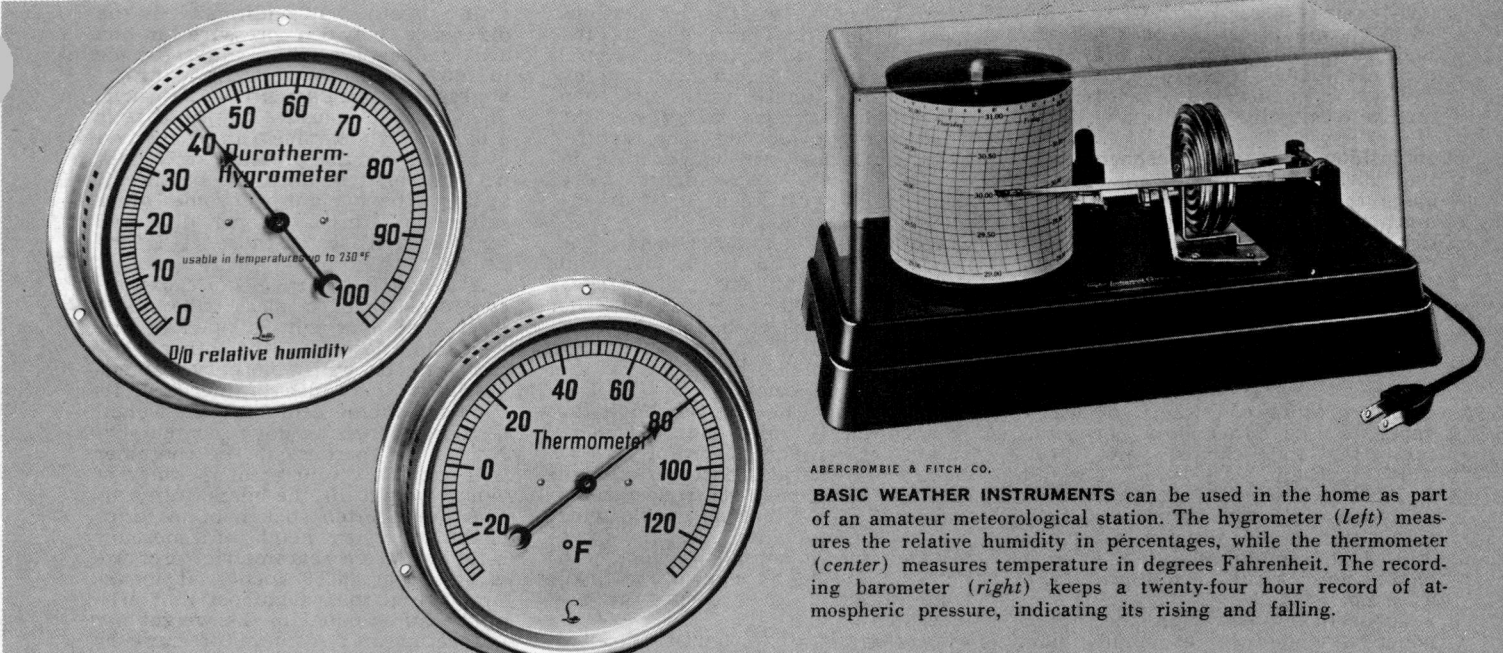

ABERCROMBIE & FITCH CO.

BASIC WEATHER INSTRUMENTS can be used in the home as part of an amateur meteorological station. The hygrometer (*left*) measures the relative humidity in percentages, while the thermometer (*center*) measures temperature in degrees Fahrenheit. The recording barometer (*right*) keeps a twenty-four hour record of atmospheric pressure, indicating its rising and falling.

One end of a bundle of hairs is fixed, and the other end is attached to a pointer that moves across a humidity scale as the hair length changes. An instrument of this type making a constant record of humidity changes, in the same manner that a thermograph records temperature changes, is called a *hygrograph.*

An instrument that measures humidity through the principle of evaporation is called a *psychrometer. Evaporation,* the process of changing a liquid into a gas, is a cooling process. As such it is used to measure atmospheric humidity. The psychrometer consists of two liquid-in-glass thermometers. The bulb of one of these, called the *wet-bulb thermometer,* is covered with a tight-fitting piece of cloth that has been dipped in water. As the water evaporates, the bulb is cooled, thus lowering the wet-bulb thermometer's temperature reading. The other thermometer records the ordinary air temperature, known in this instance as the *dry-bulb temperature.* Due to the evaporative cooling, the temperature of the wet-bulb thermometer is normally lower than that of the dry-bulb thermometer—the lower the relative humidity, the greater the difference between wet-bulb and dry-bulb temperatures. Using these readings, the relative humidity is then determined by reference to *psychrometric tables.*

An instrument that utilizes condensation in measuring the water vapor content of the atmosphere is called a *dew-point hygrometer.* Just as liquid water can be evaporated into the air, water vapor can also be drawn from the air in the form of a liquid. This process is called *condensation.* As air is cooled, a temperature is reached at which condensation occurs. This is known as the *dew-point temperature.* For every value of water vapor content (humidity) there exists a corresponding dew point. The point at which condensation begins and dew forms is the *dew point*—the more water vapor in the air, the higher the temperature at which the vapor will begin to condense. The dew-point hygrometer usually consists of a piece of highly polished metal arranged so that its temperature can be measured as it is cooled to the dew point. An advanced type of this instrument consists of an electronically cooled mirror that is automatically monitored by a photoelectric cell, which signals the point at which condensation occurs.

■HUMIDITY UNITS.—The amount of water vapor in the air at a given temperature has a certain maximum value. When that value is reached, the air is said to be *saturated* or to have reached its water-vapor capacity—the point at which the water vapor begins to condense into a liquid or a solid, and fog, clouds, rain, snow, frost, or dew begin to form. It is important, therefore, to know just how close the air is to saturation. The amount of water vapor in a unit volume of air is called the *absolute humidity.*

Relative humidity defines the ratio of absolute humidity to capacity—a measure of how close the air is to saturation at a given temperature.

$$\text{relative humidity (per cent)} = \frac{\text{absolute humidity}}{\text{capacity}} \times 100$$

Since capacity depends upon temperature, relative humidity also depends upon temperature. Thus, even if the absolute humidity remains the same, the relative humidity will change; it will be higher at lower temperatures. In other words, although the actual amount of water vapor in the air remains the same, the relative humidity will fall during the day as the temperature rises and increase at night as the air cools. Atmospheric pressure is another factor to be considered because as the pressure changes, the volume of air will also change, thus affecting both absolute and relative humidity.

A humidity unit that remains constant although pressure or temperature varies is defined as *specific humidity,* the amount of water vapor per unit *mass* of air. Specific humidity is usually expressed as grams of vapor per kilogram of air. One kilogram of air containing 15 grams of water vapor at a given temperature and pressure has a specific humidity of 15 grams per kilogram. If the water vapor content remains the same, this value will likewise remain the same for all temperatures and pressures because the mass of air is not affected by temperature and pressure changes.

Clouds.—Weather conditions on the earth's surface are often governed by conditions at higher altitudes. In the past, cloud observations were the only available means of determining conditions in the upper atmosphere. They are still useful indicators of weather changes.

U.S. DEPARTMENT OF COMMERCE, WEATHER BUREAU

RADIOSONDE is carried aloft by a balloon.

■CLOUD TYPES.—The highest clouds are *cirrus clouds.* "Cirrus," which means "curl" in Latin, describes the characteristic hooks or curls these clouds have at their borders (sometimes called "mares' tails"). Cirrus clouds are feathery and white, and range to heights at which temperatures are well below freezing. These clouds are therefore usually composed of ice crystals. When the cirrus clouds remain feathery or slowly disappear, fair weather is indicated. When they grow thicker and blanket the sky, it is likely that lower clouds will form, followed by rain or snow.

Cirrostratus clouds take the form of a continuous white sheet and often give the sky a milky appearance. Enough sunlight penetrates this sheet to cast shadows on the ground. Like cirrus clouds, the cirrostratus are made up of ice crystals, and generally produce a halo or ring around the sun or moon; only clouds composed of ice crystals produce such a ring. When cirrostratus clouds increase and thicken, rain or snow can be expected within 24 hours.

Cirrocumulus clouds appear at high levels as small, white patches. When arranged in rows or waves, they produce what is sometimes called a "mackerel sky." Cirrocumulus, cirrus, and cirrostratus clouds are usually classed together. They all form at altitudes exceeding 20,000 feet, and are sometimes called *high clouds.*

Altostratus clouds form a heavy, gray sheet across the sky. The sun is usually visible as a bright spot, but is not bright enough to cast shadows on the ground. These clouds are composed of water droplets, even at temperatures below freezing, and therefore do not form halos. The appearance of altostratus clouds usually means that rain or snow will follow shortly.

Altocumulus clouds appear in closely spaced patches and are white or gray. They are similar in appearance to the cirrocumulus variety, but are larger and usually at lower levels. When they are in the proper position between the sun and the earth below, beautiful colors often appear around their edges as the sunlight passes through the water droplets. Alto-type clouds usually range from 6,500 to 20,000 feet above the earth and are called the *middle clouds.*

Stratocumulus clouds are irregularly shaped, appearing in rolls or patches that often blend together. They are larger and thicker, and appear at lower levels than altocumulus clouds. Sometimes only a few thousand feet above the ground, stratocumulus clouds often appear just after a storm, but before complete clearing sets in. Light showers of rain or snow may fall from these clouds.

Stratus clouds are low-level gray sheets located from a few hundred to a few thousand feet above the ground. They are relatively thin, and sometimes produce light drizzle.

Nimbostratus clouds are low, dark, gray clouds. They are thicker and darker than the stratus variety and often are the result of a thickening and lowering of altostratus clouds.

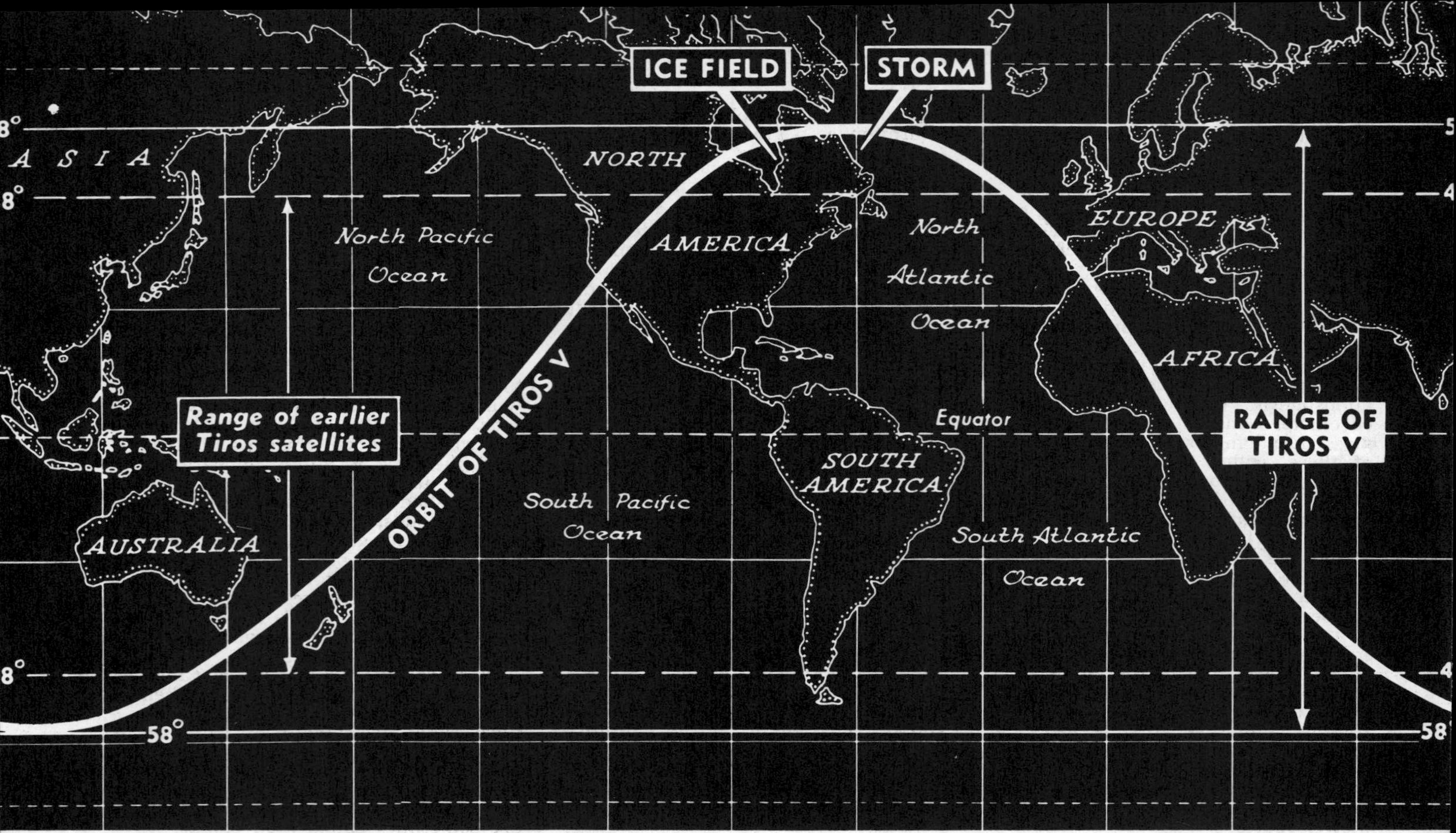

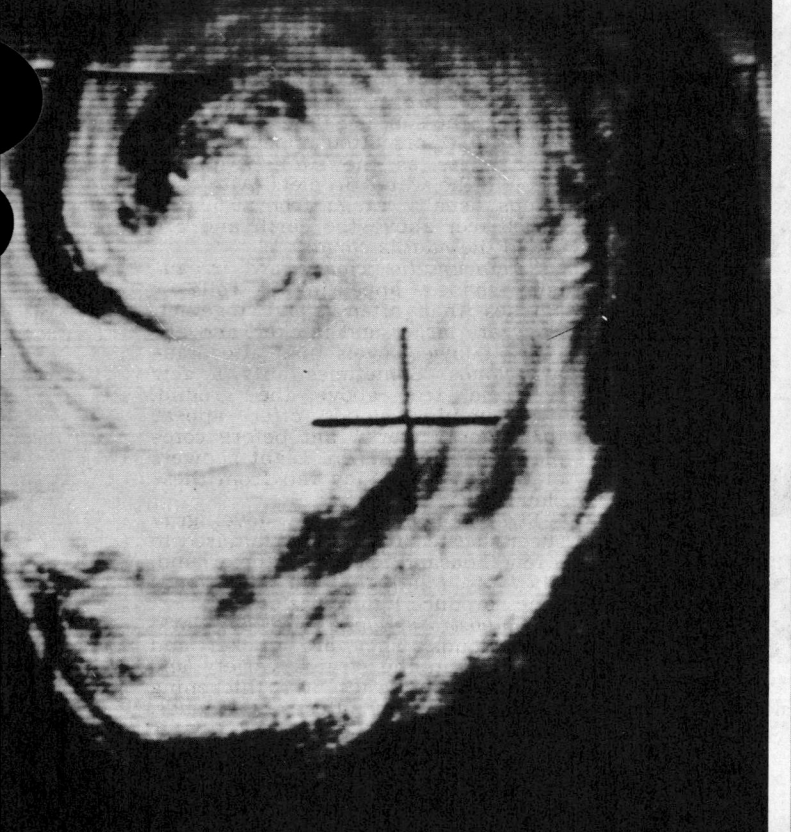

ICE FIELD   STORM

ASIA

NORTH

North Pacific Ocean

AMERICA

North Atlantic Ocean

EUROPE

AFRICA

Range of earlier Tiros satellites

ORBIT OF TIROS V

Equator

RANGE OF TIROS V

South Pacific Ocean

SOUTH AMERICA

South Atlantic Ocean

AUSTRALIA

58°

58°

THE NEW YORK TIMES

NASA

Weather eyes on the world watch, predict and warn

FROM 400 MILES above the earth, artificial satellites like Tiros V, whose orbital path is shown above, look down on the globe through the eyes of their television cameras. The pictures they transmit enable meteorologists to keep constant track of weather all over the world. Left, a glimpse into the vortex of an Atlantic storm sheds light on the origin, development and movement of storms, to warn against their approach and perhaps, eventually, to tame them. Right, photograph of an ice field in Hudson Bay helps predict future icebergs which menace shipping lanes.

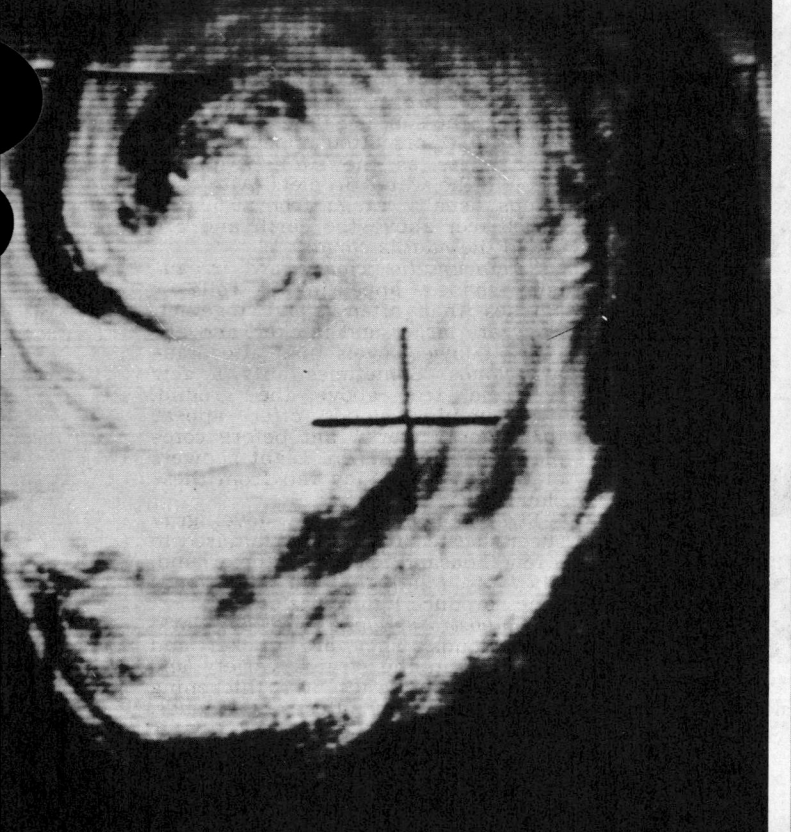
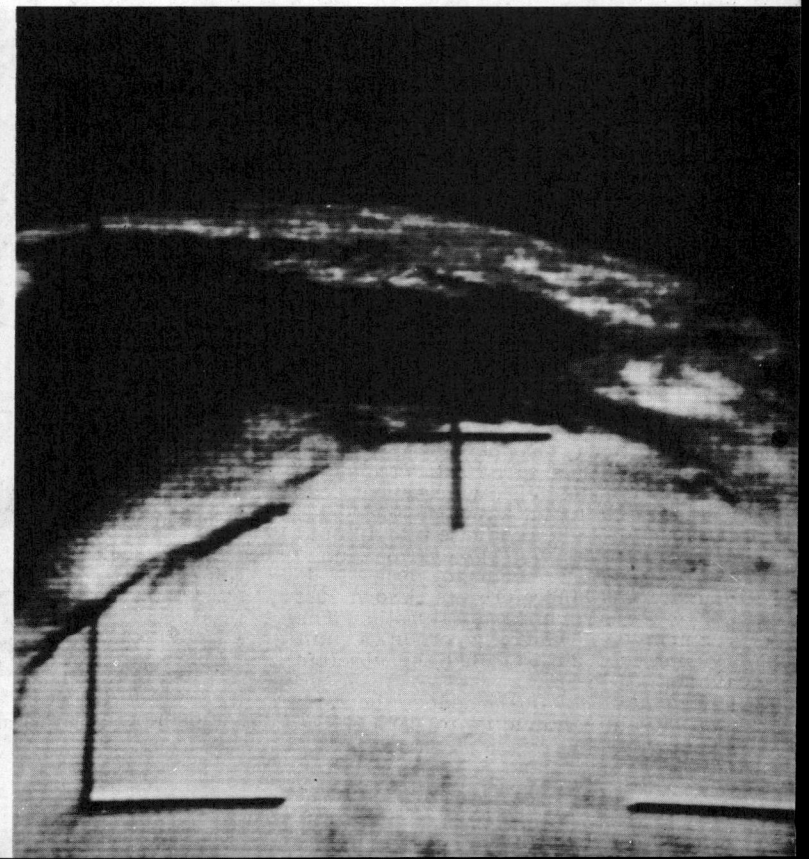

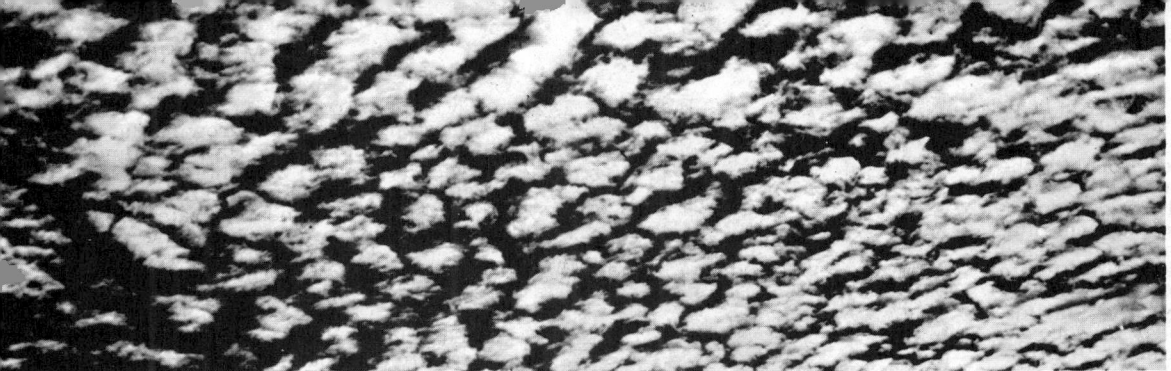
TUFTED PATCHES of Altocumulus water clouds spread across the sky

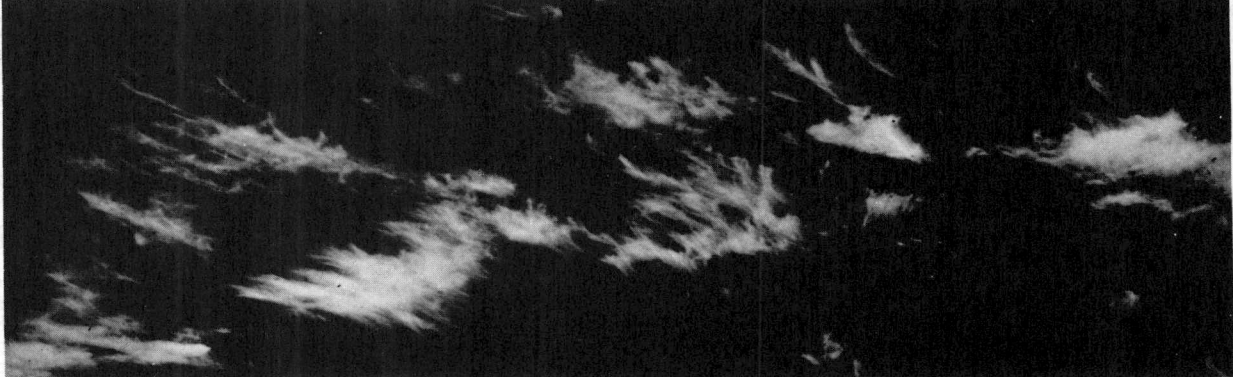
CIRRUS, high ice clouds, may portend rain or snow

CUMULUS, usually seen on sunny days, can develop into rain-clouds

CIRROCUMULUS, merging with Cirrostratus, are harbingers of rain

CUMULONIMBUS, towering over the landscape in great thunderheads

ALTOCUMULUS LENTICULARIS, named for their strange lens-like shape

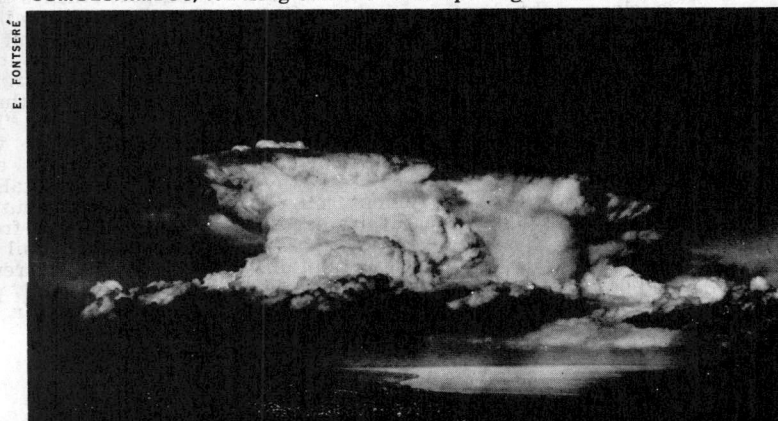

E. FONTSERÉ

When nimbostratus clouds appear, heavy rain or snow usually follows immediately.

Cumulus clouds are probably the most familiar. They are fluffy, white, flat-based, puff-sided, and round-topped, and usually result from surface heating of the earth. Over land they form most frequently in the late morning and early afternoon. They are essentially fair-weather clouds. If they slowly disappear as the sun begins to set, the weather will probably remain fair throughout the night. The air inside cumulus clouds is in a continuous state of up-and-down motion; so much so, in fact, that airplanes flying through them often experience a bumpy ride. Cumulus clouds change size and shape very rapidly.

Cumulonimbus clouds are the largest clouds in the sky. They are actually overgrown cumulus clouds, often extending to more than five miles above the earth. At the top of these clouds the rounded edges break into a flattened, anvil-shaped layer. Cumulonimbus clouds are the familiar thunderclouds that produce heavy showers, lightning, thunder, and often hail and high winds. As cumulus clouds grow in the process of becoming cumulonimbus clouds, but before the anvil-shaped top appears, they are known as *cumulus congestus*.

The accompanying illustration shows the forms and relative heights of the main cloud types. There are two main divisions based on shape. Cumulus-type clouds have a heaped-up, or bulging, appearance. Stratus-type clouds are spread out in a layer. There are four main divisions based on height. Cirrus-type clouds appear at the greatest heights; alto-type clouds appear at middle levels; stratus and stratocumulus are at low levels; and nimbostratus, cumulus, and cumulonimbus occur in more than one level. The nimbus-type clouds usually produce large amounts of rain.

Condensation and Precipitation

■**CONDENSATION.**—When the air becomes *saturated* (relative humidity reaches 100 per cent), the water vapor in it usually condenses into a liquid. The drops form upon small airborne particles of sea salt, dust, and other matter, known in this instance as *condensation nuclei*. Air may become saturated by the addition of water vapor or through cooling. Condensation in the atmosphere is most often due to cooling, which may take place in a number of ways.

Radiative cooling occurs when, on a clear night, heat from the earth's surface is radiated into space; air near the ground is cooled by contact with the earth. Air may also be cooled by *expansion*. Since atmospheric pressure decreases with each increase in altitude, air rising from a lower level expands. In so doing, its temperature decreases.

An upward air movement can result from the heating of the earth's surface by the sun. Air may also be forced upward by hills or mountains over which it flows, or may be displaced by a heavier mass of air.

SNOWFLAKES are symmetrical hexagons.

Condensation sometimes results in the formation of small drops of water near the ground, called *fog*. These drops are so tiny it would take billions to fill a teaspoon. If the drops formed by this near ground-level condensation grow large enough to fall to the ground, they produce *drizzle* or *mist*, although drizzle most often falls from low clouds. If condensation forms directly on the ground or on some other surface, it is called *dew*. Dew that forms on a surface whose temperature is below freezing will become small ice needles called *frost*. Condensation that is produced by the expansion of rising air and takes place above ground level will result in the formation of *clouds*.

■**PRECIPITATION.**—When cloud drops grow big enough to fall from a cloud and reach the ground, the condition produced is known as *precipitation*. Very few clouds produce precipitation unless the interior temperature first falls below freezing, and ice crystals form. Thus, most precipitation begins as ice. The small cloud drops begin to condense on the ice crystals, forming larger drops. As the drops grow in size, they begin to fall through the cloud, collecting still more cloud drops. The average rain drop equals about one million cloud drops.

■**TYPES OF PRECIPITATION.**—Precipitation that reaches the ground in liquid form is called *rain* or *drizzle*. If the liquid freezes on coming in contact with the ground, it is known as *freezing rain* or *freezing drizzle*. Precipitation that falls through the air as ice is called *sleet*. These ice crystals sometimes have very complex and beautiful shapes and are known as *snow*. Snow crystals are always hexagonal in shape, but no two are alike. *Hail* is formed from raindrops that freeze. Often hail is carried up and down by air currents within a cloud, collecting liquid water drops as it falls and is again carried aloft. This process is sometimes repeated many times, the *hailstones* growing larger with each passage. Hail is almost always associated with thunderstorms.

■**PRECIPITATION MEASUREMENT.**—All that is needed to measure rainfall is a large, open can to catch the rain-water and a ruler to measure the depth of the water collected. A rainfall measurement, therefore, represents the height to which rainwater accumulates on a level surface. The *standard rain gauge* used by the U.S. Weather Bureau is a cylindrical can 24 inches high and 8 inches across. A funnel channels the rain water into a measuring tube with cross-sectional area exactly one-tenth that of the catching can. The depth of rain water measured is, therefore, ten times its actual depth. In other words, one inch of rain in the catching can is measured as ten inches in the tube. The height of rainwater in the measuring tube is divided by ten to find the actual reading. This allows for more accurate measurement—to 1/100 of an inch. The funnel minimizes evaporation because it covers the collected water, except a very small opening.

Snowfall is measured in terms of both depth and weight. The depth is determined by choosing a level area where there has been no drifting and inserting a ruler into the snow until it reaches the ground. Several depth measurements are taken at different points in the area, and the average of these is used. Weight is determined by melting a volume of snow and then measuring the depth of the resultant water. This is known as the *water equivalent* of snow. A standard rain gauge, with the measuring tube and funnel removed, is used to catch the snow. The snow collected in the can is then melted, and the water depth is measured. On the average, ten inches of snow will melt down to approximately one inch of water, but the water equivalent (weight) of snow varies widely.

Wind

■**PRESSURE GRADIENTS.**—*Wind*, which is air in motion, sharply influences the weather by transporting heat and moisture. If the temperature of the atmosphere were the same all over the world, atmospheric pressure would also be the same and air would not move—there would be no wind. Heat from the sun, however, is distributed unevenly over the earth. The variations in temperature produce the differences in atmospheric pressure that, in turn, produce air movement. (The greater the difference in pressure, the faster the air will move.) The force producing this air movement is known as the *pressure-gradient force*. If this were the only force acting on the atmosphere, winds would always blow directly from areas of high pressure to areas of low pressure.

■**CORIOLIS EFFECT.**—The rotation of the earth deflects the wind; instead of flowing in a straight line from high to low, winds flow *around* pressure centers. This *Coriolis force* turns the wind to the right (clockwise) in the Northern Hemisphere and to the left (counterclockwise) in the Southern

METEOROLOGY

Hemisphere. If a person stands with his back to the wind in the Northern Hemisphere high pressure will be on the right; low pressure on the left. In the Southern Hemisphere, it would be just the opposite; low pressure on the right, high on the left. In the Northern Hemisphere, winds blow counterclockwise around a low-pressure center (*cyclone*) and clockwise around a high-pressure center (*anticyclone*). In the Southern Hemisphere, winds blow clockwise around a low-pressure center; counterclockwise around a high-pressure center. Friction with the earth's surface also affects the wind, making it spiral *in* toward the center of a low-pressure area, *out* from a high-pressure area.

■**WIND SYSTEMS.**—The distribution of heat over the surface of the earth results in world-wide pressure patterns and relatively steady wind systems. These *prevailing winds* are known as *polar easterlies* in polar latitudes, *prevailing westerlies* in middle latitudes, and *trade winds* in tropical regions. Smaller cyclones and anticyclones migrate within these large-scale wind systems.

■**MONSOONS.** — Localized temperature variations sometimes create small-scale wind systems. The *sea breeze* is one example. During the day the air over the land becomes hot and rises, reducing the air pressure near the ground. The cooler (higher-pressure) air over the water flows toward the land. A wind system produced in this manner is called a *monsoon*. The most famous monsoon circulation occurs over India.

■**JET STREAM.**—A special, high-altitude wind system, generally found from 30,000 to 35,000 feet above the earth, just below the tropopause, is known as the *jet stream*. Winds in the jet stream average 75 miles per hour, but

speeds as high as 200 miles per hour have been recorded.

■**WIND MEASUREMENT.**—In some localities, the direction from which the wind blows can be associated with a particular kind of weather. For example, in many sections of the United States a south wind signals the approach of warmer weather, while a north wind indicates the opposite. A wind from the west will most often bring fair weather; an easterly wind, rain or snow. A change in wind direction can therefore serve as a useful indicator of a change in the weather.

Wind speed is expressed in either knots or miles per hour and can be estimated on the basis of constant observations. The first wind scale was devised in 1805 by the British admiral, Sir Francis Beaufort. The *Beaufort Scale* is still used in a modified form.

An instrument that shows wind direction is called a *wind vane*. The most common wind vane is an arrow with a large tail. This arrow rotates freely on a fixed base and points *into* the wind—in the direction from which the wind blows.

The instrument used to measure wind speed is called an *anemometer*. The *cup anemometer* is made up of three or four hollow, hemispherical cups attached to horizontal arms extending from a vertical axis. The force of the wind on the cups causes the apparatus to turn on the axis—the higher the wind speed, the faster the cups turn. The spinning apparatus is linked mechanically to a pointer that moves over a scale and indicates speed in knots or miles per hour.

There are some instruments designed to measure wind direction and wind speed simultaneously. One of these looks like a wind vane, but has a hollow tube in the head of the

arrow. The wind speed is measured in terms of the pressure of the air blowing into the tube. Another instrument that measures wind speed and direction simultaneously is the *aerovane*, which looks like a miniature airplane without wings. A tail fin keeps the instrument facing into the wind, and the wind speed is determined by a spinning propeller.

■**WIND VELOCITY.**—*Wind velocity* encompasses both wind speed and wind direction. It should never be used to indicate wind speed alone. *Wind direction* is specified in compass degree points and indicates the direction *from* which the wind is blowing. An east (90°) wind blows from east to west; a south (180°) wind blows from south to north.

Weather Control.—Since all of us participate in outdoor activities of some sort, we must at times be concerned about the weather. Man has therefore always thought about the possibility of exercising some control over it. The *smudge pots* (pots of burning oil) used by citrus growers to prevent their crops from freezing are one example of small-scale weather control. Weather, of course, also affects indoor environment.

■**RAINMAKING.**—In most cases, precipitation is the kind of weather we want to regulate. In the past, ritual ceremonies were performed to conjure up, or to stop, rainfall. The most famous of these is the *rain dance* of the North American Hopi Indians.

The modern era of rainmaking began in 1946, when it was discovered that dropping small particles of dry ice into a cloud could initiate precipitation by converting some of the small water drops in the cloud to ice crystals. (Natural precipitation usually begins with the formation of ice

HURRICANES periodically lash the Florida coast with high winds and heavy rain (*left*). As part of the hurricane-surveillance program, a photographic plane flies above a hurricane (*right*); the clouds circle into the storm's eye, visible above the tail of the aircraft.

crystals.) This process became known as *cloud seeding*. Later it was discovered that if large amounts of dry ice were dropped into thin clouds, the resulting rain drops would be so small they would evaporate before reaching the ground. A hole could thus be cut in a cloud without causing precipitation. Even later it was found that crystals of silver iodide could produce the same effect as the dry ice. This was important because it enabled scientists to "seed" clouds from the ground by burning a solution containing silver iodide and allowing the vapor to float up into the clouds—a much less expensive method than flying above a cloud to drop dry ice into it.

Clouds must be present before rainmaking activities can begin. No one has yet devised a way to form clouds in clear, dry air. Thus, it is very difficult to determine whether cloud seeding really produces rainfall, over and above that which would have occurred naturally. This question will be answered only after years of experiment and observation.

■**STORM CONTROL.**—Experiments have been performed to determine whether seeding special types of clouds can prevent damaging storms. The idea is that seeding thunderstorm clouds before they develop fully may start premature precipitation and eliminate the clouds before they reach the thunder, lightning, and hail stage. It is believed that such early seeding may prevent tornadoes and that seeding hurricanes early in their development may stop them from maturing.

■**REGULATING SOLAR ENERGY.**—Future efforts to control the weather will most likely be concerned with discovering a way to influence and control the distribution of solar energy. This will really be going to the heart of the matter because it is the sun's energy that conditions the earth's atmosphere, producing most of the conditions we call "weather." A number of devices have already been suggested to capture or reject the sun's energy, thereby producing very extensive weather modification. If more solar energy, for instance, could be concentrated on the polar regions, it would increase the rate at which the ice and snow in these regions melt. This would result in a rise in the level of all the oceans. Winters would become much milder, and precipitation in the middle latitudes might be drastically reduced.

Special Storms

■**HURRICANES.**—High-speed winds sometimes occur near the surface of the earth in conjunction with some types of cyclones. One of these is the most destructive of all weather systems, the *hurricane*. Hurricanes are seasonal storms (most prevalent in August and September) that originate over the tropical regions of the Atlantic Ocean. Sometimes more than 300 miles in diameter, these storms move at 10 to 20 miles per hour and have winds of over 75 miles per hour. (A hurricane generates more energy in one hour than all the electric power generated in the United States in one year.) At the center, or *eye*,

of a hurricane is an area about five miles wide where the winds are usually calm and the sky above is sometimes clear. Hurricanes usually last from 5 to 10 days. They lose force rapidly when they move over land. On the average, two hurricanes strike the United States each year. No hurricane has ever been observed south of the equator.

The most destructive element of a hurricane is the extraordinarily high tides it drives before it. The hurricane of 1938 caused 500 deaths in New England, most of them drownings. The tragic Galveston hurricane of 1900 swept a 15-foot wall of water out of the Gulf of Mexico and across the city, killing over 5,000 people.

■**TYPHOONS.**—A *typhoon* is the Pacific version of a hurricane. It occurs mainly during February and March.

■**TORNADOES.**—Although limited in size and duration, *tornadoes* are the most violent and deadly of all storms. Ranging from 100 to 500 feet wide, they move at from 25 to 40 miles per hour for up to 50 miles. Tornadoes are characterized by a dark funnel shape descending from a low cloud.

A tornado presents a double hazard —high-speed winds and low pressure. Wind speeds have been estimated to be as high as 500 miles per hour. The air pressure at the center of a tornado is very low—perhaps two-thirds that of the surroundings. Thus, closed houses over which a tornado passes usually explode—the pressure within the house pushes against the abnormally low pressure outside. Tornadoes have played many curious tricks, such as driving boards through utility poles and carrying children and animals through the air for miles without harming them. A tornado occurring over water is a *waterspout*.

Most tornadoes occur in Australia and in the southern and the western sections of the United States. More than 100 tornadoes, killing more than 200 people, are recorded every year in the United States.

■**THUNDERSTORMS.**—One of the most common and spectacular storms is the *thunderstorm*, a composite of high winds, heavy rain, loud noises, and flashing light. *Thunder* is the result of a weather phenomenon called lightning. *Lightning* is untamed electricity that shoots across the sky, causing intense heating along its path. This heating causes the air to expand suddenly. When the air surfaces separated by the expansion come together again, a series of vibrations causes the violent crash known as thunder. Thunder in itself is not dangerous. Many thunderstorms sometimes travel together, forming what is known as a *squall line*.

Sound waves travel about one mile in five seconds, while light travels at more than 186,000 miles per second. Lightning is therefore seen practically at the instant it occurs, while the thunder is heard somewhat after the flash of light appears in the sky. Hence, the distance of a thunderstorm can be calculated by counting the seconds between the time the lightning flash is seen and the time the thunder is heard, allowing five seconds per mile.

THUNDERSTORMS, caused by electrical discharges in the atmosphere, are characterized by streaks of lightning and thunder.

More than 1,800 thunderstorms occur in the atmosphere every hour. Every year about 400 people in the United States are killed by lightning. While the chances of being struck by lightning are very small, the following precautions should be taken. Indoors, the center of a room is the safest spot, provided it is not under a light fixture. Radiators and corners near outside rainspouts should be avoided. Outdoors, isolated trees, tops of hills, and metal fences should be avoided. The inside of an automobile is one of the safest places to be during a thunderstorm. If you are caught on open water in a small boat, or on a wide expanse of flat land, the best precaution is to lie down.

Air Masses.—Weather in any area depends greatly upon the characteristics of the air mass over the area. An *air mass* is a large portion of the atmosphere with relatively uniform properties throughout. An air mass develops when a large section of the atmosphere remains relatively stationary over a surface area with uniform properties. Such a surface area is known as a *source region*.

Movements and interactions among different air masses also affect the weather.

Air masses are classified primarily by source region or place of origin. The principal air-mass source regions are those areas where high pressure centers tend to develop—over the land in high latitudes and over the ocean in low latitudes. The principal air masses are classified as *polar* and *tropical*, identified P and T on a weather map. Classifications *arctic* (A) and *equatorial* (E) are also used.

A secondary classification distinguishes whether the air mass formed over land or over water, designated *continental* (c) and *maritime* (M) respectively. In general, maritime-tropical air (MT) is warm and humid, continental-tropical (cT) warm and dry, maritime-polar (MP) cold and moist, and continental-polar (cP) cold and dry.

■ **FRONTS.**—Major weather changes occur at the boundaries separating air masses, called *fronts*. When cold air is advancing at the boundary, the boundary line is called a *cold front*. Cold fronts are usually accompanied by heavy showers and followed by lower temperatures. When warm air is advancing at the boundary, the boundary line is called a *warm front*. Gentle rains usually precede a warm front, followed by higher temperatures. A boundary line that is not moving is called a *stationary front*.

Frontal boundaries are shown as lines on a weather map, but they really extend upward from the ground. Since cold air is heavier than warm air, the surface slopes; and the cold air forms a wedge underneath the warm air. When cold and warm fronts meet, one of the air masses is lifted from the ground, thus forming an *occluded front*.

Climate.—The condition of the weather at a given time and place is the sum total of temperature, air pressure, relative humidity, wind velocity, precipitation, and cloudiness. Although changes in the weather in one particular area are many and varied, it is possible to arrive at a composite picture of the weather by averaging these variations. Such a generalization is called the *climate* of an area.

The climate of an area, however, is not determined solely by the long-term annual averages of the meteorological elements. Edinburgh, Scotland, and Boston, Massachusetts, for example, have nearly the same annual average temperature (48°F. or 9°C.), but the temperature extremes during the year are markedly different. At Edinburgh average temperatures range from 38°F. to 58°F. (3°C. to 14°C.), and at Boston, from 27°F. to 70°F. (−3°C. to 21°C.). Thus, to characterize climate it is first necessary to consider the regular variations the meteorological elements are subjected to, particularly seasonal changes. But temperature is not the only element to be considered. Cairo, Egypt, and New Orleans, Louisiana, have about the same mean temperature (68°F. or 20°C.) and similar temperature variations, but the annual 1.3-inch rainfall at Cairo and the 56.5-inch rainfall at New Orleans make their climates quite different. Climate thus can be defined as the mean state of the atmosphere at a given place and the variations to which that mean state is subjected.

In general, climates are classified according to the effect they have on animal and plant life. Temperature and precipitation are the two principal elements in most classifications because heat and water are the two factors most profoundly affecting living organisms. They are also the two variables most regularly and generally observed. Evaporation, ground temperature, radiation, and winds are also important, but the distribution of these elements is reflected in temperature and precipitation.

Climate is governed by a number of geographic factors. The most important are latitude, altitude, topography, and proximity to an ocean. Latitude influences average temperatures. Warm climates are generally nearer the equator than cold climates, and vice versa. Altitude and topography influence average temperatures and precipitation—the higher the altitude, the colder the climate. The average midsummer temperature on Pike's Peak in Colorado is more than 30° lower than at Denver, which is 9,000 feet lower. The topographical location of an area in relation to mountains is also important. Air flowing up the windward side of a mountain is cooled, and the water vapor condenses to form clouds and rain. The air flowing down the leeward side of the mountain is heated as it descends and thus is dry. The climate therefore is often cool and wet on the windward side of a mountain range, warm and dry on the lee side. Mountains can also block the flow of air. The Rocky Mountains in the United States, for instance, act as a barrier preventing cold winter air masses from reaching the Pacific Coast.

Finally, oceans are relatively cool in the summer and relatively warm in the winter. Thus they tend to stabilize the climates of nearby land areas, particularly if the prevailing winds are from the ocean to the land. Such climates (*maritime*), on the average, change very little in temperature from season to season. Amid large land masses, temperature variations are usually more pronounced; winters are frequently very cold and summers very hot. This type of climate is called a *continental climate*.

—Francis K. Davis, Jr.

WEATHER

The *National Weather Service*, a division of the *National Oceanic and Atmospheric Administration* in the U.S. Department of Commerce, provides forecasts and storm warnings for the general public, agricultural, aviation, and other interests.

History.—The *National Weather Service*, first organized in 1870, was operated by the U.S. Army Signal Corps. In 1891 it was transferred to the newly formed Weather Bureau, an agency put under the jurisdiction of the Department of Commerce in 1940. In 1965 it was placed under the *Environmental Science Services Administration* in that department; in 1970 it was made part of its National Oceanic & Atmospheric Administration.

Operations.—Today, weather observations are made at stations located in cities, at airports, in oceans, and additional reports come from military stations, other federal agencies, avia-

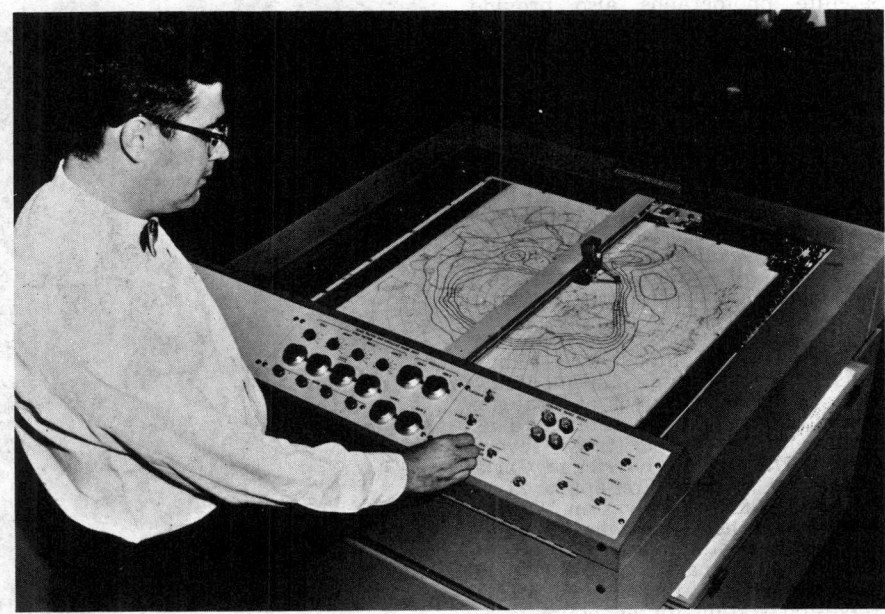

U.S. DEPARTMENT OF COMMERCE, WEATHER BUREAU

ELECTRONIC COMPUTER-PLOTTER automatically draws contours of the pressure surface of the atmosphere at specified altitudes above the Northern Hemisphere in under three minutes.

tion interests, merchant vessels of all nationalities, and from foreign countries under international agreement. In addition, there are almost 13,000 private citizens in the United States who assist the Service by making daily weather observations.

Weather information collected by this vast network is transmitted to the Weather Service's *National Meteorological Center* near Washington, D.C. Meteorologists there use the collected data to analyze the current weather situation and in turn issue comprehensive forecasts covering areas as large as the entire Northern Hemisphere. Much of this work is done with the help of electronic computers and other automatic equipment. One such machine is capable of drawing weather maps automatically. The completed forecasts and maps are then transmitted to area Weather Service offices and military field stations.

Using the guidance material provided by the National Meteorological Center, the Weather Service's *Area Forecast Offices* issue forecasts and storm warnings covering their specific areas of responsibility. Each local station in turn adapts the forecasts prepared by the Area Forecast Offices to its particular locality. Local weather information is then distributed by the press, radio and television stations, and automatic telephone answering devices.

Modern Observational Instruments

■ SATELLITES.—Since 1960, a variety of weather satellites have been launched by the *National Aeronautics and Space Administration.* The cloud pictures taken by cameras in these satellites are used by the Weather Service to supplement other reports. The satellites have been of great value to forecasters by providing information about vast areas of the earth where few weather observations are made. Satellite photographs also provide early storm warnings. Since their inception orbiting satellites have demonstrated their effectiveness by identifying and tracking storms. When significant weather developments, such as hurricane and typhoon formations, are detected by the satellites, the Weather Service issues special international bulletins to the nations that may be affected. Several weather satellites have carried sensors that measure the radiation balance of the earth and its atmosphere, thereby yielding valuable information that will aid in understanding the atmosphere and predicting its behavior.

■ RADAR.—The Weather Service maintains many long-range, and medium-range, radar installations at strategic points in the United States. This equipment is used to track severe storms. The eye of hurricane Carla (1961), for example, first appeared on the scope of the Galveston, Texas, radar when the storm was 220 nautical miles south, over the Gulf of Mexico. This particular hurricane was tracked continuously by the Galveston station for 46 hours.

■ AUTOMATIC STATIONS.—In addition to manned installations, the Weather Service also maintains automatic stations to provide weather information from remote, inaccessible locations. These automatic stations observe cloud height, runway visual range for pilots, air pressure, and other weather conditions, transmitting these observations over teletype circuits. A marine automatic meteorological observation station is now operating in the Gulf of Mexico. For extremely remote locations, an atomic-powered weather station was developed through the efforts of the Atomic Energy Commission and the Weather Service. One such station was installed in the Canadian Arctic during the summer of 1961, and has been operating satisfactorily ever since.

■ COMPUTERS.—To aid the weatherman in assembling and analyzing the wealth of weather data received, high-speed electronic computers have been installed at the *National Meteorological Center,* the *National Environmental Satellite Service,* and the *National Hurricane Center* at Coral Gables, Florida, and at various other research and forecast centers.

Weather Research.—Much of the progress made in hurricane forecasting is the result of intensive studies made by the Weather Service's *National Hurricane Research Project.* Basic information for this research is gathered by a fleet of flying laboratories and networks of upper-air observational stations. In 1961, under the joint sponsorship of the Weather Bureau, the Navy, and the *National Science Foundation,* a series of experiments began to explore the possibilities of modifying hurricanes by releasing silver iodide into the cloud tops near the area of maximum hurricane winds.

The Weather Bureau also initiated the *National Severe Storms Project* in 1961. This project is designed to collect detailed and comprehensive information on the behavior of tornadoes and severe local storms, using aircraft, radar, and observational networks in Oklahoma, Texas, and Kansas—the heart of the tornado belt. The program has received the active cooperation of many government agencies, including the Air Force, the *Federal Aviation Administration,* and the National Aeronautics and Space Administration. Many universities and private agencies have also cooperated in the project.

Weather Service Publications.—The Weather Service publishes the *Daily Weather Map;* the *Weekly Weather and Crop Bulletin, Climatological Data,* the *Mariners Weather Log,* the *Average Monthly Weather Resumé and Outlook,* and the *Monthly Weather Review.* Its research findings are published in the *Research Paper Series,* the *Monthly Weather Review,* and various scientific journals.

—Robert M. White

For Further Reference

Blumenstock, David I. *Ocean of Air.* Rutgers University Press, 1959.

Day, John A. *The Science of Weather.* Addison-Wesley, 1966.

Lutgens, Frederick K., and Edward J. Tarbuck. *Atmosphere: An Introduction to Meteorology* (3rd Ed.). Prentice-Hall, 1986.

Powers, Edward, and James Witt. *Traveling Weatherwise in the U.S.A.* Dodd, Mead, 1972.

Riehl, H. *Introduction to the Atmosphere.* McGraw-Hill, 1965.

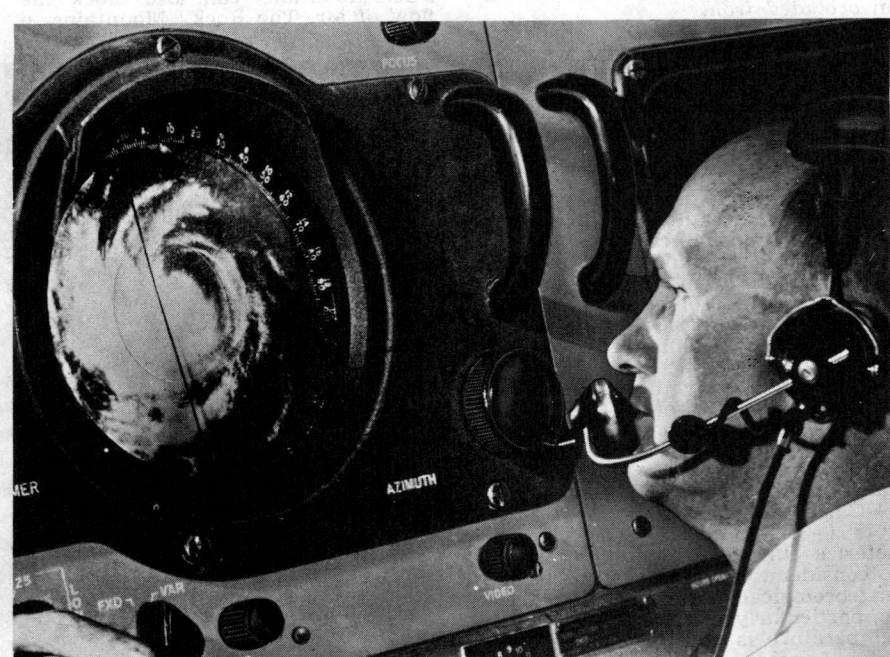

U.S. DEPARTMENT OF COMMERCE, WEATHER BUREAU

RADAR has become a valuable tool to meteorologists for the tracking of storms. The storm vortex, presented on this radarscope, can be tracked at distances of up to 250 miles.

AA. Hawaiian term for a lava flow whose surface has broken into rough, jagged blocks bristling with sharp points. Also called block lava.

ABLATION. Reduction of the surface of a glacier or snow field through evaporation and melting.

ABNEY LEVEL. An instrument with a tube containing a movable bubble; used to measure the steepness of a slope or a vertical angle. It resembles a carpenter's level.

ABRASION. The wearing down of land surfaces by the frictional action of solid particles moved by ice, wind, water, or gravity.

ABSOLUTE ATMOSPHERE. A unit of pressure equaling 1 million times the pressure produced on a square centimeter by a force of one dyne.

ABSOLUTE TIME. Measurement of a sequence of events in geological time in years rather than in chronological sequence, which indicates only relative time.

ABYSSAL. Referring to the deepest parts of the oceans, generally below 2,000 fathoms (12,000 feet). See *Ocean depth zones.*

ABYSSAL DEPOSITS. Solid material covering the floor of ocean basins lying at a depth of more than 2,000 fathoms (12,000 feet).

ACCRETION. The process by which inorganic masses become larger through the addition of new matter to the outside. *Natural accretion* is the gradual buildup of land over time by the deposit of material carried by water or air. *Artificial accretion* is the same buildup caused by human action.

ACIDIC. A term describing igneous rocks containing a large proportion of silica, usually more than 66 percent.

ADIABATIC RATE. The change in temperature of a rising or falling body of air due to its expansion or compression. Rising, expanding air loses about 1.6°F per 300 feet, and the temperature of falling bodies of air increases at the same rate.

ADOBE. Heavy clay and silt surface soils found in desert and dry areas, as in the U.S. southwest. Also, the sun-dried bricks made from the clay and silt.

ADVECTION. Horizontal movement of parcels of air, such as sea fog, and the flow of sea water, as a current.

AERATION ZONE. See *Zone of aeration.*

AEROLOGY. The scientific study of the atmosphere.

AFFLUENT. A stream or river flowing into a larger river or other body of water; a tributary.

AFTERGLOW. Radiance seen in the sky when the sun is below the horizon.

AFTERSHOCK. An earthquake following a larger earthquake. Major earthquakes are usually followed by several aftershocks.

AGATE. A varied-colored waxy quartz, or silica, with bands of chalcedony; commonly found embedded in limestone or in rock cavities.

AGGLOMERATE. A mass of coarse, volcanic rock fragments. The fragments are usually slightly rounded in shape and larger than volcanic ash.

AGGLUTINATE. A volcanic deposit consisting of fragments fused at their point of contact. It is distinguished from agglomerate by the presence of glassy cement and bits of scoria or cinders between the blocks, and the absence of ash.

AGGRADATION. The building up of a land surface by the deposit of loose materials as by a stream or river.

AGGREGATE. A grouping or mixture of particles of earth material, as a rock, which may be separated into its components by mechanical means.

AGONIC. No magnetic declination. An agonic line connects points on the earth's surface at which the needle of a magnetic compass points to true north and magnetic north simultaneously.

A HORIZON. See *Soil profile.*

AIR MASS. A large body of air generally homogeneous with respect to temperature and moisture, vertical variations being about the same throughout its horizontal extent.

ALLUVIAL FAN, land counterpart of a delta, is formed of debris from the cliff face.

ALBEDO. The ratio between the amount of light falling on a surface and the amount reflected. The albedo of earth is about 0.4, which means that 4/10 of the sun's radiation is reflected by the earth's surface.

ALEUTIAN LOW. A semipermanent center of low pressure that develops during the winter in the North Pacific Ocean in the vicinity of the Aleutian Islands.

ALIDADE. A straight-edge ruler mounted with a sighting device, such as a telescope; used to measure horizontal angular distances.

ALKALI FLAT. A broad, barren, flat plain into which desert streams drain. As accumulated water evaporates, it deposits fine sediment and dissolved minerals, thus forming a salt surface.

ALLOTROPIC. Pertaining to a substance which may exist in two or more structural forms, such as carbon as graphite and as diamond.

ALLUVIAL FAN. A fan-shaped, or cone-shaped, mass of soil deposited by a stream.

ALLUVIUM. Loose stream or river-borne deposits of sand, silt, and gravel.

ALPIDES. A great structural belt extending eastward from the Alps in Europe to the Himalayas and related mountains in Asia; formed in the Tertiary period, between 60 million and 1 million years ago.

ALPINE. Referring to a mountain region above the timberline but below the snowline.

ALTIMETER. An instrument used to measure height above ground level or sea level.

ALTITUDE. The vertical distance above sea level or the angular distance above the horizon plane.

AMORPHOUS. Without a distinctive form. The absence of a definite crystalline structure in rocks or minerals.

AMPHIBOLE. A group of common rock-forming minerals. The most important is hornblende.

AMYGDULE. A vesicle, or gas cavity, in igneous rock which has been filled with some mineral such as calcite, chalcedony, or quartz.

ANABATIC. A local, upward-flowing wind found in mountainous areas. It is caused by the convectional rise of air that has been heated.

ANCHOR ICE. Ice formed on the bottom of a stream or river which is not frozen solid.

ANDESITE. A fine-grained volcanic rock composed largely of plagioclase feldspars.

U.S. DEPARTMENT OF THE INTERIOR NATIONAL PARK SERVICE

ANTECEDENT RIVER. The Colorado cuts through the rocks to form the Grand Canyon.

ANALEMMA. A chart giving the declination of the sun, on the vertical scale, and the equation of time, on the horizontal, for every day of the year. It forms a figure "8" on the globe.

ANEMOGRAPH. A self-recording instrument that traces a curved line showing the speed or force of the wind.

ANEMOMETER. An instrument measuring the speed of wind.

ANEROID. See *Barometer*.

ANGLE OF REPOSE. The maximum angle at which material such as sand, soil, or loose rock can remain stable. If the angle is exceeded, the material will slide.

ANGULAR UNCONFORMITY. An unconformity in which older, lower, beds of rock tilt at a different angle than the later, upper layers.

ANHYDROUS. Essentially without water, as opposed to hydrous.

ANIMATE ENERGY. Energy or work created by living organisms such as a man or a horse. The opposite of inanimate energy.

ANISOTROPIC. Having different physical properties when tested in different directions, as opposed to isotropic. Characteristic of most crystalline structures.

ANNULAR DRAINAGE PATTERN. A circular pattern of stream paths developed on the weaker sedimentary rocks of dome or basin structures.

ANOMALY. An area which differs in gravitational pull from its surroundings, often associated with valuable mineral deposits such as petroleum.

ANORTHITE. See *Feldspar*.

ANTARCTIC CIRCLE. The parallel of latitude 66½° South.

ANTECEDENT RIVER. A river, or stream, that has maintained its original course by cutting through land that rose in its path.

ANTHRACITE. Hard, black, highly metamorphosed lustrous coal containing a high percentage of carbon and a low percentage of volatile matter. It burns with little smoke and gives great heat.

ANTHROPOGEOGRAPHY. The study of the distribution of human societies on the earth in relation to their environment.

ANTICLINAL THEORY. The theory that water, petroleum, and natural gas accumulate in up-bowed strata in the order named (water lowest), provided that the structure contains reservoir rocks in proper relation to source beds and is capped by an impervious barrier.

ANTICLINE. A fold of stratified rocks that was arched upward. It is the reverse of a syncline.

ANTICLINORIUM. A series of anticlines and synclines forming a general anticline covering an extensive area.

ANTICYCLONE. A high-pressure air mass, generally circular in shape, around which winds spiral outward in a clockwise direction in the northern hemisphere and counterclockwise in the southern hemisphere. It is often called a "high" and is characterized by clear or clearing skies.

ANTIPODES. Two points on diametrically opposite sides of the earth's surface. A line drawn between them passes through the center of the earth.

ANTITRADES. Upper air winds moving in a direction opposite that of surface trade winds.

APHANITIC. Referring to a fine-grained igneous rock, such as basalt, in which the crystals are too small to be seen with the unaided eye. The material cooled too rapidly to form large mineral crystals.

APHELION. The position of a planet in its orbit when it is farthest from the sun.

APOGEE. The position of a celestial body or satellite in its orbit when it is at its greatest distance from the body around which it is revolving.

APPARENT TIME. Solar time, or time based on the apparent motion of the sun as seen by an observer on the earth.

AQUEOUS. Pertaining to water and the sediment it deposits. Used to describe ripple marks made by waves and water currents, as opposed to eolian, or those made by the wind.

AQUICLUDE. A porous sedimentary rock that does not readily transmit water.

AQUIFER. A porous layer of sedimentary rock that freely transmits water.

AQUIFUGE. A nonporous rock that neither absorbs nor transmits water.

ARCHIPELAGO. A cluster of related islands; often tops of submerged mountains.

ARCTIC AIR MASS. An air mass originating over northern Canada.

ARCTIC CIRCLE. The parallel of latitude 66½° North.

ARCTIC PACK. The drifting ice floes of the Arctic Ocean. Also, nearly salt-free sea ice more than two years old.

ARENACEOUS. Referring to rocks derived from or composed largely of sand or other small particles.

ARÊTE. A sharp mountain ridge carved by a glacier. It can be the crest of a mountain range, a subsidiary ridge between two mountains, or a spur between two rock basins.

ARGILLACEOUS. Rocks composed primarily of clay.

ARID. Deficient in moisture. A territory where rainfall is insufficient to support vegetation (less than 10 inches of rain a year) or where it is subject to great evaporation.

ARKOSE. Sandstone containing a large proportion of quartz and feldspar.

ARROYO. A stream bed, usually dry for all or most of the year; found in semi-arid and arid regions.

ARTESIAN WATER. Ground water confined in an aquifer between two impermeable layers and under sufficient pressure to rise above the level at which it is first encountered. It does not necessarily rise to the surface.

ASBESTOS. Also called "rock wool." Fibrous form of various minerals. It is fire resistant and is a poor conductor of heat. Some types of asbestos have fibers long enough to be woven.

ASH. Inorganic residue left after combustion. Also, the small particles of matter, or dust, thrown up during a volcanic eruption.

ASPHALT. A brown to black solid or semisolid bituminous substance. A combination of hydrocarbon compounds, it occurs in nature and is also obtained by distillation in the refining of certain petroleums, when it is known as artificial asphalt.

ASSAY. Analysis of ores to determine the proportion of metals they contain.

ASSIMILATION. The incorporation into a pool of molten rock of material originally present in the surrounding wall rock, resulting in "hybrid" rock.

ASTEROID. A minor planet, or planetoid, of the solar system, revolving between the orbits of Mars and Jupiter.

ATMOSPHERE. The gaseous envelope surrounding a heavenly body and bound to it by gravitational attraction. Earth's atmosphere, which is also called air, consists chiefly of nitrogen (about 76 percent) and oxygen (about 23 percent), with small amounts of carbon dioxide, argon, hydrogen, helium, neon, krypton, xenon, ozone, water vapor, dust, and gaseous impurities.

At the earth's surface the atmosphere has a density of about 1/800 that of water and exerts a pressure of 14.7 pounds per square inch at sea level. Earth's atmosphere may extend more than 1,000 miles above the land and water surface, but one-half its mass lies below 3.46 miles. There are three major divisions: the *troposphere*, *stratosphere*, and *ionosphere*.

The *troposphere*, or lowest layer, extends from the earth's surface to about 5 miles at the poles and about 11 miles at the equator, and contains the eddies and convection currents (caused by uneven heating and cooling) that create most of the earth's weather.

The *stratosphere*, the next higher region, is approximately 50 miles deep and has relatively uniform temperatures and wind, although jet streams appear at high midlatitudes. It contains a layer of ozone which absorbs most of the sun's ultraviolet rays.

The *ionosphere*, or highest layer, has a lower limit of about 35 miles during the day and about 60 miles at night. It consists of a series of constantly changing layers of highly ionized molecules, which reflect radiowaves back to earth, thereby making possible radio transmission around the earth's curvature.

In polar regions, the ionosphere contains the edges of the Van Allen belt, which, when it dips to an altitude of about 50 miles above the earth in subpolar latitudes, may cause aurora borealis (northern lights) in the northern hemisphere and aurora australis (southern lights) in the southern hemisphere.

ATOLL. A circular coral reef enclosing a lagoon.

AUGEN. Large, lenslike mineral grains or aggregates of minerals, usually occurring in metamorphic rocks.

AUREOLE. A zone surrounding an igneous intrusion in which contact metamorphism has taken place.

AURORA. Light, in streaks or arcs, seen in the atmosphere in the northern and southern hemispheres most frequently in spring and autumn, when the sun reaches both the Arctic and Antarctic circles. Auroras are believed to occur when negative electrons from the sun are trapped in the magnetic field of the earth and ionize the atoms of such gases as oxygen, nitrogen, helium, neon, ozone, hydrogen and krypton. They may range from 50 to 600 miles in height.

The aurora borealis, or northern lights, is visible in North America between the 40th and 60th parallels and in Europe and Asia between the 50th and 70th parallels. The aurora australis, or southern lights, is visible only between the 40th and 55th parallels in South America.

AVALANCHE. A large mass of snow, ice, or loose earth material sliding rapidly down a mountain slope. It can also be called a landslide when primarily composed of earth and loose rock.

AXIS. A straight line, real or imaginary, passing through a body or system, around which the parts are symmetrically arranged. The polar diameter of the earth around which the earth rotates. The place of sharpest folding of an anticline or syncline.

AZONAL SOILS. A group of young soils without well-developed profile characteristics. See also *Soil*.

BACKING. The counterclockwise change of direction of a wind (e.g., the wind goes from east through northeast to north). The opposite of veering.

BACKSET BEDS. Layers of sand developed on the gentler, windward slope of a dune.

BACKSET EDDY. Small current revolving in a direction opposite that of the great eddies of the ocean.

BADLANDS. A region of soft rock and dry soil where erosion has cut an intricate maze of narrow ravines and sharp crests. The name refers to the difficulty of travel across such areas, as the South Dakota Badlands.

U.S. DEPARTMENT OF THE INTERIOR NATIONAL PARK SERVICE

BADLANDS, a barren region of South Dakota and Nebraska, has an eroded land surface.

BARRIER REEF, a coral reef separated from the mainland by a lagoon. Heron Island, a coral cay, is part of Australia's Great Barrier Reef.

BAJADA. A sloping fringe of coarse material, such as gravel, in a desert basin or along a mountain range.

BAND. A layer of rock or soil differing in color from adjacent layers.

BANK. The sloping land border of a stream, designated as right or left as it would appear facing downstream. Also, a raised but underwater portion of a sea or ocean bed.

BAR. A unit of atmospheric pressure, commonly expressed in millibars (1/1000 of a bar) and equal to the mean atmospheric pressure at about 100 meters, or some 328 feet, above mean sea level. Standard atmospheric pressure is 1,013.3 millibars. Also, a ridge of sand, gravel, or mud deposited by streams, currents, or waves.

BARCHAN, or barkhan, a crescent-shaped sand dune whose horns point downwind. Barchans are sometimes migrating, or moving. The convex, or windward, side of the dune is the gentler slope.

BAROMETER. An instrument for measuring the pressure of the atmosphere. The *mercury barometer* is a calibrated glass tube, closed at one end, the other resting in a cup of mercury. The *aneroid barometer* is a corrugated vacuum box sensitive to external pressure; its expansion or contraction is indicated on a graduated dial by mechanical devices. When it is self-recording it is called a barograph.

BARRAGE. An artificial barrier placed across a stream to increase the depth of the water.

BARRANCA. A deep gully made by heavy rain.

BARRANCO. An amphitheater-shaped valley on the side of a volcano in which streams converge to pass through a narrow exit.

BARRIER REEF. A coral reef generally parallel to the coast and separated from the landmass by a lagoon, too deep for coral growth, that is open to the sea through passes in the reef.

BARYSPHERE. See *Earth structure.*

BASAL CONGLOMERATE. A coarse, usually homogeneous rock deposit above an eroded surface or unconformity, formed by a rising sea level.

BASALT. A dark-colored, finely-grained extrusive igneous rock composed primarily of plagioclase feldspars.

BASE LEVEL. The lowest level to which a land surface can be reduced by running water. For a region, the base level is a plane extending inland from the sea and sloping upward from sea level. For a stream, the base level is usually sea level, athough there may be "temporary base levels," such as lakes or resistant rock layers, along its course.

BASE LINE. An accurately surveyed line on the earth's surface used as a base for further surveys.

BASEMENT COMPLEX. A mass of igneous or metamorphic rocks, generally with complex structure, underlying the oldest identifiable rocks in any region.

BASIC. A term describing a rock low in silica and high in ferromagnesians.

BASIN. A depression in the earth's surface formed by faulting, folding (in which case a circular or eleiptical syncline tilts the beds inward to a central

low point), erosion by water or a glacier, or by volcanic flows or landslides that dam valleys. The opposite of dome. Also used to describe the area drained by a river.

BASIN FLOODING. A method of irrigation in which a stream is permitted to overflow its banks during flood stage and is controlled to inundate large areas with its floodwaters.

BATHOLITH. A large, coarse-textured, irregularly dome-shaped mass of igneous rock which, when molten, penetrated older formations. It may be "concordant" (having pushed up overlying beds and being composed of granite gneiss) or "discordant" (having cut through overlying beds and being composed of granite). It may form the backbone of a mountain range.

BATHYAL. See *Ocean depth zones.*

BATHYSPHERE. A vehicle for investigating the deeper portions of the ocean basin.

BAUXITE. A hydrated aluminum oxide, the chief ore of aluminum.

BAY. An indentation in the shore line or an inlet of a sea or lake between two headlands. A bay is smaller than a gulf and larger than a cove.

BAYMOUTH BAR. A sandbar extending partially or fully across the mouth of a bay.

BAYOU. A sluggish stream or creek in a swamp or river delta.

BEACH. The gently sloping, narrow strip of land bordering a lake or sea, formed by wave or tidal action. Beaches consist of silt, sand, gravel, or rocks.

Because of the water's constant action the structure of a beach changes continuously.

BEADED DRAINAGE. The pattern of small pools connected by short streams characteristic of an area underlain by permafrost.

BEAUFORT WIND SCALE. A series of numbers used to designate wind velocities.

No.	Description	Mph	Knots
0	Calm	1	1
1	Light air	1- 3	1- 3
2	Light breeze	4- 7	4- 6
3	Gentle breeze	8- 12	7- 10
4	Moderate breeze	13- 18	11- 16
5	Fresh breeze	19- 24	17- 21
6	Strong breeze	25- 31	22- 27
7	Moderate gale	32- 38	28- 33
8	Fresh gale	39- 46	34- 40
9	Strong gale	47- 54	41- 47
10	Whole gale	55- 61	48- 55
11	Storm	62- 72	56- 63
12	Hurricane	73- 80	64- 71
13		81- 91	72- 80
14		92-101	81- 89
15		102-112	90- 99
16		113-124	100-109
17		125-134	110-118

BED. The smallest division of a series of rock layers, clearly separated from the older rock layers below and the younger rock layers above. It lies parallel to the stratification. Also, the bottom or floor of a body of water, such as a river, lake, or sea.

BEDDING PLANE. The surface on which material forming sedimentary rock was originally deposited.

BED LOAD. The loose material moved by a stream along its channel floor, as compared to silt load, which is material carried in suspension.

BEDROCK. Solid rock exposed at the earth's surface or covered by soil or unconsolidated weathered material, or regolith. Also, the parent material in the soil profile.

BEHEADED STREAM. A stream, or river, from which the upper portion of its watercourse has been captured by a stronger stream. See also *Stream capture*.

BEN. In Scottish, a peak or mountain. The term is often used as a prefix in names of mountains, such as Ben More-Mt. More.

BENCH MARK. A special mark indicating a point on the earth's surface whose elevation and location have been accurately found by surveying.

BENTHIC. See *Ocean depth zones*.

BERGSCHRUND. A crevasse or series of open fissures at the head of a mountain glacier, between the moving glacial ice and snow and the immobile ice and snow on the headwall of the valley, or cirque.

BERG WIND. A warm dry wind of the foehn type that occurs in South Africa.

BERM. A terrace formed when an erosion cycle is interrupted with the rejuvenation of a stream in its mature stage, leaving remnants of the earlier valley floor above flood level. Also, a storm-built beach terrace whose seaward edges are low ridges built by waves.

BEVELING. The wearing down or planing by erosion of outcropping edges or tops of ridges or hills.

B HORIZON. See *Soil profile*.

BIGHT. A bend in a shore line between comparatively distant headlands, forming a shallow opening toward the sea.

BIOCLIMATOLOGY. The study of climate in relation to living organisms and their distribution.

BIOGEOGRAPHY. The study of the geographical distribution of plants and animals on the earth.

BIOSPHERE. All living organisms on the earth's surface, as distinguished from those living only in the atmosphere, hydrosphere, or lithosphere.

BIOSTRATIGRAPHY. Differentiation of rocks on the basis of the fossils they contain.

BIOTA. The collective plant and animal life of a region.

BIOTITE. See *Micas*.

BISE. A cold, dry wind from the north, northeast, or northwest occurring in southern France, Switzerland, and northern Italy. It is accompanied by heavy clouds.

BITUMINOUS. A type of soft coal with a blocky structure that has experienced intermediate metamorphosis.

BLACKBODY. An ideal body whose surface completely absorbs all radiation that falls upon it.

BLACK EARTH. Dark-colored soils high in humus. See *Soil*.

BLIND VALLEY. A feature in limestone areas where a stream disappears underground at the closed end of a valley.

BLIZZARD. A heavy, blinding snowstorm, usually accompanied by a freezing wind. Blizzards result from the action of a high wind on dry, powdery snow.

BLOCK DIAGRAM. A technique for showing the topography of a region by sketching the surface features on a perspective block to give a three-dimensional effect.

BLOCK LAVA. See *Aa*.

BLOCK MOUNTAINS. Mountains formed by uplifted and tilted earth-blocks and bounded by fault scarps or cliffs.

BLOWOUT. A hollow made by wind in sandy soil or in a dune. Its size may vary from a few feet to several miles in diameter.

BLUE MUD. A deposit on the ocean floor having a blue-gray color. The color is the result of incomplete oxidation because of rapid deposition.

BLUFF. A headland or high, steep cliff with an almost perpendicular front.

BODY WAVE. A seismic wave that travels through the interior of a medium, as distinguished from a surface wave. See *Earthquake*.

BOG. A poorly drained, spongy land composed of decaying vegetation, or peat.

BOGAZ. Narrow, deep chasms in a limestone area caused by water penetrating a fault, bedding plain, or joint.

BOHOROK. A warm, dry wind occurring in Southeast Asia during the winter (the northeast monsoon season) caused by the descent of air on the lee side of mountains.

BOLSON. A basin, depression, or wide mountain valley drained by a stream flowing through canyons at either end; found in arid or semiarid regions.

BOMB, VOLCANIC. Lava thrown up during a volcanic eruption and solidifying before reaching the ground. The round rock masses formed range up to several feet in diameter.

BORA. A cold, dry northeasterly wind that blows across the Yugoslav Adriatic coast and northern Italy, mainly during the winter season.

BORE. A huge wave moving upstream (in opposition to the current) in funnel-shaped bays or narrow estuaries.

BOREAL FOREST. A regional plant cover consisting of coniferous trees found in the subarctic climate zone.

BOSS. A knob-like or dome-shaped mass of rock, circular in shape and often about 40 square miles in area.

BOTTOM LAND. See *Floodplain*.

BOTTOMSET BEDS. The layers of fine sediment deposited on the bottom of a sea or lake beyond the advancing edge of a growing delta. As the delta advances they are covered by thick foreset beds. Above this, where erosion and deposition alternate with the fluctuation of the stream current, thin topset beds are deposited.

BOULDER CLAY. A mass of silty and clayey materials containing matter ranging in size from rock flour to boulders; formed by glacial action. The material is dragged along the foot of a glacier and left behind when the ice melts.

BOWEN'S REACTION SERIES. Two orders of crystallization of silicate minerals in which any early-formed phase tends to react with the melt that remains, yielding a new mineral further along in the series.

In the continuous feldspar series, comprising the plagioclase minerals, early-formed crystals react with the

A CAPE is a pointed headland extending into the sea or a lake. Cape Cod extends from Massachusetts into the Atlantic Ocean.

remaining liquid without abrupt changes. In the discontinuous ferromagnesian series, including the minerals olivine, augite, hornblende, and biotite, each change represents a different crystalline structure and composition.

Fractionation is an interruption in the series, occurring when crystals settle out of the melt and do not enter into further reactions.

BOX CANYON. A steep-sided, flat-floored valley with a zigzag course; formed in dry regions. It appears to have four almost vertical walls.

BRACKISH. Referring to water with a salt content between that of freshwater and seawater.

BRAIDED STREAM. A stream flowing in several separating and reuniting channels divided by sediment the stream has deposited.

BRASH ICE. Fragment of sea or river ice less than 6.6 feet in diameter.

BREAKER. A wave that breaks into foam as it moves toward the shore, or a wave that breaks against a rock or other obstacle.

BREAKWATER. See *Jetty*.

BRECCIA. Rock composed of cemented angular fragments and thereby distinguished from conglomerates, which contain waterworn fragments.

BRODEL. A bulbous mass of silt, without horizontal continuity and enclosed by clay except at "necks," which connect with overlying silt beds.

BROOK. A small stream, one of the smallest branches of a drainage system. In the northeastern United States it is considered smaller than a creek.

BROWN COAL. See *Lignite*.

BULK MODULOUS. Volume elasticity of a body or number of pounds per square inch required to cause a specific change in volume. A body under increasing force per unit area will decrease in size but increase in density.

BUSH. A type of vegetation region having a dense undergrowth, with or without trees.

BUTTE. A small, flat-topped, steep-sided mountain standing above an adjacent plain.

BUYS BALLOT'S LAW. A general law of storms. It states that when standing with one's back to the wind in the northern hemisphere, the low pressure center will be on the left; in the southern hemisphere, the low pressure center will be on the right. Therefore, winds move counterclockwise around low pressure centers in the northern hemisphere and clockwise in the southern hemisphere. See also *Cyclone*.

CAATINGA. A type of vegetation region composed of thorny scrub and stunted, sparse forest in an area of slight rainfall. It is found in parts of northeastern Brazil.

CADASTRAL SURVEY. A large-scale survey of land to show accurately the property lines of every plot.

CALCAREOUS. Containing calcium carbonate ($CaCO_3$).

CALCITE. One of the commonest minerals and the principal constituent of limestone. It is composed of calcium carbonate ($CaCO_3$) and effervesces freely upon the application of acid.

CALDERA. A great, basin-shaped depression with a diameter at least three times its depth, as contrasted with a crater. It is formed by explosion or, more often, by the collapse of the peak of a volcano.

CALICHE. Gravel, sand, or desert debris cemented by calcium carbonate. It is found in dry regions. Also, the hardpan deposit of calcium carbonate found close to the surface.

CALVING. The formation of icebergs by the breaking off of a large block of ice from a glacier where it reaches into the sea. A piece of ice which rises to the surface after breaking away from the submerged portion of its parent body is called a calf.

CAMBRIAN PERIOD. The earliest period of the Paleozoic era in geological time. It began approximately 550 million years ago and ended approximately 450 million years ago.

CAMPOS. The tropical grasslands, or savanna, of interior Brazil.

CANAL. An artificial watercourse cut through a narrow stretch of land separating two bodies of water.

CANYON. A steep-walled, relatively narrow gorge, chasm, or ravine formed by the down cutting of a river.

CAPE. A headland, generally pointed, jutting out beyond the ordinary coastline into the sea or a lake. It differs from a peninsula in that it narrows as it projects into the water. It is usually larger than a point.

CAPILLARY FRINGE. A soil belt above the zone of saturation and composed of pores filled with water, held there by capillarity, or the ability to hold water by molecular attraction.

CAP ROCK. A layer of resistant rock overlying a layer of less resistant material.

CARBONATION. A chemical weathering process in which air or rain-borne carbon dioxide reacts with rock constituents to form carbonates.

CARBON 14. A radioactive isotope of carbon with a half life (time required for half the radioactive particles present to disintegrate into stable atoms) of about 5,700 years. It is used to date carbonaceous material younger than 50,000 years.

CARBONIFEROUS PERIOD. See *Mississippian period* and *Pennsylvanian period*.

CARDINAL POINTS. The four main directions of the compass: north, south, east, west.

CARTOGRAPHY. The art and science of representing in charts and maps the visible physical features—both natural and man-made—of the earth's surface.

CASCADE. A small waterfall, or a series of falls.

CATACLASTIC. A texture in metamorphic rocks in which brittle minerals have been broken and flattened in a direction at a right angle to the pressure stress.

CATARACT. A large waterfall. Also, a series of steep falls or rapids in a river.

CATASTROPHISM. The theory that certain geologic events were caused by sudden and violent disturbances of nature.

CATAZONE. The deepest zone of rock metamorphism. It is marked by very high pressures and high temperatures.

CATCHMENT BASIN. Drainage basin or area from which a stream draws its water.

CATS–PAW. An occasional feeble wind in the doldrums.

CAVE. A natural opening or underground cavity formed by the dissolution of limestone or gypsum by ground water, wave action against a cliff, faulting, or earthquakes.

CAVERN. A large cave or group of connected caves.

CAVITATION. Local reduction of a stream's pressure (by contraction or curvature) to a point at which partial vacuums are formed. As these vacuums collapse, the solid surfaces they contact are worn away in the process called cavitation erosion.

CAY. A low, flat island slightly above high tide level.

CELESTIAL SPHERE. A sphere whose center lies at some point within the solar system, most commonly the center of the earth. All members of the solar system may be projected onto this imaginary sphere.

CEMENTATION. The precipitation of a binding mineral matter, commonly calcite, silica, and iron oxide, in the spaces between the individual particles of an unconsolidated deposit.

CENOZOIC ERA. The "Era of Recent Life," the Cenozoic, or Caenozoic, is the latest of the three main eras of geological time. It began approximately 60 million years ago and continues into the present. Also called the Age of Mammals.

CENTRIFUGAL FORCE. The force which pulls a moving body out from its center of rotation. It is the opposite of gravitation, with which it combines to form gravity.

CENTROSPHERE. See *Earth structure.*

CHAIN. In the United States, the legal unit of length (66 feet) for the survey of public lands; ten square chains equal one acre. Also, a series of related or connected natural features such as mountains or lakes.

CHALCEDONY. An extremely fine-grained (cryptocrystalline) quartz, often deposited by aqueous solutions in a rock cavity, such as a geode, and having a hardness of 7.

CHALK. A soft, fine-grained variety of weakly cemented limestone. It is white, yellowish, or gray in color.

CHANNEL. The deepest part of a body of water (stream, bay, or strait) through which the main volume or current flows. Also, a narrow sea lane between two landmasses and connecting two larger bodies of water. The navigable part of a river or harbor.

CHAPARRAL. A dense thicket of stiff or thorny shrubs or dwarf trees, found in an area of Mediterranean climate—dry, sunny summers and moist winters.

CHASM. A deep cleft in the earth, often made by an earthquake.

CHEMICAL WEATHERING, or Chemical erosion. The decomposition of rock materials by oxidation, carbonation, hydrolysis, and chemicals in solution which transform the original material into new chemical combinations.

CHEMOSPHERE. The zone of the atmosphere from 40 to 160 miles above the surface of the earth containing a concentration of ozone.

CHERNOZEM. A zonal great soil group classified in the United States under the order *Mollisols.* It is a very dark, or black, soil, rich in humus and high in calcium, formed under cool subhumid grassland climatic conditions, as in the East European region between the Ural and Carpathian mountains.

CHERT. Cryptocrystalline varieties of silica often occurring in limestone as compact massive rock or as nodules. Flint is a darker, less brittle, and finer-grained variety of chert.

CHESTNUT SOIL. A zonal great soil group classified in the United States under the order *Mollisols.* It has a moderately thick top layer, high in organic matter, above a zone of calcium carbonate. It develops in the semiarid grasslands of the middle latitudes.

CHINOOK. A warm, dry wind, or foehn, blowing down the eastern side of the Rocky Mountains in the winter and early spring.

CHLORITE. A group of green minerals, the hydrous silicates of aluminum, magnesium, and ferrous iron, related to the micas.

C HORIZON. See *Soil profile.*

CHUTE. A narrow waterway between the mainland and an island. For a stream, a quick drop.

CIENAGA. An area where the water table is at or near the surface. It is covered with grass or heavy vegetation and sometimes short springs flow from it. In the southwestern United States, an elevated marsh with springs.

CINDER CONE. A cone of volcanic ash and small fragments formed around the mouth, or vent, of a volcano.

CIRQUE. A saucer-shaped, steep-walled hollow formed in rock by a mountain glacier and the alternate melting and freezing of the ice, or nivation. When glacier ice has melted from a cirque and the basin is filled with water, the lake formed is called a tarn. When two or more cirques gnaw into a ridge from opposite sides, an arête, or sharp, jagged ridge is formed.

CLASTIC ROCK. A class of sedimentary rocks, such as sandstone and shale, composed of particles produced by the disintegration of previous rocks by weathering processes.

THE AMERICAN MUSEUM OF NATURAL HISTORY

CLAY, a fine-textured earth material, goes into the composition of shale.

CLAY. A fine-textured earth material, one of the commonest materials in the mantle. It goes into the composition of shale, the most abundant type of sedimentary rock. See also *Wentworth grade scale.*

CLEAVAGE. In minerals, the characteristic of breaking in certain directions along smooth plane surfaces, being governed by the atomic structure of the material.

In rocks, the property of breaking along parallel planes or surfaces. There are four degrees of rock cleavage: *slaty,* the planes are separated by microscopic distances; *phyllitic,* the distance is barely visible; *schistose,* the distances are clearly visible; and *gneissic,* the distance is as great as ½ inch.

CLIFF. A high, steep rock face caused by weathering or wave action.

CLIMATE. The average weather conditions of an area as characterized by temperature, humidity, wind, and atmospheric pressure, and controlled by latitude, altitude, topography, distribution of land and sea, ocean currents, and prevailing winds.

CLIMATIC ZONE. An area having a distinctive climate. See *Frigid zone, Temperate zone, Torrid zone.*

CLIMATOLOGY. The study of the formation, distribution, and characteristics of earth climates.

CLIMAX. The plant cover believed to be in equilibrium with its environment. It is stable for the site.

CLIMOGRAPH. A graphic representation of the relation of two climatic elements in a region, such as temperature and rainfall, plotted at monthly intervals throughout the year.

CLINOMETER. An instrument for determining vertical angles, particularly dips, in a surface. It is essentially a pendulum swinging through a graduated arc.

CLOUD. A mass of visible vapor or collection of water or ice particles formed in the atmosphere by the condensation of water vapor at various elevations. Clouds are found in a variety of forms.

CLOUDBURST. A very heavy downpour of rain, averaging 3.94 inches per hour, usually of short duration and accompanied by thunder.

CLOUDINESS. An estimate of the amount of sky covered by clouds and expressed in tenths of sky covered. When the sky is up to 3/10 clouds, weather is considered clear; 3/10 to 7/10, partly cloudy; 7/10 to 9/10, cloudy; 9/10 or more, overcast.

COAL. A series of sedimentary rocks in which vegetable matter has been disintegrated, decomposed, and compacted, increasing in carbon content and, thus, increasing in effectiveness as fuel.

There are four types of coal, classified according to composition, degree of change, and hardness: peat, the softest, with about 60 percent carbon; lignite; bituminous; and anthracite, the hardest, with 92 to 98 percent carbon.

COAL MEASURES. The series of strata containing coal seams or minable deposits of coal and other sedimentary rocks, such as shale.

COAST. The edge of land bordering the sea, extending from the shoreline inland to the first major change in surface features.

COASTAL PLAIN. A low-lying level region or plain composed of sand, gravel, silt, and clay bordering the seacoast and extending inland to the first elevated land surface. Coastal plains represent a falling sea level or emerging sea bottom.

COASTLINE. The outline of a landmass where it meets the sea.

COBBLE. See *Wentworth grade scale.*

COKE. A hard, porous residue produced by the baking of bituminous coal. The heat drives off volatile constituents leaving a fuel useful in blast furnaces.

COL. A gap across a ridge or between two peaks; a high pass through a mountain range.

COLD POLE. The point on the earth's surface where the lowest winter temperatures are recorded. It is in the vicinity of Verkhoyansk, in the Siberian region of the Soviet Union.

COLD WAVE. A burst of cold polar air that causes a sudden drop in temperature.

COLLOID. A substance resulting from submicroscopic, yet larger than molecular, subdivision of one substance in another. When apparently dissolved in a liquid, it diffuses through a membrane very slowly or not at all, as contrasted with a crystalloid.

COLLUVIUM. A mixture of loose and incoherent material moved down a slope by gravity and usually found at the foot of a slope or cliff.

COLUMNAR JOINTING. A pattern of cracking breaking igneous rocks into columns. It is caused by contraction during cooling.

COMPACTION. A decrease in the volume of sediments by the reduction of the space between individual grains. It is the result of the evaporation or pressure of later deposits above or from earth movements.

COMPASS. An instrument indicating direction, usually by the pointing of a magnetized needle free to rotate in a horizontal plane. The needle responds to variations in the earth's magnetic field. Also, an instrument used for drawing circles and transferring measurements.

COMPETENCE. The maximum size of particles of given specific gravity that can be moved by a transporting agency such as a stream, glacier, or wind moving at a given velocity.

COMPLEX. A complicated assemblage of rocks of any age or origin.

COMPOSITE CONE, or stratovolcano. A volcanic cone, usually large with steep sides, built up over time by a number of eruptions.

CONCORDANT PLUTON. An igneous body lying parallel to the layering of the rocks into which it was intruded, as opposed to a discordant pluton.

CONCRETION. A rounded mass, or nodule, of material harder than the rock in which it is found. It is formed within sedimentary rocks by the concentration of cementing material around a nucleus such as a fossil or grain of sand.

CONDENSATION. The change of a substance from a gaseous state into a liquid or solid state. Condensation is the opposite of evaporation.

CONDUCTION. The transmission of energy through matter (the conductor) away from the source of energy.

CONE OF DEPRESSION. A dimple, or drop, in the water table surface produced by pumping or artesian outflow greater than the replacement of water.

CONE SHEET. A concentric set of dikes forming a funnel-shaped zone around an igneous intrusion.

CONFLUENCE. The point at which two streams meet.

CONFORMABLE. Referring to conformity—the parallel order of strata lying one above the other in unbroken geologic sequence.

CONGLOMERATE. A sedimentary rock composed of pebble-sized, waterworn rocks (generally of some durable material such as quartz) mixed with sand and cemented together with a mineral such as calcium carbonate. Conglomerate is distinguished from breccia, which is composed of angular rock fragments.

CONNATE WATER. Water trapped in the pores or interstices of sedimentary or extrusive igneous rock at the time the rock material was deposited, and therefore not participating in the hydrologic cycle.

CONSEQUENT STREAM. A stream whose course is a direct consequence of the original slope of the surface on which it developed.

CONTACT METAMORPHISM. Metamorphism at or near the point of contact between an intrusive igneous body and the surrounding rocks. Contact metamorphism occurs in relatively narrow zones called aureoles, in contrast to regional metamorphism.

CONTEMPORANEOUS DEFORMATION. Deformation, especially folding and faulting, that takes place during the time sedimentary rocks are being deposited.

CONTINENT. A large, unbroken landmass rising abruptly above the deep ocean floor. The earth's six major landmasses (Eurasia, Africa, North America, South America, Australia, and Antarctica), with islands, make up about 30 percent of the earth's surface, or an area of some 55 million square miles.

CONTINENTAL AIR MASS. A large, dry panel of air originating over a land surface. The air mass may be either hot or cold.

CONTINENTAL CLIMATE. A type of climate found in the interior of large landmasses. It is characterized by a wide range of temperature difference between winter and summer.

CONTINENTAL DRIFT. The idea that continents can shift, or drift. Proponents of the concept cite as an example the matching continental margins of western Africa and eastern South America.

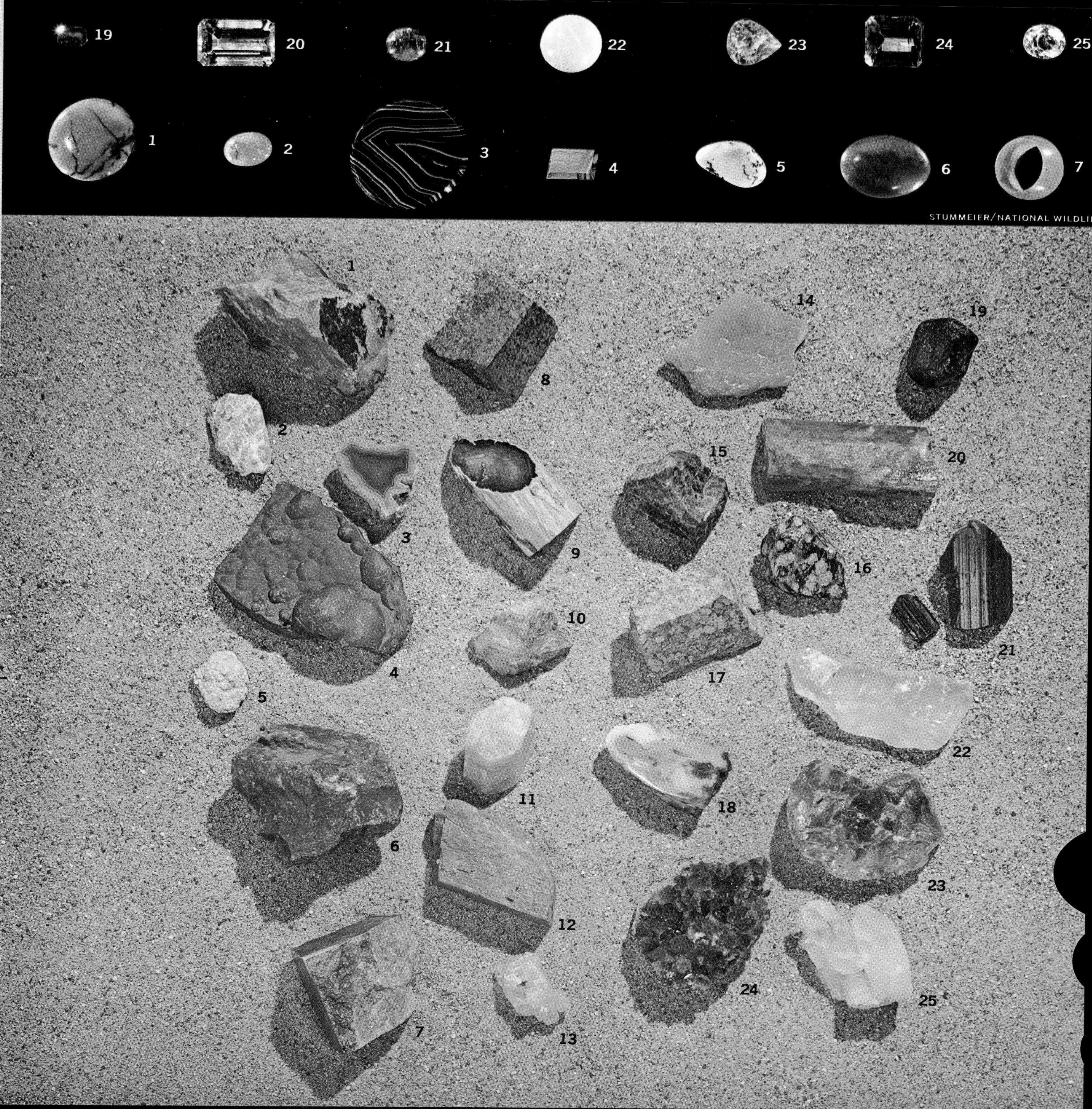

STUMMEIER/NATIONAL WILDLIFE

1. RHODENITE with cabochon.

2. TURQUOISE with cabochon.

3. FORTIFICATION AGATE with flat cabochon.

4. MALACHITE with square cabochon.

5. VARISCITE with tumbled specimen, also called Utahite.

6. JASPER with oval cabochon; usually red, also brown and green, sometimes banded.

7. JADE with carved ring.

8. EPIDOTE.

9. PETRIFIED WOOD; minerals are opal, agate, and jasper.

10. CHRYSOCOLLA; soft, but gem value if evenly colored.

11. BERYL EMERALD when dark green and clear.

12. AMAZONITE, also Amazon stone.

13. SULPHUR CRYSTALS; too soft to cut, but sought as beautiful specimens.

14. SMITHSONITE; most valuable in sea green.

15. SODALITE; bright, deep blue most valuable.

16. OBSIDIAN, a volcanic glass, here with white "snowflakes."

17. UNIKITE, a form of epidote with feldspar blotches.

18. MOSS AGATE, another popular agate type; note "madonna" pattern in this piece.

19. GARNET with faceted stone.

20. AQUAMARINE with faceted stone; a popular light green beryl.

21. TOURMALINE with faceted rubellite.

22. ROSE QUARTZ with deep cabochon; popular pinkrose quartz.

23. CITRINE with faceted stone; another popular quartz variety.

24. AMETHYST with faceted stone; another quartz.

25. CLEAR QUARTZ with faceted stone, called rock crystal.

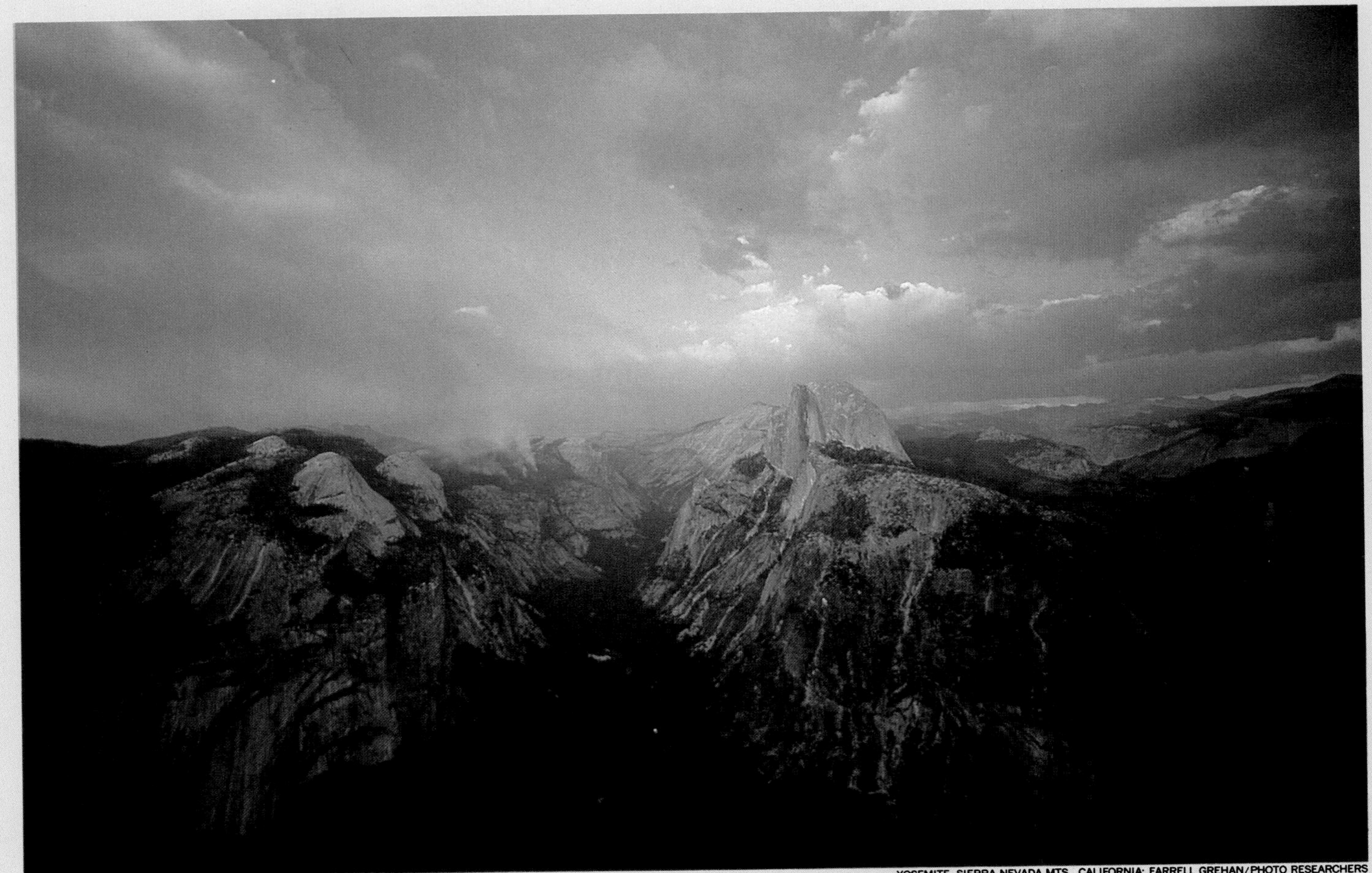

YOSEMITE, SIERRA NEVADA MTS., CALIFORNIA: FARRELL GREHAN/PHOTO RESEARCHERS

Water, in its many forms, is the leveler of the land. Rivers of water have helped to wear away the peaks and valleys of Yosemite (*above*). Rivers of ice (*below*) gouge out their own deep valleys.

GLACIER, CHILEAN ANDES: EARL DIBBLE/PHOTO RESEARCHERS

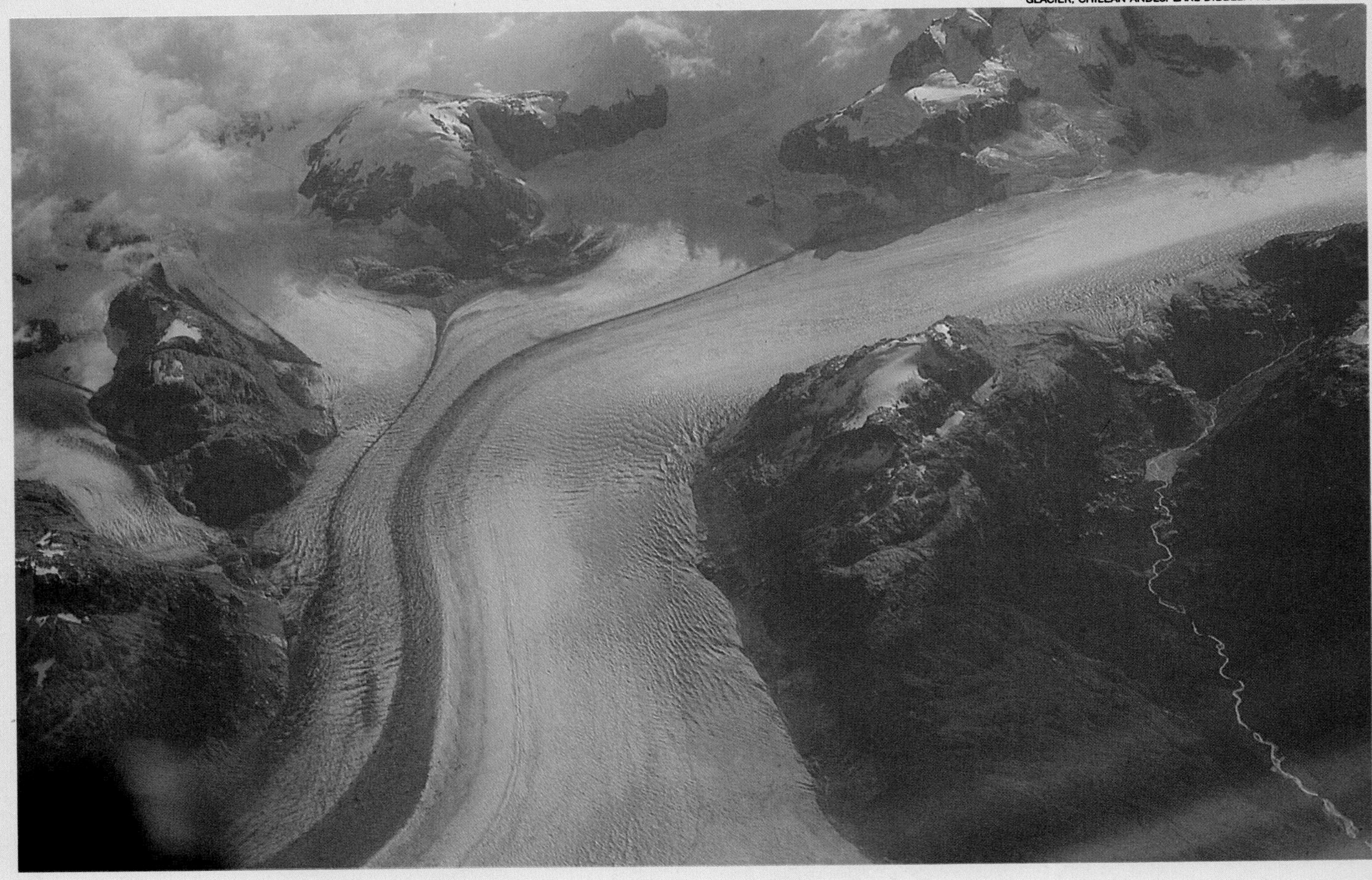

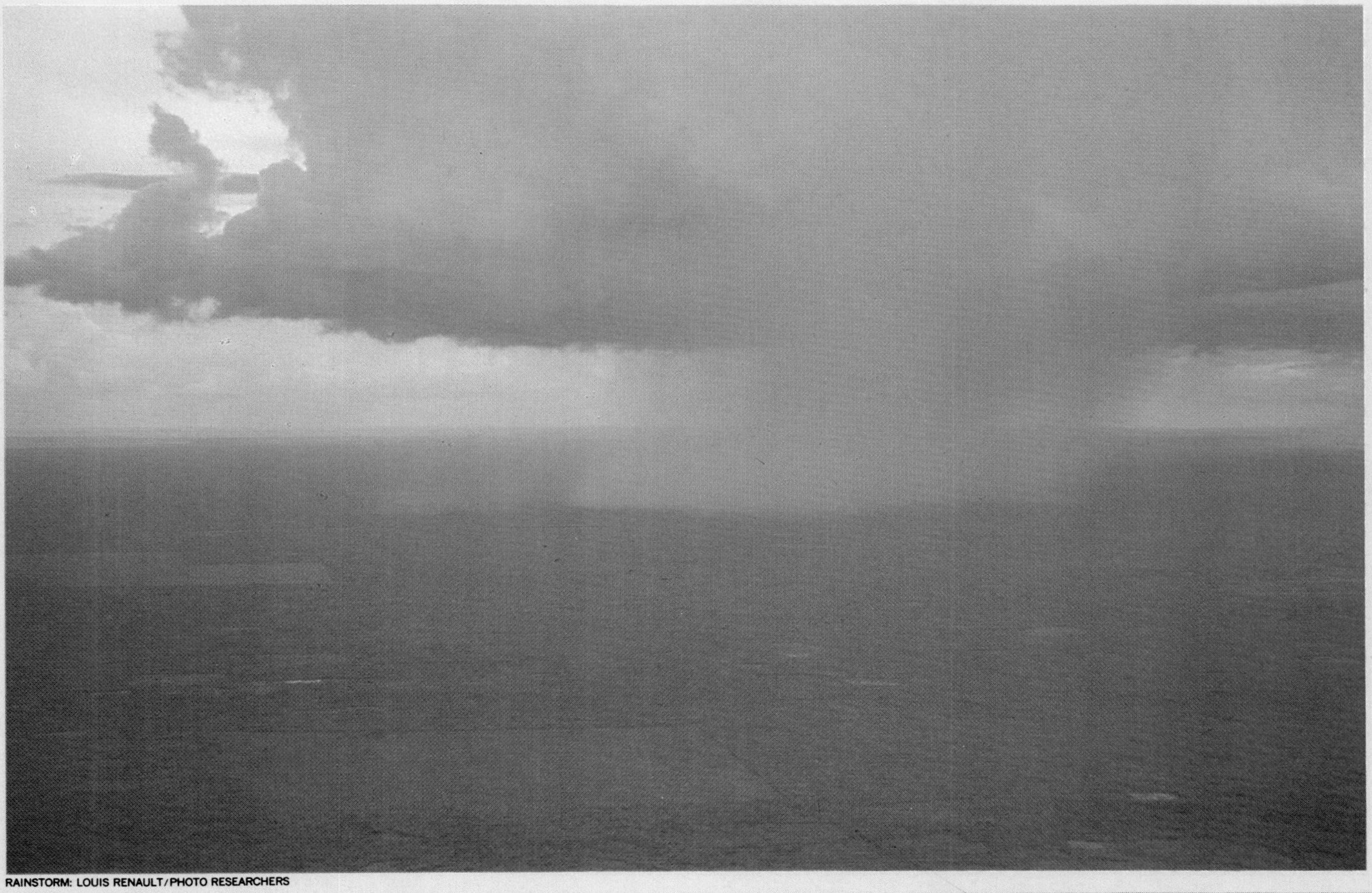

RAINSTORM: LOUIS RENAULT/PHOTO RESEARCHERS

Ice and water between them cover about 70% of the earth's surface, whether in the form of oceans, rivers, icebergs (*below*), glaciers, or snow. There is much water, too, in the atmosphere, especially during a rainstorm (*above*).

ICEBERGS, ANTARCTICA: WILLIAM CURTSINGER/PHOTO RESEARCHERS

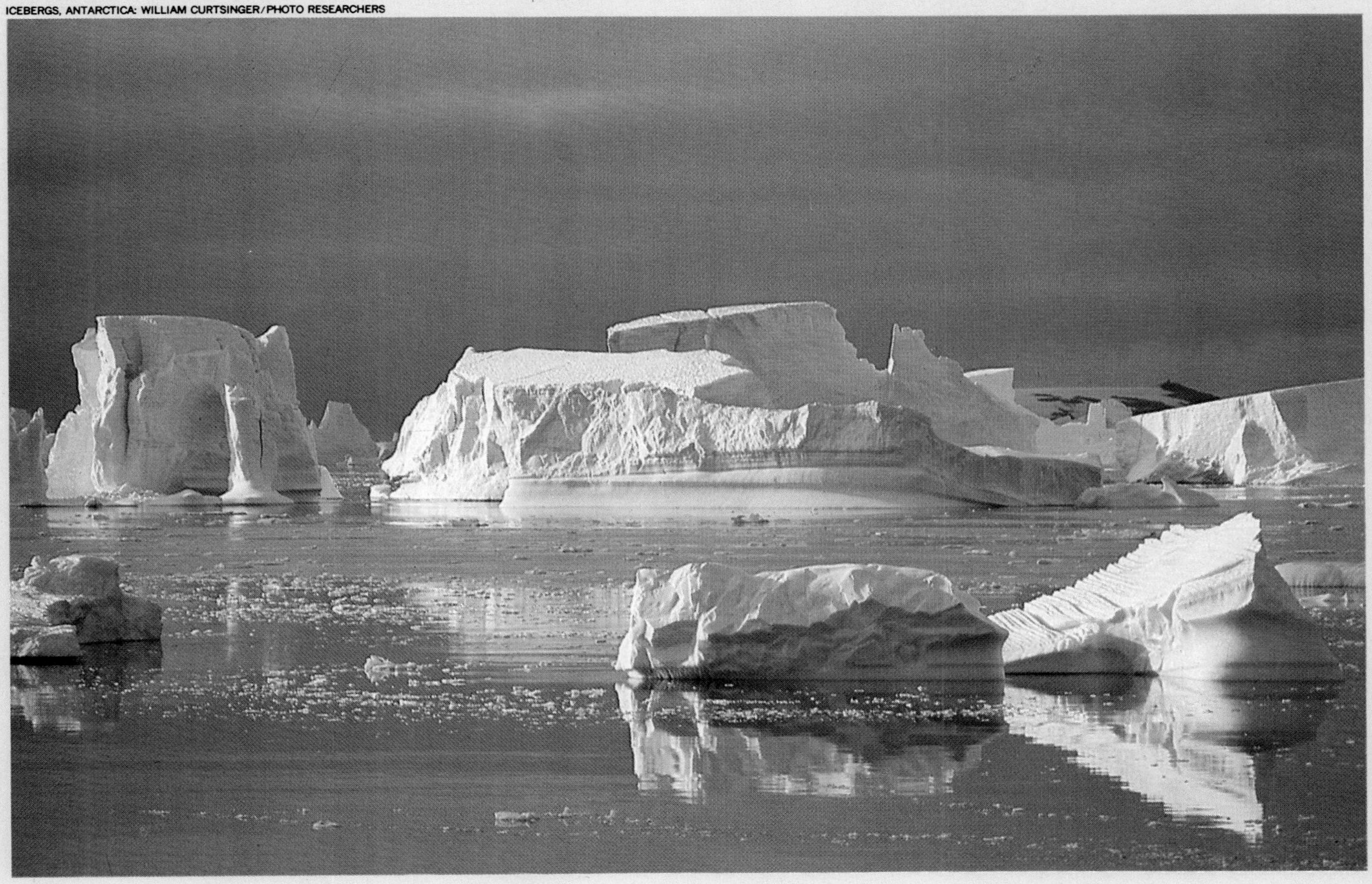

TAHANDS FALLS, MT. HOOD, OREGON: JOHN V.A.F. NEAL/PHOTO RESEARCHERS

CARIBBEAN ISLAND: DON LORIMER

DEATH VALLEY, CALIFORNIA: NED HAINES/PHOTO RESEARCHERS

Water, the most abundant liquid on earth, carves out rivers, tumbles over waterfalls, and fills the oceans. Without water life fails,
the earth turns to desert, and even rivers can be lost.

AMARGOSA RIVER. DEATH VALLEY. CALIFORNIA: WILLIAM BELKNAP/PHOTO RESEARCHERS

CONTINENTAL GLACIER. An ice sheet covering a large part of a continent, obscuring mountains and plains, such as the glaciers on Greenland and in Antarctica.

CONTINENTAL SHELF. The gently sloping extension of a continent beneath its bordering seas. The shelf extends from the low-water mark to the point where there the continental slope begins its drop to the ocean floor. It may range in width from less than 10 to more than 200 miles.

CONTINENTAL SLOPE. The sharply sloping portion of the continental margin extending from the continental shelf to the ocean floor.

CONTINUOUS FELDSPAR SERIES. See *Bowen's reaction series.*

CONVECTION. The transmission of heat in a gas or liquid by the movements of the particles themselves. A temperature rise in one area of air, for example, will decrease its density and, therefore, its pressure. The denser portion surrounding that area moves into the low-pressure area, thus producing a convection current. A pair of such convection currents is known as a convection cell.

COPROLITE. Petrified excrement, or fecal pellets, found in Paleozoic, Mesozoic, and Tertiary strata.

COQUINA. A soft, coarse-grained porous limestone composed of cemented shell fragments.

CORAL. Various sessile (lacking voluntary mobility) marine animals that excrete an external skeleton of calcium carbonate, which they extract from sea water. They are usually found in colonies. Most corals require warm water and although they may grow as far below the ocean surface as sunlight penetrates, they are usually found where the water is 200 feet deep or less.

CORAL REEF. An accumulation of coral skeletons in three types of shore lines: *fringing reef,* which grows directly out from a landmass; *barrier reef,* which is separated from the landmass by a lagoon; and *atoll,* which is a ring of low coral islands around a central lagoon.
 The term "coral" island for many tropical islands is often incorrect. In many cases they are made up largely of calcareous algae.

CORDED LAVA. See *Pahoehoe.*

CORDILLERA. A unified belt or series of mountain systems extending over considerable distances and including such intermontane features as valleys, plains, rivers, and lakes.

CORE. The innermost zone of the earth. See *Earth structure.*

CORIOLIS FORCE. The force exerted on freely moving bodies by the earth's rotation. It deflects a moving body, or currents of air or water, to the right in the northern hemisphere and to the left in the southern hemisphere.

CORN BELT CLIMATE. The type of climate found in the corn belt region of the United States and other similar areas in Europe and Asia. It is a type of humid continental climate with a long summer.

CORONA. Concentric luminous circles around the sun or moon. Also, a zone of minerals around another mineral or at the point of contact between two minerals.

CORRASION. The mechanical erosion, or wearing away, of the bed or bank of a stream by the abrasive action of loose material carried in suspension.

CORRELATION. The process of establishing the equivalence in geologic age and stratigraphic position of rocks or events in one area with rocks or events in another area.

CORRIE. See *Cirque.*

CORROSION. The erosion, or wearing away, of rocks by chemical action. It is an oxidizing process.

COSMIC RAYS. Streams of subatomic particles with enormous energy surrounding the earth. Although their activity increases with the altitude above the earth, their effects are measurable not only at the earth's surface, but well below the surface of bodies of water.

COSMOGONY. The science of the origin and development of the universe and its components.

A CORAL COLONY consists of marine animals and the calcium carbonate skeletons they excrete. The shells may be white, pink, or red.

COSMOLOGY. The study of the universe, its origin, structure, and space-time relationships.

COTTON BELT CLIMATE. A type of climate found in the cotton belt area of the United States and other similar areas in Asia, Africa, Australia, and South America, It is a humid, subtropical climate.

COULEE. A steep-sided gulch. Also, a congealed lava flow.

COUNTER–TRADE WINDS. See *Antitrades.*

COUNTRY ROCK. A general term for rock penetrated by mineral veins or invaded by an igneous intrusion.

COVE. A small, baylike recess or hollow along a shore or in a mountain.

CRAG, A rough, steep, rock outcrop or broken cliff.

CRATER. A bowl-shaped, steep-sided basin such as in the top or side of a volcano or a depression in the earth caused by the impact of a meteor.

CREEK. A small stream tributary, larger than a brook but smaller than a river. Also, a small, narrow bay longer than it is wide.

CREEP. A slow but continuous downward and outward movement of slope-forming soil or rock carrying its plant cover with it unbroken.

CRETACEOUS PERIOD. The third and latest period of the Mesozoic era in geologic time. It began about 125 million years ago and lasted some 65 million years.

CREVASSE. A deep, vertical crack, or fissure, in a glacier.

CROSS–LAMINATION. Layers of deposits tranverse or oblique to the general plane of stratification of the rocks above and below. It is found in granular sedimentary rocks. Also called bedding.

CRUDE OIL. Oil as it comes from a pool in the earth before refining and treatment.

CRUST. The outermost layer of the earth. See *Earth structure.*

CRYPTOCRYSTALLINE. Having a structure so fine that although crystalline, it cannot be seen with an ordinary microscope.

CRYPTOZOIC EON. The eon of "hidden life" which preceded the Phanerozoic eon and includes perhaps as much as 9/10 of the history of earth. Its rocks range in age from less than 600 million years to almost 3 billion years. It lacks fossils to aid correlation and is not divisible into units of more than local application.

    During the Cryptozoic, magma was intruded in great areas which stabilized by the beginning of the Phanerozoic eon. These areas are gently arched interior plains, called shields, and they

are found in each of the continents. There is a fossil record only of calcareous algae, fungi, and the trails of wormlike creatures.

CRYSTAL. A solid (e.g., most minerals) with a definite, orderly internal arrangement of atoms.

CRYSTALLINE ROCK. Rock containing minerals of crystalline form. Applied to igneous and metamorphic rocks but not to sedimentary rocks.

CRYSTALLIZATION. The formation of crystals from solution, a fluid that is evaporated or cooled; fusion, a viscous substance that is cooled; or sublimation, a gas that is condensed as a solid without passing through the liquid state.

CRYSTALLOBLASTIC. A crystalline texture in which the essential constituents are included in all the others. The result is simultaneous crystallization. See also *Metamorphic facies.*

CRYSTALLOID. A substance that forms a true solution in which it diffuses readily through a membrane and is capable of being crystallized.

CUESTA. An asymmetrical ridge with one steep slope, or scarp, and one long, gentle slope generally parallel to the dip of the resistant sedimentary rock beds that form it.

CURRENT. The vertical motion of the air, wind being the horizontal movement. Also the horizontal movement of water. See also *Ocean current.*

CURRENT METER. An instrument used to determine the velocity of streams.

CYCLE OF EROSION. See *Geographical cycle.*

CYCLONE. A low-pressure air mass, nearly circular, around which winds spiral inward, turning counterclockwise in the northern hemisphere, clockwise in the southern. It is commonly referred to as a low. It tends to produce cloudiness and precipitation, sometimes severe storms, such as a hurricane, tornado, or typhoon.

DACITE. A group of dense volcanic rocks, the extrusive equivalent of quartz diorite, consisting of plagioclase, quartz, pyroxene, or hornblende, with some biotite and sanidine. Structurally they are either glassy or crystalline.

DALLES. The nearly vertical walls of a canyon or gorge, usually containing a rapid. Also, the plural of dell.

DAM. A natural or man-made obstruction across a stream raising the level of water in the stream channel.

DARCY'S LAW. An equation expressing the rate of flow of water through permeable rock. In a rock of constant permeability (P), the velocity (V) of water will increase as the hydraulic gradient ($\frac{h}{l}$), or slope of the water table, increases: $V = P\frac{l}{h}$.

DATUM LEVEL. The base level against which the altitudes of land surfaces are measured, usually mean sea level.

DAUGHTER ELEMENT. An element formed from another element through radioactive decay.

DEBRIS. Loose, or unconsolidated, surface material containing larger rock fragments than detritus, or pulverized rock.

DECLINATION. The declination of the sun is the angular distance, covering a range of 47° (from 23½° north of the equator to 23½° south of the equator), in which the sun attains a zenith position. See also *Magnetic declination.*

DEEP. A narrow, troughlike depression found along some margins of the ocean basins, generally more than 3,000 fathoms (18,000 feet) deep. Also called the hadal zone. See *Ocean depth zones.*

DEFLATION. An erosive process in which material is removed from a land surface by wind action.

DEFORMATION OF THE EARTH'S CRUST. See *Diastrophism.*

DEFORMATION OF ROCKS. Changes in the volume and shape of rocks. There are three types of deformation—*elastic, plastic,* and *rupture.*

    In *elastic* deformation, a rock changed by stress will return to its original shape or volume when the stress is removed (see also *Hooke's law*). In *plastic* deformation, a rock will flow at a certain intensity of stress and accompanying heat and will not recover its original shape or volume. In *rupture,* the rock is actually cracked or broken.

DEGRADATION. The process of wearing down the land and transporting the material elsewhere, usually by a river.

DEGREE–DAY. The number of degrees Fahrenheit the mean temperature drops below 65°F in one day. It is used to estimate heating fuel needs.

DELL. A small wooded valley or hollow.

DELTA. A plain or extension of land at the mouth of a river, often roughly triangular in shape, resembling the Greek letter delta (△). Deltas result from the deposit of material carried in suspension by a stream whose velocity is suddenly reduced upon entering more quiet waters. See also *Bottomset beds.*

DENDRITIC DRAINAGE PATTERN. A system of streams in which tributaries join the mainstream at all angles, thus resembling the branching of a tree when shown on a map.

DENDROCHRONOLOGY. The study of tree rings to determine the past climatic history of an area and to date events in the past.

DENSITY. The ratio of mass to volume, showing the quantity of a substance in grams per cubic centimeter or pounds per cubic foot. The ratio between the density of a substance and that of water at 39.2°F is specific gravity.

DENSITY CURRENT. A current which may be colder, more salty, or muddier, and therefore more dense, than the water through, over, or under which it flows. It does not mix with the surrounding water. A muddy density current is called a turbidity current.

DENUDATION. The wearing away of a land surface by natural agencies such as streams, glaciers, frost, wind, rain, and the sea.

DEPOSITION. The laying down of solid material transported from one part of the earth's surface to another by a natural agency, such as wind (eolian deposits), ice, rainfall, and earth movements. Also, the precipitation of mineral matter from solution.

DEPRESSION. An area of lower elevation than the surrounding land surface with no natural outlet for surface drainage. Also, a region where the atmospheric pressure is lower than that of the surrounding area.

DESALINIZATION, or desalination. The removal of salt from water or soil, or the reduction of salt content.

DESERT. A region in which vegetation is too sparse to support any but specialized animals. A *cold desert,* such as the wastes of Antarctica, is caused by perpetual snow and temperatures too low to permit plant growth. A *hot* or *tropical desert,* such as the Sahara, is caused by low rainfall and tempera-

tures and winds so high that evaporation exceeds precipitation.

A "topographic" desert, such as the Takla Makan in Asia, is caused by a rainfall deficiency either because it is located far from the oceans in the center of a continent, or because it is ringed by high mountains that deprive it of rain-bearing winds.

DESERT PAVEMENT. The layer of stone or pebbles fitted closely together in desert regions after wind action has removed the fine dust and sand.

DESICCATION. The loss of water from pore spaces of sediments by evaporation or compaction. Also, the drying up, or increasing aridity, of an area of the earth as a result of long-term changes in climate.

DETRITUS. Loose, pulverized pieces of earth material; the product of mechanical weathering.

DEVONIAN PERIOD. The fourth period of the Paleozoic era in geological time. It began 355 million years ago and lasted 43 million years. During that time trees grew in swamps, amphibians developed, and fish became common in the sea and in freshwater. Also called the Age of Fishes.

DEW. Moisture condensed onto objects on or near the earth's surface. It is caused by the objects having cooled below the dew point of the adjacent air through radiational cooling during the night.

DEW POINT. The temperature at which air becomes saturated with water

vapor. Condensation will occur when the air temperature falls below the dew point.

DIALYSIS. A method of separating mixed substances — crystalloids from colloids — in solution by diffusion through a membrance. The crystalloid particles will pass through the membrane, but the colloid particles are too large and are retained.

DIAMOND. A form of carbon. It is the hardest substance known (10 on Moh's Hardness Scale). It is insoluble, inert at ordinary temperatures, and has perfect cleavage. Its specific gravity is 3.52.

DIASTROPHISM. The process by which the earth's crust is bent, folded, broken, or warped, producing continents, ocean basins, plateaus, and mountains.

DIATOMACEOUS OOZE. A soft siliceous deposit, chiefly composed of the frustules, or shells, which diatoms, or one-celled marine algae, have built by extracting mineral matter from sea-water. It is found on the deep-sea floors. See also *Ooze.*

DIFFERENTIAL WEATHERING. The process in which different sections of a rock mass weather at different rates. It is caused by variations in the composition of the rock itself and differences in the intensity of weathering from one section to another in the same rock.

DIKE. A mass of igneous rock. Also, a bank of earth materials used to protect lowlying areas from flooding by the sea or a river.

GEORGE HUNTER/OTTAWA

DELTA on the Mackenzie River in northwestern Canada. Slowed crossing the delta, the river meandered and formed a series of oxbow lakes.

DINOSAURS

Reptilia—cold-blooded, scaly-skinned, egg-laying animals.

Archosauria—distinguishing bony arch in skull.

Thecodontia—teeth in sockets in the jaw.

Pterosauria—flying reptiles.

Phytosauria—primitive crocodiles.

Pseudosuchia (false crocodiles)—fast-running, bipedal reptiles.

Dinosauria (terrible lizards)—originally bipedal and rarely more than 15 feet long.

Saurischia (lizard-hipped)—originally carnivorous bipeds; late in the Triassic diverged into two suborders.

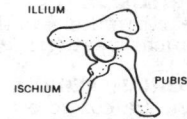

ILLIUM / ISCHIUM / PUBIS

TYRANNOSAURUS

Theropoda (beast-footed)—earliest dinosaurs; carnivorous bipeds; provided the stock from which Sauropoda arose; late in the Cretaceous culminated in Tyrannosaurus, the 50-foot-long "King of Dinosaurs."

BRONTOSAURUS

Sauropoda (reptile-footed)—giants among terrestrial reptiles; became herbivorous quadrupeds in the Jurassic; had long necks and tails; probably spent most of their time in shallow water for protection from enemies and support for their enormous weight; culminated in Brontosaurus, often more than 80 feet long.

Ornithischia (bird-hipped)—dominant terrestrial reptiles of the late Cretaceous; herbivorous; in general, more advanced than Saurischia, with many specializations.

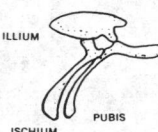

ILLIUM / ISCHIUM / PUBIS

TRACHYDON

Ornithopoda · (bird-footed)—bipedal, but could assume quadrupedal stance; some had webbed feet; culminated in the duck-billed Trachydon.

STEGOSAURUS

Stegosauria—plated dinosaurs; herbivorous quadrupeds; one member, Stegosaurus, was over 20 feet long with alternating bony plates on either side of the backbone, a walnut-size brain and a nerve center near its hip 20 times as large as the brain.

SYRMOSAURUS

Ankylosauria—armored dinosaurs; herbivorous quadrupeds; best-known member is the Syrmosaurus, which resembled a large horned toad.

TRICERATOPS

Ceratopsia—horned dinosaurs having a bony frill extending from the back of the skull; herbivorous quadrupeds; best-known member, Triceratops, was 20 feet long, with a horn over each eye and on the snout.

DINOSAUR. Any of the large, extinct reptiles that dominated the earth for more than 100 million years, during the Mesozoic era. They ranged in size from less than 10 pounds to over 85 tons. They were herbivorous and carnivorous and could be found on land and in the water. They are classified as shown in the chart at left.

DIORITE. A coarse-grained, equigranular igneous rock composed of about 75 percent plagioclase feldspars and the balance ferromagnesian silicates.

DIP. The maximum slope of an inclined rock layer, or fault surface, measured from the horizontal and stated in terms of angle and direction (e.g., 15° west). Also, the angle between the direction of the earth's magnetic field and the horizontal plane at any point on the surface of the earth as shown by a compass needle.

DISCHARGE. The volume of water or ice flowing through a river, fjord, or harbor during a unit of time. It is usually expressed in terms of cubic feet per second.

DISCONFORMITY. An unconformity in which the older and newer beds of rock are parallel, as opposed to angular unconformity; indicates that the older beds were uniformly uplifted and eroded before deposit of the newer beds.

DISCONTINUITY (in the earth's interior). Sudden or rapid changes with depth in the physical properties of the material constituting the earth, as shown by seismic data. See *Earth structure.*

DISCORDANT PLUTON. An intrusive igneous body cutting across the layers of the rocks into which it was intruded, as contrasted with a concordant pluton.

DISINTEGRATION. See *Mechanical weathering.*

DISSECTION. The erosion of a land surface into ravines and valleys by the action of streams.

DISTRIBUTARY. A branch of a river that does not rejoin the mainstream, as in a delta.

DIURNAL RANGE. The range, or difference, between the maximum and minimum value of any property, such as temperature or humidity, during a 24-hour period.

DIVIDE. A ridge separating two drainage basins.

DOLDRUMS. The equatorial belt of calm or light, fitful winds where the northeast and southeast trade winds converge. In addition to the absence of sustained wind, the area is subject to heavy downpours, thunderstorms, and squalls. Temperature and humidity are high.

DOLINEN. Closed, rounded depressions found in limestone regions. They vary from 30 feet to 3,000 feet in diameter and from 6 feet to over 300 feet in depth, and may be dish, funnel, or well shaped. Dolinen contain sinkholes into which runoff surface water disappears.

DOLOMITE. A common rock-forming mineral, the carbonate of calcium and magnesium.

DOME. An anticlinal fold in rock layers in which the beds dip in all directions from a central area. The opposite of basin.

DOWN. An undulating, grassy, and generally treeless upland with sparse soil.

DRAG. Minor folding of rock layers near a fault surface. It indicates the direction of faulting.

DRAINAGE BASIN. An area within which all precipitation flows toward one collection point.

DREDGING. The process of excavation in shallow water or swamps to recover mineral deposits or to create or maintain a channel.

DRIFT. The loose material transported and deposited by glaciers. Also, the motion of sea, ice, or vessels as a result of ocean currents and wind. See also *Continental drift.*

DRIFT–ICE. Detached portions of icebergs carried by currents into the open sea.

DRIPSTONE. Calcite precipitated by subsurface water. An inclusive term for stalagtite and stalagmite.

DROUGHT. Long period of dry weather.

DROWN. To submerge land, whether by a rise in the water level or by a sinking of the land.

DRUMLIN. An elongated, oval-shaped hill deposited by glaciers. A drumlin may be up to 300 feet high. It resembles an inverted teaspoon bowl. The axis of a drumlin is parallel to the direction in which the ice sheet moved and may be more than a mile long. Drumlins are composed of unstratified clayey till.

DRY. A state of ground in which pore spaces to the depth of 3 inches or more are essentially free of water.

DRY FARMING. A method of agriculture in areas of low rainfall without irrigation. A system of crop fallowing and other moisture-conserving practices are followed.

DRY HOLE. A drill hole that has failed to produce oil or gas in commercial quantity.

DRY SNOW. Snow at a temperature below the freezing point.

DRY VALLEY. A valley in an area high in chalk and limestone without a permanent stream.

DUN. See *Downs.*

DUNE. A low ridge or hill of shifting, loose sand transported and formed by wind. See also *Barchan, Longitudinal dune,* and *Parabolic dune.*

DUST. Finely divided organic and inorganic matter easily carried by wind.

DUST BOWL. A dry area in which the wind removes the surface soil.

DUST DEVIL. A whirling pillar of sand or a sand spout which moves across the country at up to 30 miles an hour. Occurring during the heat of the day, it is caused by strong convection in hot, dusty regions.
   Although only a few yards in diameter, it may extend upward to 3,000 feet.

DUST STORM. A storm in which the wind carries a large volume of dust or silt.

DYNE. A force which produces on a one-gram mass an acceleration of one centimeter per second per second.

U.S. DEPT. OF THE INTERIOR NATIONAL PARK SERVICE

DOME STRUCTURE exposed by erosion, showing beds dipping outward from the center. An example of the effects of differential weathering.

EARTH. The third planet in order of distance from the sun and the fifth in size in our solar system. A flattened sphere, or oblate spheroid, it is somewhat flattened at the poles and bulges slightly at the equator. The equatorial diameter is 7,926.68 miles and the polar diameter is 7,899.99 miles.

The earth rotates on its axis, at a velocity of 1,037 miles per hour (mph) at the equator, once every 23 hours, 56 minutes, 4.09 seconds, or one sidereal day. It completes one elliptical orbit, or revolution, around the sun, at a speed of 66,000 mph, every 365 days, 6 hours, 9 minutes, 9.54 seconds, or one sidereal year, at a mean distance of 92.9 million miles which, because of the elliptical orbit, varies 3 million miles in the course of a year.

The earth is tilted on its axis 23 degrees, 26 minutes, 40.15 seconds. This causes the seasons. The sun's rays are perpendicular to the tropic of Cancer (23½°N) on about June 21 and to the tropic of Capricorn (23½°S) on about December 21. When perpendicular to the tropic of Capricorn, the sun's rays make an obtuse angle with the northern hemisphere, providing less heat.

The precession, or gyration of the earth's axis around the (imaginary) perpendicular to its orbit, is caused by the gravitational pull of the sun and moon on the earth's equatorial bulge. It completes one cycle every 25,800 years, and 12,000 years from now Vega will be the North Star.

While the earth is rotating, revolving, and precessing, the entire solar system is traveling toward Vega at a velocity of nearly 40,000 mph. Thus, in one year the earth ascends approximately 400 million miles along a spiral in the general direction of Vega.

The earth is generally believed to be 5 billion years old. It is composed of a series of concentric shells—crust, mantle, and core. See *Earth structure.*

EARTHFLOW. The gravitational movement down a slope of a mass of water-saturated soil, mantle, or weak bedrock. It is common in humid regions.

EARTHQUAKE. A sudden movement or tremor in the earth's crust resulting from the creation and transmission of waves in the earth caused by the faulting of rocks or by volcanic activity. The focus, or source, of a given set of earthquake waves may be near the surface or more than 400 miles down (1/10 of earth's radius). The epicenter is on the surface directly above the focus.

Earthquakes occur most often in regions of weak rocks where volcanic activity is most pronounced and where high mountains and ocean deeps are close together. Almost 80 percent of all earthquakes occur around the edge of the Pacific Ocean. Another belt of earthquakes runs along the north shore of the Mediterranean Sea, extending into Central Asia.

An earthquake begins with minor tremors, or body waves, which are generated simultaneously and travel through the earth. P waves are longitudinal, or push-pull, waves which travel several miles a second, pushing particles along the line of their travel.

S waves are transverse, or shake, waves which travel at about half the speed of P waves, moving particles across the line of their travel.

The interval between the arrival of P and S waves at a seismograph is proportional to the distance traversed, which is the radius of a circle. Comparable information from seismographs in three different locations describes three different circles, their intersection being the epicenter of the earthquake. See also *Seismology.*

At the epicenter, body waves generate long surface, or L, waves which travel along the earth's surface, causing at least one major, violent shock. This is followed by aftershocks or vibrations of decreasing intensity which eventually fade out.

The total energy of an earthquake at its source is indicated by the Richter Magnitude Scale. A magnitude of 2.5 is just large enough to be felt nearby; a magnitude of 4.5 causes slight local damage; 6 is moderately destructive; and 8.6 is the largest earthquake known.

EARTH STRUCTURE. The earth is composed of concentric shells. The outermost shell is the crust, or lithosphere, beneath the crust is the mantle, or asthenosphere, and at the center is the core, or centrosphere.

The crust varies in depth from more than 20 miles under the continents to as little as 3 or 4 miles under the oceans. It consists of two layers of approximately equal thickness—a sialic (silica and aluminum), or granitic, layer and a simatic (silica and magnesium), or basaltic, layer. The sialic layer is thinner under the oceans, disappearing completely in areas under the Pacific Ocean. The surface separating the crust from the mantle is called the Mohorovičić discontinuity.

The mantle, about 1,800 miles in depth, is a relatively solid region that probably consists of ferromagnesian minerals, or sima, and may be glassy in its upper portion.

The earth's core, or centrosphere, is also called the barysphere. It is approximately 2,100 miles from the lower edge of the mantle to the center of the core. It has two parts—an outer zone 1,300 miles thick, probably in a plastic

EARTH STRUCTURE shown in cross section.

or liquid state, and an inner core with a radius of 800 miles, probably composed of solid iron mixed with about 8 percent nickel and some cobalt.

EBB CURRENT. The tidal current generally flowing seaward after high tide and before low tide.

ECOLOGY. The study of the interrelationships of organisms, both plants and animals, and their environment.

EDAPHOLOGY. The study of the influence of soil properties on organisms.

EFFLUENT. Outflow, such as lava through fissures in a volcano or water in a stream forming the outlet of a lake. Also, liquid discharged as waste.

EJECTA. Material thrown out by a volcano, such as cinders and other pyroclastic rocks.

ELEMENT. A substance whose atoms have the same atomic number and which cannot be broken down by ordinary chemical methods.

ELEVATION. The altitude or angular height of a body or object above a general level. In the U.S. it generally refers to the vertical distance in feet above mean sea level.

ELUVIATION. The removal of material in solution or suspension from a layer of soil by percolating water through earth material. Soil horizons that have lost material through eluviation are termed eluvial; those that have gained material are termed illuvial (see *Illuviation*). Distinguished from leaching, which refers to the complete removal of material in solution.

ELUVIUM. Deposits of sand, silt, and gravel accumulated in a place or shifted by wind, as contrasted with alluvium.

EMERGENCE. A term implying that a portion of the ocean floor has become dry land. It does not distinguish between a lowered water level and a raised land level.

ENDOGENETIC. Refers to a rock formed by solidification from fusion, the separation of minerals from a solution (*precipitation*) or from a vapor (*sublimation*), as contrasted with *exogenetic.*

ENTRENCHED MEANDER. A mature stream that has cut deeply into underlying bedrock.

EOCENE EPOCH. The second epoch of the Tertiary period of the Cenozoic era. It began about 50 million years ago and lasted some 10 million years. During this time, mammals became prominent on the earth.

EOLIAN. Relating to or caused by the action of wind, as eolian erosion or deposition. Subaerial was often used in much the same sense.

EON. One of the grand divisions in geological time, such as the Phanerozoic eon, which includes the Paleozoic, Mesozoic, and Cenozoic eras.

THE STRATOSPHERE

Top of Troposphere and Base of Stratosphere approximately 37,300 feet above sea level

The Troposphere — (region of dust and clouds)

Ground Horizon

Ground Horizon

The First Photograph Ever Made Showing the Actual Curvature of the Earth

EPEIRIC SEAS. Almost landlocked seas less than 250 meters (820 feet) deep.

EPEIROGENY. Large-scale movements of uplift and subsidence which affect vast areas of the earth's crust.

EPHEMERAL STREAM. A stream that flows only during and shortly after precipitation in the immediate locality. Its channel is always above the water table. See also *Intermittent stream.*

EPICENTER. The point on the surface of the earth directly above the focus, or origin point, of an earthquake.

EPICONTINENTAL. Located on or overlying a continent or continental shelf.

EPICONTINENTAL SEA. A shallow sea or portion of the sea on the continental shelf.

EPIDOTE. A common mineral in metamorphic rocks. It is a silicate of aluminum, calcium, and iron and is characteristic of low-grade metamorphism.

EPIGENE. Geological processes occurring at or near the surface of the earth, as opposed to hypogene.

EPOCH. A small division of time in geological time, a subdivision of a period. A time unit corresponding to a series in time-stratigraphic units.

EQUATOR. The imaginary parallel lying midway between the poles of rotation of a celestial body, determining northern and southern latitudes (its own latitude being everywhere 0°).

ERA. In geological time, one of the major divisions of an eon. A time unit corresponding to a group in time-stratigraphic units.

ERG. A vast desert sand region. Also, a unit of energy equal to that expended when a force of one dyne acts through a distance of one centimeter in the direction of the force.

EROSION. The wearing away of the land surface by natural agencies such as water and the acids it may contain, wind, waves, frost, and glaciers. Erosion includes the processes of weathering, solution, corrasion, and transportation. If man-induced, the wearing away process is termed accelerated erosion.

ERRATIC. A large rock or rock fragment transported by a glacier from its place of origin to rest on or near bedrock of different composition.

ERUPTION. The discharge of solid, liquid, or gaseous material from the interior of the earth onto the earth's surface.

ESCARPMENT. A cliff or steep slope.

ESKER. A type of glacial drift. It is a long, narrow, sinuous ridge of stratified gravel and sand deposited by the action of glacial streams. It may range from 10 feet to 100 feet in height and from a fraction of a mile to more than 100 miles in length.

ESTUARY. A tidal bay formed by the sinking or drowning of a river mouth by the sea. Because of the effect of river and tidal currents, estuaries may be quite deep and provide good harbors.

EUSTASY. Simultaneous, worldwide changes in sea level.

EVAPORATION. The change of a substance from a liquid to a gaseous state.

EVAPORITE. A sedimentary rock precipitated or separated from a solution as a result of the evaporation of a watery solution, such as rock salt or gypsum.

EVAPOTRANSPIRATION. The loss of water from a body both by evaporation and by transpiration of plants.

EVERGLADE. A tract of swampy land with tall grass and some trees. In peninsular Florida, the Everglades refers specifically to the oblong basin of approximately 4,000 square miles which is the largest saw-grass marsh in the world.

EXFOLIATION. A weathering process in which thin surface layers of a rock peel.

EXOGENETIC. Refers to a rock composed of fragments of older rocks and owing its origin to erosion or metamorphism through contact with an adjacent igneous intrusion, as contrasted with endogenetic. An exogenetic sedimentary rock may also be called a clastic rock.

EXOTIC RIVER. A river flowing through an arid region whose headwaters are in a humid area.

EXPLOSION CRATER. A volcanic crater formed by violent explosion on the flanks or at the summit of a large volcano. There is no lava outflow.

EXTRATROPICAL CYCLONE. An atmospheric low-pressure center that develops outside the tropics.

FELDSPAR, a group of common minerals that decompose into clay with weathering.

EXTRUSIVE ROCK. An igneous rock formed from the cooling of magma at the earth's surface.

FABRIC. The characteristic pattern of a rock produced by the shape of mineral grains and their orientation to each other. A factor of rock texture.

FACIES. The mineral, rock, or fossil features which reflect the specific environment in which a rock was formed. A sedimentary rock may grade from a sandstone facies into a shale facies. Although the two facies were deposited at the same time, they reflect an environment of quiet water where the shale was formed and water of some velocity where the sandstone was formed.

A particular fossil found in one area of a rock and not in another reflects favorable conditions for that animal in that area and a change of those conditions in the rest of the rock. A metamorphic rock may have one to four facies, according to the temperature-pressure conditions under which it was formed. See *Metamorphic facies.*

FALL LINE. An imaginary line connecting a number of streams where they make a sudden descent, as at the edge of a highland. Also, the natural downward course between two points on a slope.

FAST ICE. Sea ice that remains where it was originally formed, whether attached to the shore or over shoals where it is held by islands or grounded icebergs.

FATHOM. A unit of measurement equal to 6 feet (1.83 meters) used mainly to measure the depth of water.

FAULT. A fracture in rock along which there has been differential movement, as opposed to a joint. The surface may be vertical, horizontal, or inclined. The line formed at the intersection of the fault and a horizontal plane is the strike; the angle between the fault surface and the horizontal plane is the dip. Near the fault surface friction causes drag, or bending, of the rock layers which serves as a clue to the direction of movement.

Faults are generally caused by excessive deformation, which results in the rupture of rocks. In igneous rocks, faults may also occur during the cooling process.

FAULT BLOCK. A body of rock bounded on at least two opposite sides by faults.

FAULT SCARP. The steep face of a rock on the uplift side of a fault.

FAUNA. All animal life of a region in a geologic time period.

FELDSPAR. A group of common nonferromagnesian rock-forming minerals, generally light-colored, composed of silicates of aluminum and potassium, calcium, and sodium.

Feldspars comprise about 60 percent of igneous rocks, are the dominant minerals in a large group of metamorphic rocks (gneisses), and are important constituents of sedimentary rocks. In weathering they decompose into clay. They have a hardness of 6.

There are two kinds of feldspar— orthoclase and plagioclase. Orthoclase feldspars are potassium aluminum silicates and are white, gray, or pink. Plagioclase feldspars are aluminum silicates. They may be white or gray, or transparent or opalescent.

FELSENMEER. A surface littered with angular blocks that accumulate at the foot of a large outcrop of rock as a result of separation and shattering. Characteristic of high mountain slopes where there is rapid disintegration.

FELSITE. An igneous rock with cryptocrystalline groundmass consisting of feldspar, quartz, and interstitial volcanic glass. It is red in color.

FEN. A low-lying, marshy area.

FERREL'S LAW. The first complete explanation of the effects of the Coriolis force.

FERROMAGNESIAN. A group of dark-colored minerals containing iron and magnesium, especially amphibole, pyroxene, biotite, olivine, and magnetite.

FERTILIZER. Any material, organic or inorganic, that is applied to the soil to increase its fertility. Generally, it furnishes one or more of the elements nitrogen, which promotes vegetative growth; phosphorus, which promotes root growth and speeds maturity; and potassium, which increases plant resistance to disease and weather.

FETCH. The distance traveled by sea waves before reaching a shore line. Also, the distance wind travels over open water or land.

FIARD. A sea-drowned valley formed by glacial action in a lowland area. It is shorter and shallower than a fiord.

FIELD CAPACITY. The amount of water a soil is able to hold by capillary attraction against gravity. It is expressed as a percentage of the dry weight of the soil.

FILL. Material deposited in the outer side of a curve where a river current has lost velocity.

FIRN SNOW, or névé. Granular snow which has become coarse and partially compacted through temperature changes, forming the transition stage to glacier ice.

FIRTH. A long, narrow arm of the sea. Also, the opening of a river into the sea.

FISSILITY. The ability to split readily along the grain or closely spaced parallel planes. A characteristic of shale.

FISSURE. In rocks, an extensive crack or fracture whose walls are distinctly separated but not otherwise dislocated.

FJORD, or fiord. A long, narrow inlet of the sea formed by rivers and glaciation. Fjords are shallow near the mouth but very deep inland, and are characterized by steep surrounding cliffs extending below the surface of the water.

FLATIRON. A triangular landform composed of sedimentary rocks adhering to the crystalline core of an eroded dome mountain. Flatirons often appear in a series on the flank of a mountain.

FLINT. Granular cryptocrystalline siliceous rock, usually dull, dark, and nodular, occurring in calcareous beds and having conchoidal fracture. It is a purer and less brittle chert.

FLOCCULATE. To collect in small lumps or loose clusters. It often applies to soils and colloids.

FLOE. See *Ice floe.*

FLOODPLAIN. A level area, or plain, in a river valley, built up by sediment from the river overflow. It may be submerged in time of flood.

FLOOD CURRENT. The current associated with a rising tide.

FLORA. All plant life of a given region in a geological time period.

FLOTATION. A method of ore concentration in which gas bubbles selectively attach themselves to particles of a particular mineral suspended in water, holding them at the surface while other particles sink.

FLOW. The movement of air, water, or lava. Of rocks, see *Deformation.*

FLUME. A deep, narrow ravine through which a stream flows forming a series of cascades.

FLUVIAL CYCLE. The geographical cycle (upheaval through reduction to base level of a region) controlled by steams and mass-wasting.

FOCUS. The point of generation of an earthquake. Earthquakes are classified by their energy and depth to focus. Shallow focus earthquakes originate within 40 miles of the earth's surface; intermediate, from 40 to 185 miles; deep, from 185 to 435 miles.

FOEHN. A warm, dry wind that blows down the leeward side of a mountain. As the air moves up the windward side of the mountain, moisture is removed by cooling and the resultant condensation. Then the air is warmed by compression as it descends the leeward slope.

FOG. A dense mass of small water droplets (much smaller than the droplets in rain-bearing clouds) forming in the lowest layers of the atmosphere. Fog is caused by condensation produced by a sudden cooling of the air, usually when a warmer air current meets a colder air current. Fog, by international definition, reduces visibility below 0.62 miles.

Ground fog, or radiation fog, is a shallow layer formed over low ground on calm, clear nights by cool air which suddenly lowers the temperature of the ground.

Advection fog results when clouds formed in moist air are blown from warm regions over cold water and ground.

Warm-front fog is caused by the saturation of the air by rain falling through it from a cloud system associated with cyclonic disturbances.

Steam fog, rare and transitory, is produced by the evaporation of relatively warm water into cold air.

FOLD. A bend in rock strata, caused by crustal movement, which may form a series of arches, upfolds or anticlines, and troughs, downfolds or synclines. When the axis of a fold is not horizontal, it is termed a *plunging fold,* the angle between the axis and the horizontal plane being the plunge. In an *isoclinal fold* the strata are so compressed that the limbs are parallel and thus have the same dip. A *monocline* is a one-limb fold; the strata on either side are horizontal.

A series of folds (anticlines and synclines) forming an arch is an *anticlinorium;* if a trough is formed, it is a *synclinorium.* Geosynclines and *geanticlines* are large-scale synclines and anticlines, respectively, and are formed by very gentle folding.

FOLIATION. The tendency of certain rocks to break in thin layers along almost parallel planes. It is caused by the parallel alignment of minerals resulting from pressure and higher than normal temperatures during regional metamorphism. Such rocks are commonly called *schists* (well-defined foliation) and *gneisses* (poorly defined foliation).

FOOTHILLS. A series of hills at the foot of a mountain or mountain range lying between the mountains and a plain.

FORAMINIFERAL OOZE. A deposit on the ocean floor containing a large percentage of calcium carbonate, being the shells of foraminifera, a single-celled, minute animal.

FORD. A shallow part of a stream or other body of water which may be crossed by wading.

FORESHOCK. An earthquake which precedes a larger earthquake, announcing that the stress has become critical. It originates at or near the focus of the larger earthquake.

FORESHORE. The part of the shoreline lying between high and low water levels.

FOSSE. A depression between a glacier and a moraine or rock wall.

FOSSIL. Animal or plant remains or impressions from the geologic past preserved in the earth's crust.

FOSSIL FUELS. Commercial sources of inanimate energy derived from the alteration of the remains of organic matter, such as coal, oil, and natural gas.

FOUCAULT PENDULUM. A pendulum demonstrating the earth's rotation on its axis, made public by J. B. L. Foucault in 1851. Each swing of the pendulum describes a plane of vibration which appears to move clockwise (counterclockwise in the southern hemisphere) around a circle drawn on the surface of the earth. Actually, the plane is constant—the circle rotates.

Because of the earth's curvature, the northern edge of the circle describes a smaller circle (or shorter line of latitude) around the earth than the southern edge.

The time required for a complete rotation varies with the degree of latitude, ranging from 5 days, 18 hours, 13 minutes at 10° latitude to one day at 90° latitude. At the equator there is no apparent movement of the plane of vibration because the north and south edges of the circle are equidistant from the earth's axis.

FRACTURE. The manner of breaking of a mineral that does not exhibit cleavage. A *conchoidal fracture* has a smooth, curved surface similar to that of a seashell. An *uneven fracture* is rough and irregular. A *fibrous* or *splintery fracture* is similar to that of wood. A *hackly fracture* has a jagged surface with sharp edges. Also, a joint, fault, or fissure.

FREE WATER. Groundwater moved by the force of gravity through the pore spaces of soil and not held by capillary attraction.

FRESHET. An area of comparatively fresh water at the mouth of a stream flowing into the sea. Also, a sudden rise in the level of a stream caused by heavy rains or melting snow.

FRESH WATER. Water containing no significant amount of salt, usually having less than 0.2 percent salinity.

FRIABLE. Referring to easily pulverized rock or easily crumbled soils.

FRIGID CLIMATE. The climate in a region of permafrost or in a region with a permanent cover of ice and snow.

FRIGID ZONE. The area north of the Arctic Circle and south of the Antarctic Circle.

FRINGING REEF. A reef attached to the shore. The outer edge of the reef is submerged.

FRONT. The boundary or zone of transition between two air masses of different density.

FROST. Small particles of frozen moisture formed by the condensation of water vapor or dew on objects having temperatures below freezing.

FROST HEAVING. The upthrusting of a surface by the internal action of frost. It generally occurs after a thaw has released water droplets into the soil, and a sudden drop in temperature to below freezing changes the water droplets into ice crystals. As freezing expands the volume of water, there is an upward and outward movement of the soil.

FROST LINE. The maximum depth to which soil can freeze.

THE AMERICAN MUSEUM OF NATURAL HISTORY

GEODES AND CRYSTALS. Geodes are hollow bodies lined with mineral crystals.

FULLER'S EARTH. Fine, claylike earth with a high percentage of water. It does not retain a form when molded.

FUMAROLE. A vent in the earth's crust emitting steam and other gases; common in volcanic regions.

FUNNEL CLOUD. See *Tornado; Waterspout.*

GABBRO. A dark, coarse-grained plutonic or intrusive igneous rock, composed of plagioclase feldspars and dark, ferromagnesian minerals such as hornblende, pyroxene, or olivine.

GAL. A unit expressing acceleration equal to one centimeter per second per second (1 cm./sec.²). The term gal honors Galileo and is not an abbreviation.

GALE. A wind with a velocity between 32 and 61 miles per hour, designated 7-10 on the Beaufort scale.

GALENA. Lead sulfide, the principal source of lead. It has a bright metallic luster, a hardness of 2.5, a specific gravity of about 7.5, and perfect cleavage in three planes at right angles to each other, forming cubes.

GANGUE. Earth material of small value enclosing valuable mineral matter.

GAP. A cut or break through a ridge, either complete, as in a water gap, or through the upper part, as in a wind gap.

GARNET. A group of silicates (iron, magnesium, aluminum, calcium, manganese, chromium, and titanium) with a vitreous to resinous luster, a hardness of 6.5 to 7.5, a specific gravity of 3.4 to 4.3, and uneven fracture. It usually has 12-sided or 24-sided fully-developed crystals. Characteristic of metamorphic rocks, it is used to define one of the zones of middle-grade metamorphism.

GAT. A natural opening through cliffs leading inland from the sea. Also, a passageway extending inland through shoals or steep banks.

GEANTICLINE. A broad uplift, formed slowly by gentle pressure and covering hundreds of miles. See *Fold.*

GEM. A general term for any cut and polished precious or semiprecious stone.

GEO. A prefix meaning earth. Also, in Icelandic, a deep, narrow coastal inlet walled by steep cliffs.

GEOCHEMICAL CYCLE. The sequence of rock change in which magma, or molten matter, is cooled and solidified or crystallized into igneous rocks, which are weathered to sediments. The sediments are compacted and hardened into sedimentary rocks, which are metamorphosed by pressure, heat, and chemicals into metamorphic rocks. They, in turn, undergo further metamorphism and are melted into magma.

GEODE. A hollow, globular body that may be an inch, or more than a foot, in diameter, lined with mineral crystals. It is formed in sedimentary deposits where a piece of organic matter is buried, decays, and leaves a water-filled pocket.

As the deposit begins to consolidate into rock, a wall of silica forms around the water and isolates it. The silica wall dries, crystallizes into chalcedony, contracts, and cracks. Later, mineral-bearing water may seep through the cracks and precipitate minerals just inside the geode wall where the crystals begin to grow toward the center. Geodes are characteristic of certain limestone beds.

GEODESY. The study of the shape, size, and gravity field of the earth.

GEOGRAPHICAL CYCLE. The relatively systematic series of changes through which a landform passes—from youth, when constructional processes define its form, through maturity, when erosion carves and molds it, to old age, when the landform is reduced to base level.

GEOGRAPHY. The study of the earth's surface and the relationship between man and his environment, with particular emphasis on the location of physical, economic, and cultural conditions.

GEOID. The figure of the earth considered as a mean sea level surface extended continuously through the continents. It is an equipotential surface in that the direction in which gravitational force acts is perpendicular to any point on the surface.

GEOLOGIC TIME. The measurement of earth's physical history through fossil evidence, the interrelationship of rock strata, and radioactive dating. Geologic time has been divided into eons, eras, periods, epochs, and sometimes ages. These intervals correspond to time-stratigraphic units in the geologic column: group (era), system (period), series (epoch), stage (age). See chart, CHRONOLOGICAL HISTORY OF GEOLOGIC TIME.

GEOLOGIC EROSION. The wearing down of land surfaces at natural rates. See *Erosion.*

GEOLOGY. The study of the composition, structure, processes, and history of the earth.

GEOMORPHIC CYCLE. The cycle of upheaval through reduction to base level of the earth's surface.

GEOMORPHOLOGY. The study of the form of the earth, the general configuration of its surface, and the changes that take place in the evolution of land-forms.

GEOPHYSICS. The physics or nature of the earth. The study of the composition and the physical processes operating on and within the earth. It makes use of meteorology, oceanography, seismology, and related sciences.

GEOSPHERE. The solid portions of the earth.

GEOSTROPHIC. Pertaining to the deflective force caused by the rotation of earth.

GEOSYNCLINE. A large syncline, or a great trough or basin of accumulated sediments which slowly downwarps.

GEOTHERMAL GRADIENT. The increase in temperature of the earth with depth.

GEYSER. A hot spring which throws hot water and steam into the air at intervals. The vent to the surface must be narrow or winding, or a boiling spring would result. Geysers are found in Yellowstone National Park, in Iceland, and in New Zealand.

GLACIAL. Referring to the existence, size, composition, and actions of glaciers (large masses of land ice).

GLACIAL MILK. Glacial meltwater carrying light-colored rock flour or rock particles of the size of silt or clay.

GLACIAL PERIOD. Generally applied to the time during the Pleistocene epoch when continental ice sheets and valley glaciers covered large areas of the continents. Other glacial periods are not so abundantly recorded, although there is evidence of extensive glaciation in the late Precambrian and Permian periods.

GLACIER. A mass of land ice moving slowly over the surface of the earth. A glacier is classified according to the way it occurs. There are three basic types, which grade into each other: *valley glaciers, piedmont glaciers,* and *ice sheets.*
  Valley glaciers are the most common type. They are formed on mountain sides along well-defined valleys. They carve precipitous walls (cirque) at their upper limit and are melting at their lower limit. They tend to be long and narrow, following valleys cut by streams and sculpting them into U-shaped profiles.
  Piedmont glaciers occur where valley glaciers emerge from the mountains to spread out onto plains. They coalesce to form a continuous thick sheet of ice.
  Ice sheets are formed on plateau areas by the accumulation of snow and the amalgamation of valley glaciers and ice caps flowing from higher places.

GLADE. A natural or man-made open area or passage in a forest.

GLASS. An amorphous solid, generally treated as a rock, which results when molten rock, or magma, is rapidly cooled. The ions are disorganized, as in a liquid, but are frozen in place by the quick change of temperature.
  Also, one of the first-made compound materials in which sand or another form of silica and a fluxing alkali, such as soda or potash, are combined and heated to about 2800° F, then gradually cooled.

GLEI. A blue-gray soil with mottled discolorations. It is somewhat sticky, often structureless, and indicates poor drainage.

GLEN. A long, narrow, steep-sided valley.

GLOBIGERINA OOZE. A chalky, or calcareous, marine deposit consisting of the shells of surface-dwelling forms of Foraminifera that reach the sea floor after death. It is found in deep water, to 12,000 feet, in the Atlantic, Pacific, and Indian oceans.

GNEISS. A metamorphic rock with alternating bands of granular and schistose minerals; commonly formed by the metamorphism of granite.

GORGE. A deep, narrow valley with steep sides and enclosed among mountains, as contrasted with a ravine, which is not necessarily enclosed.

GRABEN. A narrow depression, or structural valley, long in comparison to its width and bounded on at least two sides by faults. The opposite of a horst.

GRADATION. The reducing of elevations and the filling of depressions to make a land surface level.

GRADED BEDDING. Sedimentary deposits with a gradation in grain size from coarse at the bottom to fine at the top. It is also called diadactic structure.

GRADED SHORE LINE. A shore line straightened by the building of bars across indentations and the cutting back of headlands.

GRADED STREAM. A stream that has eliminated irregularities, such as falls, and adjusted its gradient, or slope, so that its velocity is sufficient to transport the load from its drainage basin.

GRADE SCALE. See *Wentworth grade scale.*

GRANITE. A coarse-grained plutonic, or intrusive, igneous rock composed largely of feldspar, quartz, and some common mica (biotite or muscovite). It is the most abundant rock in the earth's crust.

GRANULE. Rounded rock fragment larger than ä coarse sand grain and smaller than ä pebble. See *Wentworth grade scale.*

GRAPHITE. A soft form of carbon, having a hardness of 1. It is black or gray, and has a metallic luster and a specific gravity of 2.25.

GRAPTOLITE. An extinct colonial organism whose remaining shell and supporting structures are important in dating Ordovician and Silurian rocks.

GRASSLANDS. Regions of the world where the natural plant cover consists of grass. In the tropics they are called savannas and steppes, and in the middle latitudes, prairies and steppes.

GRAVEL. A loose mixture of rounded stones, composed of granules, pebbles, cobbles, and boulders. See *Wentworth grade scale.*

GRAVITATION. The mutual attraction between bodies or masses of matter, directly proportional to the product of their masses and inversely proportional to the square of the distance between them. It is the opposite of centrifugal force and a component of gravity.

GRAVITATIONAL THEORY. The theory that, because of buoyancy, or lower specific gravities, oil will rise to the top of water and gas will rise to the top of oil. See also *Anticlinal theory.*

GRAVITY. The attraction of earth's mass for other bodies at or near earth's surface (gravitation), as modified by earth's rotation (centrifugal force).

GRAYWACKE. A hard, dark sandstone marked by large angular fragments of quartz and feldspar and small rock fragments (chert, quartzite, slate, and phyllite).

GREENHOUSE EFFECT. The heat resulting from the fact that incoming shortwave solar radiation freely penetrates the atmosphere to be absorbed at the earth's surface, while outgoing longwave terrestrial radiation passes upward with difficulty, thus heating the area in which it is contained.

GREENWICH MEAN TIME (GMT). A system of international time based on the local mean time at the meridian that passes through Greenwich, England (the prime or zero meridian).

GROIN. A low wall built out into the sea, roughly perpendicular to the coastline, for a particular purpose, such as to change a current or protect a coast.

GROOVES. Scour marks, or large striations, cut into hard rocks by the movement of glacial ice over their surface.

GROTTO. A small cave often found in a limestone region. It also refers to a small cave eroded in the wall of a larger cave.

GROUNDWATER. Water passing through or standing in the soil and the subsoil layers.

GROUP. A time-stratigraphic unit corresponding to an era in geological time.

GROVE. A small group of trees in an open area.

GROWING SEASON. The interval of time between the last spring frost and the first fall frost in any given area.

GRUS. An accumulation of fragments derived from the weathering of granite.

GUANO. A deposit of partially decomposed excrement of fish-eating creatures. It is rich in nitrogen and phosphorous and is used as fertilizer.

GULCH. A narrow, steep-sided ravine.

GULF. A large, deep inlet of the sea. The entrance generally is wider than a bay and smaller than a sea.

GULF STREAM. A major ocean current originating in the Gulf of Mexico, where the Florida and Antilles currents meet. It is a warm, swift (3 to 4 miles per hour), and relatively narrow current. It flows out of the gulf between Florida and Cuba, turns north to join the North Equatorial Current, and then flows generally parallel to the U.S. coast, bending northeast off Norfolk, Virginia.

Southeast of Newfoundland it separates into two main streams. One stream flows northeast to the Grand Banks, where it joins with the cold Labrador Current to form the North Atlantic Current, which flows north to Sweden and the Soviet Union. There its force and warmth are dissipated.

The other branch flows eastward to Europe and bends south. Off the coasts of Portugal and northwestern Africa it merges with the Canary Current, which eventually joins the North Equatorial Current.

GULLY. A relatively small, narrow channel, or a miniature valley, carved out of the earth's surface by intermittent running water, usually during and following a heavy rain.

GUMBO. A term used in the southern and western United States for fine-grained, silty soils which yield a sticky mud when wet.

GUMBOTIL. A dark, thoroughly leached, unlayered deposit resulting from the complete chemical decomposition of clay-rich glacial till. It is very hard when dry, sticky when wet.

GUT. A narrow channel or strait.

GUYOT. A flat-topped mountain beneath the sea.

HEMATITE, an oxide of iron, in botryoidal (grape) form is commonly known as *kidney ore.*

GYPSUM. A common mineral in sedimentary rocks, composed of calcium sulfate and hydrated water molecules. It is usually white or colorless and has a hardness of 2. It is one of the first minerals to crystallize with the evaporation of seawater.

GYRE. A closed circulatory system in major ocean basins, larger than an eddy or whirlpool.

HAAR. A cold, wet sea fog which sometimes invades eastern Scotland and parts of eastern England, especially during summer.

HABITAT. The natural characteristics of a region; the environment.

HACKLY. A fracture having a jagged, irregular surface with sharp edges.

HADAL ZONE. Referring to the greatest depths of the oceans. See *Ocean depth zones.*

HALF–LIFE. The average time required for one-half the atoms of a sample of a radioactive substance to decay.

HALITE. A mineral, sodium chloride (common salt), which has cubic cleavage, a hardness of 2.5, and occurs in thick beds with layers of sedimentary rock. It is also called rock salt.

HALMYROLYSIS. The chemical rearrangement, replacement, and weathering of sedimentary rocks on the sea floor.

HALO. A ring of light which surrounds the moon, sun, or other heavenly bodies when their light is refracted by ice crystals in the atmosphere, usually in the form of a thin veil of cirrostratus clouds.

HALOGENS. Any of four elements—chlorine, bromine, iodine, and fluorine—found as ions in seawater.

HALOMORPHIC. A soil with a high content of salts.

HAMMADA. A plateau or rocky upland in a desert whose surface has been swept clear of sand by the wind.

HANGING GLACIER. A small glacier protruding from a high mountain slope and from which pieces continually break off.

HANGING VALLEY. A tributary valley whose floor is higher than the valley into which it leads.

HARDNESS SCALE. A means of determining the relative hardness of a mineral by comparing it with Mohs' scale, in which each mineral is harder than those that precede it: (1) talc; (2) gypsum; (3) calcite; (4) fluorite; (5) apatite; (6) orthoclase; (7) quartz; (8) topaz; (9) corundum; (10) diamond.

HARDPAN. A hardened soil layer caused by the cementation of soil particles with relatively insoluble materials which will not become plastic when mixed with water.

HARD WATER. Water with dissolved calcium and magnesium compounds.

HARMATTAN. A strong, dry wind blowing from the Sahara in the direction of the western coast of Africa.

HAWAIIAN PHASE. See *Volcano.*

HAZE. An accumulation of fine dust or salt particles in the atmosphere sufficient to reduce visibility.

HEADLAND. A high, steep projection of the shoreline into a body of water. Usually called "head" when coupled with a specific name.

HEADWALL. A steep cliff at the back of a cirque.

HEADWARD EROSION. The action of a stream in lengthening its valley by cutting back into its source area or upper end. Also, the action of a glacier in gnawing into the mountain above and beside it by frost heaving, creating a cirque.

HEADWATER. The upper reaches of a stream; also the water area at or near the source of a stream.

HEAT GRADIENT. See *Geothermal gradient.*

HEATH. An open tract of level, uncultivated ground covered with small shrubs.

HEMATITE. An oxide of iron (Fe_2O_3), the principal source of iron ore.

HIGH. A high-pressure air mass. See *Anticyclone.*

HIGH WATER. The highest level reached by rising tide.

HILL. A prominence on the earth's surface rising less than 1,000 feet above the surrounding country, as contrasted with a mountain.

HILLOCK. A small hill or mound.

HINGE FAULT. A fault whose displacement dies out gradually.

HINTERLAND. Literally, the land behind. The area inland from a coastline to a distance of about five miles, or the land beyond a mountain range which is relatively undisturbed by folding.

HOGBACK. A sharp ridge of rock with steeply sloping sides.

HOMEOBLASTIC. In metamorphic rocks, an equigranular texture caused by recrystallization.

HOMOCLINE. Rock strata sloping in the same direction over a large area.

HOMOPYCNAL INFLOW. Literally, equally dense inflow. Refers to a sediment-laden stream entering a body of water of comparable density.

HOMOSEISMAL LINE. A line drawn on a map through points affected by an earthquake at the same time; used to locate the epicenter of the quake.

HOOK. A spit or narrow cape of sand or gravel whose end turns sharply landward.

HOOKE'S LAW. Within the limits of elastic deformation, a solid whose physical properties are the same in all directions is subject to deformation (strain) in proportion to the force per unit area acting on it (stress).

HORIZON. The physical limit to vision imposed by the curvature of the earth's surface. It is a circle bounding the portion of the earth's surface visible from a given point. Also, a layer in the soil profile.

HORN. A high pyramid peak with steep sides formed by the headward erosion of a ring of cirques around a single high mountain.

HORNBLENDE. A rock-forming mineral, a variety of black or greenish black aluminous amphibole containing a considerable amount of iron.

HORNFELS. A fine-grained silicate resulting from contact metamorphism.

HORSE LATITUDES. A belt of high pressure and variable light winds and calms formed by descending air near 30°-35° N and 30°-35° S latitudes (between trade winds and prevailing westerlies). It moves north and south south by about 5° following the sun.

HORST. A rock body, long in comparison to its width and bounded on at least two sides by faults, elevated relative to the adjacent rock bodies. The opposite of graben.

HOT SPRINGS. The discharge of water hotter than 98°F from the ground. Found commonly, although not exclusively, in volcanic regions.

HUMIDITY. The amount of water in the atmosphere in vapor or gaseous form.

HUMMOCK. A small elevation or mound.

HUMUS. Partly decomposed organic matter found in the soil or in sediment under water.

HURRICANE. A severe cyclonic storm. See *Meteorology.*

HUYGENS' PRINCIPLE. A principle applying to wave motion which states that every point on an advancing wave front at a given time may be regarded as a source of secondary wavelets. A moment later, the position of the front is as an envelope for all the secondary wavelets.

HYDRAULIC GRADIENT. The slope of the water table, found by dividing the head, or vertical, distance between intake and discharge by the length of the flow between those two points.

HYDROGRAPH. A chart showing the level, flow, velocity, or other property of water through time.

HYDROGRAPHY. The description and mapping of the distribution of the waters of the earth's surface.

HYDROLOGIC CYCLE. The cycle through which water passes—atmospheric water vapor passing into liquid and solid form as precipitation, then to the surface of the earth, where evaporation and transpiration through plants return it to the atmosphere as water vapor.

HYDROLOGY. The study of the properties, distribution, and circulation of the waters of the earth and how they are affected by precipitation and evaporation.

HYDROLYSIS. A chemical process whereby a substance is decomposed by water.

HYDROSPHERE. The water portion of the earth, as distinguished from the solid portion, or lithosphere, and the gaseous envelope, or atmosphere. It includes liquid and solid water (ice) in the oceans, seas, lakes, and streams groundwater, and water vapor in the atmosphere. It comprises 139.5 million square miles of the earth's surface, as compared with the lithosphere, which comprises 57.5 million square miles.

HYDROTHERMAL. Relating to the action of heated water in the earth's crust.

HYGROMETER. An instrument used to measure the relative humidity of the atmosphere.

HYGROSCOPIC WATER. Water held so tightly by the attraction of soil particles that it cannot be removed except as a gas, by raising the water temperature above the boiling point. Such water is unavailable to plants.

HYPABYSSAL. Refers to fine-grained igneous rocks formed in minor intrusions, such as sills and dikes. These rocks are crystallized under conditions intermediate between plutonic (slow cooling) and extrusive (rapid cooling) and are distinguished from them by texture or mode of occurrence.

HYPERPYCNAL INFLOW. An inflow so dense that the sediment-laden fluid flows down the side of the basin and then along the bottom as a turbidity current. Vertical mixing is inhibited by the tendency of the dense fluid to stay at the lowest possible level. It forms deltas at the mouth of submarine canyons. It is the opposite of hypopycnal inflow.

HYPOGENE. Originating or lying below the earth's surface, as opposed to epigene.

HYPOPYCNAL INFLOW. Inflow less dense than the fluid filling a basin and therefore flowing out over the surface of the basin. If the discharge is small, a crescent-shaped bar will form off the point of inflow. If it is moderate to large, a birdfoot delta, such as the Mississippi delta, will form. It is the opposite of hyperpycnal inflow.

HYSTERESIS. A lag in a body's return to its original shape after elastic deformation.

ICE. The solid form of water. Ice is formed at 0°C (32°F) by the freezing of water, by the compaction of snow, and by condensation of atmospheric water vapor directly into ice. Ice has a density of 0.917, whereas water has a density of 1.0 and therefore ice floats. But ice is only slightly less dense and as much as 9/10 of its bulk may be below the surface of the water.

ICE AGE. See *Glacial period.*

ICEBERG. A mass of ice that has broken off the seaward edge of a glacier and floats in the sea.

ICE CAP. A large mass of permanent ice and snow covering an extensive land area.

ICE CAP CLIMATE. The type of climate found over large ice sheets, such as in Greenland and Antarctica, where the mean annual temperature is estimated to be below 0°F.

ICE FLOE. An extensive, generally flat mass of free-floating ice.

ICELANDIC LOW. A low-pressure area that develops in the vicinity of Iceland during the winter season.

ICE SHEET. A vast extent of ice and snow covering a large area. Ice sheets are very thick. A floating ice sheet permanently attached to a land mass is called an *ice shelf.*

IGNEOUS ROCK

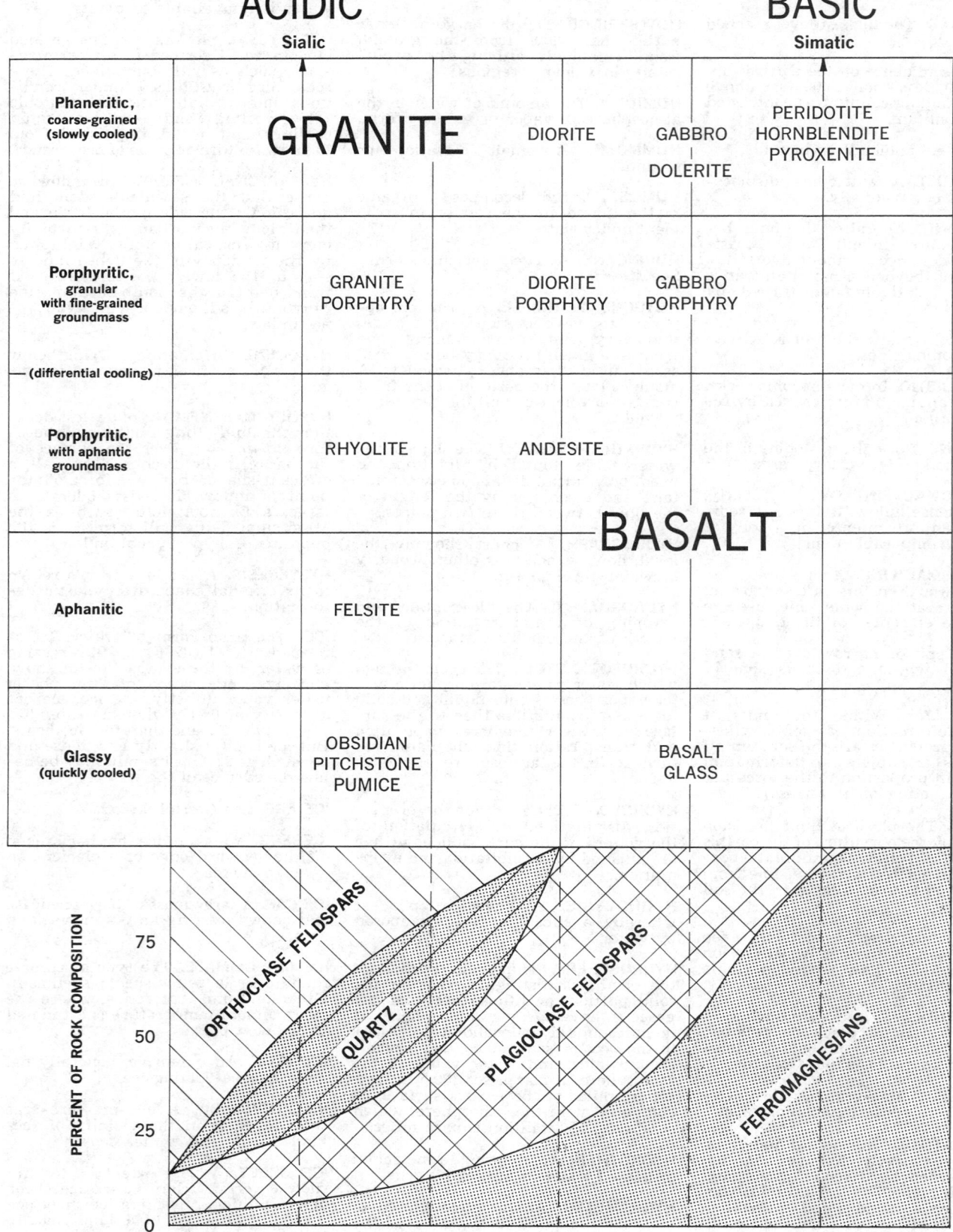

IGNEOUS ROCK. One of the three principal groups of rock, the others being sedimentary and metamorphic rock. Igneous rock is formed by the solidification or crystallization of molten material, or magma. An igneous rock is classified by texture, the minerals present and their proportions, and feldspar content.

ILLITE. A family of hydrous aluminous silicates. Illite is the most common clay mineral in clayey rocks, marine sediments, and many soils.

ILLUVIATION. The deposition in a soil horizon of material in solution or suspension which has been leached out of an overlying horizon by percolating water. The opposite of eluviation.

ILMENITE. A mineral ($FeTiO_3$), the principal ore of titanium.

IMPERMEABLE ROCK. Rock that does not permit the free passage through it of water, petroleum, or natural gas.

INANIMATE ENERGY. Energy derived from nonliving materials, such as water power, nuclear fuels, coal, or oil. The opposite of animate energy.

INCISED MEANDER. See *Entrenched meander.*

INDIAN SUMMER. A spell of mild weather occurring in late autumn, especially after a frost. It is characterized by a cloudless sky and a haze on the horizon.

INDURATED. Refers to rocks hardened by heat, pressure, and cementation.

INFILTRATION RATE. The maximum rate at which loose earth material such as soil can absorb surface water. It is measured in inches per hour. Infiltration refers to flow into soil; percolation refers to flow through soil.

INFLUENT STREAM. A stream whose channel lies above the water table and therefore loses much of its water to the zone of saturation.

INLET. A small opening into the coastline which may connect a bay or lagoon with the sea.

INLIER. A mass of old rock surrounded by younger rocks; often the crest of an anticline which has been exposed by erosion. The opposite of outlier.

INSEQUENT STREAM. A minor stream whose course is determined by minor surface irregularities of rock resistance and not by the slope of the surface.

IN SITU. Latin for "in place." Refers to a rock, soil, or fossil found in the situation in which it was originally formed or deposited.

INSOLATION. Contraction of "incoming solar radiation." It refers to radiation from the sun received at the earth's surface.

INSULATED STREAM. A stream separated from the zone of saturation by impermeable rock. It therefore does not contribute to or receive water from the water table.

INTERFLUVE. The area between adjacent streams.

INTERGLACIAL PERIOD. The time between two glacial periods when climates grew warm and the ice retreated.

INTERIOR. The country extending indefinitely inland of the hinterland.

INTERMITTENT STREAM. A stream that flows only at certain times, such as after a rainstorm or during a spring thaw.

INTERMONTANE. Lying between mountains.

INTERNATIONAL DATE LINE. The line roughly approximating the 180th meridian of longitude (exactly opposite the prime meridian) used to adjust for the necessary difference of one day in traveling the full circumference (360°) of the world. It is made necessary by the hour change with each 15° of longitude covered. Crossing the date line from east to west adds one day; crossing it west to east subtracts one day.

INTERRUPTED STREAM. A stream that flows only at certain places and not at others, either because portions of it are ephemeral, or intermittent, or because it drains into an underground channel. See also *Lost river.*

INTERSTICE. A pore in soil or rock.

INTERSTITIAL WATER. Water contained in the pore spaces between the grains in rock and sediments.

INTRAMONTANE. Situated or acting within a mountain.

INTRATELLURIC. Refers to the crystallization of molten matter, or magma, before its outflow as lava. It is represented in volcanic rocks by large crystals, or phenocrysts, which form under comparatively deep conditions.

INTRAZONAL SOIL. One of the three orders in soil classification. A group of soils whose formation is influenced strongly by local factors, such as the nature of the parent material or age, which prevail over such normal soil-forming factors as climate and vegetation. See also *Soil.*

INTRUSIVE ROCK. An igneous rock which, while molten, invaded other rocks and solidified below the surface. It is also called plutonic rock.

INVERSION. Reversal of the normal order of succession, whether referring to the folding back of rock layers on themselves, as in an overturned fold, or an increase of temperature with elevation above the earth's surface.

IONOSPHERE. See *Atmosphere.*

ISLAND. A landmass, smaller than a continent, surrounded by water.

ISOBAR. A line on a map or chart joining places on the earth that have the same atmospheric pressure.

ISOGONIC LINE. A line on a map or chart joining places having an equal magnetic declination.

ISOSEISMIC LINE. A line on a map joining points on the earth's surface where an earthquake shock is of the same intensity.

ISOSTASY. The theory that the crust of the earth is in a state of equilibrium because the lighter, less-dense continental masses float on heavier, denser material. The continental masses consist primarily of silica and alumina, or sial, which has a specific gravity of about 2.7. Under this is a layer consisting of silica and magnesium, or sima, which has a specific gravity that may be as high as 3.3.

ISOSTATIC COMPENSATION. The process in which mountains are eroded and the material deposited on the ocean floor, which sinks under the weight. In sinking, the floor pushes down on the sima under it. The sima compensates by pushing up under the portion of sial where the mountain stood.

ISOTROPIC. Having the same physical properties in all directions. Isotropism is characteristic of amorphous substances.

ISTHMUS. A narrow strip of land joining two larger landmasses.

JAPAN CURRENT. See *Kuroshio.*

JET STREAM. A narrow band of very fast westward moving winds, or westerlies, that develops in the upper troposphere. The winds average 75 miles per hour (mph) in winter and 35 mph in summer, although they have been known to exceed 200 mph.

JETTY. A structure, such as a wharf, pier, or low wall, so located as to influence water current or to protect the entrance to a harbor or river. A jetty extending into the sea to protect the coast from erosion is called a *groin.* A jetty which breaks the force of the sea at any place is called a *breakwater.* A jetty built to direct or confine the flow of a river or tidal current is called a *training wall.*

A jetty or a wall along a waterfront to resist the encroachment of the sea is called a *sea wall.*

JOINT. Cracks in a rock mass which form along planes of weakness. There is no relative movement of the rock around the cracks.

JUNGLE. Uncultivated land with a dense undergrowth, usually applied to the tropical rain forest.

JURASSIC PERIOD. The second, or middle, period of the Mesozoic era in geologic time. It began 158 million years ago and lasted 33 million years. During this period the first birds appeared in Europe and dinosaurs flourished.

BUREAU OF RECLAMATION—DEPARTMENT OF THE INTERIOR

CRATER LAKE, formed by water accumulated in an almost perfect example of a caldera. Volcanic activity built the small cone, Wizard Island.

JUVENILE WATER. Water from molten material, or magma, either brought to the surface by an eruption or added to underground water after magma crystallizes. This water was not previously part of the hydrologic cycle.

KAME. A steep, irregular ridge or hill of stratified glacial drift.

KAME TERRACE. A body of stratified glacial drift deposited between a wasting glacier and an adjacent valley wall. It stands as a terrace along the valley wall after the ice melts.

KANAT. See *Qanat*.

KAOLINITE. A common clay mineral, hydrous aluminous silicate, that develops from the weathering of plagioclase feldspars.

KARST TOPOGRAPHY. A type of landscape with numerous surface depressions, unsystematic drainage patterns, caverns, and disappearing streams. It occurs in an area underlain by limestone which has been dissolved by rain or rivers. Named for a limestone plateau area in Yugoslavia.

KATABATIC WIND. A cool wind blowing downhill. Also, the flow of cold air off ice caps.

KETTLE. A depression, frequently containing a pond, formed in glacial deposits by an isolated mass of glacier ice that later melted.

KEY. A low island chain formed by a sandbank or reef.

KLIPPE. A block of rocks, generally older than the underlying rocks and separated from them by a fault with a gentle dip. It may be the remnant of an overthrust layer of rock.

KNOB. A rounded hill or mountain, especially an isolated one.

KNOLL. A small, rounded hill. Also, an undersea hill less than 1,000 meters (about 3,280 feet) above the sea floor and of limited extent across its summit. It is smaller than a seamount.

KNOT. A unit of speed equal to one nautical mile (6,076.12 feet) per hour.

KUROSHIO. A warm, fast (2 to 4 knots) ocean current, the Pacific counterpart of the Atlantic Gulf Stream. It is also called the Japan Current. It originates in the Pacific North Equatorial Current, which divides east of the Philippines. It flows northeastward from Taiwan, close to Japan, ultimately joining with the Oyashio to form the North Pacific Current.

KYMATOLOGY. The science of waves and wave motion.

LABRADOR CURRENT. A cold ocean current flowing southward from Baffin Bay and southeastward along the coasts of Labrador and Newfoundland. East of Newfoundland it meets the Gulf Stream, and the two flow eastward as the North Atlantic Current.

LACCOLITH. A landform caused by the intrusion of a mass of molten material, or magma, into the crust of the earth to produce a dome-shaped surface of overlying rock.

LACUSTRINE. Referring to a lake.

LADU. An avalanche of glowing volcanic debris.

LAGOON. A shallow body of water partly or completely separated from the sea by a narrow strip of land, such as a reef or bar.

LAKE. A standing body of inland water formed when a substantial amount of water collects in a depression in the earth's surface. It may be fed by surface and groundwater.

LAMINAR FLOW. A smooth and relatively slow movement, or flow, of a liquid in which the fluid moves in straight-line paths parallel to the channel.

LAND BREEZE. A light wind blowing from the land to the sea. It is caused by unequal cooling of land and sea at night. The cooler, denser air over the land moves into an area of warm, less dense air.

LANDLOCKED. A body of water enclosed, or nearly enclosed, by land.

LANDSCAPE. A portion of the earth's surface having a complex of natural and cultural features which gives it a distinctive character.

LANDSLIDE. The downward movement of a large mass of loose earth material containing varying amounts of water.
   A *debris slide* is the rapid movement of rock fragments, such as gravel. It produces a surface of low rounded hills. A *rockslide* is the sliding of sheets of bedrock along planes of weakness and the tumbling of rocks and boulders down a slope. It produces a dam-like structure in the valley below. A *slump*, or slope failure, is the downward and outward movement of rock or unconsolidated material. It produces a scarp, or cliff, above it.
   Other relatively slower movements are creep, earthflow, mudflow, and solifluction.

LAPIES. Furrows and sharp crests on a limestone surface. The furrows can be more than 40 feet deep.

LAPILLI. Small cinder fragments ejected from a volcano.

LAPSE RATE. The rate of decrease in the temperature of the atmosphere with increase in height.

LATERITE. A red-colored soil high in iron and aluminum found in tropical regions.

LAVA. Molten material reaching the surface from a pool of magma, or molten rock, in the interior of the earth. Also, the same material when cooled and solidified. It may be called pumice if light in color and weight, or scoria if dark and heavy.

LAVA FLOW. A stream of lava. A basic lava flow usually erupts gently, is relatively fluid, and may flow for miles. A silicic lava flow usually erupts explosively and is more viscous or gluey. A silicic lava flow usually piles up around the volcano.

LAW OF CROSS–CUTTING RELATIONSHIPS. Any rock is younger than any rock it cuts across.

LAW OF SUPERPOSITION. The basis of geologic chronology in that if a series of sedimentary rock has not been overturned, the underlying strata must be older than overlying strata.

LEACHING. The removal or washing away of soluble material by water percolating through layers of soil or shattered bedrock.

LEAD. A soft, heavy metallic element (Pb) with a boiling point of $1,750°C$ and a specific gravity of 11.34.

LEAD–URANIUM RATIO. As the radioactive element uranium disintegrates, lead is formed. On the basis of the relative amounts of these two elements in a rock or mineral the geologic age can be computed. See also *Radioactive decay*.

LEAN ORE. A mineral deposit in which the ore content is low.

LEE. The sheltered side of an object, as a mountain.

LEEWARD. The direction toward which the wind is blowing, as opposed to windward.

LENTICULAR. A body of ore or rock thick in the middle and thinning toward the edges, thus resembling a double convex lens.

LEVEE. A natural or man-made river bank higher in elevation than the land running parallel to the stream.

LEVEL, or spirit level. An instrument for establishing a true horizontal. It consists of a hermetically sealed small glass tube nearly filled with a nonfreezing liquid, but with enough space left for the formation of an air bubble. The tube is mounted horizontally in a form with a straight edge, which provides a reference to the surface being tested. The bubble will always find the top of the tube.

LIGHT YEAR. The distance light can travel in one year, about 6,000 billion miles.

LIGNITE. An intermediate form of coal.

LIMB. The side of a fold.

LIME. Calcium Oxide, CaO.

LIMESTONE. A sedimentary rock formed from calcareous remains of plants and animals or precipitated from solution. It is natural calcium carbonate ($CaCO_3$) and will yield lime when heated.

LIMNOLOGY. The study of freshwater lakes and ponds.

LIMONITE. A brown hydrous iron oxide derived from the weathering of dark-colored minerals.

LITHIFICATION. The processes of cementation, compaction by pressure, and crystallization which convert magma, or molten material, and sediments into rock.

LITHOLOGY. The study and description of rocks.

LITHOSOLS. A great soil group of azonal soils consisting of partially weathered rock fragments. They are largely confined to steep hillsides.

LITHOSPHERE. The solid crust of the earth. See also *Earth structure*.

LITTORAL. Refers to a narrow strip of land along the coast between high and low water marks. See also *Ocean depth zones*.

LLANO. An extensive tropical grassland plain. The term is generally applied to vast savanna regions of South America.

LOAD. The solid material carried by a stream in suspension or rolled along the bed. The quantity of material depends upon the discharge and velocity of the stream and the particle size.

LOAM. A soil in which there is 28 to 55 percent silt, 7 to 27 percent clay, and less than 52 percent sand.

LOCH. A lake or an arm of the sea, especially when narrow or nearly landlocked.

LODE. A deposit of economically valuable mineral lying within definite boundaries, as in a fissure in country rock. The term may also refer to a system of closely spaced veins.

LOESS. An unconsolidated, unstratified deposit of silt and fine sand or clay, probably carried by the wind.

LONGITUDINAL DUNES. Long ridges of sand running in the general direction of wind movement. Longitudinal dunes are formed by two alternating wind directions or by the funnel-effect of valleys as wind sweeps sand through them. In the Libyan Desert they may be 60 miles long and are called seif (sword) dunes.

LONGITUDINAL VALLEY. A mountain valley parallel to the main trend of the range.

LONGSHORE CURRENT. A current moving roughly parallel to the shore. It is usually generated by waves breaking at an angle to the shoreline.

LOST RIVER. A surface stream that has lost its trunk and tributaries either because of increased aridity, in which evaporation exceeds precipitation, or because it drains into an underground channel, as may occur in a region of karst topography.

LOW. A parcel of air of lesser atmospheric pressure than the surrounding air.

LOW WATER. The lowest level reached by a falling tide.

LUNAR DAY. The interval of time between two successive passes of the moon across the same meridian. It is equal to approximately 24 hours, 50 minutes. Also called *tidal day*.

LUNAR MONTH. The period of time in which the moon makes one complete revolution around the earth, or from new moon to new moon. It is approximately equal to $29\frac{1}{2}$ days.

LUSTER. A means of identifying a mineral according to its appearance in reflected light. There are several kinds of luster: *metallic*, having the luster of a metal (selective surface absorption with strong reflection); *vitreous*, having the luster of glass; *resinous*, having the luster of yellow resin; *pearly*, having the iridescence of a pearl; *greasy*, appearing to be covered with a thin layer of oil; *silky*, appearing like silk, with a finely fibrous structure; *adamantine*, having the brilliance of a diamond.

LYSIMETER. An instrument for measuring the percolation of water through soil and for determining the materials removed in solution by the drainage.

MAAR. A relatively shallow, flatfloored crater at a volcanic vent which is coneless or nearly so. It is formed by a violent explosion not accompanied by lava or ash. If it intersects the water table, the maar will be occupied by a lake.

MACCHIA. See *Maquis*.

MAGMA. Molten rock material (primarily silicates) existing deep within the earth. It cools and crystallizes to form igneous rock. When extruded it is called lava. It may be forced to the surface either by gases imprisoned within the magma or by the gross weight of the overlying solid rock on the basaltic layer below the crust.

MAGMATIC DIFFERENTIATION. The process by which initially homogeneous magma results in rocks of various textures and compositions. As magma cools, certain minerals crystallize more readily than others. Some of these crystals settle out of the magma, the rest react with the remaining melt (see *Bowen's reaction series*).

The rate of cooling affects the texture of the resultant rock. If rapidly cooled, it will have an extremely fine or glassy texture. If it cools slowly, it will have a coarse-grained texture.

MAGNETIC DECLINATION. The angle between geographic, or true, north and magnetic north.

MAGNETIC POLE. One of the two ends of the bipolar magnet at which magnetic properties appear to be concentrated, thus establishing the earth's magnetic field. These poles do not coincide with the geographic poles, as the axis connecting them passes approximately 750 miles from the earth's center.

MAGNETIC STORM. A large, temporary, often sudden variation in the earth's magnetic field. It is frequently associated with sunspots.

MAGNETITE. Iron oxide (Fe_3O_4), an important ore of iron. It is black and strongly magnetic.

MAGNETOMETER. An instrument for measuring the intensity and direction of the earth's magnetic field.

MALLEE. A shrubby vegetative cover consisting mostly of low eucalyptus bushes. It is found in Australia's dry regions.

MAGNETITE, an iron oxide, is black, strongly magnetic, and an important ore of iron.

MANGROVE SWAMP. A salty, or brackish, marsh found in the coastal regions of tropical and subtropical climates in which mangrove trees develop aerial roots, forming an almost impenetrable tangle.

MANTLE. The interior portion of the earth lying between the core and the crust. See *Earth structure*.

MAQUIS. A low, thick, shrubby vegetation consisting of drought-resistant trees found along the shores of the Mediterranean Sea. Maquis is the French term, macchia the Italian.

MARBLE. The metamorphic equivalent of limestone or dolomite with grains large enough to be seen by the unaided eye. Commercially, any limestone that can take a polish.

MARINE. Of, or relating to, the sea.

MARINE CLIMATE. A climate under the predominant influence of the sea. It is characterized by small daily and annual temperature ranges and high relative humidity. It is found where the prevailing winds blow onshore, such as ocean islands and continental shores.

MARITIME. On, or near, the sea.

MARITIME CLIMATE. See *Marine climate*.

MARL. A calcareous clay. A sedimentary deposit of silt or clay and calcium carbonate, of marine or freshwater origin.

MARSH. An area of soft, wet, and poorly drained land, usually covered with grasses.

MARSH GAS. Methane (CH_4), the chief constituent of natural gas. It also results from the partial decay of plants in swamps.

MASSIF. A mountainous mass or group of uplands with relatively uniform characteristics. It may break up into peaks near the summit.

MASS–WASTING. The wearing down of the land surface by the downward movement of large masses of earth material directly controlled by gravity. It includes such gradual movements as creep and solifluction and such rapid movement as landslides.

MATTERHORN. A sharply pointed mountain peak resembling the Swiss peak of that name. See *Horn*.

MEADOW. A level grassland that is used generally for hay.

MEANDER. A loop, or curve, in a mature stream. It is formed when the current is turned against one bank by an obstruction and then is deflected against the other. A meander grows and migrates downstream by erosion on the outside of the bend and deposition on the inside. If the base level is lowered the stream will resume downward cutting and form an entrenched meander.

MEAN SEA LEVEL. The mean surface water level determined by averaging heights at all stages of the tide over a 19-year period.

MECHANICAL WEATHERING. The disintegration of rock material by expansion and contraction during temperature change, frost heaving, exfoliation, and the action of plant roots, streams, wind, glaciers, and ocean waves. There is no chemical change involved. See *Geology*.

MEDITERRANEAN CLIMATE. A type of climate characterized by hot, dry summers and cool, moist winters.

MELT. A liquid solution of ions at high temperature. A naturally occurring silicate melt is called magma.

MELTWATER. Water derived from the melting of snow or glacial ice.

MERCALLI INTENSITY SCALE. A system of registering the intensity of an earthquake on a scale ranging from 1, only barely detectable, to 12, force great enough to demolish large buildings. It has been replaced by the Richter magnitude scale.

MESA. A tablelike, flat-topped mountain with steep sides.

MESOTHERMAL. Referring to warm temperature.

MESOZOIC ERA. The "Era of Middle Life," the second of the three eras into which the Phanerozoic eon is divided. It began 185 million years ago and lasted 125 million years.

METAMORPHIC FACIES. A group of rocks characterized by particular mineral associations that indicate an origin under specific temperature-pressure conditions.

Four metamorphic facies have been identified: *hornfels* facies, formed at temperatures greater than 700°C (1,300°F); *amphibolite* facies, formed at temperatures from 450°C (850°F) to 700°C; *epidote-amphibolite* facies, formed at temperatures from 250°C (500°F) to 450°C; *greenschist* facies, formed at temperatures from 150°C (300°F) to 250°C. The hornfels facies are formed by contact metamorphism, the other facies by regional metamorphism.

METAMORPHIC ROCK. One of the three principal groups of rock, the others being sedimentary and igneous rock. Metamorphic rock is formed when solid rock is physically or chemically changed by deforming pressures, heat, and chemically active fluids. See also *Geochemical cycle*.

METASOMATISM. The changes in the composition of rock as a result of the replacement of one mineral by another. It is a process of almost simultaneous solution and deposition by which a mineral of differing chemical composition may grow within another mineral or mineral aggregate.

METASTASIS. Lateral shifting of the earth's crust, such as continental drift.

METEOR. A small body of matter traveling through space and which may enter the atmosphere. In the atmosphere it is heated by friction and is either wholly or partially consumed. If only partially consumed, it reaches the earth's surface as a meteorite.

METEORIC WATER. Water derived from the earth's atmosphere.

METEORITE. See *Meteor.*

METEOROLOGY. The scientific study of the atmosphere and its phenomena.

METHANE. The simplest paraffin hydrocarbon (CH_4) and the principal constituent of natural gas. Also called marsh gas.

MICA. A group of minerals with flat or perfect sheetlike structures composed of aluminum silicate with iron, calcium, magnesium, potassium, sodium, or lithium. The two most common types are biotite, or ferromagnesian black mica, and muscovite, or potassic white mica.

MICROSEISM. A disturbance of the earth's crust of very low intensity and short duration that may be produced by such factors as atmospheric storms or the activities of man.

MIDNIGHT SUN. A phenomenon seen in the high latitudes, above 63½°, during the summer season, when the sun does not fall below the horizon plane and is visible for 24 hours.

MIDOCEAN RIDGE. A great median arch or sea bottom swell extending the length of an ocean basin roughly parallel to the continental margins.

MIGMATITE. A mixed rock produced by the injection of granitic magma between the layers of a rock.

MILE. A unit of linear measurement. A *geographic* mile is 1/60 of a degree measured along the equator, or 6,087 feet. A *nautical* mile is equal to 1/60 of a degree of a great circle on a sphere whose surface is equal to that of earth. One international nautical mile equals approximately 6.076 feet. A *statute* mile is equal to 5,280 feet.

MILLIBAR. A unit of atmospheric pressure equal to 1/1000 of a bar. In meteorology, it is equal to a force of 1,000 dynes per square centimeter.

MINERAL. A naturally occurring inorganic substance with distinctive physical and chemical properties and a tendency to assume a crystal form. A mineral is classified according to its structure, cleavage, and fracture; its luster, hardness, and specific gravity; and its color and the color of the streak it makes on unglazed porcelain.

MINERALOGY. The study of the origin, chemical composition, and physical characteristics of minerals.

MINUTE. A unit of time equal to 1/60 of an hour. Also, a unit of angular measurement equal to 1/60 of a degree.

MIOCENE EPOCH. The fourth epoch of the Tertiary period of the Cenozoic era. It began 30 million years ago and lasted 15 million years. During this time such major mountain ranges as the Alps, the Andes, and the Himalayas were raised and certain ruminating animals, such as cows, developed. Also, there arose the Hominidae (which later gave rise to the Homo sapiens).

MIRAGE. An optical illusion seen on deserts, at sea, and in polar regions. It is caused by layers of air that have been unequally heated, and therefore, have differing densities. If the difference in density between two layers is great enough, the common surface will act as a mirror. In this way distant objects may appear magnified, distorted, and often inverted. Because the surface is not smooth there is continual shimmering.

MISSISSIPPIAN PERIOD. The fifth period of the Paleozoic era in geologic time. It began 310 million years ago and lasted 40 million years. During this time, coal beds were formed and reptiles and amphibians developed. Formerly, the Mississippian with the Pennsylvanian composed the Carboniferous period. This grouping is now considered obsolete in the United States, and the Mississippian and Pennsylvanian are each ranked as periods.

MIST. A parcel of air containing dispersed water droplets that reduce visibility. It is less severe than a fog.

MISTRAL. A cold, dry, and gusty north or northwest wind that blows from a high pressure area in snow-covered mountains to the low pressure area extending along the Mediterranean coast of France.

MOHO, or Mohorovičić discontinuity. See *Earth structure.*

MOHOLE. a U.S. scientific project to dig a deep borehole to penetrate the earth's crust and on into the mantle below the Mohorovičić discontinuity. The site chosen was in the ocean, 100 miles northeast of Maui, Hawaii, where the crust is thinner. By analyzing the material brought up from the hole and then lowering instruments to record temperature, magnetism, and other factors, scientists hoped to answer some questions about the structure of the inner earth. The project was abandoned.

MOHS' SCALE. See *Hardness scale.*

MONADNOCK. An isloated residual mass of resistant rock that stands above the surrounding land.

MONOCLINE. See *Fold.*

MONSOON. A wind system characterized by a complete reversal of direction from winter to summer. In winter it is a dry, offshore wind formed in high pressure areas over cold continents. In summer, it is a damp onshore wind blowing toward the heated interior of the continents.

MIDNIGHT SUN at North Cape on Magery Island, Norway, during the summer.

MOON. The only natural satellite of the earth, traveling at a mean distance of 238,866 miles from the earth at an average speed of almost 2,300 miles per hour. The moon makes a complete revolution around the earth every 27 days, 7 hours, 43 minutes, 11.47 seconds—one sidereal month. It moves into the same relationship with the earth and sun every 29 days, 12 hours, 44 minutes, 2.8 seconds—one synodic month.

The moon's diameter is 2,160 miles or slightly more than ¼ that of the earth; its mass is 1/81 that of the earth. The moon's temperature ranges from over 200°F in the sun to below −250°F in complete shadow. The moon has no atmosphere.

Because the moon completes one rotation about its axis in the same time it takes to complete one revolution around the earth, the same side of the moon always faces the earth. The phases of the moon are new moon (invisible from the earth), first quarter, full moon, and last quarter.

MOOR. An extensive area of open rolling land covered with heather or wild grasses, with or without marshy patches.

MORAINE. Unconsolidated, disordered rock material, or debris, deposited by a glacier. *Lateral moraines* are built along the lateral, or side, margins of a glacier. These merge to form a *medial moraine* at the meeting of two valley glaciers. *Terminal,* or *end, moraines* are formed at the farthest advance of a glacier.

Recessional moraines are formed at temporary positions during the retreat of a glacier. *Ground moraines* are formed as the main body of a glacier melts, creating gently rolling plains across a valley floor. *Superficial moraines* are formed on a glacier as the ice melts and the drift it had contained accumulates on the surface.

MOTE. A large dust particle visible in a beam of light.

MOUNTAINS are elevations in the earth's surface caused by a variety of geological factors.

MOUNTAIN. A natural elevation, usually of at least 2,000 feet, formed as a fold, fault, volcano, or as the remnant of erosion. A single mountain is a peak; connected peaks, a ridge; an elongated ridge, a chain or range; a series of ranges, often parallel, a system; a number of systems, including intervening valleys, rivers, and plains, a cordillera.

MOUNTAIN BUILDING. See *Orogeny*.

MOUNTAIN CLIMATE. A type of climate whose properties are mostly determined by relief and altitude rather than latitude and proximity to the ocean.

MOUTH. The place of discharge of a stream into a larger body of water.

MUCK. A dark-colored soil high in organic matter, usually formed in wet places.

MUD CRACKS. Irregular polygonal cracks formed by shrinkage as a mud deposit dries. On further exposure they bake and harden so that the polygonal form is preserved through repeated flooding.

MUDFLOW. A downward moving, thick mixture of rock fragments, soil, and water. It produces a widening tongue of rock when dried and solidified. It occurs in the canyons of desert regions after a rainstorm or on the slopes of a volcano.

MUDSTONE. A fine-grained sedimentary rock consisting of an indefinite mixture of clay, silt, and sand particles. The term also refers to a clay rock, or shale, without fissility (ready breaking along closely spaced parallel planes).

MUSCOVITE. See *Mica*.

MUSKEG. A moss-covered swamp in northern North America.

NAPPE. A faulted, overturned fold thrust over other rocks.

NATURAL BRIDGE. An arch of rock or earth spanning a gorge or other depression. It is formed by erosion.

NATURAL GAS. A mixture of gaseous hydrocarbons that occurs in nature.

NAUTICAL MILE. See *Mile*.

NEAP TIDE. The tide with the smallest range between high water and low water. Neap tides occur about every two weeks when the moon is in the first or third quarter, the sun and moon being at right angles to each other with respect to a place on the earth (quadrature).

NECK. A mass of hardened lava which has filled the conduit or vent of a volcano and which has been exposed by erosion of the surrounding material. Also, a narrow strip of land connecting a peninsula with the mainland or a narrow channel connecting two larger bodies of water.

NECK CUTOFF. A channel cut by a stream across the neck of land between two meanders. The abandoned loop is called an oxbow.

NERITIC. See *Ocean depth zones*.

NÉVÉ. Granular snow, the intermediate stage between snow and ice in a glacier. It is also called firn.

NITRATES. A group of nitrogen fertilizers in which the nitrogen is available as a salt of nitric acid—a compound containing the radical of nitrogen and oxygen (NO_3).

NIVATION. Frost heaving and erosion beneath and around a snowbank.

NODULE. An irregular, knobby-surfaced body of mineral matter whose composition differs from the sedimentary rock in which it was formed. Silica, in the form of chert or flint, is the major component of a nodule.

NONCONFORMITY. An unconformity in which igneous rocks were partially eroded and then covered by sedimentary rocks.

NORTHERN LIGHTS. See *Aurora*.

NORTH POLE. See *Poles*.

NOTCH. A deep cut, or notch, in the base of a sea cliff made by breaking waves. Also, a narrow pass between two hills or mountains.

NUÉE ARDENTE. A cloud of hot gas and ash ejected horizontally from beneath a lava plug in a volcano. The cloud travels swiftly down the side of the volcano.

NUNATAK. An isolated mountain peak projecting through the surface of a glacier.

OASIS. An area in a desert where water is permanently available. Oases range in size from a small patch with a few palm trees to an area of several hundred square miles.

OBLATE. Flattened at the poles. For example, the earth is an oblate spheroid.

OBSEQUENT STREAM. A stream flowing in a direction opposite to that of the dip of the strata or the tilt of the surface. It occurs in rock beds of differing resistance. Also called a reversed stream. It is the opposite of a consequent stream.

OBSIDIAN. Volcanic glass. An extrusive igneous rock containing a large proportion of silica.

OCEAN. The great body of salt water that occupies the depressions in the earth's surface.

OCEAN CURRENT. A large stream moving continuously through the ocean in approximately the same path, distinguished chiefly by temperature and salinity from the water through which it flows.

OCEAN DEPTH ZONES. The primary divisions of ocean depths are the *pelagic*, the entire mass of water, and the *benthic*, the ocean floor.

The *pelagic* division is composed of the neritic province, which extends from the low water point to a depth of 100 fathoms (600 feet), and the oceanic province, which includes water deeper than 100 fathoms. The upper 50 fathoms of the pelagic division comprise the photic zone, where there is ample sunlight for plants to carry on photosynthesis. Below that is the aphotic zone.

The *benthic* division includes the supralittoral zone, or land just above the high water level kept moist by waves and spray; the littoral zone, between high water and low water levels; the sublittoral zone, from the low water level to 100 fathoms (underlying the neritic province); the bathyal

OASIS, in the Sahara, consists of a group of date palms watered by underground springs.

zone, between 100 and 2,000 fathoms; and the abyssal zone, below 2,000 fathoms. The hadal zone comprises the greatest depths, over 3,000 fathoms.

OCEANOGRAPHY. The study of the ocean, including its physical boundaries, the chemistry and physics of the sea, and marine biology.

OFFSHORE WIND. A wind blowing from the land toward the sea, a land breeze, as contrasted with an onshore wind, or sea breeze.

OIL. See *Petroleum*, p. 560.

OLIGOCENE EPOCH. The third epoch of the Tertiary period of the Cenozoic era. It began 40 million years ago and lasted 10 million years.

OLIVINE. A dark green mineral consisting of silicates of magnesium and iron which crystallizes early from magma, or molten material, and weathers readily at the earth's surface.

ONSHORE WIND. A wind blowing from the sea toward the land, a sea breeze, as contrasted with an offshore wind, or land breeze.

OÖLITE. A rock made up of spherical, sand-sized grains, usually composed of calcium carbonate.

OOZE. Wet mud or slime. Also a fine-grained deep-sea deposit, 30 percent or more of which is composed of the hard parts of small organisms.

ORDOVICIAN PERIOD. The second period of the Paleozoic era in geologic time. It began 450 million years ago and lasted 70 million years.

ORE. A mineral deposit of economic value.

OROGENY. The process of forming mountains by folding, faulting, and thrusting.

OROGRAPHIC RAIN. Rainfall produced when a mountain deflects moist air upward. The moist air cools at the higher elevation and the moisture falls as rain.

OROGRAPHY. The branch of physical geography concerned with the study of mountains and mountain systems.

OUTCROP. A naturally protruding portion of a rock formation, most of which is covered by overlying material.

OUTLIER. A mass of younger rocks separated by erosion from the main mass and surrounded by older rocks. The opposite of inlier.

OUTWASH PLAIN. A plain formed of material deposited by streams flowing from a melting glacier.

OVERBURDEN. The loose earth material lying over other material, such as an ore deposit.

OXBOW. A crescent-shaped lake formed in a meander cut off from the main stream.

OXYSPHERE. A proposed synonym for lithosphere on the basis that 60 percent of the atoms in the earth's crust are oxygen and these atoms occupy more than 90 percent of the volume of the familiar rocks.

OYASHIO. A cold ocean current flowing south along the Kuril Islands. It meets the Kuroshio and with it forms the North Pacific Current.

PACK ICE. Any area of sea ice other than fast ice. Specifically, an area of floating ice which has been driven together. It is often referred to as drift ice.

PAHOEHOE. Hawaiian term for a lava flow whose surface is smooth, billowy, or ropy. Also called corded lava. The opposite of aa.

PALEOCENE EPOCH. The first epoch of the Tertiary period of the Cenozoic era. It began 60 million years ago and lasted 10 million years.

PALEOGEOGRAPHY. The study of the distribution of land and water masses during earlier periods of geologic time.

PALEONTOLOGY. The study of extinct plant and animal organisms based on their fossil remains.

PALEOZOIC ERA. The "Era of Old Life," the earliest era of the Phanerozoic eon. It began approximately 550 million years ago and lasted approximately 350 million years.

PALISADE. An extended rock cliff rising abruptly from the margin of a stream or lake.

PALUDAL. Referring to swamps or marshes and to material deposited in a swamp.

PALUSTRINE. Pertaining to material deposited in a swamp or marsh.

PAMPA. A treeless grassland plain. Specifically, the extensive grassland area around the River Plate (Río de la Plata) in South America.

PAMPERO. A strong, cold, west or southwest wind which sweeps over the pampas of South America.

PARABOLIC DUNE. A U-shaped sand dune whose tips point upwind and whose concave, or windward, side is the gentler slope. It is formed in sandy areas along coasts and is often covered with sparse vegetation which limits its advance.

PARAMO. A high, bleak plateau with scattered, stunted vegetation, as in the Andes of South America.

PASS. A narrow gap or low break in a mountain barrier.

PATER NOSTER LAKES. A chain of small lakes along a glaciated valley where ice-plucking and gouging have scooped out a series of basins.

PEAK. The summit of a mountain.

PEAT. The semisolid remains of decayed marsh plants. It is the first stage in the formation of coal.

PEBBLES. See *Wentworth grade scale*.

PEDALFER. A soil type characterized by the accumulation of iron and aluminum salts. Such soluble materials as calcium carbonate or magnesium carbonate generally do not occur in a pedalfer. It is found in humid climates, beneath forest vegetation.

PEDIMENT. A gently sloping rock surface at the base of a highland in arid and semiarid regions.

PEDOCAL. A soil type characterized by the accumulation of calcium carbonate. It is commonly found in temperate climates with low rainfall, below brush or grass growth.

PEDOLOGY. The study of the origin, character, and use of soils.

PEGMATITE. A small pluton or dike of very coarse texture with crystals up to 40 feet long, usually associated with a batholith of finer texture.

PELAGIC. See *Ocean depth zones.*

PENEPLAIN. An extensive level land surface close to base level formed by a long period of erosion.

PENINSULA. A body of land nearly surrounded by water and connected to a larger body of land by a neck.

PENNSYLVANIAN PERIOD. The sixth period of the Paleozoic era in geological time. It began 270 million years ago and lasted 45 million years. During this time large insects developed. Cockroaches achieved a length of 3 or 4 inches, and the period is also called the "Age of Cockroaches." Formerly, with the Mississippian, it comprised the Carboniferous period.

PERCHED WATER TABLE. A body of groundwater held above the main water table by a layer of impermeable rock.

PERCOLATION. The downward passage of water moved by its own weight through the crevices or pores of rock or soil.

PERIDOTITE. A group of coarse-grained intrusive igneous rocks, such as granite, containing ferromagnesian silicates and little or no feldspar.

PERIOD. In geologic time, a subdivision of an era; a time unit corresponding to a system in time-stratigraphic units.

PERMAFROST. Permanently frozen subsoil.

PERMEABILITY. The ability of earth material to transmit liquids.

PERMIAN PERIOD. The seventh and last period of the Paleozoic era in geologic time. It began some 225 million years ago and lasted for approximately 40 million years.

PETROGRAPHY. See *Lithology.*

PETROLOGY. The study of the origin, present conditions, and alterations of rocks, including ore and mineral deposits.

pH. A means of expressing the relative acidity and alkalinity of a soil in terms of a scale in which complete acidity is 0 and alkalinity is 14 (7 is neutral).

PHANERITIC. Refers to equigranular, coarse-grained (hence visible), and therefore slowly cooled rock.

PHANEROZOIC EON. The "Time of Visible Life." It began 550 million years ago with the Cambrian period of the Paleozoic era and continues into the present.

PHENOCRYST. A large, conspicuous crystal in an aphanitic, or fine-grained, groundmass.

PHENOLOGY. The study of the relationship between seasonal climate change and animal and plant life.

PHOROGENESIS. The slipping of the earth's crust over the mantle.

PHOSPHATES. Salts of phosphoric acid used as fertilizers to supply phosphorous compounds to the soil. A compound containing the chemical radical of phosphorus and oxygen, such as PO_4.

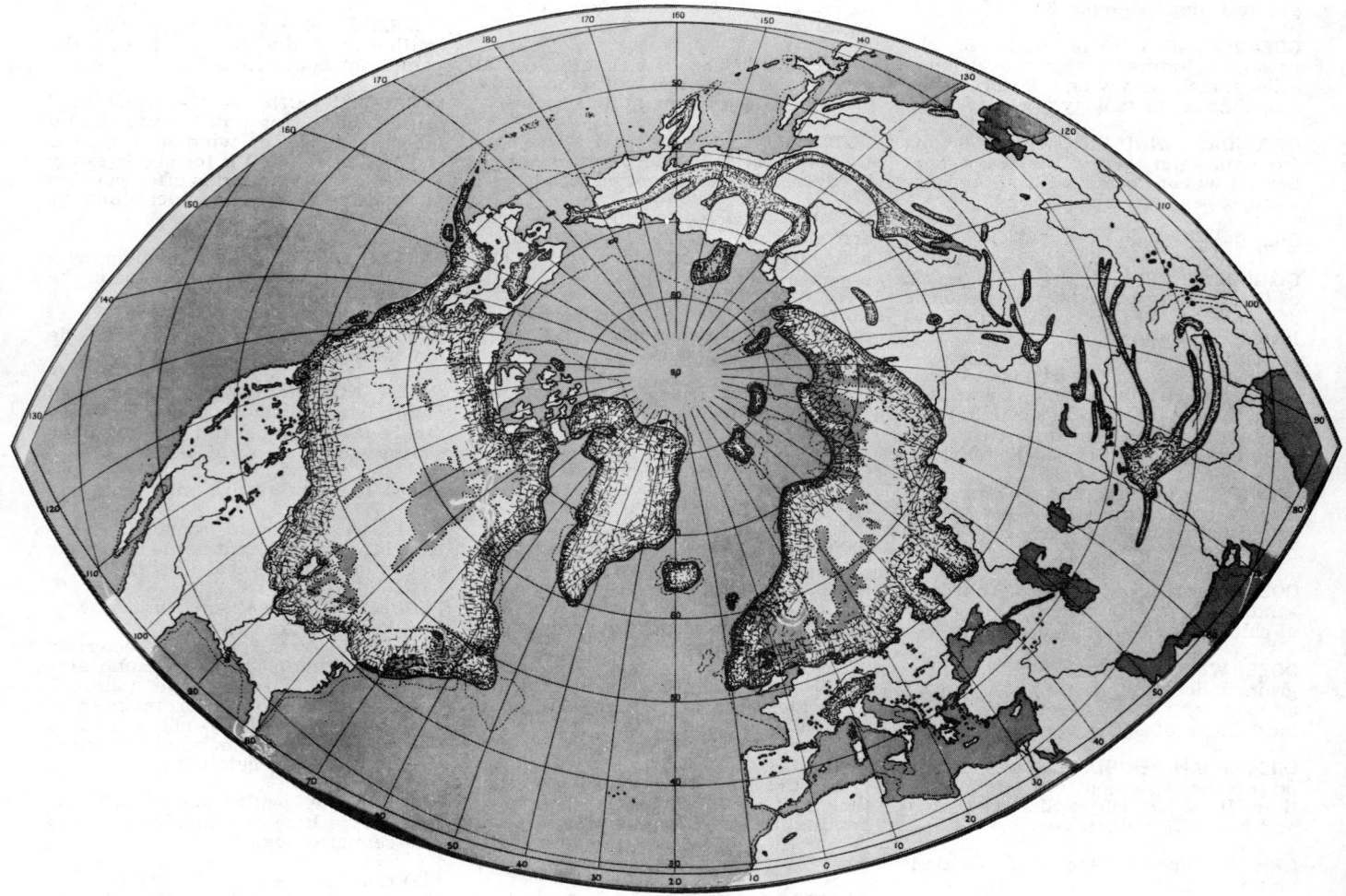

AMERICAN MUSEUM OF NATURAL HISTORY
PLEISTOCENE GLACIATION at its maximum extent covered northern Europe, the British Isles, and North America as far south as the Ohio River.

PHREATIC. Pertaining to groundwater.

PHYLLITE. A clayey metamorphic rock with cleavage coarser than slate and finer than schist.

PHYSIOGRAPHY. The study of the physical features of the earth.

PICACHO. A large, pointed mountain or hill with steep sides.

PIEDMONT. Refers to any feature lying or formed at the base of a mountain.

PIEZOMETRIC SURFACE. The imaginary surface corresponding to the level to which groundwater will rise under hydrostatic pressure in wells or springs.

PILLOW LAVAS. Rounded masses of lava occurring in basic lava, such as basalt.

PIRACY. See *Stream capture.*

PITCH. See *Rake.*

PITCHSTONE. A dull, pitch-lustered variety of volcanic glass containing more water than other glassy rocks.

PLACER DEPOSIT. A mass of gravel or similar material containing particles of valuable minerals, such as gold or platinum.

PLAIN. A large area of level or gently undulating land not broken by any great elevations or depressions.

PLANETARY WINDS. The major winds of the earth—the polar easterlies, trade winds, westerlies.

PLANOSOL. A great soil group of intrazonal soils consisting of eluviated surface horizons, overlying compacted B horizons.

PLATEAU. An extensive, comparatively flat surface rising sharply above adjacent land on at least one side and often dissected by canyons.

PLATEAU BASALT. A vast horizontal lava flow.

PLAYA. A shallow central portion of a basin floor where water gathers after a rain and is evaporated, leaving an alkali flat.

PLAYA LAKE. A temporary lake in a playa.

PLEISTOCENE EPOCH. The first epoch in the Quaternary period of the Cenozoic era in geologic time. It began 1 million years ago and, according to some authorities, ended with the beginning of history, 10,000 to 25,000 years ago. During this epoch, glaciers made several advances and retreats, at times covering almost one third of the earth's land surface. It is thus also called the Ice Age.

PLIOCENE EPOCH. The fifth and latest epoch in the Tertiary period of the Cenozoic era in geologic time. It began 15 million years ago and lasted 14 million years.

PLUCKING. The chief process in glacial erosion by which meltwater freezes around pieces of rock, incorporates them into the glacier, and, by the pressure of the thick moving glacier, breaks off or quarries blocks of bedrock.

PLUTON. A mass of igneous rock that has solidified within the earth by the crystallization of magma.

PLUVIAL. Pertaining to rain.

PODZOL. A great soil group consisting of soils formed in temperate, humid climates under coniferous or mixed coniferous and deciduous forests. It is characterized by an ashy-gray, highly leached layer.

POINT. The extreme end of a cape.

POLAR FRONT. The boundary, or front, between cold, polar air and the warm air of temperate or tropical regions. The majority of atmospheric depressions of temperate latitudes develop there.

POLAR WIND. An extremely cold wind blowing out of the high-pressure zone around the poles.

POLDER. An area of flat land at or below sea level, or the level of the nearest river, which has been drained.

POLES. The intersections of the extremities of the earth's axis with the earth's surface, located at 90°N and 90°S latitudes.

POLJE, or polye. An extensive depression with a flat floor and steep walls in a region of karst topography.

POLYGONAL GROUND. See *Mud cracks.*

POND. A small, rather deep body of water, usually fresh. Also, an underground accumulation of oil or gas in a natural reservoir composed of such porous rock as sandstone or limestone and bounded by impermeable strata of rock.

PORE. An interstice or void in rock or soil.

POROSITY. The ratio between the volume occupied by pores in a material to its total volume.

PORPHYRY. An igneous rock containing conspicuous crystals, or phenocrysts, in a fine-grained, or aphanitic, groundmass.

POTASH. Potassium salts, used as a source of potassium fertilizer.

POTHOLE. A hole in rock, generally deeper than it is wide, caused by the abrasive action of rock fragments. Potholes are commonly found in the bed of a stream or at the base of a waterfall.

PRAIRIE. An extensive, undulating to flat, grassland area. Also, a zonal great soil group composed of soils formed under grass cover in cool to temperate, humid regions.

PRECAMBRIAN. Refers to the Cryptozoic eon, preceding the Cambrian period of the Palezoic era in geologic time.

PRECIPICE. A very steep cliff, particularly one that is almost perpendicular or overhanging.

PRECIPITATION. The deposit of water on the earth from the atmosphere. It occurs when water vapor particles grow large enough to fall to the earth and the moisture content of the air exceeds the saturation point. Precipitation may be in the form of rain, snow, sleet, hail, dew, frost, or fog. Also, the separation of minerals from a solution by evaporation, centrifugal force, or fractionation.

PRESSURE GRADIENT. See *Hydraulic gradient.*

PREVAILING WIND. The wind direction at a given place with the greatest frequency of occurrence.

PROFILE. A cross section or outline. A longitudinal section of a stream showing its change in elevation. A soil profile is a vertical section through the soil showing the nature and sequence of the different layers.

PROMONTORY. A headland or high cape projecting into a body of water.

PSYCHROMETER. An instrument which measures the humidity of the atmosphere.

PUMICE. A light, porous volcanic glass filled with gas-bubble holes.

PUNA. A treeless, windswept tableland in the higher Andes mountain system of South America.

P WAVE. See *Earthquake.*

PYRITE. Iron sulfide (FeS_2). An important ore of sulfur. Because of its brassy color, it is often called "fool's gold."

PYROCLASTIC ROCK. Fragmental extrusive volcanic rock, including bombs (rounded fragments), blocks (angular), cinders (coarse, slaglike), ash (dust-sized), tuff (consolidated ash), and pumice (bombs or blocks with gas-bubble holes).

PYROMETER. An instrument for measuring temperatures beyond the range of mercurial thermometers by means of the change of electric resistance, the production of thermoelectric current, the expansion of gases, the specific heat of solids, or the intensity of heat or light radiated.

PYROXENE. A group of common rock-forming minerals, calcium and magnesium silicates with varying amounts of aluminum, iron, and sodium.

PYRRHOTITE. Iron sulfide. An important nickel ore.

QANAT. An underground channel, or tunnel, used to divert water for irrigation.

QUADRATURE. The position of the moon at a 90° angle from the sun in respect to a point on earth. It causes neap tides.

QUAGMIRE. An area of soft, wet land that gives way under foot. A bog or marsh.

QUARRY. An open cut into the earth for the extraction of stone.

QUARRYING. The removal of earth and rock by a glacier or a stream. See also *Plucking.*

QUARTZ. A common mineral, silicon dioxide (SiO_2), usually colorless or white, although it may be colored by impurities. It has a vitreous luster, conchoidal fracture, and a hardness of 7. There are several varieties of quartz, including rock crystal, amethyst, chalcedony, and agate.

QUARTZITE. A rock formed by the metamorphism of sandstone. Quartzite has no cleavage, breaking through grains instead of around them as in sandstone.

QUATERNARY PERIOD. The second period in the Cenozoic era and the most recent in geologic time. It began 1 million years ago and continues into the present.

QUICKSAND. A mass of loose, wet, unstable sand that readily yields to pressure, thus engulfing any heavy object resting on its surface.

RACE. A very fast current flowing through a relatively narrow channel.

RADIAL DRAINAGE PATTERN. A system of streams flowing outward from a central area.

RADIATION. The process by which a body emits energy in the form of waves.

RADIOACTIVE AGE DETERMINATION. The establishment of the age of a rock or sediment by measuring the proportion of the radioisotope Carbon 14 in the organic material it contains.

RADIOACTIVE DECAY. The disintegration of the nucleus of an unstable atom by the spontaneous emission of charged particles, the original element thus becoming a new element. For example, Uranium 238 (an isotope of uranium) disintegrates into helium and lead; its half-life is 4.56 billion years. Therefore, it can be used to date very old igneous and metamorphic rocks and some sedimentary rocks.

RADIOACTIVITY. The spontaneous and continuous breakdown of the nucleus in such elements as uranium, thorium, and radium by the emission of alpha, beta, and gamma rays.

RADIOLARIAN OOZE. A siliceous ooze composed of the hard parts of minute marine protozoa called Radiolaria. The greatest concentration of this siliceous mud occurs in a long east-west belt in the Pacific Ocean just north of the equator.

RADIOSONDE. A miniature radio transmitter with recording instruments carried aloft, usually by a balloon. Every few seconds it broadcasts signals giving temperature, humidity, and pressure.

RAIN. See *Precipitation.*

RAINBOW. An arc with bands of the various colors of the spectrum formed by the refraction and reflection of sunlight by water drops.

RAIN SHADOW. An area of low rainfall on the lee side of a mountain or mountain range.

RAISED BEACH. A beach elevated above the present shoreline resulting from uplift or change in sea level.

RAKE. The angle between a line in a plane and a horizontal line in that plane. Preferred over pitch in structural geology.

RAMP. A normal, or gravity, fault at the surface, curving or dipping at depth in the opposite direction. Also, an accumulation of snow forming an inclined plane between land or land ice and sea ice.

RAND. A low, marshy border around a lake or lagoon.

RANGE. An elongated ridge or chain of mountains. An open region over which livestock graze. Also, a unit of measurement, used in surveying, equal to 6 miles along a parallel.

RAPID. A turbulent portion of a stream where velocity is increased by a slope of more than one foot every 200 feet or where the current is diverted by successive outcrops of resistant rock.

RAVINE. A small, narrow, steep-sided depression in the earth, larger than a gully and smaller than a canyon.

REACTION SERIES. See *Bowen's reaction series.*

RECENT. The latest, or most recent, epoch in geological time, beginning 10,000 to 25,000 years ago and continuing to the present.

RECTANGULAR DRAINAGE PATTERN. A system of streams in which tributaries join the mainstream at 90° angles because of the right-angled faulting of rocks.

RECURVED SPIT. A hook developed as the end of a spit is turned toward the shore by the current or by the opposing action of two or more currents.

RED AND YELLOW SOILS. A combination of Red Podzolic and Yellow Podzolic zonal great soil groups formed in humid climates under forest cover.

RED CLAY. A widespread fine-grained deposit, or ooze, on the ocean floor at depths exceeding 13,000 feet, especially in the Pacific Ocean. Its red color probably results from oxidation during its slow rate of accumulation, one inch in 3,000 years.

REEF. A ridge of rocks at or near the surface of the sea, narrower than a shoal.

REFRACTORY. Refers to a mineral or compound that resists the action of heat and chemicals.

REG. A desert surface covered with tightly-packed gravel.

REGELATION. The process by which ice is melted under pressure and the meltwater is refrozen on the release of that pressure. It is believed to play a role in the movement of a glacier.

REGIMEN. In glaciers, the balance between accumulation and wastage. In streams, the stability of a stream and its channel, including seasonal fluctuations.

REGIONAL METAMORPHISM. Metamorphism on a large scale, usually unrelated to obvious igneous bodies.

REGOLITH. The layer of loose rock material resting on bedrock. It forms the surface of the earth nearly everywhere.

REGOSOLS. An azonal soil consisting primarily of soft and imperfectly consolidated material, such as sand or recent volcanic ash.

REGUR. A group of dark soils high in clay formed mainly from rocks with low quartz content. It is found extensively on the Deccan Plateau of India.

REJUVENATION. The renewal of the erosion of a land surface. It usually is caused by uplift or an increase in the discharge of a stream following an increase in precipitation.

RELATIVE TIME. Measurement of a sequence of events in geological time in terms of position in a chronological order of occurrence.

RELIEF. The difference in elevation between the highest and lowest points in a given area.

RESIDUAL SOIL. A soil formed by the disintegration and decomposition of the rocks on which it rests.

REVERSED STREAM. See *Obsequent stream.*

REVOLUTION. A time of major crustal deformation, or orogeny.

RHYOLITE. The extrusive equivalent of granite. It has a fine-grained, or aphanitic, texture.

RIA COAST. An irregular coastline with many short, funnel-shaped bays which broaden and deepen seaward, although not reaching the depth of fiords.

RICHTER MAGNITUDE SCALE. See *Earthquake.*

RIDGE. A long, narrow elevation. An elongated crest.

RIFT. A large strike-slip fault parallel to the regional structure, such as the San Andreas rift in California.

RIFT VALLEY. See *Graben.*

RILL. A very small, shallow, often temporary stream.

RIPARIAN. Pertaining to the banks of a stream.

RIP CURRENT. A strong, narrow surface current which returns to the sea the water piled up on shore by incoming waves and wind.

RIPPLE MARK. A system of small waves produced on unconsolidated material, such as sand, by wind, water current, or wave action.

RISE. A long, broad elevation rising gently and smoothly from the sea floor.

RIVER. A large stream flowing to progressively lower levels in a natural channel.

ROARING FORTIES. A belt of strong, often stormy, prevailing westerly winds which blow throughout the year in the oceans of the southern hemisphere between 40° and 60° South latitude.

ROCHE MOUTONNÉE. An exposed knob of bedrock that has been smoothed and striated by a glacier on the upstream side and left with a rugged, steeper slope on the downstream side.

ROCK. A consolidated, relatively hard, naturally formed mass of mineral matter.

ROCK FLOUR. Finely ground rock material resulting from the abrasive action of a glacier.

ROCK GLACIER. A glacierlike tongue of angular boulders usually found in cirques. In many cases a rock glacier grades into a true glacier.

ROCK MANTLE. See *Regolith.*

ROCK SALT. See *Halite.*

ROCKSLIDE. See *Landslide.*

ROCK–STRATIGRAPHIC UNIT. A group of sedimentary rocks identified by structural features without regard to fossils or time boundaries.

ROCK WOOL. See *Asbestos.*

ROPAK. A slab of sea ice standing vertically on edge.

ROPY LAVA. Corded pahoehoe.

ROSSI–FOREL INTENSITY SCALE. A scale for rating earthquake intensity replaced in 1931 by the Modified Mercalli intensity scale, which in turn was generally replaced by the Richter magnitude scale.

ROTARY FAULT. A fault which has rotated or pivoted one side of the fault away from the other.

RUNOFF. The portion of precipitation falling on a surface that runs downslope to join streams, neither evaporating nor sinking into the ground.

SADDLE. A mountain pass or low point on a ridge.

ST. ELMO'S FIRE. A luminous electrical discharge with the appearance of a brush of red or blue fire which may occur during storms at the extremities of tall objects, such as the tops of trees or steeples, or at prominent points on an airplane or ship.

SALINITY. The measure of the quantity of dissolved salts in a substance.

SALT. Halite, sodium chloride (NaCl). Also, a substance obtained when the hydrogen of an acid is displaced by a metal. Also, a compound formed from an acid and a base.

SALTATION. The bouncing movement of sand particles. In deserts, wind pushes particles of sand along the surface. When one grain collides with another the impact lifts it into the air where wind and gravitation combine to push it forward through the air and pull it back to the ground in a parabolic path from its former position. Saltation also occurs in streams; however, instead of wind, the activating force is a current of turbulent water.

SALT DOME. A mass of rock salt which has been forced to flow plastically and intruded into overlying sedimentary rock. It tends to be cylindrical and have a top diameter of about a mile.

SALT GLACIER. Generally, an exposed salt dome. It is found only in extremely arid regions.

SALT LAKE. A lake containing a predominant amount of sodium chloride and other salts. It occurs in arid regions where evaporation exceeds precipitation and runoff.

SALT MARSH. A flat, poorly drained coastal swamp often covered at high tide.

SALT PAN. A shallow basin lined with salt and often containing a salt lake.

SALT PLUG. See *Salt dome.*

SAND. Earth material (often pure silica) finer than gravel and coarser than silt. See *Wentworth grade scale.*

SANDBAR. See *Bar.*

SAND DUNE. See *Dune.*

SAND SPOUT. See *Dust devil.*

SANDSTONE. A porous sedimentary rock composed of cemented sand-sized grains, predominantly quartz.

SANDSTORM. A strong wind carrying relatively coarse sand. It rarely extends to more than 100 feet above the ground.

SAPROLITE. Residual clay, silt, or other substance from rock decomposed in situ. It is commonly red or brown and found in warm, humid climates.

SAPROPEL. An ooze, or sludge, that accumulates in swampy areas. It is rich in organic (carbonaceous or bituminous) matter.

SASTRUGI. Irregularities or wave formations caused by persistent winds on a snow surface.

SAVANNA. A plain covered with tall grasses and scattered low trees. It is found in tropical regions of alternate rainfall and drought.

SCHIST. A foliated metamorphic rock dominated by fibrous or platy minerals, such as mica. See also *Foliation.*

SCORIA. Pieces of dark, heavy, partly glassy basaltic lava with many large, irregular cavities. A pyroclastic rock.

SCOUR AND FILL. A stream in flood scours out its channel (degradation) and, as it subsides, refills its channel (aggradation).

SCREE. A heap of debris at the base of a cliff or a sheet of debris covering a mountain slope. It is distinguished from talus, which occurs only at the base of a cliff.

SCRUB. A thick vegetation consisting of stunted trees and shrubs. It grows in poor soil or in sand.

SEA. A body of salt water secondary in size to an ocean. It may be partially or completely surrounded by land. Also, waves generated or sustained by

ARABIAN AMERICAN OIL COMPANY

SAND. Blown by the wind, particles of sand are constantly forming new surface patterns.

winds within their fetch, or generating area, as opposed to swell, which refers to more regular, longer waves that have traveled out of their generating area.

SEA BREEZE. A light wind blowing from the sea to the land. It is caused by unequal heating of land and sea during the day. The cooler, denser air over the water moves into an area of warm, less dense air.

SEA LEVEL. See *Mean sea level.*

SEA MILE. A nautical mile. See *Mile.*

SEAMOUNT. An elevation rising 500 fathoms (3,000 feet) or more from the sea floor and of limited extent across its summit.

SEDIMENTARY ROCK. One of the three principal groups of rock, the others being igneous and metamorphic. Sedimentary rock is formed by the compaction of such sediments as rock fragments, the remains of plants or animals, or the products of chemical action or evaporation which water, ice, or wind have deposited. See also *Geochemical cycle.*

SEICHE. A variation in the surface of a body of water occurring every few minutes or hours. It is believed to be caused by variations in atmospheric pressure, by earth movements, or by wave action, and aided by winds and tidal currents. Tides are considered seiches caused primarily by the gravitational pull of the sun and moon.

SEISMICITY. Seismic activity, the phenomenon of earth movements.

SEISMIC SEA WAVE. See *Tsunami.*

SEISMOGRAPH. An instrument for measuring and recording earthquake vibrations and other earth tremors.

SEISMOLOGY. The study of earthquakes, their force, duration, direction, frequency, and other characteristics.

SEMIARID. Having 10 to 20 inches of precipitation a year. A semiarid region is characterized by the growth of short grasses.

SERACS. Jagged ice pinnacles on the surface of a glacier formed by the intersection of two or more sets of crevasses.

SERIES. The time-stratigraphic unit corresponding to an epoch in geologic time.

SHALE. A fine-grained sedimentary rock composed of cemented silt and clay-sized particles. Metamorphosed shale is slate.

SHEET EROSION. The erosion of the earth's surface by the slow removal of thin layers of material from an extensive area.

SHEETING. A series of closely spaced joints essentially parallel to the surface. They grow farther apart with depth.

SHIELD. A stable, continental block of the earth's crust primarily composed of Precambrian rocks, which may have undergone gentle warping in contrast to the strong folding of the geosynclines at its borders.

SHINGLE. A mass of rounded, often flat waterworn rocks.

SHOAL. A submerged ridge, bank, or bar covered with mud, sand, or gravel. It is near enough to the water surface, at 10 fathoms (60 feet) or less, to be a danger to navigation.

SHORE. The narrow strip of land in immediate contact with the sea, including the zone between high and low water.

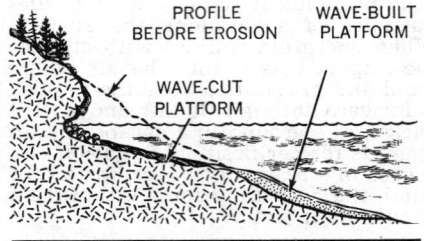

SHORE PROFILE shows how the constant action of water will erode a shoreline.

SHORELINE. The line of intersection of the sea at mean high water and the land. The region landward of the shoreline is the coast, that seaward is the shore.

SHOTT. A shallow salt lake in a desert region.

SIAL. The layer of rocks high in silica and aluminum underlying all continents. It ranges from granitic at the top to gabbroic at the bottom, where it grades into sima. It may be approximately 20 miles thick but thins out under the Pacific Ocean. It has a specific gravity of 2.7.

SIDEREAL DAY. See *Earth.*

SIERRA. A chain of jagged mountain peaks whose outline resembles the teeth of a saw.

SIKUSSAK. Very old (at least 25 years) sea ice.

SILICA. Silicon dioxide (SiO_2). It commonly comprises 40 to 80 percent of igneous rocks. It is an acid-forming oxide.

SILICEOUS. Pertaining to or containing or having the character of silica.

SILICON. The second most abundant element in the earth's crust. It occurs in all ordinary rocks except limestone.

SILL. An intrusive sheet of igneous rock lying parallel to the surrounding rock layers. It is formed when magma, or molten matter, forces its way between two layers of sedimentary rock. Also, a ridge at a relatively shallow depth separating two ocean basins.

SILT. See *Wentworth grade scale.*

SILT LOAD. The loose material carried in suspension by a stream, as opposed to bed load.

SILTSTONE. A fine-grained, consolidated clastic rock composed predominantly of silt-size particles.

SILURIAN PERIOD. The third period of the Paleozoic era in geologic time. It began 380 million years ago and lasted 15 million years.

SIMA. The basic outer shell of the earth, primarily composed of silica and magnesium. Sima underlies the sial of continents but directly underlies the water of the Pacific Ocean. It has a specific gravity of 3.3.

SIMOOM. A hot, dry, violent wind laden with hot sand and dust. It occurs during spring and summer in Asian and African deserts.

SINKHOLE. A funnel-shaped depression through which surface water drains, found within dolinen in limestone regions.

SINTER. A mineral substance deposited by hot or cold springs. Siliceous sinter is also called geyserite and fiorite. Calcareous sinter is also called tufa, travertine, and onyx marble.

SIROCCO. A hot, dust-laden wind, similar to a simoom, which blows on the northern Mediterranean coast. Blowing over the sea it becomes moist and enervating; blowing over land it becomes dry, dusty, and irritating.

SKARN. Lime-bearing silicates with large amounts of silicon, aluminum, iron, and magnesium.

SLACK WATER. Refers to the period of reversal between ebb and flood currents when the velocity of the current is very weak or zero.

SLAKING. The breaking up of dried clay when saturated with water.

SLATE. A fine-grained metamorphic rock formed from shale by regional metamorphism. It is harder, more lustrous than shale and when split yields approximately plane surfaces.

SLEET. Precipitation in the form of hail or snow mingled with rain. It is produced at the same time as hail but is partially melted in an upper layer of air, refreezing as it falls.

SLICKENSIDE. A fault surface smoothed and striated or scratched by friction from the pressure and motion of fault blocks.

SLOUGH. An area of deep mud or mire.

SMOG. A contraction of smoke and fog. A condition in the atmosphere when a high concentration of smoke particles and water droplets reduces visibility.

SNOW. Precipitation consisting of six-sided ice crystals formed directly from water vapor.

NEW YORK JOURNAL-AMERICAN

SMOG, particularly serious in midtown Manhattan, almost obscures the Empire State Building.

SNOWDRIFT. Snow that has been driven by the wind to form a bank.

SNOWFIELD. An area with a permanent snow cover.

SNOWLINE. The lower limit of a snowfield, rising from near sea level in polar regions to more than 20,000 feet in the Andes and Tibet.

SOAPSTONE. An impure variety of talc.

SOFT COAL. Bituminous coal.

SOFT WATER. Water with virtually no dissolved calcium or magnesium salts.

SOIL. The unconsolidated, or loose, material at the earth's surface that can support rooted plants. It is formed from rocks and plants by physical, chemical, and biological processes. Climate, vegetation, bedrock, relief of the land surface, and time combine to develop three soil orders—zonal, intrazonal, and azonal soils. The orders are divided into suborders.

There are six suborders of zonal soils—(1) soils of the cold zone; (2) light-colored soils of any region; (3) dark colored soils of semiarid, subhumid, and humid grasslands; (4) soils of the forest-grassland transition; (5) light-colored podzolized soils of the timbered regions; and (6) lateritic soils of forested warm-temperate and tropical regions.

The intrazonal order includes three suborders—(1) halomorphic soils of imperfectly drained arid regions and littoral deposits; (2) hydromorphic soils of marshes, swamps, seep areas and flats; and (3) calcemorphic soils. There are no suborders of azonal soils.

SOIL PROFILE. A vertical section through layers, or horizons, of soil from the surface to the limit of plant roots or bedrock.

The A horizon forms at or near the surface. It is the zone of eluviation or leaching. Soluble salts and colloids are washed from it and organic matter accumulates in it, grading downward from fresh or partially decomposed organic matter (O horizon), undecomposed vegetable litter (O1, or Aoo, horizon) to pure humus (O2, or Ao, horizon).

The B horizon is the zone of accumulation, containing clayey material and soluble minerals deposited by water percolating down from the A horizon and water evaporating from the C horizon.

The C horizon is the zone of unconsolidated material, little influenced by organisms. It consists of partially decomposed parent material or bedrock and grades down to unweathered bedrock, the R horizon.

SOLAR CONSTANT. The rate at which solar radiation is received normally at the outer layer of the earth's atmosphere at the earth's mean distance from the sun.

SOLIFLUCTION. The downslope flowage of loose earth material under saturated conditions in high latitudes where soil is affected by alternate freezing and thawing. It occurs during periods of thaw when the water released from the surface cannot percolate into the still frozen soil and rock beneath.

SOLUM. "True soil," the A and B horizons in the soil profile.

SOUND. An arm of the sea connecting two larger bodies of water, wider and more extensive than a strait.

SOUNDING. The determination of the depth of a body of water, either by a pressure-sensing device or by measuring the time required for sound waves to reflect from the bottom.

SPALLING. The disintegration of rock by the successive peeling of shells from the surface. See *Exfoliation*.

SPAR. A transparent or translucent, readily cleavable, crystalline mineral with a vitreous luster.

SPATHIC. Resembling spar in having good cleavage.

SPECIFIC GRAVITY. The ratio of the density of a substance to that of water at 4°C (39.2°F).

SPELEOLOGY. The study or exploration of caverns and related features.

SPHALERITE. The principal ore of zinc. It is composed primarily of zinc sulfide, but it often contains iron, manganese, or other elements. It is commonly yellow to dark brown and has a resinous to almost metallic luster, a hardness of 3.5 to 4, and a specific gravity of 3.9 to 4.1. It is also called false galena.

SPHEROID. An ellipsoid of revolution—a figure formed by rotating an ellipse around one of its axes. The earth is called an oblate, or flattened, spheroid because it bulges at the equator and is flattened at the poles.

SPILLWAY. A channel or passageway for surplus water to flow over or around a dam.

SPIT. A long, narrow deposit of sand or gravel projecting into a body of water from the land.

SPLASH EROSION. Erosion caused by the downslope movement of loose surface material resulting from the beating effect of falling raindrops.

SPRING. A continuous or intermittent natural flow of water from the ground. It occurs where a water table intersects the earth's surface.

SPRING TIDE. A tide which rises highest and falls lowest from its mean level about every two weeks at the new moon, when the moon is directly between the sun and the earth (conjunction), and at the full moon, when the moon and the sun are directly in line with, but on opposite sides of the earth (opposition).

SPUR. A subordinate elevation, ridge, or rise projecting outward from a larger feature.

SQUALL. A sudden violent wind of brief duration. It may be accompanied by thunder, lightning, and precipitation.

STACK. A rock mass cut off from the mainland by wave erosion. It first becomes a sea cave, then a sea arch, and finally an isolated stack.

STALACTITE. A deposit of minerals, usually calcite, precipitated by water on the ceiling of a cavern. In appearance, it resembles an icicle. A type of dripstone.

STALAGMITE. A deposit of minerals, usually calcite, precipitated by water on the floor of a cavern. In appearance it resembles an inverted, broad-based stalactite. A type of dripstone. Where a stalactite meets a stalagmite a column is formed.

STATUTE MILE. See *Mile*.

STEPPE. An extensive treeless, grassy plain found in semiarid regions.

STOPING. The process by which magma, or molten matter, detaches and engulfs blocks of the overlying country rock, thus working its way upward toward the surface.

STORM. A disturbance of the ordinary conditions of the atmosphere. It includes meteorological disturbances, such as wind, rain, snow, hail, and thunder. Also, a wind force of 11 on the Beaufort scale.

STOSS. Facing the direction from which a glacier moved.

STRAIN. Deformation of matter in response to force per unit area, or stress. Within elastic limits, strain is proportional to stress.

STRAIT. A narrow waterway connecting two larger bodies of water or separating two landmasses.

STRAND. A beach.

STRATH. A broad river valley.

STRATIFIED. Having layers.

STRATIFIED DRIFT. Drift deposited in layers.

STRATIGRAPHIC TIME. See *Time-stratigraphic unit*.

STRATIGRAPHIC TRAP. A natural reservoir that traps petroleum or natural gas because of variation in the permeability of the rock. The termination of an inclined reservoir on the higher side.

STRATIGRAPHY. The study of rock strata, including their origin, composition, order of sequence, and distribution.

STRATOSPHERE. See *Atmosphere*.

STRATUM. A single sedimentary layer of generally homogeneous rock, regardless of its thickness.

STREAK. A means of identifying a mineral by the color of the powder obtained by rubbing the mineral on an unglazed porcelain surface, such as a dish. The color of the streak may be similar to the color of the mineral or quite different.

STREAM. Any body of flowing water, from a rill to a river.

STALACTITES are deposits of calcium carbonate that grow downward from cave ceilings.

STREAM CAPTURE (or piracy). The diversion of the upper part of a stream by headward erosion of another stream.

STRENGTH. The amount of stress a solid can withstand without rupturing or flowing.

STRESS. Force per unit area required for the deformation of rocks.

STRESS–STRAIN LAW. See *Hooke's law*.

STRIAE (or striations). Minute parallel grooves and scratches on a rock, produced by rocks trapped in a glacier grinding against other rocks.

STRIKE. The direction of a line formed at the intersection of the horizontal plane with a tilted bedding plane or a fault surface. The strike is always perpendicular to the dip.

STROMBOLIAN PHASE. See *Volcano*.

STRUCTURAL GEOLOGY. The branch of geology concerned with the form, arrangement, and internal structure of rocks.

STRUCTURE. The attitude and relative position of a rock mass. In soils, the combination of primary particles into units forming a distinctive pattern that is classified on the basis of such factors as size and shape.

SUBAERIAL. Formed, existing, or taking place on the land surface.

SUBAQUEOUS. Formed, existing, or taking place beneath a body of water, as on the ocean floor.

SUBARCTIC. Referring to a climate similar to that immediately south of the Arctic Circle, where the mean temperature is less than 50°F in the warmest month and 32°F in the coldest month.

SUBHUMID. Referring to a climate too dry for natural forest growth, such as a prairie or pampa region. It is characterized by the growth of tall grasses.

SUBLIMATION. The direct transition of a substance from a solid state into a gaseous state, or the reverse, without an intervening liquid stage.

SUBLITTORAL. See *Ocean depth zones.*

SUBMARINE CANYON. A steep underwater depression, or trench, crossing the continental shelf. It may be as much as 10 miles wide and more than 6,000 feet deep. Some submarine canyons appear to be extensions of valleys on the land.

SUBSEQUENT STREAM. A tributary stream developed along a belt of weak rock after a consequent stream has removed the overlying resistant rock.

SUBSIDENCE. The sinking of a large part of the earth's crust.

SUBSOIL. The B and C horizons of the soil profile.

SUBSURFACE WATER. Water below the surface of the earth. If it is between the surface and the water table it is vadose water. If it is below the water table it is groundwater.

SUBTROPICAL. Referring to the regions between the tropic of Cancer and 40°N latitude and the tropic of Capricorn and about 40°S latitude, including their climate and vegetation.

SUPERIMPOSED STREAM. A stream that has eroded, or cut through a younger rock formation to its present level, where its course has no direct relation to the rock structure.

SUPERPOSITION. See *Law of Superposition.*

SUPRALITTORAL. See *Ocean depth zones.*

SURF. The foam, splash, and sound of waves breaking into turbulent water between the shoreline and the outermost limit of breakers.

SURFACE WAVE. A wave that travels on the surface, as distinguished from a body wave. See *Earthquake.*

SWALE. A marshy depression in level land. Also, a depression in a glacial ground moraine.

SWAMP. Low, spongy land, generally saturated or even covered with water.

S WAVE. See *Earthquake.*

SWELL. Regular, long waves which have traveled out of their generating area, or fetch.

SYENITE. An intrusive igneous rock with a composition similar to granite but containing little or no quartz.

SYMMETRICAL FOLD. A fold whose axial plane is vertical, the limbs dipping at similar angles.

SYNCLINE. A fold of stratified rocks in the form of a trough. The reverse of anticline.

SYNCLINORIUM. A series of anticlines and synclines so arranged structurally that together they form a general trough, or syncline, covering an extensive area.

SYNOPTIC. Relating to atmospheric conditions as they exist simultaneously over an extended region.

SYNTHETIC FAULTS. Subsidiary faults parallel to the master fault.

SYSTEM. A time-stratigraphic unit corresponding to a period in geological time.

SYZYGY. Two points in the moon's orbit where it is aligned with the sun and earth, in conjunction (between the sun and earth) and in opposition (on the opposite side of the earth from the sun).

TABLELAND. A comparatively level tract of upland bounded by relatively steep sides.

TABLEMOUNT. A type of seamount having a comparatively smooth, flat top.

TABULAR PLUTON. A pluton that is thin in comparison to its other dimensions. A tabular concordant pluton is a sill; a tabular discordant pluton is a dike.

TAIGA. A cold, humid vegetation zone with a coniferous forest cover. It lies in the northern hemisphere south of the tundra.

TALC. A mineral, hydrous magnesium silicate. It occurs in foliated, granular, or fibrous masses. It has a greasy feel, a hardness of 1, a pearly luster, a specific gravity of 2.6 to 2.9, and is usually gray, green, or white. An impure variety is called soapstone.

TALUS. A mass of rock fragments accumulated at the foot of a cliff.

TARN. A small lake in the bottom of a cirque. It is formed after the glacier has disappeared.

TECTONIC. Relating to the deformation of the earth's crust, the forces producing it, and the resultant structure.

TECTONO–PHYSICS. The study of stress and strain in relation to earth structure.

TEKTITE. Small, rounded, black or green glassy objects with a composition similar to that of clay, found in the earth's surface.

TELLURIC CURRENT. An earth current or natural electric current flowing on or near the earth's surface in a large sheet. By means of these currents the resistance, and therefore the composition, of various portions of the earth may be surveyed.

TEMPERATE ZONE. A general term for the middle latitude climatic zone lying between the tropical and cold zones.

TEMPERATURE GRADIENT. The rate of change of temperature with distance in a specified direction. If the direction is into the earth's crust, it increases with depth and is called geothermal gradient; if it is into the atmosphere, it decreases with height and is called lapse rate.

TEPHRA. A collective term for all materials ejected from a volcano during an eruption. It includes dust, ash, cinders, lapilli, scoria, pumice, bombs, and blocks.

TERRACE. A level band of land cut into a sloping surface either by natural forces, as in the case of a stream terrace, or by man, as in the case of a rice terrace.

TERRA ROSSA. A shallow, red, clayey soil developed from limestone in warm-temperate climates.

TERRIGENOUS. Derived from the earth. Specifically, it refers to material from above sea level, such as volcanic ash, which has been deposited on the ocean floor.

TERRITORIAL WATERS. A portion of the sea adjoining the coast considered to be under the jurisdiction of the country occupying that coast. It is measured outward from the mean low watermark on the shore.

TERTIARY PERIOD. The first period in the Cenozoic era of geologic time. It began 60 million years ago and lasted 59 million years.

TETHYS. The elongated east-west trough separating Europe and Africa and extending across southern Asia in pre-Tertiary time.

TETON. A rugged, rocky mountain crest.

TEXTURE. The general physical appearance of a rock as determined in the size, shape, and arrangement of the particles that compose it. If the grains can be seen by the unaided eye, the rock is phaneritic; if they cannot be seen by the unaided eye, the rock is aphanitic.

The shape of mineral grains and their arrangement with respect to one another produce a characteristic pattern or fabric. In igneous rocks texture is influenced by the gas content of the magma and the rate of cooling.

Also, the dissection of a land surface by streams and runoff from rainfall.

THAW LAKE. A lake or pond in a permafrost area whose basin is formed by the melting, or thawing, of ground ice.

THEODOLITE. A surveyor's instrument for measuring horizontal and vertical angles. It consists of a telescope mounted to swivel vertically and secured to a table that revolves.

THERMAL EQUATOR. A line drawn around the earth connecting places with the highest mean temperature for any particular period. The position of the thermal equator varies with the seasons.

THERMAL GRADIENT. See *Geothermal gradient.*

THERMAL SPRINGS. See *Hot springs.*

THERMAL STRATIFICATION. The division into three layers of the water of deep lakes on the basis of temperature. The upper layer, or epilimnion, has an almost uniform temperature because it is stirred by wind and convection currents. The middle layer, or thermocline, has a rapid decrease in temperature with depth. The bottom layer, or hypolimnion, is relatively stagnant, low in oxygen, and has a uniform but lower temperature than the upper layers.

THERMOGRAPH. A self-recording thermometer.

THICKET. A dense growth of shrubs and trees.

THORN FOREST. A dense growth of small, thorny trees found in hot, relatively dry areas.

THROW. The vertical displacement caused by a fault.

TIDAL CURRENT. The alternating horizontal movement of water caused by the attraction of the sun and moon. It is associated with the vertical movement, or tide.

TIDAL DAY. See *Lunar day.*

TIDAL FLAT. A marshy coastal area covered by the tide at high water and uncovered at low water.

TIDAL MARSH. A tidal flat.

TIDAL RANGE. The difference between the level of water at high water and low water.

TIDAL WAVE. The wave motion of the tides. Often used for a very high tide.

TIDE. The periodic rising and falling of the earth's oceans and atmosphere caused by the gravitational attraction of the sun and moon.

TIERRA CALIENTE. The lowest and hottest of three vertical climate zones in the tropics. It is found at elevations of less than 3,000 feet.

TIERRA FRIA. The highest and coolest of three vertical climate zones in the tropics. It lies at elevations above about 7,000 feet.

TIERRA TEMPLADA. The middle of three vertical climate zones in the tropics. It lies between 3,000 and 7,000 feet.

TIGHT FOLD. A fold whose limbs are virtually parallel.

TILL. A glacial deposit of loose, unsorted earth material.

TILLITE. A sedimentary rock composed of cemented till.

TIMBERLINE. The upper limit of tree growth. It varies with latitude and climate.

TIME—STRATIGRAPHIC UNIT. Describes sedimentary rocks deposited during a specific interval of geologic time, regardless of their composition or conditions of origin. The units, in descending order, are: group (era), system (period), series (epoch), stage (age).

TOMBOLO. A bar or spit connecting an island to the mainland or to another island.

TOPOGRAPHY. The study and description of physical features, such as heights, depressions, slopes, and other surface forms, on the surface of the earth.

TOR. An isolated mass of rock standing above the surrounding land and usually weathered into an odd shape.

TOREVA—BLOCK SLIDE. A large-scale, slump-type landslide found in arid and semiarid regions. It consists of an undisturbed mass of material which has rotated backward toward the parent cliff during its descent.

TORNADO. A relatively short-lived violent cyclonic storm (see *Cyclone*) with winds as high as 500 miles an hour. It is common in the central Mississippi Valley. It is associated with a fall in atmospheric pressure so rapid that structures may be lifted and burst by the air within them.

TORRENT. A stream of water or lava flowing with great velocity or turbulence.

TORRID ZONE. A general term for the high temperature region of the earth found in the equatorial belt.

TRADE WINDS. The almost constant, mild (10 to 15 miles per hour) winds which blow toward the equator from the northeast in the northern hemisphere and from the southeast in the southern hemisphere. Their point of convergence is called the doldrums.

TRANSPIRATION. The passage of water through a plant to be emitted as vapor from the leaves.

TRANSVERSE DUNE. A dune crossing the path of the wind. The leeward slope is at or near the angle of repose; the windward slope is comparatively gentle.

AUSTRALIAN NEWS AND INFORMATION BUREAU
VALLEYS are depressions in the earth's surface, often separating high elevations. A stream usually flows through and deepens a valley.

TRANSVERSE VALLEY. A valley which cuts across a mountain range.

TRAVERTINE. A light-colored, compact form of calcium carbonate ($CaCO_3$) deposited from solution in water. It forms the stalactites and stalagmites in limestone caves or the incrustations around the mounts of calcareous springs. Also called dripstone, tufa, or calcareous sinter.

TRELLIS DRAINAGE PATTERN. A stream system in which tributary streams flow at almost right angles into the mainstreams.

TREMOR. An earthquake of low intensity.

TRENCH. A long, narrow, and deep depression in the sea floor with relatively steep sides. A trench is narrower and deeper than a trough.

TRIASSIC PERIOD. The first, or earliest, period of the Mesozoic era in geologic time. It began 185 million years ago and lasted for about 27 million years.

TRIBUTARY. A stream which contributes its water to a larger stream or to a lake.

TROPICAL CYCLONE. A hurricane or cyclonic storm of great intensity which forms over tropical oceans. It is called a hurricane in the West Indies, a typhoon in the West Pacific, and a willy-willy in the area west of Australia.

TROPICAL ZONE. The region of the earth lying between the tropic of Cancer and the tropic of Capricorn.

TROPIC OF CANCER. The parallel of latitude at 23½° north of the equator. It marks the northernmost point at which the noon sun can be directly overhead.

TROPIC OF CAPRICORN. The parallel of latitude at 23½° south of the equator. It marks the southernmost point at which the noon sun can be directly overhead.

TROPOSPHERE. See *Atmosphere.*

TROUGH. A long depression of the sea floor, wider and shallower than a trench.

TSUNAMI. A great sea wave produced by a submarine earthquake, landslide, or volcanic eruption. A tsunami may go unnoticed for thousands of miles across the ocean building up to great heights over shallow water and causing widespread destruction on shore. Tsunamis are also called seismic sea waves.

TUFA. See *Travertine.*

TUFF. A rock composed of cemented or compacted volcanic ash.

TUNDRA. The undulating treeless plain characteristic of the arctic region. It has permanently frozen subsoil, and its vegetation consists primarily of mosses, lichens, some grasses, and dwarf shrubs.

TURBIDITY CURRENT. A density current carrying large quantities of clay, silt, and sand down an underwater slope through less dense water.

TURBULENT FLOW. An irregular movement of a liquid in which the velocity at any given point varies in magnitude and direction with time. It is characteristic of most stream flow.

TWILIGHT. The faint light between sunset and full night and between full night and sunrise. It is caused by the diffusion of sunlight through the dust in the atmosphere.

TYPHOON. A severe tropical cyclone which occurs in the western Pacific Ocean region.

ULTIMATE BASE LEVEL. The level, sea level or below, beyond which land cannot be eroded.

UNCONFORMITY. An erosion surface separating two rock masses. See *Angular unconformity, Disconformity, Nonconformity.*

UNDERTOW. A seaward flow near the bottom of a sloping beach. Also, the undersurface return of the water carried up on shore by waves or breakers.

UNIFORMITARIANISM. The theory that all changes in the earth's crust in the past were caused by processes that are observable today, such as erosion and volcanic activity.

UNPAIRED TERRACES. Terraces formed on one side of a stream but not on the other. They are formed by differential erosion caused by resistant rock.

UVALA. A large, broad depression in a limestone, or karst, region formed by the breaking down of the walls between a series of dolinen. It is considered intermediate between a dolina and a polje in that it is larger than a dolina and its floor is more uneven than that of a polje.

VADOSE WATER. Subsurface water above the water table.

VALE. A broad, level valley.

VALLEY. A long depression in the earth's surface, usually containing a stream. A structural valley is formed by folding or the subsidence of an area with subterranean drainage or with volcanic activity. An erosional valley is formed by the removal of material by a stream.

VALLEY TRAIN. A long, narrow outwash plain or deposit of material carried by a stream from a glacier.

VARVE. A sedimentary deposit, or bed, representing a year's deposition in lakes fringing a glacier. The winter deposit is a dark-colored clay layer. The summer deposit is a light-colored silt layer.

VEERING. A clockwise change of direction of a wind (for example, east to southeast to south). The opposite of backing.

VEIN. A long, thin body of ore with a sharp difference from the rock enclosing it. A fissure vein is formed by deposition from solution by underground water in a rock fissure or crack. A vein may also be formed by chemical replacement, ore-forming solutions changing rocks into ore. Several veins spaced closely enough to be mined as a unit may be called a lode.

VELD. An upland, relatively level area covered with scattered shrubs or trees.

VELOCITY. The distance traveled in a specific direction per unit of time. It differs from speed in that it includes direction.

VENT. The opening through which gases and molten lava leave a volcano enter its crater from a body of magma.

VENTIFACT. Any stone shaped by the abrasive action of wind-driven sand.

VESICLE. A small, round cavity in an aphanitic, or glassy, igneous rock formed by the expansion of a gas bubble during the solidification of the rock. If the vesicle becomes filled with some mineral, the filling is called an amygdule.

VITREOUS. See *Luster.*

VLEI. A temporary lake or marshy depression formed where water collects during the rainy season.

VOLCANO. A vent in the earth's crust through which gas, ash, rock, and molten lava reach the earth's surface from a body of magma, or molten matter, 20 to 60 miles below. Also, the cone-shaped mound formed of material discharged through a vent.

One means of classifying volcanoes is by form. A *shield volcano* is a gently sloping dome built up by a series of lava flows. It may have several vents in addition to the central vent. A *composite volcano*, or stratovolcano, is a steep, conical structure built up over time by successive eruptions. It is formed from rock fragments interspersed with lava flows. A *compound volcano* has two or more cones or an associated dome. *Pyroclastic cones*, consisting of ash, cinders, bombs, and blocks, have no strength and are fissured by explosions and the pressure of the lava during successive eruptions.

The stage or phase of a volcano is determined by the proportion of gas, molten lava, and solid fragments it ejects. During the mildest or *Hawaiian phase*, hot, fluid lava is discharged, unaccompanied by the explosive escape of gases or the ejection of rock fragments. During the *Strombolian phase*, clots of incandescent lava are ejected and the magma in the crater does not crust over between explosions. During the *Vulcanian phase*, fragments of old rock along with a cloud of ash and gas are ejected. Lava in this phase is extremely viscous and consolidates in the crater.

During the *Peléan* phase, the most violently explosive stage, great clouds called *nuées ardentes* are ejected horizontally from beneath the lava plug in the summit. These peléan clouds are extremely hot, travel at great speeds, and carry a great quantity of gas-charged lava fragments, often many yards in diameter.

Volcanic activity is found in the same areas as earthquake activity, around the Pacific basin, in the mid-Atlantic, and the Mediterranean.

VUG. A cavity of any size in a rock, usually lined with a crystalline incrustation of minerals which differ in composition from the surrounding rock.

WADI. A ravine in an arid region, dry except in the rainy season.

WARPING. The gentle bending of the earth's crust without forming pronounced folds or dislocations.

WATER. An odorless, colorless, tasteless liquid compound (H_2O) whose specific gravity of 1 is the standard for comparison of all liquids and solids.

WATER CYCLE. See *Hydrologic cycle*.

WATERFALL. A steep fall in the course of a stream where the water descends perpendicularly, or nearly so.

WATER GAP. A gap, or notch, in a mountain ridge through which a stream flows.

WATERSHED. See *Divide*.

WATERSPOUT. A tornado or cyclone occurring at sea, comparable to a dust devil over land, common over tropical and subtropical waters.

WATER TABLE. The upper surface of the zone of saturation. Its slope or shape is determined by the quantity of groundwater and the permeability of the earth materials. Generally, it is higher under hills and lower under valleys. A prolonged drought will lower the water table.

WEATHER. The condition of the atmosphere at a given time defined by the measurement of air temperature, barometric pressure, wind direction and speed, humidity, clouds, and precipitation.

WEATHERING. The disintegration of rock material through chemical means, such as rainwater or plants and bacteria, and mechanical means, such as

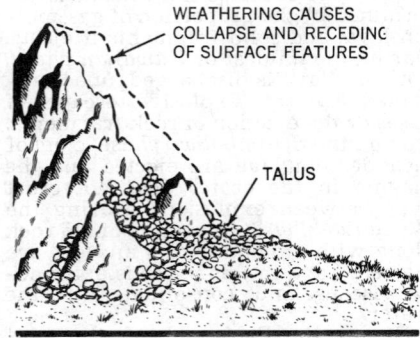

WEATHERING CAUSES COLLAPSE AND RECEDINC OF SURFACE FEATURES

TALUS

WEATHERING is one natural process of changing the earth's structural features.

abrasion and temperature variation, which change its color, texture, composition, and form.

WELDING. Consolidation by pressure caused by the weight of overlying material or earth movement.

WELL. A hole drilled into the earth to obtain water, gas, or oil.

WELT. A sharp, narrow uplift.

WENTWORTH GRADE SCALE. A scale for the classification of sediment particles:

Size limit	fragment		Consolidated equivalent
256 mm.	boulders		
64 mm.	cobbles	gravel	conglomerate
4 mm.	pebbles		breccia
2 mm.	granules		
	sand		sandstone
0.0625 mm.	silt		siltstone
0.0039 mm.	clay		shale
0.00024 mm.	colloids		

WESTERLIES. The prevailing winds in the temperate zones, between the polar easterlies and the trade winds, or between 30° and 60° latitude.

WET. The state of ground in which the pore spaces to a depth of 3 or more inches are largely or completely filled with water.

WHIRLPOOL. A circular eddy in the sea or in a stream caused by the shape of the channel or the meeting of two currents. It has a depression in the center into which floating objects may be drawn.

WHIRLWIND. A small rotating windstorm marked by an inward and upward spiral motion in the lower air followed by an outward and upward spiral motion.

WILLIWAW. A sudden violent gust of cold land wind, common along mountainous coasts in high latitudes.

WILLY–WILLY. A tropical cyclone originating west of Australia.

WILTING POINT. The point at which soil moisture becomes unavailable to plants and permanent wilting ensues. It is caused by the lowering of the water table, as may happen during a prolonged drought.

WIND. The horizontal component of air motion. Current is the vertical component. Planetary winds form the generalized surface wind pattern of the earth. They are polar easterlies, westerlies, and trade winds.

Monsoon winds are characterized by a complete reversal of direction from winter to summer. Foehn winds are warm, dry winds warmed by compression in flowing down the lee side of a mountain. Foehn-type winds include the bohorok and the chinook as well as the Swiss foehn.

Bora winds are cold, katabatic winds, flowing from a continental interior toward warm seashores. The mistral and the williwaw are two examples of this type.

There are also winds produced by outbreaks from an atmospheric source region. If the region is hot, a sirocco may develop, if cold, a pampero.

WIND-CHILL FACTOR (or **INDEX**) the effect of low temperatures and high winds on exposed skin, expressed as a loss of body heat.

WIND GAP. A notch, or gorge, cutting through the upper part of a ridge.

WIND ROSE. A diagram showing the proportionate distribution of winds by direction and speed at a given place.

WIND SHADOW. A portion of a scarp or slope protected from the direct action of the wind blowing over it.

WIND SPEED. See *Beaufort scale*.

WINDWARD. The direction from which the wind is blowing, as opposed to leeward. The side of an object facing the wind.

XENOLITH. A rock fragment included in a body of igneous rock.

YARDANG. A sharp-crested ridge between round-bottomed troughs. It is formed by wind erosion from a soft deposit, such as clayey sand.

YAZOO STREAM. A tributary stream on a flood plain flowing parallel to the mainstream.

YIELD POINT. The point at which stress exceeds the plastic limit, causing a solid to flow or rupture. See *Deformation*.

ZEOLITE. A group of hydrous aluminosilicates of sodium, calcium, barium, strontium, and potassium, characterized by their easy and reversible loss of water and tendency to swell when heated. They have a hardness between 3.5 and 5.5 and a specific gravity between 2.0 and 2.4.

ZONE. A region set off from the surrounding area by climate, landforms, time, or other distinctions.

ZONE OF AERATION. The zone in which the pores of permeable rocks are not filled, except temporarily, with water. The water is under pressure less than that applied by the atmosphere on the earth's surface.

ZONE OF ELUVIATION. The A horizon in the soil profile.

ZONE OF OXIDATION. The area above the water table where water provides a good supply of oxygen.

ZONE OF SATURATION. The zone in which permeable rocks are saturated with water. Its upper surface is the water table. The water is under pressure equal to or greater than atmosperic pressure.

For national flags see VOLUME 12: GOVERNMENT AND LAW.

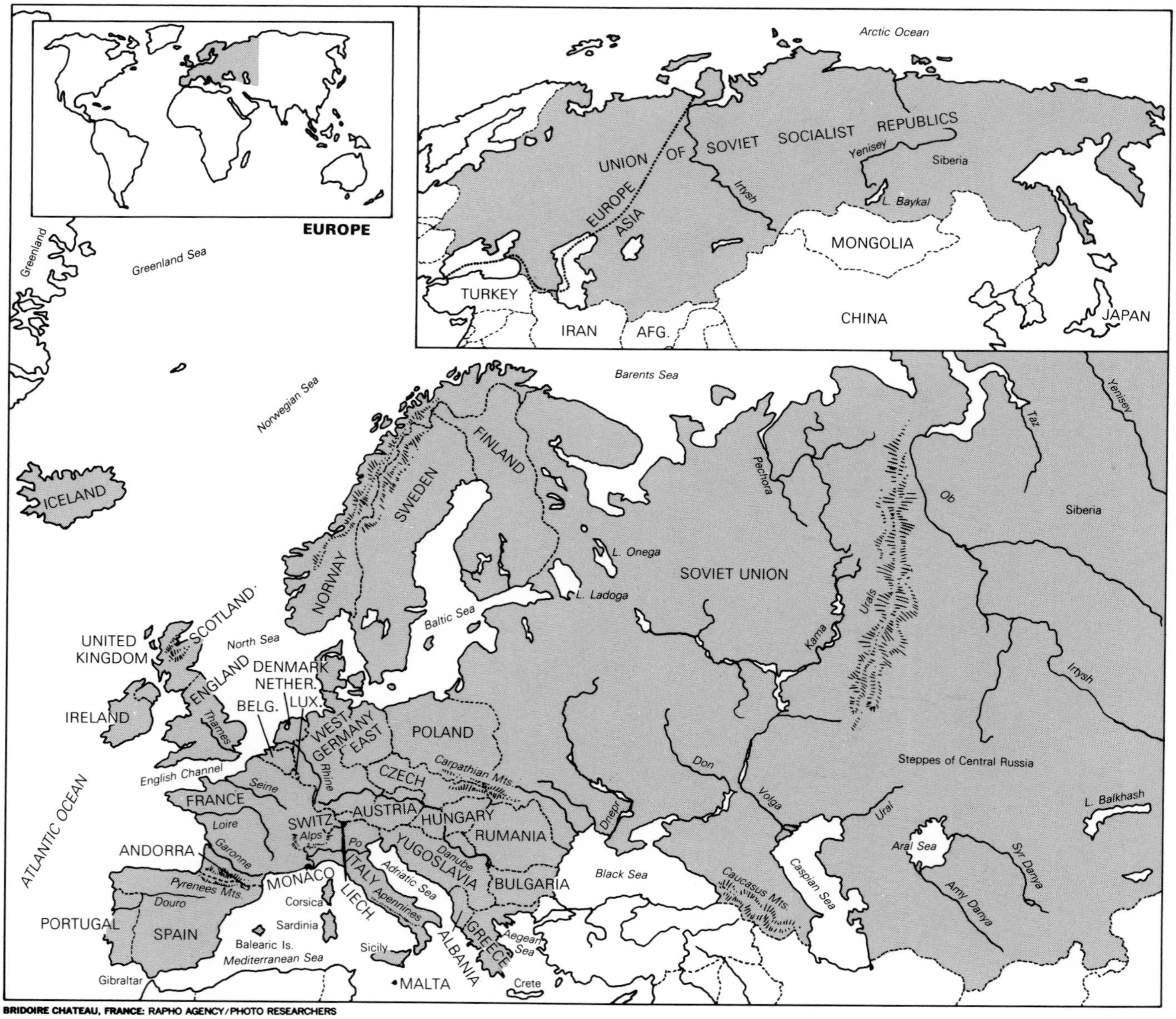

CULVER PICTURES

EUROPE

Soviet Union map (inset)

Arctic Ocean

UNION OF SOVIET SOCIALIST REPUBLICS

EUROPE ASIA

Yenisey

Irtysh

Siberia

L. Baykal

TURKEY

IRAN

AFG.

MONGOLIA

CHINA

JAPAN

Europe map

Greenland

Greenland Sea

Norwegian Sea

Barents Sea

ICELAND

NORWAY

SWEDEN

FINLAND

L. Onega

L. Ladoga

Baltic Sea

SOVIET UNION

Taz

Yenisey

Ob

Siberia

Urals

Pechora

Kama

Irtysh

SCOTLAND

UNITED KINGDOM

North Sea

ENGLAND

DENMARK

NETHER.

BELG. LUX.

IRELAND

Thames

WEST GERMANY

EAST

POLAND

Carpathian Mts.

Don

Steppes of Central Russia

Ural

English Channel

Rhine

CZECH

Seine

FRANCE

Loire

Garonne

SWITZ.

Alps

AUSTRIA

HUNGARY

RUMANIA

Dnepr

Volga

L. Balkhash

ATLANTIC OCEAN

ANDORRA

Pyrenees Mts

Douro

MONACO

Po

ITALY

YUGOSLAVIA

BULGARIA

Black Sea

Caucasus Mts.

Caspian Sea

Aral Sea

Amu Darya

Syr Darya

PORTUGAL

SPAIN

Corsica

Apennines

Adriatic Sea

LIECH.

Sardinia

Balearic Is.

Mediterranean Sea

Sicily

ALBANIA

GREECE

Aegean Sea

Gibraltar

MALTA

Crete

BRIDOIRE CHATEAU, FRANCE: RAPHO AGENCY / PHOTO RESEARCHERS

Europe

NEW YORK PUBLIC LIBRARY

BARBARA PFEFFER / PETER ARNOLD

25 NORGE ØRE POST

TRANS WORLD AIRLINES PHOTO

AMERICAN SWEDISH NEWS EXCHANGE

INGEBORG LIPPMAN

The land. Europe's eastern boundary is indefinite, but for the purpose of this volume all of the Soviet Union is included, while Turkey and Cyprus may be found in the volume on the Middle East.

The Arctic Ocean bounds Europe in the north, touching on the Soviet Union, Scandinavia, Iceland, and Greenland. The Barents and Norwegian seas bound Scandinavia in northern Europe; to the west the Atlantic Ocean washes Europe from the United Kingdom to Portugal. In the south, the Mediterranean and Black seas, the Caucasus Mountains, and the southern border of the Soviet Union, all bound Europe from Spain to the Soviet Union. The Tyrrhenian, Adriatic, Ionian, and Aegean seas are also a part of this boundary. Europe is connected to Asia on the southeast, but everywhere else it is separated from other continents by massive oceans. However, Africa lies only eight miles from Europe at the Strait of Gibraltar, off southern Spain.

Europe has many coastal indentations and peninsulas that have facilitated its role as the commercial and colonial leader of the world throughout modern history. The Scandinavian peninsula is the most imposing of these peninsulas, while the Italian and Balkan peninsulas in the Mediter-

ranean, and the Iberian Peninsula separating the Atlantic from the Mediterranean, have all played significant roles in the cultural, political, and economic history of Europe.

Europe's many coastal indentations have resulted in the establishment on the Continent of some of the world's greatest ports. These include the great North Sea and Atlantic ports of Copenhagen, Göteborg, Oslo, Hamburg, Lübeck, Bremen, Rotterdam, Antwerp, London, Newcastle, Dublin, Glasgow, and Southampton. These ports represent mostly Great Britain, Scandinavia, the Low Countries, and northern Germany. Le Havre, Bordeaux, and Lisbon are important ports in the southwest, while the Mediterranean ports include Barcelona, Marseille, Nice, Genoa, Naples, Venice, and Piraeus. Odessa on the Black Sea and Leningrad on the Baltic are the Soviet Union's major ports.

Europe has highland regions that extend from the northwest to the southeast. Much of Scandinavia is highland, especially along the Norway-Sweden border, but the great highland arc is generally considered to begin in the United Kingdom, where the Scottish highlands and the Cambrian (Welsh) mountains are imposing. There are highland regions along the western coast of France, and the

Iberian Peninsula includes the Pyrenees and, especially, the great Sierra Nevada chain, which is part of the Alpine region. Moving eastward, the Alps, Carpathians, Apennines, Dinaric, and Pindus ranges dominate southern Europe all the way to the Black Sea. The Urals and the Caucasus form the major highland regions of the Soviet Union.

Besides the highlands, a major feature of Europe is its great central plain. The lowlands are the part of this plain that appear in northwestern Europe, in France's Aquitaine and Paris basins, in the Brabant Lowland in central Belgium, and across the English Channel, running through central Britain as far north as the Pennines. There are also lowlands in southern Scandinavia and northern Germany, but the most famous lowland region in Europe is that which dominates the so-called Low Countries, named for it, especially Belgium and the Netherlands.

The Low Countries were once the center of the greatest commercial and colonial enterprises in the world, owing largely to their location in these lowlands, which made them so readily accessible to the great waterways of the West. The more elevated portions of the central plain extend, on the Continent, from the Low Countries eastward through the Soviet Union. They are bordered on the south by the great Mediterranean highlands and the Caucasus, and on the east by the Urals.

There are many important rivers in Europe, especially those that rise in the Alps and flow toward the northern and southern seas. These rivers have been important routes for the spread of culture in ancient times, and as commercial waterways in modern times. The Rhine with its tributaries is probably the greatest of the continental river systems, and the Volga in central Russia is the longest. Most of the other important rivers are in Western Europe. They include the Thames in Britain, the Rhône and Seine in France, the Meuse in the Low Countries, and the Po and Tiber in Italy. The Oder is a major river in East Germany and Poland.

Climate. Europe has a basically moderate climate. The Continent is protected from chilling northern winds by its great southern Alpine mountain system. Its climate is further moderated by westerly winds. The western Atlantic moderate marine climate extends throughout Europe and even into the Soviet Union, but the northern Soviet Union and Scandinavian peninsula have little rain, severe winters, and a generally arctic climate.

Eastern Europe has severe winters and little precipitation, but its growing season is warm, wet, and sustained enough to produce good grain harvests. The central portion of the Soviet Union is in this semimoderate zone.

Southwestern Europe has an extremely moderate Mediterranean climate, while northwestern Europe has a mild, wet, western Atlantic climate.

The only dry areas of Europe, generally receiving under 15 inches of rain a year, are the inner Iberian Peninsula and the southeastern part of the Soviet Union.

The people. Europe is the most densely populated continent in the world and it contains one-fifth of the total world population. It has a high literacy rate and its population provides a wealth of skilled workers. Education has played a prominent role in European civilization for centuries, especially in Western Europe.

Europe was populated by emigrants from Asia and Africa in ancient times. It is now generally composed of several ethnic groups, including the Nordic of Scandinavia and northern Europe; the Alpine of France and south-central Europe; the Mediterranean of southwestern Europe, including the Iberian Peninsula; the Atlanto-Mediterranean of Britain and west and southwest Europe; the Dinaric of France, Italy, and southeastern Europe; and the Slavs of Eastern Europe and the Soviet Union.

Europeans speak many languages,

SWEDISH ROOSTERS *for Easter, typical of Scandinavian folk art and design.*

most of them belonging to the Indo-European group. The Indo-European subgroups include the Germanic languages of English, German, Dutch, and Scandinavian; the Romance languages derived from Latin, spoken mostly in the Mediterranean countries; and the Slavic languages spoken by Eastern Europeans and Russians. Most people in Europe know several languages in addition to their own.

Christianity is Europe's dominant religion. Most people in the Mediterranean countries are Roman Catholic. Those in northwestern Europe are predominantly Catholic or Protestant, and those in Eastern Europe and the Soviet Union are Eastern Orthodox, although religion in general is often sup-

pressed by the communist regimes of these countries.

Most Europeans live in urban areas where cultural and commercial activity is high. Rural life is diminishing more and more as industrialization continues to rise throughout Europe. Since World War II, inter-European economic, political, and cultural organizations have tended to unify the nations of Europe, but they have been split between the Eastern European nations that are primarily communistic and socialistic, and the Western European nations that are largely democratic and capitalistic.

The economy. The continent of Europe is believed to be more productive than any other. It creates even more wealth than Asia, and in the northwestern portion mining and manufacturing are developed to a very high degree.

Europe leads the continents in the production of more than half of the world's principal commodities. The importance of northwestern Europe in population and industrial activity is due in large part to the fact that it is one of the few regions in the world with an ideal climate—one in which the average temperature for the coldest month does not go below freezing and for the hottest month is not above 70°. The climate is cyclonic in nature, bringing the stimulation of rapid but considerable short-range changes in temperature and in humidity.

In northwestern Europe, industrial civilization has grown to great levels.

Before the recent development of the European Economic Community (or Common Market), Europe's political divisions, with accompanying tar-

STEEL WORKS IN CARDIFF, WALES. *Although Britain's steel industry, once a world leader, is ailing, the country as a whole has benefited from its entry into the Common Market in 1973.*

**MEMBERS OF THE
EUROPEAN ECONOMIC
COMMUNITY
(COMMON MARKET)**
As of 1981

Belgium
Denmark
France
Greece
Ireland
Italy
Luxembourg
Netherlands
United Kingdom
West Germany

iffs and import quotas, made it impossible for natural geographic regions to operate as economic units. Neighboring European nations often discriminated against one another's goods to their mutual disadvantage, on the narrow grounds of protectionism. Because of this, ailing industry was perpetuated, and countries cut themselves off from their best markets, sources of materials, and labor forces.

The Marshall Plan successfully rehabilitated European national economies after the devastation of World War II. The next step for Europe was a customs union and the free flow of goods and services across the old political boundaries. This was finally effected by the Treaty of Rome, signed in March, 1957, by Belgium, France, Italy, Luxembourg, the Netherlands, and West Germany.

The spectacular economic success of the Common Market in a few short years made Britain abandon its historic isolation from the Continent and join the Market in 1973. In that same year Ireland and Denmark joined, and other nations are hopeful of allying themselves with this dynamic forward-looking community.

Among the continents, Europe exceeds only Australia in size. European vegetation may be divided roughly into (1) the Mediterranean region, which includes Spain, Italy, and the southern coast bordering that sea; (2) the deciduous forests that cover an extensive area from Britain and northwestern Europe eastward across to the Soviet Union; (3) the coniferous forests that extend from Norway and Sweden eastward over northern Europe and Asia.

About one-third of the world's coal is produced by Britain and West Germany. Rumania and Poland are the big oil producers of Europe, and all European countries except the Soviet Union, Rumania, and Poland are large importers of mineral oil. Fortunately, European waterpower is located in regions with coal deficits, and waterpower supplements coal as a source of power for most of the great industries of Europe.

France, Sweden, and Britain have considerable iron ore reserves, and the bulk of the iron and steel produced in the world is made in six countries, five of which are located in Europe.

Development of modern transportation has rendered the close natural association of iron and coal unnecessary for industry. Britain produces only about half of its ore requirements and consequently imports large quantities. Spain is one of the major sources, as are the Lorraine fields in France. Spain exports large quantities of the ore to such countries as Britain and Germany.

More than half of the world's supply of zinc comes from the European countries (Belgium, Poland, France, and Germany). These countries are

also large producers of lead. Aluminum is produced largely by countries with hydroelectric power—hence Norway's importance as an aluminum producer, although it imports the bauxite required.

The Mediterranean countries, with their cool moist winters and hot dry summers, must overcome climatic handicaps as well as poor soils. Wheat, the hardy universal cereal, is the most important crop in this region. The countries of this area are also outstanding producers of raw silk. France is one of the largest centers of raw silk and also has a great wool-manufacturing capacity. It is one of the world's greatest wine producers and has enormous iron ore reserves in the world-famous Lorraine deposits.

France ranks, with the United States, as a great producer of bauxite; it formerly was a large producer of antimony. The chief imports of France are coal and machinery and the exports consist largely of iron and steel products, silk, cotton, and various woven fabrics.

Agriculture is the chief occupation of the people living in the Danube basin in southeastern Europe. Austria leads the other countries in this region in wool production. In the last few years, these countries have all increased their industrial output. The Danube countries also produce potatoes, sugar beets, barley, tobacco, and orchard fruits. Cattle, as well as sheep and horses, are bred.

West-central Europe includes the Netherlands, Germany, Switzerland, and Poland. The Netherlands is famous for scientific dairying and exports of cheese, butter, margarine, eggs, and meat. The chief occupations are dairying, shipbuilding, and ocean fishing. The Dutch are traditionally a seafaring and commercial people, but increasingly they are becoming a manufacturing people.

Germany is a nation of great scientific industrial activity, with a vast production of potash, phosphates, and nitrates. West Germany has become one of the world's most wealthy industrial states. Its export trade is chiefly with the neighboring countries of Britain, the Netherlands, Czechoslovakia, and Switzerland, and includes factory products such as steel manufactures, cotton, wool, silk fabrics, beet sugar, chemicals, and dyes. The United States ranks high in supplying Germany's imports and in buying its goods, but German trade is heaviest with its partners in the European Economic Community.

Switzerland is world famous for its scenery and its specialized manufacture of watches, clocks, and jewelry. It is among the leading countries in per capita foreign trade. Poland is a valuable mineral region, with great coal reserves and the most productive zinc mines in Europe.

In spite of its great crops, Europe

must import food. This is because of the geographic specialization of agricultural production and also because all of Europe lies in the Temperate Zone and cannot produce the variety of foods needed.

Europe grows about one-third of all the wheat in the world (excluding the Soviet Union); but all the big importers of wheat, except Brazil and Japan, are European countries, with Britain in the lead. Of wheat, dairy products, and meat, Europe produces more than all the rest of the world; of barley, more than twice as much as the rest of the world; and of rye, 20 times as much. Europe formerly produced more than 40 percent of the world's sugar. Despite all this, Europe imports more food than the rest of the world combined.

The North Sea region is one of the world's great fisheries. More than 3.3 million tons of fish are caught every year, over 70 percent of which is taken by Norway, Denmark, and Britain.

Europe is self-sufficient in timber products. Except for British-U.S. trade, most European timber trade is among the countries of the Continent and not across seas. Europe has about ten percent of the world's forest areas, three-fourths of which is coniferous forest. Finland, Sweden, Poland, Russia, Norway, Czechoslovakia, Austria, and Rumania are important exporters of timber. The Soviet Union has the greatest potential capacity.

Scandinavia (Norway, Sweden, and Finland) is a part of Eurasia's great northern forest belt. Norway is noted for its waterpower, timber, and particularly its fisheries. Fish and fish products represent a large proportion of Norway's exports. It is said that Norway is the only country in the world whose people could all get in their boats with all their household goods and sail away.

Coal represents nearly 90 percent by value of all the mineral products of the British Isles. The mineral next in value is iron ore. Britain no longer exports coal, except in negligible amounts, because reserves are only sufficient to meet domestic needs. Though an important iron and steel industry exists, Britain has to import much of the iron ore used. This is received mainly from Spain and from Algeria.

In value, Britain's agriculture is second to its manufactures. Agricultural products of importance include potatoes, sugar beets, barley, oats, and wheat. Manufactured goods total about 80 percent of British exports. These include mainly cotton goods and woolens, and heavy goods, such as machinery, iron, and steel. Food accounts for about half of the imports. Britain's trade balance is unfavorable, but this excess of imports over exports has traditionally been balanced by invisible exports such as credits and tourist trade.

HISTORY OF EUROPE

Ancient Civilization

Greece

Civilization derived from the Near East, especially from Egypt, came to the island of Crete as early as 2500 B.C. From Crete it gradually spread to the Aegean Islands and the mainland of Greece.

Archaeology has revealed a typical Bronze Age culture still imperfectly known because of a scarcity of written records. Thus, the detailed historical information available from Mesopotamia, Egypt, and the Near East in general is lacking in Crete and Greece, and the nature of Aegean culture can be learned only indirectly from its material remains.

Aegean civilization. Enormous palace complexes, particularly at Knossos in Crete, show that the skills of Aegean craftsmen were the equal of those in the Near East. Painted pottery and wall paintings were produced in a lively and elegant style. Marine motifs occurred frequently as a reminder of the importance of the sea rather than the river valley on the island of Crete.

Monumental sculpture, a usual feature of Bronze Age art, is curiously missing from the finds.

In the early 1900's A.D., when archaeology began to reveal Bronze Age Crete, historians were sure that the society uncovered must have grown powerful through sea trade and naval power. Further study cast grave doubts on this view, and it is now generally held that although the sea was important to the islanders, their economy, like that of most Near Eastern people, was based upon agriculture and controlled by the palace.

The view of Cretan political power has also undergone revision. The idea of a "thalassocracy," or sea power, dominating the islands and coastal lands of the Aegean has begun to give way to a view of localized political power exercising a cultural influence rather than territorial control over the Aegean lands. Information gained from the small number of inscribed clay tablets that are the only written records from the Aegean region in the Bronze Age has contributed to this view.

A few hundred of these tablets, written in a script called Linear A, are found only on Crete and date from about 1500 B.C. Another 3000, brief and mostly fragmentary, written in a somewhat different script called Linear B, have been found at sites on both Crete and the Greek mainland. They date from about 100 years after the Linear A tablets.

Linear A is still a puzzle, but Linear B was deciphered in 1953, and its language proved to be an early, primitive form of Greek. The tablets contain records that testify to the high degree of organization in the palace economies of the Cretan and Greek cities. Although it is not known to what linguistic group the Cretans belonged, they are known to have been a different people from the mainland Greeks.

The Linear B tablets, being in Greek, confirm both the archaeological finds and the later Greek tradition that mainland domination of Crete, at least culturally and perhaps politically as well, occurred shortly after 1500 B.C. Evidence of considerable destruction of the Cretan palaces about that time is variously interpreted as having been caused by an earthquake or by war.

The final 300 years of the Bronze Age in the Aegean are known as the Mycenaean Period, named for wealthy "golden" Mycenae, the leading Greek city of the time, where modern archaeology has uncovered the finest examples of the crafts of the late Bronze Age, especially jewelry and decorative articles of solid gold buried in the royal tombs.

The Dark Age. The Bronze Age in Greece and Crete came to an end with barbarian invasions in about 1200 B.C. In the Aegean, the invaders were the Dorian Greeks. The destruction they wrought was total, and for 400 years afterward the material level of culture was so low that the period is called the Dark Age. Along with the splendor of the Mycenaean palaces, the art of writing was also lost, and the memory of the past remained only in oral poetry.

Contacts with the Phoenicians gradually stimulated a revival of civilized life. When the Greeks borrowed the alphabet from their Eastern neigh-bors in about 800 B.C., they were already on the road to the brilliant achievements that laid the foundations of Western culture. The earliest written literature, the *Iliad* and the *Odyssey* of Homer, which recount the great deeds of Bronze Age heroes, was produced at that time.

The Greek city-state. It was also at the end of the Dark Age that the city-state, or polis, which was to become the characteristic political unit of Greece, began to appear. Greece at its height consisted of more than a thousand of these autonomous units, most of them no more than towns, each with its small area of fertile farmland and separated from its neighbors by the rugged mountains that typify the Greek landscape.

The loyalty of the citizen to his polis was fierce, and in antiquity Greece was never voluntarily unified. The polis dominated every aspect of life, both public and private.

The city-state was so essential a part of the Greek way of life that it was thought to be part of the natural world. Aristotle's famous axiom that man is by nature "a political animal" is more correctly and meaningfully rendered as man is by nature "an animal who lives in a polis."

An era of growth. The political and economic development of Greece in the 600's and 500's B.C. was very rapid. Stimulated by population growth as well as trade, the Greek cities sent boatloads of colonists throughout the Mediterranean, where they established scores of new city-states.

The main areas settled by the Greeks were the shores of the Black Sea, Sicily, and southern Italy. Sicily and southern Italy were so heavily colonized that the region became known as Magna Graecia, or Greater Greece.

Overseas expansion was accompanied by the evolution of most Greek city-states from simple agrarian societies ruled by a small, hereditary, landowning nobility, through a stage of violent dictatorship, to aggressive trading and manufacturing communities, with armies and navies, usually ruled under written constitutions by a fairly large class of prosperous people.

A remarkable cultural growth also took place during this period. Lyric poetry was written that, in the variety of its meters, subject matter, and imagery, was far more original than any produced in the Near East. It was this poetry that was to form the poetic tradition of the West.

Two of the three classic architectural orders—the Doric and the Ionic—were developed. Sculpture and vase painting advanced rapidly and soon broke away from their Eastern models and developed characteristically Greek styles.

Birth of philosophy. Perhaps the most important achievement of the period, however, was the birth of philosophy (literally, "love of wisdom"). It first appeared during the early 500's in the cities along the Ionian coast of the Aegean, where it was stimulated by close contact with the older cultures of Asia.

It was at Miletus, the most prominent of the Ionian cities, that Thales (whom tradition calls the first philosopher), along with a group of other pioneers, initiated the process of systematic thought that led to the later political and moral philosophy of Plato and Aristotle, as well as to the philosophical and scientific explorations of the Hellenistic period.

The attempt of these men to find a rational explanation for all phenomena, without reference to the supernatural, has been called "the discovery of the mind," and is one of the momentous achievements in the history of civilization.

The classical period.

Ancient Greece reached its height in the classical period, the 400's and 300's B.C. Although "the glory that was Greece," or "the Greek miracle," as succeeding ages have called this epoch, was primarily intellectual and cultural, it can be understood only within its political setting. The independent Greek city-state, the polis, provided the dynamic element.

The polis permitted a wide variety of governmental forms, customs, institutions, and attitudes, and thereby nourished freedom and a spirit of adventurous experiment. At the same time, its very smallness inspired an intense devotion in its citizens.

In the Greek polis, public and private life were tighly interwoven. Religion, recreation, and entertainment, which are private concerns for us, were usually public activities.

The Persian wars. The Greek cities, each immersed in its own relatively isolated development, became aware of themselves as powers in a larger world as the result of a series of invasions in the early 400's, when Persia attempted to add Greece to its empire.

The motives for the Persian attempts are by no means clear. Recent historians have sought for economic

METROPOLITAN MUSEUM OF ART

GREEK SPHINX *of the sixth century* B.C. *once graced a gravestone in Attica.*

reasons, but earlier generations were perhaps on firmer footing in looking for political causes, principally the sheer momentum of expansion on the part of a huge empire.

The original historian of the wars, the Greek writer Herodotus, attributed the first impulse toward the invasion of Europe to the whim of the Persian queen. In any case, the crushing defeats that Greece inflicted on the enormous forces launched against it by Persia are historic examples of human courage and skill.

Sparta and Athens. Two cities, Sparta and Athens, emerged from the wars as the leading powers in Greece. Both were much larger and more powerful than any of the other Greek cities. But Sparta and Athens were diametrically opposed in their economic and political institutions, as well as in their cultural lives and in their goals, and the history of classical Greece is generally viewed as the story of the struggle between them.

Sparta had long been recognized as the most powerful military state in Greece. Spartan life was rigid and austere, as the term "spartan" signifies. It was entirely dedicated to military strength as the means of maintaining an authoritarian society.

That society was supported by the agricultural labor of the surrounding peoples, called Helots, who were completely enslaved. Spartan cultural life was narrow, as indicated by the term "laconic" (Laconia was the region in which Sparta was situated) to describe very plain speech.

Athens, on the other hand, had developed into a culturally brilliant society. Trade was encouraged, opening the city to the arts and crafts of the whole world. At the close of the 500's B.C., Athens had begun one of the most venturesome political experiments in history with the creation of a direct democracy. All adult male citizens, aris-

tocrats or peasants, rich or poor, ignorant or learned, had an equal share in guiding the affairs of state, and all public matters were decided by a majority vote of citizens in the assembly, which met every ninth day.

Both the vigorous character and expansionist tendencies of Athens were expressed in the navy built a few years before the final Persian attack. This navy proved to be the deciding factor in the repulse of Persia, and after the war it became the most powerful fleet in the Mediterranean.

As Sparta retired to its traditional defensive isolation, Athens grasped the opportunity to grow, and in the guise of a maritime alliance it rapidly built an empire over the Greek cities and islands of the Aegean. Athenian ambition seemed insatiable, and the Spartans reluctantly decided to fight.

The Peloponnesian War was fought for 27 years, on land and sea, from the Aegean to Sicily. It engaged the entire Greek world. Neither side was able to prevail, and the balance was finally tipped by the intervention of Persia, which provided Sparta with the funds to build a fleet. In 404 B.C., the Athenian fleet was destroyed and Athens unconditionally surrendered.

Decline of Greece. For the next 70 years, Greece was engaged in useless and destructive warfare as each of the other major Greek cities in turn attempted to gain leadership, only to be met by a coalition that it could not defeat. The principle of the independent polis would not permit a voluntary national unity, nor could any single polis accomplish it by force. The Greeks were steadily destroying themselves.

The inevitable conclusion—conquest by an outside power—occurred in 338 B.C., when Philip II of Macedon defeated the Greeks at the Battle of Chaeronea. Greece's "Golden Age" came to an end, and all its cities were subjected to Macedonian rule.

Culture of classical Greece. In the 150 years from the Persian wars to the Battle of Chaeronea, Greece produced Western civilization's most precious intellectual, artistic, and literary heritage. Most of this achievement not only originated in Athens but found its most brilliant expression there.

The Acropolis, the flat-topped hill in the center of Athens where the temples to the gods were located, had been destroyed by the Persians in 480 B.C. The rebuilding of the Acropolis represented not only the height of Athenian ambition but of Greek artistic expression in sculpture and architecture.

The Parthenon, superbly designed and executed, with its elegant proportions and magnificent sculptural decoration, is the finest example of the architecture of the 400's. The other buildings, never completed because of the Peloponnesian War, demonstrate the range and variety, as well as the quality, of classical art.

Athenian vase painting was raised

to the level of a fine art, and Athenian pottery, numerous examples of which can be seen in the museums of Europe and America, was prized throughout the Mediterranean world.

Greek literary and intellectual accomplishments during this period were equally dazzling. The drama originated in Athens, where it developed not as commercial entertainment but as part of the civic and religious festival of the god Dionysus.

The tragedies written in the 400's by Aeschylus, Sophocles, and Euripides, with the grandeur of their language and subject matter, created a standard for serious literature that remains unshaken. When performed today, these plays are as capable of enthralling an audience as when they were first written.

The comedies of Aristophanes, in addition to gusto and bawdy humor, introduced the great tradition of political satire. To understand what freedom of speech and opinion meant in democratic Athens, one has only to read one of Aristophanes's antiwar plays, with its ferocious lampooning of Athens's leading politicians, and to realize that it was originally produced as part of a state festival.

The writing of history also originated in Athens in the 400's B.C. The accounts of Herodotus, the "father of history," are still widely read. They were followed by Thucydides' *History of the Peloponnesian War,* one of the most celebrated historical works ever written. It is distinguished by the powerful style of its narrative and the intellectual force of its analysis.

In philosophy, the early accomplishments of the Ionian thinkers came to maturity in the writings of Plato and Aristotle in the 300's. They raised and systematically examined the questions that men have probed ever since: the nature of the universe, of man, of God; the meaning of life; the relation of the individual to the state, and the whole range of scientific, metaphysical, aesthetic, and ethical inquiry.

Hellenistic Greece. In the centuries that followed, Greek culture continued, but with a difference that reflected its changed environment. Greece's conqueror, Philip II of Macedon, was soon assassinated and was succeeded by his son, Alexander. It was Alexander, called "the Great," who drastically altered the Greek world.

In the mere 13 years from his accession to the Macedonian throne at the age of 20 in 336 B.C. to his death at 33 in 323, Alexander's combined Greek and Macedonian army conquered the Persian Empire, thereby giving the Greeks mastery of the civilized world and bringing about the reciprocal influence of Greek and Near Eastern culture throughout the immense territory that stretched from the central Mediterranean to India.

The epoch following Alexander's death is called the Hellenistic period. His empire was fought over by his generals, who ultimately divided it among themselves and set up several hereditary monarchies.

To match these powerful territorial states, the old Greek city-states, recognizing the ineffectiveness of the polis in the international sphere, united in leagues. The political history of the Hellenistic period consists of wars and alliances, the usual pattern of balance-of-power politics, among the monarchies and leagues.

Two important political developments occurred before the entire Greek world fell to Rome in the 100's B.C. The first was the universal acceptance of the claim of divinity, similar to that of the Egyptian pharaohs, made by the Hellenistic monarchs.

The second development came about within the Greek leagues. It involved the first significant experiments in representative government in world history. Although these experiments bore no immediate fruit, their record was studied and at least some of their techniques were imitated by the Founding Fathers of the United States.

Hellenistic culture. The most important contributions of the Hellenistic era were made in cultural life. Literature produced no giants to match the earlier writers, but with the spread of education and literacy, new forms of literature arose: the comedy of manners and situation, of which the major poet was Menander; pastoral poetry; didactic poetry; and the prose romance of adventure, which was the ancestor of the modern novel.

Historical writing became more professional, and histories, most of which have been lost, were written to cover all the countries newly opened to Greek curiosity. The only major historian of the period whose work has come down to us is Polybius.

In art, there was a tendency toward a more ornate and decorative style. In architecture, temples were built on a larger and more lavish scale than ever before, but the characteristic buildings were nonreligious and were typified by great tombs and by the Pharos, the huge lighthouse that stood in the harbor of the Hellenistic world's most cosmopolitan city, Alexandria. Sculpture emphasized the exotic and the expression of violent emotion.

Science made the most spectacular

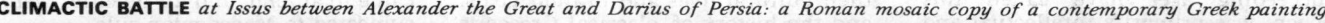

CLIMACTIC BATTLE *at Issus between Alexander the Great and Darius of Persia: a Roman mosaic copy of a contemporary Greek painting.*

ALINARI/EPA

progress in any period of history until modern times. The scientific inquiry of Aristotle's later work was continued, and in Alexandria the kings of the Ptolemaic dynasty founded the Museum, which was the first scientific institute in history.

At the Museum scholars were maintained at the expense of the state. A huge library was collected, laboratories and dissecting rooms were provided, and zoological and botanical collections were organized. Literary scholarship, textual criticism, and library science were developed.

Enormous strides were made in mathematics, physics, astronomy, geography, botany, biology, and medicine. The properties of air were demonstrated; the heliocentric theory of Earth's relation to the sun was advanced; the circumference of Earth and the degrees of latitude were calculated; the motor and sensory nervous system were discovered; the properties of cubes, cylinders, cones, and spheres were analyzed; and the techniques for the measurement of curved surfaces were developed.

In philosophy, the formal schools focused their attention on ethics and their teachings began to emphasize a divine sanction for moral behavior. The most influential philosophy of the period was Stoicism, which eventually became as much a religion as a rational philosophy. The Stoics taught the immortality of the soul, the importance of doing one's assigned duty on Earth, and the brotherhood of man.

There were numerous movements in religion that created a receptive environment for the growth of Christianity. Syncretism, the fusion of the gods of one people with those of another, became prevalent and resulted in the almost universal concept of a single deity.

Most important, the Greek world absorbed the "mystery" cults of the Near East, and thereby shifted drastically from their worship of local patron gods. These mystery religions focused upon the individual and his direct, emotional communion with the divine. They taught belief in a god who had suffered, died, and been reborn. The communicant, through sacramental union with the deity, could himself achieve rebirth and salvation in the life after death.

Rome

The Hellenistic world's political stalemate was ultimately broken by conquest. The conqueror was Rome, the last and greatest organizer of the ancient world.

The early history of Rome was "invented" by the romantic propaganda of a world-state in the first century B.C. and the first century A.D. out of a combination of legend, tradition, and the desire to provide a suitable pedigree for the new rulers of the world.

Modern analysis of this "history," based on extensive archaeological research, indicates that the Romans were a local group of the Latins, one of the many Indo-European tribes who entered Italy shortly after 1000 B.C. These tribes are known collectively as the Italic peoples.

The Romans were the inhabitants of a town that had a potentially advantageous location at the last point upstream navigable by seagoing vessels on the Tiber River. Their basic institutions appear to have been like those of other Indo-European peoples, notably the Greeks.

The Romans were first ruled by a monarchy, which soon gave way to an oligarchy composed of hereditary aristocrats (patricians). The patricians, like their counterparts in the early Greek polis, ruled by means of a permanent council of elders (the Senate), and a monopoly of the state's judicial, executive, and religious offices.

The mass of citizens (plebeians) met in their assemblies (Comitia), whose principal function was the ratification of acts promulgated by the patricians. The formula that embodied this relation between the patricians and the plebeians and represented the authority for decisions of state was SPQR (the Senate and the Roman People).

Early development of Rome.
Until the late 300's B.C., Rome was an insignificant state, largely agricultural and almost entirely illiterate. For a long period the Romans were culturally influenced and even ruled by the Etruscans, their neighbors across the Tiber River.

The Etruscan language is only partially understood, and thus detailed knowledge of the Etruscans is lacking. Nevertheless, it is certain that at their height in the 600's and 500's B.C., they were far more advanced politically and culturally than the Romans.

At that time there were three powers in the western Mediterranean: the Etruscans, the Greeks of southern Italy and Sicily, and the Phoenicians, whose major commercial city was Carthage, in North Africa. In the three-way struggle for land, trade, and power, the Etruscans were the losers, and Rome's independence (traditionally dated at 509 B.C.) was a consequence of the decline of Etruscan power.

The most lasting mark made by the Etruscans was in the sphere of religion, and the Etruscan heritage can be seen in the complex structure and extreme ritualism of Roman religious institutions.

Roman expansion.
Following its independence from the Etruscans, Rome's development was at first inconsequential. As late as 390 B.C., a tribe of barbaric Gauls from northern Italy sacked the city. Probably as a direct result of this event, Rome began to cultivate the military prowess that was responsible for its remarkable growth. By 338 B.C., the Romans controlled the surrounding region of Latium, whose inhabitants had long been organized for military purposes in the Latin League, which Rome took over.

By the end of the 300's, they ruled the entire peninsula south of the Po River. In the following 150 years of uninterrupted military advance, Rome rose from a local power in Italy to the unchallenged ruler of most of the Mediterranean world and arbiter of the rest, over which it continued to extend its direct control.

A series of wars with Carthage began in 264 B.C., and with the destruction of Carthage in 146 B.C., Rome ruled absolute over the western Mediterranean. In the same year, the sack and the destruction of Corinth, the outcome of another series of wars that had begun in 215 B.C., completed the Roman conquest of the Greek mainland.

The rest of the Hellenistic East was subjugated piecemeal. For practical purposes, the task was completed when Rome added the last Hellenistic monarchy, Egypt, to its dominions in 30 B.C.

The Roman Republic.
The nearly 500 years from Rome's independence to its total control of the Mediterranean mark the period of the Roman Republic. In theory, the structure of the republic emphasized the joint power of all classes in a unified citizen body. But the gaining of equal rights for the plebeians with the patricians, the subject of much of the legendary early history of Rome, is illusory.

In actuality, the political and judicial equality gained by the plebeians resulted in the formation of a joint patrician-plebeian aristocracy. It was composed of a few score of the wealthiest families in Rome, who intermarried among themselves and rigorously excluded outsiders. This aristocracy maintained a monopoly over the higher offices of state, and the holders of these offices filled vacancies in the Senate.

A man who managed to break into this charmed circle was a *novus homo,* a "new man" whose ancestors had never held high office or been a member of the Senate. In 63 B.C., when Cicero was elected consul—the highest executive office in the Roman state, to which two men were elected each year—he was the first novus homo to hold that state post in over 30 years.

The tightly knit oligarchy that presided over and directed the triumphant territorial expansion of Rome was motivated by a combination of patriotism and greed. Without any ideals or guiding philosophy, it treated conquest merely as an opportunity to gain unlimited wealth and power. Its improvised techniques of provincial government acknowledged little in the way of responsibility to the governed, who were simply fleeced.

No better was its treatment of the citizen-farmers, whose endless military service had won the empire. Long years in the army caused neglect of small landholdings, which were taken over and consolidated into large estates by the senatorial aristocracy. These profitable enterprises were worked by gangs of slaves, available in whatever number was desired from the unfortunate populations defeated by Rome in war.

Popular unrest. By the end of the 100's B.C., the dispossessed small farmers, formerly the backbone of Rome's citizenry, had become a landless, rootless, unemployed mob in the city of Rome. Permanently discontented, they became a chief source of the political violence that brought the republic to its end in the first century B.C.

Equally alienated were the wealthy businessmen, the equestrians, whose fortunes had been made by Rome's military victories but who were denied entry into the closed circle of the senatorial rulers of the state.

Beginning in 133 B.C., class antagonisms resulted in increasing pressure on the Senate to institute reforms in the interests of one or another group. The Senate refused to yield, however, and there was a gradual breakdown of the constitutional order. More and more frequently, issues were decided by violence, and it was not long before the army, as the primary wielder of force, became the arbiter of Roman politics.

Ambitious demagogues exploited the general discontent to circumvent the Senate, gain control of an army, and exercise personal power. Roman territorial expansion continued, however, and even increased as reckless politicians realized the surest way to power was the command of a victorious army with which they could coerce the Senate.

Julius Caesar. After 100 years of intermittent civil strife, military coups, assassinations, and violent rioting, it is merely convention to call only the final episode in the destruction of the republic a civil war. The victor, Julius Caesar, took the office of permanent dictator, but in reality, in the few months between elimination of organized resistance and his assassination in 44 B.C., he wielded the absolute power of a Hellenistic monarch.

Of all the remarkable political figures of the first century B.C.—Tiberius and Gaius Gracchus, Marius and Sulla, Pompey, Crassus, Cicero, and the rest—Caesar appears to have been the first to realize that however pleasurable power might be, its pursuit was not self-justifying, and that the issue at stake was how Rome's vast domain was to be governed.

The arrangements Caesar completed or launched before his sudden death made it clear that he had decided on monarchic rule aided by a Hellenistic-style centralized, permanent officialdom. The aim of empire he enunciated—eternal peace and stability, fair and equal treatment of conquered peoples, and only such taxation as proved necessary for the maintenance of a government and army to guarantee and extend these goals—goes back to the great tradition of the Persian Empire and Alexander the Great.

Caesar's death brought about a brief resumption of civil war. The victor was Caesar's nephew and heir, Octavian, who, under the title of Augustus (the Revered), realized Caesar's aims and established the governmental structure of the Roman Empire.

Roman culture. The dramatic rise of the Roman Republic and its equally dramatic self-destruction and transformation into the Roman Empire are important in world history because of the cultural development that accompanied those transformations.

The Rome that embarked upon world conquest after 300 B.C. was extremely primitive. It was a nation of simple and illiterate farmer-soldiers. There was no Latin literature at all until 250 B.C., when the first written work was produced—significantly, it was a translation into Latin of Homer's *Odyssey* by Livius Andronicus, a Greek from southern Italy.

The key to Rome's cultural achievements lay in its ability to absorb, adapt, preserve, and transmit the mighty cultural achievements of Greece. In the famous line of the Roman poet Horace, "Captive Greece captured her barbarian captor."

As Rome moved relentlessly forward on its course of conquest, its simple rustic culture was lost in that of Hellenistic Greece. Rome quickly absorbed Hellenistic religious cults and ideas, philosophies, art, literature, and political institutions—all the tastes and habits and ways of life of a highly sophisticated people.

The Roman ideal. In vain did conservatives like Cato in the 100's B.C. inveigh against the corrupting influence of Greece. For centuries thereafter Romans continued to exhort their fellow Romans to return to the

THE ROMAN EMPIRE, *founded in effect by Julius Caesar* (below), *boasted in later years magnificent cities like Leptis Magna in Libya* (right).

NEW YORK PUBLIC LIBRARY

B.O.A.C.

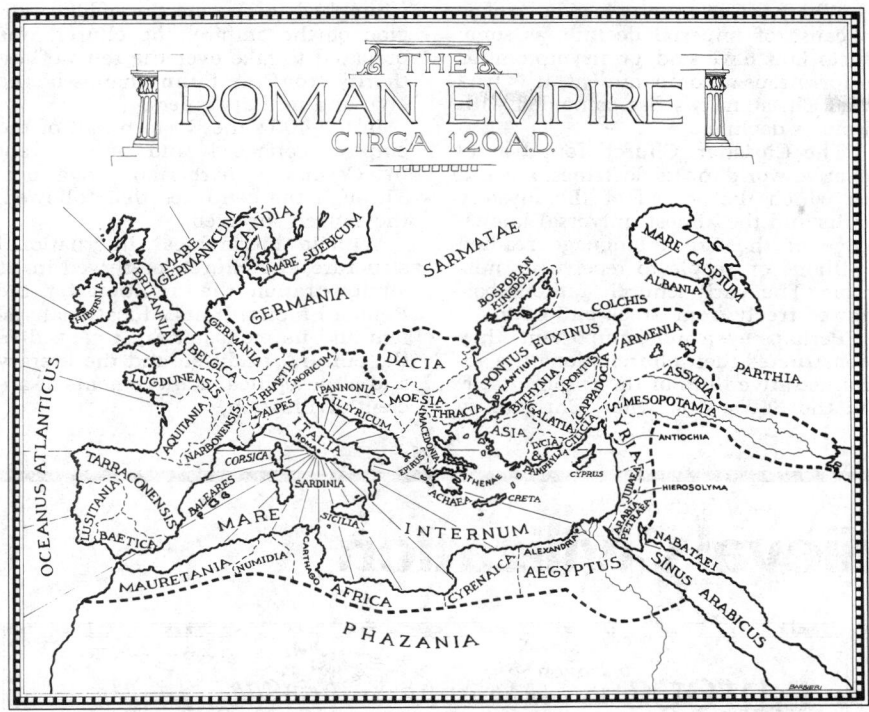

THE ROMAN EMPIRE CIRCA 120 A.D.

straightforward, homely virtues of their ancestors. They succeeded in shaping a Roman ideal based on the way of life of these legendary ancestors: grave, austere, simple, courageous, honest; loyal and obedient to family, religion, and state. It was conspicuously lacking in subtlety, cleverness, frivolity, and intellectuality.

While giving way to the persuasive influence of Greece, Romans, to the end of ancient times, continued to try to hold themselves to this ideal. At his best the cultivated Roman of the late republic and early empire combined the urbane, sophisticated, flexible way of the Greek with the serious, dedicated simplicity of the Roman.

Roman literature reached maturity only in the first century B.C., with the poetry of Catullus and Lucretius and the prose of Cicero. The two poets succeeded in transforming the Latin language into a subtle vehicle capable of expressing all the variety of mood, emotion, thought, and color of 500 years of Greek poetic achievement.

The immense literary productivity of Cicero performed a similar service for prose. He gave Rome a language capable of expressing the complexity of Greek philosophy and Western civilization, a prose style that remained an educational model until our day.

Under the Roman Empire, the assimilation of Greek culture was accelerated and its Roman adaptation was carried into the newly conquered barbarian lands of central and western Europe as well as to the island of Britain. With Romanization, these lands received the heritage that was to become the foundation of their own cultural tradition.

The Roman Empire. The Roman Empire placed the civilized world under a single monarchic rule, although it persisted for centuries in using the political terminology of the Roman Republic and carefully preserved such obsolete institutions as the Senate. The empire tended toward authoritarianism and military despotism, but it was centuries before its autocratic nature became absolute and by then it had begun its decline.

Its accomplishment is still unmatched in history, however. It created a system of government that enabled a vast territory and a population of about 100 million people of different races, languages, cultures, and traditions to enjoy centuries of security, stability, peace, rational and disinterested administration, and almost impartial law.

Although the early emperors of the first century A.D. led scandalous private lives, the empire they ruled actually prospered, and the centralized bureaucracy that made Rome a synonym for the art of government evolved during their reigns. By the middle of the 100's, that government consisted of a permanent, highly organized civil service leading from the lowest levels to the emperor, who considered himself the servant of his demanding office.

The "good emperors" of the 100's created the Pax Romana, or Roman Peace, an epoch that Edward Gibbon, the great English historian of the 1700's, described as the period in the world's history when "the condition of the human race was the most happy and prosperous."

Civilization spread throughout the vast realm of the Roman Empire as scores of cities were built where formerly there had been only barbarism. A Greek lecturer who came to Rome in the 150's A.D. praised Rome's accomplishment. He stated that the new unwalled cities were meant for a world at peace—for the first time in history cities needed no local defense.

Decline and fall of the empire. The empire at its height already contained the seeds of its decay and its eventual fall. The decline and fall of the Roman Empire is one of the classic problems of history. Interpretation of the fall has ranged over the whole spectrum of causes that historians have developed to explain historical events.

The moral explanation has emphasized such matters as the private wickedness of individual emperors, the decadent luxury in which the wealthy lived, indifference to the misery of the masses, and the general malaise of a civilization that had somehow lost its dynamism and its capacity to innovate. This theory also points out that citizens sought escape from sheer boredom and tameness of life in the other-worldly promises of religious cults.

The social-political explanation has emphasized the divisions and conflicts of interest that developed—rich and poor, urban and rural, governmental bureaucracy and citizenry, military and civilian.

The control of the armed forces remained a problem for centuries. Army commanders always presented the threat of coups, and at various critical times made war upon each other with the control of the empire as the prize for victory.

The need for large military forces was always present because of the pressure of outside powers upon the imperial borders—in the East a revived Persian Empire, in Europe a succession of partly civilized Germanic tribes. The threat in Europe was met in the 200's by admitting whole tribes into the empire, settling them along the frontiers, and using them as defensive troops against the continuing waves of attack by other tribes still on the outside.

The sheer magnitude of the problems that beset the empire in the 200's, and its decreasing power to deal with them, brought about an administrative revision from about 300 on that in effect divided the empire into an eastern Greek-speaking half and a western Latin-speaking half.

Despite the myth that the empire was still one, and in spite of the efforts of individual emperors to restore unity, the two halves tended to grow further apart. By about 400 they were not only separate, but, beneath the surface of brotherhood, hostile.

Modern study of the problem of decline and fall, while retaining these traditional explanations as contributing causes, has tended to emphasize economic factors. Among these are the failure to develop an expanding economy and an improved technology, the drain on the empire's money supply as luxury items continued to be imported from as far away as China, to be paid for in cash, and the consequent devaluation of currency.

Also included among economic factors is the increasing burden of an ever-growing bureaucracy and an armed service not balanced by increased production but paid for by a growing burden of taxation. Clearly all these "causes" are interlocked. Together they describe the Roman Empire and its fate, whether or not they satisfactorily explain it.

Whether Christianity is to be seen as a cause of imperial decline, as some historians have said, or a symptom, or a fortuitous accompaniment, it is true that Christianity's rise coincided with Rome's decline.

The Christian Church found a receptive world for its doctrines, a world in which the spread of the mystery cults and the almost universal knowledge of the Greek language readied millions of people to receive its mission. The early church fathers borrowed freely from Greek philosophy.

Perhaps even more important, they constructed their church along the administrative lines of the empire itself. In the 300's A.D., when Christianity

triumphed to become the official religion of the empire, the church was prepared to take over the reins of authority from the failing hands of the civil and military rulers.

In the 400's the western half of the empire collapsed and was swept by Germanic barbarian invasions. Through the centuries that followed, the church survived.

With its hierarchical, international structure, the church preserved in its administration the traditions of the Roman Empire. In its educational system and its monasteries, it kept alive the cultural tradition and the literary and philosophical achievements of ancient civilization.

Medieval Civilization

The concept of a "Middle Age" belongs to the Italian humanists of the 1400's. Looking back, they realized that between their own time, in which they had so much pride and hope, and the classical antiquity they admired so much, lay a radically different kind of civilization.

The humanists saw this Middle Age as 1000 years of barbarism and superstition. Although this view is no longer accepted, the existence of a distinct civilization between the ancient world and the Renaissance is recognized.

Medieval civilization, unlike ancient or modern civilization, was largely self-contained. It was confined to northwestern Europe and had little contact with the Byzantine and Arab worlds. Its economic organization, social and political institutions, religious attitudes, moral values, and intellectual viewpoint were all different from those of the civilizations that preceded and followed it. The question is how this civilization came into being.

THE FINAL PARTITION of Charlemagne's great empire in 888 A.D. ushered in the Middle Ages.

Making of the Middle Ages

Historians agree that the Middle Ages began with the disintegration of the Roman Empire in the West and its replacement by a series of Germanic successor states between roughly 400 and 600 A.D. The classical world that the Germanic barbarians ventured into was in a state of decay or at least change.

The economy of the Roman Empire had always been primarily agricultural. During the empire's last days, especially in the West, it became more so, a development that included the increased importance of large landed estates worked by a servile peasantry,

or serfs. Similarly, commerce in the western half of the Roman Empire, which had never been very lively, gradually became less so.

The Latin language had changed a great deal from what it had been in the 100's B.C. at the time of Cicero and Vergil in ways that pointed toward the development of the Romance languages. Classical Latin, because it remained the language of the church, became the language of law, government, and learning.

Germanic influences. The German tribes moved into a world already in flux. Their presence only served to reinforce economic and intellectual tendencies already in progress.

The Germans destroyed the western

Roman Empire as a political entity, but they did not destroy its civilization. They took over the administrative system, the taxes, the law, and the language of the culture they conquered. They had very little immediate effect upon agriculture, commerce, or society in the areas they occupied.

On the other hand, the Germans did not play a completely passive role in the formation of the Middle Ages. The independent political states they created in Western Europe were ruled by a warrior aristocracy whose social ethic became dominant in European society and literature.

The Germans also introduced important technological innovations, each of which contributed to a minor social revolution. The heavy plow made possible the cultivation of the rich bottom lands of northern Europe and may have determined the development of some features of the medieval manor, or landed estate.

The stirrup and the spur contributed to the preeminence of the heavily armed cavalryman in medieval warfare. In turn, the importance of the heavily armed cavalryman led to a radical social differentiation between the class that fought on horseback and the serfs who tilled the soil.

Isolation of Europe. One further step remains in the emergence of the Middle Ages: its isolation from the Mediterranean world. The earliest Germanic states founded in the West—Visigothic Spain, Vandal Africa, and Ostrogothic Italy—were on the fringes of the Mediterranean. In these kingdoms a promising beginning had been made toward the fusion of Roman and German culture.

Two circumstances contributed to the failure of these Germanic states. The first has to do with the Byzantine, or East Roman, Empire, and the second with the spread of Islam.

Byzantine Empire. The Roman Empire had been divided culturally into a Greek East and a Latin West. The East had a much larger population, many more cities, more commerce, industry, and wealth; and a richer heritage of art, literature, and philosophy.

In 286 the Roman Empire had been divided for administrative purposes into eastern and western halves by the emperor, Diocletian, who established the eastern capital at Nicomedia, in Asia Minor. In 330 Emperor Constantine transferred the capital to Byzantium, a small city strategically located on the European side of the Bosporus that had been founded by Greek colonists in the 600's B.C. The new capital soon came to be called Constantinople in honor of the emperor.

In 395, on the death of Emperor Theodosius I, the Roman Empire became completely divided and was ruled by two separate emperors. During the 400's, barbarians increased their pressure along the frontiers of both empires. The East Roman Empire was able to withstand the onslaught but the West Roman Empire collapsed in 476 when the emperor was deposed.

During the 500's, the emperor Justinian (527–565) attempted to reconquer the west. Under the able generals Belisarius and Narses, the east was able to regain Italy, North Africa, and southeastern Spain. Justinian also fought a long war against the Persians, who had invaded the empire from the east.

Justinian. Justinian was one of the greatest of the Byzantine emperors. He reorganized government administration and fortified the frontiers. In order to clarify the law, he had the entire body of Roman law codified. The Code of Justinian became the ba-

BYZANTINE IVORY *from 700 A.D., when Western Europe was in the "Dark Ages."*

sis of French, German, and Italian law.

Justinian also made a major attempt to ensure the unity of the eastern and western churches, which had been steadily growing apart. Justinian suppressed heresy and paganism and sent out numerous missionaries. This action temporarily healed the breach but the two churches quarreled continually, and by 1054 the split between western Christianity, or Roman Catholicism, and eastern Christianity, or Eastern Orthodox Christianity, became irrevocable.

A project of more permanent value was Justinian's enormous public building program. Two of the most famous Byzantine structures still standing, the churches of Hagia Sophia in Constantinople and San Vitale in Ravenna, date from his reign.

Barbarian and Persian threat. Justinian was succeeded by a series of weak and ineffective emperors whose reigns were marked by internal unrest and renewed barbarian and Persian invasions. Between 568 and 571, the Lombards conquered all of Italy except areas around the cities of Rome, Naples, and Ravenna.

In 616 Spain was lost to the Visigoths. Between 606 and 622 the Persians overran Syria, Asia Minor, Palestine, Mesopotamia, and Egypt. Slavs moved into the Balkans and the Avars raided almost as far south as Constantinople.

In 610 Heraclius I, the son of the provincial governor of North Africa, seized the imperial throne and became the founder of a new dynasty. Heraclius reorganized the army and launched three brilliant campaigns against the Persians. By 628 the Persians were decisively defeated and the territory they had won regained.

The Arabs. The Byzantine Empire, however, had been weakened by the war and when the Arabs, who had recently been converted to Islam, embarked on a program of conquest in 634, the Byzantines were unable to stand against them. The Arabs conquered the lands that Heraclius had won from the Persians, and between 673 and 678, and in 717 and 718, besieged the city of Constantinople itself. In 698 the Arabs seized Carthage. Byzantine rule in North Africa also ended.

Isaurians and Macedonians. In 717 Leo III, the first emperor of the Isaurian dynasty (717–802), came to the throne. The first Isaurians were able leaders who managed to defeat the Arabs in Asia Minor and were successful in several campaigns against the Bulgars, a Turkic people that threatened from the northeast.

In 802 the Isaurian dynasty ended, to be followed in 820 by the Amorian, or Phrygian, dynasty, which ruled until 867. The last of the Amorian emperors, Michael III, was murdered by the grand chamberlain Basil, who subsequently founded the Macedonian dynasty (867–1056).

Under the Macedonians, the Byzantine Empire experienced its golden age. The Macedonian emperors were intelligent and responsible rulers who had both administrative and military ability. Byzantine culture reached its peak and Constantinople became the artistic center as well as the marketplace of the Mediterranean.

Basil II, the ablest of the Macedonian emperors, extended the empire to its greatest territorial limits. A cruel and capable general, he waged highly successful campaigns against the Arabs and Bulgars. Syria, parts of Palestine, Crete, and Cyprus were added to the empire. Bulgaria was conquered and divided into provinces.

Decline of Byzantium. After the death of Basil II in 1025, Byzantium entered a period of decline that lasted until 1080. The empire was ruled by a succession of weak and inept emperors, and its territory was whittled away by Turkic raiders in the north, Normans in Italy, and Seljuk Turks in Asia Minor, who won most of Asia Minor at the disastrous battle of Manzikert in 1071. Internally, Byzantium was weakened by a conflict between the administrative nobility in Constantinople and the feudal nobility outside the capital and in the provinces.

In 1081 this decline was partially checked by the advent of the Commenian dynasty, which ruled until 1185. While the Commenians were unable to regain the territory that had been lost, they were able to prevent further encroachments. The preservation of the remainder of the empire was accomplished mainly through diplomatic means, by turning the enemies of Byzantium against one another, not through military conquest.

The decline of the empire was accelerated, however, under the weak Angelus dynasty (1185–1195; 1203–1204). The Angeli lacked the ability to prevent internal schisms and the power to stand against foreign enemies. As a result, the West, which had grown envious of the wealth of the Eastern empire that it had witnessed during the Crusades, found an easy opportunity to turn against Byzantium.

The Latin Empire. In 1204, during the fourth Crusade, Venetian and French leaders attacked Constantinople on the pretext of intervening on behalf of Emperor Isaac II, who had been deposed by his brother Alexius III. After a siege of one month, the city fell to the Crusaders and was thoroughly sacked.

The Crusaders set up a feudal state under Baldwin of Flanders that was known as the Latin Empire. Under the empire the French controlled most of the former Byzantine mainland possessions and the Venetians held most of the islands and coastal regions. Byzantine princes, however, managed to retain control of Epirus in northwest Greece, and Nicaea and Trebizond in Asia Minor.

Byzantine restoration. These Byzantine princes continued to struggle against the Crusaders, and finally in 1261 Michael VIII Palaeologus of Nicaea recaptured Constantinople and overthrew the Latin Empire. He founded the Palaeologian dynasty, which ruled for almost 200 years over a substantially reduced Byzantine Empire, consisting of the area around Constantinople and parts of Greece.

Under the Palaeologi the Byzantine Empire enjoyed a cultural renaissance, although it gradually diminished physically and grew weaker politically. During the 1300's inroads into Byzantine domains were made by the Serbs in the north and the increasingly powerful Ottoman Turks in the east, while the empire was divided internally by civil war and religious controversy. By about 1400, Byzantium had become financially dependent on Venice and Genoa and was reduced to paying tribute to the Ottoman Turks.

Final collapse. In May, 1453, Constantinople fell to the Ottoman Sultan Muhammad II and the last of the Byzantine emperors, Constantine XI, was killed in the battle. Athens and the Peloponnesus continued to hold out against the Turks, but within a few years they were defeated. Trebizond fell in 1461. Constantinople, for more than 1100 years the capital of Byzantium, became the Ottoman capital.

Spread of Islam. The other circumstance that contributed to the isolation of the early medieval world was the

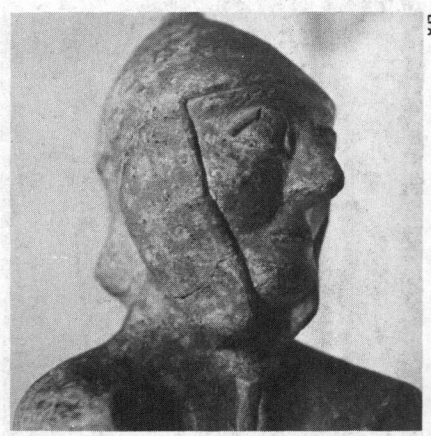

HEAD OF CHARLEMAGNE *dating from about 845* A.D., *not long after his death.*

spread of Islam. What distinguished the spread of Islam was its political success. Within a generation of the death of the prophet Muhammad, in 632 A.D., the Arabs conquered the southern shore of the Mediterranean.

In scarcely more than 100 years the Muslims held almost all of Spain and most of the Mediterranean islands, had threatened the existence of the Frankish kingdom in southwestern Europe, and had besieged Constantinople, the capital of the Byzantine Empire. As a result, the diverse peoples of the southern Mediterranean became united through Islam and use of the Arabic language.

The spread of Islam was the last step in the emergence of the Middle Ages in that it made western Europe's isolation from the old Mediterranean world complete. Henceforth, western Europe looked out on a Mediterranean world that was superior to it culturally and hostile to it politically. Not until the 1100's, during the Crusades, and then only temporarily, would there be much contact between the two.

After the initial period of transition, medieval civilization developed in northwestern Europe, above all in the broad area between the Loire and the Rhine rivers. Therefore, the next phase of medieval history began with the people who gave that area its modern name, the Franks.

Frankish Kingdom

The Franks were one of many tribes inhabiting the North Sea coast of Germany. As the Roman defenses on the Rhine gradually collapsed, Frankish war bands, each under an individual king, moved into northern Gaul.

Merovingians. The Franks first became politically significant under the Merovingians, the family of Clovis, who became the king of all Franks about 481 A.D. The practice of dividing the kingdom among surviving sons was the leading cause of the civil wars that plagued Frankish history.

By the mid-700's the Merovingians had declined. They were replaced by the Carolingians, who inaugurated the most significant period in Frankish history. Charlemagne the Great (ruled 768–814), the outstanding Carolingian king, unified a vast empire and the Roman Catholic church under his leadership. In 800 he was crowned in Rome "Emperor of the Romans," thus reviving the Roman Empire and establishing a special relationship between its "holy" emperor and the papacy. Charlemagne's rule also inspired a revival of learning and literacy, and the copying of Latin texts to preserve knowledge of classical antiquity.

By the mid-800's, the empire consisted mostly of a landed society united by a loose and decentralized political system. Internal struggles for power and land ensued, and in 843 the empire was partitioned into three portions by the Treaty of Verdun. Thus weakened, it was attacked by various barbarian groups: the Vikings from Scandinavia and the Magyars from Asia. By the early 900's, Charlemagne's empire had been shattered into more than 50 political units.

Feudalism. Feudalism emerged from the failure of the Frankish monarchy in the west to protect the kingdom from Viking invaders. It was initially an improvisation for solving on a local basis the need for military protection that the larger political units were unable to provide. It was the result of a weak central government, a time of military necessity that brought about a professional fighting class, and a predominantly rural society. The towns had not yet recovered.

Feudalism had several distinct features. The principal one was vassalage, a relationship in which one man placed himself at the service of another in return for maintenance and protection. The vassal was originally maintained by his lord's household. Later, as the position of the vassal rose in the social scale, he was supported by a grant of property, or a fief.

Feudalism was established by the mid-900's, at least in its homeland of northern France. In the 1000's it spread from France to England and 100 years later to Germany. Spain and Italy, however, remained largely untouched.

Manorialism. The institution of feudalism was inseparable from its economic base, manorialism. Normally the fief consisted of a large landed estate or estates called villas or manors, cultivated by a peasantry in varying degrees of economic and legal servitude. It was from the villa or manor that the vassal derived his income and over which he exercised his political jurisdiction.

In its simplest definition, the manor was a village community of peasants tilling the soil by means of the open field system. In the open field system, arable land and meadows are divided into strips, each peasant possessing several strips in the various fields.

Revival of commerce.

One of the first signs of revival in medieval Europe was the development of towns and commerce. Although trade had never quite died out along the coast of the North Sea in Europe, the source of commercial revival was Italy.

The revival of Italian commerce was given impetus by the Crusades. Beginning at the end of the 1000's, western Europeans spent 200 years vainly attempting to wrest the Holy Land from its Muslim conquerors. The Italians were in a splendid position to profit from the Crusades. They transported armies of Crusaders and pilgrims to the Holy Land and provisioned them while they were there.

The Italians also imported exotic goods from Africa and the East that were in great demand in medieval Europe: spices, cloth, precious stones, and perfumes. In return they exported woolen cloth that was woven in towns like Bruges, Ypres, and Ghent in the Low Countries. The wool itself came from England, and the fine finished products were traded at the famous fairs of Champagne in France. Later, however, the Italians began to eliminate the middlemen in this prosperous trade by manufacturing their own woolen cloth.

Growth of towns.

The revival of commerce stimulated the development of towns. In the initial stages of the revival of commerce, merchants were itinerant, often traveling in caravans for mutual protection. Naturally, they sought out fortified centers as places of refuge and as markets for their goods.

At a later stage, merchants began to settle down in the most strategically located places. In due course they were surrounded by people who catered to their needs, such as blacksmiths, bakers, and cobblers. As the population expanded, houses were built outside the original fortified center and it became necessary to protect them with another wall. Simultaneously, independent municipal governments were formed.

Thus, along with the rise of towns and commerce came the origins of a merchant class. The medieval merchant class and the social forms it produced were alien to the economic and social ethic of early medieval society. The feudal class resented its wealth and independence and the church took a long time to recognize the activities of the marketplace and the counting house as Christian.

Medieval church.

Another aspect of revival was the change that began to take place within the medieval church. The first manifestation of change was the emergence of religious reform.

During the 900's the increasing stability of medieval life made it possible for the ordinary Christian to live a life somewhat closer to the Christian ideal

than had been previously possible. In turn, he demanded that the clergy live a life superior to his own.

One of the fundamental convictions of medieval popular Christianity was that the clergy ensured the salvation of the laity by leading moral lives and by administering the sacraments.

The Cluniac reform movement, which began at the French monastery of Cluny in the early 900's, was an attempt to purify the church by restoring monastic discipline as exemplary of the Christian life, and by eliminating prevailing abuses in the church.

The Gregorian reform movement of the 1000's not only restored papal and church influence, but it greatly expanded the authority of the pope while calling for state subordination to the church.

Later, popular sects arose that challenged the assumptions of the church. These sects believed these assumptions to be based on worldliness and wealth rather than spiritual salvation. These "heresies" not only rejected the authority of the papacy, but also the intermediacy of the priesthood in administering the sacraments. They believed, instead (thus heralding the Reformation), that the true church was a priesthood of believers who were saved through their individual religious experiences.

The Franciscan and Dominican mendicant orders also developed outside of the formal church. The Franciscans preached world renunciation and the value of manual labor. The Dominicans constructed an intellectual defense of church dogma, and in the 1200's developed into probably the greatest intellectual force in Europe.

IN THE EARLY MIDDLE AGES *the church was a major force in cultural life. The French monastery of Cluny* (below, right), *founded in 910 A.D., became a European center of religious reform and learning. Much knowledge was preserved by monks* (below) *who copied books by hand.*

TWO MEDIEVAL SAINTS. *Thomas Aquinas was a noted philosopher and theologian, while King Louis IX of France was known for his participation in the seventh and eighth Crusades.*

Revival of learning. During the 1000's there was also a revival of learning. The intellectual reawakening of Europe began in the monasteries, but in time it was taken over by cathedral and then secular schools.

The new learning was not only intellectually stimulating, it was immensely practical. The expanding bureaucracies of the church and government demanded men who could reason as well as read and write.

In the 1200's there was a renewed interest in the philosophy of Aristotle, insofar as it revealed religious truth as being compatible with human reason. St. Thomas Aquinas became a leading scholastic thinker of this age, arguing that Christian faith was a kind of supernatural knowledge.

Feudal Monarchies

Although the political prospect everywhere looked bleak in Europe at the beginning of the 900's, by the end of the century a revival began to take place. By the end of the 1200's France and England had become something

like modern nation-states, and Germany only narrowly missed. Paradoxically, it was Germany that originally seemed to be the most likely to become a unified state.

Germany. Beginning with Otto the Great (ruled 932–973), the Saxon kings ruled Germany until they were replaced by the Salian dynasty (1024–1125). The Saxons delegated great authority and power to the church, thus gaining the support of this prestigious and wealthy institution while limiting the power of the nobles. In 962 Otto was crowned Holy Roman Emperor, a title held by German kings for the next 300 years.

But the power of the church soon overshadowed that of the German state. The last two Salian kings, Henry IV and Henry V, fought bitterly with the church over the issue of lay investiture. The nobility used this struggle to improve its own situation, even though an agreement known as the Concordat of Worms supposedly settled the issue in 1122.

During the Hohenstaufen dynasty (1152–1250), the German kings tried to unify Germany under a strong monarchy, but they met unmovable resistance from northern Italy, which was

then part of the Holy Roman Empire, and from the church. Germany thus remained politically fragmented and weak.

France. France did not have the dynastic problems of Germany. The Capetian kings ruled France from 987 to 1328. A powerful, unified national state arose during this period.

The Capetians maintained good relations with the church, preserving their just rights while enriching the church with buildings and lands. They increased their own kingdom through marital and hereditary arrangements.

Philip II (ruled 1180–1223) wrested former English holdings in France from the English under King John, Louis IX (ruled 1226–1270) centralized the administration of the kingdom in Paris, and Philip IV (ruled 1285–1314) began the Hundred Years War (1338–1453) with England. The financial demands of the war prompted Philip to tax the French clergy, thus causing a conflict with Pope Boniface VIII, who believed adamantly in papal supremacy over the state and clerical independence under it. The outcome of this conflict, decidedly in favor of the French monarchy, was the election of a French pope (or antipope), thus dividing the church itself in what came to be called the Great Schism (1378–1417).

England. By the early 900's England had achieved a territorial unity and an administrative sophistication unmatched in western Europe. One hundred years earlier, Anglo-Saxon England had been the intellectual leader of western Europe.

By the 1000's, however, England had fallen behind. It had not kept up with the intellectual revival, economic progress, and religious reforms that were sweeping the Continent at the time.

In 1066 William of Normandy invaded England and captured the throne at the Battle of Hastings. The Norman Conquest of England resulted in the establishment of a feudal system far more systematic and effective than any existing in Europe. The feudal aristocracy resented the power of the monarchy, but all benefited from the subsequent establishment of unified codes of law and general order. English medieval history thereafter became a record of attempts by the nobility to limit arbitrary monarchical power while preserving the benefits of strong central government.

Henry I (ruled 1100–1135) consolidated an English system of justice and provided the foundations of English Common Law. Henry II (ruled 1154–1189), who inherited large French possessions, held his great empire together by greatly strengthening the royal power and the machinery of central government in England. The increased legal power of the monarchy brought him into open conflict with the English church, which not only had its own ecclesiastical law but often permitted its clergy to violate English civil law. When the Archbishop of Canterbury, Thomas à Becket, was assassinated in 1170, during the church-state struggle, Henry performed public penance for it. Nevertheless, the royal courts continued to diminish the jurisdiction of the ecclesiastical courts.

King John (ruled 1199–1216) not only lost England's possessions in France, but was forced to yield to the papacy, and finally, in 1215, was impelled by the barons to sign the Magna Carta. This document, limiting the king's power over the aristocrats, led eventually to the emergence of Parliament, a baronial body of political representatives that first rose to power briefly during the reign (1216–1272) of Henry III.

End of the Middle Ages

In the year 1270 the saintly Louis IX of France died while participating in the last Crusade. His successor, Philip IV, was a different kind of monarch. As we have seen, Philip fought Pope Boniface VIII and established the supremacy of the French crown over the French church.

In 1272, the pious Henry III of England was succeeded by Edward I, who similarly effected the dominance of secular over spiritual power in England. The last three decades of the 1200's thus mark the triumph of secularism in politics and the beginning of a weakening papal authority.

In theology and philosophy, there was a similar breakdown after 1270. The major intellectual achievement of the 1200's had been the integration of Christian theology with the natural philosophy of Aristotle. In the late 1200's there was general retreat from this attempt at synthesis. In the 1300's the choice was either faith or reason, rather than a harmony between the two.

Finally, the period of expanding population and economic growth that began in the 1000's came to a halt in the early 1300's. Although the fundamental cause of this economic decline is unknown, one cause was the black death (1347–1351), a plague that halved the population of Europe.

Europe, however, was to survive this crisis without being plunged into another age of barbarism. The 1300's saw the end of a period of European history and the beginnings of a new one, and form a bridge between the Middle Ages and the Renaissance.

BURYING THE DEAD *during the black death, in Tournai, Belgium, 14th century. The plague is estimated to have killed possibly half of Europe's population in three or four years.*

KONINKLIJKE/BIBLIOTHEEK, BRUSSELS

Early Modern Europe

Historians refer to the three or four hundred years before the French Revolution in 1789 as the "early modern" period of European history. Most of those elements that make modern civilization seem very different from medieval civilization developed during those centuries. But it is impossible for historians to be precise about when the Middle Ages actually ended and the "early modern" period began.

Modern institutions, modern attitudes, and other things we think of as "modern" clearly had their roots in still earlier centuries. The developments in arts and letters known as the Renaissance, the great explorations and expansion of Europe overseas, the commercial revolution, the rise of centralized monarchies (the forerunners of the modern "nation-state"), and the breakup of the religious unity of Europe during the Protestant Reformation, all had earlier origins.

The Renaissance

In the usual traditional sense, the term "Renaissance," which literally means rebirth, denotes the revival of classical learning and culture in Italy (the Italian Renaissance), mainly in the 1300's and 1400's, and its spread to other parts of Europe (the Northern Renaissance), mainly during the 1400's and 1500's.

The Renaissance was the first period

in which men really considered themselves to be "modern"—that is, they believed their own age to be not only different from the preceding one but superior to it. The "Renaissance man" rejected the "barbarisms" and "corruptions" of the centuries since the decline of ancient Greece and Rome. He considered the intervening period decadent, and contemptuously labeled it the "Middle Ages"—thinking it a dismal, uncultured period separating the classical age from his own.

Renaissance scholars scorned medieval "dog-Latin," and eagerly searched for old manuscripts from which they could recover the pure Latin of the ancient Romans. On a smaller scale, the study of ancient Greek was enthusiastically taken up, as was Hebrew.

The medieval scholar had been concerned with the harnessing of reason in the defense and service of religion. The Renaissance scholar was more concerned with the secular side of things. He was more concerned with form than with content—for example, the correct use of words, the purification of style, the restoration of classical languages. Poets and philosophers concerned themselves with this world, not the next; with the world of nature, not that of theology; with men, not angels.

Painters and sculptors sought to capture real people rather than general types and individual personalities rather than universal human traits.

In fact, the spirit of the Renaissance was above all secular. Even the papal throne was usually occupied in this period by "Renaissance popes." Nicholas V (ruled 1447–1455) created the Vatican Library. Pius II (ruled 1458–1464) had himself been a leading classical scholar under his own name, Aeneas Silvius.

Julius II (ruled 1503–1513) divided his time between making war (as ruler of the Papal States) and sponsoring enormous art projects by Michelangelo and other masters. Leo X (ruled 1513–1521) launched so ambitious a rebuilding of St. Peter's Basilica that its financing helped trigger the Lutheran revolt.

The universities were also more secular. As centers of the "new learning," they not only concentrated heavily upon secular subjects but also produced large numbers of educated laymen, not just clergy. Even the "universal man" (one who is adept at a variety of pursuits, from scholarship and poetry to the art of war), who was the Renaissance ideal, was concerned mainly with secular activities.

Renaissance literature includes some of the greatest literary figures in history: Dante (1265–1321) who wrote *Divine Comedy;* Petrarch (1304–1374) who was famous for his sonnets and poems; and Boccaccio (1313–1375) who wrote *Decameron.*

One of the greatest Renaissance achievements was the development of a superb vernacular literature that furthered the development of native languages like Italian. This was helped along as books printed in the vernacular began to replace hand-copied classical manuscripts, thereby reaching a greater number and variety of people.

Renaissance art of both religious and secular subjects became more proportional, natural, and realistic.

Among a host of great painters of the High Renaissance that followed were the versatile Leonardo da Vinci (1452–1519), best known for his paintings *Mona Lisa* and *The Last Supper;* Raphael (1483–1520), a remarkable master of color; and Michelangelo (1475–1564), most famous for his fresco covering the entire ceiling of the Sistine Chapel in St. Peter's Basilica in Rome.

The Northern Renaissance in Europe was conspicuous during the 1300's for its growing religious mysticism. This was fostered early in Germany by the writings of Meister Eckhart (c 1260– c 1327) and Thomas à Kempis (1380–1471). Humanism was also influential, especially through the writings of Erasmus of Rotterdam (c 1466–1536) and Sir Thomas More (1478–1535) of England. Flemish painters popularized the use of oils in the 1400's, while Albrecht Dürer (1471–1528) of Germany became one of the greatest painters of the period.

The greatest literature of the Northern Renaissance came from England. Geoffrey Chaucer (c 1340–1400) wrote *The Canterbury Tales* and Edmund Spenser (c 1552–1599) wrote *The Faerie Queene.* Perhaps the greatest literary achievements of all came in the form of English drama written by Christopher Marlowe (1564–1593) and the more famous William Shakespeare (1564–1616).

Rabelais (c 1494–1553) and Michel de Montaigne (1553–1592) represented French literary development in the Northern Renaissance, while Cervantes (1547–1616), who wrote *Don Quixote,* became Spain's master literary figure.

Age of discovery.

As important as any other development during the Renaissance was Europe's expansion overseas. The first area reached was the Orient. Europeans had considerable knowledge of the Orient at the end of the Middle Ages. They had received this from ancient writers, from the experience of the Crusaders in the Near East, from travelers to the Far East (of whom Marco Polo was only the most famous), and from the commerce of Venice and other Italian cities with Muslim ports in the eastern Mediterranean and the Black Sea.

The Portuguese prince Henry the Navigator (1394–1460) sponsored a long series of voyages that steadily advanced down the west coast of Africa. Bartholomeu Dias and Vasco da Gama rounded the southern cape to reach India, and thereafter Portugal maintained a monopoly of trade with Africa and Asia for a century. In the 1600's the Dutch and English East India companies wrested most of this trade from Portugal.

The Genoese navigator Christopher Columbus sailed westward in 1492 and discovered the Americas, the New World. In 1518 the Spanish soldier Cortés began the conquest of the Aztec empire in Mexico, and in the 1530's Pizarro toppled the Inca empire in Peru. Spanish America soon became one of the richest of colonial ventures.

In North America the Spanish, English, Dutch, and French seized and colonized vast territories in the 1600's, although the long-sought water route to the east by sailing west was never to materialize as a significant trade route.

Commercial revolution.

During the Middle Ages the overwhelming majority of the people of Europe were

THE LUSTY RENAISSANCE *started in Italy. The climactic 16th century saw Michelangelo's great art* (below, left), *as well as American conquests like that of Cortés* (right).

METROPOLITAN MUSEUM OF ART, PURCHASE, 1924, JOSEPH PULITZER BEQUEST

NEW YORK PUBLIC LIBRARY

engaged in agriculture, and this was only slightly less true centuries later at the time of the French Revolution in 1789. Still, enormous changes had taken place within the economy during the early modern period.

Important urban commercial centers, which had begun to flourish in the late Middle Ages, particularly in northern Italy and the Low Countries, continued to grow in size and number throughout Europe. Local and regional self-sufficiency was increasingly replaced by a geographical division of labor, in which areas concentrated to a large extent on what they did best or what they seemed best suited for—growing foodstuffs, producing raw materials, or manufacturing.

Long-distance commerce was inevitably stimulated by western Europe's penetration of overseas areas, which expanded the source of goods in demand and provided new markets, although both did not necessarily occur in the same area. The East, for example, had little desire for Europe's primitive exports, and demanded coined money in exchange for its spices, fine cloths, and other products. Overland trade routes in Europe became safer, which led to the even more important development of large-scale maritime commerce along the Atlantic coast.

Overseas shipping, banking, and commerce to handle increased trade volumes, stock companies to finance commercial ventures, and government protection of business and industry, all increased dramatically.

By the middle of the period referred to here as "early modern," small-scale medieval trading had evolved into fully developed commercial capitalism. A commercial revolution had taken place.

The Renaissance state. The decline of imperial and papal domination left Italy a scene of incessant war among independent states. The greater states absorbed the lesser states until only a few remained, among which a balance of power—a new and modern concept in international affairs—was manipulated for 40 years (1454–1494) through the rapidly developing institutions of diplomacy.

The Renaissance state, in many ways a forerunner of the centralized, omnipotent modern state, developed rapidly, particularly in northern Italy's cities. Medieval republican city governments, which also ruled outlying territories, gave way to rule by an individual despot in Milan, by a wealthy oligarchy in Venice, by both in Florence, and by the pope in the Papal States around Rome.

Elsewhere, larger territorial states were being consolidated under strong monarchical rule, most importantly in England, France, and Spain. By the

LUTHERAN PREACHER *in Switzerland brings religion to the people. From an early woodcut.*

early 1500's, each of these countries had achieved, in rough form, its modern boundaries. Although each developed differently, royal power was markedly increased, and the centralized institutions characteristic of modern government swiftly developed.

In England, strong government was established by the Tudor dynasty, especially by Elizabeth I (ruled 1558–1603). In France, centralization was slowed by almost constant foreign wars in the first half of the 1500's, and by religious civil wars in the second half. The Valois dynasty ended in 1589, and Henry IV (ruled 1589–1610), the first of the Bourbons, brought about religious peace with the Edict of Nantes in 1598, which granted religious tolerance to the Protestants.

In 1469, Spain was united under the strong rule of Ferdinand and Isabella, patrons of Columbus. Maximilian I (ruled 1493–1519), the Hapsburg Holy Roman Emperor, inherited the Netherlands and Austria, and married his son into Spanish royalty. The resulting vast empire, the greatest in Europe, was split in 1556 between the Austrian lands under Ferdinand I (ruled 1556–1564) and the Spanish lands under Philip II (ruled 1556–1598), who brought the power of the Spanish crown to its highest peak.

The rivalry between the French crown and the Hapsburgs—especially the Spanish branch—continued until the Treaty of Pyrenees was signed in 1659, by which time French predominance had replaced Spanish. Meanwhile the Protestant Reformation had added religion to the issues states fought over.

The Reformation

By the early 1500's the church was in a serious condition. There was secularism in its hierarchy, ignorance among the lower clergy, and widespread abuses, such as simony (sale of church offices), pluralism (holding more than one church office), and violation of vows of celibacy. Papal authority had been undermined, and many heresies since the 1200's, which had been put down, had left dangerous traditions.

Mysticism, especially popular in northern Europe, favored direct worship of God without an intervening priesthood. This undermined the doctrine of "works," according to which the sacraments were necessary to salvation. The Neoplatonist vogue, which disparaged material things, undermined the visible church and its rituals and symbols.

NEW YORK PUBLIC LIBRARY

CATHOLICS MARCH *in Paris in the 1580's, part of the Counter Reformation in France.*

Humanists pointed to errors of translation in the official Vulgate Bible. These errors destroyed the scriptural basis for some doctrines and opened the way for attack on others. In earlier periods of decline, the church had found the inner resources to reform itself; under the Renaissance papacy it did not.

The Protestant Reformation.
The matter was brought to a crisis by Martin Luther in 1517, when he posted a list of grievances against the church, the "95 theses," on the Wittenberg, Germany, church door. The Lutherans were joined by followers of Zwingli in Zurich and Calvin in Geneva, who also preached against church dogma, ritual, and pomp. The still more extreme Anabaptists were active in Münster.

Many of the German princes adopted the new religion and prevented the emperor, Charles V, from stamping it out. Lutheranism was recognized by the Religious Peace of Augsburg (1555) under the principle *cuius regio, eius religio* ("whose region, his religion"). The ruler's religion was to be the legal religion of each German state. As migration to another state was allowed, Germany had two generations of religious peace, but France and the Netherlands were torn with strife.

Bloody civil wars raged in France and the Netherlands, where Calvinism was particularly popular. In France, thousands of Protestants were butchered in the St. Bartholomew's Day Massacre in 1572. Noble families were forced to choose between the Catholic League, part of the Catholic Counter Reformation effort, and the Huguenot (French Calvinist) armies. The matter was temporarily settled, with tolerance for the Protestant position, by the Edict of Nantes in 1598.

In the Netherlands, unpopular Spanish rule created a Protestant reformation that became as political as it was religious, so that the Protestant rebels, led by William of Orange, were eventually joined by the Catholics of the Low Countries in opposing Spanish rule. In 1581 the northern provinces, aided by the British, who were already at odds with Spain, separated from the southern provinces to form the United Provinces. This continued the civil war against the Spanish Netherlands.

In 1588, Philip II of Spain, incensed at British intervention, sent the great Spanish fleet—the Invincible Armada—to conquer England and depose Queen Elizabeth. The elaborate and costly undertaking was a dismal failure, and when Henry IV took the throne in France, Catholic Spain lost its last ally in its attempt to reconquer the rebel United Provinces. To forestall defeat, Spain agreed to the Truce of Antwerp (1609–1621), and granted the full independence of the Netherlands in the Peace of Westphalia (1648).

Thirty Years' War.
In Germany the Catholic Counter Reformation had gained strength, and in 1608–1609 German princes began to form rival military alliances, grouping themselves in the Protestant Union and the Catholic League. Religious and political hostility erupted into three decades of war (1618–1649), widely considered to be Europe's most destructive conflict. The four main phases of the Thirty Years' War began with revolt in Bohemia in 1618 and successive intervention by Denmark in 1625–1629, Sweden in 1630–1635, and France in 1635–1648.

In 1635, five years after Sweden's king Gustavus Adolphus had joined the Protestant cause in the war, peace was reached. But Cardinal Richelieu of France, wishing to destroy Austrian and Spanish Hapsburg power, plotted to prolong the war. He allied France with Sweden, the Dutch princes, Savoy, and numerous German princes in successfully weakening the Hapsburg strength.

The war ended in Germany and the Netherlands in 1648 with the Peace of Westphalia, which gave France important territories on its German frontier and made the German states practically independent of the empire, and most vulnerable to French influence. Secularized church lands were returned to their 1624 holders, while Calvinists were tolerated. Spain recognized the independence of the United Provinces. The war between France and Spain, however, dragged on until 1659.

The Age of Absolutism

While the development of strong monarchical government progressed during the 1500's in Spain and England, and in lesser states such as Sweden, it was badly interrupted in France by civil war. Yet France is the classic example of the development of absolute monarchy in the 1600's. The effectiveness of the Spanish crown declined with the power of Spain itself, and in England royal power lost ground to Parliament.

In France, Cardinal Richelieu served as chief minister to Louis XIII (ruled 1610–1643) with zealous dedication. Strongly supported by Louis, he gave firm and effective rule to France, strengthening Louis' absolute royal control over a centralized government, which he helped to make dominant in Europe. He ruthlessly checked the political power of the nobles, and destroyed the military power of the Huguenots, though he allowed them religious tolerance to regain their loyalty. His aim was to weaken the Hapsburgs and thus make France the supreme power in Europe.

Spain's strength during this period was exhausted by long wars. Hapsburg rule ended in 1700 and was replaced by Bourbon rule after the War of the Spanish Succession, which further split and weakened the empire.

France continued to be ruled by strong ministers in succession to Richelieu. Mazarin continued Richelieu's basic policies while putting down nobles' unrest caused by the curbs he imposed on the independence of the *parlements*. Two risings, or *frondes*, in 1648 and in 1651–1653, were finally subdued.

Louis XIV (ruled 1643–1715) established an imposing and powerful royal scene at his lavish palace at Versailles. Colbert, his minister of finance, tried to establish French economic self-sufficiency through a policy known as "mercantilism." According to this scheme, France was to export more than it imported, thus maintaining a favorable balance of trade. The surplus, paid for in gold, would enrich the national treasury. This program was only partly successful since other, more industrialized nations responded with anti-French mercantilist policies of their own.

The French economy was dangerously exhausted by Louis' constant wars. Louis spent many years trying to conquer the Dutch United Provinces, but he was always met by strong resistance from the European powers. The Netherlands, Sweden, and England formed a Triple Alliance against him in the 1660's, and the Austrian Hapsburgs, Brandenburg, Spain, and Denmark joined the alliance in the next decade.

Louis next conquered the Rhine Palatinate in 1687, precipitating the War called after the League of Augsburg (1688–1697). In 1700 he attempted to extend Bourbon control over Spain, precipitating the War of the Spanish Succession (1701–1714). These wars also failed because of staunch opposition from European allies, who were determined never to allow the French and Spanish crowns to be united.

Eighteenth Century Europe

By the end of the "Age of Louis XIV," Europe was much changed, and would continue to change. Bourbon Spain retained its American and Italian lands and was busy in foreign affairs, but it remained a minor power. The United Provinces gave way to England as the dominant commercial state. Denmark's importance was past, and Sweden's would soon fade. The extensive kingdom of Poland would be divided among its neighbors.

The Holy Roman Empire continued to exist as a political entity, but had lost all importance. The Hapsburgs drew on their patrimonial lands for power and prestige, while a powerful rival, Brandenburg-Prussia, rose in northern Germany. Meanwhile, a strong Russian state was emerging. The major roles in European affairs were to be shared by France, England, Austria, Prussia, and Russia.

Rise of Prussia. The nucleus of the future kingdom of Prussia was the electorate of Brandenburg, ruled by the Hohenzollern family. Its strength grew steadily in the 1600's through inheritance and the acquisition of new territories during the long and successful reign of Frederick William, the "Great Elector" (ruled 1640–1688). This military state became even more powerful and better organized under the able Frederick William I (ruled 1713–1740).

Emergence of Russia. From the 800's, the political center of a loose grouping of Russian states was Kiev, on the Dnieper River. The Kievan state was destroyed by Mongol invaders in the 1200's, and the center of political development shifted to new settlements in the northern forests. These grew into feudal principalities, of which Muscovy, or Moscow, was the most important by the 1400's.

In this period Prince Ivan III (the "Great"; ruled 1462–1505) increased the territory and central position of Moscow, reduced the threat of the Mongols to the south, and laid the foundations of modern Russia. Ivan considered himself the heir of the Byzantine Empire, now lost to the Ottoman Turks, and an actual successor to the Byzantine and Roman emperors. He assumed the title of czar, or Caesar.

Successive czars strengthened their power within the increasingly centralized state, while extending its territory. Ivan IV ("the Terrible"; ruled 1533–1584) ruthlessly subdued the nobles, or boyars, and created a centralized state administration. He also expanded the empire considerably eastward and westward.

Following a century of relative stagnation and political turbulence, the westward advance was renewed by Peter I ("the Great"; ruled 1682–1725), who westernized many Russian institutions and cultural ideas.

His modernized, strong, centralized administration enabled Peter to seek "windows to the west." After two decades of war, Russia absorbed all of Sweden's Baltic lands, from Karelia to the Polish frontier, by the terms of the Treaty of Nystadt in 1721. In 1715 St. Petersburg became the new capital and Peter made advances into Turkish territories to the south in search of a Black Sea outlet. Westernization continued during the reign of Elizabeth (1741–1762).

National rivalries. During the half century 1733–1783, there occurred a series of wars fought neither in the name of religion nor against a predominant power. They were, rather, the result of colonial rivalries, territorial ambitions, and a desire to preserve a balance of power.

In the War of the Polish Succession (1733–1735), France, Spain, Italy, and Sardinia fought Poland and Russia over the election of a successor to Augustus II, king of Poland.

FREDERICK THE GREAT *of Prussia, the imperious face of an enlightened despot.*

In the War of Austrian Succession (1740–1748), France, Spain, Saxony, and Bavaria attacked Prussia under Frederick the Great to force the succession of Maria Theresa, the rightful heir to the Austrian Hapsburg throne. Britain was already at odds with Spain and France over their respective colonies in the New World. It fought Spain in the War of Jenkins' Ear (1739–1748). It then joined Prussia in the Seven Years' War (1756–1763), a continuation of the continental power struggle, to prevent France from upsetting the European balance of power.

Britain took over most of France's colonial empire in Canada and India, and then withdrew from the continental conflict. Prussia's remarkable military machine continued to roll up victories as Frederick won Silesia. In 1772 he engineered the first of three partitions of Poland, whereby Austria, Prussia, and Russia acquired substantial Polish territory. In 1793 and 1795 Poland was split again among these powers and disappeared entirely. The Prussian empire emerged massive and dominant on the continent. Both France and Spain were weakened by their colonial struggles with Britain.

Enlightenment

For France, 1715–1789 was a period of social and political decay and intellectual ferment that ended with the overthrow of the Old Regime.

Absolutism had given France an effective government, but the system developed by Louis XIV required a vigorous and able monarch. Under his less capable successors, Louis XV (ruled 1715–1774) and Louis XVI (ruled 1774–1792), France lacked a dominant central force to unify the activities of ministers and councils. Government at all levels became a labyrinth of delay and resistance to change that stifled occasional attempts at reform.

Peasant resentment of aristocratic privilege and feudal dues, including enforced service, was perhaps exceeded by that of the bourgeoisie— merchants, bankers, and professional men—who by education and wealth had a claim to the political voice denied them. From this class came a group of vigorous dissenters and critics of the Old Regime known as the *philosophes.* They applied ideas from the Age of Reason to the new call for social and political revolution in France. Voltaire and Diderot were among the most influential of the *philosophes,* while the great Romanticist, Rousseau, supported many of their claims.

Enlightened despots. Frederick the Great of Prussia and Catherine the Great of Russia (ruled 1762–1796) were the foremost of a group of monarchs, "benevolent despots," who applied some reason, progressiveness, and justice to their rule. Both attempted to reform government to make it more responsive to their subjects'. Their aims, however, were political rather than idealistic.

Modern Europe

Europe on the eve of the French Revolution presented a deceptively tranquil appearance. Social life among the highborn had never been so brilliant. A young man of good family traveling from London to Moscow could expect to be received in much the same way everywhere.

The topics of conversation were the same everywhere—the latest literature or scientific discovery, the proper form for an enlightened government to take or, more specifically, the American Revolution. The language of educated Europeans was also universal. French was spoken in polite society in London and Moscow, as well as in Paris.

This society rested upon a firm and prosperous economic base. The Seven Years' War (1756–1763) had ended a century-long struggle between France and Britain for imperial supremacy. Britain's wealth was increasing rapidly as goods and raw materials poured in from the empire. Although the French had lost much to Britain, they still had an empire left to exploit, and France was the richest land in all of Europe.

Prussia, newly consolidated and reformed by Frederick the Great, drew strength from the efficiency of its army and civil service. The Hapsburg domains, in east-central Europe, combined the agricultural riches of the great Hungarian Plain with the urbanity of Vienna and Prague. Even Russia, which was the most backward and the least developed of the great powers, was ruled by an "enlightened" sovereign, Catherine the Great.

Aristocracy. The wealth that was so evident in the social world was firmly held by the aristocracy in all the states of Europe. It is traditional to view the French Revolution as the final conflict of power between a vigorous, intelligent middle class, the bourgeoisie, and a decadent, incompetent nobility whose only strength lay in its determination to cling to the last vestiges of its feudal heritage. Nothing could be further from the truth.

The aristocracy, far from being exhausted in the 1700's, had discovered a new vigor that permitted it to challenge both the monarchy and the rising middle class. The revolutionary movements that shook the very foundations of the traditional governments throughout the 1800's were a response to this aristocratic resurgence.

In both Switzerland and Belgium, between 1789 and 1792, aristocrats inaugurated reigns of terror against middle-class democrats who fought for equal human and political rights and independence from aristocratic con-

MARIE ANTOINETTE, *Queen of France—a proud woman—on her way to execution in 1793.*

trol. Similar events occurred all over Europe—in Poland, Holland, Italy, Prussia, and Britain.

In France, the aristocrats were finally defeated, and the Third Estate, comprising the middle class of French society, rose to power. Other Europeans watched in horror as the ruling mobs, acting with confused and savage displays, seemed to confirm their inability to exercise mature judgment in government.

The deputies of the Third Estate had formed a National Assembly and swept away the old order. But the deputies split into factions, and the split eventually contributed to making the French Revolution a general European affair.

The Girondists, the party of moderate, well-to-do burghers, in an attempt to rally the country to them and gain ascendancy over their more radical colleagues, the Jacobins, decided on war against the European powers they believed to be conspiring against the revolution.

Revolutionary Wars

On April 20, 1792, the French Revolution was internationalized when war was declared on the House of Hapsburg. By summer, the war had expanded to include Prussia and Sardinia. By 1793, Britain, the Dutch republic, and Spain were involved. It was a war that, with only brief interludes of peace, was to last until 1815—the year of the final defeat of Napoleon Bonaparte at Waterloo.

The victorious armies of the French Revolution led to the creation of republics in Italy and the Netherlands. Napoleon rose to power in France in 1799 as a champion of the revolution, but by 1804 he had proclaimed himself emperor and proceeded to expand his empire by military might. Napoleon's mighty attempt to unify all of Europe under his rule was stalled by the arousal in Germany, Russia, and elsewhere, of a national consciousness that militated against incorporation into a foreign-ruled empire. Napoleon's dream finally fell apart when he failed to capture Russia, and his army returned home, crippled and disoriented.

Congress of Vienna

It is incredible that those who had witnessed the power of unleashed nationalism and the struggle between aristocracy and democracy could, once the fighting with France was over, feel that nothing had changed. Nevertheless, at the Congress of Vienna (1814–1815), which ended the period of the revolutionary and Napoleonic wars, this was the prevalent feeling.

The participants, led by the representatives of the Big Five—Austria, Britain, France, Prussia, and Russia—all remembered the days of the old regime, the *ancien régime,* and were determined to return to them.

Except for the genius of the French diplomat, Talleyrand, who argued convincingly for a return to the previous balance of power in Europe, France would have been destroyed by partitioning among the victors.

The congress finally recreated a Europe with a proper balance of power that would supposedly permit freedom, security, and prosperity for all. France was "buffered" by the creation of the Kingdom of the Netherlands. Austria, which lost territory to the Netherlands, gained Lombardy and Venetia in Italy, and was permitted to preside over a newly organized loose confederation of 39 German states. This last concession had been insisted on by Austria's genius statesman, Metternich, who feared a strong, united Germany.

The balance of power was maintained by shuffling territories and alliances so that no one state could dominate the others. The success of the Congress of Vienna is evidenced by the fact that no major European war was fought from 1815 to 1854, a record that has hardly been equaled.

Despite its relative success, the congress totally ignored the vital issues of nationalism and liberalism. It was this shortsightedness that eventually destroyed the peace effected for some years by the settlement.

The liberal aspirations that had been created during the revolutionary era could not be eradicated by a stroke of the pen. As the groups to which liberalism appealed grew stronger, their challenge to the constituted governments became sharper, until they exploded into revolution.

Similarly, the nationalism that had been aroused by French occupation could not be turned off with the departure of the French. This was particularly true in Italy and Poland, where the withdrawal of the French was followed by occupation by the Austrians and the Russians.

Another factor that had not been taken into account was the industrial revolution. As rapid industrialization changed the social composition of Europe, it altered the bases of government and contributed to the internal instability that marked the mid-1800's.

As industrialization increased at different rates in different countries, it also altered the balance of power. At the Congress of Vienna, international power was measured by counting a country's population. By the end of the 1800's, power was measured by counting the tons of steel produced.

Industrial Revolution

The industrial revolution grew from very humble beginnings in Britain, where its first impact was felt in the area of cotton textile manufacture.

During the 1770's and 1780's a burst of inventive genius revolutionized the textile industry. From hand operations on simple machines, such as spinning a single thread or weaving only one bolt of cloth at a time, the industry progressed to multiple spindles and complicated looms.

As the machines grew larger and more complicated, they could no longer be run by human power. Instead they were run by waterpower. Ultimately, even waterpower became insufficient. The development of the steam engine by the end of the 1700's had provided a solution to the power problem by the 1800's. Its application in the steam locomotive was to revolutionize transportation.

Areas rich in natural resources but without easy access to water transportation, the only economical method of transport before the railroad, were stagnant. When rail transportation was brought to those areas, they became centers of industrial activity.

Social effects. The many social effects of the industrial revolution were as important as the material effects. It was through industrialization that western Europe was transformed from a rural to an urban civilization. Factories drew formerly rural peoples together to one spot for the purpose of production. Men, women, and children worked long hours for a salary, and labor abuse became prevalent.

THE NEWCOMEN ENGINE *of 1712 was a primitive steam engine designed to pump out flooded mines. It proved to be one of the prime movers of the Industrial Revolution in England.*

NEW YORK PUBLIC LIBRARY

This abuse, including child labor, unsafe conditions, overworking, and underpayment, led to the growth of socialism.

Cities sprang up everywhere and grew in size by leaps and bounds. Urbanization increased political awareness and activity among the masses, who, as rural peasants, had been traditionally isolated and disunited. The new industrial classes in Britain and France began gradually to undermine the power of the landed aristocracy. This was particularly true in Britain, the supreme industrial power of the world, where human labor became an important and valued resource.

France industrialized much more slowly, and in Prussia, Austria, Russia, and most of the other nations of Europe, the time for industrialization had not yet come. Most nations feared the emergence of a proletarian class that might clamor for equal rights, and of subversive democracies resembling those of the tumultuous French Revolution. Moreover, the world economy was not yet ready for industrialization, as it would be by the end of the century.

Liberalism and Nationalism

With the defeat of Napoleon and the conclusion of the Vienna settlement in 1815, Europe settled down to enjoy the calm of peace. Although each nation reacted differently to the absence of war, the essential dynamic forces in every country were the same.

In the period 1815–1848, it was the challenge of liberalism that tended to provide the greatest impetus to change. After 1848 the situation became more complicated. In some countries, notably Britain and Italy, liberalism retained its vigor. In other countries, such as France, its suppression led to the rise of socialism. In Austria and Germany liberalism was submerged in a wave of nationalism.

In Britain, the new class of industrial workers demanded representation in Parliament. The situation came to a crisis following passage of the Corn Laws, which worked to the advantage of the landed aristocracy and led to more misery for the industrial class. In 1819 riots broke out and several people were killed by government troops in the so-called "Peterloo Massacre."

In the following years, though, Parliament was finally brought around to reform. The Reform Bill of 1832 gave the industrial class much greater representation in Parliament, and by 1884 the urban workers had finally been enfranchised.

In France, the industrial class was small and weak, but tension grew when the Bourbons were restored to the monarchy by the Congress of Vienna in 1815. Both peasants and bourgeoisie were angered by the return to power of the monarch and the émigré aristocrats. When Charles X (ruled 1824–1830) sought to restore the prerevolutionary full power of church and state by revoking the liberal Constitutional Charter, revolution broke out again. The "July Revolution" of 1830 only succeeded in turning the monarchy over to Louis Philippe of the House of Orléans, although the revolution of 1848 eventually led to the establishment of the Second Republic in 1851.

The benefits of the new government of 1848 went to the bourgeoisie rather than to the industrial workers, who still lacked unity and influence. The working class, whose demands derived from the socialist, Louis Blanc, were put down by brutal force during the "June Days" slaughter. This marked the origin of socialism as an active and potent force in French politics.

In 1852, Louis Napoleon, elected president in 1851, declared himself emperor of the Second Empire. The empire worked hard to establish an industrial base, but it suffered diplomatic catastrophes, was decisively defeated in the 1870 Franco-Prussian War, and was generally unpopular and weak.

The rise of nationalism in Germany posed a constant threat to Metternich of Austria, who was trying to maintain Austrian rule over a weak and loosely organized German Confederation. The Hungarians, Italians, and Poles ruled by the Austrian Empire also seethed with discontent as nationalistic fervor rose to oppose foreign rule, especially that of Metternich's oppressive brand.

Metternich responded with determination. To keep the empire intact, he created a virtual police state and held back the growth of industrialism for fear that it would breed revolutionary discontent among the urban workers.

News of the French revolt of 1848 electrified all of Europe, and revolutions broke out everywhere. The Hungarians seized the opportunity to break away from Vienna; the Romans overthrew papal power; the Italians in northern Italy felt their day of liberation had come; revolution broke out even in Vienna.

The Metternich system appeared to be in ruins. Yet it survived. It survived because the Austrian government called for aid from the Russian czar who was only too happy to help put down a revolt. The Hungarian revolution was crushed by him, the Vienna revolutionaries were successfully intimidated, and the Austrian army was left free to punish insurgents in other parts of the empire.

The Austrian Empire remained in a state of precarious equilibrium for the rest of its life. Although it made concessions to the national spirit, it never made enough to prevent nationalistic opposition.

In Prussia, a state without a middle or industrial class, the efficient and powerful military machine was operated by both king and nobles, working together. Following the French Revolution, the state embarked on a liberal course, allowing the abolition of serfdom and granting various concessions to the free peasantry. The result was a liberal Prussian state that elicited fierce patriotism, national pride, and loyalty from all classes of people.

National Unification

A major aspect of European development in the mid-1800's was the creation of two new national states in major geographical-cultural regions—the forging of modern Germany and Italy.

An industrial middle class began to emerge in Germany in the 1840's, and in 1848 it was powerfully affected by the French revolution of that year. At the Frankfurt Assembly, which resulted, popular representation in a unified Germany was called for—but Prussian assistance would be needed to break Austria's control.

Otto von Bismarck, becoming the prime minister of Prussia in 1862, began to build a liberalized state to enlist the support of the growing working and industrial classes. A constitution, a broad franchise, and progressive social legislation followed. In 1866 he forced Austria out of German affairs, and in 1870 he rallied the nationalistic southern German states in the Franco-Prussian War against the French, who were easily beaten. Germany was at last united under strong Prussian influence.

In Italy, Cavour, prime minister of Sardinia, forged the unification of much of Italy, using liberalism as a tool for popular support in much the same way that Bismarck had done. In inciting Austria, which controlled large portions of Italy, to war in 1859, Cavour was aided by Napoleon III of France. Austria was soundly defeated, and the national patriot, Garibaldi, then succeeded in forcing Sicily and south Italy into the new union. The new nation of Italy was proclaimed in 1861, with Victor Emmanuel of Sardinia its new king.

Rebalancing of Power

The unification of Germany and Italy and the industrialization of Germany destroyed the pattern of the balance of power upon which the Vienna settlement had been made. In the years following the Franco-Prussian War, this imbalance led to a somewhat frantic search for a means to restore the former balance.

The result was a diplomatic realignment among the nations of Europe and the race for overseas wealth known as imperialism. Out of this diplomatic reshuffling came a new balance of power. It was exquisitely adjusted, but instead of preventing war it merely insured that when war came it would be long and bloody.

Germany and Austria.

It was Germany under Bismarck that first realized the full extent of the changes it had itself wrought in the European state system. Bismarck had already laid the groundwork for the decisive shift in foreign policy that he knew was necessary.

What Germany needed above all was protection against a resurgent France, which was intent on recovering Alsace-Lorraine, lost in the Franco-Prussian War. The nightmare of the Germans was the prospect of a two-front war, with Germany caught between Russia and France.

To insure his southern flank, Bismarck made a defensive treaty with Austria, which he had carefully refrained from humiliating in the Seven Weeks' War of 1866. The alliance was concluded in 1879 in secret. It guaranteed Austria-Hungary German support if attacked by Russia, and it gave Germany a similar assurance if Russia moved offensively.

Russia was Bismarck's major diplomatic concern and the most difficult country to keep within the circle of German friendship. The loss of Austria's Italian territories had turned Austrian ambitions toward the Balkans, where they collided directly with Russian interests. Russia therefore found it against its national interests to become friendly with any ally of Austria.

All that Bismarck could gain was the Reinsurance Treaty in 1887, under which Russia agreed not to support France if Germany would support Russia in the Balkans. Bismarck was dismissed in 1890, and the Reinsurance Treaty was allowed to lapse.

France and Russia.

France had learned the necessity of allies with its defeat by Prussia in 1870, and it set out to remedy the lack. France's natural ally was Russia, for the two had no areas of real conflict.

In imperial concerns, Britain was the enemy of both. In Europe, the new power of a united Germany loomed ominously before both. Furthermore, Russia was desperately seeking capital to invest in the industrial plant it was belatedly trying to build. France was as eagerly looking for good investments for its wealth.

As long as Bismarck was on the scene, he was able to prevent a Franco-Russian alliance. But as soon as he was dismissed in 1890 the two rushed to negotiate. In 1894 the Dual Alliance, bringing France and Russia together, became a reality.

Britain and Italy.

The two major states on the periphery of Europe—Britain and Italy—proved to be the most difficult to deal with diplomatically. The British felt secure behind their powerful navy and desired no permanent entanglements on the Continent.

Only when its colonial empire was threatened did Britain begin to cast about for allies. This occurred with the rapid buildup of the German navy in the 1890's and the constant German attempts to win a colonial foothold in North Africa.

By the end of the 1800's, the imperialist race had just about run its course, with France and Britain emerging the winners. Germany, demanding its place in the sun, was a threat to both these colonial empires, and it was natural for Britain and France to turn to each other. In 1904 the Entente Cordiale between Britain and France came into being, reversing a diplomatic pattern in existence since the 1300's.

Italy proved to be a special problem. Unification had brought more frustrations than achievements, and the Italians turned outward and entered the contest for colonies. The Italians were willing to sign treaties with everyone as long as they were permitted to create a colonial empire of their own.

This was the golden age of secret diplomacy, and it was not hard to become enmeshed in conflicting alliances. Italy finally allied itself with Germany and Austria-Hungary in the Triple Alliance in 1882. But a few years later, Italy's other obligations were practically to nullify its promise to support Germany and Austria.

Military plans.

The new system of alliances forced certain changes in military strategy. Germany realized that it might face a two-front war. To counter this, the Germans adopted the Schlieffen Plan.

The plan was based on two basic assumptions. The first was that the Germans could muster their armies some six weeks faster than the Russians. This would give the Germans a short but essential period in which they could fight on one front alone. The second was that France would fall rapidly if a massive assault were directed down the Atlantic coast, blocking any British intervention attempt, to strike at Paris from the rear.

These two assumptions imposed two conditions that had to be followed without fail. First, the Germans must march the moment the Russians began to mobilize; second, communications on the German right flank had to be maintained.

World War I

By the early 1900's two great power blocs faced each other. Germany and Austria-Hungary were allied in central Europe, and a French-Russian alliance, supported by British participation, faced the center of Europe.

The alliances were defensive, although there were militant parties on both sides. The French were not prepared to accept the permanent loss of Alsace-Lorraine, and there were Germans who knew this and felt that Germany should seize an advantageous moment to hammer home once more the lesson of 1870.

The Austrians were experiencing difficulties in the Balkans, where a series of petty wars had more than once brought Austria and Russia to confrontation. The Balkans were a hotbed of nationalism, and a number of small groups pledged to national liberation saw their mission in an almost messianic light.

One such group in Austrian-held Bosnia, headed by a Serbian patriot and secretly backed by Serbia, assassinated the Austrian archduke, Francis Ferdinand, on June 28, 1914, in the city of Sarajevo.

The Austrians interpreted this as the first move in a new nationalist attack on the Austro-Hungarian Empire, with Serbia playing the part Sardinia had played in Italy. Austria felt it had no alternative, if its empire was to survive, but to declare war on Serbia.

WORLD WAR I: 1914–1918

ALLIED POWERS			CENTRAL POWERS
France (1914)	Rumania (1916)	Siam (1917)	Germany (1914)
Great Britain (1914)	Portugal (1916)	China (1917)	Austria-Hungary (1914)
Russia (1914)	United States (1917)	Guatemala (1918)	Turkey (1914)
Belgium (1914)	Greece (1917)	Nicaragua (1918)	Bulgaria (1915)
Serbia (1914)	Panama (1917)	Costa Rica (1918)	
Montenegro (1914)	Cuba (1917)	Haiti (1918)	
Japan (1914)	Brazil (1917)	Honduras (1918)	
Italy (1915)	Liberia (1917)		

SOPHIA SMITH COLLECTION

DOUGHBOYS IN THE TRENCHES. *The Americans entered combat late in World War I. During the war about 10 million men were killed, mostly in the trenches.*

Outbreak. In spite of a conciliatory Serbian reply to a stiff Austrian note, the Austrians continued in their aim and declared war on Serbia on July 28. Russia, tied by treaty to Serbia, ordered a general mobilization of its armed forces. Germany felt it then had no choice, if the Schlieffen Plan was to be effective, but to throw its military machine into gear.

Germany declared war on Russia on August 1, 1914, and on France on August 3. To insure the vital communications with the right flank of the German army and to speed the attack to the English Channel, the Germans had to march through Belgium.

Belgium, a neutral, refused permission for German armies to cross its territory. The Germans denounced the treaties guaranteeing Belgium neutrality and marched into Belgium. This brought Britain into the war on August 4.

Stalemate. During the first few weeks of the war, the Germans seemed about to prove the brilliance of the Schlieffen Plan. But French armies held at the Marne River, and the war on the western front settled down to static slaughter. An advance of 100 yards was hailed as a great victory and was purchased at a cost of thousands of dead and wounded.

Machine guns and barbed wire proved a match for the infantry and artillery. All that could be done was to wait and see which side bled to death first.

In the east the situation was some-

what more fluid. The Russian military machine began to collapse, and the incredible inefficiency and unpreparedness of the Russian imperial regime became evident to all. There were shortages of munitions and supplies, and a lack of organization.

For three years it was only because the main German force was tied down in the west and the Russian peasant was willing to die for his country that catastrophe was staved off. Finally, even the peasants could take no more. The Russian armies dissolved at the front and revolution broke out in the Russian cities.

The deepest desire of most Russians was for peace, and Vladimir Lenin, leader of the Bolshevik wing of the Russian Social Democratic Party, promised peace. With brilliant tactical insights, Lenin was able to outmaneuver rivals for power and bring the Bolsheviks to control of the Russian state. The net effect of the Russian Revolution in 1917 was to remove Russia from the war and permit the Germans one more year of battle.

Victory. In early April, 1917, the United States, angered by Germany's unrestricted submarine warfare, entered the conflict on the side of the Allies, led by Britain, France, and Russia. This, together with the cumulative effects of a British blockade, brought Germany to its knees.

On November 11, 1918, the war ended and the German Empire ended with it. It remained for the victors to pick up the pieces and to try to put

Europe together again. To this end, a peace conference was convened in the great Palace of Versailles, outside of Paris.

Versailles settlement. When the representatives of the great powers met at the Palace of Versailles on January 18, 1919, it was, with few exceptions, in a grim spirit of revenge. This reflected the changes both in governments and in warfare since the Congress of Vienna had met a century before. Then wars had been made by governments, not by whole peoples, and had been considered instruments of national policy. Defeat merely closed off one avenue temporarily until the game could be played again.

World War I, in contrast, was waged on a mass basis by governments dependent on the support of their people. To gain this support, governments had to arouse mass emotions. No people could be expected to sacrifice its most vigorous generation just for some diplomatic goal or dynastic gain.

War on such a scale had to have a high moral justification, such as "to make the world safe for democracy," and it had to be directed against the forces of "evil." Only in such an atmosphere of intense and unreasoning emotion could so many millions be persuaded to believe that they were not to die in vain.

Such emotions cannot be turned on and off at will, and no statesman at Versailles could have survived if he had suggested that the past be forgotten and forgiven. The greatest bloodletting in the history of Europe had just ended, and someone had to be found guilty and punished.

The obvious candidate at Versailles was Germany, and the Treaty of Versailles contained a "guilt clause," under which the Germans were to assume ultimate responsibility for the war. All else followed from this. Germany was loaded with a reparations debt that it could not possibly pay and was stripped of its colonies. Territory in Europe was taken from Germany and given to the newly created states of Czechoslovakia and Poland.

The Treaty of Versailles was a bitter pill for the Germans to swallow, but they had no choice. The British refused to lift their blockade until Germany accepted the terms of the treaty. In June, 1919, the German representatives signed.

The recognition of the principle of nationalism was the one pure principle embodied in the treaty, but this too proved to be a failure. Instead of removing the pressures caused by intense nationalism that had served so long to disturb the equilibrium of Europe, the terms of the treaty merely served to aggravate the pressures in such nations as Germany and Italy. Both saw their nationalist ambitions thwarted by the peace settlement.

Interwar Europe

The Europe that emerged from the Versailles settlement was vastly different from the one that had gone in a carefree manner into the summer of 1914. In Russia a civil war raged that was to decimate further the Russian population. At a critical moment, Lenin suffered a fatal stroke and died in 1924. Gradually, power was gathered into the hands of Joseph Stalin, and the country sank into a new time of tyranny.

Stalin ruthlessly drove the Soviet people to industrialize the vast country. On the international front, Stalin abandoned the world crusade to carry the revolution to all countries. All energies were devoted to making the Soviet Union safe for the development of Communism.

Intellectual mood. The interwar years in both Britain and France, the two great democracies of Western Europe, were marked by a general feeling of disillusionment. Deprived of the generation that should have provided fresh leadership in the 1920's and 1930's, the two countries pursued listless and cynical courses.

The war "to make the world safe for democracy," as World War I had been proclaimed, clearly had not done so. There were still social injustices, political corruption, and national rivalries. Moreover, a new dimension had been added. World War I had to a large degree destroyed faith in reason and in the democratic process, itself founded on reason.

How could one believe in reason, given the spectacle of millions of young men being led to the slaughter by "reasonable" leaders? To buttress this despair there was the work of a generation of important thinkers who had emphasized the darker side of human nature.

Sigmund Freud had suggested before the war that man's rational nature was but a facade created to shield him from the powerful undertow of his irrational and subconscious self. Vilfredo Pareto, an Italian sociologist, had pointed out that a crowd made up of rational men did not necessarily act in a rational way. And the German philosopher Friedrich Nietzsche had declared that God was dead and that anyone who still believed in divine justice or good must be hopelessly confused.

The general mood was thus not one calculated to inspire confidence in the future of democracy. To many, the new system of the Soviet Union was a portent of the future. This in turn stimulated a reaction among those who felt that communism meant the death of civilization.

Western European society polarized into left and right, and the bitterness between the two grew more intense with time. In the center were the democrats, those who still believed that the people were capable of ruling themselves through the ballot box. The democratic faith was a delicate thing, however.

Effects of the war. World War I redrew the map of Europe. It also left bitterness and disillusionment.

Austria. The Austro-Hungarian Empire was destroyed by World War I. Hungary became a separate nation, but its new boundaries made it a relatively small one. The large non-Hungarian territories once controlled by prewar Hungary were lost.

Bohemia became part of Czechoslovakia, and the southern Slavs of the empire united with those of Serbia to form the new nation of Yugoslavia. Only the kernel of the old empire, the archduchy of Austria, was left.

Without large-scale industry, commerce, or any national resource other than the once glittering capital of Vienna, the Austrians were suddenly plunged from the position of a world power to that of a fourth-class nation easily ignored by everyone. All that was left was the bitterness of defeat and humiliation, and a strong desire by many for union with Germany.

Italy. Italy emerged from the war in frustration. In 1915 the country had finally decided to throw in its lot with Britain and France. The Italian soldier had fought bravely, but poor leadership and inadequate supplies had made the Italian front more of a liability than an asset to the Allies.

At the Versailles conference, Italy's demands were submerged in the demands of others. The Italians left Versailles convinced that they had been cheated of their just due only because they were not as powerful as Britain, France, or the United States.

This feeling of national humiliation, combined with the failure of unification to achieve any significant national or international goals, led to the rise to power in 1922 of Benito Mussolini, a young former socialist leading a national fascist movement.

At the heart of fascist political theory was a belief in the inability of the individual to run his own life satisfactorily. The leader, *il duce* in Italian, must assume the heavy burden of responsibility for the individual. As a consequence, the sickness of society would be cured.

Germany. The road back to a semblance of normal life seemed incredibly long and difficult in Germany. After a series of short but violent revolutions, the country settled down under the ill-fated Weimar Republic.

The experiment in democratic republican government suffered from a dire lack of the most essential ingredient—believers in a democratic republic. The upper classes sneered, and the lower classes looked to socialism for salvation.

Small splinter parties appeared like mayflies in the intense heat of opposition to the Weimar Republic. Among these small splinter groups was the National Socialist German Workers Party, the Nazis. Its only real resource was the oratorical talent of its leader, or *führer*, Adolf Hitler, who was an Austrian by birth.

During the 1920's the German people attempted to dig out of the ruins of defeat. Fortunes had been wiped out, savings of the solid middle class had disappeared in inflation, and the threat of socialism seemed ever present. In a class-conscious society such

HITLER VISITS MUSSOLINI *in Rome in 1938. The two dictators were uneasy partners in World War II. Italy entered the war late and surrendered to the Allies long before Germany.*

LOOK

SIGNAL CORPS PHOTO

AMERICAN TROOPS *with full equipment wade ashore on a beach in Normandy, France, on June 7, 1944, as part of the immense invasion of the Continent that led to Germany's defeat. Italy had surrendered in September, 1943, after the Allies, fighting through North Africa and Sicily, landed in southern Italy. In August, 1944, southern France was invaded.*

as that of Germany, loss of social status was the ultimate evil and to be avoided at all cost.

The great achievement of the Weimar Republic was that it staved off this possibility for a decade. But the drain of reparations payments on Germany's financial resources prevented the creation of a stable business class, and a financial collapse in 1929 that marked the beginning of the world economic depression of the 1930's effectively sealed the doom of the Weimar Republic.

Hitler drew broad support from the desperate middle class that was rapidly being absorbed into the lower echelons of society. But in spite of inflation, chaos, the weakness of the Weimar Republic, and the fear of the dissolution of society itself, Hitler and the Nazis did not win a majority of votes in the elections held in November, 1932. In fact, the Nazis actually lost seats in the German parliament, the *Reichstag.*

Hitler was brought to power by a right-wing cabal of men high in government who persuaded the president of Germany, the aged Paul von Hindenburg, to appoint Hitler chancellor. Once in power, Hitler lost no time in bringing his Nazi underlings into positions of control.

Prelude to war. Although few people realized it at the time, Hitler's advent to power was the decisive moment in the history of the first half of the 1900's. He had spelled out his pro-

gram in the 1920's in his book *Mein Kampf (My Struggle)*, in which he underlined the necessity of a German military victory in Europe to restore the honor and integrity of Germany.

National expansion was a constant theme of Nazi ideology. Its thrust rose from the dogma that the Nordic, or Germanic, peoples were scientifically a superior race, and that it was the destiny of this race to rule mankind. The Jews, according to this racist doctrine, were at the opposite end of the racial ladder, an inferior race and an obstruction to the conquering path of Nazism. As a result, Jews were excluded from social and political activities, had their religious observances outlawed, and, eventually, were taken in large numbers to specially constructed extermination centers where over 6 million of them were murdered.

Hitler boasted that his Third Reich, as he called his regime, would last a thousand years. In 1933 most people

felt that this was only bombast intended to raise popular support. After all, the Versailles settlement had created an international body, the League of Nations, to prevent just the kind of aggression that Hitler extolled.

The failure of the United States to join the league was regretted but not deemed fatal. But in the 1930's the league was tested and found wanting. Its existence did not deter Hitler from satisfying his ambitions for Germany.

Hitler saw clearly that the opposition to him was weak. Many hated him and all he stood for, yet few were willing to go to war to stop him. It was on this unwillingness to fight that Hitler based his foreign policy.

In defiance of the Versailles settlement, Hitler sent his military forces into the Rhineland. No country moved against him. Nazi war weapons were tested in support of the rebels led by Francisco Franco in the Spanish Civil War of 1936–1939. No one moved. Austria was united with Germany, and no one took action. The Sudetenland was taken from Czechoslovakia, and the Allied powers accepted it.

World War II

By 1939, it was clear that a line had to be drawn somewhere or Hitler would swallow all of Europe. Britain and France finally took a stand on the issue of Poland's territorial integrity.

Stalin recognized that Russia was unprepared for a Nazi assault should Hitler turn farther to the east and so signed a nonaggression pact with Germany that profoundly shocked and shook the communist parties throughout Europe. That pact sealed Poland's fate. On September 1, 1939, German and Russian forces began the dismemberment of Poland; on September 3, France and England declared war on Germany.

It took Hitler only a short time to defeat Poland. Then, in May, 1940, he turned against the West. The *Wehrmacht* swept by the Maginot Line in France, defeated the French armies, and forced France to surrender on June 22, 1940. The English managed to escape at Dunkirk but watched helplessly as the Nazi tide, helped by

---

WORLD WAR II: 1939-1945
Principal Combatants

ALLIED POWERS	AXIS POWERS
France	Germany
Great Britain	Italy
and the Commonwealth	Japan
Belgium	Hungary
Netherlands	Rumania
United States	Bulgaria
Soviet Union	

Italy, spread over Greece, Crete, Norway, and North Africa. The Royal Air Force fought the gallant Battle of Britain in September and October of 1940, in which Hitler and Goering had hoped to force the British to their knees. They failed.

In 1941, Hitler invaded Russia and committed the better part of his armies to this new conquest. In the same year, the Japanese attacked the United States at Pearl Harbor and thereby brought America into the war. Although the Germans and the Japanese won some sweeping early victories, the tide began to turn as American industrial might and productivity began to make itself felt. The armies of the Soviet Union, aided by winter, halted the German advance and began to push the *Wehrmacht* back. In 1944, the British and Americans invaded France. On May 7, 1945, Germany surrendered. Japan followed suit on August 14, after atomic bombs had been dropped on Hiroshima and Nagasaki on August 6 and 9.

Aftermath of war. Peace came in 1945 to a Europe that had suffered more than at any time since the barbarian invasions of Rome. A new word, genocide, was coined to describe the Nazi attempts to wipe out the Jews and other "inferior" races of Europe. The discovery that 6 million Jews and 6 million Slavs and others had actually been killed in special extermination camps shocked a world that thought it had seen every imaginable kind of cruelty. The moral foundations of Europe had been severely battered by this display of barbarism.

The physical state of Europe was no better. Strategic bombing had leveled cities, destroyed industries, and disrupted communications. Everything had to be rebuilt, including the structure of governments.

There was no coherent or unified plan for postwar Europe. The Allies held a number of meetings at Teheran, in Iran, and at Yalta, in which Churchill, Roosevelt, and Stalin discussed the problems of postwar Europe. The question of what to do with Germany was left open. All that was decided was that there would be occupation zones. The Russians were to occupy eastern Germany, whereas Britain, the United States, and France would share the western part. The occupation zones hardened into two new countries. In 1949 the German Democratic Republic was established in the east under the Russian aegis, and the German Federal Republic was created in the west, guarded by the British, French, and Americans. The creation of the two Germanies marked a larger phenomenon, the consolidation of effective Soviet rule in Eastern Europe which, in effect, became a Soviet dependency. As Winston Churchill remarked, an Iron Curtain had fallen across Europe dividing it into a communist east and a democratic west.

The political reorganization of Europe took place at the same time that attempts were being made to revive the European economy. In 1947, George C. Marshall, President Truman's secretary of state, proposed a plan for the economic recovery of Europe that involved heavy American subsidies. It was offered to all the nations that had suffered from World War II, including the Soviet Union and the countries of Eastern Europe. The Soviet Union declined and forced her satellites to go with her. The rest of Europe eagerly accepted the helping hand. The results were dramatic.

Western Europe made a rapid economic recovery, although at a different pace in different countries, and by the 1950's normalcy had been regained.

Things were quite different on the other side of the Iron Curtain. The Soviet Union was determined to compensate itself for its terrible losses in the war, and this it could do only by exploiting the lands that had fallen under its control. The countries behind the Iron Curtain were drawn into a close economic embrace, and their economies were subordinated to Russian needs. The standard of living rose with glacial slowness, a pace that was in contrast to the incredible rapidity with which the standard of living in the West shot up.

Contemporary Europe

The economic recovery of Europe had a number of important effects. The most dramatic was the move to bring some kind of economic unity to the European community of nations. In 1957, the Treaty of Rome was signed by representatives of Belgium, France, West Germany, Italy, Luxembourg, and the Netherlands, establishing a common market, a coal and steel pool, and a joint atomic energy development project. The old economic walls that had served to separate the countries of Europe began to tumble down. They did not, however, crumble in a day. France, under the leadership of Charles de Gaulle, played a leader's role, and was able to exclude Great Britain from the Common Market, although the British were not terribly eager for continental entanglements when the Common Market was first created. But, as the years went by and Britain found itself increasingly incapable of competing with her European neighbors, entry to the Common Market became more attractive. Not until 1973, however, did Britain finally join the European community.

The existence of the Common Market cast into sharp relief those countries that were not members. Spain and Portugal had been excluded because their regimes were repugnant to the original members. Fascists were simply not welcome. In 1968, Antonio de Oliveira Salazar, the dictator of Portugal for 30 years, suffered a stroke from which he did not recover. In 1974, a full-fledged revolution overthrew the authoritarian Portuguese regime and, within a year, a democratic republic emerged. Events were not so dramatic in Spain. Francisco Franco died in 1975. Spain is now a monarchy moving toward parliamentary democracy at a rapid rate. Elections in 1977 were the first free ones since the Spanish Civil War of 1936.

BOMBED HOUSES in Cologne, Germany, in 1945. The massive Allied aerial assault on Germany did great damage, but postwar studies showed that it was less effective than thought.

The economic recovery of Europe took place against the background of another worldwide and fundamentally important movement. World War II spelled the end of European imperialism. Great Britain divested itself with relative grace and ease of its once magnificent empire, which had reached the height of its glory in the late 19th century. It granted independence to its vast possessions in Asia, particularly on the great subcontinent of India (now India and Pakistan), with a minimum of military hostility between mother country and colony. The Suez Canal was relinquished, and countless small islands in the Pacific, Mediterranean, and Caribbean have been granted independence since 1960.

For France, decolonialization was much more painful. Bitter fighting occurred in Indochina until the French recognized the futility of the struggle and let it go in 1954. Algeria, which had been incorporated into metropolitan France and which sent deputies to the French Chamber of Deputies was not even considered a colony, but it, too, had to be set free. All of French Africa disintegrated into independent states in the two decades following the war. The winds of change in Africa blew hard, forcing the Portuguese, too, to free Mozambique and Angola. Decolonialization, however, did not seem to affect economic recovery. As a matter of fact, it appeared to accelerate it. Mother countries no longer had to maintain expensive armed forces or supply colonies with subsidies, and money that had previously been spent in colonial development could now be used in domestic investment.

In spite of the economic and political recovery of Europe after the war, there are serious clouds on the European horizon. The largest is the threat of Russian invasion. The Russians have maintained a serious and massive military presence in Eastern Europe since 1945. To counter this presence, the North Atlantic Treaty Organization was created in 1949. It has remained the major shield for Europe. NATO (supported by the United States) was countered by a Soviet bloc military alliance created in 1955 under the terms of the Warsaw Pact. Soviet-dominated Warsaw Pact troops are stationed throughout Eastern Europe to protect its interests.

The split between communistic Eastern Europe and democratic/capitalistic Western Europe is also economic. East European nations have coordinated their mutual economic planning as well as trading interests through the Council for Mutual Economic Assistance (Comecon). Created in 1949, it is Soviet-dominated. West European nations draw mutual economic support not only through the European Economic Community (the Common Market or EEC), but also through the European Free Trade Association (EFTA), a trading bloc cre-

TWO MARINES *on a NATO exercise, one Italian and one American, discuss a weapon.*

ated in 1960, and the Organization for Economic Cooperation and Development (OECD), developed in 1961 to promote mutual economic interests and to expand worldwide trade.

Although there is a marked political, economic, and cultural separation between Eastern and Western Europe, since the mid-1960's there have been increasing attempts to minimize these divisions, especially in the arena of international trade. Trade between the Soviet bloc nations and the Common Market has increased steadily, and in the early 1970's Willy Brandt led West Germany in its bold policy of restoring closer political ties between East and West. Other nations, in both East and West Europe, have taken steps toward breaking the boundaries, often imposed by self-interested superpowers, that have separated Europe into the two camps.

Another source of unrest in Europe is the failure to achieve a satisfactory balance between social justice and affluence. The standard of living in Europe is higher now than it has ever been, but there are still serious gaps in the distribution of wealth and welfare. The workers in England and France, not to mention Spain, Portugal, Italy, and Greece, feel cheated by the results of the economic recovery. The communist parties throughout Europe are able to exploit this feeling. Very recently, the leaders of the communist parties in Spain and Italy have insisted that they are independent of Russia and, indeed, wish to pursue a separate road to real socialism. This Eurocommunism clearly appeals to many in Europe who resent the injustices of the old system but are suspicious of Soviet Communism and its totalitarian ways.

Communist bloc nations, meanwhile, have suffered from problems of their own. In 1956, citizens and workers of Hungary agitated for more human freedoms, consumer products, and a standard of living that could compare with that of peoples in the democratic Western nations. Again in 1968, Czechoslovakia rose against its government for the same reasons. Although Soviet military force suppressed both revolutions, other Eastern nations have continued the struggle. Albania, Yugoslavia, and Rumania have followed political and economic courses that have often been at variance with the wishes of the Soviet Union. Czechoslovakian factions renewed their human rights movement in the late-1970's, and national workers' strikes have posed serious and foreboding problems in Poland since 1980. Meanwhile, a divisive controversy concerning ideological differences between Soviet and Chinese forms of communism has intensified.

The roots of discontent in contemporary Europe are overwhelmingly economic. Western European nations, highly industrialized, suffer increasingly from the higher and higher prices of imported oil, as that essential industrial fuel becomes more and more scarce. The result has been increased trade deficits as the cost of imports (derived largely from oil from the Arab states of the Middle East) rises faster than the revenues from exports (mostly manufactured goods), which become increasingly expensive to produce and ship. This has led, in turn, to a decrease in industrial investment and, consequently, output. Inflation, unemployment, and insecurity have accordingly intensified.

Eastern European nations have additional problems. Their dependence on foreign oil has led them to an increased dependence on the Soviet Union, their major supplier of fuel. The high demand for oil in these nations is the result of the extremely rapid industrialization that has taken place since World War II. Moreover, industrialization in the East has progressed largely at the expense of agricultural production and planning. Importing food, therefore, has become an additional burden on the economies of many of these nations.

The nations of Europe, broadly divided since World War II into two political camps, are discovering the need for economic cooperation in the face of worldwide recession and inflation. Moreover, the frightening threat of nuclear holocaust has come closer. Political division, colonialism, self-interest, and warfare has characterized European, as well as world, history. As the 21st century approaches, the greatest challenge directed at European governments is now to reverse these courses for the sake of mutual prosperity, and even more critically, mutual safety.

COUNTRIES OF EUROPE

Albania

Official name: *People's Socialist Republic of Albania*
Area: *11,100 sq. mi., 28,748 sq. km.*
Population: *(1980) 2,734,000*
Capital: *Tiranë (Pop., 1978, 169,300)*
Language: *Albanian*
Religion: *Islam, Orthodox Christian, Roman Catholic*
Currency unit: *Lek*
National holiday: *Liberation Day, Nov. 29*

Albania, a small nation in southeastern Europe, lies along the western coast of the Balkan peninsula. It is bounded on the north and northeast by Yugoslavia, on the southeast and south by Greece, and on the west by the Adriatic Sea. Albania is separated from southern Italy by the narrow Strait of Otranto, at the entrance to the Adriatic. Albanians call their country *Shqiperia,* or "Eagle's land."

The land. Albania is a mountainous land, and mountains cover more than two-thirds of the country. Level land is found only along rivers and near the coast. Albania's rivers are few and short, and they flow westward, to the Adriatic. Three large lakes lie astride Albania's borders—Scutari, in the northwest, and Ohrid and Prespa, in the east.

The climate along the coast is Mediterranean, with warm, dry summers and mild, damp winters. The vegetation there is of the *maquis* type—dry evergreen bushes and small trees. Farther east the rainfall is considerably higher, and part of the original forest of oak, beech, and evergreens still stands.

The people. Almost all of the people are Albanians, but there is a small Greek minority in the south, along the Albanian-Greek border. About 1 million Albanians live across the border in Yugoslavia's Kosovo-Metohija region, and about 200,000 live in Greece. The population of Albania is increasing faster than anywhere else in Europe. Between 1975 and 1980 it rose 2.4 percent. Over 60 percent of the population is rural.

The Albanians are divided into two main groups, each with its own dialect. The Ghegs live in the northern half of the country, and the Tosks live in the southern half. Most Albanians are Muslims. About 20 percent of the people are Orthodox Christians, and ten percent are Roman Catholics.

Economy. Albania's economy is controlled by the government, which directs economic life through a series of five-year plans. The government has sought to transform the country from an agricultural to an agricultural-industrial nation. Up to the early 1960's, Albania depended on the Soviet Union for economic and technical aid. Since then, it has depended on China alone.

Agriculture is the major employer of Albania's people, although there is little land that can be cultivated and soils are poor. Wheat and corn are the principal grain crops, and cotton, tobacco, and sunflowers are the main industrial crops. Large quantities of fruit are produced. Livestock includes cattle, goats, and sheep. Sheep are the most important.

Albania has considerable mineral resources, but the rough landscape makes it difficult to exploit them. The major minerals include oil, lignite, chromium, and copper.

The exploitation of minerals and also the development of hydroelectric power is essential to the nation's industrial growth, which is based on the processing of Albanian agricultural and mineral products. Oil extraction has increased rapidly since 1960, with 2.1 million metric tons of crude being extracted in 1973.

In 1976 Albania's exports earned $200 million and its imports cost $250 million. The major exports are minerals and metals and agricultural products—such as fruit, wine, and tobacco. Imports consist largely of machinery and transportation equipment. Coking coal, required in metal processing, is also an important import. Albania trades heavily with China, but trade with Czechoslovakia, East Germany, and Poland is also important.

Government. Political life in Albania is dominated by the Communist Party, officially called the Albanian Labor Party. The political bureau, or politburo, of the party's central committee determines national policy, and the first secretary of the Communist Party is actually the key figure in the government.

The Albanian constitution provides for a popularly elected legislature of one house, the People's Assembly. Assembly candidates are nominated by the Albanian Democratic Front, which is controlled by the Communist Party. The assembly chooses a small committee, or presidium, to act for it between its relatively short sessions.

The chairman of the presidium is the head of state. A council of ministers functions as a cabinet. Its chairman is equivalent to a prime minister.

Albania is a member of the United Nations.

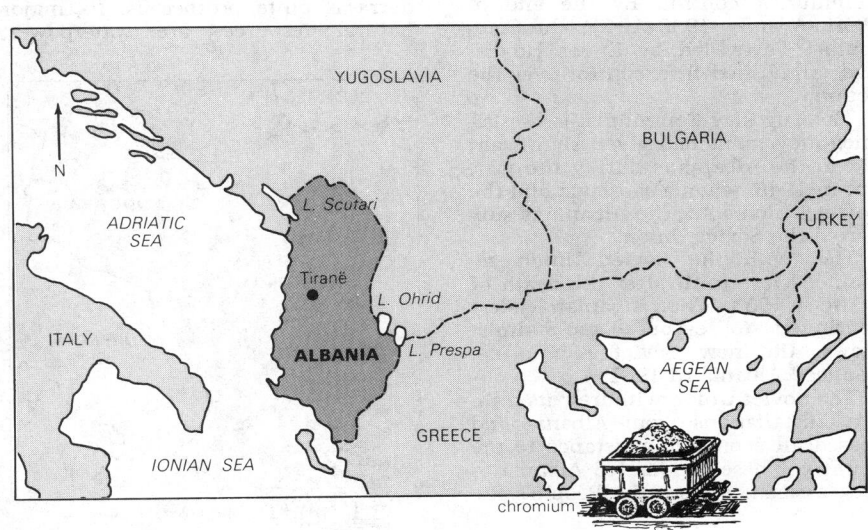

chromium

History. Illyrian tribes from central Europe migrated into the area of present-day Albania in about 2000 B.C. The region was called Epirus by the Ancient Greeks, who established colonies along the coast. In the 200's B.C., Pyrrhus of Epirus built a powerful state and in 280 he invaded Italy. He was defeated, and internal unrest led to the disintegration of the state.

Roman era. Rome conquered the Illyrian states by 167 B.C., and the region became fairly prosperous from its geographic position astride Rome's trade routes to the East. Many Albanians became prominent in Roman life, and the towns generally became Roman in culture. In 395 the Roman Empire was divided into eastern and western halves, and Albania became part of the Eastern Empire.

During the 400's A.D. a number of barbarian tribes invaded the region, and during the 600's and 700's Slavic peoples began to settle in the lowland areas. During the 800's and 900's the region was included in a Bulgarian state, but Byzantine rule was reestablished in 1018.

In 1054, a schism in the Christian Church led to a new era of conflict. Normans and Crusaders, representatives of the Western, or Roman Catholic, Church, invaded the country and fought against adherents of the Eastern, or Orthodox, Church.

The decline of Byzantium in the 1100's was accompanied by the establishment of Albanian principalities, and in 1230 by the reimposition of Bulgarian rule. During the later 1200's, the Anjou rulers of Sicily established themselves in parts of Albania, and in the mid-1300's the region was part of a Serbian empire.

Ottoman rule. The Ottoman Turks began the conquest of Albania in the 1300's, and by 1389 most of the country was under Ottoman control. Albania remained under Turkish control until 1912. There were many risings against Ottoman rule during the 1400's, and in 1443 a major rising was led by Gjergj Kastrioti (George Castriota), popularly known by his Turkish name, Skander, and title, beg ("Skanderbeg").

In 1444 a general assembly of Albanian notables created an Albanian league with Skanderbeg as president. The Albanian state collapsed after the death of Skanderbeg in 1468.

During the period of Ottoman rule, local officials, often Albanians, gained control of large areas, and they made these lands hereditary possessions. The population came to be divided into three main groups—Muslims, educated in Turkish; Orthodox Christians, educated in Greek; and Roman Catholics, educated in Italian.

In the 1800's the Ottoman Empire was near collapse, and Albania became a focal point for the ambitions of several states. Serbia and Montenegro, both part of present-day Yugoslavia,

and Greece, staked out claims to Albanian lands.

In 1912 the first Balkan War was fought against Turkey by Bulgaria, Greece, Serbia, and Montenegro. The Greeks, Serbs, and Montenegrins planned to divide Albania among themselves. But the Albanians proclaimed their independence in the city of Vlonë in November, 1912, and petitioned the great powers of Europe for recognition.

The powers agreed to the establishment of an autonomous Albanian state under the suzerainty of the Ottoman sultan, and set out the boundaries of the new state. The boundaries included only about one half the area and one half the people traditionally considered Albanian by the Albanians.

Independence. In 1913 the powers recognized Albania as an independent nation with the stipulation that it be under a ten-year period of control by them. The new nation was to be a monarchy, and the powers chose a German prince, William of Wied, to head the new state. World War I broke out in 1914, and William left the country.

After the war, Italy, Serbia, Greece, and Montenegro all put forth claims to Albanian territories. But in 1920 Albania won recognition of its full independence and membership in the League of Nations.

The new Albanian government was weak. The country was poor, most of the people were illiterate, and neighboring nations interfered in the country's troubled politics. In 1928 a regional chieftain proclaimed himself King Zog I. In 1939 Italian troops invaded Albania and on April 12 incorporated the economically depressed country into the Italian empire. Traditionally, Albanian areas in Yugoslavia (Kosovo) and in Greece (Cameria) were added to the puppet Albanian state. But Italian efforts to win Albanian support met with little success.

Communist rule. In 1942 a national resistance movement, the National Liberation Front, was organized under Communist control. By the end of World War II (1939–1945), the Communist Party, led by Enver Hoxha, had established firm control over the country.

The Yugoslav Communist-led resistance movement had given significant aid to the Albanians during the war, but in 1948, when Yugoslavia and the Soviet Union split, the Albanians supported the Soviet Union.

Ties with the Soviet Union remained close until after the death of Stalin in 1953. When Albanian leaders continued to espouse pro-Stalinist views, the new Soviet regime denounced Albania in 1961.

The Soviet Union withdrew its military installations from Albania and ceased all economic assistance to the country. These actions led Albania to seek assistance from the People's Re-

public of China. China offered extensive financial aid and trading rights to Albania, and close ties resulted.

With the death of China's leader, Mao, in 1977, however, came a clash of ideologies. The new Chinese government sought better relations with the West and Albanians charged that this moderate line was compromising the communist goal of international revolution. By 1978 China had cut all financial and military aid to Albania.

Albania withdrew from the Warsaw Pact when the Soviet army invaded Czechoslovakia in 1968. Since then, closer ties have been developing with Yugoslavia and Greece.

Andorra

Official name: *Andorra*
Area: *175 sq. mi., 453 sq. km.*
Population: *(1980) 31,000*
Capital: *Andorra la Vella*
(Pop., 1971, 8000)
Language: *Catalan*
Religion: *Roman Catholic*
Currency units: *French franc, Spanish peseta*

Andorra, one of Europe's smallest states, is a principality lying high in the eastern Pyrenees between Spain and France.

The land and people. Andorra has a rugged landscape dominated by mountains rising from 6500 to over 9000 feet and cut by steep gorges. The climate is dry and rather mild.

Andorrans are descendants of a people known to the ancient Romans. They speak Catalan, the language of Catalonia, a region in northeastern Spain. The population is 60 percent Spanish, 30 percent Andorran, and includes a French minority. Andorra la Vella, the capital, is the only large town.

Economy. Although tiny, Andorra is quite prosperous. Its major natural resources are waterpower,

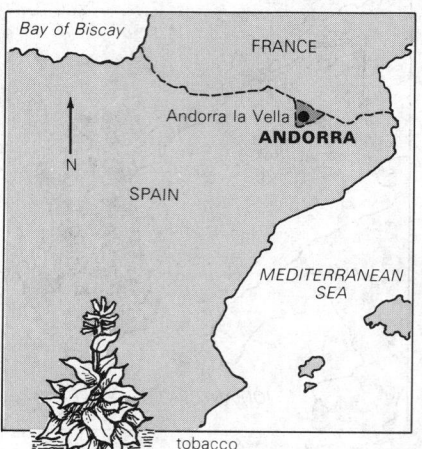

tobacco

from several lakes and the Valera River; small deposits of iron and lead; and timber. Only a small part of the land can be farmed. Rye, wheat, vegetables, and a valuable tobacco crop are grown, but Andorra depends on Spain and France for most of its food.

Tourism and trade contribute heavily to the economy. Andorra exports chiefly tobacco, cigarettes, and timber, especially to Spain and France.

Government. Sovereignty over Andorra is exercised jointly by the Roman Catholic bishop of Urgel, in Spain, and by the head of the French state. Each is represented locally by a delegate called a *viguier.* Actual government is administered by a general council elected every four years by heads of households. The council chooses a nonmember as *syndic,* or chief executive.

History. Andorra's history as a state traditionally extends back to Charlemagne, who is said to have driven the Muslims from the region. The country gained semi-independent status in 1278, when the bishop of Urgel and the French counts of Foix assumed joint sovereignty over the "Valleys of Andorra," with the right to collect tribute.

The arrangement endured, but the counts were replaced by the princes and kings of Navarre, the kings of France, and then the presidents of France. Nominal tribute is still paid to the co-sovereigns.

Because of its small size and geographic isolation, Andorra escaped involvement in modern European wars. In the 1950's and 1960's, however, the increasing importance of the tourist trade led to fuller involvement in European affairs.

Since the early 1960's, Andorra has been meeting formally with other small European states, including Liechtenstein, Monaco, and San Marino, to discuss various matters of mutual concern.

Austria

Official name: *Federal Republic of Austria*
Area: *32,374 sq. mi., 83,850 sq. km.*
Population: *(1980) 7,481,000*
Capital: *Vienna*
(Pop., 1978, 1,592,000)
Language: *German*
Religion: *Roman Catholic*
Currency unit: *Schilling*
National holiday: *Oct. 26*

Austria, a landlocked nation in central Europe, is bounded on the north by Germany and Czechoslovakia, on the east by Hungary, on the south by Yugoslavia and Italy, and on the west

MOZART'S BIRTHPLACE *in Salzburg, Austria, a charming example of Baroque architecture.*

by Switzerland and Liechtenstein. Although Austria today is a small republic, it was once the center of the mighty Holy Roman and Austro-Hungarian empires, and Vienna was until recently a cultural and intellectual capital of the entire world.

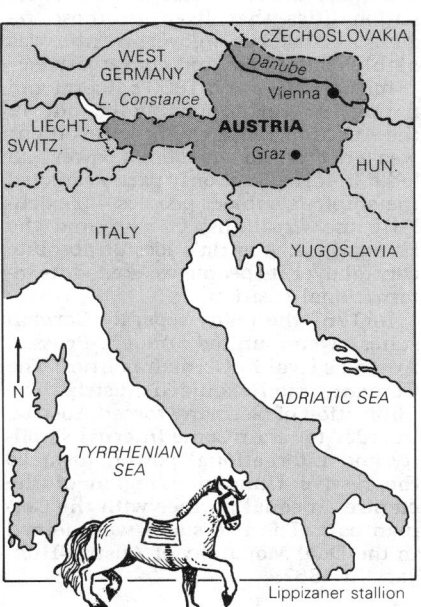

Lippizaner stallion

The land. Austria is a mountainous land. The Austrian Alps run west to east from the Swiss border and occupy nearly all of central and southern Austria. Aside from a few prosperous valleys, the Alps are rugged and barren, with many ice-covered peaks rising above 10,000 feet.

North of the Alps lies the crescent-shaped Alpine Foreland, a hilly area that grades into a forested plateau region between the Danube River and the Czech border. In the northeastern corner of the plateau is the fertile and heavily populated Vienna basin. The navigable Danube crosses northern Austria on its way to the Black Sea, and its many tributaries thread the country.

The Austrian climate varies greatly from region to region. For the country as a whole, the average temperature in January is 22°F, and in July 64°F. The Alps, however, are much colder in winter and cooler in summer than the rest of Austria. Rainfall averages between 30 and 40 inches a year.

The people. The people of Austria are almost entirely German-speaking, but there are some who speak other languages, including Croatian, Czech, and Slovene. Ninety percent of the people are Roman Catholic, and about six percent are Protestant. There is a small Jewish minority.

The most densely populated areas are on the northern and southern edges of the Alps, especially along the Danube River in the north. Vienna, in the northeast, is Austria's largest city, with over 20 percent of the country's total population. The mountainous central part of the country is sparsely settled.

The economy. Austria is a prosperous nation with an extremely low unemployment rate. Industry is the most important part of the Austrian economy, contributing 35 percent of the national product.

After World War II, heavy industry (iron, steel, and chemicals) gained steadily in importance. The overall economy, helped by financial aid from the United States under the Marshall Plan, recovered slowly until the 1970's, when it advanced sharply. Large-scale nationalization also became a postwar trend, but since the war-torn economy has recovered, private enterprise has increased.

An important factor in industrial growth has been the availability of hydroelectric power, large quantities of which are exported to neighboring nations. Austria's moderate mineral resources include iron, magnesite, lead, and copper. In 1978 1.8 million metric tons of oil were produced.

Agriculture and forestry are important in the economy. Dairying is the leading farm activity, and wheat, corn, barley, oats, sugar beets, and potatoes are the principal crops. Austria produces 85 percent of its domestic food supply.

Trade, mainly with West Germany and other western European nations, is vital to Austrian prosperity. In 1979 the country imported $20.3 billion worth of goods and exported goods valued at $15.5 billion. Imports consist mainly of machinery, foodstuffs, vehicles, electrical equipment, and textile raw materials. Exports include iron and steel, machinery, wood and wood products, and textiles. Tourism is an important source of income.

Government. Austria is a federal republic made up of nine provinces. A president, elected to a six-year term, is head of state. He appoints the chancellor, or prime minister, who heads the cabinet. The chancellor and cabinet are responsible to the lower house of the legislature. Members of the lower house are popularly elected; those of the upper house are chosen by provincial legislatures.

By the 1955 treaty restoring its sovereignty, Austria may possess only defensive weapons and must maintain neutrality in world affairs. It is a member of the United Nations and the Council of Europe, and Vienna is the headquarters of the International Development Organization of the United Nations.

History. The Danube basin was an important roadway for peoples migrating from the east many centuries ago. The Romans established military posts and settlements in the area, but by the 400's A.D. migrating Germanic tribes had forced the Romans out of the region. By about 800 the area had become part of the vast empire of Charlemagne, who made it the eastern kingdom, the "Ostmark" or "Osterreich," of his realm.

In 1282 Austria, then part of the Holy Roman Empire, became a possession of the Hapsburg family. The Hapsburgs, Holy Roman emperors for 400 years, ruled Austria for over 600 years. Through the strength of their dynasty the country achieved a position of leadership in Europe during the 1500's, 1600's, and 1700's. During that time Austria was the center of a Hapsburg empire that controlled territory throughout Europe.

The empire. In 1804, two years before the Holy Roman Empire was dissolved, Hapsburg emperor Francis II declared himself emperor of Austria and Austria itself became an empire. In the following 50 years, the Austrian Empire, led by its foreign minister, Prince Klemens von Metternich, played a major role in the series of military and political alliances that characterized European affairs during the Napoleonic and later eras.

The Austrian Empire included Galicia, Bohemia, Hungary, northern Italy, and part of the Balkan peninsula, and the many different and often restless nationalities that lived in those regions. Austria's government was highly centralized and conservative.

In the 1840's and 1850's liberal and nationalist revolutions broke out in the Austrian Empire. These rebellions weakened the government's power and led to reforms that only partly satisfied the empire's subject peoples—particularly the Croatians, Czechs, and the Hungarians. Austria's loss of absolute control over its people weakened its international position.

In 1867 the many separate German states were united under Prussia, Austria's rival in German politics. The German union excluded Austria. The unification of Germany forced Austria, in order to retain some internal stability and international power, to make the restive Hungarian region of the empire an equal partner with the German part. The two states were joined in the Dual Monarchy of Austria-Hungary in 1867.

METTERNICH, *Austrian prince and foreign minister, became the arbiter of Europe.*

Creation of the Dual Monarchy, controlled by the Germans of Austria and the Magyar people of Hungary, left the Slavic subject peoples in Bohemia and the Balkans dissatisfied. The discontent of the Slavs was an important cause of World War I, which began when a Slav from Serbia assassinated Archduke Francis Ferdinand, the heir to the Austro-Hungarian throne. Austria-Hungary declared war on Serbia, and was joined by Germany.

The German allies were defeated, and at the end of the war in 1918 the Hapsburg empire lay in ruins. In 1918 the emperor abdicated and was replaced by a provisional government. The provisional assembly declared its desire to unite with Germany, but the Allied powers prohibited Austrian-German unification by the Treaty of St. Germain (1919).

The Allies divided much of Austria's old territory among Italy, Hungary, a restored Poland, and the new states of Czechoslovakia and Yugoslavia. The treaty also proclaimed Austria a republic.

The first republic. In 1920 a permanent government was formed, and its members drafted a constitution. Austria, now a small, overwhelmingly German-speaking nation, was made a federal state with a president as chief of state and a cabinet led by a chancellor. A two-house legislature was to be elected democratically.

Two political parties dominated the republic—the Christian Socialists and the Social Democrats. The Christian Socialist Party drew its principal support from the wealthy landowners and manufacturers, the clergy, and the farmers. It favored some form of authoritarian government. The Social Democrats mainly represented the urban workers and followed a socialist program. A small, nationalistic faction favoring union with Germany grew rapidly in size during the 1920's.

The first republic faced serious difficulties from its earliest years. In 1920 the government had to use force to prevent parts of the country from seceding and joining Germany. Pressure for unification with Germany, or *Anschluss,* was to plague the republic continually. The Austrian economy was weak. It avoided total collapse only by receiving financial grants from the League of Nations between 1922 and 1925.

Party politics created the most severe problems, however. In 1926 a serious conflict opened between the Christian Socialist national government and the Social Democrats. The Social Democrats governed the province that included the capital city, Vienna, where one quarter of the country's population then lived.

In Vienna the Social Democrats had financed experimental social welfare programs for the workers by heavily taxing the rich. The conservative Christian Socialists objected strongly to these programs. The conflict, centered in Vienna, led to frequent riots. Each party had its own private army, and the riots were usually bloody.

A new Christian Socialist national government elected in 1929 set the restoration of order as its primary goal. It outlawed the bearing of arms and banned the political parties. In 1930 it signed a treaty of friendship and protection with Benito Mussolini's fascist government of Italy.

To strengthen Austria's economy the government, in 1931, tried to enter a customs union with Germany. Both countries gave up the attempt when the World War I Allies protested. Without the agreement, the Austrian state bank collapsed. The League of Nations granted funds again in 1932 on the condition that Austria would form no economic union of any kind for 20 years.

The financial crisis had seriously weakened the national government, which proved unable to handle the continuing political conflicts. The National Socialist (Nazi) Party's growing power in Germany inspired the Austrian nationalists. They held demonstrations in Austria, and in 1932 nearly succeeded in taking over the government of one province. The nationalists' strongest opposition came from the Social Democrats, and the conflict between the two parties grew violent.

Dictatorship. A Christian Socialist cabinet formed in 1932 by Chancellor Engelbert Dollfuss determined to restore order. In 1933 Dollfuss dissolved the legislature and restricted the rights of free speech, press, and assembly. He tried to ban the Austrian Nazis in 1933, but was met with firm German opposition.

Faced with the threat of a German invasion, Dollfuss made himself dictator in 1934 to strengthen his position, and in 1935 he entered into an alliance with Hungary and Italy. On July 25, 1935, however, he was assassinated by Austrian Nazis.

Kurt Schuschnigg continued the dictatorship, which relied on heavy economic aid and military protection from Italy, its only buffer against a German takeover. Domestic disorder crippled the nation, however, as nationalists and socialists bitterly attacked each other over political ideologies.

As Hitler gained the friendship of Mussolini, Nazi activity increased in Austria. In 1938 Schuschnigg was forced to recognize the Austrian Nazi party.

Anschluss. In a last effort to save Austria, Schuschnigg tried to show the world that Austrians did not want to join Germany. Hitler then began massing troops on the Austrian border. Schuschnigg resigned, and Seyss-Inquart, the Nazi minister of the interior, replaced him as chancellor. In March, 1938, Seyss-Inquart announced Austria's union with Germany and invited the German army into the country. The *Anschluss* had been accomplished.

The Allies hoped to avoid a second war by letting Hitler take Austria. In 1939, when World War II did begin, Austria, as part of Germany, shared Germany's fate. The early years of victory ended in 1945 with the defeat of the Axis, the German allies.

Contemporary Austria. After the war, Austria was divided into four zones, each occupied by one of the major Allied powers—the Soviet Union, Britain, France, and the United States.

The democratic constitution of 1920 was restored, and the Socialist and the People's parties, the more moderate successors of the prewar Social Democratic and Christian Socialist parties, formed a coalition government. The coalition avoided the destructive political conflicts of the first republic, and, with Allied aid, Austria rebuilt and expanded its economy.

Full independence was achieved in 1955 when the Austrian State Treaty was signed with the Allies, after the Soviet Union, seeking large war damage payments, was forced to withdraw its occupation troops from the nation's rich industrial regions.

Elections in 1975 gave a slight majority of legislative seats to the Socialist Party.

Belgium

Official name: *Kingdom of Belgium*
Area: *11,781 sq. mi., 30,513 sq. km.*
Population: *(1980) 9,920,000*
Capital: *Brussels (Pop., 1978, urban area, 2,216,938)*
Language: *Flemish, French*
Religion: *Roman Catholic*
Currency unit: *Franc*
National holiday: *Independence Day, July 21*

Belgium, a small nation in western Europe, is bounded on the north by the Netherlands, on the east by West Germany and Luxembourg, on the south by France, and on the west by the North Sea.

In 1922 Belgium and Luxembourg formed an economic union that abolished the customs frontier between them. The union was dissolved in 1940, but was reestablished in 1945. In 1948 a customs union went into effect linking Belgium and Luxembourg with the Netherlands, which is known as the Benelux Customs Union. Full economic union of the three countries has existed since 1960.

The land. Most of Belgium consists of low-lying plains. In the southeast, however, the country is quite hilly, and this highland wood and pasture zone—the Ardennes—is rather sparsely settled. The main rivers in Belgium are the Schelde, the Sambre, and the Meuse.

Belgium has little variation in climate. Its mild winters and cool summers are characterized by light rainfall, high humidity, and partial cloudiness. In the southwest, however, the higher elevations cause somewhat cooler summers and distinctly colder winters, and the precipitation is much heavier.

The people. The country can be nearly evenly divided linguistically, and, to a certain extent, culturally, by an east-west line. In the north are Flemings, who make up about 55 percent of the population. They speak Flemish, a language closely related to Dutch. In the south, French-speaking Walloons are dominant. Brussels is bilingual. Flemish and French are the official languages, and both are used for highway and other signs, public

announcements, and official documents. Belgium is overwhelmingly Roman Catholic.

The relatively stable population is one of the densest in the Western world, with 842 people per square mile. It is 95 percent urban.

Economy. Belgium is an important industrial nation that manufactures significant amounts of refined copper, pig iron, steel, and textiles. While there are important coal mines in Belgium, the nation is overly dependent on expensive foreign oil imports. **Industry.** The western cities, of which Ghent is the largest, specialize in textiles and food processing. Antwerp's industries, with access to the endless variety of raw materials unloaded at its great port, range from diamond cutting to smelting and shipbuilding.

Brussels concentrates on a wide variety of light industries. The coal-rich Sambre-Meuse area contains the country's heavy industry. Metallurgy and metal fabrication are important and cement, glass, chemicals, rubber goods, and paper are all produced there in large quantities.

Agriculture. Although agriculture now plays a secondary role in Belgium's economic life, employing only a small share of the labor force, the country's farms meet about 80 percent of domestic food requirements and provide an important share of raw materials for industry.

Trade. International trade is of great importance to the country, and Belgium has a sizable merchant fleet. Antwerp, on the river Schelde, is one of Europe's busiest ports. Belgium and Luxembourg trade as a unit, and in 1979 their exports earned $56.3 billion, and their imports were valued at $60.4 billion.

Major exports include iron and steel products, machinery, chemicals and pharmaceuticals, and textiles. Major imports include textiles, chemicals, machinery, and petroleum. Exports go chiefly to the Netherlands, West Germany, France, the United States, Britain, Italy, and Switzerland. The principal suppliers of imports are West Germany, France, the Netherlands, the United States, and Britain.

Government. Belgium is a constitutional monarchy. The king is head of state. Executive power is exercised by the king and his ministers. No act of the king is effective, however, unless countersigned by a minister. Ministers are appointed by the king from among the members of the majority party in Parliament, and they are responsible to Parliament. Since World War I, the government has been headed by a prime minister, who coordinates national policy.

Legislative power is exercised by the Parliament, which consists of two

houses, the Senate and the Chamber of Representatives, and by the king, who sanctions and promulgates the laws. Members of the Chamber of Representatives are popularly elected on the basis of proportional representation. The Senate members are partly directly and partly indirectly elected every four years.

Belgium is a member of the United Nations, the Common Market, the North Atlantic Treaty Organization (NATO), the Organization for Economic Cooperation and Development (OECD), and the Western European Union.

History. The Belgae, or Belgians, were one of the Gallic tribes conquered by Julius Caesar in the first century B.C., and the area that is now Belgium became part of the Roman Empire. Roman occupation was followed by invasions of Franks between the 200's and 400's A.D. After 476 Belgium was ruled by the Merovingians, and later it became part of Charlemagne's empire (800–843).

During the Middle Ages, Belgium existed as a group of duchies, which in 1384 came under the control of the dukes of Burgundy. Belgium passed to the Hapsburgs through marriage in 1477 and subsequently became part of the Holy Roman Empire. On the resignation of the Holy Roman Emperor Charles V in 1556, Belgium, along with the Netherlands, passed to Philip II of Spain.

The northern provinces of the Netherlands, or Holland, formed the Union of Utrecht and declared their independence in 1581. But the provinces that constitute modern Belgium continued to be ruled by Spain and then by Austria (1713) until conquered by France in 1792.

Belgium became part of Napoleon's empire in 1801. The Congress of Vienna (1814–1815), which redrew the map of Europe after Napoleon's defeat, united Belgium with Holland in the Kingdom of the Netherlands.

The union failed to take into consideration the difference in character between the two regions, however. Holland was Protestant, Germanic, agricultural, and commercial, whereas Belgium was Roman Catholic, French-oriented, and industrial. Holland favored a policy of free trade, and Belgium sought high tariffs to protect its industry.

Independence. In 1830 the Belgians revolted. King William I sent Dutch troops into Brussels to suppress the revolution, but they were unsuccessful. A provisional government was established, and Prince Leopold of Saxe-Coburg-Gotha was elected king. Within a year, after several conferences, the Great Powers recognized the independence of Belgium and in 1839 guaranteed its neutrality.

Under Leopold I, who ruled from

1831 to 1865, Belgium's economy expanded rapidly, and under Leopold II (1865–1909) Belgium acquired a vast empire in Africa. By the end of the 1800's, Belgium had transformed itself from an oligarchy governed by a small middle class to a democracy based on universal suffrage with very advanced social welfare programs.

Belgian neutrality was violated by Germany during both World War I and World War II. German troops first entered Belgium on August 4, 1914, after Germany repudiated the treaty guaranteeing Belgian neutrality. The resulting destruction and death toll were enormous, and the country was plundered to the extent that the people were reduced to starvation.

Belgian war damage amounted to more than $7 billion. The tremendous cost of reconstruction after the war caused a rapid rise in the national debt, inflation, and other financial problems that were to plague the country for almost 20 years. Economic problems increased demands for social legislation, and popular dissatisfaction was expressed politically. As a result, the interwar period was characterized by a series of short-lived governments.

During World War II, the Germans attacked Belgium on May 10, 1940. On May 28, King Leopold III surrendered to avoid further bloodshed. It was felt, however, that his early surrender weakened Allied strategy. The patriotic feelings of many Belgians were outraged, and Leopold was deposed. The second German occupation was far worse than the first. Material damage was more extensive and many more lives were lost.

After World War II, the Belgians voted, on March 12, 1950, to recall King Leopold to the throne. Socialist opposition proved so bitter, however, that Leopold abdicated on June 16, 1951, in favor of his son, who became King Baudouin.

Contemporary Belgium. Early during the postwar period, Belgium recognized the pressing need for economic cooperation among the nations of Europe. It was a founding member of the European Monetary Agreement (1950), the European Coal and Steel Community (1951), and the European Economic Community (1958). In 1957 Belgium, along with five other nations, signed the treaty establishing the Common Market.

One of the main concerns of the government during the 1950's was the increasing political unrest in the mineral-rich Belgian Congo. Independence was granted to the Congo on June 30, 1960, and the loss of this important market and source of raw materials dealt a severe blow to the Belgian economy.

Since the early 1970's, nearly two-fifths of the national labor force has been employed in manufacturing, and half of the national product has come from exported manufactured goods.

High imported oil prices have brought high unemployment rates (over seven percent in recent years) and increasing trade deficits for Belgium, which boasts one of the highest trade volumes per capita in the world.

The long-standing hostility between French and Flemish-speaking Belgians, which caused the resignation of several governments in the 1960's, have resulted in a reversal of the government's original centralization policy. Three autonomous and politically equal regions were created by constitutional revision in 1971—French-speaking Wallony, Flemish-speaking Flanders, and the bilingual Brussels region.

Bulgaria

Official name: *People's Republic of Bulgaria*
Area: *42,823 sq. mi., 110,912 sq. km.*
Population: *(1980) 9,007,000*
Capital: *Sofia (Pop., 1978, 976,015)*
Language: *Bulgarian*
Religion: *Orthodox Christian*
Currency unit: *Lev*
National holiday: *National Liberation Day (anniversary of the socialist revolution), Sept. 9*

The People's Republic of Bulgaria, a nation in southeastern Europe, occupies the northeastern corner of the Balkan peninsula. It is bounded on the north by Rumania, on the east by the Black Sea, on the south by Turkey and Greece, and on the west by Yugoslavia.

The land. Mountains and plains alternate in Bulgaria to form four major geographical regions. In the north is the Danube basin, a low, fertile plateau crossed on the north, at the Bulgarian-Rumanian boundary, by the Danube River.

At the eastern end of the Danube basin is the Dobruja, a large limestone plateau region. To the south of the basin, arching southeastward from Bulgaria's northwestern corner to the Black Sea, are the Balkan Mountains (the Stara Planina), ranging from 3000 feet to over 7000 feet in elevation. The entire southwestern corner of the country is also mountainous, with the Rila, Pirin, and Rhodope ranges rising to over 9000 feet.

Between the two mountainous regions, in central Bulgaria, is the basin of the Maritsa River. At its eastern end, the basin widens and opens into the Black Sea. At its western end is the heartland of Bulgaria, the Sofia Basin. The basin is one of the great crossroads of the Balkan peninsula, connected by river valleys to the Danube on the north, the Morava River in Yugoslavia on the west, and the Aegean Sea on the south.

The Bulgarian climate varies from region to region. The Danube plateau has cold, snowy winters and hot summers. The Maritsa basin, farther south, is protected by the mountains to the north and has milder winters. The mountains throughout the country tend to have harsher weather, with yearly variations in temperature and rainfall.

The people. Nearly 90 percent of the people are Bulgarians. They speak Bulgarian, a south Slavic language, and use an alphabet similar to the Russian. The larger minority groups include Turks, Macedonians, Rumanians, Armenians, and gypsies. Most of the people belong to the Bulgarian Orthodox Church, an independent Eastern Christian body. Islam is the largest minority religion.

Population is densest in the Sofia Basin, especially around Sofia, the capital, which is a rapidly growing industrial center as well as the administrative and intellectual heart of the

country. Other large urban centers are Plovdiv in the Maritsa valley; Varna and Burgas, the leading Black Sea ports; and Ruse, the largest Danubian port.

Economy. Bulgaria's economy, traditionally based on agriculture, was industrialized rapidly under Communist leadership in the post-World War II era. This process, aided by the nation's good supply of natural resources (including coal, uranium, iron ore, lead, zinc, copper, and manganese) has led to a serious decline in agricultural output without a significant rise in the national standard of living.

Agriculture, almost entirely collectivized now, has dropped sharply in significance. By 1975 it accounted for only 20 percent of the national product and 24 percent of the labor force. These figures were 33 percent and 55 percent, respectively, in 1960. Part of the problem is the relatively low yields that even the rich soils of the Danube and Maritsa basins now produce. Since 1970, agricultural-industrial complexes have become a major target of Bulgaria's economic planning.

Wheat and corn are the leading cereal crops, while tobacco, sugar beets, cotton, and soybeans are also important crops. Livestock, fishing, tourism, and forestry are other significant contributors to the economy.

Industry, totally nationalized since 1947, now accounts for over half of the national product. Close economic ties have existed with the Soviet Union since 1947, and Bulgaria's industry is dependent on Soviet-imported petroleum, which is rising tremendously in price.

The nation's leading industries include metalworking, oil refining, iron and steel production, machinery manufacture, chemical production, and electricity production. The traditionally important light industries, including textiles and weaving, leather

BULGARIA, *of all the iron curtain countries of Eastern Europe, is the most fervently Communist, and perhaps the least known to the West. Yet like all Russia's satellites, it has rapidly modernized itself, as this striking view of a Black Sea resort suggests.*

tooling, woodworking, and tobacco processing, thrive on a smaller scale.

Bulgaria's international trade increased greatly since the 1950's, and in 1979 imports cost $8.5 billion and exports earned $8.8 billion. Farm products, especially tobacco, are the leading exports, and clothing, fruits, and ship parts are also important. Leading imports are machinery, fuel, minerals, metals, and raw materials.

Over 75 percent of Bulgaria's trade is with other communist countries, but since 1970 economic ties with the West, especially Britain, have increased considerably.

Government. The Communist Party dominates Bulgarian political life. At the head of the party is a central committee, whose political bureau, or politburo, determines policy. The first secretary of the party is normally the key figure in government.

The constitution formally vests governmental powers in the popularly elected National Assembly. But assembly candidates are nominated by the Fatherland Front, a mass organization controlled by the Communist Party. The National Assembly elects an executive committee, or presidium, to function for it between its short sessions. The chairman of the presidium is the official head of state. The assembly also elects a council of ministers, or cabinet, and its chairman, the prime minister.

Bulgaria is a member of the United Nations, the Council for Mutual Economic Assistance (Comecon), and the Warsaw Pact.

History. Bulgaria's location has made the country subject to competing Slavic, Byzantine, Ottoman Turkish, and West European influences, and Bulgaria's history has been marked by frequent conquest and domination by foreign powers. Present-day Bulgaria was part of the Roman Empire by the middle of the first century A.D. By the 500's, a variety of Slavic tribes had settled in the region.

In the 600's the Bulgars, a warlike people from the northern shores of the Black Sea, conquered the Slavs and settled in the territory. By the 700's the Bulgars had organized a state, the first Bulgarian Empire, and for the next 100 years they resisted conquest by the Byzantine Empire. In 817 a Bulgarian-Byzantine treaty established peace between the two nations.

During the mid-800's, under Emperor Boris, the Bulgarian Empire reached its height. Boris consolidated his power by putting down rebellious nobles, and his armies conquered new territory. During that time the Bulgars were converted to Christianity. In the late 900's Bulgarian territory began to fall to Byzantine armies, and by 1018 the entire nation had been conquered.

During the 1100's, when the Byzantine Empire had begun to disintegrate, a second Bulgarian empire was established. By the 1200's it had become a great power.

Ottoman rule. The brief period of brilliance and expansion of the second empire was followed by 500 years of rule by the Ottoman Turks. Under the Ottomans, Bulgaria was isolated from both the Western and the Slavic worlds. Ottoman control of the country was complete, and only those Bulgarians who became Muslims could achieve positions of authority. But life for the peasants—the bulk of the population—was probably no more difficult than under Bulgarian rulers.

During the second half of the 1800's, Bulgarian nationalism became an active force. The Ottoman Empire had become weak, and Bulgarians were able to assume greater control over their own affairs. They established a national school system, an active press, and a newly independent Bulgarian church. In 1876 a revolt against the Turks was crushed with vicious ferocity. This provided Russia, an enemy of the Ottomans, with an excuse to go to war with Turkey in 1877.

Independence. Russia was victorious, and in 1878 the Treaty of Berlin granted independence to the principality of Bulgaria, the northern section of present-day Bulgaria. The southern two-thirds, known as Eastern Rumelia, received independence separately. The area remained the center of international political and territorial disputes, however, until 1885, when the two regions were united as Bulgaria.

The new nation was governed by nationalist leaders until 1908, when Prince Ferdinand proclaimed it a kingdom. In the years between 1886 and 1912, Bulgaria made substantial economic and political progress under a democratic constitution. Domestic progress was jeopardized by territorial quarrels, however. Bulgaria claimed Macedonia from Serbia and Greece, Thrace from Greece and Turkey, and southern Dobruja from Rumania.

These territorial disputes led, in 1912, to the first Balkan War, which Bulgaria and its Balkan allies won against Turkey. In the second Balkan War, in 1913, Bulgaria lost territories to its former allies, Greece and Serbia, and to Rumania and Turkey. When Germany and Austria promised the return of these territories, Bulgaria sided with them in World War I. Germany and its allies lost the war, and the 1919 Treaty of Neuilly forced Bulgaria to cede still more territory—to Yugoslavia, Greece, and Rumania.

The losses embittered Bulgaria's domestic politics and foreign relations during the decades between the two world wars. Relations with Greece and Yugoslavia were especially uneasy, and border disputes were frequent. Resentment within Bulgaria led to the loss of many social and economic gains. Premier Aleksandr Stamboliski, the effective political leader of the time, instituted many reforms, but his methods were unpopular and aroused further resentment.

In 1923 a militant nationalist organization, IMRO (Internal Macedonian Revolutionary Organization) helped overthrow the Stamboliski government. IMRO played a large part in precipitating a series of government crises during the next ten years. After a decade of disorder, the military seized control in 1934.

A second coup staged by the king took place in 1935. The king suspended the constitution and made himself a dictator. Bulgaria's continuing territorial ambitions and close trade ties with Germany brought it into World War II on the German side in 1941.

Communist rule. Toward the end of the war, in September, 1944, the Soviet Union declared war on Bulgaria, and within a week Soviet forces occupied the country. In 1945 elections were held under Communist rule, and a government dominated by the Communist-controlled Fatherland Front came to power.

Bulgarians voted in 1946 to abolish the monarchy, and by the end of 1947 Communist rule was absolute. The nationalistic Bulgarian Communists who had organized the republic gradually were replaced by those controlled from the Soviet Union.

Under close Soviet scrutiny, Bulgaria was rapidly converted into a modern industrial state. Although close political and economic ties remain with the Soviets, relations with the West have vastly improved in recent years.

In November, 1989, Todor I. Zhivkov, the head of Bulgaria's Communist Party since 1954, was removed as president and party chief. His successor, Petar T. Mladenov, called for restructuring of Bulgaria's political and economic systems. Most of Bulgaria's old-line Communists were subsequently removed from power, and in early 1990 the Bulgarian parliament voted to end the Communist Party's political monopoly.

Czechoslovakia

Official name: *Czechoslovak Socialist Republic*
Area: *49,370 sq. mi., 127,870 sq. km.*
Population: *(1980) 15,300,000*
Capital: *Prague
(Pop., 1978, 1,173,031)*
Language: *Czech, Slovak*
Religion: *Protestant, Roman Catholic*
Currency unit: *Koruna*
National holiday: *Liberation Day,
May 9*

The Czechoslovak Socialist Republic is a landlocked nation in east-central Europe. It is bounded on the north by Poland, on the east by the Soviet Union, on the south by Hungary and Austria, and on the west by West Germany and East Germany.

The country consists of three historic regions—Bohemia, or Czečy, in the west, Moravia in the center, and Slovakia in the east. These regions were united in 1918 to form the state of Czechoslovakia.

The land. Uplands predominate in Czechoslovakia's terrain. In Bohemia, the western third of the country, the rolling plateau of the Bohemian Quadrangle is rimmed with mountains. The Bohemian Forest in the southwest, the Erz (Ore) Mountains in the northwest, and the Sudeten range in the north all rise above 4000 feet, and the hills of the Czech-Moravian Uplands (Ceskomoravskă Vysočina) form the eastern limit of the plateau. The Elbe River and its tributaries drain the entire region. Flowing northwest, the Elbe provides a route to the North Sea.

Moravia, in central Czechoslovakia, is a wide passageway of river valleys and low hills drained by the Morava and Oder rivers. The Morava flows south toward the Danube River, which provides access to the Black Sea. The Oder flows north toward the Baltic.

Higher mountains rise in Slovakia, the eastern third of the country. The Carpathian range reaches a peak of more than 8000 feet. From this mountainous core a series of lower ranges, hills, and plateaus descends toward lowlands in the southeast.

Czechoslovakia's climate is moderate, with temperatures averaging about 70°F in summer and 20°F in winter. Between 20 and 40 inches of rain fall each year, most of it in the winter.

The people. Slightly less than two-thirds of the people are Czech, and just under one-third are Slovak.

RICHLY DECORATED HOUSE *in Slovakia, the easternmost and least developed region of Czechoslovakia. The people speak Slovak, one of the two official languages. The other is Czech.*

There are small groups of Hungarians, Ukrainians, Germans, and Poles. Czech and Slovak, the official languages, are West Slavic tongues.

Slovaks are concentrated in the east, Czechs in the center and west. Friction between the two groups has created serious problems.

Population is densest in central Bohemia, especially around Prague, the capital, largest city, and cultural and economic center of the country.

Economy. Czechoslovakia is one of the most prosperous countries in eastern Europe. Its prosperity stems largely from industry, which is based on the country's location along many excellent transportation routes, its industrious and skilled population, and its rich natural resources.

Agriculture. Although there is rich soil, agriculture is limited to the lowland areas and contributed only ten percent to the national product in 1975. Most of the land is cultivated by collective farms. The limited amount of good farmland is partially compensated for by the use of advanced agricultural techniques.

Wheat, rye, barley, oats, sugar beets, and potatoes are the leading crops. Meadows and fields devoted to fodder crops support large herds of livestock.

Industry. Czechoslovakia is one of eastern Europe's most industrialized nations, and in 1975 industry contributed 63 percent of the national product. All large-scale industries and businesses are government-operated.

Chemicals, iron and steel, heavy machinery, and electricity are the country's major products.

The country has rich mineral resources, especially coal and pitchblende (used to process uranium and radium). Jachymor is Europe's leading source of pitchblende. There is also a direct oil pipeline from the Soviet Union to Czechoslovakia, with a second one under construction. Czechoslovakian industry relies heavily on this Soviet oil, but its price is rising sharply.

Trade. In 1979 imports cost $14.3 billion, and exports earned $13.2 billion. Iron, steel, machinery, and chemicals are the leading exports, and fuel oil, raw materials, and foodstuffs are imported. The Soviet Union is the country's leading trading partner, followed by other eastern European states. In the early 1960's, however, trade began to be expanded with some western European, Asian, and African countries.

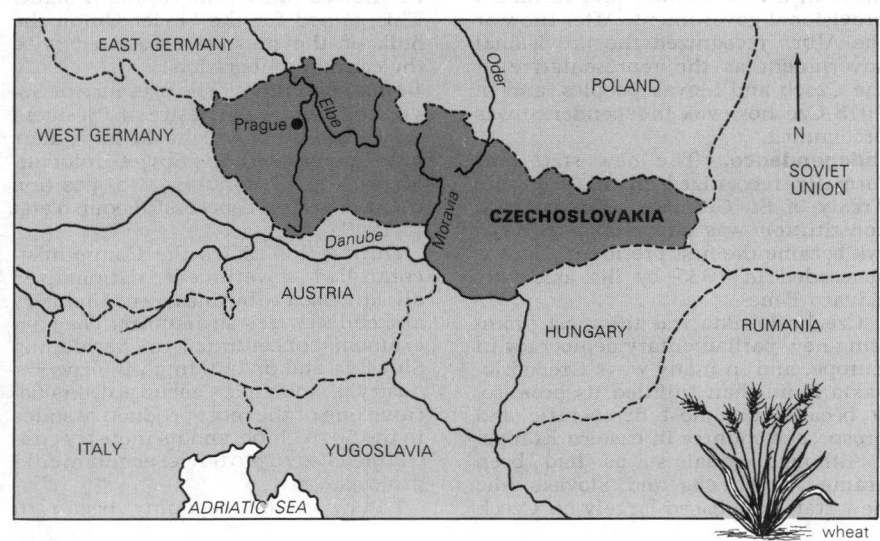

EAST GERMANY
WEST GERMANY
Prague
Elbe
Oder
POLAND
N
SOVIET UNION
Morava
CZECHOSLOVAKIA
Danube
AUSTRIA
HUNGARY
RUMANIA
ITALY
YUGOSLAVIA
ADRIATIC SEA
wheat

Government. The Czech Communist Party dominates political life. At the head of the party is a central committee whose presidium, or executive committee, determines national policy. The first secretary of the central committee is the key political figure in the country.

In 1969 a new constitutional law established a federal republic composed of the Slovak Socialist Republic and the Czech Socialist Republic. Each has its own prime minister and cabinet. Both republics send representatives to the bicameral national legislature, made up of The House of People and The House of Nations.

Czechoslovakia is a member of the United Nations, the Council for Mutual Economic Assistance (Comecon), and the Warsaw Pact.

History. Czechoslovakia first came into existence as a single independent state in 1918. Prior to that, the history of the Czechs of Bohemia and Moravia and that of the Slovaks differed, but each was characterized by domination by other nations.

The basins of the Elbe, Oder, and Morava rivers, protected by the surrounding mountains, had been settled by Slavic peoples by the 500's. By the 600's some tribal and geographical distinctions had been made between Czechs, Moravians, and Slovaks.

Moravia developed most quickly, and by the end of the 800's Moravian princes ruled an empire that included Slovakia and parts of present-day Austria and Hungary. Moravian subjects became Christians during the 800's. In the early 900's, the Moravian empire was conquered by the Magyar people of Hungary.

Hungary ruled Slovakia and the eastern part of old Moravia for 1000 years, until the defeat of Austria-Hungary in World War I. The Czech tribes of Bohemia were gradually united during the 800's and 900's. By the end of the 900's, one leader ruled Bohemia and western Moravia.

In the 1000's the kingdom of Bohemia became part of the Holy Roman Empire, but its military power and political strength were great enough to permit the state a great deal of independence. Its wealth, prestige, and cultural and political leadership reached a peak in the 1300's, when Prince Charles of Bohemia became Holy Roman Emperor.

Hapsburg rule. During the 1400's, especially after the execution in 1415 of a Bohemian religious reformer, John Hus, conflict within Bohemia and between Bohemia and the empire led to a gradual decline in the kingdom's prestige. In 1526 a Hapsburg of Austria was elected king of Bohemia, and in 1547 the Bohemian crown became the hereditary possession of the Hapsburgs, who ruled Bohemia together with Austria and Hungary. The

Hapsburgs also ruled the Holy Roman Empire.

The Bohemian nobles resented the Hapsburg king, not only because he was not a Czech, but also because he was a Roman Catholic and during the late 1500's many Bohemians had become Protestants. In 1618 the Bohemian nobles rebelled. The rebellion raged for two years, until 1620, when the Bohemian rebels were defeated at the Battle of White Mountain, near Prague.

Through the 1600's and 1700's Bohemia was included in the Hapsburg Holy Roman Empire, which was succeeded by the Hapsburg-ruled Austrian Empire. Catholic German rule impoverished Bohemia and crushed Czech spirits and Czech prospects. In the early 1800's the pan-Slav movement developed in Bohemia and Slovakia, and in 1848 it contributed to a Slavic revolt against the German-speaking Austrians.

The rebellion was put down by 1849, but the movement gained strength as Austria lost power to Prussia and gradually relaxed its rule. In 1867 Austria's reception of the Magyars of Hungary into an equal partnership in a dual Austrian-Hungarian monarchy served to spur the Slavic independence movement. By the last decades of the 1800's, Austria-Hungary's encouragement of industrialization in Bohemia had made the Czechs among the most prosperous people of Europe.

Austria-Hungary went to war with Serbia in 1914, and World War I began. The Czechs were economically, emotionally, and politically ready to take advantage of the turmoil the war caused in Austria-Hungary. Czech and Slovak soldiers surrendered independently to the Allied armies and fought against Austria-Hungary, thus winning support in the Allied countries for their independence movement.

During the war Tomáš Masaryk, the leader of the Czech national movement, and Slovak leaders agreed to unite in a new country and formed a provisional government. After the war the Allies recognized the provisional government as the representative of the Czech and Slovak peoples, and in 1918 Czechoslovak independence was proclaimed.

Independence. The new state was formally recognized in 1919 in the Treaty of St. Germain. A democratic constitution was adopted, and Masaryk became the first president. He was succeeded in 1935 by his associate, Eduard Beneš.

Czechoslovakia was the most promising new parliamentary democracy in Europe, and in many ways Czechoslovakia more than fulfilled its promise. It became the most democratic and prosperous country in eastern Europe.

Although equal status had been granted to Czechs and Slovaks, the new state was based largely on Czech

political and economic leadership centered in Prague. The Slovaks, after 1000 years of rule by Hungary, were not as advanced as the Czechs politically or economically.

Friction between Czechs and Slovaks mounted over political, economic, religious, educational, and social issues. To these difficulties was added the dissatisfaction of a sizable German minority included in the new state. The Germans, concentrated in the strategic Sudeten region of northwestern Czechoslovakia, resented rule by Czechs and Slovaks, whom they had dominated for centuries. They charged discrimination and claimed they had no real voice in government.

The problems of Czechs and Slovaks and of Slavs and Germans might have been solved if Adolf Hitler and the Nazi party of Germany had not taken advantage of the German minority's dissatisfaction. Suffering the effects of the world economic depression of the 1930's and excited by Hitler's brand of German nationalism, Sudeten Germans served as German agents within Czechoslovakia. Their complaints and Hitler's diplomatic and military pressures created a severe international crisis that led in 1938 to the Munich agreement.

Britain and France agreed at Munich to the division of Czechoslovakia and the transfer of one-third of its population and its vital defenses to Germany. Poland and Hungary also took areas they had long claimed. In return, Hitler promised to leave untouched the remainder of Czechoslovakia. In 1939, despite this promise, German troops occupied the rest of Czechoslovakia.

During the war, a major Czechoslovakian resistance movement was organized in which Czechoslovakian Communists played a prominent role. In 1944–1945 Soviet troops liberated Slovakia, Moravia, and most of Bohemia from the Germans. U.S. forces liberated western Bohemia in 1945, but the Soviets insisted that Soviet troops be allowed to free the capital, Prague. This gained for the Soviet Union the bulk of the prestige associated with the country's liberation.

Communist rule. The presence of Soviet troops and the desire of President Beneš and other Czechoslovak leaders to cooperate with the Soviet Union allowed the Communists to position themselves for a successful coup d'etat in 1948.

During the 1950's the Communist-controlled government nationalized all large-scale business and industry and collectivized agriculture. The government concentrated on developing Slovakia and on building up heavy industry in Bohemia. Czechoslovakia became one of the most productive states in the Soviet bloc, and its industry contributed heavily to Soviet economic aid projects.

Later, as the economy began to

slump, Czech Communist Party Chairman Alexander Dubcek led a movement in the 1960's to establish a humanistic-socialist democracy in which Slovakian autonomy would be recognized. As the movement reached its height in 1968, Soviet and other Warsaw Pact forces invaded, and the reform movement was crushed.

In the late 1980's, a movement for political and economic reform swept through Eastern Europe. In November, 1989, massive demonstrations held throughout Czechoslovakia forced the resignation of the hard-line Communist leadership. The new party leadership called for free elections, paving the way for a multiparty democracy. Vaclav Havel, a playwright and opposition leader, became the new president. Alexander Dubcek was chosen by the Czechoslovak parliament to be its new chairman.

Denmark

Official name: *Kingdom of Denmark*
Area: *16,629 sq. mi., 43,069 sq. km.*
Population: *(1980) 5,101,000*
Capital: *Copenhagen*
(Pop., 1978, 699,300)
Language: *Danish*
Religion: *Protestant*
Currency unit: *Krone*
National holiday: *Birthday of the queen, April 16*

Denmark, a small kingdom in northern Europe, lies between the North Sea, to the west, and the Baltic Sea, to the east. Its only land boundary is with West Germany, to the south. Denmark consists of the Jutland Peninsula, four main islands—Fyn, Sjaelland, Lolland, and Bornholm, and 478 smaller islands, 99 of which are inhabited. The self-governing Faeroe Islands and Greenland are the dependencies of Denmark.

Denmark occupies a strategic position in northern Europe controlling

the Kattegat and the Skagerrak, the waterways that connect the Baltic Sea with the North Sea. The narrow Sound, the only easily navigable waterway between the Kattegat and the Baltic, passes between Sjaelland and Sweden and is the major route for shipping between the Baltic and North seas.

The land. Denmark has a long, deeply indented coastline with many fine harbors. Almost all of Denmark is low plains. The highest point, on hilly east Jutland, is less than 600 feet above sea level. There are many small lakes, ponds and streams throughout Denmark.

Denmark's climate is generally mild and moist. Average temperatures range from about 32°F in January to 62°F in July, and rainfall averages about 24 inches a year in the east, and about 30 inches in the west. In the western part of the country, winters are slightly warmer, summers cooler, fog more frequent, and the humidity higher.

The people. The Danish population is quite homogeneous. Danish is the universal language, and 97 percent of the Danes belong to the Danish Lutheran Church.

Overall population density is high, but the rate of population growth is low. The most heavily populated regions are northern Fyn, East Jutland, and eastern Sjaelland, especially the Copenhagen area, where almost 20 percent of the population lives. Western Jutland, which is rather barren, is sparsely settled.

Economy. Denmark's prosperity is based on its very efficient farming, light industry, and commerce. There are few mineral resources other than building stone, sands, and clays.

Over half of Denmark's land is cultivated. Agriculture employs about 8.5 percent of the population, and in 1974 it contributed seven percent to the national product. Farms are small and privately owned, but farmers are organized into cooperative societies for purchasing, for processing and marketing their produce, and for improving production.

Dairying and the production of meat, especially pork, are the most important farm activities. Cereals, particularly barley, account for about 50 percent of the cultivated land. Fishing is also an important activity.

Manufacturing employs about 44 percent of the labor force, and production has increased rapidly in the last two decades. Processed foods, textiles, chemicals, and light machinery are leading industrial products. Tourism and shipping are also significant sources of income.

Denmark has experienced serious trade deficits in recent years. It has joined international organizations to establish new markets for its exports, but as the problem persists there is an increasing public protest against the social welfare levies and high taxes that have been part of the Danish economy for many years.

In 1979 Denmark's exports earned $14.6 billion, while its imports cost 18.5 billion. Most of its trade is with Western Europe and the United States. Leading imports are heavy machinery, iron and steel products, and oil. The high cost of imported oil has contributed heavily to the inflationary prices that have hurt the balance of trade. Leading exports are meat, fish, dairy products, and light machinery.

Government. Denmark is a constitutional monarchy with the queen as head of state. A prime minister and a state council wield executive power and are responsible to the parliament, the Folketing. The parliament has one house and is popularly elected. Greenland and the Faeroe Islands are represented in the Folketing.

Denmark is a member of the United Nations, the North Atlantic Treaty Organization (NATO), the Organization for Economic Cooperation and Development (OECD), and the Common Market.

History. Archaeological evidence indicates that the region of present-day Denmark has long been inhabited by man. Primitive societies may have existed there as early as 10,000 years ago, and beginning about 2500 B.C. a society based on agriculture developed in the area. Early Danish peoples may have included the Cimbri and Teutons, warlike tribes described in Roman histories as inhabiting the region in the first century B.C.

By the 800's A.D., Danish Vikings had developed a society with a complex social organization. The Viking period, between about 800 and 1050, was turbulent. Scandinavian adventurers—raiders, merchants, and eventually settlers—visited the Caspian Sea, Iceland, Greenland, and possibly even North America, and raided England and western Europe. During the 900's Christianity was introduced into the region, and by about 1035 it had become the dominant religion.

The inhabitants of Denmark remained divided into separate communities until about 950, when one chieftain, Harold Bluetooth, began uniting the tribal kingdoms. The consolidation continued gradually until the 1000's, when King Canute (1014–1035) ruled a single Danish kingdom. Canute also expanded his power over England and Norway, but this Anglo-Scandinavian empire did not survive his death.

By the mid-1200's a highly organized, semifeudal society had developed, with a strong central monarchy limited by a council of royal advisers firmly based on a middle class of farmers and artisans. During the 1200's and 1300's Denmark took over territory in the Baltic area, Norway, and Sweden.

Union. By 1388 both Norway (with its possessions—the Faeroe Islands, Greenland, and Iceland) and Sweden were united under the Danish crown. This union survived, at least in form, for over a century. At the beginning of the Protestant Reformation in the early 1500's, Scandinavia was torn by religious disputes and social conflicts. As a result, Sweden in 1523 asserted its independence, but Norway remained under Danish rule.

Wars with Sweden were frequent well into the 1600's. A peace settlement was finally reached in 1660, by which Denmark surrendered to Sweden the southern part of the Scandinavian peninsula. In the same year, the monarchy became absolute as the result of a rebellion among townsmen and the clergy in support of the throne. Led by several strong rulers, Denmark-Norway regained lost territory from Sweden.

In the 1700's, however, the monarchy weakened and a form of parliamentary government was introduced. Many other liberal reforms followed, and industry and trade expanded. During the Napoleonic period of the early 1800's, the monarchy of Denmark-Norway allied itself with France against England and Sweden, and as a result of the defeat of Napoleon, Denmark lost Norway to Sweden.

Nationalism and reform. After the Napoleonic wars a nationalist and liberal movement developed in Denmark that was directed toward rebuilding and reforming the country. Representative local government was introduced in the 1830's, and in 1849 a constitution was adopted that limited the monarchy, created a national assembly, and guaranteed civil liberties.

The Danish nationalist movement was partly responsible for attempts to bring under Danish rule the duchies of Schleswig and Holstein, at the southern end of the Jutland Peninsula. Although the duchies had once been ruled by Danes, all but the predominantly Danish northern section of Schleswig was German in language and loyalty, and the German states disputed Danish claims to the territory. The conflict led to two Danish-German wars, one in 1848–1850 and another

in 1864. An 1864 settlement forced Denmark to relinquish all claims to the duchies.

The latter half of the 1800's was an era of continuing reform in Denmark. The cooperative movement was organized, and broad social welfare measures were gradually introduced. The constitution underwent several revisions, and by 1914 Denmark had already achieved a fully democratic parliamentary government.

Modern Denmark. Denmark remained neutral during World War I. In 1918 Iceland was granted independence, but it remained united with Denmark under the Danish crown. In 1920, in a plebiscite required by the Treaty of Versailles, the Danes of northern Schleswig voted to rejoin Denmark.

Denmark faced a series of economic crises in the years following World War I. Attempts at recovery were thwarted by the worldwide depression of the late 1920's and early 1930's. In the mid–1930's, however, Denmark made an excellent recovery, enacting advanced social legislation that remained in effect long after the depression had ended.

Denmark again proclaimed its neutrality at the beginning of World War II, but in April, 1940, German forces invaded and occupied the country. King Christian X refused to go into exile or to yield to the Germans, and the Danes governed themselves until 1943, when the Germans assumed direct control. In 1945 the country was liberated.

Denmark's economy had been badly damaged during the German occupation, but by the early 1950's prosperity had returned. In 1953 a new constitution was adopted. It removed Greenland from colonial status, and it substituted a unicameral for a bicameral legislature.

Danish politics since the 1950's have been complex, though changes have taken place gradually. The existence of a large number of political parties has made compromise an essential element in Danish political life; since 1945 no single party has been able to command a majority in the Folketing.

Denmark ended its long-standing policy of isolation when it joined the North Atlantic Treaty Organization (NATO) in 1949 and the European Economic Community, or Common Market, in 1972.

The nation, today, is plagued with economic problems caused largely by the fact that 90 percent of its energy comes from price-inflated oil imports. Demands for easing social programs in the face of unemployment and inflation led to significant gains by nontraditional parties in the elections of 1973. Since traditional parties have begun to respond to these demands, however, they have regained their prominent position.

Finland

Official name: *Republic of Finland*
Area: *130,119 sq. mi., 337,009 sq. km.*
Population: *(1980) 4,828,000*
Capital: *Helsinki*
  (Pop., 1978, 496,263)
Language: *Finnish, Swedish*
Religion: *Protestant*
Currency unit: *Markka*
National holiday: *Independence Day, Dec. 6*

Finland is a republic in northern Europe. It is bounded on the north by Norway, on the east by the Soviet Union, on the south by the Gulf of Finland, and on the west by the Gulf of Bothnia and Sweden. The Åland Islands, between the Baltic Sea and the Gulf of Bothnia, belong to Finland.

The land. The name Finland means "land of fens and marshes," and much of Finland is quite low and swampy. Ten percent of the land area is occupied by about 50,000 lakes, most of which are concentrated in the central third of the country. The southwestern third of Finland lies on a low coastal plain. Elevations rise to above 1000 feet only in the northern third of the country where densely forested uplands extend into the barren Lapland region of the far north.

About one-third of Finland lies north of the Arctic Circle, but the sea moderates the climate, especially in the south. Finland has long, cold winters and short, warm summers. Snow covers the ground for from four months of the year in the south to almost eight months in parts of the north. Rainfall averages about 30 inches in the southwest and decreases generally toward the north.

The people. Finland is rather sparsely populated. Population is concentrated in the southwestern third of the country, especially along the coast near Finland's largest cities, which include Helsinki, the capital, Turku, and Tampere.

The majority of the people speak Finnish, a language related to Estonian and Hungarian. Swedish is a second language, spoken by fewer than ten percent of the people. Most Finns are Lutheran, but there are Orthodox Christian, Jewish, and Roman Catholic, as well as other Protestant groups.

The seminomadic Lapps of the far north make up about 0.5 percent of the population. They remain generally isolated from Finnish life.

Economy. Finland's economy is based on the exploitation of its rich forests and considerable mineral resources. Almost two-thirds of the country is forested, and deposits of

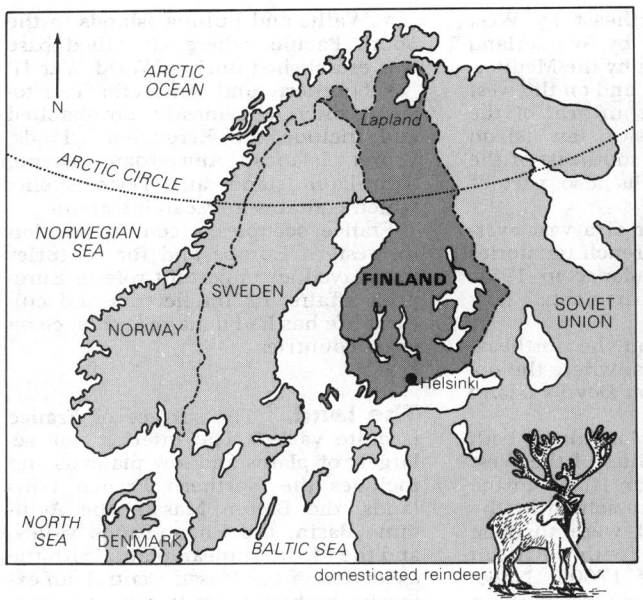

FINNISH NATIONAL TRAVEL OFFICE

FINLAND, LAND OF THE MIDNIGHT SUN, *shown* (below) *shining over a typical Finnish landscape; home of the tribal Lapps* (above).

copper, nickel, lead, zinc, and iron are mined. Abundant water is available for power.

Manufacturing contributed 39 percent to the gross national product in 1976, with wood and paper products the principal manufactured goods. Copper smelting and iron and steel production are also important. Shipbuilding and shipping are valuable industries.

Agriculture is of decreasing importance in Finland, and agriculture and forestry together employ under 15 percent of the labor force, compared with nearly 50 percent after World War II. Less than ten percent of the land is under cultivation, and farming is confined almost entirely to the south. Dairying is a major activity, and such hardy crops as hay, fodder, and cereals are grown. Minks and foxes are raised for their fur, and coastal fishing is prosperous.

The Finnish economy depends heavily on foreign trade, which increased sharply in value during the 1960's and 1970's. In 1979 exports earned $11.2 billion and imports cost $11.4 billion.

Finland's exports include paper and wood pulp, timber and wood products, machinery, and transportation equipment. The major imports are heavy machinery and vehicles, finished consumer goods, fuels, chemicals, and foodstuffs. Most of Finland's trade is with Great Britain, West Germany, the Soviet Union, and Sweden.

Government. Finland is a republic, with a president as head of state. Executive power is wielded by a prime minister and cabinet responsible to Parliament. Members of Parliament, which has one house, are popularly elected to four-year terms.

Finland is a member of the United Nations, the Nordic Council, the Organization for Economic Cooperation and Development (OECD), and the European Free Trade Association.

History. Finland contains archaeological evidence of human settlement as early as the Stone Age, over 50,000 years ago. Modern Finland was settled by people who migrated from the eastern Baltic region in about 100 A.D. For many centuries they lived in a tribal society based on hunting, trapping, and fur trading.

In the 1100's Sweden conquered the Finnish tribes and converted them to Christianity. The Finns absorbed a

great deal of Western culture through Swedish influence, and with Sweden adopted Lutheranism in the 1500's. For most of the 600 years that Sweden controlled Finland, the Swedes and the Russians competed for control of the Baltic region, and Finland was often their battleground.

Finally, in 1808, during the Napoleonic wars, Sweden lost Finland to Russia. Emperor Alexander of Russia made Finland an autonomous grand duchy and allowed it to govern itself. The Finns enjoyed a great deal of autonomy throughout the 1800's. During the reign of the last czar, Nicholas II (1904–1917), however, Russian imperialism resulted in the loss of Finnish home rule.

Independence. Finland took advantage of the turmoil caused in Russia by the 1917 revolutions and proclaimed its independence. In January, 1918, civil war broke out in Finland between the Communists and socialists, called the Reds, and conservative factions, called the Whites. Aided by German troops, the Whites won and established a republic.

In 1920 the Soviet government ceded to Finland a navigable port. Finland joined the League of Nations in 1920 and in 1921 was given sovereignty over the Åland Islands.

In the 1920's and 1930's the Finns passed legislation for advanced social and economic reforms. But the young republic was harassed by extremist organizations and some attempted coups throughout the 1930's. A socialist coalition finally restored order in 1937.

In 1939 the Soviet Union invaded Finland. The war resumed between the two nations during World War II, at the end of which Finland found itself burdened with heavy reparation payments and territorial losses.

Since the end of the war, Finland has sought to maintain neutrality in international affairs, promoting good relations with the Soviet Union and with both East and West European nations. In 1948 it signed a long-term mutual aid treaty (renewed in 1970) with the Soviet Union, and in 1977 the two nations endorsed a mutual trade agreement. Finland imports a significant amount of Soviet oil today.

Finland's proportional representation system encourages a multitude of political parties and has resulted in a number of short-lived coalition governments.

A national emergency arose in the mid-1970's. Inflation was coupled with a rapidly and suddenly rising unemployment rate, which rose from less than three percent in the early 1970's to six percent by 1977.

A new five-party coalition came to power in 1977 to deal with this crisis. It is headed by the Social Democratic Party, supported mainly by the urban workers; but it is strongly influenced by the Communist Party, the People's Democratic League.

France

Official name: *French Republic*
Area: *211,208 sq. mi., 547,026 sq. km.*
Population: *(1980) 53,500,000*
Capital: *Paris (Pop., 1975, urban area 8,547,625)*
Language: *French*
Religion: *Roman Catholic, Protestant*
Currency unit: *Franc*
National holiday: *Bastille Day, July 14*

France, the largest country in western Europe, is bounded on the north by the English Channel, Belgium, and Lux-

embourg; on the northeast by West Germany; on the east by Switzerland and Italy; on the south by the Mediterranean Sea and Spain; and on the west by the Bay of Biscay, an arm of the Atlantic Ocean. Corsica, an island lying about 100 miles southeast of the Mediterranean coast, is also part of France.

France, once master of a vast overseas empire, offered French territories the choice of independence in 1958. French "overseas departments" now include the following:

• French Guiana, on the northeast coast of South America, where the notorious penal station on Devil's Island was closed in 1944.

• Guadeloupe and Martinique, both part of the Lesser Antilles of the West Indies, and Réunion, an island in the Indian Ocean. All were settled by the French by 1635, and were thriving plantation colonies with African slaves throughout the 1700's. Napoleon's Empress Josephine was born on Martinique.

• Mayotte, in the Mozambique Channel, part of Comores before 1976 when it voted to become a French department.

• St. Pierre and Miquelon, small islands off the southern coast of Newfoundland. They are all that remains of the once vast French North American empire.

French "overseas territories" include the following:

• French Polynesia, which placed itself under French protection in the early 1800's. It includes the "Society Archipelago" (the Windward and Leeward Islands), Tuamotu Archipelago, Gambier Islands, the Austral or Tubuai Islands, and Marquesas Islands.

• New Caledonia, which includes Loyalty Islands, Isle of Pines, Huon Islands, and Chesterfield Islands.

• Wallis and Futuna Islands in the South Pacific, where an Allied base was established during World War II.

• Southern and Antarctic Territories, which are mostly uninhabited and include the Kerguelen Islands, Crozet Islands, Amsterdam Island, Saint-Paul Island, and Terre Adélie, which contains a research station.

France occupies a central position in western Europe and for centuries has played an important role in European affairs. Its intellectual and cultural life has had a major influence on other countries.

The land. The surface of France is quite varied. The interior consists largely of plains and low plateaus and includes the Northern French Lowlands, the Breton Massif, the Aquitaine Basin, the Rhône-Saône valley, and the Mediterranean plain. With the exception of the Massif Central, an extensive highland area in the south central part of France, the upland and mountain regions are found on or near the borders of the country.

The Alps, in the southeast, separate France from Italy. The Jura and Vosges mountains in the east run along France's boundaries with Switzerland and Germany. The Pyrenees form France's boundary with Spain in the south, and in the north the Ardennes cross the border with Belgium.

France's major rivers are the Seine, the Loire, the Garonne, and the Rhône. The Rhine River forms part of the eastern border with Germany.

Climate. Most of France has a maritime climate, with cool winters and mild summers. The southern coast has a typical Mediterranean climate, with hot, dry summers and mild, rainier winters. The greatest seasonal variations in temperature occur in the east and in the highland areas.

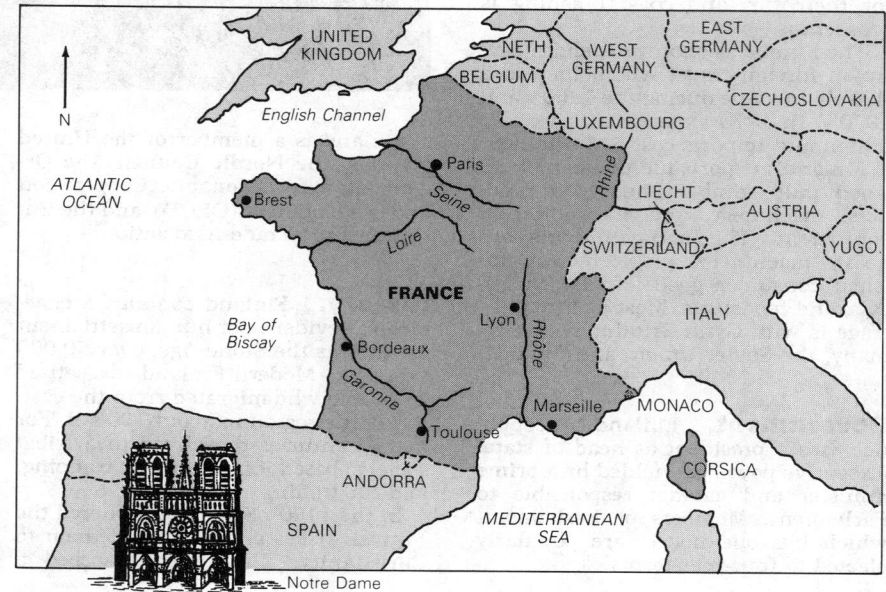

Notre Dame

The people.

France has one of Europe's most homogeneous populations. There is a strong feeling of cultural unity, and France has been troubled very little by minority unrest.

French is the universal language, and more than 95 percent of the people are Roman Catholic. Breton, Flemish, German, Catalan, and Basque are spoken in the border areas by relatively few people. The only substantial linguistic minority is the German-speaking population in Alsace.

The population has grown sharply since World War II, but this increase has become more moderate in recent years. In addition to the native population, there are 4 million foreign residents, most of whom have come from four Mediterranean countries—Algeria, Italy, Portugal, and Spain. These countries provided workers during the economic expansion of the 1960's and 1970's, but since the later 1970's this immigration has been more and more strictly controlled because of an increase in unemployment.

France's population is fairly evenly distributed throughout the country. Only a few areas, such as the high Alps and parts of the infertile Landes district, near the Spanish border, are sparsely populated, and only a few industrial areas are densely settled.

Paris, the capital, has one of the densest concentrations in the world. This concentration has contributed to the predominance of the city in the administrative, economic, and cultural life of the country; however, in recent years there has been a movement to the suburbs and smaller centers. The government has also tried to encourage regional development.

Other major cities include the industrial city of Lyon, France's principal seaport, Marseille, the seaport and industrial center of Bordeaux, the manufacturing and marketing center of Toulouse, and Nice.

Economy.

France's economy has moved ahead briskly since World War II, sharing fully in the remarkable economic resurgence of Western Europe. Membership in the European Coal and Steel Community and the European Economic Community, the EEC or Common Market, has given a tremendous impetus to French industrial and agricultural growth.

Part of this economic growth has been the result of the revamping of much of the nation's transportation and communications systems, and heavy investments in the modernization of French mines and factories. Additionally, France has had the advantage of possessing relatively rich iron ore, bauxite, and coal deposits.

Strong governmental direction of the economy under a series of formal development plans also contributed greatly to France's economic growth. The plans involve close cooperation between government and private business and have been successful in channeling resources and the balancing of economic growth.

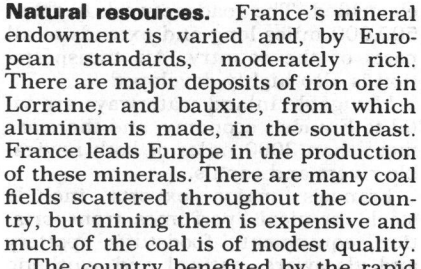

THE FRENCH FARMER *loves both his café* (left) *and his fertile land, which includes the rich Champagne wine country* (below).

Natural resources.

France's mineral endowment is varied and, by European standards, moderately rich. There are major deposits of iron ore in Lorraine, and bauxite, from which aluminum is made, in the southeast. France leads Europe in the production of these minerals. There are many coal fields scattered throughout the country, but mining them is expensive and much of the coal is of modest quality.

The country benefited by the rapid development in the late 1950's and the 1960's of huge, French-controlled North African oil and natural gas deposits. Other mineral resources of much importance are lignite, sulfur, and potash.

The abundant waterpower of the Alps, Pyrenees, and Massif Central place France second in Europe in developed hydroelectric capacity. However, the sharp rise in oil prices poses problems for future growth, and consequently France is actively searching for alternatives such as atomic, solar, and tidal power.

Agriculture.

France leads Europe in agricultural production, and exports more farm products than any other European country. France has always had the advantage of large tracts of fertile soil and a varied climate, but has often been handicapped by overly small farms and outmoded techniques. However, larger units, increased mechanization, chemical fertilizers, extended irrigation, and the stimulus of the Common Market have increased production dramatically. France ranks high in the production of grain, meat, milk, cheese, wine, and fruit.

Industry.

France has become one of the world's most important industrial nations, and French industry produces many different products. Between 1968 and 1978 the French national product increased 56 percent. Only Japan (102 percent) and Spain (65 percent) did better. The image of France as primarily an exporter of fashions, perfumes, and wines is no longer correct. France is also a major exporter of automobiles, trucks, airplanes, electronic equipment, and other modern products.

France's manufacturing is concentrated in five major industrial regions: Le Nord, Paris, Lorraine, Alsace, and Lyon-St. Étienne.

Paris and its suburbs form France's most important industrial district. The city's large reservoir of highly skilled workers, concentrated market with high-buying capacity, and position as France's government and chief cultural center have led to the development of a great variety of industries. Paris is the major center of the important French automotive industry and is also world renowned for the manufacture of women's clothing.

French industry is enhanced by a well-planned transportation network. There are about 25,000 miles of railroad track, about one-fifth of which is electrified. The road network is about 500,000 miles long and extends to all parts of the country. Air transportation is also highly developed.

Navigable inland waterways are vital to France's economy, and there are more than 3000 miles of both navigable rivers and canals.

France's major exports include steel, chemicals, perfumes, transportation equipment, foodstuffs, pottery and glassware, natural and synthetic rubber, and textiles. The principal imports include petroleum products and fuels, ores, raw textiles, and machine tools.

Two-fifths of French trade is within the Common Market, but France also trades extensively with Algeria, Switzerland, and the United States. In addition, France has made a determined effort to open up trade with Eastern Europe, the Soviet Union, Communist China, and the developing countries of Asia, Africa, and Latin America. French exports earned $94.9 billion in 1983, while imports cost $105.4 billion.

Government.
France is a democratic republic. The head of state and chief executive is the president, who is directly elected to a seven-year term. The president appoints a prime minister and council of ministers, or cabinet, as well as all other officials.

The constitution grants the president the right to dissolve the powerful lower house of the legislature, the National Assembly, after conferring with the prime minister, and the right to call new elections. In a national emergency, the president may assume all executive and legislative powers.

Legislative authority is vested in the Parliament, which consists of the National Assembly and the Senate. The stronger of the two houses is the National Assembly, whose 487 deputies are popularly elected to four-year terms. The 274 members of the Senate are elected by regional and city electoral colleges to nine-year terms.

In 1958, under the constitution of the Fifth Republic, French overseas territories were offered the choice of becoming independent, of becoming departments of France, or of keeping their dependent status. Other French overseas settlements elected, in 1958, to adopt the status of "overseas territories." As such they are administered by a governor who presides over a government council and a territorial assembly.

France is a member of the United Nations, the Common Market, and the Council of Europe. In 1966 it withdrew its military forces from the North Atlantic Treaty Organization (NATO), though it remains a member.

History.
The territory of France, known in ancient times as Gaul, was inhabited by Celtic tribes when Julius

MONT ST. MICHEL, *the famous medieval abbey built on a rock in the Gulf of St. Malo, dates from the 13th century. A causeway links the tourist attraction to the mainland.*

TRANS WORLD AIRLINES PHOTO

Caesar led his Roman legions into the region in 58 B.C. By 51 B.C. Caesar had brought all of Gaul under his control. The Romans introduced the Latin language and Christianity to the Gauls.

For over 200 years the region was prosperous, but as the Roman Empire began to disintegrate, the Visigoths, Franks, and Burgundians established themselves in various parts of Gaul.

The Merovingians. In the late 400's the Franks, led by Clovis I, the first of the Merovingian kings (ruled 481–511), succeeded in conquering Gaul and western Germany. Clovis conquered most of what had been Roman Gaul, established the Merovingians as the ruling dynasty of the Franks, and was instrumental in converting his people to Christianity.

Clovis, however, regarded the Frankish kingdom not as a state but as his private property, and he divided it among his four surviving sons when he died. This practice, which continued to be maintained by the Frankish monarchy, was the leading cause of the chronic civil wars that plagued Frankish history.

By the middle of the 600's, continual civil strife had taken its toll on the power and prestige of the Merovingian kings. At about the same time their wealth had dwindled due to their lavish grants of land to the church and to their noble retainers in return for government service.

As the Merovingians became poorer they became weaker. On the other hand, the church and leading noble families gained enormously in wealth and political power.

In the 600's the Carolingians, who were the royal stewards of the Merovingians, assumed most of the royal authority. In 732 the Carolingian, Charles Martel, thwarted Muslim invaders at Tours—halting the Muslim threat to France and enhancing the prestige of his house. But Charles did not depose the Merovingians, who continued as nominal rulers of the Franks until 751, when Charles's son, Pepin the Short, seized the throne.

The Carolingians. Pepin's son, Charlemagne, or Charles the Great, who ruled from 768 to 814, won control of most of western Europe. He created a powerful empire, which he administered efficiently. Charlemagne was a patron of learning, and scholars from all of western Europe came to his capital, Aachen. Charlemagne cooperated closely with the church, and in 800 Pope Leo III crowned him emperor of the Romans, which legitimized his rule over the former Western Roman Empire.

The strength of the Carolingian empire was dependent on the genius of Charlemagne. His son, Louis the Pious (ruled 814–840), was incapable of maintaining a strong hold over the kingdom. The centralized administration collapsed, and Louis' three sons struggled among themselves for supremacy. In 843 they signed the Treaty of Verdun, which divided the Carolingian empire into three parts.

The eastern region, Germany, was awarded to Louis the German; the western region, France, went to Charles the Bald; and the middle strip, which included northern Italy and Alsace-Lorraine, was given to Lothair I, who also retained the title of Emperor of the Romans. The partition of 843 marked the beginnings of modern France and Germany.

Throughout the Middle Ages France remained a separate kingdom. Carolingian rule declined rapidly in the 800's and 900's. New barbarian invasions shook Europe, and political power fell into the hands of feudal lords. Economic life shrank and became centered on the self-sufficient manor.

The Capetians. The Carolingian dynasty died out in 987, and the powerful nobles chose Hugh Capet as king. The Capetian kings—Hugh and his descendants—brought authority and prestige to the French crown. They used force sparingly and built up their power and possessions by the strategic marriages of their sons and daughters to the great feudal families of France, waiting patiently until they inherited their lands. They were careful to preserve their just rights over the French church but at the same time they enriched it with buildings and lands. France became the largest, richest, and most populous kingdom in medieval Europe.

The first important French king was Louis VI (ruled 1108–1137), whose principal achievement was to gain complete control of the royal patrimony itself, the Isle de France. He also married his son and heir to Eleanor of Aquitaine, the duchess of the largest feudal principality in France.

After 15 years, Louis VII (ruled 1137–1180) divorced Eleanor, ostensibly because they were too closely related, but, in fact, because she had not produced a male heir. Louis then married a daughter of the King of Castile, who died childless. Within five weeks of her death he married the Countess of Champagne, who did produce a male heir, the future Philip II.

Philip II (ruled 1180–1223) was determined to regain the territory gained through marriage by Henry II of England and unify all of France with himself as absolute monarch. Philip succeeded in wresting control of Normandy, Anjou, Maine, Poitou, and Touraine from the English between 1202 and 1204.

To carry royal power to the newly acquired territories, he organized administrative districts *(bailliages)* governed by royal agents *(baillis)*.

During the reign of Louis IX (1226–1270) the royal court began to evolve into a central bureaucracy. Louis established a high court of justice, known as the *parlement,* and reorganized the royal treasury into a more workable body of government.

The last great Capetian king was Philip IV (ruled 1285–1314), who completed the administrative organization and territorial development of the French medieval state. He also taxed the French clergy, who had been exempt from direct royal taxation. This in turn led to a conflict with Pope Boniface VIII, who held the most extreme views of any medieval pope concerning papal supremacy and clerical independence.

In his confrontation with the papacy Philip was completely victorious. He gained the right to tax the French clergy and after the death of Boniface secured the election of a French pope. For over 70 years—an era called the "Babylonian Captivity"—the popes reigned from Avignon under the supervision of the French monarchs.

For 300 years the continuity of the Capetian kings and their policies had run like a bright thread through French history. When Philip IV died in 1314 the French monarchy was at its height. Moreover, Philip left three adult sons behind him. In a little more than a decade, however, they were all dead and the medieval French monarchy died with them.

The Valois kings. The throne passed to one of Philip's nephews, Philip VI (ruled 1328–1350), who was the first of the Valois dynasty. Under the Valois, royal power continued to grow, despite some major setbacks.

In 1337 the right of Philip VI to the throne was challenged by his distant cousin, Edward III of England. This led to a long, complex dynastic conflict from 1337 to 1453 known as the Hundred Years' War. During this war the French crown also faced a revolt of French peasants, the *Jacquerie* of 1358; a Parisian insurrection; and bitter civil strife among powerful French nobles, particularly between those of Armagnac and Burgundy.

In 1420 Henry V of England, who had defeated the French at Agincourt in 1415, forced the Valois king, Charles VI, to disown his own son and make Henry the heir to the French throne. However, the dauphin, as the French heir to the throne was known, fought back. With the help of Joan of Arc, who escorted him to Reims, where in 1429 he was crowned Charles VII (ruled 1422–1461), he managed to drive the English out of all of France except Calais by 1453.

During the Hundred Years' War the French kings had begun to create a more effective army by placing it under royal control, supporting it with royal funds, and selecting its officers. They also obtained a special direct tax on land, called the *taille,* which they did not give up at the end of the protracted conflict.

Louis XI (ruled 1461–1483) inherited a monarchy that had almost absolute power and that was no longer threatened by foreign intervention. Louis destroyed the power of the remaining feudal lords and brought most of present-day France under royal control. Louis continued to reinforce the strength of the monarchy,

and sought ways to ally the throne with the growing middle class.

Louis XI's son, Charles VIII (ruled 1483–1498), introduced a French policy of expansion abroad with campaigns in Italy. Although they were unsuccessful, they succeeded in stimulating French interest in Italian Renaissance culture. Charles's cousin, Francis I (ruled 1515–1547), continued the Italian campaigns and initiated French support of German Protestants as a means of weakening the rival Hapsburg dynasty.

Henry II (ruled 1547–1559) won a foothold in Lorraine by seizing the bishoprics of Toul, Metz, and Verdun from the Holy Roman Emperor Charles V. The French also captured Calais, the last English possession in France, and ended the Italian wars.

Religious conflict. After Henry's death, his three sons ruled France in succession—Francis II (1559–1560), Charles IX (1560–1574), and Henry III (1574–1589). During most of that period, the queen mother, Catherine de Medici, dominated political life.

Catherine and her sons were unable to maintain control in the face of Calvinism, rivalry between the powerful Catholic Guise and Protestant Bourbon families, and the intervention of Hapsburg Spain in French affairs.

The Huguenots, as the French Calvinists were called, created the greatest problems for the three Medici monarchs. During their reigns the royal army was intermittently engaged in a fierce civil war with Huguenot forces.

The struggle reached its bloodiest point in 1572, when Catherine incited Parisian Catholics against a large assemblage of Huguenots gathered in the capital to attend the wedding of Margaret of Valois, Catherine's daughter, and the Huguenot, Henry of Bourbon, king of Navarre. The Massacre of

JOAN OF ARC, *the "Maid," who rallied the French against the English, is captured outside Compiègne. She was burned at the stake as a witch, but was later canonized.*

EPA

St. Bartholomew's Day ensued, resulting in the death of many Protestants.

The leadership of the Huguenots fell to Henry of Navarre, who had successfully escaped the massacre. When the Valois line ended in 1589 amid the confusion of civil and religious strife, Henry returned to Paris to ascend the throne as the famous Henry IV (ruled 1589–1610), the first of France's Bourbon kings.

Bourbon rule. The Bourbons made France a relatively centralized state and a world power. Henry IV took several steps to bring order to divided France. He became a Roman Catholic to consolidate his position as king, but in 1598 he issued the Edict of Nantes, which gave the Huguenots religious rights and political guarantees. He defeated or bought off rebellious nobles and rebuilt the economy.

After initial difficulties, his successor, Louis XIII (ruled 1610–1643), was able to continue the expansion of royal power by delegating authority to Cardinal Richelieu. Richelieu, an important force from 1624 to 1642, crushed rebellious Huguenots while allowing them religious privileges; forced the nobles to demolish fortifications that did not protect the frontiers; developed the technique of sending out royal inspectors, or *intendants,* to supervise local administration; and ruthlessly suppressed conspiracies against the regime.

Richelieu had increased royal power and improved administration through a central bureaucracy of competent experts, who owed their fortunes and loyalty to him and the king. He also placed the government of the provinces under royal officials, or *intendants,* who had arbitrary authority to take over many of the duties and powers of traditional local officials. His innovations greatly improved the effectiveness of government, especially law enforcement and the administration of justice. Increased taxes and more efficient tax collection helped to strengthen the crown financially and politically.

Outside France, the cardinal intervened in Germany's religious conflict, the Thirty Years' War, on the side of the Protestant princes to prevent the consolidation of Hapsburg power.

After Richelieu's death in 1642, Cardinal Mazarin carried on his work, surviving a series of revolts—called the *Fronde*—by the nobility and *parlements,* who sought greater participation in government. They were put down with great difficulty, but proved to be the nobility's last rebellion in defense of medieval privileges.

Mazarin also brought the Thirty Years' War to an end in 1648 with the Peace of Westphalia. This settlement strengthened the French foothold in Lorraine and won France most of Alsace. Although the Austrian Hapsburgs had conceded defeat, the Spanish Hapsburgs continued to fight

CULVER PICTURES

LOUIS XIV, *the famous king of France, in costume as the "sun king" when young.*

until 1659, when they yielded some territories in the Pyrenees and the Lowlands.

Louis XIV. With the death of Cardinal Mazarin in 1661, Louis XIV (ruled 1643–1715) began to rule France personally. By that time France was already the most unified, most populous, and wealthiest state in Europe. Louis, known as "the Sun King," further strengthened the power of the monarchy and reinforced French hegemony in Europe.

Louis excluded the great nobles from his councils in favor of reliable middle-class officials, domesticated the troublesome aristocracy in his splendid palace at Versailles, silenced opposition from the *parlements,* used *intendants* to enforce his will in the provinces, and avoided convening the Estates-General, or national assembly.

Jean Baptiste Colbert, his controller general of finance, encouraged the development of industry with favors and protection; the Marquis de Louvois, minister of war, reorganized the army; and the Marquis de Vauban, a military engineer, improved military fortifications. In North America, French explorers and soldiers built an empire extending from the St. Lawrence River and the Great Lakes to the mouth of the Mississippi River on the Gulf of Mexico.

The work of modernizing France was only half completed, however. The tax system remained riddled with exemptions and inequities; internal customs barriers still impeded commerce outside of central France; and underneath the royal superstructure

lay a confusion of local administrative organs, courts, and laws inherited from the past.

Louis, moreover, weakened French economic life when he revoked the Edict of Nantes in 1685, suppressing the remaining Protestant rights. This led to the emigration of thousands of Huguenots, large numbers of whom were merchants, manufacturers, and craftsmen.

Colbert, meanwhile, was establishing an economy based on "mercantilism." This policy aims at economic self-sufficiency and a favorable balance of trade, in which exports exceed imports and the surplus is paid for in gold, which increases national wealth and power. Colbert's mercantilist tactics—protective tariffs and prohibitions, subsidies and monopolies to stimulate native industries, shipping, and so forth—were only partially successful.

Other nations were more advanced industrially and commercially. They responded with anti-French mercantilist policies of their own, while the king's wars crippled the program by draining the economy.

Louis' wars, inspired primarily by a desire for glory, drained French resources and made his reign unpopular. As a result of the first three wars (War of Devolution, 1667–1668; Dutch War, 1672–1678; and War of the League of Augsburg, 1688–1697) France acquired bits of the Spanish Netherlands, the Franche-Comté, in east-central France, and Alsace.

After the War of the Spanish Succession (1701–1714), however, waged against a Grand Alliance of European powers, France had to recognize English claims to Newfoundland, Nova Scotia, and Hudson Bay territory in North America. Although one of Louis' grandsons became Philip V of Spain, the Spanish and French thrones were never to be united.

At Louis' death in 1715, France was economically exhausted—but the economy was more fully developed and sounder than it had been before Colbert.

ELEGANT FRENCH PORCELAIN. *In the 18th century, French culture dominated Europe.*

METROPOLITAN MUSEUM OF ART

Decline of the monarchy. In the 1700's the French monarchy began to lose its power and prestige. Louis XV (ruled 1715–1774) preferred private pleasure to the tasks of government. French intellectuals of the Enlightenment, a contemporary philosophic movement characterized by its emphasis on the idea of universal human progress, campaigned for social and political reform.

Although their ideas influenced large numbers of the bourgeoisie and many European "enlightened despots" of the period, Louis XV chose to ignore them. Ministers quarreled, necessary reforms were defeated, and the *parlements* repeatedly challenged royal authority on behalf of vested interests.

France also became involved in several new wars. The War of the Polish Succession (1733–1735) assured France of eventual acquisition of the rest of Lorraine, but the War of the Austrian Succession (1740–1748) ended in stalemate. Finally, the Seven Years' War (1756–1763), fought after a "diplomatic revolution" in which France became allied with its old rival, Hapsburg Austria, resulted in the loss of French Canada to the British.

Louis XVI (ruled 1774–1792) was a well intentioned ruler, but he, too, lacked determination. Early in his reign he was faced with the problem of the public debt, swelled by war costs and aid to the American rebels against England. The antiquated tax system could not provide enough funds to balance the budget, and the nation faced bankruptcy.

A series of reform ministers who saw the need to tax the upper classes were dismissed. Finally, as the crisis mounted, a program was proposed that would force the aristocracy to assume their share of the tax burden. They rebelled, maintaining that the Estates-General alone had the authority to approve new taxes. In 1789, hopeful of consolidating their position, the aristocracy compelled the king to summon the Estates-General for the first time in 175 years.

The Revolution. The three estates were to sit separately, with one vote apiece, giving the first two estates (the nobility and the clergy), which represented a tiny minority, a two-to-one advantage. But the aristocratic Third Estate proclaimed itself the National Assembly, and swore that it would not be dissolved until it had written a constitution for France. With this famous "Tennis Court Oath" made on June 20, 1789, and the storming of the Bastille on July 14, the French Revolution was clearly at hand.

The revolutionaries then destroyed the remnants of feudalism, swept away antiquated laws and local institutions, guaranteed certain basic civil rights, and created a constitutional monarchy with a fairly democratic legislative assembly.

They antagonized many Frenchmen

THE STORMING OF THE BASTILLE, *the royal prison, in Paris on July 14, 1789 (now the national holiday), marked the opening of actual hostilities in the French Revolution.*

when they seized church property to gain revenue and proceeded to turn the church into a government department with elected priests paid by the state and virtually detached from Rome. The revolution also produced economic disorder and high prices, which kept the country unsettled. Even more serious for the new constitutional monarchy was the public distrust of Louis XVI and his queen, Marie Antoinette.

Even before the constitution went into effect in the autumn of 1791, the royal family had tried to escape the country. The leaders of the legislative assembly became convinced that reactionary European rulers were allying against them and on April 20, 1792, they declared war on Austria, inaugurating the wars of the French Revolution, which were to last until 1815. The monarchy was overthrown by a Parisian insurrection on August 10.

The First Republic. On September 21, 1792, a new revolutionary assembly, the National Convention, announced the establishment of the First Republic. The convention delegates, elected by universal suffrage, were republicans, and they proceeded to draft a republican constitution. In the convention, the radical Jacobin Party, which was allied with the Parisian populace, gradually defeated the moderate Girondists.

A reign of terror occurred in 1793–1794, when the Jacobin leaders of the convention formed a Committee of Public Safety to conduct the government. Faced with foreign invasion, serious threats of counterrevolution, and grave economic problems, the commit-

tee created a "revolutionary government" designed to crush its enemies and prepare the way for the establishment of a democratic republic.

This revolutionary government, led by Maximilien de Robespierre, featured a centralized dictatorship, a single party, a police regime, a dictated economy, and attempts at mass propaganda. Thousands of Girondists and counterrevolutionaries, as well as Louis XVI and Marie Antoinette, were executed.

To win the war—which had expanded by the spring of 1793 to include Prussia, Sardinia, Britain, the Dutch Republic, and Spain—the government drafted the entire able-bodied male population. With the largest army ever organized in Europe, the French Republic turned the tide of war in its favor.

The Directory. In July, 1794, Robespierre was overthrown by the more moderate members of the convention. A reaction against the terror followed, culminating in 1795 in the establishment of a conservative republic called the Directory, because executive authority was shared by five directors.

Under the Directory (1795–1799), France experienced ineffective and unstable government at home, but enjoyed marked military success abroad. France won control over Belgium, the Rhineland, and much of Italy. In 1799 Napoleon Bonaparte, the republic's most successful general, overthrew the Directory and proclaimed himself consul. In 1802 he made himself consul for life, and in 1804, emperor. Each change was approved by the people in a plebiscite.

Napoleonic period. Within France Napoleon created a political system that was an amalgam of the old monarchy and the revolution. He made himself a hereditary, divine-right ruler and formed a new aristocracy composed of those who served the state well. He made peace with the Roman Catholic Church in 1801 in a concordat with the pope, although he did not return the clergy's confiscated lands.

Napoleon issued a new civil law code, usually known as the Code Napoleon, which assured all citizens equality under the law. He introduced a tax system that was more efficient and equitable than that of the old regime and he instituted administrative reforms that gave France a modern highly organized and fully centralized bureaucracy.

Abroad, France absorbed Belgium, Holland, the Rhineland, and part of Italy. Napoleon set up puppet states in western Germany, Switzerland, Italy, and Poland, and forced Austria, Prussia, and Russia into an alliance. However, failure to crush Britain either militarily or economically, a costly war in Spain, and a disastrous campaign in Russia led in 1814 to Napoleon's defeat by a European coalition. Napoleon's attempt to regain control—known as the Hundred Days—ended in his final defeat at Waterloo, Belgium, in 1815.

Restoration. Under the terms of the peace agreement concluded at the Congress of Vienna in 1815, France's territory was reduced to what it had been in 1792 and the Bourbons were restored to the French throne. The Bourbons could not restore the old regime, however, and in 1814 Louis

NAPOLEON BONAPARTE, *the adventurer from Corsica who created a French empire.*

FRENCH EMBASSY PRESS & INFORMATION DIVISION

XVIII (ruled 1814–1824) issued the Constitutional Charter to win the support of the bourgeoisie and the peasants, while limiting the power of the ambitious émigré aristocrats who had recently returned to France from their exile. The charter guaranteed basic liberties and created a constitutional monarchy like the British system.

The king headed a chamber of peers whom he appointed and a chamber of deputies chosen by a small electorate.

When Charles X (ruled 1824–1830) succeeded Louis, he immediately made it clear that he wished to reestablish the prerevolutionary order.

Charles chose reactionary ministers, granted indemnities to the nobles whose lands had been confiscated during the revolution, and entrusted public education to the clergy. The chamber, dominated by the bourgeoisie, opposed the king's actions.

Charles dissolved the chamber and called for new elections, but the majority of the electorate failed to support his policies. He retaliated by promulgating the July Ordinances, which restricted the freedom of the press, reduced the size of the electorate, and again dissolved the chamber of deputies.

Fearing that the ordinances were a prelude to a coup d'état, liberal intellectuals incited the Parisians to revolt in the July Revolution of 1830. Charles abdicated, and a constitutional monarchy was established. A cousin of the deposed ruler, Louis Philippe, duke of Orléans, became the new king.

The July Monarchy. To the disappointment of the republicans, the liberal middle class, and the workers, the "July Monarchy," as Louis' reign was called, proved to be as opposed to social and economic reforms as the previous regime.

The revolution had merely shifted the power from one small group to another—the upper middle class, or *haute bourgeoisie,* had replaced the nobility. Like their aristocratic predecessors, the bourgeoisie refused to widen voting privileges, and they used their newly acquired power to develop industries and businesses for their own material gains.

Many groups opposed the "July Monarchy." The "Legitimists" wanted Charles X or his grandson, the duke of Bordeaux, restored to the throne, and the republicans wanted universal suffrage and a republic. The workers demanded better working conditions and a voice in the government.

The workers joined with the republicans, both groups believing that only a radical change in the country's political structure could bring about improved social conditions. On February 22, 1848, rioting broke out in Paris, and two days later Louis abdicated.

The Second Republic. A provisional government headed by the poet Alphonse de Lamartine and the journalist Louis Blanc was established. Blanc, strongly in favor of social reform, established National Workshops to provide jobs for the unemployed. He was unable to provide enough work for everyone, however, and in the ensuing dissension dissolved the workshops. The closing of the workshops was followed by rioting, which was finally suppressed by the army.

In November, 1848, an assembly completed the drafting of a new constitution, which provided for a legislature of one house and a president with strong powers to be elected by universal suffrage. In December, 1848, the first presidential election under the Second Republic was held. The vote made Louis Napoleon, a nephew of Napoleon Bonaparte, president, and revealed that the country as a whole, especially the French peasantry, was much more conservative than the vocal Paris populace.

Second Empire. In an almost bloodless coup d'état in 1851, Louis Napoleon declared the national legislature dissolved. The liberal dreams of a generation were dissipated on December 2, 1852, when Louis Napoleon became by plebiscite Emperor Napoleon III.

The Second Empire witnessed feverish attempts to create an industrial base. It was hoped that by using state funds for industrial enterprises and by encouraging technological innovation a true industrial revolution could be accomplished.

But France still remained woefully behind both Britain and the rising state of Prussia. Just how far behind became clear in 1870, when Prussia inflicted a surprising and humiliating defeat on Napoleon III's France in the Franco-Prussian War.

The news of Napoleon III's surrender on September 4, 1870, to the Germans was the last straw for a nation that had already been embarrassed by a series of diplomatic catastrophes in the 1860's.

The Third Republic. On September 4, 1870, the Third Republic was born. A provisional government of national defense raised an army to try to prevent the Germans from occupying the city of Paris, but the Parisians were defeated after a four-month siege. Under the terms of the peace treaty negotiated between Bismarck and Adolphe Thiers, the head of the National Assembly, France was forced to cede Alsace and part of Lorraine to Germany and to pay a huge indemnity.

Before the treaty was signed, the Third Republic was confronted by an insurrection in Paris, which evolved into a civil war. Unwilling to concede defeat to the Prussians, the Parisians drove the French government troops out of the capital in March, 1871, and formed their own municipal regime—the Paris Commune. Civil war raged for two months until the supporters of the National Assembly managed to suppress the commune.

Although the Third Republic started badly, it survived until 1940. The republic, headed by Thiers, was provisional at first since a majority of deputies in the National Assembly favored a monarchy. But the monarchists were badly divided between supporters of the Bourbon and Orleans lines, and gradually the voters turned to conservative republican candidates.

During the Third Republic there was a rapid change in cabinets—more than 50 before World War I. Since presidents did not call elections when ministries were voted out, deputies were not afraid to overthrow a cabinet. More important, France did not develop large, disciplined political parties such as those in Britain. Instead, after a century of ideological conflict, there was a multitude of small parties.

This system, which continued into the Fourth Republic, was not as unstable as it seemed, however. Changing ministries were composed of many of the same men who represented coalitions of center parties. Also, behind the shifting ministries stood the Napoleonic administrative structure, with its centralized bureaucracy.

The republic weathered a number of crises—such as a threatened coup in 1889 and the Dreyfus affair in the late 1890's. In 1894 Alfred Dreyfus, a Jewish army officer, was convicted of treason. Later evidence pointed to his innocence, but the army refused to reopen the case. Monarchists, conservatives, and militarists as well opposed reopening the case, wishing not only to stand behind the army but to disgrace the republic. The country was bitterly divided.

In 1898 the case was reopened, and the following year Dreyfus was pardoned. In 1906 he was fully exonerated. Thus the scandalous Dreyfus affair ultimately discredited the monarchists and strengthened the republic.

The Third Republic proved politically radical but socially conservative. Republicans led by Jules Ferry restricted the role of the church in education, and the schools were to turn out loyal republicans.

In social welfare legislation, however, the republic lagged behind Germany and Britain. The Radical Socialists, who held the balance of power in the chamber before World War I, proved radical in name only.

Industry expanded, but not as rapidly as in other nations, and the population barely increased at all. Yet French trade grew considerably as a result of extensive colonial expansion in Africa and Southeast Asia (Indochina). By 1914 France's colonial empire was second only to Britain's.

To protect its colonial interests and to secure its position against Germany, France strengthened its army and navy, formed the Dual Alliance with Russia in 1894, and entered the Entente Cordiale with Britain in 1904.

Rather than risk losing a vital ally, France supported Russia in the Balkan crisis that precipitated World War I.

World War I. In August, 1914, German troops drove westward through Belgium to invade France, and soon most of Europe was involved in the conflict. Britain supported France, and the United States entered the conflict on their side in 1917. For four years most of the fighting on the western front was carried out in northeastern France, costing the lives of over 1 million French soldiers and untold physical damage.

Although the Allies eventually defeated Germany, France still faced a powerful German state, and after the 1917 Bolshevik Revolution Russia was lost as an ally. Under the terms of the Treaty of Versailles (1919) France was granted a 15-year occupation of the Rhineland, which was to be permanently demilitarized.

Germany was disarmed, and France was given Alsace-Lorraine, large war reparations, and some former German colonies. The period from 1919 to 1925 was marked by labor unrest and serious inflation, and French foreign policy was based on a tough line against Germany. France occupied the Ruhr in 1923 to force reparation payments from Germany, and in 1921 formed an alliance with Poland.

Interwar France. From 1925 to 1932 France pursued a more conciliatory German policy, although France allied itself with the nations of the Little Entente—Czechoslovakia, Rumania, and Yugoslavia. The Locarno treaties of 1925, guaranteeing the Versailles frontiers and providing for arbitration of disputes, seemed to ensure European stability. At home, prosperity obscured the need for social legislation, although a modest social security system was approved. The world economic depression of the 1930's and the rise of Adolf Hitler in Germany ended this quiet interlude.

Unemployment, growing insecurity, and a succession of ineffective ministries gave rise to extreme right-wing groups, who were as militant, antirepublican, and antidemocratic as their prototypes in Italy and Germany. In 1934, when the government was alleged to be involved in a financial scandal, the rightists staged antiparliamentary riots.

In response to the right-wing threat, the Socialist, Radical Socialist, and Communist parties formed a political bloc, known as the Popular Front, which came to power in 1936. The Popular Front's premier, Léon Blum, promised moderate reforms which were well within a capitalistic economic system.

Blum won parliamentary approval to establish collective bargaining, a 40-hour work week, paid vacations, closer government control over national financial affairs, nationalization of the arms industry, and cultural programs for the lower classes. But in 1938 France returned to economic and social conservatism under Premier Edouard Daladier.

With its finances exhausted, lacking British support, preoccupied with internal politics, and with an influential right wing sympathetic to Mussolini, France avoided taking action against the growing aggressiveness of Nazi Germany.

France failed to halt German rearmament in 1935, remilitarization of the Rhineland in 1936, or the annexation of Austria and the dismemberment of Czechoslovakia in 1938. A Nazi-Soviet nonaggression pact, signed in 1939, left France without a powerful ally on Germany's east.

World War II. In 1939 World War II began with Germany's attack on Poland. France was economically stagnant, politically badly divided, and militarily unprepared. In May, 1940, France collapsed before the German *blitzkrieg,* and on June 22 an armistice was signed with the Nazis.

Northwestern France was occupied by the Germans. In the southeast the Germans set up a puppet government headed by Marshal Henri-Philippe Pétain, which was known as the Vichy regime after the town that was its capital.

General Charles de Gaulle and a handful of Frenchmen escaped to London and formed the French Committee of National Liberation (the Free French). At first the committee functioned to recruit Frenchmen to continue the fight against Germany, but eventually it took the form of a provisional government ready to take control of France after the defeat of Germany.

CHARLES DE GAULLE, *a dynamic leader who resurrected France after World War II.*

France was liberated in August, 1944, by Allied forces, which included contingents of the Free French under General de Gaulle. During the immediate post-liberation period, de Gaulle presided over a provisional government, but he resigned in 1946 because of Communist and socialist opposition to a constitution providing for a strong executive.

After the resignation of de Gaulle, a coalition of Communists, socialists, and members of the MRP (the Catholic Popular Republican Movement) carried through various social reforms and nationalized the country's most important power, transportation, and banking facilities.

The Fourth Republic. Soon, however, the coalition broke up over ideological differences and Cold War tensions, and France once more returned to social and economic conservatism. Beset by inflation, strikes, and foreign exchange problems, the French economy was modernized and production increased with the help of U. S. aid under the Marshall Plan, which was inaugurated in 1947.

The most serious problem facing the Fourth Republic was the struggle to maintain the French colonial empire. France waged a losing war in Indochina from 1946 to 1954, when it was forced to withdraw. A few months later France was engaged in a costly colonial war in Algeria, where there were many French settlers.

Finally, weakened by the old pattern of changing ministries, the Fourth Republic was destroyed in 1958 by an attempted coup led by French soldiers and settlers in Algeria determined to forestall an agreement with the nationalists.

The Fifth Republic. De Gaulle returned to power as head of France's Fifth Republic, which placed extensive powers in the hands of the president, and in 1962 he recognized Algerian independence. Meanwhile, France had granted independence to most of its numerous other African dependencies.

During the first decade of the Fifth Republic France enjoyed stability and prosperity, and played an ambitious role in foreign affairs. De Gaulle worked to build France into a major power free from the constraint or influence of other nations, particularly the United States. Under his leadership, France developed its own nuclear atomic force.

The Gaullist regime tottered in 1968 when a student rebellion touched off a national strike. De Gaulle resigned in 1969 after the defeat of a referendum for his proposals for constitutional reform, and died a year later. His successor, Georges Pompidou, initiated reforms to benefit blue-collar workers, but died in office in 1974. In May of 1974, Giscard d'Estaing, a conservative, was elected president.

As France's economic recession and inflation worsened, political analysts predicted Socialist-Communist victories in the 1978 elections, but the conservative Gaullists and Republicans retained a healthy majority in Parliament.

In the 1981 presidential elections, however, the Socialist Francois Mitterrand was elected, and later that year the Socialist Party won an absolute majority in the National Assembly.

Germany

West Germany

Official name: *Federal Republic of Germany*
Area: *95,929 sq. mi., 248,454 sq. km.*
Population: *(1980) 61,100,000*
Capital: *Bonn (Pop., 1977, 284,000)*
Language: *German*
Religion: *Protestant, Roman Catholic*
Currency unit: *Mark*
National holiday: *Proclamation of the Republic Day, June 2*

East Germany

Official name: *German Democratic Republic*
Area: *41,766 sq. mi., 108,174 sq. km.*
Population: *(1980) 16,860,000*
Capital: *East Berlin (Pop., 1978, 1,111,398)*
Language: *German*
Religion: *Protestant, Roman Catholic*
Currency unit: *Mark*
National holiday: *Republic Day, Oct.7*

Germany is a divided nation in north-central Europe. German territory is bounded on the north by the North Sea, Denmark, and the Baltic Sea; on the east by Poland and Czechoslovakia; on the south by Austria, Liechtenstein, and Switzerland; and on the west by France, Luxembourg, Belgium, and the Netherlands.

After World War II, Germany was divided among the four major Allied powers—Britain, France, the United States, and the Soviet Union. Its capital city, Berlin, was also partitioned into four zones. Each zone was occupied by one of the Allied powers. Pre-World War II territories of Germany lying east of the Oder and Neisse rivers were placed under Polish administration. The West German government now recognizes the Oder-Neisse line as a permanent frontier and has given up all claims to a revision of this demarcation. East Prussia, a separate territory on the east coast of the Baltic, was annexed by the Soviet Union.

In 1949 the Soviet zone was established as the German Democratic Republic, with the eastern sector of Berlin as its capital. The other Allies merged their three zones into the Federal Republic of Germany. The line separating East Germany, as the Communist sector is called, from West Germany, the non-communist sector, runs an irregular course south from Lübeck, on the Baltic Sea, to Adorf, on the Czechoslovakian border. The North Sea island of Helgoland belongs to West Germany.

The land. The political division of Germany is arbitrary, for East and West Germany form a geographical unit containing two distinct and strikingly different regions—northern Germany, low and flat, and southern Germany, hilly and of complex relief. The North German Plain, south of a low, sandy northern coastline, is low and dotted with swamps and lakes, especially in the northeast. Toward the interior are hummocks and low hills.

The elevation begins to rise in central Germany, the *Mittelland,* a region of uplands with plateaus and low mountains broken by broad river val-

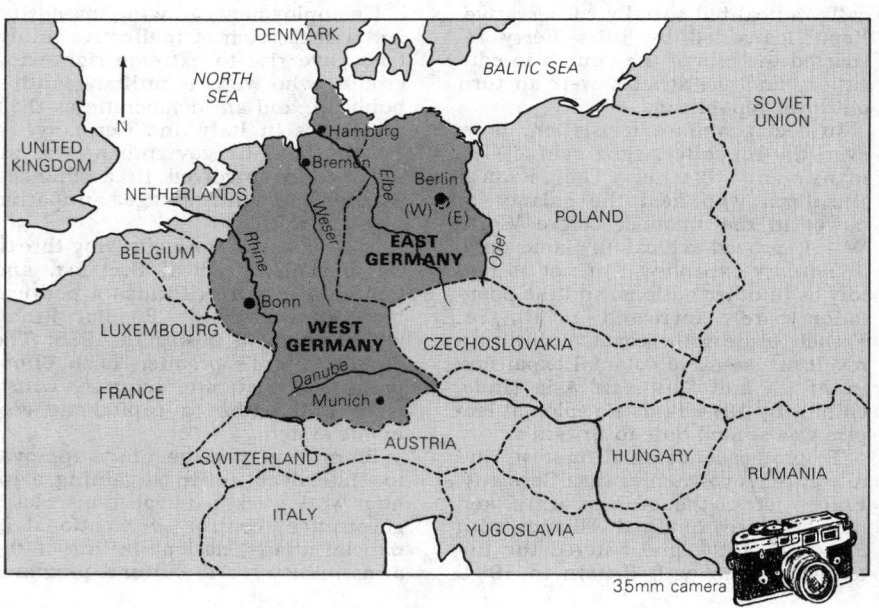

35mm camera

leys. These uplands rise into the Bohemian forest, the Black Forest, and the Bavarian Plateau until, near the southern border, the Alps reach almost 10,000 feet.

Several major European rivers cross Germany. The Rhine, with its tributaries, including the Main and the Moselle; the Ems; the Weser; and the Elbe all flow through central Germany, many into the North Sea. The Oder crosses eastern Germany and empties into the Baltic. The Danube and the Inn drain southern Germany and flow toward the Black Sea.

Germany's climate is temperate. Warm ocean currents moderate the cold of the far north, and high elevations counteract warmer tendencies toward the south. Winter temperatures average below 20°F in the south and about 30°F in the north. Summer temperatures average in the mid-60's throughout the country. Rainfall is moderate, averaging about 30 inches for the country as a whole and generally decreasing toward the south.

The people. The population of both Germanys is quite homogeneous. German is the universal language. A majority of the people are Protestant, accounting for 80 percent of the population in East Germany, and almost half in West Germany. Roman Catholicism ranks second and accounts for 47 percent of the West German population. There are no major minority groups. A large Jewish community that lived in Germany before World War II was brutally destroyed by the Nazi regime.

Since World War II, West Germany has received a steady flow of refugees from East Germany. The western population was also swollen by an influx of foreign workers, mostly from southern Europe, who were attracted by West Germany's manpower shortage. As a result of these migrations, West Germany, with 637 people per square mile, is one of Europe's densest nations. East Germany, the victim of steady emigration, is much sparser. Both countries have very small growth rates.

Both nations are three-quarters urbanized, but West Germany has more and larger cities. Hamburg and Munich are the largest cities in West Germany; Dresden and Leipzig, after East Berlin, are the largest in East Germany. Divided Berlin as a whole is the largest city in all Germany.

Economy. Both East and West Germany are prosperous countries, although West Germany is by far the wealthier of the two. Germany's prosperity is based on a long tradition of industry and on a highly skilled, well disciplined, and industrious labor force. Industry makes the greatest contribution to the German economy.

BUSY HARBOR AT BREMEN *exemplifies West Germany's postwar economic miracle, despite recent defeat. In fact, the rebuilding of Germany's bombed industry promoted the miracle.*

The economies of both Germanys expanded rapidly after 1945. In West Germany, the expansion consisted of rebuilding and developing industries destroyed in World War II. West Germany has become the leading industrial nation in Europe, and the fourth largest in the world. In East Germany, the expansion consisted largely of developing new industries. East Germany has lately become the most industrialized of the East European countries other than the Soviet Union. Both Germanys concentrate on heavy industry.

Germany has some excellent farmland, especially in the river valleys of the *Mittelland,* but agriculture is of much less importance than industry in both East and West. It contributes a greater proportion of the East German national product than of the West German product.

International trade is of more importance in the economy of West Germany than in that of East Germany. West Germany is fully integrated into the West European economy through the Common Market. Its tremendous volume and surplus value have made it a keen rival of the United States as the most prosperous and active commercial nation in the world.
West Germany. West Germany's principal natural resource is high-

grade coal, which provides 20 percent of the nation's energy needs. Imported oil provides over 50 percent, however, because of the excessively high energy demands of the heavily industrialized economy.

There are also deposits of petroleum, potash, iron, copper, and zinc, and waterpower is abundant. The leading West German industries are iron and steel production, mining, chemical manufacture, machinery and vehicle production, shipbuilding, and power production. The older light industries of textile weaving, brewing, food processing, and precision tool manufacture still prosper, however.

West German industry is concentrated in the Saar and the Ruhr regions near the western border, on the northern plain, and in the middle Rhine valley.

While West German manufacturing employs almost two-fifths of the labor force, less than ten percent is absorbed by agriculture. Only three percent of the national product comes from agriculture, while nearly 50 percent comes from industry.

West Germany is Western Europe's leading producer of rye and potatoes. Wheat, barley, and sugar beets are also important crops. Tobacco, nuts, and fruits—especially wine grapes—are grown in the lower Rhine valley. Dairy

THE POSTWAR ECONOMIC MIRACLE *extends to both Germanys, which share a common geography. Scenes like this could be duplicated all along the north German coast, east or west.*

cattle and other livestock, particularly pigs, are important.

West German exports earned $171.9 billion in 1979, and imports cost $159.7 billion. West Germany is the second-ranked trading nation in the world. Machinery and equipment, automobiles, and chemicals are the leading exports, and foodstuffs and raw materials are imported. Most West German trade is with other West European countries and the United States.

East Germany. East Germany's main natural resource is low-grade brown coal, and it produces one-third of the world's supply. Electricity is the nation's main energy source, and natural gas is gaining in importance. A gas pipeline from the Soviet Union was completed in the mid-1970's. Uranium, cobalt, iron, copper, potash, and zinc are also available, and waterpower is abundant. All East German industry is nationalized, and the state has concentrated on developing heavy industry. Iron and steel production, as well as mining, machinery and vehicle production, chemical manufacture, shipbuilding, and power production are the main industries. Industry provides nearly two-thirds of the national income.

Agriculture has made great strides since its large-scale collectivization beginning in the 1960's, followed by rapid technological advances in the 1970's. East Germany now leads all East European nations in agricultural output.

Wheat, rye, barley, sugar beets, and potatoes are the leading crops. Livestock, especially pigs, are extensively raised, and dairying is also important to the economy.

East Germany has an equitable balance of trade. In 1978 exports earned $13.3 billion and imports cost $14.6 billion. Machinery and vehicles, textiles, and chemicals are the leading

exports, and foodstuffs and raw materials are imported. Most East German trade is with other communist-dominated East European countries, particularly the Soviet Union.

Government. The Federal Republic of Germany is a democracy; the German Democratic Republic is a totalitarian state.

West Germany. West Germany is a federal union of eleven *Länder,* or states. The city of West Berlin has close political ties with West Germany. A president is head of state. Actual executive power rests with a chancellor, or prime minister, who is elected by the *Bundestag,* the larger house of the legislature. He and the cabinet he leads are responsible to the legislature.

Members of the *Bundestag* are popularly elected to four-year terms. Members of the *Bundesrat,* the smaller, less powerful upper house, are chosen by the governments of the individual *Länder* for indefinite terms. Representatives of West Berlin sit as members of the West German legislature.

The Federal Republic is a member of the United Nations, the Organization for Economic Cooperation and Development (OECD), the Common Market, the North Atlantic Treaty Organization (NATO), and the Council of Europe.

East Germany. Political life in the German Democratic Republic is dominated by the East German Communist Party, officially called the Socialist Unity Party. The politburo, or political bureau, of its central committee determines national policy, and the first secretary of the party is usually the key figure in the government.

The East German constitution provides for a popularly elected legislature. Candidates for the legislature are

nominated under party control. The legislature chooses a council of state to act for it between its short sessions, and the chairman of the council serves as head of state. Actual executive power rests with a council of ministers, or cabinet, and its chairman, who is equivalent to a prime minister.

Most noncommunist countries did not recognize the Democratic Republic until West Germany did so in 1972. In 1973 it became a member of the United Nations; diplomatic relations with the United States were established in 1974. East Germany is also a member of the Warsaw Pact and of Comecon.

History. Political division is not new to Germany. With no major natural boundaries save the Alps, the territory has been open to invasion from east, north, and west. In ancient times there were many small, tribal states, all subject to easy conquest. Among the earliest settlers were the Teutons, a Germanic people.

The territory was divided among several Teutonic tribes—the Franks, the Saxons, and the Thuringians—led by elective kings. Beginning in the 200's A.D., other Germanic peoples from the east settled in the area—notably the Goths and the Burgundians. The Romans made several unsuccessful attempts to conquer the Germanic tribes, but no single ruler gained control of the entire region until the 300's, when the Huns swept across the land.

Both the Huns and the Vandals, who followed soon after, were migratory, warlike peoples whose main goal was conquest, and their rule over the settled tribes was brief. It was only the Franks, who settled in the Rhine valley in the late 300's, who eventually attempted to unite permanently the Germanic peoples.

Frankish kingdom. The Franks expanded westward from the Rhine into Gaul, driving out the Roman legions stationed there. They adopted Christianity and won the support of the popes, whose power by the 500's was greater than that of Rome. They defeated the other Germanic tribes and in 732 they fought off a Muslim invasion of Europe.

The Franks reached the height of their power under Charles the Great, or Charlemagne, who became king in 768. Under Charlemagne, the Franks controlled a vast territory ranging from central Italy on the south to the Baltic Sea on the north, and from the Pyrenees on the west to the Elbe River on the east. Charlemagne accepted the role of protector of the popes, and in 800 he was crowned emperor in Rome, an act that laid the religious and political foundations for the later Holy Roman Empire.

The unity Charlemagne achieved did not long survive him. Several dec-

KLAUS D. FRANCKE/PETER ARNOLD

ades of disunity followed his death in 814, and in 843 the Treaty of Verdun divided his territories into three parts. The eastern, predominantly Teuton, portion, between the Rhine and the Elbe rivers, went to Louis the German, and became the core of modern Germany while the west remained French.

The Saxons. The tribal loyalties and ambitions born before Charlemagne's time had not been forgotten. Each major tribal unit had formed a country, and the dukes and princes who led them vied for control of the German throne. By the early 900's one Teuton clan, the Saxons, had emerged dominant. Its first ruler, Henry the Fowler, extended German territory to the Oder River and defended it against attacks from Magyar and Slavic peoples to the south.

A Saxon king, Otto I, in 962, was given the crown of Italy and became the first Holy Roman Emperor as a reward for aiding the pope. The Holy Roman Empire revived, at least in name, the old Roman Empire and gave to Germany the empire's prestige as well as the support of the papacy.

By about 1030, the Holy Roman Empire was a prosperous feudal nation with thriving towns and vigorous trade. Henry III, who became emperor in 1039, probably held more actual power than any other.

Henry was the last emperor with such power, however. After his death in 1056 a regent ruled for his young heir, and the period of the regency was fatal for the strength of the German throne. Both the church and the nobility had become dissatisfied with their lack of power. By the 1070's the pope and the emperor were in open conflict over the distribution of political and religious power. The local princes sided with the papacy to reduce the strength of the emperor.

The conflict continued into the mid-1200's, and although both emperors and popes won victories, the final result of the struggle was a great loss of power for both. The empire disintegrated into a state of anarchy in the 1250's. For a 20-year period known as the "Great Interregnum," no one man ruled Germany, although many tried. Moreover, as each faction grew in power—the princes, the dukes, the bishops, and the towns—a tradition of disunity was firmly established, and it became even harder to consolidate political power.

It was only in 1273, at the insistence of Pope Gregory X, who feared the growing power of France, that the German princes elected one of their number to be Holy Roman Emperor. Their choice was Rudolf of the House of Hapsburg in Austria, which was then a minor princely house. Rudolf took steps to insure the continuance on the throne of members of his family, and later Hapsburg emperors became powerful.

The Hapsburgs. During the Middle Ages, the Hapsburg emperors added to the territory under their control, but the unification of the German states did not follow the Hapsburg rise to power. The German emperor was an elected king by tradition and by a law enacted in 1356. As he could rule only with the consent of the princes who elected him, the German emperor constantly had to make concessions to them, and he was unable to rule as firmly as a hereditary monarch could. Because of the weakness of the central government, the German states were less an empire than a federation dominated by the stronger states. Nearly constant competition for power kept the German states in turmoil from the 1300's to the 1800's, but the Hapsburg family remained the dominant power through the 1700's.

Administrative and economic policies initiated during the 1100's had encouraged the development of towns. By the middle of the 1300's, these policies, coupled with a renewed interest in the arts and an expanding economy, had transformed many towns into "free cities" — large, autonomous units free from the control of local princes. From the middle of the 1200's to the middle of the 1400's, the influence of German cities rivaled that of German princes.

Despite the fragmentation of the Holy Roman Empire, it reached the height of its power and size in the early 1500's under Emperor Charles V, who, by inheritance and marriage, ruled Spain, Portugal, Belgium, and the Netherlands as well as the German states. It was during his reign, however, that religious controversy flared, contributing to the final disintegration of the empire. In 1517 Martin Luther, an Augustinian monk, called for reforms in the Roman Catholic Church.

DÜRER'S MOTHER, *a superb portrait by the supreme master of the German renaissance.*

GERMAN INFORMATION CENTER

Reformation. The Lutheran "Reformation" attracted many more radical social, political, and religious reformers, and they became a threat to both the church and the empire. Charles V led a diet, or council, at Worms in 1521 to try Luther. The council banned the spread of any new doctrines. The reformers continued, however, encouraged by power-seeking princes, who adopted their reforms as a means of opposing the emperor.

The progress of the Reformation was speeded by Charles's involvement in a series of wars with France. In Germany, disputes among the proliferating Protestant sects and between Protestants and Roman Catholics led to a series of religious wars, which were ended in 1555 by the Peace of Augsburg.

The peace settlement marked the final collapse of the emperor's real power. It granted to each prince within the empire the right to determine the religion of his subjects. In 1556 Charles abdicated, leaving his Spanish possessions to his son Philip, and his German dominions to his brother, Ferdinand.

The Peace of Augsburg had not finally settled the religious disputes, and it had only aggravated Germany's political confusion. In 1618 fighting began again in the Thirty Years' War. At first the war was confined to the Roman Catholic-Protestant conflict, but almost immediately the old issues of prince versus emperor, and federation versus empire, were renewed.

The war spread and eventually involved most of continental Europe as well as England and Sweden. The Peace of Westphalia, which settled the war in 1648, formalized German disunity by giving the local princes more power than the emperor. Each of the 300 separate German states received the right to conduct its own diplomacy, determine the religion of its people, and vote on the emperor's right to collect taxes, raise an army, or conduct foreign policy.

Germany's enemies, notably France, gained from German fragmentation, which greatly diminished its international power.

Rise of Prussia. During the latter half of the 1600's, Prussia, known then as Brandenburg, began to grow from a small duchy into the most powerful state in Germany. Prussia's ruling Hohenzollern house increased the territory within its domain and, at the same time, established an efficient, centralized administration to control it. The army, officered by the nobility, became the central institution of the state.

Decisive in Prussia's ascendancy to power within Germany was the succession to the throne in 1740 of Frederick II, called the Great, a man of driving force and shrewd statesmanship. Immediately upon assuming the throne he invaded Silesia, a large and wealthy

Austrian territory. Finally, in 1763, Prussia won the disputed Silesian territory, which doubled Prussia's population and natural resources. Germany was then polarized between northern Germany, dominated by Prussia, and southern Germany, led by Austria.

Prussia's rapid rise to power had been due in large part to Frederick the Great, and after his death in 1786, the system he had built could not function effectively. Thus in 1806, when the French armies of Napoleon were conquering Europe, Prussia offered little resistance and fell to Napoleon after the Battle of Jena.

Napoleonic era. By 1806 Napoleon controlled most of the German states, which he organized into the Confederation of the Rhine. He persuaded the Austrian emperor, Francis I, formally to dissolve the Holy Roman Empire. In 1809 Austria itself yielded to the French, and Napoleon's troops occupied all of Germany.

The French occupation ended in 1813, after Austria reluctantly joined forces with Prussia and Russia in a war of liberation that pushed Napoleon's armies west of the Rhine. But the fairly brief French occupation had wrought changes in Germany more significant than the formal dissolution of the Holy Roman Empire.

Germany was still a loose collection of states, but the Napoleonic Confederation of the Rhine had reduced their number and the Congress of Vienna, held in 1815 after Napoleon's defeat, accepted the reduction by setting up the Germanic Confederation, a loose grouping of 38 independent German states.

Prussia had pressed for a more unified Germany, but the congress encouraged the autonomy of the states as sought by the Austrian foreign minister, Prince Klemens von Metternich. Metternich's shrewd leadership led to tightened monarchical control over the social, political, and economic life of Austria. This "Metternich system" dominated the south German states.

In Prussia, too, the movement for reform—which before 1815 had resulted in tax and administrative reforms and the abolition of serfdom—began to lag as reactionary forces triumphed over liberalism throughout Germany.

The Napoleonic wars had awakened democratic and nationalistic movements that the German governments felt must be repressed. Under the leadership of Austria's Metternich, the German states imposed tight controls on all civil liberties, especially on the activities of the universities. These controls only spurred the liberals and nationalists to resist, and in 1848 they rebelled against Metternich's reactionary government.

Risings of 1848. Inspired by a similar revolution in Paris, large numbers of Austrians, mostly in Vienna, organized and demanded a constitution.

Metternich fled Austria, and the emperor granted a constitution and abdicated in December, 1848.

The rebellion had spread from Vienna to the Hapsburg's Hungarian and Slavic subject peoples, who demanded the establishment of independent Slavic and Magyar states. The Slavs organized a Pan-Slav Congress to lead their nationalistic movement. A new Austrian emperor, Francis Joseph I, concentrated on crushing the rebellions in Hungary and the Slavic areas, ignoring the more peaceful rebellion among the Germans.

The rebellious Germans were demanding not only political and social liberties, but the political union of Germany. Most German states elected liberal local governments, which in turn elected liberal representatives to a national assembly that met in Frankfurt in May, 1848, to establish a republic. In 1849 the assembly drafted a democratic constitution for a unified German state and elected Prussia's ruler, Frederick William IV, emperor of the new nation.

Some of the states opposed the new organization, however, and Austria, which with Russia's help had quelled the Hungarian and Slavic revolutions in early 1849, refused to join the unification movement that would have forced it to give up its non-German territories in joining Germany.

Frederick William IV, unwilling to accept the throne from an elected assembly, refused the imperial crown, and by 1850 the old constitution of the Germanic Confederation had been readopted and the unification and reform efforts of the assembly had failed. Austria was once more able to impose a superficial calm on Germany after putting down the 1848 rebellions, but it could not stem the movement for German unification.

Unification. In 1844 Prussia had encouraged unification by organizing a customs union, the *Zollverein,* among more than half the German states, excluding Austria. The unification efforts gathered strength after 1862 under the leadership of Otto von Bismarck, Prussia's chief minister, who followed a stern policy of "blood and iron" in leading Germany to European dominance.

Bismarck had soon centralized and strengthened Prussia's government and pressed the development of the army and expansion into new territory. Prussia annexed the two predominantly German duchies of Schleswig and Holstein, which Denmark claimed. Austria aided Prussia to drive out the Danes, but Bismarck's subsequent attempt to control Holstein angered Austria, and war between the two was only narrowly averted.

War did break out between them for seven weeks in 1866. In the Seven Weeks' War Prussian forces easily defeated Austria, and in 1867 as a result a constitution was adopted for a new

OTTO VON BISMARCK, *the iron chancellor, creator of the modern, unified Germany.*

confederation excluding Austria and several south German states.

Constitutionally a federal state, the new North German Confederation was actually under Prussian control. Austria, having lost control of Germany, was forced to admit Hungary as an equal partner in a dual monarchy, and Austrian history diverged from that of Germany.

German Empire. Prussia quickly became the greatest power in Europe and had soon roundly defeated France in 1870–1871 in a war over dynastic claims to the throne of Spain. Prussia forced France to accept a harsh, cruel and humiliating settlement—France ceded the industrially rich territories of Alsace and Lorraine, paid a large indemnity, and supported a German army of occupation.

Now the leader of all Europe, Bismarck also succeeded in 1871 in bringing the south German states except Austria into the North German Confederation. He became the first chancellor of this German Empire.

The new Prussian state was a curious mixture of democratic and authoritarian institutions. Advanced social welfare laws existed side by side with legislation curbing the Roman Catholic Church and suppressing the socialists. Both the central government and the 25 states constituting the union had monarchical forms of government.

Each state enjoyed a large degree of autonomy, although the federal government, or *Reich,* was empowered to administer a common communications system, maintain an army, and conduct foreign affairs. In addition to the Kaiser, or emperor, the federal government had a legislature with two houses—the *Bundesrat,* where the states received representation, and the *Reichstag,* where the people were represented through a system of universal suffrage.

The economic growth of the new empire was astounding. In 1860, for example, German steel production did not even equal that of France; by 1900 it exceeded that of both England and France combined. By 1900, moreover, German naval power rivaled that of Great Britain, the traditional "mistress of the sea."

Germany's political prestige also grew, as a result not only of its strengthened economic and military position but also of the capable leadership of the "iron chancellor." Bismarck consolidated the new Germany's continental position by arranging alliances in 1882 with Austria-Hungary and Italy, in the Triple Alliance, and in 1887 with Russia.

Bismarck fell from power in 1890, when the young emperor, William II, who opposed his authoritarian measures and his diplomatic techniques, decided to conduct German diplomacy personally.

Under William, Germany followed a policy of aggressive imperialism that divided Europe into two opposing camps—pro-German and anti-German. William antagonized Britain by enlarging the German navy, enraged his ally Russia by competing with it for territory in the Near East, and made no attempt to improve relations with France, which had been poor since the loss of Alsace-Lorraine.

German aggressiveness drew France and Britain, traditional enemies, closer together. In the Entente Cordiale of 1904 the two settled several long-standing disputes and united in opposition to Germany. In 1905 William tested the entente by openly urging independence for the French protectorate of Morocco.

The entente proved solid, and in 1906 France and Britain led the Algeciras Conference of European powers, which berated Germany for its insult to France. In 1907 Russia, Germany's former ally, entered the British-French alliance, forming the Triple Entente. In 1911 Germany precipitated a second "Moroccan Crisis" and was again rebuked.

World War I. The European powers were able to settle the incidents of 1905 and 1911 peacefully, but crisis followed crisis in the Balkan region. Bulgaria and Turkey, having lost territory in Balkan wars in 1912 and in 1913, joined Germany, Austria-Hungary, and Italy to form the alliance of Central Powers in opposition to the Triple Entente.

In 1914 a crisis caused by the assassination of Archduke Francis Ferdinand, heir to the Austrian throne, led to World War I. Bosnia, where the assassination occurred, was an Austrian territory, but as the assassin was Serbian, and as Serbia had led Pan-Slav activity in Bosnia, Austria threatened reprisals against Serbia. Germany supported Austria, while Russia backed Serbia.

Both sides misjudged the seriousness of the situation, and the war that resulted involved the allies of Germany and Russia and eventually all of Europe as well as the United States, Japan, and the Middle East. Germany had predicted that the war would be short, but the war lasted four years, and Germany was unable to maintain the strength of its forces.

In 1918, with defeat imminent, rebellions broke out in the German territories, resulting in the abdication of the emperor and the declaration of a German republic. The peace settlements exacted huge reparations; confiscated German overseas possessions and non-German-speaking European territories, including Alsace and Lorraine; and disarmed the country.

Weimar Republic. A republic was formally established in July, 1919, when the Weimar constitution was adopted. The new German state faced difficulties from its establishment, especially in dealing with the humiliation of the dictated peace and in bearing the heavy burden of reparations, which led to inflation and a currency collapse.

The lack of a tradition of unity and of parliamentary democracy provided a shaky foundation for the new government, made more unstable by attacks from the Communists on the extreme left and authoritarian nationalists on the extreme right.

In 1929, just as the government had begun to solve its economic and political problems and had begun to be reintegrated into Europe by joining the League of Nations, the worldwide economic depression struck. Unemployment increased and with it came widespread resentment against the existing German government. The heavy victories of extremist parties in elections held in 1930 reflected the growing popular discontent.

On the left, the Communists scored heavily, and on the right, Adolf Hitler's National Socialist, or Nazi, Party, gained enough seats to become the second largest party in the *Reichstag*. In 1932 elections, the Nazis became the largest single party in the *Reichstag*, and in 1933 Adolf Hitler was appointed chancellor.

Nazi era. Hitler came to power partly by heading a highly organized political party, and partly because the brand of nationalism that he preached was attractive to the Germans, who were humiliated by defeat in the war, impoverished by the depression, and fearful for their property in the face of Communism.

He promised to create a revitalized,

NAZI YOUTH RALLY. *Germans of the 1930's, humiliated by defeat, dismayed by inflation and disunity, easily fell under the spell of the authoritarian bombast of Adolf Hitler.*

strengthened Germany—a Germany stronger than the First Reich, the Holy Roman Empire, or the Second Reich, Bismarck's empire. He assured Germans that they were capable of greatness because they were descended from the strong, pure, "Aryan race" of Teutons, and he directed their hostility toward the Jews and non-Germans, especially the Slavs.

Although the Nazi party received only 44 percent of the vote in elections held in late 1933, Hitler proclaimed that the elections had made him the spokesman of all Germany. The *Reichstag* granted him dictatorial powers and suspended the constitution. Germany was transformed from a federal state into a highly centralized state. The office of president was abolished, and Hitler assumed all powers of state.

Economic policy was determined by the central government, and unemployment was reduced by public works projects and massive rearmament. All opposition parties were banned and strict censorship was imposed. The legal system was reorganized to place the needs of the state above accepted standards of justice, and concentration camps were opened to imprison and often kill Hitler's "convicted" political opponents.

The camps came to be used primarily for the imprisonment and murder of Jews, as anti-Semitism became an increasingly important part of the Nazi program. Jews were forbidden to teach, hold office, attend universities, or engage in many businesses, and non-Jews were ordered to ostracize them and to boycott Jewish businesses. Between 1935 and 1945 Hitler's regime killed some 6 million European Jews.

At the basis of Hitler's foreign policy was hostility to the conditions imposed on Germany by the Versailles treaty system that ended World War I. In 1933 Germany ended its membership in the League of Nations. Hitler abrogated German agreements to remain neutral, and in 1935 began openly to rearm the country.

In 1936 and 1937 Germany entered into treaties with Japan and Italy. Italy, led by the Fascist dictator Benito Mussolini, became an especially close ally, forming one half of the "Rome-Berlin Axis." One common feature of these treaties was their declaration of opposition to communism, but in 1939 Hitler entered a nonaggression pact with the Communist government of the Soviet Union.

Hitler also refused to obey the territorial limits set by the Versailles settlement. Using the desire to unite all German-speaking peoples as an excuse, Hitler annexed Austria in 1938 and in 1939 he took part of Czechoslovakia. The World War I allies did not strongly object to his actions, hoping to appease him and prevent a second world conflict.

World War II. Until 1939 Hitler had gained territory and allies bloodlessly, but in that summer he demanded that the Free City of Danzig, within Poland's borders, be "restored" to the Reich. When he was refused, Germany invaded Poland and occupied Danzig. Britain and France, bound by treaty to protect Poland and realizing that Hitler could not be appeased, declared war on Germany on September 3, 1939.

The major German offensive against the west began in 1940, when German

THE HOLOCAUST. *General Eisenhower at the Gotha concentration camp in 1945. About 6 million Jews and others died in these camps.*

troops overran the neutral states of Denmark, Norway, the Netherlands, and Belgium, and invaded France. In June, 1941, German armies broke the nonaggression pact and invaded the Soviet Union.

In December, 1941, the United States entered the war against Hitler, and in 1942 Soviet troops began a counteroffensive. Before the tide turned in favor of the Allies, Hitler controlled by conquest or alliances almost all of continental Europe as far east as the outskirts of Moscow and territories in North Africa and the Middle East.

The main Allied counteroffensive began in June, 1944, when British, Canadian, and U. S. troops landed on the beaches of Normandy. By September, 1944, the Allies had reached the German border. When Soviet troops reached the outskirts of Berlin from the east in May, 1945, and the fall of the city seemed imminent, Hitler committed suicide. The Germans surrendered, and the war was over.

Occupation. The leaders of the four major allied nations met at Potsdam, Germany, in July, 1945, and agreed to partition Germany into four zones of occupation. The Soviet Union occupied the portion east of the Elbe River and the United States, Britain, and France divided the territory to the west.

Portions of Germany east of the Oder and Neisse rivers were placed under the administration of Poland, which was dominated by the Soviet Union. The Allies also divided Berlin into four occupation zones and established the Allied Control Council to coordinate the occupation.

The Soviets did not cooperate with the other members of the council, and in 1948, after several policy disputes with the Soviet Union, France, Britain, and the United States merged their sectors and gave the new zone a large measure of self-government.

Later in the same year, elections were held in western Germany and a federal constitution was agreed upon. The Soviet Union responded in October, 1949, by establishing the Soviet zone of occupation as the German Democratic Republic.

Germany was thus divided again. The Soviet Union tried to force the Allies to leave Berlin and to allow unification on Soviet terms by blockading Berlin in 1949, but a massive airlift broke the blockade.

Britain, France, and the United States maintained nominal control over West Germany until 1955, when the Federal Republic of Germany became fully sovereign. In 1955 the Soviet Union recognized the sovereignty of the German Democratic Republic, in the east.

Divided Germany. In the early 1950's both Germanys concentrated on repairing the destruction wrought by the war, and both worked to develop

CHILDREN PLAY *under the Berlin Wall, built to stem the flow of refugees to the West.*

and expand their industry. By the mid-1960's West Germany had become one of the world's leading industrial nations. Its political recovery paralleled its economic recovery.

Under the leadership of Konrad Adenauer and his Christian Democratic Party, West Germany became integrated into Western Europe as a staunch ally of the West. A resurgence of extreme right-wing nationalism in the mid-1960's disturbed the government and led in 1966 to the formation of an alliance of the Christian Democrats and their traditional opponents, the Social Democrats. Willy Brandt, leader of the Social Democratic Party, became chancellor in 1969.

He inaugurated a new foreign policy, *Ostpolitik,* which sought accomodation with the Soviet Union and other communist nations. Friendship treaties were signed with the Soviet Union and Poland in 1970, with East Germany in 1972, and with Czechoslovakia in 1973. For these efforts Brandt received the Nobel Peace Prize in 1971, but he resigned in 1974 following the discovery that one of his aides was an East German spy.

Helmut Schmidt succeeded him in time to face an economic recession induced by oil-import shortages, which resulted in high unemployment and inflation. By 1975 the crisis had passed and prosperity resumed.

West Germany has relatively low unemployment and inflation, and one of the strongest economies in the world. In 1982, however, the worsening economic climate and a general trend toward conservatism led to the ousting of Schmidt by a parliamentary no-confidence vote. He was replaced by conservative Helmut Kohl.

The United States, France, and Britain still have military troops stationed in parts of West Germany.

East Germany made somewhat slower progress in rebuilding its economy. Despite a serious workers' revolt in 1953, which was suppressed only with the help of Soviet forces, relative prosperity was attained by the early 1960's. Severe economic problems in the mid-1960's resulted in some decentralization of economic administration and increased tolerance of the profit motive in industry. By the 1970's the economy had expanded significantly, giving East Germans the highest standard of living in Eastern Europe.

East Germany was made a socialist state, separate from the Soviet Union, by the terms of its 1968 constitution. However, a 1974 amendment to the constitution asserted the nation's eternal allegiance to the Soviet Union. East Germany is fully integrated into the Soviet bloc, and its industry is a vital factor in the economies of other Soviet satellites.

In 1961 the government of East Germany built a wall in Berlin separating the two sectors of the city to halt the flight of refugees to the west through West Berlin. However, by 1972, with tensions easing, an agreement was signed providing for civilian travel in the two sectors of Berlin.

In the late 1980's, the steady flow of young skilled workers from East Germany became a flood, crippling the East German economy and helping to fuel mass demonstrations for major economic and political reforms. In late 1989, Erich Honecker, long-time Communist Party chief and head of state, was removed from power along with many old-line Communist leaders. The new leadership began the dismantling of the Berlin Wall and the East German secret police, and opened the way for multiparty democracy and the possible reunification of Germany.

Greece

Official name: *Hellenic Republic*
Area: *50,944 sq. mi., 131,944 sq. km.*
Population: *(1980) 9,317,000*
Capital: *Athens (Pop., 1971, 867,023)*
Language: *Greek*
Religion: *Orthodox Christian*
Currency unit: *Drachma*
National holiday: *Independence Day, Mar. 25*

Greece, the southernmost state of the Balkan peninsula, is a mountainous country with many small peninsulas that jut out into the Mediterranean Sea. Almost one-fifth of the total land area consists of islands, the largest of which are Crete, Rhodes, Lesbos, Chios, and Samos. Mainland Greece is bordered on the northwest by Albania, on the north by Yugoslavia and Bulgaria, and on the northeast by Turkey. To the east is the Aegean Sea; to the west, the Ionian Sea; and to the south, the open Mediterranean.

The land. The surface of Greece is mainly rough and hilly, and there is very little flat land. The rugged Pindus Mountains dominate the landscape of western mainland Greece from the northern border to the southern coast. Plains are few and lie mostly along the eastern coast. They are isolated by intervening highlands. Rivers are short and usually dry in summer.

The climate varies from region to region. In general, the south and east have hot, dry summers, and mild, moist, windy winters. In the north and west winters are rather cold, summers are hot, and rainfall is more abundant than in the south and east.

West of the mainland are the Ionian Islands. To the east, in the Aegean, are the Cyclades, Sporades, Dodecanese, and other island groups.

BOYS WHITEWASHING THE STREETS *on the Greek island of Mykonos. Dazzling white houses and streets seen against blue skies make the Aegean islands a tourist paradise.*

The people. Almost the entire population of the country is Greek, but there are small minorities of Bulgarians, Turks, Slavs, and Albanians in the border areas.

Population is densest along the eastern coast, in the Athens region, in the major towns of Macedonia in the north, and on a few of the islands. The southern Peloponnesus and the more mountainous interior are sparsely populated. Greece has traditionally had a high rate of emigration, and Greeks have settled throughout the world. Those who do well often help support their relatives back home in Greece.

Economy. Greece is not a prosperous country by Western standards, but its economy has industrialized and generally improved significantly since World War II. Agriculture employs about one-third of the labor force. It is the mainstay of the economy, despite the fact that less than 30 percent of the land is suitable for cultivation.

Since mining is insignificant (although lignite and bauxite extraction is somewhat prosperous), the impressive gains of recent years in hydroelectric production have been insufficient to fulfill the nation's energy needs.

Greece's generally poor soils are suitable for only a limited variety of crops, including olives, grapes, cotton, tobacco, and grains. Sheep and goats are herded in the northwest hills.

In 1979 Greece's imports cost more than $9.7 billion and its exports earned only $3.9 billion. The expenditures of tourists in Greece, and the remittances of Greeks abroad, partially offset the large deficit.

The chief exports are tobacco, fruits, cotton, wine, olives and olive oil, and mineral ores. The main imports are machinery and vehicles, lumber, textiles, manufactured consumer goods, foodstuffs, chemicals, and petroleum. Greece's leading trading partner is West Germany, followed by Japan, Italy, and France.

Parthenon

THE ROCKS OF METEORA *in Thessaly in central Greece hold ancient monasteries, built high up for seclusion and defense. Meteora has few monks left, but many tourists visit the site.*

Government.
By popular referendum, Greece has a republican form of government, with a president elected by Parliament, and a premier as chief of government. The monarchy, abolished in 1973, was replaced by a republic in 1974, and a new constitution was adopted in 1975.

Greece is a member of the United Nations, the Council of Europe, the Common Market, and the North Atlantic Treaty Organization (NATO).

History.
Modern Greece has roots in the classical Greek civilization that flourished on the Hellenic peninsula in ancient times. Between about 800 B.C. and 300 B.C., the Greeks developed a culture that laid the foundation for much of later Western civilization.

In 338 B.C. Greece was conquered by its northern neighbor, Macedonia. Greek culture was spread throughout Macedonia's vast Middle Eastern and Mediterranean empire, all of which, including Greece itself, eventually came under the control of Rome.

In 285 A.D. the Roman Empire was divided, and Greece became part of the eastern section, ruled from Byzantium. In 330 Byzantium, renamed Constantinople, became the capital of all that remained of the Roman Empire. As a part of what later became the Byzantine Empire, the Greeks were still the cultural and intellectual leaders of the eastern Mediterranean.

While western Europe struggled with the disorder produced by barbarian invasions, the Orthodox Christian, Greco-Roman civilization of the eastern empire maintained its stability. Greek cultural influence was dependent on Byzantine political strength, however, and the eastern empire was unable to withstand the onslaught of a new power in Asia Minor, the Ottoman Turks.

In the 1000's, the Turks began to attack the Byzantine Empire. Over a perior of 400 years they conquered Byzantine territory bit by bit, until in 1453 they captured Constantinople.

Ottoman rule.
The Greeks did not fare badly under the Ottomans. They enjoyed some self-government, and Greeks in Constantinople, called Phanariots, filled many high positions in the Ottoman administration. The Turks did not force the Greek Christians to convert to Islam, although those who did enjoyed a higher status in the Muslim society.

For the most part, the Ottoman government ignored Greeks living outside Asia Minor, and in many cases neglected them. What remained of Classical Greek culture decayed, and the people of Greece sank into poverty.

The Greeks were far from content under Turkish rule, however. In the 1700's those who still lived in the Hellenic peninsula began to develop a feeling of national pride and a desire for independence. Moreover, in the 1700's the Ottoman government began to loosen control over its more distant territories.

The Greek economy, exhausted since Roman times, began to revive, and Greek trade, industry, and shipping expanded. At the same time self-government began to develop on the local level. The spirit of nationalism swept Europe in the early 1800's, and Greek nationalism took the form of a desire for full freedom from Turkey and included the goal of uniting all Greek-speaking people into one nation.

Independence.
The Greek struggle for independence began in 1821, when Alexander Ypsilanti, a leader of a secret revolutionary organization, *Hetairia Philikê,* or Society of Friends, led a revolt in the Phanariot-governed principalities of Moravia and Walachia.

Ypsilanti had hoped for aid from neighboring Russia, but he received no support and was defeated. Uprisings also broke out in the south of Greece, however, and continued despite severe Turkish reprisals.

By 1822 the rebellion was countrywide, and the Greeks declared their independence. Over the next few years, Greek guerrilla forces won control of much of their territory from the Ottoman Turks. In 1825, however, Turkey gained the support of Egypt, nominally a part of the Ottoman Empire. The untrained Greek guerrillas could not stand up against the power and organization of the Turkish-Egyptian army, and the Greeks steadily lost the land they had won.

The rebels would have met total defeat if they had not received help in 1827 from Britain, France, and Russia. All three had interests in the Balkans, and all opposed Turkish domination of the region. The European nations agreed to join in finding or forcing a solution to the war. They tried to impose an armistice and urged Turkey to grant independence to Greece.

When the Turks refused, the European powers ordered a blockade to enforce a truce and to prevent the Turkish forces from receiving supplies. In enforcing the blockade, ships from Britain, Russia, and France destroyed most of the Egyptian fleet when it tried to bring troops and supplies into the port of Navarino in October, 1827.

In 1828 Russia declared war on Turkey, and by so doing aided the Greeks. Although the war grew out of a Russo-Turkish territorial dispute, Russia also saw an advantage in weakening Turkey by driving the Turks from Greece.

Russia defeated Turkey in August, 1829, and the Treaty of Adrianople, which ended the war, contained a provision granting independence to Greece. Turkey agreed to accept the London Protocol of March, 1829, in which the three European powers decided that Greece—which then included only the Peloponnesus, the Cyclades, and Central Greece—would be an autonomous state under a king to be chosen from among the royal families of Europe.

The Greeks, however, already had a government. In 1827 they had chosen an assembly and elected a president, Ioannes Kapodistrias. He was assassinated in 1831, however, and Greece then accepted the powers' choice of a Bavarian prince, Otto, as king.

A new nation. The new state faced great problems. Many Greeks wished to continue fighting to liberate territory that was inhabited by Greeks but not governed by Greece. The economy, severely damaged by the revolution, was weak—there was little manufacturing and agricultural techniques were old-fashioned and inefficient. A sense of local pride hindered administration by a national government.

Otto's attempts to solve these problems led to a highly centralized, bureaucratic government that was too clumsy to be effective and too complex for the people to deal with. In addition, the European powers still had great influence in Greek politics.

In 1843 two political factions, one supported by the British and one by the Russians, rebelled against the king. The rebels demanded a constitution and an elected assembly. Otto agreed to these demands and established a constitutional monarchy. The new system worked almost as poorly as absolute rule had, and in 1862 Otto was deposed.

In the following year a Danish prince was named king as George I of Greece (ruled 1863–1913). The Greeks had selected another leader, but accepted the powers' choice of George when Britain turned over to Greece the Ionian Islands, which had been a British protectorate.

George's attempts to transform Greece into a country governed by the most advanced parliamentary institutions were only partly successful. The Greeks' lack of education and their inexperience with parliamentary government resulted in a rapid turnover of governments.

The first leader to have any success in establishing an efficient Greek government was Eleutherios Venizelos, who became prime minister in 1910. Venizelos won a strong majority in parliament in 1911 and was able to pass a revised constitution that allowed for more stable parliamentary government.

Venizelos reorganized and simplified the bureaucracy and reduced the power of the army in government affairs. During his first years in office, the educational system was broadened and large estates were divided among small farmers.

Expansion. During the reign of George I, Greece made many additions to its territory. The European powers exerted great efforts to prevent this expansion from resulting in a clash with Turkey that could lead to a general European war. In 1881 the powers forced Turkey to yield most of Epirus and Thessaly to Greece as part of the

settlement of the Russo-Turkish War of 1877.

In 1896 Greece, trying to aid a rebellion in Crete against Turkish rule, did go to war against Turkey, and was soundly defeated. But Britain, France, and Russia forced Turkey to evacuate Crete, which was then occupied by the three powers and by Italy. Crete successfully rebelled in 1905, and in 1908 declared its union with Greece. The European alliance withdrew its forces the following year.

Greece entered another territorial war before World War I. In the spring of 1912 Premier Venizelos made an alliance with Bulgaria, and in the following fall Greece and Bulgaria—with its ally, Serbia—declared war on Turkey over conflicting territorial claims. Greece and its allies won this First Balkan War, and in 1913, by the Treaty of London, Turkey gave up its claims to Crete and ceded Macedonia to the Balkan allies.

Another Balkan War in the summer of 1913, fought by Greece, Serbia, and Rumania against Bulgaria, determined which state would receive what part of the territory. By the Treaty of Bucharest, Greece gained part of Macedonia and another section of Epirus.

In World War I, Premier Venizelos urged Greek intervention on the side of the Allies (Britain, Russia, and France). King Constantine, who had come to the throne after his father's death in 1913, preferred to remain neutral. It was not until 1917, after an Allied ultimatum forced Constantine to yield the throne to his son, Alexander, that Greece entered the war against Germany.

Greek troops fought primarily in the Balkans, and at the end of the war the Treaty of Sèvres gave Greece eastern Thrace, the Turkish islands in the Aegean, and a mandate to occupy a part of Turkey's mainland. Turkish nationalists opposed the treaty, however, and in 1920 a Greek army invaded Turkey, only to meet disastrous defeat in 1922. King Constantine, who had regained the throne after Alexander's death in 1920, was forced to abdicate again.

Search for stability. Constantine's son became king as George II, but his government was forced out of office in 1923 by a powerful faction that favored a republican form of government. In 1924 this faction formed a revolutionary government that proclaimed Greece a republic. The republic was a failure. The leaders of the new government could not agree on policy, and after a rapid succession of governments, George II was restored to the throne in 1935.

Greece's extreme political instability left the nation helpless in the face of serious problems. The greatest difficulties were economic. Weak industry, unproductive agriculture, and an extremely high birthrate kept the people in poverty. The world economic depression of the 1930's was particularly

severe for Greece because of its dependence on exporting such costly items as wine and olive oil.

In 1936 King George appointed General Ioannes Metaxas as premier after a parliamentary election gave no party a majority. Metaxas dissolved Parliament and made himself dictator. His fascistlike regimentation of society was unpopular, but he relieved some of the country's economic problems.

World War II ended the Metaxas dictatorship, but brought enormous economic, social, and political problems. The Greeks successfully fought off an Italian invasion attempt in 1940, but in 1941 German forces conquered the country and occupied it until 1944.

During the war George Papandreou, a leader of the Greek Parliament, formed a government in exile. After the war, however, his government remained in office for only three months, in 1945. Its rivals for power were two opposing political organizations formed during the war.

A Communist-led resistance group had political and economic control of the countryside, and a right-wing royalist faction dominated Parliament. An election in 1946 restored the monarchy, but by the time King George returned a few weeks later, a civil war had broken out between the right and the left.

Greece's desperate political and economic troubles inflamed the war, which continued with support from Yugoslavia for the Communist guerrillas and with U.S. aid for the governments forces. In 1947 Yugoslavia withdrew military assistance from the rebels and the United States gave large-scale financial and military aid to the country under the Truman Doctrine. By 1949 Greek government troops were able to subdue the rebels.

Contemporary Greece. Between the years 1963 and 1967, Greece endured almost continual government crises. No one party succeeded in winning a majority in Parliament, and George Papandreou led a series of coalition cabinets that were bogged down in endless disputes with King Constantine, who had inherited the throne in 1964.

In 1967 military leaders staged a coup to avert a leftist rebellion allegedly being planned by Papandreou's son, Andreas.

Conservative and reactionary policies ensued until a new but bloodless military coup in 1973 paved the way for civilian government; Constantine Karamanlis became prime minister in 1974. By popular referendum in that year, the monarchy was replaced with a republic.

The new republican government has tried to convert the basically small-scale nature of Greece's industry into larger enterprises to strengthen the nation's economic base. But energy shortages and worldwide economic recession in the mid-1970's led to unpopular government intervention aimed at stopping inflation. In the 1977 elections strong socialist gains were made, and in 1981 Andreas Papandreou, leader of the Panhellenic Socialist Party, was elected premier.

When the Turkish army invaded Cyprus in 1974, Greek residents of the island were caught in bitter fighting. This, with disputes over Aegean oil rights, nearly led to war between Greece and Turkey in 1974. Tensions with the United States have also grown because of its apparent tolerance of Turkey's activities, while relations with the communist world have been improving.

Hungary

Official name: *Hungarian People's Republic*
Area: *35,919 sq. mi., 93,030 sq. km.*
Population: *(1980) 10,760,000*
Capital: *Budapest*
(Pop., 1978, 2,085,615)
Language: *Hungarian*
Religion: *Roman Catholic, Protestant*
Currency unit: *Forint*
National holiday: *Liberation Day, April 4*

The Hungarian People's Republic, a nation in central Europe, occupies the middle basin of the Danube River. It is bounded on the north by Czechoslovakia, on the northeast by the Soviet Union, on the east by Rumania, on the south by Yugoslavia, and on the west by Austria.

The land. Most of Hungary is flat land less than 600 feet in elevation. The lowlands fall into two main areas, the Lesser Hungarian Plain and the Greater Hungarian Plain, divided by the Central Hungarian Uplands.

In the northwest lies the very fertile, triangular Lesser Hungarian Plain, drained by tributaries of the Danube.

The Greater Hungarian Plain occupies the southeastern half of the country and is crossed on the west by the Danube. West of the Danube, the Greater Hungarian Plain is characterized by rolling land that rises gradually toward the south, culminating in the Mecsek uplands in the southernmost part of Hungary. East of the Danube the plain is almost completely level, drained toward the south by tributaries of the Danube, and dotted with lakes.

The central uplands consist of several ranges of hills and low mountains. West of the Danube, in the region known as Transdanubia, are the mineral-rich Bakony and Vértes ranges. East of the Danube, in the north-central part of the country, are the higher, heavily forested, Börzsöny, Cserhát, Mátra, and Bükk ranges, which reach a height of over 3000 feet near the northern border.

The Danube, Hungary's largest river, forms part of the boundary between Hungary and Czechoslovakia and cuts through the Hungarian upland. The Danube's important tributaries in Hungary are the Drava (Drau) in the south and the Tisza in the east. Lake Balaton, along the southwestern edge of the central uplands, is Hungary's largest lake.

Hungary's climate varies from region to region. For the country as a whole, summer temperatures average 71°F and winter temperatures average 31°F. About 25 inches of rain falls each year. The greater plain tends to be hotter and drier, and the uplands somewhat colder and wetter than the average.

The people. Over 95 percent of the population is Magyar, or Hungarian. The Hungarian, or Magyar, language is similar to Estonian and Finnish, and is unrelated to any of the languages spoken in neighboring countries. About two-thirds of the people are Roman Catholic, and most of the rest are Protestant. There are small minorities of Germans, Slovaks, Serbs and Croats, and Rumanians.

About 40 percent of the people are urban dwellers and half of these live in the capital, Budapest, which is the political, cultural, economic, and intellectual center of the country. Other important cities are Miskolc, an industrial center in the northeast, Debrecen, an eastern university town, Pécs, near the center of an important southern mining district, and Szeged, a southeastern city known for its textiles and food products and especially for its strong paprika.

Economy. The Hungarian economy, traditionally based on agriculture and light industry, became industrialized under the Communist regime that took power in 1947. Industrialization was based largely on development of the country's natural resources.

Natural resources. Bauxite, found mainly in the western part of the central upland, is the most important mineral, and Hungary is one of the world's largest producers, mining over 2.9 million metric tons in 1976. Uranium is mined in the southwest, and there are also deposits of iron ore and manganese.

Coal is Hungary's prime source of energy, but the reserves are mostly of low quality. There is some natural gas and hydroelectric power. In 1979 2.9 million metric tons of oil were produced in Hungary, but Soviet oil imports are still considerable.

Agriculture. Hungary's soil is quite rich and is especially suitable for raising grains. Corn, the leading crop, and wheat, barley, and rye represent about half of the total crop acreage. Potatoes, sugar beets, sunflowers, and tobacco are the main industrial crops. Warm summers enable Hungary to produce table and wine grapes, fruit, and vegetables. Almost all agriculture has now been collectivized.

Industry. Under the Communist regime there has been a distinct shift from light to heavy industry. Nearly half of the national product now

EAST GERMANY

WEST GERMANY

N

POLAND

SOVIET UNION

CZECHOSLOVAKIA

AUSTRIA

Danube

Miskolc

HUNGARY •Debrecen

Budapest

L. Balaton

Pécs

Drava

Szeged

RUMANIA

Tisza

ITALY

YUGOSLAVIA

ADRIATIC SEA

bauxite

comes from industry. More recent developments have been aimed at an increased output of consumer goods.

Iron, steel, chemicals, machinery, and textiles are the major industrial products. Aluminum and computers have become significant additions to this list in recent years.

Trade. Hungary generally has an equitable balance of trade. In 1979 exports earned $8.0 billion and imports cost some $8.7 billion. Raw materials, farm products, processed food, and some machinery are exported. Oil, raw materials, textiles, and machinery are imported.

Most of Hungary's trade is with the Soviet Union and East Europe.

Government. Political activity in Hungary is dominated by the country's Communist Party, officially called the Hungarian Socialist Workers Party. The political bureau, or politburo, of its central committee determines national policy, and its first secretary is usually the key figure in the government.

The Hungarian constitution places supreme government power in a one-house legislature, the National Assembly. All candidates for assembly seats are sponsored by the Communist Party, and all legislation is proposed by the party.

Hungary is a member of the United Nations, the Council for Mutual Economic Assistance (Comecon), and the Warsaw Pact.

History. The Hungarian plains and the Danube valley lie along a major ancient European migration route and offered good settlement sites for early European peoples. The territory, known to the Romans as Pannonia, was inhabited by a succession of Germanic and Slavic tribes and by the Huns between about 1000 B.C. and the 800's A.D. In the late 800's the Magyars, a people from the Ural Mountains, arrived on the Pannonian plains and conquered and mixed with the Slavic people settled there.

The Magyars were a seminomadic and warlike people. Under their leader, Prince Árpád, they expanded their territory at the expense of nearby Germanic and Slavic kingdoms. In 955 they were defeated by the Germans, and the Magyars, by then a mixture of Magyar, Slavic, and Germanic peoples, retreated to territory in the Danube basin and settled into an agricultural way of life.

The Hungarian kingdom. By the end of the 900's, the Magyars had developed a stable government and a well organized feudal society. In 997 Stephen, a descendant of Árpád, became Hungary's first king. Stephen established strong ties with Western, rather than Eastern, Europe and with the Roman Catholic Church.

During Stephen's reign, the Magyars became Christian. Stephen began what was to be a long struggle to weaken the great nobles and centralize Hungary's government. During Stephen's reign, Hungary's territory was greatly expanded.

Several decades of dynastic warfare followed Stephen's death in 1038, but order was restored in 1077, when Ladislas, also of Árpád's line, became king. For the next 150 years Hungary's territory grew, its prosperity increased, and its ties with the West strengthened.

Hungary was unable to resolve the conflict between the king and the nobles, however. The nobles' feuds and rebellions against the king threatened the stability of the nation and left the country unprotected, as the nobles were responsible for its defense.

In 1241 Mongol armies swept across Hungary, meeting little opposition. The destruction they wrought was repaired, but by the end of the 1200's no solution had been found to the dispute between the king and the nobles. Their rivalries for power permitted a foreigner, Charles of Anjou, to take the throne in 1308.

Hungary's new rulers also held thrones in other countries, and as a result of the foreign involvements of Charles and his descendants during the 1300's and early 1400's, Hungary became increasingly active in the diplomatic affairs of Western Europe.

Hunyadi. In the early 1400's the Ottoman Turks posed a threat to Europe, and Hungary assumed the role of protector of the West. Between 1437 and 1456 Hungarian armies led by a powerful nobleman, János Hunyadi, blocked attempted Turkish invasions of Europe.

Hunyadi's son, Matthias, became king of Hungary in 1458 and led the country to its peak of greatness. He broke the power of the great nobles, organized an efficient centralized administration, and introduced the art and learning of the Renaissance into Hungary.

In an attempt to become leader of a united central Europe that could crush the Ottoman Turks, Matthias conquered territory in Bohemia, where he was named king, and in Silesia, Moravia, and Austria. At his death in 1490, Hungary was the most powerful state in western Europe. Matthias's successors were weak men. They lost most of his political and territorial gains, and they took no action against the Turks.

Ottoman era. In the early 1500's the Turks began to move toward Hungary, and in 1526 they overwhelmed the country. Although the Turks were the nominal overlords of all Hungary, in fact the country was divided into three parts.

Northern and western Hungary were ruled by the Hapsburgs of Austria, who succeeded to the throne of Hungary in 1526. In the northeast, the

principality of Transylvania grew so powerful that it was independent in all but name. The Turks controlled central Hungary.

Throughout the country there was turmoil. The Magyars resented Austrian and Turkish rule; Hungary's Slavic peoples resented the Austrians, the Turks, and the Magyars; and the Magyar nobility was split between those who had gained power by supporting the Turks and those who had fought against the Turks.

To these frictions was added religious strife arising from the Protestant Reformation. The Hungarians were unable to resolve their differences or to throw off Turkish rule.

Austrian rule. In 1686 Austria's armies drove the Turks out of the region, and Austria assumed complete rule over the Magyar and Slavic peoples of Hungary. Austria did little to rebuild the country, which was still laboring under an outmoded feudal structure and which had been ravaged by years of warfare. Austrian rule was harsh and autocratic at first, and was unpopular with all Hungarians.

The Austrian rulers of the latter half of the 1700's were more liberal, however. They improved the economy and expanded the educational system, which in turn stimulated efforts for more radical reforms. Organizations were formed by democratic, progressive nationalists, and in the late 1700's and early 1800's, inspired by the French Revolution, they led demands for social, economic, and governmental reforms.

The Austrian emperor, with the support of the conservative Hungarian nobility, refused the demands and harshly repressed the movement. Repression only intensified the revolutionary spirit. In 1848, when liberal, democratic rebellions were breaking out all over Europe, Hungarian nationalistic reformers led an uprising against the Austrian Empire and demanded independence as a democratic state. The emperor yielded, the Hungarian nobles fled, and a republican government was established.

The new regime abolished the country's feudal, social, and economic organization, but the republic was short-lived. In 1849, under orders from a new emperor, Austrian and Russian troops crushed the republic, and Hungary once more became a subject state. The old order could not be restored by force, however, and Hungary remained the most independent of all of Austria's territories.

The Dual Monarchy. After 1848 Austria steadily lost power to Prussia, and in 1867 Prussia organized a union of German states that excluded Austria. The Hungarians took that opportunity to demand independence. In the same year, 1867, Austria and Hungary arrived at a compromise by which the Dual Monarchy of Austria-Hungary was formed.

The two states shared control of foreign policy, finance, and defense. Hungary, however, was a self-governing state that ruled Slavic subjects as well as Magyars. The Slavs resented Magyar rule, which was no better than Austrian rule had been.

Austria-Hungary had joined the series of alliances creating the Central Powers, and in 1914 entered World War I. In 1918 Hungary went down to defeat with its allies. When defeat was imminent, a rebellion broke out in Hungary, and in November, 1918, a republic was proclaimed. But in 1919 the Communist Party assumed control. Communist rule was overthrown at the end of 1919 by monarchists, who chose Admiral Miklós Horthy as regent in 1920.

The regency. In June, 1920, the Hungarian government signed the Treaty of Trianon, which officially ended World War I for Hungary and which stripped Hungary of much of its territory and power. Under the treaty, Hungary ceded almost three-quarters of its land and two-thirds of its population to Austria, Rumania, and the new states of Czechoslovakia and Yugoslavia. In 1921 Hungary's king, who attempted to return, was exiled.

The regency remained in power throughout the 1920's and 1930's. It was a conservative and authoritarian government, and all efforts at reform were stifled. Hungarian foreign policy was based on opposition to the Treaty of Trianon, and the government sought to recover the lands and peoples lost under the treaty.

The regency was bitterly hostile to the "Little Entente" of the new Slavic states and to their western patron, France. It was equally hostile to the Soviet Union, because of the brief but violent and destructive Communist dictatorship of 1919.

The government of the regency thus was attracted by the political and territorial aims of Adolf Hitler of Germany and Benito Mussolini of Italy. Despite strong opposition within Hungary from monarchists, Communists, and democratic liberals, right-wing nationalists prevailed in the government. In 1934 Hungary entered a political and economic alliance with Italy and Austria and thereafter moved closer to the National Socialist (Nazi) government of Germany.

In 1939 and 1940 Adolf Hitler restored to Hungary parts of its former territories in Rumania and Czechoslovakia. In November, 1940, Hungary formally allied itself with the Axis powers, although Hungarians did not fight in the war at first.

The Germans used the country as a base to delay Soviet advances into central Europe, and in 1944 took direct control of the government. In the winter of 1944–1945, Soviet troops invaded and occupied Hungary, and when the war ended they were in firm control of the country.

Communist rule. After the war a Communist dictatorship with close ties to the Soviet Union was established under the leadership of Mátyás Rakosi. The regime used repression and terrorism to stay in power. Its efforts to transform Hungary's economy from agriculture to state-owned heavy industry seriously damaged the country's economic life.

Economic, political, and social grievances fanned Hungarian nationalism and desire for independence from Soviet control. After the death of Joseph Stalin in 1953, the Hungarian Communist Party split between advocates of continuing tight controls over all aspects of life and those seeking a more moderate course.

In October, 1956, demonstrations against the government erupted and led to a popular rising that had wide support, even from the Communist prime minister, Imre Nagy; but it was crushed by Soviet troops and tanks.

Janos Kadár became prime minister and first secretary of the Communist Party. In 1958, after a secret trial, Nagy was executed. The Hungarian Communist Party, which had disintegrated during the revolution, was completely reorganized.

The methods used by Kadár to consolidate power were repressive, but when the government's position was more secure Kadár began to relax controls and allow an increasing measure of freedom. Under Kadár's administration, economic programs were reorganized to achieve greater efficiency and a better balance between agriculture and industry.

Some free enterprise was permitted, consumers and producers were given a greater voice in the economy, and trade with non-Communist countries was expanded. The standard of living rose, and by the mid-1960's Kadár's regime was among the least repressive of the governments of Eastern Europe.

An economic downturn in the 1980's, coupled with growing demands for political and economic reforms, led to Kadár's retirement in 1988. In 1989 Hungary opened its border with Austria. Increased pressure for major changes led to the disintegration of the Communist Party and the scheduling of multiparty elections in 1990.

SOVIET TANKS *enter Budapest, Hungary's capital, to quell the uprising of 1956. The Soviet Union treated Czechoslovakia in the same way in 1968, when a westward-looking, liberal government threatened the hold of the Communist Party.*

Iceland

Official name: *Republic of Iceland*
Area: *39,800 sq.mi., 103,000 sq. km.*
Population: *(1980) 231,000*
Capital: *Reykjavik*
    (Pop., 1978, 83,887)
Language: *Icelandic*
Religion: *Lutheran*
Currency unit: *Króna*
National holiday: *Anniversary of the
    establishment of the republic,
    June 17*

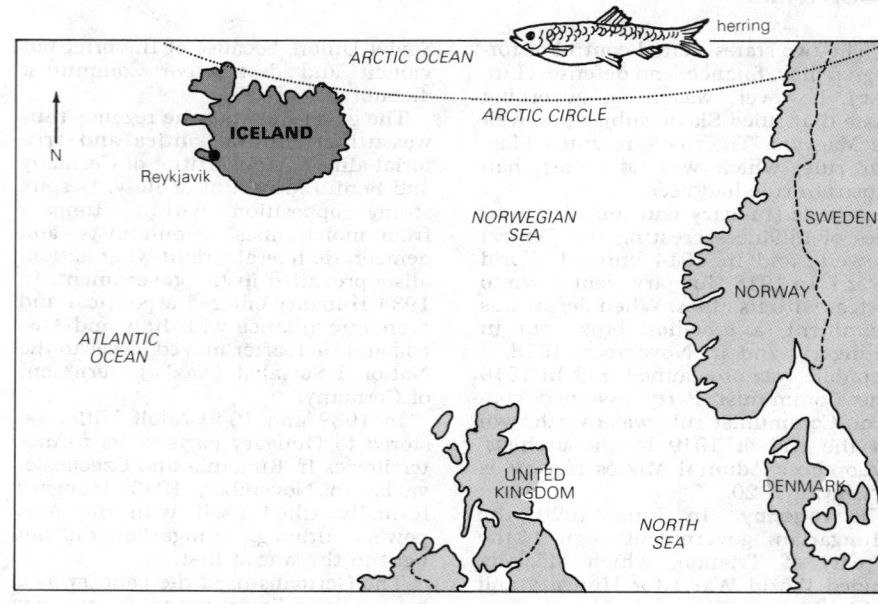

Iceland is an island republic in the North Atlantic Ocean, less than 200 miles southeast of Greenland. The Arctic Circle just touches the northern tips of Iceland.

The land. Iceland is a forbidding land, with a rugged, barren terrain. The island is quite mountainous, with a central core of highlands rising above 5000 feet. Glaciers cover large areas, and many swift rivers rush down from the glaciers.

Iceland is of volcanic origin, and some volcanoes are still active. Hot springs are common in the volcanic areas. In the early 1960's two new volcanic islands rose in Iceland's coastal waters.

The island's northerly climate is moderated by a section of the Gulf Stream that warms its coasts. Average temperatures range between 30°F and 52°F throughout the year. Almost 50 inches of rain a year falls in the southern lowlands. The mountains are much wetter, but the far north receives only an average of 15 inches.

The people. Iceland is rather sparsely settled, with only five people per square mile. Its rapidly rising population is found mostly on the southwest coast, with almost half of it centered around Reykjavik. Almost 90 percent of the population is urban.

Iceland's population is quite homogeneous. Almost all the people are Scandinavian in origin, and Icelandic, a Scandinavian tongue, is the universal language. Over 95 percent of the population is Lutheran.

Economy. Despite its barrenness, Iceland is a moderately prosperous country with an economy based largely on fishing and trade. The chief natural resources are its rushing rivers, which provide hydroelectric power, its thermal springs, and its geographic position near rich fishing banks and along a major route between Europe and North America.

Less than one percent of the land is cultivated, and only hay, root crops, and other hardy crops can be grown. Grazing land is available and dairying is of some importance.

Fishing and related activities make the greatest single contribution to the Icelandic economy. Cod and herring, from coastal waters and from the Grand Banks near Canada, are the chief catches. Fishing and fish processing constitute the bulk of Iceland's industrial activity.

To diversify its economy, Iceland rapidly developed new industries in the 1950's and 1960's. The aluminum industry is particularly prosperous now, but most of the aluminum ore is imported.

Farm, business, and manufacturing cooperatives are common in Iceland.

Trade is vital to the Icelandic economy. In 1979 exports earned $705 million and imports cost $738 million. Fresh and processed fish and fish products accounted for over 70 percent of the country's exports in the mid-1970's. Raw materials, foodstuffs, machinery, manufactured goods, petroleum products, and ships must be imported. Most of Iceland's trade is with Great Britain, the United States, West Germany, the Soviet Union, and the Scandinavian countries.

Government. Iceland is a republic, with a president as head of state. Actual executive power rests with a prime minister and cabinet responsible to the legislature. Members of the bicameral legislature, the *Althing,* are popularly elected. The Althing chooses one-third of its members to sit as an upper house; the remaining two-thirds forms the lower, more powerful, house.

Iceland is a member of the United Nations, the North Atlantic Treaty Organization (NATO), the Nordic Council, the Council of Europe, the Organization for Economic Cooperation and Development (OECD), and the European Free Trade Association.

History. Iceland was settled in the late 800's by Norwegian Vikings. Immigration increased through the 900's, with settlers coming from the British Isles as well as from Norway. By the end of the 900's, the descendants of these first settlers had established their own system of representative government, with a constitution, a court system, and the Althing.

The yearly Althing, the meeting of chieftains and popular representatives, soon became the social and cultural center of Icelandic life, as well as the country's legislature and supreme court. In 1000 the Althing adopted Christianity as the religion for the entire country. During the 900's and 1000's, Vikings from Iceland made many voyages of exploration. They

ICELAND'S FIRST SETTLER: *statue in Reykjavik of a ninth-century Viking.*

MONKMEYER

discovered and settled Greenland and visited North America.

Dissension among the Icelanders during the early 1200's led to the breakdown of government, and in 1262 Iceland joined with Norway and submitted to the rule of the Norwegian king, although nominally remaining self-governing. In 1387 Denmark and Norway were united, but Iceland remained legally Norwegian until 1814.

Between the 1300's and the 1700's the island was struck by many natural disasters, including volcanic eruptions, plagues, and floods. Denmark-Norway did little to alleviate the resulting famine. Moreover, trade monopolies and other commercial regulations of the 1600's and 1700's served to further the interests of Norway and Denmark rather than those of Iceland. **Danish rule.** Norway was separated from Denmark in 1814, but Iceland remained under Danish sovereignty. In the early 1800's Iceland began to recover from the effects of natural disaster, and a spirit of nationalism spread through the island, leading to demands for independence. The first step toward increased autonomy was the restoration of some authority to the Althing in 1843.

In 1854 Denmark relaxed its trade restrictions and Iceland's economy began to improve. In 1874 Iceland was granted a new constitution, which provided for Icelandic self-government under the supervision of a Danish minister. The island became completely self-governing in 1904.

Independence. After World War I Iceland demanded the self-determination that had been granted to other nations by the Treaty of Versailles. In 1918 a Danish-Icelandic treaty recognized Iceland's independence within a personal union with the Danish crown, and Denmark remained responsible for Iceland's foreign affairs and defense.

During the 1920's and 1930's Iceland was generally isolated from the rest of the world. During World War II, however, Iceland was of great strategic importance as an Allied air and naval base. After its occupation by Germany in 1940, Denmark was unable to handle Icelandic affairs. In 1944 Iceland proclaimed itself a sovereign republic.

During the 1940's and 1950's Iceland concentrated on expanding and balancing its economy. The island began to participate more fully in world affairs, and it became increasingly dependent on international trade agreements and defense pacts. It was also an important link on international air routes as well as a strategically important NATO base.

In the early 1960's, at Iceland's request, the United States withdrew most of its troops from Iceland. This trend was reversed under the direction of a new conservative coalition that came to power in Iceland following the 1974 elections. There are now nearly 3000 U.S. NATO military personnel stationed in Iceland.

In 1972 Iceland extended its fishery limit from twelve to 50 miles, and in 1975 it extended the limit to 200 miles. The government said that the extension was necessary to protect the fish stocks, because the fishing industry is vital to the nation's economy. Tensions mounted between Iceland and Great Britain over this issue, until the British finally consented to Iceland's extended fishing rights in 1976.

Ireland

Official name: *Republic of Ireland (Irish Republic)*
Area: *27,136 sq. mi., 70,283 sq. km.*
Population: *(1980) 3,037,000*
Capital: *Dublin (Pop., 1979, 543,563)*
Language: *Irish (Gaelic), English*
Religion: *Roman Catholic*
Currency unit: *Pound*
National holiday: *St. Patrick's Day, Mar. 17*

The Republic of Ireland, or Eire, is an independent country that occupies the southwestern five-sixths of the island of Ireland, one of the two main British Isles. The northeastern sixth of the island makes up Northern Ireland, which is part of the United Kingdom. The North Atlantic lies to the west and south, and the Irish Sea to the east, separating Ireland from Britain.

The land. Ireland is an old, low, glaciated plateau with few elevations above 2000 feet. There is a central plain, opening more widely on the east, fringed by higher and more rugged land, especially in the north and southwest. Drainage is a problem, and much of Ireland is covered by odd-shaped lakes, marshes, and peat bogs.

The combination of damp, acid soils, a very damp climate, and uncertain drainage has restricted forest growth and greatly limited the variety of agriculture. More than one-third of Ireland is classified as moor and heath, although there are sizable tracts of excellent grassland suitable for raising livestock.

The climate is dominated by maritime influences. Winters are mild, and summers are quite cool. The humidity is high, rain is abundant and frequent, and it is often cloudy or foggy. Dublin has a temperature range of only 20°F, with August averaging 62°F and January 42°F.

The people. The Irish people are culturally quite homogeneous. Irish, a Celtic Indo-European language related to Gaelic, is the official first language and is spoken in the southern and western coastal regions of Cork, Kerry, Mayo, and Donegal. English, however, is universally spoken, and official documents are printed in English and Irish. About 94 percent of the population is Roman Catholic. Most of the remainder is Anglican or Protestant.

Ireland's population declined steadily from the late 1840's until the 1960's. In the 1840's potato diseases began to attack the country's principal crop, and famine precipitated a flood of emigrants to North America and other areas. A high rate of celibacy and a low birthrate contributed to the decline in population, a trend reversed since the 1960's.

Dublin, the capital, is by far the largest city, and one-fifth of the entire population of Eire resides in the Dublin area.

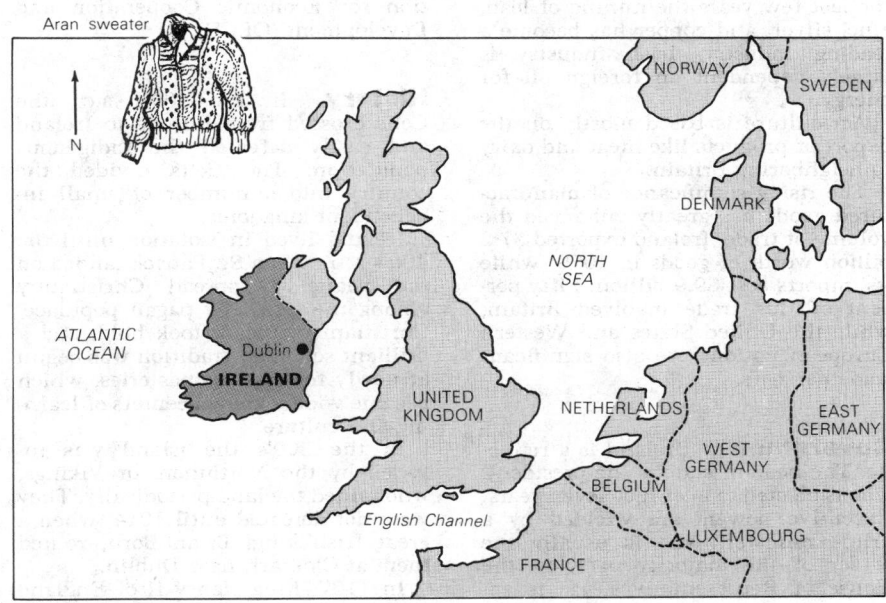

Aran sweater

THE IRISH TRADITION: *schoolchildren playing the tin whistle, and a page from the eighth- to ninth-century hand-illuminated Book of Kells* (right).

Economy.

Ireland's economy has become increasingly diversified in the last two decades. Traditionally an agricultural state, Ireland now has a labor force that is composed of 30 percent manufacturing workers and only 23 percent agricultural laborers.

The slow growth rate of agricultural products, with the nation's determined efforts to industrialize, has created a national product in which the value of manufactured goods has doubled over that of agricultural goods. In the last few years the mining of lead, zinc, silver, and copper has become a leading industry. Irish industry is largely dependent on foreign oil for energy.

Agriculture is based mostly on the export of products like meat and dairy to neighboring Britain.

The rising significance of manufactured goods has greatly enhanced the volume of trade. Ireland exported $7.2 billion worth of goods in 1979, while its imports cost $9.9 billion. Fifty percent of this trade involved Britain, while the United States and Western European nations are also significant trade partners.

Government.

Ireland is a republic. The head of state is the president, who is elected to a term of seven years. Executive powers are wielded by a prime minister, who is usually the leader of the majority party in the House of Representatives. He is appointed to a five-year term by the president, on the recommendation of the House of Representatives.

Legislative power is vested in the Parliament, which includes the House of Representatives, elected on the basis of proportional representation, and the Senate, which is partly elected and partly appointed by the incumbent prime minister.

Ireland is a member of the United Nations, the Common Market, the Council of Europe, and the Organization for Economic Cooperation and Development (OECD).

History.

In the 300's B.C., the Celts crossed from Europe to Ireland and easily defeated the indigenous population. The Celts divided the country into a number of small independent kingdoms.

Ireland lived in isolation until the 400's A.D., when St. Patrick landed on the island to spread Christianity among the generally pagan populace. Christianity quickly took hold, and a brilliant scholarly tradition was begun at newly founded monasteries, which became widely known centers of learning and culture.

In the 800's the island was invaded by the Northmen, or Vikings, who raided the land periodically. They were not defeated until 1014, when a great Irish king, Brian Boru, routed them at Clontarf, near Dublin.

In 1167, King Henry II of England invaded Ireland upon the invitation of a deposed Irish king, Dermot MacMurrough. The Irish were defeated, and in 1171 Henry established his personal rule over the country.

English rule.

In time, England relaxed its control, partly because its attention was almost totally given to the Hundred Years' War (1338–1453) with France and to the internal Wars of the Roses (1455–1485). A considerable degree of autonomy had gradually been obtained by the local aristocracy, and the era is known as the period of "aristocratic home rule." Direct English control was actually reduced to an area around Dublin known as the Pale.

It was not until 1494, under the first of the Tudors, Henry VII, that English power was reestablished throughout the island. During the Tudor dynasty, the major issues that were to poison relations between the two countries—religion, land ownership, and home rule—began to arise. Henry VIII broke with the papacy in 1534 and attempted to eradicate Roman Catholicism from Ireland.

Mary I, Henry's daughter, tried to force the assimilation of the Irish by confiscating the lands of the Irish lords who refused to conform and distributing them to English settlers. Elizabeth I continued this system, which came to be known as "plantation," and excluded the Irish from any significant role in the administration.

A great rebellion—known as the "Tyrone Wars"—finally broke out in

1597, and its leaders became two of the most celebrated Irish heroes—Hugh O'Neill, earl of Tyrone, and Hugh O'Donnell. After a series of victories, they were finally defeated in 1601 by the English at Kinsale.

Under England's Stuart king, James I, Scottish settlers were given lands in Ulster. As a result, a new rebellion started in 1641, when the Ulstermen massacred many of the usurpers of their lands. Terrible revenge was taken in 1649 by England's Puritan dictator, Oliver Cromwell. The population of the town of Drogheda in eastern Ireland was slaughtered, and most of the land still remaining in Irish hands was confiscated.

Conditions were better under Charles II, and they improved greatly under James II, who was a Roman Catholic. The Glorious Revolution of 1688, however, soon removed him from the throne, and he was finally defeated on Irish soil at the battle of the Boyne in 1690.

Eventually the Penal Laws—a series of laws first formulated under James I that sought to reduce the power of the Irish—were made more stringent, and economic measures ruinous to the Irish nation were enacted. Tension mounted steadily.

It was only in 1798, however, that a major revolution, led by Wolfe Tone, was attempted. The effort failed, and England then deprived Ireland of its own parliament. In 1800 Ireland was united to England and allowed representation in the English Parliament.

The period of union. A great disaster, the "potato famine," struck the island in 1845, causing about 1 million deaths in a few years. A massive emigration then began, directed chiefly to the United States.

Emigrants living in the United States founded the Fenian Society to continue the struggle against Britain. In 1873 the Home Rule League was formed in Ireland. Its outstanding figure was Charles Stewart Parnell, a brilliant and also an extremely popular leader.

Later, a more active movement, the Sinn Féin, came to the fore. On Easter Monday, 1916, in the middle of World War I, several hundred of its members rose in Dublin, but the rebellion was put down by British troops. In the following years, another organization, the IRA (Irish Republican Army) harassed the British.

Free state and republic. After the war, the Sinn Féin triumphed in elections held in 1918, winning most of the Irish seats in the British Parliament. These candidates refused to go to England, however, and instead set up their own Parliament in Dublin, declaring Ireland an independent republic.

A period of political upheaval followed, during which the British tried to maintain order by pouring troops into the country. But in 1922 Britain

EASTER MONDAY: *British troops face the Irish rebels in Dublin in 1916. Continued insurrection finally led to recognition of the Irish Free State in 1922, now the Irish Republic.*

recognized the Irish Free State and granted it dominion status. The six northern, predominantly Protestant, counties of Ulster chose to remain part of the United Kingdom. The new situation provoked profound and violent dissension among the Irish.

Under Prime Minister (later president) Eamon de Valera, a new constitution was promulgated in 1937, whereby the sovereign country of Ireland or Eire, was proclaimed. In 1948 the last ties with the British Commonwealth were cut and Ireland became a republic on April 18, 1949. Eamon de Valera served as prime minister and then as president until 1973.

Ireland faced severe economic problems in the mid-1970's partly because of the recession in Britain and partly because of the energy crisis brought on by the inflated price of imported oil. The energy crisis became especially severe in 1979.

As inflation in the early 1970's climbed to over 20 percent and unemployment went above ten percent, Ireland entered the European Common Market in 1973 to ease the crisis.

The violence in Northern Ireland caused by Protestant-Catholic discord has spread to Ireland recently. In 1976 the British ambassador to Ireland was assassinated by IRA terrorists. The Irish government has taken a tougher stand against the IRA since then.

Italy

Official name: *Italian Republic*
Area: *116,304 sq. mi., 301,225 sq. km.*
Population: *(1980) 57,000,000*
Capital: *Rome (Pop., 1978, 2,897,505)*
Language: *Italian*
Religion: *Roman Catholic*
Currency unit: *Lira*
National holiday: *Anniversary of the republic, June 2*

Italy, a republic in southern Europe, is bounded on the north by Switzerland and Austria; on the east by Yugoslavia and the Adriatic and Ionian seas; on the south by the Mediterranean Sea; on the southwest by the Tyrrhenian Sea; and on the northwest by the Ligurian Sea and France.

The country is a boot-shaped peninsula measuring about 750 miles in length and averaging about 125 miles in width. Its territory includes two large islands—Sicily, lying just off the toe of the boot, and Sardinia, lying 130 miles off the southwest coast—as well as a number of smaller islands. Of these the most important are Elba, Capri, Ischia, Capraia, Giglio, and the Lipari Islands.

Although Italy was not politically unified until 1870, it has since Roman times made basic contributions to the cultural life of Europe.

The land.

Much of Italy is hilly or mountainous, and the amount of land suitable for agriculture is limited. The Alps run along the entire northern border. In the northeast they curve south to form the Apennines, which extend down through the peninsula into the toe of the boot and across to Sicily. The only sizable plain is the valley of the Po River, in the north, although there are coastal plains and numerous interior basins.

Italy's major rivers are the Po, the Adige, the Arno, and the Tiber. Many shorter streams originate in the Apennines and flow toward the Adriatic or Tyrrhenian coasts.

Italy's climate is varied. The north has a continental climate, with warm summers and cold winters, which are often accompanied by heavy snowfall in the more mountainous regions.

Southern Italy has a typically Mediterranean climate, with hot, dry summers and mild, rainy winters.

Rainfall varies, generally decreasing toward the southeast. The north averages over 30 inches a year, but parts of Apulia, at the heel of the boot, receive less than 15 inches.

The people.

The country is densely settled with nearly 500 people per square mile. Overpopulation has long plagued Italy and has led to a heavy outflow of Italians to the rest of Europe and to many other parts of the world. The currently modest rate of population growth has helped make the economy more manageable.

Italian is the nearly universal language. There are a few small linguistic minority groups. More than 99 percent of the people are at least nominally Roman Catholic.

Italy is traditionally urban, and over half of the population lives in cities and towns. Rome, Milan, Turin, and Naples have more than 1 million inhabitants and over 40 other Italian cities have populations of more than 100,000.

Economy.

Before the mid-1950's, the Italian economy was largely dependent on agriculture and tourism. Although both are still important, their relative weight in the economy has declined in the wake of industrial expansion since then. Industry now accounts for nearly half of both the labor force and the national product.

An important factor in the Italian economy is the tremendous difference in the standard of living between the north and south. The north is highly industrialized and has the country's more fertile farmland, which is the most intensively cultivated in southern Europe. The south is heavily populated and suffers chronically from high unemployment. It is much poorer and far less developed, having little industry and small, inefficient farms. Since 1950 the government has actively sought to bring economic and industrial development in the south up to the level enjoyed in the north.

Italy joined the European Monetary System in 1980.

Natural resources. Italy is poor in natural resources. Sulfur and mercury are mined in quantity and large amounts of limestone and marble are quarried. Italy is essentially dependent on foreign oil to supply energy for its industries, but it has four nuclear plants and a good supply of hydroelectric power. It hopes to increase these capacities further.

Agriculture. Agriculture employs about 15 percent of the labor force, and it accounts for less than ten percent of the national product. In recent years, production has improved with land consolidation, increased mechanization, and improved agricultural methods.

The Po Valley, which has an extensive irrigation system, raises all the nation's rice, most of its wheat, and three-fourths of its corn. Yields per acre compare favorably with those of northwestern Europe and rank among the world's highest. The region also supports many cattle and produces substantial quantities of wine.

Southern Italy grows a variety of vegetables, fruit, and nuts. Among the most important of these are olives, peas, beans, grapes, citrus fruits, and almonds. Livestock is also raised in the south, but sheep and goats are more numerous than cattle.

THE STRENGTH OF ITALY, *from Roman times when the mighty Colosseum was built* (right) *to the present, has always resided in her sturdy peasants* (below).

ITALIAN STATE TOURIST OFFICE

SAM FALK/MONKMEYER

Industry. The government plays an important role in Italian industry. Three state-owned holding companies—the Industrial Reconstruction Institute, the National Hydrocarbons Agency, and the National Power Authority—control a major part of the country's industrial capital. Government holdings are heavily concentrated in iron and steel, engineering, telecommunications, shipbuilding and shipping, petroleum, gas, and electric power.

Most of Italy's industry is concentrated in the northwestern part of the Po Valley, particularly in the triangle formed by the cities of Milan, Turin, and Genoa. Textiles, refined and fabricated metals, machinery, vehicles, and electrical equipment are the most important manufactures.

Trade. Italy's exports in 1979 earned $72.2 billion and its imports cost $78.0 billion. Italy's main exports are textiles, vehicles, electrical equipment, machinery, chemicals, fruits and vegetables, and wine. Principal imports include iron and steel, petroleum, coal, chemicals, foodstuffs, timber and paper products, and raw cotton and wool.

The nation's most important trading partners are West Germany, the United States, France, the Benelux countries, Britain, and Switzerland.

Government. Italy is a democratic republic with a parliamentary form of government. The chief of state is the president, who is elected to a seven-year term by the legislature. The president has the power to dissolve the legislature and call for new elections. He also nominates the prime minister, who must then also be approved by the legislature.

The prime minister chooses the ministers who form his cabinet from among the members of the legislature.

The legislature consists of the 630-member Chamber of Deputies and the 315-member Senate. Both chambers are directly elected on the basis of proportional representation to five-year terms. The Senate also includes five lifetime members and former presidents of the republic. Legislation may originate in either house and must be passed by a majority of both.

Italy is a member of the United Nations, the Common Market, and the North Atlantic Treaty Organization (NATO).

History. Italy has been inhabited since very early times, and traces of Paleolithic and Neolithic cultures have been found throughout the peninsula. In about 2000 B.C. a group of people closely related to the ancient Greeks entered Italy from the north and gradually established themselves throughout the peninsula.

Approximately 1100 years later the

METROPOLITAN MUSEUM OF ART/FLETCHER FUND, 1946

THE GENIUS OF ITALY: *a 1480's dish* (above) *bears the arms of the rulers of Milan. Leonardo da Vinci's engineering drawings show only one side of this brilliant artist.*

Etruscans, who may have come from Asia Minor, settled in north-central Italy, and subjugated the local inhabitants. In the 700's and 600's B.C., the Greeks colonized parts of southern Italy and Sicily. They dominated the area to such an extent that it was known as *Magna Graecia,* or Greater Greece.

In 388 B.C. Rome, an insignificant city-state that until 100 years earlier had been dominated by the Etruscans, gained control of the surrounding area of Latium. By 270 B.C. the Romans had conquered all of Italy, and the history of Italy from the 200's B.C. to the 400's A.D. is largely the history of Rome and the Roman Empire.

In the 400's Italy was invaded by peoples from central and eastern Europe, including the Visigoths, Ostrogoths, Heruli, and Huns. In 476 the last Roman emperor in the west, Romulus Augustulus, was deposed by Odoacer, a Heruli chieftain. Odoacer ruled until 493, when he was killed by Theodoric, king of the Ostrogoths. Theodoric established a kingdom that lasted until 553, when Italy was conquered by the emperor of the east, who ruled from Byzantium.

The Byzantines were unable to defend Italy, and in 568 it was invaded by the Lombards. The Lombards gained control of most of the peninsula except Rome, Ravenna, and Naples. Furthermore, in 726 Pope Gregory II, who had quarreled with the Byzantine emperor over ecclesiastical matters, declared Rome and the Roman church independent.

Rome's independence was continually threatened by the Lombards, and the popes began to turn to the Carolingian kings of the Franks for help. In 756 Pepin subdued the Lombards and forced them to cede part of central Italy to Pope Stephen II, creating the nucleus of the Papal States.

Pepin's son Charlemagne deposed the last Lombard king in 774, and in 800 Charlemagne was crowned Emperor of the Romans by Pope Leo III. Italy was ruled by the Franks until

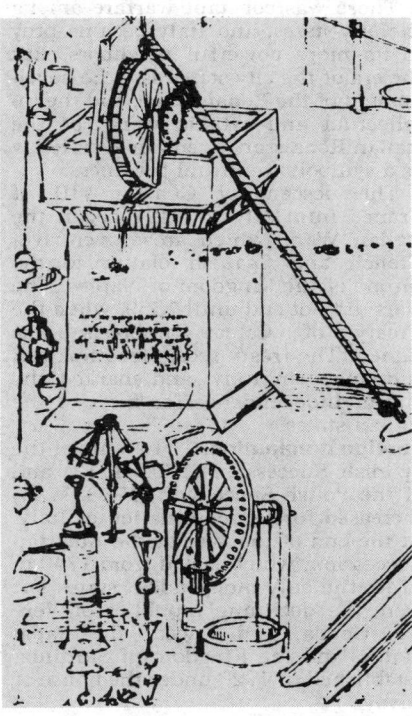

887, when the Carolingian empire disintegrated.

A century of turmoil followed, during which Muslims established themselves in southern Italy and Sicily. Order was restored in 962 with the coronation by Pope John XII of Otto I of Saxony as emperor of Italy and Germany. This union of Italy and Germany marked the beginning of the Holy Roman Empire.

The German emperors, who were mainly concerned with domestic affairs, rarely visited Italy, and the northern and central parts of the country were ruled by warring feudal lords. In the south the Normans wrested Sicily from the Muslims and Apulia and Calabria, at the tip of the peninsula, from the Byzantines. The Normans then established the Kingdom of the Two Sicilies.

City-states. During the 900's cities began to develop, particularly in north-central Italy, and by the 1000's and 1100's they had become independent communes. The Italian cities prospered as a result of the Crusades and increased trade with the Muslim world. Venice and other cities in the north became Europe's marketplaces and banking centers.

Strong rivalries existed between these cities and prevented even partial national unification. By the end of the 1200's Italy was divided into several hundred city-states. In the 1300's and 1400's several republics, such as Genoa and Venice, and the ruling princes of a number of other cities, including the Medici of Florence, the Visconti and Sforza of Milan, and the Este of Ferrara, grew extremely rich and powerful through trade.

There was constant warfare among the city-states, and Italy became prey to its more powerful neighbors. But the era of the city-states saw the development of the Renaissance, and the intellectual and artistic works of the Italian Renaissance remain even today as a symbol of cultural greatness.

The descent of Charles VIII of France into Italy in 1494 began the Italian Wars, which arose over rival French and Spanish claims to the throne of the Kingdom of Naples. The wars did not end until 1559, when the Treaty of Cateau-Cambrésis was signed. The treaty recognized Spanish supremacy in Italy, and marked the end of independence for most of the Italian states

Foreign domination. The wars of the Spanish Succession (1701–1713) and of the Polish Succession (1733–1735) increased foreign domination of Italy. At the end of the War of the Austrian Succession, which lasted from 1740 to 1748, the only independent states left were the declining republics of Venice, Genoa, and Lucca; the Papal States; and the Kingdom of Sardinia, established in 1720 under the house of Savoy.

Although divided and under foreign domination, Italy during the 1700's enjoyed enlightened rule. The rulers of Italy, inspired by the principles of rationalism, which emphasized the idea of universal human progress, embarked on a program of government reform.

By about 1790, however, the French Revolution had caused a reactionary spirit. Nonetheless, many Italians had become familiar with progressive ideas, and when the French emperor, Napoleon Bonaparte, won Lombardy from the Austrians in 1796, a movement for independence and unity developed and spread throughout the peninsula of Italy.

Under the protection of Napoleon, several republics were created. In 1799 Napoleon was driven out of Italy by Russian and Austrian armies of the Second Coalition, formed the previous year between Russia, Britain, Austria, Naples, Portugal, and the Ottoman Empire. But Napoleon returned in 1801 and was crowned king of Italy in 1805.

The government of Napoleon was one of enlightened despotism. Although the Italians had little political freedom, many economic, administrative, and educational reforms were carried out.

The Napoleonic empire collapsed in 1814, and the Congress of Vienna, which met to redraw the map of Europe, restored the old regimes in Italy. Austrian influence was dominant in the peninsula. By and large the restoration was reactionary, and most of Napoleon's reforms were repealed.

Risorgimento. Many Italians, especially those of the middle class who had benefited the most under Napole-onic government, realized how advantageous a strong central government could be. This realization, the memory of the earlier reform governments of the 1700's, the recent republican experiments, and a growing feeling of nationalism, all contributed to the development of the *risorgimento,* or resurgence, and the desire for a united and independent Italy.

Some of the more daring patriots joined secret societies whose aim was to overthrow the existing governments. The most important of these societies was the Carbonari. The Carbonari staged a revolution in Naples in 1820 that overthrew the monarchy there and set up a constitutional government. But Austrian troops defeated the rebels the following year.

The Carbonari also led a number of less successful revolutions—in Piedmont in 1821 and in Modena, Parma, and the Papal States in 1831–1832. Soon after the failure of these uprisings, the Carbonari began to decline. It was largely replaced by *Giovine Italia,* Young Italy, founded in 1831 by Giuseppe Mazzini, a former member of the Carbonari.

Mazzini believed that God's will was an independent Italy that would take the lead in the spiritual and political regeneration of Europe. During the 1840's and 1850's Mazzini incited numerous revolts throughout Italy, all of which were unsuccessful.

Unification. Italian unification was finally brought about by Count Camillo Benso di Cavour, prime minister of the Kingdom of Sardinia. Cavour understood that foreign aid was needed to free Italy from Austrian domination. In 1858 Cavour met secretly with Napoleon III of France at Plombières and promised him Nice and Savoy in return for military assistance against the Austrians.

War broke out in 1859 and the Austrians were defeated, but the Sardinians were able to gain only Lombardy. Meanwhile, however, Tuscany, Modena, Parma, and Romagna had declared their independence and formed provisional governments. Under the sanction of Napoleon III, plebiscites were held in March, 1860, and the four states voted for union with Sardinia in a larger kingdom.

In May, 1860, Giuseppe Garibaldi, a nationalist leader, landed in Sicily with 1000 volunteers. By September he had won not only Sicily, but Naples as well. Sardinian troops then marched into the Papal States, but France intervened on behalf of the pope.

Nonetheless, the Kingdom of Italy, excluding Rome, was proclaimed in 1861 under Victor Emmanuel, the king of Sardinia. In 1870 French troops were withdrawn from Rome when war broke out between France and Prussia, and the Papal States and Rome were added to the new kingdom.

The Kingdom of Italy was a consti-tutional monarchy with a parliamentary form of government. The two major political forces were the Right, which was conservative, and the Left, which was radical. From 1860 to 1876 the government was controlled mainly by the Right. A highly centralized government was formed, which set about establishing national armed forces, restoring the country's finances, modernizing the transportation system, encouraging industry, and improving agriculture.

This program was continued and expanded by the Left, which held power from 1876 to 1891. The right to vote was extended, elementary education was made compulsory, administrative and legal reforms were instituted, and the army and navy were strengthened.

Expansion. In the late 1800's and early 1900's many Italians felt that the acquisition of colonies was necessary to Italy's international prestige, and Italy embarked on a program of colonial expansion in Africa. In 1885 Italy began the occupation of Eritrea, and in 1889 southern Somaliland was obtained. Territory in present-day Libya was added to Italy's African possessions in 1912. These colonies, for the most part desert, proved to be a heavy drain on Italy's economy.

In 1882 Italy, with Germany and Austria-Hungary, formed the Triple Alliance against France. A year earlier France had occupied Tunisia, where there was a large Italian population. The Triple Alliance was renewed in 1887, 1891, 1902, and 1912.

World War I broke out in July, 1914, and Italy proclaimed its neutrality in the conflict, which pitted the Central Powers, led by Germany and Austria-Hungary, against the Allied Powers, led by Britain, France, and Russia. Italy maintained that it was not bound by the terms of the Triple Alliance inasmuch as Austria was an aggressor.

Within Italy feelings were divided as to whether the country should remain neutral throughout the course of the conflict. Many Italians felt that they should not let the war end without trying to secure territory in the Balkans and firmly establish the border with Austria, which was open to question.

To secure these ends, Italy began negotiations with Austria. The Austrians proved evasive, and on April 26, 1915, Italy concluded the secret Treaty of London with the Allies. In the event of Allied victory, the treaty promised Italy Trentino, the south Tyrol, Istria, Gorizia, Gradisca, and the city of Trieste, some of the Dalmatian Islands, sovereignty over the Dodecanese Islands, part of Germany's African colonies, and the seaport of Adalia on the coast of Asia Minor.

Italy declared war on Austria-Hungary in May, 1915, and in August, 1916, declared war on Germany. Italian troops fought the Austrians and

BOMBASTIC MUSSOLINI *and his Black Shirts. He was shot by partisans in 1945.*

Germans along the northern frontier for four years with varying degrees of success. In 1918 they held firm against a major offensive launched in June, and in November won a decisive victory at Vittorio Veneto.

Fascism. At the 1919 Versailles Peace Conference, which ended the war, Italy won little of what it had been promised. The resulting popular discontent, together with postwar social and political unrest, contributed to the development of an extreme nationalistic movement, Fascism, led by Benito Mussolini. Fascism was embraced primarily by discontented members of the lower middle class.

On October 28, 1922, the Fascists staged a march on Rome. King Victor Emmanuel III, rather than use the military to put down the revolt, asked Mussolini to form a government. Mussolini was named prime minister and gradually created a dictatorial regime. Parliament became his puppet, and in 1938 the lower house, the Chamber of Deputies, was replaced by the Chamber of Fasces and Corporations, whose members were appointed by the Fascist Party.

Fascist foreign policy was imperialistic. In defiance of the League of Nations, Mussolini invaded Ethiopia in October, 1935, and following the conquest of Ethiopia, Victor Emmanuel assumed the title of emperor of Ethiopia. In 1937 Italy withdrew from the League of Nations, and in 1939 Italy conquered Albania and Victor Emmanuel was named its king.

Mussolini also supported fascist movements abroad. He aided General Francisco Franco in the Spanish Civil War of 1936–1939, and supported Adolf Hitler in Germany's annexation of Austria and Czechoslovakia. Finally, on May 22, 1939, he concluded an alliance with Germany, establishing the Rome-Berlin Axis.

World War II. Following the outbreak of World War II in September, 1939, Mussolini declared Italy's neutrality. But in June, 1940, when France was on the verge of defeat, he invaded southern France, bringing Italy into the war. The Italian troops were ill-prepared and were soon demoralized by disaster after disaster. General discontent grew as the war continued, and German troops moved into Italy.

On July 25, 1943, the king dismissed Mussolini as head of the government, and a new government was formed by Marshal Pietro Badoglio. The Allies invaded Sicily in July and August of 1943, and in September Italy surrendered. Mussolini proclaimed a "social republic" in the German-controlled north, which lasted until the country was completely liberated in 1945.

On May 9, 1946, Victor Emmanuel abdicated in favor of his son, who became King Humbert II. But the monarchy had lost its popularity as a result of its cooperation with Mussolini, and a referendum held in June made Italy a republic. A new constitution was adopted in 1947, and in 1948 Luigi Einaudi became president.

Republic. Italy soon developed three major political parties—the Christian Democrats, the Socialists, and the Communists. Center-right coalitions ruled Italy through most of the postwar era. The nation began to industrialize and improve its economy as it cooperated closely with the United States and the nations of Western Europe in the postwar revival.

Economic problems, which worsened after 1973, are rooted in Italy's dependence on inflated foreign oil imports. High unemployment and widespread workers' strikes have resulted.

Amid this turmoil, the Communist Party, disavowing its ties with the Soviet Union, made strong gains in the elections of 1976 and 1980. It now ranks closely behind the Christian Democrats as the most influential party of the center-left coalition.

The government has been harassed since 1977 by neofascist terrorist activities. In 1978 former prime minister Moro was assassinated by the Red Brigade terrorists, who are alleged to have set the bomb at the Bologna train station where 76 people were killed in 1980.

In 1976 the Concordat of 1929, which determines Italy's relations with the Vatican, was revised to end the Catholic Church's standing as the national religion.

Liechtenstein

Official name: *Principality of Liechtenstein*
Area: *61 sq. mi., 159 sq. km.*
Population: *(1979) 26,000*
Capital: *Vaduz (Pop., 1977, 4,704)*
Language: *Alemannic*
Religion: *Roman Catholic*
Currency unit: *Swiss franc*
National holiday: *Jan. 23*

Liechtenstein is a very small independent principality located on the border between Austria and Switzerland. It extends no more than 16 miles from north to south and seven miles from east to west.

The land. The Alps dominate the country's landscape in the east, rising to over 8000 feet. Western Liechtenstein lies in the valley of the Rhine River, which flows along the country's western border. Winters are long and cold, but summers are mild.

The people. Liechtenstein's small population is concentrated in the Rhine Valley, where Vaduz, the capital and only large town, is located. The people speak Alemannic, a Germanic dialect. More than 90 percent of the population is Roman Catholic.

Since the nation began to industrialize, after 1950, it has attracted large numbers of foreign workers, who account for one-third of the population.

Economy. Liechtenstein's economy was once based almost entirely on agriculture, but by the mid-1900's industry had become the main source of income. In 1930, for instance, 70 percent of the nation's labor force was involved in agriculture. Today that figure is less than two percent. Cattle, dairy, corn, fruit, and potatoes are the leading farm products.

Vaduz Castle

Liechtenstein's hydroelectric power resources, good transportation facilities, and skilled labor force combine to attract industry. Major manufactured products include precision instruments, small machine parts, pharmaceuticals, and false teeth. Textiles, ceramics, leather goods, and processed foods are also produced.

A large portion of the country's income consists of registration fees paid by foreign companies that incorporate in the principality because of its favorable tax policies. Sales to collectors of postage stamps also contribute to the economy, as does tourism, which increased greatly after 1950.

Liechtenstein has a favorable balance of trade, as its exports earn a great deal and it imports only a few items. It trades heavily with Western Europe and the United States, and it has a customs union with Switzerland.

Government.
Liechtenstein is a constitutional monarchy ruled by a prince of the house of Liechtenstein. A head of government, an assistant head, and two councilors, all appointed by the prince, are responsible to a 15-member, popularly elected Parliament. Switzerland represents the country's interests abroad.

Liechtenstein is a member of the International Court of Justice, the Council of Europe, and the European Free Trade Association.

History.
In ancient times, Liechtenstein's territory was part of the Roman province of Rhaetia. During the 1300's and 1400's the Holy Roman Empire's county of Vaduz and barony of Schellenburg were united under a single count, and by 1712 this feudal state had come into the possession of the Liechtenstein family.

In 1719 the Holy Roman Emperor granted the fief to the family as the Principality of Liechtenstein, and at the dissolution of the Holy Roman Empire in 1806, it became fully independent. Since then, to secure protection, diplomatic representation, and trade advantages, it has become associated with several states, including the Flemish Confederation, the German Confederation, and Austria-Hungary.

In 1919, after Austria-Hungary's defeat in World War I, Switzerland agreed to represent Liechtenstein abroad. In 1921 Liechtenstein established a democratic form of government, adopted Swiss currency, and entrusted postal and telecommunications services to Switzerland. In 1924 they formed a customs union.

Liechtenstein avoided involvement in World War II. The country concentrated on developing its economy, and today its people enjoy a high standard of living. Since the 1960's Liechtenstein has been seeking closer cooperation with other small European states.

Luxembourg

Official name: *Grand Duchy of Luxembourg*
Area: *998 sq. mi., 2,586 sq. km.*
Population: *(1980) 358,000*
Capital: *Luxembourg*
  (Pop., 1978, 78,400)
Language: *Letzeburgesch (Luxembourgish), French, German*
Religion: *Roman Catholic*
Currency unit: *Franc*
National holiday: *Grand duke's birthday, June 23*

Luxembourg, one of the smallest countries of Europe, is bordered on the north and west by Belgium, on the east by West Germany, and on the south by France.

In 1922 Luxembourg and Belgium formed an economic union that abolished the customs frontier between them. The union was dissolved in 1940, but was reestablished in 1945. In 1948 a customs union went into effect among Luxembourg, Belgium, and the Netherlands, which is known as the Benelux Customs Union. Full economic union of the three countries has existed since 1960.

The land.
The southern third of Luxembourg is part of the Lorraine Plateau and consists of rolling plains. The northern two-thirds of the country is part of the Ardennes and is hilly and wooded. Its principal river is the Sauer.

Luxembourg has a cool, temperate, rainy climate. Winters are mild and summers cool, with summer temperatures averaging 60°F. Precipitation averages about 30 inches a year.

The people.
Luxembourgers are a mixture of nationalities—primarily French, Dutch, German, and Belgian. The official language is French, but German and Letzeburgesch, a Germanic dialect, are very widely spoken.

More than 95 percent of the population are Roman Catholic. The only important urban center is the capital, Luxembourg.

Economy.
The main support of Luxembourg's economy is the iron and steel industry. There are large iron ore deposits in southwestern Luxembourg, and there is coal nearby in Germany. This combination has made Luxembourg one of Western Europe's major iron and steel producers. Other important industries include distilling and tanning.

About six percent of the labor force is employed in agriculture, which is troubled by low yields. Livestock is raised, and the principal crops are potatoes, wheat, barley, and wine grapes. Domestic production meets most of Luxembourg's food needs.

The iron and steel industry provides about 70 percent of Luxembourg's exports. Major imports include fuels, motor vehicles and parts, machinery, and a variety of manufactured goods. Luxembourg's major trading partners are Belgium, West Germany, France, and the Netherlands.

Government.
Luxembourg is a constitutional monarchy with a grand duke as chief of state. Executive power is exercised by the grand duke and the Council of Government. The council, or cabinet, is headed by a minister of state, or prime minister.

Legislative power rests with the Chamber of Deputies, which is directly elected to a term of five years. The Council of State, an advisory body of elder statesmen appointed by the grand duke, deliberates on proposed legislation and expresses its opinion on other matters referred to it, but its decisions can be overruled by the Chamber of Deputies.

Luxembourg is a member of the United Nations, the Common Market, the Organization for Economic Cooperation and Development (OECD), the North Atlantic Treaty Organization (NATO), the Council of Europe, and the Western European Union.

History.
The name Luxembourg is derived from the castle of Lützelburg, the seat of Count Siegfried I, under whose sway several lands were united in the 900's. The size of the country gradually increased under a series of able rulers. In 1308 Count Henry of Luxembourg became Holy Roman Emperor. In 1354 his grandson, Emperor Charles IV, expanded Luxembourg's territories considerably and made it a duchy.

Luxembourg was conquered by Philip the Good of Burgundy in 1443. In 1477 it passed to the Hapsburgs through marriage, and in 1555 Philip II of Spain received it from Charles V as part of the Low Countries. Luxembourg was conquered by Louis XIV and ruled by France until 1697, when it was restored to Spain.

It was ruled by Austria from 1714 until 1795, when it again came under French rule. Luxembourg was annexed to the French Republic and subsequently became a part of the Napoleonic empire. At the Congress of Vienna (1814–1815), Luxembourg was made a grand duchy, ruled by William I, who was also king of the Kingdom of the Netherlands.

Luxembourg was associated with Belgium when it seceded from the Netherlands in 1830, but in 1839 part of the country merged with Belgium and the rest remained an independent grand duchy under the personal rule of the Netherlands' king.

Lacking economic ties with the Netherlands, Luxembourg became associated with the German states, and in 1866, upon dissolution of the German Confederation, Luxembourg was neutralized, and the crown passed to Grand Duke Adolphe of Nassau.

Modern Luxembourg. Luxembourg was invaded by the Germans in 1914, at the outbreak of World War I, and it remained under German occupation throughout the war. Luxembourg's neutrality was violated again in World War II, when German troops occupied the Low Countries in 1940. Grand Duchess Charlotte and the cabinet carried on a government in exile in London and Montreal, Canada. The country was liberated in 1944.

In 1949 Luxembourg abandoned its neutrality and joined NATO. It cooperates closely with Western European countries in economic matters.

Malta

Official name: *Malta*
Area: *122 sq. mi., 316 sq. km.*
Population: *(1980) 340,000*
Capital: *Valletta (Pop., 1977, 14,096)*
Language: *Maltese, English*
Religion: *Roman Catholic*
Currency unit: *Pound*
National holiday: *Independence Day, Sept. 21*

Malta is an island nation in the Mediterranean Sea, about 60 miles south of Sicily. The country includes the islands of Malta, Comino, and Gozo, and two uninhabited islands.

The land. The Maltese islands are flat and consist of limestone rock covered with a thin layer of soil. There are few trees and no rivers or lakes.

The climate is semitropical, with mild winters and hot summers. An average of 20 inches of rain a year falls on the islands, but the amount varies greatly from year to year.

MALTA ◗ Valletta

The people. The Maltese are a Mediterranean people who speak a Semitic language. The population is almost entirely Roman Catholic. Malta's density of population is extremely high—about 2800 persons per square mile. Emigration, especially since the end of World War II, has been high and directed mainly to Australia, Britain, and Canada.

Economy. Malta is in the process of developing its economy. Its only resources are its people, its geographic location, and its limestone.

Tourism has become one of the nation's leading sources of income in recent years. Manufacturing began on Malta in the early 1960's, and it now employs nearly one-quarter of the labor force. Significant manufactured products include textiles, rubber products, and processed foods. Shipbuilding is the main industry.

Agriculture is relatively insignificant to the economy. Potatoes, tomatoes, grapes, and wheat are the main crops. Fishing is important.

Malta's imports cost about $609 million in 1965 and exports earned only about $363 million. The leading exports are potatoes, wines, processed foods, textiles, and cut flowers. The leading imports are textiles, machinery, foodstuffs, and consumer goods.

Government. Malta became a republic within the Commonwealth on December 13, 1974. The popularly elected Parliament has one house, the House of Representatives, of 55 members. The cabinet, consisting of the prime minister and appointed ministers, derives authority from the House.

Malta is a member of the Commonwealth, the United Nations, and the Council of Europe.

History. Malta, called Melita in ancient times, and its small sister island, Gozo, were inhabited in prehistoric times by people whose great stone monuments are still in existence. An important refuge for ships following Mediterranean trade routes, the islands were visited by early Phoenicians and Greeks, and in the 200's B.C. they passed under Carthaginian rule. Malta became a Roman possession in 216 B.C. During the first century A.D. the Maltese adopted Christianity.

After the dissolution of the Roman Empire, Malta passed successively to the Byzantine Empire, the Arabs, Sicily, the kingdom of Aragon, and then to the united kingdoms of Aragon and Castile. In the early 1500's the Holy Roman Emperor received Malta from Spain by inheritance, and in 1530 he granted it to the Order of the Hospital of St. John of Jerusalem.

The knights, who served as protectors of religious pilgrims, regarded Malta as an outpost for the defense of Christianity. They withstood attacks by the Muslim Turks, including a long siege in 1565. The island under the knights was supported and protected by the nations of Europe, and it grew prosperous from Mediterranean trade.

The military strength and effectiveness of the order declined during the 1600's and 1700's, and in 1798 Napoleon Bonaparte of France occupied Malta. Two years later, with the aid of the Maltese, a British force drove out the French, and the Maltese requested permanent British protection. In 1814 Malta became a British crown colony and a vital British naval base.

British rule. The islanders had partial self-government during the 1800's. They were self-governing during the 1920's and 1930's, but two issues sharply divided the island—the choice of Maltese or Italian as an official language and church-state relations. The conflict grew so bitter that home rule was abolished in 1936.

During World War II, Malta had great strategic value. It withstood heavy German and Italian air bombardments and was a base for the Anglo-U.S. invasion of Sicily in 1943. In 1942 Britain awarded the George Cross to the Maltese people for their bravery during the bombardments.

Independence. After the war, the country worked to achieve sufficient unity to allow restoration of complete internal self-government, which it received in 1962. Maltese and English were made the official languages, and Roman Catholicism was declared the official religion. In 1964 the British granted the country full independence. In 1974 it became a republic.

Malta concentrated on expanding its economy to end its dependence on the British naval base, which had been its major source of income and which was being closed down. By 1979 the British had abandoned the base, ending nearly two centuries of British military presence on the island.

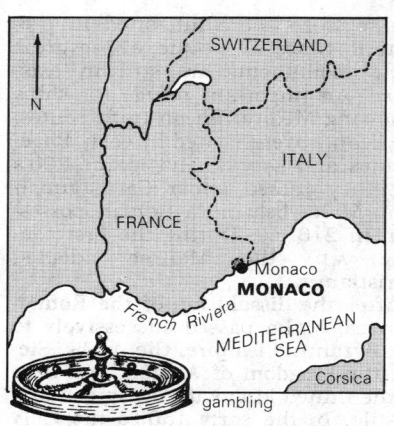

TINY MONACO, *ruled since the 1200's by an ancient family—Prince Rainier is the present ruler—is known as a resort, with beautiful beaches and a world-famous gambling casino.*

Monaco

Official name: *Principality of Monaco*
Area: *0.6 sq. mi., 1.6 sq. km.*
Population: *(1979) 26,000*
Capital: *Monaco-Ville*
  (Pop., 1979, 1700)
Language: *French*
Religion: *Roman Catholic*
Currency unit: *French franc*
National holiday: *Nov. 19*

Monaco is a tiny principality on the French Riviera. It is bounded on the north, east, and west by France and on the south by the Mediterranean Sea.

The land and people. Monaco is set into steep cliffs surrounding an excellent harbor. Its climate is mild and rather dry.

There are three sections in the principality—Monte Carlo, La Condamine, and Monaco-Ville, which lies atop a rocky promontory jutting into the Mediterranean.

A majority of the people are from other European countries, and in the mid-1960's only slightly more than one-tenth of the people were native Monagasques. French is the official language, and Roman Catholicism the predominant religion.

Economy. Tourists, attracted by Monaco's scenery, beach resorts, and gambling casino, are the major source of Monaco's income. The sale of postage stamps to collectors is important. The country also has light industries producing pharmaceuticals, precision tools, and luxury consumer items.

Monaco has no income tax, and it long served the wealthy as a refuge from taxes.

Government. Monaco is governed by a prince, who is assisted by a small appointed cabinet. An elected council shares legislative power with the prince. France is responsible for Monaco's foreign affairs and defense,

but the principality maintains consulates and missions throughout the world.

History. The ancient Phoenicians, Greeks, Carthaginians, and Romans all used Monaco's harbor. In the 600's and 700's, Monaco was occupied by the Lombards, who built a fortress on its rocky promontory. In the 800's the fortress fell to the Saracens.

Monaco became part of the Holy Roman Empire, and in the 900's Monaco was granted to a leading family of Genoa, which later took the name Grimaldi. The Grimaldis did not exercise their rights over the territory until the late 1200's, when they were driven from Genoa as a result of political feuds.

The tiny state was in constant danger of being overwhelmed by its larger neighbors. With its fortress and its excellent harbor and port facilities, Monaco was coveted by Genoa, Savoy, Florence, France, and Spain. Monaco managed to maintain its independence, however, and in 1512 the right of the Grimaldis to rule Monaco was

formally acknowledged by the king of France.

After the French Revolution, in 1793, France annexed the principality. The sovereignty of the Grimaldis was restored in 1814, and in 1815 the Treaty of Vienna made Monaco a protectorate of the Kingdom of Sardinia. In 1861 the principality once more came under the protection of France. In 1911 Monaco adopted a constitution ending the absolute rule of the princes.

During the early 1900's, the principality developed into a fashionable resort. It is well known for its gambling casino at Monte Carlo, which accounts for about three percent of the government's revenue.

Netherlands

Official name: *Kingdom of the Netherlands*
Area: *15,770 sq. mi., 40,844 sq. km.*
Population: *(1982) 14,350,000*
Capital: *Amsterdam*
  (Pop., 1983, 936,000)
Language: *Dutch*
Religion: *Protestant, Roman Catholic*
Currency unit: *Guilder*
National holiday: *Birthday of the queen, April 30*

The Netherlands, a small nation in western Europe, is bounded on the north and west by the North Sea, on the east by West Germany, and on the south by Belgium. The Frisian Islands separate the mainland from the open sea in the north. Holland, which is a name often used in referring to the nation, properly refers to two coastal provinces.

The Netherlands Antilles, a fully autonomous part of the kingdom, is all that remains of a once vast overseas empire controlled by the Dutch.

In 1948 a customs union went into

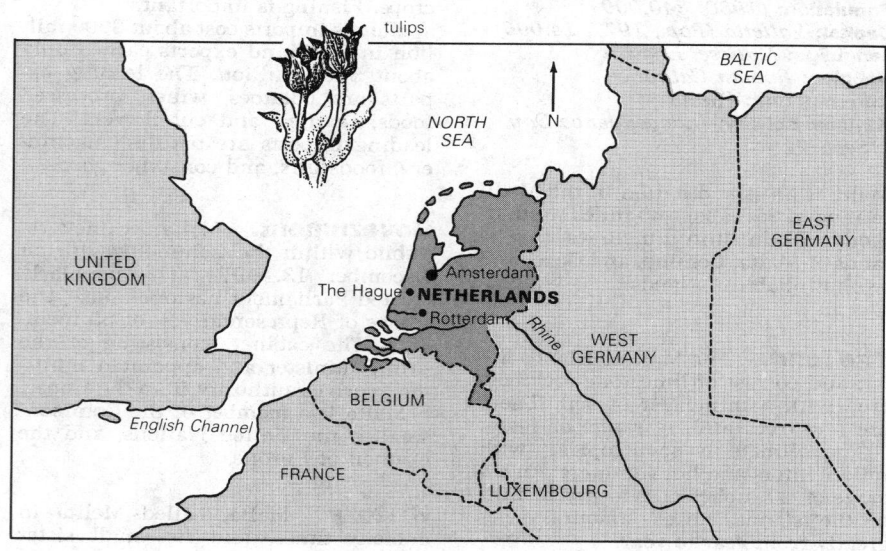

effect, known as the Benelux Customs Union, linking Belgium, Luxembourg, and the Netherlands. Full economic union of the three countries has existed since 1960.

The land.

The Netherlands consists mostly of low plains, although there are some hilly sections in the east. Much of the land along the coast lies below sea level. It is protected by dikes and kept dry by drainage and pumping systems. The Dutch have a much higher percentage of reclaimed land than any nation in Europe.

The climate is maritime, with cool summers, mild winters, and high humidity. Rainfall is ample and reliable.

The people.

The Netherlands is one of the most densely settled of the world's developed nations, with some 970 people per square mile. The population is densest in the western half of the country. The largest city is Amsterdam. Other major cities include Rotterdam, The Hague, Haarlem, Utrecht, and Eindhoven.

The population is homogeneous. There are no large ethnic minorities, although religious differences have been the basis of past friction. About 40 percent of the population is Roman Catholic, and 40 percent is Protestant.

Economy.

The Netherlands is located along the heavily trafficked North Sea coast, and commerce is a mainstay of the Dutch economy. The Dutch merchant fleet is one of Europe's largest, and Rotterdam is the continent's leading port.

The Netherlands industrialized considerably after World War II, although mostly without the aid of industrial raw materials. Since 1960 great quantities of oil and natural gas have been discovered. Europe's largest natural gas field, in Groningen Province, provides for almost half of the country's energy needs. Forty-five percent of this gas is exported. One and a half million metric tons of oil a year are produced in the Netherlands, with most of the refining done at Pernis, near Rotterdam. The nation's coal mines have been closed since 1975.

Agriculture, hindered by poor soil and climate, accounts for under five percent of the national product and only six percent of the labor force. Despite this, Dutch agriculture uses intensive and highly efficient methods, and yields per acre and per animal are among the highest in the world.

Twenty-three percent of the labor force is engaged in manufacturing. Major industrial products include steel and other finished metals, transportation equipment, machinery, chemicals, refined petroleum, radios, textiles, ships, and a wide variety of processed foodstuffs. The chief industrial cities are Rotterdam, Amsterdam, Utrecht, Eindhoven, Limburg, and Groningen.

In 1983 exports earned $65.5 billion, and imports cost $62.5 billion. Industrial exports include chemicals, refined petroleum, metal and electrical goods, and textiles. Major imports are industrial raw materials, which make up about one-third of the total; foodstuffs; fuels; and a variety of consumer goods.

The Netherlands' chief trading partners are West Germany, Belgium, Luxembourg, the United States, Britain, and France.

Government.

The Netherlands is a constitutional monarchy. The sovereign is head of state, but executive power is exercised by a prime minister and cabinet. The prime minister must normally be able to command a majority of votes in the legislature.

Legislative power is held by the States-General, which consists of two houses. The upper house is called the First Chamber, and its members are chosen by provincial legislatures for six-year terms. Members of the lower house, the Second Chamber, are directly elected and serve four-year terms.

The Netherlands is a member of the United Nations, the Common Market, the Organization for Economic Cooperation and Development (OECD), the Council of Europe, and the North Atlantic Treaty Organization (NATO).

History.

When Roman legions led by Julius Caesar first advanced into the Netherlands in 57 B.C., the area was inhabited by Celtic and Germanic tribes. The region south of the Rhine became a part of the Roman Empire, and remained so until 400 A.D., when the Netherlands came under the control of the Franks. The Netherlands was part of Charlemagne's empire from 800 to 843. After the breakup of the empire, it emerged as a group of duchies, most often under the control of German princes. After 1384 they were ruled by the dukes of Burgundy.

Mary of Burgundy married the future Holy Roman Emperor Maximilian I in 1477, and in 1493 the Netherlands became part of the Holy Roman Empire. After the resignation of Emperor Charles V in 1555, the empire was divided, and the Netherlands passed to Philip II of Spain.

During the second half of the 1600's, many of the Dutch accepted Calvinism. Philip, a devout Roman Catholic, saw the suppression of Protestantism as a paramount goal and introduced the Inquisition into the

LOW-LYING LAND *characterizes the Netherlands. Much of it lies below sea level and some has been reclaimed from the sea by the industrious Dutch. Three large islands have been joined to the mainland, and part of the old Zuider Zee is being turned into fields.*

CONSULATE GENERAL OF THE NETHERLANDS

LADY WITH A PINK *by Rembrandt, the great Dutch artist of the 17th century.*

Netherlands. Religious persecution intensified the existing conflict between the Dutch and the Spaniards. In addition to religious freedom, the Dutch desired economic independence and self-government, and they strongly resented foreign rule.

Independence. In 1579 the seven northern provinces formed the Union of Utrecht, and two years later they proclaimed their independence. A bloody civil war was fought until 1609, when a twelve-year truce was signed. Under the leadership of William of Orange, the Dutch Netherlands achieved *de facto* independence.

At the end of the truce, Spain resumed the war, but the Dutch were more than able to hold their own, and in 1648 the Treaty of Westphalia formally recognized the independence of the United Netherlands. The southern provinces continued to be ruled by Spain, and then by Austria until the end of the 1700's.

During the 1600's, the Dutch nation reached its political and cultural height. The Dutch established a colonial empire, and for a brief time the Netherlands was the leading commercial power in Europe. Dutch supremacy was broken by a series of naval wars fought with England (1652–1654; 1665–1667), that soon reduced the Netherlands to the status of a second-rate power.

During the second half of the 1600's, the Dutch were also engaged in trying to stem the expansionist tendencies of France under King Louis XIV. Although successful, they were never able to recover from the strain of the effort, and after the War of the Spanish Succession (1702–1713), the Dutch economy declined.

In 1795 the Netherlands was conquered by France and made into the puppet state of the Batavian Republic. In 1806 Napoleon created the Kingdom of Holland, which was incorporated into his empire in 1810. After Napoleon's defeat in 1814, the Congress of Vienna restored the Netherlands' independence.

Union. The Congress of Vienna also joined the Austrian and former Spanish provinces with the Dutch Netherlands to create the Kingdom of the Netherlands, which was intended to serve as a bulwark against future French expansion. But the union between Belgium and Holland was shortlived.

Holland was Germanic in orientation, Calvinistic in religion, and favored a policy of free trade, whereas Belgium was French in orientation, predominantly Roman Catholic, and sought high tariffs to protect its growing industry. In 1830 a revolution broke out in Belgium that eventually resulted in the separation of the two countries.

Modern Netherlands. The Netherlands remained neutral in World War I, but was invaded by the Germans during World War II. It suffered greatly during German occupation. Queen Wilhelmina escaped to London, where she led a government in exile. After the liberation in 1944, she was restored to her throne. In 1948, after a reign of 50 years, she abdicated in favor of her daughter, Juliana, who turned the throne over to her daughter, Beatrix, in 1980.

During the postwar period, the Netherlands lost a large portion of its colonial possessions. A nationalist rebellion broke out in Indonesia in 1945, and in 1949 the Dutch granted the country its independence. In 1954 the American colonies of Dutch Guiana and the Netherlands Antilles gained internal self-government, but they remained in the kingdom as equal partners of the Netherlands. In 1962 Netherlands New Guinea (West Irian) was transferred to Indonesia and, in 1975, Dutch Guiana, or Surinam, became independent.

There were massive emigrations into the Netherlands from Indonesia after 1949, and from Surinam after 1975. In recent years, terrorist activity in the Netherlands has been carried on by a group supporting the independence of the South Moluccan islands from Indonesia.

The Netherlands has played a prominent role in bringing about closer ties among the countries of Western Europe. In 1967 the Netherlands met with Belgium and Luxembourg to discuss extending the integration between their countries beyond the field of economics, hoping thus to encourage closer cooperation between France, Italy, West Germany, and the other members of the West European community.

Norway

Official name: *Kingdom of Norway*
Area: *125,182 sq. mi., 324,219 sq. km.*
Population: *(1980) 4,075,000*
Capital: *Oslo (Pop., 1982, 450,386)*
Language: *Norwegian*
Religion: *Lutheran*
Currency unit: *Krone*
National holiday: *Constitution Day, May 17*

Norway, a kingdom in northern Europe, occupies the entire western side of the Scandinavian peninsula. It is bounded on the north by the Arctic Ocean, on the east by Sweden, on the northeast by the Soviet Union and Finland, on the south by the Skagerrak Strait and the North Sea, and on the west by the Norwegian Sea, an arm of the North Atlantic Ocean.

The land. Norway is a long, narrow country described as being "all mountains and sea." It is almost totally devoid of plains. Most of the terrain is rugged and mountainous, but there is a high, hilly plateau region in the center of the country.

A mountainous ridge follows the border with Sweden. It rises to about 8000 feet in the south-central region, and steep slopes plunge into the Skagerrak along the coast.

Norway's long coastline is penetrated by almost innumerable deep, sheltered, navigable inlets, or fjords, and is protected from the open sea by a fringe of islands. Many lakes lie scattered throughout Norway, and many rivers and streams rush down from the mountains.

More than one-third of the country lies north of the Arctic Circle, and two arctic islands, Jan Mayen and Spitsbergen (Svalbard), are part of Norway.

Norway's climate is varied. The south has a temperate marine climate, with cool summers, mild winters, and much cloudiness. The warm North Atlantic drift keeps the entire coast ice-free all year. In the north and in the higher elevations, the climate is colder and more severe. Precipitation is plentiful, particularly in the mountainous areas.

The people. Norway has one of Europe's smallest populations, with about 33 persons per square mile. The population is increasing very slowly, at 0.3 percent a year between 1975 and 1980.

The interior and the northern two-thirds of the country are sparsely inhabited, and most of the people live along the southern coast, where Norway's main cities, Oslo, Bergen, and Trondheim, are located.

Almost all of the people are Norwegian. Norwegian is the universal lan-

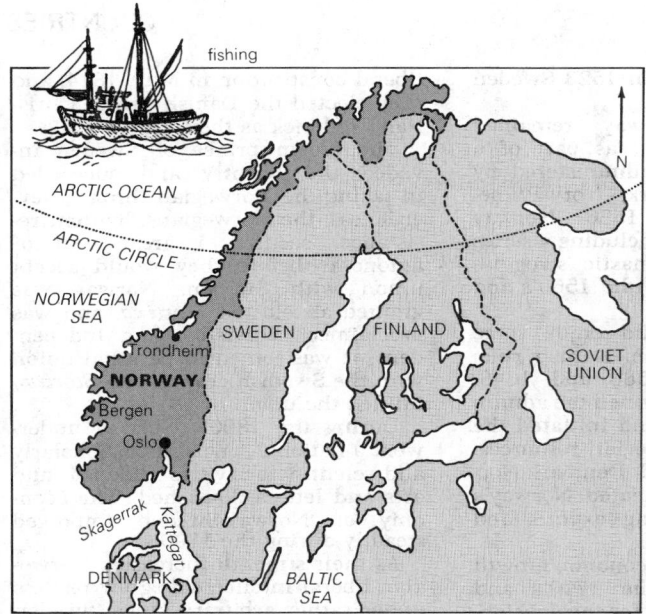

THE LONELY FJORDS OF NORWAY, *reaching from the sea far into the rugged mountains, have made Norwegians a seafaring people.*

guage and Evangelical Lutheranism is the established religion. In the far north there is a minority (about 0.5 percent of the population) of seminomadic Lapps, who have their own language and culture.

Economy. Norway's economy traditionally was based on merchant shipping, fishing, forestry, and agriculture. In the 1900's the country began to expand its industry by developing and utilizing its natural resources.

Although its economy operates on a comparatively small volume, Norway was one of the world's richest countries per capita even before its oil and gas reserves began to be exploited in the 1970's.

Hydroelectric power was Norway's main domestic energy source before the discovery of great oil reserves and natural gas fields in the North Sea. Hydroelectric power is still important, though, especially since gas and oil reserves are expected to decline sharply as the new century approaches. In 1979, 18 million metric tons of oil were produced in Norway. New refineries were opened in the same year.

Commercial fishing, though of less importance than formerly, still prospers, and forestry is important in the economy.

Norway has the world's fourth largest merchant fleet, nearly 28 million gross registered tons in 1976. Income from the fleet accounts for about one-third of the country's foreign exchange earnings.

Agriculture. Less than five percent of Norway's land is cultivable, and in 1976 agriculture contributed only six percent to the domestic product. Agriculture employs about 17 percent of the labor force and meets a large part of the country's food requirements. The major emphasis is on livestock

raising and dairying. Hardy grains, potatoes, and some fruits and vegetables are also grown.

Manufacturing. Norwegian industry received a tremendous boost in the 1950's and 1960's from the rapid development of hydroelectric power, which now supplies the nation with half its energy needs. The other half, supplied by foreign oil imports prior to 1975, is now supplied by domestic oil.

In 1976 construction and manufacturing contributed 35 percent of the national product. Among the newer industries made possible by cheap and abundant electricity are the electrometallurgical and electrochemical industries. Major industrial products include ships, machinery, and vehicles. Lumber and pulp and paper mills are also important, and fish processing plants produce some of Norway's major exports.

Trade. Norway's new status as a major oil supplier has improved its volume as well as its balance of trade considerably. In 1983 imports cost $13.4 billion and exports earned $17.9 billion.

Major imports are ships and boats, machinery, petroleum products, textiles, and foodstuffs. Metals and ores, pulp and paper, and fish and fish products are the leading exports. Sweden, Britain, West Germany, the United States, and Denmark are Norway's major trading partners.

Government. Norway is a constitutional monarchy, with a king as head of state. Actual executive power is wielded by a prime minister and cabinet responsible to Parliament.

The Parliament, called the *Storting,* is popularly elected every four years. It elects one-quarter of its membership to sit as an upper house, the *Lagting.* The remainder of the *Storting* is called the

Odelsting. Most legislative actions are taken by the united *Storting.*

Norway is a member of the United Nations, the North Atlantic Treaty Organization (NATO), the European Free Trade Association, the Organization for Economic Cooperation and Development (OECD), the Council of Europe, and the Nordic Council.

History. Archaeological evidence indicates that man lived in Norway as early as 8000 years ago. Beginning about 7000 years ago, a variety of wandering tribes from the north and south appeared in Scandinavia. Germanic tribes, the main forebears of the present Norwegian people, had established themselves in the land by about 500 B.C.

For the next 1000 years, during the eras of the Roman Empire and the barbarian migrations, tribal groups in Norway shifted and resettled, competing for dominance over the region.

During the 800's A.D. the tribal communities were gradually united, and Harold Fairhair (Harald Haarfager) became Norway's first king. The united tribes began to expand their territory, and from the late 800's through the early 1000's, Norwegian Vikings explored and colonized the shores of Britain, Ireland, the Faroe Islands, Iceland, Greenland, and probably North America.

During several brief intervals in the late 900's and early 1000's, the country was under Danish rule, but Norwegian kings always regained control, and by the mid-1000's the monarchy was quite strong.

Early kingdom. Through the efforts of King Olaf Tryggvesson and King Olaf Haraldsson in the late 900's and early 1000's, Christianity was introduced into Norway. As the church gained influence, it challenged royal power and was supported by members of the land-owning aristocracy, whose power was growing.

Civil wars filled the period between the mid-1100's and the mid-1200's, but the strength of the monarchy was maintained, and the 1200's marked the high point of Norwegian power and prosperity. Between 1217 and 1263, during the reign of King Haakon IV, Iceland and Greenland were added to the realm. Norwegian art and literature flourished, and King Magnus VI sponsored a codification of law for the entire country in the 1270's.

This era of greatness was short-lived, however. In the mid-1300's the plague killed half of Norway's population and crippled the country. The merchants of the German Hanseatic League gained a firm grip on Norwegian economic life. Moreover, the Norwegian royal succession became entangled with that of Sweden and Denmark.

In 1380 King Olaf V, the last of Harold Fairhair's dynasty, became king of both Norway and Denmark. When he died in 1387, his mother, Queen Margaret of Denmark, combined the thrones of both kingdoms. In 1397 Sweden was added to form the Kalmar Union, which was completely dominated by Denmark.

Norway was the weakest member, and its territory, prestige, and autonomy declined steadily in the 1400's. The union was frequently torn by internal struggles, and in 1523 Sweden broke away.

Danish union. Norway remained linked with Denmark, as part of a kingdom ruled and administered by Danes. With Denmark, Norway became Lutheran in 1536. Norway shared Danish wars, including a series of territorial and dynastic struggles with Sweden between the 1560's and the 1720's.

The Norwegians did enjoy some economic benefits from Danish rule, however, between 1588 and 1648. King Christian IV reformed the administration of Norway and initiated the development of Norwegian resources. Absolutists who ruled Denmark-Norway after 1660 stimulated Norway's economy by expanding exports and founding new towns.

Modest but steady economic growth continued through the 1700's and helped to lay the basis for the development of a Norwegian national consciousness. In 1807 Denmark granted Norwegian requests for a degree of self-government. The French Revolution and the hardships endured during the Napoleonic Wars stimulated Norwegian nationalism. In 1814 Sweden, which had opposed Napoleon and had won a victory over Denmark, forced Denmark to cede Norway.

Swedish union. The Norwegians rose in protest and refused to recognize Swedish rule. They convened a national assembly, which adopted a liberal constitution in May, 1814, and they elected the Danish prince Christian Frederick as their king.

The crown prince of Sweden invaded the country and succeeded in taking the Norwegian throne. Nevertheless, the Norwegians, by their resistance, secured a great deal of autonomy before they would accept union with Sweden. Norway was granted an elected *Storting,* and was proclaimed indivisible and independent; it was joined in personal union with the Swedish crown. The *Storting* ratified the union in 1815.

During the 1800's Norway underwent a national renaissance. Scholarly and scientific activities widened, and arts and letters flourished. The economy of Norway-Sweden improved steadily during the 1800's.

As their strength increased, Norwegian liberal intellectuals grew restless under rather arbitrary kings. Sweden granted concessions, including a system of free education, complete religious freedom, and expansion of voting rights.

The reform movement accelerated, and in 1872 the first Norwegian trade union was formed. In the 1880's a parliamentary government was introduced, based on universal manhood suffrage. In the 1890's Norwegian demands for complete independence grew, led by Johan Sverdrup. The economies of both Norway and Sweden were booming, with Norway's merchant fleet serving as the basis of the prosperity.

Renewed independence. As Norway's international trade expanded, the Norwegian *Storting* requested permission to handle Norway's consular affairs under its own flag. When the Swedish king refused, the Norwegian *Storting* declared Norway independent in June, 1905. Norway elected the Danish prince Charles to be king as Haakon VII. Sweden accepted Norway's declaration of independence in October, 1905.

Norway was well prepared for independence by its material progress, political activism, and social reforms of the late 1800's. Democratic reform continued in Norway after independence. The royal veto over the *Storting* was abolished, the vote was extended to women, and social welfare programs were initiated.

Norway remained neutral in World War I, but its vital merchant fleet was severely damaged. After the war, the nation suffered an economic depression that was intensified by the world economic depression of the 1930's.

Economic and social reforms initiated during the 1920's and 1930's included the formation of cooperative enterprises, the institution of national collective bargaining, and the expansion of social welfare legislation under the leadership of Liberal, Labor, and left-wing farmers' party governments. A Labor government elected in 1935

A STAVE CHURCH, *an early medieval type of church made of wood, and reminiscent of Viking ships with their upturned dragons on the gables. A handful survive, all in Norway. Norway was converted to Christianity only in the 900's, so pagan influences were strong.*

was successful in ending Norway's economic crisis by expanding the government's economic role.

In 1940, during World War II, Germany invaded Norway, and despite stiff Norwegian resistance Nazi troops conquered and occupied the country. King Haakon rallied resistance to the Germans, and the Norwegian home front played a prominent part in Norway's liberation from the Germans in 1945.

Contemporary Norway. Norway participated actively in postwar international affairs. In 1945 it became a charter member of the United Nations and a Norwegian, Trygve Lie, became the first UN secretary general. Although its neighbors pressed for a Scandinavian defense union, Norway joined NATO in 1949. At the same time it encouraged the social, economic, and cultural unity of the Scandinavian nations. In 1952 Norway joined the Nordic Council, formed to encourage Scandinavian cooperation.

Sharing a common border with the Soviet Union, Norway has had to be circumspect in its foreign policy during the era of the Cold War between the Soviet Union and the United States, but it remained anti-Communist in domestic politics and tended to be pro-Western in international affairs. In 1957 King Haakon died and was succeeded by his son, Olav V.

Since 1950 Norway has concentrated on expanding and modernizing its economy and developing its natural resources, particularly its waterpower. The growth of industry was not rapid enough to support Norway's broad social welfare programs, and in the early 1960's the economy began to falter. The Labor government, which is Marxist in theory but permissive toward the development of free enterprise, bore the brunt of popular dissatisfaction because of the many social welfare programs it had introduced.

Coalition governments have ruled since 1965, with the Labor and Conservative (with a more capitalistic orientation) parties sharing most of the power.

In a national referendum in 1972, Norwegians rejected membership in the European Economic Community. Subsequently, in July, 1973, a free-trade agreement for manufactured goods was negotiated with the EEC.

Poland

Official name: *Polish People's Republic*
Area: *120,725 sq. mi., 312,677 sq. km.*
Population: *(1980) 35,800,000*
Capital: *Warsaw*
    (Pop., 1978, 1,474,200)
Language: *Polish*
Religion: *Roman Catholic*
Currency unit: *Zloty*
National holiday: *National Liberation Day, July 22*

Poland, a communist-controlled nation in eastern Europe, is bounded on the north by the Baltic Sea, on the east by the Soviet Union, on the south by Czechoslovakia, and on the west by East Germany.

Following World War II, Poland underwent major territorial changes. In 1945, as a result of the Potsdam Agreement among the leading Allied Powers—Britain, the Soviet Union, and the United States—the country lost nearly 45 percent of its territory, in the east, to the Soviet Union. In compensation Poland was given German lands east of the Oder and Neisse rivers. Permanent determination of the German-Polish frontier, however, was to be decided by a future peace treaty.

The land.   The greatest part of Poland is level to rolling lowland, although there are local variations in relief.

Central Poland is a flat plain and the only noticeable relief features are deeply cut river valleys. The Vistula, Poland's largest and longest river, crosses the eastern part of this plain and flows north to the Baltic. The Oder flows north along the western border.

Southern Poland is mountainous. To the west lies the Sudeten range, to the east, the Carpathian Mountains. The two mountain systems are separated by the uppermost valley of the Oder River, which is known as the Moravian Gate.

Most of Poland has a distinctly continental climate, characterized by wide yearly temperature variation. Winters are cold and snowy, and summers are warm and dry.

The people.   Before World War II Poland was a state with substantial

minorities—Byelorussians, Germans, Jews, and Ukrainians. After World War II and its turmoil it became largely homogeneous.

The former religious and linguistic minorities were either exterminated during the wartime German occupation, or were forced to leave Poland after 1945. The Byelorussians and Ukrainians had been concentrated in the eastern regions annexed by the Soviet Union. The population is now nearly all Polish-speaking and Roman Catholic, though there are small Greek Orthodox and Protestant groups.

Warsaw, Poland's capital, suffered greater destruction during World War II than almost any other city in Europe. Warsaw had more than 1 million people in 1939, but in 1945 it had only about 20,000 inhabitants living in bombed-out ruins.

Other major cities include Łódź, which is primarily industrial, and Kraków, which was untouched by the war and is full of monuments to Poland's past. Gdańsk (Danzig), at the mouth of the Vistula, on the Baltic, is Poland's first port for freight traffic. Nearby Gdynia specializes in passenger traffic.

Economy.   Before World War II Poland was primarily an agricultural country. As a result of the Potsdam Agreement in 1945, however, Poland gained industrial areas in Silesia in the west and lost farmland in the east, and thus emerged with the resources for a more balanced economy.

Agriculture, employing 28 percent of the labor force, remains important to the economy. Industry employs 24 percent of the labor force, but it has not been developed fast enough to raise sufficiently living standards and employment rates.

Natural resources. Coal is Poland's most valuable mineral resource, and

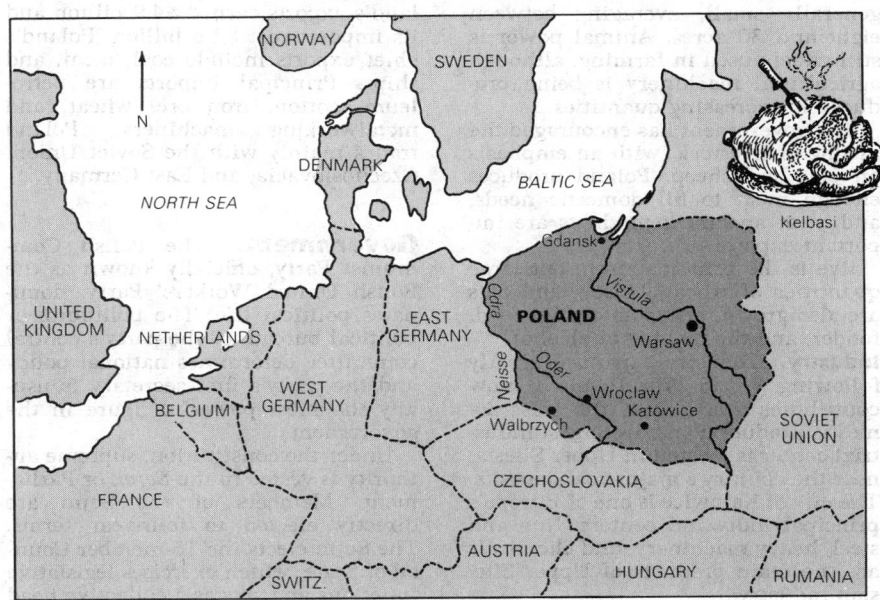

NATIONAL CATHOLIC NEWS SERVICE

UPI

TWO POLISH LEADERS, *Pope John Paul II* (right) *is of Polish birth, and Lech Walesa, head of the labor union Solidarity. The union and the Catholic Church oppose the Communist Party.*

its major source of energy. Polish coal deposits, located largely in Upper and Lower Silesia, the middle and upper valley of the Oder River, are extensive. Poland is one of the world's largest coal producers.

After World War II the Soviet Union annexed Poland's major petroleum-producing areas in what was then southeast Poland. Today Poland imports most of its petroleum, the second most important national energy source, from the Soviet Union.

Agriculture. Polish agriculture differs fundamentally from that in most other communist-controlled countries, for little land is collectivized. Nearly nine-tenths of Poland's agricultural land is privately cultivated. Farms are generally small, averaging between eight and 30 acres. Animal power is still widely used in farming, although agricultural machinery is being produced in increasing quantities.

The government has encouraged the raising of livestock, with an emphasis on pigs and sheep. Poland produces enough meat to fill domestic needs, and meat and meat products are important exports.

Rye is the principal crop, but large quantities of wheat, barley, and oats are also grown, and potatoes for food, fodder, and the making of alcohol.

Industry. Industry expanded greatly following World War II and it now contributes over half of the gross domestic product. Poland's largest industrial center is located in Upper Silesia, near the country's major coal deposits. The city of Katowice is one of Europe's principal industrial centers. Iron and steel, heavy machinery, and chemicals are the main products of Upper Silesian industry.

A second, smaller industrial center is in Lower Silesia, around the cities of Wroclaw, Walbrzych, and Jelenia Góra. This area contains mostly light industry and produces some consumer goods.

Most Polish industry has been nationalized under Communist rule. Production has not met expectations, however, and in 1970 new wage incentive laws were attempted. Workers, already troubled by price rises, unemployment, and low incomes, rioted. The government reversed its policy, and since then has tried to appease workers by investing more in housing and consumer production.

Trade. Poland's trade is chiefly a state-operated enterprise. In 1982 Poland's exports earned $4.9 billion and its imports cost $4.6 billion. Poland's chief exports include coal, meat, and ships. Principal imports are petroleum, cotton, iron ore, wheat, and metalworking machinery. Poland trades mainly with the Soviet Union, Czechoslovakia, and East Germany.

Government. The Polish Communist Party, officially known as the Polish United Workers' Party, dominates political life. The politburo, or political bureau, of the party's central committee determines national policy and the party's first secretary is usually the most powerful figure in the government.

Under the constitution, supreme authority is vested in the *Sejm,* or Parliament. Members of the Sejm are directly elected to four-year terms. The Sejm elects the 15-member Council of State, which exercises legislative functions and acts as a collective head

of state, and the Council of Ministers, which performs executive functions.

Poland is a member of the United Nations, the Council for Mutual Economic Assistance (Comecon), and the Warsaw Pact.

History. The Poles were originally one of several Slavic tribes that settled between the Oder and Vistula rivers before the 700's. During the 900's they joined with neighboring peoples to fight off a series of invasions by Germanic tribes and became unified under the Piast dynasty.

In 966 one of the early Piast rulers, Prince Mieszko, accepted Christianity. Mieszko's successors expanded Polish domains, especially to the east. In 1138, with the death of Boleslav III, Poland entered a period of political disintegration that was worsened by attacks from the Mongols.

Under Casimir the Great (ruled 1333–1370), however, Poland revived. Casimir strengthened the central government, consolidated Polish territory, developed agriculture, and constructed roads and bridges. In 1364 he founded the University of Kraków, one of the oldest institutions of higher learning in Eastern Europe.

On the death of Casimir in 1370, the Piast dynasty died out and the crown passed to Louis I of Hungary, Casimir's nephew. Louis was succeeded by his daughter Jadwiga, who in 1386 married Ladislas Jagello of Lithuania. Under the Jagellons, cultural activity reached a peak and Poland greatly extended its territory, which by the mid-1500's stretched from the Baltic to the Black Sea.

The Jagellon dynasty ended in 1572 with the death of Sigismund Augustus, and for 200 years the succession to the Polish throne was contested by the various ruling houses of Europe. The succession was further complicated by the fact that the king was elected by the Polish Parliament, which was composed of the nobility.

Any noble could block any measure by his one vote. This practice, known as the *liberum veto,* not only made the election of a new monarch extraordinarily difficult, but almost paralyzed the central government.

Partition. In 1764 a pro-Russian Polish nobleman, Stanislas Poniatowski, was made king through pressure exerted by Russia. This interference by Russia was resented by the Polish nobles, who rebelled in 1768. Russian troops crushed the rebellion, but Prussia and Austria feared that Russia would absorb Poland to their disadvantage. As a result, in 1772, the three countries agreed to partition Poland. Russia, Prussia, and Austria annexed territories adjoining them, and Poland lost approximately one-third of its land.

Alarmed, the Poles sought to strengthen their government and institute various reforms. Russia, however, invaded Poland again in 1793 and the country was once more partitioned, with Russia and Prussia each annexing more land. A third partition by Russia, Prussia, and Austria took place in 1795, and Poland was wiped off the map.

In 1807 Napoleon I of France created the Grand Duchy of Warsaw out of the Polish territories that had been annexed by Prussia. Although nominally independent, the Grand Duchy was really a puppet state. After Napoleon's defeat, the Congress of Vienna, held in 1814–1815, divided the Grand Duchy among Russia, Prussia, and Austria. Thousands of Polish intellectuals left the country for other nations in Western Europe, where they kept the spirit of Polish nationalism alive.

Life for Poles in the three territories varied. In Russian Poland, despite some persecution, Poles took part in Russian national life. In Austrian Poland, the Poles gained important political privileges and frequently held posts in the Austrian government service. In Prussian Poland, the Poles were politically oppressed but became strong economically.

Throughout the 1800's, however, all Poles sought to rid themselves of foreign rule. Uprisings in Russian Poland took place in 1830 and 1863 but were brutally crushed.

Independence. At the turn of the century the movement for independence gained momentum. A few years before the outbreak of World War I, Józef Piłsudski, a nationalist leader, secretly trained an army to fight for a reconstituted Polish nation. During World War I, exiled Polish leaders formed the Polish National Committee in Paris, which was recognized by the Allies as the spokesman for Poland. When U.S. President Woodrow Wilson enunciated his Fourteen Points in 1918, he called for the establishment of an independent Polish nation.

The Central Powers were defeated in 1918, and Piłsudski established an independent Polish government in Warsaw. Under the terms of the Treaty of Versailles in 1919, Poland regained most of Polish territory from Prussia and much of Upper Silesia. The region around the Lithuanian city of Vilna, which both countries claimed, was granted to Lithuania in 1920 but seized by Poland in 1922.

Poland gained access to the sea through the Polish Corridor, a narrow strip of land that cut through Germany to the port of Danzig, which was made a free city under the supervision of the League of Nations. Poland's claim to territories in the east, however, soon resulted in a clash with the Soviet Union.

The Allies had suggested a border between Poland and the Soviet Union based on ethnic lines, with the non-Polish territories in the east going to the Soviet Union. This suggested border, known as the Curzon Line, was rejected by the Poles, and in 1920 fighting broke out between Poland and the Soviet Union. A peace treaty signed at Riga in 1921 made Poland's frontier much the same as it had been before the partition in 1795.

Interwar era. In the same year Poland adopted a democratic constitution that provided for a parliamentary form of government. The new republic, lacking a strong executive and subject to the conflicting demands of many different political parties, was unable to deal effectively with the myriad problems caused by bringing together territories that had been parts of other states for more than 100 years, and large minorities of other nationalities, including Ukrainians, Byelorussians, and Germans.

In 1926 Józef Piłsudski headed a military coup that overthrew the existing government and established himself as dictator. On his death in 1935, a group of army colonels continued the dictatorship.

World War II. The rise to power of Adolf Hitler in Germany, the disintegration of the League of Nations, and the collapse of the various efforts within Europe to establish regional security arrangements led, on September 1, 1939, to World War II. The war began with a German invasion of Poland from the west, and two weeks later the Soviet Union invaded from the east. The Poles fought bravely, but were quickly overwhelmed. A government in exile was established in London, and Polish units fought with the Allies throughout the war. During the war the large Jewish minority in Poland was virtually exterminated by the Nazis.

In April, 1943, the Soviet government broke relations with the Polish government in London, and in July, 1944, created the Polish Committee of National Liberation on conquered Polish territory. In January, 1945, the Soviet Union reorganized the committee as the government of Poland.

British and U.S. efforts to ensure the active participation of democratic groups in this government and to guarantee free elections in Poland were unsuccessful, and after controlled elections in January, 1947, a Communist government was firmly in power.

Communist rule. The history of Poland under communism followed that of the other states of Eastern Europe: repression, industrialization, forced collectivization of agriculture, and domination of the Polish state by the Soviet Union.

This pattern was broken in the summer of 1956, when riots for "bread and freedom" in Poznań sparked a successful revolt. Władysław Gomułka, the new head of the Polish Communist Party, led Poland into an era of Polish-style socialism, distinct from that of the Soviet Union.

Collectivization was sharply reduced, industry was somewhat decentralized, and consumer production was increased. But as the people were given more freedom, and as relations with the West improved, there were increased demands for better living and working conditions. Gomułka, faced with a cultural revolution, resorted to repression.

In 1970 workers' strikes forced Gomułka's resignation in favor of Edward Gierek. Gierek had little success in appeasing the populace. In 1976 workers led a new series of strikes in response to new price rises. Incensed by constitutional amendments that favored the Soviet position in Poland, the workers began a human rights and working peoples' movement that gained momentum.

ORTHODOX JEWS *of Warsaw build barricades against German attack in 1939. After the German occupation of Warsaw (1939-1945), only about 200 Jews survived out of 500,000.*

The government made mild concessions to the strikers, but a new massive series of strikes paralyzed the national economy in 1980. Party leadership changed hands again. The workers were given the right to strike, and the promise of gradual wage increases. The independent labor organization, Solidarity, was officially recognized.

Tension persisted, however, and in 1981 party leadership changed hands again, as the strike-torn nation faced economic chaos and possible Soviet intervention. In December the new government banned Solidarity and imposed martial law.

Wojciech Jaruzelski, president of Poland and head of the Communist Party, lifted martial law in 1982, but Solidarity remained outlawed.

In 1988, faced with monumental economic problems and encouraged by ongoing reforms in the Soviet Union, the Polish government opened talks with Solidarity leaders. In an open parliamentary election in June, 1989, Solidarity scored a sweeping victory. In August, Tadeusz Mazowiecki became the first non-Communist prime minister of Poland since the 1940's. In January, 1990, the Polish Communist Party voted itself out of existence.

Portugal

Official name: *Republic of Portugal*
Area: *35,553 sq. mi., 92,082 sq. km.*
Population: *(1980) 9,894,000*
Capital: *Lisbon (Pop., 1978, 829,900)*
Language: *Portuguese*
Religion: *Roman Catholic*
Currency unit: *Escudo*
National holiday: *Day of Portugal, June 10*

Portugal, a republic occupying the western part of Europe's Iberian Peninsula, is bounded on the north and east by Spain and on the south and west by the Atlantic Ocean. The Ma-

deira islands and the Azores, lying respectively, about 1000 and 750 miles to the southeast in the Atlantic Ocean, are administered as integral parts of Portugal.

The land. Portugal has three major geographic regions. In the northeast the western fringe of the high tablelands of central Spain produces a fairly rugged terrain. Narrow mountain ranges rise to elevations of more than 3000 feet above sea level and extend almost to the Atlantic. In the west is a broad coastal plain, which widens toward the south. The southeast is covered by low, rolling hills.

Portugal's principal rivers are the Douro in the north; the Tagus, which divides the country almost equally into northern and southern regions; and the Guadiana in the southeast. The wide, protected mouth of the Tagus gives the city of Lisbon one of the world's finest natural harbors.

Portugal has a temperate maritime climate. Winters are generally mild, except in the highland areas where they are cold and snowy. Summers are warm in the north and hot in the south. North of the Tagus rainfall is abundant, averaging nearly 30 inches annually, but it decreases toward the southeast and is less than 20 inches along the southern coast.

The people. Portugal has no significant minority groups. Portuguese is the universal language, and the overwhelming majority of the people are Roman Catholic.

The population is concentrated in the north along the coast from the region of Setúbal to the Spanish border, and is especially dense in the lower

Tagus and in the lower and middle Douro River valleys. The country is sparsely settled south of the Tagus and along the entire eastern border.

Portugal has the highest birthrate in Europe next to Iceland. Substantial emigration, however, keeps the average net population increase low.

Portugal's population is nearly two-thirds rural. Lisbon and Porto are the largest cities.

Economy. Portugal is one of Europe's poorest countries. As industry has steadily increased, however, the gross national product and its per capita value have risen significantly.

One of Portugal's main economic problems is its lack of energy and mineral resources. Wolfram, from which tungsten is produced, is the most important mineral mined. Hydroelectric power has increased recently, but as industry becomes more important, Portugal becomes more dependent on oil, all of which is imported.

Portugal is 25 percent forested, and forest products (cork, turpentine, rosin, and timber) are major export items.

Fishing, particularly for tuna and sardines, is an important and prosperous economic activity.

Portugal is traditionally an agricultural country, but its labor force today is slightly more dependent on manufacturing jobs than agricultural ones. Industry and agriculture are both hindered by a poor, although improving, transportation system. Portugal's major agricultural product is wine; the country is known both for its port and for its Madeira.

Fruits and nuts, produced in the south, are also important exports and include oranges, lemons, figs, grapes,

WOMEN OF THE ALGARVE, *the extreme southern region of Portugal. The land is picturesque, and the people friendly, but Portugal is still one of the poorest countries in Europe.*

and almonds. Olives are grown throughout the country and rice, the principal cereal crop, is raised in the Tagus River valley.

Portugal's small but expanding industrial sector produces tomato paste, canned seafood, olive oil, textiles, electronic equipment, steel, woodpulp and paper, and petrochemical products. The expanding ship repair and shipbuilding facilities promise to add significantly to the economy.

Trade. In 1978 Portugal's exports earned about $2.4 billion and imports cost $5.2 billion. A large part of the deficit is made up by tourism.

Portugal's major exports include wine, cork, pulpwood, and rosin. Principal imports are manufactured goods, machinery, transportation equipment, coal, petroleum, wheat, sugar, cotton, and other raw fibers.

The country's chief trading partners are the countries of Western Europe.

Government.
Portugal is officially a republic but it was actually a dictatorship from 1932 to 1968 when Dr. António de Oliveira Salazar was premier and concentrated power in his own hands.

Under the constitution, the president is elected to a seven-year term by an electoral college composed of members of the National Assembly, the Corporative Chamber, and representatives from overseas legislatures. The president appoints the premier and a cabinet, which are responsible to him.

The legislature consists of the National Assembly, whose 263 members are directly elected to four-year terms. There is also an advisory group made up of representatives from various commercial, industrial, religious, and cultural groups.

Following World War II, Portugal's "colonies" were changed to "provinces." In 1961 India seized Portugal's Indian territories of Goa, Damão, and Diu, and nationalist rebellions broke out in the African territories.

In the mid-1970's the provinces of Cape Verde Islands, Portuguese Guinea, São Tomé and Principe, Angola, and Mozambique became independent nations. In 1976 Portuguese Timor was made a province of Indonesia. This leaves Macao as Portugal's only remaining overseas territory. It has internal administrative autonomy.

Portugal is a member of the United Nations, the European Free Trade Association, the Organization for Economic Cooperation and Development (OECD), and the North Atlantic Treaty Organization (NATO).

History.
The history of Portugal is inseparable from that of Spain until the 1000's. In 1055 Ferdinand I of León and Castile began to reconquer from the Muslims, or Moors, the northern part of present-day Portugal and organize it as a country. In 1094 Ferdinand granted the country of Portugal to Henry of Burgundy, who had distinguished himself in the campaign against the Muslims.

Afonso Henriques of the Burgundian dynasty became count in 1128 and declared Portugal independent of Castile. In 1143, in the Treaty of Zamora, Castile formally recognized Portuguese independence, and Afonso Henriques was proclaimed king.

Afonso continued to push the Muslims southward, and in 1147 he captured Lisbon and established a frontier on the Tagus River. Afonso's immediate successors, Sancho I, Afonso II, and Sancho II, extended Portugal to its present boundaries, which were attained in 1249.

Avís dynasty. Afonso's direct descendants reigned until 1385, when John I of Avís seized the throne and successfully defended Portugal against Castilian invasion. During the 1400's the Portuguese kingdom consolidated its power and began to expand overseas.

Under the direction of Prince Henry the Navigator (1394–1460), the third son of King John I, Portugal discovered and colonized the Madeira Islands, the Azores, and the Cape Verde Islands, and explored far down the west coast of Africa.

John II (1481–1495) further advanced Portuguese exploration, and in 1488 Bartholomeu Dias reached the Cape of Good Hope. During the reign of Manuel I (1495–1521), the Portuguese sailed to India, discovered Brazil, and began to establish a vast empire through the acquisition of territories in the East Indies and Southeast Asia.

During the 1500's Eastern trade brought great profits for a time, but holding such extensive territories proved difficult and eventually the empire proved a disastrous drain. Reckless spending, persecution of the Jews, who were prominent in banking and finance, and the introduction of the Inquisition further weakened the small kingdom.

Bragança dynasty. In 1580 the Portuguese throne fell vacant and was seized by Philip II of Spain. Philip and his son and grandson ruled for 60 years, during which time Portugal was little more than a conquered province. The kingdom regained its independence in 1640, when the Portuguese revolted and elected John of Bragança to the throne, but most of Portugal's Eastern empire had been lost to the Dutch and the English.

The 1700's brought a revived prosperity, largely due to the trade and newly discovered wealth of Brazil. In the mid-1700's the country was ruled by the Marquis of Pombal, a powerful minister of Joseph Emanuel (ruled 1750–1777).

Although he was often ruthless, Pombal sought to strengthen the monarchy, develop trade and agriculture, and reorganize the army and navy. He also attempted to break the power of the church and nobility in order to weaken class differences. The Braganças proved unable to cope with the international problems raised by the French Revolution of 1789, and in 1807 the country was conquered by Napoleon I of France.

The Braganças fled to Brazil and did not return until 1822, seven years after Napoleon's final defeat at the battle of Waterloo. In the same year Brazil declared its independence and Portugal was beset by a series of political and constitutional struggles that lasted until the mid-1800's.

The reigns of Peter V (1853–1861) and Louis I (1861–1889) brought some measure of political calm. Portugal attempted to balance the budget and reduce poverty, but little progress was made and discontent with the monarchy grew.

The reign of Carlos I (1889–1908) brought no improvement. The king was financially extravagant and licentious. Popular discontent increased and Carlos was assassinated in 1908. His son Manuel II was also financially irresponsible, and following an insurrection in Lisbon in 1910, he was forced to flee the country. Portuguese leaders immediately proclaimed a republic but political conditions remained extremely chaotic and a total of 18 revolutions took place during the next 16 years.

Republic. During World War I Portugal fought on the side of the Allies, but the government was continually threatened by pro-German factions, which attempted to seize power.

In 1926 a junta of military officers, headed by General António Oscar de Fragoso Carmona, seized power. In 1928, unable to handle economic problems, the generals appointed a professor of economics, António de Oliveira Salazar, finance minister. In 1932 Salazar became premier, or prime minister, and soon established a long-lasting dictatorship. Although he did not assume the presidency, he arranged for the successive election of figureheads while firmly holding power himself.

Portugal remained neutral in World War II, but provided Britain with raw materials from its African possessions and the right to establish a military base in the Azores.

Salazar retired in 1968, and in 1974 there was a military takeover. Leftist factions forced further changes in the government's leadership. In the elections of 1975, the democrats won the most seats, but the socialists and Communists made strong gains.

Socialism became increasingly influential in the next four years, and the Socialist Party won a plurality in the 1976 elections. The following years were chaotic, and the democrats regained the plurality in 1979.

Rumania

Official name: *Socialist Republic of Rumania*
Area: *91,699 sq. mi., 237,500 sq. km.*
Population: *(1980) 22,270,000*
Capital: *Bucharest
(Pop., 1978, 1,807,044)*
Language: *Rumanian*
Religion: *Orthodox Christian, Roman Catholic, Protestant, Jewish*
Currency unit: *Leu*
National holiday: *Liberation Day, Aug. 23*

Rumania is a Communist-controlled country in southeastern Europe, bordered on the north and northeast by the Soviet Union, on the east by the Black Sea, on the south by Bulgaria, and on the west by Yugoslavia and Hungary.

The land. The land surface of Rumania is dominated by the great arc-shaped mountain system formed by the Carpathians and the Transylvanian Alps. The Carpathians run from the northwest to the southeast, where they meet the Transylvanian Alps. The Transylvanian Alps run across the country from the southeast to the southwest, ending at the Danube River.

West and north of these mountains lies Transylvania. This triangular plateau is drained by the Mures and Somes rivers, which flow northeast toward Hungary. The Transylvanian plateau is separated from the Hungarian plain by the low Bihor Mountains. Beyond the Bihor, Rumania controls a long, narrow strip of the Hungarian plain.

The region between the Carpathians and the Prut River, which forms the border with the Soviet Union, is known as Moldavia. The area between the Transylvanian Alps and the Danube is Walachia. Between the Danube and the Black Sea lies the Rumanian portion of the Dobruja Plateau.

The Danube is Rumania's largest river, although for much of its course it forms the border with Bulgaria and Yugoslavia. The Oltul and Siret, which cross the lowlands of Walachia and Moldavia, are the Danube's most important tributaries.

Most of Rumania has a continental climate with hot, dry summers and cold, windy, snowy winters.

The people. Rumanians represent about 86 percent of the total population. Approximately nine percent of the population is Hungarian and two percent is German. Other small minority groups include Ukrainians, gypsies, Russians, and Yugoslavs (Serbs and Croatians). The minorities are concentrated in western Rumania.

The Rumanian language, which is derived from Latin, belongs to the Romance group. Its vocabulary, however, contains substantial borrowings from the Slavic languages.

The population is divided almost equally between rural and urban areas.

Bucharest, the capital, is the country's political, artistic, and intellectual center. It is a large sprawling metropolis that contains only a few relics of its long history. The second largest city is Cluj, in Transylvania. Timişoara, in the southwest, and Braşov, in eastern Transylvania, are important regional trade centers. Ploieşti is the oil center of Walachia. Iaşi, in Moldavia, is known for its university.

Economy. Before World War II Rumania was largely an agricultural nation, but under the Communist regime great emphasis has been placed on industrial development. Agriculture and industry each employ about one-third of the nation's labor force, but industry accounts for about two-thirds of the national income.

Natural resources. Oil is Rumania's most important resource, and Rumania ranks second among European oil producers, with about 13.5 million metric tons produced annually. While Rumania's self-sufficiency in oil is rare in Europe, its reserves are expected to be nearly exhausted by the end of this century.

The principal oil fields are located along the southern and eastern flanks of the main mountain system, in Walachia and Moldavia.

Rumania also has major deposits of natural gas near its oil fields and in Transylvania. The production of natural gas has been growing rapidly and its current annual production rate is about 30 billion cubic meters, making Rumania one of the world's leading producers.

Coal is increasing rapidly in importance. It now supplies 40 percent of the nation's energy and is expected to supply two-thirds by the 1990's.

Rumania also mines iron, manganese, gold, silver, and uranium, but it is dependent on Soviet-imported iron ore and coking coal.

Agriculture. Ninety percent of Rumanian agriculture is collectivized. While production has increased in recent years, it has been at a much slower rate than that of industrial production. Cereals, especially corn (for food and fodder), and wheat are the country's major crops. Potatoes, fodder, and sunflowers are also grown.

ANCIENT CHURCH (right) *at Curtea de Arges, former capital of Wallachia. Built in the 1300's, the church has a distinct Rumanian flavor.*

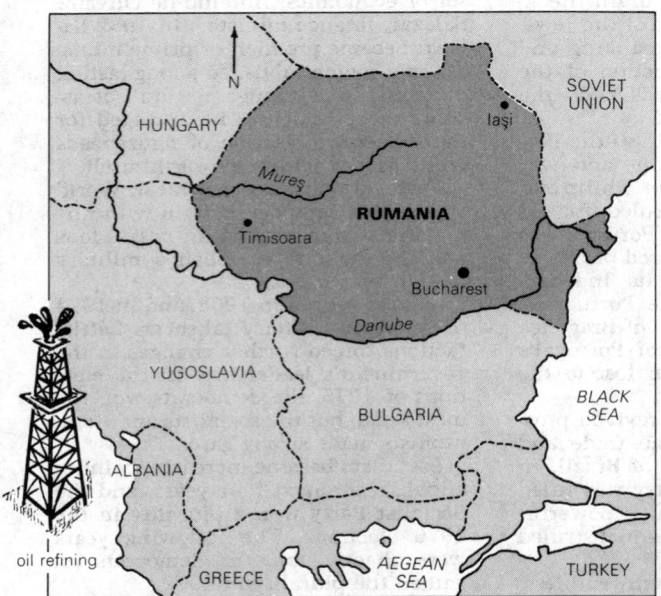

Industry. Although Rumanian industrialization has been rapid, it has been directed toward the development of heavy industry rather than the production of consumer goods. In 1979 Rumania produced almost 13 million metric tons of steel, almost 35 times as much as in 1948.

Substantial progress has also been made in the production of iron, machinery, and chemicals, as well as in nonferrous metallurgy. Textiles and food processing are the most important light industries.

The country's chief industrial centers are Bucharest, Ploieşti, Braşov, Timişoara, Reşiţa, and Hunedoara.

Trade. In 1978 Rumanian exports earned $8.2 billion and imports cost $9.1 billion. The country's trade is mostly a state-controlled enterprise. Its relatively small volume is slowly increasing. Rumania's chief exports include electric motors, petroleum products, window glass, wood products, ball bearings, and transformers. Major imports include automobiles, iron ore, finished rolled metal, coking coal and industrial coke, and industrial equipment.

About one-third of Rumania's trade is with the Soviet Union. Other important trading partners are West Germany, Czechoslovakia, East Germany, Italy, and France.

Government. Political life in Rumania is dominated by the Rumanian Communist Party, and the party's leading role is written into the constitution. Under the constitution the legislature, the Grand National Assembly, is the supreme organ of state. Its 369 members are popularly elected to five-year terms.

The assembly meets for only a few days a year, however, and when not in session its functions are carried out by the Council of State, which is elected by the assembly from among its members. The president of the council is Rumania's chief of state. The assembly also appoints a council of ministers to carry out executive functions.

Rumania is a member of the United Nations, the Warsaw Pact, and the Council for Mutual Economic Assistance (Comecon).

History. During the 300's B.C., what is now Rumania was settled by the Dacians, a people related to the Thracians in Greece. In about 60 B.C., the Dacians were united by Burebistas. The Roman Emperor Trajan conquered the Dacian kingdom in 105–106 A.D., and in 107 made it a Roman province. Roman rule lasted until 271, when the Emperor Aurelian, who was faced with the threat of barbarian invasions and various problems within the empire, withdrew Roman troops together with a substantial part of the population.

For the following 700 years Rumania was swept by successive waves of barbarian invaders, including the Visigoths, Huns, Lombards, Avars, Slavs, and Magyars. These invasions all but obliterated the original Dacian population, though their language survived.

During the 1200's two chief principalities, Moldavia and Walachia, emerged. The principalities were prevented from gaining power, however, by the strength of their neighbors, Poland, Hungary, and the Ottoman Empire. By the 1500's the Moldavian and Walachian princes were reduced to paying heavy tribute to the Ottoman Turks.

For a brief period during the late 1500's, Michael the Brave of Walachia succeeded in defeating the Turks and uniting the two principalities. But on his death in 1601 the Turks regained control of the area. Early in the 1700's Moldavia and Walachia allied themselves with Peter the Great of Russia in his campaign against the Turks, but the joint effort failed.

Phanariot rule. The Turks appointed Phanariots, wealthy Byzantine Greeks, to the thrones of Moldavia and Walachia. The Ottoman sultan usually sold the throne to the highest bidder, and the Phanariot princes sought to extort enough money from the populace to show a profit over their original investment. The Phanariot period was one of misery for the Rumanians.

From 1802 to 1812, as the result of wars between the Russians and Turks, the principalities were occupied by the Russians. The Peace of Bucharest in 1812 restored Ottoman control, but the Moldavian province of Bessarabia remained in Russian hands.

In 1821 revolts against the Phanariots took place in Moldavia and Walachia. Although the revolts failed, the Turks replaced the Greeks with native princes. In 1829, as a result of the Russo-Turkish War of 1828–1829, the Russians once again occupied the principalities.

Autonomy. Russia withdrew in 1834, and Moldavia and Walachia were granted autonomy under Ottoman suzerainty. During the following 14 years, the principalities made progress in education, agriculture, and trade.

In 1848 Rumanian intellectuals staged revolutions in Moldavia and Walachia to secure social and political reforms. The revolt in Moldavia was quickly put down, but in Walachia the rebels established a republic. The Russians and Turks both intervened to suppress the republican government, and the princes were restored under an arrangement whereby they were elected to seven-year terms of office.

As a result of the Crimean War (1854–1856), in which the Russians were soundly defeated by the British, French, Sardinians, and Turks, it was decided that a commission would determine the future status of the princi-

TWO PEASANT WOMEN in traditional Rumanian costume pose by their wooden house.

palities. Elections were held in 1857, and Moldavia and Walachia voted for union under one prince. But the Convention of Paris, held in 1858, decided that the principalities were to have a central control commission but separate legislatures and separate princes. Both Moldavia and Walachia then elected the same prince, Alexander Cuza.

In 1861 the principalities succeeded in having their union recognized by the Turks and the European powers, and in 1862 they established a single legislature and cabinet. Cuza, however, proved to be unpopular and in 1866 he was forced to abdicate.

Independence. Cuza was replaced by Charles of Hohenzollern-Sigmaringen, who reigned as Carol I. After the Russo-Turkish War of 1877–1878, in which Rumania sided with Russia, the Turks were forced to recognize Rumanian independence, which was recognized internationally by the Treaty of Berlin in 1878. In 1881 Carol became Rumania's first king.

In the years following independence, Rumania was governed by a conservative and authoritarian landowning class that allied the country and its economic and political development with Germany and Austria-Hungary. Nonetheless, the desire to gain Transylvania and Bukovina from Austria-Hungary led Rumania to enter World War I on the side of the Allies in 1916.

Rumania emerged from the war

having gained not only those two territories but also Bessarabia from the Soviet Union, and eastern Banat from Austria-Hungary, which had a large Magyar (Hungarian) population.

In the postwar period, the government remained conservative and authoritarian. In the 1930's the world economic depression brought financial hardship to the Rumanians, especially to the peasantry. Dissatisfaction was expressed politically and the Rumanian Communist Party and the strongly pro-German fascist Iron Guard grew in strength.

Dictatorship. In 1938 several factors, including a mounting agricultural crisis and a need to control the power of the Iron Guard in the face of increasing pressure from Nazi Germany, led King Carol II to establish a royal dictatorship. Nonetheless, in 1940 Germany and Italy forced King Carol to cede Transylvania to Hungary and southern Dobruja to Bulgaria in an agreement known as the Vienna Award. The Rumanians were outraged and the king was forced to abdicate.

Carol was succeeded by his son Michael, and the government was taken over by Gen. Ion Antonescu, the former prime minister under Carol, who had strong Iron Guard leanings and who continued to maintain a complete dictatorship.

During World War II Rumania was occupied by the Germans and participated in Germany's campaign against the Soviet Union. In August, 1944, King Michael overthrew Antonescu's dictatorship and entered the war on the side of the Allies. Rumania restored Bessarabia and Bukovina to the Soviet Union, which in turn nullified the Vienna Award.

Communist rule. Following World War II, despite the presence of an Allied Control Council in the country, the Soviet Union managed to take control of Rumania. King Michael abdicated in December, 1947, and Rumania was proclaimed a People's Republic. By 1952 nationalist Communist leaders had been replaced by pro-Soviet Rumanian Communists, who gave the nation a Soviet-style constitution. A state-controlled program of agricultural collectivization and forced industrialization followed.

In the mid-1960's Rumania began to act independently of Soviet control in both domestic and international concerns. It formally declared its independence in 1964, and in 1965 it adopted a new constitution that made it a socialist republic.

Rumania followed a policy of neutrality between the Soviet Union and China, while cooperating economically with both. It maintained close economic ties with Comecon nations, but it also established strong ties with non-Communist nations, including Israel.

In 1965 Nicolae Ceausescu became head of Rumania's hard-line Communist government. Ceausescu held

power largely through repression. New austerity measures instituted in the 1980's, aimed at eliminating Rumania's foreign debt, led to great hardship and greater repression. In December, 1989, a bloody revolution led to Ceausescu's overthrow and execution. The new government called for major economic reforms and for multiparty elections to be held in 1990.

San Marino

Official name: *Most Serene Republic of San Marino*
Area: *23.6 sq. mi., 39 sq. km.*
Population: *(1980) 21,000*
Capital: *San Marino*
(Pop., 1978, 4,628)
Language: *Italian*
Religion: *Roman Catholic*
Currency unit: *Italian lira*
National holiday: *Anniversary of the foundation of San Marino, Sept. 3*

San Marino is a tiny republic in the north of the Italian peninsula. It is entirely surrounded by Italy.

The land. San Marino consists almost entirely of one mountain, the three-peaked Mt. Titano, which rises over 2700 feet. Several rivers rush down the mountain. The most important rivers are the Fumicello and the San Marino.

San Marino's climate is mild, with rather cold winters and warm summers. Rainfall is moderate.

The people. Almost all of San Marino's population is of Italian descent.

Most of the population is concentrated in twelve towns lying around the base and on the peaks of Mt. Titano. The largest town, Borg Maggiore, is on one peak of the mountain. The capital, San Marino, is on the highest peak.

Economy. San Marino is a moderately prosperous country. Its chief natural resources are building stone, which is quarried, farm and pasture land, and magnificent scenery, which attracts many tourists.

Farming is the main occupation. Grapes and wheat are the leading crops, and dairying is important. San Marino's industries produce textiles, paper, leather goods, pottery, bricks, cement, wine, and candy. Tourism and the sale of postage stamps contribute heavily to the country's income. San Marino has a customs union with Italy and uses Italian currency.

Government. San Marino is a republic. Legislative power is vested in a 60-member assembly, the Grand and General Council, which is popularly elected every five years.

Twice yearly the council appoints from among its members two regents who, with the Council of State, or cabinet, wield executive power. San Marino is represented diplomatically abroad by Italy.

History. According to tradition, San Marino was founded in the 300's A.D. by Marinus, a Christian stonemason from Dalmatia who was fleeing from religious persecution. Marinus is said to have been later made a saint, San Marino. The earliest document definitely establishing San Marino's existence as an independent commune, however, is dated 885. San Marino was apparently self-governing at that time.

San Marino's rugged terrain and its political and economic insignificance protected it from destruction by medieval invaders of Italy and helped to keep it generally aloof from violent political and religious feuds that disrupted Italy during the 1200's and 1300's.

In the 1400's and 1500's San Marino avoided incorporation into the Papal States and was able to expand its territory somewhat. In the 1500's it was controlled for a brief period by the powerful Italian Borgia family, but in 1549 Pope Paul III proclaimed its independence and sovereignty.

When Napoleon I of France conquered Italy in the late 1700's, he spared the tiny republic. When the many states of Italy were united in 1861, San Marino did not join the new nation. In 1862 it entered a customs union with Italy, and in 1879 San Marino and Italy signed a lasting treaty of friendship.

San Marino entered World War I as an ally of Italy, and in the 1930's, when Benito Mussolini led the fascist government of Italy, San Marino adopted a fascist form of government. In World War II, it proclaimed its neutrality and was a haven for refugees, but it was bombed by Allied planes and suffered damage from ground fighting.

After the war, in the late 1940's, a Communist-socialist coalition government was elected. It held power until 1957, when the more conservative Christian Democratic Party took control. In 1978 the Christian Democrats finally lost control of the assembly when a Communist-led coalition won 31 of 60 seats. San Marino has the only West European government ruled by Communists.

Soviet Union

Official name: *Union of Soviet Socialist Republics*
Area: *8,649,540 sq. mi., 22,402,200 sq. km.*
Population: *(1980) 267,000,000*
Capital: *Moscow (Pop., 1977, 6,941,961)*
Language: *Russian*
Religion: *Orthodox Christian, Islam*
Currency unit: *Ruble*
National holiday: *Anniversary of the revolution, Nov. 7*

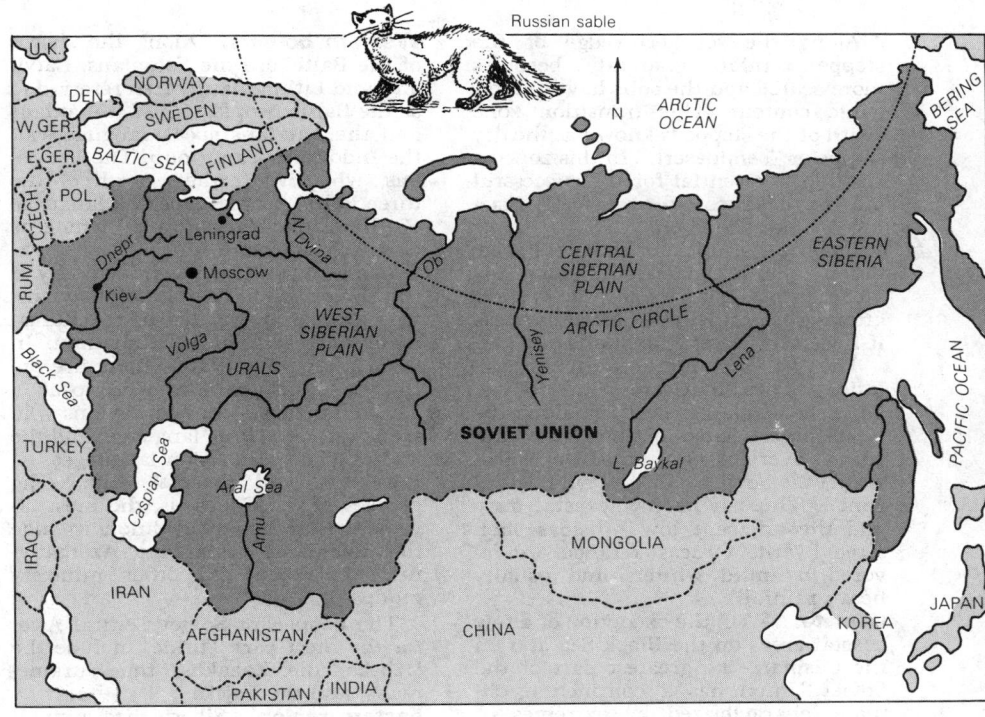

The Union of Soviet Socialist Republics (also referred to as the U.S.S.R. or the Soviet Union), the world's largest sovereign state in territory, was called Russia before the Revolution of 1917. It is bounded on the north by the Arctic Ocean; on the east by the Pacific Ocean; on the south by North Korea, the Mongolian People's Republic, China, Afghanistan, Iran, the Caspian Sea, Turkey, and the Black Sea; and on the west by Rumania, Hungary, Czechoslovakia, Poland, the Baltic Sea, Finland, and Norway.

The land. The Soviet Union covers one-sixth of the land surface of Earth and extends over two continents, occupying much of eastern Europe and all of northern Asia. A natural boundary between the European and Asian parts of the country is formed by the Ural Mountains, the Ural River, and the Caspian Sea.
Physical regions. The Soviet Union may be divided into five major land regions. The European-West Siberian plain is the great plain that extends from the European border into Siberia, broken only by the Ural Mountains. The great majority of the Soviet people live within the confines of this plain. It stretches northward all the way to the Arctic Ocean and eastward to the Yenisey River.

Beginning at the Yenisey, the Central Siberian Plateau extends to the Lena River. Covered almost entirely by forest, it is sparsely settled. Beyond the Lena, stretching eastward to the Pacific Ocean and the Bering Strait, is Eastern Siberia. Vast mountain chains divide this desolate area into subregions, most of which are drained by

rivers that flow into the Arctic Ocean.

The Soviet Far East, separated from the Central Siberian Plateau and Eastern Siberia by the Stanovoy and Yablonovvy Mountains, is the Soviet Union's link with China, Japan, and the Pacific Ocean. East of the Caspian Sea and south of Siberia is Soviet Central Asia, consisting of a northern plateau, central and southern lowlands, and arid deserts.
Mountain systems. The mountains of the Soviet Union vary greatly in size, elevation, and characteristic features. The Ural Mountains are for the most part a low, worn-down range, highly mineralized, and one of the principal centers of Soviet mining and manufacturing.

In the southwest the Caucasus Mountains run some 700 miles from the Black Sea to the Caspian Sea. They form the traditional boundary between European Russia and the countries of the Near East. From the eastern shores of the Caspian Sea to eastern Siberia the borders of the Soviet Union are dominated by a series of mountain systems. Farthest west are the Kopet Dagh Mountains and the foothills of the Hindu Kush chain, which separate the Soviet Union from Iran and Afghanistan. Beyond the valley of the Amu River, which flows into the Aral Sea, lie the Pamir Plateau and the Alai Mountains.

The mountains north of the Pamir and Alai form the boundary between the Soviet Union and China. The principal components of this complex range are the Tien Shan, Ala Tau, Tarbagatay, Altai, and Sayan mountains. The Sayan Mountains lie in southern Siberia and overlook the deepest lake in the world, Lake Baykal.

Vegetation zones. The combined result of the influences of surface features, climate, and soils on the land of the Soviet Union is several different vegetation zones, which extend in a general east-west direction across Soviet territory.

In the far north, along the shores of the Arctic Ocean, on the Arctic islands, and inland for a distance varying from 100 to 400 miles, is the tundra zone. This is an arctic desert, where low year-round temperatures inhibit the growth and variety of vegetation. During the greater part of the year it is an empty, storm-swept place, covered with snow and ice.

South of the tundra and stretching across the entire width of the Soviet Union is the northern forest zone, or taiga. The taiga is composed mostly of coniferous evergreen trees—pine, fir, and larch—interspersed with clumps of birches.

South of the taiga, in the European part of the Soviet Union, is a triangle-shaped mixed forest zone with its points located near the cities of Leningrad in the northwest, Kiev in the southwest, and Perm, in the Urals.

Much of the original mixed forest has long since been cut, and substantial areas are under the plough. Moscow, Leningrad, and Kiev, the three largest Soviet cities, are located within this zone, as are some of the leading Soviet industrial areas and the bulk of the population.

South of the mixed forest is the grassland zone, or steppe. This area is covered with black earth, one of the most fertile soils known to man. Virtually all of the steppe in the European part of the Soviet Union and in western Siberia is now under cultivation.

Along the southern edge of the steppe rainfall gradually becomes more scarce and the soils have less organic content. This transition zone south of the steppe is known as the dry steppe or "semidesert." In this zone irrigation is essential for the successful growing of crops; otherwise only grazing can be carried on.

The southernmost of the great vegetation zones is the desert region of Soviet Central Asia. Its unusually long growing season will yield rich harvests if irrigation water is available.

The one exception to the great vegetation zones that cross the Soviet Union is a small area, lying along the westernmost flanks of the Great Caucasus overlooking the Black Sea, which the Soviets call the "subtropical zone." There a narrow coastal strip and the adjacent low hillsides sheltered by the Caucasus range are favored by mild winters and usually heavy rainfall.

Climate. With the exception of a few coastal areas on the Black Sea and on the Caspian, the greatest part of the Soviet Union has a continental climate, characterized by extremes of temperature and rainfall.

Winter temperatures throughout most of the Soviet Union are well below freezing, but it is coldest in the northeast. Summers, on the other hand, are likely to be warm, except in the far north.

Rainfall ranges from an annual average of 70 to 80 inches in the western Caucasus to less than eight inches in Soviet Central Asia. Over 40 percent of the area of the Soviet Union is covered by permafrost, or permanently frozen soil that varies in depth from one foot to several hundred feet and thaws only a few inches during the summer months. Agriculture, as well as road and railroad building, can be carried out only with extreme difficulty and at great expense on this permanently frozen ground.

The people. The Soviet Union is a multinational state, with over 100 officially recognized ethnic groups. About 70 percent of the population, however, belong to the East Slavic language group.

Slavs. The East Slavic group has three major subdivisions—Russian, Ukrainian, and Belorussian (White Russian). The Russians are the largest Slavic subgroup, as well as the country's largest national group. They are represented in every region of the Soviet Union. Russian is the official language of the Soviet Union.

The Ukrainians are the second largest subgroup and second in size among all national groups. They inhabit the southern European part of the Soviet Union, and have a separate historical and cultural heritage. The third group, the Belorussians, live north of the Ukrainians.

Western borders. Along the shores of the Baltic are the Estonians, Latvians, and Lithuanians, often referred to as the Baltic peoples. The Lithuanians and the Latvians speak languages of the Indo-European group. The Estonians, who live farthest north of the three Baltic peoples, speak a language of the Finno-Ugric group, which is closely related to Finnish.

Along the southwestern boundary of the Soviet Union live the Moldavians, who are closely related to the Rumanians and who speak Rumanian. In the Middle Volga Valley there are the Chuvash and Bashkirs who speak a Turkic language, the Mordovians who speak a Finno-Ugric language, and the Tatars who speak Asian languages.

Caucasus and Central Asia. The peoples of the Caucasus, the most diverse within the Soviet Union, include the Georgians, Armenians, Azerbaijanis, and about 25 other minority groups.

The peoples of Soviet Central Asia, for the most part Turkic, include the Uzbeks, the Kazakhs, the Turkmenians, and the Tajiks.

Eastern region. Siberia has a small but diverse native population. Except for the Yakuts, a Turkic-speaking people of the Lena valley in eastern Siberia, none of the surviving native groups of Siberia has a population of over 25,000.

Koreans are found in the Soviet Far East, and Buryats, related to the Mongols of neighboring Mongolia, live in southern Siberia.

Jews. The census of 1959 listed 2.3 million Soviet citizens as Jews, a decrease of nearly one-half since the previous census of 1939. This loss was chiefly caused by the persecution of Jews in German-occupied parts of the Soviet Union in World War II. By the end of the 1970's the number of Jews was estimated at between 3 and 4 million, despite some emigration to Israel.

Distribution. Owing to climate and geography, the distribution of population is very uneven in the Soviet Union. The majority of the people live within the European part of the country, but there has been a marked increase in the population east of the Urals and the Caspian Sea. During and immediately after World War II, there was considerable migration to Siberia, and in the 1960's and 1970's several million migrants settled in Kazakhstan, Soviet Central Asia, and the Soviet Far East.

There has also been a substantial migration from the countryside to the cities. In 1940, 67 percent of the population was rural. In 1979 only 38 percent of the people lived in nonurban areas, although this is still a considerably larger proportion than is found in most of Western Europe and North America. According to the 1979 census, the Soviet Union had 272 cities with populations of over 100,000 and 45 cities of over 500,000. Three cities—Moscow, Leningrad, and Kiev—had more than 2 million inhabitants, and fifteen others had populations of over 1 million.

Economy. In the 50 years following the Russian Revolution, the Soviet Union made significant economic progress, changing from an agricultural to an industrial nation with a gross output second only to that of the

RED SQUARE, *the heart of Moscow, with Lenin's tomb in the foreground close to the Kremlin.*

United States. Soviet gains, however, were made by concentrating on heavy industry at the expense of consumer goods, services, and agriculture.

In the 1960's and 1970's the rate of economic growth slowed considerably. Despite reforms designed to decentralize industrial management and to raise productivity, the economy remained sluggish and the basic problems continued. Soviet technology lags behind that in the West, the central system of planning and management is cumbersome, and agriculture is relatively unproductive.

The five-year economic plan for 1976–1980 called for slower overall growth, but increased modernization of industrial plants, more agricultural investment, greater production incentives, and increased production of consumer items.

Natural resources. The Soviet Union is extremely rich in many natural resources. Most metals and minerals are produced in such quantities that imports from abroad are of minor importance.

There are large deposits of iron ore, copper, lead, zinc, nickel, chrome, manganese, bauxite, and mercury. The Soviet Union produces substantial quantities of gold, and following the discovery of a large deposit of diamonds in Siberia the country became one of the world's leading diamond producers.

The Soviet Union also has abundant fuel resources. Coal is the major fuel used in Soviet transportation, homes, and factories, and in 1978 coal production amounted to 724 million metric tons. The Donets basin, in the southern European part of the Soviet Union, is first in coal production and has the largest reserves.

The Kuznetsk basin of southern Siberia is second in production, eastern Siberia is third, and the Karaganda area of Soviet Central Asia is fourth. Other important coal deposits are in the Urals and in the Moscow area.

The oil fields of the eastern Caucasus, near the city of Baku on the Caspian, have been working for more than 75 years and until the mid-1950's were the leading producers in the Soviet Union. A major shift in oil production occurred during World War II, and after 1954 the oil fields between the Ural Mountains and the middle Volga River became first in output. It is now estimated that the Volga-Ural fields represent four-fifths of known Soviet oil reserves.

Other major oil fields are found along the northern edge of the Caucasus, along the Soviet-Polish boundary, in Soviet Central Asia, and in the Soviet Far East. Pipelines not only connect the Volga-Ural fields with the major industrial areas in the European and Siberian parts of the Soviet Union, but with Poland, East Germany, Czechoslovakia, and Hungary. In 1978 crude oil production reached 572 million metric tons.

The most important natural gas deposits lie near the Arctic Circle, north of the West Siberian lowlands in the Urengory fields. Other sources are in the southern part of Soviet Central Asia and in deposits overlying existing oil fields.

Although Soviet hydroelectric development has generally been far removed from major cities and industrial areas, there is a spectacular hydroelectric project on the Volga River, where five dams have transformed the Volga into a series of enormous reservoirs. The Yenisey and Angara rivers in Siberia are additional sources of hydroelectric energy.

Agriculture. Use of arable land in the Soviet Union is severely limited by cold in the north and drought in the south. As a result, fully tillable farmland is confined to an area known as the Fertile Triangle, with its corners in Leningrad on the Baltic Sea, Odessa on the Black Sea, and the lowland of Western Siberia.

Soviet cropland equals the combined sown areas of the United States and Canada. The northerly location of the country (the bulk of the Fertile Triangle lies north of the U.S.-Canadian boundary), however, results in a shorter growing season, and the distances separating Soviet cropland from warm seas are reflected in limited and undependable rainfall.

These severe handicaps are responsible for the low yields that have characterized Soviet agriculture. They have not been compensated for by the extension of cropland into areas of marginal rainfall, nor by attempts to develop varieties of plants that could mature quickly in areas farther north, where growing seasons are very short.

To these environmental difficulties the Soviet system added manmade ones. The fact that virtually all cultivatable land is under either collective or state farms has deprived the Soviet farmer of the incentive present when men work on land they own. The reluctance of the Soviet government to offer farm workers sufficient rewards for their labor, and the policy of directing investments into industry while ignoring the needs of agriculture, have added further difficulties.

In the 1970's, about 30 percent of the active population of the Soviet Union was engaged in agriculture, as opposed to less than ten percent in the United States. But yields, productivity, and farm income are much lower in the Soviet Union, and the output of foods has risen only very slowly over the past 40 years.

An interesting characteristic of Soviet farming is the significance of the "private sector" in the production of certain essential foods. Although farmland is owned by collective and state farms, farm workers are entitled to small plots of land, usually about half an acre in size but never more than one acre. The produce of these plots is either consumed by the worker's family or, more frequently, sold directly to consumers, without state control.

More than one-third of the meat and milk and two-thirds of the eggs produced in the Soviet Union come from these tiny private plots. In the 1970's the government increased investments in agriculture, provided more fertilizer and machinery, and raised the material incentives for farmers, but all

LONELY SIBERIA: *laying the Northern Lights pipeline across the flat and frozen wasteland.*

SOVFOTO

WOMEN CONSTRUCTION WORKERS *man the jackhammers on a street repair job. Traditionally, Russian women did much heavy labor and still do under the Communist regime.*

with only modest success in increasing agricultural output and productivity.

Grains, the leading crop of Soviet farms, include wheat, rye, and barley. The Soviet Union grows virtually all the cotton it needs, exports considerable amounts of flax, and produces part of the hemp its industry consumes. Sugar beets and oilseeds—sunflower, rapeseed, and castor beans—are among the leading industrial crops.

Soviet livestock suffered severe losses during the drive for collectivization (1929–1933), when nearly half the cattle and two-thirds of the hogs in the country were destroyed by farmers unwilling to turn over their animals to collective ownership.

The livestock levels of 1929 were not regained until 1956, and further growth, with the exception of hogs, has been very slow. The output of meat, milk, eggs, and other dairy products remains well below that of the United States and Western Europe.

Industry. Iron and steel production is a general indicator of industrial strength, and since 1945 the Soviet Union has ranked next to the United States as the world's largest producer of pig iron and steel. In 1978 the Soviet Union produced more than 151 million metric tons of crude steel and almost 111 million metric tons of pig iron.

Two regions, the Ukraine and the Urals, account for more than four-fifths of the iron and more than three-fourths of the steel produced. A third major region of iron and steel production has recently been developed in the Kuznetsk basin in Siberia.

Before the Revolution of 1917, Russian industry was concentrated in the European part of the country. St. Petersburg (renamed Leningrad in 1924) and Moscow were among the leading centers of light industry. Heavy industry was concentrated in the Ukraine.

The temporary loss of much of Russia's industrial capacity during World War I and the civil war that followed led to efforts to decentralize industry and develop new centers further removed from the vulnerable western borders of the Soviet Union.

Four major regions now dominate Soviet industry. The Central Industrial Region, in the Moscow area, contains the country's most valuable industries, producing electrical equipment and automobiles, as well as a number of consumer goods, including textiles.

The Ukraine is noted for iron and steel, heavy machinery, and chemicals. It is a less concentrated area than the Central Industrial Region.

The Ural industrial region owes its present large-scale development to Soviet planning. It produces iron and steel, petroleum and its byproducts, heavy machinery, and chemicals.

Also largely a creation of the Soviet government, the Siberian lowlands and adjacent river valleys near the Soviet-Chinese border produce coal and a variety of metals.

In accordance with its policy of industrial decentralization, the Soviet government has developed other, smaller industrial centers to lessen the dependence of its farflung territories on the major industrial areas and thereby reduce the burden on its transportation system. Some of the more important smaller industrial centers are located in Transcaucasia, Soviet Central Asia, and the Soviet Far East.

Trade. In 1980 the Soviet Union's exports earned $66.29 billion and its imports cost $59.19 billion. Major exports include petroleum, coal, timber, iron ore, industrial equipment, and iron and steel. Principal imports are ships, wheat, sugar, clothing, metal ores, and industrial machinery.

The Soviet Union carries on 55 percent of its trade with the communist bloc nations, and 33 percent with the West.

Government. The Communist Party of the Soviet Union (CPSU) dominates political life. The presidium, formerly the politburo, or political bureau, of the party's central committee, determines national policy. The party's first secretary is the most powerful figure in the government and in the country.

Formally, the highest authority in the Soviet Union is the national legislature, the Supreme Soviet. It has two houses, the Soviet of the Union, elected on the basis of population, and the Soviet of Nationalities, elected on the basis of territorial units. The two houses have equal powers and the members of both are directly elected to five-year terms.

The Supreme Soviet elects a presidium to act as the supreme state authority in between its relatively short sessions. The chairman of the presidium serves as head of state. The Supreme Soviet also appoints a council of ministers, or cabinet, which is the highest executive and administrative organ of the government.

The Soviet Union is a member of the United Nations and the Council for Mutual Economic Assistance (Comecon). It heads the Warsaw Pact.

History. Archaeological evidence indicates that various societies existed in European Russia before there were written records. The earliest Slavic inhabitants probably arrived there from an unknown point of origin several hundred years before the birth of Christ. Their settlements tended to concentrate in the south, near the Black Sea, and along the river systems that stretch inland from the Baltic and Black seas.

The river routes made it possible for groups of Scandinavian Vikings, or "Varangian," warriors and traders to move through the same regions. From this composite of Slavs, Scandinavians, and the remnants of earlier populations, the oldest Russian state emerged during the 800's A.D. "Kiev Rus" was a confederation of principalities. Its two most important cities, Kiev and Novgorod, were located along the major river trade routes, and the Kievan principalities contained a mixture of merchants, peasants, and warrior-politicians.

Kievan Russia. Kiev's power and wealth, and its social and political structure, were rooted in an agrarian as well as a commercial economy. This duality made for complex patterns of political administration. Kievan society was eventually undermined by strife among claimants to the princely thrones that characterized the administrative system. Kiev finally fell in 1240 to the Mongols who invaded from the East.

Three centuries earlier, Orthodox Christianity had been introduced into Kievan Russia from the Byzantine Empire. It was destined to make a deep and lasting impression on Russia.

Rise of Moscow. The Mongol conquerors permitted religious and political autonomy in Russia, as Kiev Rus disintegrated into a number of tiny principalities (appanages) whose rulers owed allegiance to the Mongol khans. The Russian Orthodox Church continued to function and serve the local population.

In the 1300's a few of the appanage princes were able to increase their holdings by purchase, marriage, or conquest. Among these was Ivan I (ruled 1325–1340), who ruled the principality of Muscovy, or Moscow. By the time of Ivan's death Moscow, an active trading center at the confluence of the Moscow and Uka rivers, had secured important advantages over its neighbors.

Ivan III (ruled 1462–1505). Under Prince Ivan III, called "the Great," Moscow succeeded in establishing its sovereign authority over important independent principalities in central European Russia, as well as over more "frontier" territories to the east and north.

The most important challenge to Muscovite expansion was the flourishing commercial principality of Novgorod. Nevertheless, the principality fell easily under Muscovite pressure in 1478. Muscovy then incorporated other independent principalities and began to challenge Mongol control.

By 1480 the Mongols had been overthrown, although Tatar heirs of the empire continued to raid and harass Moscow. The main sources of conflict in the early 1500's were with the Baltic countries of Poland, Lithuania, and Sweden. Meanwhile, serious internal problems had developed.

To ensure continued support from their boyar warriors and administrators, the Muscovite princes had often rewarded them with special privileges and large grants of land. As a result, the power of the boyars increased and some members of this Muscovite aristocracy began to challenge the authority of the sovereign prince himself.

Muscovite Russia. Ivan IV (ruled 1533–1584), wishing to continue the expansionist policies of his predecessors and determined to preserve and increase sovereign authority, met these problems aggressively. Sometimes called "the Terrible," he was one of the most brutal and bloody figures in Russian history. Taking for himself the title of czar (caesar), he proceeded to wield the absolute political power of an autocrat.

During the first years of Ivan IV's reign, the young czar undertook reforms generally regarded as enlightened and necessary. Muscovy was a patchwork of formerly independent principalities and separate local units of varying independence, and the Muscovite state was badly in need of administrative reorganization and legal reform.

Among Ivan's measures were a codification of laws (*Sudebnik* of 1550) and a reorganization of local administration. In 1549 Ivan ordered the convocation of the first national assembly, or *Zemski Sobor.*

IVAN THE TERRIBLE, or *Ivan IV. A bloody autocrat but an able administrator, he built up the power of his Muscovy state.*

During the 1550's Ivan also became deeply involved in wars of territorial expansion. At first Muscovite military campaigns were concentrated against khanates at Kazan on the middle Volga River, at Astrakhan, and against others in the Crimea.

A much more serious campaign began in 1557 against the inhabitants of the eastern Baltic region who blocked Russian access to the Baltic Sea and northern Europe. This conflict gradually expanded until Ivan IV's armies were involved in an exhausting war with the large and powerful states of Poland and Sweden.

Centralization. At the same time the czar's policies of expansion and domestic reform ran into mounting opposition, particularly from the boyars, who felt themselves threatened by administrative reforms and who bore the burden of the military campaigns. This political struggle came to a crisis in the early 1560's, when Ivan IV re-

nounced the throne and retired to a monastery. Ivan returned only after the boyars and the church agreed to meet certain of his demands.

The victorious czar then organized the central territories of Muscovy as a separate administrative unit subservient to his will. Using handpicked men, called *oprichniks,* Ivan began to punish as "evildoers," anyone who objected to his policies of expansion and creating a centralized state.

A virtual reign of terror was unleashed against the boyars, and Muscovy was plunged into near civil war. Crushing most opposition, Ivan IV became far more powerful than any previous Muscovite prince.

Theodore I (ruled 1584–1598), Ivan IV's successor, was too weak to master the legacy of power and antagonism bequeathed him by his father, and real authority began to fall into the hands of court favorites. When Theodore died, the ancient Muscovite dynasty died with him.

The period immediately following the death of Theodore, featuring increasing domestic strife, foreign wars and, finally, Polish invasion, is known as the Time of Troubles (1598–1613). Poland was eventually defeated, and peasant uprisings and other social disorders were suppressed. The Time of Troubles ended in 1613 with the accession to the throne of the new Romanov dynasty.

Romanovs. Physically exhausted and verging on economic ruin, Russian society only slowly regained the international independence and domestic order that had characterized it in the early days of Ivan IV. The first Romanovs were unable to claim the prestige and authority of the earlier rulers of Moscow.

Nevertheless, Czar Michael Romanov (ruled 1613–1645) and his successor, Czar Alexis (ruled 1645–1676), managed to reassert and extend centralized autocratic authority, and to restore some measure of prosperity.

Serfdom. By the 1600's the institution of serfdom had become central to the functioning of the state. Exploitation of the large areas of land granted by the czars to their royal servitors since the early days of Muscovite expansion was feasible only through the use of serf labor.

A community of interest between the warrior landowners and the czar known as the *pomiestie* system developed. The noble landowner became responsible not only for providing soldiers and military leadership during times of war, but also for administering the land under his control.

Gradually the landowner became the immediate representative of authority over the peasant who worked the land. To insure social stability and to placate an increasingly demanding nobility, the state made it legally more difficult for the peasant to escape bondage to land and lord.

Renewed expansion. By the mid-1600's Russia had largely regained the territory it had lost during the Time of Troubles. With the decline of Poland and Sweden, the west was again open to Russian expansion. In the south, the power of the Turks, who had captured Constantinople in 1453, was also waning.

Despite a major schism in the Russian Orthodox Church and the peasant rebellion of Stenka Razin, Russian society prospered in this period. Trade with Western Europe grew, and educated Russians became increasingly attracted to Western organization and technology. It was Peter the Great, however, who initiated an era of rapid modernization and reform.

Peter the Great (ruled 1689–1725). Peter's reign inaugurated the Imperial period of Russian history. One of Peter's major goals was to modernize Russia as quickly as possible. He made the church subordinate to the state, reorganized the central government and provincial administration, and introduced a new military and civil service based on merit. Peter also required the nobility to serve the state, undertook tax and financial reforms, and developed trade and industry.

Following the acquisition of the eastern Baltic coastlands from Sweden in 1703, Peter built a new capital, St. Petersburg, on the Gulf of Finland. He called the city Russia's "window to the West." The Great Northern War against Sweden dragged on, however, until 1721.

Peter launched a vigorous program of reforming and westernizing Russian ideas, manners, and customs. This, like his military efforts and centralizing policies, was often unpopular. By the end of his reign in 1725, it was clear that Russia had become a major power in Europe, and that old Muscovy had been transformed into the Russian Empire.

Early empire. Certain of Peter's reforms remained largely intact under the czars of the 1700's. The nobility pressed for and eventually received greater and finally absolute authority over their serfs, while owing fewer and fewer obligations to the state. Finally, in 1762, the nobility was freed entirely from compulsory state service.

The emergence of the nobility from the service position it had occupied under Peter was partly due to the weakness or indifference of his successors. Lax leadership allowed groups such as the Guards' Regiments in St. Petersburg, which were composed exclusively of nobles, to gain power. During the reign of the powerful, brilliant Catherine II "the Great" (1762–1796), the nobles suffered no loss of power. Catherine, who had come to the throne through a coup d'etat, needed their political backing and administrative talents. On the other hand, public office and thus public power came to be held by a group of

CATHERINE THE GREAT *of Russia, under whose strong rule the country became a major power.*

individuals drawn from an increasingly smaller professionalized reservoir of nobles and civil servants.

The bureaucracy continued to be dominated by the nobility, but many nobles settled into a life of apathy and indolence on their estates. As a result, in the 1800's, men of various classes, or *raznochintsi,* began to fill the lower ranks of the administration, and the direct authority and influence of the nobility was gradually reduced.

Imperial expansion. By the end of Catherine the Great's reign in 1796, Russian control of the Ukraine had been consolidated, and areas north of the Black Sea that had been protectorates of the Ottoman Empire had been added to the Russian state.

All of Siberia to the Pacific Ocean and more and more of Central Asia had also been incorporated into the Russian Empire, which had become by far the largest land state in the world. Most important, however, Russian expansion brought with it direct and constant contact with the great European powers—France, Britain, Austria, and Prussia.

Contact with the powers resulted in Russian involvement in major European wars of the 1700's, and Russian participation between 1772 and 1795 in the partitions of Poland. Thus, the Russian Empire found it difficult to escape involvement in the wars of the French Revolution and the Napoleonic wars (1789–1815).

Alexander I (ruled 1801–1825). In 1812, despite efforts by Alexander I to hold Russia aloof from the Napoleonic

struggle in the west, Napoleon invaded Russia. After heroic resistance and great suffering, the Russian armies forced the French to retreat. Russia joined Austria and Prussia in a coalition that helped defeat Napoleon in 1813–1814, thus exalting Russia to new heights of European importance.

During the first years of his reign, Alexander welcomed the possibility of undertaking extensive reforms, including the easing or abolition of serfdom and the drawing up of a constitution for the empire, but the projects themselves were never effectively realized.

When real reform failed to materialize, a protest movement was formed by educated Russians who had been inspired by the ideals of the French Revolution. By the mid-1800's demands for radical social and economic reform had grown into a chorus of opposition to the government.

Nicholas I (ruled 1825–1855). Unfortunately, Alexander's successor, Nicholas I, was naturally conservative and did not favor reform. Furthermore, his accession to the throne was immediately followed by the Decembrist Revolt, an attempted seizure of the government by a group of liberal and reform-minded officers and nobles. The rising made Nicholas determined to dominate not only the actions, but the thoughts, of his subjects.

The government attempted to protect society from "radical" political and social influences, and it viewed most proposals for change with great suspicion. It practiced strict censorship and instituted an early form of the secret police. These policies were disastrous for Russia. They not only allowed severe problems to go unsolved, but also stifled Russia intellectually, technologically, and economically at a time when Europe was being transformed by the profound changes resulting from the industrial and the French revolutions.

Despite the repression carried out by Nicholas, a small band of intellectuals continued to oppose the government, some from exile in Western Europe. Brilliant writers like Tolstoy and Dostoevsky and a number of fine musicians and painters rose to prominence.

Nicholas intervened several times against revolutions in Europe and tried to expand Russian influence in the Balkans. This latter policy led to a major conflict with Britain, France, and the Ottoman Empire in the Crimean War (1853–1856). The resulting defeat of Russian armies, on Russian soil, by countries supplying their troops by sea over many thousands of miles led many Russians to conclude that a major overhaul of their society and government was needed.

Reform. On Nicholas's death in 1855 the new czar, Alexander II (ruled 1855–1881), realized that the time for action on reforms had come. In 1861 the serfs were freed.

Additional reforms encouraged economic growth and social change, which were seen as essential to Russia's survival in the modern European world. They included reforms in state finance, in local government, in the judicial system, and in military administration. But the inertia of a tradition-bound society, combined with the conservatism of the landed nobility and the government bureaucracy, prevented rapid social change.

As a result, liberal critics were not stilled by Alexander's reforms, and they became increasingly frustrated and isolated from society as a whole. After the 1860's their dissatisfaction was manifested by the formation of groups dedicated to overthrowing the autocracy. In 1881 one of these groups assassinated Alexander II, hoping thereby to touch off a revolution.

Alexander III (ruled 1881–1894). Although Alexander III succeeded in crushing his father's assassins, the revolutionary movement continued to grow. It grew not only inside Russia, but also among the many Russian émigrés in Western Europe.

Alexander III determined to meet the problems of Russian society with force and more thorough bureaucratic control. But this extreme reaction could not prevent industrialization and urbanization and the social changes that accompanied them.

Consequently, in the 1880's government policy became ambivalent. The ministry of finance promoted rapid change, while the ministry of the interior remained extremely conservative. At the same time Russia's position in international affairs was delicate, and in contrast to its most powerful European neighbors, Russia became politically and militarily weaker.

Nicholas II (ruled 1894–1917). The situation was not improved when the weak and indecisive Nicholas II succeeded Alexander III in 1894. Nicholas pursued the same domestic policies as his predecessor and continued his conservatism and repression. But a major social and political crisis was brewing. The peasantry, deprived of land and burdened by taxes, were angry and restless. Marxists and other intellectuals spread revolutionary ideas among the newly urbanized workers, who were poorly paid and badly housed. Several non-Russian ethnic groups within the empire developed a nationalist spirit and began to seek greater autonomy. Russian liberals demanded civil freedoms and a more responsible government. Before long a disaster in foreign affairs touched off Russia's first modern revolution.

The Revolution of 1905. Conflicting interests in East Asia led to war (1904–1905) between Russia and a recently strengthened and Westernized

Japan, and the Russians experienced a series of humiliating defeats on land and sea.

The domestic repercussions were serious. In addition to the burdensome and unimaginative rule of Nicholas II, basic changes taking place in the social and economic structure of Russia, and the disastrous war with Japan, resulted in the rapid growth of a broadly based revolutionary movement.

In January, 1905, Imperial troops opened fire on a crowd of unarmed workers trying to present a petition of grievances to the czar. This incident, known as "Bloody Sunday," fanned the fires of revolution which spread widely in the cities and countryside, and even to some units of the armed forces.

The czar offered minor concessions, but they failed to stem the tide. By the autumn of 1905, peasant riots and seizure of their landlords' estates, together with a general strike, virtually paralyzed the government. With the situation out of control, Nicholas II reluctantly endorsed reform. He issued the October Manifesto, which promised basic civil liberties and the convocation of a national assembly, the Duma.

The Duma did not have full parliamentary powers, and its members were chosen by indirect and unequal suffrage. Moreover, the czar retained

NAPOLEON'S INVASION OF RUSSIA *of 1812 is shown in a realistic scene from the film version of Leo Tolstoy's novel,* War and Peace.

CULVER PICTURES

sovereignty over the country, and when the first two Dumas elected turned out to be critical of the government, he dissolved them.

In 1906 Nicholas dismissed the somewhat liberal Count Witte as prime minister and appointed Peter A. Stolypin, who promptly revised the electoral laws to weight the franchise even more heavily in favor of the propertied classes.

As a result, Duma deputies on the right supported the czar and his policies, and liberal leaders and parties of the center tried to work within the Duma.

The liberals and moderates worked to achieve necessary reform and to extend gradually the Duma's authority and influence so that it might become a representative parliament like those of Western democracies. The few deputies of the extreme left, primarily Social Democrats (Marxists), continued to oppose the government wholeheartedly.

In 1907 the continued restlessness of the peasantry, caused by land hunger and general economic hardship, led Prime Minister Stolypin to introduce agrarian reforms. He sought to break up the traditional peasant commune, under which land was owned collectively, and to encourage individual peasant proprietors.

It was hoped that if the peasants became property owners they would have a stake in the existing social order and develop a less revolutionary attitude. The transfer of land belonging to the state and to the nobles into peasant hands was also stepped up. World War I interrupted these reforms before their full impact could at all be measured.

World War I. In the years after the Revolution of 1905, the Russian economy generally prospered and limited social and educational reforms were initiated, but at the same time dissatisfaction among the workers increased. Whether Russia was at that period headed for a new social crisis or for a peaceful evolution is unclear. In any case, the war cut off these developments and made a revolution much more likely.

For several decades before 1914 Russia and Austria-Hungary had been vying for influence in the Balkans. Russia aspired to serve as protector of the Slavic peoples there, and in August, 1914, when Serbia, under pressure from Austria-Hungary, turned to Russia for help, the Russians decided to back Serbia, even though many Russian leaders realized that Russia was ill-prepared for war and might not be able to withstand the strain on its resources.

Russia's leaders hoped the war would be short and victorious, and that they would receive substantial territorial gains in the Balkans. These hopes were to be bitterly disappointed. The war soon proved disastrous for the Russians as German and Austro-Hungarian armies battered the Russians.

Losses in men and equipment were high, mismanagement of supplies and of the general war effort was common, and morale sagged badly, both at the front and at home. By 1916 the economy as a whole had begun to collapse, and there were severe food and fuel shortages in the cities.

The situation was complicated by a general disintegration in leadership at the upper level. Gregory Rasputin, a charlatan "holy man," had acquired considerable influence over Empress Alexandra as a result of his success on several occasions in preventing her only son, the heir to the throne, from dying of hemophilia.

In 1915 Nicholas II decided to go to the front to take personal command of the armies. Rasputin, through his hold on Alexandra, began to have a strong influence on the appointment of ministers and the formation of government policy. Although Rasputin was murdered in 1916 by a group of patriotic noblemen, the weakness, inefficiency, and political ineptitude of the government persisted.

Revolution. The situation became critical in March, 1917. Quite unexpectedly, food riots, coupled with strikes, lockouts, and general labor unrest, led to a mass demonstration in the capital, St. Petersburg (Petrograd), against which the government proved powerless. Within one week the czar had been toppled from the throne.

With the collapse of the government there was no legally constituted authority, but two centers of power sprang up. One was the Provisional Government, a temporary committee formed by members of the Duma to rule until elections could be held for a constituent assembly. The other was the Petrograd Soviet (Council) of Workers' and Soldiers' Deputies, an institution that had existed briefly during the Revolution of 1905.

Provisional government and Soviet. The Soviet was more representative of the Russian people than the Provisional Government. The Soviet fell at first under the domination of doctrinaire socialists, primarily Mensheviks (moderate Marxists) and Social Revolutionaries (agrarian socialists). At that time the extreme wing of the Marxists in Russia, the Bolsheviks, constituted only a tiny minority of the Soviet.

A compromise between the Soviet and the Provisional Government was reached, and the Soviet agreed to let the Provisional Government run the basic governmental system, provided that civil liberties and other democratic guarantees were maintained. The Soviet retained control over certain services, such as communications,

THE TURNING POINT *in the Russian Revolution: Bolshevik troops attack the Winter Palace, headquarters of the Provisional Government in Petrograd (now Leningrad), in 1917.*

UPI

and exerted a strong influence in the army. The resulting "dual power" system provided a rather shaky government for a society wracked by revolution and war.

Moreover, there were a number of basic social and economic issues on which the Provisional Government and the Soviet disagreed. The leaders of the Provisional Government wanted to continue the war until victory could be achieved. The leaders of the Soviet wanted a rapid end to the war, and opposed annexations of territory by the victors.

For the masses, the key issues were the ending of the war, distribution of land, and better living conditions. The general population wanted immediate peace and instant reform. V. I. Lenin, leader of the Bolshevik, or extremist, faction of the Russian Marxists, stepped into this breach.

Bolsheviks. Taking advantage of the basic desires as well as the growing radicalism of the masses, Lenin propounded the slogan, "Peace, Land, and Bread," and saw that the Soviet might be the means by which his Bolshevik party could seize power. As a result, after an abortive popular uprising in the summer of 1917, Lenin, with the brilliant assistance of Leon Trotsky, seized power in Petrograd (now Leningrad) on October 25–26, 1917, and shortly thereafter in most of Russia. This "October Revolution," which became the November Revolution when the Russian calendar was changed, easily overthrew the existing moderate regime and instituted sweeping changes in Russia.

Soviet Union. After the Bolshevik seizure of power, Lenin turned to the tasks of consolidating the authority of his government and meeting the basic demands of the people. He called for peace and nationalized all land, although he permitted the peasants to use the acreage they had seized during the revolution. Lenin also decreed the separation of church and state, and nationalized major industries and banks.

Lenin also promulgated a new, "socialist," constitution for the Russian Soviet Federated Socialist Republic (R.S.F.S.R.). He encouraged the formation of separate but closely allied socialist republics under Bolshevik control in non-Russian areas of the former czarist empire, and between 1922 and 1924 these were joined to the R.S.F.S.R. to form the Union of Soviet Socialist Republics (U.S.S.R.).

Dictatorship. Lenin suppressed opposition parties and ended freedom of expression. He also dissolved the Constituent Assembly, which he had allowed to be elected in November, 1917, when it convened with the Bolsheviks in a minority, and established the Cheka, the forerunner of the secret police, to ferret out and punish "counterrevolutionaries."

Despite considerable opposition not only within the Bolshevik party but

LENIN, *leader of the Bolshevik Revolution in Russia, an implacable revolutionary.*

throughout the country, Lenin finally forced through his policy of obtaining peace for Russia. On March 3, 1918, the war with Germany and Austria-Hungary was ended by the Treaty of Brest-Litovsk.

Under the terms of the treaty, Russia suffered heavy territorial and economic losses. The treaty outraged many patriotic Russians and contributed to the outbreak of civil war between Bolshevik supporters (Reds) and those opposed to the new Soviet government (Whites). The treaty also helped lead to intervention in Russia by U.S. and Allied troops.

The Western powers, furious at what they considered Russia's betrayal of the common cause against German militarism, and desperately anxious to reestablish an eastern front against Germany, sent small forces to northern Russia and Siberia and money, supplies, and advisers to various anti-Bolshevik forces.

After the end of World War I, in November, 1918, the Allies continued half-hearted intervention in the hope of overthrowing the Bolshevik regime. But by the end of 1920 the Soviet government had succeeded in defeating its internal and external foes, although the country was exhausted, near starvation, and demoralized.

Ruthlessly putting down peasant protests and disorders, as well as a serious popular uprising at the city and naval base of Kronstadt, Lenin made it clear that the Bolsheviks would not tolerate opposition from the people. In

addition, at the tenth party congress in 1921, Lenin crushed dissent within the party itself, making it clear that the leadership would not tolerate opposition from the rank and file. Thus the foundation was laid for dictatorship over Russia by the Communist Party.

NEP. Lenin began reconstruction of the devastated country by launching the New Economic Policy, or NEP, under which some of the controls and centralization that had characterized the previous period of wartime Communism were abandoned.

Considered a temporary expedient from the start, the NEP did not solve the problem of how to increase Russia's productive forces and build an economy firm enough to support the socialist society envisaged by the Communist leaders. By 1927, however, the economy had been restored to its 1913 level and Soviet leaders were faced with the problem of establishing new goals.

This situation was complicated by a power struggle within the Communist Party following Lenin's death in 1924. Joseph Stalin, the general secretary of the party, emerged victorious, first defeating Leon Trotsky and his "Left" supporters, and then the so-called Right opposition. Stalin established one-man rule over both the party and the country.

Stalinism. After expelling Trotsky from the party's politburo, Stalin then adopted Trotsky's domestic policy, which called for rapid and extensive industrialization. To achieve this, the first five-year plan was begun in 1928, and completed ahead of schedule in 1932. To obtain the labor and capital for industrialization, Stalin found it necessary to force the peasants onto state-owned collective farms.

Massive peasant resistance bordered on civil war, and an estimated 5 to 10 million peasants were killed, died of starvation, or were exiled to Siberia and Central Asia. But by 1933 Stalin had won.

He established complete party control over every aspect of private and public life and instituted a rigid totalitarian regime, known as "Stalinism." At the cost not only of lives but of an almost total loss of freedom, Soviet society thus achieved remarkable industrial growth during the decade of the 1930's.

Fearing that critics of his program were springing up within the party, Stalin began a "great purge" in 1936, starting with former party colleagues and rivals. The elimination of alleged "traitors to the party" soon spread to all levels of the party and to people in all walks of Soviet life.

Many thousands were arrested, imprisoned, exiled to slave labor camps, or executed. The blood bath finally ended in 1938, but by then terror had become a major ingredient of Soviet daily life under the Stalinist regime.

DICTATOR STALIN (left) *ruled by terror, cruelly enforcing industrialization, exploiting his allies. The Soviet is still a police state. A Jewish demonstrator* (above) *is arrested in 1973.*

Foreign policy. During the 1920's Soviet foreign policy had been directed toward gaining recognition and support for the new Soviet state and preventing the possibility of Western intervention in Russia, as had occurred during the revolution. Soviet leaders proposed disarmament and the formation of alliances against Nazi Germany and Fascist Italy. But Stalin finally became disillusioned with the "appeasement" policies of France and England and in August, 1939, ignoring communist ideology, which decried fascism, and the anguished protests of millions of communists and Soviet sympathizers around the world, Stalin signed a nonaggression pact with Hitler. In so doing he bought time and some territory in Eastern Europe, but he also permitted Hitler to conquer Poland and France, which meant that by June, 1941, Hitler was able to launch a major offensive against the Soviet Union.

World War II. After sweeping initial successes, facilitated by inadequate Soviet preparations, the Nazi armies were checked before Moscow and Leningrad (formerly Petrograd) in the late fall of 1941. Britain and the United States furnished considerable aid to the Soviet Union, and all three nations subscribed to general war aims set forth in the Atlantic Charter.

Despite the considerable successes of the Germans in 1942, the Soviet forces remained intact and inflicted a major defeat on the Nazi armies in the last months of 1942 at the hard-fought battle of Stalingrad, the present-day city of Volgograd.

From that time on, Soviet troops began to push the Germans back, a pro-

cess assisted by the British-U.S. landing in France in June, 1944. Attacked on two fronts, the Germans surrendered in May, 1945. The Soviet Union attacked Japan on August 8, 1945, and easily occupied Manchuria.

Cold War. After victory the Soviet Union faced two major problems: reconstruction and its relationship with its Western allies. Despite attempts in a series of wartime conferences to work out cooperative arrangements for the postwar period, friction soon arose between the Western powers and the Soviet Union, marking the beginning of the "Cold War."

The chief issues were Germany and Eastern Europe. The Soviet Union, which had agreed to joint four-power occupation of Germany, began to extract unilateral reparations to assist its own reconstruction effort. As a result, Germany soon became divided into a pro-Allied West Germany and a Soviet-dominated East Germany.

In Eastern Europe the Soviet Union, whose armies had liberated much of the area from German domination, exerted pressure to insure the emergence of pro-Soviet governments despite Soviet promises at the Yalta Conference (1945) that free elections would be held in those countries.

Between 1946 and 1948 one country after another in Eastern Europe came under Soviet domination over the protests of the Western nations.

Stalin clearly intended not only to ensure the security of the Soviet Union, but also to aid the spread of "socialist" revolutions in the world. The opportunity for Soviet expansion in Western Europe arose through the disorder left by the war and the large

Communist parties that existed in France and Italy.

The Western powers responded with military and massive economic aid to Western Europe, hoping to "contain" Soviet and communist expansion.

The Iron Curtain. At home, Stalin launched a renewed program of industrialization and totalitarianism. The mild freedom of thought and activity that had been permitted during the war was ended, and strict adherence to anti-Western and nationalistic dogma was demanded in all areas of Soviet life.

To keep out Western influence, Stalin drew an "Iron Curtain" between Western and Eastern Europe, cutting off all contacts and normal interchange. At the same time he forced the Soviet people to make even greater sacrifices to rebuild the country and to further advance the process of industrialization. The Soviet Union was determined to compensate itself for its terrible losses in the war, and this it could do only by exploiting the lands that had fallen under its control. The countries behind the Iron Curtain were drawn into a close economic embrace, and their economies were subordinated to Russian needs. The standard of living rose with glacial slowness, a pace that was emphasized by the incredible rapidity with which the standard of living in the West shot up.

Post–Stalin era. When Stalin died in 1953, there was a change in Soviet foreign and domestic policy. At home, the new leaders were anxious to eliminate the worst abuses of Stalinism without undermining their own control. After a brief struggle for power, Nikita S. Khrushchev emerged as the strongest figure, and soon began a daring experiment in "de-Stalinization."

Blaming the evils of the Soviet system on Stalin personally, Khrushchev attempted to reduce substantially the use of terror and to increase material incentives to achieve higher economic performance. To do this meant encouraging initiative, providing a higher standard of living, and permitting a slightly wider range for intellectual and artistic creativity.

Khrushchev was deposed in 1964, largely because of the personal and arbitrary nature of his rule, but his successors, Leonid Brezhnev and Aleksei Kosygin, followed the same policies.

Although skilled Soviet cosmonauts achieved a number of successes in space, following the launching of the first Soviet space vehicle, *Sputnik,* in 1957, and although housing and living conditions improved, Soviet society faced severe problems in the late 1960's and 1970's. The rate of industrial growth slowed and the economy was sluggish, partly because of the difficulties involved in planning centrally for such a large and complex industrialized society. The agricultural sector performed erratically, and

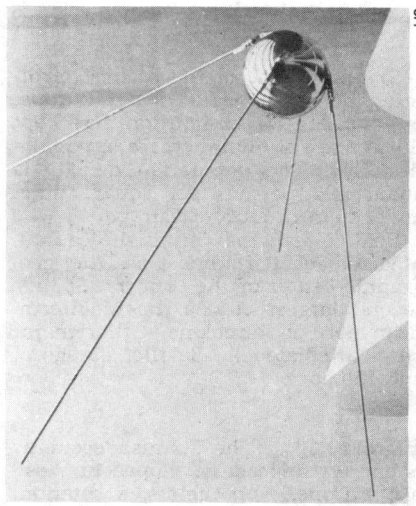

RUSSIA TODAY: *A poster for the Moscow circus* (right), *and the Sputnik* (left), *the first satellite in orbit. Despite a repressive system, the Russians are a talented and capable people.*

in years of poor weather, notably in 1973–1974, the Soviet Union was forced to buy millions of tons of wheat abroad, primarily from the United States.

In this period a small number of intellectuals and scientists began openly to criticize the party and government in what came to be known as the "dissident movement." Although the government exiled some prominent dissidents, such as the writer, Alexander Solzhenitsyn, and permitted some Jewish dissidents to emigrate, the movement was not eliminated and remained a thorn in the side of the government. Moreover, the commitment to Communism of many citizens, particularly young people, seemed more and more formalistic or nonexistent, despite the adoption of a new constitution and extensive discussions about the future Communist society.

Peaceful coexistence. In foreign policy, the Soviet leaders accepted the realities of the nuclear age and espoused a policy of "peaceful coexistence" with the West.

Improved Soviet-American relations during this era of "détente" resulted in agreements on nuclear nonproliferation (SALT I, 1972), joint space missions, trading arrangements, and cultural and educational exchanges.

These efforts countered low points in U.S.-Soviet relations, such as the crisis in 1962 over Soviet missiles in Cuba. The American government also criticized Soviet support to revolutions in Ethiopia, Angola, and elsewhere, and Soviet encouragement of Palestinian ambitions in the Middle East. For its part, the Soviet government opposed American policy in Vietnam and denounced normalization of U.S. relations with the People's Republic of China.

From the 1950's through the 1970's, the Soviet Union faced a series of challenges within the Communist camp. Yugoslavia, expelled from the socialist bloc in 1948, continued to pursue an independent course throughout the period. In 1956 the Soviet government intervened by force to put down a revolt in Hungary, and in 1968 it used Warsaw Pact forces to crush a reform movement in Czechoslovakia.

More critical dissension arose between the Soviet Union and China, where a Communist regime had won power in 1949 with little Soviet aid. Taking a hard line, the Chinese denounced what they termed Soviet revisionism and appeasement. Soviet leaders accused the Chinese of adventurism and warmongering.

The Soviet Union clashed with China in 1969 over possession of an island in the Ussuri River. In 1973 it sent heavy shipments of arms to Egypt and Syria, which were attacking Israel. Also in the 1970's, the Soviets sent massive aid to North Vietnam.

Détente suffered an especially severe setback when Soviet armies launched a surprise invasion (December, 1979) of Afghanistan to "protect" it from internal political turmoil. The United States reacted by discontinuing SALT II talks, restricting trade, and initiating a boycott of the 1980 summer Olympic Games held in Moscow.

In 1982 Brezhnev died, and power passed in quick succession to two of his contemporaries, Yuri Andropov, who died in 1984, and Konstantin Chernenko, who died in 1985. It was considered the start of a new ruling generation when Mikhail Gorbachev, a much younger man, was chosen.

Gorbachev, consolidating power as general secretary of the Communist Party and president of the Soviet Union, introduced major political and economic reforms. Soviet forces withdrew from Afghanistan in February, 1989. Gorbachev announced deep cuts in Soviet military spending, began major troop withdrawals from Eastern Europe, and promoted serious political and economic reforms. Despite increased democratization and new business incentives, the Soviet economy remained stagnant, and long-suppressed nationalist movements threatened to plunge the Soviet Union into a period of chaos. In February, 1990, recognizing the need for even greater change, the Communist Party Central Committee, at Gorbachev's urging, voted to end the party's 70-year monopoly on political power.

SOVIET LEADERS *(Brezhnev is third from left) gather on the balcony of Lenin's tomb in Moscow for the usual ritual appearance.*

Spain

Official name: *The Spanish State*
Area: *194,897 sq. mi., 504,782 sq. km.*
Population: *(1980) 37,380,000*
Capital: *Madrid*
     (Pop., 1978, 3,520,320)
Language: *Spanish*
Religion: *Roman Catholic*
Currency unit: *Peseta*
National holiday: *June 24*

Spain occupies the bulk of the Iberian Peninsula in southwestern Europe. It is bounded on the north by the Bay of Biscay and France, on the east and southeast by the Mediterranean Sea, on the south by the Strait of Gibraltar, and on the west by Portugal and the Atlantic Ocean.

The Canary Islands, which lie in the Atlantic about 800 miles off the southwest coast, and the Balearic Islands, in the Mediterranean just off the east coast, are also part of Spain.

The land.   Most of Spain consists of a high tableland, the Meseta, which has an average elevation of more than 2500 feet above sea level. Most of the Meseta is flat, but it has many hilly and mountainous areas.

The principal mountain ranges of the Meseta are the Sierra de Gata, the Sierra de Gredos, and the Sierra de Guadarrama, to the west and north of Madrid; the Sierra Morena in the south-central area; and the Cantabrian Mountains in the north.

Northeastern Spain is dominated by the rugged Pyrenees, which run along the border with France, isolating the Iberian Peninsula as a whole from the rest of Europe.

There is a relatively narrow coastal plain in the east, along the Mediterra-nean, which widens substantially only in the lower Ebro River valley. This plain is broken in many places by mountains that extend to the sea. In southwestern Andalusia, along the Atlantic shore, the coastal plain is fairly wide.

Spain's major rivers are the Ebro, the Douro, the Tagus, the Guadiana, and the Guadalquivir. The Guadalquivir is the only river navigable for any significant distance.

Climate.   The climate of Spain is varied. The southern and eastern coasts have a Mediterranean climate, with long, hot, dry summers and short, cool, moderately rainy winters.

The interior has a continental climate, with very hot summers and cold winters. It is generally quite dry. Galicia and the northern coast have a maritime climate, by far the rainiest in Spain. The higher elevations experience cooler summers and much colder winters.

The people.   The Spanish people tend to reflect strong regional differences because of the country's historical development and the mountainous terrain, which helps isolate one part of the country from another.

The official language is Castilian Spanish, which is generally understood throughout the country. Numerous regional dialects are spoken, however, including Galician in the northwest and Andalusian in the south. Catalan, spoken in the northeast, and Basque, spoken in the mountains of the north, differ greatly from Castilian.

The state religion is Roman Catholicism, and more than 99 percent of the population is at least nominally Roman Catholic. There are small minorities of Jews, Muslims, and Protestants.

Spain has one of the highest birthrates and lowest death rates in Europe, but substantial emigration has kept the average annual increase in population low. The population density is about 192 persons per square mile, lower than in most of Europe.

Spain's principal city is the capital, Madrid, located almost at the geographic center of the country. Spain's second largest city is the Mediterranean port of Barcelona. Other major cities are Valencia, Seville, Zaragoza, and Bilbao.

Economy.   The Spanish economy is one of the least developed in Western Europe. Nonetheless, substantial improvement has taken place since 1960.

Between 1960 and 1975 Spain sought to increase the national income and to improve production efficiency in order to compete in the world market. The result of this planning has been a general rise in the standard of living and a rapid growth of industry, which now accounts for 37 percent of the labor force, and one-third of the national product. Agriculture, which employed 41 percent of the 1960 labor force, now provides for only 23 percent of labor, and for less than ten percent of the national product. Foreign investment and tourism rose significantly during this period.

Since 1975, worldwide recession has slowed Spain's industrial growth and has reduced foreign investment. High oil prices have damaged the national balance of trade, decreased exports, and contributed heavily to rising unemployment.

Natural resources.   Spain's mineral resources compare favorably with those of the rest of southern Europe, but the production of some materials,

THE ALHAMBRA IN GRANADA (below). *Moorish influence, with Spain's isolation within Europe, goes far to explain the Spanish character.*

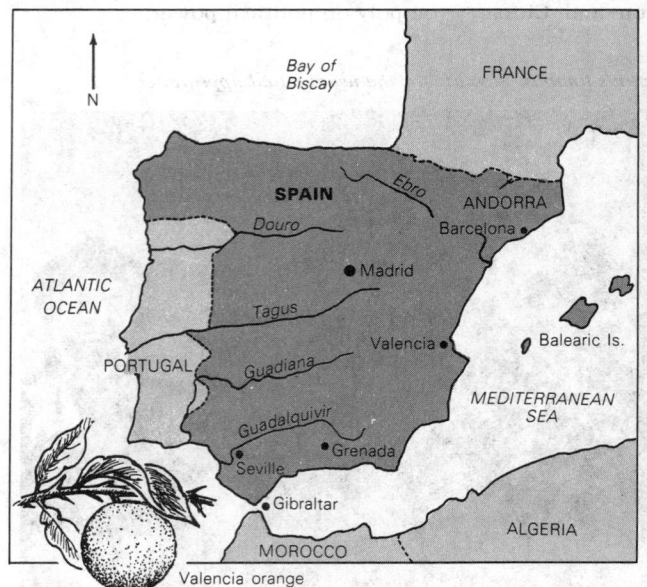

such as mercury, pyrites, and potash, has decreased considerably because quality deposits of these have been nearly exhausted.

Spain's mineral industry does produce substantial quantities of coal (anthracite), lignite, iron ore, lead, manganese, tin, zinc, and wolfram.

Oil has been discovered in recent years, but most of Spain's oil is still imported. Hydroelectric capacity is small, while nuclear energy is gaining in importance.

Agriculture. Spain is traditionally an agricultural nation, but low levels of technical progress, poor land distribution, and the careless depletion of national forests, have decreased the importance of agriculture in the economy as compared with industry.

Grains, fruits, and vegetables are the chief products. These include grapes, olives, and oranges. Sheep, goats, and cattle are raised, and Spain is one of the world's leaders in cork production.

Industry. The industrial sector has grown steadily since 1960, but it is still largely undeveloped and is unable to meet domestic requirements.

The port of Barcelona is the most advanced industrial area, while the Bilbao-Santander district, Avilés, and Oviedo, are also important. Textiles, chemicals, ships and automobiles, and iron and steel are the major industrial products.

Trade. In 1979 Spain's imports cost $25.4 billion and its exports earned $18.2 billion. The country's principal exports are oranges, nuts, fresh and dried fish, vegetables, wine, textiles, olive oil, and cork. The chief imports include machinery, foodstuffs, chemicals, manufactured goods, and petroleum. Spain's major trading partners are the United States, West Germany, France, Britain, and Saudi Arabia.

Government. Ruled from 1939 to 1975 by Franco's dictatorial regime, Spain has since adopted a parliamentary form of government, free elections, and guaranteed human rights.

According to Spain's 1978 constitution, the monarch is now a figurehead, although the present king, Juan Carlos, personally wields great influence. Actual power under the constitution lies with the bicameral Cortes, with a 350-member Chamber of Deputies and a 208-member Senate. All legislative members are elected to four-year terms. The Cortes is headed by a prime minister. In the first election, in 1979, the Center Democratic Party won a majority in both houses.

Spain is a member of the United Nations, the Organization for Economic Cooperation and Development (OECD), and the North Atlantic Treaty Organization (NATO).

History. Spain was peopled in prehistoric times by primitive Basques and Iberians. In about 900 B.C. Celts began entering the peninsula from the north.

The Phoenicians began founding trading colonies on the southeastern coast in about 800 B.C., and the Greeks followed suit from about 500 B.C. The Phoenician city of Carthage, in North Africa, acquired control over southern Spain during the 200's B.C. In 202 B.C. Rome defeated Carthage in the Second Punic War and completed the conquest of Spain. By the beginning of the first century A.D., Roman control over the peninsula was undisputed.

Under Roman rule, classical civilization entered Spain, which soon became one of the most Romanized provinces of the empire. Spain made significant contributions to Latin literature and produced one of Rome's greatest emperors, Trajan. Spain was also one of the first parts of the empire to accept Christianity.

In 409 A.D. Spain was overrun by the Vandals, who were in turn driven out by the Visigoths. In 419 the Visigoths established a kingdom that included Spain and southern France. They contributed little to Spain culturally, and put up little resistance when Arab and Berber Muslims from North Africa invaded the country in 711. The Muslims, or Moors as they were called, ruled most of Spain from Córdoba, which became the center of a brilliant civilization.

Reconquest. A small Christian nucleus survived the Muslim invasions in the Asturian Mountains, which in 722 became the kingdom of Asturias. The establishment of this kingdom marked the beginning of the Reconquest, the 800-year struggle of the Christians in the north to rid Iberia of the Muslims.

In addition to Asturias, which evolved into the kingdom of León in the 1000's, there arose the Christian kingdoms of Aragon and Navarre, the county of Catalonia, and the county—later the kingdom—of Castile. Each of these medieval Christian states had its own body of laws and feudal customs. Each also had a *côrtes,* or representative assembly.

For 300 years these kingdoms waged unsuccessful wars with the Caliphate of Córdoba, the ruling power of Muslim Spain. In the 1000's civil war among the Muslims shattered the unity of the caliphate. Its disintegration aided the Reconquest, and by 1300 the Christians had reduced the Muslim hold to a narrow strip in southern Spain known as the kingdom of Granada.

Aragon and Catalonia had merged in the 1100's, and Castile and León had done the same in the 1200's, but Portugal separated from Castile in 1143 and became an independent kingdom. Further unification of Christian Spain was brought about by the marriage in 1469 of Ferdinand of Aragon (ruled 1479–1516) and Queen Isa-

CULVER PICTURES

FERDINAND AND ISABELLA *united Spain, backed Columbus, and expelled the Moors.*

bella of Castile (ruled 1474–1504).

In 1478 they supported the Inquisition, whose stern ecclesiastical courts sought out the thousands of converted Jews and Muslims living in Spain whose allegiance to Roman Catholicism was doubted.

In 1492 Ferdinand and Isabella conquered Granada, the last Muslim stronghold, and to unify the country completely they expelled the remaining Jews and Muslims. In the same year, Christopher Columbus discovered the New World and claimed it for Spain, thus opening up vast new territories for colonization.

The Hapsburgs. Joanna, the daughter of Ferdinand and Isabella, married Philip of Hapsburg, the heir to the Holy Roman Empire and to much of northern Europe. Their son, Charles I of Spain (ruled 1516–1556), became the Holy Roman Emperor Charles V in 1519.

Charles encouraged Spanish colonial expansion, and during his reign Spain gained control of most of Middle America and northwestern South America. In his role as emperor, however, he embroiled Spain in a series of wars against France. A devout Roman Catholic, he made an unsuccessful attempt to defeat Lutheranism in Germany and engaged in a long struggle against the Muslims of North Africa.

Philip II. Charles's son, Philip II (ruled 1556–1598), did not succeed to the Holy Roman Empire, but he did inherit Spain, the New World possessions, Franche-Comté, Milan, Naples, and the Netherlands. As staunch a Roman Catholic as his father, Philip's foreign policy was often largely the result of his religious feelings.

Philip was determined to suppress Protestantism among his subjects in the Netherlands, but his attempts failed and the Netherlands declared their independence from Spain in 1581. His greatest failure, however, was his attempt to conquer England, which was not only Protestant but also Spain's rival for control of the seas.

In 1588 Philip launched the Spanish Armada against the English. The

PICASSO'S GUERNICA, *famous painting commemorating the Nazi bombing of Guernica in the Spanish Civil War, the first modern bombing.*

armada was largely destroyed; its destruction marked the beginning of the end of Spanish sea power. Philip's only notable success in foreign affairs was the acquisition of Portugal in 1580.

Decline and renewal. Spain declined rapidly in the 1600's, partially as a result of mediocre and indolent kings who left governing to inferior ministers. The country grew poorer, government revenue proved insufficient despite heavy gold imports from Spain's American colonies, and the population declined. The Dutch and English crippled Spanish trade on the seas, and Portugal regained its independence in 1640.

The nation was at its weakest when Charles II (ruled 1665–1700) died without heirs and the throne passed to Philip V (ruled 1700–1746) of the French Bourbon line. Under the Bourbons, Spain underwent a revival in the 1700's. Trade and industry grew, the population increased, colonial administration improved, and the Spanish army and navy regained some of their former strength. These gains, however, were swept away during the Napoleonic era.

Spain in the 1800's. In 1807 Napoleon I of France seized the Spanish throne for his brother Joseph, and the Spanish monarch, Ferdinand VII, was forced to abdicate. The Spanish carried on guerrilla warfare against the French, and in 1813, aided by the British, they finally drove Napoleon's troops from the peninsula.

In 1814 Ferdinand VII was restored to the throne, but Spain had been seriously weakened. The mainland American colonies, which had proclaimed their independence during Ferdinand's reign, were completely lost by 1825, and a family quarrel among

Spanish Bourbons over the throne led to a fierce civil war, the Carlist struggle, that raged from 1834 to 1839.

The reign of Isabella II, who had come to the throne in 1833 as an infant, was marked by political unrest and internal disorder. In addition, she was personally unpopular and in 1868 was forced to abdicate.

After an experiment with an imported Italian monarch, Amadeo I (ruled 1871–1873), a republic was established in 1873. The following year, however, Isabella's son, Alfonso XII (ruled 1875–1885), came of age and was recalled to the throne.

Alfonso XII died in 1885 and was succeeded by Alfonso XIII (ruled 1885–1931), who was born after his father's death. In 1898 Spain fought a disastrous war with the United States, the Spanish-American War. In the war it lost Cuba, Puerto Rico, the Philippines, and Guam, reducing Spain's colonial empire to a few minor holdings in Africa.

Instability. Spain was neutral in World War I, but the wartime demand for goods led to an expansion of Spanish industry. In the postwar period, when the demand for goods and munitions ceased, Spain suffered labor problems and political instability. The country was also burdened with the financial and military problem of putting down uprisings in Spanish Morocco, where a Spanish zone had been established in the early 1900's.

In 1921 a military disaster in Morocco seriously threatened the monarchy. The political situation grew steadily worse, and in 1923 General Miguel Primo de Rivera seized power with the king's consent and established a dictatorship. Primo de Rivera resigned in 1930, and the republicans took advantage of the overwhelming

majority they had won in parliamentary elections in 1931 to proclaim a republic.

The Second Spanish Republic, which attempted liberal reforms, was unpopular with the Roman Catholic Church and the aristocracy. General dissatisfaction with the republic increased as the world economic depression of the 1930's began to affect Spain.

The armed forces, the monarchists, the land-owning aristocracy, and the church were united in their opposition to the republic. The republic was supported, on the other hand, by socialists, Communists, republicans, and various liberal groups.

Civil war. Following a republican victory in elections held in 1936, violence broke out and the army, led by General José Sanjurjo, rose against the government. General Sanjurjo was killed in a plane crash, and General Francisco Franco assumed leadership of the rebels.

Soon after the outbreak of hostilities, foreign nations began to intervene. The Loyalists, as the supporters of the government were called, were aided by sympathizers in the United States and other countries, as well as by the Soviet Union. Franco received large-scale aid from Nazi Germany and Fascist Italy, and by 1939 the Loyalists were defeated.

Franco set up a dictatorship and governed with the title "El Caudillo," or "the leader," aided by the Falangists, the Spanish equivalent of the Italian Fascists.

Contemporary Spain. Although he was openly favorable to the Axis powers in World War II, Franco remained neutral. In 1947 Franco promulgated the Law of Succession, which restored the monarchy by providing for the election of a king by a Regency Council after his death.

In 1953, during the Cold War, the United States changed its previously unfavorable attitude toward Franco's government and obtained military bases in Spain.

Franco's government became somewhat less reactionary in the mid-1960's and it granted a new constitution in 1966.

Since Franco's death in 1975, Spain has improved relations with East European nations and has reasserted its close ties with Latin America and the Arab states. It has reorganized its government along democratic lines under the new constitution of 1978.

In parliamentary elections in 1982, the Socialist Party won a majority of the seats in the Cortes, bringing into power the first left-wing government since the civil war.

Terrorists, demanding the total independence of the Basque region, remain active, although both Catalonia and the Basque area were granted autonomy in 1980.

As the Spanish people continue to gain personal freedoms, they are victimized by an increasingly inflationary economy with high unemployment.

Sweden

Official name: *Kingdom of Sweden*
Area: *173,649 sq. mi., 449,750 sq. km.*
Population: *(1980) 8,253,000*
Capital: *Stockholm*
   (Pop., 1978, 661,258)
Language: *Swedish*
Religion: *Lutheran*
Currency unit: *Krona*
National holiday: *Birthday of the king;*
   Flag Day, June 6

Sweden, a kingdom in northern Europe, occupies the eastern half of the Scandinavian peninsula. It is bordered on the north by Norway and Finland; on the east by Finland, the Gulf of Bothnia and the Baltic Sea; on the south by the Baltic; and on the west by the Kattegat and the Skagerrak, and Norway. Gotland and Öland islands in the Baltic are part of Sweden.

The land. Sweden may be divided into two geographic regions—the Norrland, the northern two-thirds of the country, and the south. Part of the Norrland lies north of the Arctic Circle. In western Norrland, Kjölen, the mountainous backbone of the Scandinavian peninsula, rises to nearly 7000 feet. The Northern Plateau occupies the center, and in the east there is a relatively narrow coastal plain. The main rivers of the region drain eastward into the Gulf of Bothnia.

The southern third of Sweden includes the broad, level Central Lowland and Skåne, a flat plain in the extreme south. These two regions are separated by a rough upland zone, the Småland plateau, which has many rivers and includes Sweden's largest lakes, Vänern and Vättern.

Each region has a distinct climate. The Norrland is subarctic, with long, cold winters and short, cool summers. The severity of the climate increases to the north and in the higher elevations. Southern Sweden has much milder winters and slightly warmer, although still cool, summers. The country as a whole is rather dry, receiving only about 20 inches of rainfall a year, most of it in the south.

The people. The Swedish people are ethnically and culturally homogeneous. Swedish is the universal language, and the dominant religion is Lutheranism. There are small minorities of Lapps and Finns in the north.

Although Sweden is one of Europe's largest countries in area, its population density, less than 50 people per square mile, is one of Europe's lowest. The population growth rate, only about 0.2 percent a year in the 1970's, is one of the world's lowest.

Over 80 percent of the Swedes live in urban areas, particularly in the southern third of the country.

Sweden's major cities include Stockholm, the capital, on the southeast coast; Göteborg, on the southwest coast; and Malmö, near the southern tip of Sweden.

Economy. Sweden has a highly industrialized economy based on rich natural resources. All of Norrland and much of the south are heavily forested, and the dense timber stands make Sweden's forestry output one of Europe's largest. Sweden's many swift rivers and streams are harnessed for electricity, and electrical production has increased steadily since the 1950's. Electricity now supplies the nation with much of its energy needs, but two-thirds of its needs are supplied by imported oil. Nuclear energy is being developed, however.

Sweden's most important mineral resources are its exceptionally large deposits of high quality iron ore. There are also modest reserves of lead, zinc, manganese, tungsten, sulfur, copper, gold, silver, and uranium.
Agriculture. Owing to poor climate, poor soil, and rough topography, only about seven percent of the land can be cultivated, most of it in the south. Agriculture employs only about five percent of the labor force. Nevertheless,

THE VERSATILE SWEDES *have developed folk arts and handcrafted items into a fine art. These amusing wooden birds are nutcrackers.*

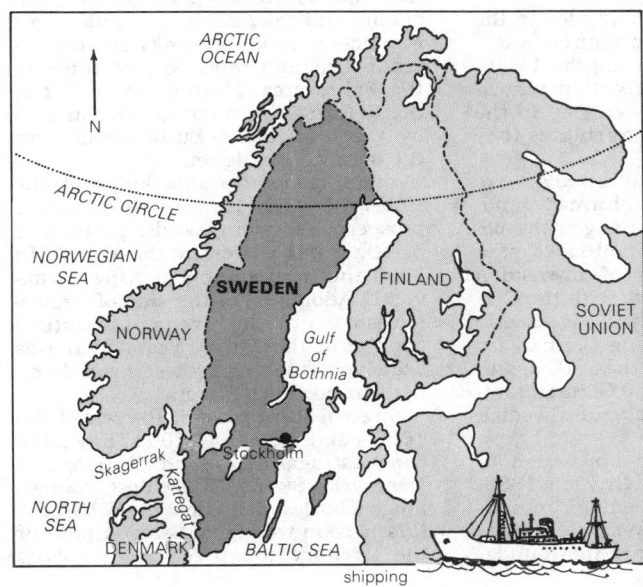

ANN AND GÖRAN WARFF

shipping

730

efficient farming techniques produce high yields per acre.

Dairying is the main agricultural activity, and dairy products account for about half of farm revenues. Oats, wheat, rye, barley, and potatoes are the main crops. Commercial fishing prospers and provides important export products.

Manufacturing and shipping. Manufacturing is the most important part of the Swedish economy. It employs 45 percent of the national labor force and contributes nearly one-third of the national product, but its rapid growth since World War I has slowed considerably since the mid-1970's. Most Swedish industry is privately owned, but the government is directly involved in the operation of many enterprises, especially the waterpower industry.

Although there is some iron and steel production, metalworking, and shipbuilding, emphasis has been placed on producing electrical machinery, vehicles, furniture, scientific instruments, paper, porcelain, and glass.

Merchant shipping makes an important contribution to the economy. Sweden's merchant fleet in 1976 totalled 8.0 million gross registered tons. The earnings of the fleet offset Sweden's otherwise unfavorable balance of trade.

Trade. In 1983 imports cost more than $25.8 billion and exports earned over $27.3 billion. The leading imports are machinery and transportation equipment, petroleum products, iron and steel products, and foodstuffs. The major exports are machinery, lumber and wood pulp, iron and steel, paper and cardboard, sawed timber, and ships. Most Swedish trade is with West Germany, Britain, the United States, Denmark, Norway, and the Netherlands.

Government. Sweden is a constitutional monarchy, with a king as head of state. Actual executive power is exercised by a prime minister and cabinet responsible to the legislature, the *Riksdag.*

A new constitution was granted in 1975 and the *Riksdag* became a unicameral body in 1971. Its 349 members are elected for three-year terms. Of these, 310 are elected by proportional representation and the other 39 seats are distributed to insure that the parties are represented according to the votes they poll.

Sweden is a member of the United Nations, the Nordic Council, and the European Free Trade Association.

History. In about 1000 B.C. Germanic peoples related to modern-day Swedes appeared in the land. The settlers remained divided into numerous small bands and kingdoms until about 600 A.D., when two large tribal groups

HISTORIC KALMAR CASTLE, *begun in the late twelfth century, but with many later additions. The castle withstood many sieges during the 16th to 17th-century wars between Sweden and Denmark.*

became dominant—the Goths, on the shores of Lake Vättern, and the Svear, in the area of Lake Mälaren, near Stockholm.

As other Scandinavian Vikings, or adventurers, sailed westward between 800 and 1050, Sweden's Vikings thrust eastward along European river systems. In the 1100's they established colonies on the eastern shore of the Baltic and governed territory between the Baltic and the Black seas in Russia.

Although the kingdoms of Gothia and Svealand were united in the early 800's, competition for power continued between the Goths and the Svear. Nevertheless, by the end of the 1100's a unified Swedish state had emerged in which Svear, or Swedish, influence tended to prevail.

Christianity spread to Sweden in the 800's, and by 1000 the church was a powerful influence. During the 1100's Christianity was an important part of the culture the Swedes carried to the Finnish peoples of the territories they conquered.

The 1200's and early 1300's were turbulent, as a newly formed landowning aristocracy challenged the political and economic dominance of a powerful middle class of townsmen and merchants. Contacts with the German merchants of the Hanseatic League introduced strong German influence into Sweden in the 1300's, and in 1363 a member of the German family of Mecklenburg took the Swedish throne.

Kalmar Union. When opposition to the king arose, the nobility, in 1388, called on Margaret, Queen of Denmark and Norway, to intervene. She became ruler of Sweden, and laid the foundation for the Kalmar Union (1397–1483), which united the three kingdoms. The union was dominated by Denmark, and throughout the 1400's Sweden remained a restless partner.

Both the peasants and the nobility rebelled against the Danish rulers in the 1400's, and Sweden gradually regained its autonomy. In 1520 Denmark, trying to reassert its supremacy, invaded Sweden and killed Swedish nationalist leaders. This sparked a nationalist revolt led by Gustavus Vasa, a young nobleman.

Vasa kings. Sweden succeeded in breaking away from the Kalmar Union, and in 1523 Gustavus became the first king of the House of Vasa. He had the strong support of the merchants and townsmen, and one of his first acts was to end the German Hanseatic League's monopoly of trade in the Baltic area. During his rule, too, the Reformation came to Sweden, and by the mid-1500's Lutheranism was the dominant religion.

Under generally able kings of the House of Vasa, Sweden developed a prosperous economy, and a position of prestige and power in the world. In 1630 the intervention of King Gustavus II Adolphus on the side of Protestantism in the religious-political conflict of the Thirty Years' War was decisive in making Protestanism dominant in northern Europe.

Sweden spent most of the rest of the 1600's and the early 1700's in wars of conquest against Poland, Russia, and Denmark. Sweden's greatest soldierking, Charles XII, died in 1718, and Russia soon won from Sweden most of the territory conquered from Poland

and Denmark in the last century.

The country returned briefly to constitutional government, but absolutism was restored in 1772 under Gustavus III, who feared that Sweden would come totally under the control of Prussia. At first he ruled as an "enlightened despot," introducing progressive and liberal measures, but in the 1780's his rule began to grow more repressive.

Gustavus invaded Russian Finland in an unsuccessful attempt to regain dominance in the Baltic. Aristocratic opposition and intrigue resulted in his assassination in 1792.

Turmoil followed the death of Gustavus. His successor, Gustavus IV, lost Sweden's Finnish provinces in still another war with Russia in 1808, and he was forced by the dissatisfied nobility to abdicate in 1809. Charles XIII was then chosen to succeed him. In 1809 a new constitution was adopted giving great power to the aristocracy.

Charles XIII had no heir and the nation was in need of a strong leader. In 1810 a French marshall, Jean Baptiste Bernadotte, was elected crown prince under the name Charles John.

Reforms and growth. In 1812 Sweden joined the coalition against Napoleonic France, and the end of the Napoleonic era brought major territorial changes. In 1814 Sweden acquired control of Norway from Denmark and the two states were joined in a personal union under the Swedish king. The aged Charles XIII continued to rule in name only until 1818, when Bernadotte came officially to power.

Bernadotte's tendency toward arbitrary rule stimulated liberal reform movements. Under his successor, Oscar I, the Liberals made some headway toward universal education and the limitation of royal power. Under Oscar's successor, Charles XV, they achieved economic and political liberalization and, in 1866, a two-chambered legislature was authorized.

During the later 1800's, Sweden underwent rapid industrialization, especially after 1872, when Oscar II came to the throne and initiated programs that made Sweden a commercial and industrial state. The social upheaval that accompanied rapid industrialization resulted in progressive social welfare and suffrage legislation, the growth of trade unionism, and the development of cooperatives.

Prosperity and political reform affected Norway, too, and by the 1890's Norwegian nationalism was a major force. In 1905, partly because of a dispute over consular service, Norway proclaimed its independence, which Sweden accepted late in the year.

Modern Sweden. Political and social progress continued in the 1900's. Under Gustavus V, who came to the throne in 1907, universal suffrage and a system of proportional representation were introduced. In 1914 Sweden's Socialist Party won about one-

third of the seats in the lower house of the legislature, and the pace of social legislation accelerated.

Sweden managed to stay neutral in World War I and suffered little from it. During the 1920's and 1930's, under continuing Socialist direction, prosperity continued. Sweden successfully combatted the world economic depression of the 1930's by heavily involving the government in the economy and introducing unemployment insurance legislation.

When Adolf Hitler's Nazi party came to power in Germany in the 1930's, Sweden armed itself but maintained its neutrality. Its neutrality was severely tested in 1939, when Finland was invaded by the Soviet Union, and later in 1940, during World War II, when Denmark and Norway were attacked and occupied by German forces. Sweden was forced to make some concessions to Germany, but it also gave asylum to refugees.

After the war, Sweden's economy continued to expand and its standard of living rose to one of the highest levels in Europe. Prosperity and a successful combination of socialism and individualism combined to produce a stable society that was at the same time dynamic and liberal.

Sweden participated actively in the international organizations of the postwar world, and used its historic position of neutrality to work for international peace. It has worked hard for tighter Scandinavian unity.

The Swedish economy has slowed down since the world recession of the mid-1970's. In 1980 it was paralyzed for several weeks by national strikes engineered by its traditionally contented industrial work force, disillusioned by the over-rigidity of an extreme welfare state.

Switzerland

Official name: *Swiss Confederation*
Area: *15,941 sq. mi., 41,288 sq. km.*
Population: *(1980) 6,310,000*
Capital: *Bern (Pop., 1978, 145,500)*
Language: *French, German, Italian, Romansch*
Religion: *Protestant, Roman Catholic*
Currency unit: *Franc*
National holiday: *Anniversary of the founding of the Swiss Confederation, Aug. 1*

Switzerland, a small, landlocked country in western Europe, is bounded on the north by West Germany, on the east by Austria and Liechtenstein, on the south by Italy, and on the west by France.

The Swiss have achieved a remarkable internal cohesiveness in spite of a rugged physical environment, a long history of decentralized government, and considerable cultural and linguistic diversity.

The land. Switzerland has three major physical regions: the Jura Mountains in the northwest, the central Swiss Plateau, and the Alps, which cover the southern three-fifths of the country.

Switzerland has many lakes, of which Lake Geneva is the largest. The principal rivers are the Rhine and the Rhône, which have their headwaters high in the Swiss Alps, only a few miles from one another.

Switzerland's climate is humid, with mild to cool summers and mostly cold winters. Winters increase in severity with altitude, and the more rugged parts of the Alps are very cold and snowy. In the south and along Lake Geneva the climate is much milder.

The people. The Swiss are descended from several different ethnic groups. Rhaetic and Celtic tribes that lived in Switzerland in Roman times were overwhelmed by the Germanic Alemanni and Burgundians in the 400's. Roman culture and the Latin language stayed strongest in the south. These ethnic differences have remained embedded in local speech.

Switzerland has four official languages—French, German, Italian, and Romansch—and most Swiss have at least a working knowledge of more than one language. About two-thirds of the population speaks German.

Nearly half the people are Protestant urbanites, the other half Roman Catholic rural dwellers.

Switzerland's natural rate of population growth is average for a European nation, but its net growth is the highest in Europe due to heavy immigration. The highest population density is found on the Swiss Plateau, in an east-west band from Zürich to Geneva, and in the Rhine corridor.

Switzerland's most heavily populated urban areas, in order, are Zürich, Basel, Geneva, Bern, Lausanne, Lucerne, and Winterthur.

Swiss watch

AROSA, AN ALPINE VILLAGE. *Though Switzerland's scenery is idyllic, the people are hardworking and have made much out of few resources.*

Economy. Switzerland has few natural resources, and agriculture is limited by the rugged terrain. But the Swiss have developed a prosperous economy based on the manufacture of high-quality, low-bulk goods that involve a high degree of skilled workmanship, such as watches and clocks. These goods have an excellent reputation and a steady market abroad.

The economy has also been aided by the country's political stability and policy of strict neutrality, which have made it a great international banking and insurance center. Switzerland also derives large revenues from international transit traffic, mainly between West Germany and Italy, and from tourism.

Natural resources. Switzerland has no important mineral deposits other than salt and stone. But the country's rivers provide an excellent source of hydroelectric power, which the Swiss have developed to compensate for the lack of fuels. It provides the nation with 30 percent of its energy needs. Imported oil supplies 60 percent, and nuclear energy is being developed to offset some of that dependency.

Agriculture. Agriculture employs about eight percent of the labor force. It is efficient but production does not meet domestic requirements.

The raising of livestock, particularly dairy cattle, is the most important agricultural activity. The major crops are wheat and potatoes, which are grown in the central plateau.

Industry. Swiss industry, employing 38 percent of the labor force, must import a large part of its raw materials. Most of its products are exported. The most important industries produce textiles, chemicals, dyestuffs, inks, pharmaceuticals, clocks and watches, and precision machinery. Printing is also important.

Trade. In 1979 Swiss exports earned $26.5 billion and imports cost $29.4 billion. The country's chief exports are watches and clocks, pharmaceuticals, chemicals, dyestuffs, textiles, and machinery. Major imports include foodstuffs, heavy machinery, iron and steel, motor vehicles, raw fibers, and petroleum.

Switzerland conducts the bulk of its trade with West Germany, France, Italy, the United States, and Britain.

Government. Switzerland is a federal republic of 23 cantons, which are roughly equivalent to provinces or states. The executive branch of government consists of the Federal Council, which is composed of seven ministers who head various administrative departments.

The head of state is the president, who is elected to a one-year term from among the members of the Federal Council by the legislature. The president has comparatively little power and cannot serve consecutive terms.

Legislative power is vested in the Council of States and the National Council. The Council of States has 46 members, two from each canton. The National Council has 200 members directly elected to four-year terms.

Women did not gain the right to vote in federal elections until 1971, and, until the passage in 1982 of a constitutional amendment guaranteeing equal rights, were still prohibited from participating in local elections.

Neutral Switzerland is not a member of the United Nations, but it does cooperate with a number of UN agencies, many of which have their headquarters in Geneva. It is a member of the Council of Europe, the European Free Trade Association, and the Organization for Economic Cooperation and Development (OECD).

The principality of Liechtenstein, on the Austrian-Swiss border, is closely associated with Switzerland. It has been united with Switzerland in a customs union since 1924. The tiny country uses Swiss currency and the Swiss postal administration and its transportation system.

History. The earliest recorded inhabitants of present-day Switzerland were a number of Celtic tribes, among them the Helvetii, who had at an earlier time probably conquered the Rhaeti, who also lived in the area. In the first century B.C. these tribes were defeated by the Romans under Julius Caesar, and Switzerland became Roman territory.

During the 400's A.D., when Roman power began to decline, the area was conquered by the Alemanni, the Burgundians, and Franks. By the early 800's, Switzerland had become part of Charlemagne's empire, although it became divided under Charlemagne's successors.

Independence. During the 1200's the area around Lake Lucerne came under the rule of the Swabian Hapsburg family. In 1291 the Swiss communities, or cantons, of Schwyz, Uri, and Unterwalden entered into a defensive league, or confederation, against the Hapsburgs, whose rule was oppressive. The Hapsburgs were decisively defeated in 1315 at the battle of Morgarten, and the cantons gained their independence.

By 1513 the confederation had expanded to include 13 cantons, and Switzerland became an important military power. Swiss expansionism, however, was permanently checked by Francis I of France, who won a crushing victory over the Swiss at Marignano in 1515.

In the 1500's the Reformation, led by Ulrich Zwingli in Zürich and John Calvin in Geneva, provoked a civil war between Roman Catholic and Protestant cantons and seriously weakened the league. Switzerland remained neutral throughout the Thirty Years' War, but was able to gain international recognition of its independence and neutrality in 1648 at the Peace of Westphalia, which ended the conflict.

For 100 years following the Peace of Westphalia, Switzerland was in a decline, which came to an end in the mid-1700's with the growth of industry and an intellectual renaissance. In 1798, during the French revolutionary wars, the confederation was replaced by the French-sponsored Helvetic Republic, which had a strong central government and abolished the sovereignty of the cantons.

Neutrality. In 1815 the Congress of Vienna, which redrew the map of Europe after Napoleon's defeat, reaffirmed Switzerland's independence and perpetual neutrality. It also drew up a federal plan for the cantons that granted them a large degree of individual autonomy. In 1848 a new constitution was adopted that strengthened the central government. It was revised in 1874 to strengthen central authority even further.

In the 1800's and 1900's Switzerland's neutrality led many international organizations to choose the country as the site of their headquarters. The country stayed neutral, although heavily armed, throughout both world wars.

Contemporary Switzerland. In 1946, in order to maintain its neutrality, Switzerland decided not to join the United Nations, but it hosts many important international conferences, and UN European headquarters are in Geneva.

Postwar prosperity, especially in the 1950's and 1960's, led to an influx of foreign workers into labor-short Switzerland. Today 20 percent of the national labor force is composed of foreign workers.

Reaction against the presence of so many foreign workers, strongest in the financial and industrial center of Zürich, led the Swiss government in 1967, 1970, and 1974 to announce referendums to impose constitutional limitations on the number of foreign workers admitted into the country. Each popular vote opposed the restrictions, but voting was close and tension continues to mount over the issue.

In 1979 Jura became the 23rd canton. It represents the French-speaking population that was formerly part of Canton Bern.

United Kingdom

Official name: *United Kingdom of Great Britain and Northern Ireland*
Area: *94,220 sq. mi., 244,019 sq. km.*
Population: *(1980) 55,900,000*
Capital: *London*
(Pop., 1978, 7,028,200)
Language: *English*
Religion: *Anglican, Protestant, Roman Catholic*
Currency unit: *Pound*
National holiday: *Queen's birthday*

The United Kingdom of Great Britain and Northern Ireland, usually referred to as Great Britain or Britain, covers most of the British Isles, off the northwest coast of continental Europe.

The major island, Great Britain, includes England, in the south and east, Wales, in the west, and Scotland, in the north. It is separated from France on the south by the English Channel and the Strait of Dover, and from northern Europe on the east by the North Sea.

Great Britain is separated from the other large island of the group, Ireland, by St. George's Channel, the Irish Sea, and the North Channel. Northern Ireland, part of the United Kingdom, shares the island with the independent Republic of Ireland.

Most of the islands near Great Britain, including the Hebrides, Shetland, and Orkney groups off Scotland and the Isle of Wight off England, are British. The Channel Islands in the English Channel and the Isle of Man in the Irish Sea are British dependencies.

The land. A complex geological structure gives the British Isles a varied topography despite their limited size. On Great Britain a moderately high highland region arches northward from the Cambrian Mountains in southwestern Wales and the Cotswold Hills in western England. It extends through the Pennine Mountains in north-central England and the Cheviot Hills, the Southern Uplands, and the Grampian Mountains of Scotland to the Scottish Highlands, where the island's and the nation's highest peak, Ben Nevis, rises to 4406 feet.

Most of England is occupied by low plains. In central England the Midlands occupy the basins of the Mersey and the Trent rivers between the Cotswolds to the south and the Pennines to the north. In the south and east the lowlands are called the Downs and Fens. The Central Lowland, in Scotland between the Southern Upland and the Highlands, is the only major lowland outside of England.

Narrow plains skirt the deeply indented coasts of Wales, northern England, and southern Scotland, but the highlands of northern Scotland drop sharply into the sea. The northern and western sections of Northern Ireland are rolling uplands, leveling off in the south and east.

Big Ben

THE UNITED

England

Northern Ireland

BRITISH OIL RIG *in the North Sea. England's economic difficulties have been somewhat eased by the profits from oil.*

SCENE IN BELFAST: *the boulders prevent booby-trapped cars from parking, an aspect of the endless civil war in Northern Ireland.*

England and The United Kingdom

The status of England within the United Kingdom is sometimes hard to grasp. The United Kingdom is made up of England, Scotland, Wales, and Northern Ireland. Great Britain consists of England, Scotland, and Wales alone. For the Commonwealth, see opposite.

KINGDOM

Scotland

SCOTS WHA HAE . . . *Scotland and Wales differ from England, but there is no civil war over independence, as in Northern Ireland.*

Wales

WELSH MINERS: (above) *the traditional heavy industry, and Prince Charles, heir to the throne, at Caernarvon Castle in Wales, where he was invested as Prince of Wales in 1969.*

The Commonwealth of Nations

A voluntary association of many former members of the British Empire, loosely united for cooperation and consultation, the Commonwealth was set up in 1931 as the British Commonwealth. All of the members recognize the British Queen as the symbolic head of the Commonwealth. There are at present 46 members.

The House of Windsor

Queen Elizabeth II heads the royal House of Windsor. Her role in United Kingdom and Commonwealth affairs is largely ceremonial. The monarch's male heir is always Prince of Wales.

The most important of Britain's rivers are the Thames and the Severn in England and the Tweed and the Clyde in Scotland. Most British lakes are in the Lake District of northwestern England and in the Scottish highlands, which are also marked by long, narrow fjordlike inlets. Britain's largest lake, Lough Neagh, lies in the center of Northern Ireland.

Climate. Britain has a temperate maritime climate. The cold temperatures usual for the islands' northerly location are moderated by the warm Gulf Stream flowing just west of the islands, and by warm winds off the Atlantic Ocean. As a result, winters are generally mild and summers cool, with few temperature extremes. Average temperatures are about 40°F in winter and 60°F in summer.

Rainfall is moderate to heavy, ranging from 20 inches a year in the southeast to 120 inches on the west coast, and averages about 40 inches a year for the country as a whole.

The people. Britain is one of the world's most densely settled countries, with 593 people per square mile. The bulk of the country's population lives in England and Wales.

Britain is also a highly urbanized nation, and most Britons live in cities or suburbs. There are six cities with urban areas of over 1 million people. London has the largest population with approximately 8 million people.

During the last decade, the population grew at the slow rate of 0.6 percent each year. The country limits immigration.

Britain's population is quite homogeneous. Most Britons are descendants of Celtic, Scandinavian, French, and Germanic peoples who settled in the islands by the 1000's.

English is the universal language, although the Celtic languages of Welsh and Gaelic are spoken in the north and west. The Church of England (Anglican) is the established church and the dominant religion, but many other Protestant denominations and Roman Catholicism are also important.

The few ethnic minority groups of any significance are made up of immigrants from member nations of the British Commonwealth of Nations. Most prominent are people deriving from the West Indies and from India and Pakistan.

Economy. The British economy, once the most stable and prosperous in the world, faced serious difficulties after World War I. Its earlier prosperity was based on commerce and England's world leadership in manufacturing and banking.

The recent development of commercial oil production has been the most favorable sign in recent years of Britain's ability to slow down the high inflationary and unemployment rates that have so damaged her economy. Rich oil deposits under the North Sea were first exploited in the early 1970's, with commercial production

beginning in 1975. In 1979 Britain produced 79 million metric tons of oil, thus cutting into the expensive importation of that fuel.

Britain's natural resources also include abundant fields of excellent coal and rich iron ore deposits, mostly in the Pennines, as well as quantities of limestone, gravel, chalk, and fine clays. There are also small deposits of zinc, tin, and lead, and bauxite is mined in northern Ireland.

Agriculture. The soils of Britain's lowlands and river valleys, especially in eastern England and northern Ireland, are quite fertile, but limited in quantity. The highlands are generally unsuitable for farming, but they provide excellent grazing land.

About 30 percent of Britain's land area is used for farming. Agriculture, though highly productive, contributes only three percent of the gross domestic product and occupies less than three percent of the labor force. Half of Britain's food supply has to be imported from abroad.

A great variety of crops are raised. Wheat and barley are important, and fruits, vegetables, and other grains are also raised. Dairy farming prospers, particularly in Wales, Northern Ireland, the Scottish lowlands, and western England. Large herds of sheep are grazed in the Highlands and the Midlands, and pigs, poultry, and beef cattle are important throughout the country.

Fishing contributes less than one percent of the gross domestic product, but it has long provided an important item in the British diet and is vital to the economies of Scotland and the northern islands.

Industry. Britain is a highly industrialized nation, and manufacturing contributes about one-third of the gross domestic product, one of the highest percentages in the world. British industry, originally based on its coal, iron, and wool, was forced to shift in the mid-1900's to keep pace with modern technology and to meet the varied demands of modern markets. Heavy industry remains central to the British economy, however.

Iron and steelworking, metal finishing, chemical production, shipbuilding, and the manufacture of machinery, machine tools, and vehicles are the most important activities. Textiles, both wool and the newer synthetics, are an important element in British industry.

The centers of British heavy industry are in the Midlands, in southern Wales, in the Scottish lowlands, and, to a lesser extent, in coastal northern Ireland and on the northern English coast. Greater London is the center of British light industry, and is also the commercial and financial center of the country.

The British government plays an active role in the economy, stimulating and regulating agriculture and

ENDLESS STRIKES *have plagued modern England. One strike left piles of rubbish in London.*

THE QUEEN AND HER PRIME MINISTER. *As queen, Elizabeth II* (right) *is considered above politics, and must accept as prime minister whoever is elected. Margaret Thatcher, the present prime minister, is shown in 1975, when she was elected head of the Conservative Party.*

industry and providing broad social services for the British people. The government owns and operates in whole or in part the country's rail and air transport systems, it coal and steel industries, and its radio, television, and telecommunications networks.

In spite of the government's extensive control over wages and prices in most areas of the economy, it has been unable to control a series of recessions and inflationary booms that have marked the economy since 1945.

Trade. International trade is vital to Britain's economy, and Britain for many years was the world's first-ranking trading nation.

After World War II, however, an increasingly poor balance of trade developed as trade imbalances, once made up by "invisible items," including foreign investment and shipping, began to increase sharply.

In 1983 Britain's exports earned $91.6 billion and its imports cost $101.1 billion. Foodstuffs constitute the largest single import classification, and fuels, industrial raw materials, and finished and semifinished consumer goods are also imported. Machinery, vehicles, and scientific instruments are the leading exports, and textiles, chemicals, metals, and other manufactured goods are important as well.

The United States, Canada, Australia, West Germany, France, the Netherlands, and the Scandinavian countries are Britain's major trading partners. As the leading member of the Commonwealth of Nations, Britain has many special trade arrangements with other Commonwealth nations.

Government. Britain is a constitutional monarchy with a parliamentary system of government. The British queen is head of state. Actual executive power is wielded by a prime minister and cabinet responsible to the legislature, the Parliament. Parliament has two houses—a popularly elected lower house, the House of Commons, and the less powerful, hereditary and appointive upper house, the House of Lords.

Britain does not have a single written constitution; rather, its government is based on a series of documents, judicial decisions, and traditions that have the force of law. These define the civil rights of British citizens and outline the powers of the organs of government.

Commonwealth and empire. Britain is the central member of the Commonwealth of Nations, a group of nations all of which were once colonies of Britain and all of which recognize the British monarch as the symbolic head of the Commonwealth. The Commonwealth nations hold frequent meetings to discuss mutual problems, and member nations provide financial, technical, and often military aid to one another.

Britain's once vast colonial empire has shrunk greatly. During the two decades following World War II, most of Britain's African and Asian colonial territories won their independence, as did many colonial areas in the western hemisphere. Moreover, Britain began withdrawing from the Middle East, where it had established many protectorates, particularly in the Persian Gulf area.

Although Britain still holds a number of territories, most are small and internally autonomous. In Europe, dependencies include Gibraltar, which has also been claimed by Spain since 1704; the Channel Islands; the Isle of Man; the Hebrides; the Orkney Islands; and the Shetland Islands, which have recently become an industrial center of Britain's developing oil industry.

In the western hemisphere, Britain retains Bermuda, once a wealthy plantation and resort colony; the Falkland Islands, which are also claimed by Argentina; St. Helena; British Antarctic Territory; Tristan da Cunha; Ascencion; and the Leeward Islands, which includes St. Kitts-Nevis-Anguilla, among others. Belize, formerly British Honduras, was, until its independence in 1981, a British dependency, though it was also claimed by Guatemala.

In Asia and the Pacific, Britain retains the important and prosperous commercial colony of Hong Kong, on the South China Coast; the British Indian Ocean Territories, formed in 1965; and Brunei, a wealthy colony on Borneo, scheduled to become independent in 1983.

International relations. Britain is a member of the Council of Europe, the Colombo Plan, the United Nations, the Common Market, the North Atlantic Treaty Organization (NATO), and the Organization for Economic Cooperation and Development (OECD).

Britain also has special treaty relations with a number of countries under which Britain is responsible for the defense and foreign relations of those countries.

History. The British Isles have been inhabited since prehistoric times. In about 600 B.C. Celtic peoples from the mainland of Europe began to settle on the island. They were divided into two groups: Gaels and Britons. The Gaels arrived first and settled in the north and west. The Britons occupied the south and east.

The Roman general Julius Caesar invaded the British Isles in 55 B.C. and found Gaels and Britons living in informal communities whose economies were based on agriculture, metalworking, and trading. But the Romans did not seriously attempt to conquer Britain until 43 A.D., when under the emperor Claudius a military expedition invaded the island and occupied part of present-day England.

The Romans established settlements, founded cities, built roads and forts, and eventually extended Roman civil and military administration up to the present-day Scottish border. There the emperor Hadrian had a wall built in the 120's to protect the Roman part of the island from the hostile Celtic and Pictish tribes that remained outside Roman control. From the 40's A.D. to the 300's, England was Roman and its history was part of that of Rome.

As England shared in Rome's greatness, it shared in its decline. In 367 the Picts and the Scots breached Hadrian's wall. Within the next 50 years Rome withdrew its troops from Britain to defend the empire in other areas. This resulted in a degeneration of culture, law, and prosperity. It left Britain vulnerable to foreign invasions. From about 450 to 600 successive waves of invaders from northern Germany—Jutes, Angles, and Saxons—conquered the Celts or forced them to retreat to the western areas of the island, into Cornwall and Wales.

The various tribes of Anglo-Saxon invaders eventually created a number of kingdoms in the various parts of the island each had settled. The most important kingdoms were Northumbria, in the northeast; Mercia, in the Midlands; and Wessex, stretching from London westward to the Severn River. The other kingdoms included East Anglia, Essex, Kent, and Sussex in the south and east.

In the 600's the Anglo-Saxon kingdoms began to be converted to Christianity through the influence of a missionary from Rome, Augustine, who baptized Ethelbert, king of Kent, and in 601 became the first archbishop of Canterbury.

Monastic life flourished in England and produced notable figures like the Venerable Bede (673–735), a monk at Jarrow, who wrote a history of the English people. Through the work of the monasteries, the Germanic Anglo-Saxon tongue became a written language, English. Church structure developed early, and religious leaders often exerted great influence, especially in Mercia and Wessex.

WILLIAM THE CONQUEROR *sails for England in 1066, from the Bayeux tapestry, dated shortly thereafter. William was descended from Norman Vikings and his ship is a Viking ship.*

Rivalries among the kingdoms prevented any real unity for many centuries. Mercia, under Offa II (ruled 757–796), and Wessex, led by Egbert of Wessex (ruled 802–839), underwent marked political development and extended their boundaries westward. By the early 800's a unique English social and political structure had taken shape, and the once warlike Anglo-Saxons had become a settled, agricultural people, enjoying peace and stability. Protected only by an army of untrained farmers, however, they were prey to more warlike peoples.

The "Danes," or Vikings, inhabitants of present-day Denmark, Sweden, and Norway, began raiding the east coast of Britain in 787. In the 850's they began a systematic conquest of the island, and by 870 all of the Anglo-Saxon kingdoms except Wessex had surrendered.

Wessex, led by King Alfred the Great (ruled 871–899), successfully resisted, and in 878 Alfred made a treaty with the Danes that divided England along a line running from London northwest to the Irish Sea. The area northeast of the line remained in Danish hands and was called the "Danelaw." The area southwest of the line was an enlarged kingdom of Wessex.

Alfred created in Wessex a strong political and cultural unit, and in 955 his grandson was able to conquer the Danelaw. Alfred's descendants ceased to be kings merely of Wessex and became the first kings of all England.

In about 980 the Danes renewed their raids. Ethelred the Unready (ruled 978–1016) attempted to buy off the Danes by paying tribute to them, but by 1017 England had fallen to the Scandinavians.

Ethelred and his son both died in 1016, and the Danish king, Canute, became the king of England (ruled 1017–1035) as well. He established an orderly system of government, but his

two sons lacked his ability and one of Alfred's descendants, Edward "the Confessor," became king (ruled 1042–1066).

During Edward's reign, two groups competed for power. One was led by Godwin, the earl of Wessex, and his son Harold. Their rivals were Normans, the descendants of a group of marauding Northmen, who in 910 had settled opposite England's south coast on the French peninsula that came to be called Normandy.

Norman conquest. On the death of the English king Edward the Confessor in 1066, the council of the realm elected Harold, earl of Wessex, king. William of Normandy, a cousin of Edward, maintained that Edward had promised him the throne. William invaded England in October, 1066, and defeated the English at the Battle of Hastings.

As the result of William's conquest, England received a new royal dynasty, a new aristocracy, a new architecture (Norman Romanesque), a new language (Norman French), and a new institution (feudalism). But William the Conqueror preserved all that was useful from the Anglo-Saxon past—the law, the courts, the tax system, the national militia, and the administrative machinery. The conquest enabled William to establish a feudal system far more systematic and effective than any existing in Europe.

By 1085 William's rule over England was firm. His Norman followers held lands throughout the kingdom and acknowledged him as their feudal overlord; his castles were built at strategic points to protect the land from internal and external violence.

The feudal aristocracy of England was resentful of the power of the monarchy from the beginning. On the other hand, the benefits of the law and order brought about by this power were obvious to everyone. The political theme of English medieval history is thus a search for ways to prevent royal power from becoming arbitrary while preserving the very real benefits of strong central government.

In religious matters, William and his successors worked to make the church in England conform to the standards of the papacy while preventing papal influence in England from becoming superior to their own.

Most important, William's conquest of England bound the island, through Normandy, to Latin Christendom and turned it away from those ties it had had with Scandinavian lands, peoples, and customs.

Henry I (ruled 1100–1135). When William died in 1087 he left the kingdom of England to his second son, William Rufus (William II, ruled 1087–1100), who lacked his father's wisdom and ruled oppressively. Another of William the Conqueror's sons, Henry I, who followed William II to the throne, showed something of his father's skill and energy in government and administration.

Because some disputed his right to the throne, Henry's first acts as king were bids for popular favor. One of the most significant was his issuance of a charter promising to remedy many grievances the people had held against his predecessor. By this limiting of the king's own powers, his charter proved a precedent for later demands upon royal prerogatives.

Henry also made legal and administrative reforms. He appointed traveling justices, or judges, who brought the legal expertness of the royal court to the shires of England. Their accumulated experience later resulted in the beginnings of English common law.

Henry established a central finance office, the Exchequer, for the fair receipt and adequate accounting of the royal revenue. He was also successful in foreign affairs, being able to reconquer Normandy and reunite it with the English crown.

Henry II (ruled 1154–1189). Many of the gains in the direction of an ordered royal government were lost when dynastic disputes followed Henry I's death in 1135. The king left no direct male heir, and the nobles' rivalry for power brought near anarchy between 1135 and 1154. In 1154 Henry I's grandson, Henry of Anjou, gained the throne as Henry II.

Through inheritance and marriage, Henry controlled nearly all of southwestern France and was thus lord of not only England, but of continental territories far larger than those directly controlled by the actual king of France. Ireland, too, came at least nominally under the English king's authority when in 1154 Pope Adrian IV allowed Henry to extend his kingdom there.

Henry II strengthened the position of the monarchy, which had been weakened during the dynastic struggle. By defining royal rights, he strengthened the position of the king over the barons. He was able to hold together his vast and diverse possessions in France, involving immense financial commitments, while he also strengthened the royal power and the machinery of the central government.

Henry II also carried forward the legal reforms of Henry I. He extended the use of the sworn testimony of "jurors" to help in arresting criminals. It is largely due to Henry II that English common law, not Roman law, and trial by jury, not trial by inquisition, became the English legal tradition.

The expansion of royal judicial activity brought Henry into conflict with the church, which was also expanding its legal system, and with his own archbishop of Canterbury, Thomas à Becket. The bitter struggle that ensued culminated in the assassination of Becket at the high altar of Canterbury Cathedral in 1170.

Although Henry did not order the assassination, he did perform public penance for it. Subsequently, the principle of "benefit of clergy," or immunity from secular courts, remained a feature of English law. In practice, however, the royal courts steadily diminished the jurisdiction of the ecclesiastical courts.

Richard I (ruled 1189–1199). Henry was succeeded by his son Richard. Richard I, "the Lionhearted," was great in legend but of little importance in fact as far as England was concerned. Throughout almost all of his reign he was engaged in the Third Crusade, which kept him out of the country.

The absence of King Richard did not cause the degeneration of royal power, largely as a result of Henry II's reforms and the work of Hubert Walter, archbishop of Canterbury, his chief minister.

By the 1100's English society was well settled into its particular pattern of feudalism. Differing from continental feudalism, the English manorial system led more to internal peace than to internal conflict, for, with armed castles required to be licensed by the king and thus few in number, the noblemen of England were more gentlemen landowners than warriors. Feudal duties to higher lords, including the king, were fulfilled more often through the courts of law than in war.

John (ruled 1199–1216). During John's reign England lost its continental Angevin possessions, including Normandy itself, to France. Moreover, John's attempts to control the nomination of the archbishop of Canterbury failed, and in 1213 he had to humble himself before the pope and acknowledge that England was a papal fief.

In his attempt to extend royal power at the expense of the barons, especially in the dispensing of justice and the levying of taxes, John was brought to heel by a revolt of the barons. In 1215, at Runnymede, the discontented nobles forced him to grant a long and detailed charter, which came to be known as the Great Charter, or *Magna Carta.*

The Magna Carta was not a charter of liberties for all Englishmen. It was a catalog of baronial grievances against the excessive financial exactions of English kings in general, and of John in particular.

The Magna Carta was not an attempt to destroy the real benefits of strong central government. It attempted to limit kingship rather than destroy it. As the first attempt to limit the authority of the king, the Magna Carta pointed toward the most important development in England during the 1200's, the growth of Parliament.

Henry III (ruled 1216–1272). The nobility increased its control over the monarchy during the reign of Henry III.

From the point of view of the English, Henry had four faults: his subservience to the papacy; his subservience to foreign favorites, the French relatives of his wife and mother; his defeats at the hands of the Welsh and Scots; and his inability to recover English possessions in France. In 1258 the barons revolted and set up their own

THE MURDER OF THOMAS À BECKET in Canterbury Cathedral in 1170. Becket was Henry's friend and minister, but as Archbishop of Canterbury opposed him over church matters.

BATTLE SCENE *in the 1200's. Under Edward I at this time there were wars with France, Wales, and Scotland. Note that the knights wore heavy helmets, but no body plate armor.*

government, and Henry III remained king in name only.

The baronial council of government called for a "Model Parliament" in 1265. It was to be attended by two knights elected from each shire and, for the first time, two representatives from each city and borough.

Under such a strong threat to their power, however, the king and the more conservative barons rallied, and late in 1265 the king's forces led by his son and heir, Prince Edward, defeated the barons in battle. The baronial rebellion and experiment with government ended. All charters granted were annulled.

Edward I (ruled 1272–1307). Edward decided that he could utilize a Parliament that brought together the greater clergy, nobility, and town leaders. Envisioning Parliament as a broad-based advisory council, he realized that it could effectively announce royal policy and influence public opinion. Moreover, Parliament could be most useful in opening to the king new sources of revenue beyond the limited and inadequate income that the crown derived from its traditional source, fixed feudal dues.

Edward needed new sources of money and support because of his ambitious foreign and domestic policies. While he was making inroads in the power of the barons and the church in England, he was at war with France on the continent to defend one of his French territories. Even more aggressive and costly were the wars he waged in Wales and Scotland.

Wales had for centuries been a troublesome and occasionally threatening land on the western frontier of the English kingdom. In the early 1200's Wales had been united under Llewelyn the Great (ruled 1194–1240) and had begun to exploit the rifts existing among English political factions.

In the late 1200's Edward I decided

that the peace of England required the conquest of Wales, and by 1284 he had conquered the kingdom. Although Welsh laws, customs, and language survived, independent Wales ceased to exist, and Edward's castles dominated the land. In 1301 Edward proclaimed his son and heir the "Prince of Wales."

Edward had less success in Scotland, the kingdom to the north. Scotland, like Wales, had had a troubled domestic history, and for centuries had been a threat to England. After the death in 1286 of its king, Alexander III, Scotland found itself without a ruler and prey to the evils arising from a disputed succession to the throne. Edward I was called in to choose a king, and in 1292 he declared John Baliol king of Scotland. Taking advantage of his position, Edward then made extensive demands on the Scots.

To resist the king's aggression, the Scots made a military alliance with the king of France. John Baliol, William Wallace, and Robert Bruce led Scotland in wars against English domination. These wars continued for over 30 years and did not end until 1328, when King Edward III recognized Bruce's title to the Scottish crown.

Edward II (ruled 1307–1327). Although Edward left his son, Edward II, the benefits of advancements in the laws and institutions of the realm, he also left a drained treasury, an exhausting war in Scotland, and a host of enemies at home and abroad. Edward II was not the man to overcome these difficulties.

In Edward II's reign, the barons sought with some success to supervise royal policy through a commission known as the Lord's Ordainers. When, in 1327, Edward, surrounded by plots and conspiracy, was deposed and murdered, it was Parliament that named

his successor, proclaiming his 15-year-old son King Edward III.

Edward III (ruled 1327–1377). The young king came to the throne during a turbulent period in England's social and political development. During the 1200's and early 1300's English cultural and economic life had quickened dramatically, and the speed of the resulting social change was increased by a long series of wars and a major epidemic during the 1300's.

English cities and towns, which had grown into thriving centers of trade, had developed a particularly active commerce in cloth with the Low Countries—Belgium, the Netherlands, and Luxembourg.

In part to insure the continuation of this commerce and to foil the attempts of the French king to interrupt it, Edward III in 1337 began a conflict with the French that lasted so long it earned the name the Hundred Years' War.

Britain enjoyed early victories, but suffered, both from financial exhaustion and from the violent onset in 1348 of the plague known as the Black Death. The plague killed perhaps one-third of the English population and about one-half of that of Europe.

By causing a manpower shortage that broke the traditional bonds of the serf to the land and the manor, the Black Death hastened the process of social change. Feudalism began to disintegrate and the position of the towns and of a newly formed middle class was strengthened. Aided by the collapse of feudal loyalties and by the new spirit of nationalism inspired by the wars with France, the English monarchy in the late 1300's was able to centralize its power at the expense of the local lords and clergy.

The new social order not only increased the power of the monarchy, it also enhanced the status of the representatives of the expanding middle class in Parliament.

Between 1339 and 1349 the knights and burgesses began to be designated as the "Commons," because they had begun electing a common speaker to represent them before the king.

The continuing wars with France also strengthened Parliament, as the growth of parliamentary power depended primarily on the control of taxation, and Edward III was continually in need of funds to wage the war. He asked Parliament to take on the burden of levying taxes, and Parliament consented to grant the funds in return for the king's remedying grievances or giving additional privileges sought by Commons.

By the end of Edward's reign, Parliament's power was great. Not only had the nobles succeeded in increasing their control over finance, but they had also secured an important role in formulating legislation, and had even exerted occasional pressures to control executive policy.

Richard II (ruled 1377–1399). In the wars with France, the English suffered many defeats. By 1375 the burdens of war and taxation had added to the discontent the lower classes felt in a time of rapid social change and economic instability. This discontent led in 1381 to a briefly successful "Peasants' Revolt."

Richard responded to foreign failures and domestic unrest by arbitrary, absolute rule. His rule made many enemies, who rallied behind Richard's cousin, Henry of Lancaster, in 1399 and forced Richard to abdicate.

Henry IV (ruled 1399–1413). The proclamation of Henry of Lancaster as King Henry IV by Parliament marked a great step in the growth of Parliament. Henry reigned as a frankly constitutional monarch. By putting down several attempted rebellions and invasions, Henry passed on to his son Henry V a kingdom more secure than the one he had taken. It looked as though stability had returned to England.

Henry V (ruled 1413–1422). Henry V was able to pursue the long war with France with remarkable success. By his victories and by his marriage to the daughter of the king of France, Henry became heir to the French throne in 1420. But two years later, he unexpectedly died, and left only an infant son, Henry VI. Both France and England were ruled by regents, and under these circumstances, both kingdoms deteriorated.

Henry VI (ruled 1422–1461). France recovered first. It improved its military position, and between 1429 and 1431 the tide of battle began to turn against the English.

England's reverses on the Continent had repercussions at home. Unfavorable terms accepted after England's losses caused the House of Commons to raise treason charges against the king's ministers. A brief rebellion by landed gentry followed and weakened Henry VI's shaky hold on the throne. In 1455 the weakness of the monarchy caused rivalries among contenders for the throne to erupt into civil war.

Henry VI's Lancastrian followers opposed the supporters of other descendants of Edward III, who were led by Richard of York, Henry's cousin. The conflicts that arose between the two houses were known collectively as the War of the Roses, because the traditional badge worn by Lancastrians was the red rose, and the Yorkists' badge was the white rose.

Bloody civil war between the houses dragged on for 30 years, with the leaders of each faction claiming the right by inheritance to be king. An end seemed to be in sight in 1461. Richard of York had been killed the year before, but his son, Edward, defeated the Lancastrians in that year.

York. Edward of York was proclaimed king as Edward IV (ruled 1461–1483). His reign and that of his brother, Richard III (1483–1485), were marked by continuing warfare and violence. Many powerful groups in England, including Yorkists, turned to Henry Tudor, earl of Richmond. Henry had only a remote claim to the throne as a Lancastrian, but he had resided safely in France during the dynastic wars. Henry invaded England in 1485 and defeated Richard III's army. As a result of Richard's death in the battle, Henry gained the crown as Henry VII.

Henry VII (ruled 1485–1509). Henry had come to the throne through military victory and parliamentary consent; hereditary right had played little part. He sought to make his throne secure for himself and his descendants and to bring peace and order back to England. To achieve both ends, in 1486 he united the formerly warring houses by marrying Elizabeth of York, the eldest daughter of Edward IV, and founded the Tudor dynasty.

Under the Tudors, England entered one of its greatest eras. Under Henry's guidance, the first royal navy was built, and the Cabots explored the coasts of North America, preparing the way for English colonies there.

NEW YORK PUBLIC LIBRARY

HENRY VIII, *a brilliant king who broke with the pope on political grounds.*

Henry VIII (ruled 1509–1547). Henry VII's son, Henry VIII, led England into participation in the diplomatic and military affairs of Europe. From 1515 to 1529, Thomas Wolsey, lord chancellor, was his brilliant adviser and agent in foreign affairs.

Henry became obsessed with a personal struggle against the Catholic Church. The papal courts at Rome, in 1529, refused to permit his divorce from Catherine of Aragon, who had failed to bear him a male heir. Moreover, Henry resented the authority of a foreign religious figure (the pope) over the political concerns of England. His predecessors had tried for centuries to limit church authority. Henry VII had come close to subordinating the nobility to the monarchy, but the church remained, with its courts, laws, taxes, and massive properties. Henry's divorce would provide the occasion for a sweeping reform of the relations between the monarchy and the church.

By 1533 Henry had an English court declare his marriage to Catherine invalid, and he married Anne Boleyn. In 1534 Henry passed an Act of Supremacy, making himself and his successors head of the church in England, and declared all appeals to Rome hereafter illegal.

Although at the time that Henry defied the church, the Protestant Reformation was sweeping Europe, the impetus for England's "reformation" was more political than religious. The Anglican Church differed little from the Roman Catholic Church, except that Henry, not the pope, was its head.

Henry's marriage to Anne Boleyn did not serve his dynastic purposes. In 1533 she bore him a daughter, Elizabeth, but no son. In 1536 he had Anne executed, and he married Jane Seymour, who died in 1537 while giving birth to a son, Edward. Two other wives preceded Henry's sixth, Catherine Parr, who survived him.

Edward VI (ruled 1547–1553). Henry's actions had made religion a vital issue in English politics, and its importance increased after Henry's death. Henry was succeeded by his ten-year-old son, Edward VI, whose policies were determined by the Duke of Somerset and the Duke of Northumberland, both of whom worked to make the English church far more Protestant than it was.

Mary (ruled 1553–1558). After Edward VI's death, the crowned passed to Mary, the devoutly Roman Catholic daughter of Henry VIII and Catherine of Aragon. Mary tried unsuccessfully to restore Roman Catholicism in England. She married Philip II of Spain, heir to the Holy Roman Empire, but their marriage was unpopular because of English fears of intervention and domination by Roman Catholic Spain.

Mary's persecution of Protestants earned her the name "Bloody Mary," although in her insistence on a single national religion she was in company with every other European ruler in the 1500's. Her death brought her half-sister, Elizabeth, to the throne.

Elizabeth (ruled 1558–1603). Elizabeth saw the importance of bringing order and peace to the realm and with the help of talented advisers she found the means and developed the policies to do so with remarkable success.

In the area of religion, Elizabeth moved cautiously, not making a decision until Parliament did. By the Act of Supremacy (1559) and Uniformity (1563), passed by Parliament, she achieved a broad religious settlement that was moderate enough to satisfy the great majority of her subjects.

Elizabeth increased royal power by gaining widespread popular support through insuring the welfare of the people. Elizabeth initiated a program of national regulation of economic and social affairs unprecedented in Europe. Currency was stabilized, and industry was stimulated by grants of patents and monopolies. The "poor laws" provided relief for the disabled and the indigent, and the Statute of Apprentices regulated the hours and conditions of labor. Laws against religious dissent were enforced only when it threatened the peace of the realm.

The economic vitality of the kingdom found expression in the formation, near the end of Elizabeth's reign, of a number of trading companies—the most famous of which was the East India Company—that established commercial relations and trading outposts in many parts of the world.

Elizabeth also used the English institutions of government to her, and England's, benefit. Under the Tudors, the Privy Council, consisting of the monarch's personal advisors, usually led Parliament, which passed into law many of the measures initiated by the council. The centralizing of these institutions, together with the elimination of older ones associated with feudalism or Roman Catholicism, made the English machinery of government more efficient.

Elizabeth's government brought England international prestige as well. By successfully facing a series of crises brought on by the Spanish king and other Roman Catholic leaders determined to restore Roman Catholicism in England, Elizabeth gained new respect for her country.

Moreover, in Elizabeth's reign English sailors broke the Spanish monopoly of trade with the New World and established England as a leading maritime nation. They plundered Spanish

galleons, raided Spanish colonial outposts, and seized Spanish treasure. These exploits increased Englishmen's national pride and their awareness of the importance of the sea to England's world position.

England's growing maritime supremacy led Philip II of Spain to build a great armada in 1586 to destroy the English fleet and to make possible the conquest of England. Faced with this great crisis, the English navy defeated the Spanish Armada in 1588, and thus opened the way for further expansion of trade and, eventually, for the building of an empire.

James I (ruled 1603–1625). Elizabeth never married, and upon her death in 1603, the crown passed to James VI of Scotland, son of her cousin, Mary of Scotland. James became the first of the Stuart kings, as James I of England. Although the crowns of England and Scotland were united in one person, the kingdoms remained separate.

Religion was one of the first issues confronting James. Dissatisfaction with the vagueness and breadth of Elizabeth's church settlement had increased in the late 1500's, and many hoped that further changes could be made in the law to eliminate vestiges of Roman Catholicism in the Church of England. The term "Puritan" came to be applied to those who were thus dissatisfied.

These Puritans turned first to Parliament for church reform, but with little effect. James, himself an Anglican, was unwilling to commit himself on the issue and gave the Puritans little more than permission to make a new translation of the Bible. The king's stubbornness was one cause for the departure of some Puritans to America,

where they established the Massachusetts Bay colony—the second English colony in the New World. "Jamestown," a settlement in Virginia, had been the first.

Roman Catholics, too, were unhappy over James's refusal to revoke the Elizabethan anti-Roman Catholic laws. In 1605 they formed a conspiracy called the "Gunpowder Plot," designed to blow up Parliament. When the plot was exposed, it inspired strong anti-Roman Catholic feeling in the general public, and resulted in further restrictions on Roman Catholics.

James was unsuccessful in dealing with Parliament, and during his reign the conflicts between king and Commons over religion, foreign policy, and economic affairs grew increasingly sharp. The central and most important issue of James's reign was the extent of royal authority.

James held to the "divine right" theory of kingship—royal authority came from God and the king was above the law. James's ineptitude in handling the institutions of government caused the Commons to become equally rigid in asserting the rights of subjects and in fixing constitutional limits upon the arbitrary use of royal power.

Unable to deal with Parliament, James ruled without it almost continuously from 1611 to 1621. Parliament's hostility toward James impelled it to develop powerful procedures and strong leaders capable of initiating and carrying through policies. The conflicts between the king and the Commons grew still sharper during the reign of James's son, Charles I.

Charles I (ruled 1625–1649). The economic and governmental policies of Charles hardened and enlarged opposition to his rule. Charles, after dissolving two Parliaments that opposed his arbitrary rule, was forced by Parliament in 1628 to grant the Petition of Right, a document that declared illegal certain royal taxes, such as forced loans, and practices, such as arbitrary imprisonment. Charles had had to reconvene Parliament and grant its demands because he needed parliamentary approval to finance English involvement in the Thirty Years' War, a European religious and political conflict that had begun in 1618.

When Parliament continued to refuse funds, Charles ruled without it between 1628 and 1640, resorting to makeshift methods of taxation and dictatorial behavior, which alienated the populace. In 1640, when the additional expense of a war with Scotland forced Charles to reconvene Parliament, the members were ready to challenge the king.

In 1641 the House of Commons formulated a program called the "Grand Remonstrance" that would have created a limited parliamentary monarchy in England and that would have

DEFEAT OF THE SPANISH ARMADA *in 1588 was a turning point for little England. Victory over Spain, Europe's most powerful nation, opened the seas for British maritime expansion.*

BRITISH WORTHIES. *Shakespeare* (right), *poet and dramatist, was the crowning glory of Elizabethan England. He died in 1616. In 1649 Oliver Cromwell* (left) *became the "Protector."*

modified the episcopal organization of the church. Charles accused the parliamentary leaders of treason.

In 1642 civil war began between the royalists, called "Cavaliers," who supported the king, and the parliamentarians, called "Roundheads." The Cavaliers were generally Anglican nobles or gentry; the Roundheads were mostly Puritan burghers and townsmen who wanted to abolish the episcopacy. Led by Oliver Cromwell, the parliamentarians finally defeated the royalists in 1648.

Commonwealth. Charles I was tried and beheaded early in 1649. The monarchy and the House of Lords were abolished and England was declared to be a commonwealth. An executive council led by Cromwell as "Protector" ran the government.

Between 1649 and 1658 Cromwell had as much difficulty with Parliament as Charles had had, and several times he found it necessary to dismiss it. His revolutionary government made little progress with the constitutional experiments it had planned. One of the few benefits of the commonwealth was the support it gave to Puritan colonists in America. In Scotland and Ireland, however, its excessive zeal only alienated the population and made future union more difficult.

Charles II (ruled 1660–1685). After Cromwell's death in 1658, the Protectorate was too weak to survive, and in 1660 Charles I's son took the throne as Charles II. Religion continued to be the central issue, and in the 1670's Parliament passed a series of laws directed against Catholic and Protestant dissenters.

Much of the parliamentary debate centered on a bill that would have excluded Charles's brother, James, from the throne because he was a Roman Catholic. During this debate the party labels "Whig" and "Tory" came into general use.

Whig designated one favoring religious toleration and the exclusion of James, that is, asserting parliamentary control over the succession. Tory designated one favoring an intolerant and exclusive Anglican Church policy and the hereditary right of kingship, even if it should involve bringing a Roman Catholic to the throne.

James II (ruled 1685–1688). The 1680's led to the firm establishment of a constitutionally limited monarchy in England.

James II followed his brother to the throne in 1685, and most Englishmen were willing to be loyal to him and accept his declaration that he would defend the Anglican Church and keep his own Roman Catholic loyalties a purely private matter. By 1688, however, James's actions, such as giving Roman Catholics high positions in his council and in the army, and his harshness toward Anglican opponents, had caused many men to contemplate acting against him.

The birth of a son to James's wife in June, 1688, brought this discontent to a head, for in the absence of a son, the throne would have gone to James's daughter, Mary. Mary, a staunch Protestant, was married to William of Orange, head of the Dutch state and leader of the Protestant forces in Europe against Roman Catholic Louis XIV of France. Thus Mary's succession and the future of Protestantism in England seemed doubtful.

In June, 1688, a small group of both Whigs and Tories invited William of Orange to invade England, and William and an army landed in England in November, 1688. Finding little support in England against this challenge, James II fled to France.

William of Orange (ruled 1689–1702). In accepting a Declaration of Rights along with the crown, William and Mary accepted constitutional limitations upon their royal authority,

which were written into the Bill of Rights. The absolutist theory of divine right was dead. The king ruled by grace of legally constituted popular representatives who could remove his authority as well as grant it.

The events of the "Glorious Revolution" were confirmed in a number of statutes. By them, the king could not suspend acts of Parliament, and was required to convene Parliament annually. In addition, Roman Catholics were excluded from the throne, but limited toleration was granted to Protestant dissenters.

As king, William had to deal with unrest in Scotland and Ireland. Scotland, though still officially ruled by the English king, was more loyal to the deposed James II than to England, and William only barely managed to maintain his position there. Roman Catholic Ireland, still smarting from harsh treatment under Cromwell, was even more rebellious, and the Protestant king responded with severity.

As soon as the political situation in England was stabilized, William brought England into the League of Augsburg, an alliance that united both Protestant and Roman Catholic Europe against the territorial aggression of Louis XIV of France. War began in 1689 and continued with brief interludes of peace until 1713.

Anne (ruled 1702–1714). Despite strong allies and Parliament's vigorous support of the war, England and its allies did not begin to win until William's successor, Mary's sister Anne, appointed John Churchill, first duke of Marlborough, as commander of the armed forces. His brilliant victories resulted in the defeat of Louis XIV's policies and led to the Treaty of Utrecht in 1713.

The terms of the treaty laid the groundwork for the expansion of England's empire. By the treaty, England received as colonies Gibraltar and Minorca in the Mediterranean and the Hudson Bay Region and Newfoundland in Canada. In addition, Britain gained trading rights with Spanish colonies and a monopoly of the slave trade in Europe for the next 30 years.

At the head of this embryonic empire was the newly formed United Kingdom. Scotland and England had been formally joined in 1707 into Great Britain. All of the British Isles were under the control of the British monarch, although Ireland's membership in the union was in little more than name.

None of Queen Anne's children outlived her, and upon her death the parliamentary rules concerning the succession operated, thus excluding from the throne the Roman Catholic Stuarts.

House of Hanover. The next in line was the head of the German state of Hanover, a descendant of James I. He ascended the throne of England as George I (ruled 1714–1727). Because

744

George I and his son, George II (ruled 1727–1760), spoke poor English, had little knowledge of British politics, and were more interested in the affairs of their German state, Britain's development into a nation governed by ministers advanced rapidly during their reigns.

Cabinet government had gradually developed from the monarchs' custom of using members of the Privy Council as their active agents in Parliament. Because it was expedient to have a united cabinet, supported by the majority in the House of Commons, the kings found it necessary to consider the desires of Parliament when choosing a cabinet. The Georges were often absent from cabinet meetings, allowing the ministers great autonomy. This custom hardened into a precedent.

Both Georges employed the political genius of their adviser, Sir Robert Walpole (1721–1742), in making the difficult machinery of government work. Walpole was the first man in British history to warrant the designation of prime minister. Walpole's policies gave England political stability, and his reforms of fiscal and commercial regulations stimulated internal industry, shipping, and foreign trade. Moreover, he refused to let England become involved in wasteful European conflicts.

During the peaceful ministry of Walpole, an aggressive war party emerged that was eager to extend English penetration of Spanish America. Spain's attempts to check English violations of the Peace of Utrecht of 1713 led to numerous incidents that were used to arouse support for a "patriotic" war. The War of Jenkins' Ear (1739–1748) was named for the most publicized atrocity, but it was really over trading interests. It soon merged with a larger war on the Continent, the War of Austrian Succession (1740–1748), which had imperial and commercial overtones, as Europe's overseas colonies and international trading privileges were at stake.

Hostilities stopped in 1748, only to resume in 1756, as the Seven Years' War, which was more directly between England and France, the leading European powers. An important part of the conflict stemmed from colonial and commercial rivalries in North America and in India.

Britain's victory in the war, directed by the war minister William Pitt, made England the most powerful nation in Europe and the foremost colonial and commercial power in the world. By the Peace of Paris of 1763, England received most French possessions in North America east of the Mississippi and increased trading power in India.

George III (ruled 1760–1820). This king's futile attempts to strengthen the ties between England and the colonies and extend his own influence through repressive legislation ended in

WASHINGTON TAKES THE SURRENDER *at the Battle of Trenton in 1776. In the 1760's Britain dominated the world. By the 1780's it had already lost its potentially richest colony— the United States of America.*

1775 with the outbreak of the American war of independence. Britain recognized the independence of the colonies in 1782.

George's policies were more successful after 1783, when he named Pitt's son, William Pitt "the Younger," as prime minister. Pitt's genius for finance led to fruitful economic reforms, and he did much to eliminate governmental corruption. Above all, he organized a massive war effort against the French empire under Napoleon in the early 1800s.

During the century following Napoleon's defeat in 1815, England enjoyed relative peace. Pitt's attempt to incorporate Ireland into the United Kingdom failed in 1801, however, when George forbade religious freedoms for Irish Roman Catholics.

English society had changed rapidly since the mid-1700's. As industrialization increased tremendously, so did the population, especially in the new industrial urban centers. By 1815 Britain was the world's supreme industrial nation, resulting in both national power and stability.

The Industrial Revolution and its emerging middle class elicited reactionary policies from the conservative, aristocratic Tories who dominated Parliament. Moreover, by the time George IV took the throne, parliamentary policy merely required royal approval, which had come to be taken for granted.

The basic problem remained the partition of power. The old aristocracy, armed with the lessons it felt it had learned from the French Revolution, was more adamant than ever in refusing to yield one iota of its control over the state.

Further, it was generally accepted, according to the theory of "virtual" representation, that a member of Parliament represented the best interests of Britain, not the specific interests of any particular locality. Some fairly liberal Tories, however, felt that public protests of injustice had validity and responded by passing legislation reforming labor, criminal, and religious toleration laws.

The Tories refused to reform electoral laws, however, which, written centuries before the radical population shifts and class changes forced by the Industrial Revolution, deprived many citizens of representation. The Tories lost the 1830 election on this issue of election reform, and the new Whig, or liberal, majority in the House of Commons gave priority to the issue, and began a gradual reform of the electoral system.

After considerable maneuvering and difficulties, the Whigs were successful in 1832, when the Reform Bill fundamentally altered the nature and philosophy of Parliament. Henceforth, the concept of actual representation was to gain steadily on that of virtual representation.

Victoria (ruled 1837–1901). Reform was achieved in other areas, as well. For the remainder of the 1800's, both Whig and Tory cabinets under Queen Victoria passed masses of legislation that radically changed the structure of English society.

Slavery in the colonies was abolished in 1833. Factory acts limited working hours and set standards for conditions and wages, while other laws regulated trade unions. Poor laws established national relief programs. As the century drew to a close, Parliament overhauled the judiciary and the educational systems and established a public health system.

During Victoria's reign many Englishmen felt that their constitution and their society had reached a perfect

British Colonialism in 1914

DOMINION OF CANADA

GREAT BRITAIN

BERMUDA

BAHAMAS

GIBRALTAR

CYPRUS

KUWAIT

INDIA

BURMA

AREAS OF INFLUENCE PORTS OF: SHANGHAI HONG KONG

BARBADOS GRENADA TRINIDAD

ANGLO-EGYPTIAN SUDAN

ADEN

AREAS OF INFLUENCE

ANDAMAN IS.

BR. HONDURAS

NIGERIA

BR. SOMALI-LAND

CEYLON MALDIVES

SARAWAK

SIERRA LEONE

GOLD COAST

UGANDA

PAPUA TERR.

BR. GUIANA

ASCENCION IS.

BR. EAST AFRICA

SEYCHELLES

SOLOMON IS.

FIJI

SAMOA

ST. HELENA

NYASALAND

CHAGOS ARCHIPELAGO

MAURITIUS

NEW HEBRIDES

TONGA

BECHUANALAND

COCOS IS.

PITCAIRN IS.

N. AND S. RHODESIA

UNION OF SOUTH AFRICA

COMMONWEALTH OF AUSTRALIA

TASMANIA

TRISTAN DA CUNHA

FALKLAND IS.

GOUGH IS.

PR. EDWARD IS.

NEW ZEALAND

S. GEORGIA IS.

S. SANDWICH IS.

BARBIERI

THE BRITISH EMPIRE *at its height in the late 1800's under Queen Victoria* (left) *was immense, covering large parts of the world. It grew quickly—and has as quickly melted away.*

balance that insured peace at home and abroad and guaranteed continued prosperity. England seemed to be at a peak of power and progress.

Industry and trade had made Britain the most prosperous state in the world. It became the leading political power after the 1850's, when it acquired colonies all over the world. Benjamin Disraeli, who became prime minister in 1868, was the guiding light of English imperialism. In 1875 he acquired a controlling interest in the Suez Canal Company. By the end of the century, Britain had gained colonies or commercial interests in the Far East, the Middle East, and Africa, in addition to its older colonies in North America and the Caribbean.

But Britain's imperial role brought the country into conflict with other colonial powers. All the major European countries were establishing colonies in Africa and Asia, and Britain sought to

compete. It became involved in a series of crises and conflicts over colonial territories, from the Afghan and Zulu wars of the late 1870's through the South African Boer War of 1899–1902.

By the end of the 1800's the optimism and confidence that had marked the mid-1800's had waned considerably in Britain. In addition to conflicts abroad, industry at home ceased to enjoy the unquestioned superiority it had once held over other nations, and agriculture began to suffer from foreign competition.

Edward VII (ruled 1901–1910). In the early years of the 1900's, during the reign of Queen Victoria's son, Edward VII, two Liberal governments passed radical social welfare legislation, including old-age pensions and national unemployment and medical insurance.

In 1909 the Liberals in the House of Commons introduced a radical "people's budget" designed to put the burden of taxes on the rich. By refusing to pass the bill, the House of Lords was deprived of its dominant position in the government.

George V (ruled 1910–1936). In 1910, the year that George V came to the throne, the House of Commons passed a law limiting the power of the Lords over the Commons on all issues.

Ireland remained a problem. In 1912 the introduction of a series of bills that would have provided home rule for Ireland led to a crisis between

the government and the people of Protestant Ulster, who declared their intention to resist home rule. A showdown was prevented only by the outbreak of war in Europe in 1914.

A series of international crises involving the great powers after 1900 had encouraged Britain to make alliances with France (1904) and Russia (1907) to counteract the Triple Alliance of Germany, Austria-Hungary, and Italy. A dispute between Austria-Hungary and Serbia in the summer of 1914 led to the outbreak of World War I. Britain declared war on Germany on August 4, 1914.

The war was costly for England and resulted in a staggering loss of men before it ended in November, 1918. The war also severely damaged the British economy and drained industrial resources. As a result, Britain lost its preeminent world economic position to newly industrialized nations that had suffered less during the war, notably the United States.

British international political power declined as well, as the nation's colonial empire began to disintegrate. At a conference in 1926, Britain and its domains agreed to form an association in which no member should have subordinate status—the British Commonwealth of Nations. The era of British imperial power was drawing to a close. The Commonwealth agreement was formalized in 1931 by the Statute of Westminster.

The United Kingdom itself lost one

PRIME MINISTER CHURCHILL *visits a bombed area of London during the German aerial blitz in 1941. This was Britain's finest hour—but nearly its last as a major world power.*

of its members when Ireland rebelled in 1920. In 1922 it became the Irish Free State, and only Ulster, in the north, remained British.

Britain's main problems in the 1900's were economic. Neither the co-alition Liberal-Conservative govern-ments, nor the first governments of the newly formed socialistic Labor Party, nor the Conservative governments in power between 1918 and 1931, suc-ceeded in improving England's poor economic situation.

The economy never fully recovered after World War I, and unemployment spread. As Britain lost colonies and fell behind in manufacturing, its trade also declined. The worldwide eco-nomic depression of the 1930's wors-ened Britain's situation.

George VI (ruled 1936–1952). In 1936 Edward VIII came to the throne and abdicated in less than a year. He was succeeded by his brother George VI. A national coalition government of Conservatives, Liberals, and Laborites, formed in 1931, held power through-out the 1930's.

The government's attempts to cope with the depression extended Britain's broad social welfare programs and in-troduced great control by the govern-ment over industry and trade. Little progress was made, however, and the depression's cure was left largely to time.

Inactivity marked the coalition's foreign policy. Britain had entered the "collective security" agreements of the League of Nations and the Locarno

Pact in the 1920's, but, in a policy of appeasement, failed to stand by these agreements when confronted by the aggressive foreign policies of Fascist Italy and Nazi Germany.

The policy of appeasement reached its peak in 1938 when Prime Minister Neville Chamberlain consented to Nazi occupation of the Sudeten Ger-man region of Czechoslovakia in meet-ings with Adolf Hitler at Munich. In March, 1939, Hitler repudiated the Munich agreements by annexing the remainder of Czechoslovakia.

World War II. Realizing the failure of Chamberlain's appeasement policy, the British and French governments reaffirmed their guarantee of the in-dependence of Poland. By the end of the summer, however, Hitler invaded Poland, and on September 3, 1939, Britain and France declared war on Germany.

Within nine months Holland, Bel-gium, and France had fallen, and Brit-ain stood virtually alone against the Germans. In May, 1940, Winston Churchill succeeded Chamberlain as prime minister, and, at the head of a coalition government, provided vigor-ous leadership in the resistance to Ger-man air attacks in 1940 and 1941.

Churchill led Britain into alliances with the Soviet Union and the United States that brought about the defeat of Italy in 1943 and of Germany in 1945. After the war, Britain took on a large measure of responsibility in the mak-ing of the peace and in the subsequent formation of the United Nations. In

July, 1945, a general election replaced Churchill with a Labor government led by Clement Attlee.

Contemporary Britain. World War II spelled the final blow for British impe-rialism. Britain divested itself with relative grace and ease of an empire upon which the sun had never set in the 19th century. The great subconti-nent of India became the two nations of India and Pakistan, the Suez Canal was relinquished after an abortive at-tempt to retain it in 1956, and Rhode-sia in Africa declared its independence in 1965, with its white-dominated gov-ernment refusing to yield to British de-mands that it agree to grant popular representation to its black citizens. Later, through a combination of guer-rilla action and British negotiation, the black state of Zimbabwe Rhodesia was acclaimed in 1979.

The 1970's and 1980's saw more longstanding colonies become in-dependent: the Windward Islands of the former British West Indies, the Gilbert Islands (now Kiribati), the El-lice Islands (now Tuvalu), the New Hebrides French-Anglo condominium (now Vanuatu), and others.

Meanwhile, Labor took advantage of its first clear majority over all other parties and carried through a sweep-ing program of economic reform be-fore it fell in 1951. It greatly expanded programs of national insurance; it cre-ated the National Health Service, which provided low cost medical care; and it nationalized the Bank of Eng-land, the coal industry, and the rail-roads, among others.

The great cost of World War II to Britain had worsened its already criti-cal economic situation. The national debt had tripled during the war, and the domestic economy was drastically dislocated. It was essential that Britain regain its all-important overseas mar-kets and increase trade to get the coun-try back on a sound economic basis.

In 1949 the pound sterling was de-valued, to stimulate exports and in-dustry. Rationing of food, fuel, and other consumer goods imposed during the war continued into the 1950's.

In 1952 George VI died. He was suc-ceeded by his daughter Elizabeth II (ruled 1952–   ). An unfavorable balance of payments, inflation, low levels of investment in industry, and militancy by certain trade unions, ac-companied by some crippling strikes, confronted several Conservative gov-ernments and, after 1964, a Labor gov-ernment led by Harold Wilson.

Labor's efforts to restore economic balance met with little early success. Wilson's government imposed tight controls on wages and prices, reduced private spending abroad, reduced over-seas defense commitments, national-ized the steel industry, and accelerated the pace of granting independence to remaining British dependencies.

The relative weakness of England's economic position, in contrast to the

CHARLES AND LADY DIANA *in 1981. They are now the Prince and Princess of Wales.*

position of other highly industrialized European nations in the Common Market, became the central issue that the Common Market had to face once England became a member in 1973. England's lagging productivity was brought to the fore by the election in 1979 of the Conservative Party under the leadership of Margaret Thatcher.

Prime Minister Thatcher promised to steer the nation away from the burdensome socialist and welfare programs that the Labor Party had imposed since World War II. She proposed to return some of England's nationalized industries to private ownership, to cut personal income taxes, and to restrict the labor unions' power to demand unreasonable and inflationary wage and benefit increases.

In April 1982 war broke out between Britain and Argentina after Argentina invaded the British colony of the Falkland Islands. The war ended two months later with the retaking of the islands by the British.

Vatican City

Official name: *State of the Vatican City*
Area: *109 acres*
Population: *(1983) 1,000*
Language: *Italian, Latin*
Religion: *Roman Catholic*
Currency unit: *Lira*
National holiday: *Celebration of the coronation of the Holy Father.*

Vatican City, located in Rome, Italy, is the world's smallest sovereign state. It is the seat of the central administration of the Roman Catholic Church and the residence of the supreme pontiff, or pope. The term "the Vatican" is frequently used to refer to both the central administration of the church and the government of Vatican City.

Vatican City lies on the west bank of the Tiber River. It includes St. Peter's Basilica, St. Peter's Square, the Vatican palaces, Belvedere Park, and the Vatican Gardens.

The Vatican also exercises extraterritorial sovereignty over a dozen buildings and some territory in or near Rome, including the basilicas of St. Mary Major, St. John Lateran, and St. Paul outside the Walls; the pope's summer residence at Castel Gandolfo; and the Vatican radio station at Santa Maria di Galeria.

The Vatican population consists of clergy of all nations, the Vatican guard, and a number of lay personnel in the service of the Vatican.

Government. The Vatican is ruled by the pope, who has absolute power. He delegates much of the actual administration of the Vatican to the Pontifical Commission for the State of the Vatican City. The commission has five members and is headed by a governor.

The Vatican's diplomatic relations with foreign countries are carried on by the Secretariat of State. The Vatican maintains diplomatic relations with about 107 countries. The pope is pledged to neutrality in political disputes between governments except when his mediation is requested by both sides. There is also a permanent observer at the United Nations.

History. The traditional seat of the papacy has always been Rome. Throughout the Middle Ages the popes controlled not only the city of Rome but large territories in central Italy, the Papal States. The popes lost most of the territory that formed the Papal States during the Italian struggle for unification in the 1850's and 1860's.

In 1849 a Roman Republic was declared, and France, intervening on behalf of the pope, sent troops to Rome. The Kingdom of Italy was formed in 1861, and in 1870, when French troops were withdrawn on the outbreak of the Franco-Prussian War, Rome was added to the new kingdom.

In 1871 the Italian government passed the Law of Guarantees granting the papacy full sovereignty over Vatican City and an annual income from the Italian treasury. The pope refused the offer. The 1929 Lateran Treaties restored relations with Italy however.

The treaties recognized the sovereignty of the papacy within Vatican City, regulated the status of the church in Italy, and arranged for an indemnity to be paid to the papacy as compensation for the loss of the Papal States. In 1947 the terms of the Lateran Treaties were incorporated into the constitution of the Italian Republic itself.

In 1976 the treaties were revised so that Roman Catholicism would no longer be recognized as Italy's official religion, and religious education would no longer be required in schools.

Yugoslavia

Official name: *Socialist Federal Republic of Yugoslavia*
Area: *98,766 sq. mi., 255,804 sq. km.*
Population: *(1980) 22,330,000*
Capital: *Belgrade (Pop., 1982, 1,250,000)*
Language: *Serbo-Croatian, Slovenian, Macedonian*
Religion: *Orthodox Christian, Roman Catholic, Islam*
Currency unit: *Dinar*
National holiday: *Proclamation of the republic, Nov. 29*

Vatican seal

corn

Yugoslavia, a nation on the west of the Balkan peninsula in southeast Europe, is bounded on the north by Austria and Hungary, on the east by Rumania and Bulgaria, on the south by Greece and Albania, and on the west by the Adriatic Sea and Italy.

The land. Yugoslavia has three major geographic regions. The first is the Dalmatian plain that extends along the irregular Adriatic coastline.

The second is the mountainous region that covers about two-thirds of Yugoslavia. The most important ranges are the Julian Alps, which form Yugoslavia's northwest border with Italy and Austria, and the Dinaric Alps, running parallel to the Adriatic coast, south to the Albanian border.

The third region is the interior lowlands, dominated by the Vojvodina lowland in northern Yugoslavia. This fertile area, formed by the Danube River and its tributaries, is Yugoslavia's chief food-producing region.

South of the Vojvodina in Serbia is the valley of the Morava River, the country's second major agricultural region. To the south, the Vardar valley separates Serbia from Macedonia. It is largely unfit for cultivation.

Climate. Yugoslavia has a varied climate. The Adriatic coast has a mild climate with cool, rainy winters and hot, dry summers. The northwest and the Dinaric Alps have warm summers and cold winters. The northeast has a continental climate with seasonal extremes of heat and cold.

The people. Yugoslavia is a multinational state. The population is about 40 percent Serbian, 23 percent Croatian, nine percent Slovene, and six percent Macedonian. There are many minorities, the largest being Albanians, Hungarians, and Turks.

There is also considerable religious diversity. About 50 percent of the population is Orthodox Christian, 30 percent Roman Catholic, ten percent Muslim, and one percent Protestant.

The majority of the population speaks Serbo-Croatian, a South Slavic language written in the Cyrillic alphabet by the Serbs and in the Latin alphabet by the Croatians. The Slovenes and Macedonians speak South Slavic languages of their own.

The country's principal city is the capital, Belgrade. Other large cities include Zagreb, the capital of Croatia, and an important industrial center; Skopje, the capital of Macedonia; Sarajevo, the capital of Bosnia-Hercegovina and a major commercial center; and Ljubljana, the capital of Slovenia and a transportation center.

Economy. Before World War II the Yugoslav economy was based on agriculture and mining. During the postwar period, however, the role played by industry increased greatly under the direction of the Yugoslav Communist Party, which had come to power during the war.

Yugoslavia's economy since then has had one of the highest growth rates in the world. Since the mid-1960's, in order to improve competitiveness in the world market—a weak link in the economy—the government has sought to decentralize the administration of the economy and to increase efficiency in industry, most of which is nationalized.

Natural resources. Yugoslavia is well endowed with minerals and has important deposits of copper, zinc, lead, iron ore, bauxite, mercury, and chromite, as well as some magnesite, asbestos, and pyrites.

Yugoslavia produced 4.1 million metric tons of petroleum in 1979, enough to supply half of the domestic energy demand. Next to petroleum, hydroelectric power is the most important energy resource. In 1978, 51.4 billion kilowatt hours of electricity were produced.

Agriculture. After a brief and not very successful experiment with collectivization in the immediate postwar period, Yugoslavia returned to a system of private land ownership. Collective farms do exist, particularly in the north, but about 80 percent of the country's arable land is privately owned.

Private holdings are limited to small 25-acre plots. This contributes to the fact that nearly half of the labor force works in agriculture. But small farms are not well suited to modern farming methods. This fact, coupled with recurrent droughts, has kept agricultural production low. Since the 1970's, however, there has been rapid technological improvement in farming in order to raise production efficiency.

Cereal grains, particularly corn and wheat, are planted on most of the land. Other major crops include potatoes, sugar beets, and hemp. Feed crops are gaining in importance. Tobacco, which is raised in Macedonia, is a leading export crop. Wine grapes are grown on the Adriatic coast and fruit is raised in Croatia and Serbia.

The raising of livestock and poultry is important, and meat is one of Yugoslavia's most valuable exports.

Industry. Yugoslavian industry was largely underdeveloped before World War II, but it now accounts for 40 percent of the national product, even though only 18 percent of the labor force is employed in manufacturing.

Growth has been greatest in heavy industry, and major increases have been made in the production of iron, steel, and chemicals. Other industries produce ships, machinery, textiles, foodstuffs, construction materials, leather, paper, rubber, tobacco, and beverages.

Yugoslavia has a thriving handicraft industry, and textiles, leather, wood, and metal goods are made in many parts of the country.

Trade. Yugoslavia is troubled by a poor balance of trade and is attempting to improve the competitiveness of its exports. In 1982 exports earned only $10.2 billion, while imports cost $13.3 billion.

Major exports are live animals, machinery and transportation equipment, minerals, chemicals, beverages, tobacco, and textiles. Principal imports are cereal grains, industrial raw materials, chemicals, coal, manufactured goods, and machinery and transportation equipment. Yugoslavia's major trading partners include the Soviet Union, Italy, East and West Germany, the United States, Britain, and Poland.

Government. Yugoslavia is officially a republic. Political life is controlled by the country's Communist Party, however, though the new constitution of 1974 was designed to give workers more representation in economic policy-making, and to give the people more representation in government. The constitution is based on the "assembly system."

Legislative power is vested in the Federal Assembly, which consists of two chambers: the Federal Chamber, and the Chamber of Representatives and Provinces. Chamber deputies, popularly elected either directly or indirectly, all serve four-year terms.

The executive organ of the Federal Assembly is a nine-member collective presidency. President Josip Broz Tito was its president-elect for a lifelong term (since 1974). Tito died in 1980, and it is supposed that leadership will rotate among the nine members. Members of this agency, representing each of the country's nine republics and provinces, are elected to one-time, five year terms. They, in turn, elect the president of the collective presidency. He is the most powerful person in the government. Yugoslavia is a member of the United Nations.

History. In the 500's the South Slavs, or "Yugo Slavs," migrated into the Balkan peninsula from territories to the east. During the Middle Ages the histories of the various tribes that composed the South Slavs began to diverge widely.

The Slovenes in the northwest became part of the Frankish empire in the 700's. They were under German rule until 1918. The Croatians in the north had an independent kingdom until they came under Hungarian domination in 1102.

The Serbs in the east were part of the Byzantine Empire until the 1100's, when they established a kingdom that reached its height in the 1300's under Stephen Dushan. It remained independent until 1389, when

TITO OF YUGOSLAVIA. *As a partisan in World War II, he won the trust and help of the Allies, though a Communist. The trust was justified by his later moderate rule as president.*

it was absorbed by the Ottoman Empire. By 1500 not only Serbia, but also Macedonia, Bosnia, Hercegovina, and Montenegro had fallen to the Ottoman Turks. After the Ottoman defeat of Hungary in 1520, most of Slovenia and Croatia were added to the Ottoman Empire.

Independence and unity. During the 1800's, with the decline of the Ottoman Empire, the South Slavs began to agitate for independence. In 1878 the Treaty of Berlin, which settled the Russo-Turkish War of 1877–1878, guaranteed the independence of Serbia and Montenegro.

These two small states, influenced by the doctrine of Pan-Slavism, or Slavic unity, enlisted the support of Russia, the most powerful Slavic state, in the struggle for complete South Slav independence and unity.

In October, 1908, Austria announced the annexation of Bosnia and Hercegovina, two Slav provinces that Serbia had hoped to bring under Serbian authority. To resist the encroachments of the Ottoman and Austrian empires, a Balkan League was organized in the spring of 1912. Balkan wars broke out in 1912 and 1913, and Serbia conquered much of Macedonia from Turkey.

In 1914 World War I was precipitated by the assassination at Sarajevo, the capital of Bosnia, of Franz Ferdinand, heir to the Austro-Hungarian throne, by a Bosnian nationalist. The defeat of Austria-Hungary and of Ottoman Turkey in the war and the sympathy of the Allies, particularly of the United States, helped the South Slavs to gain full independence.

In November, 1918, Montenegro declared itself united with Serbia, and on December 1, 1918, the Kingdom of the Serbs, Croats, and Slovenes was proclaimed. King Peter of Serbia became king under the regency of Prince Alexander. In January, 1921, a new constitution providing for a centralized government was proclaimed. In August, King Peter died and was succeeded by Alexander.

Internal dissension. This success in bringing all Yugoslavs into the new kingdom was soon overshadowed by the enormous problems facing the new state. The Yugoslavs had been ruled for hundreds of years by empires with varying cultures, and they not only had different traditions but different religions. The Yugoslavs who had been under Austria-Hungary were Roman Catholic, whereas those ruled by the Turks were either Orthodox Christian or Muslim.

National and religious diversity presented a serious difficulty, particularly because the 1921 constitution reflected the centralistic wishes of the Serbs, who dominated the new state. The kingdom of Serbia was the nucleus of Yugoslavia, whose army and bureaucracy were generally dominated by Serbia. This, combined with Serbian insensitiveness to the feelings of the other groups, especially the Croatians, led to animosity and friction.

In 1929 King Alexander established a dictatorship, and changed the name of the country to Yugoslavia. Alexander was assassinated by a Macedonian revolutionary associated with Croatian extremists in 1934. Peter II, only eleven years old, became king under the regency of Prince Paul. In 1939 Paul permitted the establish-

ment of a democracy that gave Croatians full economic and cultural freedom. But his pro-German position was unpopular and pro-Allied Serbs, led by Peter II, staged a successful military coup on March 27, 1941.

World War II. Following the coup, on April 6, Germany invaded Yugoslavia. King Peter fled the country and set up a government in exile in London. Pro-German puppet states were established in Croatia and Serbia, and the rest of the country was divided among Germany, Italy, Hungary, Italian-ruled Albania, and Bulgaria.

Yugoslavia became one of the bloodiest battlefields of the war, as liberation guerrilla armies fought each other as well as foreign occupying forces. The two major liberation forces were the Communist Partisans, led by Josip Broz, who came to be known by his single guerrilla pseudonym, Tito; and the Chetniks, led by General Draza Mihajlović.

Although the Chetniks were the official Yugoslav resistance movement, supported by the exiled government, after 1943 the Allies began to support the Partisans, enabling them to gain control of the country after the war.

Communist control. Following Communist-controlled elections in 1945, the Federal People's Republic of Yugoslavia was proclaimed on November 29 by Tito and his Partisans.

During the immediate postwar period, Yugoslavia was a firm supporter of the Soviet Union. In 1948, however, Joseph Stalin, who had been disturbed by Tito's independence in foreign and domestic policy, broke with Yugoslavia. The other Communist-controlled states of Eastern Europe followed the Soviet lead and severed ties with Yugoslavia.

Following the break, Yugoslav leaders began to reevaluate their economic policies. Agricultural collectivization was abandoned as unworkable in the early 1950's, central controls were somewhat relaxed by a revised constitution in 1953, and workers' and producers' councils were formed to allow workers a greater degree of responsibility in policy-making.

Yugoslavia, under Tito, steered a middle course in international affairs, supporting the Soviet Union at times, while accepting economic, military, and technical aid from the West, particularly the United States. Tito was opposed to the Soviet invasion of Czechoslovakia in 1968.

In the 1970's and 1980's, Yugoslavia's economy began to show serious problems, including a growing international debt and soaring inflation. After Tito's death in 1980, a resurgence of nationalist sentiment and ethnic strife increased the difficulties facing the central government. In 1989 the government introduced a number of important economic and political reforms in an effort to prevent the country's disintegration.

DEPENDENCIES IN EUROPE

Danish Dependencies

The Faeroe Islands (540 square miles) is a group of 18 islands, including Streymoy, Eysturoy, and Váagar. The islands are located in the Atlantic Ocean, 300 miles northeast of the Shetlands. The Faeroes, with a population of 43,000 (1979), are self-governing, but as an integral part of the Danish kingdom they also have two representatives in the Danish Parliament. The islands have been Danish since 1340. Fishing, whaling, and sheepherding are the most important economic activities.

Greenland (840,000 square miles), the largest island in the world, is located in the North Atlantic Ocean and the Polar Sea. It became a Danish province in 1953 and was granted internal self-rule in 1979. With 49,000 people (1979), it has two representatives in the Danish Parliament. It was Norwegian from 1261 to 1814, when it first became Danish. There is some mining on the island, although most of its resources are unexplored. Fishing and fur hunting are its main economic activities. Nuuk, formerly called Gothab, is its capital.

Norwegian Dependencies

Jan Mayen (143 square miles) is an uninhabited island, 300 miles northeast of Iceland, in the Arctic Circle. Originally discovered by Henry Hudson in the early 1600's, it has been a Norwegian dependency since 1929. An Icelandic-Norwegian dispute concerning part of its offshore area was settled in 1980. A research station is located here.

Svalbard (23,957 square miles), a group of islands in the Arctic Ocean, has a population of 3431 (1975). It has been a Norwegian dependency since 1925. Spitsbergen is the most important of these islands, which also include North East Land, Barents Island, and Edge Island. There are rich coal deposits here, particularly on Spitsbergen. They are exploited by Soviet and Norwegian mining camps.

United Kingdom Dependencies

Gibraltar (2.3 square miles), a massive, rocky headland on the southern coast of Spain, at the entrance to the Mediterranean Sea, has 29,000 people (1979). It has been a British crown colony since 1704. Although in 1966 Spain demanded its independence, in 1967, by popular referendum, it chose to remain British. In 1969, the United Nations requested Britain to liberate it. Spanish-British negotiations have gone on sporadically since 1972. Gibraltar's economy revolves around its flourishing tourism industry, and the needs of its British naval base.

THE COLONIAL POWERS *built their empires in Asia, Africa, and the Americas. There never were many dependencies in Europe. Today the largest European-owned dependency is Greenland (the harbor at Julianehaab,* below left), *the most interesting Gibraltar* (right), *with its apes.*

CITIES OF EUROPE

Amsterdam, the capital of the Netherlands, located in the province of North Holland. The city lies at the junction of the Amstel and IJ rivers near the IJsselmeer (formerly the Zuider Zee). It is connected by canal with the North Sea and the Rhine River.

Amsterdam is the commercial and industrial center of the Netherlands and one of its busiest ports. Its most important manufactures include iron and steel, machinery, chemicals, paper, printed matter, and beer. Amsterdam also is a center of the diamond-cutting industry. Pop., 933,593.

Antwerp, the second largest city in Belgium and the country's chief port. It is located on the Scheldt River about 50 miles (80 km.) inland from the North Sea. Antwerp has one of the world's largest harbors and is among the busiest ports in Europe.

Antwerp's major industries include shipbuilding, metallurgy, brewing, distilling, lacemaking, sugar refining, and diamond cutting. The city has many historic buildings and art treasures. Pop., 673,111.

Arkhangelsk, or Archangel, a seaport on the northwestern coast of the Soviet Union, near the mouth of the Northern Dvina River. Owing to its northern location, Arkhangelsk is blocked by ice for six months of the year, although it is kept open longer by icebreakers. The port has numerous sawmills, and timber is its chief export. Railroads connect the city with Moscow and Leningrad. Pop., 391,000.

Athens, the capital and largest city of Greece, located on the Attic plain, about five miles inland from its port of Piraeus on the Saronic Gulf. Named after the classical Greek goddess of wisdom, Athens was the cultural center of ancient Greece. The flat-topped hill of the Acropolis, which overlooks the city, contains the ruins of some of the most beautiful buildings of ancient Greece.

Modern Athens is the center of Greece's political, cultural, and economic life. The products of its wide variety of industries include ships, food, steel, chemicals, beverages, and textiles. Athens is one of the busiest ports on the Mediterranean Sea, and lies on major railroad and airline routes. Pop., 867,023.

NETHERLANDS INFORMATION SERVICE

AMSTERDAM *and one of its canals. The city, laced with canals that are still heavily used, has a rich past as a commercial and agricultural center, particularly in the 1600's.*

Barcelona, on the northeast Mediterranean coast of Spain, the capital of Barcelona Province and the second largest city in the country. Barcelona is Spain's leading manufacturing center and its largest port. Its major industries produce textiles, chemicals, machinery, electrical equipment, office machines, and automobiles. Pop., 2,750,000.

Basel, in northern Switzerland, situated on the Rhine River near the French and West German borders. It is the second largest city in Switzerland and a major river port. Basel is also an important railroad junction and travel center. The chief local industries produce dyes, chemicals, silk textiles, and pharmaceuticals. Pop., 367,000.

Belfast, the capital of Northern Ireland, located on the east coast, at the mouth of the Lagan River. The city is Northern Ireland's leading port and manufacturing center. Belfast's industries produce linen and other textiles, ships, aircraft, processed foods, tobacco, and whiskey. Many educational institutions are located in Belfast, including Queen's University. Pop., 494,032.

Belgrade, the capital of Yugoslavia, located on the Danube River, about 50 miles (80 km.) from the Rumanian border. The city is an active port and a transportation and industrial center. Belgrade's industries produce chemicals, machine tools, electrical equipment, paper, textiles, and processed foods. It is the seat of the University of Belgrade and has many museums. Pop., 746,105.

Berlin, in East Germany, located on the Spree and Havel rivers, about 100 miles (160 km.) inside East Germany. Berlin was the capital of Germany until the end of World War II, when it was divided into four zones and occupied by the United States, France, Britain, and the Soviet Union.

In 1949 the American, British, and French zones became West Berlin and the Soviet zone became East Berlin. East Berlin is now the capital of East Germany and West Berlin, although it has close ties with West Germany, is not a constitutional part of the latter. East and West Berlin are financial, commercial, and manufacturing centers whose chief products are chemicals, electrical equipment, machinery, and foodstuffs. Pop., West Berlin,

1,926,826; East Berlin, 1,111,398.

Bern, the capital of Switzerland and of Bern Canton, located in the west-central part of the country, on the Aare River. Its varied manufactures include chemicals, precision instruments, machinery, and chocolate. It is a cultural, educational, banking, and commercial center. Pop., 145,500.

Birmingham, in south-central England, located in the West Midlands. The second largest city in England, Birmingham is one of the world's leading industrial centers. The city specializes in the manufacture of motor vehicles, bicycles, machinery, and electrical products. The production of iron, steel, and nonferrous metals is also important. Pop., 2,437,000.

Bologna, in north-central Italy, at the foot of the Apennines, about 50 miles (80 km.) north of Florence. Bologna is the capital of the political region of Emilia-Romagna. The city is an industrial, commercial, and educational center. Manufactures include machinery, chemicals, electric motors, and shoes. Bologna is also a tourist center and an important agricultural market. Pop., 481,120.

Bonn, the capital of West Germany, situated on the Rhine River, 15 miles (24 km.) south of Cologne. Long an educational and cultural center, the city is noted for its architecture, its museums, and its university. After it became the West German capital in 1949, Bonn expanded rapidly. The city's industries produce electrical equipment, chemicals, pharmaceuticals, and precision instruments. Pop., 284,000.

Bordeaux, in southwestern France, located on the Garonne River. The city is an important seaport and a leading commercial and cultural center. Its principal industries are oil refining, shipbuilding, and food processing. It produces and exports red and white wines that are world famous. The history of Bordeaux dates back to Roman times, and in old sections there are Roman ruins and medieval buildings. Pop., 591,447.

Bristol, a port on the west coast of Britain, located at the junction of the Avon and Frome rivers, near the Bristol Channel. The city is one of Britain's most important ports. The leading industry is the design and manufacture of aircraft, but nuclear engineering, chemicals, food processing, and printing are also important. Bristol is an ancient city and has many historic buildings. It is the seat of several fine secondary schools and of Bristol University. Pop., 409,900.

Brussels, the capital and largest city of Belgium, located near the center of

CANTERBURY CATHEDRAL, *seat of the Archbishop of Canterbury, primate of the Anglican Church. Here Thomas à Becket was murdered. His martyr's shrine attracts countless pilgrims.*

the country, on the Senne River. Brussels is an important administrative, financial, and cultural center. The city manufactures chemicals, machinery, textiles, electrical equipment, and rubber goods. Brussels is famous for its lace and carpets. Pop., 2,216,938.

Bucharest, the capital and largest city of Rumania, located in central Walachia, on the Dimbovita River. The city is the country's commercial, industrial, and cultural center. Its industries produce machinery, electrical equipment, textiles, clothing, chemicals, and processed foods. Bucharest is known for its many cultural and educational institutions. Pop., 1,807,044.

Budapest, the capital and largest city of Hungary, on the Danube River, in the north-central part of the country. As Hungary's largest industrial center, Budapest produces iron and steel, textiles, electronic equipment, pharmaceuticals, machinery, and processed foods. The city is also the cultural and educational center of Hungary and has several museums and libraries. It is the seat of the Academy of Sciences. Pop., 2,085,615.

Cambridge, in eastern England, on the Cam River, about 50 miles (80 km.) north of London. It is the home of Cambridge University and contains many medieval and Renaissance churches. Pop., 101,700.

Canterbury, in southeastern England, on the Stour River, about 55 miles (89 km.) southeast of London. The cathedral of Canterbury is the seat of the Church of England's ranking prelate, the archbishop of Canterbury. The city has many other churches and buildings of historic interest. Pop., 117,400.

Cardiff, the capital and largest city of Wales, on the Taff River, near the Bristol Channel in western Britain. Cardiff is the cultural and educational center of Wales. Its major industries include food processing, iron and steel manufacture, and ship repairing. Pop., 278,900.

Chelyabinsk, a city in the west-central Soviet Union, in the eastern foothills of the Urals, on the Mias River. It is a major metallurgical and industrial center that produces iron and steel, industrial and agricultural machinery, tractors, machine tools, and bulldozers. It lies on the Trans-Siberian Railroad. Pop., 1,007,000.

Cologne, or Köln, in western West Germany, on the Rhine River in the state of North Rhine-Westphalia. The Rhineland's most important industrial center, Cologne manufactures iron and steel, railroad cars, diesel engines, machinery, and textiles. It is a busy river port and has extensive shipyards. It is also a leading cultural and educational center. Cologne Cathedral is the city's most famous landmark. Pop., 976,761.

Copenhagen, or København, the capital and largest city of Denmark, lying on Sjaelland and Amager islands. An important industrial center, the city produces ships, machinery, and chemicals. It has an excellent natural harbor and is a major European port. The city is the seat of Copenhagen University and the cultural center of Denmark. Pop., 699,300.

Córdoba, or Cordova, a city of south-central Spain, situated on the Guadalquivir River at the foot of the Sierra Morena. The city is an industrial, commercial, and tourist center. The manufacture of leather goods, traditionally Córdoba's most important industry, has been surpassed by textile mills, distilleries, and heavy industries.

Once a center of Arab power, Córdoba shows strong Muslim influence in its architecture. Notable are the Cathedral of Córdoba, formerly a Muslim mosque, an alcazar, and a Moorish bridge. Pop., 253,632.

Donetsk, a city in the southern European Soviet Union, in the Ukraine, on the Kalmius River. It is the leading industrial center of the Donets Basin, with coal mines, foundries, metallurgical plants, chemical works, and machinery plants. It has a university and a number of technical colleges. Pop., 984,000.

Dresden, an East German industrial city situated on the Elbe River. Its manufactures include chemicals, machinery, optical instruments, and glass. It is also an important river port. The city's buildings include some excellent examples of Baroque architecture. Pop., 512,490.

Dublin, the capital, largest city, and chief port of the Republic of Ireland, located on Ireland's east coast at the mouth of the Liffey River.

Dublin is a major transportation, commercial, and administrative center. Its industries include brewing and distilling, flour milling, and textile weaving. The city is Ireland's cultural and educational center, containing a large university, a cathedral, and many museums and libraries. Pop., 543,563.

Düsseldorf, the capital of the West German state of North Rhine-Westphalia, situated on the Rhine north of Cologne. One of the largest and most industrialized cities of the Rhineland, Düsseldorf manufactures iron and steel, chemicals, textiles, and glass. The city has a large harbor and an excellent railroad system. Pop., 607,560.

Edinburgh, the capital of Scotland and the seat of Midlothian county. It is located on the south shore of the Firth of Forth in southeastern Scotland. Edinburgh is a residential and administrative city. It is noted for its cultural and educational activities and historic buildings. The principal industries are printing, papermaking, chemicals, brewing, and distilling. Pop., 463,923.

Florence, in central Italy, on the banks of the Arno River, in the western Apennines. It is the capital of Tuscany and a center of commerce and light industry. One of the world's foremost art centers, Florence attracts many tourists. Handicrafts include textiles, pottery, jewelry, and leather goods. A flood in 1966 damaged many art treasures and buildings. Pop., 464,020.

Frankfurt-am-Main, in central West Germany, on the Main River, about 100 miles (160 km.) southeast of Cologne. A leading industrial city, Frankfurt's manufactures include machinery, electrical equipment, and chemicals. The city is a commercial and financial center and its location makes it the transportation hub of West Germany. Frankfurt is also an educational and cultural center. Pop., 632,565.

Gdańsk, formerly Danzig, a Polish seaport situated on the Baltic Sea, on the delta of the Vistula River. The port of Gdańsk handles coal, lumber, and grain. Products of the city's varied industries include ships, processed foods, and chemicals. Pop., 444,000.

Geneva, the capital of Geneva canton in southwestern Switzerland, located on the Rhône River at the southern end of Lake Geneva. The city serves as a banking center and as the headquarters for a number of international organizations. Its industries include tourism and the manufacture of clocks, jewelry, precision tools, surgical and optical equipment, leather goods, and textiles.

Geneva is an ancient city that became important during the Reformation. It is an intellectual and cultural center with many schools, museums, libraries, and old buildings. Pop., 322,900.

Genoa, a port in northwestern Italy on the Gulf of Genoa in the Mediterranean Sea. It is the capital of the province of Genoa and the region of Liguria. Genoa's exports include food-

stuffs, marble, and silk. Among the many products of the city's industries are steel, metal goods, and cement. Pop., 795,027.

Glasgow, a port and industrial city of west central Scotland, lying on the Clyde River. Glasgow is the largest city in Scotland with extensive docks and shipyards. Its principal industries are shipping and shipbuilding, followed by the production of chemicals, electronic equipment, carpets, and textiles. Pop., 1,079,000.

Granada, the capital of the province of Granada, situated in southern Spain on the Genil River. The city is the commercial and industrial center for the region. Its chief industries are food processing, brewing and distilling, chemical production, and leather and metal handcrafting. Granada is the site of the Alhambra, an ancient Moorish fortress and palace, and other Moorish and Renaissance buildings. Pop., 190,429.

Graz, a city in southeastern Austria, on the Mur River. It is the second largest city in Austria and is a rail, industrial, and cultural center. Its manufactures include iron and steel, textiles, leather goods, and paper. Pop., 250,893.

Hague, The, the seat of the Netherlands' legislature and royal residence, and the capital of the province of South Holland. The Hague lies near the country's west coast. It is the site of many international conferences and the headquarters of several international organizations. The Hague is mainly a residential city. Pop., 673,391.

Hamburg, the capital of the West German state of Hamburg, with which it is coextensive, situated at the confluence of the Elbe, Aster, and Bille rivers, near the North Sea. Hamburg is Germany's largest seaport and an important industrial center. Shipping and shipbuilding are the city's major industries, followed by the manufacture of machinery, chemicals, and metal products. Hamburg also has important food processing industries. Pop., 1,680,340.

Heidelberg, in southwestern West Germany, on the Neckar River. Its manufactures include machinery, printing presses, protective clothing, precision instruments, and metal goods. It is a major tourist center and is famous for its university. Pop., 129,179.

Helsinki, the capital and largest city of Finland. It is situated on the southern coast, on the Gulf of Finland. Helsinki is a major seaport and the country's chief trading center.

Shipbuilding is Helsinki's leading

industry. The production of textiles, foodstuffs, paper and wood products and ceramics is also important. Helsinki is an educational center with a university and several colleges. Pop., 496,263.

Kiev, a city in the western Soviet Union, the capital of the Ukrainian Soviet Socialist Republic. It is situated on the Knepr River about 450 miles (725 km.) southwest of Moscow. Kiev is a commercial, industrial, and transportation center. Its industries produce electric motors, agricultural machines, radio and telephone equipment, and cables.

Kiev was the capital of a Russian principality in the 800's, and the first seat of the Russian Orthodox Church. It was a sacred place of pilgrimage. It is an educational and cultural center, with museums, old churches and monasteries and a national library. Pop., 2,079,000.

Kraków, or Cracow, a city in southern Poland on the Vistula River. It is a rail and commercial center that manufactures machinery, construction materials, chemicals, paper, and clothing. The city is also a cultural and educational center, with medieval buildings, a Gothic cathedral, a castle, and a university. Pop., 713,000.

Leeds, in north-central England, on the Aire River, about 165 miles (266 km.) northwest of London. It is the center of England's wool industry. Manufactures include textiles and clothing, iron and steel, machinery, chemicals, and leather goods. The city is an important cultural and educational center. Pop., 734,000.

Le Havre, an important seaport on the northern coast of France, at the mouth of the Seine River on the English Channel. Le Havre handles imports and exports for Paris and northwestern France. The city's diverse industries include shipbuilding and the manufacture of machinery, electrical equipment, and chemical products. Le Havre also has an important oil refinery. Pop., 263,978.

Leningrad, the second largest city in the Soviet Union, located at the mouth of the Neva River on the Gulf of Finland, an inlet of the Baltic Sea. The city was known as St. Petersburg until 1914 and as Petrograd until 1924.

Leningrad is a major industrial center. Its industries produce electrical equipment, precision tools, machinery, chemicals, textiles, and paper. It is also an important shipbuilding center. The city has many cultural and educational institutions, including the Hermitage art museum and the University of Leningrad. Pop., 4,425,000.

Lille, in northern France, near the Belgian border, about 130 miles (210 km.) north of Paris. It is one of the largest conurbations in France and a cultural, commercial, and manufacturing center. Lille has long been the textile center of France, and its manufactures include iron and steel, machinery, processed foods, and chemicals. It has a large university and one of the most famous art museums in the world. Pop., 928,569.

Lisbon, the capital and largest city of Portugal, located at the mouth of the Tagus River on the Atlantic Ocean. It is Portugal's leading port, and it exports the country's fish, olive oil, and wine. Lisbon contains most of the country's industry and produces ships, refined oil, textiles, chemicals, processed foods, and tile. The city has many beautiful churches and a number of interesting Moorish and Renaissance buildings. Pop., 829,900.

Liverpool, the second largest seaport in Britain, situated on the Mersey River, near the Irish Sea. The city's economy is based on shipping and warehouse storage, especially of cotton, wool, tobacco, and grain. Liverpool is a rail and distribution center. Its industries produce flour, refined sugar, electrical equipment, chemicals, and rubber. Pop., 1,262,467.

Łódź, the second largest city of Poland, about 75 miles (120 km.) southwest of Warsaw, in the central part of the country. It is an important industrial center and produces textiles and machinery, also electrical equipment, chemicals, and processed foods. Pop., 818,000.

London, the capital of the United Kingdom, and one of the world's largest cities, located on the Thames River about 40 miles (65 km.) from the North Sea. London is Great Britain's major port and commercial center. Its industries produce mostly finished consumer goods, including clothing, metal and electrical goods, chemicals, processed goods, plastics, and cigarettes. London is also a major center for banking, insurance, publishing, and printing.

A city since Roman times, London has many points of historical interest. Its fine educational institutions, libraries, and museums make it an important cultural and intellectual center. London is joined to other parts of Great Britain and the world by an excellent network of land, sea, and air transportation. Pop., 7,028,200.

Luxembourg, capital of Luxembourg, located in the south-central part of the country. The city is an industrial, commercial, and cultural center. Luxembourg's industries produce iron and steel, textiles, leather goods, machinery, and processed foods. Pop., 78,400.

ST. PAUL'S CATHEDRAL, *London, designed by the great Sir Christopher Wren in the 1600's.*

BRITISH TRAVEL ASSOCIATION

TWO GREAT CITIES. *Beer wagon parades in Munich* (left); *the ornate Gum department store, the pride of Moscow.*

Lyon, city in France, situated at the confluence of the Saône and Rhône rivers, in the southeastern part of the country. Lyon is a major commercial and industrial center.

The leading industry is the manufacture of silk textiles, but the city also produces chemicals, drugs, dyes, and electrical machinery. A stock exchange and international banks make it a financial center, and yearly international trade fairs are held in the city. Over 2,000 years old, Lyon has many sections of historical interest. Pop., 1,152,863.

Madrid, the capital and largest city of Spain. The city is located in the region of New Castile, at the geographical center of the Iberian Peninsula. Madrid is situated on a plateau on the Manzanares River. It is Spain's leading administrative, financial, and cultural center. It is also among the nation's chief educational and tourist centers. Manufactures include machinery, leather goods, optical and electrical equipment, plastics, and chemicals. Pop., 3,520,320.

Manchester, in northwestern England, on the Irwell River in Lancashire, about 30 miles (48 km.) northeast of Liverpool. Manchester, Britain's leading manufacturing center, is among the world's chief producers of cotton goods. Other products include plastics, electronic equipment, machinery, chemicals, and rubber goods. Manchester is a railroad junction and an ocean port, linked to the Irish Sea by the deepwater Manchester Ship Canal. Pop., 2,674,000.

Marseille, or Marseilles, in southeastern France, its chief port on the Mediterranean Sea. It is located on the Gulf of Lions, about 25 miles (40 km.) east of the mouth of the Rhône River. It is the capital of the department of Bouches-du-Rhône and a leading industrial center. Manufactures include machinery, sugar, textiles, and olive oil. Pop., 1,004,536.

Milan, in northern Italy, located between the foothills of the Alps and the Po River, near the border with Switzerland. Milan is the second largest city in Italy and the nation's leading industrial and commercial center. Manufactures include aircraft, motor vehicles, heavy machinery, chemicals, and textiles. Pop., 3,817,873.

Minsk, in the far western Soviet Union, the capital of the Belorussian Soviet Socialist Republic. The city is located on a branch of the Berezina River, about 150 miles (240 km.) east of the border with Poland. Minsk is a leading industrial, cultural, and transportation center. Manufactures include trucks, tractors, television sets, and radios. Pop., 1,231,000.

Moscow, the capital and largest city of the Soviet Union. It is located on both banks of the Moscow River, about 400 miles (640 km.) southeast of Leningrad. Moscow is the Soviet Union's industrial, political, and transportation center. Manufactures include motor vehicles, machinery, electrical equipment, chemicals, textiles, and steel.

Moscow is the headquarters of the Communist Party of the Soviet Union and the administrative and cultural center of the nation. Landmarks include the Kremlin, Red Square, St. Basil's Cathedral, and Lenin's tomb. Pop., 6,941,961.

Munich, or München, capital of the state of Bavaria and the third largest city in West Germany. Munich is situated on the Isar river, about 25 miles (40 km.) north of the Bavarian Alps in southeastern West Germany. The city is an important industrial, commercial, and transportation center.

In addition to beer, for which the city is famous, Munich manufactures vehicles, machinery, chemicals, and textiles. The city is also a major cultural, educational, and tourist center. Pop., 1,313,939.

Nantes, in western France, at the head of the estuary of the Loire River, about 35 miles (56 km.) from the Atlantic. It has more than two miles of quays, and shipbuilding is an important industry. It is a major shipping and industrial center, and its leading manufactures are processed foods, agricultural equipment, clothing, metal products, machine tools, appliances, motor vehicles, and fertilizers. Its museum houses a very important collection of paintings, and it has many educational facilities. Pop., 437,566.

Naples, or Napoli, a major seaport in Italy on the Bay of Naples, off the Tyrrhenian Sea. It is 10 miles (16 km.) northwest of Mount Vesuvius. It is a port and industrial center and important for the manufacture of ships, engines, textiles, glass, gloves, wine, and machinery.

Naples was founded several hundred years before the birth of Christ. Many relics from the ruins of Pompeii are in the National Museum. Naples has medieval and Renaissance buildings, as well as a university, libraries, and museums. Pop., 1,225,227.

PRAGUE, *the Czech capital. The Old Town and Prague Castle, from Charles Bridge.*

Nice, an ancient city in southern France on the Mediterranean Sea near the Italian border. The Maritime Alps lie to the north, and the city's beautiful location and climate make it a world-renowned resort. The tourist trade is the city's chief industry but also important are the manufacture of perfume oils, soap, and clothing, and the preparation of olive oil. Flowers and olive trees are cultivated, and there is significant trade in cut flowers. Pop., 438,000.

Odessa, a city in the southwestern Soviet Union, situated on the Black Sea near the mouth of the Knestr River. The city is one of the major seaports of the Soviet Union. Its excellent harbor handles a variety of exports, including grain, wood, wool, and foodstuffs. Imports include coal, cotton, and tea. Odessa manufactures such products as machinery, auto parts, fertilizer, and processed foods. Pop., 1,039,000.

Omsk, a city in the west-central Soviet Union, at the junction of the Irtysh and Om rivers, on the Trans-Siberian Railroad. It is a major river port and industrial center that produces textiles, farm machinery, flour, timber, wood pulp, synthetic rubber, and petrochemicals. It has several research and educational institutes. Pop., 1,026,000.

Oslo, the capital of Norway, lying at the northern end of Oslo Fjord, near the Skaggerak. The largest city in Norway, Oslo is also the country's principal port and its administrative, commercial, and industrial center. Industrial activities include shipbuilding and the manufacture of textiles, paper products, and chemicals. The city has many historic sites and cultural institutions, and is the seat of the University of Oslo. Pop., 461,437.

Oxford, a city in central England, situated on the Thames River. Oxford is the seat of Oxford University, which was founded in the 1100's. Oxford's industries include the production of steel and automobiles, and printing and publishing. Pop., 123,400.

Padua, in northeastern Italy, 22 miles (35 km.) west of Venice. The city is an agricultural, transportation, commercial, and industrial center. Its manufactures include motor vehicles, machinery, textiles, soap, and processed foods. It has many notable medieval and Renaissance buildings and churches, and the University of Padua is the second oldest in Italy. Pop., 241,983.

Palermo, an Italian port, the capital of the Province of Palermo and of Sicily. The city has shipyards and warehouses, and its industries produce wine, chemicals, textiles, and cement. Palermo, which is thought to be over

WOMEN'S FASHIONS *in Paris, satirized in a Parisian magazine as early as 1910.*

2,500 years old, has many historical and architectural monuments. Pop., 679,493.

Paris, the capital of France, situated in east-central France on the Seine River. The city is the administrative and commercial hub of France, and one of the cultural and intellectual centers of the world. Its collections of art and architecture are outstanding, and its excellent educational facilities attract students from all over the world.

Among the best known points of interest in Paris are the Louvre, Notre Dame Cathedral, the opera, and the Eiffel Tower. Paris is also a thriving industrial city that produces machinery, electronic equipment, and a variety of luxury consumer goods. Pop., 8,547,625.

Pisa, in north-central Italy, on the Arno River, near the Tyrrhenian Sea. The city is a commercial and industrial center whose manufactures include textiles, glass, pharmaceuticals, machine tools, and processed foods. It has many art treasures and notable buildings, including the famous Leaning Tower. Pop., 103,570.

Porto, or Oporto, the second largest city of Portugal, situated on the Atlantic coast at the mouth of the Douro River. Porto is known for the export of port wine. Its industries produce beverages, textiles, clothing, and pottery. Pop., 693,170.

Prague, the capital of Czechoslovakia, situated in the west-central part of the country on the Vltava (Moldau) River. The city is an educational center and a transportation hub. Its manufactures include machinery, steel, automobiles, chemicals, and textiles. Prague has many historic monuments representing Romanesque, Gothic, Italian Renaissance, and Baroque styles. Pop., 1,173,031.

Reykjavík, the capital of Iceland, located on the southwestern coast of the country. It is the country's leading seaport and only major city. Reykjavík has a large fishing industry, busy shipyards, and publishing houses. It is the site of a university. Pop., 83,887.

Rome, the capital of Italy, located in the west-central part of the country, on the Tiber River, 17 miles (27 km.) inland from the Tyrrhenian Sea. Rome has been a major center of civilization for over 2000 years. It was the capital of the Roman Empire and retained its importance during the Middle Ages as the seat of the papacy. In the 1500's and 1600's Rome became the center of the Italian Renaissance, and many magnificent palaces and churches, decorated with beautiful sculptures and paintings, were built.

Modern Rome is the cultural, financial, and transportation center of Italy. Its industries include leathercrafting, metalworking, motion pictures, food processing, printing, and publishing. The city attracts many tourists and is an international center for the arts and fashion. Pop., 2,897,505.

Rostov, a city in the southeastern European Soviet Union, on the Don River, about 30 miles (48 km.) from its mouth at the Gulf of Taganrog. It is an important port, transportation, and industrial center whose manufactures include farm machinery, barges, ball bearings, electrical equipment, chemicals, road-making machinery, clothing, and processed foods. It has a university and several institutions of higher learning. Pop., 921,000.

Rotterdam, city in the Netherlands, on the New Maas River, an outlet of the Rhine River, near the North Sea. The districts of Maavlakte, Botlek, and Europoort to the west are also part of the port. With easy access to both the North Sea and Rhine River, Rotterdam is one of the busiest ports in Europe. Shipping and shipbuilding are Rotterdam's leading industries, but chemicals, paper, furniture, refined petroleum, clothing, and proc-essed foods are also produced. Pop., 1,017,136.

Ruse, on the Danube River, about 40 miles (65 km.) south of Bucharest. The city is Bulgaria's largest port on the Danube and an important transportation center. Ruse's major industries produce textiles, leather, processed foods, refined petroleum, and agricultural implements. Pop., 163,012.

Samarkand, an ancient city of Soviet Asia, located in central Uzbek Soviet Socialist Republic, on the slopes of the Alai mountains. Samarkand is one of the oldest cities in the world, and it still prospers on commerce and light industry, especially the weaving of cotton and silk textiles. Pop., 312,000.

Sofia, the capital and largest city of Bulgaria, situated in the western foothills of the Balkan Mountains. It is the economic center of the country, with industries producing machinery, electrical equipment, textiles, and processed foods. Sofia is the home of the country's main educational institutions. Pop., 976,015.

Stockholm, the capital and largest city of Sweden. It is situated in the Southeast, on Mälaren Lake near the Baltic Sea. The city is Sweden's chief port and its industries include shipyards, food-processing plants, chemical and machinery factories, and paper and textile mills. It is an important commercial and financial center, and its many schools, museums, libraries, and theaters give it great cultural importance. Pop., 661,258.

Syracuse, or Siracusa, an Italian seaport in southeastern Sicily, on the Ionian Sea. Its chief industries are food processing and tourism. It was settled about 734 B.C. by Greek colonists from Corinth and became one of the great centers of Greek culture and power in the fifth century B.C. Among its archaeological remains are a Greek theater and temple, a Roman amphitheater, and many catacombs. Pop., 122,534.

Tampere, in southwestern Finland, on Lake Nasijarvi. The city is a cultural, transportation, and industrial center and the second largest city in Finland. It is a leading textile center, and its industries include lumber mills, machinery, and leather-processing plants. It is notable for its modern architecture. Pop., 271,207.

Tashkent, a city in the southwest-central Soviet Union, the capital of the Uzbek Soviet Socialist Republic. Tashkent, an oasis settlement, lies on a small tributary of the Syr Darya. The city has good rail facilities and is an industrial and commercial center.

Textiles, leather goods, metal products, and farm machinery are manufactured, and cotton and grain are traded. Tashkent is also the focus of cultural and educational activities in central Soviet Asia. Pop., 1,689,000.

Tbilisi, or Tiflis, a city in the southwestern Soviet Union, capital of the Georgian Soviet Socialist Republic. The city, which lies on the Kura River, is a resort with thermal springs. It is also an agricultural and economic center. Tbilisi's industries produce textiles and clothing, wood products, machinery, plastics, and industrial equipment. Pop., 1,042,000.

Tiranë, or Tirana, the capital of Albania. Tiranë is served by Durrës, an Adriatic seaport. The city is a commercial and industrial center in an agricultural region well known for the production of olives. Tiranë's manufactures include building materials, metal products, and textiles. Tiranë is the seat of a university, a science institute, and museums. Pop., 169,300.

Toulon, in southeastern France, on the Mediterranean Sea, 30 miles (48 km.) southeast of Marseille. Toulon is France's principal naval base with extensive docks and shipyards. Other important industries are fishing and winemaking. Cork, machinery, vegetable oils, and chemicals are also produced. Toulon is a winter resort. Pop., 378,609.

ANCIENT SAMARKAND, *one of the world's oldest cities—it was once Greek, then Arab, then Mongol, and is now Russian.*

LOOK

Tours, in the Loire Valley of France, about 130 miles (210 km.) southwest of Paris. The city's manufactures include textile products, chemicals, electrical goods, silk, and printed matter. Tours is the commercial center for the surrounding agricultural region, handling products such as wine, grain, and dried fruit. Tours was the capital of a Roman province in France and the site of a decisive battle in 732 A.D. when Charles Martel defeated an invading Moorish army. Pop., 235,059.

Trieste, a port in northeastern Italy, situated on the Adriatic Sea, near the border with Yugoslavia. Trieste serves as a port for Czechoslovakia, Austria, Hungary, Yugoslavia, and Italy. Following World War II, the city was made part of a free territory, but in the 1950's it was incorporated into Italy and surrounding territory into Yugoslavia. The main industry is shipbuilding, but there are also steel mills and oil refineries. Pop., 265,453.

Turku, a seaport in southwestern Finland, on the Baltic Sea. It is the third largest city in Finland, and it produces textiles, processed foods, steel, machinery, and clothing. Turku has a Finnish and a Swedish university. Pop., 239,672.

Uppsala, in eastern Sweden, 40 miles (64 km.) northwest of Stockholm. It is a railroad and industrial center whose manufactures include clothing, processed foods, machinery, and printed materials. The city is a cultural and educational center with a world-famous university and many academic institutions. Pop., 141,444.

Utrecht, in central Netherlands, on the Oude Rijn River, 20 miles (32 km.) southeast of Amsterdam. The city is a finance, transportation, and industrial center whose manufactures include machinery, aluminum, chemicals, cement, and processed food. Utrecht has many museums and splendid medieval churches. The university is the largest of the Dutch state universities, with many specialized schools and a large library. Pop., 471,897.

Vaduz, capital of the European principality of Liechtenstein, situated on the banks of the Rhine River. As the country's chief city, it is primarily an administrative center. Tourism is important. Pop., 4,704.

Valencia, capital of Valencia Province in eastern Spain, situated on the Turia River near the Mediterranean. It is an important commercial and industrial city. It manufactures chemicals, textiles, glazed tiles, metal products, and furniture and processes grains, fruits, tobacco, and vegetables grown nearby. Pop., 653,690.

Venice, or Venezia, the capital of the province of Venezia, in northeastern Italy. Occupying more than 100 islets in a lagoon off the Adriatic Sea, the city is built on a foundation of sunken piles and is connected with the mainland by bridges. Transportation in the city is by boat along numerous canals.

Venice is noted for its outstanding architecture in a variety of styles, and it has long been an artistic center for Italy and the world. The city's chief source of income is tourism. Its few light industries produce glass, jewelry, textiles, furniture, and handicrafts. Pop., 360,293.

Vienna, the capital of Austria, located in the northeastern part of the country on the Danube River. Vienna is Austria's major commercial and industrial city, producing chemicals, textiles, machinery, beer, handicrafts, and food products. As capital of the Austrian Empire, Vienna was for centuries a European cultural center. With its state university, technical schools, and music, drama, and fine arts academies, Vienna is still an important intellectual center. Pop., 1,592,000.

Vladivostok, a port on the Sea of Japan, in southeastern Siberia in the Soviet Union. It is the most important Soviet port on the Pacific Ocean and is kept open in the winter by icebreakers. The city is the eastern terminus of the Trans-Siberian Railroad. Fishing fleets are based in Vladivostok. The city's industries include fish canning, shipbuilding, and mineral refining. The city is also the chief Soviet naval base in the Pacific. Pop., 536,000.

Warsaw, the capital and largest city of Poland. It is located on both banks of the Vistula River, in the east-central part of the country. Warsaw is the commercial, political, educational, and cultural center of Poland. Manufactures include machinery, chemicals, electrical equipment, textiles, clothing, and food products. Warsaw is a river port and the communications and transportation center of Poland. Pop., 1,474,200.

Wrocław, in southern Poland, on both banks of the Oder River, about 190 miles (300 km.) southwest of Warsaw. Wrocław, German Breslau, is a river port and railroad junction. Manufactures include machinery, chemicals, textiles, and food products. Pop., 593,000.

Zagreb, in northwestern Yugoslavia, on the Sava River. Zagreb is the second largest city in Yugoslavia and a major commercial and financial center. It is the capital and cultural and educational center of Croatia. Manufactures include machinery, textiles, chemicals, paper and metal products. Pop., 602,058.

Zaragoza, or Saragossa, in northeastern Spain, on the Ebro River. The city is a commercial, railway, and industrial center. Its manufactures include machinery, textiles, chemicals, paper, and processed foods. It is also a cultural center with many famous works of art, several Gothic churches, and a university. Pop., 479,845.

Zürich, in Switzerland, at the mouth of the Limmat River, at the northwest end of Lake Zürich. It is the capital of the canton of Zürich and the largest city in Switzerland. The city is the industrial, commercial, and financial center of the country, with many banks and financial institutions. Manufactures include machinery, textiles, machine tools, turbines, radios, and paper. The city is also a leading cultural, educational, and tourist center. Pop., 707,500.

THE CHARM OF VENICE. *Once a powerful city-state, its canals are lined with palaces.*

GLOSSARY OF EUROPE

Achaean League, two confederations of ancient Greek city-states formed in Achaea, a region in the northern Peloponnesus bordered by the gulfs of Corinth and Patrai. The first league was established before the 400's B.C. when twelve Achaean cities united to defend themselves against attacks by pirates. The confederation disintegrated in the early 300's.

The second league was formed in 280 B.C. By 225 B.C. it included all of the northern and central Peloponnesus except Sparta.

The second league developed the nearest equivalent to a modern democratic federal government that was created in ancient times. Each state was internally self-governing, but the league acted as a unit in foreign policy and the members combined their forces in time of war. In 146 B.C. the League was defeated by Rome, and Achaea became a Roman province.

Adriatic Sea, an arm of the Mediterranean Sea lying between Italy on the southwest and Yugoslavia and Albania on the northeast. The Adriatic is about 500 miles (800 km.) long and 100 miles (160 km.) wide. To the south, the Strait of Otranto links it with the Ionian Sea.

Aegean Sea, an arm of the Mediterranean Sea between Greece and Turkey. The Aegean is about 400 miles (645 km.) long and 200 miles (320 km.) wide, and flows into the Sea of Crete in the south. It contains a great many dry, rocky islands, including those in the Cyclades, Sporades, and Dodecanese groups.

Agincourt, a famous battle of the Hundred Years' War between England and France. It was fought on October 25, 1415, at Agincourt, in northern France. An invading English army commanded by King Henry V defeated a French force more than twice its size.

The English victory demonstrated the superiority of the English longbow over the medieval cavalry of the French and the cumbersome armor worn by the knights on horseback. The victory at Agincourt won Henry England's confidence. He was then able to secure the support of Parliament for a large-scale invasion of the Continent in the following year.

THE BATTLE OF CRÉCY *in 1346 preceded Agincourt. Here English bowmen were first effective.*

Alps, an extensive and complex mountain system in central Europe, extending about 700 miles (1130 km.) from southeastern France east through Switzerland and southwestern Austria, and south into western Yugoslavia. The highest peak is Mont Blanc, which towers 15,781 feet (4813 m). The range is narrow in the west and widens toward the east.

A variety of regional names are applied to the Alps. Some of the more important sections are the Maritime Alps, in France; the Dolomites and Pennines in northern Italy; the Dinaric Alps in Yugoslavia; and the Leopontines, in Switzerland.

Apennines, a mountain range that forms the backbone of peninsular Italy. The Apennines extend in a long arch from the Ligurian Alps in northwestern Italy to Calabria in the south, about 850 miles (1370 km.). The highest peak, Monte Corno, is 9560 feet (2916 m). Pastures and forest cover the upper slopes, and fruits and grains are grown in the valleys.

Arno, a river in Italy that rises in the Apennines in central Italy, passes through Florence, and flows about 150 miles (240 km.) west to empty into the Ligurian Sea near Pisa. It is navigable but subject to sudden flooding.

Atlantic Charter, a World War II joint declaration of policy and war aims agreed upon by U.S. President Franklin D. Roosevelt and British Prime

Minister Winston Churchill on August 14, 1941, after a meeting held at sea off the coast of Newfoundland.

The charter gave full expression to President Roosevelt's doctrine of the Four Freedoms—freedom of speech and religion and freedom from want and fear. The charter pledged the two nations to seek no territorial aggrandizement or territorial changes contrary to the freely expressed wishes of the peoples concerned.

The charter also called for the right of peoples to determine their own form of government and for the restoration of self-government to those who had been forcibly deprived of it. Other aims were to achieve greater economic and trade opportunities, to foster international cooperation in labor and social security, to secure freedom of the seas, and to realize a system of world security that would include in it a measure of disarmament.

The principles of the Atlantic Charter were confirmed in the Declaration of the United Nations, signed by 26 World War II allies in Washington, D.C., on January 1, 1942. Much of the Atlantic Charter was included in the Charter of the United Nations.

Babylonian captivity of the church (1309–1376), the period during which the popes resided in Avignon, a city in southern France, rather than in Rome. Avignon was papal territory from 1348 to 1791.

Clement V (1305–1314) was the first pope to take up residence in Avignon. His move was the result of a quarrel between King Philip IV of France (1285–1314) and Pope Boniface VIII (1294–1303) over the power of the state to tax the clergy and the issue of church supremacy over the state. In 1302 Boniface issued a bull, the *Unam sanctam,* stating that all men were subject to the pope. Philip was so enraged by the bull that he sent soldiers to arrest Boniface, who died shortly thereafter.

Boniface's successor, Pope Benedict XI, died in 1304, and Philip secured the election to the papal throne of a Frenchman, Bertrand de Got, who took the name Clement V. The Avignonese popes were regarded as tools of France. As a result, the prestige of the Holy See declined.

In 1377 Pope Gregory XI (1370–1378) returned to Rome, and his successor, Urban VI (1378–1389), established a line of popes in Rome. However, a rival line of popes established themselves in Avignon, beginning a period of church history known as the Great Schism (1378–1417), during which the Western church was divided in its allegiance between the two lines of popes.

Baltic Sea, an arm of the North Atlantic Ocean separating the Scandinavian peninsula and Finland from the rest of continental Europe. It flows into the North Sea to the west through the Kattegat and the Skagerrak.

The Baltic is the world's largest body of brackish water. It covers an area of 160,000 square miles (415,000 sq. km.). The Baltic has two large branches—the Gulf of Bothnia in the north and the Gulf of Finland in the east.

Black Death, an epidemic that swept Europe in the first half of the 1300's, killing an estimated one-half to one-third of Europe's population.

The Black Death caused vast social and economic changes in medieval Europe. Labor became scarce, and wages and food prices rose to unprecedented heights. Many serfs seized the opportunity to bargain with their masters for better conditions and, whenever possible, for their freedom. Unsuccessful attempts to fix wages and prices generated discontent among workmen, and unwillingness to concede improved conditions to serfs eventually led to peasant revolts.

Black Forest, a mountainous region in southwestern West Germany. The mountains reach summits of nearly 5000 feet (1525 m) and are thickly forested. They contain the sources of the Danube and Neckar rivers.

Black Sea, a large inland sea between southeastern Europe and Asia, lying north of Asian Turkey, west and south of the Soviet Union, and east of Rumania, Bulgaria, and European Turkey. About 170,000 square miles (440,000 sq. km.) in area, it receives the Danube, the Dnester, the Dnepr, and other major rivers. The Sea of Azov, a small arm of the Black Sea, lies to the north. The Bosporus, the Sea of Marmara, and the Dardanelles link the Black Sea with the Aegean.

Bosporus, a strait between European and Asian Turkey. It joins the Sea of Marmara with the Black Sea, and is 19 miles (31 km.) long.

Bothnia, Gulf of, the northern arm of the Baltic Sea. It lies between Sweden on the west and Finland on the east.

Brest-Litovsk, a World War I peace treaty signed at Brest, in the present-day Soviet Union, on March 3, 1918, by the newly established Bolshevik government of Russia and the Central Powers, led by Germany and Austria-Hungary.

Russia stalled for as long as it could before signing the treaty, but after revolution, economic collapse, and a succession of military defeats, it was impossible for Russia to continue fighting. On February 9, 1918, the Central Powers signed a peace treaty with a Ukrainian government in which they recognized the independence of the Ukraine, a part of the pre-war Russian Empire. On March 3, 1918, Russia finally signed the treaty.

The treaty required Russia to pay a large indemnity, and to give up territories including the Baltic states (Estonia, Latvia, Lithuania), large areas of Belorussia (White Russia), Finland, Poland, large areas of the Transcaucasian region (Azerbaijan, Armenia, and Georgia), and the Ukraine.

By concluding a separate peace with Russia, Germany hoped to win the war quickly by transferring to the western front troops that had been tied down on the eastern front. Germany also expected to receive food and other supplies from the former Russian territories. By later peace settlements with the Allies, led by Britain, France, and the United States, Germany was forced to renounce the Treaty of Brest-Litovsk.

Carlists, supporters of the claims to the Spanish throne of Don Carlos María Isodro de Borbón (1788–1855) and his descendants. Following the death of his brother, King Ferdinand VII, in 1833, Don Carlos claimed the throne on the basis of the Spanish Salic Law of 1713, which prohibited females from succeeding to the throne. In 1830 King Ferdinand had formally abrogated the Salic Law, and in 1833 his infant daughter became Queen Isabella II.

The Carlists fought two wars, 1834–1839 and 1873–1876, and staged several uprisings in support of Don Carlos's claim. The movement was strongest among the conservative elements of society, and its activities were centered in the north of Spain. The Carlists continued to exert a traditionalist influence in Spanish politics into the early 1900's.

Carpathian Mountains, a mountain system of central and eastern Europe extending more than 1000 miles (1610 km.) through Czechoslovakia, Hungary, Poland, Rumania, and the Soviet Union. Although a continuation of the Alps, the Carpathians are more rounded and lower than the Alps; the highest peak, Mt. Gerlach, is 8711 feet (2657 m).

The Carpathians contain the sources of many rivers, including the Vistula and the Dnestr.

Caspian Sea, the world's largest inland sea, between the Soviet Union and Iran, at the border of Europe and Asia. It is about 750 miles (1208 km.) long and averages 200 miles (320 km.) in width. There are no outlets, but the Ural, Volga, Kura, Terek, and Atrek rivers flow into the Caspian.

Caucasus Mountains, an extensive mountain range between the Black and Caspian seas, often considered as part of the boundary between Europe and Asia.

The Greater Caucasus, in the north, is about 750 miles (1208 km.) long and the highest peak, Mt. Elbrus, is 18,481 feet (5637 m). Volcanic in origin, this chain has hot springs and occasional earthquakes.

The Lesser Caucasus, in the south, is a mountain system formed in part by the northern ranges of the Armenian Highland.

Chartism, an English working-class movement that advocated parliamentary reform between 1836 and 1848.

The movement originated in 1836 when an association of workers in London prepared a six-point program known as the People's Charter. They demanded annual parliaments, universal male suffrage, vote by secret ballot, equal electoral districts, abolition of property requirements for membership in the House of Commons, and salaries for members.

The People's Charter was published in 1838, and the Chartist movement assumed political importance in 1839, when the Chartists held mass meetings and threatened violence if their demands were not met. In May, 1839, they submitted to Parliament a petition that incorporated their charter, but their demands were refused. Rioting in Birmingham and other cities was put down by force.

A second petition presented to Parliament in 1842 was also rejected, and in 1848, when revolutionary activity disturbed much of Europe, the English Chartists made another unsuccessful attempt to have their petition accepted by Parliament.

After 1848, economic conditions improved in England and the movement gradually lost influence. Most of the objectives of the Chartist movement were ultimately realized.

Concert of Europe, an agreement among the leading nations of Europe in the early 1800's to join in a loose union for political and military action to protect their mutual interests.

The idea of the Concert of Europe was developed under the guidance of the Austrian foreign minister, Klemens von Metternich. Austria joined Prussia, Russia, and Britain in the Quadruple Alliance of 1815. The alliance was aimed primarily against France and was designed to return Europe to its pre-Napoleonic status.

The Concert of Europe grew out of the Quadruple Alliance and was dedicated to maintaining the balance of power in Europe. France joined the other powers in 1818, but by 1820 Britain had left the alliance, which because of its loose organization was to prove ineffectual in dealing with the political upheavals of the late 1800's.

Congress of Berlin, a meeting of the major European powers—Austria-Hungary, England, France, Germany, Italy, the Ottoman Empire (Turkey), and Russia—held at Berlin, Germany, from June 13 to July 13, 1878. The purpose of the congress was to revise the Treaty of San Stefano, which Russia had imposed on Turkey on March 3, 1878, after Russian victory in the Russo-Turkish War of 1877-1878.

The treaty terms had increased Russian influence in the Balkans, and had provoked an international crisis. Austria-Hungary and Britain were especially alarmed, and they called the congress. Otto von Bismarck, chancellor of the German Empire, served as chairman of the discussions.

Many of the resolutions of the congress had been worked out beforehand in secret bilateral agreements between the major powers. They considerably reduced Russian gains in the Balkans. Bulgaria proper, north of the Balkan mountains, was to be an autonomous principality. Eastern Rumelia, the area south of the Balkan mountains, was to be administered by a Christian prince chosen by the Ottoman ruler, who would have political and military control of the province.

Other settlements reached at the Congress of Berlin included authorization of Austria-Hungary's occupying and administering the Ottoman provinces of Bosnia and Hercegovina and garrisoning the Sanjak of Novi Pazar, a strip of land between Serbia and Montenegro. Montenegro, Rumania, and Serbia were recognized as independent states.

Rumania received Dobruja, a region between the Danube River and the Black Sea, and ceded southern Bessarabia (a region in the present-day Soviet Union between the Prut and Dnestr rivers) to Russia. Turkey ceded the island of Cyprus to Britain, and Batumi (in the present-day Soviet Union) as well as Ardahan and Kars (in present-day northeastern Turkey) to Russia. France was granted the right to occupy Tunis when it saw fit.

Continental System, the attempt by Emperor Napoleon I of France to blockade England and to prevent England from trading with the Continent. He sought to create a European economy centered on France and to force England into economic collapse and eventual surrender.

The Berlin Decree of November, 1806, the Treaties of Tilsit of July, 1807, and the Milan Decree of December, 1807, formally instituted the Continental System. By these and later decrees, the ports of France, its allies, and neutrals were to be closed to England as well as to neutrals who traded with England.

After 1806 Napoleon expected all governments that signed peace treaties with him to comply with the system. At Tilsit, for example, both Prussia and Russia agreed to close their ports to British shipping.

The Continental System worked well at first, but it became increasingly difficult to enforce. The system proved unpopular with the French middle and upper classes, who resented the commercial restrictions and the blocking of imports of luxury goods.

Other European countries began to feel that the Continental System was designed to increase French prosperity, often at their expense. Russia partially withdrew from the system in December, 1810, having become increasingly distrustful of France. In 1811 Russia withdrew further, and in 1812 a peace treaty between England and Russia effectively marked the end of the Continental System.

Corsica, a French island in the Mediterranean, about 100 miles (160 km.) southeast of the French coast and 3352 square miles (8682 sq. km.) in area. It is mountainous; the highest is Mont Cinto, 8891 feet (2710 m).

Crimean War, 1854-1856, a war fought against Russia by Britain, France, Sardinia (Piedmont), and the Ottoman Empire (Turkey). The main fighting was in the Crimean peninsula, in the present-day Soviet Union.

CRIMEAN WAR CAMP, *a rare and very early view by Roger Fenton, a pioneer photographer.*

The general cause of the war was Russia's desire to gain territory in the eastern Mediterranean at the expense of the declining Ottoman Empire.

EPA

A FANCIFUL VIEW OF JERUSALEM *from a medieval manuscript. The Crusaders held Jerusalem with its holy monuments for 88 years.*

tually sold into slavery. Another section of the Children's Crusade started in Germany. Thousands died of exposure, disease, and hunger, and few ever reached their homes.

The Fifth Crusade (1218–1221) began with the capture of Damietta, Egypt, by the Christians, but ended with their defeat and retreat. The Sixth Crusade (1228–1229) resulted in the regaining of Jerusalem by Frederick II (1194–1250), Holy Roman Emperor and King of Sicily as Frederick I. Frederick made a treaty with the sultan of Egypt in 1229 that gave him a grant of lands including Nazareth, Bethlehem, Jerusalem, and a strip of land from Jerusalem to the sea. In 1244 the treaty was broken, and the Muslims recaptured Jerusalem, which they retained until World War I, when it was taken by the British.

The Seventh Crusade (1248–1254) retook Damietta, but the Christians were unable to hold it.

The Eighth Crusade (1270) was inspired by the fall of Antioch and Jaffa

to the Muslims in 1268, but it accomplished nothing. In 1289 Tripoli fell to the Muslims, and in 1291 Saint-Jean-d'Acre, the last stronghold of the Latin kingdom of Jerusalem, fell. The major Crusades had ended.

Danube, a major river of central and southeastern Europe. It rises in the Black Forest of West Germany and flows for some 1775 miles (2858 km.) through or along the borders of eight countries before emptying into the Black Sea. Its major tributaries include the Drava, Sava, Tisza, and Prut.

Dardanelles, a strait separating parts of European and Asian Turkey. It links the Aegean Sea and the Sea of Marmara and is 38 miles (61 km.) long and three-quarters to four miles (1.2 km. to 6.4 km.) wide. Its ancient name was the Hellespont.

Declaration of the Rights of Man and of the Citizen, a document adopted by

the French Constituent Assembly on August 27, 1789, and used later as the preamble to the French Constitution of 1791. The declaration stated that men have inalienable rights and are born and remain free and equal.

The declaration guaranteed the rights of life, liberty, security, property, and resistance to oppression. It further declared that the nation is sovereign, that law should be an expression of the general will, that the same law should be applicable to all people, and that taxes should be raised only by common consent.

The Declaration of the Rights of Man and of the Citizen was based on the principles of the Enlightenment and the American Declaration of Independence. It expounded the basic philosophy of the French Revolution and was a call for liberal reform throughout Europe in the 1800's.

Delian League, created in 478 B.C., a defensive alliance of Greek city-states. It included Athens, the islands in the Aegean Sea, and the Ionian cities of Asia Minor, against the Persians. At its height, the league had over 200 members. Although the Greeks had defeated the Persians in 492, 490, and 480–479 B.C., they were still a threat.

The members of the league contributed funds, ships, and troops in varying degrees. In the first decades, the league's treasury and general assembly were located on the island of Delos. Athens soon dominated the league, however, and the league treasury, military force, and ships served to enhance Athenian power.

In 467 B.C. Naxos attempted to withdraw from the league. Athens quelled this and future attempts by members to withdraw and imposed a tributary status on the recalcitrant city-states. In 454 B.C. the league's treasury was moved from Delos to Athens. By 440 B.C. the Aegean islands of Chios and Lesbos were the only autonomous members. The league was formally ended in 404 B.C., when Athens was defeated by Sparta and its allies in the Peloponnesian War (431–404 B.C.).

A brief revival of Athenian sea power led to the creation of a second league from 377–338 B.C.. This association succumbed to Macedonian conquest in 338 B.C. at the Battle of Chaeronea, when Philip II of Macedon (382–336 B.C.) defeated the allied armies of Athens and Thebes.

Delphic Oracle, the shrine of Apollo at Delphi in Phocis, Greece. In ancient times it was believed that Apollo communicated with mortals at Delphi through his priestess, who was reputed to have special prophetic powers. The word "oracle" refers to the site of Apollo's temple at Delphi as well as to the messages transmitted by the priestess. Anyone, commoner or statesman, could consult the priestess, who could reveal the future.

ROUND TEMPLE AT ANCIENT DELPHI *in Greece, a sacred area for over 2000 years. The oracle played a large part, early in its career, in encouraging and directing Greek colonization.*

Although there were many shrines in ancient Greece, the Delphic Oracle was the most famous. It served as one of several cultural bonds uniting the politically fragmented Greeks. In 390 A.D. the Roman Emperor Theodosius I (c 346–395) silenced the oracle when he adopted Christianity.

Dnepr, a major river of the western Soviet Union. It rises near Smolensk and flows southwest and south for over 1400 miles (2255 km.), emptying into the Black Sea. Its tributaries include the Sozh, Desna, and Berezina rivers.

The Dnepr is navigable for most of its course, and it is an important producer of hydroelectric power. It drains an area of 195,000 square miles (505,000 sq. km.).

Don, a major river of the western Soviet Union. It rises in the Central Russian Upland, southwest of Moscow. It flows in a generally southerly direction between the Dnepr and the Volga rivers for about 1225 miles (1972 km.) before emptying into the Gulf of Taganrog of the Sea of Azov.

Tributaries of the Don include the Donets, Medveditsa, Sal, and Manych rivers. Seagoing ships can travel as far as Rostov, and the entire course is navigable by smaller vessels.

Donation of Pepin, a tract of land in central Italy extending from Ravenna down the Adriatic coast. In 756 it was ceded to Pope Stephen II (752–757) and his successors by Pepin the Short, king of the Franks (751–768).

In 751 the Lombards seized Ravenna from the Byzantine Empire, and a year later they became a serious threat to Rome itself. In 754 Pope Stephen II went to France and appealed to Pepin for aid against the Lombards. Pepin agreed to become the pope's protector and give him armed assistance. In return for this assistance, the pope personally crowned Pepin.

In 754 and again in 756, Pepin marched into Italy and defeated the Lombards. After his second victory he ceded the lands he had conquered to the papacy.

The Donation of Pepin strengthened the temporal power of the popes. Ravenna and Rome, under the rule of the popes, formed the nucleus of the Papal States. These remained in papal hands until 1870, when they were added to the newly united kingdom of Italy. The present-day Vatican City is all that remains of the Papal States.

Enclosure Movement, part of the agricultural revolution in Britain, by which great landowners between 1790 and 1820 achieved private control over the land. New techniques to improve agricultural production had been discovered, and landowners sought full control of the land to put the new techniques into practice.

The old village system of common lands and open fields was part of the common law and could only be changed by an act of Parliament. Since the great landowners controlled Parliament, they managed to pass many "enclosure acts," which permitted the enclosure, by fences or other means, of common lands and open fields.

English Channel, a body of water between England and France that joins the Atlantic Ocean and the North Sea. It is 21 miles (34 km.) wide at its narrowest extent, the Strait of Dover, and 112 miles (180 km.) at its greatest.

Fashoda crisis, a diplomatic dispute in 1898 between Britain and France over control of the Sudan that brought the two nations close to war. In July, 1898, French troops, led by Captain Jean Baptiste Marchand, marched eastward from Lake Chad and reached Fashoda (present-day Kodok) on the Nile River in southern Sudan. Marchand claimed Fashoda for France.

In September, 1898, British forces under General Horatio Herbert Kitchener advanced southward up the Nile and met the French at Fashoda. The British claimed the area for Egypt, a British protectorate since 1882.

Sudan was of strategic importance to both French and British plans for expansion in Africa. France envisaged a solid French belt from Dakar in the west to the Gulf of Aden in the east. Britain wanted to create an empire stretching from Cairo in the north to the Cape Colony in the south. Furthermore, French penetration of Sudan was regarded by the British as a threat to their position in Egypt.

Neither side would yield, until the British threatened war. Then the French, concerned about internal problems and unprepared for a naval confrontation, withdrew from Fashoda in November, 1898. In March, 1899, France gave up all claims to territory along the Nile.

Franco-Prussian War, a conflict in 1870–1871 between France and the German states led by Prussia. The war, in which Germany was the victor, completed the unification of the German states and brought the end of the second Napoleonic dynasty in France.

The war was touched off by a dispute over the succession to the Spanish throne. The Prussian chancellor, Otto von Bismarck, supported the claim of Leopold of Hohenzollern-Sigmaringen, a Prussian prince. France, fearful of having a Prussian on the Spanish throne, demanded that Leopold repudiate his claim. Leopold refused, and soon France declared war.

The Germans were successful from the start and within a year the French army had been defeated. The defeat of France's Emperor Napoleon III led to the establishment of the Third Republic under Adolphe Thiers.

The war ended with the Treaty of Frankfurt in 1871. France was forced to cede the province of Alsace and part of the province of Lorraine to Germany and to pay heavy reparations.

Geneva, or Léman, a crescent-shaped lake on the border of France and Switzerland, 224 square miles (580 sq. km.) in area.

Golden Horde, a Mongol khanate that dominated Russia during the 1200's and 1300's. In 1237 a group of Mongols led by Batu Khan, the grandson of Genghis Khan, swept westward, conquering Kiev in 1240 and advancing into Poland, Silesia, and Hungary. The Mongols defeated Henry II, duke of Silesia, at Liegnitz (Legnica, Poland).

Although the Mongols won the battle, they suffered heavy losses and retreated to Sarai on the lower Volga, where they established their capital. It was at Sarai that Batu's splendid tent gave the Mongols their name of the Golden Horde.

The Mongols ruled from Sarai, extracting tribute from the Russian princes until the mid-1300's, when the last of Batu's direct descendants died and the empire began to split up. The Russian princes began to regain their autonomy, but in 1378 Toqtamish, of the eastern Qipchaq, united the divided empire and regained much of its former strength. In 1391 Toqtamish was defeated by Tamerlane, and the Golden Horde disintegrated into smaller khanates.

Greenland, the largest island in the world, 840,000 square miles in area. A dependency and former colony of Denmark, it lies northeast of North America and is washed by the North Atlantic and Arctic oceans and by the Greenland Sea. About three-quarters of its area lies above the Arctic Circle, and almost seven-eighths of Greenland is covered by ice.

Guelphs and Ghibellines, opposing political factions important in Italy during the late Middle Ages, when popes and emperors vied for political supremacy. The names of the papal (Guelph) and imperial (Ghibelline) parties derive from two rival factions of the German nobility in the 1100's.

The Italian conflicts involved not only questions of allegiance to the pope or emperor, but also economic and social differences within communities and political differences among them. The nobility tended to be Ghibelline and the communes Guelph, but individual communes were often split internally, and neighboring communes frequently fought against one another. The use of these names to denote political factions ended in the 1400's.

Hague peace conferences, two international meetings held at the Hague, the Netherlands, to discuss means to prevent war. The first conference was called in 1899 by Russia. Conventions were signed providing for the peaceful settlement of international disputes and the definition of the laws of war. A permanent court of arbitration was established.

The second conference was called in 1907 by U.S. President Theodore Roosevelt. The conference rejected agreements providing for limitation of armaments and compulsory arbitration of disputes among nations, but the machinery for voluntary arbitration was enlarged. Conventions were concluded dealing with the rights and obligations of neutrals and on action to collect international debts.

Hanseatic League, a commercial confederation of cities in northern Germany formed in the 1200's to protect merchants and their goods from robbers and pirates and to secure trading privileges abroad.

At the height of its power in the late 1300's the league was composed of 80 or 90 member cities and controlled almost all northern European trade. Although some Hansa towns were located in eastern Europe, the most important were in Germany and included Lübeck, Hamburg, Bremen, Cologne, as well as Hanover. League merchants also established branches in other European cities, the most important of which were in Bruges, Belgium; Bergen, Norway; and London.

In the commercial centers of Western Europe, Hansa traders exchanged their goods for products from the Mediterranean and Near East carried by Italian merchants. By the 1500's the league was in decline due to the shift of commercial routes to the Atlantic and to the growth of national monarchies, which suspended Hansa trading privileges in order to support their own merchants.

Holy Alliance, an agreement drawn up by Czar Alexander I of Russia and signed September 26, 1815, by Austria, Prussia, and Russia. It contained a declaration of Christian principles of conduct by which the rulers were to abide.

The compact was ultimately signed

ROMANTIC VIEW *of the Franco-Prussian War. Those nice Germans sing for the delighted French, whose house in Paris they have seized.*

CZAR ALEXANDER I *of Russia, original author of the Holy Alliance of 1815.*

by all European rulers except the English king, the pope, and the sultan of Turkey. The document itself was vague, but it came to symbolize the reactionary policies followed by Austria, Prussia, and Russia.

Hundred Days, the period of March 20—June 29, 1815, during which former emperor Napoleon I of France attempted to reestablish his rule. Escaping from exile on the island of

Elba, Napoleon landed in the south of France on March 1, 1815, with a few hundred followers. He rapidly gained support, and troops sent to arrest him joined his ranks. On March 20, 1815, he reentered Paris and took control of the government.

Austria, England, Prussia, and Russia, the powers that had just defeated Napoleon, were assembled at the Congress of Vienna to conclude a European settlement after the long and costly Napoleonic Wars of 1792–1815. Once again they renewed their coalition against him. After several smaller battles, Napoleon faced the armies of the coalition at Waterloo, in Belgium, on June 18 and suffered a disastrous defeat.

Napoleon was driven back to Paris, and on June 22 he abdicated and fled. He finally surrendered to the British, and was again exiled.

Iberia, a peninsula in the southwestern corner of Europe, between the Mediterranean Sea and the Atlantic Ocean, occupied by Spain and Portugal. It is ringed with the Pyrenees and the Cantabrian Mountains on the north, the Sierra da Estrella on the west, and the Cordillera Penibética on the southeast.

The interior is also mountainous, with the Sierra Morena and Sierra de Guadarrama the most important chains. The major rivers crossing the peninsula are the Duero, the Tejo (Tagus), the Guadiana, the Ebro, and the Guadalquivir.

Inquisition, a medieval Roman Catholic tribunal first established by Pope Gregory IX (1227–1241) to investigate the Albigensian heresy in southern France.

The inquisitors, usually Dominicans, later sought out heretics of all kinds in France, Italy, Germany, Burgundy, and Spain. The accused, subject to anonymous accusations and often torture, were usually punished by fines, imprisonment, and the confiscation of property, although the death penalty was sometimes used.

In 1542 Pope Paul III (1534–1549) revived the medieval Inquisition by establishing the Roman Inquisition under a committee of cardinals called the Holy Office. Its investigations were confined to Italy.

In the late 1400's the Spanish monarchs Ferdinand and Isabella tried to create a unified national state. They asked the pope to establish the Inquisition in Spain, planning to use the machinery of the Roman Catholic Church to help them unify the country. Since

there was little Spanish national feeling in Spain, the monarchs tried to make national feeling synonymous with Roman Catholic feeling.

The Spanish Inquisition began to function about 1480. Unlike the medieval and Roman inquisitions, which were under ecclesiastical control, the Spanish Inquisition was an instrument of a secular power, the crown.

The goal of the Spanish Inquisition was to search out Marranos (converted Jews) and Moriscos (converted Moors) suspected of practicing their original religions. Those who were not good Catholics were considered disloyal to the crown. The Spanish Inquisition was later used against political opponents. The Inquisition lasted in Spain until the 1800's.

Jacobites, the name given to partisans of the descendants of James II, the Stuart king of England who was forced to flee the country in the Glorious Revolution of 1688.

James II died in exile in 1701, and the Stuart claim to the British throne was taken up by his son, known as James III to his supporters, the Jacobites. He is usually called by historicans "the Old Pretender," the name given him by opponents of his claim.

In 1714 the German elector of Han-

THE INQUISITION IN SPAIN. *Relatively mild in the rest of Europe, the Spanish Inquisition—a political weapon—was pernicious.*

CULVER PICTURES

over became king of Great Britain as George I. Shortly thereafter the Pretender landed in Scotland. Aided by followers from the Scottish Highlands, he tried to organize a revolt. The uprising was badly organized and it failed.

In 1745 the Pretender's son, called the "Young Pretender" or "Bonnie Prince Charlie," landed in Scotland. This new attempt at revolt was also crushed, and the British government decided to destroy Jacobitism in the Scottish Highlands once and for all by breaking up the Highland clans.

Junkers, originally some 12,000 to 15,000 families descended from the Saxon knights who took Prussia from the Slavs in the early 900's. The term has come to be applied to the Prussian landed aristocracy and to the militarism, nationalism, and authoritarianism associated with them.

Kattegat, a strait between Sweden on the east and the Danish Jutland Peninsula on the west. It connects the Baltic Sea to the Skagerrak and the North Sea.

Kellogg–Briand Pact, or the Pact of Paris, an international declaration in 1928 renouncing war as an instrument of national policy and advocating the peaceful settlement of international disputes. It was signed in Paris, France, on August 27, 1928, by 15 nations, including Britain, France, Germany, and the United States. It was eventually endorsed by more than 60 nations.

The pact did not prohibit defensive wars, and many nations added reservations to their ratifications indicating that there were areas, especially in their colonies, where it would not apply. Since it did not provide for methods of enforcement or punishment of aggression, the pact was ineffectual. The ultranationalist regimes of the 1930's, such as those of Germany, Italy, and Japan, were the first to repudiate it.

League of Nations, an international governmental organization devoted to the preservation of world peace and the promotion of international cooperation. It was in existence from 1920 to 1946. The league dissolved itself in April, 1946, after World War II, and passed on its heritage to the United Nations.

The league was one of the 14 points upon which U.S. President Woodrow Wilson sought to base the peace following World War I, and the league covenant was written into the 1919 peace treaty with Germany. The covenant stated that members were to protect each other against aggression and submit disputes to arbitration.

The main league organs consisted of an assembly, in which all members were represented; a council with the great powers holding permanent seats and four other nations holding temporary membership; and a secretariat consisting of civil servants drawn from all member states. An international court and an international labor office were also established.

The league began to function in January, 1920, in Geneva, Switzerland, but it was weakened from the outset by the refusal of the United States to join. The league was also weakened by the belated admission of such important nations as Germany, not a member until 1926, and the Soviet Union, which joined only in 1934. Moreover, three major powers later withdrew—Germany, in 1933; Italy, in 1937; and Japan, in 1933.

The league peacekeeping machinery was limited. The league had no armed forces and every member had veto power over resolutions. The league could not agree on a general disarmament policy and was unable to halt Japanese aggression in China, which began in 1931, or Italy's invasion of Ethiopia in 1935, although sanctions were voted against Italy.

Nor could the league prevent German reoccupation of the Rhineland in 1936, a violation of the peace agreements ending World War I. It also was unable to act in regard to German and Italian participation in the Spanish Civil War (1936–1939), German annexation of Austria in 1938 and of Czechoslovakia in 1938–1939, or Germany's sudden invasion of Poland in September, 1939, which launched World War II.

Although the league was ineffective in maintaining peace, its work in social and economic affairs was considerable. Gains werre made in education and public health work, refugee assistance, and trade liberalization.

The league also sponsored the mandate system, which placed pre-World War I colonial possessions of the defeated Central Powers under the administration of Allied nations. These areas later became independent or UN trust territories.

Lepanto, Battle of, a great naval battle fought off the coast of Greece on October 7, 1571, between the Spanish, Venetian, and Papal fleets commanded by Don Juan of Austria, brother of King Philip II of Spain, and the Ottoman Turkish fleet under Ali Pasha.

The Turkish fleet was almost entirely destroyed, shattering the naval power of the Ottoman Empire, which had been threatening to make the Mediterranean Sea a Turkish lake. But the Christian allies did not effectively follow up on their victory, and the Turks rebuilt their fleet while Spain and Venice were disputing among themselves.

Locarno Conference, a meeting in 1925 of representatives of Belgium, Britain, Czechoslovakia, France, Germany, and Poland held at Locarno, Switzerland. The conference sought to bring peace and security to Western Europe and resulted in the Locarno Pact, a series of international treaties.

Germany signed treaties with France and Belgium guaranteeing its frontiers with them and agreed not to attack or invade either country. Britain and Italy agreed to give military aid to France and Belgium if they should be attacked. Also guaranteed was the continued demilitarization of the Rhineland as specified in the Treaty of Versailles.

Germany signed arbitration treaties with Poland and Czechoslovakia in which it agreed that any changes in its eastern frontiers would be made only after discussion and arbitration. France signed treaties of mutual assistance with Poland and Czechoslovakia against the possibility of a German attack.

For the first time in history, the great powers surrendered their absolute "right to make war." But in 1936 the Locarno treaties became scraps of paper when Germany fortified the Rhineland.

Loire, the longest river of France. It rises in the Cevennes Mountains in the southeast, flows northwest and west for 634 miles (1020 km.) and empties into the Bay of Biscay through a wide estuary at St. Nazaire.

Lombard League, a military coalition formed by the towns of Lombardy, in northern Italy, against the German emperor, Frederick I (Barbarossa, 1152–1190). The league was formed after Frederick's fourth expedition to Italy (1166–1168) and was composed of the Lombard towns, joined by Venice and the Normans of Sicily.

Frederick invaded northern Italy again in 1174, and in 1176 he was defeated by the league at Legnano. This was the first time since the fall of Rome that an experienced, professional cavalry was defeated by an army of nonprofessional foot soldiers. By the Peace of Constance drawn up in 1183, the independence of the Lombard towns was recognized.

A second Lombard League was formed about 1230, when German Emperor Frederick II renewed German claims on Italy.

Long Parliament, a British Parliament that theoretically sat for 20 years, from November, 1640, to March, 1660, without holding new elections.

The Stuart king, Charles I, had decided to rule without Parliament in 1629. In 1640, however, he was forced to convoke Parliament to raise funds to crush a revolt in Scotland. The Parliament was a revolutionary body. One of its leaders was the Puritan, Oliver Cromwell. It abolished certain royal courts and insisted on the execution of the king's chief advisers.

In 1642 war broke out between Parliament and the king. In return for Scottish army support, Parliament passed the Solemn League and Covenant in September, 1643, establishing Presbyterianism as the official religion of England, Ireland, and Scotland.

The parliamentary forces defeated the royalists, and Cromwell wanted Charles I executed. But about 100 members of Parliament protested, and Cromwell used the army to exclude them from Parliament. Parliament then consisted of about 50 members, known as the Rump Parliament. The Rump had Charles I executed in January, 1649.

Lucerne, a roughly cross-shaped lake in central Switzerland, 44 square miles (114 sq. km.) in area, bounded by the cantons of Lucerne, Unterwalden, Uri, and Schwyz.

Marathon, Battle of, a battle fought in 490 B.C. on the plain of Marathon, about 20 miles northeast of Athens, in which the Athenians and their allies defeated an invading Persian army led by Darius I. Although greatly outnumbered, the Greeks were led to victory by the Athenian general Miltiades.

The Athenian victory saved Athens from Persian conquest. Although the Persians organized a larger expedition against Greece ten years later, the victory had given the Greeks time to prepare for the attack.

Marne, a river that rises in eastern France and flows north and west for about 325 miles (525 km.) into the Seine at Charenton.

Marne, Battle of the, the name given to two major World War I battles fought along the Marne River in northern France, on September 6–9, 1914, and July 15–August 6, 1918.

In the first battle, British and French troops forced invading German troops to retreat, thereby breaking the German Schlieffen Plan, which had called for the rapid defeat of France by an invasion through Belgium. The Germans were also defeated in the second battle, by British, French, and U.S. troops. The second battle was a prelude to Germany's final defeat.

Marshall Plan, the unofficial name given to the European Recovery Program (ERP), a project in which the United States gave economic assistance to certain war-devastated European countries after World War II.

The plan was proposed by U.S. Secretary of State George C. Marshall in June, 1947. It called for a cooperative effort by the European countries to assess their common needs and resources before the arrival of U.S. aid. Marshall intended U.S. aid to be extended to all European countries, but the Soviet Union refused to allow its

WAR CRIMES TRIALS *at Nuremberg, Hitler's show town, opened with lesser fry in the dock, as shown here. Ten leaders were executed.*

satellites to participate in the program.

To draw up an economic recovery program, 17 countries formed the Organization of European Economic Co-operation (OEEC) in April, 1948. In the same month, Congress established an agency called the Economic Cooperation Administration (ECA), headed by Paul G. Hoffman, to administer the Marshall Plan.

The plan, which cost the United States about $12 billion in aid, was so successful that it was ended in 1951, six months ahead of schedule. An important effect of the plan was the containment of Soviet influence in Western Europe.

Mediterranean Sea, the largest inland sea in the world, 2400 miles (3865 km.) long and up to 1000 miles (1600 km.) wide. It separates the continents of Europe to the north, Asia to the east, and Africa to the south. The Mediterranean is linked with the Atlantic Ocean by the Strait of Gibraltar and with the Red Sea by the man-made Suez Canal.

The irregularly shaped sea is divided into two deep basins by the Italian peninsula, the island of Sicily, and a submarine ridge joining Sicily and Tunisia. There are islands in each basin. The eastern basin, connected to the Black Sea by the Bosporus and the Dardanelles, has two northern extensions, the Adriatic and Aegean seas.

The climate of the Mediterranean basin consists of hot, dry summers and warm, wet winters.

Meuse, a river that rises in northeastern France and flows through Belgium and the Netherlands for 580 miles (935 km.) into the North Sea. In the Netherlands, the Meuse becomes the Maas.

North Sea, an arm of the North Atlantic Ocean, separating Britain from the northwestern European mainland.

Nuremberg laws, decrees promulgated in 1935 by Adolf Hitler's Third Reich depriving all Jewish Germans of the rights of citizenship. The laws also forbade intermarriage between Jews and non-Jews. The same laws became applicable in Austria in 1938, when Germany annexed that country.

Nuremberg trials, the prosecution of German leaders in 1945–1946 by an international tribunal for war crimes and crimes against humanity.

The tribunal was established by Britain, France, the Soviet Union, and the United States after World War II. The trials were held in Nuremberg, Germany, where Adolf Hitler's National Socialist (Nazi) Party had held its party congresses.

The charges included launching aggressive warfare and genocide, the extermination of entire peoples. By the end of the war, some 6 million European Jews had been systematically murdered by Germany's Nazi regime. In 1946, after the trials, ten of the accused were executed.

Oder, a river in central Europe, about 560 miles (900 km.) long. It rises in Czechoslovakia, flows north through western Poland, is joined by the Neisse River, and continues north to the Baltic Sea. The Oder forms a major part of the border between East Germany and Poland.

Old Regime, or, in French, *ancien régime,* the term used to describe French society and government in the period before the French Revolution of 1789. The phrase refers to a society in which many characteristics of medieval life persisted.

French society before the revolution was divided into three "estates," or classes. The first and second estates, the clergy and nobility, had many privileges, rights, and immunities denied to the third, the common people.

The tax structure under the Old Regime was complex and inequitable, and the system of weights and measures was irregular. Society was regulated by conflicting legal codes and government was headed by an absolute monarch.

Olympus, a mountain range in Greece, near the coast of Thessaly. Mt. Olympus, 9570 feet (2917 m), the highest point in the range and in Greece, was thought in ancient times to be the home of the gods.

Pan–Slavism, an Eastern European movement during the 1800's that believed in the uniqueness of the Slavic peoples and worked for cultural and political unity among them.

In 1848, a year of revolutionary ferment in Europe, the Czechs called an all-Slav congress at Prague. Most of the Slavs represented at the congress were citizens of the Austrian Empire.

Opposed to czarist Russia and unwilling to be incorporated into a German state (the Frankfurt Assembly was simultaneously trying to create a unified Germany), the Slavs believed that they could best develop a Slavic national life by demanding local autonomy within the Hapsburg domains. This idea of constitutional rights for the Slavic peoples within the Austrian Empire was known as Austro-Slavism.

The Austrian emperor Ferdinand was opposed to national movements in his empire, however, and by 1849 all hopes for Austro-Slavism and internal autonomy were crushed.

By 1870 Pan-Slavism was becoming popular in Russian intellectual circles. In 1875 and 1876 Slavs in the Ottoman Empire utilized Russian Pan-Slavism to fight against their Turkish rulers. Revolts broke out in Bosnia and Bulgaria, and in 1877 Russia declared war on Turkey.

A congress held in Berlin in 1878 gave independence to Serbia and Rumania, and gave full autonomy to Montenegro. Bulgaria, however, was kept within the Ottoman Empire, and Bosnia was occupied by Austria-Hungary. Both Russian Pan-Slavs and Balkan Slav nationalist partisans were dissatisfied by the treaty, and Slavic discontent helped ignite World War I.

Peloponnesus, or Peloponnese, a peninsula and province of southern Greece, connected with the mainland by the narrow Isthmus of Corinth. The Peloponnesus is the site of ancient Corinth and Sparta.

Popular Front, the name often given to a coalition of left-wing parties or of left and center parties. The term refers specifically to the French government of Léon Blum and his successors, Camille Chautemps and Édouard Daladier, formed in 1936 and renewed in 1937 and again in 1938.

The Popular Front government at-

tempted to institute a wide program of social and economic reforms to combat the threat of fascism and to meet the challenge of the world economic depression of the 1930's. But the Popular Front foundered over methods to remedy basic economic problems.

The left-wing parties demanded radical changes, but the center parties demanded austerity and the use of traditional economic measures. The Daladier government finally broke with the left-wing parties in October, 1938, thus ending the Popular Front.

A similar Popular Front government under President Manuel Azaña took over in Spain in 1936 and led the Loyalist forces of the republic in Spain's civil war of 1936–1939.

Potsdam Conference, a meeting held in July, 1945, in the German city of Potsdam by Britain, the Soviet Union, and the United States to determine policy in regard to defeated Germany and toward Japan. It was attended by the leaders of the World War II Allies–British Prime Minister Winston Churchill, who was succeeded by Clement Attlee; Soviet Premier Joseph Stalin; and the current U.S. President Harry Truman.

The conference demanded unconditional surrender from Japan and established the terms for the partition of Germany into zones of occupation. There was also Allied agreement to try Axis leaders for war crimes.

Pragmatic Sanction, a statement or decree relating to affairs of state issued by the head of a government with the force of law. The one best known in European history was issued by Holy Roman Emperor Charles VI in 1713. It declared that in the absence of male heirs, the emperor's domain would be inherited by his daughter Maria Theresa.

Most of the powers of Europe agreed to the Pragmatic Sanction, but after the death of Charles in 1740 they tried to prevent Maria Theresa's accession. Her efforts to win her rights in the

MARIA THERESA *of Austria. The Pragmatic Sanction gained her a shaky throne.*

NEW YORK PUBLIC LIBRARY

face of several claims to her domain led to the War of the Austrian Succession (1740–1748).

Pyrenees, a major European mountain range extending some 270 miles (435 km.) along the entire Spanish-French border, from the Bay of Biscay to the south coast of the Gulf of Lions. The highest peak is Pico de Aneto, 11,168 feet (3404 m).

Rhine, a West European river that rises in the Swiss Alps and flows north and west, forming parts of the boundaries of Liechtenstein, Switzerland, France, and West Germany. In Germany it crosses a rich, densely populated, and highly industrialized region before turning west into the Netherlands, where it divides into two branches, the Nederrijn and the Waal, which empty into the North Sea near Rotterdam.

The Rhine is 820 miles (1320 km.) long, and its major tributaries include the Neckar, Main, Ruhr, Lippe, and Moselle rivers. It is navigable for most of its course, and is connected by many canals with other major European river systems.

Rhône, a west European river that flows some 500 miles (800 km.) through Switzerland and France. It rises in the Swiss Alps, passes through Lake Geneva and crosses into France. Joined at Lyon by the Saône River, it turns south and empties into the Mediterranean Sea west of Marseille.

Riviera, a Mediterranean seacoast in southern France and northwestern Italy. Its blue water and white beaches have made it one of the world's most popular resort areas.

Scandinavia, a peninsula of northwestern Europe washed by the Arctic Ocean on the north, the Norwegian Sea on the west, the North Sea, Skagerrak and Kattegat straits on the south, and the Baltic Sea and Gulf of Bothnia on the southeast. It is shared by Norway and Sweden.

Seine, a river of northern France that rises in the highlands northwest of Dijon. It flows through Paris and empties into the English Channel at Le Havre after a course of 482 miles (776 km.).

Seven Years' War, a struggle fought from 1756 to 1763 between Britain, Hanover, Portugal, and Prussia against Austria, France, Russia, Sweden, Spain, and a few German principalities. It was a contest for dominance in central Europe and for control of colonies in North America and India. In America the struggle began in 1755 and was known as the French and Indian War.

The immediate cause of the war in Europe was Austria's desire to reclaim the rich territory of Silesia that it had ceded to Frederick the Great of Prussia in 1742. The war was a contest between Austria and Prussia, the two greatest German powers.

By a complicated series of alliances, known as the diplomatic revolution, Austria allied itself with France, its traditional enemy. Austria also formed alliances with Saxony and Poland. Britain, fearing a French or Prussian attack on its royal province of Hanover, allied itself with Prussia. This alliance enabled Austria to win Russia as an ally and to bring France to declare war on Britain in June, 1756.

Frederick, aware of these Austrian moves, struck first by invading Saxony in August, 1756. In January, 1757, Austria declared war on Prussia in the name of the Holy Roman Empire.

During the early stages of the war, Frederick was generally successful in Europe and Britain stripped away the French colonial empire. But after 1760 the pressure on Prussia began to tell. In 1762, the Russian empress Elizabeth died and was succeeded by Peter III, who admired Frederick. Russia then withdrew from the war. This enabled Prussia to hold off the French and Austrians until 1763, when the Treaty of Hubertusburg ended the war in central Europe between Austria and Prussia.

By the terms of the treaty, Prussia retained Silesia and other European boundaries remained essentially as they were before the war. The Treaty of Paris (1763), which settled colonial matters, gave most of French North America to Britain and forced France to withdraw from India. France was, however, allowed to keep a few small trading stations on the eastern coast of India.

Sicily, the largest island of the Mediterranean. A part of Italy, it is separated from the southwestern tip of the mainland by the narrow Strait of Messina. Most of Sicily is mountainous and rugged, and the climate is dry and mild.

Skagerrak, a strait between Norway and Denmark, about 150 miles (240 km.) long and 80 miles (130 km.) wide. It leads into the North Sea in the southwest and the Kattegat in the northeast, and forms an important link in the North Sea-Baltic waterway.

Tagus, the longest river of the Iberian Peninsula. It rises in Spain's eastern mountains, flows west across Spain, and forms a small section of the border with Portugal before turning southwest to enter the Atlantic at Lisbon after a course of 626 miles (1008 km.).

Thames, a river 210 miles (338 km.) long in southern Britain. It rises in Gloucestershire, flows east into the densely settled fertile English Lowlands, through London, and empties into the North Sea.

Toleration Acts, a group of laws dealing with religious freedom in Britain. The Toleration Act of 1689, passed under the reign of William and Mary following the Glorious Revolution, allowed greater freedom to Protestants who were not members of the Church of England, or Anglicans.

Statutes passed in 1778, 1791, and 1829 provided freedom of worship for Roman Catholics, and statutes passed in 1846, 1851, and 1858 granted religious freedom to Jews. A statute of 1888 allowed the admission of atheists to Parliament.

Tours, Battle of, battle in 732 in which invading Muslims from Spain were decisively defeated by the Franks, led by Charles Martel. Tours is about 130 miles southwest of Paris.

In 711 an army of Arabs and Berbers from North Africa had begun the Muslim conquest of Spain. The Battle of Tours effectively ended the threat of Muslim domination in Europe north of the Pyrenees.

Trafalgar, Battle of, a British naval victory on October 21, 1805, over combined French and Spanish fleets during the Napoleonic wars. The British fleet, led by Lord Horatio Nelson, caught and destroyed the main body of the enemy fleet off Cape Trafalgar, on the Spanish coast. Not one British ship was destroyed, but Nelson was killed. The victory ensured British naval supremacy for the next century.

Tyrrhenian Sea, an arm of the Mediterranean Sea. It lies between Italy on the east, Corsica and Sardinia on the west, and Sicily on the south.

Ural, a river in the west-central Soviet Union. It rises in the southern Ural Mountains and flows southwest, and south again, emptying into the Caspian Sea. The river is about 1500 miles (2415 km.) long.

Ural Mountains, a mountain system in the Soviet Union that extends for about 1300 miles (2100 km.) from the Kara Sea to the Ural River, forming the traditional geographic boundary between Europe and Asia. The Urals can be divided into three sections—the Northern Urals, which contain the highest peaks; the Central Urals, which are gently rounded; and the Southern Urals, which are formed by a

Versailles, Treaty of, the most important of the treaties ending World War I. The Treaty of Versailles was framed by Britain, France, Japan, and the United States, although the United States did not ratify it.

The treaty dealt with Germany's responsibility for the war and its obligations in defeat. Among the most significant provisions were the separation of a number of territories from Germany, the requirement that Germany pay substantial reparations, and limitations on German rearmament.

NAPOLEON AT WATERLOO. *The battle in 1815 was Napoleon's last fling, after escaping from exile on Elba. He lost by a hairsbreadth, after the Prussian, Field Marshall Blücher, turned the tide at the end of the day in favor of the Allies. Napoleon abdicated and was again exiled, this time to the island of St. Helena far off in the South Atlantic.*

In addition, the treaty provided for the demilitarization of the Rhineland.

One of the most significant provisions of the treaty was the establishment of the League of Nations. Although the United States did not join the league, which soon proved ineffective, the idea of a world organization endured and established the basis for the United Nations.

Much of the Treaty of Versailles was based upon the 14 points proposed by U.S. President Woodrow Wilson during the final stages of the war. Many of the more liberal provisions, such as covenants openly arrived at, freedom of the seas, and impartial adjustment of colonial claims were ignored, however.

Vesuvius, an active volcano in Italy, lying on the eastern shore of the Bay of Naples. Vesuvius is about 4000 feet (1220 m) above sea level, but its exact height varies with each eruption. In 79 A.D. it buried Roman Pompeii.

Volga, the longest river of the Soviet Union and of Europe, 2293 miles (3692 km.) long. It rises in the Valdai Hills northwest of Moscow and follows a winding course to the Caspian Sea. The volga flows first east and southeast to Kazan, and then generally south to Astrakhan, where it forms an extensive delta.

An extensive series of canals joins the Volga to the Baltic and Black Sea river systems.

Waterloo, Battle of, the last engagement of the armies of Napoleon Bonaparte against the forces of the allied powers of Europe led by England's Arthur Wellesley, Duke of Wellington.

The battle began on June 18, 1815 just south of the Belgian town of Waterloo. The battle raged all day without decisive result. Late in the day the Prussian General Gebhard Leberecht von Blücher arrived with reinforcements for Wellington. The struggle was renewed immediately, and the allies were then victorious. The battle marked Napoleon's final defeat.

Westphalia, Peace of, the treaties that ended the Thirty Years' War in 1648. Its most important effects were the disintegration of the Holy Roman Empire, and the ending of the religious wars accompanying the Reformation.

Under the treaties, each of the German states was given a large degree of autonomy and the border states of the Holy Roman Empire, such as Switzerland, the Netherlands, and parts of Alsace and Lorraine, broke away entirely from the confederation. The peace also granted to each of the states the right to determine its own religion.

Yalta Conference, a meeting held in February, 1945, in the Soviet city of Yalta, by Britain, the Soviet Union, and the United States to determine policy in regard to Eastern Europe, Germany, and the Far East. The conference was attended by the leaders of the World War II Allies—British Prime Minister Winston Churchill; Soviet Premier Joseph Stalin; and U.S. President Franklin D. Roosevelt.

Stalin, whose troops were occupying Eastern Europe, promised to allow free elections in the occupied states at the soonest possible date. Poland's eastern frontier, with the Soviet Union, was moved farther west and its western boundary, with Germany, was moved farther west, in effect moving the whole country westward.

The three powers agreed that Germany would be disarmed and divided into four occupation zones, each to be administered by one of the big three powers and France. It was also agreed that German reparations would go to those countries that had suffered the heaviest losses, with the Soviet Union receiving half the total. The three leaders also agreed on plans to create an international organization, the United Nations.

The Soviet Union, which had signed a nonaggression treaty with Japan in 1941, agreed to enter the war against Japan about three months after Germany's defeat. In return, Stalin demanded from Japan the southern half of Sakhalin Island and the Kuril Islands; from China special concessions in the port of Dairen, the lease of Port Arthur as a Soviet naval base, and joint control over the railroads leading to those ports; and the continuation of Soviet control over Mongolia.

Yenisey, a major river of Asia, located in central Siberia. It is formed from the Greater Yenisey, rising in the Sayan Mountains of Mongolia, and the Lesser Yenisey, rising in the Siberian highlands. They meet at Kyzyl to form the Yenisey proper. It is over 2500 miles (4000 km.) long.

Major tributaries of the Yenisey include the Lower Tunguska, Stony Tunguska, Angara, and Abakan rivers. The Yenisey empties into the Yenisey Gulf of the Kara Sea.

For Further Reference

General

Adams, Arthur et al. *Atlas of Russian and East European History.* Frederick A. Praeger, 1966.

Atkinson, William C. *A History of Spain and Portugal.* Penguin, 1960.

Bisselle, Walter C. *The Peoples of Eastern Europe.* Cliffs, 1978.

Brinton, Crane, John B. Christopher and Robert L. Wolff. *A History of Civilization* (3rd Ed.). 2 volumes. Prentice-Hall, 1967.

Charques, Richard D. *A Short History of Russia.* E. P. Dutton, 1958.

Chew, Allen F. *An Atlas of Russian History.* Yale University Press, 1967.

Cobban, Alfred. *History of Modern France* (Revised Ed.). 3 volumes. Penguin, 1961–1963.

Dmytryshyn, Basil. *The U.S.S.R.: A Concise History.* Charles Scribner's Sons, 1965.

Dopsch, Alfons. *Economic and Social Foundations of European Civilization.* Gordon Press, 1979.

Drachkovitch, Milorad, editor. *East Central Europe: Yesterday, Today, Tomorrow.* Hoover Institute Press, 1980.

Dukes, Paul. *History of Europe, Sixteen Forty-Eight to Nineteen Forty-Eight: The Arrival, the Rise, the Fall.* Sheridan House, 1985.

Dunlop, John K. *Short History of Germany,* Dufour Editions, 1966.

Eyck, F. Gunther. *The Benelux Countries.* Van Nostrand Reinhold, 1959.

Fischer, Eric. *Passing of the European Age.* Russell, 1967.

Gottmann, Jean. *A Geography of Europe* (3rd Ed.). Holt, Rinehart & Winston, 1954.

Grindrod, Muriel. *Italy.* Oxford University Press, 1964.

Hoffman, George W., et al. *Geography of Europe.* Ronald Press, 1963.

Holborn, Hajo. *History of Modern Germany.* 3 volumes. Alfred A. Knopf, 1958–1968.

Hume, David. *History of England.* 6 volumes. Liberty Fund, 1985.

Livermore, Harold. *A New History of Portugal.* Cambridge University Press, 1966.

O'Callaghan, Joseph F. *A History of Medieval Spain.* Cornell University Press, 1983.

Palmer, Doris M., editor. *Sources of Information on the European Communities.* Merrimack Book Service, 1979.

Palmer, R. R., and Joel Colton. *A History of the Modern World* (3rd Ed.). Alfred A. Knopf, 1966.

Peters, D. J. *Short History of France.* Pergamon Press, 1967.

Sharp, Samuel L. *Soviet Union and Eastern Europe* (8th Ed.). Stryker-Post, 1979.

Stearns, Peter N. *The Face of Europe.* Forum Press, 1977.

Trevelyan, Janet P. *Short History of the Italian People from the Barbarian Invasion to the Present Day.* Pitman, 1956.

Tuma, Elias H. *European Economic History: Tenth Century to Present.* Pacific Books, 1979.

Wolff, Robert L. *The Balkans in Our Time.* W. W. Norton, 1967.

Wuorinen, John H. *Scandinavia.* Prentice-Hall, 1965.

Prehistory

Bruce-Mitford, Rupert, editor. *Archaeological Excavations in Europe.* Routledge & Kegan, 1975.

Collins, Desmond, editor. *The Origins of Europe: Four New Studies in Archaeology and History.* Crowell, 1976.

Phillips, Patricia. *The Prehistory of Europe.* Indiana University Press, 1980.

Piggott, Stuart. *Ancient Europe.* Aldine, 1968.

Ancient Civilization

Burns, Edward M. *Western Civilization* (8th Ed.). W. W. Norton, 1974.

Crawford, Michael. *Ancient Greece and Rome.* Cambridge University Press, 1984.

Lopez, Robert, et al. *Civilization: Western and World.* 2 volumes. Little, Brown, 1975.

Rostovtzeff, M. I. *Greece.* Oxford University Press, 1963.

Rostovtzeff, M. I. *The Social and Economic History of the Roman Empire.* 2 volumes. Oxford University Press, 1941.

Medieval Civilization

Artz, Frederick B. *The Mind of the Middle Ages* (2nd Ed.). Alfred A. Knopf, 1968.

Bloch, Marc. *Feudal Society.* 2 volumes. Phoenix Books, 1961.

Brooke, Christopher. *Medieval Church and Society.* New York University Press, 1972.

Hollister, Warren C. *Medieval Europe: A Short History* (5th Ed.). Random House, 1982.

Leff, Gordon. *Medieval Thought.* Quadrangle Books, 1960.

Lopez, Robert. *The Birth of Europe.* M. Evans, 1967.

Mathew, Donald. *The Medieval European Community.* St. Martin's, 1977.

Painter, Sidney. *The Rise of the Feudal Monarchies.* Cornell University Press, 1951.

Pirenne, Henri. *Economic and Social History of Medieval Europe.* Harvest Books, 1956.

Setton, Kenneth, editor. *A History of the Crusades.* 3 volumes. University of Wisconsin Press, 1969–1975.

Early Modern Europe

Ashley, M. P. *Louis XIV and the Greatness of France.* Macmillan, 1965.

Bainton, Roland. *Here I Stand: A Life of Martin Luther.* Abingdon Press, 1959.

Bainton, Roland. *The Reformation of the Sixteenth Century.* Beacon Press, 1956.

Benians, Sylvia. *From Renaissance to Revolution.* Kennikat, 1970.

Bruun, Geoffrey. *The Enlightened Despots* (2nd Ed.). Holt, Rinehart & Winston, 1967.

Clark, George. *Early Modern Europe From About 1450 to About 1720.* Oxford University Press, 1960.

Cunningham, James V., editor. *The Renaissance in England.* Harcourt, Brace & World, 1966.

Dunn, Richard S. *Age of Religious Wars, 1559–1715.* W. W. Norton, 1979.

Durant, Will, and Ariel Durant. *The Story of Civilization: Rousseau and Revolution. Volume 10.* Simon & Schuster, 1967.

Elliot, J. H. *Imperial Spain, 1469–1716.* St. Martin's, 1963.

Friedrich, Carl J. *Age of the Baroque: 1610–1660.* Harper & Row, 1952.

Gilmore, Myron P. *World of Humanism: 1453–1517.* Harper & Row, 1952.

Grimm, Harold J. *The Reformation Era, 1500–1650* (Revised Ed.). Macmillan, 1965.

Hale, John R. *Age of Exploration.* Silver Burdett, 1966.

Hay, Denys. *The Italian Renaissance in Its Historical Background.* Cambridge University Press, 1961.

Jensen, DeLamar. *Reformation Europe: Age of Reform and Revolution.* D. C. Heath, 1981.

Manuel, Frank. *The Age of Reason.* Cornell University Press, 1951.

Mattingly, Garrett. *The Armada.* Houghton Mifflin, 1959.

Morison, Samuel Eliot. *Christopher Columbus, Mariner.* Little, Brown, 1955.

Rowen, H. H., and C. J. Ekberg. *Early Modern Europe: A Book of Source Readings.* Peacock Publishers, 1973.

Wolf, John B. *Early Modern Europe: 1500 - 1789.* AHM Publishing, 1972.

Modern Europe

Alocroff, Derek. *European Economy: 1914–1970.* St. Martin's, 1978.

Baldwin, Hanson W. *World War I.* Harper & Row, 1962.

Bendersky, Joseph W. *A History of Nazi Germany.* Nelson Hall, 1984.

Black, C. E., and E. C. Helmreich. *Twentieth Century Europe* (3rd Ed.). Alfred A. Knopf, 1966.

Boutwell, Jeffrey, and Paul Doty, editors. *The Nuclear Confrontation in Europe.* Auburn House, 1985.

Clissold, Stephen, editor. *A Short History of Yugoslavia.* Cambridge University Press, 1968.

Clough, S. B., et al. *European History in a World Perspective.* 3 volumes. D. C. Heath, 1975.

Coffey, Joseph I. *Arms Control and European Security: A Guide to East-West Negotiations.* Frederick A. Praeger, 1977.

Craig, Gordon. *Europe Since 1815* (2nd Ed.). Holt, Rinehart & Winston, 1966.

Dornberg, John. *Eastern Europe: A Communist Kaleidoscope.* Dial Press, 1980.

Furdson, Edward. *The European Defense Community: A History.* St. Martin's, 1980.

Gay, Peter, and Robert Webb. *Modern Europe.* 2 volumes. Harper & Row, 1973.

Goodwin, Albert. *The French Revolution* (5th Ed.). Hutchinson, 1984.

Hohmann, Hans-Hermann, et al., editors. *The New Economic Systems of Eastern Europe.* University of California Press, 1975.

Hussey, W. D. *The British Empire and Commonwealth, 1500–1961.* Cambridge University Press, 1963.

Kitchen, Martin. *Europe Between the Wars.* Longman, 1988.

Laqueur, Walter. *Europe Since Hilter: The Rebirth of Europe* (Revised Ed.). Penguin, 1982.

Lieberman, Sima. *The Growth of European Mixed Economics 1945–1970: A Concise Study of the Economic Evolution of Six Countries.* Wiley, 1979.

Maier, Charles S. *Recasting Bourgeois Europe: Stabilization in France, Germany, and Italy in the Decade After World War I.* Princeton University Press, 1975.

Paskins, Barrie, editor. *Ethics and European Security.* Auburn House, 1986.

Paxton, Robert O. *Europe in the Twentieth Century* (2nd Ed.). Harcourt Brace Jovanovich, 1985.

Pool, Ithiel. *Satellite Generals: A Study of Military Elites in the Soviet Sphere.* Greenwood Press, 1975.

Riasanovsky, Nicholas V. *A History of Russia* (2nd Ed.). Oxford University Press, 1969.

Rodney, Walter. *How Europe Underdeveloped Africa.* Howard University Press, 1974.

Strahan, Hew. *European Armies and the Conduct of War.* Allen & Unwin, 1983.

Stavrianos, L. S. *The Balkans Since 1453.* Holt, Rinehart & Winston, 1958.

Sumner, B. H. *Peter the Great and the Emergence of Russia.* Macmillan, 1950.

Taylor, Telford. *Munich: The Price of Peace.* Random House, 1980.

Thompson, Samuel H. *Czechoslovakia in European History.* Princeton University Press, 1953.

Wagner, Francis. *Toward a New Central Europe.* Danubian, 1970.

Webb, R. K. *Modern England.* Dodd, Mead, 1968.

Wegs, J. Robert. *Europe Since 1945: A Concise History.* St. Martin's, 1984.

Wright, Gordon. *France in Modern Times.* Rand McNally, 1974.

Food and Agriculture

METROPOLITAN MUSEUM OF ART/DICK FUND, 1926

WORLD FOOD CONSUMPTION IN CALORIES

Figures from the World Bank for the early 1970's dramatize the disparity in living standards between the developed and the underdeveloped nations. Given below is the caloric intake per person per day for the top 20 out of 118 countries listed; in way of contrast, the caloric intake of the 20 countries lowest on the list is also given. The daily minimum consumption of calories of food per person recommended by specialized agencies of the United Nations is 2600. This minimum is far exceeded by 34 developed countries, almost all in Europe and the western hemisphere, except for three in Asia. The rest of the world eats less well, with black Africa as a whole at the bottom of the list.

Highest Country	Calories	Lowest Country	Calories
Ireland	3410	Dominican Republic	2120
Belgium	3380	South Yemen	2070
Luxembourg	3380	Chad	2060
United States	3330	Zaire	2060
Austria	3310	Mozambique	2050
Australia	3280	Botswana	2040
Turkey	3250	Burundi	2040
Denmark	3240	Guinea	2040
West Germany	3220	Liberia	2040
Netherlands	3220	Yemen Arab Republic	2040
France	3210	Ecuador	2010
New Zealand	3200	Angola	2000
Greece	3190	Mauritania	1970
Switzerland	3190	Rwanda	1960
United Kingdom	3190	Upper Volta	1940
Yugoslavia	3190	El Salvador	1930
Canada	3180	Bolivia	1900
Italy	3180	Somalia	1830
Argentina	3060	Algeria	1730
Finland	3050	Haiti	1730

Food and Agriculture

Agriculture and Civilization.—Civilization began when man started farming some ten thousand years ago. Before that, for perhaps a million years, people lived a wandering, precarious existence, hunting seeds and nuts and killing small wild animals for food. Agriculture permitted men to live settled lives and encouraged the development of industries and cities, necessary attributes for modern civilization.

Very likely one of mankind's greatest achievements—planting and harvesting crops—resulted from chance observation. A primitive woman may have noticed that grain-bearing plants grew up where grain had been spilled or stored. She then took the vital step of planting seeds, protecting the growing plants, and harvesting the crop.

Keeping animals probably began when primitive man tamed wounded or trapped animals, or when women saved and tamed young animals. Farming and animal husbandry developed together for a long period of time. The nomadic herding of livestock was a later development.

■ **ORIGINS.**—Agriculture originated first in the Middle East, probably in the grassy uplands where the wild grains and the wild animals first to be domesticated were found. By 5000 B.C., crops included wheat and barley, while sheep, goats, pigs, horses, and cattle had all been domesticated. The first farmers used tools of polished or chipped flint and obsidian.

Agriculture spread from the Middle East to the Danubian Basin, the shores of the Black Sea, the fertile crescent bordering the Arabian desert, and the valleys of the Indus River in India and the Hwang Ho in China. The crops, animals, and tools were much the same except in America, where agriculture probably was discovered independently.

Prehistoric man, drawing upon wild stock, developed all the major food plants and animals used today. Wheat and barley were domesticated in the Middle East. Rice and bananas were developed later in southeast Asia, and sorghum and millets in Africa. The New World saw the domestication of maize (corn) and potatoes. Food animals were domesticated first in the Middle East. Chickens were developed in southeast Asia, and turkeys domesticated in the New World.

■ **EARLY TOOLS.**—The first farming tool was a pointed stick, the digging stick. The food gatherers had used it to dig roots; the first farmers used it to dig holes for seeds. The spade was invented by the man who added a crossbar to his digging stick so that he could use his foot to drive it deep-

ABOUT TEN PER CENT of the world's land is under cultivation today. Much of the growing area is north of the equator.

er into the soil. A stick with a sharp branch at one end was the first hoe. Later, a sharp stone or shell was tied to the branch to give it a more effective cutting edge. Sharp stones set along one edge converted a stick into a sickle.

After animals were domesticated for food, they were soon trained to become beasts of burden. The next step, never taken by the American Indians, was to train animals to pull a heavy hoe through the earth—the beginning of plowing and cultivating by animal power. The Indians, perhaps because they had no animals for plowing, never adopted a *clean field* agriculture. Instead, they planted seeds in hills a few feet apart and cut the weeds only around the hills.

Nearly all prehistoric farmers in arid regions developed some method of irrigating their crops. Many also discovered the advantages of various types of fertilizer, from using farmyard manure to planting fish in hills of maize. They stored grain, seeds, and nuts for winter and also preserved meat and fish by salting and drying.

The discovery of metal and its uses, marking the end of the Neolithic period, enabled farmers to have sharper, stronger blades for hoes, plow points, and sickles. The change came slowly and in some areas, particularly in America, did not take place until Europeans introduced the new tools.

When agriculture first appeared in recorded history, it already was well developed—all the basic advances in domesticating major crops and animals had been made. The rules men followed were based upon longtime observations and trial and error. For centuries, few changes took place.

Advances in Agriculture.—The transformation in English agriculture which took place during the eighteenth century paved the way for modern farming. The key to the change was the enclosure of former open-field farms and the conversion of much arable land into pasture. The rights of villagers to use certain lands in common were largely revoked, and many small landowners and laborers were forced out of farming. At the same time, many improvements in farming were made. Improved methods of cultivation were adopted and machines were more widely used. New crops and more productive varieties were introduced, and controlled animal breeding became possible.

Not all the improvements originated in England. Clover was introduced in Spain, turnip cultivation in Flanders, and new grasses in France. The Rotherham plow, with a coulter and share made of iron, may have originated in Holland.

■ **AGRICULTURAL LEADERS.**—The adoption of advanced practices was encouraged by a number of English agricultural leaders. For 150 years, British farmers learned from such men as Jethro Tull (1674-1740), Charles Townshend (1674-1738), Robert Bakewell (1725-1795), Arthur Young (1741-1820), Sir John Sinclair (1745-1835), and Thomas Coke (1752-1842).

Tull invented a grain drill and advocated more intensive cultivation and the use of animal power. Townshend improved crop rotation and stressed the field cultivation of turnips and clover. Bakewell developed better breeds of livestock. Young and Sinclair were influential writers, and corresponded with American leaders such as George Washington and Thomas Jefferson. Coke developed a model agricultural estate, working particularly with wheat and sheep.

■ **THE NEW WORLD.**—British technological improvements in agriculture gradually spread through western Europe and to the United States. Members of such groups as the Philadelphia Society for Promoting Agriculture and the South Carolina Society for Promoting and Improving Agriculture, both founded in 1785, were familiar with the new English practices and followed some of them. Longhorn cattle, developed by Robert Blakewell, were imported into the United States in 1783, while Henry Clay imported Hereford cattle in 1817. The first agricultural journal appeared in 1810, and John Stuart Skinner began publishing the influential *American Farmer* in 1819. Such periodicals brought some of the English advances to the knowledge of a wider group of American farmers.

The most important technological advance in American agriculture dur-

WORK-SAVING INVENTIONS that raised farm production are the McCormick reaper (*left*), Whitney cotton gin (*right*), and Deere steel plow (*insert*).

ing this period, however, had no relation to English agricultural change. It was, instead, English demand for cotton that led Eli Whitney in 1793 to invent the cotton gin. This practical device for separating the seed from the lint of short-staple cotton revolutionized Southern agriculture. Production of cotton increased from an estimated 10,500 bales in 1793 to 4,486,000 bales in 1861.

Extensive commercial production of cotton, made possible by the cotton gin, led to the expansion of the plantation system, with its use of slave labor. It also led to dependence upon the single staple crop. Cotton cultivation led to the rapid settlement of the region and returned large sums of money to the planters. It also encouraged the economic development of the entire nation by providing large sums for use in foreign exchange.

■IMPROVEMENT OF PLOWS.—Technical ingenuity was not confined to cotton. Many Americans were attempting to build better plows, fundamental to an improved agriculture. In 1793, Thomas Jefferson developed a moldboard, made according to a mathematical plan, that would offer little soil resistance.

The first patent for a plow was issued to Charles Newbold of New Jersey in 1797. The plow, except for the handles and beam, was to be of solid cast iron. Farmers distrusted the new plow, believing that the iron poisoned the soil and made weeds grow.

The next great improvement in the plow was Jethro Wood's cast-iron model, first patented in 1814 but greatly improved in 1819. The moldboard, share, and landside were cast in three parts. The interchangeability of the parts was one of Wood's major contributions to the development of the modern plow.

The cast-iron plow was successful in New England and the Middle Atlantic states. But it would not scour in the prairies; the heavy, sticky soil would cling to the moldboard instead of sliding by and turning over. The steel plow was the answer to this problem. In 1833, John Lane, a blacksmith of Lockport, Ill., began covering moldboards with strips of saw steel. These plows succeeded in turning the prairie soil. In 1837, John Deere, a blacksmith of Grand Detour, Ill., began making a one-piece share and moldboard of saw steel. Deere became a successful manufacturer of steel and wrought-iron plows, which by 1860 had largely displaced the cast-iron plow in the prairies.

■DEVELOPMENT OF THE REAPER.—The mechanical reaper was probably the most significant single invention introduced into American farming between 1800 and 1860. It replaced much human power at a critical point in grain production where the work must be completed quickly to ensure saving the crop. By the American Revolution, the cradle had generally replaced the sickle and ordinary scythe for cutting grain. The cradle was a scythe with a light framework which gathered the stems and laid the grain down evenly.

Many inventors worked on animal-powered machines for harvesting grain. The first such machines in America efficient enough to find a market were patented by Obed Hussey in 1833 and Cyrus H. McCormick in 1834. In the struggle for business that followed, McCormick emerged dominant.

The Marsh harvester, patented in 1858, used a traveling apron to lift the cut grain into a receiving box where men riding on the machine bound it into bundles. Early in the 1870's, an automatic wire binder was perfected, but it was superseded by a twine binder late in the decade.

Other horse-drawn machines fol-lowed the improved plows and the grain reapers. Threshing machines were first brought from Scotland, then a practical thresher was patented in the United States in 1837. Other American patents were granted in the 1840's and 1850's for an improved grain drill, a mowing machine, a disk harrow, a corn planter, and a straddle row cultivator. At the same time, improved crop varieties were being introduced from abroad, and the commercial fertilizer industry was just beginning.

American Agricultural Revolution.—The Civil War led to the first American agricultural revolution. Farmers found that the demand for farm products was so great and the labor shortage so pronounced that it seemed both possible and profitable to adopt the new machines and techniques developed in the preceding decades. The establishment of the land-grant colleges to teach agriculture and mechanical arts and of the Department of Agriculture, the provisions for Western settlement in the Homestead Act, and the chartering of the Union Pacific Railroad, all in 1862, were also made immediately possible by the war. Together, these changes marked a transition from subsistence to commercial agriculture and from hand power to animal power.

The first state agricultural experiment station was established in Connecticut in 1875. Congress provided in 1887 for a yearly grant to each state for the support of an agricultural experiment station. These stations, the state colleges, and the Department of Agriculture together brought science to farming. As a result, farmers obtained improved or new varieties of plants and breeds of animals, learned how better to fertilize their crops, feed their animals, and control many plant and animal diseases and pests. This became more prevalent after 1914, when Congress, by the Smith-Lever Act, provided for a county agent in each agricultural county. The county agent, college-trained, carried scientific knowledge directly to the farmers.

The farm machinery widely adopted after the Civil War was mostly horse-drawn, while various devices were used to transmit horse-power to such stationary machines as threshers. A considerable number of steam engines were built for farm use. These usually were mounted on wheels and could be moved from place to place by horses. By 1900, self-propelled steam tractors were being sold for use in agriculture, but their weight made them unwieldy.

The internal-combustion engine, which had been invented in Europe, was a more practical answer to the search for mechanical power. By 1890, a number of American companies were manufacturing stationary engines, some of which were mounted on wheels. John Froelich of Iowa built the first gasoline tractor on record that was an operating success. In 1892 he mounted a gasoline engine on a running gear equipped with a traction arrangement of his own manufacture. The tractor completed a 50-day threshing run. The first company in the United States devoted exclusively to the manufacture of tractors was established in Iowa City, Iowa, about 1903.

The change from animal power to mechanical power came slowly. Farmers already had horses and could grow the feed necessary to maintain them. It took another crisis, World War II with its manpower shortage and seemingly unlimited demand for farm products, to give impetus to the change.

Advances in Technology.—Technological changes, in most instances, resulted from the application of scientific theories to practical problems. This was true of hybrid corn, one of the greatest agricultural innovations in modern times. The theories of two European scientists, Gregor Mendel and Charles Darwin, were applied to the problem. In 1865, Mendel discovered and announced the basic laws of inheritance of specific characteristics, but the importance of his work was not recognized until about 1900. Darwin pointed out in 1876 that inbreeding usually reduced plant vigor while crossbreeding restored it.

■IMPROVEMENTS IN GRAINS.—A number of American scientists built upon the work of Darwin and Mendel. Those who contributed directly to the development of hybrid corn included William James Beal, George Shull, Edward Murray East, H. K. Hayes, and Henry A. Wallace. In 1914, Donald F. Jones, who had been appointed to the Connecticut Agricultural Experiment Station, devoted himself to developing a method for making hybrid corn practical. Within three years, drawing upon the work of his predecessors, he developed the technique called double-crossing. It has been used by commercial firms since. The first seed company devoted to the commercial production of hybrid corn

was organized in 1926. Mainly because of the use of hybrid seed, the per-acre yield of corn rose from an average 23 bushels in 1933 to 87 bushels in 1976.

The techniques used in breeding hybrid corn were successfully applied to grain sorghum in the 1950's and to semidwarf winter wheat for the Pacific Northwest in the 1960's. There have been gains, less spectacular, for other crops.

■ADVANCES IN ANIMAL HUSBANDRY.—Similar breeding techniques have been successfully applied to chickens, both as broilers and egg producers. Productive work has also been done with developing hybrid hogs. Crossbreeding has resulted in the development of new, useful breeds of beef cattle and sheep.

The dairy industry in the United States underwent a major change in the 1940's and 1950's. The changes have been due to several factors, such as the influence of markets, prices of milk and feeds, better knowledge of feeding, and the conquest of many pests and diseases. However, one of the most important has been the increased use of artificial insemination.

Artificial insemination as the best means of speeding up livestock improvement was demonstrated in Russia in the 1920's. The first dairy artificial-breeding cooperative in the United States was organized in New Jersey in 1938. It was found that instead of breeding only about 40 cows a year, artificial insemination made it possible for one bull to impregnate thousands of cows a year. Sires of proven ability to get high-producing offspring could be used to improve a dairy herd quickly. In 1943, the average American dairy cow produced 4,598 pounds of milk and 183 pounds of butterfat. In 1976, the figures were 10,893 and 399 pounds, respectively.

■FERTILIZERS.—The growth of the worldwide chemical fertilizer industry, able to supply farmers with the

elements needed for more effective production at reasonable cost, has helped bring about major changes in agriculture in many nations. It has been an important factor in what might be called the second American agricultural revolution. The Department of Agriculture has estimated that the increased use of fertilizer was responsible for 55 per cent of the increase in productivity per crop-acre from 1940 to 1955.

■INCREASES IN PRODUCTIVITY.—The unparalleled demand for farm products, a doubling of prices, and the shortage of manpower during World War II were basically responsible for the tremendous upsurge in production. The specific changes making up this technological revolution included the displacement of animal power by mechanical power, widespread progress in mechanization, greater use of lime and fertilizer, irrigation, adoption of conservation practices, use of improved varieties, better balanced feeding of livestock and poultry, and more effective control of insects and disease. The widespread use of agricultural chemicals has led some to label the contemporary period in agriculture the *age of chemurgy*.

The major key to progress in farming, with increases in productivity per acre and man-hour, was that technological innovations were adopted in combination. The farmer became a skilled manager and businessman, constantly seeking to find the most efficient and profitable combinations of technology. His success can be measured by the fact that in 1860 the American farmer produced enough food and fiber for 4.5 people; in 1940, for 10.7 people; and in 1976, for 56 people. In the 100 years from 1870 to 1970, the proportion of America's working population engaged in agriculture declined from 53 percent to 4.6 percent, and by 1976 to 3.7 percent, but that percentage was providing abundantly for all Americans and millions of people overseas.

—Wayne D. Rasmussen

U.S. DEPARTMENT OF AGRICULTURE

HENRY AGARD WALLACE (*left*) developed hybrid corn and, as secretary of agriculture, aided other advancements in farming methods. Through research into new products and processes, George W. Carver (*right*) made contributions to the field of scientific agriculture.

FOOD IN THE HISTORY OF MANKIND

THE IMPORTANCE OF FOOD *in history goes far beyond the product alone—such as the loaves of bread baked for a hospital* (left), *or the turtles awaiting the pot in Indonesia. The need for food lies behind wars, migrations, trade—and the birth of civilization itself.*

Eating. A person eats because he is hungry. That is the basic reason for eating, but not the only one. The feeling of hunger is the body's way of reminding us that it is necessary to eat in order to stay alive, but eating also gives a sense of security, relieves tension, and imparts a sense of well-being. This sense of well-being is increased if we get pleasure from the appearance, taste, smell, and even the feel of food.

Food and society. Eating is not only a physical process of absorbing enough nourishment to stay alive and healthy; it is a social occasion as well. We dine in company for sociability; consuming food is only a part of the process. Man, in fact, is said to be the only animal that invites his own kind into his lair (his home) to share his food.

Ethnic backgrounds, national traditions, and religious beliefs can also be factors in determining what and how one eats. A child growing up where it is customary to consume a great deal of pasta will be surprised when first learning that rice is served at nearly every meal in another part of the world. Sheeps' eyes are considered a delicacy in some parts of the Middle

East, but not in Wichita, Kansas. Until fairly recent years, hot dogs would have seemed strange indeed in Yemen.

Food as a gift or weapon. Nations use food as a weapon to influence the behavior of other nations. When Russia invaded Afghanistan in December, 1979, the American government refused to sell any more badly needed wheat to the Soviets as a way of putting pressure on them, and of showing its displeasure.

On the brighter side, food has long been a welcome gift. People take food to friends on happy occasions such as holidays, and on sad occasions, as when there is a death in the family. A gift of food—especially if home prepared—is a very personal way of showing friendship, pleasure, or deep sympathy.

Since the very earliest times, human beings have shown fear, respect, and love toward their gods by making offerings or gifts of food to them. In many times and places, animals have been sacrificed on the altars of the local gods, and priests and soothsayers consulted parts of animals, especially organs such as the liver, to find portents for the future.

Food of the First Men and Women

The first period of human development began about 2 million years ago and continued until somewhere between 40,000 and 10,000 years ago. From this Paleolithic, or Old Stone, Age come the earliest remains of man, some stone tools. The people of this long period were hunters and food gatherers. They probably first ate meat, and ate it raw, when they came upon the bodies of dead animals. They hunted animals with crude weapons—rocks, spears and clubs—to trap them, or to drive the quarry over a cliff. As time went on, hunters must have learned to work cooperatively to kill large, fierce animals. More weapons were developed, such as nooses, nets, snares, and blowguns.

Another source of food for prehistoric man was fish and other marine life. Fish were caught by hand, club, spear, net, and, in time, with hooks. Fish was an important part of early man's diet, especially if he lived on a river, lake or ocean, and fish is still one of mankind's three primary sources of food, with cereals and meat.

HUNTING DEER, *from a prehistoric painting in a cave shelter in eastern Spain.*

Prehistoric peoples also depended on food gathering to supply part of their needs. The work was probably done mostly by the women and children, who sought roots, nuts, berries, and wild grains. Many of the vegetables they gathered are eaten today—turnips, onions, radishes, and cabbages, for example.

Food and fire. When man first discovered fire, he most likely used it for warmth and to warn off wild animals. It is impossible to say exactly when humans began to use fire to cook their food instead of eating it raw. Probably it was not less than 500,000 years ago. Perhaps the roasting of meat was discovered accidentally when a raw piece fell into a fire or onto some hot coals. In any event, people found that it tasted better, and increased the range of digestible foodstuffs.

The first farmers. The first crops cultivated were most likely various grains, which supplied food for humans and fodder for animals. Man had settled in areas where grains were growing wild. By accident he discovered that he could get grain again the next year if he left some of the seeds on the ground.

Either barley or millet seems to have been the first cereal cultivated and eaten by early man, closely followed by wheat. Barley originated in the highlands of Ethiopia, but spread rapidly once man began to make use of it. It was the chief bread grain of the ancient Hebrews and of the oldest Greeks and Romans. In fact, barley remained the main bread grain in Europe until the 16th century, when it was displaced by wheat because yeast does not act well with barley.

Millet originated in Africa or Asia and is known to have been grown by the Stone Age lake dwellers of Switzerland. To Americans, millet is almost unknown, but it remains an important food for millions of people in India, China, and Africa.

The oldest records in many parts of the world indicate that wheat was also an early primary ingredient in man's diet. Originating in Asia Minor, wheat spread rapidly and remains today, with rice, one of the two basic cereal food sources. A Sumerian record in Mesopotamia about 3100 B.C. indicates it was being used not only to make bread but also beer.

For sweetening and seasoning, Stone Age man had honey and salt. A painting of the period in a cave in Spain shows honey being gathered. It remained the chief sweetening agent for most people until the 17th century, when sugar from cane became generally available. There is some evidence that early man mined salt and also extracted it from seawater.

Domestic animals. Beginning perhaps as far back as 40,000 B.C., and continuing for thousands of years, man accomplished another major change in controlling his food supply by domesticating wild animals. The sheep or the goat seems to have been the first, followed by the pig and the dog. The dog was eaten as well as used as an aid in hunting. The horse and the camel were similarly domesticated, at first for food rather than transportation. Even though camels disappeared from North America long ago, American Indians appear to have been the first to have eaten them, nearly 25,000 years ago. The cow was the last major food animal to be domesticated. Many of the wild and domesticated animals provided milk as well as meat, both for nomads wandering with their herds and for settled peoples.

As people acquired more and different kinds of food, they needed better cooking and eating utensils. Basket weaving was inspired at least in part by the need to have something in which to collect and store seeds, nuts, and fruits. The invention of pottery was spurred by the need for containers that would hold water and other liquids and that could be subjected to high heat. Pottery remains dating from the Neolithic period have been found in many parts of the world. For the most part, prehistoric man's eating implements were his hands. Spoons, however, were devised fairly early, for serving as well as eating. Horn, wood, and flint were used as the materials.

As man began to exercise more control over his food supply by farming and keeping domestic animals, he also began to settle down. He did not need to keep on the move and spend almost all of his time looking for food. He thus had time to do other things, such as working at arts and crafts. Furthermore, his surplus food made it possible for some members of the tribe or settlement to be paid in food for their work as artisans and craftsmen.

Food of the Ancient Empires

The 4000 years from about 3500 B.C. to 500 A.D. witnessed the discovery, dissemination, cultivation, and consumption of a variety of foods over wide areas. Among the most generally known foods were butter, cheese, and oats. Churning to produce butter may have been discovered by accident when someone transported milk and jiggled it too much. Butter was known by 2000 B.C., but it was used more as an ointment or medicine, or for illumination, than for food. The early Greeks made cheese from mares' and goats' milk.

AFTER HUNTING *came the growing of crops, here being harvested by ancient Egyptians.*

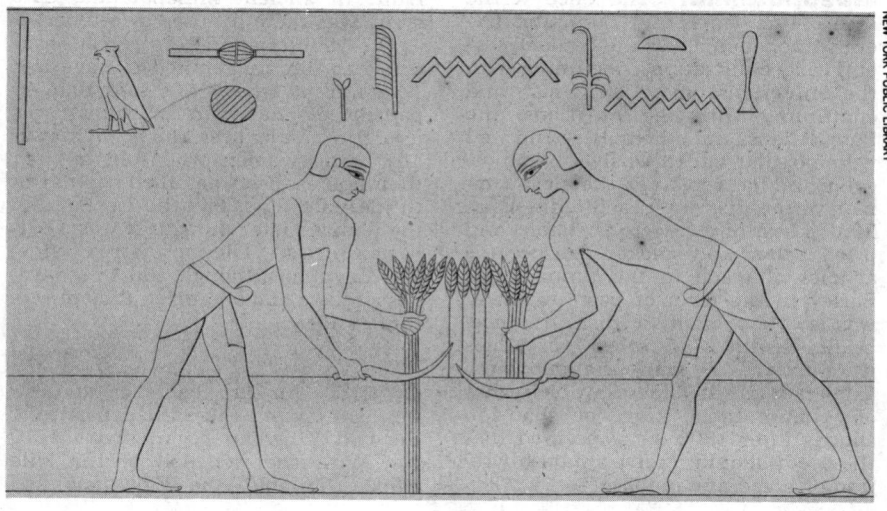

FOOD AND RELIGION *have always been inseparable, from ritual fasting to offerings for the gods, as in this ancient Egyptian relief.*

Oats were domesticated about 2500 B.C., considerably later than wheat, barley, and millet. Oats originated in central and northern Europe in the Bronze Age, before spreading south to the Mediterranean. The Romans did not like oats. The Scots, however, are reputed to have long been fond of them, which caused Samuel Johnson, the famous dictionary compiler, to write in the 18th century of oats: "A grain which in England is generally given to horses, but in Scotland supports the people." Nevertheless, quite a bit of oatmeal is still eaten.

Mesopotamia. The once fertile area of the Tigris and Euphrates rivers, Mesopotamia was the home of several early civilizations, beginning with the Sumerians' about 3000 B.C., and continuing with the Assyrians, the Babylonians, and others. Beef and veal were popular but expensive. Lamb became and has remained the most common meat dish in the Middle East. Many kinds of fish were available, and dried, salted and smoked fish became articles of trade in the Bronze Age. Barley in the form of paste or bread was a Mesopotamian dish. Lettuce, beans, lentils and other vegetables were grown. We know the onion was eaten because the oldest law code, that of Hammurabi, king of Babylon shortly after 1800 B.C., specified that the needy should receive a monthly ration of bread and onions.

Pears, melons, figs, and dates were consumed. The pear, a native of western Asia, was one of the earliest fruits cultivated, but really good eating pears were not developed until the 18th and 19th centuries in Europe. Melons, of which there are many varieties, suited to different climates and native to Asia, are first heard of in Sumer. Figs were eaten as early as 3000 B.C.; they later were grown in the Hanging Gardens of Babylon. Wild dates were eaten 50,000 years ago and have been cultivated since at least 3000 B.C. in the Middle East. Their original home was Iraq and that country today is the largest producer and exporter of the fruit. In ancient Mesopotamia, date syrup was the most used sweetener.

The Sumerians were great beer drinkers and are reputed to have had 19 different types. It is said that 40 percent of the grain in Sumer was used for making beer, the brewers usually being women who sold it from their homes. Beer remained popular in the Middle East, but the Greeks and the Romans later thought it was a barbarian drink. They preferred wine. The Egyptians, though, did a big business in beer and organized the brewers into guilds.

Egypt. An early center of civilization was Egypt, where the dynasties of the Old Kingdom began about 3110 B.C. With the rich soil of the Nile banks available, the Egyptians had

many different foods to choose from, although the basic diet of the peasants was most likely bread, onions, and beer, and a bean cake, called *tamia,* made from broad beans. Richer Egyptians might sit down to a banquet that included cabbage (which was said to delay drunkenness) as an appetizer, roast goose, legs of small calves, gazelles, wild duck or quail, fish (which might be served raw or grilled), together with lettuce, endive, peas, onions, leeks, beans, parsley, and radishes. This would be topped off with fruits, cakes, and melons.

The Egyptians most likely were the first to discover how to make leavened bread. The discovery may have been made by accident, but it is known that they cultivated yeast and that the kind of wheat they raised was suitable for leavening. There were combined bakeries and breweries by 2000 B.C., and at one period workers were paid in bread. The daily wage of a servant was three loaves of bread and two jugs of beer.

Salt also played an important part in Egyptian life. There was great concern for preserving the bodies of the dead and sometimes salt was used. Thus it also came to be used for preserving food, and was sold in lumps or bricks. Access to a supply of salt has been a primary concern of man ever since he discovered its uses. Nations have gone to war to control sources of salt; it has been used as money, and at times Roman soldiers were paid in salt. Our

English word salt comes from the Latin word for salary, *salarium*. Salt has played a part in religious ceremonies, and in the biblical story of the destruction of the wicked city of Sodom, near which rock salt was obtained. Lot's wife was turned into a pillar of salt because she took a forbidden look backward. Centuries later, in Christian Europe, salt was used to preserve fish so that it would be available the year round to eat on Fridays and during Lent.

Egypt may also be the land where the apple, the fruit that stands for all fruits, was first cultivated. Pharaoh Ramses II had some apple trees planted in the 13th century B.C. Of course, the apple, which was apparently a native of the Caucasus Mountains in western Asia, had also been enjoyed by prehistoric man. One reason for the apple's popularity is that it keeps well and, until recent times, was the only fresh fruit that could be on hand all winter.

Biblical lands.

A region that, like Egypt, contributed significantly to the food of the world is the eastern end of the Mediterranean, which in ancient times was described generally as Palestine and Syria. Here there were herders and farmers by the fourth millennium B.C., and towns not much later. The great contribution of these people was to cultivate the olive and to produce olive oil. The olive tree may have originated on the not-far-distant island of Crete, and it was cultivated there by about 3500 B.C.

Since then the olive has shaped the cuisines of many lands. The olive branch, which a dove brought to Noah at the end of the deluge, according to the Bible, has been a symbol of peace for centuries. Perhaps this is because olive oil has a healing quality and because oil calms troubled waters. In the ancient world, olive oil was used for lighting and ritual anointing, as a lubricant, preservative, and cosmetic, and for cooking.

In the 13th century B.C., Moses led the Hebrews out of Egypt; eventually they reached the Promised Land—Palestine. Here they enjoyed the richness of the "land of milk and honey." The milk came mostly from goats and the honey was wild. The ancient Hebrews' diet included wheat, barley, bean flour bread, rice, vegetables of various kinds, and a thick lentil soup called pottage. They were also fond of the pomegranate, which they had known in Egypt. This fruit represented abundance and fertility because of the number and size of its seeds. It was also associated with fertility in Greek mythology. It may have come originally from Afghanistan, and although never much eaten in the United States, it was as important as the grape and the fig to the people of the ancient world.

Chinese food.

In the Far East a very old civilization contributed to the variety of mankind's food. In China a unique and unified culture existed by the second millennium B.C. Here the first dynasty, that of the Shang, began about 1523 B.C. The Chinese had a concept of "five flavors": bitter, salt, sour, hot, and sweet. As in all countries, though, the poor had to be content with a simple diet: curd soup, rice, onions, bamboo shoots, and beans. Fish has always been important in China; the Chinese raised carp at an early date. By the second century B.C., the primary food animals were pigs, ducks, goats, and hens. Pork has remained popular in China; the words for meat and pork are synonymous.

Although when one thinks of China and food one automatically thinks of rice, China is not its original home. The earliest traces known have been found in Thailand, but rice may also be native to the deltas of large Asian rivers such as the Ganges or Yangtze. Still, the Chinese have cultivated rice for several thousand years and it long ago became the staple of their diet. Probably half the population of the world today depends wholly or in part on rice for existence.

The growth and consumption of rice spread in all directions. It is as central to Japan's diet as to China's, and in Japan the word for rice means a full meal. The Japanese make wine, *saki*, from it. The Muslim Moors brought rice to Spain when they invaded that country in the eighth century A.D. Later, Italy became Europe's biggest consumer and invented *risotto*, a tasty rice dish. By the late 17th century rice was being grown in the American colonies. Actually what we call wild rice in the United States is not rice at all but an aquatic grass.

China and tea are also closely associated. Tea seems to have appeared first in the Assam section of India and in China. It was cultivated in China in prehistoric times, and at first it was probably used as a vegetable relish. It was also thought to have medicinal value and to aid longevity. By the eighth century A.D. it was being grown on a commercial scale. Tea was introduced to Japan in the ninth century and became that country's national drink. In turn, the tea ceremony of Japan was brought to China in the 15th century by Buddhists.

China was the center of cultivation of a vegetable with a history going back 5000 years. But the soybean, a most versatile legume, was hardly appreciated by much of the world until the 1940's. Native to tropical and warm temperate climates of Asia, it was cultivated for centuries chiefly in China and Manchuria. It is a most important food product, eaten by the people of Korea, Japan, and Malaysia as well. It is also the most important member of the bean family because its edible oil is used in salads, margarine, and for cooking, while the bean itself is converted to high protein flour.

The Chinese eat bean sprouts from soybean seedlings. The plant and residual oilseed is fed to livestock. Outside the food field, the soybean is used in the manufacture of soap, linoleum, paint, plastics, printing ink, and numerous other products. Although the United States now produces more soybeans than any other country, hardly any American consumes them, except in processed forms.

The world is indebted to China for three of its favorite fruits: oranges, peaches, and apricots, all of which began to be eaten there in the third millennium B.C. To the Chinese the peach was a symbol of immortality, and it was used as a gift to show affection.

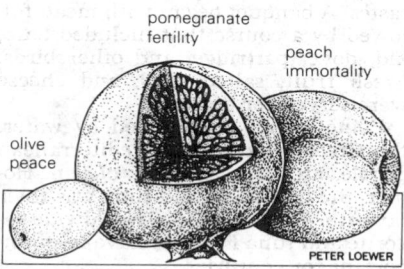

FRUITS *in the ancient world were much esteemed and often had symbolic meanings.*

All three fruits moved westward and all were very popular with the Romans around the beginning of the Christian era. The Moors introduced oranges to Spain and by 1290 A.D. they had reached England, where they have always been highly regarded. Like so many other foods, these were taken to the New World by the Spaniards, and oranges were growing in Florida by 1565. Today the orange is the most important fresh fruit in international commerce.

The Indus Valley.

Another of the early civilizations was that of the Indus River valley, in what is now Pakistan. Here, between about 2500 and 1500 B.C., there flourished a sophisticated, urban civilization that boasted a well developed agricultural system. The people ate dishes prepared from wheat and barley, and peas cooked with sesame oil. The lemon may have been native to this area at this time, but there is still some mystery as to just where that fruit first grew. Like other Asian fruits, it spread to Rome, to other parts of Europe, and eventually to the Americas.

Our great debt to the Indus Valley civilization is that it gave the world the chicken and the egg. The people here domesticated the chicken, a wild jungle fowl, about 2000 B.C. The chicken is now, worldwide, the most universally eaten meat, while one authority estimates that humans consume 250 billion eggs a year.

Greece. Greece and the Roman Republic and Empire were the last of the ancient civilizations, and were of particular importance in forming the culture of the later Western world of which we are a part.

The diet of the Greek peasants consisted mostly of bread, fish, cheese, goat's milk (they thought cow's milk unwholesome), vegetables, and wine. Meat, especially beef, was expensive and was eaten mainly by the upper classes. Bread was such a staple that the Greek word *artos* meant both bread and food in general. The Spartans, whose name has come to stand for a grim, stark way of life, ate a black broth made of pork, blood, and vinegar. The wealthier Greeks, especially in Athens when it was at the height of its power, developed more refined tastes. A banquet began with meat, followed by a course that included hare, kid, dove, partridge, and other birds. Fresh fruit, salted nuts, and cheese were served for dessert.

Being nearly surrounded by water, the Greeks, like other Mediterranean people, ate large amounts of fish. Homer, the epic poet, said tuna was their favorite. Tuna is now a worldwide favorite and tuna fisheries have been important for centuries.

Greece became the center of olive growing, partly because its soil was better suited to this use than to growing crops, or even for pasturage. As a result the Greeks not only ate large quantities of olives and used great amounts of olive oil, but also depended on the sale of exported olives and oil to be able to buy foreign grains. The cultivation of olives reached Rome after 580 B.C. and the Romans became addicted to them. Cato the Elder, a noted Roman statesman, said olives and bread were the staple diet of peasants and workers.

Peas and carrots were known to the Greeks and Romans. The former is so ancient a plant that no one knows where it originated, but it was one of the few vegetables grown in Greece. At the time of Pericles, in the fifth century B.C., hot pea soup was sold in the streets of Athens. Mostly, though, the Greeks and Romans ate peas in cooked, dried form and the pea was not used as a fresh table vegetable until the late Middle Ages.

Although there is mention of the carrot in Greece about 500 B.C., neither the Greeks nor the Romans seemed to care much for it. It is a native of Afghanistan. It was a favorite in Europe for use in soups and stews for a long time, and is now used all over the world, but eating carrots raw or in salads did not become widespread until this century.

The Greeks and Romans were noted wine drinkers, although they had nothing to do with its first discovery and production. In fact, wine making is so ancient that its origin is unknown. It was probably discovered by accident and vineyards were most likely first cultivated in the Aegean area of the Mediterranean in the early Bronze Age. Wine is mentioned in early Egyptian inscriptions; it was used first only in temple rituals. There were wine shops in Greece. Originally wine was always diluted with water, probably because it was much stronger than later wine. Greek wine spread north to Europe and the Romans carried it with them into western Europe.

Rome. The diet of common Romans in the days of the republic included a thick porridge made with wheat, millet, or bean flour, cheese, milk, and vegetables, such as peas, turnips, and onions. In short, the diet was mostly vegetarian. As time went on and Rome's size and power grew, some important changes took place. Rome had to import a great deal of wheat, mostly from North Africa. By the second century, poverty was such that the rulers began to distribute free grain to the populace; this turned into a means of gaining political favor with the masses. Later, bread and pork, and even wine, were distributed free.

Meanwhile, the rich and powerful lived extravagantly and indulged their taste for rich foods and lavish entertainment. They often imported luxury foods, such as oysters from Britain. They brought snow and ice from the mountains to preserve such delicacies. Rare fish and wild boars were served, as well as peacocks, which were garnished with their own feathers after being cooked. Lucullus, a Roman general of the first century B.C., spent huge sums on banquets and other ostentations. He is said to have introduced the cherry to Europe. His extravagance was so outstanding that the phrase "Lucullan feast" is used today to describe lavish dining.

DELICACIES *artfully arranged on a silver platter appealed to the Romans.*

RONNY JAQUES/PHOTO RESEARCHERS

The author Petronius, who died in 66 A.D., satirized this kind of living in his imaginary account, "Trimalchio's Feast." Here was served a hare with wings affixed so that it presumably looked like Pegasus, the winged horse of Greek mythology; a wild sow with its belly full of live birds; quinces stuck with thorns so they looked like sea urchins; and roast pork carved to look like fish.

As to poultry, the Romans enjoyed chicken, duck, and goose. The chicken, though, did not catch the Roman fancy until the second century B.C. A hundred years or so later, the poet Horace reported that a fowl drowned in wine had an especially fine flavor. The duck, which had been known to the Egyptians, was a Roman luxury. Only the breast and the brains were eaten. Sometime after the Romans conquered Gaul in the first century B.C., they began to import fat geese, which the people of Gaul had been enjoying for some time.

In the later days of the empire, more meat was eaten than earlier. Pork, lamb (mostly in the form of mutton), goat, and veal were preferred in that order. Beef was rare and expensive. As to fish, the Romans developed a craze for red mullet, and in the time of the emperor Caligula, one fish brought the equivalent of $400. Another Roman paid as much for a mullet as four oxen would have cost him.

The Romans were associated in one way or another with a number of vegetables. Lentils, one of the oldest cultivated leguminous crops, and known in Egypt, where it helped to sustain the poorer classes, was a favorite of the Romans. They imported it by the shipload from Egypt. Parsley, a member of the carrot family that originated in the Mediterranean area, has been cultivated since Roman times. The naturalist, Pliny the Elder, in the first century A.D., said no sauce or salad should be without it. It was also used for chaplets and as a funeral decoration. Asparagus, whose place of origin is unknown, was and still is considered a luxury. Julius Caesar liked it, Pliny claimed he saw one that weighed three pounds, and Cato, in his book *On Farming,* in the second century B.C., gave instructions for growing it.

Vegetables. The beet is native to the Mediterranean area and probably to Italy. The early Romans ate only the leaves but later the root also. Cabbage (whose family includes broccoli, Brussels sprouts, cauliflower, and kale) first grew in northern Europe. Although cabbage in various places and at various times has been a basic food for poor people because it is so common, this was not true in Rome, where it was so much in demand that it was expensive. Mark Twain said of cauliflower that it "is nothing but cabbage with a college education." The Greeks and Romans were the first to make much use of celery, treating it as a vegetable dish, not just something to be nibbled on.

The bean of ancient Europe was the broad bean, probably the descendant of a North African wild species. The Greeks and Romans used beans for balloting the way we use voting machines today. Later, in England, beans were used to elect the king and queen for Twelfth Night celebrations. The remains of cucumber seeds, going as far back as 7750 B.C., have been found in Southeast Asia. From there the cucumber spread westward and Romans were fond of it. It was not until the 14th century, though, that it reached France and England. Garlic played a much more prominent role in Greek and Roman diet than it does today. It was eaten as a vegetable, not just as a seasoning. Garlic oil was thought to be a stimulant and so the Romans fed it to their soldiers and slaves. The Romans probably introduced leeks (part of the onion family, along with garlic and chives) to England.

Spices and herbs.
Most of the major spices come from the East Indies, at least originally. In ancient times they had to be brought overland by caravan from China and India, and this made them expensive. Later, in the eleventh and twelfth centuries, the Crusades, Christian Europe's attempt to retake the Holy Land from the Muslims, stimulated new interest in spices, which the Crusaders came upon. In those days, as well as earlier, strong seasonings were appreciated to preserve meat, or at least to kill the smell and taste of meat that was not as fresh as it might be. Later, when the Mongols and the Turks cut off the land route from Asia, the nations of western Europe were stimulated to seek sea routes to the Far East in order to secure these desirable products. An indirect result was the discovery of the New World in 1492.

Pepper was a great luxury in Greece and Rome after it reached the Mediterranean area in the fourth century B.C. from its place of origin, Java. At first it was used more as medicine than as food. Pepper was so expensive that it became the equivalent of money. As part of the ransom for not sacking Rome in 408 A.D., Alaric, the Visigoth king, demanded 3000 pounds of pepper. Nearly half a century later, Rome bought off Attila the Hun with gifts that included both pepper and cinnamon. In the Middle Ages, peppercorns could be used to pay taxes, tithes, and customs duties. Even today, British legal documents still sometimes refer to a peppercorn rent to signify a legal acknowledgment of the ownership of a piece of property.

Cinnamon, which originated in Ceylon (now Sri Lanka and still the chief producing country), was known in

NEW YORK PUBLIC LIBRARY

IN CIVILIZED ROME, *food was important in religion as well as in society. A wall painting from Pompeii may show an initiation in the Dionysiac mysteries involving food. A delicate Roman silver strainer* (left) *attests to sophisticated cooking.*

China by 2000 B.C. and in Egypt about 1450 B.C. It was very expensive in Greece and Rome, where it was often used to flavor wine. It was not until the early 16th century, when the Magellan expedition found the Spice Islands (the Moluccas in eastern Indonesia), that cinnamon became very widely available in Europe. The Spice Islands were the original home of nutmeg, clove, and other spices, and by seizing them in the 17th century the Dutch acquired a monopoly of the clove and nutmeg trade.

The Romans were fond of mustard, but it was known earlier to prehistoric man. It was used in Sumer, and the ancient Hindus believed it aided fertility. In Egypt and Rome, mustard seed was chewed along with meat. In the New Testament the mustard seed is a symbol of what can be created by faith, because a very large plant grows from such a very small seed. The mustard greens of the American South is a dish brought from Africa by slaves.

Caraway and cumin are easily confused, the former originating in northern Europe and Asia and the latter in Asia. Cumin is mentioned in the Bible. Marjoram and oregano are also much alike, and both come from the Mediterranean area. The Greeks and Romans used marjoram to make bridal wreaths as well as for a seasoning, while in the Renaissance high-born ladies made sachets of it to perfume their linen.

Many kinds of mints are or have been used in food. Followers of Bac-

chus, the god of wine in Greek and Roman mythology, made wreaths of mint to ward off the effects of drunkenness. Saffron seems to have originated in Asia Minor and Greece, and was cultivated before the second millennium B.C. on the island of Crete. It is mentioned in the Bible in the Song of Solomon, and is important today in the cooking of many regions, including the Pennsylvania Dutch region. The people here grow it for their own use. In the past it was considered a spice, a dye, a cosmetic, and a medicine.

Sage is said to have received its name because in classical times it was thought that it increased wisdom and strengthened the memory. The Greeks used it as a medicine, and it was more popular in the Middle Ages than now. In the United States today it is found primarily in stuffing. Thyme, first used by the Sumerians, also served a number of purposes. The Greeks treated it as a medicine and as incense in their temples. The Egyptians employed it as an ingredient in embalming, while the Romans thought it promoted bravery.

Cooking and serving food.
From prehistoric times to the height of Greek and Roman culture, many changes took place in cooking methods and in cooking utensils. The Romans had a wide variety of kitchen equipment: a crescent-shaped blade with a handle for mincing; strainers and colanders of different sizes; and a device for shelling shrimp. Large platters and

bowls of pottery, silver, and bronze were used for serving food.

At banquets the guests ate on couches in reclining positions, propping themselves on their left forearms. Most eating was done with the fingers, possibly aided by fingerbowls or napkins. If these were not available, bread was used to wipe the hands and then thrown on the floor. The Romans thought that nine was the right number of guests, and they arranged the couches in a U form. The position of a guest on the couches indicated his importance. Apparently, tablecloths were not provided and shells, fruit pits, and stones were simply thrown on the floor for the servants to clean up.

Fast food shops.
When prehistoric men and women cooked food, they did it for themselves or their small group. Later food was bartered for other goods and services. By ancient times food stores began to appear. There were bread shops in Egypt in the twelfth century B.C., and in sixth century B.C. Babylon, in King Nebuchadnezzar's time, one could buy cooked food "to go." Men who were combination millers and bakers appeared in Rome about 170 B.C., and a wall painting in Pompeii shows a baker's shop.

In the fourth century B.C. in Greece, there were professional cooks, some of whom operated independently and some of whom were employed by wealthy households. Some specialized as pastry cooks. Professional chefs were comparatively well paid and the chef might be invited to have a drink with the guests if they thought he had done extremely well. There were restaurants in Rome, but according to one observer they were not very clean. The famous public baths of Rome attracted vendors who offered sausages, eggs, and cakes to the bathers.

Tropical foods.
While the empires of the Middle East and the Mediterranean region were rising and falling, other peoples on the tropical Pacific islands were also experimenting with foodstuffs and spreading certain foods into new areas. On the islands were the screwpine and the breadfruit. The screwpine bears an edible fruit, but the fruit of the breadfruit is a more important staple. It was while the notorious British ship *Bounty* was in the South Seas in the late 18th century, in the process of gathering breadfruit saplings to be transported to the West Indies, that the crew mutinied against Captain William Bligh. Nevertheless, Bligh returned, and in 1793 brought breadfruit to Jamaica. It is now grown in the West Indies and on much of the South American continent. The Polynesians who colonized some of the South Sea islands from Southeast Asia

took with them the coconut palm, taro, and yams.

To Americans, coconut is a treat associated mostly with candy or cake, but for millions of people it is a basic food, used everywhere from Thailand to Hawaii. The coconut and the olive were two of the earliest sources of vegetable oil, but the coconut was not known to the Western world until the sixth century A.D.

Taro is a very starchy plant and from its roots come a staple food of the Pacific. This is *poi,* a slightly fermented, sticky paste. The yam, often confused with the sweet potato, may have been native to Africa or Asia. It is commercially important in the Far East, but in the United States it is grown only in the South.

Food in the Middle Ages

From about 500 to 1000 A.D., Europe was in a period of decline, labeled for convenience the Dark Ages. After the fall of Rome, trade, communication, and transportation were disrupted, so that only high-priced foods, such as spices, were carried from place to place. Man existed mainly by growing his own food, and he ate considerably more grain than meat.

The later Middle Ages in Europe, from approximately 1000 to 1500 A.D., saw a revival of urban life, an increase in population, and an improvement in agricultural methods. More food was available and the growing cities provided a market for it as they became centers of a more dynamic life.

The diet of the peasants and of the urban poor was monotonous, although it improved as the centuries passed. The masses usually had only two meals a day, mainly vegetables, but with some dark bread, perhaps porridge, a bowl of curds, and occasionally some meat or poultry. Among the vegetables they ate were turnips, radishes, onions, carrots, and leeks. (The leek, incidentally, provides an example of the way in which food can become symbolic. The Welsh wear a leek on St. David's Day to commemorate the victory of their semilegendary King Cadwallader over the Saxons in 640 A.D. Before that battle, the Welsh soldiers picked leeks from a nearby garden and wore them in their hats so as to avoid mistaken identity when the battle was being fought.)

Buckwheat, millet, and oats were the cheaper grains. Water and milk were the usual beverages. By the 15th century, the workers and peasants were better off and could sometimes have wheat bread, mutton, pork, and goat. Wages were often paid in food, such as three herrings and a loaf of bread for a day's work.

The nobility, the lords of the man-

ors, and the urban merchants and bankers ate better. They could afford more meat and better bread, as well as wine. Pastry was expensive because of the fats needed, but there were all kinds of pies—fish, fowl, meat, fruit, or vegetable—baked with a crust of pastry.

The importance of rye.
In a large part of medieval Europe, rye was the main grain crop. Rye was not known to the civilized world until the first millennium B.C.; it originated either in Asia Minor or northeastern Europe. It was important chiefly in central and northern Europe, partly because it is a hardy grain that can be grown north of the Arctic Circle and in poor soil. In many places rye came up with wheat and the two were harvested and ground together to produce maslin. From the 14th to the 16th century, maslin was the most common flour used in making bread. At one time pumpernickel, a coarse, slightly sour bread, was the major product of rye.

One disadvantage of rye is that it is susceptible to a fungus disease called ergot, and this disease can be fatal. It can also have the same effect as LSD. The first recorded outbreak of ergotism is from 857 A.D.. Some 40,000 people are said to have died in Aquitaine in southwest France in 995, and as late as the 18th century there were two serious outbreaks of the disease within six years. During the Middle Ages, Europe sometimes suffered from famine, when crop growing conditions were bad, or, in some times and places, when war such as the ravages of the Vikings destroyed crops. There are said to have been 20 serious famines in the course of the ninth and tenth centuries.

Another grain not in use in Europe before the Middle Ages was buckwheat, which may have been brought

A LEEK, *an emblem of the Welsh, is forced on Pistol in Shakespeare's* Henry V.

to Europe by the Moors, through Spain. It was used to make porridge and grown as a honey plant, but many people think the only really tasty dish it provides is the buckwheat pancake. Eastern Europeans use it to make a dish called *kasha*.

Fish.

The medieval Europeans consumed large quantities of fish, partly because it was readily available, partly because it was one of the few foods of the time that could be preserved and transported, and partly because the practice of Christianity, almost universally, called for some fasting, as in Lent, when no meat could be eaten. The cod and the herring were the most important fish foods. Cod could be preserved by salting, or simply by drying. Preserved cod played an important part in the growth of Viking power between the ninth and eleventh centuries. Cod provided the Vikings with food for their voyages and could be used to barter for other goods. In later times, cod was used to buy African slaves to be transported to the Americas, and it was a factor in the economic life of New England. The cod is still the emblem of the state of Massachusetts today.

The herring was a staple by the twelfth century, and was at its peak of use in the 16th, when it was served to armies, in schools and hospitals, and to prisoners. It more than once saved people from famine. The Dutch prospered the most from the demand for herring, and today they are the biggest consumers of herring. The American Indians fertilized their corn fields with herring. Mackerel and pike were the other two types of fish most eaten in medieval Europe, the latter being highly esteemed by gourmets.

Turnips and spinach.

Turnips were known in prehistoric times, and the Romans ate them, although they considered them a lowly vegetable. The turnip, however, came into its own in the Middle Ages, when it was very important in the diet of the peasants. The rutabaga, or Swedish turnip, originated in this period as a cross between the white turnip and cabbage. Parsnips also enjoyed their heyday, although the Romans had known them and had imported them from Gaul and Germany. Because they were starchy and filling, they were favored during fasting times, along with salted cod. During the Middle Ages, better, fleshier parsnips were developed. Much later, in an 1819 novel, Sir Walter Scott quoted what he cited as a common saying: "Fine words butter no parsnips." Spinach, which is of Persian origin, was also eaten in Europe in medieval times. A mid-14th-century list recommended it to monks on fast days; by the 16th century it was a favorite Lenten food.

Sugar and spices.

As already noted, medieval cooks made wide use of spices to the extent they were available, and they liked their spices hot. They also had tarragon and nutmeg, which were not known to the ancients. Tarragon probably came via Asia, brought westward first by the Mongols and then into western Europe by the Crusaders. The nutmeg is first mentioned in Europe in 1190, about a century after a Persian physician referred to it. Connecticut is known as the Nutmeg State because of the reputation of some ingenious Yankee peddlers of the past who were said to palm off wooden nutmegs on unsuspecting housewives.

Most of the human race has always seemed to have had a sweet tooth, and the people of the Middle Ages were no exception. Until the end of that period, honey was the general sweetener, although in some countries date or fig syrup was used. In classical times it was also discovered that an alcoholic drink could be made with fermented honey. It was called mead.

Confectionery had been known in the Orient and in Egypt for centuries in the form of preserved or candied fruits. Before the 14th century, though, it was used chiefly to disguise medicine and was sold mainly by physicians. Marzipan, made of almonds or other nuts pounded to a paste and blended with sweetening and egg white, is one of the earliest forms of confectionery. By the Middle Ages it was being molded into fancy shapes. It was not until the 19th century, however, that candy making became a big business. By the mid-19th century there were 380 small factories manufacturing candy in the United States.

The most common sweetener today, sugar made from sugar cane, was a rare commodity in medieval times and was not known to the Greeks and Romans. Sugar cane has been cultivated since prehistoric times, but for many centuries only in Asia. It may have originated around the Bay of Bengal. It seems to have been introduced into Persia in the fifth century B.C., but only the very rich could afford it. From the Middle East it got to Europe in small quantities in the Middle Ages, where it was sold by druggists as medicine and was a great luxury. If a wealthy person wanted to show off, he decorated his table with figures molded from sugar.

The situation changed completely after sugar cane was taken to the New World in the 16th century by the Portuguese, British, Dutch, and French; production began there, especially in the West Indies. As the demand and the market for sugar grew, a shortage of labor developed. This shortage prompted the importation of black slaves from Africa on a large scale. Molasses and rum, as well as sugar, were products of the cane, and thus they became involved in the slave trade. In effect, rum was traded for

COUGH SYRUP *being prepared from fruit by a doctor, from an Islamic manuscript.*

slaves to produce more cane, to produce more sugar and rum.

Dining at table.

Cooking utensils in the Middle Ages were little changed from ancient times. In use were a device to raise and lower cauldrons (the basic piece of equipment), and a jack to allow spits to be turned. Forks were used for kitchen work, or to move food from a pot to a plate, but not to eat with. Earthenware and metal dishes were used for baking food, but glass was not usually found in kitchens. Cooking pots hung over the fire in the fireplace.

Noble and wealthy families dined well and in state, although some of their customs seem rather haphazard today. The table was probably really a trestle, and tablecloths do not seem to have been used until the 13th century. Even then, it was all right to wipe one's hands on the edges. A large number of dishes were put on the table at once, rather than a course at a time, and diners selected what they wanted. The richer the family, the greater the number of dishes. A thick slice of bread served as a plate until, by the end of the period, wood or pewter trenchers came into use. When bread was used as a trencher, it became soaked with meat and vegetables in the course of the meal. Afterward it would be given to the dogs or the poor.

Much use was made of fingers in eating, and most people carried their own knives for cutting up food. Forks were not common at all until the 18th century, although spoons were in general use. Sometimes two people shared the same trencher, so it was considered courteous not to do such things as scratch oneself while sharing food.

SALT CELLAR *of gold and enamel, made for the King of France by Benvenuto Cellini.*

When napkins were provided, it was not proper to wipe off perspiration with them or to blow one's nose in them.

Salt and salt cellars had symbolic and meaningful parts in dining. To the Romans, salt, together with the salt cellar, was an indication of hospitality and friendship. The salt cellar was a prized possession; it was often made of silver in the shape of a bowl rather than a shaker. From Roman times, through the medieval period and into modern times, it was a matter of prestige as to where a person was seated in relation to the salt cellar. To be "below the salt" was to be put in the class of children, servants, or unimportant guests.

The East. While Europe was advancing out of the Dark Ages, a rich civilization had developed in the Middle East. The Arabs had been a nomadic people who ate much meat, mostly mutton, along with dates and sheeps' milk. Then, in the seventh century A.D., Muhammad, the founder of Islam, united them under the banner of his new faith. In about a century, the Arab armies had subjugated North Africa and southwest Asia, and had gained control of Spain. They were stopped from further advances in Europe by the Franks in 732.

In succeeding centuries a culture developed that drew well ahead of Europe in learning and fine living. By the tenth century diners in Baghdad listened to poetry as they ate. They enjoyed roast meat with spices and sauces; wheat, millet, and rice dishes; raisins, olives, and apples; and almonds, walnuts, and pistachio nuts to thicken sweet dishes.

Farther east, in the Hindu civilization of India, religion called for a rather simple lifestyle. Two meals a day were eaten and each was to be accomplished in 32 mouthfuls. The food was boiled rice, bean soup, cakes, and fruit, with water and milk. Only the right hand was used in eating, and one never touched food with the left. Each person had his own flask to drink from, and one did not touch the flask

with the lips, or ever let anyone else drink from it. Richer tables held better rice, as well as curries, meat dishes, and sweets. Only kings could afford to import grape wine, but beer was made from rice.

Later, after the Islamic Mughals conquered most of India in the 16th and 17th centuries, the new court introduced the Persian royal style of dining. Food included kebabs and pilafs in a cuisine based on mutton and chicken. Fruit was mixed into meat dishes and sweetmeats were popular.

When Europeans began to penetrate India in force in the 17th century, they took to some of this cuisine with great pleasure, enjoying such dishes as chickens stuffed with rice, almonds and raisins, and beef or mutton kebabs. Small pieces of the meat were salted, peppered, and dipped in oil and garlic, then roasted on a spit with sweet herbs between the pieces of meat.

China. Rice, vegetables, and pork remained mainstays of the diet in China. It is said that in the 13th century the people of Hangchow ate an average of 37 ounces of rice every day. They had their meals at dawn, noon, and sunset. At grand banquets so many dishes were served that a person was not expected to try them all.

One of the principal and most interesting sources of information about China in the Middle Ages is Marco Polo and the book he wrote. Polo was a Venetian who, with his father and uncle, started overland for China in 1271, reaching Peking in 1275. He visited other parts of the Far East as well, and arrived back in Venice in 1295. At this time China was ruled by Kublai Khan, the fabled Mongol conqueror

who founded the Yuan dynasty. Polo recounted how, at feasts, the khan was seated higher than anyone else, his sons seated so their heads were at the height of his feet, and so on down, row after row, in order of importance. The emperor also gave 13 feasts a year, one for each lunar month, with 12,000 barons as his guests.

Kublai Khan, Polo further said, fed 30,000 poor people every day. He is also noted for having reestablished public granaries and for rebuilding canals to bring rice to the capital more easily. Polo noted restaurants, teahouses, fish markets, and men selling cakes and candied fruits from a bamboo stall.

Food in Modern Times

The Middle Ages blended into the Renaissance period, which began in Italy in the 14th century, and elsewhere in Europe went on to the mid-17th century. It was a transition period from the medieval era to modern times, marked by new movements in learning, the arts, and science. Nation-states emerged. The period was, most of all, an era of exploration and discovery in Asia and the Americas.

Food from the Americas. Although not considered of primary importance at the time compared with gold, one of the greatest benefits Europe and all the world received from the discovery of the New World by Columbus and his successors was the many foods discovered there and spread around the globe.

INDIAN CORN, *America's gift to the world, displayed before an Apache Indian woman in Arizona. Of the common cereals of the world, corn alone is native to the Americas.*

BOB ADELMAN/MAGNUM

The potato. The most important of these new foods was the unglamorous potato. It had been cultivated in the Andes Mountains of South America for at least 2000 years before the Spaniards arrived in the 16th century and took it to Spain. The potato reached North America by being brought back by English colonists around 1600. The Portuguese carried it to western Africa, and Ferdinand Magellan is believed to have passed it on to the Philippines and the East Indies. Gradually it spread over Europe and became essential in feeding the growing population when the Industrial Revolution took place.

Nowhere, though, did it play a more fundamental role in diet than in Ireland, where it was introduced in the 1580's. The Irish became so dependent on it that when there was a blight in 1845, leaving no seed potato for the next crop, famine set in. The country was devastated, and the result was a great flow of Irish to the United States, where today the vegetable is still often referred to as the Irish potato.

Corn. Next in importance to the potato was corn. (In general, corn is used to name the leading cereal crop of a nation. For example, in England wheat is called corn. America's corn is sometimes called Indian corn, or maize, to avoid confusion.) The only native cereal of the Americas, corn was seen by Columbus on his first voyage. Soon taken to Europe, corn spread over southern France, Italy, the Balkans, Asia Minor, and North Africa. The Spanish conquistador Cortés found the Aztecs eating corn tortillas and tamales. Corn saved the first settlers in Virginia from starvation. Taken to Africa by the Portuguese, it improved the diet in that food-short continent to such an extent that the population increased, ironically providing more slaves to be shipped to the Americas. The Indians surprised and delighted early white settlers with popcorn.

The sweet potato. The sweet potato goes back at least to 750 B.C. in Peru. It was also cultivated by the Aztecs. The sweet potato was introduced to Europe in the 16th century, and later to Asia, where it is now the most important root crop in the diet of millions.

The cassava (also known as manioc), which resembles the sweet potato, is a native of Brazil, long cultivated there by the Indians. Although it contains the deadly poison prussic acid, this can be eliminated by cooking. In flour form, cassava is widely eaten in South and Central America, the West Indies, Africa, and some parts of India. A product manufactured from its roots is tapioca, much of which used to be consumed in puddings in the United States.

The tomato. The tomato, so popular today, made slow progress originally in the United States. It is a native of the low Andes, from whence it spread to Mexico. Taken to Europe by the Spaniards, it was called the golden apple because the first ones were that color. It was also considered poisonous and was grown only as an ornamental plant. However, this mistaken belief was overcome and Thomas Jefferson was growing tomatoes by 1781. They were being eaten in New Orleans by 1812.

Pumpkin. The pumpkin, which in the form of pie is an all-American dish, may be a native of Asia, but if so it was introduced to America in early prehistoric times. This, and other squashes, were among the most important crops of pre-Columbian Indians. Pumpkin, of course, was served at the Pilgrims' first Thanksgiving dinner.

The lima bean. The lima bean, which also goes back to prehistoric times, and which Columbus may have been the first white man to see, was important in the diet of North American Indians. Combined and stewed with corn, it made succotash, into which the Indians sometimes, so it is said, put a little dog meat. The Pilgrims used salt beef instead.

The peanut. One of the most popular foods of New World origin is the peanut, which was cultivated in South America by pre-Columbian Indians. Actually, it is not a nut but a legume, related to the pea. It is also known as goober, pinder, earthnut, groundnut, ground pea, and monkey nut. It reached North America by way of Africa after Portuguese slave traders had taken it there. In the United States, it is eaten mostly in candy or in peanut butter sandwiches, but it is a more basic item of diet in other parts of the world and is the 15th most important food crop.

The pecan is also a New World product, perhaps native to Texas, where it is still more popular than anywhere else. Pecan is an Indian word, and while in the United States it is the most popular nut after the peanut, it is not much eaten in the rest of the world.

Fruit. The strawberry is one of the most popular fruits in the world. Wild ones were eaten in prehistoric times. The Romans knew the strawberry, and it was sold on the streets of London in the 15th century. It is native to many temperate regions, but it is the American species, introduced to Europe shortly after 1600, that is grown and eaten almost everywhere now.

The grapefruit, the most popular citrus fruit after the orange, is an oddity: a new species that appeared in America after European colonization began. It seems to have been found first in Jamaica as a mutant, and was not recognized as a species until 1830. It was not much eaten in the United States until after World War I, and in Europe not until after World War II.

The pineapple was cultivated by American Indians. The early explorers of the New World found it very tasty and began to spread it around the world. The cranberry, usually thought of as purely and typically American, is a native of Europe and northern Asia as well as North America. However, the American cranberry is the biggest. The American Indians invented cranberry sauce, a dish that many prefer with turkey.

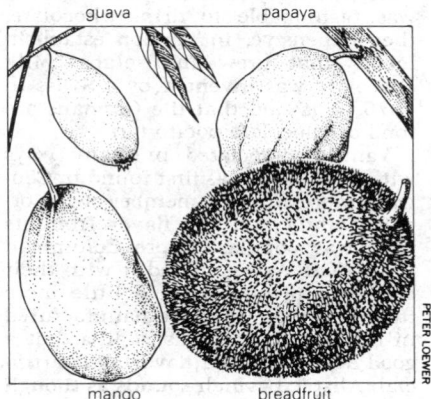

TROPICAL FRUITS *are now eaten around the world, regardless of their origin.*

There are more than 100 species of the plum, of which 30 are native to North America, but it is the European plum tree, imported to the United States, whose fruit we eat. The Pilgrims had wild plums along with their first Thanksgiving dinner. The papaya, or pawpaw, is native to tropical America. It was carried to Africa and Asia by traders. It is now grown in all tropical regions and is the most popular fruit in the hot regions of the western hemisphere.

The turkey. This bird is considered the most American of all creatures that supply meat. Benjamin Franklin suggested that it, rather than the eagle, should be the national bird of the United States. However, the turkey also has a very long history in Mexico, and was domesticated by the Aztecs. Europeans took to the turkey in Europe in the 16th century, and in the 18th the roasted turkey, stuffed with the expensive truffle, was the rage of France. (The truffle is an edible fungus found chiefly in western Europe.) The turkey, wild in the northeastern part of North America, was apparently brought by the Indians to the first Thanksgiving dinner.

The buffalo. Although no longer available as wild game, the American buffalo was once an important source of meat for the western Indians and for white explorers in the West. The creature is more correctly called bison, and is related to some African and Asian mammals of the cattle family. The Indians made use of almost every part of the buffalo, but red man and white alike considered the tongue the great delicacy. Around 1800 there were some 60 million buffalo in North America, but by 1900 they had been hunted down, leaving only two herds. Since then they have been protected and have increased.

Cocoa. The source of one of the most popular drinks and candies is the cacao tree, native to South America. The Aztecs in Central America grew it and prized it highly. From the cacao comes the cocoa bean and, eventually, chocolate. By the mid-17th century it was fashionable to drink chocolate, then expensive, in London establishments that grew into clubs. Milk chocolate was invented by a Swiss in 1876. It is said that the Germans are fond of chocolate potato tart.

Vanilla, associated in many ways with chocolate, was first found in Central America. It is a member of the orchid family and the flavor from its fruit was popular in pre–Columbian times. The Aztecs mixed it with their chocolate drink. Today a little more than half the ice cream manufactured in the United States is vanilla, but a good deal of vanilla flavoring is artificial. Allspice, which sounds as though it were a mixture, is the berry of the allspice tree, native to Central America and the West Indies. Another name for it is pimento.

Maple syrup. Sweet maple syrup and maple sugar have the distinction of being not only food products native to America, but the only ones that are produced nowhere else. Only in the northeastern United States and Canada are conditions just right for the growth of the sugar maple tree, from whose sap these products come. The Indians depended on maple syrup, and it was the staple sweetener of the colonists, maintaining its importance until about 1875, when cane sugar at last became cheap and available.

WILD GAME *such as the rabbit was included in most diets until very recent times.*

BETTMANN ARCHIVE

The Old World to the New.

The traffic in foods was not all one way between the New World and the Old. The Europeans brought to America some basic foodstuffs, including wheat and rye. The Spaniards introduced wheat to Mexico about 1520, and Virginia colonists did so in North America in the early 17th century. Vegetables came, too, among them the carrot, brought by English colonists. Carrot that escaped and now grows wild in the countryside is our Queen Anne's lace.

Okra, a native of Africa and still not much eaten in the United States, came with the slaves. It is an important item, as a vegetable and in soups and stews, in the developing nations. Mango was taken to Brazil about 1700, but is still not much known or eaten in temperate zones. However, its importance in other parts of the world is indicated by its description as "the apple of the tropics." Even hogs were new to the western hemisphere, being introduced first in the 16th century by the Spaniards and later in the American colonies from England.

Changing times.

In the approximately 400 years since Europe discovered the New World, great changes have taken place in the production of food, in methods of preparation, and in the eating habits of people all over the world.

In the late 17th century, in much of western Europe, barley bread was replaced by rye and wheat. Butter was more common and the peasant diet improved with more milk and pork. In winter, though, only the rich had meat, smoked or salted.

The general cuisine in China in the 18th century was rather different. Most of the population existed on rice or noodles, bean curd, pork, and the traditional vegetables. The rich, however, enjoyed bird's nest soup, dried and smoked sea cucumber, plover's eggs, shark fins, and roast snails. The very poor had to make do with dog and cat meat.

The American colonies.

The American colonists of the 17th and 18th centuries had rather different problems with their food supply. All kinds of wild game and fruit were available for the taking, but each family, for the most part, had to do its own hunting and farming to provide for its own sustenance.

Deer, bears, squirrels, rabbits, possums, and pigeons could be shot and eaten. The Indians were said to cook wildcats, moose noses, and beaver tails. Berries could be picked, and in the fall children were sent out to gather nuts such as chestnuts and black walnuts. Fish and even lobsters were cheap and plentiful. Out of the products on hand, the New England colonists made such dishes as Indian pudding, a baked mixture of cornmeal, butter, eggs, spice, and molasses; or hasty pudding, also based on cornmeal and eaten with milk, or if cooled and solidified, with maple syrup. Hominy was more of a southern than a northern dish. Corn had to be soaked in a weak solution of wood lye to loosen the hulls. It was then boiled and could be shaped into patties and fried. The colonists produced beer, but the most common drink was cider or apple brandy.

Black slaves had to make do with whatever their owner gave them to eat, plus a small garden patch they were sometimes allowed. They may have raised a few hens, too, and occasionally they did some hunting. George Washington's slaves in 1797 received a peck of corn a week per adult and 20 salt herring a month. There was salt meat at harvest time. Slaves got leftovers from the "big house," and ate a lot of black-eyed peas, turnip tops, ham hocks, and chitterlings (the small intestines of a pig).

The 19th century.

In the United States and in western Europe, there was a fairly steady improvement in the food available during the 19th century, although the situation was far from ideal as far as the average factory worker was concerned. In England he and his family ate a lot of bread and drank lots of tea, and had a piece of cheap meat or bacon on Sunday. There might be a pudding on Sunday, too. Some existed mainly on potatoes, with some bread, cheese, and porridge. The growth in population made it necessary to import large amounts of food, chiefly grain.

The middle class in England, which was increasing, ate better. A family would have soup, several kinds of meat, and some cakes and custards. Equivalent French families in the 19th century had six to eight courses, but in time this was reduced to three. The meal began with appetizers such as soup and fish; then came meat, game birds or poultry, with salads and vegetables; and finally, cold meats, aspics, and sweets.

At the upper levels, as witnessed by a dinner the prince regent of England gave in 1817, food was more than plentiful. His meal began with four soups, followed by four fish dishes, four meat dishes, 36 other entrees, from chicken to oysters, followed by cakes, pastries, and much more.

Not quite so lavish, but more than filling, was the Sunday dining of a well-to-do New York family in the 1840's. Their day began with a breakfast of beefsteak or chops, potatoes, hot rolls, griddle cakes with maple syrup, hot corn bread or muffins, eggs, and coffee. In the evening, after a very big dinner, supper offered hot biscuits, cold meat, game, salad and sweets.

In the United States urban residents, mostly in the East, lived much like their counterparts in Europe. The same was true on the farms, except that the farther west one lived, the more one could still rely on hunting game, while accepting a smaller selection of fruits and vegetables. But springs and wells could be used to keep farm foods cool. In the city people had to depend for milk, for example, on delivery by cart, with little attention to hygiene. The milk was quite likely watered as well. Drinking spruce beer and chewing spruce twigs helped prevent scurvy. One of the chief pleasures of American cuisine, though, was the prevalence of pies, stemming from an abundance of fruit.

The principal meats.
Cattle were domesticated in Egypt by 3500 B.C. Veal, the meat of a two- to three-month old calf, is first noted in Sumerian records of about 2500 B.C. Italians are the greatest veal eaters, consuming about four times as much per person as Americans. Pork has been one of the most widely eaten meats in the world for centuries, except where religion forbids it. Pigs, as scavengers, are economical to raise. They roamed the streets of Athens and Rome, later London, and still later, New York City. China, though, is probably the leading nation in pork consumption, and it was the most important meat in the United States until after the Civil War.

Sheep were domesticated about 7000 years ago (for wool as well as meat). Lamb, or mutton, is the foremost meat dish in the Middle East and North Africa. In the Western world, mutton is more important to the menus of Great Britain than elsewhere. In the United States, less lamb is eaten per person now than in 1900, while France's consumption of it is half as much again, Britain's five times as much.

Seafood.
A wide assortment of seafood provides a great deal of nourishment for people all over the world. The salmon has been widely eaten for centuries. In fact, it was so common in colonial times that servants resisted having it fed to them too often. Nevertheless, both the colonists and the Indians ate a great deal of Atlantic salmon, and on the Pacific coast the Indians of the northwest depended on Pacific salmon for about half their food. Char and trout are part of the salmon family, and the latter originated in the mountain streams of central and western Europe. France and Japan raise large numbers of trout, while in the United States the rainbow trout of the West is favored.

The carp, probably native to China, may be the most important freshwater food fish today. It was taken from Asia to Europe in the 16th century and to

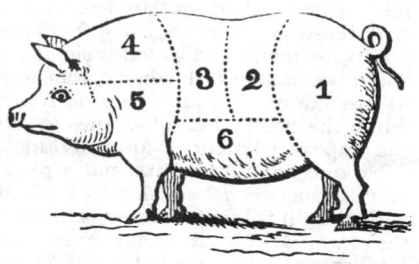

BUTCHERING *to obtain the best cuts is an art that differs from country to country.*

CULVER PICTURES

America in the 17th. Carp have long been raised in Asia and Europe.

Remains of oyster shells show that the oyster goes back to Neolithic times, and it was eaten in quantity by American Indians. The Romans loved oysters, and 17th-century Europe developed a craze for them. King Louis XIV of France ate them by the dozen. In the same way, the United States took to them in the 19th century. They were then plentiful and cheap and fashionable parties featured them. Oyster bars flourished, and one advertised "all you can eat for 6 cents."

From the sea also comes kelp, a form of seaweed that is an important modern food source. The Japanese are the greatest seaweed eaters and it accounts for about ten percent of their food intake. The Japanese make foods known as *kombu* from kelp. The Irish boil it into a green gruel and serve it with boiled mutton.

A variety of plants.
Americans developed a taste for broccoli, a form of cabbage, only in this century, although it was brought here in the late 18th century. The Romans knew it and the Chinese have adopted it. Eggplant, a native of Southeast Asia, was imported into North America by Thomas Jefferson. Europe seems to have received it earlier from the Moors, by way of Spain, and Louis XIV sponsored the first cultivation of it in France. To most people, the dandelion is a lawn pest, but some still eat the leaves as greens. The ancient people of the Mediterranean appreciated dandelions, but in the Renaissance they were considered only an aid to women's complexions. The French seem to be the only ones who actively cultivate dandelions. The roots, when roasted and ground, make a coffee substitute, and many Americans in the past made wine of the flower heads.

A native of Europe, the herb dill is widely used in the eastern and colder parts of Europe, in countries such as Poland, Russia, Hungary, and in the Scandinavian nations. The Romans wore wreaths of it at feasts and fed it to the gladiators because they thought it was a tonic. It has also seen use as a charm against witchcraft. In the United States, however, its main function seems to be to make dill pickles.

The mushroom has become very popular in recent times, but it has a long history. Hippocrates, the early Greek physician, used it as both medicine and food. For a long period it was a delicacy available only to the rich, but now it is grown commercially on a large scale.

Tea.
Despite its long history in the Orient, tea did not reach Europe until 1609, via the Dutch East India Company. Germany and England probably first tasted it in the 1630's. The first public tea sale in England was held in 1657. The tea was very expensive, but only 100 years later it was cheap and a widely popular drink, the British East India Company by then sending in large quantities of it. Russia also took to tea with enthusiasm and made famous the samovar, on top of which there was always a teapot.

The English consume about ten pounds per person per year. After water, more tea is drunk than any other beverage in the world. The Shakers, an American religious sect, may have invented iced tea. They were known to like ice and they drank large amounts of iced tea in the 19th century.

Coffee and ice cream.
Coffee was first used in Ethiopia before 1000 A.D. It spread from there to the Middle East. It was popular in Arab lands, in the 1400's, and there was a coffeehouse in Constantinople in 1554. Oxford, England, had a coffeehouse in 1650, Marseille, France (the first on the Continent apparently), in 1671. By 1693 there were 250 coffeehouses in Paris. In London, which saw its first coffeehouse in 1652, they became such popular institutions that they evolved into men's clubs.

Ice cream, thought of as being as American as apple pie, is an import. The Roman Empire had water ices and Marco Polo brought back to Italy a report of ice-flavored foods. From Italy, which seems to be where ice cream was invented, it spread to France and England, and then to America in the early 18th century. It was available at the popular entertainment spot, the Vauxhall Gardens, in New York City soon after 1800, and was first manufactured on a commercial scale in Baltimore in 1851. The first ice cream sodas are said to have appeared at the American exhibit at the Paris Universal Exposition in 1867.

From stoves to sandwiches.
There was a general improvement in cooking in the Western world in the course of the 19th century. For one thing, a greater variety of food products became available, and more cookbooks were published to guide the ambitious. One of the most important

improvements was in stoves. It was about the middle of the century that iron, coal-burning stoves almost completely replaced fireplaces. The stoves had removable lids, and the James cookstove, patented in Troy, New York, in 1815, became standard equipment. There were some experiments with gas stoves early in the century, but it was not until the 1880's that they became common. The great advantage of gas in cooking was that it made it possible to control the amount of heat more accurately than a fireplace or coal stove.

The practice of eating mostly with the fingers was gradually abandoned, and the use of the spoon spread in the 16th century. Italians seem to have been the first to use the fork as an individual eating instrument. The custom spread and three- and four-pronged forks appeared in the 17th century. By this time, too, guests were provided with knives and were not expected to carry their own. Glass drinking vessels were now common. In China, chopsticks had been used since the fourth century B.C. and had spread into Southeast Asia and to Japan.

In the mid-18th century, upper-class families had their main meal in late afternoon, with a light lunch before, and tea after. The English afternoon tea can still be a heavy meal. In rural areas the biggest meal of the day was served at noon, whereas city people ate their main meal in the evening, as most still do. Europeans, in contrast to most Americans of the past and some of the present, eat a light breakfast to start the day and have a second one later in the morning. By the mid–19th century, the practice of putting everything on the table at once had been mostly abandoned. At formal meals waiters handed dishes around in rotation, a service known as "a la Russe." The Japanese made a practice of serving different foods in small pieces, in different dishes, to emphasize and contrast color and texture.

Today's picnic, a meal eaten outdoors, was originally a social gathering at which each person brought some of the food, but it was eaten indoors. The word picnic comes from the French *pique-nique,* which for a time in England, where a sponsoring society was formed in the early 19th century, was spelled Pic Nic.

The term barbecue comes to us from the Caribbean area, where meat was smoke dried on lattices of green wood built over a fire. In Spanish the frame was a *barbacoa.* The term was used in Virginia before 1700. At first a barbecue implied the roasting of a whole animal, but now smaller cuts are often used. In the United States, it began as a southern custom. In any case, it is a reversion to the practices of our Neolithic ancestors.

When first visited by white men, some Indian tribes of the American northwest Pacific coast held ceremonial feasts called potlatches. Along with feasting, the host gave gifts to his guests, as many and as valuable as he could possibly afford. The custom was for the guests, at a later date, to try to outdo the host. This sometimes led to the impoverishment of an individual.

No one knows who first put a piece of meat between two slices of bread and ate it. It is known, however, where the term sandwich came from. An Englishman, the fourth Earl of Sandwich, was such a devoted gambler that he once refused to leave the gaming table for 24 hours. While he played, he had brought to him some slices of cold roast beef inserted between slices of toast. In 1778, Captain James Cook, the explorer, named the Sandwich Islands in the Pacific for him.

Technology and Food

What humans have eaten at any given time or in any given place has been determined, to some extent, by the technology available to preserve and transport food. It is only within the last 200 years that the problems of preservation and transportation have been solved. Today most foods can be preserved for very long times and transported anywhere—even to the moon. The development of such techniques became essential as the world population in the course of these 200 years increased greatly and millions moved to cities from farms.

Butter and wheat are two contrasting examples of how technology can affect the diets of millions of people. For centuries, butter was made without the aid of much in the way of machinery. In 1878 a Swedish engineer and scientist, Gustav de Laval, invented the centrifugal cream separator, which made it easier and cheaper to produce large quantities of butter. In the case of wheat, new milling methods in the 19th century produced grain that made whiter bread; but in the process the wheat germ was lost. This damaged the diet of the poor the most, because bread made up a large part of their diet.

Before about the mid-19th century, the only way to refrigerate food was with natural ice. Such ice could be harvested in the winter and used in cities in the summer, and the iceman was a familiar figure in towns and cities until well into the 20th century. The first patent for artificial refrigeration was issued in Great Britain to an American inventor, Jacob Perkins, in 1834. By the mid-1880's, refrigerated railroad cars, using natural ice, were running on railroads. Mechanically refrigerated cars became available in the late 1880's. Mechanical refrigerators for homes, the final step in food preservation, appeared about 1920 and rapidly became standard household equipment.

Faster transportation, in the form of railroads and steamships, began to develop even before refrigeration, and the combination of the two allowed food to be shipped from one place on the globe to any other place. Frozen mutton was shipped from Argentina to France in 1877, and two years later a ship brought 40 tons of frozen mutton all the way from Australia to Great Britain. By 1892 a butter factory in Australia was producing for export, and after 1900 Argentina became a leading exporter of beef. The railroad made it possible to bring fresh vegetables and milk from the country to the city without any form of preservation. The quality of milk improved when given by country instead of city cows.

The popular banana is another example of a food whose distribution and consumption in many areas of the world was made possible by technology. The banana, actually a giant herb, is a native of tropical Asia. In its wild form it was eaten in the Indus valley 4000 years ago. It was not known in Greece or Rome and not planted in the western hemisphere until a Spanish friar brought it to the West Indies in 1516. It began to reach Europe in the 1870's, and had been available in the United States sometime before that.

However, its universal availability as a moderately priced fruit arrived only in the late 19th century, when special refrigerator ships were built. It is now cultivated in all tropical areas, and in east Africa one kind of banana, cooked, is a staple food for millions. It is also used there to make beer. The exported dessert banana eaten in the United States is picked green and ripened after it arrives here. Ecuador is the largest single exporting country, while Europe is supplied from West Africa.

SAFETY TIPS ON FOOD STORAGE

DON'T store food under the sink—there may be leaks and bugs there.

DON'T buy dented cans—they may be contaminated.

DON'T forget to clean dust off stored cans—the dust has harmful bacteria in it.

DON'T store food near a heat source—the stove for instance.

DON'T taste old food to see if it's bad—you may poison yourself.

DON'T drink milk or other liquids from the container—you may contaminate it.

DON'T cram things helter skelter into the refrigerator—it makes for spoiled and forgotten items.

DON'T push foods that should be used quickly to the back of the refrigerator—they'll be forgotten and will soon spoil.

Canning foods.

Although most canned foods never taste quite the same as fresh foods, the invention of canning methods has been a great boon to mankind in making fruits, vegetables, and meats available anytime, anywhere. A French chef won a prize in 1810 for developing a practical canning process based on the principle that heat destroys the ferments that cause spoilage. The first tin can was patented the same year, and two years later British sailors serving in the War of 1812 were eating canned soups and meat.

In 1858 John L. Mason perfected the glass mason jar. This made home canning safe and practical. The Civil War stimulated the canning industry, as the Union armies ate large quantities of canned tomatoes and meat.

Freezing and drying.

Frozen foods as we know them today are a recent development, even though commercial freezing operations were tried in the United States as early as 1865. The resulting product then was of poor quality because the freezing was done too slowly and at temperatures that were not low enough. A Brooklyn-born American, Clarence Birdseye, began experimenting in 1916, seeking a better process. By 1924 he had developed a practical way of freezing fish, but his important breakthrough came in 1949, when he perfected a system that cut the freezing time from 18 to one and a half hours.

Preserving food by drying it is one of the earliest processes man discovered, but doing it commercially and on a large scale is a fairly recent development. Modern methods involve changing the form of the food, by turning it into a powder or by reducing its volume. A patent for dried eggs was issued in the United States in 1865, but a full-scale plant did not operate until 1878. World wars I and II stimulated the dried food business to provide less bulky meals for troops on the move in far away places. Instant coffee was one such product.

Milk, as a very basic food, came in for early attention from those who sought to make it safer, longer lasting, and easily transportable. A patent for dried milk was given in 1855 in England. Gail Borden, an American, produced condensed milk in 1856. It contained added sugar and was popular with soldiers in the Civil War. A Swiss immigrant to the United States, J.B. Meyenberg, about 1880, found a process for sterilizing and evaporating milk without sweetening it.

After Louis Pasteur, the French chemist, proved the modern theory of germ infection, he developed a process for pasteurizing foods and this was applied to milk, beginning in 1890. At that time its main purpose was to prevent tuberculosis, which can be transmitted by infected cows.

MAKING BUTTER *the hard way, by churning cream, was common until recent times.*

Substitutes for butter and sugar.

Margarine, once called oleomargarine, was developed in the 1860's in France by a chemist, Hippolyte Mège–Mouries, in a contest sponsored by Napoleon III. Beef fat, known as oleo oil, was the main base of it at that time. The early margarine had a wavy texture, not much taste, and no color. Later, vegetable oils, such as corn, cottonseed, and soybean, were used. By the end of the 19th century, millions of people were using margarine, much to the distress of the dairymen who produced butter.

The sugar beet, as a variety of beet, was known for a long time, but it was only in the late 18th century that a German chemist found a practical way to extract sugar from it. The first sugar beet factory was built in Silesia, in eastern Europe, in 1801. The sugar beet became an important crop in France and Germany in the early 19th century, when Napoleon I urged its use to offset the British blockade of the Continent that shut off the supply of cane sugar from the West Indies and other tropical areas. Today about one-third of the world's sugar supply comes from this beet.

Packaged and "invented" foods.

As cities grew, a large proportion of the people had no way of obtaining food except in retail stores. They became willing to let food processors do much of the work formerly done in the home, and to buy foods that were canned, frozen, ready-mixed, precooked, heat-and-serve, and "instant." Manufacturers and retailers found that thousands if not millions of people were willing to buy these products. This made possible the production of large quantities of the same foods, and it meant, among other things, less difference in the way the

various social and economic classes lived.

Before the day of national brands, retailers received food in large containers, such as barrels of crackers. When a customer bought crackers, the grocer, or general store proprietor, picked some out by hand and put them in a paper bag. On a national scale, however, food needed packaging to protect it and to label it. It was soon discovered that attractively labeled packages, whether of glass, paper, or tin, caught a customer's eye and helped sell the product. At first Americans took to this kind of selling more than people of other countries. With standard names and packages, a customer also knew what to expect in the way of quality and price.

The 19th century also witnessed the start of what might be called "invented foods." Sylvester Graham, an early 19th-century Presbyterian clergyman and temperance lecturer, advocated the use of coarsely ground wheat flour, to be included in a vegetarian diet that, he thought, would promote temperance. Today we have graham crackers. John Kellogg, a young physician in Battle Creek, Michigan, where he ran a health institute, devised a flaky, dried preparation of wheat. He meant it as a vegetable snack but his patients liked it for breakfast, with milk. He also offered granola, a sort of ground zwieback.

Charles W. Post then brought out Grapenuts and, to compete with cornflakes, which had been invented by a brother of Kellogg, Post Toasties. He was also responsible for a coffee substitute called Postum, based on bran, wheat, and molasses. Since then there has been a flood of breakfast foods, snacks, and soft drinks invented and promoted to sell nationwide and sometimes worldwide.

Supermarkets and vending machines.

As food processing was done by larger and larger businesses, so too did retailing become vastly different from the original system of thousands of small stores, independently and locally owned. The Great Atlantic and Pacific Tea Company (The "A.& P.") started in 1858. By 1870 it operated eleven stores and by 1880, 100. Other chains sprang up and grew. These were still grocery stores where clerks waited on customers. The first supermarket, where the customer roams the store picking out what he wants, appeared in the United States in the 1930's, but the concept did not spread to Europe until the 1950's. Customers liked the opportunity to handle the brightly labeled cans and packages. Also, the supermarket could presumably offer lower prices because its overhead was reduced by eliminating clerks. Not the least attraction of the modern supermarket is that one can do all one's shopping there without the necessity of going to the fruit and vegetable store, the butcher, and the baker. By 1976, three-quarters of all grocery sales in the United States were made in supermarkets.

Another development of modern times that has had great influence on eating habits is the rise of restaurants, followed by cafeterias, fast-food outlets, and vending machines. In the 16th century, English inns served one meal a day at a set time, the meal consisting of one dish which everyone ate, all sitting at the same table. This was called the "ordinary," and soon places that served such meals were known as ordinaries. Lloyd's, the famous marine insurance syndicate, got its name from an eating place where men interested in shipping matters gathered.

The word restaurant was first used in about 1765 in Paris. *Restaurer,* in French, means to restore, and the original idea of these eating places was to serve a light dish that would restore one's energy and perhaps one's spirits. Another French word, *chef,* meaning in general "chief," was first taken into English in 1842 to mean a professional cook in 1842.

In the United States, the first modern restaurant was opened in New York City about 1834 by Lorenzo Delmonico, and was soon widely imitated.

A rather different approach to eating was taken by the cafeteria, which was first devised by organizations trying to provide low-priced meals for working women. Like the supermarket, it cut costs by making the customer do some of the work. In recent years, the cafeteria has been largely replaced by fast-food outlets, drive-ins, and vending machines. The fast-food

FINE RESTAURANTS, *found around the world, elevate cooking and eating to a fine art.*

KRATH/WOHL/STOCK BOSTON

outlets combine some of the features of the cafeteria and the restaurant, but by offering a small choice of dishes they can serve many customers in a short time.

The drive-in was made possible by the automobile. If millions of people went driving, many could be induced to stop to eat if they did not even have to get out of the car to do it. The vending machine has been adapted to serve almost any kind of prepacked food, including hot dishes, and liquids. In many office and factory canteens, the impersonal machines have replaced the cafeteria.

Traveler's food. The Mongols of the Asian steppes are said to have eaten meals while riding their horses, but dining while traveling did not come into its own until the arrival of the passenger train, the ocean liner, and, finally, the airplane.

The American Indian traveled with pemmican, which the early colonists learned about. This general kind of dried food goes far back in time. The Chinese 2000 years ago thought dried snake was delicious and other Asians carried dried fish. Pemmican consisted of slices of venison or buffalo, dried in the sun. It was pounded to shreds and mixed with melted fat. Sometimes dried berries were included. Pemmican would not spoil, was easy to carry, and was very nourishing.

In the late 19th and early 20th centuries, the food served on the best trains and best ocean liners, together with the luxurious surroundings and attentive service, gave them a reputation for the utmost in gracious dining. With the virtual disappearance of such trains and ships, the late 20th century traveler is left with the precooked, reheated meal, served on plastic trays in the cramped spaces of the plane. But these meals are improving.

Protection of food. Ever since one human being sold food or drink to another, there have been complaints of short weight and of adulteration. Greek and Roman writers told of dealers who sold colored and flavored wine. In medieval times, as markets in towns grew, the first steps in inspection were taken. Except for weighing food, such inspection had to be done on the basis of sight, smell, and taste, since there was no knowledge available that made any other kind of inspection or testing possible. It was believed that bad odors transmitted disease.

Not much could be done about most adulterated food until the 19th century, when advances in chemistry made it possible to find adulterants and to determine which were harmful. The science of chemistry also provided the knowledge with which the dietary value of foods could begin to be judged. The first book on the subject

INGREDIENTS: CHICKEN STOCK, ENRICHED EGG NOODLES, CHICKEN, WATER, SALT, CARROTS, CORN STARCH, MONOSODIUM GLUTAMATE, UNBLEACHED PALM OIL, VEGETABLE OIL, YEAST EXTRACT AND HYDROLYZED PLANT PROTEIN AND NATURAL FLAVORING

CAMPBELL'S SOUP LABEL. *By law, ingredients must be listed to protect the consumer.*

of adulteration was published in 1802.

In the United States, the first steps in food protection laws came in 1906 with the passage, with the strong support of President Theodore Roosevelt, of the Pure Food and Drug Act. The enactment of this law was stimulated by the activities of two men. One of them was Upton Sinclair, whose novel *The Jungle,* published in 1906, revealed the horror, adulteration, and neglect of all sanitary precautions, at the stockyards and meat-packing plants of Chicago. The other man was Dr. Harvey W. Wiley, chief chemist of the Department of Agriculture, who showed how preservatives and adulterants were being used in canned food without the public's knowledge. The original act was strengthened in 1938 and has been amended several times. A new section having to do with color additives has been included. The Food and Drug Administration was formed in 1927 and is now part of the Department of Health and Human Services.

Cookbooks. Almost as soon as people began taking a serious interest in the way food was prepared, cookbooks began to appear. Marcus Gabius Apicius, a Roman gourmet of the first century, is given credit for writing a cookbook that was actually compiled 100 years later. One recipe for a sauce for a roast required a quarter ounce of each of twelve different spices. Apicius was a rich merchant who fell on hard times and who is said to have poisoned himself because he could no longer live in the style he required. Another Roman cookbook was translated into English as recently as 1958.

During the Han dynasty in China (202 B.C.-220 A.D.) there appeared a handbook called *Li-chi,* which included among other things recipes for the "Eight Delicacies" that were to be prepared for the elderly on ceremonial occasions. One dish included the liver of a dog, while another was a suckling pig stuffed with dates.

One of the first known cookbooks of the Middle Ages appeared in France in 1375. Its title was *Le Viandier de Taillevent* and its author was Guillaume Tirel, who was chef to King Charles V. One of the earliest English cookbooks, published in 1508, was the *Boke of Keruynge* (book of carving). By the 17th century the cooking of France was beginning to be noted as outstanding, and *Le Patissier François,* written by François de la Varenne, formalized its practices in 1655.

The number of cookbooks increased as time went on. Queen Victoria's chief cook wrote one in 1845. The best known English cookbook of the 19th century was Isabella Beeton's *Book of Household Management* (1861). That same year in the United States, Mrs. Horace Mann, wife of the noted educator, produced a cookbook whose theme was "Christianity in the kitchen." One of the most famous and successful cookbooks was published in 1896. It was the *Boston Cooking-School Cook Book,* then and now known familiarly as "Fanny Farmer." It started the practice of giving exact measurements for ingredients instead of simply calling for a "pinch" of something.

Today the number and variety of cookbooks is almost unlimited. Depending on your culinary interests, you can buy such guides as *Chinese Vegetarian Cooking, The Ebony Cookbook, Jewish Low Cholesterol Cookbook, Fearless Cooking for Men,* and *Spoonbread and Strawberry Wine.* There is even one devoted solely to various ways to cook zucchini.

National Foods

There can be no doubt that we associate certain dishes with certain countries. Sometimes we seem to picture everyone in a given country eating the same dish at the same time every day, though we know this really is not so.

We all have impressions about "national foods": Australians are said to like fried eggs or oysters with their steak, and they have a dessert called pavlova that is a crisp meringue shell on the outside, filled with whipped cream and fruit. Austrians, on the other hand, praise wiener schnitzel, very thin slices of veal, coated with egg and white bread crumbs, fried quickly. Austria is also famous for its pastries, especially apfelstrudel. Waterzoie, chicken broth that includes dry white wine, is a favorite of the Belgians. For the feast of St. Nicholas they bake spicy cookies, cut in animal shapes and iced pink and white.

Brazil is the home of yerba de maté, usually called just maté. The beverage is made from the leaves of a small tree. It contains a small amount of caffeine and is mildly stimulating. In the Caribbean countries they serve a dish called *arroz con pollo,* which is rice with chicken, with a number of other ingredients. The Chinese, of course, have exported some of their national foods, such as egg roll, bamboo shoots, and soy sauce. They use the latter the way Americans use ketchup. The litchi (sometimes spelled litchee or lychee) is a fruit long savored in China but not well known to the Western world. It is mostly eaten fresh as the last course of a traditional Chinese dinner, but it can become a nut by being dried.

French cuisine. France is synonymous with the best foods—the "haute cuisine" that restaurants all over the world try to imitate. French is the language of menus that want to impress the customer, and French cooking traditionally makes much of rich sauces, using many kinds of herbs. In the past few years French chefs have begun to offer a "nouvelle cuisine," food that is somewhat lighter for an era in which people are very weight conscious. The French also do such simple things as croissants and hot chocolate very well.

Britain. Great Britain, on the other hand, has a poor reputation, not entirely deserved, when it comes to cooking. Those who disparage British cooking contend that the British boil everything before doing anything else with it. Perhaps not, though, with roast beef. In the 18th century a British poet, looking backward "when mighty roast beef was the Englishman's food," ended with the lament, "Oh! the roast beef of old England!" Yorkshire pudding, a thin batter baked in a bit of hot fat, is appreciated. As to seasonings, in the British Isles they stick mostly to salt and pepper.

Germany. German food is tasty and nourishing—and rather on the heavy side. The Germans like sweet sauces and garnishes on their meat and poultry. A traditional dish is hasenpfeffer, which is rabbit soaked in vinegar, onions, and spices, and browned in butter. The Germans are also said to make a soup out of beer.

Greece. Lamb is the favorite meat in Greece, which has a good reputation for eatable food. Moussaka is a national dish, prepared by first frying minced meat in oil. Eggplant is added, everything is covered with cheese sauce, and then baked in an oven. Hungary, of course, means goulash, either as a soup or as a stew. It includes beef, onions, paprika, tomato puree, and caraway seeds.

India. The cuisine of India does not include a great deal of meat, partly because of religious beliefs, partly because of the poor state of the economy. *Chapati* is a bread made from whole wheat flour that is mixed into a stiff dough with water, then rolled out like a pancake and baked on a griddle. The butter of India, called ghee, is also used as a medicine and is an ancient sacrificial material of Hinduism. It is made from the milk of both cows and

CHINESE CUISINE, *subtle and complex, uses a wide variety of ingredients.*

苔 條 炸 黃 魚
Fried Whole Fish with Seaweed

蝦 子 大 烏 参
King Sea Cucumber with Shrimp Seeds

buffaloes and is clarified by boiling so that only the oil of the butter is left. It will keep for a long time. In India, and elsewhere in the Orient, a great deal of curry is used in combination with meat, rice, and other dishes. Curry is made of such spices as tumeric, fenugreek, cloves, cumin, ginger, black and cayenne pepper, coriander, and caraway.

Italy. The favorites of the Italian cuisine are almost as well known in the United States as in their homeland. Pizza is perhaps the best example, but there is also minestrone, the thick vegetable soup, and zabaglione. The latter consists of egg yolk, sugar, and Marsala wine, beaten together and served as a dessert. Less known is vitello tonnato, veal with tuna fish sauce.

Japan. Japanese cooking, on the other hand, tends toward being plain and simple, including much fish, some of it eaten raw. Sukiyaki, made of beef, chicken, or pork, and containing vegetables, soy sauce, and bean curd, is well known in the United States.

Mexico. Mexican food is hot and many Americans like it for that reason. The dish called tamale is a good example, its meat being highly seasoned and put in cornmeal dough before being cooked. Tortilla is an unleavened bread that is cooked quickly on a hot, ungreased griddle; huachinango soup is made from fish.

Netherlands. The people of the Netherlands eat a great deal of fish, being by tradition a nation of seafarers and fishermen. They like cheese (a Dutch speciality) and favor eggs for breakfast.

Northern Europe. A Polish dish apparently little known here is chlodnik, a cucumber soup with sour cream. Russia gave us beef stroganoff, lean beef cooked in cubes and served with a sauce of mushrooms and sour cream. Russians eat lots of borscht, containing beets and usually cabbage, and served with sour cream. The Russians also have more caviar (the eggs of sturgeon) than most countries. The Scandinavian countries consume a great deal of fish, and herring is supposed to be the basis of Sweden's diet. Sweden is also known for the assortment of appetizers served under the name smorgasbord, which in Denmark is smorrebrod. Danes also eat a giblet soup made with vegetables and called Kraasesuppe, and dine on roast goose on Christmas Eve.

Favorite foods. Gourmet tours never include Scotland, where they eat oatmeal and also haggis, which is a boiled pudding made from sheep or calf's heart, liver, and lungs, minced and mixed with onions, suet, and oatmeal, then boiled in the animal's stomach.

Spain's *paella* is by now well and favorably known in the United States. It can be made with chicken alone or with meat and seafood, too, and includes rice, garlic, saffron, and other seasonings. From Turkey and other countries of the same region comes kebab, always served with rice in the form of pilaf. In Uganda a staple food is called *matoke,* steamed plantains, while in coastal West Africa there is a very large black snail that is so highly thought of it is eaten at festival times.

The USA. The United States is so diversified geographically, ethnically, and culturally that no one food dish can claim to be *the* national dish. Outside observers might nominate the hot dog. Germans are said to have brought over the meat part in the mid-19th century, and a German who sold it was the "wiener wurst man." Hence the "weenie." It may have been a Coney Island baker, named Charles Feltman, who first put it in a roll and created the hot dog.

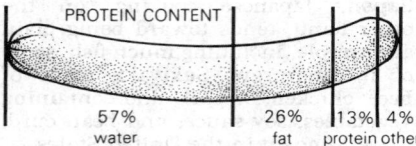

PROTEIN CONTENT

57% water   26% fat   13% protein   4% other

THE BELOVED HOT DOG, *like most American junk food, is far from nutritious.*

There are many American dishes with regional connections: Boston baked beans, Philadelphia scrapple (actually invented by the Pennsylvania Dutch who blended cornmeal and headcheese), Shaker loaf, New England clam chowder, Louisiana chicken creole, Southern fried chicken, Virginia smoked ham, key lime pie, spoonbread, cowpoke beans, hush puppies (so-called because they are often fed to dogs), jambalaya, pandowdy, and Swedish meatballs. The list could easily be extended.

Food and Religion

Religious beliefs and practices, as well as national and ethnic considerations, play an important role in determining what foods will be eaten or not eaten. In some cases, rules about food may have been imposed for a nonreligious reason and later transferred to the religious domain. A prejudice against an alien group of people may extend to the food they eat. In ancient times, one way of protecting people against a disease such as trichinosis, which can come from raw or inadequately cooked meat, especially pork, was to forbid eating the food in question. In general, such rules and taboos are not as strong today, at least in the Western world, as they once were.

The two extremes of gluttony and fasting are prominent in religious rules and practices. Gluttony is one of the seven deadly sins, while partial or temporary abstinence from eating is a common practice imposed on believers of various faiths. Fasting is undertaken for many reasons. The Crow In-

dians, for example, fasted in order to produce visions.

Among Christian groups, the Roman Catholic Church, until about 15 years ago, required its members to abstain from meat on Fridays and to eat fish instead. The observance of Lent, the period of 40 days before Easter, beginning on Ash Wednesday, goes back to the fourth century A.D. It is a period of fasting and penitence. Ember days, whose origin is very old but uncertain, are various days in the course of the year marked by fasting, although the practice has generally ceased.

Christmas feasts. Christmas, when Christians observe the birth of Jesus Christ, comes near the winter solstice, when many ancient cultures celebrated the occasion, principally by feasting. Christmas did not become the great popular festival it is today until the Middle Ages. In England the goose was considered the proper dish for yuletide. Mince pie has long been a feature of Christmastime, but the Puritans called it "superstitious pie" because they thought it was connected with a pagan way of celebrating the season.

Mincemeat in such a pie includes a finely chopped mixture of raisins, currants, apples, suet, sugar, spice, with, sometimes, meat, brandy or cider, and perhaps other ingredients. Twelfth Night, which is January 5, the twelfth night after Christmas, has long been a popular festival in England, with much feasting and parties.

Vegetarianism. As a general movement, without necessarily having any connection with religious belief, vegetarianism began in the mid-19th century and has attracted many followers in the United States and Great Britain. Its practice may be based on ethical, economic, or nutritional beliefs. There are companies that produce foods for vegetarians that take the place of the meat portion of a meal. These are vegetable protein products, made mainly from wheat and soybeans. In recent years, vegetarianism has become associated with the so-called "health foods," and "organic foods," containing, as is usually stated, "only natural ingredients."

Orthodox and Jewish. In the Eastern Orthodox Church, the Great Lent fast is broken on Easter Sunday with mageritsa, a soup made with the internal organs of the lamb. The traditional food of Easter is lamb. Greek custom is to bake Easter bread, thick, round loaves decorated with hard-boiled and colored eggs, which are dyed bright red and are tokens of good luck.

The dietary laws of Judaism, as practiced by Orthodox Jews, are very

precise and complicated. The most sacred writing of the Jews is the Torah, the first five books of the Old Testament, and in one of them, Leviticus, are laid down a series of rules about what may and may not be eaten. It is permitted to eat any animal that has a divided hoof and also chews its cud, but not those that meet only one of the requirements. This means that the cow, sheep, ox, and goat are clean and can be eaten, but not the pig or the camel.

Only fish with both fins and scales are allowed, which rules out shellfish and eels. It is forbidden to eat many kinds of birds, and "all teeming winged creatures that go on four legs," unless they have legs jointed above their feet. Meat and dairy foods may not be eaten at the same meal.

The term kosher, meaning proper or fit for use, is applied not only to the permitted foods, but also to the way they are prepared. There are rules regulating the slaughter and preparation of poultry and animals. The appearance of a great variety of processed foods has complicated matters for Orthodox shoppers, but this problem has been solved by putting symbols on those packages that have been certified as properly prepared.

In autumn come the ten most solemn days of the Jewish year. The period begins with Rosh Hashanah, the Jewish New Year, and ends with Yom Kippur, the day of fasting. For Rosh Hashanah a bread called challah is prepared and decorated with ladders or birds baked on top. These are intended, symbolically, to carry prayers to heaven. As a symbolic wish for sweetness in the new year, bread and apple slices are dipped in honey.

In the spring comes the eight-day festival of Passover, which celebrates the flight of the Israelites from Egypt under the leadership of Moses, as described in the book of Exodus. This is the most important and elaborate of Jewish festivals. It begins with the ceremonial Seder meal, eaten on either of the first two evenings of the festival. There are dishes symbolizing the hardships that the Jews underwent in Egypt. Only unleavened bread, matzo, is eaten during the period. It is unleavened because the Jews, on leaving Egypt, had no time to leaven their bread. Special dishes and utensils are used for the Seder. The Seder plate, used only on the first two nights of Passover, contains other symbolic food.

Islam. The youngest of the world's major religions, Islam also has rules about fasting and foods that cannot be eaten. These rules are stated in the Koran, the sacred book of Islam. Five duties are specified and one of them is to keep the fast of Ramadan, the ninth month of the lunar Muslim year. During that month a person may not eat, or drink water, or smoke between sunrise and sunset. Even then the meals eaten are supposed to be light. A special type of leavened bread is prepared. Like the Jews, the Muslims are forbidden to eat pork and there is a strict ritual for slaughtering animals.

Hinduism. One of the oldest of the world's religions, most Hinduism exists in India and nearby areas. The caste system, which has to some extent been broken down in recent years, divides society into four groups. An individual is born into one of the four castes and can never belong to another. Each caste abides by definite rules, including some pertaining to what a person may eat. The original castes have been subdivided, and there are also the untouchables. The cow is a sacred animal in Hinduism; it is allowed to roam at will and must not be killed.

A Hindu is supposed to be a vegetarian, partly because meat cannot be obtained without injuring a living creature, a violation of Hindu beliefs. The coconut is a sacred food because it is a symbol for Shiva, one of the greatest of Hindu gods. The higher castes are not supposed to eat onions, garlic, turnips, mushrooms, or salted pork. There are many days of fasting and prayer, called Vratas, when a person is expected to eat nothing, or at least to abstain from cooked foods.

Buddha. Buddhism, which originated during the sixth century B.C. and which to some extent is an outgrowth of Hinduism, is a religion practiced almost entirely in the Far East. It calls for vegetarianism in general, but in Buddhist Thailand farm families eat a few chickens and supplement their rice diet with fish. They do not kill the fish, they say; they simply remove them from the water and they die. Buddhism is the religion of a very large number of monks who are entirely dependent on gifts for their food.

Food and ceremonies. In different countries there are special occasions other than strictly religious ones that call for something extra in the way of food. In the United States, for example, there is still a feeling that "Sunday dinner" is more important and more festive than meals on other days. Several generations of a family might be assembled at table on Sunday, and there is a little more and a little better food than on, say, Thursday. The American holiday of Thanksgiving is primarily an eating festival, to give thanks for having had enough to eat all year. Weddings call for some kind of breakfast, or dinner, or buffet at a reception after the ceremony. The occasion is marked by a wedding cake, cut by the bride with the assistance of

HYDROPONIC GARDENING, *shown here—the growing of vegetables in water treated with chemicals, but using no soil—is but one of the many horticultural advances of recent years.*

JOHN COLWELL/GRANT HEILMAN

the groom as a way of showing that they are now united. If they stay married for 50 years, the chances are their children and friends will tender them a special dinner to mark that event as well.

Birthdays, especially for children, are occasions for parties, usually marked by a cake, with icing and candles to blow out, one for each year being celebrated. In American life funerals, too, are often followed by a gathering of relatives and friends of the deceased, to sympathize with one another and to partake of food to sustain one after an ordeal—and, perhaps, to show the unity of the living in the face of death.

Food and the Future

More food is being produced in the world today than ever before, and yet millions of people are undernourished, if not on the verge of starvation. The areas of great food shortages are chiefly in parts of Africa and Asia. There are a number of reasons for this shortage. For one thing, the population of most countries involved has increased faster than the food supply. There have been droughts, and political and military revolutions in recently independent countries have driven people from their own regions, or from the cities to the country. It is estimated that famine in Ethiopia in the 1973 up to 1975 period caused 200,000 deaths; *The New York Times* reported in March, 1981, that 150 million people in Africa face starvation.

Food and agricultural experts say that more drought-resistant crops, such as sorghum, yams, and potatoes, must be grown. Sorghum is native to Africa and is the leading grain grown there. Overall, sorghum is one of the

three or four most important cereals in the world and is basic to the diet of 300 million people. Besides in Africa, it is grown on a large scale in India, China, and Manchuria. There are arid regions where sorghum and millet are the only grains that can be grown. A coarse bread is made from sorghum in China. Sorghum came to the United States from Africa and most of the crop here is used to feed livestock.

The palm, the common name for a large family of trees that grow chiefly in tropical areas, is the source of several food products that help sustain the people of some of the less fortunate parts of the world. Oil can be derived from many palms and used for many purposes. In countries such as Nigeria, it is used in all kinds of cooking. The oil palm originated in western tropical Africa and the biggest producers now are Nigeria, the Congo, Malaysia, and Indonesia. From the pith of the sago palm can be made a flour that is eaten in the tropics.

The chickpea is a very ancient vegetable that today is consumed in large quantities in the food-needy parts of the world, especially in India and Africa. In India it is called Bengal gram.

The growing, selling, buying, cooking, and eating of food are so fundamental to life that food has played a part in almost every aspect of world affairs ever since men in tribes or other units came in contact with other groups. In one way or another, food has affected population growth and the expansion of cities; it has expanded commerce and has caused fierce competition, even wars; not to mention its part in religion. There is danger that the shortage of food in some parts of the world will cause problems in the near future, not only for those threatened with starvation but for the richer nations, who must correct the situation or, possibly, face the revolt of suffering peoples.

—*Fon W. Boardman, Jr.*

FOOD AND AGRICULTURE GLOSSARY

Agricultural Chemistry, the application of chemistry to the efficient production and utilization of plants and animals of economic importance. While the definition refers mainly to farm crops and livestock, it may be extended to include forest and marine products, and indeed, to anything else that grows and is useful to mankind.

Together with genetics, improved farm equipment, and improved cultural practices, chemistry has played an important part in advancing modern agriculture to the status of big business. Various agencies of the Federal government are engaged in fundamental and applied chemical research, and in analytical and regulatory activities, that are of service to producers, handlers, processors, and consumers of agricultural commodities. Likewise engaged in this field are various state departments of agriculture, universities, and agricultural experiment stations; private institutions that conduct or foster chemical research and development; industrial processors of agricultural products; and manufacturers of agricultural chemicals.

Among the fields of application of agricultural chemistry are crop production; livestock and poultry production; storage, transportation, and marketing; food utilization; and industrial utilization of by-products.
—S. B. Detwiler, Jr.

Agricultural Engineering, the application of engineering principles to agricultural problems. The divisions are power and machinery, structures, electric power, processing, and soil and water.

The strong position of the United States in today's world is due to a prospering mechanized agriculture— an agriculture that produces food and fiber in abundance with only about 6 per cent of the gainfully employed labor force. The millions of workers thus released to other industries, services, and professions contribute to the remarkable industrial expansion and high standard of living.

Crops once thought next to impossible to be harvested mechanically have been mechanized recently. Typical examples are sugar beets, cotton, tomatoes, figs, peaches, prunes, and nuts. Research will extend mechanization to many other crops.

Production structures contribute to increased efficiency. A well-designed milking parlor permits one machine milker to handle up to 60 cows. A crew of 10 can feed 20,000 beef animals in a mechanized feed lot. Dehydrators and fruit and vegetable packing houses prepare products for final consumption.

Fully 95 per cent of the farms in the United States are electrified. In addition to the general improvement in living conditions, electricity operates much of the farmstead equipment. Pumping and heating water, brooding chickens and pigs, milking, refrigerating, and feed processing are now done electrically.

Other engineering contributions are in irrigation and drainage and soil conservation. The western third of the United States depends upon an irrigated agriculture. Drainage is as important in irrigated areas as in regions with abundant rainfall. Soil erosion, a menace to the land, can be controlled to a large extent by agricultural engineers.   —Roy Bainer

Agricultural Science, an interdisciplinary science that provides information on biological, physical, and socio-economic problems in the production, marketing, processing, and use of crops and livestock for food and clothing. Generally, it is divided into several separate but related sciences, each with its own professional groups. These include: plant sciences, animal sciences, engineering sciences, soil sciences, entomology, parasitology, and social and behavioral sciences.

Many persons who are agricultural scientists are also biologists, chemists, physicists, mathematicians, engineers, or economists. Agricultural science consists of portions of these and other basic sciences applied to crop and livestock production, marketing, and use.

Agricultural science includes *molecular biology*, the study of how viruses, bacteria, and molds change virulence due to changes in RNA or DNA, the chemical bases of living materials. Such changes must be understood in order to combat these organisms. It also includes *radio biology*, the use of isotopes to follow the physiology of nutrient assimilation, and of radiation to induce genetic change or insect sterility.

Systems engineering and *electronic data processing* have become a part of agricultural science. The combination of soil moisture, fertility, probability of rainfall, hours of sunshine, and known plant characteristics may be used to determine the best time to plant peas in Wisconsin or the amount, formula, and time of fertilizer application for Indiana corn. Automated equipment places the feed formulated to provide all nutrient requirements at least cost before Delaware broilers. The least-cost formulated feed may have been selected by means of linear programming, a method also used by economists to determine the best use of resources by an individual farmer to increase his income.

■**EDUCATION AND RESEARCH.**—Agricultural science results from research in the laboratories of national governments, of universities, and of private institutions in many countries. In the United States, about 5,000 agricultural research scientists in the U.S. Department of Agriculture conduct research in many locations; about 10,000 do research in state agricultural experiment stations in the 50 states and Puerto Rico; about 10,000 do research in universities and col-

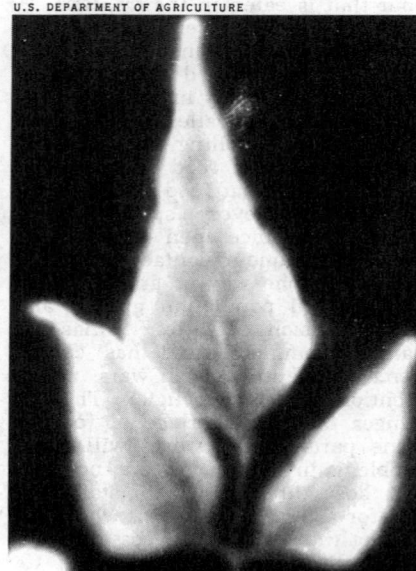

RESEARCH brings agricultural knowledge as a scientist (*above*) studies chemicals' effects on plant development. At *left*, radioactivity records and controls plant growth.

SEAGRAM AND SONS, INC.

A SAMPLE of whiskey is drawn for quality checking by a tester using a "whiskey thief," which reaches to the center of the barrel.

JOSEPH SCHLITZ BREWING COMPANY

MALTING, initial step in brewing beer, begins with "steeping." *Above,* oxygen bubbles through barley and water in "steep tanks."

leges and in private research institutions, including the laboratories of many manufacturers of chemicals, food products, and textiles.

Many more agricultural scientists are engaged in teaching, extension service, regulatory work, and production. They take the technical information developed in research to the farms and factories where it is put to use. This has resulted in yields, per acre and per animal unit, double those of a hundred years ago. It has made fresh meat, milk, and eggs available the year round.

■**PEST CONTROL.**—*Entomologists, plant pathologists,* and *weed scientists* have developed means of controlling many insect pests, diseases, and weeds that limit the productivity of crop plants, trees, grasses, flowers, and shrubs. The wheat crop depends on the continued development of wheat stocks resistant to old virulent rusts and new virulent ones as they occur. Weeds are controlled on 75,000,000 acres in the United States by effective chemicals. Used according to prescription, these chemicals are innocuous to man and animals. Dramatic control of an animal pest, the screwworm fly, has been achieved by the production and distribution of radiation-sterilized males. Development of power machinery for planting, cultivation, and harvest has led to the displacement of the horse as a source of power, greatly reducing the amount of manual labor required for crop and forest production and livestock care.

Research in animal nutrition has led to the formulation of efficient diets that have cut in half the feed cost of producing broilers. *Nutrition research* has contributed to the improved health and production efficiency of all our livestock.

Research in animal disease has developed diagnostic tests and immunization methods that have made possible the control of such diseases as *pullorum* in poultry, *brucellosis* and *tuberculosis* in cattle, *cholera* in swine. Research has developed effective parasiticides that protect our livestock against protozoan and worm parasites.   —T. C. Byerly

Alcoholic Beverages, potable liquids containing ethyl alcohol produced by enzyme action on sugars. There are three kinds of drink containing alcohol: wine, spirits, and beer. *Wine* is fermented from grapes or other berries and plants; *spirits* are distilled; *beer* is malted. Wine was first made by the ancient Egyptians. Grapes were later carried by the Romans to France, Spain, parts of Germany, and even to Britain. More recently, grapes have been grown in the United States, South Africa, and Australia. The cereals used to make spirits, except those made from wine, have spread over the world with the Caucasian population. Beer, known in the ancient East, was also made by the ancient inhabitants of northern Europe.

■**WINE.**—Grapes are used to make wine in commercial quantities. Other materials are generally used for home winemaking only. The grapes are crushed to express the juice, which ferments naturally because of the presence of skin fungi on the fruit, producing a chemical reaction. Two broad differences result from the color of the fruit—white and red grapes each produce wine of their own color with many intermediate and varying shades. The flavor varies from dry—that is, rather sour—to very sweet. The alcoholic content ranges between 9 and 18 per cent by volume and up to 25 per cent in fortified wines.

Champagne is a sparkling or bubbling wine, the sparkle being caused by bottling before fermentation is finished. Like many other wines, it is named after the place where it is made: Champagne, Marne, France. *Asti spumante* is a sparkling wine made in Italy. Other French wines are *claret* from Bordeaux and burgundy from the province of the same name. Some light white wines are also made in France, but the German white wines, *moselle* and *rhenish,* from the grapes grown along the banks of these rivers, are perhaps best known of this kind. *Tokay* is a famous Hungarian wine. *Chianti* and *lacrima christi* are well-known Italian products. Sherry comes from Spain, and *port* from Oporto, Portugal. The last is a fortified wine, that is, one to which brandy or alcohol is added. There are many other fortified wines. Wines of all these types are now made in the United States, principally in California and New York; in Australia, and in South Africa. Light white wines of the German type are now exported from Yugoslavia, as are Greek, Cyprian, and other wines formerly consumed locally.

■**SPIRITS.**—Brandy, whisky, rum, gin, and vodka are the best known spirits. Besides these, there is a variety of liqueurs, usually consumed after a meal. These drinks have a higher alcoholic content than wine, 25 to 50 per cent or more. Spirits are made by distillation; brandy from fermented grape juice, and the others from grain or potatoes.

Brandy, said to be first known in the East, was carried to Italy in the thirteenth century and known as *aqua di vita.* After this, it was made in the Netherlands, where it was known as *brandewijn,* the origin of its modern name. *Cognac* and *Armagnac* are made in those parts of France from which they take their names. Distilled drinks are made from the juice of other fruits, such as apples and cherries.

Whisky (or whiskey) originated in Scotland as *usquebaugh.* It has a high alcoholic content, ranging from about 40 to occasionally 75 per cent. It is made from cereals (rye, barley, maize, etc.) or potatoes. The grain is boiled to mash; then malt is added. Malt is grain sprouted in water, a process that changes the starch content to sugar. When the two are mixed, a chemical change from sugar to alcohol takes place, and this is separated by distilling.

Rum, which originated in the West Indies, is distilled from the fermented juice of sugarcane or from fermented molasses. All rums are colorless when distilled, but acquire color from the casks in which they are aged or from the addition of a coloring agent, such as caramel.

Gin is also distilled from cereals, chiefly barley. Various flavorings are added, the most favored being juniper oil. Gin contains from 25 to 50 per cent alcohol. It is the easiest spirit to fake, and substitutes (the renowned bathtub gin) are often sold.

Vodka is a Russian drink that is now being exported and becoming popular in western Europe and the United States. The materials used are roughly the same as those for other spirits, but the process and mixing are rather different.

■**BEER, ALE, AND STOUT.**—These beverages are brewed, using barley or other cereal grain for malting, and then boiled with hops, after which yeast is added to the liquor to cause it to ferment. *Beer* is sometimes made from maize, and there is a story that Columbus was given maize beer by American Indians. Maize is also used by the natives of South Africa for making beer. *Lager* beer, a light beer, introduced to the United States by German immigrants in the nineteenth century, is the most popular type. A *dark lager* is made in southern Germany. *Ale* made in England is stronger and more bitter than lager. *Porter* is dark ale, and *stout* is a stronger ale. The color of the liquor is said to depend upon the tint of the barley used, though varied grain is often mixed before malting.

—G. E. Fussell

Alfalfa, a perennial *legume* sometimes referred to as the "queen of forage crops." It is the most nutritious of the commonly-grown hay crops, and richer in protein, minerals, and vitamins than either clover or timothy. It is utilized as pasture, hay, or meal.

Alfalfa is a particularly hardy plant, being drought-resistant as well as resistant to extreme heat and cold. It grows best in deep loam soils with porous subsoils that contain lime. If lime is not present in the soil, as is the case in most areas east of the Mississippi River, it must be added.

Alfalfa grows 2 to 3 feet high, with trifoliate leaves, purple or yellow flowers, and a long tap root that may extend 25 or 30 feet into the ground. It is subject to attack by *bacterial wilt, spotted alfalfa aphids,* and *alfalfa weevil.*

The center of production in the United States is the Middle West, with California, Idaho and Washington excelling in seed production.

—Robert G. Dunbar

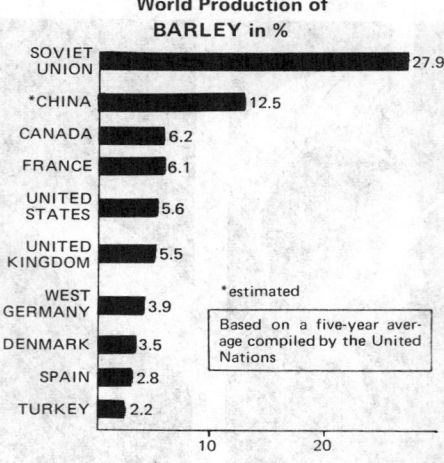

World Production of BARLEY in %

SOVIET UNION	27.9
*CHINA	12.5
CANADA	6.2
FRANCE	6.1
UNITED STATES	5.6
UNITED KINGDOM	5.5
WEST GERMANY	3.9
DENMARK	3.5
SPAIN	2.8
TURKEY	2.2

*estimated

Based on a five-year average compiled by the United Nations

Barley, first brought into cultivation by prehistoric man, one of the two *cereals* that supplied the food necessary to allow civilization to develop, the other being wheat. There are two kinds of barley, two-row and six-row. Another, *Bere,* is called four-row, but its appearance is misleading. Today, barley is grown all over the world in subtropical and temperate climates. It will flourish in high altitudes, in poor soils, and in areas of low rainfall. Owing to its chemical composition, it does not make a satisfactory loaf, but can be made into a hard bread, which English consumers used to call *Barley bangers.*

The principal modern use of this cereal is malting for brewing. Pot and pearl barley are prepared for use in cooking, thickening soups, etc. The protein dissolves in water, and the solution (barley water) is often used in infant and convalescent diets. Barley grain and straw are used for feeding livestock, especially pigs.

There are several different strains useful for growing in particular places, some of which have been bred from a single ear. A good deal of work on breeding strains suitable for cultivation in the widely varied conditions of the United States has been done by the Bureau of Plant Breeding, Soils, and Agricultural Engineering.

—G. E. Fussell

Beekeeping or **apiculture,** the industry and hobby of raising bees and collecting the honey and wax they produce. Just how long man has kept bees is not known, but a cave painting in Spain, estimated to be at least 8,000 years old, shows a man robbing a bee cave. Not until the twentieth century, however, did man learn to control *swarming,* the bees' natural method of increase. Swarm prevention helps him harvest more honey from the bees.

When swarming occurs, the queen, a few drones, and 5,000 to 40,000 worker bees leave their home in a mass flight. They establish a new home in a hollow tree, a cave, the wall cavity of a building some distance away, or a man-made beehive.

The first step in the preparation of the new home is wax construction. Hundreds of worker bees gorge themselves with nectar from flowers, then

wax glands on the underside of their abdomens convert the nectar into *white wax.* This is the structural material of the cells of the *comb,* which constitutes the framework of the hive.

Honey is also prepared from nectar. Ripe honey, which is sealed in the wax cells, consists largely of a mixture of sugars. The honey serves as food for the bees.

Other cells are filled with pollen, or *beebread,* which is also collected from flowers and carried in pellets packed ingeniously by the bee on its hind legs.

Propolis, a resinous material on buds and scars of trees, is also collected and carried like pollen on the bees' hind legs into the hive. It is used to seal cracks and holes too small for the bee to pass through, and to keep out rain and wind.

Within the hive, the queen lays about a thousand eggs a day, one to a cell. After three days, the eggs hatch into *larvae,* after five days of feeding, these are sealed in their cells to pupate, or change into adult form. The entire process takes about three weeks.

Eventually, the queen ages sufficiently so that she no longer can continue her egg-laying at the required pace. The worker bees then select a few tiny larvae, enlarge their cells, and feed them a special glandular food called *royal jelly.* These larvae, which would have become worker bees after their pupal stage, instead develop into virgin queens. The first one to emerge, however, seeks out and kills the other virgins before they complete their pupation.

When the surviving virgin is about ten days old, she goes on her mating

U.S. DEPARTMENT OF AGRICULTURE

BEES SWARM by the thousands on a branch, before going to a new hive.

flight, and in the air mates with one to six drones, who exist primarily for this duty. She returns home to begin her lifetime task of egg-laying, never to leave the hive again except with a swarm. The now-ignored mother queen may remain several weeks before she finally disappears.

During all this time, the bees have been storing honey and pollen for winter use. The amount stored depends on the flowers in the area, the weather, and many other factors, but there should be at least 50 pounds of honey and several pounds of pollen.

With approaching winter, the flowers disappear, the drones die, and the queen reduces her egg-laying or ceases altogether. When the temperature goes below about 57° F, the bees form a tight cluster to conserve heat, maintaining a cluster temperature of about 92° F, even when outside temperature falls below zero.

This is the natural way of increase for bees, but it may not always be the best way from the beekeeper's point of view. The swarm may escape. It may leave at the beginning of a good period for storing honey, and before the colony is strong with bees again. Strong colonies are essential if much honey is to be stored.

The beekeeper has found that bees can be kept in multiunit hives with movable frames. These can be taken apart for examination, and if the bees are crowded, more room can be provided. If more colonies are desired, the hive can be divided after the main honey crop has been stored. The part of the hive that lacks a queen will promptly rear another.

When frames containing sheets of wax with embedded cell bases are placed in the hive, the bees will construct straight combs in them. When these combs are filled with honey, they can be cut out, or the honey can be centrifuged from the cells and the empty comb replaced in the hive to be filled again. The average amount of honey to be expected from a colony is about 50 pounds, although trained beekeepers often harvest many times that amount.

Persons unfamiliar with bees should always wear a veil or screen over head and face. When one is working with bees, smoke should be blown into the entrance hole and over the frames as they are exposed. Although the reason is unknown, smoke tends to keep bees away from the worker and discourage stinging.

With movable-frame hives, smoker, and veil, the beekeeper can regulate the colony so it will produce the maximum amount of honey for him, and he can increase the number of colonies as he desires.

—Samuel E. McGregor

Breeding, Animal, the improvement of the quality of domestic animals through breeding, observation, and selection. Little effective progress was made until the rediscovery (1900) of Mendel's laws of heredity and their application in animal breeding. Knowledge of genetics has rapidly increased since then. With this has improved our knowledge of *cytology* (the study of chromosome

PIONEER HI-BREED CORN COMPANY

COMPUTER REPORTS help cattle raisers to select the best animals for breeding purposes.

behavior), statistics, and interdisciplinary science, providing tools for describing populations and developing experimental methods and chemistry. Applied to the fundamental laws of genetics, such knowledge provides the basis for today's science of animal breeding.

■**SELECTION.**—In animal breeding, the basic problem is to identify those animals that have desirable characteristics and to use these in producing superior animals. The application of statistical theory to the fundamental laws of heredity has resulted in the development of techniques to establish the best procedures for selecting animals having the greatest genetic value for specific objectives. These procedures provide bases for evaluating the probability that differences observed will be repeated.

■**GENETIC IMPORTANCE.**—The expression of most traits of economic importance is determined by the combined efforts of *genotypic* (hereditary determiners) and environmental effects. Therefore, the degree to which the expression of a trait is determined by genetic versus environmental factors must be considered in deciding how to design the most efficient animal-breeding programs. Furthermore, procedures must be devised to estimate the genetic value of groups selected for reproduction.

■**MATING SYSTEM.**—Individuals selected in an animal-breeding program can be mated together in many different ways to reproduce a population. Thus, *mating system* refers to any set procedure used to mate selected individuals to reproduce a population. Where relationships have been established within a population, matings based upon these relationships may be carried out. Examples of mating systems based upon matings between individuals more closely related than the average of a population are *full-sib* or *half-sib* matings. Mating sys-

tems between individuals that appear more like each other or less like each other than the average of the population, ignoring relationships, are called *assortative* and *disassortative mating systems,* respectively.

■**ARTIFICIAL INSEMINATION.**—The practice of placing sperm cells in the female genitalia of animals by instruments rather than by natural service is known as artificial insemination. This method has been used widely in dairy breeding for animal improvement. Here it is possible to collect large amounts of semen from proven sires and to use this semen in producing calves from a very large number of females. Where rare bulls can be naturally mated to only about 100 cows a year, use of artificial insemination makes it possible for individual bulls to sire more than 10,000 calves a year. Management conditions have made this practice especially worthwhile for dairy cattle in the United States. In some situations this technique is worth considering for beef cattle, sheep, swine, horses, poultry, and fur-bearing animals. It may, someday, also be considered important from a eugenic standpoint for application to human populations.

■**PROBLEMS.**—It should be realized that there are problems in the application of breeding procedures in animal populations that are not apparent. Where breeding procedures are used to improve animals of economic significance, all groups (germ-plasm sources) which *may* have, but do not now have, significance must be reproduced each generation. If this is not done, sources that may be invaluable for adaptation to conditions of the future may be lost. Artificial breeding, specifically, storage of sperm cells and ova, may in the future provide cheaper ways of overcoming this problem.

—Laurence Baker

A HONEY BEE leaves a cotton flower coated with the plant's pollen. Flying to other plants, the bee cross-pollinates the cotton.

Breeding, Plant, the improvement of the quality of crop plants through reproduction, observation, and selection. Little progress was made until the rediscovery (1900) of Mendel's laws of heredity and their application in plant breeding. Since then, knowledge of genetics and related sciences has increased rapidly.

■**CROSS-POLLINATING SPECIES.**—The most extensive plant-breeding efforts to cross-pollinate crops of economic significance have been applied to corn, or maize. The basic procedures that have been applied to corn include the application of various mating systems, such as *self-pollination,* the development of inbred lines from open pollinated varieties; mass selection in improving germ-plasm sources prior to inbreeding; and the production and evaluation of test crosses.

Due to differences in response to different environmental conditions, corn must be developed for each area that differs in length of day. Due to the increased yield obtained by crossing different sources of material, hybrid corn provides the main source of improved seed corn available today. With few exceptions, the primary objective in corn breeding has been to develop new crosses (hybrids) that yield more grain. Though disease and insect resistance is important and sometimes constitutes a problem, it has usually been provided through selection among indigenous sources of material.

■**SELF-POLLINATING SPECIES.**—Until recently, breeding techniques for improving self-pollinating species were limited. The main sources of variability for traits requiring improvement were exotic materials or crosses of related species with existing species. Most self-fertilizing crops are not completely self-fertilized; therefore, limited crossing is possible to provide sources of new material.

Self-pollinating crops that received attention were bread wheats, durum wheat, barley, rice, oats, and grain sorghum. Until recently, the potential value of first-generation hybrids of self-fertilized cereals was given little consideration. However, evidence now exists that increases of 30 per cent in yield may be possible through the development of such crosses. Other advantages, such as increased ease in improving quality, could be more important than increases in yield. A major obstacle still to be overcome in all small grains except sorghum is that cross-fertilization under field conditions must be possible before crosses can be produced in seed for wheat, rice, and barley. The problems are solvable, and first-generation hybrids of many more normally self-fertilized cereals will be available. Increased emphasis is being placed on breeding for nutritive quality in economically important feed grains.

—Laurence Baker

Cacao, the dried and fermented seeds of a green-leafed evergreen tree used in making cocoa and chocolate. Cacao, or cocoa, beans *(Theobroma cacao)* grow along the trunks and some branches of the cacao tree. The tree thrives in hot, rainy climates and is generally cultivated in lands 20 degrees north to 20 degrees south of the equator, where temperatures average between 65° and 75° **F.**

The tree is grown in shady areas, sometimes as an intercrop sheltered by leguminous trees or, as in some areas in Africa, by banana or rubber trees. In its early growth, the cacao tree is sometimes protected from winds by windbreaks. Most strains bear fruit from 3 to 5 years and produce for an average of 40 years, although some varieties have lived 200 years. The cacao tree bears its fruit, or pods, throughout the year, but the harvest is seasonal. The pods are cut by hand from the tree, and are then split. A machette wielder can open up to 500 pods an hour.

Of the many varieties of cacao, the main classifications are the *Criollo,* which produces a light-colored, thin-skinned bean used for fine chocolate; the *Forastero,* which is easier to cultivate on varied soils; and the *Trinitario,* a cross of the other two types. On plantations in the Western Hemisphere, it is rare to find only a single species.

■**COCOA AND CHOCOLATE.**—The most important products of the cacao bean are chocolate and cocoa. Before processing, the beans are weighed and blended, then roasted for one to two hours in large rotary cylinders. The beans turn a rich, brown shade and lose about 20 per cent of their weight. The remaining cracked *nibs* are conveyed to the mills, where they are crushed between large, heated steel discs. The remaining viscous mass is called *chocolate liquor.* This liquor in a solidified state is used for cooking and is familiar as *bitter chocolate.* About 53 per cent of the liquor is the practical vegetable fat, *cocoa butter.* It lasts for years and melts at low temperatures, but re-

mains solid at room temperatures. The 47 per cent residual is cocoa powder, used in chocolate-flavored foods and beverages. In manufacturing confectioneries, cocoa butter is added as an enriching agent. Breakfast cocoa contains 22 per cent fat; fine-quality chocolate requires a higher proportion of butter.

Cocoa, which is native to the American continent, was grown and used by the Aztecs, Incas, Mayans, and Toltecs. Spanish explorers popularized it in Europe, and by the 1600s cocoa had spread throughout African colonial possessions. In about 1828, a Dutchman, C. T. van Houten, developed a rich, palatable chocolate powder by removing some cocoa butter and adding an alkali to the mixture. About 50 years later, a Swiss invented milk chocolate.

Ghana, the largest producer of cocoa, turned out in 1975–76 about one-fourth (397,000 tons) of the world total of 1,521,000 tons and exports almost all of its domestic production. The United States is the world's top-ranking consumer of cocoa, accounting for about 25 percent of the world total. The West European countries, led by the United Kingdom, the Netherlands, and France, import about 40 percent of the world total.

Although West Africa continues to be the main cocoa-producing region, responsible for two-thirds of the world's cocoa crop, Brazil is emerging as an important producer since the government has initiated plans to expand production, particularly in the basin of the Amazon River. The Brazilian government hopes to boost output to 700,000 tons by 1985, more than double 1975–76 output. Among West African producers, the Ivory Coast today has the greatest potential for an increase in output. Production could reach 300,000 tons by 1980, or 75,000 tons above 1975–76, because of the opening of new growing areas.

—Marshall H. Cohen

CACAO was known to ancient Mayans, as the fossil below two modern beans shows.

Camel, a large herbivorous mammal used for riding, transport, meat, hides, and hair. The *Bactrian,* a two-humped camel, has heavy hair in the winter, hard foot pads, and short legs which fit it for cold and mountainous country. It is found in central Asia from the Black Sea to Manchuria, but cannot stand prolonged spells of great heat. The *Dromedary* has one hump, short hair, a long neck, long legs, and foot pads that hold the animal up in sand. It travels best on level sandy land and cannot move in mud. Dromedaries are found in North Africa, Egypt, Arabia, and India. They have also been successfully introduced into Spain and the Canary Islands, but unsuccessfully into Australia and the Americas.

Camels can metabolize the fat in their hump to get some water, but store most of their emergency water supply in one of their stomachs. They can go up to a week without water if they move slowly. Thick skin inside the mouth allows camels to eat nearly anything, including thorns, although they prefer brush, tree leaves, and fruit. Camels mate at any season and have a gestation period of about 12 months. The female usually produces one foal every other year. The working life of a camel is around 20 years. Camels are susceptible to *rabies, anthrax, tuberculosis, tetanus,* and *foot-and-mouth disease.* All these diseases can be prevented with vaccines. In addition, camels are particularly susceptible to the incurable and frequently fatal *trypanosomiasis* (sleeping sickness).

Camels are ruminants of the genus *Camelus,* which has two species, *C. Bactrianus* and *C. Dromedarius.*

—John T. Schlebecker

Casein, a heterogeneous compound protein derived from amino acids and containing primarily calcium, nitrogen, and phosphorus. Although the lack of uniformity limits its industrial applications, the casein compound is used in a wide variety of processes ranging from cheese-making to plastic manufacture. Casein constitutes the bulk of the curd of milk, and makes up about 3.15 per cent of the whole fluid cow's milk. It can be transformed into cheese, or *paracasein,* by the action of the enzyme *rennin.* For industrial uses, skim milk is treated with sulfuric acid, hydrochloric acid, lactic acid, and the casein is then washed, dried, and pressed. Dried casein is essentially a granulated jelly. It can be used to make a water-resistant wood glue, or a binder for various oil and latex paints. Lacquers sometimes also use a casein binder. Formerly large amounts of casein were used as a binder of paper coatings, but recently the use of casein for high-gloss paper has been declining in the United States. Casein can be hardened with formaldehyde to make plastics, but lately other chemicals have largely replaced casein. Since 1957, United States production of industrial casein has virtually ceased, although casein has been imported, chiefly from Argentina.

—John T. Schlebecker

AMERICAN ANGUS ASSOCIATION

BEEF CATTLE, such as the Angus breed (*above*) are, like dairy cattle, grazers. Angus cattle are highly adaptable to various climatic conditions and they produce high quality beef. They are popular especially in the United States, Argentina, and in Scotland.

Cattle, herbivorous, horned, bovine mammals. The male is called a *bull,* the female a *cow,* a young cow a *heifer,* a castrated male a *steer,* and a young animal a *calf.* In the United States, cattle are raised for milk, meat, and hides. Cattle furnish the bulk of dairy products in the United States, as well as cattle meat, called *beef* or *veal.* Beef, the most popular of all meats in the United States, can be readily preserved, although most of it is sold as red (fresh) meat. Livestock and livestock products rank third as a source of farm income in the United States.

Most cattle are now sold at country selling points; central markets, such as Chicago and Omaha, handle only about 30 per cent of the total marketed. Beef slaughtering and processing have also been decentralized. Chain stores have been directly buying and slaughtering large percentages of cattle. Dairy processing has concentrated in fewer companies, both private and cooperative.

In the United States, the chief beef cattle have derived from British and Indian breeds, such as the English *Devon, Hereford, Red Poll, Shorthorn,* and *Sussex,* and the Scottish *Aberdeen Angus, Highland,* and *Galloway.* The Indian cattle include several *Zebu* breeds which Americans lump together under *Brahman.* Zebus have also been crossed with other cattle to produce various new fixed breeds, including the *Santa Gertrudis, Beefmaster,* and *Brangus.* The French *Charolaise,* and crosses from it, are becoming more important as beef cattle in the United States. The several breeds are valued for their adaptability to climatic and regional differences within the United States.

The dairy breeds of the United States all originated in Europe. The *Guernsey* and *Jersey* came from the Channel Islands, and the most popular, the *Holstein-Friesian,* came from the Netherlands. Dual-purpose cattle provide both beef and milk in commercial quantities. The *Brown Swiss,* the Scottish *Ayrshire,* the *Holsteins,* and the *Milking Shorthorns* are often considered to be dual-purpose.

Cattle are grass grazers, but high milk and meat yields are achieved by feeding silage. Dairymen and beef raisers increasingly supplement feeds with minerals, vitamins, and antibiotics. Antibiotics, however, should not be used as a feed supplement for lactating dairy cows for the drugs may enter the milk. Cows reach maturity in a year and can be bred about every three weeks thereafter, although breeding should not be permitted before the cow is 18 to 24 months old. The period of gestation averages 283 days, and the cow produces one calf, or infrequently two. The cow comes in heat 30 to 60 days after calving.

Some fatal cattle diseases, such as *anthrax* and *blackleg,* can be prevented by vaccination. *Tick fever,* once highly virulent in some places, has been controlled by dipping or spraying to kill the ticks. Dips and sprays have also been effective against arthropod-borne *anaplasmosis.* Vaccines can control *contagious abortion* (brucellosis) and *tuberculosis,* although the slight incidence of tuberculosis in the United States makes slaughter of diseased animals more practical. *Pneumonia* and *shipping fever,* although very common, can be cured with antibiotics. Dairy cattle particularly suffer from *mastitis,* which antibiotics can cure. Cattle succumb to a large variety of poisonous plants, for which the only prevention is poison-free pastures.

Cattle are ruminants of the genus *Bos,* with two living species, *B. longifrons* and *B. indicus.*

—John T. Schlebecker

AMERICAN JERSEY CATTLE CLUB

DAIRY CATTLE BREEDS originated in Europe and were brought to the U.S. by early settlers. The Jersey breed (*above*) gives the richest milk but the quantity produced is only half that of the Holstein, the first-ranking milk producer in America.

—has made it nature's greatest provider to mankind in the tropics. Second only to the grasses among plants useful to man, it thrives in low-lying areas near the coast, 20° to 25° from the equator. The stem of the coconut palm rises to a height of 60 to 100 feet, with leaves growing only at its upper extremity. Within the graceful crown of leaves, the fruit ripens. A single tree may produce as many as 100 coconuts. Inside the outer husk of the fruit is found the familiar hard-shelled *nut*. It contains firm white meat and a white liquid, or *milk*. Dried coconut meat, which is known as *copra*, yields one of the world's most important vegetable oils.

Coconut oil is a product of importance in the modern technology of advanced nations. It is used in making candles, soap, shampoos, and detergents; as an element in synthetic rubber and in brake fluid for airplanes; and in the manufacture of tin cans, roofing plate, margarine, and shortenings. Shredded coconut meat supplies the coconut ingredient in cakes, pies, and confections. The husk surrounding the nut yields *coir*, a tough fiber that has many uses. Finally, young stalks produce a sweetish sap that is a source of sugar, alcohol, and alcoholic beverages. —Charles E. Rogers

Chicken, an edible bird that is probably the most widely domesticated fowl in the world. Almost all *broilers*, or young meat chickens, have white plumage; they are crossbreds, produced from matings of special meat males and females. Usually one breeder produces the male line and another breeder, the female line. All chicks are produced in large incubators, some of which can incubate more than 50,000 eggs at one time. Many chicken producers have an integrated system, controlling the entire process from producing the hatching eggs to marketing the ready-to-cook broilers, TV dinner, or chicken pie. The margin of profit per bird is very small, but integration and large volume make it possible for the producer to market a product of excellent quality at a low cost to the consumer.

Poultry processing and marketing have benefited from technological development. Live birds are placed on a moving conveyor at one end of a plant, and when they reach the other end the birds are in ready-to-cook form. In a short period of time, the poultry is slaughtered, picked, eviscerated, washed, and chilled. Most of the operations are completely automatic and it is not unusual for plants to process 40,000 to 50,000 birds per day. Poultry is offered to today's consumer at an attractive price and in a variety of forms—chilled, frozen, canned, parts, boneless, cooked, and in combinations with other ingredients. (*See also,* Egg Production, page 806.) —Carl W. Hess

Chicory, an annual that grows from seed planted in the spring and best known for the use of its root as a coffee substitute or supplement. Although often regarded as a roadside weed in the eastern United States and Canada, chicory has long been cultivated in America. The base of the chicory plant resembles the dandelion, but the stalk is longer, sometimes rising to a height of 5 feet, and its narrow, flat blossom is blue. Its spreading branches develop coarse-toothed and lobed leaves. These are valued as greens, used raw in salads or boiled. But the plant's long, fleshy root constitutes its most prized portion. Roasted and ground, it gives body, color, and long-lasting flavor to coffee. The plant originated in Europe and spread to other continents. It has been cultivated in the United States since the latter part of the nineteenth century. —Charles E. Rogers

Chocolate. See *Cacao.*

Clover, an important group of annual and perennial plants of the *pea family* having trifoliate leaves and dense flower heads. There are several species, some of which can be recognized by the color of their flowers—red, crimson, or white. All are used as forage crops. Growing clover for forage brought about great progress in farming: livestock were fed better, especially in winter, and became more productive; the extra manure they produced was used to fertilize the land, increasing grain yield; clover root bacteria add nitrogen to the soil, an aid to fertility. This crop is very ancient; its uses were known in southern Europe in Roman times. However, it was neglected until the sixteenth century, when it began to be grown again in Spain. From there it was carried to Holland, and then to Germany and England about 1650. European settlers took the crop to the United States, where it became a grazing and hay crop. —G. E. Fussell

Cocoa. See *Cacao.*

Coconut Palm, a tall tree with feather-like leaves, whose fruit—the coconut

Coffee, a large, broad-leafed evergreen shrub, its seeds, and a beverage brewed from the roasted, ground seeds. The shrub belongs to the genus *Coffea* of the madder family. In plantations, its height is generally kept at 6 feet, although it can reach 14 to 20 feet. Coffee grows best in the temperate, tropical highlands. The fruit of the plant, the *cherry*, which ripens about six months after the plant's blossoming, is dried and depulped, and its green seed or bean is transported to consumer countries, where it is roasted and distributed.

The word *coffee* is from the Arabic *Qahwah*, and legend depicts the first user of coffee as an Arab physician named Rhazes around the tenth century. However, mention is made of its cultivation in Ethiopia as early as the sixth century. Its use as a stimulating beverage was popularized by Muslim priests, who found it beneficial during prolonged prayer ritual.

Coffee use was confined to the Middle East and Turkey until the seventeenth century, when traders, explorers, and patrons to the court of Louis XIV introduced it on the Continent. *Coffee houses* became a social institution in the seventeeth century, especially in England and Austria. Until then, all coffee was cultivated in Yemen and Ethiopia. About 1690, Dutch and French explorers introduced planting methods to Java and to the Western Hemisphere from Martinique to Brazil, which today is the world's leading coffee-producing country.

■**GROWING.**—Of about 25 species of coffee, the principal one is *Coffea arabica*, which grows best at altitudes between 2,000 and 6,500 feet in a rich terra cotta soil. Arabica coffees are grown in 58 of the 70 major coffee producing countries, but the most sought-after is the Brazilian *Santos*. Arabicas are subclassified into *Brazils*

COFFEE BEANS must be sorted and graded by hand after they are dried and processed. Once this operation has been completed, the coffee is then packed for export and roasting.

and *Milds,* an example of the latter being the high-quality Colombian bean. Other species are the hardy *C. robusta* and the *C. liberica,* the former indigenous to Congolese Africa and the latter to West Africa. They are grown at low altitudes, from sea level to 2,000 feet. Robustas are primarily used in producing instant coffee due to their lower cost and high caffeine content.

The coffee seed is frequently planted in nurseries under careful temperature control. The young tree is transplanted and shaded by corn plants or banana trees. The tree is pruned after two years and matures in six years. Average trees produce for 15 to 20 years, and yield about 2,000 cherries. The cherries are hand-picked, dried, sorted, and bagged with little mechanization. However, Colombian Milds are depulped by a *wet process* in mechanically operated tanks. The *dry process* (sun-drying) is extensively used elsewhere.

■**PROCESSING.**—Coffee should always be commercially roasted shortly before it is marketed and distributed. The green beans are placed in large, revolving cylinders for 15 minutes at 390°–422° F (some new machinery can do this operation at 500° F for 5 minutes). One process, called *wet roast,* includes a water-spraying operation. Cooling and further cleaning, or *stoning,* follow, and occasionally the rich brown beans are preserved with a light coat of molasses. Grinding and packing are the final operation. *Instant* coffee requires a dehydration of the ground coffee, leaving the tiny soluble crystals. A pound of instant coffee requires three times as many beans as regular coffee. Coffee is finally bagged or canned in vacuum tins.

The economic importance of coffee is responsible for a high percentage of gross national product, employment, and export earnings in many South American and African countries. Brazil, the major coffee exporting country, normally exports about one-third of the world's coffee and Africa about one-fourth. Consumption in the U.S. has declined for several years, probably because of consumer preferences for tea and soft drinks, but the sharp decline in recent years was due to a severe frost in Brazil which sent wholesale prices to record levels of $3.40 cents per pound in April, 1977.   —Marshall H. Cohen

Corn or **maize,** a cross-fertilizing *cereal grain* that originated in Central and South America. The common hybrid *dent* corns of the United States Corn Belt were developed first by American farmers and then by plant breeders during the nineteenth century. However, they differ in morphology and performance from forms prevalent in other parts of the world. It is of interest to note that corn still furnishes 80 per cent of the calories and 70 per cent of the protein of certain Central American indians.

■**CULTURAL PRACTICES.**—Until recently, corn was planted for the purpose of harvesting the grain primarily for animal feeding. Under these conditions, corn was usually planted in rows spaced 40 inches apart, and 12,-000 to 14,000 plants were planted per acre. With changes in the importance of various forms of livestock raising and crop production in the United States, the extent of the corn-growing area has changed. At the same time, innovations in growing conditions and harvesting methods have been applied. Today it is not uncommon to find corn planted in rows spaced 20 to 30 inches apart and planted in concentrations of 25,000 to 30,000 plants per acre.

■**PHYSICAL CONDITIONS.**—Hybrid corn is now available to fit a range of maturity requirements. The growing season can range from 120 to 170 days. Warm humid weather is desirable, with 30 to 50 inches of rainfall evenly spaced during the growing season. However, although warm weather is desirable, consistent temperatures higher than 90° F can cause more damage than good to growing corn when large amounts of moisture are not available. Though rich loam is the best soil, any well-drained piece of land can be used to produce corn if it is in a good climate and is properly fertilized to provide the needed soil nutrients.

■**VARIETIES.**—Several hundred varieties of yellow *dent* corns are now in use in the U.S. Corn Belt. The majority (80 to 90 per cent) is used for animal feeding, with a small amount (4 to 5 per cent) for starch and alcohol production.

Flint corns are harder and not as desirable for animal feeding. Even so, many varieties are still produced in the United States for special purposes and even more by many countries in South America, Africa, and the Middle East.

Pod corns, which are not cultivated extensively, have grains (kernels) enclosed in individual husks.

Sweet corn has a higher sugar content than other varieties and is more palatable for human consumption. It is produced throughout the U.S. Corn Belt and is marketed fresh, frozen, or canned.

Flour corns, which are soft and starchy, are grown chiefly in South America.

Popcorn is a type of corn with a hard surface and high moisture content in the endosperm. Steam generated in each kernel by quick heating causes it to explode, thus making it pop. It is also produced throughout the Corn Belt for human consumption.

■**DISTRIBUTION.**—Most of the corn grown in the United States results from planting hybrid seed produced and distributed by commercial companies or released by universities. Such seed is made available throughout the corn-growing area of the United States through seedsmen. Corn is now grown in most areas of North America from Georgia to central Canada and from Colorado to the east coast. In addition, it is an important crop in Central and South America, South Africa, Europe, and the Middle East. Except for the United States, most countries of the world import some form of corn to be used as food by their people or livestock.

■**TRADE.**—Corn has taken on a new level of importance in the world market. Though second to wheat for human consumption, it is a cereal feed grain of primary importance. The United States, Argentina, and South Africa are the major exporters of corn. The major importers are countries in western Europe and the Middle East, and Japan.

—Laurence Baker

WORLD PRODUCTION OF CORN 1980		
COUNTRY	METRIC TONS	% OF WORLD
United States	168,855,000	43.0
China	59,705,000	15.2
Brazil	20,377,000	5.2
Rumania	11,180,000	2.9
Mexico	11,081,000	2.8
South Africa	10,230,000	2.6
Soviet Union	9,700,000	2.5

Cotton, a plant of the genus *Gossypium*, its fiber, and the fabric produced from the fiber. The plant belongs to the mallow family, which includes the okra, hisbiscus, and the rose of Sharon. Although cotton is a perennial shrub in climates where it is not killed by frost, its commercial production in nearly all areas necessitates planting a new crop annually for optimum quality and yield.

Boll segments and fiber found in caves of the Tehuacán Valley of southern Mexico indicate cotton was grown at least 7,000 years ago. And in India, seat of the ancient cotton industry, artisans many centuries ago achieved an unsurpassed degree of skill in spinning and weaving the fiber.

The comfort, launderability, and durability of cotton fabrics are due to the absorbency and strength of the fiber. It is formed when a hollow tube emerges from a cell in the seed wall—one tube from each of thousands of cells. Layers of cellulose fibrils build up in an orderly series of spirals within the tube. The fiber matures and, after the cotton boll opens, it dries into a flat, twisted, ribbonlike shape. The fibers interlock to form a fluffy white mass ideal for spinning into yarn.

While it is estimated that cotton has more than 10,000 uses, apparel and household items account for approximately 85 per cent of the total U.S. consumption. Large quantities of cotton are used also for making thread, bags, machinery belts, and medical supplies, and in automobiles.

Seed separated from the lint during the ginning process was once a waste product. Now all components—*linters* (short fibers, clinging to the seed after ginning), *hulls,* and *meats*—are important by-products. Linters are a major source of cellulose for plastics and artificial fibers and are used for cushioning in furniture and mattresses. Oil is crushed from the meats. Refined cottonseed oil products include salad and cooking oils, mayonnaise, salad dressing, margarine, and shortening. Seeds also yield a high-protein flour.

■**GROWING.**—There are many types of cotton, but cultivated varieties fall into two general categories—*upland* and *barbadense.* Upland cottons account for a major share of the world's production. Their fiber is shorter and coarser than that of barbadense cottons, such as Egyptian and Peruvian, and clings tightly to the seed.

Cotton is a commercial crop within limits of approximately 37° north latitude and about 32° south latitude in the New World. In the Old World, these extremes range from 47° north in the Ukraine to 30° south in Africa and Australia. With these wide variations, it is possible to find cotton being planted, cultivated, or harvested somewhere in the world practically every day of the year.

A growing season of at least 180 frost-free days is required for cotton. In the United States, planting dates range from early February in the Rio Grande Valley to late May or early June in North Carolina, Oklahoma, and Missouri, which are the upper limits of the Cotton Belt.

Within a week or two after planting, depending on temperature and moisture conditions, young seedlings emerge from the soil. A month to six weeks later, squares (flower buds) appear. In another three weeks the cotton blossom appears. After three days, the blossom withers and falls, leaving the young ovary attached to the plant. The ovary ripens, enlarges, and forms a pod called a *boll.* Inside the boll, the moist fibers grow and push out from the coating of the newly formed seed. Although the boll enlarges rapidly up to maturity, some time elapses before it opens and the fluffy cotton bursts forth. The interval from bloom to open boll is 45 to 60 days, depending on variety, soil fertility, moisture, and climate.

Cotton production has usually required a very large labor force, particularly during the peak seasons of weeding and harvesting. An exodus of workers from the farms of the U.S. Cotton Belt after World War II speeded mechanization. Man-hours required to produce a bale of cotton (500 pounds of lint) were reduced from 145 in 1947 to fewer than 20 in 1977, while the yield per acre has increased to over 500 pounds, compared with 252 pounds in 1940. Nevertheless, insect pests and diseases still cause great damage to the cotton crop, for, in an average year, 2 out of every 15 bales are lost to their inroads.

■**HARVEST.**—In the 1976–77 crop year, tractor power was used for virtually all of the land preparation, planting, and cultivation of cotton in the United States. Chemicals for weed control were used on more than 80 per cent of the acreage, and 99 per cent of the crop was harvested mechanically.

World cotton production increased from a pre-World War II average of about 32 million bales to about 58 million bales for the 1976–77 growing season. The United States harvests about 11 million bales of cotton annually. The Soviet Union, the second largest producer, harvests a little more than 9 million bales per year. Significant quantities of cotton are also grown in mainland China, India, Mexico, Brazil, Egypt, Pakistan, and Turkey.

Cotton is grown in 19 states and is a major crop in 14 of them. Texas leads in cotton production, averaging about 4 million bales annually. Mississippi and California each produce an average of almost 2 million bales annually. Other major producing states are Alabama, Arizona, Arkansas, Georgia, Louisiana, Missouri, New Mexico, North Carolina, Oklahoma, South Carolina, and Tennessee.

Although textile consumption has been rising throughout the world since World War II, cotton has not shared proportionately; its percentage of the market declined from 72 to 51 between 1946 and 1967. Cotton's share of the U.S. market declined from 51 per cent of the total in 1947 to 30 per cent in 1976. Cotton's inability to compete effectively has been attributed by industry leaders to rising costs and greater research and promotion expenditures by competitors. However, recent fuel shortages favor a growth in the market for cotton whose principal energy source is sunlight. Competing fibers are made from petroleum products.

—Wilmer L. Foreman

Cover Crops, grains grown to cover the soil and protect it against erosion. Their cultivation is an ancient farm practice, mentioned in the literature of pre-Christian Greece and Rome, as well as in ancient China. Buckwheat, oats, and rye were used as cover crops by colonial farmers in America. Such plants as blue lupine are grown only as cover crops because they are poisonous to livestock and, thus, cannot be used either as bedding material or as a forage food.

NATIONAL COTTON COUNCIL

COTTON PRODUCTION in the United States depends on mechanical power. Pickers here dump their loads into trailers for transport to the gin.

Some crops among a score or more now widely used for the purpose are crimson clover, rye, and vetch.

Cover crops are often plowed under or disked into the soil as *green manure*. They add organic matter and often put nitrogen into the soil as well as improve its physical conditions. Millions of acres of cover crops are grown for green manure annually in southeast United States. Cover crops commonly utilized as green manure are alfalfa, soybeans, cowpeas, vetch, red clover, sweet clover, rye, buckwheat, and lespedeza. Colorful and exotic names of other cover crops often give us a clue to their origin, use, or appearance. Some of these are kudzu, sudan grass, Australian winter peas, hairy indigo, beggarweed, and the lupines—blue, yellow, and white.

While the main purpose of a cover crop is to prevent or reduce erosion, it may provide temporary grazing or a supply of grain. Cover crops are not as widely grown in summer as in winter, for land is more often used to grow cash crops. Annual rainfall of 20 inches or more is considered essential to the growth of a cover crop.

Agricultural experiment stations in all sections of the United States have supplied evidence of the effectiveness of cover crops. The U.S. Department of Agriculture offers cost-sharing payments through the Agricultural Conservation Program to encourage farmers to use cover crops. Also, in some surplus-reduction programs, farmers replace grains with such crops. Funds of the Commodity Credit Corporation are used to maintain reserve stocks of cover crop seed and to help the seed industry increase newly developed seed varieties for sale to farmers. —Charles E. Rogers

SCHAFFER AND SEAWELL. BLACK STAR

CAMEMBERT CHEESE is exposed to air during the many-day curing, or ripening, stage.

Dairy Products, any products derived from milk, chiefly cow's milk, but including the milk of goats, sheep, horses, reindeer, camels, and yaks. Organized dairying dates back to the third millenium B.C. in the Mesopotamian city-states, but it was unknown to the American Indian until 1607, when cows arrived with the Jamestown colonists. However, the growth of cities and the Industrial Revolution contributed to making it a full-fledged industry by 1900. In the United States, the leading dairy products—other than fluid milk—by volume of milk used in production are: 1) butter; 2) nonfat dry milk; 3) cheese; 4) ice cream; and 5) evaporated and condensed milk. In the United States during the past decade, per capita consumption of butter, evaporated and condensed milk, fluid milk and cream has decreased, while consumption of ice cream, cheese, and nonfat dry milk has increased. The consumption of cottage cheese has increased impressively because of its inclusion in many special diets. Although the per capita consumption of several products has declined, the total amount of milk used has risen steadily for many years. For the farmers of America, cattle and calves alone have produced more total income than have the various dairy products taken together. Dairy products brought substantially more income than any other major commodity, including bread grains, feed grains, and other livestock products.

Dairy-product processing was among the first of the industries to employ automation. Automation not only allowed economies, but more importantly, it allowed a marked increase in sanitary handling of an

Principal Varieties of Cheese

Name	Place of Origin	Type of Milk
Brick, Muenster	Germany	Cow
Brie	France	Cow
Caciovallo e.g. Provolone	Italy	Cow
Camembert	France	Cow
Cheddar	England	Cow
Cottage	America	Cow
Cream	America	Cow
Edam	Holland, Denmark, France	Cow
Emmentaler, Swiss	Switzerland	Cow
Gouda	Holland	Cow
Hand	Germany, Austria	Cow
Limburger	Germany, Belgium	Cow
Neufchâtel	France	Cow
Parmesan	Italy	Cow
Process	America, Denmark	Cow
Romano	Italy	Sheep
Roquefort, Gorgonzola (blue cheeses)	France, Italy	Sheep
Sapsago	Switzerland	Cow
Trappist	Canada, America	Cow
Whey-albumin cheeses e.g. Primost,	Netherlands,	
Ricotta	Italy	Goat, Cow

Source: Cheese Unlimited, N.Y.C.

easily contaminated food product. Nearly all milk, whatever its ultimate processing destination, is drawn from the cow by machine, pumped into stainless-steel tanks, cooled, and then pumped into bulk tank trucks with no human contact in the process and nearly no exposure to air. Tank trucks deliver the milk to automated processing plants where the milk is pasteurized and either delivered to the consumer as fluid milk or cream or changed into some other of the dairy products. Many creameries (butter factories) use a continuous process of butter manufacture wherein the milk, cream, skim milk, and buttermilk are untouched by humans except for testing and quality control. Many of the continuous processes no longer use churns in the strict sense of that term. Many cheese factories pump milk, curd, and whey from one process to another, and move the solid product about by conveyor belts. To some extent, however, cheese making still requires human handling at various stages of manufacture. In all manufacturing most of the equipment is made of stainless steel, and pasteurization is an important element. Ice cream and evaporated milk manufacture can be and often is fully automated, even to quality control by electronic devices.

In addition to the leading dairy foods, a variety of other products are made from milk. Some of these are: buttermilk, the liquid and solids left over after the butter has formed; casein, most of the solid element in milk, used in industry chiefly for glues and paints; whey, the liquid and solids left over after cheese has formed from curd; lactic acid, produced by the fermentation of milk sugar and used in food and industrial processes; and yogurt, a fermented milk with a consistency much like sour cream. —John T. Schlebecker

Duck, a web-footed swimming bird related to the goose and swan. Ducks are raised primarily for meat production in the United States, although in some European countries they are kept for egg production. The Khaki-Campbell duck reportedly lays as many as 350 to 360 eggs per year. The Pekin is the most popular breed in the United States. Others include the Rouen, Aylesbury, and Muscovy. Twenty-eight days of incubation are required for *ducklings* to hatch, except for Muscovy eggs which require 35 to 37 days. With proper care, ducklings grow very rapidly, reaching about 7 pounds at 8 weeks of age. A mature duck, or female, weighs about 8 pounds; the *drake*, or male, 9 pounds. At maturity and when fully feathered the drake, but not the female, has a few curled feathers at the base of the tail. The duck also has a much louder voice than the drake, except in the Muscovy breed. Ducks are not as susceptible to disease as most other types of poultry. Ducks are difficult to defeather in the home. They may be scalded by immersing them for 3 minutes in water heated to 140° F. The ratio of meat to bone is lower in ducks than in other types of poultry. —Carl W. Hess

Egg Production, the growing of fowl, principally chickens, for the primary purpose of laying eggs. The great majority of hens used are crosses of strains, of breeds, or of inbred lines. Under proper management, a hen can lay 240 or more eggs per year. The hens are usually kept in artificially lighted and ventilated houses on a litter floor or slatted floor or in cages holding from one to ten or more birds.

While many chicken breeds were used 20 to 30 years ago; today, only a few are used for commercial egg production. Leghorn or Leghorn-type chickens lay white-shelled eggs. Heavies, such as Rhode Island Reds and Plymouth Rocks, lay brown-shelled eggs. Although some consumers prefer one or the other color, there is no nutritional or other difference between these eggs. The color of the yolk will also vary, depending on the feed used. For example, although complete, well-balanced commercial feeds are commonly used, large amounts of yellow corn or alfalfa in the diet will result in a deeper yellow.

Eggs are marketed by grade and size. Grade refers to quality (AA, A, B) and size refers to weight per dozen. Eggs weigh approximately 2 ounces each. Top quality eggs have a large amount of thick albumen (white) and high upstanding yolks, while low quality eggs spread when broken. In many modern egg-packing plants, eggs are automatically washed, graded, sized, and packed.

Eggs are also marketed as frozen or solid (dried) whole eggs, albumen, yolks, and various blends. These products are used in large quantities by institutions, bakers, and other food manufacturers.   —Carl W. Hess

Fats and Oils, organic chemical compounds found in plants and animals and, therefore, in foods. As discussed here, fats and oils are *glyceride oils,* in contrast with mineral or petroleum oils. *Fat* is often used to signify a solid or semisolid product, such as that obtained from steam rendering of the fatty tissue of slaughtered animals, mainly cattle and pigs. *Oil* is often used to signify the liquid product obtained from vegetable seeds—such as soybeans, cottonseed, corn, peanut, safflower, linseed, or coconut—by heating and pressing or by extraction with a solvent, which is then evaporated. Purification by treatment with alkalai and bleaching earths and deodorizing under vacuum are usually applied to the crude oil to produce a bland edible oil. Since a semisolid fat will melt when heated, and a liquid oil will solidify when cooled, fats and oils are often considered together as glycerides. This is because they are both made up of chemical combinations known as esters of *glycerine* and *fatty acids,* or as *glycerides* of fatty acids.

Glycerine, or *glycerol,* is a viscous, water-soluble, colorless liquid containing three carbon atoms. Each carbon atom has a hydroxyl group attached to it that can combine with one fatty acid. Glycerine can therefore combine with three fatty acids to

U.S. DEPARTMENT OF AGRICULTURE

EGG PRODUCTION for one carefully bred and housed hen may total 240 a year.

make a *triglyceride ester* which is insoluble in water. The three fatty acids may be the same, but usually are different.

These fatty acids are made up of many carbon atoms joined together in a chain, with an acid group at one end. Each acid group is united with one hydroxyl group of the glycerol to make the ester group, as found in fats and oils.

The unsaturated fatty-acid glycerides of liquid vegetable oils, such as cottonseed or soybean oil, can be changed to saturated glycerides by adding hydrogen to the double bonds —a process known as *hydrogenation.* The resulting glyceride has more saturated glycerides, is semisolid, and is also more stable in resisting oxidation and rancidity. Such plastic shortenings are widely used commercially and domestically in baked and fried foods. Certain chemicals known as *antioxidants* may be added to fats and oils in minute amounts to retard oxidation and rancidity.

The liquid unsaturated vegetable oils are used for making salad dressings and mayonnaise, which are emulsions of the oil and water with vinegar, spices, and flavorings. A semisolid or plastic shortening, however, would not give the desired texture.

Fats and oils have the highest caloric value as a food, 9.0 calories per gram, carbohydrates and proteins each having only 4.0 calories. In addition, fats and oils are highly digestible. The body can synthesize fats from carbohydrates, but the fats that are eaten as such also become a part of the body fat.

Certain polyunsaturated acids are considered essential to proper nutrition, and the body cannot synthesize these essential fatty acids from carbohydrates. Linoleic acid, the most common essential fatty acid, is present in sufficient amounts in ordinary diets.

Water can react with oil to break the ester group to form glycerine and fatty acids. *Soaps* are made by reacting the fatty acids with an alkali, such as sodium or potassium hydroxide, or by having it present during the reaction with water. Certain soaps, when mixed with mineral lubricating oils, form greases.

Fatty acids differ as to the number of carbons joined in the chain (usu-ally 12 to 18) and the way they are joined. Shorter chains make the acids and the oils lower melting. If each carbon in the fatty acid chain is joined to the next one in the chain by a single chemical bond, the fatty acid is said to be *saturated*—this makes the acid and the oils higher melting. If certain adjacent carbons are joined with two chemical bonds (a double bond), the acid is *unsaturated*—this makes the acid and the oil lower melting. For example, linoleic acid, which has two double bonds and 18 carbons, is lower melting than oleic acid, which has one double bond and 18 carbons. Oleic acid, in turn, is lower melting than the saturated stearic acid (18 carbons) or palmitic acid (16 carbons).

The animal fats have more saturated fatty-acid glycerides (mostly 18 and 16 carbons), which makes them semisolid at room temperatures, while the vegetable oils usually have more unsaturated acid glycerides, which makes them liquid.

The unsaturated acid glycerides are much more readily oxidized by the oxygen in air than the saturated glycerides. This is especially true if there are fatty-acid glycerides with two or more double bonds (*polyunsaturated acids*). Oxidation in edible fats and oils causes unpleasant tastes and odors.

Many authorities believe that a diet in which the unsaturated vegetable oils replace the more saturated animal fats is desirable in lowering blood cholesterol and preventing atherosclerosis and coronary thrombosis. Others feel that this effect has not been adequately proven for humans.

Unsaturated oils—particularly linseed, soybean, and tung oil—find extensive use in paints, enamels, and varnishes. These oils all contain glycerides of fatty acids with two or three double bonds. The oils, often combined with a resin, and with pigments ground into them, dry on contact with the oxygen of the air due to oxidation and polymerization of the unsaturated acid groups. The polymerized oil becomes solid and holds the pigments as a strong paint film, which is used to protect and decorate wood and metal surfaces.

—Donald H. Wheeler

Fertilizer, a substance used in the cultivation of plants to enhance their growth. In addition to carbon dioxide and water, which green plants convert to carbohydrates, plants need a number of chemical elements for their growth. The plant obtains these essential elements through its roots from the soil. But a particular soil seldom contains as much of each of these essential elements as the plant requires. Even if a soil is extremely fertile, continuous harvesting of crops removes essential elements that have been taken up by the plants. Placing additional amounts of the essential elements in the soil in the form of fertilizer will thus improve the fertility of soil, or maintain it in fertile crop lands.

Organic fertilizers, such as animal manures, dead fish, and guano, have been used as fertilizers since ancient times. These materials are still used, but today most commercial fertilizers are synthetic products.

Nitrogen, phosphorus, and potassium are the three most important plant food elements. The percentage of each is usually specified for each lot of fertilizer sold. For example, a 4-10-6 grade fertilizer contains 4 per cent nitrogen, 10 per cent phosphorus pentoxide equivalent, and 6 per cent potash (potassium oxide equivalent). The designation of phosphorus and potassium by their oxide equivalents is a long established practice.

Three other elements are sometimes called secondary plant nutrients: calcium, magnesium, and sulfur. Boron, copper, iron manganese, molybdenum, zinc, and several other elements needed by plants in very small quantities are frequently added to fertilizers as trace elements.

Nitrogen is essential to plants, since it is a component of many chemical compounds made by the plant, including amino acids, the materials of which proteins are composed. Uncombined, or free, nitrogen makes up about 78 per cent of the volume of air, but in its free state nitrogen cannot be used by plants. It must first be combined with other elements to form compounds which can be used. Certain bacteria living in the soil are able to take nitrogen from the air and "fix" it into compounds available to higher plants.

Nearly all industrial processes for fixing nitrogen from the air involve making ammonia. This is done by combining nitrogen with another gas, hydrogen, at pressures as high as 1,000 atmospheres, in the presence of a catalyst. The ammonia formed is a gas at room temperature, but it can be compressed to form a liquid that can be stored if kept refrigerated or under pressure. With proper equipment, ammonia can be used directly as a fertilizer by injection into the soil. Much ammonia is converted into solution materials to make solid fertilizers, such as *ammonium nitrate, ammonium sulfate, ammonium phosphate,* or *urea.*

Phosphorus is a component of some of the key chemical compounds in all living cells. The chief source of phosphorus for fertilizers is phosphate rock, mined in Florida, Tennessee,

WORLD PRODUCTION OF NITROGENOUS FERTILIZERS 1979–80		
COUNTRY	METRIC TONS	% OF WORLD
United States	11,180,000	18.7
China	9,095,000	15.2
Soviet Union	9,074,000	15.2
India	2,224,300	3.7
France	1,780,000	3.0
Rumania	1,738,000	2.9

PHOSPHATE FERTILIZERS 1979–80		
COUNTRY	METRIC TONS	% OF WORLD
United States	9,083,000	27.2
Soviet Union	5,930,000	17.7
China	1,869,900	5.6
France	1,364,000	4.1
Brazil	1,306,000	3.9
Poland	931,000	2.8
Australia	919,000	2.7

ALLIED CHEMICAL CORPORATION

NITROGEN compounds raise corn yield. Unfertilized plot (*left*) **produced a** small crop.

Idaho, Montana, Wyoming, and North Carolina. Outside the United States, the most important phosphate mining operations are in North Africa, West Africa, the Soviet Union, and various islands in the Pacific and Caribbean. Phosphorus in phosphate rock is in the form of *tricalcium phosphate,* which is often combined with calcium fluoride. Ground phosphate rock can be used as a fertilizer, but tricalcium phosphate is almost completely insoluble in water, so that phosphorus is not readily available to plants.

Treating ground phosphate rock with sulfuric acid to form a slurry, allowing it to harden, and then storing the mixture for a few weeks yields a solid product called *normal superphosphate.* In this mixture, the tricalcium phosphate has been converted into more soluble forms of phosphate that are readily available to the plant. *Triple superphospate* is a more concentrated phosphatic fertilizer, as is *diammonium phosphate.*

Potassium, essential to a number of chemical activities in the growing plant, is obtained from potassium compounds (collectively known as potash) mined in New Mexico, Canada, Germany, France, and elsewhere. It is also obtained from brines in California and Utah. *Potassium chloride,* often called *muriate of potash,* is the most common potassium material in fertilizers.

Today the world could not feed itself without chemical fertilizers. The use of these is growing rapidly worldwide, but chemical fertilizers will become more expensive as their nonrenewable raw materials, natural gas and petroleum (used for the production of ammonia), phosphate rock, and potash are gradually used up. Eventually a system of recycling wastes to put usable nutrients back into the soil will have to be adopted.

Recycling has always been done to some extent by plowing under the unused parts of plants and by the use of manures. Increasing use of sewage sludge as a fertilizer is a more recent development. But with existing technology only a portion of the world's fertilizer requirements can be met

this way. Much of the nutrients applied to soil is lost or washed away to cause stream pollution. Research directed at cutting these losses has produced some breakthroughs, as has the work on duplicating the natural process by which certain bacteria convert nitrogen from the air into usable nutrients without the need for expensive processing plants.

—Albert S. Hester

Fiber Crops, providers of the basic materials for the manufacture of clothing, household goods such as sheets and towels, and commercial products such as bags, rope, and twine. Cotton is the leading fiber crop grown in the United States. Other fibers that are significant in world trade are flax, hemp, henequen, and sisal.

About 30 per cent of the world's cotton is grown in the United States. It ranks second among all U.S. cash crops. The fiber is used to make thread and cloth, and the kernel of the seed is crushed for oil, which is used for salad dressing, in cooking, and in making margarine, soap, paints, and lubricants. Cottonseed cake is a cattle feed, and cottonseed hull is utilized for roughage, fertilizer, and making fiberboard. Flax and hemp are also grown in the United States. The leading product of flax is linen thread. Linseed oil is made from the crushed seed of flax, and its straw is employed in papermaking. Hemp, a coarse, strong, and durable fiber, was used in pioneering times to make "homespun" cloth; today it is commonly used to make twine, rope, bagging, rugs, and sailcloth.

—Charles E. Rogers

Fish and Seafood, edible and industrially useful marine life. From a commercial standpoint, fish can be grouped into food fish, including shellfish, and industrial fish. Food fish provides about 10 per cent of the world's animal protein used directly for human consumption. Industrial fish are utilized in the manufacture of fish meal, fish oils, pet food, and fertilizers.

Tuna, salmon, and sardines are

among the important food fish consumed in canned form throughout the world. In the more developed countries, such food fish as ocean perch, haddock, flounder, redfish, herring, and cod are marketed either in fresh or frozen form as fillets, steaks, or dressed whole fish. In countries where refrigeration and other modern preservation methods are not as widely used, food fish in smoked, dried, or pickled, and cured forms are more prevalent.

Shrimp, lobsters, crabs, oysters, and clams are the principal shellfish species. These are distributed mainly in fresh or frozen form.

Industrial, or trash, fish include such species as menhaden, alewives, and anchovies. These, along with minor nonedible species of trash fish and the trimmings and waste from the preparation of food fish, provide the raw product for this growing segment of the fishing industry.

Today, U.S. commercial fishermen average an estimated 4.5 billion pounds of all species. Of this amount, 35 per cent was landed on the northeastern and mid-Atlantic coasts, primarily in New England, 26 per cent in Alaska, Hawaii, and the Pacific coast states, and 36 per cent in the South Atlantic and Gulf states, with the remainder coming from inland lakes and rivers.

The world catch had been doubling every ten years for several decades prior to 1970. Since then, however, the catch has leveled off at about 150 billion pounds per year, and conservationists predict that a continued, often unrestricted, heavy take will seriously deplete the annual yield.

In the United States, direct use of seafood for human consumption is considerably less important than the use of meats and dairy products. The annual per capita consumption is only about 10 to 11 pounds, compared with over 150 pounds of meat products. Nevertheless, the seafood industry is an important segment of the total food industry, both because of the present volume and because of its potential for satisfying future needs.

Because the production of food fish in the United States has remained relatively stable over the last 10 years, an increasing part of the U.S. supply of edible fish products is being supplied by imports. The population growth and purchasing power of the United States has provided a lucrative market for high-priced species sold by so many other fishing countries. Imports now amount to about 40 per cent of domestic consumption.

Commercial fishermen in the United States employ a variety of gear, methods, and seagoing vessels to catch fish and other marine species. Fish which tend to live in surface waters, such as salmon, tuna, and mackerel, are caught by means of nets, or hooks and lines. Bottom-dwelling species are caught with a variety of gear including nets, dredges, lines, and traps. The ships and boats used in the commercial fisheries also vary in design, tonnage, and size of crew.

The major problems in handling fishery products prior to consumption are to minimize undesirable changes

in quality and to prevent spoilage. Ideally, therefore, the catch should be held for the shortest possible period prior to processing. Some fisheries, including some of the Soviet and the Japanese fleets, solve this problem by processing the fish on factory ships equipped for the heat-processing or freezing of seafood. Freezing at sea is used in the United States only to a very limited extent in some Alaskan fisheries.

The usual method of preservation is by icing, that is, surrounding the fish with sufficient ice to keep them at low temperatures for the period needed to bring the catch in. Some marine products, especially crabs and lobsters, must be delivered alive to shore plants. For this purpose, fishing vessels are equipped with holds flooded with circulating fresh sea water in which the lobsters or crabs may be kept alive for several days.

■PROCESSING OF SEAFOODS.—Seafoods used for human consumption are sold in one of the following forms: fresh-refrigerated, frozen, precooked frozen, canned, cured or dehydrated. Fresh products are usually sold by the pound, without prepackaging, in locations close to the port of entry. Lobsters must be sold alive, and are therefore shipped in refrigerated containers filled with seaweed, and kept at a low temperature. Transportation by air has made it possible to market lobsters at great distances from where they are caught.

Much seafood is marketed as frozen products. These may be frozen fresh, as fillets, steaks, and individually quick-frozen shellfish, or precooked prior to freezing as fish sticks, various fish dishes, and precooked frozen shrimp.

Canning is the method of preservation applied to most of the fishery

TUNA RESEARCH FOUNDATION

TUNA, hauled by net onto fishing boats, is an important commercial fish. Most processed tuna goes to consumers in cans.

products processed in the United States. Products which are preserved in this manner include tuna meat, salmon, sardines, oysters, crab, and chowders based on fishery products.

Curing of fish by addition of salt and smoking is an old method of preservation, but is used in the United States only for a few specialty products. Dehydration by conventional drying methods is also used to a very limited extent, but recently there has been developed a considerable interest in freeze-dehydration, which is capable of producing high-quality dehydrated products. Shrimp, various precooked seafoods, and fish sticks and fillets are preserved by this method. Another new development is the use of atomic radiation to pasteurize fish products. Foods pasteurized in this manner may be kept at refrigerated temperatures for weeks. Unpasteurized fish products are stable only a few days.   —Marcus Karel

Flax. See MACHINES AND PROCESSES: *Rope,* in the INDUSTRY AND TECHNOLOGY volume.

Food Additives, chemicals that do not occur naturally in foods but are introduced in the course of food production, processing, or packaging. *Intentional additives* are chemicals added in controlled amounts with the purpose of achieving some desirable results. *Nonintentional additives* are contaminants introduced into foods as a result of manufacturing operations.

■INTENTIONAL ADDITIVES.—These are introduced in order to improve the safety, palatability, or nutritional value of foods. Additives inhibiting microbial spoilage are called *chemical preservatives.* Salt, organic acids, and certain other chemicals are used for this purpose.

Chemical reactions producing undesirable changes in foods are often controlled by addition of chemicals. Reactions with atmospheric oxygen are controlled by addition of *antioxidants,* notably ascorbic acid (vitamin C), tocopherol (vitamin E), certain phenolic compounds, and other reducing chemicals. Darkening of fruits and vegetables may be controlled by sulfites, and by ascorbic acid. Reactions involving metals present in foods may be minimized by the use of chemicals that tie up the metals in a nonreactive form. Chemicals effective for this purpose, called *chelating agents,* include salts of citric and phosphoric acids. Undesirable textural changes in certain types of foods may be prevented by addition of colloidal materials, such as carboxymethyl cellulose, which are known as *stabilizers.*

Additives may be used not only to prevent changes, but also to improve the initial quality of foods. Texture of meats, for instance, may be improved by adding plant enzymes such as papain (derived from the papaya plant), or bromellin (derived from pineapple). These enzymes tenderize meat, that is, they partially hydrolyze or digest it.

Taste and flavor may be adjusted to suit consumer preferences by means of synthetic sweetening agents, synthetic or natural flavor mixtures, and by flavor enhancers or potentiators. The last-mentioned category of additives has no characteristic flavor of its own, but is capable of enhancing natural flavors.

Color of foods may be improved by agents that stabilize or desirably alter natural pigments as the addition of sodium nitrite to meats or by addition of synthetic dyes.

Additives are often used to supplement the nutritional value of foods deficient in some vitamins, minerals, or other nutrients. For instance, bread, cereals, milk, and some baby foods are enriched with selected vitamins and minerals. Table salt is enriched by addition of iodides, which not only improve its handling characteristics but are also an important source of iodine, an element needed in the synthesis of the hormone thyroxin (produced by the thyroid gland).

■NONINTENTIONAL ADDITIVES.—These may arise from agricultural practices—residues from pesticides, antibiotics for treating cattle, and similar agents; from manufacturing practices—as, metallic substances acquired from equipment used in processing foods; or packaging procedures—as, plasticizers or adhesives absorbed by foods from packaging materials. These additives serve no useful function, and their occurrence must be prevented or substantially inhibited to avoid possible health hazards.

—Marcus Karel

Food Engineering, the branch of engineering that deals with the development and operation of industrial processes aimed at the production of predictable and controlled changes in the chemical composition, physical characteristics, and biological properties of foods. These industrial processes and the associated controlled transformation of raw materials form the basis of food manufacturing and food preservation.

In designing and analyzing food processes, food engineering makes use of the concept of *unit operations.* A unit operation is an operation that may occur in any of a number of processes, often using different kinds of equipment, but that has a single physical basis and a single set of scientific principles, which apply independently of the process in which the operation is applied.

The purpose of engineering analysis of food processes is the quantitative determination of data needed for equipment design, for control of process variables, and for accurate prediction of process costs. The data obtained by the engineer may be the time needed to achieve a given effect under a given set of conditions, the size of equipment needed, or the specification of conditions such as temperature and pressure for a given process.

The complexity of the composition and structure of foods, and the stringent requirements with respect to wholesomeness and appeal of processed foods, present the food engineer with problems that call for extensive knowledge of scientific principles and the properties of foods. Food engineering must be concerned at all times not only with the efficiency of operations, but also with the effects of these operations on the foods and on the people who consume these foods. For this reason, graduate food engineers are not only trained in mathematical, physical, and chemical subjects, but are also prepared to consider the biological and biochemical problems that may arise in food processing. —Marcus Karel

Food Manufacturing, the process of preparing farm produce for the consumer. This includes the slaughter of meat, fowl, and seafood, and the packaging of eatable foodstuffs.

■MEAT-PACKING.—The conversion of livestock to meat, as well as to edible and nonedible by-products.

Most of the livestock used in the industry is produced west of the Mississippi River, and the major industry centers are located in Midwestern cities. The industry originated, however, on the East coast. At that time, the locally raised animals were slaughtered in nearby market cities, and surplus meat was salted and packed in barrels for export to the West Indies. This practice gave the industry its name, even though this method of "packing" is no longer practiced to any significant extent. During the nineteenth century, livestock raising moved progressively westward, and so did the industry. By mid-century the major meat-packing center was Cincinnati, Ohio. In the second half of the nineteenth century, with the rapid development of railroads, meat-packing plants were relocated at rail centers. The preeminence of Chicago as the meat-packing capital dates from that period. Chicago, Kansas City, Kans., Kansas City, Mo., and Omaha, Neb., are among the most important industry centers today.

Operations of the meat-packing industry include buying the livestock, slaughtering the animals, converting the carcasses to meat cuts and by-products, and selling these products. The animals are shipped to stockyards by railroad or truck and are held in pens. Prior to slaughter they are stunned. After slaughter the animal is eviscerated, and the carcass divided into two *sides,* which are then moved into a refrigerated room to allow rapid chilling. The viscera and other organs from each animal are collected in a separate container for inspection by a qualified representative of the Meat Inspection Division of the Bureau of Animal Industry of the United States Department of Agriculture. All meat that is moved in interstate commerce must be inspected, and the government inspection stamp guarantees that the animal was free from disease, was slaughtered under sanitary conditions, and that the carcass was wholesome at the time it left the packing plant. In addition, trained government graders may stamp carcasses with one of the official grades, which are based on the eating quality of the meat. The government grading is done only at the packer's request.

After chilling, the sides are divided into wholesale cuts. These are various portions of the carcass from which the retail cuts are prepared. The wholesale cuts for beef include round, sirloin, short loin, flank, rib, plate, chuck, brisket, and foreshank. For pork, they include hind foot, ham, side pork, loin, spareribs, shoulder, and jowl. The wholesale cuts are then shipped, leaving the final preparation of retail portions to the stores. Sometimes the sides are shipped, and all the cutting is done at the retail level. Most fresh meat is shipped at refrigerated temperatures; freezing is also used to some extent. Refrigeration at temperatures slightly above freezing is used also for preservation of meat products such as fresh ground meats, sausages, and a variety of cured products.

Other methods of preservation include heat processing, used for a variety of canned meats; freezing, used for many types of sausages and for certain precooked meat products; chemical preservation by salt, which is usually used in combination with refrigeration; and, more recently, irradiation and freeze dehydration.

A large variety of products forms the category of cured meats, that is, meats to which certain materials known as curing agents are added, frequently over a period of time, to alter the meat products with respect to their keeping qualities, flavor, and appearance. Originally the main purpose of curing was to allow meat to be stored at room temperature. With the advent of refrigeration, this purpose became secondary to the production of characteristic flavor and color. Curing processes vary greatly from product to product, and the curing agents vary according to the different processes. In most of the processes, however, the major components of curing mixtures are salt, nitrite, sugar, and flavoring agents. Some cured products are smoked to impart a characteristic and desirable flavor. Recently it has become possible to produce in meats a smokelike flavor without subjecting the products to actual smokehouse conditions.

In addition to the production of meats and meat products, the meat-packing industry is engaged in the production of a large variety of by-products. These include industrial raw materials, such as hides; chemicals derived from various nonedible portions of the animals, such as gelatin; and pharmaceuticals derived from the glandular organs of the slaughtered animals, such as dried thyroid glands of sheep which are used in treatment of goiter and other thyroid disorders in humans. Another important by-product of meat processing is animal fat, which is used for production of edible fats, such as lard, as well as for industrial greases.

■POULTRY PRODUCTS.—Among meat products, poultry ranks third in quantity, surpassed by beef and pork products.

Poultry production centers are located in every major region of the United States. Modern poultry farming is based on scientific principles, utilizing technological advances in housing, disease control, sanitation, and feeding. The feeding practices are based on knowledge of nutritional requirements of birds, and the feed formulas include nutritional supplements, such as high-protein meals and vitamins.

Poultry is classified in accordance with the weight and age of the bird at the time of slaughter. Thus chickens may be classified as broilers or fryers, roasters, fowl, and cocks or old roosters. Turkeys are classified as fryer-roasters, young hens and toms, yearlings, and mature turkeys. The quality of individual birds is expressed by standards, ranging from A to C quality, established by the U. S. Department of Agriculture.

At a modern processing plant, the birds are put through a series of operations conducted in production-line fashion, with the birds carried on overhead conveyors. The major steps in processing include weighing, slaughter and bleeding, scalding (dipping in hot water to facilitate defeathering), defeathering, usually by automatic equipment, eviscerating, chilling, and grading. Additional steps depend on the manner in which the products are to be sold—fresh, frozen, cooked, canned, or dehydrated.

A large proportion of poultry is shipped fresh to retail channels. Fresh poultry is stored and distributed under refrigeration, packaged in boxes or in plastic bags. The storage life of refrigerated fresh poultry is limited, but recent research on the application of ionizing radiations and on the use of antibiotic dips indicates that the shelf life may be considerably extended.

Poultry to be stored for longer periods of time than are permitted by refrigeration is usually frozen. Birds to be frozen are usually placed in tightly fitting plastic bags, for proper packaging is necessary to maintain high quality in frozen storage. Freezing is usually done in air or by immersion in liquids.

In addition to uncooked poultry, processed as described above, large quantities are sold cooked. Cooked poultry products include a variety of canned items, such as chicken in broth, various stews and soups, and many others. A smaller quantity of cooked poultry items is available frozen; recently, interest has developed in the production of precooked freeze-dehydrated poultry dishes.

■FRUIT AND VEGETABLE PRODUCTS.—Most of the fruits and vegetables grown in the United States are harvested within a relatively short season. In order to assure a year-round supply, therefore, a large proportion of these crops is processed before delivery to consumers. Canning, freezing, pickling, and dehydration are the common methods of processing.

Modern production methods are aimed at maximizing the output per man-hour, which requires the introduction of mechanical devices for harvesting, and the mechanization of much of the processing operation. The mechanization of the agricultural practices, in turn, requires the use of herbicides, insecticides, fertilizers, and growth promoters. The efficiency of agricultural operations depends also, to a large extent, on selective breeding of suitable varieties of commercial crops. In recent years, the selection of varieties has been based not only on high yields and resistance to environmental hardships but also on suitability for mechanical harvesting and for processing. Suitability for mechanical harvesting requires a degree of sturdiness and, most important, uniform maturation times. Scheduling of the planting and harvesting operations is often based on the *heat unit system* in which each day of plant growth is credited with a certain number of units depending on the mean temperature of the day.

Generally, vegetables grown for processing are processed soon after harvest, thus minimizing post-harvest deterioration. Whenever delays occur, steps are taken to minimize deterioration, principally by rapid cooling of the crop and storage at low temperature. Some fruits, such as strawberries, are very susceptible to deterioration after harvest and must be cooled and processed rapidly. Other fruits, such as apples, pears, and oranges, may be stored for long periods of time without processing. In order to maximize their storage life, however, they are stored under strictly controlled conditions of temperature, relative humidity, and gas composition in the storage chambers. The preparation for processing of vegetables includes the following operations, most of which are also used in processing of fruits:

Cleaning: This involves washing with water containing disinfectants, brushing, and rinsing with water of potable quality.

Conveying: In most operations, conveying is mechanized. Depending on the nature of the material, this may include belt conveyors, vibrating conveyors, and many other devices.

Grading: Grading for size, appearance, and lack of defects requires some degree of manual labor. Many mechanical sorting devices for size grading, however, are used, and equipment has recently been developed for automatic color sorting and grading.

Peeling and Shelling: Many different methods may be used for this purpose. The simplest is manual peeling. Mechanical devices operate on the abrasion principle, chemical peeling methods (lye peeling), and loosening of the peels by steam with subsequent removal of the peel. Certain vegetables are flame-peeled. In this process, the product is exposed briefly to high-temperature combustion gases, which puffs and loosens the skins so they can then be removed by high-pressure water sprays.

Size Reduction: The fruits and vegetables are reduced to the desired form (slices, halves, purée) by various manual or mechanized methods.

In juice preparation, a number of different processes are available for pressing the raw material to release the juice, and for removing the undesirable components extracted with the juice. In some cases, the juices may be concentrated by the removal of a portion of the water. Vacuum evaporators of high heat-transfer efficiency are usually used, but some newer processes are based on removal of water as ice crystals in a process known as freeze concentration. The most modern process, not as yet completely developed, involves removal of water by diffusion through a membrane permeable to it but not to the dissolved sugars, flavor compounds, and other juice components.

The final processing and packaging of the fruit and vegetable products varies with the method of preservation. Products preserved by heat processing are usually packaged in cans.

Internal linings of the cans are chosen to assure best taste and appearance of the products and to prevent or minimize corrosion. Some fruit products may be packaged in aluminum cans or in plastic packages. Usually, the heat processing is conducted on the packaged product but, in the case of fluid products, it is often possible to heat the product in heat exchangers, and then to fill presterilized containers while the liquid is hot. This last method is known as *aseptic canning*. The amount of heat required to assure stability and safety varies with the product. Nonacid products, such as peas and many other vegetables, require the most heat since they are capable of allowing the growth of potentially deadly microorganisms, such as *Clostridium botulinum*, the causative agent of botulism—a form of food intoxication with high mortality rates. Most fruits, and some vegetables with high acidity, require only heating to temperatures close to boiling.

Other methods of preservation include freezing, dehydration, and fermentation. Fermentation is one of the oldest methods of preservation, and is still important in the preservation of cucumbers (pickles), tomatoes, peppers, and cabbage (sauerkraut). The fermented products are usually pasteurized in glass jars or cans.

Distribution of fresh fruits and vegetables without processing requires a degree of control of temperature and suitable packaging. Packages for fresh fruits and vegetables must allow gas exchange, since the plant materials are still "alive"—that is, they possess an active enzyme system that produces a high rate of respiration. When the normal respiration is inhibited by interference with gas exchange, the plants are subject to rapid spoilage. In the case of very actively respiring plants, the packages are perforated with holes to allow adequate gas exchange. —Marcus Karel

Food Preservation, the application of a process or processes that permit a normally perishable food to be stored for long periods without spoilage. Food spoilage means the loss of edibility due to formation of offensive changes in taste, flavor, texture, or appearance; loss of wholesomeness due to formation of toxins, extensive loss of nutritive value, or development of high concentrations of microorganisms. Spoilage may occur through chemical and physical processes, or through the growth and activity of microorganisms, such as bacteria, molds, and yeasts. Microbial spoilage is of greatest concern because it usually is rapid, and is most likely to result in conditions adversely affecting the health of consumers. Food preservation, therefore, is aimed primarily at the inhibition of microbial spoilage. Additional measures, such as exclusion of air and addition of chemical agents, may inhibit chemical deterioration.

Microbial spoilage may be prevented by *sterilization* of foods, that is, complete destruction of microorganisms present in foods, or by *inhibition* of growth of microorganisms by producing conditions unfavorable to their growth. Food may be sterilized by heating (thermal sterilization), by exposure to radiation (radiation sterilization), or by treatment with chemical agents (chemical sterilization).

Thermal sterilization is usually performed by exposing foods, packaged in hermetically sealed metallic containers, to temperatures of 240 to 250° F in pressurized vessels (canning) or by heating foods prior to packaging, and then packaging them under conditions preventing recontamination with microorganisms (aseptic canning). Newer methods of canning are aimed at improving the quality of foods, often by heating at very high temperatures for short periods of time.

Radiation sterilization is achieved by exposing packaged foods to radiations such as gamma rays from radioactive isotopes, X-rays, or high-energy electrons produced by electron accelerators. The type and amount of radiation used for food preservation are controlled to achieve sterilization without the production of any radioactivity in the food, and without impairing the safety of food. Radiation preservation, an outgrowth of postwar research interest in atomic energy, has recently received full recognition as a safe method of food preservation by the U. S. Food and Drug Administration.

Chemical sterilization is only rarely applied to food products. It is usually reserved for such items as clothing.

Food preservation without sterilization may be achieved by producing conditions unfavorable to microbial growth. Processes based on this principle include freezing, refrigeration, dehydration, chemical preservation, and fermentation.

Refrigeration, or storage of foods at temperatures slightly above freezing, is effective in slowing down microbial growth, but does not prevent such growth entirely. It is used, therefore, in combination with chemical preservation, or partial destruction of microbes (pasteurization) for products expected to have only a short storage life. Freezing prevents bacterial growth by crystallization of water and by low temperatures of storage. Although freezing can preserve foods with little impairment of their quality, it requires facilities for low temperature distribution and storage.

Dehydration reduces the water content of foods to low levels at which microbial activity ceases and chemical processes are greatly slowed down. It may be performed by a number of processes, ranging from the ancient technique of sun-drying to the most modern freezing dehydration.

Chemical preservation is based on addition to the food, or production in the food, of chemical agents that prevent microbial growth. The most commonly used agents include salt, acetic acid (vinegar), lactic acid, and other organic acids, and in some types of foods, high concentrations of sugar.

Fermentation, which in principle is identical to chemical preservation, is based on production of organic acid (usually lactic acid) by bacteria or molds either naturally present in the food, or introduced to it as a fermentation starter. Production of cheese, various sour milk products, pickles, and numerous other food products is based on fermentation, which is also vitally important in production of antibiotics.

■**FROZEN FOODS.**—The crystallization of water and the low temperatures of storage produce conditions that prevent spoilage of the food by microorganisms. These conditions are also effective in greatly slowing down most of the chemical reactions and physical changes that adversely affect the eating quality and nutritional value of stored foods. Best results are obtained when high-quality foods are selected for freezing, the food is frozen rapidly, and packaged in containers that prevent loss of water and of volatile flavors, and when the food is kept at temperatures below 0° F throughout its distribution and storage cycle. The food-spoiling microbes are not destroyed by freezing. It is essential, therefore, that after thawing, such foods be stored for only brief periods, preferably at refrigerator temperatures.

Freezing of foods by exposure to natural low temperatures is an old art, but modern food preservation by freezing began in the 1920's with the development of equipment for rapid freezing. At the present time, foods are frozen by one of the following methods:

Blast freezing in tunnels in which the food is exposed to air at temperatures below −20° F and air velocities of several thousand feet per minute; *plate freezing*, in which the food is cooled by contact with plates maintained at low temperatures; *immersion freezing*, in which foods are immersed in liquids such as brine or water-glycol mixtures maintained at temperatures of −20° to −40° F. Superior quality is claimed for foods frozen at these low temperatures.

Chief among foods preserved by freezing are concentrated orange juice, fruits and berries, vegetables, poultry, seafood, and a variety of precooked dinners. The growth in volume has been most spectacular for frozen juices, which increased in consumption from approximately two million pounds in 1946 to close to a billion pounds in 1960, and for precooked frozen dinners, which account for a billion pounds annually. This revolution in home food management involved the inclusion of a freezer, some very large, in almost every household today.

—Marcus Karel

Fruit, any one of a large number of cultivated edible flower parts. Botanically, a fruit is usually considered the ripened ovary (or ovaries) of a flower (or flowers), with or without closely related parts. Some botanists prefer to designate it as basically the enlarged pistil of a flower. These definitions, however, include some plants that are classified as vegetables in economic terms (as, tomatoes and melons). We shall consider fruit to include perennial tree fruits and nuts, berries, and grapes. The main types of tree fruits are *citrus* (as, oranges), *pome* (as, apples), and *stone* (as, peaches).

The fruit industry in the United States is perhaps the most highly developed in the world. No other country produces such a quantity and variety of fruit so efficiently, and few, if any, have such an efficient fruit marketing system.

Fruit production is now a highly specialized agricultural industry in the United States. While nearly every farm produced some fruit in 1900, today commercial production is concentrated on specialized farms in fruit districts. These districts are usually endowed with a favorable climate, deep and fertile soils, and adequate rainfall or easy access to water. Mechanization is increasing; labor shortages and legislation have led to the upsurge in mechanical harvesting.

In recent years, the value of this crop at farm level has been between

FLORIDA CITRUS COMMISSION

ORANGE PRODUCTION, a major part of the large, highly-developed U.S. fruit industry.

$2.5 billion and $2.9 billion. The retail value (including marketing charges and processing) is several times this figure. The leading fruit-producing states in terms of farm value are California (with about 40 per cent of the total), Florida (about 20 per cent), Washington, New York, and Michigan. Other important states include Hawaii, Oregon, Pennsylvania, New Jersey, and Virginia. The five most important U.S. fruits, in decreasing order of farm value, are oranges, grapes, apples, peaches, and strawberries. Walnuts and pecans are the most valuable nut crops. Other leading fruits include grapefruits, pears, prunes, lemons, and cherries.

The 25 million tons of fruit produced in the U.S. are utilized either fresh or processed. About 65 per cent of the crop is processed, enabling us to have fruit throughout the year. The major form of processing is canning, but freezing and drying are also important, particularly for certain crops, notably, frozen concentrated orange juice. A number of new processing techniques, such as freeze-drying, dehydro-freezing, and radiation treatments may become more significant in the future. Controlled atmosphere (called CA storage) for apples has made it possible to have high-quality, fresh apples all year.

Total fruit consumption has averaged nearly 220 pounds per capita annually, excluding nuts. Spoilage and deterioration in the quality of fruit have been reduced by improved handling techniques and by the increased use of the various forms of processing. Indeed, processed fruit is gaining ever greater acceptance in the marketplace, since such fruit as well as fresh fruit are important sources of minerals and vitamins.

—Dana G. Dalrymple;
Robert A. Wearne

Fungicide. *See* PESTICIDES in this section.

Fur Farming, the raising of fur-bearing animals in captivity under conditions of controlled breeding, feeding, and care. Fur farming, sometimes called *fur ranching,* started in Canada at the end of the nineteenth century. Today most of the pelts from North America come from fur farms.

Fur farming is possible only with animals that breed well in captivity and present minimum problems in care and feeding. Beaver and muskrat, for example, require too much water to be profitably raised in captivity. Silver foxes and mink were the first animals to be raised on farms. Other fur farm animals are the fisher, marten, sable, nutria, skunk, raccoon, and chinchilla. The best chinchilla fur comes from wild Andean animals, but generally the fur of ranch or farm animals is superior to that of wild animals. Rabbits (conies) have long been raised for food, and more recently for fur.

Animals in captivity can be selectively bred to develop special colors of furs, such as the various mink mutations of pinks and even lavenders. In addition, furs from animals kept in captivity are more uniform in size and quality and can be used more easily in the garment industry.

Generally, the animals are kept in cages with wire mesh bottoms for ease of cleaning. The animals are usually separated to keep them from injuring one another. Some animals, notably mink, will kill their young if excited, so great care must be taken not to alarm them. All animals, if excited, are likely to damage their fur.

In captivity the animals are fed raw meat, poultry, and fish, with added supplements of cereals, citrus fruits, vitamins, and minerals. Fish of the carp family contain thiamine-destroying elements. Therefore, carp should be fed sparingly, if at all, for supplements cannot make up the thiamine deficiency, which results in *Chastek's paralysis.* Diseases such as distemper, abortion (*salmonellosis*), pneumonia, tularemia, and streptococcic septicemia either respond to antibiotics or can be prevented by vaccination. Some diseases, such as tularemia in mink, are difficult to treat because antibiotics can kill the animals. Anthrax is too dangerous to cure or treat and is too rare to require vaccination; it should be controlled by using great care in feeding and tending the animals. Avian tuberculosis has become increasingly damaging among rodents, but it can be controlled by making sure that the animals are fed uninfected pork or poultry. Most fur-bearing animals mate in the winter, although some, such as the muskrat and rabbit, produce several large litters a year.

When their fur is of best quality and size, the animals are killed painlessly by injection or electricity. The pelts are then removed, stretched, scraped, dried, and stored until sold.

—John T. Schlebecker

NATIONAL FUR NEWS

MINK farming began in the nineteenth century. Today, a good brown pelt may bring $75; a pastel mutation as much as $125.

Gelatin, a purified form of glue, produced principally by the acid treatment of pork skin and the lime or alkaline treatment of calf hides and demineralized cattle bones. It is an easily digestible but nutritionally incomplete protein that is not coagulated by heat. In water, it forms gels that are easily dispersed by the addition of heat.

The properties of gelatin in water render it useful in gelation, emulsion stabilization, water-binding, foaming, solution clarification, and inhibition of crystal formation. These functions are utilized in various applications. In foods, gelatin is used in the preparation of desserts, confections, ice cream, whips, and jellied meats. Pharmaceutically, it is used in the formulation of emulsions, capsules, lozenges, suppositories, and cosmetic preparations, and as a treatment for nail defects.

Gelatin has a number of applications in the photographic, printing, electroplating, and tanning industries. It is also used to size (stiffen) paper and textiles, to fine (clarify) beverages, and to provide culture media for microorganisms.

—Isaac J. Wahba

Gibberellic Acid, one of an expanding group of natural plant growth-regulating substances known as gibberellins. The nine closely related compounds that originally constituted this group are designated A_1 through A_9, the most widely known being A_3, or gibberellic acid. Gibberellins, produced by the fungus *Gibberella fujikuroi,* are obtained commercially by growing the fungus in a liquid culture medium and then extracting the gibberellins in a manner similar to that used in the production of antibiotics. In its natural habitat, the fungus attacks rice plants, causing abnormally long stems to develop, a disease known as *bakanae* or *foolish seedling.* The growth-accelerating factors were isolated in 1938 from infected rice plants in Japan. Responses to gibberellic acid have been studied widely in research with plants, since the acid accelerates stem elongation and induces other growth responses. It is used in crop production mainly to increase the size of some varieties of grapes, to improve the quality of navel oranges, and to increase the production of the enzyme alpha-amylase in malt.

—John W. Mitchell

Goat, a hollow-horned, hoofed mammal that is similar to sheep. Males are called *bucks,* females *does,* and the young *kids.* Goats are kept for milk, meat, hides, hair, and sometimes work. In the United States, goats are kept primarily for milk, although some *angora* goats are kept for their hair. Goat's milk is easy to digest and is generally safe from tuberculosis, since goats rarely get this disease. The milk breeds used in the United States include the *Toggenburg, Nubian, Saanen, British Alpine,* and *French Alpine.* Goats usually mate in the fall or winter, but can mate anytime, and produce one or two young, with a gestation period of five months. The doe may be bred at eight months. Goats are browsers rather than grazers and will eat almost anything.

They can be especially destructive to young plants and trees because they eat bark. Goats suffer from *milk fever* and *mastitis*, both of which may be controlled by antibiotics. Pneumonia is usually cured with antibiotics, and anthrax can be prevented by vaccination. *Goat pox* and *brucellosis* are especially contagious and incurable, but they can be prevented by sanitation and the removal of diseased animals. Sulfa drugs work well on *actinomycosis*, an inflammation caused by a fungus. Worm parasites respond to treatment by vermifuges, such as copper sulfate, nicotine sulfate, and phenothiazine.

Goats are ruminants of the genus *Capra*, with four wild species, three domesticated species, and one species both wild and domesticated. In addition, *Capra ibex*, with several species, has never been domesticated.

—John T. Schlebecker

Goose, a web-footed swimming bird, related to swans and ducks, raised mainly for its meat. There is a limited demand for geese, probably due to the fatness of the meat. Geese are often kept by some to alert against intruders, or to weed cotton and berry fields. If not more than 5 to 7 geese per acre are used, and are removed before the berries ripen, they will not damage the crop. Of the numerous breeds, the Toulouse and Emden geese are the most popular. It is generally difficult to distinguish between the male and female. However, in Pilgrim geese the *gander*, or male, is white and the female, or goose, light gray. Goose eggs require 28 to 31 days of incubation for hatching. *Goslings* grow rapidly and reach 10–12 pounds at 10 weeks of age, and up to 25 pounds at maturity, depending on the sex and breed. The gander is usually several pounds heavier than the goose. Geese are long-lived—some up to 100 years—but females are normally not useful after 8 or 10 years. Ganders may have two or more mates but they usually remain faithful to the same one for life. Geese are costly, mainly because of low egg production and hatchability.

—Carl W. Hess

Grape, a vine-grown *fruit* ranging in colors from white to red to black. Grapes are the most important fruit produced in the world in terms of tonnage. Most of the production is concentrated in the Mediterranean area. On the basis of individual nations, Italy and France are the leaders, followed by Spain and the United States.

The U.S. produces over 4 million tons annually, most of which is concentrated in California. In recent years, California has accounted for approximately 90 per cent of the crop, followed by New York, Michigan, Washington, Pennsylvania, and Ohio. Botanically, most of these grapes are of European varieties; however, American types are also grown.

About one-ninth of production is sold for fresh consumption and the remainder for processing. The main forms of processing are: crushing for wine or juice; drying into raisins; and canning of white grapes. Crushing takes a little over half of production, drying about a third, while canning is of relatively minor importance.

—Dana G. Dalrymple

Guinea Fowl, an edible bird characterized by a small, partially unfeathered head and a curved body. The Pearl guinea, with grayish plumage dotted with white, is the most popular variety of domestic guinea. Other varieties are the White and the Lavender. Guinea eggs hatch after 26 to 28 days of incubation. Young guineas, or *keets*, reach about 2½ pounds at 14 weeks of age, and at maturity weigh 3 to 3½ pounds. Guineas are used frequently in rural areas as guardians of the farmstead, for they produce harsh shrieks whenever strangers appear. They are used as a specialty food.

—Carl W. Hess

Herbicide. *See* PESTICIDES in this section.

Horse, a domesticated, four-legged, herbivorous mammal best known for its use as a beast of burden, although its flesh is eaten in some cultures. Horses range in size from a few hundred pounds to more than a ton. Although a type of prehistoric horse once existed in North America, all horse stocks today are descended from animals that originated on the high plateaus of eastern Russia and Siberia. The currently accepted date for the domestication of the horse is approximately 5,000 B.C. From their native habitat they spread to the south and west. Successive invasions of the Arabs and the Moors brought these native strains into Spain, from which was developed the *Andalusian horse*. This was the horse brought to North and South America by the Spanish conquistadores and from which the South American *Criollo* and the North American *Mustang* are descended. English and Dutch settlers on the Atlantic seaboard brought horses from England and Holland to complete the basic stocks for the North American breeds, while a number of French horses were brought to eastern Canada.

Horses played a major part in the advancing American frontier, U.S. cavalry regiments eventually subduing the mounted Indian. In the wake of these battles came horse-drawn covered wagons, which in turn were followed by the horse-drawn plows that broke the plains to facilitate the sowing of food crops.

The peak of North American horse population was reached before World War I. After that, trucks began to replace horsepower in the cities. By the end of World War II, tractors had virtually driven horses off the farms. Today, the great majority of horses are used for sport—*thoroughbreds* for running and racing, *standardbreds* for harness racing, and *quarter horses* for working cattle, rodeo performances, trail riding, and pleasure riding. The standardbred horse is the only breed exported extensively by the United States; these horses are sent all over the world to provide breeding stock for harness racing. Other American breeds include the *American saddle horse*, both three- and five-gaited, and the *Tennessee walking horse*, both of which are primarily horse show breeds. American breeds characterized by their color are the golden-colored *palomino* and the spotted *appaloosa*. Descended from the horse of conquistadores are horses of the *pinto* breed, which are marked in patches rather than in spots. One of the oldest American breeds is the *Morgan horse*, descended from Justin Morgan, a stallion foaled in the late eighteenth century and belonging to a Vermont school teacher of the same name. These horses are noted for their versatility in being able to perform all types of work.

Ponies are also bred extensively in this country, but the majority of them are imported from England, particularly the *Welsh* and the *Shetland;* the *Connemara* comes from Ireland. A native American breed is the *Pony of the Americas*, a small type of Appaloosa.

The gestation period of the horse is approximately 11 months. Given reasonable care, horses are generally free from disease, although they are subject to a number of respiratory ailments, most of them not fatal. Horses are also subject to sleeping sickness.

There has been a strong revival of interest in riding of all kinds in North America, and in fact throughout the Occident.   —Alexander Mackay-Smith

Hydroponics, the science of growing plants in water or sand culture. In *water culture*, the plants grow with their roots suspended in a dilute solution of the essential mineral elements, contained in shallow tanks. They are supported above the water by wire netting or hardware cloth, which is covered with wood shavings, peat moss, or similar material in order to exclude light from the solution and maintain a high humidity around the upper roots. The solution must be renewed at intervals as water and elements are absorbed. It must be aerated to supply oxygen to the roots. In *sand culture*, the nutrient solution is applied frequently to containers of sand, or other inert media (vermiculite, perlite, haydite), in which the plants are growing. This method has been widely used in experimental studies of plant nutrition for many years.

A variation of the sand culture method, known as *sub-irrigation culture* is the only commercial application of hydroponics. Watertight beds are filled with a coarse medium, such as washed gravel. The nutrient solution is pumped into the beds or allowed to flow into them from overhead reservoirs, until the beds are filled to within an inch of the surface. The solution then flows out of the gravel to a storage tank. Since the only source of water and nutrients for the plants is from the films of moisture around the gravel particles, the cycle of filling and draining the beds must be repeated frequently.

The major handicap to economic food production by hydroponics is the cost of the installation. Some technical training and considerable experience are necessary for the efficient management of soilless culture crop production. Soilless culture was used to produce vegetables at certain United States Army bases overseas during World War II. Hydroponics continues to be an absorbing hobby for the home gardener. —Neil Stuart

Irrigation, the practice of making available to crops, pasture, lawns, and turfs a greater quantity of water than that retained from natural rainfall. It thus includes various flooding or ditching techniques for direct water application, called *gravity* or *low-pressure irrigation; overhead sprinkling* or *high-pressure systems* of varying design; *diking* of fields to obstruct the natural draining away of rainfall, as in rice paddies; and situations where groundwater tables are or can be made sufficiently shallow to permit the wetting of root zones from below.

Irrigation has played an important role in agricultural production since the dawn of history, as evidenced by the early civilizations in the Tigris and Euphrates valleys and the dynasties of ancient Egypt supported by the floodwaters of the Nile. Today about 415 million acres—about one-eighth of the world's arable agricultural land—are irrigated. Three-fourths of the total is in Asia, especially China, India, and Pakistan. North and Central America account for about 45 million acres, led by the United States with about 42 million acres of irrigated land. About 35 million acres of this is in crops, and 7 million acres in pasture. It has been estimated that the U.S. total eventually could reach about 75 million acres.

About 92 per cent of the irrigated land in the United States lies in the 17 western states, where the practice originated with aboriginal Indians, was taken up by the Spanish missionaries and by colonists from both Spain and Mexico, and was put on a sustained basis by the Mormon settlers who arrived in Utah in 1847. Rapid expansion through the West began about 1870 from a 32,000-acre project supported by Horace Greeley, near present-day Greeley, Colorado. Other large projects were started in about the same period near Riverside and Anaheim, California. But irrigation is also important in the Mississippi Delta states, in Hawaiian sugarcane areas, in Florida citrus groves, and on truck farms in New Jersey. Also, it is increasing in importance through most of the eastern states.

■GRAVITY IRRIGATION.—Methods of irrigation vary considerably from area to area and are closely related to the nature and proximity of water supplies. Gravity methods utilizing ditches, furrows, border dikes, and flooding are still employed on 88 per cent of the acreage in the older irrigated areas—the West, the Mississippi Delta, and Florida. About 52 per cent of this acreage is served by diversions from streams or reservoirs. Most of the remainder is supplied by pumping water from wells. While limited to nearly flat terrain and requiring considerable expense for land-shaping as well as considerable

BUREAU OF RECLAMATION, U.S. DEPARTMENT OF THE INTERIOR

FLOOD CONTROL in the Missouri River Basin Project of Montana performs the secondary function of aiding sugar beet production by diversion of water through irrigation systems.

volumes of water, gravity irrigation has the special advantage of requiring a comparatively small investment for irrigation equipment. Operating costs are largely for labor. Most of the needed reservoirs, canals, and land preparation were arranged through mutual irrigation companies or in recent years by the Department of the Interior's Bureau of Reclamation.

■OVERHEAD IRRIGATION.—Overhead or sprinkler irrigation is gaining rapidly in importance in all areas of the United States and in other countries too. More than 15 per cent of the irrigated acreage in the United States is now sprinkled, compared with 2 per cent in 1950. The most common system lifts water from wells or adjacent streams and forces it at high pressure into a main pipeline having several portable lateral lines, each with its own series of nozzles or sprinklers. The lateral lines are periodically disconnected and moved to a new valve point on the main line until the field is irrigated completely. To avoid uncoupling of lateral sections, the complete lateral may be mounted on large wheels and rolled to its new position. Or there may be a combination main and delivery line on lugged wheels in which some of the water pressure itself is used to inch the system along automatically. This is called a *hydraulic-move system.* Still another sprinkler system consists of a single large boom, or perhaps several booms, mounted on a trailer with giant nozzles along the booms and at the ends, operating much like an ordinary rotating lawn sprinkler. Some of these rigs can irrigate up to 5.5 acres per setting. Sprinkler systems are well adapted to both level and moderately sloping land but require a considerable investment in equipment. Their special advantages are complete control over rates of water application to match absorptive capacity of soils, uniform application to all areas, and portability.

■SUBIRRIGATION.—Subirrigation is possible with little expense under conditions where ground water tables are naturally shallow, as in the cranberry

bogs of Massachusetts and Michigan. Favorable conditions also can be created if the subsoil is impervious at a depth of 6 feet or more and if the surface soil is relatively permeable. A common technique is to surround large blocks of land with levees to prevent flooding, to install drainage systems, and then to pump excess water in wet seasons over the levees into the streams. In dry periods, the river water is siphoned or pumped back over the levees into ditches about one foot wide, 2 or 3 feet deep, and up to several hundred feet apart. The water is diffused through the root zone by capillary action, with downward percolation restricted by the impervious subsoil. Subirrigation can be very efficient as expenses for labor and operation are relatively small.

The role of irrigation in the U.S. farm economy is indicated by the fact that irrigated crops account for about one-fifth of the value of all harvested crops but only 8.5 per cent of the total crop acreage. In the order of their market value, the leading irrigated crops are cotton, vegetables, tame hay, potatoes, sugarbeets, corn, sorghums, barley, and wheat. Citrus and other orchard and vineyard crops also rank high. The 7 million acres of irrigated pasture is part of the feed base on many dairy farms and cattle ranches. —George A. Pavelis

Jute. *See* MACHINES AND PROCESSES: *Rope,* in the INDUSTRY AND TECHNOLOGY volume.

Meat Packing. *See* FOOD MANUFACTURING in this section.

Oats, a grain of the grass family, widely used as a source of human and animal food and an important source of straw. Oats rank fourth among the grain crops, next below wheat, corn, and grain sorghum. Despite the inroads of motor-propelled machines on farms, displacing the horses and mules that formerly were the main consumers of oats, this grain retains a prominent place in the farm economy. Now the oat crop is fed largely to dairy cattle, poultry, hogs, and sheep.

About 8 per cent of the annual United States crop, which totals about 700 million bushels, goes into the manufacture of breakfast foods, particularly oatmeal. Some oats are pastured and cut for hay or livestock bedding.

The oat originated in eastern Europe or western Asia. Among its principal growers today are the United States, the Soviet Union, Canada, West Germany, Poland, and France. The type that is generally grown, known as the *common oat,* develops an upright pinnacle with branches falling about equally to all sides. Another type, known as *side oats,* has branches that fall to one side. Oat hulls vary in color according to variety. Some are white or gray, others are yellow, red, or black. The hulls are most often white in the sections of predominant U.S. production—the Corn Belt, the Great Lakes states, and the northern Plains. These areas taken together grow about 60 per cent of the 17 to 20 million acres seeded annually in the United States. In the south, oats are usually red or gray. Most oats in cool climates are sown in the spring, but a fall-seeded crop will winter over in the warmer Southern states. Oat straw is a good fertilizer.

—Charles E. Rogers

Peanuts, a legume of the pea family, deriving the "nut" part of the name from the fact that the plant ripens its product within a shell. Though the peanut originated in South America, probably in Brazil, it has migrated to many parts of the world. China, India, West Africa, and the United States are leading producers. Except in the United States, peanuts are mainly crushed for oil, but here about 50 per cent of the crop goes into peanut butter. Most of the remaining nuts are roasted for direct consumption, used in candy and bakers' goods, or left in the soil to be rooted out by swine. *Peanut vines* produce hay equal in feeding value to clover. In the United States, the peanut is an annual plant grown mainly in the Southern states. Planted from the hulled seed in the spring, it develops *pegs* after blossoming. The pegs elongate and go into the soil where they produce the *groundnut,* as the peanut is sometimes called.

—Charles E. Rogers

Pesticides, any of various substances used to control plant or animal pests. Most modern pesticides are manufactured chemicals. These may be lethal to particular pests, but they can also cause indiscriminate destruction of plant and animal life, create ecological imbalances, and produce unanticipated side effects in the environment and in man himself.

The pesticides include insecticides, herbicides, and fungicides, each of which is named to indicate the specific class of organisms that they are primarily designed to control. *Insecticides* are substances that are poisonous to insects, and their proper application should kill pest species while doing minimal damage to beneficial and neutral species. Comparatively few insects are harmful, for the majority are neutral in that they neither harm nor aid man. However, nearly all insecticides, if used im-

properly, will also kill plants and animals and, even if employed with the greatest care, will produce some injurious effects. *Herbicides* and *fungicides* are substances that are specific poisons for plants and fungi respectively, but they, too, cause unwanted harm.

■INSECTICIDES.—Prior to World War II only a limited number of chemical insecticides, such as Paris green (copper acetoarsenite), lime-sulfur solution, and lead arsenate, were in general use, along with some poisonous substances of plant origin, such as nicotine, rotenone, and pyrethrum. During and immediately after the War, chemical research uncovered many substances that were effective in destroying insect pests. Two groups of such substances that have since been most widely used are the *chlorinated hydrocarbons* and the *organo-phosphorus compounds.* In 1939 the chemical *dichlorodiphenyl   trichloroethane* (DDT), which belongs to the first group and which had first been synthesized in 1874, was found to be very toxic to insects and relatively safe to man. During the War it probably saved millions of lives in the West by controlling diseases, such as louse-borne typhus, which were spread by insects. But in the 1950s indiscriminate applications of DDT, especially in the United States, resulted in such heavy concentrations in some food chains that animals at the end of the chain were fatally poisoned. Also, many pest species, as flies, mosquitoes, and lice, developed resistance to DDT. In the light of these discoveries and from a pervasive fear of many other undesirable effects, the use of DDT was banned for most purposes in the U.S. by the EPA in 1972. Other chlorinated hydrocarbons, such as aldrin, dieldrin, chlordane, and heptachlor, were found to be even more poisonous and more dangerous and have now been banned also except for minor uses, as for the control of termites.

The *organo-phosphorus* insecticides appear to disrupt the transmission of nerve impulses, but the method of action varies with different animals, and, as with most poisons, a complete understanding of their effects is yet to be

U.S. DEPARTMENT OF AGRICULTURE

SPRAYING soft-jet pesticides prevents or destroys various tree diseases.

discovered. Indeed, the organo-phosphorus chemicals pose a grave danger in that a member of this group may potentiate another member. For example, the seemingly harmless chemical malathion, may be extremely hazardous to a person who has recently used parathion.

Insecticides of plant origin, such as nicotine, rotenone, and pyrethrum, break down quickly. These are still widely used because they are not poisonous to plants, and, even though toxic to mammals and birds, proper use minimizes their potential dangers.

■HERBICIDES.—Chemicals of a nonselective type, as arsenic compounds, are usually inorganic and have been used as herbicides for many years. Such total weed killers, however, are very toxic to man and to wildlife, and their residues persist for many years. Selective herbicides which are usually organic and which for the most part kill unwanted species, especially broadleaf weeds, have been exploited only since about 1940. Some of these, as the *dinitro compounds,* are very poisonous to all living things and, therefore, must be used when the plant species to be protected is in a dormant stage. The dinitro compounds have been largely replaced today by much less poisonous herbicides, as *2,4-dichlorophenoxyacetic acid* (2,4-D). These less toxic compounds function as natural hormones that stimulate the rapid growth and destruction of pest plants. Grass and cereal plants are not usually adversely affected.

■FUNGICIDES.—Fungicides containing copper or sulfur have long been widely used, and wildlife has seldom been endangered by their application. However, these compounds do produce stable residues in the soil, the effects of which have not yet been sufficiently studied. Modern *organo-mercury compounds* are very poisonous to fungi and have been extensively used in the treatment of seeds before planting. In 1976, however, the EPA banned the production of almost all pesticides containing mercury, because nervous system disorders caused by mercury poisoning had been rising. It was estimated that this ban would reduce the amount of mercury entering the environment by 98.5 per cent.

—Paul B. Murry

Pheasant, an edible bird having a compact body, short unfeathered legs, and short rounded wings. The Ringneck is the most common of the pheasants. There are other popular breeds, such as Mongolian and Chinese, and ornamental breeds including Golden, Silver, Lady Amherst, and Reeves. In many sections of the country pheasants are popular as game birds and are raised for sports clubs. They are also used as a specialty food. Pheasant eggs hatch after 22 to 24 days of incubation. Pheasants are highly nervous and may injure their heads when raised in confinement. This is true even when the wing feathers of one wing are clipped or the last joint of one wing is removed to prevent flying. Most states in the United States restrict the raising of game birds, and require a permit or license for the raising or hunting of pheasants.

—Carl W. Hess

Pigeon, a bird with dense fluffy plumage, a stout body and short neck, a small head, and a square or rounded tail. Young pigeons are called *Squab*. Of the many pigeon breeds, the King, Carneau, and Homer are the ones used for squab production. Squabs grow very rapidly and reach market age in about 4 weeks, depending on the size of the breed. *Homing pigeons* are raised by pigeon fanciers for racing. About 17 days of incubation are required for pigeon eggs to hatch.

—Carl W. Hess

Poultry Products. See *Food Manufacturing,* page 809.

Rice, a native grass of tropical Asia and the cereal food mainstay of the peoples of China, Japan, the mainland of southeast Asia, and the islands of the southwest Pacific. This is the *rice bowl,* where 95 per cent of the world's supply of the cereal is produced and consumed. There are thousands of known varieties, more than of any other crop.

Alone among the world's great crops, rice grows typically in a field of standing water, but the land must slope enough to allow a slight movement of the water. Irrigation is the prime requisite. Upland rice, grown without irrigation, constitutes a negligible part of the total harvest.

Most rice is grown in coastal plains and tidal deltas in tropical, semitropical, and temperate climates. Relatively high humidity and an average temperature of 70° F during the growing season of 4 to 6 months are necessary for best results. Heavy soil is desirable, and the subsoil must be impervious to water. Except in technically advanced countries like the United States, rice cultivation is done almost entirely by hand.

Seed is sown broadcast, and the seedlings that emerge are transplanted when they are 6 to 8 inches in height. They are planted in water 2 to 4 inches deep, in rows about one foot apart, to permit intensive cultivation. From the time the seedlings are transplanted until the harvest, they are supplied with heavy fertilization. Harvested rice is threshed by flailing or beating. It is then winnowed and the hulls removed. Afterward the clean rice is polished.

China leads the world in rice production—about 120 million metric tons annually, according to an estimate made by the Food and Agricul-

RICE CULTIVATION remains unchanged despite technological improvements in most of Asia, and many farmers still employ the primitive methods used by their ancestors for centuries.

and Indonesia is in third place with 27 million. Some rice is grown on every continent. North America produced 5.8 million metric tons in 1974–75, the largest part—5.18 million tons—in the United States. The leading rice-producing states are Louisiana, Texas, Arkansas, and California.

About two-thirds of the world's exports of rice in 1974–75 were from six Asian countries: Thailand, Burma, South Vietnam, Cambodia, Taiwan, and South Korea. The principal importing countries also were Asian—Indonesia, India, Japan, Malaysia, the Philippines, and Pakistan. The United States exported a record 2.2 million tons in 1974–75. India was the largest importer of U.S. rice. Increases in both acreage and yield among the principal importing countries of Asia have failed to bring about sufficient production to satisfy growing domestic needs.

—Charles E. Rogers

Rye, a cereal of the grass family. Like many others, it probably originated from a wild species growing in the Near East. It is used largely as a bread grain in the Soviet Union and Germany. It flourishes in a variety of conditions, but when grown on good soil yields less profit than other crops. It is therefore cultivated mainly on the poor, light, dry land un-

crop to be consumed at an early stage of growth. If allowed to reach maturity, it is hard, dry, and unpalatable to stock. The straw is used for thatching, packing, and similar purposes. The crop is not important in the United States, where its annual production is comparatively small and is used chiefly to give flavor to the so-called rye bread. The grain is malted to make rye whiskey, and the straw is used for packing.

Rye is subject to a fungus disease, *ergot,* and if infected grain is made into bread, it can be a dangerous poison, sometimes causing death. Ergot is used, however, as an ingredient of drugs for medical purposes.

—G. E. Fussell

Seafood. See *Fish and Seafood,* page 807.

Sheep, horned, woolly mammals that are similar to goats. Males are called *rams,* females *ewes,* castrated males *wethers,* and the young *lambs.* Domesticated sheep are kept for wool, meat, fur, and hides. Outside the United States, ewes are sometimes kept for milk. Some sheep breeds produce higher-quality wool than others, and some produce meat more abundantly and rapidly. Meat animals must be raised comparatively near the point of consumption, because mutton cannot be pickled or smoked. Lambs are preferred for meat in the United States. Various breeds differ in their gregariousness. Sheep that are range-grazed should be gregarious, while sheep kept in farm pastures need not flock. The mutton types are best kept separate and need not be very gregarious.

Various crosses of breeds can be achieved to secure other desired characteristics, such as hardiness, rapid lamb growth, large lamb crops, and dual production of wool and meat. Wool breeds, sufficiently gregarious for herding, include the Rambouillet, Merino, Corriedale, Romeldale, Panama, Columbia, Targhee and the long-

World Production of RICE in %

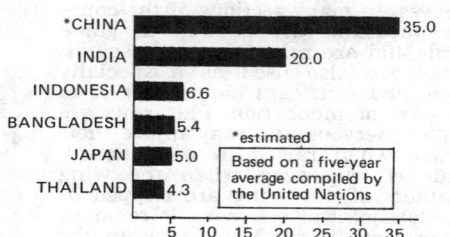

*CHINA	35.0
INDIA	20.0
INDONESIA	6.6
BANGLADESH	5.4
JAPAN	5.0
THAILAND	4.3

*estimated

5 10 15 20 25 30 35

Based on a five-year average compiled by the United Nations

ture Organization of the United Nations. The second largest producer is India with 65 million metric tons,

World Production of RYE in %

SOVIET UNION	35.7
POLAND	28.7
WEST GERMANY	9.6
EAST GERMANY	6.3

10 20 30 40

Based on a survey compiled by the United Nations

suited to producing high yields of wheat, characteristic of northeastern Europe. It is extremely winter-hardy and drought-resistant.

In Great Britain, rye is grown as a forage crop, sometimes as a spring

wooled Lincolns, Cotswolds, and Romneys. The meat breeds include the Hampshires, Suffolks, Oxfords, and Southdowns.

Sheep usually mate in the fall, and the lambs are born in the spring. The gestation is about five months, and the breeding life of a ewe averages seven years. Several of the most deadly sheep diseases, such as anthrax, blackleg, tetanus, and rabies, have effective vaccines. Crippling or fatal diseases, such as foot-and-mouth, listerellosis (circling disease), mastitis, and shipping fever respond well to antibiotics. Black disease, caused by liver flukes, can be prevented by chemical destruction of the intermediary snail hosts. Brucellosis and tuberculosis in sheep are very rare, and slaughter eradication works well. Liver flukes, long worms, and tapeworms all succumb to phenothiazine or other vermicides. Dips and sprays are effective against disease-carrying ticks and insects.

Sheep are ruminants of the genus *Ovis,* with four wild species-groups, one domesticated species-group, and many subspecies.

—John T. Schlebecker

Sisal. See *Rope,* page 1137.

Soils, earth composed of inorganic particles, organic matter, water, and air. They are formed by the weathering of rocks and the decay of organic material.

The parent materials of soils determine their classification into ten orders. Soils which have been recently formed such as those on the alluvium of rivers are classified as *Entisols.* Somewhat more developed are the cracking, swelling, clayey *Vertisols,* of which examples are found in Texas and India. The *Inceptisols* include the arctic tundra soils, the soils of northern Appalachia, and the volcanic soils of the Pacific Northwest. The *Aridisols* are the desert soils, while the *Mollisols* are the grassland soils of the North American prairies, the Argentine pampas, and the Russian steppes. The *Alfisols* and *Spodosols* of northeastern United States and eastern Canada are forest-made soils as are the reddish *Ultisols* of the southeastern States. *Oxisols* are the lateritic, leached soils of the tropics, and the *Histosols* or bog soils, from organic material, include the peat soils of northern Europe.

■**CHEMICAL CONTENT.**—Plants need at least 16 chemical elements for growth and seed production: carbon, hydrogen, oxygen, calcium, nitrogen, phosphorus, potassium, sulfur, magnesium, iron, manganese, zinc, copper, molybdenum, boron, and chlorine. Of these, the first nine are the most essential. Carbon, hydrogen, and oxygen are obtainable from water and air, but the other elements or nutrients must be obtained from the soil.

The forest-derived soils of eastern United States are usually deficient in calcium and consequently are more acid than alkaline. Since many plants are sensitive to acidity, these soils need the addition of calcium in the form of lime. To designate the soil condition, a pH scale from 0 to 14 is used. A pH factor below 7 indicates acidity; above it, alkalinity.

Nitrogen and sulfur are needed in the production of proteins, while phosphorus is necessary for photosynthesis and seed formation. Potassium is essential for such physiological processes as cell growth and the formation of starch and sugars.

These and other nutrients are added to soils deficient in them by means of crop rotation, green manuring, and the application of animal manures and commercial fertilizers. The inclusion of clover or alfalfa in a *rotation cycle* enriches the soil because of the action of nitrogen-fixing bacteria, which live in nodules on the roots of these plants. *Green manuring* is the plowing under of a growing, leafy crop, usually leguminous. Farmers have long used *animal manures,* but recently they have increased greatly their use of *commercial fertilizers.*

■**MOISTURE.**—The *moisture content* of the soil is of major concern to farmers. If there is too much, they must provide surface drainage by grading, terracing, and ditching or subsurface drainage by the construction of *tile* or *mole drains.* If the rainfall is normally sufficient, they try to retain it by cultivation and by the destruction of weeds. If there is not enough, they must either conserve it or supplement it by irrigation.

In the United States, on the Great Plains and in the intermountain valleys farther west where annual rainfall is less than 20 inches, farmers and agronomists have developed a type of moisture-conserving agriculture known as *dry-land farming.* It consists of the culture of drought-resistant crop

varieties and of a system of alternate cropping known as *summer fallowing* in which every other year the land lies fallow in order to store moisture. Excessive storage of moisture by this method has led in some places to a destructive salinization of the soil known as *saline seep.*

In arid regions, water is diverted from streams into ditches or pumped from wells and applied to the land by methods called *flooding, furrow, border, basin,* and *sprinkler irrigation.*

■**TILLAGE.**—Through the centuries, crop production has required tillage, with loose, granulated seedbeds prepared by plowing and harrowing. Seeds are sown by means of drills and planters and, in the case of intertilled crops, the growing plants are cultivated to reduce competition from weeds. Recently developed *minimum-tillage* or *no-till* methods reduce or eliminate tillage and rely upon herbicides to control weeds.

These new methods lessen *erosion* by wind and water. On the Great Plains, where wind erosion is a problem, it has been checked by strip cropping and the creation of a stubble or trashy mulch. *Strip cropping* is the planting of grain in strips alternating with fallow, while stubble mulch is created by chisels and sweeps, loosening and granulating the soil but retaining the stubble from the previous crop on the surface. Erosion by water is retarded by *terracing, contour plowing,* and the planting of *cover crops.*

—Robert G. Dunbar

Soybeans, an Asian legume or its seed. Soybeans originated in the Orient; in China they have been a staple food for thousands of years, being consumed in various forms, such as bean curds, bean milk, soy sprouts, and soy sauce. Introduced into the United States in the nineteenth century, the U.S. Department of Agriculture encouraged the culture of soybeans during the early years of this century and promoted the development of domestic production by the importation of hundreds of Asiatic varieties. Soybeans, however, did not become a major crop in this country until after World War II, when, encouraged by government restrictions on the planting of corn and cotton, acreage exploded. Whereas in 1945 farmers planted almost 14 million acres to this crop and harvested about 200 million bushels, thirty years later they seeded nearly 55 million acres and harvested 1.5 billion bushels, a seven-fold increase. Because of this spectacular expansion, soybeans have been called the "miracle crop." Today, farmers' income from it, more than $7,000,000,000, is exceeded only by the income from corn and wheat.

Initially grown for hay, pasture, and green manure, soybeans today are harvested largely for their oil and meal. Soybean oil is the most popular of the edible animal and vegetable oils, supplying 60 per cent of the national consumption. It is used in shortening, margarine, mayonnaise, and cooking and salad oils. The oil is also in demand for industrial uses, particularly as an ingredient of paints, varnishes, enamels, soaps, and

PRIMARY SHEEP PRODUCTS are wool and mutton. The Hampshire breed (*right*) is more suitable for mutton, while the fine-fleeced Merino (*left*) is best used for wool.

M. FELDMAN

SUGAR CANE being dropped into a waiting wagon by a loader that crops a quarter-ton of cane. The new tractor, dubbed "Sugar Babe," has the capacity to pull four loaded trucks, or 65,000 pounds, to a sugar mill. This harvest is part of Florida's expanding sugar industry.

cleaning compounds. Soybean meal, which is the residue after the extraction of the oil, enters the market as a constituent of high-protein livestock and poultry feeds, but it is also used in breakfast foods and in meat substitutes, as well as in the manufacture of adhesives and plastics.

Soybean culture in the United States is concentrated in the Corn Belt where one-half of the national production is grown. Illinois is the premier soybean-growing State, accounting for one-fifth of the national total. Another fifth is grown in the States of Louisiana, Mississippi, Alabama, Tennessee, and Arkansas. The United States grows about 75 per cent of the world's production.

The soybean plant resembles the garden varieties of the stringbean, with trifoliolate leaves but with taller stems. In the Corn Belt, the crop is planted in May or June in rows 36 to 42 inches apart, cultivated during the summer, and harvested with combines in September or October. It is subject to a number of fungal and bacterial diseases such as stem canker and bacterial blight.   —Robert G. Dunbar

Spices, aromatic vegetable products used primarily for seasoning and preserving food, and to a lesser extent for making perfumes, soaps, and lotions. The "true" spices, so designated by spice specialists, are pepper, vanilla, cloves, cinnamon, nutmeg, and ginger. Some spices come from the seeds, buds, flowers, and fruits of plants; others, from the bark, leaves, or roots. The harvested substance is usually ground, as is pepper, the most widely-consumed spice.

All true spices grow in the tropics, particularly in Asia and Africa. Cinnamon, cloves, nutmeg, pepper, and opium have been cultivated since medieval times in Ceylon, Malacca, and the Malabar Coast. For centuries these areas were exploited by Arabia, Venice, and Portugal, who amassed a great wealth by importing flavoring, meat preservative, and luxury spices to western Europe.

Measured by use and world trade, *pepper* is the leading spice and the United States is the leading consumer. Both black and white pepper are derived from a berry, known as *peppercorn,* that grows on a vine. India and Indonesia produce two-

thirds of the world's supply.

Vanilla comes from an *orchid,* which also grows on a vine. About two-thirds of the world production originates on islands off the southeast coast of Africa. Besides its well-known use as a flavoring, it is employed in the manufacture of chocolate, perfumes, and soap.

Cloves grow on trees that are native to Indonesia, though the bulk of world production now comes from Tanzania and the Malagasy Republic. While cloves have been used for centuries to flavor and decorate foods, two-thirds of the world's crop is now ground and mixed with cigarette tobacco.

Cinnamon, a popular flavoring, is derived from the bark of a tree grown in Asia. Its cousin *cassia* is similar, but is usually regarded as somewhat inferior. Trees that supply these spices belong to different but related species.

Nutmeg and *mace* grow on an evergreen tree—nutmeg is the seed, and mace is the membrane around it. Indonesia and the West Indies are the chief sources. Ground nutmeg has many uses in the food and beverage trade, and the oils of nutmeg and mace find their way into soaps, cosmetics, perfumes, confections, and pharmaceutical products.

Ginger, a pungent spice used widely for making ginger ale and for medicinal preparations, is derived from a root native to Asia. About one-half of the world's supply comes from India. Other sources are the west coast of Africa and Jamaica.

In addition to the true spices, there are many herbs and other plants that are commonly regarded as spices. Included among these are oregano, anise, caraway, cardamon, coriander, cumin, fennel, and mustard seed.

—Charles E. Rogers

Sugar, one of the carbohydrates, an important source of energy. Technically known as *sucrose,* it is produced commercially from sugarcane and sugarbeets. There are many types of sugar, notably *dextrose,* produced from corn, and *lactose,* produced from milk. Other sources of sugars are *honey, sugar maple trees, palm trees,* and *sorghum.* Sugars are produced in the leaves of green plants by photosyn-

thesis. Sugarcane and sugarbeets, which store sugar abundantly, have become the primary sources of sugar.

Sugarcane is a large perennial grass, which is produced in tropical and semitropical climates. Cuttings of the cane stalk, rather than seed, are used to propagate the crop. The cane attains heights of 10 to 20 feet. It is normally harvested 12 to 24 months after planting. For centuries, sugarcane was laboriously harvested by hand; today, the crop is often harvested by machine. The stalk is cut near the ground, and the top and the leaves are removed. The stalk or cane is shipped to a nearby sugar mill for processing. Normally, a number of crops may be cut from the same roots. It is not necessary, therefore, to replant every year.

The sugarbeet, a biennial plant, is produced in temperate climates. Normally, the crop is planted in the spring and harvested in the fall. Sugar is produced in its leaves and stored in its root. The crop is harvested by lifting the beet from the ground and removing the tops or leaves. Sugarbeet tops are fed to livestock. The root, or beet, is shipped to a nearby factory for processing.

Sugarcane is believed to have originated in the Orient, where its juice was valued hundreds of years before the birth of Christ. People are believed to have learned to produce sugar from sugarcane sometime about the fifth century. Much early trade revolved around sugar. Columbus introduced sugarcane to the New World on his second voyage.

The production of sugar from sugarbeets is a relatively recent development. In 1747, Andreas Marggraf, a German chemist, proved that sucrose could be extracted from sugarbeets. The world's first beet sugar factory began operating in Europe in 1802. The first successful sugarbeet operation was started in America in 1879.

Approximately 60 per cent of the sugar consumed in the United States is processed from sugarcane and sugarbeets produced by American farmers. The remaining 40 per cent is imported and then refined in the United States.

Per capita consumption of sugar in the United States is approximately 100 pounds a year. One-third of the sugar consumed is distributed through retail stores. The other two-thirds is distributed to food processors—bakers, bottlers, canners, confectioners, ice-cream manufacturers, and others—who use sugar as an ingredient in their products.

Sugar is an essential ingredient in many processed foods. In addition to its contribution as a sweetener, sugar can enhance the flavor, appearance, and texture of many foods. It performs many other purposes, one of which is that of a preservative.

—Nicholas Kominus

Sweeteners, Artificial, chemical compounds that are used for sweetening. They are also known as *synthetic, nonnutritive,* or *noncaloric sweeteners*. Artificial sweeteners have no nutritional value. They are primarily produced for people suffering from diabetes and other diseases that prohibit the consumption of sugar, and for dieting.

Saccharin, the first commercial artificial sweetener, is produced from coal tar. It was discovered by Ira Remson, an American chemist, in 1879. Its sweet taste, however, was discovered by Constantin Fahlberg, a German chemist working in Remson's laboratory, who obtained a patent on a process to manufacture saccharin. Commercial production began in 1901 in the United States.

The sweetening power of saccharin is 500 times that of cane sugar, while the cyclamates are about 30 times sweeter.

Sodium cyclamate and *calcium cyclamate* were once widely used in the United States as sugar substitutes, but both were banned from general use in 1969 by the Food and Drug Administration after laboratory research produced evidence that they could endanger the health of users. Today both are available only by prescription.

Questions have also been raised about the safety of saccharin, so a wide search has been stimulated to discover nonhazardous sugar substitutes.

Swine, omnivorous hoofed mammals that are a domesticated form of wild hog. The male is called a *boar,* the female a *sow,* the young female a *gilt,* the castrated male a *barrow,* the young a *pig.* In the United States, swine are kept primarily for meat and lard, with hides and bristles as side products. Hogs are especially desirable meat animals because pork can readily be preserved by pickling or by smoking. Furthermore, swine eat almost anything and can be raised under a variety of conditions. The animals also mature quickly and reproduce frequently with large litters,

WORLD PRODUCTION OF SOYBEAN 1980		
COUNTRY	METRIC TONS	% OF WORLD
United States	49,454,000	59.2
Brazil	15,153,000	18.1
China	10,026,000	12.0
Argentina	3,500,000	4.1
Canada	713,000	.8
Paraguay	600,000	.7
Indonesia	600,000	.7
North Korea	340,000	.4
Rumania	330,000	.4

WORLD PRODUCTION OF SUGAR 1978		
COUNTRY	METRIC TONS	% OF WORLD
Soviet Union	9,353,000	10.1
Brazil	7,913,000	8.6
Cuba	7,662,000	8.3
India	7,103,000	7.7
United States	5,133,000	5.6
China	4,000,000	4.3
France	3,740,000	4.1
Mexico	3,131,000	3.4
West Germany	2,997,000	3.2

so that they provide a large and steady supply of meat. Currently, hogs reach market weight in five or six months, and with recent advances in pig weaning and feeding, sows can be bred three times a year. The gestation period averages 114 days, and sows come in heat about once every three weeks.

Various breeds of swine have different characteristics, although crosses are frequently preferred. Some breeds tend to produce more meat than others, but there are no distinctive meat or lard breeds. In general, the breeds which produce the most meat are the Yorkshire, Poland-China, Duroc, Tamworth, and Danish Landrace, and the recently developed American Landrace, Maryland #1, Minnesota #1, Minnesota #2, Beltsville #1, Beltsville #2, Montana #1, and Palouse. Other swine with varying advantages in size and hardiness are the Chester White, Berkshire, Hereford, and Spotted-Swine.

Swine gain best on formula rations containing corn, barley, sorghum, and alfalfa, with heavy supplements of vitamins, proteins, minerals, and antibiotics. Supplements should be added even when the swine are on pasture. Swine are susceptible to a wide range of diseases which, even when not fatal, sharply reduce rates of gain. Some diseases, such as brucellosis (abortion), atrophic rhinitis, influenza, and virus pneumonia, must be controlled by sanitation and sometimes by the slaughter of infected animals. Other diseases, such as erysipelas, leptospirosis, and hog cholera, can be prevented with vaccines. Swine parasites are mostly worms such as flukes, tapeworms, and roundworms. Roundworms cause the most trouble in the United States. Group treatment of swine produces the best

results. Treatment requires the use of dangerous chemicals. Effective vermifuges include phenothiazine, sodium fluoride, piperazine, and hydrocyin. *Trichina* are not serious in swine because recovery occurs rapidly as the worms enter the cyst state.

Swine belong to the genus *Sus,* with three species groups and several species subgroups.

—John T. Schlebecker

Tea, an evergreen shrub, its leaves, and the beverage brewed from these leaves. The tea plant, *Camellia sinensis,* whose leaves contain caffeine and tannin, grows in the humid tropics. Frequent rainfall, plentiful sunshine, and good soil fertility—conditions natural to Ceylon and India—produce the best yields and quality. In Japan, rapid yield increases have resulted from the use of organic fertilizers as plant nutrients.

Tea is grown at varied elevations and on different terrains. Indian tea grows at elevations from 200 to 6,000 feet, mainly in the Darjeeling hill district. It is commonly grown on flat foothills in Latin America. In China, tea has been cultivated for centuries on almost vertical terraced banks, where frequent rainfall results in natural irrigation. Tea is regarded as a plantation crop, but it is often cultivated on small holdings and estates in Africa, Asia, and Latin America.

The three major varieties of tea are green, black, and oolong. Green, an unfermented leaf, is immediately toasted, while the black is fermented before being machine-toasted (Ceylon black dominates U.S. tea imports). Oolong is a semifermented leaf.

The tea plant reaches maturity 4 to 6 years after planting. Replanting is customary after about 60 yields per plant. The leaves are graded by size: the fine leaves near the end of the twig produce a high-quality tea, in contrast to coarse plucking.

India and Ceylon (Sri Lanka) together produce nearly 60 per cent of the world's tea. In 1975 India produced approximately one billion pounds of tea and Ceylon about 500 million pounds, most of which was exported. Japan, the USSR, Kenya, Indonesia, Turkey, Bangladesh, Taiwan, and Argentina are also important producers. China is the world's largest tea grower, but exports comparatively little of its crop. Traditionally,

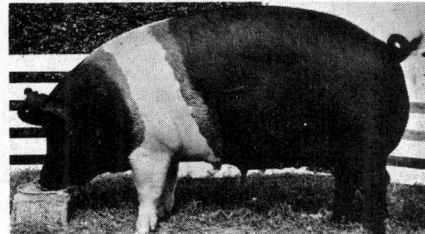

HAMPSHIRE SWINE REGISTRY

AMERICAN YORKSHIRE CLUB

SWINE provide a variety of pork and pork products. The Hampshire sow (*left*) is recognized as an excellent lard producer. The Yorkshire hog (*right*) is prized for its quality bacon.

U.S. DEPARTMENT OF AGRICULTURE

VEGETABLES are always available in U.S. markets. Cabbages (*right*) are grown in a suitable climate year-round, and snap beans (*center*) are bred for adaptability to fresh, frozen, or canned sales. Potato fields (*left*) produce the largest-selling crop.

Asia has produced 85–90 percent of the world's tea and has supplied 70–75 per cent of the exports.

The supply and demand for tea in the world's markets of 1975 and 1976 was estimated to be in near balance. However, tea consumption has been given a boost in recent years because high coffee prices have induced many consumers to drink tea.

In the United Kingdom—the world's largest importer of tea and second only to India in consumption—tea consumption averaged 8 lbs. per person for the years 1970–1975. Although the United States is the second largest tea importer, Americans consumed only about 0.8 pound per person in 1975. However, with the prospect of continued high coffee prices consumption is expected to rise. In fact tea sales in 1976 approximated a record $539 million. Imports were also a record 124,264,000 pounds, with Ceylon, India, and Kenya, the major suppliers.

—Marshall H. Cohen

Tobacco, a herbaceous plant of the nightshade family whose leaves are used extensively for smoking and chewing and as snuff. The origin of tobacco was well symbolized by the cigar-store Indian, a hallmark of tobacco shops in earlier generations. The American Indian introduced tobacco to the first white colonists in North America in the fifteenth and sixteenth centuries. He taught the Europeans how to use the leaf in forms common today—for smoking, chewing, and snuff.

Today tobacco is grown in 22 states of the United States. Three-quarters of the crop comes from five states: North Carolina, Kentucky, South Carolina, Georgia, and Virginia. There are six main classifications of tobacco leaf, according to the U.S. Department of Agriculture: flue-cured, fire-cured, air-cured, cigar-filler, cigar-binder, and cigar-wrapper. The United States leads the world in tobacco production, followed by China, India, the Soviet Union, and Japan. The world's annual harvest amounts to about 12 billion pounds.

Labor input to grow an acre of tobacco is about 300 man-hours, contrasted with only 3 for wheat. Seeds are planted in seedbeds protected by cloth covering, and the seedlings that emerge are transplanted to the field in the spring, from March to May. After 90 to 100 days, the crop is harvested, then cured and sold at auction. It takes 1.45 billion pounds of domestic tobacco to manufacture the number of cigarettes produced annually in the United States—a total of 650 billion in all.

—Charles E. Rogers

Turkey, an edible game bird native to North America, now almost entirely raised on farms. Of the many turkey varieties, only the Broad-Breasted Bronze, the Broad-Breasted Large White, and the Beltsville Small White are raised in commercial quantities. Much emphasis has been given by turkey breeders to wide breasts and overall meatiness. The Beltsville Small White is a relatively small, broad-breasted bird raised for use by small families. Marketed at about 5 months, the live *hens,* or females, weigh about 9 pounds; the *toms,* or males, about 16. The large

U.S. DEPARTMENT OF AGRICULTURE

BELTSVILLE TURKEYS, bred for small ovens, have extra meat on their bodies.

broad-breasted varieties weigh about twice as much or more when marketed. Turkeys were traditionally popular, chiefly for holiday consumption, although they are now available and used throughout the year. Reproduction in turkeys is relatively low due to poor egg production, fertility, and hatchability. Eggs hatch after 28 days of incubation. *Blackhead,* a major disease in turkeys, especially when kept with chickens, is caused by a microscopic parasite which attacks the cecum and liver. Pullorum and fowl typhoid used to cause heavy losses but these diseases now have been largely eliminated through blood testing. To help prevent losses from diseases and parasites, sanitary practices should be followed and chickens and turkeys should not be raised together.

—Carl W. Hess

Vegetable, any one of a large number of herbaceous plants cultivated for food. The precise definition of a vegetable is troublesome. No single botanic or economic description is adequate or clear-cut. We shall consider vegetables as annual or semiannual crops (excepting asparagus or artichokes) that have an edible fleshy portion. Thus, some plants that botanically are fruit (as tomatoes and melons) are included.

As in few other nations of the world, fresh domestic vegetables are available the year-round in the United States. This is due to two factors: a wide range of climate, which permits vegetables to be harvested every day of the year somewhere in the country, and an efficient marketing system.

Vegetable production, like other phases of agriculture, is becoming more specialized. Therefore, production is becoming concentrated in fewer but larger farms. These generally are found in areas of temperate climate (excepting potatoes), good soil, and ample supplies of rain or other sources of water. Production is also becoming more mechanized; labor problems have led to special interest in mechanical harvesting.

The farm value of the U.S. commercial vegetable crop ranges widely over the years, but its present annual value is more than $3 billion. The major vegetable producing States are California, Florida, Texas, Arizona, New York, and Michigan. While traditionally Idaho and Maine were the leading States in potato production, Washington has now supplanted Maine in the second position. Other leading vegetable-producing States are Oregon, Wisconsin, New Jersey, Washington, Minnesota, North Dakota, and Ohio. The most important single crop is the white potato, followed by tomatoes and lettuce. Other vegetables in approximate order of importance include snap beans, string beans, corn, onions, cantaloupes, celery, cucumbers, carrots, cabbage, green peas, and sweet potatoes.

Vegetables are either marketed fresh or shipped for processing. Some potatoes are also used for feed and seed. While more than half of the vegetable crop has been sold fresh in the past, processing is becoming more important. The most common forms of processing are canning and freezing; dehydration is of lesser importance. Potato products such as chips, shoestrings, and frozen French fries are of special significance. New techniques, such as freeze-drying, may play a greater role in the future.

Total vegetable consumption, or apparent use, is about 364 pounds per person per year; nearly one-third of this figure is represented by potatoes (these figures are in farm-weight terms, but allow for imports and exports). Consumption of fresh vegetables is decreasing while that of processed vegetables is increasing. Trends for the many individual vegetables vary: consumption of cabbage, for example, appears to be decreasing while that of salad vegetables, such as lettuce, has been increasing. Potatoes had been going through a long downward trend until a few years ago, when consumption leveled off.

—Robert A. Wearne

Wheat, the most widely cultivated *cereal.* It is grown around the world, with the Soviet Union, United States, China, Canada, and France leading in production. From 1971 to 1975 the average world production was 12.7 billion bushels, grown on 533,786,000 acres. Since wheat is a cool-season crop, most of these acres are situated

WHEAT, the most widely cultivated cereal, is grown primarily in the climates of the Northern Hemisphere. Here, combines completely process a Kansas wheat crop.

WORLD PRODUCTION OF WHEAT
1980

COUNTRY	METRIC TONS	% OF WORLD
Soviet Union	98,100,000	22.0
United States	64,492,000	14.5
China	54,158,000	12.2
India	31,564,000	7.1
France	23,668,000	5.3
Canada	19,131,000	4.3
Turkey	17,455,000	3.9
Pakistan	10,805,000	2.4
Australia	10,800,000	2.4

in the Northern Hemisphere. The leading producers in the United States are Kansas, North Dakota, Montana, Oklahoma, and Washington.

Botanists count 15 species of wheat, of which three are generally grown in the United States—*common, durum,* and *club.* However, 95 per cent of the wheat produced in the United States belongs to the first-named species.

There are two principal types of wheat: *winter wheat,* planted in the fall, and *spring wheat,* planted in the spring. Another classification divides wheat into soft and hard varieties.

The soft varieties are grown in the eastern half of the United States and in the states of Washington, Oregon, and Idaho; the hard winter wheats account for most of the production on the central plains, while most of the wheat grown on the northern plains is of the hard spring varieties. When it was realized in the late nineteenth century that soft wheats could not withstand the temperatures and droughts of the plains, plant breeders sought adaptive varieties. Cerealists such as Mark A. Carleton of the U.S. Department of Agriculture learned that the hard winter wheats grown on the steppes of southern Russia were adaptable. He visited Russia and brought back a winter variety known as *Kharkov,* as well as a spring-grown durum wheat. In Canada, William Saunders and his sons bred a hard spring wheat known as *Marquis.* Using these varieties and others as parent stocks, wheat breeders have developed the wheats that now account for much of the nation's production.

Whatever the variety, the wheat plant consists of a root system, leaves, stem, and heads or spikes. The roots ordinarily reach to a depth of 5–6 feet, while the stems vary from 2 to 5 feet. The heads bearing the kernels are usually 2 to 4 inches in length; the kernels are small and oval, consisting of a protective coating, a starchy endosperm, and the germ.

Wheat grows best on well-drained medium-to-heavy soils, especially silt and clay loams. Farmers living in humid areas prepare a seedbed by means of moldboard plows, spiketooth harrows, and disks; in the more arid Western states, they use adapted cultivators and blades. Farmers in both areas sow wheat by means of tractor-drawn drills.

Winter wheat, which is planted in September or October, is harvested in June and July, while spring wheat, planted in April, is harvested in July and August. Whereas 40 years ago most of the wheat crop was cut with a binder and threshed by a thresher, now more than 95 per cent of the crop is cut and threshed by combines.

Wheat is subject to attack by rusts and smuts. Stem rust, which has been particularly destructive on the Great Plains, has been checked by the development of rust-resistant varieties, such as *Thatcher,* which was developed by the Minnesota Agricultural Experiment Station. Insect enemies include the Hessian fly, wheat jointworm, grasshopper, and the wheat-stem sawfly. To combat the attacks of the latter, Canadian cerealists developed the *Rescue* variety with solid rather than hollow stems.

Wheat is used principally for human consumption. The hard varieties, richer in protein than the others, produce flour that is used in the making of bread. Flour from the soft wheats is suitable for pastries, crackers, biscuits, and cakes. Durum wheat is used for the manufacture of macaroni, spaghetti, and vermicelli. Some wheat is converted into breakfast foods.

Wheat is nutritious. The average kernel contains about 70 per cent carbohydrates, 12 per cent protein, 2 per cent fat, 12 per cent water, 1.8 per cent mineral matter, and 2.2 per cent cellulose. The protein content of the hard wheats of the Great Plains may be as high as 15 per cent. A kernel also contains vitamins of the B-group, such as thiamine, riboflavin, and niacin.

Wheat is an important article of international trade. The United States exports more than half of its crop; in 1975 this amounted to approximately 1.173 billion bushels. The other leading exporters are Canada, Australia, and France. Major importers are the United Kingdom, India, Japan, the Soviet Union, Egypt, and Brazil. (See also *Flour Milling*, p. 1122.)

—Robert G. Dunbar

Wool, a major textile fiber derived from the soft coat of a domesticated sheep. Its chief use is in outer apparel and household articles, such as blankets, with the manufacture of carpets and rugs utilizing a lesser amount. Wool is broadly classed as apparel or carpet quality. It is the seventh largest commodity in world trade.

SOUTH AFRICAN INFORMATION SERVICE

SHEARING SHEEP BY MACHINE enables sheep raisers to shear up to 250 sheep a day.

In the decade after 1955, world production of wool gained about 15 per cent to approximately 5.75 billion pounds (grease basis). Consumption rose by about one-fourth. Wool's share of total world fiber consumption dipped slightly, however, as the overall total rose and the use of newly developed man-made fibers increased.

Australia, which grows more than 1.7 billion pounds (grease basis) annually (almost entirely of apparel wool), is the world's largest producer, and has nearly 160 million sheep. Other leading producers of apparel-class wool, in order of importance, are New Zealand, Argentina, South Africa, the United States, Uruguay, and Great Britain. The Soviet Union is considered the second largest producer, and while its wool has been coarse, the output of apparel types is believed to be growing. Others in the coarse-wool category are The People's Republic of China, India, and Pakistan.

Wool has natural crimp and elasticity. It absorbs water vapor readily, but many wool articles resist wetting by liquid water. Wool dyes easily in a wide variety of fast colors. Wool garments impart a feeling of warmth, yet lightweight wool apparel is comfortable in hot weather. It has been said that if a fiber with wool's attributes had just been invented, it would lead the list of so-called miracle fibers. Also regarded as wool-type fibers are the specialty hairs such as mohair, cashmere, camel's hair, and vicuña.

Sorting of fleeces and scouring (washing) of the wool are the first steps in processing that leads to spinning. There are two spinning systems: woolen and worsted. The woolen system makes use of the shorter fibers. Woolen yarns are usually soft and lofty with relatively little twist and the individual fibers lie in all directions. In the worsted system, the aim is to lay the fibers as parallel as possible. The resulting yarn is firmer or harder and is given more twist than woolen yarn. Fabrics made of these two types of yarns are called woolens and worsteds.

Woolens, often used in sportswear and coats, lend themselves to a variety of colors and often have a woolly or hairy surface, which mutes and diffuses the colors and patterns. Fabrics usually made with woolen yarns include tweeds, meltons, coverts, and fleeces. Worsted fabrics, which usually are crisp and springy with little or no surface fiber, include serge, gabardine, and whipcord.

The United States, Great Britain, Italy, and Japan are among the largest manufacturers of wool. Though there has been a severe decrease in the number of mills and amount of wool machinery and a decline in cloth production since World War II, the American industry is regarded as the most efficient in the world, and it leads in the development of products made of wool blended with the new noncellulosic man-made fibers. For example, polyester/wool tropical cloth is the basic quality fabric for summer clothing. Producers make man-made

fibers especially for the various systems of textile processing, so the trend to blends is expected to continue. (See also, *Sheep*.)

—Gordon F. Graham

Yeast, a fungus growth consisting of tiny cells of vegetable matter that collect in a frothy, yellowish cluster. There are hundreds of species, widely distributed in nature, each strain possessing distinctive characteristics, properties, and uses. The most familiar species, *Saccharomyces cerevisiae*, is used to prepare cultures adapted specifically for the baker, the brewer, and the manufacturer of primary food yeast. Yeast has been utilized since ancient times as a leavening property in baking, as a fermenting agent in alcoholic beverages, and as a medicine and food. The ability of yeast to change sugar to alcohol makes it indispensable to brewers and distillers.

The yeast organism is grown in a suitable medium and harvested when a sufficient crop of cells has appeared. In former times it was grown from *wort* (an Old English word meaning herb, plant, or root) prepared from grains mashed in water. More recently, primary yeast has been cultivated from refuse material.

—Charles E. Rogers

For Further Reference

Anderson, Arthur L., and James J. Kiser. *Introductory Animal Science.* Macmillan, 1963.

Bear, Firman E., editor. *Chemistry of the Soil* (2nd Ed.). Reinhold, 1964.

Bushey, Jerry. *Farming the Land: Modern Farmers and their Machines.* Carolrhoda Books, 1987.

Freeman, Orville L. *World Without Hunger.* Frederick A. Praeger, 1968.

Harrison, S. G., et al. *The Oxford Book of Food Plants.* Oxford University Press, 1969.

Leonard, Warren H., and John H. Martin. *Cereal Crops.* Macmillan, 1963.

Lowenberg, Miriam E., et al. *Food and People* (3rd Ed.). Wiley, 1979.

Mallis, Arnold. *Handbook of Pest Control; the Behavior, Life History and Control of Household Pests* (4th Ed.). MacNair-Dorland, 1964.

Porter, A. R., J. A. Sims, and C. F. Foreman. *Dairy Cattle in American Agriculture.* Iowa State University Press, 1965.

Revel, Alain, and Christophe Riboud. *American Green Power.* Johns Hopkins University Press, 1987.

Richey, C. B., editor. *Agricultural Engineers' Handbook.* McGraw-Hill, 1961.

Root, Waverly. *Food.* Simon & Schuster, 1980.

Taylor, Norman. *Taylor's Encyclopedia of Gardening, Horticulture and Landscape Design* (4th Ed.). Houghton Mifflin, 1961.

U. S. Department of Agriculture. *Science for Better Living; Yearbook of Agriculture, 1968.* U.S. Government Printing Office, 1968.

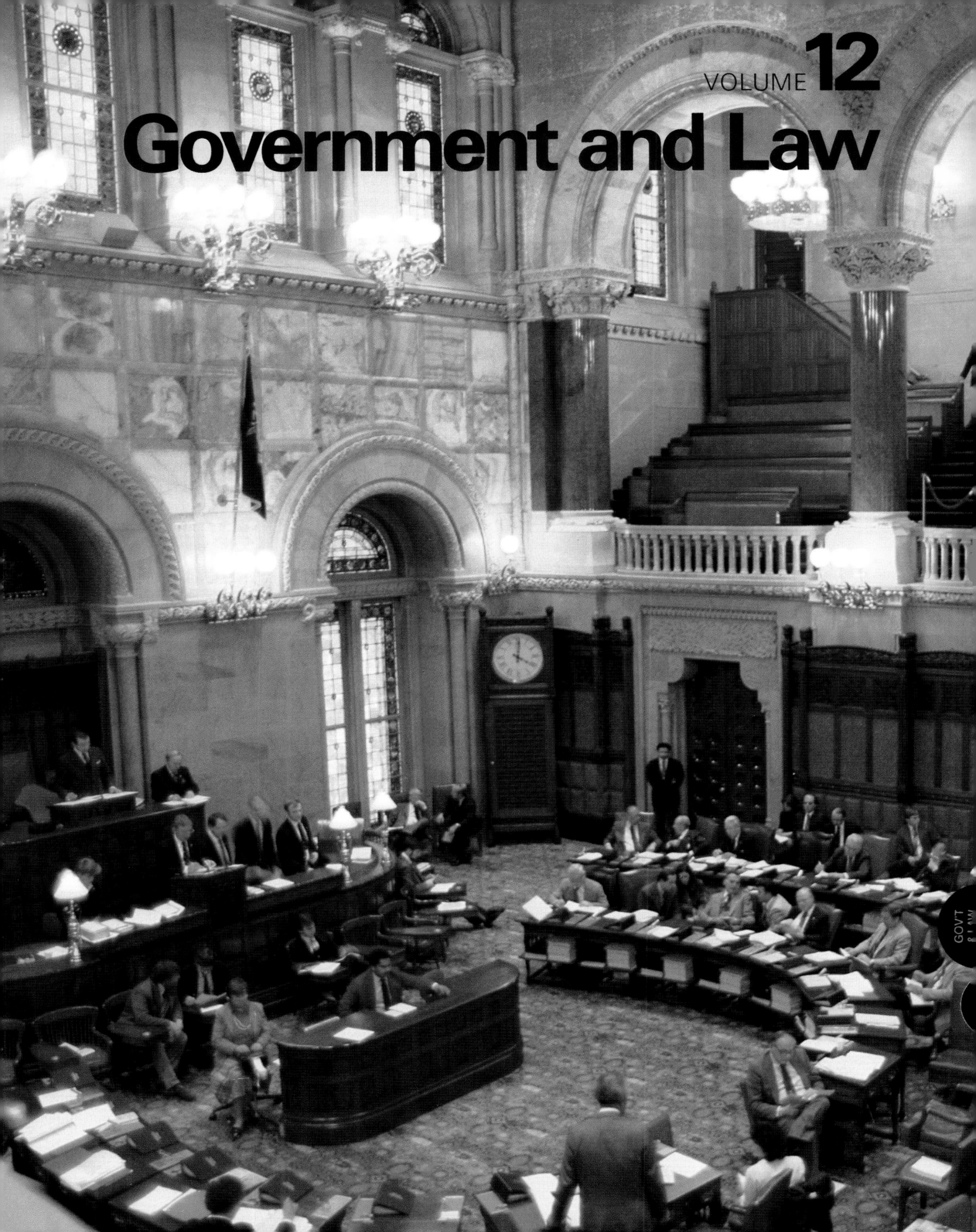

NATIONAL PARK SERVICE

THE GOVERNMENT OF THE UNITED STATES

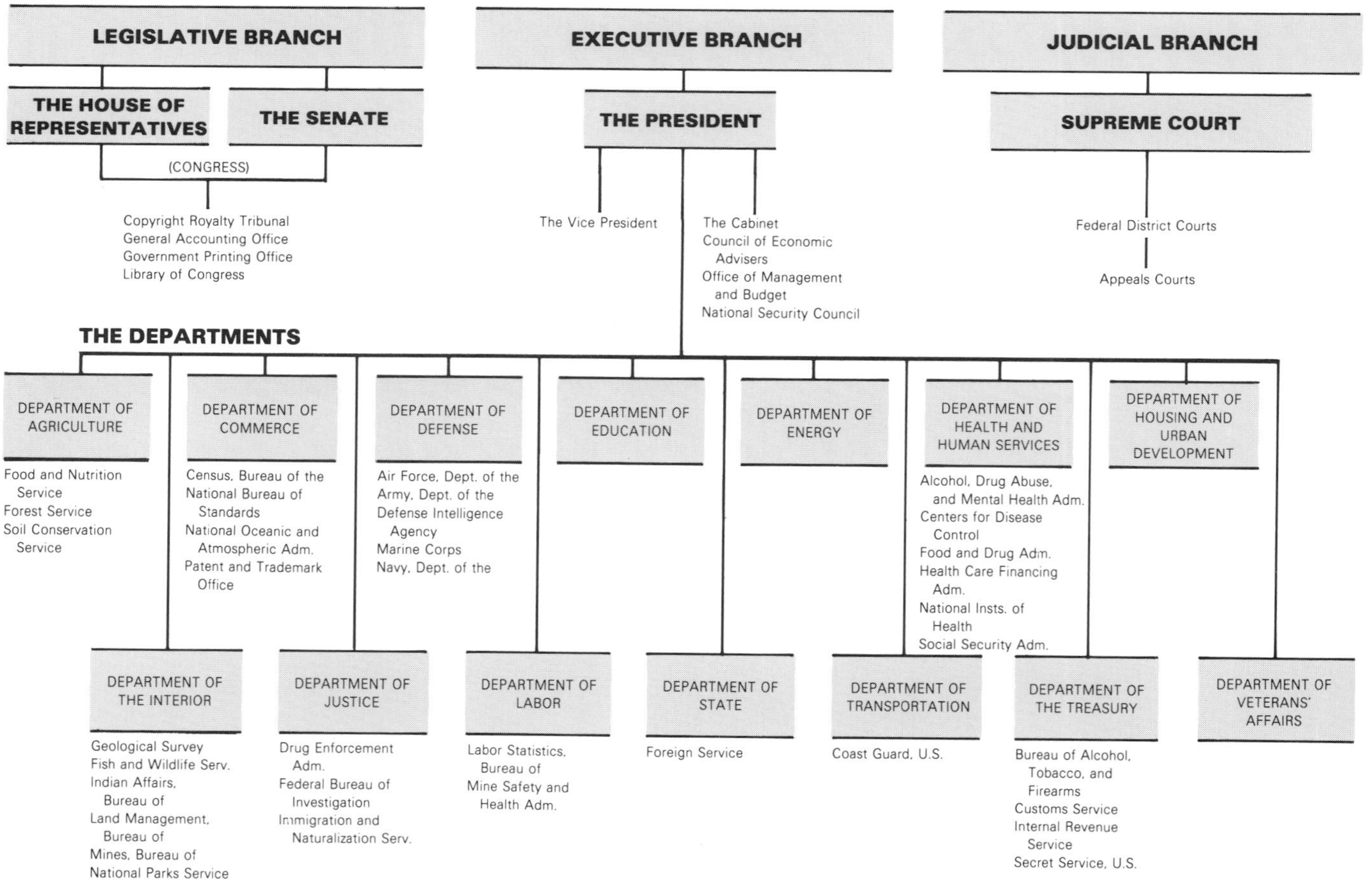

LEGISLATIVE BRANCH	EXECUTIVE BRANCH	JUDICIAL BRANCH

THE HOUSE OF REPRESENTATIVES	THE SENATE	THE PRESIDENT	SUPREME COURT

(CONGRESS)

Legislative Branch (Congress):
Copyright Royalty Tribunal
General Accounting Office
Government Printing Office
Library of Congress

Executive Branch:
The Vice President

The Cabinet
Council of Economic
  Advisers
Office of Management
  and Budget
National Security Council

Judicial Branch:
Federal District Courts

Appeals Courts

THE DEPARTMENTS

DEPARTMENT OF AGRICULTURE	DEPARTMENT OF COMMERCE	DEPARTMENT OF DEFENSE	DEPARTMENT OF EDUCATION	DEPARTMENT OF ENERGY	DEPARTMENT OF HEALTH AND HUMAN SERVICES	DEPARTMENT OF HOUSING AND URBAN DEVELOPMENT

DEPARTMENT OF AGRICULTURE
Food and Nutrition
  Service
Forest Service
Soil Conservation
  Service

DEPARTMENT OF COMMERCE
Census, Bureau of the
National Bureau of
  Standards
National Oceanic and
  Atmospheric Adm.
Patent and Trademark
  Office

DEPARTMENT OF DEFENSE
Air Force, Dept. of the
Army, Dept. of the
Defense Intelligence
  Agency
Marine Corps
Navy, Dept. of the

DEPARTMENT OF HEALTH AND HUMAN SERVICES
Alcohol, Drug Abuse,
  and Mental Health Adm.
Centers for Disease
  Control
Food and Drug Adm.
Health Care Financing
  Adm.
National Insts. of
  Health
Social Security Adm.

DEPARTMENT OF THE INTERIOR	DEPARTMENT OF JUSTICE	DEPARTMENT OF LABOR	DEPARTMENT OF STATE	DEPARTMENT OF TRANSPORTATION	DEPARTMENT OF THE TREASURY	DEPARTMENT OF VETERANS' AFFAIRS

DEPARTMENT OF THE INTERIOR
Geological Survey
Fish and Wildlife Serv.
Indian Affairs,
  Bureau of
Land Management,
  Bureau of
Mines, Bureau of
National Parks Service

DEPARTMENT OF JUSTICE
Drug Enforcement
  Adm.
Federal Bureau of
  Investigation
Immigration and
  Naturalization Serv.

DEPARTMENT OF LABOR
Labor Statistics,
  Bureau of
Mine Safety and
  Health Adm.

DEPARTMENT OF STATE
Foreign Service

DEPARTMENT OF TRANSPORTATION
Coast Guard, U.S.

DEPARTMENT OF THE TREASURY
Bureau of Alcohol,
  Tobacco, and
  Firearms
Customs Service
Internal Revenue
  Service
Secret Service, U.S.

LEGISLATIVE ASSEMBLY: GEOFFREY CLIFFORD/WHEELER PICTURES

Government and Law

CULVER PICTURES

K. JEWELL

WIDE WORLD PHOTOS

Whenever humans gather together, there is a need for government: a mutually understood system that will allow decisions to be made efficiently and allow a division of responsibilities to ensure the survival of the group. In this sense, even the most isolated family develops the basic elements of a government, and along with that organization comes a kind of law—rules for behavior that contribute to the survival and comfort of the group. Study of this kind of elementary government is a part of the social sciences and is of special concern to the disciplines of sociology and anthropology (see SOCIAL SCIENCES).

With the growth of more complicated societies—agricultural settlements, cities, and finally nation-states—government became a subject of great interest in itself. Among the earliest surviving written documents we find codes of law for early civilizations. The most famous of these are the Codes of Hammurabi, a king of Babylon around 1800 B.C.

Later, the leaders and thinkers of the city-states of Greece provided some of the most influential documents for all later studies of government as they sought to understand how a perfect state should be organized. The Roman Empire succeeded Greece as a great

power. Its representatives spread important ideas about civil law and administration to many parts of Europe and the Middle East.

The modern study of government began a thousand years after the fall of Rome, in the growing nation-states of Europe. The kings of these states claimed to rule by divine right and jealously guarded their powers against lesser nobles. But their arbitrary actions created opposition from noblemen, merchants, and small landowners. They justified their opposition by proposing new doctrines of government, stressing the rights of the governed to have a say in their government. Gradually, in a series of civil wars and revolutions, a variety of new governments were formed.

This volume is primarily concerned with government and law in today's world. It has four main sections. The first, "Theories of Government," surveys the major types of world governments. The second, "Intergovernmental Organizations," considers the United Nations and other modern efforts at cooperation among independent governments.

The third section, and by far the longest, is "United States Government." It outlines governmental structure and activities on the local, state,

and federal levels. In addition, it contains the full text of the U.S. Constitution, a table of U.S. Presidents, and a glossary of important federal agencies.

The fourth section discusses law. It explains the branches of the law, describes common court procedures, and provides a glossary of common law terms.

Other information on government can be found in other sections of the *Volume Library*. In each regional volume (ASIA AND AUSTRALASIA, EUROPE, etc.) entries on individual countries show the country's form of government and its political history. The histories and political subdivisions of the United States and Canada are treated at length in UNITED STATES AND CANADA.

The volume SOCIAL SCIENCES describes sociological and anthropological approaches to government and ways in which the social sciences are applied to government operations. Activities of government in such areas as business, agriculture, and education are further described in volumes concerned with those subjects. In addition, the volume PEOPLE contains brief biographies of many important political leaders and thinkers. See the INDEX (volume 28) for additional references to government and law.

THEORIES OF GOVERNMENT

A government is a group or organization that is responsible for making decisions and carrying out policy for a larger group. This general definition applies to governments of churches, business corporations, labor unions, social clubs, and other organizations. A government's responsibilities are usually formally defined in a set of laws, though these responsibilities may amount to no more than increasing membership and income or maintaining the buildings or social programs of the organization.

The government of a country fits this definition, but three additional characteristics must be added. First, a national government is *sovereign*: either there is no authority higher than the government, or the government rules in the name of an ultimate authority. In the United States, for example, formal sovereignty belongs to the people; they delegate their sovereign power to the government every four years.

Second, a national government exercises sovereignty *within a specific territory*. Third, every sovereign government has the ultimate power of *coercive force*: in extreme situations, it can use physical force to compel citizens or political subdivisions to accede to its rulings.

Such a sovereign government is called a State. In much of the world the word government may also refer to those presently in power, for example, "the Labour government" in Britain or "the Mitterand government" in France. In the United States, the word administration is more common, as in "the Roosevelt administration" or "the Republican administration."

A State exercises its powers within the restraints of a constitution or body of laws. These may be written or unwritten, easily changed or rigid. The laws may apply to all residents equally or there may be exceptions, privileges, and burdens for various groups and classes. Social customs and expectations play a large role in determining the power of the State and the application of the laws. Even in the United States, which has a written Constitution and a long tradition of written law, a large body of custom further defines what the government may or may not do.

DIPLOMACY TO SNOW REMOVAL: *modern government is responsible for a wide variety of tasks.* Left, *President Reagan greets a Saudi Arabian leader.* Right, *a New York City sanitation team cleans the streets during a blizzard.*

Why Government?

Different kinds of government are expected to perform different tasks but, roughly speaking, all governments are founded to carry out certain essential duties. The Preamble to the United States Constitution provides a convenient way to think about the various purposes of government. Those purposes are
- "to form a more perfect union"— coordinate resources
- "establish justice"— mediate between citizens
- "ensure domestic tranquility"— protect citizens
- "provide for the common defense"— conduct foreign affairs
- "promote the general welfare"— provide services for citizens
- "secure the blessing of liberty"— promote prosperity.

Coordination of resources.

Before a government can do anything else, it must coordinate the resources of the nation. It can do this in many different ways, from appealing to the population's self-interest to using force. By granting honors (titles, medals, privileges) and patronage (jobs, monopolies), governments are able to call on the talents and energies of capable administrators and specialists and to encourage citizen responsibility and generosity. Through appeals or propaganda, governments can mobilize the population to help repel invaders, provide relief after natural disasters, or make major sacrifices for the good of the whole nation.

Through the power to tax, governments can take financial resources from one group and use them to benefit the whole (defense spending in times of war) or another group (the unemployed). Through the right of eminent domain, a government can take title to private land (in most cases with "just compensation") and put it to use for roads, reservoirs, or schools. Finally, a government can use armed force, if need be, to take land, money, or people to carry out the tasks it believes necessary.

Mediation.

Perhaps the first task of the earliest government was to settle disputes within the society. Any society, no matter how well ordered, has to deal with conflicting interests within it. For example, conflicts between citizens, between citizens and corporations (including local and regional governments), between corporations themselves, or between any of these groups and the State must have means for resolution.

Mediation is accomplished first through laws and regulations that define the rights and duties of each segment of the society with respect to the other segments. Since law must be interpreted, the government establishes courts to hear disputes and resolve them in a way that supports the interests of the society as a whole.

Because it is better to enforce laws before a violation causes some injury or inequity, governments set up a variety of enforcement bodies—from highway police to tax auditors—to remind citizens of their duties. Public knowledge of penalties for violating laws or obligations serves as a deterrent.

Protection of citizens.

Another task of early governments was to ensure civil order, protecting the weak from the strong and the law-abiding from the lawless. It is for this purpose that the State insists on a monopoly of coercive force. A store owner who shoots a robber will be tried for homicide and may be punished for taking the law—the use of coercive force—into his own hands.

In order to further ensure domestic tranquility, governments establish police forces, criminal courts, and prisons to enforce criminal laws. Violations range from petty misdemeanors, such as "public drunkenness" and "disturbing the peace," to more serious crimes, such as "inciting to riot," murder, and treason. These serious offenses may be punishable by death, the State's ultimate penalty.

Foreign affairs.

The final purpose of early governments was to deal with foreign governments through diplomacy and war. Diplomacy seeks to advance national interests through the peaceful resolution of disputes and the making of alliances (economic, cultural, or military). Diplomacy may include negotiations to improve inter-national order and cooperation in matters ranging from mail delivery and currency exchange to control of disease and of nuclear power.

A sovereign government reserves to itself all rights to deal with other sovereign governments. A private person or corporation in one country may not make any agreement with a foreign government without the approval of its own government. This approval may be given in advance for many activities, but it can be withdrawn without notice. The U.S. government, for example, may abruptly suspend a contract between IBM and the Soviet Union for the sale of a special computer. The government need not compensate IBM for any loss it may suffer as a result.

When peaceful methods for settling disputes are exhausted, a sovereign State claims the right to settle disagreements by force of arms and to counter with armed force any threat to its territory or vital interests. A government may impose special taxes and forcibly draft manpower to defend the nation. It may confiscate supplies and housing for troops and commandeer civilians to work on special defense projects.

These government powers were a major issue in the development of modern democracy. Kings did not usually have enough money to wage war on their own. They had to appeal to wealthy nobles and merchants or else confiscate what they needed. Too often, however, the kings' wars were not in the national interest; they served only the kings' private or dynastic interests. Nobles and merchants came to resent military adventures at their expense and began to refuse to cooperate unless they were consulted in advance. This was the beginning of the demand that there be "no taxation without representation." It was also the basis of the U.S. constitutional provision that only Congress may declare war.

Provide services for citizens.

In modern times, governments have increasingly come to recognize that the State is strengthened if it takes some responsibility for supporting the poor, improving public health, and educating all citizens. In the past, such activities were usually left to religious, charitable, and communal organizations, and to the family. But since 1900, promoting the general welfare has become a major activity of the State in most Western countries. A vast array of government regulations and agencies have developed to carry out this task.

Activities in this area range from the regulation of working conditions to the provision of subsidized housing and financial support for the poor, the unemployed, and the disabled. Most governments today require a certain number of years of school attendance and some specify in detail what is to be taught. Most governments also set educational or training standards for professions (law, medicine) and crafts (welding, carpentry). Another body of regulations seeks to ensure that food is of good quality and uncontaminated, that sanitary conditions are maintained, and that dangerous products are not sold to the public or released in the environment.

Many societies today have also come to feel that wide differences in wealth damage the general welfare and add to social disorder. They hold that great wealth and poverty are not simply the result of differences in talent, hard work, and thrift, but are also caused by larger social forces that ought to be controlled by government so that all may have an equal opportunity to enjoy the best. Therefore, taxation in some nations is designed not just to finance the government and keep the poor from starving, but also to redistribute wealth by reducing the income of the rich and using it to provide the less favored with free or inexpensive housing, medical care, legal services, education, and other benefits.

Promotion of prosperity.

In most modern democratic countries, "the blessings of liberty" have usually been taken to mean the freedom to pursue wealth and to exchange goods and ideas. In authoritarian systems, the free exchange of goods and ideas is often seen as a disorderly process that is detrimental to prosperity, equality and justice, public order, and the security of the State.

To promote prosperity, governments build and maintain the economic infrastructure of the country: highways and railroads to transport goods to markets, power networks to run machinery, and research and communications networks to develop and publicize improved production methods and materials. (The U.S. Agricultural Extension Service is a very successful example of such government-sponsored research and communication.)

Governments may provide special benefits to protect vital economic activities from market fluctuations and imbalances (farm subsidies or tariffs to penalize cheap foreign products). Governments have also developed elaborate systems to protect the rights of discoverers, inventors, thinkers, and manufacturers to profits from their work (patent and copyright law, trademark regulation).

Finally, the entire economic process of production, trade, and finance usually comes under some degree of government regulation. This is to discourage cutthroat competition, monopolies, and practices that might disrupt the smooth running of the economic system by giving one group unfair advantage and power.

Elements of Government

All governing can be divided into three parts: executive, legislative, and judicial. Regardless of the kind of government—totalitarian, democratic, or mixed—every government makes laws (legislative), carries them out (executive), and interprets them in individual cases (judicial). These functions may be separated, as in the United States; partly unified, as in Great Britain, where the Parliament is both legislative and executive; or unified, as in the Politburo of the Communist Party of the Soviet Union.

In the history of government, these elements have seldom been completely unified by one ruler, and they have seldom been altogether separate. Effective government requires both leadership and cooperation. When power is divided among too many groups, there is no leadership to carry out major, and often unpopular, projects that would benefit all. Totalitarian rulers, on the other hand, lack the knowledge and self-restraint necessary to encourage the free cooperation of people to achieve a common purpose. Attempts to establish either extreme have been short-lived and often disastrous.

Most governments, therefore, are mixtures in which the elements of government are more or less spread among several groups and institutions. These bodies may be centrally controlled, as in totalitarian and authoritarian governments, or they may act relatively independently, as in democratic systems. Even in the United States, where the Constitution spells out a sharp separation of powers, the President has considerable judicial and legislative power, the Congress now and then takes over some executive functions, and the Supreme Court occasionally makes new laws.

Executive. The executive develops policy and makes decisions. This role is usually played by the head of government and his or her advisers. The executive defines problems, outlines government policy toward problems, and decides on solutions. During this process, the executive may be influenced by demands from interested parties. The solutions may have to be submitted to a legislature for approval, but the executive usually has the advantage of starting the process and defining the issues. Sometimes, a legislature or court may take the initiative, in which case it can be seen as playing an executive role.

The second role of the executive is the administration of laws. To accomplish this, most executive bodies have a relatively large bureaucracy that analyzes laws, writes regulations to govern their applications, and sets up

CONSTITUTION		
EXECUTIVE	**LEGISLATIVE**	**JUDICIAL**
● Propose plans, policy ● Make day-to-day decisions ● Administer and enforce laws	● Make laws ● Set long-term policies ● Respond to individual and group concerns	● Interpret existing laws, policies ● Apply laws to individual cases

THREE AREAS OF GOVERNMENT: *these terms were first used in the 1700's, but political thinkers had used similar concepts for centuries.*

the machinery (report forms, review boards) to see to it that the laws are applied. The decisions made in this process of application can dilute or strengthen the effects of laws. On occasion, a bureaucracy may virtually nullify a law or, through its regulations, create a new one (administrative law).

Legislative. The legislative element engages primarily in debate over policy—which policy to adopt and how best to put it into law. This debate may be carried out in a special body designed for that purpose—a legislature, congress, parliament, or council of advisers. The debate may also take place among a narrower group of leaders, or within the mind of an autocrat. Whatever the forum—whether public debate or interior monologue—the debate is influenced by forces in the society as a whole. Even the most powerful dictator cannot make decrees that directly strike at powerful forces that can effectively oppose him. So the views of the economic community, the army, and other more or less powerful groups must usually be taken into account. The bureaucracy and the masses also cannot be ignored. Within each of these general groups, special interest groups (regional, economic, social, etc.) must be considered.

In public debate in a legislature, these interest groups will usually speak for themselves directly or through elected representatives. An open process of compromise and conciliation usually determines the shape of the resulting laws. In less demo-

cratic systems, the debate may turn on strategy: how to carry out an action by dividing, immobilizing, or manipulating potential opposition.

Judicial. The judicial element of government exists to apply laws to specific cases. This application of law may be a relatively open and public process in established courts operating according to a detailed set of procedures within a legal tradition. It may also be a private and often arbitrary process that depends entirely upon an autocrat's needs at the moment. An autocrat may well ignore the public law if its application in a specific case is seen as a threat to the State.

In most countries, the judiciary is best understood as an extension of executive power. Legal decisions are usually made in accordance with the general policy aims of the executive and with particular concern for domestic tranquility. Judicial officers have an interest in the preservation and welfare of the State and are usually sworn to uphold its vital interests. Yet in some cases, courts may also act to protect individuals against arbitrary government action.

In the United States, the judicial branch also has the power of constitutional review. The Supreme Court can strike down a law or executive decree if it violates the Constitution, the basic law of the nation. Only in a very few other countries is such judicial power recognized in practice, though many countries have included it in their constitutions.

A powerful and fully independent judiciary is rare because courts have

TRADITION *may take the form of uniforms and group discipline, as with these Canadian Guards. Flags,* background, *are also potent symbols of political tradition.*

no real physical power of their own, usually depending on the executive to carry out judicial decisions. A determined executive, perhaps with the support of an aroused people and their legislature, could choose to ignore a significant court decision. This would restrict the court's power in other areas for years afterward. Thus, courts usually find it good politics not to challenge a strong executive. In the United States, the Supreme Court depends for its power on a strong tradition of support from all sections of society.

What Gives Government Its Authority?

If a State is to be both permanent and stable, it must be acknowledged as legitimate. Its citizens must recognize the State's authority and right to exercise its powers. In the United States, the State's authority is clearly defined in the Constitution, but where did the Constitution get *its* authority?

The sources of legitimacy are usually obscure, hidden in a mist of history, special circumstances, popular feeling, and, above all, time. Nevertheless, these sources can be roughly divided into three categories: tradition, ideas, and effectiveness.

Tradition. The most binding and powerful of these sources is tradition. Tradition has special strength because

it is associated with emotional attachments to family, religion, race, language, and folk history. Tradition appears to be spontaneous and timeless, the way of nature or the gods. "That's just the way things are," and "It's always been done that way," are the essential ingredients of tradition. In many societies, government and law are deeply rooted in religion and social custom.

Tradition is often expressed through symbols—flags, slogans, oaths, anthems, holidays, shrines (the Statue of Liberty, the Alamo), and public rites and ceremonies (a Presidential inauguration, a Fourth of July parade). In some cases a living person may serve as a powerful symbol of the authority of government—the Queen of England and other constitutional monarchs are still powerful symbols, even if their practical power is small. Symbols bring out feelings of solidarity with and loyalty to the government among the citizens of the State.

In many newly independent countries there are no effective symbols appealing to national solidarity. A government in that situation must continually struggle to maintain its legitimacy against the competing claims of tribes or other regions and their symbols. These governments often put a great deal of effort into glorifying their national leader or emphasizing unity in the distant past in order to create a strong tradition. Any new government that deviates greatly from the old must set to work creating new symbols to evoke feelings of solidarity and loyalty.

Objects of hatred often serve a short-term purpose in providing legitimacy.

In Iran in 1980, vilification of the shah and America served to legitimize a new government. In Hitler's Germany, a racial division—the "virtuous" Aryans and the "degenerate" Jews—served to legitimize and justify the excesses of the Nazi regime.

Whether based on religion, race, or custom, national traditions and symbols arouse emotion and create feelings automatically, without requiring thought or learning on the part of the populace. The traditions need not be rational, moral, or practical, only generally accepted and, usually, old. Even those symbols that originally had a practical or moral purpose lose that purpose in the popular mind over a period of years. In the United States, for example, the Bill of Rights calls forth spontaneous feelings of unity and loyalty. But when citizens actually read what the Bill says, they tend to disagree, sometimes violently, over the meaning, morality, and practicality of its contents.

Ideas. A second important source of authority is ideas. The teaching of Jesus, "Give unto Caesar that which is Caesar's and unto God that which is God's" (Mark 12:17), probably helped to undermine the authority of pagan Rome and to increase that of the early bishops. The Protestant Christian idea that individuals are responsible directly to God tended to deprive bishops and monarchs of special status and to justify popular participation in government.

In the Declaration of Independence, America's Founding Fathers justified the Revolution and the new government with ideas they said were "self evident": that all men are created equal and are granted certain "unalienable" rights by the highest authority of all, God. Among these rights is the right to change or abolish any government that tries to take those rights away.

In Russia, the Bolshevik revolution and the establishment of a Communist government was justified with the ideas of Karl Marx. Marx taught that the natural process of history would lead inevitably to the overthrow of monarchs and capitalists, to government by the working class, and finally to the "withering away" of the State. Lenin, the leader of the revolution, added an amendment. Between the time of the revolution and the decay of the State, he said, the working class would govern through a "revolutionary vanguard" that would establish a "dictatorship of the proletariat" through the Communist Party and its leaders.

The governments of modern Western democracies base much of their authority on the ideas of Jeremy Bentham. In 1789, this Englishman argued that the test of a moral society is whether it strives to create the "greatest good for the greatest number" of people. Using this idea, people argued that a legitimate government had to consult with the greatest number of people and had to seek the maximum social benefit for all citizens.

Effectiveness. Finally, governments gain and lose legitimacy simply on the basis of their effectiveness. The ancient Chinese conception of the Mandate of Heaven puts the idea in mythological form. According to the Chinese, a ruler or an entire dynasty receives the Mandate of Heaven to govern. Under that mandate prosperity in the land will increase, wars will be few and successful, sickness mild, and floods rare. If the people became poor, war and violence common, and sickness and natural catastrophes frequent and devastating, it was clear to the Chinese that the ruler's Mandate of Heaven had been withdrawn. Disobedience to the central government then became common, and the regime could be overthrown. If a new leader could restore order, this would be a sign that a new mandate had been granted to him.

In the 1950's, to cite another example, France's parliamentary government showed itself unable to make important decisions; it faced the loss of France's most important colony (Algeria) and the possible revolt of the French army. The government collapsed peacefully, and the French soon voted overwhelmingly for a new constitution that took many powers away from the parliament and granted them to a greatly strengthened presidency. (The Russian revolution sprang from the inability of the old czarist government to carry out *any* task of government effectively.)

On the other hand, the legitimacy of reasonably effective governments is seldom questioned. Great Britain, for example, has been a limited monarchy for nearly 300 years. During that time the government has adapted to a variety of different circumstances. It has not always been perfectly efficient or responsive, but it has performed the essential functions of government—including the modifying of its own procedures. As a result, there has been no serious governmental crisis since 1688.

Measuring Government

There are many different ways to measure governments. Political scientists study their economic policies, administrative organization, cultural aims, and many other aspects. But there are two scales of measurement that seem especially important, and they will help to characterize existing governments into several distinct types.

The first measure is the kind of authority the government claims for itself. Some governments, including that of the United States, claim only *conditional* authority. Others, including those of China, the Soviet Union, and many newly independent nations, claim *unconditional* authority.

The second measure has to do with the way the government is organized. Who makes policies and carries them out? When the policies are made and imposed from the highest level, the government is *centralized*. When policy making is done at many levels (local, regional, national) and by many groups, the government is *decentralized*.

Conditional authority.
A government that claims conditional authority is one that does not claim to represent a final truth. It sees itself as a means to some purpose besides its own power. Such a government depends for its survival on the approval of its citizens. These citizens, either as individuals or as groups, hold basic values that the State cannot usually examine or condemn. The primary role of the State is to protect the rights and values of its citizens.

In a crisis, a government with conditional authority may change its organization and methods to suit new situations. Since the government claims no ultimate values of its own, it must remain ready and willing to change to meet the needs of its individual citizens. Thus, its effectiveness and flexibility is essential to its survival.

The most serious danger faced by a government claiming conditional authority is a dissatisfied citizenry that wants the State to adopt a set of religious or philosophical principles and claim *unconditional* authority (as happened in Germany in 1933). For a State with conditional authority to survive, its citizens must be tolerant of people with widely varying views and must be willing to support a government that offers no ultimate answers.

Unconditional authority.
Where government bases its authority on a sacred tradition or body of ideas (ideology), we can describe the government's authority as *unconditional*. The leaders of such a State and most of its citizens must believe that the ultimate values of the State are part of the unchangeable nature of things.

The best example of unconditional authority can be seen in the government of ancient Egypt. The Pharaoh was not simply installed by the gods, he was a god. To doubt the Pharaoh's right to rule was as unthinkable as to doubt that the sun was hot. A current example of unconditional authority can be seen in the government of the Soviet Union. The ideas of Marx and Lenin are accepted there as scientific

descriptions of the truth. To doubt these truths in the Soviet Union is to be either criminal or insane.

When a government claims unconditional authority, the State is the source of all values. Individuals have no real rights; only the society as a whole has rights, and they are defined by the State. Sacred tradition or ideology decree the ultimate goals of government, and those goals justify the use of any means the State wishes to take to achieve them. The government can do anything it chooses—except change its basic ideology.

In face of a serious crisis, such a government cannot ask if its ideology is wrong. Serious failure must be blamed on outside forces—angry gods, demonic powers, foreign intrigue, or domestic conspiracy and sabotage. Thus, governments claiming unconditional authority do not have to be as effective as those whose authority is more limited. Effectiveness becomes important only in extreme situations, when massive disorder, hunger, or overwhelming incompetence cause a majority of the people to doubt the State's ideology.

Centralized government.
Governments that impose policies on their citizens are *centralized*. Such governments decide what constitutes a problem and choose the remedy. A centralized government manages society.

THE PHARAOH of Egypt had the unconditional powers of a god.

COURTESY THE BROOKLYN MUSEUM

Modern centralized governments usually try to control all phases of society. They may decide who will go to college and, in some cases, what will be studied. They decide what will be manufactured, where it will be manufactured, and how much it will cost at the retail level. They may even decide what each town's budget will be and what the money will be spent on. People learn to look to the top for a definition of their problems and for solutions. The government requires its citizens to support and obey major government policies.

Decentralized government.

Governments that permit policy to be made at the regional or local level are *decentralized*. Such governments allow individuals and local authorities as much freedom of choice as possible on the assumption that the free play of many different interests will result in the most effective policies.

The hallmark of decentralized government is the existence of many centers of independent authority—states, cities, community bodies, business and labor organizations, political parties, special interest groups, and individuals. The United States and other federal governments are good examples of decentralized systems. They are less easy to direct than centralized regimes. Society helps to manage a decentralized government; by contrast, society is managed by a centralized government.

Kinds of Government

Measuring governments on these two scales—centralized vs. decentralized and unconditional vs. conditional—we can divide them into four basic kinds:

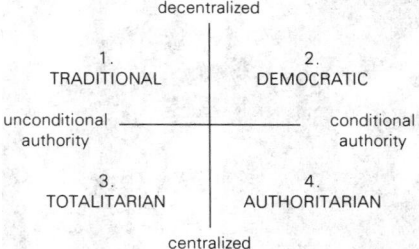

Type 1 we will call *traditional* government; it is represented by most of the governments in recorded history, including many ancient empires and all feudal governments. Type 2 includes the modern *democratic* governments. Type 3 are *totalitarian* governments, and type 4 are *authoritarian* governments, represented today especially by the new countries of Africa and Asia.

It is important to note that there may be considerable variation in any of these categories, and that a particular government may change over a period of time. For example, a demo-

cratic State may become authoritarian over specific issues (such as race in South Africa). During wartime, it may adopt a fixed ideology (for example, anti-Japanese ideology in the United States in 1942 "justified" the internment of Americans of Japanese origin). A totalitarian State may move toward decentralization or toward acknowledgment of individual citizens' needs and desires (for example, the emphasis on consumer goods in the Soviet Union in the 1960's).

But no State can stray far from its basic nature. Political or economic pressure may push a government toward its opposite pole, but if this shift is extreme, the State becomes unstable and severe political turmoil will result. A shift from conditional to unconditional authority or *vice versa* can cause civil war (Russia 1918–1920 or France 1789–1795, respectively). A shift from centralized to decentralized government may cause revolution (America 1776–1781) or major social unrest and disorder (Poland 1980), while a shift from decentralized to centralized will bring severe political repression (Germany 1930–1935) if not civil war. Each type of government can operate only within certain *limits of variation*; a period of government weakness and intense political conflict follows any violation of those limits. Political scientists are particularly interested in the stresses caused by change from one of these forms to another.

RADICAL CHANGES IN GOVERNMENT *can produce violence and repression.* Left, *Chilean troops search suspects during the military coup in 1973.* Right, *Poles protesting military repression in 1981 seek to disarm soldiers by putting flowers in the muzzle of their tank.*

TRADITIONAL RULERS *include divine right kings such as Louis XIV of France and modern corporatist rulers such as Francisco Franco of Spain (ruled 1936–1975).*

Traditional government.
Decentralized government based on unconditional values, usually religious, is the most common form of government in world history. From the empires of the ancient Near East through the Roman Empire to early czarist Russia, more or less decentralized governments have been the most common.

Populations under such governments were seldom politically active, leaving government to local or institutional leaders such as nobles, provincial governors, priests, or tribal chiefs. These political leaders brought the society's problems to the attention of the sovereign and attempted to influence his decisions to the benefit of their constituencies.

Kings and emperors were seldom able to control and direct all the operations of the government, even when the government was autocratic. True centralized government was all but impossible: communication was slow and moving an armed force over any great distance even slower. Under these circumstances, it was practical for the central authority to delegate power to trusted administrators and accommodate local or institutional leaders. The unity of the State, in most circumstances, was based on shared religious values that frequently supported the spread of power among local groups.

The prime example of this kind of government in today's world is in Saudi Arabia. The monarch is recognized as the supreme guarantor of Islamic virtue, but even with all modern means of communication, he cannot centralize his power. Islam, the state religion, is relatively egalitarian: before Allah, all men are equals and the king has no special standing. The

faith also requires the existence of an independent body of religious scholars and judges who hold wide-ranging powers. Finally, the Saudi kingdom grew from alliances between the Saudi tribe and other tribes in the Arabian Peninsula. The leaders of the other tribes continue to hold the primary allegiance of their peoples; they deal with the Saudi king from secure bases of authority.

Feudalism. The Saudi government replaced a feudal system in which there was no central government. Feudalism is the extreme form of the unconditional decentralized type of government. It has appeared in many places—notably Japan—but the usual model is that of Europe in the Middle Ages (about 500 to 1500 A.D).

Feudalism is based on a rigorously defined caste system (nobility, clergy, artisans and merchants, peasantry). Position and land are held by grant from a lord (nobleman) to whom the vassal (a lesser noble) swears an oath of loyalty and owes goods and services. In an ideal feudal system, all the land would be the property of the king, who would parcel it out among the top nobility, who, in turn, would grant much of it to lesser nobles. Each major landholder was sovereign in his own domain and ruled according to local custom. The primary function of the central government was to defend the land, and each noble in the system was obliged to provide troops and supplies for that purpose. In practice, the greater nobles were free to do nearly as they pleased, shifting their allegiances to suit their own advantage and often withholding payment of goods and services to coerce the monarch into granting additional land or privileges.

In times of crisis, feudalism proves unstable. The central government

gains greater power and the powers of the nobility are gradually curtailed. In Europe, the growing merchant class in the late Middle Ages demanded an end to arbitrary local taxes on goods in transit. They also called for a regular currency and protection from highway robbery. At the same time, increased conflict between church and state began to erode the religious underpinnings of feudalism's authority. People began to seek secular and centralizing solutions to government inefficiency.

Kings took advantage of this trend. They began to claim a "divine right" to rule, thus deriving their authority directly from God rather than from the church. They next began to "nationalize" the church, asserting greater authority over it in their realms. This development went furthest in England, where the monarch became head of the church and denied the pope any jurisdiction whatsoever. Finally, the Protestant Reformation brought a new emphasis on self-control, community responsibility, and effective stewardship over wordly resources. This prepared the ground in Northern Europe for the rise of governments based on law rather than religion, and on individual representation.

Corporatism. The old religious bases of the feudal system remained in Southern Europe. There, the idea of unconditional decentralized government called "corporatism" developed in the 1900's. Corporatists criticized modern secular governments as too materialistic and too reliant on the individual. They stressed ideal relationships between family members, workers, employers and workers, and the people and government.

In the ideal corporatist State, functional groups rather than individuals would be represented in government. Trade unions, employer associations, the clergy, and organizations of writers, teachers, farmers, etc., would be responsible for the interests and welfare of their members and exercise some authority over their lives. The independence of these organizations would serve as a check against arbitrary actions by the central government.

In practice, however, attempts to establish corporatist governments, as in Italy under Mussolini (1922–1943) and in Spain under Franco (1936–1975), have produced dictatorships with many features of centralized government.

Christian democracy, Christian socialism, and democratic socialism are more democratic variations on the corporatist idea. These movements criticize modern secular governments for reducing human relationships to rational arrangements of self-interest. They say that unrestrained individualism results in the exploitation of the poor by the rich and in the violation of religious or moral values for the sake of expedience.

In these Christian (almost exclusively Roman Catholic) and socialist variations on democracy, the State intervenes to protect religious and moral values through laws designed to achieve greater economic equality and security. These socialist experiments have taken place within democratic governments of secular societies such as Sweden and West Germany. The result has generally been a growth in public welfare systems. But the societies have remained democratic and relatively individualistic.

Democratic government.

Modern Western democratic systems developed out of traditional governments. England was one of the first societies to go through this evolution and remains the best example of a process that was repeated in most Western European countries. The English experience was also passed on to its former colonies: the United States, Canada, Ireland, Australia, New Zealand, and South Africa, and in a lesser degree, to India and Anglophone black Africa.

The evolution of democracy. The Magna Carta (1215) is often taken to be the beginning of the democratic impulse. In fact, the Magna Carta was a conservative document designed to keep the king from abridging the rights and privileges of feudal barons. Nevertheless, the document is an early example of limiting the arbitrary use of central power. It guaranteed certain rights to a few subjects, and set a valuable precedent.

By the end of the reign of Elizabeth I (1603), the idea of national sovereignty was firmly established. Divided allegiances, in which an Englishman might be a vassal to both the French and English monarch because he held land from both, no longed existed. Englishmen were part of a sovereign England that had national interests above and beyond the interests of any individual Englishman, including the monarch. After Elizabeth's time, political debate in England turned not on whether king or Parliament was sovereign, but on which was to exercise the power of the sovereign nation.

That debate was largely settled in 1688–1689. Parliamentary leaders put the absolutist king, James II, to flight. In his place, they installed a foreign prince (William) and his English royal wife (Mary) to take the throne under strict conditions. The new English monarchs gave up the right to suspend laws and were unable to impose taxes without the consent of Parliament. Parliamentary supremacy was never again a major issue.

From 1689 to 1832, political debate turned on how parliamentary powers should be exercised and on how members of Parliament should be chosen. During this period, the English developed the institution of a cabinet of

DEMOCRATIC GOVERNMENT *owes much to English history. The first constitutional monarchs were William and Mary, shown here as parliamentary leaders offer them the crown. Below,* the chamber of the House of Commons in Canada is based on the English model in design and purpose.

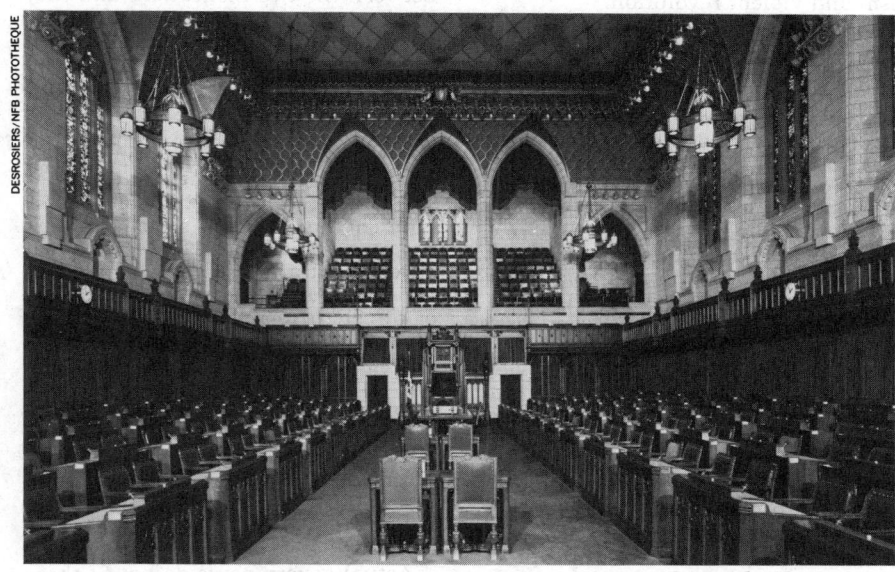

ministers to manage policy debates and oversee government administration. To control this new institution and subject it to the will of Parliament, coalitions of special interests, that is, political parties, began to form. They sought to take majority control of Parliament, then select a cabinet of party members. The party leader became the prime minister. Cabinets were required to refer major decisions back to Parliament for approval, thus making the cabinet responsible to the parliamentary majority.

Prime ministers gained considerable power, but they were strictly accountable to Parliament. If a majority of Parliament voted against the prime minister on an important matter, he was required to dissolve Parliament, resign, and call for new elections.

During this period, the English electorate was comprised of a small percentage of the country, made up of aristocrats, landed gentry, and their political hirelings. Seats in Parliament represented not people but traditional districts, many of them sparsely populated and left over from feudal days. Seats representing the sparsely populated "rotten boroughs" were openly bought and sold, while major new industrial centers were not represented at all. Agitation for fairer representation began in the 1760's. Finally, in 1832, a reform bill extended the franchise to most of the middle class and abolished some of the worst inequities of representation. Subsequent reform bills extended the vote to the working class and corrected most of the inequities in the representation of districts. By 1885, England had installed a rational system in which communities were represented in proportion to their population.

Prerequisites of democracy. These democratic developments were dependent on several social factors. The first prerequisite of democracy is an interested and well-informed electorate. Second, individuals must feel free to consider alternatives rationally and to choose those that serve their own interests; they must be relatively free of undue pressure to vote according to the dictates of landlords, employers, churches, parties, or community customs. Third, a high degree of tolerance for minority opinion must have developed and such opinion must be protected by custom and/or law. Fourth, individuals and groups with political aims must perceive that they have a fair chance of success within the democratic system and little or no chance at all outside of it. Political customs must be so entrenched as to make the rewards for moderation and patience greater than the price of such adventurist alternatives as terrorism and violent revolution.

If a democracy fails to develop any one of these prerequisites, it is in danger of instability. For example, government secrecy and press censorship may keep voters from informed considerations of their self-interest and force them to vote as dependents of other, more powerful, forces. Suppression of minority opinion not only removes potentially useful alternatives from consideration, but suggests that the majority opinion has fixed authority. Although democracies must not tolerate the political adventurism that invites demagogues and ambitious political or military leaders, they also must not rule out particular political creeds for fear that their adherents will feel they have nothing to lose by resorting to extremist tactics.

Forms of democracy. Democratic governments come in two forms—parliamentary and presidential. In parliamentary government as practiced in England, Israel, West Germany, Italy, Scandinavia, and other countries, parliament is supreme. The head of parliament, the prime minister, is the chief executive officer or head of government, but he is responsible to parliament and serves at its pleasure. There is little or no division of powers between the executive and legislative branches of the government. The head of State, whether monarch or president, is little more than a figurehead, a national symbol.

In a presidential system, as in the United States and France among other countries, the president is the chief executive officer, head of government *and* State, and wields a great deal of power. He is elected by the people and is responsible only to them. The legislature is also responsible to the people. There is a sharp division of powers

VOTING *is an important responsibility in any representative government. This voter is voting in a local election in Ottawa, Ontario, the capital of Canada.*

between the two institutions and they may come into serious conflict over policy, a development that is impossible in the parliamentary system.

Democratic governments may also be classified according to their administrative structure. In a *unitary* government, regional and, in some cases, even local government comes under the direct control of the central government. In a federal system, powers not expressly granted to the national government are reserved to the lower jurisdictions, which are not controlled or directed from the center. Most democracies in Europe (West Germany excluded) are unitary; most democracies outside of Europe are federal. Another variation, the *confederal* system, in which sovereign units create a weak central government to deal with a very limited range of common problems, is highly unstable and very rare; it has often been a transitional stage on the way to a federal system.

Actual governments do not fit these forms of classification perfectly. A government may have a formal constitution that appears to make it a federal system, but it may be very close to a unitary government in practice if the federal government exercises a great deal of control over state and local options. Canada, for example, has a constitution that calls for a fairly strong federal government, but in fact, time and custom have created a system that is nearly confederal.

Totalitarian government.

While the fixed centralized form of government has existed in the past in some theocratic states (ruled by God or a priestly order), the truly totalitarian state is a modern development. True centralization, especially in a large

country, depends on rapid communication and transportation systems.

The hallmark of a totalitarian government is an elaborate ideology, a set of ideas that gives meaning and direction to the whole society. To date, totalitarianism has always been associated with a new government that has arisen after a revolution or the achievement of national independence. Totalitarian governments have so far appeared in two forms—democratic centralist (communist) and fascist (national socialist).

Democratic centralism (communism). The concept and practice of democratic centralism was developed by V. I. Lenin, leader of the Russian Bolshevik revolution, to ensure the control of the Communist Party. Government is charged with the task of transforming the material and mental condition of the society in order to create the ideal socialist system. Government legitimacy is derived from this high moral aim and any excesses of the totalitarian system are justified by it.

This goal is sought under the leadership of an elite group, the party, the "vanguard of the proletariat," which exercises national sovereignty in the name of the working class. The party in turn is led by the Politburo (political bureau), a small group that selects its own members. The Politburo, in turn, selects a first secretary or secretary-general who holds all the reins of party and government power.

Democratic centralist systems are marked by such an overlap of party and government roles that it makes sense to speak of the party-state. The secretary-general of the party can and often does serve as the president and/or prime minister of the government. Many Politburo members are also

All candidacies for political office are approved by the party. All publications and other sources of information and opinion are managed by active party members. Every military unit has a political officer, a party member. Every key economic organization—factory, trade union, distributor, major retailer—has party members as employees in key positions. This system, called *nomenklatura* in the Soviet Union and its satellites, is designed ostensibly to make sure that all elements of society are working properly to fulfill the goals laid down by the party leadership. In practice, its function is to see that nothing escapes party control. It also provides employment for obedient, but otherwise mediocre, party members.

In the Soviet Union, a few noncommunist institutions, notably the Russian Orthodox Church, are allowed to function, but they have been stripped of most of their physical and human resources and are closely supervised by the government. Where a communist party-state has been forced to compromise with a rival institution, as in Poland with the Roman Catholic Church, the party-state is far less able to formulate and carry out a coherent policy. The rival institution is able to promote a competing ideology and to protect anti-party activists.

Two other communist nations, Yugoslavia and Hungary, have sharply decreased the centralized management of industry. While these party-states still closely control all political activity, factory management (which includes workers as real participants) is free to plan production and set prices according to its best understanding of the relatively free market. In both countries, *nomenklatura* no longer plays a significant role in industry or commerce.

This development may in time create a class of relatively independent, energetic, and able entrepreneurs who will demand a greater role in political policy making within the party-state. This trend could be a serious challenge to communism.

Fascism (National Socialism). While communism traces its legitimacy to a modern "scientific" theory of political economy, the National Socialist (Nazi) government of Germany (1933–1945) appealed to ancient feelings of racial and national identity. The emotional attraction of its elemental ideas of Aryan racial supremacy and German national destiny gave the Nazi Party a great following. It did not have to exercise quite the degree of control required in communist parties in East Europe. The Nazis retained a free market economy, though industry and commerce were highly regulated, primarily in preparation for war. Both Catholic and Protestant churches continued as relatively strong organizations, and active Christians were left alone as long as they raised no serious

TOTALITARIAN GOVERNMENT: *Nikolai Lenin was an important theorist of totalitarian communism as the dictator of the Soviet Union from 1919 to 1921. Even today, Soviet citizens wait for an hour or more to visit Lenin's tomb in Moscow.*

members of the cabinet. Members of the legislature are members of the party or its associated organizations.

Ideally, all policy debate originates and is settled in the Politburo. Decisions made there are referred to the central committee of the party and to the legislature (in the Soviet Union, the Supreme Soviet) for approval. The function of both groups is not to debate or amend the decisions, but to demonstrate the "obvious" correctness of the decisions by approving them unanimously. This is the extent of the "democratic" in democratic centralism.

In practice, both the party and the government contain a variety of special interest groups (industry, agriculture, military, police, scientists, ethnic groups, etc.) whose views may be considered in the Politburo and may influence the final shaping of policy. On the other hand, if the secretary-general manages to totally dominate the Politburo, as Stalin did, he may arrive at decisions with little or no consultation.

In the ideal form of democratic centralism, the ruling party permits no competing institutions or sources of independent power. As in other totalitarian systems, the party's main line of defense against such a development is an elaborate network of police surveillance and informers. The party also inhibits the development of independent power by placing loyal party members in important positions in all institutions.

AUTHORITARIAN GOVERNMENTS *include those of Napoleon III of France (ruled 1852–1870) and such modern dictators as Anastasio Somoza of Nicaragua (ruled 1967–1979).*

objections to the existing regime.

On the other hand, all mass media and educational institutions came under strict management by the party-state. Labor was reorganized into militarylike groups. Military leaders who showed the least signs of independence were retired. Leaders of non-Nazi political parties and other political institutions were silenced by fear, imprisoned, or killed. The German legislature was used only occasionally to rubber-stamp the regime's decrees.

Fundamental to the Nazi system was the Leader Principle (*Führer Prinzip*) expressed in the slogan "One People, One State, One Leader." Führer Adolph Hitler was the sole source of power, the only policy maker. His personal viewpoints were official state philosophy: his book (*Mein Kampf*) and speeches were treated as holy writ. Press, film, and radio trumpeted his praises. Army officers were required to take an oath of loyalty not to the nation or the government, but to Hitler personally. The national salute and even common greetings—hello, goodby—were replaced by "Heil Hitler."

The excesses of the system were justified by the racial ideology. According to the Nazi view, the "master race," the Aryans (a vague concept that included most of the peoples of northwest Europe), were being threatened and undermined by the "slave races" (mostly Slavs) and the "degenerate races" (Jews and gypsies). Communism was a Slavic-Jewish conspiracy, and capitalism was controlled by a secret Jewish cabal. It was the German national destiny to conquer the "slaves" and rid Europe of the "degenerates." This theory "explained" the necessity for the extensive and brutal

police network, the massive war effort, and the extermination camps.

Both Italian and Spanish fascism had many features in common with Nazism, particularly the idolization of the national leader. Both fascist governments, however, glorified a particular period of national grandeur (the Roman and Spanish empires) rather than a myth of racial supremacy. In neither State did the party acquire the degree of control that the Nazis did in Germany. The Spanish party, the Falange, was sharply downgraded in importance after the mid-1940's. In both Spain and Italy, the Roman Catholic Church remained a powerful independent force; in Spain, the Catholic faith was a fundamental element of the regime's ideology.

Authoritarian government.

Authoritarian regimes are centralized like totalitarian regimes, but they lack an ultimate tradition or ideology that could provide the government with a sound base of authority.

In many respects, modern authoritarian regimes resemble totalitarian states. Power is concentrated in the hands of a single person or small group, and there is often a single major party that may be a small elite or a mass party with an elite leadership. If there is a legislature, it is powerless. The election system does not allow for public policy debate or competition between candidates.

An authoritarian regime usually permits some independent institutions—churches, labor unions, political organizations, etc.—providing they pose no immediate threat to government security. Such institutions are kept under control by random and

often arbitrary repression. In many cases, the regime cannot totally repress such institutions because the people are more loyal to the institutions than to the government.

Another characteristic of instability is a high incidence of political corruption. All political systems have problems with corruption, but without any ideology or tradition to restrain them, authoritarian leaders may use the State simply as a means to get rich or to establish personal empires.

Among governments in the authoritarian class are many European monarchies of the 1800's that had lost their religion-based authority as society became more secularized; modern military regimes (for example, South Korea, Brazil, Syria); and some civilian-led governments, particularly in former colonies.

Many of the governments in former colonies are authoritarian. At first, most of them claimed their authority from the ideology of national liberation. But when these governments failed to bring prosperity and social order, they lost their claim to unconditional authority. Some other new nations began hopefully as decentralized democratic systems, but they lacked the prerequisites that ensure the success of democracy. Their governments have been forced to revert to the centralized style and techniques of the former colonial masters.

Authoritarian governments are inherently unstable. They find it extremely difficult to manage an orderly succession of power or to work out regular systems for managing disagreements within the ruling elite. On the death of a leader or the development of a crisis, the regime faces collapse. In Europe, such governments usually evolved into representative, decentralized governments. The electorate then conferred legitimate (if conditional) authority on its leaders in periodic elections. Notable exceptions to this trend were in Germany and Italy, where the collapse of authoritarian systems led to the triumph of totalitarian ideologies.

Throughout the former colonial world, including Latin America, nations that have not been able to develop the prerequisites for democracy are faced with a choice between continuing instability or the adoption of a fixed ideology to legitimize the national government. The resurgence of an Islamic political ideology (beginning in Libya in 1969) is one approach to this dilemma; the spread of socialist ideology is another. The democratic option is often unrealistic, because of widespread poverty, illiteracy, and ethnic intolerance.

The future of such unstable authoritarian governments is one of the great problems of the 1980's. Continued small wars and revolutions threaten to involve major powers in this struggle.

—George DeLury

INTERGOVERNMENTAL ORGANIZATIONS

Just as the U.S. government consists in part of amalgamated state governments and federal representatives, so the world is in part governed by amalgamations of countries in intergovernmental organizations. Social, industrial, and agricultural patterns seldom conform to national boundaries, so intergovernmental organizations are needed to address concerns shared by nations. This need has increased in modern times because of the "shrinking world" created by 20th-century improvements in communication and transportation.

The most famous intergovernmental organization is the United Nations. Although the UN has become the most important forum for international discussion, there is a continuing need for organizations devoted to specialized needs or to specifically regional concerns.

The modern world has produced a network of customs organizations,

THE SEA *is a major concern of intergovernmental agencies because its use affects nearly all peoples.*

commodity groups, development commissions, monetary funds, and regional banks. The majority of these organizations address economic interests only, but there are a number of diplomatic and defense organizations that, like the UN, are international in their membership and essential to world welfare. Along with the UN, the most important of these organizations are described below.

A detailed description of the UN appears first because its complex structure provides the pattern followed by most intergovernmental organizations. Most international bodies have a central council similar to the General Assembly of the UN, economic and social councils, administrative secretariats, and defense arms, like the UN Security Council. Following the section on the UN, individual intergovernmental organizations appear under world or regional headings according to their membership.

The United Nations

The United Nations is the largest, most important, and most famous of all intergovernmental organizations. Some nations, such as Switzerland, choose to remain outside the UN, while other states, such as San Marino, have no real need for membership. For all practical purposes, the current membership of 156 nations establishes the UN as a truly global community.

The organization designates Arabic, Chinese, English, French, Russian, and Spanish as its official languages. Its actions are so sweeping that they now affect all regions of the world. The UN draws worldwide attention when national leaders gather at its headquarters in New York for debate, or when its peacekeeping forces enter a combat zone. The UN also operates numerous research, economic, and humanitarian programs that make a large contribution to world welfare with long-term, relatively unpublicized activities.

The idea of a League of Nations was proposed first by U.S. President Woodrow Wilson during World War I. The organization did come into existence, but it failed to attract sufficient membership for effective operation. The continuing need for a community of all nations became apparent again at the outbreak of World War II. The origins of today's UN can be traced to the Inter-Allied Declaration of June 12, 1941. The declaration called for worldwide "economic and social security"; it was signed by five British Commonwealth countries and eight European governments forced into exile by the war.

The spread of the Axis threat, and the U.S. entry into World War II later in 1941, increased the urgency for a world organization and broadened the base of interested countries. On January 1, 1942, 26 Allied nations gathered in Washington, D.C., and issued the United Nations Declaration, the first document to employ the title of the current organization. Toward the end of the war, peace talks led by the United States, the United Kingdom, and the Soviet Union began to focus on specific proposals for the structure of a world organization.

The key concern was insuring democratic participation by all countries while providing the superpowers with rights commensurate with their international stature. At the Dumbarton Oaks Conference in 1944, and the Yalta Conference in 1945, the problem

was resolved by granting permanent membership in the Security Council to the Big Five: China, France, the United States, the United Kingdom, and the Soviet Union.

The United Nations Charter that emerged from these conferences was signed by 50 nations at the San Francisco Conference on June 26, 1945. Poland was not represented, but it signed the charter soon after and is considered one of the 51 original members. The U.N. charter has been amended many times in subsequent years by a process similar to that used to amend the U.S. Constitution. The charter took effect on October 24, 1945, the date now celebrated as United Nations Day.

At the first General Assembly meeting in London, on January 10, 1946, a U.S. invitation to establish permanent UN headquarters in New York City was accepted. The first building in the huge UN complex was completed in 1951. The entire headquarters enjoys special diplomatic legal status, and it has its own international post office.

The UN has four stated goals: to maintain international peace and security; to develop friendly relations among countries; to achieve international cooperation on economic, social, cultural, and humanitarian problems;

ORGANIZATION OF THE UNITED NATIONS

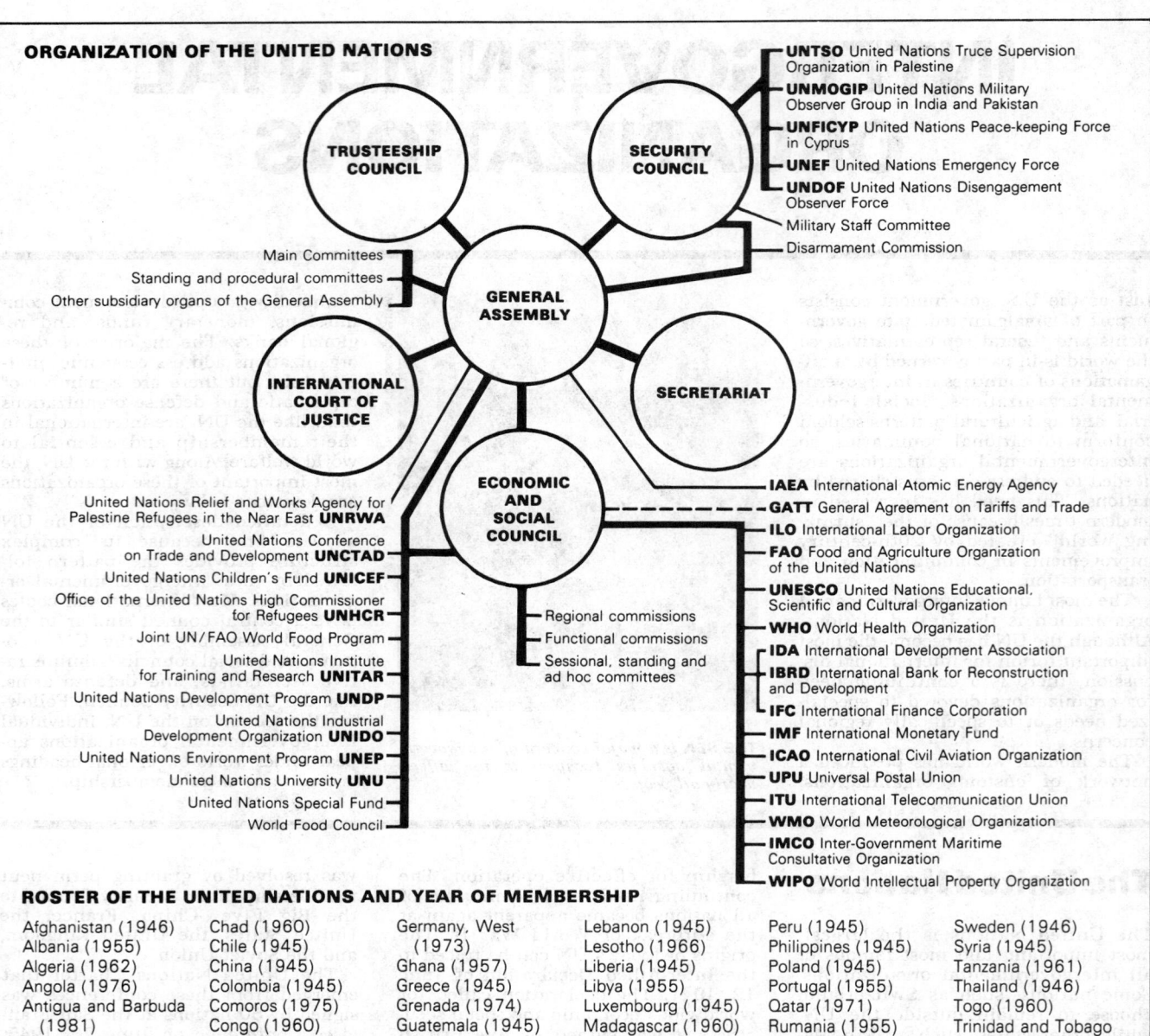

UNTSO United Nations Truce Supervision Organization in Palestine
UNMOGIP United Nations Military Observer Group in India and Pakistan
UNFICYP United Nations Peace-keeping Force in Cyprus
UNEF United Nations Emergency Force
UNDOF United Nations Disengagement Observer Force
Military Staff Committee
Disarmament Commission

TRUSTEESHIP COUNCIL

SECURITY COUNCIL

Main Committees
Standing and procedural committees
Other subsidiary organs of the General Assembly

GENERAL ASSEMBLY

INTERNATIONAL COURT OF JUSTICE

SECRETARIAT

ECONOMIC AND SOCIAL COUNCIL

United Nations Relief and Works Agency for Palestine Refugees in the Near East **UNRWA**
United Nations Conference on Trade and Development **UNCTAD**
United Nations Children's Fund **UNICEF**
Office of the United Nations High Commissioner for Refugees **UNHCR**
Joint UN/FAO World Food Program
United Nations Institute for Training and Research **UNITAR**
United Nations Development Program **UNDP**
United Nations Industrial Development Organization **UNIDO**
United Nations Environment Program **UNEP**
United Nations University **UNU**
United Nations Special Fund
World Food Council

Regional commissions
Functional commissions
Sessional, standing and ad hoc committees

IAEA International Atomic Energy Agency
GATT General Agreement on Tariffs and Trade
ILO International Labor Organization
FAO Food and Agriculture Organization of the United Nations
UNESCO United Nations Educational, Scientific and Cultural Organization
WHO World Health Organization
IDA International Development Association
IBRD International Bank for Reconstruction and Development
IFC International Finance Corporation
IMF International Monetary Fund
ICAO International Civil Aviation Organization
UPU Universal Postal Union
ITU International Telecommunication Union
WMO World Meteorological Organization
IMCO Inter-Government Maritime Consultative Organization
WIPO World Intellectual Property Organization

ROSTER OF THE UNITED NATIONS AND YEAR OF MEMBERSHIP

Afghanistan (1946)
Albania (1955)
Algeria (1962)
Angola (1976)
Antigua and Barbuda (1981)
Argentina (1945)
Australia (1945)
Austria (1955)
Bahamas (1973)
Bahrain (1971)
Bangladesh (1974)
Barbados (1966)
Belgium (1945)
Belize (1981)
Benin (1960)
Bhutan (1971)
Bolivia (1945)
Botswana (1966)
Brazil (1945)
Brunei (1984)
Bulgaria (1955)
Burma (1948)
Burundi (1962)
Byelorussia (1945)
Cameroon (1960)
Canada (1945)
Cape Verde (1975)
Central African Republic (1960)

Chad (1960)
Chile (1945)
China (1945)
Colombia (1945)
Comoros (1975)
Congo (1960)
Costa Rica (1945)
Cuba (1945)
Cyprus (1960)
Czechoslovakia (1945)
Denmark (1945)
Djibouti (1977)
Dominica (1978)
Dominican Republic (1945)
Ecuador (1945)
Egypt (1945)
El Salvador (1945)
Equatorial Guinea (1968)
Ethiopia (1945)
Fiji (1970)
Finland (1955)
France (1945)
Gabon (1960)
Gambia (1965)
Germany, East (1973)

Germany, West (1973)
Ghana (1957)
Greece (1945)
Grenada (1974)
Guatemala (1945)
Guinea (1958)
Guinea-Bissau (1974)
Guyana (1966)
Haiti (1945)
Honduras (1945)
Hungary (1955)
Iceland (1946)
India (1945)
Indonesia (1950)
Iran (1945)
Iraq (1945)
Ireland (1955)
Israel (1949)
Italy (1955)
Ivory Coast (1960)
Jamaica (1962)
Japan (1956)
Jordan (1955)
Kampuchea (1955)
Kenya (1963)
Kuwait (1963)
Laos (1955)

Lebanon (1945)
Lesotho (1966)
Liberia (1945)
Libya (1955)
Luxembourg (1945)
Madagascar (1960)
Malawi (1964)
Malaysia (1957)
Maldives (1965)
Mali (1960)
Malta (1964)
Mauritania (1961)
Mauritius (1968)
Mexico (1945)
Mongolia (1961)
Morocco (1956)
Mozambique (1975)
Nepal (1955)
Netherlands (1945)
New Zealand (1945)
Nicaragua (1945)
Niger (1960)
Nigeria (1960)
Norway (1945)
Oman (1971)
Pakistan (1947)
Panama (1945)
Papua New Guinea (1975)
Paraguay (1945)

Peru (1945)
Philippines (1945)
Poland (1945)
Portugal (1955)
Qatar (1971)
Rumania (1955)
Rwanda (1962)
St. Kitts-Nevis (1983)
St. Lucia (1979)
St. Vincent (1980)
Samoa (1976)
São Tomé and Principe (1975)
Saudi Arabia (1945)
Senegal (1960)
Seychelles (1976)
Sierra Leone (1961)
Singapore (1965)
Solomon Islands (1978)
Somalia (1960)
South Africa (1945)
South Yemen (1967)
Spain (1955)
Sri Lanka (1955)
Sudan (1956)
Surinam (1975)
Swaziland (1968)

Sweden (1946)
Syria (1945)
Tanzania (1961)
Thailand (1946)
Togo (1960)
Trinidad and Tobago (1962)
Tunisia (1956)
Turkey (1945)
Uganda (1962)
Ukraine (1945)
Union of Soviet Socialist Republics (1945)
United Arab Emirates (1971)
United Kingdom (1945)
United States (1945)
Upper Volta (1960)
Uruguay (1945)
Vanuatu (1981)
Venezuela (1945)
Vietnam (1977)
Yemen (1947)
Yugoslavia (1945)
Zaire (1960)
Zambia (1964)
Zimbabwe (1970)

and to harmonize the actions of nations to realize these goals.

The UN consists of five principal bodies: the General Assembly, the Security Council, the Economic and Social Council, the Trusteeship Council, and the International Court of Justice. Each of these bodies is described below, with some indication of their many subsidiary organs. There are also a number of autonomous specialized agencies and related agencies within the UN, some of which are also described below. The total number of subsidiary organs and agencies changes from year to year according to need; in 1980 the UN maintained approximately 125 such bodies, many of them working in collaboration with each other.

The General Assembly.
The General Assembly is the most prominent of all UN bodies. It has the primary responsibility for harmonizing the actions of member nations; for this reason it has been given the broadest powers by the original UN Charter. All nations in the UN are represented by a single vote in the General Assembly. The Assembly meets at a regularly scheduled session each year to consider resolutions and to oversee the UN budget. Special sessions may also be convened on single topics by a majority vote of member nations or at the request of the Security Council.

At its regular meeting, the General Assembly elects its own officers and approves an agenda by assigning topics for discussion to main, procedural, or standing committees. Recommendations on these topics are then returned from committee to the General Assembly for a vote. On most recommendations, a simple majority is required for approval; very important topics, such as peace resolutions or the admission of new members, require a two-thirds majority for approval.

The General Assembly regularly elects representatives to the other principal UN bodies: the ten nonpermanent members of the Security Council, the 54 members of the Economic and Social Council, the elected representatives to the Trusteeship Council, and (with the Security Council) the 15 judges of the International Court of Justice. It also appoints the UN secretary-general on recommendations from the Security Council.

To realize its humanitarian, economic, and research goals, the General Assembly operates fourteen subsidiary organs that range from temporary committees to permanent administrative boards. The UN Office of the High Commissioner for Refugees (UNHCR) addresses humanitarian needs. It has been assisting displaced people since 1949. Economic assistance is provided by the UN International Children's Emergency Fund (UNICEF), the UN Development Program, and the World

Food Council, among other organs. Important research activities sponsored by the General Assembly are carried out by organs such as the UN Fund for Population Activities and the UN University, both of which make publications available to the public. These subsidiary organs usually pave the way for the more visible activities of the entire General Assembly.

The Security Council.
The first stated goal of the UN is to maintain peace, and this is the function of the Security Council. Its membership of 15 includes permanent representation from the world's chief military powers (China, France, the United States, the United Kingdom, and the Soviet Union) and ten representatives from other countries elected to two-year terms by the General Assembly.

The Security Council's jurisdiction extends to any threat to peace identified by any UN nation. It is empowered to act to preserve peace on behalf of the entire UN, and all member nations are required to cooperate with such actions.

Decisions on procedural matters within the Security Council require nine affirmative votes. All other matters, however, require nine affirmative votes including five from the permanent members. Hence, a permanent member can veto a resolution supported by 14 other Security Council members. Security Council members that are a party to the dispute in question are required to abstain from voting.

By right of the original UN Charter, the Security Council operates a Military Staff Committee and a Disarmament Commission. Its most visible subsidiary organs, however, are peacekeeping forces composed of military personnel from member nations. Peacekeeping forces to maintain truces are currently stationed in Cyprus, on the India-Pakistan border, and on Israel's borders with Syria, Egypt, and Lebanon.

The Economic and Social Council.
The Economic and Social Council (ECOSOC) is the body given primary responsibility for the economic, social, cultural, and humanitarian goals of the UN. The original UN Charter established an ECOSOC membership of 18 to provide assistance to European and Asian areas damaged by World War II. Since then, ECOSOC activities have become more complex; for this reason the membership has been increased by amendment to 54 nations. One-third of the seats are assigned each year by a vote of the General Assembly, with elected members serving three-year terms.

Because so many UN activities touch on UN responsibilities, the

ECOSOC has a complex network of ties to other UN bodies, especially the General Assembly. There are also a number of subsidiary organs that meet regularly and report to the ECOSOC; these are classified as standing committees, functional commissions, and regional commissions.

Standing committees are convened at the opening of ECOSOC sessions if their services are required. Eight standing committees are currently active, including the Committee on Natural Resources, the Committee on Science and Technology, and the Committee on Crime Prevention and Control.

Functional commissions address specific concerns of a permanent nature; there are currently eight functional commissions. These include the Commission on Human Rights, which monitors civil liberties; the Commission on the Status of Women, which promotes equal rights; and the Commission on Transnational Corporations, which protects countries from exploitation by foreign investors.

Regional committees study the economic needs of specific areas of the world and make recommendations to individual countries as well as to the ECOSOC. There are currently five regional commissions, for Africa, Europe, Latin America, western Asia, and Asia and the Pacific.

The Trusteeship Council.
The original UN Charter provides for a Trusteeship Council to administer territories until they are economically and socially prepared for complete independence. In 1945 there were eleven trust territories. Since then, ten have become independent countries; the last to become independent was Papua New Guinea, in 1975, formerly called New Guinea and administered by Australia.

The only remaining trust territory is the Trust Territory of the Pacific Islands, which is administered by the United States. These islands require special consideration because they have been designated strategic military areas. Recently, however, Belau, the Northern Marianas, Micronesia, and the Marshall Islands have received preliminary mandates for independence. When negotiations for independence are completed, the Trusteeship Council will become inactive until its services are again required.

By UN Charter the Trusteeship Council is composed of countries administering trust territories, all remaining permanent members of the Security Council, and "enough" representation from other UN members to provide a voice for smaller countries.

The International Court of Justice.
Commonly referred to as the World Court, the International

Court of Justice (ICJ) was created by the original UN Charter to encourage friendly relations between nations. It sits in The Hague, Netherlands, and is the only principal body of the UN not located in New York City. The court membership consists of 15 judges elected for renewable nine-year terms by vote of the General Assembly and the Security Council. In addition to all UN members, participants in the ICJ include the nonmember nations of Switzerland, Liechtenstein, and San Marino.

The jurisdiction of the ICJ extends to any matter submitted to it by participating countries. Verdicts, usually involving border disputes, are reached by a majority decision of the 15 judges. The decisions are binding on the nations involved; they can, however, be appealed to the Security Council.

Among other activities, the ICJ has been involved since 1950 in establishing the legal independence of Namibia, currently a western province administered by South Africa.

The Secretariat. The Secretariat is the central administrative body of the UN. Its chief officer is the UN secretary-general, who is elected to a five-year term by the General Assembly on recommendation of the Security Council. There are a number of other appointed officers, including secretaries-general, for departments such as legal affairs, political affairs, and economic and social affairs, and assistant secretaries-general for departments such as general services, financial services, personnel, and public information.

The Secretariat takes primary responsibility for overseeing UN budgets, which are approved by the General Assembly. The current UN budget of $1.25 billion is provided by allocations from member nations based on ability to contribute. The United States makes the largest contribution—25 percent of the total; there are many countries that make the minimum contribution of .02 percent of the total budget, or approximately $250,000.

It is crucial to the effective operation of the UN that the secretary-general, who reports to the General Assembly, provide objective leadership free of political allegiance. This objectivity was successfully maintained by the most prominent of past secretaries-general, including Dag Hammarskjöld of Sweden, U Thant of Burma, and Kurt Waldheim of Austria.

Specialized and related agencies. There are a number of autonomous international organizations operating under the auspices of the UN. Each has its own separate membership, budget, headquarters, and individually negotiated working

relationship with UN headquarters. The arrangement is beneficial because it increases UN activity without placing additional demands on its budget and because it opens UN diplomatic channels to small organizations that would be otherwise cut off.

There are currently 15 specialized agencies working in cooperation with the UN. Among the most prominent are the World Health Organization (WHO), devoted to improving health standards through the research of its 157-nation membership based in Geneva, Switzerland; and the International Bank for Reconstruction and Development (the World Bank), devoted to international financing through its 121-nation membership based in Washington, D.C. Other important specialized agencies include the World Meteorological Organization in Geneva, the Universal Postal Union in Berne, Switzerland, and the Food and Agriculture Organization (FAO) in Rome, Italy.

There are two international organizations with ties to the UN that have the special status of related organization. The first is the General Agreement on Tariffs and Trade (GATT), instituted by treaty in 1947 to regulate international commerce; the second is the International Atomic Energy Agency, established by the UN in 1956 to explore the potential of nuclear power plants.

Other Intergovernmental Organizations

The UN is the most famous intergovernmental organization, but there are a number of other important organizations that fulfill the same need for collaboration on concerns that cross national boundaries. Most intergovernmental organizations exist to serve the needs of a specific region, but there are some that are global in membership and activities.

Worldwide organizations. Groups with worldwide membership include one of the oldest intergovernmental organizations, the Permanent Court for Arbitration, dating from 1899, and one of the newest, the Nonaligned Movement, formed in 1961. There are also a number of worldwide monetary funds, development commissions, and customs organizations. The five organizations described below are representative of the political, defense, economic, and judicial functions of such bodies.

The Commonwealth. As the possessions within the global empire of the United Kingdom began to move toward independence, the need for a

body to encourage continuing cooperation among them became apparent. This need was first served by the dominion status granted to Canada and Australia in the 1800's, but the British Commonwealth was not formalized until December 31, 1931.

Originally consisting of six sovereign states and the mother country, the Commonwealth now includes the 46 nations that were once territorial possessions of the United Kingdom. Some former colonies, such as South Africa, have chosen not to join the Commonwealth, and some, like the Republic of Ireland, have withdrawn from it. British involvement in member states ranges from a ceremonial presence in some cases to complete control of defense and international relations in others. To supervise these various political relationships, a Commonwealth Secretariat was established at Marlborough House, London, in 1965.

The Nonaligned Movement (NAM). Because the modern political world has increasingly polarized toward either the United States or the Soviet Union, NAM was established to protect the rights of countries pursuing courses outside the realm of "bloc politics." Twenty-five such countries met for the first Conference of Nonaligned Heads of State in Belgrade, Yugoslavia, on September 1, 1961. Since then, membership in the organization, which has no fixed headquarters, has risen to 94, with twelve observer nations and eight guest nations bringing the total to 114. The organization functions through irregularly scheduled conferences.

The North Atlantic Treaty Organization (NATO). Formed by a treaty signed on April 4, 1949, NATO is a defense alliance that consolidated Western European and North American countries against the threat of the Soviet bloc. NATO has 15 member nations, all of them located in Europe except the United States, Canada, and Turkey. To foster the collective defense of its members, NATO operates a North Atlantic Council, a Military Committee, and a Defense Planning Committee, each with representation from all members. NATO also sponsors a variety of economic and technological agencies not specifically related to military defense.

Organization of Petroleum Exporting Countries (OPEC). Created on November 14, 1960, on the initiative of Venezuela, OPEC has become the world's most important commodity group because of the rapid increase of petroleum fuel prices in the 1970's. Most of the 13 member nations are located in Africa and the Middle East, but OPEC also includes Indonesia in Asia and Ecuador and Venezuela in South America. OPEC meets twice each year to address issues surrounding price regulation and equitable distribution of fuel oil.

NATO NATIONS	OPEC NATIONS
Belgium	Algeria
Canada	Ecuador
Denmark	Gabon
France	Indonesia
Germany, West	Iran
Greece	Iraq
Iceland	Kuwait
Italy	Libya
Luxembourg	Nigeria
Netherlands	Qatar
Norway	Saudia Arabia
Portugal	United Arab
Turkey	Emirates
United Kingdom	Venezuela
United States	
Total: 15	Total: 13

Permanent Court for Arbitration.

Dating from the first International Peace Conference at The Hague, Netherlands, in 1899, the Permanent Court for Arbitration became the preeminent world judicial body following its reorganization in a charter effective January 26, 1910. Its membership now numbers 74 nations, and it functions as an alternative legal body to the International Court of Justice of the UN. The great majority of international judicial decisions are now handled by the UN body, but the International Court's judges are still recommended to the UN by the Permanent Court for Arbitration.

Asian and Australasian organizations.

The intergovernmental organizations within Asia and Australasia consist primarily of island and coastal nations. These organizations have all been formed since World War II to face the actual or threatened destruction of the member nations.

Intergovernmental organizations are especially useful in this region because a large part of the geography of the area consists of small land masses separated by great expanses of Pacific Ocean. In addition to the important political organizations described below, the region is also connected by numerous commodity groups, such as the Asian and Pacific Coconut Community, and regional banks, such as the Asian Development Bank.

The Tripartite Security Treaty Between the Governments of Australia, New Zealand, and the United States (ANZUS).

The ANZUS pact was signed on September 1, 1951, in San Francisco. It was devised as part of the post-World War II security arrangements for the South Pacific, and it binds the member nations as allies in case of attack within the region by an outside country. War has never been a threat, but the pact serves as an effective forum for political discussions among the three members. The need for continued annual meetings was reaffirmed by the members in 1976.

Association of Southeast Asian Nations (ASEAN).

ASEAN was formed in Thailand on August 9, 1967, by the current membership of Indonesia, Malaysia, the Philippines, Singapore, and Thailand. It replaced the Association of Southeast Asia as a body for the economic, political, and cultural cooperation of the noncommunist nations in this subregion of Asia. The foreign ministers of member nations occupy seats on a standing committee that supervises the activities of specialized agencies devoted to areas such as agriculture, transportation, and social development. Since a major summit meeting in 1976, ASEAN has been actively interested in becoming a bilateral forum by improving relations with communist countries, such as Vietnam, in Southeast Asia.

The South Pacific Commission (SPC).

The SPC was established by a treaty signed in Australia on February 6, 1947. Its purpose is to oversee the economic and social welfare of Pacific territories and the policies of colonial authorities such as the United States, the United Kingdom, and Australia. Membership currently consists of 18 Pacific dependencies. Recent activities have included an evaluation of the members' educational facilities.

The South Pacific Forum (SPF).

Because the South Pacific Commission is prohibited by its original treaty from entering defense debates, the SPF was organized in New Zealand in 1971 to address this particular concern of South Pacific nations. Membership consists of Australia, New Zealand, and eleven smaller island nations. The most important efforts of the SPF to date have focused on banning nuclear tests and weapons in the South Pacific.

Middle Eastern and African organizations.

Africa and the Middle East have been subject to severe sovereignty and border disputes throughout most of modern history. In Africa, a receding colonial empire left new nations with sudden responsibility for long-standing domestic and international problems. In the Middle East, the creation of the State of Israel in 1948 disrupted the configuration of the very center of the region. Consequently, many African and Middle Eastern nations have joined into intergovernmental organizations to protect their sovereignty and to address shared domestic concerns.

In addition to the principal diplomatic bodies described below, there are within the region a number of development commissions, such as the West African Economic Community, and commodity groups, such as the African Groundnut Council. The Organization of Petroleum Exporting Countries (OPEC) is often associated with this region, but it was in fact formed on the initiative of Venezuela and includes Indonesia among its members; it is described above as a world organization.

Organization of African Unity (OAU).

Newly independent African nations first joined in the Conference of Independent African States in 1958. Their common concerns led to the creation of the OAU on May 25, 1963, at Addis Ababa, Ethiopia, which remains OAU headquarters. The current membership of 50 African nations excludes neocolonial states such as South Africa. The principal OAU body is the Assembly of Heads of State, consisting of all members; its many subsidiary commissions and agencies have a selected membership.

The primary goal of OAU is to protect the rights of native African people by ending institutionalized racial discrimination. In recent years, the OAU has served as the principal African forum for political discussions of international scope, one of which resulted in OAU protests against Cuban troops in Angola.

The Council of the Entente.

Consisting of countries formerly within French West Africa, the Council of the Entente is a subregional organization formed on May 29, 1959, to assist in the development of Benin, the Ivory Coast, Niger, and Upper Volta. Togo became the fifth member in 1966. Its activities focus on the shared development of port, railroad, telecommunications, and tourist facilities.

League of Arab States (LAS).

The LAS was established on May 22, 1945, to protect Arab rights after the end of British colonial influence in the Middle East. At present, the LAS has 21 members, including the Palestine Liberation Organization (PLO). Egypt was excluded in 1980 because of its peace treaty with Israel, which is not a member or participant. In addition to fostering political and cultural ties between member nations, the LAS is deeply involved in discussions on the borders of Israel and the future of Palestinian refugees displaced by the creation of Israel.

Organization of the Islamic Conference.

Founded by a summit meeting of Muslim leaders on September 25, 1969, the Islamic Conference is intended to increase solidarity among countries joined by Islamic religions but separated by geographic, economic, and political barriers. Membership consists of 40 countries in Africa and the Middle East, Malaysia in Asia, and the Palestine Liberation Organization. The Islamic Conference has a tripartite structure consisting of a Conference of Foreign Ministers, a Conference for Economic Cooperation, and a Secretariat. Its most important activities to date have been the creation of the Islamic News Agency in 1972, the Islamic Development Bank in 1974, and the Islamic Solidarity Fund in 1977.

European organizations.

The European countries share so many political, social, and economic concerns that they are sometimes described as essentially a confederation of states. Plans for formalizing such a confederation have been proposed, but they have never approached acceptable form. The European countries rely, instead, on an extensive system of intergovernmental organizations to address their common needs. These include the sort of commodity groups, development commissions, and subregional pacts common elsewhere in the world, as well as unique river commissions for the Rhine, Danube, and Moselle rivers, and the European Space Agency, the only regional organization of its kind.

The Council of Europe (CEUR).

The first and most consequential of the many "United States of Europe" proposals, the CEUR was established by an agreement signed by ten Western European nations on August 3, 1949, in London. The membership has risen since to 21 nations, including all major European countries not affiliated with the Soviet Union. The CEUR operates with a Committee of Ministers, including all members, a Parliamentary Assembly, with proportionate representation, and a central Secretariat. Defense concerns are excluded from the CEUR's deliberations. CEUR's most important recent activity was the ratification of human rights resolutions, which led to the exclusion of Greece from 1969 to 1974.

The European Communities (EC).

The EC was established in 1967 to consolidate the operations of three existing organizations. The most famous of the three is the European Economic Community (EEC), generally known as the Common Market, created in 1957 to coordinate economic aid and price supports for member nations. The oldest of the three is the European Coal and Steel Community, a specialized commodity group formed in 1951 to regulate prices and improve the distribution of coal and steel. The third organization is the European Atomic Energy Commission (EURATOM), established in 1957 to enforce safety standards on nuclear power plants. Membership in the consolidated EC consists of ten industrialized European nations, with applications pending from Spain and Portugal. A Council of Ministers, a Coordinating Commission, and a European Parliament preside over the operations of the three EC agencies, each of which is itself organized into similar bodies.

The Western European Union (WEU).

The WEU is a defense pact signed on May 6, 1955, in Paris to replace the older Brussels Treaty Organization. It exists as the Western European equivalent of the Eastern European Warsaw Treaty Organization; both have seven members. The

EUROPEAN ORGANIZATONS

COUNTRY	CEUR	EC	WEU	WTO
Austria	•			
Belgium	•	•	•	
Bulgaria				•
Cyprus	•			
Czechoslovakia				•
Denmark	•	•		
France	•	•	•	
Germany, East				•
Germany, West	•	•	•	
Greece	•	•		
Hungary				•
Iceland	•			
Ireland	•	•		
Italy	•	•	•	
Liechtenstein	•			
Luxembourg	•	•	•	
Malta	•			
Netherlands	•	•	•	
Norway	•			
Poland				•
Portugal	•			
Rumania				•
Spain	•			
Sweden	•			
Switzerland	•			
Turkey	•			
United Kingdom	•	•	•	
Union of Soviet Socialist Republics				•
Totals	21	10	7	7

WEU is organized into a Permanent Council of all member nations and an Assembly with proportionate representation. Its activities focus entirely on political and military relations between East and West Europe.

The Warsaw Treaty Organization (WTO).

The WTO was created in Poland on May 15, 1955, by a treaty commonly referred to as the Warsaw Pact. Its formation was an immediate and direct response to the creation of the West European WEU. The WTO has a membership of seven, like the WEU, and it includes the Soviet Union along with East European nations. The principal bodies of the WTO are the Political Consultative Committee, the Permanent Committee of Foreign Ministers, and the Committee of Defense Ministers. WTO provides mutual defense for members, and its activities center on the balance of power between East and West Europe.

Organizations in the Americas.

The intergovernmental organizations in the Americas serve functions related to the isolation of North and South America and to colonization by European countries. Hence, priority is given to solidarity among member states in case of intervention from outside the hemisphere. Assisting former colonial possessions to emerge into full independence is also a major concern.

In addition to the principal bodies described below, there are also a number of American development commissions, such as the Latin American Free Trade Association, and commodity groups, such as the Group of Latin American and Caribbean Sugar Exporting Countries.

The Organization of American States (OAS).

The oldest and largest organization in the hemisphere, the OAS has roots extending back to 1890. Once called the Union of American Republics, the organization took its present form under a charter signed in Bogotá, Colombia, on April 30, 1948; the charter was substantially amended at a conference in Buenos Aires, Argentina, on February 27, 1967.

The current membership is 28 nations, including Cuba, which has been excluded from formal OAS activities since 1962 on ideological grounds. The structure of the OAS includes a General Assembly of all members, which meets each year, a Permanent Council of all members, which meets as needed, and economic, educational, and judicial committees of selected membership.

The OAS acted together in 1964 to establish a trade embargo with Cuba (lifted in 1975), and in 1965 to establish a peacekeeping force from member nations to restore order in the Dominican Republic. Recent OAS activities include negotiating the treaty by which the United States will cede the Panama Canal and speaking for human rights in South America.

The Organization of Central American States (ODECA).

ODECA was established by a charter adopted at San Salvador, El Salvador, on October 14, 1951. Its stated aims are to unify Central America as a political and economic community and to insure its rights in the balance of power between the larger countries to the north and south. There are five members: Costa Rica, El Salvador, Guatemala, Nicaragua, and Honduras, the latter having withdrawn from active participation because of a 1969 dispute with El Salvador. ODECA's principal bodies are a Meeting of Heads of Governments and a Conference of Foreign Ministers, with several subsidiary councils. Its recent activities have concentrated on border disputes and internal conflicts in member nations.

The Caribbean Community and Common Market (CARICOM).

CARICOM became the successor to the Caribbean Free Trade Association by a charter signed in Trinidad on July 4, 1973. The current membership of eleven states includes territorial possessions within the Caribbean, such as the British dependencies of Montserrat and St. Kitts and Nevis. CARICOM's principal body is a Secretariat comprised of planning, legal, trade, and service subdivisions. The organization operates numerous subregional commerce and customs commissions.

UNITED STATES GOVERNMENT

Although we seldom think about it, government touches each of our lives every day. When we consider government at all, we think of the President sitting in the Oval Office contemplating national policy or of the local mayor dealing with problems such as budgets or crime. Such visions give a very misleading picture of government as a whole. The heads of governments are actually tiny parts of much larger and more pervasive institutions.

Administrations come and go. Policies and procedures change. But most of the functions of government remain. The postman still brings the mail. The state trooper still patrols the highways. The roads are still cleared of snow. The traffic light still blinks. The schools are still open from fall to late spring. And inevitably, the tax bills still come due.

These, and many other functions that we take for granted, are the essence of government. They are the details of the overall contract a government makes with the governed to provide certain services at a tolerable cost. That contract is very broad and general. Government is not like a supermarket, where someone can buy a case of this service or a box of that service and pay for each individually. A citizen may not have children in the public schools, but he must pay school taxes. He may never use a state park, but part of his tax dollar will nonetheless go to pay for park maintenance. He may be a pacifist and oppose a large military establishment, but a healthy percentage of his income tax payments will be spent in support of the military.

In all governments, a citizen's effect on its operations and services is limited. The government of the United States was organized to give the individual maximum power over government. The U.S. system encourages its citizens to help choose its leaders, and to help determine government policies, through voting, writing to elected officials, and direct political action—campaigning and demonstrating.

Citizen protest is an honored tradition in the United States. The basic principle of American government is popular sovereignty: the people hold the ultimate power and merely delegate it to their elected representatives. Sometimes elected and appointed officials behave as if the people are nothing but a nuisance. Sometimes they

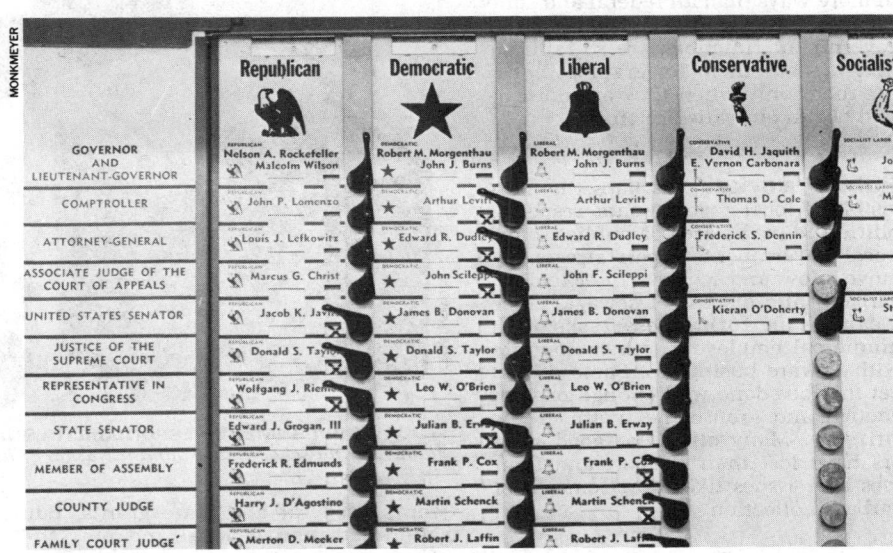

VOTING in a New York State election gives the voter a choice between many parties and candidates for statewide and local offices. The voting machine records the results.

get away with outrageous behavior. But when the people choose to use their power, it can be formidable. The people called for an end to the war in Vietnam well in advance of most congressmen. They cried out for President Richard Nixon's resignation prior to official action. They begged for tax relief long before most of their representatives.

Obviously, it is impossible to get everything we want from government. The interests of various groups often are opposed, and government is slow to move to meet new needs or redress grievances. But nearly all governments do change, gradually and almost imperceptibly.

To take an obvious example, the modern Presidency is a far different office, with far different powers and prerogatives, than it was when George Washington filled it. It has far more resources than it did two centuries ago. The Founding Fathers could not have conceived of a White House staff numbering in the hundreds. (Washington got by with a few clerks to handle his correspondence.)

The constitutional framework of the U.S. government has allowed these changes. Despite changes there has been a remarkable degree of continuity, especially in comparison with other countries. When Washington was President, Italy and Germany

were collections of small states and principalities; France was in the throes of a revolution to topple its monarchical government; Austria and Russia had emperors; Turkey had a sultan; and Japan had an emperor who was worshiped as a god. Revolutions and civil strife have brought radical changes to many countries since the 1790's, but the U.S. Constitution and its provision for government by popular democracy is unchanged in its essentials. We are fortunate that the men who met at the Constitutional Convention in 1787, to revise a hopelessly deficient system of government, were wise enough to draft a document strong enough to survive two centuries, yet flexible enough to permit solutions to problems they could not imagine.

The Constitution created an entirely new form of government that balanced local interests against the need for a potent central government. It is vague in many areas and silent in many more. But it has worked at least as much because of the things it does not say as because of the things it does say. Its silence has made possible creative solutions to the problems of a society far different from the one for which the document was written. That capacity for change without disruption is the genius of American government.

Local Government

Functions

Despite all the attention showered on national and state politics, local government probably affects more people in more ways than all federal and state government combined. Many local government functions are so familiar that we take them for granted, noticing them only when they are not carried out to our satisfaction.

Public works. Perhaps the most visible of local governments' responsibilities lie in the area of public works. Local governments repair streets, remove snow and ice in winter, collect garbage, and dispose of sewage. Some localities perform these tasks with municipal employees; others contract with private businesses. Some do not get the jobs done well enough or soon enough and arouse the wrath of the citizenry. Many otherwise good mayors have lost their support and their jobs over issues like snow removal or garbage collection.

Public safety. One of local governments' most important jobs is promoting public safety through police and fire protection. Not only must local governments prevent crimes, catch lawbreakers, and limit fire damage, they must do so publicly and visibly so that citizens feel secure. This holds true for the one-man constable force as well as for the largest urban police department. Local office-holders and police supervisors continually seek new techniques to reassure the public: one-man patrol cars, restoration of foot patrolmen, adjustments in shifts, and hiring more policemen are typical responses to public outcries. Police professionals often feel overworked and unappreciated, claiming most people take police protection for granted. Fire fighting, too, involves more than responding to alarms. Fire fighters worry that a bad piece of equipment or a badly trained fireman could lead to disaster.

Human services. Most local governments also provide important human services. Many operate public hospitals and medical clinics. Nearly all have health departments that enforce codes governing the cleanliness of restaurants, proper sewage disposal, inoculation against contagious diseases, and other public health concerns. Cities and counties also administer a variety of welfare services for the poor. These services are often paid

JEROME WEISMAN

LOCAL GOVERNMENT RESPONSIBILITIES *include fire and police protection, operation of libraries and schools, and administration of hospitals and clinics.*

for by federal and state grants, but administration is local and may include construction of public housing, aid to families and individuals, and special programs for children, the aged, and the handicapped.

Culture and recreation. Many local governments operate public libraries. No country in the world boasts so large and diverse a group of libraries, where books can be borrowed without fee or membership requirements, as the United States. Many of these libraries were built with the help of private contributions and local fund-raising efforts, but their basic operating budgets come from local governments. Public libraries range from tiny one-room buildings to major research institutions. The New York Public Library is among the largest in the world. Local governments may also sponsor museums and keep up local historic structures.

Local governments also develop and maintain parks and other recreational facilities for local residents. Parks may range from small town squares to thousands of acres; they may include boating facilities, tennis courts, zoos, beaches, bicycle paths, or golf courses. Funds for special activities may be raised by charging use fees, but the operating budget is a local responsibility.

Regulation. Zoning, the determination of how land will be used, is one of the most far-reaching powers of

local government. At first the jargon of local planning and zoning boards may seem far removed from everyday life, but these boards have the power to revitalize a community or destroy a neighborhood.

Zoning officials prepare master plans for their community, deciding if each new house shall sit on a half-acre plot or a 50- by 100-foot plot; they mark out certain areas for industrial or commercial use; and they reserve land for municipal buildings, parks, and other public uses. They may also grant variances, exceptions to the master plan; for example, a variance might allow a high-rise apartment in a neighborhood of single-family dwellings.

Local communities also enforce various building, housing, plumbing, electrical, health, and fire codes. These codes spell out minimum standards for the construction and maintenance of dwelling units and commercial and industrial establishments. The general public is well served when they carry out their duties honestly and impartially.

Education. Of all the services provided by local government, perhaps the most important is education. In the United States, elementary and secondary education have traditionally been a local concern. Some large city school systems have enrollments of hundreds of thousands. In less populated areas, small towns may consolidate to pool resources and provide better instruction and equipment. In many areas, education costs more than all other local government activities combined. Some towns and cities also operate municipal junior or senior colleges with low tuition to give a majority of local students an opportunity to attend college.

Local education is almost always supervised by a board of education that is separate and distinct from all other government units. This board is responsible only for educational policy and the upkeep of schools. The members of a school board may be elected or they may be appointed by the mayor or city council. The board then appoints a superintendent of schools, usually a professional educator, and supervises his or her work. In rapidly growing communities, new school facilities may be urgently required to keep up with rising enrollment. In stable communities, a declining birthrate may cause the opposite problem: unused school buildings and the need to reduce teaching staffs and budgets.

Acquiring Resources

All these governmental responsibilities cost money, and a large part of local officials' time is spent raising the necessary funds. Most funds come from direct taxes on local residents, but municipalities may also collect fees, receive grants, or borrow money for large projects.

Taxation. Local governments rely heavily on property taxes for their funds. The taxation of property works best when a community has a healthy mix of industrial and residential areas. In less diversified areas, the tax burden falls disproportionately on one group or another. In "company towns," the dominant industry pays

the largest share of the taxes; in turn, it usually dictates the philosophy and activities of local government. In exclusive suburbs, homeowners assume a heavy tax load, having no industrial taxpayers to help pay for local services.

Serious problems arise with property taxes in middle-class suburbs and in older urban areas. In the suburbs, annual tax bills may be almost as large as the original purchase price of the house. In older cities, business and industry may have moved away to other more promising towns, taking their well-paid employees with them. Inner cities may have a high proportion of retired persons living on fixed incomes, the poor, and the unemployed. These groups have a high need for social services—housing, medical care, income supplements—but the city has few taxpayers and so must reduce services or face bankruptcy.

Property taxation is among the most complicated issues for local government. Generally, a tax assessor from the state, the county, or the municipality assigns a value to each piece of property. This is called its *assessed valuation*. The total assessed valuation of property in a locality is its *tax base*.

The local government prepares an estimate of the amount needed from property taxes. This total is divided by the total assessed valuation of all properties to produce the *tax rate*, which is usually expressed in terms of a certain amount per $100 (or per $1000) of assessed valuation. When the tax rate is $3 per $100 of assessed valuation, a taxpayer with a house assessed at $40,000 owes $1200. The process is so complicated that many property owners pay attention only to the final bill.

Property taxes are not the only source of funds available. Some large cities have a sales tax, a payroll tax, or an income tax. One danger of high tax rates is that businesses or wage-earners may choose to move away rather than pay the high rates.

Fines, penalties, and fees. Fines and penalties provide varying degrees of financial support for local governments. Traffic tickets, penalties for doing construction work without a permit, citations for health and sanitation code violations, and even library fines fall into this category. In most instances, these are fair levies, but there are abuses. For example, some small communities on heavily traveled highways have perfected the speed trap, requiring huge fines of travelers while leaving local drivers unmolested.

Perhaps the fairest form of revenue production is user fees for specific services. Parking meters, application fees for building or plumbing permits, and charges for other services, all ask payment from those who seek the benefit. Unfortunately, such user fees often fall short of the cost of the service. Many services simply defy the imposition of direct fees. Who should be charged for police protection? For fire protection?

Nevertheless, there have been experiments with direct fees for more and more local services. In 1978, the voters of California passed Proposition 13, a referendum that froze property assessments for three years and limited increases to 2 percent a year after that in most situations. As a result, local governments had to cut services or find new revenue. Many municipalities imposed new direct fees for such services as fire inspections and the use of local paramedic corps. Many of these fees were rescinded, however, after public protest by the very people who had voted for Proposition 13.

The fundamental lesson for all governments is that most people want both lower taxes and increased services, contradictory desires that challenge public officials regardless of political philosophy.

Grants. While local governments may be efficient at delivering basic

<table>
<tr><th colspan="2">LOCAL FUNDS: WHERE EACH DOLLAR COMES FROM AND WHERE IT GOES</th></tr>
<tr><th>Revenue</th><th>Expenditures</th></tr>
<tr><td>$ .20 property tax</td><td>$ .26 sanitation and utilities</td></tr>
<tr><td>.15 other taxes</td><td>.17 health, housing, recreation</td></tr>
<tr><td>.18 state grants</td><td>.14 police and fire protection</td></tr>
<tr><td>.14 other grants</td><td>.12 general administration</td></tr>
<tr><td>.16 utility charges</td><td>.11 education and libraries</td></tr>
<tr><td>.17 other</td><td>.07 highways and airports</td></tr>
<tr><td>$1.00 total</td><td>.13 other</td></tr>
<tr><td></td><td>$1.00 total</td></tr>
</table>

HOW LOCAL GOVERNMENTS ASSESS PROPERTY TAXES

A small town has
Total assessed value of property of — $26,000,000
Budget needs from property tax of — 1,000,000

To find tax rate
divide total assessed property value by budget needs from property tax
$1,000,000 ÷ $26,000,000 = .0385
The rate is usually expressed in dollars per $100 of assessed value: $3.85 per $100

A home owner with a house assessed at $40,000 must pay
$40,000 × .0385
or 400 × $3.85
The tax bill comes to — $1540

services, they are, unfortunately, often far less efficient at gathering the resources necessary to do their job. Since state and federal governments are better at collecting taxes and local governments are better at spending them, one popular theory holds each should do what it does best. In the 1960's and 1970's, when the price of local government was soaring, state and federal governments developed an elaborate system of grants to local communities. There were grants for drug prevention, safe streets, hot lunches, and many other programs.

Some communities received grants far out of proportion to their tax contributions, while others received much less than they felt they deserved. In addition, administrative costs ate into the grants. When the federal government cut back grant programs in the early 1980's, local groups had to discontinue programs that citizens had come to rely on.

Borrowing. Capital projects—the construction of buildings, sewer lines, and schools, and the purchase of heavy equipment such as fire engines—are almost always financed through borrowing. When a local government needs a large sum of money for a capital improvement, it issues bonds for the amount. Individuals and institutions lend the government money by buying these bonds, which represent the government's promise to pay back the amount of the loan with interest after a specified period of time. Governments are very careful to keep their bond ratings high in order to make their bond issues more salable. Bonding is virtually the only means available to local governments for raising substantial amounts of money quickly. But many local budgets are heavily encumbered with funds for "debt service," repayment of bonds issued in the past.

Who Runs Local Government?

Forms. Four basic forms of government dominate municipalities. The *strong mayor-council form* is a miniature of state and federal government. The mayor acts as chief executive, appoints the heads of most major departments, drafts the budget, and has veto power over acts of the city council, which serves as a legislature. The advantages of this system include its division of powers and system of checks and balances.

Under the *weak mayor-council form*, the power of the mayor is severely curtailed. The council appoints administrators and drafts budgets. The mayor lacks veto power and

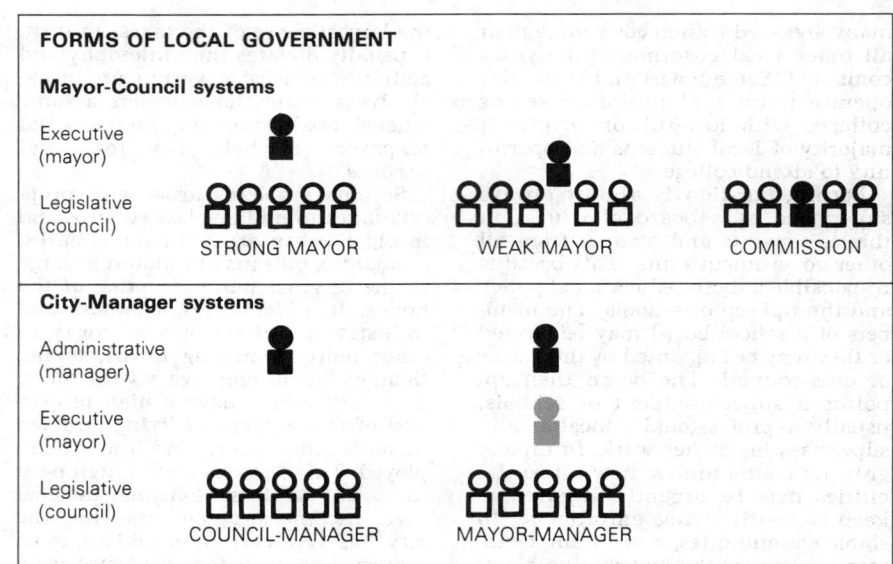

LOCAL GOVERNMENTS *offer various divisions of responsibility between legislative, executive, and administrative functions. In small towns, legislative power may be in the hands of citizens at regular town meetings.*

sits at council meetings only as a moderator.

The *commission form* of government is a curious blending of administrative and legislative functions in one body. The commissioners—usually five in number—are elected at large and each assumes executive control of a department (public safety, public works, revenue, parks and recreation, public affairs). While they usually choose one of their number to be titular mayor, each runs his or her department separately. The commissioners also serve as a legislature, adopting budgets and ordinances. This system was first implemented in Galveston, Texas, in 1903 to rebuild the city after a terrible hurricane. Reformers encouraged its adoption in hundreds of localities, but its popularity has decreased in recent years. The major weakness of the system is that each commissioner is equal to the others, and competition among them can cripple the government.

The *council-manager system* usually consists of an elected council, which

passes ordinances and sets broad policies, and a professional manager, who is appointed by the council to administer the daily business of government and give advice to the council on matters of policy. The obvious model for this system is the corporation, with the council serving as board of directors and the city manager as an appointed president.

A variation of the council-manager system is the *mayor-manager system*, in which the mayor, as chief executive officer, appoints the city manager to be chief operating officer. In this model the manager serves at the mayor's pleasure rather than the council's. The voters can get rid of a manager whose actions are unpopular by voting against the mayor.

The city manager system began as a reform in the early decades of the 20th century. This system can be relatively efficient, but no system can assure clean government. Kansas City, Missouri, had a city manager for most of the reign of the infamously corrupt Pendergast machine.

All cities with 1 million or more inhabitants use one or the other of the mayor-council systems; this form is also prevalent in very large cities (500,000 to 1 million people) and some small towns (5000 to 10,000 people). About half the municipalities between 10,000 and 500,000 use the city manager system, about 40 percent employ mayors and councils, and about 10 percent retain commissions.

Elected officials.
The American political system employs several different methods of electing local governing bodies. Mayors are always elected at large by the entire population of the municipality. Most of the largest cities allow mayoral candidates to run on party lines, but about two-thirds of municipalities with more than 50,000 people—including cities as large as Detroit and Houston—hold nonpartisan elections. The nonpartisan system was adopted to eliminate voter confusion between local issues and the policies of national parties, but voters are often left bewildered by a long list of candidates. Also, nonpartisan candidates are often local Democratic or Republican leaders, nonpartisan only for the election.

Councilmen or aldermen are elected either at large (that is, by all the voters of the city or town) or from individual wards (that is, in districts with roughly equal populations). At-large elections tend to bolster the dominant political party and the traditional centers of power, such as downtown business interests. The election district system gives some voice to racial, ethnic, and political minorities who live in cohesive neighborhoods. In many places municipal clerks, judges, and comptrollers are elected; in others, they are appointed by the mayor or council.

Appointees.
In almost all municipalities of any size appointed officials bear most of the daily workload of administering the government. Police commissioners, fire commissioners, public works directors, superintendents of schools, parks commissioners, directors, deputies, deputy assistants, and assistants are generally political appointees. Often they are supporters of victorious candidates for high local office. The right to make appointments, called *patronage*, has been under attack for a century. Some appointed commissioners have terms in office that do not coincide with the mayor's tenure to make them less subject to political pressure.

Competing interests.
Perhaps the most difficult job of municipal officials is to balance the competing interests of various groups. Every municipality of any size must take into account the needs of the downtown business community, for example. Businesses pay high taxes and want to maintain the vitality of Main Street in the face of threats by suburban shopping malls. The local newspaper, which depends heavily on downtown stores for advertising, is usually allied with the chamber of commerce and supports the businesses' regular demands for more parking and safer streets.

Residential neighborhoods have other concerns. They may seek better police protection or oppose housing projects for low-income tenants. They may want more money for local schools, and almost certainly they will want lower taxes.

Local elected officials often are less respected than their colleagues in state and federal governments. The pressure of conflicting demands, many by their neighbors and friends, may make their jobs the most difficult of all.

Other Jurisdictions

There are several other levels of local government that affect the lives of most citizens. In most states, the county is the most important unit of government. The 50 states contain over 3000 counties. In the South and the West, the sheriff is the preeminent county official, while in the Midwest and the East, county commissioners or legislators exercise both executive and legislative power. In some places these commissioners are called judges although they have no judicial function.

The powers of counties vary from state to state and even within states. In New England, counties have little or no responsibility. In other states, where towns are small, the county provides most services. Even within a state, practice may vary.

The growth of suburbs across the nation has greatly complicated the overall picture of local government. Suburbs have lured taxpayers away from the inner cities, creating serious deficits in the cities. The suburbs themselves, in their desire to keep government units small, have created a patchwork of overlapping jurisdictions that can only serve to confuse residents. It is entirely possible for a family to live in a town that has an elected council, send its young children to a local grade school run by an elected board of education, send its older children to a regional high school run by a different elected school board, have the road in front of its house repaired by a county governed by an elected board of commissioners, and receive its water and sewage disposal from separate regional boards with trustees elected in still another geographical district.

Since there are over 80,000 local governmental jurisdictions in the United States, only the most diligent citizen can be sure which unit of government is supposed to do what for whom. Consequently, most people look to the most visible local public official, usually the mayor, to redress all grievances, whether they are his direct responsibility or not. A mayor may actually lose his office because of inefficiency or incompetence in a government unit over which he has no control.

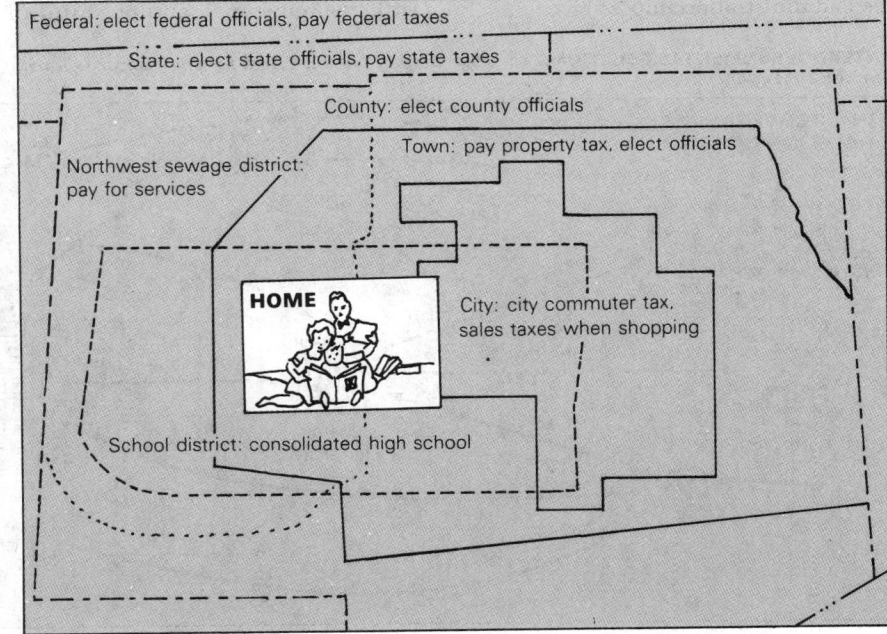

OVERLAPPING JURISDICTIONS *may require a single household to exercise duties in (and pay for) many local governmental organizations.*

Federal: elect federal officials, pay federal taxes

State: elect state officials, pay state taxes

County: elect county officials

Town: pay property tax, elect officials

Northwest sewage district: pay for services

HOME

City: city commuter tax, sales taxes when shopping

School district: consolidated high school

Problems of Local Government

There are tremendous variations in the size of local governments. Loving County, Texas, has about 100 people, while Harris County, in the same state, has over 2 million. Howe's Cave, New York, has about 120 people, while New York City has about 7 million.

The smallest communities are often without any significant resources. Most rely on the counties to fill their needs, but counties are often willing to ignore their smallest subdivisions. Often several towns operate under the umbrella of a township to provide services.

The largest cities have difficulty remaining responsive to their citizens' needs and wishes. Some of the largest have made efforts to decentralize control of vital services. These experiments—such as district school boards and local planning boards in New York City—have only been moderately successful, however.

Ironically, many cities have tried to solve the problems of overlapping jurisdictions by risking the problems of large size. Houston, Texas, has traditionally incorporated small communities on its fringes. Jacksonville, Florida, was a pioneer in regional or metro government, which unifies the delivery of services in a metropolitan area. While this approach seems to make sense, there is great resistance to it. Similar county and municipal departments are more interested in rivalry than in unity. Suburbanites resist sharing the high costs of inner city government with its poor population, large payroll, and small tax base. In addition, many metropolitan areas spill over state borders, making a unified administration impossible.

Relation to the states.

It is difficult to discuss local governments without discussing their lack of standing in the U.S. Constitution, the basic law of the nation. Local governments, both incorporated urban giants and small villages, are the creatures of the states. Dillon's Rule, accepted by most courts, restricts the rights of local governments to those states allow in their constitutions and statutes.

While home rule is a tradition engraved in the laws of about half the states, even the powers granted to the municipalities under this principle are circumscribed. State legislatures keep a short leash on the municipalities, offering a privilege here but withholding a request there.

Larger towns and cities have made significant gains in the state legislatures since the early 1960's, when the Supreme Court ordered legislative bodies to reapportion themselves according to the "one man–one vote" criterion. Previously, many state senates consisted of districts based on county lines rather than on population. This resulted in some absurd disparities, the most glaring of which was in the California Senate, where the most populous district had over 400 times more people than the least populous. To make matters worse, legislatures often neglected to change district lines with shifting populations. The decision that "legislators represent people, not trees or acres" gave many more legislative seats to the cities and suburbs. Minorities won greater representation, and state legislation took a decided turn toward the concerns of large population centers.

Relation to federal government.

It is not only the states that limit the powers of local governments. The federal government, with its sometimes abrupt shifts in

policy, restricts the ability of local jurisdictions to plan for the future. In the 1960's, the Great Society policies of Lyndon Johnson initiated numerous programs to benefit the cities. Money poured out of Washington not only to the urban centers but to smaller towns as well. It continued to come through the 1970's. Then, in 1980, President Ronald Reagan's New Federalism sought to dismantle the entire structure of federal support for local government. Voters approved of the general aims of the program, but many were likely to miss the benefits that federal grants made possible.

A prime example is the Comprehensive Employment Training Act (CETA) and its predecessor, the Emergency Employment Act (EEA). These programs sought to alleviate unemployment by using federal funds to put people to work in local governments. Staffs for libraries, police departments, and parks departments swelled. EEA and CETA employees made it possible for towns and counties to provide additional services. People grew accustomed to those services.

When the federal government eliminated public service jobs from the CETA program in the early 1980's, local funds were insufficient to maintain the CETA employees. Services suffered and unemployment rose. Local officials—*not* the federal lawmakers—took the blame.

Any discussion of local government ultimately returns to a discussion of insufficient resources. City hall is probably condemned to an eternal struggle to balance what it wants to do with what it can afford to do. Liberals and conservatives alike want local government to do more. Yet without the assistance of the states and the federal government there is little likelihood that U.S. counties, cities, and towns can meet all of the demands placed on them.

INTERGOVERNMENTAL RELATIONS *are very complex, as illustrated by this diagram showing the flow of funds to and from a state university branch in Anytown.*

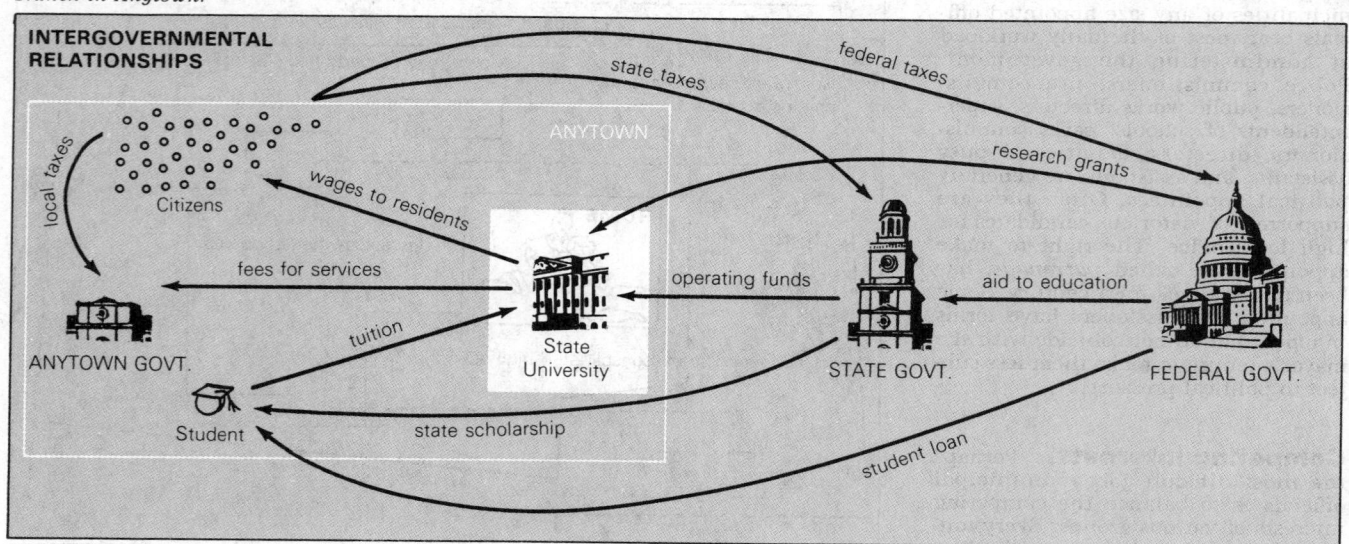

State Government

Functions

The states affect citizens' lives in a variety of ways. They charter corporations, and oversee banks, insurance companies, railroads, public utilities, and the liquor industry. In addition, they maintain highways, license drivers, and register motor vehicles. Some of them operate mass transportation systems, including bus and rail routes. Many states have established offices to protect consumers and the environment and to encourage energy production.

All states are active in education. States regulate and help fund local public schools and operate state university systems. Some university systems, including those in California, New York, and Texas, serve hundreds of thousands of students on campuses spread across the state. States operate hospital systems (especially for the mentally ill), state park systems, and a variety of support services for agriculture and business. They also serve as conduits for federal grants to local governments.

In recent years, the states have created public authorities in increasingly greater numbers. These authorities develop or manage affairs for port facilities, airports, bridges, housing units, parkways, sports arenas, reservoirs, and university dormitories. They can borrow money more cheaply than the states and can act more quickly than the state bureaucracies. But they are only indirectly accountable to voters. A poorly run public authority can threaten a state's financial standing, as happened when the failure of New York's Housing Authority almost precipitated the bankruptcy of the state in the 1970's.

Finally, states have broad responsibility for maintaining law and order. State laws define crimes and prescribe punishments, set minimum ages for operating vehicles and drinking alcoholic beverages, and establish rules concerning marriage, divorce, inheritance, and other matters of personal conduct. Among the more difficult issues states must handle are regulations covering abortion, drug use, and the distribution of "adult" books, magazines, and films.

Each state has a state police department, which patrols unincorporated areas and cooperates with local law enforcement officials. State courts try most defendants accused of serious crimes. Those convicted of criminal charges are kept in a network of correctional institutions ranging from reform schools to maximum security prisons.

STATE GOVERNMENT RESPONSIBILITIES *include licensing of motor vehicles, administration of justice, and provision of higher education and recreation facilities.*

Acquiring Resources

The major source of revenue in every state but one is the state income or sales tax. Some 44 states (all except Florida, Nevada, South Dakota, Texas, Washington, and Wyoming) levy some sort of income tax. Most of these income taxes are graduated: those with higher incomes pay higher percentages. Some 45 states (all but Alaska, Delaware, Montana, New Hampshire, and Oregon) have a sales tax. The percentage of this tax varies between 3 and 7.5 percent, and each state has its own list of excluded purchases.

In addition, 45 states tax the net income of corporations. The exceptions are Nevada, South Dakota, Texas, Washington, and Wyoming. Nineteen states tax some estates and inheritances. Every state taxes gasoline sold at the pump.

Nevada is unique in having neither an income nor a sales tax. Legalized gambling, which attracts millions of visitors, is taxed, and the proceeds provide a majority of the state's revenue. New Jersey is the only other state with legalized casino gambling. There, gambling is allowed only in Atlantic City and the proceeds go toward property tax relief for the elderly and veterans.

The states also collect revenue through fines imposed for criminal penalties and from fees charged for drivers' licenses, corporate registrations and filings, motor vehicle registrations, hunting and fishing and other licenses, and park admissions.

A popular innovation in recent years has been the creation of state lotteries. The lottery proceeds are usually budgeted for specific purposes. Some states permit horse racing, dog racing (Florida), and jai alai (Connecticut), and New York allows off-track betting on racing and sports events in state betting shops. States take a share of all legal gambling on these sports.

Like local governments, states borrow large amounts of money by issuing bonds for large public works programs. The ultimate problem for all states is balancing their budgets. The federal government can print new money and run up huge deficits, but states cannot. Thus, they are asked to provide more services while keeping tax rates low, often an impossible task.

STATE FUNDS: WHERE EACH DOLLAR COMES FROM AND WHERE IT GOES

Revenue
$ .48 taxes
.21 fed. govt. grants
.12 charges and misc.
.13 insurance trust
.06 borrowing
$1.00

Expenditures
$ .34 education
.24 welfare and health
.13 highways, police, prisons
.27 administration and misc.
.02 debt reduction
$1.00 total

Structure

Each of the states is unique. The differences among them—in geography, demography, and history—are so great that to generalize about them is risky. Texas is more than 250 times larger than Rhode Island in area, and Alaska is more than twice the size of Texas. Ninety percent of North Dakota's surface is farmland; 80 percent of Rhode Island's population live in urban areas. Wyoming has under five people per square mile; New Jersey has nearly 1000. In 1980, the per capita income in Mississippi was only 57 percent of that in Connecticut. Virginia was first settled by English planters, Arizona by Spanish missionaries, and Louisiana by French colonists.

Despite all these differences, the governments of the 50 states are remarkably similar in structure both to each other and to the federal government. Each has a governor, who serves as chief executive; a legislature, which has an upper and a lower house (except in Nebraska); and a judiciary, which may review legislation for its adherence to the state constitution.

Executive branch. The governors are the chief executives of their states, but they are usually far less powerful in their realms than the President is in his. The governors face a variety of restrictions that severely curtail their powers.

In four states (Arkansas, New Hampshire, Rhode Island, and Vermont) governors serve only two-year terms. In five states (Kentucky, Mississippi, New Mexico, South Carolina, and Virginia) governors may not succeed themselves; in three others (Delaware, Georgia, and North Carolina) a governor may serve only two terms, successive or otherwise; and in ten more a governor may serve only two consecutive terms.

Many governors must share executive responsibilities with many officials. They may sit on budget drafting committees comprised of other state elected officers or legislators or both. Or they may work directly with an elected or appointed budgetary official. In North Carolina, the governor has no veto power over legislation.

A few governors have considerably more power to act. New Jersey's governor, for example, is the only state official elected statewide. He appoints every state department head, including the attorney general and the secretary of state, and also appoints numerous county officials, including the county prosecutors. Finally, he has the power of line item veto: he can veto individual items in the state budget, yet leave the rest standing.

All limitations affect governors' ability to carry out their programs. State governments often seem indeci-

STATE LEGISLATURES *are very similar despite varying sizes and terms.* Above, *the Colorado Senate deliberates.* Below, *a table shows the sizes and terms of the 50 state legislatures.*

STATE GOVERNMENTS

Unless otherwise noted, governors and upper house have 4-year terms, lower house 2-year terms.

Membership in legislature
(Medium size: Upper house 40, Lower house 100)

	UPPER HOUSE	LOWER HOUSE		UPPER HOUSE	LOWER HOUSE
Alabama[1]	35	105	Montana	50	100
Alaska	20	40	Nebraska	49	—
Arizona[2]	30	60	Nevada	20	40
Arkansas[3]	35	100	New Hampshire[3]	24	375–400
California	40	80	New Jersey[4]	40	80
Colorado	35	65	New Mexico	42	70
Connecticut[2]	36	151	New York[2]	60	150
Delaware	21	41	North Carolina[2]	50	120
Florida	40	120	North Dakota	50	100
Georgia[2]	56	180	Ohio	33	99
Hawaii	25	51	Oklahoma	48	101
Idaho[2]	35	70	Oregon	30	60
Illinois[4]	59	118	Pennsylvania	50	203
Indiana	50	100	Rhode Island[3]	50	100
Iowa	50	100	South Carolina	46	124
Kansas	40	125	South Dakota[2]	35	70
Kentucky	38	100	Tennessee	33	99
Louisiana[1]	39	105	Texas	31	150
Maine[2]	33	151	Utah	29	75
Maryland[1]	47	141	Vermont	30	150
Massachusetts[2]	40	160	Virginia[3]	40	100
Michigan	38	110	Washington	49	98
Minnesota	67	134	West Virginia	34	100
Mississippi[1]	52	122	Wisconsin	33	99
Missouri	34	163	Wyoming	30	62

[1] Both houses have 4-year terms   [3] Governor and both houses have 2-year terms
[2] Both houses have 2-year terms   [4] Upper house has two 4-year and one 2-year terms each decade

sive and slow to act, but this is partly due to states' preferences for a weak, rather than a strong, chief executive.

Forty-two states have an elected lieutenant governor (Arizona, Maine, New Hampshire, New Jersey, Oregon, Utah, West Virginia, and Wyoming are the exceptions). The powers of this office vary from state to state. If the lieutenant governor is elected on a unified ticket with the governor, he or she resembles the U.S. Vice President, merely presiding over the state senate and remaining ready to replace the governor in case of death, disability, or

resignation. In other states, the lieutenant governor is elected separately from the governor, and is a powerful force in state politics, often engaging in serious rivalry with the governor himself. This situation has occurred in California, Texas, and other states.

Most states also elect an attorney general, who is the state's attorney and the representative of the people in civil actions; and a secretary of state, who oversees elections, licensing, corporate registrations, and other administrative functions. Many states elect a treasurer, an auditor, or a controller, with various fiscal responsibilities. A few elect commissioners of education, agriculture, or public lands. One or two states even elect members of state regulatory boards.

Legislatures. With the single exception of Nebraska, each state's legislature is a miniature of the U.S. Congress in that it has an upper and a lower house. (Nebraska has a one-house legislature called the Senate with 49 members.) Beyond this general similarity, diversity is the rule. State legislatures differ widely in their sizes, powers, and even their names.

In 17 states the entire legislature is called the general assembly. In North Dakota and Oregon it is the legislative assembly. In Massachusetts and New Hampshire it is the general court. Elsewhere it is the legislature. In all states the upper house is the state senate; but the lower house is variously known as the assembly (California, Nevada, New York, and Wisconsin), the house of delegates (Maryland, Virginia, and West Virginia), the general assembly (New Jersey), or the house of representatives (every other state).

Upper houses range in size from 20 (Alaska and Nevada) to 60 (New York). Lower houses vary in membership from 40 (Alaska and Nevada) to 400 (New Hampshire). Most state senators serve four-year terms, although in twelve states they serve for two years. (Illinois and New Jersey state senate seats are up for election three times each decade—twice for four-year terms and once for a two-year term.)

In most states, the legislature meets annually, although some meet every two years. In California, the legislature convenes only in December of even-numbered years, but the session lasts two years. The Minnesota legislature meets for only 120 days every two-year span.

Payment to legislators varies considerably. Few expect to make an independent living on a legislator's salary alone, but large states like California and New York pay comfortable amounts. Rhode Island, however, pays only a few dollars for each day the legislature is in session plus travel expenses. New Hampshire pays its legislators only a few hundred dollars per year. New Hampshire's huge general court (400 members), its low salaries, and infrequent sessions make it unique. Some members are professional politicians, but many are senior citizens or students who seem willing to contribute to the legislative process for very little money or recognition.

The state legislatures play essentially the same role in state government that the U.S. Congress plays in the national government. They pass legislation to create or amend programs, hold the power to appropriate

money, and (at least in the upper houses) vote to approve gubernatorial appointments to cabinet offices and independent agencies. In practice, however, most legislatures have less real power than it appears. Sessions tend to be brief and confusing. Some legislatures are limited to 90 days or less of deliberation in each two-year period, too little time to conduct the business of the state in a deliberative manner. Even where legislative sessions go on almost nonstop, there is often a scramble at the end of each session to vote on many bills, leaving legislators little time to read them all. (New York even engages in the practice of stopping the clock a few minutes before midnight on the last day of a session to complete its work before the legal deadline.)

The low pay of most state legislators is matched by insufficient staff allowances. Legislators are usually part-time officials and rarely have time to develop personal expertise on the complex issues they face. They cannot hire staffs like those of U.S. congressmen to assist them in researching and drafting bills.

As a consequence, individual legislators are left at the mercy of the governor, the legislative leaders, and the lobbyists. Governors have the support of larger staffs and of cabinet officers; these assistants can make compelling cases for the legislation that a governor wants passed. In addition, a governor may offer political favors to individual legislators and benefits to their districts in return for a favorable vote.

The leaders of the legislature include the lieutenant governor or senate president in the upper house, the speaker in the lower house, and the majority and minority leaders in both houses. All but the lieutenant governors are elected by the legislators themselves. Leaders can offer choice committee assignments and help pass legislation favorable to a legislator's district in return for support. Most state legislators understand the famous remark of Sam Rayburn, former Speaker of the U.S. House of Representatives: "To get along you have to go along."

Lobbyists may also take advantage of state legislatures. Large businesses have time and money to research issues of importance to them. Passage of a bill in the legislature may be so important to a business that its lobbyist may provide legislators with elaborate entertainment (which is legal), large campaign contributions (which may be legal depending on the circumstances), or even cash payments (which are decidedly illegal), in hopes of a favorable vote. Lobbyists often have a distinct advantage over the legislators just by being better prepared and informed. The packet of information a utilities lobbyist offers to a legislator may not only convince

the legislator to vote for a rate increase; it may also give him the arguments to explain his vote to his constituents back home.

Even with all their disadvantages, state legislators may sometimes vote against the wishes of the governor, their leaders, and the lobbyists. They may vote in the interests of the state as a whole, of the region they represent, or of a political philosophy they believe in.

The judiciary. Every state has a court of last resort, usually called the Supreme Court. The size of these courts varies slightly. Eighteen states' highest courts have five members, 24 have seven, and five have nine. Connecticut has six and Oklahoma and Texas have unique systems in which civil and criminal cases are heard in different courts. The terms of the justices vary considerably as well. Some receive life tenure, but most are elected to terms ranging from six to fourteen years.

There are two basic systems for selecting justices—direct election and gubernatorial appointment. Alaska and Indiana have a dual system. Judges are appointed to a trial period, then elected on an approval-rejection basis to a ten-year term.

Neither system succeeds in removing politics from judicial appointments. Judges themselves nearly always gain their judicial status through political activity. Whether they run for a judgeship or are appointed, politics is likely to play a role. Fortunately, a person may be both political and fair-minded as a judge. In the best circumstances, such people are the ones appointed or elected to high political office.

The lowest level of the judiciary may be either a justice of the peace without legal training or a municipal judge drawn from the ranks of local lawyers. These justices handle relatively minor civil cases, criminal misdemeanors, and traffic violations. Their courts are those with which the average citizen deals almost exclusively, yet these courts have been seriously hampered by lack of funds, heavy loads, and sometimes biased or unscrupulous judges.

State district courts hear the bulk of all serious criminal cases and civil suits (including family court proceedings). Their decisions are subject to appeal to an intermediate appellate court or to the state Supreme Court. (See also Law section.)

State courts suffer from two chronic ills. One is their caseload, which has increased far more rapidly than funds or court staff. The other is that they themselves decide what is legal. Since they have jurisdiction over their own actions, they have assumed more responsibility at the expense of the legislative and executive branches.

Limitations and Opportunities

One limitation on state government's effectiveness is the inconsistencies between state law and policies. This can lead to inconvenient and even dangerous situations. Trucks traveling across state borders must meet the weight and size standards of each state, often at great expense. Worse, one state may give a driver's license to someone whose license has been revoked in another state for serious and chronic violations there.

A second and more serious limitation is the imposition of federal regulations, restrictions, and standards in many areas that were once the province of the states.

The relationship between the national government and the states has changed dramatically since the early days of the republic. The balance of power has tipped decisively in favor of the central government since the 1930's. The states are by no means powerless, however. Some have, in fact, been far in advance of the federal government in making policy. Wyoming gave women the right to vote almost 30 years before the passage of the constitutional amendment extending the franchise nationally. Wisconsin had a program of assistance to the elderly long before Social Security

became the law of the land in 1935. And Minnesota and Colorado passed far-reaching civil rights legislation long before the enactment of the 1964 Civil Rights Act.

Even today some states lead the federal government in outlook. Arkansas' restrictions on nuclear power plants are more severe than those of the federal Nuclear Regulatory Commission. The California State Supreme Court banned capital punishment earlier and more sweepingly than the U.S. Supreme Court.

Reforms. The Populist movement in the late 1800's and early 1900's produced the greatest innovations in state government. Three reforms, experiments in direct democracy, continue to play a significant role in the politics of some states.

Initiative. The ability to put a provision on the ballot by petition and to vote it into law without the involvement of politicians is called initiative. Slightly less than half the states provide for it. Initiative is particularly popular in California, where Proposition 13 is only the most celebrated of the dozens of propositions placed on the ballot in recent years.

Referendum. The right to review laws by subjecting them to a vote of the electorate before they go into effect is called referendum. It exists in some form in almost 40 states. Often this

right of review applies only to amendments to the state constitution, but it is nonetheless a valuable tool for keeping some measure of power in the hands of the people.

Recall. The ability to remove or recall elected officials between regularly scheduled elections exists in different forms in different states. The general rule is that a specified number of signatures on a petition will place the recall on the ballot. Sometimes an election for a replacement is held the same day, sometimes not. Thirteen states currently have a provision for recalling the governor, but recall is usually limited to local officials. The most sensational recall in recent years occurred in Madison, Wisconsin. In 1977 a judge excused a rapist by placing the blame on the permissiveness of society; the voters promptly excused the judge from office.

There are serious problems with each of these experiments in direct democracy. Well organized single-issue groups can use initiative and referendum to force their views on the entire society. A vocal political opposition can use recall to harass an elected official. There are, however, tremendous benefits to letting politicians know that the people are watching what they do. Public awareness—and public willingness to respond—is necessary for maintaining creative and productive relations among local, state, and federal governments.

The Federal Government

The Preamble to the Constitution of the United States describes the purposes of the new central government and the federal system: "to form a more perfect union, establish justice, insure domestic tranquility, provide for the common defense, promote the general welfare, and secure the blessings of liberty. . . ."

The men who wrote the Constitution at the Constitutional Convention of 1787 created a national government with considerable powers because the existing system was completely inadequate. The Articles of Confederation, which determined the relationship between the states and the central government from 1776 to 1787, gave the national government few real powers. It had to rely on the goodwill of the states for its money and for the enforcement of its edicts.

In the late 1700's and early 1800's the new central government tried out its new powers. It was able to carry out its constitutional duties with a small number of officials. Beginning with several early decisions of the Supreme Court, however, the central government began to expand. The Court de-

fended the powers of the federal government *implied* in the Constitution, opening the way for a gradual shift of power from the states to the federal establishment in Washington.

The 1900's brought even more astonishing growth to the federal government. Areas such as education and police protection, once the exclusive domain of the states and local governments, have become federal obligations, at least in part. At the same time, however, state and local governments have grown. Government at every level has become both more active and larger. Although the balance of power has shifted toward the central government, for the most part, relations among local, state, and federal governments have been harmonious. Instances of disagreement receive publicity, but day-to-day cooperation between governments is the rule rather than the exception.

The genius of the federal government is that it has been so adaptable to changing circumstances. A system designed to govern a small, coastal, agrarian nation of fewer than 4 million people has, without revising its

basic structure, proven adequate for a transcontinental, industrialized, urban country of a quarter of a billion people.

Acquiring Resources

Financing the operations of the federal government is extraordinarily complex. Annual federal budgets climbed from $250 million a century ago to almost $65 billion in 1955; then, in less than 30 years, they grew tenfold, to nearly $650 billion in 1982. Government revenues have not matched expenditures since the early 1960's, and deficit spending has become the ordinary way of doing business.

Almost 47 percent of the federal government's revenue comes from personal income taxes, with another 12.5 percent coming from corporate income taxes. Other major sources of federal revenue are excise taxes (4.5 percent), interest on deposits (2.25 percent),

The Executive Branch

Most people think of the President as the executive branch of the government. Constitutionally this is accurate. There is no mention in the Constitution of the White House staff, Cabinet, executive departments, or independent agencies. The President commands the nation's attention as Chief Executive, and he represents the rest of the executive establishment, which employs some 2.8 million government workers.

Electing a President. The President and the Vice President are the only two officials elected by the entire nation. Technically, they are elected indirectly. Each voter casts his ballot not for a Presidential and Vice Presidential candidate but for his state's share of 538 unnamed electors pledged to vote for those candidates. The votes are counted at a joint session of Congress presided over by the president of the Senate.

Each state has a number of electors equal to the size of its congressional delegation (senators plus representatives), and each state's votes are awarded on a winner-take-all basis to the candidates who receive the highest number of popular votes in that state. The size of each state's electoral vote changes after each decennial census. As a result of the 1980 census, California has the largest electoral vote (47) and Alaska, Delaware, North Dakota, South Dakota, Vermont, Wyoming, and the District of Columbia have the smallest (3).

This system allows candidates to forge election strategies based on individual states and regions in an effort to reach a winning total of 270 electoral votes (half of the total votes plus one). The results of the electoral college vote are often quite different from those of the popular vote. In 1980, for example, Ronald Reagan took 51 percent of the popular vote (to 41 percent for Jimmy Carter) but he carried most states and received 489 electoral votes (to Carter's 49). Twice—in 1876 and 1888—the winner in the popular vote actually lost the election in the electoral college vote.

In the event of a tie in the electoral vote, the House of Representatives chooses the President from among the three candidates with the highest total electoral votes. In such a case, each state has one vote, and a majority is necessary for victory. Similarly, the Senate chooses the Vice President if no one emerges from the electoral college with a majority, although in this situation each senator votes individually. Twice—in 1800 and in 1824—the President has been chosen in the House of Representatives.

PRESIDENTIAL ELECTIONS: A SCHEDULE

POPULAR ELECTION 2nd Tuesday in November	Candidate with plurality in each state wins that state's electoral votes.
ELECTORAL COLLEGE MEETINGS 1st Monday after 2nd Wednesday in December	Electors meet in state capitals to cast their votes. States certify the votes and send them to Congress.
COUNTING THE ELECTORAL VOTE January 6	Results of the electoral college vote are tallied by the President of the Senate (usually the U.S. Vice President) at a joint session of Congress. If there is a tie in the electoral vote, the House of Representatives must elect the President, each state receiving *one* vote.
INAUGURATION January 20	The President-elect is sworn in at noon and takes office.

---

customs duties (1.5 percent), and estate and gift taxes (1.25 percent). Minor sources of income—from charges for passports to admissions fees to the Smithsonian Institute—amount to less than .2 percent of the federal government's income. These sources account for nearly 70 percent of annual revenues, and constitute the general fund, which goes to pay the ordinary operating expenses, from welfare payments to new missiles.

The remaining 30 percent of federal income is designated for specific purposes, including Social Security payments, unemployment taxes, federal employees' retirement funds, and other retirement and disability funds. These funds are held in trust to provide benefits for those who have paid into the systems. For example, Social Security payments are a major source of income for many retired persons.

The largest portion of expenditures goes to Social Security and related payments (34 percent). Next comes expenditures for the national defense (23 percent), followed by interest on the national debt (11 percent). Health programs account for 10 percent, and aid to education for 5 percent. All other government programs, from veterans' benefits to agriculture, account for 17 percent. The budgets of Congress, the federal judiciary, and the White House and executive offices combined account for less than half of 1 percent.

FEDERAL SPENDING *has increased enormously since 1930 as government has taken on new responsibilities. About a third of federal revenues and expenditures are for social insurance.*

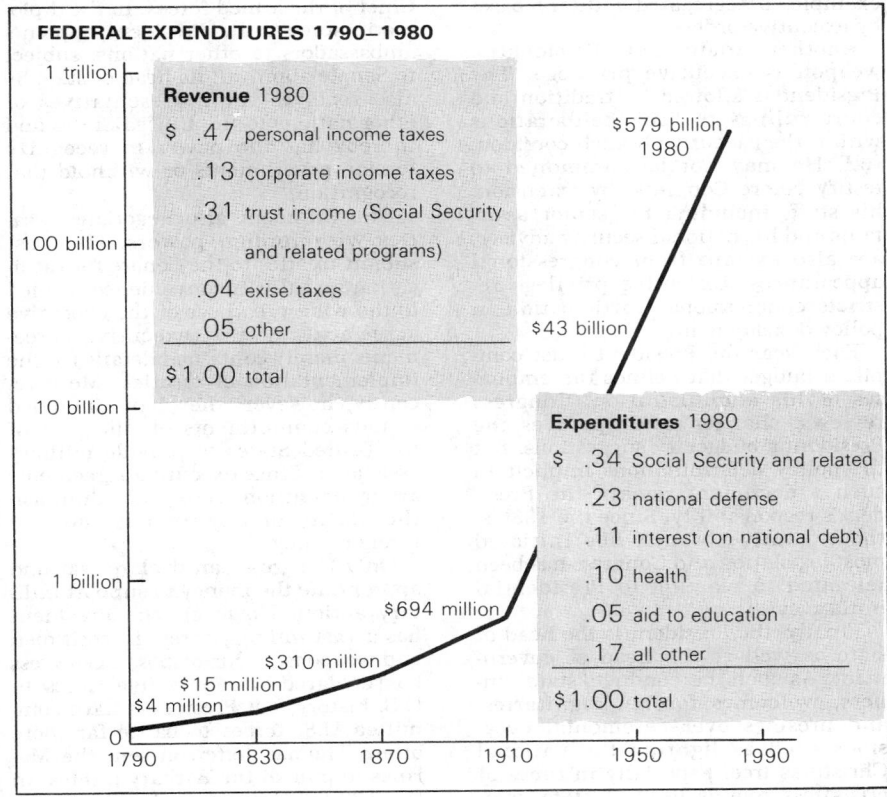

FEDERAL EXPENDITURES 1790–1980

Revenue 1980

$ .47 personal income taxes

.13 corporate income taxes

.31 trust income (Social Security and related programs)

.04 exise taxes

.05 other

$1.00 total

$579 billion 1980

$43 billion

Expenditures 1980

$ .34 Social Security and related

.23 national defense

.11 interest (on national debt)

.10 health

.05 aid to education

.17 all other

$1.00 total

$694 million

$310 million

$15 million

$4 million

(y-axis: 1 trillion, 100 billion, 10 billion, 1 billion, 0)
(x-axis: 1790, 1830, 1870, 1910, 1950, 1990)

CHIEF EXECUTIVE, HEAD OF STATE, COMMANDER IN CHIEF: *these main Presidential roles are illustrated by President Reagan signing a bill into law, President Nixon on a state visit to China, and President Carter reviewing American troops.*

There has been considerable criticism of the electoral college in recent years. Because the Constitution does not bind electors to vote for the candidate with a plurality in his state, electors can vote for someone else. This has happened, although it has never affected the result of an election. The most recent example was in 1976, when an elector from the state of Washington cast his vote for Ronald Reagan instead of for Gerald Ford, the Republican nominee.

Presidential power at home.
The President is designated by the Constitution as the Chief Executive, with responsibility for executing the laws of the land. Given the numerous laws that regulate almost every facet of our lives, this is an overwhelming responsibility. The vast number of federal programs and laws makes it necessary for each President to choose carefully the areas on which he will concentrate.

The President has a variety of tools available to accomplish his purposes. He has the power of appointment for top officials. He can prepare a legislative program for passage by Congress. He can veto acts of Congress. He can convene special sessions of Congress. He can mold public opinion through appeals directly to the electorate.

The executive order has become an essential Presidential tool for implementing policy. Executive orders are directives interpreting laws or modifying regulations. They allow a President to virtually make his own laws within certain limits. Congress has

surrendered a part of its law-making power because it cannot possibly debate and vote on every change dictated by circumstances. Most executive orders are relatively innocuous, but Presidents have made sweeping changes in government policy through this means. President Kennedy, for example, desegregated military bases by executive order.

Another traditional Presidential weapon is executive privilege. The President is allowed by tradition and court rulings to keep deliberations within the executive branch confidential. He may not be summoned to testify before Congress; by extension, his staff, including his senior assistants and his national security adviser, are also exempt from congressional appearances. Executive privilege restricts congressional participation in policy development.

Each year the President must compile a budget that defines the emphases of his administration. Congress reviews, changes, and approves the President's budgetary suggestions, but the policy determinations implicit in such a document remain the President's responsibility. Since the 1930's, the executive branch has initiated most legislation and Congress has been relegated to reacting to Presidential initiatives.

Finally, the President is the head of state as well as the head of government. As such, he conducts state dinners, welcomes foreign dignitaries, and presides over ceremonial occasions such as lighting the national Christmas tree. Especially in times of crisis, his role as head of state gives

him immense power in the interests of national unity.

Presidential power abroad.
The President, according to the Constitution, is the chief diplomat for the United States and the Commander in Chief of the armed forces. In the diplomatic sphere, the President appoints ambassadors to other nations, subject to Senate approval. As head of state he also receives the representatives of other nations to the United States and thereby has the power to recognize foreign governments or withhold that recognition.

The President also negotiates treaties with foreign powers. He must submit treaties to the Senate for ratification and this inconvenience has led to the widespread use of the executive agreement. At first executive agreements merely contained details for the implementation of treaties. More recently, however, they have included serious commitments on the part of the United States to provide military assistance. Since executive agreements are by definition secret, they diminish the ability of Congress to monitor foreign policy.

Only Congress can declare war and appropriate the money to support military action. However, the President has a vast military force, in both men and weapons, at his disposal. Congress has declared war only five times in U.S. history, but Presidents have committed U.S. forces to battle far more often. Thomas Jefferson sent the Marines to punish the Barbary pirates. In the 1800's, U.S. troops fought in the

Philippines and Mexico. In the 1900's, troops were sent to China (1900), Russia (1918–1920), various countries in the Caribbean, Korea (1950–1953), Lebanon (1958), and Southeast Asia (1964–1972).

U.S. involvement in Vietnam was so controversial that in 1974 Congress passed the War Powers Act over a Presidential veto. This act requires the President to notify Congress of any foreign military action within two days and to withdraw the troops involved within 60 days unless Congress authorizes the action. The act restores some of the balance between the executive and the legislature, but in practice, Congress would support a President's commitment of military force under most circumstances.

Limitations. Many of the President's actions are subject to congressional approval, including major appointments and treaties. Only Congress can appropriate money, even though the President prepares the budget. And only the Supreme Court can ultimately interpret the law, even though Presidential actions often involve interpretations of his powers and prerogatives.

The President is more able to lead than to drive the government to action. In order to be effective, he requires the support of Congress, the Cabinet, the bureaucracy, the media, and the public. Opposition by any of these groups can cripple his policies. Many Presidential programs have been effectively killed by lack of support from one or more of these groups.

Perhaps the most severe limitation on the Presidency is the complexity of modern problems. No one can know enough about energy, nuclear weapons, the economy, the right to exploit the ocean bed, and all the other issues the President must confront.

The Presidency seems to have taken on imperial proportions in this century. But from another perspective, the growing complexity of both foreign and domestic affairs has severely curtailed the President's ability to offer actual solutions.

The Cabinet. For the most part, the Presidential Cabinet consists of his appointed heads for the 13 federal departments. These secretaries (of defense, state, treasury, etc.) oversee the operations of the huge executive bureaucracy and advise the President on the formulation of policy. Each administration also gives Cabinet rank to selected officials who are not department heads. At various times the director of the Office of Management and Budget, the assistant to the President for national security affairs, and the ambassador to the United Nations, among others, have held Cabinet rank.

The duties and organization of the

ORDER OF SUCCESSION TO THE PRESIDENCY *
(in case of death or disability)

1. Vice President
2. Speaker of the House
3. President Pro Tempore of the Senate
4. Secretary of State
5. Secretary of the Treasury
6. Secretary of Defense
7. Attorney General
8–16. Other Cabinet secretaries

* The 25th Amendment to the Constitution provides a means by which a Vice President who has succeeded to the Presidency may nominate a new Vice President with the advice and consent of the Senate. The order of succession above would take effect only if the Vice President died at the same time as or soon after the President.

---

executive departments are described in the Glossary of Federal Agencies following this section. A brief summary of their responsibilities appears in the table on this page.

Each President deals with his Cabinet as he sees fit. Early Presidents used the Cabinet officers as advisers. But as the bureaucracy grew, the secretaries became spokesmen for their departments' constituencies. Dwight Eisenhower was the last President to hold weekly Cabinet meetings at which a wide range of issues was discussed.

Since then Presidents have tended to deal with each secretary individually and to choose "experts" to head the Cabinet departments rather than politicians with constituencies the President wishes to woo.

The Executive Office of the President. The composition of the White House Office is decided by each President. The Executive Office usually includes a legal staff, a press relations office, a congressional relations office, advisers in specific policy areas, and liaisons with state and local governments and with various constituent groups.

In addition to the actual White House staff, a number of agencies fall under the Executive Office. Four of these are especially important.

Office of Management and Budget. The OMB is the agency through which the President develops the federal budget, which defines the priorities of an administration in the most precise manner possible—by determining where the federal dollars go. The director of the OMB has played an increasingly prominent role in policy formulation.

Council of Economic Advisers. The council consists of a chairman and two members, all professional economists. Their role is exclusively advisory. They assess the impact of existing or proposed policies on all aspects of the economy—on inflation, business conditions, employment, balance of payment, etc.

National Security Council. The NSC includes the President, the Vice President, and the secretaries of state and defense. The director of central intelligence and the chairman of the Joint Chiefs of Staff advise the NSC by statute. The assistant to the President for national security affairs presides over a staff that evaluates the impact of government policy on national security. Most foreign policy and military

---

THE CABINET

Department	Year Founded	Responsibilities
State	1789	Foreign affairs
Treasury	1789	Monetary affairs: produce currency, collect taxes, etc.
Defense	1789[1]	Provide for national defense, supervise armed forces
Justice	1789[2]	Represent government in courts of law
Interior	1849	Supervise government lands and natural resources
Agriculture	1862	Assist and advise farmers, regulate agricultural production
Commerce	1903[3]	Assist and advise business, support economic development
Labor	1913[3]	Assist and advise labor, support fair labor practices
Health and Human Services	1953[4]	Provide assistance for elderly, handicapped, disabled, poor; assist medical research
Housing and Urban Development	1965	Support community development; administer housing programs
Transportation	1967	Assist and regulate air, rail, highway transportation systems
Energy	1977	Coordinate national energy policies
Education	1980[4]	Coordinate national education programs and policies

1 Originally Departments of War and Navy; consolidated 1947.
2 Directed by attorney general, an original Cabinet position; Department of Justice established 1870.
3 Originally Department of Commerce and Labor; Labor made separate department in 1913.
4 Originally Department of Health, Education and Welfare; Education made separate department in 1980.

decisions are based on NSC evaluations. The advisory role of the NSC staff often duplicates that of the State Department, with which it may be in conflict.

Central Intelligence Agency. The CIA collects and interprets intelligence from around the world. It is a powerful and secretive organization, and has been accused of interfering directly in the political and economic affairs of foreign countries.

The independent agencies. In addition to the Cabinet departments and the Executive Office, there are about 3000 independent agencies whose members are appointed by the President but which function independent of his authority. These bodies range in importance from the American Battle Monuments Commission and the President's Council on Physical Fitness and Sports to the powerful Board of Governors of the Federal Reserve System and the regulatory agencies.

Some agencies are like corporations, accomplishing major tasks on their own. The U.S. Postal Service employs nearly 700,000 workers and provides a major governmental service. Among other such agencies are the Export-Import Bank, the Smithsonian Institution, and the Tennessee Valley Authority.

Other agencies are purely administrative. The Federal Reserve System, the National Aeronautical and Space Administration, the Office of Personnel Management, the Veterans Administration, and the U.S. Arms Control and Disarmament Agency fall into this category.

Among the powerful independent agencies are those charged with regulating private enterprise. The Environmental Protection Agency, the Federal Communications Commission, the Federal Trade Commission, the Interstate Commerce Commission, the Securities and Exchange Commission, the Nuclear Regulatory Commission, the National Labor Relations Board, and the Equal Employment Opportunities Commission have vast powers over the industries they oversee. Many critics would like to see the powers of these agencies curtailed. Other critics claim that regulation is not effective enough because the regulatory agencies have fallen captive to the industries they are supposed to regulate.

The independent agencies are governed by commissioners appointed by the President for fixed terms of up to 14 years. These terms overlap and prevent any President from appointing a majority of members of any board.

The executive branch of the federal government is so large and various that it is often at war with itself. Agencies and departments may have conflicting viewpoints and policies. In the 1980's, for example, a Federal Reserve

Board chairman supported high interest rates that discouraged investment while White House policy was to stimulate investment. A successful administration can only seek to resolve such conflicts in areas it has chosen to emphasize.

The Legislature

The Congress of the United States is a unique manifestation of the federal system. One of the great debates at the Constitutional Convention of 1787 was whether the legislature of the new government should reflect the size or the sovereignty of each state. The eventual compromise—a lower house based on population and an upper house with equal membership for each state—was an expedient solution to a thorny problem for the new nation. The House of Representatives thus has 435 voting members, apportioned to the states by population; the Senate has 100 members, two from each state.

The Congress was probably intended to be the preeminent branch of government. The Constitution is very specific about its powers, which include levying taxes, borrowing money, coining money, declaring war, supporting a military establishment, and passing laws it sees as "necessary and proper" to fulfill its responsibilities.

In the 1900's, the Congress lost its preeminence, giving the executive branch the right to initiate legislation. The Congress is hardly a rubber stamp for Presidential programs, but in large

measure it has become a body that reacts rather than acts.

Legislative powers. The power of Congress begins with its ability to make laws on almost any facet of life. The executive branch may draft new laws, but the Congress must pass them, and this seldom happens without thorough scrutiny and extensive rewriting.

In its deliberations and votes the Congress takes regional and ideological interests into account. A powerful congressman with strictly regional concerns may delay or even prevent passage of legislation unfavorable to his or her constituents. For this reason, the Congress is often seen as obstructionist. The pace of legislative work is slow, and many citizens complain that more efficiency is necessary. But the system was never intended to be speedy. Deliberation and care in formulating legislation were the intent; haste could only lead to bad legislation and possibly despotism.

Congress also has the responsibility of legislative oversight. In order to see that the executive branch is accomplishing its statutory tasks, the Congress monitors the conduct of the hundreds of executive bureaus, agencies, and offices. If Congress is dissatisfied, it can withhold funds or even pass new legislation to force its intentions on the executive.

In order to scrutinize the executive branch more carefully, the Congress created the General Accounting Office (GAO). This agency, under the Comp-

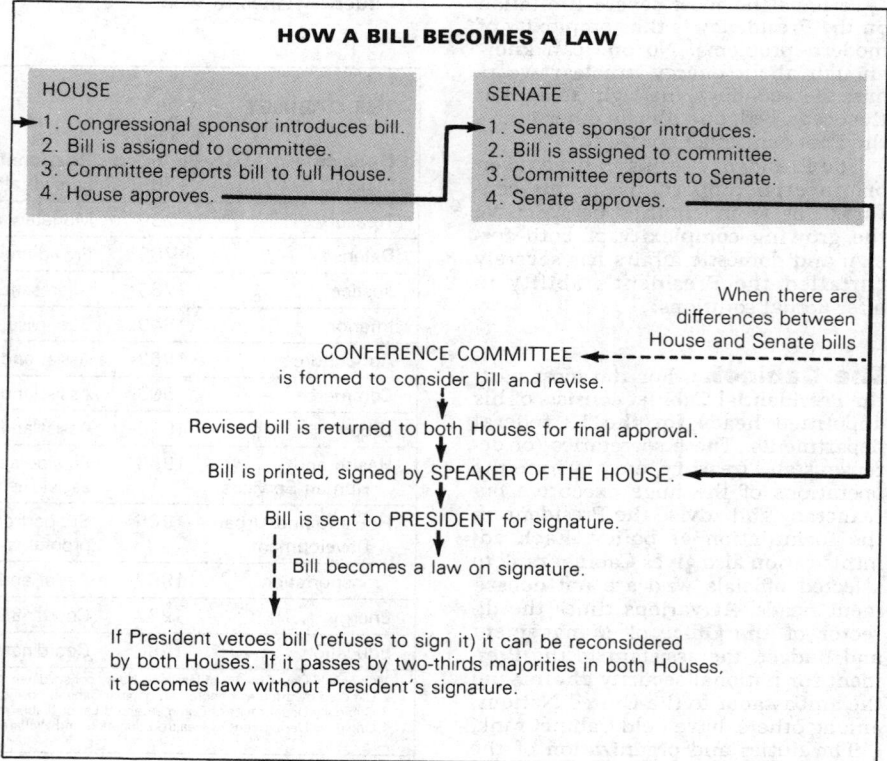

HOW A BILL BECOMES A LAW

HOUSE
1. Congressional sponsor introduces bill.
2. Bill is assigned to committee.
3. Committee reports bill to full House.
4. House approves.

SENATE
1. Senate sponsor introduces.
2. Bill is assigned to committee.
3. Committee reports to Senate.
4. Senate approves.

When there are differences between House and Senate bills

CONFERENCE COMMITTEE is formed to consider bill and revise.

Revised bill is returned to both Houses for final approval.

Bill is printed, signed by SPEAKER OF THE HOUSE.

Bill is sent to PRESIDENT for signature.

Bill becomes a law on signature.

If President vetoes bill (refuses to sign it) it can be reconsidered by both Houses. If it passes by two-thirds majorities in both Houses, it becomes law without President's signature.

troller General, can hold investigations into the use of all funds appropriated by Congress and into the administration of any federal program. GAO reports are often the basis of new legislation or budget changes.

The committee system.
Both chambers of the Congress are divided into smaller groups for preliminary consideration of new laws. The resulting committee system has become an essential instrument for the conduct of congressional business.

Partisan committees are the Republican and the Democratic steering committees and campaign committees in each House. The steering committees set broad outlines of party policy and the campaign committees collect and distribute campaign funds.

Select committees are formed to study specific problems for a limited length of time. They do not recommend legislation. The House Select Committee on Aging is one example.

Joint committees of the House and Senate deal primarily with housekeeping matters. They oversee the Government Printing Office, the Capitol Building and grounds, and a variety of other matters.

Standing committees are those in which the actual business of the Congress takes place. These committees approximate the structure of the executive branch with separate committees for individual functions. Thus, the House and Senate Armed Services committees hold hearings on defense policy and monitor the activities of the Pentagon; the two Judiciary committees consider revisions in the federal criminal laws and oversee the Justice Department; and so forth.

Passing a bill.
A new bill must be introduced in each House, where it is assigned to a standing committee and perhaps reassigned to one of its subcommittees. First the subcommittee holds hearings and votes on the bill. If it reports favorably, the bill goes to the full committee, where the process is repeated. If the subcommittee recommends against the bill, the full committee will usually follow suit. Either the subcommittee or the full committee may table the bill, thereby killing it until someone reintroduces it in the next Congress. Once the bill is "marked up," it goes to the floor for debate, possible amendments, and a vote.

Most bills with committee approval pass on the floor with relative ease. If, however, the bill passes in different forms in the House and Senate, the standing committees involved select between three and nine conferees from among their members to form a conference committee, which negotiates a resolution of the differences in the two versions of the bill. Sometimes

THE SENATE *sat as a court of impeachment for a President only once, against Andrew Johnson in 1868. It failed to convict him by a single vote.*

these differences are simple, but often they are substantial and the members of the joint committee must find a compromise that will be acceptable to a majority of both Houses. If the conferees fail to compromise, the bill dies. If they reach a solution, each House must pass the revised bill without amendment. Most conference committee reports have little trouble on the floor of either chamber. The bill is then sent to the President for his signature. If he signs, the bill becomes law. If he refuses to sign, he has *vetoed* the bill and it dies unless both House and Senate pass it again with two-thirds majorities.

Committee assignments are important to congressmen and senators. Committee assignments are made by party leaders through the partisan committees in each House.

Committee and subcommittee chairmen are chosen by seniority. The majority party member with the longest service on that committee usually becomes chairman. Until 1971 the seniority system was absolute. This absolutism favored congressmen from single-party districts and gave chairmen virtual dictatorial control over their committees. Reforms in the 1970's placed limitations on the seniority system, forcing chairmen to compromise and seek consensus.

The Senate.
The Senate (or upper House) consists of two members elected from each state. The framers of the Constitution saw the Senate as a body of elder statesmen whose age and experience would bring wisdom to the councils of government. Until 1913, senators were not directly elected by voters but elected by the legislatures of their states. The 17th Amendment to the Constitution provided for the state-wide election of both senators.

Senators must be 30 years old. They serve six-year terms, and approximately one-third are up for election every two years. The presiding officer of the Senate is the Vice President of the United States. His title in this role is president of the Senate, but he has no vote unless the vote of the senators results in a tie.

The majority party elects a president pro tempore (Latin: for the time being), who presides in the absence of the Vice President. In actual practice any senator may preside, and president pro tempore is an honorary position. The two parties elect floor leaders, called the majority and minority leaders, and two deputy leaders, called the majority and minority whips.

The Senate has certain prerogatives that distinguish it from the House of Representatives. The Senate sits as a court in impeachment proceedings, and approves judicial, Cabinet, and other Presidential appointees. Usually approval is readily granted for major appointments—for Cabinet officers, Supreme Court justices, and major ambassadors. For lesser offices, such as federal district court judge and U.S. marshal, the tradition of senatorial courtesy requires the President to ask prior approval from the senators from the state where the appointee will serve. This applies only to the senators from the President's party, but without this approval the senator can declare the nominee personally abhorrent and the rest of the Senate will refuse to confirm the appointment.

Another important tradition of the Senate is the filibuster, the privilege of a handful or even of one senator to delay indefinitely a vote on any issue by engaging in unlimited debate. By holding the floor, a minority can so delay the business of the Senate that the proponents of a filibustered bill will often give up and withdraw the proposal. Since 1975 new rules have made filibusters more difficult to carry on.

The greatest differences between senators and representatives are the length of their terms and the size of the bodies in which they sit. Six-year terms give senators a greater degree of freedom; they need not always be concerned with reelection. Further, as one of 100 rather than one of 435, a senator commands more prestige and more visibility. Senators from small states are especially important to their constituents. Six states have only one representative in the House (compared with California's 45); but even the smallest state has two votes in the Senate.

House of Representatives.

The House of Representatives (or lower House) consists of 435 members apportioned to the states according to population and reapportioned after each decennial census. Since representatives, who must be at least 25 years old, are elected in districts that are often homogeneous, and since they must run for reelection every two years, they are usually closer to the opinions of their constituents than are senators.

The presiding officer is the Speaker of the House, who is chosen from among the membership by the majority party. Each party also elects a floor leader and as many whips as it deems necessary.

The House has the constitutional authority to initiate all revenue bills and the traditional authority to initiate all appropriations bills.

The House Rules Committee has no parallel in the Senate. The Rules Committee writes the rules under which the House operates and may change those rules at the beginning of each new Congress. It decides when each bill (except those reported by the Ways and Means and Appropriations committees) will go on the calendar and how much floor time can be spent debating it. The Ways and Means Committee originates all legislation concerning taxes and other revenue, and the Appropriations Committee originates legislation concerning the budgeting of funds for executive departments and agencies. These two committees are extremely powerful.

The limitations of Congress.

The Constitution limits the Congress in a variety of ways. The President may veto a law, blocking its passage. The laws are subject to review by the Supreme Court. Congress is specifically prohibited from passing legislation that abridges freedoms granted in the Bill of Rights and from passing legislation designed to punish citizens or to convict them for acts committed before passage of a law.

APPORTIONMENT IN HOUSE OF REPRESENTATIVES, 1982

	NUMBER	CHANGE FROM 1972
Alabama	7	—
Alaska	1	—
Arizona	5	+1
Arkansas	4	—
California	45	+2
Colorado	6	+1
Connecticut	6	—
Delaware	1	—
Florida	19	+4
Georgia	10	—
Hawaii	2	—
Idaho	2	—
Illinois	22	−2
Indiana	10	−1
Iowa	6	—
Kansas	5	—
Kentucky	7	—
Louisiana	8	—
Maine	2	—
Maryland	8	—
Massachusetts	11	−1
Michigan	18	−1
Minnesota	8	—
Mississippi	5	—
Missouri	9	−1
Montana	2	—
Nebraska	3	—
Nevada	2	+1
New Hampshire	2	—
New Jersey	14	−1
New Mexico	3	+1
New York	34	−5
North Carolina	11	—
North Dakota	1	—
Ohio	21	−2
Oklahoma	6	—
Oregon	5	+1
Pennsylvania	23	−2
Rhode Island	2	—
South Carolina	6	—
South Dakota	1	−1
Tennessee	9	+1
Texas	27	+3
Utah	3	+1
Vermont	1	—
Virginia	10	—
Washington	8	+1
West Virginia	4	—
Wisconsin	9	—
Wyoming	1	—
	435	

THE HOUSE IS REAPPORTIONED *after each federal census to assure that states are represented in proportion to their population.*

Most of the limitations on Congress are institutional rather than constitutional. Senators and representatives are answerable to specific constituencies that have the power to vote them out of office. They are charged both with passing legislation in the interests of the country as a whole and with representing the particular interests of their state or district. When these two concerns are in conflict, officeholders face difficult decisions. If they vote for the national interest (and against the interests of their constituents), they may not be reelected. Yet if every congressman always followed the advice to "vote your district," little useful legislation would ever get passed.

Serving constituents is an important job of congressmen. Every citizen with a problem—a lost Social Security check, an unprocessed grant proposal, a desire for a special tour of the White House—writes or calls his congressman. Political expediency dictates that these requests receive prompt attention, but they take time away from considering legislation and reviewing programs.

Staffs—both personal and committee—help legislators perform their varied responsibilities. But as congressmen rely more and more on staff work, they place inordinate power in the hands of relatively young and ambitious people who are not directly accountable either to the voters or the Congress.

The Judicial Branch

The Constitution is vague in defining the responsibilities of the federal courts. It stipulates that federal judges will sit for life and that their salaries may not be reduced while they sit. It requires a Supreme Court of undetermined size and such lower courts as Congress may establish. Much of the structure and procedure of the federal courts today is based on tradition and on decisions of the Supreme Court itself.

Structure. There are three levels to the federal court system. The lowest level, where most federal cases originate, is the district court. There are 95 district courts with about 450 judges serving in them. Each state has at least one district court and some states have as many as four. Workload determines the number of judges, ranging from one to 24, in each district court. Federal magistrates assist the judges in the early stages of each case. Each federal court district has a U.S. attorney who serves as the prosecutor in that district's court.

The court of appeals is the second level of federal courts. Currently there are eleven appeals circuits with 120 judges. These judges hear cases on appeal from the district courts and command a great deal of respect.

The Supreme Court of the United States, which since the 1860's has consisted of a chief justice and eight associate justices, is the ultimate authority in questions of constitutionality. Some cases originate in the Supreme Court. These include suits by one state against another or against the federal government or aliens, as well as matters involving ambassadors and other diplomatic personnel.

Most of the Supreme Court's workload, however, involves hearing appeals of cases from lower federal courts or from state courts. Those opposing a Supreme Court decision have only two choices: they may bring another suit on a similar case in the hope that the Court will reverse itself, or they may campaign for an amendment to the Constitution. Both of these approaches have worked, but both take a great deal of time—running into decades—to accomplish. The 16th Amendment, ratified in 1913, authorizes the Congress to impose an income tax, overturning an 1895 Supreme Court ruling. *Brown v. Board of Education*, in 1954, declared that "separate but equal" facilities assigned on the basis of race were unconstitutional, reversing *Plessy v. Ferguson*, which found such facilities constitutional in 1896.

The Congress has also established certain special federal courts to hear cases in very specific areas of the law. These so-called legislative courts include the Court of Claims, the Court of Customs and Patent Appeals, the Court of International Trade, the Tax Court, and the Court of Military Appeals.

Judicial appointments.
The appointment power of all federal judges belongs to the President, with the advice and consent of the Senate. The process has developed into a complex one, however, with the attorney general, the Federal Bureau of Investigation (FBI), and the American Bar Association (ABA) possessing advisory, investigatory, and screening authority respectively.

The President and the Senate Judiciary Committee, which makes recommendations on nominees to the full Senate, both give serious weight to any negative factors that may be included in the FBI's background checks and the ABA's evaluations of possible nominees. Ordinarily, the Senate is willing to give the President's choice the benefit of the doubt.

Presidents use Supreme Court appointments in a number of ways. In 1953 Dwight Eisenhower appointed Earl Warren as chief justice. Warren had been the Republican governor of California and the Republican Vice Presidential candidate in 1948. His views were noncontroversial and seemingly conservative enough to harmonize with Eisenhower's. Ironically, Warren's record as chief justice proved to be far more activist and progressive than Eisenhower had any reason to expect.

Other Presidents have used Supreme Court appointments toward symbolic ends. Lyndon Johnson appointed the first black, Thurgood Mar-

THE SUPREME COURT: *Thurgood Marshall,* front left, *was the first black to be appointed to the Court in 1967. Sandra Day O'Connor, the first woman, was appointed in 1981.*

shall, in 1967, using his selection as a symbol of the new age of civil rights for minorities. Ronald Reagan appointed the first woman, Sandra Day O'Connor, in 1981, to demonstrate his support for equal rights for women even though he was opposing the proposed Equal Rights Amendment to the Constitution.

Presidents pay careful attention not only to the symbolic nature of their appointments but also to the political beliefs of appointees. They seek to shape the philosophy of the Court to approximate their own. The Court's political complexion changes very gradually, however, since justices serve for life and no President ever makes more than a few appointments. (There have, in fact, been only slightly more than 100 Supreme Court justices since 1789.) Further, justices are virtually free from interference by those who appoint them and often strike out on their own ideological paths once on the bench.

Appointments to the lower federal courts are more a matter of patronage. Presidents almost always follow the recommendations of senators from the state where the appointment will be made and those recommendations are nearly always partisan in nature. Senatorial courtesy, by which the Senate traditionally rejects a nominee not approved by the senator from the state involved, virtually assures the President's cooperation.

Judicial procedure.
The federal district courts are trial courts where accused violators of federal laws are prosecuted before a jury and where citizens or the government may bring civil actions of various kinds. Citizens may challenge administrative

behavior or the constitutionality of laws; the government may bring antitrust actions.

The appellate courts, including the Supreme Court, do not have juries. Judges decide issues on the basis of constitutionality. The Supreme Court receives between 3000 and 4000 appeals each year. The chief justice circulates each of these appeals among the justices, who review them and vote on whether to grant a hearing. The overwhelming majority of cases are disposed of by denying a hearing, allowing the decision of the lower court to stand. In cases granted a hearing, attorneys for both sides submit written briefs stating their positions.

Only about 150 cases a year reach the stage of oral argument, in which attorneys from both sides make their cases before all nine justices. Oral arguments are usually limited to one hour for each side. Justices may question the attorneys to bring out additional information.

The justices meet in conference to discuss current cases under circumstances of utmost confidentiality. After a vote, the chief justice (if he is in the majority) or the most senior judge in the majority assigns one of the justices to write the majority opinion. Written decisions are circulated to each of the justices. Each justice may either sign the decision, supporting his vote, or, if he agrees with the decision but not the reasoning, he may write a concurring opinion setting forth his own viewpoint. No decision is final until this highly private process is complete because justices may change their votes after reading written opinions.

The politics of the Supreme Court.
Supreme Court decisions

have had at least as great an effect on life in the United States as Presidential and congressional actions. The Marshall Court (1801–1835) gave the courts the right to declare acts of Congress unconstitutional and established the supremacy of the central government in the federal system. The Taney Court (1836–1864) helped bring about the Civil War with its Dred Scott decision, asserting that slaves are not citizens. After the Civil War the Court severely restricted congressional authority, especially in the regulation of interstate commerce.

President Franklin D. Roosevelt labeled the Court of the 1930's "nine old men" and sought to increase its size from 9 to 15 members because the Court was striking down much of his New Deal legislation. He failed, however, and later dropped his plan.

The Warren Court (1953–1969) had a decisive impact in several areas. It struck down "separate but equal" facilities, ordering an end to segregated schools, mandated reapportionment of state legislatures on the basis of one man–one vote, broadened the concept of freedom of speech, expanded the protections available to those accused of crimes, and extended several constitutional rights to include proceedings in state courts.

Finally, the Burger Court (1969 to date), despite its retreat from some of the Warren Court's controversial positions on criminal law, struck down state abortion statutes and granted women the qualified right to terminate a pregnancy.

Judicial principles. Three extra-Constitutional principles guide the Supreme Court in its decision making: passivity, precedent, and judicial restraint.

The principle of passivity means that while the President and Congress may initiate solutions to problems, the federal courts may react only when actions are brought before them. On rare occasions the High Court has seized the initiative and defined the issue before it more broadly than the litigators have suggested, but this is exceptional.

Precedent compels the Supreme Court to consider similar cases from the past and generally to base its decisions on the rulings in these cases. The Court ignores precedent only when a majority of its members determine that society has changed sufficiently to allow the overturning of past decisions.

Judicial restraint limits the areas in which the courts may exercise their powers. While the courts will, for example, hear cases involving the interpretation of a specific tax law or the application of that law to an individual taxpayer, they will almost never hear cases claiming that a particular tax law or appropriation is unconstitutional. As an extension of this restraint, the Supreme Court steadfastly refused to hear cases involving the legality of the war in Vietnam.

While the average citizen may regard the authority of the courts as unlimited, these three principles severely curtail the authority of the judiciary and leave a good deal of public policy in the hands of the elected branches of the federal government. (See also Law section.)

Checks and Balances

The men who wrote the American Constitution had a fundamental fear of government that led them to distribute the powers of the federal government among three branches, with separate and distinct duties and responsibilities for each. In addition, the Constitution provides for checks and balances that offer each branch protection against the others.

The President, for example, has the power of veto over acts of Congress; he may simply refuse to sign into law a bill Congress has passed. The Congress, in turn, may override a Presidential veto; if both the House and the

---

LANDMARK DECISIONS OF THE SUPREME COURT

1803 Marbury vs. Madison. Chief Justice Marshall asserted the Court's right to judicial review—to overturn a law as unconstitutional. This decision became a central part of American governmental practice.

1857 Dred Scott vs. Sandford. Court ruled 6-3 that black slaves were to be considered property; that they had no rights of citizenship; and that Congress could not abolish slavery in a U.S. territory. The decision sharpened divisions that led to the Civil War. It was nullified by the 13th and 14th Amendments.

1896 Plessy vs. Ferguson. Court ruled that "separate but equal" facilities for blacks and whites were constitutional. The decision was reversed in 1954 (see below).

1919 Schenck vs. United States. Free speech is protected unless authorities can prove it presents a "clear and present danger" of violence or harm to others.

1932 Powell vs. Alabama. A person on trial for a capital crime is entitled to legal counsel even if the state must provide it. This ruling was broadened in 1963 and 1972 to include persons on trial for any crime that could involve a jail term.

1954 Brown vs. Board of Education of Topeka. Separate but equal schools for blacks and whites are unconstitutional.

1962 Engel vs. Vitale. Public schools cannot constitutionally require students to recite prayers.

1964 Reynolds vs. Sims. The U.S. House of Representatives and both houses of state legislatures must create election districts of roughly equal population. This decision forced most of the U.S. state legislatures to redistrict.

1973 Doe vs. Bolton and Roe vs. Wade. Broad state prohibitions of abortion during a women's first six months of pregnancy are unconstitutional.

1974 Nixon vs. United States. The President cannot withhold information required in a criminal trial; his right to keep executive matters confidential—called "executive privilege"—is limited.

CHIEF JUSTICES

CULVER PICTURES   UPI   UPI

JOHN MARSHALL   EARL WARREN   WARREN BURGER

EXECUTIVE BRANCH

may veto acts of Congress, delay execution of congressional programs

may override President's veto, refuse or reduce budget appropriations, delay consideration of executive initiatives

nominates all federal judges, may delay enforcement of judicial decrees

rules on constitutionality of executive acts

CHECKS AND BALANCES

approves court appointments, budgets

rules on constitutionality of acts of Congress

LEGISLATIVE BRANCH

JUDICIAL BRANCH

Senate vote to override by a two-thirds majority, a vetoed bill becomes law despite the President's objections. The judiciary determines the constitutionality of laws passed by Congress and signed by the President.

The ultimate check in this system is that the President, the Vice President, and federal judges are subject to impeachment and removal for violation of their oaths of office. Impeachment, while uncommon, is a potent threat to the overly ambitious. Impeachment itself is the drawing up of charges against a federal official. This is done by the House, and if it votes to impeach, the official is tried in the Senate with the chief justice of the Supreme Court presiding as judge. No President has ever been removed from office in this way but President Andrew Johnson was tried by the Senate in 1868, and the vote was only one short of the two-thirds majority required to convict. In 1974, President Richard Nixon resigned in the face of almost certain impeachment and conviction.

The major complaint against separation of powers is that it breeds inefficiency. It is not uncommon for one political party to control the Presidency while the other controls the Congress, or even for the House and the Senate majorities to be in the hands of different parties. This may lead to a frustrating stalemate on occasion, but the system was designed specifically to impose limitations on power. Inefficiency is a price we pay

for protection against irresponsible use of power by any branch of the government.

The President and the Congress. Power in the federal government has shifted back and forth between the President and Congress throughout the history of the United States. The Constitution seems to give preeminence to the Congress, but the Congress itself is too unwieldy to govern directly. The institution of the Presidency, on the other hand, is the perfect vehicle for accumulating power, since one man, elected by all the people, symbolizes the power of the institution.

In foreign affairs, Presidents have more ways of circumventing Congress than in domestic affairs. An appeal to national honor or prestige can force Congress to any number of specific actions. In the 1960's, Congress passed the Gulf of Tonkin Resolution, giving President Johnson virtual war powers in Vietnam even though a later investigation found that the incident on the Tonkin Gulf had been exaggerated.

The congressional weapon against the President is usually that of delay. Congress, because it is so cumbersome, can hold off on a specific matter for years. Committee chairmen can hold endless hearings—or, worst yet, hold no hearings at all. The leadership can put off a vote. Individuals can filibuster.

With all these tactics available on both sides, the obvious solution is compromise—which is precisely what the authors of the Constitution intended. As a result, the constitutional weapons of veto and override are used relatively seldom. The checks and balances are so strong that neither the executive nor the legislature is eager for confrontation.

Judicial review. The principle of judicial review, the ability of the federal courts to negate laws they find unconstitutional, is nowhere mentioned in the Constitution. The principle was first enunciated in 1803 by Chief Justice John Marshall in *Marbury v. Madison*, and it has since become one of the foundations of our system of government.

Since the 14th Amendment to the Constitution, in 1868, the courts have also had the authority to review state statutes, but this power was seldom exercised until the Warren Court (1953–1969), which struck down numerous state laws that restricted civil rights, civil liberties, freedom of speech, and the rights of those accused of crimes.

The federal courts, and especially the Supreme Court, do not exercise judicial review with any great regularity, but the mere possibility of such action keeps legislators and executives conscious of the limitations of their roles.

Changing the Constitution.

While the Constitution is the ultimate authority in all matters of law, it is not an unchanging document. In about two centuries of existence, it has been amended 26 times to reflect changing demands on government. The first ten amendments, the Bill of Rights, guarantee basic individual liberties and are the price the states extracted for their approval of the Constitution itself. Of the other amendments, some correct glaring deficiencies in the original document. Among these are changes in the electoral college's method of choosing the President and Vice President (12th Amendment, 1804) and a provision for filling a vacancy in the Vice Presidency (25th Amendment, 1967). Other amendments extend the rights of citizenship to formerly excluded groups. Among these are the 14th Amendment (1868), granting citizenship to former slaves regardless of "previous condition of servitude," and the 19th Amendment (1920), enfranchising women.

The 16th Amendment, which in 1913 gave the federal government the power to levy an income tax, set an

---

CONSTITUTIONAL AMENDMENTS

Procedure 1 (used for Amendments 11–26)
A. Amendment passed by two-thirds majorities in both House and Senate.
B. Amendment ratified (within time limit) by three-quarters of the states (38 of 50). Ratifying body is usually the state legislature.

Procedure 2 (never used)
A. Two-thirds of state legislatures call on Congress to convene a constitutional convention to propose an amendment or amendments.
B. The proposed amendment(s) ratified by three-quarters of the states.

AMENDMENT *of the Constitution has only been accomplished by the first of the two methods.*

important precedent. This amendment represents the triumph of the system of checks and balances since it overturned a specific Supreme Court deci-

sion, *Pollock v. Farmers' Loan and Trust Co.* (1895), which denied to the government the power to tax incomes.

There are two possible methods of amending the Constitution, but only one has ever been used. The unused method calls for a constitutional convention, which Congress must assemble if two-thirds of the state legislatures request it. From time to time there have been efforts to call a second constitutional convention—most recently to limit the spending powers of the federal government—but this approach is riddled with problems. Most experts agree that a convention called to consider a single issue could decide to rewrite the entire Constitution, including the Bill of Rights.

The common method of adding to the Constitution is by a congressional proposal passed by a two-thirds majority in both the House and the Senate and ratified by three-fourths of the states. Congress in its proposal states the length of time the states have to ratify and the procedure they shall use. In every instance but one the Congress has specified the state legislatures as the approving agents.

The Unofficial Government

Parties

Political parties serve some useful purposes in the U.S. political system. They are, in fact, handy vehicles for accomplishing one essential purpose of politics—winning elections. They recruit candidates, collect money, and spend money, sometimes lavishly. They offer a banner under which candidates can run. The legends on those banners may be vague and sometimes even contradictory, but the voters have become so accustomed to them that it is almost impossible for a candidate to win unless he is a Democrat or a Republican.

The Founding Fathers deplored the development of what they called "factions," but during the Presidency of George Washington the merchants and urban classes banded together as Federalists under the leadership of Alexander Hamilton, while the farmers of the South joined with less affluent urban dwellers in the North to form the Democratic Republicans with Thomas Jefferson as their leader.

The two-party system. American politics has had a two-party system almost without interruption ever since. The two modern parties—the Democratic and the Republican—de-

veloped after the Civil War. Each of the parties attracted a broad spectrum of political philosophies. The agrarian Democrats of the South tend to be more conservative than the urban Democrats of the North, while the populist Republicans are more progressive than the business-oriented Republicans.

In Presidential elections intraparty differences rarely matter. Once the party's candidate is nominated, all branches of the party usually unite since the Presidency is too big a prize to risk losing over ideological squabbles. Only rarely will a significant faction in a party desert a Presidential candidate. Moderate Republicans

CAMPAIGN BUTTONS *and slogans are part of the vast effort by political parties to get their candidates elected. These Presidential campaign buttons are for (left to right) Eisenhower, 1952; Taft, 1908; Theodore Roosevelt, 1912; and Kennedy, 1960. The button at far right is a modern rendering of the Republican elephant.*

PHILLIP JONES

abandoned Barry Goldwater in 1964 and conservative Democrats refused to support George McGovern in 1972. In both cases the divisions within the party led to resounding electoral defeats. But in most other modern campaigns the partisans of each party united behind even lackluster candidates rather than sacrifice power.

Although there are recognizable differences between the two main parties, the parties do not exact conformity from their adherents. There is no ideological test for membership in parties, and no central committee that issues membership cards. When a party holds the Presidency, it can sometimes reformulate its ideology in support of its leader. But in the long run, the national parties are loose coalitions of scores of state and local parties whose principles are often at odds. The factions cooperate to elect candidates, and when they win, they share the power and patronage the victory brings. They also continually seek new party members—usually by making their ideology broad enough (or vague enough) to attract a wide variety of supporters.

How candidates are chosen.

There are two basic methods each party employs to choose candidates to represent it in general elections; the primary system and the convention system.

The primary was one of the numerous reforms advocated by the Populist movement in the late 1800's and early 1900's. In a primary election, registered Republicans and Democrats choose their parties' candidates at the polls. In a closed primary, only the registered members of a party may vote for their party's candidates. In areas where one party dominates, the primary actually decides who will hold office. The problem is that primaries attract a comparatively low turnout of voters.

In an open primary, a voter may select the party primary in which he chooses to participate. In a wide open primary, introduced in Washington State, a voter may cast a ballot in each party's primary. The objection to open primaries is that members of one party may vote in the other party's election for its weakest candidate.

The convention method of selecting candidates calls for assembling party loyalists to choose the party's standardbearers. The party convention, whether state or national, also writes party platforms and prepares for general elections. The drawback of this system is that delegates to the conventions are often chosen by party leaders. Thus they have almost complete power over the whole nominating process.

The nominating process of the national parties involves a national convention whose delegates are chosen partly through primaries and partly through state conventions. In Presidential primaries, the voters select delegates pledged to one of the Presidential candidates for one or more ballots. Convention states choose their delegates through gatherings of the party's faithful in increasingly larger areas, sometimes beginning at the election district level.

Recent reforms in the Democratic Party particularly have tried to make the delegate selection process more open. Delegates are selected at the congressional district level rather than statewide, and delegates are chosen in proportion to the results of the Presidential primary. (Formerly, the winner of the state primary got to name all the states delegates.) However, no

PARTY CONVENTIONS *were revolutionized by radio and television coverage. What began as a meeting of "bosses" to nominate candidates has become a show for home viewers. Conventions are held in the summer of Presidential election years and last for four or five days.*

reform has satisfied all party activists and the Democrats have continued to search for a formula that will be as inclusive as possible without eliminating the voice of their elected officials.

Third parties.

Since the solidification of the two-party system, third parties have had little effect on the outcome of national elections. They have, however, had a profound effect on the policies of the major national parties.

The Populist or People's Party, for example, ran its own candidate in 1892 and collected 22 electoral votes. In the next two elections, the Populists supported the losing Democratic candidate, William Jennings Bryan. While their electoral successes were all local, some of the major tenets of their program—direct election of senators, a graduated income tax, and the eight-hour work day—eventually became the law of the land.

Most other national third parties— the Socialist Party, the LaFollette Progressive Party in 1924, and the American Independent Party of George Wallace in 1968—have had similar long-term effects. Parties formed primarily to further the ambitions of a single political figure have been less successful.

Third parties have had their greatest successes in local elections. In the 1890's the Populists elected state legislators, congressmen, and governors in several Western states. Some third parties are entirely local. The Liberal and Conservative parties in New York State have a permanent place on the ballot, but they exist almost exclusively to pressure the Democrats and Republicans by granting or withholding their endorsements for major party candidates.

New third parties must earn a line on the ballot by getting signatures on petitions. Since the major parties control the electoral apparatus in every state, gathering and validating these signatures is seldom a simple matter. The independent Presidential campaigns of Eugene McCarthy in 1976 and John Anderson in 1980 spent a disproportionate amount of time, money, and energy getting on the ballot. Their major party opponents were spared this difficulty. The major parties remain the sole means to high political office.

Parties and personalities.

As institutions, the major parties have not fared well in recent years. More and more voters consider themselves independents. Party organizations can no longer "deliver" votes the way they once could. Public financing of Presidential elections has reduced the necessity for fund-raising.

Until the mid-1900's, powerful party bosses were able to pick a candi-

BIG CITY BOSSES *have become notorious for high-handed methods and corruption. The most notorious, Boss Tweed of New York was exposed by cartoonist Thomas Nast.*

date for President behind closed doors. The candidate then relied on the local party organizations to bring voters to the polls. After the election, the victorious candidate owed the local organizations favors, which he repaid in jobs, contracts, and public works.

Today candidates for every office from city councilman to President have come to rely increasingly on television, direct mail, and telephones as a means of reaching voters directly. These tools circumvent local party leaders; thus, after the election, the successful candidates owe nothing to the party leaders, further weakening the party structure. Candidates no longer need to develop and maintain friendly relations with party leaders. What they need instead is an "image" suitable for television.

This revolution has created a new class of political technicians, consultants who know how to make television commercials and use other technological tools—direct mailings, telephone campaigns, and sophisticated opinion polls.

Party organizations are not altogether dead, of course. They can still exert sufficient influence to control local and sometimes even statewide primaries. At the state level, they may flex their muscles on behalf of a candidate for governor, seeking the power and patronage a governor can offer. By contrast, U.S. senators control very few jobs. They run without strong party support, and an increasing number are photogenic millionaires. The danger for the American political system is that as the parties grow weaker,

candidates with appealing smiles and access to vast wealth, personal or otherwise, could come to dominate government at every level.

Centrism and extremism.

Political debate in the United States is conducted in a fairly narrow range, from slightly left of center to slightly right of center. There are no small but powerful parties on the far ends of the political spectrum as there are in most European countries. Major American parties may seem far apart on some issues, but the gap is small compared with that in Italy, for example, between the neo-Fascists or monarchists on the right and the radical parties to the left of the Communists.

The social goals of most Americans—Democrats and Republicans, liberals and conservatives—are actually surprisingly similar. The means may vary and emotions may sometimes run high, but there is no serious politician calling for a one-party dictatorship to obtain the greatest good for the greatest number.

For this reason there are seldom the wild fluctuations of policy that come with a change of government in countries where the parties are more ideological. In Great Britain the Labour Party often nationalizes an industry only to have the Conservatives denationalize it when they resume power. Because the American parties are centrist by nature, the initiatives of each can be accepted by the other with modest changes and modifications. Republicans in the 1930's opposed Social

Security legislation, for example, but when they returned to power in the 1950's they supported the system and even enlarged it. In a similar way, Democrats in the 1980's came to support reduced government spending, a policy long associated with Republicans.

Differences remain, of course, and during election campaigns, feelings run high. But the large area of agreement between the parties remains an important ingredient of governmental stability in the United States.

A Fourth Branch of Government?

Although the Constitution provides for only three branches of government, there have been repeated suggestions that some unofficial group or interest plays a role that approximates that of a fourth branch. The three most commonly mentioned candidates for that role are the bureaucracy, the media, and pressure groups.

The bureaucracy. A great deal of what goes under the name of government is actually the bureaucracy. The federal government alone employs some 2.8 million people who are engaged in tasks ranging from interpreting satellite pictures of Soviet missiles to collecting entrance fees in national parks. State and local governments employ some 11 million more.

Theoretically, the bureaucracy exists to carry out the policies set by elected officials, but most government bureaus and agencies have self-serving goals as well. Often they can circumvent or stall even the wishes of the President. They can do this because each bureau or agency has its own constituency both in the Congress and in the country. Each federal agency maintains a close relationship with the Senate and the House committees that review its programs and provide its funds.

Each bureau performs a function that some segment of the population wants. Defense contractors want an ever larger Defense Department budget. The Sierra Club wants unspoiled national parks. The National Education Association even persuaded President Carter to create a separate Department of Education with Cabinet status. Any effort to disrupt an agency's function will bring forth threats of retaliation.

President Andrew Jackson initiated the spoils system, which gave government jobs to his loyal supporters. This system prevailed until the late 1800's, when civil service reform gave rise to modern bureaucracy. Civil service employees are hired and promoted on the basis of competitive examinations and

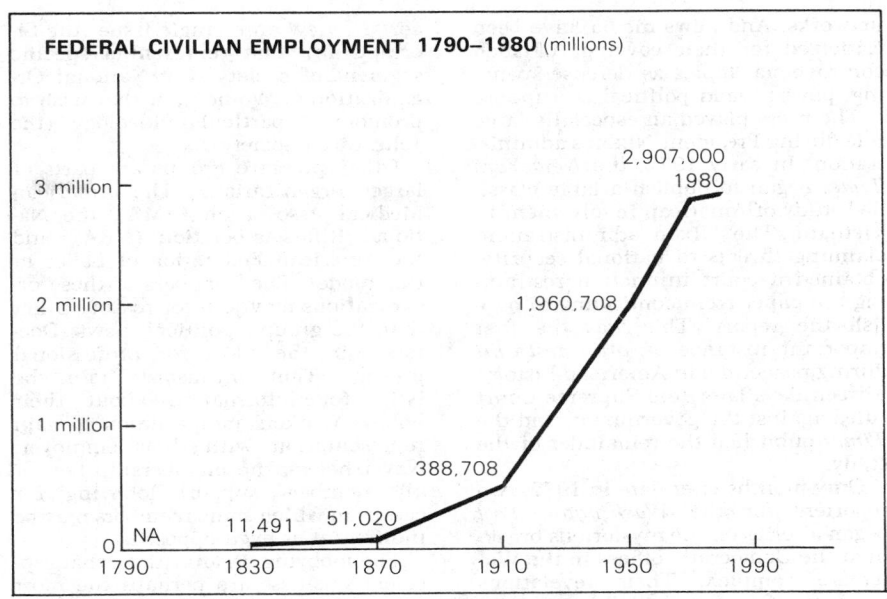

FEDERAL CIVILIAN EMPLOYMENT 1790–1980 (millions)

FEDERAL CIVILIAN EMPLOYMENT *grew rapidly between 1930 and 1970, but it has remained steady since. About 3 percent of civilian jobs are with the federal government today.*

are protected from dismissal for political reasons. Unfortunately, they may also be willfully unresponsive to changes in policy and procedure.

When the New Deal increased the size of the government beyond anything dreamed of before, the bureaucracy began to assume a position of power that has come to rival that of the executive branch—its employer—and the legislature—its provider. In recent years, there have been efforts to control the self-perpetuating permanence of government bureaucracies. A number of states have adopted sunset laws that require regular reviews of every government program in order to end or change those that are ineffective.

A bureaucracy tends to be secretive—both to increase its importance and to cover up mistakes or corruption. The Freedom of Information Act of 1967 sought to make it easier for the public to gain access to information about what government is doing. Most of the requests for information have come from businesses, however, since the ordinary citizen does not know what kinds of information are available under the new law.

Despite all the flaws of the system, most government employees carry out their responsibilities diligently and honestly. On balance, civil service employees are probably more able and honest than those who ran the government under the unrestrained spoils system. Much of the public's fear of the bureaucracy is brought on by its great size and complexity, problems individual workers are nearly helpless to solve.

The media. The press is one of the few extra-governmental institu-

tions mentioned specifically in the Constitution. The Bill of Rights prohibits the government to abridge free expression of opinion on the theory that the press serves as a watchdog on government.

Government and the press often work as adversaries. Government would prefer that news come from official sources. Elected officials appeal to reporters' and editors' sense of patriotism. By granting private interviews, they encourage reporters to become "insiders" who will not jeopardize a good source by criticizing him.

The government possesses a particularly potent weapon against radio and television, since the Federal Communications Commission, whose members are appointed by the President, licenses all radio and television stations. No station has ever lost its license for its news reporting, but the threat is implicit.

The press comes in for its own share of criticism. Candidates for office and elected officials complain bitterly that newsmen are biased in their reporting. National elections seem at times to be staged and controlled by the television

DEBATES *between Presidential candidates began in 1960 with Richard Nixon and John Kennedy.*

networks. And news media have been criticized for their coverage of such controversial topics as defense spending, poverty, and political corruption.

The press played an especially large role during President Nixon's administration. In early 1972, the *New York Times* began to publish a large classified study of American involvement in Vietnam. The Nixon administration, claiming threats to national security, obtained a court injunction restraining the paper from continuing to publish the report. This was the first important instance of *prior restraint* during peacetime in American history. Fifteen days later, the Supreme Court ruled against the government, and the *Times* published the remainder of the study.

Only months later, late in 1972, two reporters for the *Washington Post* began a series on the mysterious break-in at the Democratic offices in the Watergate complex. Their revelations prompted Congress and the courts to investigate further, and the resulting scandal led to the conviction of high government officials and finally to President Nixon's resignation.

Pressure groups. Any group of individuals or institutions organized to influence public policy is a pressure group. Some pressure groups exist solely for the purpose of lobbying. Among these are groups that hold a

certain view on a single issue (the Sierra Club), that represent a specific segment of society (the National Organization of Women), or that wish to promote a particular ideology (the John Birch Society).

Other pressure groups are parts of larger organizations. The American Medical Association (AMA), the National Rifle Association (NRA), and the American Federation of Labor fit this model. The members of these organizations may join for reasons other than the group's political views. Doctors join the AMA for professional prestige. Gun enthusiasts join the NRA for information about their hobby. Workers join a union to gain representation with their employer. Nevertheless, the membership fees of all members support lobbying for causes to which some members may be indifferent or even opposed.

The lobbying organizations that represent business are perhaps the most active. There are umbrella organizations such as the National Association of Manufacturers and the National Association of Businessmen that represent a variety of business interests. In addition, almost every industry, from mining to toy manufacturing, has an association representing its interests in Washington. The wealth of business lobbyists gives them considerable access to the seats of power.

Public institutions also form organizations for their mutual benefit. The

National Conference of Cities, which looks out for the interests of urban areas, is such a group. Among the most effective lobbying efforts are those that combine the activities of public and private institutions. The highway lobby, for example, includes state highway departments as well as the paving contractors, automobile manufacturers, the tire and glass industries, and even some labor unions. Their combined influence can be formidable in opposing any reduction in highway funds.

More recently, powerful public interest groups have been formed. Common Cause and Ralph Nader's diverse organizations profess to represent the general public on a wide range of political and consumer issues.

The lobbyist derives his name from his predecessors, who waited in the lobbies of legislatures to meet and try to influence legislators. Techniques are more sophisticated today but the principle remains the same. Lobbyists use information, the promise of votes in the next election, or money to achieve their ends. They may seek to influence legislators, policy makers, or government administrators; they may even bring suit against the government to further their purposes.

No legislator can ever know everything he needs to know about all the issues on which he must vote. Lobbyists often perform the legitimate function of providing information vital to the drafting or passage of legislation. Pressure groups that represent large numbers of people make effective use of the power of numbers. Their most potent weapon is the implicit threat that their members will punish the uncooperative at the polls.

The seamier side of lobbying involves money. Some legislators and officials can be "bought"—their vote for an important bill can be determined by an offered payment. Such corruption is probably less prevalent—at least in the Congress—than it once was. But it is unlikely that corruption will ever be completely ended. Legislation has limited the amount any contributor may give a candidate for federal office; but Political Action Committees, usually representing interest groups with very precise political goals, have made it easier to circumvent this restriction.

Lobbyists have a legitimate role, however, continually letting government officials know how one segment of society feels on issues that concern them. Reformers have continually tried to take "influence" and even "politics" out of government. But government without them would be both sterile and inhuman. The American brand of government is sometimes nasty and sordid, sloppy and inefficient, slow and cumbersome, but it can also be responsive and creative. Therein lies its potency.

—*Nick Acocella*

LOBBYISTS AT WORK

In the "lobby" outside the Senate Chamber in Albany, New York. In recent years special interest pressure groups of all kinds have grown enormously in number and importance. Among the wide variety of organizations maintaining their own lobby offices in Washington or hiring the services of professionals are:

Actors Equity Association
Air Force Sergeants Association
American Farm Bureau Federation
Campbell Soup Company
Exxon Corporation

Federation of American Hospitals
National Rifle Association of America
National Right to Life Committee
Nez Perce Indian Tribe
United Steelworkers of America

CONSTITUTION OF THE UNITED STATES

Preamble

We the people of the United States, in order to form a more perfect union, establish justice, insure domestic tranquility, provide for the common defense, promote the general welfare, and secure the blessings of liberty to ourselves and our posterity, do ordain and establish this Constitution for the United States of America.

Article I

Section 1. All legislative powers herein granted shall be vested in a Congress of the United States, which shall consist of a Senate and House of Representatives.

Section 2. The House of Representatives shall be composed of members chosen every second year by the people of the several States, and the electors in each State shall have the qualifications requisite for electors of the most numerous branch of the State legislature.

No person shall be a Representative who shall not have attained to the age of twenty-five years, and been seven years a citizen of the United States, and who shall not, when elected, be an inhabitant of that State in which he shall be chosen.

Representatives and direct taxes shall be apportioned among the several States which may be included within this Union, according to their respective numbers, which shall be determined by adding to the whole number of free persons, including those bound to service for a term of years, and excluding Indians not taxed, three-fifths of all other persons. The actual enumeration shall be made within three years after the first meeting of the Congress of the United States, and within every subsequent term of ten years, in such manner as they shall by law direct. The number of Representatives shall not exceed one for every thirty thousand, but each State shall have at least one Representative; and until such enumeration shall be made, the State of New Hampshire shall be entitled to choose three; Massachusetts, eight; Rhode Island and Providence Plantations, one; Connecticut, five; New York, six; New Jersey, four; Pennsylvania, eight; Delaware, one; Maryland, six; Virginia, ten; North Carolina, five; South Carolina, five; and Georgia, three.

When vacancies happen in the representation from any State, the executive authority thereof shall issue writs of election to fill such vacancies.

The House of Representatives shall choose their Speaker and other officers, and shall have the sole power of impeachment.

Section 3. The Senate of the United States shall be composed of two Senators from each State, chosen by the legislature thereof for six years; and each Senator shall have one vote.

Immediately after they shall be assembled in consequence of the first election, they shall be divided as equally as may be into three classes. The seats of the Senators of the first class shall be vacated at the expiration of the second year, of the second class at the expiration of the fourth year, and of the third class at the expiration of the sixth year, so that one-third may be chosen every second year; and if vacancies happen by resignation, or otherwise, during the recess of the legislature of any State, the executive thereof may make temporary appointments until the next meeting of the legislature, which shall then fill such vacancies.

No person shall be a Senator who shall not have attained to the age of thirty years, and been nine years a citizen of the United States, and who shall not, when elected, be an inhabitant of that State for which he shall be chosen.

The Vice-President of the United States shall be President of the Senate, but shall have no vote, unless they be equally divided.

The Senate shall choose their other officers and also a President pro tempore, in the absence of the Vice-President, or when he shall exercise the office of President of the United States.

The Senate shall have the sole power to try all impeachments. When sitting for that purpose, they shall be on oath or affirmation. When the President of the United States is tried, the Chief Justice shall preside; and no person shall be convicted without the concurrence of two-thirds of the members present.

Judgment in cases of impeachment shall not extend further than to removal from office, and disqualification to hold and enjoy any office of honor, trust, or profit under the United States; but the party convicted shall nevertheless be liable and subject to indictment, trial, judgment and punishment, according to law.

The Legislative Branch

HOUSE OF REPRESENTATIVES

This section set up the national census to determine how many representatives in Congress each state would have. Originally, slaves and Indians were not counted "whole persons" in the census, but the 14th Amendment gave former slaves the full rights of citizenship. The number of congressmen from each state is still determined by the number of people in the state, but the total membership of the House is limited to 435.

"Impeachment" means accusing an official of wrong conduct in office. The House of Representatives makes these charges, and the Senate acts as the court where they are tried (see Section 3).

SENATE
Since the 17th Amendment was passed in 1913, senators have been chosen by direct popular vote, not by the legislatures.

This clause set up a system of staggered elections to the Senate. All senators now have six-year terms, but the terms expire at different times. In one election year, only one-third of the senators are up for election; the others still have two or four more years to serve. This gives the Senate more continuity than the House, where all members are up for election every two years.

Since there are always an even number of senators, tie votes are possible, and so the Vice President was given the power to break ties.

CONGRESSIONAL ELECTIONS

The 20th Amendment changed this meeting time to noon, January 3.

PROCEDURES

In addition to the Congressional Record, which is published every day, both Houses of Congress keep a record of their proceedings.

PAYMENT AND PRIVILEGES
These privileges are called "congressional immunity."

"Emoluments" are salaries. This section prevents federal officials from being members of Congress at the same time.

RELATION TO EXECUTIVE

This section describes the President's veto power. Even if a bill has been passed by both the Senate and the House, the President can veto it, or turn it down, instead of signing it and making it a law. However, a two-thirds vote by both Houses can pass the bill over his veto. Simply holding the bill when Congress is about to adjourn is a "pocket veto."

SPECIFIC POWERS

Section 4. The times, places, and manner of holding elections for Senators and Representatives shall be prescribed in each State by the legislature thereof; but the Congress may at any time by law make or alter such regulations, except as to the places of choosing Senators.

The Congress shall assemble at least once in every year, and such meeting shall be on the first Monday in December, unless they shall by law appoint a different day.

Section 5. Each House shall be the judge of the elections, returns, and qualifications of its own members, and a majority of each shall constitute a quorum to do business; but a smaller number may adjourn from day to day, and may be authorized to compel the attendance of absent members, in such manner, and under such penalties, as each House may provide.

Each House may determine the rules of its proceedings, punish its members for disorderly behavior, and with the concurrence of two-thirds, expel a member.

Each House shall keep a journal of its proceedings, and from time to time publish the same, excepting such parts as may in their judgment require secrecy, and the yeas and nays of the members of either House on any question shall, at the desire of one-fifth of those present, be entered on the journal.

Neither House, during the session of Congress, shall, without the consent of the other adjourn for more than three days, nor to any other place than that in which the two Houses shall be sitting.

Section 6. The Senators and Representatives shall receive a compensation for their services, to be ascertained by law and paid out of the Treasury of the United States. They shall, in all cases except treason, felony, and breach of the peace, be privileged from arrest during their attendance at the session of their respective Houses, and in going to and returning from the same; and for any speech or debate in either House they shall not be questioned in any other place.

No Senator or Representative shall, during the time for which he was elected, be appointed to any civil office under the authority of the United States, which shall have been created, or the emoluments whereof shall have been increased during such time; and no person holding any office under the United States shall be a member of either House during his continuance in office.

Section 7. All bills for raising revenue shall originate in the House of Representatives; but the Senate may propose or concur with amendments as on other bills.

Every bill which shall have passed the House of Representatives and the Senate shall, before it become a law, be presented to the President of the United States; if he approve he shall sign it, but if not he shall return it, with his objections, to that House in which it shall have originated, who shall enter the objections at large on their journal and proceed to reconsider it. If after such reconsideration two-thirds of that House shall agree to pass the bill, it shall be sent, together with the objections, to the other House, by which it shall likewise be reconsidered, and if approved by two-thirds of that House, it shall become a law. But in all such cases the vote of both Houses shall be determined by yeas and nays, and the names of the persons voting for and against the bill shall be entered on the journal of each House respectively. If any bill shall not be returned by the President within ten days (Sundays excepted) after it shall have been presented to him, the same shall be a law, in like manner as if he had signed it, unless the Congress by their adjournment prevent its return, in which case it shall not be a law.

Every order, resolution or vote to which the concurrence of the Senate and House of Representatives may be necessary (except on a question of adjournment) shall be presented to the President of the United States; and before the same shall take effect shall be approved by him, or being disapproved by him, shall be repassed by two-thirds of the Senate and the House of Representatives, according to the rules and limitations prescribed in the case of a bill.

Section 8. The Congress shall have power to lay and collect taxes, duties, imposts and excises, to pay the debts and provide for the common defense and general welfare of the United States; but all duties, imposts and excises shall be uniform throughout the United States;

To borrow money on the credit of the United States;

To regulate commerce with foreign nations, and among the several States, and with the Indian tribes;

To establish an uniform rule of naturalization, and uniform laws on the subject of bankruptcies throughout the United States;

To coin money, regulate the value thereof, and of foreign coin, and fix the standard of weights and measures;

To provide for the punishment of counterfeiting the securities and current coin of the United States;

To establish post offices and post roads;

To promote the progress of science and useful arts by securing for limited times to authors and inventors the exclusive right to their respective writings and discoveries;

> This section allows Congress to pass laws about patents and copyrights.

To constitute tribunals inferior to the Supreme Court;

To define and punish piracies and felonies committed on the high seas, and offenses against the law of nations;

To declare war, grant letters of marque and reprisal, and make rules concerning captures on land and water;

> Only Congress can declare war, but the President, as Commander in Chief, can order the armed forces to act.

To raise and support armies, but no appropriation of money to that use shall be for a longer term than two years;

To provide and maintain a navy;

To make rules for the government and regulation of the land and naval forces;

To provide for calling forth the militia to execute the laws of the Union, suppress insurrections, and repel invasions;

To provide for organizing, arming and disciplining the militia, and for governing such part of them as may be employed in the service of the United States, reserving to the States respectively the appointment of the officers, and the authority of training the militia according to the discipline prescribed by Congress;

To exercise exclusive legislation in all cases whatsoever over such district (not exceeding ten miles square) as may, by cession of particular States and the acceptance of Congress, become the seat of government of the United States, and to exercise like authority over all places purchased by the consent of the legislature of the State in which the same shall be, for the erection of forts, magazines, arsenals, dockyards, and other needful buildings;

> This gave Congress the authority to establish and govern the District of Columbia.

To make all laws which shall be necessary and proper for carrying into execution the foregoing powers, and all other powers vested by this Constitution in the Government of the United States, or in any department or officer thereof.

> This is sometimes called the "elastic clause" because it can be interpreted to give many powers not actually mentioned in the Constitution.

Section 9. The migration or importation of such persons as any of the States now existing shall think proper to admit shall not be prohibited by the Congress prior to the year one thousand eight hundred and eight, but a tax or duty may be imposed on such importation, not exceeding ten dollars for each person.

> LIMITATIONS ON CONGRESS
> This paragraph set up a waiting period for action on the slave trade; Congress did abolish it in 1808.

The privilege of the writ of habeas corpus shall not be suspended, unless when in cases of rebellion or invasion the public safety may require it.

No bill of attainder or ex post facto law shall be passed.

No capitation or other direct tax shall be laid, unless in proportion to the census or enumeration hereinbefore directed to be taken.

> *Habeas corpus* guards against unjust imprisonment by requiring a judge or court to decide whether a person may be held.
> An *ex post facto* law applies to acts committed *before* the law was passed.
> The 16th Amendment allowed the income tax, which is not related to the census.

No tax or duty shall be laid on articles exported from any State.

No preference shall be given by any regulation of commerce or revenue to the ports of one State over those of another; nor shall vessels bound to or from one State be obliged to enter, clear or pay duties in another.

No money shall be drawn from the Treasury but in consequence of appropriations made by law; and a regular statement and account of the receipts and expenditures of all public money shall be published from time to time.

No title of nobility shall be granted by the United States; and no person holding any office of profit or trust under them shall, without the consent of the Congress, accept of any present, emolument, office, or title of any kind whatever from any king, prince, or foreign state.

> In fact, Presidents often exchange gifts with important foreign visitors, but the gifts are considered as gifts to the country.

Section 10. No State shall enter into any treaty, alliance, or confederation; grant letters of marque and reprisal; coin money; emit bills of credit; make anything but gold and silver coin a tender in payment of debts; pass any bill of attainder, ex post facto law or law impairing the obligation of contracts, or grant any title of nobility.

> LIMITATIONS ON STATES

No State shall, without the consent of the Congress, lay any imposts or duties on imports or exports, except what may be absolutely necessary for executing its inspection laws; and the net produce of all duties and imposts, laid by any State on imports or exports, shall be for the use of the Treasury of the United States; and all such laws shall be subject to the revision and control of the Congress.

No State shall, without the consent of Congress, lay any duty of tonnage, keep troops or ships of war in time of peace, enter into any agreement or compact with another State or with a foreign power, or engage in war, unless actually invaded or in such imminent danger as will not admit of delay.

Article II

Section 1. The executive power shall be vested in a President of the United States of America. He shall hold his office during the term of four years, and together with the Vice-President, chosen for the same term, be elected as follows:

Each State shall appoint, in such manner as the legislature thereof may direct, a number of Electors, equal to the whole number of Senators and Representatives to which the State may be entitled in the Congress; but no Senator or Representative, or person holding an office of trust or profit under the United States, shall be appointed an Elector.

The Electors shall meet in their respective States and vote by ballot for two persons, of whom one at least shall not be an inhabitant of the same State with themselves. And they shall make a list of all the persons voted for, and of the number of votes for each; which list they shall sign and certify, and transmit sealed to the seat of the government of the United States, directed to the President of the Senate. The President of the Senate shall, in the presence of the Senate and House of Representatives, open all the certificates, and the votes shall then be counted. The person having the greatest number of votes shall be the President, if such number be a majority of the whole number of Electors appointed; and if there be more than one who have such majority, and have an equal number of votes, then the House of Representatives shall immediately choose by ballot one of them for President; and if no person have a majority, then from the five highest on the list the said House shall in like manner choose the President. But in choosing the President the votes shall be taken by States, the representation from each State having one vote; a quorum for this purpose shall consist of a member or members from two-thirds of the States, and a majority of all the States shall be necessary to a choice. In every case, after the choice of the President, the person having the greatest number of votes of the Electors shall be the Vice-President. But if there should remain two or more who have equal votes, the Senate shall choose from them by ballot the Vice-President.

The Congress may determine the time of choosing the Electors and the day on which they shall give their votes, which day shall be the same throughout the United States.

No person except a natural-born citizen, or citizen of the United States at the time of the adoption of this Constitution, shall be eligible to the office of President; neither shall any person be eligible to that office who shall not have attained to the age of thirty-five years, and been fourteen years a resident within the United States.

In case of the removal of the President from office, or of his death, resignation, or inability to discharge the powers and duties of the said office, the same shall devolve on the Vice-President, and the Congress may by law provide for the case of removal, death, resignation, or inability, both of the President and Vice-President, declaring what officer shall then act as President, and such officer shall act accordingly until the disability be removed or a President shall be elected.

The President shall, at stated times, receive for his services a compensation, which shall neither be increased nor diminished during the period for which he shall have been elected, and he shall not receive within that period any other emolument from the United States or any of them.

Before he enter on the execution of his office he shall take the following oath or affirmation:

"I do solemnly swear (or affirm) that I will faithfully execute the office of President of the United States, and will to the best of my ability preserve, protect, and defend the Constitution of the United States."

Section 2. The President shall be Commander-in-Chief of the Army and Navy of the United States, and of the militia of the several States when called into the actual service of the United States; he may require the opinion, in writing, of the principal officer in each of the executive departments, upon any subject relating to the duties of their respective offices, and he shall have power to grant reprieves and pardons for offenses against the United States, except in cases of impeachment.

He shall have power, by and with the advice and consent of the Senate, to make treaties, provided two-thirds of the Senators present concur; and he shall nominate, and, by and with the advice and consent of the Senate, shall appoint ambassadors, other public ministers and consuls, judges of the

The Executive Branch
THE PRESIDENT

The system for electing the President has been changed a great deal since the Constitution was written, primarily because of the rise of political parties. The so-called "electoral college" still meets, though under the 12th Amendment electors vote separately for the President and Vice President. Originally, the candidate who came in second in the Presidential race became Vice President. Since electors now are pledged to support a party's candidates, election results are actually known before the electors meet.

The 25th Amendment (1967) makes further provisions for succession to the Presidency and for cases when the President is ill.

PRESIDENTIAL POWERS
This is the only mention of the Cabinet made in the Constitution; the first three Cabinet secretaries—state, treasury, and war—were named in 1789.

The Senate must approve Presidential appointments to important posts, such as Cabinet members, ambassadors, and Supreme Court justices.

Supreme Court, and all other officers of the United States whose appointments are not herein otherwise provided for, and which shall be established by law; but the Congress may by law vest the appointment of such inferior officers, as they think proper, in the President alone, in the courts of law, or in the heads of departments.

The President shall have power to fill up all vacancies that may happen during the recess of the Senate, by granting commissions which shall expire at the end of their next session.

Section 3. He shall from time to time give to the Congress information of the state of the Union, and recommend to their consideration such measures as he shall judge necessary and expedient; he may, on extraordinary occasions, convene both Houses, or either of them, and in case of disagreement between them with respect to the time of adjournment, he may adjourn them to such time as he shall think proper; he shall receive ambassadors and other public ministers; he shall take care that the laws be faithfully executed, and shall commission all the officers of the United States.

Section 4. The President, Vice-President and all civil officers of the United States shall be removed from office on impeachment for and conviction of treason, bribery, or other high crimes and misdemeanors.

Article III
Section 1. The judicial power of the United States shall be vested in one Supreme Court, and in such inferior courts as the Congress may from time to time ordain and establish. The judges, both of the Supreme and inferior courts, shall hold their offices during good behavior, and shall, at stated times, receive for their services a compensation, which shall not be diminished during their continuance in office.

Section 2. The judicial power shall extend to all cases, in law and equity, arising under this Constitution, the laws of the United States, and treaties made, or which shall be made, under their authority; to all cases affecting ambassadors, other public ministers, and consuls; to all cases of admiralty and maritime jurisdiction; to controversies to which the United States shall be a party; to controversies between two or more States; between a State and citizens of another State; between citizens of different States; between citizens of the same State claiming lands under grants of different States, and between a State, or the citizens thereof, and foreign states, citizens, or subjects.

In all cases affecting ambassadors, other public ministers and consuls, and those in which a State shall be party, the Supreme Court shall have original jurisdiction. In all the other cases before mentioned the Supreme Court shall have appellate jurisdiction, both as to law and fact, with such exceptions and under such regulations as the Congress shall make.

The trial of all crimes, except in cases of impeachment, shall be by jury; and such trial shall be held in the State where the said crimes shall have been committed; but when not committed within any State, the trial shall be at such place or places as the Congress may by law have directed.

Section 3. Treason against the United States shall consist only in levying war against them, or in adhering to their enemies, giving them aid and comfort. No person shall be convicted of treason unless on the testimony of two witnesses to the same overt act, or on confession in open court.

The Congress shall have power to declare the punishment of treason, but no attainder of treason shall work corruption of blood or forfeiture except during the life of the person attainted.

Article IV
Section 1. Full faith and credit shall be given in each State to the public acts, records, and judicial proceedings of every other State. And the Congress may by general laws prescribe the manner in which such acts, records, and proceedings shall be proved, and the effect thereof.

Section 2. The citizens of each State shall be entitled to all privileges and immunities of citizens in the several States.

A person charged in any State with treason, felony, or other crime, who shall flee from justice, and be found in another State, shall, on demand of the executive authority of the State from which he fled, be delivered up, to be removed to the State having jurisdiction of the crime.

RELATION TO CONGRESS
The President traditionally delivers his "State of the Union" message at the start of each session of Congress. He can suggest legislation at any time.

IMPEACHMENT
All federal court judges are appointed for life and can be removed only by impeachment and conviction or by resigning.

The Judicial Branch
COURTS

JURISDICTION

Certain kinds of cases are taken directly to the Supreme Court. The Court can also review cases that have been tried in other federal or state courts.

TREASON

Relations Between the States
FULL FAITH AND CREDIT
Contracts and other legal documents written in one state are valid in all other states; but not all states have identical laws.

OTHER OBLIGATIONS
Extradition is the process by which a fugitive from justice in one state is handed over to the state in which the crime was committed. States usually permit extradition, but they can refuse.

This paragraph provided that runaway slaves should be returned; the 13th Amendment abolished slavery.

No person held to service or labor in one State, under the laws thereof, escaping into another, shall, in consequence of any law or regulation therein, be discharged from such service or labor, but shall be delivered up on claim to the party to whom such service or labor may be due.

NEW STATES

Section 3. New States may be admitted by the Congress into this Union; but no new State shall be formed or erected within the jurisdiction of any other State; nor any State be formed by the junction of two or more States or parts of States, without the consent of the legislatures of the States concerned as well as of the Congress.

The Congress shall have power to dispose of and make all needful rules and regulations respecting the territory or other property belonging to the United States; and nothing in this Constitution shall be so construed as to prejudice any claims of the United States or of any particular State.

FEDERAL GUARANTEES

Section 4. The United States shall guarantee to every State in this Union a republican form of government, and shall protect each of them against invasion, and on application of the legislature, or of the executive (when the legislature cannot be convened) against domestic violence.

Constitutional Amendments

Article V

The Congress, whenever two-thirds of both Houses shall deem it necessary, shall propose amendments to this Constitution, or, on the application of the legislatures of two-thirds of the several States, shall call a convention for proposing amendments, which, in either case shall be valid to all intents and purposes as part of this Constitution, when ratified by the legislatures of three-fourths of the several States, or by conventions in three-fourths thereof, as the one or the other mode of ratification may be proposed by the Congress; provided that no amendment which may be made prior to the year one thousand eight hundred and eight shall in any manner affect the first and fourth clauses in the Ninth Section of the First Article; and that no State, without its consent shall be deprived of its equal suffrage in the Senate.

Federal Supremacy
John Marshall, the first chief justice, gave broad interpretations to many sections of the Constitution during his tenure from 1801 to 1835. This clause was interpreted by Marshall to mean that the Supreme Court had the power to review the constitutionality of acts of Congress, since, as stated here, the Constitution is the "supreme law of the land."

Article VI

All debts contracted and engagements entered into, before the adoption of this Constitution, shall be as valid against the United States under this Constitution as under the Confederation.

This Constitution, and the laws of the United States which shall be made in pursuance thereof, and all treaties made, or which shall be made, under the authority of the United States, shall be the supreme law of the land; and the judges in every State shall be bound thereby, anything in the constitution or laws of any State to the contrary notwithstanding.

The Senators and Representatives before mentioned and the members of the several State legislatures, and all executive and judicial officers both of the United States and of the several States, shall be bound by oath or affirmation to support this Constitution; but no religious test shall ever be required as a qualification to any office or public trust under the United States.

Ratification
The Constitution was signed by 39 delegates to the Constitutional Convention, representing 12 of the 13 colonies—all except Rhode Island.

Article VII

The ratification of the conventions of nine States shall be sufficient for the establishment of this Constitution between the States so ratifying the same.

Done in convention by the unanimous consent of the States present, the seventeenth day of September in the year of our Lord one thousand seven hundred and eighty-seven, and of the independence of the United States of America the twelfth. In witness whereof we have hereunto subscribed our names.

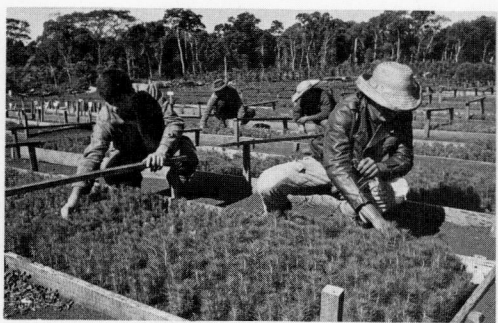

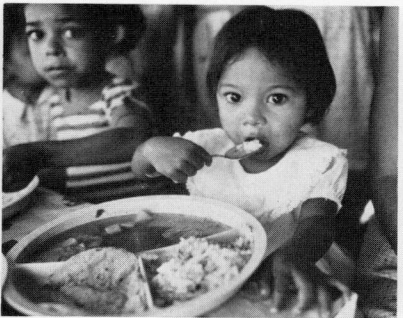

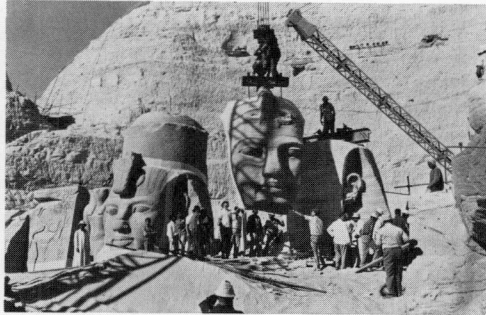

THE WORK OF THE UN includes meetings of the General Assembly (*below*) as well as varied activities throughout the world. The UN helps improve the forests of Paraguay (*left, above*), feeds children in Honduras (*middle*), and relocates threatened temples in Egypt (*right*).

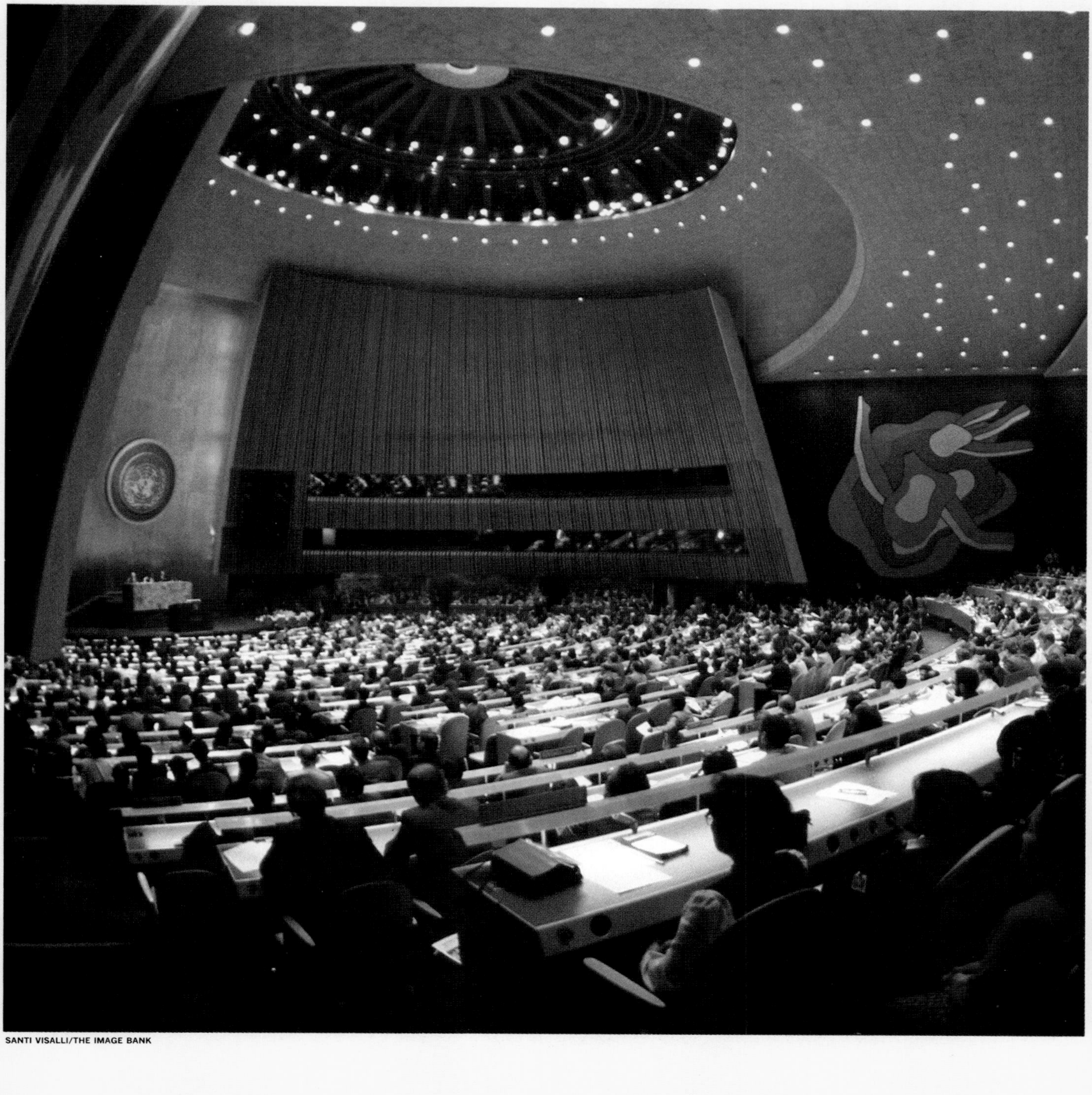

SANTI VISALLI/THE IMAGE BANK

Afghanistan	Albania	Algeria	Andorra	Angola	Antigua and Barbuda
Argentina	Australia	Austria	Bahamas	Bahrain	Bangladesh
Barbados	Belgium	Belize	Benin	Bhutan	Bolivia
Botswana	Brazil	Brunei	Bulgaria	Burkina Faso	Burma
Burundi	Cambodia	Cameroon	Canada	Cape Verde	Central African Republic
Chad	Chile	China	Colombia	Comoros	Congo
Costa Rica	Cuba	Cyprus	Czechoslovakia	Denmark	Djibouti
Dominica	Dominican Republic	Ecuador	Egypt	El Salvador	Equitorial Guinea
Ethiopia	Fiji	Finland	France	Gabon	Gambia

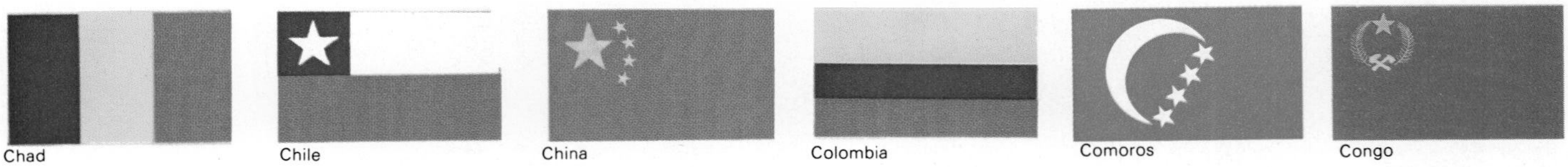

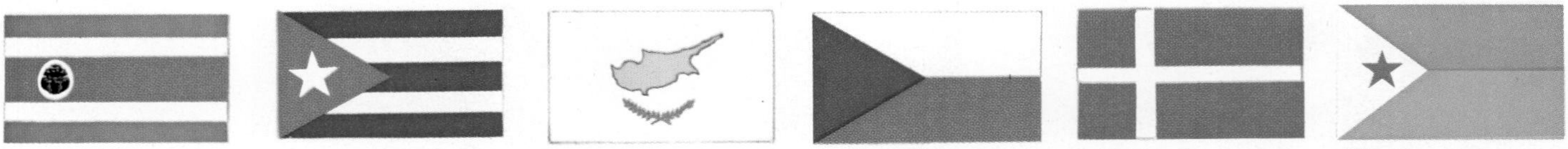

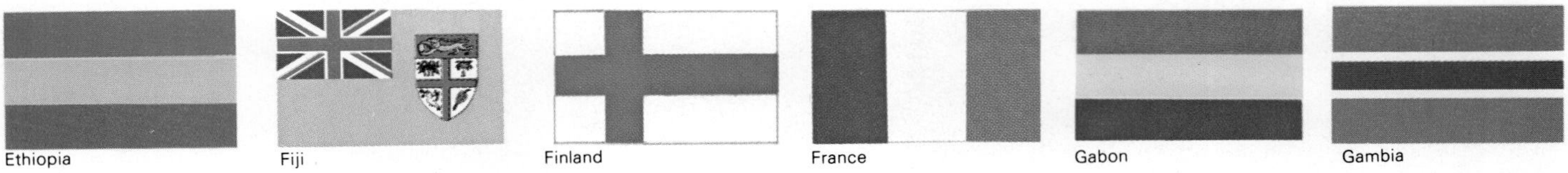

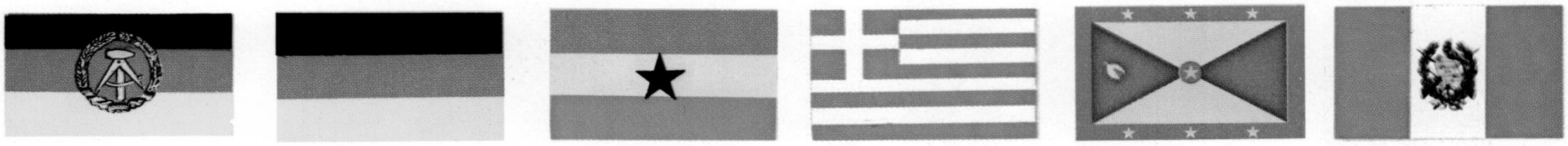

Germany, East  Germany, West  Ghana  Greece  Grenada Guatemala

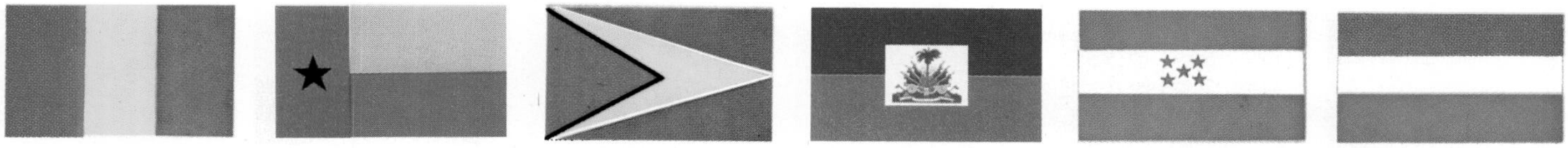

Guinea	Guinea-Bissau	Guyana	Haiti	Honduras	Hungary
Iceland	India	Indonesia	Iran	Iraq	Ireland
Israel	Italy	Ivory Coast	Jamaica	Japan	Jordan
Kenya	Kiribati	Korea, North	Korea, South	Kuwait	Laos
Lebanon	Lesotho	Liberia	Libya	Liechtenstein	Luxembourg
Madagascar	Malawi	Malaysia	Maldives	Mali	Malta
Mauritania	Mauritius	Mexico	Monaco	Mongolia	Morocco
Mozambique	Nauru	Nepal	Netherlands	New Zealand	Nicaragua
Niger	Nigeria	Norway	Oman	Pakistan	Panama
Papua New Guinea	Paraguay	Peru	Philippines	Poland	Portugal

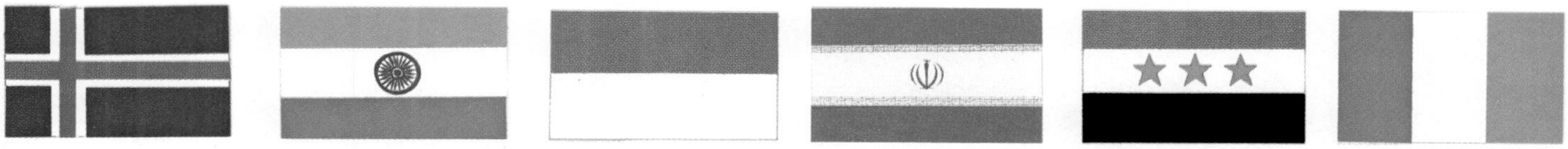

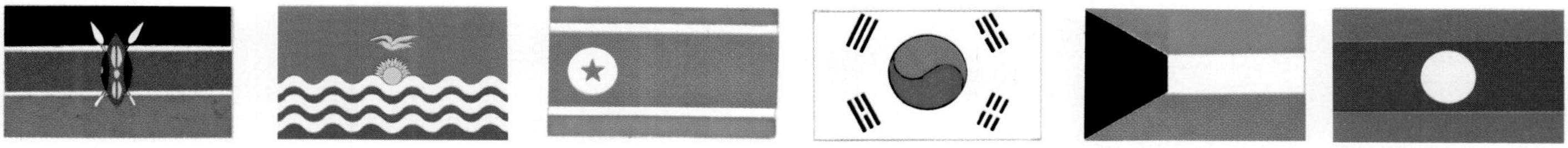

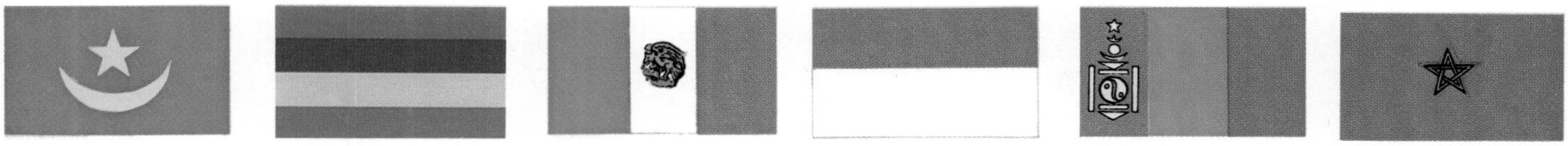

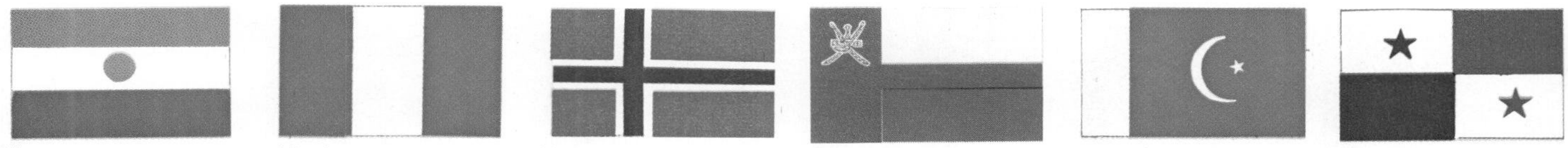

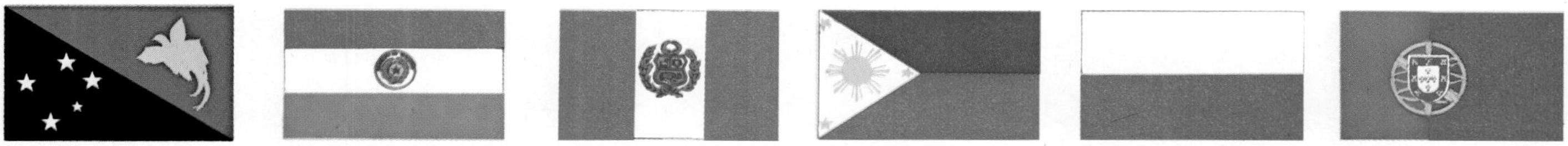

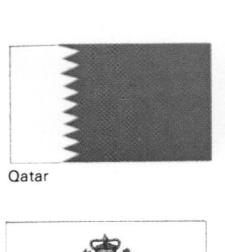 Qatar

 Romania

 Rwanda

 St. Christopher-Nevis

 St. Lucia

 St. Vincent and the Grenadines

 San Marino

 São Tomé and Principe

 Saudi Arabia

 Senegal

 Seychelles

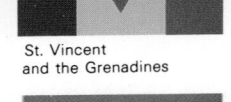 Sierra Leone

 Singapore

Solomon Islands

 Somalia

South Africa

 Spain

 Sri Lanka

 Sudan

Suriname

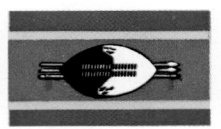 Swaziland

 Sweden

Switzerland

 Syria

 Taiwan

Tanzania

 Thailand

 Togo

Tonga

 Trinidad and Tobago

 Tunisia

 Turkey

 Tuvalu

 Uganda

 Union of Soviet Socialist Republics

 United Arab Emirates

 United Kingdom

 United States

 Uruguay

 Vanuatu

 Vatican City

 Venezuela

 Vietnam

 Western Samoa

 Yemen (South)

 Yemen Arab Republic

Yugoslavia

 Zaire

 Zambia

 Zimbabwe

Flags of International Organizations

 United Nations

NATO

Arab League

Organization of American States

SEATO

Central Treaty Organization

AMENDMENTS TO THE CONSTITUTION

The conventions of a number of the States having, at the time of their adopting the Constitution, expressed a desire, in order to prevent misconstruction or abuse of its powers, that further declaratory and restrictive clauses should be added, and as extending the ground of public confidence in the Government will best insure the beneficent ends of its institution;

Resolved, by the Senate and House of Representatives of the United States of America, in Congress assembled, two-thirds of both Houses concurring, that the following articles be proposed to the Legislatures of the several States, as amendments to the Constitution of the United States; all or any of which articles, when ratified by three-fourths of the said Legislatures, to be valid to all intents and purposes as part of the said Constitution, namely:

The Bill of Rights (1791)
The first ten amendments to the Constitution were proposed—and adopted—together at the request of the states. This Bill of Rights has become an integral part of the Constitution, and its guarantees to individuals are still significant today.

Amendment 1. Congress shall make no law respecting an establishment of religion, or prohibiting the free exercise thereof; or abridging the freedom of speech or of the press; or the right of the people peaceably to assemble, and to petition the government for a redress of grievances.

FREEDOM OF RELIGION, SPEECH, PRESS, ASSEMBLY, AND PETITION

Amendment 2. A well-regulated militia, being necessary to the security of a free State, the right of the people to keep and bear arms shall not be infringed.

RIGHT TO BEAR ARMS
This amendment is often cited by those opposed to gun-control laws.

Amendment 3. No soldier shall, in time of peace, be quartered in any house without the consent of the owner, nor in time of war, but in a manner to be prescribed by law.

QUARTERING SOLDIERS

Amendment 4. The right of the people to be secure in their persons, houses, papers, and effects, against unreasonable searches and seizures, shall not be violated, and no warrants shall issue but upon probable cause, supported by oath or affirmation, and particularly describing the place to be searched, and the persons or things to be seized.

SEARCHES AND SEIZURES
This amendment requires police and other officials to have specific search warrants when they make investigations of people, homes, or private property.

Amendment 5. No person shall be held to answer for a capital, or otherwise infamous crime, unless on a presentment or indictment of a grand jury, except in cases arising in the land or naval forces, or in the militia, when in actual service in time of war or public danger; nor shall any person be subject for the same offense to be twice put in jeopardy of life or limb; nor shall be compelled in any criminal case to be a witness against himself, nor be deprived of life, liberty or property, without due process of law; nor shall private property be taken for public use without just compensation.

RIGHTS OF DEFENDANTS
Several legal protections are included here—the need for a grand jury hearing; protection against "double jeopardy"; and the right not to testify against oneself in a trial or hearing. The right of the government to take private property for public use is called the "right of eminent domain."

Amendment 6. In all criminal prosecutions, the accused shall enjoy the right to a speedy and public trial, by an impartial jury of the State and district wherein the crime shall have been committed, which district shall have been previously ascertained by law, and to be informed of the nature and cause of the accusation; to be confronted with the witnesses against him; to have compulsory process for obtaining witnesses in his favor, and to have the assistance of counsel for his defense.

JURY IN CRIMINAL CASES
A 1963 Supreme Court decision ruled that the basic constitutional right to legal counsel in felony cases applies whether or not the accused person can afford a lawyer. If the accused cannot, the court must appoint a lawyer.

Amendment 7. In suits at common law, where the value in controversy shall exceed twenty dollars, the right of trial by jury shall be preserved, and no fact tried by a jury shall be otherwise re-examined in any court of the United States, than according to the rules of the common law.

JURY IN CIVIL CASES

Amendment 8. Excessive bail shall not be required, nor excessive fines imposed, nor cruel and unusual punishments inflicted.

EXCESSIVE PENALTIES

Amendment 9. The enumeration in the Constitution of certain rights shall not be construed to deny or disparage others retained by the people.

OTHER RIGHTS
Amendments nine and ten protect against a too-powerful federal government.

Amendment 10. The powers not delegated to the United States by the Constitution, nor prohibited by it to the States, are reserved to the States respectively, or to the people.

ADDITIONAL AMENDMENTS

SUITS AGAINST STATES (1798)

Amendment 11. The judicial power of the United States shall not be construed to extend to any suit in law or equity, commenced or prosecuted against one of the United States by citizens of another State, or by citizens or subjects of any foreign state.

PRESIDENTIAL ELECTIONS (1804)
This amendment changed the election process so that electors voted separately for President and Vice President.

Amendment 12. The Electors shall meet in their respective States and vote by ballot for President and Vice-President, one of whom, at least, shall not be an inhabitant of the same state with themselves; they shall name in their ballots the person voted for as President, and in distinct ballots the person voted for as Vice-President, and they shall make distinct lists of all persons voted for as President and of all persons voted for as Vice-President, and of the number of votes for each; which lists they shall sign and certify, and transmit sealed to the seat of the government of the United States, directed to the President of the Senate. The President of the Senate shall, in the presence of the Senate and House of Representatives, open all the certificates and the votes shall then be counted. The person having the greatest number of votes for President shall be the President, if such a number be a majority of the whole number of Electors appointed; and if no person have such majority, then from the persons having the highest numbers not exceeding three on the list of those voted for as President, the House of Representatives shall choose immediately, by ballot, the President. But in choosing the President the votes shall be taken by States, the representation from each State having one vote; a quorum for this purpose shall consist of a member or members from two-thirds of the States, and a majority of all the States shall be necessary to a choice. And if the House of Representatives shall not choose a President whenever the right of choice shall devolve upon them, before the fourth day of March next following, then the Vice-President shall act as President, as in the case of the death or other constitutional disability of the President.

The person having the greatest number of votes as Vice-President shall be the Vice-President, if such number be a majority of the whole number of Electors appointed; and if no person have a majority, then from the two highest numbers on the list the Senate shall choose the Vice-President; a quorum for the purpose shall consist of two-thirds of the whole number of Senators, and a majority of the whole number shall be necessary to a choice. But no person constitutionally ineligible to the office of President shall be eligible to that of Vice-President of the United States.

ABOLITION OF SLAVERY (1865)
The 13th and 14th Amendments were added after the Civil War. The 13th abolished slavery in the United States. The 14th gave the rights of citizenship to former slaves.

Amendment 13
Section 1. Neither slavery nor involuntary servitude, except as a punishment for crime whereof the party shall have been duly convicted, shall exist within the United States, or any place subject to their jurisdiction.

Section 2. Congress shall have power to enforce this article by appropriate legislation.

RIGHTS OF CITIZENS (1868)
This section extends the rights guaranteed in the Bill of Rights to matters under jurisdiction of the states. It is the basis for important Supreme Court decisions and legislation protecting civil rights of minorities.

Amendment 14
Section 1. All persons born or naturalized in the United States, and subject to the jurisdiction thereof, are citizens of the United States and of the State wherein they reside. No State shall make or enforce any law which shall abridge the privileges or immunities of citizens of the United States; nor shall any State deprive any person of life, liberty or property, without due process of law; nor deny to any person within its jurisdiction the equal protection of the laws.

This section gave the right to vote to black men; later, the 19th allowed women to vote, and the 26th lowered the voting age to 18.

Section 2. Representatives shall be apportioned among the several States according to their respective numbers, counting the whole number of persons in each State, excluding Indians not taxed. But when the right to vote at any election for the choice of Electors for President and Vice-President of the United States, Representatives in Congress, the executive and judicial officers of a State, or the members of the legislature thereof, is denied to any of the male inhabitants of such State, being twenty-one years of age, and citizens of the United States, or in any way abridged except for participation in rebellion or other crime, the basis of representation therein shall be reduced in the proportion which the number of such male citizens shall bear to the whole number of male citizens twenty-one years of age in such State.

The idea of this clause was to keep former Confederate officials out of the federal government. Special acts of Congress later allowed some to serve.

Section 3. No person shall be a Senator or Representative in Congress, or elector of President and Vice-President, or hold any office, civil or military, under the United States or under any State, who, having previously taken an oath as a member of Congress, or as an officer of the United States, or as a member of any State legislature, or as an executive or judicial officer of any State, to support the Constitution of the United States, shall have engaged in insurrection or rebellion against the same, or given aid or comfort to the enemies thereof. But Congress may, by a vote of two-thirds of each House, remove such disability.

Section 4. The validity of the public debt of the United States, authorized by law, including debts incurred for payment of pensions and bounties for services in suppressing insurrection or rebellion, shall not be questioned. But neither the United States nor any State shall assume or pay any debt or obligation incurred in aid of insurrection or rebellion against the United States, or any claim for the loss or emancipation of any slave; but all such debts, obligations, and claims shall be held illegal and void.

This clause forbade both the federal government and the states to pay any debt the Confederacy owed.

Section 5. The Congress shall have power to enforce, by appropriate legislation, the provisions of this article.

Amendment 15
Section 1. The right of citizens of the United States to vote shall not be denied or abridged by the United States or by any State on account of race, color, or previous condition of servitude.

BLACK VOTING RIGHTS (1870)
This amendment was added to strengthen the 14th Amendment.

Section 2. The Congress shall have power to enforce this article by appropriate legislation.

Amendment 16.
The Congress shall have power to lay and collect taxes on incomes, from whatever source derived, without apportionment among the several States, and without regard to any census or enumeration.

INCOME TAXES (1913)
An amendment was needed because the Constitution did not allow any direct tax.

SENATORIAL ELECTIONS (1913)

Amendment 17
Section 1. The Senate of the United States shall be composed of two Senators from each State, elected by the people thereof, for six years; and each Senator shall have one vote. The electors in each State shall have the qualifications requisite for electors of the most numerous branch of the State legislatures.

Section 2. When vacancies happen in the representation of any State in the Senate, the executive authority of such State shall issue writs of election to fill such vacancies: Provided, that the legislature of any State may empower the executive thereof to make temporary appointments until the people fill the vacancies by election as the legislature may direct.

Section 3. This amendment shall not be so construed as to affect the election or term of any Senator chosen before it becomes valid as part of the Constitution.

Amendment 18
Section 1. After one year from the ratification of this article the manufacture, sale or transportation of intoxicating liquors within, the importation thereof into, or the exportation thereof from the United States and all territory subject to the jurisdiction thereof, for beverage purposes, is hereby prohibited.

PROHIBITION (1919)
The Prohibition amendment was ineffective and so was repealed in 1933 by the 21st Amendment.

Section 2. The Congress and the several States shall have concurrent power to enforce this article by appropriate legislation.

Section 3. This article shall be inoperative unless it shall have been ratified as an amendment to the Constitution by the legislatures of the several States, as provided in the Constitution, within seven years from the date of the submission hereof to the States by the Congress.

Amendment 19
Section 1. The right of citizens of the United States to vote shall not be denied or abridged by the United States or by any State on account of sex.

WOMEN'S SUFFRAGE (1920)

Section 2. Congress shall have power to enforce this article by appropriate legislation.

Amendment 20
Section 1. The terms of the President and Vice-President shall end at noon on the 20th day of January, and the terms of Senators and Representatives at noon on the 3d day of January, of the years in which such terms would have ended if this article had not been ratified; and the terms of their successors shall then begin.

TERMS OF OFFICE (1933)
This is known as the "lame duck" amendment because it shortened the time between congressmen's elections and the date they took office. "Lame ducks" were defeated members who, under the old system, remained in Congress long after being defeated in an election.

Section 2. The Congress shall assemble at least once in every year, and such meetings shall begin at noon on the 3d day of January, unless they shall by law appoint a different day.

Section 3. If, at the time fixed for the beginning of the term of the President, the President-elect shall have died, the Vice-President-elect shall become

President. If a President shall not have been chosen before the time fixed for the beginning of his term or if the President-elect shall have failed to qualify, then the Vice-President-elect shall act as President until a President shall have qualified; and the Congress may by law provide for the case wherein neither a President-elect nor a Vice-President-elect shall have qualified, declaring who shall then act as President, or the manner in which one who is to act shall be selected, and such person shall act accordingly until a President or Vice-President shall have qualified.

Section 4. The Congress may by law provide for the case of the death of any of the persons from whom the House of Representatives may choose a President whenever the right of choice shall have devolved upon them, and for the case of the death of any of the persons from whom the Senate may choose a Vice-President whenever the right of choice shall have devolved upon them.

Section 5. Sections 1 and 2 shall take effect on the 15th day of October following the ratification of this article.

Section 6. This article shall be inoperative unless it shall have been ratified as an amendment to the Constitution by the legislatures of three-fourths of the several States within seven years from the date of its submission.

Amendment 21

REPEAL OF PROHIBITION (1933)

Section 1. The eighteenth article of amendment to the Constitution of the United States is hereby repealed.

Section 2. The transportation or importation into any State, territory, or possession of the United States for delivery or use therein of intoxicating liquors, in violation of the laws thereof, is hereby prohibited.

Section 3. This article shall be inoperative unless it shall have been ratified as an amendment to the Constitution by conventions in the several States, as provided in the Constitution, within seven years from the date of the submission hereof to the States by the Congress.

Amendment 22

PRESIDENTIAL TERMS (1951)
This amendment was passed after the death of Franklin D. Roosevelt, who had been elected four times. Its purpose was to prevent subsequent Presidents from serving more than two terms.

Section 1. No person shall be elected to the office of President more than twice, and no person who has held the office of President, or acted as President, for more than two years of a term to which some other person was elected President shall be elected to the office of President more than once. But this Article shall not apply to any person holding the office of President when this Article was proposed by the Congress, and shall not prevent any person who may be holding the office of President, or acting as President, during the term within which this Article becomes operative from holding the office of President or acting as President during the remainder of such term.

Section 2. This article shall be inoperative unless it shall have been ratified as an amendment to the Constitution by the legislatures of three-fourths of the several States within seven years from the date of its submission to the States by the Congress.

Amendment 23

DISTRICT OF COLUMBIA VOTING RIGHTS (1961)
Before this amendment, residents of the District of Columbia could not vote.

Section 1. The District constituting the seat of Government of the United States shall appoint in such manner as the Congress may direct:

A number of electors of President and Vice-President equal to the whole number of Senators and Representatives in Congress to which the District would be entitled if it were a State, but in no event more than the least populous State; they shall be in addition to those appointed by the States, but they shall be considered, for the purposes of the election of President and Vice-President, to be electors appointed by a State; and they shall meet in the District and perform such duties as provided by the twelfth article of amendment.

Section 2. The Congress shall have power to enforce this article by appropriate legislation.

Amendment 24

POLL TAX PROHIBITED (1964)
This amendment was passed in 1964 because poll taxes had been used in some states to prevent or discourage black voters from registering or voting.

Section 1. The right of citizens of the United States to vote in any primary or other election for President or Vice-President, for electors for President or Vice-President, or for Senator or Representative in Congress, shall not be denied or abridged by the United States or any State by reason of failure to pay any poll tax or other tax.

Section 2. The Congress shall have power to enforce this article by appropriate legislation.

Amendment 25

Section 1. In case of the removal of the President from office or of his death or resignation, the Vice-President shall become President.

Section 2. Whenever there is a vacancy in the office of the Vice-President, the President shall nominate a Vice-President who shall take office upon confirmation by a majority vote of both Houses of Congress.

Section 3. Whenever the President transmits to the President pro tempore of the Senate and the Speaker of the House of Representatives his written declaration that he is unable to discharge the powers and duties of his office, and until he transmits to them a written declaration to the contrary, such powers and duties shall be discharged by the Vice-President as Acting President.

Section 4. Whenever the Vice-President and a majority of either the principal officers of the executive departments or of such other body as Congress may by law provide, transmit to the President pro tempore of the Senate and the Speaker of the House of Representatives their written declaration that the President is unable to discharge the powers and duties of his office, the Vice-President shall immediately assume the powers and duties of the office as Acting President.

Thereafter, when the President transmits to the President pro tempore of the Senate and the Speaker of the House of Representatives his written declaration that no inability exists, he shall resume the powers and duties of his office unless the Vice-President and a majority of either the principal officers of the executive department or of such other body as Congress may by law provide, transmit within four days to the President pro tempore of the Senate and the Speaker of the House of Representatives their written declaration that the President is unable to discharge the powers and duties of his office. Thereupon Congress shall decide the issue, assembling within forty-eight hours for that purpose if not in session. If the Congress, within twenty-one days after receipt of the latter written declaration, or, if Congress is not in session, within twenty-one days after Congress is required to assemble, determines by two-thirds vote of both Houses that the President is unable to discharge the powers and duties of his office, the Vice-President shall continue to discharge the same as Acting President; otherwise, the President shall resume the powers and duties of his office.

Amendment 26

Section 1. The right of citizens of the United States, who are eighteen years of age or older, to vote shall not be denied or abridged by the United States or by any State on account of age.

Section 2. The Congress shall have power to enforce this article by appropriate legislation.

PROPOSED AMENDMENTS: Amendments proposed by Congress (passed by two-thirds majorities in both Houses) never take effect if they fail to gain ratification by three-quarters of the states (38 of 50) within the time limit set by Congress. Two recent examples are the Equal Rights Amendment (ERA) and the District of Columbia Representation Amendment.

ERA. The Equal Rights Amendment, favored by a wide range of women's groups, provided that "equality of rights under the law shall not be denied or abridged by the United States or any State on account of sex." It was passed by Congress in March, 1972, with the provision that it be ratified within five years. Thirty states ratified the amendment within a year, but only five more ratified it within the remaining four years. During this period five original ratifying states rescinded ratification.

In 1978, Congress extended the deadline for ratification to June 30, 1982, ten years and three months after it was originally proposed. But no additional state ratified the amendment during the additional time. The amendment was voted down in the Illinois and Florida legislatures in June, 1982, ending all hope of ratification. Even if three other states had ratified, the status of the amendment would have been unclear until the courts decided whether the five states that rescinded ratification should be counted among the 38 ratifying states.

D.C. Representation. This amendment, proposed by Congress in August, 1978, would provide representation for residents of Washington, D.C., in the Senate and the House of Representatives (Washington presently has one representative who serves on House committees and who can speak on the floor but cannot vote). After four years, only eight of the required 38 states had ratified this amendment. It seems nearly certain that it, like the Equal Rights Amendment, will never take effect.

PRESIDENTIAL ELECTIONS AND INAUGURATIONS

YEAR	PRINCIPAL PRESIDENTIAL CANDIDATES	STATE	PARTY	VOTE TOTAL	ELECTORAL	POPULAR	VICE-PRES. CANDIDATES NAME	STATE	FACTS CONCERNING INAUGURATION	AGE AT INAUG.
1789	George Washington	Va.	. . . . . .	73	69[1]	. . . . . .	John Adams	Mass.	I. **George Washington** was inaugurated President of the United States on a portico in front of the Senate chamber, April 30, 1789, in the federal building, facing Broad Street, in New York. The oath of office was administered by Robert R. Livingston, chancellor of the state of New York.	57
	John Adams	Mass.	. . . . . .		34	. . . . . .				
	John Jay	N.Y.	. . . . . .		9	. . . . . .				
1792	George Washington	Va.	Fed.	135	132[1]	. . . . . .	John Adams	Mass.	II. **George Washington**, for a second term, in the Senate chamber, March 4, 1793, in the Old Federal Hall, in Philadelphia. Oath of office administered by William Cushing of Massachusetts.	
	John Adams	Mass.	Fed.		77	. . . . . .				
	George Clinton	N.Y.	Rep.		50	. . . . . .				
1796	John Adams	Mass.	Fed.	138	71[1]	. . . . . .	Thomas Jefferson	Va.	III. **John Adams**, in the chamber of the House of Representatives, Congress Hall, March 4, 1797, in Philadelphia. Oath of office administered by Oliver Ellsworth, Chief Justice of the United States.	61
	Thomas Jefferson	Va.	Rep.		68					
	Thomas Pinckney	S.C.	Fed.		59					
	Aaron Burr	N.Y.	Rep.		30					
	Samuel Adams	Mass.	Rep.		15					
1800	Thomas Jefferson	Va.	Rep.	138	73[1]	. . . . . .	Aaron Burr	N.Y.	IV. **Thomas Jefferson**, in the Senate chamber of the Capitol, March 4, 1801, in the city of Washington. Oath of office administered by John Marshall, Chief Justice of the United States.	57
	Aaron Burr	N.Y.	Rep.		73					
	John Adams	Mass.	Fed.		65					
	C. C. Pinckney	S.C.	Fed.		64					
1804	Thomas Jefferson	Va.	Rep.	176	162	. . . . . .	George Clinton	N.Y.	V. **Thomas Jefferson**, for a second term, in Senate chamber, Washington, March 4, 1805, by Chief Justice John Marshall.	
	C. C. Pinckney	S.C.	Fed.		14		Rufus King	N.Y.		
1808	James Madison	Va.	Rep.	176	122	. . . . . .	George Clinton	N.Y.	VI. **James Madison**, in the chamber of the House of Representatives, Washington, March 4, 1809. Oath of office administered by Chief Justice John Marshall.	57
	C. C. Pinckney	S.C.	Fed.		47		Rufus King	N.Y.		
	George Clinton	N.Y.	Rep.		6		John Langdon	N.H.		
1812	James Madison	Va.	Rep.	218	128	. . . . . .	Elbridge Gerry	Mass.	VII. **James Madison**, for a second term, March 4, 1813. Oath was administered by Chief Justice Marshall.	
	De Witt Clinton	N.Y.	Fed.		89		Jared Ingersoll	Pa.		
1816	James Monroe	Va.	Rep.	221	183	. . . . . .	D. D. Tompkins	N.Y.	VIII. **James Monroe**, March 4, 1817. Oath administered by Chief Justice John Marshall in front of the eastern portico of the Capitol in Washington.	58
	Rufus King	N.Y.	Fed.		34		John E. Howard	Md.		
							James Ross	Pa.		
1820	James Monroe	Va.	Rep.	235	231	. . . . . .	D. D. Tompkins	N.Y.	IX. **James Monroe**, for a second term, in the House of Representatives, March 5, 1821. As March 4 came on Sunday, he took the oath, administered by Chief Justice Marshall, at noon on Monday.	
	John Q. Adams	Mass.	Rep.		1		Richard Stockton	N.J.		
1824	John Q. Adams	Mass.	Rep.	261	84[2]	108,740	John C. Calhoun	S.C.	X. **John Quincy Adams**, in the hall of the House of Representatives, March 4, 1825. Oath of office administered by Chief Justice Marshall.	57
	Andrew Jackson	Tenn.	Dem.		99[2]	153,544	Nathan Sanford	N.Y.		
1828	Andrew Jackson	Tenn.	Dem.	261	178	647,286	John C. Calhoun	S.C.	XI. **Andrew Jackson**, on the eastern portico of the Capitol, March 4, 1829. Oath administered by Chief Justice Marshall.	61
	John Q. Adams	Mass.	Nat. Rep.		83	508,064	Richard Rush	Pa.		
1832	Andrew Jackson	Tenn.	Dem.	288	219	687,502	Martin Van Buren	N.Y.	XII. **Andrew Jackson**, for a second term, in the hall of the House of Representatives, March 4, 1833. Oath administered by Chief Justice Marshall.	
	Henry Clay	Ky.	Nat. Rep.		49	530,189	John Sergeant	Pa.		
1836	Martin Van Buren	N.Y.	Dem.	294	170	762,678	R. M. Johnson	Ky.	XIII. **Martin Van Buren**, on the eastern portico of the Capitol, March 4, 1837. Oath administered by Chief Justice Taney.	54
	Wm. H. Harrison	Ohio	Whig		73		Francis Granger	N.Y.		
	Hugh L. White	Tenn.	Whig		26	735,651	John Tyler	Va.		
	Daniel Webster	Mass.	Whig		14		William Smith	Ala.		
1840	Wm. H. Harrison	Ohio	Whig	294	234	1,275,016	John Tyler	Va.	XIV. **William Henry Harrison**, on the eastern portico of the Capitol, March 4, 1841. Oath administered by Chief Justice Taney. **John Tyler**, April 6, 1841, at Brown's Indian Queen hotel, Washington. Oath administered by Judge William Cranch.	68 / 51
	Martin Van Buren	N.Y.	Dem.		60	1,129,102	R. M. Johnson	Ky.		
1844	James K. Polk	Tenn.	Dem.	275	170	1,337,243	George M. Dallas	Pa.	XV. **James Knox Polk**, on the eastern portico of the Capitol, March 4, 1845. Oath administered by Chief Justice Taney.	49
	Henry Clay	Ky.	Whig		105	1,299,062	T. Frelinghuysen	N.J.		
1848	Zachary Taylor	La.	Whig	290	163	1,360,099	Millard Fillmore	N.Y.	XVI. **Zachary Taylor**, on the eastern portico of the Capitol, March 5, 1849. March 4 came on Sunday. Oath administered by Chief Justice Taney. **Millard Fillmore**, in the House of Representatives, July 10, 1850. Oath administered by Judge William Cranch.	64 / 50
	Lewis Cass	Mich.	Dem.		127	1,220,544	Wm. O. Butler	Ky.		
	Martin Van Buren	N.Y.	F.S.		. . .	291,263	Chas. F. Adams	Mass.		
1852	Franklin Pierce	N.H.	Dem.	296	254	1,601,274	William R. King	Ala.	XVII. **Franklin Pierce**, on the eastern portico of the Capitol, March 4, 1853. Oath administered by Chief Justice Taney.	48
	Winfield Scott	N.J.	Whig		42	1,386,580	Wm. A. Graham	N.C.		
1856	James Buchanan	Pa.	Dem.	296	174	1,838,169	J. C. Breckinridge	Ky.	XVIII. **James Buchanan**, on the eastern portico of the Capitol, March 4, 1857. Oath administered by Chief Justice Taney.	65
	John C. Fremont	Calif.	Rep.		114	1,341,264	Wm. L. Dayton	N.J.		
	Millard Fillmore	N.Y.	Amer.		8	874,534	A. J. Donelson	Tenn.		
1860	Abraham Lincoln	Ill.	Rep.	303	180	1,866,452	Hannibal Hamlin	Me.	XIX. **Abraham Lincoln**, on the eastern portico of the Capitol, March 4, 1861. Oath administered by Chief Justice Taney.	52
	J. C. Breckinridge	Ky.	Dem.		72	847,953	Joseph Lane	Ind.		
	Stephen A. Douglas	Ill.	Union D.		39	1,375,157	H. V. Johnson	Ga.		
1864	Abraham Lincoln	Ill.	Rep.	314	212	2,213,665	Andrew Johnson	Tenn.	XX. **Abraham Lincoln**, for a second term, on the eastern portico of the Capitol, March 4, 1865. Oath administered by Chief Justice Chase. **Andrew Johnson**, in his rooms at the Kirkwood House, Washington, D.C., April 15, 1865. Oath administered by Chief Justice Chase.	50
	Geo. B. McClellan	N.J.	Dem.		21	1,802,237	G. H. Pendleton	Ohio		
1868	Ulysses S. Grant	Ill.	Rep.	317	214	3,012,833	Schuyler Colfax	Ind.	XXI. **Ulysses Simpson Grant**, on the eastern portico of the Capitol, March 4, 1869. Oath of office administered by Chief Justice Chase.	46
	Horatio Seymour	N.Y.	Dem.		80	2,703,249	F. P. Blair, Jr.	Mo.		
1872	Ulysses S. Grant	Ill.	Rep.	366	286	3,597,132	Henry Wilson	Mass.	XXII. **Ulysses Simpson Grant**, for a second term, on the eastern portico of the Capitol, March 4, 1873. Oath administered by Chief Justice Chase.	
	Horace Greeley	N.Y.	D. & L.		. . .	2,834,125	B. Gratz Brown	Mo.		
	Charles O'Conor	N.Y.	Dem.			29,489	John Q. Adams	Mass.		
1876	Rutherford B. Hayes	Ohio	Rep.	369	185	4,036,298	Wm. A. Wheeler	N.Y.	XXIII. **Rutherford Birchard Hayes**, privately in the White House, March 3, 1877. Oath administered by Chief Justice Waite.	54
	Samuel J. Tilden	N.Y.	Dem.		184	4,300,590	T. A. Hendricks	Ind.		
1880	James A. Garfield	Ohio	Rep.	369	214	4,454,416	Chester A. Arthur	N.Y.	XXIV. **James Abram Garfield**, on eastern portico of the Capitol, March 4, 1881. Oath administered by Chief Justice Waite. **Chester Alan Arthur**, at his residence, N.Y., Sept. 20, 1881. Oath administered by Jno R. Brady, justice of the N.Y. Supreme Court. Oath repeated at the Capitol, September 22, 1881; administered by Chief Justice Waite.	49 / 50
	Win'd S. Hancock	Pa.	Dem.		155	4,444,952	Wm. H. English	Ind.		
1884	Grover Cleveland	N.Y.	Dem.	401	219	4,874,986	T. A. Hendricks	Ind.	XXV. **Grover Cleveland**, on the eastern portico of the Capitol, March 4, 1885. Oath administered by Chief Justice Waite.	47
	James G. Blaine	Me.	Rep.		182	4,851,981	John A. Logan	Ill.		
1888	Benjamin Harrison	Ind.	Rep.	401	233	5,439,853	Levi P. Morton	N.Y.	XXVI. **Benjamin Harrison**, on eastern portico of the Capitol, March 4, 1889. Oath administered by Chief Justice Fuller.	55
	Grover Cleveland	N.Y.	Dem.		168	5,549,309	A. G. Thurman	Ohio		

YEAR	PRINCIPAL PRESIDENTIAL CANDIDATES	STATE	PARTY	VOTE TOTAL	ELECTORAL	POPULAR	VICE-PRES. CANDIDATES NAME	STATE	FACTS CONCERNING INAUGURATION	AGE AT INAUG.
1892	**Grover Cleveland**	N.Y.	Dem.	444	277	5,554,437	A. E. Stevenson	Ill.	XXVII. **Grover Cleveland**, on eastern portico of the Capitol, March 4, 1893. Oath administered by Chief Justice Fuller.	55
	Benjamin Harrison	Ind.	Rep.		145	5,175,287	Whitelaw Reid	N.Y.		
	James B. Weaver	Iowa	People's		22	1,041,028	James G. Field	Va.		
1896	**William McKinley**	Ohio	Rep.	447	271	7,104,779	Garret A. Hobart	N.J.	XXVIII. **William McKinley**, on the eastern portico of the Capitol, March 4, 1897. Oath administered by Chief Justice Fuller.	54
	William J. Bryan	Neb.	Dem.		176	6,502,925	Arthur Sewall	Me.		
	William J. Bryan	Neb.	People's				Th. E. Watson	Ga.		
1900	**William McKinley**	Ohio	Rep.	447	292	7,219,101	Theo. Roosevelt	N.Y.	XXIX. **William McKinley**, for a second term, on the eastern portico of the Capitol, March 4, 1901. Oath administered by Chief Justice Fuller. **Theodore Roosevelt**, at residence of Ansley Wilcox, Buffalo, N.Y., September 14, 1901. Oath administered by Judge John R. Hazel of the United States district court.	42
	William J. Bryan	Neb.	Dem. & P.		155	6,357,054	A. E. Stevenson	Ill.		
1904	**Theodore Roosevelt**	N.Y.	Rep.	476	336	7,623,486	Chas. W. Fairbanks	Ind.	XXX. **Theodore Roosevelt**, on the eastern portico of the Capitol, March 4, 1905. Oath administered by Chief Justice Melville W. Fuller.	
	Alton B. Parker	N.Y.	Dem.		140	5,077,971	Henry G. Davis	W. Va.		
	Eugene V. Debs	Ind.	Soc.			402,283	Benjamin Hanford	N.Y.		
1908	**William H. Taft**	Ohio	Rep.	483	321	7,637,676	James S. Sherman	N.Y.	XXXI. **William Howard Taft**, in the chamber of the United States Senate, Washington, March 4, 1909. Oath administered by Chief Justice Fuller.	51
	William J. Bryan	Neb.	Dem.		162	6,393,182	John W. Kern	Ind.		
	Eugene V. Debs	Ind.	Soc.			420,393	Benjamin Hanford	N.Y.		
1912	**Woodrow Wilson**	N.J.	Dem.	531	435	6,282,542	Thos. R. Marshall	Ind.	XXXII. **Woodrow Wilson**, on eastern portico of the Capitol, March 4, 1913. Oath administered by Chief Justice Edward D. White.	56
	Theodore Roosevelt	N.Y.	Prog.		88	4,114,585	Hiram Johnson	Calif.		
	William H. Taft	Ohio	Rep.		8	3,480,479	James S. Sherman	N.Y.		
1916	**Woodrow Wilson**	N.J.	Dem.	531	277	9,129,606	Thos. R. Marshall	Ind.	XXXIII. **Woodrow Wilson**, on eastern portico of the Capitol, March 4, 1917. Oath administered by Chief Justice Edward D. White.	
	Chas. E. Hughes	N.Y.	Rep.		254	8,538,221	Chas. W. Fairbanks	Ind.		
1920	**Warren G. Harding**	Ohio	Rep.	531	404	16,152,200	Calvin Coolidge	Mass.	XXXIV. **Warren Gamaliel Harding**, on the eastern portico of the Capitol, March 4, 1921. Oath administered by Chief Justice Edward D. White. **Calvin Coolidge**, at home of his father, John C. Coolidge, Plymouth, Vt., August 2, 1923. Oath administered by his father.	55
	James M. Cox	Ohio	Dem.		127	9,147,353	Franklin D. Roosevelt	N.Y.		50
	Eugene V. Debs	Ind.	Soc.			919,799	Seymour Stedman	Ill.		
1924	**Calvin Coolidge**	Mass.	Rep.	531	382	15,718,789	Chas. G. Dawes	Ill.	XXXV. **Calvin Coolidge**, on plaza of the Capitol, March 4, 1925. Oath administered by Chief Justice and former President William H. Taft.	
	John W. Davis	W. Va.	Dem.		136	8,378,962	Chas. W. Bryan	Neb.		
	Robt. M. LaFollette	Wis.	Prog. & F.L.		13	4,822,319	Burton K. Wheeler	Mont.		
1928	**Herbert C. Hoover**	Calif.	Rep.	531	444	21,943,328	Chas. Curtis	Kan.	XXXVI. **Herbert C. Hoover**, on eastern portico of the Capitol, March 4, 1929. Oath administered by Chief Justice William H. Taft.	54
	Alfred E. Smith	N.Y.	Dem.		87	15,430,718	Joseph T. Robinson	Ark.		
	Norman Thomas	N.Y.	Soc.			267,420	Jas. A. Maurer	Pa.		
1932	**Franklin D. Roosevelt**	N.Y.	Dem.	531	472	22,815,785	John N. Garner	Tex.	XXXVII. **Franklin D. Roosevelt**, on rostrum in front of Capitol, March 4, 1933. Broadcast over radio. Chief Justice Hughes administered oath.	51
	Herbert C. Hoover	Calif.	Rep.		59	15,759,266	Chas. Curtis	Kan.		
	Norman Thomas	N.Y.	Soc.			881,951	Jas. A. Maurer	Pa.		
1936	**Franklin D. Roosevelt**	N.Y.	Dem.	531	523	24,476,673	John N. Garner	Tex.	XXXVIII. **Franklin D. Roosevelt**, on east portico of the Capitol, January 20, 1937. Chief Justice Hughes administered the oath.	54
	Alfred M. Landon	Kan.	Rep.		8	16,679,583	Frank Knox	Ill.		
	William Lemke	N.D.	Union			882,479	T. C. O'Brien	Mass.		
	Norman Thomas	N.Y.	Soc.			187,720	George Nelson	Wis.		
1940	**Franklin D. Roosevelt**	N.Y.	Dem.	531	449	27,243,466	Henry A. Wallace	Iowa	XXXIX. **Franklin D. Roosevelt**, on the steps of the Capitol, January 20, 1941. Oath administered by Chief Justice Hughes.	58
	Wendell L. Willkie	Ind.	Rep.		82	22,304,755	Charles L. McNary	Ore.		
	Norman Thomas	N.Y.	Soc.			99,557	Maynard C. Krueger	Ill.		
1944	**Franklin D. Roosevelt**	N.Y.	Dem.	531	432	25,610,946	Harry S. Truman	Mo.	XL. **Franklin D. Roosevelt**, on south portico of the Capitol, January 20, 1945. Chief Justice Stone administered the oath. **Harry S. Truman**, in the red-draped Cabinet Room of the White House, April 12, 1945. Oath administered by Chief Justice Stone.	62
	Thomas E. Dewey	N.Y.	Rep.		99	22,018,177	John W. Bricker	Ohio		60
	Norman Thomas	N.Y.	Soc.			74,787	Darlington Hoopes	Pa.		
1948	**Harry S. Truman**	Mo.	Dem.	529	304	24,104,836	Alben W. Barkley	Ky.	XLI. **Harry S. Truman**, on east portico of the Capitol, Jan. 20, 1949. Oath administered by Chief Justice Vinson.	64
	Thos. E. Dewey	N.Y.	Rep.		189	21,969,500	Earl Warren	Cal.		
	Norman Thomas	N.Y.	Soc.			132,138	Tucker P. Smith	Mich.		
1952	**Dwight D. Eisenhower**	N.Y.	Rep.	531	442	33,938,285	Richard M. Nixon	Cal.	XLII. **Dwight D. Eisenhower**, on steps of Capitol, Jan. 20, 1953. Oath administered by Chief Justice Vinson.	62
	Adlai E. Stevenson	Ill.	Dem.		89	27,312,217	John J. Sparkman	Ala.		
	Vincent W. Hallinan	Cal.	Prog.			140,138	Charlotta A. Bass	Cal.		
	Darlington Hoopes	Penn.	Soc.			20,189	Samuel H. Friedman	N.Y.		
1956	**Dwight D. Eisenhower**	Pa.	Rep.	531	457	35,582,236	Richard M. Nixon	Cal.	XLIII. **Dwight D. Eisenhower**, on the east steps of the Capitol, Jan. 21, 1957. Oath administered by Chief Justice Warren.	66
	Adlai E. Stevenson	Ill.	Dem.		73	26,028,887	Estes Kefauver	Tenn.		
1960	**John F. Kennedy**	Mass.	Dem.	537	300	34,226,925	Lyndon B. Johnson	Texas	XLIV. **John F. Kennedy**, on the steps of the Capitol's east portico Jan. 20, 1961. Oath administered by Chief Justice Warren. **Lyndon B. Johnson**, aboard Presidential jet at Dallas airport. Oath administered by Judge Sarah T. Hughes.	43
	Richard M. Nixon	Calif.	Rep.		223	34,108,662	Henry C. Lodge	Mass.		55
1964	**Lyndon B. Johnson**	Texas	Dem.	538	486	43,126,218	Hubert Humphrey	Minn.	XLV. **Lyndon B. Johnson**, on the steps of the Capitol's east portico, Jan. 20, 1965.	
	Barry M. Goldwater	Ariz.	Rep.		52	27,174,898	William Miller	N.Y.		
1968	**Richard M. Nixon**	N.Y.	Rep.	538	301	31,770,237	Spiro T. Agnew	Md.	XLVI. **Richard M. Nixon**, on the steps of the Capitol's east portico. Jan. 20, 1969.	56
	Hubert H. Humphrey	Minn.	Dem.		191	31,270,533	Edmund S. Muskie	Me.		
	George C. Wallace	Ala.	Am. Ind.		46	9,906,141	Curtis E. LeMay	Calif.		
1972	**Richard M. Nixon**	N.Y.	Rep.	538	521	39,295,257	Spiro T. Agnew	Md.	XLVII. **Richard M. Nixon**, on the steps of the Capitol's east portico, January 20, 1973. **Gerald R. Ford**, in the East Room of the White House, Aug. 9, 1974. Oath administered by Chief Justice Burger.	60
	George McGovern	S.D.	Dem.		17	23,739,708	R. Sargent Shriver	Md.		61
1976	**James E. Carter**	Ga.	Dem.	538	297	40,287,283	Walter F. Mondale	Minn.	XLVIII **James E. Carter**, on the steps of the Capitol's east portico. Jan. 20, 1977. Oath administered by Chief Justice Burger.	53
	Gerald R. Ford	Mich.	Rep.		241	38,557,855	Robert Dole	Kans.		
1980	**Ronald W. Reagan**	Cal.	Rep.	538	489	43,899,248	George Bush	Mass.	XLIX. **Ronald W. Reagan**, on the west steps of the Capitol, Jan. 20, 1981. Oath administered by Chief Justice Burger.	69
	James E. Carter	Ga.	Dem.		49	35,481,435	Walter F. Mondale	Minn.		
1984	**Ronald W. Reagan**	Cal.	Rep.	538	525	52,609,797	George Bush	Me.	L. **Ronald W. Reagan**, in the White House, Jan. 20, 1985. Oath administered by Chief Justice Burger.	73
	Walter F. Mondale	Minn.	Dem.		13	36,450,613	Geraldine A. Ferraro	N.Y.		
1988	**George H. Bush**	Texas	Rep.	538	426	47,946,422	J. Danforth Quayle	Indiana	LI. **George H. Bush**, on the west steps of the Capitol, Jan. 20, 1989. Oath administered by Chief Justice Rehnquist.	64
	Michael S. Dukakis	Mass.	Dem.		112	41,016,429	Lloyd Bentsen	Texas		

[1] Prior to 1804 each elector was entitled to vote for two candidates for President. The candidate with the greatest number of votes was declared elected President; the candidate with the next highest vote was declared elected Vice-President.

[2] As there was no election the choice was decided by the House of Representatives.

PRESIDENTS OF THE UNITED STATES

NO.	PRESIDENT'S NAME AND NUMBER OF ADMINISTRATION	BORN DATE	BIRTHPLACE	PARENTS FATHER	MOTHER	EDUCATION *Date indicates graduation	EARLY VOCATION	RELIGIOUS FAITH	MARRIED
1.	George Washington, 1-2	Feb. 22, 1732	Bridges Creek, Va.	Augustine	Mary Ball	Common School	Surveyor	Episcopalian	1759
2.	John Adams, 3	Oct. 30, 1735	Quincy, Mass.	John	Susanna Boylston	Harvard College, 1755*	Teacher	Unitarian	1764
3.	Thomas Jefferson, 4-5	Apr. 13, 1743	Shadwell, Va.	Peter	Jane Randolph	William and Mary College, 1762	Lawyer	Liberal	1772
4.	James Madison, 6-7	Mar. 16, 1751	Port Conway, Va.	James	Nellie Conway	Princeton College, 1771	Lawyer	Episcopalian	1794
5.	James Monroe, 8-9	Apr. 28, 1758	Westmoreland Co., Va.	Spence	Elizabeth Jones	William and Mary College	Lawyer	Episcopalian	1786
6.	John Quincy Adams, 10	July 11, 1767	Quincy, Mass.	John	Abigail Smith	Harvard College, 1787	Lawyer	Unitarian	1797
7.	Andrew Jackson, 11-12	Mar. 15, 1767	near Monroe, N.C.	Andrew	Elizabeth Hutchinson	Self taught	Lawyer	Presbyterian	1791
8.	Martin Van Buren, 13	Dec. 5, 1782	Kinderhook, N.Y.	Abraham	Mary Hoes (Goes)	Kinderhook Academy	Lawyer	Reformed Dutch	1807
9.	William Henry Harrison, 14	Feb. 9, 1773	Berkeley, Va.	Benjamin	Elizabeth Bassett	Hampden-Sidney College, 1790	Doctor	Episcopalian	1795
10.	John Tyler, 14	Mar. 29, 1790	Greenway, Va.	John	Mary Armistead	William and Mary College, 1807	Lawyer	Episcopalian	1813 1844
11.	James Knox Polk, 15	Nov. 2, 1795	Mecklenburg Co., N.C.	Samuel	Jane Knox	University of North Carolina, 1818	Lawyer	Presbyterian	1824
12.	Zachary Taylor, 16	Nov. 24, 1784	Orange Co., Va.	Richard	Mary Strother	Common School	Soldier	Episcopalian	1810
13.	Millard Fillmore, 16	Jan. 7, 1800	Summer Hill, N.Y.	Nathaniel	Phebe Millard	Common School	Woolcarder	Unitarian	1826 1858
14.	Franklin Pierce, 17	Nov. 23, 1804	Hillsborough, N.H.	Benjamin	Anna Kendrick	Bowdoin College, 1824	Lawyer	Episcopalian	1834
15.	James Buchanan, 18	Apr. 23, 1791	near Mercersburg, Pa.	James	Elizabeth Speer	Dickinson College, 1809	Lawyer	Presbyterian	. . .
16.	Abraham Lincoln, 19-20	Feb. 12, 1809	Hardin Co., Ky.	Thomas	Nancy Hanks	Self taught	Farmer	Liberal	1842
17.	Andrew Johnson, 20	Dec. 29, 1808	Raleigh, N.C.	Jacob	Mary McDonough	Self taught	Tailor	Liberal	1827
18.	Ulysses Simpson Grant, 21-22	Apr. 27, 1822	Point Pleasant, Ohio	Jesse Root	Hannah Simpson	West Point Military Academy, 1843	Tanner	Methodist	1848
19.	Rutherford Birchard Hayes, 23	Oct. 4, 1822	Delaware, Ohio	Rutherford	Sophia Birchard	Kenyon College, 1842	Lawyer	Methodist	1852
20.	James Abram Garfield, 24	Nov. 19, 1831	Orange, Ohio	Abram	Eliza Ballou	Williams College, 1856	Teacher	Disciples	1858
21.	Chester Alan Arthur, 24	Oct. 5, 1830	Fairfield, Vt.	William	Malvina Stone	Union College, 1848	Teacher	Episcopalian	1859
22.	Grover Cleveland, 25	Mar. 18, 1837	Caldwell, N.J.	Richard Falley	Anne Neal	Academy	Teacher	Presbyterian	1886
23.	Benjamin Harrison, 26	Aug. 20, 1833	North Bend, Ohio	John Scott	Elizabeth F. Irwin	Miami University, 1852	Lawyer	Presbyterian	1853 1896
24.	Grover Cleveland, 27	Mar. 18, 1837	Caldwell, N.J.	Richard Falley	Anne Neal	Academy	Teacher	Presbyterian	1886
25.	William McKinley, 28-29	Jan. 29, 1843	Niles, Ohio	William	Nancy Allison	Allegheny College	Teacher	Methodist	1871
26.	Theodore Roosevelt, 29-30	Oct. 27, 1858	New York City	Theodore	Martha Bulloch	Harvard University, 1880	Writer	Reformed Dutch	1880 1886
27.	William Howard Taft, 31	Sept. 15, 1857	Cincinnati, Ohio	Alphonso	Louise M. Torrey	Yale University, 1878	Lawyer	Unitarian	1886
28.	Woodrow Wilson, 32-33	Dec. 28, 1856	Staunton, Va.	Joseph Ruggles	Janet Woodrow	Princeton University, 1879	Lawyer	Presbyterian	1885 1915
29.	Warren Gamaliel Harding, 34	Nov. 2, 1865	Corsica, Ohio	George Tryon	Phoebe E. Dickerson	Ohio Central College	Editor	Baptist	1891
30.	Calvin Coolidge, 34-35	July 4, 1872	Plymouth, Vt.	John Calvin	Victoria J. Moor	Amherst College, 1895	Lawyer	Congregationalist	1905
31.	Herbert Clark Hoover, 36	Aug. 10, 1874	West Branch, Iowa	Jesse Clark	Huldah R. Minthorn	Stanford University, 1895	Engineer	Quaker	1899
32.	Franklin Delano Roosevelt, 37, 38, 39, 40	Jan. 30, 1882	Hyde Park, N.Y.	James	Sara Delano	Harvard University, 1904	Lawyer	Episcopalian	1905
33.	Harry S. Truman, 40-41	May 8, 1884	Lamar, Mo.	John Anderson	Martha Ellen Young	Kansas City Law School, 1925	Businessman	Baptist	1919
34.	Dwight D. Eisenhower, 42-43	Oct. 14, 1890	Denison, Texas	David Jacob	Ida E. Stover	U.S. Military Academy, 1915	Soldier	Presbyterian	1916
35.	John F. Kennedy, 44	May 29, 1917	Brookline, Mass.	Joseph P.	Rose Fitzgerald	Harvard University, 1940	Reporter	Roman Catholic	1953
36.	Lyndon B. Johnson, 44-45	Aug. 27, 1908	Stonewall, Texas	Samuel Ealy	Rebekah Baines	Southwest Texas State Teachers College, 1930	Teacher	Disciples of Christ	1934
37.	Richard Milhous Nixon, 46-47	Jan. 9, 1913	Yorba, Calif.	Francis Antony	Hannah Milhous	Duke University School of Law, 1937	Lawyer	Quaker	1940
38.	Gerald R. Ford, 47	July 14, 1913	Omaha, Neb.	Gerald R.	Dorothy Gardner	Yale Law School, 1941	Congressman	Episcopalian	1948
39.	James E. Carter, 48	Oct. 1, 1924	Plains, Ga.	James Earl	Lillian Gordy	U.S. Naval Academy, 1946	Naval officer	Baptist	1946
40.	Ronald W. Reagan, 49-50	Feb. 6, 1911	Tampico, Ill.	John Edward	Nellie Wilson	Eureka College	Actor	Disciples of Christ	1940 1952
41.	George H. Bush 51	June 12, 1924	Milton, Mass.	Prescott S.	Dorothy Walker	Yale University	Businessman	Episcopalian	1945

WIFE'S NAME	CHILDREN M	F	RESIDENCE WHEN ELECTED	TERM OF OFFICE FROM	TO	SUBSEQUENT CAREER	DIED	CAUSE OF DEATH	AGE AT DEATH	PLACE OF BURIAL
Mrs. Martha (Dandridge) Custis (1732-1802)	0	0	Mt. Vernon, Va.	Apr. 30, 1789	Mar. 4, 1797	Agricultural pursuits; appointed commander-in-chief (1798) because of threatened war with France.	1799	Acute laryngitis	67	Mt. Vernon, Va.
Abigail Smith (1744-1818)	3	2	Quincy, Mass.	Mar. 4, 1797	Mar. 4, 1801	Member of Massachusetts Constitutional Convention of 1820.	1826	Natural decline	90	Quincy, Mass.
Mrs. Martha (Wayles) Skelton (1748-1782)	0	6	Monticello, Va.	Mar. 4, 1801	Mar. 4, 1809	Retired to his plantation at Monticello, Va.; devoted much time to the University of Virginia.	1826	Chronic diarrhea	83	Monticello, Va.
Mrs. Dolly (Payne) Todd (1772-1849)	0	0	Montpelier, Va.	Mar. 4, 1809	Mar. 4, 1817	Retired to Montpelier, Va.; maintained active interest in education and politics.	1836	Natural decline	85	Montpelier, Va.
Eliza Kortwright (1768-1830)	0	2	Oakhill, Va.	Mar. 4, 1817	Mar. 4, 1825	Retired to Virginia; served in Virginia Constitutional Convention in 1830.	1831	Natural decline	73	Richmond, Va.
Louisa Catherine Johnson (1775-1852)	3	1	Quincy, Mass.	Mar. 4, 1825	Mar. 4, 1829	Member House of Representatives from 1830 to his death.	1848	Paralysis	80	Quincy, Mass.
Mrs. Rachel (Donelson) Robards (1767-1828)	0	0	Hermitage, near Nashville, Tenn.	Mar. 4, 1829	Mar. 4, 1837	Retired to the Hermitage; maintained great interest in politics.	1845	Dropsy	78	Hermitage, Tenn.
Hannah Hoes (1783-1819)	4	0	Kinderhook, N.Y.	Mar. 4, 1837	Mar. 4, 1841	Renominated 1840 and 1848, for the presidency.	1862	Asthma	79	Kinderhook, N.Y.
Anna Symmes (1775-1864)	6	4	North Bend, Ohio	Mar. 4, 1841	Apr. 4, 1841	Died in office.	1841	Pneumonia	68	North Bend, Ohio
1st, Letitia Christian (1790-1842); 2nd, Julia Gardiner (1820-1889)	3 / 5	4 / 2	Williamsburg, Va.	Apr. 6, 1841	Mar. 4, 1845	Retired to his estate in Virginia; presided at the peace convention held in Washington in 1861.	1862	Liver trouble	72	Richmond, Va.
Sarah Childress (1803-1891)	0	0	Nashville, Tenn.	Mar. 4, 1845	Mar. 4, 1849	Died within 3 months.	1849	Chronic diarrhea	53	Nashville, Tenn.
Margaret Smith (1788-1852)	1	5	Baton Rouge, La.	Mar. 4, 1849	July 10, 1850	Died in office.	1850	Indigestion	65	near Louisville, Ky.
1st, Abigail Powers (1798-1853); 2nd, Mrs. Caroline (Carmichael) McIntosh (1813-1881)	1 / 0	1 / 0	Buffalo, N.Y.	July 10, 1850	Mar. 4, 1853	Chancellor, University of Buffalo.	1874	Natural decline	74	Buffalo, N.Y.
Jane Means Appleton (1806-1863)	3	0	Concord, N.H.	Mar. 4, 1853	Mar. 4, 1857	Traveled in Europe; retired to Concord, N.H.	1869	Stomach trouble	64	Concord, N.H.
Unmarried	...	...	Lancaster, Pa.	Mar. 4, 1857	Mar. 4, 1861	Wrote defense of his administration.	1868	Rheumatic gout	77	Lancaster, Pa.
Mary Todd (1818-1882)	4	0	Springfield, Ill.	Mar. 4, 1861	Apr. 15, 1865	Died in office.	1865	Assassinated	56	Springfield, Ill.
Eliza McCardle (1810-1876)	3	2	Greenville, Tenn.	Apr. 15, 1865	Mar. 4, 1869	Chosen United States senator in 1875.	1875	Paralysis	66	Greenville, Tenn.
Julia Dent (1826-1902)	3	1	Washington, D.C.	Mar. 4, 1869	Mar. 4, 1877	Made tour of the world and retired to write his memoirs.	1885	Cancer	63	New York City
Lucy Ware Webb (1831-1889)	7	1	Fremont, Ohio	Mar. 4, 1877	Mar. 4, 1881	Devoted his time to education, reforms and charity.	1893	Heart disease	71	Fremont, Ohio
Lucretia Rudolph (1832-1918)	4	1	Mentor, Ohio	Mar. 4, 1881	Sep. 20, 1881	Died in office.	1881	Assassinated	49	Cleveland, Ohio
Ellen Lewis Herndon (1837-1880)	2	1	New York City	Sep. 20, 1881	Mar. 4, 1885	Died the year following his retirement.	1886	Apoplexy	56	near Albany, N.Y.
Frances Folsom (1864-1947)	2	3	Buffalo, N.Y.	Mar. 4, 1885 / Mar. 4, 1893	Mar. 4, 1889 / Mar. 4, 1897	Retired to New York to practice law; at end of second term, retired to Princeton, N.J.	1908	Debility	71	Princeton, N.J.
1st, Caroline Scott (1832-1892); 2nd, Mrs. Mary (Lord) Dimmick (1858-1948)	1 / 0	1 / 1	Indianapolis, Ind.	Mar. 4, 1889	Mar. 4, 1893	Actively practiced law.	1901	Pneumonia	67	Indianapolis, Ind.
Frances Folsom (1864-1947)	2	3	Buffalo, N.Y.	Mar. 4, 1885 / Mar. 4, 1893	Mar. 4, 1889 / Mar. 4, 1897	Retired to New York to practice law; at end of second term, retired to Princeton, N.J.	1908	Debility	71	Princeton, N.J.
Ida Saxton (1844-1907)	0	2	Canton, Ohio	Mar. 4, 1897	Sep. 14, 1901	Died in office.	1901	Assassinated	58	Canton, Ohio
1st, Alice Lee (1861-1884); 2nd, Edith Kermit Carow (1861-1948)	0 / 4	1 / 1	Oyster Bay, N.Y.	Sep. 14, 1901	Mar. 4, 1909	Headed scientific expeditions; wrote; active in politics.	1919	Heart trouble	60	Oyster Bay, N.Y.
Helen Herron (1861-1943)	2	1	Cincinnati, Ohio	Mar. 4, 1909	Mar. 4, 1913	Chief justice of U.S. Supreme Court.	1930	General breakdown	72	Arlington, Va.
1st, Ellen Louise Axson (1860-1914); 2nd, Mrs. Edith (Bolling) Galt (1872-1961)	0 / 0	3 / 0	Princeton, N.J.	Mar. 4, 1913	Mar. 4, 1921	Lawyer and writer.	1924	Heart trouble	67	Washington, D.C.
Florence Kling (1860-1924)	0	0	Marion, Ohio	Mar. 4, 1921	Aug. 2, 1923	Died in office.	1923	Apoplexy	57	Marion, Ohio
Grace A. Goodhue (1879-1957)	2	0	Northampton, Mass.	Aug. 2, 1923	Mar. 4, 1929	Writer.	1933	Heart disease	60	Plymouth, Vt.
Lou Henry (1875-1944)	2	0	Stanford Univ., Cal.	Mar. 4, 1929	Mar. 4, 1933	Retired to private life.	1964	Natural decline	90	West Branch, Iowa
Anna Eleanor Roosevelt (1884-1962)	4	1	Hyde Park, N.Y.	Mar. 4, 1933	Apr. 12, 1945	Died in office.	1945	Cerebral hemorrhage	63	Hyde Park, N.Y.
Bess Wallace (1885-1982)	0	1	Independence, Mo.	Apr. 12, 1945	Jan. 20, 1953	Writer.	1972	Natural decline	88	Independence, Mo.
Mamie Geneva Doud (1896-1979)	2	0	New York, N.Y.	Jan. 20, 1953	Jan. 20, 1961	Retired to private life.	1969	Heart disease	79	Abilene, Kan.
Jacqueline Lee Bouvier (1929-)	1	1	Boston, Mass.	Jan. 20, 1961	Nov. 22, 1963	Died in office.	1963	Assassinated	46	Arlington, Va.
Claudia Alta Taylor (1912-)	0	2	Johnson City, Tex.	Nov. 22, 1963	Jan. 20, 1969	Rancher.	1973	Heart attack	64	LBJ Ranch, Texas
Thelma Patricia Ryan (1916-)	0	2	New York City	Jan. 20, 1969	Aug. 9, 1974	Resigned from office.				
Betty Bloomer (1920-)	3	1	Grand Rapids, Mich.	Aug. 9, 1974	Jan. 20, 1977	Retired to private life.				
Rosalynn Smith (1927-)	3	1	Plains, Ga.	Jan. 20, 1977	Jan. 20, 1981	Businessman.				
1st, Jane Wyman (1914-); 2nd, Nancy Davis (1923-)	1 / 1	1 / 1	Los Angeles	Jan. 20, 1981	Jan. 20, 1989					
Barbara Pierce (1925-)	4	2	Washington, D.C.	Jan. 20, 1989						

Federal Departments

The 13 departments of the federal government are extensions of the executive branch, and the heads of these departments have Cabinet rank (the departments of the Air Force, Army, and Navy are branches of the Department of Defense). The activities of these departments demonstrate the vast responsibilities of the federal government. An organizational chart of the U.S. government is found on page 824.

Agriculture, Department of (USDA).

The Department of Agriculture, a Cabinet-level executive department, establishes policy and carries out all programs affecting agricultural production, land use and conservation, crop prices, and nutrition. The department provides loans for rural development, enforces regulations to protect plant and animal health, and conducts research relating to food and agricultural practices.

Department programs for rural development are administered by the Farmers Home Administration and the Rural Electrification Administration. The **Farmers Home Administration** provides loans to small farmers and rural homeowners for farm improvements, land purchases, and home repairs. Loans are also made to communities and cooperative organizations for the installation of water, waste disposal, irrigation, and drainage systems, and for the conservation and development of land and water resources. The **Rural Electrification Administration** finances electric and telephone facilities in rural areas through loans and loan guarantees to local companies and subscriber-owned cooperatives.

Marketing and transportation services include the **Agricultural Cooperative Service**, which conducts research and provides technical support to cooperatives marketing farm products; and the **Agricultural Marketing Service**, which sets standards and grades for products, administers marketing programs, and provides grants to states for marketing improvements.

The **Animal and Plant Health Inspection Service** administers federal laws and regulations affecting animal and plant health. These include quarantine and humane treatment of animals and the control and eradication of pests and diseases. The service cooperates with local agencies in restricting the entry into the United States of foreign plants and animal products that may be diseased or carry pests. Veterinary programs include monitoring outbreaks of communicable diseases in livestock and poultry.

The **Federal Grain Inspection Service** studies and regulates methods for han-

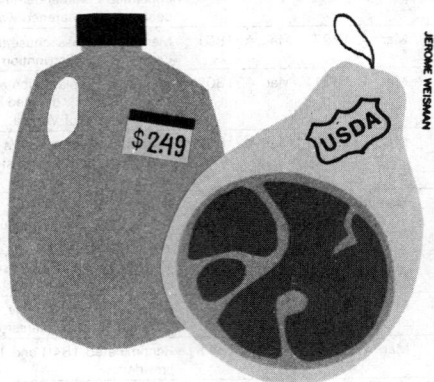

AGRICULTURE DEPARTMENT *supports prices of milk, inspects meat, and issues food stamps for the poor.*

dling grain. It carries out the official inspection, weighing, and certification of grain for export or domestic use on request.

USDA's **Food and Nutrition Service** administers food assistance and nutrition programs in cooperation with state and local agencies.

The **Food Quality and Safety Service** inspects all meat, poultry, and processed meat products, and inspects processing plants for compliance with federal sanitation standards. It also develops grade standards for food and farm products and conducts inspections to certify quality on request.

The **Agricultural Stabilization and Conservation Service** helps control the production of many farm commodities through a voluntary system of land use, acreage allotment, and marketing quotas. This control helps stabilize farm prices.

The **Federal Crop Insurance Corporation** provides insurance for crop failure owed to unavoidable causes such as disease, insect infestation, and weather variations.

The **Forest Service** manages the National Forest System and protects forests and grasslands from natural disasters and environmental hazards. The **Soil Conservation Service** develops soil and water conservation programs.

The **Science and Education Administration** conducts research on animal and plant production, soil, food processing, nutrition, and food safety. The administration makes grants for agricultural research and provides fellowships for studies in fields related to food and agriculture.

Air Force, Department of the. The Department of the Air Force, a military arm of the Department of Defense, is responsible for the airborne defense of the United States. It also provides air transport, defense, and support for the other U.S. military services. The service is organized on a functional basis in the United States and on an area basis overseas.

The Air Force includes logistics, systems, training, security, communications, and Air Force Reserve units. The Alaskan Air Command coordinates joint administrative matters in Alaska and conducts aerospace defense operations assigned by the North American Air Defense Command (NORAD).

The **Military Airlift Command** provides worldwide air transportation for personnel and cargo from all military services. The **Strategic Air Command** carries out space surveillance and maintains missile and reconnaissance forces.

The Department of the Air Force operates the United States Air Force Academy, which is in Colorado Springs, Colorado. The academy offers a four-year course leading to a Bachelor of Science degree and a commission in the Air Force.

Army, Department of the. The Department of the Army, a military branch of the Department of Defense, is responsible for the deployment and use of military forces in land operations. The Army also administers programs that concern all waterway navigation, beach erosion, and water resource development. It provides military assistance and emergency medical air transportation to state and local governments.

Army program areas include military operations and communications, training, and management of the Army National Guard and the U.S. Army Reserve.

The Army Corps of Engineers is responsible for engineering projects for the Army and the U.S. Air Force. The corps carries out the Army Civil Works Program. This program involves the engineering and management of water resource projects such as dams, reservoirs, harbors, and waterways; it also protects the navigable waters of the United States.

The Department of the Army operates the United States Military Academy at West Point, New York. The academy offers a four-year course of study leading to a Bachelor of Science degree and a commission in the Army.

Commerce, Department of. The Department of Commerce, a Cabinet-level executive department, sets policy and administers federal programs that promote economic growth and international trade, encourage regional development, and provide statistical analyses for use by American industry. The department also supervises the merchant marine and monitors the geophysical environment.

International economic and commercial programs developed by the **International Trade Administration (ITA)** encourage the expansion of world markets for U.S. goods and provide advice on foreign trade zones, quotas, and other import/export issues. The ITA establishes policies affecting trade, finance, and investment.

Regional action planning commissions promote the development of multistate regions, providing funding for industry, resources, transportation, and recreational development.

The department carries out scientific and technical research and provides standards for physical measurements. It encourages increased productivity through the standardization of techniques. The **Patent and Trademark Office** encourages investment in research by issuing patents protecting the rights of inventors. Trademarks protect the names, logotypes, or other distinctive identifications used by companies in selling their products or services.

The **National Oceanic and Atmospheric Administration** provides needed weather reports, forecasts, and warnings of destructive natural events; services for the protection of fish and other marine resources; nautical and aeronautical charts; and grants for marine research and coastal development. Through the **National Telecommunications and Information Administration**, the department regulates the use of public service satellites and the construction of public telecommunications facilities, provides grants to public service users, and protects communications security and user privacy.

The **Bureau of Economic Analysis** calculates the gross national product (GNP), a widely used measure of economic activity; it also keeps track of the U.S. balance of payments, foreign investments, and changes in industrial markets. The bureau conducts surveys and forecasts business conditions using econometric models. Industrial forecasting and productivity studies are carried out by the **Bureau of Industrial Economics.**

The department's **National Technical Information Service (NTIS)** develops information and makes available federal computer software, programs and data files, and unpublished foreign technical reports of interest to U.S. industry. Statistical research is done by the **Bureau of the Census**, which conducts a federal census of the population every ten years as well as periodic economic surveys.

The **Maritime Administration** conducts programs to aid in the development of the merchant marine, providing assistance for the reconditioning or construction of ships, ports, and other marine facilities. The Merchant Marine Academy at Kings Point, New York, is operated by the Maritime Administration.

Defense, Department of (DOD). The Department of Defense, a Cabinet-level executive department, sets policy affecting national security and political-military affairs. It also manages the U.S. military forces. The department develops and evaluates new telecommunications, intelligence, command, and weapons systems.

The DOD includes the Organization of the Joint Chiefs of Staff; the service departments of the Army, Navy (including the Marine Corps), and Air Force; the unified commands, such as the U.S. Readiness Command; and military support agencies and joint service schools.

The **Joint Chiefs of Staff** are the commanding officers of the Army, Navy, Air Force, and Marines, and their chairman. The organization's joint staff is drawn from the military service departments and organized in directorates responsible for operations, logistics, all plans and required policy, communications, and control systems. The Joint Chiefs prepare strategic plans and programs for military mobilization; establish unified commands and assign support responsibilities; and suggest policy affecting foreign military aid programs and industrial mobilization plans.

The **Defense Nuclear Agency** manages the DOD nuclear stockpile, simulations facilities, as well as all field experiments; coordinates nuclear weapons development and testing with the Department of Energy; and conducts investigations of the safety of tactical nuclear forces.

The department supervises the joint service military schools. The **National Defense University (NDU)** provides professional military education in national security, preparing graduates for senior policy, command, and staff positions. The NDU includes the National War College and the Industrial College of the Armed Forces. The **Armed Forces Staff College**, operated under the direction of the Joint Chiefs of Staff, conducts a program in combined organization planning for officers serving in joint and unified commands.

Education, Department of. The Department of Education, a Cabinet-level executive department, establishes educational policy, administers and coordinates federal assistance to education, and oversees the implementation of legislation affecting the rights of minority and handicapped students.

The **Office of Bilingual Education and Minority Affairs** supports programs to assist students with limited English language proficiency and assists in the development and implementation of desegregation plans for public schools.

The **Office of Civil Rights** enforces compliance with laws affecting education of the handicapped in programs receiving federal financial assistance. The department supports special programs for handicapped children and for the rehabilitation of all handicapped persons.

Department programs provide assistance to state and local agencies for the education of Indians, migrant workers' children, and neglected and delinquent students; and work toward the elimination of racial discrimination in schools an colleges.

Vocational and adult education programs provide assistance for technical education, professional development, and rural family education. Postsecondary education programs provide assistance for international studies programs and aid for the construction of academic facilities. Student financial assistance programs administered by the department include Basic Educational Opportunity Grants, Work Study, and the Guaranteed Student Loan Program. Regional offices of the department provide information and technical assistance to state and local agencies as well as to institutions.

Energy, Department of (DOE). The Department of Energy, a Cabinet-level executive department, establishes energy policy, administers research and development programs in energy conservation and new technologies, and regulates the sale and transportation of fossil fuels. The department also manages the nuclear weapons program and supervises the operationsof federal power administrations.

Program areas of the department focus on energy research; the use of fossil fuels; international developments affecting U.S. energy supply; conservation; environmental protection; and the development of renewable and nuclear energy sources.

As part of the Federal Emergency Preparedness Program, the DOE manages the national Strategic Petroleum Reserve and the Naval Petroleum and Oil Shale Reserves. The DOE also

THE SEAL *of the Department of Defense.*

WIDE WORLD PHOTOS

CONSUMERS *are helped by Department of Energy weatherization programs.*

cooperates with the Department of Defense in directing nuclear weapons research and testing, and in the development of fusion reactors.

The **Federal Energy Regulatory Commission**, an independent agency of the Department of Energy, sets rates for the transportation and sale of natural gas, for the transport of oil by pipeline, and for the transmission and sale of electricity. The commission also licenses hydroelectric power plants.

Five power administrations that market electricity from federal hydroelectric projects operated by the Army Corps of Engineers are managed by DOE.

Health and Human Services, Department of. The Department of Health and Human Services, a Cabinet-level executive department, establishes policy affecting health and other human services concerns, and administers national health, welfare, and income-security programs. The services and administrations of the department provide financial assistance to the needy, financing for health care, and public health and research programs.

The **Office of Human Development Services** administers programs for the elderly, the young, native Americans, disabled persons, and public assistance recipients. Programs for the aging provide senior citizens with advice and assistance in addition to advising state-administered, community-based social services. Child, youth, and family programs promote sound child development and fund research projects to demonstrate new approaches to human services. The Administration for Native Americans conducts projects for American Indians, Alaskan natives, and native Hawaiians to encourage their social and economic development; it also administers grant programs to foster native American

enterprises. The Administration on Developmental Disabilities helps to develop programs for treatment and rehabilitation services.

The **Public Health Service** assists states and communities in the development of health services and education; conducts research in medicine and the health sciences; provides services to protect public health against unsafe and impure foods, drugs, cosmetics, and other potential health hazards; and promotes programs to prevent and control communicable diseases. The service operates the National Center for Health Statistics, the National Center for Health Services, and the National Center for Health Care. Other components of the Public Health Service are the Alcohol, Drug Abuse and Mental Health Administration; the National Centers for Disease Control; the Food and Drug Administration; the Health Resources and Health Services administrations; and the National Institutes of Health.

The **Health Care Financing Administration** manages Medicare and Medicaid, the national health insurance programs. Medicare provides basic health care benefits to Social Security recipients.

The **Social Security Administration** administers the nation's social insurance program. Employers, employees, and self-employed persons contribute a percentage of their yearly earnings to the Social Security trust funds. Upon retirement, or in the case of disability or death, monthly cash payments are paid to an individual or surviving family members to partially replace the income the family has lost.

The **Office of Child Support Enforcement** administers programs that, in cooperation with state agencies, help locate absent parents, establish paternity, and obtain child support payments. The office oversees regulations requiring states to enforce the child support obligations owed to children by their absent parents.

Housing and Urban Development, Department of (HUD). The Department of Housing and Urban Development, a Cabinet-level executive department, establishes policy on housing and community needs and coordinates federal programs affecting urban, suburban, and metropolitan development. The department conducts programs that provide mortgage insurance, rental subsidies, and aid for neighborhood rehabilitation, and that preserve urban centers.

HUD programs offer grants and other assistance for community planning and development. Urban development action grants to stimulate private-sector investment are awarded to severely distressed cities and urban counties for economic development projects. Relocation assistance programs provide property owners displaced by federally assisted projects with reimbursement for moving costs and sales-related expenses, and fair market value payments.

Community block grant assistance to local governments is available for eliminating slums and hazardous housing conditions, for property preservation and conservation, and for increasing the amount of low- and moderate-income housing.

HUD housing programs provide assistance for the repair, rehabilitation, or improvement of low-income housing, health facilities, housing for the elderly, and independent living facilities for the disabled. The department insures mortgages and loans for the purchase of single-family housing; private, cooperative, and rental housing; and mobile homes. Assistance is available to private and public housing agencies for construction or rehabilitation of housing for low-income families and the elderly.

Interior, Department of the. The Department of the Interior, a Cabinet-level executive department, establishes policy on the use of federally owned

HEALTH AND HUMAN SERVICES *include assistance for the elderly and the poor. This office helps people apply for such benefits as Medicare (see card inset).*

public lands and the protection of natural resources. The department administers programs for the conservation and development of minerals, water resources, fish, and wildlife; manages the national parks and historic areas; and promotes economic and social development in the territories of the United States and the Trust Territory of the Pacific Islands. Department progams also provide services to native Americans through the Bureau of Indian Affairs.

The **United States Fish and Wildlife Service** manages the national wildlife refuges and the national fish hatcheries; protects endangered species and wildlife habitats; and coordinates marine environmental quality and biological resource programs. The **National Parks Service** manages a nationwide system of parks, historic sites, monuments, and scenic and recreation areas; maintains the National Trails System; and supports historic preservation and archaeological studies.

Land and water programs include land use and water planning, public land management, land leasing for mineral production, and development of water resources and facilities. The **Office of Water Research and Technology** develops methods of producing water suitable for agriculture, industry, and municipalities from the sea and other saline or chemically contaminated sources. The office helps train water scientists and engineers, and administers a cooperative program with university water resource institutes. The **Bureau of Land Management** oversees the use and development of natural resources on publicly owned lands and arranges for the sale, leasing, and establishment of rights of way on federally owned property.

Programs to develop and reclaim arid lands in Western states are administered by the **Bureau of Reclamation**, which helps states develop irrigation systems and hydroelectric projects and conducts research on water basins, wind and solar power, and weather modification.

The department's energy and mineral management programs include development of ocean resources, surface mining and reclamation, metallurgical and mining research, and analyses of mining data. The **Geological Survey** classifies land by mineral, water, and energy characteristics, prepares topographical maps of the United States, and conducts chemical and physical research.

The **Bureau of Mines** conducts research on mineral extraction and the recycling of mineral resources and compiles statistical and economic data on all phases of mining and mineral development. The Office of Surface Mining Reclamation and Enforcement establishes standards for regulating the surface effects of coal mining and develops programs for the reclamation of previously mined areas.

INTERIOR DEPARTMENT *protects national historic sites and wildlife and assists in development of wind and solar power.*

The **Bureau of Indian Affairs** administers economic and social programs for native Americans, including education and training, resource development, and community services; it also has trust responsibility for reservation lands. Department responsibilities for U.S. territorial lands involve the promotion of economic, social, and political development in Guam, American Samoa, the Virgin Islands, and the Trust Territory of the Pacific Islands.

Training and employment for young people are coordinated by the **Office of Youth Programs**, which manages the Job Corps Civilian Conservation Program, the Youth Conservation Corps, and the Young Adult Conservation Corps. The office cooperates with the departments of Agriculture and Labor in providing opportunities for young people to work in the national parks, forests, and historic areas.

Justice, Department of. The Department of Justice, a Cabinet-level executive department, is the principal law enforcement agency of the United States and serves as legal counsel to the federal government. The department enforces drug, immigration, and naturalization laws; and supervises the Federal Bureau of Investigation, the Bureau of Prisons, and the U.S. marshals. Department activities are carried out by divisions and offices responsible for specific legal areas.

The **Antitrust Division** investigates violations of federal antitrust laws and conducts suits to restore competitive conditions and prevent trade monopolies. The division also prepares reports on bank mergers and identical bidding in public procurement.

The **Civil Division** consists of three branches responsible for separate areas of civil litigation. The Torts Branch conducts suits involving medical malpractice, aviation disasters, bank failures, shipping, navigation,

and workmen's compensation. The Commercial Branch handles cases involving contracts, grants, subsidies, and insurance; customs, patent, and copyright issues; and civil fraud or bribery. The Federal Programs Branch conducts suits concerning the validity of statutes, constitutionality of acts of Congress, and claims under the Freedom of Information and Privacy acts.

The **Civil Rights Division** enforces laws prohibiting discrimination in voting, education, housing, credit, and the use of public facilities, and in the administration of federally assisted programs on the basis of race, national origin, religion, age, or handicap. The division also enforces laws prohibiting discrimination on the basis of sex in education, employment, and housing. Cases concerning deprivation of constitutional rights by enactment of discriminatory laws or resulting from conspiracy and interference with federally protected activities are also prosecuted by the division.

The **Criminal Division** enforces federal criminal statutes, including those involving national security and foreign relations. The division coordinates nationwide activities to suppress organized crime and the manufacture, shipment, and distribution of illegal drugs.

The **Land and Natural Resources Division** conducts suits relating to property, natural resources, and environmental protection. Cases involve property condemnation, boundary determination, mineral rights, wildlife protection, navigable waters, and air, water, and noise pollution. The division represents American Indians and Indian tribes in matters not related to trust property.

The **Tax Division** conducts litigation involving internal revenue laws and proceedings in the U.S. Tax Court. Disputes handled by the division involve mortgage foreclosures for federal tax liens, foreclosures of tax liens, tax claims in bankruptcies, receivership or probate, tax evasion, failure to file returns, and filing of false returns.

The **Federal Bureau of Investigation** compiles evidence and conducts investigations for cases in which the federal government may be involved. The **United States Marshals Service** maintains custody of federal prisoners and trial evidence, transports federal prisoners, and disburses funds for government obligations. Marshals protect witnesses, federal judges, and jurors and attorneys, and provide security in federal courtrooms.

The **Immigration and Naturalization Service** administers laws affecting the admission, naturalization, exclusion, and deportation of aliens, and guards against illegal entry. The Board of Immigration Appeals hears appeals of decisions of the Immigration and Naturalization Service.

The **Federal Bureau of Prisons** is responsible for the care and custody of persons convicted of federal crimes and sentenced to federal prisons. The bureau operates a nationwide system of maximum, medium, and minimum security prisons, halfway houses, and community programs. The bureau's National Institute of Corrections assists state and local corrections authorities in upgrading facilities and services and training correctional personnel. The **United States Parole Commission** may grant or revoke parole for eligible federal prisoners. It also supervises parolees and other released prisoners until the expiration of their terms.

Labor, Department of. The Department of Labor, a Cabinet-level executive department, establishes labor policy and enforces federal laws relating to wage earners, working conditions, and employment opportunities. The department sponsors job training programs, and provides job placement and unemployment insurance services. The Wage Appeals Board decides disputes concerning wage rates, large groups of employees, or unusual situations. Administrative law judges hear cases involving such matters as minimum wages, overtime payments, compensation benefits, and health and safety regulations.

The **Employment and Training Administration** conducts programs providing employment services, work experience, training, and unemployment insurance. The administration's employment service provides job placement services and special counseling for veterans, migrant workers, youths, and handicapped persons. The service conducts a cooperative school program for youths aged 16 to 24, and provides certification for aliens seeking employment as immigrants or temporary workers. The Employment and Training Administration also operates an apprenticeship program, provides technical information on training methods, and works closely with labor unions, vocational schools, and community groups in managing their apprentice programs.

The **Office of Comprehensive Employment and Development** develops training and work experience programs and provides public service employment for disadvantaged, unemployed, and underemployed persons. The office administers the Summer Youth Employment Program, which tries to provide employment during the summer months for economically disadvantaged youths aged 14 to 21. The **Office of National Programs** manages training programs for native Americans, providing grants to Indian tribes, Alaskan native villages, and nonprofit organizations to establish training centers and public service employment opportunities. The **Senior Community Program** subsidizes part-time community service jobs for persons aged 55 or older.

The **Labor-Management Services Administration** provides assistance to collective bargaining negotiators and to state and local governments. It conducts research in the field of labor-management relations and helps veterans, reservists, and National Guard members reestablish seniority and rates of pay in jobs held prior to military service. The administration also enforces regulations concerning the election of union officers, the rights of members, and the handling of union funds.

The **Employment Standards Administration** enforces minimum wage and overtime standards, registers farm labor contractors, determines wage rates to be paid on government contracts, and oversees affirmative action employment programs for veterans, minorities, women, and handicapped workers. The Wage and Hour Division conducts programs to protect wage earners, discourage excessively long hours detrimental to workers' health, and minimize income losses caused by indebtedness. The Office of Federal Contract Compliance establishes policies to discourage discrimination in federally assisted construction projects and ensure affirmative action in the employment of veterans and handicapped persons.

The **Occupational Safety and Health Administration** develops standards for occupational health and safety and conducts investigations and inspections to ensure compliance with federal safety and health regulations. The **Mine Safety and Health Administration** develops regulations aimed at preventing mine accidents and occupational diseases in the mining industry.

The **Bureau of Labor Statistics** is the government's principal fact-finding agency in the field of labor economics.

Navy, Department of the. The Department of the Navy, a military department of the Department of Defense, is responsible for defense activities at sea and, with its Marine Corps component, the protection of all U.S. naval bases. The department consists of the U.S. Navy, the U.S. Marine Corps, and (in time of war or national emergency) the U.S. Coast Guard as well.

The **Military Sealift Command** provides ocean transportation for personnel and cargo from all military services and logistics support units to combat fleets. The Atlantic and Pacific fleets and the Naval Forces, Europe, together form the naval component of the unified U.S. military commands.

The Department of the Navy operates the United States Naval Academy at Annapolis, Maryland. The academy offers a four-year program of academic, military, and professional instruction leading to a Bachelor of Science degree and a commission in the Navy or the Marine Corps.

State, Department of. The Department of State, a Cabinet-level executive department, formulates as well as carries out U.S. foreign policy and conducts U.S. foreign relations, including negotiations for treaties and agreements with foreign nations. The department represents the United States in the United Nations, in other international organizations, and at international conferences; it also manages the Foreign Service.

The Department of State directs and supervises U.S. foreign relations and coordinates the activities of other federal agencies overseas in areas such as security and defense, trade, energy, aid and technology, and international currency. The department's activities are managed on a regional basis by the bureaus of African, European, East Asian and Pacific, Inter-American, and Near Eastern and South Asian affairs. The bureaus work closely with the ambassadors in their geographic areas and carry out U.S. policies toward the countries in their regions.

The **Bureau of Oceans and International Environmental and Scientific Affairs** coordinates the scientific and technological aspects of U.S. foreign relations and manages policy issues involving oceans, population, and nuclear and energy technology.

The **Bureau of Consular Affairs** enforces immigration and nationality laws concerning the State Department and the Foreign Service, and issues passports and visas for American citizens traveling overseas. The bureau's Passport Office issues over 3 million passports a year.

The State Department's responsibilities for the implementation of policy on human rights are carried out by the **Bureau of Human Rights and Humanitarian Affairs**. The bureau cooperates with nongovernmental human rights organizations and advises the Immigration and Naturalization Service on applications for political asylum by foreign nationals.

U.S. EMBASSIES *in most countries of the world are run by the State Department. This one, in London, was designed by architect Eero Saarinen.*

WIDE WORLD PHOTOS

The **Office of the Chief of Protocol** is the principal adviser to the U.S. government on diplomatic procedures governed by law or international customs. The office examines the credentials of foreign diplomats and consular representatives and grants diplomatic privileges and immunities. This office also conducts official ceremonial or public events, including arrangements for visits to the United States by foreign heads of state.

Transportation, Department of. The Department of Transportation, which is a Cabinet-level executive department, establishes overall transportation policy and administers programs affecting highways, railroads, urban mass transit, aviation, oil and gas pipelines, and port and waterway safety. The operating administrations are organized by mode of transport and by regulatory and safety concerns. Their work includes administration of the United States Coast Guard, except in time of war or national emergency, when this service operates as a part of the Department of the Navy.

The **Federal Highway Administration** manages federal aid programs to the states for the construction and maintenance of the 42,500-mile National Interstate and Defense Highways.

The **National Highway Traffic Safety Administration** enforces regulations on fuel economy standards, vehicle safety equipment, and uniform maximum speed limits on U.S. highways.

The **Urban Mass Transportation Administration** assists in the development of urban transit systems and their equipment, and facilities. It also provides financial assistance to state and local governments for mass transit.

The **Federal Railroad Administration** enforces federal safety regulations affecting equipment standards and operation of the nation's rail system, administers all programs that provide assistance for regional and local service, and operates the Alaska Railroad. The administration's Transportation Test Center, which is located near Pueblo, Colorado, is used by the U.S. and Canadian governments and by private industry to test rail systems, equipment, and techniques under appropriately controlled conditions.

The **Federal Aviation Administration** regulates air commerce and the use of navigable air space and operates the air traffic control and navigation system. The administration enforces regulations affecting the manufacture and operation of aircraft, aircraft registration, and the certification of airports. It also performs inspections of air navigation facilities.

The **St. Lawrence Seaway Development Corporation** is responsible for the development and maintenance of the seaway between Montreal and Lake Erie, coordinating its activities with the St. Lawrence Seaway Authority of Canada. The corporation maintains the seaway to provide an effective water artery for maritime traffic through the Great Lakes system.

The **United States Coast Guard** enforces federal laws, treaties, and other international agreements on the high seas and in U.S. waters, conducts investigations, and works with other federal agencies in the protection of marine resources and the suppression of smuggling and illegal drug traffic. The Coast Guard carries out search and rescue actions, engages in flood relief, and helps in the removal of navigational hazards.

The **Research and Special Services Administration** conducts many programs affecting materials transportation and the transport of oil and gas through interstate pipeline facilities. The administration is responsible for transportation preparedness in case of natural disasters, regional emergencies, and other crises.

Treasury, Department of the. The Department of the Treasury, a Cabinet-level executive department, establishes economic, financial, tax, and fiscal policy, and acts as financial agent for the U.S. government. The department collects taxes, manufactures coins and currency, enforces regulations for the sale of firearms and explosives, manages the Federal Law Enforcement Training Center, and supervises the Secret Service. The offices and bureaus of the department are responsible for federal, municipal, and corporate finance; customs regulations; Federal Reserve Banks; and exchange markets.

The **Bureau of Alcohol, Tobacco and Firearms** enforces firearms and explosives laws, regulates the production and distribution of alcohol and tobacco products, and collects taxes due from the alcohol and tobacco industries. Duties, taxes, and other revenue from imports are collected by the **Customs Service**, which also enforces customs regulations.

The **Internal Revenue Service** enforces federal revenue laws affecting taxation, except those pertaining to alcohol, tobacco, and firearms. The service collects excise, estate, gift, and corporate and individual income taxes; and prepares forms, schedules, and instructions used in filing tax returns.

The Treasury Department's **Office of the Comptroller of the Currency** supervises the activities of the national banks that form the basis of the Federal Reserve System. The office approves the organization of new national banks, the establishment of new branches, the consolidations or mergers of existing national banks, and the regulations governing their operations.

The **Bureau of Government Financial Operations** maintains a central accounting and reporting system for the monetary assets and liabilities of the U.S. Treasury. The bureau issues monthly payments to individuals

TREASURY DEPARTMENT *collects income, tobacco, and other taxes, and prints stamps and money.*

under federal benefits programs and U.S. savings bonds through the Federal Payroll Savings Plan.

The **Bureau of the Public Debt** establishes regulations for public securities issues and maintains accounting control over public debt receipts and expenditures, securities, and interest costs. The bureau authorizes payment of principal and interest, and handles claims for lost, stolen, destroyed, or mutilated securities, including savings bonds, savings notes, and retirement bonds.

The Treasury's currency and coin manufacturing is done by the **Bureau of the Mint** and the **Bureau of Engraving and Printing.** The Mint of the United States produces domestic and foreign coins, national medals, proof and uncirculated coin sets, and other numismatic items. The Mint supervises gold and silver disbursements, the movement and custody of bullion, and the distribution of coins to Federal Reserve Banks. The Bureau of Engraving and Printing designs, engraves, and prints financial items issued by the U.S. government; produces paper currency and Treasury bonds and certificates; and issues postage, revenue, and customs stamps.

The **United States Savings Bonds Division** promotes the sale of U.S. savings bonds, primarily through payroll savings plans.

The **Federal Law Enforcement Training Center** is an interagency training facility serving 37 federal law enforcement organizations.

The **United States Secret Service** is authorized to arrest any person violating laws relating to coins, currency, or securities of the United States and foreign governments. The special and particular duty of the Secret Service is protection of the President and other important officials.

CANADIAN GOVERNMENT

The history of the growth of government in Canada differs from that of all the rest of the western hemisphere, even though exploration and settlement began more or less at the same time in all parts of the New World. South of what became the United States of America, to the tip of South America, Spanish and Portuguese rule prevailed, with some small enclaves and islands ruled by other nations. Spanish and Portuguese rule was monarchical, centralized, and stiflingly bureaucratic, with a complete absence of democracy. Although these Spanish and Portuguese colonies won their independence early in the 19th century, democratic governments in their successor nations have been unstable and dictatorships and military rule have been common.

By contrast, the English colonies on the Atlantic seaboard from Georgia to Canada exhibited an early tendency to wish to run their own affairs, although most of these colonies had royal governors appointed by the king. Except for a period of Dutch rule in New York that ended in 1664, these colonies had a common heritage of language, culture, and government that came from England. This background made for unity and consensus.

Canada, on the other hand, was unique in its division between the English and French backgrounds of its people. England and France fought for control of Canada for nearly 100 years before Great Britain triumphed in 1763. Even then the strength of the French part of Canada was so great that England could not insist on anglicizing its new subjects. This fact was recognized in the Quebec Act of 1774, by which Protestant England allowed French-Canadians to continue their practice of the Roman Catholic religion. The need to recognize French-English differences has continued into the Canadian governmental system to this day.

Although the Canadian and American systems of government stem basically from that of Great Britain, they exhibit certain differences. Canada's governmental structure is almost an exact copy of that of the mother country, with its parliament, prime minister, elected House of Commons, and appointed Senate, which is similar to the unelected British House of Lords. On the other hand, the United States, as a result of its armed revolt to win independence from England, avoided establishing a government with any connection to monarchical rule.

Nevertheless, over the years the governments of the two countries have developed along similar lines and have faced similar problems. The original 13 states have become 50, while the original four provinces of the Dominion of Canada have become ten. In both nations, the march westward of people and their local governments have led to conflicts with the original states and provinces. Wide regional differences in economic interests and in attitudes toward central governments have caused serious problems for both countries in federal legislatures and executive departments.

Canada, the smaller and less powerful of the two nations, for a variety of reasons, has shown no interest in a union with the United States. By contrast, the United States, or at least certain American factions, has sometimes eyed its neighbor with a view to a takeover. Whether this union would be more desirable than the present situation of two somewhat different but basically alike nations is debatable.

The Federal Government

Canada today is a parliamentary democracy comprising ten provinces and two territories, with its capital in Ottawa. At the formal head of the government, after the British monarch, is the governor-general, who is appointed by the monarch on advice of the Canadian prime minister. Most actions of the government are performed in the name of the governor-general, so assent by that official is required and normally automatically given.

The governor-general's duty is to see to it that the country has a government at all times. When a prime minister resigns, dies, or is voted out in an election, the governor-general fills the office. In practice, that official abides by the principle of majority rule in naming a new prime minister, but there can be complications requiring tact and diplomacy when no political party has a clear majority in the House of Commons. The governor-general also can dissolve parliament, doing this on the advice of the prime minister. On rare occasions this action is refused.

Until 1952 all governors-general of Canada had been British, but since then all have been native-born Canadians. The first was Vincent Massey, who took office on February 28, 1952. Massey was also the first Canadian minister to Washington, from 1926 to 1930, and high commissioner for Canada in London, from 1935 to 1946. As of late 1986, the position was held by Jeanne Sauvé, the first woman governor-general; she took office on April 26, 1984. Born in Quebec Province, Sauvé had been a member of the House of Commons since 1972 and speaker since 1980.

Among earlier governors-general were a number of interesting and notable figures, such as Lord Monck (1867–1868), Lord Minto (1898–1904), Lord Grey (1904–1911), Lord Byng (1921–1926), Lord Tweedsmuir (1935–1940), and Lord Alexander (1946–1952).

Lord Monck (1819–1894), governor of the province of Canada from 1861 to 1866, did much to bring about confederation in 1867; he then became the first governor-general of the new Dominion. He also helped prevent a breakdown of peaceful relations between England and the United States during the American Civil War.

Lord Minto (1845–1914) was a successful and innovative colonial administrator. As governor-general he was popular. Minto went on to become viceroy of India (1905–1910), Great Britain's highest colonial post; as such, he introduced reforms that started India on the way to self-government.

Lord Grey (1851–1917) had served in the British House of Commons and had been a member of the House of Lords before becoming governor-general. His popularity and success in Canada were such that the Canadian government twice asked to have his term extended.

Lord Byng (1862–1935) was a military figure who commanded the Canadian troops in World War I when they captured Vimy Ridge in April of 1917. He was created a viscount for his war service. Lord Tweedsmuir (1875–1940) is better known to many as John Buchan, author of adventure novels. The best known of these is *The Thirty-Nine Steps* (1915), which was made into an exciting movie in 1935. Tweedsmuir was popular in Canada and did much to promote friendly relations with the United States.

Lord Alexander (1891–1969) is best remembered as Field Marshal Harold Alexander, a top Allied commander in World War II. He led the invasion of Sicily in 1943 and commanded in Italy during the protracted and desperate fighting that led to the capture of Rome in June of 1944.

The Privy Council.
The Queen's Privy Council for Canada fills an important, though largely formal, function in the government. It is a very large group, including former cabinet ministers, the chief justice and former chief justices, former speakers of parliament, and, on occasion, provincial premiers, members of the royal family, and other distinguished persons. Membership is for life. The group usually meets only on ceremonial occasions. The portion of the Privy Council that actually advises the government is the sitting cabinet, which constitutes a committee. When the cabinet takes an action there, that action becomes an order-in-council and is approved by the governor-general.

The prime minister.
The most powerful member of the government is the prime minister, who is leader of the party holding a majority of seats in the House of Commons. On rare occasions, the part of the prime minister may not command an absolute majority of seats; it may be the largest party combined with a smaller party to create a majority. By custom, although not by law, the prime minister is a member of the House of Commons. If the prime minister does not hold a seat on taking office, he soon seeks one in a safe constituency. In the 20th century all have been from the lower house.

After a general election the governor-general will ask the leader of the majority party to become prime minister, form a government, and select a cabinet. If there is no clear majority after an election, the sitting prime minister may try to continue in office, but he must meet the new parliament promptly and secure its confidence. Otherwise, the governor-general will ask the leader of the major opposition party to try to form a government. Usually, if a major bill is defeated in the House of Commons, or if a straight vote of no-confidence carries, the prime minister will resign and a new election will be held speedily. The prime minister can ask the governor-general to call an election at any time, and usually this is approved without question. Sometimes, a prime minister and his party may choose to hold an election in the belief that voters will give them an even larger majority of the seats.

The cabinet.
The prime minister names the members of the cabinet, which usually has between 25 and 30 members. Cabinet departments are not rigidly set by law, so a prime minister may decide the number of ministers and their functions. By custom, although not by law, cabinet members hold seats in the House of Commons or the Senate. Also by custom, each province is represented in the cabinet, and Ontario and Quebec have ten or twelve members, depending on how many supporters of the party in power are elected from those provinces. One cabinet minister from Quebec will be an English-speaking Protestant, while another, usually from Ontario or New Brunswick, will be a French-speaking Catholic. A prime minister also may choose a minister for personal or geographic reasons.

There are three types of cabinet ministers: those who head a department with a given function, such as finance or agriculture; those who have special parliamentary responsibilities; and those without portfolio, meaning no specific responsibility for any area of the government. In addition, there are two types of ministers of state, ranking somewhat below full cabinet members: those named for a designated purpose, such as a new or urgent project or policy; and those who assist a departmental minister.

The cabinet has sole power to introduce tax measures to parliament and to introduce bills that call for the expenditure of public money. Such bills usually are introduced by the cabinet member whose department is concerned. With many issues facing a cabinet, it is customary for cabinet committees to be named so that the entire body does not have to deal with all matters. As a committee of ministers, the cabinet submits matters to the governor-general for approval, which usually is not withheld.

In late 1986, in addition to the cabinet departments, there were 24 independent federal boards, agencies, commissions, Crown corporations, and councils. They deal with a variety of government functions and include Canada Post, which employs 62,000 people and handles 7 billion pieces of mail a year; the Advisory Council on the Status of Women; the Commissioner of Official Languages, who deals with complaints and tries to improve understanding between the two language groups; and the International Joint Commission on the boundary water treaty of 1909 between the U.S. and Canada, which governs the quantity and use of water in streams and rivers that cross the border between the two nations.

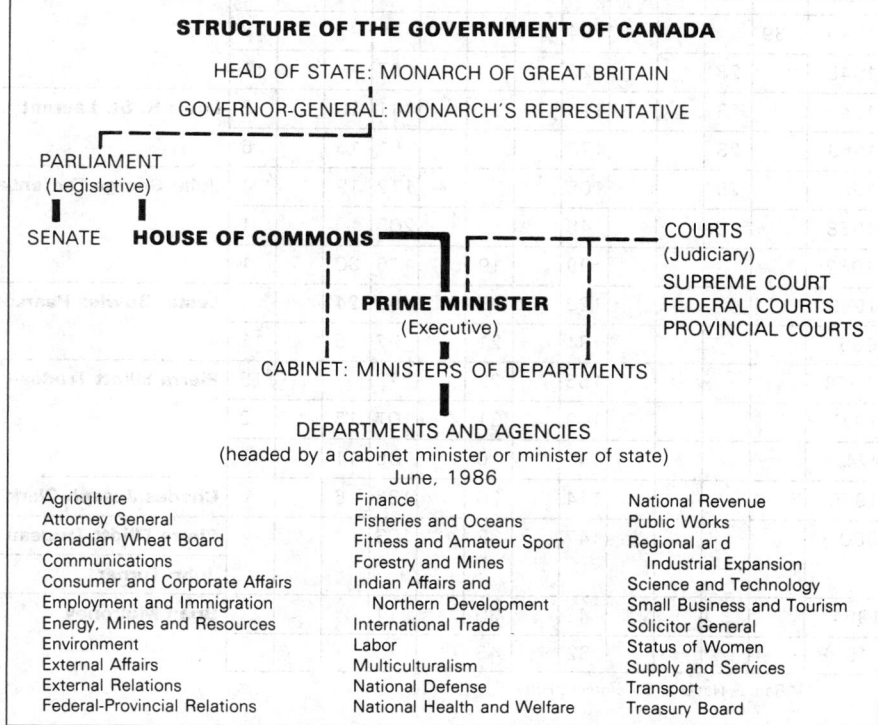

STRUCTURE OF THE GOVERNMENT OF CANADA

HEAD OF STATE: MONARCH OF GREAT BRITAIN

GOVERNOR-GENERAL: MONARCH'S REPRESENTATIVE

PARLIAMENT (Legislative)

SENATE **HOUSE OF COMMONS** COURTS (Judiciary) SUPREME COURT FEDERAL COURTS PROVINCIAL COURTS

PRIME MINISTER (Executive)

CABINET: MINISTERS OF DEPARTMENTS

DEPARTMENTS AND AGENCIES
(headed by a cabinet minister or minister of state)
June, 1986

Agriculture	Finance	National Revenue
Attorney General	Fisheries and Oceans	Public Works
Canadian Wheat Board	Fitness and Amateur Sport	Regional ar d
Communications	Forestry and Mines	Industrial Expansion
Consumer and Corporate Affairs	Indian Affairs and	Science and Technology
Employment and Immigration	Northern Development	Small Business and Tourism
Energy, Mines and Resources	International Trade	Solicitor General
Environment	Labor	Status of Women
External Affairs	Multiculturalism	Supply and Services
External Relations	National Defense	Transport
Federal-Provincial Relations	National Health and Welfare	Treasury Board

CANADIAN NATIONAL ELECTIONS AND PRIME MINISTERS, 1867–1986

Parties:
C–Conservative
CCF–Cooperative Commonwealth Federation
I–Independent
La–Labour
L–Liberal
LL–Laurier Liberals
NDP–New Democratic
P–Progressive
PC–Progressive Conservative
SC–Social Credit
U–Unionist
O–Other

DATE OF ELECTION	C	CCF	I	La	L	LL	NDP	P	PC	SC	U	O
Aug. 7, 1867–Sept. 20, 1867	101				80							
July 20, 1872–Oct. 12, 1872	103				97							
Jan. 22, 1874	73				133							
Sept. 17, 1878	137				69							
June 20, 1882	139				71							
Feb. 22, 1887	123				92							
Mar. 5, 1891	123				92							
June 23, 1896	89		7		117							
Nov. 7, 1900	78				128							8
Nov. 3, 1904	75				139							
Oct. 26, 1908	85		3		133							
Sept. 21, 1911	132				86							
Dec. 17, 1917						82					153	
Dec. 6, 1921	50		3		116			65				
Oct. 29, 1925	116	2		2	99			24				
Sept. 14, 1926	91	2	3		116			13				20
July 28, 1930	137	2	1		88			2				13
Oct. 14, 1935	39	7	1		171					17		10
Mar. 26, 1940	39*				184							28
June 11, 1945		28			125				67			11
June 27, 1949		13			190				41	10		8
Aug. 10, 1953		23			170				51	15		6
June 10, 1957		25			105				112	19		4
Mar. 31, 1958		8			48				208			1
June 18, 1962					99		19		116	30		1
April 18, 1963					129		17		95	24		
Nov. 8, 1965					131		21		97	5		11
June 25, 1968					155		22		72			15
Oct. 30, 1972					109		31		107	15		2
July 8, 1974			1		141		16		95	11		
May 22, 1979					114		20		136	6		
Feb. 8, 1980					147		32		103			
Sept. 4, 1984			1		40		30		211			
Nov. 21, 1988					82		43		170			

* Ran as National Government Party

PRIME MINISTER	PARTY	SERVED
Sir John Macdonald	C	July 1, 1867 – Nov. 5, 1873
Sir Alexander Mackenzie	L	Nov. 7, 1873 – Oct. 9, 1878
Sir John A. Macdonald	C	Oct. 17, 1878 – June 6, 1891
Sir John J. C. Abbott	C	June 16, 1891 – Nov. 24, 1892
Sir John S. D. Thompson	C	Dec. 5, 1892 – Dec. 12, 1894
Sir Mackenzie Bowell	C	Dec. 21, 1894 – Apr. 27, 1896
Sir Charles Tupper	C	May 1, 1896 – July 8, 1896
Sir Wilfrid Laurier	L	July 11, 1896 – Oct. 6, 1911
Sir Robert L. Borden	C	Oct. 11, 1911 – July 10, 1920
Arthur Meighen	C	July 10, 1920 – Dec. 29, 1921
William Lyon Mackenzie King	L	Dec. 29, 1921 – June 28, 1926
Arthur Meighen	C	June 29, 1926 – Sept. 25, 1926
William Lyon Mackenzie King	L	Sept. 25, 1926 – Aug. 6, 1930
Richard Bedford Bennett	C	Aug. 7, 1930 – Oct. 23, 1935
William Lyon Mackenzie King	L	Oct. 23, 1935 – Nov. 15, 1948
Louis S. St. Laurent	L	Nov. 15, 1948 – June 21, 1957
John George Diefenbaker	PC	June 21, 1957 – Apr. 22, 1963
Lester Bowles Pearson	L	Apr. 22, 1963 – Apr. 20, 1968
Pierre Elliott Trudeau	L	Apr. 20, 1968 – June 4, 1979
Charles Joseph Clark	PC	June 4, 1979 – Mar. 3, 1980
Pierre Elliott Trudeau	L	Mar. 3, 1980 – June 30, 1984
John Turner	L	June 30, 1984 – Sept. 17, 1984
Brian Mulroney	PC	Sept. 17, 1984 –

PRIME MINISTER *Brian Mulroney confers with Jeanne Sauvé, the first woman to serve as governor-general of Canada. The parliament building in Ottawa houses the Senate and the House of Commons.*

THE CANADIAN PARLIAMENT

Seats held by provinces and territories

PROVINCE	HOUSE OF COMMONS	SENATE
Alberta	21	6
British Columbia	28	6
Manitoba	14	6
New Brunswick	10	10
Newfoundland	7	6
Nova Scotia	11	10
Ontario	95	24
Prince Edward Island	4	4
Quebec	75	24
Saskatchewan	14	6
Northwest Territories	2	1
Yukon Territory	1	1
TOTAL	282	104

Parliament

Parliament consists formally of two chambers, the House of Commons and the Senate, but parliament often is used to refer only to the House of Commons. By law, parliament must meet at least once a year. Legislation must pass both houses and then be given the royal assent, conveyed by the governor-general.

The House of Commons comprises 282 members, elected by popular vote from constituencies, sometimes called ridings, based on population. Quebec has a fixed number of seats and each of the other provinces a number in relation to Quebec's (see table). Members are elected for terms not to exceed five years, but the parliament is often dissolved for an election before five years are up. Members of the House of Commons need not reside in the province they represent, or even the constituency from which they are elected.

The Senate has 104 members, who are appointed by the governor-general.

GOVERNORS-GENERAL OF CANADA, 1867–1986

GOVERNOR-GENERAL	SERVICE
Lord Monck	July 1, 1867– Nov. 14, 1868
Sir John Young	Feb. 2, 1869– June 21, 1872
Lord Dufferin	June 25, 1872– Oct. 19, 1878
Lord Lorne	Nov. 25, 1878– Oct. 22, 1883
Lord Landsdowne	Oct. 23, 1883– May 25, 1888
Lord Stanley	June 11, 1888– July 15, 1893
Lord Aberdeen	Sept. 18, 1893– Nov. 12, 1898
Lord Minto	Nov. 12, 1898– Nov. 18, 1904
Lord Grey	Dec. 10, 1904– Oct. 12, 1911
Duke of Connaught	Oct. 13, 1911– Oct. 11, 1916
Duke of Devonshire	Nov. 11, 1916– July 19, 1921
Lord Byng	Aug. 11, 1921– Sept. 29, 1926
Lord Willingdon	Oct. 2, 1926– Jan. 16, 1931
Lord Bessborough	Apr. 4, 1931– Sept. 29, 1935
Lord Tweedsmuir	Nov. 2, 1935– Feb. 11, 1940
Lord Athlone	June 21, 1940– Mar. 16, 1946
Lord Alexander	Apr. 12, 1946– Jan. 28, 1952
Vincent Massey	Feb. 28, 1952– Sept. 15, 1959
Georges Philias Vanier	Sept. 15, 1959– Mar. 5, 1967
Daniel Roland Michener	Apr. 17, 1967– Jan. 14, 1974
Jules Leger	Jan. 14, 1974– Jan. 22, 1979
Edward R. Schreyer	Jan. 22, 1979– May 14, 1984
Jeanne Sauvé	May 14, 1984–

They serve indefinite terms but must retire at age 75. Membership is based roughly on population.

The House of Commons is by far the more important of the two bodies. All legislation having to do with government finance must originate there. The Senate, in theory, can amend a bill or refuse to pass it, but as with the House of Lords in Great Britain, this usually means, at most, a delay or minor amendment.

When a bill is introduced, it goes through three readings. First, the minister concerned requests permission to introduce it, which is almost never refused. The bill is then printed and distributed to the legislators, after which there is debate. If the bill meets with approval, it is turned over to the appropriate committee, which may amend it. Finally, it is brought to a vote and passed or rejected.

The House of Commons elects a speaker, who must be a member and who usually represents the party in power. The speaker presides over sessions and rules on procedures. The cabinet appoints a speaker for the Senate. By custom the speakers alternate between English- and French-speaking members.

Political Parties

Political parties have existed in Canada since there were popularly elected assemblies. From 1867 on, the two major parties have been the Liberals and the Conservatives, now known as Progressive Conservatives. Other parties, usually of a more or less radical nature, or with some special interest, arise from time to time, but most have not lasted long or had much influence. At present the New Democratic Party is the only third party of consequence. Political parties were not created by law but are recognized by it. The position of leader of the opposition in parliament is officially recognized.

The Judiciary

The judicial system of Canada derives from the common law of England, except in Quebec where it is of French origin. The highest court is the Supreme Court of Canada, established in 1875, which sits in Ottawa. At its head is the chief justice of Canada. There are eight other judges known as puisne (junior or associate) judges. Three of the judges must be from Quebec. This court has general appellate jurisdiction in criminal and civil cases for the entire Dominion. Supreme Court judges are appointed by the governor-general and hold office during good behavior. Retirement age is 75. The governor-general can remove a judge on request of the House of Commons and Senate.

Next in standing is the Federal Court of Canada, which in 1970 replaced the Exchequer Court of Canada. It has equity, admiralty, civil, and criminal jurisdiction. This court has two divisions: the Court of Appeal with 11 judges, one of whom is chief justice of the Federal Court; and the Trial Division with 14 judges, one of whom is the associate chief justice of the court. These judges also are appointed by the governor-general.

Each province has a superior court and other lower courts. All the judges are named by the governor-general except for the probate courts of New Brunswick and Nova Scotia.

Law enforcement is mostly in the hands of the Royal Canadian Mounted Police (RCMP), established in 1873. As well as being a federal force, the RCMP provides police forces for all the provinces except Ontario and Quebec, which have their own. Municipal police forces are independent.

Provincial Government

Each of the ten provinces has a system of government that is essentially the same as that of the federal system. The lieutenant governor, appointed by the governor-general, is formally the chief executive. Each provincial government also has a political leader and a de facto executive, called premier; the premier represents the majority political party. In addition, there is a cabinet of department ministers.

The provinces have one-house legislatures. The membership varies considerably from province to province (see table). Legislators are elected for terms of four years. Legislation must pass three readings and then have the assent of the lieutenant governor. The last time assent was refused was in 1945.

PROVINCIAL LEGISLATURES
Number of seats in each

Alberta	79
British Columbia	57
Manitoba	57
New Brunswick	58
Newfoundland	52
Nova Scotia	52
Ontario	125
Prince Edward Island	32
Quebec	122
Saskatchewan	64

Municipal governments are established by provincial laws that provide for mayors and other governing units. There now are about 5000 municipalities. In the field of education, boards or commissions are elected under provincial laws.

Territorial Government

The two territories, the Northwest Territories and the Yukon Territory, have less self-government than the provinces. In large part this is due to their vast expanses of land and small populations. Also, while there are many natural resources, they have not yet been developed and do not provide a basis for government support. The federal government controls all Crown lands and nonrenewable resources, such as oil.

The Northwest Territories are governed by a federally appointed commissioner and a 22-member elected legislative assembly. The commissioner has final authority over legislation. On April 14, 1982, in a plebiscite, 56 percent of the voters favored separating the land into east and west units. On November 26, 1982, the federal government accepted this decision. The government noted, however, that the final division depends on the settlement of four Inuit land claims and a negotiated boundary. As of December, 1986, the Inuit have been unable to agree on a boundary. The Inuit constitute about a quarter of the 43,200 people residing in the Northwest Territories—a third of Canada's land mass.

The Yukon Territory has a commissioner and a 16-member assembly, with all members appointed by the Dominion government.

That Canada, despite many governmental changes, still has an English–French problem, along with problems common to late 20th-century democracies, was demonstrated as recently as 1986. On December 22 the Quebec Court of Appeals struck down a provision in a nine-year-old provincial language law requiring that public signs be written in French only. This was seen as a victory for store owners but it is considered likely that this change will arouse anti-English feeling on the part of extremist French elements.

Another recent and vigorous debate centered on Sunday shopping laws. On December 18, 1986, the Supreme Court upheld an Ontario law that requires most retailers to close on Sunday. This was not expected to be the end of the matter. The history and government of Canada are still developing as we move toward the final years of the 20th century.

THE CANADIAN CONSTITUTION

Address to Her Majesty

THAT,WHEREAS in the past certain amendments to the Constitution of Canada have been made by the Parliament of the United Kingdom at the request and with the consent of Canada;

AND WHEREAS it is in accord with the status of Canada as an independent state that Canadians be able to amend their Constitution in Canada in all respects;

AND WHEREAS it is also desirable to provide in the Constitution of Canada for the recognition of certain fundamental rights and freedoms and to make other amendments to that Constitution;

A respectful address be presented to Her Majesty the Queen in the following words:

To the Queen's Most Excellent Majesty: Most Gracious Sovereign:

We, Your Majesty's loyal subjects, the House of Commons of Canada in Parliament assembled, respectfully approach Your Majesty, requesting that you may graciously be pleased to cause to be laid before the Parliament of the United Kingdom a measure containing the recitals and clauses herein-after set forth:

An Act to give effect to a request by the Senate and House of Commons of Canada

Whereas Canada has requested and consented to the enactment of an Act of the Parliament of the United Kingdom to give effect to the provisions hereinafter set forth and the Senate and the House of Commons of Canada in Parliament assembled have submitted an address to Her Majesty requesting that Her Majesty may graciously be pleased to cause a Bill to be laid before the Parliament of the United Kingdom for that purpose.

Be it therefore enacted by the Queen's Most Excellent Majesty, by and with the advice and consent of the Lords Spiritual and Temporal, and Commons, in this present Parliament assembled, and by the authority of the same, as follows:

1. The *Constitution Act, 1981* set out in Schedule B to this Act is hereby enacted for and shall have the force of law in Canada and shall come into force as provided in that Act. *Constitution Act, 1981 enacted*

2. No Act of the Parliament of the United Kingdom passed after the *Constitution Act, 1981* comes into force shall extend to Canada as part of its law. Termination of power to legislate for Canada

3. So far as it is not contained in Schedule B, the French version of this Act is set out in Schedule A to this Act and has the same authority in Canada as the English version thereof. French version

4. This Act may be cited as the *Canada Act.* Short title

CONSTITUTION ACT, 1981

Part I, Schedule B
Canadian Charter of Rights and Freedoms

Whereas Canada is founded upon principles that recognize the supremacy of God and the rule of law:

Guarantee of Rights and Freedoms

1. The *Canadian Charter of Rights and Freedoms* guarantees the rights and freedoms set out in it subject only to such reasonable limits prescribed by law as can be demonstrably justified in a free and democratic society. Rights and freedoms in Canada

Fundamental Freedoms

2. Everyone has the following fundamental freedoms: Fundamental freedoms
(*a*) freedom of conscience and religion;
(*b*) freedom of thought, belief, opinion and expression, including freedom of the press and other media of communication;
(*c*) freedom of peaceful assembly; and
(*d*) freedom of association.

Democratic Rights

3. Every citizen of Canada has the right to vote in an election of members of the House of Commons or of a legislative assembly and to be qualified for membership therein. Democratic rights of citizens

4. (1) No House of Commons and no legislative assembly shall continue for longer than five years from the date fixed for the return of the writs at a general election of its members. Maximum duration of legislative bodies

(2) In time of real or apprehended war, invasion or insurrection, a House of Commons may be continued by Parliament and a legislative assembly may be continued by the legislature beyond five years if such continuation is not opposed by the votes of more than one-third of the members of the House of Commons or the legislative assembly, as the case may be. Continuation in special circumstances

5. There shall be a sitting of Parliament and of each legislature at least once every twelve months. Annual sitting of legislative bodies

Mobility Rights

6. (1) Every citizen of Canada has the right to enter, remain in and leave Canada. Mobility of citizens

(2) Every citizen of Canada and every person who has the status of a permanent resident of Canada has the right Rights to move and gain livelihood
(*a*) to move to and take up residence in any province; and
(*b*) to pursue the gaining of a livelihood in any province.

Limitation

(3) The rights specified in subsection (2) are subject to

(*a*) any laws or practices of general application in force in a province other than those that discriminate among persons primarily on the basis of province of present or previous residence; and

(*b*) any laws providing for reasonable residency requirements as a qualification for the receipt of publicly provided social services.

Affirmative action programs

(4) Subsections (2) and (3) do not preclude any law, program or activity that has as its object the amelioration in a province of conditions of individuals in that province who are socially or economically disadvantaged if the rate of employment in that province is below the rate of employment in Canada.

Legal Rights

Life, liberty and security of person

7. Everyone has the right to life, liberty and security of the person and the right not to be deprived thereof except in accordance with the principles of fundamental justice.

Search or seizure

8. Everyone has the right to be secure against unreasonable search or seizure.

Detention or imprisonment

9. Everyone has the right not to be arbitrarily detained or imprisoned.

Arrest or detention

10. Everyone has the right on arrest or detention

(*a*) to be informed promptly of the reasons therefor;

(*b*) to retain and instruct counsel without delay and to be informed of that right; and

(*c*) to have the validity of the detention determined by way of *habeas corpus* and to be released if the detention is not lawful.

Proceedings in criminal and penal matters

11. Any person charged with an offence has the right

(*a*) to be informed without unreasonable delay of the specific offence;

(*b*) to be tried within a reasonable time;

(*c*) not to be compelled to be a witness in proceedings against that person in respect of the offence;

(*d*) to be presumed innocent until proven guilty according to law in a fair and public hearing by an independent and impartial tribunal;

(*e*) not to be denied reasonable bail without just cause;

(*f*) except in the case of an offence under military law tried before a military tribunal, to the benefit of trial by jury where the maximum punishment for the offence is imprisonment for five years or a more severe punishment;

(*g*) not to be found guilty on account of any act or omission unless, at the time of the act or omission, it constituted an offence under Canadian or international law or was criminal according to the general principles of law recognized by the community of nations;

(*h*) if finally acquitted of the offence, not to be tried for it again and, if finally found guilty and punished for the offence, not to be tried or punished for it again; and

(*i*) if found guilty of the offence and if the punishment for the offence has been varied between the time of commission and the time of sentencing, to the benefit of the lesser punishment.

Treatment or punishment

12. Everyone has the right not to be subjected to any cruel and unusual treatment or punishment.

Self-crimination

13. A witness who testifies in any proceedings has the right not to have any incriminating evidence so given used to incriminate that witness in any other proceedings, except in a prosecution for perjury or for the giving of contradictory evidence.

Interpreter

14. A party or witness in any proceedings who does not understand or speak the language in which the proceedings are conducted or who is deaf has the right to the assistance of an interpreter.

Equality Rights

Equality before and under law and equal protection and benefit of law

15. (1) Every individual is equal before and under the law and has the right to the equal protection and equal benefit of the law without discrimination and, in particular, without discrimination based on race, national or ethnic origin, colour, religion, sex, age or mental or physical disability.

Affirmative action programs

(2) Subsection (1) does not preclude any law, program or activity that has as its object the amelioration of conditions of disadvantaged individuals or groups including those that are disadvantaged because of race, national or ethnic origin, colour, religion, sex, age or mental or physical disability.

Official Languages of Canada

Official languages of Canada

16. (1) English and French are the official languages of Canada and have equality of status and equal rights and privileges as to their use in all institutions of the Parliament and government of Canada.

Official languages of New Brunswick

(2) English and French are the official languages of New Brunswick and have equality of status and equal rights and privileges as to their use in all institutions of the legislature and government of New Brunswick.

(3) Nothing in this Charter limits the authority of Parliament or a legislature to advance the equality of status or use of English and French. — Advancement of status and use

17. (1) Everyone has the right to use English or French in any debates and other proceedings of Parliament. — Proceedings of Parliament

(2) Everyone has the right to use English or French in any debates and other proceedings of the legislature of New Brunswick. — Proceedings of New Brunswick legislature

18. (1) The statutes, records and journals of Parliament shall be printed and published in English and French and both language versions are equally authoritative. — Parliamentary statutes and records

(2) The statutes, records and journals of the legislature of New Brunswick shall be printed and published in English and French and both language versions are equally authoritative. — New Brunswick statutes and records

19. (1) Either English or French may be used by any person in, or in any pleading in or process issuing from, any court established by Parliament. — Proceedings in courts established by Parliament

(2) Either English or French may be used by any person in, or in any pleading in or process issuing from, any court of New Brunswick. — Proceedings in New Brunswick courts

20. (1) Any member of the public in Canada has the right to communicate with, and to receive available services from, any head or central office of an institution of the Parliament or government of Canada in English or French, and has the same right with respect to any other office of any such institution where (*a*) there is a significant demand for communications with and services from that office in such language; or — Communications by public with federal institutions

(*b*) due to the nature of the office, it is reasonable that communications with and services from that office be available in both English and French.

(2) Any member of the public in New Brunswick has the right to communicate with, and to receive available services from, any office of an institution of the legislature or government of New Brunswick in English or French. — Communications by public with New Brunswick institutions

21. Nothing in sections 16 to 20 abrogates or derogates from any right, privilege or obligation with respect to the English and French languages, or either of them, that exists or is continued by virtue of any other provision of the Constitution of Canada. — Continuation of existing constitutional provisions

22. Nothing in sections 16 to 20 abrogates or derogates from any legal or customary right or privilege acquired or enjoyed either before or after the coming into force of this Charter with respect to any language that is not English or French. — Rights and privileges preserved

Minority Language Educational Rights

23. (1) Citizens of Canada — Language of instruction

(*a*) whose first language learned and still understood is that of the English or French linguistic minority population of the province in which they reside, or

(*b*) who have received their primary school instruction in Canada in English or French and reside in a province where the language in which they received that instruction is the language of the English or French linguistic minority population of the province,

have the right to have their children receive primary and secondary school instruction in that language in that province.

(2) Citizens of Canada of whom any child has received or is receiving primary or secondary school instruction in English or French in Canada, have the right to have all their children receive primary and secondary school instruction in the same language. — Continuity of language instruction

(3) The right of citizens of Canada under subsections (1) and (2) to have their children receive primary and secondary school instruction in the language of the English or French linguistic minority population of a province — Application where numbers warrant

(*a*) applies wherever in the province the number of children of citizens who have such a right is sufficient to warrant the provision to them out of public funds of minority language instruction; and

(*b*) includes, where the number of those children so warrants, the right to have them receive that instruction in minority language educational facilities provided out of public funds.

Enforcement

24. (1) Anyone whose rights or freedoms, as guaranteed by this Charter, have been infringed or denied may apply to a court of competent jurisdiction to obtain such remedy as the court considers appropriate and just in the circumstances. — Enforcement of guaranteed rights and freedoms

(2) Where, in proceedings under subsection (1), a court concludes that evidence was obtained in a manner that infringed or denied any rights or freedoms guaranteed by this Charter, the evidence shall be excluded if it is established that, having regard to all the circumstances, the admission of it in the proceedings would bring the administration of justice into disrepute. — Exclusion of evidence bringing administration of justice into disrepute

General

Aboriginal rights and freedoms not affected by Charter

25. The guarantee in this Charter of certain rights and freedoms shall not be construed so as to abrogate or derogate from any aboriginal, treaty or other rights or freedoms that pertain to the aboriginal peoples of Canada including

(*a*) any rights or freedoms that have been recognized by the Royal Proclamation of October 7, 1763; and

(*b*) any rights or freedoms that may be acquired by the aboriginal peoples of Canada by way of land claims settlement.

Other rights and freedoms not affected by Charter

26. The guarantee in this Charter of certain rights and freedoms shall not be construed as denying the existence of any other rights or freedoms that exist in Canada.

Multicultural heritage

27. This Charter shall be interpreted in a manner consistent with the preservation and enhancement of the multicultural heritage of Canadians.

Rights guaranteed equally to both sexes

28. Notwithstanding anything in this Charter, the rights and freedoms referred to in it are guaranteed equally to male and female persons.

Rights respecting certain schools preserved

29. Nothing in this Charter abrogates or derogates from any rights or privileges guaranteed by or under the Constitution of Canada in respect of denominational, separate or dissentient schools.

Application to territories and territorial authorities

30. A reference in this Charter to a province or to the legislative assembly or legislature of a province shall be deemed to include a reference to the Yukon Territory and the Northwest Territories, or to the appropriate legislative authority thereof, as the case may be.

Legislative powers not extended

31. Nothing in this Charter extends the legislative powers of any body or authority.

Application of Charter

Application of Charter

32. (1) This Charter applies

(*a*) to the Parliament and government of Canada in respect of all matters within the authority of Parliament including all matters relating to the Yukon Territory and Northwest Territories; and

(*b*) to the legislature and government of each province in respect of all matters within the authority of the legislature of each province.

Exception

(2) Notwithstanding subsection (1), section 15 shall not have effect until three years after this section comes into force.

Exception where express declaration

33. (1) Parliament or the legislature of a province may expressly declare in an Act of Parliament or of the legislature, as the case may be, that the Act or a provision thereof shall operate notwithstanding a provision included in section 2 or sections 7 to 15 of this Charter.

Operation of exception

(2) An Act or a provision of an Act in respect of which a declaration made under this section is in effect shall have such operation as it would have but for the provision of this Charter referred to in the declaration.

Five year limitation

(3) A declaration made under subsection (1) shall cease to have effect five years after it comes into force or on such earlier date as may be specified in the declaration.

Re-enactment

(4) Parliament or a legislature of a province may re-enact a declaration made under subsection (1).

Five year limitation

(5) Subsection (3) applies in respect of a re-enactment made under subsection (4).

Citation

Citation

34. This Part may be cited as the *Canadian Charter of Rights and Freedoms.*

Part II   Rights of the Aboriginal Peoples of Canada

Recognition of existing aboriginal and treaty rights

35. (1) The existing aboriginal and treaty rights of the aboriginal peoples of Canada are hereby recognized and affirmed.

Definition of "aboriginal peoples of Canada"

(2) In this Act, "aboriginal peoples of Canada" includes the Indian, Inuit and Métis peoples of Canada.

Part III   Equalization and Regional Disparities

Commitment to promote equal opportunities

36. (1) Without altering the legislative authority of Parliament or of the provincial legislatures, or the rights of any of them with respect to the exercise of their legislative authority, Parliament and the legislatures, together with the government of Canada and the provincial governments, are committed to

(*a*) promoting equal opportunities for the well-being of Canadians;

(*b*) furthering economic development to reduce disparity in opportunities; and

(*c*) providing essential public services of reasonable quality to all Canadians.

Commitment respecting public services

(2) Parliament and the government of Canada are committed to the principle of making equalization payments to ensure that provincial governments have sufficient revenues to provide reasonably comparable levels of public services at reasonably comparable levels of taxation.

Part IV   Constitutional Conference

37. (1) A constitutional conference composed of the Prime Minister of Canada and the first ministers of the provinces shall be convened by the Prime Minister of Canada within one year after this Part comes into force.

Constitutional conference

(2) The conference convened under subsection (1) shall have included in its agenda an item respecting constitutional matters that directly affect the aboriginal peoples of Canada, including the identification and definition of the rights of those peoples to be included in the Constitution of Canada, and the Prime Minister of Canada shall invite representatives of those peoples to participate in the discussions on that item.

Participation of aboriginal peoples

(3) The Prime Minister of Canada shall invite elected representatives of the governments of the Yukon Territory and the Northwest Territories to participate in the discussions on any item on the agenda of the conference convened under subsection (1) that, in the opinion of the Prime Minister, directly affects the Yukon Territory and the Northwest Territories.

Participation of territories

Part V   Procedure for Amending Constitution of Canada

38. (1) An amendment to the Constitution of Canada may be made by proclamation issued by the Governor General under the Great Seal of Canada where so authorized by

General procedure for amending Constitution of Canada

(*a*) resolutions of the Senate and House of Commons; and

(*b*) resolutions of the legislative assemblies of at least two-thirds of the provinces that have, in the aggregate, according to the then latest general census, at least fifty per cent of the population of all the provinces.

(2) An amendment made under subsection (1) that derogates from the legislative powers, the proprietary rights or any other rights or privileges of the legislature or government of a province shall require a resolution supported by a majority of the members of each of the Senate, the House of Commons and the legislative assemblies required under subsection (1).

Majority of members

(3) An amendment referred to in subsection (2) shall not have effect in a province the legislative assembly of which has expressed its dissent thereto by resolution supported by a majority of its members prior to the issue of the proclamation to which the amendment relates unless that legislative assembly, subsequently, by resolution supported by a majority of its members, revokes its dissent and authorizes the amendment.

Expression of dissent

(4) A resolution of dissent made for the purposes of subsection (3) may be revoked at any time before or after the issue of the proclamation to which it relates.

Revocation of dissent

39. (1) A proclamation shall not be issued under subsection 38(1) before the expiration of one year from the adoption of the resolution initiating the amendment procedure thereunder, unless the legislative assembly of each province has previously adopted a resolution of assent or dissent.

Restriction on proclamation

(2) A proclamation shall not be issued under subsection 38(1) after the expiration of three years from the adoption of the resolution initiating the amendment procedure thereunder.

Idem

40. Where an amendment is made under subsection 38(1) that transfers provincial legislative powers relating to education or other cultural matters from provincial legislatures to Parliament, Canada shall provide reasonable compensation to any province to which the amendment does not apply.

Compensation

41. An amendment to the Constitution of Canada in relation to the following matters may be made by proclamation issued by the Governor General under the Great Seal of Canada only where authorized by resolutions of the Senate and House of Commons and of the legislative assembly of each province:

Amendment by unanimous consent

(*a*) the office of the Queen, the Governor General and the Lieutenant Governor of a province;

(*b*) the right of a province to a number of members in the House of Commons not less than the number of Senators by which the province is entitled to be represented at the time this Part comes into force;

(*c*) subject to section 43, the use of the English or the French language;

(*d*) the composition of the Supreme Court of Canada; and

(*e*) an amendment to this Part.

42. (1) An amendment to the Constitution of Canada in relation to the following matters may be made only in accordance with subsection 38(1):

Amendment by general procedure

(*a*) the principle of proportionate representation of the provinces in the House of Commons prescribed by the Constitution of Canada;

(*b*) the powers of the Senate and the method of selecting Senators;

(*c*) the number of members by which a province is entitled to be represented in the Senate and the residence qualifications of Senators;

(*d*) subject to paragraph 41(*d*), the Supreme Court of Canada;

(*e*) the extension of existing provinces into the territories; and

(*f*) notwithstanding any other law or practice, the establishment of new provinces.

(2) Subsections 38(2) to (4) do not apply in respect of amendments in relation to matters referred to in subsection (1).

Exception

Amendment of provisions relating to some but not all provinces

43. An amendment to the Constitution of Canada in relation to any provision that applies to one or more, but not all, provinces, including

(*a*) any alteration to boundaries between provinces, and

(*b*) any amendment to any provision that relates to the use of the English or the French language within a province,

may be made by proclamation issued by the Governor General under the Great Seal of Canada only where so authorized by resolutions of the Senate and House of Commons and of the legislative assembly of each province to which the amendment applies.

Amendments by Parliament

44. Subject to sections 41 and 42, Parliament may exclusively make laws amending the Constitution of Canada in relation to the executive government of Canada or the Senate and House of Commons.

Amendments by provincial legislatures

45. Subject to section 41, the legislature of each province may exclusively make laws amending the constitution of the province.

Initiation of amendment procedures

46. (1) The procedures for amendment under sections 38, 41, 42 and 43 may be initiated either by the Senate or the House of Commons or by the legislative assembly of a province.

Revocation of authorization

(2) A resolution of assent made for the purposes of this Part may be revoked at any time before the issue of a proclamation authorized by it.

Amendments without Senate resolution

47. (1) An amendment to the Constitution of Canada made by proclamation under section 38, 41, 42 or 43 may be made without a resolution of the Senate authorizing the issue of the proclamation if, within one hundred and eighty days after the adoption by the House of Commons of a resolution authorizing its issue, the Senate has not adopted such a resolution and if, at any time after the expiration of that period, the House of Commons again adopts the resolution.

Computation of period

(2) Any period when Parliament is prorogued or dissolved shall not be counted in computing the one hundred and eighty day period referred to in subsection (1).

Advice to issue proclamation

48. The Queen's Privy Council for Canada shall advise the Governor General to issue a proclamation under this Part forthwith on the adoption of the resolutions required for an amendment made by proclamation under this Part.

Constitutional conference

49. A constitutional conference composed of the Prime Minister of Canada and the first ministers of the provinces shall be convened by the Prime Minister of Canada within fifteen years after this Part comes into force to review the provisions of this Part.

Part VI   Amendment to the Constitution Act, 1867

Amendment to *Constitution Act, 1867*

50. The *Constitution Act, 1867* (formerly named the *British North America Act, 1867*) is amended by adding thereto, immediately after section 92 thereof, the following heading and section:

"Non-Renewable Natural Resources, Forestry Resources and Electrical Energy

Laws respecting non-renewable natural resources, forestry resources and electrical energy

92A. (1) In each province, the legislature may exclusively make laws in relation to (*a*) exploration for non-renewable natural resources in the province;

(*b*) development, conservation and management of non-renewable natural resources and forestry resources in the province, including laws in relation to the rate of primary production therefrom; and

(*c*) development, conservation and management of sites and facilities in the province for the generation and production of electrical energy.

Export from provinces of resources

(2) In each province, the legislature may make laws in relation to the export from the province to another part of Canada of the primary production from non-renewable natural resources and forestry resources in the province and the production from facilities in the province for the generation of electrical energy, but such laws may not authorize or provide for discrimination in prices or in supplies exported to another part of Canada.

Authority of Parliament

(3) Nothing in subsection (2) derogates from the authority of Parliament to enact laws in relation to the matters referred to in that subsection and, where such a law of Parliament and a law of a province conflict, the law of Parliament prevails to the extent of the conflict.

Taxation of resources

(4) In each province, the legislature may make laws in relation to the raising of money by any mode or system of taxation in respect of

(*a*) non-renewable natural resources and forestry resources in the province and the primary production therefrom, and

(*b*) sites and facilities in the province for the generation of electrical energy and the production therefrom,

whether or not such production is exported in whole or in part from the province, but such laws may not authorize or provide for taxation that differentiates between production exported to another part of Canada and production not exported from the province.

"Primary production"

(5) The expression "primary production" has the meaning assigned by the Sixth Schedule.

(6) Nothing in subsections (1) to (5) derogates from any powers or rights that a legislature or government of a province had immediately before the coming into force of this section."

Existing powers or rights

51. The said Act is further amended by adding thereto the following Schedule:

Idem

"The Sixth Schedule   Primary Production from Non-Renewable Natural Resources and Forestry Resources

1. For the purposes of section 92A of this Act,

  (*a*) production from a non-renewable natural resource is primary production therefrom if

      (i) it is in the form in which it exists upon its recovery or severance from its natural state, or

      (ii) it is a product resulting from processing or refining the resource, and is not a manufactured product or a product resulting from refining crude oil, refining upgraded heavy crude oil, refining gases or liquids derived from coal or refining a synthetic equivalent of crude oil; and

  (*b*) production from a forestry resource is primary production therefrom if it consists of sawings, poles, lumber, wood chips, sawdust or any other primary wood product, or wood pulp, and is not a product manufactured from wood."

Part VII   General

52. (1) The Constitution of Canada is the supreme law of Canada, and any law that is inconsistent with the provisions of the Constitution is, to the extent of the inconsistency, of no force or effect.

Primacy of Constitution of Canada

  (2) The Constitution of Canada includes

    (*a*) the *Canada Act,* including this Act;

    (*b*) the Acts and orders referred to in Schedule I; and

    (*c*) any amendment to any Act or order referred to in paragraph (*a*) or (*b*).

Constitution of Canada

  (3) Amendments to the Constitution of Canada shall be made only in accordance with the authority contained in the Constitution of Canada.

Amendments to Constitution of Canada

53. (1) The enactments referred to in Column I of Schedule I are hereby repealed or amended to the extent indicated in Column II thereof and, unless repealed, shall continue as law in Canada under the names set out in Column III thereof.

Repeals and new names

  (2) Every enactment, except the *Canada Act,* that refers to an enactment referred to in Schedule I by the name in Column I thereof is hereby amended by substituting for that name the corresponding name in Column III thereof, and any British North America Act not referred to in Schedule I may be cited as the *Constitution Act* followed by the year and number, if any, of its enactment.

Consequential amendments

54. Part IV is repealed on the day that is one year after this Part comes into force and this section may be repealed and this Act renumbered, consequential upon the repeal of Part IV and this section, by proclamation issued by the Governor General under the Great Seal of Canada.

Repeal and consequential amendments

55. A French version of the portions of the Constitution of Canada referred to in Schedule I shall be prepared by the Minister of Justice of Canada as expeditiously as possible and, when any portion thereof sufficient to warrant action being taken has been so prepared, it shall be put forward for enactment by proclamation issued by the Governor General under the Great Seal of Canada pursuant to the procedure then applicable to an amendment of the same provisions of the Constitution of Canada.

French version of Constitution of Canada

56. Where any portion of the Constitution of Canada has been or is enacted in English and French or where a French version of any portion of the Constitution is enacted pursuant to section 55, the English and French versions of that portion of the Constitution are equally authoritative.

English and French versions of certain constitutional texts

57. The English and French versions of this Act are equally authoritative.

English and French versions of this Act

58. Subject to section 59, this Act shall come into force on a day to be fixed by proclamation issued by the Queen or the Governor General under the Great Seal of Canada.

Commencement

59. (1) Paragraph 23(1)(*a*) shall come into force in respect of Quebec on a day to be fixed by proclamation issued by the Queen or the Governor General under the Great Seal of Canada.

Commencement of paragraph 23(1)(*a*) in respect of Quebec

  (2) A proclamation under subsection (1) shall be issued only where authorized by the legislative assembly or government of Quebec.

Authorization of Quebec

  (3) This section may be repealed on the day paragraph 23(1)(*a*) comes into force in respect of Quebec and this Act amended and renumbered, consequential upon the repeal of this section, by proclamation issued by the Queen or the Governor General under the Great Seal of Canada.

Repeal of this section

60. This Act may be cited as the *Constitution Act, 1981,* and the Constitution Acts 1867 to 1975 (No. 2) and this Act may be cited together as the *Constitution Acts, 1867 to 1981.*

Short title and citations

LAW

The law surrounds, guides, protects and restricts all of us from birth to death in a myriad of ways. For example, the law dictates what we must do if we wish to marry; it establishes certain obligations toward husbands, wives, and children. It tells us how close we can build our house to that of our neighbor or how much rent we must pay our landlord. It demands that professionals such as doctors and lawyers maintain standards of competence. The law requires healthful conditions for workers in factories and specific structural regulations in the construction of theaters and office buildings. Even after death, the law disposes of our estates.

The object of law is to enforce standards of social behavior so that fairness prevails and conflict is avoided. When disputes occur, the courts provide the means of peaceful settlement. In carrying out its objective, law functions as a part of government and is backed by the power of the state.

Legal proceedings can be divided into two major categories: criminal and civil. A criminal case always involves an offense, called a crime, by an individual. The state prosecutes criminal cases to protect society at large. A civil proceeding can involve a dispute between individuals, corporations, or even governments. The courts adjudicate the dispute, deciding for one side or the other.

The American judicial system has a dual state-federal court structure. State courts operate as the judicial arm of state governments, while fed-

THE UNIVERSITY OF THE STATE OF NEW YORK
EDUCATION DEPARTMENT

BE IT KNOWN THAT

HAVING GIVEN SATISFACTORY EVIDENCE OF THE COMPLETION OF PROFESSIONAL AND OTHER REQUIREMENTS PRESCRIBED BY LAW IS QUALIFIED TO PRACTICE

IN THE STATE OF NEW YORK
IN WITNESS WHEREOF THE EDUCATION DEPARTMENT GRANTS THIS LICENSE
UNDER ITS SEAL AT ALBANY, NEW YORK

LICENSE NUMBER

00211

EXIT

LAW AIMS TO *protect the public by licensing certain professions and by requiring "exit" signs and other safety measures in public places.*

eral courts operate as part of the federal government. An individual may bring certain types of cases in either a state or federal court. Other types of cases must be brought only in a state

court or only in a federal court. In both state and federal systems, a hierarchy of courts exists. The lowest courts are the state trial or "inferior" courts, and the highest are the state or federal supreme or appeals courts.

Inferior courts try civil cases involving small sums of money and light penalties. Higher courts hear more serious cases, and supreme or appeals courts are occupied with appeals, disputes on cases that have already been tried in lower courts.

The courts employ certain procedures to try criminal and civil cases. These procedures help reconstruct the issues accurately and ensure fairness to the parties in a dispute. Many procedures vary from state to state, but some are guaranteed by the U.S. Constitution. Among the guaranteed procedural safeguards are protection against unreasonable searches and seizures, self-incrimination, and excessive bail or unusual punishment. In civil proceedings, cases are decided upon a preponderance of evidence, while in criminal ones, proof of guilt must be "beyond a reasonable doubt."

In the following pages we will briefly consider how the law functions in the United States. First, we will look at the origins of the American legal system. Then we will examine various branches of the law: property law, business law, family law, tort law, and constitutional law. The next section considers the state and federal court structure and outlines criminal and civil procedure. Finally, the legal profession in the United States will be considered.

U.S. Law
Common Law

The national legal systems of the Western world can be divided into two major categories, those based on *civil law* and those based on *common law*. The civil law system originated in Roman law and was expressed in comprehensive codes such as the Code Napoleon, the basic law of France and other European states. The common law tradition may have originated among the the tribes of Northern Europe; it has developed most fully in England and was carried by emigrants to other English-speaking nations.

Common law originated in the grants made by the kings of England to their justices in the 1000's and 1100's to settle disputes. Gradually, royal jurisdiction extended beyond the monarch's personal presence, and a new and more rational method of trial emerged. The decisions made by the king's "officers in court" were considered precedent. When a court laid down a principle of law, it later adhered to that principle and applied it

to all cases where facts were substantially the same. Following past decisions in judging present controversies became the working rule of the common law courts. Early Parliaments rarely intervened to change laws.

The English colonists who came to America brought with them the principles of the common law judicial tradition. English common law was adopted as the basis of the legal system in each of the original colonies. However, the American legal system has diverged from that of England in several respects.

The common law tradition was modified by America's unique form of federalism. Precedents dealing with new situations developed independently in the various colonies. The judges of New York, for example, knowing little about decisions in Connecticut or elsewhere, sometimes reached different decisions in similar cases. Thus, each colony developed its own precedents and rules.

The Constitution recognized this divergence among the states by establishing a central government with limited powers, leaving all residual judicial and legislative powers to the individual states. Today 51 systems of law are in operation in the United States, one for each state and another for the federal government.

Codes

The common law tradition was further modified in the United States by several major efforts at codification. A code is a complete written system of law unified and promulgated by legislative action.

In 1824 Louisiana adopted a comprehensive civil code based on the Code Napoleon, drawn up in France in 1800. The Code Napoleon was the first great modern codification of the law. In 1847, largely because of the efforts of David Dudley Field, the constitution of New York State required that a commission codify the law. The 1847 commission, and another appointed in 1857, drafted five codes called the Field codes. New York adopted the penal code and codes of civil and criminal procedure. These codes were widely adopted in other states as well.

The most important recent attempt at codification has been the Uniform Commercial Code drafted by the uniform state law commissioners and the American Law Institute in 1951. The code was adopted in more than half the states.

Judicial Supremacy

There are other contrasts between the English legal system and that of the United States. In England there is no written constitution; the decisions of Parliament are supreme. The courts can interpret the decisions of Parliament but they cannot invalidate them. In the United States, Congress is not supreme. Its decisions can be annulled by the Supreme Court if they are in violation of the Constitution. The acts of any state legislature can also be judicially invalidated as being inconsistent with either the state constitution or the U.S. Constitution.

The framers of the Constitution may not have intended to delegate this immense power to the Supreme Court.

Yet, the famous case of *Marbury* v. *Madison* (1803) firmly established the concept of judicial supremacy. In this case, Chief Justice Marshall stated: "The powers of the legislature are defined and limited. . . . It is emphatically the province and the duty of the judicial department to say what the law is." The Constitution was thus established as a legal document subject to interpretation only by the courts.

The concept of judicial supremacy has subtly transformed the doctrine of precedent in the United States. Because the Constitution is difficult to amend, the Supreme Court has occasionally felt impelled to revise earlier interpretations of the document, particularly when these interpretations appeared to be obsolete or mistaken. In the process, the High Court overruled some of its prior decisions. Thus, earlier precedents were no longer treated as binding. This has proved true in other appeals courts as well. For example, the Court ruled in 1895 that racial segregation in public facilities was constitutional but reversed itself in 1954 in *Brown* v. *Board of Education of Topeka.*

While the lower courts still feel constrained to abide by the precedents established by the tribunals above them, these higher tribunals feel free to depart from their own precedents whenever they seem to have outlived their usefulness.

JUDGMENT *has been a function of the state from Egyptian times* (left) *to the present. It consists of applying general law to specific cases and weighing the evidence on both sides, as symbolized by the scales. Today, lawyers for two parties appear before a judge to argue for their clients* (below left). *The judge* (below) *sits near the seal of the government he represents, a symbol of the law's authority.*

Branches of the Law

Criminal Law

Legal cases can be divided into two major categories, criminal and civil. The distinction between these proceedings rests on the issue of origination. Civil actions may be initiated through governmental or private means. Criminal cases, however, must be initiated by the state, which represents society as a whole. Criminal actions are prosecuted by the government on behalf of the public. Even the victim of a crime does not have the power to bring a criminal case to trial. The victim must register a complaint with the police or the district attorney, who, in turn, have the responsibility to initiate prosecution.

Classification of crimes.

In the United States there are two types of crimes, felonies and misdemeanors. Felonies are punishable by at least one year's imprisonment in a state or federal prison accompanied by the loss of civil rights. In certain cases, felonies may be punishable by death. Misdemeanors are punishable by fines, shorter terms of imprisonment, or both. Sometimes a third category of crimes is recognized, that of offenses. Offenses are comparatively minor crimes, carrying very light penalties.

Felonies include murder and non-negligent manslaughter, rape, robbery, aggravated assault, burglary, larceny (including theft of any amount over $50), and auto theft. Misdemeanors include other assaults, arson, forgery and counterfeiting, fraud, embezzlement, vandalism, prostitution and other sex offenses, violations of narcotics and liquor laws, gambling, drunkenness, disorderly conduct, vagrancy, and various other offenses.

Criminal procedure.

The system of criminal procedure used in the United States is known as "accusatory" or "adversary." In this system, the prosecution, represented by an elected government official known as the district attorney, and the defense attorney, participate throughout the proceedings, mainly producing evidence. The judge plays the role of an umpire to ensure that the trial is carried on according to prescribed rules. The jury, rather than the judge, judges questions of fact and renders the verdict.

In a criminal proceeding, the accused is guaranteed certain constitutional rights. He must be provided with an attorney if he desires one and cannot afford one; he is entitled to bail and to a speedy trial by a jury; he may not be forced to testify at his own trial; and he may not be tried twice for the same crime.

Penalties.

Penalties vary from time to time and place to place. The traditional theory decrees that the punishment shall fit the crime. The modern view holds that punishment should also reform the criminal and serve as a deterrent. Fines and imprisonment are the most common penalties, but sentences vary from state to state.

In the United States there are prisons of many types and sizes. Some are large, high-security institutions; others are small institutions providing less restriction for the inmates. In some systems, the term of imprisonment is fixed by the judge, subject to time off for good behavior in prison. In other systems, the sentence is determined by prison officials.

Probation and parole are important substitutes for imprisonment as methods of rehabilitation. An offender on probation remains at liberty under the guidance of a probation officer. If, during the time prescribed, the offender stays out of trouble and observes the conditions of his probation, nothing further is done in his case. If he does not comply, he may be imprisoned.

Parole is a system of releasing an offender earlier than the expiration of his sentence. The time when a prisoner becomes eligible to be considered for parole is ordinarily fixed by statute. The release of prisoners is generally controlled by a parole board. The board interviews the prisoner shortly before he becomes eligible for parole and also considers information from outside sources. If released, the prisoner is supervised by a parole officer, who sees that the conditions of his release are observed and guides him in his readjustment to community life. Parole may be revoked for a violation of its conditions, and the parolee returned to prison. This kind of conditional release is provided by the laws of every state and the federal government.

Civil Law

Civil proceedings encompass all actions concerning noncriminal matters. They may involve the adjudication of disputes between two individuals, between an individual and a government, an individual and a corporation, or even between two branches of government. A single incident may give rise to both a civil claim and a criminal prosecution. However, in such situations two separate proceedings are conducted.

In a civil suit, the plaintiff is the person or organization that files a complaint with the court against another person or group. The defendant is the person or group against whom the suit is brought.

Property law.

Property is one of the oldest and most basic institutions of society. In modern society, the law of property considers the buying and selling of property, and the rights of property users (renters) as well as property owners.

Legal distinctions.

U.S. law distinguishes between immovables (land and structures permanently affixed to it) and movables. Special rules apply to the acquisition, possession, transfer, and encumbrance of land that do not apply to movables. For example, the sale of land must be publicly regis-

CRIMINAL AND CIVIL LAW: *Criminal law is a proceeding of the state against one suspected of a crime; civil law settles disputes between two or more parties.*

JEROME WEISMAN

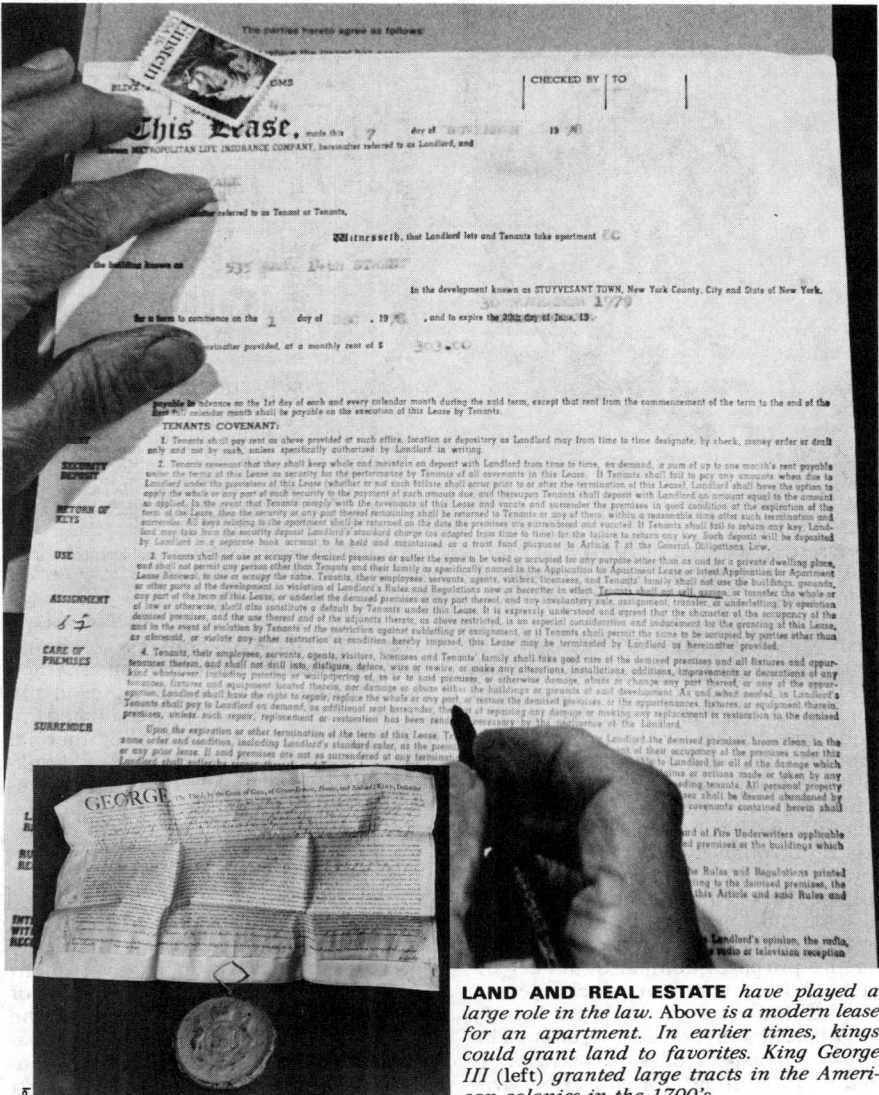

LAND AND REAL ESTATE *have played a large role in the law. Above is a modern lease for an apartment. In earlier times, kings could grant land to favorites. King George III (left) granted large tracts in the American colonies in the 1700's.*

tered. Land is also subject to special rules in the areas of family law, inheritance, contracts, and taxation.

A legal distinction is also made between tangible and intangible property. Tangible property includes land and certain possessions such as houses, automobiles, and furniture. Intangible property includes property that can only be claimed by legal action and not by physical possession. Examples of intangible property are bank accounts, debts, stocks and shares, copyrights, patents and trademarks; and certain rights to the use of land or property, such as leases, easements, and rights of way.

Disposition of property. One of the most prevalent methods of transferring property is through the contract of sale. A sale involves the transfer of something for a sum of money, or the promise of a sum of money. Real estate law sets out the guidelines for procedures required in the legal transfer of property. In the United States, as in most Western countries, the sale of

land must be recorded. One of the essential elements in the transfer of land is "title to land." Possession of title to land gives a person legal ownership of a particular plot and the right to transfer that plot to another person.

Under the title system, land is recorded in public registeries where evidence of title is preserved. When purchasing land, the buyer must conduct a title search to ensure that the seller has rightful ownership to the land. It is customary to employ a surveyor to examine the described borders of the land in order to determine any discrepancies or encroachments upon the property. A title searcher, who may be a lawyer or a professional reader of records, is then employed to trace the history of the land title and to abstract the records. Finally, a lawyer is employed to read the abstracts and to prepare an opinion as to the state of the title. A title insurance company may also investigate the history of a title. On the basis of its investigation,

it may sell insurance against loss resulting from mistakes in the abstract of the public record or from forgery or other irregularities.

Also involved in the legal sale of land is the drawing up of a contract, known as a deed, conveying the property to the new owner. The deed includes such information as the surveyors' calculations, descriptions of any structures affixed to the property, and the amount, method, and date of payment for the property. It is the responsibility of the buyer to register the purchase with the office of a recording agency, usually a county or town office.

Inheritance law. Another method of legal disposition of property occurs through inheritance. A *will* or *testament* is the legal transaction by which an owner of property disposes of his assets in the event of death. In most jurisdictions, a will must be in written form, except in emergency cases, as in the death of a soldier at war. In the United States, a will must be signed and the signature attested to by two or three witnesses.

A will is not valid if at the time of its execution the testator was mentally incompetent, or acting under coercion or fraud. It has no effect until the testator's death, and it can be revoked or changed by him at any time. In many states of the United States, a will is revoked automatically if the testator marries after its execution.

In the United States a will is filed with a probate court. The person named executor by the will, or some other interested person, petitions for the admission of the will to probate. The court appoints someone to administer the will. The administrator collects the assets of the estate, ascertains and pays the taxes and debts, and distributes the remainder to those named in the will.

If a person dies without leaving a will, his property is placed under the authority of an administrator who pays all debts and charges and provides the legal heirs with their share. (See Family law below.)

Leaseholds. In all legal systems, an owner of property may grant certain rights to others, as when a landlord rents or leases an apartment.

The rights of landlords and tenants vary widely from state to state, but some laws affecting this relationship are fairly uniform. The rights are defined by "covenants" or "promises" that are written into leases, regulated by statutes, or sanctioned by general usage. For example, tenants have the right of "quiet enjoyment" of the apartment, free from disturbance by the landlord. A landlord has a duty to make ordinary repairs, but not those resulting from damages caused by the tenant or by others not connected with the landlord. The landlord must usually pay all taxes and assessments and insure the premises. Ordinarily, the nonpayment of rent is grounds for termination of the lease and reentry by the landlord. If a tenant is evicted, he is discharged from the payment of rent.

Many states have laws requiring that landlords provide premises that are fit for habitation and free from conditions that are harmful to health and safety. Most states have laws requiring that certain safety codes be met, such as those stipulating that public places provide a certain number of fire exits or extinguishers.

Business law.
In general, business or commercial law deals with the rights of property and the relations of persons engaged in commerce.

Contracts.
The law of contracts is the basis of almost all business law. A contract is a promise that the law recognizes as binding. For the breach of such a promise, the law offers a remedy.

The most fundamental issue regarding contracts is the legal distinction between a serious contract, enforceable by the courts, and a mere expression of intent never meant to have binding obligation. In order to distinguish between the two, the common law system developed the "doctrine of consideration." Consideration is something given or promised by one party to a contract and accepted by the other party in return for the sale of a property, product, or service. A contract, to be legally enforceable, must be supported by consideration.

Contracts are considered void when they are illegal; contrary to public interest; made under duress or fraudulent conditions; made impulsively; or entered into by minors.

With the exception of special kinds of contracts covered by the statute of frauds, oral contracts are as binding as written contracts. The statute of frauds provides that certain types of promises are enforceable only if made in writing and signed by the person to be charged. These include promises by executors and administrators to pay a debt of the deceased out of their own money; promises in consideration of marriage; agreements that by their terms cannot be concluded in one year; and contracts for the sale of land.

If a contract has not been fulfilled, the court may grant monetary compensation or other relief to the injured party. The defendant is required by law to pay such damages.

Modern commercial practice relies to a growing extent on arbitration to handle disputes, especially those that arise in international transactions. Arbitration is generally less complicated than a suit at law, is decided sooner, and is less expensive.

Business organization.
In American society, many businesses act as agents for others. Two important aspects of

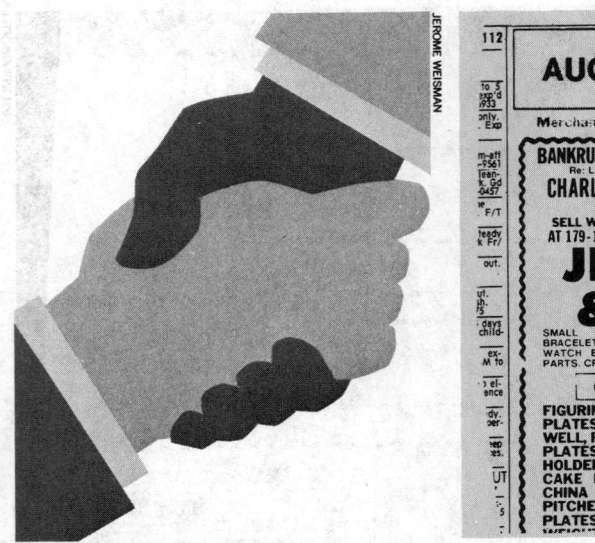

CONTRACTS AND BANKRUPTCY: *A contract may be based on a handshake and need not be written down if other criteria are met. If a business cannot pay its debts, it may declare bankruptcy; often it auctions off its assets in order to pay its creditors.*

business law are that of "agency" and "business organization."

Agency is the body of commercial law regulating the legal relationships when one person or group represents another. Business organization refers to the manner in which this representation is conducted. One may conduct business as a sole proprietor, personally or through agents. One may also conduct business by way of a partnership or corporation. Legally, a corporation can be defined as an artificial body created under authority of law for the purposes defined by its certificate of incorporation or charter. A corporation acts through its legally constituted officers and agents. The important aspect of a corporation is that while it allows for collective ownership, it retains an independent legal personality that can claim such rights as ownership of property and the ability to transfer that property. A corporation can also enter into legally binding contracts.

Commercial law.
Commercial law is the body of law relating to business transactions. It encompasses sales, commercial paper and banking, letters of credit, bulk sales, documents of title, investment securities, and secured transactions. Commercial law is one of the few areas of U.S. law that have been embodied in a comprehensive codified set of laws, the Uniform Commercial Code.

The Uniform Commercial Code covers all business transactions from the time raw materials are purchased until finished merchandise is sold to a consumer. It also deals with many related transactions, such as the movement of merchandise from one point to another, the storage of goods, and the financing of commercial transactions. Its provisions cover payments for merchandise and the deposit and collection of checks, notes, and drafts.

Bankruptcy.
The law of bankruptcy provides an important method for settling the debts of a person unable to pay them. It gives the bankrupt an opportunity to start his commercial life afresh. Jurisdiction over bankruptcy proceedings is vested exclusively in the federal courts. The National Bankruptcy Act, passed by Congress, supersedes all state laws on the subject.

Tax law.
Tax law is the body of rules under which a government may require taxpayers to pay part of their income or their property for the support of the government. Corporations and individuals are most concerned with the laws governing tax assessment, enforcement, procedure, coercive measures, and administrative and judicial appeal. Other aspects of tax law are part of administrative law (see below).

Copyrights, patents, and trademarks.
Copyright is the legal recognition of rights to control or benefit from literary or artistic productions. The author or originator of such productions has for a certain period the sole privilege of multiplying copies of his work and publishing and selling them. Literary, musical, dramatic, pictorial, and sculptural works, as well as motion pictures and other audiovisual material, are covered by copyright law.

According to the Copyright Act of 1977, an author and his heirs maintain the right to profit from a work for the author's lifetime plus 50 years. The act also regulates conditions under which authors may grant rights to publishers, film producers, or others, and under which the public may copy, perform, or otherwise use the work. If

LABOR LAW *has developed to protect workers from reprisals by employers. Here labor leader Walter Reuther is menaced by auto company police in 1937.*

a book, song, or performance is reproduced or copied without the creator's permission, he may sue the producers for infringement of copyright and collect damages. Copyright coverage has been extended to cover certain kinds of computer programs.

Patent laws grant an inventor the exclusive right to make, use, and sell his invention for a certain number of years. A valid patent generally requires the invention of something that is both novel, in the sense of never having existed before, and unobvious, in the sense of being beyond the ordinary skill of an expert in the field.

A trademark is a symbol that a manufacturer affixes to the goods he produces as a means of identifying them in the marketplace. Trademark law prevents such symbols from being appropriated by others.

Administrative law.
Administrative law refers to the law regulating public administration. This includes the organization, powers, duties, functions, and limitations of public officials and agencies of all kinds, their relations with each other and with citizens and nongovernmental bodies, such as corporations; legal methods of controlling public administration; and the rights and liabilities of officials.

The best known federal administrative agencies are the independent regulatory commissions created by Congress (see Glossary of Government Agencies above). Typical agencies at the state level include public utilities commissions, zoning boards, workmen's compensation boards, and tax commissions.

Adminstrative law helps determine the powers and limitations of government agencies and regulates their dealings with corporations, other government bodies, and individuals. For example, an individual landowner may challenge the decision of a zoning board in court. Court functions are limited, however. Not all administrative irregularities are within judicial authority.

Labor law.
Labor law refers to a varied body of law applied to such matters as employment, remuneration, working conditions, trade unions, labor-management relations, and old age and disability insurance. Labor law deals with individual contractual relationships between employers and employees and with statutory requirements and collective contractual relationships.

Individuals and groups are protected by law in such matters as work hours, health and safety conditions, right to collective bargaining, etc. They are also protected against discrimination on the basis of race, color, religion, age, or sex unless an employer can prove one of these criteria are required by the nature of the position.

Tort law.
Tort law is the body of laws that deals with private wrongs. The law of torts is concerned with the prevention of, or compensation for, harm sustained by a person through the unlawful or dangerous activity of others. Tort law regulates a wide variety of behavior ranging from physical attack and dangerous negligent conduct to more subtle violations, such as damage to social reputation. Tort suits are brought by injured persons as private plaintiffs. Often, however, the same wrong constitutes a crime against the state as well as against an individual. In some cases, the same names, such as "trespass," "assault," and "battery," and the same acts, may give rise to both civil and criminal proceedings. Under common law, torts are distinguished between those that are intentional and those that are merely negligent.

Intentional personal injury. Personal injury falls under several specific torts. *Battery* is physical contact (often a blow) with the plaintiff without his or her consent. *Assault* is threatening physical harm. *False imprisonment* is confinement against one's will to a vehicle, house, prison, or even a city. *Mental suffering* is harm suffered from abuse other than physical violence.

Intentional violation of property rights. A defendant is liable for *trespass* when he intentionally enters or causes damage to land possessed by another. Activities that produce excessive dust, noise, stench, insects, fumes, gases, seepage, smoke, vibrations, or severe emotional disturbances may give rise to an action for *nuisance*. Interference with a person's movable property gives rise to the tort of *trespass to chattels*. This action arises from any intentional physical interference with a chattel in the possession of another. The tort of *conversion* constitutes an intentional interference with a chattel in a manner that is seriously inconsistent with the right of the person entitled to it. Theft may give rise to a tort of conversion.

Negligence. The greatest number of civil actions for tort are brought by injured persons to recover compensation for damages suffered through the negligent conduct of the defendant. Negligence may be described as a failure to comply with that standard of care that would be expected of a reasonable man of ordinary prudence. The plaintiff must show that the defendant was under an obligation to take reasonable care for the plaintiff's benefit and that the defendant failed to comply with this duty of care. It must also be shown that there is a cause-and-effect connection between the defendant's carelessness and the damage suffered by the plaintiff.

Traffic accidents constitute a large number of civil actions for torts of negligence. In such cases, the conduct of the driver against whom a suit is brought is compared with that of a motorist of ordinary sense, exhibiting ordinary care and skill. However, these guidelines are often difficult to apply and leave wide room for interpretation. By law, any motorist is considered to be under an obligation to take reasonable care for the benefit of all persons on the road.

In medical malpractice suits, a plaintiff alleges that his doctor failed to exercise that degree of skill and learning commonly applied by a prudent member of the profession. These suits are a large and growing area in civil proceedings and have led to huge increases in the cost of medical malpractice insurance.

Defamation. The protection of intangible personal interests is also covered by the law of torts. Damaging the reputation and good name of a person is called *defamation,* and it is covered by the torts of *libel* and *slander.* A libel suit is generally brought to remedy damaging and untrue statements in writing (or in print or broadcast). The plaintiff need not prove that damage has actually occurred. Slander is the oral defamation of a person, and in slander suits, proof of damage is required.

Insurance law. Liability insurance arises mainly from the operation of the law of negligence. There are at least four major types of liability insurance contracts:

1. liability arising out of the use of automobiles;
2. liability arising from professional negligence;
3. liability arising out of conduct of a business;
4. personal liability, as in one's private home.

Practically all liability contracts falling in these four categories have some common elements. One is the insuring clause, in which the insurer agrees to pay on behalf of the insured all sums that the insured shall become legally obligated to pay because of bodily injury, sickness or disease, wrongful death, or injury to another person's property. It is often necessary to resort to legal or court action to determine the amount of the damages, although in a vast majority of cases the damages are settled out of court by negotiations between the parties.

All liability insurance contracts contain clauses that obligate the insurance company to conduct a court defense and pay any settlement and other costs. The insured is required to cooperate with the insurer in all court actions by appearing in court, and if necessary, giving testimony. Practically all liability insurance policies contain limitations on the maximum amount of a judgment payable under the contract.

Family law. Personal legal relationships as well as property relations are formed by the "marriage contract." In law, husband and wife are bound to each other by rights and obligations. Among the obligations are sexual relations, companionship, cohabitation, and a husband's financial support of his wife.

Marriage laws. Marriage laws specify the age at which one can legally marry. Generally, the minimum age of marriage without the consent of parents is 21 for men and 18 for women. Even with the consent of parents, marriages are generally not permitted for men under 18 or women under 16. Pregnancy may give a judge the right to waive minimum age requirements.

In all states, formalities attending

DEFAMATION *may injure a person's reputation by the printing of falsehoods (libel) or by the speaking of falsehoods (slander). The victim may sue for damages.*

marriage are prescribed by statute. Licenses to marry must be obtained, witnesses are usually required, and the persons who perform the ceremony are designated. The clerk issuing the license must be satisfied by affidavit or otherwise that there are no legal impediments to the marriage and that, in the case of minors, the consent of parents has been granted.

Common law marriages, recognized in some states, require no license or ceremony. In these states, a verbal agreement to marry, followed by cohabitation as man and wife, constitutes a legal marriage. State statutes also govern prohibitions on marriage. Prohibitions include marriage between close relatives and between those with venereal disease.

Property. In the past, women who married gave up almost all rights to personal property. Today, in almost all states, a woman's property is her own. In addition, a married woman may freely make contracts. Her liabilities as well as her rights of action are also her own.

Several states have adopted the policy of "community property." Under this principle, the property of the husband and wife is divided into three funds. What each spouse owns at the time of marriage, or acquires separately, remains the property of that individual. A third fund is created out of all other property acquired by either after marriage.

Divorce law. *Divorce* is the legal dissolution of marriage. An *annulment* declares a marriage void from the time of its inception. Marriages may be annulled for such causes as impotence, bigamy, force, fraud, or insanity.

Divorce laws are under the authority of the state legislatures. All of the states recognize adultery and bigamy as grounds for divorce and almost all

recognize mental or physical cruelty as just cause. Other grounds recognized in various states include alcoholism, impotency, nonsupport, adultery, fraud, and duress.

Some states permit divorce on the grounds of separation or absence, ranging from one to ten years. Although there has been a liberalizing tendency in divorce laws in recent years, most courts adhere to the theory that each divorce is a "contest" in which one party is guilty.

Alimony. One of the crucial problems of divorce is the determination of the property and alimony rights of the wife. If the parties can agree on financial terms, a property settlement may be entered into and the divorce will be uncontested. In cases where parties are unable to come to terms, a contested divorce ensues. It is then the duty of the court to determine the division of property and terms of support.

It is customary for the court to divide marital property between the divorced couple and to award to the wife alimony, or allowance, for the support of herself and the children of the marriage. Alternatively, the father may agree or be ordered to pay *child support* for as long as the children remain minors. Factors to be considered in the determination of alimony or child support include the number of children and the resources and earning potential of both husband and wife.

Child custody. In principle, both father and mother have equal rights of child custody. They can jointly control the actions and residence of the children. If, however, they cannot agree, a court may award custody to one parent.

Custody of the child is supposedly based on the "best interests of the child," however, "best interests" may be difficult to define. In most states, courts tend to award the custody of children to the mother, unless there are strong indications that she is unfit.

Child laws. A parent is required to shield a child from evil influences and a parent may not injure a child or treat him in a cruel manner. The conduct of any adult that tends to deprave the morals of a child or endanger his health or well-being is punishable as a criminal offense.

The principle that parents have an obligation to secure their children's education gave rise to both compulsory school attendance laws and child labor legislation. Modern education laws require school attendance of children from 6 to 18 years of age with the upper limit most commonly set by statute at 16. Parents and guardians may be penalized for failure to comply. State and federal child labor laws bar the employment of children in dangerous occupations or during periods of required school attendance. Sixteen is a usual minimum age allowed for the full-time employment of a child.

As already noted, the courts award custody, in principle, according to the welfare of the child. Both parents, or one parent, may be deprived of custody because of conduct harmful to the child. If one of the parents dies during the child's minority, the surviving parent assumes full control. If a child becomes an orphan, or if his parents prove unfit to care for him, he may be committed to the guardianship of a suitable person or social welfare agency.

In cases of parental neglect, some states provide for a termination of parental rights, freeing the child for adoption or foster home placement. By a decree of adoption, the child becomes the lawful child of his adoptive parents. In order to prevent abuses arising out of the casual transfer of children from their natural parents to irresponsible substitutes, many states require guardianship or adoption proceedings and commitment orders from a juvenile court.

Inheritance laws. In all legal systems, the property of a person who dies without a will goes to those related to him by blood. Laws relating to intestacy vary widely among the states.

Even where a will does exist, the surviving spouse is protected against complete disinheritance in every state. In most states, any real estate owned by a married couple is specifically protected. Each spouse has an "estate" in the real property of the other; if one dies, a portion of such real property is reserved for the surviving spouse, who cannot be deprived of it without his or her consent. In those states that have adopted the community property system, the surviving spouse is entitled to one-half of the community property, which generally consists of the property acquired during the marriage through the activities of either spouse.

In almost all states, surviving families are protected by one or more of the following:

1. laws that require that a will expressly state the disinheritance of a close family member;
2. laws that provide that a child born after the making of a will receive a share unless a contrary intention is stated in the will;
3. laws that provide that no more than a certain fraction of an estate may be given to charity by a person who is survived by close relatives; and
4. laws that limit or prohibit deathbed bequests to charities.

Constitutional law. Constitutional law is the law that determines the governmental organization of a state, defines its powers, and limits the use of those powers. In the United States, a formal written Constitution is interpreted and enforced by the judiciary. The Constitution is the supreme law, also applying to the states, and the federal judiciary (ultimately the Supreme Court) has express jurisdiction over all cases involving the Constitution.

In the United States there are two bodies of constitutional law, national and state. National constitutional law consists of the Constitution and its amendments, together with the interpretations of the federal judiciary, usage, and custom. State courts have the final word as to the interpretation of their own constitutional provisions. Federal courts will accept such interpretations when dealing with strictly state matters. Federal courts have the last word, however, when a question arises under the federal Constitution.

Two important areas have developed as a result of federal judicial interpretation: government prerogatives and civil liberties. Government prerogatives include the right of the federal government to acquire and administer dependent territories; the immunity of the national government from taxation by the states; the right of the federal government to issue paper currency; and the exclusive power of Congress to regulate foreign and interstate commerce. In the present century, the federal government has greatly expanded its power through the courts' liberal interpretations of the interstate commerce clause.

In the area of civil liberties, federal courts have interpreted constitutional guarantees to include the prohibition of officially prescribed prayers or Bible reading in public schools; the invalidity of laws closing retail stores on Sundays; the prohibition of segregation in schools or public accommodations; the prohibition of laws outlawing interracial marriage; and the abolishment of devices, such as poll taxes, to restrict voting rights.

Evidence acquired during the search of a suspected person, or of his immediate vicinity, without a search warrant is not admissible in court. A confession is excluded as evidence if the police did not advise the suspected person of his right to remain silent and of his right to have an attorney. Neither the prosecution nor the judge can comment on the silence of an accused person who has taken advantage of the guarantee against self-incrimination.

The 14th Amendment extended judicial protection of civil liberties in a broad sense to the states. The Supreme Court has extended coverage of the Bill of Rights to state court actions, including some or all of the provisions

CONSTITUTIONAL LAW *has helped define and extend the civil liberties of all citizens. Here blacks register to vote in 1965; many had been kept from voting before.*

ENVIRONMENTAL LAW *protects water and air in the interest of all citizens.*

of the 1st Amendment (freedom of religion, speech, press, assembly, and petition); the 4th (search and seizure); the 5th (self-incrimination); the 6th (speedy trial, impartial jury, confrontation of witnesses, right to counsel); and the 8th (protection from cruel and unusual punishment).

Antitrust law. Antitrust laws are designed to combat business monopolies and unfair commercial practices and to preserve competition.

During this century, the very large corporation has become a common type of business enterprise. Large corporations may acquire the financial power to put their smaller competitors out of business; ending competition in this way, and establishing a monopoly or "trust," the corporations could then raise their prices to greatly increase profits.

In 1890, the Sherman Antitrust Act was enacted by Congress. In 1914, the Federal Trade Commission (FTC) was created and granted the power to investigate suspected violations of the law regarding unfair methods of competition in commerce.

The Clayton Antitrust Act prohibits, under certain conditions, price discrimination, exclusive dealing contracts, tying arrangements, mergers, and interlocking corporate directorates. The FTC and Justice Department enforce antitrust provisions.

Environmental law. Environmental law is designed to combat the pollution, abuse, and neglect of air, earth, and water resources; its central concern is the impact of human activity on natural resources. It also addresses such concerns as pesticides, radiological hazards, and highway and power plant location.

Legal techniques for environmental control include the purchase or reservation of natural areas such as parks or wildlife sanctuaries; the control of environmental hazards by means of tax laws; the requirement of permits for hazardous operations; and the imposition of penalties on violators of environmental protection laws. Private individuals or groups may also bring suit against violators, claiming a legally enforceable right to a healthy environment.

International Law

International law is the body of rules, principles, and standards to which independent nations are bound by common consent. In the United States, matters of international law are in the jurisdiction of the federal judiciary. Areas covered by international law are treaties with other nations, commerce conducted with foreign nations, the acquisition of new territories, and the administration of those territories.

International law is based in large part on the consent of independent states. The International Court of Justice adjudicates disputes between countries, but is limited to cases where both sides agree to be bound by the verdict. International law is also backed by the United Nations, which can vote for sanctions against a nation accused of serious violations.

Admiralty law. Admiralty or maritime law consists of rules regarding the ownership and operation of sea vessels, the rights and obligations of masters and crews, and the transportation of goods and passengers by water.

In the United States, many aspects of maritime law are regulated by statute. The United States has joined other countries in accepting as part of its own law a large number of international conventions designed to bring uniformity to numerous local shipping regulations. As a result, the contents of ocean bills of lading, international rules for preventing collisions, minimum standards for the safety of life at sea, salvage, load lines, whaling, and many other subjects are now governed by agreements ratified by the major ship-owning states.

Court Structure and Procedure

State Courts

State courts handle most of the nation's judicial work. Their jurisdiction is broader than that of the federal courts, which are limited by the Constitution. Congress does not have the power to define crime for the nation as a whole, for example, or to pass laws regulating divorce, torts, or contracts. Such matters fall within the authority of the states.

Jurisdiction. A criminal prosecution based on state law must be brought in a court of the state where the alleged offense was committed. A civil action based on state law can be brought in several different places: in

the state where the event giving rise to the claim took place; in the court of another state; or in a federal court (when the controversy is between citizens of different states and involves $10,000 or more). Because most criminal prosecutions are based on state law and most civil cases are local affairs involving one person suing another in the same community, state courts handle the majority of civil and criminal cases. State courts also have concurrent jurisdiction to handle almost all civil cases that are within the jurisdiction of the federal courts.

Minor courts. Despite variations from place to place, a general pattern of state court structure can be outlined. At the bottom of the judicial

hierarchy are the "minor" courts, also known as "inferior" courts. They handle criminal prosecutions where the maximum penalty cannot exceed a modest fine or a short term of imprisonment (such as cases involving traffic violations, vagrancy, or disorderly conduct); and civil cases involving small sums of money or property of limited value (such as cases involving small bill collections).

In more serious criminal offenses, the minor courts conduct preliminary hearings to determine whether the prosecution has sufficient evidence to warrant holding the defendant for trial in a higher court. If the court decides there is sufficient evidence, it may fix bail, release the defendant on his promise to return for trial, or keep the defendant in custody.

Minor courts are found in most cities, towns, and villages. In urban areas, minor courts are usually staffed by full-time professional judges. In rural areas, they are likely to be manned by elected part-time officials known as justices of the peace, usually laymen without legal training. No jury is used in the minor courts.

General trial courts.

Above the minor courts are those with jurisdiction extending to larger and more serious cases. These courts are known by various names, such as county, circuit, superior, or district court. They handle criminal cases (such as murder and larceny) carrying heavy penalties, and civil cases involving large sums of money (such as actions for serious personal injury).

The majority of the work of these courts consists of trying new cases. But they may also hear *appeals* on cases originally tried in the minor courts. These appeals, however, differ from those taken to the genuine appellate courts and can more accurately be described as retrials conducted at a higher level.

Some criminal prosecutions never reach these courts, being eliminated by the preliminary hearings conducted by the minor courts. Others are eliminated by *grand juries*. A grand jury consists of a body of 16 to 23 lay citizens drawn from the community. In secret session, a grand jury hears evidence presented to it by the district attorney and determines whether the accused person should stand trial. Because the work of the grand jury is identical to that done in the minor courts by preliminary hearings, grand juries have been eliminated in many states.

General trial courts are usually organized so that one court operates for each county. In metropolitan areas, one or more judges are permanently assigned to a county. In rural areas, a judge may serve several counties and travel between them "on circuit" (hence the name circuit court).

These county judges are almost invariably full-time professionals. In many states, they are popularly elected, while in others they may be appointed by the governor. The tenure of county court judges varies between states; some have a short term of office subject to reappointment or reelection, others hold office for life or for a long period of time.

State Supreme Courts.

In every state there is at least one multi-judge tribunal, usually called the Supreme Court, whose duty is to hear appeals of cases tried in general trial courts. These rehearings determine whether any errors in the original trial require the reversal or modification of lower court judgments.

MINOR COURTS *in local areas operate more informally than higher courts. Here a local judge hears testimony from an officer and a defendant concerning a traffic summons.*

In the state Supreme Courts, lawyers submit written arguments called "briefs" to the judges. Lawyers are also entitled to deliver oral arguments, usually limited to one hour for each side. The court renders its opinion in writing some weeks or months later.

In more populous states, such as California, New York, and Illinois, where the volume of litigation is high, intermediate appellate courts sometimes function between the general trial courts and the state Supreme Courts. These courts are organized on a regional basis; each hears appeals from trial courts within its territory.

Appellate and Supreme Court judges are usually selected by the same political processes (election or appointment) that govern the selection of judges in the general trial courts of their respective states.

Federal Courts

The system of federal courts parallels that of the states. The jurisdiction of the federal courts is limited by the Constitution to cases based on federal law and to controversies between citizens of different states. As designated by the Constitution, the legal authority of the federal government extends to such areas as interstate commerce, foreign relations, postal service, customs, and currency. Criminal prosecutions based on federal laws must be brought in the federal courts. Some civil cases based on federal laws are required to be brought in the federal courts; but many others may be brought either in state or federal courts.

The structure of the federal judicial system is similar to that in the various states. There are three levels of courts: district courts, appeals courts, and the Supreme Court. All judges, from the district to Supreme Court level, are appointed by the President and confirmed by the Senate. In practice, senators have considerable power in appointing district judges with jurisdiction over their home states.

District courts.

There are over 90 federal district courts. Every state has at least one. States with large populations are likely to comprise several districts.

Federal district courts parallel state general trial courts, but they are generally limited to three types of cases: prosecutions for federal crimes; claims based on federal law; and claims between citizens of different states.

Whether a district court is manned by a single judge or several judges depends on the population of the district. The Court for the Southern District of New York has 24 judges.

Courts of appeal.

There are eleven intermediate appellate courts called United States Courts of Appeal, one for each of the circuits into which the nation is divided. Each of the circuits embraces several states, except the District of Columbia.

These courts handle criminal and civil appeals that come from the lower federal courts and from federal administrative agencies; they do not have the power to review decisions of the state courts. Decisions of the courts of appeal are subject to review only by the United States Supreme Court. The number of courts of appeal judges in a circuit varies from three to nine. Usually they sit in panels or divisions of three to hear appeals. Thus, the work is distributed between varying combinations of judges.

The Supreme Court.

The U.S. Supreme Court is the highest federal court; it hears appeals from the lower federal courts and from the highest state courts (insofar as they involve federal questions).

A litigant seeking review in the Supreme Court must show that the issue to be resolved is a "substantial federal question," deserving of consideration by the highest court. The Court grants or denies review of the case. Less than 10 percent of the petitions are granted. In cases refused review, the decision of the lower court stands.

The Supreme Court consists of nine judges. These judges, as all others in the federal court system, are appointed by the President and confirmed by the Senate.

Criminal Procedure

In attempting to determine the guilt of a person accused of a crime, the courts rely on certain legal procedures. These procedures vary slightly from state to state, and from court to court, but a general pattern of procedure can be discerned. Procedures for prosecuting a minor violation are usually more informal than those for prosecuting a more serious one. The following section considers the common procedure in prosecuting a felony.

Arrest. The first step in a criminal proceeding is usually arrest, where the accused is physically taken into custody. In cases involving crimes such as embezzlement, or where the accused has disappeared, the district attorney or a grand jury may conduct a preliminary hearing and issue a warrant for the arrest of the accused.

As already noted, criminal prosecutions are conducted on behalf of the public rather than private individuals. The decision to prosecute must therefore be exercised by government officials. In most situations, the impetus to prosecute is provided by the police officers who make the arrest. A district attorney may, however, refuse to undertake a questionable prosecution.

A serious crime is ordinarily brought to trial in the district court of the state in which the crime occurred. If the criminal has fled to another state, *extradition proceedings* may come into play. Extradition is the procedure by which a state formally requests the surrender of an individual from another state.

Arraignment. An arraignment is a hearing at which charges against the accused are read in an open court, and the accused is given the opportunity to plead guilty or not guilty. If the accused pleads guilty, the judge or state penal authorities will consider proper

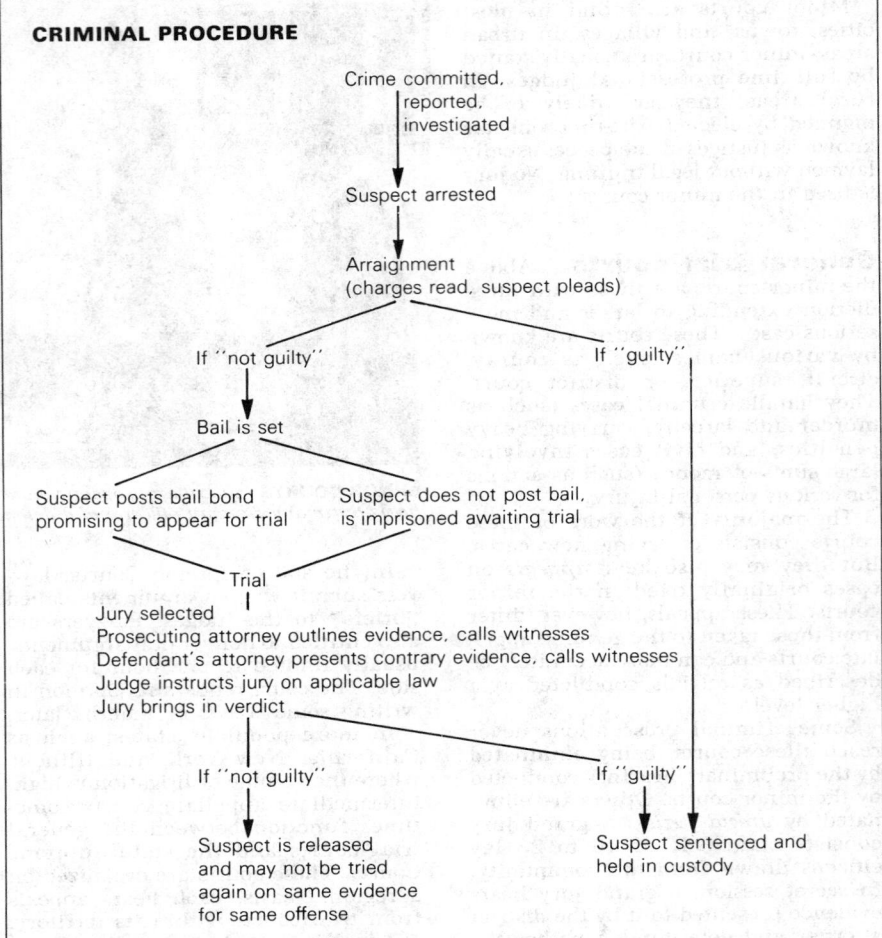

CRIMINAL PROCEDURE

Crime committed, reported, investigated

Suspect arrested

Arraignment (charges read, suspect pleads)

If "not guilty"   If "guilty"

Bail is set

Suspect posts bail bond   Suspect does not post bail,
promising to appear for trial   is imprisoned awaiting trial

Trial

Jury selected
Prosecuting attorney outlines evidence, calls witnesses
Defendant's attorney presents contrary evidence, calls witnesses
Judge instructs jury on applicable law
Jury brings in verdict

If "not guilty"   If "guilty"

Suspect is released   Suspect sentenced and
and may not be tried   held in custody
again on same evidence
for same offense

punishment. If the accused pleads not guilty, *bail* is set. Bail is security given in the form of a bond or cash as a guarantee that a released prisoner will present himself for trial. The right to bail is guaranteed by the Bill of Rights, under the theory that no one may be deprived of his liberty unless proven guilty. The amount of bail, however, is left to the judge's discretion. The accused is formally advised of his right to have a lawyer. If he cannot afford one, the court provides one—either a public defender, who is a salaried government employee, or a legal aid lawyer paid by a private legal aid society. The Constitution guarantees the right to counsel in all criminal cases.

Trial. The trial begins with the selection and swearing in of the jury, consisting of twelve laymen drawn from the community. Juror qualifications vary from state to state, but potential jurors are generally chosen by lot from a group of people who have met minimal qualifications of citizenship. Those chosen for a case are questioned about their qualifications and about any prejudices they might have both by the defending lawyer and the

prosecuting attorney. By this process, the jurors are finally chosen. The right to trial by jury for serious crimes is guaranteed by the Constitution.

Once the jury has been sworn in, the trial begins. The prosecuting attorney makes an opening speech outlining the evidence he expects to produce. The defense counsel also has the right to make such a speech. The witnesses for the prosecution are then examined by the prosecuting attorney and cross-examined by the defense. The witnesses for the defense are also examined and cross-examined. Questions asked of witnesses by either side are subject to objections by the other; the judge must decide on the propriety of the questions.

In the United States, the accused, also called the defendant, need not testify at his own trial. This is a constitutionally guaranteed protection against self-incrimination. At the end of the prosecution's case, the defendant may make a motion for acquittal if the evidence produced is clearly insufficient for conviction. If the judge grants this motion, the trial ends and the defendant is released.

At the close of the trial, both the defense and the prosecution deliver their closing speeches to the jury. The

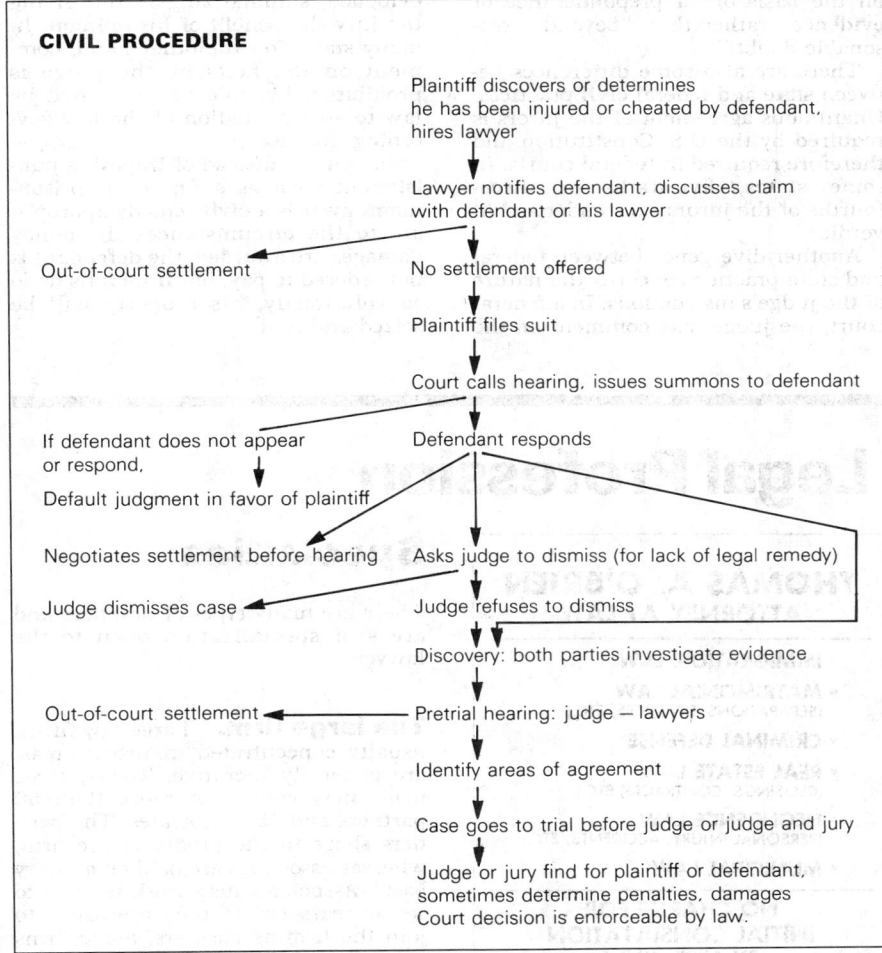

CIVIL PROCEDURE

Plaintiff discovers or determines
he has been injured or cheated by defendant,
hires lawyer

Lawyer notifies defendant, discusses claim
with defendant or his lawyer

Out-of-court settlement   No settlement offered

Plaintiff files suit

Court calls hearing, issues summons to defendant

If defendant does not appear   Defendant responds
or respond,

Default judgment in favor of plaintiff

Negotiates settlement before hearing   Asks judge to dismiss (for lack of legal remedy)

Judge dismisses case   Judge refuses to dismiss

Discovery: both parties investigate evidence

Out-of-court settlement ←──── Pretrial hearing: judge — lawyers

Identify areas of agreement

Case goes to trial before judge or judge and jury

Judge or jury find for plaintiff or defendant,
sometimes determine penalties, damages
Court decision is enforceable by law.

judge gives instructions, called the "charge," to the jury. The main purpose of the charge is to outline the legal basis on which the verdict should be rendered. Jurors must be convinced of guilt "beyond a reasonable doubt," and the verdict must be unanimous.

Jury deliberations are carried on behind closed doors. The jury is the sole judge of the facts of the case, and it follows the judge's charge in matters of law.

If the jury finds the accused innocent, the trial ends and the defendant may not be tried again on the same charge. If the jury finds the accused guilty, his lawyer may move for a new trial if he believes the law has been misapplied, or rules of procedure have been violated. If the jury cannot reach a unanimous verdict, the trial ends with a "hung jury," and a new trial may be ordered with a new jury.

Juveniles, those under 18 in certain states and 16 in others, are treated different from adult offenders. A juvenile, if taken into custody, is held in a special detention facility apart from adults. He may be returned to his parents' custody without bail pending an investigation by a caseworker employed by the court. An informal hearing is held. The juvenile is usually represented by counsel, the public is excluded, and no jury is used. The court does not decide whether the youth is guilty or not guilty but whether he is a "juvenile delinquent." If deemed a delinquent, the court prescribes treatment, which might be confinement in a rehabilitative institution. The proceedings do not leave a permanent mark on a juvenile's record, for he is not technically convicted of a crime.

Civil Procedure

When a person brings a civil suit against another individual, he first hires a lawyer. In a civil case involving a personal injury, for example, the plaintiff's lawyer usually interviews his client, and makes an investigation into how the accident happened and the nature and extent of injuries. He may attempt to settle the case with the defendant's insurance company. If the claim can be settled, the matter is ended. If a settlement cannot be reached, the lawyer will initiate a civil suit. Civil cases may be brought in a state court or federal district court, depending on the nature of the case.

In order to initiate the suit, the plaintiff's attorney must file a complaint with the court. This document states briefly the nature of the plaintiff's claim and what has occurred, and requests an appropriate remedy. The complaint is filed in the clerk's office of the federal court, which issues a summons. This summons notifies the defendant that he is being sued, fixing a time for him to appear in court and warning him that if he fails to appear, a judgment will be rendered against him by default. Ordinarily, a summons is good only in the state where the court that issues it sits.

If the defendant fails to respond to the summons and a default judgment is entered against him, he will be notified of the amount of damages he is required to pay the plaintiff. In civil suits involving damages that are not easily measured mathematically, an inquiry by a jury or by a judge is conducted to determine the amount of damages.

The defendant may respond to the summons with a "motion to dismiss" on the grounds that the allegations of the plaintiff, even if they are true, do not entitle him to a remedy against the defendant. This question is decided by the judge. If he grants the motion, the case is dismissed. If the judge denies the motion, the defendant submits an "answer" to the judge which contains his version of the facts, admitting or denying the plaintiff's allegations.

In a very clear case, where there is no dispute of the facts and where the allegations of one of the parties are demonstrably false, the judge may award a *summary judgment* to the party in the right. Otherwise, both parties to the dispute undertake the procedure known as *discovery,* in which both investigate evidence in preparation for trial. Either party can question the other party or third parties, orally or in writing, outside of court. These questionings result in *depositions.* Either party can obtain a court order permitting him to inspect or copy documents relevant to the controversy. Either side can demand admissions from the other as to the authenticity of relevant documents.

When discovery is complete, both lawyers are usually called for a pretrial conference with the judge. The purpose of this conference is to settle the case if possible, and, if not, to streamline the case for trial by agreeing as to matters not in dispute and precisely defining the remaining issues.

Approximately 90 percent of personal injury actions are settled before trial. If, however, the case cannot be settled, trial is begun, either before a jury or before a trial judge.

The trial in a civil case is carried out in much the same manner as that in a criminal case. However, there are some differences. In a civil case, either side can move for a directed verdict, which will be granted if the evidence is so clear that "reasonable" men could reach only one decision; either side can also move for a new trial after an adverse verdict. In a civil case, the defendant is not allowed to refuse to take the witness stand, as he is in a criminal case; he may be called and examined by the plaintiff's attorney. The privilege against self-incrimination may, however, be invoked by the defendant on specific questions.

The burden of proof also is different from that in a criminal case. In a civil case, the jury must evaluate the case

on the basis of "a preponderance of evidence" rather than "beyond a reasonable doubt."

There are also some differences between state and federal civil practices. Unanimous agreement of the jurors is required by the U.S. Constitution and therefore required in federal courts. In some states, five-sixths or three-fourths of the jurors can render a civil verdict.

Another divergence between federal and state practice concerns the nature of the judge's instructions. In a federal court, the judge may comment on the

evidence, summarizing it and giving the jury the benefit of his opinion. In many states, on the other hand, comment on the facts by the judge is prohibited, his role being limited by law to an explanation of the law governing the case.

Judgment, instead of imposing punishment such as a fine or imprisonment, awards a civil remedy appropriate to the circumstances. If money damages are awarded, the defendant is not ordered to pay, but if he fails to do so voluntarily, his property will be seized and sold.

The Legal Profession

The lawyer of the 19th century was a rugged individualist who represented individual clients. He was usually best known for his performance in court. The shift from a rural to an urban society brought with it the growth of large corporations. After 1870, lawyers began to organize themselves to meet the needs of these large corporations. After 1933, the profession further organized to meet the needs of an expanded government and an organized labor force.

The shift in the functions of lawyers brought with it both a change in legal education and in the legal profession. The apprenticeship system was abandoned and legal education was regulated and standardized under the guidance of the American Bar Association, established in 1848.

Legal Education

Today, law schools must be accredited by the American Bar Association. In order to obtain accreditation, schools must require that their students have a college degree for admission and follow a three-year course of study. Some schools provide evening programs, which students attend part-time while working during the day. Four years of law study are required to complete the course on a part-time basis. Students completing their law school study receive the degree Juris Doctor (Doctor of Law), abbreviated J.D.

In general, law schools approach the study of law by the "case method." Rather than studying general principles and then deducing specific conclusions, the student studies many real cases and infers principles from them. The case method has the advantage of emphasizing the fundamental feature of common law, the evolution of principles from decisions in actual cases.

Certain subjects basic to legal education are constitutional law, contract

LEGAL ADVERTISING, *forbidden by custom for years, is now widely accepted.*

law, tort law, property law, and criminal law. The primary sources used in law schools are codes, legislation, government and other public reports, textbooks, and articles in periodicals.

Qualifications for Practice

Generally, students are required to pass an examination in each subject in order to graduate from law school. Upon graduation, one must pass the bar examination of the state in which one wishes to practice. Each state examination deals to a large degree with the laws of that particular state. If a lawyer has passed a bar exam in one state and wishes to practice in another, he is required to pass the bar examination of the other state to practice there.

Specialties

There are many types of practices and areas of specialization open to the lawyer.

The large firm. Large law firms, usually concentrated in urban areas, are generally lucrative. Today, large firms may consist of more than 50 partners and 150 associates. The partners share in the profits of the firm, whereas associates are paid on a salary basis. Associates may work for five to seven years before they are asked to join the firm as partners. Some firms are dominated by one senior partner, while others have partners at several different levels of authority.

The advantage of the large firm is its ability to specialize to meet all the needs of large corporate clients. Large firms cover such areas of specialization as taxation, trusts, litigation (trial work), government regulations, monopolies, corporate financing and reorganization, and real estate.

The small firm. Small firms may consist of two to four partners and several associates and specialize in one or two areas. Some small firms work in a special area for large corporate clients, but most furnish legal services for clients of more modest means, whether they be small businesses or individuals.

The corporate legal department. The legal department of a large corporation may employ scores of lawyers. Insurance companies, banks, title companies, trade associations, universities, and other large corporations of all types employ in-house counsel. These corporations often retain outside law firms to handle litigation and specific legal problems and rely on in-house counsel for

LEGAL REPRESENTATION *for individuals may be offered by a local law firm* (left), *by a legal aid society* (right), *or even by a mobile law office* (above). *The tradition of confidence in one's family lawyer depends on continuing adherence to the long-established ethical principles of the legal profession.*

everyday legal advice and assistance. In-house legal departments handle such diverse matters as planning and corporate policy, finances, taxation, patents and copyrights, contracts for purchases and sales, government regulations, employer-employee relations, and real estate transactions.

The solo practitioner. Another possibility for the lawyer is to have his own private practice. Generally, solo practitioners are among the lowest paid group in the profession. Ordinarily, they serve individuals rather than corporations or businesses and may specialize in divorce, real estate, probate, malpractice, or criminal law. Much of the work of a solo practitioner involves drafting legal documents such as divorce settlements, wills, and deeds.

The labor lawyer. The term "labor lawyer" is ordinarily used to describe the lawyer who is hired by a labor union or by management to handle labor disputes and labor arbitration.

The government lawyer.
There are a large number of lawyers in federal government service. Most enter the area of government law immediately after graduating from law school. They are employed by such bodies as the Department of Justice, the Federal Communications Commis-

sion, and the Securities and Exchange Commission. Government law includes work in the fields of labor, social services, public works, banking, housing, public power, and taxation. The work of a government lawyer involves processing statements and reports, drafting and interpreting statutes, preparing opinions, investigating and enforcing statutes, and making court appearances.

Lawyers may also find employment in the legal department of city or county government. The legal department of a city government handles such matters as slum clearance, housing, land management, real estate assessments, safety and sanitary regulations, zoning ordinances, bond issues, and taxation.

The criminal lawyer. Criminal lawyers may find employment in several capacities. While the Constitution guarantees all those accused of serious crimes the right to counsel, it is the responsibility of the individual states to find the means to provide this service. Many municipal or county governments provide public defenders, salaried defense lawyers who provide legal aid for indigent defendants. Public defenders are selected in a variety of ways, depending on the local government. They may be selected by appointment by a judge, by election, by appointment of a special commission, or by passing a civil service examination.

Other criminal lawyers are employed by legal aid societies, which provide aid in criminal and civil cases to those unable to pay for private attorneys.

The criminal lawyer may also find employment as a district attorney. A district attorney is in charge of prosecuting criminal cases and is a government employee. District attorneys are usually elected officials.

Other areas. Another area open to the lawyer is that of the law professor. Professors of law do much of the critical writing of textbooks and law journals. They also research legal issues and are active in the drafting of legal reforms, uniform codes, and restatements of law.

A lawyer may also become a judge or a magistrate. Such a position is usually a promotion by means of election or appointment from the ranks of the bar; there is no special training required for the exercise of judicial functions.

Many lawyers enter the political arena. They have always been well represented in executive, legislative, and administrative positions. It is generally assumed that the lawyer has special training, interests, and skills that make him suited to a career in politics. In carrying out his duties, a lawyer may distinguish himself within his community, thereby accomplishing the first step toward running for public office.

Law Glossary

Abstract of title. A statement or memorandum, usually prepared for a purchaser or mortgagee of property, summarizing all documents, such as deeds or wills, and facts that appear on public records affecting the title.

Accessory (before and after the fact). An accessory before the fact is one who is not present at the time a felony is committed, but who instigates, plans, advises, contrives or persuades another to perpetrate it. An accessory after the fact is one who, knowing that a felony has been committed, shelters, receives, relieves, comforts or assists the felon.

Acquittal. The verdict in a criminal trial in which the defendant is found not guilty.

Action. The formal legal demand of one's rights from another person brought in court.

Act of God. An act occasioned exclusively by nature without human interference.

Adjudication. The formal pronouncing or recording of a judgment by a court.

Administrator. *See* Executor.

Affidavit. A written statement of fact made voluntarily by one who is not subjected to cross-examination. It is sworn to before a person authorized by law to administer oaths.

Agency. A legal relationship created by mutual consent wherein one party, the principal, authorizes another party, the agent, to represent him in business dealings with others.

Aid and abet. To assist knowingly in the perpetration of a crime by supporting, encouraging, counseling, inciting, or instigating.

Alimony. Payment made for the sustenance or support of a wife by her divorced husband.

Amicus curiae. One who acts as a "friend of the court" by offering, with the court's permission, legal advice and suggestions regarding an action pending before it, even though he is not a party to the proceedings.

Amnesty. An act of forgiveness granted by the government to a group of persons who might otherwise be subject to punishment for past criminal acts. Amnesty differs from pardon, which is given to individuals.

Annulment of marriage. The dissolving, by judicial decree, of a purported marriage that was void at its inception on the basis of, among other things, mental incompetence, lack of age of legal consent, physical cause, duress, fraud, or bigamy.

Answer. The pleading filed by a defendant in response to a complaint.

Antitrust acts. Federal and state statutes protecting trade and commerce from unlawful restraints, price fixing, and monopolies.

Appeal. A proceeding designed to review the merits of a court decision by a superior court.

Appellant. The party who requests that a higher court review the actions of a lower court.

Appellee. The party against whom an appeal is taken.

Arbitration. The hearing and settlement of a dispute between opposing parties by a third party outside of court proceedings. The decision is often binding by prior agreement of the parties.

Arraignment. The preliminary stage of a criminal proceeding in which the charges are read in open court to the accused, who is given the opportunity to plead guilty or not guilty.

Assault. Simple assault is the unlawful act of threatening with force or violence to do physical harm to another person. When bodily harm is inflicted as a result of an assault, it is called *battery*. If there is intent to commit an additional crime, such as rape, murder, or robbery, it is called *aggravated* or *felonious assault*.

Attachment. The procedure whereby either the defendant in an action at law or his property is taken into custody as security in order to satisfy the judgment of the court.

Attorney-client privilege. The client's privilege to refuse to disclose, and to prevent other persons from disclosing, confidential communications between him and his attorney.

Attorney general. The head of the Department of Justice and chief law officer of the federal government. Most states also have attorneys general.

Attractive nuisance doctrine. The principle that an owner is responsible for damages if he maintains an inher-

ently dangerous condition or object attractive to children (such as a pond) and fails to prevent injury to them from that danger.

Bad debt. A debt that has not been collectible.

Bail. Security given, in the form of a bail bond or cash, as a guarantee that a released prisoner will present himself for trial. This security may be forfeited if the released person does not appear in court at the appointed time.

Bailiff. A court officer or attendant who has charge of a court session; he keeps order, custody of the jury, and custody of prisoners while in court.

Bankruptcy. A condition in which the property of a debtor who is unwilling or unable to pay his debts is distributed to his creditors under court supervision.

Battery. *See* Assault.

Beneficiary. One who receives proceeds from another's estate or property as an heir under a will or under the provisions of a trust.

Bill of sale. A formal written document passing title to goods and other personal property from a seller to a buyer.

Blackmail. The unlawful obtaining of money or property from a person by means of threats.

Blue sky laws. State statutes providing for the regulation and supervision of securities, offerings, and sales in order to protect against investment in fraudulent companies.

Bona fide. Literally, "in good faith"; a bona fide purchase of property is a real or valid purchase without fraud or deceit.

Breach of contract. The failure to perform any of the terms of an agreement.

Breach of peace. A disturbance of public order by an act of violence or by an act likely to incite violence; also called "disturbing the peace."

Breaking and entering. The use of force to enter a dwelling or place of business for the purpose of committing a felony.

Brief. A written statement by counsel arguing a case in court containing the essential facts, legal propositions, questions in dispute, and arguments showing how the law applies to the facts.

Burden of proof. The obligation of a party in a trial to establish, by a preponderance of evidence, a proposition or the material facts that are essential to a decision or verdict.

Burglary. Unlawful entry, with or without force, into a dwelling or other building, with the intent to commit a felony.

Caveat emptor. Literally, "let the buyer beware"; indicates that purchasers buy at their own risk.

Certificate of title. A written document indicating ownership of property and identifying liens and encumbrances upon the property. The purpose of the certificate is to protect against fraud or theft.

Certiorari. A writ or legal document issued by a superior court to an inferior court, requiring the inferior court to produce the records of a specific case so that the higher court can review and correct any legal errors. It is also known as a writ of error, and is only issued on the showing of sufficient cause. It is most commonly used in connection with the U.S. Supreme Court, which uses the writ of certiorari to help choose the cases it wishes to hear.

Challenge. A right given to parties to a trial to reject a juror; such factors as bias or prejudice may be cited as reasons for rejection.

Charge. (1) A formal accusation of a wrong or offense against a person in the preliminary stage in the prosecution of a crime. (2) A judge's instructions to a jury, usually given at the end of a trial.

Charter. A document issued by a government entity that gives a corporation legal existence.

Chattel. Personal property other than freehold land (fully owned land), such as livestock, furniture, and automobiles.

Chattel mortgage. A conditional transfer, by written agreement, of personal property as security for the payment of a debt or for the performance of some other act.

Chose. Any article of personal property.

Circumstantial evidence. Indirect evidence, or proof of facts, from which other facts can be logically inferred.

Citation. (1) A court summons for a person to appear and answer, or to perform a specified act. (2) A reference to an authoritative case, previously decided, or to a pertinent statute.

Citizen's arrest. An arrest made by a private citizen, which is allowed under certain circumstances for a felony or misdemeanor.

Civil action. A court proceeding involving the enforcement or protection of some private or civil right, or for the redress or prevention of some wrong.

Civil law. (1) One of the two great legal systems of the Western world. Civil law was derived from early Roman law and was adopted by many modern nations. (*See also* Common law.) (2) The law concerning noncriminal matters.

Claim. The formal assertion of a right as to money or property; also used to identify the right itself.

Class action. A means by which, where a large group of people have an interest, one or more may sue or be sued as representatives of the class without needing to involve every member of the class.

Codicil. A testamentary writing that amends, alters, qualifies, or revokes specific provisions of an existing duly executed will.

Codification. The process of compiling, arranging, and revising the laws of a country or a specific jurisdiction into an ordered code.

Collusion. An agreement between two or more persons designed to defraud another person or to deceive the court.

Commercial law. The branch of law that governs property rights and relations of persons engaged in commercial transactions.

Common law. One of the two great legal systems of the Western world. Its legal principles, drawn from the actual decisions of earlier courts, evolved in England. These were applied and modified by the courts of the United States in the development of the American judicial system. (*See also* Civil law.)

Common-law marriage. A marriage without ceremony entered into by mutual agreement of the parties for the purpose of establishing the relationship of husband and wife; it is legally recognized in some states, usually if the couple has lived together for a specified number of years and carried out marital duties and obligations.

Community property. Property that is acquired by husband and wife during marriage. In some states, such property is considered to be jointly owned by husband and wife, on the assumption that both spouses have worked for mutual benefit; gifts and inheritances are excluded.

Complainant. One who brings suit against another.

Complaint. The plaintiff's initial pleading containing a statement of the cause of action against the person named therein.

Concurrent jurisdiction. The jurisdiction over a given type of case that is shared by two or more courts.

Concurring opinion. A statement by an appellate court judge agreeing with the decision reached by a majority of his colleagues but disagreeing with their reasoning.

Condemnation proceeding. A proceeding to compel the sale of property for public use by the right of eminent domain. (*See also* Eminent domain.)

Consideration. Something given or promised by one party to a contract, and accepted by the other party in exchange for some act or promise. Consideration is an essential element of a contract. A promise, to be legally enforceable, must be supported by consideration.

Conspiracy. An agreement of two or more persons designed to result in an illegal act.

Contempt. An intentional act, which is subject to punishment, in defiance of the authority and dignity of a court or legislative body.

Contingent fee. A fee for a lawyer dependent on his achieving a successful result for his client.

Contract. Usually a written agreement, enforceable in a court of law, made by two or more persons to do or not to do a particular thing.

Conveyance. A transfer of the legal title to land or property from one person or legal entity to another.

CONSIDERATION *may consist of a single symbolic dollar bill.*

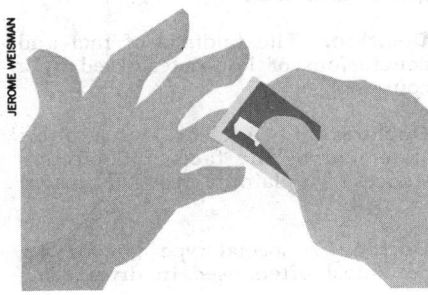

Copyright. A right granted by statute to the author or originator of literary or artistic productions, by which he has, for a limited time, the exclusive privilege of copying, publishing, and selling his work.

Corporation. A body created under authority of law for designated purposes defined by its certificate of incorporation or charter. A corporation acts through its legally constituted officers and agents.

Corpus delicti. Literally, "the body or essential elements of a crime"; proof that the crime charged in a prosecution has been committed.

Cosigner. A term designating one who signs his name to a commercial instrument, such as a promissory note, along with the originator, and thereby becomes bound to meet its obligations if the originator should default.

Count. A separate and independent claim. A civil petition or criminal indictment may contain several counts.

Counterclaim. A claim made by a defendant against the plaintiff in a civil lawsuit; it constitutes a separate cause of action.

Court decision. The disposition of a case by the court. (*See also* Opinion.)

Court of first instance. A court in which a controversy is heard and determined for the first time.

Court of last resort. A court from which there is no appeal.

Court of record. A court whose proceedings are recorded "for a perpetual memorial and testimony," thereby giving a record to which later judges may refer.

Cross-examination. The examination of a witness during a trial by the attorney of the other party. The purpose is to test, or cast doubt on, the testimony given by the witness on direct examination.

Damages. Monetary compensation awarded by a court to a party who has suffered loss or injury through the unlawful act or failure to act or negligence of another.

Decision. The findings of fact and conclusions of law determined by a court.

Declaration. A clear and explicit statement of the facts and circumstances of a plaintiff's cause of action in a suit.

Decree. A special type of court order, most often used in divorce ac-

tions, where the court sets out certain details such as the conditions of alimony, custody, support, and visitation rights. It is also used in probate courts.

Deed. A signed document that passes title to land, or to an interest therein, from one person or corporation to another.

De facto. Literally, "actually existing, in reality or in fact"; a de facto corporation, for example, is one that was defectively organized but is transacting business in good faith. (*See also* De jure.)

Defamation. The holding up of a person to ridicule, scorn, or contempt in order to injure his reputation or the confidence of others in him. It includes both libel and slander.

Default. The failure to do what is required by law, such as the nonappearance of a party in court at the appointed time.

Default judgment. Judgment entered in a civil case where the defendant does not contest the claim asserted against him. Thus, uncontested, the case is won by the plaintiff.

Defendant. The party against whom a criminal or civil action is brought.

De jure. Literally, "lawful, or by right"; a de jure officer, for example, is one whose authority rests on his having been lawfully and properly elected or appointed to office.

Demurrer. A pleading in which one party claims that there are no grounds for continuance of a legal case even if the allegations of fact are true.

Deposition. The written or oral testimony under oath of a witness, usually before trial.

Desertion. The abandonment, without justification and without consent of the party abandoned, of a relationship or service in which a duty is owed by the deserting party.

Direct examination. The first interrogation of a witness in court by the party calling him to testify.

Directed verdict. A decision by a trial judge that the evidence is not sufficient to go to the jury.

Discovery. The process of obtaining facts and information about a case by one party from the other party in preparation for trial. Discovery includes obtaining depositions and the request for and production of documents.

Dissenting opinion. The opinion of an appellate judge in which he gives

his reasons for disagreeing with the majority decision.

District attorney. The officer who represents a city or state government as a prosecuting attorney in criminal proceedings.

District court. In the federal system, the only type of trial court that exists; in state systems, a court with jurisdiction over a geographical area.

Disturbing the peace. *See* Breach of peace.

Docket. The record of the list of cases waiting to be tried.

Domicile. The place where a person maintains his permanent home.

Double jeopardy. The prosecution of an individual more than once for the same offense. The 5th Amendment prohibits such an action.

Due process of law. A constitutional provision that guarantees a defendant a fair trial according to applicable procedures and that requires that the law shall not be unreasonable, arbitrary, or capricious.

Duress. Actual or threatened violence, intimidation, or force that is intended to compel an individual to perform an act against his will.

Easement. A permanent right, created by deed or prescription, that permits one person to make use of the land of another for a specific purpose, or that requires an owner to refrain from some act.

Eminent domain. The right of the state to take private property for public use, without the owner's consent, on payment of just compensation to the owner.

Escheat. A procedure whereby property reverts to the state when there is no legal owner to claim it.

Escrow. A formal written document or a sum of money that is delivered by a party to a contract to a third party. It is kept by the third party until the performance of certain conditions, when it is returned to the original party.

Estate. Everything owned by a person. It is also the right or interest one has in real or personal property. In probate proceedings, it is all the property left by a deceased person.

Evidence. Testimony that is admissible during a trial to prove or disprove the allegations that are in dispute.

Exclusionary rule. A rule whereby evidence that has been obtained in

EMINENT DOMAIN *allows a government to tear down a house in the path of a highway.*

AN EXHIBIT *includes any object introduced as evidence in court.*

violation of the privileges guaranteed by the U.S. Constitution, such as that obtained during unreasonable search and seizure, must be excluded at trial.

Executor or administrator. An officer appointed by a probate or surrogate court to administer and settle the estate of a person who has died. An executor is often named in the will. If a decedent has not left a will, the court appoints an administrator.

Exhibit. A document or object produced and exhibited to a court during a trial or hearing, or deposition, as a proof of facts. If it is accepted, it is marked for identification and thus made a part of the case.

Expert witness. A person who possesses special skill or knowledge in some science, profession, or business and is called to testify on a subject of dispute in an action at law.

Ex post facto law. A law that has retroactive effect, punishing acts that were not punishable when committed. Such legislation is prohibited by the U.S. Constitution.

Expropriation. *See* Eminent domain.

Extortion. *See* Blackmail.

Extradition. The surrender by one state to another of a person duly accused or convicted of a crime.

Felony. A serious crime that is punishable by death or imprisonment. Felony crimes include murder, manslaughter, larceny, robbery, burglary, and arson.

Fiduciary. A person who has accepted the duty to act primarily for another's benefit in a particular undertaking.

Freehold. Full ownership of land that is transferable and inheritable.

Full faith and credit clause. A U.S. constitutional guarantee that requires a state of the United States to give force and effect to the public laws, records, and judgments of a sister state.

Gag order. A court order, in a case involving a great deal of notoriety, directing attorneys and witnesses not to discuss the case with the press in order to assure the defendant of a fair trial.

Garnishment. An action in which a creditor may attach the property or money of a debtor. Wages payable to a debtor are often garnished.

Grand jury. A body of citizens that investigates criminal acts committed within its jurisdiction and determines whether evidence warrants the trial of a suspect.

Guaranty. A contract in which a person, the guarantor, becomes liable for the payment of some debt if the principal debtor defaults.

Habeas corpus. Literally, "you have the body"; a writ in which a person in custody questions the legality of his imprisonment and asks the court that he be released or granted bail.

Hearing. A court proceeding for the purpose of examining witnesses, determining facts, considering proof and arguments presented, and resolving issues raised between the adversaries.

Hostile witness. A witness who surprises the party calling him by giving evidence against that party's interests. The party calling such a witness may cross-examine him and cast doubt on his reliability.

Hung jury. A jury so divided in opinion that they cannot agree upon a verdict.

Immaterial. Evidence that neither proves nor disproves the issues at hand.

Impeach. To question the truthfulness of a witness's testimony.

In camera. A hearing before a judge in his private chambers, or when all spectators are excluded from the courtroom.

Indemnity. The obligation of one person to reimburse or compensate for an injury, loss, or damage caused to another by a specified event.

Indictment. A formal accusation of a minor criminal charge against a person by a public prosecutor rather than by a grand jury.

Infringement. In copyright law, an unauthorized copying or performance of a copyrighted work. In patent law, the unlawful use of a patented invention. Also, the unauthorized use of a trademark or name.

Injunction. A writ issued by a court directing a person to refrain from acting in a certain way in order to prevent future wrongful acts. It is issued only if there is no adequate remedy at law.

Intestate. A state in which one dies without leaving a will.

Issue. The point to be tried, which is affirmed by one party and denied by another.

Judgment. The official decision of a court in a controversy submitted to it; the adjudication of guilt and the fixing of punishment.

Jurisdiction. The scope of a court's or law officer's authority; jurisdiction may be limited geographically or by type of case. In some cases, two or more courts may have concurrent jurisdiction.

Jurisprudence. The science or philosophy of law.

Jury. A body of citizens, usually twelve, selected and empaneled after questioning by counsel, who decide on the facts in civil and criminal trials. This is often referred to as a petit jury as distinguished from a grand jury. (*See also* Grand jury.)

Justice of the peace. A judicial officer of limited jurisdiction. In the United States, he is usually limited to the trying of misdemeanors or minor civil suits.

Juvenile delinquent. *See* Youthful offender.

Larceny. The fraudulent and unauthorized taking of the personal property of another.

Leading question. A question asked of a witness that suggests a conclusion and is therefore inadmissible.

Lease. A contract for possession of lands or houses or apartments for a defined period of time.

Legal signature. A person's name or mark written on a formal document in order to authenticate it.

Liability. An obligation to do or to refrain from doing something arising out of the law of contracts or the law of torts; responsibility for an act that injures or damages another.

Libel. A malicious and unjustified publication of false and defamatory statements in order to degrade, ridicule, or injure someone's character and reputation. (*See also* Slander.)

License. Formal permission granted by a governmental authority to carry on some business, profession, or activity; for example, permission to practice medicine or to operate an automobile.

Lien. A charge or encumbrance imposed on the specific property of a debtor, with his consent, as security for the payment of debts and obligations.

Limitations, statute of. A law prescribing a period of time within which an action must be brought to enforce certain rights or claims. After this period, action cannot be taken.

Litigants. The parties to a suit.

Litigate. To bring a civil action in court.

Loitering. Lingering aimlessly in or around a given public place with no legitimate reason. Loitering is considered a form of disorderly conduct.

Magistrate. A judicial officer authorized to order the arrest of persons charged with the commission of a public offense. Justices of the peace and other inferior judicial officers are also called magistrates.

Malfeasance. The doing of a wrongful and unlawful act by a public officer in his official capacity.

Malicious mischief. The willful or reckless destruction of property because of hatred or resentment toward its owner.

Malpractice. Professional misconduct or unreasonable lack of skill. This term usually refers to the conduct of doctors and lawyers.

Mandamus. Literally, "we command"; a writ issued by a court in the name of the state ordering a corporation, officer, or inferior court to perform an official act or duty required of it by law.

Manslaughter. The killing of a person without premeditation or malice. It may occur voluntarily during a moment of passion, unintentionally during an unlawful but not felonious act, or while performing a lawful act with gross negligence. (*See also* Murder.)

Memorandum. An informal written discussion of the merits of a matter, usually written by a law clerk or junior associate.

Memorandum of law. A formal document prepared by an attorney and submitted to the court expounding on all the points of law pertaining to a particular case.

Miranda rule. A rule requiring that prior to the questioning of a person taken into custody, he must be warned (1) that he has the right to remain silent; (2) that any statement he makes may be used as evidence against him; (3) that he has a right to the presence of an attorney; and (4) that if he cannot afford an attorney, he will be appointed one.

Misdemeanor. A minor crime or offense, such as simple assault, fraud, or forgery. Under federal law, a misdemeanor may be punishable by imprisonment for a term not exceeding one year. Under state law, misdemeanors are not punishable by imprisonment in the state penitentiary.

Misfeasance. The negligent performance of a lawful act.

Mistrial. A trial that is invalid because of the occurrence of an extraordinary event or a significant error before or during the trial. A mistried case may or may not be tried again.

Mortgage. The conditional transfer of property by the mortgager, or debtor, to the mortgagee, or creditor, as security for the performance of an obligation or payment of a debt.

Motion. An application during the course of a trial, made by one of the litigants, requesting a rule or order granting some form of relief.

Municipal court. A court empowered to try minor cases. The jurisdiction of such a court varies from state to state and from city to city.

Murder. Murder in the first degree is the premeditated, willful, deliberate, and malicious killing of a person. The killing of a person during the commission of a certain type of felony, such as robbery, arson, burglary, and rape, is known as a felony murder. Murder in the second degree is killing with malice, but without willful, deliberate, and premeditated intent. Murder in the third degree in some states denotes killing without intent to commit murder. It may occur during the perpetration of a felony other than those named above, or in a moment of passion, but in a cruel and unusual manner. (*See also* Manslaughter.)

Negligence. The failure to exercise due care.

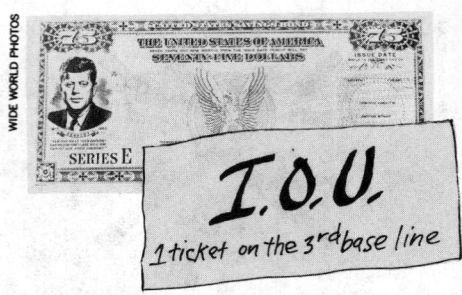

I.O.U. 1 ticket on the 3rd base line

NEGOTIABLE INSTRUMENTS *include any documents—from IOU's to government bonds—that promise a specific payment from one party to another.*

Negotiable instrument. A commercial paper, such as a bill of exchange, promissory note, or bond, that is payable for a definite sum to the bearer or to a specifically identified person. Payment may be on demand, or within a certain period of time, or on the occurrence of a designated event.

Nolle prosequi. Formal entry upon the record by the prosecutor that he "will not further prosecute" the case.

Nolo contendre. Literally, "I do not wish to contend"; a plea by an accused that he will not contest the prosecution of his case. The plea implies confession of guilt and is usually made in the hope of a lenient sentence.

Nonfeasance. The failure of a public officer to perform a duty that is legally required of him in his official capacity.

Note. A written instrument acknowledging the existence of a debt and promising to pay a certain sum of money to an identifiable person on a specified date.

Nuisance. A wrongful act that inconveniences, annoys, offends, or endangers life or health, or that adversely affects the enjoyment of or damages property.

Objection. A means used during a trial to oppose the introduction of certain testimony, or to call to the attention of the court alleged improper action of the other party. The purpose is to obtain a ruling of the court against the testimony or action. If an objection is not upheld, it may later become grounds for an appeal.

Offense. A breach of criminal law that may be a felony or a misdemeanor. The term offense, or petty offense, is also used in some states to denote a crime of a lesser degree than a misdemeanor. The maximum punishment for an offense is generally a fine or a short term of imprisonment.

Opinion. (1) In the law of evidence, an inference or conclusion drawn by a witness from a factual situation. It is generally admissible as testimony. (2) A statement of the court expressing its reasons for arriving at a particular judgment or verdict.

Ordinance. A rule established by a local authority for the regulation of some activity not covered by federal or state law.

Out-of-court settlement. An agreement or transaction between parties to a pending suit that results in the settlement of the suit without court action or approval.

Parole. The conditional release of a prisoner at the discretion of a parole board after the prisoner has served part of his sentence.

Perjury. A false statement made by a witness under oath, deliberately and willfully, with reference to a material fact, opinion, belief, or knowledge.

Petition. A formal, written request to a court for judicial action on a particular matter.

Petit jury. *See* Jury

Plaintiff. The complaining party, or one who initiates the lawsuit.

Plea. The answer given by the defendant to the accusation against him—usually guilty or not guilty.

Plea bargaining. A process whereby the accused and the prosecutor in a criminal case work out a mutually satisfactory disposition of the case. It usually involves the defendant's pleading guilty to a lesser offense in return for a lighter sentence.

Pleadings. The claims and defenses of the litigants to a case.

Power of attorney. An arrangement in which one person, the principal, authorizes another, the agent, to act on his behalf in certain legal or financial matters.

Precedent. A prior decision or authority that guides a court in deciding a case before it.

Preliminary hearing. A proceeding to determine whether there is sufficient evidence to warrant holding the accused for trial.

Presentment. In criminal law, an accusation of crime that is made independently by a grand jury. Based on presentment, the public prosecutor must frame a bill of indictment.

Prima facie. Literally, "on the face of it"; evidence that is considered to be sufficient in law to establish the presumption that a certain fact is true.

PROPERTY *may be* real *(land, buildings, and the like) or* chattel *(all movable personal property from lifestock to aircraft).*

A prima facie case is one in which there is clearly sufficient evidence to bring it to court.

Probate. All matters pertaining to the administration, settlement, and distribution of a dead person's estate.

Probation. A sentence releasing the defendant into the community on the condition that he conduct himself in a manner approved of by a probation officer, to whom the defendant must make periodic reports.

Procedural law. That part of the law that controls the mechanics of bringing, conducting, and deciding a lawsuit.

Process, service of. A procedure whereby a court obtains jurisdiction over an action at law. Its purpose is to notify a defendant of the allegations made against him and to force him to appear in court and answer. A summons is served personally on the defendant.

Property. That which is owned. (*See also* Chattel; Chose; Real property.)

Prosecution. The bringing and conducting of a criminal proceeding; the authority conducting such a proceeding.

Proximate cause. In tort law, an act that, in a natural sequence and without any intervening cause, results in an event or injury.

Public defender. A government officer whose duty is to furnish constitutionally guaranteed counsel to indigent persons charged with crime.

Rape. Unlawful sexual intercourse with a woman against her will by force or by threats of violence. Statutory rape is sexual intercourse with a female who is under the age of consent, usually 18 years, with or without her consent.

Real property. All interests in realty, such as land, and all buildings or improvements erected on, or affixed

to, the land, as well as all other rights and privileges belonging to it.

Reasonable doubt. The doubt that could arise in the mind of an ordinary, impartial, honest, reasonable, and cautious persons with reference to an accused's guilt.

Reciprocity. An understanding between nations or between states of the United States, whereby they interchange certain advantages and privileges. For example, states may agree to allow lawyers licensed in the other state to practice.

Recovery. A judgment of a court of law awarding damages to a party.

Remand. To send back for further proceedings, as when a higher court sends a case back to a lower court.

Respondent. The party contending against an appeal from a lower court to a higher court.

Reverse. To decide, in an appellate court, for the opposite side in a case earlier decided in a lower court.

Robbery. The taking and carrying away of money or other property belonging to, or in the care of, a person by means of force or the threat of harm. Robbery is a felony.

Sanction. (1) To assent to another's actions. (2) A penalty for violating a law.

Search warrant. *See* Warrant.

Sentence. In a criminal case, the punishment imposed on the defendant by the judge.

Sequester. The act of isolating jurors from contact with the public during the course of a trial.

Slander. The malicious and unjustified oral expression of false and defamatory statements in order to degrade, ridicule, or injure someone's character and reputation. (*See also* Libel.)

Small claims court. A special court that provides expeditious, informal, and inexpensive adjudications of small claims.

Stare decisis. Literally, "to stand by the decided things"; the principle that points of law established earlier by a court are binding as precedent. This applies to the same court or to inferior courts in the same jurisdiction in subsequent cases that deal with substantially similar facts.

Stay. A temporary suspension of legal proceedings in a lawsuit until a certain event or action takes place.

Stipulation. An agreement reached by opposing attorneys in the course of litigation that certain facts or events are not in dispute.

Subpoena. A court order directing a person to appear as a witness and give testimony or suffer punishment for contempt of court.

Summary judgment. An action of a court determining that no issue of material fact actually exists between the parties to a lawsuit. The court disposes of the case summarily by entering a final judgment.

Summons. A notice issued by a plaintiff's attorney, or sometimes by the court itself, that directs a defendant to appear in court and defend an action brought against him.

Supreme Court. (1) The court of last resort in the federal judicial system (it also has original jurisdiction in some cases). (2) In most states, the highest appellate court or court of last resort. Sometimes known as Court of Appeals.

Surrogate. In some jurisdictions, a judicial officer who has authority over the administration, settlement, and distribution of decedents' estates, and who may appoint guardians of infants and incompetents.

Term of court. Signifies the time during which a court holds session.

Testator. One who makes a valid will; he is said to have died testate.

Testimony. The giving of evidence by a witness under oath.

Title. In real estate, a combination of legal rights that bestows ownership to property and the right to possession.

Tort. An act of wrong, usually between private individuals, or a breach of legal duty that results in actual or legal damage to the person or property of another.

Trial. The examination by a judge, with or without a jury, and the adjudication of factual and legal issues raised between the parties in a civil or criminal case.

True bill. An indictment endorsed by a grand jury indicating that a majority of the jurors found sufficient evidence to warrant the criminal prosecution directed in the indictment.

Trust. A fiduciary relationship in which legal title to property is vested in and accepted by a trustee (either a person or a corporation) for the benefit of another.

Trustee. One who holds legal title in property for the benefit of and subject to the rights of another.

Vagrancy. An unlawful status or conduct classified as an offense in criminal statues. Types of persons usually classified as vagrants include prostitutes, professional gamblers, beggars, and habitual drunkards.

Venue. The district or county in which a crime or injury is alleged to have occurred.

Verdict. The decision or conclusion of the jury in a criminal proceeding.

Waiver. The intentional surrender or relinquishment of a right either voluntarily or by failure to assert it.

Ward of the court. An infant or legal incompetent, such as a person of unsound mind, who is involved in a lawsuit pertaining to his property rights. The court examines any transaction that might result in financial loss to a ward of the court.

Warrant. A writ or order issued by a court to a police officer that authorizes him to perform a certain act. A search warrant authorizes an officer to search for and seize any property that constitutes evidence of the commission of a crime.

Will. A document duly executed and witnessed, by which a person of legal age disposes of his estate, to take effect after his death. A will may be altered or revoked by the testator during his lifetime.

Witness. One who testifies or gives evidence under oath in an action before a court.

Writ. A written order of a court directing an officer to do something or refrain from doing something.

Youthful offender. A youth varying in age from about 16 to 19 who has committed a crime not punishable by death or life imprisonment and has not previously been convicted of a felony. Such a youth may be adjudged a youthful offender by the court; the purpose is to keep proceedings secret, to protect the youth's name, and to provide rehabilitation for him.

For Further Reference

Abbot, David W., and Edward T. Rogorisky. *Political Parties.* Houghton Mifflin, 1978.

Bain, J. S., and R. B. Jain, editors. *Contemporary Political Theory.* Humanities Press, 1980.

Barone, Michael, and Grant Ujifusa. *The Almanac of American Politics.* Barone, biannual.

Barry, Norman P. *An Introduction to Modern Political Theory.* St. Martin's, 1980.

Commager, Henry Steele. *The Defeat of America: Presidential Power and the National Character.* Simon & Schuster, 1975.

Cox, Archibald. *The Role of the Supreme Court in American Government.* Oxford University Press, 1976.

DeConde, Alexander. *The History of American Foreign Policy.* Charles Scribner's Sons, 1978.

Edwards, David. *The American Political Experience: An Introduction to Government.* Prentice-Hall, 1982.

Farnsworth, Edward A. *An Introduction to the Legal System of the United States.* Oceana, 1975.

Gray, Lee L. *How We Choose a President.* St. Martin's, 1980.

Grilliot, Harold J. *An Introduction to Law and the Legal System.* Houghton Mifflin, 1979.

Henderson, Gordon. *American Democracy: People, Politics, and Policies.* Little, Brown, 1979.

Hofstadter, Richard. *The American Political Tradition.* Random House, 1954.

Jacobsohn, Gary J. *The Supreme Court and the Decline of Constitutional Aspiration.* Rowman, 1986.

Keefe, William T. *Congress and the American People.* Prentice-Hall, 1981.

Leach, Richard. *American Federalism.* W. W. Norton, 1950.

McDonald, Forrest. *Constitutional History of the United States.* Krieger, 1986.

Morlan, Robert L., and David L. Marlir. *Capital, Courthouse, and City Hall.* Houghton Mifflin, 1981.

Mott, Kenneth F. *The Supreme Court and the Living Constitution.* University Press of America, 1981.

Nummo, D., and J. Combs. *Subliminal Politics: Myths and Mythmakers in America.* Prentice-Hall, 1980.

Parrington, Vernon L. *Main Currents in American Thought.* 3 volumes. Harcourt Brace Jovanovich, 1955–1963.

Reid, T. H. *Congressional Odyssey: The Saga of a Senate Bill.* W. H. Freeman, 1980.

Wiser, James L. *Political Theory: A Thematic Inquiry.* Nelson Hall, 1986.

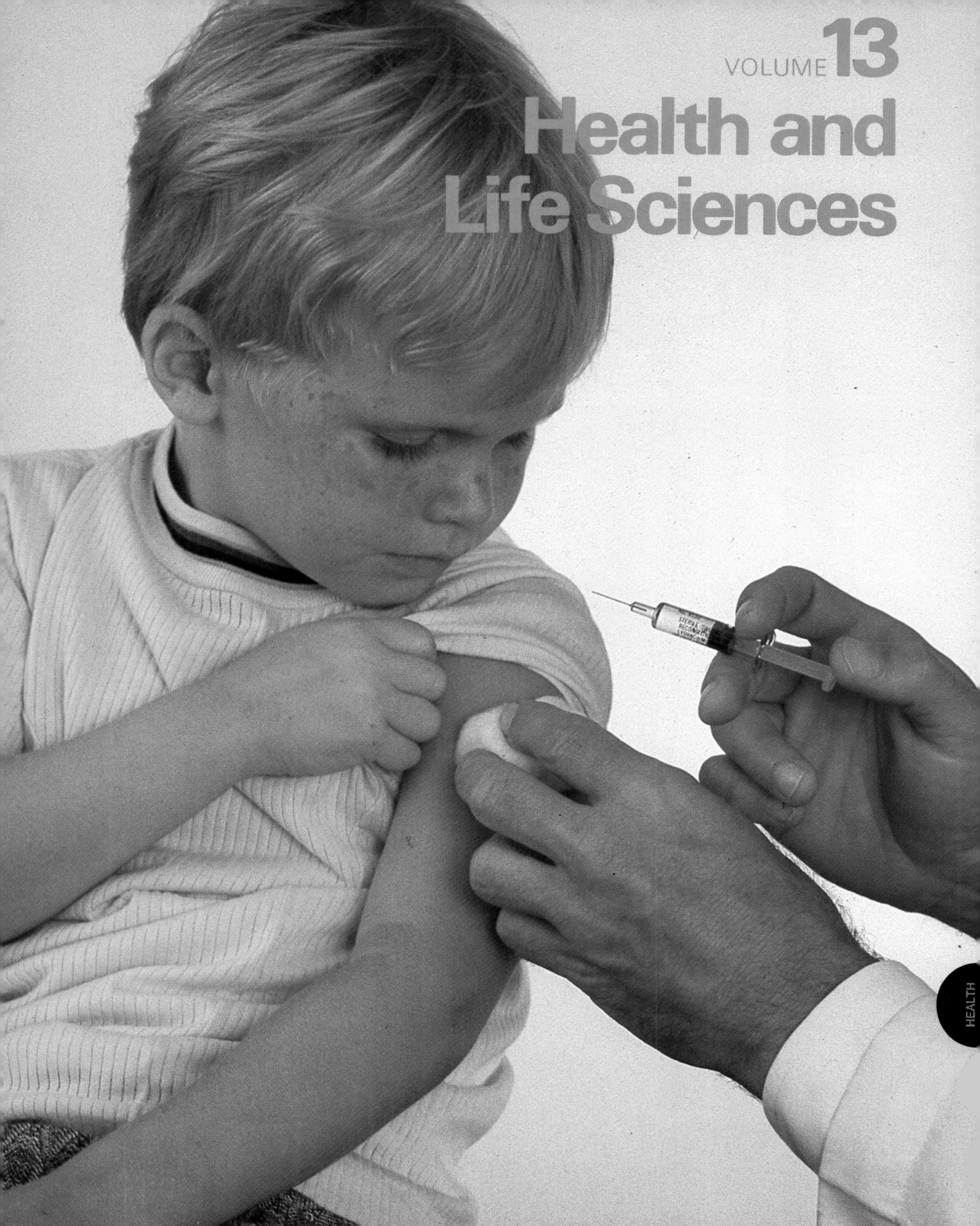

VOLUME **13**

Health and Life Sciences

HEALTH

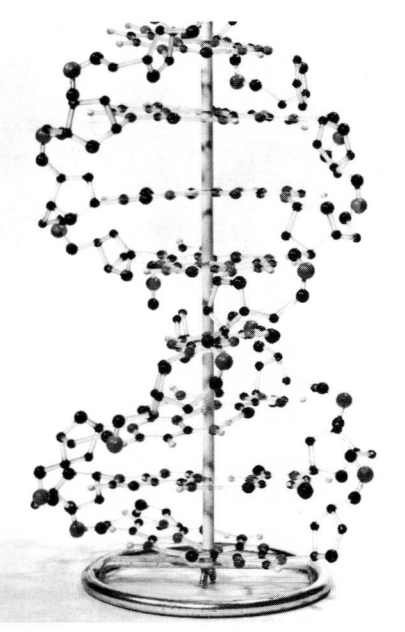

ALFRED OWCZARZAK/TAURUS PHOTOS

LIFE EXPECTANCY IN THE UNITED STATES 1900–1982

During the course of the 20th century the average life expectancy in the United States rose more than 25 years. The average age of death for people born in 1900 was 47.3 years. In 1982 the average was 74.5 years. A large part of this increase is due to vastly improved medical care.

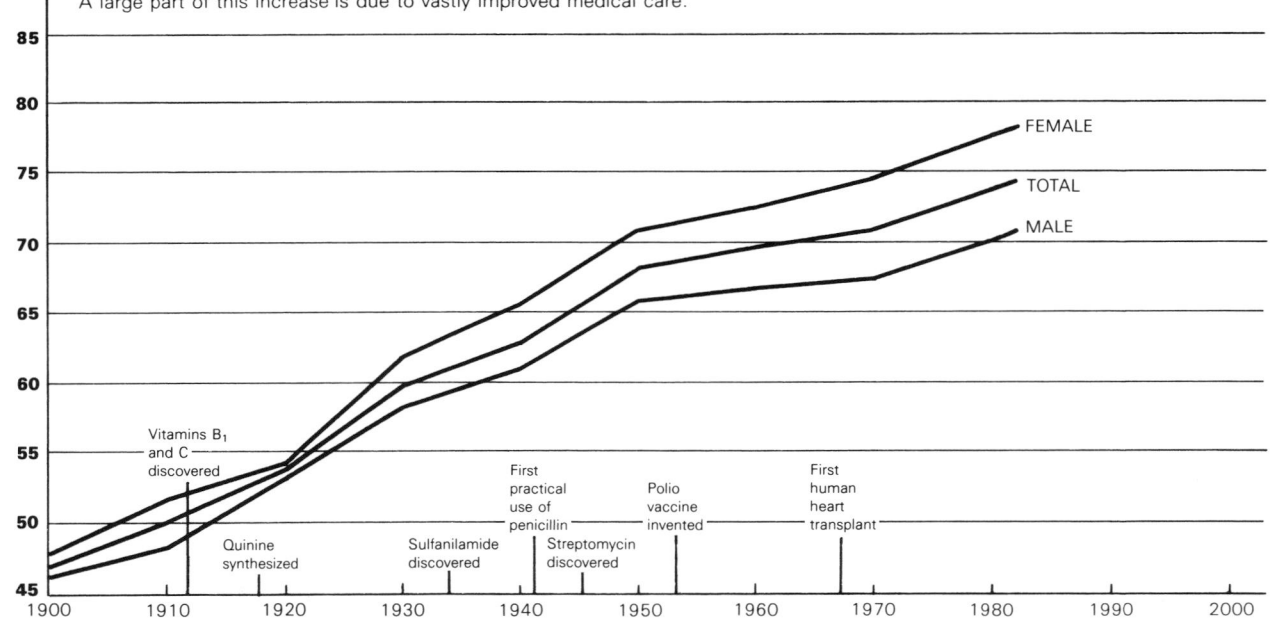

INOCULATION: EDWARD LETTAU/PHOTO RESEARCHERS

VOLUME 13
Health and Life Sciences

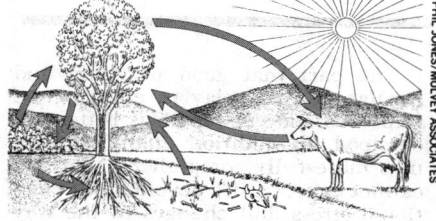

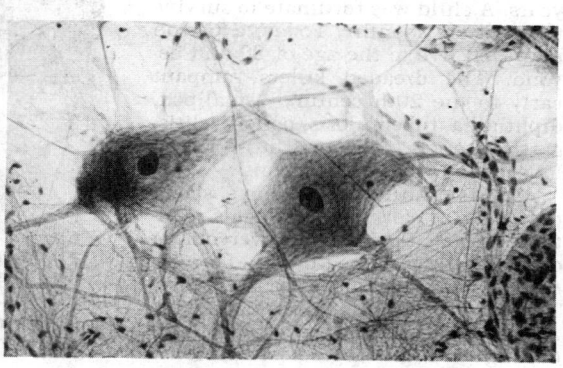

CAROLINA BIOLOGICAL SUPPLY

It is difficult to think of a subject of more concern to most Americans than good health, how to maintain it, and how to know when it is threatened. Attention to proper diet and exercise is seen in the proliferation of health food stores and exercise salons, and in the increase in popular participation in sports. Good nutrition, the importance of physical fitness, and the nature of illness and how to avoid it are subjects receiving more attention in schools and colleges as well.

But there is no knowing how to keep healthy the body's life systems without an understanding of the functioning of the life systems in the world of plants and animals. The essential elements of other forms of life are to a great degree the same as the essential elements of human life.

This volume is divided into two parts. The first, HEALTH AND NUTRITION, covers physiology, health, nutrition, and fitness. The second, LIFE SCIENCES, covers life processes, the cell, the gene, the classification of plants and animals, and ecology.

Physiology. This section provides a detailed account of that marvelous machine, the human body. It describes the skeleton and all the major biological systems, with an emphasis on their roles in a healthy body.

Nutrition. Carbohydrates, fibers, proteins, vitamins, and minerals are discussed in this section. Information about diet and cancer, diet and heart attacks, and fats and cholesterol are included. The section also shows how to plan a sensible diet, and it contains charts listing foods and their vitamin and mineral contents.

Fitness. This section is concerned with weight control, exercise, eating, stress, and sleeping habits.

Health Problems. Here, in understandable terms, are discussions of the major diseases, such as hypertension, diabetes, arthritis, alcoholism, and AIDS.

Throughout HEALTH AND NUTRITION are valuable "Health Care Alerts," which either describe what to avoid to maintain good health or list the signals of the onset of disease.

The second part of this volume begins with a description of the various theories that seek to explain the origin of life.

The Cell. Cells perform the basic functions that support all plants and animals. Understanding the cell's structure, how it works, how it is controlled, and how cells are organized in multicelled organisms is essential to understanding the human body, in sickness and in health.

Five Kingdoms of Life. This section gives an overview of the diversity of life forms, both plant and animal.

The Gene. Here is described how traits of individual plants and animals are transmitted from one generation to the next. The recent discovery of DNA and the importance of the study of human genetics, especially as it is related to inheritable disease, are covered. Genetic engineering and biotechnology are described.

Ecology. The importance of this science is explained. It is vital to know how communities sustain themselves and how to keep them healthy. It is also necessary to understand that human beings depend on these communities for survival. This section ends with a discussion of the dangers to people when their environment becomes polluted.

HEALTH AND LIFE SCIENCES concludes with a glossary of terms and books in which the reader can find more information about each subject covered. The reader may also wish to consult the volumes on SPORTS AND RECREATION for further information on ways to achieve fitness; on CHILD AND FAMILY for information on family health and on PLANTS and ANIMALS for detailed descriptions of the natural world.

HEALTH AND NUTRITION

In 1900, life expectancy was about 50 years. A child was fortunate to survive the first six months. Today, a person may well live to the age of 80 and beyond. The dreaded killers rampant early in the 20th century—smallpox, diphtheria, tuberculosis, poliomyelitis, gastroenteritis (intestinal flu)—are no longer major health problems.

A vast number of researchers, scientists, and health professionals continue to make progress in overcoming or controlling such often-fatal conditions as cancer and heart disease. There has never been a better time for Americans to make great strides in attaining a high degree of personal health. It is an achievable goal from two standpoints: scientific, providing more and more highly sophisticated diagnostic techniques, medicines, and treatment methods; and individualis-

WELL-CHOSEN ACTIVITY *improves the quality of life for everyone.*

tic, with an increasing number of people accepting a greater share of responsibility for their own health and general well-being.

The part that good nutrition and regular exercise play in ensuring an improved state of health is better understood. In addition, many individuals more fully comprehend that one cannot expect a life devoid of all emotional stress, but changes in the way one lives can help ease or avoid the damaging effects of unmitigated stress. People are also more knowledgeable about choosing their physicians, and about asking for explanations of their health problems and prescribed medications. Indeed, many with chronic health problems (for example, diabetes and high blood pressure) are—with medical supervision—monitoring their conditions with simple home medical tests and equipment. All of these important issues are discussed in this section on comprehensive health care.

Physiology

Modern science has created many engineering marvels but none can surpass, or even parallel, the incredible human machine. Our knowledge of the structure and function of the human body has been greatly expanded in the recent past with the development of sophisticated tools and techniques. Much is known about the intricate, versatile, and adaptable organism that is a human being; however, much more remains to be explored and explained. In the opinion of some scientists, some mechanisms of the human body will forever remain beyond our full comprehension.

The text and accompanying illustrations are intended to help you understand the basic structure and function of the body. Full-color anatomical drawings, together with explanatory notes, shown in the color insert of Human Anatomy, offer additional visual aids.

Skeletal System

A bony, flexible framework, the skeleton lends shape to the body, serves as a scaffolding to protect vital organs,

and, activated by the muscles, facilitates body movement (see Human Anatomy color insert). There are about 206 bones in the adult body, of varying shapes and sizes. The bones in a skeleton are often thought of as hard and dry, but, in fact, water makes up about one-quarter of the weight of human bone. Another quarter consists of organic matter: collagen (connective tissue, a type of protein) fibers. The remaining half consists of inorganic compounds: calcium, phosphorus and

STRUCTURAL COMPLEXITY *and daily demands often add up to kneecap pain (for example, runner's knee).*

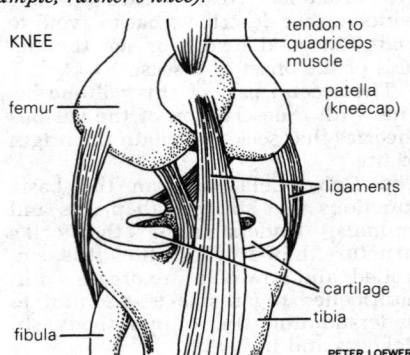

KNEE

femur

tendon to quadriceps muscle

patella (kneecap)

ligaments

cartilage

tibia

fibula

PETER LOEWER

other minerals. Bone contains living cells, osteocytes, that manufacture the connective tissue as well as form mineral matter, which is deposited in the organic framework to harden and give it strength.

The curved spinal column with its flexible vertebrae supports the head and trunk of the body, and shields the spinal cord. Cranial bones of the skull form the dome-shaped casing for the brain. The facial bones form the features, and protect the eyes and the oral and nasal passages. The cylinderlike rib cage is designed to shelter the heart, lungs, liver, and spleen. Pelvic bones protect other internal organs.

Bones are attached to each other by a series of tissues: cartilages (smooth tissues that reduce friction), which make possible bending and twisting of the back; and ligaments (strands of elastic, fibrous tissue), which hold together the ends of bone, keeping them properly aligned. The knee, a long and complex body joint, is held together by a complicated array of cartilages and ligaments acting as shock absorbers. A blow to the knee of an athlete may stretch or tear a ligament or cause the cartilage to chip, leaving bones rubbing painfully, one against another.

Sports injuries in the young.

It is estimated that 20 million American children and adolescents take part in various forms of organized sport. Significantly, 31 percent of all sports injuries occur in children between five and 14 years of age. Orthopedists and others involved in sports medicine have expressed concern about bone injuries that may occur in children who enter into highly competitive sports too early, sometimes at the urging of their parents.

Stress fractures—tiny bone cracks caused by the strain of repeated activity—are common. A typical case in point is "Little League elbow," caused by a repeated pitching motion that places tremendous strain on bones of the elbow joint. Such repeated motions, as may also occur in swimming (swimmer's shoulder), and running (runner's knee), can result in stress fractures. Constant arching of a young gymnast's back can lead to spondylolysis, a stress fracture at the base of the spine.

For these reasons, it is recommended that parents and athletic coaches consider skeletal development, rather than age or body weight and size alone, in judging the fitness of a sport for a youngster. Relative skeletal maturity can be determined by analyzing the rate of development at the 29 individual growth centers located in the wrist and hand; these are visible on x-rays.

"Out-of-place" disk.

A slipped disk is one in which the shock-absorbing cartilage tissue between vertebrae is forced out of place. Actually, the

CHILDREN BETWEEN 10 AND 16 *are especially vulnerable to sports injuries. Cartilage does not harden completely until the late teens.*

MIKE L. WANNEMACHER/TAURUS PHOTOS

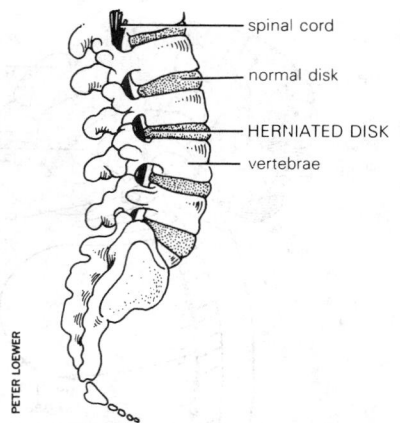

PETER LOEWER

A **BULGING DISK,** *pressing against the spinal cord, causes excruciating back and leg pain.*

disk has not slipped but has ruptured, bulging out to one side or the other. This may result from a sudden wrenching action, as during the picking up of a heavy box, in which the lower lumbar vertebrae suffer the brunt of muscle strain. Such an action can pinch together the two affected vertebrae hard enough to push the disk out of its normal position. Slowly developing degenerative changes in the disks, with gradual loss of their spongelike consistency, may also cause disk problems. Typical indications of such deterioration include:

- Unremitting pain, beginning in the lower back region and generally extending into the buttocks and thighs.
- Pain, usually limited to one side, that may be relieved by lying down on the unaffected side.
- Worsening of pain from coughing, sneezing, or a bowel movement.
- Weakness of the thigh, leg, or foot.

Muscular System

The more than 600 muscles throughout the human body, almost all in pairs, provide agility and power movement. Skeletal, or striated, muscles are voluntary, contracting when a person wills, as, for instance, when throwing a ball or walking up an incline. Visceral muscles, controlling movements in the stomach and intestine, are involuntary. A person has no direct control over them. These muscles, also called smooth muscles, activate not only the digestive functions, but also breathing and blood circulation, vital for health (see Human Anatomy color insert).

Bones are moved at the joint by the contraction and relaxation of the skeletal muscles attached to them. The exact mechanism of contraction and relaxation is an exceedingly complex electrochemical/mechanical process that still is not understood fully. Like the bones, skeletal muscles come in a variety of shapes and sizes, depending on the work they do. The deltoids, or shoulder muscles, which raise the arms, owe their name to their shape: they resemble the triangle-shaped Greek letter delta.

Another important shoulder muscle is the trapezius, which raises the shoulder and pulls back the head. Most facial muscles work together to help express emotion, a smile or frown, or the raising of an eyebrow; many make it possible for us to bite, chew, or speak. The upper arm biceps and triceps move the arm, the one to bend, the other to straighten the elbow.

FLEXING ELBOW

PETER LOEWER

The muscle team moving the arm is formed of the biceps (the flexor) and triceps (the extensor). Biceps can bend the elbow but cannot by itself extend the arm. Biceps contract and triceps relax to flex the elbow. When the elbow is straightened, the reverse takes place: biceps relax and triceps contract.

biceps

triceps

humerus

ulna

flexed

radius

extended

At the hip, and in the lower extremities, are several large muscles, including the gluteal muscles in the buttocks, and the sartorius and the quadriceps in the thigh. Gluteus medius (middle of the buttock) and gluteus maximus (largest of the buttocks) contract to move us from a sitting to a standing position, or to help us when we walk upstairs or run. Sartorius, the longest muscle in the body, together with the quadriceps, helps us bend knees, move legs, and keep our balance when standing. About mid-center in the body is the main muscle involved with breathing, the dome-shaped diaphragm. This thin muscular partition between the chest and abdominal cavities is also used in such actions as laughing, coughing, and sneezing. The muscles in back of the thigh, the hamstrings (biceps femoris, semitendinous and membranous tendons), are used in bending the knee joint as well as in straightening the hip joint.

Protecting the back.
Four out of five Americans experience low back pain at some time, owed in large part to the sedentary lives they live. According to experts, most backaches can be prevented by avoiding undue stress on injury-prone back tissues, and by performing muscle-strengthening exercises. There are many measures available for the alleviation of chronic backache. Whether pain-relieving ointments, special exercises, new types of chairs, and the like are of value is best discussed with a physician or other health professional. For a strong and healthy back, however, several factors must be considered:

Obesity. Normal weight should be maintained; added pounds make for added stress on soft back tissues.

Posture. It is important to stand straight and tall, with stomach held in, and pelvis tilted back. When standing for long periods, one foot should be placed on a stool or other object about 4 to 6 inches off the floor.

Sitting position. It is important to sit back in your chair with feet flat on the floor, knees slightly higher than the hips. Prolonged sitting should be avoided; for example, on long car trips, it is good practice to make frequent stops. A pillow or "lumbar roll" may be used to increase comfort while sitting.

Lifting technique. It is best to squat close to objects to be picked up; the back is kept straight, and the knees are bent. After grasping the object to be lifted, it is best to stand up slowly, with heavy objects kept close to the body. One should never bend from the waist, even in picking up the smallest object.

Exercise. Any exercise that tightens abdominal muscles can be helpful, for example, lower back stretch and bent-leg situps.

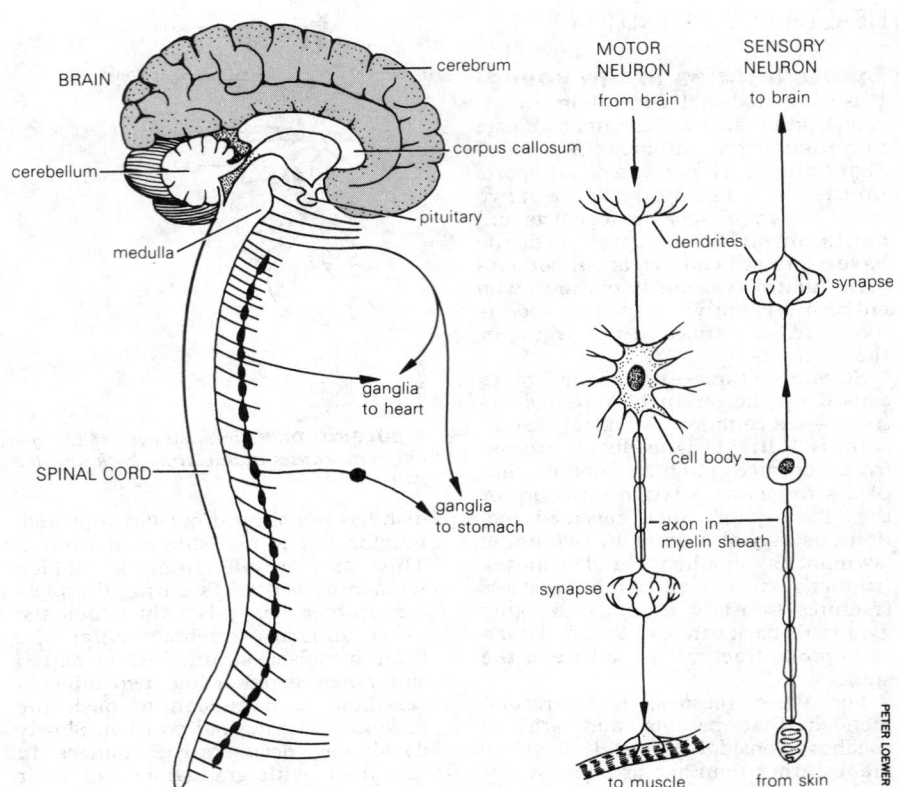

THE NERVOUS SYSTEM *serves to integrate and control all bodily functions. Sensory nerve fibers carry messages to the brain or spinal cord from tissues and organs. Motor nerve fibers carry messages from the brain or spinal cord to tissues and organs.*

Nervous System

The brain, spinal cord, and a complex system of nerves constitute the nervous system. This communications network, operated by electrochemical impulses, controls and coordinates all bodily functions. The prodigious network of nerves from the brain and spinal cord reaches every inch of the body, from head to toe (see Human Anatomy color insert). There are two main divisions of the nervous system: the central, including the brain and the spinal cord, which controls voluntary acts; and the autonomic, sympathetic, and parasympathetic, which controls involuntary functioning of glands and smooth muscle tissues. This self-governing network is concerned mainly with such functions as respiration and digestion.

The key organ of the nervous system is the brain, which weighs less than 3 pounds and which is 80 percent water. It is in three main sections: cerebrum, cerebellum, and medulla oblongata. The cerebrum, largest division of the brain, is positioned over the brain stem and cerebellum. The gray matter, which gives the cerebrum its color, is about $\frac{1}{8}$-inch thick; it forms the outer layer, called the cerebral cortex, which is convoluted into many folds. The cortex contains billions of nerve cells (neurons). These cells extend into an area below the cerebral hemispheres, which control conscious mental activity. The cerebellum lies on either side and in back of the brain stem. It aids in maintaining body balance and coordination of muscle movement. The medulla, located at the upper end of the spinal cord, contains vital reflex centers that help to control heart rate, blood pressure, and respiration.

Neurons serve as local headquarters for the nerve unit. Each neuron has one or more nerve fibers extending from its center. These fibers vary in length from a fraction of an inch to 3 or more feet, depending on their function and location in the body. Axons, the longer fibers, carry nerve impulses away from the cell body. Dendrites, the shorter fibers, carry nerve impulses toward the cell body. Nerve impulses travel by a kind of chain reaction, one neuron triggering the next along the nerve pathway. When the nerve impulse reaches a nerve junction, or synapse, it causes the release of a chemical substance at the nerve endings. This substance enables the impulse to bridge the gap and go on to the next neuron.

Sensory neurons carry messages from various parts of the body through the spinal cord or directly to the brain. These signals produce sensations of heat, cold, sight, sound, touch, pain, and pressure. From the brain or spinal cord, motor neurons carry messages to tissues and muscles in fingers, toes, heart, and elsewhere. Sensory neurons relay information to the brain via sensory pickup units called receptors. In general, each sensory receptor responds strictly to its own kinds of stimuli, which must be converted into signals before transmission to a body part. Such electrochemical impulses may be mechanical (for example, triggered by a pinprick on the skin), or chemical (perhaps triggered by the smell of roses in bloom). In either event, these nerve impulses travel along a nerve fiber at speeds up to 350 feet per second, depending on the size and type of the nerve fiber, and on the thickness of its myelin coating.

The fibers of the motor neurons terminate in motor end plates, which are very small flat plates coming in close contact with individual muscle fibers. When the nerve impulse arrives at the motor end plate, the nerve ending releases acetylcholine, a chemical substance that acts as a neurotransmitter to trigger muscle cell activity. As the muscle contracts, an enzyme called cholinesterase begins to break down and clear away the accumulated acetylcholine, making way for the next chemical cycle.

Cells of the nervous system are highly active, so they require a great deal more oxygen and glucose than do other cells. Without a continuous, rich supply of blood, which carries these vital substances, the neurons would quickly die. Neurons in the brain use up as much as 20 percent of all available oxygen in the adult body around the clock. Normally, within a 24-hour period, a small number of neurons, too few to have any noticeable effect, wear out and die. In time, however, total loss mounts up and this, as some contemporary neurologists believe, may be the basis of senility. We are born with all the neurons we will ever have: those destroyed can never be replaced.

Brain block of pain. According to current scientific thinking, the brain is capable of blocking out pain. In late 1975, molecular configurations discovered in the brains of pigs gave further credence to an earlier observation that morphine duplicated the action of a pain-killing substance inherent in the brain. It was found that neurotransmitters, called enkephalins, proved to be peptides, short chains of amino acids similar to those already known to influence the release of hormone from the pituitary gland. It is conjectured that enkephalins may play an important role in body control of pain. Final evaluation of the theory depends on extended research, which may take many years to complete.

Disturbances in neurotransmitters are a major factor in certain neurological diseases. For example, schizophrenia may involve deranged serotonin metabolism; injury to neurons producing dopamine almost certainly causes Parkinson's disease; and malfunction in neuronal systems containing GABA (gamma-aminobutyric acid) may be implicated in epilepsy.

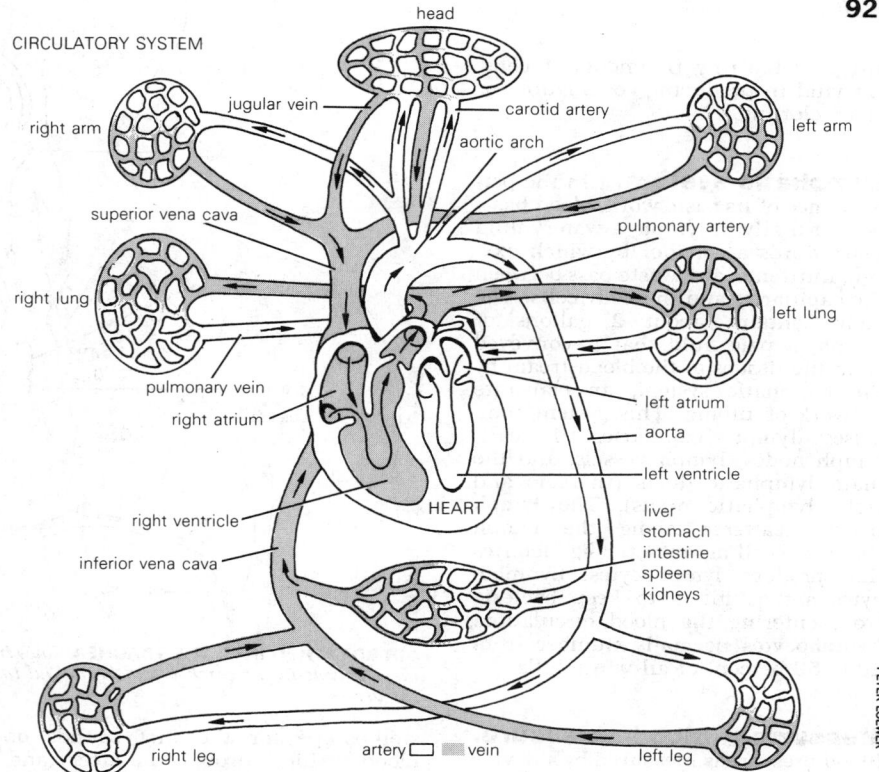

CIRCULATORY SYSTEM

PETER LOEWER

THE HEART IS THE PUMP *of the circulatory system; it drives blood throughout a closed and vast network of tubes, the blood vessels. Blood travels from the heart to body tissues via the arteries, and returns to the heart via the veins.*

Circulatory System

The major transport system making possible blood circulation comprises the heart, arteries, arterioles, capillaries, and veins (see Human Anatomy color insert). Taken together, the blood vessels extend an estimated distance of 60,000 miles, through which blood and its cargo move in endless activity—in and out of the heart, throughout the body, and back to the heart again to start another cycle.

The heart is a bundle of muscles, about the size of a fist and weighing less than a pound. On an average, the heart contracts and dilates at a rate of 72 beats a minute, each cardiac cycle lasting about 0.85 second. This adds up to about 100,000 times a day, or nearly 40 million times a year without rest. The only pause a heart takes is the fraction of a second between heartbeats. In the average adult, the heart pumps so steadily and powerfully that, in one minute, it forces 10 pints of blood through more than 1000 complete circuits. This amounts to 5000 to 6000 quarts of blood in a single day.

The heart has four chambers: the upper left and right atria are the receiving chambers, while the lower left and right ventricles are the pumping chambers. Each atrium is separated from the ventricle beneath it by a valve. A wall of muscle, called a septum, separates the left and right side

of the heart. In a healthy heart, blood cannot pass through the system from one side to the other, but moves by way of the lungs, considered part of the respiratory system (see pages 928–929). Blood flows from the right atrium down into the right ventricle, which forces blood into the lungs via the pulmonary artery. From the lungs, oxygenated blood flows back to the left atrium, down into the left ventricle, and then out to the body via the aorta, or great artery. Blood is sent to the arteries, arterioles, and a vast network of capillaries, which are smaller in diameter than a hair.

The blood has four main components, 55 percent being plasma, a straw-colored liquid consisting of 92 percent water. The remaining 8 percent contains nutrients, special inorganic materials, proteins, antibodies, and hormones. The other 45 percent of blood contains three kinds of cells: red blood cells (erythrocytes), white blood cells (leukocytes), and platelets (thrombocytes). All these cellular components, with the exception of one kind of white blood cells, are manufactured in bone marrow. The disklike red cells outnumber white cells 700 to one. They carry oxygen from the lungs to all parts of the body, and carry off waste carbon dioxide. Red cells live for about three to four months, being replaced by new recruits sent into the bloodstream from bone marrow. White cells protect the body against the invasion of toxic organisms by engulfing and destroying them. Platelets, which are platelike tiny fragments of cells, are vital in producing coagulation, or blood clotting.

Lymphatic system. In the performance of its basic work, blood has a powerful ally in lymph, a watery fluid that affords a corridor by which oxygen, nutrients, and waste pass between the capillaries and the body cells. The body contains about 2 gallons of lymph, a pale fluid that is conveyed from the tissues to the bloodstream by the lymphatic system, an elaborate network of tubing. This system comprises lymph capillaries, lacteals, lymph nodes, lymph vessels, and the main lymphatic ducts (thoracic and right lymphatic ducts). The lymph nodes, scattered along the lymph route, are cell manufacturing factories that produce lymphocytes. Lymphocytes act as filters to keep bacteria from entering the blood circulation. Lymphocytes normally number from 20 to 50 percent of all white cells.

Measuring blood pressure.
Blood pressure is measured by a device called a sphygmomanometer, an instrument that provides accurate measurement when used correctly. It includes a blood pressure cuff of appropriate size, an accurate pressure gauge, and a stethoscope capable of adequately amplifying blood pressure sounds. (This is important for anyone considering the purchase of home equipment. Before use, a competent medical professional should be consulted for step-by-step instructions.)

In taking blood pressure, a physician wraps the cuff securely around the upper arm and inflates the cuff with enough air to stop circulation in an artery. As the air is gradually released, the examiner listens with the

THE LYMPHATIC SYSTEM includes all structures carrying lymph from the tissues to the blood.

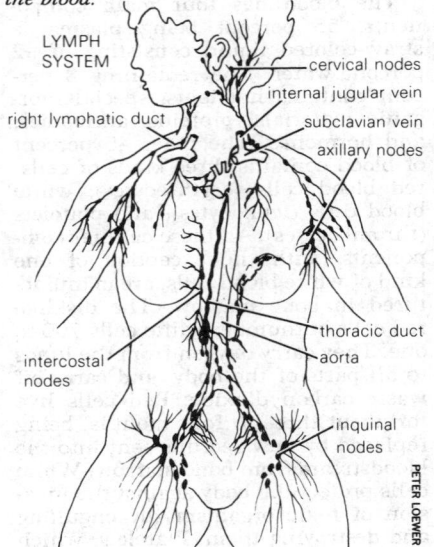

LYMPH SYSTEM
— cervical nodes
internal jugular vein
right lymphatic duct
subclavian vein
axillary nodes
thoracic duct
intercostal nodes
aorta
inguinal nodes

PETER LOEWER

stethoscope for the first sounds of blood rushing through the artery and notes the number registered on the gauge. This is the systolic pressure, the pressure when the heart is actively pumping. Continuing the gradual release of air in the cuff, the examiner listens carefully for the last muffled sounds to disappear. The number registered on the gauge at this point is the diastolic pressure, the pressure when the heart is at rest between beats.

Blood pressure may vary with such factors as age, general health, and condition of the arteries. As an average guideline, 120/80 mm Hg (120 millimeters of mercury systolic, over 80 millimeters of mercury diastolic) may be considered normal blood pressure. Any person 40 years or under with a blood pressure of 140/90 mm Hg or higher, and any person over 40 years of age with a blood pressure of 160/90 mm Hg or higher, is usually considered to have high blood pressure, and treatment may be indicated.

Respiratory System

The lungs, which weigh about 2½ pounds, perform a twofold function: breathing in (inspiration) to deliver oxygen to the blood, and breathing out (expiration), to rid the blood of waste carbon dioxide received from cells throughout the body (see Human Anatomy color insert). The vital capacity of an individual refers to the total volume of air the lungs can hold, ranging from 3 to 5 quarts. Air entering the breathing system goes first to the upper respiratory tract, which in-

cludes the nose, pharynx, and larynx (voice box), where it is filtered, warmed, and moistened.

The lower respiratory tract begins with the trachea (windpipe), at the end of which it divides into two bronchi, one entering the left lung and the other the right lung. Inside the lung, these bronchi continue to subdivide into smaller bronchi, then into bronchioles, and finally into tiny thin-walled, balloonlike air sacs, the alveoli, which constitute the bulk of lung tissue. There are an estimated 300 million of these air sacs in a man of average size. It is these alveoli, rather than the chest, that actually expand or contract during breathing, and provide the vital surface needed for intake of oxygen into the blood. When the alveolar spaces are filled with air, the lungs look somewhat like large sponges.

Each lung, as well as the inner walls of the chest, is covered by an airtight membranous sac, called the pleura. It secretes a lubricating fluid that prevents the pleural layers from rubbing against the chest wall. In a mechanical sense, the lungs act like a pair of bellows. As the diaphragm (a thin musculomembranous wall) contracts, a sheet of muscle fibers is drawn downward, creating a partial vacuum in the chest cavity. This allows air to rush in and fill the trachea, bronchi, and alveoli. With the drawing in of air, the alveoli expand. Relaxation of the diaphragm muscles forces the air out again. With the expulsion of air, the alveoli contract.

The rate and depth of breathing are controlled by respiratory centers in the brain, one being located in the medulla oblongata. These centers are remarkably sensitive to the chemical content of the blood, especially to the

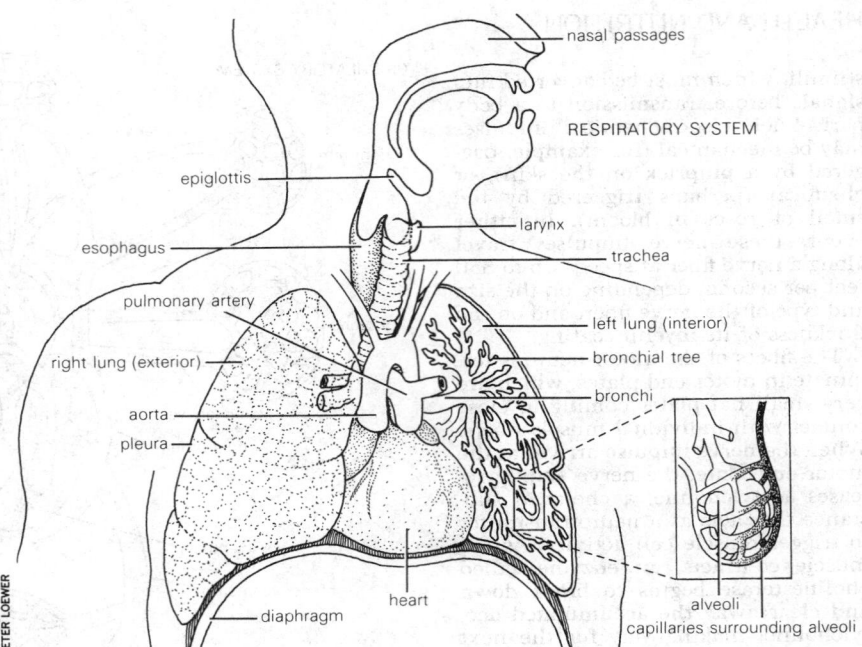

nasal passages
RESPIRATORY SYSTEM
epiglottis
larynx
esophagus
trachea
pulmonary artery
left lung (interior)
right lung (exterior)
bronchial tree
aorta
bronchi
pleura
alveoli
diaphragm
heart
capillaries surrounding alveoli
PETER LOEWER

AIR BREATHED INTO THE TRACHEA *flows into the bronchial tubes within the lungs. Defense mechanisms in the trachea and bronchial tubes help keep bacteria and viruses from entering the alveoli.*

presence of carbon dioxide. During sleep, the amount of carbon dioxide in the blood is low, and the respiratory centers slow down the breathing rate. During vigorous exertion in the waking hours, there is an increased amount of carbon dioxide in the blood; this automatically stimulates deep and rapid breathing.

Self-help in acute bronchitis.
Normally, the bronchial tubes are cleansed and lubricated by their mucus-producing membranes. When, as in the case of a viral infection, these membranes try to rid themselves of the invaders by secreting an overabundant amount of mucus, the tubes become clogged and may create breathing problems. Most acute bronchitis is said to be due to a viral infection that does not respond to treatment with antibiotics. The patient must wait for the body's own defenses to take over. In the meantime, however, much can be done to relieve the troublesome symptoms.

Loosening a cough. Use of an expectorant to thin mucus will aid a "productive cough" (one bringing up mucus) and reduce chest congestion.

Easing wheezes. Heat and moisture may also be used to thin the mucus, as well as to ease the wheezing often accompanying cough. Vaporizers, preferably using water only, can be used to humidify the air in rooms.

Draining secretions. To loosen secretions, it will help to raise the bronchial tubes above the level of the mouth and windpipe. The patient lies face down with a pillow under the abdomen, or face up with a pillow under the hips, for 10 to 20 minutes.

Fever, aching. If fever is present, relief may be obtained with rest and aspirin or aspirin substitutes. If chest soreness is caused by persistent coughing, use of a heating pad may bring some relief.

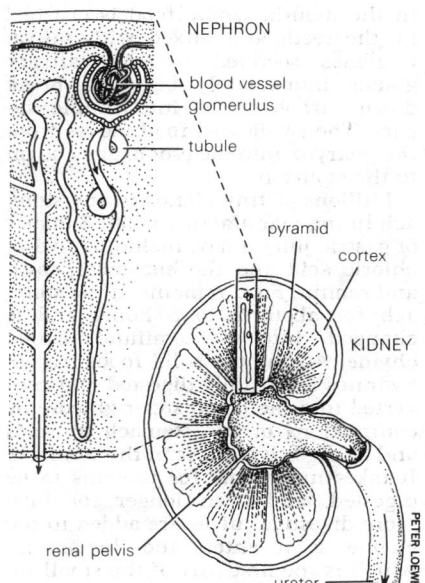

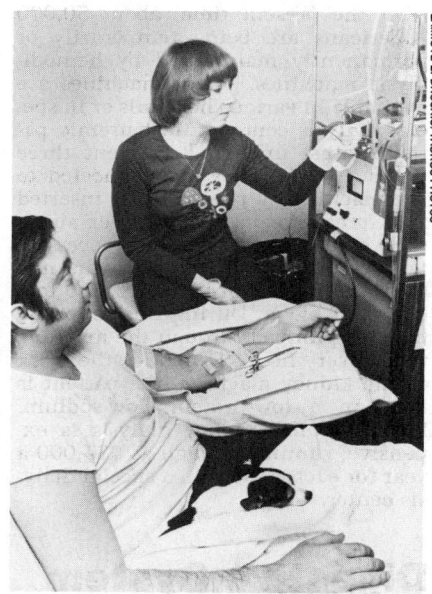

KIDNEYS EXCRETE WASTE PRODUCTS *from the blood. When kidneys no longer work, hemodialysis is used to perform their function. The procedure, once learned, can be carried out at home.*

Urinary System

The kidneys, purplish–brown and shaped like oversized lima beans, lie at the back of the abdominal cavity on each side of the spinal column (see Human Anatomy color insert). Only about 4 to 5 inches long and weighing about 5 ounces, these organs function as a filtering system for the blood, and as an important aid in regulating the body's internal environment: fluid volume, blood composition, and blood pressure. The kidneys dispose of the body's metabolic wastes and excess water as urine. Formation of urine is a continuous process, the rate of filtration depending on the daily fluid intake and on blood pressure in the glomeruli, clusters of blood capillaries within the kidneys. Each glomerulus marks the beginning of a nephron, the absorbing, filtering, and secreting unit. There are a million or so of these miniscule nephrons in each kidney, and if they were laid end to end, the nephrons would stretch out to about 50 miles.

As blood courses through the glomeruli, a considerable amount of its fluid filters out through the membranes and into the tubules (little tubes). These long-twisting tubules extract and return to the bloodstream a variety of useful substances, such as glucose, amino acids, ions, minerals, and a great deal of water. Dissolved waste materials, such as urea (a constituent of urine), are kept from returning to the bloodstream. It is estimated that 42 gallons of water daily soak into the tubules from the glomeruli to dissolve waste products. However, because the body cannot afford to lose so large an amount of fluid, it must be drawn back and

nearly 99 percent of water filtering out through the nephrons is reabsorbed into the bloodstream via the tubules. The remaining 1 percent, together with the wastes, is converted into urine and drained from the nephrons into collecting ducts, transported to the renal pelvis (center of the kidney), into the ureters to the bladder, and finally into the urethra for elimination.

Stand-ins for failing kidneys.
When one kidney fails to work, the other enlarges and picks up its load. When both kidneys fail, either temporarily or permanently, the blood becomes uremic, filled with poisonous nitrogenous waste. Uremia kills about 7000 persons yearly whose lives might have been saved by either a kidney transplant or by a kidney machine.

HEALTH CARE ALERT
Acute Bronchitis

A sensible preventive measure is to stay away from people with coughs and sneezes. The tiny droplets released into the air may cause viral infections. Smoking and smoke-filled areas can be irritating and make the bronchial tubes more susceptible to infection. It is advisable to see a doctor if any of the following symptoms are noted:
- Wheezing (often accompanying a cough) that continues for longer than a week.
- Body temperature over 101° F, chills, and sweating; aching.
- Persistent coughing with thick greenish-yellow mucus, or spots of blood in mucus coughed up.
- Breathlessness during activity.

HEALTH CARE ALERT
Kidney Disease

Malfunctioning kidneys may result in high blood pressure, anemia, and uremia. Prompt medical examination is indicated with any of these signs or symptoms:
- Painful or burning sensation in the course of urination.
- Passage of blood-tinged or tea-colored urine.
- Increased need to urinate, especially at night.
- Lowback pain just below the ribs that is not made worse by movement.
- Eye puffiness or swelling of hands and feet, especially in children.

At the present time, about 50,000 Americans are being temporarily or permanently maintained by hemodialysis machines. These machines are available in various hospitals or in special dialysis centers. Most uremic patients must undergo treatment three times a week. They are connected to the machine by plastic tubes inserted in a forearm vein that has been surgically enlarged to permit easy access. It takes about 4 to 5 hours for the machine to clear all of the person's 5 to 6 quarts of blood. During this time, the blood is pumped through the machine twice every hour. To reduce the work of the kidney machine, the patient is kept on a low-protein, low-sodium, low-fluid diet. Kidney dialysis is expensive, running as high as $35,000 a year for each patient in a special dialysis center.

Digestive System

The digestive system consists of a flexible mucus-lined muscular tube (24 to 36 feet long) beginning in the mouth and ending at the anus (see Human Anatomy color insert). During much of the trip through the digestive tract, food is either squeezed or pushed by muscles, and dissolved by digestive juices and enzymes. These delicate chemical substances act as catalysts, producing chemical changes in food but not becoming part of the chemical produced. Digestion begins in the mouth, where food is crushed by the teeth and mixed with saliva. Enzymes secreted by the salivary glands immediately begin to break down carbohydrates into simple sugars. The swallowed food moves from the pharynx into the esophagus and on to the stomach.

Millions of tiny glands in the stomach lining manufacture about 3 quarts of gastric juice a day, including hydrochloric acid and the enzymes pepsin and rennin. Food remains in the stomach for about 2 to 5 hours and is changed into a semifluid called chyme. Among the solid foods, carbohydrates are readily digested and converted into the blood sugar glucose by contractions of the stomach muscles and by digestive juices in the stomach. It takes more time for proteins to be digested, and even longer for fats. More digestive juices are added to the chyme as it enters the duodenum, which is the first part of the small intestine, a coiled tube about 20 feet long. Here, too, the chyme is acted upon by fluids from the pancreas and by bile from the liver. Bile does not contain any enzymes, but its salts aid in the digestion of fats. Pancreatic juices contain a number of enzymes that act on a variety of foods. Proteins are broken down into amino acids; complex sugar molecules are broken down into simple sugars; and fats are reduced to fatty acids prior to absorption into the blood or lymph vessels.

Projecting from the inner lining of the small intestine are thousands of microscopic, fingerlike projections called villi. These absorb the broken-down food particles, conveying them to the bloodstream for distribution to the rest of the body. By the time food has traveled along the conveyor belt of the chemical refinery to the end of the small intestine, the process of digestion has been completed. All that remains of ingested food are water and waste products, which pass into the large intestine, where much of the water is absorbed. In the meantime, food products are transported by blood vessels from the walls of the small intestine to the liver.

The liver, although weighing only about 4 pounds, is an important chemical plant. The largest gland in the body, the liver has many functions. It manufactures bile, numerous enzymes, and blood proteins; it stores fat products and makes them available as fuel; it neutralizes some of the poisons entering the bloodstream; it processes iron for the blood system; and it delivers glycogen to the body tissues on demand, providing needed fuel or energy to carry out their manifold activities.

Ulcer pain. Peptic (relating to the stomach) ulcers afflict people in all walks of life, with men affected more often than women. Although peptic ulcers may occur in the stomach and esophagus, most such breaks in the mucous membrane are duodenal, occurring in the first part of the small intestine; they are associated with excessive production of stomach acid. Why certain people are ulcer-prone is not clear. Irritating foods or medicines—coffee, alcohol, aspirin—are thought to contribute to the formation of ulcers, yet many chronic abusers of these substances do not develop ulcers. The likelihood of a genetic origin has general acceptance: ulcers are noted more often among the relatives of ulcer sufferers than among the general population. There is less acceptance of the theory of an "ulcer personality," yet many people unable to deal with high-stress situations seem more likely than others to be ulcer candidates.

The most common symptom of an active ulcer is a burning or gnawing pain that is definitely related to eating. It usually occurs from half an hour to several hours after meals, and is often relieved by the ingestion of protein foods, such as milk. Pain is accompanied sometimes by nausea and vomiting. When symptoms worsen, a person may experience fatigue, weakness, and weight loss. Continued pain often makes a person tense and anxious, and it interferes with rest and sleep. Ulcer pain should not be ignored. Untreated, there is the potential for serious complications: bleeding, obstruction, or perforation. If pain is severe and prolonged, a doctor should be consulted for diagnosis and treatment.

FOOD IN THE ALIMENTARY CANAL *is subjected to many chemical changes before it is absorbed and assimilated. About 80 percent of stomach ulcers occur in the duodenum.*

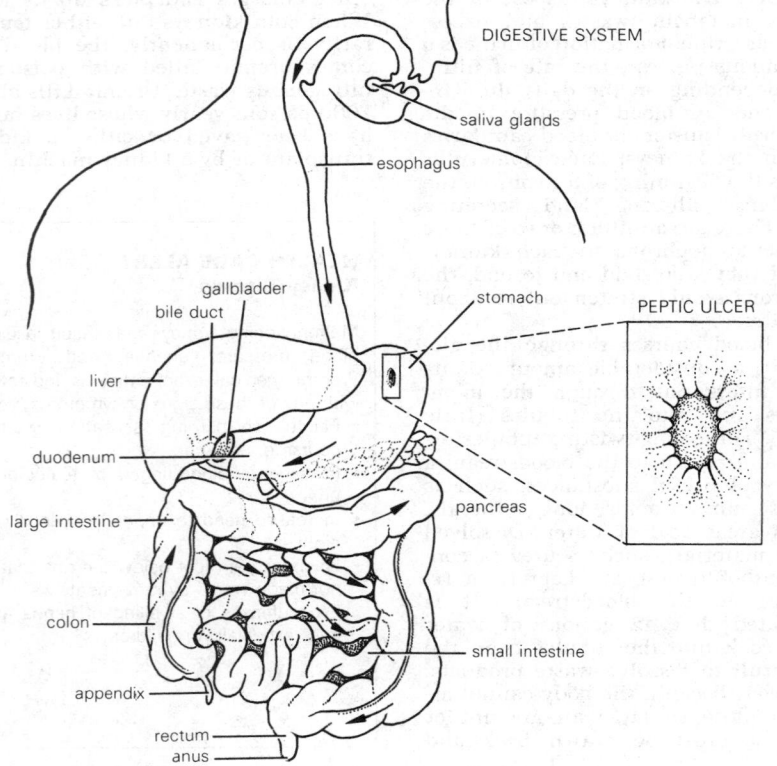

DIGESTIVE SYSTEM

saliva glands

esophagus

gallbladder

bile duct

liver

duodenum

large intestine

colon

appendix

rectum

anus

stomach

PEPTIC ULCER

pancreas

small intestine

Reproductive System

In both males and females, the reproductive system comprises the gonads, a general term referring to the sex glands forming the cells necessary for human reproduction: the male sex glands, or testes; and the female sex glands, or ovaries (see Human Anatomy color insert). In the male, spermatozoa form in the testes, where testosterone, the male sex hormone, is also produced. Sperm cells, produced in millions upon millions during the lifetime of an average man, are stored in the epididymis, a coiled tube alongside each testis. The sperm then travels into the vas deferens, a straight muscular tube that joins with the urethra, the passageway through the penis for both semen and urine. Semen consists of a mixture of sperm and secretions derived from the seminal vesicles, prostate gland, and Cowper's glands.

The primary organ of the female reproductive system is the ovary, which produces egg cells (ova) as well as the female sex hormones, estrogen and progesterone. These hormones prepare the uterus to receive and sustain a fertilized ovum, which can be described as a bit of protoplasm no bigger than a microscopic dot (about 1/175 of an inch in diameter). One ovum, released from one of the two ovaries, merges with just one sperm cell, usually in the Fallopian tube. The fertilized ovum travels through the Fallopian tube, descending to the wall of the uterus, where it is implanted for development into an embryo. If an ovum is not fertilized, as happens with most of the 400 or so ova released during the lifetime of an average woman, it is expelled from the uterus during menstruation. The vagina, serving as the passageway through which sperm cells are supplied, also acts as the birth canal.

When fertilization takes place, tissues from the mother and the embryo form the placenta, the spongy organ through which the embryo is nourished and through which waste products are eliminated. During the first trimester of pregnancy, the embryo, even though little more than a tiny piece of grayish-white tissue, has the beginnings of a brain, heart, nervous system, and eyes. By the second month, features, including ears, begin to form. At three months, fingers and toes are fully formed, and sex can be determined. The fourth month marks the start of the second trimester. By this time, the mother can feel movement, and heartbeats can be detected. In the third trimester, at the end of eight months, the fetus is nearly fully developed. At term (9 months), the average newborn infant weighs 7 pounds 5 ounces and is about 20 inches long.

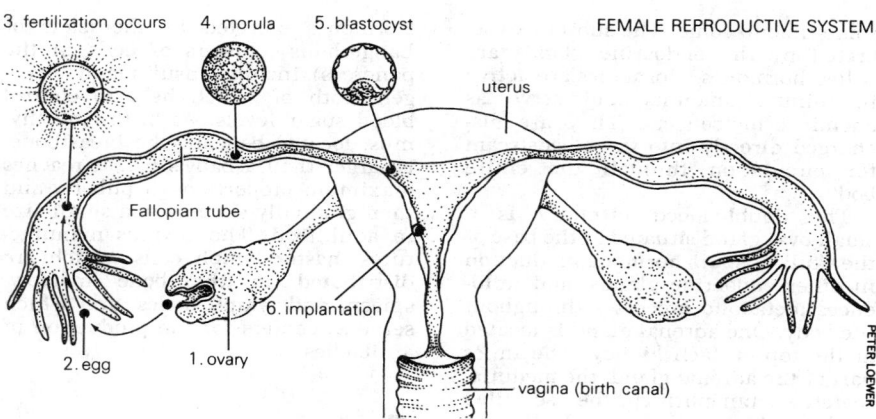

3. fertilization occurs   4. morula   5. blastocyst   FEMALE REPRODUCTIVE SYSTEM

uterus

Fallopian tube

6. implantation

2. egg   1. ovary

vagina (birth canal)

PETER LOEWER

THE STATE OF PREGNANCY *extends for a period of about 40 weeks, from conception to delivery.*

In the fertilized ovum, within a period of 12 hours, 23 chromosomes from the spermatozoa of the father merge with 23 chromosomes from the nucleus of the ovum of the mother. About 36 hours later, the new nucleus divides into two cells and continues to multiply, through the process of cleavage, at a more rapid rate into four, eight, and sixteen cells. A week or so after fertilization, the fertilized ovum enters the uterus with 64 to 128 cells, almost the start of an embryo. The bodily characteristics of the new individual are determined by both the paternal and maternal chromosomes within each cell. Each chromosome has many genes responsible for the development of a variety of physical features, such as the color of eyes and hair, body size and shape of limbs, form of the skull and bone length. Sex is determined by the constitution of the chromosomes (see The Gene, pages 966–976).

Telltale test for the unborn.

Many scientists are engaged in developing sophisticated techniques that will detect diseases and possible delivery problems in fetuses. Ultrasound examinations, for example, are presently said to be used to monitor about 50 percent of all pregnancies and deliveries in the United States. This method of taking pictures of the fetus in utero beams sound waves into the abdomen of the pregnant woman. The pictures, or sonograms, help the doctor see the fetus, evaluate growth and development, check for abnormalities, and determine sex as early as the fourth month of pregnancy. In the early stages of pregnancy, ultrasound can determine the presence and location of one or more fetuses. Toward the middle stage, it can indicate a safe area for amniocentesis when a decision is made to employ this more complicated technique. Amniocentesis, which involves a slight risk, may be used to determine whether serious metabolic disorders or chromosomal abnormalities are present. Just before

birth, use of ultrasound can indicate the position of the infant's head, the umbilical cord, and the placenta.

Endocrine System

Endocrine glands are tiny by comparison with the heart, for example, but they are veritable giants in the work they perform: regulating and integrating separate body functions. The known endocrine glands of the human body include the adrenals, gonads, islets of Langerhans, parathyroids, pituitary, and thymus. In the past hundred years, our understanding of the complex nature of the endocrine glands has increased. Yet the precise mechanism of action of the endocrine glands, and even how many there really are, may remain the subject of research for

ENDOCRINE GLANDS *make hormones that are secreted and circulated in the bloodstream.*

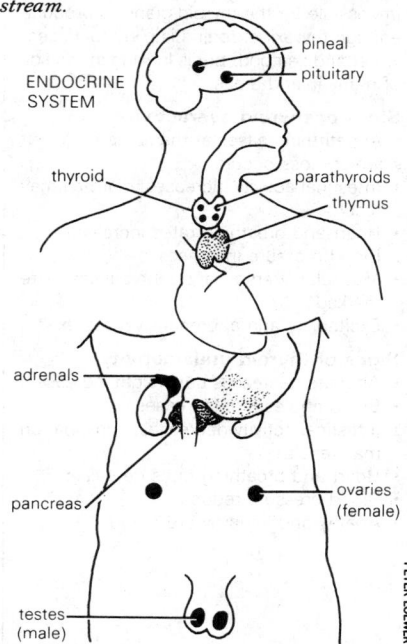

ENDOCRINE SYSTEM

pineal
pituitary

thyroid

parathyroids
thymus

adrenals

pancreas

ovaries (female)

testes (male)

PETER LOEWER

some time to come. The substances secreted by the endocrine glands are called hormones. Hormones are active in minute amounts and serve as chemical messengers. They are discharged directly into the bloodstream for circulation through the entire body.

The double-lobed pituitary is a small oval gland situated at the base of the skull. It spurs hormone production in other endocrine glands, and influences metabolic processes throughout the body. One adrenal gland is located at the top of each kidney. The inner part of the adrenal gland, the medulla, secretes epinephrine, the so-called "fight or flight" hormone. It also secretes norepinephrine, which, like epinephrine, constricts blood vessels. The cortex, the outer part of the adrenal gland, produces entirely different sorts of hormones, adrenocortico-steroids, often called corticoids. These adrenal cortical hormones help the kidneys regulate salt and water balance, aid in protein metabolism, and form antibodies against bacteria and viruses.

The thyroid gland produces the important iodine-protein compounds thyroxin and triiodothyronine, which regulate the rate at which food is converted into heat and energy in body cells. A hormone secreted in the parathyroid glands regulates the level of calcium and phosphorus in the blood.

Hormones secreted by the islets of Langerhans (clusters of cells in the pancreas) include insulin and glycogen, both of which help to control blood sugar levels. At birth, the thymus, located beneath the breastbone, is larger than a baby's fist. It reaches maximum proportions at puberty and then gradually shrinks to a small size in adulthood. The thymus manufactures master lymph cells, which are distributed to the bone marrow, spleen, and lymph nodes, and which serve as centers for the production of antibodies.

Cutaneous System

In the average adult, the skin covers a surface area of 3000 square inches, and receives one-third of all the blood circulating throughout the body. The skin is no more than $\frac{3}{16}$ of an inch in thickness at any point in the body. Several distinctive layers of tissue make up this complex structure. The epidermis, or outer surface—the portion of the skin we actually see—is composed of several layers. Topmost are dead cells, the so-called horny layer, where cells are continuously shed and replaced by new cells pushed up from the deeper, or germinative, layer of the skin. The several layers of the dermis, or true skin, lie beneath the epidermis. This living tissue, tough and fibrous, is rich in nerve endings, blood vessels, and glands. It has undulating surfaces that penetrate into the epidermis above and the subcutaneous tissue below. These undulations form ridges, especially on the hands or feet, which create the pattern that makes each individual's fingerprints unique.

The skin covering forms a barrier against invasion by harmful bacteria. It houses nerve endings that receive sensory stimuli from the external environment. It is the regulator of body temperature, providing the mechanism by which heat is retained or dissipated. There are about 2 million sweat glands over the body surface, with the largest number found on the palms of the hands and the soles of the feet. The moisture secreted by the sweat glands, controlled by a heat regulator in the brain, cools the body by evaporation.

A practically waterproof enclosure, the skin prevents the body contents from drying out. The skin not only helps maintain health, it also warns of many disorders that may affect the body. For example, abnormal skin dryness may indicate thyroid dysfunction or diabetes. Cold sweats may be a sign of heat prostration, fear, or depressed spirits. Edema, a condition in which body tissues contain an excessive amount of fluid, may be seen in heart or kidney decompensation. Local redness is seen in inflammation and fever, while jaundice or liver disorders may be indicated by a yellow skin.

Getting to the bottom of an itch. Itching may often be nothing more than a momentary annoyance that responds to self-treatment with simple remedies. When itching, perhaps from a rash or infection, becomes severe, a general physician or dermatologist should be consulted. Knowing what to do is based on identification of the itch. The following are major causes of itching.

External agents. Itches caused by insects, many of which inject irritating venoms into the skin when they bite.

Contact dermatitis. A red, itchy reaction occurring on contact with irritating substances such as turpentine, paint sprays, fabric softeners, and strong soaps.

Dryness of the skin (winter itch). The low water content of frigid outdoor air (or overheated indoor air) may cause dehydration and microscopic flaking of the top layers of the skin.

Allergy. A hypersensitivity dermatitis, usually a rash or hives, caused by touching, inhaling, or eating something to which a person is allergic. For example, eating citrus fruits, strawber-

SKIN HAS THREE LAYERS OF TISSUE: *the epidermis (horny layer), the dermis ("true skin"), and the subcutaneous (hypodermis). It is a highly protective and functional body organ.*

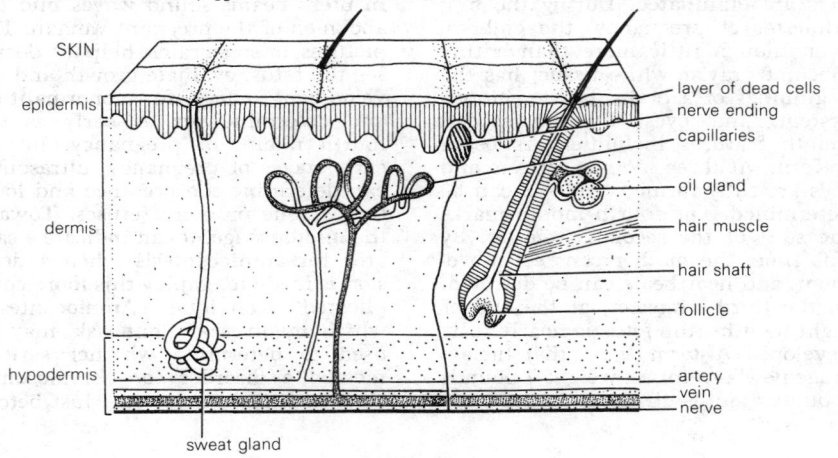

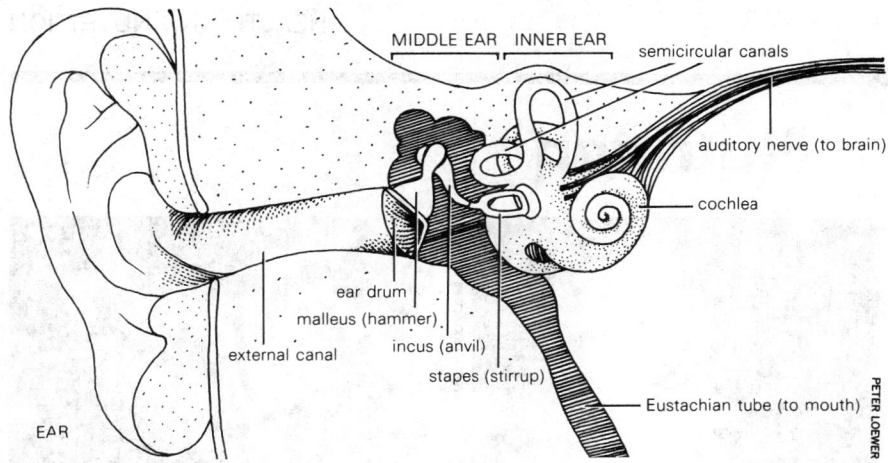

THE HUMAN EAR *is remarkably sensitive. Such high sensitivity can be a prime factor in developing tinnitus, a ringing or buzzing sound in the ear.*

ries, seafood, chocolate, or nuts will often cause hives; skin contact with poison ivy, hair dye, or nickel will often cause a rash.

Constitutional disposition. There are people who seem to be disposed to itching. For example, atopic dermatitis apparently begins with an itch, and scratching produces a rash. One spot on the skin may become the focus for an intensifying scratch/itch cycle.

Sense Organs

The principal sense organs that enable us to perceive the external world are the eyes, ears, nose, mouth, and skin. The eye is like a camera, in that it is a light-tight container with dark inside walls. Protective covering is provided by a tough, fibrous tissue called the sclera. Instead of film, the eye contains a layer of light-sensitive nerve cells, the retina. The retina contains specialized nerve cells called rods, to register black and white, and cones, which are sensitive to color. The iris at the front of the eye regulates the amount of light entering the eye. The curvature of the cornea serves to correct visual errors produced by edges of the crystalline lens of the eye. The outer edges of the lenses bend rays of light at different angles from those bent by the center parts of the lenses.

A human being can hear sounds when a vibrating object pushes air molecules at a rate between 5000 and 15,000 vibrations per second. Vibrations enter the ear canal, beat against the eardrum, and travel through the middle ear, which contains three tiny bones: the malleus (hammer), incus (anvil), and stapes (stirrup). These bones, each in turn, relay the vibrations to the oval window behind the third bone, which then sends waves through the fluid in the inner ear, the snail-shaped cochlea, where thousands of hairs are agitated to transmit vibrations along the auditory canal to the brain. Another part of the inner ear consists of three semicircular canals,

which are essential in giving us our sense of balance.

The sense of smell is provided by the olfactory organ located at the top of the inner surface of the nose. The olfactory receptors are a type of chemical detector. To be smelled, an odor must first be dissolved in the mucus covering of the olfactory membrane. The odorous molecules promptly stimulate tiny hairs in the mucus to send signals to the olfactory bulb, which in turn relays the signals to the brain.

There are only four basic distinguishable taste sensations: sweet, salty, sour, and bitter. Most receptors for taste are located on the tongue. The taste buds at the tip of the tongue transmit sweet and salty sensations, buds at the sides of the tongue transmit sour sensations, and buds toward the back of the tongue transmit bitter sensations.

In its role as sense organ, the skin records and reports a variety of touch sensations to the brain. The human hand has up to 1300 nerve endings per square inch, with the fingertips being twice as sensitive as other parts of the hand. Most touch sensations combine several of five stimuli: cold, heat, pain, pressure, and contact.

DISTANCE RECEPTORS *is a term sometimes applied to the eyes. Both eyes, observing together, can help us tell how far away objects are.*

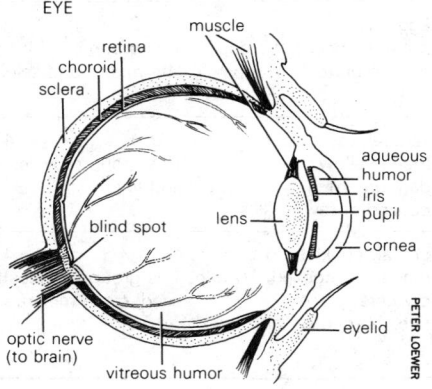

HEALTH CARE ALERT
Dizziness

Dizziness, a disturbing sensation to all who experience it, occurs in various forms and is often a transient feeling readily explained. In certain situations, however, it may indicate an underlying medical problem requiring a professional opinion. A clear description of symptoms will help in arriving at a diagnosis on which treatment may be based.

Lightheadedness. Anxiety or depression may occasion an ill-defined lightheadedness. Rapid and deep breathing (hyperventilation) may worsen the condition.

Unsteadiness (disequilibrium). In this condition, there is a feeling of falling. It may be due to a brain tumor, excessive use of alcohol, or use of a drug, such as an anticonvulsant. In older people, unsteadiness may indicate some hearing loss, or a developing cataract.

Faintness. Medically called syncope, faintness is a commonly reported type of dizziness. The cause may be dehydration brought on by heat, excessive sweating, or a stringent diet, or it may be caused by hypotension, a sudden drop in blood pressure upon standing up. It may occur with low blood pressure, certain heart conditions, shock after severe blood loss, or an overdose of medication, such as an antihypertensive. In times of great stress, some persons may experience a type of fainting known as vasovagal syndrome, in which blood pools suddenly somewhere in the body and is therefore in decreased supply in the brain.

Vertigo. A sensation of movement, either a feeling that one is spinning or that the room is spinning, often caused by some problem with the inner ear. One explanation may be labyrinthitis, inflammation of the inner ear. Other inner ear problems may be due to an overdose of aspirin, sedatives, certain antibiotics, antimalarial medications, or alcohol. Symptoms, such as tinnitus (sensation of noise) or some hearing loss, may occur, but they usually disappear when the drug is discontinued. One of the most familiar forms of vertigo is Ménière's disease, which is due to accumulation of fluid in the membranous labyrinth of the inner ear. The dizziness that ensues may last only a few minutes or go on for hours, with attacks recurring for days and sometimes even weeks. Symptoms may include tinnitus and loss of hearing.

Nutrition

Increased public awareness of the value of good nutrition in the early 1960's resulted in a change in dietary habits for many Americans. People began to follow recommendations to consume less fat and cholesterol, refined sugar, salt, alcohol, and calories, and to consume more complex carbohydrates and roughage, now called fiber. Although saturated fat intake is still high for most Americans, more polyunsaturated foods have found a place in the daily diet. The major food deficit may be found in the overconsumption of soft drinks, or sugar-sweetened drink mixes, and so-called junk foods. Junk foods, in general, are high-sugar, high-fat foods that provide plenty of calories but little protein and few vitamins or minerals. One cannot give total assurance that a sensible diet will prolong life or eradicate disease, but a diet that consists of proper food and careful regulation of how much one eats can be the basis of good health and general well-being.

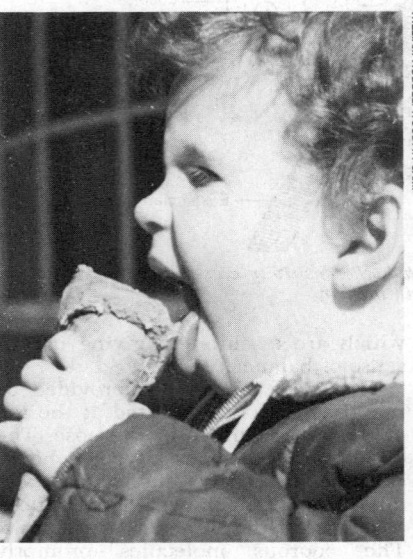 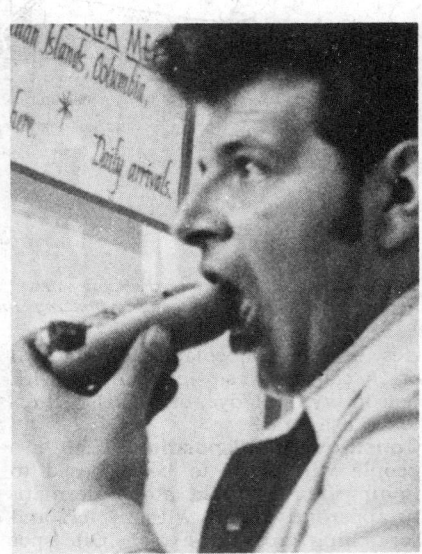

HEALTHY EATING HABITS *should be learned early in life. Poor eating patterns learned as a child may last a lifetime.*

Nutritionally adequate food plan.

Good nutrition becomes an achievable goal by observing one simple rule: Plan healthful, well-balanced meals to include servings from each of the basic four food groups. Diet should be varied in this way, because no one food contains all the nutrients needed to keep the body functioning properly. The following chart will help in the selection and use of basic foods in quantities that will provide necessary nutrients.

Diet and cancer.

Researchers of the Division of Cancer Prevention and Control at the National Cancer Institute believe that diet may be related to 35 percent of all cancer deaths in the United States. This assertion is based on the findings of three recent studies on diet and cancer prevention. There is no common agreement on which factors are most important, but one consensus reached agrees with the diet guidelines set earlier by the American Cancer Society and the National Academy of Sciences. People should eat less fat, more fruits and vegetables, and more whole grains. In particular, this includes fresh dark green, orange, and yellow vegetables (broccoli, carrots, squash, spinach, and others), which are rich in a substance called beta-carotene that is converted by the body into Vitamin A. Carotene, the precursor of Vitamin A, appears to be of value in reducing the risk of lung, bladder, and breast cancers. Cabbage-family vegetables (Brussels

FOOD GROUPS			NUMBER OF DAILY SERVINGS				
	SELECT FROM (AMOUNT PER SERVING)		CHILDREN 1–10	ADOLESCENTS	ADULTS	PREGNANT WOMEN LAST TRIMESTER	LACTATING WOMEN
Dairy products	milk, 1 cup (8 oz) yogurt, 1 cup pudding, 1 cup	*hard cheese, 1½ oz cheese spread, 2 oz *ice cream, 1½ cups cottage cheese, 1½ cups	2½	4	2	4	4
			Dairy products are important sources of calcium, protein, and Vitamins A and D.				
Meat/protein	cooked meat, 2–3 oz fish, 2–3 oz dried beans, 2–3 oz nuts, seeds, 4–6 tbsps	eggs, 2 cottage cheese, ½ cup *peanut butter, ¼ cup	2	2	2	2	2
			This group provides protein, iron, and trace elements such as zinc, chromium, and selenium.				
Fruits/vegetables	fruit, ½ cup (orange, grapefruit) cooked, raw, or juice	vegetables, ½ cup (deep yellow, dark green) cooked or raw	4	4	4	4	4
			This group provides Vitamins A and C, B vitamins, trace elements, and fiber.				
Breads/cereals	bread, 1 slice bagel/hamburger bun, ½	cereal, cooked, ½ cup macaroni, cooked, ½ cup dry cereal, 1 oz rice, ½ cup	4	4	4	4	4
			This group provides B vitamins, iron, and, if whole-grain products are used, trace minerals and fiber.				

*Relatively high fat content.

sprouts, cauliflower, kale) contain several chemicals that have been found to inhibit cancer in animals. Plentiful use of these vegetables appears to be associated with reduced risk of certain cancers, especially cancer of the colon.

Laboratory studies have shown that foods rich in Vitamin C, especially citrus fruits (oranges, grapefruits, tangerines, lemons), red fruits (strawberries, watermelon), and dark green vegetables (broccoli, collard greens) may arrest the formation of certain cancer-causing chemicals. According to studies of persons at high risk of cancer, Vitamin C reduces the incidence of stomach or esophageal cancer.

When dietary intake of fiber (whole grains, fresh fruits, and vegetables) amounts to 40 grams a day or more, there is possible protection against colon and rectal cancer. Both saturated fats (for example, animal fats, butterfat, palm oil, and coconut oil) and polyunsaturated fats (mostly vegetable oils) have been linked with increased cancer, particularly of the breast and colon. It is recommended by the American Cancer Society that all dietary fats be cut by 25 percent, by eating lean instead of fat meats, poultry without skin, low-fat dairy products, little or no fried food, and reduced amounts of hard cheese, nut butters, and salad dressings.

It has been noted that populations consuming a great amount of cured, pickled, and smoked foods have a high incidence of cancer of the esophagus and stomach. Such processed foods can introduce nitrosamines, chemicals that are potent carcinogens (agents known to cause cancer). It is recommended, therefore, that intake of cured meats, smoked fish and ham, pickles, olives, and sauerkraut and other salt-pickled foods be limited.

To restate the American Cancer Society and National Academy of Sciences dietary guidelines: avoid obesity, reduce total fat intake, eat more foods high in fiber and rich in Vitamins A and C, include the cabbage family of plants, and be moderate in the consumption of alcoholic beverages and of salt-cured and smoke-cured foods.

Diet and heart attacks.
In the opinion of the American Heart Association, reduction of fat intake is one of the most important steps to take in order to lower the risk of heart disease. Only 30 percent of total daily calories should come from fat. In general, fats are made up of three types of fatty oils: saturated fats, which tend to increase cholesterol, especially the kind that aids formation of fatty plaques that clog arteries; polyunsaturated fats, which tend to decrease cholesterol blood levels by enhancing excretion of cholesterol in the feces; and monounsaturated fats, which have no apparent effect on blood cho-

NUTRITIONAL GUIDELINES *aimed at reducing certain cancers include eating more green vegetables, citrus fruits, and whole grains, cutting down on fats, and avoiding smoked or salt-cured products.*

lesterol and therefore are considered by physicians to be neutral as related to heart disease.

It is further recommended by the American Heart Association that fats in the diet be equally divided among the three types of fats. All natural fats contain a mixture of the three fats, and the ratio of polyunsaturated to saturated fats categorizes a fat source as predominantly one or the other. For example, butter is about 64 percent saturated fat; soybean oil is about 60 percent polyunsaturated fat.

HEALTH CARE ALERT
Cancer
Seven signals

1. **C**hange in bowel or bladder habits.
2. **A** sore that does not heal.
3. **U**nusual bleeding or discharge.
4. **T**hickening of lump in the breast or any other part of the body.
5. **I**ndigestion, or difficulty in swallowing.
6. **O**bvious change in a wart or mole.
7. **N**agging cough or hoarseness.

Having any of these signs does not necessarily mean that cancer is present, but something may be wrong, and it is advisable to have a medical examination.

CIGARETTE SMOKING *is considered to be a major cause of lung cancer. For more than a decade, the number of women smokers has been increasing steadily. Today, lung cancer will kill more women than will breast cancer.*

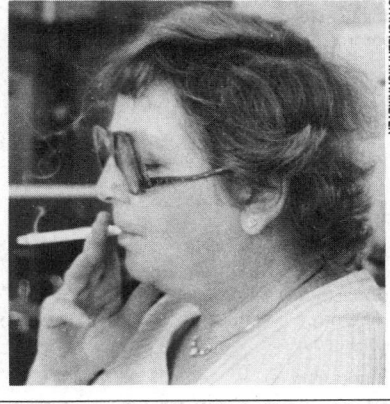

TYPES OF FATS

Saturated	butter
Avoid use of	cheese
(tend to raise	coconut
blood cholesterol)	coconut oil
	egg yolks
	lard
	meat
	milk chocolate
	palm oil
	vegetable shortening
	whole milk

Monounsaturated	avocados
Use occasionally	cashews
(have no effect on	olives
blood cholesterol)	olive oil
	peanut butter
	peanut oil
	peanuts

Polyunsaturated	almonds
Good to use	corn oil
(tend to lower	cottonseed oil
blood cholesterol)	filberts
	fish
	margarine
	pecans
	safflower oil
	salad dressing
	soybean oil
	sunflower oil
	walnuts

RIC DELROSSI/MULVEY ASSOCIATES

Carbohydrates. Carbohydrates, both simple (containing sugars) and complex (containing starches), are the main source of the fuel the body burns to meet its energy requirements. Carbohydrates are made by plants, which use photosynthesis to combine carbon, hydrogen, and oxygen into simple sugars such as those found in sugar cane and fruit. Substances called starches contain longer chains of these sugars. They include beans, grains, and potatoes. Ounce for ounce, starchy foods (those laden with complex carbohydrates) contain no more calories than pure protein, and only half the calories found in fat. If eaten without butter or sour cream, a 5-ounce potato contains 110 calories, but a 5-ounce T-bone steak contains 550 calories.

If the body is inadequately supplied with carbohydrates, it must utilize fats and proteins for energy. Since fats do not burn efficiently when carbohydrates are unavailable, an added burden is placed on the kidneys, forcing excretion from the kidneys of large amounts of toxic metabolic chemicals. Called ketones, these chemicals can build up in the blood, resulting in nausea, fatigue, and apathy, effects often experienced by those on low-carbohydrate diets. When protein is used for energy, the body cannot use this vital nutrient for building and replacing tissues, and the kidneys must eliminate the nitrogen that remains unused. This explains why it is necessary on high-protein diets to drink great amounts of water to help flush out the kidneys.

In contrast to the typical American diet, currently made up of 45 percent carbohydrates, it is recommended that 60 percent of daily calorie intake come from carbohydrates, especially the complex starches and naturally occurring sugars in fruits and vegetables.

Selecting carbohydrates.
Bread. Whole grain (unrefined); whole wheat.
Cereals. Hot, whole grain (farina enriched) oatmeal; cold, whole grain (shredded) wheat.
Fruits and vegetables. Fruits and many vegetables contain simple carbohydrates, but since they are good sources of vitamins and minerals and are relatively low in calories, they are not considered to be "empty" calories (for example, a medium-size apple contains 80 calories; a carrot, 30). Potatoes, which can provide 50 percent of the Vitamin C needed in an adult's daily diet, among other important nutrients, supplies only 4 to 5 percent of the calories. Baked, steamed, or boiled, potatoes are an excellent food.
Legumes and seeds. Dried peas, beans, seeds, and nuts are rich sources of protein, vitamins, and minerals. Seeds and nuts contain fairly large amounts of fat (polyunsaturated vegetable oils), which add to their calorie content. Fat content varies in beans and peas.
Milk products. Simple carbohydrates provide the bulk of calories in skimmed milk, buttermilk, and low-fat yogurt. These foods are excellent sources of protein.
Pasta. Enriched spaghetti and noodles can be bought in various forms. Many are high-protein varieties, and spinach pasta contains more vitamins and minerals than white enriched pasta.
Rice. Brown rice contains almost all nutrients found in the original rice grain. Polishing removes the brown coat as well as the germ containing most of the B vitamins and minerals. Still, parboiled or white rice has more nutritional value than instant or minute rice.

Fiber. Dietary fiber is derived only from plants. Fibers are the chemical substances in cell walls that give plants their structure. There are various fibers, including cellulose, hemicellulose, lignin, pectins, and gums.

Cellulose, hemicellulose, and lignin possess a remarkable ability to absorb water, making stools bulky and easy to eliminate. The facilitated passage of food to the intestine leaves less time for harmful substances to breed. It also speeds up the transit of certain body toxins, which may help prevent the development of cancer of the colon. Lignin helps the digestion of all other fibers and, by binding bile salts (which turn into cholesterol), helps reduce blood cholesterol levels. In like manner, pectins and gums help to lower blood cholesterol and influence the conversion rate of carbohydrates to sugar in the blood.

SELECTING FIBER-RICH FOODS

	FIBER (GRAMS)	SERVING SIZE
Breads and cereals		
100% bran	23	1 cup
cornflakes	2.75	1 3/4 cups
whole-wheat bread	2.4	1 slice
Fruit		
apple (unpeeled)	3.1	1 small
figs (dried)	18	2
grapefruit	2.6	1/2 medium
grapes (green)	1	20
orange	1.8	1 small
pear (unpeeled)	2.8	1 medium
peach, raw	1.3	1 medium
plums, raw	1.6	2 small
raisins	5.0	1/2 cup
strawberries, fresh	2.6	1/2 cup
tangerines	2.1	1 medium
Vegetables		
beans, (baked)	18	1 cup
beans, green	2.4	1 cup
beans, kidney, cooked	4.5	1/2 cup
beets, cooked	2.1	2/3 cup
broccoli, cooked	1.6	3/4 cup
cabbage, cooked	2.2	3/4 cup
cabbage, raw	2.1	3/4 cup
carrots, cooked, raw	2.2	1/2 cup
corn (canned)	4.75	1/2 cup
peas, frozen, raw	5.5	1/2 cup
potatoes, cooked	3.1	2/3 cup
spinach	3.5	1 cup
tomatoes	3.0	1 medium
Nuts		
almonds (shelled)	1.0	10
brazil nuts	5.5	10
peanut butter	2.0	2 tbsp
peanuts	1.0	10

VEGETARIAN DIETS

There are three basic types of vegetarian diets.
Vegetarian (strict or pure vegetarian). Restricted to foods of plant origin, seeds, grains, nuts, fruits, and vegetables.
Lacto-vegetarian. Includes all foods of plant origin; also foods made of milk, such as cheese, cream, and yogurt.
Lacto-ovo-vegetarian. Includes all foods of plant origin; also dairy foods and eggs.
A vegetarian diet is no threat to good health as long as it includes dairy products or animal flesh. Plant foods, with the possible exception of soybeans, cannot supply adequate amounts of essential amino acids to meet body demands for usable protein. Vegetarians must add legumes and nuts to their diets, and obtain sufficient iron, calcium, and B vitamins.

Complementary Vegetable Proteins
For complete protein from plant foods,
  combine any mature legume, such as

lentils	soybeans or soy products	peanuts
lima beans	garbanzos (chickpeas)	pinto beans
navy beans	kidney beans	

with any of the following

barley	rice (white or brown)
corn	seeds (sesame, pumpkin, sunflower)
oats	wheat (bread, pasta, cereal, grains)
	(or combine rice or corn with
	wheat germ or seeds)

BILL COLRUS/MULVEY ASSOCIATES

FOR PROPER PROTEIN INTAKE, *reduce amounts of animal protein and increase amounts of vegetable protein.*

On the whole, the American diet is thought to be relatively low in fiber, mainly because of the consumption of processed foods. Many Americans would probably benefit by doubling their average daily fiber intake, from an average of 10 to 20 grams to 40 grams, especially since foods rich in fiber also supply vitamins and minerals. Fiber is best added as an integral part of the diet: two servings of fresh vegetables and two servings of whole grains daily will usually provide enough fiber for the average person. Adding fibrous foods to the diet gradually will help avoid such undesirable effects as bloating and flatulence.

The chief dietary fiber components and good food sources for them are:

Cellulose: apples, beans, carrots, cereals, eggplant, peas, radishes, and whole-grain bread.

Hemicellulose: bran cereals, eggplant, radishes, and whole-grain bread.

Lignin: pears, fried or browned potatoes, toast made from whole-grain bread.

Pectin: apples, bananas, cabbage, carrots, grapes, grapefruit, potatoes, oranges.

Proteins.

Proteins are a vast family of complex molecules that play a major role in body chemistry. Proteins come in a variety of forms, including enzymes, hormones, and antibodies, and are a prime component of the human cell, making up more than half its dry weight. Protein makes it possible for muscles to contract, and for blood vessels to expand and contract in maintaining normal blood pressure. It is needed for growth and tissue replacement, for the regulation of water and acid-base balance in the body, and for the production of antibodies.

Large protein molecules are made up of smaller molecules that contain nitrogen and that are called amino acids, considered to be the building blocks of all proteins. In one protein, there may be as many as 200 amino acid molecules strung together. The

human body is able to produce all but nine of the 22 different amino acids that are found in nature, using carbohydrates and nitrogen derived generally from dietary proteins. The nine, called essential amino acids, must be obtained in the diet in order for the body to be able to make the hundreds of different proteins it needs. Most animal proteins contain all the essential amino acids, while most vegetable proteins lack one or another of them. This fact makes it desirable to combine several different vegetables in one meal, or to add animal protein to a vegetable diet.

RECOMMENDED DAILY DIETARY ALLOWANCES FOR PROTEIN

	AGE (IN YEARS)	PROTEIN (GMS PER LB IDEAL BODY WEIGHT)
Infants	0-0.5	1.00
	0.5-1	.90
Children	1-3	0.81
	4-6	0.68
	7-10	0.55
	11-14	0.45
	15-18	0.39
Adults	19 and over	0.36
	Pregnant women	0.62
	Nursing women	0.53

Sample calculations for a day's protein needs:
For a five-year-old child weighing 50 pounds:
  0.68 × 50 = 34 grams.
For a 110-pound twelve-year-old:
  0.45 × 110 = 49.5 grams.
For a 125-pound pregnant woman:
  0.62 × 125 = 77.5 grams.
For a 160-pound man:
  0.36 × 160 = 57.6 grams.

According to the Food and Nutrition Board of the National Academy of Sciencies—National Research Council, the amount of protein determined in this fashion should be adequate to meet the needs of virtually all healthy persons.

In general, a person's age and size determine the amount of protein required. According to the Food and Nutrition Board of the National Research Council, the recommended daily allowance (RDA) of protein for a 150-pound adult is about 54 grams. This need could be met by eating, for example, three ounces of cooked beef or chicken (about 24 grams), a cup of broccoli (6 grams), two tablespoons of peanut butter (8 grams), and a cup of cooked dried beans (16 grams). Actually, most Americans eat at least twice as much protein as needed, much of it fat protein, which adds up to extra calories. In an overall diet plan, nutritionists may recommend that total protein constitute no more than 10 to 15 percent of daily calories; fats, no more than 30 percent; and carbohydrates, 55 to 70 percent. Moderate consumption of protein not only will reduce fat/calorie intake but will spare the kidneys the work of ridding the body of unneeded protein, and guard against possible loss of bone calcium, which may result from diets excessively high in protein.

Cholesterol.

Cholesterol belongs to the sterol group of fats, a different type from the saturated and unsaturated fats. This waxy yellowish substance, a normal and essential component of cells throughout the body, plays a vital part in the production of nerve tissue, digestive bile, and sex hormones. In the average person, about 80 percent of cholesterol is produced in the liver. Typically, the liver manufactures the 1000 mg of cholesterol required by the body daily. If a diet is too rich in cholesterol, which is found in egg yolks, butter, and fats, the liver cuts back production, but not always enough to avoid an increase in cholesterol level in the blood. An excessive amount of cholesterol circulating in the blood can leave deposits, or plaque, on the lining of the artery walls. Continued accumulation of these deposits can result in atherosclerosis, impeding blood flow and eventually shutting it off in an artery. If the artery is one leading to the heart, a heart attack will occur. Stroke, the equivalent in the brain of a heart attack, occurs when plaque causes blockage of the carotid arteries in the head and neck.

According to a statement issued by the American Heart Association, there would eventually be a 50 percent lower incidence of heart disease if Americans reduced their blood cholesterol levels by 25 percent. Such a statement finds confirmation in a 1984 report released by the National Heart, Lung and Blood Institute on the results of its ten-year study on cholesterol. It showed that for every 1 percent of lowered blood cholesterol, the chances of having a heart attack are reduced by 2 percent. The average

American consumes about 400 to 600 mg of cholesterol, with typical blood cholesterol readings averaging 210 to 220 mg/dl (deciliter). According to experts at the National Institutes of Health (NIH), serum level counts (the amount of cholesterol circulating in the blood) should be under 200 in adults 30 years of age and over.

Serum cholesterol level is considered a prime indicator of whether a person is at risk for heart disease. Adjustment in diet offers the best attack on this problem and mainly involves

TO EAT OUT WISELY AND ENJOYABLY, *watch out for hidden fats. A cheese quiche has more fat than red meat. Fish and poultry instead of meat can help cut calories.*

CHOLESTEROL CONTENT OF COMMON FOODS

TYPE OF FOOD	SERVING SIZE	APPROX. CONTENT
Meat (cooked)		
bacon	2 slices	15 mg
beef, lean	3 oz	107 mg
beef liver	3 oz	370 mg
lamb	3 oz	112 mg
pork, ham	3 oz	100 mg
pork sausages	3 oz	80 mg
veal	3 oz	115 mg
Fish (cooked)		
haddock	3 oz	68 mg
halibut	3 oz	57 mg
herring	3 oz	96 mg
mackerel	3 oz	108 mg
salmon	3 oz	53 mg
trout	3 oz	62 mg
tuna	3 oz	62 mg
Shellfish (cooked)		
clams	3 oz	40 mg
oysters	3 oz	57 mg
scallops	3 oz	45 mg
shrimp	3 oz	170 mg
Poultry (cooked)		
chicken (light meat with skin)	3 oz	65 mg
egg white	any amount	0 mg
egg yolk	1 egg	240 mg
turkey (light meat with skin)	3 oz	68 mg
Milk products		
American cheese	1 oz	30 mg
butter	½ oz (1 tbsp)	30 mg
cottage cheese (creamed)	8 oz (1 cup)	45 mg
cottage cheese (uncreamed)	8 oz (1 cup)	16 mg
Edam cheese	1 oz	30 mg
Muenster cheese	1 oz	25 mg
Parmesan cheese	1 oz	25 mg
provolone cheese	1 oz	27 mg
ricotta cheese	1 oz	14 mg
skim milk	8 oz (1 cup)	5 mg
Swiss cheese	1 oz	28 mg
whole milk	8 oz (1 cup)	32 mg
Cooking oils		
lard	½ oz (1 tbsp)	12 mg
margarine	any amount	0 mg
vegetable oils	any amount	0 mg

the reduction of saturated fats, especially animal fats and dairy products. In general, this means restricting the dietary intake of larded meats, liver, and shellfish. Lean meats, fish, and poultry are better choices. No more than three eggs should be consumed in a week. One egg yolk amounts to 240 mg of cholesterol, as can be seen on the chart.

Cholesterol carriers. Because cholesterol is not soluble, it must be carried through the bloodstream in packets of fat and protein called lipoproteins. There are two types: high-density lipoprotein (HDL) and low-density lipoprotein (LDL). HDL may remove cholesterol from circulation, carrying excess cholesterol in the bloodstream back to the liver for disposal, but high levels of LDL have been linked to atherosclerosis. LDL transports cholesterol to the cells and, when there is more cholesterol circulating than can be used by the cells, the LDL carriers deposit the excess on the artery walls.

According to The National Institutes of Health, consuming less fatty food will lower LDL levels in the blood. In addition, recent medical data show that a diet rich in fatty fish (mackerel, salmon, sardines, tuna) may help prevent heart disease. The oil of fatty fish, called eicosapentaenoic acid, is one of the polyunsaturated fats the body uses to synthesize prostaglandins. These hormonelike substances are very active in body functions, as in the contraction of blood vessels.

In one ongoing study of more than 20 years, involving 852 men, it was found that men who ate more than an ounce of fish a day were only half as likely as other men to incur heart attacks. Another study demonstrated that a diet rich in fish oil helps reduce high levels of triglycerides, a combination of fatty acids which, together with cholesterol are considered by some medical experts to be one of the leading factors in the cause of heart disease.

Hidden fats. Many people, although aware of the nutritional value of limiting dietary fats, fail to realize the amount of hidden fat in favorite foods: red meat with its deep marbling and hard and cream cheeses top the list. Deep-fried foods, cream soups and sauces, chocolate, ice cream, seeds, and nuts are also high on the list. Sunflower seeds contain 75 percent of fat calories; nuts, at least 85 percent. People may unwittingly choose substitutes that have an even higher fat content, such as a quiche made with cheese, in which all but 25 percent of the calories are derived from fat more saturated than that of red meat. When dining out, it is well to remember that creamed dishes (soups, gravies, and sauces) are loaded with hidden fat. So too are processed and packaged foods. It is important to check the labels carefully. Ingredients are listed by weight, so when fat is among the first few ingredients, the food is likely to be high in fat content.

To calculate the fat content of a packaged food that lists nutritional information, *multiply* the number of grams of fat in a serving by nine (the number of calories in one gram of fat); *divide* this total by the number of calories per serving; and *multiply* this result by 100. This procedure will give the percentage of fat calories.

Example: whole milk:

Fat, 9 grams;
serving size, 8 oz.;
calories, 165.
Percent of calories from fat per serving:

$$9 \times 9 = 81;$$
$$\frac{81}{165} = 0.49;$$
$$0.49 \times 100 = 49 \text{ percent fat per serving.}$$

Food additives. A food additive may be a preservative, flavor, emulsifier, moisturizing agent, antioxidant (a substance preventing oxidation), nutrient, or any other of the many classifications of substances considered by food technologists as useful for their special purposes. One primary reason for the use of additives is to make food taste better; another is to keep processed foods fresh as they go from producer to consumer. Many additives are chemicals that are derived from natural substances:

alpha-tocopherol (a substance with Vitamin E activity)
ascorbic acid (Vitamin C from citrus fruits)
caffeine (from coffee and tea)
carrageenin (from seaweed)
gelatin (from bones)
glycerol (from fats)
gum tragacanth, guar gum (from trees)
lecithin (from plants)
monosodium glutamate (MSG, the salt of a natural amino acid)
sodium casenate (the protein in milk)
sorbic acid (from berries)

Other additives are synthetic chemical copies of natural substances, such as that for vanillin, the flavoring from the vanilla bean. Among the entirely synthetic additives are chemicals such as butylated hydroxyamisole (BHA), saccharin, sorbitan monostearate, and sodium bisulfite. Cyclamate, a widely used nonnutritive artificial sweetener, was banned by the Food and Drug Administration (FDA) in 1969 after studies showed that it caused cancer in rats. The FDA Cancer Assessment Committee has since stated that cyclamate is not a carcinogen.

The most commonly used food additives are natural substances: sugar, corn syrup, dextrose, and fructose. "Natural" does not automatically imply "good" any more than "artificial" means "unhealthy." For example, colas and other soft drinks have a natural additive, caffeine, which may cause sleeplessness and anxiety in some persons; and some people may experience severe allergic reactions to gum tragacanth.

Many people are demanding the removal of nitrates and nitrites from cured meats on the basis that they may produce cancer-causing nitrosamines in humans. Yet these same people may be unaware that very high levels of nitrates are present in commonly eaten foods: beets, carrots, spinach, celery, lettuce, eggplant, and radishes. Conversely, iodine added to salt prevents goiter in people living in areas where iodine is lacking in the soil, and synthetic vitamins and minerals added to bread increase its nutritive value. With additives, as with other health matters, it is wise to look at both sides of the issue, weighing the advantages against the potential risks before deciding how to proceed. There is another option: reduce consumption of food additives and processed foods, and increase consumption of unrefined and fresh foods.

Vitamins. Vitamins are essential for good health. These organic compounds act as regulators in helping to process other vital nutrients: proteins, fats, and carbohydrates. Thirteen compounds are considered to be vitamins. Four of them—A, D, E, and K—are soluble in fat. The eight B vitamins and Vitamin C are soluble in water. The fat-soluble vitamins, stored in body fat, are not readily excreted and do not necessarily have to be consumed every day. On the other hand, the body does not store water-soluble vitamins, so the B vitamins and Vitamin C must be included in the daily diet in adequate amounts to fulfill bodily demands.

The latest report by the National Academy of Sciences Committee on Dietary Allowances contains many valuable suggestions. These suggestions can help the average person to meet his or her nutritional needs as established by the recommended daily allowances (RDA). The recommended daily consumption of each vitamin is based on the amount needed to avoid signs of a deficiency in the average person. At the same time, the recommended amount allows for varying individual needs and for the capability of the body to absorb the consumed vitamins. It has often been said that anyone on a well-balanced diet, that is, anyone who eats a variety of foods based on the four food groups (see page 934), does not need additional vitamins. However, adequate amounts of vitamins may not be obtained by those who are picky eaters, those who eat mostly processed and canned foods, or those who are on a highly restricted low-calorie diet. In such instances, a physician may advise that a multivitamin supplement be taken.

At times, there may be increased need for a specific vitamin: for example, Vitamin C after operations, extensive burns, or serious illness. Poorly nourished elderly persons or heavy smokers may benefit from additonal Vitamin C. While specific vitamin supplementation may be indicated for specific needs, too great a reliance on vitamin pills, or on an added intake of fortified foods, may give one a false sense of nutritional adequacy. It may, therefore, be better to obtain essential nutrients by improving one's daily diet.

Megadose vitamins. The term "megadose" is not a scientific term, but when vitamins are taken in amounts ten times higher than the RDA, the action is druglike, and harmful effects may occur. Vitamins in greater than RDA amounts should not be taken without medical approval. The chart of vitamins and good food sources for them (on the next page) summarizes the functions of each vitamin and possible effects of excessive use.

HOW TO READ FOOD LABELS

The wise consumer will heed these pointers.

Nutrient listing. This is only demanded if a manufacturer makes a nutritional claim such as inclusion of vitamin or mineral supplements, or a low cholesterol content.

Natural foods. There is no single term to define use of the word "natural." Therefore, a food so labeled may still contain artificial preservatives.

Serving size. Lack of an industry standard makes it impossible to compare the caloric content of different brands. Also, serving sizes have become smaller, which may mislead the purchaser into thinking that calories, fat, or sodium content is lower. Certain foods, such as diet foods, must provide nutrition labeling: servings, calories per serving, protein content, and amount of carbohydrates.

Artificial colors. Only one food coloring is required to be listed by name: yellow dye number 5, because it causes an allergic reaction in many people. Any other coloring is simply referred to as an "artificial color."

Artificial flavors. Foods promoted as having no artificial flavors may often contain artificial colors and preservatives. A "sugar free" food may not contain sucrose, but it may have such high-calorie sweeteners as honey or corn syrup. Of the few thousand artificial flavors on the market, only a handful are legally required to be included on the product label.

Low calorie. Indicates that the product contains no more than 40 percent calories per serving (0.4 calories per gram).

Reduced calories. Means that a product contains at least one-third fewer calories than the standard form. Label should include a comparison of calories with the original food.

Lean or low fat meat. Applies to a meat product having 25 percent less of either breading, sodium, cholesterol, or fat. The standard of comparison is varied; for example, comparison may be with the leading brand of that particular kind of product, be a government market sample, or be the manufacturer's total fat and calorie content together with the regular sodium level or regular breading content version of the same product.

"Flex-labeling." Means that an ingredient list may state "contains one or more of the following ingredients." For instance, consumers may be informed that the product contains safflower seed and coconut oils, but not that the former is polyunsaturated, the latter a saturated oil.

VITAMINS

FAT-SOLUBLE

	GOOD FOOD SOURCES	PRIMARY FUNCTIONS	EFFECTS OF EXCESSIVE AMOUNTS
Vitamin A **Retinol**	Yellow, orange, and dark green vegetables; liver; cheese; milk; eggs; butter.	Known as the "growth vitamin." Essential in maintaining healthy skin, hair, mucous membranes, and bone. Provides visual pigments that aid vision in dim light.	May cause headache, poor appetite, nausea, vomiting, damage to the liver and blood cells, skin rashes, hair loss, injury to brain and nervous system.
Vitamin D **Calciferol**	Egg yolks; butter; fortified milk; liver; fish liver oils; tuna; salmon; herring; sardines; oysters.	Known as the "sunshine vitamin." Aids normal growth of bones and teeth. Important in intestinal absorption of calcium and phosphorus. Protects against rickets.	May cause excessive calcium deposits in the blood; kidney stones, nausea, fragile bones, loss of appetite, high blood pressure, high blood cholesterol.
Vitamin E **Alpha tocopherol**	Lettuce and other leafy green vegetables; seed oils; whole grains; dried beans; liver.	Helps in production of red cells and in strengthening of muscle tissue. Protects Vitamin A and fats from reacting with oxygen.	May cause blood clotting problems; may destroy some Vitamin K in the intestines. May interfere with conversion of beta carotene into Vitamin A.
Vitamin K	Liver; potatoes; green leafy vegetables; cabbage; cauliflower; peas; cereals.	Aids in synthesis of substances needed for blood clotting; helps maintain normal bone metabolism. Made by bacteria in human intestine, except in newborns.	May cause blood clotting problems. May cause jaundice in infants.

WATER-SOLUBLE

	GOOD FOOD SOURCES	PRIMARY FUNCTIONS	EFFECTS OF EXCESSIVE AMOUNTS
Vitamin B$_1$ **Thiamin**	Whole wheat grains; wheat germ; liver; kidney; pork; peas; beans; peanuts; oranges; various fruits and vegetables.	(All B vitamins play a similar role in the body; they help enzymes do their work.) Assists in function of 24 enzymes, helping cells to utilize carbohydrates. Assists in proper function of nervous system and digestive tract.	Not known; it is known that B vitamins are interdependent, so an excess of one may produce a deficiency of another.
Vitamin B$_2$ **Riboflavin**	Liver; kidney; lamb; beef; veal; eggs; whole wheat products; yeast; asparagus; beets; peas; dark green vegetables.	Cofactor in enzymes helping cells to use carbohydrates, proteins, and fats, and to produce energy. Promotes growth, healthy skin, and healthy mucous membranes.	None known.
Vitamin B$_3$ **Niacin** **Nicotinamide** **Nicotinic acid**	Lean meat; fish; liver; yeast; eggs; whole-grain breads; cereals; peas; beans; nuts.	Essential component of enzymes that contribute to production of energy in cells. Assists in the breakdown of fats.	Sweating, palpitations, circulatory problems, inability to digest carbohydrates, duodenal ulcer, abnormal liver function, excessive uric acid in blood.
Vitamin B$_6$ **Pyridoxine** **Pyridoxal**	Poultry; fish; liver; whole grains; cereals; breads; tomatoes; yellow corn; spinach; green beans; bananas; yogurt.	An enzyme activator; aids in breakdown of protein and carbohydrates, and in forming hormones such as adrenalin and insulin. Also helps regenerate red blood cells and produce antibodies.	Liver dysfunction; dependency on high dose can lead to deficiency symptoms on return to normal amounts.
Vitamin B$_{12}$ **Cobalamin**	Liver; kidney; fish; dairy products; brewer's yeast; wheat germ.	Assists in production of red blood cells, functioning of the nervous system, and building of genetic material.	None known.
Folic acid **(a B vitamin)**	Liver; kidney; green leafy vegetables; dried legumes.	Needed for formation of red and white blood cells. Aids in protein metabolism and in creating some components of DNA molecule.	None known; however, because it is stored in the body, it is potentially dangerous and can mask a B$_{12}$ deficiency.
Vitamin C **Ascorbic acid**	Abundant in most fruits and vegetables, especially citrus fruits, tomatoes, potatoes, green peppers, and dark green vegetables.	Enhances activity of certain enzymes. Aids body in use of iron and in blood clotting. Helps formation of teeth, gums, and bones. Aids in healing of bone fractures and wounds.	Diarrhea, formation of kidney and bladder stones, increased tendency for blood to clot, urinary tract irritation; may induce B$_{12}$ deficiency.

Macrominerals and micro-minerals (trace elements).

Minerals are inorganic substances that carry out some functions similar to those performed by vitamins—assisting in bringing about biochemical reactions. Minerals also serve as structural components in tissues, for example, calcium and phosphorus in bone, and as raw materials or chief participants in chemical reactions. Thus, sodium is needed to pump water in and out of cells, and iron is the constituent of hemoglobin carrying oxygen to the cells.

Macrominerals, such as calcium and phosphorus, are required in large amounts for proper body function. Microminerals, or trace minerals, such as copper, zinc, and iron, are needed by the body in very small amounts. Dietary deficiencies of major minerals are rare, but dietary shortages of trace minerals do occur. A shortage of iron, for example, represents the most widespread nutritional deficiency seen in the United States.

MINERALS

MACROMINERALS	CHIEF FOOD SOURCES	CHIEF BODY FUNCTIONS
Calcium	Milk; dairy products; yogurt; hard cheeses; sardines; green leafy vegetables: collard and dandelion greens.	Supports growth of bones and teeth; helps maintain cell membranes; essential for proper blood clotting; helps regulate ions in and out of cells; aids muscle contraction and relaxation; essential for functioning of several important enzymes.
Phosphorus	Meat; fish; poultry; milk; nuts; legumes; whole grain breads; cereals.	Important in formation of bones and teeth, and the functioning of several B vitamins; transports fats throughout the body; necessary for release of energy from carbohydrates; present in every cell as part of nucleic acids.
Magnesium	Meat; fish; milk; whole grains; salad greens; nuts (especially almonds and cashews).	Essential for release of energy from glycogen, production of proteins, regulation of body temperature, and proper functioning of nerves and muscles.
Potassium	Bananas; orange juice; dried fruits; meat; peanut butter; potatoes; coffee.	Aids in transmission of nerve impulses; buffers body fluids; catalyzes release of energy from carbohydrates, proteins, and fats; regulates amount of water in cells and so aids proper cell function.

MICROMINERALS (Trace minerals)		
Chromium	Liver; beef; dried beans; cheese; whole-grain breads and cereals; peanuts; brewer's yeast; molasses; beets.	Aids the body, together with insulin, in deriving energy from blood sugar; plays an important role in the synthesis of fatty acids and cholesterol in the liver.
Copper	Oysters; fish; nuts; dried peas; beans, beef and pork liver; organ meats; eggs; spinach; asparagus; corn oil margarine.	Aids in the manufacture of red blood cells, and helps body store iron. A component of several respiratory enzymes, copper is also part of the enzyme that helps make melanin (skin pigment).
Fluorine (fluoride)	Fish; tea; most animal foods; fluoridated water; foods grown with or cooked in fluoridated water.	Helps form strong teeth and resistance to decay, aids in maintaining bone strength.
Iodine	Seafood; saltwater fish; seaweed; sea salt; iodized salt.	A component of thyroid hormones, which control metabolism. Aids in development and functioning of the thyroid gland, and in the prevention of goiter.
Iron	Liver (especially pork, then calf, beef, and chicken); kidney; red meat; egg yolks; green leafy vegetables; dried raisins; apricots; prunes; dried beans; peas; potatoes; blackstrap molasses; enriched and whole-grain cereals.	Helps form red blood cells and myoglobin in muscles that supply oxygen in cells. Found in enzyme systems, including one that works to produce energy in the body.
Manganese	Nuts; whole grains; fruits; vegetables; tea; instant coffee; cocoa powder.	Aids in proper functioning of the nervous system, normal bone structure, and reproduction; extremely important in many vital enzyme systems in the body; needed for utilization of iron.
Molybdenum	Legumes; cereal grains; liver; kidney; some dark green vegetables.	Required by three important enzymes. May aid in prevention of tooth decay; associated with carbohydrate metabolism.
Selenium	Seafood; whole-grain cereals; meat; egg yolks; chicken; milk.	Prevents breakdown of fats and other body chemicals; interacts with Vitamin E in protecting cell membranes.
Zinc	Beef; liver; eggs; poultry; seafood, especially oysters; peas; carrots; whole grains; pure maple syrup.	A component of as many as 100 enzymes in the body. Involved in wound healing; needed for growth and development.

Fitness

Physiologists state that about 3500 calories equal 1 pound of fat: 100 unburned calories daily for 35 days add 1 pound of fat. At this rate, weight gain at the end of a year would amount to 10 pounds. Often, the added pounds go unnoticed in what has been called "creeping obesity." Many Americans average between 15 and 30 pounds of excess weight, and spend billions of dollars annually on diet books, low-calorie foods, and weight-loss programs of all types.

As most dieters have learned, there is no substitute for basic health habits that include good eating, regular exercise, and proper rest and relaxation. Staying active and keeping a positive outlook on life will go a long way in increasing the chances of enjoying a fuller and richer life at any age.

Weight Control

Height and weight tables. Ideal body weight may be determined by checking a table of suggested desirable weights. Such tables give no absolute answers on what constitutes ideal weight, but they can be helpful in determining advisable weight range. Compared with figures revised in 1959, the latest update on height and weight tables issued by the Metropolitan Life Insurance Company shows that adults can acceptably weigh more than previously thought. Since 1959, there has been an average increase in weight of 13 pounds for short men, and 10 pounds for short women; 7 pounds for men of medium height, and 3 pounds for women of medium height; and 2 pounds for tall men, and 3 pounds for tall women. The height and weight tables shown here apply to people ages 25 to 59. Weight is stated in pounds, according to body frame size, and including the wearing of indoor clothing (5 pounds for men and 3 pounds for women in shoes with 1-inch heels).

Body mass index. Some experts at The National Institutes of Health consider debatable the value of charts of desirable weights, preferring a body mass index instead as an indicator of body fitness. To obtain a body mass index, body weight (in pounds) is multiplied by 703, and the product is divided by height (in inches). The quotient is then divided by body height once again, yielding the body mass index. A final answer showing a value of 20 to 25 is considered normal; between 26 and 30, many experts advise losing weight; and a value over 30 is

HEIGHT/WEIGHT TABLES

Men

HEIGHT	SMALL FRAME	MEDIUM FRAME	LARGE FRAME
5'2"	128-134	131-141	138-150
5'3"	130-136	133-143	140-153
5'4"	132-138	135-145	142-156
5'5"	134-140	137-148	144-160
5'6"	136-142	139-151	146-164
5'7"	138-145	142-154	149-168
5'8"	140-148	145-157	152-172
5'9"	142-151	148-160	155-176
5'10"	144-154	151-163	158-180
5'11"	146-157	154-166	161-184
6'0"	149-160	157-170	164-188
6'1"	152-164	160-174	168-192
6'2"	155-168	164-178	172-197
6'3"	158-172	167-182	176-202
6'4"	162-176	171-187	181-207

Women

HEIGHT	SMALL FRAME	MEDIUM FRAME	LARGE FRAME
4'10"	102-111	109-121	118-131
4'11"	103-113	111-123	120-134
5'0"	104-115	113-126	122-137
5'1"	106-118	115-129	125-140
5'2"	108-121	118-132	128-143
5'3"	111-124	121-135	131-147
5'4"	114-127	124-138	134-151
5'5"	117-130	127-141	137-155
5'6"	120-133	130-144	140-159
5'7"	123-136	133-147	143-163
5'8"	126-139	136-150	146-167
5'9"	129-142	139-153	149-170
5'10"	132-145	142-156	152-173
5'11"	135-148	145-159	155-176
6'0"	138-151	148-162	158-179

© 1983 Metropolitan Life Insurance Company. Source of basic data: 1979 Build Study, Society of Actuaries and Association of Life Insurance Medical Directors of America, 1980.

usually regarded as an indication of medically significant obesity.

To lose weight, reduce calories. On the whole, commercial diet plans are nutritionally unbalanced, and seldom result in permanent weight loss. Repeated cycles of weight loss, gain, loss, and gain again, are considered by some professionals to have a more damaging effect upon health than consistent and moderate overweight. In sensible weight loss, calorie intake should be reduced, but without a cutback on the nutrients needed for proper body function.

To gain 10 pounds in one year, for example, takes no more than an extra 100 calories a day. This amount is easily obtained with one extra tablespoonful of butter, one pear, a plain muffin, or a biscuit of shredded wheat. Such additional calorie consumptions may easily occur at more than one meal. In an entire day, during which a total of 2000 or more calories may be con-

sumed, just an extra spoonful of cereal at breakfast, several more bites of cheese at lunch, a sweet snack in the afternoon, and an extra helping of meat at dinner will add up to many extra calories. It is worthwhile to consider the effects of extra calories and what can be done to overcome them. In calculating calorie intake from a meal or dietary plan, these facts will be of help: an ounce of pure protein or carbohydrate produces 110 calories; an ounce of fat produces 250 calories.

To gain weight, add calories. Some people who wish to gain weight are thin because of inherited body build. Many cannot gain an ounce of weight no matter how much calorie-rich food they consume. In some cases, medical problems such as hyperthyroidism or diabetes must be corrected before considering any program to gain weight. In general, a person who desires to gain weight needs to eat more nutritious foods and to increase

EVALUATING DIETS

A person deciding upon a weight-loss plan would do well to ask a few pertinent questions: Is the person promoting the diet a qualified nutritionist, or simply someone wanting to make money on the diet? Has the diet been thoroughly and scientifically tested? Has it survived for at least five years? Most of all, "let the buyer beware" of a diet based on some nonexistent "secret." For effective weight loss—lost pounds that stay lost—no fad diet will prove successful. A well-balanced diet is one that is based on up-to-date medical and nutritional information and that is good for a lifetime. It includes selections from the basic food groups and provides high-quality protein (at least 60 grams); no more than 30 percent of fat (mostly unsaturated, accounting for one-third of the day's calories), and at least 60 grams of carbohydrates. Such diet plans as the U.S. Senate Diet, Weight Watchers Diet, and Prudent Diet meet these criteria.

Low-calorie diets (the Nibbling Diet, the Freedom Diet, and others) consider that proteins, carbohydrates, and fats are needed in equal amounts, and do not differentiate between saturated and unsaturated fats.

Low-carbohydrate diets (the Doctor's Metabolic Diet and others) restrict carbohydrate intake and also limit calories. However, little is said about fats, an important consideration since saturated fats and cholesterol may adversely affect the heart and arteries.

High-protein diets (the Complete Scarsdale Medical Diet, Natur Slim, and others) result in an unusually high intake of protein as well as cholesterol. Even those in good health must drink plenty of water to eliminate the ketone bodies formed in the blood by incomplete burning of fat. A high-protein diet may cause fatigue and bad breath.

High-fat diets (such as Dr. Atkins' Superenergy Diet) suggest that no carbohydrates be eaten during the first week and, after that, only the barest minimum. Body requirements for all but four fatty acids are rather low. In particular, saturated fats pose a potential of heart disease in men and postmenopausal women.

Potential health-risk diets (Fasting, Calories Don't Count, and others) do not meet the criteria for safe and continued use. To lose fat and keep it off, one needs a diet that is nutritionally and medically acceptable, and that can be maintained for as long as required.

---

the total number of calories in the daily diet. Proper living habits also are important: regular meals, moderate exercise, sufficient sleep and rest, and avoidance of unnecessary tension. A physical checkup may be indicated to determine the underlying cause of being underweight, or of having continued weight loss.

Eating disorders. In the United States, concern mounts for the growing number of adolescent girls and young women who suffer from a bizarre disorder called anorexia nervosa, the so-called starvation disease. It can also occur in some older women as well as in men, although less than 10 percent of reported cases involve males. In many instances, the anorexic sees herself as repulsively fat, and is constantly fighting off the urge to eat. Food intake may be limited to between 300 and 600 calories a day. Such food restriction becomes a way for the anorexic to exert control over her body and to avoid the real issues at hand. These may include an anxiety state that is fostered by lack of communication with family members, fear of the future, or ambivalent feelings about one's sexuality. Anorexia nervosa can be fatal. Estimates indicate a mortality rate between 5 and 15 percent. Individualized treatment, including psychotherapy, often is indicated, and hospitalization may be ordered if a person is extremely malnourished.

In a related eating disorder, bulimia, individuals starve for a period of time and then go on an eating binge. Episodes of gorging on huge quantities of food may be interspersed with drastic purging by self-induced vomiting, abuse of laxatives, or an excessive amount of strenuous exercise.

Eating disorders are hazardous to the health, exacting a heavy toll on physical as well as mental well-being. On the whole, eating disorders are extremely difficult to treat, and only about 30 percent of all victims recover completely. A first step in treatment usually is psychotherapy, especially group therapy, which offers support from peers at a crucial time. Various hospitals have undertaken treatment programs for eating disorders, utilizing a team approach that may include a psychiatrist, psychologist, psychiatric and medical nurses, social workers, and other specialized personnel.

HEALTH CARE ALERT
Anorexia Nervosa

In children and young women, various behavioral and physical changes may signal a developing anorexia.

- **Extreme weight loss.** One diagnostic indication is weight loss of at least 25 percent of body weight before dieting; weight loss may be 15 to 20 percent in some women.
- **Obsession with body weight.** Fear of becoming obese; often, this exists even though the anorexic appears emaciated. A feeling of security as long as weight loss continues.
- **Excessive exercise.** The anorexic exercises compulsively in a desire to burn off calories.
- **Dieting and calorie counting.** The anorexic refuses to maintain body weight within normal limits for age and height. Knows good from bad foods, based on calorie count; becomes extremely upset if forced to eat a so-called forbidden food. May eat only certain foods, and painstakingly cuts food into small pieces before eating.
- **Other symptoms.** Starvation can produce such symptoms as insomnia, constipation, dry skin, hair loss, brittle nails, and a feeling of always being cold. There may be withdrawal from social contact, especially if a situation involves eating.

SUSAN ROSENBERG/PHOTO RESEARCHERS

MANY FAST FOODS *are nutritional booby traps, but some can be easily avoided.*

BILL COLRUS/MULVEY ASSOCIATES

FOOD VALUES OF FAST FOODS

FAST FOOD	CALORIES	PROTEIN (GRAMS)	CARBO-HYDRATES (GRAMS)	FATS (GRAMS)	SODIUM (MG)
Burger Chef Hamburger	258	26	39	31	962
Burger King French Fries	214	3	28	10	5
Burger King Vanilla Shake	332	11	50	11	159
Burger King Whaler	486	18	64	46	735
Burger King Whopper	606	29	51	32	909
Dairy Queen Banana Split	540	10	91	15	N.A.*
Dairy Queen Cheese Dog	330	15	24	19	N.A.*
Dairy Queen Onion Rings	300	6	33	17	N.A.*
Kentucky Fried Chicken Extra Crispy Dinner (3 pieces)	950	52	63	54	1915
Kentucky Fried Chicken Original Recipe Dinner	830	52	56	46	2285
Long John Silver's Fish (2 pieces)	318	19	19	19	N.A.*
McDonald's Apple Pie	300	2	31	19	414
McDonald's Big Mac	541	26	39	31	962
McDonald's Chocolate Shake	364	11	60	9	329
McDonald's Egg McMuffin	352	18	26	20	914
McDonald's Filet-o-Fish	402	15	34	23	709
Pizza Hut Thick 'n Chewy Pepperoni Pizza (1/2 of 10-inch pie)	560	31	68	18	N.A.*
Pizza Hut Thin 'n Crispy Cheese Pizza (1/2 of 10-inch pie)	450	25	54	15	N.A.*
Taco Bell Taco	186	15	14	8	79
Arthur Treacher's Coleslaw	123	1	11	8	266
Arthur Treacher's Fish Sandwich	440	16	39	24	836

Source: Data supplied by the above companies to the Senate Select Committee on Nutrition and Human Needs.   *N.A.—not available.

Fast foods. Fast food, available nearly everywhere, and processed or convenience foods, steadily growing in number and variety, have had a profound effect on the eating habits of millions of Americans. Many of these foods can be thought of as junk foods—soft drinks, snack foods, candies—which contain nothing more than so-called empty calories, offering a high sugar content with no nutritional value. While meals of such foods can hardly be considered balanced, a number of experts think they are better than one might be led to believe. Fast foods contain ample amounts of protein; for example, a burger, fries, and a shake supply 42 percent of the recommended daily allowance for protein.

Except for drinks and desserts, fast-food meals contain little sugar. However, it would be well to choose milk or fruit juice rather than the typical fast-food shake, which may have from 8 to 14 teaspoons of sugar in it. Considering the nutritional value they offer, however, fast foods are laden with too many calories. A Kentucky Fried Chicken Dinner, for example, with a 12-ounce soft drink, may amount to about 1100 calories, or more than half the daily calorie needs for many individuals. Further, fast foods on the whole contain too much fat, mostly in the cheese, the sauce added to burgers—the meat is generally rather lean—the deep-fried potatoes, and the shakes, which are made with vegetable oils.

Fast foods are lacking in fiber and in vitamins A and C. It is a good idea, therefore, to include fruit, salad, a green or yellow vegetable, and whole or enriched grains in other meals on days when a fast-food meal has been eaten. Most fast foods are extremely high in sodium: a typical meal may contain as much as three-fourths of the daily recommended intake (about 2200 milligrams a day). Those on a restricted salt diet had best eat burgers plain, without pickles, and use no salt on French fries. The information in the following chart can help diners intending to eat fast foods.

Exercise

Moderate and regular exercise offers benefits: a feeling of well-being, with increased self-confidence and reduced irritability and fatigue. Above all, research studies have shown a person who exercises becomes noticeably healthier.

For example, the more physically active a person is, the lower the risk of suffering a heart attack. Continued physical activity throughout life helps ward off osteoporosis, a leading cause of disability in people past 50. Exercise can also help relieve anxiety and tension found in high-pressure work or in difficult life circumstances.

In weight control, exercise offers a double benefit: it not only uses up calories directly, but extra calories continue to be burned up by the body up to 15 hours after the exercise. Any type of exercise, including the doing of house chores or a repair job, or weeding in the garden, can help control weight. The more activity, the greater the number of calories expended. In general, exercise decreases appetite, helping the body to readjust food intake to energy expenditure.

EXERCISE
Energy Expenditures

This table gives approximate energy expenditures by a 150-pound person in performing various activities

ACTIVITY	CALORIES PER HOUR
Bicycling, 5½ mph	210
Bicycling, 13 mph	660
Bowling	270
Domestic work	180
Driving an automobile	120
Gardening	220
Golf	250
Lawn mowing	250
Roller skating	350
Running, 10 mph	900
Sitting	100
Skiing, 10 mph	600
Sleeping	80
Square dancing	350
Squash and handball	600
Standing	140
Swimming (moderate speed)	300
Tennis	420
Volleyball	350
Walking, 2½ mph	210
Walking, 3¾ mph	300
Wood chopping or sawing	400

Source: Material prepared by Robert E. Johnson, M.D., Ph. D., and colleagues, University of Illinois.

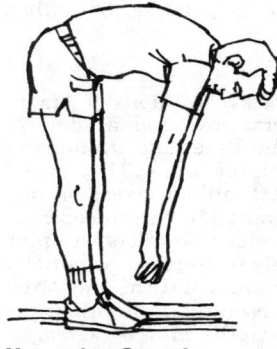
Hamstring Stretch

Side Stretch

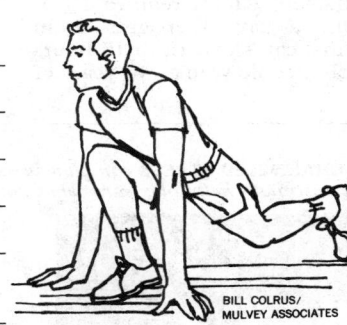
Leg Stretch

BILL COLRUS/ MULVEY ASSOCIATES

FRANCINE KEERY/LEO DE WYS

STAYING FIT *and maintaining body weight depends in great part on regular exercise, proper foods, and regulated caloric intake. The greater the physical activity, the greater the caloric expenditure. Stretching exercises, done slowly and gently, help to keep the body flexible. For maximum benefit, start off a walking program slowly, too.*

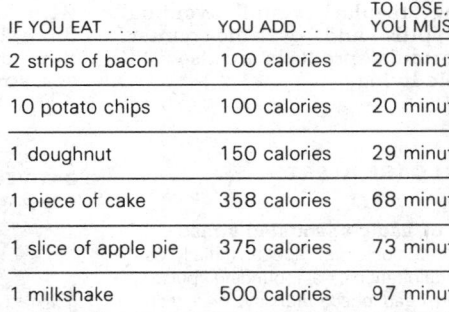

IF YOU EAT . . .	YOU ADD . . .	TO LOSE, YOU MUST WALK
2 strips of bacon	100 calories	20 minutes
10 potato chips	100 calories	20 minutes
1 doughnut	150 calories	29 minutes
1 piece of cake	358 calories	68 minutes
1 slice of apple pie	375 calories	73 minutes
1 milkshake	500 calories	97 minutes

Choice of exercise depends on a number of factors: age, physical condition, body build, capabilities, and manner of living. Thus, before plunging into physical activity, it is wise to make certain that one's body is in condition to undertake the contemplated exercise program. It is advisable for anyone with a chronic health problem, or anyone over 35 and long inactive, to have medical advice before launching an exercise program.

Walking is considered by many health authorities to be the best overall nonstrenuous activity for the heart and legs. A brisk walk lasting 20 to 30 minutes each day can help take weight off and keep it off. Walking, cross-country skiing, swimming, running, and bicycling are aerobic exercises, so-called because they increase the demand for oxygen for prolonged periods. Such physical activity strengthens the heart and lungs, and increases muscular endurance. It has been determined that aerobic exercise, when combined with a healthful diet, is probably the most effective way to lose weight. Calistenics and gymnastics improve strength, agility, and muscle tone. To be of utmost benefit, any exercise program must be done regularly, and this is more likely to happen if the activity is enjoyed.

Stretching exercises. Stretching exercises improve flexibility. Ten to 15 minutes a day of stretches can benefit both body and mind, reduce muscle tension, improve coordination, and promote circulation. After exercising for a while, there is a tendency for muscles to shorten. For this reason, such activity should be followed by gentle exercises that relax and stretch the muscles. If this is not done, the shortened muscles are more likely to go into muscle spasm, a common cause of post-exercise stiffness.

Stress

Stress is an unavoidable part of life, and people react differently to it: some thrive on stress, feeling motivated under pressure to do their best; others feel thwarted by the smallest obstacle in their path.

Turning stress into positive energy.

There are many ways of dealing with stress; some work better for some people than for others. Those who resort to the use of tranquilizers, sleeping pills, alcohol and cigarettes will probably add to their health problems. Overall, it is agreed that everyone should be familiar with a variety of stress-reducing techniques, such as the following:

Setting priorities. It is best to do essential tasks and forget about trivial matters. It is best to do as good a job as can be done in given circumstances, even if the job is not perfect. It is best to learn how to say no when demands on one's time are impossible to meet.

Learning to relax. It is advisable to take up a hobby. Deep breathing exercises are an excellent means of relaxation. Short breaks during the day, brief changes of pace, and regular vacations provide a beneficial effect.

Living sensibly. Regular, well-balanced meals with plenty of high-energy foods such as whole grains, fruits, and vegetables are part of sensible living, as is moderation in coffee or alcohol intake. Keeping physically fit; exercising regularly, and avoiding sleeping pills and over-the-counter "stress formula" products are also part of sensible living.

Getting moral support. A burdensome problem can be talked out with a trusted friend or relative, or with a professional.

Better sleep. Millions of Americans are victims of insomnia, some 25 million all the time, and millions of others part of the time. They spend well over $100 million a year on prescription sleeping pills. In the opinion of experts on sleep disorders, sleeping pills are largely ineffective, potentially dangerous to one's health, and often the cause of insomnia rather than the cure. Sleeping pills may be a *temporary* solution at a time of unusual stress, such as following the death of a loved one. Underlying medical problems, on the other hand (for example, asthma, ulcers, arthritis, migraine), psychological problems (most commonly anxiety and depression), and behavioral problems (excessive intake of harmful substances) should first be diagnosed and then specific treatment should be instituted.

People differ greatly in the amount of sleep they usually get. Some appear to need only 4 to 5 hours a night, while others may need 8 hours or more. It remains for each person to decide how much sleep is needed. If one is well rested and ready to face the day ahead after 5 hours of sleep, then that is the correct amount for that person. If 7 hours of sleep are needed to function properly, then that is the right amount. As most people grow older, they appear to be able to get along with less sleep. Babies require 18 or more hours a day. Teenagers, from time to time, can sleep 12 to 15 hours at a stretch. People who at 40 years of age appear to need 8 hours of sleep may require only 7 hours at age 50, and only 6 hours at age 60. If one occasionally has less than the usual amount of sleep, there is generally nothing to worry about. It has been shown repeatedly that people can usually function quite well for short periods of time on a limited amount of sleep, even 3 or 4 hours. Chronic sleeplessness is an annoying problem, but many insomniacs have found welcome relief through observing some simple strategies.

Retiring at regular hours. The body functions best when it establishes rhythms: a time to eat, a time to exercise, a time to relax, and a time to go to bed.

Peace of mind. Problems of work, finances, family, etc., have no place in bed. Pleasant relaxing thoughts help one fall asleep.

Bedroom comfort. The bedroom should be dark. For some people, the quieter the room the better; others may prefer some sound, perhaps a radio at low volume, tuned to soothing music or monotonous talk. Of course, a comfortable bed with a mattress of the degree of desired firmness is also conducive to good sleep.

Exercise. Studies have shown that exercising in the late afternoon seems to improve sleep more than exercising in the morning. Exercise appears to increase the depth of sleep, if not necessarily the amount.

Bedtime snacks. Some people find a cup of herb tea or a glass of warm milk relaxing at bedtime. Others have a little snack, such as a cup of ice cream. However, there can only be ill effects from the use of too much tea or coffee, or from indigestible food.

HEALTH CARE ALERT
Stress

Signals of badly channeled stress

- Stress reactions may appear initially as heart palpitations, a pounding pulse, nagging headache, irritability, or a feeling of tightness in the chest, neck, or shoulders.
- Other early symptoms may be difficulty in falling asleep, back pain, upset stomach, loss of appetite, lack of concentration, or general fatigue.
- With increased stress, the reactions intensify and signal greater damage to the body. A person may find it impossible to unwind or enjoy physical relaxation, become impatient or depressed, do more drinking or smoking than usual, spend sleepless nights, or have frequent headaches and stomach disturbances.
- If negatively channeled stress continues for a long time, the accumulated effects may contribute to such serious ailments as asthma, heart disease, migraine headaches, high blood pressure, stomach ulcers, alcoholism, and drug addiction.

NEGATIVELY CHANNELED STRESS *can play havoc with the emotions, and even cause illness. Setting priorities straight helps one learn what not to worry about and how to cope.*

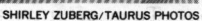

SHIRLEY ZUBERG/TAURUS PHOTOS

LEO DE WYS

Health Problems

Decisions for health. Taking responsibility for one's own health can help ensure better health for the entire family. This means not only knowing the preventive measures to be taken in maintaining health, but also the steps to be taken when serious illness strikes, or an accident or other emergency arises. Despite every effort to prevent emergencies, they can and do happen. It is wise to be prepared to deal with an emergency situation, whether it involves calling a doctor, poison control center, hospital, ambulance, or for other assistance.

A wise first step is to select a family doctor and other health professionals while in good health. A list of names can be obtained by calling the nearest hospital or medical school, or by checking with a local pharmacist or reliable friends or neighbors. One should also become familiar with services available at local and state health departments, and with information available from local and state medical societies. Community and social services, such as a visiting nurse or homemaker's service, are usually found in the local telephone book. A list of these numbers should be kept with other important telephone numbers.

Everyone needs a primary care physician or internist for supervision of family health care. It is wise to check

EMERGENCY CARE *can be speeded with the medical information on this card.*

a doctor's credentials thoroughly, making certain that he or she is board certified, which means the doctor has completed specialty training and passed specialty examinations. Not every medical doctor qualifies: of the 500,000 licensed physicians in the United States, only 62,000 are certified in family practice.

Besides primary care physicians, there are two other licensed branches of health care in this country: doctors of osteopathy, and doctors of chiropractic. Osteopaths, recognized as fully licensed physicians, place particular emphasis on a manual technique that involves examination of subtle changes in muscles and bones. Chiropractors, who cannot prescribe

medicine or perform surgery, rely entirely on a system of manipulative treatment of body disorders. A doctor's receptionist or office nurse can give information about the doctor's credentials, as well as describe such practical matters as office hours, routine appointments, and fee schedules. All these things should influence one's final selection of a doctor.

Other alternatives for health care include group-practice arrangements, in which there may be two or more family practitioners and certain specialists, and Health Maintenance Organizations (HMOs). In general, HMOs offer a wide range of services in preventive health and medical care for groups of people who enroll voluntarily. To obtain the desired quality of medical care, it is wise to consider the benefits and costs of each service before making a final decision. Regardless of choice, it is important to realize that a satisfactory association between an individual and a doctor depends on clear communication. Before a visit, it is useful to write down questions to ask. During examinations, be specific about symptoms. Information of any kind that will help the doctor make a proper diagnosis should not be withheld. If asked, the doctor will give a full explanation of any medical question that needs clarification.

Radiology and disease. It is worthwhile to learn as much as one can about the value and possible hazards of x-ray equipment used in medical diagnosis and treatment. X-rays are waves of energy that radiate constantly through the environment, in the same way as beams of microwaves and visible light. The essential difference is the wave frequency. At one end of the radiation spectrum is visible light, which is low frequency; at the other end are x-rays, which are high frequency. The latter kind of radiation is called ionizing radiation. Scientists measure radiation in the amount of energy an organism absorbs in terms of rads (radiation absorbed doses) and millirads, or mrads (1/1000th of a rad). Everyone in the United States is exposed to radiation from natural sources, such as from cosmic rays and radioactive elements in rocks and soil, amounting to an average of about 100 mrads a year, and to radiation from manmade sources such as uranium or thorium in brick houses, and radium or tritium in wrist watches.

Most people obtain the greatest amount of radiation exposure from x-rays, since about three-fourths of Americans have at least one x-ray examination a year. An ordinary chest x-ray needs about 30 mrads to reveal abnormalities, and a single dental x-ray requires 300 mrads to obtain a good look at fine tooth structure. Chest x-rays are no longer performed routinely. The American College of Radiology recommends that a chest x-ray be taken only when indicated by a person's history or by physical examination or risk group (for example, many doctors advise heavy smokers to have annual chest x-rays).

Many radiologists agree that no dose of radiation can be considered to be absolutely safe. With this in mind, the trend is toward using lower doses of radiation, and toward using methods other than x-rays to view the inside of the body. For example, ultrasound equipment uses high-frequency sonar waves to create an image. It now is being used almost routinely in obstetrics and gynecology and it is finding regular application in some other areas of medicine. Magnetic resonance imaging (MRI) is a preferred method of imaging in the detection of certain forms of brain and spinal disorders, including multiple sclerosis. Improved mammography (breast examination with x-ray imaging) has made possible the use of greatly reduced radiation doses penetrating the breasts. A single mammogram now exposes a woman to less than one rad. Microdose digital radiography (DR) uses computers to enhance the images obtained, thus requiring only a fraction of the conventional exposure. It was found at one health center that only one-hundredth to one-thousandth of the usual x-ray dose is required to obtain sharp images (for example, only two mrads for abdominal examinations that use 700 to 1000 mrads of the conventional abdominal x-rays).

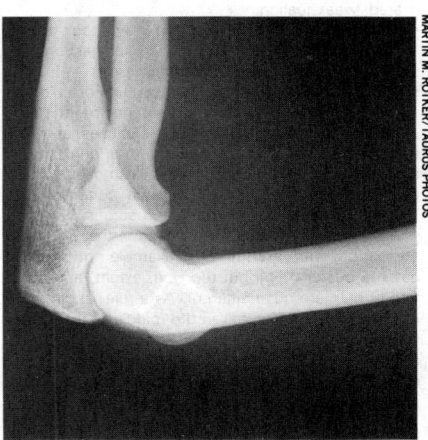

X-RAYS *are important as diagnostic tools and in treatment of certain diseases. They should, however, be administered with caution. This x-ray clearly shows the bones forming the human elbow.*

Monthly breast self-examination

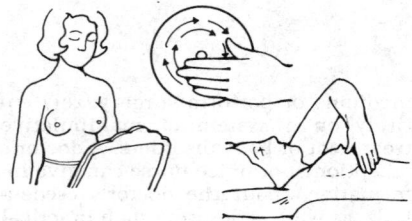

Lumps are not the only warning sign of breast cancer. Women, in examining their breasts once a month, should also note changes in breast color or contour, dimpling of the skin, scaliness (especially around the nipple), and discharges. These changes, as with a lump or thickening, may not necessarily be signs of malignancy, but they should be checked promptly.

1. With fingers flat and together, every part of both breasts is massaged in a circular motion, and checked for lumps, hard knots, or thickening.
2. The breasts should be examined while the woman is standing before a mirror, with hands on hips and muscles tensed.
3. The arms should then be raised above the head, and breasts checked for dimpling or changes in shape.
4. While lying on the back, with a pillow under the right shoulder and the right hand behind the head, each breast in turn should be pressed gently with the flat of the fingers. This is done first all around the outside in a clockwise direction, then in several small circles, ending at the nipple area.
6. Each nipple should be pressed gently to determine whether discharge results.

HEALTH CARE ALERT
Heart Attack

A key signal: chest pain

In a heart attack, pain may range from a feeling of slight pressure in the chest to a crushing sensation behind the breastbone. It may radiate to shoulder, neck, or arms.

- Pain generally lasts for hours.
- Pain does not respond to rest or nitroglycerin.
- Face turns ashen gray, and cold sweat appears. There may also be shortness of breath and a nauseated, weak feeling.
- Retching, belching, or vomiting may occur, which can be confused with an attack of indigestion.
- Pain responds only to a narcotic drug.
- **Act promptly:** call for medical help or take victim to the nearest hospital emergency room.

Chest pain may be due to various causes, some of a minor nature, such as chewing gum or drinking too much carbonated water, or excessive smoking. Chest pain may also be caused by such conditions as bruised or fractured ribs or angina pectoris.

Angina is similar to a heart attack in that it usually comes on with exertion (for example, running to catch a bus or train), but the type, extent, and duration of pain are quite different. As a rule, angina is a constrictive sensation felt in the middle of the chest, often radiating to the left arm. In contrast to a heart attack, pain usually lasts only a few minutes and responds quickly to rest as well as to ingestion of a nitroglycerin tablet.

Cancer.
Current statistics indicate that one in four Americans will have some form of cancer during his or her lifetime. The incidence rate for blacks is higher than for whites, and blacks have a higher death rate than whites as a result of this disease. Cancer may develop at any age, but it strikes more often with advancing age. The incidence of colon cancer, for example, rises considerably after age 40, and peaks around age 75. Cancer at present is not considered to be a single disease with a single cause, curable or preventable by a specific vaccine, drug, or diet. Knowledge gained from a vast amount of research has shown that cancer may be as many as 120 different diseases, each with its own complex causes—anything from radiation to toxic chemicals in the food chain.

In cancer certain cells begin a process of uncontrollable growth and spread. These abnormal cells divide and redivide until they grow into masses of tissue called tumors. Some tumors are said to be benign: they may interfere with body function and require surgical treatment, but they are usually localized and seldom pose a threat to life. Tumors that are said to be malignant (cancerous) invade and destroy normal tissue. They may also metastasize, that is, spread to other parts of the body via the blood or lymph systems, where they form new growths. If the original tumor is not completely removed by surgery before metastasis occurs, the cancer becomes advanced and may prove fatal. It is this tendency of cancer to spread throughout the body that makes early detection so important.

Many experts believe that most people develop cancer primarily through repeated and prolonged contact with carcinogens (cancer-causing agents), such as sunlight, x-rays, tobacco smoke, and chemicals, manmade as well as natural, that are found in small quantities in air, water, food, and the workplace. About 30 agents have been identified as human carcinogens on the basis of population studies. For example, studies of people who had long been exposed to tobacco smoke or asbestos found a higher occurrence of cancer of the lungs and other organs than in unexposed people. Many such cancers are believed to be preventable. In other types of cancer, early diagnosis and prompt treatment may greatly improve the outlook for survival. X-rays, radioactive substances, chemicals, hormones, immunotherapy, and surgery are the current measures available for the treatment of cancer. Management of the treatment will differ from individual to individual, and highly sophisticated diagnostic and treatment procedures have been shown to improve the statistical averages. Leukemia, especially childhood leukemia, was an insidious form of cancer just a generation ago, but it is now highly treatable. Another outstanding example is the improved management of Hodgkin's disease, a cancer of lymph glands, resulting in an increase in survival rates from 68 to 90 percent in early cases and from 10 to 70 percent in advanced cases. Deaths from uterine cancer have decreased by more than 70 percent since 1940. In large part, these encouraging statistics have come about by early detection and the use of research-developed treatment.

Heart disease.
More than 17 million Americans, or about 7 percent of the population, have some form of heart damage or disease. There are three major types of heart disease, the most common being atherosclerosis, which leads to heart attack. In this disease, there is progressive hardening of the arteries, including the coronary arteries, the blood vessels that surround and nourish the heart. It is believed that atherosclerosis begins early in life, and it is found present at death in about half of all Americans. While the cause is unknown, it is understood that the build-up of plaque (composed of fatty substances) in a blood vessel causes the artery walls to harden and thicken. The passage gradually narrows, and blood flow to the heart is restricted, and in time completely blocked. This blockage is known as myocardial infarction, commonly referred to as heart attack (see Health care alert, page 935). When this happens, a part of the heart muscle loses its nourishing supply of blood and dies. A similar situation is created when blood platelets cling to fat deposits and form a clot that eventually cuts off blood supply. If enough muscle dies, the output of the heart is greatly reduced and, unless prompt medical attention is given, the patient dies. Even when small areas of the muscle die, there may be serious consequences. The electrical signals that ensure normal pumping become altered: the heart may begin to fibrillate (twitch uncontrollably); if this happens in the ventricles, the heart no longer pumps enough blood to sustain life.

Cardiomyopathy is a disease of the heart muscle itself. In this disease, the heart is weakened and tries to compensate for its impaired pumping action by growing larger and larger. Damage to the heart increases. There is also increasing danger of clotting and cardiac arrhythmia, a disturbance in the function of the heart's electrical system. Frequently, a patient with cardiomyopathy is a candidate for a heart transplant.

A third major form of heart disease involves damage to the heart valves as a result of infection or a congenital defect. A strep throat infection, untreated or improperly treated, can pave the way for rheumatic fever, which may result in damage to the heart valves. Despite the fact that rheumatic fever is well controlled in the United States, the disease is responsible for 7000 deaths each year. Congenital heart defects claim an equal number of victims; however, only a certain number of the 25,000 babies born yearly with heart defects have damaged valves. One known cause for abnormal heart development in a child is German measles incurred by the mother early in pregnancy.

Hypertension.
Hypertension, or high blood pressure, affects an estimated 55 to 60 million Americans, about half of whom are unaware of their condition. In the early stages of the disease, most people are able to go about their daily duties as usual. Because there is no pain or discomfort, hypertension has been called the silent killer. Yet it is a prime factor in the 1.5 million heart attacks occurring each year, and the major cause of stroke, which annually claims 160,000 lives. In hypertension, the arterioles, or small arteries, become constricted, slowing down blood

flow and making the heart work harder. This increases the pressure of blood against the artery walls. As a result, the blood vessels may be damaged, leading to atherosclerosis or enlargement of the heart. The kidneys, finding it impossible to function under the increased pressure, cease to filter out waste products from the blood, and there is a potential for serious renal impairment. Visual disturbances, and even blindness, can develop as tiny retinal arteries swell up and hemorrhage.

In about 10 percent of cases, the cause of hypertension is determinable (for example, kidney abnormalities and brain tumor). More than half of the people who fall into the other 90 percent category have a family history of high blood pressure. Other risk factors are age, as shown by an increased incidence rate after 65, and race. Various studies indicate that blacks are more susceptible, and at an earlier age, than whites. Smokers have been shown to have a 70 percent greater chance of succumbing to a heart attack than nonsmokers. Populations that consume foods low in sodium and high in potassium have been found to maintain a lower blood pressure than those who have a high sodium intake. Being overweight and not exercising can have deleterious effects on health in general, and on certain organs, such as the heart, in particular. There is no cure for high blood pressure, but in a majority of cases it can be controlled through reduction of such risk factors as smoking, stress, lack of exercise, overweight, and dietary inadequacies. Periodic medical check-ups may provide early detection of hypertension.

Living with high blood pressure

1. Smoking, especially cigarette smoking, should be stopped.
2. Regular exercise should be taken, and weight should be controlled.
3. Excessive use of salt and stimulants should be eliminated.
4. Undue stress and overexertion should be avoided.
5. Regular rest and relaxation should be obtained.

Diabetes mellitus.   Diabetes and its complications afflict about 11 million Americans, about half of whom do not know they have the disease. Symptoms are often nonexistent or undramatic in appearance, suggesting no reason to consult a physician until a complication arises. Such complications are often more serious than diabetic coma or insulin shock. For example, diabetic retinopathy, a complication occurring with some frequency, is the leading cause of blindness in people between 45 and 65. Victims of diabetes may develop circulatory and kidney problems; diabetic women may not carry their babies to term; and men may become impotent.

In Type I diabetes, the insulin-dependent or juvenile type, the disease may start at any age, although it is generally first noted during childhood or early adolescence. In this type of diabetes, the body stops producing insulin and, with a few possible exceptions, all Type I diabetics need insulin injections in order to live. In Type II diabetes, the noninsulin-dependent or adult-onset type, the body still produces some insulin, which may even be present in above normal levels. However, body tissues may not be able to utilize the insulin properly, a condition termed insulin resistance. Why or how this happens is not known, although it seems that too much or too little insulin production contributes to this condition. In general, Type II diabetics can control their disease by diet alone or with the addition of oral drugs. Any type of diabetes interferes with the ability of the body to utilize sufficient insulin, the hormone produced in the pancreas that enables body cells to take up and use glucose (sugar) for energy. If there is too little or no insulin, or if the body cannot react to an appropriate insulin level, then the cells will not obtain sufficient glucose and will starve for nourishment even though there is a high blood sugar level. This state is called hyperglycemia and it is a typical sign of diabetes, as is glycosuria, the spilling of unused sugar into the urine.

A family history of diabetes (no matter which relative has had the disease) puts an individual at high risk. Other risk factors in Type II diabetes include obesity (80 to 90 percent of the victims are overweight), being 40 or older (40 percent of diabetic Americans are over 65), and sex (females develop diabetes twice as much as males). People with Type II diabetes often experience none of the usual symptoms of diabetes. They may, however, develop such symptoms are recurring infections of the gums, skin, or urinary tract; blurred vision; pain or cramps in the extremities; or intense itching, drowsiness, and fatigue. Today, diabetes can be controlled to curb its symptoms and reduce its complications. A diabetic can live a fuller, longer, and more nearly normal life than was possible before the availability of a wide range of insulins and oral drugs.

HEALTH CARE ALERT
Diabetes

It has been estimated that 5 million Americans do not know they have diabetes. Undiagnosed, they remain untreated. Heeding the warning signs given below can lead to early detection and appropriate medical treatment.

The four most important symptoms of diabetes are:
1. Frequent, copious urination.
2. Abnormal thirst.
3. Rapid weight loss.
4. Weakness and tiredness.

Other symptoms include:
5. Drowsiness and fatigue.
6. Increased appetite; craving for sweets.
7. Itching of the skin, particularly in the genital area.
8. Disturbances of vision (for example, blurring).
9. Irritability, nervousness, or nausea.
10. Skin disorders such as boils, carbuncles, and infections.

Alcoholism.   The mounting statistics on alcoholism make clear the gravity of this affliction. Many physicians and health experts regard alcoholism as the most urgent health problem in the United States, a view borne out by current estimates of 10 million adult alcoholics and 3.3 million teenage alcoholics. It is considered that one out of ten people who drink will become alcoholic, with almost half being women drinkers. For every alcoholic, the lives of at least four or five other persons are affected. Children of alcoholics are more likely to develop alcoholism than children of people who do not drink. It has also been observed that alcohol abusers having alcoholic relatives are two to three times more likely to have such well-defined symptoms of alcoholism as blackouts and drinking in the morning.

Alcohol is involved in half of the family dispute cases that are handled by the police. Twenty to 30 percent of first admissions in state mental hospitals are for alcoholism, and every day about 30 percent of adult patients in American hospitals are likely to have alcohol-related problems. In addition to inflammation of the liver and pancreas, the alcoholic is in danger of incurring other major health problems: anemia, vitamin deficiencies, digestive disorders, pneumonia, and impotence. Although a 1982 Gallup poll showed that 79 percent of Americans considered alcoholism to be a disease, they still pictured the alcoholic as a skid row derelict, although no more than 5 percent of alcoholics are derelicts. Alcoholism remains a baffling affliction for which no specific cause has yet been found. Researchers approach the problem of alcoholism as multifaceted, organizing it into three areas: biological, how alcohol affects the body; psychological, how alcohol affects behavior; and sociological, how alcohol is provided and consumed in society. From a biological standpoint, it is fairly clear that what goes on inside the body of an alcoholic differs from that of the rest of the population. It may be that research, for example, blood chemistry analysis, will help find methods for the early intervention and possible prevention of this disease.

Some warning signs of alcoholism

1. Drinking increasing amounts of alcohol and becoming intoxicated often.
2. Being preoccupied with drinking, to the exclusion of other activities.
3. Making promises to quit but breaking them.
4. Being unable to remember what was said or done while drinking.
5. Experiencing personality changes.
6. Denying, hiding, or making excuses for drinking.
7. Beginning to drink alone, in the morning, or before a party.
8. Refusing to admit excessive drinking and becoming angry if the subject is raised.
9. Beginning to have trouble at work. Arriving late or missing work altogether.
10. Changing jobs frequently, usually a demotion rather than a promotion.
11. Losing interest in personal appearance or hygiene.
12. Suffering from poor health, with loss of appetite, respiratory infections, or nervousness.
13. Suffering marital and economic hardships.

HEALTH CARE ALERT
Osteoporosis

Research has shown that various risk factors contribute to development of osteoporosis: white women, especially those with a small thin frame, women who have had an early menopause, and people with a family history of osteoporosis are at high risk. Recommendations to help minimize risk factors include the following:

1. The daily diet should include sufficient calcium and Vitamin D.
2. Regular exercise should be obtained.
3. Alcohol, coffee, and soft drinks should be used in moderate amounts.
4. Smoking should be avoided.
5. For those on medication, it is important to check with one's physician to make certain the medication (for example, cortisone and some laxatives) will not interfere with calcium absorption.

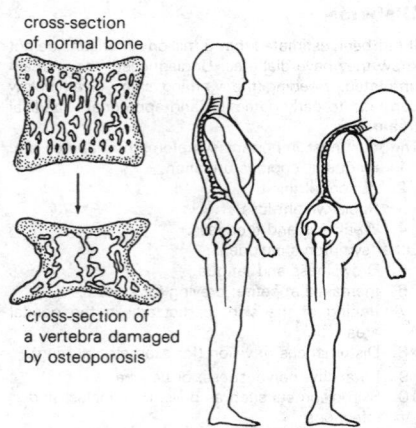

cross-section
of normal bone

cross-section of
a vertebra damaged
by osteoporosis

Osteoporosis.

Osteoporosis is the twelfth leading cause of death in the United States, affecting 15 to 20 million Americans, white women primarily. It is a principal reason for nursing home admissions and currently accounts for an annual medical expenditure of billions of dollars. Osteoporosis exists to some degree in almost half of all American women over 45; it is a major cause of spinal fractures in one out of four women over age 60. By 60, almost 40 percent of American women have lost all their teeth due in part to bone loss in the jaw. Beyond 65, one out of three women can expect to incur hip fractures because of osteoporosis. Men are not generally immune, but it is estimated by medical authorities that only one in ten cases of the disease affect men.

In osteoporosis there is a thinning and softening of the bones, making them more susceptible to fracture. Calcium is consistently being added to the bones by bone-building cells; it is then reabsorbed by bone-dismantling cells. Usually, this dynamic process continues unchanged until, at age 30 or 35, both men and women begin to lose bone. Women are the chief sufferers, especially those who have had many children and have breast-fed them without replenishing the supply of dietary calcium. Women are also subject to a hormonally related osteoporosis after the menopause, when estrogen levels diminish. Recent findings by the National Institutes of Health indicate that an increase in dietary calcium to 1000 to 1500 mg daily will reduce the incidence of osteoporosis in postmenopausal women. Men, having more bone to begin with, are not found to experience bone loss as rapidly. However, increased calcium may also be helpful in preventing bone disease in men. Black women, apparently having denser bone, are found by physicians less likely to be afflicted.

Good food sources of calcium include dairy products, canned sardines and salmon, and oysters; also broccoli, kale, and mustard and turnip greens. Coffee, meat, salt, alcohol, and soft drinks should be used in moderation because they block calcium absorption. If dietary calcium cannot supply a daily amount of 1000 to 1500 mg, experts suggest taking a calcium supplement in the form of calcium carbonate, calcium lactate, or calcium gluconate.

Osteoporosis is a subtle disease, a debilitating process that may go on for 20 to 30 years before it is diagnosed by an x-ray for an unrelated problem; or it may appear without warning or trauma: a woman may feel dizzy, fall, and break one or more bones. Often, these are compression fractures, pressing together spinal vertebrae, which eventually cause the victim to shrink in size, and possibly develop painful curvature of the upper spine, called dowager's hump. Unfortunately, irreversible bone loss is an especially serious problem because standard x-rays can distinguish bone loss of only 30 percent or more. More reliable, sophisticated techniques are becoming available, including a device called the dual photon absorptiometer, which is an x-ray-like mechanism that measures bone density, using extremely low levels of radiation. Such new techniques may make possible detection of bone loss of only 2 to 7 percent. Researchers believe that bone health can be promoted with a properly conceived regimen of good nutrition, regular exercise, and sound medical therapy.

Side effects of cocaine abuse

In addition to the brief pleasurable effects produced by cocaine, users can expect to experience any of a number of unpleasant side effects. For long-term users of cocaine, or for those who inject cocaine in solution or smoke crack, the toxic effects of cocaine are especially severe. Among the chief side effects are:

1. Irritation or ulceration of nasal membranes if cocaine is taken by sniffing.
2. Digestive problems.
3. Weight loss.
4. Sleeplessness.
5. Inability to concentrate on work, studies, or everyday tasks.
6. Mood changes. Feelings of anxiety, irritability, or depression.
7. Hallucinations.
8. Paranoia.
9. Cardiac or respiratory failure from drug overdose.

Drug abuse.

For decades, the misuse of alcohol, prescription drugs, and over-the-counter drug preparations has been a serious problem. In recent years, however, this type of drug abuse has been dwarfed by a surge in the use of illegal substances such as heroin, cocaine, and synthetic drugs. The most commonly used of these is heroin, which is physically and psychologically addicting. It is estimated that some 90 percent of the drug addicts in the United States are heroin addicts. In addition to the devastating cumulative effects of heroin use, such addicts face the risk of contracting serious diseases when, in the process of getting a "fix" by injection, they use unsterile needles or share needles with other addicts. The biggest danger is that of contracting AIDS—Acquired Immune Deficiency Syndrome—a disease that destroys the immune system, the body's natural defense against disease and infection. There is no known cure for AIDS, which is ultimately fatal.

The use of cocaine, a stimulant that produces a sense of euphoria, has risen to epidemic proportions in the 1980's. Out of the estimated 20 million Americans who have tried cocaine, it is thought that about 5 million are habitual users. Cocaine, a white, crystalline powder, is refined from the coca plant, which is grown in Peru, Bolivia, and other countries. After the coca crop has been harvested and processed, it usually is shipped to Colombia and there refined into cocaine. Virtually all the cocaine shipped to the United States comes from South America by way of Florida and the U.S.–Mexican border.

Cocaine users commonly sniff—or snort—the powder, which is absorbed by the mucous membranes in the nostrils. Cocaine also can be taken by injection. Cocaine injections magnify the drug's toxicity and can cause death.

A new form of cocaine, called crack, made its appearance about 1983. Crack is highly refined, highly addictive, and easily obtainable. A dose of crack looks like a tiny white crystalline ball and generally is sold by dealers in a small plastic vial. Users smoke the crack to attain an intense but extremely brief sense of euphoria. Virtually all crack users become psychologically dependent on the drug. Like most heavy cocaine users, those who use crack soon focus all their energies on buying the drug and getting high.

Perhaps the most insidious drugs available today are the so-called designer drugs, manufactured chemicals whose molecular structures closely resemble those of naturally occurring drugs. These drugs can produce the sense of euphoria associated with cocaine and other natural drugs, but they can also destroy a user's central nervous system. Victims can acquire symptoms similar to those of advanced Parkinson's disease, or they can be permanently paralyzed. Just one dose can make a user a prisoner for life within his or her own body, truly a fate worse than death.

Sexually transmitted diseases.

In the United States, the four leading sexually transmitted diseases (STDs) are chlamydia trachomatis, gonorrhea, genital herpes, and syphilis. Chlamydia trachomatis is a name unfamiliar to most people, yet it is the leading STD in this country: five times more common than gonorrhea, and 50 times more common than herpes. As many as 10 million Americans will contract the disease during 1985; up to 10 percent of all college students already have it. One reason for the growing incidence of chlamydia is that detection of symptoms may be difficult. In men, the symptoms may be mild; in women, there may be no symptoms. Unchecked chlamydia in men may not have permanent ill effects, but in women the disease can lead to sterility, tubal pregnancy, and premature or stillbirths.

Genital herpes is an infection of the genital skin and mucous membranes, marked by blisterlike lesions that erode and produce painful ulcers. In gonorrhea, most women have no symptoms; men generally experience a puslike urethral discharge and painful urination. Both gonorrhea and chlamydia often exist in a person at the same time. Syphilis has three phases: primary, secondary, and tertiary. The primary phase is characterized by a painless genital sore (chancre). In the secondary phase, the chancre disappears, and a rash generally develops. In the tertiary phase, years after the primary and secondary phases, untreated syphilis can cause brain or heart damage, or both, and may end in death.

Communicable disease.

Infection can only be conveyed by contact with the infecting organism. Direct contact means actually touching, or being touched by, the person having the infection or the natural source of the infection. Such contact also includes inhaling air exhaled by the person within a range of 3 feet or less. Indirect contact occurs mainly by means of contaminated vehicles of infection (food, clothing, etc.), air convection, and insects or animals.

Some communicable diseases

METHOD OF TRANSFER	DISEASE
Respiratory discharges (droplet infection) and/or contact	chicken pox, common cold, diphtheria, German measles (rubella), mumps, pneumonia/influenza, streptococcal sore throat, tuberculosis, whooping cough
Discharge from intestines (hence, often by contaminated soil/water)	cholera, dysentery (amoebic and bacillary), hookworm, paratyphoid fever, typhoid fever
Contaminated food or milk	botulism, cholera, food infections (salmonellosis), intestinal worms, streptococcal infections, tuberculosis, typhoid fever, undulant fever, anthrax, plague (for example, from rats), tularemia (for example, from rabbits), undulant fever (for example, from cows), sleeping sickness (tsetse fly), dengue and yellow fevers (mosquitoes), plague (rat-flea), typhus (louse), gonorrhea, syphilis
Intimate contact or, usually, sexual intercourse	gonorrhea, syphilis, herpes (genital)

Immunization schedule for children*

AGE	VACCINE
2 months	DTP (a combined inoculation for diphtheria, tetanus, and whooping cough): first dose. Oral polio (first dose).
4 months	DTP (second dose). Oral polio (second dose).
6 months	DTP (third dose).
15 months	Measles, rubella (German measles), mumps. These three may be given in a single injection.
18 months	DTP (fourth dose). Oral polio (third dose).
4 to 6 years	DTP (fifth dose). Oral polio (fourth dose).
14 to 16 years and every 10 years thereafter	Tetanus-diphtheria booster.

* Recommended by the Immunization Division of the Centers for Disease Control in Atlanta, a part of the United States Public Health Service.

Immunity to disease.

Within the last few decades, scientists have begun to understand the body's ingenious network of defense against infection and disease. The immune system, as presently understood, is a collection of organs, vessels, and circulating white blood cells, with the lymphocytes the principal agents in immune defense. The majority of these specialized cells are scavengers that devour foreign particles. Every second of the day, more than 200,000 lymphocytes are produced in the bone marrow, and an equal number grow old and are eliminated. For all its complexity and elaborate interconnections, the human immune system consists of relatively few basic components: a number of specialized cells and substances produced by cells. One such cell group, called phagocytes (cell eaters), is constantly on the alert for foreign cells. Phagocytes have the ability to engulf and destroy invading viruses, bacteria, fungi, protozoa, and helminths. But when the enemy is attacking in great numbers very quickly, phagocytes may be unable to keep up with the rapid cell destruction. They are then aided by more powerful white blood cells, called T lymphocytes or T cells, which are capable of identifying specific antigens (antibody producers) by their shape.

When an immune cell detects an invading antigen, a complex reaction is set in motion for destruction of the invader and protection of the body against further attack. Such a situation could begin with the piercing of the skin by a sharp object, permitting bacteria to pour in through the puncture. Or, it could begin with exposure of the body to substances to which the body is allergic—a particular food, pollen, or bee venom. In either case, the lymphocytes are alerted. Other situations might involve transfused blood or transplanted organs. The T cells, like all immune cells, form in the bone marrow and then travel to the thymus, where additional processing produces "killer" T cells, "helper" T cells, and "suppressor" T cells. The two helpers and suppressors interact with the B lymphocytes in the process of detecting and destroying foreign matter. B lymphocytes, also called B cells, are formed in the bone marrow. B cells produce chemical weapons, called antibodies. These complex proteins are constructed of amino acids and can neutralize and destroy a wide range of disease-producing microbes.

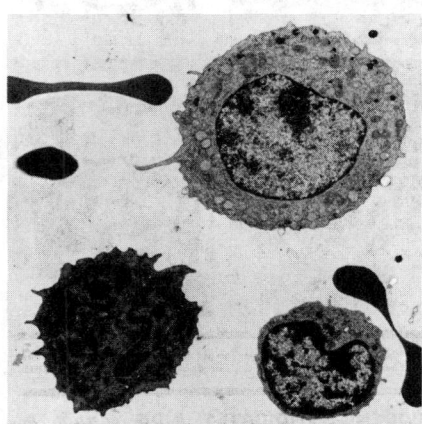

MARTIN M. ROTKER/TAURUS PHOTOS

LYMPHOCYTES RANGE IN SIZE *from an average of 10 to 12 microns to 20 microns in diameter.*

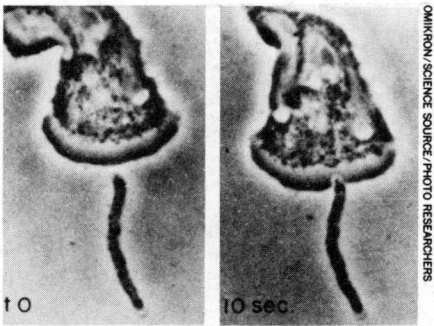

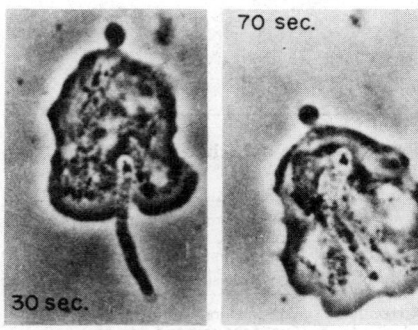

t 0

10 sec.

70 sec.

30 sec.

INGESTION/DIGESTION *of bacterium,* Bacillus megaterium, *by human white blood cell takes place in 70 seconds.*

Killer T cells and antibodies are the most potent weapons of the body against viral infection and against certain types of cancer cells. Killer T cells and antibodies are joined in the body's defense by yet another type of cell, the natural killer cell, about which very little is presently understood. Natural killer cells, killer T cells, and phagocytes constitute the body's major strategy of defense against disease: cellular immunity. In this form of immune response, immune cells are pitted against invading microorganisms in direct combat. The principal agents of humoral (derived from "humor," referring to any functioning fluid in the body) immunity are antibodies, also called immunoglobins.

Basically, the theory and method of all vaccines is the same: injection of either attenuated viruses (weakened or killed by chemical toxins) or inactivated viruses (live strains rendered harmless in the laboratory) into the body to trigger a response from the immune system. With injection of the viruses into the body, the process of infection begins, but because the injected viruses are attenuated or inactivated, they are far less virulent and therefore pose no real danger. The immune system, detecting the invaders, starts to produce active immune cells and circulating antibodies. After the viruses are destroyed, circulating memory cells are produced that render the body immune to subsequent attack against the same viruses (for example, injection with a rabies vaccine protects against other invasions of the rabies virus). The immune system goes into action whenever the circulating lymphocytes detect invading cells or material, for example, when bacteria enter the body through a skin cut, or when virus particles hidden in water droplets on the rim of a glass are swallowed and begin to multiply, or when one is subjected to substances to which the body is allergic.

In persons with autoimmune disease, the body's defense network turns protective forces against itself. Such diseases as multiple sclerosis, rheumatoid arthritis, myasthenia gravis, Hashimoto's disease, and systemic lupus erythematosus are among the diseases that are classified as autoimmune diseases. In each of these diseases, the immune system overresponds and attacks itself while invading bacteria and viruses or cancer cells. In multiple sclerosis, the immune system attacks tissues of the central nervous system; in rheumatoid arthritis, the tissues of the joints come under attack; in myastenia gravis, the voluntary muscles; in Hashimoto's disease, the thyroid gland; in systemic lupus erythematosus, the brain, kidneys, lungs, and joints may all be attacked and severely damaged.

Research immunologists the world over are engaged in studying the immune system in its parts, in its relationship to other body systems, and to the body as a whole. They are also exploring the potential of various substances, such as lymphokines (proteins secreted by immune cells) and immunotoxins (a specific monoclonal antibody attached to a toxic drug), that may offer hope in the treatment of a wide range of diseases.

None of these will give you AIDS.

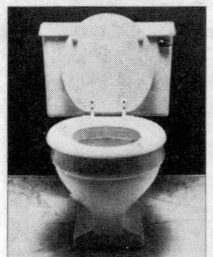

There is no evidence that a person can get AIDS from handshakes, dishes, toilet seats, door knobs or from daily contact with a person who has AIDS.

EVIDENCE INDICATES AIDS *cannot be spread by casual contact, or ways shown here.*

AIDS (Acquired Immune Deficiency Syndrome). In the United States, the first cases of AIDS are believed to have appeared during the second half of 1979. The incidence of reported cases of AIDS has doubled every six months since then and, since 1981 (according to the Centers for Disease Control), AIDS has afflicted 11,871 Americans and killed half of them. AIDS is thought to be transmitted primarily through sexual contact and through blood and blood products. Scientists do not think that AIDS can be transmitted by casual contact, such as a handshake, or through the air (coughing, sneezing). The group at highest risk is homosexual or bisexual men, amounting to 70 percent of patients (this finding may be premature). Intravenous drug abusers account for 17 percent of patients. One percent of patients have hemophilia. Another 11 percent are Haitians, or sexual partners of individuals within other risk categories, or persons who had been given blood or blood products within the past five years. By 1985, according to a leading researcher, as many as 300,000 people had already been infected by AIDS, and about 30,000 were thought likely to develop the disease in the next five years. On the average, there is an unusually long latency period between the time of infection and the development of symptoms. Some investigators suggest this to be as long as two years.

The name given this disease—Acquired Immune Deficiency Syndrome—can be interpreted as follows: "acquired" because its victims did not inherit the disease; "immune deficiency" because the common denominator is the breakdown of a patient's immune system; and "syndrome" to indicate the group of rare but often devastating diseases taking advantage of the body's collapsed defense system. These opportunistic (secondary to the disease state) disorders include an extremely rare form of skin cancer, Kaposi's sarcoma; a lethal form of pneumonia, Pneumocystis carini; and other life-threatening infections, which include multiple viral infections and severe fungal infections. In itself, as some researchers have indicated, AIDS can be considered an opportunistic infection, since it preys on people whose immune systems have already been severely compromised or damaged, leaving them exposed to a wide range of viral, fungal, bacterial, and protozoal infections. Latest findings offer evidence that an HTLV virus (human T cell leukemia virus) is the basic cause of AIDS. HTLV is an example of a retrovirus, a group of viruses known to cause tumors in a number of animals and also suspected of causing certain types of human leukemias. On the medical front, while laboratory researchers have been trying to determine the cause of AIDS, physicians throughout the world have been struggling with little success to treat patients who have the disease. There is as yet no effective way to restore the immune response in these patients. Physicians, in effect, have no alternative but to limit treatment to each opportunistic infection and cancer as it occurs. Treatments rely on the use of conventional antibiotic, antifungal, and antiprotozoal drugs. Medical understanding of AIDS can be expected to change rapidly over the next few years, perhaps giving new and better approaches to the treatment and prognosis for this disease.

—*Frances F. Barth*

LIFE SCIENCES

Scientists sometimes have a difficult time trying to draw a line between the living and nonliving world, but they do agree that all living organisms share certain basic characteristics:

1. They exhibit a higher degree of internal structure and functional organization than are found in nonliving matter.
2. They are able to use energy from the environment to maintain life by carrying out various chemical processes, collectively called metabolism.
3. They demonstrate irritability, the ability to respond to environmental stimuli.
4. They are able to adapt to changes in the environment.

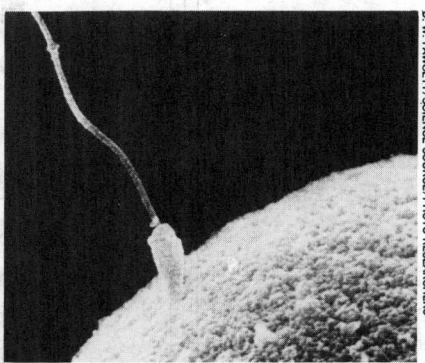

CONCEPTION CLOSE-UP—*a sperm cell, greatly magnified in this scanning electron microphotograph, begins to penetrate an egg cell.*

5. They can reproduce themselves and in so doing pass on to the resulting identical or nearly identical new organisms all the information they possess for growth, development, maintenance of life, and reproduction.

What all highly organized, energy-utilizing, irritable, adaptable, reproduction-capable organisms also have in common is the cell. Every living thing on Earth is either a single cell or composed of cells. And every cell in every organism possesses, at one time or another, all the characteristics common to living organisms. The cell is the basic unit (in the case of single-celled organisms) or subunit (in the case of multicelled organisms) of life.

The Origin of Life and Life Processes

Earth, according to most educated estimates, is between 4.5 and 5 billion years old. Scientists familiar with the fossil record believe that life first appeared on our planet a little over 3 billion years ago. When humans first began to wonder how they and the life around them originally got here is more open to speculation.

Theories of the Origins of Life

Biology is the study of living things, and modern biologists are virtually unanimous in their agreement that scientific investigation will one day solve the mystery of how living things came to populate a once lifeless Earth. There are many individuals, however, who believe that the question is adequately answered by the biblical description of the creation of our world and the things in it. Such a view lies outside the scope of scientific inquiry and, therefore, cannot be addressed here. What follows, then, is material that deals only with those scientific theories offered to date.

Vitalism. Vitalism is the belief that something other than the laws of

physics or chemistry, a mysterious vital force, brought about life originally and is still at work within all living things. Vitalist thinking is untestable by scientific means and is, therefore, neither provable nor disprovable.

Spontaneous generation.

While vitalism is not testable, scientists have managed to discredit the idea of spontaneous generation, a long-held theory that depended on vitalism. This notion, proposed as early as the fourth century B.C. by Aristotle, held that life could arise spontaneously from organic matter, as well as by sexual and asexual reproduction. The evidence put forward for spontaneous generation was the common observation that insects and small animals arose from decaying meat and rotting grain. In 1668, Italian naturalist Francesco Redi conducted an experiment to prove the evidence wrong. He placed meat in a flask and then covered the flask with muslin to keep flies from depositing their eggs in the meat. No maggots (fly larvae) developed in the meat as long as the flask remained covered. This was considered convincing proof that higher organisms do not arise spontaneously, but the concept persisted regarding microorganisms. In 1765, Lazarro Spallanzani, an Italian priest, conducted a similar experi-

ment, demonstrating that microbes would not appear in a nutrient broth if it were boiled in a sealed flask. However, skeptics argued that the boiling had destroyed the vital force necessary for spontaneous generation.

Louis Pasteur finally disproved the theory of spontaneous generation in 1862. He placed a nutrient broth in a flask with a long, S-shaped neck that permitted air to pass freely into and out of the flask but prevented dust, molds, and bacteria from entering. The broth was boiled to kill all microorganisms already present, and then the flask was allowed to cool. Since air could still pass freely in and out of the flask, and the broth subsequently could be shown capable of growing microorganisms, Pasteur's experiment demonstrated that no vital force in the broth or air had been destroyed.

Panspermy. In 1908, Swedish physical chemist Svante August Arrhenius, a Nobel Prize winner in 1903, writing in a book entitled *Worlds in the Making,* theorized that life on Earth developed as a result of the arrival of a spore or similar life form from outer space, either in a meteorite or driven by the pressure of sunlight. This theory has come to be called panspermia. One form of this theory assumes that life, like matter, always

FORMATION OF THE PRIMORDIAL SOUP

Stanley Miller and Harold Urey were able to prove, using the apparatus pictured here, that simple organic compounds could have been created spontaneously from the components of the atmosphere.

They passed a mixture of hydrogen, ammonia, methane, and water vapor between two electrodes discharging 60,000 volts, simulating lightning. Any of the mixture that condensed was collected and any organic material trapped. The process was repeated continuously for one week. When the material that had collected in the trap was examined, it was found that the amino acids glycine, alanine, glutamic acid, and aspartic acid had been created. These amino acids are important in the synthesis of proteins.

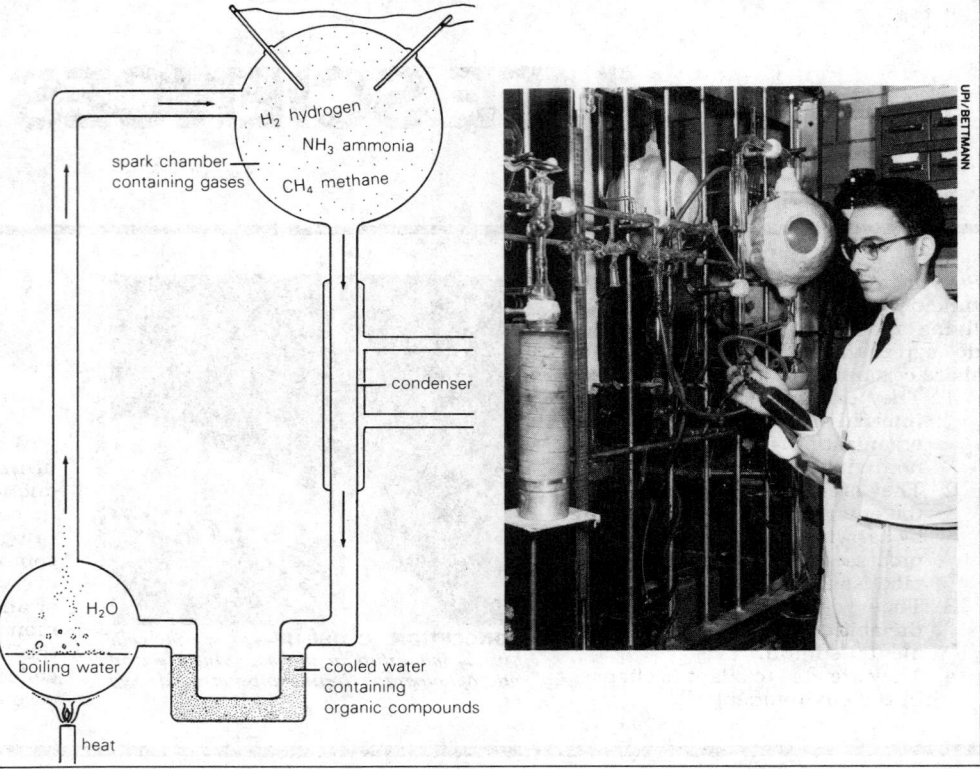

existed. Another assumes that life was first formed on another planet; however, this avoids the problem of how life originally came about. In any case, most scientists doubt that any known form of life could survive such a journey. Notable among present-day doubters are another Nobel Prize winner, British biochemist Francis Crick, and British astronomer Fred Hoyle.

Darwin's influence on modern theories.
Even before Charles Darwin published *The Origin of Species* in 1859, a number of 18th- and early 19th-century scientists and thinkers proposed the idea that more complex life forms evolved from simpler forms. These early evolutionists included Pierre Louis Moreau de Maupertuis, Jean Baptiste Lamarck, Georges Louis Leclerc de Buffon, and Darwin's own grandfather, Erasmus Darwin. What Darwin's theory had, and the others lacked, was an evolutionary mechanism—natural selection. Simply stated, natural selection works as follows: Individual organisms produce more offspring than are necessary for survival of the species. As a result of environmental factors, such as predators and limited food supply, only some of the offspring can survive. Variations occurring in some offspring may improve their fitness to survive and reproduce. Fitter offspring are thus able to pass their favorable variations on to their offspring, which in turn are more fit for survival. In this way, beneficial characteristics are

spread over successive generations to an entire species. An accumulation of such characteristics as genetic variations may result in the evolution of new species.

Darwin's theory simplified the problem of the origin of life, for its acceptance meant that concern could be shifted to how the earliest organism arose on Earth.

Oparin-Haldane hypothesis.
In 1924, the Russian biochemist Alexander I. Oparin suggested that the first living organism arose out of the large quantities of organic chemicals that he proposed were present in the oceans of the primitive Earth. Oparin's theory maintained that a combination of lightning and ultraviolet light from the sun caused a reaction of the materials in an atmosphere containing hydrogen (H_2), ammonia (NH_3), methane (CH_4), and water (H_2O) to form simple organic compounds. These compounds collected in clouds and were carried down to the primordial ocean by precipitation. The simple organic molecules in that so-called primordial mixture then reacted to form structures of greater and greater complexity, until finally something was formed that could be characterized as having life. British biologist J. B. S. Haldane independently came to the same conclusion in 1929.

Miller-Urey experiments.
In 1953, Stanley Miller and Harold Urey,

of the University of Chicago, conducted a series of experiments to determine whether organic compounds like those called for in the Oparin-Haldane model could have been created from the inorganic compounds under conditions that might have existed early in Earth's history. They circulated methane, ammonia, water, and hydrogen for one week past an electric discharge that simulated lightning. Amino acids, which are the basic building blocks of proteins, and a number of other organic compounds, including purine and pyrimidine bases found in nucleic acids, were successfully synthesized.

The Miller-Urey experiments and the Oparin-Haldane model assumed that the primitive atmosphere was rich in hydrogen. Recent geological findings suggest that molecular hydrogen might actually have been quite scarce, and that carbon dioxide (CO_2) was in abundance instead. Employing an atmosphere that took this new evidence into account, Cyril Ponnamperuma of the University of Maryland has achieved results similar to those of Miller and Urey.

Graham Cairns-Smith clay-life hypothesis.
Recent experimental findings have renewed interest in a theory first proposed during the 1960's by Graham Cairns-Smith of the University of Glasgow. This theory holds that life developed not in the early oceans but in deposits of clay. Researchers studying common

ceramic clay have discovered many unusual, previously unknown properties suggesting that the material would have acted as a chemical catalyst in, and might even have directed, the evolution of molecules from simple to complex. It is now known that clays trap and store light energy in their internal crystalline structure, energy that can move to a site where it might alter trapped compounds. It has even been suggested that defects commonly found within the crystals of a clay could have acted not unlike genes in living organisms that code for the synthesis of proteins.

Nature and Evolution of Early Organisms

Just how simple was the first living system? Was it a true organism? Or was it some sort of lifelike intermediate, or protocell, that formed a tenuous bridge between the nonliving world around it and the living world that was to be? How did the first true organisms begin to evolve? These are questions to which scientists are still seeking answers.

Protocells. It has been proposed that the first living system was a strand of DNA (deoxyribonucleic acid), the nucleic acid molecule found in every living cell as the principal constituent of chromosomes, which carry biological information for the synthesis of the entire organism. In the presence of the necessary enzymes (proteins that function as chemical catalysts), such a strand of DNA could duplicate. This primeval organism would be similar to a present-day virus, except that it would possess the enzymes required for reproduction. A virus, which consists of DNA—or, in some viruses, RNA (ribonucleic acid)—surrounded by a coat of protein, is capable of duplication, but only within a living cell containing the necessary enzymes.

Oparin proposed that a complex organic coercevate droplet immediately preceded the development of the first living organism. A coercevate (from the Latin *coacervare,* meaning to cluster together) is a type of colloid, a substance that consists of very small particles suspended in solution. These droplets would accumulate organic material from their environment, grow in size, and then split into two or more fragments. In time, the coercevate droplets would develop the ability to form fragments more and more like themselves. Later, they would develop a genetic apparatus to carry out accurate duplication.

Another first-organism candidate is

the protenoid microsphere. Sidney W. Fox and colleagues at the University of Miami's Institute for Molecular and Cellular Evolution heated a mixture of amino acids to produce large proteinlike molecules called proteinoids. When these macromolecules are dissolved in boiling water and then allowed to cool, they form tiny spheres that bear a strong resemblance to spherical bacteria. These microspheres exhibit a form of primitive internal metabolism. They also do something that looks disarmingly similar to what yeast will do when it reproduces—form buds.

First true organisms. The first true organisms were probably heterotrophs (from the Greek *heteros,* meaning different, and *trophos,* feeder). Heterotrophs are organisms that must obtain the complex organic molecules required for metabolism from a source outside the organism. Most present-day bacteria are heterotrophic. One of the problems these first heterotrophic organisms probably encountered was what might have been the world's first food shortage: rapid depletion of the available supply of complex organic compounds. By the mechanism of natural selection, organisms then developed that took

much simpler compounds and from them manufactured the more complex compounds their metabolism required.

These new organisms were primitive autotrophs (from the Greek *autos,* meaning self). When this occurred, there was little, if any, free oxygen in the primordial oceans and atmosphere. Like today's anaerobic (not dependent on oxygen in the air) bacteria and yeasts, these primitive autotrophs broke down relatively simple organic compounds to obtain the energy they required. The process used was fermentation, which releases carbon dioxide. The carbon dioxide-rich atmosphere that resulted provided a hospitable environment for the evolution of autotrophs that developed photosynthesis, a process that uses CO_2 as a source of carbon and the energy from sunlight to form complex organic compounds from inorganic compounds. The photosynthetic process released oxygen gas (O_2). Reacting with other atmospheric gases, the oxygen released by the first photosynthetic organisms played a crucial role in the development of our atmosphere. These new organisms and the complex compounds they produced also provided a new source of nutrients—themselves—for newly evolved aerobic (oxygen-dependent) organisms, and evolution was well on its way.

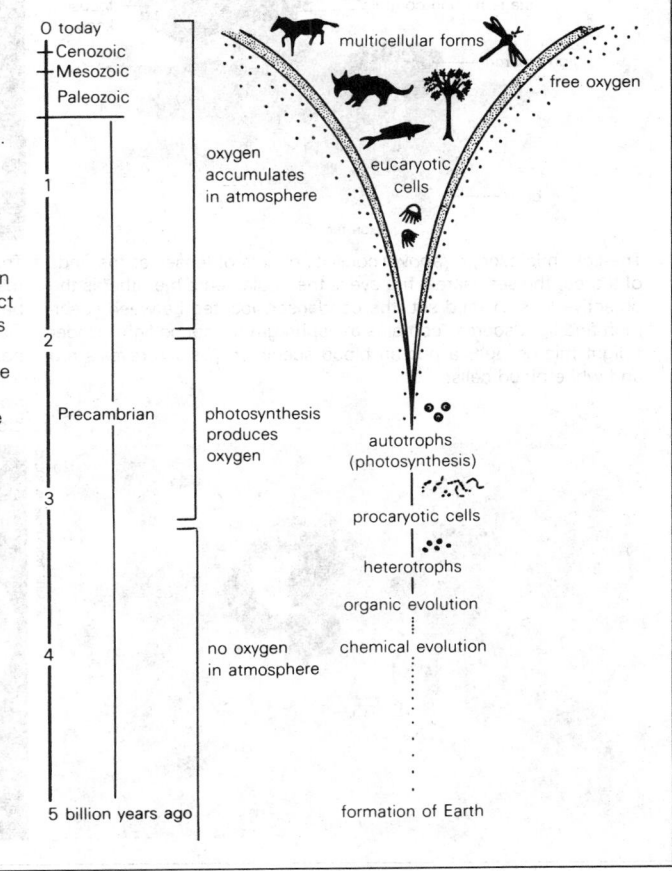

FREE OXYGEN

The amount of free oxygen in the atmosphere had a direct effect on the rise of life on Earth. The earliest organisms used photosynthesis to produce the nutrients they needed from carbon dioxide. A byproduct of photosynthesis is the release of oxygen. This release allowed both the development of the ozone shield in the upper atmosphere and of more complex aerobic organisms.

0 today
Cenozoic
Mesozoic
Paleozoic

1

2

Precambrian

3

4

5 billion years ago

oxygen accumulates in atmosphere

photosynthesis produces oxygen

no oxygen in atmosphere

multicellular forms

free oxygen

eucaryotic cells

autotrophs (photosynthesis)

procaryotic cells

heterotrophs

organic evolution

chemical evolution

formation of Earth

PETER LOEWER

The Cell

Cells are the basic units of all life, every living organism being either a single cell or a collection of many interdependent cells. Bacteria are examples of single-celled, or unicellular, organisms. Multicellular organisms, composed of many cells, include most plants, fungi, and animals.

While some cells—frog eggs and certain nerve cells, for example—can be seen with the naked eye, inspection of the vast majority of cells requires magnification. The discovery and initial inspection of cells, therefore, depended on the refinement of magnifying lenses and the invention of the microscope.

The term "cell" was coined by English physicist Robert Hooke in 1665, after observing that a thin section of cork he was examining through a primitive microscope was made up of tiny chambers, like cells in a monastery. Later in the 17th century, Dutch naturalist and microscope-maker Anton van Leeuwenhoek made the first observation of unicellular organisms, calling the bacteria and protozoa he saw "animalcules."

Today, many different scientific specialists study the cell. Cell biologists deal with cells on every level. Cytologists study cell structure. Cell physiology, or function, is investigated by biochemists and biophysicists. Histologists study tissues, collections of similar cells, such as muscles and blood. There is, of course, considerable overlapping among these disciplines.

MICROSCOPES

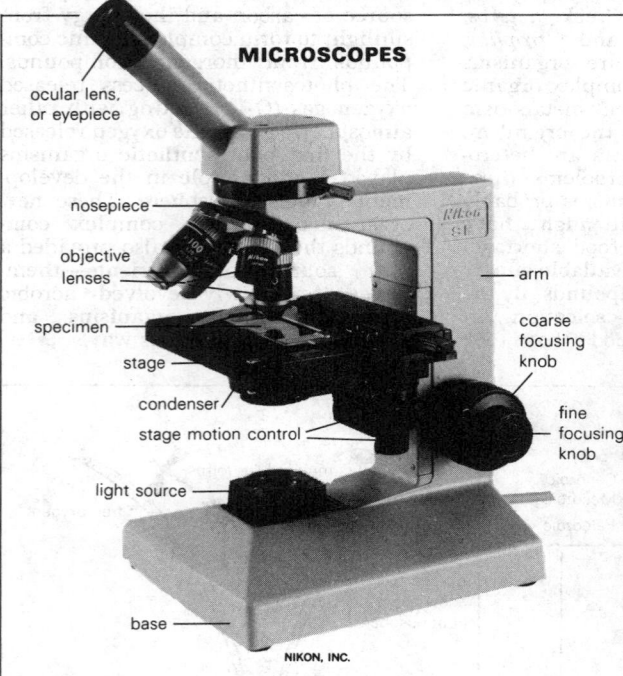

ocular lens, or eyepiece

nosepiece

objective lenses

specimen

stage

condenser

stage motion control

light source

base

NIKON, INC.

arm

coarse focusing knob

fine focusing knob

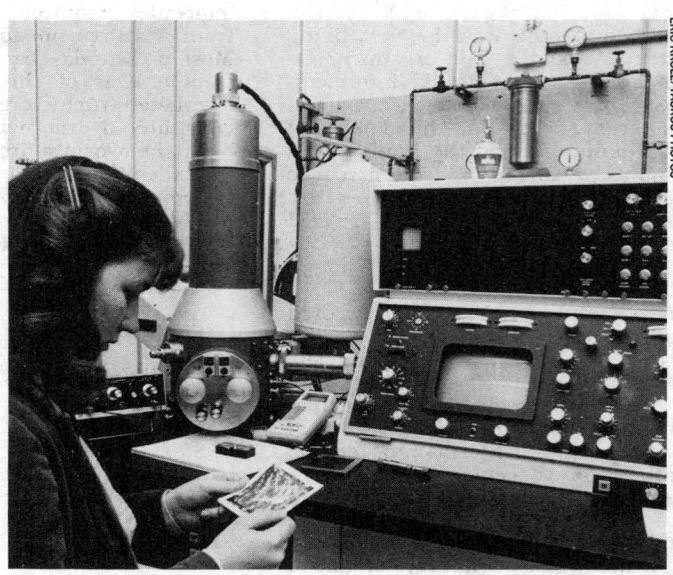

ERIC KROLL/TAURUS PHOTOS

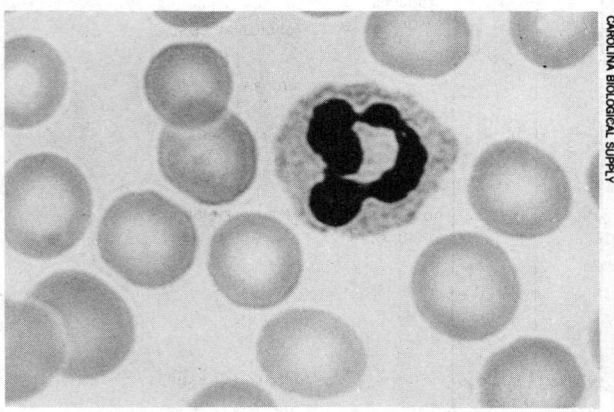

The light microscope *(above)* consists of sets of lenses at the ends of a tube; the set nearest the eye is the ocular lens; the other is the objective lens. A third set, the condenser, located between specimen and light source, contains a diaphragm to reduce light. Under a light microscope, a human blood specimen *(below)* reveals red and white blood cells.

CAROLINA BIOLOGICAL SUPPLY

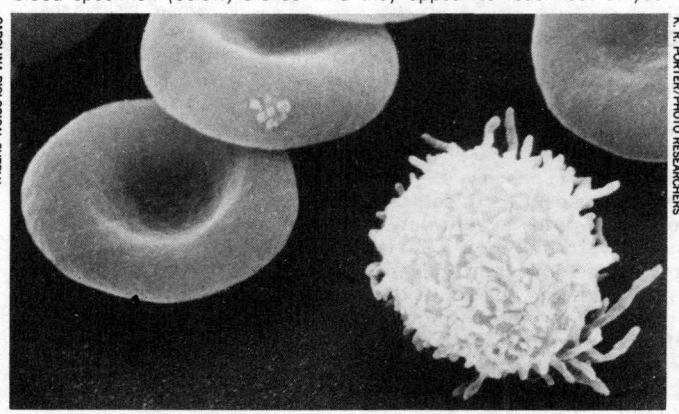

The transmission electron microscope (not shown), or TEM, uses electromagnets to magnify and focus and "illuminates" an object by means of a beam of accelerated electrons in a vacuum; because of extremely short wavelengths of electrons, magnifications of from 50X to 800,000X are possible. The scanning electron microscope *(above)*, or SEM, can produce a three-dimensional image of its subject. It has a range of magnification from 10X to 200,000X. Under an SEM, the surface features of the human blood specimen *(below)* are so vivid they appear to reach out at you.

K. R. PORTER/PHOTO RESEARCHERS

Cell Theory

The idea that every form of life is made up of cells was first stated, in 1805, by the German naturalist Lorenz Oken. However, two of Oken's countrymen, botanist Matthias Jakob Schleiden and zoologist Theodor Schwann, who came to the same conclusion in 1838 and 1839 respectively, are generally credited with translating Robert Hooke's 1665 observation of a slice of cork into what now is called cell theory.

The first two principles of cell theory—in effect a single principle stated two different ways—are that (1) the cell is the fundamental unit of all life, and (2) all living organisms are made up of cells. Another German, physician Rudolf Virchow, added a third principle in 1858: every cell is the product of the division of a previously existing cell.

Characteristics of a Cell

Strictly speaking, there is no typical cell. Cells exist in a wide variety of sizes, shapes, types, even colors and life spans. All cells, however, provide the spatial structures and protective physical limits within which are carried out the biological functions necessary to maintain and perpetuate life and the vital life processes.

Chemical composition of cells. There are 92 naturally occurring chemical elements, but only a small percentage (about 25 percent) of them occur either always or occasionally within living cells.

Hydrogen (H), carbon (C), oxygen (O), nitrogen (N), phosphorus (P), and sulfur (S) are required for life. Such elements as sodium (Na), calcium (Ca), potassium (K), magnesium (Mg), iron (Fe), chlorine (Cl), manganese (Mn), zinc (Zn), selenium (Se), molybdenum (Mo), cobalt (Co), iodine (I), and copper (Cu) are necessary for performance of specific functions in certain cells and organisms. Not all the roles these and other chemical elements play in the chemistry of life are well known.

Most of the weight of a cell is provided by water, the exact percentage depending on the type of cell. In the human body, for example, red blood cells are approximately 60 percent water, while the cells that make up muscle are about 85 percent.

Carbon is the element most closely associated with living organisms. Most molecules (arrangements of atoms linked together by chemical bonds) containing carbon, in fact, are found only in living cells and are aptly called

organic molecules or organic compounds. Small and relatively simple organic compounds, called monomers, link together to form larger and more complex compounds, called polymers or macromolecules.

The most important classes of organic compounds are the carbohydrates, the lipids, the proteins, and the nucleic acids.

Carbohydrates, which may be either monomers or polymers, are composed of carbon, hydrogen, and oxygen. Starches, sugars, and cellulose are common carbohydrates. Green plants synthesize starches from CO_2 and H_2O by photosynthesis, storing the light energy required for the process in the chemical bonds of the molecules manufactured. Breaking starches down to sugars is a major source of energy in both plant and animal metabolism. Cellulose, used for protection of plant cells and the support of the entire organism, is a polymeric carbohydrate.

Lipids are nonwater-soluble monomeric or polymeric molecules composed of carbon, hydrogen, and oxygen, and sometimes other elements as well. Fats, oils, waxes, and such steroids as cholesterol, lanolin, and some of the hormones are lipids. Lipids perform a wide range of functions.

Proteins, which account for about 50 percent of the nonwater weight of a cell, contain carbon, hydrogen, oxygen, and nitrogen, and almost always sulfur as well. Zinc, copper, iron, and phosphorus are also found in some proteins. Proteins are long, chainlike molecules consisting of as many as 22 different smaller molecules, amino acids, linked end to end. Some proteins are composed of hundreds of amino acids, and the order in which they occur determines the function a given protein will serve. Hemoglobin is the protein in blood that carries oxygen to the cells of our body. Collagen, the fibrous material in bones, tendons, and ligaments, is a very long protein containing thousands of linked amino acids. Enzymes, which act as chemical catalysts in countless different chemical reactions performed in cells, are also proteins.

Nucleic acids, in the form of DNA and RNA, are the macromolecular material that carries the hereditary message that makes it possible for one cell or organism to beget another exactly or almost exactly like it. Nucleic acids are composed of carbon, oxygen, hydrogen, nitrogen, and phosphorus. The capability of these five elements properly arranged may be the greatest wonder in all of nature.

ELEMENTS NECESSARY FOR LIFE PROCESSES

ELEMENT	EXAMPLE OF ROLE IN BIOLOGY	APPROXIMATE PERCENTAGE OF THE HUMAN BODY; TRACE = LESS THAN 0.1
Calcium	bone; muscle contraction	1.5
Carbon	constituent of organic molecules	18.5
Chlorine	HCl in digestion	0.2
Cobalt	part of vitamin B_{12}	trace
Copper	part of oxygen-carrying pigment of mollusk blood	trace
Fluorine	necessary for tooth enamel development	trace
Hydrogen	part of water and of all organic molecules	9.5
Iodine	part of thyroxine, a hormone	trace
Iron	hemoglobin, oxygen-carrying pigment of many animals	trace
Magnesium	part of chlorophyll; essential to some enzyme action	0.1
Manganese	essential to some enzyme action	trace
Molybdenum	essential to some enzyme action	trace
Nitrogen	constituent of proteins and nucleic acids	3.2
Oxygen	molecular oxygen in respiration; constituent of water and nearly all organic molecules	65.0
Phosphorus	high energy bond of ATP	1.0
Potassium	generation of nerve impulses	0.4
Selenium	essential to many enzyme actions	trace
Silicon	diatom shells; glass sponge exoskeleton; grass leaves	trace
Sodium	salt balance; nerve conduction	0.2
Sulfur	constituent of most proteins	0.3
Vanadium	oxygen transport in tunicates	trace
Zinc	essential to workings of alcohol oxidizing enzyme	trace

Cell types. Cells are either procaryotic (from the Greek *pro,* meaning before and *karyon,* nut) or eucaryotic (*eu* meaning good in Greek).

Procaryotic cells. All procaryotic cells are unicellular organisms, although some occur in colonies. True bacteria and blue-green bacteria (also called cyanophytes and formerly called blue-green algae) are the most recognizable procaryotes. The less familiar mycoplasmas are the smallest organisms known—smaller even than some of the very small viruses.

Procaryotic cells lack a true membrane-enclosed nucleus—a standard eucaryote feature—having instead a nuclear region, or nucleoid, with a single large strand of DNA. Also lacking are many of the membrane-bounded organelles (little organs) found in eucaryotic cells. Common to both cell types but considerably smaller in procaryotes are ribosomes, structures within the cell that function as sites for protein synthesis. Procaryotic cells are surrounded by a protective double-layered cell wall that in composition and physical characteristics is completely different from the membrane that surrounds eucaryotic cells. Procaryotes reproduce by a simple fission process.

Eucaryotic cells. Eucaryotic cells are much larger than procaryotic cells and far more complex. Single-celled algae and fungi and all protozoa are eucaryotic unicellular organisms. All multicellular organisms, such as plants, animals, and all multicelled fungi and algae, are composed of eucaryotic cells.

Eucaryotic cells have a true membrane-bounded nucleus containing the genetic information of the cell in structures called chromosomes. Surrounding the nucleus are numerous and varied organelles with a wide range of specialized functions.

Cell size and diversity. Eucaryotic cells are rarely smaller than 10 microns (millionths of a meter) in diameter, or larger than 100 microns. Procaryotic cells are considerably smaller, the largest measuring no more than about 3 microns across. The smallest procaryotes, the mycoplasmas, generally are well under a micron in size. Among eucaryotic cells, those of plants tend to be larger than those of animals.

Cells vary greatly in shape and appearance. A side-by-side comparison of, say, a bacterium; a long, thin, macroscopic nerve cell; an animal muscle cell; and a typical plant cell would make that fact abundantly clear. The dramatic differences that are visible suggest a diversity of internal organization and activity. There is, however, quite a bit that even cells as different as these have in common.

Cell structures and their functions. Because cells vary so greatly, it is not possible to describe a typical cell, especially since the organizations of procaryotic and eucaryotic cells are so different. Certain components, however, are commonly found in all cells.

All cells have cytoplasm, an outer membrane, and either a nucleus or a less distinct nuclear region. The nucleus, or nuclear region, is the most important of the cell's specialized internal structures, or organelles. All cells also have various kinds of organelles outside the nucleus or nuclear region. Procaryotes have only a few. In eucaryotic cells, they can be quite numerous. Plant cells, most procaryotes, and some other unicellular organisms also have external cell walls.

Cell membrane and cell wall. Surrounding every cell is a thin, double-layered membrane that gives the cell structural integrity and determines the substances that can enter and exit. These flexible, elastic membranes frequently have pouchlike protrusions and indentations that increase the surface area to facilitate the inflow and outflow of materials. Most of the organelles within a cell are also bounded by membranes. Made up mainly of protein, lipid, and carbohydrate, the typical cell membrane is less than a millimicron (one 1000th of a micron) in thickness.

Plant cells, most procaryotes, and some unicellular eucaryotes have a relatively thick and rigid cell wall surrounding the outer cell membrane. In unicellular organisms, the cell wall acts as a protective barrier against the surrounding environment. Cell walls around individual plant cells create support for the entire organism. Plant cell walls are composed mainly of carbohydrates in the form of cellulose. Procaryotic cell walls are made up primarily of murein, a macromolecular arrangement of sugars and amino acids.

Cytoplasm. The term "cytoplasm" refers to all of the cell material between the outer membrane and the nucleus. Most of the cytoplasm consists of water with proteins, carbohydrates, lipids, smaller organic molecules, and inorganic salts and minerals in colloidal suspension. Contained within the cytoplasm, and considered part of it, are the many and varied discrete organelles that perform many of the vital functions of the cell.

Nucleus and nucleolus. Bounded by a porous membrane that allows substances to move between it and the cytoplasm, the usually centrally located nucleus, the largest organelle, is ultimately responsible for direction and control of the life processes of a cell. Within the nucleus, the nucleolus, a

---

VARIOUS CELL SIZES

human nerve cell	up to 2 m in length
chicken egg cell	approx. 30 mm in diameter
frog egg cell	approx. 1 mm in diameter
human egg cell	approx. 100 μm* in diameter
human red blood cell	approx. 8 μm in diameter
average eucaryotic cell	approx. 10-100 μm in diameter
average plant body cell	approx. 30-50 μm in diameter
average animal body cell	approx. 10-20 μm in diameter
average true bacteria	approx. 1 μm in diameter by several μm in length
average procaryotic cell	approx. 1-10 μm in diameter or length
mycoplasma	approx. 0.16 μm in diameter (the smallest cell)
virus (not a cell)	approx. 0.001-0.2 μm in size

* μm = micron

BLOOD CELLS
red blood cells

white blood cells
basophil
eosinophil
lymphocyte
monocyte
neutrophil

MUSCLE CELLS
striated (voluntary)

smooth (involuntary)

cardiac

NERVE CELL

BONE CELL

REPRODUCTIVE CELLS
ovum
sperm

GLAND CELL

PETER LOEWER

discrete body composed of RNA and protein, produces the ribosomes that direct protein synthesis in the cell.

Chromatin, loosely coiled fibers of protein and DNA in the nucleus, carries the information that directs the activities of a cell. During reproduction, the nuclear chromatin condenses to form chromosomes that pass the hereditary information of the cell on to the next generation of cells.

Some cells are multinucleated, that is, they have more than one nucleus, and some nuclei have more than one nucleolus.

Endoplasmic reticulum. The endoplasmic reticulum is an intricate system of membrane-bounded flattened tubules and interconnecting channels that winds its way through the cytoplasm. The endoplasmic reticulum acts as a transport system for distribution of molecules from one part of a cell to another. In many cells, the tubules and channels are attached to the cell membrane and continuous with the nuclear membrane and certain other organelles.

Ribosomes. Attached to membranes of the endoplasmic reticulum, ribosomes are the extremely small sites within the cytoplasm where proteins are synthesized. The number of ribosomes in a cell varies with the amount of protein the cell is required to produce. In some cells there are millions of ribosomes. They attach themselves to messenger RNA from the nucleus and construct proteins from amino acids according to the coded instructions of the messenger RNA.

Golgi apparatus. Located near the nucleus and continuous with the endoplasmic reticulum, the Golgi apparatus is a stacked arrangement of small, flattened membrane-bounded sacs. Their function is to synthesize carbohydrates and to package proteins in membranous sacs, or vesicles, for transport to the surface of the cell, where they are secreted. The Golgi apparatus is sometimes called the Golgi complex or Golgi bodies.

Mitochondria. Mitochondria are relatively large, sausage-shaped, fluid-filled sacs scattered throughout the cytoplasm. They provide the cell with its supply of chemical energy in the form of adenosine triphosphate (ATP). Each mitochondrion is separated from the surrounding cytoplasm by an outer-limiting, double-layered membrane encapsulating an inner membrane that is highly convoluted to form partitions called cristae. The cristae provide a large surface area on which chemical reactions take place.

Mitochondria have their own DNA, RNA, and ribosomes and are able to reproduce by simple division, which leads some scientists to speculate that they are formerly independent procaryotic organisms living within the cell symbiotically.

Lysosomes. Lysosomes are small membranous sacs of varying size and

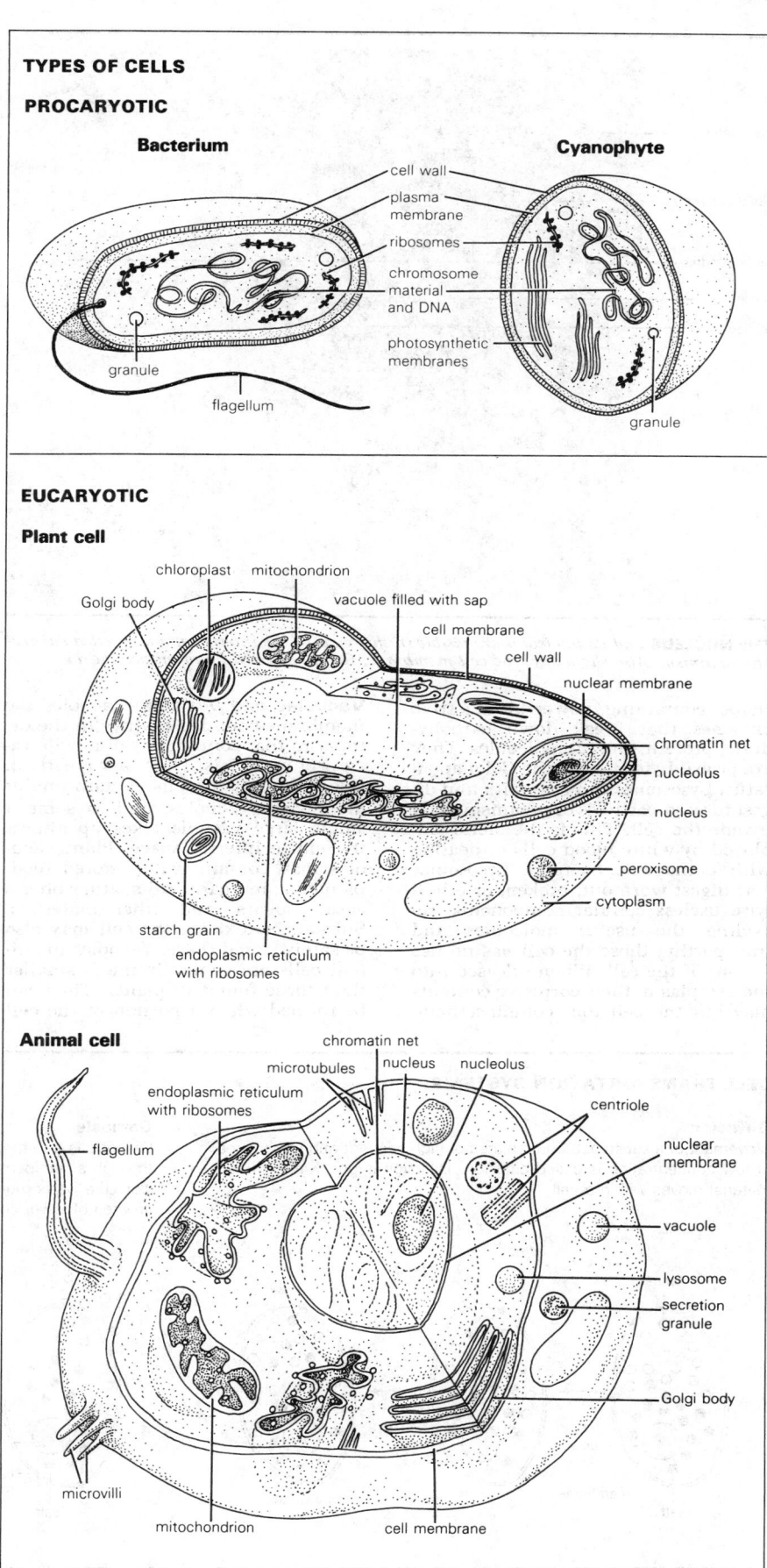

TYPES OF CELLS

PROCARYOTIC

Bacterium   Cyanophyte

cell wall
plasma membrane
ribosomes
chromosome material and DNA
photosynthetic membranes
granule
flagellum
granule

EUCARYOTIC

Plant cell

chloroplast   mitochondrion
Golgi body   vacuole filled with sap
                      cell membrane
                      cell wall
                      nuclear membrane
                      chromatin net
                      nucleolus
                      nucleus
                      peroxisome
                      cytoplasm
starch grain
endoplasmic reticulum with ribosomes

Animal cell

                chromatin net
            microtubules   nucleus   nucleolus
        endoplasmic reticulum
        with ribosomes   centriole
flagellum   nuclear membrane
                                      vacuole
                                      lysosome
                                      secretion granule
                                      Golgi body
microvilli
mitochondrion   cell membrane

PETER LOEWER

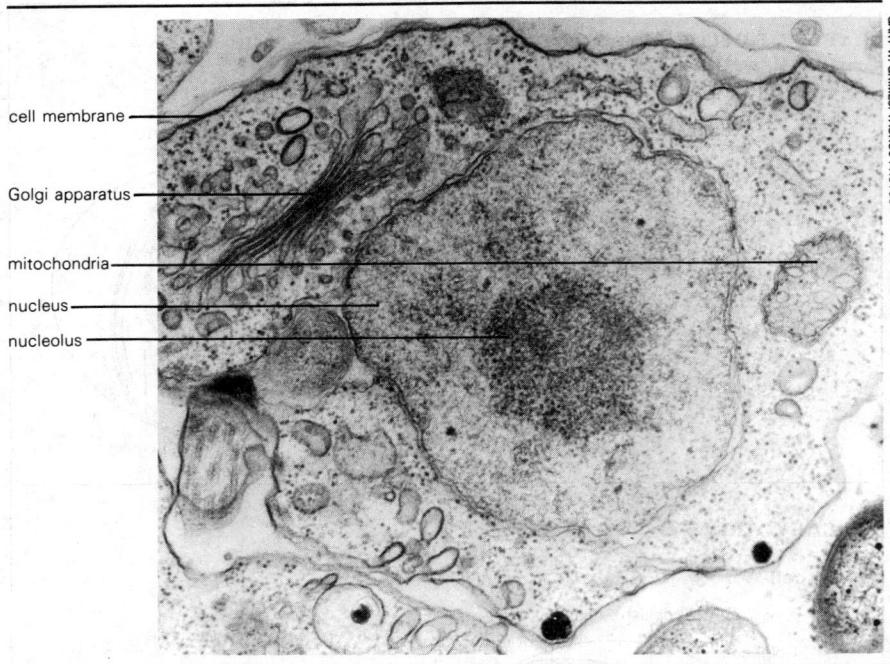

GARY W. GRIMES/TAURUS PHOTOS

THE NUCLEUS *and its nucleolus are visible in this view of the interior of a one-celled eukary-otic organism. Also shown are the cell membrane, Golgi apparatus, and mitochondria.*

membrane indents and pinches off, becoming a bubblelike cavity in the cytoplasm. Materials may enter and leave the cell by way of vacuoles. Relatively small vacuoles are sometimes called vesicles.

Plastids. Found in most plant cells and in photosynthetic unicellular organisms, plastids are highly intricate, organized, self-replicating organelles containing their own DNA, RNA, and ribosomes. The most important plastids are the chloroplasts, where photosynthesis occurs in plants.

Centrosome and basal bodies. Located near the nucleus and found in the cells of animals, most unicellular eucaryotes, fungi, and lower plants, the centrosome consists of a pair of small, rodlike bodies called centrioles. Lying at right angles to each other, the centrioles assist in the distribution of the chromosomes during the process of cell reproduction.

In motile unicellular eucaryotic organisms, centrioles give rise to basal bodies, or kinetosomes. These structures appear to anchor the cilia and flagella used by the organism for the purpose of locomotion.

Microtubules and microfilaments. Microtubules are small tubes composed primarily of the protein tubulin. They are found throughout the cytoplasm. In addition to providing internal structural support for the cell, microtubules are thought to play a role in the sorting out of chromosomes during cell division. They are the basic components of centrioles, basal bodies, cilia, and flagella.

Microfilaments, or fibrils, thought to be composed of fibers of protein, are much thinner than microtubules. They are found in some plant and animal cells and may account for the movement, or streaming, of the cytoplasm and the movement of the cell itself.

shape containing powerful digestive enzymes that break down carbohydrate, protein, and fat molecules. They are probably formed by the Golgi apparatus. Lysosomes can fuse with and digest foreign particles or organisms that invade the cell. This is the tactic employed by white blood cells in dealing with pathogenic bacteria. Lysosomes also digest worn out, broken, or otherwise useless cellular components, recycling the useful molecules and transporting those the cell has no use for out of the cell. When released into the cytoplasm, their corrosive contents may kill the cell that contains them.

Vacuoles and vesicles. Vacuoles are membrane-bounded cavities in the cytoplasm that contain any of a wide variety of materials. They vary greatly in size. Many plant cells contain one or more large vacuoles, and in some a single large vacuole takes up almost the entire interior space. Plant vacuoles may contain water, stored food, pigments, inorganic salts, atmospheric gases, sugars, and other materials. Substances toxic to the cell may also be safely stored there. Vacuoles in animal cells are generally much smaller than those found in plants. They can be formed when a portion of the cell

CELL TRANSPORTATION SYSTEMS

Diffusion

Movement of a substance from an area of high concentration to an area of low concentration is called diffusion. Diffusion is one way in which material moves within a cell.

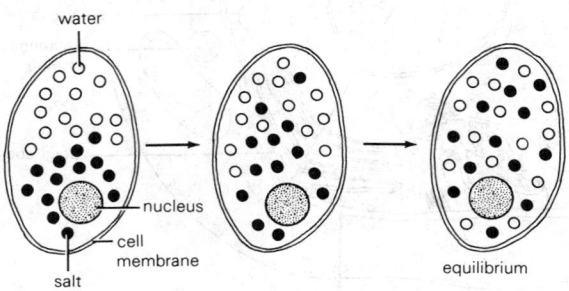

Osmosis

Osmosis is a form of diffusion in which water or another solvent moves through a semipermeable membrane such as a cell wall. As with diffusion, the water moves from an area of higher concentration of water to an area of lower concentration.

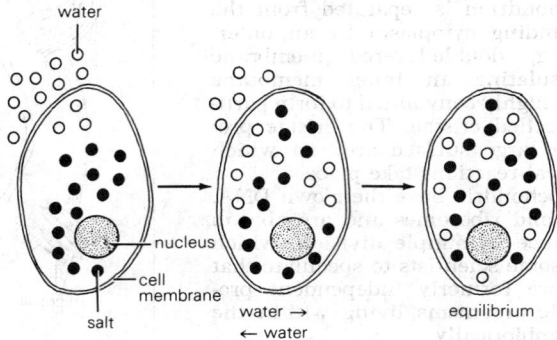

Cell Processes

Every cell takes the raw materials it needs for life from its outside environment, uses those materials to carry out chemical processes within its interior, and then returns waste products generated by those processes back into the environment.

The cell membrane, the only boundary between the cell and its chemically dissimilar environment, plays a key role in maintaining the harmonious balance required for functioning.

Passive and active processes.

The movement of materials into and out of the cellular medium through the cell membrane is accomplished by any of several processes that are considered either active or passive.

Passive processes, influenced by physical laws of nature and requiring no output of energy from the cell, include diffusion and osmosis. Active processes, which do call for the expenditure of energy and the contribution of certain chemical substances by the cell, include active transport, pinocytosis, and phagocytosis.

Diffusion. Molecules move in the environment outside a cell from areas of higher concentration to areas of lesser concentration according to the dictates of the natural physical law of diffusion. During movement, molecules will attempt to pass through the cell membrane if doing so will achieve uniformity of distribution.

Most cell membranes are selectively permeable, that is, they permit some materials to enter readily while denying entry to, or slowing down, others. Whether a molecule can pass through the membrane, or the degree of ease with which it can pass through, is de-

termined by the size of the molecule and its solubility in lipid, the major component of the membrane. Water, oxygen, carbon dioxide, small ions (such as those of sodium, chlorine, and potassium) move through with relative ease. Small organic monomers (such as glucose and amino acids) pass through more slowly. Large organic polymers (such as fats and proteins) do not enter by means of diffusion.

The same factors apply to the movement of materials out of the cell through the cell membrane. In either case, the rate of passage is determined by the relative difference in concentration on either side of the cell membrane of the substance involved.

Osmosis. Water, a major cell component, enters and exits a cell by the special form of diffusion known as osmosis, which involves the passage of a solvent through a semipermeable membrane. In osmosis, water moves through the membrane from a more dilute solution to a more concentrated solution. The solutes in a solution, dissolved or suspended solids, do not pass through the membrane.

Active transport. Cells do not rely exclusively on the effects of physical laws to regulate the passage of substances into and out of the cytoplasm. Active transport mechanisms, either augmenting or working against the effects of those laws, are constantly occurring as well.

For example, many cells actively maintain a lower concentration of sodium inside the cell than outside the cell, and a higher concentration of potassium inside than outside. Under these conditions, sodium passively diffuses into the cell and potassium naturally diffuses out. The cell, therefore, has to actively "pump" the unwanted sodium back to the outside, and the desired potassium back in—against the prevailing concentration gradients.

This active transport process calls on the cell to supply energy, certain enzymes, and a so-called carrier molecule. The carrier molecule, using the energy supplied and assisted by the enzyme, binds with the molecule that needs to be transported through the membrane and then carries it in or out by chemically opening the membrane to effect passage.

Molecules that move across membranes by active transport include glucose, amino acids, ions of sodium, potassium, and hydrogen, vitamins, and small proteins.

Pinocytosis and phagocytosis. Two somewhat similar processes by which cells actively take in substances are pinocytosis and phagocytosis.

Pinocytosis involves taking large molecules and small particles of material into a cell by enclosing them in intracellular vesicles. A deep indentation forms in the membrane. When the substance to be taken in enters the indentation, the membrane pinches off to form a bubblelike vesicle with the ingested material inside.

Instead of forming indentations, cytoplasmic extensions are produced that literally reach out and surround material to be taken in. This is called phagocytosis. Large particles of material and even entire organisms, such as bacteria, are acquired by cells in this fashion.

Control of Cell Activity

All of the many processes carried out by cells, such as cell growth, reproduction, repair, maintenance, and movement, require the production of chemical substances. The chemical

---

Phagocytosis
Cells take in large particles of material using a process called phagocytosis. The particle is engulfed by the cell and enclosed in a pocket, called a vesicle, to be digested.

Pinocytosis
Pinocytosis is similar to phagocytosis. In pinocytosis the cell also engulfs the object to be ingested, but the material is usually a fluid or very small particle.

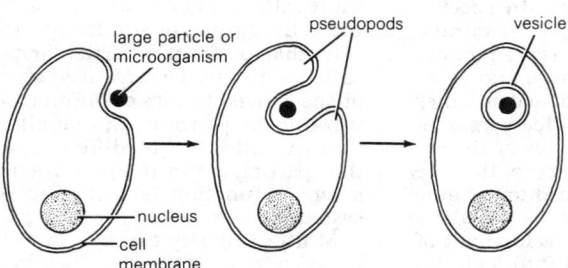

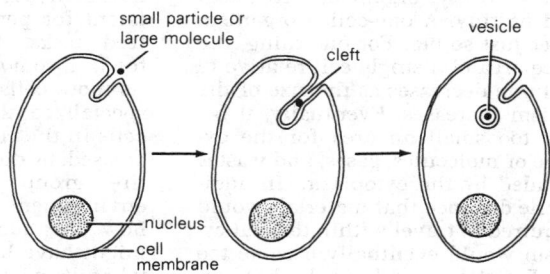

work needed to produce these essential compounds is performed by way of set sequences of chemical reactions, all of which require energy. The source of energy in all cells is found in the chemical bonds of the ATP (adenosine triphosphate) molecule. ATP, sometimes called the energy molecule, is manufactured by all cells.

To initiate chemical reactions in cells, specific enzymes are necessary. Sets of sequences of chemical reactions in cells are referred to as cycles or pathways. The information that directs production of chemical substances in a cell is provided by the genetic code of the cell, which is kept by the DNA (deoxyribonucleic acid) in the nucleus or nuclear region of the cell. The chemical substances produced in turn conduct the chemical activities that keep the system going. A change, or mutation, in the genetic code of the cell can affect production of chemical substances and thus alter the normal activity of the cell. There also are chemical substances, the hormones, that direct and coordinate certain cell activities. Hormones can influence cell membrane transport, enzyme action, and protein synthesis, and control the production and release of certain small molecules that influence cell activity.

All the activity performed to control the processes that take place in the cell cannot be accomplished without a steady supply of energy. Energy is made available to living organisms through the metabolism of any of the organic food molecules, namely carbohydrates, fats, and proteins. It is through photosynthesis (see PLANTS volume, Plant Life section) and cellular respiration that energy is processed and utilized by living organisms according to their individual needs and capabilities.

Multicellular Organization and Diversity

Until about 600 million years ago, unicellularity was a fact of life. If that situation had persisted until the present day, every organism on Earth would be tiny. A one-celled organism can get just so big. For one thing, the surface area of a single cell relative to its volume decreases as the size of the organism increases. Eventually, it becomes too small an area for the exchange of molecules, gases, and wastes demanded by the cytoplasm. In addition, the distance that materials would be required to travel within the cell cytoplasm would eventually become too great. For these and several other reasons, therefore, the size to which a single-celled organism could evolve was limited.

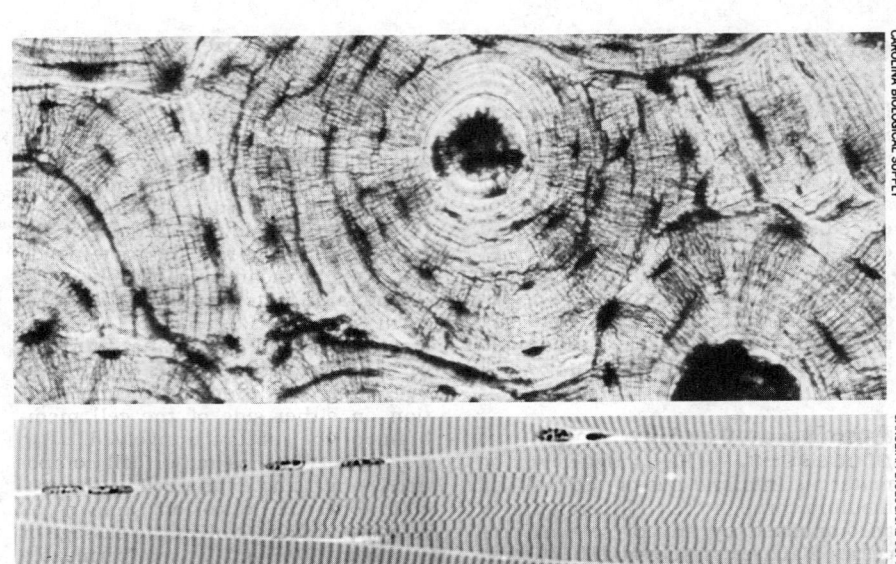

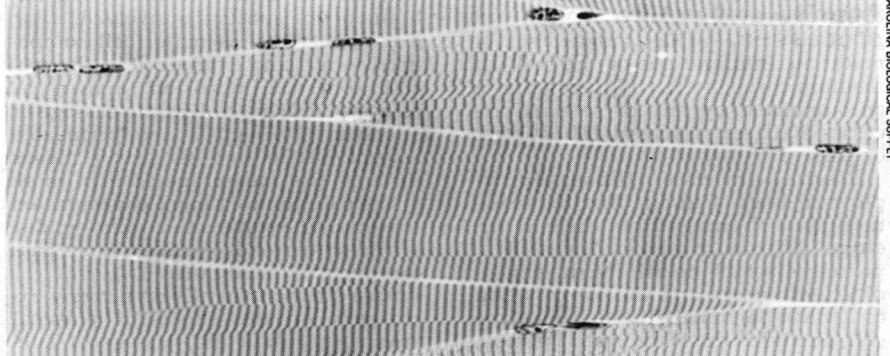

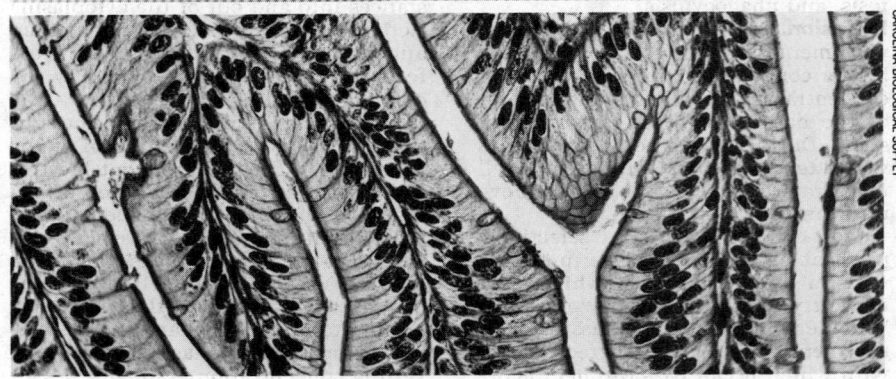

TISSUES OF MULTICELLULAR ORGANISMS *are adapted for specialized tasks. Some examples of the range of cell diversity are shown in the above microphotos of animal tissue. They are ground bone* (top), *skeletal muscle* (middle), *and simple columnar epithelium* (bottom).

Some time before 600 million years ago, some unicellular organisms adopted the strategy of living together in colonies. By doing so they became partially dependent on one another and, of course, achieved a collective increase in size. Eventually, some cells living in colonies acquired a special talent for performing certain specialized tasks, for example, obtaining food, locomotion, and reproduction. As more cells became more and more specialized, their dependence on other cells in the colony, and vice versa, increased, as did the efficiency of the entire group in dealing with the environment. It is not hard to imagine how the success of such a colony might have led to the development of what we now define as a multicellular organism.

The individual cells of a multicellular organism are so specialized and mutually dependent as to be incapable of independent survival outside the organism. Strictly speaking, a multicellular organism consists of specialized cells that cooperate to carry out all the functions required for maintenance of the life of the entire organism.

The level of organization of any multicellular organism begins with the cell. A group of similar specialized cells that perform a particular task is called a tissue. Organs are composed of specialized tissues of different kinds working to perform an overall function. A collection of different organs that participate in the performance of a single function is called an organ system.

Multicellularity can be found today in every one of the five kingdoms of life—in the Plantae, the Animalia, the Fungi, and even in the characteristically unicellular Monera and Protista.

Five Kingdoms of Life: A Survey of Key Characteristics

Recorded attempts to classify living organisms go back as far as the ancient Greek philosophers Plato and Aristotle. Aristotle developed a rudimentary system of classification that some say provided the foundation for present-day schemes. Both established a concept of species—the basic unit of classification of living organisms.

Not until the advent of the microscope, and Anton van Leeuwenhoek's observations of microscopic forms in the mid-17th century, did scientists recognize that the living world is composed of more than what the naked eye can see, and that macroscopic nonmotile plant and motile animal life forms represent only a part of that world.

Some scientists now estimate that about 10 million different species of living organisms exist. The number of extinct organisms is even greater. Some 1.5 million living organisms have been classified by taxonomists. Taxonomy is the scientific discipline that deals with the identification, naming, and classification of organisms. Systematics concentrates on phylogeny of organisms as a major factor in their classification.

Perhaps the best-known taxonomist is the Swedish naturalist Carolus Linnaeus (1707–1778). He wrote very extensively on plant and animal classification. His classic works include *Systema naturae* (1735) and *Genera plantarum* (1737). Among his most noteworthy achievements are the development of a practical system for naming organisms and for classifying all living organisms. His many accomplishments ultimately earned him the title of father of modern taxonomy.

In the Linnaean classification scheme, living organisms are grouped according to similar visible and anatomical structures. These groups are arranged in a hierarchical order, beginning with the most inclusive and largest group, the kingdom, and ending with the smallest unit of classification, the species. (Species are groups of interbreeding natural populations that are reproductively isolated from other such groups.)

For Linnaeus, all organisms fell in either of two kingdoms—one for plants, Kingdom Plantae, and one for animals, Kingdom Animalia. Below the level of the kingdoms were classes, orders, genera (singular, genus), and species. Later classification further subdivided the groups to include other groups, such as phyla (singular, phylum) and families. Subspecies, varieties, and races represent subdivisions below the species level. Today a simple hierarchical system of classification includes the following groups, from the largest to the smallest: kingdoms, phyla, classes, orders, families, and species. Each of these groups is called a taxon (plural, taxa), or taxonomic group.

According to the Linnaean system of naming organisms, called the binomial system of nomenclature, each species is given its own unique scientific name consisting of two Latinized words. The first part of the scientific name, called the generic name, identifies the genus, a group of closely related species to which the organism belongs; the second part, the specific name, identifies the particular species. When writing the binomial, the first letter of the genus is always capitalized, and both genus and species names are always italicized, or underlined if written by hand. The scientific name for humans is *Homo sapiens*. The genus *Homo* means man in Latin; *sapiens*, wise. The classification for humans is as follows:

> Kingdom Animalia,
> Phylum Chordata,
> Class Mammalia,
> Order Primata,
> Family Hominidae,
> Genus *Homo,*
> Species *sapiens.*

Although there are many different classification schemes in use today, there is one that has steadily gained recognition in the scientific community. Proposed by R. H. Whittaker of Cornell University in 1959, it diverges from traditional two-kingdom classification by placing bacteria, protozoans and unicellular algae and slime molds, fungi, plants and multicellular algae, and animals in five separate kingdoms, respectively: Monera, Protista, Fungi, Plantae, and Animalia. Each of these kingdoms is divided into the familiar taxonomic groups: phyla, classes, orders, etc. The evolutionary history and relationships of organisms is a major factor in the formulation of Whittaker's five-kingdom system of classification. Viruses are widely considered to be nonliving entities and as such are not included in the five-kingdom system of classification.

Following are descriptions of the major, or best-known, phyla, subphyla, and classes. Information on classification can also be found in the ANIMALS and PLANTS volumes.

Kingdom Monera

(approximately 4500 species)

All monerans are procaryotic; most are microscopic in size and exist as solitary single cells. Others form chains, filaments, or colonies of single cells to form a multicellularlike body. Most reproduce asexually by fission or budding and obtain food directly by absorbing it from the environment. Others derive energy from the sun or inorganic molecules to make their own sustenance. Most are nonmotile and possess a cell wall. Some possess a green photosynthetic pigment, chlorophyll.

Phylum Eubacteriae: true bacteria
Phylum Myxobacteriae: slime, or gliding, bacteria
Phylum Chlamydobacteriae: mycelium bacteria
Phylum Spirochaetae: spirochetes
Phylum Mycoplasmae: mycoplasmas
Phylum Cyanophyta: blue-green bacteria, or cyanophytes (formerly called blue-green algae)

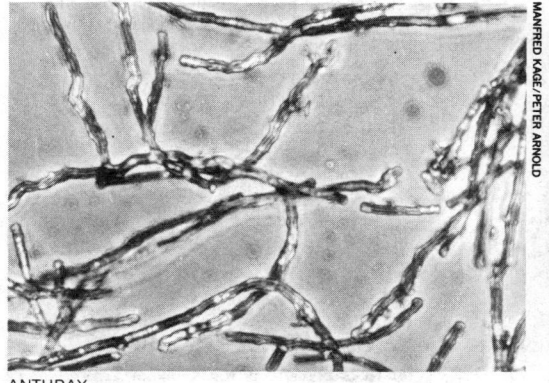

ANTHRAX

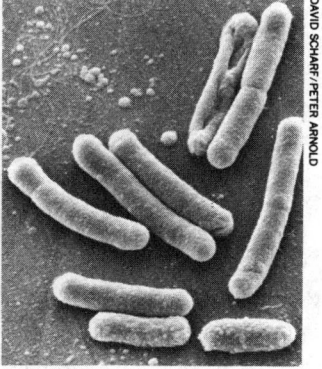

E. COLI

Kingdom Protista
(approximately 65,000 species)

All protists are eucaryotic and are among the smallest and most diverse of the eucaryotes. Most exist as solitary single cells, while others form colonies of single cells. Reproduction is asexual and sexual. Many protists are motile. Some possess chlorophyll; some have a cell wall. Protists have various methods of obtaining food, including directly absorbing nutrients from their environment, using the energy of the sun to manufacture their own food, ingesting food whole and digesting it in their bodies, or using a combination of these methods. Some algae are protists. All protozoans are protists. There are also a few fungilike protists.

Phylum Pyrrophyta: dinoflagellates
Phylum Euglenophyta: euglenoids
Phylum Chrysophyta: diatoms, yellow-green algae, and golden-brown algae
Phylum Mastigophora: flagellates (protozoans with flagella)
Phylum Sarcodina: sarcodines (protozoans with pseudopodia), including amoebas, foraminiferans, heliozoans, and radiolarians
Phylum Ciliophora: ciliates (protozoans with cilia)
Phylum Sporozoa: sporozoans (parasitic protozoans)

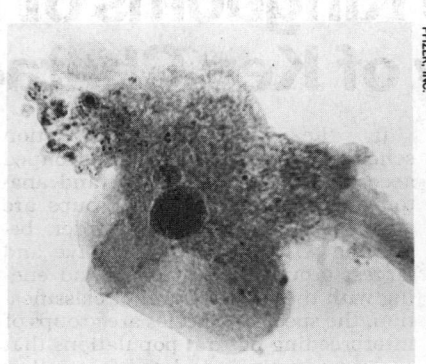

AMOEBA

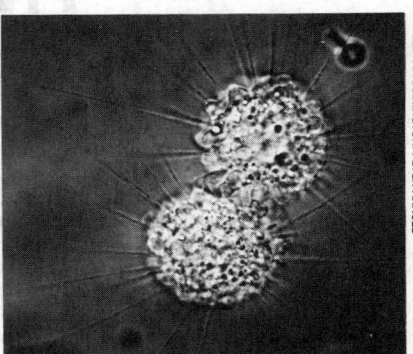

PROTOZOA

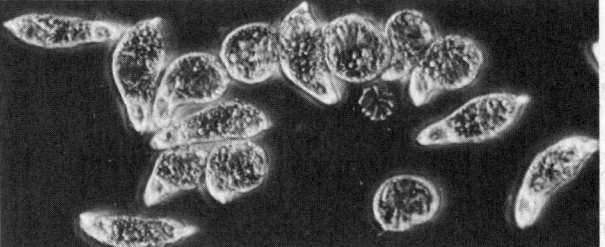

EUGLENA

Kingdom Fungi
(approximately 63,000 species)

All fungi are eucaryotic. Many have multicellular bodies composed of thin filaments, and some exist as single cells. Complex reproduction cycles often include both asexual and sexual processes. All obtain food by absorbing nutrients from their environment, some decomposing dead organic matter, some parasitizing living matter, and some doing both. Most fungi are nonmotile. None possesses chlorophyll within cells. Most fungal cells have cell walls, which are composed of either chitin or cellulose.

Phylum Ascomycota: ascomycetes, or sac fungi, including powdery mildews, blue-green, red, and brown food molds, yeasts, truffles, morels
Phylum Basidiomycota: basidiomycetes, or club fungi, including mushrooms, shelf and bracket fungi, puffballs, rusts, smuts, stinkhorns, coral fungi, earthstars, bird's nest fungi
Phylum Zygomycota: zygomycetes, or conjugating molds, including black bread mold

Phylum Deuteromycota: deuteromycetes, or imperfect fungi, a somewhat provisional taxonomic group of fungi, including fungi whose sexual stage of the life cycle is not presently known. New evidence has caused this group to be reclassified and placed with either the ascomycetes or basidiomycetes. Some of the better-known deuteromycetes are the species of Penicillium used in the production of the antibiotic penicillin; Penicillium is also used to produce the familiar blue, Roquefort, and Camembert cheeses. A species of Aspergillus, a common food mold, is used in the fermentation process of beans in the manufacture of soy sauce. There are also deuteromycetes that can cause animal and plant diseases; for example, Epidermophyton floccosum is the cause of athlete's foot, and Fusarium culmorum causes root rot of wheat.
Phylum Mycomycota: lichens, a group of fungi that live in close harmony with certain algae. The algae produce nutritive substances that the fungi absorb and use as a source of food.

PENICILLIN MOLD

AMANITA MUSCARUS

LICHEN

Kingdom Plantae
(approximately 315,000 species)

With rare exceptions, all plants are multicellular organisms with specialized cells that form tissues and organs that perform independent yet cooperative functions. All are eucaryotic and possess a cell wall, usually of cellulose, and chlorophyll. Almost all make their own food by photosynthesis, a few obtaining food by absorbing it from the environment. Most are nonmotile. The primary reproductive phase is sexual.

The nonvascular plants lack specialized cells for transporting food and water. Some are grouped as follows:

Phylum Rhodophyta: red algae
Phylum Phaeophyta: brown algae
Phylum Charophyta: stoneworts
Phylum Chlorophyta: green algae
Phylum Bryophyta: mosses, liverworts, hornworts

The vascular plants are organized under a single phylum as follows:

Phylum Tracheophyta: vascular plants
  Subphylum Psilophyta: psilopsids
  Subphylum Lychophyta: club mosses
  Subphylum Sphenophyta: horsetails
  Subphylum Pterophyta: ferns
  Subphylum Spermophyta: seed plants
    Class Gymnospermae: ginko, cycads, conifers
    Class Angiospermae: flowering plants

GREEN ALGAE

L. M. CHASE/NATIONAL AUDUBON SOCIETY/PHOTO RESEARCHERS

MAPLE SEED

CLUBMOSS

VERNA JOHNSON/NATIONAL AUDUBON SOCIETY/PHOTO RESEARCHERS

JACK DERMID/PHOTO RESEARCHERS

Kingdom Animalia
(approximately 1,000,000 species)

All animals are eucaryotic multicellular organisms whose highly specialized cells perform a variety of independent yet cooperative functions. Nutrition is primarily obtained by ingesting whole food and digesting it in the body. Reproduction is primarily sexual. Generally, no cell walls exist and no chlorophyll is present within cells. All are usually motile. Major phyla and classes are:

Phylum Porifera: sponges
Phylum Coelenterata: coelenterates, including hydroids, jellyfish, corals, anemones
Phylum Ctenophora: comb jellies
Phylum Platyhelminthes: flatworms, including planaria, flukes, tapeworms
Phylum Nemertinea: proboscis worms
Phylum Aschelminthes: roundworms and rotifers
Phylum Ectoprocta: ectoprocts, or bryozoans
Phylum Brachiopoda: brachiopods (lamp shells)
Phylum Phoronida: phoronids

Phylum Annelida: annelids, or segmented worms, including earthworms, marine worms, leeches
Phylum Mollusca: mollusks
  Class Amphinura: chitons
  Class Gastropoda: single-shelled mollusks, including snails, whelks, limpets, abalone, slugs
  Class Pelecypoda: two-shelled mollusks, including clams, mussels, scallops, oysters
  Class Cephalopoda: cephalopods, including squid, octopuses, chambered nautiluses
Phylum Onychophora: onychophorans
Phylum Arthropoda: arthropods
  Class Arachnida: arachnids, including true spiders, ticks, mites, scorpions
  Class Crustacea: crustaceans, including marine and freshwater crabs, crayfish, lobsters, shrimp, copepods, water fleas, barnacles, sow bugs, isopods
  Class Chilopoda: centipedes
  Class Diplopoda: millipedes
  Class Insecta: insects, including beetles, butterflies, moths, bees, ants, flies, bugs, wasps, grasshoppers, lice, termites, fleas, dragonflies

Phylum Ecinodermata: echinoderms, including sea lilies, sea cucumbers, sea urchins, sand dollars, sea stars, serpent and brittle stars
Phylum Hemichordata: acorn worms
Phylum Chordata: chordates
  Subphylum Urochordata: urochordates, including sea squirts
  Subphylum Cephalochordata: cephalochordates, or lancelets
  Subphylum Vertebrata: vertebrates
  Class Agnatha: jawless fish
  Class Chondrichthyes: cartilagenous jawed fish, including sharks, skates, rays
  Class Osteichthyes: bony fish
  Class Amphibia: amphibians, including salamanders, frogs, toads, caecilians
  Class Reptilia: reptiles, including turtles, alligators, crocodiles, lizards, snakes, tuatara
  Class Aves: birds
  Class Mammalia: mammals

EARTHWORM   MARTIN M. ROTKER/TAURUS PHOTOS

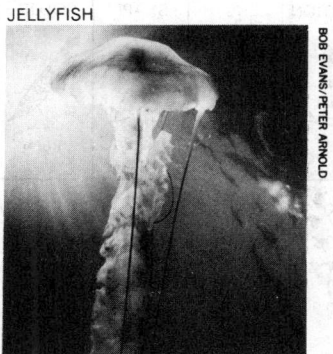

JELLYFISH

BOB EVANS/PETER ARNOLD

GIRAFFES

MARC & EVELYNE BERNHEIM/WOODFIN CAMP

The Gene

All living organisms have the inherited ability to transmit to their offspring all that characterizes life. Their offspring, in turn, pass the ability on to successive offspring. The characteristics that are transmitted are expressed as traits bearing close resemblance to those possessed by the previous generation. The continuity of life that exists can be perpetuated for many generations through time. A major factor underlying this phenomenon is the biological structure called the gene. The scientific study of the gene is called genetics. The molecular nature of genes is dealt with in molecular genetics. Given the intimate association of genes with all life processes, the science of genetics has served to integrate and act as a foundation for many diverse areas of biological and medical science.

The gene is not the only factor influencing the development of an individual; the environment also plays a key role in this transformation. Ultimately, it is the interaction between an organism's genetic constitution and its environment that is responsible for shaping the organism.

Classical Genetics

In 1866, just seven years after the appearance of Darwin's *Origin of Species,* Gregor Mendel published the results of his own experimental work based on breeding the garden pea. Darwin believed that characteristics were transmitted from one generation to the next, but he knew nothing about how this happened; nor did he ever learn of the far-reaching work of Mendel, which provided the explanation.

The mechanism by which genetic traits are transmitted from one generation to the next is the basis of classical, or Mendelian, genetics.

By the 19th century, biologists knew that an embryo developed from the fusion of an egg cell and a sperm cell, and that the organism resulting from that union was the product of materials contributed by each parent. However, biologists of the day believed that the hereditary materials supplied by the parents were bloodlike fluids that blended in the offspring. It was from that erroneous assumption that the terms "half-blooded" and "full-blooded" arose.

In 1866, Gregor Johann Mendel (1822–1884), an Austrian monk, demonstrated patterns of inheritance in the garden pea, *Pisum sativum,* and in so doing showed that hereditary traits are transmitted by distinct units, one from each parent, later called genes.

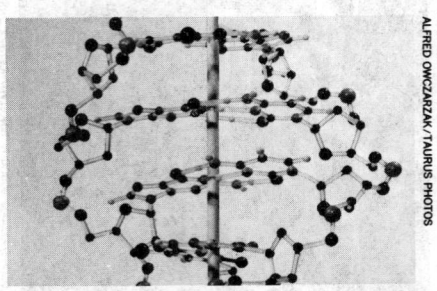

DISCOVERY OF DNA'S *molecular structure unlocked the mystery of inheritance.*

The genes reshuffle, segregate, and redistribute, rather than blend, in the resulting offspring.

Mendel used garden peas in his experiments because they hybridize easily. When he crossed a purebred tall plant with a purebred short plant, all the hybrid offspring were tall, no matter which type was the mother and which the father. In addition, the hybrids self-fertilized, and Mendel counted the offspring. He found 787 tall plants and 277 shorter plants, a ratio of approximately three to one. When the short plants self-fertilized, they produced only short offspring, but when the tall plants self-fertilized, there were two types of offspring: one-third had only tall offspring; two-thirds produced both tall and short offspring in a ratio of three to one. Mendel crossed six other characters: round and wrinkled peas, colored and uncolored flowers, and yellow and green peas. The results obtained were approximately the same.

Mendel's law of segregation.
From his results Mendel formulated the law of segregation. Today this principle states that hereditary traits, such as tallness or shortness, are transmitted by way of zygotes (fertilized eggs). One member of the pair of traits comes from the male parent; the other, from the female. These paired genes segregate during the formation of gametes (sperm cells and egg cells) so that only one of the pair is transmitted by a particular gamete. The gamete has just one gene of each pair and is called haploid. When the male and female gametes unite to form the zygote, it is called diploid.

Mendel's studies showed the principle of dominance. In garden peas, the trait of tallness is dominant over shortness. Thus, when there is a gene for tallness and one for shortness, all peas are tall. The unexpressed factor, shortness, is said to be recessive.

An individual with unlike paired genes can be represented as *Tt*. (*T* here represents the dominant gene for tallness, and *t* the recessive gene for shortness.) Such an individual is called a heterozygote. If both genes are alike, either *tt* or *TT,* the individual is a homozygote. The genetic makeup is called the genotype; the character determined by this genotype and expressed in the individual is the phenotype. If the genotype is *TT,* the phenotype is tallness. Another genotype that can give the phenotype tallness is *Tt*. The alternative forms of a gene are called the alleles.

Mendel concluded that dominant and recessive genes do not affect each other: gametes are haploid and have only one of a pair of genes; each type of gamete is produced in equal numbers by a hybrid parent; and combination between gametes depends on chance, with the frequency of each class of offspring depending on the frequency of the gametes produced by each of the parents.

DOMINANT AND RECESSIVE CHARACTERISTICS OF PEA PLANTS

	SEED TEXTURE	SEED COLOR	FLOWER COLOR	FLOWER POSITION	STEM LENGTH	POD SHAPE	POD COLOR
Dominant	smooth	yellow	red	axial	long	inflated	green
Recessive	wrinkled	green	white	terminal	short	constricted	yellow

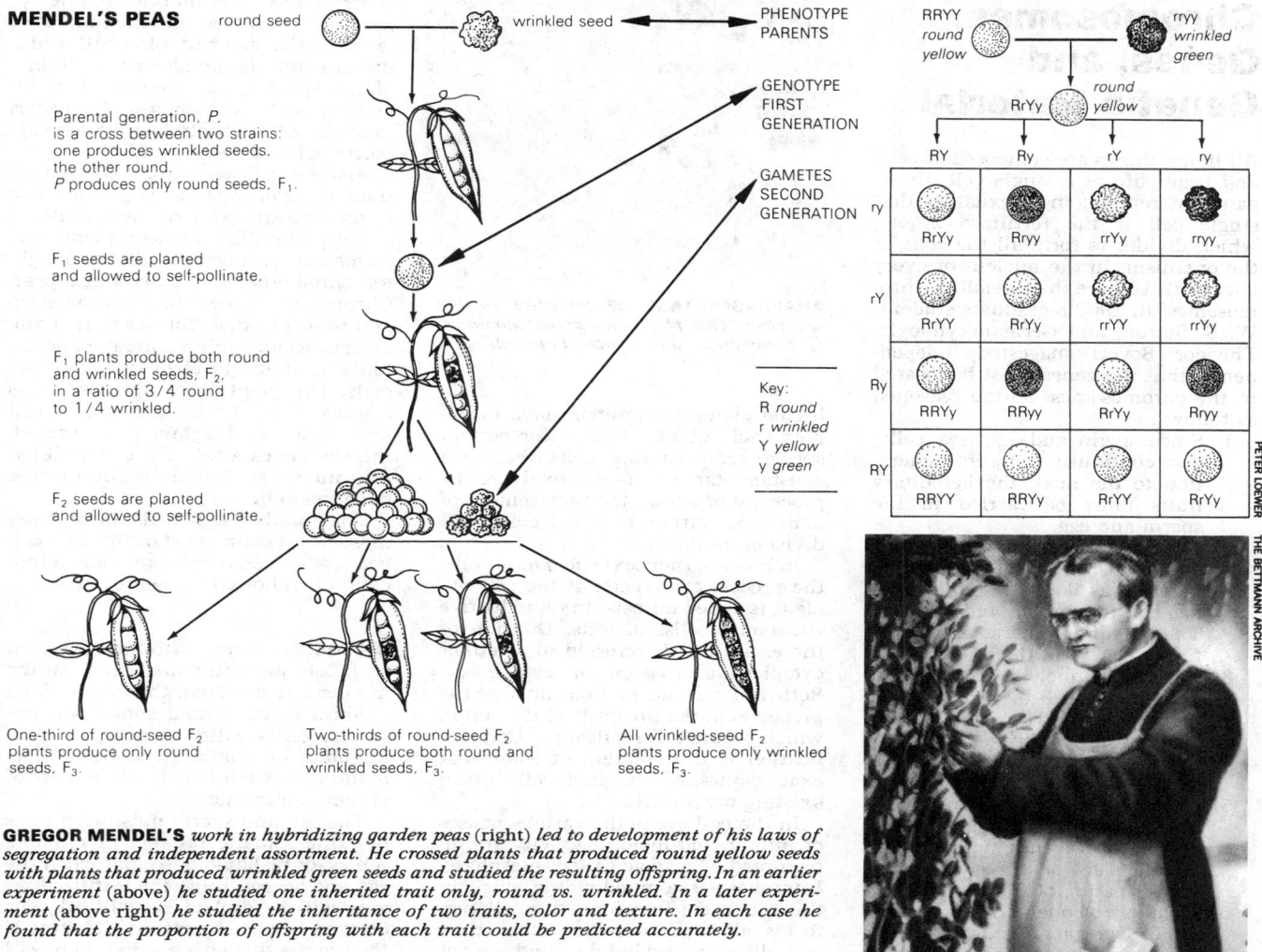

MENDEL'S PEAS

round seed ○ ⟷ ◯ wrinkled seed → PHENOTYPE PARENTS

Parental generation, *P*, is a cross between two strains: one produces wrinkled seeds, the other round. *P* produces only round seeds, *F₁*.

GENOTYPE FIRST GENERATION

F₁ seeds are planted and allowed to self-pollinate.

GAMETES SECOND GENERATION

F₁ plants produce both round and wrinkled seeds, *F₂*, in a ratio of 3/4 round to 1/4 wrinkled.

Key:
R *round*
r *wrinkled*
Y *yellow*
y *green*

F₂ seeds are planted and allowed to self-pollinate.

One-third of round-seed F₂ plants produce only round seeds, *F₃*.

Two-thirds of round-seed F₂ plants produce both round and wrinkled seeds, *F₃*.

All wrinkled-seed F₂ plants produce only wrinkled seeds, *F₃*.

RRYY *round yellow* ⟷ ◉ rryy *wrinkled green*

RrYy *round yellow*

RY · Ry · rY · ry

PETER LOEWER

GREGOR MENDEL'S *work in hybridizing garden peas* (right) *led to development of his laws of segregation and independent assortment. He crossed plants that produced round yellow seeds with plants that produced wrinkled green seeds and studied the resulting offspring. In an earlier experiment* (above) *he studied one inherited trait only, round vs. wrinkled. In a later experiment* (above right) *he studied the inheritance of two traits, color and texture. In each case he found that the proportion of offspring with each trait could be predicted accurately.*

THE BETTMANN ARCHIVE

Mendel's law of independent assortment.

Mendel next determined how two or more pairs of genes would behave in crosses. He crossed plants having round, yellow seeds with plants having wrinkled, green seeds. He knew a cross between round (*R*) and wrinkled (*r*) seeds produced round seeds in the F_1 (first filial) generation, and three round to one wrinkled seed in the F_2 (second filial) plants. He also knew that crossing yellow (*Y*) with green (*y*) produced all yellow seeds in the F_1, and three yellow to one green seed in the F_2 generation. This showed the dominance of roundness and yellowness over their respective contrasting alleles. When Mendel crossed round-yellow with wrinkled-green, the F_1 produced all round-yellow seeds. In the F_2 generation, the following seed types and proportions were obtained:

Type	Proportion
round-yellow	9/16
round-green	3/16
wrinkled-yellow	3/16
wrinkled-green	1/16

Two combinations of offspring appeared in Mendel's experiment: round-green and wrinkled-yellow, neither one present in either the parental generation or the F_1 generation. This result can be explained by Mendel's law of independent assortment. The law of independent assortment states that the members of a single pair of genes segregate independently of other pairs.

Mendel also tested his F_2 plants to determine whether all of a single phenoclass, such as round-yellow, were alike in genotype. According to his hypothesis, there should be four different genotypes in this group: *RR, YY; RR, Yy; Rr, YY;* and *Rr, Yy.* When F_2 plants self-fertilized, he found four classes of round-yellow seeded plants; the ratios fitted expectations. The breeding behaviors of F_2 round-green, wrinkled-yellow, and wrinkled-green were in accordance with the hypothesis that each pair of genes segregates independently from other pairs of genes and each pair of genes also is transmitted independently to the next generation.

Mendel's inheritance rules were later found to apply to other plants and animals, and some seeming exceptions to his rules were explained in this later work.

In all characters studied by Mendel, the heterozygote was phenotypically identical with the homozygote dominant. In some cases, however, the heterozygote is intermediate. In the case of the flower known as the four o'oclock, for example, if a red parent is crossed with a white, all F_1 hybrids are intermediate in color, one-quarter of the F_2 offspring are red, one-quarter white, and one half intermediate. In some cases, both alleles are equally dominant, as are those that determine antigenic factors of blood. For example, if one parent is, say, *M* and the other *N*, all children will be *MN*. If both parents are *M* or both are *N*, all children will be *MM* or all will be *NN*. If both parents are *MN*, one-quarter of the children will be *M*, one-quarter of them *N*, and one half of them *MN*. To understand other exceptions, one must take into full account the chromosomal basis of heredity.

Chromosomes, Genes, and Genetic Material

All living things are composed of cells and begin life as a single cell. In organisms reproducing sexually, that single cell is the fertilized zygote, which divides to form all the cells of the organism. In the nucleus of every eucaryotic cell are the threadlike chromosomes. In 1902 a graduate student, W. S. Sutton, and German cytologist Theodor Boveri suggested independently that the genes must be located in the chromosomes. Sutton reasoned as follows:

1. Since sperm and egg (sex cells) give continuity from one generation to the next, the hereditary traits must be carried in the sperm and egg.
2. The sperm is almost all nucleus and yet contributes as much to heredity as does the egg, which has both cytoplasm and nucleus. The hereditary characters, therefore, must be in the nucleus.
3. The visible nuclear parts that divide during cell division are the chromosomes. The genes, then, must be in the chromosomes.
4. Chromosomes occur in pairs, as do genes.
5. Chromosomes segregate during maturation of the egg and the sperm, as do genes, according to Mendel's law of segregation, during formation of the gametes.
6. Members of one pair of chromosomes segregate independently of other chromosome pairs, following Mendel's law of independent assortment.

Accumulated evidence has proved the truth of Sutton's hypothesis, and the molecular nature of the hereditary chromosomal material has been identified as well.

Transmission of Hereditary Characteristics

Not until 1900 was Gregor Mendel's work on the mechanism of transmission of hereditary characteristics given the credit it deserved. By 1903, Mendel's hereditary factor became known as the gene. And around 1910, the chromosomal theory of inheritance was advanced by American zoologist Thomas Hunt Morgan.

Cell cycle. Unlike the procaryotic cells of bacteria and blue-green bacteria, which have a comparatively simple life cycle, eucaryotic cells of

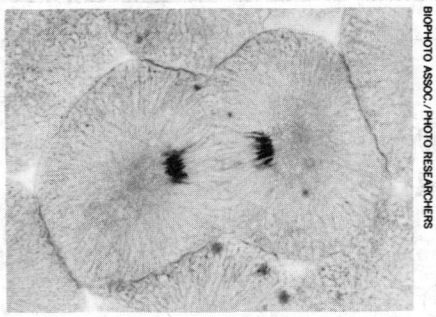

ANAPHASE STAGE OF MITOSIS *in the whitefish. This photomicrograph shows sister chromatids moving toward opposite poles of the cell.*

higher plants and animals have a complex cycle of life. Except for certain specialized eucaryotic cells, there is a constant state of change involving the processes of aging: the replacement of damaged, worn-out, or old cells; cell division; or death.

In somatic (nonsex) eucaryotic cells, the process of division of the cell nucleus is called mitosis; in reproductive eucaryotic cells, meiosis. Division of the entire cell is referred to as either cytoplasmic division or cytokinesis. Both mitosis and meiosis involve the processes in the life cycle of the cell in which occurs cell replication. Cell replication is the creation of somewhat exact copies, or daughter cells, of an existing parent cell.

In the cell cycle, the various phases of mitotic and meiotic activity are interrupted by a stage called interphase. Interphase is a nondividing stage in the cell cycle in which the cell performs all vital activities other than cell division, including synthesis of DNA, RNA, and protein; overall increase in cell size; and doubling of certain organelles. Upon completion of interphase, mitosis and meiosis can begin again.

Mitosis. Chromosomes are accurately reproduced and transmitted in a process that ensures that each new cell formed receives one of each chromosome. The number of chromosomes characteristic of each species remains constant. Every human somatic cell, for example, has 46 chromosomes; the somatic cell of every garden pea, 14.

Although mitosis is a continuous process, it may be described in terms of five phases:

Interphase. Chromosomes exist as a tangled mass of threads of chromatin. The nuclear membrane and nucleoli are evident. Each chromosome makes an exact copy, a chromatid, of itself.

Prophase. The chromatin condenses to form visible chromosomes having pairs of sister chromatids, each pair held together by a single centromere. The nuclear membrane and nucleoli disappear, and spindle fibers denser than the cytoplasm begin to appear.

Metaphase. The mitotic spindle apparatus, composed of microtubules, takes on the shape of a football. Chromatid pairs line up along the midline of the spindle, and spindle fibers attach to their centromeres. Centrioles may appear and begin to migrate to opposite poles of the spindle.

Anaphase. Sister chromatids split at their centromeres and begin to move to the opposite poles of the spindle.

Telophase. The nuclear membrane forms around a complete set of daughter chromosomes. Nucleoli reappear. Chromosomes become uncondensed and return to their former state. Cytokinesis occurs: cell membrane and cytoplasm divide to form two daughter cells. (In plant cells, cytokinesis is completed by the formation of a cell plate between daughter cells, preceding the appearance of a cell wall.) A new interphase is then begun in each daughter cell.

The number and makeup of chromosomes remain constant in each cell because successive chromosome duplication is followed by cell division.

Meiosis. The chromosomes of each cell occur in pairs, one from the mother and one from the father. Each member of the chromosomal pair has similar genes, called homologous chromosomes or homologues. Human somatic cells have twenty-three pairs of chromosomes each.

The egg and sperm must each have half the somatic number of chromosomes, or be haploid, so that when the egg and sperm unite, the fertilized zygote will be diploid, as will all cells derived from it by mitosis. Meiosis is the process that ensures that there will be one member of each chromosome pair in each gamete and that the chromosome number of somatic cells of the species will remain constant from generation to generation. Meiosis has two divisions:

First meiotic division. In this phase, each chromosome copies itself once, creating two chromatids held together by a centromere. The homologous chromosomes move toward each other and pair tightly, so that similar genes, or alleles, lie alongside each other. This makes a bundle of four chromatids and two centromeres. During this time, the matching strands twist around one another, break, and then reunite, thus exchanging homologous sections. As a result, chromosomes consist of parts from both paternal and maternal chromosomes. The centromere of each of the homologous chromosomes is pulled to an opposite pole of the cell, pulling the attached chromosome with it. The cell divides. Each new cell now has the haploid chromosome number, with either a maternally or paternally derived member of each chromosomal pair, depending on chance and the random attachments of each centromere to the spindle fi-

MITOSIS

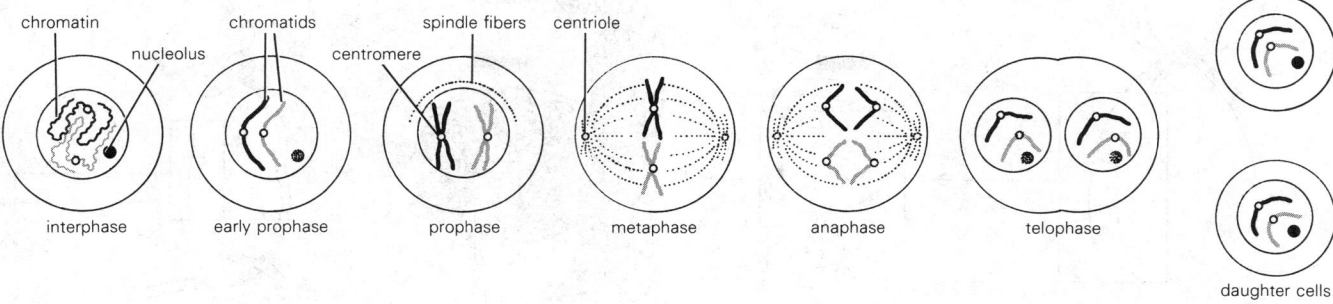

MEIOSIS

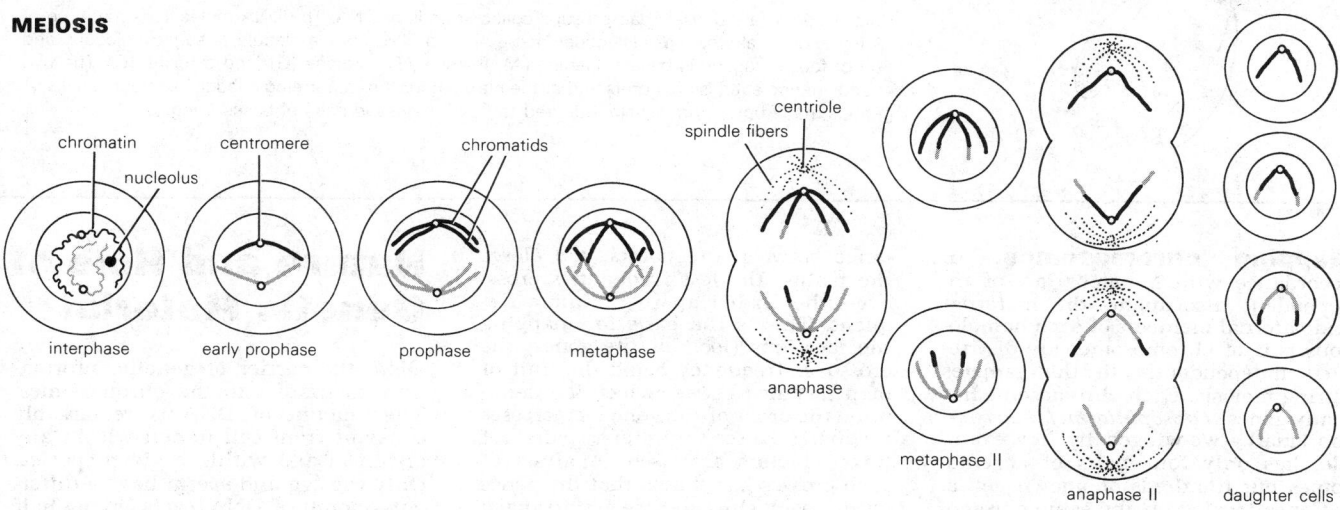

PETER LOEWER

bers. This is the chromosomal basis for the independent assortment of each member of a pair of chromosomes with respect to the other.

Second meiotic division. In this phase, the centromeres divide so that each chromatid separates from its duplicate. Another division, much like ordinary mitosis, follows, and two duplicate cells are formed.

Because of the two meiotic divisions, four cells are formed from a single original cell, each having a haploid number of chromosomes, one of each homologous pair.

Human sex chromosomes.
Chromosomes occur in pairs, one maternal chromosome and one paternal chromosome. The chromosomes of all but one pair are identical in both sexes. In one sex, usually the male, there is one pair of unidentical chromosomes—X and Y.

In the human male, there are 22 pairs of identical nonsex chromosomes, called autosomes, and one X and one Y chromosome. The X and Y

chromosomes are called sex chromosomes. The human female has 22 pairs of autosomes and one pair of X chromosomes. If an egg is fertilized by a sperm bearing an X chromosome, it becomes female (XX). If it is fertilized by a sperm bearing a Y chromosome, it becomes male (XY). Thus, sex determination occurs at fertilization. Since segregation of the sex chromosomes takes place during meiosis, as does segregation of the other chromosomes, and is completely random, the chance is even that any sperm will contain a Y chromosome. Because all eggs contain one X chromosome, the probability of

COLORBLINDNESS *is a common sex-linked trait in humans. A colorblind male passes his recessive trait to a male grandchild through his daughter.*

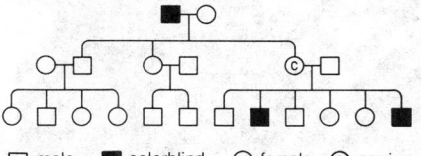

□ male   ■ colorblind   ○ female   ⓒ carrier

the offspring's being either a boy or a girl is exactly 50:50.

Y chromosomes of organisms contain few or no genes. (None are known to occur in human Y chromosomes.) X chromosomes contain many genes. Because of this, these genes are segregated differently in the two sexes, resulting in the phenomenon called sex-linkage.

In humans, red-green color blindness is the most common sex-linked trait, occurring in about 8 percent of men and about .5 percent of women. The difference in occurrence is explained by the hypothesis that the recessive gene responsible is contained in the X chromosome and that there is no corresponding allele in the Y. A woman heterozygous for the trait mated with a normal male would have daughters with normal vision, but half of her sons would probably be colorblind. The children of a homozygous (normal) woman and a colorblind man would all be normal, but half of the daughters would probably be heterozygous and would transmit the trait to half their sons.

UNRAVELING A CHROMOSOME

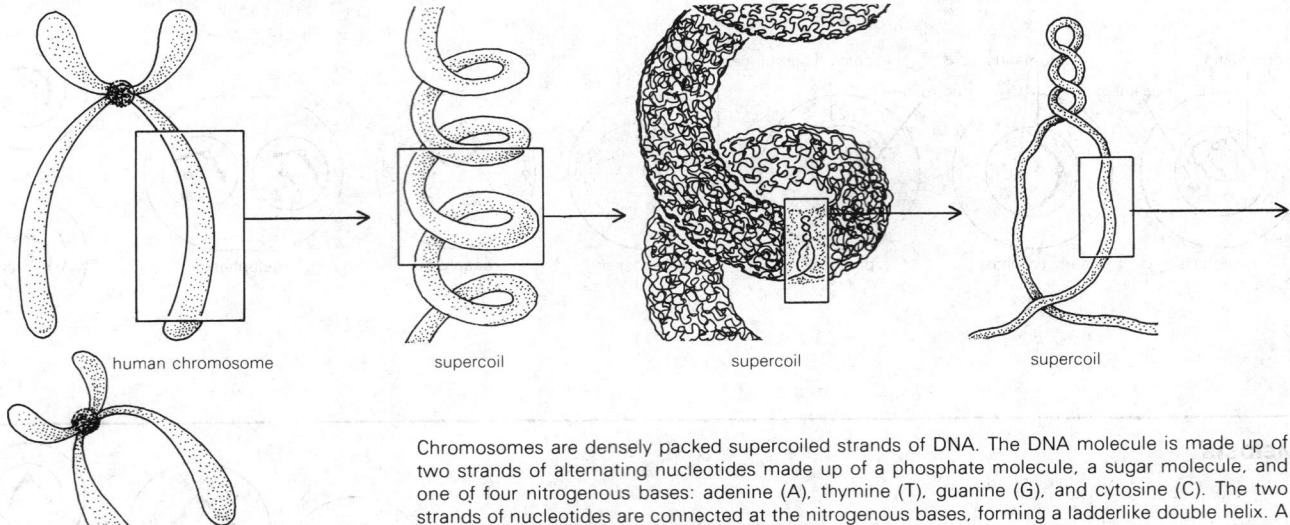

human chromosome   supercoil   supercoil   supercoil

Chromosomes are densely packed supercoiled strands of DNA. The DNA molecule is made up of two strands of alternating nucleotides made up of a phosphate molecule, a sugar molecule, and one of four nitrogenous bases: adenine (A), thymine (T), guanine (G), and cytosine (C). The two strands of nucleotides are connected at the nitrogenous bases, forming a ladderlike double helix. A gene is made up of from several hundred to a few thousand pairs of bases (rungs).

PETER LOEWER

Mapping chromosomes.

In accordance with Mendel's law of independent assortment, the maternal and paternal members of each homologous pair of chromosomes are distributed independently to the gametes during meiosis. Each chromosome has many genes. *Drosophila melanogaster,* the small, two-winged fly, for example, has only four pairs of chromosomes but hundreds of known genes.

Genes located on the same chromosome tend to be inherited together and are said to be linked. When homologous chromosomes pair during meiosis, they twist around each other, break, and reunite. As a result, some parts of a chromosome segregated to the new cell can be either maternal or paternal. This process of chromosomal recombination, called crossover, occurs at the stage of meiosis when there are four chromatids held together by the undivided centromeres.

Crossover occurs at random sites along the chromosome. The frequency of crossover is determined by the distance between the points: the closer the points, the less frequent is crossover; the farther apart, the more frequent. This is the basis for mapping the locations (loci) of the genes, the crossover frequency being the unit of map distance between loci. To determine the order of the gene loci, crosses involving three different pairs of linked factors are used. Analysis of such crosses has shown that the genes within each chromosome are arranged linearly in a definite serial order of fixed loci.

Genetic maps of chromosomes are graphic representations of the relative distances between genes in each linkage group, as determined by the percentage of recombination (crossover) among the genes. The chromosomes of *Drosophila* have been intensively mapped, as have those of pink bread mold (*Neurospora*), the colon bacillus (*Escherichia coli*), and the mouse. New techniques in tissue culture have recently made possible the mapping of all human chromosomes.

INDIVIDUAL GENES *are seen in a photo of radioactive nucleotides.*

LILA VODKIN

Nature and Role of Genetic Material

DNA, the carrier of genetic information, is unique to the chromosomes. The amount of DNA is remarkably constant from cell to cell within any organism and within a given species. Only the egg and sperm have a different amount of DNA, each having half the amount found in somatic cells, half the number of chromosomes. Proteins and RNA, also found in chromosomes and associated with DNA in carrying and transferring genetic information, vary in the amount found in tissues within a species.

Direct evidence that DNA is the genetic material grew out of experiments in transformation of certain bacteria showing that DNA is the so-called transforming principle. Work done by O. T. Avery, C. M. MacLeod, and M. McCarty in 1944 was based on earlier observations that when an extract from dead cells of one strain of *Pneumococcus* was added to living cells of another strain, it transformed some characters of the living cells so that they were identical with the extract strain. The new characters inherited by the transformed strain were then passed on to their offspring. Avery's group analyzed the extract and proved that the active part of the transforming extract was pure DNA.

Further evidence that DNA transmits genetic information was obtained by the 1952 studies of Alfred Hershey and Margaret Chase on viral infection of *Escherichia coli.* Bacterial viruses, or bacteriophages, consist of a protein

HUMAN ANATOMY

This section on Human Anatomy is designed to show the various structures of the body and their exact location in relation to each other. Many of the labels in these illustrations not only identify a structure, but give additional information about the structure and its function. The illustrations are based on the famous wall charts by Professors Franz Frohse of the University of Berlin and Max Brödel of Johns Hopkins Medical School. Professor Frohse reproduced his charts for the first time just prior to World War I.

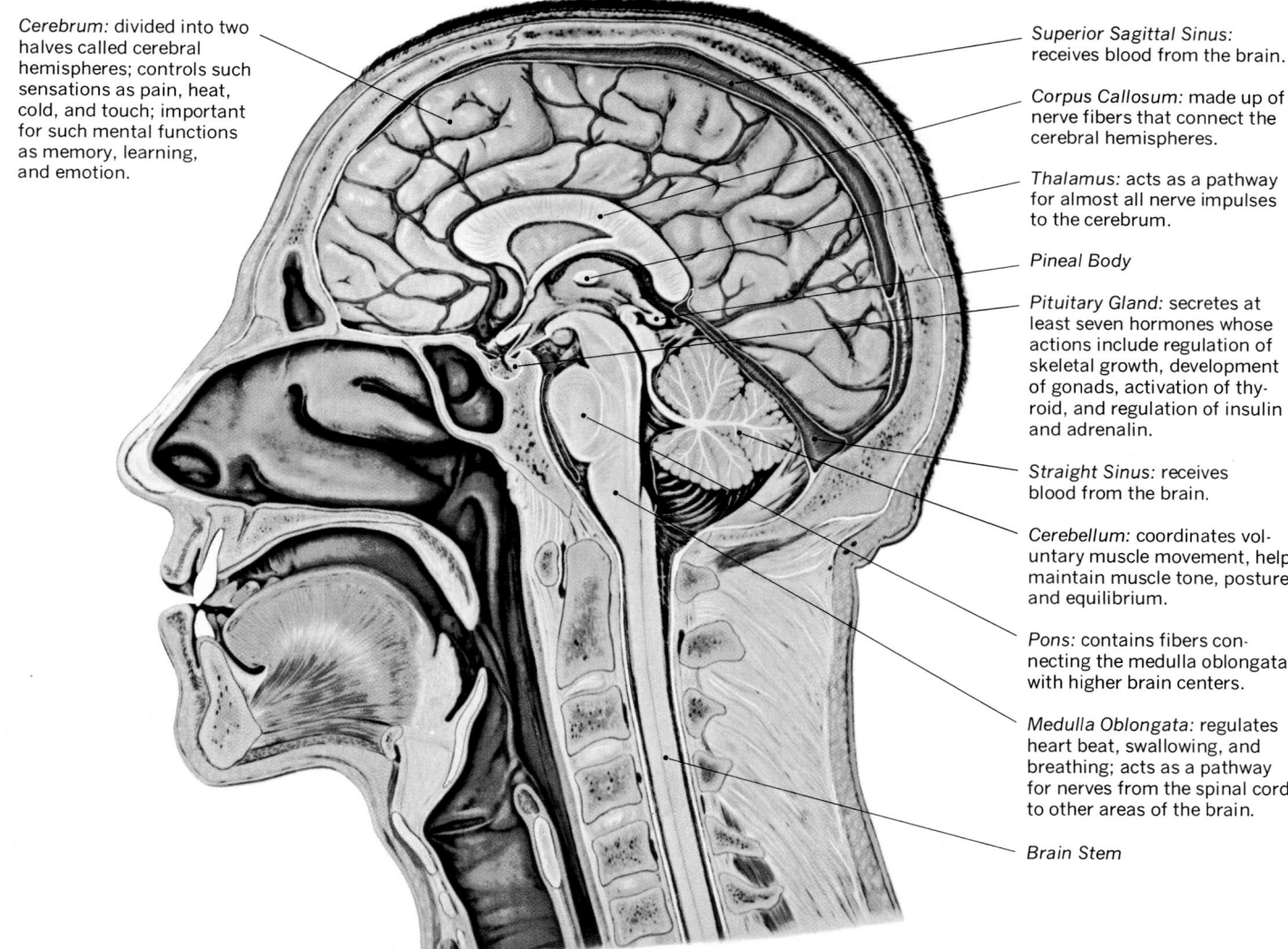

Cerebrum: divided into two halves called cerebral hemispheres; controls such sensations as pain, heat, cold, and touch; important for such mental functions as memory, learning, and emotion.

Superior Sagittal Sinus: receives blood from the brain.

Corpus Callosum: made up of nerve fibers that connect the cerebral hemispheres.

Thalamus: acts as a pathway for almost all nerve impulses to the cerebrum.

Pineal Body

Pituitary Gland: secretes at least seven hormones whose actions include regulation of skeletal growth, development of gonads, activation of thyroid, and regulation of insulin and adrenalin.

Straight Sinus: receives blood from the brain.

Cerebellum: coordinates voluntary muscle movement, helps maintain muscle tone, posture, and equilibrium.

Pons: contains fibers connecting the medulla oblongata with higher brain centers.

Medulla Oblongata: regulates heart beat, swallowing, and breathing; acts as a pathway for nerves from the spinal cord to other areas of the brain.

Brain Stem

Illustration Consultant,
Diane L. Nelson, A.M.I.

Anatomical Illustrations Courtesy of A. J. Nystrom & Co.

The Nervous System

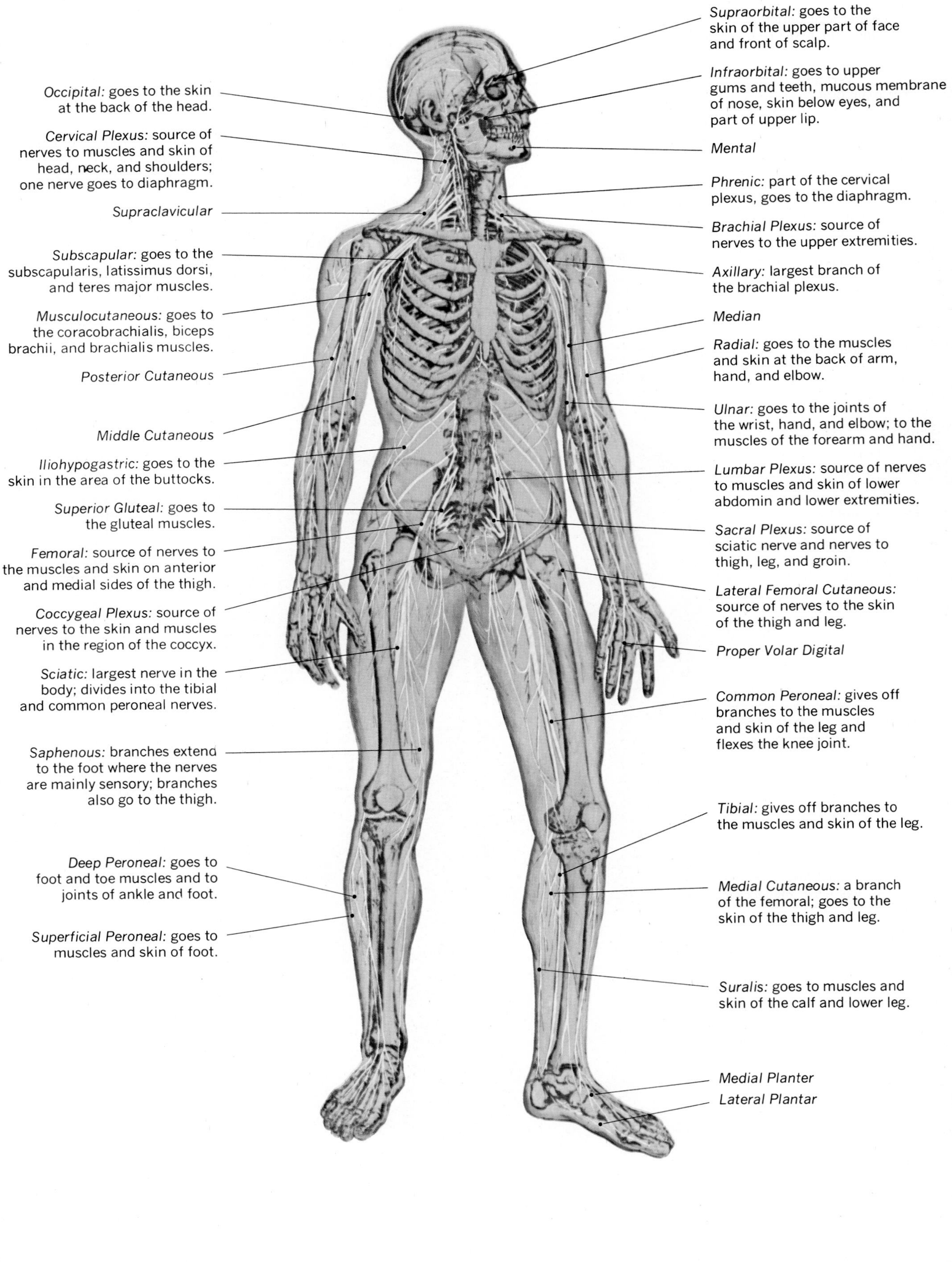

Supraorbital: goes to the skin of the upper part of face and front of scalp.

Infraorbital: goes to upper gums and teeth, mucous membrane of nose, skin below eyes, and part of upper lip.

Mental

Phrenic: part of the cervical plexus, goes to the diaphragm.

Brachial Plexus: source of nerves to the upper extremities.

Axillary: largest branch of the brachial plexus.

Median

Radial: goes to the muscles and skin at the back of arm, hand, and elbow.

Ulnar: goes to the joints of the wrist, hand, and elbow; to the muscles of the forearm and hand.

Lumbar Plexus: source of nerves to muscles and skin of lower abdomin and lower extremities.

Sacral Plexus: source of sciatic nerve and nerves to thigh, leg, and groin.

Lateral Femoral Cutaneous: source of nerves to the skin of the thigh and leg.

Proper Volar Digital

Common Peroneal: gives off branches to the muscles and skin of the leg and flexes the knee joint.

Tibial: gives off branches to the muscles and skin of the leg.

Medial Cutaneous: a branch of the femoral; goes to the skin of the thigh and leg.

Suralis: goes to muscles and skin of the calf and lower leg.

Medial Planter

Lateral Plantar

Occipital: goes to the skin at the back of the head.

Cervical Plexus: source of nerves to muscles and skin of head, neck, and shoulders; one nerve goes to diaphragm.

Supraclavicular

Subscapular: goes to the subscapularis, latissimus dorsi, and teres major muscles.

Musculocutaneous: goes to the coracobrachialis, biceps brachii, and brachialis muscles.

Posterior Cutaneous

Middle Cutaneous

Iliohypogastric: goes to the skin in the area of the buttocks.

Superior Gluteal: goes to the gluteal muscles.

Femoral: source of nerves to the muscles and skin on anterior and medial sides of the thigh.

Coccygeal Plexus: source of nerves to the skin and muscles in the region of the coccyx.

Sciatic: largest nerve in the body; divides into the tibial and common peroneal nerves.

Saphenous: branches extend to the foot where the nerves are mainly sensory; branches also go to the thigh.

Deep Peroneal: goes to foot and toe muscles and to joints of ankle and foot.

Superficial Peroneal: goes to muscles and skin of foot.

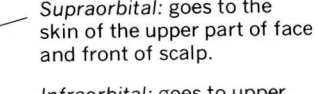

The Circulatory System

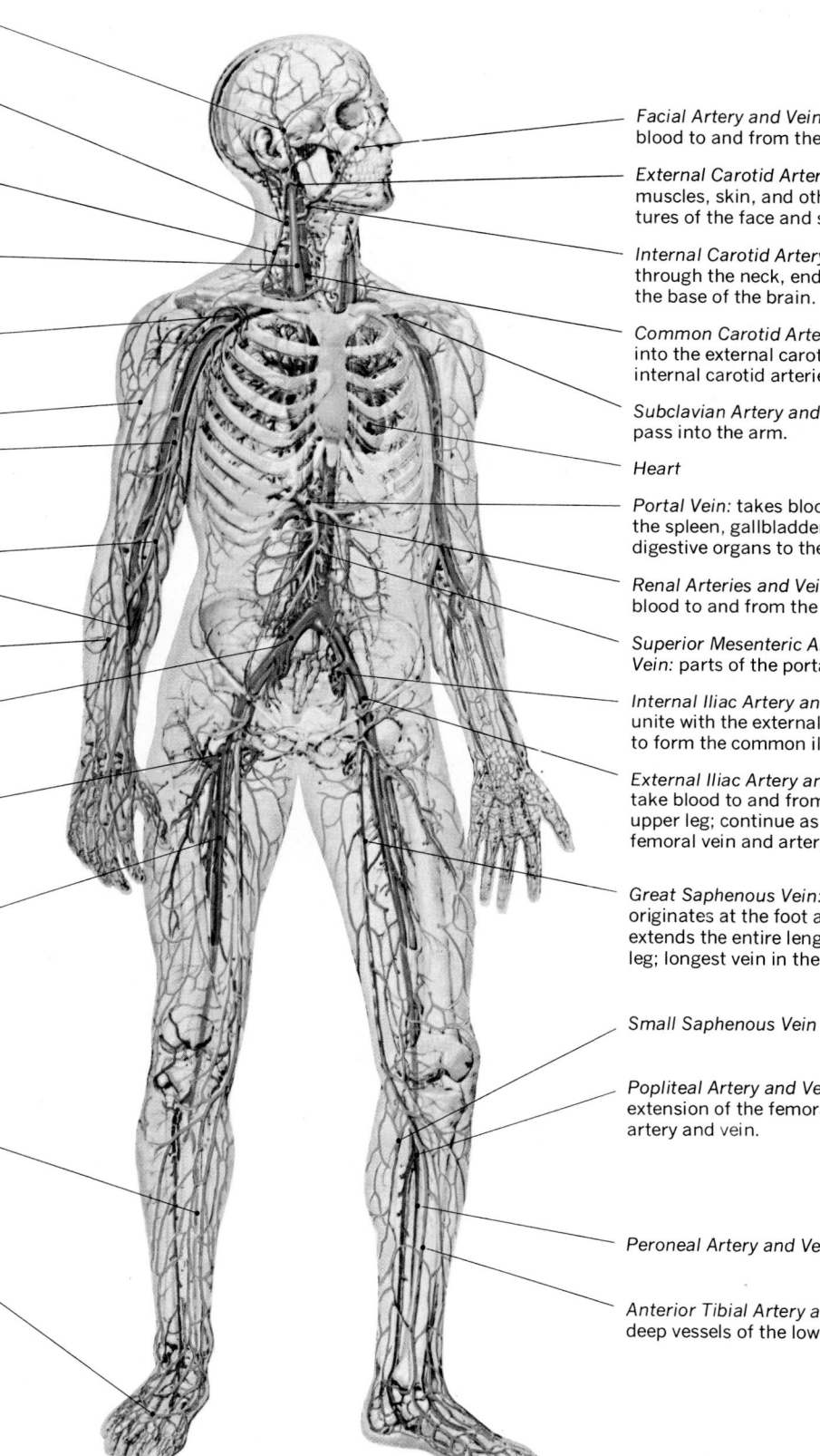

Superficial Temporal Artery and Vein: take blood to and from the side of the head.

Vertebral Artery: one of two main branches arising from the subclavian artery.

External Jugular Vein: drains the surface areas of the head, scalp, and face.

Internal Jugular Vein: receives blood from all parts of the head and neck.

Axillary Artery and Vein: form many branches that take blood to and from the arm.

Cephalic Artery and Vein

Brachial Artery and Vein: branch from the axillary; divide into the ulnar and radial arteries and veins.

Basilic Vein

Ulnar Artery and Vein: take blood to and from the lower arm.

Radial Artery and Vein: take blood to and from the lower arm.

Common Iliac Artery and Vein: the two arteries merge to form the abdominal aorta; the two veins form the inferior vena cava.

Deep Femoral Artery and Vein

Femoral Artery and Vein: pass through the thigh as an extension of the external iliac.

Posterior Tibial Artery and Vein: deep vessels of the lower leg.

Plantar Arterial and Venous Arch: main vessels of the foot.

The blue vessels represent veins; the red vessels represent arteries.

Facial Artery and Vein: take blood to and from the face.

External Carotid Artery: supplies muscles, skin, and other structures of the face and scalp.

Internal Carotid Artery: extends through the neck, ending at the base of the brain.

Common Carotid Artery: divides into the external carotid and internal carotid arteries.

Subclavian Artery and Vein: pass into the arm.

Heart

Portal Vein: takes blood from the spleen, gallbladder, and digestive organs to the liver.

Renal Arteries and Veins: take blood to and from the kidneys.

Superior Mesenteric Artery and Vein: parts of the portal system.

Internal Iliac Artery and Vein: unite with the external iliac to form the common iliac.

External Iliac Artery and Vein: take blood to and from the upper leg; continue as the femoral vein and artery.

Great Saphenous Vein: originates at the foot and extends the entire length of the leg; longest vein in the body.

Small Saphenous Vein

Popliteal Artery and Vein: extension of the femoral artery and vein.

Peroneal Artery and Vein

Anterior Tibial Artery and Vein: deep vessels of the lower leg.

The Muscular System

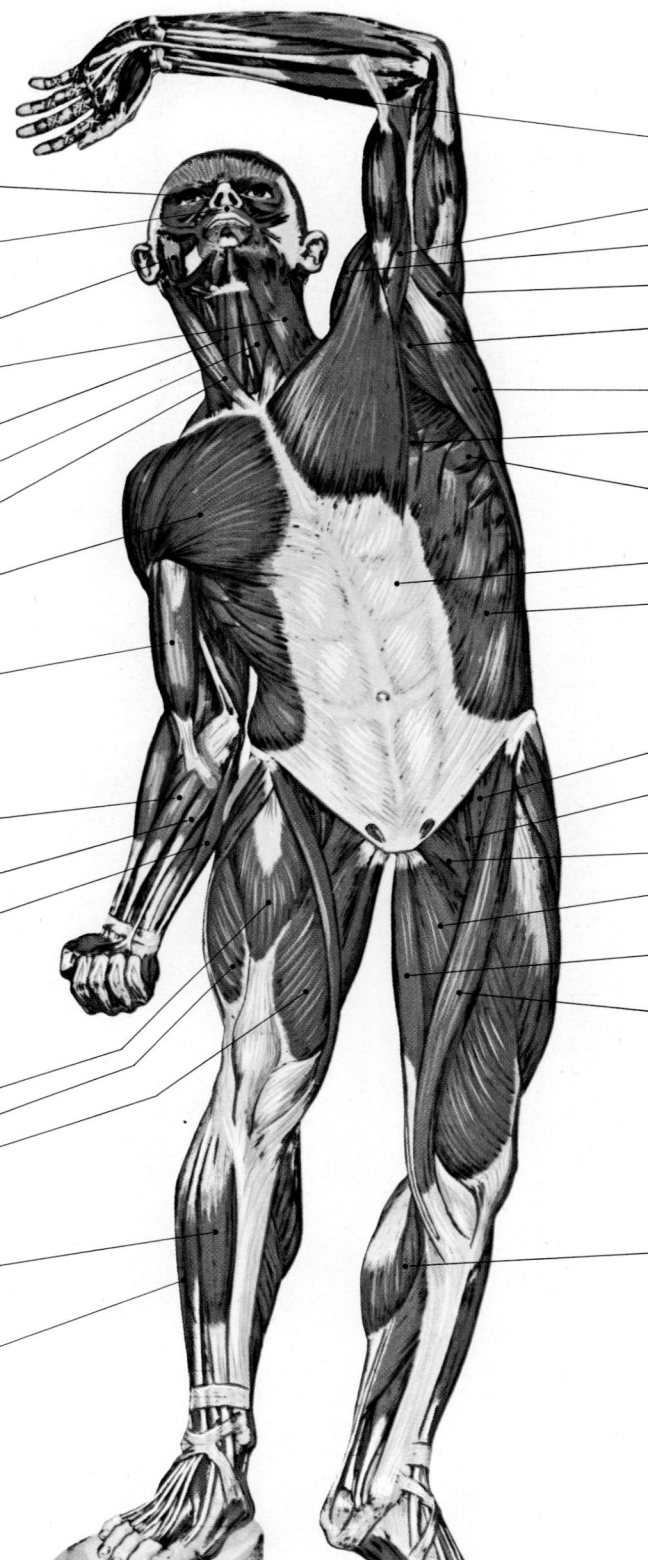

Orbicularis oculi: circles the eye.

Orbicularis oris: forms the fleshy portion of the lips; circles the mouth.

Masseter: moves the lower jaw up.

Platysma: aids in lowering the lower jaw.

Omohyoideus

Sternohyoideus

Sternocleidomastoideus: stands out when the head is rotated.

Pectoralis major: flexes and rotates the arm.

Biceps brachii: flexes the forearm.

Flexor carpi radialis: flexes the hand at the wrist.

Palmaris longus

Flexor carpi ulnaris: flexes the hand and forearm.

Quadriceps femoris: largest and most powerful muscle of the body, made up of:

Rectus femoris

Vastus lateralis

Vastus medialis

Vastus intermedius (lies next to femor under rectus femoris)

Tibialis anterior: flexes the foot.

Peroneus longus: flexes the foot.

Brachioradialis: flexes the forearm.

Coracobrachialis

Deltoid

Teres major

Subscapularis: rotates the humerus.

Latissimus dorsi

Pectoralis minor: lies under pectoralis major.

Serratus anterior: aids in elevating the ribs.

Rectus abdominis

External oblique: aids in rotating the vertebral column.

Iliacus

Pectineus: adducts and flexes the femur.

Psoas major

Adductor longus: adducts and flexes the femur.

Gracilis: flexes and rotates the thigh.

Sartorius: flexes the leg at the knee; flexes the thigh at the hip.

Gastrocnemius: flexes the leg at the knee.

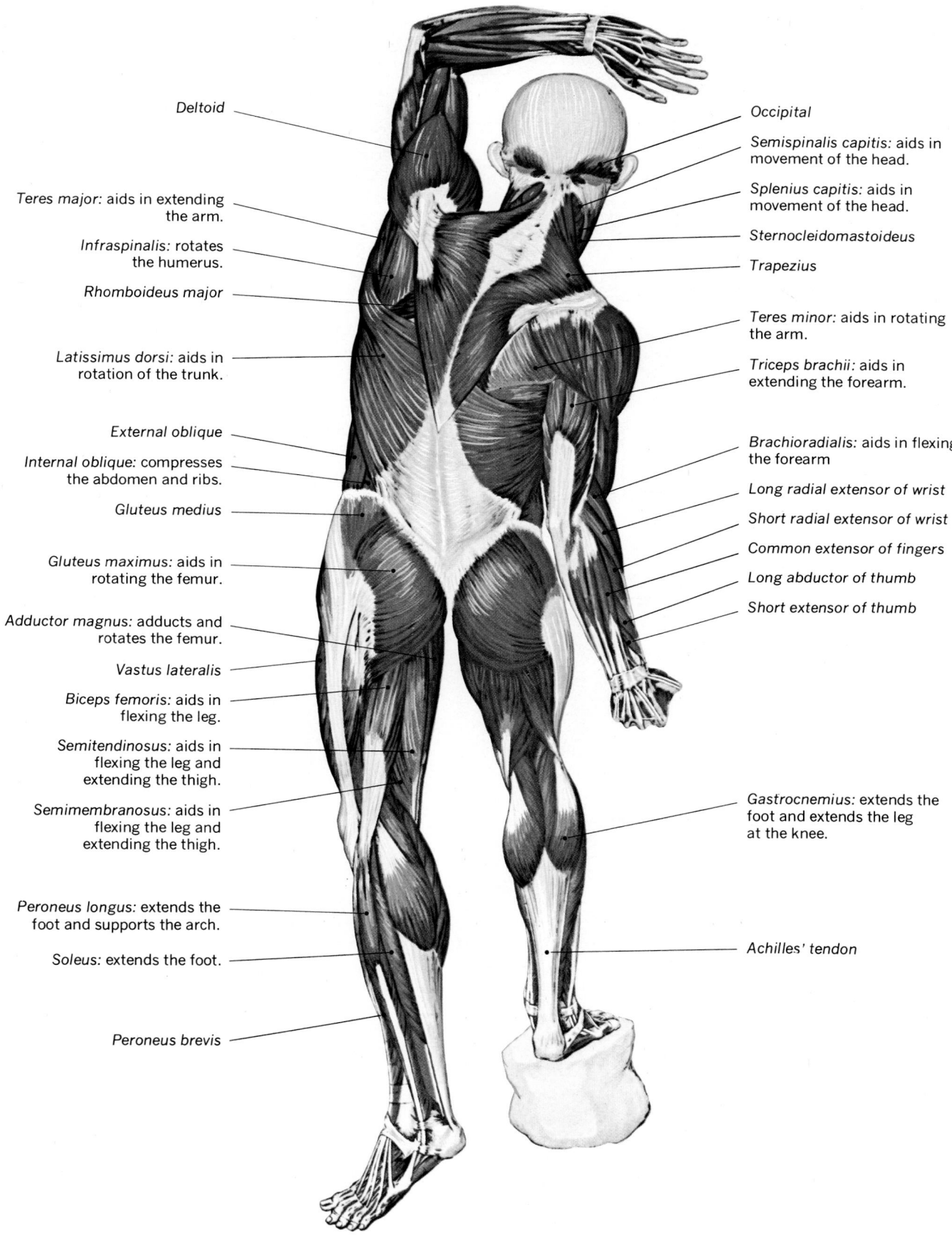

Deltoid

Teres major: aids in extending the arm.

Infraspinalis: rotates the humerus.

Rhomboideus major

Latissimus dorsi: aids in rotation of the trunk.

External oblique

Internal oblique: compresses the abdomen and ribs.

Gluteus medius

Gluteus maximus: aids in rotating the femur.

Adductor magnus: adducts and rotates the femur.

Vastus lateralis

Biceps femoris: aids in flexing the leg.

Semitendinosus: aids in flexing the leg and extending the thigh.

Semimembranosus: aids in flexing the leg and extending the thigh.

Peroneus longus: extends the foot and supports the arch.

Soleus: extends the foot.

Peroneus brevis

Occipital

Semispinalis capitis: aids in movement of the head.

Splenius capitis: aids in movement of the head.

Sternocleidomastoideus

Trapezius

Teres minor: aids in rotating the arm.

Triceps brachii: aids in extending the forearm.

Brachioradialis: aids in flexing the forearm

Long radial extensor of wrist

Short radial extensor of wrist

Common extensor of fingers

Long abductor of thumb

Short extensor of thumb

Gastrocnemius: extends the foot and extends the leg at the knee.

Achilles' tendon

The Organs of the Body

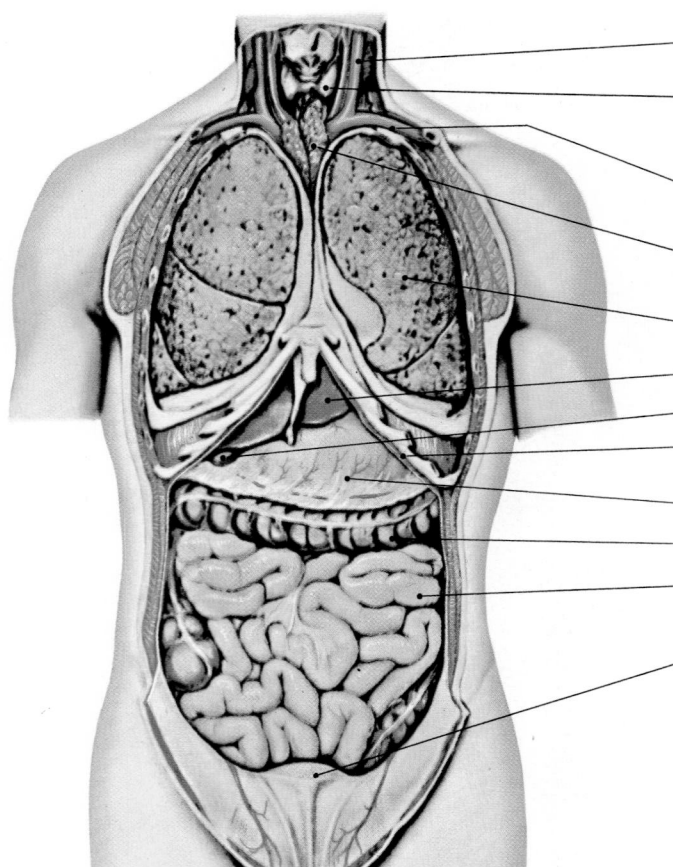

Plate One: Outer layer

Internal Jugular Vein: receives blood from head and neck.

Thyroid Gland: endocrine; influences body growth, basal metabolism, development of teeth, muscle tone, body temperature, and function of gonads and adrenal glands.

Subclavian Vein: receives blood from the arm and hand.

Thymus Gland: lymphoid organ that produces lymphocytes.

Lung: main site of respiration.

Liver: see also Plate Two.

Gall Bladder: stores bile secreted by the liver.

Diaphragm: aids in expanding and contracting the lungs.

Stomach: see also Plate Two.

Transverse Colon

Small Intestine: contains pancreatic and intestinal juice and bile that aid in digestion.

Bladder: collects and stores urine from the kidneys.

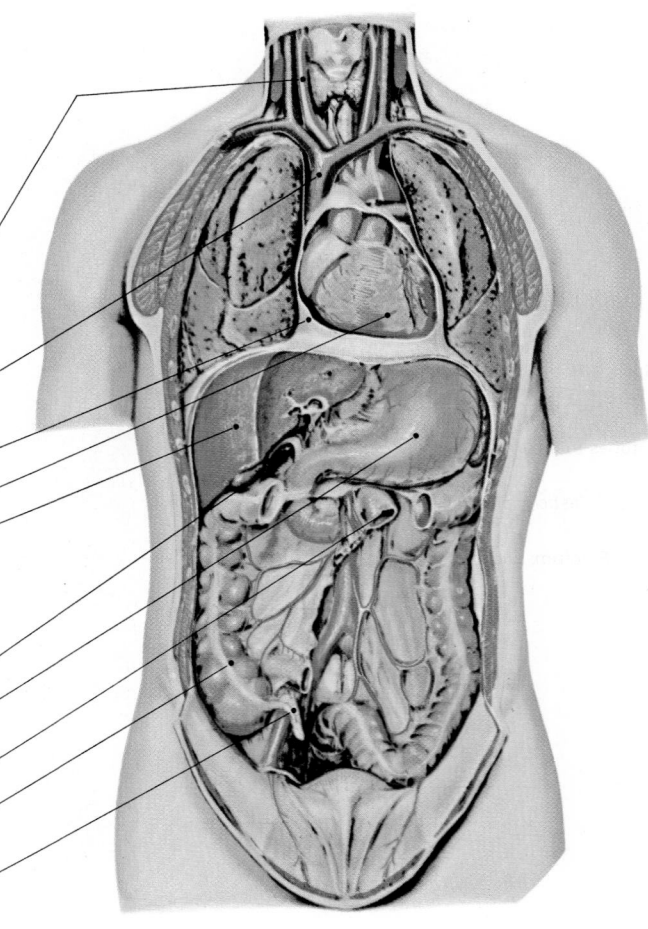

Plate Two: Middle layer

Common Carotid Artery: supplies blood to the head and neck.

Superior Vena Cava: returns blood to the heart from head, neck, thorax, and upper extremities.

Pericardium: sac that encloses the heart.

Heart

Liver: largest gland in the body; secretes bile; forms blood cells; regulates bloodvolume; metabolizes carbohydrates, fats, and proteins; stores iron, copper, and vitamins A, D, and B_{12}; forms vitamin A; detoxifies some poisons; activates some hormones.

Gall Bladder; see also Plate One.

Stomach: contains hydrochloric acid, pepsin, mucin, and inorganic salts that aid in digestion.

Duodenum: passage from stomach to small intestine.

Colon or large intestine: absorbs water from digested food and eliminates waste.

Appendix

Plate Three: Inner layer

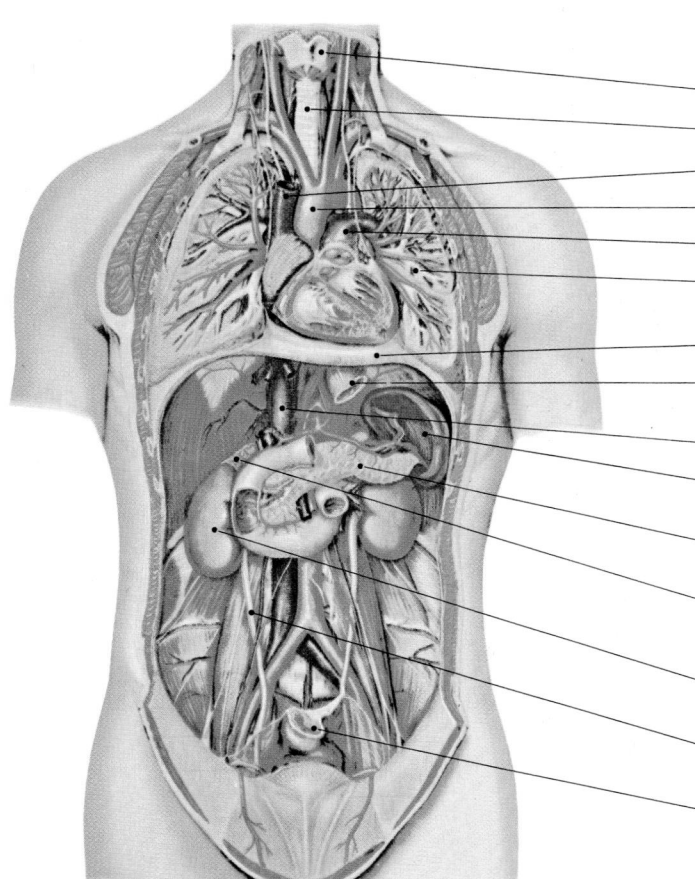

Thyroid Cartilage: main cartilage of the larynx.

Trachea or windpipe: air passage to the lungs.

Superior Vena Cava

Aortic Arch

Pulmonary Artery

Pulmonary Vessels and Bronchi: extend into the lungs to carry out respiration.

Pleura: separates thoracic from abdominal cavity.

Cardiac End of Stomach: leads from the esophagus, which lies behind the trachea.

Inferior Vena Cava

Spleen: lymphatic organ that produces blood cells and antibodies, and stores blood and iron.

Pancreas: produces the hormones insulin and glucagon, and secretes enzymes into the stomach.

Adrenal Gland: endocrine gland, regulates salt metabolism, kidney function, muscular activity, carbohydrate metabolism, and basal metabolism.

Kidney: excretes the waste products of metabolism (urine) and toxic substances; maintains proper water balance and salt concentration.

Ureter: carries urine from kidneys to bladder.

Rectum

Plate Four: Reproductive Systems of the Body

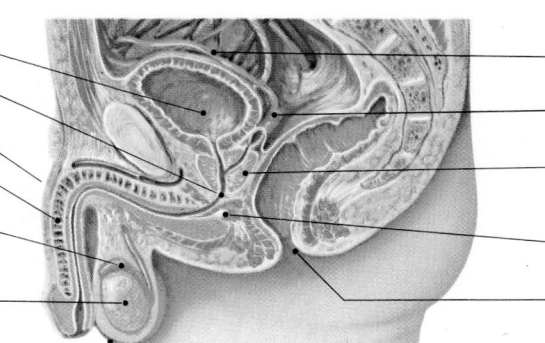

Bladder

Urethra: leads from the bladder to the penis.

Penis

Spongy Body: spongy-like tissue that fills with blood to produce erection.

Epididymus: collection of tubes that carry sperm from testes to the vas deferens.

Testicle: produces sperm and some hormones.

Scrotum: encloses the testicles.

Vas Deferens or ductus deferens: carries sperm from the testes to the urethra.

Seminal Vesicle: produces viscid fluid that is added to the sperm.

Prostate Gland: secretes alkaline fluid that alkalinizes the urethra and activates the sperm.

Cowper's Gland: secretes a mucous-like substance that acts as a lubricant.

Anus

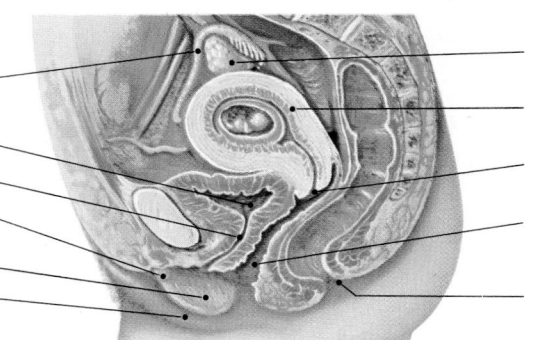

Fallopian Tube: carries the ovum to the uterus.

Bladder

Urethra

Clitoris: sensitive structure homologous to the male penis.

Labia Minor

Labia Major

Ovary: site of ova production, also produces some hormones.

Uterus: where fertilization occurs and fetus develops.

Cervix of the Uterus: leads from the uterus to the vagina.

Vagina: passage from the uterus to the outside of the body; the birth canal for the fetus.

Anus

The Skeletal System

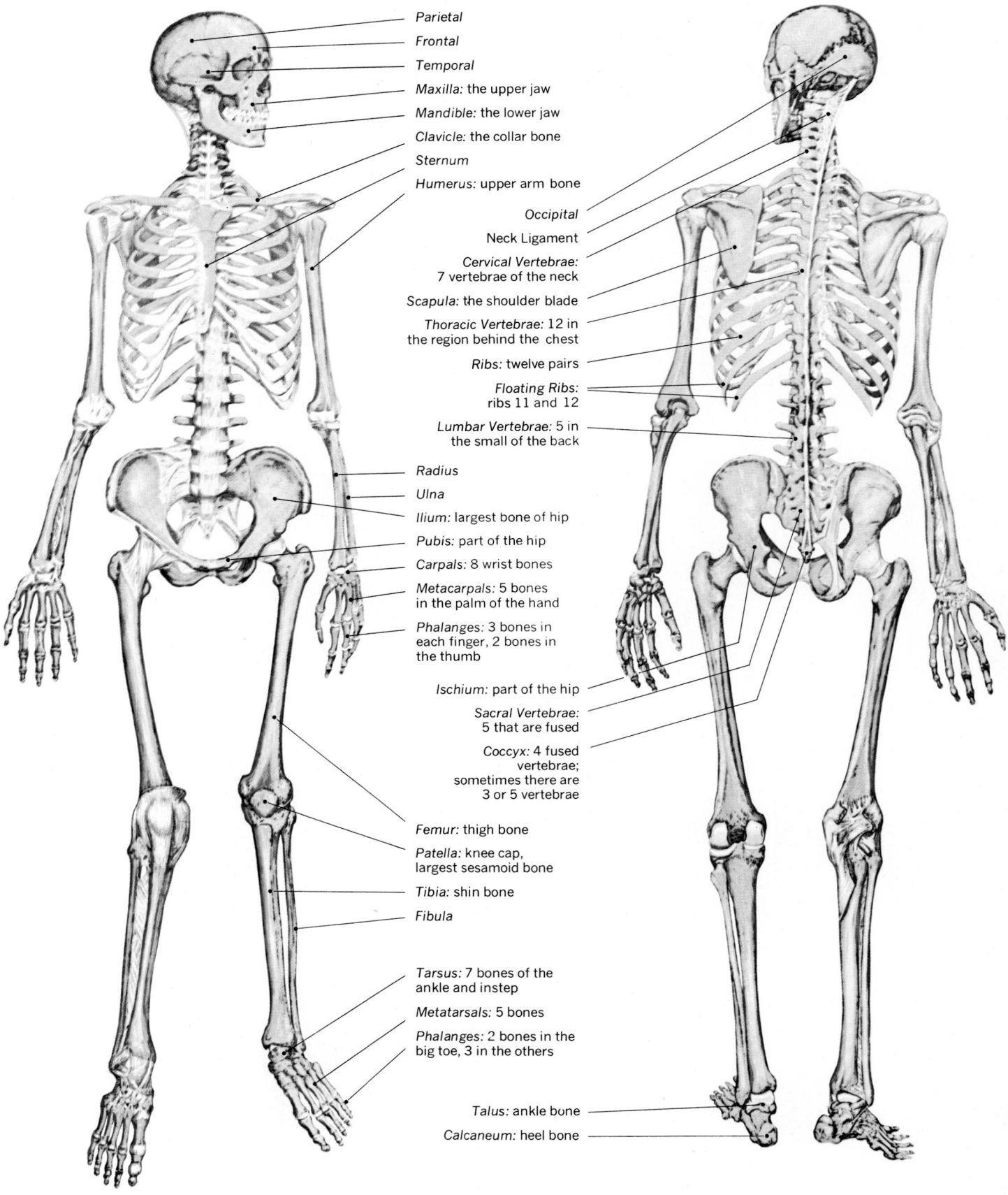

Parietal

Frontal

Temporal

Maxilla: the upper jaw

Mandible: the lower jaw

Clavicle: the collar bone

Sternum

Humerus: upper arm bone

Occipital

Neck Ligament

Cervical Vertebrae:
7 vertebrae of the neck

Scapula: the shoulder blade

Thoracic Vertebrae: 12 in
the region behind the chest

Ribs: twelve pairs

Floating Ribs:
ribs 11 and 12

Lumbar Vertebrae: 5 in
the small of the back

Radius

Ulna

Ilium: largest bone of hip

Pubis: part of the hip

Carpals: 8 wrist bones

Metacarpals: 5 bones
in the palm of the hand

Phalanges: 3 bones in
each finger, 2 bones in
the thumb

Ischium: part of the hip

Sacral Vertebrae:
5 that are fused

Coccyx: 4 fused
vertebrae;
sometimes there are
3 or 5 vertebrae

Femur: thigh bone

Patella: knee cap,
largest sesamoid bone

Tibia: shin bone

Fibula

Tarsus: 7 bones of the
ankle and instep

Metatarsals: 5 bones

Phalanges: 2 bones in the
big toe, 3 in the others

Talus: ankle bone

Calcaneum: heel bone

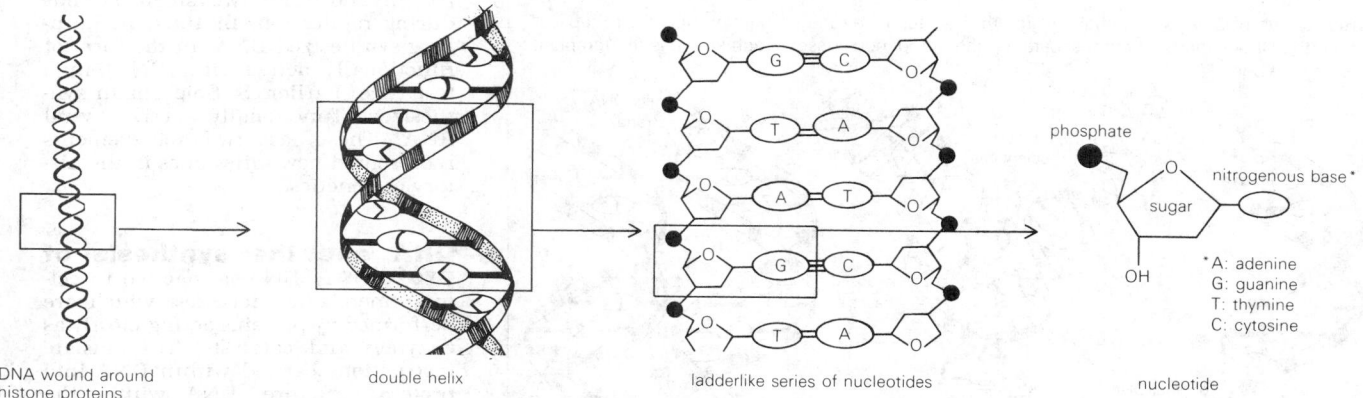

DNA wound around
histone proteins

double helix

ladderlike series of nucleotides

phosphate

nitrogenous base*

sugar

OH

*A: adenine
G: guanine
T: thymine
C: cytosine

nucleotide

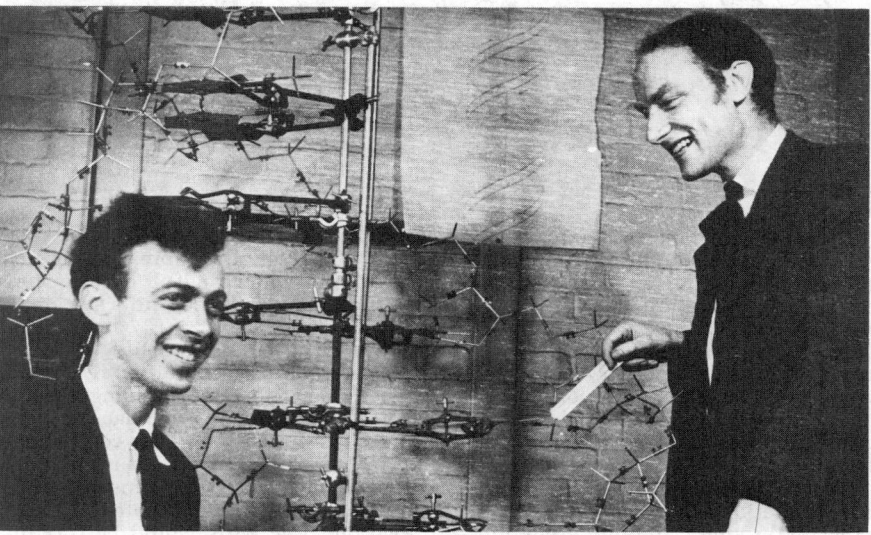

THE NOBEL PRIZE *in physiology or medicine was awarded in 1962 to James Watson (left),* Francis Crick (right), *and Maurice Wilkins for work relating to DNA's structure and function.*

OMIKRON/PHOTO RESEARCHERS

coat and a DNA core. When viral protein is labeled with a radioactive isotope of sulfur and the DNA with radioactive phosphorus and each is allowed to infect the bacterial host, the sulfur isotope remains outside the host and the phosphorus isotope inside the host. The latter is found in the new viruses released when the bacteria open. Since the viral part (phage) within the bacterium contains genetic information that directs its host to make more phage (both DNA and protein), it follows that DNA must be the genetic material.

In 1951, N. Zinder and J. Lederberg discovered bacterial transduction, providing more proof that DNA transmits genetic information. In transduction, a hereditary trait can be transferred from one bacterial cell to another via a virus that infects first one cell and then the other. The viral DNA picks up a tiny bit of the DNA of the host. When the host cell ruptures and the virus infects a new host, the virus carries the genes of the first host with it. These genes are expressed in the new host and its offspring. A bacterium resistant to streptomycin, for example, may be infected with a temperate bacteriophage (a viral strain of low virulence). The virus may multiply within the bacterium, and some viral particles may pick up the streptomycin-resistant gene. If the virus is allowed to infect a streptomycin-sensitive bacterial strain, some of the bacteria and their progeny are then found to be resistant to streptomycin. If two or more genes are transduced simultaneously, they are always closely linked. Transduction is indirect evidence that DNA is genetic

material. Assuming that the part of the virus that enters the host is DNA and that the bacterial material carried by the virus is also DNA, then transduction is like transformation, except that instead of a human transferring the DNA from donor to recipient, a temperate bacteriophage does so.

Watson-Crick model of the DNA molecule.

DNA is a very large, high-molecular-weight polymer that is formed from a few simple molecules linked repeatedly by chemical bonds. Each repeating unit, called a nucleotide, consists of a phosphate group: a five-carbon sugar (deoxyribose); and one of four different nitrogenous bases. The four bases are adenine (A) and guanine (G), both of which are purines; and cytosine (C) and thymine (T), both of which are pyrimidines. The nucleotides are connected by chemical bonds between their sugar and phosphate groups. This arrangement creates a deoxyribose-phosphate backbone with bases projecting inward and perpendicular to the axis.

Several years before the molecular model of DNA was formally worked out, Erwin Chargaff and coworkers showed that the ratio of adenine to thymine, and of guanine to cytosine, is about 1:1 in any DNA preparation. However, the ratio of adenine (or thymine) or guanine (or cytosine) varies. Chargaff and his coworkers thought that since A = T and G = C, each was associated with the other in DNA.

Using this ratio and the results of Maurice Wilkins' x-ray diffraction studies of DNA, James D. Watson and Francis H. C. Crick in 1953 proposed a structure for DNA. (Watson, Crick, and Wilkins shared a Nobel Prize in 1962 for their work.) The proposed structure essentially describes a twisted ladder, or double helix, with sugar-phosphate side rails and rungs of bonded bases. The base sequence in one strand of DNA determines the base sequence in the complementary strand—an A must always be matched with a T, and a C with a G. Weak hydrogen bonds hold A to T and G to C, giving the ladder firmness and the ability to separate when replication takes place during mitosis.

DNA REPLICATION

Replication of DNA is essential for growth, maintenance, and production of cells. In replication, the DNA strands unwind, separating the nitrogenous bases. Each strand is the template for a new one.

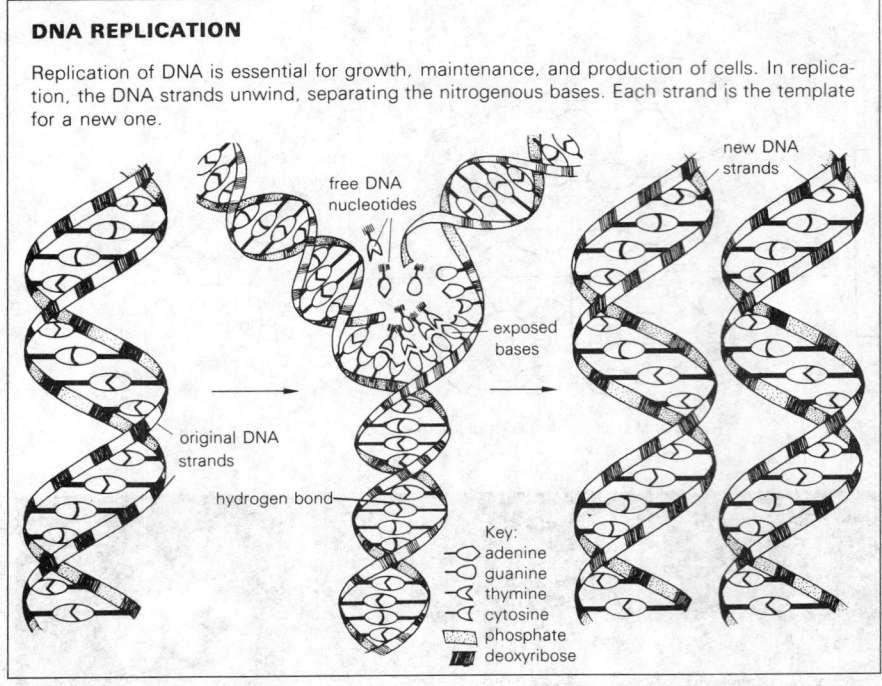

free DNA nucleotides

new DNA strands

exposed bases

original DNA strands

hydrogen bond

Key:
⬦ adenine
⬭ guanine
◁ thymine
◁ cytosine
▨ phosphate
▮ deoxyribose

1958 by M. Meselson and F. Stahl, who showed that the DNA double helix unwinds into two single strands during replication. In 1967, A. Kornberg synthesized DNA (in the form of functionally active DNA) in a test tube. Earlier, S. Spiegelman synthesized functionally active viral RNA. These last two achievements represented new milestones in the history of genetics.

DNA and the synthesis of proteins.
DNA is inactive in cellular metabolic processes, which are performed by proteins acting mostly as enzymes and catalysts. To translate instructions carried within DNA into protein structure, DNA within the chromosomes gives its message to a form of RNA called messenger RNA, or mRNA, present in the nucleus. Messenger RNA transmits the information received from the DNA to the ribosomal RNA, or rRNA, of the ribosomes, the sites of protein synthesis within the cytoplasm. On the ribosome, an RNA template is formed according to the code of the messenger RNA.

Proteins are long chains of amino acids hooked together linearly by peptide bonds. The chains are called polypeptides. Twenty amino acids occur in proteins. The smallest protein, ribonuclease, has a molecular weight of 13,500 and is a single chain of 124 amino acids. Many amino acids are repeated several times, and all do not have to be present in an individual protein. Proteins take a definite shape on which their function depends. Polypeptide chains form a helix that folds into a characteristic shape. The amino acid sequence is believed to determine the nature of this folding.

To synthesize proteins on the RNA template on the ribosome, the amino acids must be brought to their proper positions. This is done by transfer RNA, or tRNA, of which there is one specific for each of the 20-odd amino acids. Transfer RNA picks up its own amino acid, which has been activated

The Watson-Crick model makes it possible to understand how genetic information is duplicated and transmitted. If double helix strands separate, each becomes a mold, or template, that is able to specify the replication of its complementary copy. This would result in the formation of two identical DNA molecules, each with an original and a newly synthesized strand.

The model explains how DNA could carry genetic information, or code, translated into protein-producing instructions. The genetic code depends on the sequence of the four bases in relation to each other; in effect, this is a four-letter alphabet. Many configurations are possible, since there are ten base pairs in each complete turn of the double helix. For each turn, which represents only a small portion of the entire molecule, the number of configurations possible would be 4^{10}, or 1,048,576. Not all combinations of nucleotides are meaningful, but the storage potential of genetic information is enormous.

The Watson-Crick model gives a chemical basis for mutation. If DNA is genetic material, then a change in the DNA molecule should change the code and cause mutation. This could happen if an error is made during replication, or if A picks up C instead of T and the error is perpetuated. At one position, base pairs would be C-G instead of A-T, upsetting the code and preventing formation of a normal protein. If a compound similar to a normal base is introduced, one that differs so slightly that the replicating DNA could easily mistake it for the normal base, mutations might occur.

Experimental work that directly supported the model was reported in

RNA: MESSENGER IN PROTEIN SYNTHESIS

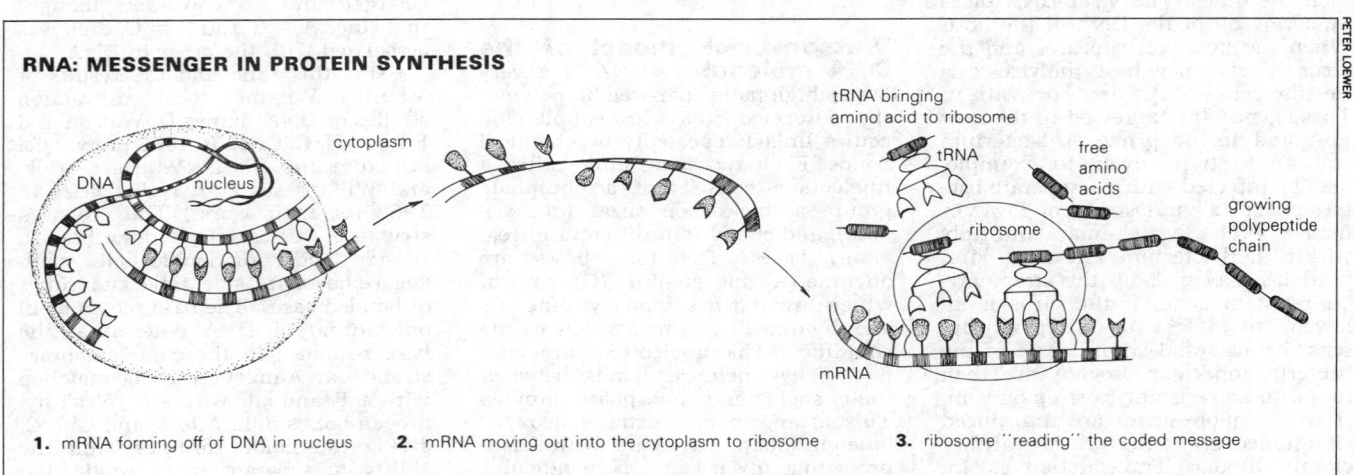

cytoplasm

DNA nucleus

tRNA bringing amino acid to ribosome

tRNA

free amino acids

ribosome

growing polypeptide chain

mRNA

1. mRNA forming off of DNA in nucleus   **2.** mRNA moving out into the cytoplasm to ribosome   **3.** ribosome "reading" the coded message

by its specific enzyme, and brings it to a specific site on the template that it is said to recognize, presumably by some kind of complementarity.

Once each amino acid has been fitted into place on the template, sequence is established, peptide bonds are formed, RNA is sloughed off, and the completed protein separates from the template and takes on the shape necessary for it to carry out its metabolic function in the cell.

Genetic code.
DNA is the carrier of genetic information, but without RNA its instructions would not be carried out.

Although less is known about RNA structure than about DNA or protein, RNA is known to be similar to DNA in that it is also a polymer containing four kinds of nucleotides. These nucleotides are similar to those of DNA except that uracil (U) replaces thymine as a pyrimidine base, and the five-carbon sugar is ribose instead of deoxyribose. The other components are the same as those in DNA. DNA transmits its information to messenger RNA through complementarity between the bases, which by their alignment in both DNA and RNA contain the key to the genetic code.

Research findings support the following model for the transmission of the genetic code:

1. The coded message of DNA is read in groups of three bases, or triplets. Each triplet is called a codon.
2. The message is read in nonoverlapping triplets.
3. Each triplet represents a specific amino acid.
4. Four bases, each combining into a group of three, produce 64 possible triplets, more than enough to code the 20 amino acids found in proteins.

Experiments with synthetic RNA have shown that more than one triplet can code the same amino acid. A code such as the genetic code, in which more than one word can signify the same object, is called degenerate. This does not imply a lack of specificity in protein structure; it simply means that more than one codon can direct the same amino acid to its specific site on the forming polypeptide chain.

Evidence suggests that the genetic code is universal. In other words, all species probably use approximately the same code to carry on the direction of their life processes.

Nature and Role of Genes

Genes are considered the basic units of heredity that determine the expression of characteristic traits in offspring, but the precise definition of a gene tends to keep changing as more is learned. On the molecular level, the gene is generally described as a segment of DNA, or sequence of nucleotides, usually found arranged in a linear order on a chromosome. The gene determines the formation of RNA or a given protein enzyme, or polypeptide chain, for controlling the structures and vital life processes of the cell.

Genes and individual development.
Each cell in an embryo, whether animal or plant, has the same chromosomal complement and the same genes, because each is derived from the original zygote by mitosis. Yet some cells become spindle-shaped muscle cells, some become pathogen-hunting white blood cells, some become glandular cells that secrete digestive enzymes, and so on

NUCLEAR TRANSPLANTATION

unfertilized egg with destroyed nucleus

nucleus from intestine cell of tadpole injected into egg

egg develops into blastula

tadpole develops

normal mature frog results

PETER LOEWER

A FROG DEVELOPS *when a tadpole cell nucleus is transplanted into a frog egg.*

through all the specialized functions performed by cells.

An experiment that proved that all genes present in the nucleus of the zygote are also present in the nucleus of each of the mature organism's differentiated cells involved the replacement of the nucleus of a frog zygote with a nucleus removed from a frog intestine cell. From the renucleated zygote, a normal tadpole and then a complete differentiated frog developed. Such an event could not have taken place unless the nucleus of the intestine cell contained the same complement of genes as the nucleus of the zygote.

An explanation proposed for how cells with identical genes can be so different is that only some of the genes of a differentiated cell are expressed, that is, turned on. Genes that are turned on in a muscle cell, for example, are turned off in a nerve cell, and vice versa. If this is in fact true, it can be inferred that the switching on and off of specific gene sequences during differentiation lies behind the differentiation of cells.

The activities of genes in directing cell differentiation can be influenced internally, as by various factors within the cytoplasm or by hormones, and externally, as by light in the germination of many plant seeds.

GENETIC CODE

The genetic code, an encoded message found in DNA or RNA, provides instructions for the synthesis of specific amino acids, the basic subunits of proteins. Each code word, or codon, consists of a triplet of any of 64 possible combinations of the 4 nitrogenous bases of DNA, represented by the code letters A (adenine), T (thymine), C (cytosine), and G (guanine).

	Second letter				
First letter	**A**	**G**	**T**	**C**	Third letter
A	AAA Phenylalanine AAG Phenylalanine AAT Leucine AAC Leucine	AGA Serine AGG Serine AGT Serine AGC Serine	ATA Tyrosine ATG Tyrosine ATT Stop ATC Stop	ACA Cysteine ACG Cysteine ACT Stop ACC Tryptophan	A G T C
G	GAA Leucine GAG Leucine GAT Leucine GAC Leucine	GGA Proline GGG Proline GGT Proline GGC Proline	GTA Histidine GTG Histidine GTT Glutamine GTC Glutamine	GCA Arginine GCG Arginine GCT Arginine GCC Arginine	A G T C
T	TAA Isoleucine TAG Isoleucine TAT Isoleucine TAC Methionine	TGA Threonine TGG Threonine TGT Threonine TGC Threonine	TTA Asparagine TTG Asparagine TTT Lysine TTC Lysine	TCA Serine TCG Serine TCT Arginine TCC Arginine	A G T C
C	CAA Valine CAG Valine CAT Valine CAC Valine	CGA Alanine CGG Alanine CGT Alanine CGC Alanine	CTA Aspartic Acid CTG Aspartic Acid CTT Glutamic Acid CTC Glutamic Acid	CCA Glycine CCG Glycine CCT Glycine CCC Glycine	A G T C

Genes and populations.

Charles Darwin's theory of natural selection, the integrating force common to all biology, is the mechanism of all biology. An appropriate place to observe this mechanism at work is in large populations.

Consider, for example, the blood groups. The most common blood group in the white population of the United States is group 0 (45 percent), followed by group A (38.5 percent), group B (13 percent), and group AB (3.5 percent). Blood groups are inherited in Mendelian fashion. One might want to know how mutations caused by exposure to radiation or certain chemicals would affect the frequency of the blood group genes, whether the same frequency occurs in different geographical locations, or whether the frequency is changing over a period of time. These questions belong to the realm of population genetics, the branch of genetics that studies the changes in gene frequencies in populations in time and place as a valid means of explaining the mechanism of evolution.

The principle of population genetics was developed by an American zoologist, W. E. Castle, in 1903; and by an English mathematician, G. H. Hardy, and a German physician, W. Weinberg, working independently, in 1908. Called the Castle-Hardy-Weinberg law, the principle states that relative gene frequencies remain constant from generation to generation in an infinitely large interbreeding population in which mating is at random, and in which there is no selection, migration, or mutation.

How, then, could evolution take place? It involves change in the genetic composition of populations. Obviously, both mutation and segregation do occur, as well as some migration and isolation of small populations. These are the factors that influence evolution.

Mutations occur spontaneously, for unknown reasons, at predictable but low rates. Most mutations are harmful, not beneficial, because the genes already present in the populations have been the most successful survivors over the millions of years that life is considered to have existed. Dominant lethal mutations are eliminated from the reservoir of genes in the population, because the individuals in whom they occur die early in life. An occasional mutation is beneficial in the sense that it confers on the recipient a better chance to survive and pass the gene on to its offspring. Such a gene is then said to have a selective advantage.

Darwin observed that in most species of plants and animals, the offspring produced are more numerous than their parents, yet most populations remain relatively stable in size. Also, many variations exist in nature, and most of these are inherited. As a

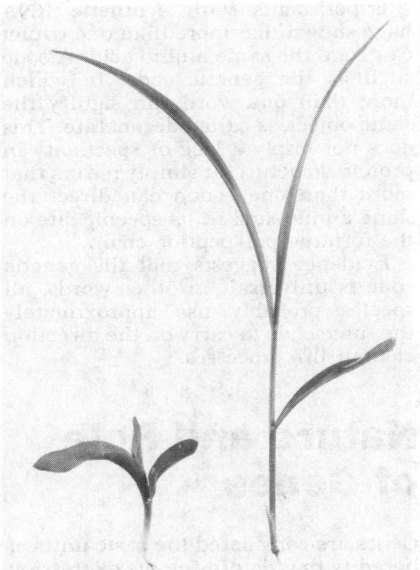

GIBBERELIN TREATMENT *of dwarf corn stimulates growth. The dwarf mutant appears to lose its ability to produce growth hormone.*

result of the great number of offspring, competition exists. Those best fitted by virtue of their variations will survive and pass on those variations to the next generation.

Beneficial genes remain in the gene pool, and dominant lethals are driven out. Unless lethal recessive genes are disadvantageous to the heterozygote in the competition for food and mates, these genes will be passed on, not eliminated, from the gene pool. If they are disadvantageous to the heterozygote, they will be eliminated slowly over many generations. Many recessive harmful genes persist in populations because they are beneficial to the heterozygote. Sickle-cell anemia is an example. The homozygote SS dies early, and the heterozygote AS has both normal and sickle-cell hemoglobin. The trait is common in central Africa, where a severe form of malaria exists. Individuals with normal hemoglobin AA readily succumb to the disease, whereas heterozygotes AS are relatively resistant to this disease and have as much as a 25 percent better chance of attaining adulthood as do normal homozygotes.

Thus, a gene is maintained in the population even though individuals homozygous for it die before reaching productive age. This is a case of balanced polymorphism, which maintains alternative genotypes in a population by a balance between forces selecting for and against the gene. It is closely related to heterosis, or hybrid vigor, exemplified in hybrid corn: A combination of genes makes hybrid corn better than any homozygous line.

Although evolution is usually too slow a process for a person to observe in a lifetime, some examples of evolu-

tionary change have been observed. One is the development of DDT-resistant strains of insects. No doubt there always were some insects that could have survived DDT, but this was not a selective advantage in a DDT-free world. Once the chemical came into wide use, DDT-resistant insects survived and reproduced, but DDT-sensitive insects died. Thus, a change in the environment (use of DDT) brought about a change in the characteristics of the insect world.

For the population geneticist, an important question is: What is the genetic basis of the origin of species? Biologists define a single species as one whose members can interbreed and produce fertile offspring. New species arise through isolation of one group from another. Within each region of different environment, the isolated population over many generations will become unique because of the selection of traits adaptively advantageous in that particular area. After a long time, individual groups will diverge to the extent that they can no longer interbreed. They then become separate species and remain separate even if they later are found to occupy the same environment.

Human Genetics

Genetic diseases and abnormalities.

When cells duplicate, the chromosomal material within them duplicates as well, usually with absolute precision. Occasionally, a mistake is made that results in a usually permanent alteration of genetic material. Such an alteration is called a mutation.

A mutation may not express itself and therefore will have no effect at all on the functioning of a cell. Or it may have so slight an effect that it goes unnoticed. A very small number of mutations are actually beneficial, improving the functioning of a cell, but many have serious, even fatal, effects.

A point mutation is the result of a change in a single base pair in the DNA of a gene representing just one of the letters in the genetic code. This seemingly minor transformation alters the coding for a single subunit of a protein, and may significantly change the functioning of that molecule.

The hereditary disease galactosemia, for example, is caused by a single recessive gene. A child homozygous for the galactosemia gene lacks an enzyme essential for conversion of milk sugar, galactose, into glucose. Accumulation of galactose in the body causes cataracts, mental retardation, and other defects. Treatment of children with galactosemia involves eliminating milk and milk products from the diet.

GENETIC INHERITANCE

RECENT PROGRESS IN GENETICS *has advanced human genetic counseling. Prospective parents can acquire information on the possibility that their offspring will inherit genetic disorders.*

ELLEN WARNER/BLACK STAR

Some traits in man that are inherited in a simple Mendelian fashion

RECESSIVE	DOMINANT
red hair	not red hair
white forelock	normal
normal	premature grayness of hair
normal	no iris
normal	glaucoma
extreme myopia	normal
night blindness	normal
normal	congenital cataract
albinism	normal
normal	no incisor teeth
normal	rootless teeth
no A or B antigens	A and B antigens
normal	sickle cell
no Rh antigen	Rh antigen
normal size	achondroplastic dwarf
St. Vitus's dance	normal
normal	Huntington's chorea
diabetes mellitus	normal

The best evidence for the precise effect of a point mutation on protein structure is seen in the abnormal hemoglobin that causes red blood cells to take on a sickle shape in sickle-cell anemia. The only difference between the defective hemoglobin, which is the result of a single recessive gene, and normal hemoglobin is the substitution of one amino acid for another in a structure containing 300 amino acids.

Certain mutations, called chromosomal aberrations or chromosomal abnormalities, result from the loss, duplication, inversion, or translocation of part of a chromosome, or from the transmission of too many or too few chromosomes during meiosis.

Perhaps the best-known chromosomal abnormality is Down's syndrome, or mongolism, which results from the production of a female gamete with an extra chromosome. The cells of individuals afflicted with Down's syndrome have 47 chromosomes instead of the normal complement of 46. Characteristics of the condition include some degree of mental retardation, abnormal body development, altered facial features, and certain heart defects.

Some other disorders transmitted genetically are Huntington's chorea, cystic fibrosis, albinism, hemophilia, and Tay-Sachs disease. Diseases for which a genetic disposition is either known or suspected include high blood pressure, obesity, heart disease, diabetes, peptic ulcers, and emphysema, among others.

Examination of chromosomes in cells during the metaphase, called karyotyping, can reveal genetic abnormalities in individuals. Karyotyping of a developing fetus to detect possible genetic abnormalities is made possible by amniocentesis, a procedure in which a sample of fetal cells suspended in the amniotic fluid is withdrawn from the uterus through a long hypodermic needle. This procedure is typically performed during the early stages of pregnancy.

Recent advances in our understanding of human genetics and genetic disorders are leading to the development of increasingly sophisticated tests for the detection of genetic disorders and promising medical procedures for their treatment.

KARYOTYPING

A karyotype is a microphoto of chromosomes organized according to shape and size. A characteristic karyotype exists for every species. Normal human male (left) and female (right) karyotypes show 46 chromosomes, the diploid number for humans. There are 22 homologous pairs, called autosomes. The remaining pair are sex chromosomes.

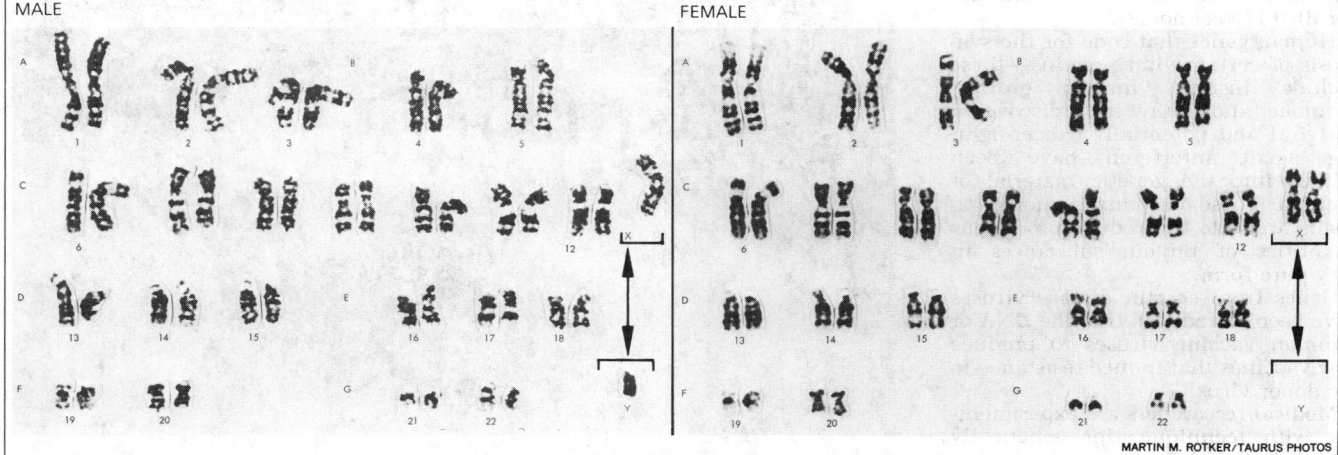

MARTIN M. ROTKER/TAURUS PHOTOS

SPLICING A GENE INTO E. COLI BACTERIUM

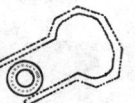

1. E. coli (on agar plate).

2. Plasmid with E. coli genetic information.

3. Plasmid broken by chemical means.

4. New gene inserted in plasmid.

5. Plasmid picked up by phage (parasite of E. coli).

6. Phage attaches to E. coli cell and inserts plasmid.

PETER LOEWER

Advances in Genetic Engineering and Biotechnology

Genetic engineering, in the broadest sense of the term, has been practiced by humans for thousands of years. Selective breeding, sometimes referred to as artificial selection, has altered the evolutionary course of numerous plant and animal species. Direct manipulation of genetic material, however, was not accomplished until the early 1970's.

Using specialized proteins called restriction enzymes, researchers developed a set of procedures that enabled them to clip specific nucleotide sequences, or genes, from the DNA of one organism and then splice such fragments into the genetic material of another strain of the same organism or into the DNA of an entirely different organism. Genetic material produced in this manner is called recombinant DNA. The methods employed in creating such hybrid DNA are called recombinant-DNA techniques or, simply and collectively, gene splicing. Today, the term genetic engineering is commonly used to refer to recombinant-DNA technology, and the practical application of recombinant-DNA techniques is called biotechnology.

Human genes that code for the synthesis of certain vital proteins—these include insulin, human growth-hormone, and the recently discovered antiviral and potentially cancer-fighting agent interferon—have been spliced into the genetic material of bacteria. These customized microorganisms are able to produce prodigious quantities of protein substances in very pure form.

Genes from certain disease viruses have been introduced into the DNA of common vaccine viruses to produce new vaccines that induce resistance to the donor virus.

Medical researchers are experimenting with techniques for genetically manipulating defective genes in human cells to correct these defects, such as sickle-cell anemia.

Nonengineered bacteria already widely used in the mining industry to leach such metals as cobalt, zinc, lead, copper, and nickel from low-grade ores may be genetically engineered to increase their metal-extracting abilities.

Genetically engineered microbes have already been employed to break down, or digest, spilled crude oil, and there is considerable optimism that similar agents may help solve the world's growing toxic waste problem.

Genetic alteration of plant cells may lead to development of crops with greater resistance to diseases and drought, improved photosynthetic efficiency, and even the ability to produce their own nitrogen fertilizers.

The list of potential and realized applications of recombinant-DNA technology grows daily, as does the concern of many individuals, both inside and outside the scientific community, that some applications pose potential dangers and ethical dilemmas. What impact might result if a microbe possessing a novel and less-than-benign gene sequence were introduced into the environment? Could a once-harmless organism, for example, with a new ability to produce a deadly toxin cause a worldwide, perhaps unstoppable epidemic? Should we be tampering with genes at all? Will we eventually be able to alter our own evolution? Should we even try?

Several scientific bodies and government agencies have issued guidelines and regulations concerning genetic research in general, and recombinant-DNA technology specifically. So far, most fears regarding potential environmental danger or damage have proven unfounded. Many of the ethical questions, on the other hand, will undoubtedly remain and probably even evolve, right along with our ability to manipulate genes.

GENETICALLY ENGINEERED MICROORGANISMS *may one day help solve one of the 20th century's environmental problems: ever-increasing accumulation of toxic wastes.*

CHRIS HARRIS/GAMMA-LIAISON

Ecology

In nature, no living thing exists alone. Rather, each is part of an intricate structure composed of other living organisms and the physical environment that encompasses them. The study of organisms in relation to each other and to their environment is known as ecology.

Ecology has been arbitrarily divided into plant ecology and animal ecology. In studying the ecology of plants, however, an involvement with animals is inevitable, and vice versa. There is fundamentally just one ecology, embracing three different concepts: population, community, and ecosystem.

Population. A population is the totality of all the individuals of a given species occupying a particular area. However, a population is more than the sum total of its individual members. Properties of a population that are of interest to ecologists are the number of individuals and their relationship to the area occupied. From these characteristics the number of individuals per unit area, or density, can be calculated. Also important is the structure of a population; this refers to the number of males in relation to females, and the age distribution of each sex. Finally, the ecologist is concerned with population dynamics of both plants and animals, changes over a period of time, and the forces that affect

AN EGRET RIDING A HIPPO *and lichen exemplify symbiotic relationships.*

these changes. These are brought about by birth rates, or natality; death rates, or mortality; and movements of individuals into or out of the population.

Investigators have found that populations of the Norway rat are essentially self-limiting in density. Even with abundant food and shelter, their numbers are restricted by social factors, particularly an aversion to crowding. Other animals, showing no such aversion and not checked by outside factors, eat all available food and so die off. Thus, populations that are not self-limiting are eventually checked by the pressures of their environment.

Every species is capable, if unchecked by mortality, of a high rate of increase—this is termed its biotic potential. Small animals, because they have a faster breeding rate, reach their biotic potential sooner than large animals. Even the largest and slowest breeders, if entirely unchecked, could overrun the Earth. No population, however, is long immune to mortality. Factors in the environment inevitably will cause losses or inhibit the birth rate: predators kill other animals, diseases and parasites decimate species,

M. W. F. TWEEDIE/PHOTO RESEARCHERS

LEONARD LEE RUE III/MONKMEYER

inclement weather causes loss or checks gains due to natality. The lack of food, water, or some other essential to sustain greater numbers will limit population growth. The sum of all agents in an environment that cause loss or arrest population growth is called environmental resistance.

A stable population is one in which the biotic potential and the environmental resistance are in balance. Interference with such a population can affect this stability and cause severe fluctuations. Certain populations, known as cyclic populations, normally fluctuate in a regular and predictable manner. The Canada lynx, for example, regularly reaches a population peak at nine- to ten-year intervals. This is followed by a marked decline. Other populations are normally stable, but occasionally show a striking increase, which is followed by a major decrease. Such population changes are called irruptions. However, most populations are relatively stable, indicating the presence of constant environmental resistance.

Community. Each species forms only a part of a biotic community, for it is dependent on other species for food or shelter, or in turn provides food or shelter for other species. Similarly, the biotic community is not an isolated entity, but bears a relationship to other communities and to the physical environment in which it is found.

A simple community would be that of hardy lichens growing on an exposed rock surface along with a few associated organisms, mostly small to microscopic in size, that can find food and shelter among the lichens. The lichen itself is an example of a close ecological relationship between species. It is not a simple plant, but consists of a combination of algae and fungi, the former manufacturing food from sunlight, water, and atmospheric gases, the latter sheltering and anchoring the algae and in turn receiving food from the algal cells. Such a close association and mutual dependence between species is an example of a relationship known as symbiosis or mutualism.

A complex community is the tropical rain forest, in which the growing conditions are so close to ideal for plants that hundreds of different species of trees sometimes occur within a small area. Associated with the trees is an even greater variety of other plants, including epiphytes (plants that grow high on tree trunks or along horizontal limbs) and giant vines, or lianas, that also depend on the trees for support. Finding food and shelter in this mass

SUCCESSION OF A GLACIAL LAKE

1. After a glacier melts, it leaves behind lakes of various depths that are devoid of life.

2. Shallow parts of the lake are soon invaded by plants that grow completely under water.

3. Debris from plant remains and silt allows water lilies to grow. These shadow out underwater plants.

4. A marsh forms, allowing cattails, reeds, and other marsh plants to grow in the muddy soil.

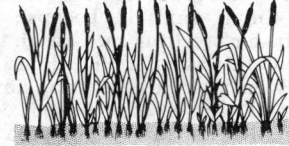

5. The plants take water from the mud and release it to the air. As the soil becomes drier, trees begin to grow.

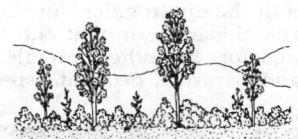

of vegetation are birds, insects, and other forms of animal life more varied than present in any other area of comparable size.

Succession. Biotic communities develop through a long process known as biotic succession. In its primary form, biotic succession occurs in areas that have not previously supported life: bare rocks and newly formed lakes or ponds. The first invaders of such areas are usually the hardiest organisms best able to survive in restricted environments. The environment is altered so that it can be occupied in turn by more demanding species. A predictable series of changes usually occurs; these changes lead to greater complexity. The soil is further built up and becomes able to support a greater variety of life. A relatively stable community, in balance with the prevailing climate and adjusted to a mature soil, eventually occupies the area until some disturbance destroys it. When disturbance occurs, succession begins again. This secondary succession may have fewer stages than primary succession, and usually resembles the later stages of primary succession. The relatively stable community resulting from a succession is known as a climax community.

Ecosystems: Basic Interacting Ecological Units

No biotic community exists apart from its physical, or abiotic, environment. Each community depends on sunlight to provide energy, soil minerals, water, and atmospheric gases, and each is influenced by all the physical and chemical forces that characterize the area in which it is found. The living portion of an ecological community and its virtually inseparable abiotic environment together form an ecosystem, the fundamental unit of study for the ecologist. Ecosystems, like the communities within them, can be simple or complex. However, even the simplest often reveals complexities that require detailed study.

Components of ecosystems.
Any ecosystem has three components:
1. Energy, usually derived from sunlight, but rarely and in small quantities derived from other sources. This energy then moves through the ecosystem, going along pathways known as food chains.

2. Abiotic factors, including water, soil minerals, and atmospheric gases.
3. Biotic factors, including producer organisms, consumer organisms, and reducer organisms. Producer organisms, usually green plants, are capable of capturing sunlight energy through the process of photosynthesis. They utilize the energy to construct the organic chemical compounds that form the plant body, or they store the energy in energy bonds and link the various atoms or molecules in these organic compounds.

Consumer organisms include some plants and all animals in the community. Consumers do not obtain their energy directly, but acquire it secondhand from the sunlight energy originally stored in green plants. All animals are completely dependent on the producers for energy and for the chemicals they require for nutrition. Consumers are subdivided into two categories: primary consumers, or herbivores, which feed directly on plants; and secondary consumers, or carnivores, which feed mainly on other animals and thus receive their energy or food chemicals after they have been processed through two other kinds of organisms.

Reducer organisms are mainly bacteria and fungi that decay and decompose the bodies of dead plants and animals. These organisms feed on the complex chemical compounds of the dead organisms and in turn release simple compounds. Through this process mineral materials that can be picked up and used once more by the roots of growing plants are eventually returned to the soil or water. Without such organisms an entire community would stagnate, choked by its own debris, and the fertility of the soil would be drained without being restored.

The nutrients required by all forms of life circulate continually between abiotic and biotic factors. Both energy and nutrients are the vital components sustaining all living organisms in all ecosystems.

Energy flow. With the exception of nuclear energy produced by humans, all of the energy on which life depends, and all of the power that makes our civilization possible, comes directly or indirectly from the sun.

In ecosystems, the source of almost all energy is sunlight, and only green plants are equipped to utilize it. (A few kinds of bacteria, the iron and sulfur bacteria, can exist without sunlight because they use energy stored in iron or sulfur compounds. They do not contribute significant amounts of energy or chemicals to ecosystems.) The mechanism by which green plants use solar energy, known as photosynthesis, is extremely complex. The presence of the green pigment chlorophyll permits

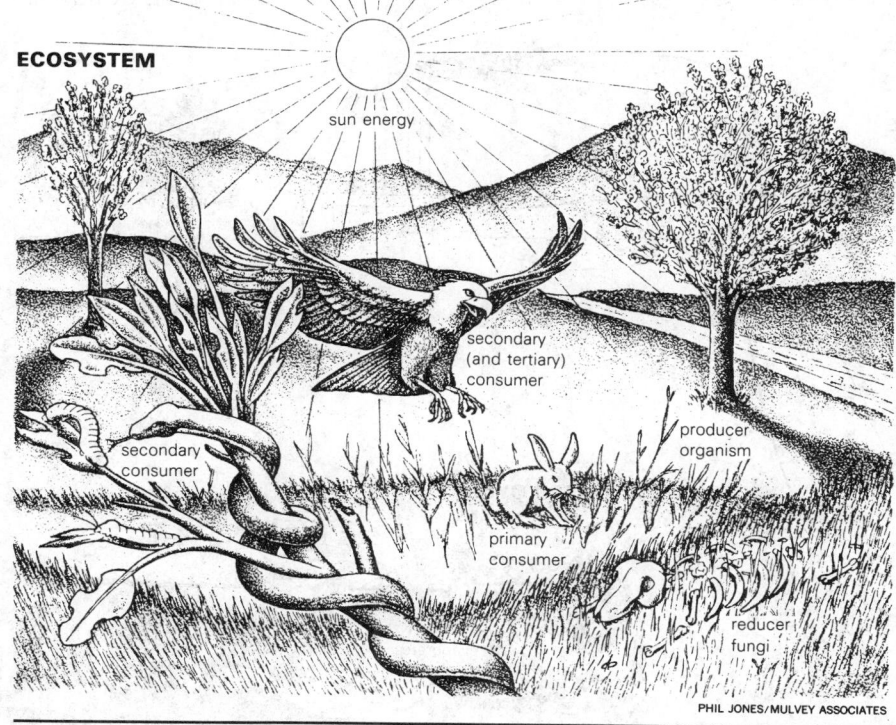

ECOSYSTEM

sun energy

secondary (and tertiary) consumer

secondary consumer

producer organism

primary consumer

reducer fungi

PHIL JONES/MULVEY ASSOCIATES

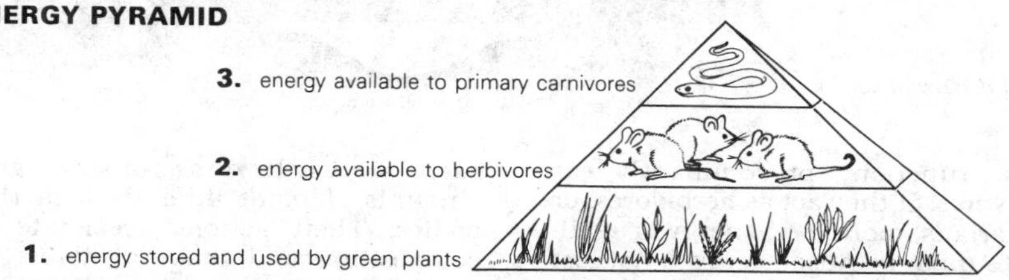

ENERGY PYRAMID

3. energy available to primary carnivores

2. energy available to herbivores

1. energy stored and used by green plants

Green plants are capable of storing large amounts of solar energy. However, only about 1 percent of the total solar energy reaching Earth is actually fixed and stored by plants. The rest is lost because it is in unusable wavelengths of light, because it is reflected away, or because it is dissipated in the form of heat. Nevertheless, the 1 percent remaining is more than adequate to maintain life on Earth.

The energy stored within plant bodies cannot be transferred to animal tissues without further loss. In herbivores, some remains in the indigested plant residue, some is lost as heat generated in the process of digestion, and some is lost during various other metabolic processes. At most, 20 percent of the energy is stored in the body tissues of herbivores. A diminished amount of energy is thus available to carnivores. Further energy is lost in eating, digesting, and metabolizing the energy stored in the body of the herbivore, resulting in only a quarter or less of that energy being stored in the body of a carnivore. Further energy is also lost when one carnivore feeds on another.

Energy follows a one-way path through the ecosystem, with the initial supply rapidly decreasing as it passes from one organism to the next. In order for the system to function, energy must be supplied continually at the green plant end of the chain.

capture of energy from the sun and storage of that energy in the chemical bonds of glucose. Through further use of sunlight energy, molecules of glucose are broken down and linked with other chemicals. This results in the formation of the various carbohydrates, proteins, vitamins, and other substances that constitute the body of a plant.

During photosynthesis, two chemical compounds, carbon dioxide from the air and water from the soil, are combined into simple sugars. In the process, oxygen is released back into the atmosphere. Without green plants or some other means of restoring atmospheric oxygen, the continued respiration by animals would eventually exhaust the supply of oxygen.

Food chains. Food chains are the pathways along which energy is transferred from one organism to another. The various levels through which energy is transferred in a community are known as trophic levels. Producers, primary and secondary consumers, and reducers represent trophic levels.

A simple predator food chain can be represented by the grass-steer-human linkage, where grass, steer, and human typify separate trophic levels and links. It is possible to have a longer food chain of this type. In a pond, phytoplankton, or plant plankton, such as the free-floating microscopic green algae, are fed upon by small floating zooplankton, or animal plankton. These in turn are eaten by aquatic insects that supply food for small carnivorous fish. These small fish may in turn support a population of large fish, for example, bass or pike. Because of the energy relationships involved, it is rare to have more than five or six links in such a chain. In addition to predator food chains, other food chains go from large animals down through small. There are also food chains composed of reducer organisms, which are involved in the breakdown of dead plant or animal tissues. Food chains are difficult to isolate in natural ecosystems because they are usually intertwined into complex food webs. Besides feeding a steer, a green plant

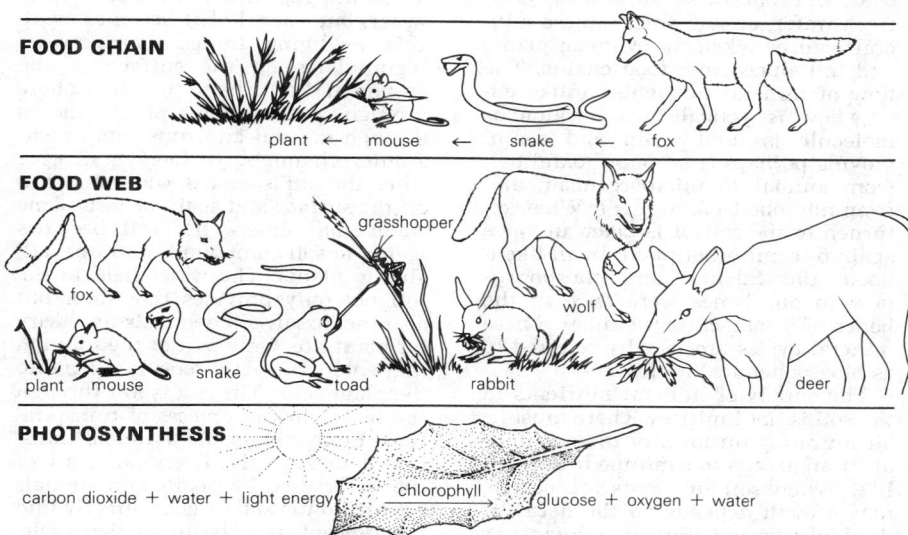

FOOD CHAIN

plant ← mouse ← snake ← fox

FOOD WEB

fox, grasshopper, wolf, mouse, snake, plant, toad, rabbit, deer

PHOTOSYNTHESIS

carbon dioxide + water + light energy → (chlorophyll) → glucose + oxygen + water

PETER LOEWER

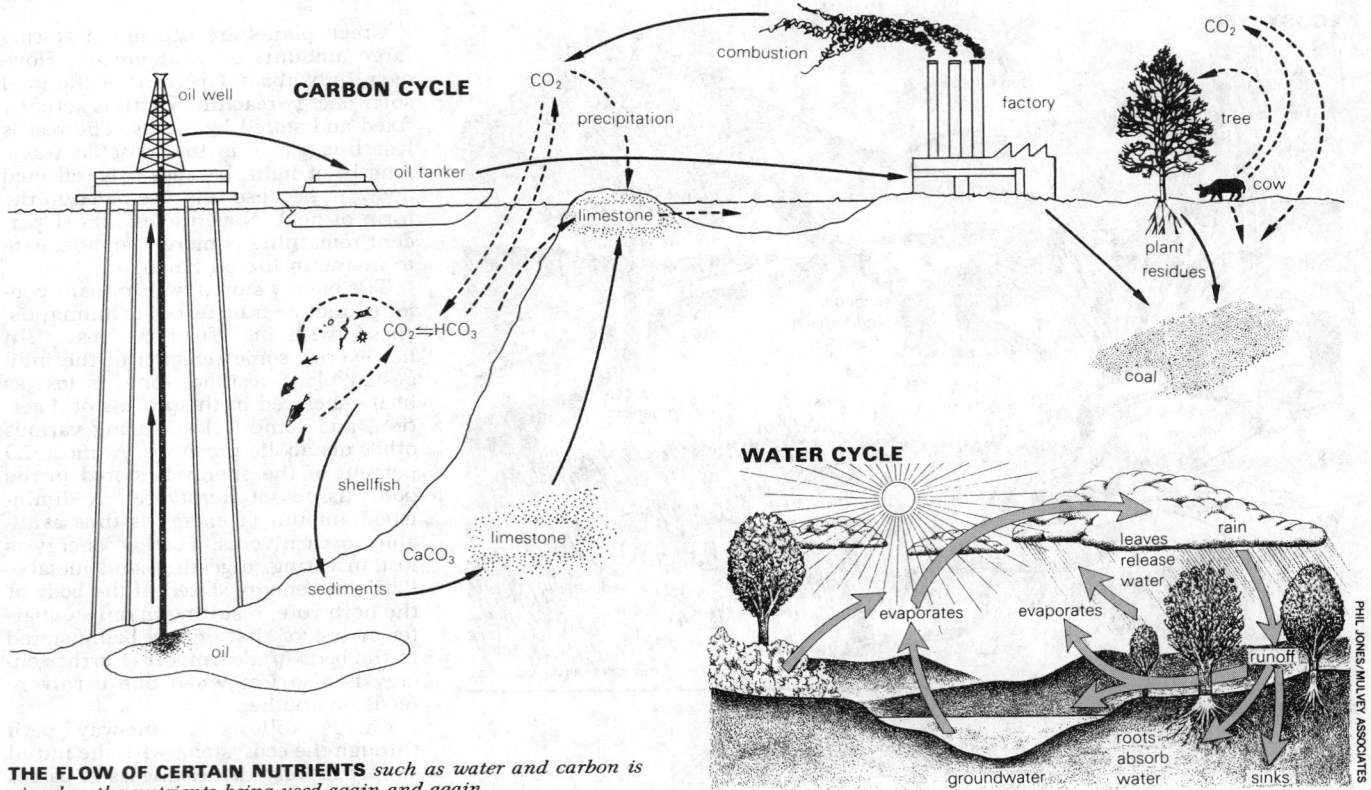

THE FLOW OF CERTAIN NUTRIENTS *such as water and carbon is circular, the nutrients being used again and again.*

may furnish food for a variety of small animals, including insects and microorganisms, which are then eaten by other species. Hence, it is difficult to unravel the chains and webs in any complex community.

The necessary loss of energy between links in each food chain directly affects the number of organisms that can be supported at any trophic level. Thus, the number of green plants upon which deer will feed is always greater than the number of deer that will be supported by the plants. The number of deer, in turn, is always greater than the number of mountain lions that may feed on them. These relationships can be diagrammed in the form of biotic pyramids, which may illustrate the number of organisms, the total weight of organisms, or the calories of energy stored in each layer of organisms. In a pyramid of numbers, there will be more green plants than herbivores supported by them, and more herbivores than carnivores. Therefore, the pyramid will show a broad base of plants and a narrow apex of carnivores. The picture would be similar if the relative weights were charted. It would take about 12,000 pounds of range forage to support a 1000-pound steer for a year, and the steer could be converted into beef to support a human weighing 170 pounds.

Humans, who are omnivorous, can support themselves on either a predominantly plant diet or animal diet. Less food, albeit food of higher nutritional quality, is available when hu-

mans function predominantly as carnivores. If they act as herbivores, or vegetarians, more food energy is available to them because energy is not lost in the transfer through another herbivore. This is a matter of more than theoretical interest to individuals and institutions involved with trying to solve the problem of feeding people in overpopulated countries.

Mineral nutrient cycles.

Food chains also provide pathways for mineral nutrients. Some of these enter the soil as rocks erode. Other minerals wash into ponds, lakes, rivers, and oceans. From these substrates—soil, fresh water, or salt water—these minerals can be taken up by green plants and introduced into food chains. The flow of mineral nutrients, unlike energy flow, is cyclical; the same atom or molecule is used again and again, moving perhaps from plant to animal, from animal to microorganism, and from microbe back to plant. When returned to the soil, it is taken up once again by some other plant. In all likelihood, the calcium and phosphorus now in our bones were once in the bones of a long-extinct animal. These mineral cycles are usually referred to as biogeochemical cycles.

The supply of mineral nutrients in the soil is not limitless. There must be a continuing turnover of these materials if an area is to continue to support life. When soil nutrients are scarce, new growth depends on the decay of dead plants and animals. Organisms

such as earthworms process great amounts of plant litter through their bodies. Their actions accelerate decomposition and make available the materials required for new growth. Such elements as nitrogen, sulfur, phosphorus, calcium, carbon, oxygen, hydrogen, magnesium, potassium, boron, chlorine, copper, iron, manganese, molybdenum, and zinc are constantly recycled through the living and nonliving dimensions. When the cycle is interrupted for any reason, the soil may become infertile.

Water, which is essential to life, is stored for the most part in oceans. Transferred through the atmosphere, it reaches vegetation and soil as rainwater, but not all of it becomes available to living things. Some water accumulates on the surface of the ground and returns to the atmosphere through evaporation. Much moves through the soil and runs into underground channels. In heavy rains, or when the soil is soaked, water may run off the surface and again be lost. Some water that enters the soil becomes bound to soil compounds and unavailable to plants. The water held in the soil not only provides the water but also the dissolved chemicals necessary for plant life. Only part of the solution that enters the plant roots is taken into the plant cells. The rest is lost through the leaves in the process of transpiration. From plants the water is transferred to animals. Eventually, all of the water used by plants and animals returns to the soil or goes directly into the atmosphere to begin another cycle.

ROGER T. PETERSON/NATIONAL AUDUBON SOCIETY/PHOTO RESEARCHERS

LEONARD LEE RUE III/TAURUS PHOTOS

RUSS KINNE/PHOTO RESEARCHERS

JEN & DES BARTLETT/PHOTO RESEARCHERS

FLORA AND FAUNA OF THE WORLD'S DESERTS—*represented above by an elf owl, a scattered stand of stately Saguaro cacti, a desert cottontail, and a Mexican beaded lizard—are well adapted for their inhospitable biome.*

Classification of Major Ecosystems

Life of many kinds is found on land; within the soil; in fresh, marine, and estuarine waters; and in the atmosphere. These regions of Earth are referred to, collectively, as the biosphere.

Classification of terrestrial ecosystems of the biosphere varies according to the emphasis ecologists place on their most distinguishing features. Because the distribution of ecosystems is determined largely by climate and topography, the kinds of ecosystems vary greatly from one part of the world to another.

Perhaps the most useful broad classification of Earth's major ecosystems is the biome system. This scheme recognizes major natural communities distributed over the world in accordance with major types of climate and vegetation. The combined plant and animal life of a particular biome is called its biota. Climate, vegetation, and animal life are so closely related that in the past, when meteorological records were relatively scarce, geographers mapped the boundaries of climatic regions according to a scheme that reflected the occurrence of major changes in vegetation.

Scientists do not all classify the biomes of the world in the same way, but they do recognize the major biomes and aquatic ecosystems described below.

Tundra. Tundra characterizes regions of arctic climate with long, cold, nearly sunless winters, short summers of constant daylight, and scant precipitation. The subsoil, permafrost, is permanently frozen. Vegetation consists of dwarf trees and shrubs; mat-like, broad-leaved herbs; grasses; sedges; and, in places, extensive stands of reindeer moss or lichen. Animals inhabiting tundra regions include the caribou, reindeer, musk ox, ptarmigan, white fox, arctic hare, and lemming.

Tundra covers the northern fringe of Canada and Alaska and extends in a band across northern Asia and Europe. It is also found above the timberline in the higher mountain ranges extending south well into the temperate zone.

Taiga. South of the tundra zone, or below the tundra zone in mountains, is taiga, a forest biome dominated by evergreen conifers, mainly spruce and fir. It covers much of Canada, Alaska, northern Europe, and Siberia. The climate is subarctic, with severe winters and summer growing seasons longer than those of the tundra. Average annual rainfall is 15 to 40 inches.

Taiga is home to the moose, snowshoe hare, northern grouse, goshawk, horned owl, red fox, and Canadian lynx.

Neither tundra nor taiga is found in the southern hemisphere. Antarctica's climate is too extreme to support tundra, and the lower portions of the southern continents are too far from the antarctic climatic regions to have the rigorous temperatures characteristic of taiga.

Temperate forests. In the northern hemisphere, temperate rain forests are dominated by dense stands of tall conifers, usually spruce, cedar, hemlock, Douglas fir, and redwood. In the southern hemisphere, a forest of similar appearance is dominated by the southern beech, and such southern conifers as *Araucaria* and *Podocarpus*. The climate in these regions presents no extremes of cold or drought. Mild temperatures and high rainfall characterize the winters; the summers are cool and seldom without moisture. Such forests support no great mass of animal life, but provide a home for a great variety of smaller species. Characteristic of the North American region are the Roosevelt elk, mountain beaver, and black-tailed deer.

In the eastern United States, western Europe, and northern China, temperate deciduous forests originally contained such broad-leaved trees as beech, maple, walnut, hickory, and oak. Extensive clearing of these regions for human occupation has radically changed the environment. Summers are warm and wet; winters are moderately cold and often snowy; and average annual rainfall is 40 to 60 inches. Most of the trees accommodate the unfavorable growing conditions by shedding their leaves and becoming dormant. Unlike the conifers, which are mostly softwoods, the broad-leaved deciduous trees are mostly hardwoods. In the United States, this biome is home, among others, to the white-tailed deer, wild turkey, gray squirrel, and cottontail rabbit.

Tropical forests.

Tropical rain forests, found in the Amazon basin of South America, in other lowland areas of South America and Central America, in the Congo basin, along the western coast of Africa, and in Southeast Asia, exist in permanently warm and humid tropical areas with plentiful, year-round rainfall. Average annual rainfall often exceeds 80 inches.

Numerous species of broad-leaved and evergreen trees occur in stands of several layers of different height. Along with a great variety of plants, the rain forest supports more birds, insects, and small tree-dwelling mammals than does any other biome.

Tropical deciduous forests occur in tropical regions that are seasonally dry. During the dry season, the country is barren, trees and shrubs leafless. In the wet season, however, the trees burst into leaf and bloom, and grasses and herbs cover the ground. Included in this biome are savanna forests, monsoon forests, and thorn forests.

Grasslands.

Sometimes there are found, interspersed among woodlands and scrub, extensive areas, called grasslands, which are dominated by grasses and other herbaceous plants. They develop best in zones between moist forests and arid deserts. Grasslands can be divided into two general categories: the more humid prairies, dominated by tall grasses; and the dry steppes, where short grasses prevail.

North American grasslands once extended unbroken from Illinois to the Rocky Mountains and beyond and supported huge herds of bison, antelope, and elk.

Mediterranean scrub forest.

This biome exists in much of California (where it is called chaparral), central Chile, the Cape of Good Hope region in South Africa, and southern Australia. It occurs most widely around the Mediterranean Sea in Europe, Asia, and Africa.

Vegetation consists of broad-leaved evergreens and is called *sclerophyll* because the leaves are hard and waxy. Live oak, madrona, and laurel are widespread in the California woodland, but brush has replaced forest or woodland over much of this biome.

Summers in a Mediterranean scrub forest are warm and rainless; winters, moderately wet and cool. Average annual rainfall is 15 to 30 inches. In California, the mule deer, gray fox, jackrabbit, and California quail are characteristic.

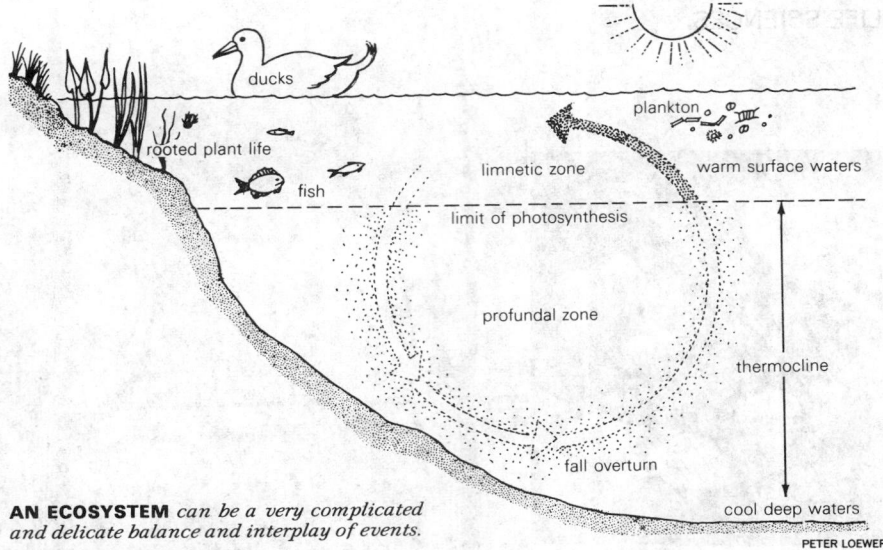

AN ECOSYSTEM *can be a very complicated and delicate balance and interplay of events.*

PETER LOEWER

Deserts.

The warm, dry areas of Earth can be considered together as the desert biome or group of biomes. In these areas, average annual rainfall seldom exceeds 5 inches, and some places go without rain for long periods. The most barren deserts are nearly lifeless, but many support an open scrub vegetation. In the American deserts, the creosote bush covers great areas in uniform, open stands. Elsewhere, various cactuses or thorny leguminous shrubs predominate. Desert fauna include the desert fox, kangaroo rat, and desert jackrabbit in North America; and the oryx, gazelle, and jerboa in Asia and Africa. Many of these animals can live drinking little or no water, obtaining most or all of their water from their food.

Aquatic environments.

Water covers just over 70 percent of Earth's surface. While there are no major aquatic biomes as such, aquatic environments, where life on Earth is most abundant, are usually considered either freshwater or marine.

In both environments, little sunlight on the water reaches any great depth. Photosynthetic algae and plants, therefore, occupy only the upper surface region, called the euphotic zone, which is lighted from above.

In the oceans, the euphotic zone produces almost all the food and supports the greatest mass of life. However, great layers of animal life have been located at depths well below the level of light penetration. Squid move to the surface to feed at night and submerge into the darkness during daylight. A great variety of other fish feed either on other organisms that move between the surface and the depths or on materials that sink from above. In the great ocean depths, animals scavenge organic material that filters down through the upper layers of life. In the open ocean, the zone below the euphotic, extending down to about 6500 feet, is called the bathyl region. Still deeper lies the abyssal region. Most

plants and animals in the open ocean are pelagic, leading a free-swimming or free-floating existence, independent of contact with land.

Around the edges of the oceans are the continental shelves, the submerged portions of the continents. Life here, in the neritic zone, is more plentiful than in the open oceans beyond. Light penetrates to support plants on the ocean floor as well as a great variety of attached or bottom-dwelling animal life. On the upper edge of the shelf is the intertidal zone. Here are found plants and animals that can withstand exposure to the air during low tide. Although narrow by comparison with the great breadth of the oceans, the productive neritic zone occupies a considerable area, following the edges of all the continents, surrounding all the islands, and occurring wherever submerged banks or reefs are near the surface.

A common classification of freshwater environments separates the oligotrophic (low nutrient) waters from the eutrophic (high nutrient) waters. At one extreme is the glacial lake of the high mountains, fed by melting ice or snow, resting on a sterile substrate of granite, and supporting few plants and animals; at the other, the farm pond in an area of rich soil, green with algae and teaming with animal life.

But life can become precarious in a farm pond. Dissolved oxygen becomes limited in fresh water more often than in the ocean. When photosynthesis occurs uninterruptedly, shallow lakes are rich in oxygen.

However, in the winter, light is screened out by ice and snow, and animal populations may exhaust the available oxygen supply. In the ocean, the environment, such as temperature, salinity, and oxygen content, changes more slowly, being governed by seasons more than by short-term weather. In freshwater ponds, the environment changes rapidly, and plants and animals must adapt or die. Life in a pond is more complicated but not more complex than in the ocean.

The Endangered Environment

At the 20th century's midpoint, the term "ecology" was seldom heard outside of a few scientific communities. The world's human population in 1950 stood at about 2.5 billion. "Ecology" has since become a household word. The fact that twice as many humans—about 5 billion—now populate our planet has a lot to do with it, but there is mounting evidence that we have been acting for far too long as if Earth were ours exclusively.

Environmental impact is—in more ways than one—a human concept. As a species we possess a unique ability to interfere with the natural workings of the environment. The ecosystem we inhabit has too often been seen by us as something to conquer rather than live with. We have viewed the natural world we inhabit as ours alone when it is not. The evidence for this lack of understanding of how the world works is all around us.

Tropical rain forests, Earth's biotically richest biome and an important source of atmospheric oxygen, are being reduced in area at the alarming rate of 1 percent per year—an area roughly the size of Denmark. This reduction is to make way for the cultivation of crops, a use to which the soil of rain forests is totally unsuited, and for the grazing of cattle, an activity that can be sustained on such land for only a short period of time. Fertilizer runoff and inflow of sewage and industrial wastes have virtually killed bodies of fresh water as large as Lake Erie by reducing their oxygen content.

Hastening the biological decline of lakes, and adversely affecting the growth and health of temperate forests as well, is acid rain, a product of airborne industrial emissions. Nuclear power plants threaten to introduce large quantities of lethal radioactivity into the environment through accidental reactor failures or by the potential mishandling of nuclear wastes. Warmed water released from nuclear reactor cookers into fragile aquatic environments has already resulted in large local fish kills. High-flying aircraft and aerosol propellants have been associated with depletion of the ozone high above Earth. Ozone shields us and other organisms from a portion of the sun's potentially carcinogenic ultraviolet radiation. Pollution of shallow coastal water and wetlands and overfishing by large stern-trawling factory ships have seriously depleted important ocean fish populations. Exploited for products for which there are synthetic equivalents, whales are threatened with extinction.

Ill-conceived agricultural irrigation projects have seriously interrupted normal nutrient cycles and produced vast tracts of infertile saline soil.

Leaks and blowouts from offshore wells and oil spills measured in hundreds of thousands of tons resulting from supertanker accidents have caused enormous damage to coastal environments. Extensive strip mining has contaminated groundwater, disrupted the landscape, and destroyed local biotic communities. Unburned hydrocarbons, lead, sulfur, and similar pollutants from automobile and airplane emissions have seriously degraded the quality of the air. (Breathing the air on an average day in Mexico City is said to be the equivalent of smoking 40 cigarettes.) Heat and carbon dioxide generated by the burning of fossil fuels, and other industrial activities, have altered the climate in some urban localities and threaten to do the same over a large portion of Earth.

This list of ecological abuses is far from complete. The list of measures thus far undertaken to correct, reverse, or lessen the impact of those abuses and more like them is even shorter. *—Diane Kender Dittrick*

ENDANGERING THE ENVIRONMENT: *ozone-depleting fluorocarbons release into the atmosphere; rain acidifies as a result of industrial emissions; oil spills pollute the sea.*

RICHARD WOOD/TAURUS PHOTOS

AP/WIDE WORLD PHOTOS

CHIP CARLIN/FPG

GLOSSARY OF HEALTH AND LIFE SCIENCES

A

Aberration. Deviation from a normal course or situation; for example, variation in the normal number of chromosomes in an individual organism.

Abiotic. Incompatible with life; incapable of living.

Abyssal region. Ocean region of great depth (3000 meters and more), where no light penetrates.

Acetylcholine. A transmitter of impulses at synapses (junctions of neurons) and myroneural junctions (nerve endings in muscle).

Acromegaly. A progressive disease producing a characteristic appearance: enlarged bones, protruding jaw, and coarsening of all features.

Addison's disease (adrenocortical insufficiency). A condition caused by inadequate secretion of the adrenal glands.

Adenine. One of two major purines (nitrogen-containing bases) found in both RNA and DNA. Also found in various free nucleotides, for example, adenosine triphosphate (ATP).

Adenosine triphosphate. A compound of adenosine containing three phosphoric acid groups. It is an enzyme found in all cells, especially muscle cells.

Adrenal. Refers to the adrenal or suprarenal gland and its secretions. There is one gland atop each kidney.

Agranulocytosis. Condition marked by greatly reduced production of white blood cells. May be due to toxic effects of drugs, for example, tranquilizers or barbiturates.

AIDS (acquired immune deficiency syndrome). An extremely serious immune deficiency disease, thought to be caused by a viral pathogen. Marked by various opportunistic infections and Kaposi's sarcoma.

Albinism. Congenital deficiency or absence of pigment in skin, hair, and eyes due to metabolic block in producing melanin.

Alcoholism. The abuse of or addiction to alcohol. Results in impairment of nervous and gastric systems. In late stages, DTs (delirium tremens), liver cirrhosis, and complete kidney failure may occur.

Algae. Chlorophyll-bearing plants that live in fresh or salt water. Used as food supplements, soil conditioners, and feed for animals.

Alleles. A pair of genes at the same positions (loci) on paired chromosomes, containing specific inheritable characteristics.

Allergen. Any substance that provokes an allergic reaction, for example, dust, pollen, metal, food, drugs, and chemicals.

Alveoli. Air cells of the lungs; the terminal saclike dilations of the alveolar ducts in the lung.

Ames test. Demonstrates the potential of a chemical substance to alter the genes of bacteria.

Amino acid. Any of a large group (20 or more) of organic compounds. All are needed for body growth.

Ammonia. A volatile gas formed by decomposition of nitrogen-containing substances such as proteins and amino acids. Converted into urea in the liver.

Amniocentesis. A diagnostic procedure used to assess various genetic defects and some hereditary disorders of a fetus. Also used to determine fetal maturity, or possible complications of Rh factor.

Anaphase. The stage of mitosis or meiosis in which the longitudinal halves of chromosomes (chromatids) separate and move toward the poles of the cell.

Anaphylaxis. A type of allergic reaction that is potentially life-threatening. May result from injection of certain drugs or diagnostic agents, bee or wasp stings, or such foods as strawberries or shellfish.

Anemia. Condition marked by loss, destruction, or faulty production of red blood cells. May be due to hemorrhaging, hemorrhoids, ulcers, cancer, pregnancy, or inadequate nutrition.

Aneurysm. Swelling of a weakened arterial wall; most dangerous when the aorta or cerebral arteries are involved. Rupturing leads to massive internal bleeding, which may be fatal.

Angina pectoris. Severe, constricting chest pain caused by a lack of blood supply to the heart muscle. Generally occurs during strenuous exertion, for example, while climbing stairs.

Angiography. An x-ray technique that makes blood vessels visible by injection of a radiopaque substance. Useful test in detecting aneurysm, tumors, and atherosclerosis.

Anorexia nervosa. A morbid condition mainly affecting adolescent girls and young women who drastically cut down on food intake. Severe nutritional deficiencies and even death by starvation may occur.

Antibiotic. Any natural or synthetic chemical used to treat infectious disease. If bactericidal, an antibiotic kills microorganisms; if bacteriostatic, it prevents growth of microorganisms.

THE IMPACT OF ANTIBIOTICS ON HEALTH

In an estimate made by the U.S. Public Health Service, modern drugs saved more than 1 million American lives during the 15-year period from 1938 to 1952. It was in 1938 that the first sulfa drug (sulfamilamide) became generally available, and in 1941 the mass production of penicillin began, ushering in the "golden age" of antimicrobial therapy.

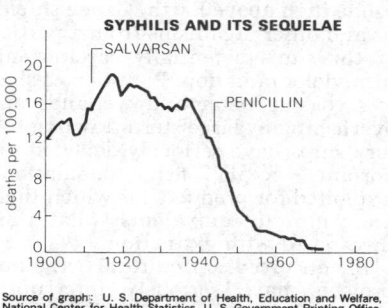

SYPHILIS AND ITS SEQUELAE

Source of graph: U. S. Department of Health, Education and Welfare, National Center for Health Statistics. U. S. Government Printing Office, Washington, D.C.

Antibody (immunoglobin). A protein substance produced by white blood cells that specifically binds to a single foreign antigen, neutralizing or destroying the invading microorganisms in the bloodstream.

Anticoagulant. The prevention of blood coagulation, or an agent that prevents coagulation.

Antigen. Any substance that elicits an immune response, producing antibodies. May be a protein or portion of a protein molecule, another large molecule, or a small molecule attached to a large one.

Antioxidant. An agent that inhibits oxidation (combination of a substance with oxygen). Prevents rancidity in fats, and deterioration of materials.

Appendicitis. Inflammation of the vermiform appendix. Perforation is a serious complication, as it can result in peritonitis.

Arrhythmia. An alteration in regular heart rhythm due to disturbances in formation or conduction of heart impulses. May be functional adjustment in heart action, or from disease.

Arteriogram. An x-ray picture of an artery after it has been injected with a contrast medium.

Arteriosclerosis. A condition commonly referred to as hardening of the arteries, in which artery walls become thickened and lose elasticity.

ARTHRITIS

Arthritis is a widespread disorder that afflicts millions of people, more than any other chronic ailment. This inflammatory disorder has many forms; the term arthritis is generally applied to diseases primarily affecting the joints.

SOME ARTHRITIC DISEASES

DISEASE	RESULT
Rheumatoid arthritis	Inflamed membrane of the joint
Gout	Chemical crystals in the joint fluid
Ankylosing spondylitis	Inflamed ligament attachment to bone
Staphylococcus, gonococcus	Bacteria in the joint fluid
Osteoarthrosis, osteoarthritis	Breakdown of joint cartilage
Polymyalgia rheumatica, polymyositis	Inflamed muscle tissues

Arthroscopy. Direct visualization of the interior of a joint by an arthroscope, a needlelike metal instrument equipped with a fiber optic light source.

Asbestos. A fibrous material made of magnesium and calcium silicate, used for fireproofing and insulation. Protracted inhalation of asbestos particles can cause asbestosis.

Asthma. Marked by difficult breathing and wheezing; may be chronic or episodic. Underlying factors may include allergy, respiratory infection, or emotional stress.

Atherosclerosis. A kind of arteriosclerosis in which the inner artery wall is made thick and irregular by deposits of fatty substances. Most often affects the heart, brain, and legs.

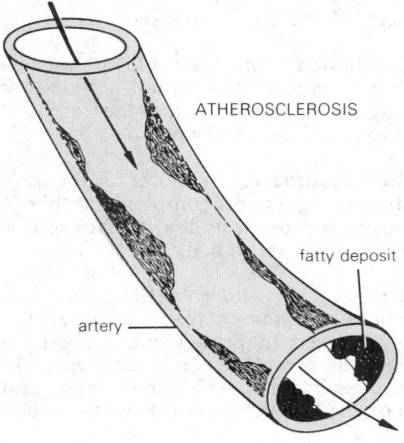

ATHEROSCLEROSIS

fatty deposit

artery

Atom. The smallest particle of an element that can exist and take part in chemical change. Atoms are composed of small particles, notably protons, neutrons, and electrons.

Atrium. A cavity or sinus. Atria of the heart comprise the upper chamber of each half of the heart.

Autoimmunity. A state of abnormal immune response in which antibodies are produced against an individual's own body tissue.

Autonomic. Self-controlling, as the autonomic nervous system, which controls involuntary bodily functions.

Autosome. Any chromosome other than a sex chromosome. Normally occurs in pairs in somatic cells, and singly in gametes.

Autotrophs. Self-nourishing plants and bacteria forming protein and carbohydrates from inorganic salts and carbon dioxide.

Axon. A process of a neuron that normally conducts nerve impulses away from the cell body.

B

Bacteria. Single-celled plantlike microorganisms lacking chlorophyll. When they appear singly, they are called micrococci; in pairs, diplococci; in irregular clusters, staphylococci; in chains, streptococci.

Bacteriophage. A type of virus that attacks and destroys bacteria by surrounding and absorbing them.

Balloon dilatation therapy. An alternative to surgery to open clogs in arteries. In some cases, an alternative to coronary bypass surgery to remove blockages in arteries feeding the heart.

Basal. Of, pertaining to, located at, or forming a base.

Bathyal region. The deeper parts of the ocean; deep sea.

BEAM (brain electrical activity mapping). Procedure in which data from an electroencephalogram are converted by a computer into colored topographical maps of the brain's electrical firings.

B cells. White blood cells producing antibodies against a specific antigen. These antibodies are effective against many bacteria, but not viruses. The "B" is for bone marrow.

Beta blockers. Drugs, also known as beta-adrenergic blocking agents, that reduce the workload of the heart and thereby lower the demand of the coronary arteries for blood.

Biochemist. One pursuing the science of biochemistry, which deals with all aspects of chemistry that apply to living organisms.

Biofeedback. The use of electronic or electrochemical instruments to measure and feed back to an individual an indication of body activities of which there is usually no awareness. The purpose is to obtain some control over these activities.

Biogeochemical. The influence of living organisms and life processes on the chemical structure and history of Earth; for example, the effects of plants on the weathering of rocks.

Biology. The science of life and living things, including botany (the study of plants), and zoology (of animals).

Biome. The total complex of biotic communities occupying and characterizing a particular area or zone, for example, the desert or a grassland.

Biophysicist. A scientist whose specialty is biophysics, the physics of biological processes.

Biopsy. Excision and microscopic examination of tissue samples and cells to determine abnormalities. Indicated when cancer or certain liver or kidney diseases are suspected.

Biosphere. The part of Earth's crust, water, and atmosphere where living organisms exist.

Biota. A collective term referring to the animal and plant life of a region or period.

Biotechnology. The relationship between man and machines.

Biotic potential. The capacity of a population of animals or plants to increase in numbers under optimum environmental conditions.

Bone marrow. The soft red (in spongy bones) or yellow (in long bones) tissue filling the inside of bone cavities. Red marrow produces both red blood cells (erythrocytes) and white blood cells (leukocytes).

Brain death. Characterized by irreversible coma and irreparable brain damage. There is lack of electrical activity for a prolonged period, no response to external stimuli, fixed pupils, and no spontaneous breathing.

Brain scan. A diagnostic technique useful in detecting brain abnormalities such as tumors. After injection of a radioactive isotope into a vein, a scintillation scanner is used to detect radioactive emissions as the tracer flows through blood vessels in the brain.

Bronchiectasis. Chronic lung disease in which air passages are abnormally, at times permanently, dilated. May be congenital or acquired.

Bronchitis. An inflammatory condition of the lungs. Acute bronchitis usually results from exposure to cold. Chronic bronchitis is slowly progressive and, if uncontrolled, may develop into serious lung problems.

Bronchoscopy. A diagnostic procedure to study the tracheobronchial tree through a bronchoscope, an illuminated tubular instrument. Also useful in obtaining biopsy specimens and in removing obstructions.

Buerger's disease (thromboangiitis obliterans). A circulatory disease affecting muscles and blood vessels of the legs. Blood clots, ulcers, or gangrene may develop.

Bulimia. A condition in which a morbid hunger alternates with periods of aversion to food.

Bursitis. Painful inflammation of a bursa (fluid-filled sac protecting a body joint against friction). May be caused by strain, injury, or internal toxic disorder.

Butylated hydroxyanisole (BHA). A food additive consisting entirely of synthetic chemicals. An antioxidant for fats and oils that has the effect of preventing rancidity.

C

Calcium. A silver-white crystalline metal. An essential component of bones, teeth, shells, and various plant structures.

Cancer. A series of diseases characterized by the irregular and uncontrolled growth of body cells. These malignant cells may remain in the area where they formed, or they may spread via the blood or lymph to other parts of the body (metastasis).

Capillaries. Minute blood vessels that connect the smallest arteries (called arterioles) with the smallest veins (called venules).

Carbohydrates. In both its forms—simple sugars and complex starches—carbohydrates provide the main source of energy for the body.

Carbon. A nonmetallic element whose compounds are found in all living things. In pure form, carbon occurs as graphite and diamond; in impure form, as charcoal, coal, and soot, and in the atmosphere as carbon dioxide.

Carcinogen. Any substance that produces cancer. The origin or production of cancer is called carcinogenesis.

Carcinoma. A malignant tumor derived from epithelium, the cellular layer covering all free surfaces, including the skin and mucous and serous membranes.

Cardiac arrest. A sudden cessation of heartbeat and breathing. This condition calls for immediate attention; that is, cardiopulmonary resuscitation (CPR) by trained personnel.

Cardiac catheterization. A procedure in which a catheter (hollow cylinder) is guided through a blood vessel into the heart, permitting an x-ray sensitive dye to be injected. This helps to determine pressure within heart chambers, and to visualize blood flow in the heart muscle.

Cardiomyopathy. Disease in the myocardium (heart muscle).

Carnivore. An order of chiefly flesh-eating mammals, including cats, dogs, bears, minks, hyenas, raccoons, and pandas.

Cartilage. A type of dense connective tissue of firm consistency, with cells embedded in a ground substance or matrix. It has no nerve or blood supply of its own.

Catalyst. A substance that speeds up the rate of a chemical reaction without being consumed itself or being permanently changed in the process.

Cataract. A condition in which the lens of the eye is no longer transparent. Loss of sight is gradual, eventually leading to blindness unless adequate medical treatment is applied.

CAT (computerized axial tomography) scan. A technique in which an x-ray camera rotates once a second around the area to be studied, producing hundreds of individual images. These data are reassembled by a computer, giving a cross-sectional image.

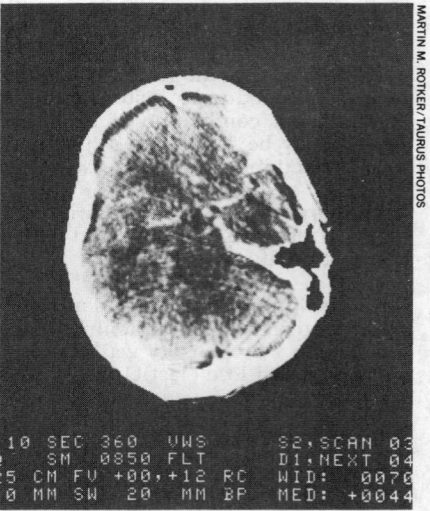

CAT SCAN

Cell. The working unit of life, comprising all tissues of the body. Cells are self-reproducing, with new cells arising by cell division.

Cellular immunity. A form of immunity involving phagocytes (cells engulfing pathogens or inert substances), T cells, and natural killer cells, which are non-T cells.

Cellulose. A fibrous form of carbohydrate that is the supporting framework of plants. Stimulates intestinal peristalsis and elimination.

Centriole. A tiny cylindrical organelle, considered a pole of the mitotic figure and located at the center of a centrosome.

Centromere. The region of a chromosome to which the spindle fiber is attached during the process known as mitosis.

Centrosome. A small mass of differentiated cytoplasm that contains the centriole.

Cerebral palsy. A condition that results from brain damage incurred before, during, or shortly after birth. Marked by uncontrollable body movements, possible speech or eye defects, mental retardation, and impaired hearing.

Chagocytosis. Process in which a cell literally reaches out and surrounds the material to be taken in. In pinocytosis, a deep indentation is formed in the cell membrane.

Chancre. The most significant lesion occurring in syphilis. It begins as a dull, red, hard papule on genitalia, the center of which becomes ulcerated.

Chaparral. A special kind of biome found in various parts of the world; for example, the West Coast of the United States and, most widely, around the Mediterranean Sea in Europe, Asia, and Africa. Vegetation consists of broad-leaved evergreens called sclerophyll.

Chemical. A substance produced by or used in a chemical process. Relating to chemistry.

Chemotherapy. In the treatment of disease, the use of drugs or chemical agents that have a specific and toxic effect upon various disease-causing microorganisms.

Chicken pox (varicella). A highly contagious but mild infectious disease, occurring mostly in children. Marked by a red, blistery, and crusting rash.

Chiropractor. One practicing chiropractic methods, which are based on the theory that disease is caused by pressure on spinal nerves. Manipulation of the spinal vertebrae is the common method of treatment.

Chlamydia. A general term that includes microorganisms causing psittacosis-ornithosis (known as parrot fever), lymphogranuloma venereum, trachoma, and conjunctivitis.

Chlorine. A highly irritating gas that is damaging to respiratory mucous membranes. It is present in gastric juice, aiding digestion and activating enzymes, and is essential to normal gastric secretion.

Chlorophyll. The green pigment essential to photosynthesis. It is present in bacteria and in all plants except fungi.

Chloroplast. A plant cell in leaves and young stems containing chlorophyll. Important in the process of photosynthesis.

Cholecystitis. Inflammation of the gallbladder, acute or chronic, usually due to obstruction of the bile duct by gallstones (cholelithiasis).

Cholecystography. X-ray study of the gallbladder; useful in detecting gallstones or gallbladder dysfunction.

Cholesterol. A sterol, this fatlike substance is found in animal fats and oils, nerve tissue, bile, blood, and egg yolk. A normal constituent of bile, cholesterol is also produced in the liver.

Cholinesterase. An enzyme needed for the hydrolysis of acetylcholine to acetic acid and choline in the body. Found in brain, nerve, and red blood cells.

Chromatin. Substance found in the cell nucleus, where it forms chromosomes, the carriers of genes.

Chromosomal genes. In bacteria, the genetic information carried on the bacteria's own chromosome (plasmid).

Chromosome. The heredity-bearing gene carrier of the living cell, derived from chromatin and consisting largely of nucleoproteins (DNA) together with other protein components (histones).

Chyme. A mixture of partly digested food and digestive secretions passed from the stomach into the small intestines during digestion.

Cilia. Microscopic hairlike projection of bone or tissue extending from an epithelial cell surface, often capable of rhythmical motion. Also, eyelashes.

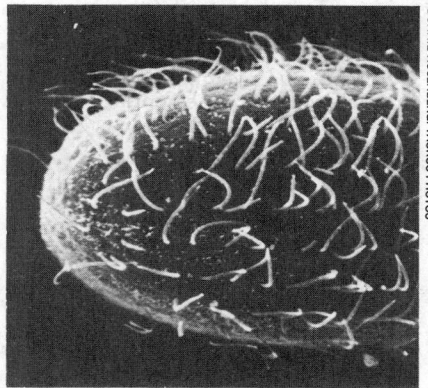

BONNIE ROSENBERG/TAURUS PHOTOS

CILIA

Cirrhosis of the liver. A chronic condition in which degenerative changes occur in liver cells and surrounding tissue thickens, interfering with normal liver function.

Clone. An identical copy obtained from a single entity; for example, a bacterium growing in a petri dish and reproducing by simple cell division produces a clone of possibly millions of identical bacteria.

Coagulation. Clotting, or the process of changing from a liquid to a solid state, especially of blood.

Cobalt. A hard, brittle, metallic element related to nickel, silver, lead, copper, and iron ores. A constituent of Vitamin B_{12}.

Codon. A sequence of three adjacent nucleotides that specifies the insertion of an amino acid in a specific structural position during the process of protein synthesis.

Coercevate droplet. A type of colloid; a complex organic substance considered to have been a forerunner of the development of the first living organism.

Colitis. Inflammation of the colon. Irritable colon (mucous or spastic colitis) produces cramplike pain, mucus in stools, constipation, or diarrhea.

Collagen. An insoluble protein that accounts for about 30 percent of total body protein. Found in the white fibers of connective tissue, cartilage, and bone.

Collagen diseases. Various conditions causing cellular changes that affect the body's connective tissue or soft skeleton. Includes lupus erythematosus, rheumatoid arthritis, and scleroderma.

Colloids. Aggregates of molecules in a finely divided state, dispersed in a gaseous, liquid, or solid medium, and resisting sedimentation, filtration, and diffusion.

Colonoscopy. Examination of the upper portion of the rectum with an elongated speculum. Also used to obtain tissue samples for biopsy and to remove polyps.

Colostomy. Surgically, a temporary or permanent opening is made from the colon through the abdominal wall, creating an artificial passage for the elimination of solid wastes.

Common cold. A communicable and infectious illness caused by one or more viruses. Involves the upper respiratory tract (eyes, ears, nose, throat).

Congestive heart failure. A condition in which the heart cannot pump enough blood to meet the body's needs and circulation becomes disturbed. As a result, fluid may accumulate in various parts of the body.

Conjugation. A bacterial process by which genetic information is exchanged between two genetically different organisms.

Copper. A metal, small quantities of which are utilized by the body. Several of its salts are used in medicine. Present in the liver at all times; excreted by the kidneys.

Cornea. A transparent membrane forming the anterior sixth of the outer fibrous coat of the eyeball.

Coronary bypass. A major operative procedure in which a blocked coronary artery is bypassed with a section of vein taken from the leg and grafted into position.

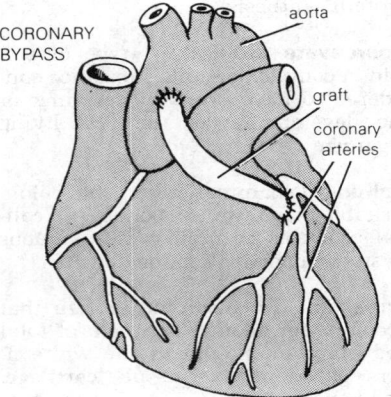

CORONARY BYPASS — aorta, graft, coronary arteries

Coronary occlusion. Blockage of vessels supplying blood to the heart muscle. May be due to plaque (fatty deposits) or a thrombus (blood clot) plugging the artery.

Corpus luteum. The ovarian follicle after it has released its ovum. Produces the hormone progesterone.

Corticosteroid. A steroid produced by the adrenal cortex; a corticoid containing a steroid.

Cretinism. A thyroid hormone deficiency occurring in the unborn child, or shortly after birth, as a result of inadequate iodine intake by the mother.

Crista. A ridge or crest; a projection, sometimes branched, of the inner wall of a mitochondrion into its fluid-filled cavity.

Cryosurgery. A surgical procedure that destroys cells by application of extreme cold (tissue is usually cooled to below 0° F). Used to treat malignant tumors and certain precancerous conditions.

Crystalline. Pertaining to, or made of, crystal, a solid of regular shape.

Culdoscopy. Examination of the female internal organs and pelvic cavity. Useful in cases of suspected abnormal uterine tissue growth, infertility, and pelvic disorders.

Cyanophytes. Blue-green algae, widely distributed in nature, that can produce complex organic molecules by photosynthesis.

Cyclamate. The group name for synthetic non-nutritive sweetening agents derived from cyclohexylamine or cyclanic acid.

Cyst. An abnormal sac or swelling filled with fluid or a semisolid material; can develop anywhere in the body.

Cystic fibrosis. A progressive disease of young people involving the exocrine glands (for external secretion through a duct).

Cystitis. Inflammation of the urinary bladder, usually due to a bacterial infection that reaches the bladder by way of infected kidneys, lymph vessels, and the urethra.

Cystoscopy. Examination of the inner bladder and urethra with a lighted tubular instrument. Indicated when there is a suspicion of bladder or urinary tract cancer or polyps.

Cytochrome. A type of iron-containing protein of importance in cell metabolism. Plays an essential part in cellular respiration.

Cytokinesis. Relates to the changes occurring in the protoplasm of the cell outside the nucleus during the process of cell division.

Cytologist. One who specializes in cytology, a branch of biology dealing with study of the formation, structure, and function of cells.

Cytoplasm. The extra-nuclear components of the living cell, containing mitochondria, plastids, and spherosomes. Together with the nucleus, constitutes the protoplasm.

Cytosine. A pyrimidine base found in nucleic acids; an essential constituent of both RNA and DNA.

D

D&C (dilation and curettage). Enlargement of the cervix to facilitate scraping of the uterine walls with a curette. Used to remove unwanted uterine tissue or polyps, or to obtain a piece of tissue for examination.

Deltoid. Musculus deltoidens, the triangular-shaped muscle that covers the shoulder prominence.

Dendrite. A branched part of a nerve cell that transmits impulses toward the cell body.

Deoxyribose. A phosphoric acid of a pentose (simple sugar); present in nucleic acid.

Dermatitis. Inflammation of the skin which, in some persons, may be due to

contact irritants such as acids and alkalis, cosmetics, fabrics, animal hair, and many other substances.

Dermis. Corium, cutis vera, or true skin. A superficial thin layer that interlocks with the epidermis and other skin layers.

Diabetes insipidus. A disease characterized by chronic excretion of large amounts of urine, accompanied by extreme thirst. Usually results from an insufficient production of the antidiuretic hormone.

Diabetes mellitus. A metabolic disease in which the body is unable to utilize carbohydrates, chiefly because of inadequate insulin production.

Dialysis. A process employed to separate or extract certain substances in solution by diffusion through a porous membrane. Used to purify the blood (hemodialysis) in persons with defective or absent kidneys.

Diaphragm. A thin musculomembranous partition separating the abdomen from the thoracic cavity.

Diarrhea. Frequent passage of loose, watery stools. May be caused by food poisoning, certain diseases, overindulgence in food, or certain drugs.

Diastole. The normal period in the heart cycle during which the muscle fiber lengthens, the heart dilates, and the cavities fill with blood. Dilation of the atria occurs before that of the ventricles.

Diffraction. Modification of the behavior of light or other forms of radiant energy (for example, x-rays, electrons, and neutrons) produced by deflection of rays of light from a straight line in passing by the edge of an opaque body.

Diffusion. Spontaneous mixing of one substance with another when in contact or separated by a permeable membrane or microporous barrier.

Digestion. The process by which food is broken down, mechanically and chemically, and is converted into absorbable forms, in the gastrointestinal tract.

Diphtheria. An infectious disease caused by *Corynebacterium diphtheriae* and its highly potent toxin. Far more severe in the unimmunized.

Diploid. Having a homologous pair of chromosomes for each characteristic except sex, the total number of chromosomes being twice that of a gamete (spermatozoa or ovum).

Discipline. A branch of knowledge or instruction.

Diverticular disease. Condition in which sacs or pockets form on the large bowel. In diverticulosis, the colon is filled with dozens of these sacs. Marked by diarrhea, colic, and abdominal pain.

DNA (deoxyribonucleic acid). A nucleic acid present in chromosomes and chromatin of the nuclei of animal and vegetable cells. Considered to be the chemical basis of hereditary characteristics and to be the carrier of genetic information.

Dopamine. The precursor of norepinephrine and epinephrine. This compound increases blood pressure; used experimentally in low blood pressure and shock.

Down's syndrome. A congenital abnormality marked by moderate to severe mental retardation. Children born with Down's have a sloping forehead, low-set ears, slanted eyes, and a generally dwarfed physique.

Dual photon absorptiometer. An x-ray-like technique that uses extremely low levels of radiation to measure bone density.

Duodenum. The first part of the small intestine, extending from the pylorus in the stomach to the junction with the jejunum (the second portion of the small intestine).

Dysplasia. Abnormal tissue development; can occur in the lungs or other parts of the body, but most often is found in the cervix.

E

Echocardiography. A diagnostic aid in detecting heart problems. Involves recording echoes of ultrasonic waves (very high frequency sound waves beyond ear range).

Ecosystem. Living organisms and plants and their environment in a defined area.

Edema. Accumulation of an excessive amount of fluid in body cells or tissues. May be local or general, and is associated with such conditions as fractures, heart failure, and urinary disorders.

Electrocardiogram (ECG or EKG). A graphic record of the electrical activity of the heart; can show if electrical conduction is normal, and if there is dead tissue due to a heart attack.

Electroencephalogram (EEG). X-ray picture of the brain. Useful in diagnosing brain tumors and other disorders.

Electroretinography. A procedure employing a special contact lens fitted

LONG-TERM, LOW-LEVEL AIR POLLUTION *has been shown to be a serious factor in contributing to chronic respiratory diseases such as bronchitis, bronchial asthma, and emphysema.*

with an electrode that records impulses produced by the retina, translating them into computerized data.

Embolism. Obstruction of a blood vessel by a transported solid (embolus); for example, a blood clot or bacterial mass.

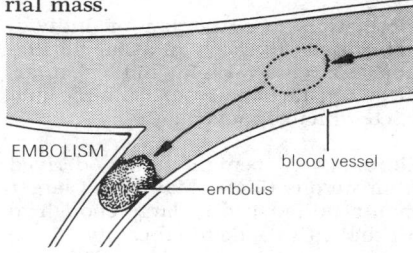

EMBOLISM

blood vessel

embolus

Embryo. A stage in prenatal development; in humans, it includes the period from the second through the eighth weeks.

Embryogenesis. Early stages of life development in every type of animal, including humans.

Emphysema. A lung disease marked by greatly distended air sacs, thinned bronchi, and, eventually, destruction of the architecture of the lung.

Chronic bronchitis or bronchial asthma, smoking, and air pollution may be implicated.

Empyema. Pus in a body cavity, caused by infection. Chills, fever, and other symptoms subside after the pus has been drained.

Endocardiography. A method used to record the site, motion, and composition of various cardiac structures, especially in detecting heart valve problems.

Endocarditis. Inflammation of the heart lining (endocardium). Most often occurs in persons with damaged heart valves.

Endocrine. An internal secretion, or a gland producing an internal secretion (for example, the thyroid gland).

Endometriosis. A nonmalignant condition in which tissue located in the uterine lining (endometrium) begins to grow elsewhere, for example, in the ovaries.

Endoscope. A flexible, fiberoptic instrument containing a light source

EPILEPSY, *disturbed brain function, can be detected by electroencephalography.* Left: *normal brain waves.* Right: *disturbed electrical activity in epileptic seizure.*

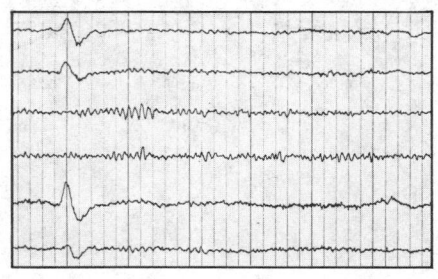
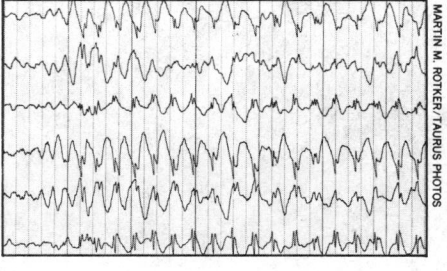

that permits direct visualization of the gastrointestinal tract.

Enkephalins. One of two closely related proteins occurring in the brain and having opiate qualities.

Environment. The aggregate of conditions, influences, and things, and their impact on the existence or development of nature or of people.

Enzyme. A biochemical catalyst. One of various complex proteins produced by living cells. Can alter the chemical changes in other substances while remaining unchanged in the process. Plays an important part in breaking down food particles into simple compounds more readily absorbed by the body.

Epidermis. Cuticle, or outer layer of the skin. Consists of four layers of skin, the stratum corneum being the outermost.

Epilepsy. A group of nervous disorders marked by either convulsive or nonconvulsive seizures.

Epinephrine. Active hormone, together with norepinephrine, produced by the adrenal medulla. Useful in arresting local bleeding and in relieving asthmatic attacks.

Epiphytes. Plants, such as orchids or ferns, growing on other plants or objects, and obtaining mechanical support but no nourishment.

Erythrocyte sedimentation rate. A laboratory test determining how fast red blood cells settle to the bottom of a long narrow tube after an anticoagulant has been added to the blood.

Estuarine. Denotes something living in an inlet or river mouth, where there is a flow of tidal waters.

ESTUARIES, rich food sources, abound in crabs, oysters, clams, and fish.

Eucaryote. An organism composed of one or more cells that contain well-defined nuclei.

Eutrophic. Relating to, characterized by, or promoting eutrophia, a state of normal nourishment and growth.

Evolution. The gradual development over a long period of time of groups of organisms and species. Consequently, descendants differ in structure and normal function from their ancestors.

F

Fallopian. The uterine tube that serves to convey the ovum from the ovary to the uterus and spermatozoa from the uterus to the ovary.

Fetus. In humans, the child in the uterus from the third month to the time of birth.

Fever (pyrexia). A body temperature above the normal (taken orally, 98.6° F). Anyone with a temperature of 101° F or more should be given medical attention.

Fiber. The threadlike process of a neuron; a neuron or the axonal portion of a neuron.

Fibrillation. Contraction of individual muscle fibers, as in atrial fibrillation. Extremely rapid and irregular, these contractions result in rapid and uncoordinated movement.

Fibroma. A benign tumor derived from fibrous tissue. May be no larger than a millet seed or large enough to fill the entire abdominal cavity.

Flagellum. A hairlike, mobile process on the extremity of a bacterium or protozoon.

PHOTOMICROGRAPH OF FLAGELLA *showing whiplike motion of microtubules.*

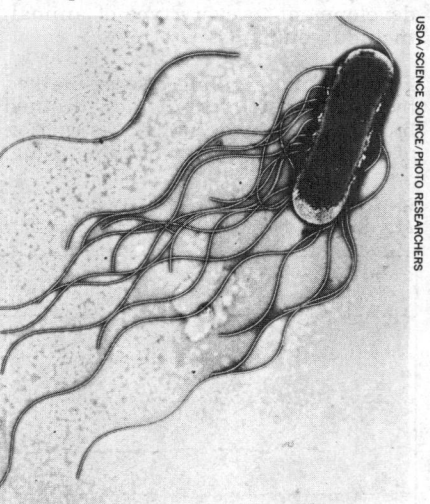

Flatulence. An excessive amount of gas in the stomach and intestines. May be caused by habitual air swallowing or indigestion.

Fluoroscopy. A technique permitting examination of inner parts of the body:
upper body: x-ray visualization of esophagus, stomach, and duodenum
lower body: x-ray visualization of large intestine.

Food chain. A succession of organisms in a community that constitutes a feeding chain in which food energy is transferred from one organism to another as each consumes a lower member and, in turn, is preyed upon by a higher member.

Food poisoning (salmonellosis). Most often, the offending organism is one of a group of *Salmonella.* A more severe and sometimes fatal food poisoning is produced by *Clostridium botulinum* (botulism).

Fracture. A broken bone:
simple: bone is broken but there is no external wound
compound: bone is broken and there is an external wound extending to the injured site.

Fungi. A division of plants, including molds, yeasts, smuts, and mushrooms, that lack chlorophyll, obtaining sustenance from organic matter.

G

GABA (gamma-aminobutyric acid). A constituent of the central nervous system that is considered a transmitter of inhibitory nerve impulses.

Galactosemia. An inborn error of metabolism marked by decreased ability to convert galactose to glucose.

Gallstones. Stonelike masses formed in the gallbladder or bile ducts. They may give little distress, or may cause painful attacks if there is inflammation of the gallbladder (cholecystitis) or bile ducts (cholelithiasis).

Gamma globulin. Various proteins found in the lymphatic system, bone marrow, and spleen. They circulate in the blood and are important to the body's defense system.

Gangrene. Death and decay of body tissue due to obstructed blood flow. May be confined to a small area or involve an entire extremity.

Gastritis. Inflammation of the mucous membrane of the stomach. May be caused by viral infection, food poisoning, or overindulgence in alcohol and other beverages.

Gastroenteritis. Acute inflammation of the intestinal lining. May be caused by a virus (intestinal flu), food allergy or poisoning, or certain drugs.

Gastroscopy. Inspection of the inner surface of the stomach with a special instrument—an endoscope.

Gene. A functional hereditary unit that occupies a fixed location in a chromosome, has a specific influence on phenotype, and is capable of mutation to various allelic forms.

Genetic engineering (gene splicing). Intentional alteration of genetic material or control of the gene process to prevent or modify hereditary defects.

Geneticist. One who specializes in genetics, the branch of science dealing with heredity.

Genome. The male or female contribution to the genetic makeup of an individual organism; in bacteria, the chromosomal genes of the organism under study.

German measles (rubella). Acute contagious disease, similar to measles and scarlet fever. Pregnant women who have not had rubella in childhood should be protected against this disease. If infected, there is risk to the fetus.

Gigantism. Excessive production of the growth hormone (somatotropin). Before the extremities are fully united, an excess of this hormone causes part of the body, or the entire body, to grow to an abnormal size.

Glandular. Relating to a gland, a secreting organ or structure. Many types of glands serve different purposes throughout the body.

Glaucoma. An eye disease marked by an unaccountable rise in the fluids within the eyeball. Unrelieved, this pressure can cause permanent eye damage and lead to blindness.

Glomeruli. A network of capillaries. In the kidney, capillary blood vessels form a cluster at the beginning of each kidney tubule.

Glomerulonephritis. A type of kidney disease in which the glomeruli (small tufts of capillary loops) are inflamed. The chronic form can result in irreparable damage to the nephrons (functional kidney units).

Glucose. An important carbohydrate in body metabolism, formed during digestion and absorbed from the intestines into the blood.

Glycogen. An animal starch that is converted into glucose when needed by body tissues.

Glycosuria. Sugar in the urine. May result from insulin insufficiency, disorders of the endocrine glands, or excessive carbohydrate intake.

Goiter (hyperthyroidism). Enlargement of the thyroid gland due to abnormal activity of the thyroid, specifically in secreting an excessive amount of hormones.

Golgi apparatus. A lamellar membranous structure near the nucleus of almost all cells.

Gonads. The female sex glands (ovaries) and the male sex glands (testes).

Gonorrhea. An inflammatory disease affecting the genitalia in either sex, transmitted primarily during sexual contact.

Gout. A familial metabolic disorder involving the joints. Basically, a problem of excessive uric acid in the bloodstream, and deposits of sodium urate crystals, mainly in the joints.

Graft. Insertion of skin, or other living substance, into similar substances to overcome a defect. For example, a piece of skin is removed from one body part and grafted onto another to cover a large superficial burn.

Gynecology. A branch of medicine that deals with diseases of women, the genital tract, and female endocrine and reproductive physiology.

H

Hamstrings. Three muscles on the back of the thigh. They flex the leg and extend the thigh.

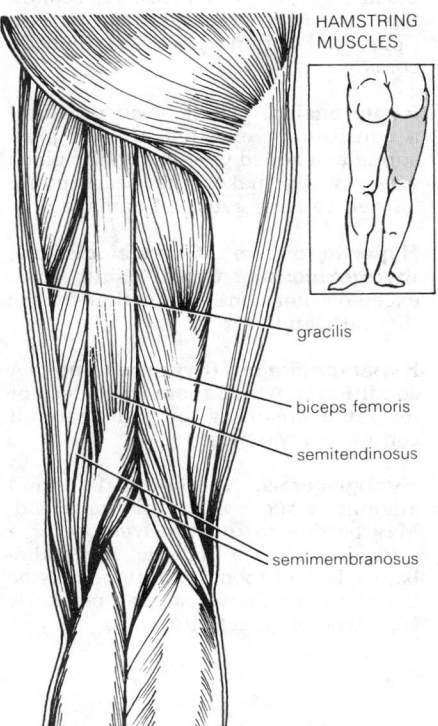

HAMSTRING MUSCLES

gracilis

biceps femoris

semitendinosus

semimembranosus

Hashimoto's disease. A chronic form of thyroiditis (inflammation of the thyroid gland). Marked by a particular type of goiter and decreased secretion of the thyroid hormone.

Heartburn. The abnormal return of acid liquid from the stomach into the esophagus. Produces a burning and tightening sensation deep in the chest.

Helix. The double helix of DNA, each half of which contains chemical compounds arranged in a specific sequence. Variations in the sequence of these compounds enable genetic information to be transmitted.

Helminth. A worm, especially an intestinal nematode or trematode.

Helper T cells. Cells that stimulate the growth of other T cells and the production of B cell antibodies; activate macrophage (immune cells) through release of specific lymphokine signals. The "T" is for thymus, where T cells mature.

Hematoma. A localized mass of blood that has escaped from a blood vessel into the tissues at the site of an injury. The blood is usually clotted, wholly or partially.

Hemodialysis. A procedure used to purify the blood of patients with kidney failure. On an average, a patient has to undergo hemodialysis for 20 hours a week.

Hemoglobin. The iron-containing pigment found in red blood cells; the transport for oyxgen from the lungs to the tissues.

Hemophilia. An inherited disorder in which the blood fails to clot and there is an abnormal tendency to bleed from a cut or other injury. Transmitted from mother to son as a sex-linked recessive condition.

Hemorrhoids (piles). Varicose (enlarged or swollen) veins of the anus and rectum. External hemorrhoids occur outside the anal sphincter; internal hemorrhoids, inside it.

Hepatitis (infectious viral type A). An acute infectious liver disease transmitted from person to person by infected food handlers, contaminated food, water, feces, or bedpans.

Hepatitis (serum viral type B). Transmitted by injection of infected blood, or by the use of contaminated needles or instruments. Caused by a virus found in blood and tissues.

Hepatitis (toxic). An inflammation of the liver caused by exposure to certain chemicals, such as carbon tetrachloride or insecticides. Also occurs in persons sensitive to drugs.

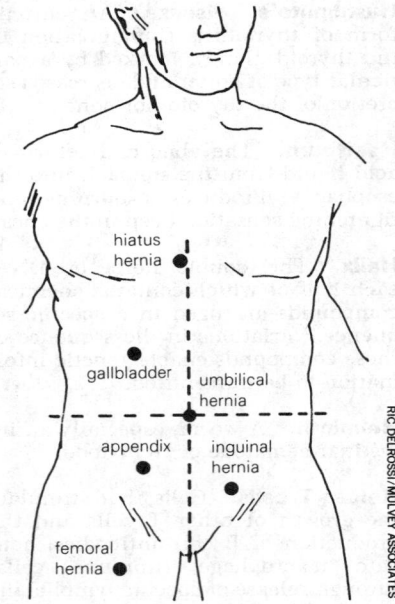

SOME COMMON HERNIA SITES

hiatus hernia

gallbladder   umbilical hernia

appendix   inguinal hernia

femoral hernia

RIC DELROSSI/MULVEY ASSOCIATES

Hernia. Protrusion of an organ from the cavity in which it is normally held. Frequently seen types include the inguinal (groin), and the umbilical (naval).

Hernia (hiatus). Protrusion of the upper part of the stomach into the chest cavity.

Herniated intervertebral disk (a slipped or ruptured disk). Cartilage disks become thick and hard, causing a disk to herniate or slip out.

Herpes simplex. A virus infection that causes painful fluid-filled blisters (cold sores). Other forms are named according to site; for example, herpes facialis (face); herpes labialis (lips).

Herpes zoster (shingles). An entirely different disease from herpes simplex, this painful vesicular eruption occurs along a nerve pathway. Caused by the same virus, Herpes varicella, as that of chicken pox (varicella).

HERPES SIMPLEX VIRUS

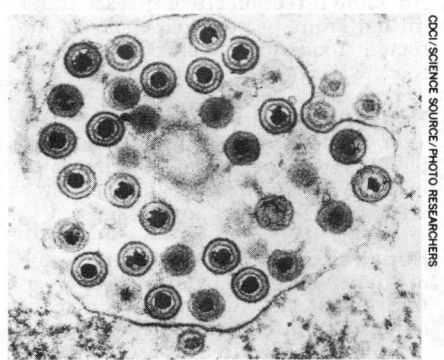

CDC/SCIENCE SOURCE/PHOTO RESEARCHERS

Heterozygote. An individual that has inherited different alleles at one or more loci.

Hodgkin's disease. A disease that is marked by progressive enlargement of lymph nodes and spleen. Symptoms such as anemia, fever, fatigue, and weight loss are common.

Homozygote. An individual developed from the union of genetically identical gametes.

Hormone. A chemical substance that begins in an organ, gland, or body part and is conveyed by the blood to another part of the body where its activity and secretion are stimulated.

Humoral immunity. A form of immunologic defense involving the action of antibodies and their complement (a group of about 15 proteins found in the blood).

Hydrocarbon. A compound made up of hydrogen and carbon only.

Hydrocephalus. Condition in which there is an increased accumulation of cerebrospinal fluid within the hollow spaces (ventricles). May result from a malformation, infection, injury, or brain tumor.

Hydrogen. An element existing as a colorless, odorless, tasteless gas; present in almost all organic compounds.

Hydronephrosis. Enlargement of the kidney pelvis with the collection of urine resulting from blockage to the flow of urine. Blocked urine may cause only slight dilation of the kidney, or serious organ damage.

Hyperglycemia. The elevation of blood sugar, as in diabetes. This condition increases susceptibility to infection, and often precedes diabetic coma.

Hypertension. High blood pressure; a consistently elevated arterial pressure. Such added pressure on the blood vessel walls makes the heart pump harder, causing eventual damage.

Hyperthyroidism (Grave's disease, thyrotoxicosis). Often results from excessive hormone production by the thyroid gland.

Hyperventilation (overbreathing). A condition in which there is too deep or too rapid breathing, or both, without conscious awareness.

Hypoglycemia. An abnormally small amount of sugar in circulating blood. May be due to insulin overdose or a missed meal by a diabetic. In nondiabetics, lack of food and fatigue may be the cause, or the cause may be excessive pancreatic activity.

Hypothermia. A technique that is used to lower body temperature and so reduce the need for oxygen during surgery, especially that involving the heart and the nerves.

Hypothesis. A theory not supported by established facts, and tentatively accepted as a basis for further investigation.

Hypothyroidism (myxedema). A state in which an underactive thyroid gland fails to secrete an adequate amount of thyroid hormones. As the condition progresses, there is puffiness of the hands and face, hair loss, muscle weakness, slowed pulse rate, and sluggish movement.

I

Immunologist. One who practices the science of immunology, the medical study of various aspects of immunity, induced sensitivity, and allergy.

Immunosuppressive agents. A wide variety of drugs that interfere with normal immune response. Used to control autoimmune diseases and to improve the chances for survival of foreign tissue in grafts and transplants.

Infarction. Death and consequent formation of scar tissue in an organ deprived of an adequate supply of blood. Myocardial infarction describes such an occurrence in the heart.

Influenza (flu). A respiratory infection caused by one of several related, yet distinct, viruses. It strikes suddenly with chills, fever, headache, muscle aches, and a dry cough.

Inoculation. Intentional introduction into the human body of the causative organism of a disease (for example, diphtheria, poliomyelitis, or rabies) as a means of preventing development of the disease.

Inorganic. Involving neither organic life nor products of organic life.

Insomnia. Wakefulness; inability to sleep. In itself, insomnia is not a disease but may be a symptom of disease, either of a slight or serious nature.

Insulin. A hormone secreted by the pancreatic islets of Langerhans. It promotes the utilization of glucose and the synthesis of proteins.

Internist. One who specializes in internal medicine, which deals with diseases that do not require surgical intervention.

Intertidal. Of, pertaining to, or being the region between the extremes of high and low tide.

Ion. An atom or group of atoms carrying a net electric charge by having gained or lost one or more valence electrons.

Irruption. An irregular increase in the aggregate number, as in population shifts.

Ischemia. State in which there is an inadequate blood supply to a part or structure of the body. There may be narrowing of the arteries, as in arteriosclerosis. May be caused by an embolism or thrombosis.

Isotope. One of a series of chemical elements having almost identical chemical properties, but differing in their atomic weights and electric charge. Many isotopes are radioactive.

J

Jaundice. An excessive amount of bile pigment, usually bilirubin, in the blood. Marked by a yellowish discoloration of the skin, eye whites, body tissue, and fluids.

K

Kaposi's sarcoma. A multifocal abnormal growth, either benign or malignant, that occurs in the skin and sometimes in lymph nodes.

Ketone. An organic chemical substance (for example, acetone).

Killer T cell. A T cell that specifically targets and destroys virus-infected cells and cancer cells.

Kinetosome. A rod-shaped or spherical structure that is posterior to the basal granule of a flagellum.

L

Laryngitis. Inflammation of the larynx. May be due to overuse of the voice, respiratory infection, inhalation of vapors or dust.

Leukemia. A form of cancer in which there is a rapid increase in white blood cells, which infiltrate body tissues and especially bone marrow. Fewer red blood cells and platelets (blood particles) cause anemia, hemorrhaging, and infection.

Leukocytes. White blood cells that act as scavengers, helping to fight infection. There are two types: granulocytes (having granules in their cytoplasm), and agranulocytes (lacking granules).

Lichens. Any one of numerous plants composed of a fungus growing in symbiotic union with certain algae.

Ligament. A band or sheet of strong, fibrous connective tissue that joins the articular ends of bones, serving to bind them together and to facilitate or limit motion.

Linkage. In genetics, a condition in which two or more nonallelic genes that are present in the same chromosome tend to stay together instead of assorting independently in the formation of gametes.

Lipid. Any one of a group of fats or fatlike substances insoluble in water. Included are true fats (esters of fatty acids and glycerol); lipoids (phospholipids); sterols (cholesterol, ergosterol); and hydrocarbons (carotene).

Lipoproteins. Conjugated (paired or joined) proteins that are made of simple proteins combined with lipid components: cholesterol, phospholipid, and triglyceride.

Lumpectomy (tylectomy). Surgical procedure in which only the primary tumor and a varying amount of surrounding breast tissue are removed. Radiation therapy may be used postoperatively.

Lymph nodes. A part of the immune system in which specific antigens activate T cells and B cells.

Lymphatic vessels. Vessels that can transport lymph (the clear fluid bathing body tissues) as well as lymphocytes (a type of white blood cell) and other substances needed for the body's immune system.

Lymphocytes. White blood cells produced in bone marrow, and maturing into B cells and three classes of T cells.

Lymphokines. Substances created naturally by various white blood cells. Serve as a communication link between immune and nonimmune cells involved in immune and inflammatory responses.

Lymphosarcoma. Morbid disorder in which excessive numbers of lymphocytes form in lymphoid tissue.

Lysosome. A small membranous sacs containing powerful digestive enzymes that break down carbohydrate, protein, and fat molecules.

M

Macromolecule. A polymer (a natural or synthetic substance formed by combining two or more molecules of the same substance), especially one composed of more than 100 repeated monomers (any molecule capable of being bound to similar molecules to form a polymer).

Macroscopic. Large enough to be seen by the naked eye; the opposite of microscopic.

Malignant. A severe condition that is growing worse and is resistant to treatment. In cancer, "malignant" denotes uncontrollable growth, and spread or recurrence of the cancer after attempted removal.

Mammography. Soft tissue x-ray that often can detect breast cancer before a lump is big enough to feel. An 85 to 95 percent cure is obtainable in such cases.

Marrow. The soft, fatty substance found in long and spongy bones. In an adult, red marrow is found in the spongy bones, and the yellow (fat) in the long bones.

Mastoiditis. An ear infection that spreads to the mastoid process (part of the temporal bone).

Measles. A highly communicable virus disease, usually occurring in early childhood. Marked by nasal discharge, fever, cough, and reddening of the eyes. Typically, there is a blotchy rash and fine white spots inside the mouth (Koplik's spots).

Meiosis. In sexually reproducing organisms, reduction of the number of chromosomes in reproductive cells by cell division.

Melanoma. A rapidly spreading, malignant tumor containing melanin, the normal skin pigment. May involve lymph nodes, liver, lungs, and brain.

Membrane. A thin layer of pliable tissue that lines a tube or cavity, covers an organ or structure, and either separates or connects one body part from another.

Ménière's disease. Disorder in which there is impairment of the balancing structure of the inner ear, resulting in vertigo, nausea, ringing or other noises in the ear, and progressive loss of hearing.

Meningitis. Inflammation of the meninges, the delicate membrane covering layers of the brain. Symptoms include fever, headache, neck stiffness, sensitivity to light, and disturbed consciousness.

Metabolism. The sum of the chemical changes influencing nutritional processes:
anabolism: energy-consuming, converting small molecules into large
catabolism: energy-producing, converting large molecules into small.

Metastasis. Movement of bacteria or body cells (especially cancer cells) from one part of the body to another.

Methane. Marsh gas. A colorless, odorless, flammable gas produced as a result of putrefaction and fermentation of organic matter.

Microbe. Minute one-celled organism in a biologically distinctive group, having a procaryotic genetic mechanism. Includes spirochetes, bacteria, rickettsiae, and viruses.

Microdose digital radiography (DR). An x-ray technique requiring only a fraction of conventional x-ray exposure to obtain sharp images (further enhanced by use of computers).

Microorganism. Living organisms too small to be seen with the naked eye. Only a relatively small number are pathogenic (capable of causing disease). Protozoa, bacteria, fungi, rickettsiae, and viruses are all microorganisms.

Microscopy. The study of minute objects by means of a microscope.

Migraine. A periodic, severe, vascular type of headache. Symptoms include vertigo, nausea, vomiting, and a sensitivity to light.

Mitochondria. Organelles of the cytoplasm of the cell; principal source of energy in the cell.

Mitosis. A sequential process in cell division by which the diploid number of chromosomes is retained in both daughter cells.

Molecule. The least amount into which a substance may be divided without losing its chemical properties. Designated by the number of atoms it contains; for example, monatonic (one atom), diatonic (two), triatonic (three).

Monoclonal antibodies. A fusion of human cancer cells and cells from another animal, resulting in cancerlike cells, hybridomas. Each hybridoma produces genetic copies, or clones, of itself (monoclonal).

Mononucleosis. An acute febrile disease thought to be due to a virus, marked by fever, sore throat, headache, and swollen lymph glands.

Mucus. The clear, viscid secretion of the mucous membranes. Consists of mucin, leukocytes, epithelial cells, and various inorganic salts suspended in water.

Multiple sclerosis. A progressive disease of the nervous system involving degeneration of the myelin (fatlike substance) sheath in the brain and spinal cord.

Mumps (epidemic parotitis). A contagious disease caused by one of the paramyxovirus group. Inflammation

of the parotid gland is the most common symptom.

Murein. Chief composition of procaryotic cell walls: a macromolecular arrangement of sugars and amino acids.

Muscular dystrophy (Duchene's disease). A hereditary disorder primarily known to afflict young men. Marked by progressive weakness and wasting of muscles.

Mutagen. Any agent that causes the production of a mutation. Includes radioactive substances, x-rays, and certain chemical substances.

Myasthenia gravis. A neuromuscular disorder caused by the defective transmission of nerve impulses to the muscles. Marked by great muscular weakness, but no wasting of muscles.

Mycoplasm. The smallest procaryote, measuring well under a micron (a millionth of a meter).

Myelin. A fatlike substance forming the primary component of the protective myelin sheath of nerve fibers.

Myelitis. Inflammation of the spinal cord or bone marrow. A potentially serious condition demanding prompt diagnosis and treatment.

Myocardial infarction. The death of part of the heart muscle when it is deprived of an adequate blood supply in the area. The muscle is gradually replaced by a fibrous scar (infarction).

Myocarditis. Inflammation of the muscular walls of the heart. A cardiac symptom present in many infections and inflammatory conditions such as rheumatic fever, meningitis, diphtheria, and typhoid fever.

Myoglobin (myohemoglobin). The oxygen-transporting protein of muscles; in function, similar to blood hemoglobin.

Myxedema. See *Hypothyroidism.*

N

Natality. The birth rate: the ratio of births to the general population.

Natural selection. The evolutionary process by which organisms best adapted to reproduce in a given environment predominate.

Nephritis. Inflammation of the kidneys. A term applied to a group of noninfectious diseases involving widespread kidney damage.

Nephrolithiasis. Calculi, or stones, formed in the kidney and urinary blad-

der. Many kidney stones eventually pass out in the urine; others must be removed surgically.

Nephron. The structural and functional unit of the kidney. Each kidney contains about 1 million nephrons.

Nephrosis. A noninflammatory condition involving degenerative changes in the kidney tubes.

Neritic zone. The continental shelf and the waters over it.

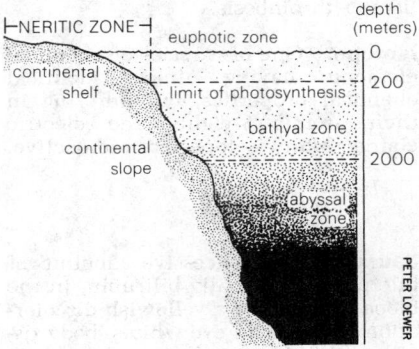

Neuritis. Inflammation of a nerve (mononeuritis) or nerves (polyneuritis), marked by pain in the affected area and various other symptoms.

Neurologist. A specialist in the treatment of diseases of the nervous system.

Neuron. A nerve cell. The structural and functioning unit of the nervous system, consisting of the nerve cell body, the dendrites, and the axon.

Neurosis. A psychological or behavioral disorder. Persons with a neurosis, unlike those with psychosis, maintain contact with reality and undergo no major personality changes.

Neurotransmitter. A substance that mediates or modulates the signals between nerve endings. Some are found only in the brain; others occur throughout the body in great numbers.

Nitrite. A salt of nitrous acid. Dilates blood vessels, lowers blood pressure, depresses centers of the spinal cord, and acts as an antispasmodic.

Nitrogen. A gaseous element occurring free in the atmosphere. An important element in all proteins, needed in plant and animal life to build tissues.

Nitroglycerin. Any nitrate of glycerol. Medically, it has the action of nitrites and dilates the blood vessels. Used specifically in angina pectoris.

Nitrosamines. Environmental cancer-causing agents. May also be produced by interaction of sodium nitrate and the normal breakdown products of protein. Sodium nitrate and sodium are used as color fixatives in cured meats.

Nonspecific urethritis. The specific organism causing inflammation of the urethra is unknown. Chlamydia trachomatis, the same microbe that causes trachoma, may be to blame.

Nuclear magnetic resonance (NMR). An extremely powerful electromagnet that "charges" the hydrogen atoms of the body's water. When weak radio waves are bounced off the charge, the structure and function of body tissue can be analyzed from a computer-generated image.

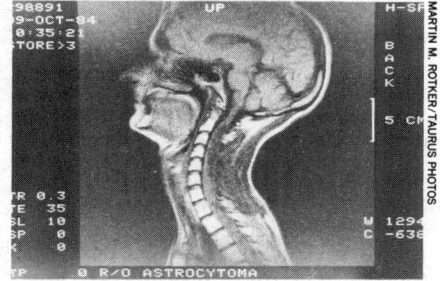

NMR IMAGE

Nucleic acids. An important group of substances of large molecular weight, found in chromosomes, nucleoli, mitochondria, and cytoplasm of all cells.

Nucleolus. A small spherical body composed of protein and ribonucleic acid (RNA) in the nucleus of a cell.

Nucleus. The essential agent in growth, metabolism, reproduction, and transmission of characteristics of a cell.

O

Oligotrophy. Inadequate or deficient nutrition.

Oncogenes. Several different types of specific genes implicated in cancer.

Organelle. A specialized part of a cell that serves for the performance of an individualized function. Includes mitochondria, Golgi apparatus, lyosomes, and cell centrioles.

Organic. Pertaining to, or derived from, animal or vegetable forms of life.

Organism. Any living thing, plant or animal, considered as a whole. May be unicellular (for example, bacteria) or multicellular (any complex organism, including man).

Orthopedist. A specialist dealing with disorders of the locomotor structures of the body, especially the spine, joints, and muscles.

Osmosis. The passage of certain fluids and solutions through a membrane or other porous substance.

Osteoarthritis. A form of arthritis marked by progressive degeneration of the joints, especially the weight-bearing joints (spinal column, hips, and knees).

Osteochondritis. Inflammation of a bone together with its cartilage, usually affecting bones of the lower extremities. Often seen in children (osteochondritis deformans juvenilis).

Osteocyte. A cell of osseous tissue occupying a small space or cavity, and having processes extending into canalicul (small canals or channels).

Osteomalacia. A disease in which bones gradually become soft due to bonelike tissue failing to calcify. Bones become brittle and flexible, causing pain and deformity.

Osteomyelitis. Inflammation of bone marrow and adjacent bone. Typically, it begins with pain in the affected bone; movement is restricted.

Osteopath. A practitioner of osteopathy, in which manipulative measures are used in addition to the diagnostic and therapeutic measures of ordinary medicine.

Osteoporosis. A condition brought on by loss of bone mass. Bone becomes thin, leading to vertebral fractures.

Otitis. Inflammation of the ear, differentiated by the affected part:
otitis externa: the outer ear
otitis media: the middle ear
otitis interna: the inner ear

Otosclerosis. Formation of spongy bone about the stapes (a middle ear bone) that results in a progressively worsening deafness.

Ovarian cyst. An abnormal fluid-filled sac that develops within an ovary. Enlarged, painful cysts are removed surgically.

Ovary. A gland in the female that produces the reproductive cell, the ovum, and the hormones estrogen and progesterone.

Oxidation. The loss of electrons in an atom (the gain of electrons is called reduction).

Oxygen. A constituent of animal, vegetable, and mineral substances that is a colorless, tasteless, and odorless gaseous element. It is the only one that enters the animal organism in a free state.

P

Pacemaker. Any rhythmic center that controls heart rhythm; normally, the sinoatrial node. An artificial pacemaker is a device that substitutes for the normal pacemaker and controls heart rhythm.

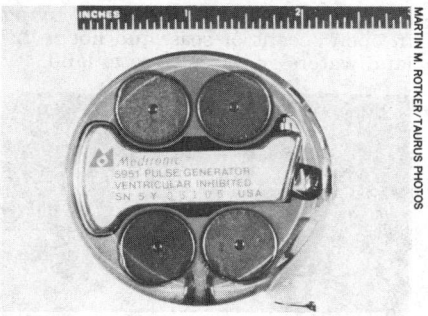

PACEMAKER

Pancreatitis. Inflammation of the pancreas that, in the acute form, can lead to tissue destruction and scattered hemorrhage.

Paralysis. Temporary or permanent loss of voluntary movement in a muscle, or a loss of sensation or of function in a part of the body.

Parasympathetic. A division of the autoimmune (self-controlling) nervous system.

Paratyphoid fever. Similar to but less severe than typhoid fever. Caused by infection of salmonella bacteria, and transmitted by contaminated food, milk, or water.

UNSAFE DRINKING WATER *exposes people to danger of typhoid and similar diseases.*

996 GLOSSARY OF HEALTH AND LIFE SCIENCES

Parkinson's disease (paralysis agitans). A chronic brain disease marked by stiffness, tremors, masklike face, and slowed movements.

Pathogen. A disease-causing microorganism; may be a virus, bacterium, protozoa, mold, yeast, or helminth.

Pelagic. Of, pertaining to, or living in open oceans or seas, and not in inland waters or water close to land.

SHARKS *are just one of the many thousands of pelagic lifeforms.*

Pelvis. Any basinlike structure or cavity; for example, the massive cup-shaped ring of bone and its ligaments at the lower end of the trunk.

Pepsin. A digestive enzyme found in gastric juice; converts proteins into proteoses and peptones.

Peptic ulcer. An ulcer of the duodenum (duodenal) or stomach (gastric) associated with a decreased ability to withstand the action of gastric juices.

Peptide. A compound of two or more amino acids in which the carboxyl group of one is united with the amino group of the other.

Perforation. An abnormal opening in a hollow organ; for example, a perforated abdominal viscera.

Pericarditis. Inflammation of the pericardium (membranous sac enveloping the heart). Often accompanied by shortness of breath and chest pain.

Peritonitis. Inflammation of the peritoneum (membranous lining of the abdominal cavity). Common causes are a ruptured appendix (appendicitis) or a duodenal ulcer.

Phagocyte. A cell, either a macrophage (an immune cell) or granulocyte (a granular white blood cell), primarily involved in engulfing pathogenic organisms.

Pharynx. A tube serving as a passageway for air from the nasal cavity to the larnyx, and for food from the mouth to the esophagus.

Phenylketonuria (PKU). Failure to break down the amino acid phenylalanine, a common constituent in nearly all proteins. If detected at birth, can be treated successfully by adjustment of the diet.

Pheochromocytoma. A tumor, usually located within the adrenal gland, causing an increased secretion of adrenal hormones. Often manifested by sustained high blood pressure.

Phlebitis. Most often noted in a leg vein, but this inflammatory condition can occur anywhere in the body. May involve injury to a vein, obesity, chronic infection, or to a condition of impaired circulation.

Phosphorus. A nonmetallic element found in combination with alkalies. Essential in converting glycogen to glucose.

Photosynthesis. The natural process by which green plants, utilizing chlorophyll and the energy of sunlight, produce carbohydrates by combining carbon dioxide from the air and water from the soil.

Pinocytosis. The cellular process of actively engulfing liquid. Minute incuppings are formed on the surface of the cell membrane, closing to form fluid-filled vesicles.

Pituitary. An endocrine gland secreting hormones that regulate important bodily processes such as growth, reproduction, and various specific metabolic activities.

Placenta. The spongy structure in the uterus through which the fetus derives its nourishment.

Plaque. Accumulation of fatty deposits in artery walls due to excessive amounts of blood cholesterol. Can result in atherosclerosis.

Plasma. The liquid part of the lymph (alkaline fluid in lymphatic vessels), and of the blood (consisting of water in which many chemical compounds are dissolved).

Plastids. One-celled, photosynthetic, self-replicating organelles consisting of chloroplasts (contain chlorophyll), leukoplasts (colorless), chromoplasts (contain pigment), and amyloplasts (store starch). Chemically active in cell metabolism.

Platelet. A round or oval disk found in blood, containing no hemoglobin or nucleus. Platelets are important in blood coagulation.

Pleurisy. Inflammation of the pleura (membranes covering the lungs). In dry pleurisy (for example, pneumonia), fluid accumulation is minimal. In wet pleurisy (for example, tuberculosis), large amounts of fluid are secreted.

Pneumococcus. A bacterium that is gram-positive, usually occurring in pairs and including 75 different serotypes capable of causing respiratory and other infections.

Pneumocystis carinii. A tiny parasite, probably a protozoa, marked by basophilic (having an affinity for dyes) dotlike form. Apparent cause of pneumocytosis.

Pneumonia. Inflammatory condition of the lungs. Causative agents are viruses, bacteria, and chemical irritants, but mainly involves the pathogenic bacterium *Diplococcus pneumoniae.*

Poliomyelitis (infantile paralysis). Inflammation of the gray matter of the spinal cord. If severe, this viral infection can lead to muscular paralysis, especially of the limbs and the muscles involved with breathing.

Polyarteritis. A condition marked by widespread inflammation of the smaller arteries. Often leads to complications such as kidney disease and high blood pressure. May involve arteries that supply the heart, brain, kidneys, liver, lungs, digestive tract, testicles, or adrenal glands.

Polycystic kidney disease. A congenital disorder that may not be evident until midlife. Many slowly enlarging cysts develop in the kidneys, which become enormous and exert undue pressure on nearby organs.

Polycythemia vera. A disease of unknown origin marked by an increased number of red blood cells. Blood clots and excessive bleeding on minor injury may be major problems.

Polyp. An abnormal, often benign, stalklike growth that usually develops in vascular organs such as the nose, uterus, and rectum.

Polyunsaturated. Long-chain carbon compounds, particularly fats that have many carbon atoms joined by double or triple bonds.

PLATELETS *help produce the meshwork that traps red blood cells forming a clot.*

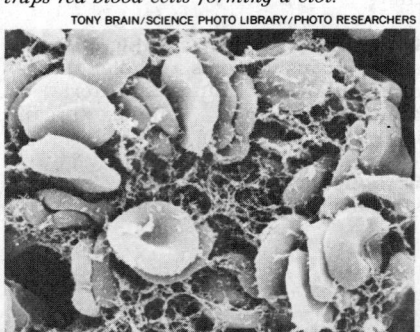

Polyuria. An excessive secretion and discharge of urine. Considered a classic symptom in diabetes, together with polydipsia (excessive thirst), and polyphagia (hunger for abnormal amounts of food).

Positron emission tomography (PET). A scanner that develops images from radioactive isotopes; the images are deciphered by means of a computer. Offers a means of visualizing dopamine receptors and other brain sites for detection of such neuropsychiatric disorders as Parkinson's disease.

Potassium. A soft, silver-white, light metallic element. Its salts are used primarily in medicine.

Pott's disease. Tuberculosis of the spine with pronounced spinal curvature due to compression of affected bones. Mainly affects children and adults up to 40 years of age.

Pregnancy tests:
slide test: simple test involving mixing urine with a solution on a slide and examining results; most accurate when done at least seven weeks after last menstrual period
tube test: typical home pregnancy test in which urine is mixed with a testing solution in a tube; slightly more accurate than slide test and can be done about a week earlier
radioreceptor assay (RRA) blood test; beta-HCG (human chorionic gonadotropin) test; monoclonal antibodies test: sophisticated tests with which accurate positive results can be obtained as early as the time of the first missed period.

Procaryotes. Unicellular microbes that lack mitochondria (organelles).

Prostaglandins. A group of fatty acid derivatives present in many body tissues. Can lower blood pressure, stimulate uterine contractions, and regulate body temperatures, and the acid secretions in the stomach lining.

Prostatitis. Inflammation of the prostate, common among elderly men. Marked by pain in the perineal region and difficult urination.

Protein. A complex nitrogenous compound. An integral part of the protoplasm of every cell and of physiological systems in multicellular organisms. Most proteins in cells are enzymes.

Prothrombin time (PT). Test that measures the time needed for a fibrin (a protein formed by the action of thrombin on fibrinogen) clot to form in a treated blood sample.

Protoplasm. Living matter; a thick viscous colloidal substance of which animal and vegetable cells are formed.

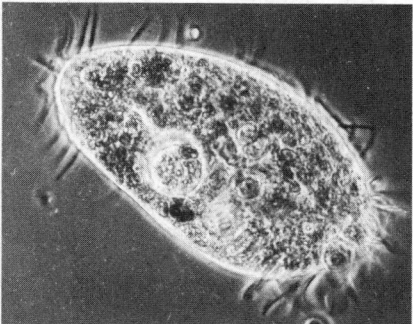
PROTOZOA

Protozoa. Mostly one-celled organisms of the phylum Protozoa, of the animal kingdom, including the simplest animals.

Pruritus. Medical term for itching. May be caused by unclean or abnormally dry skin; sensitivity to foods or drugs; insect bites or heat rash; or emotional reactions.

Psoriasis. A skin condition marked by reddish, silvery-scaled patches. These lesions usually occur on elbows, knees, back, and scalp.

Psychiatry. A medical specialty dealing with the diagnosis and treatment of mental illness. Psychotherapy employs mental rather than physical means; for example, hypnotism.

Psychosis. Severe form of mental disorder in which there is disturbed thought, disintegration of personality, and lack of touch with reality. Schizophrenia is the most common type of psychosis.

Psychosomatic illness. An illness that originates in the mind.

Psychotropic. All that affects the mind and its processes. Psychotropic drugs have an effect on psychic function, behavior, or experience.

Pulmonary embolism. A clot in an artery of the lung, often due to a detached clot from a leg vein.

Pyelography. X-ray examination of the renal pelvis and ureter. Indicated in recurrent kidney or bladder infection, or severe prostate enlargement.

Pyelonephritis. Inflammation of the kidney and renal pelvis, usually considered a bacterial infection. Often associated with pregnancy, diabetes, or other disease states.

Pyrimidine. The parent substance of several heterocyclic nitrogen compounds (uracil, thymine, cytosine).

Quadriceps. Four-headed, as quadriceps femoris, a large muscle on the outer thigh surface composed of four muscles.

R

Rabies. A viral infection attacking the nervous system. Transmitted from the saliva of an infected animal (dog, cat, cattle, etc.) through a bite, scratch, or tear in the skin.

Radiation sickness. Illness resulting from chronic or prolonged exposure to excessive quantities of high-energy radiation.

Radioactive. Possessing radioactivity, which results from the spontaneous emission of radiation directly from an atomic nuclei or as a consequence of a nuclear reaction.

Radioisotope scanning. A process that allows the study of the function and condition of internal organs, vessels, or body fluids. Uses radioactive forms of chemicals, such as iodine, which emit high-energy radiation.

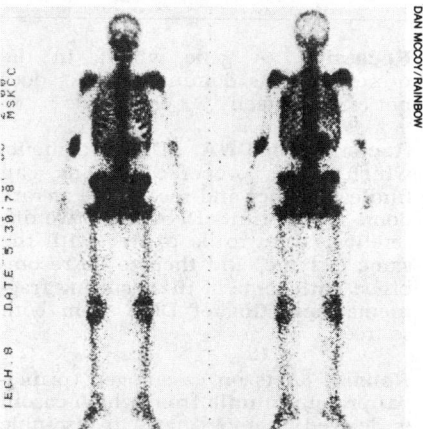
RADIOSCAN

Radiology. The branch of science dealing with the use of ionizing radiation for medical diagnosis, especially the use of x-rays in medical radiography or fluoroscopy.

Radiopaque substance. When injected into a blood vessel, swallowed, or given as an enema prior to x-ray examination of a body area, permits clear visualization of the area on x-ray film or a fluoroscope screen.

Radiotherapy. Treatment of disease by use of roentgen rays (x-rays), radium, and ultraviolet. May be used alone or combined with surgery or drug therapy.

Raynaud's disease. Disorder in which there is spasm in the blood vessels of the extremities, especially in response to cold temperatures that would not normally affect a person. Often occurs in the fingers.

Receptor. Sensory nerve endings found in the skin, deep tissue, viscera, and special sense organs.

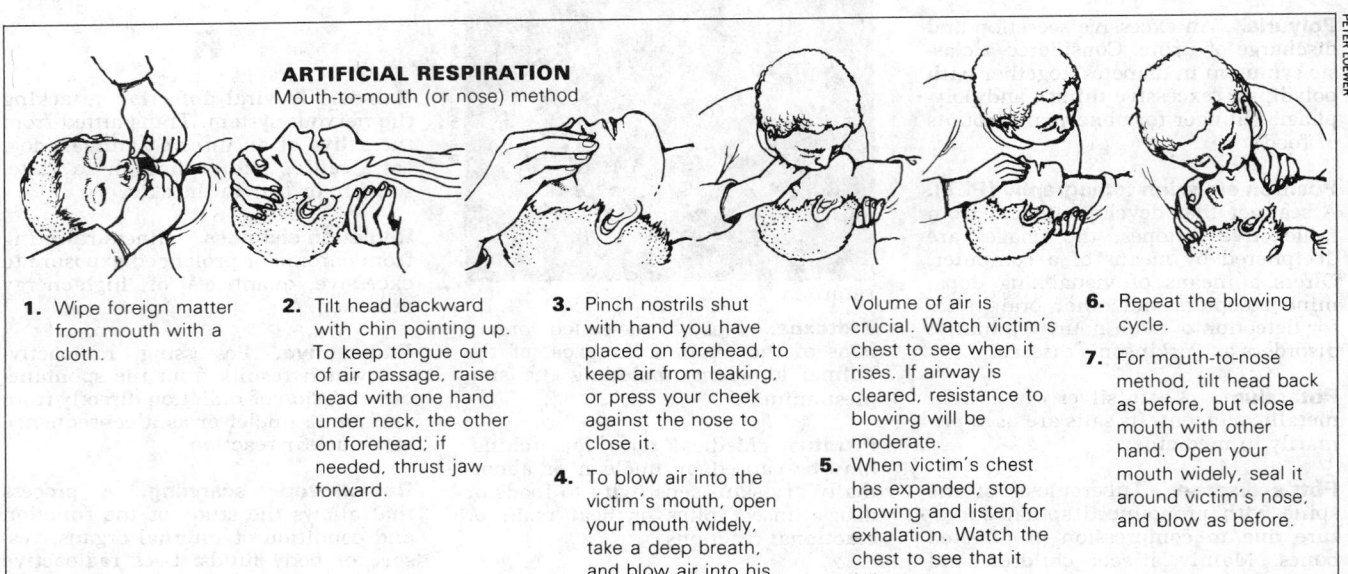

ARTIFICIAL RESPIRATION
Mouth-to-mouth (or nose) method

1. Wipe foreign matter from mouth with a cloth.

2. Tilt head backward with chin pointing up. To keep tongue out of air passage, raise head with one hand under neck, the other on forehead; if needed, thrust jaw forward.

3. Pinch nostrils shut with hand you have placed on forehead, to keep air from leaking, or press your cheek against the nose to close it.

4. To blow air into the victim's mouth, open your mouth widely, take a deep breath, and blow air into his mouth.

5. Volume of air is crucial. Watch victim's chest to see when it rises. If airway is cleared, resistance to blowing will be moderate.

6. When victim's chest has expanded, stop blowing and listen for exhalation. Watch the chest to see that it falls.

6. Repeat the blowing cycle.

7. For mouth-to-nose method, tilt head back as before, but close mouth with other hand. Open your mouth widely, seal it around victim's nose, and blow as before.

PETER LOEWER

Recessive. A gene which, in the presence of its dominant allele, does not express itself.

Recombinant DNA. DNA fragments which, under proper conditions, can find each other and recombine at random. This permits DNA from two different sources to be treated with the same enzyme, and then to be recombined with some of the resulting fragments consisting of DNA from both sources.

Rennin. Acts on caseinogen (principal protein in milk from which casein is derived), converting it to insoluble casein in the presence of calcium ions.

Replication. The act of reproducing one cell from another (division).

Respiration, artificial. The use of artificial methods to restore or maintain breathing until medical help can be obtained.

Resuscitation (by mouth-to-mouth breathing). A process used when a person has stopped breathing (as a result of drowning, electric shock, gaseous poisoning, heart disease, etc.). (See illustration.)

Reticular activating system (RAS). A complex system of nerve cells and fibers in the brain stem, hypothalamus, and adjacent areas. Plays an important part in maintaining alertness or wakefulness.

Retina. The innermost membrane of the eye; receives images formed by the lens and acts as the immediate instrument of vision.

Retinitis pigmentosa. Slowly progressive childhood disease. Marked by retinal degeneration, by widespread changes in retinal pigmentation, by wasting of the optic nerve, and by defective night vision.

Retrovirus. Belonging to a group of viruses known to cause tumors in some animals; suspected of causing certain types of human leukemias.

Reye's syndrome. A potentially fatal disease generally afflicting those under 18 years of age, and following a viral infection such as type B influenza or chicken pox.

Rh blood factor (rhesus factor). A factor present in about 85 percent of the human population who are said to be Rh positive (Rh+). Those not having this inherited factor in the blood are Rh negative (Rh-).

Rheumatic fever. Occurs in children and young adults, usually following a streptococcal throat infection. Marked by pain, fever, lassitude, and swelling of the joints.

Rheumatoid arthritis. A chronic, usually progressive inflammatory disease of the joints, affecting more women than men. Pain and swelling of the joints restrict movement.

Ribonuclease. Any of various enzymes that decompose ribonucleic acid.

Ribosome. A spherical cytoplasmic RNA-containing particle that is active in protein synthesis.

Rickets. A childhood disease that is mainly due to a lack of dietary Vitamin D or inadequate exposure to sunlight, or both. Interferes with normal deposition of calcium.

RNA (ribonucleic acid). The "message" molecule that carries information from the nucleus (vital body in cell protoplasm) to cytoplasma (cell protoplasm outside the nucleus) sites.

S

Sac. A pouch or pouchlike structure in a plant or animal.

Salmonellosis. The most common form of food poisoning; caused by ingestion of food contaminated with bacteria of the genus *Salmonella*. Results in inflammation of the stomach lining and intestines (gastroenteritis).

Salpingitis. Inflammation of a Fallopian tube, usually caused by a bacterial infection spreading upward from the uterus, cervix, or vagina.

Sarcoma. A tumor, usually malignant, occurring in connective tissue, such as bone or muscle. The bladder, kidneys, lungs, liver, spleen, and nearby tissue may be involved.

Sartorius. Longest muscle in the body. Located in the thigh.

Saturated. Carbon compounds in which all the atoms are linked by single bonds. A saturated compound (for example, any methane) is one incapable of additional products.

Scabies. An infectious skin disease caused by the female itch mite, *Sarcoptes scabei*. In general, affects the hands, between the fingers, forearms, armpits, breasts, and inner thighs.

Schizophrenia. A group of mental disorders marked by disturbances in thinking, mood, and behavior.

Sciatica. A severe pain involving the sciatic nerve, extending from the back of the thigh through the inner leg. Causative factors include osteoarthritis and a ruptured disk.

Scleroderma. A systemic disease of connective tissue that may affect skin, muscle, bone, heart, and lungs.

Scoliosis. An abnormal sideways curvature of the spine. There may be just one curve, or a compensating curve in the opposite direction. May be due to a congenital defect, injury, disease, or poor posture.

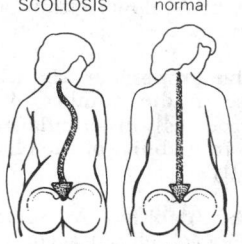

SCOLIOSIS   normal

Senile dementia (senility). A wide range of mental and emotional changes afflicting the elderly. Signs may be memory loss, short attention span, irritability, and loss of humor.

Sensory. Relating to impulses carried from sense organs to reflex centers; for example, an afferent nerve conveys sensory impulses to the brain.

Septicemia (blood poisoning). A general term describing various conditions due to infective organisms or their toxins in circulating blood.

Septum. A thin membranous wall that divides two cavities or masses of softer tissue.

Serotonin. An organic compound found in blood serum, mast (connective tissue) cells, gastric mucosa, and carcinoid tumors.

Shingles. See *Herpes zoster.*

Shock. Impaired blood circulation due to a precipitate drop in blood pressure. Various causes may include severe injury, effects of major surgery, extensive bleeding, infection, drug reaction, poisoning, and heart damage.

Sickle cell anemia. An inherited blood disorder marked by sickle-shaped red blood cells that die more rapidly than they should.

Sigmoidoscopy. A process that permits inspection through a speculum of the interior of the sigmoid colon. Indicated for the detection of polyps, cancer, or other abnormalities in the lower 12 inches of the bowel.

Sinusitis. Inflammation of any sinus membrane, especially the nasal passages. The common cold, nasal polyps, or a deviated septum are believed to be involved.

Sleeping sickness (encephalitis lethargica). A disease marked by lethargy, drowsiness, and muscular weakness. Another form, African trypanosomiasis, is caused by the bite of a blood-sucking tsetse fly.

Smallpox (variola). A contagious disease caused by a virus found in oral and nasal secretions, and in skin lesions of infected persons. Pustules leave permanent pitted scars in the skin (pock marks).

Spermatozoa. The mature male sex or germ cells formed within the tubules of the testes.

Sphygmomanometer. The familiar instrument used for measuring arterial blood pressure.

Spina bifida. A congenital abnormality in which the membranes of the brain or the spinal cord are pushed through a defect in the skull or spinal column (meningocele).

Spinal tap. Lumbar puncture, used in cases of suspected meningitis and in certain types of spinal cord or brain damage. May also be used together with other tests in diagnosing neurological diseases.

Splenic anemia (Banti's syndrome). An anemic condition marked by an enlarged spleen, irregular episodes of gastric bleeding, and a cirrhotic fever.

Spondylitis (Marie Strümpell spine). A rheumatoid condition in which part of or the entire spinal column becomes fused.

Spondylolysis. The breaking down of a vertebral structure.

Spore. A reproductive cell, usually unicellar and asexual, produced by nonflowering plants such as fungi, mosses, or ferns, and some protozoa.

Staphylococcus. A genus of micrococci comprised of gram-positive bacteria, including many pathogenic species that cause suppurative infections and that can release toxins destructive to tissues and cells.

Steroids. A large family chemically related to sterols (fats). Includes various hormones, D vitamins, bile acids, other body constituents, and certain drugs.

Sterol. Any of a group of chiefly unsaturated solid alcohols of the steroid group (for example, cholesterol and ergosterol); occur in the fatty tissues of plants and animals.

Stethoscope. An instrument used to aid in hearing vascular or other sounds produced anywhere in the body.

Still's disease (juvenile rheumatoid arthritis). A disorder that develops in infants and young children, and is associated with enlargement of the spleen and lymph nodes. May cause crippling deformities.

Stokes-Adams syndrome. A condition marked by lightheadedness or sudden loss of consciousness, and associated with various heart conditions. There is impairment of normal cardiac pumping action and output of blood.

Streptococcus. A genus of gram-positive bacteria, usually occurring in chains, that includes species pathogenic to humans, especially children.

STREPTOCOCCI *form a large group of bacteria, many of which cause infections.*

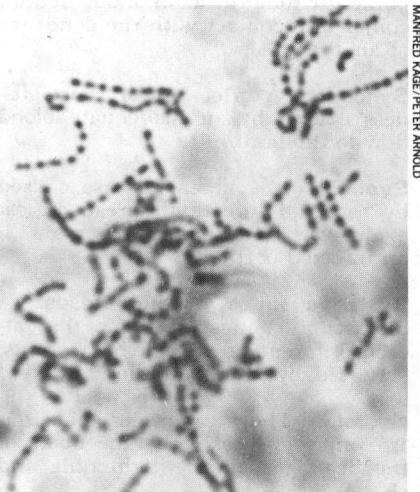

MANFRED KAGE/PETER ARNOLD

SIGNS OF SHOCK	FIRST AID FOR SHOCK
• Cold, clammy, pale skin. • Rapid, faint pulse. • Irregular breathing. • Nausea and vomiting.	• Call a doctor at once. • Make person comfortable. Loosen tight clothing. • Do not move person unnecessarily. Keep him quiet and lying down. • Keep person comfortably warm. Do *not* use electric blanket or hot water bottle. • Do not give anything to drink.

WARNING SIGNALS OF STROKE

- Sudden, temporary weakness or numbness of the face, arm, and leg on one side of the body.
- Slurred speech, or temporary loss of speech.
- Temporary dimness or loss of vision, especially in one eye.
- Unexplained dizziness or unsteadiness.

HELPING THE STROKE VICTIM

- Call a doctor at once.
- Get victim to bed and watch him carefully until help arrives.

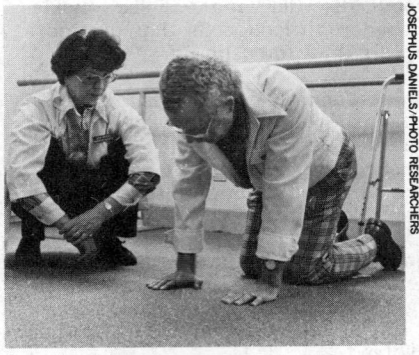

JOSEPHUS DANIELS/PHOTO RESEARCHERS

PHYSICAL THERAPIST *helping a stroke victim with exercises designed to bring back the use of an affected arm.*

Stroke (apoplexy). Condition in which there is sudden loss of consciousness and usually some degree of paralysis. Due to rupture or clogging of a blood vessel in the brain.

Substrate. Any layer or stratum lying beneath another. Also, the substance acted upon and changed by the action of an enzyme.

Suppressor T cells. Cells that provide a control for the immune system. Absence of these cells may be the underlying cause of certain autoimmune diseases.

Symbiosis. Two organisms of different species living together in close association. If both benefit from the association, it is mutualism; if one is benefited and the other is harmed, it constitutes parasitism.

Sympathetic. Referring to the sympathetic part of the autonomic (involuntary) nervous system.

Synapse. A juncture between two neurons in a neural pathway, the point at which the axon of one neuron comes into contact with the dendrites of another.

Syncope. A brief loss of consciousness caused by an inadequate blood flow to the brain.

Syphilis. A venereal disease caused by bacterial infection, spread almost exclusively by sexual intercourse with an infected partner.

Systemic lupus erythematosus. A disease of connective tissue that affects different parts of the body: joints, skin, kidneys, lung, and heart.

Systole. The heart cycle when it is in contraction, or when the fibers of the heart muscle are tightening and shortening.

T

T cells. The most active of the three types of T cells (helper, killer, and suppressor). Produces lymphokines, which draw other lymphocytes and macrophages to the scene of infection. Effective against viruses and other microorganisms.

Tabes dorsalis (locomotor ataxia). A late manifestation of syphilis, occurring in persons having had inadequate or no treatment in the early stage of this disease.

Tachycardia. An abnormally fast heartbeat (over 100 beats per minute). May be brought on by an overactive thyroid gland or some form of heart disease.

Tay-Sachs disease. Hereditary disorder caused by transmission of an abnormal gene, resulting in a specific enzyme deficiency. Marked by progressive mental and physical retardation, and typically by paralysis, blindness, and convulsions.

Temporal arteritis. An inflammation of the arteries supplying temporal arteries (sides of the scalp). Increasingly recognized in the elderly.

Testosterone. The male hormone, the most potent naturally occurring androgen. Stimulates and promotes growth of male sexual characteristics.

Tetanus (lockjaw). Caused by bacteria (*Clostridium tetani*) that live in soil, dust, and the intestinal contents of man and animals. Bacteria enter the body through a scratch or wound, releasing toxins.

Tetany. A nervous disorder marked by intermittent muscle spasms, and involving the extremities. May be due to gastric and intestinal disorders, or a lack of calcium salts.

Tetralogy of Fallot. A cyanotic congenital heart disease involving malformations of heart chambers. Most afflicted children have a bluish skin, retarded growth, and labored breathing after exercise.

Thalassemia. Hereditary form of anemia, marked by the development of abnormally thin and fragile red blood cells.

Thermography. A process used to detect, record by a sensitive scanner, and interpret the significance of radiant heat thrown off by tissues affected by disease. The technique has been used to study blood flow in limbs and to detect cancer.

Thrombocytopenia. An abnormal decrease in the number of platelets (thrombocytes) in circulating blood. Results in inability of the blood to clot efficiently.

Thrombophlebitis. An inflammation of a vein (phlebitis) accompanied by clot formation (thrombosis). May develop after major surgery, after hip or other fracture, in pregnancy, or during prolonged illness.

Thymine. A constituent of thymidylic acid, and a nitrogen-containing base in DNA; it is always paired with adenine.

Thymus. An organ of the immune system in which T cell precursors from bone marrow mature into active helper, killer, and suppressor T cells.

Thyroid. A gland of internal secretion in the neck. Thyroid extracts (natural or synthetic) are used to treat cases of deficient action of the gland.

Thyroiditis. Inflammation of the thyroid gland, the most common cause of goiter and of inadequate thyroid secretion. A common form is Hashimoto's disease.

Tinnitus. Ringing, buzzing, or other sounds in one or both ears not caused by external sound vibrations. May be due to wax in the ear, drug overdose, ear infection, or Ménière's disease.

Tonsillitis. Inflammation of tonsillar tissue, in which the tonsils appear enlarged and red, and are painful on swallowing. A streptococcal infection, it is seen most often in children.

Torticollis. Stiff neck, a contraction of neck muscles that is often spasmodic. May be congenital or be caused by traumatic injury or inflammatory conditions.

Trachoma. A contagious inflammation of the conjunctiva (mucous membrane lining the eyelids), caused by the virus *Chlamydia trachomatis.*

Traction. A technique applied in bone fractures to keep the broken bones in proper alignment; for example, suspension traction, using weights and pulleys.

Transduction. The process whereby genetic material is carried from one bacterium to another by a virus or viruslike agent.

Transformation. Genetic change resulting from genetic material being directly incorporated into a bacterial cell's chromosome.

Transpiration. The act of exhaling water, gas, or vapor through the skin or a membrane.

Trapezius. A flat, triangular-shaped muscle covering the posterior surface of neck and shoulder. Draws the head back and to the side; rotates the shoulder blade.

Triceps. Three-headed; for example, triceps muscle of the arm and calf.

Trichinosis. A parasitic disease that is caused by eating raw or insufficiently cooked meat, especially pork, infected with *Trichinella spiralis*.

Trigeminal neuralgia (tic douloureux). Disorder in which there is unbearable pain in the trigeminal nerve, usually in spasms along one or more branches of the nerve.

Triglycerides. Glycerol that is combined with three fatty acids (stearic, oleic, palmitic); found in most animal and vegetable fats.

Trophic. Of, or pertaining to, nutrition or to the nutritive processes concerned with nourishment.

Tuberculosis. Disease caused by *Mycobacterium tuberculosis;* occurs most commonly in the lungs. Generally acquired by contact with infected person, or milk from infected cow.

Tumor. A benign or malignant growth. Benign tumors do not invade and destroy surrounding tissue. Malignant tumors metastasize (spread to other parts of the body).

Turner's syndrome. An abnormality of the sex chromosomes. Deviations include dwarfism, webbed neck, elbows bent outward, shield-shaped chest, and premature, infantile sexual development.

Typhoid fever. Disorder caused by the bacillus *Salmonella typhosa*. There is usually continued fever, eruption of rose-colored spots on chest and abdomen, and an enlarged spleen.

Typhus (epidemic and endemic). One of a group of rickettsial infectious diseases. Epidemic typhus fever is louse-borne. Endemic, or murine, typhus is spread to man by rats or the mouse flea.

U

Ulcer. A necrotic lesion of the stomach or duodenum (usually a peptic ulcer) due to the action of gastric juices.

Ultrasound. High-frequency sound waves bounced off a body organ or tissue, and converted into an image or photograph for the study of abnormalities otherwise difficult to observe.

Ultraviolet. Of, or pertaining to, the actinic or chemical rays beyond the violet end of the visible spectrum.

Unicellular. One-celled.

Uracil. A pyrimidine base found in ribonucleic acid.

Uremia. Kidney failure. Marked by an excess of urea and other substances in the blood when the kidneys fail to function as purifiers.

Urethritis. Inflammation of the urethra. May be secondary to a bladder infection or may be a sexually transmitted disease.

Uropathy. Any disease affecting the urinary tract; for example, urethritis or pyelonephritis. Obstructive uropathy results from obstruction of the urinary tract.

V

Vaccine. Attenuated (weakened) or dead microorganism that is used as an antigen to produce desired long-term immunity to the pathogenic form of a microorganism.

Vacuole. A clear space in the protoplasm of a cell filled with fluid or air.

Vaginitis. Inflammation of the vagina, most often caused by *Trichomonas vaginalis* or *Candida albicans*.

Varicose veins. Swollen, twisted veins due to incompetent venous valves that allow blood to seep backward and collect in the veins instead of being returned to the heart. Usually noted in lower extremities.

Ventricle. Either of two lower chambers of the heart. When filled with blood, the ventricles contract to propel blood into the arteries.

Vertebrae. The 33 bony segments of the spinal column comprised of 7 cerebral, 12 thoracic (dorsal), 5 lumbar, 5 sacral, and 4 coccygeal vertebrae.

Vertigo. A sensation of falling or whirling, either of oneself or of external objects, with difficulty in keeping one's balance. May be caused by middle-ear disease, alcohol or drug intoxication, head injuries, or physical exertion.

Vesicle. Small blisterlike elevation on the skin that contains serous fluid.

Villi. Hairlike surface projections, especially of a mucous membrane. A minute projection from a cell surface is a microvillus.

Viruses. Minute organisms not visible with ordinary light microscopy. Responsible for a very wide variety of diseases.

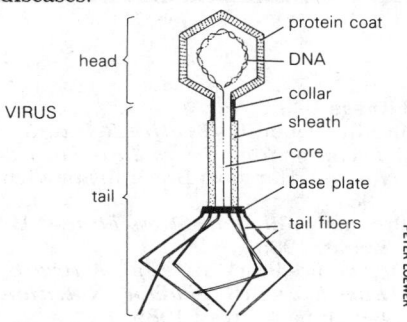

Vital capacity. Breathing capacity; the greatest volume of air that can be forcibly exhaled from the lungs following a full inspiration.

PATIENT BEING TESTED *for vital (breathing) capacity.*

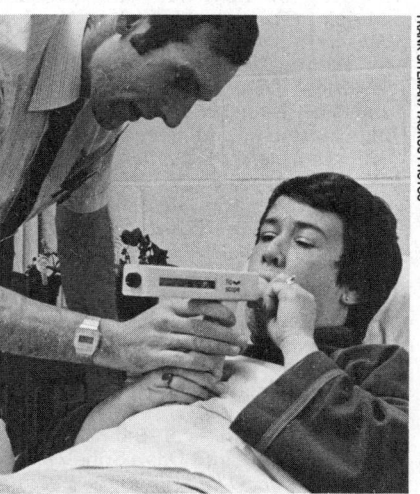

Vitalism. The theory that animal functions are dependent upon a special form of energy or source, the vital force, which is distinct from the physical forces.

Volvulus. Condition in which there is a twisting upon itself of a section of intestine, causing a serious obstruction. Prompt treatment is indicated, as delay may lead to gangrene, peritonitis, and death.

W

Wetlands. Lowland areas, such as a marsh or swamp, that are saturated with moisture. In particular, pertains to the natural habitat of wildlife.

Whooping cough (pertussis). Usually, the causative organism is *Bordetella pertussis*. Coughing is sporadic and is continued during each attack until breath is exhausted.

Wilm's tumor. A malignant kidney tumor found in young children. It is spread by the blood and lymph systems, with the lungs being the usual site for early metastases.

Wilson's disease. Predominantly, a metabolic disease of young persons. It is inherited in an autosomal recessive fashion, and is considered to result from the abnormal transport and storage of copper within the body.

X

X-ray. Electromagnetic radiation of a wavelength shorter than visible light or ultraviolet radiation. Has the ability to penetrate the body and most other solids and to act on photographic film. Valuable in diagnosing diseases.

Z

Zinc. A bluish-white, lustrous metallic element, found as a carbonate and silicate known as calamine.

Zooplankton. Floating, often microscopic, aquatic animals that live near the surface of the ocean.

Zygote. The fertilized ovum. A cell formed by the union of two gametes.
—*Frances F. Barth*

For Further Reference

Fitness
Bright, Deborah: *Creative Relaxation: Turning Your Stress Into Positive Energy.* Harcourt Brace Jovanovich, 1981.
Brown, Millie. *Low-Stress Fitness.* HP Books, 1985.
Drews, Frederick R., et al. *A Healthy Life: Exercise, Behavior, Nutrition.* Benchmark Press, 1986.
Kuntzleman, Charles T., and the editors of *Consumers Guide. The Complete Book of Walking, Total Fitness, Step-By-Step.* Simon & Schuster, 1978.

Health Problems and Maintenance
American Medical Staff and Jacques Melek. *Cancer and All You Need to Know to Avoid It.* J. Melek, 1984.
Amsterdam, Erza A., and Ann M. Holmes. *Take Care of Your Heart.* Facts on File, 1984.
Dolger, Henry, and Bernard Seeman. *How to Live With Diabetes* (5th Ed.). W. W. Norton, 1985.
Galton, Lawrence. *Medical Technology, The Lay Person's Guide to Today's Medical Miracles.* Harper & Row, 1985.
Hurdle, J. Frank. *A Medical Doctor's Home Guide for Arthritis, Muscle and Bone Ailments.* Parker Publishing, 1980.
Hyde, Margaret O., and Lawrence E. Hyde. *Cloning and the New Genetics.* Enslow Publishers, 1984.
Klein, Arthur C., and Dava Sobel. *Backache Relief, The Ultimate Second Opinion From Back-Pain Sufferers Nationwide Who Share Their Successful Healing Experiences.* Random House, 1985.
Kra, Siegfried J., and Robert S. Boltax. *Is Surgery Necessary?* Macmillan, 1981.
Levenson, Frederick B. *The Causes and Prevention of Cancer.* Stein and Day, 1985.
Reese, Michael K. *The Complete Family Guide to Living With High Blood Pressure.* Prentice-Hall, 1980.

Nutrition
Bosco, Dominick. *The People's Guide to Vitamins and Minerals, From A to Zinc.* Contemporary Books, 1980.
Calabrese, E. J., and Michael W. Dorsey. *Healthy Living in an Unhealthy World.* Simon & Schuster, 1984.
Davis, Adelle. *Let's Stay Healthy: A Guide to Lifelong Nutrition.* Harcourt Brace Jovanovich, 1981.
Gibney, Michael J. *Nutrition, Diet, and Health.* Cambridge University Press, 1986.
Morgan, Brian L. G. *The Lifelong Nutrition Guide, How to Eat for Health at Every Age and Stage of Life.* Prentice-Hall, 1983.

Physiology
Hixson, Joseph. *The History of the Human Body.* Cooper Square Publishers, 1966.
McNaught, Ann. B., and Robin Callander. *Illustrated Physiology* (3rd Ed.). Churchill Livingstone, 1975.

The Cell
Crick, Francis. *Life Itself, Its Origin and Nature.* Simon & Schuster, 1981.
Darwin, Charles. *The Illustrated Origin of Species* (abridged and introduced by Richard E. Leakey). Hill and Wang, 1982.
Ford, Brian J. *Single Lens: The Story of the Simple Microscope.* Harper & Row, 1985
Gould, Stephen Jay. *Ever Since Darwin, Reflections in Natural History.* W. W. Norton, 1977.
McMahon, Thomas A., and John Tyler Bonner. *On Size and Life.* Scientific American Books, 1983.
Medawar, P. B., and J. S. Medawar. *Aristotle to Zoos: A Philosophical Dictionary of Biology.* Harvard University Press, 1983.
Miller, Jonathan, and Borin Van Loon. *Darwin for Beginners.* Pantheon Books, 1982.
Montagu, Ashley. *Science and Creationism.* Oxford University Press, 1984.

Schrödinger, Erwin. *What Is Life? Mind and Matter.* Cambridge University Press, 1983.
Stebbins, Ledyard G. *Darwin to DNA, Molecules to Humanity.* W. H. Freeman, 1982.

Five Kingdoms of Life
Margulis, Lynn, and Karlene Schwartz. *Five Kingdoms* (2nd Ed.). W. H. Freeman, 1987.

The Gene
Dillon, Lawrence S. *The Gene: Its Structure, Function, and Evolution.* Plenum, 1987.
Elkington, John. *The Gene Factory.* Carroll and Graf, 1985
Garber, Edward D. *Genetic Perspectives in Biology and Medicine.* University of Chicago Press, 1985.
Lampton, Christopher. *DNA and the Creation of New Life.* Arco, 1985.
Nossal, G. J. V. *Reshaping Lives: Key Issues in Genetic Engineering.* Cambridge University Press, 1985.
Olby, Robert. *Origins of Mendelism* (2nd Ed.). University of Chicago Press, 1985.
Watson, J. D. *The Double Helix.* Atheneum, 1968.
Watson J. D., and John Tooze. *The DNA Story.* W. H. Freeman, 1981.

Ecology
Barlett, Donald, and James B. Steele. *Forevermore: Nuclear Waste in America.* W. W. Norton, 1985.
Colinvaux, Paul. *Ecology.* Wiley, 1986.
Friday, Adrian, and David S. Ingram. *The Cambridge Encyclopedia of Life Sciences.* Cambridge University Press, 1985.
Howard, Robert West. *The Vanishing Land.* Villard Books, 1985.
McIntosh, Robert P. *The Background of Ecology: Concept and Theory.* Cambridge University Press, 1985.
Ridgeway, James. *Powering Civilization: The Complete Energy Reader.* Pantheon Books, 1982.

VOLUME **14**

Invention and Technology

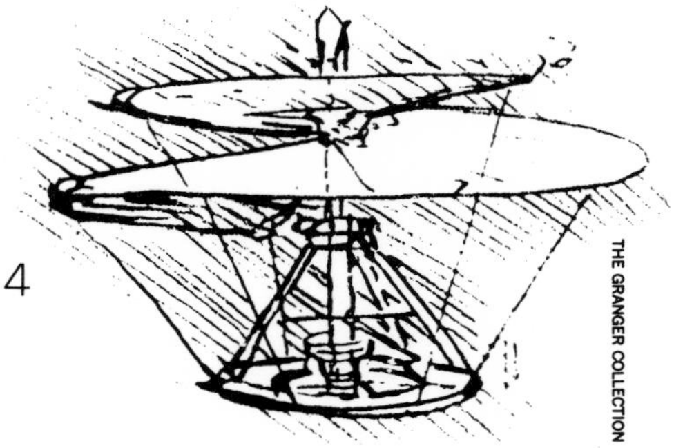

THE GRANGER COLLECTION

NOTEWORTHY INVENTIONS (U.S. and Canadian inventors)

Invention	Inventor	Date
AC electric motor	Tesla	1888
Air brake	Westinghouse	1869
Airplane	Wright Brothers	1903
Bakelite	Baekeland	1909
Camera, Kodak	Eastman	1888
Cash register	Ritty	1879
Cotton gin	Whitney	1793
Dental plate, rubber	Goodyear	1855
Elevator, steam-powered	Otis	1861
Evaporated milk	Borden	1856
Fiber optics	Armour Research	1960
Fountain pen	Waterman	1884
Garbage disposal	Merrill	1935
Harvester–thresher	Matteson	1888
Heart, artificial	Cooley	1969
Helicopter	Sikorsky	1939
Incandescent light	Edison	1879
Insulin	Banting, Best, and MacLeod	1922
Integrated circuit	Kilby	1958
Laser	Townes and Schawlow	1958
Lawn mower	Hills	1868
Lightning rod	Franklin	1752
Linotype typesetter	Mergenthaler	1884
Machine gun	Gatling	1861
Malaria vaccine	Nussenzweig	1981
Measles vaccine	Enders and Peebles	1954

Invention	Inventor	Date
Microprocessor	Hoff	1969
Mimeograph	Edison	1876
Movies, silent	Edison	1893
Movies, sound	Edison	1913
Nylon	Carothers	1935
Phonograph	Edison	1877
Polio vaccine	Salk	1953
Polio vaccine (oral)	Sabin	1955
Radar	Taylor and Young	1922
Radio, FM	Armstrong	1939
Radio, superheterodyne	Armstrong	1918
Railroad sleeping car	Pullman	1858
Reaper	McCormick	1834
Refrigerator	Goss	1913
Revolver	Colt	1835
Rocket, liquid fuel	Goddard	1926
Rubber, vulcanized	Goodyear	1839
Sewing machine	Howe	1846
Streetcar, electric	Sprague	1887
Submarine	Bushnell	1776
Telegraph	Morse	1837
Telephone	Bell	1876
Television	Zworykin	1934
Transistor	Shockley, Brattain, and Bardeen	1948
Triode vacuum tube	DeForest	1906
Xerography	Carlson	1938

SATELLITE DISH ANTENNA: GERARD RANCINAN/SYGMA

Invention and Technology

AP/WIDE WORLD PHOTOS

THE BETTMANN ARCHIVE

CRITON/SYGMA

BELL LABORATORIES

The 20th century is sometimes characterized as a technological era. Most people find this description easy to accept because within their lifetimes they have seen a dramatic proliferation in the kinds of goods and services that are readily available in advanced societies.

This abundance can be attributed to rapid development of science and technology. Yet, one must ask how these advances in science and technology were achieved. Who did the work? What processes where used? In a broader sense, from the point of view of society, how are science and technology supported and controlled?

The technology of a society is the sum of its tools, methods, experience, skilled and trained people, knowledge, and the employment of all these factors for the benefit of the society.

For most of history, those who added to technology were primarily ingenious and inventive mechanics, people we now refer to as technologists. Today, however, a true technologist must also be something of a scientist.

Technologists use scientific knowledge to develop a preconceived product, technique, or service. Moreover, they are involved in many of the same types of activities that scientists pursue in their work. For example, they

perform many tests to make sure that a procedure leading to a new product is refined and reliable.

They also test the materials they plan to use in order to determine the effectiveness of the materials in the planned application. They test the completed product in prototype to make certain it performs as predicted, and they incorporate further refinements in the product that will make it perform even better. Finally, they test the first manufactured item to ascertain that mass-produced units perform to specifications.

All this testing is planned and executed in accordance with scientific principles. Science and technology are thus interdependent. Often, the same person will be involved in both pure science and its application, even when working on a single project.

For instance, people working to develop a new form of bacterium by means of genetic engineering seek evidence of the structure of the genetic material of the original organism. In this activity, technologists use the same approach used by scientists. On the other hand, the same people are working as technologists when, using both knowledge of bacteria and the techniques of gene splicing, they develop a new form of the organism.

Impact of technology on society.

The fruits of technology usually have a strong impact on society. In turn, society responds to technological advances by regulating their impact. These responses are sometimes formal actions carefully planned and publicly announced. At other times, grass-roots belief or popular understanding will generate responses by enough people that, taken together, they may control technological activity. The discussion that follows will consider the interaction between society and technology from the perspectives of economics, politics, social attitudes, and societal needs.

Economic interactions. Throughout most of the world there is competition for the sale of goods and services. Competitors strive to produce a product that will be in high demand and readily exchanged or sold at a profit.

Technologists, therefore, require as much information as possible about present and future products in order to overcome their limitations, control their quality, and reduce the cost of their production. At the same time, as a result of the increasing insistence of society, technologists strive to reduce the negative effects that old and new products may have on the world's environment. Meeting these two broad challenges—making a better product and reducing its possibly harmful impact—requires research and development, for which large industrial organizations typically allocate a major part of their income.

When experimental science appeared after the Middle Ages, it was possible for individuals to design their own experiments, make or acquire their own research tools, compile their own data, and make or invent something to be used for a specific, immediate task. Within the last 50 years, the situation has changed. This change has been due to the increase in cost of conducting experiments. Sophisticated equipment, precisely controlled laboratory conditions, and highly trained personnel are essential. All of this adds enormously to the cost of research. As a result, the old independence of people engaged in scientific research has shifted to a dependence on financial support.

Since the cost of research and development today is too great to be borne by individuals, it is paid for by large industrial companies or by governments. Eventually, of course, the cost is passed on either directly to the consumer or indirectly to the taxpayer.

Such financial dependence tends to determine the direction science and technology take, since industry and government ultimately respond to the demands of consumers or the votes of constituents. New procedures are carefully guarded, and new products become patented property.

Political interactions. From earliest times, political strength has usually depended on exploiting natural resources. When a nation has control of a unique and precious resource, other nations are placed in a poor bargaining position and must make concessions to get a share of the resource, do without it, or use power to secure it. The most desired resources usually have been those that enriched governments and, therefore, made them more powerful; have-not governments often became subservient.

Several types of natural resources produced political strength. Plentiful food, for example, and the technology needed to cultivate and store it, have always been important. The availability of transportation in the form of horses and ships, for example, has often been a major factor. The availability of copper and, later, the technology needed to make bronze, provided a source of wealth and power. In all instances, however, the natural resource itself could not have established controlling political influence without the presence of the technological means required to exploit what nature provided. This interaction between the availability of natural resources and the development of technology has been the major ingredient in establishing and maintaining a world balance of political and military power.

A modern example of this interaction may be seen in the development of nuclear energy, which was achieved by an advanced technology exploiting fissionable materials. One result has been the atomic bomb, which helped make some nations very powerful.

Another result has been the utilization of nuclear energy to generate electricity and to power huge ships. Nations with limited supplies of fossil fuels, especially oil, have been attracted to developing nuclear energy. If these nations can end their dependence on nations that control the fossil energy resources, they may improve their economies and strengthen their political power.

Technology stimulated by military needs has resulted in achievements in many other areas. The military development of airplanes for offensive and defensive purposes as well as for transport has helped make possible a worldwide system of air transport of people and cargo. Radar, an electronic development in World War II, is another example. Radar has become essential to safe water, air, and space travel. The practice of medicine has also benefited, for example, from wartime sulfa drugs, specialized field supplies, and methods for collecting, storing, and using human blood.

Space exploration, stimulated by competing world powers, has been another major factor in the 20th-century advance of science and technology. The first Russian satellite in space in 1957 stirred the United States to establish the National Science Foundation for the dual purpose of sponsoring science and technology research and accelerating the education of American scientists and engineers. The space program, more than any other factor, has generated a whole new world of very powerful microcomputers. Among other innovations that have come from the space program are important advances in the fuel cell, a kind of battery that produces potable water as a byproduct; solar panels; and new materials such as thermal tiles and special lubricants.

Political interaction with technology cannot be separated from economic involvement nor from the demands of people to meet prevailing social needs. Yet, the requirement that nations use their natural, financial, and human resources to compete politically has had immeasurable impact on the progress of both science and technology.

Social interactions. Though economic and political interactions tend to support rapid and competitive development in science and technology, the attitudes and beliefs of the general public act as controls.

For example, during the recent period of nuclear testing above ground, a growing public concern centered on the belief that weather patterns were changing. Some felt that winters were

colder; others, on the contrary, feared that the polar ice caps were melting. The public demanded that scientists be sued for billions of dollars because of the climatic changes they believed had been caused by the bomb tests. Although the actual banning of aboveground testing was based mostly on proven environmental damage, the effect of general, nonscientific concerns by a large number of people could not be ignored by the various regulating agencies of government.

In the 20th century there has been a large-scale modification of values and attitudes about science and technology. From almost universal acceptance and approval of technological advances, most elements of society have moved toward a growing distrust of many kinds of technology.

This uneasiness is coupled with ever-deepening concern for the perceived irreversible degradation of the environment. These changes in the perceptions of the general public have placed science and technology, and especially modern industry, under closer public scrutiny than at anytime since the beginning of the Industrial Revolution.

It is open to question whether the attitudes and beliefs of society provide the ultimate control over science and technology. The British writer and philosopher C.P. Snow is credited with the observation that once scientific knowledge exists and the techniques for technological application have been developed, a new product *will* be used and the changes caused by that use *will* occur. The question, Snow said, is not whether, but when.

Societal needs. Some discoveries that have improved the lot of people were made before the general public perceived a need for them. That is, the need was felt only after the need had been met. For example, the horse was considered adequate before the automobile was invented, and oil and gas lamps were considered adequate before the invention of electric lights. In similar manner, the telegraph was considered adequate before the invention of the telephone, radio, and television. Thus, there is not only a dependence of technology on public support, but there is a dependence, almost a reliance, of society on technology to anticipate the larger needs of society and provide for them before they become major problems.

Problems of technology. Life for most people throughout the world has changed dramatically since the beginning of the 20th century, mostly because of the rapid pace of technological advance. For example, food products have become available in packages that greatly extend the shelf life of perishable products. As a result the diet of many segments of the world's population has become more varied and nutritious. Medical tech-

GOVERNMENT-FINANCED RESEARCH PROJECTS, such as one at NASA to build a space station, can lead to technical advances that are of general benefit. Technical knowledge is often transferred to developing countries. However, the most appropriate technology for a developing country often is one that does not require use of materials or skills not available locally.

nology has also vastly improved the health of much of the world's population. Modern transportation and communications have made the world smaller and more accessible, thus helping backward people enjoy some of the benefits of 20th century life.

No one would deny that the technological advances of the past two centuries have brought great benefits to mankind. Many of these changes, however, individually and as a whole, have had undesirable side effects.

Unbalanced development. Unfortunately, the advantages of advanced technology have not benefited all parts of the world equally. Technologically advanced countries maintain a much higher standard of living than do undeveloped countries. The rapid pace of technological change, generated by increased wealth and political stability, tends to widen the gap between developed and undeveloped countries.

One of the ways in which this disparity can be overcome is by the transfer of technology to less developed regions of the world. It is to the economic advantage of both developed and undeveloped countries that technology raise the standard of living throughout the world. Only in countries with relatively high standards of living can there be markets for many of the products of a technological society.

There are problems, however, in transferring technology to undeveloped countries. The most efficient machinery for a particular job is sometimes inappropriate in an undeveloped country. For example, modern farm machinery will rust if there are no spare parts, no skilled mechanics to

use them, or insufficient fuel to keep the machines running. Instead of a large tractor pulling complicated equipment, an improved type of animal-drawn plow might produce more benefits.

Waste. One of the problems that technology has created but society has been unable or unwilling to solve is that of safe disposal of waste products. Every industrial process involves a certain amount of production of waste and pollution. These wastes gradually build up and result in the degradation of our soil, water, and air. In some parts of Europe and the United States, for example, the contamination of local water supplies has already become a serious problem.

Often it is not only the making of a product that creates a waste problem, but the product itself that becomes the waste. Plastic, for example, is not biodegradable and cannot be burned safely. Its rising use since World War II has created a huge solid waste problem.

The growing nuclear power industry also creates waste disposal problems. No way has yet been found to render nuclear waste harmless, so dumps for both high- and low-level radioactive waste must be found. Yet no one wants to live near a nuclear dump, principally because technology has not yet developed a completely safe and long-lasting way of storing radioactive waste.

Many of the problems caused by advancing technology are subtle and go hand in hand with the benefits technology brings.

Medical technology, for example, has greatly reduced the number of

children who die at birth or in early childhood. It has also extended the average human life span by several years. This has contributed to a population increase worldwide that is anticipated to cause huge problems by the end of the century unless dramatic advances are made in the production of food and housing.

Another dilemma caused by advances in medical technology involves medical ethics. Doctors now have the technology to prolong life long after the patient would have died naturally, and sometimes long after the quality of life has so diminished that the patient may feel that he or she no longer wishes to live. Should doctors do everything they can to keep patients alive at all costs? Or should doctors reduce their efforts to keep their patients alive for the sake of relieving suffering? This problem in medical ethics is debated continually by clergymen, physicians, and philosophers.

Making choices. Living in an age of technology involves a tradeoff of risks and benefits. A balance must be found in which the possible harm of a technology does not outweigh the advantages. For instance, many people in the United States believe that the benefits of electricity produced by nuclear power plants, such as lower cost, less dependence on imported oil, and lower levels of air pollution, outweigh such risks as occasional emissions of small amounts of radiation, the seemingly insoluble problem of disposing nuclear waste, and the possibility of an accident like the one the occurred at Chernobyl.

—Kenneth W. Dowling

TIMELINE OF TECHNOLOGY

Construction

30,000 B.C.–1 B.C.

2800 B.C. The first version of Stonehenge is constructed on the Salisbury Plain, England; it consists of an earthen bank, a ditch, 56 pits known today as the Aubrey Holes after John Aubrey, who discovered them, and only three stones, including the Heel Stone.

2600 B.C. The megalithic stonework at Avebury, near Stonehenge, is started, to be completed in its present form about 2000 B.C.
The Great Pyramid of Giza is built as a tomb for Egyptian Pharaoh Cheops.

2200 B.C. Eighty bluestones are set up at Stonehenge in the form of two concentric circles.

2170 B.C. Queen Semiramis orders construction of the first tunnel to be built under a river (the Euphrates), linking the Royal Palace in Babylon with the Temple of Jupiter.

1550 B.C. Stonehenge achieves the form in which it is known today.

600 B.C. King Sennacherib of Assyria orders construction of a 50-mile canal at Nineveh.

530 B.C. Greek engineer Eupalinos builds an aqueduct on Samos that requires a tunnel .75 mile long.

438 B.C. Phidias, working with Actinus and Callicrates, completes the Parthenon in Athens.

350 B.C. Celtic chiefs begin building Maiden Castle in south Dorset.

312 B.C. Appius Claudius Caecus launches construction of the Appian Way, a highway from Rome to Brindisi by way of Capua.
The Aqua Appia aqueduct is started by Appius Claudius to bring water to Rome from springs 16 kilometers (10 miles) away.

270 B.C. Eqyptian King Ptolemy II commissions Sostrastos of Cnidos to build the Pharos, the great lighthouse at Alexandria.

246 B.C. Construction on the Great Wall of China begins, to be completed in 209 B.C.

215 B.C. Ling Ch'u launches construction of a canal 145 kilometers (90 miles) from Ch'ang-an to the Yellow River.

170 B.C. The first paved roads are built in Rome.

19 B.C. Agrippa orders construction of the Aqua Virgo aqueduct to supply baths in Rome.

1 A.D.–1799 A.D.

1 The aqueduct Aqua Alsientina is built to supply water for an 1181-foot by 1800-foot artificial lake designed for mock sea battles to amuse the Romans.

50 Emperor Claudius of Rome has a 3.5-mile tunnel constructed to drain Lake Fucino.

70 Construction of the Grand Canal of China begins, eventually 600 miles long.

75 Emperor Vespasian orders construction of the Colosseum in Rome; it will be the largest amphitheater in the world until construction of the Yale Bowl in 1914.

120 Romans build Hadrian's Wall to protect Britain from northern tribes.

124 The Pantheon is completed in Rome.

452 Venice is founded by refugees trying to escape Attila the Hun.

532 Eastern Roman Emperor Justinian orders construction of Santa Sophia, the first building with a dome large enough to cover a square.

600 The building of Arles Cathedral, France, begins.

602 Chinese engineers relocate the bed of the Huang Ho to reduce flooding.

607 The Horyuji temple in Japan is completed; now the oldest wooden building.

674 Glass windows are introduced in English churches.

900 Construction begins at Chichen Itza, one of the great cities of the Maya.

976 Work is started on St. Marks in Venice, to be completed in 1094.

984 On the Grand Canal of China, the first practical lock is built.

1052 Edward the Confessor orders construction on Westminster Abbey, in London.

1078 Work begins on the Tower of London.

1100 The first examples of Gothic architecture appear in Europe.

1113 The Church of St. Nicholas in Novgorod, Russia, is built, one of the earliest Russian churches with the characteristic onion dome.

1129 The Abbé Suger orders construction on the St. Denis Cathedral, France, the first Gothic church with flying buttresses.

1135 Work begins on a bridge over the Danube at Ratisborn, completed in 1145.

1137 Work begins on the western facade of Chartres Cathedral, France.

1174 The Leaning Tower of Pisa is built.
William of Sens supervises rebuilding of Canterbury Cathedral, using pointed-arch Gothic style.

1260 Chartres Cathedral, France, is completed.

1283 A northern branch of the Grand Canal of China, 700 miles in length.

1295 The Castle of Beaumaris on the shores of Menai Straits is the last of the Welsh castles to be started; it is completed in 1320.

1364 The Aztecs build Tenochtitlan on the site that is now Mexico City.

1368 The Great Wall is restored in China.

1369 The Bastille is built in Paris.

1408 A windmill is used in Holland to pump water from inland areas out to sea.

1481 The first European lock on a canal is built by Pietro and Dionysius Domenico.

1546 Michelangelo designs the dome for St. Peter's in Rome.

1578 Work is begun on the Pont Neuf, Paris.

1584 The oldest wave-swept lighthouse still standing is built at mouth of the Gironde River in France.

1590 Giacomo della Porta and Domenico Fontana complete the dome of St. Peter's in Rome, still the largest church in the world.

1611 The 186-foot Tour de Condonan at the mouth of the Garonne River, France, becomes the first lighthouse to have a revolving beacon.

1628 At Le Havre, France, sluices are built to control the flow of water in the harbor.

1642 The Briare Canal is opened, linking the Loire and Seine rivers.

1650 At Agra in India, the Taj Mahal is completed.

1666 The Great Fire destroys much of the city of London, which will be rebuilt in its present form mostly by Sir Christopher Wren.

1700 Eddystone Lighthouse, England, is completed, later destroyed by storm in 1703.

1738 Charles Dangeau de Labelye develops the caisson for a bridge over the Thames at Westminster, England.

1779 The world's first iron bridge is built, spanning the Severn River, England.

Energy, Machines, and Transportation

30,000 B.C.–1 B.C.

23,000 B.C. The bow and arrow is invented.

21,000 B.C. The sewing needle is in use in southwestern France.

15,000 B.C. About this time, or by 13,000 B.C., the spear thrower and harpoon are invented.

3500 B.C. The potter's wheel is introduced in Mesopotamia.
Wheeled vehicles come into use in Sumer.

3000 B.C. People begin to manufacture iron objects.
Sumerians begin to use oil-burning lamps.

2500 B.C. Chariots are in use by Sumerian armies.

2000 B.C. The Cretan palace of Minos introduces interior bathrooms with a water supply.
Spoked wheels come into common use.

700 B.C. Glaucus of Chios invents soldering.

600 B.C. Theodorus of Samos invents ore smelting and casting, the bubble level, locks and keys, the carpenter's square, and the lathe.

250 B.C. Archimedes works out the principles of the lever and other simple machines; he demonstrates the lever by single-handedly pulling a large ship onto land.

200 B.C. The development of gears leads to invention of the ox-powered water wheel.

MODEL OF
SUMERIAN CHARIOT

N.Y. PUBLIC LIBRARY

1 A.D.–1799 A.D.

100 In Illyria, water-powered mills begin to be used for grinding corn.
Hero, an Alexandrian mathematician, develops a primitive steam engine.

700 Tapestry weaving becomes popular in Peru.

851 The crossbow is introduced in France.

1090 A water-driven mechanical clock is constructed in Beijing, China.

1328 The sawmill is invented.

1416 Dutch fishermen begin to use drift nets.

1500 Leonardo da Vinci designs the first helicopter, which was never built and probably would not have flown if built.

1530 The spinning wheel is in general use in Europe.

1535 Diving bells are invented.

1564 The horse-drawn coach is introduced from Holland to England.

1581 While watching hanging lamps in church, Galileo discovers that a pendulum of a given length always takes the same amount of time for a single swing.

1589 The Reverend William Lee of Cambridge invents the first knitting machine.

1596 Admiral Visunsin of Korea develops the first ironclad warship.

1608 Dutch scientist Johann Lippershey invents the telescope.

1643 Evangelista Torricelli, on a suggestion from Galileo, develops the first barometer.

1654 Otto von Guericke, in Magdeburg, demonstrates that a vacuum in a sphere formed by two hemispheres is so powerful that horses cannot pull it apart.

1663 The Marquis of Worcester claims discovery of the power of steam to raise water from wells and to rupture cannons.

1670 Francesco de Lana designs an airship——never built——that would be lifted by four copper spheres containing a near vacuum.

1679 Denis Papin develops a "digester engine for softening bones."

1699 Thomas Savery demonstrates before the Royal Society the first machine since the time of Hero to be powered by steam; although crude in concept, his "Miner's Friend" showed that it could pump water by using steam power.

1712 Thomas Newcomen produces steam engine, used to pump water from mines.

1745 The Leyden jar, the first practical way to store static electricity, is invented.

1764 James Hargreaves introduces the spinning jenny; his first model is able to spin eight threads at once, later models 120 threads, especially suited for wefts.

1765 James Watt develops his basic idea for improving the steam engine while walking on the Glasgow Green (not while watching his mother's teakettle).

1769 Joseph Cugnot, a French military engineer, builds a steam carriage that can carry four people at speeds up to 3.6 kilometers per hour (2.25 mph).
Richard Arkwright develops the water-frame spinning machine.

1776 The first two of Watt's steam engines are installed.

1779 Samuel Crompton develops the spinning mule, a cross between the spinning jenny and the water-frame spinning machine.

1781 The Marquis of Jouffroy (later builds) the Pyroschape, a steam-powered paddleboat; it is tested on the River Saône near Lyons in 1783.
James Watt patents a way to change steam power to rotary motion.

1782 James Watt patents a double-acting steam engine.

1783 Thomas Bell develops cylinder printing for fabrics.
Joseph-Michel and Jacques-Etienne de Montgolfier demonstrate their first hot-air balloon on June 5 at Annonay, France.

1784 William Murdock, an employee of steam-engine manufacturer Boulton & Watt, builds a working model of a steam-powered carriage.

1785 The English Channel is crossed for the first time by a manned balloon.

1786 John Fitch successfully tests his steamboat on the Delaware River; by 1790 one of his steamboats is in regular service for several weeks during the summer.

1797 Some roadways in Shropshire, England, are converted to iron rails along which wagons are drawn by horses.
Henry Maudslay perfects the slide rest for lathes; it permits the lathe operator to operate the lathe without holding the metal-cutting tools in his hands.

1798 William Murdock demonstrates the use of coal gas for lighting.

Medicine

500 B.C. The Pythagorean physician Alcmaeon is the first person known to dissect human bodies for scientific purposes; about this time he notes the optic nerve and the Eustachian tubes, differentiates veins from arteries, and recognizes the brain as the seat of intellect.
In India, Susrata performs the first eye cataract operations.

450 B.C. Greek philosopher Empedocles recognizes that the heart is the center of the system of blood vessels, but concludes wrongly that the heart is also the seat of the emotions, a notion that has persisted into modern times.

400 B.C. Hippocrates becomes known as the father of medicine by founding a medical school at Cos that treats diseases on a rational basis.

300 B.C. Greek physician Diocles, a student of Aristotle's, writes the first anatomy book and also the first book of herbal remedies.
Greek physician Herophilus flourishes in Alexandria, performing dissections in public; he describes the liver, spleen, retina, duodenum, ovaries, Fallopian tubes, and prostate gland.

275 B.C. Greek physician Erasistratus comes close to recognizing the circulation of the blood, especially by noting the relationship of the lungs to the circulatory system.

40 Dioscorides' *De materia medica*, written about this time, deals with the medical properties of about 600 plants and nearly 1000 drugs.
1266 Theodoric Borgognoni of Lucca's *Chirurgia* [Surgery] advocates cleansing of wounds and use of stitches to mend cuts, as well as narcotics for anesthesia.
1286 The first known postmortem is conducted in Cremona, Italy.
1299 The first clear reference to spectacles for farsightedness appears in a Florentine manuscript.
1316 Mondino de'Luzzi writes the first book in history to be devoted entirely to anatomy.
1450 Nicholas Krebs, known as Nicholas of Cusa, suggests timing the pulse to help in diagnosis.
1451 Nicholas of Cusa constructs spectacles for the nearsighted.
1500 Jakob Nufer of Switzerland performs the first recorded Caesarean operation.
1520 Paracelsus introduces tincture of opium, which he names laudanum, into medicine.
1542 Jean François Fernel's book on anatomy is the first to describe appendicitis and peristalsis, the waves of contraction in the digestive system that move food through the alimentary canal.
1543 Andreas Vesalius' *De corporis humani fabrica* [On the structure of the human body] is the first accurate work on human anatomy.
1545 Ambroise Paré advocates abandoning the practice of treating wounds with boiling oil and suggests using soothing ointments instead.
1579 The first glass eyes are manufactured.
1603 Santorio Santorio describes his device that uses a pendulum for counting pulse beats.
1609 Hans Lippershey and Zacharias Jansen invent the compound microscope.
1626 Sanctorius measures human temperatures with a primitive thermometer, called a thermoscope.
1655 Johann Shultes's *Armamentarium chirurgicum* [The hardware of the surgeon] describes a procedure for removing the breast of a woman.
1701 Giacomo Pylarini inoculates children with smallpox in the hope of preventing development of more serious cases of smallpox later in life.
1728 Pierre Fauchard's *Le chirurgien dentiste, ou traité des dents* [The surgeon dentist, or treatise on the teeth] describes how to fill a tooth infected with dental caries.
1756 Philipp Pfaff's *Abhandlung von den Zähnen* [Treatment of the teeth] describes how to make false teeth.
1774 Franz Mesmer uses hypnotism to help combat disease.
1775 William Withering introduces digitalis to cure the dropsy associated with heart disease.
1796 Edward Jenner develops the system of vaccinating a person with cowpox to prevent smallpox.

Communication

30,000 B.C. People in ice-age Europe mark ivory, bone, and stone with patterns that can be used to keep track of time based on a lunar calendar.
14,000 B.C. The first known artifact with a map on it is made from bone at what is now Mezhirich, U.S.S.R.
3000 B.C. Writing is developed by the Sumerians.
2772 B.C. Calendar of 365 days introduced in Egypt.
2500 B.C. Egyptians discover the use of papyrus as a writing surface.
600 B.C. Sundials come into use in China.
520 B.C. Anaximander introduces the sundial to Greece; he also makes the first attempt to model Earth according to scientific principles.
400 B.C. Hecataeus develops map showing Europe and Asia as semicircles surrounded by ocean.
375 B.C. Eudoxus improves the map of Earth, going beyond the primitive concepts of Hecataeus.
300 B.C. Dicaerchus, a student of Aristotle's, develops map of Earth that is on a sphere and has lines of latitude based on the lines where noonday sun is at given angle on a particular day.
250 B.C. Ctesibius of Alexandria improves the Egyptian clepsydra, or water clock, making it the most accurate timepiece for the next 1800 years.
46 B.C. Acting on the advice of Greek astronomer Sosigenes, Julius Caesar decrees that the calendar will henceforth follow a four-year cycle—three years of 365 days followed by one of 366.

105 Cai Lun invents paper for use in writing; the Chinese had been making coarse paper for packing since about the second century B.C.
271 In China, the first form of a compass is in use.
300 The Maya develop the day-count calendar, which combines the 365-day Olmec calendar, having a 52-year cycle, with the tzolkin, having a year of 260 days in 13 months of 20 days.
527 First paddle boats are built, drawn by animals.
700 The earliest known printed document, a Buddhist sutra translated into Chinese, is produced in Korea.
748 First printed newspaper appears in China.
868 The *Diamond Sutra* is printed, the earliest complete book, actually a scroll still extant.
1000 The churchman Gerbert, later Pope Sylvester II in 999, introduces abacus to Europe.
1050 Chinese books are printed with movable type.
1080 Alexander Neckam makes first known reference in Europe to use of a compass for directions.
1250 The quill is used for writing.
1269 French engineer Petrus de Maricourt, known as Petrus Peregrinus, describes how to make a compass with the needle pivoted and pointing to a graduated circular scale.
1434 Leone Battista Alberti's book on drawing includes laws of perspective.
1453 Johann Gutenberg prints the 42-line Bible, the first book printed with movable type in Europe.
1492 Martin Behaim of Nuremberg constructs the first globe map of Earth.
1494 Luca Pacioli's book on arithmetic and geometry includes the first description of double-entry bookkeeping.
1568 Gerard Kremer, better known as Gerardus Mercator, introduces the Mercator map projection.
1582 On the advice of astronomer Christoph Clavius, Pope Gregory XIII announces the reform of the calendar, which drops the 11 days between October 4 and October 15 of 1582; in the new Gregorian calendar, century years not divisible by 400 will no longer be leap years, as in the Julian calendar.
1614 John Napier invents the device for multiplying that comes to be known as Napier's bones.
1639 William Gascoigne invents micrometer, placing it in the focus of a telescope to enable it to measure angular distance between stars.
1646 Athanasius Kircher invents the magic lantern.
1656 Christiaan Huygens develops a type of pendulum that keeps accurate time.
1710 Jacob Le Blon invents three-color printing.
1780 The first fountain pen is made.
1792 Claude Chappe invents the semaphore, an optical system using flags for the transmission of messages.
1798 Aloys Senefelder invents lithography.

Materials

28,000 B.C. Beads, bracelets, pendants worn by people.
13,000 B.C. Cord is in use at Lascaux, France.
4000 B.C. The potter's wheel begins to be used.
The Egyptians and Sumerians begin using copper alloys and smelting silver and gold.
3000 B.C. Wrought iron is produced by smelting.
Metal mirrors begin to be used in Egypt.
1000 B.C. Dyes made from the purple murex are introduced by the Phoenicians.

N.Y. PUBLIC LIBRARY

EGYPTIAN GOLD FIGURE

300 Greek alchemist Zosimus summarizes the work of Egyptian alchemists; he describes what apparently are arsenic and lead acetate.
671 Kallinikos of Byzantium invents Greek fire, a missile weapon made of sulfur, resin, rock salt, and petroleum that can set targets on fire.
720 Abu Masa Dshaffar discovers sulfuric acid, nitric acid, aqua regia, and silver nitrate.
750 Arabian alchemist Jabir, known as Geber, describes the preparation of aluminum chloride, white lead, nitric acid, and acetic acid.
900 Persian physician and alchemist Al-razi, known as Rhazes, describes the preparation of plaster of Paris and metallic antimony.
1000 The Chinese develop gunpowder.
1020 Arabian physicist Al-Haytham, known as Alhazen, explains how lenses work and develops parabolic mirrors.
1250 English scientist Roger Bacon is the first European to mention gunpowder.
1298 Marco Polo describes such substances as coal and asbestos for the first time in Europe.
1320 German monk Berthold Schwarz determines the mixture of chemicals to form gunpowder.
1340 In or near Liège, Belgium, the first blast furnaces for producing iron are developed.
1597 Libavius' *Alchemia* describes the preparation of hydrochloric acid and ammonium sulfate.
1664 Cast iron is used for the pipes supplying water to the gardens at Versailles.
1679 Johannes Kunckel invents the artificial ruby, actually a form of colored glass.
1707 E.W. von Tschirhands and Johann Friedrich Böttger discover how to make Dresden china.
1717 Abraham Darby succeeds in making iron with coke, a derivative of coal.
1735 Georg Brandt discovers cobalt.
1751 Axel Fredrik Cronstedt discovers nickel.
1766 Henry Cavendish discovers hydrogen.
1772 Daniel Rutherford discovers nitrogen.
1774 Joseph Priestley discovers oxygen.
Johann Gottlieb Gahn discovers manganese. Karl Wilhelm Scheele discovers chlorine; Humphry Davy will be first to recognize it is a new element.
1778 Peter Jacob Hjelm discovers molybdenum.
1782 Franz Joseph Müller discovers tellurium.
1783 Don Fausto D'Elhuyar discovers tungsten.
Oxymuriatic acid is introduced for bleaching.
1784 Henry Cort, in England, develops puddling method of turning coke-smelted iron into wrought iron.
1789 Martin Klaproth discovers uranium, zirconium.
1791 William Gregor discovers titanium.
1794 Johann Gadolin discovers yttrium.
1797 Louis Vauquelin discovers chromium, beryllium.

(continued)

TIMELINE OF TECHNOLOGY *(continued)*

Construction | **Energy, Machines, and Transportation**

1800–1899

Construction

1801 James Finney of Pennsylvania builds the first modern suspension bridge.

1824 The Erie Canal from Albany to Buffalo, New York, is completed; it had been started in 1817.

1825 Thomas Telford's suspension bridge over Menai Straits in Wales, with a single span of 176 meters (579 feet), inaugurates the age of modern bridge construction.

1843 Joseph Fowle develops the first tunnel drill to use compressed air for power.

Isambard Kingdom Brunel builds the first tunnel under the Thames at London; the tunnel is opened for use on March 25.

1848 The Illinois–Michigan canal is completed, linking the Great Lakes with the Mississippi.

1851 London's Crystal Palace, built by James Paxton, is opened by Queen Victoria; it is one of the highlights of the Great Exhibition in London.

1854 Elisha Otis installs the first safe and workable elevator, in New York's Crystal Palace.

1859 Ferdinand de Lesseps turns over the first shovelful of earth to start construction of the Suez Canal, which is completed ten years later on August 15, 1869.

1870 Germain Sommeiller's Mont Cenis Tunnel through Alps completed, the first major railroad tunnel.

1882 The first attempt to build a tunnel beneath the English Channel is halted for political reasons.

1883 The Brooklyn Bridge, which introduces a revolutionary method of cable spinning, is dedicated on May 24.

1884 Washington Monument completed.

1889 Gustave Eiffel builds the 993-foot tower in Paris named for him.

1894 Manchester Ship Canal completed.

Energy, Machines, and Transportation

1801 Richard Trevithick builds a steam-powered carriage; it runs well for four days, but burns up when all water in boiler evaporates.

1804 Richard Trevithick develops a steam locomotive that runs on iron rails and hauls 10 tons of iron 16 kilometers (10 miles).

1807 The era of steamboat travel begins when Robert Fulton tests the boat later named the *Clermont* on the East River in New York City on August 9; the steamboat starts service on the Hudson later in the year and is a commercial and an engineering success.

1808 Humphry Davy develops the arc light, the first electric-powered lamp; while it produces a great deal of smoke and heat, it also produces a brilliant bright light so long as the two carbon rods can be kept apart at the proper distance.

1809 George Cayley's "On Aerial Navigation" is published, the first scientific study of the principles of heavier-than-air flight.

1812 The London Gas Light & Coke Company is formed, leading to the lighting of the city of London by coal gas.

1814 British engineer George Stephenson introduces his first steam locomotive, capable of hauling 30 tons at speeds faster than a horse-drawn system can achieve.

1819 The paddle steamer *Savannah* becomes the first steamship to cross the Atlantic (27 days, 100 hours).

Hans Christian Oersted discovers that a magnetized needle is deflected by a nearby electric current, leading to the practical application of electric motors and generators as well as the theoretically important unification of the electric and magnetic forces.

1821 Michael Faraday creates the first two motors that are powered by electricity.

1825 George Stephenson's Locomotion No 1 makes first trip, the first steam locomotive to carry passengers and freight regularly.

1829 Regular railway passenger service is inaugurated in the United States by The Best Friend of Charleston.

George Stephenson's steam locomotive Rocket easily bests four rival locomotives in competition.

1830 The opening of the Liverpool and Manchester rail line, equipped with George Stephenson's Rocket locomotives, inaugurates age of the railroad.

1831 Michael Faraday develops first electric generators by reversing direction of electric motors he had developed ten years earlier.

1833 The *Royal William* crosses the Atlantic under steam power in 17 days.

1836 Swedish inventor John Ericsson patents the screw propeller for use with steamships.

1838 James Nasmyth designs the steam hammer, essential to construction of large vessels from iron.

1841 Joseph Whitworth introduces the first set of standards for parts in his paper "On a Uniform System of Screw Threads."

1845 The steamship *Great Britain* becomes the first ocean vessel made of wrought iron.

In England, J.W. Starr, an American from Cincinnati, patents the first incandescent lamp.

1850 John Wilkinson develops a method for boring the interiors of cylinders that is greatly superior to previous methods.

1852 Henri Giffard builds and flies the first dirigible.

1858 The Foreland lighthouse in Kent, England, is the first to be equipped with electrically powered arc lights.

1862 *Monitor*, designed by John Ericsson, defeats but does not sink *Merrimac* in first naval engagement between ironclad ships.

1867 U.S. engineer George Westinghouse solves a major problem of the railways by inventing the air brake.

1869 The golden spike is hammered at Promontory Point, Utah, completing the first railway line from the Atlantic to the Pacific.

1872 In Germany, George M. Pullman introduces the sleeper car to railroad travel.

1876 Paul Jablochkoff develops the electric candle, which will burn for 2 hours with no mechanical adjustment.

1879 Thomas Edison in America and Joseph Swann in England develop incandescent lights that use a filament in a partial vacuum.

1880 Thomas Edison's first electric generation station, designed mainly for lighting, is opened in London.

1882 The Pearl Street power station in New York City brings electric lighting to the United States for the first time.

1883 Albert and Caston Tissandier design the first dirigible capable of being steered along a designated course.

1884 Charles Algernon Parsons designs and installs the first turbogenerator for electric power.

1885 The first transcontinental rail link across Canada is opened.

1889 The first dam is built to produce hydroelectric power for a plant on the Willamette River at Oregon City.

1890 William Kemmer becomes the first person to be executed in the electric chair, a device that uses alternating current.

1893 Rudolf Diesel describes the engine that will come to be named for him.

1895 Gustav and Otto Lilienthal design and fly a glider that can soar above the altitude of takeoff.

1897 Charles Algernon Parsons' ship *Turbinia* is the first steamship to be powered by a steam turbine.

1900–1986

Construction

1900 The first offshore oil wells are drilled.

1902 First dam at Aswan, in Egypt, is completed.

1904 Work begins on the Panama Canal.

1906 The Dutch begin to drain the Zuider Zee; work is completed in 1932.

The 12.5-mile Simplon Tunnel joins Italy and Switzerland.

1908 The A.E.G. turbine factory in Berlin is the first building to be constructed of steel and glass.

1911 The first escalators anywhere are introduced at Earl's Court subway station in London; a man with a wooden leg is hired to ride up and down regularly to demonstrate their safety.

1913 Grand Central Terminal opens in New York City.

1914 The first modern sewage plant, designed to treat sewage with bacteria, opens in Manchester, England.

The first ships pass through the newly completed Panama Canal, linking the Atlantic and Pacific oceans.

Yale Bowl opens and becomes the largest amphitheater in the world, seating 80,000.

1916 Frank Lloyd Wright designs the earthquake-proof Imperial Hotel in Tokyo.

1919 The Bauhaus, an influential school of design, is founded by Walter Gropius in Weimar, Germany.

1927 An 8000-foot well in Orange County, California, sets a new depth record.

1929 Construction begins on the Empire State Building in New York City; it will be finished in 1931.

Energy, Machines, and Transportation

1900 The first Browning revolvers are manufactured.

1901 King Camp Gillette and William Nickerson patent the first safety razor.

Motor-driven bicycles are introduced.

1902 The first practical airship, *Le Jaune*, is launched in France by the Lebaudy brothers.

1903 Konstantin Tsiolkovsky details the principles of using rockets to reach outer space.

The first successful airplane is launched at Kitty Hawk, North Carolina, by the Wright Brothers on December 17.

1904 J.P.L. Elster devises the first practical photoelectric cell.

Ultraviolet lamps are introduced.

1906 The tungsten-filament light bulb is introduced.

1907 French bicycle dealer Paul Cornu builds the first helicopter that can take off vertically while carrying a human.

1908 The Hughes Tool Company develops the steel-toothed rock-drilling bit, enabling drilling through hard rock.

The Holt Company of California develops the first tractor to use moving treads.

Henry Ford introduces the prototype of the assembly line for production of his Model T automobile.

1909 Enrico Forlanini develops the hydrofoil ship, which reduces drag by using winglike foils to lift the main hull out of the water.

English aviator Henri Farman completes the first airplane flight of 160 kilometers (100 miles).

On July 25 Louis Blériot of France becomes the first human to fly across the English Channel.

1910 Eugene Ely becomes the first person to take off in an airplane from the deck of a ship.

F. Cotrell invents the electrostatic precipitator to reduce air pollution from factory smokestacks.

Georges Claude introduces the neon light in Paris.

1913 Henry Ford introduces the first true assembly line, with cars carried along a conveyor belt at a speed slow enough for workers to assemble them, but fast enough to reduce assembly time from $12\frac{1}{2}$ hours to $1\frac{1}{2}$ hours.

Hans Geiger invents a radiation detector for detecting alpha particles.

1914 U.S. engineer Robert H. Goddard starts developing experimental rockets.

1915 Fokker aircraft become first airplanes to be equipped with machine gun that can fire between blades of moving propeller.

1917 The 100-inch telescope is installed at Mount Wilson, California; it will be the world's largest for 30 years.

1918 The electric beater is introduced for mixing foods.

1919 English physicist F.W. Aston builds the first mass spectrograph.

John Alcock and Arthur Whitten-Brown become the first human to fly the Atlantic nonstop.

1920 Retired U.S. Army officer John T. Thompson patents his submachine gun, later famous as the tommy gun.

1921 Playwright Karl Capek coins the term *robot* to describe the mechanical people in his play *RUR*.

1923 Spanish inventor Juan de la Cierva develops the basic idea of the autogiro.

1924 The self-winding watch is patented.

1926 The pop-up toaster is introduced in the United States.

Robert Hutchings Goddard fires the first successful liquid-fueled rocket on March 16.

1928 U.S. inventors J.W. Horton and W.A. Marrison develop the first quartz crystal clock.

Joseph Schick invents the electric razor.

1929 Robert Jemison Van de Graaf builds his first electrostatic generator from tin cans, a silk ribbon, and a small motor; two years later he builds the first high-voltage version, an early form of particle accelerator.

German engineer Felix Wankel patents a rotary engine, although it will not become practical until 1951.

TIMELINE OF TECHNOLOGY

Medicine

1800 English chemist Humphry Davy discovers nitrous oxide and suggests its use as an anesthetic.
1816 René Laënnec invents the stethoscope.
1827 Achromatic microscopes are introduced by several inventors to rid the microscope of color distortion.
1829 Vincenz Priessnitz develops the method now called hydropathy of using water to treat illnesses.
1842 U.S. surgeon Crawford Long uses ether as an anesthetic to perform an operation on a human.
1843 Thomas Watson suggests use of rubber gloves while performing surgery.
Oliver Wendell Holmes suggests that physicians disinfect themselves during obstetrical procedures to avoid spreading childbed fever.
1844 U.S. dentist Horace Wells introduces nitrous oxide for use in removing diseased teeth.
1847 Ignaz Semmelweis finds that childbed fever is spread by physicians performing obstetrical procedures who do not disinfect their hands and tools.
1851 Hermann von Helmholtz invents the ophthalmoscope.
1865 Joseph Lister introduces antiseptic surgery.
1877 Robert Koch develops a way of obtaining pure cultures of bacteria.
1880 Louis Pasteur's On the Extension of the Germ Theory to the Etiology of Certain Common Diseases develops the germ theory of disease.
1881 Carlos Finlay suggests the mosquito carries yellow fever.
1882 Robert Koch discovers the bacterium that causes tuberculosis, the first association of a germ with a disease.
1887 Louis J. Girard, of Baylor College of Medicine, develops the first form of contact lens, which covers the white of the eye as well as the cornea.
1890 Surgeons at Johns Hopkins Hospital in Baltimore begin using rubber gloves during surgery.
1891 An antitoxin for diphtheria is tested for the first time on humans.
1892 Russian biologist Dmitri Ivanovsky demonstrates the existence of a virus.
1893 U.S. surgeon Daniel Williams performs the first open-heart surgery on a patient.
1898 Ronald Ross shows that the anopheles mosquito can transmit malaria.

1900 Austrian doctor Karl Landsteiner shows that there are at least three different types of human blood, some of which are incompatible with others.
1901 The hormone adrenalin is isolated.
Dutch scientist Gerrit Grijns shows that a substance missing from the diet causes beriberi.
1902 Millar Hutchinson of the United States invents the first electrical hearing aid.
1903 Willem Einthoven in the Netherlands develops the string galvanometer, the forerunner of a device used to produce an electrocardiogram.
German surgeon George Perthes discovers x-rays inhibit growth of tumors.
1905 J. B. Murphy of the United States develops first artificial joints for use in hips of an arthritic patient.
Alexis Carrel develops techniques for rejoining severed blood vessels.
Austrian ophthalmologist Eduard Zirm performs the first cornea transplant.
1906 August von Wasserman creates the blood test for syphilis, later named after him.
1907 German bacteriologist Paul Ehrlich discovers a dye that will kill the parasites that cause African sleeping sickness, the first specific chemical for a specific disease.
1910 Major Frank Woodbury, U.S. Army, introduces use of tincture of iodine as a disinfectant for wounds.
Paul Ehrlich discovers a chemical to cure syphilis.
1911 English physician William Hill develops the first gastroscope, a tube that can be swallowed by a patient so that a physician can look through the tube at the inside of the patient's stomach.
1913 German surgeon A. Salomen develops mammography, a technique for diagnosing breast cancer.
John J. Abel develops the first artificial kidney.
1914 Alexis Carrel performs the first successful heart surgery on a dog.
1919 Fish are added to reservoirs to eat mosquito larvae in order to prevent mosquito-borne diseases.
1922 Frederick Banting and a team of doctors including Charles Best use insulin injections against diabetes.

Communication

1805 Joseph Marie Jacquard develops a method of controlling the operation of a loom based on punched cards, an idea later used in early computers.
1822 Joseph Niepce, using silver chloride, produces the first object that can be called a photograph.
1831 Charles Wheatstone and William Fothergill create the first primitive telegraph, a machine with an arrow that points to letters of the alphabet.
1832 Charles Babbage conceives of the first computer; strikingly novel in concept, his computer was never built in a workable form.
1833 Karl Friederich Gauss, a German mathematician, develops a form of electric telegraph.
1834 Heinrich Lenz discovers the phenomenon of self-induction in electromagnetic devices.
1835 Joseph Henry invents a relay that enables an electric signal to be sent distances over a wire as a dot or dash; in effect, this is the telegraph, but not until Henry's work is applied by Wheatstone (1837) and Morse (1843) does telegraphy become practical.
1837 Samuel F.B. Morse patents his version of the telegraph, a machine that sends letters in codes made up of dots and dashes.
1843 Samuel F.B. Morse uses his telegraph system to send a famous message from Washington to Baltimore: "What hath God wrought?"
1846 Alexander Bain develops a method of sending telegraph messages using punched paper tape, greatly increasing the speed of transmission.
1866 The first cable across the Atlantic Ocean is successful in transmitting messages.
1876 Alexander Graham Bell patents the telephone.
1890 Herman Hollerith develops system based on punched cards that is used in counting the U.S. census.
1895 Radio signals are first transmitted.

TELEGRAPH KEY

1900 U.S. scientist R.A. Fessenden transmits human speech via radio waves.
1901 Guglielmo Marconi receives the letter "S" in St. Johns, Newfoundland, transmitted from England; first transatlantic telegraphic radio transmission.
The first electric typewriter is produced, the Blickensderfer Electric.
1904 Arthur Korn telegraphs photographs from Munich to Nuremberg.
1905 The radio tube, a diode, is introduced.
U.S. undertaker Almon Brown Strowger invents the dial telephone.
1907 The radio amplifier is introduced.
The triode radio tube is introduced.
1913 The cascade-tuning radio receiver is introduced.
The heterodyne radio receiver is introduced.
1914 Radio transmitter triode modulation introduced.
1915 The radio tube oscillator is introduced.
U.S. physicist Manson Benedicks discovers that germanium crystal can convert A.C. to D.C., a discovery that leads to development of microchip.
French scientist P. Lagevin invents sonar, mainly as a means enabling ships to detect icebergs.
The first North American transcontinental telephone call is made, between Alexander Graham Bell in New York and Thomas A. Watson in San Francisco.
1918 The radio crystal oscillator is introduced.
1919 The shortwave radio is developed.
1923 The first photoelectric cell is produced.
1928 The radio beacon is introduced.
1929 FM radio is first used.
1930 Vannevar Bush develops a differential analyzer, a machine that is the first analog computer.
The tape recorder, using magnetized plastic tape, is developed in Germany.
1932 U.S. engineer Karl Jansky discovers that radio waves are coming from space, leading to the development of radio astronomy.
1935 British scientists, led by Robert Watson-Watt, develop the first radar.

Materials

1801 Ándrés Del Rio discovers vanadium.
Charles Hachett discovers niobium.
1803 Smithson Tennant discovers iridium and osmium.
1804 Nicolas Appert invents food canning.
William Wollaston discovers palladium, rhodium.
1807 Humphry Davy discovers potassium on October 6 and sodium on October 13.
1808 Joseph Louis Gay-Lussac discovers the element boron on June 21.
Humphry Davy discovers barium, strontium, calcium, and magnesium.
1811 Bernard Courtois discovers iodine in seaweed.
1817 Friederich Strohmeyer discovers cadmium.
August Arfvedson discovers lithium.
1818 Selenium is discovered.
1819 John Kidd derives naphthalene from coal tar.
1823 Silicon is discovered.
1825 Bromine is discovered.
1828 Aluminum and thorium are discovered.
1830 Vanadium is discovered.
1839 Lanthanum is discovered.
1843 Terbium and erbium are discovered.
1844 Ruthenium is discovered.
1856 English inventor Henry Bessemer develops the Bessemer process for producing steel.
1860 Cesium is discovered.
1861 Rubidium is discovered.
1862 Alexander Parkes displays in London items made from what later is called celluloid.
1868 William H. Perkin synthesizes coumarin, a scent and flavoring used in foods until 1954.
1875 Gallium is discovered.
1879 Samarium and scandium are discovered.
1884 Louis Marie Hilaire Bernigaud begins to produce fibers made from cellulose, later known as rayon.
1885 Neodymium and praseodymium are discovered.
1886 Germanium, fluorine, dysprosium discovered.
1894 Argon is discovered.
1896 Europium is discovered.
1898 Radium, neon, krypton, and xenon are discovered.
1899 Actinium is discovered.

1901 The first synthetic vat dye, indanthrene blue, is manufactured.
1902 Carl von Linde discovers how to liquefy air, producing both liquid oxygen and liquid nitrogen.
1904 French scientist Leon Guillet develops the first stainless steels, but fails to note that they resist corrosion.
F.S. Kipping discovers silicones.
1905 Safety glass is introduced.
1907 The paint spray gun is invented.
Louis Lumière develops color photography.
1908 Fritz Haber, in Germany, develops the Haber process for extracting nitrogen from the air and making ammonia for use as a cheap fertilizer.
H. Kamerlingh Onnes liquefies helium.
1909 Leo Baekeland patents Bakelite, the first plastic that solidifies on heating; it was the first plastic to be widely used to replace more traditional materials such as wood, ivory, and hard rubber.
1910 Rayon stockings are manufactured in Germany.
1911 Dutch physicist Kamerlingh Onnes discovers superconductivity in mercury that is cooled close to absolute zero.
German scientist P. Monnartz becomes the first to realize that stainless steels resist corrosion.
1912 Edwin Brandenberger develops cellophane.
1915 The Corning Glass Works develops Pyrex, a heat-resistant glass.
1917 Clarence Birdseye develops freezing as a way of preserving foods.
1921 U.S. scientist Thomas Midley synthesizes the gasoline additive tetraethyl lead.
Cultured pearls are introduced.
1923 John B. Tytus develops hot-strip rolling of steel.
1924 Kimberly Clark introduces the first version of Kleenex, known then as Celluwipes.
Insecticides are used for the first time.
1925 German chemist Carl Bosch invents a process for manufacturing hydrogen.
1928 Minnesota Mining and Manufacturing Corporation introduces Scotch Tape.

(continued)

TIMELINE OF TECHNOLOGY (continued)

Construction

1900–1986 *(continued)*

1931 Construction of Rockefeller Center, New York City, begins.
   The George Washington Bridge, over the Hudson River, opens, with double the span of the previous record holder.

1936 The Hoover Dam—it is sometimes known as Boulder Dam—is completed on the Colorado River; for 22 years. At 577 feet, it will be the highest dam in the world, and the reservoir behind it, Lake Mead, will be the largest.

1937 The Golden Gate Bridge in San Francisco opens.

1940 Collapse of the four-month-old Tacoma Narrows Bridge impels engineers for the first time to consider aerodynamic stability in designing bridges and buildings.

1942 United States Army Engineers build the Alcan Highway, the 1470-mile link between the 48 states and Alaska.

1943 The Grand Coulee becomes the largest dam in terms of amount of concrete used; 3,360,000 cubic meters (4,400,000 cubic yards) were used in its construction.

1945 Frank Lloyd Wright designs the Guggenheim Museum, which will not open until 1958.

1952 Lever House in New York City is completed, setting the style for office buildings for years to come.

1959 The St. Lawrence Seaway opens, linking the Great Lakes and the Atlantic Ocean.

1964 The Verrazano Bridge, the longest suspension bridge in the world at the time, opens to traffic in New York City.

1970 The High Dam at Aswan is completed, eventually flooding the Nile Valley for 400 miles upstream.

1975 The C.N. Tower in Toronto's Metro Centre, at 555 meters (1822 feet), becomes the tallest tower anywhere, although some television antennae are taller.

1977 The trans-Alaska pipeline from Prudhoe Bay to Valdez begins delivering oil.

1981 The world's longest suspension bridge opens over the estuary of the Humber, England.

1986 Agreement is reached between the United Kingdom and France to build the Chunnel, a 31-mile-long railroad tunnel under the English Channel.

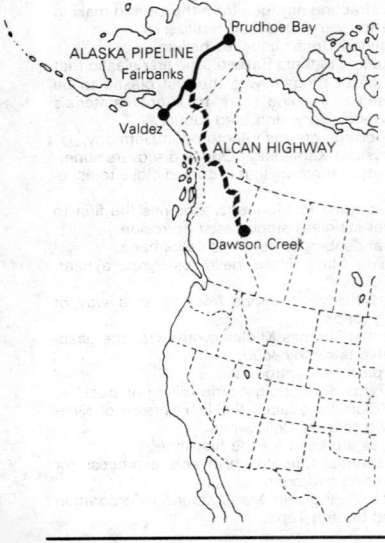

Energy, Machines, and Transportation

1930 Estonian optical instrument maker B.V. Schmidt builds the first Schmidt telescope, a type that will come to dominate much of astronomy because it is free from the aberrations called coma.
   William Beebe and Otis Barton dive to 417 meters in their new submersible, the bathysphere.
   British engineer Frank Whittle patents the jet engine.

1932 American physicist Ernest O. Lawrence develops the first workable particle smasher, the cyclotron.
   John Cockcroft and Ernest Walton become the first to use a particle accelerator to break apart an element.
   Auguste Piccard becomes the first human to enter the stratosphere; his balloon climbs to 16,201 meters.

1934 A liquid-fuel rocket launched by German engineer Werner von Braun achieves an altitude of 2.4 kilometers (1.5 miles).
   The first streamlined car, the Chrysler Airflow, is introduced.
   German engineers Ernst Ruska and Max Knoll develop the first functioning electron microscope.

1936 German engineer Heinrich Focke develops the first practical helicopter.
   Fluorescent lighting is introduced.

1938 U.S. engineer T. Ross develops the first machine that can learn from experience, that is, find its way through mazes.
   German physicist Otto Hahn is the first to split the atom of uranium, opening up the possibility of a chain reaction.
   German engineer Ferdinand Porsche introduces the prototype of the Volkswagen beetle.

1939 Pan-American Airways institutes the first regular commercial flights across the Atlantic Ocean.
   German engineer Pabst von Ohain's jet engine becomes the first such engine actually to propel an airplane, the He-178.
   French scientists Frédéric and Irène Joliot-Curie demonstrate that fission of the uranium atom can lead to a chain reaction.
   Igor Sikorsky constructs the first helicopter.

1940 The Radio Corporation of America demonstrates the first electron microscope.

1941 German scientist Konrad Zuse's Z_2 computer is the first to use electromagnetic relays and a punched tape for data entry.

1942 The first electronic digital computer is developed in the United States.
   At the University of Chicago, a team led by Enrico Fermi starts the first controlled chain reaction.

1943 The world's first operational nuclear reactor is activated at Oak Ridge, Tennessee.

1944 The Greenwich Royal Observatory installs its first quartz-crystal clock, providing ten times the accuracy of the previous pendulum system.
   Early in the year, the German armed forces begin to use the V-1 flying bomb, propelled by a jet engine and controlled by an autopilot, against the United Kingdom; in September the V-2, a liquid-fueled rocket-propelled bomb, also goes into operation.

1945 The first nuclear bomb is detonated near Alamogordo, New Mexico, by the United States on July 16.

1947 The tubeless tire is introduced by Goodyear in the United States.
   Chuck Yeager flies the Bell X-1 rocket plane faster than the speed of sound in level flight on October 14.

1948 The atomic clock is introduced.
   The 200-inch (5-meter) Hale telescope is dedicated at Mount Palomar Observatory; when it goes into full operation in 1949, it will serve as the most effective optical telescope on Earth for 40 years.

1951 The United Kingdom introduces the zebra street crossing, a striped area, an important contribution to pedestrian safety.

1952 The first accident at a nuclear reactor occurs at Chalk River, Canada. Technician's error causes nuclear core to explode.
   The first fusion (hydrogen) bomb is exploded by the United States at Eniwetok Atoll, Marshall Islands, on November 6.

1953 Michelin of France and Pirelli of Italy introduce radial-ply tires.

1954 The first nuclear-powered submarine, the U.S.S. *Nautilus*, is launched.
   Bell Telephone scientists Chapin, Fuller, and Peterson develop the photovoltaic cell, to produce electric power from sunlight.

1955 Christopher Cockerell develops the first practical hovercraft.
   Commercial electric power from a nuclear reactor is produced for the first time in the United States.

1957 The first nuclear-powered surface ship, the Soviet icebreaker *Lenin*, is launched.
   The Soviet Union launches the first Earth-orbiting artificial satellite, *Sputnik 1*, on October 4.

1959 The first U.S. nuclear-powered surface ship, the merchant ship *Savannah*, is launched.
   The Soviet Union's *Lunik 2* becomes the first manmade object to hit the moon when it crash lands on September 12.

1960 Jacques Piccard and U.S. Navy Lt. Don Walsh descend in the bathyscaphe *Trieste* to the bottom of the Challenger Deep, in the Marianas Trench in the Pacific Ocean, 35,800 feet below the surface.
   Geothermal power is produced for the first time in the United States at The Geysers, near San Francisco.

1961 On April 12, Soviet Cosmonaut Yuri Gagarin becomes the first human to orbit Earth.

1962 The U.S. spaceprobe *Mariner 2* becomes the first manmade object to voyage to another planet.
   Unimation markets the world's first industrial robot in the United States.

1965 Container ships are introduced, simplifying international trade.
   Soviet astronaut Aleksey Leonov becomes the first human to move out of a space capsule in a spacesuit.

1966 Fuel injection for automobile engines is developed in the United Kingdom.

1968 The *Queen Elizabeth II* is launched.
   Surveyor 7 becomes the first space vehicle to land undamaged on the moon.
   The Soviet spacecraft *Zond 5* becomes the first manmade object to travel around the moon and return to Earth.
   The first supertankers for carrying petroleum are put into service.
   U.S. space vehicle *Apollo 8* is the first to make a flight carrying human passengers around the moon and back.
   Regular hovercraft service across the English Channel begins.
   The first supersonic airliner, the Soviet Tupolev TU-14, goes into service.

1969 The scanning electron microscope reaches practical use after 15 years of development.
   Neil A. Armstrong and Edwin E. (Buzz) Aldrin of the United States, as part of the Apollo 11 mission, on July 20 become the first human beings to land safely on the moon.

1970 Carbon dioxide lasers are introduced for industrial cutting and welding.

1971 The U.S. spacecraft *Mariner 9* becomes the first to orbit another planet, in this case Mars.
   In Canada, the first nuclear power station that is cooled by ordinary water goes into service.

1972 The first Earth-resources satellite, *Landsat 1*, is launched.
   In Germany, an experimental power station uses coal that is converted to gas before being burned.
   Soviet spacecraft *Venera 8* soft-lands on Venus.
   U.S. space probe *Pioneer 10* is launched; on June 13, 1983, it will become the first manmade object to leave the solar system.
   Apollo 17 lands on the moon, the last of the series.

1974 A Soviet space probe lands on Mars.

1975 The Soviet airplane Tupolev-144 becomes the first supersonic airliner to make regularly scheduled flights.

1976 *Viking 1* soft-lands on Mars; expected to transmit information for about 90 days, it will transmit for $6\frac{1}{2}$ years.
   The French-English Concorde becomes the first supersonic airliner to operate a regularly scheduled passenger service.

1977 *Voyager 1* and *2* are launched to Jupiter; *Voyager 2* later will fly by Saturn and Uranus, heading out toward Neptune.

1981 The world's largest solar-power station is completed, Solar One, in the Mojave Desert, California, generating up to 10 megawatts of electricity.
   Columbia, the first U.S. space shuttle, is successfully launched on April 12, John Young pilot and Robert Crippen copilot.

1982 Soviet *Venera 13* and *Venera 14* spacecrafts make the first successful soft landings on Venus.

1983 A team of German and U.S. scientists develops a wet solar cell with an energy conversion efficiency of 9.5 percent.
   IRAS, a U.S. satellite designed to detect infrared radiation from objects in space, is launched on January 25; in the course of its mission, it will discover evidence of planet formation around stars outside the solar system.
   U.S. space shuttle, *Challenger*, is successfully launched. On January 28, 1986, *Challenger* will explode shortly after launch, killing all seven of its crew.

1985 The Tevatron particle accelerator at Fermilab in Batavia, Illinois, begins operation.

1986 Chernobyl nuclear reactor Number 4, near Kiev, U.S.S.R., explodes at 1:23 A.M. local time on April 26, leading to a catastrophic release of radioactivity that kills dozens of people within a few weeks.

Medicine

1927 P. Drinker and L. A. Shaw develop the iron lung.
1928 Alexander Fleming discovers penicillin.
U.S. medical scientist George Papanicolaou develops the Pap smear for diagnosing uterine cancers.
1929 German psychiatrist Hans Berger develops the electroencephalogram (EEG).
1934 U.S. biochemist J.P. Lent discovers the anticoagulant now known as coumarin in spoiled clover.
1935 John Gibbon and his wife develop the first prototype of the heart-lung machine.
German chemist Gerhard Domagk develops the first sulfa drug, Prontosil.
1936 Alexis Carrel, working with Charles A. Lindbergh, develops a form of artificial heart.
1937 Italian pharmacologist Daniel Bovet develops the first antihistamine.
Italian physicians Ugo Cerletti and Lucio Bini develop the first form of electroconvulsive therapy (ECT) for treating schizophrenia.
1938 English surgeon Philip Wiles develops the first totally artificial hip replacement, using stainless steel.
1942 U.S. microbiologist Selman Waksman discovers streptomycin in a soil fungus and coins word *antibiotic* to describe medicines that kill bacteria.
Dutch doctor Wilhelm Kolff develops the first kidney dialysis machine.
1945 Fluoridation of a water supply to prevent dental decay is introduced in the United States.
1949 X-rays from a synchrotron are used for the first time in medical diagnosis and treatment.
1951 J. Andre-Thomas and U.S. surgeon John Gibbon develop heart-lung machines.
1954 Frederick Sanger determines the molecule-by-molecule structure of a protein, insulin.
1956 Birth-control pills are used in a large-scale test by John Rock and Gregory Pincus in Puerto Rico.
1958 Ian Donald of Scotland is the first to use ultrasound to examine unborn children.
1961 Jack Lippes introduces an inert plastic intrauterine device (IUD) for birth control.
1964 Home kidney dialysis is introduced in the United Kingdom and the United States.
1965 Soft contact lenses are invented.
1967 U.S. surgeon Rene Favaloro develops the coronary bypass operation.
South African surgeon Christiaan Barnard performs the first heart transplant.
1969 In the United States, Denton Cooley and Domingo Liotta replace the diseased heart of Haskell Karp with the first artificial heart used in human being.
1970 Scientists at the University of Wisconsin announce the first complete synthesis of a gene.
1972 In United Kingdom, CAT-scan imager is introduced.
1973 Scientists in United Kingdom introduce the nuclear magnetic resonance (NMR) scanner for diagnosis.
1975 The discovery of how to produce monoclonal antibodies is announced from United Kingdom.
1976 U.S. scientists announce construction of a functional synthetic gene.
1981 Ruth and Victor Nussenzweig of New York University apply for a patent on a malaria vaccine.
The U.S. Food and Drug Administration approves a vaccine for hepatitis B made from human blood.
1982 A gene from one mammal functions for the first time in another as the gene for rat growth hormone is transferred to mice; some of the mice grow to double normal size because of the hormone.
A team of surgeons led by William DeVries implants the first Jarvik 7 artificial heart; the patient, Barney Clark, lives on for 112 days.
1983 The immunosuppressant cyclosporine is approved for use by the U.S. Food and Drug Administration, increasing the safety of transplants of organs.
The first field test of a bacteria with artificially altered genetic structure is stopped by a lawsuit; the test is delayed for several years as a result.
John Buster and Maria Bustillo of the Harbor-UCLA Medical Center in Torrance, California, perform the first successful human embryo transfers.
1984 Allan Wilson and Russell Higuchi of Berkeley clone genes from an extinct species.
Surgeon William H. Clewall of the University of Colorado Health Sciences Center at Denver performs the first successful surgery on a fetus.
The first clinical trials begin on June 1 of a vaccine against hepatitis B produced by yeast that has been given genes for a molecule of the hepatitis virus.
1985 Lasers are used in the United States for the first time to clean out clogged arteries.

Communication

1939 American engineer Edwin Armstrong perfects FM (frequency modulation) radio.
1942 LORAN (long range navigation) begins operation for the first time along the Atlantic seaboard.
1944 The first general purpose digital computer, Mark I, is completed by Howard Aiken and IBM engineers; it uses punched paper tape and vacuum tubes to calculate problems and breaks down frequently as a result of problems with the tubes.
1946 U.S. law student Chester Carlson invents xerography, a practical method of photocopying.
1948 U.S. inventor Edwin Land invents a camera and film system that develops pictures inside the camera.
U.S. inventor Peter Goldmark develops the first long-playing record.
Scientists at Bell Laboratories, led by William Shockley, invent the transistor.
1949 EDSAC, a computer, is developed in Cambridge, England; it is six times faster than ENIAC and can accept input and produce output on paper tape.
1950 Commercial color television broadcasts begin in the United States.
1952 British radar expert W.A. Dummer develops the concept of the integrated circuit.
Sony develops the pocket-sized transistor radio.
1953 U.S. physicist Charles H. Townes develops the maser, precursor of the laser.
1955 The first optical fibers are produced by Narinder Kapary in London.
1956 FORTRAN, a computer language, is invented.
The first transatlantic telephone cable is put into operation on September 25.
1957 Bernard Lovell supervises construction and operation of the first major radio telescope at Jodrell Bank, England.
1958 Texas Instruments produces first integrated circuit.
1959 COBOL, a computer language designed for business uses, is invented.
1960 U.S. scientists develop the first laser.
Echo, the first passive communications satellite, is launched on August 12.
1962 *Telstar*, the first active communications satellite, is launched on July 10.
1963 *Syncom*, the first communications satellite to be placed in a geosynchronous orbit, is launched.
1967 R.M. Dolby develops a method to eliminate background sound in recordings.
1969 Bubble-memory devices are created for use in computers; unlike conventional memory devices, bubble memory continues to remember when the computer is off.
1970 The floppy disk is introduced.
1971 Direct telephone dialing, as opposed to operator-assisted calls, begins between parts of U.S. and Europe.
The first microprocessor is introduced by Intel in the United States.
1974 Hewlett-Packard introduces the pocket calculator.
1975 First liquid-crystal displays for pocket calculators and digital clocks marketed in the United Kingdom.
Altair, the first home computer that has serious applications, is marketed in the United States.
1976 IBM develops the ink-jet printer.
The Apple computer is introduced, the first truly successful home computer.
1977 The first video-cassette recorder able to show a whole feature length motion picture on tape becomes commercially available.
1979 The first electronic spreadsheet program, VisiCalc, makes the personal computer a useful tool instead of a toy.
1980 Philips in The Netherlands and Sony in Japan introduce the compact disk, an audio system that uses a laser to access digitally recorded sound.
1981 IBM introduces the PC, the first personal computer to use a 16-bit microprocessor.
1984 Hewlett-Packard introduces a laser printer that is directed by a personal computer.
1985 AT&T Bell Laboratories achieves the equivalent of sending 300,000 simultaneous telephone conversations or 200 high-resolution television channels at once over a single optical fiber.
Construction of the world's largest telescope, the Keck, begins on Mauna Kea in Hawaii; the Keck telescope's mirror will be 10 meters (33 feet) in diameter, but it will not be cast as a single piece.

Materials

1929 Dunlop Rubber Company produces foam rubber.
1930 W.L. Semon of the B.F. Goodrich Company invents polyvinyl chloride.
The Postum Company begins marketing frozen foods.
Sliced bread is introduced.
1931 The first Freons are produced by the Kinetic Chemical Corporation; much later, they will be considered possible causes of destruction of the ozone layer that protects Earth from ultraviolet radiation.
Julius A. Nieuwland develops synthetic rubber.
1932 U.S. engineer Edwin Land invents a synthetic substance that will polarize light.
1934 French physicists Frédéric and Irène Joliot-Curie develop the first artificial radioactive element, a radioactive form of phosphorus.
1935 W.H. Carothers patents nylon.
1938 The beer can is introduced in New Jersey.
Roy Plunkett discovers the first form of Teflon.
1939 DuPont begins to market nylon.
British firm ICI manufactures polyethylene.
Swiss chemist Paul Müller discovers DDT.
The first precooked frozen foods are marketed under the Birds Eye label.
1940 Freeze drying is used for food preservation for the first time in the United States.
Philip Abelson and Edwin McMillan create the first element with an atomic number higher than that of uranium; element number 93 is named neptunium.
1941 I.G. Farbenindustrie begins to produce polyurethanes, developed between 1937 and 1939 by Otto Bayer.
English chemist E. Whinfield discovers Dacron.
U.S. scientists L.D. Goodhue and W.N. Sullivan develop the aerosol spray for insecticides.
Glenn T. Seaborg and Edwin McMillan create element 94, named plutonium.
1942 U.S. chemist Louis Fieser develops napalm.
1943 Continuous casting of steel is developed by German engineer S. Junghans.
Dow Corning Corporation begins to manufacture the first silicones.
1944 British biochemists A.J.P. Martin and R.L.M. Synge develop paper chromatography, an important new tool in identifying the chemistry of organic compounds.
1945 The herbicide 2,4-D is introduced.
1946 Willard Libby introduces the radioactive carbon-14 method of dating objects.
1949 General Mills and Pillsbury both begin marketing prepared cake mixes.
1950 The artificial sweetener cyclamate is introduced.
1954 TV dinners are introduced in the United States.
1955 Deep freezers capable of freezing fresh food go on sale in the United States.
The first artificial diamonds for industrial use are produced in the United States.
Velcro is patented.
1959 DeBeers of the Union of South Africa manufactures the first artificial diamond.
1960 Astroturf, a replacement for sod, is used to cover the playing field at the Astrodome in Houston, Texas.
1964 The International Rice Research Institute starts the so-called green revolution with new strains of rice that double the yield of previous strains.
1969 The first home yogurt maker is marketed.
1972 In the United States, the use of DDT is restricted to protect the environment, especially birds, whose shells are thinned, lowering the birds' reproductive rate.
1973 The push-through tab on soft drink and beer cans is introduced.
1976 The United States National Academy of Sciences reports that Freon used in spray cans can deplete the ozone layer in the atmosphere, increasing ultraviolet radiation in the atmosphere.
1982 West German scientists announce on August 29 the creation of a single atom of element 109.
1983 Scientists develop a method for dating ancient objects based on chemical changes in obsidian.
Aspartame is approved for use as an artificial sweetener in soft drinks.
1984 West German scientists announce on the creation of three atoms of element 108.
1985 Information about lanxides, crosses between ceramics and metals, is released when the U.S. Defense Department declassifies the subject.

MODERN TECHNOLOGY

Construction

Construction refers to the creation of many types of structures, all of which are affected by rapid developments in technology. This section deals with the technology of constructing buildings, dams, canals, bridges, tunnels, and roads.

Buildings

Buildings, fixed structures for human use, are designed to support loads that are carefully calculated to ensure the safety of the building's occupants. Buildings also must be able to withstand such pressures as the force of wind, the weight of snow on the roof, and the jolts caused by earthquakes.

Frames. A critical feature of a strong, safe building is the construction of its frame. One of three types of framing systems usually is chosen to support the roof and floors: bearing walls, skeleton frames made of beams or slabs and columns, or long-span roof systems.

Bearing walls not only divide a building into rooms but also support the ends of the roof and floor beams. They can be either interior or exterior load-bearing walls. Materials used for this type of wall include bricks, concrete blocks, concrete that is poured into molds and reinforced with steel bars, and prefabricated concrete panels. Bearing-wall construction is used for houses, low-rise industrial and commercial buildings, and skyscrapers up to 75 stories high.

STEEL BEAM CONSTRUCTION, *as was used in the Hancock Building in Chicago, enables the use of lightweight curtain walls. The use of heavy concrete or stone bearing walls limits the height of a building.*

Skeleton frames are made of either steel or reinforced concrete. The greatest development in construction technology since the Industrial Revolution is that of the steel-frame building, in which the weight is carried by the frame and the walls are merely "curtains." The tallest buildings in the world have skeleton frames.

Long-span construction is used for auditoriums, gymnasiums, hangars, and other buildings in which a great deal of open floor space is needed. Construction techniques include the use of arches, trusses, suspended cables, and domes. Domes, once widely used, reappeared in the 20th century as a means of covering large areas at relatively low cost. Ways were devised for combining curtain walls and roofs by stretching aluminum, fiberglass, or other sheet material over a metal shell.

The geodesic dome has become popular in the past three decades. In a

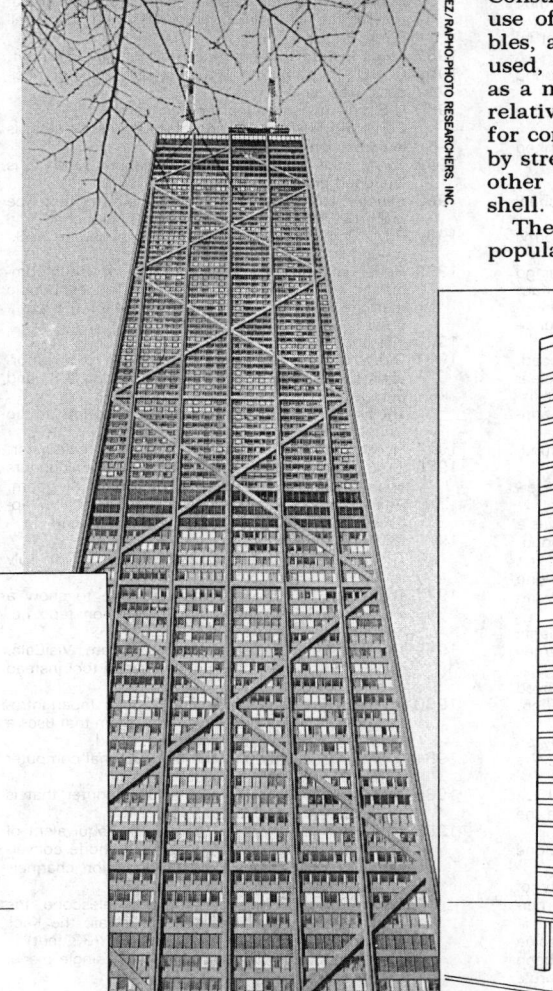

BEARING WALL

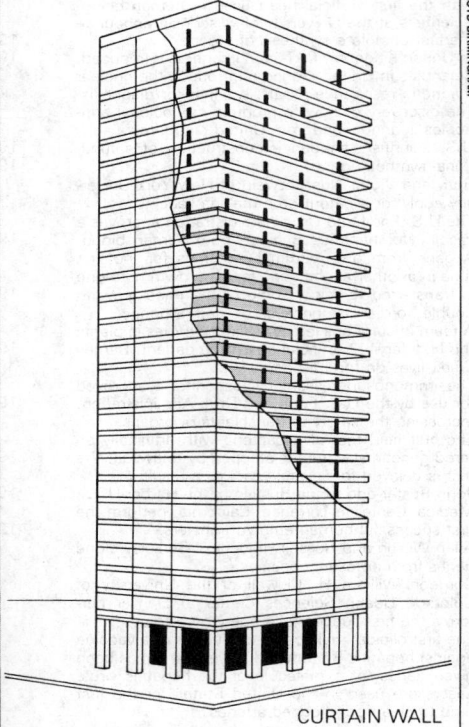

CURTAIN WALL

NOTEWORTHY NORTH AMERICAN BUILDINGS

BUILDING	HEIGHT	FLOORS
Sears Tower, *Chicago*	1454 ft.	110
World Trade Center, *New York*	1377	110
Empire State, *New York*	1250	102
Standard Oil, *Chicago*	1136	80
John Hancock Center, *Chicago*	1127	100
Chrysler, *New York*	1046	77
Texas Commerce Tower, *Houston*	1002	75
Allied Bank, *Houston*	985	71
Columbia Center, *Seattle*	954	76
First Canadian Place, *Toronto*	952	72
American International, *New York*	952	66
Northwest Center, *Minneapolis*	950	66

geodesic dome, lightweight, inexpensive rods replace the heavy metal ribs of a conventional dome. A strong, rigid frame is created by arranging the rods in triangles and hexagons.

Skyscrapers. The taller a building, the stronger its beams and columns must be to remain rigid against wind pressure. Some skyscrapers are built with belts of rigid steel-beam trusses part way up the exterior and around the top, to join the outside and inside columns. The trusses also may be diagonal to join the vertical columns together. Other skyscrapers have steel or reinforced concrete frames shaped like tubes. Some buildings are themselves tubes within tubes, with the exterior of concrete and the interior of steel frame.

Prefabrication. One of the greatest postwar changes in the construction industry has been the emergence of prefabricated buildings or parts of buildings. Box systems include walls, floors, and roof, made and finished to some degree in a factory. The box is transported to a site, where it may be combined with other box systems. Panel systems are made in small sections or in room-sized exterior or interior load-bearing walls. Frame systems, or entire buildings with curtain walls, are commonly used for apartment houses, commercial buildings, and dormitories.

Dams

Dams are structures that stop or slow the flow of water mainly to control floods, regulate water supply, provide water for hydroelectricity, or provide lakes for recreation. Most modern dams are constructed of concrete or earth, though they may be built of masonry, timber, or steel.

Concrete dams. The types of concrete dams are gravity, arch, and buttress. A gravity dam has heavy walls to prevent overturning or sliding. In cross section, a gravity dam is triangular, with narrow top and broad base. An arch dam has relatively thin walls, and it curves upstream so the pressure of the water is deflected to the sides. Such dams are usually built in narrow valleys with rock sides. Several variations of buttress dams have been developed, but they all slope upstream and have buttresses on the downstream side. The weight of the water on the slopes and the weight of the structure keep the dam from sliding or overturning.

In building a dam, the first task is to dry out the site by erecting a cofferdam, a watertight box made of wood or metal. A cofferdam may provide a work area within its walls, or it may force water away from the work area through diversion ditches or tunnels.

To provide a safe base for the dam, workers usually carve a trench in the bedrock. The trench may be as much as 100 feet deep; it often has grooves built lengthwise along the bottom to keep the dam from sliding downstream. The concrete for the dam itself is poured into a series of wooden frames that build up the dam in blocks from the bedrock. When construction is complete, the cofferdam is removed and the water allowed to return.

Earthen dams. Earthen dams, which may be built of a combination of clay, silt, sand, gravel, and rock, are still the most common type of dams. The material is packed down firmly by rollers to make it watertight. Riprap, a layer of closely fitted stones, is placed on the upstream side of the dam.

Controlling water flow. Spillways are troughs or pipes that allow excess water to escape before it can wear away or dislodge the dam. Many spillways have gates to control the amount of water that passes through.

Dams that have hydroelectric plants near them also have penstocks, large steel pipes up to 15 feet in diameter to carry water through the dam to turbines that generate electricity. Fish and debris are kept out of the penstocks by filters, called trashracks, placed on the upstream side of the dam.

Many dams have scouring galleries. These are tunnels built through the lower portion of the dam. Water flows freely through the scouring galleries, carrying with it mud and silt that tend to build up on the upstream side of the dam.

Mammoth new projects. The new Itaipú Dam, on the border of Brazil and Paraguay, went into operation in 1982. When the last of its 18 planned generators starts up in 1988, Itaipú Dam will produce 12,600 megawatts of electricity, making it the largest hydroelectric project in the world.

In 1982, the Thames Barrier was completed. It is a new type of dam, intended to protect London, England, from the devastating tides that occasionally surge up the Thames River. It consists of ten 200-foot-long floodgates arranged end to end across the river. In normal times, the floodgates rest on the river bottom. If a surge tide approaches, the floodgates can be raised by steel arms to form a dam more than 50 feet high.

A similar concept is being used in the Netherlands for the Delta Project, a 17-mile-long series of floodgates across the estuary of the Rhine River.

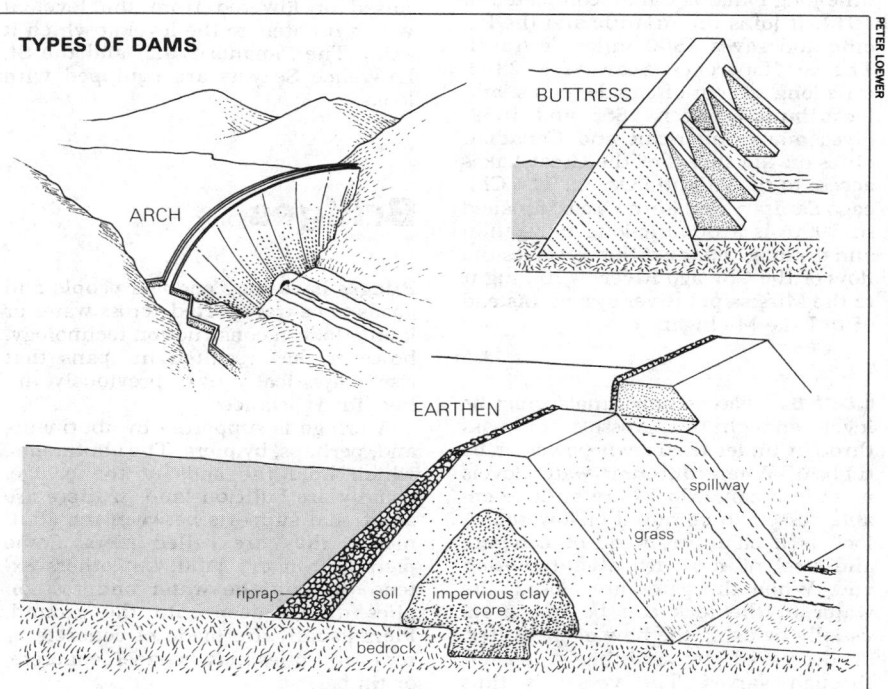

TYPES OF DAMS

ARCH

BUTTRESS

EARTHEN

spillway

grass

riprap   soil   impervious clay core

bedrock

PETER LOEWER

Canals

Canals, open channels or large ditches, are used for carrying drinking water to towns or cities, irrigating crops, controlling floods, draining water, supplying power, or providing a means of navigation. Some canals must pass through mountains in tunnels. Others are carried across rivers or gorges by steel, wood, or concrete structures called aqueducts.

Many canals are lined with concrete, stones, bricks, or synthetic materials. A lining reduces seepage from the canal and weeds that grow in it. A lining also enables water to pass swiftly, making the canal efficient.

The sides of a canal usually slant inward, so the canal is wider at top than at bottom. This makes the walls less likely to cave in. Canals used to transport water or provide power must be designed so that they slope downhill enough for water to flow but not so steeply that the lining is washed away. Many canals must be dredged from time to time to remove mud and silt.

An ambitious canal project of the 20th century is the 220-mile-long Jonglei Canal in southern Sudan. When it is completed, the White Nile River will have been diverted to irrigate 600,000 acres of desert.

Navigation canals. Historically, the largest and most costly canals in the world were navigation canals, built for barges or ships. Some link two bodies of water; others give inland cities access to the ocean.

Several famous canals are still in use in the Americas. One is the 51-mile-long Panama Canal, completed in 1914; it joins the Atlantic and the Pacific and saves 7800 miles of travel. The St. Lawrence Seaway, a 2342-mile-long system of canals, dams, and locks built between 1855 and 1959, gives many American and Canadian cities on the shores of the Great Lakes access to the Atlantic Ocean. The Chicago Sanitary and Ship Canal, finished in 1900, is a 30-mile-long navigation and drainage channel that reverses the flow of the Chicago River by linking it to the Mississippi River system instead of to Lake Michigan.

Locks. Navigation canals must be level enough for vessels to pass through under their own power or by tugboat. Where different water levels meet in a canal, locks are built to enable vessels to be raised or lowered. A lock is a chamber made of concrete and steel piling, with a gate at each end. When the gates are closed, the water in the lock can be increased, usually by using the flow of the water, or decreased, by draining water off through valves. The vessel is thus

THE WELLAND CANAL, *part of the St. Lawrence Seaway, links Lake Erie and Lake Ontario. To keep the canal level, it was necessary in places to build it above ground level and then tunnel roads and railroad tracks under it.*

HOW A LOCK WORKS

A lock consists of one or more basins sealed off from a canal by gates that prevent flow of water in the canal. When a ship moves from the upper level of the canal to the lower, it enters the basin, gates are closed behind it, and water in the basin drains out until the level in the basin is the same as that in the lower level of the canal. Then the lower gates are opened and the ship exits. When a ship travels from the lower to the upper level of the canal, the process is reversed.

raised or lowered from the level at which it enters to the level at which it exits. The Panama Canal and the St. Lawrence Seaway are equipped with locks.

Bridges

Bridges have long enabled people and goods to be transported across water or land. Modern construction technology, however, has resulted in spans that rise majestically over previously unimagined distances.

A bridge is supported by abutments and, perhaps, by piers. The abutments, which hold the ends of the bridge, usually are built on land. If there are additional supports between the abutments, they are called piers. Some piers are on dry land, but others extend through the water and rest on piles driven deep into the ground. Piers usually are made of concrete or rock, and piles may be steel, concrete, or timber.

In shallow water, cofferdams are built to provide a dry work area. In water up to 150 feet deep, bridge builders work inside caissons, large watertight boxes into which air is forced to prevent their collapse. In deeper water, machines do the digging and the pouring of concrete.

Fixed bridges. Bridges can be classified as fixed or movable. The beam bridge, which is a fixed bridge, has a series of rolled steel beams placed on abutments or piers. Without piers, beam bridges are seldom longer than 50 feet if they are to carry trains. They may reach 100 feet if they are for highway traffic. A girder bridge is similar but may extend up to 700 feet. Slightly more complex is a truss bridge, which has triangular supports.

A special form of beam bridge is the cantilever bridge, typically built outward from each side and called double-leaf. Some, called single-leaf, are built outward from one side only. From the point of attachment on the shore, the anchor section of the bridge stretches to a tower built on an abutment. From there an arm reaches out toward the section extending from the opposite shore.

Another type of fixed bridge is the arch bridge. Today's arch bridges are constructed of steel or of hollow concrete wedges reinforced with networks of heavy wire. In these bridges, the roadway is placed on top of the arch. A modern variant is a large steel arch that goes from one end of the bridge to the other.

A suspension bridge can rise higher above water and can cover greater distances than any other type of bridge. Two towers, sometimes hundreds of feet tall, are built first. Then huge steel cables are firmly anchored in concrete and fastened to solid rock on the shore. The cables are strung up and over the towers and anchored on the far shore. Smaller cables, known as hangers, are suspended from the main cables. Hangers hold sections of truss, providing a framework for the stringers, or large steel beams, forming the roadbed.

N.Y. PUBLIC LIBRARY

A SUSPENSION BRIDGE *is often the only practical way of spanning a great distance, even when the materials and design are somewhat primitive.*

Movable bridges.
Most movable bridges span waterways that have only occasional traffic. One type of movable bridge is the bascule bridge, usually used for highway bridges less than 175 feet long or railroad bridges less than 250 feet long. A bascule bridge is a single-leaf or double-leaf cantilever span with heavy concrete weights at the shore end to balance the weight of the span. A motor moves the shore end of the span downward, and the end over the water rises upward so that ships can pass through.

Another kind of movable bridge is the vertical lift bridge. A system of ca-
bles and pulleys enables a portion of the span between two towers to be raised and lowered without tilting. In a swing bridge, a section of the roadway rests on a pivot pier. The entire section can swivel 90 degrees to permit passage of vessels.

Pontoon bridges, which consist of planking laid on floating bases, are usually temporary, but they can be permanent. In the latter case, the roadway is built on floating hollow concrete boxes or metal cylinders. In the case of the permanent pontoon bridge built in Seattle, Washington, a 200-foot-long section was made to slide aside to form a shipping channel.

NOTEWORTHY NORTH AMERICAN BRIDGES

BRIDGE	LENGTH OF MAIN SPAN	TYPE
Astoria	1232 feet	Truss
Astoria, Ore.		
Bayonne	1675	Arch
Bayonne, N.J.		
Commodore John Barry	1644	Cantilever
Chester, Pa.		
Croton Reservoir	1052	Truss
Croton, N.Y.		
Golden Gate	4200	Suspension
San Francisco, Calif.		
Jesse H. Jones Memorial	1500	Arch
Houston, Tex.		
Mackinac Straits	3800	Suspension
Mich.		

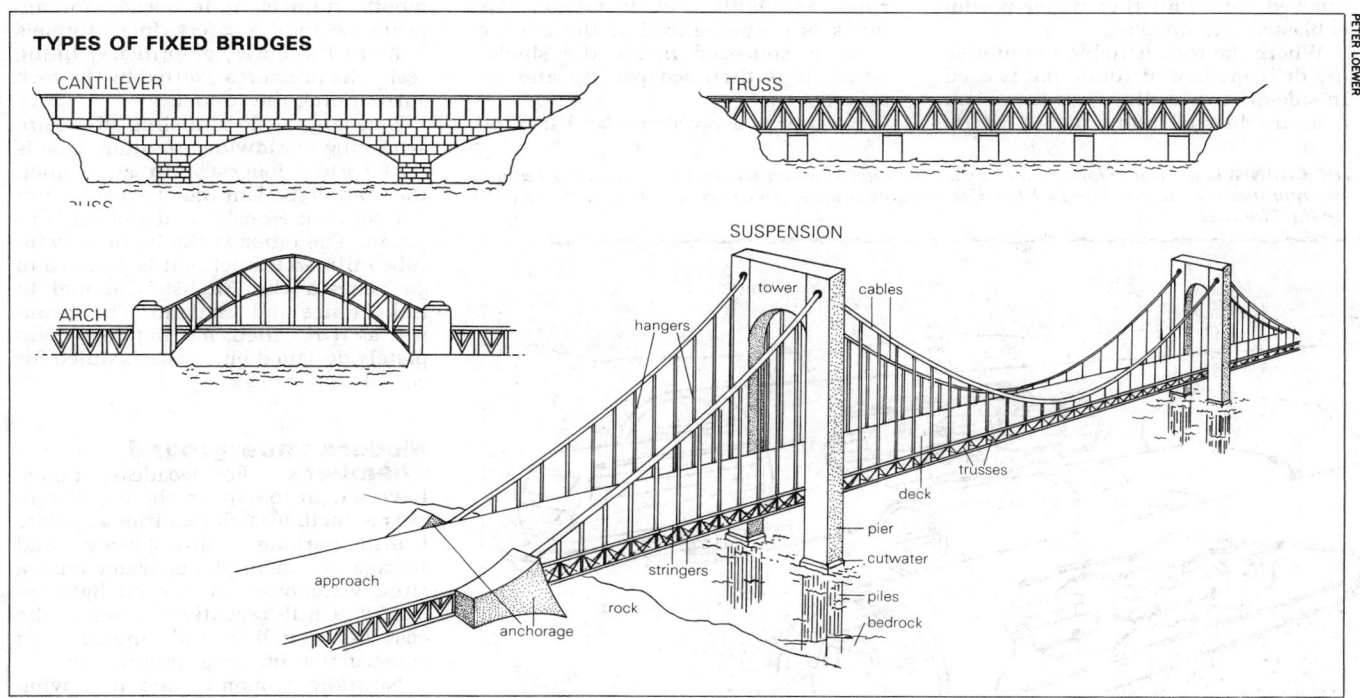

PETER LOEWER

TYPES OF FIXED BRIDGES

CANTILEVER

TRUSS

ARCH

SUSPENSION

hangers — tower — cables

trusses

deck

approach — pier — cutwater

rock — piles

anchorage — stringers — bedrock

Tunnels

Some tunnels are used for trains or automotive vehicles. Others transport water, and some transport sewage. The technology used varies with the type of material the tunnel goes through, as well as with the purpose, length, and depth of the tunnel. There are three main methods of tunneling: hard-rock, soft-ground, and trench-type.

Hard-rock tunneling.

Tunneling through hard rock requires blasting and mucking; that is, removing broken rock and dirt. A large platform carrying several drills and mounted on wheels or rails, called a jumbo, is brought up to the face, or the surface, to be blasted. Carefully positioned holes are drilled, and dynamite is pushed deep into the holes. After the blast, fresh air is pumped into the tunnel, and smoke and fumes are drawn out. A mucking machine scoops up the debris and drops it onto a conveyor belt or a muck train for removal.

The fastest and most economical way to drive a tunnel through solid rock is called full-face tunneling. In this method, each round of blasting carves out a section that is the full diameter of the tunnel. This method can be used where the roof and sidewalls of the tunnel will not collapse after blasting and mucking. In some cases, a method known as top-heading must be used. Here the entire upper portion of the tunnel, or heading, is blasted and mucked first; then the bottom portion, or bench, is driven. A variation on this method is the heading-and-bench technique, in which an upper portion and then a lower portion is blasted out and mucked before another upper portion is blasted and mucked.

Where the rock is liable to crumble, the drift method of tunneling is used. In side-drift tunneling, two small tunnels are blasted and mucked at the lower, outer edges of what will become the main tunnel. Supports are installed, and then the rest of the tunnel face is blasted. In especially poor rock, multiple-drift tunneling is used. First the side drifts are cleared and then the arch drift, or upper portion, of the tunnel. When all of that has been opened up, the remaining core is excavated.

Blasting is not always necessary. If the rock is soft enough, a machine called a mole can be used instead. At the front of the mole is a cutter head that is the full diameter of the tunnel. The cutter head has steel teeth that rotate as the mole bores into the tunnel face. Rock ground up by the cutter head drops onto a conveyor belt or a muck train.

Once the muck is cleared away, measures are taken to prevent collapse. Where the rock is solid enough, bolts are inserted into holes drilled in the roof of the tunnel. A bolt can hold rock in place because the inner end expands when the bolt is twisted and the outer end is secured with a steel plate. Arch ribs made of steel also provide primary support for the tunnel; the spaces between the ribs are lined with timber, concrete, stone, or steel plates.

Soft-ground tunneling.

Driving a tunnel through soft ground requires special techniques and precautions against cave-ins. The full length of the tunnel must be supported with circular rings. One means of doing this employs a shield, a steel cylinder slightly larger than the support rings that are to be installed. Imagine a tin can with its ends removed that is pushed forward by jacks. As the cutting edge of the shield moves ahead, the jacks are removed and the support rings are built and installed. The muck is pushed ahead of the cutting edge or squeezed inside the shield, where it is then scooped up and removed.

If water is a problem—and it often is—a bulkhead is built just inside the edge of the shield. Air is forced in to balance the pressure of the water. Workmen enter and leave through an air lock, and muck is removed through a muck lock. Because people cannot work when the air pressure is great, tunnels built under air pressure are seldom more than 110 feet deep.

Trench-type tunneling.

Trench-type construction often is used to avoid the difficulties of building an underwater tunnel under air pressure. In this method, a trench is dredged in the bottom of the river, lake, or sea to be tunneled. Steel or concrete sections of the tunnel then are lowered into the trench, where they are joined together by divers. The linked segments are covered with fill, and the inside of the tunnel is pumped dry.

Tunnels are given an inner, or secondary, lining of reinforced concrete, which is poured over removable steel forms and allowed to set. The lining enables a greater volume of flow through water-supply tunnels. In automobile tunnels, it is needed for appearance and for safety. In all tunnels it helps the outer, or primary, lining resist the pressures exerted by the rock surrounding the tunnel.

Two large-scale tunneling efforts are attracting worldwide attention. One is the world's longest railroad tunnel, the 33-mile Seikan undersea rock tunnel between Honshu and Hokkaido in Japan. The other is the 31-mile twin-tube railroad tunnel that is planned to go beneath the English Channel to link France and England. The Chunnel, as it is called, has not been completely designed but it is scheduled for completion in 1993.

Modern underground chambers.

For decades, planners have sought to expand the use of tunnels to include such facilities as public transit, parking, utilities, water- and sewage-treatment plants, water storage sites, warehouses, and even light industry. Until recently, however, the cost of tunneling and underground construction has been prohibitive.

Now the economics are improving

NOTABLE TUNNELS

Seikan *(Japan, railroad)*	33.5 miles
Dai-shimizu *(Japan, railroad)*	13.0
Simplon *(Italy-Switz., railroad)*	12.3
Kanmon *(Japan, railroad)*	11.0
Apennine *(Italy, railroad)*	11.0
St. Gotthard *(Switz., vehicular)*	10.2
St. Gotthard *(Switz., railroad)*	9.3
Lötschberg *(Switz., railroad)*	9.1
Mont Cénis *(France, railroad)*	8.5
Cascade *(U.S., railroad)*	7.8

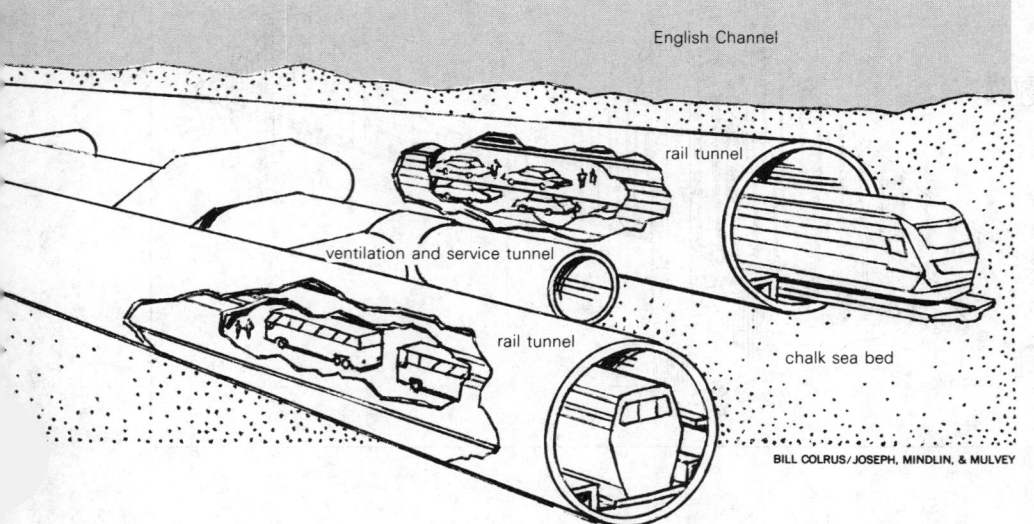

THE CHUNNEL, *a 31-mile-long tunnel under the English Channel between Dover and Calais, was approved for construction in 1986. Car-carrying shuttle, passenger, and freight trains will use the Chunnel.*

English Channel

rail tunnel

ventilation and service tunnel

rail tunnel

chalk sea bed

BILL COLRUS/JOSEPH, MINDLIN, & MULVEY

as underground construction costs are being reduced, especially in comparison with above-ground construction costs and as competition for scarce surface land increases.

Planners are working on potential underground interurban rapid transit systems, possibly stretching from Boston to Washington, D.C.; on underground shopping malls, such as the one in Montreal; on additional underground hydroelectric plants; and on the use of mined-out space such as that near Kansas City, Missouri. There, old limestone quarries have been turned into laboratories, cold storage sites for food, and other facilities that require careful control of temperature and humidity.

Such novel uses of underground areas are becoming more feasible because of improvements in the technology of many aspects of underground construction. Better ways of studying the kinds of rock, soil, and water at specific sites have been developed. So have more effective and efficient rock cutters, some of which involve the use of lasers. Faster ways of removing and disposing of muck exist now, as do better methods of protecting underground chambers against water seepage and collapse.

Roads

The technology of road and highway construction has developed rapidly and spectacularly. Giant, efficient machines have increased capacity per unit. Automation has reduced the number of workers needed. Aerial photographs linked to computers speed the work of siting and designing the roadway.

The basic steps involved in building roads and highways remain the same.

Once an exact route has been determined, bulldozers remove all vegetation from the area. Bridges, culverts, overpasses, and tunnels are built. If necessary, earth-moving machines move rocks and soil from sections that have been cut out of hills to sections in which valleys must be filled in. The materials are layered and compacted by giant rollers, and drainage is devised to maintain the correct amount of moisture.

Control of water is of prime concern in constructing roads and highways. Drains must be adequate to carry streams under the roadway and to remove rain. Roads and highways are built with crowns, slight elevations in the middle, and sloping shoulders to ensure that water runs off to the sides. There it collects in ditches, designed today with flat side slopes to reduce injury and damage to vehicles. The ditches are linked together in a system of storm drains.

Water that rises into the roadbed through capillary action and is imprisoned by surface tension cannot be drained and may cause serious problems. To protect the roadbed, thick layers of waterproof road surfaces are used, and care is taken to ensure that the base and subbase drain well. Sometimes the water table must be lowered by installing underground pipes.

Flexible pavements. Roadway pavement is either flexible or rigid. In a flexible pavement, the surface layer consists of sand and gravel or of crushed stone mixed with a tarry material such as asphalt. In dry areas where traffic is not heavy, a method called surface treatment is used. First the base of the roadway is spread with a thin layer of asphalt to fill in small cracks. On top of this is laid one or more layers of harder asphalt, topped

with gravel or stone chips.

Another kind of flexible road surface is macadam. In macadam construction, a layer of gravel or uniform crushed stone between 1 and 3 inches is placed directly on the base. Heavy rollers then compact the stone layer, which is sprayed or sprinkled with any one of a number of substances, including heated asphalt or tar, to hold it in place.

Some flexible pavements are plant mixes. In this method, stone or gravel of various sizes, from particles the size of dust to pieces the size of walnuts, is dried and heated to 300° to 400°F in a central plant. While the stone or gravel is still hot, it is mixed with a carefully measured amount of tar or asphalt cement. The macadam mix then is trucked to the roadbed, spread out, and rolled before it cools. Such pavement offers a smooth ride and is strong and waterproof enough to carry a large volume of traffic even in extreme climates.

Rigid pavements. Rigid pavements consist of a surface layer of Portland cement concrete, 6 to 12 inches thick, placed directly on a subbase of compacted gravel. One problem with rigid pavements is that concrete tends to shrink when it is cold and to expand when it is hot, creating cracks. Cracks are controlled by form joints and by leaving space for expansion and contraction.

Another problem with cement pavement is the difficulty of joining one section smoothly with another. This problem is solved by embedding a continuous layer of steel bars in the cement. The steel holds the concrete tightly together, so that cracks cannot open up and let water pass through.

—*Sarah K. Myers*

Energy

This article surveys the use of energy technology in the industrialized world, especially in the United States. Energy technology in the modern world must take into consideration efficiency, the environment, and economy. Aware of such considerations, engineers and planners are developing energy systems that are in keeping with the needs of the biosphere.

A petroleum-based civilization. For more than a hundred years, petroleum and its by-products have fueled the industrialized world. The so-called energy crisis of the 1970's was really an oil crisis: supply of available petroleum declined

while prices skyrocketed. When the Organization of Petroleum Exporting Countries (OPEC) cartel began to limit production, gasoline prices in the United States rose from about 30 cents a gallon to more than a dollar. Home heating bills also increased rapidly, causing much hardship.

The energy crisis led engineers and others to take a hard look at the rate at which the industrialized world was gobbling up resources that nature had taken millions of years to produce. Coal, petroleum, and natural gas are called nonrenewable fuels because once extracted from the earth and burned, they cannot be replenished for millions of years. Alternative fuels, such as solar and wind energy, are

termed renewable because they exist in seemingly unlimited abundance and are not depleted by daily use.

Black diamonds. Coal generally contains carbon, hydrogen, oxygen, and nitrogen, plus other elements. In its purest form (that is, when it is closest to pure carbon or anthracite, or is hard), coal is found in abundance in the deep coal mines of eastern Pennsylvania. Soft or bituminous, coal is generally found in western Pennsylvania, West Virginia, and Kentucky. It has a carbon content of about 80 to 90 percent. Bituminous coal is especially suitable for use in blast furnaces and power plants. In recent years, extraction of eastern coal has declined considerably in favor of coal reserves in the western states, which are generally surface mined.

It was just 100 years ago that coal surpassed wood as the dominant American fuel. In that era, nearly half the coal mined in the United States was used as fuel for steam locomotives and to make coke for the steel industry. (Coke is the solid left after coal gas and coal tar have been extracted from coal.) The remainder was used for other industries and for decentralized home heating.

Industrial processes over the past 20 years have used energy more efficiently and in different forms. For example, the steel industry began to phase out the old open-hearth steel furnaces. Such innovations cut in half the amount of energy needed to make a ton of steel.

Environmental considerations, both in mining and combustion, have made coal a less popular fuel since World War II, though it continues to be a major fuel for many electric power plants. Critics claim that coal-burning plants have added significantly to atmospheric pollution, especially to the acid rain problem that has been affecting lakes and forests throughout Canada and the northern United States. In recent years, engineers have proposed new technologies for cleaning up coal emissions and for using the vast coal reserves of the United States to produce liquefied petroleum products as well as synthetic gas.

Uses of coal. After the energy crisis of the 1970's, the United States sponsored new approaches to the use of coal as a replacement for the much scarcer oil and gas. One of these was the Cool Water Coal Gasification Project in Daggett, California. The Cool Water plant is a demonstration power plant that each day converts 1000 tons of low-grade, subbituminous coal into more than 100 megawatts of electricity. An oil-fired power plant of the same size would use 4300 barrels of oil in a day. The efficiency at Cool Water comes from the manufacture of synthesis gas, a more energetic form of coal gas that is used as fuel for the plant.

Not only does Cool Water replace oil with subbituminous coal, but it does so with a significant reduction in air pollution. The gasification process permits removal of 95 percent of the sulfur dioxide, the principal offender in coal-caused air pollution. To achieve that kind of reduction in sulfur with scrubbers attached to the chimneys of a regular coal-fired power plant would reduce the power production of the plant by about 10 percent. At Cool Water, the sulfur is taken out without loss of power. The Cool Water demonstration achieved its purpose. A year after it opened, at least a dozen electric

utilities were planning larger power plants based on the same design.

Coal gasification, however, may not turn out to be the most popular new way to get energy from coal without air pollution. About 65 years ago, the concept of a fluidized bed was developed. The idea is to create a dry fluid that consists of solid particles and air. This is done by pumping compressed air into a bed of sand. If the air is pumped fast enough, the sand is lifted from its bed and becomes a fluid, but it is a fluid filled with air in which anything can burn. If the bed of sand is hot enough, anything introduced to it will burn, completely and with maximum energy production.

Specifically, coal can be introduced into the fluid. Along with the coal, powdered limestone can be injected. The limestone effectively removes the sulfur from the coal so that the smoke from the coal is relatively free of pollution. Three major utility companies are turning to the fluidized bed system instead of coal gasification. Their plants, scheduled for operation in the late 1980's, will either prove or disprove the theoretical advantages of fluidized beds.

In the meantime, it is increasingly unlikely that electric power plants will be built in the future to consume coal in the manner of the past—in an ordinary fire.

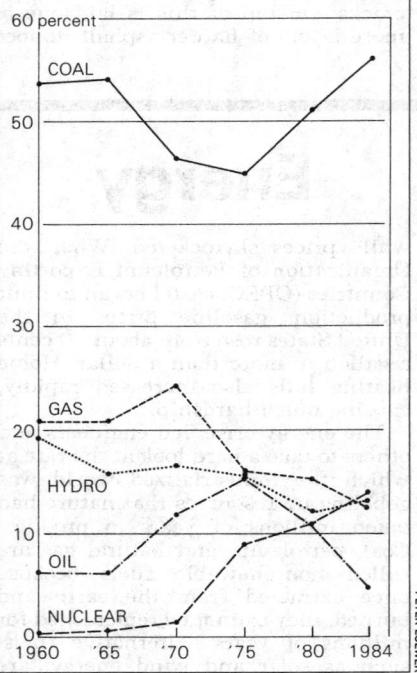

U.S. ELECTRICITY PRODUCTION BY ENERGY SOURCE, 1960–1984

Coal is by far the most important energy source for electricity production in the United States. Oil has declined sharply as a source since the energy problems of the 1970's. Nuclear power has increased.

PETER LOEWER

Power from Atomic Processes

Since the early 1950's, one of the alternatives to coal, oil, and gas has been nuclear, or fission, power, often called atomic power. Certain radioactive substances, when assembled in bulk, create a self-perpetuating reaction, just as a match touched to paper creates a self-perpetuating fire. When the process occurs as a result of radioactive decay, it is called a *chain reaction.*

In a chain reaction, neutrons from the regular decay of uranium bump into other atoms of uranium and speed up the decay process. Each atom that decays produces more neutrons, so the number of atoms decaying increases with lightning speed. To produce nuclear power, the chain reaction is controlled by slowing down the neutrons.

Like fire, a chain reaction produces heat. Unlike fire, it can do so without releasing chemicals into the air. When the heat from a chain reaction is used to produce steam that is used to produce electricity, the central heat-producing source is called a nuclear reactor. The entire complex is called a nuclear power plant.

Nuclear power is nonpolluting. Although it does not use fossil fuels, most nuclear power does use uranium as fuel. Not much fuel is needed for the chain reaction, so the rarity of uranium is only a minor cause for concern. The major causes for concern are unrelated to the problems of fossil fuels.

While nuclear power normally does not create air pollution, it produces solid and liquid waste that is radioactive. It is not clear that such waste can be disposed of safely. Nuclear waste in the Soviet Union is known to have started its own chain reaction and exploded, although such an explosion might have been avoided with better planning. The United States is planning to bury its waste deep underground. Warnings will need to be left at the burial sites that will be readable for thousands of years, since the waste will be dangerous for that many years.

Some nuclear power plants have had accidents that have killed people, although not as many people as in other types of industrial accidents. The worst nuclear accident in the United States, at the Three Mile Island power plant near Harrisburg, Pennsylvania, killed no one. The worst nuclear accident ever, the Chernobyl explosion in the Soviet Union in 1986, killed dozens of people, but it may have affected many more in ways that will not be known for years. There is concern that a nuclear power plant in a densely populated region will explode and release even more radioactivity than at Chernobyl.

Furthermore, the radioactivity from a nuclear accident does not go away

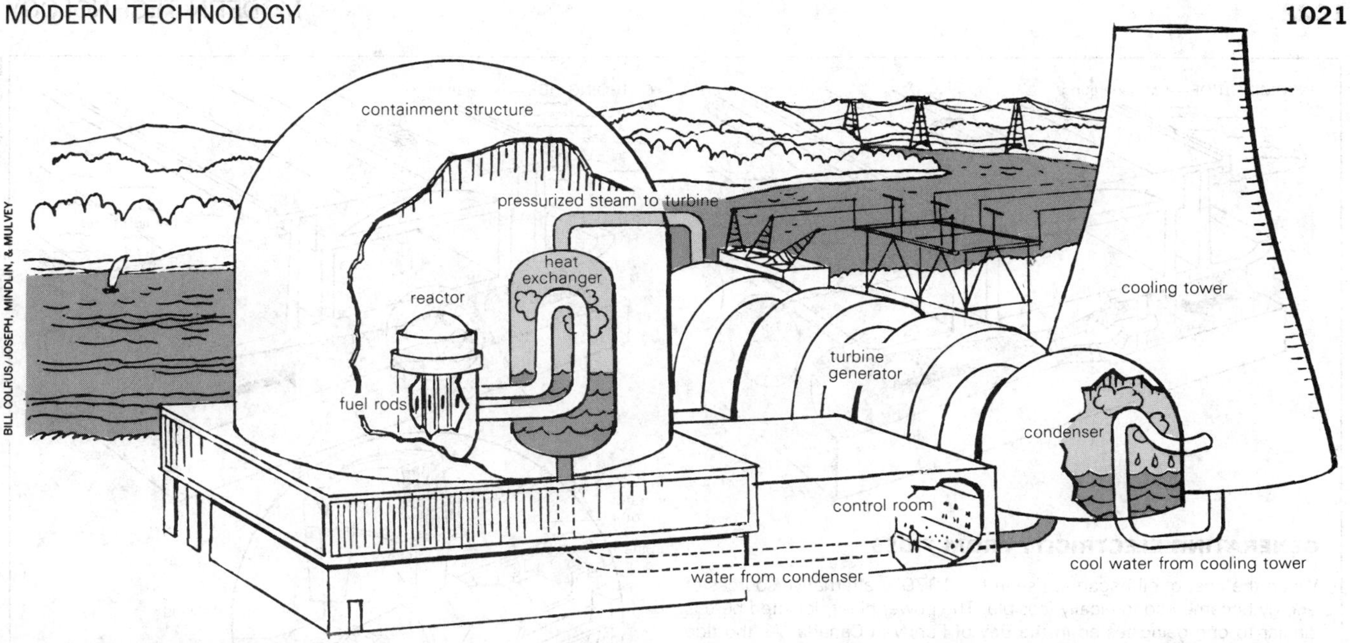

THE NUCLEAR POWER STATION *shown here is typical of a pressurized water reactor. It has three separate water systems. Water used to cool the reactor passes through a heat exchanger, where water in the second system is changed into steam. This steam drives a turbine and then is changed back into water in a condenser that is cooled by water from a nearby water source.*

quickly. It is doubtful that the ruins of the Three Mile Island and Chernobyl reactors will be visited by people without protective clothing for hundreds of years.

Fusion power.   One consequence of nuclear accidents is that many people are looking for different energy sources. One is fusion power, the power source of the sun and other stars. Fusion does not depend on a chain reaction. Power comes from putting atoms together so closely in a place with such high energy that they begin to fuse; that is, to merge with each other. Such merging can produce an explosion, for each merging releases energy. In fact, fusion power is the basis of the hydrogen bomb, known as a thermonuclear weapon. But in the hydrogen bomb, the high energy needed to start fusion is supplied by a chain reaction. Unlike a chain reaction, a thermonuclear, or fusion, reaction cannot sustain itself without help.

If a fusion plant that produces electric power is ever built, it is unlikely that the plant will blow up as a result of a fusion reaction. In the sun and stars, fusion reactions occur because of the immense gravity of such large bodies; on Earth, gravity is not nearly strong enough to start or sustain a fusion reaction.

Fusion also has other advantages over fission. Fusion uses hydrogen, two atoms of which are found in every molecule of water in the ocean. It is true that the most effective form of fusion uses a rare form of hydrogen, called deuterium or heavy hydrogen, combined with an artificial radioactive hydrogen, called tritium. In principle, however, any form of hydrogen

could be used. The products of a fission plant include high-level radioactive substances, but the radioactivity of fusion byproducts is very low.

Fusion power has yet to become a reality. A fission reaction begins when enough of the right material is put together. A fusion reaction begins only when the material is so hot that it will destroy any solid substance, and a great deal of it must be put in a very small place. No one has yet conceived of a way to do this all at once.

The most nearly successful efforts contain deuterium or deuterium mixed with tritium in a so-called magnetic bottle. The heat and pressure are so great that an ordinary container would melt, but powerful magnetic fields can be used to hold and squeeze the ionized gases. Another approach uses laser beams to squeeze the fuel. While a reaction that produces more power than it takes to start it has not yet been achieved, scientists are getting closer to a solution. Commercial production of fusion power may become a reality in the early 21st century.

Water Power

In the past century, falling water has been harnessed to turn the massive turbines in hydroelectric plants. In many parts of the United States, notably the Pacific Northwest and the Tennessee Valley, water power is the major source of electricity.

New techniques.   Since the energy crisis of the 1970's, more impetus has been given to new approaches to using water power, tapping the energy of ocean waves or temperature differ-

entials between warm and cool layers of water. In addition, as previously mentioned, efforts have been made to extract hydrogen from the water molecule to fuel power plants.

Modern waterwheel technology employs pipes and nozzles to release concentrated streams of water to the wheel. This same principle is used for massive hydroelectric plants as well. In addition, more efficient turbines have been developed for hydroelectric plants, such as the Pelton wheel, the Francis turbine, and the Deriaz turbine. Turbines are classified as either impulse or reaction. Impulse turbines reverse the direction in which the water is flowing. Reaction turbines have blades that move at the same rate as the water.

Hydroelectric engineers must calculate supply and demand carefully to take maximum advantage of water availability. For example, during dry seasons, water is released from storage reservoirs where it has accumulated during rainy weather. In addition, the design and siting of hydroelectric plants take into consideration flood control, ecological balance, and the potential of using water reserves for other purposes, such as irrigation or human or industrial consumption.

Using the tides.   The past decade has witnessed the revival of proposals to harness the tides of the oceans or river estuaries as sources of power. Since the 1960's, a sizable tidal-power installation has been operating in the estuary of the Rance River near Saint-Malo, France. A large seawall built across the estuary contains reversible turbines that produce about 350 megawatts of power as the tide rises and as it recedes. Another large

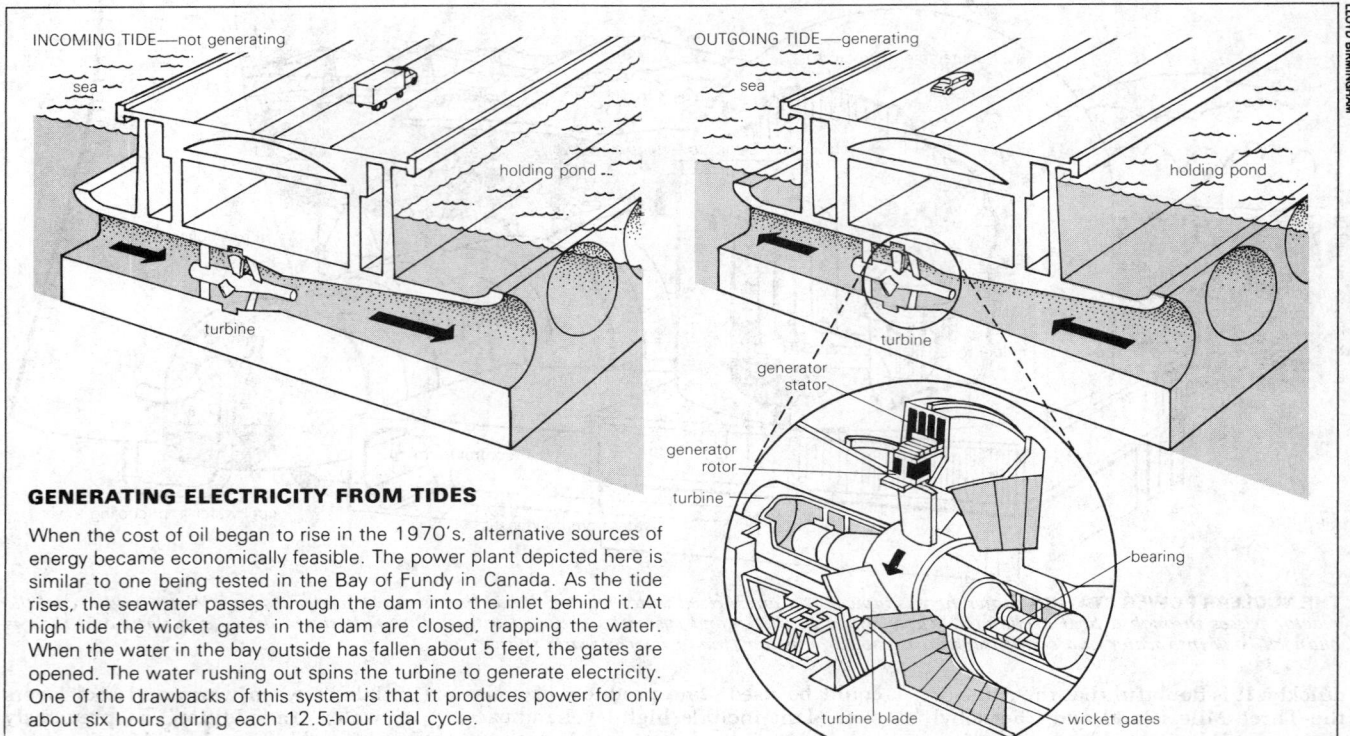

LLOYD BIRMINGHAM

INCOMING TIDE—not generating

sea

holding pond

turbine

OUTGOING TIDE—generating

sea

holding pond

turbine

generator stator

generator rotor

turbine

bearing

turbine blade

wicket gates

GENERATING ELECTRICITY FROM TIDES

When the cost of oil began to rise in the 1970's, alternative sources of energy became economically feasible. The power plant depicted here is similar to one being tested in the Bay of Fundy in Canada. As the tide rises, the seawater passes through the dam into the inlet behind it. At high tide the wicket gates in the dam are closed, trapping the water. When the water in the bay outside has fallen about 5 feet, the gates are opened. The water rushing out spins the turbine to generate electricity. One of the drawbacks of this system is that it produces power for only about six hours during each 12.5-hour tidal cycle.

plant of this type has been operating in the Soviet Union for nearly 20 years.

Canadian and American engineers would like to build a wave-energy plant in the Bay of Fundy off Nova Scotia, or in Passamaquoddy Bay, between Maine and New Brunswick. A bilateral commission in the 1950's recommended construction of a number of tidal plants in this region, estimating that nearly 3 billion kilowatt-hours of electricity could be generated each year. At the time, the idea did not engender much enthusiasm because power was relatively abundant and cheap.

Temperature gradients. Another revolutionary scheme for using ocean power is the thermal energy, or temperature-gradient, concept. In the oceans, cool dense water tends to sink beneath currents of warm, thin water. Experiments in the early part of the century proved it was possible to extract energy from that temperature differential. The French scientist Georges Claude successfully demonstrated the technique in the 1920's at Matanzas, Cuba, where he produced electricity by drawing cold water up through a pipe more than a mile beneath the surface of the water. The amount of power produced was negligible, and the idea was dismissed in an era of cheap and abundant power.

In recent years, researchers have proposed a 100-megawatt floating barge that would use ammonia as the working fluid; ammonia has greater

efficiency at the small temperature differential of seawater. The barge would be anchored offshore and make use of boilers 300 feet below the surface. Scientists also have proposed using the plant to mine previously inaccessible minerals from the sea, and have suggested that the plant would provide fishing opportunities by creating a nutrient-rich environment around it.

In the 1970's, a researcher developed plans for an ocean-thermal plant, supplemented by offshore wind generators, that would be located in the Gulf Stream off the coast of Florida. The 400-megawatt plant would separate seawater into hydrogen and oxygen for use as fuel.

Although little in the way of practical work has been done in building plants on these criteria, many researchers believe that the era of exploitable ocean energy will open the way to cheap and abundant power by the 21st century.

Wind Power

Throughout history, wind power has been used primarily for mechanical purposes, such as grinding grain, pumping water, or running sawmills. Dutch and English mills, for example, drove huge grooved millstones that turned grain into flour with a minimum of muscle power. The American pinwheel device helped pump water for crop irrigation and cattle feeding. Later, in the days before rural electrification, farmers were able to produce

small amounts of power through the use of power turbines.

New and more efficient turbines have been developed in recent years; they use lightweight materials and airfoil shapes. The federal government financed several large demonstration projects and erected so-called megawind plants in New Mexico, Ohio, and North Carolina.

While the familiar two- or three-bladed horizontal-axis rotors continue to be in vogue, a number of innovative vertical-axis designs have been developed. The Savonius rotor looks like a drum cut in half and placed off center on a vertical axis. It catches wind in "buckets," transferring rotary motion

THE VERTICAL AXIS WIND TURBINE *is one of several new types of windmills designed to harness the power of the wind efficiently.*

through gears to an alternator. The Darrieus rotor, or eggbeater wind generator, is constructed of thin ribbons of metal or fiberglass to minimize weight and drag.

Siting problems. While wind plants offer practically no environmental pollution, they have a major disadvantage in terms of site selection. Wind power is capricious. While many areas of the country guarantee fairly steady winds, it is not always possible to match supply with demand. Smaller generators always have made use of storage batteries to store wind-produced electricity for use in periods of high demand. In general, wind plants must be placed to take advantage of prevailing winds, usually far from urban areas, where demand is greatest.

In recent years, wind farms have been developed, notably in the western portion of the United States. Hundreds of small windmills are sited over several hundred acres to generate a total of several megawatts of electric power.

Some experts project that wind power will decline in cost per kilowatt as more efficient devices are mass produced. However, few believe that wind will provide more than 2 or 3 percent of the nation's total energy needs by the year 2000, quite a drop from the mid-19th century, when wind power provided more than 10 percent of the nation's power.

Solar Power

The sun is the ultimate source of all energy, whether in the form of direct sunlight or of coal, petroleum, or wind power. By promoting photosynthesis, the sun creates organic reactions in vegetable matter that sustain life on Earth. Since petroleum and coal are composed of decayed animal and vegetable matter under pressure, these fossil fuels can be termed stored solar energy. The sun produces winds by heating air currents, so wind energy is also a form of solar energy.

For practical purposes, however, solar energy refers to a more direct and immediate phenomenon: the use of the sun's rays for heating buildings, for generating steam for electricity, or for producing electricity directly from photovoltaic cells.

Trillions of kilowatts bombard Earth from the sun, but only a fraction are used directly in space heating or electrical applications. It is estimated that each square yard of Earth daily receives an average of 1000 watts of solar energy.

Practical applications. Building construction uses solar energy in two forms: passive and active. Passive

THIS ARRAY OF SOLAR REFLECTORS *focuses the sun's rays on a boiler on top of the tower in the center of the array. Steam produced in the boiler drives a turbine to produce electricity.*

solar heating refers to heating in buildings designed and situated to take full advantage of the sun's rays. For example, a building with windows on the south and heavy insulation on the north, together with heat-sink materials like slate or eutectic salts beneath the south-facing windows, is an example of good passive solar construction. An active solar system, which can be designed into a building or retrofitted to an existing building, employs an array of pumps, ducts, and rooftop solar collectors to heat water or air for circulation in a building's heat-distribution system.

Innovative applications. Backyard inventors have fabricated collector panels out of everything from black-painted troughs to arrays of aluminum cans. The most efficient collectors are usually manufactured from copper or aluminum tubing sealed under glass or plexiglass panels. Other materials have been tried, such as rubber tubing, which permits the home owner to expand the collector area or to repair damaged sections quickly.

Many solar collectors are used successfully in both northern and southern climates for heating water or space. It is not so much the temperature of the air as the intensity and duration of sunlight that make the difference. Thus, solar power can be a good source of energy even in northern New England or the Pacific Northwest. Frequently, home solar systems are used as supplements or preheaters for existing hot-water or space-heating plants, thereby reducing the load on conventional gas, oil, or electric systems. A typical installation feeds water at 80 or 90 degrees to the boiler, where it is raised to 140 degrees.

Typical flat-plate collectors circulate water or air to an insulated storage tank for use when needed. For a water-heating system, a 35-gallon tank encased in fiberglass insulation is effective. Air-storage systems sometimes are large bins filled with rocks that re-

tain heat for circulation through a house at night or when the sun is not shining.

Innovative architects have developed solar homes that use unconventional techniques to capture and circulate solar energy. The Hay solar roof concept includes a large plastic bag of water on a steel ceiling. During the day, the water absorbs the sun's rays. At night or during cloudy weather, the water is covered by sliding insulated panels to trap the heat and distribute it through the house. Other systems use glass or fiberglass walls covered or filled with insulation as required. Despite the claims of efficiency, most home builders have not incorporated these devices, preferring to use retrofit collectors.

Recent advances in solar collector technology promise to produce electricity directly from the photovoltaic effect of sunlight on certain crystal materials. In the 1950's, the first silicon solar cells were produced by Bell Laboratories. Over the past 20 years, engineers have attempted to make more efficient cells to reduce costs. The use of cadmium sulfide and gallium arsenide has brought down the cost per kilowatt substantially, though direct solar conversion to electricity is still not cost competitive with conventional energy technologies. Recently, the Solar Energy Research Institute announced a major effort to improve solar cell technology through the use of amorphous silicon, which will make solar cells thinner, cheaper, and easier to manufacture.

In recent years, solar experts have been experimenting with the concept of the solar power tower to produce electricity on a large scale. Such a system, ideal for remote desert areas, focuses hundreds or thousands of rotating mirrors on a tall tower with solar cells or a water tank. In the world's largest such system, SEGS I near Daggett, California, the mirrors focused on the water tank turn the water into steam that drives the turbines in an otherwise conventional plant.

Energy from Earth

Miners learned long ago that Earth's interior is hot. Depending on the type of rock beneath the surface, the temperature can rise 36° to 85°F for each kilometer of penetration through Earth's crust. The deepest mine of any kind on Earth is more than 3 kilometers deep, and the temperature at the bottom is more than 123.8°F. This heat is produced in large part by the decay of radioactive elements in rock.

Some places are hotter than others. These are places where molten rock from deep in Earth has moved up near the surface. In such places, it has been common for years to use this energy for heating homes or producing electricity. This *geothermal energy* is most common in Iceland, where there are many volcanoes.

Although some places are hotter than others, every place is hot if one drills deep enough. Thus, geothermal energy could be used anywhere. Geothermal power is completely clean. It is also virtually inexhaustible, since there is much more heat in Earth's interior than could be siphoned off in producing all the world's power.

On June 21, 1985, this idea was tested by a commercial power producer. An experimental geothermal power plant was started up in California's Imperial Valley, a region that is not volcanic. The plant is essentially a heat exchanger. A cool brine is pumped down a well to depths of about 2.5 kilometers. The hot rock raises the temperature of the brine to about 400°F. The well has a loop at the bottom that brings the brine back up to the surface, where it is used as the energy source for a generator. The plant generates 70 megawatts of power, about enough for 350,000 households.

Other experimental plants use technology that is cheaper but less efficient. Scientists from Los Alamos National Laboratory tried this technology on a small scale in the mid-1970's and on a larger one in 1986. They pumped water into the natural cracks in hot, previously dry rock. The water was heated enough to produce about 4 megawatts of electricity. After demonstrating that the method would work, the scientists turned the system off without actually producing electric power. They plan further tests.

Although the Imperial Valley plant has shown that the concept works, it is not clear how practical it is. For example, while the overall heat of Earth is practically inexhaustible, that might not be true at a given spot. If the Imperial Valley geothermal plant extracts heat equivalent to 30,000 megawatts of power over the next 30 years, will the rocks where the well is built still be hot? No one knows for sure.

Hydrogen Power

In all the energy systems discussed so far, except for the system using photovoltaic cells for some forms of solar power, the actual electricity is made from steam-powered turbines turning a generator. An energy producer called the *fuel cell* can make electricity directly. This is important because steam turbines produce only about 30 percent of the energy that is fed into them. A fuel cell, on the other hand, can make energy with an efficiency of 40 to 80 percent.

The concept of a fuel cell was developed in 1839, even before the rechargeable storage battery. When hydrogen and oxygen are in the presence of an appropriate chemical, they combine to form water. In the process, electrons that can be directly siphoned off are released. As long as enough hydrogen and oxygen are available, the fuel cell will keep producing power. The difficulty has been in making practical cells that stand up to continuous power production. Not until the 1950's were fuel cells made that were more than laboratory curiosities. Fuel cells were then used in U.S. space programs as clean sources of power, with drinking water as a byproduct.

Commercial fuel cells have been tested but they are not yet available for purchase. The two largest tests were in New York City and Tokyo in the mid-1980's. They employed a process that used natural gas as a source of hydrogen, and air as a source of oxygen. The natural gas first was converted to hydrogen and carbon dioxide, so these fuel cells had carbon dioxide as a byproduct as well as water. Concern about the contribution of carbon dioxide to so-called greenhouse warming may limit the application of this process in the future. Two companies are planning to introduce fuel cells for electric power production in the 1990's. Each fuel cell would generate from 7.5 to 11 megawatts of energy, but they could be treated as modules to produce additional electricity.

Although these fuel cells run on natural gas, it would be simple to convert the process to run on coal gas. In that case, there would be unwanted carbon dioxide as an additional byproduct.

Ideally, it would be useful to have a pure source of hydrogen to run fuel cells. Such a source may be on the way. Elias Greenbaum, a scientist at Oak Ridge National Laboratory, announced in 1985 that he had succeeded in making hydrogen by photosynthesis, the process that plants use to make starches and sugars. Greenbaum mixed chloroplasts, the plant parts in which photosynthesis takes place, with ultrafine particles of platinum. When exposed to sunlight, the combination split water into hydrogen and oxygen. Although a long way from realization, this experiment suggests a fuel cell in which the ultimate source of energy is the sun.

Hydrogen would be useful in other ways. Although the main concern has been production of electric power, over half the oil used in the United States is not involved with the production of electricity. Although various new storage batteries offer some hope for electric automobiles and trucks, at present they are not practical. What might be practical is an engine that burns hydrogen. Cars with such an engine have been built, but the costs so far have been prohibitive. If a cheap source of hydrogen were available, the situation might change. One advantage of hydrogen as a fuel is that its combustion with oxygen produces only water as a byproduct, so such an engine would be totally nonpolluting.

Interest in these new energy sources rises when oil becomes scarce and falls when oil is plentiful. Ultimately, however, oil is a finite resource. It is used up completely when burned. Furthermore, oil is the basis for the vast petrochemical industry. At some point it will become important to society to keep the remaining oil as a base for other chemicals and to turn to other energy sources. Technology is capable of doing so whenever the economic motivation arises.

—Bryan H. Bunch and Edward Moran

GEOTHERMAL ENERGY *is another source of electricity with possibilities that are only just beginning to be explored at plants like this one in California.*

Transport

Before the invention of the wheel and axle, in Sumer about 3000 B.C., land transport was limited to walking, riding animals, and using humans and animals as beasts of burden to carry loads or pull them along on wooden skids. The wheel and axle made land transport easier but still left it dependent on muscle power. During the late 18th and early 19th centuries, windmills and sails were tried as a means of propulsion, with limited success.

From earliest times, water transport was easier than land transport. The first ships were crude river barges that traveled downstream with the help of river currents. Traveling upstream was hard work, however, requiring human rowers or polers or human and animal pullers to move the craft along. It was not until 3000 B.C. that the sail was invented by Egyptians. For many centuries thereafter, wind power together with human muscle power for rowing were the only means of propelling ships.

With the relatively recent development of the turbine, steam engine, and internal combustion engine it became possible to power land and water transport by burning fuel.

fueled by coal, oil, or nuclear power produce approximately 80 percent of the electricity in the United States. Turbines in jet engines, whose exhausts are directed at the blades of multistage turbines, use the energy produced by the combustion of jet fuel. The spinning turbine blades channel gases from the combusted fuel through a cylindrical metal housing the length of the engine to produce the thrust necessary for propulsion.

Steam engines. At the heart of a steam engine is the boiler. Its function is to contain the pressure created as water is boiled into steam, increasing in volume. The first boilers often exploded from the nearly two-thousandfold increase in volume. But even a strong-walled boiler was of little use alone. Steam energy had to be harnessed to power machinery.

Thomas Savery, an English military engineer, invented the Miner's Friend in 1698 to pump water from mine shafts. Steam from a boiler rushed into a long, oval tank that was sprayed with cold water released by a valve. The condensing steam created a partial vacuum in the tank. Water from

the mine shaft rushed into the tank and was then released by opening an outlet valve. The Miner's Friend was unable to pump water from shafts more than 25 feet deep. In a confined and narrow mine shaft, the pump was dangerous because it was fire-powered.

In 1712 Thomas Newcomen of England invented a steam-powered pump containing a cylinder and piston mechanism. By heating the cylinder with steam, then cooling it with a spray of cold water, the piston was kept moving by the alternation of steam pressure and vacuum. Although Newcomen's pump was an improvement on the Miner's Friend, it required huge amounts of coal to operate.

James Watt invented the condensing steam engine in 1765. By channeling the steam into a separate condensing chamber, Watt was able to eliminate much heat loss, making the engine more efficient by burning less fuel. By the 1780's, Watt's steam-condensing engine had been improved to the point where it used one-third less coal to do the same work as Newcomen's engine.

With a sun-and-plant gear system, which Watt had devised, the up and

Types of Engines

Turbines. The turbine, a machine that spins, can be the power plant that runs a lumber mill, generates electricity for transmission, or powers a jet engine. The Greek inventor Hero of Alexandria is credited with having built the first simple steam turbine, the *aeolipile*, nearly 2000 years ago. It was a hollow copper globe with two angled nozzles. The globe was filled with water and suspended over a fire. As the water boiled into steam, it expanded and was forced out through the nozzles, causing the globe to spin.

Examples of early turbines include the waterwheel and windmill with their paddles or vanes angled to intercept the flow of water or air currents. For centuries, these simple turbines have provided power for grinding grain, pumping water, and running mills.

In the late 1890's, the hydropower of Niagara Falls turned the blades of turbogenerators to produce electricity for transmission to sites many miles away. In the same era a Swedish engineer, C.G.P. de Laval, developed the first modern steam turbine. Today's large steam turbines generally have more than 20 wheels, each with hundreds of blades, to generate more than 30,000 horsepower. Steam turbines

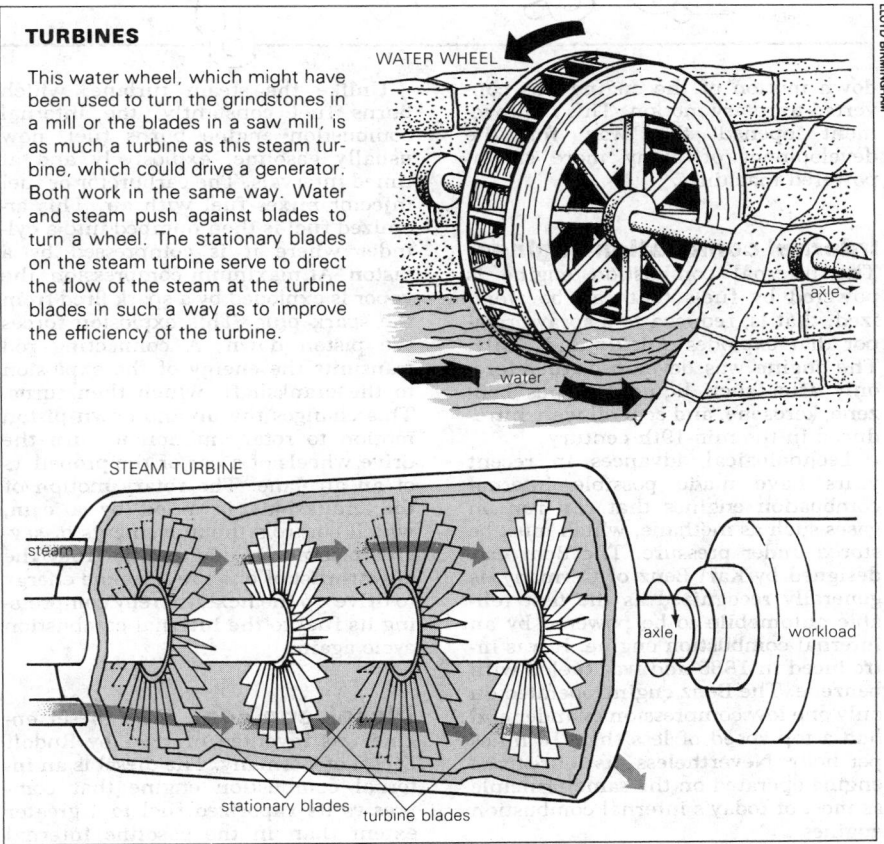

TURBINES

This water wheel, which might have been used to turn the grindstones in a mill or the blades in a saw mill, is as much a turbine as this steam turbine, which could drive a generator. Both work in the same way. Water and steam push against blades to turn a wheel. The stationary blades on the steam turbine serve to direct the flow of the steam at the turbine blades in such a way as to improve the efficiency of the turbine.

WATER WHEEL

axle

water

LLOYD BIRMINGHAM

STEAM TURBINE

steam

axle   workload

stationary blades   turbine blades

STEAM ENGINE

The steam locomotive uses the principle of expansion of heated water to achieve motion: when a volume of water is heated to its boiling point, a greater volume of steam is produced. The water in the locomotive is heated in a boiler through which run pipes containing the hot exhaust gases from a coal fire. A great deal of pressure is created by the steam in the boiler. This pressurized steam is led to each side of a piston alternately, where the steam expands, driving the piston back and forth, to turn the wheels of the locomotive.

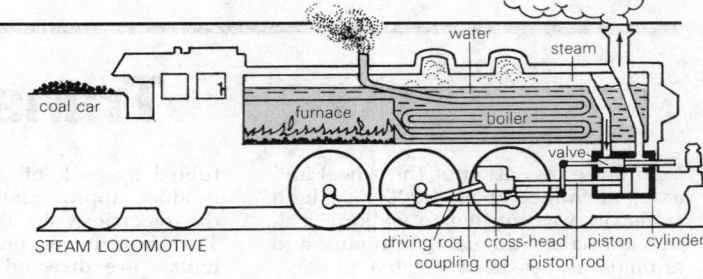

STEAM LOCOMOTIVE

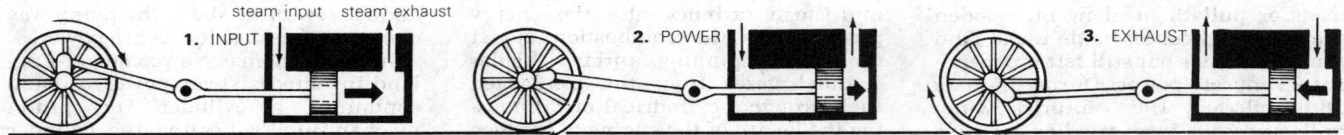

1. INPUT   steam input   steam exhaust   2. POWER   3. EXHAUST

FOUR-STROKE INTERNAL COMBUSTION ENGINE

During the intake stroke, the piston moves down, allowing fuel-air vapor from the carburetor to enter the cylinder. The compression stroke is caused by the piston being forced back up by the turning of the crankshaft. When the fuel is compressed, it is ignited by the spark plug. This is the power stroke. In the typical automobile engine, the opening and closing of the valves is controlled by the rotation of a camshaft. The up and down movement of the piston is transformed into rotary motion by the crankshaft.

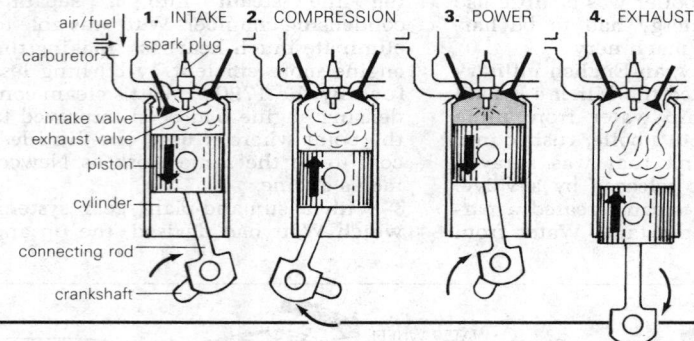

1. INTAKE   2. COMPRESSION   3. POWER   4. EXHAUST

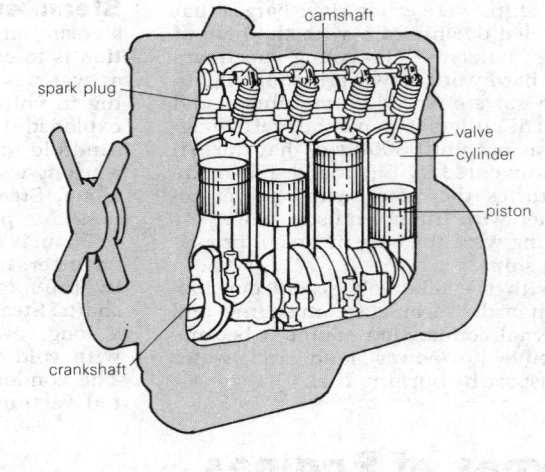

LLOYD BIRMINGHAM

down motion of the engine was converted to rotary motion. This improvement opened the way for the development of many more steam-powered machines.

Internal combustion engines.
The internal combustion engine is powered by fuels that can be atomized; that is, reduced to a spray or vapor that explodes quickly and easily. The engine was developed, therefore, only after such liquid fuels as benzene, kerosene, and coal oil were introduced in the mid-19th century.

Technological advances in recent years have made possible internal combustion engines that can run on gases such as methane, which must be stored under pressure. The Benz car, designed by Karl Benz of Germany, is generally recognized as the first reliable automobile to be powered by an internal combustion engine. It was introduced in 1885 and was fueled with benzene. The Benz engine operated on only one low compression cylinder and had a top speed of less than 10 miles per hour. Nevertheless, its four-stroke engine operated on the same principle as most of today's internal combustion engines.

Unlike the steam turbine, which burns fuel constantly, the internal combustion engine burns fuel, now usually gasoline, explosively and at timed intervals. The carburetor or fuel injector mixes fuel with air. This atomized fuel is then pumped into a cylinder where it is compressed by a piston. At maximum compression, the vapor is exploded by a spark fired from the spark plug. This explosion forces the piston down. A connecting rod transmits the energy of the explosion to the crankshaft, which then turns. This changes the up and down piston motion to rotary motion to turn the drive wheels of a car or the propellers of an airplane. The rotary motion of the crankshaft is aided by a cam, which controls the movements of several pistons so that power from the downthrust of one provides the energy to drive up the next, thereby compressing its fuel to the internal combustion cycle again.

Diesel engines.
The diesel engine was invented in 1892 by Rudolf Diesel of Germany. The diesel is an internal combustion engine that compresses its vaporized fuel to a greater extent than in the gasoline internal

combustion engine. Thus, it gets more power from the same amount of fuel. Instead of gasoline, the diesel engine uses lightweight oil similar to kerosene. A diesel cylinder pulls in air and raises the air temperature to over 550°F by means of compression. At this point, a small amount of fuel is sprayed in and spontaneously ignites—without need of a spark—because of the high temperature inside the cylinder. The resulting explosion forces the piston down. This is the power stroke. As in the gasoline-powered internal combustion engine, the piston rod in a diesel engine rotates the cam-bearing crankshaft, which controls the movement of the other pistons.

Diesel engines now come in many sizes. They are used to power electric generators, air compressors and pumps, boats, large ships and submarines, trucks, trains, buses, and automobiles.

Electric motors.
An electric motor converts electrical energy into rotary mechanical energy. The first electric motor, built by the British scientist Michael Faraday in 1821, consisted of a single wire suspended from

one end, with the other end in a vessel of mercury containing a magnet. When a current was run through the wire, the end in the vessel began moving around the magnet. Faraday's motor had no practical application but was followed, in 1837, by Thomas Davenport's motor, different in design and capable of powering a small locomotive. Until the 1870's, electrical power came only from heavy batteries. The first direct current (DC) generator was built in 1873, followed by the alternating current (AC) generator in the 1880's. Generators and improved batteries paved the way for the development of better electric motors.

Direct current motors. Direct current was the first electrical source available to inventors. The simple DC motor consists of three elements: a stationary field magnet, either permanent or electromagnetic; an armature, rotating electromagnet; and a commutator, which switches the direction of the electric current many times each second. Without the commutator, the armature would come to rest between the poles of the field magnet after half a turn, as the opposing poles of the field magnet and armature become aligned. The commutator, made of two copper half rings separated by insulation, receives current through small carbon blocks (brushes) wired to a power line. The commutator is turned by the armature so that with each half turn, the brushes are in contact with one or the other of the two halves. This produces a reversed electric current to the armature in each half turn.

Simple DC motors can operate more smoothly with more coils of wire around the rotor. The simplest two-pole motor, described above, has just two coils wound around the rotor and so requires a commutator with only two segments. Additional sets of coils require additional sets of commutator segments. Most standard DC motors have between six and twelve poles and can power items such as toys and household fans. The series and shunt motors are designed for heavier work.

In the series motor, current travels through coils around the field magnet, which is an electromagnet connected in series with the coils of the armature. This design enables the series motor to start with considerable force and to speed up once it is in motion, making it an ideal motor for elevators, subways, cranes, and the like.

Shunt motors are constructed with the armature and field coils each receiving part of the current. The armature gets the major part of the current. This design enables the shunt motor to operate at a fairly constant speed, independent of the load. Rheostats are used to control the current entering the motor, thereby increasing current to increase motor speed. Shunt motors are used in machines that must operate at controllable, constant speeds, such as lathes and adjustable fans.

DC MOTOR

A D.C. motor uses a commutator, or split ring, to cause current to flow through the rotor and reverse direction at each half rotation.

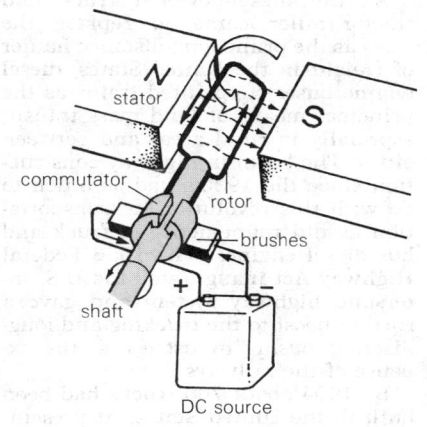

AC MOTOR

In an A.C. motor, the current is already constantly reversing direction, so two slip rings are used to provide current to the motor.

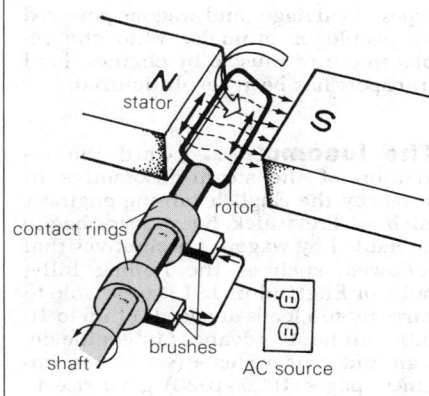

LLOYD BIRMINGHAM

Compound motors are basically a combination of series and shunt motors. The armature coils are connected in series with a number of the field coils and connected in parallel with the rest. The compound motor turning force is midway between that of series and shunt motors. Its ability to start and stop quickly and to maintain desired constant speed despite changes in load makes compound motors very useful in such applications as powering conveyor belts, textile machinery, and elevators.

The universal motor is built like a series motor and operates like one when on DC. Unlike the other motors discussed, however, the universal motor also can operate on AC power, which alternates the direction of the current in the electromagnetic field coil on every half cycle. Since the field and armature are wired together in series, the current direction in the coils of the armature changes at the same time as it changes in the field magnet coils.

Direct current motors have a major drawback. DC power, whether from batteries or DC generators, is more expensive than AC power. Furthermore, AC motors are generally more efficient and less expensive to build than DC motors. Though AC motors cannot change speeds or reverse motion, as DC motors can, they power many types of factory machines as well as household appliances such as refrigerators, which operate at constant speed.

Alternating current motors. A simple AC motor looks much like a DC motor but has no commutator, since the current already alternates. When the field magnet is an electromagnet, it is pow-

ered by a small DC generator, built as a component of the larger AC motor. Thus, the electric field of the field magnet, or stator, does not alternate. Carbon brushes supply AC current to two metal slip rings, insulated from each other but each connected to one pole of the armature. In household current, the armature poles are reversed 120 times per second.

A basic AC motor is already a synchronous motor, as it operates synchronously with alternations of current produced by a generating plant. The simplest synchronous motors operate clocks and have a simple mechanism such as a magnetized disk that spins between the poles of an electromagnet stator, making a half turn with each alternation of current. Other synchronous motors have more complex mechanisms to power recording, film, and video equipment, which require precise operating speeds.

An induction motor is built with the stator, or field magnet, around the rotor. The stator receives the full current, generated here as a special three-phase current, which enables the stator to produce a powerful magnetic field. The drum-shaped rotor, sometimes called a squirrel cage rotor, receives no current. It is turned by the magnetic field of the stator.

The induction motor has the advantage of requiring no brushes. Brushes are expensive and wear out quickly, requiring periodic replacement. The induction motor also produces sufficient turning power to operate most types of industrial and construction machinery. As a result, this motor is more widely used than any other electric motor.

Land Transportation

Until the mid-19th century, land transport was accomplished by human porters, laden animals, or various types of carriages and wagons powered by people or animals. With the replacement of muscle by engines, land transport has been revolutionized.

The locomotive. Until the invention of the steam locomotive in 1804, by the English mining engineer Richard Trevithick, heavy loads had to be hauled by wagon. Locomotives that followed, such as the Puffing Billy, built in England in 1813, were able to carry 50-ton loads at speeds of up to 10 miles an hour. Advances in engine design and gear systems (see Steam engines, pages 1025–1026) gave rise to steam locomotives that could haul more tonnage at much greater speeds.

The electric locomotive appeared in 1895. It had the advantage of producing no direct exhaust from combustion. Electric locomotives first operated in electrified urban areas in the early 20th century. Some, such as the trolley, drew their power from overhead electrical lines. Others used an electrified third rail.

The diesel electric locomotive, developed by Hermann Lemp in 1924, and perfected during the 1930's and 1940's, has largely replaced the steam locomotive on most main rail lines in the United States. The diesel electric is a self-contained power-generating system that does not depend on overhead cables or electrified third rails. Its diesel engine powers electric generators that, in turn, supply power to the electric traction motors that move the locomotive wheels. Diesel electric locomotives can achieve speeds 20 times greater than the Puffing Billy and can haul hundreds of times more tonnage.

Trucks and buses. Many of the advances in diesel technology that resulted in the dominance of diesel electric locomotives over steam locomotives also made trucks with diesel engines the principal means of land transport for heavy loads in the United States.

As the diesel-powered truck and tractor-trailer came to replace the train as the prime long-distance hauler of freight in the United States, diesel engine buses supplanted trains as the principal means of land mass transit, especially in rural areas and between cities. The boom in highway construction since the 1930's had as much to do with this revolution in transportation as did refinements in truck and bus diesel engines. The 1956 Federal Highway Act inaugurated the U.S. interstate highway system and gave a further boost to the trucking and long-distance busing industries, at the expense of the railways.

By 1904 about 700 trucks had been built in the United States. At present, more than 3 million are produced annually. The heaviest trucks can weigh more than 13 tons, supply nearly 700 horsepower, and carry more than double their net weight.

Recent developments in the harnessing of magnetism have resulted in the development of magnetic guide rail systems. The Maglev train system, currently being tested in West Germany and Japan, travels less than an inch above electromagnetic guide rails. An electric current produced by a generator on the train supplies the current necessary to run through the magnetic field of the electromagnetic rails, propelling the train. Since the Maglev train moves without direct track contact, hence without friction, it has the potential for greater speed and efficiency than conventional trains.

The automobile. The first automobiles, such as the Benz car of 1885, used the gasoline internal combustion engine. The diesel engine, developed seven years later, was not in general use in automobiles until the mid-20th century. Modifications in diesel design over the past two decades have eliminated much of the noise, thick exhaust, and slow pick-up associated with diesel-powered automobiles.

Essential components of the power train of an automobile are the crankshaft, which translates the up and down piston motion to rotary motion; the geared transmission, which controls the speed and direction of engine power to the drive wheels; and the differential, which enables the drive wheels to turn at different speeds, as they do when an automobile is making a turn.

An unfortunate byproduct of the automobile has been increased air pollution from exhaust gases. In addition to more efficient, high-compression engines, which burn fuel more completely and produce cleaner emissions, the catalytic converter was introduced in the 1970's to further reduce harmful exhaust emissions.

The catalytic converter is a box of chemicals—catalysts that initiate and speed up chemical reactions—located in the automobile exhaust system. Engine exhaust, containing unburned hydrocarbons and other pollutants, passes through the catalytic converter and is broken down to carbon dioxide, water vapor, and a relatively small amount of soot.

Water Transportation

With the invention of the steamboat by an American, John Fitch, in 1790, the era of machine-powered ships began. By the end of the 19th century, the steam engine, steam turbine, internal combustion engine, and diesel turbine were available to power boats and ships.

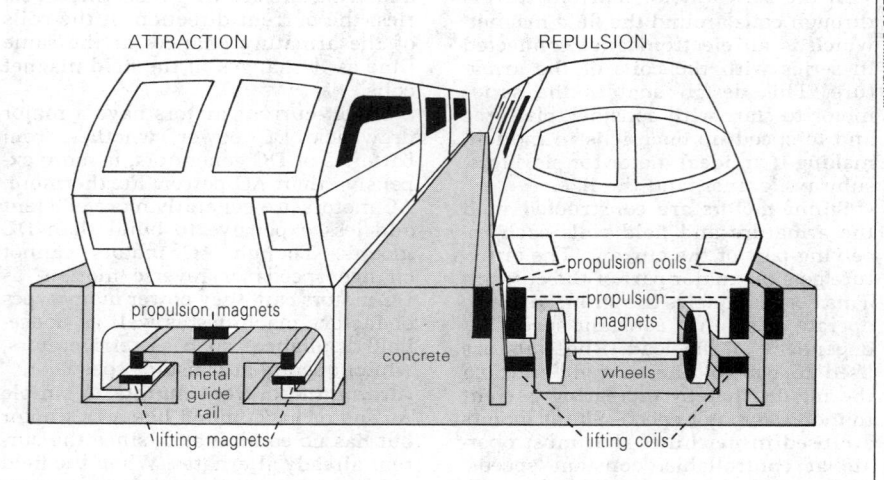

MAGLEV TRAINS

Maglev (magnetic levitation) trains use a magnetic field to provide a cushion on which the trains can ride. The magnetic field helps reduce energy loss and maintenance costs resulting from friction. There are two main kinds of maglev trains: attraction system and repulsion system. In the attraction system, arms attached under the train curve around under each side of a T-shaped center rail. Electromagnets on the underside of the rail crossbar and on the arms of the train attract each other, thereby lifting the train. In the repulsion system, magnets on the train and in a center rail repel each other, thereby lifting the train. This system works only at high speeds, so wheels are needed as well.

ATTRACTION   REPULSION

propulsion magnets   propulsion coils
                        propulsion magnets
metal guide rail   wheels
concrete
lifting magnets   lifting coils

LLOYD BIRMINGHAM

The *Great Western* was the first steamship, in 1838, to cross the Atlantic. In 1845 the *Great Britain* became the first of the large iron transatlantic steamships to make use of the screw propeller.

By the 1850's and 1860's, transatlantic sail ships began to give way to faster, safer steamships. The *Monitor* and *Merrimac*, which battled inconclusively in 1862, set the model for steel warships that followed.

The *Turbina*, in 1897, was the first turbine-powered ocean liner. By 1900 the sail ship had all but disappeared from commercial use.

Conventional boats and ships.

Despite advances in methods of propulsion, most ships continue to use a single-hull design. The single hull is subject to pitching and rolling in even moderately high seas. The small waterplane area twin hull (SWATH) is a much more stable sea craft because its hulls, attached to the main ship body by means of narrow struts, are submerged below wave level. SWATH aircraft carriers, built recently, provide a more stable takeoff and landing surface for aircraft than single-hull designs.

Stewart Way, an American engineer, experimented in the 1960's with submarines that could be propelled electromagnetically, but the so-called magship exists only as a prototype at this time. Until recently the superconducting magnets necessary for operating such a vessel were too expensive to be practical. Yoshiro Saji, a Japanese physicist, has used many of Way's magnetic propulsion concepts for his present magship prototype. Although it travels at less than 2 knots, Saji expects that it can be made 50 percent more efficient, in time, than any conventional ship.

The magship design calls for no moving parts. During the last quarter of a century, great advances have been made in the production of superconducting magnets, which are also used in atomic particle accelerators. On ship, these magnets produce a powerful electromagnetic field that extends through the seawater, which is an excellent conductor. The generator of the magship sends a strong electrical current through the water, from one electrode near the front of the hull to a second, which is closer to the rear. This current flows through the electromagnetic field and causes the magship to be propelled.

Hovercrafts.

A hovercraft, rather than floating in water, rests on a cushion of air produced by turbine or internal combustion engines that drive fans aimed to blow directly downward. Propulsion is accomplished by additional sets of jets or fans, positioned perpendicularly to the thrust of the hovering jets or fans. Because hovercraft ride on an air cushion rather than on the surface of the water, they are not impeded by shallows or wetland waters. The hovercraft air cushion makes it an amphibious vehicle as well as a watercraft. Military hovercraft can travel over land and water, as can hovercraft operated by the Department of the Interior in such areas as the Everglades National Park.

Submersibles.

In the fourth century B.C., Alexander the Great explored beneath the surface of the sea in a barrel equipped with glass portholes. The barrel was lowered and raised from above. In the 17th century, Cornelis van Drebbel, a Dutchman, sailed a self-propelled submarine made with a hull of greased leather in the Thames River in London.

David Bushnell, an American, is credited with having built, in 1776, the first submarine used for war. The *Turtle* had room for a crew of one. It was propelled by a hand-cranked, 24-inch wooden propeller that could be turned by the operator for forward or reverse motion at a top speed of 3 knots. It was steered by means of a hand-controlled rear-mounted rudder. The operator worked a hand pump that let in water for submerging and forced it out for surfacing. Bushnell's *Turtle* attempted to sink with British warship *Eagle* on September 7, 1776, by use of a time bomb on a spike. The spike was unable to penetrate the *Eagle's* copper-plated hull, however, and the bomb drifted away without causing damage.

During the Civil War, the Confederate submarine *Hunley*, powered by a crew of eight turning a hand-cranked propeller, became the first submarine to sink an enemy ship. Despite sinking during several tests, the *Hunley* was launched against the Union gunboat *Housatonic* in 1864. The submarine was armed with a time bomb on a rod extending from the bow. It was designed to be rammed into the enemy hull, then detonated as the *Hunley* pulled away. The *Hunley* did sink the *Housatonic*, but the detonation sank both vessels.

It was not until the end of the 19th century that the submarine became relatively safe and practical. An American inventor, John Holland, designed an improved submarine in the 1890's. In 1895 he built the *Holland*, the Navy's first submarine.

The *Holland* benefited from developments in submarine propulsion. In the 1880's, a steam-powered submarine was built by Garrett of England and Nordenfeldt of Sweden. In 1887 Isaac Peral, a Spanish naval officer, built a submarine powered by storage batteries. The French submarine *Gymôte*, built in 1888, was powered by a 55-horsepower electric motor. The *Holland* was powered by a 45-horse-power gasoline engine when it surfaced. The engine recharged storage batteries, which were used for power when the craft was submerged.

The basic submarine power plant design of a gasoline engine and storage batteries was in use throughout World War I, most effectively in German U-boats. By World War II, diesel engines replaced the gasoline engines of earlier submarines. Modern conventional submarine design includes a cylindrical pressure hull, compartments separated from each other by strong metal bulkheads with screw-lock doors, more complex ballast systems, and many other refinements.

The U.S.S. *Nautilus*, built in 1955, was the first nuclear-powered submarine. Its reactor was water cooled. The coolant water, kept under pressure at approximately 600°F, expends its energy driving the steam turbines, generators, and other systems of the submarine. The nuclear-powered generators and the steam turbines powered by steam from the reactor coolant water run while the craft is submerged, keeping batteries charged and other systems operating. Because a nuclear reactor does not consume oxygen in producing energy, a nuclear submarine has more oxygen available for

A SUBMARINE *maneuvers and maintains trim using a system of ballast tanks that are filled with water to dive and filled with air to surface.*

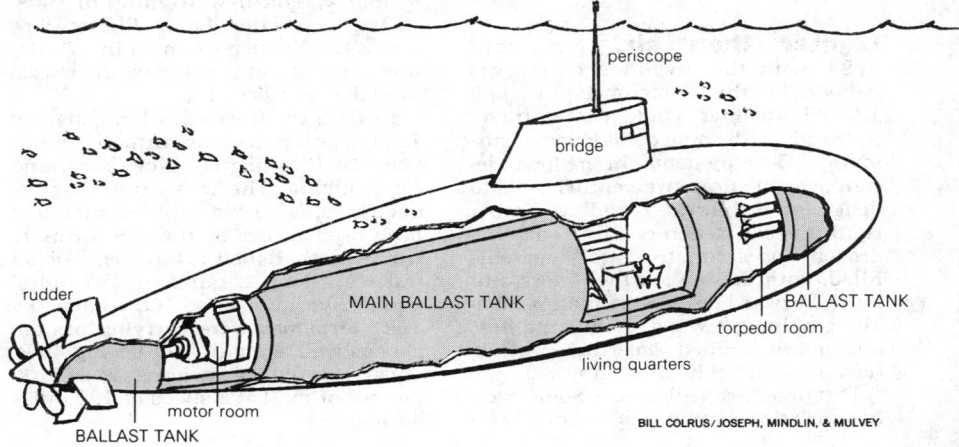

periscope

bridge

rudder

MAIN BALLAST TANK

BALLAST TANK

torpedo room

living quarters

motor room

BALLAST TANK

BILL COLRUS/JOSEPH, MINDLIN, & MULVEY

longer periods of submersion than does a diesel-powered submarine, which uses oxygen to burn fuel. The nuclear submarine, therefore, can remain underwater for long periods of time, traveling at speeds of over 30 knots and at depths of as much as 5000 feet.

Other types of submersibles, unlike submarines, are used mainly for research. The bathyscaphe, built in 1948 by Auguste Piccard of Switzerland, is a thick-walled, ball-shaped craft able to withstand the tremendous pressure at 35,000 feet below sea level. The Sedco/BP 471 is a submersible used for undersea drilling at depths of up to 27,000 feet.

Other submersibles, such as the *Alvin*, which is manned, and the *Vega*, which is not, operate at depths of a few thousand feet to explore the ocean floor of continental shelf areas. Equipped with conventional and video cameras, floodlights, and mechanical arms, these submersibles are carried by a support ship to the area where they are needed. Once released by the support ship, the *Alvin* submerges by taking water into its ballast tanks. Its titanium pressure hull is 2 inches thick. All available space is filled with high-density foam, resistant to collapse from outside pressure yet buoyant. Two electric motors power a rear-mounted propeller. Two side propellers give it maneuverability. Three banks of batteries and an independent air supply give the *Alvin* ample opportunity to explore. It carries over 2 tons in weights, which it releases in order to surface.

Air Transportation

It seems man always has dreamed of being able to fly, as suggested by the Greek myth of Daedalus and Icarus. Leonardo da Vinci even designed a flying machine based on the skeleton of a bird. But it was the Wright brothers who flew the first powered airplane less than a hundred years ago.

Lighter than air. Not until 1783, with the invention of the gas balloon by the Frenchmen J.E. and J.M. Montgolfier, could people travel in the air with some confidence of surviving. Developments in balloon design over the next two centuries led to dirigibles, or blimps. Dirigibles have a rigid interior structure filled with hydrogen and later, for safety reasons, filled with helium, which does not burn. Forward propulsion motors, usually gasoline powered, stabilizing fins, and more refined steering controls have kept the balloon with us.

Dirigibles are still in use. Some even have carried commuters in such met-

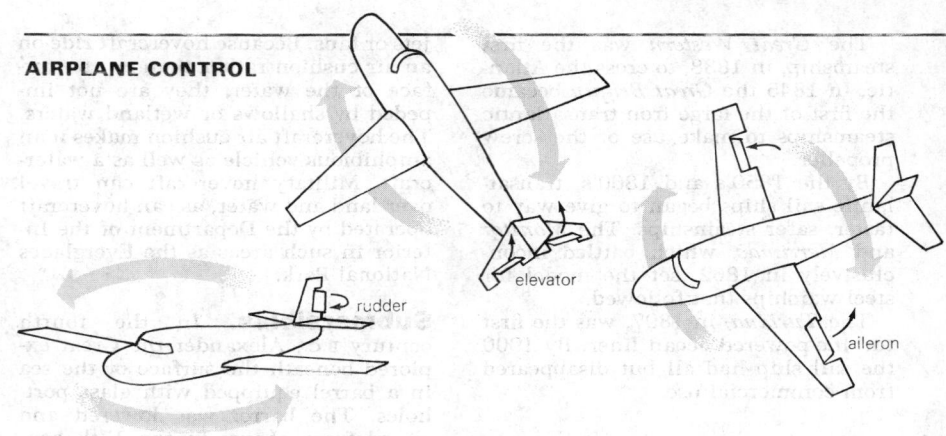

AIRPLANE CONTROL

elevator

rudder

aileron

Control of an airplane is achieved through manipulation of flaps on the wings and tail of the plane. When one of the flaps is moved so that it impedes the flow of air past the wing or tail, the pressure on the flap turns the plane on the corresponding axis. For instance, when the aileron on a wing is raised, that wing is pushed down and the plane rotates so that the other wing rises.

ropolitan areas as New York City. Meteorological instruments are still sent aloft, carried by high-altitude weather balloons, and hot-air ballooning is currently a popular sport.

Conventional aircraft. Powered heavier-than-air flight was considered an impossibility by most people until the 20th century. Thanks to the work of Otto Lilienthal, Octave Chanute, S.P. Langley, and others, the curved-wing design emerged, making the Wright brothers' successful airplane a possibility.

The Wrights' first successful powered airplane flew for 12 seconds on December 17, 1903. Pitched propellers, with blades angled to move air over the curved wings, provided sufficient air flow to lift the airplane and keep it aloft. The plane had a four-cylinder, twelve-horsepower engine, a bicycle-style chain and sprocket drive, and a delicate, but unwieldy, appearance. Nevertheless, it made four flights that same day, setting a record of 59 seconds for powered flight. By 1905 the Wrights had built another aircraft powered by a 24-horsepower engine. It flew 24 miles in 38 minutes. Wilbur Wright flew 76 miles in 1908, and a year later Louis Blériot flew across the English Channel in 37 minutes. Speed and distance increased over the next decades.

In 1918 the Curtis JN-4, nicknamed Jenny, began regular airmail service between Washington, New York, and Philadelphia. The Jenny was a single-engine, single-prop biplane that had been used earlier by the U.S. Army to train pilots. It had a top speed of 93 miles an hour, a range of 230 miles, and a payload of up to 150 pounds. By 1927 airplanes were carrying passengers as well as mail. The Boeing 40-B-4 carried four passengers and 1200 pounds of mail at a speed of 125 miles an hour.

Increased range, cargo capacity, and speed were achieved by adding more engines. The Ford trimotor, built in 1927, could carry a pilot, copilot, 13 passengers, and cargo at a cruising speed of 120 miles an hour. The Ford trimotor was a high-wing monoplane and was among the first aircraft to be built with a metal skin.

From the 1930's on, most passenger and transport aircraft had switched from a biplane design to a monoplane wing design and achieved greater speeds, ranges, and load capacities by the use of three, and later four, powerful engines. The 1954 Douglas DC-7, for example, one of the last propeller-driven passenger planes built in the United States, had four engines, a cruising speed of 365 miles an hour, and a range of nearly 4500 miles. The Boeing 707, the first jetliner, was put into service in 1954.

The jet propulsion turbine was developed in England in 1930. With continued advancements in design, this turbine engine enabled manned aircraft eventually to break the sound barrier. To achieve speeds of Mach 2 and greater, the turbojet was replaced by the ramjet and rockets.

Helicopters. The possibility of flight was inspired by nature, but human attempts to imitate the forward flight of birds have not been successful. Scientists recently tested a model they constructed of the flying reptile, the *Pterodactyl;* it flew successfully. Plants, rather than birds or insects, provided the first observable example of slow, hovering descent. Seed capsules, such as that of the maple, with its double wings, provided an example of slow aerodynamics. Such capsules may have inspired the design of the boomerang, a prehistoric invention that still is used. The boomerang was the first device capable of both horizontal flight and brief hovering.

HOW AN AIRPLANE FLIES

An airplane is able to fly because of the lift created as air rushes past its wings. The shape of a wing causes air to follow a longer path over the top of the wing than under the bottom of the wing. This causes the pressure of air on the underside of the wing to be greater than that on the top of the wing, pushing the wing—and airplane—up.

As a plane puts its nose in the air, the angle at which the air hits the wing—called the angle of incidence—increases, and the path the air takes across the top of the wing increases. This causes greater pressure on the underside of the wing, producing greater lift.

If the angle of incidence become too great, however, the air on top of the wing ceases to follow the wing, creating turbulence. The plane will then stall and begin to fall.

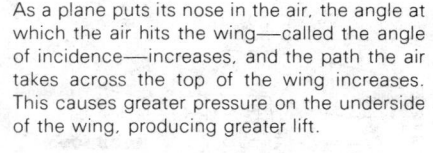
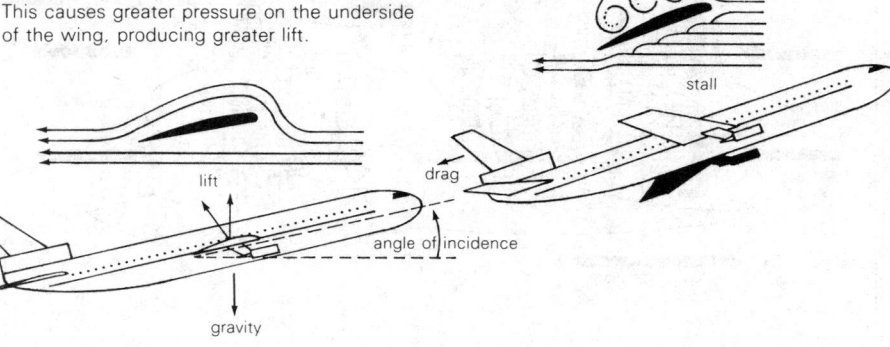

LLOYD BIRMINGHAM

The secret of seed descent is in the inclination, or slant, of the wings. Winged seeds spin as they fall and create a cushion of air beneath them to slow their descent. The lift blades of the helicopter, which enable it to leave the ground and hover, also are inclined so as to push air downward.

The first machine-powered helicopter was built by a French engineer, Louis Breguet, in 1907. It had four sets of blades, each 26 feet long, driven by a 45-horsepower engine. Breguet's helicopter managed to hover at an altitude of about 5 feet, but it was unable to move horizontally and had to be controlled by cables moved by assistants on the ground. In modern helicopters, horizontal movement is achieved by the use of adjustable main rotor blades and rear-mounted rotors with vertical blades. Smaller helicopters are powered by internal combus-

tion engines. Larger, higher speed helicopters are powered by turbojets.

Igor Sikorsky, a Russian-born American, built his first working helicopter in 1939. His name is still nearly synonymous with the modern helicopter. Today's helicopters still depend on various rotor designs, but they contain a host of other controls and refinements to give them added stability, reduced vibration, and increased controllability and power.

In 1962 Sikorsky and Boeing introduced turbojet-powered helicopters able to produce much greater forward speeds and carry much more cargo. Helicopters today can lift more than 20 tons and travel at speeds of over 200 miles per hour.

V/STOL aircraft. Vertical/short takeoff and landing aircraft (V/STOL)

were designed to overcome a major drawback of conventional and jet aircraft: the need for long runways for takeoff and landing. V/STOL aircraft are able to achieve vertical and/or short takeoff by the use of tilt rotors, tilt wings, special flaps, and movable jet nozzles.

British Harrier jets, often launched from aircraft carriers, rotate their jet engines 90 degrees downward from forward flight position to lift the aircraft straight up. Once the Harrier is aloft, its jets rotate to forward flight position, enabling the aircraft to travel at speeds above 500 miles per hour.

Short takeoff and landing aircraft (STOL) depend on extra long wings for added lift, in addition to powerful engines. The resulting increased lift enables the STOL to take off and land on far shorter runways than those used by conventional aircraft.

MODERN AIRCRAFT DESIGN

BURRI/MAGNUM

FISHMAN/WOODFIN CAMP

The Voyager (left) was designed as an extremely efficient airplane. It proved itself in 1986, when it made a nonstop around-the-world flight on one tank of fuel. The Harrier jet (right) can take off and land vertically, making it very useful on aircraft carriers.

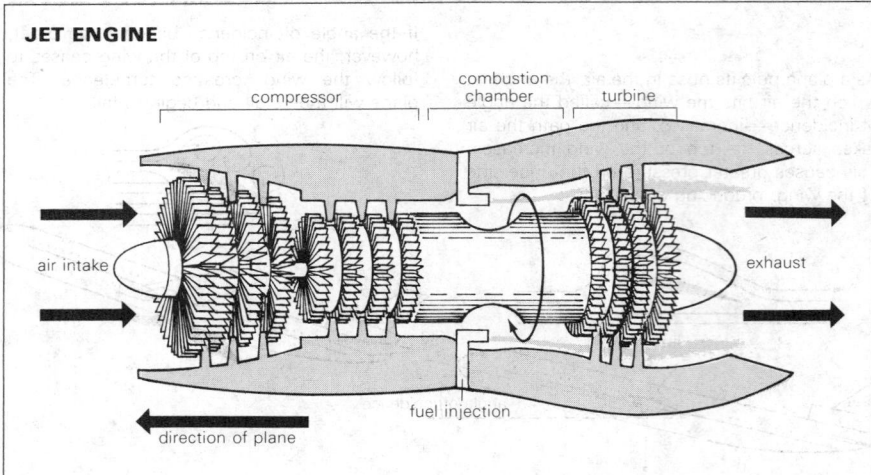

JET ENGINE

compressor — combustion chamber — turbine

air intake — exhaust

direction of plane

fuel injection

The basic propulsion of a jet engine comes from the expanding gases exhausting from the rear of the engine. To increase the expansion of the gases as they exhaust, and thereby increase the propulsion, the air taken in at the front of the engine is passed through a compressor before it reaches the combustion chamber. The compressor is driven by a turbine impelled by the exhaust as it leaves the engine.

Rockets and jets. The liquid fuel rocket, developed by an American, Dr. Robert Goddard, in 1926, was followed in the next decade by German V-2 liquid fuel rockets able to travel at supersonic speeds over hundreds of miles. The liquid-fuel rocket remained a means of propulsion for unmanned craft only until the late 1940's.

Multistage rockets, powered by solid and liquid fuels, have been in use for more than a quarter of a century. They provide the only propulsion system powerful enough to take manned and unmanned spacecraft free of Earth's gravitational pull.

But long before a rocket or jet engine is flown, its components must be tested. Wind tunnels were built and used by the earliest airplane designers, including the Wright brothers, for just such testing. Factors such as vehicle velocity, expected wind speeds, altitude, air density, humidity, and more are considered in aircraft aerodynamics. A space shuttle has design requirements different from those of a Harrier jet or a Piper Cub. Wind tunnels are designed to produce appropriate simulations of flight demands.

Today powerful computers are used in the preliminary design of flight vehicles to simulate the environments to which the vehicles will be subjected.

For more information on rockets, the space shuttle, and space flight, see the ASTRONOMY AND SPACE volume.

—*Marc Sacerdote*

Medicine

Medical technology is moving forward at a pace that outstrips the ability of most people to keep up. Medical technology never reaches an end point; it is part of a continuing search for better ways of diagnosing and treating disease. But along with the potential for solving many complex medical problems comes controversy over costs and benefits, and new questions about medical ethics. Notwithstanding the ultimate resolution of this controversy, technology will play an increasingly important role in helping to prolong and improve life.

Body Imaging Techniques

Thermography. Thermography employs sensing devices to detect heat, or infrared radiation, produced by the body. Heat from the body strikes a mirror and is reflected onto the lens of a special camera. More heat causes more electricity to be produced by the camera. Computers transform these varying intensities into multicolored heat maps that enable physicians to locate tumors and inflammations, which give off more heat than normal tissue.

Ultrasonography. Ultrasonography uses high-frequency sound to perceive the internal organs of the body. The ultrasound technologist touches a transducer—a device that changes electrical energy into sound waves—to a patient's skin in the area being studied. When the waves contact tissue, they are reflected to the transducer as echoes. The echoes produce a picture of the patient's organs on a video monitor. The technologist can make a photograph, a sonogram, of what appears on the monitor.

Ultrasound makes possible a painless, noninvasive procedure and produces images without the use of harmful radiation. Ultrasound cannot penetrate bone, so it is not used for imaging organs that are located inside the skeleton.

A sonogram can be used to detect gallstones, for example, which do not show up on x-rays. It also can be used to examine the prostate gland and to detect plaque build-up in the carotid arteries. Ultrasound cannot be used to detect plaque build-up in the coronary arteries, since the heart is behind the rib cage. Ultrasound is being used experimentally to emulsify tumors near the brain or along the spinal cord and also to pulverize kidney stones.

The most widespread use of ultrasound is in obstetrics, where it is employed to monitor half of all pregnancies and deliveries. It enables diagnosis of prenatal conditions and multiple births.

Computerized tomography scans. The development of advanced computers in the early 1960's has made possible a number of body imaging techniques such as computerized tomography (CT) scans, positron emission tomography (PET) scans, and nuclear magnetic resonance (NMR). At the core of these techniques is the computer, which can rapidly accept, process, store, and display information to actively help in seeking patterns of health and disease.

A conventional x-ray photograph, called a tomograph, is produced by placing the patient against a piece of x-ray film. The x-rays are sent through the patient's body. The amount of x-rays that can penetrate the body and strike the film depends on the density of the body tissue. Dense tissue in the path of the radiation absorbs more x-rays than less dense tissue. Thus, a tomogram represents the various densities of tissues lying between the x-ray machine and the film. Bone tissue, which absorbs most of the x-rays, appears as light areas on the exposed film. Soft tissue, such as heart, cartilage, and connective tissue, absorbs fewer x-rays and shows up as dark areas on a tomogram.

Computerized tomography, also often called computer assisted tomography (CAT), makes use of a computer to store and manipulate information from x-rays. CAT scans produce cross-sectional images rather than two-dimensional images. This is accomplished by rotating the x-ray source around the patient. An x-ray detector on the other side of the patient rotates synchronously. Variations in the absorption of radiation by the tissues are fed to a computer, which manipulates the data to produce images of cross sections. The resulting images can be viewed on a television monitor, photographed, or stored on disks.

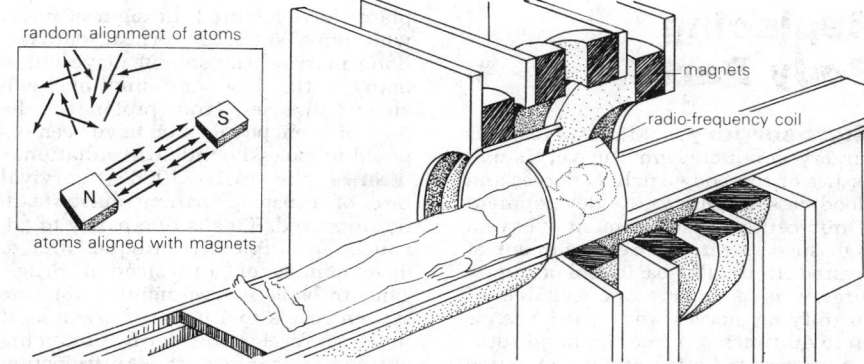

IN NUCLEAR MAGNETIC RESONANCE, *atoms in the body align themselves with the magnets. Radio waves of the proper frequency can cause the atoms to flip their alignment.*

Digital subtraction angiography.

Digital subtraction angiography makes use of CT scans and angiography. Information gathered by CT scans is translated into computer language so that it can be manipulated in various ways and displayed on a monitor. This technique can be used to light the artery figuratively out of the body so it can be studied in isolation. First, a regular CT scan (a mask image) is taken of the patient's tissues. Then a contrast material is injected into the veins. The computer subtracts the mask image from the relatively faint dye-producing image, producing an unobstructed image of the arteries as defined by the contrast material. The process enables studies of heart and major blood vessels with minimum risk.

Positron emission tomography (PET).

The PET scanner uses radioactive isotopes that emit positrons, positively charged atomic particles that are otherwise the same as negatively charged electrons. When a positron and an electron collide, they are annihilated, and two gamma rays are emitted. The PET scanner is an array of detectors that detect gamma rays and thus pinpoint the location of the positron-omitting isotope. A computer is used to construct a three-dimensional picture of the distribution of gamma rays.

PET scanners, developed in the 1970's, record human metabolism at work. A patient inhales or is injected with a substance, such as glucose, that is tagged with positron-emitting isotopes. The glucose travels to the parts of the body that are using energy, and hence are using more glucose. Thus, PET scans enable physicians to see where and how cells are using glucose. Live, healthy cells, which are using glucose at a normal rate, show up on a PET scan as a bright glow. Cells that have been damaged are still partially functioning are less bright, and dead cells register a dark patch. This

means, for example, that for the first time physicians can see the exact extent of damage caused by a stroke in a patient's brain. PET scans also can be used to get information on how much heart tissue can be saved in a coronary bypass operation.

With a PET scanner, it is possible to watch the brain think. A patient can be asked to think about moving a hand without moving it, and researchers can see, using PET and glucose, if the specific area of the brain that is in control of movement becomes activated.

Nuclear magnetic resonance (NMR).

NMR makes use of the tendency of some atomic nuclei placed in a magnetic field to become aligned with that field. Atomic nuclei that have an odd number of protons and neutrons rotate around their own axes, just as Earth rotates on its axis. The rotation of the nuclei creates a magnetic field, with a north and south pole. In other words, the spinning nuclei act like tiny magnets.

In the absence of an outside magnetic field, the nuclear magnets are oriented in all different directions. When a strong enough external magnetic field is applied, however, the nuclei became oriented parallel with this field. If the nuclei then are exposed to radio waves of exactly the right frequency, called the resonant frequency, some of the nuclei will absorb energy from the radio waves and flip to oppose the outside magnetic field. When the radio signal is turned off, the nuclei flip back to their original positions, in alignment with the outside magnetic field, and release radio waves at the resonance frequency. In other words, the nuclei are made to resonate at their own natural frequencies. This is similar to the way a soprano can make a wine glass ring if she sings a note at exactly the right pitch—the natural vibration frequency of the glass—she can make a wine glass resonate. When she stops singing, the glass continues to resonate at the same frequency.

In the case of NMR, a radio wave of exactly the right frequency will cause

hydrogen nuclei to line up in a different direction from that of the outside magnetic field. As each nucleus returns to a position in line with the large magnetic field, it transmits a resonant radio wave. The resonant frequencies of the nuclei and the time it takes them to realign with the outside magnetic field depend on the environment around the nuclei. This varies from one type of body tissue to another, producing carrying signals picked up by a radio frequency receiving coil that are used to produce computer-generated pictures.

NMR has several advantages over CAT scans. CAT scans use x-rays, which are absorbed by bone tissue. Therefore, images of soft tissue can sometimes be obstructed by bone tissue on CAT scans. NMR signals depend on the amount and environment of hydrogen nuclei. Most soft tissue has a high water content, and therefore a higher density of hydrogen nuclei than hard tissue, such as bone. Therefore, NMR produces excellent images of soft tissue unobstructed by bone. CAT scans reveal only differences in density. Some brain tumors may have the same density as surrounding brain tissue that is swollen. CAT scans cannot distinguish between these two areas, but NMR can. Another advantage of NMR is that it does not rely on potentially harmful x-rays. For these reasons, NMR has become the preferred method for imaging the brain. Multiple sclerosis produces characteristic NMR images. Tumors, aneurysms, cysts, hemorrhages, and infarctions of the brain also can be detected with NMR.

Because it takes longer to receive NMR signals, nuclear magnetic resonance cannot easily be used to image moving body parts. Respiratory motion, for example, degrades the sharpness of the image in the chest and upper abdomen. Other disadvantages are the expense and lack of availability of NMR equipment, and its unsuitability for certain patients, such as those with pacemakers, which would be affected by the strong magnetic fields and the radio waves that the machine generates.

Replacing Body Parts

Microsurgery. Microsurgery is surgery conducted on the very small tissues of the body, such as nerves and blood vessels. Due to the development of microsurgery, surgeons now have a high success rate for reattachment of severed limbs. The basic tool of microsurgery is a microscope capable of magnifying nerves and blood vessels up to 40 times. To free the hands during surgery, the microscope is operated with zoom pedals. The microscope often is connected to TV screens so that members of the operating team can see what the surgeon is doing. Other microsurgical instruments include scissors with tiny blades, miniature forceps, and surgical thread so thin it can barely be seen with the naked eye. With more understanding of the complicated structure of nerves, microsurgeons can successfully graft partially damaged nerves onto other nerves, thus greatly increasing the success of reattachments.

Organ transplantation. About 25 human organs can now be transplanted. The most commonly performed transplantations are kidney (over 5000 per year), cornea, and bone marrow transplants. Corneal transplants have restored the sight of many who have suffered corneal damage. Bone marrow transplants have cured many with blood and immune deficiency diseases, and prolonged the lives of some people who have been exposed to excessive nuclear radiation.

Since the early 1980's, survival rates of transplant patients have steadily improved. This is due partly to advances in surgical techniques and to development of antirejection drugs. The transplant recipient's immune system reacts to a donated organ as if it were a foreign invader by producing antibodies against it. Antirejection drugs suppress the immune system to prevent rejection of the new organ. One widely used antirejection drug was isolated from a soil fungus. This drug selectively suppresses the production of cells known as T-lymphocytes without damaging other cells. Transplant patients must take this drug for the rest of their lives. The lifelong suppression of the immune system means the continuing threat of infection.

Artificial organs. The advantage of artificial organs over transplants is that they are not rejected. The first artificial organ was the artificial kidney, or dialysis machine. Blood from a patient's artery goes through a system of tubing, which is immersed in a bath of fluid. Waste products from the blood pass through the membrane of the tubing into the bath of fluid. The cleansed blood then passes back into the patient through a tube inserted into a vein. A newer technique provides continuous portable cleansing of the blood. A plastic bag worn around the abdomen delivers the filtering solution into the abdominal cavity. Waste collects in this solution, and the fluid then drains back into the plastic bag. A fresh solution then is put into the bag.

Development of the heart-lung machine, which takes over the function of both heart and lungs, has made it possible to perform open-heart surgery. The heart-lung machine has the twofold function of keeping the blood in circulation by means of a pumping system and enriching the blood with oxygen. The blood from the vena cava, which leads to the heart, is diverted through tubes into an artificial lung. In the artificial lung, the blood is exposed to a stream of oxygen. The oxygenated blood then is pumped back into the patient's body.

A recently developed artificial pancreas regulates changes in levels of blood glucose by injecting tiny amounts of insulin into the bloodstream. A current model looks like a large stove on wheels. It can monitor glucose levels in a diabetic patient and, when it senses too much deviation, dole out tiny amounts of insulin for up to four days. The artificial pancreas currently is being used to help diabetic women during childbirth. Smaller, more portable units are under development.

The artificial heart has received a great deal of publicity in recent years. The device is used in patients suffering from nonoperable congestive heart failure, or patients whose hearts fail while undergoing cardiac surgery. The artificial heart consists of two pumping chambers that correspond to the two pumping chambers (ventricles) of the natural heart. Pulses of compressed air squeeze the two diaphragms that push the blood through valves leading to either the lungs or the aorta. Patients with an artificial heart have limited mobility, since they must be connected to a pneumatic pump that sends compressed air through tubes into the chest. Researchers are attempting to design models that will give patients more mobility.

Recent advances in microelectronics, which uses tiny silicon chips that provide memory and logic functions, have made possible many of the most spectacular developments in artificial organs. One device that now is being used is the Utah arm, which can be controlled, with the help of microelectronics, by the muscles. For a lower-arm prosthesis, electrodes are placed on the biceps and triceps muscles in the upper arm. To flex the artificial arms, amputees flex their biceps muscles just as they would if they had

ARTIFICIAL HEART

The Jarvik-7, an artificial heart named for its inventor, Robert Jarvik, replaces most of the natural human heart. It uses air that is supplied from an external compressor to manipulate pumps that simulate the desired action of a normal heart. When implanted into Barney Clark, a retired 62-year-old dentist from Seattle, Washington, the Jarvik-7 beat more than 13 million times, keeping Clark alive from December, 1982, to March, 1983, when he died of organ and tissue failure. Doctors reported that without the Jarvik-7, Clark would have died within hours or days. With it, he survived for an additional 112 days.

DR. WILLIAM DEVRIES, *seen here holding models of a human heart and the Jarvik-7, was the first surgeon to implant an artificial heart in a human being.*

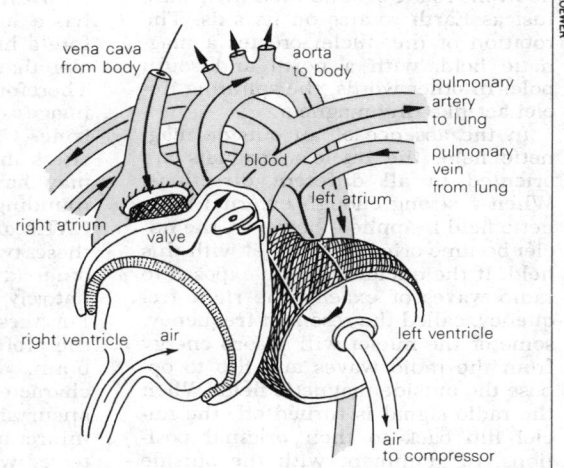

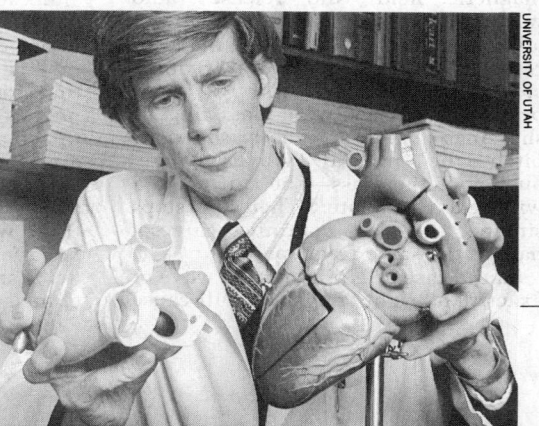

natural arms. Electrodes pick up the electrical signal generated by the biceps muscle and send the signal to a microcomputer located in the elbow. The microcomputer translates the signal command to flex the elbow. For upper arm amputees, the electrodes are placed on the deltoid muscles at the shoulder. Artificial arms now under development will allow motion not only at the elbow joint, but also at the wrist, hand, and upper arm.

Artificial vision also makes use of computer technology. When the visual cortex of the brain is electrically stimulated, a blind person can perceive discrete points of light, called phosphenes. When several electrodes are used, volunteer subjects see letters and geometric shapes. One subject could read Braille patterns made up of phosphenes at a rate five times faster than he could read tactile Braille. Eventually, it may be possible to mount a fingernail-size camera inside an artificial eye and attach a microcomputer to an eyeglass frame. This system would produce a halftone picture similar to the cartoons seen on an animated scoreboard.

Artificial hearing also relies on the stimulation of an implanted electrode. In a normal ear, the cochlea in the inner ear stimulates thousands of delicate hair cells. In turn these cells produce an electrical current in the auditory nerve leading to the brain. Hearing impairment often is caused by

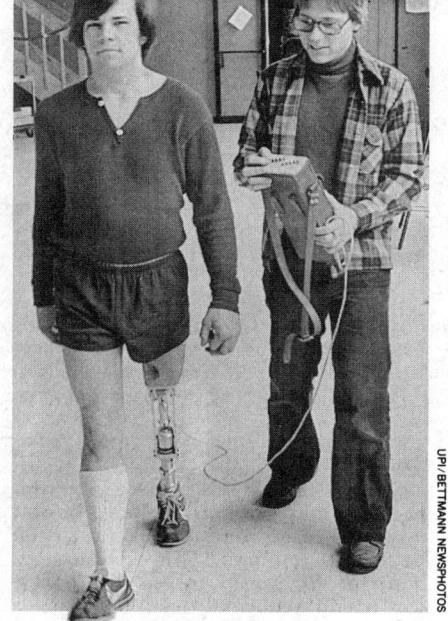

UPI/BETTMANN NEWSPHOTOS

ADVANCES IN ELECTRONICS *have made possible the development of controllable prostheses, such as artificial knees.*

the destruction of these hair cells. Artificial hearing devices use a small microphone, which changes sound into an electrical current. The current is transmitted to an electrode that replaces the function of the hair cells. Patients who have the device can hear sounds such as traffic noises and telephones. When the device is perfected, patients may hear well enough to carry on telephone conversations.

ROBOT SURGERY

Robots now are being used to make surgical procedures, such as biopsies, safer, faster, and far less invasive than conventional procedures. Biopsies are performed to extract tissue samples from suspected tumors. In conventional biopsy surgery on the brain, the surgeon must seek the best way to point the probe to reach the suspected tumor. Each pass of the probe increases the risk of brain damage. Since the robot is programmmed to know exactly where the target is, it can find the suspected tumor with just one pass of the probe. This greatly reduces trauma to the brain.

The robot knows exactly where the suspected tumor is because the information is fed into the robot before the surgery is performed. The patient's head is held steady. A CAT scanner is used to locate the exact position of the suspected tumor. A track ball device, similar to the kind used in video arcades, is used to roll the computer cursor to the exact spot of the suspected tumor. The computer calculates this location in x, y, and z coordinates. The target coordinates are fed via computer keyboard into the robot memory. Thus the robot "knows" exactly where to drill a hole through the skull, where to insert the biopsy needle, and how deep the probe should go. The robot is accurate to within one two-thousandth of an inch.

Robots have been used thus far mainly to help surgeons perform biopsy surgery. In the future, they may be used to drain abscesses, implant radioactive pellets directly into tumors, repair blood vessels, guide laser beams to tumors, or help surgeons repair ruptured disks, torn ligaments, and damaged cartilage.

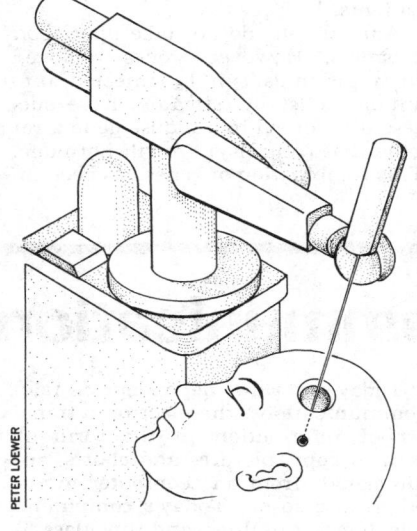

PETER LOEWER

Radioactive Isotopes

Radioactive isotopes have many uses in medicine. For example, radioactive iodine can be used to check the functioning of the thyroid gland. The thyroid uses iodine to produce thyroxine, a hormone that controls metabolism. Iodine does not concentrate in any other body tissue. Thus, a patient can be given a drink of an iodine compound that contains radioactive iodine. The physician then can use a Geiger counter to monitor the amount of radioactive iodine that goes to the gland. In this way, the physician can tell whether the thyroid is producing too much or too little thyroxine.

Radiation therapy. Radioactive isotopes also destroy cells with radiation. Doses of radioactive iodine can be used to destroy cells in an overactive thyroid gland with minimal harm to the rest of the body. The radioactive iodine, administered orally, concentrates in the thyroid, where it bombards the gland with radioactive particles, destroying some of the gland tissue. Radioactive cobalt is used to treat cancer patients. Cancer cells, which divide rapidly, are readily killed by radiation because cells are more vulnerable when they are dividing. Radiation therapists give patients the exact dosages they need to kill cancer cells without causing extensive damage to normal tissue. Particle accelerators such as the synchrotron also are used to produce streams of particles in the same way as radioactive elements. The particles are aimed at the cancerous tissue to destroy it.

Advances in Genetics

Genetic testing. All living cells contain genes, the chemical units made of DNA (deoxyribonucleic acid) that carry hereditary traits and give cells day-to-day instructions for their reproduction, growth and development. Genes are part of larger structures, called chromosomes, which are dark, rodlike bodies found in the nucleus. Humans have 23 pairs of chromosomes. Thus, for each trait we have two genes, one on each half of a chromosome pair. For a more complete explanation of genetics, see the HEALTH AND LIFE SCIENCES volume.

Sometimes genes are defective. It is estimated that everyone carries eight to ten defective genes. Usually they do not produce any harmful effects because the other gene in the pair is not defective. In some cases, however,

MONOCLONAL ANTIBODY PRODUCTION

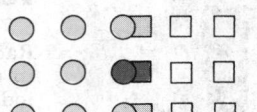

1. The immune system of a mouse is stimulated to produce a particular antibody. Tumor cells, noted for their rapid growth rate, are grown in culture.

2. The antibody-producing cells from the mouse and the tumor cells are fused to form a hybrid cell.

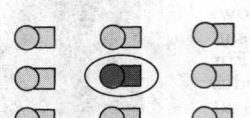

3. The hybrid cells are examined for the desired characteristics of the parent cells: antibody production and rapid growth.

4. The hybrid cells with the proper characteristics are grown in culture to produce large quantities of the antibody.

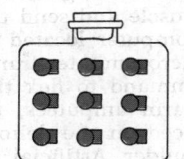

both good genes are needed for a trait, and both genes are defective. This may cause birth defects and health problems. Sickle cell anemia and cystic fibrosis are examples of diseases caused by defective genes. Down's syndrome is a genetic disease that is caused by an extra chromosome. Instead of the usual 46 chromosomes, people with Down's syndrome have 47.

Carrier tests are available for a large number of genetic diseases. A carrier is a person who has one gene for a disease. Since the other gene in the pair is normal, a carrier does not have the disease. However, carrier parents can pass on a gene for a genetic disease to their offspring. If their children inherit two genes—one from each parent—for a genetic disease, the children will acquire the disease.

When a woman is pregnant, it is possible to collect and test the cells of the developing baby. People who are at high risk for having children with genetic defects are advised to have this test. Amniocentesis is a technique used during the 16th week of pregnancy to detect genetic defects of the developing fetus. Guided by ultrasound, the physician inserts a hollow needle into the amniotic sac of the mother. A small amount of the amniotic fluid is withdrawn through the needle, which contains cells that have sloughed off from the developing fetus. These cells then can be tested for genetic defects.

A new technique, called chorionic villi sampling, enables physicians to collect cells as early as the fifth week of pregnancy. The chorion is a membrane surrounding the fetus, and cho-rionic villi are small projections from the chorion. Cells from the chorion have the same genetic makeup as the developing embryo. This technique is superior to amniocentesis in that it can detect abnormalities much earlier in a pregnancy.

Recombinant DNA. Scientists have discovered a way to introduce new DNA into an organism. Certain bacteria, such as *E. coli,* have DNA, which is found in rings called plasmids. Plasmids can be extracted from the bacteria and sliced into fragments. After this is done, DNA taken from other sources can be attached to these fragments; that is, recombined before the plasmid is hooked back together. The reattached plasmids are introduced into other *E. coli* bacteria, which then multiply in nutrient cultures. As the *E. coli* multiply, the spliced gene also multiplies. This procedure has been used to cause *E. coli* to produce various useful products, including the human insulin hormone, which can be used to treat diabetics, and a growth hormone, which can be used to treat dwarfism. Another useful product produced by recombinant DNA is interferon, a chemical that stimulates the immune system and may prove helpful in treating cancer patients.

Animal cells do not take up *E. coli* plasmids. However, genes removed from plasmids can be injected into animal cells. Investigators have successfully joined to a mouse gene a rat gene that controls a growth hormone. This combination of genes has been in-jected into mouse embryos; they successfully carried the genes. This experiment and others like it have spurred hope that it may eventually be possible to cure many human genetic diseases.

Monoclonal antibodies. Antibodies are proteins the body produces to combat foreign protein invaders. Artificial clones, colonies of cells all of the same kind, have been produced, giving rise to the hope that someday it will be possible to manufacture antibodies commercially by cloning them in large numbers. Antibodies against cancer cells are produced in a similar way. Cancer cells taken from a human patient are injected into mice. After the mice have been given time to make antibodies against the cancer cells, their spleens are removed and cells containing the antibodies are extracted. These cells are fused with cancer cells. Cancer cells are used because of their ability to multiply very quickly.

The resulting cell has the traits of the two parent cells, producing large numbers of antibodies and reproducing rapidly. As the cells multiply, they produce clones that make monoclonal antibodies. The antibodies, injected into the cancer patient from whose cancer cells their production was stimulated, will be specific for destroying the particular cancer. The antibodies also might be tagged with toxic drugs that would then be delivered to cancer cells but not healthy cells.

—Sharon Kakonen

Communications

Recent years have accounted for more advances in communications than the previous 6000 years. Overall use of modern communications is expected to increase by more than 500 percent by the year 2000. The term has come to mean more than telephone, radio, and television.

Today's world is dependent on telecommunications, the electronic transfer of information in the form of printed copy, pictures and charts, audio signals from one computer to another, and so on. Today's computers, telephones, satellites, and tiny glass fibers convey data at speeds once con-sidered unattainable. Megabit chips enable transmission speeds measured in nanoseconds, billionths of a second.

This revolution in communications has not only drastically changed the way many industries do business, but has had effects that are beginning to be seen in many aspects of daily life.

Radio Wave Transmission

Radio communication, used since the 1920's, is the wireless transmission and reception of signals sent through space as electromagnetic waves. These waves are part of the electromagnetic spectrum, traveling through empty space at the speed of light.

Radio waves are measured according to their rate of oscillation, or regular fluctuation. Since all waves travel at the same speed, long waves oscillate only a few times in a given length of time; short waves oscillate more often in the same period of time.

Early radio communications traveled at low frequencies. Waves travel great distances, curving according to Earth's contour, bending around mountains or buildings. But as the frequency of waves increases, so does their information-carrying capacity. Higher frequency waves are less subject to interference. In recent decades technology has concentrated on developing communications for very high frequencies, thereby improving quality and capacity.

Radio wave transmissions include telegraphy, telephony, television, and radar. Each differs in the method by which the signal is transmitted and received. Information may be either analog or digital. Analog transmission, usually from a microphone, is the varying of a continuous signal. It has been commonly used for voice transmission. Digital transmission, using the binary digits 0 and 1, converts voice signals to digits and transmits them as *off* or *on* pulses.

Because radio frequencies, like any path or route, can accommodate only a given amount of traffic, frequencies are allocated carefully. International

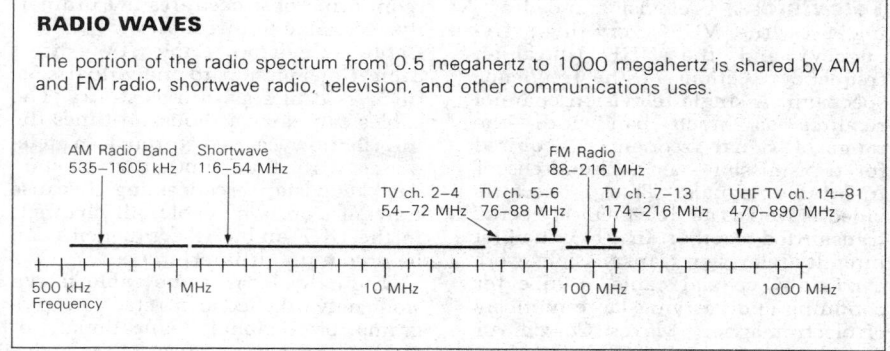

RADIO WAVES

The portion of the radio spectrum from 0.5 megahertz to 1000 megahertz is shared by AM and FM radio, shortwave radio, television, and other communications uses.

and domestic regulations deal with frequency allocations. The International Telecommunications Union, a specialized branch of the United Nations since 1947, works to enable use of the radio spectrum by all countries.

Radio. Radio is broadcast in either AM (amplitude modulation) or FM (frequency modulation). AM transmission, using low-frequency waves, sends information by varying or modulating the amplitude of the power wave. FM sends information by varying the frequency of the wave, while its amplitude remains the same. FM transmissions travel shorter distances than AM, and FM waves are straighter and more focused. But FM can carry more information and is free from atmospheric interference.

Stereophonic radio first was used experimentally in the early 1960's. Two FM signals from microphones placed on the right and on the left are transmitted together. The receiver separates them to be fed to separate speakers. Stereo sound is in widespread use today in television and AM radio, as well as in FM radio.

Cellular radio is a mobile radiotele-

phone system used in vehicles. A procedure known as handing off enables a call being made from a vehicle in one geographic spot, or cell, to be transferred automatically when the vehicle enters a new spot. Because there are many small cells in any given area, radio frequencies do not become overloaded. The computerized equipment monitoring the signals enables an instant switch from cell to cell.

Radio, like all communications, is now transmitted by microwave and satellite technologies. Microwaves, unlike longer radio waves, do not bounce off the ionosphere, so they travel essentially on straight lines. They can reach only as far as the horizon from where they are broadcast.

Microwave radio, using digital transmission, is expected to be used in the Federal Communications Commission (FCC) Digital Terminal System (DTS), a network for intracity communications. Several major companies have received FCC permission to begin developing DTS equipment. Radio transmissions via satellite began in August, 1982: the Satellite Music Network transmits two 24-hour programs via RCA's Satcom 1 to radio stations for local broadcast.

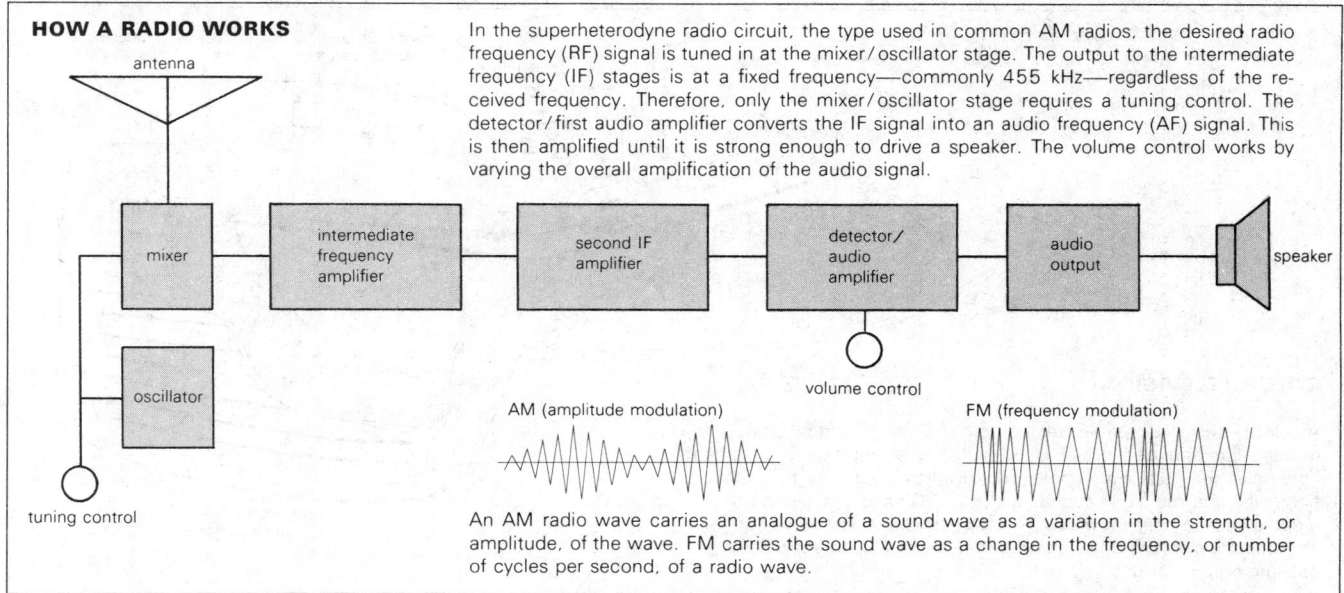

HOW A RADIO WORKS

In the superheterodyne radio circuit, the type used in common AM radios, the desired radio frequency (RF) signal is tuned in at the mixer/oscillator stage. The output to the intermediate frequency (IF) stages is at a fixed frequency—commonly 455 kHz—regardless of the received frequency. Therefore, only the mixer/oscillator stage requires a tuning control. The detector/first audio amplifier converts the IF signal into an audio frequency (AF) signal. This is then amplified until it is strong enough to drive a speaker. The volume control works by varying the overall amplification of the audio signal.

An AM radio wave carries an analogue of a sound wave as a variation in the strength, or amplitude, of the wave. FM carries the sound wave as a change in the frequency, or number of cycles per second, of a radio wave.

Television. Television broadcasting uses the VHF (very high frequency) and the UHF (ultrahigh frequency) sections of the frequency spectrum. A single television channel requires as much bandwidth—the range of signal frequencies required for transmission—as do hundreds of AM radio signals. This is because video as well as audio signals are being transmitted together. In 1946, the first intercity television transmissions were carried by coaxial cable, a tube for confining and carrying large numbers of electromagnetic waves. Coaxial, or broadband, communication can use the entire width of the VHF and UHF frequency ranges because there is no interference within the cable.

Television screens are cathode ray tubes containing electron guns that shoot electrons at phosphor-coated screens. The phosphors illuminate when radiated. A picture is created 30 times a second by changing the intensity of the electron beam. Color television, which was first commercially available in the early 1960's, uses three kinds of phosphors (red, green, and blue) and three electron guns, one activating each color. By combining them, all colors can be achieved. In modern television sets, electronic chips control the gun and the intensity, functions that used to be handled by vacuum tubes. The same chips also have improved quality and color by computerized filtering of the images.

The first television transmission by microwave was in 1947. In 1951, the microwave relay system (see below) transmitted a television broadcast across North America.

CCTV. Programming transmitted by wire within a building or other confined area is called closed circuit television (CCTV). It is in wide use in medicine and education. CCTV enables transmission of information or monitoring of procedures not ordinarily accessible to direct view.

Cable television. Cable TV, direct cable transmission to individual sets, involves cables as thin as straws. The cables can carry a thousand times the information carried through a telephone wire, four times that of standard television broadcasting. Because transmission is by cable, all channels in the UHF and VHF frequencies can be used without interference.

Originally local, some cable television networks concentrated on programs of regional, educational, or public service interest. But today many cable television networks are nationwide. Cable television is also useful in areas with poor standard broadcast reception. A predicted 90 percent of television viewers will be on cable systems within the next ten years, with much of the programming transmitted by satellite.

Cable TV has the potential for viewer interaction. The Subscriber Response System (SRS) may be a future means of casting ballots in an election or expressing opinions in public referendums. Zenith's new space phone, introduced in 1982, enables viewers to communicate through a television set. The audio part of the programming is replaced by the callers' voices. Future uses may include linking people with libraries, police, and medical services.

Telephone

Modern telephone equipment enables a user to put a call on hold, forward a call to another number, and automatically dial frequently used numbers. Telephones can signal the user that another call is coming through. Phones for offices have such sophisticated built-in devices as calculators, calendars, and screens for viewing data. These and other telephone models, such as those that look up and dial telephone numbers and take messages electronically, make ample use of microchips.

Because there are at least 132 million telephones in the United States, more than a million billion different connections must be achievable rapidly. Automated devices not only accomplish the switching in seconds but also record the billing information. Other improvements in central office switching include the Integrated Services Digital Network (ISDN), introduced in the United States in 1986. ISDN is a digital telecommunications network used with special telephone switching equipment to channel three kinds of information: voice, data, and control information, such as dialing codes, switching codes, and busy signals. Video also can be transmitted. Such a network eventually will eliminate separate transmission equipment for different kinds of communications.

Private branch exchanges (PBX) are central switching systems contained within individual buildings or complexes. Modern PBX systems convert signals into digital form. Computer data as well as audio signals can be transmitted, enabling many computer programs and peripherals to be used within a single system.

Interactive videotex enables subscribers to see, on their television screens or on lap-held monitors, information they have requested via telephone from data banks. In France, telephone books, as well as other sources of information, can be accessed by interactive videotex.

Pulse code modulation (PCM), introduced in the 1960's, enables transmission of twelve telephone conversations over a single pair of wires. The transmission of so many conversations at

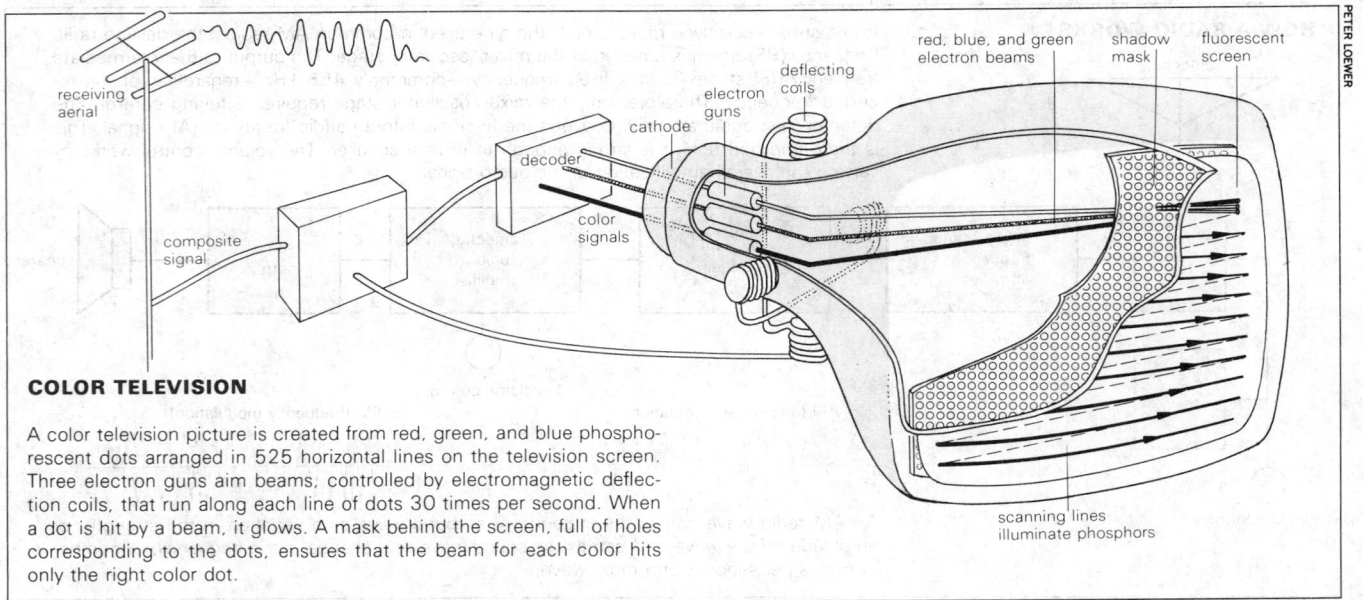

COLOR TELEVISION

A color television picture is created from red, green, and blue phosphorescent dots arranged in 525 horizontal lines on the television screen. Three electron guns aim beams, controlled by electromagnetic deflection coils, that run along each line of dots 30 times per second. When a dot is hit by a beam, it glows. A mask behind the screen, full of holes corresponding to the dots, ensures that the beam for each color hits only the right color dot.

receiving aerial · decoder · composite signal · cathode · color signals · electron guns · deflecting coils · red, blue, and green electron beams · shadow mask · fluorescent screen · scanning lines illuminate phosphors

PETER LOEWER

PULSE CODE MODULATION *enables a number of telephone conversations to be sandwiched in pulses on the same line, thus greatly reducing the number of telephone wires needed.*

one time can be compared to twelve decks of cards being shuffled so perfectly that single cards from all the decks in turn fall consecutively into one deck. To unscramble the cards exactly requires separating the batch, again consecutively, into twelve equal piles. Conversations are similarly overlapped in transmission. PCM equipment at the receiving end separates the pulses to reconstruct the original conversations. Multiplex transmission, an improvement over PCM, is the sharing of circuits in one of two different ways. Frequency-division multiplexing transmits different messages at slightly different frequencies. Amplified every few miles, frequency-division signals can be transmitted via underground and submarine cables. The L5 coaxial-cable system delivers nearly 11,000 telephone channels through a single pipe.

Time-division multiplexing is the transmission of different signals over a single channel, each varied slightly in time of transmission. Voice signals are converted to digital form, and each message is sampled 8000 times per second. The messages then are transmitted and neatly stacked or overlapped on one frequency, to be separated and decoded at destination. Costs are lower with time-division multiplexing, and its digital nature enables much of the work to be done with integrated circuits.

New Transmission Technology

Telecommunications today is dominated by microwave, laser beam, and fiber optics transmission.

Microwave relay system.
Microwaves are shorter than low-frequency radio waves, travel in a straighter line, can be more focused, and limit energy waste. By 1950, the microwave relay system, involving placement of receiving/transmitting towers approximately 30 miles apart, was in use in the United States.

Broadband signals capable of carrying large amounts of information are caught by tower antennae, amplified, and then sent on to the next tower. Because there are no physical links between towers, problems such as right of way are avoided. Lightning and high winds do not affect microwaves, but clouds and rain do.

In 1975, more than half of all U.S. long-distance calls and almost all interstate television broadcasts were transmitted by microwaves. Overcrowding of the microwave system plus the constant need to amplify the waves soon presented problems.

Laser beams.
Light is a form of electromagnetic energy that can carry information. Like radio waves and microwaves, light travels in a vibrating wave, but it also can be used as the flow of units of energy, called photons. Photons travel at the speed of light in a vacuum. They can travel through plastic, glass, and other media and can be manipulated by reflective surfaces, such as mirrors, lenses, and prisms.

A laser (light amplification by stimulated emission of radiation) is a gas, liquid, or solid medium within a tube-shaped chamber with mirrors at either end. One mirror, only partially reflective—like a surveillance mirror in a police station—allows the most powerful light to pass through. The rest is reflected. Introduction of an intense burst of energy into the chamber, either electric or light, charges the atoms in the medium with extra energy. Excess energy is released as a single light wavelength. It is reflected back and forth, building up additional energy. The light eventually breaks through the partially reflective mirror as a laser beam.

Laser light is monochromatic (composed of a single wavelength, or color) and coherent (polarized, a group of waves traveling in the same wavelength and frequency). Laser beams can focus great energy on a target area. Low-power laser beams can carry vast amounts of information.

Unfortunately, laser beams are subject to interference by weather: smog, fog, and snow can break up a light wave and absorb parts of it. Protective glass fibers clear enough to transmit light waves over long distances solve this problem.

Fiber optics.
Fiber optic cable, along with a laser beam, transmits light without need for amplification. The pure glass fiber, called a light guide, protects the light wave from interference. According to a principle called total internal reflection, the light waves are reflected into the center of the fiber when they strike the edge of the glass, thus manipulating the light around corners and bends. For sending telephone messages, sound waves converted to digital electrical signals are transmitted as light pulses. Time-division multiplexing within the fiber carries many messages. The capacity of a pair of optical fibers is equivalent to 24,000 telephone conversations.

In 1985, the Southern New England Telephone Company joined with CSX, a transportation corporation, to lay 8000 kilometers of optical fiber along railroad rights of way, reaching more than half of the United States. Similar networks followed.

TAT-8, an undersea fiber optic cable scheduled for use by 1986, is an inexpensive link between the United States and Europe. Compared with the first transatlantic cable, which was made of copper, TAT-8 carries a thousand times the information at a quarter of the weight and a fraction of the cost.

Light guides are helpful in photography and the observation of living organs during medical procedures. The endoscope, a modern medical instrument, is a fiber optic "eye," recording information for physicians.

Communications Satellites

Geosynchronous satellites positioned 22,000 miles above Earth are in widespread use today. Each can reach 40 percent of Earth's surface, so three satellites together have worldwide accessibility. The earliest communications satellites were satellites already in orbit that contained communications equipment and antennae.

In 1960, Echo I was launched into space, a satellite as tall as a ten-story building. Echo was a balloon made of Mylar, a material thinner than cellophane. A thin coating of aluminum on the surface of Echo reflected radio signals. Echo was a passive satellite, serving to reflect signals from Earth only when it was in the right position to do so.

In 1962, the Bell System launched Telstar, an active satellite (one that is part of a communications relay system). It carried transponders (radio or radar receivers that automatically transmit replies to certain signals) that amplified radio signals thousands of times before returning them to Earth. In 1965, the 85-pound Early Bird was sent into space and parked over the Atlantic in geostationary orbit, relaying 240 telephone conversations at a time and carrying a television station as well. This was the first space link for Intelsat (International Telecommunications Satellite Organization), an organization of 109 nations with 15 communications satellites in operation as of 1986. The organization has reduced telecommunication costs to about 5 percent of what they were in the 1960's. The sixth generation of Intelsat satellites, Intelsat VI, will have at least five solar-powered satellites, each carrying 30,000 voice circuits and several color television channels.

Ground terminals with 85-foot antennae receive transmissions from Intelsat satellites. Any country with one of these ground stations and membership in Intelsat can take part in worldwide telecommunications. Argentina and Chile, for example, despite sharing a 2000-mile border, had no direct communication, because of the Andes Mountains, before Intelsat gave them the means. An agreement in 1986 with the Soviet Union may mean a merger

A SATELLITE in geosynchronous orbit can reach 40 percent of Earth's surface.

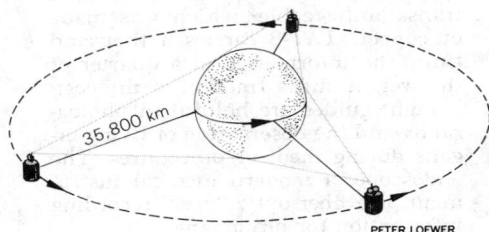

35,800 km

PETER LOEWER

RADAR uses the reflection of radio waves off an object to create an image of the object.

between Intelsat and the Soviet Intersputnik system of satellites. The International Telecommunications Union, a UN agency, now is structured to handle certain satellite functions: establishment of policies concerning major telecommunications issues, allocation of radio frequencies, planning for international satellite communications needs, and more.

For transmission of information between computers, satellites are 160 times faster than land transmission. A communications satellite can operate for years on the amount of energy required by a small light bulb. Cable television operators use satellite transmissions. Satellite dishes, huge satellite-receiving antennae, are seen even in backyards and on rooftops.

The 1985 Live Aid rock concerts broadcast by satellite from London and Philadelphia reached 1.5 billion people in 110 nations and raised tens of millions of dollars for African famine relief. NASA's communications satellite ATS3 provided essential support following the September, 1985, Mexican earthquake, when all other contact with the country had been lost. The hotline between the White House and the Kremlin now is transmitted via satellite and has been modernized to include transmission of charts, maps, etc.

In the future, direct broadcast satellite (DBS) will broadcast directly to homes. Programming received by inexpensive dish antennae less than 3 feet in diameter is expected to begin before 1990.

New communications satellites are launched into the geostationary belt as frequently as permitted by launching conditions. These satellites include privately owned satellites, such as Westar and Satcom. Domestic satellites such as Canada's Anik join others launched by Indonesia, Japan, Mexico,

Saudi Arabia, Australia, and the U.S.S.R. The geostationary orbit is a resource that is finite in terms of available space. Like radio frequencies, its use must be controlled and allocated.

Scientists say the technology of satellite communications is increasing and improving faster than any other. Citizens worldwide witness meetings between world leaders, dramatic ocean recoveries of astronauts and spacecraft, and Olympic Games. For example, an estimated 2 billion viewers watched the 1984 Olympic Games, which were transmitted by Intelsat.

Radar and Navigation

Radar (radio detection and ranging), invented in Britain in 1924, uses the reflection of radio waves to detect solid objects. Originally, long low-frequency radar waves gave little definition to objects located. Like radio and telephone transmission, modern radar has moved into the higher frequencies with improved results.

Invention of the klystron tube in 1939, which used the microwave portion of the radio spectrum, produced short, powerful radar waves capable of great accuracy.

The oceanographic satellite SEASAT, launched in 1978, used microwave wavelengths capable of penetrating cloud cover. Although it failed after 100 days, scientists had great success with two important radar devices installed on SEASAT. The radar altimeter, similar to one that had flown on Skylab, gave precise readings of sea surface height, thus enabling easy detection of ocean eddies, currents, and so on. It functioned perfectly to within 10 centimeters at altitudes of 790 kilometers. Synthetic-aperture radar (SAR) provided high-resolution imaging of surface waves, so scientists were able to detect patterns in the development of ocean eddies. SAR also has been used to measure ocean ice in climate studies.

The flight path of the space shuttle *Columbia* in November, 1981, passed over Egypt's Selima sand sheet, among the most barren land expanses in Africa. Shuttle-imaging radar, reflecting from bedrock beneath the sand, yielded pictures of river valleys buried below layers of sand. The area had obviously once been a major source of water.

In 1984, the U.S. Federal Aviation Authority began a ten-year modernization of airport radar and air traffic control systems, an estimated $10 billion project. New solid-state units to replace the existing vacuum-tube system will transmit weather and aircraft data simultaneously. Airport Surveillance Radar (ASR-9) will deliver weather information at six intensity levels.

Doppler radar.

Doppler radar is a pulsed carbon dioxide infrared device that monitors atmospheric properties such as the thickness of volcanic dust and wind variations. It measures the backscattering of certain radar waves, including laser waves from tiny water droplets and aerosols in the atmosphere. Also called wind-sensing coherent infrared radars, Doppler systems create global mapping of winds, and also can be used to detect downdrafts, perhaps helping to prevent wind shear-related aviation accidents.

Use of two Dopplers results in three-dimensional descriptions of winds and their velocities. A Doppler system developed in 1984, called NEXRAD (next generation radar), will collect data for predicting future amounts of rain and snow.

Navigation.

A navigator uses LORAN (long-range navigation) to calculate an exact position from radio signals transmitted by separate LORAN radio stations. Modern LORAN systems include computers that turn the antenna equipment toward the stations, collect and measure the intensities of their signals, and access maps from memory to display the exact location of the ship.

SARSAT (search and rescue satellite-aided tracking) is the project of nine countries that use U.S. and Soviet satellite-transmitted data to pinpoint emergency situations. In 1985, the United States and the U.S.S.R. signed an agreement to maintain satellites with SARSAT transponders.

NavStar, the U.S. global positioning system, will have 18 orbiting satellites by the late 1980's designed to transmit three-dimensional navigation data for use in air traffic control, search and rescue, and worldwide navigation.

Modern navigation equipment includes the laser gyroscope, first used in 1982 as a sensor for aircraft navigation systems. Because a laser beam is not diffuse, its reflection from solid objects results in precise distancing. Modern sextants are computerized and use tiny television cameras to scan the sky for the sun. The instruments use this location and the angle of rotation to calculate latitude.

Publishing

Preparation and printing of material for publishing have been affected enormously by automation. From the word processing programs used in almost all editorial and newspaper offices to light pens for corrections to programs that automatically check spelling, justify, compose, hyphenate, and print clean copy, to computer-assisted printing operations, the publishing world has become electronic.

Manuscripts are read on cathode-ray tubes, and corrections made swiftly and automatically. Charts, maps, graphs are added easily. Transmission to another office, another city, even across the world, is almost instantaneous. Information sources for checking facts are accessed easily. Artwork can be simulated, changed, made larger or smaller, and moved about. There are programs that help prepare indexes, tables of contents, maps, and bibliographies.

At the production end, automation has virtually eliminated manual typesetting. In 1968, the first electronically typeset novel was published. When a reduction in line length and narrower format were required, both were done easily by computer and at almost no additional expense. Now, when a manuscript is ready for typesetting, it can be run through a computer system in which an electronic beam writes it onto a cathode-ray tube at over 600 characters a second. The characters are simultaneously exposed on sensitized film. An entire book can be typeset and printing begun within minutes.

Newspapers such as the *Wall Street Journal* are transmitted electronically for printing in local areas. In 1967, an experimental transmission of the London *Daily Express* front page to Puerto Rico used telephone transmission, communications satellite (the Early Bird), and submarine cables to travel 50,000 miles in less than 15 minutes. Today the same trip takes only a few seconds.

MAGAZINE PUBLISHING

The time required to publish a magazine has been reduced dramatically by increased use of computers and digital communication. For example, an article can be written one day and published the next day simultaneously in many countries around the world. **1.** Portable computers are used to transmit stories over telephone lines from almost anywhere in the world to editorial offices. **2.** The stories are edited on computer terminals. **3.** The computer sets the text in type and a designer works on a terminal to fit together type and photographs to make up pages. **4.** Digitized images of the pages are sent to printing plants around the world where the magazine is quickly printed and distributed.

Advanced Information Storage

Computer output microfilming (COM) is a means of storing data in digital form without the previous existence of printed material. In some libraries, COM data have replaced printed book catalogs. The Library of Congress now offers COM-generated microfiche and microfilm, as do other independent companies. Libraries with computer equipment can prepare their own COM data.

A hologram is a laser-created picture containing a thousand times the information of a single photograph. Laser light reflected from an object exposes photographic film, creating a three-dimensional image. With a hologram, each data point can have other data points stacked above it. The hologram's immense capacity for information storage gives it the potential for storing up to 500 million words.

In compact disk read-only memory (CD-ROM), a powerful digital information storage device, the surface of the disk is etched with tiny marks that the CD-ROM drive reads by focusing a laser on the surface.

CD-ROM can be used with a computer. Information can be viewed on the cathode-ray tube screen or printed. Recent examples of data storage on a CD-ROM disk include the recording of an entire 20-volume encyclopedia on one-tenth of a disk. CD-ROMs for information storage are expected to include graphics and sound.

—Ann Marr

Materials

Plastics that can bind a 747 jet together better than steel rivets, ceramics that are able to withstand heat that would liquefy steel yet are rugged enough for use in automobile engines, molecule-cracking catalysts, and semiconductors many times faster than silicon are materials once thought to be the stuff of science fiction.

Four major categories of materials dominate modern research and development: ceramics, polymers, catalysts, and semiconductors. In addition, there is research on metals, new materials, and superconductors. More information on these subjects can be found in the CHEMISTRY AND PHYSICS volume.

Recent Advances

The present period of chemical technology is the era of the electronic revolution. Computers and other electronic instruments now collect, compile, compare, and transmit much more information in the laboratory and on the production line than was ever possible before. Information that provides more insights into the functioning of chemical processes and equipment spurs improved performance with respect to quantity, quality, and safety.

In the late 19th century, some chemical technologists began to note the common aspects of the operations required to make products. While various other disciplines were advancing, chemical knowledge was also expanding, especially in understanding the properties of matter, thermodynamics, chemical kinetics, and catalysis. Expanding knowledge made it possible to produce a large number of products from one material and to produce one product from many different starting materials.

Increased knowledge of building materials and development of construction skills made it possible to construct big, interconnected plants and systems to achieve production on a large and efficient scale. But comparable attention was not directed to the cyclical connection between natural resources and the disposal of wastes produced by these increasingly efficient plants. The criteria for plant efficiency generally failed to include or anticipate the possibility of costs beyond those of the most obvious methods of waste disposal.

Chemicals and Dyes

Chemical technology refers to the means, based on the science of chemistry, by which raw materials are converted into industrial and commercial products. Although there is a chemical nature to all materials, the term *chemical* usually refers to products derived, extracted, or synthesized from natural sources in commercial quantities to be used in the preparation of other products. Most modern chemicals of importance are obtained from organic materials and are called organic chemicals.

Until well into the 20th century, coal and wood were the major sources of such chemicals. Beginning about the 1920's, rapid growth in the use of motor fuels produced large quantities of relatively inexpensive byproducts of petroleum. From these byproducts, chemical companies developed over 3000 individual petrochemicals, constituting well over 80 percent of all organic chemicals. Coal, however, still forms the world's largest reserve of concentrated raw material from which chemicals can be extracted, so plans for the expanded use of coal continue to be updated. It is considered to be only a matter of time before the diminishing reserves of oil will necessitate the use of coal if an economy based on organic materials is to be sustained.

Chemicals from Coal

Initially, most chemicals from coal were obtained by destructive distillation. Coal was pyrolyzed to produce a variety of solid, liquid, and gaseous products depending on the temperature used in the pyrolysis and the type of coal used. The principal product by weight was solid coke, but liquids, called coal tar, also were produced along with gases.

Coal tar and coal-tar products were considered to be wastes until 1856, when Sir William Perkin, an English

PETROLEUM REFINING

| Separation |

gas
gasoline
naphtha
DISTILLATION
kerosene
farm
CRUDE OIL
gas oil
water   solid contaminants
residue
ATMOSPHERIC OR VACUUM DISTILLATION — heavy gas oil
asphaltic
VACUUM DISTILLATION — heavy gas oil, asphalt
lubricating oil
VACUUM DISTILLATION — heavy gas oil, lubricating distillates

chemist, synthesized the first coal-tar color, a brilliant violet dye, and coal tar became a commercial product of increasing value. Today petroleum supplies so many of the chemicals formerly derived from coal tar that producing coke has once again become the major reason for distilling coal.

The coal is pyrolyzed in long narrow chambers, called byproduct ovens, that hold about 15 to 25 tons. The volatile substances leaving the oven contain gases usable as fuel as well as condensable coal-tar vapors. After condensation, the coal tar is distilled to separate the chemicals, oils, and hard pitches used for electrode binders, road tar, or roofing material. The chief products are benzene, toluene, xylene, naphthalene, and methynaphthalenes. These products are known as aromatics and consist of ring structures of carbon with hydrogen. They are starting materials for dyes, medicinals, flavors, perfumes, resins, rubber chemicals, and thousands of other products.

Chemicals from Petroleum

The story of petroleum parallels that of modern civilization. Gasoline, once discarded as waste, grew to be the major product derived from petroleum. Waste gases from the production of fuel oil and gasoline became the starting materials for more than 3000 petrochemicals. From these petrochemicals came what seems to be an almost unlimited supply of raw materials for expanding industry: antifreeze, lubricating oil additives, resins for plastics, synthetic fibers, protective coatings, fertilizers, and pesticides. The petroleum/chemical industry even displaced the coal industry as a source of 98 percent of the aromatic chemicals. At first, oil companies sold their waste gases from petroleum refining operations to chemical companies, which separated and converted them to useful products. Now many petroleum refiners and chemical producers have combined operations.

Crude oil refining.
Thousands of chemical substances make up crude petroleum. They include gases, liquids, and solids and range from methane to asphalt. Although there are significant numbers of compounds containing nitrogen, sulfur, and oxygen, most constituents of petroleum are hydrocarbons. Refining does not usually separate crude oil into pure chemical compounds. Most petroleum products are mixtures of compounds separated on the basis of distillation; that is, boiling points. They are identified by the ultimate uses for which they are best suited.

Petrochemical production.
The mixtures produced by crude oil refining are treated further to obtain the precursors to petrochemical products. Olefins, which are unsaturated hydrocarbons, and aromatics are separated by such operations as distillation, absorption, solvent extraction, crystallization, encapsulation, and adsorption plus fluid flow and heat transfer unit operations. These products are reformed by a variety of chemical conversions. About 70 percent of the crude oil processed in the United States is subjected to conversion processes. The major conversion processes include the following.

Cracking. The major conversion process, for which the industry is best known, is cracking, or pyrolysis, in which large hydrocarbon molecules are broken down into smaller molecules by heat or catalytic action.
Polymerization. Similar molecules are linked, and light (low molecular weight) olefins are joined together.
Alkylation. Olefins are joined with an aromatic or paraffinic hydrocarbon.
Hydrogenation. Hydrogen is added to an olefin.
Isomerism. The position of atoms in a molecule is altered without changing the number of atoms.
Reforming or aromatization. Naphthas (refining products with boiling ranges between gasoline and kerosene) are converted to obtain products of higher octane number. Reforming is similar to cracking except that the starting materials are more easily vaporized and the catalysts usually contain rhenium, platinum, or chromium.
Esterification and hydration. Esterification is the reaction of alcohol and an organic acid to form a single molecule by eliminating a water molecule between them. Hydration is the addition of a water molecule to the molecular structure of an organic molecule.

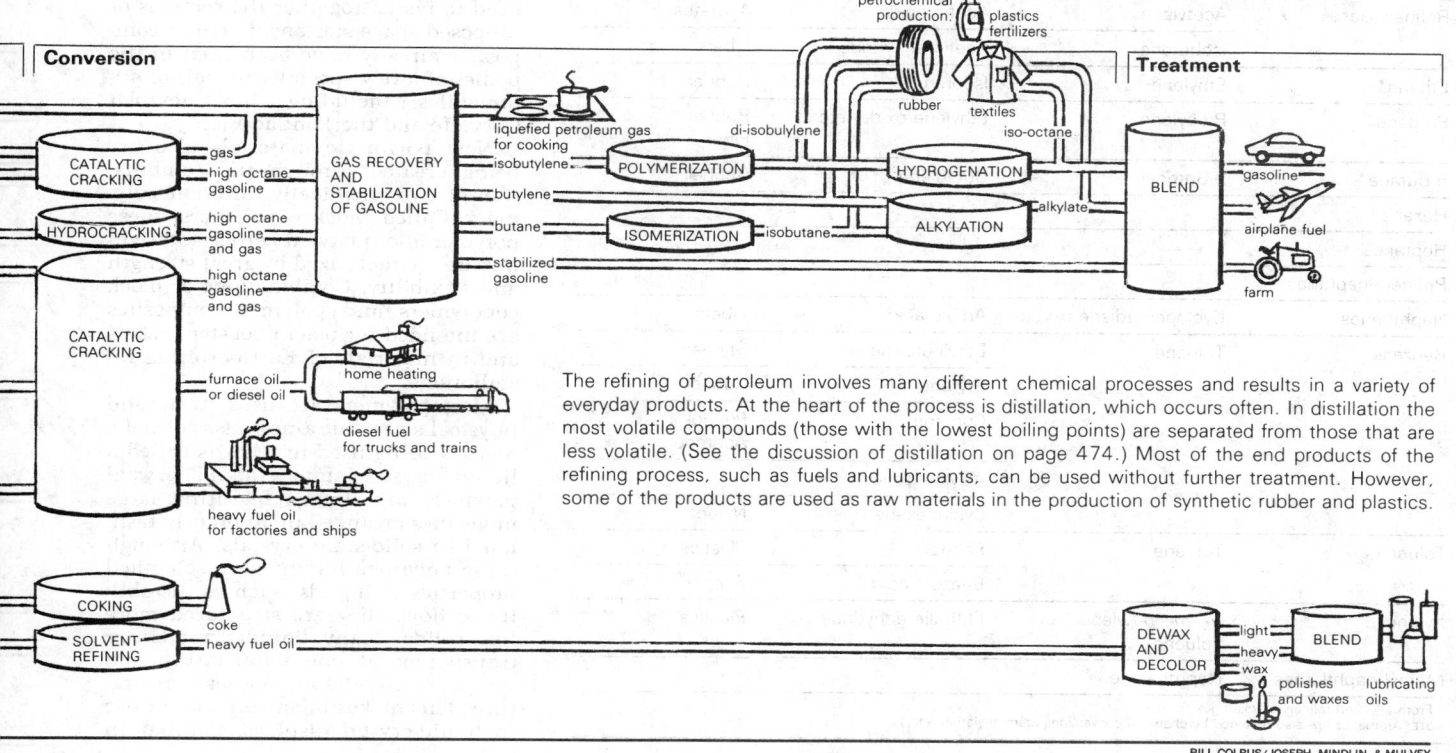

The refining of petroleum involves many different chemical processes and results in a variety of everyday products. At the heart of the process is distillation, which occurs often. In distillation the most volatile compounds (those with the lowest boiling points) are separated from those that are less volatile. (See the discussion of distillation on page 474.) Most of the end products of the refining process, such as fuels and lubricants, can be used without further treatment. However, some of the products are used as raw materials in the production of synthetic rubber and plastics.

BILL COLRUS/JOSEPH, MINDLIN, & MULVEY

Petrochemicals. Products obtained from the separation and chemical conversion of crude oil or natural gas form the precursors of petrochemicals. In turn, theses precursors are treated by various unit operations and chemical conversions to form end products.

Many different kinds of products are derived from petroleum, and new ones are being discovered all the time. Petrochemical end products include the adhesives; agrichemicals; alcohols; ammonia; antifreeze and antiknock; detergents; dyes, lakes, and toners; electrical insulation; explosives; fertilizers and pesticides; flavors and perfumes; the flotation agents; the food additives; industrial carbon; industrial gases; lubricants and additives; medicinal products; nitrogen industries; paints, varnishes, etc.; plastics, polymers, and plasticizers; rubber, rubber chemicals; solvents; sulfur and sulfuric acid; surface coatings; synthetic fibers; synthetic motor fuels.

Polymers

Polymers are materials composed of large molecules that are themselves formed from chains of smaller molecules, called monomers. Monomers are assembled, or grown, in a sequence that may be repeated thousands of times to produce a single polymer. Polymers are both natural and synthetic. Cellulose, for example, is a natural polymer, occurring in the cell walls of plants. The main constituent of wood, cellulose is a repeating chain of monomers consisting of carbon, hydrogen, and oxygen atoms. Proteins, starches, fingernails, and hair are also natural polymers.

Synthetic polymers are more commonly known as plastics. The monomers used to construct synthetic polymers are made from the chemicals in raw materials, primarily petroleum. Alexander Parkes, an English chemist, created in 1862 the first synthetic

POLYMERS *are being used in the construction of some automobiles, like the Pontiac Fiero.*

polymer, a cellulosic plastic, but it was not until two years later that a usable product was invented by an American, John Wesley Hyatt, who called the material celluloid. Synthetic polymers have become increasingly popular in recent times. Materials such as polyethylene, a long chain of simple ethylene molecules, have joined nylon, polyvinyl chloride, and polystyrene on the international marketplace.

A high strength-to-weight ratio is the prime virtue of all polymers. Industrial-strength polymers surpass titanium in tensile strength. To strengthen the material even further and improve its flexibility, polymers are sometimes fortified with chopped short-fiber additives, most commonly fiberglass. The material is called a polymer composite. One new polymer composite has three times the strength of tempered steel and is being used in bulletproof vests. Another composite, a graphite reinforced epoxy, will be used to fasten together the sections of proposed space stations. Polymer composites already have been used in the bodies of a few specialty models of automobiles, including the Chevrolet Corvette and the Pontiac Fiero.

New polymeric materials also are being created through the combination of two chemically different polymers. Called block copolymers, these polymer alloys have no other additives but are characterized by great strength and flexibility. Combinations of block copolymers and polymer composites are intended for use in booster rockets and in materials of Earth-orbiting installations.

Most polymers are used in a solid physical state, but a new class of polymers is being used in what is called a liquid crystal state. Liquid crystal polymers are liquids featuring large molecules arranged in an orderly fashion like solid-state crystals. Although these polymers retain the mechanical properties of liquids, such as the ability to flow, they are structured more like solids. Many liquid crystals are transparent at one temperature and opaque or colored at another temperature. This makes them suitable for use in liquid-crystal displays, familiar in

PRIMARY PRECURSORS: PETROLEUM-PETROCHEMICAL COMPLEX

RAW MATERIALS BY DISTILLATION	PRECURSORS BY CONVERSION	INTERMEDIATES BY CONVERSION	FINISHED PRODUCTS BY CONVERSION
Paraffins Cyclics	Olefins Diolefins Acetylene Aromatics	Various inorganics and organics	Inorganics and organics
Natural gas			Carbon black
Sulfides	H_2S	S, H_2S	H_2SO_4
Hydrogen		Synthesis gas	NH_3
Methane			Methanol Formaldehyde
Refinery gases	Acetylene	Acetic acid	Acetates
	Isobutene	Acetic anhydride	Fibers
Ethane*	Ethylene	Isoprene	Rubber
Propane*	Propylene	Ethylene oxide, etc.	Rubber Fiber
n-Butane*	n-Butenes	Butadiene	Rubber
Hexane			
Heptanes			
Refinery naphthas			
Naphthenes	Cyclopentadiene	Adipic acid	Fibers
Benzene	Toluene	Ethylbenzene	Styrene
		Styrene	Rubber
		Cumene	Phenol Acetone
		Alkylbenzene	
		Cyclohexane	Nylons
Toluene	Toluene	Phenol	Plastics
		Benzoic acid	Phenol
Xylenes	o-, m-, p-Xylene Toluene	Phthalic anhydride	Plastics
Methyl naphthanes	Naphthalene		

* From LPG and refinery cracked gas.
NOTE: Aromatics are also obtained by chemical conversions (demethylation. etc.).

digital watches, hand-held calculators, and most lap-top computers.

A new type of liquid polymer, loaded with a mixture of powdered iron and nickel, is being used to make metallic inks, which can be stenciled onto almost any kind of surface, including glass, paper, and other polymers. The first application of this material will be to make printed circuits on electronic circuit boards.

The properties of a polymer are determined by its microstructure, which in turn is a product of the chemical composition of the material plus changes that occur during processing. Polymers usually are processed while the material is in a liquid state, with fiber additives forming flow patterns that are much like logs floating on a river. The material then is cooled and solidified, except for liquid crystal polymers. During the processing, the orientation of the long molecules within a polymer or polymer composite is established. This orientation determines the solid-state properties of the polymer. A new technique still in the developmental stage, called coprocessing, is the simultaneous processing of two polymers to form a single material. This technique should result in the creation of new high-performance polymer materials.

Despite the extensive development and widespread use of polymers, and despite their tremendous promise for the future, scientific understanding of polymers is still sketchy. Polymer development through the years has generally come piecemeal, from trial and error. Such scientific shortcomings are becoming more apparent in the search for polymer materials that can meet the demands of high technology. In the past, scientific research has concentrated on the microstructures of polymers after they have been processed and cooled into a solid state. The new focus is on polymer microstructure while the material is still in the liquid state; the purpose is to learn how the solid-state structure is established. The ultimate goal is to be able to predict properties that will be obtained from a specific material under a given set of processing conditions.

Catalysts

Polymerization, the assembling of monomers into a polymer, is triggered by the application of heat, a catalyst, or both. Catalysts initiate, speed up, or slow down chemical reactions without undergoing chemical changes themselves. A society's standard of living can be said to be directly related to its catalytic technology because all industrial manufacturing processes begin with catalysis. Catalysts, like polymers, occur naturally and can be synthesized. Though many catalytic materials have been known and exploited for years, new demands created by the latest industrial technologies have called for new catalysts, as well as improvements in the properties of those already in use.

Zeolites. Generating the most industrial excitement today are porous crystalline catalysts, called zeolites. They are made from alumina silicates found in virtually all soil.

The pore structure of zeolite surfaces enables these catalysts to function as molecular sieves. Any molecule passing through the pores of a zeolite can undergo bond-breaking chemistry; that is, the electrical force holding together the atoms of the molecule can be overcome. If a molecule is small enough to enter the holes, it will be absorbed by the zeolite. If the molecule is too big to pass through the holes, it will be rejected. This selective absorption or rejection enables zeolites to separate liquids or gases, or to speed up refining processes by breaking the molecular bonds of organic molecules, such as those of petroleum. Speeding up the petroleum refining process can significantly reduce the cost of the production of gasoline.

Projected future roles of zeolites in the energy industry include their use in producing synthetic gasoline from natural gas, in cleaning spent nuclear fuel, and in drying natural gas for use in heating. Zeolites may also be used in timed-release capsules and to simplify manufacture of certain pharmaceutical drugs, such as L-dopa, which is used in treating Parkinson's disease.

Only a dozen zeolite catalysts have ever been developed to commercial significance, even though hundreds are possible. Currently, zeolite catalysts are made by following established chemistry recipes, but the recipes are not sufficiently understood to know how much more effective these catalysts could be, or how many other useful variations are possible.

Transition-metal catalysts. An important future also is suggested for transition-metal catalysts, compound materials consisting of a nonmetal and a metal that include the carbides (compounds of carbon and a metal), nitrides, sulfides, and borides. These materials have an arrangement of electrons that gives them unique electronic properties. It is believed by many materials scientists that transition-metal catalysts could become inexpensive replacements for expensive rare metal catalysts not found in the United States.

Other new catalysts. Organometallic compounds—materials composed of metal atoms sandwiched between organic molecules—can be used to make catalysts that may help in converting coal to liquid or gaseous fuel. Organometallic catalysts also may help in the recovery of metals from the aqueous waste of oil shale.

Since all catalysis takes place on the surfaces of materials—both of the catalyst and the material with which it is reacting—scientists are exploring the relationship between microscopic surface structures and catalytic activity. In the past, catalysis research was pursued with a specific purpose in mind. Today the hope is that by obtaining a better understanding of the catalytic process, new applications of catalysts, as well as new catalytic materials, will be discovered.

Semiconductors

In the electronics industry, the search is on for a semiconductor that is faster and that can perform a greater variety of functions than silicon.

Silicon. How fast a microprocessor can take an incoming electrical signal and send it out to a circuit component depends on how fast electrons can move through the semiconductor material of the chip. The first integrated circuit was fashioned from germanium. Use of germanium was limited by an inability to function at high temperatures, so it was quickly replaced by silicon. Silicon crystals, doped with an impurity such as aluminum or boron, are easy and inexpensive to produce and can withstand heat and handle large numbers of transistors and other circuit components on their surfaces. They also have swift electrons.

As fast as silicon is at processing electrical signals, it is not fast enough to handle the requirements of supercomputers. Devices called junctions, which route electrical signals on a microprocessor chip by permitting or denying the flow of electrical current, have been developed; they can switch on or off 100 million times a second. At this rate of data transmission, information would soon become seriously bottlenecked on a silicon microprocessor chip.

Gallium arsenide. Bottlenecks would be far less likely using microprocessor chips made of gallium arsenide, a crystalline compound of gallium and arsenic. Gallium arsenide provides high electron velocity at low electric fields because its electrons travel in a unique wave motion and have a smaller effective mass than that of silicon. Under equal electrical force, therefore, it takes a hundred times more electrical power for a silicon chip to attain about half the speed of a comparably sized gallium arsenide integrated circuit. At such power levels, adequate cooling becomes an insurmountable problem for the silicon chip.

Gallium arsenide also can be used to make light-emitting devices, such as lasers, for optical-fiber transmissions. Offering about 30 times the capacity of copper wiring, fiber optics are playing an increasing role in telecommunication. Light waves travel in a straight line, but when carried through filaments of polymer fibers, they can be bent around corners or wound along twisted paths. By varying the amount of light sent through these fibers, sound and images can be transmitted across great distances almost instantaneously. For the potential of fiber optics to be fully realized, a means of efficiently converting electrical signals into light is needed. Light-emitting diodes (LEDs) are a possibility for local transmission, but they lack the power for long-distance communication. Lasers must be used for long distance.

Use of gallium arsenide has been hampered by problems that occur when crystals of the material are fabricated into chips or other usable devices. For example, during the various heating cycles used in most manufacturing processes, arsenic can readily leave the crystal unless special precautions are taken. The problem stems from the fact that unlike silicon, which has a very stable oxygen compound (silicon oxide) to protect the surface structure of its crystal during processing, gallium arsenide has no protective oxide of its own. To protect the crystal, gallium arsenide must be capped with another substance, such as silicon nitride. This can open up new problems.

Supercomputers, the next generation of computers, will demand very large-scale integrated circuits (VLSIs). Such circuits require bulk crystals, 2 to 3 inches in diameter, of a semiconductor material. It is difficult to grow structurally perfect gallium arsenide crystals of this size, and the superb electronic properties of a gallium arsenide crystal can be reduced markedly by defects. For a gallium arsenide crystal to perform properly, gallium and arsenide must be present in precisely equal amounts. If they are not, gallium arsenide will not function as a semiconductor.

Electromagnetic pulse. Microprocessor chips made from gallium arsenide crystals are far less sensitive to radiation than are silicon crystals. For this reason, gallium arsenide semiconductor devices are relatively immune to electromagnetic pulse, the nuclear explosion-generated radiation effect that defense strategists fear could knock out many of the silicon-based communications networks and computers in the United States.

Wiring. Although components required for an electric circuit are chemically processed into a semiconductor chip, wiring is still needed to connect the components. Unfortunately, wires will not be able to withstand the heat and intensity of the powerful electrical current passing through VLSIs of the supercomputer. Techniques now are being developed to eliminate the need for wiring. One technique involves deposition of a film of tungsten only a few molecules thick on the surface of the microprocessing chip. Electrical signals then are transported through the tungsten film.

Another possibility being investigated would combine gallium arsenide with silicon to obtain the high performance of gallium at the price and strength of silicon. By depositing a layer of gallium arsenide on a silicon surface, electronic devices in an integrated circuit can be connected by superquick, tough, and efficient optical fibers.

A drawback is that it is difficult to align atoms of silicon and gallium arsenide. Mismatches create problems for the accurate transmission of electrical signals. Tilting the silicon base creates atomic steps that may compensate for mismatches.

Metals

Metals are outstanding conductors of electricity and heat. These qualities, combined with strength, malleability, and ductility ensure that metals will continue to be significant materials.

Receiving the most attention at this time is the possibility of creating metal materials with the heat endurance of ceramics and the elasticity of polymers. For example, a stretchable stainless steel has been made that can be molded into a variety of shapes with almost no size limitations. The stretchability is provided by a carbon steel core sandwiched between thin stainless steel veneers.

Refining metals. A few metals exist naturally in elemental form: copper, gold, silver, platinum, and bismuth. Metals occur most commonly as oxides or sulfides in ores containing variable amounts of gangue; that is, worthless earth, rock. A variety of methods are used to reduce the oxides or sulfides to the metal form. Some sulfides can be reduced by heating in air, others by heating with oxides.

Smelting. By far the greatest tonnage of metals, mainly iron, is produced by reduction at high temperatures with carbon or carbon compounds in a process called smelting. Copper, zinc, cadmium, antimony, tin, nickel, cobalt, and molybdenum also are produced in this way.

Electrolysis. Many metals, including aluminum, sodium, magnesium, and potassium, are produced or refined by electrolysis in aqueous or molten salt baths. The English chemist Sir Humphry Davy prepared potassium and sodium for the first time in the early 1800's using electrolysis. In this method, electricity is used to split a chemical compound into its constituent elements, either when it is in solution or in the molten state.

Aluminum, for example, is produced by electrolysis from purified bauxite, an oxide ore, from a molten solution. In the process, pure alumina (aluminum oxide) is dissolved in molten cryolite (another aluminum mineral). This permits the temperature to be reduced to about 950°C—pure alumina melts above 2000°C. Electricity is passed through the molten solution between carbon rods, which act as the anode, and the graphite lining of the cell, which acts as the cathode. The purified molten aluminum collects in the cathode floor. Oxygen is produced at the anodes.

Metals such as sodium, magnesium, aluminum, and calcium have so powerful a reducing action that they can be used in the preparation of other metals. Hydrogen also is used to reduce some metal ores.

Leaching. A third major process for producing metals is leaching, the treatment of ores by chemical solutions. Certain copper oxide ores, such as cuprite, are treated in this way. When washed with a sulfuric acid solution, the copper oxide dissolves to form copper sulfate, leaving the insoluble gangue behind. After purifying the copper sulfate solution, copper metal is obtained by electrolysis. Sulfuric acid also is used to extract uranium, and sodium cyanide is used to leach gold and silver.

Modern Metal Processes

Modern research has concentrated on how to process materials in bulk amounts while retaining their intrinsic properties. These properties include strength and melting point, which are measured or otherwise observed in individual crystals or small segments of materials. These desirable properties often are degraded in bulk amounts because of the presence of impurities or other difficulties arising from the fabrication process.

Beryllium in space. Although the strength-to-weight ratio of aluminum is generally adequate for aircraft, the space shuttle orbiters require beryllium for certain uses because of its high stiffness-to-density ratio.

Critical structures in the windshield retainer, inertial measurement unit, and umbilical doors are made of beryllium. A weight saving of 172 pounds was made on a total of 20 parts at a cost increase of $1350 per pound. It is important to note that putting an extra pound into orbit from the space shuttle costs $1500 to $3000.

Porous aluminum. Manufacturing techniques for most porous metals rely on sintering by use of a pressure-forming machine. In 1978, Japanese researchers, using a new technique, started a pilot plant that manufactured porous aluminum. By 1983, the product was in use as standard soundproofing by TV companies, in office buildings, and on high-speed train lines.

Porous aluminum has low specific gravity, good flexibility with a great capacity for elongation, and comparatively low cost of manufacture because of its low sintering temperature. In a 3-mm thick sheet, it provides sound absorption equivalent to that of a 50-mm thick sheet of other sound absorbents. Water drains rapidly from it and barely affects its acoustic properties. It has good ventilation and radiation properties, resists heat and corrosion when painted, and can be used for decoration because it can be patterned before sintering.

The key to the successful sintering was the use of a low-pressure method instead of a pressure-forming machine. By the same process, aluminum powder can be sintered onto a solid aluminum plate to create a material useful for nucleate boiling and for radiation plates.

Alloys. The classifications of alloys reflect the extent of miscibility of the constituents in the liquid and solid states. By far the most important group of alloys consists of those that are miscible over a considerable range of composition and temperature. Alloys are made to obtain desirable properties that the pure components do not have or to obtain required properties at lower cost.

Rapid solidification. In rapid solidification processing (RSP), molten metal is quenched rapidly by spraying it onto a cold rotating wheel or another surface in an oxygen-free atmosphere. Quenching conditions can be controlled to produce either an amorphous (noncrystalline) or a microcrystalline form. Variations of the technique are used to produce composite structures with specific properties, such as magnets with high energy, great resistance to demagnetization, and, when they are magnetized, higher strength of magnetic field. These advanced techniques make possible the use of much smaller magnets in electric and magnetic devices that help to achieve desired reductions in the size of motors by a factor of as much as 40 to 50 percent.

In a plasma deposition technique, fine powdered alloys (30 to 40 micrometers) of almost any composition are injected into a stream of high-energy ionized gases (plasma) heated to a temperature of 11,000°C, or 20,000°F. The alloys melt instantaneously and are propelled away from the gun nozzle at about 800 km an hour. After a flight of less than a second, the liquid droplets hit a substrate where they are quenched at a rate close to 500,000°C per second (1 million°F/second). After the metal is built up layer by layer to the desired shape, size, and composition pattern—by spraying different alloys at specific sites to achieve specific properties—the substrate is etched or machined away to leave an almost finished part. This process has been used to fabricate turbine blades with a corrosion-resistant alloy for the outer skin and with high structural strength for the inner core. This plasma deposition technique is still in its developmental stage and is more expensive than powder metallurgy and casting, but it is expected to rival both of them in importance.

Lanxides. Also in development is an entirely new category of metal materials called lanxides. Lanxides are formed when a molten metal reacts with a vapor-phase oxidant, such as oxygen in the air. By controlling the temperature of the molten metal and slightly doping the metal with other metals, it is possible to grow an inch-thick layer of a metal oxide composite on the surface of the molten metal. When the molten metal cools and hardens, it has a protective coating that makes it sufficiently heat-resistant for use in rocket engines yet tough enough to be used as armor plating.

Other new metallurgical techniques still in the experimental stage, such as the implantation of atoms from one metal onto the surface of another metal, may result in metals and metal alloys never before achievable.

Nonequilibrium materials. Explorations are beginning on the next materials frontiers, the nonequilibrium materials and high-temperature superconductors.

Nonequilibrium materials exist in an unnaturally energetic or ordered state. They possess physical, chemical, and electrical properties that may be entirely different from the properties the same materials would possess in

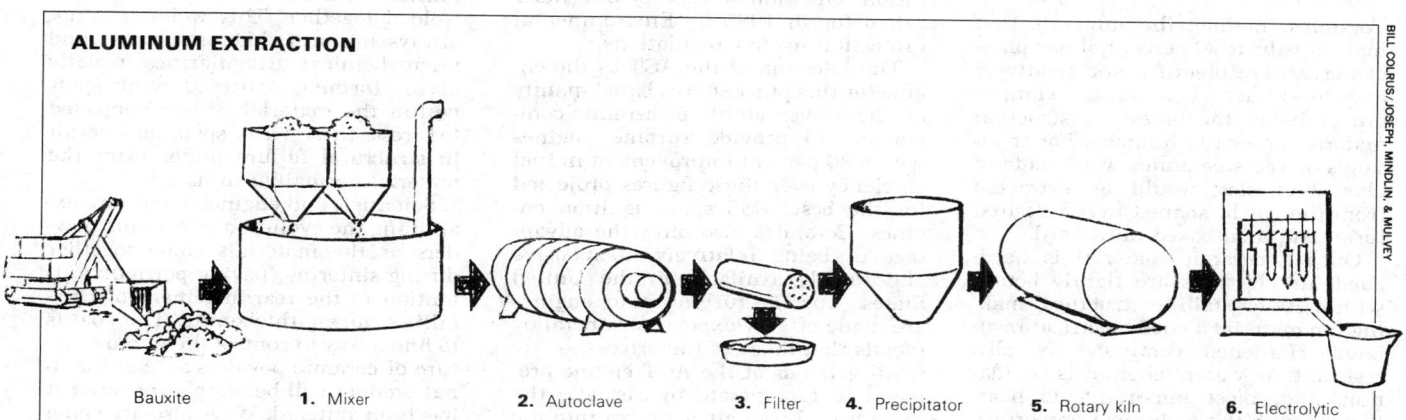

ALUMINUM EXTRACTION

Bauxite — **1.** Mixer — **2.** Autoclave — **3.** Filter — **4.** Precipitator — **5.** Rotary kiln — **6.** Electrolytic furnace

BILL COLRUS/JOSEPH, MINDLIN, & MULVEY

1. Aluminum-rich bauxite is mixed with lime, soda ash, and water to form a caustic soda solution. **2.** With the addition of heat in an autoclave, the alumina (aluminum oxide) is dissolved into the solution. The impurities remain solid. **3.** The solids are filtered from the solution. **4.** The alumina is precipitated from the solution in crystalline form. **5.** Water is removed from the alumina crystals in a rotary kiln. **6.** Finally, the alumina crystals are dissolved into molten cryolite, and electrolysis is used to remove pure aluminum from the solution. (See the CHEMISTRY AND PHYSICS volume, pages 412–413, for an explanation of electrolysis.)

their natural energetic state. A familiar example of such a material that is produced by natural processes is the diamond, which is graphite that has been forced into a perpetually excited state by exposure to the intense heat and pressure deep below Earth's surface. Scientists are trying to duplicate the natural processes by forming a material at high temperature and pressure, then keeping it stable for use at ambient temperatures and pressures.

High-temperature superconductor.

If a high-temperature superconductor ever becomes a reality, the global energy situation will be significantly improved. In a superconducting state, a material loses all electrical resistance. This means that unlike today's inefficient electrical transmission wires, wires made from a superconductor could transmit electricity over vast distances with no loss of power. To date, however, making a superconductor has meant chilling a material nearly to absolute zero (−273°C), an operation far too expensive to be of commercial value.

The break-even point for commercially useful superconducting wires is estimated to be about 70°K (−203°C). Since the highest temperature superconducting material currently in use is a niobium-germanium compound that becomes superconducting at about 23°K at atmospheric pressure, it appears that new materials will have to be found. Work is under way by scientists around the world to find the fundamental ingredients required for high-temperature superconductivity.

Ceramics

Ceramics, nonmetallic minerals that make up about 70 percent of our planet's crust, are plentiful and relatively easy to extract. As a result, ceramics are probably the oldest construction material known to humans. For thousands of years ceramics were made of clay. Wet clay would be extracted from the earth, shaped into a desired form, and then baked until hard.

Once a ceramic material is hardened, its electrons are tightly bound within its crystalline structure, making the material a good electrical insulator. Hardened ceramics are also resistant to water, chemicals, oxidation, and, most important, to heat. Blessed with these physical properties, ceramics are well suited for the production of a wide variety of items, including bricks and tiles, cooking and eating ware, sanitary equipment, and electrical insulation. Ceramic materials are used as furnace liners by the steel and pulp industries, as cladding materials for the nuclear fuel ele-

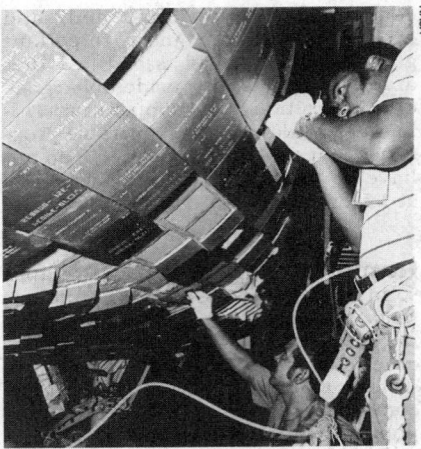

CERAMIC TILES, *because of their high resistance to heat, are used as heat shields on space shuttles.*

ments in gas-cooled fission reactors, and in textile machinery.

Modern ceramics are not made from clay, but from powders of complex chemical compounds. Projected uses for modern ceramics include high-energy storage batteries that are able to maintain constant voltage through their discharge cycles, artificial human hips, and microprocessing chips.

Advanced gas turbine.

The most immediate new use of ceramics will be in the advanced gas turbine (AGT) automobile engine, an engine being jointly sponsored by the U.S. Department of Energy and the National Aeronautics and Space Administration. All major U.S. automobile makers are involved in the project, which calls for development of advanced automotive power trains capable of promoting fuel conservation through improved efficiency. Such power trains also are required to reduce pollution emission levels below those called for in 1985 by Environmental Protection Agency regulations.

The selection of the AGT as the engine for this purpose was based mainly on the proven ability of ceramic components to provide turbine engines with a 30 percent improvement in fuel efficiency over those figures projected for the best 1985 spark ignition engines. Ceramics also offer the advantage of being relatively inexpensive and readily available in the United States. Current turbine auto engines are made of very expensive superalloy metals that must be imported.

All versions of the AGT engine proposed so far operate in basically the same way. Fresh air is drawn into the engine and pressurized. The highly compressed air passes through a regenerator, where it receives waste heat recovered from the engine exhaust. The heated air then enters the combustor. Fuel is added and the mixture burns, raising its temperature for expansion in the turbine. When the hot, expand-

ing gases of the mixture are channeled into the turbine, the thermal energy of the gases is converted by a bladed rotor into kinetic energy, providing power to both the compressor and the automobile drive shaft. (See also the discussion of internal combustion engines on page 1026.)

Current AGT engine plans call for the bladed rotor, combustor, compressor, and regenerator to be made of ceramics. These ceramic components will enable the AGT engine to operate at temperatures of 1300°C or more (2300°F). Since the higher the temperature at which the fuel is burned, the more efficiently the engine will perform, the AGT engine should outperform any engine on the road today.

If the AGT engine or any of the other projected applications of modern ceramics are to be realized, manufacturers will need to know more about ceramic microstructures and the relationship between these microstructures and ceramic properties. Despite the extensive use and development of ceramics, a basic understanding is lacking of why ceramics are what they are. In the further development of ceramics, more knowledge is needed to cope with brittleness, the most serious deficiency.

Brittleness is not a major problem when a material is being used to make a heat shield for a space shuttle, or a liner for a blast furnace. However, under the massive stresses that the components of an AGT automobile engine must endure, brittleness can be a fatal flaw.

The nature of chemical bonding in ceramics ensures that these materials will always suffer from brittleness to some extent, but current ceramic manufacturing technology aggravates the problem. When ceramic powders are sintered, that is, caused to become a coherent mass by heating, the crystallites (grains) of the material are welded together. This welding is not always uniform. Microstructural and microchemical irregularities usually occur, forming scattered weak spots within the material. When subjected to stress, these weak spots may result in structural failure under loads the material normally can handle.

Scientists and engineers now are examining the evolution of ceramic powders as the materials come together during sintering, paying particular attention to the rearrangement of crystallites during thickening. The goal is to find a way to control the microstructure of ceramic powders so that the final product will be more stable after it has been sintered. Ways also are being sought to avoid adding new flaws and imperfections to ceramics during processing, and to reduce the effects of wear caused by erosion, corrosion, and abrasive actions in order to ensure a strong final ceramic product.

—Frederick I. Scott and Lynn Yarris

GLOSSARY OF TECHNOLOGY

Abrasives. Materials of extreme hardness that are used to shape other substances by wearing them away. Abrasives are central to modern industry, especially in preparing metal surfaces by precision grinding. In the home, the most familiar abrasives are various grades of sandpaper or emery cloth, used to smooth wood.

Adhesives. Materials that can bond other materials together by sticking strongly to the surfaces of the materials to be bonded. To be effective, an adhesive must not only bond strongly to materials but also must be strong itself. See also *Cement; Glue.*

Airships. Lighter-than-air vehicles that are powered and can be steered. Large airships with rigid frames are called *dirigibles* or *Zeppelins.* The many crashes these vehicles have experienced have discouraged dirigible technology, and none have been built since World War II. A nonrigid type of airship, the blimp, continues in use.

Alternating current (A.C.). Electric current that continuously reverses direction. In the United States and Canada, there are 60 reversals each second, while in most of the rest of the world, 40 reversals per second is the rule. The principal advantage of alternating current is that it can be sent over wires for great distances.

Amplifier. Any device that changes a weak signal to a strong one. In an amplifier, the strong signal is made to vary when changes occur in the weak signal. The most familiar amplifiers are those that convert a weak electric signal to a strong audio signal, but amplifiers also are employed in long-distance transmission of other types of signals.

Assembly line. Manufacturing system in which a belt or track moves a partly built product past workers as the product is being constructed. As the product passes each worker, the worker performs the same operation on the same product over and over again—bolting on the same part, for instance. Assembly lines greatly speeded up production of automobiles and lowered prices when autos were first introduced. Today assembly lines are gradually being replaced by more efficient production systems.

Automation. Automatic handling of parts or processes in manufacturing with little or no human intervention. Automation requires feedback, the return of information from the process in order to make corrections. Although the first feedback device was James Watts's governor in the 1700's, modern automation depends on computers and computer-directed robots.

Bearings. Friction-reducing support for rotating shafts or spindles. There are two main types of bearings, ball bearings and roller bearings. In each type, balls or cylindrical rotors are housed in a circular frame, called a *race.* Since only a small portion of the surface of the ball or roller is in contact with the rotating shaft and the race, friction is greatly reduced.

Breeder reactor. A nuclear reactor that produces fuel at the same time that it produces power. Reactor fuel is generally uranium 238, enriched with either uranium 235 or plutonium. The basic type of breeder reactor creates plutonium from uranium 238. Breeder reactors produce more enriching materials than they use in making energy.

Cam. One of the most common tools used to make machines work, converting rotary motion into the type of motion needed by a given system. Most familiar are the cams used to open and close valves in an internal combustion engine.

Cathode-ray tube. A device that produces a beam of electrons to draw a picture on a fluorescent surface. The most familiar cathode-ray tube is the picture tube found in a television set or computer monitor.

Cement. Adhesives thought of as cements include those that bond together many small particles to form a solid. Portland cement is a mixture of chalk and clay that has been heated and then crushed. When it is wetted it crystallizes into a hard mass that can be used to bind sand and gravel together to form concrete.

Coal tar. A black, viscous mixture of complex organic compounds that has been condensed from gases released by coal that is heated in an oxygen-free environment. Coal tar is converted into various synthetic chemicals that are used as drugs, vitamins, water repellants, fungicides, weed killers, and food additives. The residue of the tar is used as pitch in electrodes, roofing materials, and fuel.

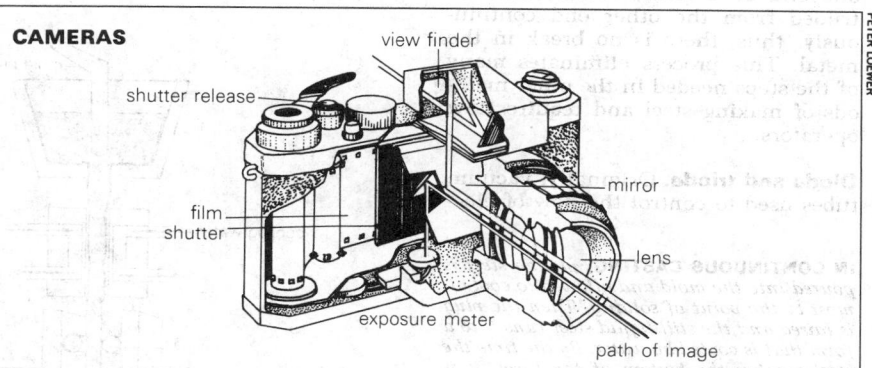

CAMERAS

view finder
shutter release
film shutter
exposure meter
mirror
lens
path of image

PETER LOEWER

Cameras are becoming increasingly electronic. By 1985, nearly every major manufacturer of 35 mm cameras was offering models with automatic focusing.

Talking cameras, which advise about focus and flash, contain voice-synthesizing computers controlled by chips. In other models, light is projected from an infrared diode. The returning light is measured and the focus set accordingly.

In 1981, Polaroid introduced a camera that corrected exposure time automatically by measuring available sunlight. The Polaroid SX-70 instant camera uses ultrasonic radar to calculate the distance to an object when adjusting the focus. Some cameras use control sensors and computer chips to collect and compare light from two images to focus lenses automatically.

THE SYDNEY, AUSTRALIA, OPERA HOUSE *is an impressive example of how reinforced concrete, because of its great ability to withstand stress, can be used to create unusual architectural effects.*

Concrete. An important construction material made by using water and cement to bind together sand and gravel. When concrete hardens, or sets, the sand and gravel are joined together by the cement to form a rocklike mass with great compressive strength. Although strong under compression, concrete is weak under tension. For use in constructing buildings and bridges, concrete is usually reinforced with steel rods that can withstand tensile stresses.

Continuous casting. A method of casting in which molten steel is poured in one end of a form, cooled, and extruded from the other end continuously; thus, there is no break in the metal. This process eliminates many of the steps needed in the other methods of making steel and requires few operators.

Diode and triode. Originally, vacuum tubes used to control the flow of elec-

tricity, but more recently semiconductor devices that perform the same functions. A diode restricts current flow to a single direction. In a triode, current flowing between the two parts of what otherwise would be a diode is further controlled by a third part, the control grid. The control grid changes the size of the current in response to changes in a small current in the control grid, enabling the triode to be used as an amplifier.

Direct current (D.C). Electric current that maintains a single direction of flow. Certain kinds of electric motors,

electroplating, and chemical refining require direct current.

Dirigibles. See *Airships.*

Dye. Coloring agent that is absorbed by the surface or into the material being colored. Most dyes used today are synthetics and are especially useful for coloring fibers, paper, leather, plastics, and foods.

Electric motor. Device that converts electrical energy to mechanical energy using the basic concept of an electric generator in reverse. Just as electric generators either produce alternating current or direct current, electric motors are also either A.C. or D.C.

Feedback. See *Automation.*

Gears. Toothed wheels used to connect rotating shafts. The ratio of the number of teeth on one gear to the number of teeth on another provides mechanical advantage. Circular gears are most commonly used, mainly to change the number of rotations in a period of time and, at the same time, to change the torque, or force, of the rotation. Noncircular gears are used as desired to provide changing velocities in various applications.

Generator. Electric device that converts mechanical energy into electrical energy. When a conductor moves through a magnetic field, an electric current is generated in the conductor. In a large electric generator, this effect is used as coils of wire are moved by steam or waterpower through powerful magnetic fields produced by electromagnets.

Glue. An adhesive classified as a glue is normally spread on surfaces in the form of a liquid, emulsion, or gel, although some glues can be applied in solid form as thin layers that become fluid upon heating. Epoxies are an important type of glue. They are resins that generally set with the application of heat and that form cross-linked polymers (plastics) upon setting.

Gravure printing. A printing method in which ink is first deposited into small depressions, or wells, on the printing surface. The raised surfaces around these wells are cleaned after the ink is deposited. The best known form of gravure printing is *rotogravure,* in which printing is accomplished by a gravure cylinder on a continuous roll of paper.

Gyroscope. A rotating wheel that can have its axis pointed in any specified direction. Conservation of rotation keeps the gyroscope pointing in the desired direction. As a result, gyroscopes are used as compasses, as components of inertial guidance systems of missiles and other vehicles, and as devices

IN CONTINUOUS CASTING, *molten steel is poured into the mold and allowed to cool almost to the point of solidity. Then the plug is raised and the still liquid steel runs into a form that is cooled by water. By the time the steel reaches the bottom of the form, it is solid. It is cooled further by sprays of water as it moves through rollers.*

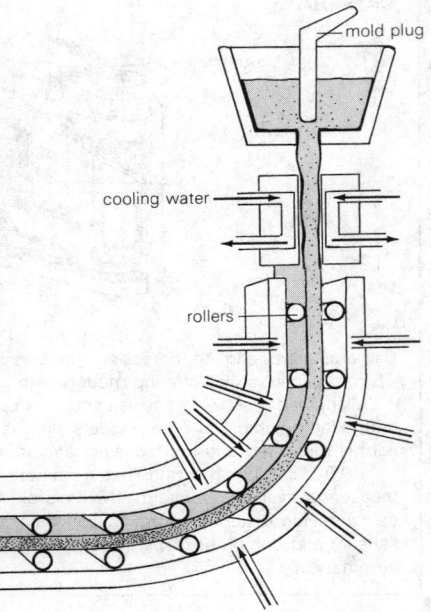

mold plug

cooling water

rollers

PETER LOEWER

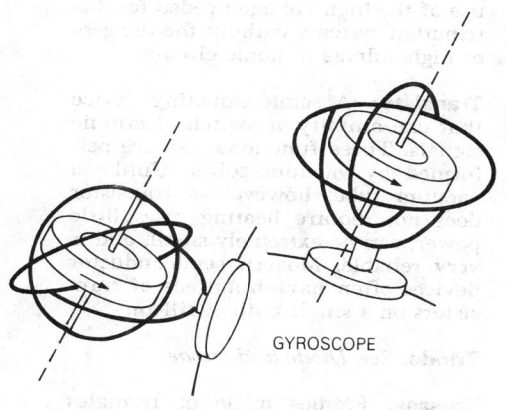

GYROSCOPE

INCANDESCENT LIGHT

An incandescent light, the common light bulb, consists of a metal filament, usually tungsten, suspended in a glass bulb. The filament glows when it is heated by a current passing through it. The glass bulb is evacuated or filled with an inert gas to prevent deterioration of the filament.

- lead-in-wires
- base contact
- socket
- screw base
- vacuum or inert gas
- supports
- filament
- glass bulb

for maintaining the stability of ships in rough waters.

Junction diode. A semiconducting device, similar in many ways to the transistor, that permits electricity to flow through it in one direction while blocking it in the other.

Letterpress printing. Printing method in which raised surfaces that pick up ink directly transfer the ink to the paper. While most people think of this form of printing when they picture how printing is done, it is no longer widely used.

Light-emitting diodes (LEDs). Semiconductors that emit light when an electric current is passed through them. LEDs have been used as displays for calculators, watches, and portable computers. They may become even more useful when optical computers and communications systems become more effective.

Machines. See *Simple machines.*

Machine tools. Power-driven devices used in making the parts of machines. Most machine tools cut or shape metals or other materials. Lathes, presses, milling machines, planers, drills, and grinding machines are the most common machine tools.

Monorail. An electrically powered transit system characterized by cars running on a single rail or beam. In some monorails the cars are on the beam, while in others the cars are suspended from the beam. Although monorails have been built since at least 1901, only recently have they shown signs of replacing conventional cars that ride on two tracks.

Offset lithography. A printing method in which the ink is attracted to areas of a plate and then passed to a rubber cylinder that does the actual printing. Inking is controlled by the principle that oil and water do not mix. The ink used in the process is oily; portions of the plate that are not to attract ink are treated with substances that will attract water but not oil.

Open-hearth steelmaking. The classic method of steelmaking that at one time accounted for 90 percent of American steel production. Recently, the method has been replaced by continuous casting and other steelmaking processes.

Paint. A liquid containing a pigment, which hardens to protect and decorate the surface to which it is applied. Although paints have been used by humans for at least 20,000 years, technical understanding of their properties, including binders, pigments, solvents, and additives, was not achieved until fairly recently.

Petrochemicals. Chemicals derived from crude oil or natural gas. Synthetic rubber, artificial fibers, plastics, detergents, and chemical fertilizers are petrochemicals used in place of natural rubber, cotton and wool, wood and metal, soap, and manure.

Photoelectric devices. Materials that become either more conductive of electricity when light shines on them, or that produce electricity in the presence of light. The first group has long been employed in "electric eyes," but more recently as the heart of photocopying, optical computer, and communications systems. The second group is used in solar cells to produce electricity from sunlight.

Plywood. An assembly of thin layers of wood glued together so that the grain in each layer is at a right angle to the grain of the layers next to it. Plywood is more uniform than ordinary wood and resists splitting and warping.

Power train. The mechanism that connects an engine to an axle or a propeller. In an automobile, this includes the drive shaft and coupling, clutch and gears or automatic transmission, and differential.

Printing. See *Gravure printing; Letterpress printing; Offset lithography.*

Radar and sonar. Devices that use emitted and reflected waves to form images of the objects that reflect the waves. Radar emits and receives radio waves. It is employed in the air and in space for both short- and long-range imaging, for example, for locating rain showers and mapping the surfaces of other planets. Sonar, which uses sound waves, is employed mostly under water.

Robot. A machine that performs tasks independently of humans, especially

THE DRIVE TRAIN *of a rear wheel drive automobile transforms the vertical motion of a piston to a rotary motion and transfers that motion to the rear wheels.*

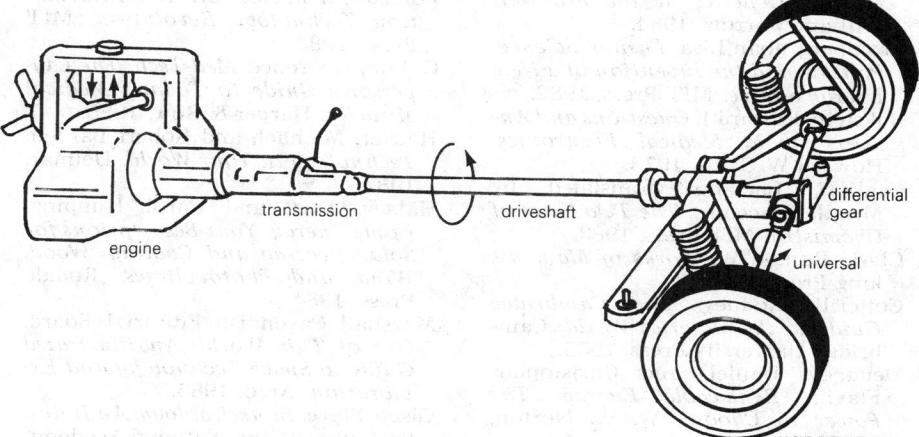

transmission

engine

driveshaft

differential gear

universal

tasks normally performed by humans. Robots often replace humans on assembly lines. Although they are often pictured as artificial humans, most robots can perform only limited tasks and look nothing like humans.

Rotogravure. See *Gravure printing*.

Servomechanism. Any device that uses feedback to control the operation of another device or machine. Examples range from household thermostats to industrial robots.

Simple machines. The lever, the inclined plane, the pulley, the wedge, the wheel, the axle, the screw, the gear, and the gear train. All simple machines are devices that change the mechanical advantage, or the ratio, of a resisting force to an applied force by amplifying or reducing motion. Simple machines also are used to change the direction of motion. (See page 438 for more information.)

Sinter. To cause a powder to become a solid without melting the material. Often heated air is passed through the powder at temperatures just below the melting point of the material. Mostly used in the past in treating metals, sintering is now being applied to new types of ceramics.

Sonar. See *Radar and sonar*.

Spinning. Twisting short fibers to make a continuous thread or yarn. Although spinning has been practiced for thousands of years, the large spinning machines developed in the 18th century often are considered to have launched the Industrial Revolution.

WATCHES AND CHRONOMETERS

Chips in wristwatches and other time devices make them cheaper, lighter, and precise. A quartz crystal in the watch oscillates over 30,000 times a second. In a quartz crystal watch, chip circuits halve the pulses repeatedly until arriving at a desired unit of time. Stopwatches use time divided into hundredths of a second. Everyday watches use units equal to one second.

The same chip controls the display in a digital watch. Liquid crystals display the numbers by changing color when an electric field is applied.

A marine chronometer, which also relies on a chip for accurate timekeeping, contains another clock. It is reset when the craft leaves port and hooked to the engine to measure distance. A chip within the clock accesses from memory oceanographic charts for display on a cathode-ray tube screen of ship position and longitude.

Transducer. Any device that converts energy from one form to another. Common transducers include loudspeakers, which transform electrical energy to sound; solar cells, which transform light into electricity; and thermionic converters, which change heat into electricity.

Transformer. A device that changes the voltage of alternating current. Most electrical appliances have one or more transformers, since some applications need high voltage and others work better at low voltage. Because transformers exist, it is possible to supply a single voltage to accomplish many tasks. Also, transformers permit

use of the high voltage needed for distribution systems without the dangers of high voltage in home circuits.

Transistor. A semiconducting device that can amplify or switch electronic signals. These functions also are performed by vacuum tubes. Unlike a vacuum tube, however, a transistor does not require heating, uses little power, can be extremely small, and is very reliable. Modern semiconductor devices often have hundreds of transistors on a single chip of silicon.

Triode. See *Diode and triode*.

Trusses. Frames made of triangles that are used to support bridges and roofs. Because a triangle theoretically cannot change shape, trusses are considered rigid and are light in weight. In practice, bending of the sides of the triangles needs to be compensated for by increasing the weight of trusses in order to maintain rigidity.

Turbine. A machine that changes the velocity or pressure of a moving fluid into rotary motion. Technically, even a water wheel is a turbine, but in practice the term is used only for machines that operate by changing high-velocity or high-pressure fluids to fluids of high-rotational speeds.

Waxes. Thick or even solid, greasy materials that are used primarily as protective coatings, although waxes also are used for candles. Familiar mainly as floor and furniture waxes, waxes also are used to coat paper and fruit, thicken some foods, and supply desirable characteristics in soaps and cosmetics.

For Further Reference

Asimov, Issac, and Karen A. Frenkel. *Robots: Machines in Man's Image.* Harmony Books (Crown), 1985.

Baskin, Yvonne. *The Gene Doctors: Medical Genetics at the Frontier.* William Morrow, 1984.

Bromberg, Joan Lisa. *Fusion: Science, Politics, and the Invention of a New Energy Source.* MIT Press, 1982.

Bukstein, Edward J. *Questions and Answers about Medical Electronics.* Howard W. Sams, 1973.

Caglioti, Luciano (translated by Mirella Giacconi). *The Two Faces of Chemistry.* MIT Press, 1983.

Clark, Ronald W. *Works of Man.* Viking Press, 1985.

Cotterill, Rodney. *The Cambridge Guide to the Material World.* Cambridge University Press, 1985.

Deudney, Daniel, and Christopher Flavin. *Renewable Energy: The Power to Choose.* W. W. Norton, 1983.

Drexler, K. Eric. *Engines of Creation.* Doubleday, 1986.

Dreyfus, H. L., and S. E. Dreyfus. *Mind Over Machine.* Free Press, 1985.

Forester, Tom, editor. *The Information Technology Revolution.* MIT Press, 1985.

Galton, Lawrence. *Med-Tech: The Layperson's Guide to Today's Medical Miracles.* Harper & Row, 1985.

Hacker, Michael, and Robert Barden. *Technology in Your World.* Delmar, 1987.

Halacy, Dan, and Carol Hupping. *Home Energy: Your Best Options for Solar Heating and Cooling, Wood, Wind, and Photovoltaics.* Rodale Press, 1984.

Marshall Cavendish Editorial Board. *Out of This World: An Illustrated Guide to Space Technology and Exploration.* Arco, 1985.

Olsen, Steve. *Biotechnology: An Industry Comes of Age.* National Academy Press, 1986.

Pacey, Arnold. *The Culture of Technology.* MIT Press, 1985.

Pagena, Kathleen D., and T. J. Pagena. *Understanding Medical Testing.* C. V. Mosby, 1983.

Panati, Charles. *The Browser's Book of Beginnings: Origins of Everything Under (and Including) the Sun.* Houghton Mifflin, 1984.

Petroski, Henry. *To Engineer Is Human.* St. Martin's, 1985.

Pierce, John R. *Signals: The Telephone and Beyond.* W. H. Freeman, 1981.

Pytlik, Edward C., et al. *Technology, Change and Society.* Davis Mass, 1985.

Stoler, Peter. *Decline and Fall: The Ailing Nuclear Power Industry.* Dodd, Mead, 1985.

Wade, Herb. *Building Underground: The Design and Construction Handbook for Earth-Sheltered Houses.* Rodale Press, 1983.

VOLUME **15**

Language

JOE DI DIO/NEA

FAMILY READING

CONVERSATION: FOUR BY FIVE

Language

When we first learn to speak, language is all one thing. It is the set of sounds that people use to communicate with each other. Only gradually do we begin to understand the importance and complexity of the subject.

In many ways the gift of language is miraculous. Despite years of study and conjecture, scholars can still not say how it first began. No other species has a set of signals and symbols that remotely resembles human language.

The miracle of language reoccurs every time a small child learns to speak. But how does the child learn? By imitating what he hears? By making use of certain patterns already imprinted on his brain? No one knows exactly.

If the human brain is imprinted with a particular language pattern, why are there so many languages? Are there ways in which all languages are alike? Did all languages grow from a single common language long before the dawn of history? Or did it develop independently in many different places?

Language is far more than a subject of study, however. It is our principal means of communicating with each other. From the moment we begin to speak, we work towards using language effectively to express feel-

ings, needs, desires, and information.

This volume concentrates on language as a tool. The first half of the volume considers the three main language skills—speaking, reading, and writing.

Many languages, even today, have no written form. But every people on Earth has a spoken language. Even in a society of readers and writers, speaking skills are of great importance in everyday life and in a wide variety of careers. Not every individual has the ability to become a great orator, but nearly everyone could benefit from improving his or her speech.

For most of man's history, only a small number of people could read at all. In the last two centuries, however, reading has become almost a necessity for people in advanced countries. In the United States today, a person who cannot read has trouble shopping, getting a driver's license, and holding a job. Although the great majority of people now read, many do not read well. As with speaking, most of us could benefit from improved reading skills.

Writing is the most difficult of the three language skills to master. A child may speak clearly at four and be able to read fluently by the age of twelve, but many people never learn

to write fluently and easily. Writing problems can be a serious handicap both in personal and business life.

The section on writing begins with the most elementary skills: spelling, basic grammar, usage, and punctuation. Then it considers the art of writing itself, suggesting ways to go beyond mechanics. Finally, the section gives guidelines for some common writing situations and briefly outlines careers in which writing is important.

The second half of this volume contains further material about language. It includes an article on language studies describing comparative and structural linguistics, phonetics, grammar, philology, and semantics. It then considers English in particular, its place among the languages of the world, and its history. This is followed by a special article on vocabulary improvement.

The volume concludes with brief introductions to three other languages: French, Spanish, and German. These introductions are designed to help those who are studying or reviewing one of the languages or who are preparing for such study.

In schools, the study of language is often combined with the study of literature. Readers who are interested in literature should refer to the Volume on Literature in the *Volume Library*.

SPEAKING

All human beings of normal intelligence know how to speak. More than any other characteristic, this is what sets humans apart from all other creatures. Parrots and myna birds can mimic human speech. Chimps have been taught to communicate a few rudimentary ideas through sign language. But no animal can do what the human child can do: speak.

The child learns to speak without special instruction. He gradually masters a set of amazingly complicated rules that allow him to communicate feelings, thoughts, and wants.

The origins of human speech are lost in antiquity, but it is clear that humans began speaking hundreds of centuries before they began writing. Students of language estimate that speech began at least 5,000 centuries (500,000 years) ago. The earliest known written language dates back only 60 centuries (6,000 years).

Studies of Language

The study of language must ultimately trace back to speech. Students of ancient languages may rely on written materials, but they do so only because writing is a representation of the spoken word. Of the thousands of languages and dialects spoken today, many have no written form. Students of these languages must either invent a written form or rely on what they hear or can record. Even in cultures where language has had written form for centuries, nearly everyone speaks the language. Fewer people can read it, and still fewer can write it. As the spoken language changes, the written language will change as well.

Some approaches to the study of speech and language follow.

Linguistics. This field concentrates on the sounds and grammatic structures of a language. *Comparative linguistics* compares languages and dialects, and has been able to identify many relationships between languages. For example, two modern languages may be shown to have developed from a common ancient language. *Structural linguistics* seeks basic similarity in *all* languages in order to understand just what language is.

Semantics. This field considers not only the dictionary meanings of words but their connotative meanings as well—what they mean in a specific situation, both to the speaker or writer and to those who hear or read them.

Communications theory. This modern elaboration on semantics and linguistics deals with nonverbal as well as verbal communication. When speaking, people communicate

INTERNATIONAL PHONETIC ALPHABET

/i/	be	/t/	tie
/ɪ/	bit	/d/	die
/e/	bate	/k/	key
	(often	/g/	gay
	/eɪ/ bay)	/m/	me
/ɛ/	bet	/n/	no
/æ/	bat	/ŋ/	wing
/a/	aisle	/f/	foe
/ʌ/	cup	/v/	vote
/ə/	above	/θ/	thin
/ɜ, ɝ/	her	/ð/	then
/ɚ/	herder	/s/	so
/u/	food	/z/	zero
/ʊ/	good	/ʃ/	ash
/o/	obese	/ʒ/	azure
	(often	/h/	he
	/ou/	/tʃ/	chest
	know)	/dʒ/	jest
/ɔ/	awe	/w/	wet
/ɒ/	hot	/ʍ/	whet
/ɑ/	ah		(also
/aɪ/	aisle		/hw/)
/au/	how	/r/	row
/ɔɪ/	boy	/j/	yet
/p/	pie	/l/	lie
/b/	buy		

through gestures, tone of voice, facial expressions, and other nonverbal means, as well as through words. A certain tone of voice and facial expression may cause a sentence to have a meaning opposite to its literal meaning. For example, a speaker may say "You're a *wonderful* friend," sarcastically, really meaning, "You're no friend at all." Communications theorists also study the cultural framework in which words exist. To one speaker of English, "I don't care," may mean, "It makes no difference to me." To another, it may mean "I don't care at all about the issue, and I wish you hadn't asked me."

Phonetics. Phonetics is a specialized study of the sounds of different languages. In written form, these sounds are represented by the International Phonetic Alphabet (IPA). The symbols in the IPA are shown at the left.

The study of phonetics has been greatly assisted by modern recording techniques. The tape recorder has allowed linguists to collect samples of every spoken language and dialect for study and comparison.

Phonetics may also have practical uses in speech therapy and for speakers or actors who wish to learn a particular accent or dialect.

Dialects. A *dialect* is a variant of a particular language. One dialect of English is spoken in England, another in the United States. Given enough time and distance, two dialects may develop into separate languages.

At any given time, a widely spoken language may exist in dozens of forms. The particular dialect a person speaks may tell a great deal about him: what region of a country he grew up in; what social status his family had; or how much education he received. In the early 1900's, a dialect specialist in England claimed to be able to tell a person's native town

THESE SPEAKERS OF ENGLISH *each speak a different dialect of the language.*

UPI

1056

or village, to within 15 miles, from his speech. Dialects in the United States are generally less distinct than in Britain, but most people would have no trouble telling the difference between a Bostonian and a Texan after listening to their speech.

Social distinctions are often based on speech. The speaker who says, "Dis chair, dat desk, dem flowers," will be less well received in an office or school than a person who says, "This, that, those."

Linguists have been able to trace the distinctive sounds of certain dialects to interesting sources. The "oi" sound, generally thought to be characteristic of a New York City native (*foist* for *first, boid* for *bird,* etc.), originated among Cockneys in East London. Large numbers of Cockneys settled in parts of Brooklyn (as well as in New Orleans and Charleston, South Carolina), and the variant pronunciation was established in local speech.

Dialects also tend to have some differences in vocabulary. For example, a bottle of *soda* in the Eastern U.S. is a bottle of *pop* in the West, and a bottle of *tonic* in Boston.

The English spoken by black Americans is an important and interesting dialect. It shares some characteristics with certain urban and Southern dialects, but has many characteristics of its own. For example, the verb *be* is used to make distinctions not possible in standard English. In black English, "She is sick" means that she has a temporary illness, such as a cold. "She be sick" means that she is chronically ill, with a serious physical or emotional ailment.

Recent studies of black English suggest that it may owe some of its differences to African languages spoken by blacks before they were brought to America as slaves. Slaves were often forbidden to speak their native tongues, but the deep structure of those languages may have survived in their English.

Right and wrong. Modern studies of speech differ from earlier language studies in that they concentrate on *how the language is spoken,* not on *how the language ought to be spoken.* Proponents of this new approach

CHESTER HIGGINS, JR./
PHOTO RESEARCHERS

contend that it is very difficult to distinguish between correct and incorrect speech. Too much depends on the setting, the speaker, and the listeners. For example, a speaker at a neighborhood meeting who does not use the local dialect may be considered affected. If the same speaker uses the local dialect on national television, he may be considered wrong again.

Most people concerned with practical speech do agree, however, that there is a kind of *standard English* that is widely understood and considered acceptable. We will return to standard English later.

Mechanics of Speech

The words we hear are produced in the same way that notes are produced by a musical instrument. Vibrations are created when air is pushed between two bands of muscle called the vocal cords. The vocal cords are about five-eighths of an inch long and are situated in the larynx or voice box. When air passes through them, they vibrate just as the strings on a guitar vibrate when they are plucked.

The vibrations are amplified and enriched by resonating through the hollows of the chest, throat, mouth, and sinuses, the way the body of a guitar enhances the strings' vibrations. Finally, the sounds are shaped by the teeth, lips, tongue, and palate.

The four functions. Speaking consists of the four functions of breath, vibration, resonance, and articulation.

Breath. The breathing done when speaking is different from normal breathing. When you are not speaking, you inhale and exhale through your nose in breaths of equal duration. When speaking, however, you inhale air rapidly and let it out more slowly through tightened vocal cords to produce sound. This is called diaphragmatic breathing.

The diaphragm is a sheet of muscle that lies above the abdominal organs and beneath the lungs. You can feel the action of the diaphragm by breathing in with your mouth open. You will feel your abdomen push out in front as the diaphragm flattens, pressing down on your stomach and other organs. As you let the air out in speaking, the diaphragm relaxes and your abdomen pulls in again. Learning to breathe from the diaphragm can help you to speak clearly and forcefully, since an adequate supply of air is necessary for clear speech.

Vibration. When you are breathing normally, the vocal cords are relaxed.

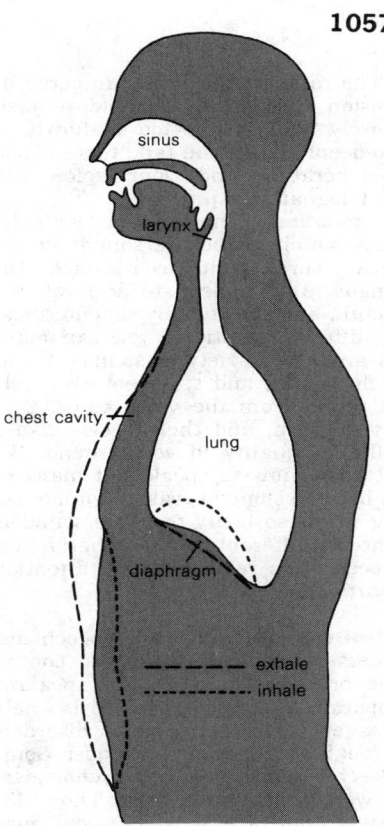

sinus

larynx

chest cavity

lung

diaphragm

— — — exhale
· · · · · · inhale

SPEECH PHYSIOLOGY: *the diaphragm and lungs produce the air, the vocal cords produce the vibration, sinuses and other hollows in the chest and head produce the resonance, and the tongue, teeth, and lips articulate the sound.*

When you are speaking, muscles in the jaw, throat, and neck lengthen the vocal cords and pull them closer together. The air rushing between them causes them to vibrate. The more tightly the cords are stretched, the higher the voice is pitched. The comfortable range of pitch in speaking is about five or six notes. A trained actor should be able to use twelve notes comfortably. Singers learn to pitch their voices over two octaves or more.

Resonance. The vocal cords provide only five percent of the volume of the voice. Much of the rest is provided by the resonators. These are the hollow spaces in the chest and head through which the sound from the vocal cords reverberates. The best way to sense the power of the resonators is to hum loudly. You will feel the vibrations in your chest and head.

If any of these hollow spaces are full of fluid or tense, both the volume and tone of the voice will be changed. When you have a cold, for example, and your sinuses are clogged, your voice sounds flat. People may ask you to speak up, which further strains your already sore throat. As a guitar would sound flat and lifeless if it were filled with water, so the voice loses volume and power if the sinuses are clogged.

The resonators can be hampered by tension as well. If you hold yourself tensely and breathe too shallowly or too deeply when you talk, there is less reverberation and your voice will sound small and pinched.

Articulation. The main articulators—which shape the sounds of the vocal cords into words—are the tongue, the upper surfaces of the mouth, and the lips. By placing these in different positions, you can make an amazing variety of sounds. Some, such as p, t, and s, do not even rely on sound from the vocal cords. Others—l, m, n, and the vowels—give a different quality to vocal sound. We all know how to speak, but many of us become sloppy speakers, pronouncing words so lazily that one sound is scarcely different from another. Better speech often requires closer attention to articulation.

Speech disorders.
Speech disorders reflect an inability to control one or more parts of the speaking apparatus. Speech therapists help speakers overcome such disorders through a variety of techniques. Some speech disorders have psychological as well as physical causes. Those disorders that are only physical may cause psychological problems if not corrected, since being unable to communicate effectively can be deeply discouraging. Many speech therapy programs combine physical training and psychological counseling.

Stuttering. Stuttering is a disorder that afflicts about one percent of the population of any country. The speaker may be unable, for seconds or minutes, to utter a sound, or the first sound of a word may be repeated over and over again. Male stutterers outnumber female by about four to one. According to tradition, such famous figures as Moses and the Greek orator Demosthenes were stutterers.

Stuttering usually begins between three and five years of age. Often, the sufferer has been fluent in speech before this time. Many stutterers outgrow their problem in adolescence, but for others it is a lifelong problem.

Despite many medical and scientific advances in the field, specialists do not agree on the exact cause of or the preferred treatment for stuttering. Physical and psychological therapies are usually combined. Most stutterers respond temporarily to therapy, especially if the therapist gains their confidence. The problem often returns, however.

Stuttering is sometimes treated as a breathing problem. Special breathing techniques may be helpful. Often, the stutterer is taught to slow down his speech, since the tendency to rush through words aggravates the problem. Stutterers may also be taught to keep their vocal cords in a constant state of vocalization by humming between words or phrases. This seems to reduce violent and frustrating attacks.

EYE CONTACT AND FACIAL EXPRESSION *help communicate, as the woman on the left and the basketball coach* (insert) *recognize.*

Improving Your Speech

Most of us speak without any particular problem, but some speakers are better than others. Nearly everyone could profit from some improvement in speaking ability. A person who communicates clearly usually has an advantage over those who do not. We have already considered some mechanical problems with speech. This section will consider other aspects of effective speaking.

Nonverbal aspects of speech.
Communication theorists tell us that people communicate not only through words but through many silent elements as well. These include the way they dress, sit and stand, use their eyes, and respond to the actions of others when they speak. As for speech itself, it is not just the choice of words that matters, but the tone of voice and cadence of speech.

Body language. Our attitudes and feelings are conveyed to others by the way we sit and stand. Experts have delineated dozens of small patterns that reveal how confident a person is, what attitude he has toward others, and what purpose he may have at a given moment.

In a typical encounter between a man and a woman, for example, the man may tighten his stomach, straighten his back, arrange his hair, smile slightly, and glance at the woman out of the corner of his eye. The woman may respond with a smile if she approves of the man's approach, or avert her eyes and turn away if she does not. A salesman who sits back in his chair and casually throws one leg up on the other while visiting the company president's office will probably not get an order, since his body language is disrespectful.

Winks and waves, hand and eye movements, frowns and smiles, posture, scratching, fidgeting, movements of the head and hips, and the distance kept from another person all say something about you and your attitudes.

We are all attuned to reading body language, even if we are not aware of it. In general, Americans respond most favorably to a strong, confident posture and a firm handshake. But the exact approach to others may vary widely from one region to another (restraint with a Vermont farmer, for example, and a more effusive approach to a rancher in the Far West) and from one setting to another (consider the differences in acceptable behavior at a college faculty meeting, a union meeting, a business lunch, and a church banquet).

Eye contact and visual cues. The eyes are a speaker's most important tool after the voice itself. Eyes both receive and send messages. In our society, looking someone in the eye is a sign of confidence and straightforwardness. Looking someone in the eye also gives you an immediate idea of the effect you are having on him. Is your message getting through? Is the listener bored and restless? If you are looking down at the floor or up at the ceiling, you may not know until it's too late.

Once a young playwright invited a famous poet to a rehearsal. The poet fell asleep during the performance. "How could you do this when you know how I value your opinion?" the playwright asked. "Sleep is an opinion," the poet replied.

Your listener expects you to look him in the eye, but beware of overdoing it. If you stare constantly at him, you suggest that you are challenging him, not befriending him. Being fixed in an unblinking stare can be very unnerving.

Gestures. Before movies and broadcasting, public speaking was a form of popular entertainment. Thousands of people would assemble to see a debate or address. Public speakers toured the country like vaudevillians. Political campaigns attracted vast crowds. A visit from a presidential candidate could draw people from hundreds of miles around.

In order to be visible at great distances, old-fashioned speakers used their hands and bodies in broad, dramatic movements. Today, we are accustomed to more subdued gestures. We prefer our speakers to be almost still by comparison.

Still, a few gestures can enhance your words. Use your hands to describe things—the shape of a spiral staircase, the length of the fish you caught, the height of the stack of papers on your desk. If you have a dramatic point to make, you might pound your fist on a table or point a finger at someone or something. Such gestures are risky, however. If they look contrived, your listeners will come to doubt your sincerity. At the same time, be careful to avoid unconscious gestures—cracking your knuckles, rocking back and forth—that can be irritating or distracting.

Your face is most important, especially if you are speaking in a small group. People will read your face to judge your mood, your attitude toward them, and your sincerity. Amusement, anger, curiosity, or any number of other feelings can be expressed with only slight changes of expression. Learning to use your facial expression will add more to your speech than any contrived repertoire of hand movements.

Pitch, tone, cadence. The sound of your voice is another nonverbal aspect of your speech. If your speech is shrill or nasal or monotonous, your words may have little effect on your listeners. By the same token, a skillful speaker can use positive qualities to give a message more impact.

Pitch is the level of your voice—high or low or middling. It is partly determined by your vocal equipment. Some people have voices pitched lower than others. If your voice is particularly

ORATORICAL STYLE *requires extravagant gestures, as shown here by President Teddy Roosevelt.*

high pitched, so that it sounds shrill (if you are a woman) or effeminate (if you are a man), you can probably lower the pitch by a whole tone. Keep in mind that shrillness is often related to nervousness. We tend to speak shrilly when we are nervous or upset. Try relaxing before you begin to speak.

Tone is the quality of your voice. Again, this will depend partly on your vocal equipment, but you can learn to improve your tone. Read something into a tape recorder or record a conversation. When you play it back, note what qualities you like about your voice and what qualities you dislike. Is it too nasal or shrill? Experiment with modifying it to be more distinct and pleasing. Also listen carefully to other people whose speaking voices you admire. How is theirs different from yours?

Finally, cadence is the rhythm and inflection of your voice, similar to a melody in music. Some people have an annoying habit of using the same inflection over and over again. They may sound whiny or depressed or groundlessly cheerful all the time. Soon their listeners stop listening simply because of the monotony. Listen to your own speech. Does it vary in speed and pitch to reflect your mood or the message you are communicating? Variety of rhythm and cadence is an important quality of good speech.

Saying what you mean. In deciding what to say on a given occasion, there are two things to consider: the listener and the subject of the speech.

Consider the listener. Aristotle said, "Of the three elements in speech making—speaker, subject, and person addressed—it is the last one, the hearer, that determines the speech's end and object."

The speaker should be aware that

his listeners have their own concerns and problems. These color and prejudice everything they hear and see. Unless great care is taken, people will not understand everything that the speaker is trying to say because they will filter it through their own perceptions. Because of this, it is useful to know as much as possible about your audience.

If you were a politician, you might address a group of landlords on one night and a tenant organization on the next night. You would certainly want to know which was which. The content of your speech might be much the same, but you would make many small adjustments in order to present the subject in the best possible light to both groups. Whether you speak to strangers or to friends, you are constantly making choices in order to present the subject in the best possible light.

What you know about your listeners will help determine what kind of language to use, what mood to adopt, and what approach to take to your subject. As you gain experience, you will make these decisions more and more deliberately. Here are some things to consider.

In speaking to friends, try to be sensitive to their mood. Are they sad, happy, introspective, or outgoing? Their mood determines what you can say to them and when you can say it. There are times when a criticism or complaint will be taken in stride, but there will be other times when the same comment might ruin a friendship.

When talking to strangers, consider their sex, age, social status, ethnic or regional identity, and politics. Pay attention to the small clues—dress, accent, manners. Every message must be "pitched" to an audience, and different audiences respond to different approaches.

Organize your remarks. To speak clearly, one must think clearly. In all but the briefest speech, some preparation is necessary, and the big part of preparing is organization.

EMOTIONAL SCENES *can make a person more eloquent than she would normally be.*

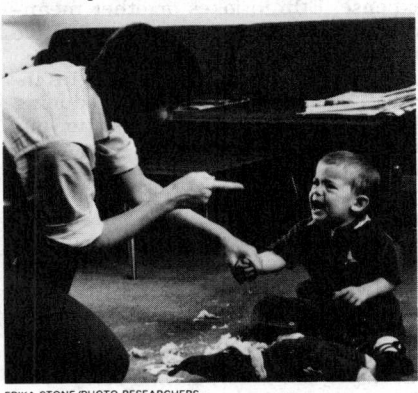

ERIKA STONE/PHOTO RESEARCHERS

Any talk has three sections, which we can think of as the beginning, the middle, and the end. For a formal address, these sections are called the introduction, the body, and the conclusion. Salespeople use the same basic structure. They divide a sales talk into the approach, the demonstration, and the close.

The beginning of a speech must be calculated to capture the listener's attention. Unless you capture his attention, your message will not matter.

There is a famous story about the owner of a small New York printing company. For some months he had been visiting the print buyer of a major magazine publisher to ask for a printing contract. Every week, the print buyer replied distantly that his printing needs were taken care of.

One day the printer realized that the buyer did not even remember him from one visit to the next. He set out to make sure that he would not be forgotten again. On his next visit, when the buyer gave his usual refusal, the printer threw his hat on the floor, jumped on it, and left. The buyer came running after him and demanded to know what was wrong. When the printer explained, the buyer gave him his first contract. Word of the printer who made such a scene even reached the chairman of the publishing company. He arranged to meet the printer and eventually lent him money to expand his business.

You can't open every talk you give with a display like the printer's, but you can resolve to find a way to keep your audience from forgetting you. Your opening impression is important in many kinds of presentations. One study of job interviews showed that the majority of interviewers made their decisions within the first few minutes of meeting an applicant.

A favorite way to open a talk is with a joke. It works for many speakers. But beware: joke telling can be disastrous if not done right. Remember that comedians work for years on their timing and delivery, so do not expect to become proficient instantly. Be sure that you know the joke well and that you have the important lines down word for word. Avoid making a joke at anyone's expense. Ethnic jokes or other mean–spirited humor mark you as insensitive or prejudiced.

Other possible opening strategies include a dramatic story introducing your theme, an informal appeal to your audience for sympathy or support, or a bold statement of your theme. At all costs, avoid the introduction that begins, "My name is . . . and I'm here to talk about. . . ."

The middle of a speech must explain the theme and establish it in the minds of the listeners. There are several useful patterns of organization.

Time. Narrate a series of events in chronological order, as in a story.

Space. Describe events or attitudes in different places—countries, regions, towns, or along a road or path.

Topic. Discuss various aspects of the theme one at a time. For example, in discussing inflation, consider its economic, social, political, and moral consequences.

Definition. Treat the subject as an extended definition. What is theosophy? What is security? What is health? What is the Red Cross? Compare your subject with a related one, give its history, explore its connotations, or examine its causes or effects.

Cause. Organize a talk from cause to effect or effect to cause. This can be particularly useful for argument or persuasion. For example: "The failings of my opponent are the reason we're in a mess today."

Logic. Proceed from a premise to a conclusion by reasoned steps. All points should be established with evidence.

Problem and solution. Follow these five steps: 1) be aware of the problem; 2) analyze the problem through the observation of facts; 3) suggest probable solutions; 4) discuss each proposed solution to gauge the results; 5) determine the best solution.

The end of a talk leaves the final impression. You want people to remember what you have said and you want them to leave in a certain frame of mind. If the purpose is to entertain, you want them to be happy. If the message is serious, you want them to feel moved. If you are campaigning for office, you want them to vote for you. If you are selling something, you want them to buy. Here are some effective types of conclusions.

Summary. Use when the speech has been lengthy and full of information. Take your subject briefly, point by point.

Abridgement. Make a paragraph-length statement of the salient points of the speech. This is easier to listen to than point-by-point summary.

Restatement. State your central idea succinctly.

Application. Call for immediate or future action, ask a challenging question, offer a service, or make a prediction.

Many inexperienced speakers want more than one conclusion. In most speaking situations, this does not work. Often, if the speech leads to more than one conclusion, it has gone astray before reaching the end.

Avoid coming to a false climax, where the speech seems to be over but is not. In a good speech, listeners know when the conclusion is approaching. One of the most frequently broken rules of speaking is, *"Not one word too many."*

Conversation. A Chinese proverb tells us, "A single conversation across the table with a wise man is worth a month's study of books." The French essayist Michel de Montaigne wrote, "It is good to rub and polish our brain against that of others."

Most of the speaking we do is conversational, the give and take of everyday life. Very few of us take conversation seriously as a source of learning and entertainment.

In order to enjoy and profit from conversation, you must first take it seriously enough to learn how to do it well. Conversation differs from formal speaking in several ways. First, it's a *dialogue* in which two (or more) speakers take roughly equal parts. Second, remarks for a conversation cannot be prepared, since the direction of the talk can scarcely be predicted ahead of time. A good conversationalist must be able to "prepare" on the spot. Finally, conversation

OUTLANDISH MANNERS AND DRESS *make Mork of TV's "Mork and Mindy" seem out of place with a solemn lawyer and a psychiatrist.*

ABC-TV

requires two skills—listening and speaking.

What topics are suitable for conversation? George Bernard Shaw said that the three best topics are religion, politics, and sex. Nearly everyone has strong feelings about such topics, and any discussion of them will be lively. Of course there are many other topics that are interesting as well. But Shaw's point was that genuine conversation differs from everyday small talk in that it considers topics that matter.

The three principal rules for conversation are these:

1. *Do not talk too much.* Good conversation is the exchange of ideas. Do not bore people by trying to say everything.

2. *Listen.* Do not use the time when others are talking to prepare your next comment. Be ready to ask questions and learn from the answers.

3. *Be considerate.* Do not mock other people's beliefs, no matter how strongly you may disagree.

Improving speech habits.

When you are among friends, your speech probably does not matter very much. You may not always say things with precision, but your friends know what you mean because they know you well.

With people you do not know, however, bad speech habits can be a serious handicap. People make all sorts of judgments about you from the way you speak. Bad speech habits may cost you a chance for a job or a promotion; they may keep you from doing things you really want to do or even keep you from getting to know a person you really like. Unfortunately, we learn bad speech habits before we know the difference between good and bad. Our first speech patterns come from our families, and these are often reinforced by our friends. Rooting out these habits can be very difficult.

You cannot expect to improve your speech by talking only with your friends and family if their speaking habits are not up to par. Try to spend more time talking with people whose speech you know to be good. Ask them for help with your grammar and pronunciation. Speech is like chess, tennis, or any other skill. You cannot improve by associating with people who are worse at it than you are. One good model for speech and pronunciation is the speech of broadcasters on national news programs.

Grammar for speech. Grammar for speech need not be as strict as written grammar. For example, many writers will write, "It is I," or "It is he." But in speech, the same writers are likely to say, "It's me," or "That's him."

The following section on grammar for writers will help if your grammar is weak. We will confine ourselves here to pointing out some of the more common spoken errors—mistakes that may mark you among strangers as less intelligent and educated than you really are.

Noun-verb agreement. Say "I don't," and "You don't." But say "He doesn't" and "It doesn't."

Adjectives and adverbs. Many adverbs are formed by adding -ly to an adjective. Use the adjective form when the word modifies a noun and the adverb form when it modifies a verb or an adjective. For example, it is correct to say, "They had a *real* fight," and "The fight they had was *really* big." Avoid such incorrect expressions as *"real"* big or *"real"* good.

Mistakes in the use of adjectives and adverbs are common in the comparative forms.

Incorrect: more louder, most loudest
more curiouser

Correct: loud, louder, loudest
curious, more curious, most curious

Negatives. Many people use *double negatives.*

Incorrect: I wouldn't never do that.

Correct: I wouldn't ever do that.
I would never do that.

Remember that two negatives can be misleading. For example, "I'm not going nowhere," could mean, "I'm going somewhere."

Pronouns. A pronoun is a word that can be used in place of another noun. Instead of using a girl's name, for example, you may use the pronoun *she.* There must be agreement between the form of the noun and the pronoun that replaces it:

The boys . . . they
The king . . . he
The woman . . . she

A major problem with pronouns arises over their *antecedents,* the nouns to which they refer. Using the same pronoun to refer to more than one person confuses the listener. Make sure that you repeat the names of the people of whom you are speaking.

Incorrect: When Harold's son came home, he was happy. (Who was happy?)

Correct: Harold's son was happy to be home. Harold was happy that his son was home.

Past tenses. When talking about past events, be careful to use the right verb forms. Verbs have three forms: the present, the past, and the past participle (for example, *go, went, gone*). Use the simple past form by itself: "I went to school." If you use a verb with *have,* you must use the past participle:

Incorrect: I *have went* to school.
Correct: I *have gone* to school.

Incorrect: They *have fell* down.
Correct: They *fell* down.
They *have fallen* down.

Other grammatical faults.

Wrong	Right
hisself	*himself*
I ain't	*I'm not*
we ain't	*we're not*
I been	*I've been*
I done	*I did*
irregardless	*regardless*
nowheres	*nowhere*
out loud	*aloud*
out of the door	*out the door*
overly	*over*
over with	*over*
supposing	*suppose*
them things	*those things*
them people	*those people*
theirselves	*themselves*
this here	*this*
thusly	*thus*
unawares	*unaware*
undoubtably	*undoubtedly*
youse	*you*

Pronunciation. Certain words are like a code. If you pronounce them correctly, you are acceptable. But make a mistake, and some people will judge you as harshly as if you came to a formal dinner in blue jeans.

Words	Incorrect Pronunciation
did you	*didja*
goodbye	*guhby*
ought to	*oughta*
want to	*wanna*
interesting	*inneresting*
government	*gummint*
hundred	*hunnert*
because	*becuzz, becoss*
strength	*strenth*
height	*heighth*
length	*lenth*
fifth	*fith*
width	*with*
often	*off-ten*
library	*liberry*
judgment	*judgament*
athletic	*athaletic*
ask	*ax*
mischievous	*mischeevious*

Other common speech faults. Most of us are impatient with our speech. Instead of saying what is really on our minds, we take shortcuts. We use interjections such as "you know" and "understand?" instead of fully expressing ourselves so that the listener will know and understand.

Instead of striving for vivid, descriptive, original language, we substitute profanity, jargon, and clichés. These shortcuts are often a substitute for thought. By using the same words over and over, we lose the ability to really express our feelings. What we say has about as much meaning as the barking of a dog.

Many people use swear words for emphasis. Overuse of swear words is not only rude, it also robs those words of any power they might once have had. If a man known never to use profanity gets angry enough to use it, his hearers understand the depth of his anger. A man who uses profanity in every other sentence would make no impression no matter how angry he was.

Clichés are words and phrases that have been used so often that they too have lost their meaning. Some examples are *fit as a fiddle, sick as a dog, high as a kite.*

Jargon is special language used in a given field. While jargon may serve to make you look like one of the crowd, it often conceals a lack of thought. Most ideas can be expressed in plain English.

We also distrust our own silence. We fill the pauses in our speech with little nonsense sounds like "uh-h-h" and "um-m-m" as well as "you know." These noises are a detriment to understanding.

Listen to yourself and try to pick up your bad speech habits. When you recognize a problem, work toward correcting it. When you find yourself uttering one of those tired words or phrases, stop and ask yourself what you really want to say. Isn't there some better way of expressing it?

Another serious problem in speech is pretentiousness, or talking up or down to people. If you try to sound more expert or informed than you really are, people will not be fooled. If you condescend to less educated audiences, they will resent you. Speak at a level that suits both you and your audience.

Above all, mean what you say. The sincere speaker is the persuasive speaker. If you are not sure that you believe your own message, you cannot expect others to believe it.

We have already discussed all the ways you communicate with others—through gestures, facial expressions, and eye contact, as well as through words. Don't forget that people are communicating with you in all the same ways. If you become too intent on talking, you may forget to listen.

Be alert for other people's nonverbal signals. Tone of voice, pitch, even eye movements can tell you important things about the other person's frame of mind or intentions. Your interest (or lack of interest) in others is visible in many small ways, and may have an important effect on your success as a speaker. Do you change the subject when someone brings up his problems? Do you "listen with one ear" when others are speaking? If so, you may be hurting your own ability to communicate. Good speakers know that communication is a two-way process, and that speakers who do not listen often fail.

Speech in Careers

Business analyst Peter F. Drucker once gave this advice to college graduates:

> As soon as you move one step up from the bottom, your effectiveness depends on your ability to reach others through the spoken word . . . .
>
> The foundations for skill in expression have to be laid early; if you do not lay these foundations during your school years, you may never have an opportunity again.

Often the top manager in a business is not a technician or an expert in a particular field, but a man or woman skilled in dealing with people. The ability to speak well is one

SPEAKING CAREERS *are represented by a network news team, evangelist Billy Graham, and actors Jessica Tandy and Hume Cronyn.*

of the most important parts of this skill. Although ability to write well may also be important, it cannot be a substitute for effective face-to-face contact. Large corporations sometimes hire speech consultants to help their managers communicate verbally.

Speaking is especially important in some occupations. For example, trial lawyers must be adept at speaking since it is their job to persuade judges and juries to see things their way.

Speech is a teacher's principal tool. A professor may lecture ten or twelve hours each week, and spend at least twice that time in preparation. Elementary school teachers must learn how to explain new concepts to young children in terms that they understand.

Clergymen, too, rely on speech, both in the pulpit and in smaller groups. Those who preach to large groups often receive professional speech training.

Speech is a major concern in the acting profession. Actors receive professional instruction in such areas as breath control, refinement of pitch, and extension of vocal range. They study dialects and accents and learn to imitate every conceivable type of speech.

Formal Speaking

Speech contests have a long tradition in schools and colleges. Among the events at such contests are:

Impromptu speaking, in which the speaker is given the topic of his talk as he steps in front of the audience.

Extemporaneous speaking, in which a serious topic is assigned to the speaker 30 minutes before he speaks.

Oratory, in which the speaker delivers a prepared address on a topic of general interest.

Oratorical declamation, in which the speaker delivers a speech written by a famous speaker.

Competing in such events can help a speaker sharpen his speaking skills.

A special speech competition is *debate.* In debate, a topic is assigned, and debaters must prepare to argue on either side of the issue. They compete in teams of two. Each team gets a chance to present its case and to rebut the arguments of the other side. Judges determine the winning side.

Still another kind of formal speaking is *banquet* or *after-dinner speaking.* After-dinner speakers usually seek both to entertain and to inform their audience. Popular professional speakers may receive fees of $1,000 or more for a single engagement, but there are many less experienced speakers who do banquet speaking for pleasure. Toastmasters' clubs in many cities and towns give members experience in speaking informally before large groups.

—*Henry Ehrlich*

WRITING

The Mechanics of Writing

Writing picks up where speech leaves off. Because we know how to speak, we feel that we should know how to write. But writing skills are somewhat different and more difficult for most people to master. Thus, it is important to recognize writing as a special discipline, and to consider its special requirements.

There are two kinds of writing: for yourself and for others. In the first kind, you are the only one who will read what you have written. In the second type, others will read it as well. The reason for your writing will dictate your writing style. For example, in a diary, you may use abbreviations that no one but you can understand. You will unconsciously use different styles to write to your best friend, your boss, your parents, and your grandmother.

You often write *for* yourself by writing *to* yourself. You make up a grocery list, note the things you must do next week, remind yourself to pick up the laundry. In addition to these functional notes, you may jot down things you have heard or read or want to remember.

You may also write for yourself by keeping a journal, log, or diary. Because these are private, you feel free to follow an idea, pursue an analogy, and speculate about people, ideas, or events without having to be convincing or perfect. Such private writing gives valuable practice in setting ideas down in your own words, without concern for how they will look to someone else. If you would like to improve your writing, consider keeping a journal. Nothing improves writing like writing.

Writing for others is what we generally think of when we think of writing at all. This kind of writing takes many forms. Informally, we write notes, leave messages or memos, and dash off personal letters. Here we are not much concerned with style. The important thing is to get the message across: "Ann, David called. Wants you to call him back." Not elegant, but it does the job.

In addition to our short informal messages, we are often obliged to put down our thoughts, instructions, or

PRIVATE AND PUBLIC WRITING: *the note will be read by only one or two people, while the novel may be read by millions.*

information in a more formal way, so that others who may not know us can understand and follow what we are saying.

Friends are likely to understand what you mean even when you do not say it clearly; a certain looseness and informality is accepted by them. In a formal situation, however, you must assume just the opposite. The reader knows nothing more of you than what he reads. You must keep in mind how your writing will sound to a total stranger. Your writing is not just a substitute for your speech; it is a substitute for you.

Learning to Write

In the primary grades, children are taught language arts, that is, a combination of reading, writing (penmanship), speech, and written composition. Children first learn to compose when they speak. They put their thoughts into words, then into sentences, and then into short speeches.

Grammar—which consists of following the rules of a certain language—is as much a part of oral communication as it is of written composition. But in speech, even young children rarely make serious grammatical mistakes.

Preschool children who speak English sometimes improperly transfer a rule of grammar. Knowing words such as "batted" and "frosted," they may use "losted" by analogy. They soon overcome this, though, usually without any formal instruction. But no native English-speaking child in the primary grades would say, "Mommie my in kitchen the is." Children learn the correct grammatical placement of words in English sentences long before they reach an English class. (Some children learn a dialect that may differ in some respects from standard English. Even then, they will not violate the basic grammar of their dialect in their speech much after the age of five or six.)

Beginning in kindergarten, the child is exposed to the new skills of reading and writing. Writing skills include what some call the *transcribing skills:* handwriting, spelling, and punctuation—and, although not completely logical, grammar as well. Grammar in this sense means more than word endings and word position; it encompasses all the rules that make writing different from speech.

Writing is different from speech in many ways. When we speak of correctness in writing, we almost always mean following the rules of *standard English.* Few of us speak pure standard English in our families, with our friends, in our communities, or on our jobs. There are many names for the language we speak—colloquial, vernacular, dialect—and our various versions of English have their place, but they do not translate into writing very well, and they do not travel well to other regions. Schools encourage students to learn to write standard English so that they can communicate effectively with a wide audience.

Many students find it strange to have to be so careful, when writing, about putting the final -s on words to make them plural. They can say, "I got ten piece of candy," and be perfectly understood. Grammatical faults are more conspicuous in the written language, and less tolerated. It is this shift from the friendly practices of speech to the rigors of standard English that causes many writing problems among adults as well as children.

In a way, written composition is like learning a foreign language. Nearly all of us use run-on sentences in speech; we are unclear in our use of pronouns, we ramble and repeat ourselves. These habits are common in speech, but are considered serious faults in writing. In order to write well, we must adopt a different standard of style and usage. The demands of written language are particularly difficult for speakers of nonstandard dialects. All their fluency and skill in spoken language suddenly become a handicap. They are scolded for making mistakes that do not *sound* like mistakes at all. Many such people give up trying to write in frustration.

Recent teaching methods emphasize a constructive approach to writing skills. Rather than concentrate on negative rules and regulations, these methods encourage students to expand short kernel sentences into larger, more complete ones by adding phrases or combining new sentences with previous ones.

Many educators urge teachers of young children to develop the children's inherent sense of language, and to stress the expressive uses of writing. Thus, early language arts activities include storytelling and the writing of "wishbooks" and poems. Gradually, more structured word and language skills are introduced. For-

mal grammar may not be presented until the child is in junior high school or later.

Handwriting, spelling, and punctuation—the "mechanical" parts of writing—are taught from the early grades on. Indeed, spelling is normally taught from first to eighth grade, and punctuation all the way to freshman year in college. The number of years of formal instruction in punctuation, in fact, is testimony to the difficulty that this subject has in "taking." Punctuation will be discussed later in this article.

Handwriting is normally not taught as a subject much after third grade. Preschoolers learn to recognize and make capital letters at home, in nursery school, and in kindergarten. In first and second grade, youngsters learn to print *manuscript* and then, as they gain the motor control necessary, to write the flowing script we call *cursive.* Learning to recognize and form the letters of the alphabet is often taught in conjunction with *phonics,* a reading method that emphasizes the sounds of the letters. However, as there is great variety in the way the sounds in English are transcribed, the correlation between sounds and letters is not exact. For this reason, spelling is a major problem for many people throughout their school careers, and sometimes beyond.

Certain physical disabilities can

teachers must be especially sensitive to emotional problems that are revealed in their pupils' writings. Often, the inexperienced writer reveals more of himself in his writing than he knows. An alert teacher may recognize signs of emotional trouble and be able to offer help.

Spelling

The so-called mechanics of writing include spelling, grammar, usage, and punctuation. These are the subjects of the following sections.

"Oh, I'm a terrible speller," is a commonly heard expression. Often it is said with mock humility, as if the speaker meant, "Well, I'm too busy to be concerned with something so trivial." Almost no one is willing to admit to being a bad driver. But there is an aura of virtue in being a poor speller.

Poor spelling can be a serious handicap, however. Misspelled words in a letter or a report cause the reader to think, "This person did not care enough to be careful." No matter how good the content, the letter or report full of misspellings may be ignored. For this reason, it is worth devoting time and energy to improving your spelling.

Unfortunately, English spelling is far more erratic than such phonetic languages as German or Italian. Many English words have long complicated histories, and there are good reasons for their being spelled so many different ways. But this is often of little help in remembering how a certain word is spelled. Through the years, teachers have developed many rules to help a speller. Some of them work, but none are foolproof: every rule seems to have a list of exceptions. So, no matter how systematically we approach the subject, learning to spell requires a fair amount of memorization.

Keeping a list of words that you know to be troublesome is an excellent way to begin. When you keep a list of words that you get wrong time after time, you will probably begin to see a pattern emerging (inability to tell whether *i* comes before *e;* not knowing when to drop a final *e;* not knowing when to double a final consonant, etc.).

Once you have a good idea of where your problems lie, you can find ways to go about correcting them. First, study rules covering your particular problem. Then, if rules do not help, simply memorize your own list of "spelling demons."

The quickest way to learn to spell a new word is to use the word often. Just as teachers sometimes have students write each spelling word five times,

CURSIVE HANDWRITING *is learned beginning in third grade. Here are examples of excellent, average, and poor handwriting at the end of third grade. At right, a hasty note written by Abraham Lincoln would probably receive a grade of poor.*

Example 1 — Excellent for Grade Three

Look in a book and you will see words and magic and mystery.

Example 3 — Average for Grade Three

Look in a book and you will see words and magic and mystery.

Example 5 — Poor for Grade Three

Look in a book and you will see words and magic and mystery.

ZANER-BLOSER CO.

CULVER PICTURES

cause young children great problems in learning to write. Seeing and hearing problems make it difficult for a child to master the transcription skills of spelling and handwriting. In addition, because writing makes something up for someone else to decode, it involves the young child in thinking about and expressing his emotions. For children who are emotionally disturbed, this can be a frightening experience. English

```
separate   → sep a rat e

necessary  → ne c e ss ary

earnest    → earn est
```

MNEMONIC DEVICES: "A rat" *in* separate, *the formula* "1 c 2 s" *for* necessary, *the* "earn" *in* earnest *each help avoid common spelling errors.*

write your own problem words over and over. Use each word in a sentence. Watch for it when reading. Soon you will be able to see at a glance whether the word looks right.

A good dictionary is your major resource when trying to improve your spelling. Unless you are looking up specialized words, it need not be a very big one. When in doubt about a word, look it up. Keep the dictionary by your side when writing, and get comfortable with it. Once in a while, you may have trouble finding a word because you are not sure of the first letter or two. But, generally, this is not a major problem. With a little practice, a dictionary becomes an easy book to use.

A dictionary can help you to become familiar with standard pronunciation, too. When you have found a word, practice pronouncing it, using the pronouncing guide. Then write it down several times and use it in a sentence. Chances are that these three steps—pronounce, write and repeat, and use in a sentence—will be enough to fix the correct spelling in your mind.

Mnemonic devices.

A mnemonic device (pronounced nĕ-MON-ik) is a memory aid. When you have trouble remembering how to spell a word correctly, make up an easily remembered, catchy sentence that gives a clue to the correct spelling. For example, "There is *a rat* in *separate.*" The key letters *a rat* will remind you to avoid the common error of spelling the word sep*e*rate.

There are many such mnemonic devices, but you will remember the ones you make up longer than those you find on a list. The following are examples of mnemonic devices.

affect is a verb with *a* for action
all right as one word is all wrong
friend comes to an *end*
meet: gr*eet* those you m*eet*
meat: we *eat* m*eat*

Paired words.

There are several kinds of paired words in English that lead to confusion:
homonyms are spelled and pronounced alike but differ in origin and meaning. For example: *pool* (water) and *pool* (game).
homophones are pronounced alike but differ in spelling, origin, and meaning. For example: *led* (go before) and *lead* (metal).

heteronyms are spelled alike but differ in pronunciation, origin, and meaning. For example: *bass* (fish) and *bass* (male voice).

Following is a list of homophones that often are mistaken for each other. If you are unsure which word is which in a pair, look the words up in a dictionary.

Spelling rules.

Although there are many exceptions to spelling rules in English, there are five rules that are worth remembering because they cover so many of the instances where misspellings occur.

1. The rule governing words with *ie* and *ei* is a familiar mnemonic verse.

> *i* before *e*
> except after *c,*
> or when sounded like *a,*
> as in n*ei*ghbor and w*ei*gh

This rule covers such common words as *friend, believe, relieve,* and *receive.* Exceptions include *height* and *sleight (of hand).* The rule does not apply when a noun ending in *-cy* is made a plural, as in *aristocracies.*

2. Plurals of nouns ending in *-y* often cause confusion.

(a) When a word ends in *y* preceded by a consonant, change the *y* to *i* and add *-es* to form the plural:

ability	→	*abilities*
tragedy	→	*tragedies*
mystery	→	*mysteries*

(b) When a word ends in *y* preceded by a vowel (*a, e, i, o, u*) keep the *y* and add *-s* to form the plural:

boy	→	*boys*
key	→	*keys*
monkey	→	*monkeys*

3. Adding suffixes to words ending in *-e* may result in creating many spelling problems.

HOMOPHONES

aisle	isle	die	dye	made	maid	sea	see
altar	alter	done	dun	mail	male	seam	seem
ant	aunt	earn	urn	meat	meet	sew sow	so
arc	ark	faint	feint	medal	meddle	shone	shown
ascent	assent	fair	fare	might	mite	sight site	cite
ate	eight	feat	feet	miner	minor	slay	sleigh
ball	bawl	fir	fur	moan	mown	sleight	slight
bare	bear	flea	flee	muscle	mussel	soar	sore
base	bass	flour	flower	night	knight	sole	soul
be	bee	fore	four	none	nun	some	sum
beach	beech	foul	fowl	one	won	son	sun
beat	beet	freeze	frieze	pail	pale	staid	stayed
been	bin	great	grate	pain	pane	stair	stare
bell	belle	groan	grown	pair pare	pear	stake	steak
berth	birth	guest	guessed	pause	paws	stationary	stationery
bier	beer	hair	hare	peace	piece	steal	steel
blew	blue	hall	haul	peal	peel	straight	strait
board	bored	heal	heel	plain	plane	suite	sweet
born	borne	hear	here	pore	pour	tail	tale
bough	bow	heard	herd	pray	prey	their	there
brake	break	heir	air	pride	pried	threw	through
buy	by	hoes	hose	principal	principle	throne	thrown
canvas	canvass	hole	whole	profit	prophet	to too	two
capital	capitol	holy	wholly	rain rein	reign	toe	tow
ceiling	sealing	hour	our	raise	raze	vail veil	vale
cell	sell	idol	idle	read	reed	vain vane	vein
cellar	seller	in	inn	read	red	vice	vise
cent sent	scent	kernel	colonel	real	reel	wade	weighed
cereal	serial	knead	need	right write	rite	waist	waste
chord	cord	knew	new	ring	wring	wait	weight
clause	claws	knot	not	road rode	rowed	ware	wear
coarse	course	know	no	role	roll	warn	worn
council	counsel	lain	lane	rose	rows	wave	waive
creak	creek	lead	led	rough	ruff	way	weigh
currant	current	lessen	lesson	rye	wry	week	weak
dear	deer	lie	lye	sail	sale	whole	hole
dew	due	loan	lone	scene	seen	wood	would

mouse	leaf	find	judge
~~mouses~~	~~leafs~~	~~finded~~	~~judgement~~
mice	leaves	found	judgment

SPELLING EXCEPTIONS *abound in English. The general rules for forming plurals of nouns, past tenses of verbs, and for adding suffixes do not always apply.*

(a) If the suffix begins with a vowel, drop the silent *-e:*

bake	→	baking
sale	→	salable
cite	→	citation
sphere	→	spherical
live	→	livable
sense	→	sensible

The silent *-e* remains in words where leaving it out might make the pronunciation or meaning of the word doubtful. In words ending *-ce* or *-ge,* for example, the *-e* is kept:

change	→	changeable
		(changable looks as if it
		should be pronounced
		with a hard *g)*
peace	→	peaceable
manage	→	manageable
dye	→	dyeing
singe	→	singeing
		(to distinguish from
sing	→	singing)

(b) If a suffix begins with a consonant, keep the silent *e:*

care	→	careful
pure	→	purely
manage	→	management
aware	→	awareness

CAUTION: There are a few common words that drop the final *e* before the suffix *-ment:*

judge	→	judgment
acknowledge	→	acknowledgment

4. Many words ending in a consonant require that you *double* the consonant when adding a suffix beginning with a vowel.

(a) If the word ends with a single vowel and a single consonant, and if the accent is on the second syllable, double the consonant when adding the suffix:

rebel	→	rebelled	→	rebelling
control	→	controller	→	controlling

(b) In most other cases, do not double the consonant:

travel	→	traveling	→	traveler

The following table will help you to determine when to double a consonant. The first column shows words

that end with a vowel and a single consonant. In these words, the vowel is short *(hop)* and the last consonant is doubled when adding a suffix *(hopping).* When a word ends with a silent *e,* the vowel is long *(hope)* and the last consonant is not doubled before a suffix *(hoping).*

Consonant Ending		Silent *-e* Ending	
hop → hopping		hope → hoping
win → winning		wine → wining
star → starring		stare → staring
scrap → scrapping		scrape → scraping
bar → barring		bare → baring
fat → fatter		fate → fated
slop → sloppy		slope → sloping

5. Most English nouns form their plurals by adding *-s* or *-es* to their singulars.

(a) When the plural keeps the same number of syllables, add *-s:*

pencil	→	pencils
jump	→	jumps

(b) When the plural makes an extra syllable over that of the singular, add *-es:*

brush	→	brushes
watch	→	watches
fox	→	foxes

Some words change their forms in the plural. This is caused by a change in sound in going from the singular form to the plural. For example, as you know, some common words ending with an *f* sound, have a *v* sound in the plural:

leaf	→	leaves
loaf	→	loaves
life	→	lives
thief	→	thieves
wife	→	wives

SPELLING DIFFICULTIES *can even bother sign makers.*

JESSE FORDE

Parts of Speech

Because writing requires a stricter handling of grammar than does speaking, this section is devoted to a review of the basic parts of a sentence and of the parts of speech found in a sentence.

Nouns. A noun is the name of a person, place, thing, or quality.

George Washington	*Chicago*
horse	*honesty*

Nouns are either common or proper. A *common noun* is the general name of a class of persons, places, or things.

A *painting* makes a wonderful *present* for the right *person.*

A *proper noun* is the name of a particular person, place, or thing. In general, proper nouns are capitalized.

Babe Ruth was known as the *Sultan of Swat.*
Millions of immigrants came to the *United States.*
The *Titanic* was sunk by an iceberg.

A *collective noun* is a noun that is singular in form but refers to a group. A collective noun is treated as singular when the group is thought of as a unit. A collective noun is treated as plural when the members of the group are considered individually. Some of the most common collective nouns are *audience, cast, choir, flock, majority, minority, opposition, squad, staff,* and *team.*

The minority is too small to make its voice heard.
(Collective noun *minority,* thought of as a unit, is treated as singular.)
The majority in our shop are satisfied with their working conditions.
(Collective noun *majority,* thought of as meaning *more than half the number of individuals* in our shop, is treated as plural.)

An *appositive* is a noun or noun substitute—also known as a *noun repeater*—placed next to another noun or noun substitute to explain or identify it. The appositive, or noun repeater, is said to be in apposition to the first noun or noun substitute.

Mr. Williams, my speech teacher, has helped me improve my diction.
(The phrase *my speech teacher* is in apposition to *Mr. Williams.*)
The prosecutor called both of them, the child and her mother, to the stand to give testimony.
(The phrase *the child and her mother* is in apposition to *them.*)

Pronouns. A pronoun is a word that is used in place of a noun. It can take any position in a sentence that a noun can take. Pronouns are classified as being *personal, relative, interrogative, demonstrative, indefinite,* or *possessive.* The last three are also classified as *adjective pronouns* because they are used as adjectives when a noun is expressed.

The *personal pronouns* are *I, you, he, she, it, we,* and *they;* their inflected forms are *me, him, her, us,* and *them.* *Compound personal pronouns* can be formed by adding *-self* or *-selves* to certain of the simple personal pronouns: *myself, yourself, himself, herself, itself, ourselves,* and *themselves.*

Relative pronouns are not only pronouns but also connecting words. A relative pronoun refers to a noun (its *antecedent*) and joins a *subordinate* (embedded) clause to its antecedent. Such words as *who, whom, whose, which,* and *that* are relative pronouns. *What* is a relative pronoun that requires no antecedent; it stands for *that which.* Relative pronouns are compounded by adding the endings *-ever* and *-soever: who, whoever, whomever; what, whatsoever.*

> The soldiers, *who* are on leave, seem very cheerful.
> The prize *that* they won was not particularly useful.

The *interrogative pronouns* are *who, whom, whose, which,* and *what* when they are used for asking questions rather than for the introduction of a subordinate clause.

> *Who* is it? *What* did you say?

Demonstrative pronouns are used to point out a specific person, place, or thing. The most common demonstratives are *this, that, these,* and *those.* Demonstratives can be used as pronouns and as adjectives.

> *That* is a great car. *(pronoun)*
> *This* is my house. *(pronoun)*
> *That* movie was exciting. *(adjective)*
> *This* cold is driving me crazy. *(adjective)*

Indefinite pronouns are used to point out persons, places, or things, but less specifically than the demonstratives do. Some common indefinite pronouns are *everybody, nobody, each, either, neither, one, none, some, other, another, few, many, all, several,* and *both.* The indefinites can be used, like the demonstratives, both as pronouns and as adjectives.

> *Many* are called but *few* are chosen. *(pronoun)*
> *Many* people are soap opera buffs. *(adjective)*
> *Few* plays are commercial successes. *(adjective)*

The *possessive pronouns* are *mine, yours, his, hers, its, ours,* and *theirs.*

> Mine is not as fast as *yours.*
> *Hers* does the job better than *his.*

The *possessive adjectives* are *my, your, his, her, its, our,* and *their.*

> My hat looks old-fashioned.
> *Your* car eats gasoline.
> *Their* motives are open to suspicion.

The antecedent of a pronoun is the word for which the pronoun stands in a sentence. Pronouns are used to replace nouns because sentences would otherwise become too repetitious.

> Ann said that Ann's car was at Ann's house. *(repetitious)*
> Ann said that *her* car was at *her* house. *(better)*

In the second sentence, the pronoun *her* replaces *Ann's* and clearly refers back to *Ann,* the antecedent.

Verbs. A verb is a word used to express action, being, or a state of being.

> The shortstop *fired* the ball to first.
> Margaret *is* president of her own company.
> Nevertheless, kindness *exists.*

Verbs may be one word or a group of words *(verb-phrase),* and can be classified as *transitive* or *intransitive,* according to their use.

Transitive verbs, sometimes called action verbs, take a direct object.

> John *completed* the income tax form.

In this sentence, *John,* the subject, is doing the action and *form* is the object of the verb *completed.*

Transitive verbs can be "turned around" by using the passive form. The receiver of the action becomes the subject of the sentence.

> The income tax form *was completed* by John.

In this sentence, the passive-voice verb is *was completed,* and the subject, which is the receiver of the action, is *form.*

Intransitive verbs do not have a receiver of the action expressed in the verb.

> The sun *rose.*

Intransitive verbs are either *complete* or *linking.* The *complete intransitive verb* is one that makes a whole statement without the need of any words other than the subject.

> Fish *swim.*
> The men *work.*
> Winter *departs.*

The *linking verb*—also called the *copulative verb*—is an intransitive verb that links or connects the subject with a noun or adjective (called a *complement*) that has the same meaning as the subject, or describes, limits, or indicates the subject.

The verb *to be (am, are, is, was, were)* is the most common of the linking verbs; other common linking verbs are *become, appear, look, remain, feel, taste, smell, sound, turn, grow, stay,* and *continue.*

> The day *is* cold.
> We *were* hungry.
> The apple *tastes* good.

A *complement* is an adjective or noun that is used to complete the meaning of a linking verb. Complements are referred to as *predicate adjectives* or *predicate nouns.*

> *My mother felt sick.*
> (Predicate adjective *sick* complements linking verb *felt.*)
> *Lucy was an accomplished flutist.*
> (Predicate noun complements linking verb *was.*)

Adjectives or nouns that complement (complete the meaning of) a noun or pronoun are called objective complements.

> *We find him objectionable.*
> (Adjective *objectionable* acts as objective complement of pronoun *him.*)
> *They named the secretary chairman as well.*
> (Noun *chairman* acts as objective complement of noun *secretary.*)

An *auxiliary verb* is a verb used with other verbs to form voice and tense.

> *Mrs. Jackson was admired by all her clients.*
> (Passive voice, *was admired.*)
> *Mr. Page was pruning his prize shrubs.*
> (Past progressive tense, *was pruning.*)

Commonly used auxiliary verbs are *be, can, do, have, may, must,* and *should.*

Adjectives. An adjective is a word or group of words used to modify—describe, define, or explain—a noun or pronoun.

> The *sleek, black* sedan cruised down the street.

Here *sleek* and *black* are adjectives modifying *sedan.*

Phrases and clauses may also be used as adjectives.

> The reports *on the desk* are finished.

(*See also* the sections on prepositions and relative clauses that follow.)

Adjectives can express degrees of a quality. The three degrees are *positive, comparative,* and *superlative.*

The positive degree of an adjective is its common form: *fast, slow, big, small,* etc. The comparative degree is used when comparing.

> Our systems analyst is *faster* than yours.
> My bicycle is *slower* than yours.

ADJECTIVES *often describe an attitude or feeling, for example,* happy, smug, foolish.

ALMOST *is an adverb that changes the meaning of a verb or adjective. These comedians aren't* falling, *or* dead *here, but they are* almost falling, almost dead.

THE MECHANICS OF WRITING

(See also the section on clauses that follows.)

Conjunctions are classified as being *coordinating, conjunctive, subordinating,* and *correlative.*

A *coordinating conjunction* connects two words, two phrases, or two clauses of equal rank. Some of the common coordinating or linking conjunctions are *and, but, for, or,* and *still.*

Some adverbs, known as *conjunctive adverbs,* also are used to connect two independent clauses or two sentences. These include *however, then, therefore,* and *thus.*

It rained all day. *Thus,* the ball game was canceled.

The *subordinating conjunction* or *embedding conjunction* is used to connect two clauses of unequal rank. It connects a less important (dependent) clause to the main (independent) clause.

Everyone was happy *until* the telephone rang.

Here *until* is a subordinating conjunction connecting *the telephone rang* to the main clause, *everyone was happy.*

Correlative conjunctions appear in pairs: *both—and; either—or; neither —nor; not only—but also.*

Neither the meat *nor* the vegetables were cooked properly.

Interjection.
An interjection is an exclamatory expression with no grammatical relation to the sentence in which it occurs.

Gosh, is she really that sick?
My, I had no idea.

In these sentences, the interjections are *Gosh* and *My.*

Article.
An article functions as an adjective. There are three articles: *a, an,* and *the. The* is the definite article; *a* and *an* are the indefinite articles. Use *a* before a word beginning with a consonant sound: *a memory, a woman.* Use *an* before a word beginning with a vowel sound: *an hour, an honest man.*

Expletive.
An expletive is the grammatical term designating *it* and *there* when these words function only to open sentences or clauses. Expletives have no meaning; they are merely introductory words.

It is later than you think.
(*It is* is merely a convenient way to open the sentence.)
There are too many unanswered questions in the investigation.
(*There are* is merely a convenient way to open the sentence.)

The superlative degree expresses a quality of the highest or lowest degree when more than two things or persons are compared.

Our systems analyst is the *fastest* in the business.
My bicycle is the *slowest* in the race.

The degrees of an adjective are formed in one of three ways:
1. Adding *-er* or *-est* to the positive (*cool, cooler, coolest*).
2. Prefixing *more* and *most* to the positive (*beautiful, more beautiful, most beautiful*).
3. Using irregular inflections for some common adjectives (*bad, worse, worst; good, better, best*). If you are not sure how to form the degrees of a particular adjective, look the adjective up in a dictionary.

Adverbs.
An adverb is a word or group of words used to modify a verb, an adjective, another adverb, a pronoun, or even a whole phrase, clause, or sentence.

He worked *steadily.*

Here *steadily* is an adverb modifying the verb *worked.*

She is a *nearly* great singer.

Here *nearly* is an adverb modifying the adjective *great.*

"Don't bother," the woman said *rather* petulantly.

Here *rather* is an adverb modifying the adverb *petulantly.*

She crawled *almost* to the top.

Here *almost* is an adverb modifying the phrase *to the top.*

The game ended *just* after I arrived.

Here *just* is an adverb modifying the clause *after I arrived.*

Almost everyone there was single.

Here *almost* is an adverb modifying the indefinite pronoun *everyone.*

Consequently, the entire operation was a failure.

Here *consequently* is an adverb modifying the entire sentence.

Like adjectives, adverbs can show three degrees of comparison: positive (*cleverly*); comparative (*more cleverly*); superlative (*most cleverly*).

Prepositions.
A preposition is a word that indicates a relationship between its object and some other word in the sentence. Some common prepositions are *above, below, before, after, to, from, in, into, between,* and *among.*

The family drove *to* Denver.

Here *to* is a preposition showing the relationship between its object, *Denver,* and the verb *drove.*

A preposition, together with its object and any modifiers of its object, forms a *prepositional phrase.* Prepositional phrases can modify nouns, pronouns, verbs, adjectives, and adverbs.

Our friends want to leave after dinner.
(*After dinner* modifies *leave.*)
A book without a cover will not last long.
(*Without a cover* modifies *book.*)

Conjunctions.
A conjunction is used to connect words or groups of words. The conjunction itself may be a word or several words.

The lion *and* the lamb shall lie down together.

Here *and* is a conjunction connecting two nouns, *lion* and *lamb.*

He was asked to attend, *but* he couldn't make it.

Here *but* is a conjunction connecting two parts, or clauses, of the sentence.

The Sentence

Although we do not always speak in sentences, the sentence is, nevertheless, the basic unit for conveying thought in our language. It is especially important in writing because the written word lacks the benefit of facial expression and bodily gesture to convey meaning.

Sentences. The sentence is a word or group of words that expresses a complete thought. It is made up of a *subject* (that about which something is said) and a *predicate* (that which is said about the subject).

> Fortune smiles.

The *complete subject* is the subject along with all its modifiers. The *simple subject* is the subject without its modifiers.

> The old man in the gray suit wept.

Here *man* is the simple subject and *The old man in the gray suit* is the complete subject.

The *complete predicate* is the predicate with all its modifiers and complements. The *simple predicate* is the predicate without any modifiers or any complements.

> Juan walked slowly to the door.

Here *walked* is the simple predicate and *walked slowly to the door* is the complete predicate.

The receiver of the action, if there is one, is called the *direct object* or *objective complement*.

> The cafeteria served peas at lunch.

Here *cafeteria* is the simple subject, *served* is the simple predicate, and *peas* is the direct object.

The subject, the predicate, and the direct object of a sentence may be compound; that is, the sentence may have two or more subjects, two or more predicates, or two or more objects.

> Paula and Ramon will come.
> *(compound subject)*
> Charlayne laughed and clapped her hands.
> *(compound predicate)*
> David sent Joey and me to see them.
> *(compound object)*

A *direct object* is the word or words that receive the action of a verb:

> The boxer fought *the contender*.
> (*Contender* is the direct object of *fought*.)
> They found their *wallets*.
> (*Wallets* is the direct object of *found*.)
> The cat ate its *food*.
> (*Food* is the direct object of *ate*.)

An *indirect object* is the word or words that receive the direct object of a verb:

> The referee gave *them* a signal.
> (The subject is *referee*. The verb is *gave*. The direct object is *signal*. The indirect object *them* receives the direct object, *signal*.)
> They told *me* tall stories.
> (The indirect object *me* receives the direct object *stories*.)
> They gave their *car* good care.
> (The indirect object *car* receives the direct object *care*.)

An *object of a preposition* is a noun, pronoun, or noun substitute that follows a preposition.

> We distributed the candy to *them*.
> We looked at the *painting*.
> (In these sentences, the prepositions are *to* and *at*. The object of *to* is *them*. The object of *at* is *painting*.)

Phrases. A phrase is a group of related words that does not contain a subject or a predicate.

> Washington wintered *at Valley Forge*.
> *(prepositional phrase)*

A *noun phrase* is a phrase that functions as a noun.

> *Round-trip tickets on a transatlantic flight* are not expensive in the spring and autumn.
> (Noun phrase *Round-trip tickets on a transatlantic flight* functions as the subject of *are*.)

An *absolute phrase* is a phrase closely related in meaning to the rest of the sentence in which it is found, but grammatically independent of it. Absolute phrases occur either before or after an independent clause.

> *Her marriage ended*, Jessica set out for the city to start a new life.
> (Absolute phrase: *Her marriage ended*.)
> Alfred went slowly toward his truck, *the rain falling gently on his head and broad shoulders*, *scarcely wetting him*, *reminding him only of the approaching winter*.
> (Three absolute phrases follow *Alfred went slowly toward his truck*.)

Clauses. A clause is a group of related words that has a subject and a predicate and that is used as part of a sentence.

> If he arrives in time, we can close the deal.

In the first clause, *he* is the subject and *arrives* is the predicate. The second clause also has a subject (*we*) and a predicate (*can close*).

Clauses may be *independent* (of equal rank) or *dependent*. An *independent clause* is a clause that makes sense when it stands alone and is grammatically complete.

A *dependent* (subordinate) *clause* is a clause that usually does not make complete sense when it stands alone, although it contains a subject and a predicate. It is a sentence embedded in another sentence, and dependent on another clause to complete its sense. Dependent clauses can be used as different parts of speech in a sentence, playing the role of a noun, an adjective, or an adverb.

> He sat down very quietly *after he made the statement*.

Here the dependent clause *after he made the statement* is used as an adverb modifying *sat*.

Verbals. There are three types of verbals, called *gerunds, infinitives,* and *participles*.

A *gerund* is a verb form ending in *-ing* and functioning as a noun, not as a verb.

> *Loafing* can be productive.

An *infinitive* is a verb form that functions as noun, adjective, or adverb.

> She loves *to study*.

A *participle* is an adjective form derived from a verb.

> No one wears a *smoking* jacket in our circle of friends.
> You act like a *trapped* animal.

Types of sentences. Sentences are also classified as being *simple, compound,* and *complex*. A *simple sentence* has only one independent clause and no dependent clauses.

> The sales figures for May were excellent.

A simple sentence remains a simple sentence even though it contains phrases or compound subjects, compound predicates, and compound objects.

A *compound sentence* has two or more independent clauses connected by a coordinating conjunction or by punctuation.

> Nathan is a born leader and he will go far.
> The roast is burning; the gas must be turned down.

A *complex sentence* is a sentence that contains one independent clause and one or more dependent clauses.

> She didn't say anything while I was there.

Here *while I was there* is the dependent clause and *She didn't say anything* is the independent clause.

Sentences are also classified by function. The four classifications are *declarative, imperative, interrogative,* and *exclamatory*.

DIAGRAMMING SENTENCES

One way to grasp all the parts of a sentence and their relationships to each other is to diagram the sentence, that is, to make a visual representation of it.

Diagram of a simple sentence: *Birds eat.*

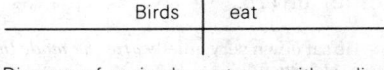

Diagram of a simple sentence with a direct object:

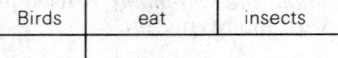

The direct object *insects* is placed above the horizontal line. Notice that the line separating *eat* (the verb) from *insects* (the direct object) does not go through the horizontal line.

Expanding the sentence to read *Wild birds usually eat many insects* results in the following diagram:

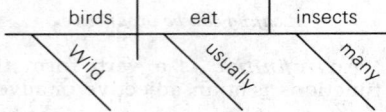

Because the subject *birds* is modified by *Wild*, the modifier *Wild* appears along a slanted line coming out of the horizontal line before *birds*. The modifiers *usually* and *many* also appear on slanted lines coming out of the horizontal line before the words they modify.

Diagram of a simple sentence with a prepositional phrase used as an adjective and with an adjective as complement: *The lady in the red dress was beautiful.*

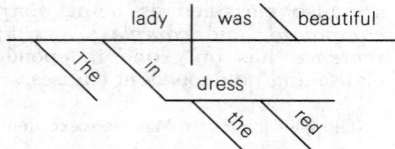

The horizontal line supplies the subject *(lady)*, the verb *(was)*, and the complement *(beautiful)*. Notice that the verb and the complement are separated by a slanted line coming down to the horizontal line. This slanted line indicates that *beautiful* is a complement. Notice also that the subject is modified by a prepositional phrase *(in the red dress)*.

Diagram of a simple sentence that contains a noun complement: *Anne recently became a physician.*

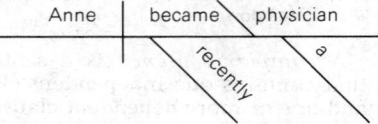

The horizontal line now supplies the subject *(Anne)*, the verb *(became)*, and the complement *(physician)*. Notice that the verb and the complement are separated by a slanted line coming down to the horizontal line. This slanted line indicates that *physician* is a complement, not a direct object. Notice also that the verb and the complement are modified.

Diagram of a simple sentence with a compound subject and a prepositional phrase used as an adverb: *Ray and Bernice sat in the rowboat.*

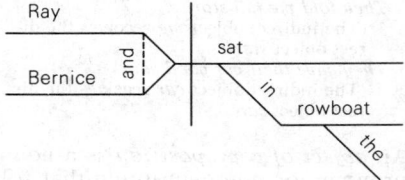

We have now shown how to treat subjects, verbs, direct objects, and modifiers. The next sentence element to be represented is the indirect object. *Joan sent us a book.*

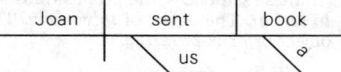

The indirect object *us* appears on a line below and parallel with the horizontal line on which appear the subject, verb, and direct object. Notice that the line for the indirect object is connected to the horizontal line by a slanted line. The fact that *us* is written on a horizontal line shows that it is an indirect object, not a modifier. Notice also that the direct object *book* is modified by *a*, written on a slanted line.

If you can diagram a simple sentence in this way, you can also diagram other sentence types. For example, the compound sentence *Jack spent his allowance, but I saved mine* may be diagrammed as follows:

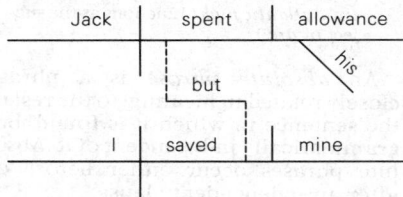

Notice that each independent clause has its own horizontal line and that the conjunction *(but)* sits between the clauses connected by broken lines to each horizontal line.

When a sentence has more than one word serving as subject, verb, object, or complement, it is diagrammed as follows. *John thoroughly enjoys school and gladly pays his tuition.*

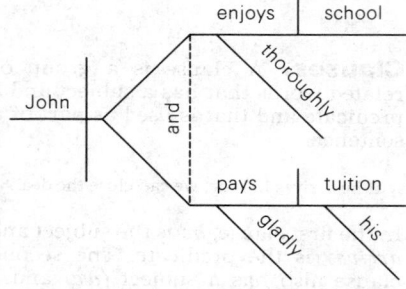

This sentence shows a compound verb *(enjoys, pays)*. The conjunction *and* is connected to the two horizontal lines by a broken line. Since each verb also has an object, two vertical lines separate the verbs from their objects.

The same system is used with compound subjects and compound objects. *Frank and Jamie pay no attention to me.*

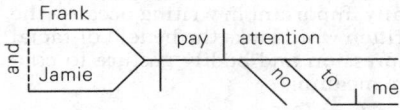

The compound subjects *(Frank, Jamie)* are connected by *and*, shown on the broken line. Notice that the object *(attention)* is modified.

Until this point, diagrams of independent clauses have been shown. A few sentences containing dependent clauses follow.

Diagram of a complex sentence: *The programmer will not run the program until she checks the input terminal.*

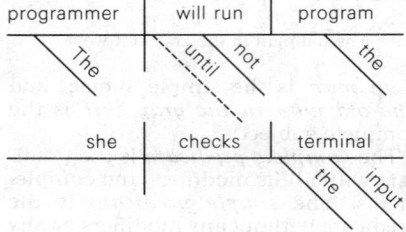

In this sentence, *until she checks the input terminal* is a dependent clause modifying the verb *will run* in the independent clause.

Diagram of a complex sentence: *That she was a beautiful woman could not be denied.*

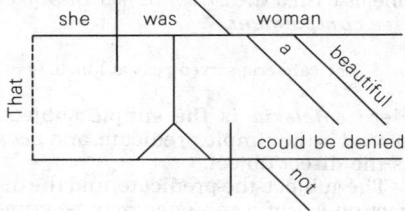

The noun clause *That she was a beautiful woman* is the subject of the sentence.

Diagram of a complex sentence: *I still deny that she gave money to me yesterday.*

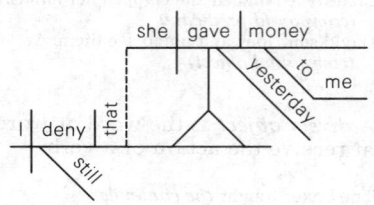

In this sentence, the noun clause *that she gave money to me yesterday* is the direct object of *deny*.

A *declarative sentence* makes a statement or asserts a fact.

> The soup tastes good.
> Trenton is the capital of New Jersey.

An *imperative sentence* gives a command or makes a request. The subject of most imperative sentences is not expressed; it is understood to be *you* (the person or persons who are being addressed).

> Leave me alone.
> Please don't walk on the grass.

Interrogative sentences are those that ask a question.

> Are you finished yet? Where's the report?

Exclamatory sentences show surprise, anger, or other strong emotion.

> How I wish I'd been there! I can't believe it!

Nearly any sentence that is said with strong emotion or emphasis can be exclamatory.

> Is the report ready? *(interrogative)*
> Is the report ready! *(exclamatory)*

Basic Usage

Errors in usage frequently occur when an inexperienced writer attempts to use the standards for spoken language in written composition. Because most people are able to communicate quite adequately when speaking, they find the discovery of errors in their written work both frustrating and baffling.

The usage problems discussed in this section are ones that often appear in the writing of educated adults as well as students. There are many fine points of usage, and some usage questions are answered differently by different experts. Here we confine ourselves to points of usage that are fairly common and on which there is wide agreement.

Nouns. Much of the trouble in using nouns comes when a writer omits adding the inflectional -*s* or -*es* endings for plurals. These endings signal a change in meaning by their presence, and their absence confuses a reader, even if the context of the sentence gives a plural meaning.

Sometimes poor speech habits are the cause of this omission. In noun plurals that end with -*sts* or -*sks* (*wrists, fists, scientists, desks*), everyday speech tends to blur the final *s*. The unwary writer then leaves it off in his written composition, writing "Scientist are always trying to prove their

work." The verb *are* shows that the writer knows that the plural is wanted, but he rejects or forgets the -*s* inflectional ending. If you find that you often write plurals without the -*s*, sensitize your ear to the sound of the -*s* ending.

Certain regional dialects and variants of standard English (including black English), omit the -*s* in certain plurals when plural meaning is clearly indicated by the modifiers:

ten gallon of gas	3 million job
many year ago	these subject
two car are needed	not enough word

These uses are not considered acceptable in written communication.

Cases of pronouns. A pronoun has the attributes of number (singular or plural), gender (masculine, feminine, or neuter), and person.

There are three classes of person: *first person,* denoting the person speaking (*I* am going); *second person,* denoting the person or thing spoken to (*you* may not); and *third person,* denoting the person or thing spoken of (*they* have not arrived).

Pronouns also may be classified by case. There are three cases in English: *nominative, objective,* and *possessive.* Pronouns often have distinct forms for all the cases. Below is a chart of the forms of personal and possessive pronouns for plural and singular number and for all three cases.

The *subject* of a verb is in the *nominative case,* whether the subject is a noun or pronoun.

> The *fish* were frightened; *they* dove deeper into the pool.

Here the noun *fish* and the pronoun *they* are in the nominative case because both are the subjects of verbs (*were frightened* and *dove,* respectively).

The *object* of a verb or a preposition is in the *objective case.*

> Ray met the *girl* but would not speak to *her.*

Girl is the object of the verb *met* and is in the objective case. *Her* is the object of the preposition *to* and is in the objective case.

The *possessive case* indicates ownership, possession, or some similar

relationship. Pronouns have their distinct possessive form; they may stand as nouns or be used as adjectives (sometimes called possessive adjectives).

> It is *my* boat; the boat is *mine.* (*adjective, noun*)

Some other pronouns have different forms for adjective and noun uses: *your—yours, her—hers, our—ours, their—theirs.*

One common fault of inexperienced writers is the failure to use the possessive form of the pronoun in cases that call for it. Often writers feel that closeness is enough to show possession and that no change in form is necessary.

> They are not ready to sacrifice in the way *they* parents did.

The correct form is *their* parents.

Agreement of pronouns. A pronoun is said to *agree with* (that is, to conform to or match) the number, gender, and person of its antecedent.

> The man worked on his project.

Here the pronoun *his* is singular, masculine, and in the third person to agree with *man.* A common mistake is to think of a singular noun as representing an abstract group.

> A young student today must work hard and keep up *their* attention because of the competition.

Here the writer sees *student* as the representative of a group (*young students*). The sentence may be rewritten correctly as

> Young students must . . . keep up *their* grades.
> or
> A young student must . . . keep up his grades.

A special group of pronouns causes trouble with agreement. They are called indefinite pronouns. One group requires plural verbs and complements: *few, some, many, all.*

> *Many* are called but *few* are chosen.

The indefinite singular pronouns include *everybody, everyone, each, ei-*

PERSONAL AND POSSESSIVE PRONOUNS

	SINGULAR			PLURAL		
	Nom.	*Poss.*	*Obj.*	*Nom.*	*Poss.*	*Obj.*
1ST PER.	I	my, mine	me	we	our, ours	us
2ND PER.	you	your, yours	you	you	your, yours	you
3RD PER.	he	his	him	they	their, theirs	them
	she	her, hers	her	they	their, theirs	them
	it	its	it	they	their, theirs	them

ther, neither, someone, no one, anyone. They require singular verbs and complements.

> *Everybody is* happy.
> *No one comes* to see me.

Another problem in pronoun agreement comes when a writer unnecessarily shifts from one person to another in the same sentence.

> Many young *people* have heard that if *they* want to succeed and get a good job, *you* have to stay in school.

Here the writer shifts from the third person *(people, they)* to the second person *(you)*. Most likely, the writer himself is changing perspective as he writes. But such shifts are very disconcerting to the reader. The corrected sentence should end, ". . . *they* have to stay in school."

Subject-predicate agreement.
The subject of a sentence must agree with the predicate in number. A plural subject takes a plural verb, and a singular subject takes a singular verb.

> The cats play. A dog runs.

A particularly common subject-predicate error is the wrong use of the contractions *don't* and *doesn't*. *Don't* is correct for first and second person (I *don't* want to go. You *don't* see the point.) and for all plurals (They *don't* care.). But for the third person singular, *doesn't* is correct.

> She *doesn't* want to go.
> He *doesn't* see the point.
> It *doesn't* matter.

Using *don't* in place of *doesn't* is incorrect.

There are several special rules that help determine whether a subject requires a singular or plural verb and complement.

A subject that is joined to a group of words introduced by *with, together with, accompanied by, as well as, including,* and the like is *not* changed in number.

> The director, together with the department managers, *was* at the meeting.
> The department managers, accompanied by the director, *were* at the meeting.

When two or more singular subjects are joined by *or* or *nor*, the verb is singular. On the other hand, when a singular and a plural subject are joined by *or* or *nor*, the verb must agree in number with the subject nearest it.

> Either *Rosita* or *Carmen is* to be in charge.
> Neither Roberta nor the *people* in the typing pool *are* to be present.
> Either the sales representatives or

Daniel is to handle telephone queries.

When a sentence begins with the words *here* or *there*, the number of the verb must agree with the subject that follows the verb.

> Here *is* the *house* I spoke of.
> Here *are* the *players* now.
> There *is* a great *deal* of grumbling among the staff.
> There *are* many *reasons* for this procedure.

In expressions like *one of the strategies that,* the verb agrees in number with the antecedent of the pronoun.

> This is one of the *strategies* that *are* employed to reduce costs.

Here the antecedent of *that* is *strategies*, hence the plural verb *are*.

> She is the only *one* of the typists who *is* capable of doing the job.

Here the antecedent of *who* is *one* (referring to *she*); hence the singular verb *is*.

Verb forms.
Some of the characteristics of verbs have already been described *(see* Parts of Speech above). Verbs take many forms to express action or state of being in various times *(tense),* in ways of acting between subject and object *(voice),* and in *mood*.

Tense is used to indicate the time of the action implied or stated in the verb. While there are traditionally six classifications of tenses in English, most simple expository writing concerns itself with two: the *present* and the *past.*

The *present tense* is most often used to express action that is going on at present.

> The orders *are* ready to ship now.
> The canoe *glides* downstream.

However, the present tense can also express future time in certain circumstances.

> The plane *departs* in five minutes.

The present tense can also be used to refer to an event that was completed in past time.

> The police *arrive* just in time to foil the robbery.

The *past tense* is used to indicate an action that was completed at a definite time in the past.

> Bob *wrote* that memo last week.
> The team *played* well in yesterday's doubleheader.

All verbs have a present and past tense. Most verbs (sometimes called

weak verbs) form the past tense by adding *-ed* or *-d* to the root.

> *jump→jumped   die→died*

Certain common verbs (sometimes called *strong* verbs) change their form in the past tense.

> *sing→sang   write→wrote*

Other tenses of verbs are formed by using *auxiliary* verbs. For example, to show action completed in the past, we use the *perfect* tense, which is formed by using the auxiliary *have* and the past participle of the verb.

Past participles of weak verbs are the same as their simple past.

> I *jumped* over the wall.
> I *have jumped* over the wall.

Strong verbs, however, have a separate form when used as past participles

> She *sang* a song.
> She *has sung* that song before.

The principal parts of a verb are its present form, past form, and past participle form. The forms of the weak verbs are *regular* and easy to predict. Below is a table of strong verbs showing their principal parts.

The table includes only a handful of the verbs, but it does contain many of the common verbs in the language. The most common of all, *to be*, is so irregular that it requires special mention. The present form differs according to person and number, as does the past form.

Present	*Past*
I *am*	I *was*
you, we, they *are*	you, we, they *were*
he, she, it *is*	he, she, it *was*

The past participle of *to be* is *been;* the infinitive form is *(to) be*.

HABITUAL OR CONTINUED ACTION *is often expressed by the simple present. These joggers* run *for exercise. At the present moment they* are *running.*

PRINCIPAL PARTS OF STRONG (IRREGULAR) VERBS

Present	Past	Past Participle
awake	awoke	awaked or awakened
bear	bore	borne
beat	beat	beaten or beat
become	became	become
begin	began	begun
bite	bit	bitten or bit
bleed	bled	bled
blow	blew	blown
break	broke	broken
bring	brought	brought
build	built	built
buy	bought	bought
catch	caught	caught
choose	chose	chosen
come	came	come
dig	dug	dug
do	did	done
draw	drew	drawn
drink	drank	drunk
drive	drove	driven
eat	ate	eaten
fall	fell	fallen
fight	fought	fought
fly	flew	flown
forbid	forbade	forbidden

Present	Past	Past Participle
forget	forgot	forgotten or forgot
freeze	froze	frozen
get	got	got or gotten
give	gave	given
go	went	gone
grow	grew	grown
hang	hung	hung
	hanged (executed)	hanged (executed)
have	had	had
hide	hid	hidden or hid
hurt	hurt	hurt
know	knew	known
lay	laid	laid
lead	led	led
leave	left	left
lend	lent	lent
let	let	let
lie	lay	lain
make	made	made
pay	paid	paid
put	put	put
ride	rode	ridden
ring	rang	rung
rise	rose	risen
run	ran	run

Present	Past	Past Participle
say	said	said
see	saw	seen
seek	sought	sought
sell	sold	sold
set	set	set
shake	shook	shaken
shrink	shrank or shrunk	shrunk or shrunken
sing	sang	sung
sink	sank	sunk
sit	sat	sat
slay	slew	slain
speak	spoke	spoken
spin	spun	spun
spring	sprang	sprung
steal	stole	stolen
sting	stung	stung
strike	struck	struck
swear	swore	sworn
swim	swam	swum
swing	swung	swung
take	took	taken
teach	taught	taught
tear	tore	torn
think	thought	thought
throw	threw	thrown
wear	wore	worn
write	wrote	written

Many writers and speakers have an ear for the correct form of irregular verbs and use the right form without thinking. Those who find themselves using the wrong forms should study the table and memorize the right forms. Two special rules may be useful in studying the table:

1. The *past* form is *never* used with such auxiliary verbs as *was, were, have,* and *had.* The following expressions are wrong:

> have *froze*
> has *swam*

2. The *past participle* is *always* used with these auxiliary verbs. The following expressions are correct:

> have *frozen*
> has *swum*

Mastering the forms of irregular verbs may correct more writing errors than any other exercise.

There are three forms of the verb with special uses. The *infinitive* consists of the root of the verb preceded by the word *to.* Infinitives are used in showing intention or desire.

> We plan *to fly* to Los Angeles.
> He wants *to go* home.

They are also used when reporting what has been said or thought.

> She told him *to be* good.

The infinitive form without the *to* is also used with the auxiliary verb *will* to express future actions or states of being.

> He *will go* to town tomorrow.
> I *will be* angry if you continue.

The second special form of the verb is the *participial* form. Participles have many uses. The *past participle,* which we have already met, is used with the auxiliary verb *have* to express actions or states of being in the past. Consider the following:

Simple past:	I *ran* fast.
Perfect:	I *have run* fast. (on past occasions)
Past perfect:	I was tired because I *had run* fast. (before becoming tired)
Future perfect:	By tomorrow at this time I *will have run* a fast race. (rarely used)

The *present participle* is formed by adding *-ing* to the verb root. It is used with forms of the verb *to be* to express actions or states of being that are continuing or habitual.

> I *am running* three times a week.
> She *was smoking* more than usual.
> They *have been sending* signals all night.

A participle may also be used as an adjective, describing the action or state of the noun it modifies.

> the *broken* doll (past participle)
> the *dripping* faucet (present participle)

The third special form of the verb is called the *gerund.* It is the same as the verb's present participle in form, but it is used as a noun.

> *Swimming* is good exercise.
> His hobbies are *singing* and *playing* the piano.

Note in the second example that the gerund can take an object as if it were a verb.

Transitive verbs (those that can take an object) also have *voice.* They use the *active voice* in the most common sentence order.

> Jack *hit* the ball hard.

They use the *passive voice* when the receiver of the action is the subject.

> The ball *was hit* hard by Jack.

The passive form of a verb is formed by using *to be* as an auxiliary with the past participle of the verb.

> The bicycle   *is being stolen.*
>   *was stolen.*
>   *has been stolen.*
>   *will be stolen.*

Mood indicates the manner in which the action of the verb takes place. The *indicative mood* makes a statement or asks a question. The *imperative mood* gives a command or makes a request. The *subjunctive mood* indicates wishfulness, doubt, or uncertainty about the action of the verb. Verb forms do not change for indicative and imperative mood. The subjunctive mood makes use of auxiliaries such as *would* and *should*. In formal writing, use of the infinitive form of the verb *to be* sometimes shows the subjunctive mood.

> If God *be* for us, who can be against us?

The subjunctive may also be shown by the use of a past form where a present form would otherwise be expected.

> I wish you *were* here now.

Today, many writers would use an alternate form to express this wish.

> I wish you *could be* here now.

The following usage guide concentrates on particular English usage problems and supplements the general comments above.

GUIDE TO USAGE

Informal English is the language you use most of the time in speaking with your friends and family and in writing friendly letters. It is also the language used in many magazines, books, and newspapers meant to be read by the general public. The words of informal English are the familiar, everyday ones. Contractions such as *don't* and *aren't* are part of this pattern.

Formal English is the language you use for formal situations—delivering a speech before a town meeting, reporting on a topic you have researched, writing a paper. In these settings, your choice of words should be the best you can manage.

Speaking or writing correctly may not guarantee that your message is sound, but correctness does guarantee that your audience will not be distracted by the form of your communication.

This glossary contains many examples of commonly misused, misspelled, incorrect, and confusing words and phrases. Being aware of them helps you avoid the pitfalls of careless speaking and writing. In addition to studying the entries in this glossary, you will find it useful to consult the bibliography at the end of this volume, which supplies titles of additional guides to correct usage.

a, an. *A* is the article used before a consonant sound (*a* dog); *an* is used before a vowel sound (*an* ant). This rule is based on the opening sound of the following word, not on its first letter. (*A* house, *an* hour.)

accept, except. *Accept* is a verb meaning to receive or approve. *Except* is a preposition that means excluding. (I *accept* all your comments *except* the last one.)

adjectives. There are many overworked and misused adjectives that should be avoided in formal writing. Something is *wonderful* if it inspires wonder; otherwise, *wonderful* is an empty adjective. When you say that something is *nice,* the reader politely yawns. Other adjectives to look out for are *awful, beautiful, incredible, terrible,* and *terrific.* If an adjective tells the reader only that one has vaguely approved or disapproved of something, a better adjective is needed. Tired adjectives can also be made into exhausted adverbs, usually by adding *-ly* to the end.

advice, advise. *Advice* is a noun; *advise* is a verb. (He *advised* me to take the doctor's *advice.*)

affect, effect. *Affect* is a verb that means to influence. (The weather *affects* my moods.) *Effect* is a noun that means result. (She did not consider the *effect* of her action; if you are *affected* by the sight of blood, a gory movie may have a nauseating *effect* on you.) *Effect* may also be a verb meaning to cause. (The new law *effected* a major change in government.)

aggravate. In formal usage, *aggravate* means to make worse. (She *aggravated* her ulcer by worrying about it.) The informal use of *aggravate* to mean to annoy, while acceptable in speech, is less so in writing.

agree to, agree with. *Agree to* something; *agree with* someone.

ain't. Not acceptable in formal speech or writing.

all of, alongside of. See *of.*

already, all ready. *Already* means by this time. (She was *already* angry when he arrived.) *All ready* means all prepared. (He was *all ready* to leave.)

altogether, all together. *Altogether* means thoroughly or completely. (That is an *altogether* different matter.) *All together* means in a group. (They played cards when they were *all together.*)

amount, number; fewer, less. *Amount* refers to quantity in bulk while *number* refers to separate units. (The *amount* of money; the *number* of dollars.) Likewise, *fewer* refers to *numbered* things while *less* refers to *amount.* (The *number* of pieces in the game was *fewer* than called for; the *amount* of sugar we needed was *less* than we thought.)

an. See *a.*

anxious, eager. In formal writing, *anxious* means apprehensive, worried, while *eager* means looking forward to. (I am *anxious* about the exam; I am *eager* to have it over.)

anybody, anyone, each, everybody, everyone, nobody, no one, none, somebody, someone. These words are all singular and always take a singular verb. (*Everybody is here.*) When a pronoun refers back to these words, *he* and *his* are most often used. (*Everyone knows* what *he* is supposed to do.) (See also *gender.*)

awful. Do not use as an adverb. (He was *awful* sorry.) (See also *adjectives.*)

beautiful. See *adjectives.*

beside, besides. *Beside* means by the side of. (They stood *beside* each other.) *Besides* means moreover. (*Besides,* what difference does it make?)

between you and me. This is the correct expression. *Between you and I* is grammatically wrong. After prepositions like *between,* use the objective pronouns *me, him, her, them,* not the subjective pronouns *I, he, she, they.*

but. See *double negatives.*

can, may. *Can* implies the ability to do something; *may* implies permission or chance. (He *can* drive; his father said he *may* go; she *may* stay or she *may* not.)

capital, capitol. A *capitol* is the main building of a government. (The *Capitol* in Washington is open to the public at certain times.) All other meanings of the word are spelled *capital*.

censor, censure. To *censor* means to prohibit or cut out objectionable material. (News coverage is strictly *censored* in the Soviet Union.) The person whose job it is to examine material for censorship is called a *censor*. To *censure* someone is to reprimand him. (He was *censured* by the principal for cheating.)

childish, childlike. Children are both lovable and annoying. Someone who is *childish* reminds one of the annoying traits of children. (His whining and *childish* obstinacy lost him many friends.) Someone who is *childlike* has the innocence and freshness associated with children. (He viewed the most ordinary things with a *childlike* wonder.)

cite, sight, site. To *cite* something means to quote or refer to it. (They *cited* the benefits derived from other projects.) *Sight* is a noun that means vision. (Her *sight* was improved by wearing glasses.) As a verb, to *sight* something means to see it. (He *sighted* the body floating on the water.) A *site* is a location. (The construction *site*.)

compare to, compare with. *Compare to* means to show the similarities between two things of different classes. (He *compared* Earth *to* a child's ball since they are both round.) *Compare with* means to show the similarities and differences of two things in the same class. (*Compare* this house *with* the other one and you'll see which is more modern.)

complement, compliment. A *complement* is that which completes; *to complement* is to complete. (The rug *complements* the room; the dessert was the *complement* to a fine meal.) A *compliment* is praise; *to compliment* means to praise. (I *complimented* him on his choice of materials; he returned the *compliment*.)

contact. This verb is overused in the sense of conversing with someone. It is better to be more specific and use words like *ask, speak, telephone,* or *write*.

could of. See *of*.

council, counsel, consul. A *council* is a meeting or a group set up to govern or advise. (The *council* voted to accept the proposition.) *Counsel* means advice or, as a verb, to advise. (I offer you my *counsel* in this matter, if you want it; she *counseled* him on what steps to take first.) *Counsel* also means a lawyer. (The *counsel* for the defense called his first witness.) A *consul* is a government official residing in a foreign country.

credible, credulous. *Credible* means believable. (He gave a *credible* excuse for being late.) *Credulous* means gullible. (The *credulous* girl believed every story she heard.) (See also *incredible*.)

criteria. *Criteria*, meaning standards of judgment, is plural and takes a plural verb. (Their *criteria* for giving her the promotion *were* sound.) The singular is *criterion*.

deduce, deduct. To *deduce* is to reach a conclusion through reasoning. (Sherlock Holmes's method was to *deduce* who the criminal was from a few facts surrounding the case.) To *deduct* is to subtract. (Don't forget to *deduct* the amount he owes you.)

dependent. It is a good idea to spell *dependent* with the -*ent* ending. This is acceptable for both the noun and the adjective. *Dependant* is an acceptable spelling for the noun (My son is my only *dependant*), but is incorrect for the adjective (She is too *dependent* on her mother).

desert, dessert. A *desert* is an arid tract of land. To *desert* means to abandon. (He *deserted* his family when they needed him.) *Dessert* is a sweet course served at the end of a meal.

device, devise. *Device* is a noun. (The ingenious *device* had several functions.) *Devise* is a verb. (He *devised* a strategy to get a promotion.)

differ from, differ with. To *differ from* means to be unlike. (Her work methods *differ from* mine.) To *differ with* means to disagree. (He *differs with* me on the best approach to the problem.)

double negatives. Double negatives occur in a sentence where two negative words are used. (I *don't* go *nowhere*.) The meaning of such a sentence is unclear. Does it mean that the person does not go anyplace, or that he goes everywhere *but* nowhere? Avoid double negatives in writing, especially such tricky ones as *but, hardly,* and *scarcely*. (I *don't* have *but* a dollar; I *can't hardly* do it; he *scarcely* knows *nobody*.)

each. See *anybody*.

eager. See *anxious*.

effect. See *affect*.

e.g. This abbreviation, which is preceded and followed by commas, is usually used in scholarly writing. It means for example. (See also *i.e.*)

either, neither. *Either* goes with *or; neither* goes with *nor*. (*Either* you go *or* I will; *neither* you *nor* I can go.) (See also *neither*.)

emigrate, immigrate. One *immigrates to* a new country and *emigrates from* an old one. People who move to another country are called *emigrants* in their former country and *immigrants* in their new country. *Migrants* travel from place to place.

eminent, imminent. *Eminent* means distinguished. (The *eminent* scholar lectured at our school.) *Imminent* means about to take place. (The collapse of the government was *imminent*.)

epitaph, epithet. An *epitaph* is an inscription on a gravestone. An *epithet* is a phrase that accompanies or replaces the name of a person. (The Little Tramp is an *epithet* for Charlie Chaplin.) *Epithet* may also mean a word of abuse.

everybody. See *anybody*.

every day, everyday. *Every day* describes an action that takes place day after day. (She went to work *every day*.) *Everyday* is an adjective meaning ordinary. (She wore her *everyday* clothes.)

everyone. See *anybody*.

except. See *accept*.

feel bad. The correct expression is *feel bad*, not *feel badly;* it means that one does not feel well or happy. (See also *good*.)

fewer. See *amount*.

former, latter. *Former* refers to the first of two things mentioned earlier; *latter* refers to the second of the two things. (He had to decide between the red tie and the blue, and he chose the *latter*.)

gender of singular pronouns. When a pronoun refers back to a singular subject, it is often difficult to determine what gender should be used. (The good writer always makes good use of *his* (or *her*) material; *one* must raise *his* (or *her*) hand when *he* (or *she*) wants to be recognized.) Traditionally, the singular pronouns *he* and *his* have been used. This may be confusing when the original noun or pronoun is indefinite. In that case, one may substitute *he or she* and *his or her*. (*One* must raise *his or her* hand when *he or she* wants to be recognized.) This solution is often cumbersome. In many cases it is best to rewrite the sentence. Often *you* and *your* can be substituted for *one* and *his*. (*You* must raise *your* hand when *you* want to be recognized.) Some authorities recommend using the plural pronoun even with a singular noun. (*One* must raise *their* hand . . .) This solution has not been widely accepted, however, and should be avoided.

good, well. *Good* is an adjective; it describes a noun (the *good* child). It also describes nouns when used with verbs of appearance, sound, taste, smell, and feel. (The dress looks *good* on her; the ice cream tastes *good*.) *Well* is the adverb equivalent of good and is used to describe actions. (He runs *well;* the chorus sings *well*.) *Well* may also be an adjective meaning healthy. (I am not sick, I am *well*.) The following uses of *well* and *good* are incorrect: the dress looks *well* on her; he swims *good*.

got to. This should be changed to *have to.* (I *have to* run; not, I *have got to* run.)

hanged, hung. The past of *hang* is *hung* except when referring to an execution by hanging. (The coat *hung* on the hook; but, the man was *hanged* at dawn.)

hardly. See *double negatives.*

i.e. This abbreviation, usually found in scholarly writing, means that is. It should be set off by commas. (Plato is concerned with the ideal, *i.e.,* the forms in the world of Idea.)

immigrate. See *emigrate.*

imminent. See *eminent.*

imply, infer. To *imply* means to suggest without actually saying so. (You *implied* that I was lying.) To *infer* means to derive a conclusion from evidence, or to surmise. (We *inferred* that she did like him from her tone of voice.)

incidence, incidents. *Incidence* means frequency of occurrence. (The *incidence* of fatal car accidents keeps rising.) *Incidents* is the plural of incident, and means events. (The three *incidents* happened in one week.)

incredible, incredulous. Something that is *incredible* is hard to believe. Someone who is *incredulous* is hard to convince, skeptical.

infer. See *imply.*

inside of. See *of.*

in the event. Use *if* instead. (*If* something should happen to me; not, *in the event.* . . .)

irregardless. The correct word is regardless. (We will go *regardless* of what you say; not, *irregardless* of what you say.)

it's, its. *It's* is the shortened form of it is. (*It's* getting late.) *Its* is the possessive form of it. (Put the toy back in *its* place.)

it's I, it's me. Formal writers prefer *It's I,* which is grammatically correct. But English speech insists on *it's me, it's him,* etc. Unless the occasion is very formal, use *me, him, her.*

-ize. Be cautious of verbs made with the *-ize* suffix in writing. Often there is another word that is more precise. Use *conceive* instead of *conceptualize;* use *complete* for *finalize;* use *perfect* for *optimize.*

later, latter. *Later* means more late or after some time. (He will not arrive until *later*.) *Latter* refers to the second of two previously mentioned things. (Of the two ideas your mentioned, I am inclined to agree with the *latter*.) (See also *former*.)

lay, lie. These two verbs are often confused. To *lay* an object down is to put it down; to *lie* down is to recline. *Lay* takes an object while *lie* does not. I can *lie* down to sleep (no object) or *lay* the pencil on the table (object). The confusion arises because the past forms of these two verbs overlap. The past forms of *lie* are *lay* and *lain*. (She *lay* back and breathed her last; he had *lain* in that position for nearly an hour.) The past form of *lay* is *laid*. (I *laid* the book down.)

lead, led. *Lead* is the present tense of the verb *to lead.* (She will *lead* the class to the auditorium.) *Led* is the past tense of the same verb. (I *led* the class yesterday.) As a noun, *lead* (pronounced *led*) is a metal.

less. See *amount.*

let's us. *Let's* already means *let us* so *let's us* means let us us. Use *let's.*

lie. See *lay.*

literally. *Literally* means in truth, really. Do not use it just to be emphatic. (When he saw me he *literally* fell through the floor, is incorrect.)

look good, look well. See *good.*

loose, lose. Something that is *loose* is slack. (My *loose* dress is cool in the summer.) If you *lose* something, you cannot find it. (Did you *lose* an earring?)

may of, might of, must of. See *of.*

mean for. In writing use *mean that.* (I didn't *mean that* you should go without me; not, *mean for* you to go without me.)

moral, morale. That which is *moral* is ethical. (He did not think it *moral* to cheat.) It is also the lesson of a tale. (The *moral* of the story was that honesty is the best policy.) *Morale* means mental outlook or spirit. (They blamed the rainy weather for their low *morale*.)

most. Do not write *most* when you mean *almost.* (I eat *almost* anything; not, *most* anything.)

neither. *Neither* and *nor* are negatives and should not be used with other negatives. Use *either* instead. (She *will* not go *either* place; or, *will* go *neither* place.) (See also *double negatives; either.*)

nice. See *adjectives.*

nobody. See *anybody.*

none, no one. See *anybody.*

number. See *amount.*

of. It is incorrect to use *of* when you mean *have:* could *have,* may *have,* might *have,* must *have,* ought to *have,* should *have,* would *have,* will *have.* (I may *have* done it; not, may *of* done it.) *Of* is also often added to expressions where it is not needed with words such as all, alongside, inside, off, and outside. (He took all my money; not, he took all *of* my money.)

on account of. *Because* is better. (I'm only going *because* of you; not, *on account of* you.)

one. Never use *one* when you mean *I.* (Should *I* raise my hand to answer the question?; not, should *one* raise *his* hand?) It sounds pretentious.

oral, aural. *Oral* refers to the mouth and hence to speaking. An *oral* examination is one in which a student speaks, rather than writes, the answers. *Aural* refers to the ear and hence to sounds. *Aural* is often opposed to *visual.* (Thunder is an *aural* experience, lightning is *visual*.)

persecute, prosecute. To *persecute* means to harass. (The dictatorship *persecuted* those whose views differed from its own.) To *prosecute* means to carry out a legal suit or to perform. (Our lawyer *prosecuted* a claim against the company for negligence; the war was *prosecuted* with ruthlessness on both sides.)

phenomena. This is the plural form of the word *phenomenon.* (These *phenomena are* strange; this *phenomenon is* strange.)

principal, principle. As an adjective, *principal* means chief. (The *principal* reason for her dismissal was frequent lateness.) *Principal* is also a noun that means capital sum. (She lived off the interest on the *principal* she'd invested.) A head person is often called a *principal.* (He is the school's *principal*.) A *principle,* on the other hand, is a general rule or assumption. (He lived by his *principles,* though they differed from the community's; it was the *principle* of the thing, not the small amount of money involved.)

raise, rise. To *raise* means to lift or grow something. It always has an object. (I *raise* my hand; I *raise* corn.) To *rise* means to get up or to increase in size. It never has an object. (I *rise* at six each day; the river *rises* in the spring.)

real. *Real* is an adjective; do not use it as an adverb. (He was *really* big; not, *real* big.)

respectfully, respectively. *Respectfully* means with respect. (She *respectfully* questioned him.) *Respec-

tively means in the mentioned order. (The oldest and middle children are nine and six *respectively*.)

rise. See *raise*.

scarcely. See *double negatives*.

set, sit. To *set* means to put (something) down. (I'll *set* the book on the table.) To *sit* is to be seated. (You may *sit* anywhere.) *Set* usually takes an object while *sit* does not. Only the sun, the moon, and hens can *set* by themselves. (See also *lay, lie*.)

should of. See *of*.

sight, site. See *cite*.

sit. See *set*.

somebody, someone. See *anybody*.

stationary, stationery. If an object is *stationary*, it is not moving. *Stationery* means writing paper.

sure and. Use *sure to*. (Be *sure to* bring your family; not, be *sure and* bring your family.) (See also *try and*.)

terrible, terrific. See *adjectives*.

than, then. *Than* means when compared with or except. (He is better equipped for it *than* you; I'd rather be anywhere *than* here.) *Then* means at that time. (*Then* I went to the store.)

theirselves. Use *themselves*. (They asked *themselves* the same question; not, they asked *theirselves*.)

their, theirs, there, there's, they're. *Their* and *theirs* mean belonging to them. (*Their* house is red; it's *theirs*.) *There* means at that place. (The blue house over *there* is mine.) *There* is also used to introduce a sentence. (*There* is nothing left of it.) *There's* is a shortened form of there is. (*There's* nothing left of it.) *They're* is a shortened form of they are. (*They're* going home.)

there is, there are. A singular noun follows *there is*; a plural noun follows *there are*. (*There is* a good reason for bicycle riding; in fact, *there are* several good reasons.)

to, too, two. *Too* means also or more than enough. (I want some, *too*; they were *too* loud.) *Two* is the number 2. In every other case, the word is *to* (*to* run, give it *to* me, *to* and fro, from New York *to* California, dance *to* the music, etc.).

try and. Use *try to*. (*Try to* make me do it; not, *try and* make me.) (See also *sure and*.)

unique. This word means the only one of a kind. Therefore, one thing cannot be more unique than another. (The desk that she built was *unique*; not, was most *unique* or was practically *unique*.)

well. See *good*.

which. Do not use *which* when you are referring to people. Use *who* instead. (The people *who* own this car are inconsiderate; not, *which* own this car.)

who, whom, whoever, whomever. Traditionally, *who* and *whoever* are the subjects of a sentence; *whom* and *whomever* are the objects. (*Who* is coming? *Whom* do you wish to see?) *Whom* and *whomever* are disappearing, however, and are being replaced by *who* and *whoever*. Many authorities consider it acceptable to write, *who* do you wish to see? Using *whom* where *who* is required is a more serious blunder. Use *whom* only when you are sure that it is the object of a sentence.

who's, whose. *Who's* is the shortened form of who is. (I need to know *who's* going.) *Whose* is the possessive form of who. (*Whose* coat is that?)

-wise. This suffix should be used in formal writing to mean in the manner or direction of, e.g., *clockwise*, *otherwise, lengthwise*. Do not use it to mean in regard to. (I'm having a bit of trouble *moneywise* is not acceptable. Write instead, I'm having some *financial trouble*.)

wonderful. See *adjectives*.

would of. See *of*.

Punctuation

Punctuation does for written language what facial expression, change of voice tone, and gestures do for speech. It keeps thoughts together, signals a break in continuity, prepares the reader for a change in thought, and keeps incidental comments separate from the mainstream of the writing. In short, punctuation acts as a road map, guiding the reader through the tangle of phrases, sentences, and paragraphs that make up a piece of writing.

In order to master punctuation, the writer must develop a sense for building logical sentences. He must know when to use words that link clauses of equal rank (*and, but, for,* etc.), and when to use words that signal embedded sentences (*when, although, because, while,* etc.), and how to punctuate so that these connective words make sense. A writer who is having trouble with correct punctuation should practice writing short simple sentences and then combine them into longer compound and complex sentences. As he builds up a fund of sentences, the writer will come to see that punctuation is an important tool for making good sense.

End stops. End–stop or terminal punctuation is a way of signaling to the reader that a sentence has ended. Inexperienced writers are often reluctant to let go of a sentence, stringing it out by using commas or a series of *ands*. Do not be carried away by the force of an idea; punctuation is most often based on grammatical structure, not on the size of the idea. Big ideas sometimes require many sentences or paragraphs to unfold.

The *period* is the most commonly used end–stop punctuation in English. It is placed after every declarative and imperative sentence, and it is used to punctuate even *elliptical sentences*. These are sentences in which either the subject or the predicate is not stated because it is understood.

> Are you going? Yes.

Here *Yes* is punctuated as a sentence because both subject and the predicate are understood: "Yes (I am going)."

The period is *not* used to punctuate a declarative or imperative sentence that is embedded parenthetically in another sentence.

> The party was attended by Dan Bates (he's the actor) and Charlayne Rogers (she's the congresswoman).

The period has uses other than as end–stop punctuation. It is placed after the initials of a person (*T. S. Eliot*) and after many abbreviations (*B.C., Ph.D.*). Accepted practice in punctuating abbreviations, however, varies widely, and a dictionary should be consulted on the correct way to write an abbreviation.

Above all, do not use a period to punctuate a clause that is subordinate to another clause. This is known as a *sentence fault* or a *sentence fragment*.

> I'm returning the file cases. *Although I like the design.*

Here *Although I like the design* is a dependent (embedded) clause introduced by the subordinating conjunction *although*. The clause has a subject and a predicate, but it does not make complete sense when it stands alone. It should read

> I'm returning the file cases, although I like the design.

On the other hand, do not run two independent clauses together without any form of punctuation. This is known as a *run-on sentence*. It is difficult to read and constitutes a serious grammatical error in written composition.

The sales reps must see the new items they will have to examine all new products carefully.

Here the reader, because there is no sign that a thought has been completed, goes right on to *all new products* before he realizes that there are *two* thoughts expressed. It should read

> The sales reps must see the new items. They will have to examine all new products carefully.

The *question mark* (?) is the end–stop punctuation for all interrogative sentences. Even though a declarative sentence in parentheses takes no end–stop punctuation, an interrogative sentence in parentheses does retain its question mark.

> Is the theater full?
> At the meeting (you'll be there, won't you?), we'll discuss the matter in full.

The *exclamation mark* or *point* (!) is used in any case where the writer wishes to indicate a sudden or strong emotion or to make a forceful statement. The exclamation mark can go after a word, phrase, expression, or sentence. An exclamatory statement in parentheses retains the exclamation mark.

> Fire! To the barricades! It was horrible!
> Some people still do not see (willful blindness!) that there is an energy problem.

Exclamation marks can be effective when used sparingly. Beware of overusing them.

Semicolons. The semicolon (;) is used in formal writing to stress the closeness or parallelism of thought between two independent clauses. The semicolon is not an end–stop punctuation, but it indicates the end of one complete thought and the beginning of another complete thought that is closely related to the first one. Semicolons are also used in compound sentences that are joined by words like *therefore, hence, however, nevertheless, accordingly, thus,* and the like. They are also used to separate items in a series when the items themselves have commas.

> The price is high; the quality is not worth it.
> I can't answer your question; however, I will call someone who can.
> We must bring fliers for curiosity seekers, students, and new prospects; samples for serious shoppers; and order forms for really serious customers.

Colons. The colon (:), like the semicolon, ends a statement that leads to a listing, a catalog, an example, a question, a series of statements,

or a long quotation. Frequently the need for a colon is indicated by the expressions *as follows, following, such as,* and *including.*

> We would like to order the following: five reams of manuscript typing paper, three packages of carbon paper, and three boxes of carbon typewriter ribbon.

Commas. The comma (,) has a number of important uses in punctuating sentences. Unfortunately, it has become a favorite of the inexperienced writer. Some unskilled writers have the mistaken notion that a comma should be used whenever you would pause for a breath while speaking. Still others feel that commas should be inserted before every *and* or *but.* Be sparing with commas.

Generally, commas are used to separate the clauses of a compound sentence, to mark off items in a series, to set off nonrestrictive or parenthetical remarks in a sentence, and to set off introductory adverbial phrases.

When separating clauses in a compound sentence, the comma is used only in the case of the clauses being joined by a coordinating conjunction (*see* Parts of Speech above). The comma does not go before *but* if the subject of the two clauses is the same.

> The train was late starting, but we got here in time anyway.
> The trucker was delayed but had a good excuse.

With *or,* the comma is used when the subject shifts from one clause to another. If the subject remains the same, the comma is not used. With *and,* the comma is used unless the subjects of the two clauses are very closely connected in thought.

> The salesclerk was careless, or we would not have found out.
> The manager looked for it carefully or said he did.
> The executive assistant wrote the memo, and she took it with her when she went to lunch.
> The executive assistant wrote the memo and she did it with great tact.

Under no circumstances should you separate two independent clauses by a comma alone. This is known as a *comma splice* or *comma fault.*

Incorrect: The personnel office issued the procedures, all the employees are expected to follow them.

On August 9, 1974, he became President.
He lived in Bangor, Maine, until last September.
Make checks payable to Henry Will, Jr., D.D.S.

SPECIAL USES FOR COMMAS *include setting off numbers in dates, separating city and state or city and country, and setting off certain abbreviations to avoid confusion.*

Correct: The personnel office issued the procedures.
All the employees are expected to follow them.

Items in a series (words, phrases, short clauses) are separated by commas.

> Sales on this product will be good in the West, in the Midwest, in the South, and in the Southwest.
> She was angry, she was frightened, she was on the verge of tears.

Commas are used to set off certain phrases and clauses embedded in a sentence. A *nonrestrictive phrase* or *clause* in a sentence is one that is not essential to the meaning of the sentence; it can be omitted and the main clause will not be changed. Commas are used to set off such nonrestrictive material.

> The accountant, who was chosen just last week, has had years of experience.

When a relative clause is *restrictive,* it is necessary to the meaning of the main clause, and is not set off by commas.

> The accountant who is out sick was taken to the hospital last night.

Remarks of a parenthetical nature in a sentence can be set off by commas. These include the names of persons addressed and *appositives* or words placed after nouns to explain them.

> Can you do this, Bill?
> *(person addressed)*
> Ed Bains, our new programmer, seems intelligent. *(appositive)*

A comma is used to set off an introductory adverbial clause. But when such a clause follows the main clause, it is not set off.

> When we get back to the office, we'll confirm the order.
> We'll confirm the order when we get back to the office.

Dashes. The dash (—) is used to indicate a sudden break or change of emphasis in a sentence. It is particularly useful for overcoming the straight–line thrust of a sentence that moves from A to B to C and so on. The dash allows for change of direction and inserted emphatic remarks.

First the orders must be checked for price, then checked for available stock in inventory, and then—be careful here—copied for shipping labels.

Apostrophes. The apostrophe (') is used for two primary purposes: to indicate missing letters in contractions and to indicate possession. In contractions, the apostrophe is inserted where the missing letter would go. In possessives, the apostrophe and *s* are added to the singular of the noun.

can't (cannot)	*Ed's* account
isn't (is not)	*bank's* rules
they're (they are)	*everyone's* problems

The possessives of plural nouns ending in *s* and singular nouns ending in *s* or *z* is formed by adding an apostrophe and an *s* after the *s* or *z*. In certain cases, proper nouns ending in *s* have two forms. (Some writers prefer to add the apostrophe only.)

businesses's interests
Ramirez's assets
James's debts

Quotation marks. The quotation mark (" ") is used to enclose words, phrases, or sentences that are taken word for word from another source (a *direct quotation*). The quoted material is set off from the main clause by commas and enclosed in quotation marks. (Quoted material printed in indented form uses neither commas to set it off nor quotation marks.) Question marks and exclamation marks are placed *inside* the quotation mark if they are part of the quote, and *outside* if they apply to the main clause. Periods and commas are always placed *inside* the quotation marks, while the semicolon is always placed *outside*. Indirect quotes are not separated by a comma and do not take quotation marks.

The night manager said, "I want the keys now."
"Do you have them?" he asked.
Was it you who said, "Let's go"?
His comment was, "I don't believe it."

A man ran up to me and said, "A boy just ran up to me and said, 'A woman just ran up to me and said, "A girl just ran up to me and said, 'Fire!'"'"

QUOTATIONS WITHIN QUOTATIONS: *the first set used is double, the second is single, the third is double. In the sentence above, each open quote is matched with its close quote.*

The manual says, "Stop when red light flashes"; we have no choice.
The instructor said that we should wait for him.

Parentheses. Parentheses ( ) are used to set off material in a sentence that is separate or apart from the main thought. The normal sentence punctuation that would be used if there were no parentheses should be used after the second or *close parenthesis* (the first parenthesis is called the *open parenthesis*).

As soon as I hear from you (it will be soon won't it?), I'll call Margaret.

Only when a complete independent sentence is placed within parentheses is the period placed inside the parentheses.

Italics. Matter to be set in *italics* is indicated in typescript or in longhand by an underline. Italics are used to single out words, phrases, or even sentences for special emphasis. Titles of books, plays, magazines, and newspapers, and the names of ships, trains, aircraft, and manmade satellites are italicized. Shorter works like poems and stories are put in quotation marks.

Maugham's *Rain* and Shakespeare's *Tempest* are discussed in this week's *New Yorker*, which also comments on Hemingway's short story "The Killers."

Russia's *Soyuz* and America's *Apollo* ushered in the age of space exploration.

Italicized words and phrases you wish to emphasize and words you wish to consider as words.

It's so *hot*.
Let's consider the derivation of *dependent*

Capitals. As you know, all proper names of persons, places, or things are capitalized (*Tom Smith, United States*). In addition, capitalize the first word of every sentence, the first word of a direct quotation embedded in another sentence, the names of groups, associations, and businesses, the letters of some abbreviations, and all historic events, buildings, monuments, and documents.

Democratic or *Republican Party*
Vermont Historical Society
Exxon Corporation
HUD, AAA, AMA
Battle of Gettysburg
Empire State Building
Lincoln Memorial
Treaty of Versailles
the *Constitution*

Titles used with proper nouns are capitalized (*Dr. Brown, Captain Fredericks*), as are the first, last, and important words in titles of printed works. Prepositions, articles, and conjunctions in titles are generally not capitalized except if they begin or end the title.

"Psalm of Life"
Through the Looking Glass
War and Peace

Consult your dictionary for the proper capitalization of words used as proper nouns and adjectives. The capitalization of certain words depends upon their usage.

a revolution; the American Revolution
a renaissance of chamber music; the Renaissance scholars

—*Harry L. Wagner*

Learning to Write

When the Wright brothers set out to make an airplane, their aim was not to make a beautiful object. Their aim was to make an object that would fly. The same is true of writing. When you sit down to write a letter, a report, or any other composition, your first concern should be whether it will fly. To be successful, your composition should carry your readers safely from your starting point to your conclusion.

Accomplishing this goal is not easy.

You will discover (as the Wright brothers did) that your knowledge of mechanics is very helpful. Correct sentences, properly punctuated, will help you carry your reader along. But you must keep the flight in mind at all times. Too many pieces of writing get off the ground and then crash into confusion.

This section will discuss ways to get your writing off the ground, keep it on course, and bring it safely to its destination.

Making a Plan

The first step in any piece of writing is to determine its destination. If you do not know where your report is going, no reader will know either. When you read a story or article that seems to wander in every direction without getting anywhere, you probably feel bored and resentful. Your reader will feel the same way unless you do your planning.

Let's consider some possible destinations. You are writing a book report. If you liked the book, you want to encourage others to read it, so your goal might be to show why a reader might like the book. If you are writing a letter to a department store, your aim might be to persuade the store to remove overcharges from a bill.

A good aim for almost any piece of writing is to persuade a reader to do something or to believe something. Such an aim encourages the writer to keep the reader in mind. Every good piece of writing is directed *to someone* and is *about something*. Whether your reader is a teacher, a complaint department, a friend, a co-worker, or a whole class, keep in mind what you want them to do or to believe.

Once you have decided on your destination or aim, you must consider how to get there. This is a more complicated problem. It involves several steps. The first is deciding where to begin. The second is deciding what route to follow (there may be dozens of possible routes). The third is knowing how to conclude (as the Wright brothers discovered, landing may be the hardest job of all).

As you can see, these three steps are related to the beginning, middle, and end of your written composition, but you must consider them all at once. A failure on any one of the steps will ruin your composition.

Where to begin.
To decide where to begin, you must consider the reader for a moment. How much does he know about the subject? How interested is he in it? If the topic is one of general interest—say, the quality of the school football team—you can begin with a general statement with which most readers will agree. For example:

All of us who follow football at Jackson High know that the team has had three losing seasons in a row.

This is a fact, and it sets up a good starting point for a discussion of reasons for the team's poor performance or for a discussion of steps that might be taken to change the situation.

If your topic is not a matter of general interest, you will have to work harder to gain your reader's attention. Say that you are writing a paper about the war in Vietnam. It happened years ago, and your readers do not know much about it.

You might begin with a human interest story illustrating the effect of the war on an individual:

Corporal William Johnson lives in a bed at the Sepulveda Veterans Administration Hospital. He has lived in that bed ever since 1971, when he was carried there from the battlefield in Vietnam.

You could start with a controversial quotation strongly favoring or opposing the war. Or you might begin with an account of the steps by which the United States became involved.

Wherever you begin, your opening should end with a question or a problem—something that will encourage a reader to go on to find the answer or the solution. Your opening should create some suspense, and leave some question or problem in the reader's mind to be answered or solved later.

What route to take.
You have decided on your destination and decided how to begin. Now, what route should you take? Students of geometry learn that the shortest distance between two points is a straight line. This may be true in mathematics, but it is not always true in writing.

In certain communications, you should take a straight-line path to your destination. If your host's house is burning down, you would have to be crazy to make a long introduction and give an elaborate explanation of the circumstances. In certain letters of complaint, a straightforward approach is best, too. For example:

Credit Department
S and S Department Store

Dear Sirs:
On my charge account bill (acct. # 48–726–37) dated February 15, I was charged for a color television set costing $716.32. I have not bought a television set or any major appliance at S and S in the past year. The charge must be an error, and I hope you will remove it from my account promptly.

In many situations, however, the straight-line approach does not work as well. Consider the case of a writer of a book report who wants to persuade his class to read the book on which he is reporting. Perhaps the straightest route he could take is this:

The Mystery of the City Dump by Harry Carey is the best mystery I have ever read. It is better than all the others I have read, so I know you will like it, too.

If we do not know the writer very well, we begin to wonder if we can trust his judgment. In what way is *The Mystery of the City Dump* better than other mysteries? What other mysteries has he read? And why is he so sure that I like the same kind of mysteries he does? The report has to take a longer route if it is to be convincing. For example:

In the past two years I have read many mystery stories. Most often, I lose interest in them long before I finish because I always know who committed the crime before the detectives do.

The Mystery of the City Dump is different. I thought I knew who the culprit was after three chapters, but I was wrong. I was still guessing when I reached the next-to-last chapter, and I was so interested that I read the whole book in two evenings.

If you like mysteries that are really mysteries, you'll like *The Mystery of the City Dump*.

This second report tells more about the book, but it also comes closer to convincing a reader than the first report.

In research papers and other longer compositions, the route must be more complicated. The map you make for yourself is called an outline.

An *outline* helps to organize your facts and thoughts about your subject and can help you plan how to get from your starting point to your destination. Often you must consider major topics in one-two-three order. These become the main headings.

A common outline would look something like this:

```
    I.   Introduction
   II.   Body
         A.  First main topic
         B.  Second main topic
         C.  Third main topic
  III.   Conclusion
```

Some outlines can become much more complicated, with 1., 2., 3. listed under A., another set of numbers under B., and so on. The most important parts of a first outline, however, are the main headings, which will help you plan your fact-gathering.

The whole process of outlining has two serious dangers. The first is that it encourages a writer to become so involved with organizing the subject that he forgets the reader and forgets to think of the writing itself as a journey from one point (the starting place) to another (the destination). Keep in mind that an outline is only a map for the trip.

The second danger of the outline is that it tends to freeze the shape of a composition too early, long before the writer has sat down to write. It is better to think of outlining as a continuing process. Make one outline before gathering facts or doing research. Revise it or make another one when your research is complete. Then, if you run into trouble in the writing itself, do still another outline.

A smooth landing.
Any reader is bound to be disappointed by a composition that ends like this:

Well, that's all I have to say about the subject. I don't know what you think about it and I don't know what I think about it, either. I hope you enjoyed it.

Such an ending really says, "I've taken you on a wild goose chase and left you out here in the wilderness; find your own way home." As a writer you get to pick the destination—that's the enjoyable part. But you also have a responsibility to get there.

The conclusion of any composition should say to the reader, "This is where we've been heading." It may summarize what has gone before or make recommendations for future action; but most important, it resolves the question or problem that was posed at the beginning.

Sometimes a conclusion looks back to the very beginning of the composition. The report on Vietnam that began with the soldier in the hospital might return to him at the end:

> The war continued for the Americans until 1974; in 1975, North Vietnamese troops overran the South, ending the conflict once and for all.
> What was the point of it all? Corporal Johnson, still confined to a hospital with his injuries, has considered the question for a long time.
> "I didn't understand the war at the time," he says, "and I'm not sure I really understand it now. But I think we had to go in there. Maybe we failed, but that doesn't mean we shouldn't have tried."

We began this section talking about having a destination. It should be the writer's first concern; as a composition comes to an end, it should also be his last.

Gathering Facts

Most writing—even most fiction—depends to some degree on gathering facts. Teachers in schools and colleges call this "doing research" and tend to think of students looking up information in libraries. A library can be a valuable source of information, but library research is only one type of fact-gathering. In this section we consider several ways of collecting information.

Personal records. Many everyday kinds of writing depend on records you keep yourself. If you have a disagreement about a bill with a department store, chances are that the necessary facts are on the bill itself or in your financial records. You must gather up your account number, the date of the bill, perhaps an order number, and so on. You may also have to put a series of events in order, telling what day you visited the store, who you talked to, etc.

This simple example suggests that there are two parts to fact-gathering. The first is keeping or finding information. The second—and often the more important—is putting the information in order for a particular purpose. Useful information is information that has been organized.

Not all records are financial. Many writers keep a diary or a journal, making entries in it every day. They can look back at this material months or years later and reconstruct what they were doing or thinking at a given time. They may get ideas for stories or articles, or even gain a piece of supporting evidence in a dispute over a telephone bill.

By nature, diaries and journals are somewhat disorganized. Only later, looking back, can we pick out the events that were really important as opposed to those that only seemed important at the time. If you use material from a diary to write an autobiographical story, you will soon see how much organizing is required.

Keeping informal notes during a research project can be an important means of fact-gathering. In addition to keeping notes on reading or other research in connection with the project, take five minutes each day to write down what you have accomplished, what problems you are having with the material, and what ideas and questions have occurred to you. When you sit down to write the research paper, these notes may give you just the hints you need.

Interviews. For many kinds of writing, the most valuable source of information is other people. Whether you are writing about your town 50 years ago or about the problems of running a small business, you will find that most people are flattered to be asked about a subject.

If you schedule a formal interview with someone who knows about your subject, it is up to you to be prepared. Have you outlined your report? What specific things are you trying to find out?

Tell the person you are interviewing what your report is about; then tell him what specific things you are trying to find out. Do not start out with a question that is so vague that it will take six hours to answer:

> *Wrong:* Well, Mr. Harrison, tell me about your business.
> *Right:* I've heard that one problem a small business owner has is the long hours he has to work. Has that been a problem for you, Mr. Harrison?

> *Wrong:* What was Centerville like during the Depression?
> *Right:* There's a photograph in the library that shows a long line of men in front of a soup kitchen, but I haven't been able to find out where the soup kitchen was or who ran it. Do you recall?

Specific questions often lead the person being interviewed to remember many other interesting facts or events. Vague, general questions often receive vague, general answers.

It may be difficult to take notes during an interview, but note-taking is very important. If you try to rely on your memory, you may remember the general content of the conversation but few of the details. It is much better to have questions written down in advance, with room underneath them to make notes. As soon as possible after the interview, go over the notes and fill them out with further details while you still remember them.

Library research. Libraries can be useful for gathering facts on almost any subject for school and business reports, political and historical studies, etc.

Unfortunately, many people find libraries intimidating and never learn to make good use of them. If you have never used a library, take an hour or two and study the library itself to help you learn how to use its many resources.

Libraries are organized to help the fact-gatherer. Nearly all of a library's material is *cataloged:* marked and placed so that it can be found easily.

Most libraries in the United States use the Dewey Decimal System or the Library of Congress System. Both are numerical systems by which books, magazines, pamphlets, and other material are classified by subject. The table below shows the broad classifications of each system.

DEWEY DECIMAL SYSTEM	
000	General Works
100	Philosophy
200	Religion
300	Sociology
400	Philology
500	Natural Science
600	Useful Arts
700	Fine Arts
800	Literature
900	History and Biography

LIBRARY OF CONGRESS SYSTEM	
A	General Works
B	Philosophy, Religion
C	History
D	Foreign History
E,F	American History
G	Geography, Anthropology
H	Social Sciences
J	Political Science
K	Law
L	Education
M	Music
N	Fine Arts
P	Language and literature
Q	Science
R	Medicine
S	Agriculture
T	Technology
U	Military Science
V	Naval Science
Z	Library Science, Bibliography

Since the books are classified, all books on a certain subject will be together. This means that if you can find the classification for the subject you are seeking, you can find the important books on the subject all on one shelf.

How can you find the classification for a particular subject or a specific book? Most libraries have a *card catalog* (or a catalog in book form). To find the classification for a subject, go to the *subject* catalog. Under the subject, specific books are listed. Make a note of particularly interesting titles, and be sure to take down their Dewey Decimal or Library of Congress number. This enables you to find the books on the shelves.

To find a particular book, go to the *title* or *author* catalog. The book will be listed both under its title and under the author's name.

The cataloging system should allow you to locate many books on your own. Certain kinds of books, however, may be kept in a separate *reference department*. These include encyclopedias, dictionaries of many kinds, indexes, and often magazines and newspapers. As a rule, reference material must be used at the library.

If you have trouble finding a book or a piece of information, ask a librarian for help. Librarians are trained to know where things are and are usually eager to assist you. Even if you want a book that the library does not have, a librarian may be able to borrow a copy from another library.

Once you have found the material you want, you will want to make the best possible use of it. If you are using a book that is in the *circulating* section of the library, you can borrow it and read it at home. Books and other materials marked *reference* must be used at the library.

One of the most difficult problems for a person doing research at a library is deciding what to read carefully. There is usually more material on a given topic than one could read in a year. Before spending hours at a library table, or borrowing a dozen books and hauling them home, make a quick survey of each book to determine how helpful it may be. The section on Reading gives some useful information on "prereading." A few minutes spent surveying possible sources can save many hours of unnecessary reading.

Gathering information efficiently from a library is an art that can only be perfected with practice. A few do's and don'ts that may help to get your research off on the right foot are shown in the table above.

Thinking. As we said at the beginning of this section, useful information is organized information. Too many writers—especially students do-

---

RESEARCH POINTERS

DO:

1. Take careful notes. Many researchers use 4 x 6 or 5 x 7 index cards, using a new card for every important piece of information.

2. Write down the full title, author, and other bibliographic information for each book you use. Nothing is more frustrating than having to find the same books over again just for a few lines of bibliography.

3. Keep in mind the rough plan for your report and what specific information you need.

DON'T:

1. Get distracted by irrelevant information. Poorly researched reports are often the result of reading the sports section of a magazine instead of the article you set out to read.

2. Waste time hunting for one particular book. If it is not essential to your report, use other books. If it is essential, ask a librarian for help in finding it.

3. Rely on your memory. Write down what you want to remember; otherwise you may have to do the same research more than once.

---

ing research papers—become robotlike, gathering up masses of information, first on cards, then on paper. If that were all there was to do, computers could write better research papers than people.

Only the human mind can organize material in interesting or useful ways, find novel connections between apparently unrelated facts, and communicate new ideas through writing.

During the fact-gathering phase of your writing, keep your mind in gear. Every fact needs to be evaluated and looked at from several different directions, and then placed in some reasonable connection to other facts. It is possible that the most creative "facts" you gather will not come from records, interviews, or libraries but from your own head. Do not be afraid to draw your own connections.

Sitting Down to Write

Starting out. No matter how carefully you prepare to write, there still comes the moment when you must sit down, stare at a blank piece of paper, and lift your hand to begin. For many writers—even those who write for a living—this is a frightening moment. How to begin? What should the first word be? How should the first sentence be framed? Suddenly it all seems hopelessly difficult.

There is probably no way to make starting out easy, but there are a few observations that will make it less difficult.

First, remember that the beginning is often the hardest part of a composition to get just right. If you are in doubt, plunge ahead and promise yourself that when the first draft is finished you will come back and improve the first few lines or paragraphs. It is a common practice for a writer to write his introduction at least twice—once

when starting out and again after finishing the whole composition.

Second, remember that the words you put down in a first draft are not graven in stone. Every writer, from the most famous novelist to the most obscure technical writer, knows that *revision is a necessary part of writing*. Do not feel that you are a failure if you do not get things right the first time. If it helps, write DRAFT 1 across the top of your first sheet just to remind yourself that you will be back to correct and improve later on.

Third, remember that you are the expert. You are the only person in the world who has gathered these particular facts or opinions and organized them in just this way. Your reader is waiting to hear from you, and he does not want to hear excuses or qualifications. Start out boldly: announce your topic and take charge. Most readers are happy to be led through a subject, especially if it is done in a confident and enthusiastic way.

There is one problem that may cause you to get stuck on the first page, however, and that is lack of preparation. If you have failed to make a plan or failed to gather sufficient information, you are like a person who is lost and does not know which way to go. If you have started a composition without proper preparation, stop trying to write and start working on a usable plan.

The middle. Once you get a good start, the writing may go well for awhile. If the whole composition is short, you may be able to write straight through to the end. But if the report or paper is longer, you may get bogged down somewhere in the middle. Perhaps you left the job half finished and returned to it a day or two later without any idea of how to continue. Or perhaps you finished one part of your plan and could not find a way to lead to the next part.

The middle of your composition is

BEGINNING, MIDDLE, END: *Like a melodrama, a piece of writing should have a shape. This story begins when the villain threatens the heroine, reaches its midpoint when the hero risks death to save her, and ends when the villain is overcome.*

the part that tests your whole design. If your design is faulty, you are likely to write yourself into a corner. Instead of following the main line of discussion, you may get sidetracked and digress onto a subject that especially interests you. Once you realize that you are far off the subject, there may be no way to get back again.

If this happens, go back through the part you have written and look for the point where you went astray. When you find that place, cross out everything that follows and start from there, paying more attention to your plan or outline.

Sometimes you may get stuck in the middle even when you are following a carefully made plan. If you just cannot make things work, sit down and look over your outline. You may have to revise it in order to make the writing go smoothly. You may find, for example, that it is difficult to discuss point B until you have introduced point C. Consider turning the two topics around so that you discuss C first.

Another problem that sometimes arises in the middle of writing is the writer's realization that there is too much material to cover. For example, if you are writing an assigned ten-page paper and you have already written ten pages when you get to the middle of your outline, some changes will be necessary. The question then is how to simplify. Can you reduce the amount of detail in the paper and cover the essential points within the assigned length? Is there one major point or topic that might be left out altogether, making room to treat the other points thoroughly?

When serious problems come up in the middle of a composition, a writer may make unwise compromises because he does not want to write the report all over again. To get around this problem, cut apart the material already written paragraph by paragraph. The paragraphs can be pasted on new pieces of paper in an improved order with space between for new transitional sentences or phrases. The re-

sulting draft will not be very handsome, but it will have saved the time and trouble of rewriting more than necessary.

Coming to the end.

There are two common problems with endings. The first is common among writers who find writing difficult. These writers get near the end of their material and realize that they have no ending. The material just runs out and the report just stops as if suspended in mid-air. There seems to be nothing left to say, yet the report seems unfinished.

This problem usually begins with the design of the whole composition. Chances are that the writer did not write much of a beginning, either; his report is probably all middle. If you get caught in this trap, consider adding a few introductory paragraphs or sentences that state your problem and a few concluding paragraphs or sentences that resolve it. Ask yourself, "What question was my middle designed to answer?" Then ask that question in the new introduction and answer it in the conclusion.

The second problem with endings is the opposite of the first and is common among people who find writing easy. They have an ending in mind, but are reluctant to use it until they have used every shred of information. In short, they do not know when to stop. The reader thinks he sees the ending coming and begins to relax. Just as the supposed ending arrives, however, the writer starts up again and presents a new fact or argument. If this happens very often, the reader loses all interest in the subject and in the writer.

The cure for this problem is *selection.* The skilled writer learns not to use every shred of information. Better to leave out a few amusing or curious details than to abuse the reader's patience. If you have this problem, ask yourself, "What facts are essential to my plan?" Keep the essential facts and begin crossing out the others. Perhaps someday you will

write something else where the discarded material will be useful. If you are a facile writer, force yourself to stick to a spare, economical plan.

Rereading and revising.

Now that the first draft is finished, it needs recopying or typing. But what else does it need? Almost certainly, it needs some revision if it is to be really good. Busy business executives often draft an important letter two or three times; magazine writers work over their articles again and again; novelists have been known to draft a whole book as many as a dozen times. If professional writers spend so much time revising, it makes sense that less experienced writers do the same.

If you have time, put the manuscript away for a week or more. Then get it out and read it as if you had never seen it before. Make believe it was written by a stranger. What are its strong points? Where is it weak? Does the organization make sense? Did it keep your interest? Was anything important left out?

Once you have answered these questions, take a pencil (use a different color if the original is in pencil) and start to make corrections and revisions. If you need to reorganize, cut paragraphs apart and paste them down in different order. If a paragraph needs rewriting, write the new draft on a fresh sheet of paper and paste it over the old paragraph. Finally, if there are unnecessary words or phrases or sentences or paragraphs, cross them out. You will be surprised at how much better a report reads when the unnecessary has been deleted.

If you do not have time to let the manuscript "cool" and to be your own editor, give your draft to a friend whose judgment you trust and ask him to suggest improvements. Do not ask if the paper is "all right" as it stands; make it clear that you want to improve it.

When your friend makes suggestions, listen with an open mind. If he misunderstood a certain passage or was con-

A Declaration by the Representatives of the UNITED STATES OF AMERICA, in General Congress assembled.

When in the course of human events it becomes necessary for one people to dissolve the political bands which have connected them with another, and to assume among the powers of the earth the separate and equal station to which the laws of nature & of nature's god entitle them, a decent respect to the opinions of mankind requires that they should declare the causes which impel them to the separation.

We hold these truths to be self-evident; that all men are created equal; that they are endowed by their creator with certain [inherent &] inalienable rights; that among these are life, liberty, & the pursuit of happiness; that to secure these rights, governments are instituted among men, deriving their just powers from the consent of the governed; that whenever any form of government

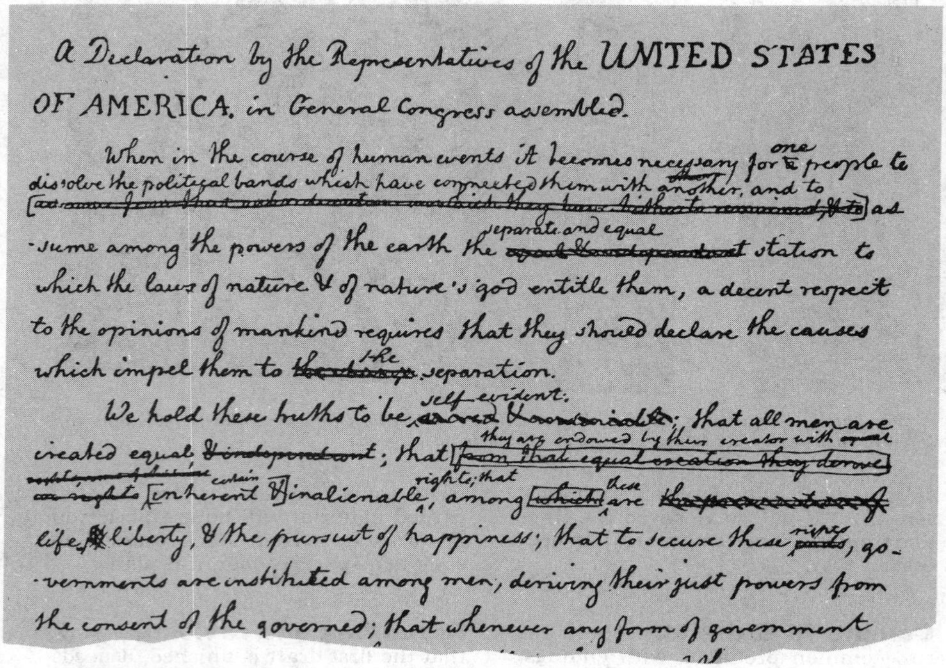

REVISE AND EDIT: *Even Thomas Jefferson had to revise his own work when composing the Declaration of Independence.*

fused by the report's organization, chances are that other readers will have the same problem. You need not take every suggestion, but your friend's reactions should be a good guide.

Most beginning writers do not revise enough, but there are a few who over-revise. It is a good thing to set high standards for yourself, but do not become a perfectionist. Perfection is very difficult to achieve in writing. For most kinds of composition, one or two careful revisions should be enough.

What Is Style?

Previous sections have concentrated on the parts of writing that are judged by standards of "correctness." The spelling of a word is almost always right or wrong; grammar is largely a question of using language correctly; even usage in standard English is most often a series of recommendations for the correct use of words or phrases.

But what about a composition that is written in perfectly correct standard English but is still tiresome or frustrating to read? Can writing be correct but still be bad?

Unfortunately, it can. Sometimes even correct writing that is clearly organized seems boring or awkward or wooden. Then we say it lacks style. Another piece of writing may have many flaws in organization and even be incorrect, yet it seems able to carry a reader along and to persuade him or to move him. Then we say that the composition has style.

Style is very real, but it is difficult to define. There is no such thing as right or wrong style; yet, there is general agreement that some writers have a distinguished style and others have none at all.

Some ingredients of style.

Even though there is no exact definition of the word, most serious readers and writers would agree on some of the ingredients of style. No one of the following ingredients is enough in itself to make a great stylist, but taken together, they go far toward defining the word.

Appropriateness. Certain ways of writing are appropriate for certain situations. We would be unlikely to approve of a lawyer who wrote his love letters in the form of legal briefs, and if he wrote his legal briefs in the form of love letters, he would soon be without a job.

Some people have an instinct for doing or saying the right thing at the right time. In the same way, a good writer does or says the right thing at the right time in his writing. The right thing may be unexpected—but it will be surprisingly right.

The look of the page. Style has something to do with the look of words, sentences, and paragraphs. Good writers may use paragraphing, punctuation, and special effects such as italics to hold a reader's attention. Good writing is rarely sensational (filled with exclamation marks and double question marks, for example). But a reader often comes to trust a good writer's visual style to point out what is especially significant.

The sound of the words. Style also has something to do with sound. We all read partly with our ears. As our eyes scan the lines, we get a sense of the rhythm and sound of the words and phrases. Readers of poetry are especially sensitive to sound, but the sound of prose—even of business reports and term papers—is important, too.

Some writing that is clear and accurate still sounds awkward. There is no simple way to improve the sound of your writing, but the first step is to listen as you write. Many writers find it helpful to read their writing aloud when they are finished. This simple exercise will reveal many awkward spots in almost any composition.

Precision. Whether a good writer uses long sentences or short, whether he writes medical articles or novels, his writing will use words precisely; that is, to mean just exactly what he wants to say, no more and no less.

You need not use big or fancy words to write with precision, but you must become sensitive to fine shades of meaning. For example, note the differences among the words in the following lists of related words:

sad	happy
depressed	manic
sorrowful	joyful
grieving	jubilant
distraught	exhilarated
unhappy	buoyant
pensive	satisfied

The mark of precision in a writer shows up when he needs a word to describe an emotion or a color or an action: he picks the exact one for his purpose and is not satisfied with an approximation.

Writers are often secret students of dictionaries, thesauruses, usage guides, and other word books. They do this not to become smarter than others but to discover new words or new meanings for words. Someday one of these words may be exactly the one they need.

Variety. Some writers begin almost every sentence the same way:

> He was a man of great talents. He lived in the 1800's, and he became famous for his great speeches. He was the son of a coal miner, and he was very poor as a boy.

The first thing we notice about this passage is that every sentence begins with "he." The long sentences are really only short sentences beginning with "he" and strung together with "and." Of all the ways to begin an English sentence, this writer chose the same way (and the most common way) every time.

Often this kind of monotony is

caused by a more serious flaw. Another look at the passage shows that each thought is given equal weight and that the facts are not organized in any clear order. Putting things in order and making some facts more important than others will help to bring variety:

> Born in 1840, he was the son of a coal miner and grew up in grinding poverty. But his great talents finally brought him the recognition he deserved. By the end of the century, his speeches had made him famous around the world.

Even experienced writers fall into bad habits. One may love dashes to set off special comments to the reader. Another may begin every other paragraph with an unanswerable question. Still another may overuse a particular word or phrase. Any one of these devices may be effective if used sparingly, but overuse makes the writing seem tired and stale.

Variety in sentence structure, punctuation, use of special devices, and choice of words are important aspects of style.

Coherence. Good writing is coherent—it holds together, making its subject more clear or understandable than it was before. In fact, good writing can be a pleasure to read for its coherence and shape, even when the reader is not interested in the subject.

By contrast, mediocre writing seems to fall apart. The more one examines it, the less convincing or enlightening it becomes. Really bad writing is nonsense and may give a reader the feeling that he knows less about the subject after reading about it than before.

Writing a coherent composition—one that seems to hold together in every respect—is a difficult task. In some ways it is the sum of all the other ingredients of style.

Improving your style. There is no simple way to become an accomplished writer overnight, but there are three activities that seem likely to improve your style.

First, *read.* Seek out authors whose work you admire and read their work. Imitate their style as an exercise. Then read authors whose work you do not admire and whose style is difficult. Read in different subject areas—good writing is not confined to the literary greats. To the alert eye, there are examples of good writing to imitate and bad writing to avoid nearly everywhere.

Second, *study the language.* Learn its history, its structure, its grammar. Compare its strengths and weaknesses to other languages. Listen to the way people around you speak. Any study that shows how language works and how it might work is worthwhile for a writer.

Finally, *write.* In many ways, writing is a skill, like swimming or playing the piano. Those who want to excel at it practice every day to remain in perfect condition to perform well.

—*Lawrence T. Lorimer*

Everyday Writing

Different writing situations require different forms and conventions. A careful writer finds it helpful to know these conventions because they help assure that a paper, letter, or invitation will be appropriate and favorably received.

The following section describes the forms and practices generally followed in common writing situations. These situations include writing a research paper (in high school or college); inquiring about and applying for a job; writing a letter of complaint or request to a large organization; and preparing wedding invitations and other formal social correspondence.

The Research Paper

Writing a research paper requires attention to detailed and specific rules and forms. In most cases, an instructor will refer beginning writers to a particular authority for setting the style for footnotes, bibliography, and other details. More advanced writers are expected to know the basic style requirements (which differ slightly from one discipline to another). If in doubt, select a manual of style. Whatever authority you choose, be consistent. (*See also* the Bibliography at the end of this volume.)

A research paper begins with the selection of a topic. Students are often tempted to choose a topic far too large for the time they have or the length they are allowed. If you are assigned a 20-page research paper on American literature, for example, it would be too ambitious to try to deal with the American novel since 1800. It would be more realistic to limit your topic to novels of the 1920's or to the work of a particular writer. Most instructors give help in choosing a topic and in preparing an outline. If you are in doubt, ask for advice.

The next step is to do the research (*see* Gathering Facts, Libraries above). Taking careful and accurate notes is essential. If you use ruled index cards, they can later be arranged according to subject. Each source you use should be listed on a separate card in correct bibliographic style. Do not rely on memory! What you remember reading today may be just a distant memory by the time you write your paper. All ideas that are not original must be credited to their source. If you quote material directly, the quoted material must be within quotation marks. Copying someone else's words and using them without acknowledgment is called plagiarism. It is the research equivalent of theft.

When the research has been completed, it is time to begin writing. Have a clear idea of the point you are about to make before beginning to write. Assemble your notes into subject order, and try to integrate those that deal with the same point.

Follow your own plan in your own words. Quote material directly only when it cannot be improved on by simplifying or rephrasing. Long, tedious quotes suggest that the writer did not take the time or trouble to think the subject out for himself. Include examples to support your points, and lead the reader logically to the concluding argument. Unless you are writing for an audience of experts, assume that your reader has only general knowledge of your subject.

NOTE CARDS *in research should be headed by the author and title of the book or article being used and the page number. Put information in a form that will be easy to refer to.*

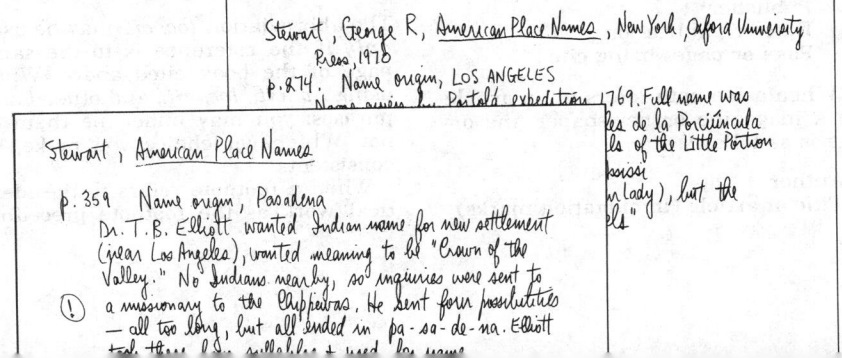

Stewart, George R., *American Place Names*, New York, Oxford University Press, 1970.
p. 274. Name origin, LOS ANGELES
Name given by Portolá expedition 1769. Full name was
...es de la Porciúncula
...ls of the Little Portion
...cissi
...r Lady), but the
...els"

Stewart, *American Place Names*
p. 359 Name origin, Pasadena
Dr. T.B. Elliott wanted Indian name for new settlement (near Los Angeles), wanted meaning to be "Crown of the Valley." No Indians nearby, so inquiries were sent to
① a missionary to the Chippewas. He sent four possibilities — all too long, but all ended in pa-sa-de-na. Elliott
...

Footnotes. Research papers and other scholarly writings use footnotes. They are usually used to document information in the body of the paper. Less frequently, footnotes offer explanatory or parenthetical remarks. They are indicated by a slightly raised number at the end of the sentence or quotation to which they refer. Until recent years, the notes themselves (numbered to correspond with the numbers in the text) had to appear at the bottom of the page where the text number appeared. Today, both in published and unpublished papers, the notes often appear at the end of the text.

When using a footnote to cite a book, follow this order: the author's name (first name first); the title of the book, which must be underlined; the name of the editor or translator, where applicable; the city of publication, publisher, and date of publication; and the page number(s) of the citation. Each of these categories is separated by a comma, except for the facts of publication, which are enclosed in parentheses and not preceded by a comma. For example:

> [1] Yevgeny Yevtushenko, *A Precocious Autobiography,* trans. Andrew R. MacAndrew (New York: E. P. Dutton & Co., 1963), p. 42.

Footnotes should be double-spaced and should always end with a period.

If a book is part of a series, the name of the series follows the title (and the name of the editor or translator, if any), and is separated from it by a comma. When the reference is to other than a first edition, this information is cited, since content and page references may vary in different editions. The number of the edition also follows the title, and is separated from it by a comma. If the book is one volume of a set, the volume number follows the title, too. "Volume" is abbreviated "vol.," and Arabic numbers are used. For complex footnotes, the following list gives the appropriate order, according to *A Manual of Style,* published by the University of Chicago Press:

> Author
> Title of work (underlined)
> Editor
> Translator
> Name of series
> Number or volume in series
> Edition number (if not first)
> Number of volumes
> City or cities where published
> Publisher
> Date of publication
> Page or pages being cited

When a footnote refers to an article in a magazine or newspaper, the order is as follows:

> Author
> Title of article (in quotation marks)

Name of periodical (underlined)
Volume and number of periodical
Date of issue
Page or pages being cited

As in the footnote for books, the sections of the citation are separated by commas. If the reference is to a scholarly journal, however, the date is given within parentheses and is followed by a colon. When giving volume and number citations, either Roman or Arabic numerals may be used. Modern usage favors Arabic numerals, which take less space and are easier to read. Below are examples of footnotes for a magazine article and a scholarly journal, respectively:

> [2] John Papanek, "Now Mexico Feels the Heat," *Sports Illustrated,* 10 December 1979, pp. 32–41.

> [3] Robert A. Moses, "Circumferential Flow in Schlemm's Canal," *American Journal of Ophthalmology* 88 (September 1979): 585–591.

In works with more than one author, each of the authors is listed in the order in which he appears on the title page. If there are more than three authors, however, the name of the first is cited, followed by the Latin phrase *et al.* (which means "and others") and a comma.

Once a work has been fully documented in a footnote, further references to the same work may use a shortened footnote form. A shortened footnote includes the author's last name, the title of the book, and the page reference. For instance, a second reference to the Yevtushenko book would read:

> [4] Yevtushenko, *A Precocious Autobiography,* p. 12.

If a book is referred to frequently, you may omit the title entirely, using only the last name of the author and the page:

> [4] Yevtushenko, p. 12.

This form is impractical, though, if more than one work by the same author is mentioned anywhere in the paper or bibliography.

The Latin terms *op. cit.* (in the work cited) and *loc. cit.* (in the place cited) may also be used in place of the title. For example, the above reference could read:

> [4] Yevtushenko, *op. cit.,* p. 12.

The abbreviation *loc. cit.* may be used *only* if the reference is to the same page of the book cited above. When using *op. cit., loc. cit.,* and other Latin phrases, you may underline them or not. Whichever choice you make, be consistent.

When a footnote refers to the identical work as the footnote preceding

it, the Latin phrase *ibid.* (the same) may be used. This should be followed by a period, then a comma and the page reference. If another reference intervenes between two citations of the same book, the short form, rather than *ibid.,* must be used. For example:

> [4] Yevtushenko, *op. cit.,* p. 12.
> [5] *Ibid.* (refers to Yevtushenko)
> [6] Papanek, *loc. cit.*
> [7] Yevtushenko, *op. cit.,* p. 15.

Footnote 7 could not be *ibid.* unless it referred to the work cited in footnote 6.

Bibliography. The bibliography appears at the end of a research paper and is a list of all works consulted by the writer, including works cited in footnotes. It is in alphabetical order, by the author's last name. The bibliography may be merely a list, compiled in accepted form, or it may be annotated with descriptive or evaluative comments.

A bibliographic entry is divided into three parts, each of which ends with a period. The parts are author, title, and facts of publication. The author's name is given last name first. The title of the book is always underlined. The facts of publication are the same as those in a footnote, but the punctuation is different. In a bibliographic entry, the city of publication is followed by a colon, after which comes the name of the publisher, followed by a comma, and the date of publication. When a work has more than one author, all the names appear. Co-authors may be listed last name first or first name first, but the style should be consistent from entry to entry.

When listing works from a periodical in a bibliography, the rules are much the same as for books. The author's name appears last name first, and is followed by a period. The title of the article is enclosed in quotation marks. A period precedes the final quotation mark. The title of the magazine or journal is underlined, followed by a comma, the date, another comma, and the pages on which the article appears. In scholarly articles, the volume number immediately follows the name of the journal, and the date is enclosed in parentheses followed by a colon and the page references. All entries end with a period. Examples of book, magazine, and scholarly journal entries follow:

Yevtushenko, Yevgeny. *A Precocious Autobiography.* Trans. Andrew R. MacAndrew. New York: E. P. Dutton & Co., 1963.

Papanek, John. "Now Mexico Feels the Heat." *Sports Illustrated,* 10 December 1979, pp. 32–41.

Moses, Robert A. "Circumferential Flow in Schlemm's Canal." *American Journal of Ophthalmology* 88 (September 1979): 585–591.

When a book is compiled by an institution or an editor, the institution or editor is listed in place of the author. The entry is inserted into the alphabetical order with the other entries.

Getting a Job

Often the first contact you have with a prospective employer is a letter (often accompanied by your résumé). Your first task in this situation is to attract the employer's attention and to arouse his interest. Thus, the letter and résumé should be correct, concise, and attractive. Since the employer does not know you and may never have seen you, the written words must represent you. Many others may be applying for the same position, so the style and appearance of your written material may determine whether you get an appointment for an interview.

The letter. Before considering the content of your letter, let us first address the question of appearance. Business letters should be written on business stationery or plain, unlined typing paper. Social stationery is not acceptable. The letter should be single-spaced, with double spaces between paragraphs. The top right hand corner should contain the writer's address and the date. Below this, beginning at the left margin, should be the name of the person being addressed, his title, organization, and address. All letters should be personally signed in ink with the name typed below the signature. Do not send carbon copies or machine-made copies. Erasures and corrections detract from the appearance of the letter, and may create a poor impression. Take the time to draft the letter carefully, to set it up attractively, and to type it perfectly.

The body of the letter should address someone *by name* when possible. If you do not know the name of anyone in the organization, make a phone call and ask to whom an inquiry should be addressed. In the first paragraph, state the kind of job that you are interested in, and explain how you learned of the open position or about the organization. If you are inquiring whether there is a vacancy, you must be specific about the kind of position you are seeking.

After making your objective clear, briefly summarize past experience that would make you a candidate for

---

Patricia Smith
344 West 76th Street
New York, New York 10023

June 12, 1980

Mr. Robert Bingham
Personnel Director
Taylor Publishing Company
12 West 41st Street
New York, New York 10022

Dear Mr. Bingham:

I understand from Mr. Howard Singleton that you have a job opening in your executive training program. I would very much like to be considered for that position.

With my recent degree in business administration and extensive summer experience selling advertising space for the Complete Publications Group, I feel I would be an ideal candidate for the position. My résumé is enclosed.

As I am frequently not at home to receive calls, may I take the liberty of phoning your secretary for an appointment? I look forward to having an opportunity to meet with you.

Sincerely,

Patricia Smith

Patricia Smith

---

the job. Specific dates, addresses, and the like, should be saved for the résumé. In the letter you must interest the reader in you and your background. Cite the experience and education you think is most relevant to your reader. If you have recently left school and have little work experience, emphasize your education. If your extra–curricular activities are related to the position, add some information about them. Finally, give a telephone number and the times at which you can be reached. Make it easy for the prospective employer to get in touch with you. If you cannot be reached by phone, ask to be reached by mail, or ask if you may phone for an appointment.

A letter of inquiry must be factual and polite, but it must also be personal and enthusiastic enough to stand out among others. Remember that employers may receive hundreds of letters of inquiry each week. Those that are too long, too short, or too dif-

ficult to read are often discarded. Try to find a balance that reflects enough of your personality to get you an interview.

The résumé. In most instances, the letter of inquiry is accompanied by a résumé, or fact sheet, with the applicant's business, educational, and personal experience summarized. The résumé, like the letter, should be typed on unlined paper and should follow a consistent form. Unlike the letter, the résumé may be duplicated or printed, as long as the copies are clear and neat.

There are many different forms for résumés, but all should contain certain basic information. Typically, the résumé begins with your name, address, and telephone number. On a separate line, write your job objective. In the next section, deal with your job experience, starting with your most recent position and working back-

```
Résumé of:                          344 West 76th Street
PATRICIA SMITH                      New York, New York 10023
                                    Phone: 212-715-5315

                           OBJECTIVE
        To enter an executive training program in which business
             and finance will be emphasized.

                           EDUCATION
1980            M.B.A., Harvard Business School,
                Cambridge, MA
                     Ranked top 10% of class
1976            B.A., State University of New York at
                Stony Brook
                     Cum laude, Dept. of Economics
1972            Bronx High School of Science, NYC

                          EMPLOYMENT
June-August     Advertising space salesperson Complete
1979            Publications Group, 723 Madison Avenue,
                NYC. Duties included calling prospective
                advertisers and convincing them to place
                their accounts with Group periodicals.

June-August     Assistant to branch manager,
1978            Bloomingdale's, White Plains, NY. Although
                duties were mostly clerical, worked
                closely with manager and observed various
                aspects of department store management.
                Was placed in control of summer stock
                inventory by August.

                        EXTRA-CURRICULAR
1978-1980       Business manager of college newspaper.
                Duties included selling advertising space,
                complete management of accounts.
                Supervised staff of 10.

                           PERSONAL
Born:           2/4/54 in NYC
Marital
  status:       Single
Health:         Excellent; no physical limitations
Residence:      Willing to relocate for proper
                opportunity; willing and eager to travel.

                          REFERENCES
Available on request
```

ward in chronological order. Then include a section with your educational credentials. (If you have little job experience and have recently left school, these two sections may be reversed.) Finally, you may add a section offering personal information. This might include the year of your birth, place of birth, marital or family status, hobbies, whether you are willing to travel, etc. The personal section is optional and should be included only when you feel that it is relevant to your application or helpful. Fair employment laws make it illegal for an employer to discriminate against an applicant because of sex, age, race, or religion.

At the bottom of the résumé you may list three or four references—people the employer might call or write to ask about you. These should be mostly business references, although one personal or character reference may be included. List only people from whom you have obtained prior permission. If you choose not to list references, you may state that references are available on request.

A résumé should be more complete than a letter. For example, it should include all jobs that you have held in recent years. Do emphasize the positive, such as positions that gave you valuable experience or increased responsibility. Summer jobs and part-time or temporary work, especially if years in the past, need not be reported unless you feel they add to your qualifications. Try to give the prospective employer a clear idea of your responsibilities in previous jobs. Above all, do not lie. Never falsify a date or claim to have held a position you did not hold. Prospective employers *do* check with past employers on dates of employment, and false claims on your application may be grounds for dismissal even after you are hired.

A sample résumé is shown below. Please remember, however, that a résumé should reflect the job seeker. It is not necessary to follow the form

exactly. Allow variations for the particular job you are seeking, and emphasize those things that will make you an attractive candidate. If you are awkward at the typewriter, it may be to your advantage to seek help from an experienced typist. Setting up the information in clear, attractive form, with proper margins and spacing, may help you get an interview.

After you have obtained an interview, it is wise, although not obligatory, to write a short note to the interviewer, thanking him for the time and consideration shown you. Say why you are even more interested in the job opening now, and end on a positive note. Such a letter may help the interviewer to remember you.

Writing to Large Organizations

As with letters inquiring about employment, your immediate objective when writing to a business or other organization is to have the letter read. This may seem unnecessary to worry about, but many business and government officials receive large volumes of mail. Letters that are not likely to bring prompt results are those that contain no easily located return address, are illegible, overly long, unclear, or abusive. Letters that are neat, clear, concise, and respectful have a much better chance. Empty threats and sarcasm usually accomplish nothing.

Let us begin with the mechanics of good letter writing. If you have a printed letterhead, use it. Otherwise use plain, unlined typing paper or stationery in a solid color. If you write by hand, your ink should contrast with the paper. Typing is preferred, however. In either instance, margins should be ample, paragraphs should be short, and pains should be taken to make the letter legible and attractive. In handwritten letters, the first line of each paragraph should be indented. In typed letters, the body should be single-spaced, and paragraphs indicated by a double space between them.

If you are not using a printed letterhead, place your address at the upper right corner of the first page. Below and beginning at the left margin, write the name, title, organization, and address of the person to whom the letter is going. The letter will be most effective if it is personally addressed. Take the time to find out who has the authority to handle your problem. A phone call to the organization being addressed can often produce that information.

In a letter of complaint, the objective is to state the problem and to have it remedied. The first paragraph of the letter should make clear to the reader what the problem is. If you are writing about defective or missing merchandise, give the style numbers, order date, shipment and invoice numbers, and other relevant information. Then explain the problem as clearly and briefly as possible.

The second paragraph of the letter should deal with the specific remedies that would be acceptable to you. It should also include data on any steps you have already taken to solve the problem. Finally, the letter should close with the expectation that the matter will be remedied promptly.

When writing to request replacement of a broken part, one might say:

Dear Mr. Jones:

In January a Washer–Maid dishwasher, series 6703, was installed in my home. The handle with which one closes the machine was cracked at the time of installation. The dealer, Kountry Kitchens of Pleasantville, claims that the responsibility is the manufacturer's; the part must, therefore, be replaced by your company.

Despite repeated telephone calls to the Washer–Maid representative in our area, I have been unable to secure a replacement for this part. The dishwasher is unusable in its current condition.

I would like an immediate replacement of the broken part, as well as a service representative to install it. Your prompt attention to this frustrating problem would be greatly appreciated.

Sincerely,

When writing about a billing problem, give your name, the number of your account, and the date of the bill. If possible, enclose a photocopy of the bill itself. If you telephone before writing, get the name and extension of the person to whom you spoke, and keep a record of the advice he gives you. Even if the person promises to straighten the matter out, a follow-up letter is wise. The letter (of which you should keep a copy) makes a record of your call, and is more difficult to forget than a phone call.

If the person to whom you spoke on the phone is of no assistance, ask for the name of his supervisor and address the letter to this new person. Be firm and insistent, but avoid personal vindictiveness or bitterness. For example:

Dear Mrs. Walker:

My telephone bill of January 6 contains a number of charges for calls made to San Francisco during the months of November and December. These charges are in error. My husband and I were out of the country during those months, and our telephone was disconnected.

Despite repeated phone calls to the business office, I have been unable to have these charges removed from my bill. On January 9, Mr. William Brading of your office promised to look into the

matter. Nonetheless, the charges appeared on my February bill. At that time I called the business office and spoke to Ms. Nina Jones, who attributed the problem to computer error and promised to rectify the mistake. My March bill not only continues to show the charges, but threatens me with discontinuation of service should I not pay it immediately.

These charges are a telephone company error and have already caused me great inconvenience. I want them removed from my bill immediately. I must further insist that my good credit rating be restored at once.

Kindly give this matter your prompt attention.

Sincerely,

Letters of request should be equally specific. State what you want at the outset and give all necessary information. Refer to serial numbers, dates, and times when appropriate. Be polite. After all, the recipient of your letter is in a position to grant or deny your petition. Below is a sample of a letter that makes a request:

Dear Mr. Thompson,

As the cultural arts representative of High Ridge School in Farmdale, I am writing to request a performance of the Power Authority's free energy program, which was recommended to me by Dr. Hiram Nelson of Central School.

We are an elementary school (grades K-6) and would like the program for our 5th and 6th grades, both of which are scheduled for assemblies on Tuesday or Thursday mornings from 10:00 to 10:45.

We would be delighted to have the program any Tuesday or Thursday during the months of February, March, or April. Please note that school is not in session during the week of April 1–7, which is our spring vacation.

Should you be able to accommodate us, our three custodians will be available to help move and assemble all equipment. Lunch will be provided for your representative in our faculty cafeteria.

Travel directions to our school will be forwarded when a date has been confirmed. We eagerly await your reply.

Sincerely yours,

Mentioning how you learned of the program is helpful. Arranging for lunch, custodians, and travel arrangements is not only courteous, but shows the reader that you are truly interested in what he or she can offer. A self-addressed return envelope is another way in which to expedite a response. Make it as easy as possible for the recipient of the letter to grant your request.

Social Letters

In general, social letters should be handwritten in ink on light-colored paper. Recent usage has made typing acceptable in many circumstances,

however, especially for long letters between friends.

There is certain social correspondence, such as wedding invitations and birth announcements, that receives more formal treatment. Some traditional forms and usages are given here, with the caution that in recent years, more people have felt free to modify or ignore these forms.

The standard wedding invitation form reads:

Mr. and Mrs. James Smith
request the honor of your presence
at the marriage of their daughter
Susan Bethany
to
Mr. Harris Johnson
on Saturday, the Fourth of July
at half past noon
St. Bartholomew's Church
New York City

R.s.v.p.

The invitation might also give the place of a reception to follow the ceremony. Some people prefer the phrase "the favor of a reply is requested" to the more common r.s.v.p. (abbreviation for *respondez, si'l vous plait*). Some invitations use English spelling, such as *honour* and *favour,* while others list the hour as "half after noon."

Formal etiquette requires such an invitation to receive a handwritten reply following the exact wording of the invitation. For example:

Miss Letitia Newsom
accepts with pleasure
the invitation of
Mr. and Mrs. James Smith
to attend the marriage of their daughter
Susan Bethany
to
Mr. Harris Johnson
on Saturday, the Fourth of July
at half past noon
at St. Bartholomew's Church
New York City

In the case of inability to attend, the same form would follow after an opening line of, "Miss Letitia Newsom deeply regrets that she will be unable to attend . . ." A less formal response is also acceptable today; a handwritten note of acceptance or regret is welcome. Many invitations now include self-addressed printed cards on which guests indicate whether they can attend.

Traditional wedding invitations are engraved in black on white or cream–colored stock with no border. But invitations are now commonly being printed instead, and tinted papers with color–coordinated inks are not uncommon.

A similar change has taken place in the forms that birth announcements take. Standard etiquette demands that the announcement be sent on a white card, perhaps bordered in blue or pink. On this card would appear the child's name, the date of birth, and the parents' names. Deviations from this formal format include patterned cards, brightly colored borders, the names of the newborn's siblings, and frequently the child's birth weight.

Traditional usage is still often followed in the writing of condolence notes. A handwritten note, on white, cream, or gray personal stationery, is the most acceptable. Printed cards purchased at the store are no substitute for a personal letter. A letter of condolence should express your sympathy for the bereaved and, if the deceased was well known to you, should mention some of the personal qualities you will miss. The letter need not be long or florid. It should be sincere and brief. For example:

Dear Sue,

How truly sorry I was to learn of your mother's death. I shall always remember her good-natured tolerance of all the noisy teenagers who so loved to congregate at your house on Saturday nights. Your mother was everybody's favorite, and you are not alone in cherishing her memory.

Please offer my most sincere condolences to your father and brother.

As always,

Gail Jamison

One may acknowledge letters of condolence either by hand or by a printed card on plain white stock. Handwritten acknowledgments should be on plain note paper and be personally addressed. A printed card might read:

The family of Gertrude Soames
wishes to acknowledge
your kind expression of sympathy.

Other personal letters may be long and newsy, perhaps to someone who lives at a great distance; thank-you notes for gifts or entertainment; congratulatory letters; notes of apology; or notes to convalescents. The kind of stationery and the form of the letter depend on the degree of intimacy you have with the recipient.

—*Phyllis R. Bocian*

Careers in Writing

When people think of professional writers, they usually think first of best-selling novelists or newspaper columnists. They never stop to think that someone must be writing all kinds of other material—scripts for television shows, advertising, fund-raising literature, catalogs, instruction manuals, employee benefit booklets, religious pamphlets, etc.

In addition, many kinds of writing are never published in any form, but are important nevertheless—business letters, memos, legal arguments, speeches, specifications for industrial products, and much, much more. Novelists and columnists are a tiny minority in the community of writers.

There are many jobs for various kinds of writers in many different businesses. Writing can also be a valuable skill in nonwriting jobs. Managers in business, government, and the professions complain that too many of their employees do not write well enough. In fact, a skilled writer often has a better chance of professional advancement because he can communicate ideas and make recommendations clearly and tactfully.

This section concentrates on careers in writing itself. These careers are in three main categories: business, advertising, and journalism.

Business Writing

Business writing takes a number of forms. Large corporations, universities, and other organizations employ writers to produce brochures, employee publications, alumni magazines, and other materials. For other projects, they may hire public relations firms that have their own staff of writers. In fact, public relations is a business that depends heavily on writing skills.

Public relations. The term public relations is a catchall for a host of services that help businesses communicate with their public and their employees.

One public relations firm might specialize in entertainment, planning campaigns for movies, for example. The firm would arrange for articles to appear in newspapers and magazines about the movie, the stars, or the director, and would plan a splashy premiere with a celebrity party to attract press coverage. The main aim of such a campaign is to attract favorable publicity and public interest. Through press releases, news and feature stories, and TV appearances, the firm helps the movie to

BUSINESS *provides many jobs for writers. The periodicals below report business news. Private studies like the one at right are commissioned by many large corporations.*

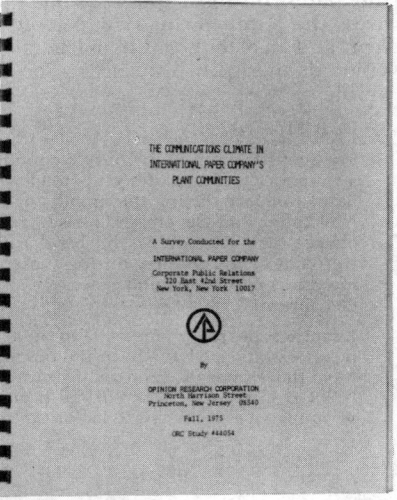

INTERNATIONAL PAPER CO.

succeed financially and may help the producer to raise money to make his next film.

Another firm might specialize in banking. A public relations campaign for a bank might be aimed at changing public policy. It would be designed to reach influential legislators and leaders in the community. For example, in many states there are laws limiting the interest a bank can charge for mortgage money. If the bank considers such laws unfair, the public relations firm could seek to have them changed by preparing articles for specialized banking journals, testimony for legislative hearings, and information for editorial writers on newspapers and magazines. The firm might help plan legislative strategy, perhaps arranging for a bill to be presented to the state legislature. The writing in such a campaign is specialized and would not appear directly before the general public.

The simplest form of writing for a public relations firm is the publicity news release, a short piece in journalistic style describing the who, what, when, and why of an item or event. It is sent to newspapers, magazines, radio and television stations, and others who may be interested in the story. Many brief articles in newspapers are based on such releases. The release always includes the name of a person to contact for additional information.

On the simplest level, a perfume manufacturer might send out a release about a new perfume, including the news that each ounce of perfume uses 20,000 roses from a special field in France. These three lines might appear all over the nation in local newspapers as "fillers" for three lines of space that the newspaper could not fill itself.

Many public relations writers also write brochures and copy for catalogs. For example, the developer of a major real estate project may need several brochures, one telling the history of the project, another describing the units for sale, and still another describing how a home purchase may be financed.

Other public relations writers specialize in preparing speeches to be given by business executives. A speech may be used to support a larger campaign (such as the bank campaign described above) or to state a company's position on an issue of public interest. For example, a large corporation that owns a gun company might want to declare its support for stronger gun control laws. The employees of the gun company disagree with this position, so small meetings are arranged to explain the company's point of view. Executives of the corporation give speeches to public gatherings on gun control. Parts of the speeches are then rewritten to be used as testimony for a congressional hearing. In a state that is to hold a referendum on gun control, the cor-

DOYLE, DANE, & BERNBACH, INC.

A STORYBOARD *for a television commercial illustrates how writers, artists, and designers collaborate to produce an advertising campaign. This one is for chocolate syrup.*

poration might prepare articles to be used by newspapers and magazines, and supply information on the issues to politicians who do not have time to research the topic themselves.

Public relations firms also do financial writing, preparing quarterly and annual reports for business that are sent to stockholders, brokerage firms, and others. Such reports are required by law to be factual. At the same time, however, the writers see that the company is presented in the best possible light.

Other business writing. Another major area of business writing is *internal communications*—newsletters, magazines, booklets, and other publications for distribution to a company's employees. The form of these communications ranges from simple newsletters, known popularly as "Bowling Scores and Baby Sheets," to daily employee news broadcasts over internal television networks. Very large corporations have their own glossy monthly magazines.

Another important kind of business writing is *technical writing*. This writing is often done by a special technical writing department. Technical writers take the results and the work of engineers and scientists and put it into a form that nontechnical readers can understand. For example, technical writers prepare the instruc-

tion manual for your TV set and repair manuals for TV repairmen. They also write manuals for salesmen explaining the features of various TV's in nontechnical terms.

In nonprofit organizations (hospitals, universities, museums, etc.) technical writers prepare grant proposals for submission to government departments and foundations. Grant writers may interview scientists, doctors, or professors, and then write up the proposed project in a form that meets the granting organization's requirements. If the grant is awarded, the same writer often prepares progress reports on the project.

Advertising

Advertising is a major business in the United States and employs thousands of copywriters. Good copywriters must know how to get a message across in the shortest possible way—sometimes in only a few words. They often work closely with artists, designers, or film makers to produce a final ad. Behind the seemingly simple copy lies weeks or months of research, planning, and preparation.

A writer who is responsible for an advertising campaign must get to know the product in detail. Often this involves trips to the manufacturer's plant to see how the product is made. The writer must also have a creative sense of how to reach the target audience and persuade it to buy the product.

Ad writers must also know the fields of *demographics* and *psychographics*. Demographics is the study of the age, sex, social, economic, and educational status of an audience. An advertising writer may learn, for example, that a particular advertisement will be seen primarily by young women under 25. This information will help determine how he writes the advertising copy. Psychographics is the study of psychological traits that cause a given audience to buy a product. When a diet beer was first introduced, ads were prepared to show that the beer would not make a beer drinker fat. No one bought the beer. Research showed that beer drinkers weren't particularly worried about gaining weight. A later campaign showing famous former athletes drinking the beer was much more successful.

Often an ad campaign includes advertisements in many different media—television, radio, newspapers, magazines. Each ad must be tailored to be effective in its own way, and advertising writers must know the characteristics of each medium.

Some large corporations do not directly sell a product in their advertising. Instead, they may emphasize the company's commitment to conservation, education, or some other public concern. Such advertisements seek to encourage a viewer or reader to think favorably about the company. This type of advertising is called *institutional*, and is closely related to public relations.

Local advertising is usually less elaborate than national advertising, yet it is very important to local businesses. A local ad can use the tone, language, and approach favored by a smaller group of people. Ads that would seem crude or laughable in one part of the country may be very effective in their own areas.

Another kind of advertising is the direct-mail response ad. Writing an effective direct-mail advertisement is a difficult task, especially when it competes with so many other direct-mail appeals. The first step—as in many forms of writing—is to gain the reader's attention. Finding a design and a message to put on the envelope may be the first step, so that people do not throw the envelope away unopened. The material inside must encourage the reader to act right away. Otherwise the recipient may forget and the ad may be lost or discarded.

Direct-mail has proved to be a good way of reaching specialized audiences. A direct-mail writer might work for a specialized book club or record club or even a "cheese of the month" club, offering people with special interests products related to these interests.

ABC-TV

BROADCAST NEWS *requires many writers. A half-hour TV news show may use 3,000 words, and an all-news radio station requires more than 100,000 words every day.*

Journalism

The field of journalism covers the news, whether on television or radio, or in newspapers, newsletters, or magazines. Although the most visible writing jobs are for national networks or publications, most journalism jobs are for small publications that most of us have never read or heard of. These include specialized newsletters, trade papers and magazines (which report on a particular business), local daily and weekly newspapers, and publications of religious groups.

Nearly every kind of journalism makes a firm distinction between the news story and the feature story. *News stories* report facts and events. The stories are often written in the form of an inverted pyramid. The opening paragraph or "lead" must tell the essentials of the story—who, what, where, when—in an eye-catching way. The following paragraphs elaborate on the story, giving further details, reporting the reactions of those involved, etc. In general, however, each paragraph is less important than the one before. This structure allows a newspaper editor to cut a story as necessary to fit a given space without needing to rewrite. And it allows a reader to get the essentials of a story by reading only the first few paragraphs. The news story is one of the few writing forms that is not composed of a beginning, a middle, and an end. It has a big beginning and a middle that tapers off to nothing.

News stories concentrate on facts and are not generally used for interpretation. Interpretation is the job of the *feature story*. For example, a news story about a policeman being shot would report what happened, who the policeman was, where and when the incident occurred, and perhaps why it happened. A feature story might take the same story and use it to show how dangerous a policeman's life is, how necessary gun control laws are, or (depending on the facts of the story) how oppressive the police force is in a certain area.

Investigative reporting is a special field in which the writer is half a detective. A year of investigation may be required before any story appears. The most famous reporters of recent years are Carl Bernstein and Bob Woodward, whose investigations of the Watergate scandal led to the resignation of President Nixon.

Journalists are expected to be fast writers and to have ingenuity in getting a story. But above all, they must be accurate. Accuracy is journalism's highest value. A badly researched story that turns out to be wrong casts doubt on the whole publication (and might cost the writer his job). If claims about the wrongdoing or misbehavior of an individual are unfounded, the individual may sue both the publication and the reporter for libel. Large newspapers and news magazines have staffs of "checkers" to check the facts of a story. In most situations, however, the writer must take personal responsibility for the accuracy of a story.

Television news reporting has special problems with accuracy. For example, the written commentary may say that John Jones gave a rousing campaign speech to a crowd of supporters this afternoon. But if the camera shows a tired person dozing off in the crowd and a section of the auditorium with empty seats, the meaning of the commentary is changed. People interviewed for TV also complain

SAN FRANCISCO CHRONICLE/BALTIMORE SUN

WRITING A HEADLINE *is an art that requires brevity. The writer must tell a story in ten words or less. The more important the story, the larger the type, and the fewer the words.*

that their views can be easily misrepresented, especially if a news program shows 90 seconds from a 20-minute interview.

There are many ways for a journalist to combine writing skills with interest in a particular business or hobby. Trade, technical, and professional journals range in subject matter from religion and recreation to accounting and sewage disposal. These journals do not appear on the newsstand, but have loyal regular readers. For example, the *Progressive Grocer* has been reaching 90,000 people a month since 1922, and the *Pipeline and Gas Journal,* a 100-page monthly magazine, goes to 25,000 readers and has been in existence since 1859.

Other Writing Fields

There are several other fields that use professional writers. The most important is the entertainment field—television, radio, films, and popular publishing.

Writing is the basis for many forms of entertainment. The general public is aware of a few writers who have made large amounts of money from best-selling novels or screenplays, but the fact is that a very small number of writers make their livings in the fields of entertainment and literature.

Most writers of entertainment material are not employed by a particular company. They are *freelancers,* selling their written material to film production companies, theater producers, or book and magazine publishers. For some material, the writer receives a flat sum of money. In other cases, he

receives a percentage of the proceeds from the resulting book, play, or movie. Established writers often have agents who help sell their work and negotiate contracts.

Many serious writers support themselves at other jobs—as teachers, editors, public relations writers, etc. If one of their productions becomes very successful, they may be able to give up other work and write full-time. But many authors are satisfied to have two callings—their regular job and their writing.

MYSTERIES, WESTERNS, AND ROMANCES *are published each year by the hundreds to entertain the reading public.*

ALLEN REUBEN

Editing. To the general reader, editors seem a mystery. Nearly every newspaper story, magazine article, and book written passes through their hands, yet it is not clear just what they do.

Technically, they are responsible for making sure that an author's work ends up in print. What they actually do depends on what kind of publication they work for and what kind of position they hold.

Many leading magazine and book editors concentrate on acquiring articles and books. Often they evaluate proposals submitted by writers. On other occasions, they may assign a particular idea to an author. Since each author is different, the same assignment given to ten different people might require ten different sets of instructions from the editor. If one author has difficulty in starting projects, the editor might provide a list suggesting several different approaches to his topic. If another author writes well and quickly but is not too good at doing detailed research, the editor might hire a researcher to help.

Traditionally, editing required no special qualifications beyond a knowledge of the written word. But today there is an increasing trend toward specialization. For example, a business editor today may have a Masters degree in business, a medical editor may have some training in medicine, and a law editor may be a lawyer.

Newspapers also employ editors. Like book and magazine editors, these editors may assign stories to different writers, but in this case the writers are often reporters who work for the paper.

The basic editing tasks are the same in most areas of publishing. Editors generally evaluate manuscripts, work with the author on any major revisions, and see the finished manuscript through the different phases of production into print.

Copy editors receive manuscripts from general editors and make sure that the manuscripts make sense and that the general rules of grammar are observed. Copy editors also edit for style. In this context, style means a set of rules for abbreviations, spellings, punctuation, and capitalization. Often they follow a company style guide and use a particular dictionary as the authority for spelling.

The manuscript then goes to a production editor, who sees it into type. Production editors coordinate the work of designers, artists, typesetters, and printers to see that the written word is properly set, accompanied by appropriate illustrations, and printed satisfactorily. The first printed form of the material is called a *proof,* and proofreaders check the printed version against the manuscript to be sure that the proof is accurate.

Research Skills

Throughout the years of formal education, students are encouraged to learn research skills. Not only is research an important means of expanding one's knowledge, but it finds direct application in many careers. Thus, it is of special importance to become proficient in developing and using the ability to locate information.

Every year countless books, scientific studies, films, articles, government reports, recordings, almanacs, surveys, and sheets of statistics add to our storehouse of information and opinions about a wealth of subjects, ranging from Indian war whoops to exploring outer space. Research is our way of tapping these vast resources and acquiring new knowledge on our own. Research can be as simple as looking up addresses in a telephone directory, or as painstaking and complex as reading the manuscripts, letters, and papers of a famous statesman in order to write his biography.

The Research Topic

The area you decide to explore will be limited by many factors. You have to ask yourself if you can realistically research a topic in the amount of time you have available. Some subjects may prove too bewildering. Unless you already know something about a field such as particle physics, for instance, you will have a difficult time reading and understanding the literature on it. Another factor is the availability of information. If few books or articles exist on your topic, or if they cannot easily be obtained, you may not be able to find what you need.

Doing research can be an endless task, particularly if you have chosen your own topic. Some scholars spend decades collecting data for exhaustive studies of scientific or historical topics. Their goal is to be as thorough as possible. Most research tasks do not require this much work. Instead, most people choose a field, gain a general overview of it, and then concentrate on one single aspect of that field to explore in depth. Your scope of inquiry will probably depend on how much material has already been written. As a rule, the more information available, the narrower your focus should be. For example, a research project in American history should be confined to individual events like the Boston Tea Party. "The American Revolution" as a topic would be altogether too broad. On the other hand, the history of the Polynesian islands as a whole could be treated in a research paper because the data available are not so extensive.

In narrowing the field of interest, it can be helpful to determine which aspects fascinate you most. If you have a general curiosity about geology, are you more eager to learn how Earth was formed or how scientists classify minerals? Does the structure of crystals intrigue you, or the methods of dating fossils?

Organizing Research

Whether your topic is your own or is given to you, you can organize your research by making a preliminary list of the specific issues you would like to cover. If you have decided on "How Was Earth Formed?" as your subject, the list might include: 1) What are the various estimates of our Earth's age? 2) How were these estimates made? 3) What arguments does each theory present? 4) What evidence supports these arguments? 5) How has scientific thinking evolved on this question? 6) What have earlier civilizations believed? In gathering material, your notetaking should concentrate on answering questions like these. This approach will save you from wasting time and energy collecting useless pieces of information. You can keep the scope of your study in mind by making an outline of it. This outline should break down your initial questions into even more detailed points of inquiry and serve as a checklist during your research.

You should decide next on the kind and quantity of information you will need. Are a few essential facts sufficient, or do you want to investigate a subject in depth? Does it matter if the information is up to date? Will you need facts and figures collected for use by specialists, or simply for the general reader? Are you interested in a book or article that imposes its own point of view or one that sticks more closely to giving the facts? Raising questions of this sort at the outset will steer you toward the research resources best suited to your project.

Resources for Research

These resources are many and varied. University libraries house several million volumes as well as issues of as many as 20,000 magazines and schol-arly journals. But if, for instance, you are trying to find out the best methods of refinishing an old desk, a knowledgeable neighbor might be the best place to start.

Research resources can be divided into primary and secondary sources. A primary source relates what people directly involved in a matter have said or written about it. Samuel Pepys's diary about life in 17th-century London and the stockholders' reports of General Motors are examples of primary sources. Their point of view is immediate and subjective. They are useful in providing a close-up perspective on a subject or event, but not in giving a wider, more balanced outlook. Secondary sources do this.

Secondary sources are commentaries written by people somewhat removed from the matters they are describing and analyzing. They deal with and evaluate primary source materials. Generally, secondary sources attempt to absorb several points of view in order to reach a more objective truth. But no source can be free of all bias. Secondary source materials include scholarly reviews, biographies, encyclopedias, dictionaries, and "popular" treatments of a subject. Most secondary sources, as well as primary sources such as newspapers, autobiographies, manuscripts, records, and reports on scientific experiments, can be located in libraries.

A good way to decide on the sources of information that will be most useful is to review the list of questions you wish to have answered. For example, if you want to discover how Americans felt about the Vietnam War, interviewing residents of your community about their personal recollections would serve as a handy and logical primary source. However, if you want to learn more about how a human embryo develops, an encyclopedia would be a better starting point.

Once you have determined which resources are appropriate for your research, you need to uncover where they are located and how you can best make use of them. Talking to people familiar with your field can be a valuable part of your research, especially if you are studying individual reactions to events. Interviews can also add an anecdotal and personal flavor usually lacking in textbook accounts. A manager of a local shoe factory can give you a more concrete picture of how automation has affected his industry than a government report can, though both would be valuable.

You can find out if a prospective interviewee is willing to talk to you by writing him a letter stating your purpose and the range of the questions

ENCYCLOPAEDIA BRITANNICA

RESEARCH *embraces primary sources, such as the interview* (left), *as well as secondary sources, such as encyclopedias* (right) *and other books.*

you would like to raise. Interviews ought to be requested well in advance. Before going to an interview, it is a good idea to outline the areas you intend to cover and to inform yourself, in a general way, about both your topic and the person you will be seeing. This is to avoid wasting the interviewee's time by asking elementary questions that could be answered by first checking a secondary source. A businessman probably does not want to be bothered by a query about when his company was founded.

During an interview, it is important to take notes, or to use a tape recorder, in order to record accurately what is said. Otherwise, you may distort the interviewee's opinions or his statements of fact.

Written primary sources include official reports of corporations, other private organizations, and government bureaus. These can usually be obtained by writing to the information office of each organization and stating your request. If you are interested, for example, in discovering the historical sites that can be visited in and around Mexico City, a letter to a Mexican consulate in the United States should produce this information.

The library. Because of the size and scope of its holdings, the library is a major source of secondary, as well as primary, research materials. There are many types of libraries in this country. The largest library in the United States—and probably in the world—is the Library of Congress, in Washington, D.C. It houses over 16 million volumes. Other government libraries, such as the National Library of Medicine, have extensive collections of books and periodicals relating to particular fields. In addition, each of the 50 states has a state library with large

reference departments. Many states also have law and legislative libraries.

Major private reference collections include the J. Pierpont Morgan Library, in New York City; the Folger Shakespeare Library, in Washington; the Henry E. Huntington Library, in California; and the John Crerar and Newberry libraries, in Chicago. These libraries are used primarily by professional researchers. Numerous private companies and industries maintain libraries of their own, containing up-to-date data on developments in their fields. There are approximately 2500 junior- and senior-college libraries in the United States that offer basic research facilities. Some 83 university libraries possess materials of major significance to scholars carrying out professional research.

The most frequently used and most easily accessible library is your local public library. Of the 7000 such libraries scattered around the country, 24 have more than 1 million volumes on their shelves. Most of these are big-city libraries. Even though a community library will contain fewer titles, it is still a perfectly adequate place to begin most research.

Many people find going to the library a confusing experience. They find themselves surrounded by stacks and stacks of information, but unsure of where to turn first. Reference librarians can provide sound initial advice on how to track down material on a specific topic. Many librarians have professional training, and they are well acquainted with the books in their library's collection. They can save you time by directing you to one or two appropriate, introductory sources. You should tell the librarian exactly what you would like to know: "Where might I find some books on learning how to sail small boats?" or "Can you suggest a source for statistics

on grain harvests in the Midwest?" A vague inquiry like "I'm writing about the American Navy—can you help me?" can only yield vague advice. A librarian can also point out where various departments—the reference section, magazine racks, microfilm viewers—are located.

Encyclopedias. A general introduction to most subjects can be gained by reading one or two articles in an encyclopedia. Encyclopedias are part of any library's reference collection. They contain brief descriptions of historical events, countries, cities, scientific processes, natural phenomena, notable figures in the arts, public affairs, and the sciences, and most other subjects of general interest. Encyclopedias vary in their depth of information. *The New Columbia Encyclopedia* is a one-volume encyclopedia containing short articles on nonspecialized topics. The *Encyclopaedia Britannica* is divided into a "Propaedia" (an "outline of knowledge" with a list of page references to articles in the other volumes), a ten-volume "Micropaedia" (containing brief pieces on specific subjects), and an 18-volume "Macropaedia" (containing lengthy articles on general subjects such as "Broadcasting" and "Sedimentary Rocks"). The *Encyclopaedia Britannica*, like many general encyclopedias, contains illustrations and drawings. Its articles end with a bibliography of books and articles that can furnish additional information. Making a note of these titles on index cards is a good way to further your research. Later, you can see if these works are listed in the library's card catalog.

It is important to make notes as you read these encyclopedia articles. Your notes should include the main points raised as well as more specific aspects covered in your research outline.

For more technical matters, you

may prefer to consult a specialized encyclopedia. A medical encyclopedia, for example, will provide the scientific definitions of parts of the body and of physical diseases. Other specialized encyclopedias would be helpful in, for example, music history, engineering, the social sciences, or the arts. Such encyclopedias are designed primarily for persons already familiar with a field and its terminology.

Encyclopedic yearbooks summarize items of contemporary interest. They are also found in the reference section.
The card catalog. Another research starting point is the card catalog. This is usually located near the circulation desk. Individual cards list every volume in the library. Works are indexed by title, author, and subject. When you are just beginning to do research and do not have particular titles in mind, the subject index is most useful. Under a listing such as "Aviation" you will find an alphabetical (by author) file of books about airplanes—their invention, development, and technology. Card catalogs generally include a number of cross-reference cards to direct you toward the proper subject. For example, under "Philately and Philatelists" you may come across a card suggesting "See Postage Stamps–Collections and Collecting."

The author card is the main entry in the catalog. It supplies the author's name, the title of the book, the publisher's name and publication date, a short statement of the book's contents and length, and information on illustrations and bibliography. Each catalog card has a classification number in the upper left-hand corner. This number indicates where the book is shelved.

There are two major systems of organizing libraries. One is called the Dewey Decimal System, after its inventor, a 19th-century American librarian. The Dewey Decimal System divides books into ten major categories, including religion, technology, and philosophy. Each of these subjects is subdivided into more particular areas of knowledge. The Dewey system runs from 000 to 999. (Fiction is an exception; it is shelved separately, by the author's last name. Biography also very often has an unclassified section of its own, the books arranged by the author's subject.)

The Library of Congress System uses 21 letters of the alphabet to classify books. Thus its major topic divisions are more specific. There is more information on the Dewey Decimal System and the Library of Congress System on page 1183 of this book.

To find a book on the shelves, you should write down the entire numerical listing. A notice posted near the card catalog will tell you where to find each individual section. In some larger libraries, where the book shelves are closed, you must turn in your card and receive your book at the desk.

HOW TO USE THE CARD CATALOG

1. THE CARD CATALOG *of books (right) is the key to the use of any library. Suppose you are looking for a book on teen-agers.*

2. INSIDE THE CATALOG *(drawer 130, above) you will find a card for the book,* Today's teen-agers *(the third card below). The book is also filed by author (middle card) and subject (top card) in different parts of the catalog.*

```
        ADOLESCENCE
301.43  Duvall, Evelyn Ruth (Millis) 1906-
D          Today's teen-agers, by Evelyn Millis Duvall.
        New York, Association Press [c1966]
           256p.  illus.  23cm.

           Bibliography: p.225-248.


           1.Adolescence.  I.Title.
                                              10/27/66
```

```
301.43  Duvall, Evelyn Ruth (Millis) 1906-
D          Today's teen-agers, by Evelyn Millis Duvall.
        New York, Association Press [c1966]
           256p.  illus.  23cm.

           Bibliography: p.225-248.


           1.Adolescence. I.Title.
                                              10/27/66
```

3. THE BOOK YOU WANT *is requested by call number, title, and author on a Book Request Card (below, right), or it can be found by call number on the open shelf (below).*

```
        Today's teen-agers
301.43  Duvall, Evelyn Ruth (Millis) 1906-
D          Today's teen-agers, by Evelyn Millis Duvall.
        New York, Association Press [c1966]
           256p.  illus.  23cm.

           Bibliography: p.225-248.


           1.Adolescence. I.Title.
                                              10/27/66
```

JESSE FORDE

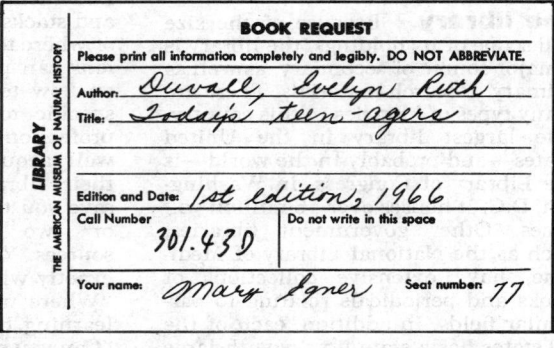

Reference guides. Additional book titles can be tracked down by using reference guides. They are part of the reference department. These guides provide extensive bibliographies on many topics. One of the most helpful is *Books in Print*. This multi-volume guide lists books currently available in the book market by subject, title, and author. It also cites the publisher's name and date of publication, in case you want to buy a particular title.

Articles in newspapers, journals, and magazines treat specific aspects of a topic usually not discussed in general reference materials or in books devoted to an entire field. They may also furnish more timely information than do encyclopedias or textbooks. Titles of articles relevant to your research can be located in various periodical guides. Thus, popular magazine articles are indexed by author and subject in *The Reader's Guide to Periodical Literature*. More technical articles are listed in guides such as the *Social Sciences and Humanities Index*. The *Public Affairs Information Service Bulletin* is a weekly listing of the titles of recently published books, pamphlets, and government publications in the areas of economic and social conditions, international relations, and public administration. A more complete listing of government publications available to the public is contained in the *Selected List of United States Government Publications*.

Some subjects have separate periodical guides of their own. *Chemical Abstracts*, which indexes articles about research and recent developments in chemistry, is one example.

Articles can also be found by turning to a guide like *N. W. Ayer & Son's Directory of Newspapers and Periodicals*. If you are researching a subject currently in the news, *The New York Times Index* is a valuable tool. This is an annotated author and subject index to articles that have appeared in *The Times* since 1851. Academic dissertations are listed by author and keyword in *Dissertation Abstracts International* and in other guides. These dissertations can supply you with statistics and data not available in published sources. A synopsis of the research findings is given.

Further brochures and pamphlets on some topics may be found in the library's so-called Vertical File. The librarian will show you where this material is.

Once you have jotted down a number of titles, it may simplify your research reading to examine a book review index. The *Book Review Digest*, for example, reprints reviews of current fiction and nonfiction works selected from several well known publications. These reviews give some idea of a book's contents and an opinion of its strengths and weaknesses. Reading these reviews may save you having to read lengthy volumes that do not add to your knowledge.

On occasion you may go to a library simply to check one or two facts. In this case, too, you should begin with the materials shelved in the reference section. Biographical information—where a famous man or woman was born, what positions he or she held—is readily available in a number of biographical dictionaries. *Chambers's Biographical Dictionary,* for one, contains summaries of the lives of 15,000 prominent men and women, while the *Dictionary of American Biography* lists important Americans. Facts about well known living Americans can also be found in *Who's Who in America.* *Current Biography* is a yearly encyclopedia of people in the news, with a cumulative index. Certain fields have their own factbooks, such as the *Dictionary of the American Indian* and *American Men of Science.*

Dictionaries and other factbooks provide varied kinds of information. Some are full of data about the world in general. *Facts on File* is a weekly world news digest, dating back to 1938, that abbreviates reports from several daily newspapers around the country. The *Statesman's Year-Book* gives detailed up-to-date data on international organizations. Almanacs such as the *World Almanac* offer hundreds of statistics on population, organizations, presidents, fishing, baseball, and countless other subjects. The *Guinness Book of World Records* is the place to look for the fastest, biggest, and longest in the animal world as well as the world of man.

Dictionaries tell us about words and language usage as well. Bilingual dictionaries provide the equivalent meanings of words in two different languages. Other word dictionaries supply definitions and guides to proper English usage. For example, the one-volume *Random House Dictionary of the English Language* cites 260,000 words in current usage, including proper names, place names, and titles of literary works. If you are interested in discovering the origins of a particular word, the 13-volume *Oxford English Dictionary* is an authoritative source. It also gives examples of how words have been used by individual authors over the centuries.

A Dictionary of Foreign Words and Phrases in Current English is another useful language handbook. A thesaurus such as *Roget's* lists synonyms for thousands of words. A reference section will usually include dictionaries of proper names and dictionaries of proper usage. Slang words may be looked up in Eric Partridge's *A Dictionary of Slang and Unconventional English*. Rhymes and abbreviations are listed in other volumes, as are quotations. *Bartlett's Familiar Quotations* is a standard compendium of well known sayings arranged chronologically from biblical times to the 20th century.

Atlases specialize in data about the physical world. They feature many kinds of maps, including historical and topographical ones. They commonly list the names and sizes of cities and major towns around the globe. The *Atlas of World Affairs* shows where wars were fought and how peoples have migrated throughout history. The *Atlas of the World's Resources* indicates where minerals, foodstuffs, forests, and other raw materials exist. Gazetteers are atlases without maps, furnishing geographical facts about towns, rivers, oceans, mountains, and countries. Information about what to see and where to stay in foreign countries and in the United States is contained in guidebooks such as *Fodor's Modern Guides*. These cover regions of the world as well as individual countries, especially those in Europe. Other well known guidebook series are the *Blue Guides* and *Nagel's*.

THE READER'S GUIDE (below) *and other useful reference books supplement the main catalog in any well equipped library.*

Other reference tools. You may discover that some of the material you would like to read is listed in the card catalog as being on microfilm or microfiche. Many libraries routinely photograph and reduce books, magazines, and newspapers on film in order to save shelf space or to preserve the material from damage or deterioration. Microfilm is put on spools and stored in file cabinets. A full two weeks of *The New York Times* can be stored on a single roll of microfilm. These films can be read by means of a magnifying viewer found in the library. Texts are even more greatly reduced on microfiche cards. A four-by-six-inch card can reproduce as many as 77 pages. Microfiche cards can also be read with special enlargers.

In many libraries, audiovisual resources supplement information available in print. Educational filmstrips in 16- and 35-mm can be borrowed for home viewing. A complete list of titles can be found in a guide like the *National Information Center for Educational Media Index to 35-mm Educational Filmstrips.*

Recordings of every type of music, from Italian opera to New Orleans jazz, can either be listened to in the library or taken out on loan. (Some large public libraries, such as the New York Public Library, have branches primarily devoted to records.) Recordings of writers and poets reading their own works as well as the speeches of famous public figures are part of many library collections.

After you have located on the shelves all the titles you have noted in the card catalog, you will have to determine which ones are useful for your research project, and which are not. Skimming the table of contents and the introduction will usually indicate if a book's scope and approach are relevant. Instead of having to read through an entire volume searching for a discussion of your topic, you may be able to identify one or two chapters that have special interest for you.

CONDENSED INFORMATION *on cards greatly enlarged on a microfiche machine.*

Evaluating the Sources

Any person doing research has to read critically, evaluating his sources as he goes along. For most projects, information exists in abundance. It would be fruitless if not impossible to read every page of every book and article treating the topic "How Earth Was Formed." A discriminating researcher narrows the possible resources down to those that further his goals and discards the rest. These are a few questions to ask yourself before setting out on your task:

• Is it essential to know current developments in the field? For example, scientific data gathered over the last few years may have generated a new theory about the origin of our planet; thus, a 15-year-old text would be outdated. Current issues of magazines like *Scientific American* might be a more valuable source for making sure that your research stays up to date.

• Is the material easy to understand? A scholarly monograph aimed at professional geologists may assume much more familiarity with scientific terms and geological research than you have. It is best to concentrate on sources written for readers at your level of knowledge.

• Is the information complete? Some writers provide a thorough treatment of a subject, while others choose to explore only a single aspect in great detail. A book on ancient myths about the universe may offer you too much information about a question that is only a small part of your inquiry. The more a book's contents coincide with the outline of your research goals, the more valuable it will be to you.

• What is the author's point of view? All writers make value judgments, consciously or unconsciously, which inevitably shape the material they present. Sometimes an author will state his perspective, or bias, in the preface. He may indicate what ideas he believes to be true and wishes to demonstrate in his book. In fact, he may well have written this book to advocate a theory or point of view of his own. Often a writer will only imply the values governing his work; thus, you should be alert for such "loaded" language.

In general, secondary sources require a more careful screening on your part since they are interpreting events, people, and primary sources for you. A primary source advertises its limitations more clearly and can be judged by how accurate it appears compared with other sources. No good researcher will rely solely on one authority. He will consult several in order to weigh their perspectives and draw his own conclusions.

• What are the author's credentials? A geologist who has made a life study of the formation of Earth and written two books on the subject is more qualified to comment on a new theory of Earth's origin than a journalist writing in a news magazine. Some authorities have better reputations than others. In some cases, the introduction to a book or the biographical data on the jacket will give you some idea of the author's relevant background. You may wish to check further by looking him up in a biographical encyclopedia.

• Is the author convincing? A writer may demonstrate his grasp of a topic by the soundness of his arguments or by the thoroughness of his research. A book on the "big bang" theory of how the universe came into being, for instance, may or may not consider conflicting theories. It may ignore or misrepresent certain facts. A source of this sort may not be reliable.

No one source can supply the final word on any topic. Research involves sifting through a great deal of material and extracting the information that is the most intelligently presented and that best increases your understanding of the topic.

While you are reading, take notes. New and unusual facts, illuminating arguments, and quotable statements should be jotted down on separate index cards so that you can rearrange them in preparing your research paper. You should copy quotations accurately, setting them off with quotation marks to distinguish them from your own paraphrases or summaries. (To reproduce a long passage in your paper, you will have to obtain permission from the author or his publisher.) It is equally important to make a note of the exact page source for each comment or quotation. This will help you in adding footnotes to your paper.

Bibliographical references at the back of a book or article should also be noted down. They may guide you to other important sources.

Hard-to-Find Titles

Frequently the printed materials you most want to consult are missing from the library shelves. Once you have double-checked the call number in the card catalog, ask the circulation librarian if he can help you. He will be able to tell you if a book has been borrowed from the library. If it has, and if you need it in a short period of time, he may be able to have the book recalled or reserved. He will also know if this material is being bound (as happens with current periodicals) or microfilmed.

Some books may have been shelved in the wrong place or put aside in a special reserve section. In many university libraries, books on the reading list of large courses are put on reserve so they will be available to large numbers of students. Reserve books may only be borrowed for short periods, if at all.

If a title you have noted is not in your library, there are several ways of trying to obtain it. The first method is to visit a library with a more extensive collection. A big-city library contains thousands of volumes that a village library does not have the space to house. A specialized library, such as a geological library, will carry many additional materials.

If this fails, find out what libraries outside your area carry the particular title you are looking for. You may borrow from these libraries on request. *The National Union Catalog* of the Library of Congress lists over 16 million titles and 2500 libraries that house many of these volumes. By writing to your state library, you can also discover the location of hard-to-come-by titles. Some state libraries can be contacted by means of a teletype hookup in major branch libraries.

Periodicals in fields such as engineering and the sciences can be found by utilizing a data base computer network.

After you know where a book is, you can have it forwarded to your local library via an interlibrary loan system. For a fee, it is also possible to have microfilm copies of books or articles made and sent to you. *Serials in Microform* is a listing of titles already on microfilm or microfiche, arranged by title and subject.

Rare books and unpublished papers, such as personal letters and diaries, may only be available in special collections, or in private libraries. They can be traced through a reference book such as *A Guide to Archives and Manuscripts in the United States.* You may have to request permission to have access to these materials.

Very recent books may not have been ordered or received by libraries. A guide like *Books in Print* will provide the information needed to order a book from a bookstore or the publisher.

If you are researching a subject in the news, following developments in a daily newspaper or television news program is a good way to keep abreast of events.

Books that are out of print, and do not appear in a guide like *Books in Print,* may be purchased by contacting bookstores that specialize in them. Some of these bookstores will write to their correspondents at your request to find your book, or will advertise for it in specialized old and rare book journals for a fee. If this does not work, you yourself can haunt secondhand bookstores in the hopes of finding that elusive volume; or you can watch out for private sales of old books advertised in newspapers.

—*John V.H. Dippel*

A SELECTIVE LIST OF RESEARCH SOURCES

Reference guides
American Reference Books Annual
Hirshberg, H.S. *Subject Guide to Reference Books*
Hutchins, Margaret, et al. *Guide to the Use of Libraries*

Bibliographies
The Bibliographic Index, 1938–present
Books in Print
Cumulative Book Index, 1933–present
Paperback Books in Print, 1955–present

Encyclopedias
Collier's Encyclopedia (multi-volume)
Encyclopedia Americana (multi-volume)
Encyclopaedia Britannica (multi-volume)
The New Columbia Encyclopedia (one volume)
World Book Encyclopedia (multi-volume)

Newspaper and magazine guides
British Union Catalogue of Periodicals
Essay and General Literature Index, 1900–1933
International Index to Periodicals, 1920–present
The New York Times Index, 1851–present
Poole's Index to Periodical Literature, 1802–1906
The Reader's Guide to Periodical Literature, 1900–present
Social Sciences and Humanities Index, 1907–present
Union List of Serials in Libraries of the United States and Canada

Dictionaries
Funk & Wagnalls New Standard Dictionary
Oxford English Dictionary
Random House Dictionary of the English Language
Webster's Third New International Dictionary

Government publications
Monthly Catalog of United States Government Publications, 1895–present
Selected United States Government Publications, 1928–present

Biographies
Biography Index
Dictionary of American Biography (multi-volume)
The International Who's Who
Webster's Biographical Dictionary (one volume)
Who's Who in America

Factbooks
Facts on File: A Weekly Digest of World Events with a Cumulative Index
Information Please Almanac
Statesman's Year-Book
Statistical Abstracts of the United States
The World Almanac & Book of Facts

Atlases
Atlas of World Affairs
Atlas of the World's Resources
Hammond World Atlas
The Times Atlas of the World

Wordbooks
Bliss, Alan Joseph. *A Dictionary of Foreign Words and Phrases in Current English*
Fowler, H.W. *A Dictionary of Modern English Usage*
Mawson, Sylvester C. *New Roget's Thesaurus in Dictionary Form*
Webster's New Dictionary of Synonyms

PRINTING

You are reading this article thanks to a process we take for granted—printing. Printing makes it possible for us to communicate ideas and pictures to millions of people in distant places and even to people of future generations. We can read what the prime minister of England said yesterday about the price of coal, and what Shakespeare wrote in the 17th century about the temptations of power. Because of printing we are able to look at a color reproduction of a canvas by Rubens, or photographs of Antarctica.

Everywhere we turn, the printed word and image bind us to a larger world and enable us to learn more about it. Printing conveys all sorts of mass information, from the nutritional value of a box of cornflakes, to the daily notices on a school bulletin board, or to the comments of a street vendor in Peking quoted in a local American newspaper.

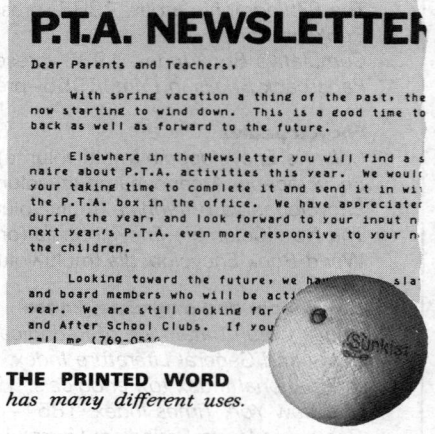

P.T.A. NEWSLETTER

Dear Parents and Teachers,

With spring vacation a thing of the past, the now starting to wind down. This is a good time to back as well as forward to the future.

Elsewhere in the Newsletter you will find a s naire about P.T.A. activities this year. We would your taking time to complete it and send it in wi the P.T.A. box in the office. We have appreciate during the year, and look forward to your input n next year's P.T.A. even more responsive to your n the children.

Looking toward the future, we ha and board members who will be acti year. We are still looking for and After School Clubs. If you all me (769-05)

THE PRINTED WORD *has many different uses.*

Before the invention of printing, information was scarce. News spread slowly, by word of mouth. Stories, legends, and history were passed on orally, too, since few people could read or write. New advances in human thought and technology reached only a small audience, usually through teaching and letter writing, or through hand-written manuscripts. During the Middle Ages, these manuscripts were preserved and copied by hand at religious centers of learning and at a few large manuscript libraries. The general public did not have access to these materials and thus did not know much about the world beyond their immediate surroundings. This ignorance and isolation meant that it was difficult for new ideas and developments to become accepted.

Printing greatly speeded up the process of scientific, political, economic, and social transformation by allowing a rapid and broad exchange of facts and opinions. It was a truly revolutionary instrument, helping to change fundamentally the structure and values of Western society.

The Invention of Printing

The art of printing originated in China. As early as the second century A.D., craftsmen in that country had developed the three essential elements for reproducing a written language: paper, ink, and a surface to print from. For a language to be printed it must, of course, first exist in a written form—in a symbolic code either in ideographs derived from simple pictures, or in an alphabet like ours, which dates back to the Phoenicians in the Near East.

At first, the surface used for imprinting was a hard material like stone or marble, but by the sixth century A.D., Chinese artisans were using wood blocks to print religious texts. The first printed books—a series of Buddhist incantations—appeared between 764 and 770.

The Chinese developed ink in the fifth century A.D. The earliest inks were a mixture of linseed-oil varnish and carbon black. The Chinese were also responsible for the invention of movable type. Instead of carving out an entire page of script, an eleventh-century alchemist made individual blocks for each ideograph out of glue and hardened clay, and then assembled them on an iron plate to form a printing surface. When he wanted to print another sheet he simply took the blocks apart and rearranged them to make new words. By having a stock of the necessary number of type pieces on hand, a printer could more quickly and easily reproduce a written work. The possibilities for printing expanded. For instance, in 1313 a Chinese treatise on technology was printed using a set of 60,000 separate type pieces of wood. The first bronze type was also cast in the 14th century, in Korea.

Paper. Printing emerged in Europe much later. A major reason for this delay was the lack of good writing materials. Animal skins were treated and made into parchment for manuscripts, but skins were expensive and hard to obtain. The use of paper spread westward slowly from China. Traders introduced a Chinese paper made of tree fiber, with linen and cotton rag fiber, to the Middle East region, and by the middle of the eighth century A.D., the Arabs had brought this invention to Europe. But Western craftsmen did not readily adopt the new product. Four hundred years

THE CHINESE *invented printing centuries ago. A Buddhist charm of the ninth century A.D*

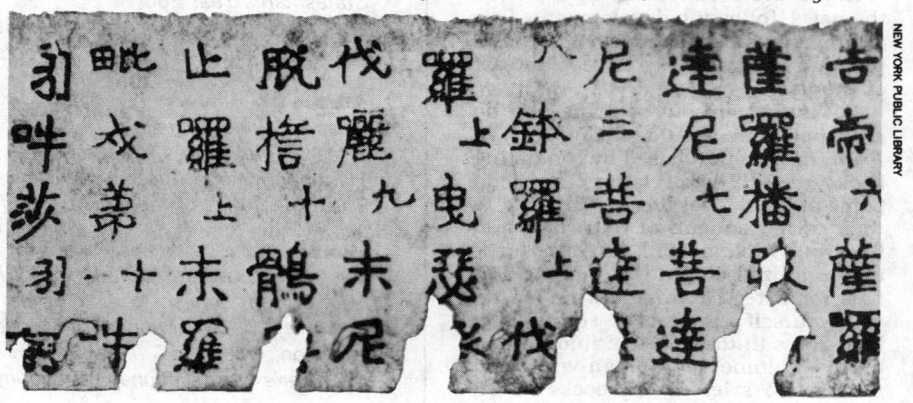

went by before paper was made in Europe—first in Spain and then in Italy, France, and Germany.

Paper was manufactured by separating various fibers—predominantly flax and hemp in Europe—and saturating them with water. This paper stock was then filtered by a screen to form a mat. The mat was pressed to squeeze out excess water and left to dry out by evaporation. More pressure was later applied to firm up the paper surface.

The first European papermaking machine was constructed in London in 1803. Since then, the manufacture of paper has been increasingly mechanized, but the principle used for making it has not changed. The use of more plentiful fibrous materials, such as wood pulp from the trunks of hard- and softwood trees, has reduced the cost of papermaking. Scrap cardboard and other wastepapers have become another major source of paper fiber. Today, mills produce paper in huge quantities for newspapers, books, and other printing purposes.

The quality of the paper produced depends on the kinds of fibers used, the refining of the paper stock, the amount of pressing to remove water and dry the paper, and the chemical additives used. Papers can be as much as half an inch thick—for example, paperboard for building construction—or extremely thin. Most printing is done on newsprint made of wood pulp, on writing papers, and on book papers. Book papers are coated for reproducing quality illustrations.

Gutenberg.

With the building of paper mills in southern Europe in the 14th century came the first Western use of movable type. Letters of the alphabet were carved in relief on wood blocks and then set in rows to form a page of text for printing—much like the method developed in China. These wood type pieces broke easily, however, and did not print letters of uniform size. It took engravers in Holland to make type that was both durable and standardized, though their product was very imperfect. They cut letters out of bronze, made molds from these, and then poured lead into the molds.

A COMPOSING STICK. *Drawing of a printing device first used in Gutenberg's time.*

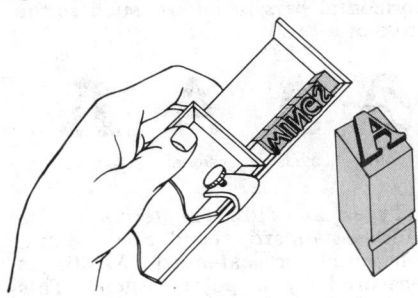

Johann Gutenberg was a German goldsmith who is generally credited with being the first European to bring the art of printing with movable type, cast in molds, up to a practical level. At first, Gutenberg used letters cut out of wood and fastened together by wires. But these wore down so quickly that he began to substitute ones made of lead. Perhaps in the 1430's, he began to carve letters out of either brass or bronze and to pour lead over these letter dies to make his printing molds. The lead type pieces Gutenberg cast from these molds also proved too soft, and he later switched to an alloy of lead, tin, and antimony for his type.

In order to print, Gutenberg and his contemporaries would select the appropriate type pieces from a rack, place them in order on a wood composing "stick," and make a line of even length by inserting spacing pieces between the letters.

Gutenberg is also regarded as the inventor of the modern printing press. Presses already existed for squeezing grapes and printing textiles. What Gutenberg did was to apply this method of pressure to transferring ink from metal type to paper. His press consisted of a metal frame that held the type pieces in place, and a plate that was tightened by a wood screw to press a sheet of paper against the inked metal letters. This manner of printing produced a sharp and uniform imprint. Once it had dried, a sheet could be printed on both sides.

The most famous work of this German inventor is the Gutenberg Bible. Copies of these Bibles—believed to be the first books printed from movable type in the Western world—were completed around 1455. Gutenberg produced both a 42-line (per column) and a 36-line Bible.

The spread of printing.

Gutenberg's printing innovations were copied by printers in other parts of Germany. Printed books illustrated with elaborate woodcuts appeared in Bamberg, Cologne, and Nuremberg. When Gutenberg's city of Mainz was sacked in 1462, workmen fled abroad, spreading the knowledge of how to make type and print books. Two German printers opened a shop near Rome in 1464. Three others established a press at the Paris Sorbonne, or university. By 1460, followers of Gutenberg were printing large volumes in Strasbourg.

William Caxton was the first person to print books in English. He learned the craft of printing in Cologne. At Bruges, in 1475, he and a colleague printed *The Recuyell of the Historyes of Troye*. This was followed by about 100 books, which appeared in England.

By the late 16th century, printing presses were in operation throughout Europe. Venice established itself as a printing center, producing more books than any other European city. In France, the Estienne family built a reputation for printing editions of Greek and Latin classics. Dutch printers produced their first books at Utrecht in 1473. The first major book printed in Spain was a multilingual Bible, written in Hebrew, Greek, Latin, and Chaldee.

A GERMAN BIBLE, *printed in Cologne in 1478, only some 25 years after Gutenberg's day, and beautifully illustrated. The picture at the bottom illustrates the adoration of the Magi.*

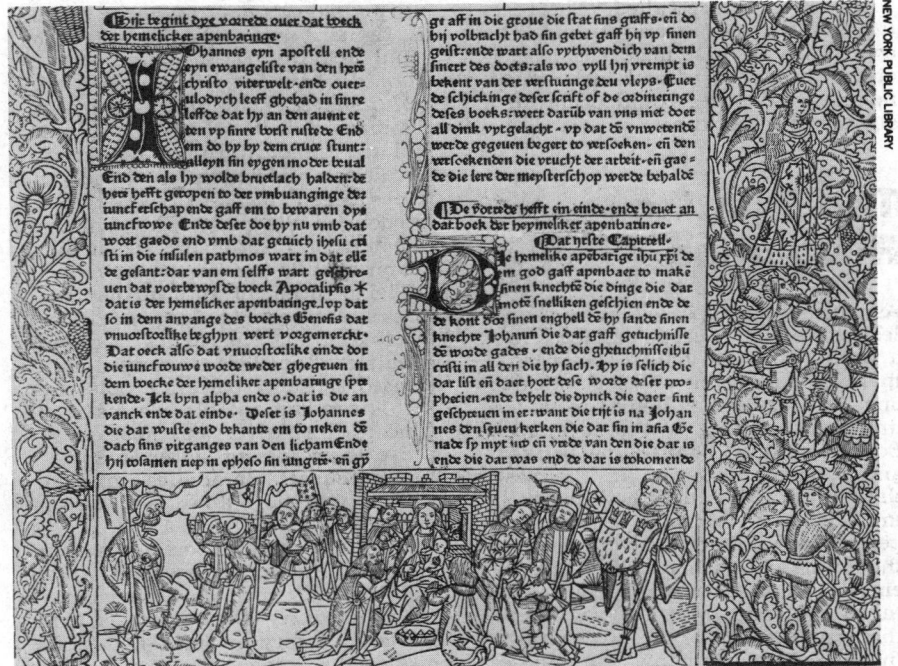

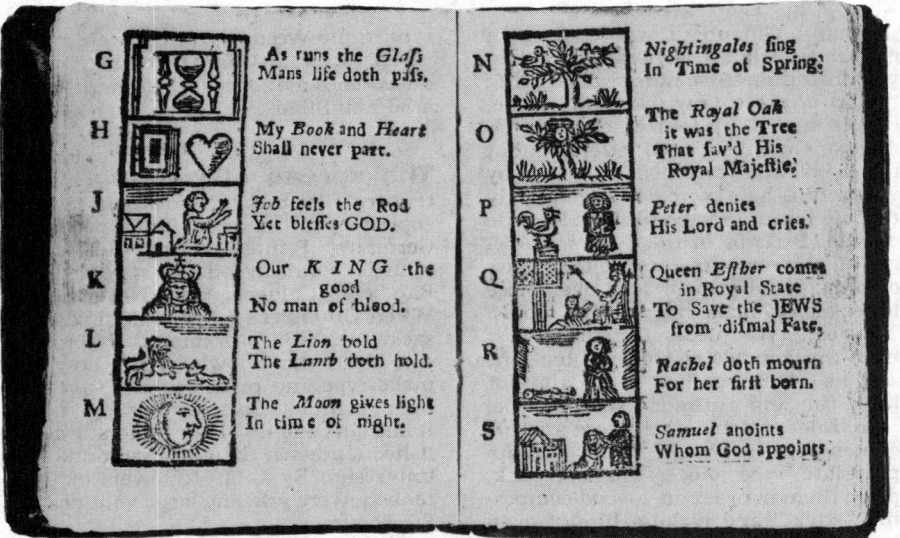

THE NEW ENGLAND PRIMER, *an example of early printing in New England, about 1690. This schoolbook, in use for nearly 100 years, attempted to teach theology and the alphabet.*

Printing came to the United States in 1638. The earliest press was set up in Cambridge, Massachusetts, and printed its first book, the *Bay State Psalm Book,* in 1640. One of the most notable printers of colonial America was Benjamin Franklin, who published both the *Pennsylvania Gazette* and *Poor Richard's Almanack* during the 18th century.

The growth of printing brought many sweeping changes. Before 1400, only a wealthy few could afford hand-copied books. Now great numbers of people were able to obtain religious works like the Bible as well as scientific and other scholarly texts. For example, the popular writings of the philosopher Erasmus were reprinted in dozens of editions before the end of the 16th century. In England, 10,000 copies of a treatise called "The Practice of Godliness" were printed. The availability of these materials accelerated a discussion of new ideas. Technological advances could occur in a shorter period of time.

The Printing Revolution

As more books appeared, more people learned to read. Europe changed from a largely illiterate feudal society to a more knowledgeable and sophisticated one. Greater literacy helped to undermine the existing power structures. Books contained challenging political and religious theories. In the past, these unorthodox ideas had had little immediate significance because few persons could read about them. Now thousands of readers could be influenced by a single work. For example, in 1517 Martin Luther posted his 95 theses on the door of the castle church in Wittenberg, Germany. These theses

are considered the beginning of the Protestant Reformation. Although they were widely distributed, they did not have nearly as great an impact as Luther's printed "Address to the Christian Nobility of the German Nation" (1520), or his later translation of the Bible. Both were read by countless German laymen.

Having access to Luther's critique of the Roman Catholic Church and to copies of the Bible meant that German Christians were less dependent on the words of their priests for spiritual guidance, a fact that encouraged the growth of the Reformation. (The printing press was also put to many effective uses by the opponents of Luther's teachings.)

The printed book also tended to weaken the power of the European nobility. Radical doctrines concerning the rights of man and political tyranny could no longer be easily suppressed. A work like Jean Jacques Rousseau's *Social Contract* greatly influenced political thought in the 18th century and laid the groundwork for the French Revolution. Meanwhile, democratic forces began to take steps to protect freedom of the press. The American Constitution was the first document to guarantee this freedom explicitly.

The printing of information on a mass scale encouraged a general social leveling trend in many European countries. Knowledge conveyed an increased sense of power. People from the lower and middle classes could educate themselves and hope to rise above their present status in society. Rigid feudal hierarchies gradually gave way to more fluid, mobile social orders.

Along with greater personal freedom arose a desire for more wealth. An entrepreneurial spirit developed among the bourgeoisie—the merchants, bankers, and factory owners—and slowly displaced the economic dominance of

the landed aristocracy. Capitalism grew out of this belief in individual initiative and mobility.

Man's sense of his place in history was also altered. Curious readers could now reach back to the writings of antiquity and see their age in a more clear perspective. The evolution of human thought could be more readily traced.

New kinds of literature came into being with cheaper printing methods. Diaries, travel journals, chivalric romances, political tracts, and collections of letters were published, along with statistical records and scientific studies. As the appetite for reading material grew, these new literary forms continued to multiply. Later genres such as the novel reflected both a vast increase in literacy and the growing prominence of the middle class in Western society.

Generally, the trend was in the direction of more secular reading: the Bible and theological writings lost the primary importance they had once had. Man became more interested in—and informed about—the world he lived in rather than in the world that might await him after death.

Typefaces

While the method of printing did not fundamentally change between Gutenberg's day and the Industrial Revolution, there were many innovations in type design. Individual printers such as the Englishman John Baskerville perfected distinctive typefaces varying in size and contour. Type was classified into several major categories. The earliest form imitated the script found in hand-copied manuscripts and was called *gothic. Roman* type was a more plain and rounded design that achieved its greatest perfection in Venice around 1470. Members of craft guilds in Europe produced a wide range of variations on these two forms.

Roman type can be divided into old-style and modern. Modern roman type has strong contrasts between its light and heavy lines, whereas old-style is more even. *Italic,* or slanted, print was first used by Aldus Manutius, a 15th-century Venetian printer. More recent type forms include *sans-serif* and *square serif.* (Serif is the term for fine horizontal bars in letters, such as the cross of a "t.")

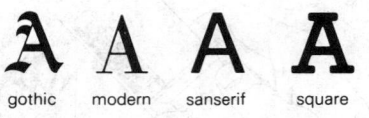

gothic   modern   sanserif   square

Type can differ in terms of its width—standard, condensed, extra-condensed or extended. Width is measured by a point system. This method of measuring was perfected by a French printer, François Ambrose Didot. American founders adapted his classification system to the inch. Under this system, one point equals .013837 of an inch. Thus, there are 72 points to one inch. This page is set in nine-point type.

standard   condensed   extended   italic

Typefaces can also have different weights, indicating the lightness or heaviness of the ink tones. The weight may be standard, lightface, boldface, or extra bold. Combinations of typefaces, weights, and widths have led to a proliferation of typefaces. Types are frequently named after their inventors, such as Kennerly, Bodoni, Janson, and Caslon. The art of type design reached its greatest height prior to the 19th century. As the making of print evolved from an artistic craft to an industrial skill, the number but not the quality of typefaces proliferated.

A A A **A**

light   standard   bold   extrabold

The Press

With the coming of industrialization, the printing press underwent many refinements. In the late 18th century, the wood-screw method of making an imprint on paper was replaced by a press method using metal joints. *Stereotype* printing grew out of an increased demand for books and newspapers in and around Paris at the time of the French Revolution. In this method, a clay impression was formed from an entire page of type. From this, several lead molds were cast, so that the same text could be printed simultaneously on a number of presses. As a result, a greater number of copies could be made available in a short period of time.

One of the most important advances was the mechanization of the raised-metal type, or *letterpress* printing process. The invention of the steam engine made this development possible. A German named Friedrich König invented a press in 1803 that used steam power to raise and lower the *platen*—the metal plate that presses the paper against the type—and to ink the metal letters held in place by a steel frame called a chase. This mechanical press was later improved so that it could print on both sides of a sheet of paper. It was further improved by two Boston printers, Isaac Adams and Daniel Treadwell. In 1882 Treadwell constructed a press that used steam power while still relying on the principle of

JOHN CLYDE OSWALD, PRINTING IN THE AMERICAS

WOODEN HAND PRESS, *thought to be the first press used in New England (1638).*

the hand press. Adams made modifications to this operation. A few of his presses are still in use at the Riverside Press in Cambridge, Massachusetts.

In 1810 König also developed the first cylinder press. Instead of a flat plate, a rotating metal impression cylinder, driven by steam, pressed the paper against a moving, horizontal type bed, or form. After a sheet had been imprinted, the cylinder was raised and moved back from the form to be reinked. This press could print 1100 sheets per hour—four times the rate that could be attained with a platen press.

The cylinder press was first used commercially by the *London Times* in 1814. At that time, it was hailed as the greatest invention since the art of printing itself. Flatbed cylinder presses today are used primarily for small printing operations, such as sheets of stationery and business cards.

The next step involved putting the type on a cylinder as well. Curved, stereotype plates made of a lead alloy

were developed by the Parisian Jacob Warms in 1848. In this rotary press, the paper was fed between the impression and the larger, inked cylinder, producing copies at the rate of 8000 an hour.

With the introduction of the Fourdrinier papermaking machine in 1803, which made paper in continuous rolls, the production rate of paper increased markedly. The web rotary cylinder press, which used paper in rolls, was in general use in England by the second half of the 19th century. It was most efficient for newspaper printing. The web press can print, dry, cut, and fold sheets of newsprint at high speeds. Up to this day, it remains the major press for printing newspapers.

For large jobs, a web rotary generally uses printing plates in place of set type pieces. A printing plate can be produced in duplicate, thus eliminating the need to frequently replace worn-out type.

There are two ways of making duplicate plates. Stereotypes utilize hardened paper mats to form a matrix. In electrotype duplicate plates, the molds are plastic and the letter imprints are transferred to copper plates by means of an electroplating cell. Electrotypes are used for high-quality printing, while stereotypes are used for newspaper printing.

The letterpress method is based on applying pressure to raised lead type known as hot type. Subsequent printing procedures moved away from relying on metal relief type. *Lithographic* printing is based on the incompatibility of grease and water. It utilizes a flat surface, usually stone or metal, and hence is also known as *planographic* printing. At the beginning, lithographic printing was developed for copying illustrations. A drawing is made on a stone or metal plate with a greasy crayon or ink. The surface is

A WEB PRESS, *a rotary cylinder type invented in the 19th century and still used today.*

THE NEW YORK TIMES

then flushed with water. When ink is applied, it will only adhere where the original grease markings have been made. The earliest lithographic printing was done on limestone by a German playwright, Alois Senefelder.

The planographic procedure was adapted for printing type by an American, Ira W. Rubel, working in Nutley, New Jersey, in 1904. He successfully transferred an imprint from a rotating metal-type cylinder onto a rubber mat, or blanket, and from there onto paper. Rubel's three-cylinder offset press operated faster and lasted much longer than metal letterpress machines, since his inked surface did not chip or wear away.

Offset printing also produces better tone qualities and sharper imprints than those achieved by letterpress. Offset presses range in size from small office machines to web offset presses for printing books at high speeds of 1000 feet of web (paper) per minute. A web offset press can print and fold a 24-page newspaper at the rate of 30,000 copies an hour.

A more recent form is dry offset, or driography, which eliminates the need for a dampening process to repel ink from the nonimage surfaces. In this type of press, imprints are made on photographic plates instead of on rubber mats.

The third major kind of printing is called *intaglio*. This derives from the art of woodcutting. Here the image to be reproduced is cut into—etched on—a metal or plastic plate. Ink fills these cavities and is then transferred to the printing surface. The depression on the etching plate can be made in two ways.

In *gravure* printing a zinc or copper plate is etched by an acid bath. These baths—known as bites—are repeated to etch the metal at varying depths.

This is a process first attempted by Karl Klič (or Klietsch), a Czech, in 1878. It is chiefly used for illustrations. The image is first photographed and then projected onto a metal plate that has been made sensitive to light. This plate is then etched in a bath of nitric acid or ferric chloride, depending on the nature of the metal used.

Two types of illustrations can be reproduced. *Line engravings* duplicate pen-and-ink drawings, hand lettering, and diagrams—illustrations consisting of solid ink lines and an uninked background. *Line plates* immersed in acid baths are eaten away leaving only the desired drawn lines in relief, ready for inking.

Screen half-tone engraving is better suited for printing photographs and pictures of varying tones. First the image is photographed through a half-tone screen. This process breaks the picture up into a crisscross pattern of tiny dots. These dots vary in size according to the intensity of tone. Dark areas are made up of concentrations of dark dots, whereas light areas have smaller, scattered dots. The film negative produced with the screen is then used to make a half-tone engraving plate. This is honeycombed by cells at different depths, which correspond to the half-tone dots.

Once the engraved plate is made, it is inked and pressed against the surface to be printed. Where the engraving lines are deep, the ink will print darker and heavier than where the lines are shallow. Thus, fine shades of tone can be duplicated in printing photographs and other pictures. Gravure plates are generally printed on cylinder presses, called rotogravure presses.

An additional printing technique called silk screen involves fine mesh screens, usually of silk or synthetic fabrics, that are similar to stencils. Ink is forced through the porous areas of the screening material, leaving a reproduced image beneath. This process is frequently applied for printing posters and for transposing patterns onto glass, plastics, and textiles.

Stencil printing of type is done by mimeograph machines. An original manuscript is typed on a typewriter, which cuts outlines of letters on a thin tissue stencil. This stencil is placed on a roller and inked. Mimeograph machines are commonly used in offices and schools.

A more recent form of printing has done away with the need for presses and printing plates. This is called *ink-jet printing*. Fine nozzles controlled by a computer spray the ink directly onto the paper.

Copying machines.
The development of photosensitive paper has also made it possible to dispense with the making of printing plates. Sheets of chemically treated paper are passed in front of a cathode ray screen, and the letters are instantly copied onto it. Photocopying machines have become widely used in offices for reproducing limited amounts of copies. The first Xerox copying machine was perfected in 1938. It was derived from a photocopying machine made in France at the end of the 19th century.

While mechanical composition and typesetting are still practiced, they are being displaced by photoelectronic methods, particularly in large-scale printing operations.

Composition

This is the process of assembling and setting type so that it can then be printed. In the early days of printing, printers did this entirely by hand, picking individual letters from racks, spacing them and arranging the type in lines of even length—a process referred to as *justification*. Setting type manually is a slow and tedious process. During the 19th century, machines were invented that were able to select type pieces and place them in the proper position at the rate of five to 12,000 an hour. But these machines produced only a single, continuous row of type; they did not justify lines. A major improvement in composition was the invention of the *Linotype* machine by the German Ottmar Mergenthaler, in Baltimore during the 1880's.

Mergenthaler's machine cast a lead slug—a solid, one-line row of type—after the lead had been pressed against metal matrices. The matrices are selected by striking the keys of a keyboard resembling that of a typewriter. This composing machine was first put to use by *The New York Tribune*.

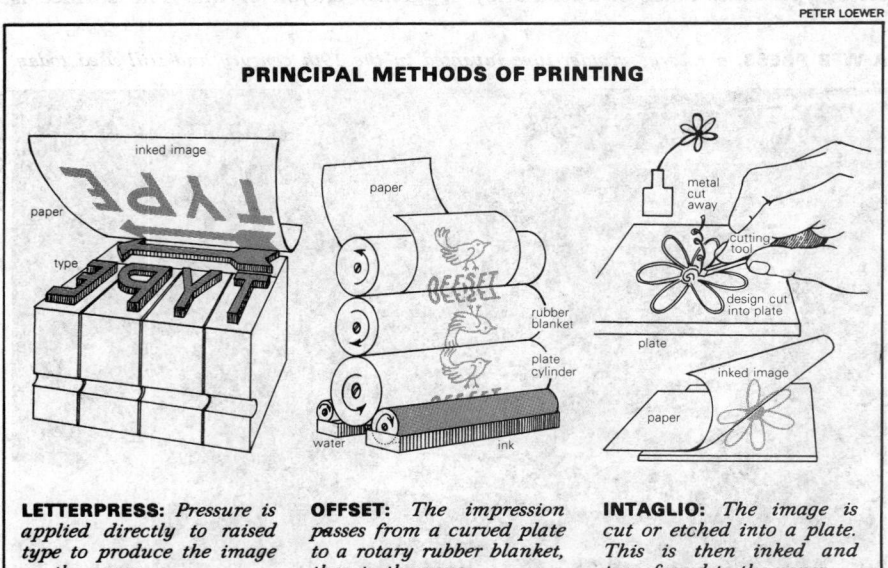

PETER LOEWER

PRINCIPAL METHODS OF PRINTING

LETTERPRESS: *Pressure is applied directly to raised type to produce the image on the paper.*

OFFSET: *The impression passes from a curved plate to a rotary rubber blanket, then to the paper.*

INTAGLIO: *The image is cut or etched into a plate. This is then inked and transferred to the paper.*

A related typesetting machine is the *Monotype,* first produced in 1897. It casts individual letters from matrices and then justifies these pieces into properly spaced lines by means of a counting system. Monotype composition is commonly used for printing texts containing large numbers of mathematical or other symbols.

In the 20th century, printing and composition have moved away from a reliance on metal type and mechanical operations toward high-speed photographic and electronic methods. Few, and sometimes no, moving parts are involved in using these methods, thus reducing the power necessary to print and making the reproduction of texts and illustrations faster and cheaper.

Electronics enables printing to occur at sites far removed from those where original type copy is prepared. For example, *facsimile transmission* enables print to be broken down by a sensor into electronic signals that can then be sent across the country by electric networks such as the telephone system. At the receiving terminal, the electrical impulses are reconverted to letters of readable type. This copy can be photographed and duplicated. Facsimile transmission allows newspapers to update stories at the last minute, before printing begins.

Composition has also been increasingly automated. Although many small presses continue to assemble type manually, most major printing operations make use of mechanical or phototypesetting methods.

After 1929, composition could be guided by remote control, replacing a Linotype operator. Copy to be printed was typed out on paper tape, with letters, capitals, and proper spacing determined by perforations in the tape. A translator device in front of the Linotype machine "read" this tape and ordered the release of the appropriate type pieces.

By the 1950's, the use of electronics further increased the speed of composition. A computer could scan the paper tape and control which typefaces were to be used, where words were to be divided at the ends of lines, and what the exact length of the lines would be. Using this method, 300,000 letters could be readied for print in one hour.

In the 1960's, magnetic tape replaced perforated paper tape. This raised the production of characters to $3\frac{1}{2}$ million per hour, for printing on offset presses. Electronic scanners performed Optical Character Recognition (OCR), reading copy directly from a typewriter and recording it on computer tape. This procedure eliminated the time-consuming task of putting printed material on paper tape.

Correcting copy has been facilitated by video-display terminals—VDTs. These resemble television screens with keyboards. They print out copy stored in the computer for possible changes or additions prior to printing. The corrected copy is fed back into the computer and then transmitted to a phototypesetting machine, thus saving much time and effort.

Photocomposition. Photocomposition machines have had a significant impact on modern printing. These devices go beyond the Linotype and Monotype methods by replacing lead-type slugs with images of print on photographic film. These films can be exposed and developed at very high speeds. Print is projected from the film onto light-sensitive paper or plates for offset printing.

One of the most sophisticated versions is the *Photon* machine, invented in France. This electronic setup makes use of an electric typewriter, a computer (for justifying lines), and a photographic apparatus for converting stored signals into film. Copy reproduced from film is the product of photolithography.

A photocomposition machine developed in 1959, the Lumizip 900, has the capacity to photograph entire lines at once, by scanning. It is controlled by magnetic tape and is able to compose 2 million characters per hour. It was first used to print the *Index Medicus,* a 600-page text. This job was completed in twelve hours; on a typecasting machine, it would have taken a full year.

Photocomposition has drastically reduced the mechanical operations involved in printing. A technique invented in the 1960's eliminated all moving parts by freeing itself from the use of light and prisms to scan the matrices. A cathode ray tube is activated by magnetic tape to release a stream of electrons. The electrons analyze the image matrix of each letter, projecting another stream of electrons onto light-sensitized photographic film. This process is based on the same principle as is television.

The *Digiset* is an advanced variation of the cathode ray scanner. It keeps the matrices on a magnetic memory and does not need to scan them. The Digiset machine can produce 30 million characters per hour, or ten times the number possible using an earlier electronic scanner.

The Digiset 50T2 can analyze an entire page of newspaper type, scanning and composing photographically by means of a binary code. It can yield 10 million characters in an hour.

To prepare copy for photocomposition, the text is first typed on machines that produce letters as they will appear in print. A page layout is made by cutting the typed text into strips and arranging these into a mockup of the printed page. The assembled page is then photographed. Photographs are also made of line drawings and halftone photographs or illustrations accompanying the written text.

Printing Today

Today the printed word, as well as pictures, can be reproduced in vast quantities and transmitted around the world in a very short period of time. Information is available to us in print in forms ranging from billboard advertisements to computerized telephone bills. Print has become our most abundant source of data, with books published in the thousands and magazines and other periodicals appearing by the hundreds of thousands each year.

But printed materials are not our sole source of information. This century has witnessed a strong challenge to print's primary role in our culture. Starting with the telegraph in the mid-19th century, telecommunication has become a competitor of the print media in supplying information at instantaneous speeds. These electronic media have the advantage of being able to transmit sounds and moving pictures. The invention of radio and television has made it possible to convey aspects of reality that the printed page or picture cannot. There are indications that these media are gradually supplanting printed materials, just as the art of printing replaced oral communications as a primary means of imparting information.

But printing will retain a valuable function in our culture. It remains the sole means of providing the general public with information that can be studied and absorbed in detail. Printed materials remain more accessible than information transmitted by radio or television. This encyclopedia is one example of how the wide use of printing still plays an important part in informing us about the world we live in.

—John V.H. Dippel

SOME PROOFREADERS' MARKS

Take out letters or words.
He marked the proof.

Start new paragraph.
reading. The printer marked

Set in lower case type.
He Marked the proof.

Transpose letters or words.
He the proof marked.

Let stand as set.
He marked the proof.

Insert comma.
Yes he marked the proof.

Reset in Italic type.
He marked the proof.

Use capital letter
he marked the proof.

LANGUAGE STUDIES

There are many different ways of looking at a language. We may look at where it comes from or where it is headed. We may wonder how it differs from other languages. We may be fascinated by its inner workings or its external written form. It may be a living language or a dead one. It may be the language of a culture similar to our own, or it may belong to a culture so different from ours that we are forced to reexamine our notions of what language can and cannot express. Since people look at language in many different ways, there are many different terms that have to do with the study of language.

Linguistics. The generally accepted term used to describe the study of language in all its various aspects is *linguistics,* also called the science of language. The word linguistics itself is derived from the Latin word *lingua,* meaning both "tongue" and that which the tongue produces, "language." The first recorded use of the word linguistics in English, according to the *Oxford English Dictionary,* occurs in 1837. There was a surge of interest in the spoken word, and not just in its written form, at about that time. This was a more radical development than it might seem at first glance.

Philology. Language study before the mid 1800's was largely study of the classics, particularly of ancient Greek and Latin classics. Since ancient Greek and Latin were no longer spoken languages, only their literary form was studied. One term used for such study was and still is, *philology.* This word comes from the Greek *phílos* (love) and *lógos* (word), that is, "love of the word." Today, scholars tend to use the word philology in relation to the study of older languages. It is therefore considered a branch of the broader study of linguistics.

Etymology. A term that sometimes gets confused with linguistics or philology is *etymology.* Etymology is the study of how individual words evolve, both in form and meaning. For example, the Old English version of the Lord's Prayer contains the verb

CULVER PICTURES

MANUSCRIPTS *written and illustrated by hand preserve the languages spoken by our ancestors. This manuscript shows a portrait of Geoffrey Chaucer (died 1400).*

syle, meaning "give." The verb does not survive in Modern English with that meaning, but it is the ancestor of Modern English *sell.* Etymological analysis allows us to understand how this word changed, both in its form and its meaning; but no word changes in isolation. Words must live within the structure of the language of which they are a part. Etymology, therefore—with its emphasis on individual words—is a branch of linguistics. Interesting and important as it may be, it is incomplete by itself.

Semantics. Fascination with meanings has given rise to another branch of linguistics, *semantics.* Semantics is concerned with why and how words signify things. The origin of the word semantics, the Greek *sēmaínein* (to signify, show by a sign), reflects the object of the field. Semantics considers the historical development of meaning in the words of a language, such as the change in *sell* noted above, but it also deals with larger issues: the theoretical limits

and possibilities of meaning in language at any given time. Semantics has attracted the interest of logicians, mathematicians, sociologists, and psychologists. These specialists have brought many new tools and points of view to language study.

Grammar. Perhaps the most confusing term we run across—probably because we take it so for granted—is the word *grammar.* This word is derived from the Greek *grammatikós* (pertaining to letters), although its modern definitions do not have to do primarily with letters.

In general, grammar refers to the formal side of language, as opposed to the world of meaning, with which *etymology* and *semantics* are concerned. When we are young, grammar is the study of the elements that make up a sentence, and indeed this is one of the most important things we learn in what is sometimes called grammar school. But the word grammar can also refer to the analysis of individual sounds; this is sometimes called *phonology*. When grammar refers to the prefixes and suffixes that often define a word's function, the study is called *morphology*.

In the 20th century, we come across the term *transformational grammar*, which has to do with the underlying structure or grammar of a language and the transformations that structure goes through to produce the actual sentences we utter. In contrast, an old term like *comparative grammar* also survives. This is a name for the study of the similarities in form among related languages. The important thing to bear in mind in all this is that grammar does not just mean the process of labeling nouns, verbs, predicates, subordinate clauses, etc. Rather, its wide range of meanings reminds us just how complex language is and how many elements there are to analyze and understand.

Other specialties. There are many other specialties in modern language study. For example, *psycholinguistics* concerns itself with the relationship between the human mind and the way it uses language. *Sociolinguistics* focuses on the ways in which the makeup of a society affects the language spoken by that society. One could go on and on listing various branches of language study, but the important thing for us to keep in mind is that language is a complex phenomenon. Whether we wish to analyze a given sentence that we utter or the long-term history of a language, there are many factors to be considered. What is the structure of the language being considered? What are the pressures in the society from which it stems? How do individual sounds interact with whole words, and words with sentences, and sen-

NOAM CHOMSKY'S *ideas about language revolutionized linguistics in the 1960's.*

tences with groups of sentences, and so on? In other words, every factor—large and small—must be considered. Defining our terms helps us focus on each of these factors in our pursuit of understanding language and its history.

The Languages of the World

For two centuries, students of language have been seeking to trace the relationship of a given language to other languages. One way of doing this is to look for systematic similarities among languages. Consider the list of words for the numbers 1, 2, and 3 in the following table. English, Old High German, Old Norse, and Gothic present forms that are very like one another. These in turn show some likeness to the forms in Latin, Greek, Old Irish, and Sanskrit (the ancient language of India). But none of these languages seems to have any similarity to Chinese and Japanese, nor do the last two present forms that are similar to each other. Thus, we may suspect from this evidence that English, German, Norse, and Gothic belong to a single family, that is, that they all come from some common ancestor language, just as brothers and sisters come from the same parents. As we will see later, this ancestor is called Germanic. We may also sus-

THE NUMBERS "ONE," "TWO" AND "THREE" IN SELECTED LANGUAGES

Modern English	Old English	Old High German	Old Norse	Gothic	Latin	Greek	Old Irish	Sanskrit	Chinese	Japanese
one	ān	ein	einn	ains	ūnus	heis	ōen	ēkas	i	hitotsu
two	twā	zwei	tveir	twai	duo	dúŏ	dāu	dvāú	erh	futatsu
three	thrie	driĕ	thrir	thri	trēs	treis	tri	tráyas	san	mittsu

pect that this group of languages belongs to a larger family that includes Latin, Greek, Irish, and Sanskrit. Indeed, all of these languages are thought to belong to a family called Indo–European, which we will examine in more detail below. As for Chinese and Japanese, the evidence suggests that they belong to other language families.

The implication here is that all languages may be organized into different

family groupings. Apparently, a particular language may produce "children" in time and die out itself. The family relationships may be shown in a diagram that resembles a family tree. The more distant the common ancestor of two languages, the more remote their similarities become, just as second cousins and cousins are less likely to resemble each other than brothers and sisters.

ALPHABET SOUP: *Unfamiliar letters in these Yiddish, Greek, and Serbo-Croatian papers keep us from even sounding out the words.*

A language creates "children" gradually. At first, its variant forms are enough alike to be mutually understood and are called *dialects*. But if there is little or no contact between two communities with the same language, the language will develop in different directions until, finally, when the communities can no longer understand one another, we say they speak two distinct languages. In fact, there is a fine line between a dialect and a separate language, and in the end they are simply two stages in a single process.

Language Families

A brief survey of the major language groupings will help show the position of English. We have already mentioned the Indo–European family, of which English is a member, and we will look at it in more detail below. Other important families include the following.

The *Afro-Asiatic* family includes the Semitic languages of the Middle East, among them Hebrew and Arabic, as well as Egyptian and lesser known languages such as Berber (the language of the North African tribe of that name) and Chad. There is a purely African family known as *Niger-Congo*, which includes languages such as Swahili and Zulu. There is also an extensive grouping in Asia called *Altaic,* deriving its name from the Altai Mountains, which stretch through central Asia from the Soviet Union into Mongolia and finally to China. This family includes Turkish in the west and Mongolian in the east.

The language family of Southeast Asia is called *Sino-Tibetan.* This family includes the languages of China, Tibet, Burma, and other lands in that area. *Malayo–Polynesian* stretches from Indonesia and Malaysia out into the Pacific as far east as Hawaii.

In Europe, we find two languages—Finnish and Hungarian—that are related to one another but are not part of the Indo–European family. In fact, there are languages that seem to defy classification throughout the world. Two examples are Basque, spoken by the people of that name who inhabit the Pyrenees Mountains of France and Spain, and Japanese.

The Americas had several large and complex language families, but many of those languages are no longer spoken. The Europeans conquered and settled most of the two continents, and their languages (especially English, Spanish, Portuguese, and French) replaced the native languages. Those surviving to this day include Eskimo in the far north and

ARABIC, *spoken in many Mideastern and North African countries, uses an alphabet of consonants only. Arabic is related to Hebrew.*

Quechua in Peru and Bolivia. Some American Indian languages also survive and provide interesting examples of just how different languages can be. For example, Fox—the language of the tribe of that name—does not show the basic differentiation between noun and verb, a concept that is very difficult for a speaker of English to grasp.

But it is with English and its history that we are primarily concerned here. To be sure, it would be interesting to know how many of the world's language families are derived from the same source. Perhaps the families of English and, say, Chinese were once related at some distant moment when language itself first arose. But the evidence we have will not take us back that far. In fact, the earliest stages of linguistic history will likely remain a mystery to us. Even for the Indo-European language, we have no written record, and must reconstruct the language from later evidence. These educated guesses give us a *prehistory* for languages in the family, including English. Let us begin by taking a closer look at the Indo-European relatives of English.

Indo-European

We can see from the corresponding number words (one, two, and three) discussed above that English is related to languages spoken as far east as India and throughout much of Europe. Because of this range, this language family has acquired the name Indo-European. Linguistic evidence suggests that there was a people or tribe who spoke a language that is the ancestor of this large language family. But who were these Indo-Europeans? Where and when did they live? Unfortunately, the answers to these questions are unknown and are likely to remain so. But various pieces

of evidence allow us to narrow down the possible answers.

For example, the Indo-European languages have no common word for "sea." Nor do they share common words for "olive tree" or "tiger." On the other hand, the descendant languages do have related words for "birch" and "fir" and for "bear" and "wolf." The word "snow" is another example of a distinct word shared by all the languages. This type of evidence leads scholars to suspect that the Indo-Europeans did not live on the seacoast and that their homeland was far enough north to have had fir trees, bears, and snow. Of course, all this still leaves many possibilities, but the best guess is that the Indo-Europeans lived in the steppes of today's U.S.S.R.

Scholars have tried to arrive at a date for Indo–European by *glottochronology,* the analysis of the rate at which languages change. There are so many variable factors in such a study that the answers are far from certain. But we estimate that Indo-European was spoken about 4500 B.C.

In the centuries since then, the Indo–European family has spread and grown. A brief tour of the language map in historical times will show just how far. Let us begin in the west of Europe and work our way east.

Celtic. All the way at the western end of Europe we find the Celtic family of languages. The Celts originally lived in Europe or Western Asia, but a large contingent migrated across the English Channel to England and Ireland. Others remained in Europe. Little survives of Continental Celtic—the language as it developed in Europe. We have a few inscriptions written in a language called Gaulish, evidently the language spoken by the Celts when the Roman Julius Caesar fought in Gaul (present-day France and Germany). There was also a dialect of this branch spoken in Spain in the 15th century A.D. called Celtiberian (the Celtic of the Iberian peninsula) but little survives of this dialect. Most of the early forms that remain—and all of the modern Celtic languages—are of the Insular branch, the form that developed in Britain and Ireland. The earliest attested form is the language called Old Irish, the ancestor of Modern Irish or what is sometimes called Gaelic. A rich literature survives in Old Irish. Some speakers of Old Irish moved to the Isle of Man (their language, Manx, was spoken until the early 1900's). Others migrated north to Scotland and their language, Scottish Gaelic, survives to this day in the north and west of Scotland. Welsh, spoken in Wales, in the western part of Britain, is another Celtic language that still flourishes. Still another, Cornish, died out in England in the 1600's. Other Celtic speakers moved across the English Channel to Brittany (now a province of France). Their language is called Breton and it survives to this day.

Italic. Before the time of Christ there were several related languages spoken on the Italian peninsula—Oscan, Umbrian, and Feliscan. As Rome grew to be an important power, its language, which we know as Latin, became predominant, and the other languages died out. Eventually Latin died, too, as a spoken language, but it was the parent of many modern languages including French, Italian, Spanish, Portuguese, and Romanian.

It is interesting to consider the history of the Italic family when imagining what Indo–European might originally have been. When we think of the Romance languages, we tend to think of the vast influence of Latin and the Roman Empire. But several hundred years before the birth of Christ, Latin was simply one of several equally limited languages spoken in Italy, and Italic itself only part of the much larger Indo–European family. In a similar way, Indo–European itself must have once been only a small dialect of a larger family. Thus, we should not be fooled by its vast spread. Like Latin, Indo–European, too, must have started as a language spoken in a very limited area that happened to spread out because of developments that are lost to history.

Greek. Farther east, we come to the Greek branch of Indo–European. The first evidence of Greek is the so-called Linear B tablets of the 12th century B.C., deciphered only in the early 1950's. We begin to find extensive texts in Greek in the 8th century B.C., the date of the famous poems of Homer, the *Iliad* and the *Odyssey*. Though Greek shows clear traces of several distinct dialects from its earliest periods, these dialects were evi-

INDO-EUROPEAN LANGUAGES

FAMILY (prehistoric)	Branch	Early Historic Languages	Modern Languages
BALTO-SLAVIC	Slavic		
	West		Polish Slovak Czech
	South	Old Church Slavonic	Slovene Serbo-Croatian Bulgarian
	East		Russian Ukrainian
	Baltic	Old Prussian	Latvian Lithuanian
GERMANIC	West	Anglo-Frisian	English Frisian
		Low German	Plattdeutsch Dutch Flemish Afrikaans
		High German	German Yiddish
	North	Old Norse	Icelandic Norwegian Danish Swedish
	East	Gothic	
CELTIC	Insular	Gaelic	Irish Scottish Gaelic (Manx)
		Britannic	Welsh (Cornish) Breton
	Continental	Gaulish	
ITALIC	Osco-Umbrian	Oscan Umbrian	
	Latino-Feliscan	Feliscan	
		Latin	Portuguese Spanish French Italian Romanian (others)
GREEK		Classical Greek	Modern Greek
ARMENIAN			Armenian
ALBANIAN			Albanian
ANATOLIAN		Luvian Palaic Hittite	
INDO-IRANIAN	Iranian	Old Persian Avestan	Persian Kurdish (others)
	Indic	Sanskrit	Hindi Bengali (others)
TOCHARIAN		Tocharian	

dently always comprehensible to one another. Indeed, there was always enough contact among the various city-states of the Greek isles so that separate languages never developed. Rather, after the classical period of the 5th century B.C., a common dialect became predominant; this gave rise to what we call Modern Greek.

Armenian and Albanian.

As we move farther east we come across two more separate branches. One is Armenian, the earliest form of which shows up before 1000 A.D. Its modern descendant is the official language of the Armenian Soviet Republic. Some scholars claim that the few traces of the languages called Thracian and Phrygian belong to this family, too. But so little remains of these languages that it is difficult to tell. A second branch of Indo–European in this area is Albanian, which first shows up only in 1462 and remains a language unto itself. It has been suggested that another scantily attested language—Illyrian—is related to Albanian, but in this case, too, there is little evidence to go on.

Anatolian.

In Asia Minor, we arrive at the earliest attested branch of Indo–European, Anatolian, the main language of which is Hittite. It was only in the 20th century that the tablets containing Hittite were deciphered and discovered to be Indo–European. The texts themselves date back almost to 2000 B.C. The contents of these texts range from mythological rituals to bureaucratic lists, and include records of Hittite dealings with Egypt that are also mentioned in the Bible. Other Anatolian languages include Lydian, Lycian, Luvian, and Palaic.

Indo–Iranian.

As we move farther into Asia, we come across the vast Indo–Iranian branch. The Iranian side of the family includes its oldest form, Avestan, in which we have the ancient hymns of the prophet Zoroaster, and a whole group of modern languages, among which are Kurdish and Persian. Speakers of Indic languages moved even farther east and south into the Indian subcontinent. The oldest version of this family is a form of Sanskrit called Vedic, the language of the Rig Vedic hymns dating before 1000 B.C. These hymns, the central holy text of Hinduism, are recited from memory in their original form to this very day. Indeed, it was Vedic Sanskrit—which has many obvious similarities to Greek—that led Sir William Jones, a British jurist, to suggest in 1786 the idea of a prehistoric Indo–European language. Modern languages from this branch include Hindi and Ben-

gali, among many others. One need only compare, for example, English and Hindi to see how different two related languages can become in the course of time.

Tocharian.

There is one other Indo–European language attested in Asia, only discovered in this century. It is called Tocharian, and our only texts date from the 7th and 8th centuries A.D. in the area now part of China's Sinkiang Province. There are no original texts in Tocharian, only translations of Buddhist tracts. One interesting fact about Tocharian is that it seems to belong, according to its linguistic features, to the western branch of Indo–European, even though it was apparently spoken in an isolated area thousands of miles to the east of Europe. Indeed, it is always important to keep in mind that linguistic affinity is not a geographic concept. In a similar way, such non-Indo–European languages as Basque, Finnish, and Hungarian are isolated in a sea of Indo–European languages.

Balto–Slavic.

We can now head north and start circling back toward Western Europe for the Balto–Slavic family of languages. The Baltic side consists of the modern languages Lithuanian and Latvian. Lithuanian is attested in an earlier form called Old Lithuanian; there is also an early form of this branch called Old Prussian. The Slavic family falls into three categories. East Slavic is represented primarily by Russian, but it also includes Byelorussian and Ukrainian, the languages of those two Soviet Republics. South Slavic appears in an early form called Old Church Slavonic, from the 10th and 11th centuries A.D., and in the modern languages Bulgarian, Serbo–Croatian, and Slovene. West Slavic consists primarily of Polish, Czech, and Slovak.

Germanic.

Finally, as we move farther back west, we come to the Germanic family, of which English is a member. It is to this branch that we now turn our attention.

Germanic

In the 19th century, the German scholar Jacob Grimm—while he was still working on his collection of stories now known as *Grimm's Fairy Tales*—noticed that what made the Germanic branch of Indo-European so distinctive was a series of consonant shifts. These changes, he pointed out, were shared by all the Germanic languages, but not by any other Indo-European language. This phenomenon, called *Grimm's Law,* helps explain different forms of many words in English, since later in its history English borrowed words from other Indo-European languages that had not undergone the shift. For example, Grimm noticed that where a *p* appears in Greek, Latin, and other Indo-European languages, an *f* appears in Germanic. Thus, English *father* corresponds to Latin *pater,* English *foot* to Greek *pod-,* and English *fish* to Latin *pisces.* Later on, English borrows these words from Greek and Latin, but at a time when Grimm's Law had stopped functioning. As a result, English is filled with pairs of words such as *fatherly* and *paternal,* and *foot doctor* and *podiatrist.* The table of numerals above suggests additional instances of this process involving other sounds. For example, the sound *d* became *t* in Germanic according to Grimm's Law, thus leaving us with a pair such as native *two* but borrowed *dual.* Similarly, *t* became *th,* giving us native *three* but the borrowed prefix *tri-.*

Germanic also developed a fixed stress. A word like *friend* can be made into *friendly, friendliest,* or *friendship,* and the stress remains on the first syllable. In their oldest forms, the other Indo-European languages had a variable pitch accent. It is, therefore, possible to distinguish by sound and stress native English words from later borrowed words. The *father* in *fatherly* is a native Germanic word, and thus has initial stress. In contrast, *paternal* has a *p* and stress on the second syllable, and we can be quite sure that *paternal* is not native to English.

FOOT AND POD *come from the same prehistoric root. Jacob Grimm (shown with his brother) demonstrated how sound shifts made them differ.*

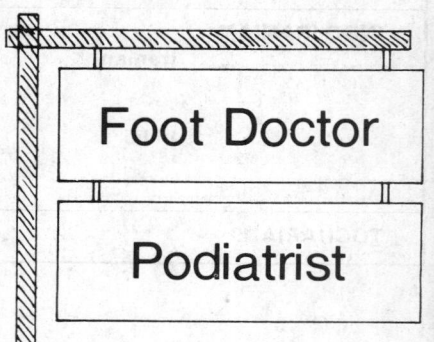

East Germanic. As for Germanic itself, it falls into three groups. The earliest to appear in any written text is East Germanic, the language called Gothic, attested in the middle of the 4th century A.D. At that time, a local bishop evidently decided that his missionary efforts would have greater success if there was a translation of the Bible in the language of the Goths, whom he was attempting to convert. As a result, the one text we have in Gothic is a selection from his translation of the Bible. By the end of the 7th century, Gothic had evidently died out, though a few individual words of a dialect called Crimean Gothic were recorded in the 1500's.

North Germanic. The other two branches of Germanic, North and West, survive to this day. North Germanic—which includes the languages of Scandinavia—appears around the 9th century in a form usually called Old Norse, though this language shows up in several different dialects. Old Norse literature has left us a rich array of sagas and myths that include stories about the Germanic gods after whom some of our days of the week are named. For example, the chief god is named Odin (or Woden as in Wednes-day); another important god is Týr (Tues-day); and a third is Thor (Thurs-day). The most important goddess was named Frigg (Fri-day). There are two main branches of North Germanic. That of the east consists of Danish and Swedish, while the western branch includes Norwegian, Faeroese,

Tyr	→	Tuesday
Woden	→	Wednesday
Thor	→	Thursday
Frigg	→	Friday

IN TUESDAY THROUGH FRIDAY *we use the names of Germanic gods long forgotten.*

and Icelandic. The last of these, Icelandic, is an interesting example of a language that developed very differently than English. Because of the isolation of Iceland, this language has changed very little in the last thousand years. By contrast, English has changed very rapidly.

West Germanic. The third branch of Germanic is called West Germanic. One branch of this group is the German branch, consisting of Low and High German. Low German (spoken mainly in the lowlands) survives today in Dutch, Flemish, Afrikaans (the language taken to Africa by the Dutch who settled there), and a language spoken in the northern lowlands of Germany called Plattdeutsch (*platt* means "low," and *Deutsch* is the German word for "German"). High German, or Hochdeutsch, attested from around 1000 A.D., is the ancestor of Modern German as well as of the language called Yiddish. At first glance, German does

not look as closely related to English as it is, since the consonants of High German went through another series of shifts. The result of this change is that many German words begin with different consonants than their English equivalents. But if we look closely, we can see that the differences are systematic. For example, in the Lord's Prayer, the word *thin* ("thine" in Early Modern English) corresponds to Old High German *dīn*. If we then look at our list of numbers, we can notice that another word beginning with *th* in English, *thrīe*, has a *d* in Old High German *drīe*. There are many such pairs in English and German. Other examples include *then* ∾ Ger. *dann; thing* ∾ Ger. *ding; thick* ∾ Ger. *dick; thunder* ∾ Ger. *donner.* The *th* in English is a *d* in German. This kind of systematic and consistent similarity helps establish the relationship between two languages.

The other branch of West Germanic is usually called Anglo-Frisian. Frisian is a language that was spoken on the Baltic Coast as far back as the 900's A.D. and is still spoken today in the Dutch province of Friesland and in certain areas of the western part of Germany. From this same area along the Baltic, tribes closely related to the Frisians—the Angles, the Saxons and the Jutes—sailed to England and settled there around 450 A.D. The language spoken by these people, called Anglo-Saxon or Old English, is the earliest form of English proper. With it, we can move out of prehistory and examine the history of English.

English

When the Angles, Saxons, and Jutes came to England, their dialect of West Germanic must have been quite similar to that of the Germans. Indeed, early Old English was fairly close to Old High German. The striking thing about English in the 1500 years since its beginning is how much it has changed—far more than any of its related languages.

Why Languages Change

Why has English changed so much? There are two major reasons for a language to change, and both help explain the development of English.

Foreign influence. When two cultures come into contact with each other, their languages tend to reflect

this contact. New words—additions to a language's vocabulary—are often the first sign of foreign influence. Traders need common terms for their bartering. Missionaries often introduce new religious terms. If a people or tribe conquers another, new words having to do with government, law, and social relations are often brought into the language of those conquered.

English has had a rich history on all these fronts. The Anglo-Saxon settlers immediately faced the problem of coexisting with the Celts, particularly the Welsh, who already inhabited England. Indeed, many place names in England are Celtic names. Christian missionaries soon arrived in England and many religious words from the Latin spoken in the church entered the language. In the 9th and 10th centuries, many Scandinavians settled along the east coast of England and intermingled with the English who proceeded to borrow many basic words from these new immigrants.

The most important event for English, however, was the Norman Conquest of 1066. In the years that followed, hundreds of French words were borrowed into English. In fact, for more than a century, it appeared that Norman French might become the language of England. The Normans finally lost their influence, and English reasserted itself. But new influences continued to change it. The European Renaissance, with its emphasis on the art and learning of classical Greece and Rome, brought new borrowings from ancient Greek and Latin.

In America, borrowing continued. The early American settlers borrowed terms from the North American natives they met when they arrived. In the northeast, there were borrowings from the neighboring French, in the southwest from the Spanish. Immigrants coming to America brought words from many of the languages of the world.

We can see, therefore, the remarkable mixture that makes up the word stock of the English language. Indeed, English has as rich and varied a vocabulary as any language in the world, precisely because of an enormous amount of borrowing. Other languages did less borrowing. For example, German borrowed few words from neighboring France; but English borrowed hundreds because of the Norman Conquest.

Structural changes. The second important reason for a language to change is much harder to grasp. Changes in the structure of a language are interrelated and seem to have a power of their own, continuing over many centuries.

We noted above that one of the most important changes that occurred in Germanic was the movement to stress on the first syllable of the root in all words. When heavy stress is placed on the beginning of a word or phrase, pronunciation of the rest of the word is weakened. For example, in speech, the phrase *going to* often sounds like *gonna.*

A similar process occurred in Early Germanic, which originally had a complex system of endings, or inflections, that conveyed a word's function and meaning within a sentence. For example, if a noun was the subject of a sentence it had one ending; if it was the object of a verb it had another; if it was the indirect object, still another; and so on. Over the course of centuries, these endings became weaker and weaker, however, because of the initial stress, until they finally disappeared. Very few remain in English. For nouns, we still use an *s* to signify that a word is plural rather than singular. For verbs, only the *s* of the third person singular (for example, *I speak, he speaks*) remains. Old English had many more such endings, but very few survive.

Heavy stress on the initial syllable of roots caused a gradual loss of word endings. Loss of these endings made certain sentences hard to understand because the function of some words was not clear. To solve this problem, English came to rely on the word order of a sentence to show word function and developed a different way of showing the tense and mood of verbs through use of *auxiliary* or *function words* such as *have, will, might,* and *could.*

This whole process illustrates how various structural changes in a language are interrelated and how such changes can alter a language in important ways. In contrast to English, changes in German took place much more slowly. Although endings in German, too, became weaker, many more survived, and the modern language still relies more heavily on the endings of words than English does, and less heavily on word order.

Another example of structural change concerns the *-ed* ending of verbs. English had inherited a system from Indo-European in which the past tense of a verb was formed by changing the vowel sound of the root. We can still see examples of this process in such forms as *sing ∼ sang ∼ sung; ride ∼ rode ∼ ridden; freeze ∼ froze;* and *tear ∼ tore.* Note that each of these sets presents us with different changes of the vowel sounds.

Originally, all of these verbs had the same pattern of change to show the difference between past and present. But this system began to break down. Many of the vowel sounds in the language began shifting, and the more they changed, the harder it was to tell a verb's past form from its present. In this situation, *-ed* came to the rescue. It was an ending that showed the past tense in less common verbs. Now it began to be used even in common verbs. Thus, the language was forced to keep this particular ending to avoid confusion. In fact, *-ed* continues to replace the older way of making past forms of verbs. Today many people are unsure whether to use *dove* (the old form) or *dived* (the new form) for the past of *dive.*

So English is a mixture on many different levels. It has a mixed vocabulary, consisting not only of native Germanic words but also of words borrowed under many circumstances. It also has a mixed set of linguistic changes, some of which seem almost contradictory.

With this overview in mind, we can step back and look at the specific developments—from old to middle to modern times—that created the mixture we call English.

Old English

Old English, as we saw above, is the language spoken by the Germanic tribes in England from their arrival before 500 A.D. until after the Norman Conquest in 1066. This is a period of over 600 years. Much can change in such a long stretch of time, and much did. Indeed, many of the changes that began in the Old English period continue even today.

Old English differs from Modern English in several important ways. Chief among these differences is the use of endings to indicate a word's function within a sentence. Modern English preserves only a few such endings, such as the *s* added to make a noun plural (sing. *land,* pl. *lands*) or the *s* used with a third person singular verb (I *land,* he *lands*). In Old English, many forms of nouns, adjectives, and verbs received such endings. Notice the endings on the words for "our" (*ūre*), "are" (*eart*), "heaven" (*heofonum*), "name" (*nama*), etc., in the Lord's Prayer.

One effect of this feature is that strict patterns of word order, such as those we use in Modern English, are not necessary. The endings themselves tell us whether a word is noun, verb, subject, direct object, etc. Again, we may use an example from the Old English version of the Lord's Prayer: *ūrne gedæghwāmlīcan hlāf syle ūs tō dæg* means "give us this day our daily bread." But the order is all wrong from our point of view: it says "our daily bread give us today." We are tempted to assume that *hlāf* (Modern *loaf,* but with the meaning "bread") must be the subject of the sentence. A speaker of Old English would not make this mistake, because the endings of "our" (*ūrne*) and "daily" (*gedæghwāmlīcan*) tell him that "bread" is the object of the sentence, regardless of its position in it. Indeed, this system of endings allowed speakers of Old English to use word order for other purposes. For example, "our daily bread"—the central idea of this sentence—is further emphasized by being placed at the beginning. But if we were to say "our daily bread give us today," the result would be merely awkward and confusing, since it would violate our notion of proper word order.

As the Old English period progressed, some of these endings became weaker. The weakening process had already begun before English split off from its Germanic relatives. We will see that this gradual loss of endings continued through Middle English times and has continued to the present day.

The second major difference between Old and Modern English has to do with vocabulary. When the Angles, Saxons, and Jutes arrived in England in the 5th century, most of their words were from their native Germanic. But just as they found England accessible by sea, so did others throughout the Old English period, in particular Christian missionaries from Rome and Scandinavian raiders whom we often call Vikings. Many of these missionaries settled in England, establishing monasteries that became famous throughout Europe in the 8th century. Also, increasing numbers of Scandinavians decided to settle down, especially in the 9th and 10th centuries, along the east coast of England.

As is often the case with languages, Old English borrowed many terms from its new speakers. Religious terms such as *devil, priest, presbyter*—most of which are either Greek or Latin in origin—were borrowed from their new Christian neighbors. At first, Old English tried to make up words for the new faith with its own vocabulary. In Old English texts we find a native term like *hēahfaeder,* literally "high Father," to refer to the head of Christendom. But we also find its borrowed equivalent *pāpa* (pope), which eventually won out.

THE LORD'S PRAYER IN ENGLISH

Old English
> Fæder ūre
> thū the eart on heofonum,
> sī thīn nama gehālgod;
> tobecume thīn rīce;
> gewurthe thīn willa on eorthan swā swā on heofonum;
> ūrne gedæghwāmlīcan hlāf syle ūs tō dæg;
> and forgyf ūs ūrne gyltas, swā swā wē forgyfath ūrum gyltendum;
> and ne gelæd thū ūs on costnunge,
> ac ālȳs ūs of yfele. Sōthlīce.

Middle English
> Oure fadir
> that art in heuenes,
> halewid be thi name;
> thi kyngdoom come to;
> be thi wille don in erthe as in heuene;
> gyue to vs this dai oure breed ouer othir substaunce;
> and forgyue to vs oure dettis, as we forgyuen to oure dettouris;
> and lede vs not in to temptacioun,
> but delyuere vs fro yuel. Amen.

Early Modern English
> Our father
> which art in heaven,
> hallowed be thy name;
> thy kingdom come;
> thy will be done on earth as it is in heaven;
> give us this day our daily bread;
> and forgive us our debts as we forgive our debtors;
> and lead us not into temptation,
> but deliver us from evil. Amen.

Modern English
> Our Father
> in heaven,
> hallowed be your Name,
> your kingdom come,
> your will be done, on earth as in heaven.
> Give us today our daily bread.
> Forgive us our sins as we forgive those who sin against us.
> Save us from the time of trial,
> and deliver us from evil. Amen.

Most such old native terms were replaced by borrowed words.

The relationship to the Scandinavians was of a different nature. The language of these foreigners, often called Old Norse, was similar to Old English. Over several centuries the two peoples mingled socially until they were indistinguishable, and the changes in Old English reflect this commingling. Many everyday words were borrowed from Old Norse. For example, such basic words as *sister* and *sky, give* (a new pronunciation) and *take, skirt* as opposed to its Old English equivalent *shirt,* and perhaps even the plural pronouns *they, them,* etc.

Other borrowings during the Old English period are more isolated. We can note borrowings from the neighboring Celts, especially for place names such as *Kent, Dover,* and *Bryn Mawr* (from Welsh *bryn* "hill" and *mawr* "great"). There are also nonreligious borrowings from Latin like *cheese, copper, mile,* and *pound,* terms no doubt borrowed as a result of commercial transactions. It is even possible that some of these words may have been borrowed by the Anglo-Saxons before they came to England.

Old English reached its height during the 700's and 800's. With the death of the most powerful Old English ruler, King Alfred, in 899, the government became weaker, and the Anglo-Saxon kingdom was besieged by attacks from within and without. With less central government, there was less communication between one region and another, and so the language began to develop in different directions in different parts of Britain. To the east and north, there were more borrowings from the Scandinavian invaders, for example.

In the middle of the 11th century, there was an invasion of England on a far grander scale. William of Normandy (later known as the Conqueror) defeated the English King Harold at the battle of Hastings in 1066, and brought Norman French rule to England. William and his successors brought French-speaking nobles to England, where they became large landholders. The government and important merchants carried on their business in French. Many native Englishmen learned the new language, and some eventually forgot their mother tongue. English did not reassert itself for 150 years after the Norman invasion, and when it did, it was quite a different language.

Middle English

The language we call Middle English begins with the predominance of French rule at the end of the 11th century. The Old English period came to an abrupt end because of a foreign invasion. This changed the status of the native language. English became a language spoken predominantly by the lower classes. At court, all matters of importance were transacted in French. As a result, whole groups of words having to do with affairs of state, religion, medicine, etc., were borrowed into English during this period. Words like *governor* and *councilor, cardinal* and *pastor, physician* and *surgeon* are typical of such borrowings. Indeed, the words *state, religion,* and *medicine* are themselves French in origin and entered the English language at this time.

We can see just how pervasive this phenomenon was by looking again at the Lord's Prayer. Notice that we find the word *dettis* (debts) instead of the Old English *gyltas, temptacioun* (temptation) instead of the Old English *costnunge,* and *delyuere* (deliver) instead of the Old English *ālȳs.* These are all borrowings from French.

There are other changes we can note in the Lord's Prayer between Old and Middle English times that are not the result of borrowing. For example, the Old English word for *kingdom (rīce)* became obsolete, but it was replaced by another native word, *kyngdom.* The Old English word for *bread (hlāf)* became more restricted in meaning (thus, Modern English *loaf*), but it was nonetheless replaced with the native *breed* (Modern *bread*). Many food words were borrowed from French, including *toast* and *biscuit,* but basic bread remained a native word.

There was a tension in the language because of the upper classes' tendency to borrow French terms and the common people's desire to remain with their native English. As the French were gradually driven out of England, after 1200, so was the process of borrowing their vocabulary. But many French words had become so familiar that they were probably not recognized as French at all. Today we use *dinner* and *appetite*, and *dress* and *fashion* without ever stopping to realize that they were originally French. In fact, our vocabulary in Modern English remains at least one-third French in origin.

English also continued to change structurally. The tendency to weaken word endings, begun in Germanic times and continued in Old English, became even stronger in Middle English. For example, consider the following line of the Middle English version of the Lord's Prayer: *be thi wille don in erthe as in heuene.* If we compare this to the same line in Old English, we can see that the endings of the words for *earth* and *heaven* have lost their final consonants and that the vowels in those endings, as in the word for *will,* have merged into a single sound written *e.* If we then think of the present-day version of this line, we can see that even this vowel has been lost in Modern English *earth, heaven,* and *will.*

This gradual loss of endings led to even greater reliance on word order and on function words. In the Lord's Prayer, we saw that in Old English *our daily bread,* the direct object of the verb meaning *give,* preceded that verb. But by Middle English times, the verb comes first, telling us that *bread* cannot be the subject. Thus, word order gradually took over the function that noun endings used to fill.

As verb endings disappeared, the English language turned to constructions that included function words. Helping verbs such as *have, will,* and *may* became more important because they helped express the tense and mood of the main verb. Indeed, English has developed this tendency to such a great extent that we can now convey a whole range of meanings through the use of such function words. Consider the differences of meaning in the following verb phrases:

I am singing
I do sing
I have sung
I have been singing
I can sing
I might sing
I would sing
I will sing

The range of possibilities is quite impressive, and extends far beyond the capacities of Old English. But again, we should note that this entire system is simply a way of compensating for the loss of verb endings.

FATHERS OF ENGLISH: *The poems of Chaucer helped establish London English in the 1300's. Four hundred years later, Samuel Johnson published the first great dictionary.*

Because of this new reliance on word order and function words, and because of the presence of the many familiar French words, late Middle English of the London area is fairly easy to read. Consider the following lines from the late 1300's, with which Geoffrey Chaucer's famous *Canterbury Tales* begin:

Whan that Aprille with his
  shoures soote
The droghte of March hath perced
  to the roote
And bathed every veyne in swich
  licour
Of which vertu engendred is the
  flour,

There is an unfamiliar word or construction every once in a while; for example, in the first line *soote* is a variant form of *sweet,* and it follows the noun it modifies rather than preceding it. Also, the spelling often seems odd, since it did not start to become standardized until the introduction of printing to England almost 100 years later. The lack of standardized spelling points to another important development in Middle English.

Many of the variations in spelling between Middle and Modern English involve vowels. Thus, we find *whan* instead of *when, shoures* for *showers, perced* for *pierced, veyne* for *vine,* etc. Yet by Shakespeare's time, only 200 years later, most of these vowels had changed to the ones we are familiar with today. The reason is that during the 1400's and 1500's there was a massive shift of the vowels of English, a change that is called the Great Vowel Shift. Sound changes happen gradually and spellings generally reflect the changes only after some delay. But right in the middle of this shift in English, the printing press came to England. The advent of printed books was a powerful force

for standardized spelling. Unfortunately, the standardization often reflected the old-fashioned pronunciation rather than the new. For example, it seems likely that by 1500 English speakers said *laf,* but the early printers still spelled the word *laugh.*

In Modern English, the spelling of vowels seems particularly confusing. Words like *great, late,* and *straight* have different spellings but the same vowel sound. Hard as the spellings may be to remember, however, they have preserved an interesting piece of language history: in Middle English, these three words had distinct vowels. On the other hand, the vowel in *great* is spelled the same as that in *breath* or *heath,* but all three are pronounced differently. Yet in Middle English, they all had the same vowel and the spelling reflects that too. Thus it is an accident of history—the coincidental timing of the Great Vowel Shift and the introduction of the printing press—that produced the written form of English that we recognize as modern. English has one of the more difficult spelling systems among European languages, but to the alert observer, English spelling provides a source of information on the history of the language.

FRENCH *gave English many food words. These animal names are Germanic; the meat names are French.*

cow	→	beef
pig	→	pork
sheep	→	mutton
calf	→	veal

Modern English

By 1600, the English language was already quite similar to the English we speak today. In the 200 years after Chaucer's death, the language was still changing, but several factors helped standardize it. We have already discussed the invention of the printing press. In addition, a strong central government under Henry VIII and Elizabeth I tended to impose a single standard—for writing more than for speech. The third factor was the rise of London as a great commercial center. In the Middle English period, regional dialects of English showed considerable differences. But with the rise of London, the London dialect became the standard for the language and remained the standard until the 1800's.

The changes in Early Modern English, though less profound, were of some importance. The growth of interest in the classical worlds of Greece and Rome brought whole new waves of borrowings as people searched for terms to describe their new interests. Words like *education* and *contemplation* were created from Latin, which was still a principal subject of study in every school. New explorations brought strange new products to England. For example, from explorations of the Americas came *tobacco* and *potato*. At the same time, the loss of endings and the spread of auxiliary or function words, discussed above, continued.

Perhaps the most significant development of Modern English is still another result of losing endings. In Old English, endings could tell us, among other things, whether a word was a noun or a verb; for example, the Old English root *luf* meaning *love*. The form *lufu* was a noun meaning *love*. But *lufian,* with the ending *ian,* was a verb meaning *to love*. By Modern English times, both of those endings had been lost. Noun and verb now have the same form, *love.* Many speakers of the language interpreted this to mean that *a noun can be made a verb* and *a verb can be made a noun.* For example, modern businessmen may *target* funds for a given purpose, creating a new verb from the noun *target.* Or, when we want to drive around on a Sunday afternoon,

LATIN *provided English with many learned words such as the adjectives at the right.*

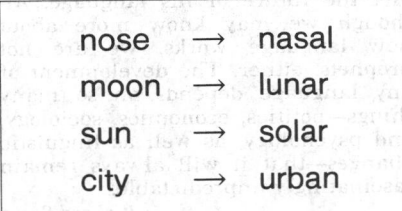

nose	→	nasal
moon	→	lunar
sun	→	solar
city	→	urban

FATHERS OF AMERICAN ENGLISH: *Noah Webster prepared an influential American dictionary in 1828. H. L. Mencken's* The American Language *(1938) is still an important guide.*

we say we are taking *a drive,* making a noun from the verb. Thus, the loss of endings has led to a whole new way to make new words.

At the same time, other procedures for coining new words resulted from different factors. From Greek and Latin we took not only whole words but also many prefixes and suffixes. For example, from Greek we borrowed the suffix *ism,* which is used to form nouns. At first, it was attached to words that were Greek in origin, such as *mystic.* Thus we get the word *mysticism.* But we also learned to make words like *truism,* though *true* itself is a native Germanic word. The dozens of borrowed prefixes and suffixes have given English still another means of creating new words.

One other historical development was to have great influence on the language. Beginning in the 1600's, the English began to establish a worldwide empire. At one time or another, the empire included most of North America, Australia, and New Zealand, large parts of Africa and the Indian subcontinent, and smaller parts of Asia. Wherever the British Empire was established, the English language was planted. It is today the official language of Australia and New Zealand, of Zimbabwe and South Africa (along with Afrikaans), of Jamaica and most of Canada, and of course of the 13 colonies that became the United States of America. English has also gained great importance as a second language. Teaching English to Europeans, Africans, and Asians has become an international business. The language has become the predominant international tongue and is used in every corner of the world for business, trade and diplomacy. Like Latin, English has grown in importance with the growth of an empire.

American English

English came to America with the settlement at Jamestown, Virginia, in 1607. To put this fact in perspective, we may note that Shakespeare was still writing his plays in 1607 and the King James translation of the Bible, filled with *thou*'s and *ye*'s, dates from 1611. The foundations of American English, therefore, lie in the relatively early forms of Modern English. If we keep this in mind, we will begin to understand what an interesting mixture American English is: on one hand it preserves some of the oldest and most unchanged features of Early Modern English, and on the other hand, it changes more quickly than any dialect in the English-speaking world.

The earliest English settlers of America were conservative in the English they spoke, and as a result all American dialects share certain old features that are rarely found in British English. For example, we have already noted the Great Vowel Shift in Middle and Early Modern English. The sounds of vowels continued to change in English, but the changes were much more rapid in England than in the American colonies. The way Americans pronounce words like *either* and *neither*—with the vowel found in *teeth*—is closer to the Early Modern English pronunciation than the British pronunciation, which uses the vowel in the word *ride.* The conservative nature of the early American settlers, or perhaps their isolation, preserved such old features in their brand of English.

Early American English did develop separate dialects. The map on the next page shows regional dialects

AMERICAN		BRITISH
trunk	↔	boot
hood	↔	bonnet
gear shift	↔	gear lever
tire	↔	tyre

BRITISH AND AMERICAN ENGLISH *have become different, as this list of car parts shows.*

INDIAN		ENGLISH
atchitamon	→	chipmunk
aposoum	→	opossum
arakunen	→	raccoon
wejack	→	woodchuck

AMERICAN INDIANS *gave English the names for common animals.*

in the mid-1900's. The southern dialects tend to be more conservative. For example, the phenomenon we refer to as "southern drawl" in fact preserves many old features of Early Modern English, particularly with respect to vowels.

In the Northeast, society changed more rapidly. Cities in particular tended to reflect this tumult in their speech patterns, so that distinctive brands of American English are easily noticed in places such as Boston and New York, at least in the speech of local inhabitants of more than a generation. But today these dialect variations seem to be fading. Why is this the case? The answers to that question provide a clue to this most distinctive feature of American English, its very lack of clear-cut dialect lines.

In England, at least until the 1900's, the great majority of people lived and died within their own small region. Thus, over a long period of time, each region developed certain distinctive speech patterns. By contrast, Americans were restless and mobile. Beginning with the westward expansion and continuing to the present day, they

move farther and more often than citizens of other countries. Naturally, this had its effect on the language. The dialect map shows that the farther west we go, the more difficult it is to distinguish dialect families. The Midwest and Far West were settled by people from all parts of the eastern United States. Furthermore, as time went on, there was much more north-south, as well as east-west, movement. We may understand what this meant for American English by pausing for a moment to again consider the very notion behind the word *dialect*.

Dialects develop as people speaking the same language have less and less contact with one another. They may be separated by geography—say, a mountain or a body of water—or by social divisions such as race, religion, or politics. Whatever the reason, the longer they are apart, the more their speech will differ, until they can no longer understand one another and their different dialects become separate languages. Conversely, when people speaking different dialects begin to live together, the differences in their speech begin to fade.

In the American West, dialect dif-

ferences tended to fade, and the same thing happened in the East as well during the 1900's. The millions of immigrants who came to America also helped break down dialect barriers. Radio, television, and the movies have also had a significant effect on breaking down dialect areas. The evening news, for example, presents us with an American speech norm, distinctive by its very lack of recognizable dialect. Since the Far West, Deep South, Northeast, and other regions are now constantly in touch with one another via telephone, television, and modern transportation, Americans tend to speak more similarly now than at any other stage in American history.

Groups that remain culturally distinct still show traces of dialectal development. For example, some groups of immigrants have largely settled together and kept to themselves. There are Chinatowns in cities throughout the United States. Some of the communities in Appalachia have remained isolated for over a century, and their residents speak a kind of antique Modern English.

Black English is also the result of social isolation, some by choice and some imposed by society. But we must not think of black—or any other form of—English as "incorrect." It is just the result of changing language, something that has always happened and no doubt always will, however much the rate of change may slow.

The melting pot phenomenon discouraged dialect development, but it encouraged more borrowing. North American Indians provided Americans with words for animals, foods, and other items: *moose* and *skunk, squash* and *pecan, canoe* and *moccasin,* and many others. Americans also made up new words to describe new ideas, ranging from *backwoodsman* to *statehouse.* Immigrants brought still more words. For example, in the realm of food, French colonists gave us *chowder,* the Dutch provided *cookies,* the Germans brought *noodles,* and the Spanish introduced *tortillas.*

Will American English ever become a separate language, different from other forms of English? Robert Burchfield, a distinguished British student of language, believes it will. Others, pointing out the increase in international communication and contact, believe it will not.

No resident of Britain in the 700's A.D. would have had any way to predict the future of his language. Although we may know more about how language works, we are not prophets, either. The development of any language depends on so many things—politics, economics, sociology, and psychology, as well as linguistic changes—that it will always remain fascinatingly unpredictable.

—*Richard Sacks*

REGIONAL DIALECTS *of English in the U.S. appear mostly in the East and South. They are not as numerous or as clearly defined as in Great Britain.*

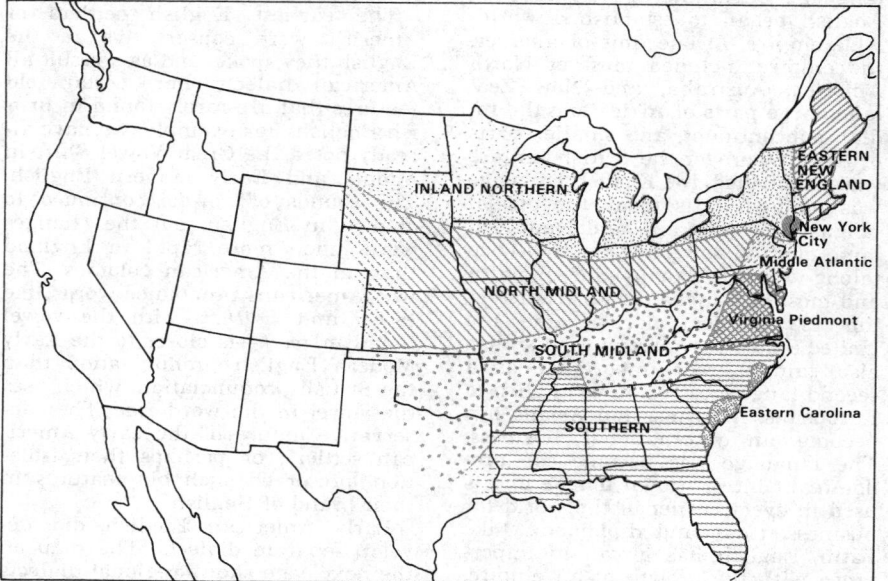

PETER LOEWER

EASTERN NEW ENGLAND
INLAND NORTHERN
New York City
Middle Atlantic
NORTH MIDLAND
Virginia Piedmont
SOUTH MIDLAND
Eastern Carolina
SOUTHERN

VOCABULARY IMPROVEMENT

There are many reasons for improving your vocabulary: to speak more effectively, to write more clearly, to read more comprehensively, and even to sharpen your thought processes. This section gives some ways to learn new words.

The best way to acquire new words is by reading for pleasure. The words that you meet in this kind of reading match your interests, and you encounter them in context, where you can see how they are used.

A word in the abstract is hard for most people to remember, but a word in a sentence can often be guessed at. Take, for example, the word *proclivity.* If you had never heard this word, would you say that it means

   a) a benign tumor
   b) an inclination or tendency
   c) a slight rise in land elevation?

You would have to guess at the answer. But if you encountered the word in a sentence, you would have a better chance to understand its meaning:

   He was a corpulent old fellow with
   a *proclivity* for strong drink and
   bad cigars.

Given the three possibilities, you could figure out that the word must mean an inclination or a tendency. The sentence also suggests that a *proclivity* is not just a tendency, but a negative one.

Next, you would look the word up in a dictionary to get its exact meaning and to see how it might be used in other senses. Think of a sentence or two in which the word seems to fit naturally. Soon, the word becomes part of your vocabulary, popping into your mind when you need it, just like *tendency, inclination,* and other related words.

When you read, you often come across words that you do not know. As in the example above, you may get the general meaning from the rest of the sentence. If you encounter the word several times, it becomes part of your reading vocabulary but not necessarily of your speaking or writing vocabulary. It would be awkward to stop reading every time you encountered a word that you did not know. But if you are interested in improving your vocabulary, mark the unfamiliar words when you read or jot them down on a slip of paper. Once you have a list of these words, take out your dictionary.

Study the definitions and pronounce the words aloud. If your dictionary shows the derivations of words, study those, too. Try to think of similar words—those with the same roots or the same suffixes or prefixes. How are the meanings of these words related? Make up sentences using the words. When you feel confident that you are using and pronouncing your new words correctly, try to use them in conversation or in writing.

Keep a list of words you have acquired in this way and sometime, when you have a few minutes, go through the list to keep the memory of the words fresh. New words can be acquired at no expense—except the time and energy it takes to learn them.

The history of words is interesting in itself and it can be a useful tool in learning new words. As the previous section (Language Studies) shows, English has a complicated history and owes its modern form and vocabulary to several earlier languages.

The science of tracing a word's history is known as *etymology.* It is the study of (*-logy*) true or original senses of a word (*etymon*). The derivation of a word can be used as a mnemonic device (a technique for remembering) in two ways. First, it presents a concise story about the word and its ancestry; second, it introduces you to related words, its modern cousins. An additional benefit can be obtained from learning the derivation of a word you already know, as it may give you new insights into the word itself.

Take the word *comprehend,* for example. We use it to mean understand thoroughly. It is derived from the Latin verb *prehendere,* meaning to take hold of or to grasp. We use the word grasp to mean understand: to have *a fine grasp of* the subject, *to grasp the meaning* of a speech or book, etc. Ideas or subjects cannot be grasped literally, of course; but both Latin and Old English (from which *grasp* comes) settled on this metaphor. *Comprehend* and *grasp* are cousins, using the same metaphor and having closely related meanings. Knowing this about *comprehend* causes us to look at the word with new insight into the workings of language and the human mind.

Our common vocabulary—the one we use every day—comes mainly from the Germanic ancestors of English. Such everyday words as *man, woman, boy, girl,* and *house* are all Germanic. Most of our intellectual vocabulary, however, that is, words dealing with thought and abstract things, comes from Latin and Greek. Since we already know the meaning of everyday English words, the task of increasing our vocabulary means largely learning the words that have their origins in Latin and Greek.

The job is made easier because many long words from these languages are *combined forms* made up of a *root* and at least one *prefix* or *suffix* that modifies the meaning of the root.

Consider the word *transportation.* The root, *port,* comes from the Latin word that means *to carry* or *bring. Trans-* is a prefix that means *across.* Thus, to *transport* means to *carry across.* The suffix *-tion* tells us that the word is a noun. So *transportation*

BY CHANGING PREFIX AND SUFFIX, *a single root can have many meanings.* Suspense *seems far from the original root meaning, yet a good suspense story is called a* cliffhanger.

ROOT: pend (Latin, *to hang*)	
with de-	**with sus-**
depend, depending	suspend
dependable	suspenders
dependent, dependence	suspension
independent, independence	suspense

must be something that carries across. It is only a small distance to the modern meaning of *transportation:* a means of getting from one place to another.

Knowing that much, we can look for other words with the same root:

import, to bring (goods) in (to a country)
export, to send (goods) out (of a country)
report, to bring (a message)
support, to bear up, sustain

In addition, there are many words that use *trans- (translate)* and hundreds that end in *-tion (translation).*

Roots

A root is the basic part of a word. It suggests the primary idea. The Latin root *loqu (locut)* has to do with speaking. We find *loqu* in ventri*loqu*ist (one who talks from the stomach). Col*loqu*ial is composed of the root *loqu* plus the prefix *col-,* which means together, and the adjective suffix *-ial,* which means pertaining to. So the literal meaning of colloquial is "pertaining to speaking together." We use the word to describe informal or conversational speech or writing, the sort of language people use in a relaxed atmosphere. A soli*loqu*y is a speech to oneself (*solus* means alone). An e*loqu*ent person is one who speaks well. If *loquacious* is a new word for you, you can now begin to guess at its meaning. *Loqu*acious, too, has to do with speaking; the *-acious* suffix means that it is an adjective. In fact, *loquacious* has a close cousin in the Anglo-Saxon word *talkative.*

The spelling of a root is not always the same. One reason for this is that roots come from different forms of the same word in the original language. For example, words with *loqu-* come from the present form of a Latin verb (meaning *talk*); those that have the *locut-* form come from the past participle (meaning *talked*). Roots may also change their spellings in order to combine more easily with suffixes or prefixes.

Sometimes a change in the spelling of a root tells a complicated story about the word's history. *Jettison,* for example, comes from the Latin root *ject,* having to do with throwing; *jettison* means to throw overboard. Most English words that come from this root (in*ject,* pro*ject,* re*ject,* etc.), keep the spelling. But jettison comes to us through French, where it lost its *c* (in

---

COMMON ROOTS

acu, acr. sharp (acute, acid, acrimony)
aesthe. feel (aesthetic, anesthesia)
ag, act. do, drive (activate, agitate, react, agility)
alg. pain (analgesic, nostalgia)
am. love (amorous, amiable)
anim. life, mind, soul (animal, inanimate, animation)
annu, enni. year (annual, bicentennial, annuities)
anthropo. humanity (anthropology, misanthrope)
aqu. water (aquarium, aqualung)
arche, archa. ancient (archaic, archaeology)
aud. hear (auditory, audience, audio-visual)
bel. war (belligerent, bellicose)
bio. life (biology, biopsy, antibiotic)
cad, cid, cas. fall, befall (accident, cadaver, occasion)
cap, cip, cept, ceiv, ceit. seize, hold (capture, anticipate, accept, receive, deceit)
carn. flesh (carnivore, reincarnation)
ced, cede, ceed, cess. yield, go (antecedent, secede, proceed, recession)
cern, cret. separate, distinguish (discern, secret)
chron. time (chronology, synchronize)
clam, claim. shout (clamor, proclaim)
clud, clus, clos. shut (conclude, seclude, inclusive, close)
cogn. know (recognize, incognito)
cord. heart (accord, concordance)
corp. body (corpse, incorporate, corporeal)
cre, cresc. grow (increase, create, crescendo)
culp. blame (culprit, culpable)
cumb, cub. lie down (succumb, incubate)
cur, curs, cours. run (current, cursory, course)
dict. say (dictator, indictment, jurisdiction)
duc, duct. lead (seduce, induct)
dyna. power (dynamite, dynasty)
fac, fic, fact, fect. make, do (facile, proficient, factory, perfect)
fal, fals. deceive, fail, disappoint (fallacious, falsify)
fer. carry, bring (transfer, ferry)
flect, flex. bend (reflect, flexible)
flu, flux. flow (influence, influx)
fring, fract, frag. break (infringe, infraction, fragile)
fus, fund, found. melt, pour (fuse, refund, foundry)
gen, genit. produce, birth, race (congenital, genealogy, generate)
gest. produce, action (gesticulate, gesture)
gno. know (agnostic, diagnosis, prognosis)
grad, gress. step (grade, graduate, progress)

grat. pleasing (gratitude, congratulate)
grav. heavy (gravity, aggravate)
jac, ject. throw (eject, adjacent, jettison)
junct. join (junction, injunction)
jur. swear, right (perjury, jury, abjure)
lect. gather, choose (collect, select)
loqu, locut. speak (eloquent, interlocutor, elocution)
mit, miss. send (transmit, missionary, emit)
mon, monit. warn, advise (admonition, monitor)
mort. death (mortuary, mortal)
mot. move (motion, motive, motor)
mut. change (mutation, immutable)
nat. born (native, natal)
neg. deny (abnegation, negative, negate)
path. feeling, suffering (sympathy, pathetic)
pel, pell, puls. push (propel, compelling, pulse)
pend. hang, weight (appendage, pendant)
pet, petit. go, seek (petition, compete)
plac. please (placate, placid, placebo)
ple, plen, plet. fill (complete, plenty, plethora)
port. carry (transport, portable)
posit, pound, pose. put, place (position, expound, transpose)
pugn. fight (impugn, pugnacious, repugnant)
pung, punct. point (pungent, compunction, punctual)
quir, quisit, quest. seek (require, inquisitive, inquest)
rog, rogat. ask (abrogate, arrogance, surrogate)
rupt. burst (interrupt, disrupt, rupture)
scrib, script. write (scribble, scripture, manuscript)
sed, sid, sess. sit, settle (sedentary, reside, possess)
spec, spic. look (spectacle, prospectus, conspicuous)
spir. breath (spirit, respiration)
tang, ting, tact. touch (tangible, contingent, contact)
temp, tempor. time (tempo, temporal, contemporary)
ten, tin, tain. hold (tenant, continue, maintain, retain)
tort. twist (contortion, torture)
tract. drag, pull (retract, tractor)
trud, trus. push, thrust (protrude, intrusion, obtrusive)
unda. wave (undulate, inundate, surround)
ven, vent. come (intervene, invent, circumvent)
ver. true (veracity, very, aver, verdict, verify)
vert, vers. turn (revert, version, controversy)
vid, vis. see (evident, televise, vision)
viv. life (vivid, vivacious)
voc, vok. voice, call (advocate, vocal, revoke)
volv, volut. roll (revolve, evolution)

SOLILOQUY AND CANDIDATE: *Both words are derived from Latin. The actor in* Hamlet *"speaks alone," and a candidate wears a white shirt, if not the toga suggested by the Latin.*

Old French it was spelled *getteson*).

The root *pung* or *punct* means point. It is found in words like *punct*ual ("on the dot"), *punct*uate ("to mark with a point"), and *punct*ure ("to prick with a sharp point"). Com*punct*ion means a sense of guilt or remorse, and is made from the root *punct,* meaning stung or pricked with a point. The prefix *com-* is an intensive, in this case, which adds power to the root as if it were saying, "thoroughly." Its literal meaning resembles such phrases in English as "stung by remorse." *Pung*ent is another word made from *pung.* It describes something penetrating, biting, or pointed, usually a taste or smell.

Some words do not translate as easily from their root meanings to their modern meanings. Such words usually have the most interesting stories of all attached to them. They tell of people long forgotten whose names we still use; myths no longer a part of our folklore; customs of different people in different times; beliefs we no longer share but which still color our language.

Inaugurate, for example, means to begin or to set a person in a high office. Literally, it means to practice augury, the reading of omens. In ancient Rome, priests called *augures* interpreted signs around them and told when it was good to start, or inaugurate, an enterprise.

Candidate comes from a Latin word, *candidus,* which means white. In ancient Rome, candidates for office would campaign wearing white togas. They were called *candidatus,* clothed in white. *Candid* comes from the same word and means honest.

A *maverick* is a dissenter, one who refuses to go along with the group. The word comes from Samuel Maverick, a 19th-century cattleman who

refused to brand his calves. The noun *jeremiad,* meaning prolonged denunciation, is from the Old Testament prophet Jeremiah, who brought God's denunciation to his people. *Tantalize* means to tease someone by presenting something desirable to him, but keeping it out of reach. In Greek mythology, this was Tantalus's punishment in Hades: to be up to his chin in water that would vanish when he tried to drink it, and to have boughs of fruit hanging over him that would disappear when he reached for them.

Such one-of-a-kind word stories help suggest the fascinations of etymology. But they are less useful for expanding your vocabulary than a study of the common roots that help make up dozens of useful words. The table at left lists the most common Latin roots and their basic meanings. In parentheses are a few English words made from them. Try to think of others that share each root. If you do not know the meanings of the words listed, look them up in a good dictionary.

Prefixes

A prefix is fastened to the front of a word and indicates attitude, number, position, or direction. Sometimes it just intensifies the meaning of the root, as if it were saying, "completely" or "very."

The prefix *intro-* means *into.* We have already learned that the root *vert* means *to turn.* So a person who is an *introvert* is one who is turned inward. To describe the opposite sort of person, we would look for a prefix that means outward, in this case *extro-,* as in *extrovert. Avert* takes the

same root. The prefix *a-* (a shortened form of *ab-*), meaning away, gives this word the meaning *to turn away* or *avoid.* Another word that means turn away is *divert.* The prefix *dis-,* as used in *dismissal* ("send away"), also means away. When it is attached to the root *vert,* the "s" is dropped. *Divert* means to turn away in the sense of directing a force in another direction; it has also come to mean to distract or amuse—to turn a person's mind away from serious or sad matters.

Many prefixes change spelling depending on the sound that follows the prefix. This makes it difficult to recognize certain prefixes in some words. Prefixes can also be disguised when two look alike but have different meanings; for example, *ante-* means *before; anti-* means *against* or *opposite to. Ante meridian,* commonly abbreviated as a.m., means *before noon.* But an *antismog* device is one that is used against smog, and an *antiseptic* is used against an infection.

Some prefixes have similar meanings. For example, both *ante-* and *pre-* mean *before.* As we saw above, *ab-* and *dis-* both mean *away.*

By studying the following list of prefixes, you will improve your ability to pick up the meaning of an unfamiliar word through understanding the meaning of its parts.

Suffixes

Suffixes are attached to the ends of words. They indicate a word's function (verb, noun, adjective, adverb), number, and/or tense. Familiar suffixes like *-ed* or *-ing* tell you that the word you are looking at is a verb in the past or present tense, respectively, for example look: look*ed;* look*ing.* An *-s* or *-es* added to the end of a noun tells you that it is probably a plural, for example, cat: cat*s;* class: class*es.*

Other endings also indicate whether a word is a verb, noun, adjective or adverb. A word can often be changed from one part of speech to another by changing its ending. For instance, a common noun suffix like *-ion* can sometimes be substituted for the verb suffix *-ate* to change a verb like moti*v*ate into the noun motivat*ion.* Substituting *-or* for *-ion* would again change the word, now into motivat*or.* If you needed an adjective, you could add *-al* to the noun suffix *-ion,* producing motivat*ional.* To make this into an adverb, you add *-ly* to motiva*tional* and come up with motiva*tionally.*

The following list of suffixes should be useful in helping you produce words that fit your needs. Always check the dictionary before using them since spelling can be tricky and unusual formations may occur.

COMMON PREFIXES

a-. without (atheism, amoral)

ab-, abs-. away, away from (abnormal, abstract, aberration, abjure, abrogate)

ad-, a-, ac-, af-, ag-, al-, an-, ap-, ar-, as-, at-. to, toward (admonition, accord, affect, aggravate, appear, assign)

an-. without (anonymous)

ante-. before (antecedent, antechamber)

anti-. against (antiseptic, antitrust)

auto-. self (automatic, automobile)

bene-. well (beneficial, benign)

circum-. around (circumference, circumstantial)

com-, co-, col-, con-, cor-. together (companion, collect, concern, correct), *intensifier* (comfort, corrode)

counter-, contra-, contro-. opposite (counterclockwise), against (contrary, controversy)

de-. down (decay), reversal (decontrol), away (defect), *intensifier* (declaim, default)

dem-. people (democracy, demagogue)

dia-. across (diagonal), apart (diagnosis, diagram), through (diarrhea, diaphanous)

dis-, dif-, di-. not (differ, dislike, discourtesy)

equ-, equi-. equal (equivalent, equation)

eu-. well (euphoria, eulogy)

ex-, e-, ef-. out (exhale, eject, effervescent)

extra-, extro-. outside of (extraordinary, extrasensory)

hyper-. over (hypercritical, hypertension)

hypo-. under (hypodermic, hypocrisy)

in-, em-, en-. in (intrude, inspect, embargo, enclave, immure), *intensifier* (enchant), against (impugn, infest)

in-, ir-, im-. not (inoffensive, irreligious, imbalance)

inter-. between (international, interact, interscholastic)

intra-, intro-. within (intravenous, introspective)

macro-. large (macrocosm, macroscopic)

mal-, male-. bad, wrongly (malign, malefactor)

micro-. small (microcosm, microscope)

multi-. many (multiple, multitude)

neo-. new (neolithic, neocolonialism)

non-. not (nonsense, nonentity)

ob-, oc-, of-, op-. to (offer), against (obtrusive, oppose), *intensifier* (occupy)

omni-. all (omniscient, omnivorous)

para-. alongside (parallel, parody)

per-. through (perfume), completely (perfect)

poly-. many (polygamy, polygon)

post-. after (posterior, postpone)

pre-. before (premature, premise)

pro-. forward (prospectus, proceed), away (prodigal), in place of (pronoun)

pseudo-. false (pseudonym)

re-. again (reopen, repast), back (receive, recall), *intensifier* (revere)

recti-. straight, right (rectitude, rectify, rectangle)

sub-, suc-, suf-, sug-, sum-, sup-, sur-, sus-. under (suffer, suggest, suppose, surreptitious, sustain), in place of (surrogate, substitute)

super-. above (superintendent, superhuman)

syn-, syl-, sym-, sys-. together (synchronize, syllable, sympathy, system)

trans-. across, over, through (translate, transcend)

un-. not (unearthly, unassailable), reversal (untie)

NUMBER PREFIXES

half. *hemi*sphere, *semi*circle, *demi*tasse

one. *mono*logue, *uni*verse

first. *proto*type, *primi*tive

two. *bi*nocular, *di*lemma, *dicho*tomy, *du*et

both. *ambi*valent

three. *ter*tiary, *tri*ad

four. *tetra*pod, *quad*rant, *quart*er

five. *penta*gon, *quint*uplet

six. *hexa*gram, *sex*tet

ten. *deca*de, *decennial*

one-tenth. *deci*mal

one hundred. *cent*ennial

one thousand. *mill*enium

COMMON SUFFIXES

Verb Endings. extri*cate*, awai*ted*, efferv*esce*, light*en*, dei*fy*, danc*ing*, demol*ish*, critic*ize*

Noun Endings (people). Republi*can*, tru*ant*, li*ar*, slugg*ard*, benefici*ary*, wait*er*, physi*cian*, intern*ist*, suburba*nite*, impos*tor*

Noun Endings (acts, conditions, results, states). lun*acy*, suff*rage*, refus*al*, radi*ance*, penit*ence*, pi*ety*, radi*ation*, hero*ism*, vera*city*, detri*ment*, matri*mony*, like*ness*, cand*or*, bigo*try*, paraly*sis*, recti*tude*, over*ture*, liber*ty*, ten*ure*, perj*ury*

Adjective Endings. cap*able*, therm*al*, hum*an*, in*ane*, ext*ant*, simil*ar*, sanguin*ary*, desper*ate*, wood*en*, lat*ent*, bigg*er*, small*est*, terri*fic*, ed*ible*, harmon*ic*, mag*ical*, ar*id*, frag*ile*, fel*ine*, gra*cious*, slugg*ish*, specula*tive*, fear*less*, anthrop*oid*, audi*tory*, numer*ous*, scar*y*

Adverb Endings. careful*ly*, down*ward*, other*wise*

The following endings act as suffixes but are called combining forms; they attach themselves easily to other combining forms, creating new words.

COMBINING FORMS

-arch (ruler). matriarch (matr:mother); patriarch (patr:father)

-archy (government). oligarchy (oligo:few); anarchy (an:without)

-cide (killer, murder). fratricide (frater:brother); genocide (genos:race); regicide (reg:king)

-cracy (government). democracy (demos:people); plutocracy (ploutos:wealth)

-crat (member of government). aristocrat (aristos:best)

-graph (writing apparatus: writing). autograph (auto: self); biography (bio:life); telegraph (tele:distance); photograph (photo:light)

-logy (study of). anthropology (anthropo:human); archaeology (arche:ancient); biology (bio:life); cardiology (cardio:heart); entomology (entomo:insect); geology (geo: earth); ophthalmology (ophthalmo:eye); ornithology (ornitho:bird); otolaryngology (oto:ear; laryngo:throat); zoology (zoo:animals)

-mania (excessive excitement or enthusiasm for). dipsomania (dipsa:thirst—alcoholism); kleptomania (kleptein:to steal); megalomania (megalo:greatness—delusions of grandeur)

-meter (measuring device). barometer (baro:pressure)

-nomy (laws governing). astronomy (astro:star); agronomy (agro:field, earth, soil)

-phile (lover). bibliophile (biblio:book)

-phobia (fear). acrophobia (acro:height); agoraphobia (agora:public places)

-scope (instrument for observing). microscope (micro: small); periscope (peri:around)

-tomy (cutting of). appendectomy; tonsillectomy

USEFUL WORDS TO KNOW

This is a list of words with short definitions and derivations. Most of the words are made from roots, prefixes, and suffixes in the previous tables. Brief derivations are given in parentheses. New roots are given in italics. The capitalized words at the end of some entries have the same root or prefix as the main entry.

VERBS

abjure. to repudiate or renounce (ab:away; jur:swear)

abrogate. to abolish by authority (ab:away; rogat:ask)

adjure. to earnestly entreat or appeal (ad:toward; jur: swear)

aver. to strongly affirm (ad:to; ver:true)

circumvent. to avoid by going around (circum:around; ven:come)

discern. to perceive differences (dis:apart; cern:distinguish)

expunge. to erase or annihilate (ex:out; pung:point)

immure. to imprison or entomb (im:in; *murus*:wall—Latin); MURAL

impugn. to oppose, criticize, refute, or make insinuations against (im:against; pugn:fight)

inundate. to flood or swamp (in:in; unda:wave)

jettison. to discard or cast overboard (ject:throw)

malign. to slander (mal:bad; gen:birth)

proscribe. to prohibit or condemn (pro:in front, publicly; scrib:write); (Notices of punishment used to be posted publicly.)

revert. to return to a former condition (re:back; vert:turn)

secede. to withdraw from membership in an organization (se:apart; cede:go); SELECT, SEPARATE

undulate. to move in waves (unda:wave; ate:verb ending)

NOUNS

abnegation. self-denial (ab:away; neg:deny)

acrimony. bitterness in speech and action (acr:sharp; mony:noun ending)

admonition. a warning or reproval (ad:to; monit:warn)

appendage. anything attached to something larger or more important (ad:to; pend:hang)

effervescence. bubbling; high spirits (ex:intensifier; *fervere*:boil); FERVOR, FERVID

martinet. a rigid disciplinarian (Jean Martinet was a 17th-century French general known for his system of military drill)

nemesis. an avenger; a just punishment; an unavoidable fate (Nemesis was the Greek goddess of retribution)

plethora. an excess (plet:fill)

surrogate. substitute (sub:in place of; rogat:ask)

veracity. truthfulness; accuracy (ver:true; ity:noun ending)

ADJECTIVES AND ADVERBS

congenital(ly). existing at birth but not hereditary (com: together; gen:birth)

diaphanous(ly). transparent (dia:through; *phainein*:to show—Greek); CELLOPHANE, PHANTOM

fallacious(ly). misleading; based on a mistake (fall:deceive; ious:adjective ending)

immutable (ly). unchangeable (in:not; mut:change)

obtrusive(ly). thrusting forward; undesirably noticeable (ob:against; trus:thrust)

proficient(ly). skillful (pro:for; fic:make); PROFIT

pugnacious(ly). ready for a fight (pugn:fight; ious:adjective ending)

rapacious(ly). greedy; plundering (*rapare*:to seize—Latin); SURREPTITIOUS, RAPE

surreptitious(ly). done in a secret, sneaky way (sub:under; *rapare*:to seize—Latin); RAPACIOUS, RAPID

MEDICAL WORDS

analgesic. a drug that reduces pain (an:without; alg:pain)

anemia. a lack of red blood cells (an:without; *haima*:blood—Greek); HEMORRHAGE

anesthetic. an agent that causes loss of sensation (an: without; aesthe:feel)

biopsy. examination of tissues from a living body (bio: life; opsy:medical examination); AUTOPSY

neurology. the study of the nervous system (*neuron*: nerve—Greek; logy:study of); NEUROTIC

placebo. an inactive substance, administered as if it were a drug, that often has a psychological effect (*placebo*:I shall please—Latin; plac:please)

prognosis. a prediction of the course of a disease (pro:before; gno:know); PROGRAM

virulent. poisonous; irritating; spiteful (*virus*:poison—Latin; ent:adjective ending); VIRUS

LEGAL WORDS

advocate. one that pleads in the cause of another before a court (ad:to; voc:voice)

affidavit. a written statement made under oath before an officer (*affidavit*:he has sworn—Latin)

arbitration. the process by which an impartial judge decides a case between disputing parties (*arbiter*:judge—Latin); ARBITRARY, ARBITRATOR

homicide. murder (homo:human; cide:murder)

inquest. a judicial investigation (in:intensifier; quest:seek)

jurisdiction. the right of authority (jur:right; dict:say)

libel. a written accusation or defamation of character (*liber*:book—Latin); LIBRARY

plaintiff. the complaining party in a lawsuit (*plangere*:to lament—Latin); COMPLAIN

BUSINESS WORDS

default. to fail to pay money when it is due (de:intensifier; fall:fail)

fiscal. of or pertaining to finances (*fiscus*:treasury, basket—Latin)

lien. the right to take property as security or payment of debt (*ligare*:to bind—Latin); OBLIGE, LIGAMENT

prospectus. a formal summary of a proposed venture (pro:forward; spec:look).

POLITICAL WORDS

abdicate. to formally give up authority (ab:away; dict: say)

autocracy. government by a single person having unlimited power (auto:self; cracy:government)

demagogue. a leader who obtains power by appealing to the base emotions of people (demos:people; agogue: lead)

detente. an easing of tensions between nations (de:apart; *tendere*:to stretch—Latin)

enclave. a country or part of a country entirely within the boundaries of another country (in:in; *clavis*:key—Latin); CONCLAVE, CLOVE, CLAVICLE

plenary. fully attended by all members (plen:fill)

—Marcia H. Golub

GUIDE TO OTHER LANGUAGES

French

French is quite easy to read. The words are arranged in sentences very much as they are in English. And many of the words have the same spelling and the same meaning as they do in English. Some French words are written with special marks called accents. For example, an acute accent is used in *littérature,* a grave accent in *poète,* and a circumflex accent in *câble.* These marks generally show how to pronounce the vowels over which they are written (*é* sounds like *a* in "late" and *è* like *e* in "let"). Sometimes they merely distinguish one word from another; for example, *a* means "has" but *à* means "to." A small hooklike mark, called a cedilla, is another special mark. It appears under *c,* in words like *garçon* (boy), to show that *c* sounds like *s.* The final vowel of certain short words like *je* (I), *de* (of), *le* (the), and *la* (the) is replaced by an apostrophe, if the following word begins with a vowel (*l'enfant,* the child), and, often, if the following word begins with an *h* (*l'herbe,* the grass).

Sentence structure.
Word order is often the same or nearly the same as it is in English. However, object pronouns (pronouns corresponding to "him," "them," etc.) are usually placed before the verb.

Declarative sentences.
A declarative sentence makes a statement:

> Elle chante la chanson.
> *She is singing the song.*

To express "not" with a verb, *ne* is put before the verb and *pas* after the verb:

> Elle ne chante pas la chanson.
> *She is not singing the song.*

Interrogative sentences.
An interrogative sentence asks a question. A declarative sentence can be made a question by beginning the sentence with *Est-ce que* (Is it that):

> Est-ce qu'elle chante la chanson?
> *Is she singing the song?*

A declarative sentence can also be made a question by adding *n'est-ce pas* (is it not) at the end:

> Elle chante bien, n'est-ce pas?
> *She sings well, is it not (so)?*

A question can also be formed by putting the verb before the subject pronoun. A hyphen then connects the verb with the pronoun:

> Il est riche.   *He is rich.*
> Est-il riche?   *Is he rich?*

In such a question, if the verb and the subject pronoun bring two vowels together, *-t-* separates the vowels:

> Il a la clef.   *He has the key.*
> A-t-il la clef?   *Has he the key?*

If the subject of such a question is a noun, the noun begins the question:

> Henri est-il riche?   *Is Henry rich?*

Imperative sentences.
An imperative sentence gives a command:

> Chantez la chanson.   *Sing the song.*

Word order.
An object pronoun is usually placed before the verb:

> Elle le voit.   *She sees him.*

The pronoun *lui* means "to him" or "to her"; *leur* means "to them":

> Elle lui parle.   *She speaks to him.*
> Vous leur parlez.   *You speak to them.*

In a negative sentence, *ne* precedes the object pronoun:

> Je ne le vois pas.   *I don't see him.*

If there are two object pronouns, both precede the verb:

> Je les lui donne.   *I give them to him.*

In a positive command, the object pronoun follows the verb and is joined to it by a hyphen:

> Parlez-lui.   *Speak to him.*

If there are two object pronouns, a hyphen connects them:

> Donnez-les-lui.   *Give them to him.*

In a negative command, the object pronouns precede the verb and no hyphens are used:

> Ne le lui dites pas.   *Don't say it to him.*

Articles.
Each noun in French is classed as masculine or feminine. There is no neuter. Nouns like *père* (father) and *fils* (son) are of course masculine. Nouns like *mère* (mother) and *fille* (daughter) are feminine. But the gender of most nouns has to be memorized.

Definite articles.
The English definite article (the) is *le* (before a masculine noun) and *la* (before a feminine noun):

> le père   *the father*
> la mère   *the mother*
> le livre   *the book*
> la maison   *the house*

If the nouns are plural, *le* and *la* are changed to *les:*

> les pères   *the fathers*
> les mères   *the mothers*

Before a vowel, and often before *h,* *le* and *la* become *l':*

> l'enfant *the child*   l'homme *the man*

When *de* (of) precedes *le,* the *de* and the *le* combine into *du:*

> du père   *of the father*

But *de* does not combine with *la* or *l':*

> de la mère   *of the mother*
> de l'enfant   *of the child*

When *de* precedes *les,* the combination is *des:*

> des pères   *of the fathers*
> des mères   *of the mothers*

If *à* (to) precedes *le,* the combination is *au:*

> au père   *to the father*

But *à* does not combine with *la* or *l':*

> à la mère   *to the mother*
> à l'enfant   *to the child*

When *à* precedes *les*, the combination is *aux*:

aux pères	*to the fathers*
aux mères	*to the mothers*

Indefinite articles. The indefinite article (a, an) is *un* (before a masculine noun) and *une* (before a feminine noun):

un père	*a father*
une mère	*a mother*
un livre	*a book*
une maison	*a house*

Partitive construction. In an English sentence like "We are eating bread," the word "some" (before bread) is understood and is sometimes expressed. Similarly, in a sentence like "We are not eating bread," the word "any" (before bread) is understood and is sometimes expressed.

Even though "some" and "any" are not always expressed in English, the idea of "some" and "any" is always expressed in French. This is done through what is called the partitive construction. The partitive construction is the use of *du, de la, de l',* or *des* to express "some" and of *de* alone to express "any":

Nous mangeons du pain.
We are eating (some) bread.

Nous ne mangeons pas de pain.
We are not eating (any) bread.

Noun plurals. In English, most nouns are made plural by the addition of *s*. This is also true of French nouns, for *s* is usually added to the singular forms:

le crayon, les crayons	*the pencil(s)*
la pomme, les pommes	*the apple(s)*

But nouns ending in *s, x,* or *z* remain unchanged in the plural:

le bas, les bas	*the stocking(s)*
la voix, les voix	*the voice(s)*
le gaz, les gaz	*the gas(es)*

Nearly all nouns that end in *-au* or *-eu* add an *x* instead of an *s* for the plural:

le bureau, les bureaux	*the office(s)*
le feu, les feux	*the fire(s)*

Some nouns that end in *-ou* add an *x*:

le chou, les choux	*the cabbage(s)*

Many nouns that end in *-al* or *-ail* change the ending to *-aux*:

le métal, les métaux	*the metal(s)*
le bail, les baux	*the lease(s)*

Some nouns have irregular plurals:

l'oeil, les yeux	*the eye(s)*

Pronouns. Pronouns (I, you, etc.) replace nouns. Like nouns, pronouns may be the subjects or objects of verbs or the objects of prepositions.

Subject pronouns. The subject pronouns are *je* (I), *tu* (you), *il* (he, it), *elle* (she, it), *nous* (we), *vous* (you), *ils* (they), *elles* (they).

The pronoun *tu* is used only within a family, or by very close friends, or in speaking to children, animals, etc. Its plural is *vous*.

The pronoun *vous* is both singular and plural. It is the pronoun used whenever *tu* would not be proper, as in formal address.

Object pronouns. The object pronouns are *me* (me), *te* (you), *le* (him, it), *la* (her, it), *nous* (us), *vous* (you), *les* (them); also, *lui* (to him, her, it), *leur* (to them).

The pronouns *me, te, nous,* and *vous* may be direct or indirect objects. The pronouns *le, la,* and *les* are direct objects only.

Two of the pronouns, *me* and *te*, change their form in a positive command:

Répondez-moi.	*Answer me.*
Lave-toi.	*Wash yourself* (Wash you).

Disjunctive pronouns. Disjunctive pronouns are pronouns that follow a preposition or that are used alone. The disjunctive pronouns are *moi* (me, I), *toi* (you), *lui* (him, he, it), *elle* (her, she, it), *nous* (us, we), *vous* (you), *eux* (them, they: masculine), *elles* (them, they: feminine):

avec moi	*with me*
avec eux	*with them*
Qui est là? Lui.	*Who's there? He (is).*

The disjunctive pronouns are often used to give emphasis to the subject of a sentence:

Moi, je le crois. *I believe it.*

They are also used after *que* in comparisons:

Vous parlez mieux que lui.
You speak better than he (does).

Elle marche plus vite que moi.
She walks more quickly than I.

And they appear after *c'est*:

C'est lui qui l'a dit.
It is he who has said it.

Reflexive pronouns. Reflexive pronouns are pronouns that are used as objects and that refer to the subject of the verb. As direct or indirect objects, they are identical with the object pronouns (*me, te,* etc.), except that *se* is used in place of all third-person object pronouns (*le, la,* etc.):

Je me lave.	*I am washing myself.*
Il se lave.	*He is washing himself.*

The pronoun *se* may also mean "oneself," as in: *s'habiller* (to dress oneself).

Even though the reflexive pronoun is omitted in English, it is always expressed in French:

Je m'habille. *I am dressing.*

A French reflexive verb usually has to be translated into an English phrase that does not include a reflexive pronoun. For example, in English *s'asseoir* means simply "to sit down," *se coucher* means "to go to bed," *se lever* means "to get up," and so on.

Il s'assied.	*He sits down.*
Couchez-vous.	*Go to bed.*
Nous nous levons.	*We get up.*

A sentence like "I am washing my hands" becomes in literal, unidiomatic English "I am washing the hands to myself":

Je me lave les mains.	*I wash my hands.*
Lavez-vous les mains.	*Wash your hands.*

Possessive pronouns. The possessive pronouns express possession:

SINGULAR

Masculine	Feminine	
le mien	la mienne	*mine*
le tien	la tienne	*yours*
le sien	la sienne	*his, hers, its*
le nôtre	la nôtre	*ours*
le vôtre	la vôtre	*yours*
le leur	la leur	*theirs*

These pronouns agree in gender and number with the noun to which they refer:

Violà sa mère.	*There is his mother.*
Où est la mienne?	*Where is mine?*

The plural of the possessive pronouns is regular: *les miens, les miennes* (mine), *les tiens, les tiennes* (yours), etc.:

Voici nos filles.	*Here are our daughters.*
Où sont les leurs?	*Where are theirs?*

Possession may also be indicated by

FRENCH STREET SIGNS *in historic Old Montreal, the center of French Canada.*

use of the preposition *à* followed by a disjunctive pronoun:

Le livre est à moi.   *The book is mine.*

Relative pronouns. In English the relative pronouns are "who," "whom," "whose," "what," "which," and "that." The relative pronouns are always expressed in French, even though they are sometimes omitted in English.

When "who," "which," or "that" is used as a relative pronoun and as a subject, it is expressed in French by *qui:*

L'homme qui est ici est mon ami.
The man who is here is my friend.

Voici un livre qui m'intéresse.
Here is a book that interests me.

To express "whom" or to express "which" and "that" used as direct objects, the relative pronoun *que* is used:

La dame que vous voyez est ma mère.
The lady whom you see is my mother.

Le livre que vous avez est à moi.
The book which you have is mine.

The pronoun *dont* expresses "whose," "of whom," and "of which":

la dame dont nous parlons
the lady of whom we speak

le livre dont j'ai besoin
the book of which I have need

In a sentence like "Tell me what happened," the word "what" could be replaced by "that which." Whenever "what" can be replaced by "that which," either *ce qui* or *ce que* is used (*ce qui,* if "that which" or "what" is used as a subject; *ce que,* if "that which" or "what" is used as an object):

Dites-moi ce qui est arrivé.
Tell me what happened.

Dites-moi ce que vous savez.
Tell me what you know.

Here are some additional relative pronouns: *lequel* (masculine; plural: *lesquels*); *laquelle* (feminine; plural: *lesquelles*). These pronouns mean "who," "whom," or "which." The prepositions *à* (to) and *de* (of) combine with *lequel, lesquels,* and *lesquelles: auquel, duquel; auxquels, desquels; auxquelles, desquelles.* They do not combine with *laquelle: à laquelle, de laquelle.*

une maison dans laquelle
a house in which

une dame à laquelle
a lady to whom

un homme auquel
a man to whom

Phrases like *une dame à laquelle*

and *un homme auquel* occur especially in spoken French. In written French *une dame à qui* and *un homme à qui* are more usual, but after a preposition a form of *lequel* is used to refer to things.

Interrogative pronouns. Interrogative pronouns are pronouns used in asking questions. They include interrogative words like "who" or "what" when these words are used alone or in independent sentences. Unlike relative pronouns, interrogative pronouns do not depend on another word or another sentence.

The interrogative "who" and "whom" are both expressed by *qui:*

Qui l'a fait?   *Who did it?*
Qui?   *Who?*
Qui vois-tu?   *Whom do you see?*
A qui écrit-il?   *To whom is he writing?*

In a sentence, the interrogative "who" is often expressed by *qui est-ce qui* and the interrogative "whom" by *qui est-ce que:*

Qui est-ce qui chante?   *Who is singing?*
Qui est-ce que tu vois? *Whom do you see?*

When "what" is the direct object of an expressed verb, either *que* or *qu'est-ce que* is used:

Que désirez-vous?
What do you want?

Qu'est-ce que vous désirez?
What do you want?

When "what" is the subject of an expressed verb, *qu'est-ce qui* is used:

Qu'est-ce qui est arrivé?   *What happened?*

When "what" occurs after a preposition, *quoi* is used:

De quoi parle-t-il?
What is he talking about?

If "what" stands alone, *quoi* is used:

Ça me gêne. Quoi?
That irks me. What (does)?

The phrase *qu'est-ce que c'est que* is used in asking for the definition of something:

Qu'est-ce que c'est que la philosophie?
What is philosophy?

Notice also these questions:

Qu'est-ce que c'est?
What is it?

Qu'est-ce que c'est que cela?
What is that?

The interrogative pronouns used for "which one(s)," referring to a definite object, already mentioned, are *lequel, laquelle, lesquels, lesquelles:*

J'aime ce livre. Lequel?
I like this book. Which one?

THE FIRST FRENCH-CANADIAN PRIME MINISTER *of Canada was Pierre Trudeau.*

Demonstrative pronouns. Demonstrative pronouns are used in pointing out a person or thing without naming the person or thing. When "this" is used in a general sense, it is expressed by *ceci; cela* is used for "that":

Ecoutez ceci.   *Listen to this.*
Cela me plaît.   *That pleases me.*

Cela is often shortened to *ça:*

Ça vous plaît?   *Do you like that?*

The pronouns used for pointing out an individual person or thing are these: *celui-ci* (this one: masculine); *celle-ci* (this one: feminine); *ceux-ci* (these: masculine); *celles-ci* (these: feminine); also, *celui-là, celle-là* (that one), and *ceux-là, celles-là* (those).

Voici six complets. Celui-ci est à moi.
Here are six suits. This one is mine.

Phrases like "the one who" or "the one that" are expressed by *celui qui, celle qui,* etc. *Celui, celle,* etc. are also used with a following preposition.

celui qui arrive
the one that arrives

mon auto et celle de Jean
my car and John's

The pronoun *ce* means "this," "that," or "it" in certain phrases; it sometimes also means "he," "she," or "they":

C'est vrai.   *That's true.*
C'est mon frère.   *It's my brother.*
Ce sont mes amis.   *They're my friends.*

Indefinite pronouns. Indefinite pronouns are pronouns that indicate, without actually pointing out, someone or something understood or already mentioned.

A common indefinite pronoun is *on.* It corresponds to "one" (in the sense of "someone," "anyone," "a person," "people in general"):

> On ne dit pas ça.   *People don't say that.*

The disjunctive pronoun used with *on* is *soi.* The same pronoun is used with an indefinite pronoun like *chacun:*

> Chacun pour soi.   *Everyone for himself.*

The pronoun *en* expresses "some" or "any" when the noun is not specified:

> Voici de l'eau. Buvez-en.
> *Here is some water. Drink some.*

In other uses *en* may mean "of it," "of them," "about it," "from there," etc.:

> J'en ai besoin.   *I have need of it.*
> Il en parle.   *He speaks about it.*
> J'en viens.   *I come from there.*

The pronoun *y* may mean "about it," "on it," "to it," etc.:

> J'y travaille.   *I'm working on it.*
> Elle y est fidèle.   *She's faithful to it.*
> Il y pense.   *He's thinking about it.*

And *y* may mean "there":

> Nous y allons.   *We're going there.*

Y also occurs in *il y a* ("there is," "there are"):

> Y a-t-il de l'eau?   *Is there any water?*
> Oui, il y en a.   *Yes, there is some.*

Adjectives. An adjective is a word that limits or qualifies a noun in some way. English adjectives (such as "wise," "tall," etc.) have the same spelling when they modify a plural noun as they do when they modify a singular noun. But French adjectives typically add an ending when they modify a plural noun.

Plurals. Usually the plural of an adjective is shown by adding an *-s* to the masculine or feminine singular form:

> le petit garçon   *the little boy*
> les petits garçons   *the little boys*

Adjectives ending in *-s* or *-x* in the masculine singular remain unchanged in the plural:

> un mauvais signe   *a bad sign*
> des mauvais signes   *some bad signs*
> le vieux vase   *the old vase*
> les vieux vases   *the old vases*

Adjectives whose masculine singular ends in *-eau* add an *-x* instead of an *-s:*

> un beau château   *a beautiful castle*
> six beaux châteaux   *six beautiful castles*

The adjectives just given are examples of adjectives that precede the noun. Most adjectives, however, follow the noun:

> une robe bleue   *a blue dress*

Adjectives that precede the noun include the following masculine singular forms: *bon* (good), *grand* (big), *jeune* (young), *joli* (pretty), *long* (long), *nouveau* (new).

Gender. An adjective used with a feminine noun must also be feminine. An adjective is made feminine by adding an *e* to the masculine singular form:

> une grande maison   *a large house*

No *e* is added if the masculine form of the adjective already ends in *e.* Thus, *jeune* (young) and *jaune* (yellow) are used to modify both masculine and feminine nouns.

An adjective like *heureux* (happy) becomes *heureuse* in the feminine; *faux* (false) becomes *fausse; doux* (sweet) becomes *douce.*

Here are a few examples of feminines that have to be learned along with the masculine form of the adjectives: *vieille (vieux,* old); *blanche (blanc,* white); *fraîche (frais,* fresh); *belle (beau,* beautiful); *nouvelle (nouveau,* new); *bonne (bon,* good); *publique (public,* public); *longue (long,* long); *pareille (pareil,* alike).

An adjective like *vif* (lively) changes the *f* to *v* and then adds the *e: vive.* An adjective like *amer* (bitter) whose masculine form ends in *-e* plus a consonant changes to *amère* which has a grave accent over this *-e* as well as the regular feminine *-e* ending. The feminine of *ancien* (old) is *ancienne; naturel* (natural) becomes *naturelle.*

The forms *bel, nouvel,* and *vieil* are alternate masculine forms of *beau* (beautiful), *nouveau* (new), and *vieux* (old). These alternate forms are used before masculine nouns that begin with a vowel and before some that begin with *h:*

> un bel enfant   *a beautiful child*
> un vieil homme   *an old man*

Comparison. The comparative degree of the English adjective "beautiful" is "more beautiful"; the superlative degree is "most beautiful." Most French adjectives are compared in a similar way: "more" is expressed by *plus,* and "most" is expressed by *le* (or *la) plus.* Thus, the comparative degree of *beau* (beautiful) is *plus beau,* and the superlative degree is *le plus beau; belle,* the feminine of *beau,* becomes *plus belle* and *la plus belle.*

To express "less" and "least" in comparisons, *moins* and *le* (or *la) moins* are used. Thus, "less beautiful" and "least beautiful" become *moins beau* and *le moins beau* (or, for the

feminine, *moins belle* and *la moins belle).*

In a phrase like "as beautiful as," the first "as" is expressed by *aussi* and the second "as" is expressed by *que:*

> Ce château-ci est aussi beau que l'autre.
> *This castle is as beautiful as the other.*

The word *que* also expresses "than" in a phrase like "more beautiful than":

> Ceux-ci sont plus beaux que ceux-là.
> *These are more beautiful than those.*

Some English adjectives have special comparative forms. Thus, the comparative of "good" is "better." Similarly, certain French adjectives have special comparative forms. The comparative of *bon* (good), for example, is *meilleur* (and of *bonne* it is *meilleure*). The superlative of *bon* is *le meilleur* (and of *bonne* it is *la meilleure*).

Possessive adjectives. The possessive adjectives are:

> mon, ma, mes   *my*
> ton, ta, tes   *your*
> son, sa, ses   *his (her, its)*
> notre, nos   *our*
> votre, vos   *your*
> leur, leurs   *their*

Mon, ton, and *son* modify masculine singular nouns (*mon frère,* my brother); *ma, ta,* and *sa* modify feminine singular nouns (*ma mère,* my mother); *mes, tes,* and *ses* modify all plural nouns, whatever their gender (*mes frères,* my brothers; *mes soeurs,* my sisters).

Notre, votre, and *leur* modify any singular noun, masculine or feminine (*votre père,* your father; *votre mère,* your mother); *nos, vos,* and *leurs* modify all plural nouns, masculine or feminine (*leurs oncles,* their uncles; *leurs tantes,* their aunts).

Demonstrative adjectives. Words like "this" in "this car" or like "that" in "that book" are demonstrative adjectives.

Before a masculine singular noun *ce* is used to express either "this" or "that" (*ce livre:* this book, that book). To distinguish "this" from "that," *-ci* is attached to the noun (*ce livre-ci,* this book); to distinguish "that" from "this," *-là* is attached to the noun (*ce livre-là,* that book).

If the masculine singular noun begins with a vowel (and often if it begins with *h*), the form *cet* is used (*cet enfant:* this child, that child; *cet homme:* this man, that man).

Before a feminine singular noun *cette* is used (*cette dame:* this lady, that lady).

The form *ces* is used before all plural nouns, masculine or feminine (*ces hommes:* these men, those men; *ces femmes:* these women, those women).

Interrogative adjectives. In a sentence like "Which book do you want?" the word "which" is an interrogative adjective. "What" may be used in the same way. When so used, both "which" and "what" are expressed by *quel* (masculine singular), *quels* (masculine plural), *quelle* (feminine singular) and *quelles* (feminine plural): *Quel étudiant?* (Which student?); *Quelle cravate?* (Which tie?); *Quels étudiants?* (Which students?); *Quelles cravates?* (Which ties?).

These forms are also used in sentences like these:

Quel est cet animal?
What's that animal?

Quel sera le premier?
Which will be first?

And the same forms are used in exclamations:

Quel film! *What a movie!*

Adverbs. An adverb is a word that modifies a verb, an adjective, or another adverb.
Formation. An English adverb is often formed by the addition of *-ly* to an adjective. Similarly, French adverbs are often formed by the addition of *-ment* to adjectives. Thus, *rapidement* (rapidly) is formed from *rapide* (rapid); *vraiment* (truly) is formed from *vrai* (true).

The *-ment* can be added only to an adjectival form that ends in a vowel. If an adjective does not end in a vowel, the feminine form of the adjective is used; thus, the adverb *joyeusement* (joyously) is derived from *joyeuse*, the feminine of *joyeux* (joyous) which does not end in a vowel.
Comparison. Adverbs are generally compared just as adjectives are: *plus rapidement* (more rapidly), *moins rapidement* (less rapidly), *aussi rapidement que* (as rapidly as).

For the superlative, *le* (never *la*) is used: *le plus rapidement* (most rapidly), *le moins rapidement* (least rapidly).

Certain adverbs have special comparative forms. For example, the comparative of *bien* (well) is *mieux* (better). The superlative of *bien* is *le mieux*.

Negatives. In addition to *ne . . . pas*, various other negatives are used. Among the most important are these: *ne . . . jamais, ne . . . personne, ne . . . rien*. The word *jamais* means "never"; *personne* (when used with *ne* or alone) means "no one"; *rien* means "nothing":

Je ne le vois jamais. *I never see him.*
Jamais? *Never?*
Tu ne vois personne. *You see no one.*
Personne? *No one?*
Nous n'avons rien. *We have nothing.*
Rien? *Nothing?*

When *personne* and *rien* are used as subjects, the *ne* follows:

Personne n'est ici. *No one is here.*
Rien n'est facile. *Nothing is easy.*

Jamais means "ever" in a sentence without *ne*:

Avez-vous jamais été en France?
Have you ever been in France?

Prepositions. Certain verbs are followed by either *à* or *de* before an infinitive that completes the sense of the verbs:

Aidez-moi à le faire. *Help me do it.*
Il promet d'écrire. *He promises to write.*

Other verbs are followed immediately by the infinitive:

Je vais étudier. *I'm going to study.*
Nous devons partir. *We must leave.*

The noun alone follows *de* when this preposition is used after most adverbs of quantity:

beaucoup de livres *many books*
trop de voitures *too many cars*

If the noun is not expressed in a sentence using such expressions, it is replaced by *en* ("of them," "of it," etc.):

J'en ai beaucoup. *I have many of them.*

Verbs. French verbs are grouped into four classes (conjugations). Verbs in the first conjugation are those with infinitives ending in *-er* (*parler*, to speak). Second-conjugation verbs have infinitives ending in *-ir* (*finir*, to finish). In the third conjugation the infinitives end in *-oir* (*recevoir*, to receive). In the fourth, the ending is *-re* (*vendre*, to sell).
Present. The present tense of the English verb "to speak" is "I speak," "you speak," "he speaks," etc. Equivalent forms are "I am speaking" or "I do speak." A form like *je parle* may be translated by whichever form of the English verb fits best.

Here is the present indicative tense of the regular verbs in the four conjugations:

je parle / nous parlons
tu parles / vous parlez
il parle / ils parlent

je finis / nous finissons
tu finis / vous finissez
il finit / ils finissent

je reçois / nous recevons
tu reçois / vous recevez
il reçoit / ils reçoivent

je vends / nous vendons
tu vends / vous vendez
il vend / ils vendent

Imperative. The second-person formal imperative is formed by the omission of the "vous" of the present tense:

Parlez. *Speak.* Recevez. *Receive.*
Finissez. *Finish.* Vendez. *Sell.*

First-person imperatives ("Let us speak," "Let us finish," etc.) omit the "nous" of the present tense: *parlons, finissons, recevons, vendons*.

Second-person *tu* imperatives omit the *tu*; in the first conjugation only, the final *s* is also dropped: *parle, finis, reçois, vends*.

The omitted *-s* of an imperative such as *parle* is restored before *en* and *y*:

Parles-en. *Speak of it.*

Present perfect. The English present perfect of "to speak" is "I have spoken," "you have spoken," "he has spoken," etc. In the same way, the French present perfect of *parler* (to speak) is formed by combining the present tense of *avoir* (to have) with *parlé*, the past participle of *parler*:

j'ai parlé / nous avons parlé
tu as parlé / vous avez parlé
il a parlé / ils ont parlé

The present perfect of the other three conjugations is formed in the same way as in the first conjugation: *j'ai fini, j'ai reçu, j'ai vendu*.

Any present perfect may be translated by a form using "did" or by a simple past tense. Thus, *j'ai parlé* may be translated "I have spoken," or "I did speak," or "I spoke."

The past participle of the present perfect (as also of the past perfect and the future perfect) agrees in gender and number with a pronoun as a direct object:

Avez-vous vendu les robes?
Did you sell the dresses?

Oui, nous les avons vendues.
Yes, we sold them.

The present perfect of some verbs, such as *entrer*, is formed by combining the present tense of *être* (to be) with the past participle. The past participle of such verbs agrees in gender and number with the subject.

je suis entré / nous sommes entrés
tu es entré / vous êtes entré(s)
il est entré / ils sont entrés

A form like *je suis entré* is translated "I have entered" (even though *suis* literally means "am").

Because *vous* may be singular or plural, an *s* is shown in parentheses at "vous êtes entré(s)."

If the subject of any part of the present perfect of *entrer* were feminine, an *e* would be added after the *é* in the past participle: *je suis entrée; elles sont entrées*.

Reflexive verbs are conjugated in the present perfect in the same way that *entrer* is conjugated. Here is the present perfect of the reflexive verb *se laver* (to wash):

je me suis lavé	nous nous sommes lavés
tu t'es lavé	vous vous êtes lavé(s)
il s'est lavé	ils se sont lavés

Imperfect. The imperfect tense of "to speak" is "I was speaking," "you were speaking," etc.

je parlais	nous parlions
tu parlais	vous parliez
il parlait	ils parlaient
je finissais	nous finissions
tu finissais	vous finissiez
il finissait	ils finissaient
je recevais	nous recevions
tu recevais	vous receviez
il recevait	ils recevaient
je vendais	nous vendions
tu vendais	vous vendiez
il vendait	ils vendaient

The imperfect indicates a continued action or condition in the past. And so *il parlait*, for example, could be translated "he was speaking," "he used to speak," or "he would speak," or, sometimes, "he spoke."

Past perfect. The past perfect of "to speak" is "I had spoken," "you had spoken," etc.

j'avais parlé	nous avions parlé
tu avais parlé	vous aviez parlé
il avait parlé	ils avaient parlé

The form *j'avais* is part of the imperfect tense of *avoir*.

The past perfect of the other three conjugations is formed like the past perfect of *parler: j'avais fini, j'avais reçu, j'avais vendu.*

Verbs like *entrer* combine the imperfect of *être* with the past participle to form the past perfect.

j'étais entré	nous étions entrés
tu étais entré	vous étiez entré(s)
il était entré	ils étaient entrés

Reflexive verbs are conjugated like *entrer: je m'étais lavé, tu t'étais lavé,* etc.

Future perfect. The future perfect of "to speak" is "I will have spoken," "you will have spoken," etc.

j'aurai parlé	nous aurons parlé
tu auras parlé	vous aurez parlé
il aura parlé	ils auront parlé

The form *j'aurai* is part of the future tense of *avoir*.

The future perfect of the other three conjugations is formed like the future perfect of *parler: j'aurai fini, j'aurai reçu, j'aurai vendu.*

Verbs like *entrer* combine the future of *être* with the past participle:

je serai entré	nous serons entrés
tu seras entré	vous serez entré(s)
il sera entré	ils seront entrés

Reflexive verbs are conjugated like

entrer: je me serai lavé, tu te seras lavé, etc.

Future. The future tense of "to speak" is "I will speak," "you will speak," etc.

je parlerai	nous parlerons
tu parleras	vous parlerez
il parlera	ils parleront
je finirai	nous finirons
tu finiras	vous finirez
il finira	ils finiront
je recevrai	nous recevrons
tu recevras	vous recevrez
il recevra	ils recevront
je vendrai	nous vendrons
tu vendras	vous vendrez
il vendra	ils vendront

Present conditional. The present conditional of "to speak" is "I would speak," "you would speak," etc. (as in "I would speak if I could").

je parlerais	nous parlerions
tu parlerais	vous parleriez
il parlerait	ils parleraient
je finirais	nous finirions
tu finirais	vous finiriez
il finirait	ils finiraient
je recevrais	nous recevrions
tu recevrais	vous receviez
il recevrait	ils recevraient
je vendrais	nous vendrions
tu vendrais	vous vendriez
il vendrait	ils vendraient

Past conditional. The past conditional of "to speak" is "I would have spoken," "you would have spoken," etc.

j'aurais parlé	nous aurions parlé
tu aurais parlé	vous auriez parlé
il aurait parlé	ils auraient parlé

The form *j'aurais* is part of the present conditional of *avoir*.

BABAR THE ELEPHANT, *created by Frenchman Laurent de Brunhoff, is a favorite both in French and in English.*

The past conditional of the other three conjugations is formed like the past conditional of *parler: j'aurais fini, j'aurais reçu, j'aurais vendu.*

Verbs like *entrer* combine the present conditional of *être* with the past participle:

je serais entré	nous serions entrés
tu serais entré	vous seriez entré(s)
il serait entré	ils seraient entrés

Reflexive verbs are conjugated like *entrer: je me serais lavé, tu te serais lavé,* etc.

Present subjunctive. The subjunctive is used after verbs expressing desire, doubt, emotion, etc.:

Il veut que nous parlions lentement.
He wants us to speak slowly.

The subjunctive is also used after certain conjunctions like *quoique* (although):

Quoiqu'elle soit ici, je ne l'ai pas vue.
Although she is here, I haven't seen her.

It is also used after an expression like *il faut* (it is necessary):

Il faut que nous finissions vite.
It is necessary that we finish quickly.

The subjunctive, introduced by *que*, expresses a third-person imperative:

Qu'il finisse vite.
Let him finish quickly.

Here is the present subjunctive of the model verbs:

je parle	nous parlions
tu parles	vous parliez
il parle	ils parlent
je finisse	nous finissions
tu finisses	vous finissiez
il finisse	ils finissent

TOUS LES MATINS JE PRENDS UNE DOUCHE

Every morning I take a shower.

I rub my arms. Je frotte mes bras.

I rub my stomach. Je frotte mon ventre.

I rub my back. Je frotte mon dos.

I rub my left leg. Je frotte ma jambe gauche.

I rub my right leg. Je frotte ma jambe droite.

And while I rub myself, **I sing.** Je chante.

Then I take **a large towel**—une grande serviette—

and **I dry myself.** Je me sèche.

And **I put on my clothes.** Je m'habille.

Then I am ready. Alors je suis prêt.

je reçoive   nous recevions
tu reçoives   vous receviez
il reçoive   ils reçoivent

je vende   nous vendions
tu vendes   vous vendiez
il vende   ils vendent

Past subjunctive. The past subjunctive expresses a completed action or a condition, as after a verb of doubt:

> Je doute qu'ils aient fini.
> *I doubt that they have finished.*

Here is the past subjunctive of *parler*:

j'aie parlé   nous ayons parlé
tu aies parlé   vous ayez parlé
il ait parlé   ils aient parlé

The form *j'aie* is part of the present subjunctive of *avoir*.

The past subjunctive of the other three conjugations is formed like the past subjunctive of *parler: j'aie fini, j'aie reçu, j'aie vendu*.

Verbs like *entrer* combine the present subjunctive of *être* with the past participle:

je sois entré   nous soyons entrés
tu sois entré   vous soyez entré(s)
il soit entré   ils soient entrés

Reflexive verbs are conjugated like *entrer: je me sois lavé, tu te sois lavé,* etc.

An imperfect subjunctive and a pluperfect subjunctive also occur, but they are relatively infrequent.

Past definite. The past definite is a special past tense used chiefly in written French, as in some kinds of narration. It is translated into English by a simple past tense:

> Il parla de toutes ces choses.
> *He spoke of all these things.*

Here is the past definite of the model verbs:

je parlai   nous parlâmes
tu parlas   vous parlâtes
il parla   ils parlèrent

je finis   nous finîmes
tu finis   vous finîtes
il finit   ils finirent

je reçus   nous reçûmes
tu reçus   vous reçûtes
il reçut   ils reçurent

je vendis   nous vendîmes
tu vendis   vous vendîtes
il vendit   ils vendirent

Past anterior. The past anterior expresses an action or condition that precedes what is expressed by the past definite. It is translated into English by the past perfect:

> Quand il eut parlé, il s'assit.
> *When he had spoken, he sat down.*

Here is the past anterior of *parler:*

j'eus parlé   nous eûmes parlé
tu eus parlé   vous eûtes parlé
il eut parlé   ils eurent parlé

The form *j'eus* is part of the past definite of *avoir*.

The past anterior of the other three

IRREGULAR VERBS

	Present	Imperfect	Future	Past Definite	Present Subjunctive	Imperative
aller (to go) **allant** **allé**	vais vas va allons allez vont	allais	irai	allai	aille ailles aille allions alliez aillent	va allons allez
avoir (to have) **ayant** **eu**	ai as a avons avez ont	avais	aurai	eus eus eut eûmes eûtes eurent	aie aies ait ayons ayez aient	aie ayons ayez
boire (to drink) **buvant** **bu**	bois bois boit buvons buvez boivent	buvais	boirai	bus	boive boives boive buvions buviez boivent	bois buvons buvez
être (to be) **étant** **été**	suis es est sommes êtes sont	étais	serai	fus fus fut fûmes fûtes furent	sois sois soit soyons soyez soient	sois soyons soyez
faire (to do, make) **faisant** **fait**	fais fais fait faisons faites font	faisais	ferai	fis fis fit fîmes fîtes firent	fasse fasses fasse fassions fassiez fassent	fais faisons faites
pouvoir (to be able) **pouvant** **pu**	peux *or* puis peux peut pouvons pouvez peuvent	pouvais	pourrai	pus pus put pûmes pûtes purent	puisse puisses puisse puissions puissiez puissent	
savoir (to know) **sachant** **su**	sais sais sait savons savez savent	savais	saurai	sus sus sut sûmes sûtes surent	sache saches sache sachions sachiez sachent	sache sachons sachez
venir (to come) **venant** **venu**	viens viens vient venons venez viennent	venais	viendrai	vins vins vint vînmes vîntes vinrent	vienne viennes vienne venions veniez viennent	viens venons venez
voir (to see) **voyant** **vu**	vois vois voit voyons voyez voient	voyais	verrai	vis vis vit vîmes vîtes virent	voie voies voie voyions voyiez voient	vois voyons voyez
vouloir (to want) **voulant** **voulu**	veux veux veut voulons voulez veulent	voulais	voudrai	voulus voulus voulut voulûmes voulûtes voulurent	veuille veuilles veuille voulions vouliez veuillent	veuille veuillons veuillez

conjugations is formed like the past anterior of *parler: j'eus fini, j'eus reçu, j'eus vendu.*

Verbs like *entrer* combine the past definite of *être* with the past participle:

je fus entré   nous fûmes entrés
tu fus entré   vous fûtes entré(s)
il fut entré   ils furent entrés

Reflexive verbs are conjugated like *entrer: je me fus lavé, tu te fus lavé,* etc.

Present participle. The present participle ends in *-ant (parlant,* speaking):

parlant   recevant
finissant   vendant

Past participle. The past participle ends in *-é* (first conjugation), *-i* (second conjugation), and *-u* (third and fourth conjugations):

parlé   reçu
fini   vendu

Irregular verbs. A sampling of irregular verbs is given here. The infinitive, the present participle, and the past participle are shown in boldface type. Five tenses of each verb

are given next, together with the imperative.

The pronouns (*je, tu,* etc.) are here omitted, to save space.

If only a single form is shown (*allais*), *je* (or *j'*) is to be understood with it (*j'allais*). The remaining forms use the same stem (as *all-* of *allais*) plus the regular endings of the tense shown (*tu allais, il allait,* etc.).

The present conditional, not shown, can be inferred from the stem of the future (thus, *j'irais* can be inferred from *j'irai,* the future of *aller*).

—*Christopher T. Hoolihan*

Spanish

Sentence structure.

Declarative sentences. In a simple declarative sentence the usual word order is: article, noun (subject), verb, article, noun (object).

El gato toma la leche.
The cat drinks the milk.

An adjective ordinarily follows the noun:

el gato blanco   *the white cat*

An adverb modifying a verb is placed as close as possible to the verb, usually immediately after it:

El gato come rápidamente.
The cat eats quickly.

A preposition precedes the noun or noun phrase used as its object:

en la cocina   *in the kitchen*

A conjunction connects two or more parts of a sentence:

El gato tomó la leche y salió.
The cat drank the milk and went out.

A subject pronoun may replace the subject noun:

Él tomó la leche.   *It drank the milk.*

Object pronouns are ordinarily placed before the verb, and the indirect object pronoun precedes the direct:

Ella me los dio.   *She gave them to me.*

The elements in a sentence are frequently shifted—sometimes for syntactic reasons, sometimes to indicate a change in meaning or emphasis, sometimes for variety, and sometimes for poetic or other stylistic effects.

The verb, for example, often precedes the subject:

Entró el profesor.   *The professor came in.*

If an adjective stresses a quality inherent in the noun it modifies, rather than simply differentiating the noun from others, the adjective usually comes first:

la triste verdad   *the sad truth*
la niña triste   *the child who is sad*

A demonstrative or possessive adjective usually precedes the noun, as does an adjective indicating quantity or sequence:

esta casa   *this house*
nuestros amigos   *our friends*
cinco perros   *five dogs*
la última clase   *the last class*

An adjective modified by an adverb ordinarily follows the noun, as do adjectives joined by a conjunction:

una persona sumamente agradable
a most agreeable person

el árbol alto y verde
the tall, green tree

Although an adverb that indicates manner or degree ordinarily follows the verb, one that indicates place or time is as likely to precede the verb as to follow it:

CESAR CHAVEZ, *a prominent spokesman for Spanish-speaking Chicanos in the Southwest U.S.*

Afuera hace calor.   *It's hot outside.*

An adverb precedes another adverb or an adjective that it modifies:

David habla muy claramente.
David speaks very clearly.

Gloria es menos lista.
Gloria is less clever.

Simple negative adverbs such as *no* and *nunca* precede the verb, but adverbs added for negative emphasis follow the verb. (Double negatives are common in Spanish.)

Ella no viene.   *She isn't coming.*
Ella no viene nunca.   *She never comes.*

Though object pronouns ordinarily precede the verb, they follow the verb and are attached to it if the verb form is an infinitive, an affirmative imperative, or a present participle. To preserve the original verb stress, written accents may be added.

Carlos va a dármelos.
Carlos is going to give them to me.

Démelos, Carlos, por favor.
Give them to me, Carlos, please.

Rosa entró saludándonos.
Rosa came in, saying hello to us.

Interrogative sentences. An inverted question mark is placed before a written interrogative sentence or sentence part. A regular question mark follows the sentence.

A question can be formed by placing the verb before the subject:

¿Tiene hambre el perro?
Is the dog hungry?

Interrogative adjectives, adverbs, or pronouns may also be used:

¿Cuántas naranjas?
How many oranges?

¿Dónde está Juan?
Where is John?

¿Quién vive aquí?
Who lives here?

¿Cuál prefieres?
Which one do you prefer?

An interrogative clause or phrase may be added to a statement:

Usted es americano, ¿no es verdad?
You're an American, right?

Imperative sentences. Commands or requests may be formal or familiar. In Spain and the Americas the third-person present subjunctive is used for formal commands. If used out of courtesy, *usted* (you: singular) and *ustedes* (you: plural) follow the verb, and *por favor* (please) is often added:

Abra usted la puerta, por favor.
Open the door, please.

Hablen ustedes más despacio.
Speak more slowly.

In Spain and the Americas the true imperative is used for familiar commands (those used with friends, relatives, children, etc.) that are affirmative and singular. Subject pronouns are not ordinarily used:

Abre la ventana, por favor
Open the window, please.

In Castilian Spanish the true imperative is also used for plural affirmative familiar commands. But in the Americas (as in plural formal commands) the plural third-person present subjunctive is used. Thus, in American Spanish, "Open the window" becomes "Abran la ventana." In Castilian the sentence becomes "Abrid la ventana."

In both Spain and the Americas, the second-person present subjunctive, singular, is used for familiar commands that are negative and singular:

No abras la ventana.
Don't open the window.

In Castilian Spanish the plural, second-person present subjunctive is used for plural, negative familiar commands. But in the Americas the plural, third-person present subjunctive is used. Thus, in American Spanish, "Don't open the window" becomes "No abran la ventana." In Castilian the sentence becomes "No abráis la ventana."

Third-person imperatives, singular and plural, are expressed in both Spain and the Americas by the corresponding present-subjunctive forms (¡Que salgan ellos! *Let them leave!*), as the first-person plural imperatives (Salgamos. *Let's leave.*). The inverted exclamation mark shown in the first example is also used in written exclamations (¡Qué sorpresa! *What a surprise!*).

Articles.

Definite articles. The definite article (the) is *el* (before a masculine noun) and *la* (before a feminine noun):

el oro   *the gold*
la pluma   *the pen*

Before plural nouns, *el* is changed to *los; la* is changed to *las:*

los burros   *the burros*
las niñas   *the girls*

Before a feminine singular noun beginning with a stressed *a* sound, the masculine article *el* is used; but *las* is used before the plural:

el águila   *the eagle*
las águilas   *the eagles*

A neuter article, *lo,* is occasionally used before adjectives; it gives adjectives the force of nouns: *lo neuvo* (that which is new).

When *a* (to) precedes *el,* the *a* and the *el* combine into *al; de* (of) and *el* become *del:*

al teatro   *to the theater*
del edificio   *of the building*

The definite article is used before clearly identified nouns:

Los maestros llegan a la escuela.
The teachers arrive at the school.

It is also used before nouns taken in a general sense:

Los payasos divierten a la genté.
Clowns amuse people.

Except in direct address, it occurs before most titles:

la señora Chávez   *Señora Chávez*
el coronel Vargas   *Colonel Vargas*

Except after the verb *ser* (to be), it is used before names of days of the week:

Hoy es lunes.
Today is Monday.

Carlos viene el martes.
Carl is coming Tuesday.

It is likewise used before names of months, seasons, and expressions of time:

el abril   *April*
la primavera   *spring*
las diez de la mañana   *ten in the morning*

The names of certain continents, countries, states, and cities are preceded by the definite article:

la América del Sur   *South America*
los Estados Unidos   *the United States*
la Florida   *Florida*
la Habana   *Havana*

The definite article is also used before the names of languages:

Me gusta el francés.   *I like French.*

However, it is not used after the verb *hablar* (to speak) unless there is an intervening word or phrase:

¿Habla usted alemán?
Do you speak German?

¿Habla usted bien el alemán?
Do you speak German well?

Nor is the definite article used before the names of languages when these names are preceded by *en* (in) or *de* (of):

en español   *in Spanish*
de inglés   *of English*

The definite article often replaces the possessive adjective used in English before a noun denoting an article of clothing or a part of the body:

Me quité el abrigo.
I took off my overcoat.

¿Le duele a usted la cabeza?
Your head hurts?

Indefinite articles. The indefinite article (a, an) is *un* (before a masculine noun) and *una* (before a feminine noun):

un disco   *a disk*
una palabra   *a word*

"Some" is expressed by *unos* (before a masculine plural) and *unas* (before a feminine plural):

unos discos   *some disks*
unas palabras   *some words*

Before a feminine singular noun beginning with a stressed *a* sound, the masculine article *un* is used; but *unas* is used before the plural:

un alma   *a soul*
unas almas   *some souls*

The indefinite article is used before nouns not yet clearly identified:

Una amiga me regaló un libro.
A friend gave me a book.

The indefinite article is ordinarily omitted before a noun of nationality, occupation, rank, or political affiliation when the noun follows the verb *ser:*

Arturo es peruano.
Arthur is a Peruvian.

Mi sobrina es médica.
My niece is a doctor.

But if such a noun is modified, the indefinite article is retained:

Borges es un escritor famoso.
Borges is a famous writer.

The indefinite article is omitted before a qualifying adjective like *mil* (thousand) and *otro* (other):

> Pasaron mil soldados.
> *A thousand soldiers passed by.*

> ¿Vendrás en otra ocasión?
> *Will you come some other time?*

It is also omitted after adjectives like *qué* (what, what a) and *tal* (such, such a) in exclamations:

> ¡Qué maravilla! *What a marvel!*

Nouns.

Gender. Each noun is classed as masculine or feminine, not necessarily because it denotes a male or female but because of grammatical gender. The neuter gender is limited to abstract nouns that are ordinarily formed by the combination of *lo* and an adjective. The gender of most nouns has to be memorized.

Nouns like *padre* (father) are of course masculine. In general, the following nouns are also masculine: those ending in *o, e, l, r,* (*libro*, book; *juguete*, toy; *sol*, sun; *favor*, favor); those of Greek origin ending in *ma, pa, ta* (*idioma*, language; *mapa*, map; *planeta*, planet); names of trees, and of days and months (*roble*, oak; *sábado*, Saturday; *enero*, January).

By natural gender, nouns like *madre* (mother) are feminine. The following nouns are also ordinarily feminine: those ending in *a, z, d* (*biblioteca*, library; *paz*, peace; *salud*, health); those ending in *-ión* and *-umbre* (*canción*, song; *costumbre*, custom); names of fruits, and of letters of the alphabet (*naranja*, orange; *una* c, a *c*).

Most masculine nouns ending in *o* change the *o* to *a* for the feminine (*muchacho*, boy; *muchacha*, girl). Most masculine nouns ending in *-ol, -or, -ón, -án,* and *és* add an *a* and, as necessary, drop a written accent (*el español*, Spaniard: *la española; el doctor*, doctor: *la doctora; el patrón*, boss: *la patrona; el alemán*, German: *la alemana; el inglés*, Englishman: *la inglesa*, Englishwoman).

Many nouns denoting persons remain unchanged in the feminine, except for the replacement of *el* by *la* (*el joven*, the youth: *la joven*).

Some nouns change gender according to their meanings (*el frente*, the front; *la frente*, the forehead). Other nouns can be either masculine or feminine, with no change in meaning (*el mar* or *la mar*, the sea).

Plurals. Nouns ending in an unstressed vowel or in a stressed *e* are made plural by the addition of *s*:

> la manzana, las manzanas   *the apple(s)*
> el bebé, los bebés   *the infant(s)*

Most nouns ending in a consonant or in a stressed vowel other than *e* add *-es*:

> el mes, los meses   *the month(s)*
> el cebú, los cebúes *the zebu(s)*

Nouns ending in *z* change the *z* to *c* and add *-es*:

> el lápiz, los lápices   *the pencil(s)*

Nouns ending in unstressed *-es* or *-is* remain unchanged:

> el jueves, los jueves   *Thursday(s)*

Most pluralized nouns retain the stress of their singular forms, even if written accents must be added or deleted:

> el joven, los jóvenes   *the youth(s)*
> la ocasión, las ocasiones   *the occasion(s)*

Pronouns.

Pronouns (I, you, etc.) replace nouns. Like nouns, pronouns may be the subjects or objects of verbs or the objects of prepositions.

PERSONAL PRONOUNS

		Subject	Direct Object	Indirect Object
1ST	SING.	yo	me	me
	PL.	nosotros nosotras	nos	nos
2ND	SING.	tú	te	te
	PL.	vosotros vosotras	os	os
3RD	SING.	usted	lo, le, la	le
		él	lo, le	le
		ella	la	le
	PL.	ustedes	los, las	les
		ellos	los	les
		ellas	las	les

Subject pronouns are frequently implied in the verb but not expressed:

> Leemos mucho. *We read a lot.*

When subject pronouns are expressed, it is usually for clarity, for emphasis, or out of courtesy.

The pronouns *usted* and *ustedes* are the formal, or polite, pronouns for "you." These pronouns are used with third-person verb forms:

> Ustedes hablan bien. *You speak well.*

The pronouns *tú* is the familiar pronoun for "you" (singular). In Castilian Spanish its plural is *vosotros* and *vosotras*, but the invariable *ustedes* is used in American Spanish.

Because all Spanish nouns are either masculine or feminine, *el* and *ella* mean "it" when referring to a thing.

The pronouns *me, te, le, nos,* and *os* may be direct or indirect objects. The pronouns *lo, la, los,* and *las* are direct objects only.

An additional object pronoun is *les. Les* is the indirect-object form of *los* and *las*. The indirect-object form of *la* is *le*.

CHINESE AND CARIBBEAN FOOD *is offered by a New York restaurant in Spanish and English.*

Either *lo* or *le* may be used as the masculine third-person singular direct-object pronoun; *lo* is more commonly used in the Americas, and *le* is more commonly used in Spain.

Both direct and indirect object pronouns precede most verb forms, but they follow and are attached to others. In either position the indirect object pronoun precedes the direct.

The third-person, indirect object pronouns *le* and *les* are changed to *se* whenever either one of them immediately precedes a direct object pronoun:

> Se lo di. *I gave it to him.*

Object pronouns used after a preposition are identical in form with the subject pronouns, except that *mí* is used in place of *yo* and *ti* is used in place of *tú*:

> para mí   *for me*
> para ti   *for you*

When *mí* and *ti* are used with *con* (with), special forms are used:

> conmigo   *with me*
> contigo   *with you*

Relative pronouns. In English the relative pronouns are "who," "whom," "whose," "what," "which," and "that." The relative pronouns are always expressed in Spanish, even though they are sometimes omitted in English.

The relative pronoun *que* means "who," "whom," "which," or "that." It refers to subjects and objects, persons and things, whatever the gender or number involved.

> el libro que   *the book which*
> la alumna que   *the pupil who(m)*
> los libros que *the books which*

The relative pronouns *quien* and *quienes* refer only to persons and mean "who" or "whom." *Quien* is singular, *quienes* plural.

> la muchacha quien   *the girl who(m)*
> los abogados quienes *the lawyers who(m)*

Other relative pronouns are these: *el cual, la cual, lo cual, los cuales, las cuales; el que, la que, lo que; los que, las que.* These pronouns mean "who," "whom," "which," etc. They refer to either persons or things, and their form changes according to the gender and number of that to which they refer.

la biblioteca en la cual pienso trabajar
the library in which I think I'll work

The pronouns *cuyo, cuya, cuyos,* and *cuyas* mean "whose" or "of which." They refer to either persons or things and distinguish gender and number.

Raúl, cuya hermana es amiga mía
Ralph, whose sister is my friend

Reflexive pronouns. Reflexive pronouns are pronouns used as objects that refer to the subject of the verb. They may be objects of reflexive verbs or objects in a prepositional phrase that modifies the verb.

As objects of verbs the reflexive pronouns are these: *me* (myself), *te* (yourself), *se* (yourself, himself, herself, itself), *nos* (ourselves), *os* (yourselves), *se* (yourselves, themselves).

Nosotros nos vestimos.
We dressed ourselves.

Even without an apparent reflexive meaning, many Spanish verbs take reflexive pronouns:

¿Por qué se fue usted?
Why did you go away?

A reflexive construction may be equivalent to the passive voice:

Se habla portugués en el Brasil.
Portuguese is spoken in Brazil.

As objects of prepositions the reflexive pronouns are these: *mí* (myself), *ti* (yourself), *sí* (yourself, himself, herself, itself), *nosotros* and *nosotras* (ourselves), *vosotros* and *vosotras* (yourselves), *sí* (yourselves, themselves). These pronouns frequently take the intensive reflexive *mismo* or one of its variations:

Ellas hablan a sí mismas.
They talk to themselves.

When *sí* is used with *con*, the special form *consigo* is used.

Interrogative pronouns. The principal interrogative pronouns are: *qué* (what); *quién, quiénes* (who); *cuál, cuáles* (which, what, which one, which ones); *cuánto, cuánta* (how much); *cuántos; cuántas* (how many). All but *qué* agree in number with the noun they replace. The various forms of *cuánto* agree in gender as well.

¿Qué es la fecha?   *What's the date?*

¿Cuál de los dos?   *Which of the two?*
¿Cuántas vienen?   *How many are coming?*

Demonstrative pronouns. Demonstrative pronouns point out a person or thing without naming the person or thing.

"This" is expressed by *éste, ésta;* "these," by *éstos, éstas:*

De todos los libros, éstos son nuevos.
Of all the books, these are new.

In referring to persons or things not very remote from the speaker, "that" is expressed by *ése, ésa*, and "those" by *ésos, ésas:*

¿Es ése el suyo?   *Is that yours?*

In referring to persons or things remote from both the speaker and the person addressed, "that" is expressed by *aquél, aquélla*, and "those" by *aquéllos, aquéllas:*

Me gustan aquéllos.   *Those please me.*

The forms *esto, eso,* and *aquello* are neuter, but, since there are no neuter nouns in Spanish, these refer only to situations, statements, or ideas:

Aquello es lo que me interesa.
That is what interests me.

Possessive pronouns. The possessive pronouns express possession:

SINGULAR

Masculine	Feminine	
el mío	la mía	*mine*
el tuyo	la tuya	*yours*
el suyo	la suya	*yours, his, hers, its*
el nuestro	la nuestra	*ours*
el vuestro	la vuestra	*yours*
el suyo	la suya	*yours, theirs*

The plural of the possessive pronouns is regular: *los míos, las mías* (mine), *los tuyos, las tuyas,* (yours), etc.

The possessive pronouns agree in gender and number with the noun to which they refer.

Third-person possessive pronouns are often replaced by *de usted, de él,* etc.

After a form of the verb *ser* (to be), the possessive pronoun is usually used without the definite article: *Es mío* (It's mine).

Adjectives. Adjectives agree in gender and number with the nouns they modify.

Gender. The feminine of adjectives ending in *o* is formed by changing the masculine ending *o* to *a: cansado* (tired), *cansada.* To adjectives of nationality ending in a consonant, an *a* is added; written accents are dropped as necessary: *francés* (French), *francesa.*

Some adjectives have the same form for both genders: *feliz* (happy), *joven* (young), *pobre* (poor), etc.

Some adjectives drop the final *o* before a masculine singular noun: *un buen amigo;* but *una buena amiga* (a good friend). The adjective *grande* (big) drops the *de* before all singular nouns: *un gran edificio* (a big building).

Number. Adjectives form the plural in the same way as nouns: *los niños contentos* (the happy children); *los días felices* (the happy days).

Comparison. The regular comparative form is shown by placing *más* (more) or *menos* (less) before the adjective: *alto* (high), *más alto* (higher). The superlative usually adds the definite article: *el más alto* (highest).

Some adjectives are irregular: *bueno* (good), *mejor* (better), *el* (or *la*) *mejor* (best).

The suffixes *-ísimo(s)* or *-ísima(s)* may be used to express "most" or "very"; *dificilísimo* (most difficult), *grandísimo* (very big).

Demonstrative adjectives. Except for having no written accents and no neuter forms, the demonstrative adjectives are identical with the demon-

BILINGUAL LABELS—*in Spanish and English—are common on specialty foods.*

BARRY FEIG

strative pronouns: *este perro* (this dog); *esa tienda* (that store); *aquellas épocas* (those epochs).

Possessive adjectives. The possessive adjectives are:

mi, mis	*my*
tu, tus	*your*
su, sus	*your, his, her, its*
neustro(s), nuestra(s)	*our*
vuestro(s), vuestra(s)	*your*
su, sus	*your, their*

These adjectives precede the noun: *su amigo* (your friend). But emphatic possessive adjectives (*mío, tuyo*, etc., identical with the possessive pronouns except for omission of the definite article) follow: *amigo mío* (my friend).

Interrogative adjectives. The most common interrogative adjectives are: *qué* (which, what); *cuál, cuáles* (which); *cuánto, cuánta* (how much); *cuántos, cuántas* (how many).

¿Qué libros?	*Which books?*
¿Cuántas veces?	*How many times?*

Adverbs. In Spanish, an adverb is always placed as close as possible to the verb, adjective, or other adverb it modifies.

Formation of adverbs. Some adverbs, especially those indicating manner or degree, are formed by adding the suffix *-mente* to the singular feminine form of the corresponding adjective or to the invariable form: *solamente* (solely), *ferozmente* (ferociously). If an adjective has a written accent, this accent is retained even though the principal stress shifts to the second-last syllable: *fácil* (easy), *fácilmente* (easily). When two or more adverbs formed with *-mente* occur together, only the last takes the suffix:

Lola contestó segura y claramente.
Lola answered firmly and clearly.

Some adverbs take the masculine singular form of the adjective, even to indicate manner or degree:

Habla despacio, por favor.
Speak slowly, please.

Some adverbs are invariable in form. This group includes affirmative adverbs like *sí* (yes), *por cierto* (surely), *sin duda* (without doubt), and *de veras* (truly); negative adverbs like *no* (no), *jamás* (never), *nunca* (never), and *tampoco* (neither, nor); and adverbs that express doubt like *tal vez* (perhaps, maybe) and *quizás* or *quizá* (perhaps).

Other adverbs that are fixed in form include adverbs of time like *ayer* (yesterday), *tarde* (late), *después* (afterward), and *mañana* (tomorrow); adverbs of place like *aquí* (here), *alrededor* (around), *debajo* (beneath, below), and *lejos* (far, far off); adverbs of quantity like *bastante* (enough, quite), *mucho* (much), *muy* (very, much), *demasiado* (too much), *más* (more, plus), and *menos* (less, minus); and interrogative adverbs like *cómo* (how), *cuándo* (when), and *dónde* (where).

¿Cuándo piensa usted volver?
When do you think you will return?

Quizás mañana.
Perhaps tomorrow.

Tarde o temprano llegaremos.
We will arrive sooner or later.

Comparison of adverbs. The comparison of adverbs is generally the same as that of adjectives. Thus, the regular comparative form is shown by placing *más* (more) or *menos* (less) before the adverb:

María maneja más cuidadosamente.
Mary drives more carefully.

¿Escribes menos despacio?
Are you writing less slowly?

The regular superlative of adverbs is shown by placing *lo más* or *lo menos* before the adverb.

Antonio se expresa lo más claramente.
Anthony expresses himself the most clearly.

Some adverbs have irregular forms for the comparative and the superlative: *bien* (well), *mejor* (better), *lo mejor* (best); *mucho* (much), *más* (more), *lo más* (the most). To form the absolute superlative the suffix *-ísimo* or *-ísima* (very) is added to the stem of adverbs that do not end in *-mente*: *muchísimo* (very much; from *mucho*, much), *tardísimo* (very late; from *tarde*, late). In order to preserve the consonant sound of the stem, a spelling change may be necessary: *cerquísima* (very near; from *cerca*, near). For adverbs that end in *-mente* the special suffix *-ísimamente* is used to add the idea of "very": *rarísimamente* (very rarely; from *raramente*, rarely).

Prepositions. A preposition is a word or phrase inserted before a noun, or before a word or phrase used as a noun, to show the relationship between such a noun and the rest of the sentence. Prepositions may be either simple or compound. Simple prepositions are prepositions that consist of just one word. Compound prepositions are prepositions that consist of two or more words.

Common one-word prepositions are: *a* (to, toward, at), *ante* (before), *bajo* (under), *de* (of, from), *en* (in, into, at, on), *entre* (among, between), *para* (for, to), *por* (by, through, for), and *sobre* (over, on, about).

Voy a la escuela en una hora.
I'm going to school in an hour.

entre la casa y la biblioteca
between the house and the library

Besides its many other uses, the preposition *a* must be placed before the direct object of a verb when the direct object is a person or a personified thing. This peculiarity of Spanish grammar is known as the "personal *a*."

¿Conoce usted a Daniel?
Do you know Daniel?

Él quiere a su gato.
He likes his cat.

Common compound prepositions include *acerca de* (about, concerning), *a causa de* (on account of), *afuera de* (outside), *antes de* (before), *debajo de* (below), *delante de* (before), *dentro de* (inside), *después de* (after), *enfrente de* (opposite, in front of), *en vez de* (instead of), *junto a* (next to), and *lejos de* (far from).

La pelota está debajo de la silla.
The ball is underneath the chair.

Conjunctions. The two most frequently used conjunctions are *y* (and) and *o* (or). The conjunction *y* is changed to *e* before a word beginning with the letters *i* or *hi*:

Juan y Eva son serios e inteligentes.
John and Eva are serious and intelligent.

The conjunction *o* is changed to *u* before a word beginning with the letters *o* or *ho*:

¿Va el avión a Roma o a Paris?
Is the plane going to Rome or to Paris?

Hay lugar para dos mujeres u hombres.
There is space for two ladies or gentlemen.

Other connecting words often used in Spanish include *aunque* (although), *cuando* (when), *como* (as, if, unless), *pero* (but), *porque* (because), *que* (that) and *si*. The connecting word *si* means "if," "whether." The form written with an accent (*sí*) is an adverb meaning "yes" or a reflexive pronoun meaning "yourself," "himself," "herself," etc.

Verbs. Spanish verbs are grouped into three classes (conjugations), according to whether the infinitive ends in *-ar* (first conjugation), *-er* (second conjugation), or *-ir* (third conjugation). Examples of verbs that are conjugated regularly are: *mandar* (to send), *beber* (to drink), *subir* (to climb). Spanish verb forms indicate not only mood and tense but also the number, and frequently the person, of the subject.

In the following sections the principal indicative, conditional, subjunctive, and imperative forms of these three common verbs are shown, and these are the forms taken by all regular verbs in each of the three conjugations. In the indicative mood the present, imperfect, and preterit tenses are formed by replacing the infinitive endings with endings that correspond to the person and number of the subject. In the future indicative and in the conditional mood the inflectional endings are added to the infinitive form.

Present. Here is the present indicative tense of the regular verbs in the three conjugations:

mando	bebo	subo
mandas	bebes	subes
manda	bebe	sube
mandamos	bebemos	subimos
mandáis	bebéis	subís
mandan	beben	suben

Imperfect. The imperfect tense indicates a continued action in the past:

mandaba	bebía	subía
mandabas	bebías	subías
mandaba	bebía	subía
mandábamos	bebíamos	subíamos
mandabais	bebíais	subíais
mandaban	bebían	subían

Preterit. The preterit expresses a simple past action:

mandé	bebí	subí
mandaste	bebiste	subiste
mandó	bebió	subió
mandamos	bebimos	subimos
mandasteis	bebisteis	subisteis
mandaron	bebieron	subieron

Future. The future tense of "mandar" is translated "I will send," "you will send," etc.

mandaré	beberé	subiré
mandarás	beberás	subirás
mandará	beberá	subirá
mandaremos	beberemos	subiremos
mandaréis	beberéis	subiréis
mandarán	beberán	subirán

Conditional. The form *mandaría* is equivalent to "I would send" (as in "I would send it if I could").

mandaría	bebería	subiría
mandarías	beberías	subirías
mandaría	bebería	subiría
mandaríamos	beberíamos	subiríamos
mandaríais	beberíais	subiríais
mandarían	beberían	subirían

Present subjunctive. The present subjunctive is formed by replacing the infinitive ending with special -e endings for -ar verbs and -a endings for -er and -ir verbs.

mande	beba	suba
mandes	bebas	subas
mande	beba	suba
mandemos	bebamos	subamos
mandéis	bebáis	subáis
manden	beban	suban

ORTHOGRAPHIC CHANGING VERB

	Present	Preterit	Present Subjunctive	Imperfect Subjunctive	Imperative
alcanzar (to overtake) **alcanzando alcanzado**		alcancé alcanzaste alcanzó alcanzamos alcanzasteis alcanzaron	alcance alcances alcance alcancemos alcancéis alcancen		
averiguar (to ascertain) **averiguando averiguado**		averigüé averiguaste averiguó averiguamos averiguasteis averiguaron	averigüe averigües averigüe averigüemos averigüéis averigüen		
convencer (to convince) **convenciendo convencido**	convenzo convences convence convencemos convencéis convencen		convenza convenzas convenza convenzamos convenzáis convenzan		
distinguir (to distinguish) **distinguiendo distinguido**	distingo distingues distingue distinguimos distinguís distinguen		distinga distingas distinga distingamos distingáis distingan		
enviar (to send) **enviando enviado**	envío envías envía enviamos enviáis envían		envíe envíes envíe enviemos enviéis envíen		envía enviad
escoger (to select) **escogiendo escogido**	escojo escoges escoge escogemos escogéis escogen		escoja escojas escoja escojamos escojáis escojan		
leer (to read) **leyendo leído**		leí leíste leyó leímos leísteis leyeron		leyera leyeras leyera leyéramos leyerais leyeran	
pagar (to pay) **pagando pagado**		pagué pagaste pagó pagamos pagasteis pagaron	pague pagues pague paguemos paguéis paguen		
producir (to produce) **produciendo producido**	produzco produces produce producimos producís producen		produzca produzcas produzca produzcamos produzcáis produzcan		
sacar (to take out) **sacando sacado**		saqué sacaste sacó sacamos sacasteis sacaron	saque saques saque saquemos saquéis saquen		

Imperfect subjunctive. The basic stem of the imperfect subjunctive is found by dropping the *-ron* ending of the third-person plural of the preterit indicative, thus: *manda-* (from *man-* daron), *bebie-* (from *bebieron*), and *subie-* (from *subieron*). There are two forms of the imperfect subjunctive. The more common form having the endings *-ra*, *-ras*, etc. is given below.

The less frequent form has these alternate endings -se, -ses, -se, ' -semos, -seis, -sen, thus: *mandase, mandases,* etc., *bibiese, bibieses,* etc., *subiese, subieses,* etc.

mandara	bebiera	subiera
mandaras	bebieras	subieras
mandara	bebiera	subiera
mandáramos	bebiéramos	subiéramos
mandarais	bebierais	subierais
mandaran	bebieran	subieran

Compound forms. Compound (perfect) tenses, in the indicative, conditional, and subjunctive, are made by combining appropriate forms of the auxiliary verb *haber* (to have) with the past participle of the main verb: *he bebido* (I have drunk).

Present participle. The present participles of the three model verbs are:

mandando	bebiendo	subiendo

Past participle. The past participles of the model verbs are:

mandado	bebido	subido

Imperative. The imperative mood is used in modern Spanish only to express familiar commands—and then only in the affirmative, never in the negative. Imperative verb forms are thus limited to the second-person familiar with the singular subject *tú* or the plural subject *nosotros* either expressed or understood. In the great majority of cases commands are expressed in the subjunctive, and today present subjunctive forms are used for familiar plural commands in American Spanish. The singular forms of the true imperative are:

manda	bebe	sube

The plural forms are:

mandad	bebed	subid

Irregular verbs. There are three kinds of irregular verbs in Spanish: the orthographic-changing verbs, in which spelling changes are made to preserve the final consonant sound of the stem; the radical-changing verbs, in which the final stem vowel undergoes a phonetic change; and a miscellaneous group of verbs that display other major irregularities in certain moods and tenses.

Orthographic-changing verbs. In orthographic-changing verbs, the final letters of the stem (that is, the letters that immediately precede the -ar, -er, or -ir infinitive ending) must be changed before certain endings are added. Otherwise, according to the rules of Spanish spelling, the final consonant sound of the stem would be lost.

In -ar verbs these changes are made before the letter e in the first person singular of the preterit indicative and in all persons of the present subjunctive: the final c of the stem becomes qu; g becomes gu; gu becomes gü; z becomes c. For examples of such changes see *alcanzar, averiguar, pagar, sacar.*

In most -er and -ir verbs the following changes are made before the letter a or o in the first person singular of the present indicative and in all persons of the present subjunctive: the final g of the stem becomes j; gu becomes g; c becomes z if cer or cir in the stem is preceded by a consonant; c becomes zc if cer or cir in the stem is preceded by a vowel. For examples of such changes see *convencer, distinguir, escoger, producir.* Other orthographic changes include changing an unstressed i between vowels to y in a few verbs, and adding a written accent to a final i or u of the stem of some verbs ending in -iar and -uar to keep the stem vowel from becoming a diphthong in certain forms of the present tenses. For examples see *leer* and *enviar.* Some typical verbs of this kind are given here. The infinitive, the present participle, and the past participle are shown in boldface type. These forms are followed by additional parts of the verb to show the spelling changes.

Radical changing verbs. These verbs fall into three classes, according to the kind of phonetic change made in the stem vowel (radical vowel) that precedes the infinitive ending -ar, -er, or -ir.

Class I (-ar and -er verbs): when the natural stress falls on the stem vowel o or e, the o becomes ue and the e becomes ie; these changes occur in the present indicative and the present subjunctive (in all persons except the first and second person plural) and in the singular of the affirmative imperative. For examples of such changes see *contar* and *perder.*

Class II (-ir verbs): when the natural stress falls on the stem vowel o or e, the o becomes ue and the e becomes ie (as in verbs of Class I): further, when the stem vowel o or e is unstressed and is followed by an ending that contains a stressed a, ie, or ió, the o becomes u and the e becomes i. These changes occur in the present participle, in the third-person singular and plural of the preterit indicative, in the first-person and second-person plural of the present subjunctive, and in all persons of the imperfect subjunctive. For examples of all these changes see *consentir* and *dormir.*

Class III (-ir verbs): when the natural stress falls on the stem vowel e, the e becomes i; even when unstressed the stem vowel e becomes i if the ending that follows contains a stressed a, ie, or ió. This change from

RADICAL-CHANGING VERBS

	Present	Preterit	Present Subjunctive	Imperfect Subjunctive	Imperative
consentir (to permit) **consintiendo** **consentido**	consiento consientes consiente consentimos consentís consienten	consentí consentiste consintio consentimos consentisteis consintieron	consienta consientas consienta consintamos consintáis consientan	consintiera consintieras consintiera consintiéramos consintierais consintieran	consiente consentid
contar (to count) **contando** **contado**	cuento cuentas cuenta contamos contáis cuentan		cuente cuentes cuente contemos contéis cuenten		cuenta contad
dormir (to sleep) **durmiendo** **dormido**	duermo duermes duerme dormimos dormís duermen	dormí dormiste durmió dormimos dormisteis durmieron	duerma duermas duerma durmamos durmáis duerman	durmiera durmieras durmiera durmiéramos durmierais durmieran	duerme dormid
medir (to measure) **midiendo** **medido**	mido mides mide medimos medis miden	medí mediste midió medimos medisteis midieron	mida midas mida midamos midáis midan	midiera midieras midiera midiéramos midierais midieran	mide medid
perder (to lose) **perdiendo** **perdido**	pierdo pierdes pierde perdemos perdéis pierden		pierda pierdas pierda perdamos perdáis pierdan		pierde perded

OTHER IRREGULAR VERBS

	Present	Imperfect	Future	Conditional	Preterit	Present Subjunctive	Imperfect Subjunctive	Imperative
dar	doy				di	dé	diera	
(to give)	das				diste	des	dieras	
dando	da				dio	dé	diera	
dado	damos				dimos	demos	diéramos	
	dais				disteis	deis	dierais	
	dan				dieron	den	dieran	
decir	digo		diré	diría	dije	diga	dijera	
(to say)	dices		dirás	dirías	dijiste	digas	dijeras	di
diciendo	dice		dirá	diría	dijo	diga	dijera	decid
dicho	decimos		diremos	diríamos	dijimos	digamos	dijéramos	
	decís		diréis	diríais	dijisteis	digáis	dijerais	
	dicen		dirán	dirían	dijeron	digan	dijeran	
estar	estoy				estuve	esté	estuviera	
(to be)	estás				estuviste	estés	estuvieras	está
estando	está				estuvo	esté	estuviera	estad
estado	estamos				estuvimos	estemos	estuviéramos	
	estáis				estuvisteis	estéis	estuvierais	
	están				estuvieron	estén	estuvieran	
haber	he	había	habré	habría	hube	haya	hubiera	
(to have)	has	habías	habrás	habrías	hubiste	hayas	hubieras	
habiendo	ha	había	habrá	habría	hubo	haya	hubiera	
habido	hemos	habíamos	habremos	habríamos	hubimos	hayamos	hubiéramos	
	habéis	habíais	habréis	habríais	hubisteis	hayáis	hubierais	
	han	habían	habrán	habrían	hubieron	hayan	hubieran	
hacer	hago		haré	haría	hice	haga	hiciera	
(to do, make)	haces		harás	harías	hiciste	hagas	hicieras	haz
haciendo	hace		hará	haría	hizo	haga	hiciera	haced
hecho	hacemos		haremos	haríamos	hicimos	hagamos	hiciéramos	
	hacéis		haréis	haríais	hicisteis	hagáis	hicierais	
	hacen		harán	harían	hicieron	hagan	hicieran	
ir	voy	iba			fui	vaya	fuera	
(to go)	vas	ibas			fuiste	vayas	fueras	ve
yendo	va	iba			fue	vaya	fuera	id
ido	vamos	íbamos			fuimos	vayamos	fuéramos	
	vais	ibais			fuisteis	vayáis	fuerais	
	van	iban			fueron	vayan	fueran	
poder	puedo		podré	podría	pude	pueda	pudiera	
(to be able)	puedes		podrás	podrías	pudiste	puedas	pudieras	
pudiendo	puede		podrá	podría	pudo	pueda	pudiera	
podido	podemos		podremos	podríamos	pudimos	podamos	pudiéramos	
	podéis		podréis	podríais	pudisteis	podáis	pudierais	
	pueden		podrán	podrían	pudieron	puedan	pudieran	
saber	sé		sabré	sabría	supe	sepa	supiera	
(to know)	sabes		sabrás	sabrías	supiste	sepas	supieras	
sabiendo	sabe		sabrá	sabría	supo	sepa	supiera	
sabido	sabemos		sabremos	sabríamos	supimos	sepamos	supiéramos	
	sabéis		sabréis	sabríais	supisteis	sepáis	supierais	
	saben		sabrán	sabrían	supieron	sepan	supieran	
ser	soy	era			fui	sea	fuera	
(to be)	eres	eras			fuiste	seas	fueras	se
siendo	es	era			fue	sea	fuera	sed
sido	somos	éramos			fuimos	seamos	fuéramos	
	sois	erais			fuisteis	seáis	fuerais	
	son	eran			fueron	sean	fueran	
tener	tengo		tendré	tendría	tuve	tenga	tuviera	
(to have, hold)	tienes		tendrás	tendrías	tuviste	tengas	tuvieras	ten
teniendo	tiene		tendrá	tendría	tuvo	tenga	tuviera	tened
tenido	tenemos		tendremos	tendríamos	tuvimos	tengamos	tuviéramos	
	tenéis		tendréis	tendríais	tuvisteis	tengáis	tuvierais	
	tienen		tendrán	tendrían	tuvieron	tengan	tuvieran	

e to *i* occurs also in all the forms affected in verbs of Class I and Class II. For examples of this change see *medir*. Some typical verbs of this kind are given here. **Other irregular verbs.** Because both orthographic-changing and radical-changing verbs follow definite patterns, they are less irregular than many Spanish verbs that have major irregularities in their forms. From this large group (which includes orthographic-changing and radical-changing verbs) a number of irregular verbs are given, with the forms in which the irregularities occur.

—*Bernice Randall*

German

Sentence structure. The primary unit of communication is the sentence, which is identified by the intonation pattern at the end. Each of the important sentence types ends with a characteristic intonation pattern. A sentence may consist of a single word, a phrase (a meaningful combination of words without an inflected verb), or a clause (a meaningful combination of words with an inflected verb).

The words that make up sentences are called parts of speech. Some words (nouns, pronouns, adjectives, verbs) are inflected. An inflected word is a word that changes form in some way so that its relationship to other words in a phrase or sentence is made clear or so that its specific meaning is made clear. Uninflected words (adverbs, prepositions, conjunctions, interjections) always remain unchanged in form, however they are used.

Nouns and pronouns may be used as the subjects or objects of verbs and as the objects of prepositions. Nouns may also serve as predicate nominatives and as modifiers of other nouns. Adjectives modify nouns, and they may also serve as nouns or pronouns. Adverbs modify verbs, descriptive adjectives, other adverbs, or whole sentences. The verb may be the entire predicate, or it may serve as a link between the subject and the rest of the predicate. Prepositions signal a relationship between a following noun or pronoun and other parts of a phrase or sentence. Conjunctions join words, phrases, or clauses. Interjections usually stand alone as whole utterances. They do not modify other words, and they themselves are not modified by other words.

Word order. Word order is of considerable importance in German sentences. Most rigidly fixed are the positions of verbal elements. Other elements tend to follow patterns; they are subject to variation, however, depending on their importance in the context.

Declarative sentences. Declarative sentences may be simple, compound, or complex. A simple sentence consists of one clause. A compound sentence is made up of two or more main clauses joined by a coordinating conjunction, such as *und* (and), *aber* (but), *denn* (for), *oder* (or).

A complex sentence consists of a main clause and one or more dependent clauses. A dependent clause may have no introductory word at all, or it may be introduced by a subordinating conjunction, such as *da* (since), *wenn* (when, whenever, if), *als* (when, as), *obwohl* (although); it may also be in-

PLEASE STAY IN LINE, *asks this German road sign. It also gives directions.*

troduced by an interrogative adverb or by a relative pronoun. In a dependent clause introduced by a conjunction or by a relative pronoun, the inflected verb is last, unless the clause contains a double infinitive. A dependent clause that has no introductory word and that follows a verb such as *sagen* (to say) or *wissen* (to know) has the word order of a main clause, in which the inflected verb must be in second place. A dependent clause in which *wenn* is merely implied has its inflected verb in first place. A variant of this word order occurs in a dependent clause of comparison that would usually be introduced by *als ob* (as if) or *als wenn* (as if); the *ob* or *wenn* may be omitted and the inflected verb placed directly after *als*.

Interrogative sentences. An interrogative sentence may be introduced by an interrogative adverb, pronoun, or adjective. The interrogative words introducing the question may be used alone or with other words. Some common interrogative adverbs are *wann* (when), *warum* (why), *wie* (how), *wo* (where), *wohin* (where, to what or which place). When a question has introductory words, the interrogative word or phrase is placed first and the inflected verb second. When there are no introductory words, the inflected verb begins the question.

Imperative sentences. An imperative sentence expresses an order or command and normally expects some action in response rather than a verbal reply. The verb of an imperative sentence is placed first, and it is in the imperative mood. In written German an imperative sentence is followed by an exclamation mark.

Articles. Articles function like

adjectives, for they agree in case, gender, and number with the nouns that they modify. Articles have their own special set of endings, and their presence or absence affects the endings of descriptive adjectives.

Definite articles. Originally a demonstrative adjective, the definite article still has demonstrative force when stressed. When unstressed, it is equivalent to the English definite article "the."

Because of their similar forms and use, the definite article, the interrogative adjective *welcher* (which), and the demonstrative adjectives make up a group called *der*-words.

DECLENSION OF THE DEFINITE ARTICLE

| | SINGULAR | | | PLURAL |
	Masc.	Fem.	Neut.	All Genders
Nom.	der	die	das	die
Gen.	des	der	des	der
Dat.	dem	der	dem	den
Acc.	den	die	das	die

Indefinite articles. Originally the numeral "one," the indefinite article still means this when stressed. When unstressed, it is equivalent to the English indefinite article "a, an." Its negative *kein* has all the forms of *ein*. It means "not any," "not a," as in *kein Mann* (not a man). But it also has plural forms which, of course, *ein* lacks.

DECLENSION OF THE INDEFINITE ARTICLE

| | SINGULAR | | | PLURAL |
	Masc.	Fem.	Neut.	All Genders
Nom.	ein	eine	ein	keine
Gen.	eines	einer	eines	keiner
Dat.	einem	einer	einem	keinen
Acc.	einen	eine	ein	keine

Because of their similar forms and use, the indefinite article *ein,* the adjective *kein,* and the possessive adjectives make up a group called *ein*-words.

Nouns. German nouns may be simple or compound (made up of several elements, as a prefix and a noun). The first letter of nouns is capitalized (*das Haus,* the house).

Plurals. Nouns are pluralized in various ways. Masculine nouns, for example, may add an *-e* (*der Freund,* the friend: *die Freunde*) or an *-er* (*der Leib,* the body: *die Leiber*) or an *-er* and, over the root vowel, a doubled dot called umlaut (*der Mann,* the

NOUN DECLENSIONS

plural formation	STRONG I ending zero		STRONG II ending -e		STRONG III ending -er		WEAK IV ending -(e)n		MIXED V ending -(e)n		OTHER VI ending -s	
number	sing.	pl.	sing.	pl.	sing.	pl.	sing.	pl.	sing.	pl.	sing.	pl.
masculine case nom.	—	—(¨)	—e	—(¨)e	—	¨—er	—	—(e)n	—	—(e)n	—	—s
gen.	—s	—(¨)	—(e)s	—(¨)e	—(e)s	¨—er	—(e)n(s)	—(e)n	—(e)s	—(e)n	—s	—s
dat.	—	—(¨)(n)	—(e)	—(¨)en	—(e)	¨—ern	—(e)n	—(e)n	—(e)	—(e)n	—	—s
acc.	—	—(¨)	—	—(¨)e	—	¨—er	—(e)n	—(e)n	—(e)n	—(e)n	—	—s
neuter nom.	—	—(¨)	—	—e	—	¨—er		—en	—	—(e)n	—	—s
gen.	—s	—(¨)	—(e)s	—e	—(e)s	¨—er	—ens	—en	—(e)s	—(e)n	—s	—s
dat.	—	—(¨)(n)	—(e)	—en	—(e)	¨—ern	—en	—en	—(e)	—(e)n	—	—s
acc.	—	—(¨)	—	—e	—	¨—er		—en	—	—(e)n	—	—s
feminine nom.	—	—¨	—	—¨e			—	—(e)n			—	—s
gen.	—	—¨	—	—¨e			—	—(e)n			—	—s
dat.	—	—¨n	—	—¨en			—	—(e)n			—	—s
acc.	—	—¨	—	—¨e			—	—(e)n			—	—s

explanatory notes

I: all have at least two syllables

add -n in dative plural, only if nominative singular does not end in -n

includes most masculine and all neuter nouns ending in -el, -er, -en

masc: der Käse

neut: diminutives ending in -chen, -lein; collectives in Ge—e; infinitives used as nouns

fem: only two nouns: die Mutter die Tochter

II: many monosyllables

masc: many take umlaut
neut: one takes umlaut: Floß
fem: all take umlaut

some polysyllables, including following suffixes: *masc.* -ig, -ling; most *neut.* and some *fem.* -nis (pl. -nisse); some *neut.* and some *fem.* -sal; *neut.* most in -ment

das Hospital das Hospiz

III: mostly monosyllables: umlaut wherever possible

masc: less than ten
neut: many
fem: none

some polysyllables, including suffix -tum (pl. tümer)
masc: Irrtum, Reichtum
neut: all others

das Regiment das Spital

IV: monosyllables and polysyllables: never umlaut

masc: nouns denoting live males take only -n (-en) in genitive singular; inanimate masculine nouns add -ns in genitive singular

neut: only one: das Herz

fem: almost all feminine nouns except die Mutter, die Tochter. Those ending in -e, -er, -el add only -n for plural; those with suffix -in, add -nen. Other feminine suffixes are: -heit, -keit, -ung, -schaft

die Regatta (pl. Regatten)

V: monosyllables and polysyllables: never umlaut

masc: only a few nouns; those in -or shift stress in plural -óren; others in -r add only -n in plural; irregular: Sporn (pl. Sporen)

neut: those ending in -e add only -s in genitive singular and -n for plural forms; a few substitute -en in plural for a foreign suffix: Museum (pl. Museen); Thema (pl. Themen); Mineral (pl. Mineralien)

fem: none

VI: nouns of foreign origin that do not fit into regular declensional patterns

all surnames

masc: a few

neut: a few, including those ending in -o; also, Schema

fem: Kamera

---

man: *die Männer*); or they may use other endings, or remain unchanged in the plural. Feminine nouns and neuter nouns also vary in the way their plurals are formed. Dictionaries indicate directly after the main entry of a noun how the plural of that noun is formed.

Gender. Nouns are classified as masculine, feminine, or neuter. The gender of most nouns has to be memorized, though nouns denoting animate beings generally have the gender corresponding to their sex. (For suffixes associated with a particular gender, see the noun table.)

Case. As has already been indicated in the section on definite articles, the cases used in German are the nominative, genitive, dative, and accusative. Sets of case endings are called declensions. The nominative case is the case form of the subject of a sentence or of a predicate complement. The genitive case shows a possessive relationship or other relationship of one noun to another, and it is also used after certain prepositions. The dative case is used for an indirect object, after certain verbs and prepositions, and in some expressions involving adjectives. The accusative case is used for a direct object, after certain verbs and prepositions, and in some expressions of time and space.

The noun table is intended to give a general view of declensional patterns. The dashes in each column stand for the nominative singular form of the noun. The umlaut sign (¨) above the dash indicates that the stem vowel, if a, o, or u, is umlauted, that is, modified in pronunciation and provided with a written symbol indicating modification. The umlaut sign in parentheses means that not all nouns with the stem vowel a, o, or u are modified. The sign does not apply to other vowels, for they do not "take umlaut" and, in fact, are never modified in the plural. (For the plurals of specific nouns, see a dictionary.)

Pronouns. Pronouns function as subjects of sentences, objects of verbs and prepositions, and as complements of certain adjectives. They may be modified by predicate adjectives, rarely by other forms. Most personal pronouns have one form when they are used as subjects and another when they are used as objects. The pronoun *du,* along with its plural *ihr,* is used only to address family members and close friends; it is the pronoun of familiar address. The capitalized pronoun *Sie* (used with a third-person plural verb) is used for both singular and plural; it is the pronoun of formal or polite address. A third-person pronoun standing for a noun previously mentioned normally takes its gender and number from that noun. In colloquial speech, however, *er* (masculine) or *sie* (feminine) may replace a neuter noun denoting a person, as in:

Wer ist das Mädchen da?
Who's that girl there?

Sie ist meine Schwester.
She's my sister.

The genitive forms of the personal pronouns are rarely used in modern German.

DECLENSION OF PERSONAL PRONOUNS

1ST PERSON

	Sing.	Pl.
Nom.	ich	wir
Gen.	meiner	unser
Dat.	mir	uns
Acc.	mich	uns

| | 2ND FAMILIAR | | 2ND FORMAL |
	Sing.	Pl.	Sing. and Pl.
Nom.	du	ihr	Sie
Gen.	deiner	euer	Ihrer
Dat.	dir	euch	Ihnen
Acc.	dich	euch	Sie

3RD PERSON

| | Sing. | | | Pl. |
	Masc.	Fem.	Neut.	All Genders
Nom.	er	sie	es	sie
Gen.	seiner	ihrer	seiner	ihrer
Dat.	ihm	ihr	ihm	ihnen
Acc.	ihn	sie	es	sie

Relative pronouns. Originally a demonstrative pronoun, the relative pronoun is used to introduce a dependent clause that describes or limits in some way a noun or pronoun antecedent in another clause. The relative pronoun agrees with its antecedent in gender and number but derives its case from its function in its own clause. It may never be omitted and must be first or be included in the first phrase in the clause.

All forms of the interrogative adjective *welcher* except the genitive may be used as relative pronouns. The interrogative pronouns *wer* and *was* are used as relative pronouns, if the relative clause itself is subject of the main clause, or if the antecedent is an indefinite pronoun such as *etwas* (something), *nichts* (nothing), or *alles* (everything), as in:

Das ist alles, was ich weiss.
That's all I know.

DECLENSION OF THE RELATIVE PRONOUN

| | SINGULAR | | | PLURAL |
	Masc.	Fem.	Neut.	All Genders
Nom.	der	die	das	die
Gen.	dessen	deren	dessen	deren
Dat.	dem	der	dem	denen
Acc.	den	die	das	die

Reflexive pronouns. Reflexive pronouns are pronouns used as objects which refer back to the subject of the verb. Since the reflexive pronouns are objects, there are no nominative forms, and the genitive is rare. They are identical with the object pronouns except that a special form, *sich* (himself, herself, itself, etc.), is used in place of all third-person object pronouns. The pronoun *sich* (uncapitalized) is also used as the reflexive form of the formal *Sie* and *Ihnen*:

Bitte, setzen Sie sich!
Please sit down!

Der Junge zieht sich an.
The boy gets dressed. (dresses himself)

A dative reflexive pronoun is used in preference to the possessive adjective with parts of the body or with articles of clothing associated with the subject of the sentence:

Ich putze mir die Zähne.
I brush my teeth.

Interrogative pronouns. Interrogative pronouns are used in asking questions and have only singular forms. These pronouns distinguish between living beings and inanimate objects or concepts. There is no genitive form for the inanimate interrogative, and *was* is now often used with prepositions taking the dative. But it may be replaced by special forms like *womit* (with what) or *worauf* (on what). The interrogative adjective *welcher* (which, what) may also be used as an interrogative pronoun.

DECLENSION OF THE INTERROGATIVE PRONOUN

	Animate "who"	Inanimate "what"
Nom.	wer	was
Gen.	wessen	——
Dat.	wem	was
Acc.	wen	was

Demonstrative pronouns. Demonstrative pronouns are pronouns used in pointing out a person or thing without naming the person or thing. Demonstrative pronouns include all the *der*-words except *welcher*—words like *dieser* (this one) and *jener* (that one), along with forms of the definite article (especially *das*). When used as a demonstrative pronoun, the definite article is identical in form with the relative pronoun but can be readily

distinguished from it by the position of the inflected verb in the sentence. Although not strictly demonstrative, the *ein*-words can also be used as pronouns, and, as pronouns, these words take the endings *-er* in the nominative masculine singular and *-(e)s* in the nominative and accusative neuter singular, but are otherwise declined like the indefinite article.

Adjectives. An adjective is a word that limits or qualifies a noun in some way. Descriptive adjectives may be used as attributive or predicate adjectives. An attributive adjective precedes and agrees with the noun it modifies:

ein guter Mann　　*a good man*
eine gute Frau　　*a good woman*

A predicate adjective follows a linking verb like *sein* (to be):

Meine Tochter ist jung.
My daughter is young.

From the examples given, it is clear that a predicate adjective is invariable, whereas an attributive adjective varies in its endings. Three sets of endings are used for attributive adjectives. If neither a *der*-word nor an *ein*-word precedes the adjective, the adjective takes a "strong" ending (*schwarzer Kaffee*, black coffee); if a *der*-word precedes the adjective, it takes a "weak" ending (*der schwarze Kaffee*, the black coffee); if an *ein*-word precedes the adjective, it takes a "mixed" ending (*ein schwarzer Kaffee*, a (cup of) black coffee).

Comparison of adjectives and adverbs. German adjectives are compared as to degree by adding suffixes. The comparative is formed by adding *-er* to the positive or stem form (*heiß*, hot: *heißer*) or just *-r* (*leise*, soft: *leiser*), the superlative by adding *-st-* or *-est-* (*schön*, beautiful: *schönst-*; *heiß*: *heißest-*). Adverbs are similarly compared (but see below).

Some adjectives in addition add an umlaut over the stem vowel in the comparative and superlative (*kalt*, cold: *kälter*, *kältest-*). And some have an irregular comparison (*gut*, good: *besser*, *best-*). When used as attributive adjectives, the comparative and superlative forms are declined like any descriptive adjective. However, the comparative may be used without inflection as a predicate adjective or as an adverb, but the superlative always has inflection. When a superlative is used purely as a predicate adjective, it is preceded by the word *am* (at the) and *-en* is added to the regular superlative stem (*am schönsten*). The superlative of adverbs is restricted to this *am* form. The following adjectives are compared irregularly; *gern* is an adverb only, but the others may be adjective or adverb.

ATTRIBUTIVE ADJECTIVE ENDINGS

	A. Strong Masc.	Fem.	Neut.	Pl.	B. Weak Masc.	Fem.	Neut.	Pl.	C. Mixed Masc.	Fem.	Neut.	Pl.
Nom.	-er	-e	-es	-e	-e	-e	-e	-en	-er	-e	-es	-en
Gen.	-en	-er	-en	-er	-en	-en	-en	-en	-en	-en	-en	-en
Dat.	-em	-er	-em	-en	-en	-en	-en	-en	-en	-en	-en	-en
Acc.	-en	-e	-es	-e	-en	-e	-e	-en	-en	-e	-es	-en

Positive	Comparative	Superlative
groß *(large)*	größer	größt-
gut *(good)*	besser	best-
hoch *(high)*	höher	höchst-
nah *(near)*	näher	nächst-
viel *(much)*	mehr	meist-
gern *(gladly)*	lieber	am liebsten

Interrogative adjective. The interrogative adjective *welcher* (which, what) is declined like the demonstrative adjective *dieser*. *Welcher* may also serve as a relative pronoun. The phrase *was für* (what kind of) is often used adjectivally, and a form of *ein* often follows it:

Was für ein Buch ist das?
What kind of book is that?

Demonstrative adjectives. *Dieser* (this), *jeder* (each, every), *jener* (that), *mancher* (many a), and *solcher* (such) are often called demonstrative adjectives. Of these *dieser* occurs most frequently and is often used to contrast with the stressed definite article. In writing it is sometimes used in the meaning "the latter" in contrast to *jener* "the former." The declension of *dieser* can serve as a model for all these words.

DECLENSION OF *DIESER* "THIS"

	Singular Masc.	Fem.	Neut.	Plural All Genders
Nom.	dieser	diese	dieses	diese
Gen.	dieses	dieser	dieses	dieser
Dat.	diesem	dieser	diesem	diesen
Acc.	diesen	diese	dieses	diese

Possessive adjectives. The possessive adjectives are *mein* (my), *dein* (your, familiar singular), *Ihr* (your, formal, singular and plural), *sein* (his, its), *ihr* (her, their), *unser* (our), *euer* (your, familiar plural). These adjectives are declined like *(k)ein*, but when endings are added, *unser* is sometimes shortened to *unsr-*, and *euer* to *eur-*.

Numerals. Cardinal numbers are used to give a specific count of the members in a collection of objects, and ordinal numbers are used to designate a position in an ordered sequence of numbers. Cardinal numbers must be classed as adjectives when they are used with nouns, although only *ein* (one) regularly shows agreement with the noun it modifies. The numerals above *null* (zero) and through 999,999 are not separated into individual words but are combined into one solid word. The major units above 999,999 are feminine nouns with singular and plural forms that are written as separate words and are capitalized. When Arabic numerals are used, German has a period or a space where English requires a comma, and a comma where English has a period.

All intermediate numerals can be deduced from the above patterns, for example, 9 876 543 210 123,456 would be read neun Billionen achthundertsechsundsiebzig Milliarden fünfhundertdreiundvierzig Millionen zweihundertzehntausendhundertdreiundzwanzig (Komma) vier fünf sechs.

Ordinal numbers correspond to the cardinal numbers and except for *erst-* (first), *dritt-* (third), and *acht-* (eighth) are regularly derived by adding the suffix -*t*- to the cardinal numbers through 19 and -*st*- to those from 20–100. The series begins again with 101 (*hundertunderst-*, etc.). As ordinals they are always inflected and take strong, weak, or mixed endings,

depending on what precedes. A period after an Arabic numeral indicates an ordinal number and is used mainly in writing dates, with the word *Tag* understood (*Heute ist der 5. (fünfte) März*, today is the fifth of March; *am 21. (einundswanzigsten) Mai*, on the twenty-first of May). Ordinals used with names of royalty follow the name and Roman numerals are used (*Wilhelm II., Wilhelm der Zweite; der Sohn Friedrichs III., Friedrichs des Dritten*).

Prepositions. A preposition governs its object, which is put in the appropriate case. Most prepositions make special compounds instead of taking a personal pronoun object, if the antecedent is inanimate (*damit*, with it; *darauf*, on it). All prepositions make these compounds except *außer*, *bis*, *ohne*, *seit* and those that take the genitive.

Among the common prepositions that take the dative are *aus* (from, of, out of), *außer* (besides, except), *bei* (near, at), *mit* (with), *nach* (after, to), *seit* (since), *von* (of, from, by), and *zu* (to, towards). Contractions of the definite article occur with some prepositions that take the dative. For example, *bei* combines with *dem* to produce *beim*; *von* and *zu* combine similarly to produce *vom* and *zum*. *Zu* also combines with *der* to become *zur*.

Among the prepositions that are followed by the accusative are *bis* (up to, until), *durch* (through), *für* (for), *gegen* (towards, against), *ohne* (without), *um* (about), and *wider* (against). *Bis* occurs by itself but is more often paired with other prepositions in phrases such as *bis an* (up to) and *bis auf* (except for). In such phrases the second preposition governs the case of the object. The accusative definite article *das* combines, principally in colloquial speech, with *durch*, *für*, and *um* to become *durchs*, *fürs*, and *ums*.

Common prepositions that take the dative or accusative include *an* (to, at), *auf* (on, at, to), *in* (in, to, at), *neben* (beside, near), *über* (over, above), *unter* (under, below, among), *vor* (before, in front of), and *zwischen* (between). These prepositions involve location or motion in space or time with reference to their objects. They take the dative if there is no motion:

auf dem Tisch　　*on the table*
im Sommer　　*in summer*

But if motion is involved or if the usage is nonliteral, they take the accusative:

Er legt das Buch auf den Tisch.
He puts the book on the table.

Er denkt an seinen Vater.
He thinks about his father.

THE CARDINAL NUMERALS

0 null	10 zehn	20 zwanzig	10^2 (ein)hundert
1 eins	11 elf	21 einundzwanzig	101 hundert(und)eins
2 zwei	12 zwölf	22 zweiundzwanzig	202 zweihundert(und)zwei
3 drei	13 dreizehn	30 dreißig	10^3 (ein)tausend
4 vier	14 vierzehn	40 zierzig	2013 zweitausend(und)dreizehn
5 fünf	15 fünfzehn	50 fünfzig	10^4 zehntausend
6 sechs	16 sechzehn	60 sechzig	10^6 eine Million
7 sieben	17 siebzehn	70 siebzig	10^7 zehn Millionen
8 acht	18 achtzehn	80 achtzig	10^9 eine Milliarde
9 neun	19 neunzehn	90 neunzig	10^{12} eine Billion

A GERMAN DIALECT *is still spoken by this Amish family in Eastern Pennsylvania.*

An and *in* combine with *das* and *dem* to *ans, ins* and *am, im,* respectively. All the others of this group of prepositions may combine with *das* in colloquial speech.

Of the prepositions that take the genitive, *anstatt* (instead of), *statt* (instead of), *trotz* (in spite of), *während* (during), and *wegen* (because of) are frequent. *Trotz* is frequently used with the dative, and the others are sometimes so used, especially in colloquial speech. Most of the less commonly used prepositions (such as *jenseits,* on the other side of, and *oberhalb,* above) and other words when used as prepositions (such as *kraft,* by virtue of, and *unweit,* near) take the genitive. When *wegen* is used with personal pronouns, a special form of the pronoun is prefixed to it, as in *meinetwegen* (for my sake).

Verbs. German verbs consist of stems that carry the central meaning of the verbs and of endings that are attached to the stems. Verbs are inflected for person, number, tense, mood, and voice. Most verbs have three persons (first, second, and third), two numbers (singular and plural), two simple tenses (present and past), four compound tenses (present perfect, past perfect, future, and future perfect), three moods (indicative, subjunctive, and imperative), one simple voice (active), and one compound voice (passive). These forms are collectively called conjugations. Verbs also form nouns (infinitives) and adjectives (present and past participles).

The infinitive form of a verb is the

form usually entered in dictionaries or referred to in discussions on grammar. The infinitive form consists of the stem plus a typical, but not exclusive, ending. Most verb stems take the ending *-en.* A few end in *-n,* such as the irregular verbs *sein* and *tun,* and verbs with stems of two or more syllables terminating in *-el* or *-er* (for example, *wandeln,* to change, and *wandern,* to roam). In many infinitive constructions the preposition *zu* is required, forming an infinitive phrase. But the term "infinitive" is used grammatically for the form without *zu.*

The person and number categories correspond to the personal pronouns and are identified by appropriate endings. The first and second persons, including the formal second person, are used exclusively with personal pronoun subjects (though the subject may be omitted in colloquial speech, especially in the present tense). Since the formal second person is third person plural in form, it is not given separately in the conjugations shown in this section; the term "second person" applies only to the familiar form, both singular and plural. The subject of a third-person verb may be any noun or third-person pronoun. In a few constructions (called impersonal constructions), the subject *es* may be omitted if something other than the subject precedes the verb. Thus, *es ist mir kalt,* "I'm cold," may have equivalent wording *mir ist kalt.*

Verbs occur most frequently in the indicative mood and in the active voice. Unless otherwise stated, verbs in this discussion will be assumed to be indicative and active.

The present and the past (the imperfect) are true tenses, in that the form of the verb that carries basic meaning varies with the tenses. The compound tenses are not true tenses, because the tense indicator is not contained in the basic verb form but is supplied by a tense form of another verb (the auxiliary verb), and the significant verb appears as an infinitive or past participle. The passive voice is also classed as compound, since it is formed with an auxiliary.

The subjunctive mood has one true tense (the present, a tense which has, however, two forms) and two compound tenses (the past and the future, each with two forms). It is used primarily to express speculation about what might be or might have been; it is also used in most indirect quotations (those in which another person's ideas are quoted without using the exact words). The commonly used subjunctive form, here called general (but also named type II), is, with a few exceptions, based on the past indicative stem. It is the form required in speculative statements that are often termed contrary-to-fact conditions or improbable conditions. The other subjunctive form, here called special

(but also named type I), is formed on the infinitive stem. Its use is severely restricted, because its forms are often identical with, and indistinguishable from, those of the present indicative. The special third-person singular, however, is never identical with the indicative and is often used in indirect discourse (indirect quotation).

Weak verbs. Verbs that form the past stem by adding a suffix to the infinitive stem are known as weak verbs. The suffix is *-t,* except for stems ending in *-d* or *-t;* such stems add *-et.*

Most German verbs are weak and regular. All their conjugational forms can be derived by adding endings and suffixes, or both, to the infinitive stem.

A few weak verbs form the past stem on a special base that is different from the infinitive stem. These are listed with their principal parts in the table of strong and irregular verbs. The present and past tenses are formed by adding appropriate endings to the infinitive and past stems, respectively.

WEAK VERB ENDINGS

	PRESENT ENDINGS		PAST ENDINGS	
	Sing.	Pl.	Sing.	Pl.
1st Person	-e	-en	-e	-en
2nd Person	-st	-t	-est	-et
3rd Person	-t	-en	-e	-en

The past endings have no variants. In the present, stems ending in *-d, -t,* or in certain consonant combinations (such as the *tm* in *atmen,* to breathe) add *-e-* before the second person singular, the third person singular, and the second person plural endings. Stems ending in *-s, -ss, -ß,* or *-z* drop the *-s-* of the second person singular ending. Two-syllable stems ending in *-el* (regularly) and *-er* (optionally) drop the *-e-* of the stem before the first person singular ending and the *-e-* of the ending in the first person and third person plural.

The endings for both forms of the subjunctive are identical with the past endings of weak verbs. The present general subjunctive of regular weak verbs is identical with the past indicative. The special subjunctive is formed regularly on the infinitive stem.

Strong verbs. Verbs that form the past stem by changing the vowel of the infinitive stem are known as strong verbs. Both the principal parts and the endings of these verbs must be known in order to derive all their conjugational forms. For most such verbs, the principal parts consist of the infinitive, the third person singular of the past tense, and the past participle. For some of these verbs the third person singular of the present tense (this also provides the stem for the second person singular) is needed; for a few other verbs the general subjunctive stem is needed.

Most strong verbs follow one of seven patterns (shown in the verb table on the next page). Each class is illustrated by two regular verbs. Some common verbs that conform to the classes (except for minor irregularities) are also given, in addition to the unclassified strong verbs and the irregular weak verbs. The examples of verb forms listed in the verb table are given in the following order: A is the infinitive; B is the third-person singular, present tense, indicative; C is the third-person singular, past tense, indicative; D is the past participle.

The present-tense endings are the same as for weak verbs. In the first three classes and in the plural of all classes the endings vary with the stem terminals, just as for weak verbs. In the remaining classes, where the stem vowel changes in the second and third person singular, stems ending in -d or -t add the regular second person singular ending (-st) but drop the third person singular ending entirely. Verbs of all classes with stems terminating in -s, -ss, -ß, or -z drop the -s- of the second person singular ending.

In the past tense, strong verbs add no ending in the first and third person singular; the second person singular ending is -st (-est, if the stem terminates in -s, -ss, -ß); the second person plural ending is -t (-et, if the stem terminates in -d or -t); the first and third person plural have the ending -en.

The subjunctive endings are the same as for weak verbs. For most strong verbs the general subjunctive stem is that of the past indicative with umlaut of the stem vowel, if possible. A few verbs of class IV and one unclassified verb have the vowel ü instead of ä. These are: helfen (to help), sterben (to die), verderben (to ruin), werfen (to throw), and stehen (to stand). The special subjunctive of strong verbs is formed regularly on the infinitive stem.

Modal auxiliaries. The verbs dürfen (to be allowed), können (to be able), mögen (to like), müssen (to be obliged), sollen (to be expected), and wollen (to want) are called auxiliaries, because they are normally used with the infinitive of a verb that carries basic meaning; they are called modal because they supplement that verb with a shade of meaning akin to mood (and, indeed, they are often used in the subjunctive mood). The verb wissen (to know), though not a modal, is included here because its conjugation parallels that of the modals. They are all irregular in the present tense. Their past-tense forms are weak, but most are formed on an irregular base.

Auxiliary verbs. The verbs haben (to have), sein (to be), and werden (to become) have their own explicit meanings, but they also serve as tense indicators for verbs that carry basic meaning (including themselves) and are called auxiliary verbs. Werden serves also as the indicator for the passive voice. These verbs form the special subjunctive regularly on the infinitive stem, except that the first person and the third person singular of sein lack the ending -e.

PRESENT TENSE OF AUXILIARIES

	haben		sein		werden	
	Sing.	Pl.	Sing.	Pl.	Sing.	Pl.
1st	habe	haben	bin	sind	werde	werden
2nd	hast	habt	bist	seid	wirst	werdet
3rd	hat	haben	ist	sind	wird	werden

PAST TENSE OF AUXILIARIES

hatte	hatten	war	waren	wurde	wurden
hattest	hattet	warst	wart	wurdest	wurdet
hatte	hatten	war	waren	wurde	wurden

GENERAL SUBJUNCTIVE STEM

hätt-	wär-	würd-

Present participle. The present participle may be formed for any verb by adding the suffix -end (-nd for two-syllable stems terminating in -el or -er) to the infinitive stem. Present participles are never used as predicate adjectives; otherwise, they follow the pattern of descriptive adjectives. The participle retains verbal character to the extent that it shows active voice, may take objects, and may have the same relationship to prepositional phrases and adverbs as the inflected verb. It normally follows all these elements.

Past participle: weak and strong verbs. Past participles are verbal adjectives formed from any verb by the addition of suffixes and, for most verbs, a prefix. The past participle is used mainly to supply the element carrying basic meaning in most compound verbal constructions. It is also used as an adjective in much the same way as the present participle. The past participles of intransitive verbs (those that do not take an accu-

sative object) are not used as predicate adjectives. The past participles of transitive verbs (those that require an accusative object) have passive force and are used as predicate adjectives in a construction sometimes called the "statal passive."

Weak verbs form the past participle by adding the suffix -t (-et, to stems terminating in -d or -t) to the infinitive stem or, if irregular, to the special past base. All strong verbs except tun (to do) add the suffix -en to the participial stem, and all verbs that stress the first syllable also add the prefix ge-.

Past participle: modals. The modals (and wissen), when used without a dependent infinitive, form weak past participles by prefixing ge- and suffixing -t to the special past base. When the past participle of a modal is used with a dependent infinitive, it takes on the form of its infinitive and follows the dependent infinitive; the construction produced is called a double infinitive. The double infinitive is the only element that follows the inflected verb in a dependent clause.

Certain other verbs (such as lassen, to allow) also have a past participle that looks like the infinitive when used with a dependent infinitive.

Compound verb constructions with auxiliaries. The present perfect, past perfect, future, and future perfect tenses are made up of auxiliaries plus a noninflected form of the basic verb. For the future the noninflected form is the infinitive; for the other tenses it is the past participle.

A synopsis using the third person singular as the inflected verb is given for machen (to make, do) and gehen (to go) to show the pattern. The relative position of the elements in an independent clause is also shown.

Present Perfect	er hat gemacht
	er ist gegangen

Past Perfect	er hatte gemacht
	er war gegangen

Future	er wird machen
	er wird gehen

Future Perfect	er wird gemacht haben
	er wird gegangen sein

PRESENT TENSE OF MODALS AND wissen

	dürfen	können	mögen	müssen	sollen	wollen	wissen
ich	darf	kann	mag	muß	soll	will	weiß
du	darfst	kannst	magst	mußt	sollst	willst	weißt
er	darf	kann	mag	muß	soll	will	weiß
wir	dürfen	können	mögen	müssen	sollen	wollen	wissen
ihr	dürft	könnt	mögt	müßt	sollt	wollt	wißt
sie	dürfen	können	mögen	müssen	sollen	wollen	wissen

PAST STEM

durft-	konnt-	mocht-	mußt-	sollt-	wollt-	wußt-

GENERAL SUBJUNCTIVE STEM

dürft-	könnt-	möcht-	müßt-	sollt-	wollt-	wüßt-

STRONG AND IRREGULAR VERBS

CLASSIFIED STRONG VERBS

	I	II	III {nd,ng} {nn,mm}	IV	V	VI	VII
Stem Vowel							
A	ei	ie	i, i	e	e	a	a
B	ei	ie	i {nk}, i	(a)i (b)ie	(a)e (b)i	ä	
C	(a)ie (b)i	ie	o	a	a	u	ie
D	ie i	o	a u	o	e	a	a

	I	II	III	IV	V	VI	VII
A	bleiben	bieten	finden	helfen	lesen	wachsen	lassen
B	bleibt	bietet	findet	hilft	liest	wächst	läßt
C	blieb	bot	fand	half	las	wuchs	ließ
D	geblieben	geboten	gefunden	geholfen	gelesen	gewachsen	gelassen
A	greifen	gießen	beginnen	stehlen	messen	fahren	raten
B	greift	gießt	beginnt	stiehlt	mißt	fährt	rät
C	griff	goß	begann	stahl	maß	fuhr	riet
D	gegriffen	gegossen	begonnen	gestohlen	gemessen	gefahren	geraten

IRREGULAR STRONG VERBS

	I	II	III	IV	V	VI	VII
A	schneiden	ziehen		nehmen	geben	schaffen	laufen
B	schneidet	zieht		nimmt	gibt	schafft	läuft
C	schnitt	zog		nahm	gab	schuf	lief
D	geschnitten	gezogen		genommen	gegeben	geschaffen	gelaufen
A	leiden	heben	erlöschen	treten	sitzen	heißen	fangen
B	leidet	hebt	erlischt	tritt	sitzt	heißt	fängt
C	litt	hob	erlosch	trat	saß	hieß	fing
D	gelitten	gehoben	erloschen	getreten	gesessen	geheißen	gefangen
A		schmelzen	saufen	essen	liegen	stoßen	hängen
B		schmilzt	säuft	ißt	liegt	stößt	hängt
C		schmolz	soff	aß	lag	stieß	hing
D		geschmolzen	gesoffen	gegessen	gelegen	gestoßen	gehangen
A		lügen	betrügen	treten	bitten	hauen	rufen
B		lügt	betrügt	tritt	bittet	haut	ruft
C		log	betrog	trat	bat	hieb	rief
D		gelogen	betrogen	getreten	gebeten	gehauen	gerufen

UNCLASSIFIED STRONG VERBS

A	kommen	gehen	stehen	tun
B	kommt	geht	steht	tut
C	kam	ging	stand	tat
D	gekommen	gegangen	gestanden	getan

IRREGULAR WEAK VERBS

A	bringen	denken	kennen	senden
B	bringt	denkt	kennt	sendet
C	brachte	dachte	kannte	sandte
D	gebracht	gedacht	gekannt	gesandt
*	brächt-	dächt-	kennt-	sendet-
			also:	*also:*
			brennen	wenden
			nennen	
			rennen	

* general subjunctive stem

NOTES: Class I verb stems ending in a vowel, change the vowel of the past tense and of the past participle to *i* before -en.

Class IV verbs, helfen, sterben, verderben, and werfen, have the umlauted vowel, *ü*, in the general subjunctive. The unclassified verb, stehen, has *ü* for *ä*.

All transitive verbs, the modals, and many intransitive verbs are conjugated in the perfect tenses with *haben.* Verbs conjugated with *sein* are intransitive verbs that express motion, such as *gehen* (to go), *aufstehen* (to get up), *laufen* (to run); or a change of condition, such as *sterben* (to die), *einschlafen* (to fall asleep), and *werden* (to become). Also conjugated with *sein* are *sein* itself, *bleiben* (to remain), and the impersonal verbs (verbs used only in the third person singular), such as *gelingen* (to succeed) and *geschehen* (to happen). A very few verbs of motion, including *ziehen* (to draw, pull) and *fahren* (to go, drive), may be used transitively or intransitively. When used transitively, they are conjugated with *haben;* when used intransitively, they are conjugated with *sein.*

The past and future tenses of the subjunctive are formed similarly, using the general or special subjunctive of the appropriate auxiliary plus the past participle or infinitive of the basic verb.

The passive voice has the same tenses and moods that the active voice has. A synopsis using the third person singular of *machen* is given to show the pattern. The subjunctives use the appropriate subjunctive forms of the auxiliaries. Note that the past participle of *werden* lacks the prefix *ge-* when it is used as an auxiliary.

Present	er wird gemacht
Past	er wurde gemacht
Present Perfect	er ist gemacht worden
Past Perfect	er war gemacht worden
Future	er wird gemacht werden
Future Perfect	er wird gemacht worden sein

Imperative mood. The true imperative is limited to second-person familiar forms, singular and plural. The singular is formed by adding -*e* to the infinitive stem of all weak verbs and strong verbs of classes I, II, III, VI, and VII, the irregulars, *werden* and *wissen. Sein* uses the infinitive stem but omits the ending. The ending is optional except for verbs with stems terminating in -*d* or -*t,* two-syllable stems terminating in -*el* (which drop the -*e-* of the stem) or -*er* (which may drop the -*e-* of the stem), and stems terminating in a consonant combination not pronounceable in one syllable. For these the ending is mandatory. Strong verbs of classes IV and V form the singular without ending, using the third-person singular present stem. The plural familiar imperative of all verbs is identical with the second-person plural present indicative. Except for special emphasis, the personal pronouns are not used with the familiar forms; if used, they follow the verb and are stressed.

The use of the third person plural as a formal second person has necessitated the development of a new imperative form. It is actually the special subjunctive, but for all verbs except *sein* it looks like the third-person plural indicative with the verb and pronoun reversed in position. The pronoun is never omitted. The formal imperative of *sein* is *seien Sie.*

Reflexive verbs. Some verbs are used frequently or exclusively with reflexive pronouns as objects. Many are true reflexives; that is, the subject acts on itself:

Er badet sich. *He bathes himself.*

But many cannot be taken literally:

Das Tor öffnet sich. *The gate opens.*

Most of these expressions are highly idiomatic and are best studied with the help of a dictionary.

Verbal prefixes. Prefixes may be added to verbs to effect changes in meaning that range from very slight (*zahlen,* to pay; *bezahlen,* to pay) to virtually complete (*kommen,* to come; *bekommen,* to receive). Prefixes are classed as separable or inseparable, depending on how the resulting compound is handled.

Separable prefixes were originally separate adverbial elements which became closely associated with the verb through frequent usage. The prefix may be almost any part of speech or occur in no other usage.

GERMAN *as a literary language was established by Martin Luther's translation of the Bible in the early 1500s.*

The word *aus* (out) may serve as such an element in addition to its use as a preposition. In the infinitive form the prefix and the verb are written as a single word *ausgehen* (to go out), and the main stress falls on the prefix. When the infinitive is used with the preposition *zu*, the preposition comes between the prefix and the verb, and the whole is written as a single word *auszugehen*. In the past participle the prefix *ge-* comes between the prefix and the verb:

Ich bin ausgegangen. *I have gone out.*

Separation occurs when these verbs serve as inflected verbs in a main clause; the verb is in second position and the prefix is last:

Ich gehe aus. *I am going out.*

In dependent clauses, when the inflected verb is last, the prefix and verb are again written together:

Er weiß, daß ich nicht ausgehe.
He knows that I am not going out.

Inseparable prefixes are unstressed elements that never occur as separate words. Though they usually produce a change in meaning in the verb stems to which they are added, the prefixes themselves have no specific meaning. The inseparable prefixes are: *be-, ge-, emp-, ent-, er-, miß-, ver-,* and *zer-.* Two examples of their use are:

kommen	*to come*
finden	*to find*
bekommen	*to receive*
erfinden	*to invent*

Verbs having inseparable prefixes never add *ge-* to the past participle, and such a prefix is never stressed.

A few words as *durch, über, um, unter, voll, wider,* and *wieder* may be used as either separable or inseparable prefixes. The compound verbs in which these prefixes are used vary in stress and meaning, depending on whether such a prefix is being used as a separable prefix or as an inseparable prefix. Thus, the compound, *übersetzen,* stressed on the first syllable, means "to transfer" and is using *über* as a separable prefix. However, when this compound is stressed on the third syllable, it means "to translate" and is using *über* as an inseparable prefix.

—*Erminnie Bartelmez*

MAJOR WORLD LANGUAGES

Spoken by	Europe and the Americas	U.S.S.R.	Middle East	Indian subcontinent	China	East Asia
More than 600 million					Mandarin	
350–400 million	English					
200–300 million	Spanish	Russian		Hindi		
100–150 million	Portuguese German French		Arabic	Bengali		Japanese Malay- Indonesian
40–70 million	Italian	Ukrainian	Turkish	Urdu Punjabi Tamil Teluga Marathi	Cantonese Min Wu	Korean Javanese Vietnamese
10–40 million	Polish Rumanian Dutch Serbo- Croatian Hungarian Czech Greek	Uzbek	Persian Pushtu	Gujarati Kannada Malayalam Oriya Bihari Rajasthani Assamese Sinhalese Sindi Nepali	Hakka	Thai Burmese Tagalog Sundamese
1–10 million*	8 others	9 others	5 others	8 others	3 others	18 others

*In addition, 45 languages in Africa; 3 in South America; and 3 (Hebrew, Yiddish, and Esperanto) spoken in several parts of the world.

READING

Imagine that you are watching someone read a letter that has just arrived by special delivery. He may burst into tears, laugh, sigh, grow pale with fear, or turn red with anger. What would cause such strong reactions? The letter itself is only a piece of paper with ink marks on it. The reader is not made sad or happy or fearful by the ink marks themselves. His emotions are triggered by the concepts and images locked into those ink marks. He can read, and the written symbols on the page can speak to him. They mean something to him.

What if the reader were looking at a letter written in an alphabet or a language that he did not know? There would be no emotional reaction. He would simply stare at the ink marks on the paper and wonder what they

IF YOU CAN'T READ *you may get into big trouble because you miss warnings and instructions.*

ALLEN REUBEN

mean because he is not able to decode the message, understand it, and react to it. Reading is the ability to decode written symbols, understand them, and react to them.

In earlier days, the vast majority of people could neither read nor write. They received information by word of mouth. Stories about their families and their leaders were passed down from generation to generation of listeners. Only the most important records were kept in writing, and anyone who could read and write was a member of a special ruling class. Today, the ability to read is necessary for nearly everyone. Adults who cannot read or who read poorly find it difficult to get a job, find housing, buy food, or receive medical care. Reading is no longer a special skill; it is a basic requirement.

Learning to Read

Everyone learns to speak and to understand his native language virtually without guidance. Reading is another matter. It must be learned over several years of guided instruction, usually by children in the elementary grades. The following sections describe the steps in learning to read and tell how to judge reading readiness.

Components of reading. Students of reading identify three important components of reading skill: word recognition, comprehension, and reaction and fusion.

Word recognition. At the heart of the reading process is the decoding of printed symbols. This involves translating these symbols into their correct analogues in the spoken language. Educators speak of this as recognizing the relationship between the *grapheme* (the written or printed word) and the *phoneme* (the oral language sound). A printed letter represents a particular sound in the spoken language; a combination of letters represents the sounds that make up a word; the word means something. Translating from symbol to sound to meaning is very complex.

Comprehension. It is not enough to just decode printed symbols into their

corresponding oral sounds; readers must also understand what is meant by the words they have just decoded. A bright youngster may be taught to decode the printed symbols "familiarity breeds contempt" into their correct oral form, but he may not understand any of the individual words or what meaning the three words have when combined. Therefore, along with decoding skills, the reader must know what the words in his language mean (vocabulary) and what they mean when they are put together in new ways (comprehension).

Reaction and fusion. Often the reading process does not end with understanding a message—it requires some physical or emotional response. *Reaction* is the reader's response to what he has read. For example, the driver who sees a stop sign is expected not just to decode and understand the word "Stop," but is also expected to stop the car at the appropriate place. *Fusion* is a more complicated kind of reaction to the reading experience. The person reading the letter in our example may be moved to laughter or tears or anger not just by the message in the letter, but also by his earlier memories and experiences. The human mind stores and interprets what it reads, fusing the new material with what has gone before and with what may come after.

Preparation for reading. In preparing young children for reading instruction, teachers and parents must consider the physical, mental, and social development of the children.

Physical health. Reading is done primarily with the eyes, so good eyesight or eyesight corrected with glasses is essential. If a child has a problem with near point vision—seeing objects clearly and sharply at a distance of 14 inches or less—he should receive attention. Otherwise, learning to read will be difficult or impossible.

Hearing problems can also be a factor in learning to read. Hearing acuity is necessary for discerning the sounds of different combinations of letters, and a child with poor hearing will not benefit from instruction pointing out such differences.

In recent years, psychologists and doctors have identified other physical or neurological problems that make reading difficult, and have coined the term "dyslexia" to describe these problems. There seems to be no hard and fast definition of dyslexia, but it does appear that some individuals who are otherwise normal have particular problems with learning to read. Special methods of instruction to assist such persons are being developed by reading specialists.

Consonant blend	Vowel sound
slide	play
slip	way
slow	say
slap	tray

SESAME STREET (left) *has introduced millions of children to letters and their sounds. Learning to recognize common sounds* (right) *is an important preparation for reading.*

Mental health. A child who has a good self-image and strong sense of self-confidence is much better able to master reading skills than one who suffers from a poor self-image, fear of failure, and frustration and doubt. The family is the place where the preschooler develops his self-image, so parents and others entrusted with child care should be especially attentive to fostering a positive self-image and feelings of worth in the young child.

Maturity. Maturity is not only a matter of age but of social growth as well. In order to learn to read, a child must be able to persist at tasks and to remain receptive to instruction. He must be able to work alone at times and with others. Parents can help their preschool children to mature by speaking and talking with them, and by seeing to it that the children are able to play with others of their age. In this way, the child grows accustomed to listening to adults and to getting along with his peers.

Social and cultural differences. Children who come from backgrounds that are culturally different from those of most of the other children often encounter reading difficulties in school. Children whose primary language is not English have particular problems. They must first learn the English language before they can read it, and many schools do offer courses in English as a second language for such students.

Children from very poor families also run into serious trouble in reading. Many such children live in homes where there are no books, magazines, or other reading materials. They often lack experiences, such as travel and exposure to educational toys and games, that they can relate to their reading. Reading comes especially hard to such children because it is a completely new task for them, one for which they have no preparation.

Early childhood programs like Head Start have sought to provide materials and experiences that will help disadvantaged children prepare for reading. Television, through such early childhood educational programs as *Sesame Street* and *The Electric Company,* has also sought to encourage reading readiness, especially among the poor.

Beginning Reading

How best to teach reading is a subject of great controversy in educational circles. Debate rages about the proper age at which to begin reading and about which approaches should be emphasized. An approach that is successful with one child may prove useless with another.

Decoding. The first major step in learning to read is learning to recognize familiar words in print. Four major approaches are used in elementary schools, either separately or in combination.

Sight method. Sight words are words that readers have learned to recognize without having to analyze them. They are common words and are learned as wholes. The young child learns to recognize them and say them aloud at a glance.

Even before 1900, some educators pointed out that it is easier—especially for young children—to recognize and remember a whole word than it is to recognize and remember the letters in a word. So, in the sight-word system, children are taught whole words—*cat, boy, girl* and the like—without knowing the relationship of individual letters to sounds.

The sight method helps a child to score early successes in reading by allowing him to recognize familiar words that he has seen over and over. Because words—not letters—express meaning, children also find that they are able to read immediately for meaning. The disadvantage of this system is that it gives a child no means of decoding an unfamiliar word, and can lead to memorizing words without understanding their meanings.

Context clues. Learning word recognition through context clues, that is, through the role the word plays in a sentence, is often an accompaniment to the sight method. The teacher presents the children with a sentence in which they know all the words but one by sight. The teacher then encourages them to make an informed guess as to what the unfamiliar word is by asking them to discern what word would fit the context of the sentence.

Context clues have the advantage of building on the child's knowledge of words and of encouraging him to think about the meaning of a sentence in order to guess the meaning of the unfamiliar word. It has the disadvantage, again, of providing no way of learning the meaning of new words in the beginning and of requiring much repetition of context to establish a new word in the reader's mind. Worst of all, the child may make a wrong guess as to meaning based on context clues and thus become confused.

Phonic approach. Phonics is the study of sounds as expressed in symbols. Because phonics is a way of breaking down a written word into its sound components, it is a powerful decoding device. It is also the most difficult to learn, requiring hours of drill on the various vowel and consonant sounds in English.

Phonics is a useful tool for developing reading skills rather than a method of teaching reading. In the beginning, phonics is frequently used in conjunction with sight words. Some educators feel that a fund of sight words should be built up first so that students can relate the study of phonics to words they already know. Indeed, most contemporary reading texts stress that a mix of approaches serves the beginning reader best, with phonics as only one element of the entire reading program.

Structural analysis. Another method of analyzing words, structural analysis, concentrates on recognizing the structure of words. The beginning student learns to recognize and pronounce root words, then learns the inflectional endings (plurals, past tenses, etc.). At a later stage, the student studies syllabication, accent, prefixes, additional suffixes, and more complex roots.

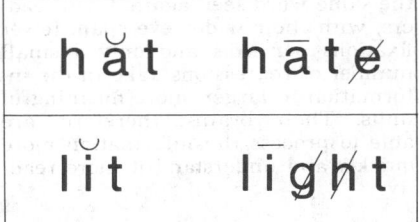

DIACRITICAL MARKS *like the short* (ˇ) *and long* (ˉ) *signs above help readers distinguish between words with similar spellings. A slash through a letter shows that it is silent.*

As with the other word-attack methods, structural analysis is best used in conjunction with other programs and with the child's grasp of oral language. For instance, in some cases the study of the context of a word in a sentence is the only way that a reader can tell how to pronounce the word. Some words have the same form but are pronounced differently to give different meanings: "Did he *refuse* to pick up the *refuse?*"

As children progress in their ability to recognize, analyze, pronounce, and understand new words, the development of their vocabulary becomes more and more important. Phonic and structural analysis of new words affords some means of discovering meaning and pronunciation, but the child can never be sure that his analysis is correct; English is just not that regular. Therefore, schools, parents, and others caring for children should encourage them to look up unfamiliar words in a dictionary. It is a habit that good readers of all ages should acquire and practice.

Other methods. Besides the foregoing, there are a number of other word-attack methods used by educators and elementary schools.

The *Montessori Method,* implemented by Maria Montessori early in the 20th century, features a structured environment for young children involving specially constructed materials such as three-dimensional and sandpaper letters. These allow young children to use their sense of touch as well as sight to learn letters.

The *Initial Teaching Alphabet* (i.t.a.) is another device to simplify the symbol-to-sound correlation. It is an expanded Roman alphabet, using 44 characters instead of the normal 26 to encode the various sounds of oral English. The sound correlation is better with i.t.a. than with the regular alphabet, but as children must learn the regular one anyway, the transition is not always easy. Also, many children find it difficult to write in the i.t.a.

Words in Color tries to do something like the i.t.a. in that it color codes words to show phonetic differences and similarities. Sounds that are similar have the same color, no matter what their spelling. The sys-tem's most serious drawback is that the transition to regularly printed material may be difficult.

The *Diacritical Marking System* uses diacritical marks to indicate the values of certain letters and letter combinations. The spelling of the word is traditional. Short vowels and consonants that are regular have no mark; a bar over a vowel indicates a long vowel sound; a slant indicates silent letters; letters combining to form a unique sound are underlined; and a dot over vowels indicates an unaccented or *schwa* (ə) sound.

Comprehension skills. Word-attack skills are all very necessary but they are scarcely the whole story in reading. The main reason for reading is to discover the meaning of the writer. The basic unit of meaning is the sentence, so many primary grade teachers stress working with writing and reading sentences. Young children learn to build sentences by combining two short sentences into one. "Jane has a bat. It is a big bat." becomes "Jane has a big bat." They also learn to expand sentences, beginning with kernel sentences. "The car was fast." What color was the car? "Red." What size was it? "Small." What kind of car was it? "Racing." How fast was it? "Fast as lightning." The children use the teacher's questions and their answers to build up a more complete sentence. "The small, red racing car was as fast as lightning."

These sentence exercises, and others like them, are designed to make young children aware of the sentence and its parts as carriers of meaning. In building sentences, they come to ask the questions: who, what, where, when, and how. They then carry over the questioning technique begun by their teacher to the reading they are doing. By asking and answering questions as they read, the children learn to recognize not only the words they are reading but their meanings as well.

Most teachers will pose a question or two before a class or child sets out to read a story. This gives the child motivation to read the selection (what is the answer to the question, can you find out?).

Reading for meaning—comprehension—in the early grades involves studying the language with word-attack methods and paying attention to the units of meaning, especially sentences. It also involves asking questions and answering them as the child reads along, which engages the child in the story, encouraging further questions and even predictions. For if the child has read well—not just for words but for understanding also—he will see that the ship is going to be caught in a storm shortly after it leaves port. This is reading for understanding, and the only real reason anyone reads anything.

Types of reading programs. Reading programs in the elementary grades are most frequently one of two types: basal or individualized.

The basal program uses a whole set of graded readers and supplementary materials, usually ranging from reading readiness programs to 8th-grade reading level materials. The series of readers, which use a controlled vocabulary and a sequential development of reading skills, guide the students through the elementary and

INDIVIDUALIZED LEARNING *has been made possible by modern teaching machines.*

middle years of instruction. As most large educational publishers publish a basal reading program, there are many such programs to choose from.

In contrast to the basal program, an individualized program normally uses a wide variety of books from many publishers to appeal to all tastes and levels. These programs place a heavy reliance on the childrens' own selection of reading materials. Word-attack skills and comprehension skills are introduced in conjunction with the individual child's own reading habits and special problems.

A more structured form of individualized reading—*Individually Prescribed Instruction (IPI)*—also relies on the availability of a wide range of reading selections. In this program, the young child is tested by a battery of aptitude, intelligence, and reading readiness tests, and then is placed in the appropriate reading level as determined by his scores on the tests.

The child progresses through the various levels of the program at his own pace. When he experiences difficulties, a "prescription" is written out for him by a teacher recommending the materials he should consult to overcome his problem.

As a supplement to the basal and individualized programs, many schools use audio–visual materials (filmstrips, television tapes, slide/tape presentations, and the like). Some schools have programmed books on reading or computer–assisted instruction that are generally used in conjunction with another more traditional program. No doubt, as technology progresses, new systems and devices will find their place in the classroom.

Learning to Read Better

This section deals with older children, college students, and adults who have mastered basic reading as taught in the elementary grades but who find that their reading skills are not adequate. These people can recognize words, can understand what the words mean, and can use words in meaningful groups such as phrases and sentences. Yet they find reading tedious and time-consuming. These people want to read better, more efficiently, faster, and with greater comprehension and retention.

The techniques, devices, and suggestions set forth here do not guarantee improvement, but they do offer several methods of improving reading, one or a combination of which should prove valuable to anyone wishing to read better.

Eye movements in reading.

Despite the fact that you feel that your eyes are continuously moving from left to right as you read this, the truth is that your eye movements are not continuous; they progress in a series of jumps from one fixed point to another. These jerky movements are called *saccadic movements*. The pauses or fixed points between movements when the eye is at rest looking at the page are called *fixations*. The fixation lasts only a fraction of a second, but this is the only time that the eye sees when reading. At the end of a line, the eyes go back in a continuous movement, called the *return sweep,* to the beginning of the next line to repeat the saccadic movement along that line.

Ideally, a reader should perceive a whole line of print in three fixations. In many cases, however, readers are obliged to stop (fixate) on every word in the line. Their *eye span* or *reading span* (the number of words recognized per fixation) is very small. The efficient reader, on the other hand, can see two or more words in a single fixation. Obviously, the more words seen per fixation, the fewer fixations needed to read the line. The efficient reader then reads more rapidly than the poor one in part because of his greater eye span. The ability to see several words in one fixation also allows the efficient reader to see groups of words as whole units; thus, he can read the line for meaning by taking in its meaningful phrases and word clusters in one fixation. The poor reader, concentrating on every word, gets them all right eventually, but then he must try to remember what all the words add up to, what they mean.

Sometimes, even in good readers, the eye moves backward along a line of type to take a second look at something. Such a backward movement is called a *regression.* Poor readers, in addition to fixating on nearly every word in a line, also tend to regress frequently. This fragments the reader's perception of the meaning of a sentence as the brain receives information word by word—and often

the same word seen again. Good readers, with their wider eye span, fewer fixations per line, and only a small number of regressions, take in the information in larger, more meaningful units. Their brains, therefore, are able to process the information more quickly and understand it more readily.

Flexibility in reading rate.

Speed is not the only factor in good reading, though. Slowness is often more a symptom than a cause of bad reading. Some material (for example, science reports, financial analyses, and sets of complex instructions) needs to be read slowly, almost word for word. But it is a waste of time to read everything in this way.

Flexibility is what the good reader aims for in reading rate. He wants to approach printed material with a reading rate that makes sense for that kind of writing: slow and detailed for difficult or unfamiliar matter like an economics text; more rapid for easier material like a newspaper; and very rapid for locating information in a telephone directory or turning the pages of an exciting whodunit to see how it comes out.

Reading rates for different kinds of material are classified below to give you an idea of the range that is available for different situations:

Skimming (very rapid) is used for locating information, a reference, or an answer to a specific question. It is good for getting the main idea of a piece of writing, for glancing through a book or magazine article to get a general idea of its contents and style, and for reviewing something that has been read before.

Scanning (rapid reading) is used to review familiar material, or to get the main idea or important point (as in a newspaper column).

Normal rate (as rapid as the reader feels comfortable with) is used to find answers to specific questions, to note details, to get the point of a piece with some supporting details, and to read material of average difficulty (as in a magazine article).

Careful rate (slow and detailed) is used to master details in a written piece, to evaluate arguments, to follow instructions, to read complex or technical material, and to appreciate literary works that demand attention to their use of language.

Poor habits are often reflected in slow reading rates, and the correction of these habits can help the reader to attain flexibility in his approach to written material.

All readers must recognize words in order to read, but *excessive word analysis,* reading each word syllable by syllable or even letter by letter, destroys the reader's ability to comprehend what he has read and makes

TOPS OR BOTTOMS? *The top halves of letters are more important to understanding than the bottom halves, as this headline illustrates.*

Twisters Hit East Oklahoma

How to read faster

By Bill Cosby

1. Preview—if it's long and hard

2. Skim—if it's short and simple

3. Cluster—to increase speed <u>and</u> comprehension

Most of us learned to read by looking at each word in a sentence—*one at a time.*

Like this:

My—brother—Russell—thinks—monsters...

You probably still read this way sometimes, especially when the words are difficult. Or when the words have an extra-special meaning—as in a poem, a Shakespearean play, or a contract. And that's O.K.

But word-by-word reading is a rotten way to read faster. It actually *cuts down* on your speed.

Clustering trains you to look at *groups* of words instead of one at a time—to increase your speed enormously. For most of us, clustering is a *totally different way of seeing what we read.*

<u>Here's how to cluster:</u> Train your eyes to see *all* the words in clusters of up to 3 or 4 words at a glance.

Here's how I'd cluster the story:

My brother Russell thinks monsters live in our bedroom closet at night. But I told him he is crazy. "Go and check then," he said. I didn't want to. Russell said I was chicken. "Am not," I said. "Are so," he said. So I told him the monsters were going to eat him at midnight. He started to cry. My Dad came in and told the monsters to beat it. Then he told us to go to sleep. "If I hear any more about monsters," he said, "I'll spank you." We went to sleep fast. And you know something? They never did come back.

Learning to read clusters is not something your eyes do naturally. It takes constant practice.

"Preview, skim, and cluster to read faster—except the things you <u>want</u> to read word for word."

GETTING BETTER: *Comedian Bill Cosby gives some tips on better reading in a national advertising campaign.*

the reading process slow and painful. Excessive analysis makes the reader unable to see the forest for the trees.

Allied with excessive word analysis is *slowness of word recognition,* in which the reader recognizes individual words so slowly that his reading rate is held back and comprehension impaired.

One of the most common causes of slow reading is the habit many readers have of mumbling or making lip movements that form the words as they read. Children all learn to read by sounding out the words they see. Adults, even ones who do not mumble or move their lips as they read, often hear themselves pronounce in their minds each word that they read. This is called *subvocal reading* or *subvocalization.*

The problem with lip reading and subvocal reading is that the reader is unable to read faster than he can speak intelligibly, which is around 200 words per minute. This might be useful for mastering a chemistry text or a Shakespearean play, but it is unsuitable for reading a television listing or an account of yesterday's football game.

Frequent regressions cause the reader to lose speed and to lose the train of thought of the written material. Even good readers will make a large number of regressions when reading material that contains many new or unfamiliar words, complex ideas, or long and highly involved sentences. However, excessive regressions, even on material that is easy to read and is well understood by the reader, causes slow reading and comprehension problems.

Improving reading rate. The practices and devices mentioned below can help a reader overcome the problems of excessive word analysis, lip reading, subvocalization, and regression. Remember, the goal is to develop a flexible reading rate that allows one to approach a piece of writing with the reading rate appropriate to it and to the purpose for which it is being read.

Flashcards. Flashcards are small cards with words printed on them. The cards are shown for only a brief period of time during which the reader tries to identify the words. Flashcards are designed to remove the necessity of detailed word analysis as the reader becomes more familiar with the words and accustomed to identifying them in a flash. Commercial books for building vocabulary, found in all bookstores, are also useful for this purpose.

Tachistoscope. The tachistoscope is a device that allows for the presentation of material for only brief moments, like the flashcard; only here the emphasis is not on words alone but on meaningful groups of words such as phrases and even short sentences. The point is to expand the reader's eye span to take in more words at each fixation. Some educators are doubtful about the carryover from recognizing words and phrases on the tachistoscope to the actual reading situation. It is doubtful that this device alone will help a reader to improve his reading speed, but it can be useful along with other methods.

Reading pacers. Reading pacers are small machines that send some sort of shutter down over the page of a book while the reader is reading it. The idea is to keep the reader's eyes moving in front of the shutter. Regressions are discouraged by this device, as is subvocalization. The speed with which the shutter moves down the page can be adjusted so that the reader can gradually increase the pace as he becomes more accustomed to higher reading speeds.

Both tachistoscopes and reading pacers are available in relatively inexpensive models.

Practice. Perhaps the best and most effective method of increasing reading speed is to do a large amount of easy reading. This means reading material in which vocabulary and content pose no problem in comprehension. There are a number of books on the market that include such high-interest/low-level material and that offer many selections suitable for timed reading with comprehension questions to be answered afterward. The reader is given a set time—usually three minutes—to read the selection, and then answers the questions. He is in competition only with himself to better both his rate and his comprehension.

Improving comprehension.

Comprehension can mean almost anything. It is best to attack the problem of what it means to have comprehended a piece by asking what purpose the reader had in reading it.

Purpose. If a reader is looking for an answer to a specific question, he will not dawdle with the material or be unsure of what it means. He wants to know how to change a washer or the date of the Battle of Waterloo. He knows he has comprehended the piece when he changes the washer successfully or can give the date of the battle. Having a clearly understood purpose, then, is one way for the reader to set up the criteria for the kind of comprehension he wants or needs, and then to know when he has achieved it.

Preread. Prereading, or surveying, is a method for familiarizing oneself with what a book or article is about, what information it contains, and how that information is organized. Readers should preread all nonfiction materials.

To preread a book, first run down the table of contents to see what the book covers and how the coverage is arranged. Then scan the preface or introductory remarks, which give further information on the content, design, and purpose of the book.

Next skim through the chapters of the book, or at least the ones of most interest. Read the main headings in the chapters and the introductory and concluding paragraphs of each chapter. Look at any illustrations (graphs, maps, tables, etc.) and read the captions accompanying them. Finally, glance at any special features indicated in the contents, such as an index, appendix, glossary, etc.

This prereading gives a very good idea of the content, scope, organization, and purpose of the book. It is a technique that is especially good for studying textbooks for high school or college or for reading reports and books for business. A reader can preread a book in a fraction of the time it would take to read the whole work and then can judge if he wants to read all of it or only parts of it. If he must read the whole book anyway, prereading will help him to place details in their proper perspective and to understand what the author is saying.

Outlining and summarizing. One way a good reader fixes what he has read in his mind is by making a summary or outline of it after he finishes. A *summary* is particularly useful when reading from a number of sources, such as newspapers, magazines, and books. To make a summary, the reader should take notes while reading, and then summarize important points that the author makes. Summarizing forces one to identify and concentrate on the important ideas.

An *outline* is a schematic organization of material that has been read. It shows the relationship of each idea or fact to the piece as a whole. Outlines can be very elaborate or not much more than a listing of important points with subordinate details indented and separately listed below the point to which they relate.

Phrase reading. When a reader has difficulty in grasping the meaning of units of thought such as phrases, clauses, and sentences, a simple procedure he can use is to mark off phrases in the material that are sense units. The reader first marks off the material and then tries to read it by taking in the phrases in one fixation. This technique is also useful for breaking the habits of subvocalizing and word-by-word reading. A line marked off might look like this:

*General Motors/will announce/
new prices/next week/
for small car models./*

SQ3R. Francis P. Robinson published in 1946 a systematic procedure for reading for meaning that is particularly useful as a study device for schoolwork and business reading. SQ3R stands for *S*urvey, *Q*uestion, *R*ead, *R*ecite, and *R*eview.

Survey, discussed under prereading, gives a quick overview of the material to orient the reader to the content, scope, tone, and organization of the material. The *question* method is to be used while reading. The reader turns each heading and subheading of the work into a question, that is, "Oil Shortage Serious," becomes "Why is the oil shortage serious?" Next, he will *read* the material that comes after the heading with a view to answering the question that the heading has been turned into. The question technique focuses the reader's mind on the material as a source of information that will yield a definite answer. The reader will then *recite* aloud or subvocally, or even note down, the answer to the question asked and the major supporting evidence. Finally, he will *review* the notes made after finishing the reading assignment. Ideally, the notes will provide a summary of what has been read, and make clear the relationship between one idea and another. The notes can be used for review before a test in classroom situations or for the preparation of a report or memo in a business situation.

Above all, the reader must concentrate on a piece of writing, thinking about what the writer is trying to say, and considering what it means. If a reader's mind wanders, if he is continuously interrupted, if he crams his reading in while doing something else, even the best skills in the world will not help him to read better. It is senseless for one to complain of not being able to hear if one is not listening. Concentrate on what is being read and—for that moment—on nothing else. It is remarkable what great dividends of understanding can be obtained from even small investments of attention.

—*Harry L. Wagner*

THE TABLE OF CONTENTS can help readers and researchers find what they are looking for quickly. It is also a valuable tool when prereading a book.

HARCOURT BRACE & JOVANOVICH

FAMILY READING

In this modern, language-oriented world it is important for people to know how to read. Imagine not being able to read a street sign, or a tax form, or the label on a bottle of medicine. Yet reading is more than an indispensable skill in everyday living. It is the key to a world of fun, adventure, and knowledge. If we can read, we can share the dreams and ideas of writers who lived long ago, and those who are living today.

There are literally millions of books to choose from, including novels, collections of short stories, volumes of poetry, biographies, and nonfiction works in virtually every field of interest. A popular type of book is the anthology, which offers the reader a selection of works by a number of authors. Anthologies make it easy for the reader to become familiar with the writings of different authors and to determine which writers' works they want to explore further.

This anthology brings together a broad selection of poems and stories. There is something here for everyone in the family, from the youngest member to the oldest. Children who have not yet learned to read will enjoy hearing the Mother Goose rhymes and the fairy tales. Young people and grownups alike will enjoy the poems and stories in this collection. Many of these works are literary classics, loved by generations of readers. Others are less well known but just as fascinating, delightful, and appealing as the more familiar pieces. Selections of special interest to beginning readers are set in larger, easy to read type.

The anthology presents poetry and fiction in five sections:

Mother Goose rhymes. These are ideal for reading to preschoolers, and for children who are just learning to read. By the time children have some skill in reading, they have already memorized many rhymes. The process of seeing in print the poems they already know by sound helps build their confidence and inspires them to improve their reading skills further. This section includes many of the best known and most popular of the several hundred Mother Goose rhymes in print in various editions.

A BROAD RANGE of reading material is represented in this volume, including such favorites as "Rip Van Winkle," Sherlock Holmes in "The Red-Headed League," and the fables of Aesop.

Fairy tales. These stories have fascinated young people and adults for generations. Almost every country has produced some fairy tales or folk tales, and collections of fairy tales abound.

Aesop's fables. These appeal to children because of their simplicity and frequent use of animals as characters. Aesop's fables are among the earliest works of literature, handed down by oral tradition for centuries before anyone thought of putting them in writing.

Poetry. A well-wrought poem is a song captured on the page. This section includes poems for youngsters and adults, including outstanding literary works as well as poems that are just plain fun.

Fiction. This section includes 17 pieces, ranging in length from the very short modern fables by James Thurber to a full-length Sherlock Holmes tale by Arthur Conan Doyle. The selections include stories for children, humor, adventure, suspense, mystery—something for everyone.

Reading is a social activity. It is fun to read the poems and stories in this anthology to oneself, but it is even more fun to read them to others. Poetry especially gains a new dimension when read aloud, because of the sound of the words and the cadence of the lines as they are spoken.

At the end of the fiction section is a bibliography listing books for further reading. It is only a hint of the many books available. For example, only one anthology is listed—an anthology of children's literature—because there are so many good poetry and fiction anthologies in existence. Also, volumes by specific authors frequently can be found in several editions. For example, at least 20 editions of *The Adventures of Tom Sawyer* are available. Works by the authors represented in this anthology can be found at good bookstores and libraries. The family reading list also includes several references to help readers identify additional books by these and other authors.

Mother Goose Rhymes

Mother Goose rhymes, also known simply as nursery rhymes, have been passed from parent to child for centuries. Nobody knows how old they really are, nor can we be certain of their exact origins. They came from many countries and appear in many versions. Some are pleasant stories wrapped up in rhyme; some are counting rhymes; some are nonsense lyrics;

some may have had their origins in actual historical events.

Whatever their original sources, they have fascinated, tickled, entertained, and enlightened generations of youngsters. Here is a perfect introduction to the delights of language. Adults reading these rhymes to children find they are a natural bridge of communication between the grown-up world of

experience and the childhood world of wonder and imagination.

Young people quickly commit any number of rhymes to memory and seem never to tire of hearing or reciting them. As soon as they learn to read, children find a new thrill in seeing their favorite rhymes in print and reading them aloud to others or even to themselves.

Rock-a-Bye Baby

Rock-a-bye baby,
In the tree top,
When the wind blows
The cradle will rock;
When the bough breaks
The cradle will fall,
And down will come baby,
Cradle and all.

Baa, Baa, Black Sheep

Baa, Baa, black sheep,
    Have you any wool?
Yes, sir, yes, sir,
    Three bags full.

One for my master,
    One for my dame,
One for the little boy
    That lives in the lane.

Baa, baa, black sheep,
    Have you any wool?
Yes, sir, yes, sir,
    Three bags full.

Pussy Cat, Pussy Cat

Pussy cat, pussy cat,
    Where have you been?
I've been to London
    To visit the Queen.
Pussy cat, pussy cat,
    What did you there?
I frightened a little mouse
    Under her chair.

Jack Sprat

Jack Sprat could eat no fat;
His wife could eat no lean.
And so betwixt the two of them,
They licked the platter clean.

Solomon Grundy

Solomon Grundy,
Born on a Monday,
Christened on Tuesday,
Married on Wednesday,
Took ill on Thursday,
Worse on Friday,
Died on Saturday,
Buried on Sunday,
This is the end
Of Solomon Grundy.

Star Light, Star Bright

Star light, star bright
First star I see tonight;
I wish I may, I wish I might
Get the wish I wish tonight.

One, Two, Buckle My Shoe

One, two,
    Buckle my shoe;
Three, four,
    Open the door;
Five, six,
    Pick up sticks;
Seven, eight,
    Lay them straight;
Nine, ten,
    A big fat hen;
Eleven, twelve,
    Dig and delve;
Thirteen, fourteen,
    Maids a-courting;
Fifteen, sixteen,
    Maids in the kitchen;
Seventeen, eighteen,
    Maids a-waiting;
Nineteen, twenty,
    My plate's empty.

Ladybug

Ladybug, ladybug,
Fly away home,
Your house is on fire,
Your children will burn.

A Diller, A Dollar

A diller, a dollar, a ten o'clock scholar,
    What makes you come so soon?
You used to come at ten o'clock,
    And now you come at noon.

Jack and Jill

Jack and Jill went up the hill
    To fetch a pail of water.
Jack fell down and broke his crown
    And Jill came tumbling after.

Up Jack got and home did trot
    As fast as he could caper.
He went to bed to mend his head
    With vinegar and brown paper.

This Little Pig

This little pig went to market,
This little pig stayed home,
This little pig had roast beef,
This little pig had none,
And this little pig cried wee-wee-wee
All the way home.

Simple Simon

Simple Simon met a pieman,
Going to the fair;
Says Simple Simon to the pieman,
Let me taste your ware.

Says the pieman to Simple Simon,
Show me first your penny;
Says Simple Simon to the pieman,
Indeed I have not any.

Humpty Dumpty

Humpty Dumpty sat on a wall,
Humpty Dumpty had a great fall.
All the King's horses
And all the King's men
Couldn't put Humpty together again.

Rub-a-Dub-Dub

Rub-a-dub-dub,
Three men in a tub,
And how do you think they got there?
The butcher, the baker,
The candlestick maker,
They all jumped out of a rotten potato,
'Twas enough to make a man stare.

Three Blind Mice

Three blind mice, see how they run.
They all ran after the farmer's wife;
She cut off their tails with a carving knife;
Did you ever see such a sight in your life,
As three blind mice?

Sing a Song of Sixpence

Sing a song of sixpence,
    A pocket full of rye;
Four and twenty blackbirds
    Baked in a pie.

When the pie was opened
    The birds began to sing;
Was not that a dainty dish
    To set before the king?

The king was in his counting-house
    Counting out his money;
The queen was in the parlor,
    Eating bread and honey.

The maid was in the garden,
    Hanging out the clothes;
When down came a blackbird
    And snapped off her nose.

Mary Had a Little Lamb

Mary had a little lamb,
Its fleece was white as snow;
And everywhere that Mary went
The lamb was sure to go.

It followed her to school one day,
That was against the rule;
It made the children laugh and play
To see a lamb in school.

And so the teacher turned it out,
But still it lingered near,
And waited patiently about
Till Mary did appear.

Why does the lamb love Mary so?
The eager children cry;
Why, Mary loves the lamb, you know,
The teacher did reply.

Mary, Mary

Mary, Mary, quite contrary,
    How does your garden grow?
With silver bells and cockle shells,
    And pretty maids all in a row.

Peter, Peter, Pumpkin Eater

Peter, Peter, pumpkin eater,
Had a wife and couldn't keep her;
He put her in a pumpkin shell
And there he kept her very well.

Little Bo-Peep

Little Bo-Peep has lost her sheep,
And can't tell where to find them;
Leave them alone, and they'll come home,
And bring their tails behind them.

Little Bo-Peep fell fast asleep,
And dreamt she heard them bleating;
But when she awoke, she found it a joke,
For they were still all fleeting.

Then up she took her little crook,
Determined for to find them;
She found them indeed, but it made her heart bleed,
For they'd left all their tails behind 'em.

It happened one day, as Bo-Peep did stray
Unto a meadow hard by
There she espied their tails side by side,
All hung on a tree to dry.

She heaved a sigh and wiped her eye,
And over the hillocks she raced;
And tried what she could, as a shepherdess should,
That each tail should be properly placed.

Little Boy Blue

Little Boy Blue, come blow your horn,
The sheep's in the meadow, the cow's in the corn.
But where is the little boy tending the sheep?
He's under the haystack, fast asleep.
Will you wake him? No, not I,
For if I do, he's sure to cry.

There Was an Old Woman

There was an old woman who lived in a shoe;
She had so many children she didn't know what to do;
She gave them some broth without any bread;
She whipped them all soundly and put them to bed.

Wee Willie Winkie

Wee Willie Winkie runs through the town,
Upstairs and downstairs in his nightgown,
Rapping at the window, crying through the lock,
Are the children all in bed, for now it's eight o'clock?

ARTHUR RACKHAM/THE GRANGER COLLECTION

Little Miss Muffet

Little Miss Muffet
Sat on a tuffet,
Eating her curds and whey;
    There came a big spider,
    Who sat down beside her,
And frightened Miss Muffet away.

Little Jack Horner

Little Jack Horner
Sat in a corner,
Eating his Christmas pie.
He put in his thumb
And pulled out a plum,
And said, "What a good boy am I."

Jack Be Nimble

Jack be nimble,
    Jack be quick,
Jack jump over
    The candlestick.

Yankee Doodle

Yankee Doodle went to town,
Riding on a pony;
Stuck a feather in his cap
And called it macaroni.

Yankee Doodle keep it up,
Yankee Doodle dandy,
Mind the music and the step,
And with the girls be handy.

Monday's Child

Monday's child is fair of face,
Tuesday's child is full of grace,
Wednesday's child is full of woe,
Thursday's child has far to go,
Friday's child is loving and giving,
Saturday's child works hard for his living,
And the child that is born on the Sabbath day
Is bonny and blithe, and good and gay.

To Market, To Market

To market, to market, to buy a fat pig,
Home again, home again, jiggety-jig.
To market, to market, to buy a fat hog,
Home again, home again, jiggety-jog.

Diddle, Diddle, Dumpling

Diddle, diddle, dumpling, my son John,
Went to bed with his stockings on;
One shoe off and one shoe on,
Diddle, diddle, dumpling, my son John.

N.Y. PUBLIC LIBRARY PICTURE COLLECTION

WHO WAS MOTHER GOOSE?

Say the name Mother Goose and most people picture a smiling old lady in colonial costume riding on the back of a goose. It is almost certain there was no person known as Mother Goose. The name originated in France, where the term *Mother Goose tale* was used to identify folk or fairy stories for children. In 1697 the Frenchman Charles Perrault published a collection entitled *Histoires ou Contes du temps passé* [Histories or tales of times past], which also carried the title *Contes de ma mère l'Oye* [Tales of Mother Goose]. However, Mother Goose was associated with stories, not with the familiar nursery rhymes that were being passed on from generation to generation through oral tradition. Perrault's book, which included the stories "Sleeping Beauty," "Puss-in-Boots," Cinderella," "Red Riding Hood," and others, was soon translated into English. *Tales of Mother Goose*, a translation of Perrault's book by Robert Samber, was published in 1729. About 1780 a volume entitled *Mother Goose's Melody; or, Sonnets for the Cradle*, a collection of the popular nursery rhymes, was published in England by John Newbery, and a U.S. edition was published by Isaiah Thomas within a few years. In 1860 it was claimed that the real Mother Goose was Mrs. Elizabeth Foster Goose (or Vergoose) of Boston, and that her son-in-law, Thomas Fleet, had collected her rhymes in a book published in 1719. No evidence of this work has ever been uncovered, but thousands visit Mrs. Goose's grave in Boston each year—a tribute to the enduring appeal of the rhymes themselves.

Fairy Tales

Fairy tales have long been an important part of childhood literature. The term *fairy tale* can be applied to a story in which magic or enchantment plays an important role. In a broader sense, a fairy tale can be a story that unlocks the imagination—for what greater magic is there than the power of imagination? And what greater imagination can there be than that of a child?

Here are five classic fairy tales. Two are by the Danish writer Hans Christian Andersen, one of the greatest storytellers of all time. Two are tales collected by the brothers Jacob and Wilhelm Grimm, who spent years gathering and studying European folk tales, most of which had never been written down. One is a Scandinavian folk tale collected by Peter Asbjörnsen and Jörgen Moe.

These stories are fun to read. Once you have become familiar with them, you will discover that these timeless tales are even more delightful when read aloud to others.

The Ugly Duckling

Hans Christian Andersen

FROM *THE COMPLETE FAIRY TALES AND STORIES OF HANS CHRISTIAN ANDERSEN* TRANSLATED BY ERIK CHRISTIAN HAUGAARD. REPRINTED BY PERMISSION OF DOUBLEDAY & CO., INC.

It was so beautiful out in the country. It was summer. The oats were still green, but the wheat was turning yellow. Down in the meadow the grass had been cut and made into haystacks; and there the storks walked on their long red legs talking Egyptian, because that was the language they had been taught by their mothers. The fields were enclosed by woods, and hidden among them were little lakes and pools. Yes, it certainly was lovely out there in the country!

The old castle, with its deep moat surrounding it, lay bathed in sunshine. Between the heavy walls and the edge of the moat there was a narrow strip of land covered by a whole forest of burdock plants. Their leaves were large and some of the stalks were so tall that a child could stand upright under them and imagine that he was in the middle of the wild and lonesome woods. Here a duck had built her nest. While she sat waiting for the eggs to hatch, she felt a little sorry for herself because it was taking so long and hardly anybody came to visit her. The other ducks preferred swimming in the moat to sitting under a dock leaf and gossiping.

Finally the eggs began to crack. "Peep . . . Peep," they said one after another. The egg yolks had become alive and were sticking out their heads.

"Quack . . . Quack . . ." said their mother. "Look around you." And the ducklings did; they glanced at the green world around them, and that was what their mother wanted them to do, for green was good for their eyes.

"How big the world is!" piped the little ones, for they had much more space to move around in now than they had inside the egg.

"Do you think that this is the whole world?" quacked their mother. "The world is much larger than this. It stretches as far as the minister's wheat fields, though I have not been there. . . . Are you all here?" The duck got up and turned around to look at her nest. "Oh no, the biggest egg hasn't hatched yet; and I'm so tired of sitting here! I wonder how long it will take?" she wailed, and sat down again.

"What's new?" asked an old duck who had come visiting.

"One of the eggs is taking so long," complained the mother duck. "It won't crack. But take a look at the others. They are the sweetest little ducklings you have ever seen; and every one of them looks exactly like their father. That scoundrel hasn't come to visit me once."

"Let me look at the egg that won't hatch," demanded the old duck. "I am sure that it's a turkey egg! I was fooled that way once. You can't imagine what it's like. Turkeys are afraid of the water. I couldn't get them to go into it. I quacked and I nipped them, but nothing helped. Let me see that egg! . . . Yes, it's a turkey egg. Just let it lie there. You go and teach your young ones how to swim, that's my advice."

"I have sat on it so long that I guess I can sit a little longer, at least until they get the hay in," replied the mother duck.

"Suit yourself," said the older duck, and went on.

At last the big egg cracked too. "Peep . . . Peep," said the young one, and tumbled out. He was big and very ugly.

The mother duck looked at him. "He's awfully big for his age," she said. "He doesn't look like any of the others. I wonder if he could be a turkey? Well, we shall soon see. Into the water he will go, even if I have to kick him to make him do it."

The next day the weather was gloriously beautiful. The sun shone on the forest of burdock

MIKE EAGLE/DILAS EVANS FINE ILLUSTRATION

All of the new brood swam very nicely, even the ugly one.

plants. The mother duck took her whole brood to the moat. "Quack . . . Quack . . ." she ordered.

One after another, the little ducklings plunged into the water. For a moment their heads disappeared, but then they popped up again and the little ones floated like so many corks. Their legs knew what to do without being told. All of the new brood swam very nicely, even the ugly one.

"He is no turkey," mumbled the mother. "Look how beautifully he uses his legs and how straight he holds his neck. He is my own child and, when you look closely at him, he's quite handsome. . . . Quack! Quack! Follow me and I'll take you to the henyard and introduce you to everyone. But stay close to me, so that no one steps on you, and look out for the cat."

They heard an awful noise when they arrived at the henyard. Two families of ducks had got into a fight over the head of an eel. Neither of them got it, for it was swiped by the cat.

"That is the way of the world," said the mother duck, and licked her bill. She would have like to have the eel's head herself. "Walk nicely," she admonished them, "And remember to bow to the old duck over there. She has Spanish blood in her veins and is the most aristocratic fowl here. That is why she is so fat and has a red rag tied around one of her legs. That is the highest mark of distinction a duck can be given. It means so much that she will never be done away with; and all the fowl and the human beings know who she is. Quack! Quack! . . . Don't walk, waddle like well-brought-up ducklings. Keep your legs far apart, just as your mother and father have always done. Bow your heads and say, 'Quack!' " And that was what the little ducklings did.

Other ducks gathered about them and said loudly, "What do we want that gang here for? Aren't there enough of us already? Pooh! Look how ugly one of them is! He's the last straw!" And one of the ducks flew over and bit the ugly duckling on the neck.

"Leave him alone!" shouted the mother. "He hasn't done anyone any harm."

"He's big and he doesn't look like everybody else!" replied the duck who had bitten him. "And that's reason enough to beat him."

"Very good-looking children you have," remarked the duck with the red rag around one of her legs. "All of them are beautiful except one. He didn't turn out very well. I wish you could make him over again."

"That's not possible, Your Grace," answered the mother duck. "He may not be handsome, but he has a good character and swims as well as the others, if not a little better. Perhaps he will grow handsomer as he grows older and becomes a bit smaller. He was in the egg too long, and that is why he doesn't have the right shape." She smoothed his neck for a moment and then added, "Besides, he's a drake; and it doesn't matter so much what he looks like. He is strong and I am sure he will be able to take care of himself."

"Well, the others are nice," said the old duck. "Make yourself at home, and if you should find an eel's head, you may bring it to me."

And they were "at home."

The poor little duckling, who had been the last to hatch and was so ugly, was bitten and pushed and made fun of both by the hens and by the other ducks. The turkey cock (who had been born with spurs on, and therefore thought he was an emperor) rustled his feathers as if he were a full-rigged ship under sail, and strutted up to the duckling. He gobbled so loudly at him that his own face got all red.

The poor little duckling did not know where to turn. How he grieved over his own ugliness, and how sad he was! The poor creature was mocked and laughed at by the whole henyard.

That was the first day; and each day that followed was worse than the one before. The poor duckling was chased and mistreated by everyone, even his own sisters and brothers, who quacked again and again, "If only the cat would get you, you ugly thing!"

Even his mother said, "I wish you were far away." The other ducks bit him and the hens pecked at him. The little girl who came to feed the fowls kicked him.

At last the duckling ran away. It flew over the tops of the bushes, frightening all the little birds so that they flew up into the air. "They, too, think I am ugly," thought the duckling, and closed his eyes—but he kept on running.

Finally he came to a great swamp where wild ducks lived; and here he stayed for the night, for he was too tired to go any farther.

In the morning he was discovered by the wild ducks. They looked at him and one of them asked, "What kind of bird are you?"

The ugly duckling bowed in all directions, for he was trying to be as polite as he knew how.

"You are ugly," said the wild ducks, "but that is no concern of ours, as long as you don't try to marry into our family."

The poor duckling wasn't thinking of marriage. All he wanted was to be allowed to swim among the reeds and drink a little water when he was thirsty.

He spent two days in the swamp; then two wild geese came—or rather, two wild ganders, for they were males. They had been hatched not long ago; therefore they were both frank and bold.

"Listen, comrade," they said. "You are so ugly that we like you. Do you want to migrate with us? Not far from here there is a marsh where some beautiful wild geese live. They are all lovely maidens, and you are so ugly that you may seek your fortune among them. Come along."

"Bang! Bang!" Two shots were heard and both the ganders fell down dead among the reeds, and the water turned red from their blood.

"Bang! Bang!" Again came the sound of shots, and a flock of wild geese flew up.

The whole swamp was surrounded by hunters; from every direction came the awful noise. Some of the hunters had hidden behind bushes or among the reeds but others, screened from sight by the leaves, sat on the long, low branches of the trees that stretched out over the swamp. The blue smoke from the guns lay like a fog over the water and among the trees. Dogs came splashing

The dog's tongue hung out of its mouth and its eyes glistened evilly.

through the marsh, and they bent and broke the reeds.

The poor little duckling was terrified. He was about to tuck his head under his wing, in order to hide, when he saw a big dog peering at him through the reeds. The dog's tongue hung out of its mouth and its eyes glistened evilly. It bared its teeth. Splash! It turned away without touching the duckling.

"Oh, thank God!" he sighed. "I am so ugly that even the dog doesn't want to bite me."

The little duckling lay as still as he could while the shots whistled through the reeds. Not until the middle of the afternoon did the shooting stop; but the poor little duckling was still so frightened that he waited several hours longer before taking his head out from under his wing. Then he ran as quickly as he could out of the swamp. Across the fields and the meadows he went, but a wind had come up and he found it hard to make his way against it.

Toward evening he came upon a poor little hut. It was so wretchedly crooked that it looked as if it couldn't make up its mind which way to fall and that was why it was still standing. The wind was blowing so hard that the poor little duckling had to sit down in order not to be blown away. Suddenly he noticed that the door was off its hinges, making a crack; and he squeezed himself through it very carefully and was inside.

An old woman lived in the hut with her cat and her hen. The cat was called Sonny and could both arch his back and purr. Oh yes, it could also make sparks if you rubbed its fur the wrong way. The hen had very short legs and that was why she was called Cluck Lowlegs. But she was good at laying eggs, and the old woman loved her as if she were her own child.

In the morning the hen and the cat discovered the duckling. The cat meowed and the hen clucked.

"What is going on?" asked the old woman, and looked around. She couldn't see very well, and when she found the duckling she thought it was a fat, full-grown duck. "What a fine catch!" she exclaimed. "Now we shall have duck eggs, unless it's a drake. We'll give it a try."

So the duckling was allowed to stay for three weeks on probation, but he laid no eggs. The cat was the master of the house and the hen the mistress. They always referred to themselves as "we and the world," for they thought that they were half the world—and the better half at that. The duckling thought that he should be allowed to have a different opinion, but the hen did not agree.

"Can you lay eggs?" she demanded.

"No," answered the duckling.

"Then keep your mouth shut."

And the cat asked, "Can you arch your back? Can you purr? Can you make sparks?"

"No."

"Well, in that case, you have no right to have an opinion when sensible people are talking."

The duckling was sitting in a corner and was in a bad mood. Suddenly he recalled how lovely it could be outside in the fresh air when the sun shone: a great longing to be floating in the water came over the duckling, and he could not help talking about it.

"What is the matter with you?" asked the hen as soon as she had heard what he had to say. "You have nothing to do, that's why you get ideas like that. Lay eggs or purr, and such notions will disappear."

"You have no idea how delightful it is to float in the water, and to dive down to the bottom of a lake and get your head wet," said the duckling.

"Yes, that certainly does sound amusing," said the hen. "You must have gone mad. Ask the cat—he is the most intelligent being I know—ask him whether he likes to swim or dive down to the bottom of a lake. Don't take my word for anything. . . . Ask the old woman, who is the clever-

est person in the world; ask her whether she likes to float and to get her head all wet."

"You don't understand me!" wailed the duckling.

"And if I don't understand you, who will? I hope you don't think that you are wiser than the cat or the old woman—not to mention myself. Don't give yourself airs! Thank your Creator for all He has done for you. Aren't you sitting in a warm room among intelligent people whom you could learn something from? While you, yourself, do nothing but say a lot of nonsense and aren't the least bit amusing! Believe me, that's the truth, and I am only telling it to you for your own good. That's how you recognize a true friend: it's someone who is willing to tell you the truth, no matter how unpleasant it is. Now get to work: lay some eggs, or learn to purr and arch your back."

"I think I'll go out into the wide world," replied the duckling.

"Go right ahead!" said the hen.

And the duckling left. He found a lake where he could float in the water and dive to the bottom. There were other ducks, but they ignored him because he was so ugly.

Autumn came and the leaves turned yellow and brown, then they fell from the trees. The wind caught them and made them dance. The clouds were heavy with hail and snow. A raven sat on a fence and screeched, "Ach! Ach!" because it was so cold. When just thinking of how cold it was is enough to make one shiver, what a terrible time the duckling must have had.

One evening just as the sun was setting gloriously, a flock of beautiful birds came out from among the rushes. Their feathers were so white that they glistened; and they had long, graceful necks. They were swans. They made a very loud cry, then they spread their powerful wings. They were flying south to a warmer climate, where the lakes were not frozen in the winter. Higher and higher they circled. The ugly duckling turned round and round in the water like a wheel and stretched his neck up toward the sky; he felt a strange longing. He screeched so piercingly that he frightened himself.

Oh, he would never forget those beautiful birds, those happy birds. When they were out of sight the duckling dove down under the water to the bottom of the lake; and when he came up again he was beside himself. He did not know the name of those birds or where they were going, and yet he felt that he loved them as he had never loved any other creatures. He did not envy them. It did not even occur to him to wish that he were so handsome himself. He would have been happy if the other ducks had let him stay in the henyard: that poor, ugly bird!

The weather grew colder and colder. The duckling had to swim round and round in the water, to keep just a little space for himself that wasn't frozen. Each night his hole became smaller and smaller. On all sides of him the ice creaked and groaned. The little duckling had to keep his feet constantly in motion so that the last bit of open water wouldn't become ice. At last he was too tired to swim any more. He sat still. The ice closed in around him and he was frozen fast.

Early the next morning a farmer saw him and with his clogs broke the ice to free the duckling. The man put the bird under his arm and took it home to his wife, who brought the duckling back to life.

The children wanted to play with him. But the duckling was afraid that they were going to hurt him, so he flapped his wings and flew right into the milk pail. From there he flew into a big bowl of butter and then into a barrel of flour. What a sight he was!

The farmer's wife yelled and chased him with a poker. The children laughed and almost fell on top of each other, trying to catch him; and how they screamed! Luckily for the duckling, the door was open. He got out of the house and found a hiding place beneath some bushes, in the newly fallen snow; and there he lay so still, as though there were hardly any life left in him.

It would be too horrible to tell of all the hardship and suffering the duckling experienced that long winter. It is enough to know that he did survive. When again the sun shone warmly and the larks began to sing, the duckling was lying among the reeds in the swamp. Spring had come!

He spread out his wings to fly. How strong and powerful they were! Before he knew it, he was far from the swamp and flying above a beautiful

He was no longer an awkward, clumsy, gray bird.

MIKE EAGLE/DILAS EVANS FINE ILLUSTRATION

garden. The apple trees were blooming and the lilac bushes stretched their flower-covered branches over the water of a winding canal. Everything was so beautiful: so fresh and green. Out of a forest of rushes came three swans. They ruffled their feathers and floated so lightly on the water. The ugly duckling recognized the birds and felt again that strange sadness come over him.

"I shall fly over to them, those royal birds! And they can hack me to death because I, who am so ugly, dare to approach them! What difference does it make? It is better to be killed by them than to be bitten by the other ducks, and pecked by the hens, and kicked by the girl who tends the henyard; or to suffer through the winter."

And he lighted on the water and swam toward the magnificent swans. When they saw him they ruffled their feathers and started to swim in his direction. They were coming to meet him.

"Kill me," whispered the poor creature, and bent his head humbly while he waited for death. But what was that he saw in the water? It was his own reflection; and he was no longer an awkward, clumsy, gray bird, so ungainly and so ugly. He was a swan!

It does not matter that one has been born in the henyard as long as one has lain in a swan's egg.

He was thankful that he had known so much want, and gone through so much suffering, for it made him appreciate his present happiness and the loveliness of everything about him all the more. The swans made a circle around him and caressed him with their beaks.

Some children came out into the garden. They had brought bread with them to feed the swans. The youngest child shouted, "Look; there's a new one!" All the children joyfully clapped their hands, and they ran to tell their parents.

Cake and bread were cast on the water for the swans. Everyone agreed that the new swan was the most beautiful of them all. The older swans bowed toward him.

He felt so shy that he hid his head beneath his wing. He was too happy, but not proud, for a kind heart can never be proud. He thought of the time when he had been mocked and persecuted. And now everyone said that he was the most beautiful of the most beautiful birds. And the lilac bushes stretched their branches right down to the water for him. The sun shone so warm and brightly. He ruffled his feathers and raised his slender neck, while out of the joy in his heart, he thought, "Such happiness I did not dream of when I was the ugly duckling." ∎

The Emperor's New Clothes

Hans Christian Andersen

FROM *THE COMPLETE FAIRY TALES AND STORIES OF HANS CHRISTIAN ANDERSEN* TRANSLATED BY ERIK CHRISTIAN HAUGAARD.
REPRINTED BY PERMISSION OF DOUBLEDAY & CO., INC.

Many, many years ago there was an emperor who was so terribly fond of beautiful new clothes that he spent all his money on his attire. He did not care about his soldiers, or attending the theater, or even going for a drive in the park, unless it was to show off his new clothes. He had an outfit for every hour of the day. And just as we say, "The king is in his council chamber," his subjects used to say, "The emperor is in his clothes closet."

In the large town where the emperor's palace was, life was gay and happy; and every day new visitors arrived. One day two swindlers came. They told everybody that they were weavers and that they could weave the most marvelous cloth. Not only were the colors and the patterns of their material extraordinarily beautiful, but the cloth had the strange quality of being invisible to anyone who was unfit for his office or unforgivably stupid.

"This is truly marvelous," thought the emperor. "Now if I had robes cut from that material, I should know which of my councilors was unfit for his office, and I would be able to pick out my clever subjects myself. They must weave some material for me!" And he gave the swindlers a lot of money so they could start working at once.

They set up a loom and acted as if they were weaving, but the loom was empty. The fine silk and gold threads they demanded from the emperor they never used, but hid them in their own knapsacks. Late into the night they would sit before their empty loom, pretending to weave.

"I would like to know how they are getting along," thought the emperor; but his heart beat strangely when he remembered that those who were stupid or unfit for their office would not be able to see the material. Not that he was really worried that this would happen to him. Still, it might be better to send someone else the first time and see how he fared. Everybody in town had heard about the cloth's magic quality and most of them could hardly wait to find out how stupid or unworthy their neighbors were.

"I shall send my faithful prime minister over to see how the weavers are getting along," thought the emperor. "He will know how to judge the material, for he is both clever and fit for his office, if any man is."

The good-natured old man stepped into the room where the weavers were working and saw the empty loom. He closed his eyes, and opened them again. "God preserve me!" he thought. "I cannot see a thing!" But he didn't say it out loud.

The swindlers asked him to step a little closer to the loom so that he could admire the intricate patterns and marvelous colors of the material they were weaving. They both pointed to the empty loom, and the poor old prime minister opened his eyes as wide as he could; but it didn't help, he still couldn't see anything.

"Am I stupid?" he thought. "I can't believe it, but if it is so, it is best no one finds out about it. But maybe I am not fit for my office. No, that is worse, I'd better not admit that I can't see what they are weaving."

"Tell us what you think of it," demanded one of the swindlers.

"It is beautiful. It is very lovely," mumbled the old prime minister, adjusting his glasses. "What patterns! What colors! I shall tell the emperor that it pleases me ever so much."

"That is a compliment," both the weavers said; and now they described the patterns and told which shades of color they had used. The prime minister listened attentively, so that he could repeat their words to the emperor; and that is exactly what he did.

The two swindlers demanded more money, and more silk and gold thread. They said they had to use it for their weaving, but their loom remained as empty as ever.

Soon the emperor sent another of his trusted councilors to see how the work was progressing. He looked and looked just as the prime minister had, but since there was nothing to be seen, he didn't see anything.

"Isn't it a marvelous piece of material?" asked one of the swindlers; and they both began to describe the beauty of their cloth again.

"I am not stupid," thought the emperor's councilor. "I must be unfit for my office. That is strange; but I'd better not admit it to anyone." And he started to praise the material, which he could not see, for the loveliness of its patterns and colors.

"I think it is the most charming piece of material I have ever seen," declared the councilor to the emperor.

TOM O'SULLIVAN/JOSEPH, MINDLIN & MULVEY, INC.

"It is very lovely. It has my approval."

Everyone in town was talking about the marvelous cloth that the swindlers were weaving.

At last the emperor himself decided to see it before it was removed from the loom. Attended by the most important people in the empire, among them the prime minister and the councilor who had been there before, the emperor entered the room where the weavers were weaving furiously on their empty loom.

"Isn't it *magnifique*, my king?" asked the prime minister.

"Your Majesty, look at the colors and the patterns," said the councilor.

And the two old gentlemen pointed to the empty loom, believing that all the rest of the company could see the cloth.

"What!" thought the emperor. "I can't see a thing! Why, this is a disaster! Am I stupid? Am I unfit to be emperor? Oh, it is too horrible!" Aloud he said, "It is very lovely. It has my approval," while he nodded his head and looked at the empty loom.

All the councilors, ministers, and men of great importance who had come with him stared and stared; but they saw no more than the emperor had seen, and they said the same thing that he had said, "It is lovely." And they advised him to have clothes cut and sewn, so that he could wear them in the procession at the next great celebration.

"It is magnificent! Beautiful! Excellent!" All of their mouths agreed, though none of their eyes had seen anything. The two swindlers were deco-

rated and given the title "Royal Knight of the Loom."

The night before the procession, the two swindlers didn't sleep at all. They had sixteen candles lighting up the room where they worked. Everyone could see how busy they were, getting the emperor's new clothes finished. They pretended to take the cloth from the loom; they cut the air with their big scissors, and sewed with needles without thread. At last they announced: "The emperor's clothes are ready!"

Together with his courtiers, the emperor came. The swindlers lifted their arms as if they were holding something in their hands, and said, "These are the trousers. This is the robe, and here is the train. They are all as light as if they were made of spider webs! It will be as if Your Majesty had almost nothing on, but that is their special virtue."

"Oh yes," breathed all the courtiers; but they saw nothing, for there was nothing to be seen.

"Will Your Imperial Majesty be so gracious as to take off your clothes?" asked the swindlers. "Over there by the big mirror, we shall help you put your new ones on."

The emperor did as he was told; and the swindlers acted as if they were dressing him in the clothes they should have made. Finally they tied around his waist the long train which two of his most noble courtiers were to carry.

The emperor stood in front of the mirror admiring the clothes he couldn't see.

"Oh, how they suit you! A perfect fit!" everyone exclaimed. "What colors! What patterns! The new clothes are magnificent!"

"The crimson canopy, under which Your Imperial Majesty is to walk, is waiting outside," said the imperial master of court ceremony.

"Well, I am dressed. Aren't my clothes becoming?" The emperor turned around once more in front of the mirror, pretending to study his finery.

The two gentlemen of the imperial bedchamber fumbled on the floor, trying to find the train which they were supposed to carry. They didn't dare admit that they didn't see anything, so they pretended to pick up the train and held their hands as if they were carrying it.

The emperor walked in the procession under his crimson canopy. And all the people of the town, who had lined the streets or were looking down from the windows, said that the emperor's clothes were beautiful. "What a magnificent robe! And the train! How well the emperor's clothes suit him!"

TOM O'SULLIVAN/JOSEPH, MINDLIN & MULVEY, INC.

"But he doesn't have anything on!" cried a little child.

None of them were willing to admit that they hadn't seen a thing; for if anyone did, then he was either stupid or unfit for the job he held. Never before had the emperor's clothes been such a success.

"But he doesn't have anything on!" cried a little child.

"Listen to the innocent one," said the proud father. And the people whispered among each other and repeated what the child had said.

"He doesn't have anything on. There's a little child who says that he has nothing on."

"He has nothing on!" shouted all the people at last.

The emperor shivered, for he was certain that they were right; but he thought, "I must bear it until the procession is over." And he walked even more proudly, and the two gentlemen of the imperial bedchamber went on carrying the train that wasn't there. ■

SOMETHING ABOUT THE AUTHORS

Up until the early 1800's there was no such thing as a collection of fairy and folk tales. In Europe the telling of such stories was quite common but few had been written down or published. Some fairy tales were well known everywhere, from the smallest towns to the largest cities. Others were popular only in certain areas. But for centuries these tales had been passed on from adult to child through the simple art of storytelling.

Then two German scholars with a love for language and literature, Jacob and Wilhelm Grimm, set out to collect all the folk and fairy tales they could find. Jacob (1785–1863) was a robust, scientifically minded man whose love in life was the study of language. His brother Wilhelm (1786–1859), in addition to being a thorough scholar, had a love of literature, particularly stories for children. Wilhelm's selection and editing preserved the stories in all their beauty and power. The Grimms did not try to change the tales in order to please readers. Even the tales that would frighten young people were left intact. In addition, they included notes about the stories—where they had been found, variations of stories, etc. In that way they handed the tales down to future generations as they had been told for centuries.

These collected tales were published in a two-volume work entitled *Kinder- und Hausmärchen* (1812–1815), then reissued (1819–1822) in a three-volume edition. The complete work was first published in English in 1884 and has come to be known popularly as *Grimm's Fairy Tales*.

The brothers Grimm were collectors of existing fairy tales. Hans Christian Andersen (1805–1875) was a creator of new ones. Born in Odense, Denmark, the son of a self-educated shoemaker, Andersen was deeply influenced by his father's love of literature and his mother's strong belief in the superstitions of the time. At first Andersen sought a career in the theater, but eventually he turned to writing. His first published work was a poem, which appeared in a journal in 1827. In 1835 his first and most successful novel, *The Improvisatore*, was published. That year also saw the publication of *Fairy Tales Told for Children*, his first collection of fairy tales. The stories, which combined elements of folk mythology with Andersen's own inventiveness, were well received, but it was years before his storytelling genius was fully appreciated. By the time of his death in 1875, Andersen had written 168 tales and had been acknowledged the greatest folklorist of the 19th century.

Hansel and Gretel

Jacob and Wilhelm Grimm

ADAPTED FROM *THE BLUE FAIRY BOOK* (1889), EDITED BY ANDREW LANG.

Once upon a time there lived on the outskirts of a large forest a poor woodcutter with his wife and two children; the boy was called Hansel and the girl Gretel. He had always little enough to live on, and once, when there was a great famine in the land, he could not even provide them with daily bread. One night, as he was tossing about in bed, full of cares and worry, he sighed and said to his wife:

"What's to become of us? How are we to support our poor children, now that we have nothing more for ourselves?"

"Early tomorrow morning," answered the woman, "we'll take the children out into the thickest part of the wood. There we shall light a fire for them, give them each a piece of bread, and go on to our work, leaving them alone. They will not be able to find their way home, and we shall thus be rid of them."

"No, wife," said her husband, "that I won't do. How could I find it in my heart to leave my children alone in the wood? The wild beasts would soon come and tear them to pieces."

"Oh," said she, "then we must all four die of hunger, and you may just as well go and plane the boards for our coffins." And she left him no peace till he consented.

Hansel dropping one of the white pebbles on the path.

THE GRANGER COLLECTION

"But I can't help feeling sorry for the poor children," added the husband.

The children, too, had not been able to sleep for hunger, and had heard what their stepmother had said to their father. Gretel wept bitterly and said to Hansel, "Now it's all up with us."

"No, no, Gretel," said Hansel, "don't fret yourself. I will find a way of escape, no fear."

When the old people had fallen asleep he got up, slipped on his little coat, opened the back door and stole out. The moon was shining clearly, and the white pebbles which lay in front of the house glittered like bits of silver. Hansel bent down and filled his pocket with as many of them as he could cram in. Then he went back and said to Gretel:

"Be comforted, my dear little sister, and go to sleep: God will not desert us." And he lay down in bed again.

At daybreak, even before the sun was up, the woman came and woke the two children, "Get up, you lie-abeds; we're all going to the forest to fetch wood."

She gave them each a bit of bread and said, "There's something for your luncheon, but do not eat it up before, for it is all you will get."

Gretel took the bread under her apron, as Hansel had the stones in his pocket. Then they all set out together on the way to the forest. After they had walked for a little, Hansel stood still and looked back at the house, and this maneuver he repeated again and again.

His father observed him, and asked, "Hansel, what are you gazing at there, and why do you always remain behind? Take care, and do not lose your footing."

"Oh, Father," said Hansel, "I am looking back at my white kitten, which is sitting on the roof, waving me a farewell."

The woman exclaimed, "What a donkey you are! That isn't your kitten, that is the morning sun shining on the chimney."

But Hansel had not looked back at his kitten, but had dropped one of the white pebbles out of his pocket on to the path.

When they had reached the middle of the forest the father said, "Now, children, go and fetch a lot of wood, and I will light a fire."

Hansel and Gretel heaped up brushwood till they had made a pile nearly the size of a small hill. The brushwood was set fire to, and when the flames leaped high the woman said:

"Now lie down by the fire, children, and rest yourselves. We are going into the forest to cut wood; when we have finished we will come back and fetch you."

Hansel and Gretel sat down beside the fire, and at midday ate their little bits of bread. They heard the strokes of the axe, so they thought their father was quite near. However, it was no axe they heard, but a bough he had tied on a dead tree blown about by the wind. And when they had sat for a long time their eyes closed with fatigue, and they fell fast asleep. When they awoke at last it was pitch dark.

Gretel began to cry, and said, "How are we ever to get out of the wood?"

But Hansel comforted her. "Wait a bit," he said, "till the moon is up, and then we will find our way sure enough."

And when the full moon had risen he took his sister by the hand and followed the pebbles, which shone like new threepenny bits and showed them the path. They walked all through the night, and at daybreak reached their father's house again.

They knocked at the door, and when the woman opened it, she exclaimed:

"You naughty children, what a time you've slept in the wood! We thought you were never going to come back." But the father rejoiced, for his conscience had reproached him for leaving his children behind by themselves.

Hansel and Gretel return home.

THE GRANGER COLLECTION

Not long afterward there was again great hunger in the land, and the children heard the woman say, "Everything is eaten up once more; we have only half a loaf in the house. We must lead them deeper into the wood this time so they won't be able to find their way out again."

The man's heart smote him heavily, and he thought, "Surely it would be better to share the last bite with one's children!" But if a man yields once he's done for.

When the old people were asleep Hansel got up and tried to go out and pick up pebbles again, as he had done the first time; but the woman had barred the door, and he could not get out. But he consoled his little sister, and said, "Don't cry, Gretel, and sleep peacefully, for God is sure to help us."

At early dawn the woman came and made the children get up. They received their bit of bread, but it was even smaller than the time before. On the way to the wood Hansel crumbled it in his pocket, and every few minutes he stood still and dropped a crumb on the ground.

"Hansel, why are you stopping and looking about you?" said the father.

"I'm looking back at my little pigeon, which is sitting on the roof waving me a farewell," answered Hansel.

"That isn't your pigeon," said the woman, "it is the morning sun glittering on the chimney." But Hansel gradually threw all his crumbs on to the path.

The woman led the children still deeper into the forest, farther than they had ever been in their lives before. Then a big fire was lit again, and the woman said:

"Just sit down, children, and if you are tired you can sleep a bit. We are going into the forest to cut wood and in the evening we shall come back to fetch you."

At midday Gretel divided her bread with Hansel, for he had strewed his all along their path. Then they fell asleep, and evening passed away, but nobody came for the poor children. They did not awake till it was pitch dark, and Hansel comforted his sister, saying:

"Only wait, Gretel, till the moon rises, then we shall see the bread crumbs I scattered along the path. They will show us the way back to the house."

When the moon appeared they searched but found no crumbs, for the thousands of birds that fly about the woods and fields had picked them all up. "Never mind," said Hansel, "we shall find a way out, you'll see."

They wandered about the whole night, and the next day, from morning till evening, but they could not find a path out of the wood. They were very hungry, for they had nothing to eat but a few berries they found growing on the ground. And at last they were so tired they lay down under a tree and fell fast asleep.

On the third morning after they had left their father's house they became even more lost, and now they felt that if help did not come soon they must perish. At midday they saw a beautiful little snow-white bird sitting on a branch, which sang so sweetly they stopped still to listen to it. And when its song was finished it flapped its wings and flew on in front of them. They followed it and came to a little house, on the roof of which it perched; and when they came quite near they saw that the cottage was made out of bread and roofed with cakes, while the window was made of transparent sugar.

"Now we'll set to," said Hansel, "and have a regular feast." Hansel stretched up his hand and broke off a little bit of the roof to see what it was like, and Gretel went to the casement and began to nibble at it. Thereupon a shrill voice called out from the room inside:

> "Nibble, nibble, little mouse,
> Who is nibbling at my house?"

The children answered:

> " 'Tis Heaven's own child,
> The tempest wild,"

and went on eating. Hansel, who thoroughly appreciated the roof, tore down a big bit of it, while Gretel pushed out a whole round windowpane, and sat down the better to enjoy it. Suddenly the door opened, and an ancient dame leaning on a staff hobbled out. Hansel and Gretel were so terrified that they let what they had in their hands fall. But the old woman shook her head and said:

"Oh, ho, you dear children! Who led you here? Just come in and stay with me, no ill shall befall you." She took them both by the hand and led them into the house and laid a sumptuous dinner before them—milk and sugared pancakes, with apples and nuts. After they had finished, two beautiful little white beds were prepared for them, and when Hansel and Gretel lay down in them they felt as if they were in Heaven.

The old woman had appeared to be most friendly, but she was really an old witch. When anyone came into her power she cooked and ate him and held a regular feast day. Now witches have red eyes, and cannot see far, but like beasts, they have a keen sense of smell, and know when human beings pass by. When Hansel and Gretel

fell into her hands she laughed maliciously, and said, "I have them now. They cannot escape me."

Early in the morning, before the children were awake, she rose, and when she saw them both sleeping so peacefully, with their round rosy cheeks, she muttered to herself, "That will be a dainty bite." Then she seized Hansel with her bony hand and carried him into a little stable, and barred the door on him. He might scream as much as he liked, it did him no good.

Then she went to Gretel, shook her till she awoke, and cried, "Get up, you lazybones, fetch water and cook something for your brother. When he is fat I shall eat him." Gretel began to cry bitterly, but it was of no use; she had to do what the wicked witch bade her.

So the best food was cooked for poor Hansel, but Gretel got nothing but crab shells. Every morning the old woman hobbled out to the stable and cried, "Hansel, put out your finger that I may feel if you are getting fat." But Hansel always stretched out a bone, and the old dame, whose eyes were dim, could not see it, and thinking always it was Hansel's finger, wondered why he fattened so slowly.

When four weeks passed and Hansel still remained thin, she lost patience and determined to wait no longer. "Hi! Gretel," she called to the girl, "be quick and get some water. Hansel may be fat or thin, I'm going to cook him tomorrow."

Oh! how the poor little sister sobbed as she carried the water, and how the tears rolled down her cheeks! "Kind Heaven help us now!" she cried. "If only the wild beasts in the wood had eaten us, then at least we should have died together."

"Just hold your peace," said the old witch, "it won't help you."

Early in the morning Gretel had to go out and hang up the kettle full of water and light the fire. "First we shall bake," said the old dame. "I have heated the oven and kneaded the dough." She pushed Gretel out to the oven, from which fiery flames were already issuing. "Creep in," said the witch, "and see if it is properly heated so we can shove in the bread." For when she had Gretel in she meant to close the oven door and let the girl bake that she might eat her up too.

But Gretel perceived her intention, and said, "I do not know how I am to do it. How do I get in?"

"You silly goose," said the witch, "the opening is big enough. See, I could get in myself," and she crawled toward it and poked her head into the oven. Then Gretel gave her a shove that sent her right in, shut the iron door, and drew the bolt. Gracious! How the witch yelled! It was quite hor-

Gretel pushes the witch into the oven.

rible, but Gretel fled, and the wretched old woman was left to perish miserably.

Gretel flew straight to Hansel, opened the little stable door, and cried, "Hansel, we are free; the old witch is dead." Then Hansel sprang like a bird out of a cage when the door is opened. How they rejoiced and fell on each other's necks and jumped for joy and kissed one another! And as they no longer had any cause for fear, they went into the witch's house, and there they found, in every corner of the room, boxes with pearls and precious stones.

"These are even better than pebbles," said Hansel, and crammed his pockets full of them.

"I too will bring something home," said Gretel, and she filled her apron full.

"But now," said Hansel, "let us go and get well away from the witch's wood." When they had wandered about for some hours they came to a big lake.

"We cannot get over," said Hansel. "I see no bridge of any sort or kind."

"Yes, and there is no ferryboat either," answered Gretel. "But look, there swims a white duck; if I ask her she will help us over." And she called out:

"Here are two children, mournful very,
Seeing neither bridge nor ferry;
Take us upon your white back,
And row us over, quack, quack, quack."

The duck swam toward them, and Hansel got on her back and bade his little sister sit beside him. "No," answered Gretel, "we should be too heavy a load for the duck. She shall carry us across separately." The good bird did this, and when they were landed safely on the other side and had gone on for a while, the wood became more and more familiar to them, and at length they saw their father's house in the distance. Then they sat off at a run, and bounding into the room fell on their father's neck. The man had not passed a happy hour since he left them in the wood, but the woman had died. Gretel shook out her apron and the pearls and precious stones rolled about the room, and Hansel threw down one handful after the other out of his pocket. Thus all their troubles were ended, and they all lived happily ever afterward. ∎

COMMON FEATURES OF THE FAIRY TALE

The story "Hansel and Gretel" contains a number of elements found in many other fairy or folk tales. For example, the wickedness of the children's mother, who instigates their abandonment in the woods, is mirrored by that of the wicked stepmother and stepsisters in "Cinderella."

The witch, a common figure in folk tales, is but one of a number of characters possessing supernatural powers. The little man Rumpelstiltskin, who had the power to turn straw into gold, is another.

Animals play an important role in many folk tales. Frequently they can talk. In the story "The Ugly Duckling" they talk to each other; in "Little Red Riding Hood" the wolf speaks as well as a human and actually tries to impersonate the heroine's grandmother.

Frequently in fairy tales animals are actually human beings turned into animal form by some enchantment, as in "The Frog Prince" and "Beauty and the Beast." Objects can be enchanted, too, as are the spinning wheel in "Rumpelstilt-

Beauty and the Beast

skin," the grinding mill in "Why the Sea Is Salt," and the mirror in "Snow White."

Finally, a number of moral themes appear again and again in fairy and folk tales: goodness, faithfulness, patience, and selfless love are rewarded; cruelty, deception, greed, and foolishness are punished. Virtue is triumphant.

Rumpelstiltskin

Jacob and Wilhelm Grimm

ADAPTED FROM *THE BLUE FAIRY BOOK* (1889), EDITED BY ANDREW LANG.

There was once upon a time a poor miller who had a very beautiful daughter. Now, it happened one day that he had an audience with the king, and in order to appear a person of some importance he told him that he had a daughter who could spin straw into gold. "Now that is a talent worth having," said the king to the miller. "If your daughter is as clever as you say, bring her to my palace tomorrow."

When the girl was brought to him he led her into a room full of straw, gave her a spinning wheel and spindle, and said, "Now set to work and spin all night till early dawn, and if by that time you have not spun the straw into gold you shall die." Then he closed the door behind him and left her alone inside.

So the poor miller's daughter sat down and did not know what in the world she was to do. She hadn't the least idea of how to spin straw into gold and at last became so miserable that she began to cry. Suddenly the door opened, and in stepped a tiny little man who said:

"Good evening, Miss Miller-maid. Why are you crying so bitterly?"

"Oh," answered the girl, "I have to spin straw into gold and I haven't a notion how it is done."

"What will you give me if I spin it for you?" asked the manikin.

"My necklace," replied the girl.

The little man took the necklace, sat himself down at the wheel, and whir, whir, whir, the wheel went round three times, and the bobbin was full. Then he put on another, and whir, whir, whir, the wheel went round three times, and the second too was full. And so it went on till the morning, when all the straw was spun away, and all the bobbins were full of gold.

As soon as the sun rose the king came, and when he perceived the gold he was astonished and delighted, but he became more greedy than ever for the precious metal. He had the miller's daughter put into another room full of straw, much bigger than the first, and bade her, if she valued her life, spin it all into gold before the following morning.

The girl did not know what to do and began to cry. Then the door opened as before, and the tiny little man appeared, and said:

"What will you give me if I spin the straw into gold for you?"

"The ring from my finger," answered the girl.

The manikin took the ring, and whir! Round went the spinning wheel again, and when morning broke he had spun all the straw into glittering gold. The king was pleased beyond measure at the sight, but his greed was still not satisfied, and he had the miller's daughter brought into a yet bigger room full of straw and said:

"You must spin all this away in the night, but if you succeed this time you shall become my wife." She's only a miller's daughter, it's true, he thought, but I could not find a richer wife if I were to search the whole world over.

When the girl was alone the little man appeared for the third time, and said, "What will you give me if I spin the straw for you once again?"

"I've nothing more to give," answered the girl.

"Then promise me when you are queen to give me your first child."

Who knows what may happen before that? thought the miller's daughter, and besides, she saw no other way out of it. So she promised the manikin what he demanded, and he set to work once more and spun the straw into gold. When the king came in the morning and found everything as he had desired, he straightaway made her his wife, and the miller's daughter became a queen.

When a year had passed a beautiful son was born to her, and she thought no more of the little man, till all of a sudden one day, he stepped into her room, and said, "Now give me what you promised." The queen was in a great state, and offered the little man all the riches in her kingdom if he would only leave her the child.

But the manikin said, "No, a living creature is dearer to me than all the treasures in the world." Then the queen began to cry and sob so bitterly that the little man was sorry for her, and said:

"I'll give you three days to guess my name, and if you find it out in that time you may keep your child."

Then the queen pondered the whole night over all of the names she had ever heard and sent a messenger to scour the land and to pick up far and near any names he should come across. When the little man arrived on the following day she began with Kasper, Melchior, Belshazzar, and all the other names she knew, but at each one the manikin called out, "That's not my name." The next day she sent to inquire the names of all the people in the neighborhood and had a long list of the most uncommon and extraordinary for the little man when he made his appearance.

"Is your name, perhaps, Sheepshanks, Cruick-shanks, Spindleshanks?"

But he always replied, "That is not my name."

On the third day the messenger returned and announced:

"I have not been able to find any new names; but as I came upon a high hill round the corner of the wood, where the foxes and hares bid each other good night, I saw a little house, and in front of the house burned a fire, and round the fire sprang the most grotesque little man, hopping on one leg, and crying:

> *"Tomorrow I brew, today I bake,*
> *And then the child away I'll take;*
> *For little deems my royal dame*
> *That Rumpelstiltskin is my name!"*

Imagine the queen's delight at hearing the name, and when the little man stepped in shortly afterward and asked, "Now, my Lady Queen, what is my name?" she asked first:

"Is your name Conrad?"

"No."

"Is your name Harry?"

"No."

"Is your name, perhaps, Rumpelstiltskin?"

FRITZ KREDEL/THE GRANGER COLLECTION

Round the fire sprang the most grotesque little man.

"Some demon has told you that! Some demon has told you that!" screamed the little man, and in his rage he drove his right foot so far into the ground that it sank in up to his waist. Then in a passion he seized the left foot with both hands and tore himself in two. ■

Why the Sea Is Salt

Peter Christian Asbjörnsen and Jörgen Ingebretsen Moe

ADAPTED FROM *THE BLUE FAIRY BOOK* (1889), EDITED BY ANDREW LANG.

Once upon a time long, long ago, there were two brothers, the one rich and the other poor. When Christmas Eve came, the poor one had not a bite in the house, either of meat or bread; so he went to his brother, and begged him, in God's name, to give him something for Christmas Day. It was by no means the first time his brother had been forced to give some food to him, and he was not better pleased at being asked now than he generally was.

"If you will do what I ask you, you shall have a whole ham," said he. The poor one immediately thanked him and promised. "Well, here is the ham, and now you must go straight to Dead Man's Hall," said the rich brother, throwing the ham to him.

"Well, I will do what I have promised," said the poor man, and he took the ham and set off. He went on and on for the livelong day, and at nightfall he came to a place where there was a bright light. I have no doubt this is the place, thought the man with the ham.

An old man with a long white beard was chopping Yule logs.

"Good evening," said the man with the ham.

"Good evening to you. Where are you going at this late hour?" asked the old man.

"I am going to Dead Man's Hall, if only I am on the right track," answered the poor man.

"Oh, yes, you are right enough, for it is here," said the old man. "When you go inside they will all want to buy your ham, for they don't get much meat to eat there. But you must not sell it unless you can get for it the hand mill which stands behind the door. When you come out again I will teach you how to stop the hand mill, which is useful for almost everything.''

So the man with the ham thanked the other for his good advice and rapped at the door. When he got in, everything happened just as the old man had said it would. All the people, great and small, came round him like ants on an anthill, and each tried to outbid the other for the ham.

"By rights my old woman and I should have it for our Christmas dinner, but since you have set your hearts upon it, I must just give it up to you,'' said the man. "But, if I sell it, I will have the hand mill standing there behind the door.''

At first they would not hear of this, and haggled and bargained with the man, but he stuck to what he had said, and the people were forced to give him the hand mill. When the man came out again into the yard, he asked the old woodcutter how he was to stop the hand mill. And when he had learned that, he thanked him and set off with all the speed he could, but he did not get home until after the clock had struck twelve on Christmas Eve.

"But where in the world have you been?'' asked the old woman. "Here I have sat waiting, hour after hour, and have not even two sticks to lay across each other under the Christmas porridge pot.''

"Oh, I could not come before. I had something of importance to see about, and a long way to go, too. But now you shall just see!'' said the man. Then he set the hand mill on the table, and bade it first grind candles, then a tablecloth, and then meat and beer, and everything else that was good for a Christmas Eve supper.

And the mill ground all that he ordered.

"Bless me!'' said the old woman as one thing after another appeared. And she wanted to know where her husband had gotten the mill, but he would not tell her that.

"Never mind where I got it. You can see it is a good one, and the water that turns it will never freeze,'' said the man. So he ground meat and drink, and all kinds of good things, to last all Christmastide, and on the third day he invited all his friends to come to a feast.

Now when the rich brother saw all there was at the banquet and in the house, he was both vexed and angry, for he grudged everything his brother had. On Christmas Eve he was so poor he came to me and begged for a trifle, and now he gives a feast as if he were both a count and a king!

thought he. "But, for heaven's sake, tell me where you got your riches from,'' said he to his brother.

"From behind the door,'' said he who owned the mill, for he did not choose to satisfy his brother on that point. But later in the evening, when he had taken a drop too much, he could not refrain from telling how he had come by the hand mill. "There you see what has brought me all my wealth!'' And he brought out the mill and made it grind first one thing and then another.

When the brother saw that, he insisted on having the mill and after a great deal of persuasion got it. But he had to give three hundred dollars for it, and the poor brother was to keep it till the haymaking was over, for he thought, If I keep it as long as that, I can make it grind meat and drink that will last many a long year.

During that time the mill did not grow rusty, and when hay harvest came the rich brother took it, but the other had taken good care not to teach him how to stop it. It was evening when the rich man reached home, and in the morning he bade the old woman go out and spread the hay after the mowers, and he would attend to the house himself that day, he said.

So, when dinner time drew near, he set the mill on the kitchen table, and said, "Grind herrings and milk pottage, and do it both quickly and well.''

So the mill began to grind herrings and milk pottage, and first all the dishes and tubs were filled, and then it covered the kitchen floor. The man twisted and turned it, and did all he could to make the mill stop, but howsoever he turned it and screwed it, the mill went on grinding, and in a short time the pottage rose so high that the man was like to be drowned. So he threw open the parlor door, but it was not long before the mill had ground the parlor full too, and it was with difficulty and danger that the man could go through the stream of pottage and get hold of the door latch. When he got the door open, he did not stay long in the room, but ran out, and the herrings and pottage came after him and streamed out over both farm and field.

Now the old woman, who was out spreading the hay, began to think dinner was long in coming, and said to the women and the mowers, "Though the master does not call us home, we may as well go. It may be he finds he is not good at making pottage, and I should do well to help him.'' So they began to straggle homeward, but a little way up the hill they met the herrings and pottage and bread, all pouring forth and winding

BEN KUTCHER/DAVID MCKAY COMPANY

"Take care that you are not drowned in the pottage," he cried as he went by them.

about one over the other, and the man himself in front of the flood.

"Would to heaven that each of you had a hundred stomachs! Take care that you are not drowned in the pottage!" he cried as he went by them as if Mischief were at his heels, down to where his brother lived. Then he begged him to take the mill back again, and that in an instant, for, said he, "If it grind one hour more the whole district will be destroyed by herrings and pottage!" But the brother would not take it until the other paid him three hundred dollars, and that he was obliged to do.

Now the poor brother had both the money and the mill again. So it was not long before he had a farmhouse much finer than his brother's, and the mill ground him so much money that he covered it with plates of gold. The farmhouse lay close by the seashore, so it shone and glittered far out to sea. Everyone who sailed by had to put in to visit the rich man in the gold farmhouse, and everyone wanted to see the wonderful mill, for the report of it spread far and wide, and there was no one who had not heard tell of it.

After a long, long time came also a skipper who wished to see the mill. He asked if it could make

salt. "Yes, it could make salt," said he who owned it, and when the skipper heard that, he wished with all his might and main to have the mill, let it cost what it might. He thought, if he had it, he would not have to sail far away over the perilous sea for freights of salt. At first the man would not hear of parting with it, but the skipper begged and prayed, and at last the man sold it to him, for many, many thousands of dollars. When the skipper had the mill he did not stay long, for he was afraid the man would change his mind, and he had no time to ask how he was to stop it grinding, but got on board his ship as fast as he could.

When he had gone a little way out to sea he took the mill on deck. "Grind salt, and grind both quickly and well," said the skipper. So the mill began to grind salt, till it spouted out like water, and when the skipper had the ship filled he wanted to stop the mill, but whichsoever way he turned it, and howsoever he tried, it went on grinding, and the heap of salt grew higher and higher, until at last the ship sank.

There lies the mill at the bottom of the sea, and still, day by day, it grinds on: and that is why the sea is salt. ■

Aesop's Fables

The fables of Aesop have been entertaining and enlightening people for some 25 centuries. Most of these short tales feature animals that can talk. Their adventures and experiences generally point to some moral or practical lesson to help people in their daily lives.

It is not known if Aesop ever existed, or if the Greeks invented him to explain the origin of the fables that had become part of their culture. It is thought, however, that Aesop lived during the sixth century B.C., that he originally came from Thrace, and was a slave on the island of Samos.

The fables ascribed to Aesop come from many sources, but most of them are based on Greek and Latin texts compiled centuries after Aesop's time. They have been reworked and retold many times, yet their simplicity and brilliance still endear them to readers young and old.

CHRISTOPHER SANDERS/THE GRANGER COLLECTION

The Dog and His Shadow

One day a dog, passing by a butcher's shop, found a beautiful piece of meat the butcher had carelessly thrown away. The dog took the meat and went to find a quiet place to eat it. On the way he crossed a footbridge over a small, quiet-flowing stream. Looking down, he saw his own reflection in the water, but he thought it was another dog with a bigger piece of meat. He decided he would take that meat too, and lunged at his reflection. In so doing, he dropped the real meat into the stream and it was lost forever. All he got for his selfishness was a mouthful of water.

Greed for more can cause the loss of all.

The Two Travelers and the Bear

Two friends were traveling along a road one day when, much to their surprise, a bear suddenly appeared. One of the travelers quickly left the other and climbed up a big, stout tree. The other was not so quick in his actions. Seeing that the bear would overtake him before he could hide, he lay down on the ground and pretended to be dead, because it is said that a bear will not touch a dead body. The bear poked him up and down, and then put its muzzle close to the man's ear for a moment. Eventually it ambled back into the woods. After it had gone away, the man who had fled up the tree climbed down and rejoined his companion. "Did the bear hurt you?" he asked. The other said, "No, he just whispered in my ear and left." While he was dusting himself off, his friend inquired, "What did the bear say to you?" "He told me," he replied, "to take care in future not to travel with friends who disappear at the first sign of danger."

A friend in need is a friend indeed.

The Boy Who Cried Wolf

There once was a shepherd boy who was fond of playing practical jokes. Each morning he drove his flock some distance from the village to graze, but he found the quiet life of a shepherd boring. One day he decided to create a little excitement. He shouted to the villagers for help, saying that wolves were attacking his sheep. The villagers ran into the fields, carrying knives and clubs, ready to drive the wolves away. But when they got there they found the sheep grazing calmly and the shepherd rolling on the ground in laughter. The boy enjoyed this trick so much that he tried it again, and yet again. Each time the villagers came to the rescue, and each time they found they had been fooled. Then one day some wolves really came, and worked their way between the shepherd boy and his flock. The boy called for help, but his friends and neighbors all thought he was up to his usual foolishness and ignored his cries. The wolves ate up all the sheep.

Those who tell lies will not be believed even when they tell the truth.

Town Mouse and Country Mouse

A field mouse invited a friend who lived in a nearby town to dine with him in the country. The other mouse accepted eagerly, and the two journeyed off to the home of the field mouse. There the town mouse learned that dinner consisted only of corn, barley, and nuts. He said to his host, "My friend, how can you live on such ordinary food and in such solitude? Come with me to the bustling city, and I will show you a good time and no end of delicious things to eat."

So the two of them set off for the town. Arriving at the house in which the town mouse lived, the two settled down to a fine meal of cheese, fruit, bread, dates, cake, nuts, and any number of other tasty morsels. The astonished field mouse began to think his country life was indeed boring and empty compared with city living. But no sooner had they begun their meal when a door suddenly opened and the two friends ran for cover. After a while they returned to eat. Just as they settled down to taste some delicious fruits, a person came into the room and they again scampered to their hiding places. A third time they began to eat, and again the sound of footsteps sent them scurrying.

ROBERT LAWSON/FROM AESOP'S FABLES, ©1941 BY THE HERITAGE PRESS

Finally the field mouse decided that he did not care for city living at all. "Good-bye, my friend," he said, hurrying off. "You may think this is the life, but I would rather enjoy my barley and corn in peace and quiet than have the choicest fare amid noise and danger."

A simple, peaceful life is better than
one of luxury touched by fear and trouble.

The Lion and the Mouse

One day a lion was sleeping peacefully at the mouth of his den when a mouse, not thinking of what he was doing, ran right up the lion's body. Waking up, the lion grabbed the mouse and decided to eat it. The mouse begged to be released, promising to repay the lion for such a kind and generous act. To the lion, the idea that the mouse could repay him—*him,* the king of beasts—was an enormous joke. He laughed and laughed and then, feeling so good, let the little mouse go.

Not long afterwards the lion was captured by hunters, who tied him with ropes to a tree. The mouse heard his roars of anger and unhappiness. Running to the spot, the mouse began to gnaw through the ropes. Soon the lion was freed of his bonds, and the two ran away to safety. Then the mouse said to the lion, "You laughed at me the other day because you did not expect me to repay your kindness. Now you know that even mice can be grateful."

There are times when even the strong
can use the help of the weak.

The Fox and the Grapes

One day a fox, tired and thirsty from his travels, came upon a vine of grapes hanging from the branch of a tree. He reached up to get some of the delicious-looking grapes, but they were too high for him to reach. He jumped up and tried to pull them down, but still he could not reach them. Again and again he tried. Finally, worn out from the effort, he went off, saying to himself, "Oh, well, they were probably sour, anyway."

Some people belittle the things they cannot have.

FROM CAXTON'S AESOP OF 1484
N.Y. PUBLIC LIBRARY PICTURE COLLECTION

Poetry

Here is a selection of poems that the whole family will enjoy. The poems are organized in ascending order of complexity and depth of subject. The poems for the youngest children begin with a selection from the beloved *A Child's Garden of Verses* by Robert Louis Stevenson, a book that has enchanted millions of children in the years since its publication in 1885.

For older children there is a wide variety of poems by such favorites as Lewis Carroll, Carl Sandburg, Langston Hughes, Edna St. Vincent Millay, and Robert Frost.

For sports fans we include the classic "Casey at the Bat" by Ernest Lawrence Thayer, probably the best-known sports poem ever written. Seafarers will be pleased to find "Sea-Fever" by John Masefield included.

The section also contains poems for young adult and adult readers, including works by such masters of the poet's craft as Edgar Allan Poe, Walt Whitman, Emily Dickinson, Robert Frost, and Carl Sandburg.

From
A Child's Garden of Verses
Robert Louis Stevenson

Time to Rise

A birdie with a yellow bill
Hopped upon the window sill,
Cocked his shining eye and said:
"Ain't you 'shamed, you sleepy-head!"

EULALIE/FROM A CHILD'S GARDEN OF VERSES. ©1929 BY THE PLATT AND MUNK CO., INC.

Looking Forward

When I am grown to man's estate
I shall be very proud and great,
And tell the other girls and boys
Not to meddle with my toys.

Rain

The rain is raining all around,
It falls on field and tree,
It rains on the umbrellas here,
And on the ships at sea.

The Cow

The friendly cow all red and white,
    I love with all my heart:
She gives me cream with all her might,
    To eat with apple-tart.

She wanders lowing here and there,
    And yet she cannot stray,
All in the pleasant open air,
    The pleasant light of day;

And blown by all the winds that pass
    And wet with all the showers,
She walks among the meadow grass
    And eats the meadow flowers.

My Shadow

I have a little shadow that goes in and out with me,
And what can be the use of him is more than I can see.
He is very, very like me from the heels up to the head;
And I see him jump before me, when I jump into my bed.

The funniest thing about him is the way he likes to grow—
Not at all like proper children, which is always very slow;
For he sometimes shoots up taller like an india-rubber ball,
And he sometimes gets so little that there's none of him at all.

He hasn't got a notion of how children ought to play,
And can only make a fool of me in every sort of way.
He stays so close beside me, he's a coward you can see;
I'd think shame to stick to nursie as that shadow sticks to me!

One morning, very early, before the sun was up,
I rose and found the shining dew on every buttercup;
But my lazy little shadow, like an arrant sleepy-head,
Had stayed at home behind me and was fast asleep in bed.

Whole Duty of Children

A child should always say what's true
And speak when he is spoken to,
And behave mannerly at table;
At least as far as he is able.

Happy Thought

The world is so full of a number of things,
I'm sure we should all be as happy as kings.

The Moon

The moon has a face like the clock in the hall;
She shines on thieves on the garden wall,
On streets and fields and harbor quays,
And birdies asleep in the forks of the trees.

The squalling cat and the squeaking mouse,
The howling dog by the door of the house,
The bat that lies in bed at noon,
All love to be out by the light of the moon.

But all of the things that belong to the day
Cuddle to sleep to be out of her way;
And flowers and children close their eyes
Till up in the morning the sun shall arise.

Escape at Bedtime

The lights from the parlor and kitchen shone out
    Through the blinds and the windows and bars;
And high overhead and all moving about,
    There were thousands of millions of stars.
There ne'er were such thousands of leaves on a tree,
    Nor of people in church or the Park,
As the crowds of the stars that looked down upon me,
    And that glittered and winked in the dark.

The Dog, and the Plough, and the Hunter, and all,
    And the star of the sailor, and Mars,
These shone in the sky, and the pail by the wall
    Would be half full of water and stars.
They saw me at last, and they chased me with cries,
    And they soon had me packed into bed;
But the glory kept shining and bright in my eyes,
    And the stars going round in my head.

The Wind

I saw you toss the kites on high
And blow the birds about the sky;
And all around I heard you pass,
Like ladies' skirts across the grass—
    O wind, a-blowing all day long
    O wind, that sings so loud a song!

I saw the different things you did,
But always you yourself you hid.
I felt you push, I heard you call,
I could not see yourself at all—
    O wind, a-blowing all day long,
    O wind, that sings so loud a song!

O you that are so strong and cold,
O blower, are you young or old?
Are you a beast of field and tree,
Or just a stronger child than me?
    O wind, a-blowing all day long,
    O wind, that sings so loud a song!

Where Go the Boats?

Dark brown is the river,
    Golden is the sand.
It flows along for ever,
    With trees on either hand.

Green leaves a-floating,
    Castles of the foam,
Boats of mine a-boating—
    Where will all come home?

On goes the river
    And out past the mill,
Away down the valley,
    Away down the hill.

Away down the river,
    A hundred miles or more,
Other little children
    Shall bring my boats ashore.

The Land of Counterpane

When I was sick and lay a-bed,
I had two pillows at my head,
And all my toys beside me lay
To keep me happy all the day.

And sometimes for an hour or so
I watched my leaden soldiers go,
With different uniforms and drills,
Among the bed-clothes, through the hills;

And sometimes sent my ships in fleets
All up and down among the sheets;
Or brought my trees and houses out,
And planted cities all about.

I was the giant great and still
That sits upon the pillow-hill,
And sees before him, dale and plain,
The pleasant land of counterpane.

EULALIE/FROM A CHILD'S GARDEN OF VERSES. ©1929 BY THE PLATT AND MUNK CO., INC.

ALLAN DANIEL/N.Y. PUBLIC LIBRARY PICTURE COLLECTION

The Owl and the Pussy-Cat
Edward Lear

The Owl and the Pussy-Cat went to sea
   In a beautiful pea-green boat.
They took some honey, and plenty of money
   Wrapped up in a five-pound note.
The Owl looked up to the stars above,
   And sang to a small guitar,
"O lovely Pussy! O Pussy, my love,
What a beautiful Pussy you are,
     You are,
     You are!
What a beautiful Pussy you are!"

Pussy said to the Owl, "You elegant fowl!
   How charmingly sweet you sing!
O let us be married! too long we have tarried:
   But what shall we do for a ring?"
They sailed away, for a year and a day,
   To the land where the Bong-Tree grows,
And there in a wood a Piggy-wig stood,
With a ring at the end of his nose,
     His nose,
     His nose!
With a ring at the end of his nose.

"Dear Pig, are you willing to sell for one shilling
   Your ring?" Said the Piggy, "I will."
So they took it away, and were married next day
   By the Turkey who lives on the hill.
They dined on mince, and slices of quince,
   Which they ate with a runcible spoon;
And hand in hand, on the edge of the sand
   They danced by the light of the moon,
     The moon,
     The moon,
   They danced by the light of the moon.

The Night Wind
Eugene Field

Have you ever heard the wind go "Yooooo"?
   'Tis a pitiful sound to hear!
It seems to chill you through and through
   With a strange and speechless fear.
'Tis the voice of the night that broods outside
   When folk should be asleep,
And many and many's the time I've cried
To the darkness brooding far and wide
   Over the land and the deep:
   "Whom do you want, O lonely night,
   That you wail the long hours through?"
And the night would say in its ghostly way:
    "Yoooooooo!
    Yoooooooo!
    Yoooooooo!"

My mother told me long ago
   (When I was a little tad)
That when the night went wailing so,
   Somebody had been bad;
And then, when I was snug in bed,
   Whither I had been sent,
With the blankets pulled up round my head,
I'd think of what my mother'd said,
   And wonder what boy she meant!
And "Who's been bad to-day?" I'd ask
   Of the wind that hoarsely blew,
And the voice would say in its meaningful way:
    "Yoooooooo!
    Yoooooooo!
    Yoooooooo!"

That this was true I must allow—
   You'll not believe it, though!
Yes, though I'm quite a model now,
   I was not always so.
And if you doubt what things I say,
   Suppose you make the test;
Suppose, when you've been bad some day
And up to bed are sent away
   From mother and the rest—
Suppose you ask, "Who has been bad?"
   And then you'll hear what's true;
For the wind will moan in its ruefulest tone:
    "Yoooooooo!
    Yoooooooo!
    Yoooooooo!"

There Was an Old Man with a Beard
Edward Lear

There was an Old Man with a beard,
Who said, "It is just as I feared!—
Two Owls and a Hen, four Larks and a Wren,
Have all built their nests in my beard."

The Night Before Christmas
Clement Clarke Moore

THOMAS NAST

'Twas the night before Christmas,
When all through the house
  Not a creature was stirring,
Not even a mouse.

The stockings were hung
By the chimney with care,
  In hopes that St. Nicholas
Soon would be there.

The children were nestled
All snug in their beds,
  While visions of sugarplums
Danced through their heads.

Mamma in her kerchief
And I in my cap
  Had just settled our brains
For a long winter's nap.

When out on the lawn
There arose such a clatter
  I sprang from my bed
To see what was the matter.

Away to the window
I flew like a flash,
  Tore open the shutters
And threw up the sash.

The moon on the breast
Of the new fallen snow
  Gave a lustre of midday
To objects below,

When what to my wondering eyes
  Should appear—
But a miniature sleigh
  And eight tiny reindeer!

With a little old driver,
  So lively and quick,
I knew in a moment
  It must be St. Nick.

More rapid than eagles,
his coursers they came,
  And he whistled and shouted
and called each by name:

"Now, Dasher, now, Dancer,
now, Prancer, now, Vixen!
  On, Comet! On, Cupid!
On, Donner and Blitzen!

To the top of the porch,
To the top of the wall,
  Now, dash away, dash away,
Dash away, all!"

As dry leaves before the wild
  hurricane fly,
When they meet with an obstacle,
  mount to the sky:

So up to the housetop
  the coursers they flew,
With the sleigh full of toys,
  and St. Nicholas, too.

And then, in a twinkling,
I heard on the roof
  The prancing and pawing
Of each little hoof.

As I drew in my head,
And was turning around,
  Down the chimney St. Nicholas came
  With a bound!

He was dressed all in fur
From his head to his foot,
  And his clothes were all tarnished
With ashes and soot;

A bundle of toys
He had flung on his back,
  And he looked like a peddler
Just opening his pack.

His eyes, how they twinkled!
His dimples, how merry!
  His cheeks were like roses,
His nose like a cherry.

His droll little mouth
Was drawn up like a bow,
  And the beard on his chin
Was as white as the snow.

The stump of a pipe
He held tight in his teeth,
  And the smoke, it encircled
His head like a wreath.

He had a broad face,
And a little round belly
  That shook when he laughed
Like a bowlful of jelly.

He was chubby and plump—
A right jolly old elf,
  And I laughed when I saw him
In spite of myself.

A wink of his eye
And a twist of his head
  Soon gave me to know
I had nothing to dread.

He spoke not a word
But went straight to his work
  And filled all the stockings,
Then turned with a jerk—

And, laying his finger
Aside of his nose
  And giving a nod,
Up the chimney he rose.

He sprang to his sleigh,
To his team gave a whistle,
  And away they all flew
Like the down on a thistle.

And I heard him exclaim
Ere he drove out of sight:
  "MERRY CHRISTMAS TO ALL,
AND TO ALL A GOOD NIGHT!"

The Sloth

Theodore Roethke

In moving-slow he has no Peer.
You ask him something in his Ear,
He thinks about it for a Year;

And, then, before he says a Word
There, upside down (unlike a Bird),
He will assume that you have Heard—

A most Ex-as-per-at-ing Lug.
But should you call his manner Smug,
He'll sigh and give his Branch a Hug;

Then off again to Sleep he goes.
Still swaying gently by his Toes,
And you just *know* he knows he knows.

The Octopus

Ogden Nash

Tell me, O Octopus, I begs,
Is those things arms, or is they legs?
I marvel at thee, Octopus;
If I were thou, I'd call me Us.

Fireflies

Carolyn Hall

Little lamps of the dusk,
 You fly low and gold
When the summer evening
 Starts to unfold.
So that all the insects,
 Now, before you pass,
Will have light to see by,
 Undressing in the grass.

But when the night has flowered,
 Little lamps agleam,
You fly over treetops
 Following a dream.
Men wonder from their windows
 That a firefly goes so far—
They do not know your longing
 To be a shooting star.

A Centipede

Unknown

A centipede was happy quite,
Until a frog in fun
Said, "Pray, which leg comes after which?"
This raised her mind to such a pitch,
She lay distracted in a ditch,
Considering how to run.

Macavity: The Mystery Cat

T. S. Eliot

Macavity's a Mystery Cat: he's called the Hidden Paw—
For he's the master criminal who can defy the Law.
He's the bafflement of Scotland Yard, the Flying Squad's despair:
For when they reach the scene of crime—*Macavity's not there!*

Macavity, Macavity, there's no one like Macavity,
He's broken every human law, he breaks the law of gravity.
His powers of levitation would make a fakir stare,
And when you reach the scene of crime—*Macavity's not there!*
You may seek him in the basement, you may look up in the air—
But I tell you once and once again, *Macavity's not there!*

Macavity's a ginger cat, he's very tall and thin;
You would know him if you saw him, for his eyes are sunken in.
His brow is deeply lined with thought, his head is highly domed;
His coat is dusty from neglect, his whiskers are uncombed.
He sways his head from side to side, with movements like a snake;
And when you think he's half asleep, he's always wide awake.

Macavity, Macavity, there's no one like Macavity,
For he's a fiend in feline shape, a monster of depravity.
You may meet him in a by-street, you may see him in the square—
But when a crime's discovered, then *Macavity's not there!*

He's outwardly respectable. (They say he cheats at cards.)
And his footprints are not found in any file of Scotland Yard's.
And when the larder's looted, or the jewel-case is rifled,
Or when the milk is missing, or another Peke's been stifled,
Or the greenhouse glass is broken, and the trellis past repair—
Ay, there's the wonder of the thing! *Macavity's not there!*

And when the Foreign Office find a Treaty's gone astray,
Or the Admiralty lose some plans and drawings by the way,
There may be a scrap of paper in the hall or on the stair—
But it's useless to investigate—*Macavity's not there!*
And when the loss has been disclosed, the Secret Service say:
"It *must* have been Macavity!"—but he's a mile away.
You'll be sure to find him resting, or a-licking of his thumbs,
Or engaged in doing complicated long division sums.

Macavity, Macavity, there's no one like Macavity,
There never was a Cat of such deceitfulness and suavity.
He always has an alibi, and one or two to spare:
At whatever time the deed took place—MACAVITY WASN'T THERE!
And they say that all the Cats whose wicked deeds are widely known,
(I might mention Mungojerrie, I might mention Griddlebone)
Are nothing more than agents for the Cat who all the time
Just controls their operations: the Napoleon of Crime!

The Walrus and the Carpenter
Lewis Carroll

The sun was shining on the sea,
   Shining with all his might:
He did his very best to make
   The billows smooth and bright—
And this was odd, because it was
   The middle of the night.

The moon was shining sulkily,
   Because she thought the sun
Had got no business to be there
   After the day was done—
"It's very rude of him," she said,
   "To come and spoil the fun!"

The sea was wet as wet could be,
   The sands were dry as dry.
You could not see a cloud, because
   No cloud was in the sky:
No birds were flying overhead—
   There were no birds to fly.

The Walrus and the Carpenter
   Were walking close at hand:
They wept like anything to see
   Such quantities of sand:
"If this were only cleared away,"
   They said, "it would be grand,"

"If seven maids with seven mops
   Swept it for half a year,
Do you suppose," the Walrus said,
   "That they could get it clear?"
"I doubt it," said the Carpenter,
   And shed a bitter tear.

"O Oyster, come and walk with us!"
   The Walrus did beseech.
"A pleasant walk, a pleasant talk,
   Along the briny beach:
We cannot do with more than four,
   To give a hand to each."

The eldest Oyster looked at him,
   But never a word he said:
The eldest Oyster winked his eye,
   And shook his heavy head—
Meaning to say he did not choose
   To leave the oyster-bed.

But four young Oysters hurried up,
   All eager for the treat:
Their coats were brushed, their faces washed,
   Their shoes were clean and neat—
And this was odd, because, you know,
   They hadn't any feet.

Four other Oysters followed them,
   And yet another four;
And thick and fast they came at last,
   And more, and more, and more—
All hopping through the frothy waves,
   And scrambling to the shore.

The Walrus and the Carpenter
   Walked on a mile or so,
And then they rested on a rock
   Conveniently low:
And all the little Oysters stood
   And waited in a row.

"The time has come," the Walrus said,
   "To talk of many things:
Of shoes—and ships—and sealing-wax—
   Of cabbages—and kings—
And why the sea is boiling hot—
   And whether pigs have wings."

"But wait a bit," the Oyster cried,
   "Before we have our chat;
For some of us are out of breath,
   And all of us are fat!"
"No hurry!" said the Carpenter.
   They thanked him much for that.

"A loaf of bread," the Walrus said,
   "Is what we chiefly need:
Pepper and vinegar besides
   Are very good indeed—
Now, if you're ready, Oysters dear,
   We can begin to feed."

"But not on us!" the Oysters cried,
   Turning a little blue.
"After such kindness, that would be
   A dismal thing to do!"
"The night is fine," the Walrus said.
   "Do you admire the view?

"It was so kind of you to come!
   And you are very nice!"
The Carpenter said nothing but
   "Cut us another slice.
I wish you were not quite so deaf—
   I've had to ask you twice!"

"It seems a shame," the Walrus said
   "To play them such a trick.
After we've brought them out so far,
   And made them trot so quick!"
The Carpenter said nothing but
   "The butter's spread too thick!"

"I weep for you." the Walrus said:
   "I deeply sympathize."
With sobs and tears he sorted out
   Those of the largest size,
Holding his pocket-handkerchief
   Before his streaming eyes.

"O Oysters," said the Carpenter,
   "You've had a pleasant run!
Shall we be trotting home again?"
   But answer came there none—
And this was scarcely odd, because
   They'd eaten every one.

SIR JOHN TENNIEL/CULVER PICTURES, INC.

Jabberwocky
Lewis Carroll

'Twas brillig, and the slithy toves
　　Did gyre and gimble in the wabe:
All mimsy were the borogoves,
　　And the mome raths outgrabe.

"Beware the Jabberwock, my son!
　　The jaws that bite, the claws that catch!
Beware the Jubjub bird, and shun
　　The frumious Bandersnatch!"

He took his vorpal sword in hand:
　　Long time the manxome foe he sought—
So rested he by the Tumtum tree,
　　And stood awhile in thought.

And, as in uffish thought he stood,
　　The Jabberwock, with eyes of flame,
Came whiffling through the tulgey wood,
　　And burbled as it came!

One, two! One, two! And through and through
　　The vorpal blade went snicker-snack!
He left it dead, and with its head
　　He went galumphing back.

"And hast thou slain the Jabberwock?
　　Come to my arms, my beamish boy!
O frabjous day! Callooh! Callay!"
　　He chortled in his joy.

'Twas brillig, and the slithy toves
　　Did gyre and gimble in the wabe:
All mimsy were the borogoves,
　　And the mome raths outgrabe.

SIR JOHN TENNIEL/THE GRANGER COLLECTION

Casey at the Bat
Ernest Lawrence Thayer

The outlook wasn't brilliant for the Mudville nine that day;
The score stood four to two with but one inning more to play.
And then when Cooney died at first, and Barrows did the same,
A sickly silence fell upon the patrons of the game.

A straggling few got up to go in deep despair. The rest
Clung to that hope which springs eternal in the human breast;
They thought if only Casey could but get a whack at that—
We'd put up even money now with Casey at the bat.

But Flynn preceded Casey, as did also Jimmy Blake,
And the former was a lulu and the latter was a cake;
So upon that stricken multitude grim melancholy sat,
For there seemed but little chance of Casey's getting to the bat.

But Flynn let drive a single, to the wonderment of all,
And Blake, the much despisèd, tore the cover off the ball;
And when the dust had lifted, and the men saw what had occurred,
There was Jimmy safe at second and Flynn a-hugging third.

Then from five thousand throats and more there rose a lusty yell;
It rumbled through the valley, it rattled in the dell;
It knocked upon the mountain and recoiled upon the flat,
For Casey, mighty Casey, was advancing to the bat.

There was ease in Casey's manner as he stepped into his place;
There was pride in Casey's bearing and a smile on Casey's face.
And when, responding to the cheers, he lightly doffed his hat,
No stranger in the crowd could doubt 'twas Casey at the bat.

Ten thousand eyes were on him as he rubbed his hands with dirt;
Five thousand tongues applauded when he wiped them on his shirt.
Then while the writhing pitcher ground the ball into his hip,
Defiance gleamed in Casey's eye, a sneer curled Casey's lip.

And now the leather-covered sphere came hurtling through the air,
And Casey stood a-watching it in haughty grandeur there.
Close by the sturdy batsman the ball unheeded sped—
"That ain't my style," said Casey. "Strike one," the umpire said.

From the benches, black with people, there went up a muffled roar,
Like the beating of the storm waves on a stern and distant shore.
"Kill him! Kill the umpire!" shouted someone on the stand;
And it's likely they'd have killed him had not Casey raised his hand.

With a smile of Christian charity great Casey's visage shone;
He stilled the rising tumult; he bade the game go on;
He signaled to the pitcher, and once more the spheroid flew;
But Casey still ignored it, and the umpire said, "Strike two."

"Fraud!" cried the maddened thousands, and echo answered, "Fraud!"
But one scornful look from Casey and the audience was awed.
They saw his face grow stern and cold, they saw his muscles strain,
And they knew that Casey wouldn't let that ball go by again.

The sneer is gone from Casey's lip, his teeth are clenched in hate;
He pounds with cruel violence his bat upon the plate.
And now the pitcher holds the ball, and now he lets it go,
And now the air is shattered by the force of Casey's blow.

Oh, somewhere in this favored land the sun is shining bright;
The band is playing somewhere, and somewhere hearts are light,
And somewhere men are laughing, and somewhere children shout;
But there is no joy in Mudville—mighty Casey has struck out.

The Tiger
William Blake

Tiger! Tiger! burning bright
In the forests of the night,
What immortal hand or eye
Could frame thy fearful symmetry?

In what distant deeps or skies
Burnt the fire of thine eyes?
On what wings dare he aspire?
What the hand dare seize the fire?

And what shoulder, & what art,
Could twist the sinews of thy heart?
And when the heart began to beat,
What dread hand? & what dread feet?

What the hammer? what the chain?
In what furnace was thy brain?
What the anvil? what dread grasp
Dare its deadly terrors clasp?

When the stars threw down their spears,
And water'd heaven with their tears,
Did he smile his work to see?
Did he who made the Lamb make thee?

Tiger! Tiger! burning bright
In the forests of the night,
What immortal hand or eye,
Dare frame thy fearful symmetry?

The Mouse That Gnawed
the Oak-Tree Down
Vachel Lindsay

REPRINTED WITH PERMISSION OF MACMILLAN PUBLISHING COMPANY
FROM COLLECTED POEMS BY VACHEL LINDSAY. COPYRIGHT 1914 BY
MACMILLAN PUBLISHING COMPANY, RENEWED 1942 BY ELIZABETH C. LINDSAY.

The mouse that gnawed the oak-tree down
Began his task in early life.
He kept so busy with his teeth
He had no time to take a wife.

He gnawed and gnawed through sun and rain
When the ambitious fit was on,
Then rested in the sawdust till
A month of idleness had gone.

He did not move about to hunt
The coteries of mousie-men.
He was a snail-paced, stupid thing
Until he cared to gnaw again.

The mouse that gnawed the oak-tree down,
When that tough foe was at his feet—
Found in the stump no angel-cake
Nor buttered bread, nor cheese nor meat—
The forest-roof let in the sky.
"This light is worth the work," said he.
"I'll make this ancient swamp more light,"
And started on another tree.

Aspiration

Langston Hughes

I wonder how it feels
To do cart wheels?
I sure would like
To know.

To walk a high wire
Is another desire,
In this world before
I go.

Heaven

Langston Hughes

Heaven is
The place where
Happiness is
Everywhere.

Animals
And birds sing—
As does
Everything.

To each stone,
"How-do-you-do?"
Stone answers back,
"Well! And you?"

Fog

Carl Sandburg

The fog comes
on little cat feet.

It sits looking
over harbor and city
on silent haunches
and then moves on.

Night

Sara Teasdale

Stars over snow
    And in the west a planet
Swinging below a star—
    Look for a lovely thing and you will find it,
It is not far—
    It never will be far.

Summer Stars

Carl Sandburg

Bend low again, night of summer stars.
So near you are, sky of summer stars,
So near, a long-arm man can pick off stars,
Pick off what he wants in the sky bowl,
So near you are, summer stars,
So near, strumming, strumming,
            So lazy and hum-strumming.

Moonset

Carl Sandburg

Leaves of poplars pick Japanese prints against the west.
Moon sand on the canal doubles the changing pictures.
        The moon's good-by ends pictures.
The west is empty. All else is empty. No moon-talk at all now.
        Only dark listening to dark.

April Rain Song

Langston Hughes

Let the rain kiss you.
Let the rain beat upon your head with silver liquid drops.
Let the rain sing you a lullaby.

The rain makes still pools on the sidewalk.
The rain makes running pools in the gutter.
The rain plays a little sleep-song on our roof at night—

And I love the rain.

Success Is Counted Sweetest

Emily Dickinson

Success is counted sweetest
By those who ne'er succeed.
To comprehend a nectar
Requires sorest need.

Not one of all the purple Host
Who took the Flag today
Can tell the definition
So clear of Victory

As he defeated—dying—
On whose forbidden ear
The distant strains of triumph
Burst agonized and clear!

Stopping by Woods on a Snowy Evening

Robert Frost

Whose woods these are I think I know.
His house is in the village though;
He will not see me stopping here
To watch his woods fill up with snow.

My little horse must think it queer
To stop without a farmhouse near
Between the woods and frozen lake
The darkest evening of the year.

He gives his harness bells a shake
To ask if there is some mistake.
The only other sound's the sweep
Of easy wind and downy flake.

The woods are lovely, dark and deep,
But I have promises to keep,
And miles to go before I sleep,
And miles to go before I sleep.

I Never Saw a Moor

Emily Dickinson

I never saw a Moor—
I never saw the Sea—
Yet know I how the Heather looks
And what a Billow be.

I never spoke with God
Nor visited in Heaven—
Yet certain am I of the spot
As if the Checks were given—

Who Has Seen the Wind?

Christina Rossetti

Who has seen the wind?
    Neither I nor you:
But when the leaves hang trembling,
    The wind is passing through.

Who has seen the wind?
    Neither you nor I:
But when the trees bow down their heads,
    The wind is passing by.

Sunsets
Carl Sandburg

There are sunsets who whisper a good-by.
It is a short dusk and a way for stars.
Prairie and sea rim they go level and even
And the sleep is easy.

There are sunsets who dance good-by.
They fling scarves half to the arc,
To the arc then and over the arc.
Ribbons at the ears, sashes at the hips,
Dancing, dancing good-by. And here sleep
Tosses a little with dreams.

Sea-Fever
John Masefield

I must go down to the seas again, to the lonely sea and the sky,
And all I ask is a tall ship and a star to steer her by,
And the wheel's kick and the wind's song and the white sail's shaking,
And a grey mist on the sea's face and grey dawn breaking.

I must go down to the seas again, for the call of the running tide
Is a wild call and a clear call that may not be denied;
And all I ask is a windy day with the white clouds flying,
And the flung spray and the blown spume and the sea-gulls crying.

I must go down to the seas again to the vagrant gypsy life,
To the gull's way and the whale's way where the wind's like a whetted knife;
And all I ask is a merry yarn from a laughing fellow-rover,
And quiet sleep and a sweet dream when the long trick's over.

Love
Langston Hughes

Love is a wild wonder
And stars that sing,
Rocks that burst asunder
And mountains that take wing.

John Henry with his hammer
Makes a little spark.
That little spark is love
Dying in the dark.

Requiem
Robert Louis Stevenson

Under the wide and starry sky,
Dig the grave and let me lie.
Glad did I live and gladly die,
    And I laid me down with a will.

This be the verse you grave for me:
Here he lies where he longed to be,
Home is the sailor, home from sea,
    And the hunter home from the hill.

Afternoon on a Hill
Edna St. Vincent Millay

I will be the gladdest thing
    Under the sun!
I will touch a hundred flowers
    And not pick one.

I will look at cliffs and clouds
    With quiet eyes,
Watch the wind bow down the grass,
    And the grass rise.

And when lights begin to show
    Up from the town,
I will mark which must be mine,
    And then start down!

I Wandered Lonely as a Cloud
William Wordsworth

I wandered lonely as a cloud
That floats on high o'er vales and hills,
When all at once I saw a crowd,
A host, of golden daffodils;
Beside the lake, beneath the trees,
Fluttering and dancing in the breeze.

Continuous as the stars that shine
And twinkle on the milky way,
They stretched in never-ending line
Along the margin of a bay:
Ten thousand saw I at a glance,
Tossing their heads in sprightly dance.

The waves beside them danced; but they
Out-did the sparkling waves in glee:
A poet could not but be gay,
In such a jocund company:
I gazed—and gazed—but little thought
What wealth the show to me had brought.

For oft, when on my couch I lie
In vacant or in pensive mood,
They flash upon that inward eye
Which is the bliss of solitude;
And then my heart with pleasure fills,
And dances with the daffodils.

The Star
Jane Taylor

Twinkle, twinkle, little star,
How I wonder what you are!
Up above the world so high,
Like a diamond in the sky.

Hymn

Sung at the Completion of
Concord Monument, April 19, 1836

Ralph Waldo Emerson

By the rude bridge that arched the flood,
Their flag to April's breeze unfurled,
Here once the embattled farmers stood,
And fired the shot heard round the world.

The foe long since in silence slept,
Alike the Conqueror silent sleeps,
And Time the ruined bridge has swept
Down the dark stream which seaward creeps.

On this green bank, by this soft stream,
We set to-day a votive stone,
That memory may their deed redeem,
When like our sires our sons are gone.

Spirit! who made those freemen dare
To die, or leave their children free,
Bid time and nature gently spare
The shaft we raise to them and Thee.

Annabel Lee

Edgar Allan Poe

It was many and many a year ago,
    In a kingdom by the sea,
That a maiden there lived whom you may know
    By the name of Annabel Lee;—
And this maiden she lived with no other thought
    Than to love and be loved by me.

She was a child and *I* was a child,
    In this kingdom by the sea,
But we loved with a love that was more than love—
    I and my Annabel Lee—
With a love that the wingèd seraphs of Heaven
    Coveted her and me.

And this was the reason that, long ago,
    In this kingdom by the sea,
A wind blew out of a cloud by night
    Chilling my Annabel Lee;
So that her high-born kinsmen came
    And bore her away from me,
To shut her up in a sepulchre
    In this kingdom by the sea.

The angels, not half so happy in Heaven,
    Went envying her and me;
Yes! that was the reason (as all men know,
    In this kingdom by the sea)
That the wind came out of the cloud, chilling
    And killing my Annabel Lee.

But our love it was stronger by far than the love
    Of those who were older than we—
    Of many far wiser than we—
And neither the angels in Heaven above
    Nor the demons down under the sea
Can ever dissever my soul from the soul
    Of the beautiful Annabel Lee:—

For the moon never beams without bringing me dreams
    Of the beautiful Annabel Lee;
And the stars never rise but I see the bright eyes
    Of the beautiful Annabel Lee;
And so, all the night-tide, I lie down by the side
Of my darling, my darling, my life and my bride
    In her sepulchre there by the sea—
    In her tomb by the side of the sea.

O Captain! My Captain!

Walt Whitman

O Captain! my Captain! our fearful trip is done,
The ship has weather'd every rack, the prize we sought is won,
The port is near, the bells I hear, the people all exulting,
While follow eyes the steady keel, the vessel grim and daring;
        But O heart! heart! heart!
            O the bleeding drops of red,
                Where on the deck my Captain lies,
                    Fallen cold and dead.

O Captain! my Captain! rise up and hear the bells;
Rise up—for you the flag is flung—for you the bugle trills,
For you bouquets and ribbon'd wreaths—for you the shores a-crowding,
For you they call, the swaying mass, their eager faces turning;
        Here Captain! dear father!
            This arm beneath your head!
                It is some dream that on the deck,
                    You've fallen cold and dead.

My Captain does not answer, his lips are pale and still,
My father does not feel my arm, he has no pulse nor will,
The ship is anchor'd safe and sound, its voyage closed and done,
From fearful trip the victor ship comes in with object won;
        Exult O shores, and ring O bells!
            But I with mournful tread,
                Walk the deck my Captain lies,
                    Fallen cold and dead.

The Chambered Nautilus

Oliver Wendell Holmes

This is the ship of pearl, which, poets feign,
    Sails the unshadowed main,—
    The venturous bark that flings
On the sweet summer wind its purpled wings
In gulfs enchanted, where the Siren sings,
    And coral reefs lie bare,
Where the cold sea-maids rise to sun their streaming hair.

Its webs of living gauze no more unfurl;
    Wrecked is the ship of pearl!
    And every chambered cell,
Where its dim dreaming life was wont to dwell,
As the frail tenant shaped his growing shell,
    Before thee lies revealed,—
Its irised ceiling rent, its sunless crypt unsealed!

Year after year beheld the silent toil
    That spread his lustrous coil;
    Still, as the spiral grew,
He left the past year's dwelling for the new,
Stole with soft step its shining archway through,
    Built up its idle door,
Stretched in his last-found home, and knew the old no more.

Thanks for the heavenly message brought by thee,
    Child of the wandering sea,
    Cast from her lap, forlorn!
From thy dead lips a clearer note is born
Than ever Triton blew from wreathèd horn!
    While on mine ear it rings,
Through the deep caves of thought I hear a voice that sings:—

Build thee more stately mansions, O my soul,
    As the swift seasons roll!
    Leave thy low-vaulted past!
Let each new temple, nobler than the last,
Shut thee from heaven with a dome more vast,
    Till thou at length art free,
Leaving thine outgrown shell by life's unresting sea!

The Road Not Taken

Robert Frost

Two roads diverged in a yellow wood,
And sorry I could not travel both
And be one traveler, long I stood
And looked down one as far as I could
To where it bent in the undergrowth;

Then took the other, as just as fair,
And having perhaps the better claim,
Because it was grassy and wanted wear;
Though as for that the passing there
Had worn them really about the same,

And both that morning equally lay
In leaves no step had trodden black.
Oh, I kept the first for another day!
Yet knowing how way leads on to way,
I doubted if I should ever come back.

I shall be telling this with a sigh
Somewhere ages and ages hence:
Two roads diverged in a wood, and I—
I took the one less traveled by,
And that has made all the difference.

Because I Could Not Stop for Death

Emily Dickinson

Because I could not stop for Death—
He kindly stopped for me—
The Carriage held but just Ourselves—
And Immortality.

We slowly drove—He knew no haste
And I had put away
My labor and my leisure too,
For His Civility—

We passed the School, where Children strove
At Recess—in the Ring—
We passed the Fields of Gazing Grain—
We passed the Setting Sun—

Or rather—He passed Us—
The Dews drew quivering and chill—
For only Gossamer, my Gown—
My Tippet—only Tulle—

We paused before a House that seemed
A Swelling of the Ground—
The Roof was scarcely visible—
The Cornice—in the Ground—

Since then—'tis Centuries—and yet
Feels shorter than the Day
I first surmised the Horses' Heads
Were toward Eternity—

My Life Closed Twice Before Its Close

Emily Dickinson

My life closed twice before its close—
It yet remains to see
If Immortality unveil
A third event to me

So huge, so hopeless to conceive
As these that twice befell.
Parting is all we know of heaven,
And all we need of hell.

JIM CRON/MONKMEYER PRESS PHOTO SERVICE

I Am the People, the Mob

Carl Sandburg

I am the people—the mob—the crowd—the mass.
Do you know that all the great work of the world is done through me?
I am the workingman, the inventor, the maker of the world's food and
   clothes.
I am the audience that witnesses history. The Napoleons come from me
   and the Lincolns. They die. And then I send forth more Napoleons
   and Lincolns.
I am the seed ground. I am a prairie that will stand for much plowing.
   Terrible storms pass over me. I forget. The best of me is sucked out
   and wasted. I forget. Everything but Death comes to me and makes
   me work and give up what I have. And I forget.
Sometimes I growl, shake myself and spatter a few red drops for history
   to remember. Then—I forget.
When I, the People, learn to remember, when I, the People, use the
   lessons of yesterday and no longer forget who robbed me last year,
   who played me for a fool—then there will be no speaker in all the
   world say the name: "The People," with any fleck of a sneer in his
   voice or any far-off smile of derision.
The mob—the crowd—the mass—will arrive then.

I Hear America Singing

Walt Whitman

I hear America singing, the varied carols I hear,
Those of mechanics, each one singing his as it should be blithe and strong,
The carpenter singing his as he measures his plank or beam,
The mason singing his as he makes ready for work, or leaves off work,
The boatman singing what belongs to him in his boat,
   the deck-hand singing on the steamboat deck,
The shoemaker singing as he sits on his bench, the hatter singing as he stands,
The wood-cutter's song, the ploughboy's on his way in the morning,
   or at noon intermission or at sundown,
The delicious singing of the mother, or of the young wife at work,
   or of the girl sewing or washing,
Each singing what belongs to him or her and to none else,
The day what belongs to the day—at night the party of young fellows,
   robust, friendly,
Singing with open mouths their strong melodious songs.

Fiction

No anthology would be complete without a generous selection of stories. Good stories tell us something about ourselves and about life, and at the same time engage the imagination.

Stories introduce us to interesting characters and show us how they deal with life situations. We also learn something about the characters through their actions. Finally, stories give us the chance to imagine ourselves in the same situations and think about how we would act. Would we do the same things the person in the story did? Would we act differently? If so, how—and why?

"The Necklace" by the French writer Guy de Maupassant depicts two ordinary people who, through their own actions, are faced with an extraordinary situation. In "The Gift of the Magi" by O. Henry, "The Town Where No One Got Off" by Ray Bradbury, and "The Apprentice" by Dorothy Canfield Fisher, the characters are again just everyday people. The thoughts, feelings, and actions of the characters in these stories are so beautifully described that we have no trouble imagining ourselves in their places and experiencing what they experience.

Stories enable us to travel in time and place—to a garden in sunny India, to the frozen wastes of the Yukon, to a semibarbaric kingdom you will never find mentioned in the history books.

A good story must be believable. A master storyteller can get the reader to accept something that seems impossible as long as the rest of the story is firmly grounded in realism. For example, the idea that a person can sleep for 20 years is ridiculous, but in the hands of a writer as great as Washington Irving it becomes the basis for the classic story "Rip Van Winkle." Even the idea that animals can talk is acceptable in a beautifully crafted tale such as "Rikki-Tikki-Tavi."

There is no compromise with realism in "Love of Life" by Jack London, the story of a man's struggle against a deadly and impersonal environment. London was a versatile writer, but whether his subject was humorous or serious, fact or fiction, he tried to find the truth. In this story the truth is that human beings have an instinct for survival that almost defies comprehension. And so, despite the grim detail and unsparing description, the story is a positive one. We struggle to live because we are so made.

Humor also has its place in fiction. Mark Twain was a careful observer of humans and their ways, and his stories derive much of their humor from the words and actions of his characters, and from the truths of existence they reveal. In the whitewashing incident from *The Adventures of Tom Sawyer*, for example, Tom reflects that "in order to make a man or boy covet a thing, it is only necessary to make the thing difficult to attain." How can we keep from smiling when we reflect that this truth applies to everyone, even ourselves?

Humor is an important element in the fables of James Thurber and the story "The Open Window" by the British writer Saki, but if there is any humor in "The Tell-Tale Heart" by Edgar Allan Poe, it is very dark indeed. Here Poe examines the mind of a madman who has committed a ghastly murder. It is the man himself, describing the logical steps he took in planning and committing the crime, who reveals his insanity.

Poe was unsurpassed in the field of what he called "tales of the grotesque and Arabesque." He has also been credited with the creation of the modern detective story. However, Sir Arthur Conan Doyle was the creator of the best-known sleuth of all time, Sherlock Holmes. "The Red-Headed League," one of the most popular Sherlock Holmes stories, presents Holmes at the peak of his powers, uncovering the scheme of a master criminal in what appears at first to be merely a bizarre prank.

From

The Wonderful Wizard of Oz

L. Frank Baum

Chapter VI
The Cowardly Lion

Here is a chapter from a classic of children's literature. Dorothy, accompanied by the Scarecrow and the Tin Woodman, is on her way to ask the Wizard of Oz to help her get back home.

All this time Dorothy and her companions had been walking through the thick woods. The road was still paved with yellow brick, but these were much covered by dried branches and dead leaves from the trees, and the walking was not at all good.

There were few birds in this part of the forest, for birds love the open country where there is plenty of sunshine; but now and then there came a deep growl from some wild animal hidden among the trees. These sounds made the little girl's heart beat fast, for she did not know what made them; but Toto knew, and he walked close to Dorothy's side, and did not bark in return.

"How long will it be," the child asked of the Tin Woodman, "before we are out of the forest?"

"I cannot tell," was the answer, "for I have never been to the Emerald City. But my father went there once, when I was a boy, and he said it was a long journey through a dangerous country, although nearer to the city where Oz dwells the country is beautiful. But I am not afraid so long as I have my oilcan, and nothing can hurt the Scarecrow, while you bear upon your forehead the mark of the good Witch's kiss, and that will protect you from harm."

"But Toto!" said the girl anxiously; "what will protect him?"

"We must protect him ourselves, if he is in danger," replied the Tin Woodman.

Just as he spoke there came from the forest a terrible roar, and the next moment a great Lion bounded into the road. With one blow of his paw he sent the Scarecrow spinning over and over to the edge of the road, and then he struck at the Tin Woodman with his sharp claws. But, to the Lion's surprise, he could make no impression on the tin, although the Woodman fell over in the road and lay still.

Little Toto, now that he had an enemy to face, ran barking toward the Lion, and the great beast had opened his mouth to bite the dog, when Dorothy, fearing Toto would be killed, and heedless of danger, rushed forward and slapped the Lion upon his nose as hard as she could, while she cried out:

"Don't you dare to bite Toto! You ought to be ashamed of yourself, a big beast like you, to bite a poor little dog!"

"I didn't bite him," said the Lion, as he rubbed his nose with his paw where Dorothy had hit it.

"No, but you tried to," she retorted. "You are nothing but a big coward."

"I know it," said the Lion, hanging his head in shame; "I've always known it. But how can I help it?"

"I don't know, I'm sure. To think of your striking a stuffed man like the poor Scarecrow!"

"Is he stuffed?" asked the Lion, in surprise, as he watched her pick up the Scarecrow and set him upon his feet, while she patted him into shape again.

"Of course he's stuffed," replied Dorothy, who was still angry.

"That's why he went over so easily," remarked the Lion. "It astonished me to see him whirl around so. Is the other one stuffed also?"

"No," said Dorothy, "he's made of tin." And she helped the Woodman up again.

"That's why he nearly blunted my claws," said the Lion. "When they scratched against the tin it made a cold shiver run down my back. What is that little animal you are so tender of?"

"He is my dog, Toto," answered Dorothy.

"Is he made of tin, or stuffed?" asked the Lion.

"Neither. He's a—a—a meat dog," said the girl.

"Oh. He's a curious animal, and seems remarkably small, now that I look at him. No one would think of biting such a little thing except a coward like me," continued the Lion sadly.

"I didn't bite him," said the Lion, as he rubbed his nose with his paw.

"What makes you a coward?" asked Dorothy, looking at the great beast in wonder, for he was as big as a small horse.

"It's a mystery," replied the Lion. "I suppose I was born that way. All the other animals in the forest naturally expect me to be brave, for the Lion is everywhere thought to be the King of Beasts. I learned that if I roared very loudly every living thing was frightened and got out of my way. Whenever I've met a man I've been awfully scared; but I just roared at him, and he has always run away as fast as he could go. If the elephants and the tigers and the bears had ever tried to fight me, I should have run myself—I'm such a coward; but just as soon as they hear me roar they all try to get away from me, and of course I let them go."

"But that isn't right. The King of Beasts shouldn't be a coward," said the Scarecrow.

"I know it," returned the Lion, wiping a tear from his eye with the tip of his tail; "it is my great sorrow, and makes my life very unhappy. But whenever there is danger my heart begins to beat fast."

"Perhaps you have heart disease," said the Tin Woodman.

"It may be," said the Lion.

"If you have," continued the Tin Woodman, "you ought to be glad, for it proves you have a heart. For my part, I have no heart; so I cannot have heart disease."

"Perhaps," said the Lion thoughtfully, "if I had no heart I should not be a coward."

"Have you brains?" asked the Scarecrow.

"I suppose so. I've never looked to see," replied the Lion.

"I am going to the great Oz to ask him to give me some," remarked the Scarecrow, "for my head is stuffed with straw."

"And I am going to ask him to give me a heart," said the Woodman.

"And I am going to ask him to send Toto and me back to Kansas," added Dorothy.

"Do you think Oz could give me courage?" asked the cowardly Lion.

"Just as easily as he could give me brains," said the Scarecrow.

"Or give me a heart," said the Tin Woodman.

"Or send me back to Kansas," said Dorothy.

"Then, if you don't mind, I'll go with you," said the Lion, "for my life is simply unbearable without a bit of courage."

"You will be very welcome," answered Dorothy, "for you will help keep away the other wild beasts. It seems to me they must be more cowardly than you are if they allow you to scare them so easily."

"They really are," said the Lion; "but that doesn't make me any braver, and as long as I know myself to be a coward I shall be unhappy."

So once more the little company set off upon the journey, the Lion walking with stately strides at Dorothy's side. Toto did not approve this new comrade at first, for he could not forget how nearly he had been crushed between the Lion's great jaws; but after a time he became more at ease, and presently Toto and the Cowardly Lion had grown to be good friends.

During the rest of that day there was no other adventure to mar the peace of their journey. Once, indeed, the Tin Woodman stepped upon a beetle that was crawling along the road, and killed the poor little thing. This made the Tin Woodman very unhappy, for he was always careful not to hurt any living creature; and as he walked along he wept several tears of sorrow and regret. These tears ran slowly down his face and over the hinges of his jaw, and there they rusted. When Dorothy presently asked him a question the Tin Woodman could not open his mouth, for his jaws were tightly rusted together. He became greatly frightened at this and made many motions to Dorothy to relieve him, but she could not understand. The Lion was also puzzled to know what was wrong. But the Scarecrow seized the oilcan from Dorothy's basket and oiled the Woodman's jaws, so that after a few moments he could talk as well as before.

"This will serve me a lesson," said he, "to look where I step. For if I should kill another bug or beetle I should surely cry again, and crying rusts my jaw so that I cannot speak."

Thereafter he walked very carefully, with his eyes on the road, and when he saw a tiny ant toiling by he would step over it, so as not to harm it. The Tin Woodman knew very well he had no heart, and therefore he took great care never to be cruel or unkind to anything.

"You people with hearts," he said, "have something to guide you, and need never do wrong; but I have no heart, and so I must be very careful. When Oz gives me a heart, of course, I needn't mind so much." ■

From
Charlotte's Web
E. B. White

This is a story about Wilbur the pig, who has been raised by a young girl named Fern. Wilbur has come to live on the farm of Fern's uncle and aunt, Mr. and Mrs. Zuckerman. He has met the hired hand, Lurvy, and a number of animals, but he is bored and lonely. That is, until Charlotte the spider arrives. . . .

The next day was rainy and dark. Rain fell on the roof of the barn and dripped steadily from the eaves. Rain fell in the barnyard and ran in crooked courses down into the lane where thistles and pigweed grew. Rain spattered against Mrs. Zuckerman's kitchen windows and came gushing out of the downspouts. Rain fell on the backs of the sheep as they grazed in the meadow. When the sheep tired of standing in the rain, they walked slowly up the lane and into the fold.

Rain upset Wilbur's plans. Wilbur had planned to go out, this day, and dig a new hole in his yard. He had other plans, too. His plans for the day went something like this:

Breakfast at six-thirty. Skim milk, crusts, middlings, bits of doughnuts, wheat cakes with drops of maple syrup sticking to them, potato skins, leftover custard pudding with raisins, and bits of Shredded Wheat.

Breakfast would be finished at seven.

From seven to eight, Wilbur planned to have a talk with Templeton, the rat that lived under his trough. Talking with Templeton was not the most interesting occupation in the world but it was better than nothing.

From eight to nine, Wilbur planned to take a nap outdoors in the sun.

From nine to eleven he planned to dig a hole, or trench, and possibly find something good to eat buried in the dirt.

From eleven to twelve he planned to stand still and watch flies on the boards, watch bees in the clover, and watch swallows in the air.

Twelve o'clock—lunchtime. Middlings, warm water, apple parings, meat gravy, carrot scrapings, meat scraps, stale hominy, and the wrapper off a package of cheese. Lunch would be over at one.

From one to two, Wilbur planned to sleep.

From two to three, he planned to scratch itchy places by rubbing against the fence.

From three to four, he planned to stand perfectly still and think of what it was like to be alive, and to wait for Fern.

At four would come supper. Skim milk, provender, leftover sandwich from Lurvy's lunchbox, prune skins, a morsel of this, a bit of that, fried potatoes, marmalade drippings, a little more of this, a little more of that, a piece of baked apple, a scrap of upsidedown cake.

Wilbur had gone to sleep thinking about these plans. He awoke at six and saw the rain, and it seemed as though he couldn't bear it.

"I get everything all beautifully planned out and it has to go and rain," he said.

For a while he stood gloomily indoors. Then he walked to the door and looked out. Drops of rain struck his face. His yard was cold and wet. His trough had an inch of rainwater in it. Templeton was nowhere to be seen.

"Are you out there, Templeton?" called Wilbur. There was no answer. Suddenly Wilbur felt lonely and friendless.

"One day just like another," he groaned. "I'm very young, I have no real friend here in the barn, it's going to rain all morning and all afternoon, and Fern won't come in such bad weather. Oh, *honestly*!" And Wilbur was crying again, for the second time in two days.

At six-thirty Wilbur heard the banging of a pail. Lurvy was standing outside in the rain, stirring up breakfast.

"C'mon, pig!" said Lurvy.

Wilbur did not budge. Lurvy dumped the slops, scraped the pail, and walked away. He noticed that something was wrong with the pig.

Wilbur didn't want food, he wanted love. He wanted a friend—someone who would play with him. He mentioned this to the goose, who was sitting quietly in a corner of the sheepfold.

"Will you come over and play with me?" he asked.

"Sorry, sonny, sorry," said the goose. "I'm sitting-sitting on my eggs. Eight of them. Got to keep them toasty-oasty-oasty warm. I have to stay right here, I'm no flibberty-ibberty-gibbet. I do not play when there are eggs to hatch. I'm expecting goslings."

"Well, I didn't think you were expecting woodpeckers," said Wilbur, bitterly.

Wilbur next tried one of the lambs.

"Will you please play with me?" he asked.

"Certainly not," said the lamb. "In the first place, I cannot get into your pen, as I am not old enough to jump over the fence. In the second place, I am not interested in pigs. Pigs mean less than nothing to me."

"What do you mean, *less* than nothing?" replied Wilbur. "I don't think there is any such thing as *less* than nothing. Nothing is absolutely the limit of nothingness. It's the lowest you can go. It's the end of the line. How can something be less than nothing? If there were something that was less than nothing, then nothing would not be nothing, it would be something—even though it's just a very little bit of something. But if nothing is *nothing*, then nothing has nothing that is less than *it* is."

"Oh, be quiet!" said the lamb. "Go play by yourself! I don't play with pigs."

Sadly, Wilbur lay down and listened to the rain. Soon he saw the rat climbing down a slanting board that he used as a stairway.

Friendless, dejected, and hungry, he threw himself down in the manure and sobbed.

GARTH WILLIAMS/HARPER & ROW

"Will you play with me, Templeton?" asked Wilbur.

"Play?" said Templeton, twirling his whiskers. "Play? I hardly know the meaning of the word."

"Well," said Wilbur, "it means to have fun, to frolic, to run and skip and make merry."

"I never do those things if I can avoid them," replied the rat, sourly. "I prefer to spend my time eating, gnawing, spying, and hiding. I am a glutton but not a merrymaker. Right now I am on my way to your trough to eat your breakfast, since you haven't got sense enough to eat it yourself." And Templeton, the rat, crept stealthily along the wall and disappeared into a private tunnel that he had dug between the door and the trough in Wilbur's yard. Templeton was a crafty rat, and he had things pretty much his own way. The tunnel was an example of his skill and cunning. The tunnel enabled him to get from the barn to his hiding place under the pig trough without coming out into the open. He had tunnels and runways all over Mr. Zuckerman's farm and could get from one place to another without being seen. Usually he slept during the daytime and was abroad only after dark.

Wilbur watched him disappear into his tunnel. In a moment he saw the rat's sharp nose poke out from underneath the wooden trough. Cautiously Templeton pulled himself up over the edge of the trough. This was almost more than Wilbur could stand: on this dreary, rainy day to see his breakfast being eaten by somebody else. He knew Templeton was getting soaked, out there in the pouring rain, but even that didn't comfort him. Friendless, dejected, and hungry, he threw himself down in the manure and sobbed.

Late that afternoon, Lurvy went to Mr. Zuckerman. "I think there's something wrong with that pig of yours. He hasn't touched his food."

"Give him two spoonfuls of sulphur and a little molasses," said Mr. Zuckerman.

Wilbur couldn't believe what was happening to him when Lurvy caught him and forced the medicine down his throat. This was certainly the worst day of his life. He didn't know whether he could endure the awful loneliness any more.

Darkness settled over everything. Soon there were only shadows and the noises of the sheep chewing their cuds, and occasionally the rattle of a cow-chain up overhead. You can imagine Wilbur's surprise when, out of the darkness, came a small voice he had never heard before. It sounded rather thin, but pleasant. "Do you want a friend, Wilbur?" it said. "I'll be a friend to you. I've watched you all day and I like you."

"But I can't see you," said Wilbur, jumping to his feet. "Where are you? And *who* are you?"

"I'm right up here," said the voice. "Go to sleep. You'll see me in the morning."

The night seemed long. Wilbur's stomach was empty and his mind was full. And when your stomach is empty and your mind is full, it's always hard to sleep.

A dozen times during the night Wilbur woke and stared into the blackness, listening to the sounds and trying to figure out what time it was. A barn is never perfectly quiet. Even at midnight there is usually something stirring.

The first time he woke, he heard Templeton gnawing a hole in the grain bin. Templeton's teeth scraped loudly against the wood and made quite a racket. "That crazy rat!" thought Wilbur. "Why does he have to stay up all night, grinding his clashers and destroying people's property? Why can't he go to sleep, like any decent animal?"

The second time Wilbur woke, he heard the goose turning on her nest and chuckling to herself.

"What time is it?" whispered Wilbur to the goose.

"Probably-obably-obably about half-past eleven," said the goose. "Why aren't you asleep, Wilbur?"

"Too many things on my mind," said Wilbur.

"Well," said the goose, "that's not *my* trouble. I have nothing at all on my mind, but I've too many things under my behind. Have you ever tried to sleep while sitting on eight eggs?"

"No," replied Wilbur. "I suppose it *is* uncomfortable. How long does it take a goose egg to hatch?"

"Approximately-oximately thirty days, all told," answered the goose. "But I cheat a little. On warm afternoons, I just pull a little straw over the eggs and go out for a walk."

Wilbur yawned and went back to sleep. In his dreams he heard again the voice saying, "I'll be a friend to you. Go to sleep—you'll see me in the morning."

About half an hour before dawn, Wilbur woke and listened. The barn was still dark. The sheep lay motionless. Even the goose was quiet. Overhead, on the main floor, nothing stirred: the cows were resting, the horses dozed. Templeton had quit work and gone off somewhere on an errand. The only sound was a slight scraping noise from the rooftop, where the weather vane swung back and forth. Wilbur loved the barn when it was like this—calm and quiet, waiting for light.

"Day is almost here," he thought.

Through a small window, a faint gleam appeared. One by one the stars went out. Wilbur could see the goose a few feet away. She sat with head tucked under a wing. Then he could see the sheep and the lambs. The sky lightened.

"Oh, beautiful day, it is here at last! Today I shall find my friend."

Wilbur looked everywhere. He searched his pen thoroughly. He examined the window ledge, stared up at the ceiling. But he saw nothing new. Finally he decided he would have to speak up. He hated to break the lovely stillness of dawn by using his voice, but he couldn't think of any other way to locate the mysterious new friend who was nowhere to be seen. So Wilbur cleared his throat.

"Attention, please!" he said in a loud, firm voice. "Will the party who addressed me at bedtime last night kindly make himself or herself known by giving an appropriate sign or signal!"

Wilbur paused and listened. All the other animals lifted their heads and stared at him. Wilbur blushed. But he was determined to get in touch with his unknown friend.

"Attention, please!" he said. "I will repeat the

"How are you? Good Morning! Salutations!"

GARTH WILLIAMS/HARPER & ROW

message. Will the party who addressed me at bedtime last night kindly speak up. Please tell me where you are, if you are my friend!"

The sheep looked at each other in disgust.

"Stop your nonsense, Wilbur!" said the oldest sheep. "If you have a new friend here, you are probably disturbing his rest; and the quickest way to spoil a friendship is to wake somebody up in the morning before he is ready. How can you be sure your friend is an early riser?"

"I beg everyone's pardon," whispered Wilbur. "I didn't mean to be objectionable."

He lay down meekly in the manure, facing the door. He did not know it, but his friend was very near. And the old sheep was right—the friend was still asleep.

Soon Lurvy appeared with slops for breakfast. Wilbur rushed out, ate everything in a hurry, and licked the trough. The sheep moved off down the lane, the gander waddled along behind them, pulling grass. And then, just as Wilbur was settling down for his morning nap, he heard again the thin voice that had addressed him the night before.

"Salutations!" said the voice.

Wilbur jumped to his feet. "Salu-*what?*" he cried.

"Salutations!" repeated the voice.

"What are *they,* and where are *you?*" screamed Wilbur. "Please, *please,* tell me where you are. And what are salutations?"

"Salutations are greetings," said the voice. "When I say 'salutations,' it's just my fancy way of saying hello or good morning. Actually, it's a silly expression, and I am surprised that I used it at all. As for my whereabouts, that's easy. Look up here in the corner of the doorway! Here I am. Look, I'm waving!"

At last Wilbur saw the creature that had spoken to him in such a kindly way. Stretched across the upper part of the doorway was a big spiderweb, and hanging from the top of the web, head down, was a large grey spider. She was about the size of a gumdrop. She had eight legs, and she was waving one of them at Wilbur in friendly greeting. "See me now?" she asked.

"Oh, yes indeed," said Wilbur. "Yes indeed! How are you? Good morning! Salutations! Very pleased to meet you. What is your name, please? May I have your name?"

"My name," said the spider, "is Charlotte."

"Charlotte what?" asked Wilbur, eagerly.

"Charlotte A. Cavatica. But just call me Charlotte."

"I think you're beautiful," said Wilbur.

"Well, I *am* pretty," replied Charlotte. "There's no denying that. Almost all spiders are rather nice-looking. I'm not as flashy as some, but I'll do. I wish I could see you, Wilbur, as clearly as you can see me."

"Why can't you?" asked the pig. "I'm right here."

"Yes, but I'm nearsighted," replied Charlotte. "I've always been dreadfully nearsighted. It's good in some ways, not so good in others. Watch me wrap up this fly."

A fly that had been crawling along Wilbur's trough had flown up and blundered into the lower part of Charlotte's web and was tangled in the sticky threads. The fly was beating its wings furiously, trying to break loose and free itself.

"First," said Charlotte, "I dive at him." She plunged headfirst toward the fly. As she dropped, a tiny silken thread unwound from her rear end.

"Next, I wrap him up." She grabbed the fly, threw a few jets of silk around it, and rolled it over and over, wrapping it so that it couldn't move. Wilbur watched in horror. He could hardly believe what he was seeing, and although he detested flies, he was sorry for this one.

"There!" said Charlotte. "Now I knock him out, so he'll be more comfortable." She bit the fly. "He can't feel a thing now," she remarked. "He'll make a perfect breakfast for me."

"You mean you *eat* flies?" gasped Wilbur.

"Certainly. Flies, bugs, grasshoppers, choice beetles, moths, butterflies, tasty cockroaches, gnats, midges, daddy longlegs, centipedes, mosquitoes, crickets—anything that is careless enough to get caught in my web. I have to live, don't I?"

"Why, yes, of course," said Wilbur. "Do they taste good?"

"Delicious. Of course, I don't really eat them. I drink them—drink their blood. I love blood," said Charlotte, and her pleasant, thin voice grew even thinner and more pleasant.

"Don't say that!" groaned Wilbur. "Please don't say things like that!"

"Why not? It's true, and I have to say what is true. I am not entirely happy about my diet of flies and bugs, but it's the way I'm made. A spider has to pick up a living somehow or other, and I happen to be a trapper. I just naturally build a web and trap flies and other insects. My mother was a trapper before me. Her mother was a trapper before her. All our family have been trappers. Way back for thousands and thousands of years we spiders have been laying for flies and bugs."

"It's a miserable inheritance," said Wilbur, gloomily. He was sad because his new friend was so bloodthirsty.

"Yes, it is," agreed Charlotte. "But I can't help it. I don't know how the first spider in the early days of the world happened to think up this fancy idea of spinning a web, but she did, and it was clever of her, too. And since then, all of us spiders have had to work the same trick. It's not a bad pitch, on the whole."

"It's cruel," replied Wilbur, who did not intend to be argued out of his position.

"Well, *you* can't talk" said Charlotte. "*You* have your meals brought to you in a pail. Nobody feeds me. I have to get my own living. I live by my wits. I have to be sharp and clever, lest I go hungry. I have to think things out, catch what I can, take what comes. And it just so happens, my friend, that what comes is flies and insects and bugs. And *further*more," said Charlotte, shaking one of her legs, "do you realize that if I didn't catch bugs and eat them, bugs would increase and multiply and get so numerous that they'd destroy the earth, wipe out everything?"

"Really?" said Wilbur. "I wouldn't want *that* to happen. Perhaps your web is a good thing after all."

The goose had been listening to this conversation and chuckling to herself. "There are a lot of things Wilbur doesn't know about life," she thought. "He's really a very innocent little pig. He doesn't even know what's going to happen to him around Christmastime; he has no idea that Mr. Zuckerman and Lurvy are plotting to kill him." And the goose raised herself a bit and poked her eggs a little further under her so that they would receive the full heat from her warm body and soft feathers.

Charlotte stood quietly over the fly, preparing to eat it. Wilbur lay down and closed his eyes. He was tired from his wakeful night and from the excitement of meeting someone for the first time. A breeze brought him the smell of clover—the sweet-smelling world beyond his fence. "Well," he thought, "I've got a new friend, all right. But what a gamble friendship is! Charlotte is fierce, brutal, scheming, bloodthirsty—everything I don't like. How can I learn to like her, even though she is pretty and, of course, clever?"

Wilbur was merely suffering the doubts and fears that often go with finding a new friend. In good time he was to discover that he was mistaken about Charlotte. Underneath her rather bold and cruel exterior, she had a kind heart, and she was to prove loyal and true to the very end. ∎

Rikki-tikki-tavi
Rudyard Kipling

This tale is set in India and concerns one young, brave mongoose, a furry little animal who is a friend to humans and a tireless enemy of the deadly cobra.

This is the story of the great war that Rikki-tikki-tavi fought single-handed, through the bathrooms of the big bungalow in Segowlee cantonment. Darzee the tailorbird helped him, and Chuchundra the muskrat, who never comes out into the middle of the floor, but always creeps round by the wall, gave him advice; but Rikki-tikki did the real fighting.

He was a mongoose, rather like a little cat in his fur and his tail, but quite like a weasel in his head and his habits. His eyes and the end of his restless nose were pink; he could scratch himself anywhere he pleased, with any leg, front or back, that he chose to use; he could fluff up his tail till it looked like a bottle-brush, and his war cry as he scuttled through the long grass was: *"Rikk-tikk-tikki-tikki-tchk!"*

One day, a high summer flood washed him out of the burrow where he lived with his father and mother, and carried him, kicking and clucking, down a roadside ditch. He found a little wisp of grass floating there, and clung to it till he lost his senses. When he revived, he was lying in the hot sun on the middle of a garden path, very draggled indeed, and a small boy was saying, "Here's a dead mongoose. Let's have a funeral."

"No," said his mother; "let's take him in and dry him. Perhaps he isn't really dead."

They took him into the house, and a big man picked him up between his finger and thumb and said he was not dead but half choked; so they wrapped him in cotton wool, and warmed him, and he opened his eyes and sneezed.

"Now," said the big man (he was an Englishman who had just moved into the bungalow), "don't frighten him, and we'll see what he'll do."

It is the hardest thing in the world to frighten a mongoose, because he is eaten up from nose to tail with curiosity. The motto of all the mongoose family is "Run and find out," and Rikki-tikki was a true mongoose. He looked at the cotton wool, decided that it was not good to eat, ran all round the table, sat up and put his fur in order, scratched himself, and jumped on the small boy's shoulder.

"Don't be frightened, Teddy," said his father. "That's his way of making friends."

"Ouch! He's tickling under my chin," said Teddy.

Rikki-tikki looked down between the boy's collar and neck, snuffed at his ear, and climbed down to the floor, where he sat rubbing his nose.

"Good gracious," said Teddy's mother, "and that's a wild creature! I suppose he's so tame because we've been kind to him."

"All mongooses are like that," said her husband. "If Teddy doesn't pick him up by the tail, or try to put him in a cage, he'll run in and out of the house all day long. Let's give him something to eat."

They gave him a little piece of raw meat. Rikki-tikki liked it immensely, and when it was finished he went out into the veranda and sat in the sunshine and fluffed up his fur to make it dry to the roots. Then he felt better.

"There are more things to find out about in this house," he said to himself, "than all my family could find out in all their lives. I shall certainly stay and find out."

He spent all that day roaming over the house. He nearly drowned himself in the bathtubs, put his nose into the ink on a writing table, and burned it on the end of the big man's cigar, for he climbed up in the big man's lap to see how writing was done. At nightfall he ran into Teddy's nursery to watch how kerosene lamps were lighted, and when Teddy went to bed Rikki-tikki climbed up too; but he was a restless companion, because he had to get up and attend to every noise all through the night, and find out what made it. Teddy's mother and father came in, the last thing, to look at their boy, and Rikki-tikki was awake on the pillow. "I don't like that," said Teddy's mother; "he may bite the child." "He'll do no such thing," said the father. "Teddy's safer with that little beast than if he had a bloodhound to watch him. If a snake came into the nursery now——"

But Teddy's mother wouldn't think of anything so awful.

Early in the morning Rikki-tikki came to early breakfast in the veranda riding on Teddy's shoulder, and they gave him banana and some boiled egg; and he sat on all their laps one after the other, because every well-brought-up mongoose always hopes to be a house-mongoose some day and have rooms to run about in, and Rikki-tikki's mother (she used to live in the General's house at Segowlee) had carefully told Rikki what to do if ever he came across white men.

Then Rikki-tikki went out into the garden to see what was to be seen. It was a large garden, only half cultivated, with bushes as big as summer houses of Marshal Niel roses, lime and orange trees, clumps of bamboos, and thickets of high grass. Rikki-tikki licked his lips. "This is a splendid hunting ground," he said, and his tail grew bottle-brushy at the thought of it, and he scuttled up and down the garden, snuffing here and there till he heard very sorrowful voices in a thorn bush.

It was Darzee, the tailorbird, and his wife. They had made a beautiful nest by pulling two big leaves together and stitching them up the edges with fibers, and had filled the hollow with cotton and downy fluff. The nest swayed to and fro, as they sat on the rim and cried.

"What is the matter?" asked Rikki-tikki.

"We are very miserable," said Darzee. "One of our babies fell out of the nest yesterday and Nag ate him."

"H'm!" said Rikki-tikki, "that is very sad—but I am a stranger here. Who is Nag?"

Darzee and his wife only cowered down in the nest without answering, for from the thick grass at the foot of the bush there came a low hiss—a horrid cold sound that made Rikki-tikki jump back two clear feet. Then inch by inch out of the grass rose up the head and spread hood of Nag, the big black cobra, and he was five feet long from tongue to tail. When he had lifted one-third of himself clear of the ground, he stayed balancing to and fro exactly as a dandelion tuft balances in the wind, and he looked at Rikki-tikki with the wicked snake's eyes that never change their expression, whatever the snake may be thinking of.

"Who is Nag?" he said. "*I* am Nag. The great god Brahm put his mark upon all our people when the first cobra spread his hood to keep the sun off Brahm as he slept. Look, and be afraid!"

He spread out his hood more than ever, and Rikki-tikki saw the spectacle mark on the back of it that looks exactly like the eye part of a hook-and-eye fastening. He was afraid for the minute; but it is impossible for a mongoose to stay frightened for any length of time, and though Rikki-tikki had never met a live cobra before, his mother had fed him on dead ones, and he knew that all a grown mongoose's business in life was

ILLUSTRATIONS BY KURT WIESE FROM *THE JUNGLE BOOK* BY RUDYARD KIPLING. COPYRIGHT 1932 BY RUDYARD KIPLING. REPRINTED BY PERMISSION OF DOUBLEDAY & CO., INC.

Then inch by inch out of the grass rose up the head and spread hood of Nag.

to fight and eat snakes. Nag knew that too, and at the bottom of his cold heart he was afraid.

"Well," said Rikki-tikki, and his tail began to fluff up again, "marks or no marks, do you think it is right for you to eat fledglings out of a nest?"

Nag was thinking to himself, and watching the least little movement in the grass behind Rikki-tikki. He knew that mongooses in the garden meant death sooner or later for him and his family; but he wanted to get Rikki-tikki off his guard. So he dropped his head a little, and put it on one side.

"Let us talk," he said. "You eat eggs. Why should not I eat birds?"

"Behind you! Look behind you!" sang Darzee.

Rikki-tikki knew better than to waste time in staring. He jumped up in the air as high as he could go, and just under him whizzed by the head of Nagaina, Nag's wicked wife. She had crept up behind him as he was talking, to make an end of him; and he heard her savage hiss as the stroke missed. He came down almost across her back, and if he had been an old mongoose he would have known that then was the time to break her back with one bite; but he was afraid of the terrible lashing return-stroke of the cobra. He bit, indeed, but did not bite long enough, and he jumped clear of the whisking tail, leaving Nagaina torn and angry.

"Wicked, wicked Darzee!" said Nag, lashing up as high as he could reach toward the nest in the thorn bush; but Darzee had built it out of reach of snakes, and it only swayed to and fro.

Rikki-tikki felt his eyes growing red and hot (when a mongoose's eyes grow red, he is angry), and he sat back on his tail and hind legs like a little kangaroo, and looked all around him, and chattered with rage. But Nag and Nagaina had disappeared into the grass. When a snake misses its stroke, it never says anything or gives any sign of what it means to do next. Rikki-tikki did not care to follow them, for he did not feel sure that he could manage two snakes at once. So he trotted off to the gravel path near the house, and sat down to think. It was a serious matter for him.

If you read the old books of natural history, you will find they say that when the mongoose fights the snake and happens to get bitten, he runs off and eats some herb that cures him. That is not true. The victory is only a matter of quickness of eye and quickness of foot—snake's blow against mongoose's jump—and as no eye can follow the motion of a snake's head when it strikes, that makes things much more wonderful than any magic herb. Rikki-tikki knew he was a young mongoose, and it made him all the more pleased to think that he had managed to escape a blow from behind. It gave him confidence in himself, and when Teddy came running down the path, Rikki-tikki was ready to be petted.

But just as Teddy was stooping, something flinched a little in the dust, and a tiny voice said: "Be careful. I am death!" It was Karait, the dusty brown snakeling that lies for choice on the dusty earth; and his bite is as dangerous as the cobra's. But he is so small that nobody thinks of him, and so he does the more harm to people.

Rikki-tikki's eyes grew red again, and he danced up to Karait with the peculiar rocking, swaying motion that he had inherited from his family. It looks very funny, but it is so perfectly balanced a gait that you can fly off from it at any angle you please; and in dealing with snakes this is an advantage. If Rikki-tikki had only known, he was doing a much more dangerous thing than fighting Nag for Karait is so small, and can turn so quickly, that unless Rikki bit him close to the back of the head, he would get the return stroke in his eye or lip. But Rikki did not know: his eyes were all red, and he rocked back and forth, looking for a good place to hold. Karait struck out. Rikki jumped sideways and tried to run in, but the wicked little dusty gray head lashed within a fraction of his shoulder, and he had to jump over the body, and the head followed his heels close.

Teddy shouted to the house, "Oh, look here! Our mongoose is killing a snake," and Rikki-tikki heard a scream from Teddy's mother. His father ran out with a stick, but by the time he came up, Karait had lunged out once too far, and Rikki-tikki had sprung, jumped on the snake's back, dropped his head far between his fore legs, bitten as high up the back as he could get hold, and rolled away. That bite paralyzed Karait, and Rikki-tikki was just going to eat him up from the tail, after the custom of his family at dinner, when he remembered that a full meal makes a slow mongoose, and if he wanted all his strength and quickness ready, he must keep himself thin.

He went away for a dust bath under the castor oil bushes, while Teddy's father beat the dead Karait. "What is the use of that?" thought Rikki-tikki. "I have settled it all"; and then Teddy's mother picked him up from the dust and hugged him, crying that he had saved Teddy from death, and Teddy's father said that he was a providence, and Teddy looked on with big scared eyes. Rikki-tikki was rather amused at all the fuss, which, of course, he did not understand. Teddy's mother might just as well have petted Teddy for playing in the dust. Rikki was thoroughly enjoying himself.

That night, at dinner, walking to and fro among the wine glasses on the table, he could have stuffed himself three times over with nice things; but he remembered Nag and Nagaina, and though it was very pleasant to be patted and petted by Teddy's mother, and to sit on Teddy's shoulder, his eyes would get red from time to time, and he would go off into his long war cry of *"Rikk-tikk-tikki-tikki-tchk!"*

Teddy carried him off to bed, and insisted on Rikki-tikki sleeping under his chin. Rikki-tikki was too well bred to bite or scratch, but as soon as Teddy was asleep he went off for his nightly walk round the house, and in the dark he ran up against Chuchundra, the muskrat, creeping round by the wall. Chuchundra is a broken-hearted little beast. He whimpers and cheeps all the night, trying to make up his mind to run into the middle of the room, but he never gets there.

"Don't kill me," said Chuchundra, almost weeping. "Rikki-tikki, don't kill me."

"Do you think a snake killer kills muskrats?" said Rikki-tikki scornfully.

"Those who kill snakes get killed by snakes," said Chuchundra, more sorrowfully than ever. "And how am I to be sure that Nag won't mistake me for you some dark night?"

"There's not the least danger," said Rikki-tikki; "but Nag is in the garden, and I know you don't go there."

"My cousin Chua, the rat, told me—" said Chuchundra, and then he stopped.

"Told you what?"

"H'sh! Nag is everywhere, Rikki-tikki. You should have talked to Chua in the garden."

"I didn't—so you must tell me. Quick, Chuchundra, or I'll bite you!"

Chuchundra sat down and cried till the tears rolled off his whiskers. "I am a very poor man," he sobbed. "I never had spirit enough to run out into the middle of the room. H'sh! I mustn't tell you anything. Can't you *hear*, Rikki-tikki?"

Rikki-tikki listened. The house was as still as still, but he thought he could just catch the faintest *scratch-scratch* in the world—a noise as faint as that of a wasp walking on a windowpane—the dry scratch of a snake's scales on brickwork.

"That's Nag or Nagaina," he said to himself; "and he is crawling into the bathroom sluice. You're right, Chuchundra; I should have talked to Chua."

He stole off to Teddy's bathroom, but there was nothing there, and then to Teddy's mother's bathroom. At the bottom of the smooth plaster wall there was a brick pulled out to make a sluice for the bathwater, and as Rikki-tikki stole in by the masonry curb where the bath is put, he heard Nag and Nagaina whispering together outside in the moonlight.

"When the house is emptied of people," said Nagaina to her husband, "*he* will have to go away, and then the garden will be our own again. Go in quietly, and remember that the big man who killed Karait is the first one to bite. Then come out and tell me, and we will hunt for Rikki-tikki together."

"But are you sure that there is anything to be gained by killing the people?" said Nag.

"Everything. When there were no people in the bungalow, did we have any mongoose in the garden? So long as the bungalow is empty, we are king and queen of the garden; and remember that as soon as our eggs in the melon bed hatch (as they may tomorrow), our children will need room and quiet."

"I had not thought of that," said Nag. "I will go, but there is no need that we should hunt for Rikki-tikki afterward. I will kill the big man and

his wife, and the child if I can, and come away quietly. Then the bungalow will be empty, and Rikki-tikki will go."

Rikki-tikki tingled all over with rage and hatred at this, and then Nag's head came through the sluice, and his five feet of cold body followed it. Angry as he was, Rikki-tikki was very frightened as he saw the size of the big cobra. Nag coiled himself up, raised his head, and looked into the bathroom in the dark, and Rikki could see his eyes glitter.

"Now, if I kill him here, Nagaina will know; and if I fight him on the open floor, the odds are in his favor. What am I to do?" said Rikki-tikki-tavi.

Nag waved to and fro, and then Rikki-tikki heard him drinking from the biggest water jar that was used to fill the bath. "That is good," said the snake. "Now, when Karait was killed, the big man had a stick. He may have that stick still, but when he comes in to bathe in the morning he will not have a stick. I shall wait here till he comes. Nagaina—do you hear me?—I shall wait here in the cool till daytime."

There was no answer from outside, so Rikki-tikki knew Nagaina had gone away. Nag coiled himself down, coil by coil, round the bulge at the bottom of the water jar, and Rikki-tikki stayed still as death. After an hour he began to move, muscle by muscle, toward the jar. Nag was asleep, and Rikki-tikki looked at his big back, wondering which would be the best place for a good hold. "If I don't break his back at the first jump," said Rikki, "he can still fight; and if he fights—O Rikki!" He looked at the thickness of the neck below the hood, but that was too much for him; and a bite near the tail would only make Nag savage.

"It must be the head," he said at last; "the head above the hood; and, when I am once there, I must not let go."

Then he jumped. The head was lying a little clear of the water jar, under the curve of it; and, as his teeth met, Rikki braced his back against the bulge of the red earthenware to hold down

He was battered to and fro as a rat is shaken by a dog.

the head. This gave him just one second's purchase, and he made the most of it. Then he was battered to and fro as a rat is shaken by a dog—to and fro on the floor, up and down, and round in great circles; but his eyes were red, and he held on as the body cartwhipped over the floor, upsetting the tin dipper and the soap dish and the flesh-brush, and banged against the tin side of the bath. As he held he closed his jaws tighter and tighter, for he made sure he would be banged to death, and, for the honor of his family, he preferred to be found with his teeth locked. He was dizzy, aching, and felt shaken to pieces when something went off like a thunderclap just behind him; a hot wind knocked him senseless and red fire singed his fur. The big man had been wakened by the noise, and had fired both barrels of a shotgun into Nag just behind the hood.

Rikki-tikki held on with his eyes shut, for now he was quite sure he was dead; but the head did not move, and the big man picked him up and said: "It's the mongoose again, Alice; the little chap has saved *our* lives now." Then Teddy's mother came in with a very white face, and saw what was left of Nag, and Rikki-tikki dragged himself to Teddy's bedroom and spent half the rest of the night shaking himself tenderly to find out whether he really was broken into forty pieces, as he fancied.

When morning came he was very stiff, but well pleased with his doings. "Now I have Nagaina to settle with, and she will be worse than five Nags, and there's no knowing when the eggs she spoke of will hatch. Goodness! I must go and see Darzee," he said.

Without waiting for breakfast, Rikki-tikki ran to the thorn bush where Darzee was singing a song of triumph at the top of his voice. The news of Nag's death was all over the garden, for the sweeper had thrown the body on the rubbish heap.

"Oh, you stupid tuft of feathers!" said Rikki-tikki, angrily. "Is this the time to sing?"

"Nag is dead—is dead—is dead!" sang Darzee. "The valiant Rikki-tikki caught him by the head and held fast. The big man brought the bang-stick and Nag fell in two pieces! He will never eat my babies again."

"All that's true enough; but where's Nagaina?" said Rikki-tikki, looking carefully round him.

"Nagaina came to the bathroom sluice and called for Nag," Darzee went on; "and Nag came out on the end of a stick—the sweeper picked him up on the end of a stick and threw him upon the rubbish heap. Let us sing about the great, the red-eyed Rikki-tikki!" and Darzee filled his throat and sang.

"If I could get up to your nest, I'd roll all your babies out!" said Rikki-tikki. "You don't know when to do the right thing at the right time. You're safe enough in your nest there, but it's war for me down here. Stop singing a minute, Darzee."

"For the great, the beautiful Rikki-tikki's sake I will stop," said Darzee. "What is it, O Killer of the terrible Nag?"

"Where is Nagaina, for the third time?"

"On the rubbish heap by the stables, mourning for Nag. Great is Rikki-tikki with the white teeth."

"Bother my white teeth! Have you ever heard where she keeps her eggs?"

"In the melon bed, on the end nearest the wall, where the sun strikes nearly all day. She had them there weeks ago."

"And you never thought it worth while to tell me? The end nearest the wall, you said?"

"Rikki-tikki, you are not going to eat her eggs?"

"Not eat exactly; no. Darzee, if you have a grain of sense you will fly off to the stables and pretend that your wing is broken, and let Nagaina chase you away to this bush! I must get to the melon bed, and if I went there now she'd see me."

Darzee was a featherbrained little fellow who could never hold more than one idea at a time in his head; and just because he knew that Nagaina's children were born in eggs like his own, he didn't think at first that it was fair to kill them. But his wife was a sensible bird, and she knew that cobra's eggs meant young cobras later on; so she flew off from the nest, and left Darzee to keep the babies warm, and continue his song about the death of Nag. Darzee was very like a man in some ways.

She fluttered in front of Nagaina by the rubbish heap, and cried out, "Oh, my wing is broken! The boy in the house threw a stone at me and broke it." Then she fluttered more desperately than ever.

Nagaina lifted up her head and hissed, "You warned Rikki-tikki when I would have killed him. Indeed and truly, you've chosen a bad place to be lame in." And she moved toward Darzee's wife, slipping along over the dust.

"The boy broke it with a stone!" shrieked Darzee's wife.

"Well! It may be some consolation to you when you're dead to know that I shall settle accounts with the boy. My husband lies on the rubbish heap this morning, but before night the boy in the house will lie very still. What is the use of running away? I am sure to catch you. Little fool, look at me!''

Darzee's wife knew better than to do *that,* for a bird who looks at a snake's eyes gets so frightened that she cannot move. Darzee's wife fluttered on, piping sorrowfully, and never leaving the ground, and Nagaina quickened her pace.

Rikki-tikki heard them going up the path from the stables, and he raced for the end of the melon patch near the wall. There, in the warm litter about the melons, very cunningly hidden, he found twenty-five eggs, about the size of a bantam's eggs, but with whitish skin instead of shell.

"I was not a day too soon," he said; for he could see the baby cobras curled up inside the skin, and he knew that the minute they were hatched they could each kill a man or a mongoose. He bit off the tops of the eggs as fast as he could, taking care to crush the young cobras, and turned over the litter from time to time to see whether he had missed any. At last there were only three eggs left, and Rikki-tikki began to chuckle to himself, when he heard Darzee's wife screaming:

"Rikki-tikki, I led Nagaina toward the house, and she has gone into the veranda, and—oh, come quickly—she means killing!"

Rikk-tikki smashed two eggs, and tumbled backward down the melon bed with the third egg in his mouth, and scuttled to the veranda as hard as he could put foot to the ground. Teddy and his mother and father were there at early breakfast; but Rikki-tikki saw that they were not eating anything. They sat stone-still, and their faces were white. Nagaina was coiled up on the matting by Teddy's chair, within easy striking distance of Teddy's bare leg, and she was swaying to and fro singing a song of triumph.

"Son of the big man that killed Nag," she hissed, "stay still. I am not ready yet. Wait a little. Keep very still, all you three. If you move I strike, and if you do not move I strike. Oh, foolish people, who killed my Nag!"

Teddy's eyes were fixed on his father, and all his father could do was to whisper, "Sit still, Teddy. You mustn't move. Teddy, keep still."

Then Rikki-tikki came up and cried, "Turn round, Nagaina; turn and fight!"

"All in good time," said she, without moving her eyes. "I will settle my account with *you* presently. Look at your friends, Rikki-tikki. They are still and white; they are afraid. They dare not move, and if you come a step nearer I strike."

"Look at your eggs," said Rikki-tikki, "in the melon bed near the wall. Go and look, Nagaina."

The big snake turned half round, and saw the egg on the veranda. "Ah-h! Give it to me," she said.

Rikki-tikki put his paws one on each side of the egg, and his eyes were blood-red. "What price for a snake's egg? For a young cobra? For a young king cobra? For the last—the very last of the brood? The ants are eating all the others down by the melon bed."

Nagaina spun clear round, forgetting everything for the sake of the one egg; and Rikki-tikki saw Teddy's father shoot out a big hand, catch Teddy by the shoulder and drag him across the little table with the tea cups, safe and out of reach of Nagaina.

"Tricked! Tricked! Tricked! *Rikk-tck-tck!*" chuckled Rikki-tikki. "The boy is safe, and it was I—I—I that caught Nag by the hood last night in the bathroom." Then he began to jump up and down, all four feet together, his head close to the floor. "He threw me to and fro, but he could not shake me off. He was dead before the big man blew him in two. I did it. *Rikki-tikki-tck-tck!* Come then, Nagaina. Come and fight with me. You shall not be a widow long."

Nagaina saw that she had lost her chance of killing Teddy, and the egg lay between Rikki-tikki's paws. "Give me the egg, Rikki-tikki. Give me the last of my eggs, and I will go away and never come back," she said, lowering her hood.

"Yes, you will go away, and you will never come back, for you will go to the rubbish heap with Nag. Fight, widow! The big man has gone for his gun! Fight!"

Rikki-tikki was bounding all round Nagaina, keeping just out of the reach of her stroke, his little eyes like hot coals. Nagaina gathered herself together, and flung out at him. Rikki-tikki jumped up and backward. Again and again and again she struck, and each time her head came with a whack on the matting of the veranda and she gathered herself together like a watch spring. Then Rikki-tikki danced in a circle to get behind her, and Nagaina spun round to keep her head to his head, so that the rustle of her tail on the matting sounded like dry leaves blown along by the wind.

He had forgotten the egg. It still lay on the veranda, and Nagaina came nearer and nearer to it, till at last, while Rikki-tikki was drawing breath, she caught it in her mouth, turned to the veranda steps, and flew like an arrow down the path, with Rikki-tikki behind her. When the cobra runs for

ILLUSTRATIONS BY KURT WIESE FROM *THE JUNGLE BOOK* BY RUDYARD KIPLING. COPYRIGHT 1932 BY RUDYARD KIPLING. REPRINTED BY PERMISSION OF DOUBLEDAY & CO., INC.

Rikki-tikki knew that he must catch her, or all the trouble would begin again.

her life, she goes like a whiplash flicked across a horse's neck.

Rikki-tikki knew that he must catch her, or all the trouble would begin again. She headed straight for the long grass by the thorn bush, and as he was running Rikki-tikki heard Darzee still singing his foolish little song of triumph. But Darzee's wife was wiser. She flew off her nest as Nagaina came along, and flapped her wings about Nagaina's head. If Darzee had helped they might have turned her, but Nagaina only lowered her hood and went on. Still, the instant's delay brought Rikki-tikki up to her, and as she plunged into the rathole where she and Nag used to live, his little white teeth were clenched on her tail, and he went down with her—and very few mongooses, however wise and old they may be, care to follow a cobra into its hole. It was dark in the hole; and Rikki-tikki never knew when it might open out and give Nagaina room to turn and strike at him. He held on savagely, and struck out his feet to act as brakes on the dark slope of the hot, moist earth.

Then the grass by the mouth of the hole stopped waving, and Darzee said: "It is all over with Rikki-tikki! We must sing his death song. Valiant Rikki-tikki is dead! For Nagaina will surely kill him underground."

So he sang a very mournful song that he made up all on the spur of the minute, and just as he got to the most touching part the grass quivered again, and Rikki-tikki, covered with dirt, dragged himself out of the hole leg by leg, licking his whiskers. Darzee stopped with a little shout. Rikki-tikki shook some of the dust out of his fur and sneezed. "It is all over," he said. "The widow will never come out again." And the red ants that live between the grass stems heard him, and began to troop down one after another to see if he had spoken the truth.

Rikki-tikki curled himself up in the grass and slept where he was—slept and slept till it was late in the afternoon, for he had done a hard day's work.

"Now," he said, when he awoke, "I will go back to the house. Tell the Coppersmith, Darzee, and he will tell the garden that Nagaina is dead."

The Coppersmith is a bird who makes a noise exactly like the beating of a little hammer on a copper pot; and the reason he is always making it is because he is the town crier to every Indian garden, and tells all the news to everybody who cares to listen. As Rikki-tikki went up the path, he heard his "attention" notes like a tiny dinner gong; and then the steady "*Ding-dong-tock!* Nag is dead—*dong!* Nagaina is dead! *Ding-dong-tock!*" That set all the birds in the garden singing, and the frogs croaking; for Nag and Nagaina used to eat frogs as well as little birds.

When Rikki got to the house, Teddy and Teddy's mother (she looked very white still, for she had been fainting) and Teddy's father came out and almost cried over him; and that night he ate all that was given him till he could eat no more, and went to bed on Teddy's shoulder, where Teddy's mother saw him when she came to look late at night.

"He saved our lives and Teddy's life," she said to her husband. "Just think, he saved all our lives."

Rikki-tikki woke up with a jump, for all the mongooses are light sleepers.

"Oh, it's you," said he. "What are you bothering for? All the cobras are dead; and if they weren't I'm here."

Rikki-tikki had a right to be proud of himself; but he did not grow too proud, and he kept that garden as a mongoose should keep it, with tooth and jump and spring and bite, till never a cobra dared show its head inside the walls. ∎

Rip Van Winkle

Washington Irving

Rip Van Winkle wakes from a 20-year nap to find his whole world changed—
for better or for worse.

By Woden, God of Saxons,
From whence comes Wensday, that is Wodensday,
Truth is a thing that ever I will keep
Unto thylke day in which I creep into
My sepulchre—
                                                    CARTWRIGHT

Whoever has made a voyage up the Hudson must remember the Kaatskill mountains. They are a dismembered branch of the great Appalachian family, and are seen away to the west of the river, swelling up to a noble height, and lording it over the surrounding country. Every change of season, every change of weather, indeed, every hour of the day, produces some change in the magical hues and shapes of these mountains, and they are regarded by all the good wives, far and near, as perfect barometers. When the weather is fair and settled, they are clothed in blue and purple, and print their bold outlines on the clear evening sky; but sometimes, when the rest of the landscape is cloudless, they will gather a hood of gray vapors about their summits, which, in the last rays of the setting sun, will glow and light up like a crown of glory.

At the foot of these fairy mountains, the voyager may have descried the light smoke curling up from a village, whose shingle roofs gleam among the trees, just where the blue tints of the upland melt away into the fresh green of the nearer landscape. It is a little village, of great antiquity, having been founded by some of the Dutch colonists in the early times of the province, just about the beginning of the government of the good Peter Stuyvesant, (may he rest in peace!) and there were some of the houses of the original settlers standing within a few years; built of small yellow bricks brought from Holland, having latticed windows and gable fronts, surmounted with weathercocks.

In that same village, and in one of these very houses (which, to tell the precise truth, was sadly timeworn and weather-beaten), there lived, many years since, while the country was yet a province of Great Britain, a simple, good-natured fellow of the name of Rip Van Winkle. He was a descendant of the Van Winkles who figured so gallantly in the chivalrous days of Peter Stuyvesant, and accompanied him to the siege of Fort Christina.

He inherited, however, but little of the martial character of his ancestors. I have observed that he was a simple, good-natured man; he was, moreover, a kind neighbor, and an obedient, henpecked husband. Indeed, to the latter circumstance might be owing that meekness of spirit which gained him such universal popularity; for those men are most apt to be obsequious and conciliating abroad, who are under the discipline of shrews at home. Their tempers, doubtless, are rendered pliant and malleable in the fiery furnace of domestic tribulation; and a curtain lecture is worth all the sermons in the world for teaching the virtues of patience and long-suffering. A termagant wife may, therefore, in some respects, be considered a tolerable blessing; and if so, Rip Van Winkle was thrice blessed.

Certain it is, that he was a great favorite among all the good wives of the village, who, as usual with the amiable sex, took his part in all family squabbles; and never failed, whenever they talked those matters over in their evening gossipings, to lay all the blame on Dame Van Winkle. The children of the village, too, would shout with joy whenever he approached. He assisted at their sports, made their playthings, taught them to fly kites and shoot marbles, and told them long stories of ghosts, witches, and Indians. Whenever he went dodging about the village, he was surrounded by a troop of them, hanging on his skirts, clambering on his back, and playing a thousand tricks on him with impunity; and not a dog would bark at him throughout the neighborhood.

The great error in Rip's composition was an insuperable aversion to all kinds of profitable labor. It could not be from the want of assiduity or perseverance; for he would sit on a wet rock, with a rod as long and heavy as a Tartar's lance, and fish all day without a murmur, even though he should not be encouraged by a single nibble. He would carry a fowling piece on his shoulder for hours together, trudging through woods and swamps, and up hill and down dale, to shoot a few squirrels or wild pigeons. He would never refuse to assist a neighbor even in the roughest toil, and was a foremost man at all country frolics for husking Indian corn, or building stone fences;

the women of the village, too, used to employ him to run their errands, and to do such little odd jobs as their less obliging husbands would not do for them. In a word, Rip was ready to attend to anybody's business but his own; but as to doing family duty, and keeping his farm in order, he found it impossible.

In fact, he declared it was of no use to work on his farm; it was the most pestilent little piece of ground in the whole country; everything about it went wrong, and would go wrong, in spite of him. His fences were continually falling to pieces; his cow would either go astray, or get among the cabbages; weeds were sure to grow quicker in his fields than anywhere else; the rain always made a point of setting in just as he had some outdoor work to do; so that though his patrimonial estate had dwindled away under his management, acre by acre, until there was little more left than a mere patch of Indian corn and potatoes, yet it was the worst conditioned farm in the neighborhood.

His children, too, were as ragged and wild as if they belonged to nobody. His son Rip, an urchin begotten in his own likeness, promised to inherit the habits, with the old clothes, of his father. He was generally seen trooping like a colt at his mother's heels, equipped in a pair of his father's cast off galligaskins, which he had much ado to hold up with one hand, as a fine lady does her train in bad weather.

Rip Van Winkle, however, was one of those happy mortals, of foolish, well-oiled dispositions, who take the world easy, eat white bread or brown, whichever can be got with least thought or trouble, and would rather starve on a penny than work for a pound. If left to himself, he would have whistled life away in perfect contentment; but his wife kept continually dinning in his ears about his idleness, his carelessness, and the ruin he was bringing on his family. Morning, noon, and night, her tongue was incessantly going, and everything he said or did was sure to produce a torrent of household eloquence. Rip had but one way of replying to all lectures of the kind, and that, by frequent use, had grown into a habit. He shrugged his shoulders, shook his head, cast up his eyes, but said nothing. This, however, always provoked a fresh volley from his wife; so that he was fain to draw off his forces, and take to the outside of the house—the only side which, in truth, belongs to a henpecked husband.

Rip's sole domestic adherent was his dog Wolf, who was as much henpecked as his master; for Dame Van Winkle regarded them as companions in idleness, and even looked upon Wolf with an evil eye, as the cause of his master's going so often astray. True it is, in all points of spirit befitting an honorable dog, he was as courageous an animal as ever scoured the woods; but what courage can withstand the ever enduring and all-besetting terrors of a woman's tongue? The moment Wolf entered the house his crest fell, his tail drooped to the ground, or curled between his legs, he sneaked about with a gallows air, casting many a sidelong glance at Dame Van Winkle, and at the least flourish of a broomstick or ladle he would fly to the door with yelping precipitation.

Times grew worse and worse with Rip Van Winkle as years of matrimony rolled on; a tart temper never mellows with age, and a sharp tongue is the only edged tool that grows keener with constant use. For a long while he used to console himself, when driven from home, by frequenting a kind of perpetual club of the sages, philosophers, and other idle personages of the village, which held its sessions on a bench before a small inn, designated by a rubicund portrait of His Majesty George the Third. Here they used to sit in the shade through a long, lazy summer's day, talking listlessly over village gossip, or telling endless sleepy stories about nothing. But it

The children of the village, too, would shout with joy whenever he approached.

would have been worth any statesman's money to have heard the profound discussions that sometimes took place, when by chance an old newspaper fell into their hands from some passing traveler. How solemnly they would listen to the contents, as drawled out by Derrick Van Bummel, the schoolmaster, a dapper learned little man, who was not to be daunted by the most gigantic word in the dictionary; and how sagely they would deliberate upon public events some months after they had taken place.

The opinions of this junto were completely controlled by Nicholas Vedder, patriarch of the village, and landlord of the inn, at the door of which he took his seat from morning till night, just moving sufficiently to avoid the sun and keep in the shade of a large tree; so that the neighbors could tell the hour by his movements as accurately as by a sundial. It is true he was rarely heard to speak, but smoked his pipe incessantly. His adherents, however (for every great man has his adherents), perfectly understood him, and knew how to gather his opinions. When anything that was read or related displeased him, he was observed to smoke his pipe vehemently, and to send forth short, frequent, and angry puffs; but when pleased, he would inhale the smoke slowly and tranquilly, and emit it in light and placid clouds; and sometimes, taking the pipe from his mouth, and letting the fragrant vapor curl about his nose, would gravely nod his head in token of perfect approbation.

From even this stronghold the unlucky Rip was at length routed by his termagant wife, who would suddenly break in upon the tranquility of the assemblage and call the members all to naught; nor was that august personage, Nicholas Vedder himself, sacred from the daring tongue of this terrible virago, who charged him outright with encouraging her husband in his habits of idleness.

Poor Rip was at last reduced almost to despair; and his only alternative, to escape from the labor of the farm and the clamor of his wife, was to take gun in hand and stroll away into the woods. Here he would sometimes seat himself at the foot of a tree, and share the contents of his wallet with Wolf, with whom he sympathized as a fellow sufferer in persecution. "Poor Wolf," he would say, "thy mistress leads thee a dog's life of it, but never mind, my lad, whilst I live thou shalt never want a friend to stand by thee!" Wolf would wag his tail, look wistfully in his master's face, and if dogs can feel pity, I verily believe he reciprocated the sentiment with all his heart.

In a long ramble of the kind on a fine autumnal day, Rip had unconsciously scrambled to one of the highest parts of the Kaatskill mountains. He was after his favorite sport of squirrel shooting, and the still solitudes had echoed and reechoed with the reports of his gun. Panting and fatigued, he threw himself, late in the afternoon, on a green knoll, covered with mountain herbage, that crowned the brow of a precipice. From an opening between the trees he could overlook all the lower country for many a mile of rich woodland. He saw at a distance the lordly Hudson, far, far below him, moving on its silent but majestic course, with the reflection of a purple cloud, or the sail of a lagging bark, here and there sleeping on its glassy bosom, and at last losing itself in the blue highlands.

On the other side he looked down into a deep mountain glen, wild, lonely, and shagged, the bottom filled with fragments from the impending cliffs, and scarcely lighted by the reflected rays of the setting sun. For some time Rip lay musing on this scene; evening was gradually advancing; the mountains began to throw their long blue shadows over the valleys; he saw that it would be dark long before he could reach the village, and he heaved a heavy sigh when he thought of encountering the terrors of Dame Van Winkle.

As he was about to descend, he heard a voice from a distance, hallooing, "Rip Van Winkle, Rip Van Winkle!" He looked around, but could see nothing but a crow winging its solitary flight across the mountain. He thought his fancy must have deceived him, and turned again to descend, when he heard the same cry ring through the still evening air: "Rip Van Winkle! Rip Van Winkle!"—at the same time Wolf bristled up his back, and giving a low growl, skulked to his master's side, looking fearfully down into the glen. Rip now felt a vague apprehension stealing over him; he looked anxiously in the same direction, and perceived a strange figure slowly toiling up the rocks, and bending under the weight of something he carried on his back. He was surprised to see any human being in this lonely and unfrequented place; but supposing it to be someone of the neighborhood in need of his assistance, he hastened down to yield it.

On nearer approach he was still more surprised at the singularity of the stranger's appearance. He was a short, square-built old fellow, with thick bushy hair, and a grizzled beard. His dress was of the antique Dutch fashion—a cloth jerkin strapped around the waist, several pairs of breeches, the outer one of ample volume, deco-

Rip meets the little man with the keg of liquor.

about the unknown that inspired awe and checked familiarity.

On entering the amphitheater, new objects of wonder presented themselves. On a level spot in the center was a company of odd-looking personages playing at ninepins. They were dressed in a quaint, outlandish fashion; some wore short doublets, others jerkins, with long knives in their belts, and most of them had enormous breeches, of similar style with that of the guide's. Their visages, too, were peculiar: one had a large beard, broad face, and small piggish eyes; the face of another seemed to consist entirely of nose, and was surmounted by a white sugar-loaf hat, set off with a little red cock's tail. They all had beards, of various shapes and colors. One seemed to be the commander. He was a stout old gentleman, with a weather-beaten countenance; he wore a laced doublet, broad belt and hanger, high crowned hat and feather, red stockings, and high-heeled shoes, with roses in them. The whole group reminded Rip of figures in a Flemish painting, in the parlor of Dominie Van Shaick, the village parson, and which had been brought over from Holland at the time of settlement.

What seemed particularly odd to Rip was that, though these folks were evidently amusing themselves, yet they maintained the gravest faces, the most mysterious silence, and were, withal, the most melancholy party of pleasure he had ever witnessed. Nothing interrupted the stillness of the scene but the noise of the balls, which, whenever they rolled, echoed along the mountains like rumbling peals of thunder.

As Rip and his companion approached them, they suddenly desisted from their play, and stared at him with such fixed, statue-like gaze, and such strange, uncouth, lackluster countenances, that his heart turned within him, and his knees smote together. His companion now emptied the contents of the keg into large flagons, and made signs to him to wait upon the company. He obeyed with fear and trembling; they quaffed the liquor in profound silence, and then returned to their game.

By degrees Rip's awe and apprehension subsided. He even ventured, when no eye was fixed upon him, to taste the beverage, which he found had much of the flavor of excellent Hollands. He was naturally a thirsty soul, and was soon tempted to repeat the draught. One taste provoked another; and he reiterated his visits to the flagon so often that at length his senses were overpowered, his eyes swam in his head, his head gradually declined, and he fell into a deep sleep.

rated with rows of buttons down the sides, and bunches at the knees. He bore on his shoulders a stout keg that seemed full of liquor, and made signs for Rip to approach and assist him with the load. Though rather shy and distrustful of this new acquaintance, Rip complied with his usual alacrity; and mutually relieving one another, they clambered up a narrow gully, apparently the dry bed of a mountain torrent. As they ascended, Rip every now and then heard long, rolling peals, like distant thunder, that seemed to issue out of a deep ravine, or rather cleft, between lofty rocks, toward which their rugged path conducted. He paused for an instant, but supposing it to be the muttering of one of those transient thundershowers which often take place in mountain heights, he proceeded. Passing through the ravine, they came to a hollow, like a small amphitheater, surrounded by perpendicular precipices, over the brinks of which impending trees shot their branches, so that you only caught glimpses of the azure sky and the bright evening cloud. During the whole time Rip and his companion had labored on in silence; for though the former marveled greatly what could be the object of carrying a keg of liquor up this wild mountain, yet there was something strange and incomprehensible

On waking, he found himself on the green knoll whence he had first seen the old man of the glen. He rubbed his eyes—it was a bright sunny morning. The birds were hopping and twittering among the bushes, and the eagle was wheeling aloft, and breasting the pure mountain breeze. "Surely," thought Rip, "I have not slept here all night." He recalled the occurrences before he fell asleep. The strange man with a keg of liquor—the mountain ravine—the wild retreat among the rocks—the woebegone party at ninepins—the flagon—"Oh! that flagon! that wicked flagon!" thought Rip, "what excuse shall I make to Dame Van Winkle?"

He looked round for his gun, but in place of the clean, well-oiled fowling piece, he found an old firelock lying by him, the barrel encrusted with rust, the lock falling off, and the stock worm-eaten. He now suspected that the grave roisters of the mountains had put a trick upon him, and, having dosed him with liquor, had robbed him of his gun. Wolf, too, had disappeared, but he might have strayed away after a squirrel or partridge. He whistled after him, and shouted his name, but all in vain; the echoes repeated his whistle and shout, but no dog was to be seen.

"These mountain beds do not agree with me," thought Rip.

BROWN BROTHERS

He determined to revisit the scene of the last evening's gambol, and if he met with any of the party, to demand his dog and gun. As he rose to walk, he found himself stiff in the joints, and wanting in his usual activity. "These mountain beds do not agree with me," thought Rip, "and if this frolic should lay me up with a fit of the rheumatism, I shall have a blessed time with Dame Van Winkle." With some difficulty he got down into the glen: he found the gully up which he and his companion had ascended the preceding evening; but to his astonishment a mountain stream was now foaming down it, leaping from rock to rock, and filling the glen with babbling murmurs. He, however, made shift to scramble up its sides, working his toilsome way through thickets of birch, sassafras, and witch hazel, and sometimes tripped up or entangled by the wild grape vines that twisted their coils or tendrils from tree to tree, and spread a kind of network in his path.

At length he reached to where the ravine had opened through the cliffs to the amphitheater; but no traces of such opening remained. The rocks presented a high, impenetrable wall, over which the torrent came tumbling in a sheet of feathery foam, and fell into a broad deep basin, black from the shadows of the surrounding forest. Here, then, poor Rip was brought to a stand. He again called and whistled after his dog; he was only answered by the cawing of a flock of idle crows, sporting high in air about a dry tree that overhung a sunny precipice; and who, secure in their elevation, seemed to look down and scoff at the poor man's perplexities.

What was to be done? The morning was passing away, and Rip felt famished for want of his breakfast. He grieved to give up his dog and gun; he dreaded to meet his wife; but it would not do to starve among the mountains. He shook his head, shouldered the rusty firelock, and, with a heart full of trouble and anxiety, turned his footsteps homeward.

As he approached the village he met a number of people, but none whom he knew, which somewhat surprised him, for he had thought himself acquainted with every one in the country round. Their dress, too, was of a different fashion from that to which he was accustomed. They all stared at him with equal marks of surprise, and whenever they cast their eyes upon him, invariably stroked their chins. The constant recurrence of this gesture induced Rip, involuntarily, to do the same, when, to his astonishment, he found his beard had grown a foot long!

He had now entered the skirts of the village. A troop of strange children ran at his heels, hooting after him, and pointing at his gray beard. The dogs, too, not one of which he recognized for an old acquaintance, barked at him as he passed. The very village was altered; it was larger and more populous. There were rows of houses which he had never seen before, and those which had been his familiar haunts had disappeared. Strange names were over the doors—strange faces at the windows—everything was strange. His mind now misgave him; he began to doubt whether both he and the world around him were not bewitched. Surely this was his native village, which he had left but the day before. There stood the Kaatskill mountains—there ran the silver Hudson at a distance—there was every hill and dale precisely as it had always been. Rip was sorely perplexed. "That flagon last night," thought he, "has addled my poor head sadly!"

It was with some difficulty that he found the way to his own house, which he approached with silent awe, expecting every moment to hear the shrill voice of Dame Van Winkle. He found the house gone to decay—the roof fallen in, the windows shattered, and the doors off the hinges. A half-starved dog that looked like Wolf was skulking about it. Rip called him by name, but the cur snarled, showed his teeth, and passed on. This was an unkind cut indeed. "My very dog," sighed poor Rip, "has forgotten me!"

He entered the house, which to tell the truth, Dame Van Winkle had always kept in neat order. It was empty, forlorn, and apparently abandoned. This desolateness overcame all his connubial fears—he called loudly for his wife and children—the lonely chambers rang for a moment with his voice, and then all again was silence.

He now hurried forth, and hastened to his old resort, the village inn, but it too was gone. A large, rickety wooden building stood in its place, with great gaping windows, some of them broken and mended with old hats and petticoats, and over the door was painted, "The Union Hotel, by Jonathan Doolittle." Instead of the great tree that used to shelter the quiet little Dutch inn of yore, there now was reared a tall naked pole, with something on top that looked like a red nightcap, and from it was fluttering a flag, on which was a singular assemblage of stars and stripes—all this was strange and incomprehensible. He recognized on the sign, however, the ruby face of King George, under which he had smoked so many a peaceful pipe; but even this was singularly metamorphosed. The red coat was changed for one of blue and buff, a sword was held in the hand instead of a scepter, the head was decorated with a cocked hat, and underneath was painted in large characters, GENERAL WASHINGTON.

There was, as usual, a crowd of folk about the door, but none that Rip recollected. The very character of the people seemed changed. There was a busy, bustling, disputatious tone about it, instead of the accustomed phlegm and drowsy tranquility. He looked in vain for the sage Nicholas Vedder, with his broad face, double chin, and fair long pipe, uttering clouds of tobacco smoke instead of idle speeches; or Van Bummel, the schoolmaster, doling forth the contents of an ancient newspaper. In place of these, a lean, bilious-looking fellow, with his pockets full of handbills, was haranguing vehemently about rights of citizens—elections—members of Congress—liberty—Bunker's Hill—heroes of seventy-six—and other words, which were a perfect Babylonish jargon to the bewildered Van Winkle.

The appearance of Rip, with his long, grizzled beard, his rusty fowling piece, his uncouth dress, and an army of women and children at his heels, soon attracted the attention of the tavern politicians. They crowded round him, eyeing him from head to foot with great curiosity. The orator bustled up to him, and, drawing him partly aside, inquired "on which side he voted?" Rip stared in vacant stupidity. Another short but busy little fellow pulled him by the arm, and, rising on tiptoe, inquired in his ear, "whether he was Federal or Democrat?" Rip was equally at a loss to comprehend the question; when a knowing, self-important old gentleman, in a sharp cocked hat, made his way through the crowd, putting them to the right and left with his elbows as he passed, and planting himself before Van Winkle, with one arm akimbo, the other resting on his cane, his keen eyes and sharp hat penetrating, as it were, into his very soul, demanded in an austere tone, "what brought him to the election with a gun on his shoulder, and a mob at his heels; and whether he meant to breed a riot in the village?"—"Alas! gentlemen," cried Rip, somewhat dismayed, "I am a poor quiet man, a native of the place, and a loyal subject of the King, God bless him!"

Here a general shout burst from the bystanders—"A tory! a tory! a spy! a refugee! hustle him! away with him!" It was with great difficulty that the self-important man in the cocked hat restored order; and, having assumed a tenfold austerity of brow, demanded again of the unknown culprit, what he came there for, and whom he was seeking? The poor man humbly assured him that he meant no harm, but merely came there in search of some of his neighbors, who used to keep about the tavern.

"Well—who are they?—name them."

Rip bethought himself a moment, and inquired, "Where's Nicholas Vedder?"

There was a silence for a little while, when an old man replied, in a thin piping voice, "Nicholas Vedder! why, he is dead and gone these eighteen years! There was a wooden tombstone in that churchyard that used to tell all about him, but that's rotten and gone too."

"Where's Brom Dutcher?"

"Oh, he went off to the army in the beginning of the war; some say he was killed at the storming of Stony Point—others say he was drowned in a squall at the foot of Anthony's Nose. I don't know—he never came back again."

"Where's Van Bummel, the schoolmaster?"

"He went off to the wars too, was a great militia general and is now in Congress."

Rip's heart died away at hearing of these sad changes in his home and friends, and finding himself thus alone in the world. Every answer puzzled him too, by treating of such enormous lapses of time, and of matters which he could not understand: war—Congress—Stony Point—he had no courage to ask after any more friends, but cried out in despair, "Does nobody here know Rip Van Winkle?"

"Oh, Rip Van Winkle!" exclaimed two or three, "oh, to be sure! that's Rip Van Winkle yonder, leaning against the tree."

Rip looked, and he beheld a precise counterpart of himself, as he went up the mountain; apparently as lazy, and certainly as ragged. The poor fellow was now completely confounded. He doubted his own identity, and whether he was himself or another man. In the midst of his bewilderment, the man in the cocked hat demanded who he was, and what was his name.

"God knows," exclaimed he, at his wit's end; "I'm not myself—I'm somebody else—that's me yonder—no—that's somebody else got into my shoes—I was myself last night, but I fell asleep on the mountain, and they've changed my gun, and everything's changed, and I'm changed, and I can't tell what's my name, or who I am!"

The bystanders began now to look at each other, nod, wink significantly, and tap their fingers against their foreheads. There was a whisper, also, about securing the gun, and keeping the old fellow from doing mischief, at the very suggestion of which the self-important man in the cocked hat retired with some precipitation. At

"Does nobody here know Rip Van Winkle?"

this critical moment a fresh, comely woman pressed through the throng to get a peep at the gray-bearded man. She had a chubby child in her arms, which, frightened at his looks, began to cry. "Hush, Rip," cried she, "hush, you little fool; the old man won't hurt you." The name of the child, the air of the mother, the tone of her voice, all awakened a train of recollections in his mind. "What is your name, my good woman?" asked he.

"Judith Gardenier."

"And your father's name?"

"Ah, poor man, Rip Van Winkle was his name, but it's twenty years since he went away from home with his gun, and never has been heard of since—his dog came come without him; but whether he shot himself, or was carried away by the Indians, nobody can tell. I was then but a little girl."

Rip had but one question more to ask; but he put it with a faltering voice.

"Where's your mother?"

"Oh, she too died but a short time since; she broke a blood vessel in a fit of passion at a New England peddler."

There was a drop of comfort, at least, in this intelligence. The honest man could contain himself no longer. He caught his daughter and her child in his arms. "I am your father!" cried he— "Young Rip Van Winkle once—old Rip Van Winkle now!—Does nobody know poor Rip Van Winkle?"

All stood amazed until an old woman, tottering out from among the crowd, put her hand to her brow, and peering under it in his face for a moment, exclaimed, "Sure enough! it is Rip Van Winkle—it is himself! Welcome home again, old neighbor. Why, where have you been these twenty long years?"

Rip's story was soon told, for the whole twenty years had been to him but as one night. The neighbors stared when they heard it; some were seen to wink at each other, and put their tongues in their checks: and the self-important man in the cocked hat, who, when the alarm was over, had returned to the field, screwed down the corners of his mouth, and shook his head—upon which there was a general shaking of the head throughout the assemblage.

It was determined, however, to take the opinion of old Peter Vanderdonk, who was seen slowly advancing up the road. He was a descendant of the historian of that name, who wrote one of the earliest accounts of the province. Peter was the most ancient inhabitant of the village, and well versed in all the wonderful events and traditions of the neighborhood. He recollected Rip at once, and corroborated his story in the most satisfactory manner. He assured the company that it was a fact, handed down from his ancestor the historian, that the Kaatskill mountains had always been haunted by strange beings. That it was affirmed that the great Hendrick Hudson, the first discoverer of the river and country, kept a kind of vigil there every twenty years, with his crew of the *Half Moon;* being permitted in this way to revisit the scenes of his enterprise, and keep a guardian eye upon the river and the great city called by his name. That his father had once seen them in their old Dutch dresses playing at ninepins in a hollow of the mountain; and that he himself had heard, one summer afternoon, the sound of their balls, like distant peals of thunder.

To make a long story short, the company broke up and returned to the more important concerns of the election. Rip's daughter took him home to live with her; she had a snug, well furnished house, and a stout, cheery farmer for a husband, whom Rip recollected for one of the urchins that used to climb upon his back. As to Rip's son and heir, who was the ditto of himself, seen leaning against the tree, he was employed to work on the farm, but evinced an hereditary disposition to attend to anything else but his business.

Rip now resumed his old walks and habits; he soon found many of his former cronies, though all rather the worse for the wear and tear of time; and preferred making friends among the rising generation, with whom he soon grew into great favor.

Having nothing to do at home, and being arrived at that happy age when a man can be idle with impunity, he took his place once more on the bench at the inn door, and was reverenced as one of the patriarchs of the village, and a chronicle of the old times "before the war." It was some time before he could get into the regular track of gossip, or could be made to comprehend the strange events that had taken place during his torpor. How that there had been a revolutionary war—that the country had thrown off the yoke of old England—and that, instead of being a subject of his Majesty George the Third, he was now a free citizen of the United States. Rip, in fact, was no politician; the changes of states and empires made but little impression on him; but there was one species of despotism under which he long groaned, and that was—petticoat government. Happily, that was at an end; he had got his neck out of the yoke of matrimony, and could go in and out whenever he pleased without dreading the tyranny of Dame Van Winkle. Whenever her name was mentioned, however, he shook his head, shrugged his shoulders, and cast up his eyes; which might pass either for an expression of resignation to his fate, or joy at his deliverance.

He used to tell his story to every stranger that arrived at Mr. Doolittle's hotel. He was observed, at first, to vary on some points every time he told it, which was, doubtless, owing to his having so recently awaked. It at last settled down precisely to the tale I have related, and not a man, woman, or child in the neighborhood but knew it by heart. Some always pretended to doubt the reality of it, and insisted that Rip had been out of his head, and that this was one point on which he always remained flighty. The old Dutch inhabitants, however, almost universally gave it full credit. Even to this day they never hear a thunderstorm of a summer afternoon about the Kaatskill, but they say Hendrick Hudson and his crew are at their game of ninepins; and it is a common wish of all henpecked husbands in the neighborhood, when life hangs heavy on their hands, that they might have a quieting draught out of Rip Van Winkle's flagon. ■

From
The Adventures of Tom Sawyer
Mark Twain

Here Tom Sawyer dabbles in the art of salesmanship, convincing his friends that work is lots of fun and making a nice little profit in the bargain.

Saturday morning was come, and all the summer world was bright and fresh, and brimming with life. There was a song in every heart; and if the heart was young the music issued at the lips. There was cheer in every face and a spring in every step. The locust trees were in bloom and the fragrance of the blossoms filled the air. Cardiff Hill, beyond the village and above it, was green with vegetation, and it lay just far enough away to seem a Delectable Land, dreamy, reposeful, and inviting.

Tom appeared on the sidewalk with a bucket of whitewash and a long-handled brush. He surveyed the fence, and all gladness left him and a deep melancholy settled down upon his spirit. Thirty yards of board fence nine feet high. Life to him seemed hollow, and existence but a burden. Sighing he dipped his brush and passed it along the topmost plank; repeated the operation, did it again; compared the insignificant whitewashed streak with the far-reaching continent of unwhitewashed fence, and sat down on a tree-box discouraged. Jim came skipping out at the gate with a tin pail, and singing "Buffalo Gals." Bringing water from the town pump had always been hateful work in Tom's eyes, before, but now it did not strike him so. He remembered that there was company at the pump. White, mulatto, and negro boys and girls were always there waiting their turns, resting, trading playthings, quarreling, fighting, skylarking. And he remembered that although the pump was only a hundred and fifty yards off, Jim never got back with a bucket of water under an hour—and even then somebody generally had to go after him. Tom said:

"Say, Jim, I'll fetch the water if you'll whitewash some."

Jim shook his head and said:

"Can't, Mars Tom. Ole missis, she tole me I got to go an' git dis water an' not stop foolin' roun' wid anybody. She say she spec' Mars Tom gwine to ax me to whitewash, an' so she tole me go 'long an' 'tend to my own business—she 'lowed *she'd* 'tend to de whitewashin'."

"Oh, never you mind what she said, Jim. That's the way she always talks. Gimme the bucket—I won't be gone only a minute. *She* won't ever know."

"Oh, I dasn't, Mars Tom. Ole missis she'd take an' tar de head off'n me. 'Deed she would."

"*She!* She never licks anybody—whacks 'em over the head with her thimble—and who cares for that, I'd like to know. She talks awful, but talk don't hurt—anyways it don't if she don't cry. Jim, I'll give you a marvel. I'll give you a white alley!"

Jim began to waver.

"White alley, Jim! And it's a bully taw."

"My! Dat's a mighty gay marvel, *I* tell you! But Mars Tom I's powerful 'fraid ole missis—"

"And besides, if you will I'll show you my sore toe."

Jim was only human—this attraction was too much for him. He put down his pail, took the white alley, and bent over the toe with absorbing interest while the bandage was being unwound. In another moment he was flying down the street with his pail and a tingling rear, Tom was whitewashing with vigor, and Aunt Polly was retiring from the field with a slipper in her hand and triumph in her eye.

But Tom's energy did not last. He began to think of the fun he had planned for this day, and his sorrows multiplied. Soon the free boys would come tripping along on all sorts of delicious expeditions, and they would make a world of fun of him for having to work—the very thought of it burnt him like fire. He got out his worldly wealth and examined it—bits of toys, marbles, and trash; enough to buy an exchange of *work,* maybe, but not half enough to buy so much as half an hour of pure freedom. So he returned his straitened means to his pocket, and gave up the idea of trying to buy the boys. At this dark and hopeless moment an inspiration burst upon him! Nothing less than a great, magnificent inspiration.

He took up his brush and went tranquilly to work. Ben Rogers hove in sight presently—the very boy, of all boys, whose ridicule he had been dreading. Ben's gait was the hop-skip-and-jump—proof enough that his heart was light and

"Does a boy get a chance to whitewash a fence every day?"

his anticipations high. He was eating an apple, and giving a long, melodious whoop, at intervals, followed by a deep-toned ding-dong-dong, ding-dong-dong, for he was personating a steamboat. As he drew near, he slackened speed, took the middle of the street, leaned far over to starboard and rounded to ponderously and with laborious pomp and circumstance—for he was personating the *Big Missouri,* and considered himself to be drawing nine feet of water. He was boat and captain and engine-bells combined, so he had to imagine himself standing on his own hurricane-deck giving the orders and executing them:

"Stop her, sir! Ting-a-ling-ling!" The headway ran almost out and he drew up slowly toward the sidewalk.

"Ship up to back! Ting-a-ling-ling!" His arms straightened and stiffened down his sides.

"Set her back on the stabboard! Ting-a-ling-ling! Chow! ch-chow-wow! Chow!" His right hand, meantime, describing stately circles—for it was representing a forty-foot wheel.

"Let her go back on the labboard! Ting-a-ling-ling! Chow-ch-chow-chow!" The left hand began to describe circles.

"Stop the stabboard! Ting-a-ling-ling! Stop the labboard! Come ahead on the stabboard! Stop

her! Let your outside turn over slow! Ting-a-ling-ling! Chow-ow-ow! Get out that head-line! *Lively* now! Come—out with your spring-line—what're you about there! Take a turn round that stump with the bight of it! Stand by that stage, now—let her go! Done with the engines, sir! Ting-a-ling-ling! *Sh't! s'h't! sh't!*" (trying the gaugecocks).

Tom went on whitewashing—paid no attention to the steamboat. Ben stared a moment and then said:

"Hi-*yi! You're* up a stump, ain't you!"

No answer. Tom surveyed his last touch with the eye of an artist, then he gave his brush another gentle sweep and surveyed the result, as before. Ben ranged up alongside of him. Tom's mouth watered for the apple, but he stuck to his work. Ben said:

"Hello, old chap, you got to work, hey?"

Tom wheeled suddenly and said:

"Why, it's you, Ben! I warn't noticing."

"Say—*I'm* going in a-swimming, *I* am. Don't you wish you could? But of course you'd druther *work*—wouldn't you? Course you would!"

Tom contemplated the boy a bit, and said:

"What do you call work?"

"Why, ain't *that* work?"

Tom resumed his whitewashing, and answered carelessly:

"Well, maybe it is, and maybe it ain't. All I know is, it suits Tom Sawyer."

"Oh come, now, you don't mean to let on that you *like* it?"

The brush continued to move.

"Like it? Well, I don't see why I oughtn't to like it. Does a boy get a chance to whitewash a fence every day?"

That put the thing in a new light. Ben stopped nibbling his apple. Tom swept his brush daintily back and forth—stepped back to note the effect—added a touch here and there—criticized the effect again—Ben watching every move and getting more and more interested, more and more absorbed. Presently he said:

"Say, Tom, let *me* whitewash a little."

Tom considered, was about to consent; but he altered his mind:

"No—no—I reckon it wouldn't hardly do, Ben. You see, Aunt Polly's awful particular about this fence—right here on the street, you know—but if it was the back fence I wouldn't mind and *she* wouldn't. Yes, she's awful particular about this fence; it's got to be done very careful; I reckon there ain't one boy in a thousand, maybe two thousand, that can do it the way it's got to be done."

"No—is that so? Oh come, now—lemme just try. Only just a little—I'd let *you,* if you was me, Tom."

"Ben, I'd like to, honest injun; but Aunt Polly—well, Jim wanted to do it, but she wouldn't let him; Sid wanted to do it, and she wouldn't let Sid. Now don't you see how I'm fixed? If you was to tackle this fence and anything was to happen to it—"

"Oh, shucks, I'll be just as careful. Now lemme try. Say—I'll give you the core of my apple."

"Well, here—No, Ben, now don't. I'm afeard—"

"I'll give you *all* of it!"

Tom gave up the brush with reluctance in his face, but alacrity in his heart. And while the late steamer *Big Missouri* worked and sweated in the sun, the retired artist sat on a barrel in the shade close by, dangled his legs, munched his apple, and planned the slaughter of more innocents. There was no lack of material; boys happened along every little while; they came to jeer, but remained to whitewash. By the time Ben was fagged out, Tom had traded the next chance to Billy Fisher for a kite, in good repair; and when *he* played out, Johnny Miller bought in for a dead rat and a string to swing it with—and so on, and so on, hour after hour. And when the middle of the afternoon came, from being a poor poverty-stricken boy in the morning, Tom was literally rolling in wealth. He had beside the things before mentioned, twelve marbles, part of a jews' harp, a piece of blue bottle glass to look through, a spool cannon, a key that wouldn't unlock anything, a fragment of chalk, a glass stopper of a decanter, a tin soldier, a couple of tadpoles, six firecrackers, a kitten with only one eye, a brass doorknob, a dog collar—but no dog—the handle of a knife, four pieces of orange peel, and a dilapidated old window sash.

He had had a nice, good, idle time all the while—plenty of company—and the fence had three coats of whitewash on it! If he hadn't run out of whitewash, he would have bankrupted every boy in the village.

Tom said to himself that it was not such a hollow world, after all. He had discovered a great law of human action, without knowing it—namely, that in order to make a man or a boy covet a thing, it is only necessary to make the thing difficult to attain. If he had been a great and wise philosopher, like the writer of this book, he would now have comprehended that Work consists of whatever a body is *obliged* to do, and that Play consists of whatever a body is not obliged to do. And this would help him to understand why constructing artificial flowers or performing on a treadmill is work, while rolling tenpins or climbing Mont Blanc is only amusement. There are wealthy gentlemen in England who drive four-horse passenger-coaches twenty or thirty miles on a daily line, in the summer, because the privilege costs them considerable money; but if they were offered wages for the service, that would turn it into work and then they would resign.

The boy mused awhile over the substantial change which had taken place in his worldly circumstances, and then wended toward headquarters to report. ■

The Moth and the Star
James Thurber

A young and impressionable moth once set his heart on a certain star. He told his mother about this and she counseled him to set his heart on a bridge lamp instead. "Stars aren't the thing to hang around," she said; "lamps are the thing to hang around." "You get somewhere that way," said the moth's father. "You don't get anywhere chasing stars." But the moth would not heed the words of either parent. Every evening at dusk when the star came out he would start flying toward it and every morning at dawn he would crawl back home worn out with his vain endeavor. One day his father said to him, "You haven't burned a wing in months, boy, and it looks to me as if you are never going to. All your brothers have been badly burned flying around street lamps and all your sisters have been terribly singed flying around house lamps. Come on, now, get out of here and get yourself scorched! A big strapping moth like you without a mark on him!"

The moth left his father's house, but he would not fly around street lamps and he would not fly around house lamps. He went right on trying to reach the star, which was four and one-third light years, or twenty-five trillion miles, away. The moth thought it was just caught in the top branches of an elm. He never did reach the star, but he went right on trying, night after night, and when he was a very, very old moth he began to think that he really had reached the star and he went around saying so. This gave him a deep and lasting pleasure, and he lived to a great old age. His parents and his brothers and his sisters had all been burned to death when they were quite young.

_____

*Moral: Who flies afar from the sphere of our sorrow
is here today and here tomorrow.*

The Notorious Jumping Frog of Calaveras County

Mark Twain

Mark Twain didn't invent the jumping frog story, but when his version of the tale was first published in 1865 the newspaperman and former riverboat pilot suddenly found himself famous.

In compliance with the request of a friend of mine, who wrote me from the East, I called on good-natured, garrulous old Simon Wheeler, and inquired after my friend's friend, Leonidas W. Smiley, as requested to do, and I hereunto append the result. I have a lurking suspicion that *Leonidas* W. Smiley is a myth; that my friend never knew such a personage; and that he only conjectured that if I asked old Wheeler about him, it would remind him of his infamous *Jim* Smiley, and he would go to work and bore me to death with some exasperating reminiscence of him as long and as tedious as it should be useless to me. If that was the design, it succeeded.

I found Simon Wheeler dozing comfortably by the bar-room stove of the dilapidated tavern in the decayed mining camp of Angel's, and I noticed that he was fat and bald-headed, and had an expression of winning gentleness and simplicity upon his tranquil countenance. He roused up, and gave me good day. I told him that a friend of mine had commissioned me to make some inquiries about a cherished companion of his boyhood named *Leonidas* W. Smiley—*Rev. Leonidas* W. Smiley, a young minister of the Gospel, who he had heard was at one time a resident of Angel's Camp. I added that if Mr. Wheeler could tell me anything about this Rev. Leonidas W. Smiley, I would feel under many obligations to him.

Simon Wheeler backed me into a corner and blockaded me there with his chair, and then sat down and reeled off the monotonous narrative which follows this paragraph. He never smiled, he never frowned, he never changed his voice from the gentle-flowing key to which he tuned his initial sentence, he never betrayed the slightest suspicion of enthusiasm; but all through the interminable narrative there ran a vein of impressive earnestness and sincerity, which showed me plainly that, so far from his imagining that there was anything ridiculous or funny about his story, he regarded it as a really important matter, and admired its two heroes as men of transcendent genius in *finesse*. I let him go on in his own way, and never interrupted him once.

"Rev. Leonidas W. H'm, Reverend Le—well, there was a feller here once by the name of *Jim* Smiley, in the winter of '49—or maybe it was the spring of '50—I don't recollect exactly, somehow, though what makes me think it was one or the other is because I remember the big flume warn't finished when he first come to the camp; but anyway, he was the curiousest man about always betting on anything that turned up you ever see, if he could get anybody to bet on the other side; and if he couldn't he'd change sides. Any way that suited the other man would suit *him*—any way just so's he got a bet, *he* was satisfied. But still he was lucky, uncommon lucky; he most always come out winner. He was always ready and laying for a chance; there couldn't be no sol-it'ry thing mentioned but that feller'd offer to bet on it, and take ary side you please, as I was just telling you. If there was a horse-race, you'd find him flush or you'd find him busted at the end of it; if there was a dog-fight, he'd bet on it; if there was a cat-fight, he'd bet on it; if there was a chicken-fight, he'd bet on it; why, if there was two birds setting on a fence, he would bet you which one would fly first; or if there was a camp-meeting, he would be there reg'lar to bet on Parson Walker, which he judged to be the best exhorter about here, and so he was too, and a good man. If he even see a straddle-bug start to go anywheres, he would bet you how long it would take him to get to—to wherever he was going to, and if you took him up, he would foller that straddle-bug to Mexico but what he would find out where he was bound for and how long he was on the road. Lots of the boys here has seen that Smiley, and can tell you about him. Why, it never made no difference to *him*—he'd bet on *any* thing—the dangdest feller. Parson Walker's wife laid very sick once, for a good while, and it seemed as if they warn't going to save her; but one morning he come in, and Smiley up and asked him how she was, and he said she was considerable better—thank the Lord for his inf'nite mercy—and coming on so smart that with the blessing of Prov'dence she'd get well yet; and Smiley, before he thought, says, 'Well, I'll resk two-and-a-half she don't anyway.'

"Thish-yer Smiley had a mare—the boys called her the fifteen-minute nag, but that was only in fun, you know, because of course she was faster than that—and he used to win money on that horse, for all she was so slow and always had the asthma, or the distemper, or the consumption, or something of that kind. They used to give her two or three hundred yards' start, and then pass her under way; but always at the fag end of he race she'd get excited and desperate like, and come cavorting and straddling up, and scattering her legs around limber, sometimes in the air, and sometimes out to one side among the fences, and kicking up m-o-r-e dust and raising m-o-r-e racket with her coughing and sneezing and blowing her nose—and *always* fetch up at the stand just about a neck ahead, as near as you could cipher it down.

"And he had a little small bull-pup, that to look at him you'd think he warn't worth a cent but to set around and look ornery and lay for a chance to steal something. But as soon as money was up on him he was a different dog; his under-jaw'd begin to stick out like the fo'castle of a steamboat, and his teeth would uncover and shine like the furnaces. And a dog might tackle him and bully-rag him, and bite him, and throw him over his shoulder two or three times, and Andrew Jackson—which was the name of the pup—Andrew Jackson would never let on but what *he* was satisfied, and hadn't expected nothing else—and the bets being doubled and doubled on the other side all the time, till the money was all up; and then all of a sudden he would grab that other dog jest by the j'int of his hind leg and freeze to it—not chaw, you understand, but only just grip and hang on till they throwed up the sponge, if it was a year. Smiley always come out winner on that pup, till he harnessed a dog once that didn't have no hind legs, because they'd been sawed off in a circular saw, and when the thing had gone along far enough, and the money was all up, and he come to make a snatch for his pet holt, he see in a minute how he'd been imposed on, and how the other dog had him in the door, so to speak, and he 'peared surprised, and then he looked sorter discouraged-like, and didn't try no more to win the fight, and so he got shucked out bad. He give Smiley a look, as much as to say his heart was broke, and it was *his* fault, for putting up a dog that hadn't no hind legs for him to take holt of, which was his main dependence in a fight, and then he limped off a piece and laid down and died. It was a good pup, was that Andrew Jackson, and would have made a name for hisself if he'd lived, for the stuff was in him and he had genius—I know it, because he

hadn't no opportunities to speak of, and it don't stand to reason that a dog could make such a fight as he could under them circumstances if he hadn't no talent. It always makes me feel sorry when I think of that last fight of his'n, and the way it turned out.

"Well, thish-yer Smiley had rat-tarriers, and chicken cocks, and tomcats and all them kind of things, till you couldn't rest, and you couldn't fetch nothing for him to bet on but he'd match you. He ketched a frog one day, and took him home, and said he cal'lated to educate him; and so he never done nothing for three months but set in his back yard and learn that frog to jump. And you bet you he *did* learn him, too. He'd give him a little punch behind, and the next minute you'd see that frog whirling in the air like a dough-nut—see him turn one summerset, or maybe a couple, if he got a good start, and come down flat-footed and all right, like a cat. He got him up so in the matter of ketching flies, and kep' him in practice so constant, that he'd nail a fly every time as fur as he could see him. Smiley said all a frog wanted was education, and he could do 'most anything—and I believe him. Why, I've seen him set Dan'l Webster down here on this floor—Dan'l Webster was the name of the frog—and sing out, 'Flies, Dan'l, flies!' and quicker'n you could wink he'd spring straight up and snake a fly off'n the counter there, and flop down on the floor ag'in as solid as a gob of mud, and fall to scratching the side of his head with his hind foot as indifferent as if he hadn't no idea he'd been doin' more'n any frog might do. You never see a frog so modest and straightfor'ard as he was, for all he was so gifted. And when it come to fair and square jumping on a dead level, he could get over more ground at one straddle than any animal of his breed you ever see. Jumping on a dead level was his strong suit, you understand; and when it come to that, Smiley would ante up money on him as long as he had a red. Smiley was monstrous proud of his frog, and well he might be, for fellers that had traveled and been everywheres all said he laid over any frog that ever *they* see.

"Well, Smiley kep' the beast in a little lattice box, and he used to fetch him down-town sometimes and lay for a bet. One day a feller—a stranger in the camp, he was—come acrost him with his box, and says:

"'What might it be that you've got in the box?'

"And Smiley says, sorter indifferent-like, 'It might be a parrot, or it might be a canary, maybe, but it ain't—it's only just a frog.'

"And the feller took it, and looked at it careful,

WALT KUHN/N.Y. PUBLIC LIBRARY PICTURE COLLECTION

"I don't see no p'ints about that frog that's any better'n any other frog."

and turned it round this way and that, and says, 'H'm—so 'tis. Well, what's *he* good for?'

"'Well,' Smiley says, easy and careless, 'he's good enough for *one* thing, I should judge—he can outjump any frog in Calaveras County.'

"The feller took the box again, and took another long, particular look, and give it back to Smiley, and says, very deliberate, 'Well,' he says, 'I don't see no p'ints about that frog that's any better'n any other frog.'

"'Maybe you don't,' Smiley says. 'Maybe you understand frogs and maybe you don't understand 'em; maybe you've had experience, and maybe you ain't only a amature, as it were. Anyways, I've got *my* opinion, and I'll resk forty dollars that he can outjump any frog in Calaveras County.'

"And the feller studied a minute, and then says, kinder sad-like, 'Well, I'm only a stranger here, and I ain't got no frog; but if I had a frog, I'd bet you.'

"And then Smiley says, 'That's all right—that's all right—if you'll hold my box a minute, I'll go and get you a frog.' And so the feller took the box, and put up his forty dollars along with Smiley's, and set down to wait.

"So he set there a good while thinking and thinking to himself, and then he got the frog out and prized his mouth open and took a teaspoon and filled him full of quail-shot—filled him pretty near up to his chin—and set him on the floor. Smiley he went to the swamp and slopped around in the mud for a long time, and finally he ketched a frog, and fetched him in, and give him to this feller, and says:

"'Now, if you're ready, set him alongside of Dan'l, with his fore paws just even with Dan'l's, and I'll give the word.' Then he says, 'One—two—three—*git!*' and him and the feller

touched up the frogs from behind, and the new frog hopped off lively, but Dan'l give a heave, and hysted up his shoulders—so—like a Frenchman, but it warn't no use—he couldn't budge; he was planted as solid as a church, and he couldn't no more stir than if he was anchored out. Smiley was a good deal surprised, and he was disgusted too, but he didn't have no idea what the matter was, of course.

"The feller took the money and started away; and when he was going out at the door, he sorter jerked his thumb over his shoulder—so—at Dan'l, and say's again, very deliberate, 'Well,' he says, '*I* don't see no p'ints about that frog that's any better'n any other frog.'

"Smiley he stood scratching his head and looking down at Dan'l a long time, and at last he says, 'I do wonder what in the nation that frog throw'd off for—I wonder if there ain't something the matter with him—he 'pears to look mighty baggy, somehow.' And he ketched Dan'l by the nap of the neck, and hefted him, and says, 'Why blame my cats if he don't weigh five pound!' and turned him upside down and he belched out a double handful of shot. And then he see how it was, and he was the maddest man—he set the frog down and took out after that feller, but he never ketched him. And—"

[Here Simon Wheeler heard his name called from the front yard, and got up to see what was wanted.] And turning to me as he moved away, he said: "Just set where you are, stranger, and rest easy—I ain't going to be gone a second."

But, by your leave, I did not think that a continuation of the history of the enterprising vagabond *Jim* Smiley would be likely to afford me much information concerning the Rev. *Leonidas* W. Smiley, and so I started away.

At the door I met the sociable Wheeler returning, and he buttonholed me and recommenced:

"Well, thish-yer Smiley had a yaller one-eyed cow that didn't have no tail, only just a short stump like a bannanner, and—"

However, lacking both time and inclination, I did not wait to hear about the afflicted cow, but took my leave. ∎

WALT KUHN/N.Y. PUBLIC LIBRARY PICTURE COLLECTION

The Apprentice

Dorothy Canfield Fisher

Here is a beautiful description of what it's like to be 13 years old,
that sometimes frustrating year between childhood and adulthood.

The day had been one of those unbearable ones, when every sound had set her teeth on edge like chalk creaking on a blackboard, when every word her father or mother said to her or did not say to her seemed an intentional injustice. And of course it would happen, as the end to such a day, that just as the sun went down back of the mountain and the long twilight began, she noticed that Rollie was not around.

Tense with exasperation—she would simply explode if Mother got going—she began to call him in a carefully casual tone: "Here, Rollie! He-ere, boy! Want to go for a walk, Rollie?" Whistling to him cheerfully, her heart full of wrath at the way the world treated her, she made the rounds of his haunts; the corner of the woodshed, where he liked to curl up on the wool of Father's discarded old windbreaker; the hay barn, the cow barn, the sunny spot on the side porch—no Rollie.

Perhaps he had sneaked upstairs to lie on her bed where he was not supposed to go—not that *she* would have minded! That rule was a part of Mother's fussiness, part too of Mother's bossiness. It was *her* bed, wasn't it? But was she allowed the say-so about it? Not on your life. They told her she could have things the way she wanted in her own room, now she was in her teens, but—her heart raged against unfairness as she took the stairs stormily, two steps at a time, her pigtails flopping up and down on her back. If Rollie was on her bed, she was just going to let him stay right there, and Mother could shake her head and frown all she wanted to.

But he was not there. The bedspread and pillow were crumpled, but not from his weight. She had flung herself down to cry there that afternoon. And then she couldn't. Every nerve in her had been twanging, but she couldn't cry. She could only lie there, her hands doubled up hard, furious that she had nothing to cry about. Not really. She was too big to cry just over Father's having said to her, severely, "I told you if I let you take the chess set you were to put it away when you got through with it. One of the pawns was on the floor of our bedroom this morning. I stepped on it. If I'd had my shoes on, I'd have broken it."

Well, he *had* told her to be sure to put them away. And although she had forgotten and left them, he hadn't forbidden her ever to take the set again. No, the instant she thought about that, she knew she couldn't cry about it. She could be, and she was, in a rage about the way Father kept on talking, long after she'd got his point, "It's not that I care so much about the chess set," he said, just leaning with all his weight on being right, "it's because if you don't learn how to take care of things, you yourself will suffer for it, later. You'll forget or neglect something that will be really important, for *you*. We *have* to try to teach you to be responsible for what you've said you'll take care of. If we . . ." on and on, preaching and preaching.

She heard her mother coming down the hall, and hastily shut her door. She had a right to shut the door to her own room, hadn't she? She had *some* rights, she supposed, even if she was only thirteen and the youngest child. If her mother opened it to ask, smiling, "What are you doing in here that you don't want me to see?" she'd say—she'd just say—

She stood there, dry-eyed, by the bed that Rollie had not crumpled, and thought, "I hope Mother sees the spread and says something about Rollie—I just hope she does."

But her mother did not open the door. Her feet went steadily on along the hall, and then, carefully, slowly, down the stairs. She probably had an arm full of winter things she was bringing down from the attic. She was probably thinking that a tall, thirteen-year-old daughter was big enough to help with a chore like that. But she wouldn't *say* anything. She would just get out that insulting look of a grownup silently putting up with a crazy unreasonable kid. She had worn that expression all day; it was too much to be endured.

Up in her bedroom behind her closed door the thirteen-year-old stamped her foot in a rage, none the less savage and heart-shaking because it was mysterious to her.

But she had not located Rollie. Before she would let her father and mother know she had lost sight of him, forgotten about him, she would be cut into little pieces. They would not scold her, she knew. They would do worse. They would look at her. And in their silence she would hear droning on reproachfully what they had repeated and repeated when the sweet, woolly collie puppy had first been in her arms and she had been begging to keep him for her own.

How warm he had felt! Astonishing how warm and alive a puppy was compared to a doll! She had never liked her dolls much, after she had held Rollie, feeling him warm against her breast, warm and wriggling, bursting with life, reaching up to lick her face—he had loved her from that first instant. As he felt her arms around him, his beautiful eyes had melted in trusting sweetness. And they did now, whenever he looked at her. "My dog is the only one in the whole world who *really* loves me," she thought passionately.

Even then, at the very minute when as a darling baby dog he was beginning to love her, her father and mother were saying, so cold, so reasonable—gosh! how she *hated* reasonableness!—"Now, Peg, remember that, living where we do, with sheep on the farms around us, it is a serious responsibility to have a collie dog. If you keep him, you've got to be the one to take care of him. You'll have to be the one to train him to stay at home. We're too busy with you children to start bringing up a puppy, too." Rollie, nestling in her arms, let one hind leg drop awkwardly. It must be uncomfortable. She looked down at him tenderly, tucked his dangling leg up under him and gave him a hug. He laughed up in her face—he really did laugh, his mouth stretched wide in a cheerful grin.

All the time her parents kept hammering away: "If you want him, you can have him. But you must be responsible for him. If he gets to running sheep, he'll just have to be shot, you know that."

They had not said, aloud, "Like the Wilsons' collie." They never mentioned that awfulness—her racing unsuspectingly down across the fields just at the horrible moment when Mr. Wilson shot his collie caught in the very act of killing sheep. They probably thought that if they never spoke about it, she would forget it—*forget* the crack of that rifle, and the collapse of the great beautiful dog! Forget the red red blood spurting from the hole in his head. She hadn't forgotten. She never would. She knew as well as they did, how important it was to train a collie puppy about sheep. They didn't need to rub it in like that. They always rubbed everything in. She had

told them, fervently, indignantly, that of *course* she would take care of him, be responsible for him, teach him to stay at home. Of course, of course. *She* understood!

And now, this afternoon, when he was six months old, tall, rangy, powerful, standing up far above her knee, nearly to her waist, she didn't know where he was. But of course he must be somewhere around. He always was. She composed her face to look natural and went downstairs to search the house. He was probably asleep somewhere. She looked every room over carefully. Her mother was nowhere visible. It was safe to call him again, to give the special piercing whistle which always brought him racing to her, the white-feathered plume of his tail waving in elation that she wanted him.

But he did not answer. She stood still on the front porch to think.

Could he have gone up to their special place in the edge of the field where the three young pines, their branches growing close to the ground, made a triangular, walled-in space, completely hidden from the world? Sometimes he went up there with her. When she lay down on the dried grass to dream, he too lay down quietly, his head on his paws, his beautiful eyes fixed adoringly on her. He entered into her every mood. If she wanted to be quiet, all right, he did too.

It didn't seem as though he would have gone alone there. Still—She loped up the steep slope of the field rather fast, beginning to be anxious.

No, he was not there. She stood, irresolutely, in the roofless, green-walled triangular hideout, wondering what to do next.

Then, before she knew what thought had come into her mind, its emotional impact knocked her down. At least her knees crumpled under her. Last Wednesday the Wilsons had brought their sheep down to the home farm from the upper pasture! She herself had seen them on the way to school, and like an idiot had not thought of Rollie. She had seen them grazing on the river meadow.

She was off like a racer at the crack of the starting pistol, her long, strong legs stretched in great leaps, her pigtails flying. She took the short cut down to the upper edge of the meadow, regardless of the brambles. Their thorn-spiked, wiry stems tore at her flesh, but she did not care. She welcomed the pain. It was something she was doing for Rollie, for her Rollie.

She was tearing through the pine woods now, rushing down the steep, stony path, tripping over roots, half-falling, catching herself just in time,

The tears ran down her cheeks in streams. She sobbed loudly, terribly.

not slackening her speed. She burst out on the open knoll above the river meadow, calling wildly, "Rollie, here, Rollie, here, boy! here! here!" She tried to whistle, but she was crying too hard to pucker her lips. She had not, till then, known she was crying.

There was nobody to see or hear her. Twilight was falling over the bare knoll. The sunless evening wind slid down the mountain like an invisible river, engulfing her in cold. Her teeth began to chatter. "Here, Rollie, here, boy, here!" She strained her eyes to look down into the meadow to see if the sheep were there. She could not be sure. She stopped calling him as if he were a dog, and called out his name despairingly, as if he were her child, "Rollie! oh, *Rollie,* where are you!"

The tears ran down her cheeks in streams. She sobbed loudly, terribly. Since there was no one to hear, she did not try to control herself.—"Hou! hou! hou!" she sobbed, her face contorted grotesquely. "Oh, Rollie! Rollie! Rollie!" She had wanted something to cry about. Oh, how terribly now she had something to cry about.

She saw him as clearly as if he were there beside her, his muzzle and gaping mouth all smeared with the betraying blood (like the Wilsons' collie). "But he didn't *know* it was wrong!" she screamed like a wild creature. "Nobody *told* him it was wrong. It was my fault. I should have taken better care of him. I will now. I will!"

But no matter how she screamed, she could not make herself heard. In the cold gathering darkness, she saw him stand, poor, guiltless victim of his ignorance, who should have been protected from his own nature, his soft eyes looking at her with love, his splendid plumed tail waving gently. "It was my fault. I promised I would bring him up. I should have *made* him stay at home. I was responsible for him. It was my fault."

But she could not make his executioners hear her. The shot rang out, Rollie sank down, his beautiful liquid eyes glazed, the blood spurting from the hole in his head—like the Wilsons' collie. She gave a wild shriek, long, soul-satisfying, frantic. It was the scream at sudden, unendurable tragedy of a mature, full-blooded woman. It drained dry the girl of thirteen. She came to herself. She was standing on the knoll, trembling and quaking with cold, the darkness closing in on her.

Her breath had given out. For once in her life she had wept all the tears there were in her body. Her hands were so stiff with cold she could scarcely close them. How her nose was running! Simply streaming down her upper lip. And she had no handkerchief. She lifted her skirt, fumbled for her slip, stooped, blew her nose on it, wiped her eyes, drew a long quavering breath— and heard something! Far off in the distance, a faint sound, like a dog's muffled bark.

She whirled on her heels and bent her head to listen. The sound did not come from the meadow below the knoll. It came from back of her higher up, from the Wilsons' maple grove. She held her breath. Yes, it came from there.

She began to run again, but now she was not sobbing. She was silent, absorbed in her effort to cover ground. If she could only live to get there, to see if it really were Rollie. She ran steadily till she came to the fence and went over this in a great plunge. Her skirt caught on a nail. She impatiently pulled at it, not hearing or not heeding the long sibilant tear as it came loose. She was in the dusky maple woods, stumbling over the rocks as she ran. As she tore on up the slope, she heard the bark again, and knew it was Rollie's.

She stopped short and leaned weakly against a tree. She was sick with the breathlessness of her straining lungs, sick in the reaction of relief, sick with anger at Rollie, who had been here having a wonderful time while she had been dying, just dying in terror about him.

For she could now not only hear that it was Rollie's bark. She could hear, in the dog language she knew as well as he, what he was saying in those excited yips—that he had run a woodchuck into a hole in the tumbled stone wall, that he almost had him, that the intoxicating wild-animal smell was as close to him—almost—as if he had his jaws on his quarry. Yip! Woof! Yip! Yip!

The wildly joyful quality of the dog-talk enraged the girl. She had been trembling in exhaustion. Now it was indignation. So that was where he had been—when *she* was *killing* herself trying to take care of him. Plenty near enough if he had paid attention to hear her calling and whistling to him. Just so set on having his foolish good time, he never thought to listen for her call.

She stooped to pick up a stout stick. She would teach him. She was hot with anger. It was time he had something to make him remember to listen. She started forward on a run.

But after a few steps she stopped, stood thinking. One of the things to remember about collies, everybody knew that, was that a collie who had been beaten was never "right" again. His spirit was broken. "Anything but a broken-spirited collie"—she had often heard a farmer say that. They were no good after that.

She threw down her stick. Anyhow, she thought, he was really too young to know that he had done wrong. He was still only a puppy. Like all puppies, he got perfectly crazy over wild animal smells. Probably he truly hadn't heard her calling and whistling.

All the same, all the same—she stood stock-still, staring intently into the twilight—you couldn't let a puppy grow up just as he wanted to. It wouldn't be safe—for *him*. Somehow she would have to make him understand that he mustn't go off this way, by himself. He must be trained to know how to do what a good dog does—not because *she* wanted it, but for his own sake.

She walked on now, steady, purposeful, gathering her inner strength together, Olympian in her understanding of the full meaning of the event.

When he heard his own special young god approaching, he turned delightedly and ran to meet her, panting, his tongue hanging out. His eyes shone. He jumped up on her in an ecstasy of welcome and licked her face.

She pushed him away. Her face and voice were grave. "No, Rollie, *no!*" she said severely. "You're *bad*. You know you're not to go off in the woods without me! You are—a—*bad—dog*."

He was horrified. Stricken into misery. He stood facing her, frozen. The gladness went out of his eyes, the waving plume of his tail slowly lowered to slinking, guilty dejection.

"I know you were all wrapped up in that woodchuck. But that's no excuse. You *could* have heard me, calling you, whistling for you, if you'd paid attention," she went on. "You've got to learn, and I've got to teach you."

With a shudder of misery he lay down, his tail stretched out limp on the ground, his head flat on his paws, his ears drooping—ears ringing with the doomsday awfulness of the voice he loved and revered. To have it speak so to him, he must have been utterly wicked. He trembled, he turned his head away from her august look of blame, he groveled in remorse for whatever mysterious sin he had committed.

As miserable as he, she sat down by him. "I don't *want* to scold you. But I have to! I have to bring you up right, or you'll get shot, Rollie. You mustn't go away from the house without me, do you hear, *never*."

His sharp ears, yearning for her approval, caught a faint overtone of relenting affection in her voice. He lifted his eyes to her, humbly, soft in imploring fondness.

"Oh, Rollie!" she said, stooping low over him, "I *do* love you. I do. But I *have* to bring you up. I'm responsible for you, don't you see."

He did not see. Hearing sternness, or something else he did not recognize, in the beloved voice, he shut his eyes tight in sorrow, and made a little whimpering lament in his throat.

She had never heard him cry before. It was too much. She sat down by him and drew his head to her, rocking him in her arms, soothing him with inarticulate small murmurs.

He leaped in her arms and wriggled happily as he had when he was a baby; he reached up to lick her face as he had then. But he was no baby now. He was half as big as she, a great, warm, pulsing, living armful of love. She clasped him closely. Her heart was brimming full, but calmed, quiet. The blood flowed strongly, steadily, all through her body. She was deliciously warm. Her nose was still running, a little. She sniffed and wiped it on her sleeve.

It was almost dark now. "We'll be late to supper, Rollie," she said, responsibly. Pushing him gently off she stood up. "Home, Rollie, home."

Here was a command he could understand. At once he trotted along the path toward home. His tail, held high, waved plumelike. His short dog-memory had forgotten the suffering just back of him.

Her human memory was longer. His prancing gait was as carefree as a young child's. She plodded behind him like a serious adult. Her very shoulders seemed bowed by what she had lived through. She felt, she thought, like an old woman of thirty. But it was all right now, she knew she had made an impression on him.

When they came out into the open pasture, Rollie ran back to get her to play with him. He leaped around her in circles, barking in cheerful yawps, jumping up on her, inviting her to run a race with him, to throw him a stick, to come alive.

His high spirits were ridiculous. But infectious. She gave one little leap to match his. Rollie took this as a threat, a pretend play-threat. He planted his forepaws low and barked loudly at her, laughing between yips. He was so funny, she thought, when he grinned that way. She laughed back, and gave another mock-threatening leap at him. Radiant that his sky was once more clear, he

He leaped around her in circles, barking in cheerful yawps.

sprang high on his steel-spring muscles in an explosion of happiness, and bounded in circles around her.

Following him, not noting in the dusk where she was going, she felt the grassy slope drop steeply. Oh, yes, she knew where she was. They had come to the rolling-down hill just back of the house. All the kids rolled down there, even the little ones, because it was soft grass without a stone. She had rolled down that slope a million times—years and years before, when she was a kid herself, six or seven years ago. It was fun. She remembered well the whirling dizziness of the descent, all the world turning crazily over and over. And the delicious giddy staggering when you first stood up, the earth still spinning under your feet.

"All right, Rollie, let's go," she cried, and flung herself down in the rolling position, her arms straight up over her head.

Rollie had never seen this skylarking before. It threw him into almost hysterical amusement. He capered around the rapidly rolling figure, half scared, mystified, enchanted.

His wild frolicsome barking might have come from her own throat, so accurately did it sound the way she felt—crazy, foolish—like a little kid, no more than five years old, the age she had been when she had last rolled down that hill.

At the bottom she sprang up, on muscles as steel-strong as Rollie's. She staggered a little, and laughed aloud.

The livingroom windows were just before them. How yellow the lighted windows looked when you were in the darkness going home. How nice and yellow. Maybe Mother had waffles for supper. She was a swell cook, Mother was, and she certainly gave her family all the breaks, when it came to meals.

"Home, Rollie, home!" She burst open the door to the living room. "Hi, Mom, what'you got for supper?"

From the kitchen her mother announced coolly, "I hate to break the news to you, but it's waffles."

"Oh, *Mom!*" she shouted in ecstasy.

Her mother could not see her. She did not need to. "For goodness' sakes, go and wash," she called.

In the long mirror across the room she saw herself, her hair hanging wild, her long bare legs scratched, her broadly smiling face dirt-streaked, her torn skirt dangling, her dog laughing up at her. Gosh, was it a relief to feel your own age, just exactly thirteen years old! ■

The Necklace
Guy de Maupassant

*Probably the best known of Guy de Maupassant's short stories, this tale is an excellent example
of the short story with a surprise ending.*

She was one of those pretty, attractive girls born, as though fate had blundered, into a family of artisans. She had no marriage portion, no expectations, no means of being known, understood, loved, and married by a man of wealth and distinction; and she let herself be married off to a little clerk in the Ministry of Education.

Her tastes were simple because she had never been able to afford any other, but she was as unhappy as though she had married beneath her; for women have no caste nor class, their beauty, grace, and charm serving them for birth or family. Their natural delicacy, their instinctive elegance, their nimbleness of wit, are their only mark of rank, and put the slum girl on a level with the highest lady in the land.

She suffered endlessly, feeling herself born for every delicacy and luxury. She suffered from the shabbiness of her house, from its mean walls, worn chairs, and ugly curtains. All these things, of which other women of her class would not even have been aware, tormented and offended her. The sight of the little Breton girl who came to do her housework aroused pangs of regret and hopeless dreams in her mind. She imagined silent antechambers, heavy with Oriental tapestries, lit by torches in lofty bronze sockets, with two tall footmen in knee breeches dozing in large armchairs, overcome by the heavy warmth of the stove. She imagined vast salons hung with antique silks, exquisite pieces of furniture supporting priceless ornaments, and small, charming, perfumed rooms, created for little parties of intimate friends, men who were famous and sought after, whose homage roused every other woman's envious longings.

When she sat down for dinner at the round table covered with a three-day-old cloth, opposite her husband, who always exclaimed, as he took the cover off the soup-tureen, "Aha! Scotch broth! What could be better?" she imagined delicate meals, gleaming silver, tapestries peopling the walls with folk of a past age and strange birds in fairy forests; she imagined exquisite viands served in marvelous dishes, murmured gallantries, listened to with an inscrutable smile while she trifled with the rosy flesh of trout or wings of asparagus chicken.

She had no clothes, no jewels, nothing. And these were the only things she loved; she felt that she was made for them. She had longed so eagerly to charm, to be desired, to be wildly attractive and sought after.

She had a rich friend, an old school friend whom she refused to visit, because she suffered so keenly each time she returned home. She would weep whole days, with grief, regret, despair, and misery.

One evening her husband came home with an exultant air, holding a large envelope.

"Here's something for you," he said.

Swiftly she tore it open and drew out a printed card on which were these words:

The Minister of Education and Madame Ramponneau request the pleasure of the company of Monsieur and Madame Loisel at the Ministry on the evening of Monday, January the 18th.

Instead of being delighted, as her husband hoped, she flung the invitation petulantly across the table, murmuring:

"What do you want me to do with this?"

"Why, darling, I thought you'd be pleased. You never go out, and this is a great occasion. I had tremendous trouble to get it. Everyone wants one; it's very select, and very few go to the clerks. You'll see all the really big people there."

She looked at him out of furious eyes, and said impatiently:

"And what do you suppose I am to wear at such an affair?"

He had not thought about it; he stammered:

"Why, the dress you go to the theater in. It looks very nice, to me. . . ."

He stopped, stupefied and utterly at a loss when he saw that his wife was beginning to cry. Two large tears ran slowly down from the corners of her eyes toward the corners of her mouth.

"What's the matter with you? What's the matter with you?" he faltered.

But with a violent effort she overcame her grief and replied calmly, wiping her wet cheeks:

"Nothing. Only I haven't a dress and so I can't go to this party. Give your invitation to some friend whose wife will be turned out better."

He was heartbroken.

"Look here, Mathilde," he persisted. "What would be the cost of a suitable dress, which you could use on other occasions as well, something very simple?"

She thought for several seconds, reckoning up prices and also wondering how large a sum she could ask without bringing upon herself an immediate refusal and an exclamation of horror from the prudent clerk.

Finally she replied with some hesitation:

"I don't know exactly, but I think I could do it for four hundred francs."

He grew slightly pale, for this was exactly the amount he had been saving for a gun, intending to get a little shooting next summer on the plain of Nanterre with some friends who went lark-shooting there on Sundays.

Nevertheless he said, "Very well. I'll give you four hundred francs. But try to get a really nice dress with the money."

The day of the party drew near, and Madame Loisel seemed sad, uneasy and anxious. Her dress was ready, however. One evening her husband said to her:

"What's the matter with you? You've been very odd for the last three days."

"I'm utterly miserable at not having any jewels, not a single stone to wear," she replied. "I shall look absolutely like a nobody. I would almost rather not go to the party."

"Wear flowers," he said. "They're very smart at this time of the year. For ten francs you could get two or three gorgeous roses."

She was not convinced.

"No . . . there's nothing so humiliating as looking poor in the middle of a lot of rich women."

"How stupid you are!" exclaimed her husband. "Go and see Madame Forestier and ask her to lend you some jewelry. You know her quite well enough for that."

She uttered a cry of delight.

"That's true. I never thought of it."

Next day she went to see her friend and told her her trouble.

Madame Forestier went to her dressing table, took up a large box, brought it to Madame Loisel, opened it, and said:

"Choose, my dear."

First she saw some bracelets, then a pearl necklace, then a Venetian cross in gold and gems, of exquisite workmanship. She tried the effect of the jewels before the mirror, hesitating, unable to make up her mind to leave them, to give them up. She kept on asking:

"Haven't you anything else?"

"Yes. Look for yourself. I don't know what you would like best."

Suddenly she discovered, in a black satin case, a superb diamond necklace; her heart began to beat covetously. Her hands trembled as she lifted it. She fastened it round her neck, upon her high dress, and remained in ecstasy at sight of herself.

Then, with hesitation, she asked in anguish: "Could you lend me this, just this?"

"Yes, of course."

She flung herself on her friend's breast, embraced her rapturously, and went away with her treasure.

———

The day of the party arrived. Madame Loisel was a success. She was the prettiest woman present, elegant, graceful, smiling, and quite beside herself with happiness. All the men stared at her, inquired her name, and asked to be introduced. All the undersecretaries of state were eager to waltz with her. The Minister noticed her.

She danced madly, ecstatically, drunk with pleasure, with no thought for anything, in the triumph of her beauty, in the pride of her success, in a cloud of happiness made up of this universal homage and admiration, of the desires she had aroused, of the completeness of a victory so dear to her feminine heart.

She left about four o'clock in the morning. Since midnight her husband had been dozing in a deserted little room, in company with three other men whose wives were having a good time.

She danced madly, ecstatically, drunk with pleasure.

LLOYD BIRMINGHAM

He threw over her shoulders the garments he had brought for them to go home in, modest everyday clothes, whose poverty clashed with the beauty of the ball dress. She was conscious of this and was anxious to hurry away, so that she should not be noticed by other women who were putting on costly furs.

Loisel restrained her.

"Wait a little. You'll catch cold in the open. I'm going to fetch a cab."

But she did not listen to him and went swiftly down the staircase. When they were out in the street they could not find a cab; they began to look for one, shouting at the drivers whom they saw passing in the distance.

They walked down toward the Seine, anxious and shivering. At last they found on the quay one of those old night-prowling carriages which are to be seen in Paris only after dark, as though ashamed of their shabbiness in the daylight.

It brought them to their door in the Rue des Martyrs, and sadly they walked up to their own apartment. This was the end, for her. As for him, he was thinking that he must be at the office at ten.

She took off the garments in which she had wrapped her shoulders, so as to see herself in all her glory before the mirror. But suddenly she uttered a cry. The necklace was no longer round her neck!

"What's the matter with you?" asked her husband, already half undressed.

She turned toward him in the utmost distress.

"I . . . I . . . I've lost Madame Forestier's necklace. . . ."

He started with astonishment.

"What! . . . Impossible!"

They searched in the folds of her dress, in the folds of the coat, in the pockets, everywhere. They could not find it.

"Are you sure that you still had it on when you came away from the ball?" he asked.

"Yes, I fingered it in the hall at the Ministry."

"But if you had lost it in the street, we should have heard it fall."

"Yes. Probably we should. Did you take the number of the cab?"

"No. You didn't notice it, did you?"

"No."

They stared at one another, dumbfounded. At last Loisel put on his clothes again.

"I'll go over all the ground we walked," he said, "and see if I can't find it."

And he went out. She remained in her evening clothes, lacking strength to get into bed, huddled on a chair, without volition or power of thought.

Her husband returned about seven. He had found nothing.

He went to the police station, to the newspapers, to offer a reward, to the cab companies, everywhere that a ray of hope impelled him.

She waited all day long, in the same state of bewilderment at this fearful catastrophe.

Loisel came home at night, his face lined and pale; he had discovered nothing.

"You must write to your friend," he said, "and tell her that you've broken the clasp of her necklace and are getting it mended. That will give us time to look about us."

She wrote at his dictation.

By the end of a week they had lost all hope.

Loisel, who had aged five years, declared:

"We must see about replacing the diamonds."

Next day they took the box which had held the necklace and went to the jeweler whose name was inside. He consulted his books.

"It was not I who sold this necklace, Madame; I must have merely supplied the clasp."

Then they went from jeweler to jeweler, searching for another necklace like the first, consulting their memories, both ill with remorse and anguish of mind.

In a shop at the Palais-Royal they found a string of diamonds which seemed to them exactly like the one they were looking for. It was worth forty thousand francs. They could have it for thirty-six thousand.

They begged the jeweler not to sell it for three days. And they arranged matters on the understanding that it would be taken back for thirty-four thousand francs, if the first one were found before the end of February.

Loisel possessed eighteen thousand francs left to him by his father. He intended to borrow the rest.

He did borrow it, a thousand from one man, five hundred from another, five louis here, three louis there. He gave notes of hand, entered into ruinous arrangements, did business with usurers and the whole tribe of moneylenders. He mortgaged the whole remaining years of his existence, risked his signature without even knowing if he could honor it, and, appalled at the agonizing face of the future, at the black misery about to fall upon him, at the prospect of every possible physical privation and moral torture, he went to get the new necklace and put down upon the jeweler's counter thirty-six thousand francs.

When Madame Loisel took back the necklace to Madame Forestier, the latter said to her in a chilly voice: "You ought to have brought it back sooner; I might have needed it."

She did not, as her friend had feared, open the case. If she had noticed the substitution, what would she have thought? What would she have said? Would she not have taken her for a thief?

Madame Loisel began to live the ghastly life of abject poverty. From the very first she played her part heroically. This fearful debt must be paid off. She would pay it. The servant was dismissed. They changed their flat; they took a garret under the roof.

She came to know the heavy work of the house, the hateful duties of the kitchen. She washed the plates, wearing out her pink nails on the coarse pottery and the bottoms of pans. She washed the dirty linen, the shirts and dishcloths, and hung them out to dry on a cord; every morning she took the dustbin down into the street and carried up the water, stopping on each landing to get her breath. And, clad like a poor woman, she went to the fruiterer, to the grocer, to the butcher, a basket on her arm, haggling, insulted, fighting for every wretched halfpenny of her money.

Every month notes had to be paid off, others renewed, time gained.

Her husband worked in the evenings at putting straight a merchant's accounts, and often at night he did copying at five sous a page.

This life lasted ten years.

At the end of ten years everything was paid off, everything, the usurers' charges and the accumulation of superimposed interest.

Madame Loisel looked old now. She had become like all the other strong, hard, coarse women of poor households. Her hair was badly done, her skirts were awry, her hands were red. She spoke in a shrill voice, and the water slopped all over the floor when she scrubbed it. But sometimes, when her husband was at the office, she

She had become like all the other strong, hard, coarse women.

LLOYD BIRMINGHAM

sat down by the window and thought of that evening long ago, of the ball at which she had been so beautiful and so much admired.

What would have happened if she had never lost those jewels? Who knows? Who knows? How strange life is, how fickle! How little is needed to ruin or to save!

One Sunday, as she had gone for a walk along the Champs Elysées to freshen herself after the labors of the week, she caught sight suddenly of a woman who was taking a child out for a walk. It was Madame Forestier, still young, still beautiful, still attractive.

Madame Loisel was conscious of some emotion. Should she speak to her? Yes, certainly. And now that she had paid, she would tell her all. Why not?

She went up to her.

"Good morning, Jeanne."

The other did not recognize her, and was surprised at being thus familiarly addressed by a poor woman.

"But . . . Madame . . ." she stammered. "I don't know . . . you must be making a mistake."

"No . . . I am Mathilde Loisel."

Her friend uttered a cry.

"Oh! . . . . my poor Mathilde, how you have changed! . . ."

"Yes, I've had some hard times since I saw you last; and many sorrows . . . and all on your account."

"On my account! . . . How was that?"

"You remember the diamond necklace you lent me for the ball at the Ministry?"

"Yes. Well?"

"Well, I lost it."

"How could you? Why, you brought it back."

"I brought you another one just like it. And for the last ten years we have been paying for it. You realize it wasn't easy for us; we had no money. . . . Well, it's paid for at last, and I'm glad indeed."

Madame Forestier had halted.

"You say you bought a diamond necklace to replace mine?"

"Yes. Hadn't you noticed it? They were very much alike."

And she smiled in proud and innocent happiness.

Madame Forestier, deeply moved, took her two hands.

"Oh, my poor Mathilde! But mine was paste. It was worth at the very most five hundred francs! . . ." ■

The Lady, Or the Tiger?

Frank R. Stockton

This story has no ending. At least, the ending is not supplied by the author. That job he left up to the reader. What do you think the ending should be?

In the very olden time there lived a semi-barbaric king, whose ideas, though somewhat polished and sharpened by the progressiveness of distant Latin neighbors, were still large, florid and untrammeled, as became the half of him which was barbaric. He was a man of exuberant fancy, and, withal, of an authority so irresistible that, at his will, he turned his varied fancies into facts. He was greatly given to self-communing; and when he and himself agreed upon anything, the thing was done. When every member of his domestic and political systems moved smoothly in its appointed course, his nature was bland and genial; but whenever there was a little hitch, and some of his orbs got out of their orbits, he was blander and more genial still, for nothing pleased him so much as to make the crooked straight, and crush down uneven places.

Among the borrowed notions by which his barbarism had become semisatisfied was that of the public arena, in which, by exhibitions of manly and beastly valor, the minds of his subjects were refined and cultured.

But even here the exuberant and barbaric fancy asserted itself. The arena of the king was built not to give the people an opportunity of hearing the rhapsodies of dying gladiators, nor to enable them to view the inevitable conclusion of a conflict between religious opinions and hungry jaws, but for purposes far better adapted to widen and develop the mental energies of the people. This vast amphitheater, with its encircling galleries, its mysterious vaults, and its unseen passages, was an agent of poetic justice, in which crime was punished, or virtue rewarded, by the decrees of an impartial and incorruptible chance.

When a subject was accused of a crime of sufficient importance to interest the king, public notice was given that on an appointed day the fate of the accused person would be decided in the king's arena—a structure which well deserved its name; for, although its form and plan were borrowed from afar, its purpose emanated solely from the brain of this man, who, every barleycorn a king, knew no tradition to which he owed more allegiance than pleased his fancy, and who ingrafted on every adopted form of human thought and action the rich growth of his barbaric idealism.

When all the people had assembled in the galleries, and the king, surrounded by his court, sat high up on his throne of royal state on one side of the arena, he gave a signal, a door beneath him opened, and the accused subject stepped out into the amphitheater. Directly opposite him, on the other side of the enclosed space, were two doors, exactly alike and side by side. It was the duty and the privilege of the person on trial to walk directly to these doors and open one of them. He could open either door he pleased: he was subject to no guidance or influence but that of the aforementioned impartial and incorruptible chance. If he opened the one, there came out of it a hungry tiger, the fiercest and most cruel that could be procured, which immediately sprang upon him, and tore him to pieces, as a punishment for his guilt. The moment that the case of the criminal was thus decided, doleful iron bells were clanged, great wails went up from the hired mourners posted on the outer rim of the arena, and the vast audience, with bowed heads and downcast hearts, wended slowly their homeward way, mourning greatly that one so young and fair, or so old and respected, should have merited so dire a fate.

But, if the accused person opened the other door, there came forth from it a lady, the most suitable to his years and station that his Majesty could select among his fair subjects; and to this lady he was immediately married, as a reward of his innocence. It mattered not that he might already possess a wife and family, or that his affections might be engaged upon an object of his own selection: the king allowed no such subordinate arrangements to interfere with his great scheme of retribution and reward. The exercises, as in the other instance, took place immediately, and in the arena. Another door opened beneath the king, and a priest, followed by a band of choristers, and dancing maidens blowing joyous airs on golden horns and treading an epithalamic measure, advanced to where the pair stood, side by side; and the wedding was promptly and cheerily solemnized. Then the gay brass bells rang forth

their merry peals, the people shouted glad hur-
rahs, and the innocent man, preceded by children
strewing flowers on his path, led his bride to his
home.

This was the king's semi-barbaric method of
administering justice. Its perfect fairness is obvious. The criminal could not know out of which
door would come the lady: he opened either he
pleased, without having the slightest idea
whether, in the next instant, he was to be de-
voured or married. On some occasions the tiger
came out of one door, and on some out of the
other. The decisions of this tribunal were not
only fair, they were positively determinate: the
accused person was instantly punished if he
found himself guilty; and, if innocent, he was
rewarded on the spot, whether he liked it or not.
There was no escape from the judgments of the
king's arena.

The institution was a very popular one. When
the people gathered together on one of the great
trial days, they never knew whether they were to
witness a bloody slaughter or a hilarious wedding. This element of uncertainty lent an interest
to the occasion which it could not otherwise have
attained. Thus the masses were entertained and
pleased, and the thinking part of the community
could bring no charge of unfairness against this
plan; for did not the accused person have the
whole matter in his own hands?

This semi-barbaric king had a daughter as
blooming as his most florid fancies, and with a
soul as fervent and imperious as his own. As is
usual in such cases, she was the apple of his eye,
and was loved by him above all humanity.
Among his courtiers was a young man of that
fineness of blood and lowness of station common
to the conventional heroes of romance who love
royal maidens. This royal maiden was well satisfied with her lover, for he was handsome and
brave to a degree unsurpassed in all this kingdom; and she loved him with an ardor that had
enough of barbarism in it to make it exceedingly
warm and strong. This love affair moved on happily for many months, until one day the king happened to discover its existence. He did not
hesitate nor waver in regard to his duty in the
premises. The youth was immediately cast into
prison, and a day was appointed for his trial in
the king's arena. This, of course, was an especially important occasion; and his Majesty, as
well as all the people, was greatly interested in
the workings and development of this trial.
Never before had such a case occurred; never before had a subject dared to love the daughter of a

king. In after years such things became commonplace enough; but then they were, in no slight
degree, novel and startling.

The tiger-cages of the kingdom were searched
for the most savage and relentless beasts, from
which the fiercest monster might be selected for
the arena; and the ranks of maiden youth and
beauty throughout the land were carefully surveyed by competent judges, in order that the
young man might have a fitting bride in case fate
did not determine for him a different destiny. Of
course, everybody knew that the deed with which
the accused was charged had been done. He had
loved the princess, and neither he, she, nor any
one else thought of denying the fact; but the king
would not think of allowing any fact of this kind
to interfere with the workings of the tribunal, in
which he took such a great delight and satisfaction. No matter how the affair turned out, the
youth would be disposed of; and the king would
take an aesthetic pleasure in watching the course
of events, which would determine whether or not
the young man had done wrong in allowing himself to love the princess.

The appointed day arrived. From far and near
the people gathered, and thronged the great galleries of the arena; and crowds, unable to gain
admittance, massed themselves against its outside walls. The king and his court were in their
places, opposite the twin doors—those fateful
portals, so terrible in their similarity.

All was ready. The signal was given. A door
beneath the royal party opened, and the lover of
the princess walked into the arena. Tall, beautiful, fair, his appearance was greeted with a low
hum of admiration and anxiety. Half the audience had not known so grand a youth had lived
among them. No wonder the princess loved him!
What a terrible thing for him to be there!

As the youth advanced into the arena, he
turned, as the custom was, to bow to the king:
but he did not think at all of that royal personage; his eyes were fixed upon the princess, who
sat to the right of her father. Had it not been for
the moiety of barbarism in her nature it is probable that lady would not have been there; but her
intense and fervid soul would not allow her to be
absent on an occasion in which she was so terribly interested. From the moment that the decree
had gone forth that her lover should decide his
fate in the king's arena, she had thought of nothing, night or day, but this great event and the
various subjects connected with it. Possessed of
more power, influence, and force of character
than anyone who had ever before been interested

She raised her hand, and made a slight, quick movement toward the right.

she had seen, this fair creature throwing glances of admiration upon the person of her lover, and sometimes she thought these glances were perceived and even returned. Now and then she had seen them talking together; it was but for a moment or two, but much can be said in a brief space; it may have been on most unimportant topics, but how could she know that? The girl was lovely, but she had dared to raise her eyes to the loved one of the princess; and, with all the intensity of the savage blood transmitted to her through long lines of wholly barbaric ancestors, she hated the woman who blushed and trembled behind that silent door.

When her lover turned and looked at her, and his eye met hers as she sat there paler and whiter than any one in the vast ocean of anxious faces about her, he saw, by that power of quick perception which is given to those whose souls are one, that she knew behind which door crouched the tiger, and behind which stood the lady. He had expected her to know it. He understood her nature, and his soul was assured that she would never rest until she had made plain to herself this thing, hidden to all other lookers-on, even to the king. The only hope for the youth in which there was any element of certainty was based upon the success of the princess in discovering this mystery; and the moment he looked upon her, he saw she had succeeded, as in his soul he knew she would succeed.

Then it was that his quick and anxious glance asked the question: "Which?" It was as plain to her as if he shouted it from where he stood. There was not an instant to be lost. The question was asked in a flash; it must be answered in another.

Her right arm lay on the cushioned parapet before her. She raised her hand, and made a slight, quick movement toward the right. No one but her lover saw her. Every eye but his was fixed on the man in the arena.

He turned, and with a firm and rapid step he walked across the empty space. Every heart stopped beating, every breath was held, every eye was fixed immovably upon that man. Without the slightest hesitation, he went to the door on the right, and opened it.

Now, the point of the story is this: Did the tiger come out of that door, or did the lady?

The more we reflect upon this question, the harder it is to answer. It involves a study of the human heart which leads us through devious mazes of passion, out of which it is difficult to find our way. Think of it, fair reader, not as if the

in such a case, she had done what no other person had done—she had possessed herself of the secret of the doors. She knew in which of the two rooms that lay behind those doors stood the cage of the tiger, with its open front, and in which waited the lady. Through these thick doors, heavily curtained with skins on the inside, it was impossible that any noise or suggestion should come from within to the person who should approach to raise the latch of one of them; but gold, and the power of a woman's will, had brought the secret to the princess.

And not only did she know in which room stood the lady ready to emerge, all blushing and radiant, should her door be opened, but she knew who the lady was. It was one of the fairest and loveliest of the damsels of the court who had been selected as the reward of the accused youth, should he be proved innocent of the crime of aspiring to one so far above him; and the princess hated her. Often had she seen, or imagined that

decision of the question depended upon yourself, but upon that hot-blooded, semi-barbaric princess, her soul at a white heat beneath the combined fires of despair and jealousy. She had lost him, but who should have him?

How often, in her waking hours and in her dreams, had she started in wild horror and covered her face with her hands as she thought of her lover opening the door on the other side of which waited the cruel fangs of the tiger!

But how much oftener had she seen him at the other door! How in her grievous reveries had she gnashed her teeth and torn her hair when she saw his start of rapturous delight as he opened the door of the lady! How her soul had burned in agony when she had seen him rush to meet that woman, with her flushing cheek and sparkling eye of triumph; when she had seen him lead her forth, his whole frame kindled with the joy of recovered life; when she had heard the glad shouts from the multitude, and the wild ringing of the happy bells; when she had seen the priest, with his joyous followers, advance to the couple,

and make them man and wife before her very eyes; and when she had seen them walk away together upon their path of flowers, followed by the tremendous shouts of the hilarious multitude, in which her one despairing shriek was lost and drowned!

Would it not be better for him to die at once, and go to wait for her in the blessed regions of semi-barbaric futurity?

And yet, that awful tiger, those shrieks, that blood!

Her decision had been indicated in an instant, but it had been made after days and nights of anguished deliberation. She had known she would be asked, she had decided what she would answer, and, without the slightest hesitation, she had moved her hand to the right.

The question of her decision is one not to be lightly considered, and it is not for me to presume to set myself up as the one person able to answer it. And so I leave it with all of you: Which came out of the opened door—the lady, or the tiger? ■

The Unicorn in the Garden
James Thurber

Once upon a sunny morning a man who sat in a breakfast nook looked up from his scrambled eggs to see a white unicorn with a gold horn quietly cropping the roses in the garden. The man went up to the bedroom where his wife was still asleep and woke her. "There's a unicorn in the garden," he said. "Eating roses." She opened one unfriendly eye and looked at him. "The unicorn is a mythical beast," she said, and turned her back on him. The man walked slowly downstairs and out into the garden. The unicorn was still there; he was now browsing among the tulips. "Here, unicorn," said the man, and he pulled up a lily and gave it to him. The unicorn ate it gravely. With a high heart, because there was a unicorn in his garden, the man went upstairs and roused his wife again. "The unicorn," he said, "ate a lily." His wife sat up in bed and looked at him, coldly. "You are a booby," she said, "and I am going to have you put in the booby-hatch." The man, who had never liked the words "booby" and "booby-hatch," and who liked them even less on a shining morning when there was a unicorn in the garden,

thought for a moment. "We'll see about that," he said. He walked over to the door. "He has a golden horn in the middle of his forehead," he told her. Then he went back to the garden to watch the unicorn; but the unicorn had gone away. The man sat down among the roses and went to sleep.

As soon as the husband had gone out of the house, the wife got up and dressed as fast as she could. She was very excited and there was a gloat in her eye. She telephoned the police and she telephoned a psychiatrist; she told them to hurry to her house and bring a straitjacket. When the police and the psychiatrist arrived they sat down in chairs and looked at her, with great interest. "My husband," she said, "saw a unicorn this morning." The police looked at the psychiatrist and the psychiatrist looked at the police. "He told me it ate a lily," she said. The psychiatrist looked at the police and the police looked at the psychiatrist. "He told me it had a golden horn in the middle of its forehead," she said. At a solemn signal from the psychiatrist, the police leaped from their chairs and seized the wife. They had a hard time subduing her, for she put up a terrific struggle, but they finally subdued her. Just as they got her into the straitjacket, the husband came back into the house.

"Did you tell your wife you saw a unicorn?" asked the police. "Of course not," said the husband. "The unicorn is a mythical beast." "That's all I wanted to know," said the psychiatrist. "Take her away. I'm sorry sir, but your wife is as crazy as a jaybird." So they took her away, cursing and screaming, and shut her up in a institution. The husband lived happily ever after.

Moral: Don't count your boobies until they are hatched.

The Open Window

Saki (H. H. Munro)

FROM *THE COMPLETE SHORT STORIES OF SAKI*, BY SAKI (H.H. MUNRO).
COPYRIGHT 1930, RENEWED (C) 1958 BY THE VIKING PRESS, INC. REPRINTED BY PERMISSION OF VIKING PENGUIN, INC.

Hector Hugh Munro, writing under the pen name Saki, produced a sizable number of short
stories before his death in World War I. His work is often found in literary anthologies.
This story involves a young lady with a remarkable talent for . . . well, read on.

"My aunt will be down presently, Mr. Nuttel,"
said a very self-possessed young lady of fifteen; "in the
meantime you must try and put up with me."

Framton Nuttel endeavored to say the correct something
which should duly flatter the niece of the moment without
unduly discounting the aunt that was to come. Privately he
doubted more than ever whether these formal visits on a
succession of total strangers would do much toward helping
the nerve cure which he was supposed to be undergoing.

"I know how it will be," his sister had said when he was
preparing to migrate to this rural retreat; "you will bury
yourself down there and not speak to a living soul, and your
nerves will be worse than ever from moping. I shall just give
you letters of introduction to all the people I know there.
Some of them, as far as I can remember, were quite nice."

Framton wondered whether Mrs. Sappleton, the lady to
whom he was presenting one of the letters of introduction,
came into the nice division.

"Do you know many of the people round here?" asked the
niece, when she judged that they had had sufficient silent
communion.

"Hardly a soul," said Framton. "My sister was staying
here, at the rectory, you know, some four years ago, and she
gave me letters of introduction to some of the people here."

He made the last statement in a tone of distinct regret.

"Then you know practically nothing about my aunt?"
pursued the self-possessed young lady.

"Only her name and address," admitted the caller. He
was wondering whether Mrs. Sappleton was in the married
or widowed state. An undefinable something about the room
seemed to suggest masculine habitation.

"Her great tragedy happened just three years ago," said
the child; "that would be since your sister's time."

"Her tragedy?" asked Framton; somehow in this restful
country spot tragedies seemed out of place.

"You may wonder why we keep that window wide open
on an October afternoon," said the niece, indicating a large
French window that opened on to a lawn.

"It is quite warm for the time of the year," said Framton;
"but has that window got anything to do with the tragedy?"

"Out through that window, three years ago to a day, her
husband and her two young brothers went off for their day's
shooting. They never came back. In crossing the moor to
their favorite snipe-shooting ground they were all three engulfed in a treacherous piece of bog. It had been that dreadful wet summer, you know, and places that were safe in
other years gave way suddenly without warning. Their bodies were never recovered. That was the dreadful part of it."
Here the child's voice lost its self-possessed note and became
falteringly human. "Poor aunt always thinks that they will
come back some day, they and the little brown spaniel that
was lost with them, and walk in at that window just as they
used to do. That is why the window is kept open every evening till it is quite dusk. Poor dear aunt, she has often told
me how they went out, her husband with his white waterproof coat over his arm, and Ronnie, her youngest brother,
singing, 'Bertie, why do you bound?' as he always did to
tease her, because she said it got on her nerves. Do you
know, sometimes on still, quiet evenings like this, I almost
get a creepy feeling that they will all walk in through that
window—"

She broke off with a little shudder. It was a relief to Framton when the aunt bustled into the room with a whirl of
apologies for being late in making her appearance.

"I hope Vera has been amusing you?" she said.

"She has been very interesting." said Framton.

"I hope you don't mind the open window," said Mrs. Sappleton briskly; "my husband and brothers will be home directly from shooting, and they always come in this way.
They've been out for snipe in the marshes today, so they'll
make a fine mess over my poor carpets. So like you menfolk,
isn't it?"

She rattled on cheerfully about the shooting and the scarcity of birds, and the prospects for duck in the winter. To
Framton, it was all purely horrible. He made a desperate but
only partially successful effort to turn the talk on to a less
ghastly topic; he was conscious that his hostess was giving
him only a fragment of her attention, and her eyes were
constantly straying past him to the open window and the
lawn beyond. It was certainly an unfortunate coincidence
that he should have paid his visit on this tragic anniversary.

"The doctors agree in ordering me complete rest, an absence of mental excitement, and avoidance of anything in
the nature of violent physical exercise," announced Framton, who labored under the tolerably widespread delusion
that total strangers and chance acquaintances are hungry
for the least detail of one's ailments and infirmities, their
cause and cure. "On the matter of diet they are not so much
in agreement," he continued.

"No?" said Mrs. Sappleton, in a voice which only replaced
a yawn at the last moment. Then she suddenly brightened
into alert attention—but not to what Framton was saying.

"Here they are at last!" she cried. "Just in time for tea,
and don't they look as if they were muddy up to the eyes!"

Framton shivered slightly and turned toward the niece
with a look intended to convey sympathetic comprehension.
The child was staring out through the open window with
dazed horror in her eyes. In a chill shock of nameless fear
Framton swung round in his seat and looked in the same
direction.

In the deepening twilight three figures were walking
across the lawn toward the window; they all carried guns
under their arms, and one of them was additionally burdened with a white coat hung over his shoulders. A tired
brown spaniel kept close at their heels. Noiselessly they
neared the house, and then a hoarse young voice chanted
out of the dusk: "I said, Bertie, why do you bound?"

Framton grabbed wildly at his stick and hat; the hall
door, the gravel drive, and the front gate were dimly noted
stages in his headlong retreat. A cyclist coming along the
road had to run into the hedge to avoid imminent collision.

"Here we are, my dear," said the bearer of the white
mackintosh, coming in through the window; "fairly muddy,
but most of it's dry. Who was that who bolted out as we
came up?"

"A most extraordinary man, a Mr. Nuttel," said Mrs. Sappleton; "could only talk about his illnesses, and dashed off
without a word of goodbye or apology when you arrived.
One would think he had seen a ghost."

"I expect it was the spaniel," said the niece calmly; "he
told me he had a horror of dogs. He was once hunted into a
cemetery somewhere on the banks of the Ganges by a pack
of pariah dogs, and had to spend the night in a newly dug
grave with the creatures snarling and grinning and foaming
just above him. Enough to make any one lose their nerve."

Romance at short notice was her specialty. ∎

The Gift of the Magi

O. Henry

William Sydney Porter, pen name O. Henry, was an acknowledged master of the short story, particularly the type of story that hinges on an ironic twist of fate. In this tale, one of his best-known works, the author uses his extraordinary sense of the ironic to examine the qualities of love and selflessness.

One dollar and eighty-seven cents. That was all. And sixty cents of it was in pennies. Pennies saved one and two at a time by bulldozing the grocer and the vegetable man and the butcher until one's cheeks burned with the silent imputation of parsimony that such close dealing implied. Three times Della counted it. One dollar and eighty-seven cents. And the next day would be Christmas.

There was clearly nothing to do but flop down on the shabby little couch and howl. So Della did it. Which instigates the moral reflection that life is made up of sobs, sniffles, and smiles, with sniffles predominating.

While the mistress of the home is gradually subsiding from the first stage to the second, take a look at the home. A furnished flat at $8 per week. It did not exactly beggar description, but it certainly had that word on the lookout for the mendicancy squad.

In the vestibule below was a letter-box into which no letter would go, and an electric button from which no mortal finger could coax a ring. Also appertaining thereunto was a card bearing the name "Mr. James Dillingham Young."

The "Dillingham" had been flung to the breeze during a former period of prosperity when its possessor was being paid $30 per week. Now, when the income was shrunk to $20, the letters of "Dillingham" looked blurred, as though they were thinking seriously of contracting to a modest and unassuming D. But whenever Mr. James Dillingham Young came home and reached his flat above he was called "Jim" and greatly hugged by Mrs. James Dillingham Young, already introduced to you as Della. Which is all very good.

Della finished her cry and attended to her cheeks with the powder rag. She stood by the window and looked out dully at a gray cat walking a gray fence in a gray backyard. Tomorrow would be Christmas Day and she had only $1.87 with which to buy Jim a present. She had been saving every penny she could for months, with this result. Twenty dollars a week doesn't go far. Expenses had been greater than she had calculated. They always are. Only $1.87 to buy a present for Jim. Her Jim. Many a happy hour she had spent planning for something nice for him. Something fine and rare and sterling—something just a little bit near to being worthy of the honor of being owned by Jim.

There was a pier-glass between the windows of the room. Perhaps you have seen a pier-glass in an $8 flat. A very thin and very agile person may, by observing his reflection in a rapid sequence of longitudinal strips, obtain a fairly accurate conception of his looks. Della, being slender, had mastered the art.

Suddenly she whirled from the window and stood before the glass. Her eyes were shining brilliantly, but her face had lost its color within twenty seconds. Rapidly she pulled down her hair and let it fall to its full length.

Now, there were two possessions of the James Dillingham Youngs in which they both took a mighty pride. One was Jim's gold watch that had been his father's and his grandfather's. The other was Della's hair. Had the Queen of Sheba lived in the flat across the airshaft, Della would have let her hair hang out the window some day to dry just to depreciate Her Majesty's jewels and gifts. Had King Solomon been the janitor, with all his treasures piled up in the basement, Jim would have pulled out his watch every time he passed, just to see him pluck at his beard from envy.

So now Della's beautiful hair fell about her, rippling and shining like a cascade of brown waters. It reached below her knee and made itself almost a garment for her. And then she did it up again nervously and quickly. Once she faltered for a minute and stood still while a tear or two splashed on the worn red carpet.

On went her old brown jacket; on went her old brown hat. With a whirl of skirts and with the brilliant sparkle still in her eyes, she fluttered out the door and down the stairs to the street.

Where she stopped the sign read: "Mme. Sofronie. Hair Goods of All Kinds." One flight up Della ran, and collected herself, panting. Madame, large, too white, chilly, hardly looked the "Sofronie."

"Will you buy my hair?" asked Della.

"I buy hair," said Madame. "Take yer hat off and let's have a sight at the looks of it."

Down rippled the brown cascade.

"Twenty dollars," said Madame, lifting the mass with a practiced hand.

"Give it to me quick," said Della.

Oh, and the next two hours tripped by on rosy wings. Forget the hashed metaphor. She was ransacking the stores for Jim's present.

She found it at last. It surely had been made for Jim and no one else. There was no other like it in any of the stores, and she had turned all of them inside out. It was a platinum fob chain simple and chaste in design, properly proclaiming its value by substance alone and not by meretricious ornamentation—as all good things should do. It was even worthy of The Watch. As soon as she saw it she knew that it must be Jim's. It was like him. Quietness and value—the description applied to both. Twenty-one dollars they took from her for it, and she hurried home with the 87 cents. With that chain on his watch Jim might be properly anxious about the time in any company. Grand as the watch was, he sometimes looked at it on the sly on account of the old leather strap that he used in place of a chain.

When Della reached home her intoxication gave way a little to prudence and reason. She got out her curling irons and lighted the gas and went to work repairing the ravages made by generosity added to love. Which is always a tremendous task, dear friends—a mammoth task.

Within forty minutes her head was covered with tiny, close-lying curls that made her look wonderfully like a truant schoolboy. She looked at her reflection in the mirror long, carefully, and critically.

"If Jim doesn't kill me," she said to herself, "before he takes a second look at me, he'll say I look like a Coney Island chorus girl. But what could I do—oh! what could I do with a dollar and eighty-seven cents?"

At 7 o'clock the coffee was made and the frying pan was on the back of the stove hot and ready to cook the chops.

Jim was never late. Della doubled the fob chain in her hand and sat on the corner of the table near the door that he always entered. Then she heard his step on the stair away down on the first flight, and she turned white for just a moment. She had a habit of saying little silent prayers about the simplest everyday things, and now she whispered: "Please God, make him think I am still pretty."

The door opened and Jim stepped in and closed it. He

MIKE EAGLE/DILAS EVANS FINE ILLUSTRATION

looked thin and very serious. Poor fellow, he was only twenty-two—and to be burdened with a family! He needed a new overcoat and he was without gloves.

Jim stopped inside the door, as immovable as a setter at the scent of quail. His eyes were fixed upon Della, and there was an expression in them that she could not read, and it terrified her. It was not anger, nor surprise, nor disapproval, nor horror, nor any of the sentiments that she had been prepared for. He simply stared at her fixedly with that peculiar expression on his face.

Della wriggled off the table and went for him.

"Jim, darling," she cried, "don't look at me that way. I had my hair cut off and sold it because I couldn't have lived through Christmas without giving you a present. It'll grow out again—you won't mind, will you? I just had to do it. My hair grows awfully fast. Say 'Merry Christmas!' Jim, and let's be happy. You don't know what a nice—what a beautiful, nice gift I've got for you."

"You've cut off your hair?" asked Jim, laboriously, as if he had not arrived at that patent fact yet even after the hardest mental labor.

"Cut it off and sold it," said Della. "Don't you like me just as well, anyhow? I'm me without my hair, ain't I?"

Jim looked about the room curiously.

"You say your hair is gone?" he said, with an air almost of idiocy.

"You needn't look for it," said Della. "It's sold, I tell you—sold and gone, too. It's Christmas Eve, boy. Be good to me, for it went for you. Maybe the hairs of my head were numbered," she went on with a sudden serious sweetness, "but nobody could ever count my love for you. Shall I put the chops on, Jim?"

Out of his trance Jim seemed quickly to wake. He enfolded his Della. For ten seconds let us regard with discreet scrutiny some inconsequential object in the other direction. Eight dollars a week or a million a year—what is the difference? A mathematician or a wit would give you the wrong answer. The magi brought valuable gifts, but that was not among them. This dark assertion will be illuminated later on.

Jim drew a package from his overcoat pocket and threw it upon the table.

"Don't make any mistake, Dell," he said, "about me. I don't think there's anything in the way of a haircut or a shave or a shampoo that could make me like my girl any less. But if you'll unwrap that package you may see why you had me going a while at first."

White fingers and nimble tore at the string and paper. And then an ecstatic scream of joy; and then, alas! a quick feminine change to hysterical tears and wails, necessitating the immediate employment of all the comforting powers of the lord of the flat.

For there lay The Combs—the set of combs, side and back, that Della had worshiped for long in a Broadway window. Beautiful combs, pure tortoise shell, with jeweled rims—just the shade to wear in the beautiful vanished hair. They were expensive combs, she knew, and her heart had simply craved and yearned over them without the least hope of possession. And now, they were hers, but the tresses that should have adorned the coveted adornments were gone.

But she hugged them to her bosom, and at length she was able to look up with dim eyes and a smile and say: "My hair grows so fast, Jim!"

And then Della leaped up like a little singed cat and cried, "Oh, oh!"

Jim had not yet seen his beautiful present. She held it out to him eagerly upon her open palm. The dull precious metal seemed to flash with a reflection of her bright and ardent spirit.

"Isn't it a dandy, Jim? I hunted all over town to find it. You'll have to look at the time a hundred times a day now. Give me your watch. I want to see how it looks on it."

Instead of obeying, Jim tumbled down on the couch and put his hands under the back of his head and smiled.

"Dell," said he, "let's put our Christmas presents away and keep 'em a while. They're too nice to use just at present. I sold the watch to get the money to buy your combs. And now suppose you put the chops on."

The magi, as you know, were wise men—wonderfully wise men—who brought gifts to the Babe in the manger. They invented the art of giving Christmas presents. Being wise, their gifts were no doubt wise ones, possibly bearing the privilege of exchange in case of duplication. And here I have lamely related to you the uneventful chronicle of two foolish children in a flat who most unwisely sacrificed for each other the greatest treasures of their house. But in a last word to the wise of these days let it be said that of all who give gifts these two were the wisest. Of all who give and receive gifts, such as they are wisest. Everywhere they are wisest. They are the magi. ■

MIKE EAGLE/DILAS EVANS FINE ILLUSTRATION

Love of Life

Jack London

Jack London went to Alaska and the Yukon during the gold rush of 1897–1899. He gathered no gold,
but he found a bonanza of literary material that was to bring him wealth and world fame.
Here is one of his finest and most powerful stories.

This out of all will remain—
They have lived and have tossed:
So much of the game will be gain,
Though the gold of the dice has been lost.

They limped painfully down the bank, and once the foremost of the two men staggered among the rough-strewn rocks. They were tired and weak, and their faces had the drawn expression of patience which comes of hardship long endured. They were heavily burdened with blanket packs which were strapped to their shoulders. Head straps, passing across the forehead, helped support these packs. Each man carried a rifle. They walked in a stooped posture, the shoulders well forward, the head still farther forward, the eyes bent upon the ground.

"I wish we had just about two of them cartridges that's layin' in that cache of ourn," said the second man.

His voice was utterly and drearily expressionless. He spoke without enthusiasm; and the first man, limping into the milky stream that foamed over the rocks, vouchsafed no reply.

The other man followed at his heels. They did not remove their footgear, though the water was icy cold—so cold that their ankles ached and their feet went numb. In places the water dashed against their knees, and both men staggered for footing.

The man who followed slipped on a smooth boulder, nearly fell, but recovered himself with a violent effort, at the same time uttering a sharp exclamation of pain. He seemed faint and dizzy and put out his free hand while he reeled, as though seeking support against the air. When he had steadied himself he stepped forward, but reeled again and nearly fell. Then he stood still and looked at the other man, who had never turned his head.

The man stood still for fully a minute, as though debating with himself. Then he called out:

"I say, Bill, I've sprained my ankle."

Bill staggered on through the milky water. He did not look around. The man watched him go, and though his face was expressionless as ever, his eyes were like the eyes of a wounded deer.

The other man limped up the farther bank and continued straight on without looking back. The man in the stream watched him. His lips trembled a little, so that the rough thatch of brown hair which covered them was visibly agitated. His tongue even strayed out to moisten them.

"Bill!" he cried out.

It was the pleading cry of a strong man in distress, but Bill's head did not turn. The man watched him go, limping grotesquely and lurching forward with stammering gait up the slow slope toward the soft skyline of the low-lying hill. He watched him go till he passed over the crest and disappeared. Then he turned his gaze and slowly took in the circle of the world that remained to him now that Bill was gone.

Near the horizon the sun was smoldering dimly, almost obscured by formless mists and vapors, which gave an impression of mass and density without outline or tangibility. The man pulled out his watch, the while resting his weight on one leg. It was four o'clock, and as the season was near the last of July or first of August—he did not know the precise date within a week or two—he knew that the sun roughly marked the northwest. He looked to the south and knew that somewhere beyond those bleak hills lay the Great Bear Lake; also he knew that in that direction the Arctic Circle cut its forbidding way across the Canadian Barrens. This stream in which he stood was a feeder to the Coppermine River, which in turn flowed north and emptied into Coronation Gulf and the Arctic Ocean. He had never been there, but he had seen it, once, on a Hudson Bay Company chart.

Again his gaze completed the circle of the world about him. It was not a heartening spectacle. Everywhere was soft skyline. The hills were all low-lying. There were no trees, no shrubs, no grasses—naught but a tremendous and terrible desolation that sent fear swiftly dawning into his eyes.

"Bill!" he whispered, once and twice; "Bill!"

He cowered in the midst of the milky water, as though the vastness were pressing in upon him with overwhelming force, brutally crushing him with its complacent awfulness. He began to shake as with an ague fit, till the gun fell from his hand with a splash. This served to rouse him. He fought with his fear and pulled himself together, groping in the water and recovering the weapon. He hitched his pack farther over on his left shoulder, so as to take a portion of its weight from off the injured ankle. Then he proceeded, slowly and carefully, wincing with pain, to the bank.

He did not stop. With a desperation that was madness, unmindful of the pain, he hurried up the slope to the crest of the hill over which his comrade had disappeared—more grotesque and comical by far than that limping, jerking comrade. But at the crest he saw a shallow valley, empty of life. He fought with his fear again, overcame it, hitched the pack still farther over on his left shoulder, and lurched on down the slope.

The bottom of the valley was soggy with water, which the thick moss held, spongelike, close to the surface. This water squirted out from under his feet at every step, and each time he lifted a foot the action culminated in a sucking sound as the wet moss reluctantly released its grip. He picked his way from muskeg to muskeg, and followed the other man's footsteps along and across the rocky ledges which thrust like islets through the sea of moss.

Though alone, he was not lost. Farther on, he knew, he would come to where dead spruce and fir, very small and wizened, bordered the shore of a little lake, the *titchin-nichilie*, in the tongue of the country, the "land of little sticks." And into that lake flowed a small stream, the water of which was not milky. There was rush grass on that stream—this he remembered well—but no timber, and he would follow it till its first trickle ceased at a divide. He would cross this divide to the first trickle of another stream, flowing to the west, which he would follow until it emptied into the river Dease, and here he would find a cache under an upturned canoe and piled over with many rocks. And in this cache would be ammunition for his empty gun, fishhooks and lines, a small net—all the utilities for the killing and snaring of food. Also he would find flour—not much—a piece of bacon, and some beans.

Bill would be waiting for him there, and they would paddle away south down the Dease to the Great Bear Lake. And south across the lake they would go, ever south, till they gained the Mackenzie. And south, still south, they would go, while the winter raced vainly after them, and the ice formed in the eddies, and the days grew chill and crisp, south to some warm Hudson Bay Company post, where timber grew tall and generous and there was grub without end.

These were the thoughts of the man as he strove onward. But hard as he strove with his body, he strove equally hard with his mind, trying to think that Bill had not deserted him, that Bill would surely wait for him at the cache. He was compelled to think this thought, or else there would not be any use to strive, and he would have lain down and died. And as the dim ball of the sun sank slowly into the northwest he covered every inch—and many times—of his and Bill's flight south before the downcoming winter. And he conned the grub of the cache and the grub of the Hudson Bay Company post over and over again. He had not eaten for two days; for a far longer time he had not had all he wanted to eat. Often he stooped and picked pale muskeg berries, put them into his mouth, and chewed and swallowed them. A muskeg berry is a bit of seed enclosed in a bit of water. In the mouth the water melts away and the seed chews sharp and bitter. The man knew there was no nourishment in the berries, but he chewed them patiently with a hope greater than knowledge and defying experience.

At nine o'clock he stubbed his toe on a rocky ledge, and from sheer weariness and weakness staggered and fell. He lay for some time, without movement, on his side. Then he slipped out of the pack straps and clumsily dragged himself into a sitting posture. It was not yet dark, and in the lingering twilight he groped about among the rocks for shreds of dry moss. When he had gathered a heap he built a fire—a smoldering, smudgy fire—and put a tin pot of water on to boil.

He unwrapped his pack and the first thing he did was to count his matches. There was sixty-seven. He counted them three times to make sure. He divided them into several portions, wrapping them in oil paper, disposing of one bunch in his empty tobacco pouch, of another bunch in the inside band of his battered hat, of a third bunch under his shirt on the chest. This accomplished, a panic came upon him, and he unwrapped them all and counted them again. There were still sixty-seven.

He dried his wet footgear by the fire. The moccasins were in soggy shreds. The blanket socks were worn through in places, and his feet were raw and bleeding. His ankle was throbbing, and he gave it an examination. It had swollen to the size of his knee. He tore a long strip from one of his two blankets and bound the ankle tightly. He tore other strips and bound them about his feet to serve for both moccasins and socks. Then he drank the pot of water, steaming hot, wound his watch, and crawled between his blankets.

He slept like a dead man. The brief darkness around midnight came and went. The sun arose in the northeast—at least the day dawned in that quarter, for the sun was hidden by gray clouds.

At six o'clock he awoke, quietly lying on his back. He gazed straight up into the gray sky and knew that he was hungry. As he rolled over on his elbow he was startled by a loud snort, and saw a bull caribou regarding him with alert curiosity. The animal was not more than fifty feet away, and instantly into the man's mind leaped the vision and the savor of a caribou steak sizzling and frying over a fire. Mechanically he reached for the empty gun, drew a bead, and pulled the trigger. The bull snorted and leaped away, his hoofs rattling and clattering as he fled across the ledges.

The man cursed and flung the empty gun from him. He groaned aloud as he started to drag himself to his feet. It was a slow and arduous task. His joints were like rusty hinges. They worked harshly in their sockets, with much friction, and each bending or unbending was accomplished only through a sheer exertion of will. When he finally gained his feet, another minute or so was consumed in straightening up, so that he could stand erect as a man should stand.

He crawled up a small knoll and surveyed the prospect.

There were no trees, no bushes, nothing but a gray sea of moss scarcely diversified by gray rocks, gray lakelets, and gray streamlets. The sky was gray. There was no sun nor hint of sun. He had no idea of north, and he had forgotten the way he had come to this spot the night before. But he was not lost. He knew that. Soon he would come to the land of the little sticks. He felt that it lay off to the left somewhere, not far—possibly just over the next low hill.

He went back to put his pack into shape for traveling. He assured himself of the existence of his three separate parcels of matches, though he did not stop to count them. But he did linger, debating, over a squat moose-hide sack. It was not large. He could hide it under his two hands. He knew that it weighed fifteen pounds—as much as all the rest of the pack—and it worried him. He finally set it to one side and proceeded to roll the pack. He paused to gaze at the squat moose-hide sack. He picked it up hastily with a defiant glance about him, as though the desolation were trying to rob him of it; and when he rose to his feet to stagger on into the day, it was included in the pack on his back.

He bore away to the left, stopping now and again to eat muskeg berries. His ankle had stiffened, his limp was more pronounced, but the pain of it was as nothing compared with the pain of his stomach. The hunger pangs were sharp. They gnawed and gnawed until he could not keep his mind steady on the course he must pursue to gain the land of little sticks. The muskeg berries did not allay this gnawing, while they made his tongue and roof of his mouth sore with their irritating bite.

He came upon a valley where rock ptarmigan rose on whirring wings from the ledges and muskegs. Ker—ker—ker was the cry they made. He threw stones at them but could not hit them. He placed his pack on the ground and stalked them as a cat stalks a sparrow. The sharp rocks cut through his pants legs till his knees left a trail of blood; but the hurt was lost in the hurt of his hunger. He squirmed over the wet moss, saturating his clothes and chilling his body; but he was not aware of it, so great was his fever for food. And always the ptarmigan rose, whirring, before him, till their ker—ker—ker became a mock to him, and he cursed them and cried aloud at them with their own cry.

Once he crawled upon one that must have been asleep. He did not see it till it shot up in his face from its rocky nook. He made a clutch as startled as was the rise of the ptarmigan, and there remained in his hand three tail feathers. As he watched its flight he hated it, as though it had done him some terrible wrong. Then he returned and shouldered his pack.

As the day wore along he came into valleys or swales where game was more plentiful. A band of caribou passed by, twenty and odd animals, tantalizingly within rifle range. He felt a wild desire to run after them, a certitude that he could run them down. A black fox came toward him, carrying a ptarmigan in his mouth. The man shouted. It was a fearful cry, but the fox, leaping away in fright, did not drop the ptarmigan.

Late in the afternoon he followed a stream, milky with lime, which ran through sparse patches of rush grass. Grasping these rushes firmly near the root, he pulled up what resembled a young onion sprout no larger than a shingle nail. It was tender, and his teeth sank into it with a crunch that promised deliciously of food. But its fibers were tough. It was composed of stringy filaments saturated with water, like the berries, and devoid of nourishment. He threw off his pack and went into the rush grass on hands and knees, crunching and munching, like some bovine creature.

He was very weary and often wished to rest—to lie down and sleep; but he was continually driven on, not so much by his desire to gain the land of little sticks as by his hunger. He searched little ponds for frogs and dug up the earth with his nails for worms, though he knew in spite that neither frogs nor worms existed so far north.

He looked into every pool of water vainly, until, as the long twilight came on, he discovered a solitary fish, the size of a minnow, in such a pool. He plunged his arm in up to the shoulder, but it eluded him. He reached for it with both hands and stirred up the milky mud at the bottom. In his excitement he fell in, wetting himself to the waist. Then the water was too muddy to admit of his seeing the fish, and he was compelled to wait until the sediment had settled.

The pursuit was renewed, till the water was again muddied. But he could not wait. He unstrapped the tin bucket and began to bail the pool. He bailed wildly at first, splashing himself and flinging the water so short a distance that it ran back into the pool. He worked more carefully, striving to be cool, though his heart was pounding against his chest and his hands were trembling. At the end of half an hour the pool was nearly dry. Not a cupful of water remained. And there was no fish. He found a hidden crevice among the stones through which it had escaped to the adjoining and larger pool—a pool which he could not empty in a night and a day. Had he known of the crevice, he could have closed it with a rock at the beginning and the fish would have been his.

Thus he thought, and crumpled up and sank down upon the wet earth. At first he cried softly to himself, then he cried loudly to the pitiless desolation that ringed him around; and for a long time after he was shaken by great dry sobs.

He built a fire and warmed himself by drinking quarts of hot water, and made camp on a rocky ledge in the same fashion he had the night before. The last thing he did was to see that his matches were dry and to wind his watch. The blankets were wet and clammy. His ankle pulsed with pain. But he knew only that he was hungry, and through his restless sleep he dreamed of feasts and banquets and of food served and spread in all imaginable ways.

He awoke chilled and sick. There was no sun. The gray of earth and sky had become deeper, more profound. A raw wind was blowing, and the first flurries of snow were whitening the hilltops. The air about him thickened and grew white while he made a fire and boiled more water. It was wet snow, half rain, and the flakes were large and soggy. At first they melted as soon as they came in contact with the earth, but ever more fell, covering the ground, putting out the fire, spoiling his supply of moss fuel.

This was a signal for him to strap on his pack and stumble onward, he knew not where. He was not concerned with the land of little sticks, nor with Bill and the cache under the upturned canoe by the river Dease. He was mastered by the verb "to eat." He was hunger-mad. He took no heed of the course he pursued, so long as that course led him through the swale bottoms. He felt his way through the wet snow to the watery muskeg berries, and went by feel as he pulled up the rush grass by the roots. But it was tasteless stuff and did not satisfy. He found a weed that tasted sour and he ate all he could find of it, which was not much, for it was a creeping growth, easily hidden under the several inches of snow.

He had no fire that night, nor hot water, and crawled under his blanket to sleep the broken hunger sleep. The snow turned into a cold rain. He awakened many times to feel it falling on his upturned face. Day came—a gray day and no sun. It had ceased raining. The keenness of his hunger had departed. Sensibility, as far as concerned the yearning for food, had been exhausted. There was a dull, heavy ache in his stomach, but it did not bother him so much. He was more rational, and once more he was chiefly interested in the land of little sticks and the cache by the river Dease.

He ripped the remnant of one of his blankets into strips and bound his bleeding feet. Also he recinched the injured ankle and prepared himself for a day of travel. When he came to his pack he paused long over the squat moose-hide sack, but in the end it went with him.

The snow had melted under the rain, and only the hilltops showed white. The sun came out, and he succeeded in locating the points of the compass, though he knew now that he was lost. Perhaps, in his previous days' wanderings, he had edged away too far to the left. He now bore off to the right to counteract the possible deviation from his true course.

Though the hunger pangs were no longer so exquisite, he realized that he was weak. He was compelled to pause for frequent rests, when he attacked the muskeg berries and rush grass patches. His tongue felt dry and large, as though covered with a fine hairy growth, and it tasted bitter in his mouth. His heart gave him a great deal of trouble. When he had traveled a few minutes it would begin a remorseless thump, thump, thump, and then leap up and away in a painful flutter of beats that choked him and made him go faint and dizzy.

In the middle of the day he found two minnows in a large pool. It was impossible to bail it, but he was calmer now and managed to catch them in his tin bucket. They were no longer than his little finger, but he was not particularly hungry. The dull ache in his stomach had been growing duller and fainter. It seemed almost that his stomach was dozing. He ate the fish raw, masticating with painstaking care, for the eating was an act of pure reason. While he had no desire to eat, he knew that he must eat to live.

In the evening he caught three more minnows, eating two and saving the third for breakfast. The sun had dried stray shreds of moss, and he was able to warm himself with hot water. He had not covered more than ten miles that day; and the next day, traveling whenever his heart permitted him, he covered no more than five miles. But his stomach did not give him the slightest uneasiness. It had gone to sleep. He was in a strange country, too, and the caribou were growing more plentiful, also the wolves. Often their yelps drifted across the desolation, and once he saw three of them slinking away before his path.

Another night; and in the morning, being more rational, he untied the leather string that fastened the squat moose-hide sack. From its open mouth poured a yellow stream of coarse gold dust and nuggets. He roughly divided the gold in halves, caching one half on a prominent ledge, wrapped in a piece of blanket, and returning the other half to the sack. He also began to use strips of the one remaining blanket for his feet. He still clung to his gun, for there were cartridges in that cache by the river Dease.

This was a day of fog, and this day hunger awoke in him again. He was very weak and was afflicted with a giddiness which at times blinded him. It was no uncommon thing now for him to stumble and fall; and stumbling once, he fell squarely into a ptarmigan nest. There were four newly hatched chicks, a day old—little specks of pulsating life no more than a mouthful; and he ate them ravenously, thrusting them alive into his mouth and crunching them like eggshells between his teeth. The mother ptarmigan beat about him with great outcry. He used his gun as a club with which to knock her over, but she dodged out of reach. He threw stones at her and with one chance shot broke a wing. Then she fluttered away, running, trailing the broken wing, with him in pursuit.

The little chicks had no more than whetted his appetite. He hopped and bobbed clumsily along on his injured ankle, throwing stones and screaming hoarsely at times; at other times hopping and bobbing silently along, picking himself up grimly and patiently when he fell, or rubbing his eyes with his hand when the giddiness threatened to overpower him.

The chase led him across swampy ground in the bottom of the valley, and he came upon footprints in the soggy moss. They were not his own—he could see that. They must be Bill's. But he could not stop, for the mother ptarmigan was running on. He would catch her first, then he would return and investigate.

Now and again the wolves, in packs of two and three, crossed his path.

He exhausted the mother ptarmigan; but he exhausted himself. She lay panting on her side. He lay panting on his side, a dozen feet away, unable to crawl to her. And as he recovered she recovered, fluttering out of reach as his hungry hand went out to her. The chase was resumed. Night settled down and she escaped. He stumbled from weakness and pitched head foremost on his face, cutting his cheek, his pack upon his back. He did not move for a long while; then he rolled over on his side, wound his watch, and lay there until morning.

Another day of fog. Half of his last blanket had gone into foot-wrappings. He failed to pick up Bill's trail. It did not matter. His hunger was driving him too compellingly—only—only he wondered if Bill, too, were lost. By midday the irk of his pack became too oppressive. Again he divided the gold, this time merely spilling half of it on the ground. In the afternoon he threw the rest of it away, there remaining to him only the half blanket, the tin bucket, and the rifle.

A hallucination began to trouble him. He felt confident that one cartridge remained to him. It was in the chamber of the rifle and he had overlooked it. On the other hand, he knew all the time that the chamber was empty. But the hallucination persisted. He fought it off for hours, then threw his rifle open and was confronted with emptiness. The disappointment was as bitter as though he had really expected to find the cartridge.

He plodded on for half an hour, when the hallucination arose again. Again he fought it, and still it persisted, till for very relief he opened his rifle to unconvince himself. At times his mind wandered farther afield, and he plodded on, a mere automaton, strange conceits and whimsicalities gnawing at his brain like worms. But these excursions out of the real were of brief duration, for ever the pangs of the hunger bite called him back. He was jerked back abruptly once from such an excursion by a sight that caused him nearly to faint. He reeled and swayed, doddering like a drunken man to keep from falling. Before him stood a horse. A horse! He could not believe his eyes. A thick mist was in them, intershot with sparkling points of light. He rubbed his eyes savagely to clear his vision, and beheld not a horse but a great brown bear. The animal was studying him with bellicose curiosity.

The man had brought his gun halfway to his shoulder before he realized. He lowered it and drew his hunting knife from its beaded sheath at his hip. Before him was meat and life. He ran his thumb along the edge of his knife. It was sharp. The point was sharp. He would fling himself upon the bear and kill it. But his heart began its warning thump, thump, thump. Then followed the wild upward leap and tattoo of flutters, the pressing as of an iron band about his forehead, the creeping of the dizziness into his brain.

His desperate courage was evicted by a great surge of fear. In his weakness, what if the animal attacked him? He drew himself up to his most imposing stature, gripping the knife and staring hard at the bear. The bear advanced clumsily a couple of steps, reared up, and gave vent to a tentative growl. If the man ran, he would run after him; but the man did not run. He was animated now with the courage of fear.

He, too, growled, savagely, voicing the fear that is to life germane and that lies twisted about life's deepest roots.

The bear edged away to one side, growling menacingly, himself appalled by this mysterious creature that appeared upright and unafraid. But the man did not move. He stood like a statue till the danger was past, when he yielded to a fit of trembling and sank down into the wet moss.

He pulled himself together and went on, afraid now in a new way. It was not the fear that he should die passively from lack of food, but that he should be destroyed violently before starvation had exhausted the last particle of the endeavor in him that made toward surviving. There were the wolves. Back and forth across the desolation drifted their howls, weaving the very air into a fabric of menace that was so tangible that he found himself, arms in the air, pressing it back from him as if it might be the walls of a wind-blown tent.

Now and again the wolves, in packs of two and three, crossed his path. But they sheered clear of him. They were not in sufficient numbers, and besides, they were hunting the caribou, which did not battle, while this strange creature that walked erect might scratch and bite.

In the late afternoon he came upon scattered bones where the wolves had made a kill. The debris had been a caribou calf an hour before, squawking and running and very much alive. He contemplated the bones, clean-picked and polished, pink with the cell life in them which had not yet died. Could it possibly be that he might be that ere the day was done! Such was life, eh? A vain and fleeting thing. It was only life that pained. There was no hurt in death. To die was to sleep. It meant cessation, rest. Then why was he not content to die?

But he did not moralize long. He was squatting in the moss, a bone in his mouth, sucking at the shreds of life that still dyed it faintly pink. The sweet meaty taste, thin and elusive almost as a memory, maddened him. He closed his jaws on the bones and crunched. Sometimes it was the bone that broke, sometimes his teeth. Then he crushed the bones between rocks, pounded them to a pulp, and swallowed them. He pounded his fingers, too, in his haste, and yet found a moment in which to feel surprise at the fact that his fingers did not hurt much when caught under the descending rock.

Came frightful days of snow and rain. He did not know when he made camp, when he broke camp. He traveled in the night as much as in the day. He rested wherever he fell, crawled on whenever the dying life in him flickered up and burned less dimly. He, as a man, no longer strove. It was the life in him, unwilling to die, that drove him on. He did not suffer. His nerves had become blunted, numb, while his mind was filled with weird visions and delicious dreams.

But ever he sucked and chewed on the crushed bones of the caribou calf, the least remnants of which he had gathered up and carried with him. He crossed no more hills or divides, but automatically followed a large stream which flowed through a wide and shallow valley. He did not see this stream nor this valley. He saw nothing save visions. Soul and body walked or crawled side by side, yet apart, so slender was the thread that bound them.

He awoke in his right mind, lying on his back on a rocky ledge. The sun was shining bright and warm. Afar off he heard the squawking of caribou calves. He was aware of vague memories of rain and wind and snow, but whether he had been beaten by the storm for two days or two weeks he did not know.

For some time he lay without movement, the genial sunshine pouring upon him and saturating his miserable body with its warmth. A fine day, he thought. Perhaps he could manage to locate himself. By a painful effort he rolled over on his side. Below him flowed a wide and sluggish river. Its unfamiliarity puzzled him. Slowly he followed it with his eyes, winding in wide sweeps among the bleak, bare hills, bleaker and barer and lower-lying than any hills he had yet encountered. Slowly, deliberately, without excitement or more than the most casual interest, he followed the course of the strange stream toward the sky line and saw it emptying into a bright and shining sea. He was still unexcited. Most unusual, he thought, a vision or a mirage—more likely a vision, a trick of his disordered mind. He was confirmed in this by sight of a ship lying at anchor in the midst of the shining sea. He closed his eyes for a while, then opened them. Strange how the vision persisted! Yet not strange. He knew there were no seas or ships in the heart of the barren lands, just as he had known there was no cartridge in the empty rifle.

He heard a snuffle behind him—a half-choking gasp or cough. Very slowly, because of his exceeding weakness and stiffness, he rolled over on his other side. He could see nothing near at hand, but he waited patiently. Again came the snuffle and cough, and outlined between two jagged rocks not a score of feet away he made out the gray head of a wolf. The sharp ears were not pricked so sharply as he had seen them on other wolves; the eyes were bleared and bloodshot, the head seemed to droop limply and forlornly. The animal blinked continually in the sunshine. It seemed sick. As he looked it snuffled and coughed again.

This, at least, was real, he thought, and turned on the other side so that he might see the reality of the world which had been veiled from him before by the vision. But the sea still shone in the distance and the ship was plainly discernible. Was it reality after all? He closed his eyes for a long while and thought, and then it came to him. He had been making north by east, away from the Dease Divide and into the Coppermine Valley. This wide and sluggish river was the Coppermine. That shining sea was the Arctic Ocean. That ship was a whaler, strayed east, far east, from the mouth of the Mackenzie, and it was lying at anchor in Coronation Gulf. He remembered the Hudson Bay Company chart he had seen long ago, and it was all clear and reasonable to him.

He sat up and turned his attention to immediate affairs. He had worn through the blanket wrappings, and his feet were shapeless lumps of raw meat. His last blanket was gone. Rifle and knife were both missing. He had lost his hat somewhere, with the bunch of matches in the band, but the

He would have some hot water before he began.

matches against his chest were safe and dry inside the tobacco pouch and oil paper. He looked at his watch. It marked eleven o'clock and was still running. Evidently he had kept it wound.

He was calm and collected. Though extremely weak, he had no sensation of pain. He was not hungry. The thought of food was not even pleasant to him, and whatever he did was done by his reason alone. He ripped off his pants legs to the knees and bound them about his feet. Somehow he had succeeded in retaining the tin bucket. He would have some hot water before he began what he foresaw was to be a terrible journey to the ship.

His movements were slow. He shook as with a palsy. When he started to collect dry moss he found he could not rise to his feet. He tried again and again, then contented himself with crawling about on hands and knees. Once he crawled near to the sick wolf. The animal dragged itself reluctantly out of his way, licking its chops with a tongue which seemed hardly to have the strength to curl. The man noticed that the tongue was not the customary healthy red. It was a yellowish brown and seemed coated with a rough and half-dry mucus.

After he had drunk a quart of hot water the man found he was able to stand, and even to walk as well as a dying man might be supposed to walk. Every minute or so he was compelled to rest. His steps were feeble and uncertain, just as the wolf's that trailed him were feeble and uncertain; and that night, when the shining sea was blotted out by blackness, he knew he was nearer to it by no more than four miles.

Throughout the night he heard the cough of the sick wolf, and now and then the squawking of the caribou calves. There was life all around him, but it was strong life, very much alive and well, and he knew the sick wolf clung to the sick man's trail in the hope that the man would die first. In the morning, on opening his eyes, he beheld it regarding him with a wistful and hungry stare. It stood crouched, with tail between its legs, like a miserable and woebegone dog. It shivered in the chill morning wind and grinned dispiritedly when the man spoke to it in a voice that achieved no more than a hoarse whisper.

The sun rose brightly, and all morning the man tottered and fell toward the ship on the shining sea. The weather was perfect. It was the brief Indian summer of the high latitudes. It might last a week. Tomorrow or next day it might be gone.

In the afternoon the man came upon a trail. It was of another man, who did not walk, but who dragged himself on all fours. The man thought it might be Bill, but he thought in a dull, uninterested way. He had no curiosity. In fact, sensation and emotion had left him. He was no longer susceptible to pain. Stomach and nerves had gone to sleep. Yet the life that was in him drove him on. He was very weary, but it refused to die. It was because it refused to die that he still ate muskeg berries and minnows, drank his hot water, and kept a wary eye on the sick wolf.

He followed the trail of the other man who dragged himself along, and soon came to the end of it—a few fresh-picked bones where the soggy moss was marked by the foot pads of many wolves. He saw a squat moose-hide sack, mate to his own, which had been torn by sharp teeth. He picked it up, though its weight was almost too much for his feeble fingers. Bill had carried it to the last. Ha-ha! He would have the laugh on Bill. He would survive and carry it to the ship in the shining sea. His mirth was hoarse and ghastly, like a raven's croak, and the sick wolf joined him, howling lugubriously. The man ceased suddenly. How could he have the laugh on Bill if that were Bill; if those bones, so pinky-white and clean, were Bill?

He turned away. Well, Bill had deserted him; but he would not take the gold, nor would he suck Bill's bones. Bill would have, though, had it been the other way around, he mused as he staggered on.

Ever the sick wolf coughed and wheezed at his heels.

He came to a pool of water. Stooping over in quest of minnows, he jerked his head back as though he had been stung. He had caught sight of his reflected face. So horrible was it that sensibility awoke long enough to be shocked. There were three minnows in the pool, which was too large to drain; and after several ineffectual attempts to catch them in the tin bucket he forbore. He was afraid, because of his great weakness, that he might fall in and drown. It was for this reason that he did not trust himself to the river astride one of the many drift logs which lined its sandspits.

That day he decreased the distance between him and the ship by three miles; the next day by two—for he was crawling now as Bill had crawled; and the end of the fifth day found the ship still seven miles away and him unable to make even a mile a day. Still the Indian summer held on, and he continued to crawl and faint, turn and turn about; and ever the sick wolf coughed and wheezed at his heels. His knees had become raw meat like his feet, and though he padded them with the shirt from his back it was a red track he left behind him on the moss and stones. Once, glancing back, he saw the wolf licking hungrily his bleeding trail, and he saw sharply what his own end might be—unless—unless he could get the wolf. Then began as grim a tragedy of existence as was ever played—a sick man that crawled, a sick wolf that limped, two creatures dragging their dying carcasses across the desolation and hunting each other's lives.

Had it been a well wolf, it would not have mattered so much to the man; but the thought of going to feed the maw of that loathsome and all but dead thing was repugnant to him. He was finicky. His mind had begun to wander again and to be perplexed by hallucinations, while his lucid intervals grew rarer and shorter.

He was awakened once from a faint by a wheeze close in his ear. The wolf leaped lamely back, losing its footing and falling in its weakness. It was ludicrous, but he was not amused. Nor was he even afraid. He was too far gone for that. But his mind was for the moment clear, and he lay and considered. The ship was no more than four miles away. He could see it quite distinctly when he rubbed the mists out of his eyes, and he could see the white sail of a small boat cutting the water of the shining sea. But he could never crawl those four miles. He knew that, and was very calm in the knowledge. He knew that he could not crawl half a mile. And yet he wanted to live. It was unreasonable that he should die after all he had undergone. Fate asked too much of him. And, dying, he declined to die. It was stark madness, perhaps, but in the very grip of Death he defied Death and refused to die.

He closed his eyes and composed himself with infinite precaution. He steeled himself to keep above the suffocating languor that lapped like a rising tide through all the wells of his being. It was very like a sea, this deadly languor, that rose and rose and drowned his consciousness bit by bit. Sometimes he was all but submerged, swimming through oblivion with a faltering stroke; and again, by some strange alchemy of soul, he would find another shred of will and strike out more strongly.

Without movement he lay on his back, and he could hear, slowly drawing near and nearer, the wheezing intake and output of the sick wolf's breath. It drew closer, ever closer, through an infinitude of time, and he did not move. It was at his ear. The harsh dry tongue grated like sandpaper against his cheek. His hands shot out—or at least he willed them to shoot out. The fingers were curved like talons, but they closed on empty air. Swiftness and certitude require strength, and the man had not this strength.

The patience of the wolf was terrible. The man's patience was no less terrible. For half a day he lay motionless, fighting off unconsciousness and waiting for the thing that was to feed upon him and upon which he wished to feed. Sometimes the languid sea rose over him and he dreamed long dreams; but ever through it all, waking and dreaming, he waited for the wheezing breath and the harsh caress of the tongue.

He did not hear the breath, and he slipped slowly from some dream to the feel of the tongue along his hand. He waited. The fangs pressed softly; the pressure increased; the wolf was exerting its last strength in an effort to sink teeth in the food for which it had waited so long. But the man had waited long, and the lacerated hand closed on the jaw. Slowly, while the wolf struggled feebly and the hand clutched feebly, the other hand crept across to a grip. Five minutes later the whole weight of the man's body was on top of the wolf. The hands had not sufficient strength to choke the wolf, but the face of the man was pressed close to the throat of the wolf and the mouth of the man was full of hair. At the end of half an hour the man was aware of a warm trickle in his throat. It was not pleasant. It was like molten lead being forced into his stomach, and it was forced by his will alone. Later the man rolled over on his back and slept.

There were some members of a scientific expedition on the whaleship *Bedford.* From the deck they remarked a strange object on the shore. It was moving down the beach toward the water. They were unable to classify it, and, being scientific men, they climbed into the whaleboat alongside and went ashore to see. And they saw something that was alive but which could hardly be called a man. It was blind, unconscious. It squirmed along the ground like some monstrous worm. Most of its efforts were ineffectual, but it was persistent, and it writhed and twisted and went ahead perhaps a score of feet an hour.

Three weeks afterward the man lay in a bunk on the whaleship *Bedford,* and with tears streaming down his wasted cheeks told who he was and what he had undergone. He also babbled incoherently of his mother, of sunny southern California, and a home among the orange groves and flowers.

The days were not many after that when he sat at table with the scientific men and ship's officers. He gloated over the spectacle of so much food, watching it anxiously as it went into the mouths of others. With the disappearance of each mouthful an expression of deep regret came into his eyes. He was quite sane, yet he hated those men at mealtime. He was haunted by a fear that the food would not last. He inquired of the cook, the cabin boy, the captain, concerning the food stores. They reassured him countless times; but he could not believe them, and pried cunningly about the lazaret to see with his own eyes.

It was noticed that the man was getting fat. He grew stouter with each day. The scientific men shook their heads and theorized. They limited the man at his meals, but still his girth increased and he swelled prodigiously under his shirt.

The sailors grinned. They knew. And when the scientific men set a watch on the man, they knew too. They saw him slouch for'ard after breakfast, and, like a mendicant, with outstretched palm, accost a sailor. The sailor grinned and passed him a fragment of sea biscuit. He clutched it avariciously, looked at it as a miser looks at gold, and thrust it into his shirt bosom. Similar were the donations from other grinning sailors.

The scientific men were discreet. They let him alone. But they privily examined his bunk. It was lined with hardtack; the mattress was stuffed with hardtack; every nook and cranny was filled with hardtack. Yet he was sane. He was taking precautions against another possible famine—that was all. He would recover from it, the scientific men said; and he did, ere the *Bedford's* anchor rumbled down in San Francisco Bay. ∎

The Tell-Tale Heart
Edgar Allan Poe

Is it possible to be a rational murderer, to be sane and commit an insane act?
The answer can be found in this delightfully gruesome tale by Edgar Allan Poe.

True!—nervous—very, very dreadfully nervous I had been and am; but why *will* you say that I am mad? The disease had sharpened my senses—not destroyed—not dulled them. Above all was the sense of hearing acute. I heard all things in the heaven and in the earth. I heard many things in hell. How, then, am I mad? Hearken! and observe how healthily—how calmly I can tell you the whole story.

It is impossible to say how first the idea entered my brain; but once conceived, it haunted me day and night. Object there was none. Passion there was none. I loved the old man. He had never wronged me. He had never given me insult. For his gold I had no desire. I think it was his eye! yes, it was this! He had the eye of a vulture—a pale blue eye, with a film over it. Whenever it fell upon me, my blood ran cold; and so by degrees—very gradually—I made up my mind to take the life of the old man, and thus rid myself of the eye forever.

Now this is the point. You fancy me mad. Madmen know nothing. But you should have seen *me*. You should have seen how wisely I proceeded—with what caution—with what foresight—with what dissimulation I went to work! I was never kinder to the old man than during the whole week before I killed him. And every night, about midnight, I turned the latch of his door and opened it—oh, so gently! And then, when I had made an opening sufficient for my head, I put in a dark lantern, all closed, closed, so that no light shone out, and then I thrust in my head. Oh, you would have laughed to see how cunningly I thrust it in! I moved it slowly—very, very slowly, so that I might not disturb the old man's sleep. It took me an hour to place my whole head within the opening so far that I could see him as he lay upon his bed. Ha!—would a madman have been so wise as this? And then, when my head was well in the room, I undid the lantern cautiously—oh, so cautiously—cautiously (for the hinges creaked)—I undid it just so much that a single thin ray fell upon the vulture eye. And this I did for seven long nights—every night just at midnight—but I found the eye always closed; and so it was impossible to do the work; for it was not the old man who vexed me, but his Evil Eye. And every morning, when the day broke, I went boldly into the chamber, and spoke courageously to him, calling him by name in a hearty tone, and inquiring how he had passed the night. So you see he would have been a very profound old man, indeed, to suspect that every night, just at twelve, I looked in upon him while he slept.

Upon the eighth night I was more than usually cautious in opening the door. A watch's minute hand moves more quickly than did mine. Never before that night, had I *felt* the extent of my own powers—of my sagacity. I could scarcely contain my feelings of triumph. To think that there I was, opening the door, little by little, and he not even to dream of my secret deeds or thoughts. I fairly chuckled at the idea; and perhaps he heard me; for he moved on the bed suddenly, as if startled. Now you may think that I drew back—but no. His room was as black as pitch with the thick darkness (for the shutters were close fastened, through fear of robbers), and so I knew that he could not see the opening of the door, and I kept pushing it on steadily, steadily.

I had my head in, and was about to open the lantern, when my thumb slipped upon the tin fastening, and the old man sprang up in bed, crying out—"Who's there?"

I kept quite still and said nothing. For a whole hour I did not move a muscle, and in the meantime I did not hear him lie down. He was still sitting up in the bed listening;—just as I have done, night after night, hearkening to the death watches in the wall.

Presently I heard a slight groan, and I knew it was the groan of mortal terror. It was not a groan of pain or of grief—oh, no!—it was the low stifled sound that arises from the bottom of the soul when overcharged with awe. I knew the sound well. Many a night, just at midnight, when all the world slept, it has welled up from my own bosom, deepening, with its dreadful echo, the terrors that distracted me. I say I knew it well. I knew what the old man felt, and pitied him, although I chuckled at heart. I knew that he had been lying awake ever since the first slight noise, when he had turned in the bed. His fears had been ever since growing upon him. He had been trying to fancy them causeless, but could not. He had been saying to himself—"It is nothing but the wind in the chimney—it is only a mouse crossing the floor," or "it is merely a cricket which has made a single chirp." Yes, he had been trying to comfort himself with these suppositions: but he had found all in vain. *All in vain;* because Death, in approaching him had stalked with his black shadow before him, and enveloped the victim. And it was the mournful influence of the unperceived shadow that caused him to feel—although he neither saw nor heard—to *feel* the presence of my head within the room.

When I had waited a long time, very patiently, without hearing him lie down, I resolved to open a little—a very, very little crevice in the lantern. So I opened it—you cannot imagine how stealthily, stealthily—until, at length a single dim ray, like the thread of the spider, shot from out the crevice and fell full upon the vulture eye.

It was open—wide, wide open—and I grew furious as I gazed upon it.

It was open—wide, wide open—and I grew furious as I gazed upon it. I saw it with perfect distinctness—all a dull blue, with a hideous veil over it that chilled the very marrow in my bones; but I could see nothing else of the old man's face or person: for I had directed the ray, as if by instinct, precisely upon the damned spot.

And have I not told you that what you mistake for madness is but over acuteness of the senses?—now, I say, there came to my ears a low, dull, quick sound, such as a watch makes when enveloped in cotton. I knew *that* sound well, too. It was the beating of the old man's heart. It increased my fury, as the beating of a drum stimulates the soldier into courage.

But even yet I refrained and kept still. I scarcely breathed. I held the lantern motionless. I tried how steadily I could maintain the ray upon the eye. Meantime the hellish tattoo of the heart increased. It grew quicker and quicker, and louder and louder every instant. The old man's terror *must* have been extreme! It grew louder, I say, louder every moment!—do you mark me well? I have told you that I am nervous: so I am. And now at the dead hour of the night, amid the dreadful silence of that old house, so strange a noise as this excited me to uncontrollable terror. Yet, for some minutes longer I refrained and stood still. But the beating grew louder, louder! I thought the heart must burst. And now a new anxiety seized me—the sound would be heard by a neighbor! The old man's hour had come! With a loud yell, I threw open the lantern and leaped into the room. He shrieked once—once only. In an instant I dragged him to the floor, and pulled the heavy bed over him. I then smiled gaily, to find the deed so far done. But, for many minutes, the heart beat on with a muffled sound. This, however, did not vex me; it would not be heard through the wall. At length it ceased. The old man was dead. I removed the bed and examined the corpse. Yes, he was stone, stone dead. I placed my hand upon the heart and held it there many minutes. There was no pulsation. He was stone dead. His eye would trouble me no more.

If still you think me mad, you will think so no longer when I describe the wise precautions I took for the concealment of the body. The night waned, and I worked hastily, but in silence. First of all I dismembered the corpse. I cut off the head and the arms and the legs.

I then took up three planks from the flooring of the chamber, and deposited all between the scantlings. I then replaced the boards so cleverly, so cunningly, that no human eye—not even *his*—could have detected anything wrong. There was nothing to wash out—no stain of any kind—no bloodspot whatever. I had been too wary for that. A tub had caught all—ha! ha!

When I had made an end of these labors, it was four o'clock—still dark as midnight. As the bell sounded the hour, there came a knocking at the street door. I went down to open it with a light heart,—for what had I *now* to fear? There entered three men, who introduced themselves, with perfect suavity, as officers of the police. A shriek had been heard by a neighbor during the night; suspicion of foul play had been aroused; information had been lodged at the police office, and they (the officers) had been deputed to search the premises.

I smiled,—for *what* had I to fear? I bade the gentlemen welcome. The shriek, I said, was my own in a dream. The old man, I mentioned, was absent in the country. I took my visitors all over the house. I bade them search—search *well*. I led them, at length, to *his* chamber. I showed them his treasures, secure, undisturbed. In the enthusiasm of my confidence, I brought chairs into the room, and desired them *here* to rest from their fatigues, while I myself, in the wild audacity of my perfect triumph, placed my own seat upon the very spot beneath which reposed the corpse of the victim.

The officers were satisfied. My *manner* had convinced them. I was singularly at ease. They sat, and while I answered cheerily, they chatted of familiar things. But, ere long, I felt myself getting pale and wished them gone. My head ached, and I fancied a ringing in my ears: but still they sat and still chatted. The ringing became more distinct:—it continued and became more distinct: I talked more freely to get rid of the feeling: but it continued and gained definiteness—until, at length, I found that the noise was *not* within my ears.

No doubt I now grew *very* pale;—but I talked more fluently, and with a heightened voice. Yet the sound increased—and what could I do? It was *a low, dull, quick sound—much such a sound as a watch makes when enveloped in cotton.* I gasped for breath—and yet the officers heard it not. I talked more quickly—more vehemently; but the noise steadily increased. I arose and argued about trifles, in a high key and with violent gesticulations; but the noise steadily increased. Why *would* they not be gone? I paced the floor to and fro with heavy strides, as if excited to fury by the observations of the men—but the noise steadily increased. Oh God! what *could* I do? I foamed—I raved—I swore! I swung the chair upon which I had been sitting, and grated it upon the boards, but the noise arose over all and continually increased. It grew louder—louder—*louder!* And still the men chatted pleasantly, and smiled. Was it possible they heard not? Almighty God!—no, no! They heard!—they suspected!—they *knew!*—they were making a mockery of my horror!—this I thought, and this I think. But anything was better than this agony! Anything was more tolerable than this derision! I could bear those hypocritical smiles no longer! I felt that I must scream or die! and now—again!—hark! louder! louder! louder! *louder!*

"Villains!" I shrieked, "dissemble no more! I admit the deed!—tear up the planks! here, here!—it is the beating of his hideous heart!" ∎

The Red-Headed League

Arthur Conan Doyle

Introducing Mr. Jabez Wilson, a London pawnbroker with a remarkable and, apparently, comical
story to tell. But behind that story Sherlock Holmes sees the sinister designs of a master criminal.
What dark crime is being contemplated, and will Holmes be able to prevent it from happening?

I had called upon my friend, Mr. Sherlock Holmes, one day in the autumn of last year, and found him in deep conversation with a very stout, florid-faced, elderly gentleman, with fiery red hair. With an apology for my intrusion, I was about to withdraw, when Holmes pulled me abruptly into the room, and closed the door behind me.

"You could not possibly have come at a better time, my dear Watson," he said cordially.

"I was afraid that you were engaged."

"So I am. Very much so."

"Then I can wait in the next room."

"Not at all. This gentleman, Mr. Wilson, has been my partner and helper in many of my most successful cases, and I have no doubt that he will be of the utmost use to me in yours also."

The stout gentleman half rose from his chair, and gave a bob of greeting, with a quick little questioning glance from his small, fat-encircled eyes.

"Try the settee," said Holmes, relapsing into his armchair, and putting his fingertips together, as was his custom when in judicial moods. "I know, my dear Watson, that you share my love of all that is bizarre and outside the conventions and humdrum routine of everyday life. You have shown your relish for it by the enthusiasm which has prompted you to chronicle, and, if you will excuse my saying so, somewhat to embellish so many of my own little adventures."

"Your cases have indeed been of the greatest interest to me," I observed.

"You will remember that I remarked the other day, just before we went into the very simple problem presented by Miss Mary Sutherland, that for strange effects and extraordinary combinations we must go to life itself, which is always far more daring than any effort of the imagination."

"A proposition which I took the liberty of doubting."

"You did, Doctor, but none the less you must come round to my view, for otherwise I shall keep on piling fact upon fact on you, until your reason breaks down under them and acknowledges me to be right. Now, Mr. Jabez Wilson here has been good enough to call upon me this morning, and to begin a narrative which promises to be one of the most singular which I have listened to for some time. You have heard me remark that the strangest and most unique things are very often connected not with the larger but with the smaller crimes, and occasionally, indeed, where there is room for doubt whether any positive crime has been committed. As far as I have heard, it is impossible for me to say whether the present case is an instance of crime or not, but the course of events is certainly among the most singular that I have ever listened to. Perhaps, Mr. Wilson, you would have the great kindness to recommence your narrative. I ask you, not merely because my friend Dr. Watson has not heard the opening part, but also because the peculiar nature of the story makes me anxious to have every possible detail from your lips. As a rule, when I have heard some slight indication of the course of events I am able to guide myself by the thousands of other similar cases which occur to my memory. In the present instance I am forced to admit that the facts are, to the best of my belief, unique."

The portly client puffed out his chest with an appearance of some little pride, and pulled a dirty and wrinkled newspaper from the inside pocket of his greatcoat. As he glanced down the advertisement column, with his head thrust forward, and the paper flattened out upon his knee, I took a good look at the man, and endeavored after the fashion of my companion to read the indications which might be presented by his dress or appearance.

I did not gain very much, however, by my inspection. Our visitor bore every mark of being an average commonplace British tradesman, obese, pompous, and slow. He wore rather baggy gray shepherd's check trousers, a not overclean black frock coat, unbuttoned in the front, and a drab waistcoat with a heavy brassy Albert chain, and a square pierced bit of metal dangling down as an ornament. A frayed top hat and a faded brown overcoat with a wrinkled velvet collar lay upon a chair beside him. Altogether, look as I would, there was nothing remarkable about the man save his blazing red head, and the expression of extreme chagrin and discontent upon his features.

Sherlock Holmes' quick eye took in my occupation, and he shook his head with a smile as he noticed my questioning glances. "Beyond the obvious facts that he has at some time done manual labor, that he takes snuff, that he is a Freemason, that he has been in China, and that he has done a considerable amount of writing lately, I can deduce nothing else."

Mr. Jabez Wilson started up in his chair, with his forefinger upon the paper, but his eyes upon my companion.

"How, in the name of good fortune, did you know all that, Mr. Holmes?" he asked. "How did you know, for example, that I did manual labor? It's as true as gospel, for I began as a ship's carpenter."

"Your hands, my dear sir. Your right hand is quite a size larger than your left. You have worked with it, and the muscles are more developed."

"Well, the snuff, then, and the Freemasonry?"

"I won't insult your intelligence by telling you how I read that, especially as, rather against the strict rules of your order, you use an arc and compass breastpin."

"Ah, of course, I forgot that. But the writing?"

"What else can be indicated by that right cuff so very shiny for five inches, and the left one with the smooth patch near the elbow where you rest it upon the desk."

"Well, but China?"

"The fish which you have tattooed immediately above your wrist could only have been done in China. I have made a small study of tattoo marks, and have even contributed to the literature of the subject. That trick of staining the fishes' scales a delicate pink is quite peculiar to China. When, in addition, I see a Chinese coin hanging from your watchchain, the matter becomes even more simple."

Mr. Jabez Wilson laughed heavily. "Well, I never!" said he. "I thought at first that you had done something clever, but I see that there was nothing in it after all."

"I begin to think, Watson," said Holmes, "that I make a mistake in explaining. 'Omne ignotum pro magnifico,' you know, and my poor little reputation, such as it is, will suffer shipwreck if I am so candid. Can you not find the advertisement, Mr. Wilson?"

"Yes, I have got it now," he answered, with his thick, red finger planted half-way down the column. "Here it is. This is what began it all. You just read it for yourself, sir."

I took the paper from him, and read as follows:

"To THE RED-HEADED LEAGUE. On account of the bequest of the late Ezekiah Hopkins, of Lebanon, Penn., U.S.A., there is now another vacancy open which entitles a member of the League to a salary of four pounds a week for purely nominal services. All red-headed men who are sound in body and mind, and above the age of twenty-one years, are eligible. Apply in person on Monday, at eleven o'clock, to Duncan Ross, at the offices of the League, 7 Pope's Court, Fleet Street."

"What on earth does this mean?" I ejaculated, after I had twice read over the extraordinary announcement.

Holmes chuckled, and wriggled in his chair, as was his habit when in high spirits. "It is a little off the beaten track, isn't it?" said he. "And now, Mr. Wilson, off you go at scratch, and tell us all about yourself, your household, and the effect which this advertisement had upon your fortunes. You will first make a note, Doctor, of the paper and the date."

"It is *The Morning Chronicle,* of April 27, 1890. Just two months ago."

"Very good. Now, Mr. Wilson?"

"Well, it is just as I have been telling you, Mr. Sherlock Holmes," said Jabez Wilson, mopping his forehead, "I have a small pawnbroker's business at Coburg Square, near the City. It's not a very large affair, and of late years it has not done more than just give me a living. I used to be able to keep two assistants, but now I only keep one; and I would have a job to pay him, but that he is willing to come for half wages, so as to learn the business."

"What is the name of this obliging youth?" asked Sherlock Holmes.

"His name is Vincent Spaulding, and he's not such a youth either. It's hard to say his age. I should not wish a smarter assistant, Mr. Holmes; and I know very well that he could better himself, and earn twice what I am able to give him. But after all, if he is satisfied, why should I put ideas in his head?"

"Why, indeed? You seem most fortunate in having an employee who comes under the full market price. It is not a common experience among employers in this age. I don't know that your assistant is not as remarkable as your advertisement."

"Oh, he has his faults, too." said Mr. Wilson. "Never was such a fellow for photography. Snapping away with a camera when he ought to be improving his mind, and then diving down into the cellar like a rabbit into its hole to develop his pictures. That is his main fault; but, on the whole, he's a good worker. There's no vice in him."

"He is still with you, I presume?"

"Yes, sir. He and a girl of fourteen, who does a bit of simple cooking, and keeps the place clean—that's all I have in the house, for I am a widower, and never had any family. We live very quietly, sir, the three of us; and we keep a roof over our heads, and pay our debts, if we do nothing more.

"The first thing that put us out was that advertisement. Spaulding, he came down into the office just this day eight weeks with this very paper in his hand, and he says:

"'I wish to the Lord, Mr. Wilson, that I was a red-headed man.'

"'Why that?' I asks.

"'Why,' says he, 'here's another vacancy on the League of the Red-headed Men. It's worth quite a little fortune to any man who gets it, and I understand that there are more vacancies than there are men, so that the trustees are at their wits' end what to do with the money. If my hair would only change color, here's a nice little crib all ready for me to step into.'

"'Why, what is it, then?' I asked. You see, Mr. Holmes, I am a very stay-at-home man, and, as my business came to

"What on earth does this mean?"

me instead of my having to go to it, I was often weeks on end without putting my foot over the doormat. In that way I didn't know much of what was going on outside, and I was always glad of a bit of news.

"'Have you never heard of the League of the Red-headed Men?' he asked, with his eyes open.

"'Never.'

"'Why, I wonder at that, for you are eligible yourself for one of the vacancies.'

"'And what are they worth?' I asked.

"'Oh, merely a couple of hundred a year, but the work is slight, and it need not interfere very much with one's other occupations.'

"Well, you can easily think that that made me prick up my ears, for the business has not been over good for some years, and an extra couple of hundred would have been very handy.

"'Tell me all about it,' said I.

"'Well,' said he, showing me the advertisement, 'you can see for yourself that the League has a vacancy, and there is the address where you should apply for particulars. As far as I can make out, the League was founded by an American millionaire, Ezekiah Hopkins, who was very peculiar in his ways. He was himself red-headed, and he had a great sympathy for all red-headed men; so, when he died, it was found that he had left his enormous fortune in the hands of trustees, with instructions to apply the interest to the providing of easy berths to men whose hair is of that color. From all I hear it is splendid pay, and very little to do.'

"'But,' said I, 'there would be millions of red-headed men who would apply.'

"'Not so many as you might think,' he answered. 'You see it is really confined to Londoners, and to grown men. This American had started from London when he was young, and he wanted to do the old town a good turn. Then, again, I have heard it is no use your applying if your hair is light red, or dark red, or anything but real, bright, blazing, fiery red. Now, if you cared to apply, Mr. Wilson, you would just walk in; but perhaps it would hardly be worth your while to put yourself out of the way for the sake of a few hundred pounds.'

"Now, it is a fact, gentlemen, as you may see for yourselves, that my hair is of a very full and rich tint, so that it seemed to me that, if there was to be any competition in the matter, I stood as good a chance as any man that I had ever met. Vincent Spaulding seemed to know so much about it that I thought he might prove useful, so I just ordered him to put up the shutters for the day, and to come right away with me. He was very willing to have a holiday, so we shut the business up, and started off for the address that was given us in the advertisement.

"I never hope to see such a sight as that again, Mr. Holmes. From north, south, east, and west every man who had a shade of red in his hair had tramped into the City to answer the advertisement. Fleet Street was choked with red-headed folk, and Pope's Court looked like a coster's orange barrow. I should not have thought there were so many in the whole country as were brought together by that single advertisement. Every shade of color they were—straw, lemon, orange, brick, Irish-setter, liver, clay; but, as Spaulding said, there were not many who had the real vivid flame-colored tint. When I saw how many were waiting, I would have given it up in despair; but Spaulding would not hear of it. How he did it I could not imagine, but he pushed and pulled and butted until he got me through the crowd, and right up to the steps which led to the office. There was a double stream upon the stair, some going up in hope, and some coming back dejected; but we wedged in as well as we could and soon found ourselves in the office."

"Your experience has been a most entertaining one," remarked Holmes, as his client paused and refreshed his memory with a huge pinch of snuff. "Pray continue your very interesting statement."

"There was nothing in the office but a couple of wooden chairs and a deal table, behind which sat a small man, with a head that was even redder than mine. He said a few words to each candidate as he came up, and then he always managed to find some fault in them which would disqualify them. Getting a vacancy did not seem to be such a very easy matter after all. However, when our turn came, the little man was much more favorable to me than to any of the others, and he closed the door as we entered, so that he might have a private word with us.

"'This is Mr. Jabez Wilson,' said my assistant, 'and he is willing to fill a vacancy in the League.'

"'And he is admirably suited for it.' the other answered. 'He has every requirement. I cannot recall when I have seen anything so fine.' He took a step backward, cocked his head on one side, and gazed at my hair until I felt quite bashful. Then suddenly he plunged forward, wrung my hand, and congratulated me warmly on my success.

"'It would be injustice to hesitate,' said he. 'You will, however, I am sure, excuse me for taking an obvious precaution.' With that he seized my hair in both his hands, and tugged until I yelled with the pain. 'There is water in your eyes,' said he, as he released me. 'I perceive that all is as it should be. But we have to be careful, for we have twice been deceived by wigs and once by paint. I could tell you tales of cobbler's wax which would disgust you with human nature.' He stepped over to the window and shouted through it at the top of his voice that the vacancy was filled. A groan of disappointment came up from below, and the folk all trooped away in different directions, until there was not a red head to be seen except my own and that of the manager.

"'My name,' said he, 'is Mr. Duncan Ross, and I am myself one of the pensioners upon the fund left by our noble benefactor. Are you a married man, Mr. Wilson? Have you a family?'

"I answered that I had not.

"His face fell immediately.

"'Dear me!' he said gravely, 'that is very serious indeed! I am sorry to hear you say that. The fund was, of course, for the propagation and spread of the redheads as well as for their maintenance. It is exceedingly unfortunate that you should be a bachelor.'

"My face lengthened at this, Mr. Holmes, for I thought that I was not to have the vacancy after all; but, after thinking it over for a few minutes, he said that it would be all right.

"'In the case of another,' said he, 'the objection might be fatal, but we must stretch a point in favor of a man with such a head of hair as yours. When shall you be able to enter upon your new duties?'

"'Well, it is a little awkward, for I have a business already,' said I.

"'Oh, never mind about that, Mr. Wilson!' said Vincent Spaulding. 'I shall be able to look after that for you.'

"'What would be the hours?' I asked.

"'Ten to two.'

"Now a pawnbroker's business is mostly done of an evening, Mr. Holmes, especially Thursday and Friday evenings, which is just before payday; so it would suit me very well to earn a little in the mornings. Besides, I knew that my assistant was a good man, and that he would see to anything that turned up.

"'That would suit me very well,' said I. 'And the pay?'

"'Is four pounds a week.'

"'And the work?'

"'Is purely nominal.'

"'What do you call purely nominal?'

"'Well, you have to be in the office, or at least in the building, the whole time. If you leave, you forfeit your whole position forever. This will is very clear upon that point. You don't comply with the conditions if you budge from the office during that time.'

"'It's only four hours a day, and I should not think of leaving,' said I.

"'No excuse will avail,' said Mr. Duncan Ross, 'neither sickness, nor business, nor anything else. There you must stay, or you lose your billet.'

"'And the work?'

"'Is to copy out *The Encyclopædia Britannica*. There is the first volume of it in that press. You must find your own ink, pens, and blotting-paper, but we provide this table and chair. Will you be ready 'tomorrow?'

"'Certainly,' I answered.

"'Then, goodbye, Mr. Jabez Wilson, and let me congratulate you once more on the important position which you have been fortunate enough to gain.' He bowed me out of the room, and I went home with my assistant, hardly knowing what to say or do, I was so pleased at my own good fortune.

"Well, I thought over the matter all day, and by evening I was in low spirits again; for I had quite persuaded myself that the whole affair must be some great hoax or fraud, though what its object might be I could not imagine. It seemed altogether past belief that anyone could make such a will, or that they would pay such a sum for doing anything so simple as copying out *The Encyclopædia Britannica*. Vincent Spaulding did what he could to cheer me up, but by bedtime I had reasoned myself out of the whole thing. However, in the morning I determined to have a look at it anyhow, so I bought a penny bottle of ink, and with a quill pen, and seven sheets of foolscap paper, I started off for Pope's Court.

"Well, to my surprise and delight everything was as right as possible. The table was set out ready for me, and Mr. Duncan Ross was there to see that I got fairly to work. He started me off upon the letter A, and then he left me; but he would drop in from time to time to see that all was right with me. At two o'clock he bade me good day, complimented me upon the amount that I had written, and locked the door of the office after me.

"This went on day after day, Mr. Holmes, and on Saturday the manager came in and plunked down four golden sovereigns for my week's work. It was the same next week, and the same the week after. Every morning I was there at ten, and every afternoon I left at two. By degrees Mr. Duncan Ross took to coming in only once of a morning, and then, after a time, he did not come in at all. Still, of course, I never dared to leave the room for an instant, for I was not sure when he might come, and the billet was such a good one, and suited me so well, that I would not risk the loss of it.

"Eight weeks passed away like this, and I had written about Abbots, and Archery, and Armor, and Architecture, and Attica, and hoped with diligence that I might get on to the Bs before very long. It cost me something in foolscap, and I had pretty nearly filled a shelf with my writings. And then suddenly the whole business came to an end."

"To an end?"

"Yes, sir. And no later than this morning. I went to my work as usual at ten o'clock, but the door was shut and locked, with a little square of cardboard hammered onto the middle of the panel with a tack. Here it is, and you can read for yourself."

He held up a piece of white cardboard, about the size of a sheet of notepaper. It read in this fashion:

"THE RED-HEADED LEAGUE IS DISSOLVED.
OCT. 9, 1890."

Sherlock Holmes and I surveyed this curt announcement and the rueful face behind it, until the comical side of the affair so completely overtopped every other consideration that we both burst out into a roar of laughter.

"I cannot see that there is anything very funny," cried our client, flushing up to the roots of his flaming head. "If you can do nothing better than laugh at me, I can go elsewhere."

"No, no," cried Holmes, shoving him back into the chair from which he had half risen. "I really wouldn't miss your case for the world. It is most refreshingly unusual. But there is, if you will excuse my saying so, something just a little funny about it. Pray what steps did you take when you found the card upon the door?"

"The door was shut and locked."

"I was staggered, sir. I did not know what to do. Then I called at the offices round, but none of them seemed to know anything about it. Finally, I went to the landlord, who is an accountant living on the ground floor, and I asked him if he could tell me what had become of the Red-headed League. He said that he had never heard of any such body. Then I asked him who Mr. Duncan Ross was. He answered that the name was new to him.

" 'Well,' said I, 'the gentleman at No. 4.'

" 'What, the red-headed man?'

" 'Yes.'

" 'Oh,' said he, 'his name was William Morris. He was a solicitor, and was using my room as a temporary convenience until his new premises were ready. He moved out yesterday.'

" 'Where could I find him?'

" 'Oh, at his new offices. He did tell me the address. Yes, 17 King Edward Street, near St. Paul's.'

"I started off, Mr. Holmes, but when I got to that address it was a manufactory of artificial kneecaps, and no one in it had ever heard of either Mr. William Morris, or Mr. Duncan Ross."

"And what did you do then?" asked Holmes.

"I went home to Saxe-Coburg Square, and I took the advice of my assistant. But he could not help me in any way. He could only say that if I waited I should hear by post. But that was not quite good enough, Mr. Holmes. I did not wish to lose such a place without a struggle, so, as I had heard that you were good enough to give advice to poor folk who were in need of it, I came right away to you."

"And you did very wisely," said Holmes. "Your case is an exceedingly remarkable one, and I shall be happy to look into it. From what you have told me I think that it is possible that graver issues hang from it than might at first sight appear."

"Grave enough!" said Mr. Jabez Wilson. "Why, I have lost four pounds a week."

"As far as you are personally concerned," remarked Holmes, "I do not see that you have any grievance against this extraordinary league. On the contrary, you are, as I understand, richer by some thirty pounds, to say nothing of the minute knowledge which you have gained on every subject which comes under the letter A. You have lost nothing by them."

"No, sir. But I want to find out about them, and who they are, and what their object was in playing this prank—if it was a prank—upon me. It was a pretty expensive joke for them, for it cost them two and thirty pounds."

"We shall endeavor to clear up these points for you. And, first, one or two questions, Mr. Wilson. This assistant of yours who first called your attention to the advertisement—how long had he been with you?"

"About a month then."

"How did he come?"

"In answer to an advertisement."

"Was he the only applicant?"

"No, I had a dozen."

"Why did you pick him?"

"Because he was handy, and would come cheap."

"At half wages, in fact."

"Yes."

"What is he like, this Vincent Spaulding?"

"Small, stout-built, very quick in his ways, no hair on his face, though he's not short of thirty. Has a white splash of acid upon his forehead."

Holmes sat up in his chair in considerable excitement. "I thought as much," said he. "Have you ever observed that his ears are pierced for earrings?"

"Yes, sir. He told me that a gypsy had done it for him when he was a lad."

"Hum!" said Holmes, sinking back in deep thought. "He is still with you?"

"Oh, yes sir; I have only just left him."

"And has your business been attended to in your absence?"

"Nothing to complain of, sir. There's never very much to do of a morning."

"That will do, Mr. Wilson. I shall be happy to give you an opinion upon the subject in the course of a day or two. Today is Saturday, and I hope that by Monday we may come to a conclusion."

"Well, Watson," said Holmes, when our visitor had left us, "what do you make of it all?"

"I make nothing of it," I answered, frankly. "It is a most mysterious business."

"As a rule," said Holmes, "the more bizarre a thing is the less mysterious it proves to be. It is your commonplace, featureless crimes which are really puzzling, just as a commonplace face is the most difficult to identify. But I must be prompt over this matter."

"What are you going to do then?" I asked.

"To smoke," he answered. "It is quite a three-pipe problem, and I beg that you won't speak to me for fifty minutes." He curled himself up in his chair, with his thin knees drawn up to his hawk-like nose, and there he sat with his eyes closed and his black clay pipe thrusting out like the bill of some strange bird. I had come to the conclusion that he had dropped asleep, and indeed was nodding myself, when he suddenly sprang out of his chair with the gesture of a man who has made up his mind, and put his pipe down upon the mantelpiece.

"Sarasate plays at St. James's Hall this afternoon," he remarked. "What do you think, Watson? Could your patients spare you for a few hours?"

"I have nothing to do today. My practice is never very absorbing."

"Then, put on your hat, and come. I am going through the City first, and we can have some lunch on the way. I observe that there is a good deal of German music on the program, which is rather more to my taste than Italian or French. It is introspective, and I want to introspect. Come along!"

We traveled by the Underground as far as Aldersgate; and a short walk took us to Saxe-Coburg Square, the scene of the singular story which we had listened to in the morning. It was a poky, little, shabby-genteel place, where four lines of dingy, two-storied brick houses look out into a small railed-in enclosure, where a lawn of weedy grass, and a few clumps of faded laurel bushes made a hard fight against a smoke-laden and uncongenial atmosphere. Three gilt balls and a brown board with "JABEZ WILSON" in white letters, upon a corner house, announced the place where our red-headed client carried on his business. Sherlock Holmes stopped in front of it with his head on one side, and looked it all over, with his eyes shining brightly between puckered lids. Then he walked slowly up the street, and then down again to the corner, still looking keenly at the houses. Finally he returned to the pawnbroker's, and, having thumped vigorously upon the pavement with his stick two or three times, he went up to the door and knocked. It was instantly opened by a bright-looking, clean-shaven young fellow, who asked him to step in.

"Thank you," said Holmes, "I only wished to ask you how you would go from here to the Strand."

"Third right, fourth left," answered the assistant, promptly, closing the door.

"Smart fellow, that," observed Holmes as we walked away. "He is, in my judgment, the fourth smartest man in London, and for daring I am not sure that he has not a claim to be third. I have known something of him before."

"Evidently," said I, "Mr. Wilson's assistant counts for a good deal in this mystery of the Red-headed League. I am sure that you inquired your way merely in order that you might see him."

"Not him."

"What then?"

"The knees of his trousers."

He curled himself up in his chair.

"And what did you see?"

"What I expected to see."

"Why did you beat the pavement?"

"My dear Doctor, this a time for observation, not for talk. We are spies in an enemy's country. We know something of Saxe-Coburg Square. Let us now explore the parts which lie behind it."

The road in which we found ourselves as we turned round the corner from the retired Saxe-Coburg Square presented as great a contrast to it as the front of a picture does to the back. It was one of the main arteries which convey the traffic of the City to the north and west. The roadway was blocked with the immense stream of commerce flowing in a double tide inward and outward, while the footpaths were black with the hurrying swarm of pedestrians. It was difficult to realize, as we looked at the line of fine shops and stately business premises, that they really abutted on the other side upon the faded and stagnant square which we had just quitted.

"Let me see," said Holmes, standing at the corner, and glancing along the line, "I should like just to remember the order of the houses here. It is a hobby of mine to have an exact knowledge of London. There is Mortimer's, the tobacconist; the little newspaper shop, the Coburg branch of the City and Suburban Bank, the Vegetarian Restaurant, and McFarlane's carriage-building depot. That carries us right on to the other block. And now, Doctor, we've done our work, so it's time we had some play. A sandwich and a cup of coffee, and then off to violin-land, where all is sweetness, and delicacy, and harmony, and there are no red-headed clients to vex us with their conundrums."

My friend was an enthusiastic musician, being himself not only a very capable performer, but a composer of no ordinary merit. All the afternoon he sat in the stalls wrapped in the most perfect happiness, gently waving his long thin fingers in time to the music, while his gently smiling face and his languid, dreamy eyes were as unlike those of Holmes the sleuth-hound, Holmes the relentless, keenwitted, ready-handed criminal agent, as it was possible to conceive. In his singular character the dual nature alternately asserted itself, and his extreme exactness and astuteness represented, as I have often thought, the reaction against the poetic and contemplative mood which occasionally predominated in him. The swing of his nature took him from extreme languor to devouring energy; and, as I knew well, he was never so truly formidable as when, for days on end, he had been lounging in his armchair amid his improvisations and his black-letter editions. Then it was that the lust of the chase would suddenly come upon him, and that his brilliant reasoning power would rise to the level of intuition, until those who were unacquainted with his methods would look askance at him as on a man whose knowledge was not that of other mortals. When I saw him that afternoon so enwrapped in the music at St. James's Hall I felt that an evil time might be coming upon those whom he had set himself to hunt down.

"You want to go home, no doubt, Doctor," he remarked, as we emerged.

"Yes, it would be as well."

"And I have some business to do which will take some hours. This business at Coburg Square is serious."

"Why serious?"

"A considerable crime is in contemplation. I have every reason to believe that we shall be in time to stop it. But today being Saturday rather complicates matters. I shall want your help tonight."

"At what time?"

"Ten will be early enough."

"I shall be at Baker Street at ten."

"Very well. And, I say, Doctor! there may be some little danger, so kindly put your army revolver in your pocket." He waved his hand, turned on his heel, and disappeared in an instant among the crowd.

I trust that I am not more dense than my neighbors, but I was always oppressed with a sense of my own stupidity in my dealings with Sherlock Holmes. Here I had heard what he had heard, I had seen what he had seen, and yet from his words it was evident that he saw clearly not only what had happened, but what was about to happen, while to me the whole business was still confused and grotesque. As I drove home to my house in Kensington I thought over it all, from the extraordinary story of the red-headed copier of the *Encyclopædia* down to the visit to Saxe-Coburg Square, and the ominous words with which he had parted from me. What was this nocturnal expedition, and why should I go armed? Where were we going, and what were we to do? I had the hint from Holmes that this smooth-faced pawnbroker's assistant was a formidable man—a man who might play a deep game. I tried to puzzle it out, but gave up in despair, and set the matter aside until night should bring an explanation.

It was a quarter past nine when I started from home and made my way across the Park, and so through Oxford Street to Baker Street. Two hansoms were standing at the door, and, as I entered the passage, I heard the sound of voices from above. On entering his room, I found Holmes in animated conversation with two men, one of whom I recognized as Peter Jones, the official police agent; while the other was a long, thin, sad-faced man, with a very shiny hat and oppressively respectable frock coat.

"Ha! our party is complete," said Holmes, buttoning up his pea jacket, and taking his heavy hunting crop from the rack. "Watson, I think you know Mr. Jones, of Scotland Yard? Let me introduce you to Mr. Merryweather, who is to be our companion in tonight's adventure."

"We're hunting in couples again, Doctor, you see," said Jones, in his consequential way. "Our friend here is a wonderful man for starting a chase. All he wants is an old dog to help him do the running down."

"I hope a wild goose may not prove to be the end of our chase," observed Mr. Merryweather, gloomily.

"You may place considerable confidence in Mr. Holmes, sir," said the police agent, loftily. "He has his own little methods, which are, if he won't mind my saying so, just a little too theoretical and fantastic, but he has the makings of a detective in him. It is not too much to say that once or twice, as in that business of the Sholto murder and the Agra treasure, he has been more nearly correct than the official force."

"Oh, if you say so, Mr. Jones, it is all right!" said the stranger, with deference. "Still, I confess that I miss my rubber. It is the first Saturday night for seven-and-twenty years that I have not had my rubber."

"I think you will find," said Sherlock Holmes, "that you will play for a higher stake tonight than you have ever done yet, and that the play will be more exciting. For you, Mr. Merryweather, the stake will be some thirty thousand pounds; and for you, Jones, it will be the man upon whom you wish to lay your hands."

"John Clay, the murderer, thief, smasher, and forger. He's a young man, Mr. Merryweather, but he is at the head of his profession, and I would rather have my bracelets on him than on any criminal in London. He's a remarkable man, is young John Clay. His grandfather was a Royal Duke, and he himself has been to Eton and Oxford. His brain is as cunning as his fingers, and though we meet signs of him at every turn, we never know where to find the man himself. He'll crack a crib in Scotland one week, and be raising money to build an orphanage in Cornwall the next. I've been on his track for years, and I have never set eyes on him yet."

"I hope that I may have the pleasure of introducing you tonight. I've had one or two little turns also with Mr. John Clay, and I agree with you that he is at the head of his profession. It is past ten, however, and quite time that we started. If you two will take the first hansom, Watson and I will follow in the second."

Sherlock Holmes was not very communicative during the long drive, and lay back in the cab humming the tunes which he had heard in the afternoon. We rattled through an endless labyrinth of gas-lit streets until we emerged into Farringdon Street.

"We are close there now," my friend remarked. "This fellow Merryweather is a bank director and personally interested in the matter. I thought it as well to have Jones with us also. He is not a bad fellow, though an absolute imbecile in his profession. He has one positive virtue. He is as brave as a bulldog, and as tenacious as a lobster if he gets his claws upon anyone. Here we are, and they are waiting for us."

We had reached the same crowded thoroughfare in which we had found ourselves in the morning. Our cabs were dismissed, and, following the guidance of Mr. Merryweather, we passed down a narrow passage, and through a side door, which he opened for us. Within there was a small corridor, which ended in a very massive iron gate. This also was opened, and led down a flight of winding stone steps, which terminated at another formidable gate. Mr. Merryweather stopped to light a lantern, and then conducted us down a dark, earth-smelling passage, and so, after opening a third door, into a huge vault or cellar, which was piled all round with crates and massive boxes.

"You are not very vulnerable from above," Holmes remarked, as he held up the lantern and gazed about him.

"Nor from below," said Mr. Merryweather, striking his stick upon the flags which lined the floor. "Why, dear me, it sounds quite hollow!" he remarked, looking up in surprise.

"I must really ask you to be a little more quiet," said Holmes, severely. "You have already imperiled the whole success of our expedition. Might I beg that you would have the goodness to sit down upon one of those boxes, and not to interfere?"

The solemn Mr. Merryweather perched himself upon a crate, with a very injured expression upon his face, while Holmes fell upon his knees upon the floor, and, with the lantern and a magnifying lens, began to examine minutely the cracks between the stones. A few seconds sufficed to satisfy him, for he sprang to his feet again, and put his glass in his pocket.

"We have at least an hour before us," he remarked, "for they can hardly take any steps until the good pawnbroker is safely in bed. Then they will not lose a minute, for the sooner they do their work the longer time they will have for their escape. We are at present, doctor—as no doubt you have divined—in the cellar of the City branch of one of the principal London banks. Mr. Merryweather is the chairman of directors, and he will explain to you that there are reasons why the more daring criminals of London should take a considerable interest in this cellar at present."

"It is our French gold," whispered the director. "We have had several warnings that an attempt might be made upon it."

"Your French gold?"

"Yes. We had occasion some months ago to strengthen our resources, and borrowed, for that purpose, thirty thousand napoleons from the Bank of France. It has become known that we have never had occasion to unpack the money, and that it is still lying in our cellar. The crate upon which I sit contains two thousand napoleons packed between layers of lead foil. Our reserve of bullion is much larger at present than is usually kept in a single branch office, and the directors have had misgivings upon the subject."

"Which were very well justified," observed Holmes. "And now it is time that we arranged our little plans. I expect that within an hour matters will come to a head. In the meantime, Mr. Merryweather, we must put the screen over that dark lantern."

"And sit in the dark?"

"I am afraid so. I had brought a pack of cards in my pocket, and I thought that, as we were a *partie carrée,* you might have your rubber after all. But I see that the enemy's preparations have gone so far that we cannot risk the presence of a light. And, first of all, we must choose our positions. These are daring men, and, though we shall take them at a disadvantage, they may do us some harm, unless we are careful. I shall stand behind this crate, and do you conceal

"It's no use, John Clay."

SIDNEY PAGET / THE STRAND MAGAZINE / THE GRANGER COLLECTION

yourself behind those. Then, when I flash a light upon them, close in swiftly. If they fire, Watson, have no compunction about shooting them down."

I placed my revolver, cocked, upon the top of the wooden case behind which I crouched. Holmes shot the slide across the front of his lantern, and left us in pitch darkness—such an absolute darkness as I have never before experienced. The smell of hot metal remained to assure us that the light was still there, ready to flash out at a moment's notice. To me, with my nerves worked up to a pitch of expectancy, there was something depressing and subduing in the sudden gloom, and in the cold, dank air of the vault.

"They have but one retreat," whispered Holmes. "That is back through the house into Saxe-Coburg Square. I hope that you have done what I asked you, Jones?"

"I have an inspector and two officers waiting at the front door."

"Then we have stopped all the holes. And now we must be silent and wait."

What a time it seemed! From comparing notes afterwards, it was but an hour and a quarter, yet it appeared to me that the night must have almost gone, and the dawn be breaking above us. My limbs were weary and stiff, for I feared to change my position, yet my nerves were worked up to the highest pitch of tension, and my hearing was so acute that I could not only hear the gentle breathing of my companions, but I could distinguish the deeper, heavier in-breath of the bulky Jones from the thin, sighing note of the bank director. From my position I could look over the case in the direction of the floor. Suddenly my eyes caught the glint of a light.

At first it was but a lurid spark upon the stone pavement. Then it lengthened out until it became a yellow line, and then, without any warning or sound, a gash seemed to open and a hand appeared, a white, almost womanly hand, which felt about in the center of the little area of light. For a minute or more the hand, with its writhing fingers, protruded out of the floor. Then it was withdrawn as suddenly as it appeared, and all was dark again save the single lurid spark, which marked a chink between the stones.

Its disappearance, however, was but momentary. With a rending, tearing sound, one of the broad, white stones turned over upon its side, and left a square, gaping hole, through which streamed the light of a lantern. Over the edge there peeped a clean-cut, boyish face, which looked keenly about it, and then, with a hand on either side of the aperture, drew itself shoulder-high and waist-high, until one knee rested upon the edge. In another instant he stood at the side of the hole, and was hauling after him a companion, lithe and small like himself, with a pale face and a shock of very red hair.

"It's all clear," he whispered. "Have you the chisel and the bags? Great Scott! Jump, Archie, jump, and I'll swing for it!"

Sherlock Holmes had sprung out and seized the intruder by the collar. The other dived down the hole, and I heard the sound of rending cloth as Jones clutched at his skirts. The light flashed upon the barrel of a revolver, but Holmes's hunting crop came down on the man's wrist, and the pistol clinked upon the stone floor.

"It's no use, John Clay," said Holmes blandly, "you have no chance at all."

"So I see," the other answered, with the utmost coolness. "I fancy that my pal is all right, though I see you have got his coattails."

"There are three men waiting for him at the door," said Holmes.

"Oh, indeed. You seem to have done the thing very completely. I must compliment you."

"And I you," Holmes answered. "Your red-headed idea was very new and effective."

"You'll see your pal again presently," said Jones. "He's quicker at climbing down holes than I am. Just hold out while I fix the derbies."

"I beg that you will not touch me with your filthy hands," remarked our prisoner, as the handcuffs clattered upon his wrists. "You may not be aware that I have royal blood in my veins. Have the goodness also, when you address me, always to say 'sir' and 'please.' "

"All right," said Jones, with a stare and a snigger. "Well, would you please, sir, march upstairs where we can get a cab to carry your highness to the police station."

"That is better," said John Clay, serenely. He made a sweeping bow to the three of us, and walked quietly off in the custody of the detective.

"Really, Mr. Holmes," said Mr. Merryweather, as we followed them from the cellar, "I do not know how the bank can thank you or repay you. There is not doubt that you have detected and defeated in the most complete manner one of the most determined attempts at bank robbery that have ever come within my experience."

"I have had one or two little scores of my own to settle with Mr. John Clay," said Holmes. "I have been at some small expense over this matter, which I shall expect the bank to refund, but beyond that I am amply repaid by having had an experience which is in many ways unique, and by hearing the very remarkable narrative of the Red-headed League."

———

"You see, Watson," he explained, in the early hours of the morning, as we sat over a glass of whisky and soda in Baker Street, "it was perfectly obvious from the first that the only possible object of this rather fantastic business of the advertisement of the League, and the copying of the *Encyclopædia,* must be to get this not over-bright pawnbroker out of the way for a number of hours every day. It was a curious way of managing it, but really it would be difficult to suggest a better. The method was no doubt suggested to Clay's ingenious mind by the color of his accomplice's hair. The four pounds a week was a lure which must draw him, and what was it to them, who were playing for thousands? They put in the advertisement, one rogue has the temporary office, the other rogue incites the man to apply for it, and together they manage to secure his absence every morning in the week. From the time that I heard of the assistant having come for half wages, it was obvious to me that he had some strong motive for securing the situation."

"But how could you guess what the motive was?"

"Had there been women in the house, I should have suspected a mere vulgar intrigue. That, however, was out of the question. The man's business was a small one, and there was nothing in his house which could account for such elaborate preparations, and such an expenditure as they were at. It must then be something out of the house. What could it be? I thought of the assistant's fondness for photography, and his trick of vanishing into the cellar. The cellar! There was the end of this tangled clue. Then I made inquiries as to this mysterious assistant, and found that I had to deal with one of the coolest and most daring criminals in London. He was doing something in the cellar—something which took many hours a day for months on end. What could it be, once more? I could think of nothing save that he was running a tunnel to some other building.

"So far I had got when we went to visit the scene of action. I surprised you by beating upon the pavement with my stick. I was ascertaining whether the cellar stretched out in front or behind. It was not in front. Then I rang the bell, and, as I hoped, the assistant answered it. We have had some skirmishes, but we had never set eyes upon each other before. I hardly looked at his face. His knees were what I wished to see. You must yourself have remarked how worn, wrinkled, and stained they were. They spoke of those hours of burrowing. The only remaining point was what they were burrowing for. I walked round the corner, saw that the City and Suburban Bank abutted on our friend's premises, and felt that I had solved my problem. When you drove home after the concert I called upon Scotland Yard, and upon the chairman of the bank directors, with the result that you have seen."

"And how could you tell that they would make their attempt tonight?" I asked.

"Well, when they closed their League offices that was a sign that they cared no longer about Mr. Jabez Wilson's presence; in other words, that they had completed their tunnel. But it was essential that they should use it soon, as it might be discovered, or the bullion might be removed. Saturday would suit them better than any other day, as it would give them two days for their escape. For all these reasons I expected them to come tonight."

"You reasoned it out beautifully," I exclaimed, in unfeigned admiration. "It is so long a chain, and yet every link rings true."

"It saved me from ennui," he answered, yawning, "Alas! I already feel it closing in upon me. My life is spent in one long effort to escape from the commonplaces of existence. These little problems help me to do so."

"And you are a benefactor of the race," said I. He shrugged his shoulders. "Well, perhaps, after all, it is of some little use," he remarked. " 'L'homme c'est rien— l'œuvre c'est tout,' as Gustave Flaubert wrote to George Sand." ∎

The Glass in the Field
James Thurber

A short time ago some builders, working on a studio in Connecticut, left a huge square of plate glass standing upright in a field one day. A goldfinch flying swiftly across the field struck the glass and was knocked cold. When he came to he hastened to his club, where an attendant bandaged his head and gave him a stiff drink. "What the hell happened?" asked a sea gull. "I was flying across a meadow when all of a sudden the air crystallized on me," said the goldfinch. The sea gull and a hawk and an eagle all laughed heartily. A swallow listened gravely. "For fifteen years, fledgling and bird, I've flown this country," said the eagle, "and I assure you there is no such thing as air crystallizing. Water, yes; air, no." "You were probably struck by a hailstone," the hawk told the goldfinch. "Or he may have had a stroke," said the sea gull. "What do you think, swallow?" "Why, I—I think maybe the air crystallized on him," said the swallow. The large birds laughed so loudly that the goldfinch became annoyed and bet them each a dozen worms that they couldn't follow the course he had flown across the field without encountering the hardened atmosphere. They all took his bet; the swallow went along to watch. The sea gull, the eagle, and the hawk decided to fly together over the route the goldfinch indicated. "You come, too," they said to the swallow. "I—I—well, no," said the swallow. "I don't think I will." So the three large birds took off together and they hit the glass together and they were all knocked cold.

———

Moral: He who hesitates is sometimes saved.

For Further Reference

Books on Language

Allport, Alan, et al., editors. *Language Perception and Production: Relationships Between Listening, Speaking, Reading and Writing.* Academic Press, 1987.

A Manual of Style (12th Ed.). University of Chicago Press, 1969.

Barzun, Jacques. *The Modern Researcher* (3rd Ed.). Harcourt, Brace, Jovanovich, 1977.

Bates, Elizabeth. *Language and Context.* Academic Press, 1987.

Baugh, Albert C. *A History of the English Language* (3rd Ed.). Prentice-Hall, 1978.

Bernstein, Theodore M. *The Careful Writer: A Modern Guide to English Usage.* Atheneum, 1965.

Bloomfield, Leonard. *Language.* University of Chicago Press, 1984.

Blumenthal, Lassor A. *The Complete Book of Personal Letter Writing and Modern Correspondence.* Doubleday, 1969.

Chomsky, Noam. *Language and Mind.* Harcourt, Brace, and World, 1968.

Crystal, David. *The Cambridge Encyclopedia of Language.* Cambridge University Press, 1987.

Dillard, J. L. *All-American English.* Random House, 1975.

Dillard, J. L. *Black English: Its History and Usage in the United States.* Random House, 1972.

Ehrlich, Eugene. *The Bantam Concise Handbook of English.* Bantam Books, 1986.

Ehrlich, Eugene, and Daniel Murphy. *Writing and Researching Term Papers and Reports: A New Guide for Students.* Bantam Books, 1968.

Elliot, Alison J. *Child Language.* Cambridge University Press, 1981.

Ewing, David W. *Writing for Results in Business, Government, and the Professions.* Wiley, 1974.

Fowler, H. W. *Dictionary of Modern English Usage.* Bern Porter, 1985.

Fromkins, Victoria, and Robert Rodman. *An Introduction to Language* (4th Ed.). Holt, Rinehart and Winston, 1988.

Frueling, Rosemary T., and Sharon Bouchard. *The Art of Writing Effective Letters.* McGraw-Hill, 1972.

Gorrell, Robert M., and Charlton Laird. *Modern English Rhetoric and Handbook* (7th Ed.). Prentice-Hall, 1988.

Harris, Albert, and Edward Sipay. *How to Increase Reading Ability* (6th Ed.). David McKay, 1975.

Harris, R. *Approaches to Language.* Pergamon Press, 1983.

Hawkins, E. *Awareness of Language: An Introduction.* Cambridge University Press, 1987.

Hayakawa, S. I. *Language in Thought and Action* (4th Ed.). Harcourt, Brace, Jovanovich, 1978.

Laird, Charlton. *You and Your Language.* Prentice-Hall, 1973.

Mencken, H. L. *The American Language.* 3 volumes. Alfred A. Knopf, 1936, 1945, 1948. Abridged edition edited by Raven McDavid, Alfred A. Knopf, 1963.

MLA Style Sheet. Modern Languages Association, 1977.

Pei, Mario. *The Story of the English Language.* Simon & Schuster, 1967.

Pooley, Robert. *The Teaching of English Usage.* National Council of Teachers of English, 1974.

Publication Manual. American Psychological Association, 1974.

Reed, Jean, editor. *Resumes That Get Jobs* (2nd Ed.). Arco, 1979.

Ross, Raymond. *Speech Communication: Fundamentals and Practice* (7th Ed.). Prentice-Hall, 1986.

Sheff, Alexandra, and Edna Ingalls. *How to Write Letters for All Occasions* (2nd Ed.). Doubleday, 1961.

Strunk, William, Jr., and E. B. White. *The Elements of Style* (3rd Ed.). Macmillan, 1979.

Turabian, Kate L. *Student's Guide for Writing College Papers* (3rd Ed.). University of Chicago Press, 1976.

Walkerdine, Valerie, et al., editors. *Language, Gender and Childhood.* Routledge Chapman and Hall, 1985.

Wanniski, Jude. *Media Guide, 1987: A Critical Review of the Media.* Harper & Row, 1987.

Family Reading

Aesop's Fables (Illustrated Junior Library Series). Grosset & Dunlap, 1947.

Andersen, Hans Christian. *The Complete Fairy Tales and Stories* (translated by Erik Christian Haugaard). Doubleday, 1974.

Arbuthnot, May Hill. *The Arbuthnot Anthology of Children's Literature* (4th Ed.). Lothrop, Lee & Shepard, 1976.

Baring-Gould, William S., and Ceil Baring-Gould. *The Annotated Mother Goose.* Clarkson N. Potter, 1982.

Baum, L. Frank. *The Wonderful Wizard of Oz.* Macmillian, 1962.

Carroll, Lewis. *The Annotated Alice.* Clarkson N. Potter, 1960.

Doyle, Arthur Conan. *The Adventures of Sherlock Holmes.* Penguin, 1981.

Field, Eugene. *Poems of Childhood.* Airmont, 1969.

Fisher, Dorothy Canfield. *A Harvest of Stories.* Harcourt, Brace, 1956.

Frost, Robert. *The Poetry of Robert Frost.* Holt, Rinehart & Winston, 1969.

Galantière, Lewis, editor. *The Portable Maupassant.* Viking Press, 1947.

Georgiou, Constantine. *Children and Their Literature.* Prentice-Hall, 1969.

Gillespie, John T., and Christine B. Gilbert. *Best Books for Children: Preschool Through the Middle Grades* (3rd Ed.). Bowker, 1985.

Grimm, Wilhelm K., and Jacob Grimm. *Household Stories of the Brothers Grimm* (translated by Lucy Crane). Dover, 1963.

Handford, S. A., translator. *Fables of Aesop.* Penguin Books, 1954.

Henry, O. *Best Stories of O. Henry.* Doubleday, 1965.

Huck, Charlotte S. *Children's Literature in the Elementary School* (3rd Revised Ed.). Holt, Rinehart & Winston, 1979.

Jacobs, Joseph, editor. *The Fables of Aesop.* Macmillan, 1950.

Johnson, Thomas H., editor. *The Complete Poems of Emily Dickinson.* Little, Brown, 1960.

Kipling, Rudyard. *The Jungle Book.* Doubleday, 1981.

Lang, Andrew, editor. *The Blue Fairy Book.* Dover, 1965.

London, Jack. *Best Short Stories of Jack London.* Doubleday, 1953.

Munro, H. H. *The Complete Works of Saki.* Doubleday, 1976.

Nash, Ogden. *The Pocket Book of Ogden Nash.* Pocket Books, 1983.

Neider, Charles, editor. *The Complete Tales of Washington Irving.* Doubleday, 1975.

Neider, Charles, editor. *The Complete Short Stories of Mark Twain.* Doubleday, 1957.

Poe, Edgar Allan. *Complete Tales and Poems.* Random House, 1975.

Prakken, Sarah L., editor. *The Reader's Adviser* (12th Ed.). 3 volumes. Bowker, 1974–1977.

Roethke, Theodore. *Words for the Wind: The Collected Verse of Theodore Roethke.* University of Washington Press, 1981.

Sandburg, Carl. *The Complete Poems of Carl Sandburg* (Revised Ed.). Harcourt, Brace, Jovanovich, 1970.

Smith, Janet Adam, editor. *Robert Louis Stevenson: Collected Poems* (2nd Ed.). Viking Press, 1971.

Stevenson, Robert Louis. *A Child's Garden of Verses* (Classics Series). Airmont, 1969.

Stockton, Frank R. *The Lady or the Tiger and Other Stories* (Reprint of 1884 Ed.). Irvington Publications, 1972.

Thurber, James. *The Thurber Carnival.* Harper & Brothers, 1945.

Twain, Mark. *The Complete Adventures of Tom Sawyer and Huckleberry Finn.* Harper & Row, 1979.

White, E. B. *Charlotte's Web.* Harper & Row, 1952.

Whitman, Walt. *The Portable Walt Whitman* (Revised Ed.). Penguin, 1977.